The
Encyclopedia
of American
Religions:
Religious
Creeds

The Encyclopedia of American Religions:

Religious Creeds

A Compilation of More Than 450 Creeds, Confessions, Statements of Faith, and Summaries of Doctrine of Religious and Spiritual Groups in the United States and Canada

FIRST EDITION

J. Gordon Melton,
Editor

Gale Research Company • Book Tower • Detroit, Michigan 48226

J. Gordon Melton, *Editor*

Gale Research Company

Amy Marcaccio, *Project Editor*

Aided by:

Denise Michlewicz Broderick, Pamela Dear, Melissa Reiff Hug,
Carol A. Schwartz, Michaela Swart Wilson

Mary Beth Trimper, *Production Manager*
Linda Davis and Anthony J. Scolaro, *External Production Assistants*
Arthur Chartow, *Art Director*

Laura Bryant, *Production Supervisor*
Louise Gagne, *Internal Production Associate*
Sandy Rock, *Senior Internal Production Assistant*
Candace Cloutier, *Internal Production Assistant*

Dennis LaBeau, *Editorial Data Systems Director*
Diane Belickas, *EDS Systems and Programming Supervisor*
Donald G. Dillaman, *System Design and Development*

Frederick G. Ruffner, *Chairman*
Thomas A. Paul, *President*
Dedria Bryfonski, *Publisher*
Ellen T. Crowley, *Associate Editorial Director*
John Schmittroth, Jr., *Director, Special Reference Directories Division*
Robert J. Elster, *Senior Editor*

Library of Congress Classification Number 87-30384
ISBN 0-8103-2132-7

Contents

RELIGIOUS CREEDS

Contents

Contents

Contents

Contents

Chapter 13: Liberal Family

Chapter 14: Latter-Day Saints Family

Chapter 18: Ancient Wisdom Family

Chapter 19: Magick Family

Contents

Contents

Introduction

Just as *The Encyclopedia of American Religions (EAR)* provided the first comprehensive study of religious and spiritual groups in the United States since the U.S. Census Bureau's last edition of *Religious Bodies* (1936), this first edition of *The Encyclopedia of American Religions: Religious Creeds* represents the first comprehensive compilation of the creeds, confessions, and statements of belief of America's religious groups in over a century. *EAR: Religious Creeds* presents more than 450 creedal texts, covering not only Christian churches, but also the hundreds of Jewish, Islamic, Buddhist, Hindu, and other traditions possessing a following in the United States and Canada. In addition, historical notes and comments are provided to help researchers, librarians, students, and other information seekers understand the context in which creeds were written, revised, or discarded.

Authentic Text Used for All Creeds

The texts of the religious creeds presented in this volume are in their authentic form, although obvious typographical errors have been corrected. The authentic wording, grammar, and punctuation of each statement remains intact. In some cases, a creed's format was altered slightly for stylistic consistency and clarity. No attempt was made to introduce foreign material or explanatory notes into the body of the creed's text. Where alternate readings of a statement's text have been available, the editor chose an English language text currently in use by the church. Further, no attempt has been made to provide theological exposition, detailed textual analysis, or variant readings of a text, except in those few cases in which contemporary Christian churches disagree over the exact wording of the older creeds.

Types of Creeds and Statements Covered

Creeds are formal statements of belief to which members of a church are expected to give their intellectual assent. The writing of religious creeds is primarily an activity of Christian churches. At the same time, some other churches publish less rigid statements of belief reflecting a consensus of church teachings, while recognizing some variance of belief among members (and even leaders). A number of religious groups publish statements with an understanding that such beliefs are entirely secondary in the life of the group; emphasis is placed more upon piety, religious experience, liturgy, behavior (ethics), or membership in an ethnic group. On the other hand, some churches are strictly anti-creedal. Nevertheless, even the most anti-creedal and experience-oriented groups usually have a small body of assumed intellectual content (a system of beliefs that can be put into words) and, on occasion, official group statements are written for members' use. Such statements are considered to fall within the scope of this work.

Each creedal statement presented in this volume is acknowledged by at least one existing church or religious group described in the second edition of *The Encyclopedia of American Religions* (or its supplement). Users familiar with that volume and its supplement will note the difference in the number of entries they contain (1,550 religious groups) and the 450 creeds presented in this first edition of *The Encyclopedia of American Religions: Religious Creeds*. This difference is due to several factors. First, many creedal statements serve a variety of individual churches. For example, the Nicene Creed is the basic statement of faith for all Eastern Orthodox groups; divisions in this tradition have been based on nondoctrinal issues such as ethnicity, language, and political allegiances. Second, some groups simply have no summary statement of belief. The Plymouth Brethren groups, for example, are noncreedal, and many Hindu and Buddhist groups are centered more on experience than doctrine. Finally, some groups' statements are not listed because the editor, after repeated attempts, could not locate those creeds.

Contemporary Focus

Unlike previous collections, *EAR: Religious Creeds* seeks to maintain a contemporary focus by presenting primarily creeds currently acknowledged by those religious groups operating in the United States and Canada. This volume makes no attempt to gather creedal statements from the various religious traditions, especially the older Christian families and, therefore, it is not intended to replace previously published works on Christian creeds, such as Philip Schaff's 1877 compilation, *The Creeds of Christendom* (Harper & Brothers, 1877); *Creeds of the Churches* (John H. Leith, editor; Doubleday, 1963); Arthur C. Cochrane's *Reformed Confessions of the 16th Century* (Westminster, 1966); Williston Walker's *Creeds and Platforms of Congregationalism* (Pilgrim, 1969); and William L. Lumpkin's *Baptist Confessions of Faith* (Judson, 1959).

Religious statements for *The Encyclopedia of American Religions: Religious Creeds,* first edition, were compiled from a variety of sources located in the files of the Institute for the Study of American Religion, including sources gathered over the years directly from the religious groups. Other material was obtained through mailings during the compilation of material for production of the most recent edition of *The Encyclopedia of American Religions.*

Contents and Arrangement

EAR: Religious Creeds is organized into 23 chapters. The first chapter covers the four ancient Christian creeds (acknowledged and used by a majority of existing Christian groups and not associated with one in particular). Chapters 2 through 23 cover the statements of the individual churches, religious bodies, and spiritual groups that constitute the major religious families operating in the United States and Canada. (With minor variations, this follows the arrangement of *The Encyclopedia of American Religions.*) Material within each chapter is arranged alphabetically by name of religious group or church, not by name of creed. Some material has been rearranged to highlight those creeds and confessions serving an entire religious family or group of churches. In addition, statements that partially define religious families or subfamilies are placed at the beginning of the appropriate chapter or subchapter. (See the detailed contents pages preceding this Introduction for an overview of the arrangement of each of the 23 chapters.)

Creeds presented in *EAR: Religious Creeds* contain the following elements:

Creed Title. The actual or descriptive title, followed by the name of the primary group related to the statement. (Where no formal title was given, a descriptive title was assigned.) Names of primary religious groups not contained in the creed's formal title are added parenthetically. (Other religious groups that acknowledge the particular statement are mentioned in the notes following the text.)

Text of Religious Creed. The full text of the creed in its authentic form.

Notes. These appear in italic type following the text of individual creeds. When applicable, these remarks provide data about the origin of the creed, call attention to particular ideas and emphases covered (or, in some cases, omitted) by the text, discuss variant readings of the text as used by different churches, and point out relationships to other religious statements. Also mentioned here are other religious groups that acknowledge the particular creed.

Name and Keyword Index Provided

To facilitate access to the material, *EAR: Religious Creeds* contains a Creed/Organization Name and Keyword Index. This index lists, in a single alphabetic sequence, full titles of all the creeds presented in the volume as well as the names of all the religious traditions and individual churches mentioned in the text and notes. In addition, creed title and church name citations also appear in the index rotated by key word in title/name. Creed names appear in italic type to distinguish them from religious organizations. Citations refer users to the page where the indexed creed or religious group appears in the main body of the book.

Institute for the Study of American Religion

The Institute for the Study of American Religion was founded in 1969 for the purpose of researching and disseminating information about the numerous religious groups in the United States. More recently, the Institute's scope has been expanded to include religious groups in Canada, making it the only research facility of its kind to cover so broad a range of activity. After being located for many years in Evanston, Illinois, the Institute moved to Santa Barbara, California, in 1985. At that time, its collection of more than 25,000 books and its extensive files were donated to the Special Collections department of the library of the University of California—Santa Barbara.

Suggestions Are Welcome

Users of this volume with inquiries, additional information, corrections of inadvertent errors, or other suggestions for improvements are invited to write the Institute in care of its director. The Institute is particularly interested in obtaining copies of statements missing from this volume for inclusion in future editions.

Dr. J. Gordon Melton
Institute for the Study of American Religion
Box 90709
Santa Barbara, CA 93190-0709

The
Encyclopedia
of American
Religions:
Religious
Creeds

Chapter 1
Ancient Creeds of the Christian Church

THE APOSTLES' CREED

I believe in God the Father Almighty, Maker of heaven and earth. And in Jesus Christ His only Son, our Lord; Who was conceived by the Holy Ghost, Born of the Virgin Mary; Suffered under Pontius Pilate, Was crucified, dead, and buried; He descended into hell; The third day He rose again from the dead; He ascended into heaven, And sitteth on the right hand of God the Father Almighty; From thence He shall come to judge the quick and the dead.

I believe in the Holy Ghost; The holy Catholic Church, the Communion of Saints; The Forgiveness of sins; The Resurrection of the body; And the Life everlasting. Amen.

Notes: *The most widely accepted summary statement of the Christian faith is the Apostles' Creed. Derived from earlier statements, some dating from the beginning of the second century C.E., the present text was standardized by the eighth century. Some churches, most especially the Roman Catholic Church, have also formally and specifically named the Apostles' Creed as an official doctrinal statement, though almost all mainline Christian churches would adhere to its affirmations regardless of any formal denominational recognition. The creed commonly appears as an integral part of the standard orders of worship of many Protestant and Free Church denominations, and it is repeated weekly by worshippers much like the Lord's Prayer.*

Within the Protestant and Free Church liturgies, numerous variations of the text occur. Most reflect an attempt to counter any misunderstanding of the meaning of the phrase "holy Catholic Church." In order to underscore the belief that the Roman Catholic Church is not the object of belief, Protestants have substituted the phrase "holy Christian Church," (common to Lutherans) or "holy universal church" (used by many Free Churches). Occasionally, even where the original phrase is kept, an explanatory footnote is added.

Many of the church bodies that have emerged in the last two hundred years, particularly those growing out of the Methodist movement, have entirely dropped the phrase affirming that Christ "descended into hell." Such churches have found it confusing for members who do not understand

the difference between hell as "hades" (the abode of the dead in Hebrew thought) and hell as the place of final judgment and torment.

Finally, there is wide variation in the use of "Holy Spirit" as opposed to "Holy Ghost," even within denominational traditions. Confusion caused by the modern use of the term "ghost" to describe the shadowy apparitions of the dead has led to the adoption of a term felt to be more in keeping with the intent of the affirmation.

*   *   *

THE NICENE CREED

I Believe in one God, the Father Almighty, Maker of heaven and earth, And of all things visible and invisible.

And in one Lord Jesus Christ, the Only-begotten Son of God, Begotten of His Father before all worlds, God of God, Light of Light, Very God of very God, Begotten, not made, Being of one substance with the Father, By Whom all things were made; Who, for us men, and for our salvation, came down from heaven, And was incarnate by the Holy Ghost of the Virgin Mary, And was made man; And was crucified also for us under Pontius Pilate. He suffered and was buried; and the third day He rose again, according to the Scriptures; And ascended into heaven, And sitteth on the right hand of the Father; And He shall come again with glory to judge both the quick and the dead; Whose kingdom shall have no end.

And I believe in the Holy Ghost, The Lord and Giver of Life, Who proceedth from the Father and the Son, Who with the Father and the Son together is worshipped and glorified, Who spake by the Prophets. And I believe one holy Christian and Apostolic Church. I acknowledge one Baptism for the remission of sins; And I look for the Resurrection of the dead; And the Life of the world to come. Amen.

Notes: *During the fourth and fifth centuries, the Christian Church went through one of its most important eras theologically, and in the process hammered out what has become the standard orthodox position on the questions of God, Christ, and the nature of the Church. During this*

THE NICENE CREED (continued)

process, a variety of creeds were developed. The most important, because of its gaining almost universal acceptance among the major Christian groupings, was the Nicene Creed. It was first promulgated by the Council of Nicea in 325 C.E. and later expanded by the Council at Constantinople in 381. It became the standard creed of both the Eastern and Western Churches during the early middle ages and is integral to their liturgies. The creed is considered the unitive statement of faith by the organizationally separate Eastern Orthodox bodies. Like the Apostles' Creed, the Nicene Creed is formally recognized as a doctrinal standard by some Protestant bodies and informally recognized by most others. For example, it is printed as an optional confession of faith to be used in worship services in both the Hymnal and the Book of Worship of the United Methodist Church.

There is only one major variation in the text of the Nicene Creed. A theological difference between the Eastern and Western Churches at the time of the Great Schism of 1054 underlies the Roman Catholic Church's addition of the so-called "filioque clause," which affirmed that, within the mystery of the Godhead, the Holy Spirit proceeded from both the Father and the Son, not just the Father. Generally, churches deriving from the Roman Catholic Church have kept the clause in their reprinting of the creed. During the nineteenth century, the filioque (i.e., Latin for "and the Son") clause became a major item of discussion for the Old Catholics.

*   *   *

THE CHALCEDONIAN FORMULA

Following the holy fathers, we all unanimously teach that one and same Son, our Lord Jesus Christ, is to be confessed:

Perfect in Deity and perfect in Humanity,
Truly God and truly Man,
Of a *rational* soul and body,
Consubstantial with the Father according to his Deity,
Consubstantial with us according to his Humanity,
Like us in all respects, apart from sin;
Before the ages begotten of the Father according to his Deity,
And in these last days for us and for our salvation was born of the Virgin Mary, *the Mother of God [Theotokos]* according to his Humanity,
One and the same Christ, Son, Lord, only-begotten,
To be acknowledged in Two Natures
    without confusion or change
    without division or separation;
The difference of the Natures being by no means removed by the union,
but rather the property of each Nature being preserved and concurring in one Person and one Subsistence,
Not parted or divided into two Persons,
but one and the same Son and Only-begotten, God the Word, the Lord Jesus Christ;
According as at first the prophets, then the Lord Jesus Christ himself, taught us concerning him,
And as the Creed of the fathers has handed down to us.

Notes: *Largely confined to theological textbooks today, the Chalcedonian Formula promulgated in 451 C.E. represents the culmination of the major controversies that occupied the Christian Church leaders during the early centuries. It defined the orthodox solution to the problems of the Trinity, the dual nature of Jesus Christ, and the role of the Holy Spirit. The importance of its determinative theological role cannot be underestimated, though its popularity for liturgical use has never approached that of the Nicene Creed.*

Because the Chalcedonian Formula has not been utilized as a liturgical confession and the Greek words used in it continue to provoke theological discussions, no standard accepted English text exists, such as exist for the Apostles' and the Nicene Creeds. The formula's several translations vary from extremely literal to free flowing and interpretive. The text presented here tends toward the literal. Notice should be taken of the formula's affirmation of Mary as "theotokos" [mother of God], an implication of Jesus's divinity that had significant influence on the latter development of understanding the Virgin Mary in the life of the Church.

The Apostles' Creed, the Nicene Creed, and the Chalcedonian Formula were by no means the only creeds of the early church. They are the ones that continue to have the most direct effect upon contemporary church bodies by their use and theological impact.

*   *   *

THE CREED OF ATHANASIUS (*SYMBOLUM QUICUNQUE*)

1. Whosoever will be saved, before all things it is necessary that he hold the Catholic [true Christian] faith,

2. Which Faith except every one do keep whole and undefiled, without doubt he shall perish everlastingly.

3. And the Catholic [true Christian] faith is this: that we worship one God in Trinity, and Trinity in Unity;

4. Neither confounding the Persons; nor dividing the Substance.

5. For there is one Person of the Father, another of the Son, and another of the Holy Ghost.

6. But the Godhead of the Father, of the Son, and of the Holy Ghost, is all one: the Glory Equal, the Majesty Coeternal.

7. Such as the Father is, such is the Son: and such is the Holy Ghost.

8. The Father uncreate, the Son uncreate: and the Holy Ghost uncreate.

9. The Father incomprehensible, the Son incomprehensible and the Holy Ghost incomprehensible.

10. The Father eternal, the Son eternal: and the Holy Ghost eternal.

11. And yet they are not three Eternals: but one Eternal.

12. As there are not three uncreated, nor three incomprehensibles: but one uncreated and one incomprehensible.

13. So likewise the Father is Almighty, the Son Almighty: and the Holy Ghost Almighty.

14. And yet they are not three Almighties: but one Almighty.

15. So the Father is God, the Son is God: and the Holy Ghost is God.

16. And yet they are not three Gods: but one God.

17. So likewise the Father is Lord, the Son Lord: and the Holy Ghost Lord.

18. And yet not three Lords: but one Lord.

19. For like as we are compelled by the Christian verity: to acknowledge every Person by himself to be God and Lord; So are we forbidden by the Catholic [Christian] Religion: to say, There be three Gods, or three Lords.

20. The Father is made of none: neither created nor begotten.

21. The Son is of the Father alone: not made, nor created, but begotten.

22. The Holy Ghost is of the Father, and of the Son; neither made, nor created, nor begotten, but proceeding.

23. So there is one Father, not three Fathers; one Son, not three Sons; one Holy Ghost, not three Holy Ghosts.

24. And in this Trinity none is before, or after other: none is greater, or less than another;

25. But the whole three Persons are coeternal together, and coequal: So that in all things, as is aforesaid: the Unity in Trinity, and the Trinity in Unity is to be worshipped.

26. He therefore that will be saved must thus think of the Trinity.

27. Furthermore, it is necessary to Everlasting Salvation; that he also believe rightly the Incarnation of our Lord Jesus Christ.

28. For the right Faith is, that we believe and confess: that our Lord Jesus Christ, the Son of God, is God and Man;

29. God, of the Substance of the Father begotten before the worlds: and Man of the Substance of his mother, born in the world;

30. Perfect God, and perfect Man: of a reasonable soul and human flesh subsisting.

31. Equal to the Father, as touching his Godhead: and inferior to the Father, as touching his Manhood.

32. Who although he be God and Man: yet he is not two, but one Christ;

33. One; not by conversion of the Godhead into flesh: but by taking the Manhood into God;

34. One altogether; not by confusion of Substance: but by Unity of Person.

35. For as the reasonable soul and flesh is one man: so God and Man is one Christ;

36. Who suffered for our salvation: descended into hell, rose again the third day from the dead.

37. He ascended into heaven; he sitteth on the right hand of the Father, God Almighty: from whence he shall come to judge the quick and the dead.

38. At whose coming all men shall rise again with their bodies: and shall give account for their own works.

39. And they that have done good shall go into life everlasting: and they that have done evil into everlasting fire.

40. This is the Catholic [true Christian] faith: which except a man believe faithfully, he cannot be saved.

Notes: *Although now thought to have been written sometime between the fourth and eighth centuries, this creed was for centuries ascribed to Athanasius (299?-373 C.E.), the fourth-century bishop who championed what became the orthodox Christian position on the nature of Christ. Even though the creed was never officially accepted by a church council (resulting in a variety of texts with different renderings, rather than one standard text), it became a widely accepted church document. Rendered into liturgical form, it was chanted in both the Roman Catholic Church and Church of England several times per year.*

The creed has lost popularity in the contemporary era, although it is still accepted and used in the Roman Catholic Church. The Lutherans included the creed in their doctrinal material as part of their broader case for catholic orthodoxy. The text reproduced here is taken from the Lutheran Book of Concord. *The creed is also found in the official materials of other churches, such as the* Psalter Hymnal *of the Christian Reformed Church. The Protestant Episcopal Church deleted the creed from its prayer book in 1785.*

The words in brackets have been inserted into the text by the Lutheran translators to explain their understanding of the word "catholic," which differs considerably from the common meaning of Roman Catholic.

Chapter 2
Western Liturgical Family

Roman Catholic Church

THE PROFESSION OF FAITH OF THE ROMAN CATHOLIC CHURCH

I, N., with firm faith believe and profess each and every article contained in the symbol of faith which the Holy Roman Church uses; namely: I believe in one God, the Father Almighty, maker of heaven and earth and of all things visible and invisible; and in one Lord Jesus Christ the only-begotten Son of God, born of the Father before all ages; God from God, light from light, true God from true God; begotten not made, of one substance with the Father; through whom all things were made; who for us men and for our salvation came down from heaven and was made incarnate by the Holy Spirit of the Virgin Mary and was made man. He was crucified also for us under Pontius Pilate, died and was buried; and he rose again the third day according to the Scriptures, and ascended into heaven; He sits at the right hand of the Father, and He will come again in glory to judge the living and the dead, and of His kingdom there will be no end. And I believe in the Holy Spirit, the Lord, and giver of life, who proceeds from the Father and the Son; who equally with the Father and the Son is adored and glorified; who spoke through the prophets. And I believe that there is one, holy, catholic, and apostolic Church. I confess one baptism for the remission of sins; and I hope for the resurrection of the dead, and the life of the world to come. Amen.

I resolutely accept and embrace the apostolic and ecclesiastical traditions and other practices and regulations of that same Church. In like manner I accept Sacred Scripture according to the meaning which has been held by the Holy Mother Church and which she now holds. It is her prerogative to pass judgment on the true meaning and interpretation of Sacred Scripture. And I will never accept or interpret it in a manner different from the unanimous agreement of the Fathers.

I also truly acknowledge that there are truly and properly seven sacraments of the New Law, instituted by Jesus Christ, our Lord, and that they are necessary for the salvation of the human race, although it is not necessary for each individual to receive them all. I acknowledge that the seven sacraments are: baptism, confirmation, Eucharist, penance, extreme unction, holy orders, and matrimony; and that they confer grace; and that of the seven, baptism, confirmation, and holy orders cannot be repeated without commiting a sacrilege. I also accept and acknowledge the customary and approved rites of the Catholic Church in the solemn administration of these sacraments. I accept and embrace each and every article on original sin and justification declared and defined in the most holy Council of Trent.

I likewise profess that in the Mass a true, proper, and propitiatory sacrifice is offered to God on behalf of the living and the dead, and that the Body and the Blood, together with the soul and the divinity, of our Lord Jesus Christ is truly, really, and substantially present in the most holy sacrament of the Eucharist, and that there is a change of the whole substance of the bread into the Body, and of the whole substance of the wine into Blood; and this change the Catholic Church calls transubstantiation. I also profess that the whole and entire Christ and a true sacrament is received under each separate species.

I firmly hold that there is a purgatory and that the souls detained there are helped by the prayers of the faithful. I likewise hold that the saints reigning together with Christ should be honored and invoked, that they offer prayers to God on our behalf, and that their relics should be venerated. I firmly assert that the images of Christ, of the Mother of God ever Virgin, and of the other saints should be owned and kept, and that due honor and veneration should be given to them. I affirm that the power of indulgences was left in the keeping of the Church by Christ, and that the use of indulgences is very beneficial to Christians.

I acknowledge the holy, catholic, and apostolic Roman Church as the Mother and teacher of all Churches; and I promise and swear true obedience to the Roman Pontiff, vicar of Christ, and the successor of Blessed Peter, Prince of the Apostles.

I unhesitatingly accept and profess all the doctrines (especially those concerning the primacy of the Roman Pontiff and his infallible teaching authority) handed down,

THE PROFESSION OF FAITH OF THE ROMAN CATHOLIC CHURCH (continued)

defined, and explained by the sacred canons and ecumenical councils, and especially those of this most holy Council of Trent (and by the ecumenical Vatican Council). At the same time, I condemn, reject, and anathematize everything that is contrary to those propositions, and all heresies without exception that have been condemned, rejected and anathematized by the Church. I, N., promise, vow, and swear that, with God's help, I shall most constantly hold and profess this true Catholic faith, outside which no one can be saved and which I now freely profess and truly hold. With the help of God I shall profess it whole and unblemished to my dying breath; and, to the best of my ability, I shall see to it that my subjects or those entrusted to me by virtue of my office, hold it, teach it and preach it. So help me God and His holy Gospel.

Notes: *The Roman Catholic Church accepts the four major ancient creeds as its doctrinal standard but has made a number of additional doctrinal commitments over the centuries. Possibly the most important statement made in the years since the standardization of the text of the Nicene Creed in the eleventh century was the Profession of Faith issued by Pope Paul IV in 1564. The profession summarized Catholic doctrine, and over the years its public confession has been required of converts and of members in the process of attaining certain high offices. The text has been modified on several occasions, most importantly in 1877 by Pope Pius IX to include the clause on papal infallibility. In the decades since Vatican II, use of the profession has diminished. New converts now go through a service receiving them into the church that includes the Nicene Creed. However, the profession remains a valid summary of Roman Catholic doctrinal distinctives.*

* * *

Old Catholicism

THE FOURTEEN THESES OF THE OLD CATHOLIC UNION CONFERENCE, BONN, GERMANY, 1874

I. We agree that the apocryphal or deutero-canonical books of the Old Testament are not of the same canonicity as the books contained in the Hebrew Canon.

II. We agree that no translation of Holy Scripture can claim an authority superior to that of the original text.

III. We agree that the reading of Holy Scripture in the vulgar tongue can not be lawfully forbidden.

IV. We agree that, in general, it is more fitting, and in accordance with the spirit of the Church, that the Liturgy should be in the tongue understood by the people.

V. We agree that Faith working by Love, not Faith without Love, is the means and condition of Man's justification before God.

VI. Salvation cannot be merited by "merit of condignity," because there is no proportion between the infinite worth of salvation promised by God and the finite worth of man's works.

VII. We agree that the doctrine of "opera supererogationis" and of a "thesaurus meritorum sanctorum," i.e., that the overflowing merits of the Saints can be transferred to others, either by the rulers of the Church, or by the authors of the good works themselves, is untenable.

VIII. 1. We acknowledge that the number of sacraments was fixed at seven, first in the twelfth century, and then was received into the general teaching of the Church, not as a tradition coming down from the Apostles or from the earliest times, but as the result of theological speculation.

2. Catholic theologians acknowledge, and we acknowledge with them, that Baptism and the Eucharist are "principalia, praecipus, eximia salutis nostrae sacramenta."

IX. 1. The Holy Scriptures being recognized as the primary rule of Faith, we agree that the genuine tradition, i.e. the unbroken transmission partly oral, partly in writing of the doctrine delivered by Christ and the Apostles is an authoritative source of teaching for all successive generations of Christians. This tradition is partly to be found in the consensus of the great ecclesiastical bodies standing in historical continuity with the primitive Church, partly to be gathered by scientific method from the written documents of all centuries.

2. We acknowledge that the Church of England, and the Churches derived through her, have maintained unbroken the Episcopal succession.

X. We reject the new Roman doctrine of the Immaculate Conception of the Blessed Virgin Mary, as being contrary to the tradition of the first thirteen centuries, according to which Christ alone is conceived without sin.

XI. We agree that the practice of confession of sins before the congregation or a Priest, together with the exercise of the power of the keys, has come down to us from the primitive Church, and that, purged from abuses and free from constraint, it should be preserved in the Church.

XII. We agree that "indulgences" can only refer to penalties actually imposed by the Church herself.

XIII. We acknowledge that the practice of the commemoration of the faithful departed, i.e. the calling down of a richer outpouring of Christ's grace upon them, has come down to us from the primitive Church, and is to be preserved in the Church.

XIV. 1. The Eucharistic celebration in the Church is not a continuous repetition or renewal of the propitiatory sacrifice offered once for ever by Christ upon the cross; but its sacrificial character consists in this, that it is the permanent memorial of it, and a representation and presentation on earth of that one oblation of Christ for the salvation of redeemed mankind, which according to the Epistle to the Hebrews (9:11,12), is continuously presented in heaven by Christ, who now appears in the presence of God for us (9:24).

2. While this is the character of the Eucharist in reference to the sacrifice of Christ, it is also a sacred feast, wherein the faithful, receiving the Body and Blood of our Lord, have communion one with another (I Cor. 10:17).

Notes: *As a result of the Roman Catholic Church's adoption of the doctrine of papal infallibility as dogma at the First Vatican Council in 1870, many members in continental Europe left the Roman jurisdiction and formed the Old Catholic Church. They felt that the Roman Catholic Church had departed from traditional Catholic faith. The Old Catholic position was spelled out in a series of documents: the so-called Fourteen Theses issued by the Old Catholic Union Conference of 1874; the statement on the filioque clause in the Nicene Creed issued in 1875; and The Declaration of Utrecht [Holland], issued in 1889. An English translation of the latter was made in 1930 and printed that year in the Report of the Lambeth Conference (Anglican). The Old Catholic Church and the Anglican Communion have enjoyed many years of cordial relationship, disturbed only by the recent ordination of women by several of the Anglican church bodies.*

* * *

THE OLD CATHOLIC AGREEMENT ON THE FILIOQUE CONTROVERSY, 1875

1. We agree in accepting the ecumenical symbols and the decisions in matters of faith of the ancient undivided Church.

2. We agree in acknowledging that the addition *Filioque* to the symbol did not take place in an ecclesiastically regular manner.

3. We give our unanimous assent to the presentation of the doctrine of the Holy Spirit as taught by the Fathers of the undivided Church.

(1) We accept the teachings of St. John of Damascus concerning the Holy Spirit, as it is expressed in the following paragraphs, in the sense of the doctrine of the ancient undivided Church.

(a) The Holy Spirit proceeds from the Father as the beginning, the cause, the fountain of the Godhead.

(b) The Holy Spirit proceeds not from the Son, because in the Godhead there is only one beginning one cause, by which all that is in the Godhead is produced.

(c) The Holy Spirit proceeds from the Father through the Son.

(d) The Holy Spirit is the image of the Son (as the Son is the image of the Father), proceeding from the Father, and resting in the Son as the power shining forth from him.

(e) The Holy Spirit is the personal production out of the Father, belonging to the Son, but not out

of the mouth of the Godhead which pronounces the Word.

(f) The Holy Spirit forms the mediation between the Father and the Son, and is, through the Son, united with the Father.

4. We reject every representation and every form of expression in which is contained the acceptance of two principles, or beginnings, or causes, in the Trinity.

* * *

THE DECLARATION OF UTRECHT, 1889

1. We adhere faithfully to the Rule of Faith laid down by St. Vincent of Lérins in these terms: "Id teneamus, quod ubique, quod semper, quod ab omnibus creditum est; hoc est etenim vere proprieque catholicum". For this reason we persevere in professing the faith of the primitive Church, as formulated in the ecumenical symbols and specified precisely by the unanimously accepted decisions of the Ecumenical Councils held in the undivided Church of the first thousand years.

2. We therefore reject the decrees of the so-called Council of the Vatican, which were promulgated July 18, 1870, concerning the infallibility and the universal episcopate of the Bishop of Rome—decrees which are in contradiction with the faith of the ancient Church and which destroy its ancient canonical constitution by attributing to the Pope all the plenitude of ecclesiastical powers over all dioceses and over all the faithful. By denial of his primatial jurisdiction we do not wish to deny the historic primacy which several ecumenical councils and the Fathers of the ancient Church have attributed to the Bishop of Rome by recognizing him as the *Primus inter pares*.

3. We also reject the dogma of the Immaculate Conception promulgated by Pope Pius IX in 1854 in defiance of the Holy Scriptures and in contradiction with the tradition of the first centuries.

4. As for encyclicals published by the Bishops of Rome in recent times, for example, the Bulls "Unigenitus" and "Auctorem fidei," and the Syllabus of 1864, we reject them on all such points as are in contradiction with the doctrine of the primitive Church, and we do not recognize them as binding on the consciences of the faithful. We also renew the ancient protests of the Catholic Church of Holland against the errors of the Roman Curia, and against its attacks upon the rights of national churches.

5. We refuse to accept the decrees of the Council of Trent in matters of discipline, and as for the dogmatic decisions of that Council we accept them only so far as they are in harmony with the teaching of the primitive Church.

6. Considering that the Holy Eucharist has always been the true central point of Catholic worship, we consider it our duty to declare that we maintain with

THE DECLARATION OF UTRECHT, 1889 (continued)

perfect fidelity the ancient Catholic doctrine concerning the Sacrament of the Altar, by believing that we receive the Body and the Blood of our Saviour Jesus Christ under the species of bread and wine. The Eucharistic celebration in the Church is neither a continual repetition nor a renewal of the expiatory sacrifice which Jesus offered once for all upon the Cross; but it is a sacrifice because it is the perpetual commemoration of the sacrifice offered upon the Cross, and it is the act by which we represent upon earth and appropriate to ourselves the one offering which Jesus Christ makes in Heaven, according to the Epistle to the Hebrews, 9.11-12, for the salvation of redeemed humanity, by appearing for us in the presence of God (Heb. 9. 24). The character of the Holy Eucharist being thus understood, it is, at the same time, a sacrificial feast, by means of which the faithful, in receiving the Body and Blood of our Saviour, enter into communion with one another (I Cor. I. 17).

7. We hope that Catholic theologians, in maintaining the faith of the undivided Church, will succeed in establishing an agreement upon questions which have been controverted ever since the divisions which have arisen between the churches. We exhort the priests under our jurisdiction to teach, both by preaching and by the instruction of the young, especially the essential Christian truths professed by all the Christian confessions, to avoid, in discussing controverted doctrines, any violation of truth or charity, and in word and deed to set an example to the members of our churches in accordance with the spirit of Jesus Christ our Saviour.

8. By maintaining and professing faithfully the doctrine of Jesus Christ, by refusing to admit those errors which by the fault of men have crept into the Catholic Church, by laying aside the abuses in ecclesiastical matters, together with the worldly tendencies of the hierarchy, we believe that we shall be able to combat efficaciously the great evils of our day, which are unbelief and indifference in matters of religion.

* * *

STATEMENT OF UNION, 1911

1. THE WAY OF SALVATION. Eternal Salvation is promised to mankind only through merits of our Saviour Jesus Christ, and upon condition of obedience to the teaching of the Gospel, which requires Faith, Hope, and Charity, and the due observance of the ordinances of the Orthodox and Catholic Religion.

2. FAITH, HOPE, AND CHARITY. Faith is a virtue infused by God, whereby man accepts, and believes without doubting, whatever God has revealed in the Church concerning true Religion.

Hope is a virtue infused by God, and following upon Faith; by it man puts his entire trust and confidence in the goodness and mercy of God, through Jesus Christ, and looks for the fulfillment of the Divine promises made to those who obey the Gospel.

Charity is a virtue infused by God, and likewise consequent upon Faith, whereby man, loving God above all things for His own sake, and his neighbor as himself for God's sake, yields up his will to a joyful obedience to the revealed will of God in the Church.

3. THE CHURCH. God has established the Holy Catholic Church upon earth to be the pillar and ground of the revealed Truth; and has committed to her the guardianship of the holy Scriptures and of holy Tradition, and the power of binding and loosing.

4. THE CREED. The Catholic Church has set forth the principal Doctrines of the Christian Faith in twelve articles as follows:

I. I believe in one God the Father Almighty, Creator of heaven and earth, and of all things visible and invisible;

II. And in one Lord Jesus Christ, the only-begotten Son of God, begotten of the Father before all Ages, God of God, Light of Light, Very God of Very God, begotten, not made of one substance with the Father, by Whom all things were made;

III. Who for us men and for our salvation came down from heaven, and was Incarnate by the Holy Ghost of the Virgin Mary, and was made Man;

IV. And was crucified also for us under Pontius Pilate, He suffered and was buried;

V. And the third day He rose again, according to the Scriptures;

VI. And ascended into heaven, and sitteth on the right hand of the Father;

VII. And He shall come again, with glory, to judge the living and the dead; Whose kingdom shall have no end;

VIII. And I believe in the Holy Ghost, the Lord, and Giver of Life, Who proceedeth from the Father, Who with the Father and the Son together is worshipped and glorified, Who spoke by the Prophets;

IX. And in One, Holy, Catholic, and Apostolic Church;

X. I acknowledge one Baptism for the remission of sins;

XI. And I look for the Resurrection of the dead;

XII. And the Life in the world to come. Amen.

5. THE SACRAMENTS. The fundamental ordinances of the Gospel, instituted by Jesus Christ as special means of conveying Divine grace and influence to the souls of men, which are commonly called

Mysteries or Sacraments, are Seven in number, namely Baptism, Confirmation, the holy Eucharist, holy Orders, Matrimony, Penance, and Unction.

THUS: Baptism is the first Sacrament of the Gospel, administered by threefold immersion in, or affusion with, water with the word, "I baptize thee in the Name of the Father, and of the Son, and of the Holy Ghost." It admits the recipient into the Church, bestows upon him the forgiveness of sins, original and actual, through the Blood of Christ, and causes in him spiritual change called Regeneration. Without valid Baptism no other Sacrament can be validly received.

Confirmation or Chrism is a Sacrament in which the baptised person, on being anointed with Chrism consecrated by the Bishops of the Church, with the imposition of hands, receives the sevenfold gifts of the Holy Ghost to strengthen him in the grace which he received at Baptism, making him a strong and perfect Christian and a good soldier of Christ.

The holy Eucharist is a Sacrament in which, under the appearances of bread and wine, the real and actual Body and Blood of Christ are given and received for the remission of sins, the increase of Divine grace, and the reward of everlasting Life. After the prayer of Invocation of the Holy Ghost in the Liturgy, the bread and wine are entirely converted into the living Body and Blood of Christ by an actual change of being, to which change the philosophical terms of Transubstantiation and Transmutation are rightly applied. The celebration of this Mystery or Sacrament, commonly called the Mass, constitutes the chief act of Christian worship, being a sacrificial Memorial or re-Presentation of our Lord's death. It is not a repetition of the Sacrifice offered once for all upon Calvary, but is a perpetuation of that Sacrifice by the Church on earth, as our Lord also perpetually offers it in heaven. It is a true and propitiatory Sacrifice, which is offered alike for the living and for the departed.

Holy Orders is a Sacrament in which the Holy Ghost, through the laying-on of hands of the Bishops, consecrates and ordains the pastors and ministers chosen to serve in the Church, and imparts to them special grace to administer the Sacraments, to forgive sins, and to feed the flock of Christ.

Matrimony is a Sacrament in which the voluntary union of husband and wife is sanctified to become an image of the union between Christ and His Church; and grace is imparted to them to fulfill the duties of their estate and its great responsibilities both of each other and to their children.

Penance is a Sacrament in which the Holy Ghost bestows the forgiveness of sins, by the ministry of the priest, upon those who, having sinned after Baptism, confess their sins with true repentance, and grace is given to amend their lives thereafter.

Unction is a Sacrament in which the priests of the Church anoint the sick with oil, for the healing of the infirmities of their souls, and if it should please God, those of their bodies also.

The efficiancy of the Sacraments depends upon the promise and appointment of God; howbeit they benefit only those who receive them worthily with faith, and with due preparation and disposition of mind.

6. HOLY SCRIPTURE. The Scriptures are writings inspired by God, and given to the Church for her instruction and edification. The Church is therefore the custodian and the only Divinely appointed interpreter of holy Scripture.

7. TRADITION. The Apostolic and Ecclesiastical Traditions received from the seven General Councils and the early Fathers of the Church may not be rejected; but are to be received and obeyed as being both agreeable to holy Scripture and to that Authority with which Christ endowed His Church. Matters of discipline and ceremony do not rank on the same level with matters of Faith or Morals, but may be altered from time to time and from place to place by the Authority of the Church, according as the welfare and greater devotions of the faithful may be furthered thereby.

8. THE COMMUNION OF SAINTS. There is a Communion of Saints in the Providence of God, wherein the souls of righteous men of all ages are united with Christ in the bond of faith and love. Wherefore it is pleasing to God, and profitable to men, to honour the Saints and to invoke them in prayer; and also to pray for the faithful departed.

9. RELIGIOUS SYMBOLS. The relics and representations of Saints are worthy of honour, as are also all other religious emblems; that our minds may be encouraged to devotion and to imitation of the deeds of the just. Honour shown to such objects is purely relative, and in no way implies a confusion of the symbol with the thing signified.

10. RITE AND CEREMONIES. It is the duty of all Christians to join in the worship of the Church, especially in the holy Sacrifice of the Mass, in accordance with our Lord's express command; and to conform to the ceremonies prescribed by holy Tradition for the greater dignity of that Sacrifice and for the edification of the faithful.

11. THE MORAL LAW. All Christians are bound to observe the Moral Law contained in the Ten Commandments of the Old Testament, developed with greater strictness in the New, founded upon the law of nature and charity, and defining our duty to God and to man. The laws of the Church are also to be obeyed, as proceeding from that Authority which Christ has committed to her for the instruction and salvation of His people.

12. THE MONASTIC ESTATE. The monastic life, duly regulated according to the laws of the Church, is a salutary institution in strict accord with the holy Scriptures; and is full of profit to them who, after

STATEMENT OF UNION, 1911 (continued)

being carefully tried and examined, make full proof of their calling thereto.

ORGANIC ARTICLES

1. HEAD OF THE CHURCH. The Foundation Head and Supreme Pastor and Bishop of the Church is our Lord Jesus Christ Himself, from Whom all Bishops and Pastors derive their spiritual powers and jurisdiction.

2. OBEDIENCE. By the law and institution of our Lord Jesus Christ in the Gospel, all Christians owe obedience and submission in spiritual things to them who have rule and authority within the Church.

3. MINISTERIAL AUTHORITY. Our Lord Jesus Christ did not commit rule and authority within the Church to all the faithful indiscriminately, but only to the Apostles and to their lawful successors in due order.

4. APOSTOLIC SUCCESSION. The only lawful successors of the Apostles are the Orthodox and Catholic Bishops, united by profession of the self-same Belief, participation in the same Sacraments, and mutual recognition and Intercommunion. The Bishops of the Church, being true successors of the Apostles, are by Divine right and appointment the rulers of the Church.

    In virtue of this appointment, each individual Bishop is supreme and independent in that part of the Church which has been committed to his care, so long as he remains in Faith and Communion with the united company of Catholic Bishops, who cannot exclude any from the Church save only them who stray from the path of virtue or err in Faith.

    By virtue of this same Divine appointment, the supreme Authority over the whole Church on earth belongs to the collective Orthodox and Catholic Episcopate. They alone form the highest tribunal in spiritual matters, from whose united judgment there can be no appeal; so that it is unlawful for any single Bishop, or any smaller group of Bishops apart from them, or for any secular power or state to usurp this authority, or for any individual Christian to substitute his own private judgement for that interpretation of Scripture or Authority which is approved by the Church.

5. CHURCH AUTHORITY. The collective body of the Orthodox Catholic Episcopate, united by profession of the Faith, by the Sacraments, and by mutual recognition and actual Inter-communion, is the source and depository of all order, authority and jurisdiction in the Church, and is the center of visible Catholic Unity; so that no Pope, Patriarch or Bishop, or any number of Bishops separated from this united body can possess any authority or jurisdiction whatsoever.

    The authority of this collective body is equally binding, however it may be expressed: whether by a General Council or by the regular and ordinary consultation and agreement of the bishops themselves.

    It is an act of schism to appeal from the known judgement of the Orthodox and Catholic Episcopate, however it may be ascertained; or to appeal from any dogmatic decree of any General Council even though such appeal be to a future Council. For the Episcopate, being a continuation of the Apostolate, is clearly a Divine institution, and its authority is founded in Divine right. But General Councils are not of themselves of direct Divine appointment; and so the Episcopate having clearly the Scriptural promise of Divine guidance into all Truth, cannot be hampered in the exercise of its authority by the necessity of assembling a General Council, which may obviously be rendered impossible through natural circumstances.

    There have been seven General Councils only, which are recognized by the Whole of Catholic Christendom, held respectively in Nicaea (A.D. 325), Constantinople (381), Ephesus (431), Chalcedon (451), Constantinople (553), Constantinople (680), and Nicaea (787). At no other Councils was the entire body of the Orthodox and Catholic Episcopate representatively assembled; and the decrees and pronouncements of no others must of themselves be accepted as binding upon the conscience of the faithful.

    The Authority of the Church can never be in abeyance, even though a General Council cannot be assembled. It is equally to be submitted to and obeyed in whatever way it may be exercised, and although it may be exercised only through the ordinary administration of their respective jurisdictions by individual Bishops.

6. HIERARCHY. All Patriarchs, Archbishops, and Metropolitans (that is to say, all Bishops who exercise any authority over other Bishops) owe that authority solely to the appointment or general consent of the Orthodox and Catholic Episcopate; nor can they ever cease from owing obedience to the collective body of the Episcopate in all matters concerning Faith and Morals.

7. THE FIVE PATRIARCHATES. There are five Patriarchates, which ought to be united and form the supreme authority in the administration and government of the Holy Catholic Church. These are Jerusalem, Antioch, Rome, Alexandria, and Constantinople. Unfortunately, owing to disputes and differences on the one hand, and to the lust for power and supremacy and domination on the other; the Patriarchs are not at present in Communion; and the welfare of Christendom is jeopardized by their disedifying quarrels, which, we pray, may soon have an end.

Notes: *In England, the Old Catholic Church was founded by Arnold Harris Mathew. In 1911, Mathew was able to work out a doctrinal statement that led to the reception into communion of his jurisdiction by the Antiochian Orthodox Church in Lebanon under Archbishop Gerassimos Messar-*

ra. The Statement of Union has joined the three nineteenth-century European Old Catholic documents as an authoritative doctrinal summary for many Old Catholic jurisdictions.

In the United States, Old Catholicism has splintered into many small church jurisdictions. Most of these Old Catholic bodies adhere to the Declaration of Utrecht, at least informally, and most would accept all four statements—the Fourteen Theses, statement on the filioque clause, Declaration of Utrecht, and Statement of Union. However, the majority of Old Catholic bodies have published no doctrinal statement beyond the Apostles' or Nicene Creeds that appear in the text of the liturgy of the mass.

* * *

STATEMENT OF FAITH OF THE ARCHDIOCESE OF THE OLD CATHOLIC CHURCH OF AMERICA

Article I. HOLY TRADITION OF THE TRUE FAITH.

Section 1. We hold that Holy Tradition (Scripture) is the true and living Word of God, and that its interpretation is to be found in the Nicene Creed, the teachings of the Seven Holy Synods of the Church and in the teachings of the Holy Fathers of the Christian Faith.

Section 2. We believe God inspired all the writers of Scripture with objective fact, free from error, for our instruction.

Section 3. The Faith as written and handed down to us through the Prophets, Apostles and the Fathers unaltered, we hold fast without additions or subtractions.

Section 4. God's truths do not rely on our acceptance or our feelings. Holy Tradition (Scripture), the Nicene Creed, the teachings of the Seven Holy Synods and the teachings of the Fathers are unchanging in our ever-changing world.

Article II. THE NICENE CREED, THE SEVEN SYNODS AND THE TEACHINGS OF THE FATHERS.

Section 1. We believe that the Nicene Creed, the teachings of the Seven Holy Synods of the Church and the teachings of the Fathers to be the true interpretation of Scriptures and the Holy Faith taught by the inspiration of the Holy Spirit.

Section 2. We hold that our salvation rests upon this Faith in Christ alone. Those of other views are of another spirit and we count them not as Christian in any sense of the word.

Section 3. We hold that traditions of men (customs), although valid expressions of Faith, are not necessarily part of the Orthodox Catholic Faith. We also hold that those who teach them as necessary are guilty of idol worship. Faith in Christ as taught by the Prophets, Apostles and the Fathers alone is necessary.

Article III. THE MYSTERIES OF THE ORTHODOX CATHOLIC FAITH (SACRAMENTS).

Section 1. We believe that Christ God did institute seven holy Mysteries as a means of sharing in the life of the Holy Spirit. They are (i) Baptism; (ii) Communion; (iii) the Keys (Absolution or Penance); (iv) Chrismation (Confirmation or the Imparting of the Holy Spirit); (v) Marriage; (vi) Ordination (Bishop, Presbyter and Deacon); and (vii) the Sacrament of the Sick (Unction).

Section 2. We believe Baptism to be valid when administered according to Christ's command, as found in the Scripture: That is, in the Name of the Holy Trinity with water.

Section 3. We believe that the true body and the true blood of Christ to be present in the Holy Eucharist as taught by Holy Scripture and all the Holy Fathers of the true Faith. In this definition we neither add nor subtract. Christ's own words suffice: "This is My Body"; "This is My Blood". Christ's words are sufficient for our faith. Additional definitions only tend to confuse and mislead; and, we hold them to be of man-made origin.

Section 4. We hold Chrismation (Confirmation) to be divinely instituted and recorded in the Epistle of I John 2: 20-27, "You have an unction from the Holy One, and You have received of Him abiding in you."

Section 5. Matrimony was instituted by God Himself in the Garden of Eden and this state was blessed and reaffirmed by Christ God at the Wedding of Cana. It has as its purpose the perpetuation of the human race, companionship, submission to God's moral law and the Christian upbringing of children. All sexual relations outside of Holy Matrimony we do hold as contrary to the Divine Law of God.

Section 6. We believe and hold the Orders of the Ministry (Bishop, Presbyter and Deacon) to be of divine origin as found in Holy Scripture and necessary to God's Holy Church. Holy Scripture and the teachings of the Fathers tell us that those who minister in the Church should be called to their station in life to teach the Word of God and administer the Sacraments according to divine institution, by laying on of hands by a bishop who is the representative of Christ and His Church. A proper ordination never takes place without the affirmation of both clergy and laity, the body of Christ.

Section 7. We believe and hold that the mystery of Holy Penance is of divine origin as found in Holy Scripture. The power of the "keys" was instituted by Christ God for the forgiveness of sin and the comfort of the penitent.

Section 8. The Sacrament of the Sick (Unction) we hold to be of Apostolic origin as found in the Epistle of St. James, for the health and consolation of the sick, by the working power of the Holy Spirit.

Article IV. THE MONASTIC STATE OF LIFE.

Section 1. We believe the monastic life to be a holy expression and witness to the Christian life, although we do not believe it to be necessary to the Church's life and we do not hold the monastic state as equal to a Sacrament.

Section 2. When monastic life is freely chosen by an individual for the honor and glory of God and in witness to the Faith, then it is a useful and holy thing in the Church. For, virginity is only preserved by the working and power of the Holy Spirit and is only of value to the Church when it is lived for God's own purposes.

Section 3. Those who claim that Matrimony is a lesser state than that of a monk and who claim Matrimony an alternative to the state of a monastic are but glory-seekers and know not the correct teachings of the Scriptures and the Fathers. Each state of life in the Christian Faith is a witness and confession of a divine call from God. God's will and purpose must be the aim of each person seeking to live a holy life.

Article V. FAITH AND GOOD WORKS.

Section 1. We believe and hold it true that salvation is a free gift of Faith in Christ Jesus.

Section 2. We believe that good works are a necessary witness of true faith in Christ Jesus.

Section 3. We hold it to be heresy to teach that any or all the saints together could merit the forgiveness of even one sin against God.

Section 4. It is through the sufferings and death of Christ our Lord that our Salvation has been granted to us.

Section 5. Faith and Salvation in Jesus Christ are free gifts from God without any merit on our part.

Section 6. The true faith is to be found in the Holy Scriptures and its true interpretation is found in the teachings of the Seven Holy Synods, the Nicene Creed and the teachings of the Fathers.

Article VI. THE VIRGIN MOTHER OF GOD AND THE SAINTS.

Section 1. We believe the Virgin Mary to be the virgin mother of Christ God, the Incarnate Word of God as taught in the Nicene Creed.

Section 2. We believe Mary to have been ever a Virgin as taught by the Scriptures indirectly and taught by history and the teachings of the Fathers directly.

Section 3. We believe in the communion of Saints, the just who have their Salvation in Faith in Christ Jesus our Lord.

Section 4. We believe that the Saints here on earth and those in heaven pray for us. Yet, we reject the teaching that the saints merit favors or salvation for us. For, they pray to God through the merits of Christ our High Priest and our only Mediator between God and Man. True veneration of the Saints is to follow their way of life and a practice of their example.

Section 5. We reject that to ask the prayers of others, living or dead, is against the teachings of the Christ God. Rather it is an affirmation of Faith in the true nature of the Church, the Body of Christ.

Article VII. THE VENERATION OF ICONS (IMAGES).

Section 1. We believe that respect, veneration and praying before icons is a good and helpful means of calling to mind Christ God and His Saints.

Section 2. Those who believe that icons are gods or alive are guilty of idol worship and those who believe we worship them as a god are guilty of the same sin for they attribute life to wood and paint and paper.

Section 3. The commandment of God forbids us to fall down and worship before any image as a god. It does not forbid us to cherish memories of the truths of our faith in the arts. Whoever says that Scripture forbids the right use of the arts denies the use of our God-given talents for God's honor and glory.

Article VIII. THE SECOND COMING OF CHRIST.

We believe that Christ will come again in the flesh as recorded in the Scripture and taught in the Nicene Creed.

Article IX. MORAL CODE.

Section 1. The moral code of the Christian life is to be found in Holy Scripture, the teachings of the Church and the Fathers.

Section 2. The Ten Commandments and the Two-fold Commandment of Jesus Christ are binding for all generations.

Article X. THE CHURCH.

Section 1. The Church is the Body of Christ, united in the true Faith handed down by the Apostles through the ages, with Christ as its head.

Section 2. We confess Christ to be the only true head of His Church and we accept no other.

Section 3. We believe the Church is guided by the Holy Spirit in all her teachings Holy Tradition (the Scriptures) and its interpretation from the Creed, the Seven Holy Synods and the teachings of the Fathers.

To these Articles of Faith we do confess of our own free will. In this faith we do live and desire to die, with the help of God.

* * *

SUMMARY OF BELIEF OF CHRIST CATHOLIC CHURCH

GOD. We believe that God is the Creator of heaven and earth. We believe that He seeks the fellowship of man that man might dwell in God and God in man.

Although God cannot be understood by the finite mind, He can be experienced. The human mind cannot grasp the significance of God, but it can come into His Presence.

At the Mass, we come to be with Jesus and to unite our hearts and minds with His, so that His Will becomes our will.

No catholic theologian would pretend that he could define God or describe His wonderous glory adequately.

The human mind is simply too small, and God is too great to be compressed or encompassed by any verbal definition.

JESUS CHRIST. We believe Jesus Christ is God and that He is living, true, and eternal. As Son of God, He is the inheritor of God's Heavenly Kingdom. He has come into this world to save us from sin and death and make us joint heirs with Him in His Heavenly Kingdom.

THE HOLY SPIRIT. We believe the Holy Spirit is God and that he dwells among men and seeks to guide and instruct men that they might direct their affairs heavenward.

THE CHURCH. We believe the Church is the Body of our Lord, Jesus Christ. It is the community of the faithful and is governed by our Lord Jesus Christ. It is made up of all those who profess the Christian faith and who faithfully and regularly participate in the celebration of the Mass and receive the blessed Sacrament. Jesus Christ is the one, infallible Head of the Church.

THE RIGHT OF PRIVATE JUDGMENT. We believe the Right of Private Judgment belongs to every member, both lay and clergy, in matters of doctrine. However, a clergyman found heterdox by the Presiding Bishop or the Holy Synod shall be deprived of faculties but shall retain all the rights and privileges of a lay member.

DOCTRINES OF THE CHURCH. The Church's doctrinal position in all matters of faith and practice shall be in accordance with the Holy Scriptures, the Ecumenical Creeds, the Seven Ecumenical Councils, and the Utrecht Confession. We further accept, because they shall conform to the above, the doctrines embodied in the official liturgy of the Church, the catechism, and the Constitution and Canons of this Holy Catholic Church.

* * *

THE LEIPSIC [LEIPZIG] INTERIM OF 1548 [EVANGELICAL ORTHODOX (CATHOLIC) CHURCH]

It is our judgment that obedience should be rendered the Roman Imperial Majesty, and such disposition should be shown that His Imperial Majesty and every one may note that we are all inclined to quiet, peace and unity. [In America, in view of complete separation of Church and State in matters dealing with spiritual authority and administration, all references to Imperial Majesty, princes and potentates have no authority upon us.] This we faithfully advise, and, as far as possible, will for ourselves always serve and admonish. For as some speak and write without cause, our mind and intention is directed to no dissension or unnecessary proceedings, but to all that already mentioned. This we testify before God himself, to whom all men's hearts are known, and this too our work shall and will prove.

Accordingly, we judge, first, that all that the ancient teachers have held in regard to *adiaphora*—i.e. matters of indifference, which may be observed without injury to the Divine Scriptures, and, on the other hand, are still in use— be henceforth observed, and that therein no burden or augmentation should be sought or applied, since this cannot occur without injury to a good conscience.

Secondly, so far as concerns the doctrine, first, of the state and nature of man before and after the fall, there is no controversy.

The Article of Justification is similar to that at Pegau. [Also they teach, that men cannot be Justified before God by their own strength, merits or works, but are freely justified for Christ's sake through faith, when they believe that they are received into favor and that their sins are forgiven for Christ's sake, who, by His death, hath made satisfaction for our sins. This faith God imputes for righteousness in his sight. Rom. 3 and 4.—AUGS. Conf.]

HOW MAN IS JUSTIFIED BEFORE GOD

As now it is said that out of God's wonderful, fathomless counsel his Son has been appointed Mediator and Saviour, and that for his sake the forgiveness of sins, the Holy Ghost, righteousness and eternal life are assuredly given, it should be known further how this exalted and great grace and blessings are received. Namely, thus:

Although God does not justify man by the merit of his own works which man does, but out of mercy, freely, without our merit, that the glory may not be ours, but Christ's, through whose merit alone we are redeemed from sins and justified, yet the merciful God does not work with man as with a block, but draws him, so that his will also co-operates if he be of understanding years. For such a man does not receive the benefits of Christ unless his will and heart be moved by prevenient grace, so that he is terrified before God's wrath and has dislike of sin. For since sin causes enmity between God and man, as Isaiah writes, no one can come to the throne of grace and mercy unless by true repentance he turn from his sins. Hence John when he prepared the way of the Lord, preached with great earnestness: "Repent, for the kingdom of heaven is at hand." And there is no doubt whatever that in conversion there must be pain and terror before God's wrath; and as long as security remains, which perseveres in sins against conscience, there is no conversion and no forgiveness. Isaiah therefore says: "With whom will God dwell? With him that is poor and of a contrite spirit, and trembleth at God's Word." Moses also says: "The Lord they God is a consuming fire"—i.e. he is truly and terribly incensed against all sin, and proclaimed his sentence shortly after the Fall by his Word and by punishments, and afterwards on this account have his law with authentic testimonials, and taught therein that death, ravages and other plagues are admonitions whereby we should recognize his wrath. Besides, he wishes that in his Church until its final redemption sin should be reproved in the heart by the Word and Holy Ghost, as it is written: "The Holy Ghost will reprove the world of sin" [John 16].

THE LEIPSIC [LEIPZIG] INTERIM OF 1548 [EVANGELICAL
ORTHODOX (CATHOLIC) CHURCH] (continued)

But God has not only revealed his wrath, but has also given with it his gracious promise—viz. the Gospel of the Son of God—and it is his immutable will, confirmed by his oath and the blood of his Son and many miracles, that he will assuredly forgive sins, bestow on us the Holy Ghost, receive, renew and make us heirs of eternal blessedness, for his Son's sake, and not because of our merit or worth, if in this terror and pain we truly believe and trust that for the sake of the Mediator sins are assuredly forgiven us.

This true faith believes all the articles of faith. For every one must acknowledge God, and, together with other articles, believe also this: I believe the forgiveness of sins, that it is imparted to me, and not merely to others. For although many who live in an evil conscience, if they also confess the Christian doctrine, boast of their faith, yet it is not a living and justifying faith. For such a heart does not believe that the forgiveness of sins is given it individually, neither does it appropriate the promise, but flees from God, and both comfort in God and true invocation of him are absent. There is no doubt that the faith of the devil, who is grievously terrified before God's judgment, is a far different thing from this true faith, which appropriates the promise and gracious comfort, as Paul clearly testifies (Rom. 4), that he speaks of that faith which appropriates the promise, which is not merely knowledge, as in the devil or in men who live in evil conscience, but this faith, together with the other articles, believes the forgiveness of sins, appropriates the promise and is at heart a true trust upon the Son of God, which works consolation, invocation and other virtues; of which faith the words of Isaiah, which Paul quotes in Rom. 10, speak: "He that trusteth in him shall not be brought to confusion." And it is sure that there is no other way to God and to attain forgiveness of sins and grace than this alone through the Son of God, as it is written: "No one cometh to the Father, but by the Son." Therefore, the Holy Ghost is likewise given in our hearts if we thus grasp by faith the divine promises, and comfort and support ourselves therewith, as is clearly expressed in Gal. 3, that we receive the promise of the Holy Ghost by faith; and the Holy Ghost then works in the heart steadfast trust and life, and enkindles all necessary virtues, firm faith, invocation, fear of God, love, good intentions, hope and other virtues. And they who have thus received the forgiveness of sins and the Holy Ghost, and in whom the Holy Ghost begins faith and trust in the Son of God, love and hope, then become heirs of eternal salvation for the Saviour's sake, as Paul writes (Rom. 6): "Eternal life is a gift of God, through Jesus Christ our Lord."

And as God has always graciously continued to build and maintain a Church ever since he received again Adam and Eve, and gave them the promise of a future Saviour, he has continued also to maintain this understanding of forgiveness and faith, although indeed among many it was often obscured, who sought forgiveness by their own works, or remained fettered by doubts, as the heathen, among whom the remembrance of the promise no longer remains; yet God has clearly expressed this meaning in his Scriptures, and continues to declare it in his Church, in order that the knowledge and honor of his Son may not be effaced, and that he may continue to collect a Church and save many men.

But in the Christian Church all men should know both parts and truly believe. He who lives in sins against conscience should assuredly judge that he is in God's wrath, and that if he be not converted he will fall into eternal punishment; so again in true conversion it is God's earnest will and command that we accept his promise, and believe that not because of our worth, but because of the Redeemer and Mediator, God is gracious to us, will forgive our sins, and will accept and help us, etc.

But as some say that this is strange language, and that every one, nevertheless, experience that much doubt concerning God still inheres and remains in the heart, this is indeed true; much doubt, struggling and fleeing from God are and remain in all men. This weakness is the injury resulting from original sin. But God, on the other hand, has given us his promise to comfort and strengthen us, that we may overcome doubt and flee to God for refuge. And when St. Paul says: "I know nothing by myself; yet am I not thereby justified," he does not teach that we should doubt, but wishes us to assuredly hold both points—viz. that the conscience should stand erect, but that therewith still many faults remain in us, and therefore we should know that we are nevertheless righteous—i.e. pleasing to God, for his Son's sake; and that is correct which Augustine says: "The certainty of entire trust should be in the precious blood of Christ." And it is divine, immutable truth that in the heart which has received through faith the forgiveness of sins the Holy Ghost, prayer, love, hope and other virtues enter, and there must be therein a good intention and a good conscience, as Paul says, that faith and a good conscience must be together. John also says: "He that loveth not abideth in death."

This is all certainly true. And although, by the help of divine grace, they are able to live without vices and mortal sins, yet at the same time it must be known that in this weak life there is still much inclination against God's commandments, much ignorance, doubt and manifold irregularities, as St. Paul says to the Romans, chap. 7: "I see another law in my members, warring against the law of my mind." And the Psalmist says: "In thy sight shall no man living be justified." And Daniel says: "We do not present our supplications before thee for our righteousness, but for thy great mercies."

Although, therefore, a new obedience has been begun, yet we must not think that one has on this account forgiveness of sins, and is thus so pure that he needs no forgiveness of sins and no Mediator. The Son of God is, and continually remains, Mediator, and in God's secret counsel stands and prays for us that the grievous wrath of God against sin may not be poured out upon us. And it is not enough to say that God will not take account of the weakness that remains, and considers the person to be without sin, thus causing false confidence in one's own righteousness; but there must be in us both—viz. a good conscience and inchoate obedience; and besides this humility and faith—viz. that we confess that we still have sin, and that there is in us serious pain and displeasure at our sins; that we also confess that we have merited punishment, and are therein subject to God, as Daniel says: "O Lord, righteousness belongeth unto thee; but unto us shame and confusion of face." Besides, there must also be a necessary confidence that God will certainly receive persons, and, for his Son's sake, be gracious. This trust that thus contemplates the Mediator in God's judgment must always in this weak life overshadow the other virtues. When, therefore, Paul says: "Being justified by faith," this expression must not be understood in such sense as that faith alone is a preparation—viz. a confession—and procures other virtues because of which the person is truly justified; but his own honor should be accorded the Son of God, that he is and remains Mediator. We should also abide in this humility, that we confess we still have sins and need grace, and that God will certainly be thus gracious to us if, in this humility, we believe he is gracious to us for his Son's sake.

And that this consolation is necessary for all the godly every one experiences in his heart. In all anxiety and with intent invocation we all exclaim: "Alas, I am a poor sinner; I am not worthy that God should hear me." In such need we should not teach a man to imagine: "I have now many excellent virtues, and therefore I am pure;" but he should flee for refuge to the Son of God, and know that he should trust in the same because of the promise, as Daniel writes: "Not for our righteousness, but through mercy for the Lord's sake"—i.e. for the sake of the promised Saviour.

From all this it is clear both that it is true that in us a new obedience should begin, and yet that faith and trust in the Son of God must continue to abide, and receive the consolation that God is gracious to us for his Son's sake; and where this faith ceases there cannot be love and refuge to God and true prayer; but this faith works consolation, love and prayer, as it is said, and is not without love.

In those thus reconciled, virtues and good works should be called righteousness, yet not in the sense that the person on this account has forgiveness of sins or that the person is, in God's judgment, without sin, but that, for his Son's sake, God regards this weak, inchoate obedience of believers in this miserable, infirm, impure nature with pleasure; and of these works as righteousness John speaks when he says: "He that doeth righteousness is righteous." And it is true that where the works are contrary to God, there is contempt of God, and no conversion to God has occurred in the heart. As is the tree, so also are the fruits; as we have still further to say.

OF GOOD WORKS

We also have no doubt that our doctrine and interpretation of good works is in agreement with the Divine Scriptures and the understanding of the Catholic Church of all times; and since our writings on this subject have been published, there is no need of a long statement here. Yet, that there may be a definite rule, we declare that those works are good and necessary which God has commanded, according to the Ten Commandments and their explanation sufficiently set forth in the writings of the apostles. According to this rule, a distinction is to be made between a good and an evil conscience. And, as before said, it is God's serious command that we should live in good

conscience, and, as St. Paul writes, hold faith and a good conscience. He who perseveres in sins contrary to conscience is not converted to God, and is still God's enemy, and God's wrath abides upon him if he be not converted. This is precisely in accord with Gal. 5: "Of that which I tell you before, as I have told you in time past, that they which do such things shall not inherit the kingdom of God." God, too, has comprised both in an oath—viz. that this conversion is necessary, and that the forgiveness of sins should be believed: "As I live, I have no pleasure in the death of the wicked, but that the wicked turn from his way and live." Therefore, where there is no conversion there is no grace. This all intelligent persons know without a long explanation.

Further, if any one who has been in God's grace acts against God's command or his conscience, he grieves the Holy Ghost, loses grace and righteousness and falls beneath God's wrath; and if he be not again converted he falls into eternal punishment, as Saul and others. This is clearly expressed in Rom. 8: "We are debtors, not to the flesh, to live after the flesh; for if ye live after the flesh ye shall die"—i.e. if ye follow your wicked inclinations contrary to conscience, ye shall fall into eternal punishment. And such sins merit not only eternal punishment after this life, but also many grievous punishments in this life, whereby their perpetrators and many others with them are surprised; as David's adultery and murder were punished.

For these reasons, to speak briefly, it is readily understood that good works are necessary, for God has commanded them; and if the course of life be in opposition thereto, God's grace and the Holy Ghost are rejected, and such sins merit eternal condemnation. But virtues and good works please God thus, as we have said, in the reconciled, because, they believe that God receives their person for Christ's sake, and will be pleased with this imperfect obedience; and it is true that eternal life is given for the sake of the Lord Christ out of grace, and at the same time that all are heirs of eternal salvation who are converted to God and by faith receive forgiveness of sins and the Holy Ghost. Nevertheless, the new virtues and good works are so highly necessary that if they were not quickened in the heart there would be no reception of divine grace. Thus, there must be in us a reception of divine grace, and its consolation is not an indolent thought, but life and deliverance from great trouble, as King Hezekiah says, Isa. 38: "God, as a lion, did break all my bones; but he hath delivered my soul, and cast all my sins behind my back." Paul says: "We will be clothed upon, so that we shall not be found naked." And Rev. 2: "Be thou faithful unto death, and I will give thee a crown of life." In these passages two things are comprised: the first, that in this life the beginning must be made of eternal salvation; the second, that before our end we must not fall away therefrom.

Thus regeneration and eternal life are in themselves a new light, fear of God, love, joy in God and other virtues; as the passage says: "This is life eternal, to know thee the only true God, and me, Jesus Christ." As, now, this true knowledge must shine in us, it is certainly true that these virtues, faith, love, hope and others, must be in us, and are necessary to salvation. All this is easy for the godly to understand who seek to experience consolation from God. And since the virtues and good works please God, as has been said, they merit also a reward in this life, both spiritual and temporal, according to God's counsel, and still more reward in eternal life, because of the divine promise.

But by this the error of the manks is in no way confirmed, that eternal salvation is merited by the worth of our works; also, that we can communicate our merit to others; but faith acknowledges our own weakness and flees for refuge to the Son of God, and receives this eternal consolation from his merit and treasure because of his gracious and exceeding abundant rich promise, and knows that we are always in conversion under obligation to believe God, who has there promised grace, and confirmed this promise with his oath, and regards despair as an affront against God, and thus the greatest sin.

Good works are adorned further in the Divine Scriptures with many temporal promises and great praise, whereof we have besides given Christian instruction at length in our writing, as we will continue always to do. For God wishes to be recognized and invoked also in temporal gifts, and that this invocation be made in faith and a good conscience.

What is to be said further of works which God has not commanded will be mentioned hereafter.

OF ECCLESIASTICAL POWER AND AUTHORITY

What the true Christian Church, which is collected in the Holy Ghost, acknowledges determines and teaches in regard to matters of faith should be taught and preached, as it neither should nor can determine anything contrary to the Holy Scriptures.

OF ECCLESIASTICAL MINISTERS

That hereafter learned men should be presented and appointed to the prebendaryships in the bishoprics who have such understanding in the Divine Scriptures that they are competent to exercise the episcopal office, and for the care of the archdiaconate and the jurisdiction of the Church, and can rightly administer the same. And that by the statutes and customs which obtain in some bishoprics only qualified persons should be made canons—godly men who would be serviceable in the episcopal office, and would not be a hindrance; but since in the Papal ordinances and decrees they have been cashiered and dismissed, and it was found that the chapters were full of idle and unlearned men, learned pastors and ministers should be ordained who are capable and fit to teach the Word of God and in a Christian way to preside over the people.

And that all other ministers should be subject and obedient to the chief and other bishops who administer their episcopal office according to God's command, and use the same for edification and not for destruction; which ministers should be ordained also by such bishops upon presentation by the patrons. These ministers also when

they transgress, and especially the priests whose life is immoral or who urge impure doctrine, should be punished by the ordinary means, as by the deprivation of their office, and finally by excommunication.

OF BAPTISM

That infant baptism, together with exorcism, the assistance and confession of sponsors, and other ancient Christian ceremonies, should be taught and retained.

OF CONFIRMATION

That confirmation should be taught and retained, and especially that the youth when they have come to mature years should be examined as to their faith by their bishops or by persons to whom this is entrusted, that they confess it, and ratify the promises and renunciation of the devil made for them at baptism by their sponsors, and thus by the aid of divine grace be confirmed and established by the laying on of hands and Christian prayer and ceremonies.

OF REPENTENCE

That repentence, confession and absolution, and what pertains thereto, be diligently taught and preached, that the people confess to the priests, and receive of them absolution in God's stead, and be also diligently admonished and urged to prayer, fasting and almsgiving. Also, that no one to be admitted to the highly-venerable sacrament of the body and blood of Christ unless he have first confessed [to the priest] and received [of him] absolution. Besides, that the people be diligently taught and instructed that in this sacrament we are united with Jesus Christ our Saviour as the Head with the members of his body, so that by it we are nursed and nourished to all good. Also, that we grow in communion with the saints. For "we, being many, are one bread and one body," as St. Paul says.

That the people should be taught also that whoever partakes of this sacrament unworthily eats and drinks damnation to himself, and should therefore be urged to forsake his sinful life and to true repentance, prayer, alms, temperance and other Christian virtues. For whoever will receive and support life must avoid the cause of death, and must follow and obey the Physician who beckons us on and has gone before.

OF [EXTREME] UNCTION

Although in this country the unction has not been in use for many years, yet since it is written in Mark and James how the apostles used it, since James says: "Is any sick among you? Let him call for the elders of the Church, and let them pray over him, anointing him with oil in the name of the Lord; and the prayer of faith shall save the sick, and the Lord shall raise him up,"—such unction, according to the apostle, may be hereafter observed, and Christian prayer and words of consolation from the Holy Scriptures be spoken over the sick; and that the people should be instructed concerning this in such way as to reach the true understanding, and that all superstition and misunderstanding be removed and avoided.

ORDINATION OF MINISTERS

Also, that, as has been said, ministers should hereafter be ordained with Christian ceremonies, upon the presentation of patrons, by such bishops as administer their episcopal office, and that no one be allowed in the ministry unless, as has been said, he be presented by the patrons and have the permission of the bishops, so that no one may unbecomingly force himself or have himself appointed in a disorderly way. And that the sham examinations whereby many unlearned and unsuitable men have become pastors and church officers, to the grievous damage of conscience, be abolished; and that the bishops earnestly and diligently examine candidates for ordination, and especially those presented by patrons for ecclesiastical offices, in all ways themselves, and with the counsel, presence and co-operation of godly and learned men, in order that they may be found so qualified and suitable in doctrine, intelligence, life and walk as to be able aright to feed the flock of the Lord with God's Word, provide it with doctrine and example, and to administer their office.

OF MARRIAGE

That in all estates in this country marriage be observed according to God's institution.

OF THE MASS

That the mass be observed henceforth in this country, with ringing of bells, with lights and vessels, with chants, vestments and ceremonies. In places where there are sufficient persons the priests and ministrants should go in a becoming way before the altar in their regular church vestments and robes, speak in the beginning the *Confiteor*, and that the *Introit*, the *Kyrie eleison*, the *Gloria in excelsis Deo, et in terra*, etc., and the *Dominus vobiscum*, the Collects, the Epistle, and all that now current in Latin, be sung. And when the Epistle is sung, it should then be also read to the people in German; the *Gradual*, the *Hallelujah*, the *Sequence*, or a *Tractus* according to the occasion of the time or festival. The Gospel to be sung in Latin, and read to the people in German. The *Credo in unum Deum* according to the Creed throughout, as is customary in the chapters. In parishes where there is no chapter, for the *Gradual* the old German hymns may be sung: at Christmas, *Ein Kindelein so lobelich*; at Easter, *Christ ist erstanden*; at Whitsunday, *Nun bitten wirden heiligen Geist*, etc.; and instead of the Creed, *Wir glauben all an einen Gott, etc*. The sermon to be on the Gospel. The *Dominus vobiscum*, the *Oremus*, the *Offertorium*, the *Praefatio*, the *Sanctus*, the *Consecratio*, the Lord's Prayer in German, the *Agnus Dei*, the *Communio* and administration of the sacrament, the *Communicatio*, or partaking, Collects, the Benediction. Amended: The Liturgy remains the same—the language to be that commonly spoken and used by the local congregation: (German, French, Spanish, and English for British and American bodies.)

OF IMAGES

The images and pictures of the sufferings of Christ and of the saints may be also retained in the churches, and the people should be taught that they are there only as remembrances, and to these things no divine honor should be attached. To the images and pictures of the saints, however, no superstitious resort should occur or be encouraged.

OF SINGING IN THE CHURCHES

In the churches where they have been formerly observed the "canonical hours," the devout Psalms, should be sung in the chapters and towns at their times and on other high festivals, and also on Sundays. And therefore the usual ancient chants also be retained, according to the time and the chief festivals. There may be singing at and after burial, at the request of those who desire it, in memory of the dead and of our promise and sure resurrection.

OF HOLIDAYS

Sunday; our Lord's Birthday; St. Stephen's Day; St. John the Evangelist's Day; the Circumcision of the Lord; Day of the Three Holy Kings; Easter and the two days following; the Ascension of the Lord; Whitsunday, with the two days following; *Corpus Christi*; the Festivals of the Holy Virgin Mary; the days of the Holy Apostles; of St. John the Baptist; of St. Mary Magdalene; of St. Michael and some others, on which there should be only Church services, with preaching and mass and communion, as, of the Conversion of Paul; of the Beheading of John; Thursday, Friday and Saturday in Passion Week.

OF THE EATING OF MEAT

Likewise, that on Fridays and Saturdays, also in fasts, the eating of meat be abstained from, and that this be observed as an external ordinance [at the command of His Imperial Majesty]. Yet that those whom necessity excuses, as hard laborers, travellers, women with child and those in childbed, old weak persons, and children, be not bound hereby.

OF THE DEPORTMENT OF MINISTERS

And we regard it becoming and good that pastors and ministers, in their dress as well as otherwise, by propriety of deportment demean themselves in a clerical and creditable way, and that with the co-operation and advice of the bishops or consistories they make an arrangement with one another, and observe it, so that in their apparel a distinction may be observed between ministers and worldly persons, and proper reverence may be paid the priestly estate. And that every one should give due consideration to his pastor, preacher and minister also with respect to doctrine and deportment, and report whatever faults may be found to the bishop or consistory, who should remedy the wrong.

CONCLUSION

In other articles we are ready to diligently observe the Scriptures and the ancient teachers, and to show our friends and gracious lords the bishops our judgment, and in a friendly and submissive manner to confer with Their Beloved and Princely Graces, and to settle our differences in a Christian way.

Notes: *One of the least-heralded statements of the Reformation Era in Germany was the Leipsic [Leipzig] Interim of 1548. It was occasioned by the temporary rule of Catholic forces in Protestant territories in the middle of the sixteenth century. Written by a group of theologians under Philip Melancthon, it retained the major affirmation of Protestant thought, justification by grace through faith, while prescribing Roman ritual and practice. The necessity of the Interim was ended by the Peace of Augsburg in 1555.*

THE LEIPSIC [LEIPZIG] INTERIM OF 1548 [EVANGELICAL ORTHODOX (CATHOLIC) CHURCH] (continued)

The Evangelical Orthodox (Catholic) Church, which considers itself a non-papal Catholic body, adopted this all-but-forgotten document in 1941 as a "clearly written declaration of their position as Catholics in the true sense of the word."

* * *

TENETS OF FAITH (MARIAVITE OLD CATHOLIC CHURCH–PROVINCE OF NORTH AMERICA)

1. The Mariavite Old Catholic Churches bases itself upon the old Catholic tenets of faith and morals. These tenets are contained in the canonical books of the Holy Scripture of the Old and New Testament as well as in the early Tradition of the Universal Church and which were defined at the first seven Ecumenical Councils.

2. The Mariavite Old Catholic Church does not enact new dogmas and also does not admit dogmas, which individual Churches enacted after the separation of Christianity in the year 1054 into Roman Catholicism and Orthodoxy, since it observes, that only an Ecumenical Council (that is: representing all of Christianity) may enact a new dogma which obligates all Christians.

3. The Mariavite Old Catholic Church does not recognize the primacy of any Bishop in the Universal Church, as well as the infallability of an individual in matters of faith and morals.

4. In the Mariavite Old Catholic Church from 1924, there does not exist an obligatory clerical celibacy—consequently there are celibates and the married. All are obligated to maintain the Franciscan spirit.

5. The Mariavite Old Catholic Church believes, that God performs miracles in the soul of an individual, but it does not recognize so-called miraculous relics, pictures, and so forth; it does not however, reject the great respect which should surround pictures of religious content as well as relics and remembrances of the Saints.

6. Auricular (private) confession before the priest obliges children and youth to age 18. Adults (at their own request) may also profit from it, but what obliges them is the general confession before Christ with the absolution of the priest. (Until the year 1930, private confession obligated everyone.)

7. The Mariavite Old Catholic Church recognizes seven Holy Sacraments, namely: Baptism, Penance, Holy Eucharist, Confirmation, Holy Orders, Matrimony, and Extreme Unction.

8. Holy Communion is distributed to the faithful under both species (from the year 1922).

9. The Mariavite Old Catholic Church bases itself likewise on the Revelation of Divine Mercy, received by the Foundress of Mariavitism, the blessed Mother Maria Franciszka Kozlowska (the first revelation August 2nd, 1893), showing, that the salvation for the world threatened by its sins is in Christ present in the Most Blessed Sacrament, in Whom it is proper to believe and adore as well as in the invocation of the Perpetual Help of the Most Blessed Virgin Mary.

10. The spiritual purpose of the Mariavite Old Catholic Church is the furtherance of devotion for Jesus Christ concealed in the Most Blessed Sacrament and pointing out the need of invoking the perpetual help of the Most Blessed Mother, "because as there are perpetual efforts against God and the Church, thus is needed the Perpetual Help of Mary."

11. The worship of the Most Blessed Sacrament in the life of the faithful is expressed in the frequent and worthy reception of Holy Communion, accordingly to the words of Christ: "Unless you eat the body of the Son of Man and drink His blood, you have no life in yourselves" (John 6:53), as well as in the performance of the Adoration of Supplication. Each of the members has an obligation to perform an hourly Adoration of the Most Blessed Sacrament once in the week and in common, solemnly once in the month as well as the participation in the Holy Sacrifice of the Mass on Sundays and Holydays. The Clergy and Religious Sisters have the obligation to perform the Adoration daily.

12. The Clergy of the Mariavite Old Catholic Church remain under the protection of the Mother of God of Perpetual Help.

13. The Mariavite Old Catholic Church bears in its name the name of Mary, indicating the indispensability of imitating Her life: of solitude, of humility, spirit of prayer, great love for neighbor and readiness to fulfill the Will of God.

14. The Holy Sacrifice of the Mass and the entire liturgy (from Christmas Midnight Mass 1907) are celebrated exclusively in the language of the people. The use of the Latin language and the Polish language are also common in the Church of the Province of North America. The Mariavite Old Catholic Church does not recognize the need for liturgical reforms or innovations which water-down or often destroy Catholic belief, as is often witnessed in the state of affairs within the Roman Catholic Church since Vatican II. Rather, the Mariavite Old Catholic Church steadfastly preserves and maintains the old and traditional manner of celebrating the Holy Sacrifice of the Mass and performing rites and ceremonies as were common in the Roman Catholic Church before Vatican II and prior to the Holy Week reforms of Pope Pius XII in the early 1950's.

15. All religious ministrations are without cost, in agreement with the recommendation of Christ: "Freely you have received, freely give" (Mat. 10:8). It is however, permissable for the clergy to accept voluntary offerings for religious ministrations, but they cannot demand them.

16. The Mariavite Old Catholic Church received the Apostolic Succession from the Old Catholic Church of Holland. The Roman Catholic Church has always recognized as valid, the Holy Orders and Sacraments of the Old Catholic Church of Holland, and those of the Mariavite Old Catholic Church.

17. The Mariavite Old Catholic Church supports the ecumenical ideal, it cooperates with all Christian denominations; it is a member of the Polish Ecumenical Council and the World Council of Churches, it may belong to organizations with ecumenical or peace aims.

Notes: *The Mariavite Old Catholic Church is an independent jurisdiction that derives its beliefs from those of the Mariavite Old Catholic Church headquartered in Plock, Poland (with whom it has no official connection). The tenets make several specific references to the Mariavites, especially their devotion to the Virgin Mary, from which the church's name is derived. Article 17 is somewhat misleading, however. Although the Mariavite Old Catholic Church of Poland is a member of the Polish Ecumenical Council and the World Council of Churches, the Mariavite Old Catholic Church–Province of North America has no such connections.*

*   *   *

DOCTRINAL STATEMENT OF THE NORTH AMERICAN OLD ROMAN CATHOLIC CHURCH

Retaining as its goal a return to the ancient Catholicity of the Church of the first thousand years the North American Old Roman Catholic Church considers the Sacred Scriptures of both the Old and New Testaments, in which are found the record of the revelation of God himself to man through his people, Israel, and in his Son, Jesus Christ, the basic rule of the Christian Faith. In interpreting this scriptural revelation, the North American Old Roman Catholic Church accepts and seeks to apply the tradition of the Apostles and Fathers of the early Church. This tradition is received according to the Vincentian Canon, which dates from the fifth century:

> *In ipsa item Catholica Ecclesia magnopere curandum est, ut teneamus, quod ubique quod semper ab omnibus creditum est. Hoc est enim vere proprieque Catholicum—quod ipsa vis nominis ratioque declarat, quod omnia fere universaliter comprehendit. Sed hoc fiet si sequimur universalitatem, antiquitatem, consensionem.* (Vincent of Lérins, Commonitorium pro Catholicae fidei antiquitate et universalitate, capitalum III.)

Based on this canon, the North American Old Roman Catholic Church perseveres in professing the faith of the ancient Church as enfleshed in the Apostles' and Niceno-Constantinopolitan Creeds, and in the decisions of the Seven Ecumenical Councils of the Undivided Church. The North American Old Roman Catholic Church, retaining traceable unbroken succession of Orders from the undivided Church, adheres to the forms and formulae established by the early Roman Church in order to preserve the deposit of faith received through Roman Tradition.

True to the ancient heritage, the North American Old Roman Catholic Church holds the catholic doctrines of the Incarnation, honoring the Virgin Mary as the Mother of God and the ancient doctrine of the Virgin birth, of the Passion, Death, Resurrection and Ascension of the Lord Jesus Christ; and the personal union in him of two natures, one human, the other divine. If further adheres to the medieval doctrine of original sin, the eternal punishment of hell and the necessity of faith for salvation. The church teaches the doctrine of the real presence of Christ in the Eucharist and the spiritual efficacy of the Mass for both the living and the dead.

The North American Old Roman Catholic Church rejects those teachings of the Roman Church which have no warrant in Scripture or ancient tradition, such as the treasury of merits, indulgences, the novel doctrine of the Immaculate Conception and Papal Infallibility. Auricular confession is not obligatory; sins may be confessed before the congregation or a priest. Celibacy is optional. Women are not eligible for the priesthood.

In order to safeguard the validity of its sacramental ministrations, the North American Old Roman Catholic Church conforms strictly to the *Pontificale*, the *Missale* and *Rituale Romanum* of Pius V 1570. Each of the seven sacraments is administered according to the canons and prescriptions of the Western Rite. Liturgical vesture is also that of the Western Rite, while sacramentals and devotions of the Western Rite, as originating from the Roman Church, are utilized while avoiding the excesses that often lead to superstition.

The belief of the North American Old Roman Catholic Church, in accord with the historic faith of the undivided Church of the first thousand years is delineated by four documents. All of which follow hereafter.

The first document is the Statement of Union which served as the basis for the reception of the Old Roman Catholic Church of Great Britain (Western Orthodox Church) into Antiochene Orthodoxy by Archbishop Gerassimos Messerah of Beirut, on August 5, 1911. The second document is referred to as the Fourteen Theses. They resulted from the Old Catholic Union Conference of 1874, held at the University of Bonn. This conference, consisting of members of the Orthodox, Old Catholic and Anglican Churches, directed itself toward a confederation of the Churches on the basis of union in essentials and freedom in non-essentials. The Union Conference of the following year, also held in Bonn, produced the third document, an agreement resolving the time-worn Filioque controversy. The last document is the profession of faith, called the Declaration of Utrecht, which was formulated by the essembled Old Catholic Bishops at Utrecht on September 24, 1889.

The North American Old Roman Catholic Church, although not a member of the historic Old Catholic Churches of the Union of Utrecht, in the light of the above, thus considers itself an orthodox church, Catholic in its retension of the historic faith derived in unbroken line from the ancient church, without any doctrinal innovations, North American in its intended field of mission, and Old Roman in the ancient tradition of the apostolic see of Rome in the undivided Church.

*　　*　　*

PROFESSION OF FAITH (OLD CATHOLIC CHURCH IN AMERICA)

I, N.N., with a firm faith believe and profess all and every one of those things which are contained in that creed which the holy Catholic Church—that is, the Old Catholic Church—makes use of. To wit: I BELIEVE in one God, the Father almighty, maker of heaven and earth and of all things visible and invisible. And in one Lord JESUS Christ, the only-begotten Son of God. Born of the Father before all ages. God of God, light of light, true God of true God. Begotten not made, being of one substance with the Father; by Whom all things were made. Who for us men, and for our salvation, came down from heaven, and was incarnate by the Holy Spirit of the Virgin Mary: and was made Man. He was crucified also for us, suffered under Pontius Pilate, and was buried. And the third day He rose again according to the Scriptures. And ascended into heaven. He sitteth at the right hand of the Father. And He shall come again with glory to judge both the living and the dead; of Whose kingdom there shall be no end. And in the Holy Spirit, the Lord and giver of life: Who proceedeth from the Father. Who together with the Father and the Son is worshipped and glorified. Who spoke by the prophets. And in one, holy, catholic and apostolic Church. I confess one baptism for the remission of sins. And I look for the resurrection of the dead. And the life of the age to come. Amen.

I most steadfastly admit and embrace the apostolical and ecclesiastical Traditions, and all other observances and constitutions of the same Church.

I also admit the holy Scriptures, according to that sense which our holy mother the Church has held and does hold, to whom it belongs to judge of the true sense and interpretation of the Scriptures; neither will I ever take and interpret them otherwise than according to the consent of the Fathers.

I also profess that there are truly and properly Seven Sacraments of the new law, instituted by JESUS Christ our Lord, and necessary for the salvation of mankind, though not all for every one: to wit, Baptism, Confirmation, the Eucharist, Penance, Extreme Unction, Holy Orders, and Matrimony: and that they confer grace: and that of these Baptism, Confirmation, and Holy Orders cannot be repeated without sacrilege. I also receive and admit the received and approved ceremonies of the Old Catholic Church used in the solemn administration of the aforesaid Sacraments.

I profess, likewise, that in the Mass there is offered to God a true, proper, and propitiatory sacrifice for the living and the dead. And that in the most holy sacrament of the Eucharist there is truly, really and substantially the Body and Blood, together with the soul and divinity, of our Lord JESUS Christ; and that there is made a conversion of the whole substance of the bread into the Body, and of the whole substance of the wine into the Blood; which Conversion the Old Catholic Church calls Transubstantiation.

I constantly hold that there is a Purgatory, and that the souls therein detained are helped by the suffrages of the faithful.

Likewise, that the Saints reigning together with Christ are to be honored and invoked, and that they offer prayers to God for us, and that their relics are to be had in veneration.

I most firmly assert that the Images of Christ, of the Ever-Virgin Mother of God, and also of other Saints, ought to be had and retained and that due honor and veneration are to be given them.

I acknowledge the Old Catholic Church to be truly the One, Holy, Catholic and Apostolic Church; and I promise true obedience to her bishops as the successors of the Apostles and of JESUS Christ.

I likewise undoubtingly receive and profess all other things delivered, defined, and declared by the sacred canons and General Councils. And I reject all things contrary thereto, and all heresies which the Church hath condemned, rejected, and anathematized.

I, N.N., do at this present time freely profess and sincerely hold this true, Catholic Faith, which I acknowledge to be essential for my salvation: and I promise most constantly to retain and confess the same entire and inviolate, by God's assistance, to the end of my life.

Notes: *The Profession of Faith of the Old Catholic Church in America is a variation of the profession of the Roman Catholic Church.*

*　　*　　*

ARTICLES OF FAITH [CONGREGATION OF ST. PAUL, THE OLD CATHOLIC CHURCH (HAMEL)]

1.　God is principal; his attributes manifest only through matter to the outer man. God is not a person, nor does he appear to the outer man in any form of cloud or glory. God is a spirit, and they who worship him must worship him in spirit and in truth.

2.　The power and glory of God's dominion neither increases nor diminishes by man's belief or disbelief; and God does not set aside his laws to please mankind.

3.　The ego in man is of God, and at one with God, and is consequently immortal and everlasting.

4.　The forms of man and woman are manifestations of the truth of God, but God does not manifest himself in the form of man or woman as a being.

5.　Man's body is the temple in which the soul resides, and from the windows of which we view God's creations and evolutions.

6. At the transition or separation of the soul and body, the soul enters that secret state where none of the conditions of the earth have any charms, but the soft breeze and great power of the Holy Ghost bring comfort and solace to the weary or the anxious who are awaiting future action. Those who fail, however, to exercise the blessings and gifts of God, and who follow the dictates of the tempter and of the false prophet and the ensnaring doctrines of the wicked, remain in the bosom of the earth until they are freed from the binding powers of materialism, purified and assigned to the secret kingdom.

7. To keep holy the one sacred day of the week, that the soul may commune in spirit and ascend to contact with God, resting from all labours, and discriminating in all actions.

8. To keep silent in disputes, to close the eyes before evil, and to stop the ears before the blasphemers.

9. To preserve the Sacred Doctrines from the profane, never to speak of them to those who are not ready or qualified to understand, and be prepared always to reveal to the world that knowledge which will enable man to rise to greater heights.

10. To remain steadfast in all friendships and all brotherly relations, even unto death; in all positions of trust never to abuse the power or privilege granted, and, in all human relationships to be kind and forgiving, even to the enemies of the Faith.

* * *

CREDO (PROFESSION OF FAITH) (POLISH NATIONAL CATHOLIC CHURCH OF AMERICA)

1. I believe in God, the Almighty, cause and reason of all existence; in the most perfect Being, whose Spirit permeates this universe, who is the source of all material and spiritual life and its development. God, in relation to man, reveals Himself by His omnipotence, His creative power, by His omniscience and with His divine providence molds the fate of every man, all nations, kingdoms, and all mankind. God, in His inimitable way, for He is the Spirit of true life, light, and good, influences chosen souls of all nations, who in epochs of the development of mankind are the creative factors in the edification of His kingdom, God's kingdom on earth. God does not limit exclusively His influence to any one nation, race, epoch, or era; but implies it for all nations and all times, giving life, nurturing its development and attainment of the highest degree of culture of each individual nation, country, and all mankind. This divine influence is the outflow or result of His godly powers over man, and fruits of His spiritual beneficence are reaped by all individuals, nations, countries, races, and mankind.

2. I believe in Jesus Christ, the Redeemer, Spiritual Regenerater and Guide of this earth. I believe that Christ, our Lord, was the Messenger of God, being of the substance with God, the Father, and was born of a poor woman, Mary; that this Master of Nazareth revealed His godly mission on earth, by His life of the most supreme of ideals of good, wisdom, and sacrifice for all mankind; especially, for those who have marred their souls with sin and for the disinherited hath He also given His life on the cross. I believe that by His labors, teachings, and martyrdom, He became the glowing ember of all true, new human life, taking His beginning, strength, and fullness in the comprehension and acknowledgment of God, the Father, by loving Him, and fulfilling His sacred will.

3. I believe in the Holy Spirit, that the spirit of God controls this universe in a natural and moral order, that all His laws in the universe, and those with which He governs the souls of individual man, as well as collective humanity, are the results flowing from His spirit of strong will-power, good, and justice.

4. From this Holy Spirit flows His grace, that is an invisible, internal, creative power, which infers that if man cooperates and coordinates with this Spirit, he will become a partisan of peace of mind and soul, until he finds himself in union with God, in eternal, sublime, good fortune.

5. I believe in the necessity of uniting all believers, confessors of the Christian faith, into one body, the church of God; that the Christian, Apostolic, Universal Church is the representation of God's congregation of mankind, so proclaimed by the Saviour for whose existence worked and labored all noble people, and for which yearns and longs the human soul, ever desiring truth, light, love, justice, and complete appeasement in God.

6. I believe the Christian church is the true teacher, preceptor of all mankind, that it is the steward of God's graces, leader and light of our temporal pilgrimage to God and salvation; inasmuch as the confessors and members of this church, both lay and clerical, are united with the Divine Founder through faith and life emanating from this sincere faith.

7. I believe that every righteous Christian should take an active part in the spiritual life of the church, and this by listening to God's Word, through worthy receiving of the holy sacraments, and through fulfilling the principles founded by Jesus Christ and His Apostles, which have been submitted to us by the Church of Christ.

8. I believe that all people, as children of one Father, our God, are equal; that privileges, flowing from a difference in the racial, sexual, and religious status, or caste, or from the possession of unlimited riches, are a great wrong and injury, they are a violation, a rupture of the principles and laws of man with which he is endowed by his Creator and a blot on the escutcheon of man's worthiness, bestowed by God: that these unmerited privileges are a detriment to man in attaining his aim in life.

CREDO (PROFESSION OF FAITH) (POLISH NATIONAL CATHOLIC CHURCH OF AMERICA) (continued)

9. I believe that all people have the same inalienable right to life, to happiness, and to those means and ways which lead to the preservation of existence, to the betterment and salvation of our souls; but I also believe that all people have sacred obligations, duties, tasks to God, themselves, their nation, government, and to all humanity.

10. I believe in the ultimate justice of God; in future eternal life, which will be a continuation of our mortal struggle and pilgrimage on this earth; as to the condition and degree of perfection and happiness, dependent as it is, upon our present life, and above all, upon the state of our soul in the last few moments of this life.

11. I believe in immortality and happiness in the life to come; in the union of people with God, all generations, and at all times; because I firmly believe in the omnipotence of God's love, mercy, justice, and nothing else do I desire, but that it might so be. Amen.

Notes: *The Polish National Catholic Church of America is the only American church in communion with the Old Catholic Church in Holland. Assent to the Profession of Faith must be given by individuals who join the church.*

* * *

Anglicanism

THE THIRTY-NINE ARTICLES OF RELIGION

I. OF FAITH IN THE HOLY TRINITY.

There is but one living and true God, everlasting, without body, parts, or passions; of infinite power, wisdom, and goodness; the Maker, and Preserver of all things both visible and invisible. And in unity of this Godhead there be three Persons, of one substance, power, and eternity; the Father, the Son, and the Holy Ghost.

II. OF THE WORD OR SON OF GOD, WHICH WAS MADE VERY MAN.

The Son, which is the Word of the Father, begotten from everlasting of the Father, the very and eternal God, and of one substance with the Father, took Man's nature in the womb of the blessed Virgin, of her substance: so that two whole and perfect Natures, that is to say, the Godhead and Manhood, were joined together in one Person, never to be divided, whereof is one Christ, very God, and very Man; who truly suffered, was crucified, dead, and buried, to reconcile his Father to us, and to be a sacrifice, not only for original guilt, but also for actual sins of men.

III. OF THE GOING DOWN OF CHRIST INTO HELL.

As Christ died for us, and was buried; so also is it to be believed, that he went down into Hell.

IV. OF THE RESURRECTION OF CHRIST.

Christ did truly rise again from death, and took again his body, with flesh, bones, and all things appertaining to the perfection of Man's nature; wherewith he ascended into Heaven, and there sitteth, until he return to judge all Men at the last day.

V. OF THE HOLY GHOST.

The Holy Ghost, proceeding from the Father and the Son, is of one substance, majesty, and glory, with the Father and the Son, very and eternal God.

VI. OF THE SUFFICIENCY OF THE HOLY SCRIPTURES FOR SALVATION.

Holy Scripture containeth all things necessary to salvation: so that whatsoever is not read therein, nor may be proved thereby, is not to be required of any man, that it should be believed as an article of the Faith, or be thought requisite or necessary to salvation. In the name of the Holy Scripture we do understand those canonical Books of the Old and New Testament, of whose authority was never any doubt in the Church.

OF THE NAMES AND NUMBER OF THE CANONICAL BOOKS.

Genesis
Exodus
Leviticus
Numbers
Deuteronomy
Joshua
Judges
Ruth
The First Book of Samuel
The Second Book of Samuel
The First Book of Kings
The Second Book of Kings
The First Book of Chronicles
The Second Book of Chronicles
The First Book of Esdras
The Second Book of Esdras
The Book of Esther
The Book of Job
The Psalms
The Proverbs
Ecclesiastes or Preacher
Cantica, or Songs of Solomon
Four Prophets the greater
Twelve Prophets the less

And the other Books (as Hierome saith) the Church doth read for example of life and instruction of manners; but yet doth it not apply them to establish any doctrine; such are these following:

The Third Book of Esdras
The Fourth Book of Esdras
The Book of Tobias
The Book of Judith
The rest of the Book of Esther
The Book of Wisdom
Jesus the Son of Sirach
Baruch the Prophet
The Song of the Three Children

The Story of Susanna
Of Bel and the Dragon
The Prayer of Manasses
The First Book of Maccabees
The Second Book of Maccabees

All the Books of the New Testament, as they are commonly received, we do receive, and account them Canonical.

VII. OF THE OLD TESTAMENT.

The Old Testament is not contrary to the New: for both in the Old and New Testament everlasting life is offered to Mankind by Christ, who is the only Mediator between God and Man, being both God and Man Wherefore they are not to be heard, which feign that the old Fathers did look only for transitory promises. Although the Law given from God by Moses, as touching Ceremonies and Rites, do not bind Christian men, nor the Civil precepts thereof ought of necessity to be received in any commonwealth; yet notwithstanding, no Christian man whatsoever is free from the obedience of the Commandments which are called Moral.

VIII. OF THE CREEDS.

The Nicene Creed, and that which is commonly called the Apostles' Creed, ought thoroughly to be received and believed: for they may be proved by most certain warrants of Holy Scripture.

IX. OF ORIGINAL OR BIRTH-SIN.

Original sin standeth not in the following of Adam, (as the Pelagians do vainly talk;) but it is the fault and corruption of the Nature of every man, that naturally is engendered of the offspring of Adam; whereby man is very far gone from original righteousness, and is of his own nature inclined to evil, so that the flesh lusteth always contrary to the Spirit; and therefore in every person born into this world, it deserveth God's wrath and damnation. And this infection of nature doth remain, yea in them that are regenerated; whereby the lust of the flesh, called in Greek, φρονημα σαρκος, (which some do expound the wisdom, some sensuality, some the affection, some the desire, of the flesh,) is not subject to the Law of God. And although there is no condemnation for them that believe and are baptized; yet the Apostle doth confess, that concupiscence and lust hath of itself the nature of sin.

X. OF FREE-WILL.

The condition of Man after the fall of Adam is such, that he cannot turn and prepare himself, by his own natural strength and good works, to faith, and calling upon God. Wherefore we have no power to do good works pleasant and acceptable to God, without the grace of God by Christ preventing us, that we may have a good will, and working with us, when we have that good will.

XI. OF THE JUSTIFICATION OF MAN.

We are accounted righteous before God, only for the merit of our Lord and Saviour Jesus Christ by Faith, and not for our own works or deservings. Wherefore, that we are justified by Faith only, is a most wholesome Doctrine, and very full of comfort, as more largely is expressed in the Homily of Justification.

XII. OF GOOD WORKS.

Albeit that Good Works, which are the fruits of Faith, and follow after Justification, cannot put away our sins, and endure the severity of God's judgment; yet are they pleasing and acceptable to God in Christ, and do spring out necessarily of a true and lively Faith; insomuch that by them a lively Faith may be as evidently known as a tree discerned by the fruit.

XIII. OF WORKS BEFORE JUSTIFICATION.

Works done before the grace of Christ, and the Inspiration of his Spirit, are not pleasant to God, forasmuch as they spring not of faith in Jesus Christ; neither do they make men meet to receive grace, or (as the School-authors say) deserve grace of congruity: yea rather, for that they are not done as God hath willed and commanded them to be done, we doubt not but they have the nature of sin.

XIV. OF WORKS OF SUPEREROGATION.

Voluntary Works besides, over and above, God's Commandments, which they call Works of Supererogation, cannot be taught without arrogancy and impiety: for by them men do declare, that they do not only render unto God as much as they are bound to do, but that they do more for his sake, than of bounden duty is required: whereas Christ saith plainly, When ye have done all that are commanded to you, say, We are unprofitable servants.

XV. OF CHRIST ALONE WITHOUT SIN.

Christ in the truth of our nature was made like unto us in all things, sin only except, from which he was clearly void, both in his flesh, and in his spirit. He came to be the Lamb without spot, who, by sacrifice of himself once made, should take away the sins of the world; and sin (as Saint John saith) was not in him. But all we the rest, although baptized, and born again in Christ, yet offend in many things; and if we say we have no sin, we deceive ourselves, and the truth is not in us.

XVI. OF SIN AFTER BAPTISM.

Not every deadly sin willingly committed after Baptism is sin against the Holy Ghost, and unpardonable. Wherefore the grant of repentance is not to be denied to such as fall into sin after Baptism. After we have received the Holy Ghost, we may depart from grace given, and fall into sin, and by the grace of God we may arise again, and amend our lives. And therefore they are to be condemned, which say, they can no more sin as long as they live here, or deny the place of forgiveness to such as truly repent.

XVII. OF PREDESTINATION AND ELECTION.

Predestination to Life is the everlasting purpose of God, whereby (before the foundations of the world were laid) he hath constantly decreed by his counsel secret to us, to deliver from curse and damnation those whom he hath chosen in Christ out of mankind, and to bring them by Christ to everlasting salvation, as vessels made to honour Wherefore, they which be endued with so excellent a benefit of God, be called according to God's purpose by his Spirit working in due season: they through Grace obey the calling: they be justified freely: they be made sons of God by adoption: they be made like the image of his only-begotten Son Jesus Christ: they walk religiously in good

THE THIRTY-NINE ARTICLES OF RELIGION (continued)

works, and at length, by God's mercy, they attain to everlasting felicity.

As the godly consideration of Predestination, and our Election in Christ, is full of sweet, pleasant, and unspeakable comfort to godly persons, and such as feel in themselves the working of the Spirit of Christ, mortifying the works of the flesh, and their earthly members, and drawing up their mind to high and heavenly things, as well because it doth greatly establish and confirm their faith of eternal Salvation to be enjoyed through Christ, as because it doth fervently kindle their love towards God: So, for curious and carnal persons, lacking the Spirit of Christ, to have continually before their eyes the sentence of God's Predestination, is a most dangerous downfall, whereby the Devil doth thrust them either into desperation, or into wretchlessness of most unclean living, no less perilous than desperation.

Furthermore, we must receive God's promises in such wise, as they be generally set forth to us in Holy Scripture: and, in our doings, that Will of God is to be followed, which we have expressly declared unto us in the Word of God.

XVIII. OF OBTAINING ETERNAL SALVATION ONLY BY THE NAME OF CHRIST.

They also are to be had accursed that presume to say, That every man shall be saved by the Law or Sect which he professeth, so that he be diligent to frame his life according to that Law, and the light of Nature. For Holy Scripture doth set out unto us only the Name of Jesus Christ, whereby men must be saved.

XIX. OF THE CHURCH.

The visible Church of Christ is a congregation of faithful men, in which the pure Word of God is preached, and the Sacraments be duly ministered according to Christ's ordinance, in all those things that of necessity are requisite to the same.

As the Church of Jerusalem, Alexandria, and Antioch, have erred; so also the Church of Rome hath erred, not only in their living and manner of Ceremonies, but also in matters of Faith.

XX. OF THE AUTHORITY OF THE CHURCH.

The Church hath power to decree Rites or Ceremonies, and authority in Controversies of Faith: and yet it is not lawful for the Church to ordain any thing that is contrary to God's Word written, neither may it so expound one place of Scripture, that it be repugnant to another. Wherefore, although the Church be a witness and a keeper of Holy Writ, yet, as it ought not to decree any thing against the same, so besides the same ought it not to enforce any thing to be believed for necessity of Salvation.

XXI. OF THE AUTHORITY OF GENERAL COUNCILS.

[The Twenty-first of the former Articles is omitted; because it is partly of a local and civil nature, and is provided for, as to the remaining parts of it, in other Articles.]

XXII. OF PURGATORY.

The Romish Doctrine concerning Purgatory, Pardons, Worshipping and Adoration, as well of Images as of Relics, and also Invocation of Saints, is a fond thing, vainly invented, and grounded upon no warranty of Scripture, but rather repugnant to the Word of God.

XXIII. OF MINISTERING IN THE CONGREGATION.

It is not lawful for any man to take upon him the office of public preaching, or ministering the Sacraments in the Congregation, before he be lawfully called, and sent to execute the same. And those we ought to judge lawfully called and sent, which be chosen and called to this work by men who have public authority given unto them in the Congregation, to call and send Ministers into the Lord's vineyard.

XXIV. OF SPEAKING IN THE CONGREGATION IN SUCH A TONGUE AS THE PEOPLE UNDERSTANDETH.

It is a thing plainly repugnant to the Word of God, and the custom of the Primitive Church, to have public Prayer in the Church, or to minister the Sacraments, in a tongue not understood of the people.

XXV. OF THE SACRAMENTS.

Sacraments ordained of Christ be not only badges or tokens of Christian men's profession, but rather they be certain sure witnesses, and effectual signs of grace, and God's good will towards us, by the which he doth work invisibly in us, and doth not only quicken, but also strengthen and confirm our Faith in him.

There are two Sacraments ordained of Christ our Lord in the Gospel, that is to say, Baptism, and the Supper of the Lord.

Those five commonly called Sacraments, that is to say, Confirmation, Penance, Orders, Matrimony, and Extreme Unction, are not to be counted for Sacraments of the Gospel, being such as have grown partly of the corrupt following of the Apostles, partly are states of life allowed in the Scriptures; but yet have not like nature of Sacraments with Baptism, and the Lord's Supper, for that they have not any visible sign or ceremony ordained of God.

The Sacraments were not ordained of Christ to be gazed upon, or to be carried about, but that we should duly use them. And in such only as worthily receive the same, they have a wholesome effect or operation: but they that receive them unworthily, purchase to themselves damnation, as Saint Paul saith.

XXVI. OF THE UNWORTHINESS OF THE MINISTERS, WHICH HINDERS NOT THE EFFECT OF THE SACRAMENTS.

Although in the visible Church the evil be ever mingled with the good, and sometimes the evil have chief authority in the Ministration of the Word and Sacraments, yet forasmuch as they do not the same in their own name, but in Christ's, and do minister by his commission and authority, we may use their Ministry, both in hearing the Word of God, and in receiving the Sacraments. Neither is the effect of Christ's ordinance taken away by their wickedness, nor the grace of God's gifts diminished from such as by faith, and rightly, do receive the Sacraments ministered unto them; which be effectual, because of Christ's institution and promise, although they be ministered by evil men.

Nevertheless, it appertaineth to the discipline of the Church, that inquiry be made of evil Ministers, and that they be accused by those that have knowledge of their offences; and finally, being found guilty, by just judgment be deposed.

XXVII. OF BAPTISM.

Baptism is not only a sign of profession, and mark of difference, whereby Christian men are discerned from others that be not christened, but it is also a sign of Regeneration or New-Birth, whereby, as by an instrument, they that receive Baptism rightly are grafted into the Church; the promises of the forgiveness of sin, and of our adoption to be the sons of God by the Holy Ghost, are visibly signed and sealed; Faith is confirmed, and Grace increased by virtue of prayer unto God.

The Baptism of young Children is in any wise to be retained in the Church, as most agreeable with the institution of Christ.

XXVIII. OF THE LORD'S SUPPER.

The Supper of the Lord is not only a sign of the love that Christians ought to have among themselves one to another; but rather it is a Sacrament of our Redemption by Christ's death: insomuch that to such as rightly, worthily, and with faith, receive the same, the Bread which we break is a partaking of the Body of Christ; and likewise the Cup of Blessing is a partaking of the Blood of Christ.

Transubstantiation (or the change of the substance of Bread and Wine) in the Supper of the Lord, cannot be proved by Holy Writ; but is repugnant to the plain words of Scripture, overthroweth the nature of a Sacrament, and hath given occasion to many superstitions.

The Body of Christ is given, taken, and eaten, in the Supper, only after an heavenly and spiritual manner. And the mean whereby the Body of Christ is received and eaten in the Supper, is Faith.

The Sacrament of the Lord's Supper was not by Christ's ordinance reserved, carried about, lifted up, or worshipped.

XXIX. OF THE WICKED, WHICH EAT NOT THE BODY OF CHRIST IN THE USE OF THE LORD'S SUPPER.

The Wicked, and such as be void of a lively faith, although they do carnally and visibly press with their teeth (as Saint Augustine saith) the Sacrament of the Body and Blood of Christ; yet in no wise are they partakers of Christ: but rather, to their condemnation, do eat and drink the sign or Sacrament of so great a thing.

XXX. OF BOTH KINDS.

The Cup of the Lord is not to be denied to the Lay-people: for both the parts of the Lord's Sacrament, by Christ's ordinance and commandment, ought to be ministered to all Christian men alike.

XXXI. OF THE ONE OBLATION OF CHRIST FINISHED UPON THE CROSS.

The Offering of Christ once made is that perfect redemption, propitiation, and satisfaction, for all the sins of the whole world, both original and actual; and there is none other satisfaction for sin, but that alone. Wherefore the sacrifices of Masses, in the which it was commonly said, that the Priest did offer Christ for the quick and the dead, to have remission of pain or guilt, were blasphemous fables, and dangerous deceits.

XXXII. OF THE MARRIAGE OF PRIESTS.

Bishops, Priests, and Deacons, are not commanded by God's Law, either to vow the estate of single life, or to abstain from marriage: therefore it is lawful for them, as for all other Christian men, to marry at their own discretion, as they shall judge the same to serve better to godliness.

XXXIII. OF EXCOMMUNICATE PERSONS, HOW THEY ARE TO BE AVOIDED.

That person which by open denunciation of the Church is rightly cut off from the unity of the Church, and excommunicated, ought to be taken of the whole multitude of the faithful, as an Heathen and Publican, until he be openly reconciled by penance, and received into the Church by a Judge that hath authority thereunto.

XXXIV. OF THE TRADITIONS OF THE CHURCH.

It is not necessary that Traditions and Ceremonies be in all places one, or utterly like; for at all times they have been divers, and may be changed according to the diversity of countries, times, and men's manners, so that nothing be ordained against God's Word. Whosoever, through his private judgment, willingly and purposely, doth openly break the Traditions and Ceremonies of the Church, which be not repugnant to the Word of God, and be ordained and approved by common authority, ought to be rebuked openly, (that others may fear to do the like,) as he that offendeth against the common order of the Church, and hurteth the authority of the Magistrate, and woundeth the consciences of the weak brethren.

Every particular or national Church hath authority to ordain, change, and abolish, Ceremonies or Rites of the Church ordained only by man's authority, so that all things be done to edifying.

XXXV. OF THE HOMILIES.

The Second Book of Homilies, the several titles whereof we have joined under this Article, doth contain a godly and wholesome Doctrine, and necessary for these times, as doth the former Book of Homilies, which were set forth in the time of Edward the Sixth; and therefore we judge them to be read in Churches by the Ministers, diligently and distinctly, that they may be understood of the people.

OF THE NAMES OF THE HOMILIES.

1. Of the right Use of the Church.
2. Against Peril of Idolatry.
3. Of repairing and keeping clean of Churches.
4. Of good Works: first of Fasting.

THE THIRTY-NINE ARTICLES OF RELIGION (continued)

5. Against Gluttony and Drunkenness.
6. Against Excess of Apparel.
7. Of Prayer.
8. Of the Place and Time of Prayer.
9. That Common Prayers and Sacraments ought to be ministered in a known tongue.
10. Of the reverend Estimation of God's Word.
11. Of Alms-doing.
12. Of the Nativity of Christ.
13. Of the Passion of Christ.
14. Of the Resurrection of Christ.
15. Of the worthy receiving of the Sacrament of the Body and Blood of Christ.
16. Of the Gifts of the Holy Ghost.
17. For the Rogation-days.
18. Of the State of Matrimony.
19. Of Repentance.
20. Against Idleness.
21. Against Rebellion.

XXXVI. OF CONSECRATION OF BISHOPS AND MINISTERS.

The Book of Consecration of Bishops, and Ordering of Priests and Deacons, as set forth by the General Convention of this Church in 1792, doth contain all things necessary to such Consecration and Ordering; neither hath it any thing that, of itself, is superstitious and ungodly. And, therefore, whosoever are consecrated or ordered according to said Form, we decree all such to be rightly, orderly, and lawfully consecrated and ordered.

XXXVII. OF THE POWER OF THE CIVIL MAGISTRATES.

The Power of the Civil Magistrate extendeth to all men, as well Clergy as Laity, in all things temporal; but hath no authority in things purely spiritual. And we hold it to be the duty of all men who are professors of the Gospel, to pay respectful obedience to the Civil Authority, regularly and legitimately constituted.

XXXVIII. OF CHRISTIAN MEN'S GOODS, WHICH ARE NOT COMMON.

The Riches and Goods of Christians are not common, as touching the right, title, and possession of the same; as certain Anabaptists do falsely boast. Notwithstanding, every man ought, of such things as he possesseth, liberally to give alms to the poor, according to his ability.

XXXIX. OF A CHRISTIAN MAN'S OATH.

As we confess that vain and rash Swearing is forbidden Christian men by our Lord Jesus Christ, and James his Apostle, so we judge, that Christian Religion doth not prohibit, but that a man may swear when the Magistrate requireth, in a cause of faith and charity, so it be done according to the Prophet's teaching, in justice, judgment, and truth.

Notes: *One of the prime documents of the Elizabethan via-media settlement of the Protestant-Catholic polarity within the Church of England was a new doctrinal statement consisting of thirty-nine articles of religion. These articles, first published in 1563, have since been doctrinally definitive of the Anglican theological heritage and are printed in the back of the Prayer Book. As has been frequently noted, they are very brief in comparison with the Lutheran and Reformed confessions. Unlike the statements of the Continental Protestants, who were trying to give a lengthy summary of their full doctrinal position, the Thirty-nine Articles merely attempted a minimal doctrinal agreement for an otherwise diverse and inclusive national church. The articles do place the Anglicans in the Western Orthodox tradition while specifically rejecting some of the peculiarities of the Roman Catholic Church.*

The American Church made a few minor revisions to the text of the articles in 1801. The text reproduced here is from the 1928 Prayer Book. The Thirty-nine Articles of Religion is the doctrinal statement of the Protestant Episcopal Church in the U.S.A., the largest Anglican body in North America; its Canadian counterpart, the Anglican Church of Canada; and almost all of the smaller Anglican splinter groups.

* * *

THE AFFIRMATION OF ST. LOUIS (1976)

In the name of the Father and of the Son and of the Holy Ghost. Amen.

THE CONTINUATION OF ANGLICANISM. We affirm that the Church of our fathers, sustained by the most Holy Trinity, lives yet, and that we, being moved by the Holy Spirit to walk only in that way, are determined to continue in the Catholic Faith, Apostolic Order, Orthodox Worship and Evangelical Witness of the traditional Anglican Church, doing all things necessary for the continuance of the same. We are upheld and strengthened in this determination by the knowledge that many provinces and dioceses of the Anglican Communion have continued steadfast in the same Faith, Order, Worship and Witness, and that they continue to confine ordination to the preisthood and the episcopate to males. We rejoice in these facts and we affirm our solidarity with these provinces and dioceses.

THE DISSOLUTION OF ANGLICAN AND EPISCOPAL CHURCH STRUCTURE. We affirm that the Anglican Church of Canada and the Protestant Episcopal Church in the United States of America, by their unlawful attempts to alter Faith, Order and Morality (especially in their General Synod of 1975 and General Convention of 1976), have departed from Christ's One, Holy, Catholic and Apostolic Church.

THE NEED TO CONTINUE ORDER IN THE CHURCH. We affirm that all former ecclesiastical governments, being fundamentally impaired by the schismatic acts of lawless Councils, are of no effect among us, and that we must now reorder such godly discipline as will strengthen us in the continuation of our common life and witness.

THE INVALIDITY OF SCHISMATIC AUTHORITY. We affirm that the claim of any such schismatic person or body to act against any Church member, clerical or lay, for his witness to the whole Faith is with no authority of Christ's true Church, and any such inhibition, deposition or discipline is without effect and is absolutely null and void.

THE NEED FOR PRINCIPLES AND A CONSTITUTION. We affirm that fundamental principles (doctrinal, moral, and constitutional) are necessary for the present, and that a Constitution (redressing the defects and abuses of our former governments) should be adopted, whereby the Church may be soundly continued.

THE CONTINUATION OF COMMUNION WITH CANTERBURY. We affirm our continued relations of communion with the See of Canterbury and all faithful parts of the Anglican Communion.

WHEREFORE, with a firm trust in Divine Providence, and before Almighty God and all the company of heaven, we solemnly affirm, covenant and declare that we, lawful and faithful members of the Anglican and Episcopal Churches, shall now and hereafter continue and be the unified continuing Anglican Church in North America, in true and valid succession thereto.

FUNDAMENTAL PRINCIPLES. In order to carry out these declarations, we set forth these fundamental Principles for our continued life and witness.

PREFACE: In the firm conviction that "we shall be saved through the grace of the Lord Jesus Christ," and that "there is no other name under heaven given among men by which we must be saved," and acknowledging our duty to proclaim Christ's saving Truth to all peoples, nations and tongues, we declare our intention to hold fast the One, Holy, Catholic and Apostolic Faith of God.

We acknowledge that rule of faith laid down by St. Vincent of Lérins: "Let us hold that which has been believed everywhere, always and by all, for that is truly and properly Catholic."

I. PRINCIPLES OF DOCTRINE

1. **THE NATURE OF THE CHURCH.** We gather as people called by God to be faithful and obedient to Him. As the Royal Priestly People of God, the Church is called to be, in fact, the manifestation of Christ in and to the world. True religion is revealed to man by God. We cannot decide what is truth, but rather (in obedience) ought to receive, accept, cherish, defend and teach what God has given us. The Church is created by God, and is beyond the ultimate control of man.

   The Church is the Body of Christ at work in the world. She is the society of the baptized called out from the world: in it, but not of it. As Christ's faithful Bride, she is different from the world and must not be influenced by it.

2. **THE ESSENTIALS OF TRUTH AND ORDER.** We repudiate all deviation or departure from the Faith, in whole or in part, and bear witness to these essential principles of evangelical Truth and apostolic Order:

HOLY SCRIPTURES. The Holy Scriptures of the Old and New Testaments as the authentic record of God's revelation of Himself, His saving activity, and moral demands—a revelation valid for all men and all time.

THE CREEDS. The Nicene Creed as the authoritative summary of the chief articles of the Christian Faith, together with the Apostles' Creed, and that known as the Creed of St. Athanasius to be "thoroughly received and believed" in the sense they have had always in the Catholic Church.

TRADITION. The received Tradition of the Church and its teachings as set forth by "the ancient catholic bishops and doctors," and especially as defined by the Seven Ecumenical Councils of the undivided Church, to the exclusion of all errors, ancient and modern.

SACRAMENTS. The Sacraments of Baptism, Confirmation, the Holy Eucharist, Holy Matrimony, Holy Orders, Penance and Unction of the Sick, as objective and effective signs of the continued presence and saving activity of Christ our Lord among His people and as His covenanted means for conveying His grace. In particular, we affirm the necessity of Baptism and the Holy Eucharist (where they may be had)—Baptism as incorporating us into Christ (with its completion in Confirmation as the "seal of the Holy Spirit"), and the Eucharist as the sacrifice which unites us to the all-sufficient Sacrifice of Christ on the Cross and the Sacrament in which He feeds us with His Body and Blood.

HOLY ORDERS. The Holy Orders of bishops, priests and deacons as the perpetuation of Christ's gift of apostolic ministry to His Church, asserting the necessity of a bishop of apostolic succession (or a priest ordained by such) as the celebrant of the Eucharist—these Orders consisting exclusively of men in accordance with Christ's Will and institution (as evidenced by the Scriptures), and the universal practice of the Catholic Church.

DEACONESSES. The ancient office and ministry of Deaconesses as a lay vocation for women, affirming the need for proper encouragement of that office.

DUTY OF BISHOPS. Bishops as Apostles, Prophets, Evangelists, Shepherds and Teachers, as well as their duty (together with other clergy and the laity) to guard and defend the purity and integrity of the Church's Faith and Moral Teaching.

THE USE OF OTHER FORMULAE. In affirming these principles, we recognize that all Anglican statements of faith and liturgical formulae must be interpreted in accordance with them.

INCOMPETENCE OF CHURCH BODIES TO ALTER TRUTH. We disclaim any right or competence to suppress, alter or amend any of the ancient Ecumenical Creeds and definitions of Faith, to set aside or depart from Holy Scripture, or to alter or deviate from the essential prerequisites of any Sacrament.

THE AFFIRMATION OF ST. LOUIS (1976) (continued)

UNITY WITH OTHER BELIEVERS. We declare our firm intention to seek and achieve full sacramental communion and visible unity with other Christians who "worship the Trinity in Unity, and Unity in Trinity," and who hold the Catholic and Apostolic Faith in accordance with the foregoing principles.

II. PRINCIPLES OF MORALITY

The conscience, as the inherent knowledge of right and wrong, cannot stand alone as a sovereign arbiter of morals. Every Christian is obligated to form his conscience by the Divine Moral Law and the Mind of Christ as revealed in Holy Scriptures, and by the teachings and Tradition of the Church. We hold that when the Christian conscience is thus properly informed and ruled, it must affirm the following moral principles:

INDIVIDUAL RESPONSIBILITY. All people, individually and collectively, are responsible to their Creator for their acts, motives, thoughts and words, since "we must all appear before the judgment seat of Christ ..."

SANCTITY OF HUMAN LIFE. Every human being, from the time of his conception, is a creature and child of God, made in His image and likeness, an infinitely precious soul; and that the unjustifiable or inexcusable taking of life is always sinful.

MAN'S DUTY TO GOD. All people are bound by the dictates of the Natural Law and by the revealed Will of God, insofar as they can discern them.

FAMILY LIFE. The God-given sacramental bond in marriage between one man and one woman is God's loving provision for procreation and family life, and sexual activity is to be practiced only within the bonds of Holy Matrimony.

MAN AS SINNER. We recognize that man, as inheritor of original sin, is "very far gone from original righteousness," and as a rebel against God's authority is liable to His righteous judgment.

MAN AND GOD'S GRACE. We recognize, too, that God loves His children and particularly has shown it forth in the redemptive work of our Lord Jesus Christ, and that man cannot be saved by any effort of his own, but by the Grace of God, through repentance and acceptance of God's forgiveness.

CHRISTIAN'S DUTY TO BE MORAL. We believe, therefore, it is the duty of the Church and her members to bear witness to Christian Morality, to follow it in their lives, and to reject the false standards of the world.

III. CONSTITUTIONAL PRINCIPLES

In the constitutional revision which must be undertaken, we recommend, for the consideration of continuing Anglicans, the following:

RETAIN THE BEST OF BOTH PROVINCES. That the traditional and tested features of the Canadian and American ecclesiastical systems be retained and used in the administration of the continuing Church.

SELECTION OF BISHOPS. That a non-political means for selection of bishops be devised, adopted and used.

TRIPARTITE SYNOD. That the Church be generally governed by a Holy Synod of three branches (episcopal, clerical and lay), under the presidency of the Primate of the Church.

SCRIPTURAL STANDARDS FOR THE MINISTRY. That the apostolic and scriptural standards for the sacred Ministry be used for all orders of Ministers.

CONCURRENCE OF ALL ORDERS FOR DECISIONS. That the Constitution acknowledge the necessity of the concurrence of all branches of the Synod for decisions in all matters, and that extraordinary majorities by required for the favorable consideration of all matters of importance.

RE-ESTABLISHMENT OF DISCIPLINE. That the Church re-establish an effective permanent system of ecclesiastical courts for the defense of the Faith and the maintenance of discipline over all her members.

CONSTITUTIONAL ASSEMBLY TO BE CALLED. That our bishops shall call a Constitutional Assembly of lay and clerical representatives of dioceses and parishes to convene at the earliest appropriate time to draft a Constitution and Canons by which we may by unified and governed, with special reference to this Affirmation, and with'due consideration to ancient Custom and the General Canon Law, and to the former law of our provinces.

INTERIM ACTION. In the meantime, trusting in the everlasting strength of God to carry us through all our trials, we commend all questions for decision to the proper authorities in each case: Episcopal, diocesan, and parochial, encouraging all the faithful to support our witness as subscribers to this Affirmation, and inviting all so doing to share our fellowship and the work of the Church.

IV. PRINCIPLES OF WORSHIP

PRAYER BOOK: THE STANDARD OF WORSHIP. In the continuing Anglican Church, the Book of Common Prayer is (and remains) one work in two editions: The Canadian Book of 1962 and the American Book of 1928. Each is fully and equally authoritative. No other standard for worship exists.

CERTAIN VARIANCES PERMITTED. For liturgical use, only the Book of Common Prayer and service books conforming to and incorporating it shall be used.

V. PRINCIPLES OF ACTION

INTERCOMMUNION WITH OTHER APOSTOLIC CHURCHES. The continuing Anglicans remain in full communion with the See of Canterbury and with all other faithful parts of the Anglican Communion, and should actively seek similar relations with all other Apostolic and Catholic Churches, provided that agreement in the essentials of Faith and Order first be reached.

NON-INVOLVEMENT WITH NON-APOSTOLIC GROUPS. We recognize that the World Council of Churches, and many national and other Councils adhering to the World Council, are non-Apostolic, humanist and secular in purpose and practice, and that under such circumstances, we cannot be members of any of them. We also recognize that the Consultation of Church Union (COCU) and all other such schemes, being non-Apostolic and non-Catholic in their present concept and form, are unacceptable to us, and that we cannot be associated with any of them.

NEED FOR SOUND THEOLOGICAL TRAINING. Re-establishment of spiritual, orthodox and scholarly theological education under episcopal supervision is imperative, and should be encouraged and promoted by all in authority; and learned and godly bishops, other clergy and lay people should undertake and carry on that work without delay.

FINANCIAL AFFAIRS. The right of congregations to control of their temporalities should be firmly and constitutionally recognized and protected.

ADMINISTRATIVE MATTERS. Administration should, we believe, be limited to the most simple and necessary acts, so that emphasis may be centered on worship, pastoral care, spiritual and moral soundness, personal good works, and missionary outreach, in response to God's love for us.

THE CHURCH AS WITNESS TO TRUTH. We recognize also that, as keepers of God's will and truth for man, we can and ought to witness to that will and truth against all manifest evils, remembering that we are as servants in the world, but God's servants first.

PENSIONS AND INSURANCE. We recognize our immediate responsibility to provide for the establishment of sound pension and insurance programs for the protection of the stipendiary clergy and other Church workers.

LEGAL DEFENSE. We recognize the immediate need to coordinate legal resources, financial and professional, for the defense of congregations imperiled by their stand for the Faith, and commend this need most earnestly to the diocesan and parochial authorities.

CONTINUATION, NOT INNOVATION. In this gathering witness of Anglicans and Episcopalians, we continue to be what we are. We do nothing new. We form no new body, but continue as Anglicans and Episcopalians.

NOW, THEREFORE, deeply aware of our duty to all who love and believe the Faith of our Fathers, of our duty to God, who alone shall judge what we do, we make this Affirmation.

Before God, we claim our Anglican/Episcopal inheritance, and proclaim the same to the whole Church, through Jesus Christ our Lord, to whom, with the Father and the Holy Ghost, be all honor and glory, world without end. Amen.

Notes: *In 1976, members and former members of the Protestant Episcopal Church in the U.S.A. and the Anglican Church of Canada gathered in St. Louis, Missouri, to protest changes within those jurisdictions. A lengthy statement was adopted by those in attendance and subsequently became a basis around which new jurisdictions, such as the Anglican Catholic Church, were formed. Although the affirmation describes and has influenced the position of many smaller Anglican bodies, most have not accepted the affirmation in any official manner.*

*   *   *

DECLARATION OF PRINCIPLES AND ARTICLES OF RELIGION (REFORMED EPISCOPAL CHURCH)

DECLARATION OF PRINCIPLES

I. The Reformed Episcopal Church, holding "the faith once delivered unto the saints," declares its belief in the Holy Scriptures of the Old and New Testaments as the Word of God, and the sole Rule of Faith and Practice; in the Creed "commonly called the Apostles' Creed;" in the Divine institution of the Sacraments of Baptism and the LORD'S Supper; and in the doctrines of grace substantially as they are set forth in the Thirty-nine Articles of Religion.

II. This Church recognizes and adheres to Episcopacy, not as of Divine right, but as a very ancient and desirable form of Church polity.

III. This Church, retaining a Liturgy which shall not be imperative or repressive of freedom in prayer, accepts The Book of Common Prayer, as it was revised, proposed, and recommended for use by the General Convention of the Protestant Episcopal Church, A. D. 1785, reserving full liberty to alter, abridge, enlarge, and amend the same, as may seem most conducive to the edification of the people, "provided that the substance of the faith be kept entire."

IV. This Church condemns and rejects the following erroneous and strange doctrines as contrary to God's Word:

First, That the Church of Christ exists only in one order or form of ecclesiastical polity:

Second, That Christian Ministers are "priests" in another sense than that in which all believers are "a royal priesthood:"

Third, That the LORD'S Table is an altar on which the oblation of the Body and Blood of Christ is offered anew to the Father:

Fourth, That the Presence of Christ in the LORD'S Supper is a presence in the elements of Bread and Wine:

Fifth, That Regeneration is inseparably connected with Baptism.

DECLARATION OF PRINCIPLES AND ARTICLES OF RELIGION (REFORMED EPISCOPAL CHURCH) (continued)

ARTICLES OF RELIGION

Whereas, This Church has, in its Declaration of Principles, proclaimed its belief in the doctrines of grace substantially as they were set forth in the Thirty-nine Articles; therefore,

RESOLVED: As the sense of this Council, that the Articles reported by the Committee on Doctrine and Worship, and accepted at this Council, be and are hereby adopted, as containing substantially the great truths known as the "Doctrines of Grace."

RESOLVED: That the foregoing preamble and resolution be printed as a Prefatory Note to the Articles of Religion.

Article I. OF THE HOLY TRINITY

There is but one living and true God, who is a spirit, everlasting; of infinite power, wisdom, and goodness; the Maker and Preserver of all things, both visible and invisible. And in unity of this Godhead, there be three Persons, of one substance, power, and eternity; the Father, the Son, and the Holy Ghost.

Article II. OF THE WORD, OR SON OF GOD, WHICH WAS MADE VERY MAN

The Son, who is the Word of the Father, begotten from everlasting of the Father, the very and eternal God, of one substance with the Father, took man's nature in the womb of the blessed virgin, of her substance: so that two whole and perfect natures, that is to say, the Godhead and manhood, were joined together in one Person, never to be divided, whereof is one Christ, very God and very man; who truly suffered, was crucified, dead and buried, to satisfy Divine justice, and to reconcile us to his Father, and to be a sacrifice, not only for original sin, but also for actual sins of men.

Article III. OF THE RESURRECTION OF CHRIST, AND HIS SECOND COMING

Christ did truly rise from death, and took again his body, with flesh, bones, and all things appertaining to the perfection of man's nature, wherewith he ascended into heaven, and there sitteth, our High Priest and Advocate, at the right hand of the Father, whence he will return to judge the world in righteousness. This Second Coming is the blessed hope of the Church. The heavens have received him, till the times of the restitution of all things. To those who look for him he shall appear a second time without sin unto salvation. Then shall he change the body of our humiliation that it may be fashioned like unto his glorious body. He will take to himself his great power, and shall reign till he have put all enemies under his feet.

Article IV. OF THE HOLY GHOST

The Holy Ghost, proceeding from the Father and the Son, is of one substance, majesty, and glory, with the Father and the Son, very and eternal God.

It is the work of the Holy Ghost to reprove and convince the world of sin, and of righteousness, and of judgment; to take of the things of Christ and show them to men; to regenerate—making men willing, leading them to faith in Christ, and forming Christ in them the hope of glory; to

strengthen them with might in their inner man, that Christ may dwell in their hearts by faith; and to secure in them that walking in the ways of God which is called the Fruit of the Spirit. The True Church is thus called out of the world, and is builded together for an habitation of God, through the Spirit.

Article V. OF THE SUFFICIENCY OF THE HOLY SCRIPTURES FOR SALVATION

All Scripture is given by inspiration of God. Holy men of God spake as they were moved by the Holy Ghost: Holy Scripture is therefore the Word of God; not only does it contain the Oracles of God, but it is itself the very Oracles of God. And hence it containeth all things necessary to salvation: so that whatsoever is not read therein, nor may be proved thereby, is not to be required of any man, that it should be believed as an article of faith, or be thought requisite or necessary to salvation. In the name of the Holy Scripture we do understand the canonical books of the Old and New Testament, viz.:

OF THE OLD TESTAMENT

Genesis	The Proverbs
Exodus	Ecclesiastes
Leviticus	Song of Solomon
Numbers	Isaiah
Deuteronomy	Jeremiah
Joshua	Lamentations of
Judges	Jeremiah
Ruth	Ezekiel
The 1st Book of Samuel	Daniel
The 2d Book of Samuel	Hosea
The 1st Book of Kings	Joel
The 2d Book of Kings	Amos
The 1st Book of Chronicles	Obadiah
	Jonah
The 2d Book of Chronicles	Micah
	Nahum
The Book of Ezra	Habakkuk
The Book of Nehemiah	Zephaniah
The Book of Esther	Haggai
The Book of Job	Zechariah
The Psalms	Malachi

OF THE NEW TESTAMENT

Matthew	1st Timothy
Mark	2d Timothy
Luke	Titus
John	Philemon
Acts of the Apostles	Hebrews
Romans	James
1st Corinthians	1st Peter
2d Corinthians	2d Peter
Galatians	1st John
Ephesians	2d John
Philippians	3d John
Colossians	Jude
1st Thessalonians	The Revelation
2d Thessalonians	

The Book commonly called "The Apocrypha" is not a portion of God's Word, and is not therefore to be read in churches, nor to be used in establishing any doctrine.

Article VI. OF THE OLD TESTAMENT

The Old Testament is not contrary to the New: for both in the Old and New Testament everlasting life is offered to Mankind by Christ, who is the only Mediator between God and Man, being both God and Man. Wherefore they are not to be heard, which feign that the old Fathers did look only for transitory promises; and although the Law given from God by Moses, as touching Ceremonies and Rites, does not bind Christian men, nor the Civil precepts thereof ought of necessity to be received in any commonwealth; yet notwithstanding, as a rule of right living, no Christian man whatsoever is free from the obedience of the Commandments which are called Moral.

Article VII. OF ORIGINAL OR BIRTH-SIN

Original sin standeth not in the following of Adam, as the Pelagians do vainly talk; but it is the fault and corruption of the nature of every man, that naturally is engendered of the offspring of Adam, whereby man is wholly gone from original righteousness, and is of his own nature inclined to evil, so that the flesh lusteth always contrary to the Spirit; and therefore in every person born into this world, it deserveth God's condemnation. Men are, as the Apostle speaks, "by nature the children of wrath." And this infection of nature doth remain, yea, in them that are regenerated. And although there is no condemnation for them that are in Christ Jesus, yet the Apostle doth confess, that concupiscence or lust in such hath of itself the nature of sin.

Article VIII. OF MAN'S CONDITION BY NATURE

The condition of man after the fall of Adam is such, that he cannot turn and prepare himself, by his own natural strength and good works, to faith, and calling upon God. Wherefore we have no power to do good works pleasant and acceptable to God, without the grace of God by Christ first inclining us, that we may have a good will, and working with us, when we have that good will.

Article IX. OF WORKS BEFORE JUSTIFICATION

Works commonly called good before the grace of Christ and the inspiration of his Spirit, have not the nature of obedience to God, forasmuch as they spring not of Faith in Jesus Christ, neither do they make men meet to deserve, or to receive grace.

Article X. OF REGENERATION, OR THE NEW BIRTH

Regeneration is the creative act of the Holy Ghost, whereby he imparts to the soul a new spiritual life.

And whosoever believeth in Christ is born again, for, saith the Scripture, "ye are all the children of God by faith in Christ Jesus."

Article XI. OF FAITH

The faith which brings justification is simply the reliance or dependence on Christ which accepts him as the sacrifice for our sins, and as our righteousness.

We may thus rely on Christ, either tremblingly or confidingly; but in either case it is saving faith. If, though tremblingly, we rely on him in his obedience for us unto death, instantly we come into union with him, and are justified. If, however, we confidingly rely on him, then have we the comfort of our justification. Simply by faith in Christ are we justified and saved.

Article XII. OF THE JUSTIFICATION OF MAN

We are pardoned and accounted righteous before God, only for the Merit of our LORD and Saviour Jesus Christ, by Faith; and not for our own Works or Deservings. He who knew no sin was made sin for us, that we might be made the righteousness of God in him. He bare our sins in his own body. It pleased our heavenly Father, of his infinite mercy, without any our desert or deserving, to provide for us the most precious sacrifice of Christ, whereby our ransom might be fully paid, the Law fulfilled, and his justice fully satisfied. So that Christ is himself the righteousness of all them that truly do believe in him. He for them paid their ransom, by his death. He for them fulfilled the Law, in his life. So that now in him, and by him, every true Christian man may be called a fulfiller of the Law. Wherefore, that we are justified by Faith only, is a most wholesome doctrine, and very full of comfort.

Article XIII. OF REPENTANCE

The Repentance required by Scripture, is a change of mind toward God, and is the effect of the conviction of sin, wrought by the Holy Ghost.

The unconverted man may have a sense of remorse, or of shame and self-reproach, and yet he may have neither a change of mind toward God, nor any true sorrow; but when he accepts Christ as his Saviour, therein he manifests a change of mind, and is in possession of repentance unto life. The sinner comes to Christ through no labored process of repenting and sorrowing; but he comes to Christ and repentance both at once, by means of simply believing. And ever afterwards his repentance is deep and genuine in proportion as his faith is simple and childlike.

Article XIV. OF THE SONSHIP OF BELIEVERS

Believers in Christ are born of God, through the regenerating power of his Spirit, and are partakers of the Divine nature; for if "that which is born of the flesh is flesh," so "that which is born of the Spirit is spirit."

And all who are thus born of God are sons of God, and joint heirs with Christ; and therefore, without distinction of name, brethren with Christ and with one another.

Article XV. OF GOOD WORKS

Good Works, which are the Fruits of Faith, and follow after justification, are pleasing and acceptable to God in Christ, and do spring out, necessarily, of a true and lively Faith; insomuch that by them a lively faith may be as evidently known, as a tree discerned by the fruit. They who truly believe will seek to do the will of God, and they who do not thus seek are not to be accounted true believers.

Article XVI. OF WORKS OF SUPEREROGATION

Voluntary Works, besides, over and above God's Commandments, which they call Works of Supererogation, cannot be taught without arrogancy and impiety. For by them men do declare, that they do not only render unto God as much as they are bound to do, but that they do more for his sake than of bounden duty is required:

Whereas Christ saith plainly, When ye have done all that are commanded to you, say, We are unprofitable servants.

Article XVII. SALVATION ONLY IN CHRIST

Holy Scripture doth set out unto us the Name of Jesus Christ only, whereby men must be saved. His was a finished work, and completely sufficient. Without any merit or deserving on our part, he has secured to believers in him pardon, acceptance, sonship, sanctification, redemption, and eternal glory. Those who believe in him are in him complete. They are even now justified and have a present salvation; though they may not at all times have the sense of its possession.

Article XVIII. OF ELECTION, PREDESTINATION, AND FREE WILL

While the Scriptures distinctly set forth the election, predestination, and calling of the people of God unto eternal life, as Christ saith: "All that the Father giveth me shall come to me;" they no less positively affirm man's free agency and responsibility, and that salvation is freely offered to all through Christ.

This Church, accordingly, simply affirms these doctrines as the Word of God sets them forth, and submits them to the individual judgment of its members, as taught by the Holy Spirit; strictly charging them that God commandeth all men everywhere to repent, and that we can be saved only by faith in Jesus Christ.

Article XIX. OF SIN AFTER CONVERSION

The grant of repentance is not to be denied to such as fall into sin after conversion: that is to say, after, by the quickening into life by the Holy Ghost, they have turned to God by faith in Christ, and have been brought into that change of mind which is repentance unto life. For after we have received the Holy Ghost we may, through unbelief, carelessness, and worldliness, fall into sin, and by the grace of God we may arise again, and amend our lives; but every such fall is a grievous dishonor to our LORD, and a sore injury to ourselves.

Article XX. OF CHRIST, ALONE WITHOUT SIN

Christ, in the truth of our nature, was made like unto us in all things, sin only excepted, from which he was clearly void, both in his flesh, and in his spirit. He came to be the Lamb without spot, who, by sacrifice of himself, made *once for ever*, should take away the sin of the world; and sin (as St. John saith) was not in him. But all we the rest, although born again in Christ, yet offend in many things; and if we say we have no sin, we deceive ourselves, and the truth is not in us.

Article XXI. OF THE CHURCH

The souls dispersed in all the world, who adhere to Christ by faith, who are partakers of the Holy Ghost, and worship the Father in spirit and in truth, are the body of Christ, the house of God, the flock of the Good Shepherd—the holy, universal Christian Church.

A visible Church of Christ is a congregation of believers in which the pure Word of God is preached, and Baptism and the LORD's Supper are duly ministered according to Christ's ordinance, in all those things that of necessity are requisite to the same. And those things are to be considered requisite which the LORD himself did, he himself commanded, and his apostles confirmed.

As the Church of Jerusalem, Alexandria, Antioch, and Rome have erred: so also others have erred and may err, not only in their living and manner of ceremonies, but also in matters of Faith.

Article XXII. OF THE AUTHORITY OF A CHURCH

A church hath power to decree Ceremonies, and to establish forms of worship, and laws for the government and discipline of its members, and to declare its own faith; yet it is not lawful for any Church to ordain or decide anything that is contrary to God's Word written, neither may it so expound one place of Scripture, that it be repugnant to another. And as the Church ought not to decree anything against the same, so besides the same ought it not to enforce anything to be believed for necessity of salvation. The Nicene Creed, as set forth in the Prayerbook of this Church, and that which is commonly called the Apostles' Creed, ought to be received and believed; for they may be proved by Holy Scripture.

Article XXIII. OF THE AUTHORITY OF GENERAL COUNCILS

General Councils (forasmuch as they be an assembly of men, whereof all be not governed with the Spirit and Word of God), may err, and sometimes have erred, not only in worldly matters, but also in things pertaining to God. Wherefore things ordained by them as necessary to salvation are not binding, as such, on a Christian man's conscience, unless it may be proved that they be taken out of Holy Scripture. No law or authority can override individual responsibility, and therefore the right of private judgment: For the individual Christian, as Christ distinctly affirms, is to be judged by the Word. The only Rule of Faith is God's Word written.

Article XXIV. OF MINISTERING IN THE CONGREGATION

Those who take upon themselves the office of public preaching, or ministering the ordinances in the congregation, should be lawfully called thereunto, and sent to execute the same. And those we ought to judge lawfully called and sent, which be moved to this work by the Holy Ghost, and are duly accredited by the LORD'S People.

That doctrine of "Apostolic Succession," by which it is taught that the ministry of the Christian Church must be derived through a series of uninterrupted ordinations, whether by tactual succession or otherwise, and that without the same there can be no valid ministry, no Christian Church, and no due ministration of Baptism and the LORD'S Supper, is wholly rejected as unscriptural, and productive of great mischief.

This Church values its historic ministry, but recognizes and honors as equally valid the ministry of other Churches, even as God the Holy Ghost has accompanied their work with demonstration and power.

Article XXV. OF THE SACRAMENTS

By the word Sacrament this Church is to be understood as meaning only a symbol or sign divinely appointed.

Our LORD Jesus Christ hath knit together his people in a visible company by sacraments, most few in number, most easy to be kept, most excellent in signification, viz.: Baptism and the LORD'S Supper.

Those five so-called Sacraments, that is to say, Confirmation, Penance, Orders, Matrimony, and Extreme Unction, are not to be counted for Sacraments of the Gospel, being such as have grown partly of the corrupt following of the Apostles, partly are states of life allowed by the Scriptures; but yet have not like nature of Sacraments with Baptism and the LORD'S Supper, for that they have not any visible sign or ceremony ordained of God.

And in such only as worthily receive Baptism and the LORD'S Supper are they of spiritual benefit, and yet not that of the work wrought (*ex opere operato*), as some men speak. Which word, as it is strange and unknown to Holy Scripture, so it gendereth no godly, but a very superstitious sense. In such as receive them rightly, faith is confirmed and grace increased by virtue of prayer to God. But they that receive them unworthily, purchase to themselves judgment, as St. Paul saith; while it is equally true that none, however conscious of unworthiness, are debarred from receiving them, if they are trusting in the LORD Jesus Christ alone for salvation.

Article XXVI. OF BAPTISM

Baptism represents the death of believers with Christ, and their rising with him to newness of life. It is a sign of profession, whereby they publicly declare their faith in him. It is intended as a sign of regeneration or new birth. They that are baptized are grafted into the visible Church: the promises of the forgiveness of sin and of adoption to be the sons of God by the Holy Ghost, are visibly set forth. The Baptism of young children is retained in this Church, as agreeable to ancient usage and not contrary to Holy Writ.

Article XXVII. OF THE LORD'S SUPPER

The Supper of the LORD is a memorial of our Redemption by Christ's death, for thereby we do show forth the LORD'S death till he come. It is also a symbol of the soul's feeding upon Christ. And it is a sign of the communion that we should have with one another.

Transubstantiation (or the change of the substance of bread and wine into the very body and blood of Christ) in the Supper of the LORD, cannot be proved by Holy Writ, is repugnant to the plain words of Scripture, overthroweth the nature of a Sacrament, and hath given occasion to many and idolatrous superstitions.

Consubstantiation (or the doctrine that Christ is veiled under the unchanged bread and wine, and that his very body and blood are present therein and separate the one from the other) is utterly without warrant of Scripture, is contradictory of the fact that Christ, being raised, dieth no more, and is productive, equally with transubstantiation, of idolatrous errors and practices.

We feed on Christ only through his Word, and only by faith and prayer; and we feed on him, whether at our private devotions, or in our meditations, or on any occasion of public worship, or in the memorial symbolism of the Supper.

The elements of the LORD'S Supper were not by Christ's ordinance designed to be reserved, carried about, lifted up, or worshipped.

Article XXVIII. OF BOTH KINDS

The Cup of the LORD is not to be denied to any of his people, for both the bread and the wine, by Christ's ordinance and commandment, ought to be ministered to all Christian men alike.

Article XXIX. OF UNWORTHY PERSONS MINISTERING IN THE CONGREGATION

Although in the visible Church the evil be ever mingled with the good, and sometimes the evil have chief authority in the ministration of the Word and ordinances: yet, forasmuch as they do not the same in their own name, but in Christ's, the believer is not deprived of the benefits of God's ordinances; because, though they be ministered by evil men, yet are they Christ's institution, and set forth his promise.

Nevertheless, it appertaineth to the discipline of the Church, that inquiry be made of evil ministers, and that they be accused by those that have knowledge of their offences: and finally, being found guilty, by just judgment, be deposed.

Article XXX. OF THE ONE OBLATION OF CHRIST FINISHED UPON THE CROSS

The Offering of Christ once made is that perfect redemption, propitiation, and satisfaction, for all the sins of the whole world, both original and actual; and there is none other satisfaction for sin, but that alone. And as there is only this one sacrifice in the Christian Church, once made, never to be repeated, so there is but the one Priest, even Jesus Christ, the Apostle and High Priest of our profession. Wherefore the sacrifices of Masses, in the which it is commonly said that the Priest offers Christ for the quick and the dead, for the remission of pain or guilt, or any representations of the LORD'S Supper as a sacrifice, are blasphemous fables and dangerous deceits.

Article XXXI. OF CERTAIN ERRONEOUS DOCTRINES AND PRACTICES

The Romish doctrines concerning purgatory, penance, and satisfaction, have no support from the Word of God, and are, besides, contradictory of the completeness and sufficiency of the redemption in Christ Jesus, of justification by faith, and of the sanctifying efficacy of God the Holy Ghost. Praying for the dead is man's tradition, vainly invented, and is in violation of the express warnings of Almighty God to the careless and unconverted. The adoration of relics and images, and the invocation of saints, besides that they are grounded upon no warranty of Scripture, are idolatrous practices, dishonoring to God, and compromising the mediatorship of Christ. It is also repugnant to the Word of God, to have public prayer in the Church, or to minister the ordinances, in a tongue not understood by the people.

DECLARATION OF PRINCIPLES AND ARTICLES OF
RELIGION (REFORMED EPISCOPAL CHURCH) (continued)

Article XXXII. OF CONFESSION AND ABSOLUTION

Private confession of sins to a priest, commonly known as Auricular Confession, has no foundation in the Word of God, and is a human invention. It makes the professed penitent a slave to mere human authority, entangles him in endless scruples and perplexities, and opens the way to many immoralities.

If one sin against his fellow-man, the Scripture requires him to make confession to the offended party; and so, if one sin, and bring scandal upon the Christian Society of which he is a member. And Christians may often, with manifest profit, confess to one another their sins against God, with a view solely to instruction, correction, guidance, and encouragement in righteousness. But in any and every case confession is still to be made to God; for all sins are committed against him, as well such as offend our fellow-man, as those that offend him alone.

Priestly absolution is a blasphemous usurpation of the sole prerogative of God. None can forgive sins as against God but God alone.

The blood of Jesus Christ only can cleanse us from our sins, and always we obtain forgiveness directly from God, whenever by faith in that blood we approach him with our confessions and prayers.

Article XXXIII. OF THE MARRIAGE OF MINISTERS

Christian Ministers are not commanded by God's Law either to vow the estate of single life, or to abstain from marriage; therefore it is lawful for them, as for all other Christian men, to marry at their own discretion.

Article XXXIV. OF THE POWER OF THE CIVIL AUTHORITY

The power of the Civil Magistrate extendeth to all men, as well Ministers as People, in all things temporal; but hath no authority in things purely spiritual. And we hold it to be the duty of all men who are professors of the Gospel, to pay respectful obedience to the civil authority, regularly and legitimately constituted.

Article XXXV. OF CHRISTIAN MEN'S GOODS

The riches and goods of Christian men are not common, but their own, to be controlled and used according to their Christian judgment. Every man ought, of such things as he possesseth, liberally to give alms to the poor, according to his ability; and as a steward of God, he should use his means and influence in promoting the cause of truth and righteousness, to the glory of God.

Notes: *The Reformed Episcopal Church's doctrinal statements were adopted in two stages, in 1873 and 1875. A brief Declaration\ of Principles professed substantial agreement with the Thirty-nine Articles of Religion of the Protestant Episcopal Church, and two years later, a text of thirty-five articles derived from these Thirty-nine Articles was adopted by the church's General Council. Both now appear at the very beginning of the Reformed Episcopal Church's Prayer Book.*

Chapter 3
Eastern Liturgical Family

Orthodoxy

DECLARATION OF FAITH OF THE AFRICAN ORTHODOX CHURCH

I. THE HOLY SCRIPTURES

The African Orthodox Church declares its belief in the Holy Scriptures of the Old and New Testaments as the Word of God and the only sufficient Rule of Faith and entreats all the faithful to read the same diligently, not only as their duty and privilege, but in obedience to Christ's command, "Search the Scriptures." For the moral instruction contained therein it accepts also the so called Apocryphal books.

II. THE CREEDS

The African Orthodox Church accepts the Nicene Creed without the "filioque" interpolation as the only one of universal obligation, but believes also the two symbols known as the Apostles' Creed and the Creed of S. Athanasius.

III. THE COUNCILS

The African Orthodox Church receives as Ecumenical the Seven General Councils whose dogmatic decrees are today accepted by all the Apostolic Churches of the East and West, Viz: (1) Nicea, 325; (2) Constantinople, 381; (3) Ephesus, 431; (4) Chalcedon, 451; (5) Constantinople, 553, (6) Constantinople, 680; (7) Nicea, 787.

IV. THE SACRAMENTS

The African Orthodox Church holds that a Sacrament is a sacred rite divinely instituted to convey grace, having a sensible or visible sign connected with prayer as the means by which the grace is conveyed. It receives as a part of the original deposit of the faith "once for all delivered to the saints" the Seven Gospel Sacraments.

i.   BAPTISM. It acknowledges Baptism as the Sacrament established by Christ to cleanse men from Original Sin and to make them members of the Christian Church. It is the Sacrament of Regeneration or the New Birth.

ii.   CONFIRMATION. It believes that Confirmation is the Sacrament in which the Holy Spirit is given with the fulness of His Gifts to the believer, and regards the Bishop as the ordinary minister of this Sacred Rite.

iii. PENANCE. It believes that in the Sacrament of Penance, Jesus Christ Himself inwardly looses from their sins those who sincerely repent of them and outwardly make confession, and that every validly ordained priest has the power to pronounce Christ's pardon to penitent sinners confessing their sins. It allows both public and private confession, the mode being optional with the penitent.

iv.   THE EUCHARIST. It holds that the Eucharist is both a Sacrament and a Sacrifice offered for the living and the dead. It believes that in this most holy Sacrament of the Altar there is the Real Presence of the glorified spiritual Body and Blood of Christ under the forms of bread and wine, the mysterious transformation being effected by the Holy Spirit. Since this is a mystery it shuns all terms of definition and description. It maintains that the Chalice should not be denied the laity in holy communion; it believes that the Liturgy ought to be said in the language of the people; and it permits in connection with this Sacrament the use of the names Eucharist, Mass, or Divine Liturgy.

v.   UNCTION OF THE SICK. It believes Unction of the Sick to be a Sacrament of the New Dispensation, instituted for the spiritual and corporal solace of the sick, to be used for the benefit of the Christian when seriously ill, and not only when approaching death. Both the mode and the efficacy of this Sacrament are indicated in the fifth chapter of the Epistle of St. James.

vi.   SACRED ORDERS. It believes that Order is a Sacrament which confers upon those who validly receive it the power to exercise special ministerial function, Bishops alone being the ministers of this Sacrament. The greater, or Holy Orders, which are of divine institution, are the Episcopate, the Priesthood, and the Diaconate. The minor orders, which

DECLARATION OF FAITH OF THE AFRICAN ORTHODOX CHURCH (continued)

are of ecclesiastical origin, and may be regarded as steps to the greater are doorkeeper, reader, exorcist, acolyte and subdeacon. It believes the episcopate necessary for the life of the Church, that all bishops are equal in power and authority by divine right and that their prerogatives of honor and jurisdiction are derived from the Church and regulated by her canons.

vii. HOLY MATRIMONY. It believes marriage, when a man and woman are joined together according to the sacred rite of the Church, to be a Sacrament, and that the civil ceremony of marriage prescribed by law in certain countries, should always be blessed by the priest. There should be no dissolution of the bonds of marriage except for adultery and malicious desertion, and no priest of this Church is permitted to perform the marriage ceremony of any person who has a divorced husband or wife living, unless such person produces satisfactory evidence from court records that he or she is the innocent party in a divorce granted for the cause of adultery or malicious desertion. In all cases involving the marriage of a divorced person, the priest must submit the facts to, and receive the consent of his Bishop, before performing the rite.

V. THE SAINTS

The African Orthodox Church believes that the departed saints are not dead, but living, and that if the prayers of the righteous on earth avail much, the prayers of our glorified brethren nearer the throne of God must be more potent. Hence we consider it a good and useful practice to invoke the prayers of the saints for us, and to pray ourselves for the repose of the souls of the faithful departed.

VI. SACRED PICTURES AND IMAGES

The African Orthodox Church holds that pictures and images of Christ and the Saints may be reverenced as sacred things, though not adored. We do not deny to any Christian the use of this pious practice if it be an aid to his worship, but we caution against abuses thereof when the picture or image is given the adoration which belongs only to God, or its veneration considered necessary to salvation or justification.

Notes: *In comparison to the Western Churches, those out of the Eastern tradition have found little reason over the centuries to compose creedal statements. Almost universally, both orthodox and heterodox Eastern Churches accept the Apostles' and Nicene Creeds, differing in their acceptance of the post-Nicene creeds. The Orthodox accept the Athanasian Creed and the Chalcedonian Formula while the other churches do not accept any creeds after the Nicene. The Nicene Creed, without the filioque clause added by the Western Church, became an integral element in all of the Eastern liturgies. Most of the Eastern churches that have congregations in the United States use the liturgy of St. John Chrysostom.*

Several of the smaller independent Orthodox bodies, all formed during the twentieth century, have found it expe-dient to author supplemental statements of faith. The African Orthodox Church adopted its Declaration of Faith in 1921. Its statement reflects an attempt to distinguish Orthodoxy from the position of the Protestant Episcopal Church (of which its founding archbishop had been a clergyman) and the Roman Catholic Church, both of which had built a following among black Americans.

* * *

DOGMATIC ARTICLES (AMERICAN CATHOLIC CHURCH, ARCHDIOCESE OF NEW YORK)

Eternal salvation is promised to mankind only through the merits of life, death, and resurrection of our Savior, Jesus Christ, upon the condition of obedience to the Gospel teachings, which require Faith, Hope and Charity, and true observance of the ordinances of the Catholic and Orthodox Church which He founded.

1. FAITH is a virtue infused into the soul at Baptism, whereby man accepts, without doubting, whatever God has revealed to the Church concerning His Church.

2. HOPE is a virtue infused into the soul by God, and following upon faith; by it man puts his entire trust and confidence in the goodness and mercy of God his Creator, through Jesus Christ, the Second Person of the Blessed Trinity, and looks for the fulfillment of the promises made to man to those who obey the Gospel.

3. CHARITY is a virtue infused into the soul by God, and likewise consequent upon faith, whereby man, loving God above all things for His Own sake, as his neighbor as himself for love of God, yields up his will to a joyful obedience to the revealed Will of Almighty God.

4. THE CHURCH. God has established the Holy Catholic Church upon earth to be the pillar and ground of the revealed truth; and has committed to her the guardianship of the Holy Scriptures and of Holy Tradition, and the power of binding and loosing.

5. THE SACRAMENTS. The fundamental ordinances of the Gospel, instituted by Jesus Christ as special means of conveying Divine grace and influence to the souls of men, which are commonly called Mysteries or Sacraments, are Seven in number, namely Baptism, Confirmation, the holy Eucharist, holy Orders, Matrimony, Penance, and Anointing of the Sick (Unction).

Baptism is the first Sacrament of the Gospel, administered by threefold immersion in, or affusion with, water with the words, "I baptise thee in the Name of the Father, and of the Son, and of the Holy Ghost." It admits the recipient into the Church, bestows upon him the forgiveness of sins, original and actual, through the Blood of Christ, and causes in him a spiritual change called Regeneration. Without valid Baptism no other Sacrament can be validly received.

Confirmation or Chrism is a Sacrament in which the baptised person, on being annointed with Chrism consecrated by the Bishops of the Church, with the imposition of hands, receives the seven-fold gifts of the Holy Ghost to strengthen him in the grace which he received at Baptism, making him a strong and perfect Christian and a good soldier of Christ.

The holy Eucharist is a Sacrament in which, under the appearances of bread and wine, the real and actual Body and Blood of Christ are given and received for the remission of sins, the increase of Divine grace, and the reward of everlasting Life. After the prayer of Invocation of the Holy Ghost in the Liturgy, the bread and wine are entirely converted into the living Body and Blood of Christ by an actual change of being, to which change the philosophical terms of Transubstantiation and Transmutation are rightly applied. The celebration of this Mystery or Sacrament, commonly called the Mass, constitutes the chief act of Christian worship, being a sacrificial Memorial or re-Presentation of our Lord's death. It is not a repetition of the Sacrifice offered once for all upon Calvary, but is a perpetuation of that Sacrifice by the Church on earth, as our Lord also perpetually offers it in heaven. It is a true and propitiatory Sacrifice, which is offered alike for the living and for the departed.

Holy Orders is a Sacrament in which the Holy Ghost, through the laying-on of hands of the Bishops, consecrates and ordains the pastors and ministers chosen to serve in the Church, and imparts to them special grace to administer the Sacraments, to forgive sins, and to feed the flock of Christ.

Matrimony is a Sacrament in which the voluntary union of husband and wife is sanctified to become an image of the union between Christ and His Church; and grace is imparted to them to fulfill the duties of their estate and its great responsibilities, both to each other and to their children.

Penance is a Sacrament in which the Holy Ghost bestows the forgiveness of sins, by the ministry of the priest, upon those who, having sinned after Baptism, confess their sins with true repentance, and grace is given to amend their lives thereafter.

Unction is a Sacrament in which the priests of the Church annoint the sick with oil, for the healing of the infirmities of their souls, and if it should please God, those of their bodies also.

The efficacy of the Sacraments depends upon the promise and appointment of God; howbeit they benefit only those who receive them worthily with faith, and with due preparation and disposition of mind.

6. HOLY SCRIPTURE. The Scriptures are writings inspired by God, and given to the Church for her instruction and edification. The Church is therefore the custodian and the only Divinely appointed interpreter of holy Scripture.

7. TRADITION. The Apostolic and Ecclesiastical Traditions received from the seven General Councils and the early Fathers of the Church may not be rejected; but are to be received and obeyed as being both agreeable to holy Scripture and to that Authority with which Christ endowed His Church. Matters of discipline and ceremonial do not rank on the same level with matters of Faith or Morals, but may be altered from time to time and from place to place by the Authority of the Church, according as the welfare and greater devotion of the faithful may be furthered thereby.

8. THE COMMUNION OF SAINTS. There is a Communion of Saints in the Providence of God, wherein the souls of righteous men of all ages are united with Christ in the bond of faith and love. Wherefore it is pleasing to God, and profitable to men, to honour the Saints and to invoke them in prayer; and also to pray for the faithful departed.

9. RELIGIOUS SYMBOLS. The relics and representations of Saints are worthy of honour, as are also all other religious emblems; that our minds may be encouraged to devotion and to imitation of the deeds of the just. Honour shown to such objects is purely relative, and in no way implies a confusion of the symbol with the thing signified.

10. RITES AND CEREMONIES. It is the duty of all Christians to join in the worship of the Church, especially in the holy Sacrifice of the Mass, in accordance with our Lord's express command; and to conform to the ceremonies prescribed by holy Tradition for the greater dignity of that Sacrifice and for the edification of the faithful.

11. THE MORAL LAW. All Christians are bound to observe the Moral Law contained in the Ten Commandments of the Old Testament, developed with greater strictness in the New, founded upon the law of nature and charity, and defining our duty to God and to man. The laws of the Church are also to be obeyed, as proceeding from that Authority which Christ has committed to her for the instruction and salvation of His people.

12. THE MONASTIC ESTATE. The monastic life, duly regulated according to the laws of the Church, is a salutary institution in strict accord with the holy Scriptures; and is full of profit to them who, after being carefully tried and examined, make full proof of their calling thereto.

Notes: *The small American Catholic Church, Archdiocese of New York, broke away from the African Orthodox Church and, like its parent, produced its own doctrinal statement.*

Non-Chalcedonian Orthodoxy

THE BELIEFS OF THE SYRO-CHALDEAN CHURCH OF NORTH AMERICA (NON-CHALCEDONIAN)

We believe that the Bible is the true Word of God. "All Scripture is inspired by God and profitable for teaching, for reproof, for correction, for training in righteousness." (II TIMOTHY 3:16)

We believe in the Trinity, God the Father, Jesus the Son, and the Holy Spirit, as specified throughout the Scriptures, the Nicene and the Apostles Creeds.

We believe in all the verities of the Faith of Jesus Christ— The Incarnation, His virginal conception, His Life and teachings, the atonement of the Cross and His Saving Blood, His mighty resurrection and victory over death, His ascension and pouring out of the Holy Spirit, His glorious coming again.

We believe in the sacramental aspect of the church. The sacraments are: Baptism and Confirmation, Holy Communion, Reconciliation, Annointing for Healing, Holy Matrimony and Holy Orders.

We believe that the major function of the church is to preach the Gospel to all of mankind and reach all with His love and message of salvation through Jesus Christ. "Go therefore and make disciples of all the nations, baptizing them in the name of the Father and the Son and the Holy Spirit, teaching them to observe all that I commanded you; and lo, I am with you always, even to the end of the age." (MATTHEW 28:19, 20)

We believe as a church we should stress the fruits of the Spirit is every Christian life. "But the fruit of the Spirit is love, joy, peace, patience, kindness, goodness, faithfulness, gentleness, self-control; against such things there is no law. If we live by the Spirit, let us also walk by the Spirit." (GALATIANS 5:22, 23, 25)

We believe God's power is still here today through the various gifts of the Spirit as were first experienced by the apostles and disciples in the upper room on Pentecost, (ACTS 2, I COR. 12) including God's power to heal in lives today—physically, spiritually, and emotionally. "Jesus Christ is the same yesterday and today, yes and forever." (HEBREWS 13:8)

Notes: *Claiming some relation to the Assyrian Church of the East, the Syro-Chaldean Church of North America has published a statement that manifests some influence of the modern Pentecostal movement in its reference to the "gifts of the spirit."*

Chapter 4
Lutheran Family

THE AUGSBURG CONFESSION (1530)

PREFACE.

Most Invincible Emperor, Cæsar Augustus, most Clement Lord:

Inasmuch as Your Imperial Majesty has summoned a Diet of the Empire here at Augsburg to deliberate concerning measures against the Turk, that most atrocious, hereditary and ancient enemy of the Christian name and religion, in what way effectually to withstand his furor and assaults by strong and lasting military provision; and then also concerning dissensions in the matter of our holy religion and Christian Faith, that in this matter of religion the opinions and judgments of parties might be heard in each other's presence, and considered and weighed among ourselves in charity, leniency and mutual kindness, to the end that the things in the Scriptures which on either side have been differently interpreted or misunderstood, being corrected and laid aside, these matters may be settled and brought back to one perfect truth and Christian concord, that for the future one pure and true religion may be embraced and maintained by us, that as we all serve and do battle under one Christ, so we may be able also to live in unity and concord in the one Christian Church. And inasmuch as we, the undersigned Electors and Princes, with others joined with us, have been called to the aforesaid Diet, the same as the other Electors, Princes and Estates, in obedient compliance with the Imperial mandate we have come to Augsburg, and, what we do not mean to say as boasting, we were among the first to be here.

Since then Your Imperial Majesty caused to be proposed to the Electors, Princes and other Estates of the Empire, also here at Augsburg at the very beginning of this Diet, among other things, that, by virtue of the Imperial Edict, the several Estates of the Empire should present their opinions and judgments in the German and Latin languages, after due deliberation, answer was given to Your Imperial Majesty, on the ensuing Wednesday, that on the next Friday the Articles of our Confession for our part would be presented.

Wherefore, in obedience to Your Imperial Majesty's wishes, we offer, in this matter of religion, the Confession of our preachers and of ourselves, showing what manner of doctrine from the Holy Scriptures and the pure Word of God has been up to this time set forth in our lands, dukedoms, dominions and cities, and taught in our churches. And if the other Electors, Princes and Estates of the Empire will present similar writings, to wit, in Latin and German, according to the said Imperial proposition, giving their opinions in this matter of religion, here before Your Imperial Majesty, our most clement Lord, we, with the Princes and friends aforesaid, are prepared to confer amicably concerning all possible ways and means, as far as may be honorably done, that we may come together, and, the matter between us on both sides being peacefully discussed without offensive strife, the dissension, by God's help, may be done away and brought back to one true accordant religion; for as we all serve and do battle under one Christ, we ought to confess the one Christ, and so, after the tenor of Your Imperial Majesty's Edict, everything be conducted according to the truth of God, which, with most fervent prayers, we entreat of God.

But, with regard to the other Electors, Princes and Estates, if they hold that this treatment of the matter of religion after the manner which Your Imperial Majesty has so wisely brought forward, namely, with such mutual presentation of writings and calm conferring together among ourselves, should not proceed, or be unfruitful in results; we, at least, leave behind the clear testimony that we decline or refuse nothing whatever, allowed of God and a good conscience, which may tend to bring about Christian concord; as also Your Imperial Majesty and the other Electors and Estates of the Empire, and all who are moved by sincere love and zeal for religion, and who will give an impartial hearing to this matter, will graciously perceive and more and more understand from this our Confession.

Your Imperial Majesty also, not only once but often, graciously signified to the Electors, Princes and Estates of the Empire, and at the Diet of Spires held A. D. 1526, according to the form of Your Imperial instruction and commission given and prescribed, caused it to be stated and publicly proclaimed, that Your Majesty, in dealing with this matter of religion, for certain reasons which were alleged in Your Majesty's name, was not willing to decide and could not determine anything, but that Your Majesty

THE AUGSBURG CONFESSION (1530) (continued)

would diligently use Your Majesty's office with the Roman Pontiff for the convening of a General Council, as the same was publicly set forth at greater length over a year ago at the last Diet which met at Spires. There Your Imperial Majesty, through his Highness Ferdinand, King of Bohemia and Hungary, our friend and clement Lord, as well as through the Orator and Imperial Commissioners, caused this, among other things, to be proclaimed: that Your Imperial Majesty had known of and pondered the resolution of Your Majesty's Representative in the Empire, and of the President and Imperial Counsellors, and the Legates from other Estates convened at Ratisbon, concerning the calling of a Council, and that this also was adjudged by Your Imperial Majesty to be of advantage; and because the matters to be adjusted between Your Imperial Majesty and the Roman Pontiff were nearing agreement and Christian reconciliation, Your Imperial Majesty did not doubt that the Roman Pontiff could be induced to hold a General Council; therefore Your Imperial Majesty himself signified that he would endeavor to secure the Chief Pontiff's consent together with Your Imperial Majesty to convene such General Council, and that letters to that effect would be publicly issued with all possible expedition.

In the event, therefore, that the differences between us and the other parties in the matter of religion cannot be amicably and in charity settled here before Your Imperial Majesty, we offer this in all obedience, abundantly prepared to join issue and to defend the cause in such a general, free, Christian Council, for the convening of which there has always been accordant action and agreement of votes in all the Imperial Diets held during Your Majesty's reign, on the part of the Electors, Princes and other Estates of the Empire. To this General Council, and at the same time to Your Imperial Majesty, we have made appeal in this greatest and gravest of matters even before this in due manner and form of law. To this appeal, both to Your Imperial Majesty and to a Council, we still adhere, neither do we intend, nor would it be possible for us, to relinquish it by this or any other document, unless the matter between us and the other side, according to the tenor of the latest Imperial citation, can be amicably and charitably settled and brought to Christian concord, of which this also is our solemn and public testimony.

I. CHIEF ARTICLES OF FAITH.

Article I.

Our Churches, with common consent, do teach, that the decree of the Council of Nicæa concerning the Unity of the Divine Essence and concerning the Three Persons, is true and to be believed without any doubting; that is to say, there is one Divine Essence which is called and which is God: eternal, without body, without parts, of infinite power, wisdom and goodness, the Maker and Preserver of all things, visible and invisible; and yet that there are three Persons, of the same essence and power, who also are co-eternal, the Father, the Son and the Holy Ghost. And the term "person" they use as the Fathers have used it, to signify, not a part or quality in another, but that which subsists of itself.

They condemn all heresies which have sprung up against this article, as the Manichæans who assumed two principles [gods], one Good, and the other Evil; also the Valentinians, Arians, Eunomians, Mohammedans, and all such. They condemn also the Samosatenes, old and new, who contending that there is but one Person, sophistically and impiously argue that the Word and the Holy Ghost are not distinct Persons, but that "Word" signifies a spoken word, and "Spirit" [Ghost] signifies motion created in things.

Article II.

Also they teach, that since the Fall of Adam, all men begotten according to nature, are born with sin, that is, without the fear of God, without trust in God, and with concupiscence; and that this disease, or vice of origin, is truly sin, even now condemning and bringing eternal death upon those not born again through baptism and the Holy Ghost.

They condemn the Pelagians and others, who deny that the vice of origin is sin, and who, to obscure the glory of Christ's merit and benefits, argue that man can be justified before God by his own strength and reason.

Article III.

Also they teach, that the Word, that is, the Son of God, did take man's nature in the womb of the blessed Virgin Mary, so that there are Two Natures, the divine and the human, inseparably conjoined in one Person, one Christ, true God and true man, who was born of the Virgin Mary, truly suffered, was crucified, dead and buried, that he might reconcile the Father unto us, and be a sacrifice, not only for original guilt, but for all actual sins of men. He also descended into hell, and truly rose again the third day; afterward he ascended into Heaven, that he might sit on the right hand of the Father, and forever reign, and have dominion over all creatures, and sanctify them that believe in Him, by sending the Holy Ghost into their hearts, to rule, comfort and quicken them, and to defend them against the devil and the power of sin. The same Christ shall openly come again to judge the quick and the dead, etc., according to the Apostles' Creed.

Article IV.

Also they teach, that men cannot be Justified before God by their own strength, merits or works, but are freely justified for Christ's sake through faith, when they believe that they are received into favor and that their sins are forgiven for Christ's sake, who, by His death, hath made satisfaction for our sins. This faith God imputes for righteousness in his sight. Rom. 3 and 4.

Article V.

That we may obtain this faith, the Office of Teaching the Gospel and administering the Sacraments was instituted. For through the Word and Sacraments as through instruments, the Holy Ghost is given, who worketh faith where and when it pleaseth God in them that hear the Gospel, to wit, that God, not for our own merits, but for Christ's sake, justified those who believe that they are received into favor for Christ's sake.

They condemn the Anabaptists and others, who think that the Holy Ghost cometh to men without the external Word, through their own preparations and works.

Article VI.

Also they teach, that this Faith is bound to bring forth Good Fruits, and that it is necessary to do good works commanded by God, because of God's will, but not that we should rely on those works to merit justification before God. For remission of sins and justification are apprehended by faith, as also the voice of Christ attests: "When ye shall have done all these things, say: We are unprofitable servants" [Luke 17:10]. The same is also taught by the Fathers. For Ambrose says: "It is ordained of God that he who believes in Christ, is saved; freely receiving remission of sins, without works, by faith alone."

Article VII.

Also they teach, that One holy Church is to continue forever. The Church is the congregation of saints, in which the Gospel is rightly taught and the Sacraments rightly administered. And to the true unity of the Church, it is enough to agree concerning the doctrine of the Gospel and the administration of the Sacraments. Nor is it necessary that human traditions, rites, or ceremonies, instituted by men, should be everywhere alike. As Paul says: "One faith, one baptism, one God and Father of all," etc. [Eph. 4:5, 6].

Article VIII.

Although the Church properly is the Congregation of Saints and true believers, nevertheless, since in this life, many hypocrites and evil persons are mingled therewith, it is lawful to use the Sacraments, which are administered by evil men; according to the saying of Christ: "The Scribes and the Pharisees sit in Moses' seat," etc. [Matt. 23:2]. Both the Sacraments and Word are effectual by reason of the institution and commandment of Christ, notwithstanding they be administered by evil men.

They condemn the Donatists, and such like, who denied it to be lawful to use the ministry of evil men in the Church, and who thought the ministry of evil men to be unprofitable and of none effect.

Article IX.

Of Baptism, they teach, that it is necessary to salvation, and that through Baptism is offered the grace of God; and that children are to be baptized, who, being offered to God through Baptism, are received into His grace.

They condemn the Anabaptists, who allow not the Baptism of children, and say that children are saved without Baptism.

Article X.

Of the Supper of the Lord, they teach, that the Body and Blood of Christ are truly present, and are distributed to those who eat in the Supper of the Lord; and they disapprove of those that teach otherwise.

Article XI.

Of Confession, they teach, that Private Absolution ought to be retained in the churches, although in confession an enumeration of all sins is not necessary. For it is impossible, according to the Psalm: "Who can understand his errors?" [Ps. 19: 12].

Article XII.

Of Repentance, they teach, that for those that have fallen after Baptism, there is remission of sins whenever they are converted; and that the Church ought to impart absolution to those thus returning to repentance.

Now repentance consists properly of these two parts: One is contrition, that is, terrors smiting the conscience through the knowledge of sin; the other is faith, which, born of the Gospel, or of absolution, believes that, for Christ's sake, sins are forgiven, comforts the conscience, and delivers it from terrors. Then good works are bound to follow, which are the fruits of repentance.

They condemn the Anabaptists, who deny that those once justified can lose the Holy Ghost. Also those who contend that some may attain to such perfection in this life that they cannot sin. The Novatians also are condemned, who would not absolve such as had fallen after Baptism, though they returned to repentance. They also are rejected who do not teach that remission of sins cometh through faith, but command us to merit grace through satisfactions of our own.

Article XIII.

Of the Use of the Sacraments, they teach, that the Sacraments were ordained, not only to be marks of profession among men, but rather to be signs and testimonies of the will of God toward us, instituted to awaken and confirm faith in those who use them. Wherefore we must so use the Sacraments that faith be added to believe the promises which are offered and set forth through the Sacraments.

They therefore condemn those who teach that the Sacraments justify by the outward act, and do not teach that, in the use of the Sacraments, faith which believes that sins are forgiven, is required.

Article XIV.

Of Ecclesiastical Order, they teach, that no one should publicly teach in the Church or administer the Sacraments, unless he be regularly called.

Article XV.

Of Rites and Usages in the Church, they teach, that those ought to be observed which may be observed without sin, and which are profitable unto tranquillity and good order in the Church, as particular holydays, festivals, and the like.

Nevertheless, concerning such things, let men be admonished that consciences are not to be burdened, as though such observance was necessary to salvation. They are admonished also that human traditions instituted to propitiate God, to merit grace and to make satisfaction for sins, are opposed to the Gospel and the doctrine of faith. Wherefore vows and traditions concerning meats and days, etc., instituted to merit grace and to make satisfaction for sins, are useless and contrary to the Gospel.

Article XVI.

Of Civil Affairs, they teach, that lawful civil ordinances are good works of God, and that it is right for Christians to bear civil office, to sit as judges, to determine matters by the Imperial and other existing laws, to award just punishments, to engage in just wars, to serve as soldiers, to make legal contracts, to hold property, to make oath when required by the magistrates, to marry, to be given in marriage.

They condemn the Anabaptists who forbid these civil offices to Christians. They condemn also those who do not place the perfection of the Gospel in the fear of God and in faith, but in forsaking civil offices; for the Gospel teaches an eternal righteousness of the heart. Meanwhile, it does not destroy the State or the family, but especially requires their preservation as ordinances of God, and in such ordinances the exercise of charity. Therefore, Christians are necessarily bound to obey their own magistrates and laws, save only when commanded to sin, for then they ought to obey God rather than men [Acts 5:29].

Article XVII.

Also they teach, that, at the Consummation of the World, Christ shall appear for judgment, and shall raise up all the dead; he shall give to the godly and elect eternal life and everlasting joys, but ungodly men and the devils he shall condemn to be tormented without end.

They condemn the Anabaptists who think that there will be an end to the punishments of condemned men and devils. They condemn also others, who are now spreading certain Jewish opinions that, before the resurrection of the dead, the godly shall take possession of the kingdom of the world, the ungodly being everywhere suppressed [exterminated].

Article XVIII.

Of the Freedom of the Will, they teach, that man's will has some liberty for the attainment of civil righteousness, and for the choice of things subject to reason. Nevertheless, it has no power, without the Holy Ghost, to work the righteousness of God, that is, spiritual righteousness; since the natural man receiveth not the things of the Spirit of God [1 Cor. 2:14]; but this righteousness is wrought in the heart when the Holy Ghost is received through the Word. These things are said in as many words by Augustine in his *Hypognosticon*, book iii.: "We grant that all men have a certain freedom of will in judging according to [natural] reason; not such freedom, however, whereby it is capable, without God, either to begin, or much less to complete aught in things pertaining to God, but only in works of this life, whether good or evil. 'Good,' I call those works which spring from the good in Nature, that is, to have a will to labor in the field, to eat and drink, to have a friend, to clothe oneself, to build a house, to marry, to keep cattle, to learn divers useful arts, or whatsoever good pertains to this life, none of which things are without dependence on the providence of God; yea, of Him and through Him they are and have their beginning. 'Evil,' I call such works as to have a will to worship an idol, to commit murder," etc.

They condemn the Pelagians and others who teach that, without the Holy Ghost, by the power of nature alone, we are able to love God above all things; also to do the commandments of God as touching "the substance of the act."

For, although nature is able in some sort to do the outward work (for it is able to keep the hands from theft and murder), yet it cannot work the inward motions, such as the fear of God, trust in God, chastity, patience, etc.

Article XIX.

Of the Cause of Sin, they teach, that although God doth create and preserve nature, yet the cause of sin is the will of the wicked, that is, of the devil and ungodly men; which will, unaided of God, turns itself from God, as Christ says [John 8:44]: "When he speaketh a lie, he speaketh of his own."

Article XX.

Our teachers are falsely accused of forbidding Good Works. For their published writings on the Ten Commandments, and others of like import, bear witness that they have taught to good purpose concerning all estates and duties of life, as to what estates of life and what works in every calling be pleasing to God. Concerning these things preachers heretofore taught but little, and urged only childish and needless works, as particular holydays, particular fasts, brotherhoods, pilgrimages, services in honor of saints, the use of rosaries, monasticism, and such like. Since our adversaries have been admonished of these things they are now unlearning them, and do not preach these unprofitable works as heretofore. Besides they begin to mention faith, of which there was heretofore marvellous silence. They teach that we are justified not by works only, but they conjoin faith and works, and say that we are justified by faith and works. This doctrine is more tolerable than the former one, and can afford more consolation than their old doctrine.

Forasmuch, therefore, as the doctrine concerning faith, which ought to be the chief one in the church, has lain so long unknown, as all must needs grant that there was the deepest silence in their sermons concerning the righteousness of faith, while only the doctrine of works was treated in the churches, our teachers have instructed the churches concerning faith as follows:

First, that our works cannot reconcile God or merit forgiveness of sins, grace and justification, but that we obtain this only by faith, when we believe that we are received into favor for Christ's sake, who alone has been set forth the Mediator and Propitiation [1 Tim. 2:5], in order that the Father may be reconciled through Him. Whoever, therefore, trusts that by works he merits grace, despises the merit and grace of Christ, and seeks a way to God without Christ, by human strength, although Christ has said of himself: "I am the Way, the Truth and the Life" [John 14:6].

This doctrine concerning faith is everywhere treated by Paul [Eph. 2:8]: "By grace are ye saved through faith; and that not of yourselves; it is the gift of God, not of works," etc.

And lest anyone should craftily say that a new interpretation of Paul has been devised by us, this entire matter is supported by the testimonies of the Fathers. For Augustine, in many volumes, defends grace and the righteousness of faith, over against the merits of works. And Ambrose, in his *De Vocatione Gentium*, and elsewhere, teaches to like effect. For in his *De Vocatione Gentium* he says as follows: "Redemption by the Blood of Christ would become of little value, neither would the pre-eminence of man's works be superseded by the mercy of God, if justification, which is wrought through grace, were due to the merits going before, so as to be, not the free gift of a donor, but the reward due to the laborer."

But, although this doctrine is despised by the inexperienced, nevertheless God-fearing and anxious consciences find by experience that it brings the greatest consolation, because consciences cannot be pacified through any works, but only by faith, when they are sure that, for Christ's sake, they have a gracious God. As Paul teaches [Rom. 5:1]: "Being justified by faith, we have peace with God." This whole doctrine is to be referred to that conflict of the terrified conscience; neither can it be understood apart from that conflict. Therefore inexperienced and profane men judge ill concerning this matter, who dream that Christian righteousness is nothing but the civil righteousness of natural reason.

Heretofore consciences were plagued with the doctrine of works, nor did they hear any consolation from the Gospel. Some persons were driven by conscience into the desert, into monasteries, hoping there to merit grace by a monastic life. Some also devised other works whereby to merit grace and make satisfaction for sins. There was very great need to treat of and renew this doctrine of faith in Christ, to the end that anxious consciences should not be without consolation, but that they might know that grace and forgiveness of sins and justification are apprehended by faith in Christ.

Men are also admonished that here the term "faith" doth not signify merely the knowledge of the history, such as is in the ungodly and in the devil, but signifieth a faith which believes, not merely the history, but also the effect of the history—namely, this article of the forgiveness of sins, to wit, that we have grace, righteousness, and forgiveness of sins, through Christ.

Now he that knoweth that he has a Father reconciled to him through Christ, since he truly knows God, knows also that God careth for him, and calls upon God; in a word, he is not without God, as the heathen. For devils and the ungodly are not able to believe this article of the forgiveness of sins. Hence, they hate God as an enemy; call not upon Him; and expect no good from Him. Augustine also admonishes his readers concerning the word "faith," and teaches that the term "faith" is accepted in the Scriptures, not for knowledge such as is in the ungodly, but for confidence which consoles and encourages the terrified mind.

Furthermore, it is taught on our part, that it is necessary to do good works, not that we should trust to merit grace by them, but because it is the will of God. It is only by faith that forgiveness of sins and grace are apprehended. And because through faith the Holy Ghost is received, hearts are renewed and endowed with new affections, so as to be able to bring forth good works. For Ambrose says: "Faith is the mother of a good will and right doing." For man's powers without the Holy Ghost are full of ungodly affections, and are too weak to do works which are good in God's sight. Besides, they are in the power of the devil, who impels men to divers sins, to ungodly opinions, to open crimes. This we may see in the philosophers, who, although they endeavored to live an honest life, could not succeed, but were defiled with many open crimes. Such is the feebleness of man, when he is without faith and without the Holy Ghost, and governs himself only by human strength.

Hence it may be readily seen that this doctrine is not to be charged with prohibiting good works, but rather the more to be commended, because it shows how we are enabled to do good works. For without faith, human nature can in no wise do the works of the First or of the Second Commandment. Without faith, it does not call upon God, nor expect anything from Him, nor bear the cross; but seeks and trusts in man's help. And thus, when there is no faith and trust in God, all manner of lusts and human devices rule in the heart. Wherefore Christ said [John 15:5]: "Without me ye can do nothing," and the Church sings:

"Without Thy power divine
In man there nothing is,
Naught but what is harmful."

Article XXI.

Of the Worship of Saints, they teach, that the memory of saints may be set before us, that we may follow their faith and good works, according to our calling, as the Emperor may follow the example of David in making war to drive away the Turk from his country. For both are kings. But the Scripture teaches not the invocation of saints, or to ask help of saints, since it sets before us Christ, as the only Mediator, Propitiation, High-Priest and Intercessor. He is to be prayed to, and hath promised that He will hear our prayer; and this worship He approves above all, to wit, that in all afflictions He be called upon [1 John 2:1]: "If any man sin, we have an Advocate with the Father," etc.

This is about the Sum of our Doctrine, in which, as can be seen, there is nothing that varies from the Scriptures, or from the Church Catholic, or from the Church of Rome as known from its writers. This being the case, they judge harshly who insist that our teachers be regarded as heretics. The disagreement, however, is on certain Abuses, which have crept into the Church without rightful authority. And even in these, if there were some difference, there should be proper lenity on the part of bishops to bear with us by reason of the Confession which we have now drawn up; because even the Canons are not so severe as to demand the same rites everywhere, neither, at any time, have the rites of all churches been the same; although, among us, in large part, the ancient rites are diligently observed. For it is a false and malicious charge that all the ceremonies, all the things instituted of old, are abolished in our churches. But it has been a common complaint that some Abuses were connected with the ordinary rites. These, inasmuch as they could not be approved with a good conscience, have been to some extent corrected.

II. ARTICLES, IN WHICH ARE REVIEWED THE ABUSES WHICH HAVE BEEN CORRECTED.

Inasmuch then as our churches dissent in no article of the Faith from the Church Catholic, but omit some Abuses

THE AUGSBURG CONFESSION (1530) (continued)

which are new, and which have been erroneously accepted by fault of the times, contrary to the intent of the Canons, we pray that Your Imperial Majesty would graciously hear both what has been changed, and also what were the reasons, in order that the people be not compelled to observe those abuses against their conscience. Nor should Your Imperial Majesty believe those, who, in order to excite the hatred of men against our part, disseminate strange slanders among our people. Having thus excited the minds of good men, they have first given occasion to this controversy, and now endeavor, by the same arts, to increase the discord. For Your Imperial Majesty will undoubtedly find that the form of doctrine and of ceremonies with us, is not so intolerable as these ungodly and malicious men represent. Furthermore, the truth cannot be gathered from common rumors, or the revilings of our enemies. But it can readily be judged that nothing would serve better to maintain the dignity of worship, and to nourish reverence and pious devotion among the people than that the ceremonies be rightly observed in the churches.

Article XXII.

To the laity are given Both Kinds in the Sacrament of the Lord's Supper, because this usage has the commandment of the Lord [in Matt. 26:27]: "Drink ye all of it"; where Christ has manifestly commanded concerning the cup that all should drink; and lest any man should craftily say that this refers only to priests, Paul [in 1 Cor. 11:27] recites an example from which it appears that the whole congregation did use both kinds. And this usage has long remained in the Church, nor is it known when, or by whose authority, it was changed; although Cardinal Cusanus mentions the time when it was approved. Cyprian in some places testifies that the Blood was given to the people. The same is testified by Jerome, who says: "The priests administer the Eucharist, and distribute the Blood of Christ to the people." Indeed, Pope Gelasius commands that the sacrament be not divided (*Dist.* ii., *De Consecratione, Cap. Comperimus*). Only custom, not so ancient, has it otherwise. But it is evident that any custom introduced against the commandments of God is not to be allowed, as the Canons witness (*Dist.* iii., *Cap. Veritate*, and the following chapters). But this custom has been received, not only against the Scripture but also against the old Canons and examples of the Church. Therefore if any preferred to use both kinds of the sacrament, they ought not to have been compelled with offence to their consciences to do otherwise.

And because the division of the sacrament does not agree with the ordinance of Christ, we are accustomed to omit the procession, which hitherto has been in use.

Article XXIII.

There has been common complaint concerning the Examples of Priests, who were not chaste. For that reason also, Pope Pius is reported to have said that there were certain reasons why marriage was taken away from priests, but that there were far weightier ones why it ought to be given back; for so Platina writes. Since, therefore, our priests were desirous to avoid these open scandals they married wives, and taught that it was lawful for them to contract matrimony. First, because Paul says [1 Cor. 7:2]: "To avoid fornication, let every man have his own wife." Also [9]: "It is better to marry than to burn." Secondly, Christ says [Matt. 19:11]: "All men cannot receive this saying," where he teaches that not all men are fit to lead a single life; for God created man for procreation [Gen. 1:28]. Nor is it in man's power, without a singular gift and work of God, to alter this creation. Therefore those that are not fit to lead a single life ought to contract matrimony. For no man's law, no vow, can annul the commandment and ordiance of God. For these reasons the priests teach that it is lawful for them to marry wives. It is also evident that in the ancient Church priests were married men. For Paul says [1 Tim. 3:2] that a bishop should be the husband of one wife. And in Germany, four hundred years ago for the first time, the priests were violently compelled to lead a single life, who indeed offered such resistance that the Archbishop of Mayence, when about to publish the Pope's decree concerning this matter, was almost killed in the tumult raised by the enraged priests. And so harsh was the dealing in the matter that not only were marriages forbidden for the time to come, but also existing marriages were torn asunder, contrary to all laws, divine and human, contrary even to the Canons themselves, made not only by the Popes but by most celebrated Councils.

Seeing also that, as the world is aging, man's nature is gradually growing weaker, it is well to guard that no more vices steal into Germany. Furthermore, God ordained marriage to be a help against human infirmity. The Canons themselves say that the old rigor ought now and then, in the latter times, to be relaxed because of the weakness of men; which it is to be devoutly wished were done also in this matter. And it is to be expected that the churches shall at length lack pastors, if marriage should be any longer forbidden.

But while the commandment of God is in force, while the custom of the Church is well known, while impure celibacy causes many scandals, adulteries, and other crimes deserving the punishments of just magistrates, yet it is a marvellous thing that in nothing is more cruelty exercised than against the marriage of priests. God has given commandment to honor marriage. By the laws of all well-ordered commonwealths, even among the heathen, marriage is most highly honored. But now men, and also priests, are cruelly put to death, contrary to the intent of the Canons, for no other cause than marriage. Paul [in 1 Tim. 4:3] calls that a doctrine of devils, which forbids marriage. This may now be readily understood when the law against marriage is maintained by such penalties.

But as no law of man can annul the commandment of God, so neither can it be done by any vow. Accordingly Cyprian also advises that women who do not keep the chastity they have promised should marry. His words are these [Book I., Epistle xi.]: "But if they be unwilling or unable to perserve, it is better for them to marry than to fall into the fire by their lusts; at least, they should give no offence to their brethren and sisters." And even the Canons show some leniency toward those who have taken vows before the proper age, as heretofore has generally been the case.

Article XXIV.

Falsely are our churches accused of Abolishing the Mass; for the Mass is retained on our part, and celebrated with the highest reverence. All the usual ceremonies are also preserved, save that the parts sung in Latin are interspersed here and there with German hymns, which have been added to teach the people. For ceremonies are needed to this end alone, that the unlearned be taught. And not only has Paul commanded to use in the Church a language understood by the people [1 Cor. 14:2, 9], but it has also been so ordained by man's law.

The people are accustomed to partake of the Sacrament together, if any be fit for it, and this also increases the reverence and devotion of public worship. For none are admitted except they be first proved. The people are also advised concerning the dignity and use of the Sacrament, how great consolation it brings anxious consciences, that they may learn to believe God, and to expect and ask of Him all that is good. This worship pleases God; such use of the Sacrament nourishes true devotion toward God. It does not, therefore, appear that the Mass is more devoutly celebrated among our adversaries, than among us.

But it is evident that for a long time, it has been the public and most grievous complaint of all good men, that Masses have been basely profaned and applied to purposes of lucre. For it is unknown how far this abuse obtains in all the churches, by what manner of men Masses are said only for fees or stipends, and how many celebrate them contrary to the Canons. But Paul severely threatens those who deal unworthily with the Eucharist, when he says [1 Cor. 11:27]: "Whosoever shall eat this bread, and drink this cup of the Lord unworthily, shall be guilty of the body and blood of the Lord." When, therefore, our priests were admonished concerning this sin, Private Masses were discontinued among us, as scarcely any Private Masses were celebrated except for lucre's sake.

Neither were the bishops ignorant of these abuses, and if they had corrected them in time, there would now be less dissension. Heretofore, by their own negligence, they suffered many corruptions to creep into the Church. Now, when it is too late, they begin to complain of the troubles of the Church, seeing that this disturbance has been occasioned simply by those abuses, which were so manifest that they could be borne no longer. Great dissensions have arisen concerning the Mass, concerning the Sacrament. Perhaps the world is being punished for such long-continued profanations of the Mass, as have been tolerated in the churches for so many centuries, by the very men who were both able and in duty bound to correct them. For, in the Ten Commandments, it is written (Exodus 20), "The Lord will not hold him guiltless that taketh His name in vain." But since the world began, nothing that God ever ordained seems to have been so abused for filthy lucre as the Mass.

There was also added the opinion which infinitely increased Private Masses, namely, that Christ, by His passion, had made satisfaction for original sin, and instituted the Mass wherein an offering should be made for daily sins, venial and mortal. From this has arisen the common opinion that the Mass taketh away the sins of the living and the dead, by the outward act. Then they began to dispute whether one Mass said for many were worth as much as special Masses for individuals, and this brought forth that infinite multitude of Masses. Concerning these opinions our teachers have given warning, that they depart from the Holy Scriptures and diminish the glory of the passion of Christ. For Christ's passion was an oblation and satisfaction, not for original guilt only, but also for all sins, as it is written to the Hebrews (10:10), "We are sanctified through the offering of Jesus Christ, once for all." Also, 10:14: "By one offering he hath perfected forever them that are sanctified." Scripture also teaches that we are justified before God through faith in Christ, when we believe that our sins are forgiven for Christ's sake. Now if the Mass take away the sins of the living and the dead by the outward act, justification comes of the work of Masses, and not of faith, which Scripture does not allow.

But Christ commands us [Luke 22:19], "This do in remembrance of me;" therefore the Mass was instituted that the faith of those who use the Sacrament should remember what benefits it receives through Christ, and cheer and comfort the anxious conscience. For, to remember Christ, is to remember his benefits, and to realize that they are truly offered unto us. Nor is it enough only to remember the history, for this the Jew and the ungodly also can remember. Wherefore the Mass is to be used to this end, that there the Sacrament [Communion] may be administered to them that have need of consolation; as Ambrose says: "Because I always sin, I am always bound to take the medicine."

Now forasmuch as the Mass is such a giving of the Sacrament, we hold one communion every holyday, and also other days, when any desire the Sacrament it is given to such as ask for it. And this custom is not new in the Church; for the Fathers before Gregory make no mention of any private Mass, but of the common Mass [the Communion] they speak very much. Chrysostom says that the priest stands daily at the altar, inviting some to the Communion and keeping back others. And it appears from the ancient Canons, that some one celebrated the Mass from whom all the other presbyters and deacons received the Body of the Lord; for thus the words of the Nicene Canon say: "Let the deacons, according to their order, receive the Holy Communion after the presbyters, from the bishop or from a presbyter." And Paul [1 Cor. 11:33] commands concerning the Communion: "Tarry one for another," so that there may be a common participation.

Forasmuch, therefore, as the Mass with us has the example of the Church, taken from the Scripture and the Fathers, we are confident that it cannot be disapproved, especially since the public ceremonies are retained for the most part, like those hitherto in use; only the number of Masses differs, which, because of very great and manifest abuses, doubtless might be profitably reduced. For in olden times, even in churches, most frequented, the Mass was not celebrated every day, as the Tripartite History (Book 9, chapt. 33) testifies: "Again in Alexandria, every Wednesday and Friday, the Scriptures are read, and the doctors expound them, and all things are done, except only the celebration of the Eucharist."

Article XXV.

Confession in our churches is not abolished; for it is not usual to give the Body of the Lord, except to them that have been previously examined and absolved. And the people are most carefully taught concerning the faith and assurance of absolution, about which, before this time, there was profound silence. Our people are taught that they should highly prize the absolution, as being the voice of God, and pronounced by His command. The power of the Keys is commended, and we show what great consolation it brings to anxious consciences; that God requires faith to believe such absolution as a voice sounding from Heaven, and that such faith in Christ truly obtains and receives the forgiveness of sins.

Aforetime, satisfactions were immoderately extolled; of faith and the merit of Christ, and the righteousness of faith, no mention was made; wherefore, on this point, our churches are by no means to be blamed. For this even our adversaries must needs concede to us, that the doctrine concerning repentance has been most diligently treated and laid open by our teachers.

But of Confession, they teach, that an enumeration of sins is not necessary, and that consciences be not burdened with anxiety to enumerate all sins, for it is impossible to recount all sins, as the Psalm testifies [19:13]: "Who can understand his errors?" Also Jeremiah [17:9]: "The heart is deceitful, who can know it?" But if no sins were forgiven, except those that are recounted, consciences could never find peace; for very many sins they neither see, nor can remember.

The ancient writers also testify that an enumeration is not necessary. For, in the Decrees, Chrysostom is quoted, who thus says: "I say not to thee, that thou shouldest disclose thyself in public, nor that thou accuse thyself before others, but I would have thee obey the prophet who says: 'Disclose thy way before God.' Therefore confess thy sins before God, the true Judge, with prayer. Tell thine errors, not with the tongue, but with the memory of thy conscience." And the Gloss ("Of Repentance," *Distinct. v, Cap. Consideret*) admits that Confession of human right only. Nevertheless, on account of the great benefit of absolution, and because it is otherwise useful to the conscience, Confession is retained among us.

Article XXVI.

It has been the general persuasion, not of the people alone, but also of such as teach in the churches, that making Distinctions of Meats, and like traditions of men, are works profitable to merit grace, and able to make satisfactions for sins. And that the world so thought, appears from this, that new ceremonies, new orders, new holydays, and new fastings were daily instituted, and the teachers in the churches did exact these works as a service necessary to merit grace, and did greatly terrify men's consciences, if they should omit any of these things. From this persuasion concerning traditions, much detriment has resulted in the Church.

First, the doctrine of grace and of the righteousness of faith has been obscured by it, which is the chief part of the Gospel, and ought to stand out, as the most prominent in the Church, that the merit of Christ may be well known, and that faith, which believes that sins are forgiven for Christ's sake may be exalted far above works. Wherefore Paul also lays the greatest stress on this article, putting aside the law and human traditions, in order to show that the righteousness of the Christian is another than such works, to wit, the faith which believes that sins are freely forgiven for Christ's sake. But this doctrine of Paul has been almost wholly smothered by traditions, which have produced an opinion that, by making distinctions in meats and like services, we must merit grace and righteousness. In treating of repentance, there was no mention made of faith; all that was done was to set forth those works of satisfaction, and in these all repentance seemed to consist.

Secondly, these traditions have obscured the commandments of God; because traditions were placed far above the commandments of God. Christianity was thought to consist wholly in the observance of certain holydays, fasts and vestures. These observances had won for themselves the exalted title of being the spiritual life and the perfect life. Meanwhile the commandments of God, according to each one's calling, were without honor, namely, that the father brought up his family, that the mother bore children, that the Prince governed the Commonwealth,— these were accounted works that were worldly and imperfect, and far below those glittering observances. And this error greatly tormented devout consciences, which grieved that they were bound by an imperfect state of life, as in marriage, in the office of magistrate, or in other civil ministrations; on the other hand, they admired the monks and such like, and falsely imagined that the observances of such men were more acceptable to God.

Thirdly, traditions brought great danger to consciences; for it was impossible to keep all traditions, and yet men judged these observances to be necessary acts of worship. Gerson writes that many fell into despair, and that some even took their own lives, because they felt that they were not able to satisfy the traditions; and meanwhile, they heard not the consolation of the righteousness of faith and grace.

We see that the summists and theologians gather the traditions together, and seek mitigations whereby to ease consciences, and yet they do not succeed in releasing them, but sometimes entangle consciences even more. And with the gathering of these traditions, the schools and sermons have been so much occupied that they have had no leisure to touch upon Scripture, and to seek the more profitable doctrine of faith, of the cross, of hope, of the dignity of civil affairs, of consolation of sorely tried consciences. Hence Gerson, and some other theologians, have grievously complained, that by these strivings concerning traditions, they were prevented from giving attention to a better kind of doctrine. Augustine also forbids that men's consciences should be burdened with such observances, and prudently advises Januarius, that he must know that they are to be observed as things indifferent; for these are his words.

Wherefore our teachers must not be looked upon as having taken up this matter rashly, or from hatred of the bishops, as some falsely suspect. There was great need to warn the churches of these errors, which had arisen from misunderstanding the traditions. For the Gospel compels us to insist in the churches upon the doctrine of grace, and of the righteousness of faith; which, however, cannot be understood, if men think that they merit grace by observances of their own choice.

Thus, therefore, they have taught, that by the observance of human traditions we cannot merit grace, or be justified; and hence we must not think such observances necessary acts of worship.

They add hereunto testimonies of Scripture. Christ [Matt. 15:3] defends the Apostles who had not observed the usual tradition, which however, seemed to pertain to a matter not unlawful, but indifferent, and to have a certain affinity with the purifications of the law, and says [9]: "In vain do they worship me with the commandments of men." He, therefore, does not exact an unprofitable service. Shortly after, he adds [11]: "Not that which goeth into the mouth, defileth a man." So also Paul [Rom. 14:17]: "The Kingdom of God is not meat and drink." [Col. 2:16]: "Let no man therefore judge you in meat, or in drink, or in respect of an holyday, or of the Sabbath day;" also [v. 20, sq.]: "If ye be dead with Christ from the rudiments of the world, why, as though living in the world, are ye subject to ordinances, touch not, taste not, handle not?" And Peter says [Acts 15:10]: "Why tempt ye God, to put a yoke upon the neck of the disciples, which neither our fathers, nor we were able to bear; but we believe that through the grace of the Lord Jesus Christ, we shall be saved, even as they." Here Peter forbids to burden the consciences with many rites, either of Moses, or of others.

And in 1 Tim. [4:1, 3], Paul calls the prohibition of meats a doctrine of devils; for it is against the Gospel to institute or to do such works that by them we may merit grace, or as though Christianity could not exist without such service of God.

Here our adversaries cast up that our teachers are opposed to discipline and mortification of the flesh, as Jovinian. But the contrary may be learned from the writings of our teachers. For they have always taught concerning the cross, that it behooves Christians to bear afflictions. This is the true, earnest and unfeigned mortification, to wit, to be exercised with divers afflictions, and to be crucified with Christ.

Moreover, they teach, that every Christian ought to exercise and subdue himself with bodily restraints and labors, that neither plenty nor slothfulness tempt him to sin, but not that we may merit grace or make satisfaction for sins by such exercises. And such external discipline ought to be urged at all times, not only on a few and set days. So Christ commands [Luke 21:34]: "Take heed, lest your hearts be overcharged with surfeiting;" also [Matt. 17:21]: "This kind goeth not out but by prayer and fasting." Paul also says [1 Cor. 9:27]: "I keep under my body and bring it into subjection." Here he clearly shows that he was keeping under his body, not to merit forgiveness of sins by that discipline, but to have his body in subjection and fitted for spiritual things, and for the discharge of duty according to his calling. Therefore, we do not condemn fasting, but the traditions which prescribe certain days and certain meats, with peril of conscience, as though works of such kinds were a necessary service.

Nevertheless, very many traditions are kept on our part, which conduce to good order in the Church, as the Order of Lessons in the Mass, and the chief holydays. But, at the same time, men are warned that such observances do not justify before God, and that, in such things, it should not be made sin, if they be omitted without scandal. Such liberty in human rites was not unknown to the Fathers. For in the East they kept Easter at another time than at Rome, and when, on account of this diversity, the Romans accused the Eastern Church of schism, they were admonished by others that such usages need not be alike everywhere. And Irenæus says: "Diversity concerning fasting does not destroy the harmony of faith." As also Pope Gregory intimates in *Dist*. xii., that such diversity does not violate the unity of the Church. And in the Tripartite History, Book 9, many examples of dissimilar rites are gathered, and the following statement is made: "It was not the mind of the Apostles to enact rules concerning holydays, but to preach godliness and a holy life."

Article XXVII.

What is taught, on our part, concerning Monastic Vows, will be better understood, if it be remembered what has been the state of the monasteries, and how many things were daily done in those very monasteries, contrary to the Canons. In Augustine's time, they were free associations. Afterward, when discipline was corrupted, vows were everywhere added for the purpose of restoring discipline, as in a carefully planned prison. Gradually, many other observances were added besides vows. And these fetters were laid upon many before the lawful age, contrary to the Canons. Many also entered into this kind of life through ignorance, being unable to judge their own strength, though they were of sufficient age. Being thus ensnared, they were compelled to remain, even though some could have been freed by the provision of the Canons. And this was more the case in convents of women than of monks, although more consideration should have been shown the weaker sex. This rigor displeased many good men before this time, who saw that young men and maidens were thrown into convents for a living, and what unfortunate results came of this procedure, and what scandals were created, what snares were cast upon consciences! They were grieved that the authority of the Canons in so momentous a matter was utterly despised and set aside.

To these evils, was added an opinion concerning vows, which, it is well known, in former times, displeased even those monks who were more thoughtful. They taught that vows were equal to Baptism; they taught that, by this kind of life, they merited forgiveness of sins and justification before God. Yea, they added that the monastic life not only merited righteousness before God, but even greater things, because it kept not only the precepts, but also the so-called "evangelical counsels."

Thus they made men believe that the profession of monasticism was far better than Baptism, and that the monastic life was more meritorious than that of magistrates, than the life of pastors and such like, who serve their calling in accordance with God's commands, without any man-made services. None of these things can be denied; for they appear in their own books.

What then came to pass in the monasteries? Aforetime, they were schools of Theology and other branches, profitable to the Church; and thence pastors and bishops were obtained. Now it is another thing. It is needless to rehearse what is known to all. Aforetime they came together to learn; now they feign that it is a kind of life instituted to merit grace and righteousness; yea, they preach that it is a state of perfection, and they put it far above all other kinds of life ordained of God.

These things we have rehearsed without odious exaggeration, to the end that the doctrine of our teachers, on this point, might be better understood. First, concerning such as contract matrimony, they teach, on our part, that it is lawful for all men who are not fitted for single life to contract matrimony, because vows cannot annual the ordinance and commandment of God. But the commandment of God is [1 Cor. 7:2]: "To avoid fornication, let every man have his own wife." Nor is it the commandment only, but also the creation and ordinance of God, which forces those to marry who are not excepted by a singular work of God, according to the text [Gen. 2:18]: "It is not good that the man should be alone." Therefore they do not sin who obey this commandment and ordinance of God. What objection can be raised to this? Let men extol the obligation of a vow as much as they list, yet shall they not bring to pass that the vow annuls the commandment of God. The Canons teach that the right of the superior is excepted in every vow; much less, therefore, are these vows of force which are against the commandments of God.

Now if the obligation of vows could not be changed for any cause whatever, the Roman Pontiffs could never have given dispensation; for it is not lawful for man to annul an obligation which is altogether divine. But the Roman Pontiffs have prudently judged that leniency is to be observed in this obligation, and therefore we read that many times they have dispensed from vows. The case of the King of Aragon who was called back from the monastery is well known, and there are also examples in our own times.

In the second place, Why do our adversaries exaggerate the obligation or effect of a vow, when, at the same time, they have not a word to say of the nature of the vow itself, that it ought to be in a thing possible, free, and chosen spontaneously and deliberately. But it is not known to what extent perpetual chastity is in the power of man. And how few are there who have taken the vow spontaneously and deliberately! Young men and maidens, before they are able to judge, are persuaded, and sometimes even compelled, to take the vow. Wherefore it is not fair to insist so rigorously on the obligation, since it is granted by all that it is against the nature of a vow to take it without spontaneous and deliberate action.

Many canonical laws rescind vows made before the age of fifteen; for before that age, there does not seem sufficient judgment in a person to decide concerning a perpetual life.

Another Canon, granting even more liberty to the weakness of man, adds a few years, and forbids a vow to be made before the age of eighteen. But whether we followed the one or the other, the most part have an excuse for leaving the monasteries, because most of them have taken the vows before they reached these ages.

But, finally, even though the violation of a vow might be rebuked, yet it seems not forthwith to follow that the marriages of such persons ought to be dissolved. For Augustine denies that they ought to be dissolved (xxvii. Quæst. I., Cap, *Nuptiarum*); and his authority is not lightly to be esteemed, although other men afterwards thought otherwise.

But although it appears that God's command concerning marriage delivers many from their vows, yet our teachers introduce also another argument concerning vows, to show that they are void. For every service of God, ordained and chosen of men without the commandment of God to merit justification and grace, is wicked; as Christ says [Matt. 15:9]: "In vain do they worship me with the commandments of men." And Paul teaches everywhere that righteousness is not to be sought by our own observances and acts of worship, devised by men, but that it comes by faith to those who believe that they are received by God into grace for Christ's sake.

But it is evident that monks have taught that services of man's making satisfy for sins and merit grace and justification. What else is this but to detract from the glory of Christ and to obscure and deny the righteousness of faith? It follows, therefore, that the vows thus commonly taken, have been wicked services, and, consequently, are void. For a wicked vow, taken against the commandment of God, is not valid; for (as the Canon says) no vow ought to bind men to wickedness.

Paul says [Gal. 5:4]: "Christ is become of no effect unto you, whosoever of you are justified by the law; ye are fallen from grace." They, therefore, who want to be justified by their vows, are made void of Christ and fall from grace. For such as ascribe justification to vows, ascribe to their own works that which properly belongs to the glory of Christ. But it is undeniable that the monks have taught that, by their vows and observances, they were justified, and merited forgiveness of sins, yea, they invented still greater absurdities, saying that they could give others a share in their works. If any one should be inclined to enlarge on these things with evil intent, how many things could he bring together, whereof even the monks are now ashamed! Over and above this, they persuaded men that services of man's making were a state of Christian perfection. And is not this assigning justification to works? It is no light offence in the Church to set forth to the people a service devised by men, without the commandment of God, and to teach that such service justifies men. For the righteousness of faith in Christ, which chiefly ought to be in the Church, is obscured, when this wonderful worshipping of angels, with its show of poverty, humility and chastity, is cast before the eyes of men.

Furthermore, the precepts of God and the true service of God are obscured when men hear that only monks are in a state of perfection. For Christian perfection is to fear God from the heart, again to conceive great faith, and to trust that, for Christ's sake, we have a gracious God, to ask of God, and assuredly to expect his aid in all things that, according to our calling, are to be borne; and meanwhile, to be diligent in outward good works, and to serve our calling. In these things consist the true perfection and the true service of God. It does not consist in the unmarried life, or in begging, or in vile apparel. But the people conceive many pernicious opinions from the false commendations of monastic life. They hear unmarried life praised above measure; therefore they lead their married life with offence to their consciences. They hear that only beggars are perfect; therefore they keep their possessions and do business with offence to their consciences. They hear that it is an evangelical counsel not to avenge; therefore some in private life are not afraid to take revenge, for they hear that it is but a counsel, and not a commandment; while others judge that the Christian cannot properly hold a civil office, or be a magistrate.

There are on record examples of men who, forsaking marriage and the administration of the Commonwealth, have hid themselves in monasteries. This they called fleeing from the world, and seeking a kind of life which should be more pleasing to God. Neither did they see that God ought to be served in those commandments which he himself has given, and not in commandments devised by men. A good and perfect kind of life is that which has for it the commandment of God. It is necessary to admonish men of these things. And before these times, Gerson rebuked this error concerning perfection, and testified that, in his day, it was a new saying that the monastic life is a state of perfection.

So many wicked opinions are inherent in the vows, such as that they justify, that they constitute Christian perfection, that they keep the counsels and commandments, that they have works of supererogation. All these things, since they are false and empty, make vows null and void.

Article XXVIII.

There has been great controversy concerning the Power of Bishops, in which some have awkwardly confounded the power of the Church and the power of the sword. And from this confusion very great wars and tumults have resulted, while the Pontiffs, emboldened by the power of the Keys, not only have instituted new services and burdened consciences with reservation of cases, but have also undertaken to transfer the kingdoms of this world, and to take the Empire from the Emperor. These wrongs have long since been rebuked in the Church by learned and godly men. Therefore, our teachers, for the comforting of men's consciences, were constrained to show the difference between the power of the Church and the power of the sword, and taught that both of them, because of God's commandment, are to be held in reverence and honor, as among the chief blessings of God on earth.

But this is their opinion, that the power of the Keys, or the power of the bishops, according to the Gospel, is a power or commandment of God, to preach the Gospel, to remit and retain sins, and to administer sacraments. For with that commandment, Christ sends forth his Apostles [John 20:21 sqq.]: "As my Father has sent me, even so send I you. Receive ye the Holy Ghost. Whosoever sins ye remit, they are remitted unto them; and whosoever sins ye retain, they are retained." [Mark 16:15]: "Go, preach the Gospel to every creature."

This power is exercised only by teaching or preaching the Gospel and administering the sacraments, according to the calling, either to many or to individuals. For thereby are granted, not bodily, but eternal things, as eternal righteousness, the Holy Ghost, eternal life. These things cannot come but by the ministry of the Word and the sacraments. As Paul says [Rom. 1:16]: "The Gospel is the power of God unto salvation to every one that believeth." Therefore, since the power of the Church grants eternal things, and is exercised only by the ministry of the Word, it does not interfere with civil government; no more than the art of singing interferes with civil government. For civil government deals with other things than does the Gospel; the civil rulers defend not souls, but bodies and bodily things against manifest injuries, and restrain men with the sword and bodily punishments in order to preserve civil justice and peace.

Therefore the power of the Church and the civil power must not be confounded. The power of the Church has its own commission, to teach the Gospel and to administer the sacraments. Let it not break into the office of another; let it not transfer the kingdoms of this world; let it not abrogate the laws of civil rulers; let it not abolish lawful obedience; let it not interfere with judgments concerning civil ordinances or contracts; let it not prescribe laws to civil rulers concerning the form of the Commonwealth. As Christ says [John 18:36]: "My kingdom is not of this world"; also [Luke 12:14]: "Who made me a judge or a divider over you?" Paul also says [Phil. 3:20]: "Our citizenship is in Heaven"; [2 Cor. 10:4]: "The weapons of our warfare are not carnal; but mighty through God to the casting down of imaginations." After this manner, our teachers discriminate between the duties of both these powers, and command that both be honored and acknowledged as gifts and blessings of God.

If bishops have any power of the sword, that power they have, not as bishops, by the commission of the Gospel, but by human law, having received it of Kings and Emperors, for the civil administration of what is theirs. This, however, is another office than the ministry of the Gospel.

When, therefore, a question arises concerning the jurisdiction of bishops, civil authority must be distinguished from ecclesiastical jurisdiction. Again, according to the Gospel, or, as they say, according to Divine Law, to the bishops as bishops, that is, to those to whom has been committed the ministry of the Word and the sacraments, no jurisdiction belongs, except to forgive sins, to discern doctrine, to reject doctrines contrary to the Gospel, and to exclude from the communion of the Church wicked men, whose wickedness is known, and this without human force, simply by the Word. Herein the congregations are bound by Divine Law to obey them, according to Luke 10:16: "He that heareth you, heareth me."

But when they teach or ordain anything against the Gospel, then the congregations have a commandment of God prohibiting obedience [Matt. 7:15]: "Beware of false

THE AUGSBURG CONFESSION (1530) (continued)

prophets"; [Gal. 1:8]: "Though an angel from heaven preach any other Gospel let him be accursed"; [2 Cor. 13:8]: "We can do nothing against the truth; but for the truth." Also [v. 10]: "The power which the Lord hath given me to edification, and not to destruction." So, also, the Canonical Laws command (II. Q. vii. Cap., *Sacerdotes* and Cap. *Oves*). And Augustine (*Contra Petiliani Epistolam*): "Not even to Catholic bishops must we submit, if they chance to err, or hold anything contrary to the Canonical Scriptures of God."

If they have any other power or jurisdiction, in hearing and judging certain cases, as of matrimony or of tithes, they have it by human law. But where the ordinaries fail, princes are bound, even against their will, to dispense justice to their subjects, for the maintenance of peace.

Moreover, it is disputed whether bishops or pastors have the right to introduce ceremonies in the Church, and to make laws concerning meats, holydays and degrees, that is, orders of ministers, etc. They that claim this right for the bishops, refer to this testimony [John 16:12, 13]: "I have yet many things to say unto you, but ye cannot bear them now. Howbeit when he, the Spirit of truth is come, he will guide you into all truth." They also refer to the example of the Apostles, who commanded to abstain from blood and from things strangled [Acts 15:29]. They refer to the Sabbath Day, as having been changed into the Lord's Day, contrary to the Decalogue, as it seems. Neither is there any example whereof they make more than concerning the changing of the Sabbath Day. Great, say they, is the power of the Church, since it has dispensed with one of the Ten Commandments!

But, concerning this question, it is taught on our part (as has been shown above), that bishops have no power to decree anything against the Gospel. The Canonical laws teach the same thing (*Dist.* ix.). Now it is against Scripture to establish or require the observance of any traditions, to the end that, by such observance, we may make satisfaction for sins, or merit grace and righteousness. For the glory of Christ's merit is dishonored when, by such observances, we undertake to merit justification. But it is manifest that, by such belief, traditions have almost infinitely multiplied in the Church, the doctrine concerning faith and the righteousness of faith being meanwhile suppressed. For gradually more holydays were made, fasts appointed, new ceremonies and services in honor of saints instituted; because the authors of such things thought that, by these works, they were meriting grace. Thus, in times past, the Penitential Canons increased, whereof we still see some traces in the satisfactions.

Again, the authors of traditions do contrary to the command of God when they find matters of sin in foods, in days, and like things, and burden the Church with bondage of the law, as if there ought to be among Christians, in order to merit justification, a service like the Levitical, the arrangement of which God has committed to the Apostles and bishops. For thus some of them write; and the Pontiffs in some measure seem to be misled by the example of the law of Moses. Hence are such burdens, as that they make it mortal sin, even without offence to others, to do manual labor on holydays, to omit the Canonical Hours, that certain foods defile the conscience, that fastings are works which appease God, that sin in a reserved case cannot be forgiven but by the authority of him who reserved it; whereas the Canons themselves speak only of the reserving of the ecclesiastical penalty, and not of the reserving of the guilt.

Whence have the bishops the right to lay these traditions upon the Church for the ensnaring of consciences, when Peter [Acts 15:10] forbids to put a yoke upon the neck of the disciples, and Paul says [2 Cor. 13:10] that the power given him was to edification, not to destruction? Why, therefore, do they increase sins by these traditions?

But there are clear testimonies which prohibit the making of such traditions, as though they merited grace or were necessary to salvation. Paul says [Col. 2:16]: "Let no man judge you in meat, or in drink, or in respect of a holyday, or of the new moon, or of the Sabbath days"; [v. 20, 23]: "If ye be dead with Christ from the rudiments of the world, why, as though living in the world, are ye subject to ordinances (touch not; taste not; handle not, which all are to perish with the using); after the commandments and doctrines of men? which things have indeed a show of wisdom." Also in Tit. [1:14] he openly forbids traditions: "Not giving heed to Jewish fables and commandments of men that turn from the truth." And Christ [Matt. 15:14] says of those who require traditions: "Let them alone; they be blind leaders of the blind"; and he rebukes such services [v. 13]: "Every plant which my Heavenly Father hath not planted, shall be plucked up."

If bishops have the right to burden churches with infinite traditions, and to ensnare consciences, why does Scripture so often prohibit to make and to listen to traditions? Why does it call them "doctrines of devils"? [1 Tim. 4:1]. Did the Holy Ghost in vain forewarn of these things?

Since, therefore, ordinances instituted as things necessary, or with an opinion of meriting grace, are contrary to the Gospel, it follows that it is not lawful for any bishop to institute or exact such services. For it is necessary that the doctrine of Christian liberty be preserved in the churches, namely, that the bondage of the Law is not necessary to justification, as it is written in the Epistle to the Galatians [5:1]: "Be not entangled again with the yoke of bondage." It is necessary that the chief article of the Gospel be preserved, to wit, that we obtain grace freely by faith in Christ, and not for certain observances or acts of worship devised by men.

What, then, are we to think of the Sunday and like rites in the house of God? To this we answer, that it is lawful for bishops or pastors to make ordinances that things be done orderly in the Church, not that thereby we should merit grace or make satisfaction for sins, or that consciences be bound to judge them necessary services, and to think that it is a sin to break them without offence to others. So Paul ordains [1 Cor. 11:5], that women should cover their heads in the congregation [1 Cor. 14:30], that interpreters of Scripture be heard in order in the church, etc.

It is proper that the churches should keep such ordinances for the sake of charity and tranquility, so far that one do not offend another, that all things be done in the churches in order, and without confusion; but so that consciences be not burdened to think that they be necessary to salvation, or to judge that they sin when they break them without offence to others; as no one will say that a woman sins who goes out in public with her head uncovered, provided only that no offence be given.

Of this kind, is the observance of the Lord's Day, Easter, Pentecost, and like holydays and rites. For those who judge that, by the authority of the Church, the observance of the Lord's Day instead of the Sabbath Day was ordained as a thing necessary, do greatly err. Scripture has abrogated the Sabbath Day; for it teaches that, since the Gospel has been revealed, all the ceremonies of Moses can be omitted. And yet, because it was necessary to appoint a certain day, that the people might know when they ought to come together, it appears that the Church [the Apostles] designated the Lord's Day for this purpose; and this day seems to have been chosen all the more for this additional reason, that men might have an example of Christian liberty, and might know that the keeping neither of the Sabbath, nor of any other day, is necessary.

There are monstrous disputations concerning the changing of the law, the ceremonies of the new law, the changing of the Sabbath Day, which all have sprung from the false belief that there must needs be in the Church a service like to the Levitical, and that Christ had given commission to the Apostles and bishops to devise new ceremonies as necessary to salvation. These errors crept into the Church when the righteousness of faith was not clearly enough taught. Some dispute that the keeping of the Lord's Day is not indeed of divine right; but in a manner so. They prescribe concerning holydays, how far it is lawful to work. What else are such disputations but snares of consciences? For although they endeavor to modify the traditions, yet the equity can never be perceived as long as the opinion remains that they are necessary, which must needs remain where the righteousness of faith and Christian liberty are disregarded.

The Apostles commanded to abstain from blood. Who doth now observe it? And yet they that do it not, sin not; for not even the Apostles themselves wanted to burden consciences with such bondage; but they forbade it for a time, to avoid offense. For, in any decree, we must perpetually consider what is the aim of the Gospel. Scarcely any Canons are kept with exactness, and, from day to day, many go out of use even with those who are the most zealous advocates of traditions. Neither can due regard be paid to consciences unless this equity be observed, that we know that the Canons are kept without holding them to be necessary, and that no harm is done consciences, even though traditions go out of use.

But the bishops might easily retain the lawful obedience of the people, if they would not insist upon the observance of such traditions as cannot be kept with a good conscience. Now they command celibacy; they admit none, unless they swear that they will not teach the pure doctrine of the Gospel. The churches do not ask that the bishops should restore concord at the expense of their honor; which, nevertheless, it would be proper for good pastors to do. They ask only that they would release unjust burdens

which are new and have been received contrary to the custom of the Church Catholic. It may be that there were plausible reasons for some of these ordinances; and yet they are not adapted to later times. It is also evident that some were adopted through erroneous conceptions. Therefore, it would be befitting the clemency of the Pontiffs to mitigate them now; because such a modification does not shake the unity of the Church. For many human traditions have been changed in process of time, as the Canons themselves show. But if it be impossible to obtain a mitigation of such observances as cannot be kept without sin, we are bound to follow the Apostolic rule [Acts 5:29], which commands us to obey God rather than men. Peter [1 Pet. 5:3] forbids bishops to be lords, and to rule over the churches. Now it is not our design to wrest the government from the bishops, but this one thing is asked, namely, that they allow the Gospel to be purely taught, and that they relax some few observances which cannot be kept without sin. But if they make no concession, it is for them to see how they shall give account to God for having, by their obstinacy, caused a schism.

CONCLUSION.

These are the Chief Articles which seem to be in controversy. For although we might have spoken of more Abuses, yet to avoid undue length, we have set forth the chief points, from which the rest may be readily judged. There have been great complaints concerning indulgences, pilgrimages, and the abuses of excommunications. The parishes have been vexed in many ways by the dealers in indulgences. There were endless contentions between the pastors and the monks concerning the parochial rites, confessions, burials, sermons on extraordinary occasions, and innumerable other things. Things of this sort we have passed over, so that the chief points in this matter, having been briefly set forth, might be the most readily understood. Nor has anything been here said or adduced to the reproach of any one. Only those things have been recounted, whereof we thought that it was necessary to speak, so that it might be understood that, in doctrine and ceremonies, nothing has been received on our part, against Scripture or the Church Catholic, since it is manifest that we have taken most diligent care that no new and ungodly doctrine should creep into our churches.

The above articles we desire to present in accordance with the edict of Your Imperial Majesty, so that our Confession should therein be exhibited, and a summary of the doctrine of our teachers might be discerned. If anything further be desired, we are ready, God willing, to present ampler information according to the Scriptures.

JOHN, Duke of Saxony, Elector.
GEORGE, Margrave of Brandenburg.
ERNEST, Duke of Lüneburg.
PHILIP, Landgrave of Hesse.
JOHN FREDERICK, Duke of Saxony.
FRANCIS, Duke of Lüneburg.
WOLFGANG, Prince of Anhalt.
SENATE and MAGISTRACY of Nuremburg.
SENATE of Reutlingen.

Notes: *When the Western Church was disrupted in the sixteenth century, those church bodies separating from*

THE AUGSBURG CONFESSION (1530) (continued)

Roman Catholic jurisdiction began to generate statements "confessing" their position on the ancient symbols (creeds) by which Christianity had defined itself for centuries and on newer issues that had led to their rejection of Rome. Thus, in the decades after Luther nailed the 95 Theses to the church door at Wittenburg, a variety of confessional statements came forth from Lutheran, Reformed-Presbyterian, Brethren-Mennonite, and Anglican leaders and representative bodies. Frequently joining the confessional statements were catechisms that became major tools for training the younger generation in the faith.

For the Lutherans, the single most definitive confession was the first one, the Augsburg Confession, produced in 1530 in response to the demand of Emperor Charles V for an explicit statement of Lutheran belief. Philip Melancthon is generally given credit as the major author, though he received the assistance and counsel of others. The original texts were in German and Latin.

Eventually, the Augsburg Confession was gathered with a selection of three ancient creeds (Apostles', Nicene, Athanasian) and several sixteenth century documents (an addenda or Apology to the Augsburg Confession produced in 1531, Luther's Smaller and Larger Catechisms, The Smalcald Articles, and the Formula of Concord) into The Book of Concord. *The Book of Concord, a sizable volume of six to seven hundred pages (depending upon which edition is consulted), has remained the common standard of Lutheran doctrine despite the organizational splintering that has occurred over the centuries since the book's original publication in 1580. In addition to the items mentioned above, various editions of* The Book of Concord *have contained the Treatise on the Power and Primacy of the Pope (a document written by Melancthon in 1537), Luther's Order of Baptism, Luther's Marriage Booklet, the Catalog of Testimonies, and the Christian Visitation Articles.*

The Augsburg Confession is generally considered the best attempt of the Lutherans to present their central teachings in terms of the core of the orthodox Western tradition. It affirms the theology of the ecumenical councils, specifically condemning the classical heretics (including the Donatists and Pelegians). It makes a point of Luther's stance on salvation by grace through faith. The majority of the confession deals with specifics of the reforms in the Roman Catholic Church sought by the Lutherans. The Augsburg Confession stands in sharp contrast to the lengthier Formula of Concord (1577), which deals in depth with many Lutheran theological distinctives.

All Lutherans would accept the Augsburg Confession. Different churches vary in the strictness with which conformity to the confession is demanded of members and leaders, as well as the relative weight given to it and the other statements in The Book of Concord.

SMALCALD ARTICLES (1537)

PREFACE OF DR. MARTIN LUTHER

When Pope Paul III. convoked a Council last year to assemble at Mantua about Whitsuntide, and afterwards transferred it from Mantua, so that it is not yet clear where he will or can fix it; and we on our part had reason to expect that we would either be summoned also to the Council or be condemned unsummoned; I was directed to compose and collect the articles of our doctrine, in case there should be any deliberation as to what and how far we could yield to the Papists, and upon what we intended finally to persevere and abide.

I have accordingly collected these articles and presented them to our side. They have also been accepted and unanimously confessed by those with us, and it has been resolved that in case the Pope with his adherents should ever be so bold as seriously and in good faith, without lying and cheating, to hold a truly free Christian Council (as indeed he would be in duty bound to do), they be publicly presented, and express the Confession of our faith.

But since the Romish court is so dreadfully afraid of a free Christian Council, and shuns the light so shamefully, that it has removed, even from those who are on its side, the hope that it will permit a free Council, and much less itself hold it, whereat, as is just, they are greatly offended and have on that account no little trouble, since they notice thereby that the Pope prefers to see all Christendom lost, and all souls damned, rather than that either he or his adherents be reformed even a little, and permit a limit to be fixed to their tyranny; I have, nevertheless, determined to bring these articles to light through the public press, so that should I die before there would be a Council (as I fully expect and hope, because the knaves by fleeing the light and shunning the day take such wretched pains to delay and hinder the Council), they who live and remain after me may thereby have my testimony and confession to produce, concerning the Confession which I had before published, whereby up to this time I still abide, and, by God's grace, will abide.

For what shall I say? How shall I complain? I am still in life, am writing, preaching and lecturing daily; and yet there are spiteful men, not only among the adversaries, but also false brethren that profess to be on our side, who attempt to represent my writings and doctrine directly contrary to myself, and compel me to hear and see it, although they know well that I teach otherwise, and who wish to adorn their venom with my labor, and under my name to mislead the poor people. How will such occurrences continually increase after my death!

Yea, it is but just that I should reply to everything while I am still living. But, on the other hand, how can I alone stop all the mouths of the devil? Especially of those (as they all are embittered) who will not hear or notice what we write, but solely exercise themselves with all diligence how they may most shamefully pervert and corrupt our word in every letter. These I let the devil answer, or at last God's wrath, as they deserve. I often think of the good person, who doubts whether anything good should be published. If it be not done, many souls are neglected who could be delivered; but if it be done, the devil is there, with malignant, villainous tongues without number which envenom and pervert everything, so that the fruit is still prevented. Yet what they gain thereby is manifest. For seeing that they have lied so shamefully against us, and by means of lies wish to retain the people, God has constantly advanced his work, and been ever making their assembly less and ours greater, and by their lies they have been and still continue to be brought to shame.

I must tell a story. There was a doctor sent here to Wittenberg from France, who said publicly before us that his king was sure, and more than sure, that among us there is no Church, no magistrate, no marriage, but all live promiscuously as cattle, and each one does as he will. Say now, how will those who by their writings have represented such gross lies to the king and to other countries as the pure truth, look at us on that day before the judgment-seat of Christ? Christ, the Lord and Judge of us all, knows well that they lie and have lied, whose sentence they must again hear; that I know certainly. God convert those who can be converted to repentance! To the rest it will be said, Woe, and, alas! eternally.

But to return to the subject. I sincerely desire to see a truly Christian Council, whereby yet many matters and persons would be helped. Not that we need it, for our churches are now, through God's grace, so illumined and cared for by the pure Word and right use of the sacraments, by knowledge of the various callings and of right works, that we on our part ask for no Council, and on such points have nothing better to hope or expect from a Council; but because we see in the bishoprics everywhere so many parishes vacant and desolate that one's heart would break. And yet neither the bishops nor canons care how the poor people live or die, for whom nevertheless Christ has died, and who cannot hear him speaking with them as the true Shepherd with his sheep. This causes me to shudder and fear that at some time he may send a council of angels upon Germany that may utterly destroy us, as Sodom and Gomorrah, because we so presumptuously mock him concerning this Council.

Besides such necessary ecclesiastical affairs, there would be also in the political estate innumerable matters of great importance to improve. There is the disagreement between the princes and the states; usury and avarice have burst in like a flood, and have the semblance of right; wantonness, lewdness, pride in dress, gluttony, gambling, idle display, with all kinds of bad habits and wickedness, insubordination of subjects, domestics and laborers of every trade, also the exactions of the peasants (and who can enumerate all?) have so increased that they cannot be rectified by ten Councils and twenty Diets. If such chief matters of the spiritual and worldly estates as are contrary to God would be considered in the Council, they would render all hands so full that the child's play and absurdity of long gowns, large tonsures [wax tapers], broad cinctures, bishops' or cardinals' hats or maces, and like jugglery would be all the while forgotten. If we first had performed God's command and order in the spiritual and worldly estate, we would find time enough to reform food, clothing, tonsures and surplices. But if we swallow such camels, and instead

strain out gnats, let the beams stand and judge the motes, we might indeed be satisfied with the Council.

Therefore I have presented a few articles; for we have without this so many commands of God to observe in the Church, the state, and the family, that we can never fulfil them. What then is the use? or wherefore does it profit that many decrees and statutes thereon are made in the Council, especially when these chief matters commanded of God are neither observed nor maintained? Just as though he were to be entertained by our jugglery while we tread his solemn commandments under foot. But our sins weigh upon us and cause God not to be gracious to us; for we do not repent, and besides wish to defend every abomination.

O Lord Jesus Christ, do thou thyself convoke a Council, and deliver thy servants by thy glorious advent. The Pope and his adherents are lost; they wish thee not. So do thou help us, poor and needy, who sigh to thee, and beg thee earnestly, according to the grace which thou hast given us, through the Holy Ghost, who liveth and reigneth with thee and the Father, blessed for ever. Amen.

PART FIRST. OF THE CHIEF ARTICLES CONCERNING THE DIVINE MAJESTY, as:

I. That Father, Son and Holy Ghost, three distinct persons in one divine essence and nature, are one God, who has created heaven and earth.

II. That the Father is begotten of no one; the Son of the Father; the Holy Ghost proceeds from Father and Son.

III. That not the Father, not the Holy Ghost, but the Son became man.

IV. That the Son became man thus: that he was conceived, without the co-operation of man, by the Holy Ghost, and was born of the pure, holy [and always] Virgin Mary. Afterwards he suffered, died, was buried, descended to hell, rose from the dead, ascended to heaven, sits at the right hand of God, will come to judge the quick and the dead, etc., as the Creed of the Apostles, as well as that of St. Athanasius, and the Catechism in common use for children, teach.

Concerning these articles there is no contention or dispute, since we on both sides confess them. Wherefore it is not necessary to treat further of them.

PART SECOND IS CONCERNING THE ARTICLES WHICH REFER TO THE OFFICE AND WORK OF JESUS CHRIST, OR OUR REDEMPTION.

I. OF THE MERIT OF CHRIST, AND THE RIGHTEOUSNESS OF FAITH.

The first and chief article is this, that Jesus Christ, our God and Lord, died for our sins, and was raised again for our justification, Rom. 4:25.

And he alone is the Lamb of God, which taketh away the sins of the world, John 1:29; and God has laid upon him the iniquities of us all, Isa. 53:6.

Likewise: All have sinned and are justified without merit [freely, and without their own works or merits] by his grace, through the redemption that is in Christ Jesus, in his blood, Rom. 3:23 sq.

Since it is necessary to believe this, and it can be acquired or apprehended otherwise by no work, law or merit, it is clear and certain that this faith alone justifies us, as St. Paul says (Rom. 3:28): "For we conclude that a man is justified by faith without the deeds of the Law." Likewise (v. 26): "That he might be just, and the justifier of him which believeth in Christ."

Of this article nothing can be yielded or surrendered, even though heaven and earth and all things should sink to ruin. "For there is none other name under heaven, given among men, whereby we must be saved," says Peter, Acts 4:12. "And with his stripes we are healed," Isa. 53:5. And upon this article all things depend, which, against the Pope, the devil and the whole world, we teach and practise. Therefore, we must be sure concerning this doctrine, and not doubt; for otherwise all is lost, and the Pope and devil and all things against us gain the victory and suit.

II. ARTICLE OF THE MASS.

That the Mass in the Papacy must be the greatest and most horrible abomination, as it directly and powerfully conflicts with this chief article, and yet above all other popish idolatries it is the chief and most specious. For it is held that this sacrifice or work of the Mass, even though it be rendered by a wicked and abandoned scoundrel, frees men from sins, not only in this life, but also in purgatory, although only the Lamb of God frees us, as has been said above. Of this article nothing is to be surrendered or conceded; because the former article does not allow this.

With the more reasonable Papists we might speak thus in a friendly way: First, why do they so rigidly uphold the Mass? since it is only an invention of men, and has not been commanded by God; and every invention of man we may discard, as Christ declares (Matt. 15:9): "In vain do they worship me, teaching for doctrines the commandments of men."

Secondly. It is an unnecessary thing, which can be omitted without sin and danger.

Thirdly. The sacrament can be received in a better and more blessed way [more acceptable to God], (yea, the only blessed way), according to the institution of Christ. Why, therefore, on account of fictitious, unnecessary matters, do they drive the world to extreme misery, when even otherwise it can be well and more blessed?

Let care be taken that it be publicly preached to the people that the Mass as a toy [commentitious affair or human figment] can, without sin, be done away with, and that no one will be condemned who does not observe it, but that men can be saved in a better way without the Mass. Thus it will come to pass that the Mass will perish of its own accord, not only among the rude common people, but also in the minds of all pious, Christian, reasonable, God-fearing hearts; and this much the more when they have heard that the Mass is a very dangerous thing, fabricated and invented without the will and Word of God.

Fourthly. Since such innumerable and unspeakable abuses have arisen in the whole world from the buying and selling of masses, the Mass should by right be relinquished for no other purpose than to prevent abuses, even though in itself it had something advantageous and good. But how much more, since it is altogether unnecessary, useless and dangerous, and without the Mass all things can be held with greater necessity, profit and certainty, ought we to relinquish it, so as to escape for ever these horrible abuses?

Fifthly. But since the Mass is nothing else, and can be nothing else (as the Canon and all books declare), than a work of men (even of wicked scoundrels), by which one attempts to reconcile to God himself and others with himself, and to obtain and merit the remission of sins and grace (for thus the Mass is regarded when it is esteemed at the very best; otherwise what would it profit?); for this very reason it must and should be condemned and rejected. For this directly conflicts with the chief article, which says that it is not a wicked or a godly celebrant of the Mass with his own work, but the Lamb of God and the Son of God, that taketh away our sins.

But if any one should advance the pretext that for the sake of devotion he wishes to administer the communion to himself, this is not in earnest. For if he would commune in sincerity, the sacrament would be administered in the surest and best way according to Christ's institution. But that one commune by himself is a human persuasion, uncertain, unnecessary, yea even prohibited. For he does not know what he does, while without the Word of God he obeys a false human opinion and invention. So too it is not right (even though the matter were otherwise plain) for one to use the public sacrament of the Church for his own private devotion, and without God's Word and apart from the communion of the Church to trifle therewith.

The Council will especially labor and be occupied with this article concerning the Mass. For although it would be possible for them to concede to us all the other articles, yet they could not concede this. As Campegius said at Augsburg that he would be torn to pieces before he would relinquish the Mass, so, by the help of God, I too would suffer my body to be reduced to ashes before I would allow a celebrant of the Mass, be he good or bad, to be made equal to Christ Jesus, my Lord and Saviour, or to be exalted above him. Thus we are and remain eternally separated and opposed to one another. They think indeed with entire correctness, that when the Mass falls the Papacy lies in ruins. Before they would permit this to occur, they would put us all to death if they could.

Beyond all things, this dragon's tail (I mean the Mass) has produced manifold abominations and idolatries.

First, purgatory. For by masses for souls, and vigils, and weekly, monthly and yearly celebrations of obsequies, and finally by the Common Week and All Souls' Day, by lustrations for purgatory, they have been so occupied that the Mass is used almost alone for the dead, although Christ has instituted the sacrament alone for the living. Wherefore purgatory, and every solemnity, rite and profit connected with it, is to be regarded nothing but a spectre of the devil. For it conflicts with the first article, which teaches that only Christ, and not the works of men, can help souls. Besides also nothing has been divinely commanded or enjoined upon us concerning the dead. Therefore all this can be safely omitted, even though there were no error and idolatry in it.

The Papists quote here Augustine and some of the Fathers who have written concerning purgatory, and they think that we do not understand for what purpose and to what end they thus spake. Augustine does not write that there is a purgatory, neither does he have a testimony of Scripture to constrain him thereto, but leaves the question as to its existence in doubt, and says that his mother asked him that she should be remembered at the altar or sacrament. Now all this is indeed nothing but the devotion of men, and that too of individuals, and does not establish an article of faith, which is a work belonging to God alone.

Our Papists, however, cite those opinions of men, in order that faith may be had in their horrible, blasphemous and cursed traffic in masses for souls in purgatory [or in sacrifices for the dead and oblations]. But they will never prove these things from Augustine. And when they have abolished the traffic in masses for purgatory, of which Augustine never dreamt, we will then discuss with them as to whether the expressions of Augustine, being without the warrant of the Word, are to be admitted, and whether the dead should be remembered at the Eucharist. For it is of no consequence that articles of faith are framed from the works or words of the holy Fathers; otherwise their mode of life, style of garments, of house, etc., would become an article of faith, just as they have trifled with the relics of the saints. We have, however, another rule, viz. that the Word of God should frame articles of faith; otherwise no one, not even an angel.

Secondly. From this it has followed that evil spirits have exercised much wickedness, and appeared as the souls of the departed, and with horrible lies and tricks demanded masses, vigils, pilgrimages, and other alms. All of which we had to receive as articles of faith, and to live accordingly; and the Pope confirmed these things, as also the Mass and all other abominations. Here there is no yielding or surrendering.

Thirdly. Hence arose pilgrimages. Instead of these, masses, the remission of sins and the grace of God were demanded; for the Mass controlled everything. But it is very certain that such pilgrimages, without the Word of God, have not been commanded us, neither are they necessary, since the soul can be cared for in a better way, and these pilgrimages can be omitted without all sin and danger. Why do they leave at home their pastors, the Word of God, wives, children, etc., attention to whom is necesary and has been commanded, and run after unnecessary, uncertain, pernicious *ignes fatui* of the devil? Besides the devil was in the Pope when he praised and established these, whereby the people, in a great number, revolted from Christ to their own works, and became idolaters; which is worst of all, for the reason that it is neither necessary nor commanded, but is senseless and doubtful, and besides harmful. Wherefore to yield or concede anything here is not permitted, etc. And it should be taught in preaching that such pilgrimages are not necessary, but dangerous; and then see what will

become of the pilgrimages. [For thus they will perish of their own accord.]

Fourthly. Fraternities [or societies], in which cloisters, chapters, and associations of vicars have bound themselves in writing, and by a definite contract and confirmed sale have made common property of all masses and good works, etc., both for the living and the dead. This is not only altogether a human bauble, without the Word of God, entirely unnecessary and not commanded, but also is contrary to the chief article, Of Redemption. Wherefore it is in no way to be tolerated.

Fifthly. The relics of the saints, about which there are so many falsehoods, trifles and absurdities concerning the bones of dogs and horses, that at such rascality even the devil has laughed, ought long ago to have been condemned, even though there were some good in them: and so much the more in that, without the Word of God, they are an entirely unnecesary and useless thing. But the worst is that they have imagined that these relies work the indulgence and forgiveness of sins [and have revered them] as a good work and service of God, as the Mass, etc.

Sixthly. Here belong the precious indulgences granted (but only for money) to the living and the dead, by which the miserable Judas or pope has sold the merit of Christ, together with the superfluous merits of all saints and of the entire Church, etc. All of which is not to be borne, because it is without the Word of God, and without necessity, and is not commanded; but conflicts with the chief article. For the merit of Christ is [apprehended and] obtained not by our works or pence, but from grace through faith, without money and merit; and is offered [and presented] not through the power of the Pope, but through the preaching of God's Word.

OF THE INVOCATION OF SAINTS.

The invocation of saints is also one of the abuses of Antichrist, which conflicts with the chief article, and destroys the knowledge of Christ. It is also neither commanded nor advised, has no example [or testimony] in Scripture, and in Christ we have everything a thousand-fold better, even though it were a precious thing, as it is not.

And although the angels in heaven pray for us (as even Christ also does), as also do the saints on earth, and perhaps also in heaven; yet it does not follow thence that we should invoke and adore the angels and saints, and for them fast, hold festivals, celebrate Mass, make offerings, and establish churches, altars, divine worship, and in still other ways serve them, and regard them as helpers in need, and divide among them all kinds of help, and ascribe to each one a particular form of assistance, as the Papists teach and do. For this is idolatry, and such honor belongs alone to God.

For as a Christian and saint upon earth, you can pray for me, not only in one, but in many necessities. But, for this reason, I ought not to adore and invoke you, and celebrate festivals, fasts, oblations, masses for your honor [and worship], and put my faith in you for my salvation. I can in other ways indeed honor, love and thank you in Christ. If now such idolatrous honor were withdrawn from angels and deceased saints, the remaining honor would be

SMALCALD ARTICLES (1537) (continued)

without danger, and would quickly be forgotten. For where advantage and assistance, both bodily and spiritual, are no more to be expected, there the worship of the saints will depart in peace, whether they be in their graves or in heaven. For without a purpose, or out of pure love, no one will much remember, or esteem, or honor them [bestow on them divine honor].

In short: Whatever the [Papal] Mass is, and whatever proceeds from it and clings to it, we cannot [in general] tolerate, but we are compelled to condemn, in order that we may retain the holy sacrament pure and certain, according to the institution of Christ, employed and received through faith.

ARTICLE III. OF CHAPTERS AND CLOISTERS.

That chapters and cloisters were formerly founded with the good intention to educate learned men and chaste and modest women, and ought again to be turned to such use, in order that pastors, preachers, and other ministers of the Churches may be had, and likewise other necessary persons for the administration of the government [or for the state] in cities and governments, and well-educated maidens for mothers and housekeepers, etc.

If they will not serve this purpose, it is better that they should be abandoned or altogether destroyed, rather than continued with their blasphemous services invented by men as something better than the ordinary Christian life and the offices and callings appointed by God. For all this also is contrary to the first chief article concerning the redemption made through Jesus Christ. In addition, that they also (as all other human inventions) have not been commanded, are needless and useless, and besides afford occasion for dangerous and vain labor [dangerous annoyances and fruitless worship], such services as the prophets call *Aven, i.e.* pain and labor.

ARTICLE IV. OF THE PAPACY.

That the Pope is not, according to divine law or according to the Word of God, the head of all Christendom (for this name belongs to Jesus Christ solely and alone), but is only the bishop and pastor of the Church at Rome, and of those who voluntarily [and of their own accord] or through a human creature (that is a political magistrate) attach themselves to him, not to be under him as a lord, but with him as brethren [colleagues] and associates, as Christians; as the ancient councils and the age of St. Cyprian show.

But to-day none of the bishops venture to address the Pope as brother [as was done in the age of Cyprian]; but they must call him most gracious lord, even though they be kings or emperors. Such arrogance we neither will, can, nor ought with a good conscience to approve. Let him, however, who will do it, do so without us.

Hence it follows that all things which the Pope, from a power so false, mischievous, blasphemous and arrogant, has undertaken and done, have been and still are purely diabolical affairs and transactions (with the exception of the administration of his civil power, where God often blesses a people, even though a tyrant and faithless scoundrel) for the ruin of the entire holy [Catholic or] Christian Church (so far as it is in his power), and for the destruction of the first and chief article concerning the redemption made through Jesus Christ.

For all his bulls and books are extant, in which he roars like a lion (as the angel in Rev. 12 indicates), crying out that no Christian can be saved unless he obey him and be subject to him in all things that he wishes, that he says and that he does. All of which is nothing else than though it were said, that although you believe in Christ, and have in him everything that is necessary to salvation, yet nothing profits you unless you regard me your god, and be subject and obedient to me; although, it is nevertheless manifest that there was a holy Church without the Pope for at least more than five hundred years, and that even to the present day the churches of the Greeks and of many other languages neither have been nor are still under the Pope. Thus it is, as has often been said, a human figment which is not commanded, and is unnecessary and useless. For the holy Christian [or Catholic] Church can exist very well without such a head, and it would certainly have remained better [purer, and its career would have been more prosperous] if such a head had not been raised up by the devil. And the Papacy is also of no use in the Church, because it exercises no ecclesiastical office; and therefore it is necessary for the Church to remain and continue to exist without the Pope.

But supposing that the Pope acknowledge that he is supreme, not by divine right or from God's command, but that for the purpose of preserving the unity of Christians against sects and heretics they should have a head to whom all the rest should adhere; and that such a head should be chosen by men, and that it also be placed within the choice and power of men to change or remove this head, just as the Council of Constance almost in this very way treated the popes, deposing three and electing a fourth; supposing (I say), that the Pope and See at Rome would yield and accept this (which, nevertheless, is impossible; for thus he would suffer his entire realm and estate to be overthrown and destroyed, with all his rights and books, a thing which, to speak in few words, he cannot do); nevertheless, even in this way Christianity would not be helped, but many more sects would arise than before.

For since obedience would be rendered this head not from God's command, but from man's free will, it would easily and in a short time be despised, and at last retain no member; neither would it be necessary that it be confined to Rome or any other place, but be wherever and in whatever church God would grant a man fit for the office. Oh, the indefiniteness and confusion that would result!

Wherefore the Church can never be governed and preserved better than if we all live under one head, Christ, and all the bishops, equal in office (although they be unequal in gifts), be diligently joined in unity of doctrine, faith, sacraments, prayer and works of love, etc., just as St. Jerome writes that the priests at Alexandria together and in common governed the churches, as did also the apostles, and afterwards all bishops throughout all Christendom, until the Pope raised his head above all. This article clearly shows that the Pope is the very Antichrist, who has exalted and opposed himself against Christ, because he does not wish Christians to be saved without his power, which nevertheless is nothing, and is neither established nor commanded by God. This is, properly speaking, to "exalt himself above all that is called God," as Paul says, 2 Thess. 2:4. This indeed neither the Turks nor the Tartars do, although they are great enemies of Christians, but they allow whoever wishes to believe in Christ, and they receive [outward or] bodily tribute and obedience from Christians.

The Pope, however, prohibits this faith, saying that if any one wish to be saved he must obey. This we are unwilling to do, even though on this account we must die in God's name. This all proceeds from the fact that the Pope has wished to be considered the supreme head of the Christian Church according to divine law. Accordingly he has made himself equal to and above Christ, and has caused himself to be proclaimed the head, and then the lord of the Church, and finally of the whole world, and simply God on earth, until he has attempted to issue commands even to the angels in heaven. And when a distinction is made between a dogma of the Pope and Holy Scripture, and a comparison of the two is made, it is found that the dogma of the Pope, even the best, has been taken from [civil] imperial and heathen law, and treats of political matters and decisions or rights, as the Decretals show; afterwards, it teaches of ceremonies concerning churches, garments, food, persons and like shows, masks and comical things above measure, but in all these things nothing at all of Christ, faith and the commandments of God; and lastly is nothing else than the devil himself, while over and against God he urges [and disseminates] his falsehoods concerning masses, purgatory, a monastic life, one's own works and [fictitious] divine worship (for this is the true Papacy, upon each of which the Papacy is altogether founded and is standing), and condemns, murders and tortures all Christians who do not exalt and honor these abominations of the Pope above all things. Wherefore just as we cannot adore the devil himself as Lord and God, so we cannot endure his apostle, the Pope or Antichrist, in his rule as head or lord. For to lie and to kill, and to destroy body and soul eternally, is a prerogative of the Papal government, as I have very clearly shown in many books.

In these four articles they will have enough to condemn in the Council. For they will not concede us even the least point in these articles. Of this we should be certain, and keep the hope in mind, that Christ our Lord has attacked his adversary, whom he will pursue and destroy, both by his Spirit and coming. Amen.

For in the Council we will stand not before the Emperor or the political magistrate, as at Augsburg (where the Emperor published a most gracious edict, and caused matters to be heard kindly and dispassionately), but we will appear before the Pope and devil himself, who intends to hear nothing, but merely [when the case has been publicly announced] to condemn, to murder and to force to idolatry. Wherefore we ought not here to kiss his feet, or to say: "Thou art my gracious lord," but as the angel in Zechariah 3:2 said to Satan: "The Lord rebuke thee, O Satan."

PART THIRD.

Concerning the following articles we will be able to treat with learned and reasonable men, or even among our-selves. The Pope and the Papal government do not care much about these. For with them conscience is nothing, but money, glory, honors, power are to them everything.

I. OF SIN.

Here we must confess, as Paul says in Rom. 5:11, that sin originated [and entered the world] from one man Adam, by whose disobedience all men were made sinners, and subject to death and the devil. This is called original or capital sin.

The fruits of this sin are afterwards the evil deeds which are forbidden in the Ten Commandments, such as [distrust] unbelief, false faith, idolatry, to be without the fear of God, arrogance, blindness, and, to speak briefly, not to know or regard God; secondly, to lie, to swear by [to abuse] God's name [to swear falsely], not to pray, not to call upon God, not to regard God's Word, to be disobedient to parents, to murder, to be unchaste, to steal, to deceive, etc.

This hereditary sin is so deep [and horrible] a corruption of nature, that no reason can understand it, but it must be [learned and] believed from the revelation of Scriptures, Ps. 51:5; Rom. 5:12 sqq.; Ex. 33:3; Gen. 3:7 sqq. Wherefore the dogmas of the scholastic doctors are pure errors and obscurations contrary to this article, for by them it is taught:

That since the fall of Adam the natural powers of man have remained entire and incorrupt, and that man by nature has right reason and a good will, as the philosophers teach.

And that man has a free will to do good and omit evil, and, again, to omit good and do evil.

Also that man by his natural powers can observe and do all the commands of God.

And that, by his natural powers, he can love God above all things, and his neighbor as himself.

Also if a man do as much as is in him, God certainly grants to him his grace.

And if he wish to come to the sacrament, there is no need of a good intention to do good, but it is sufficient if he have not a wicked purpose to commit sin; so entirely good is his nature and so efficacious the sacrament.

Also that it is not founded upon Scripture that, for a good work, the Holy Ghost with his grace is necessary.

Such and many similar things have arisen from want of understanding and learning concerning both sins and Christ our Saviour, and they are truly heathen dogmas which we cannot endure. For if these dogmas would be right, Christ has died in vain, since there is in man no sin and misery for which he should have died; or he would have died only for the body, not for the soul, inasmuch as the soul is entirely sound, and the body only is subject to death.

II. OF THE LAW.

Here we hold that the Law was given by God, first to restrain in by threats and the dread of punishment, and by the promise and offer of grace and favor. But all these miscarried, on account of the wickedness which sin has wrought in man. For thereby a part were rendered worse, who are hostile to the Law, because it forbids those things which they do willingly, and enjoins those things which they do unwillingly. Therefore, if they were not restrained by punishment, they would do more against the Law than before. For these are rude and wicked [unbridled and secure] men, who do evil wherever they have the opportunity.

The rest are blind and arrogant, and think that they observe and can observe the Law by their own powers, as has been said above concerning the scholastic theologians; thence come the hypocrites and false saints.

But the chief office or power of the Law is that it reveal original sin with all its fruits, and show man how very low his nature has fallen, and that it has become utterly corrupted; as the Law must tell that man neither has nor cares for God, and adores other gods, a matter which before and without the Law would not have been believed. In this way he becomes terrified, is humbled, desponds, despairs and anxiously desires aid; neither does he know whither to flee; he begins to be enraged at God, and to murmur, etc. This is what Paul says (Rom. 4:15): "The Law worketh wrath." And Rom. 5:20: "Sin is increased by the Law." [The Law entered that the offence might abound."]

III. OF REPENTANCE.

This office [of the Law] the New Testament retains and exercises, as St. Paul (Rom. 1:18) does, saying: "The wrath of God is revealed from heaven against all ungodliness and unrighteousness of men." And 3:19: "All the world is guilty before God." "No man is righteous before him." And Christ (John 16:8) says: "The Holy Ghost will reprove the world of sin."

This therefore is a thunderbolt of God, by which he strikes manifest sinners and hypocrites in one mass, and declares no one righteous, but forces them all together to terror and despair. This is the hammer, as Jeremiah says (23:29): "Is not my Word like a hammer that breaketh the rock in pieces?" This is not *activa contritio,* or manufactured repentance, but *passiva contritio* [torture of conscience], true sorrow of heart, suffering and sense of death.

For that is the beginning of true repentance; and here man must hear such a sentence as this: "You are all of no account, whether you be manifest sinners or saints [in your own opinion]; you all must become different and do otherwise than you now are and are doing, be you great, wise, powerful and holy as you may. Here no one is [righteous, holy], godly," etc.

But to this office the New Testament immediately adds the consolatory promise of grace through the Gospel, which must be believed, as Christ declares (Mark 1:15): "Repent and believe the Gospel," *i.e.* become different and do otherwise, and believe my promise. And before him John is named a preacher of repentance, but "for the remission of sins," *i.e.* John was to accuse all, and prove that they were sinners, that they might know what they were before God, and might acknowledge that they were lost men, and might thus be prepared for the Lord, to receive grace, and to expect and accept from him the remission of sins. Thus

Christ also (Luke 24:47) himself says: "That repentance and remission of sins should be preached in his name among all nations."

But when the Law alone, without the co-operation of the Gospel, exercises this, its office is death and hell, and man must despair, as Saul and Judas; just as St. Paul (Rom. 7:10) says that through sin the Law killeth. On the contrary, the Gospel brings consolation and remission, not only in one way, but through the Word and sacraments and the like, as we will hear afterward that "with the Lord is plenteous redemption," as Ps. 130:7 says, against the dreadful captivity of sin.

We will next contrast the false repentance of the sophists with true repentance, in order that both may be the better understood.

OF THE FALSE REPENTANCE OF THE PAPISTS.

It was impossible that they should teach correctly concerning repentance, since they did not rightly know what sins are. For, as has been shown above, they do not believe aright concerning original sin, but say that the natural powers of man have remained unimpaired and incorrupt; that reason can teach aright, and the will can accordingly do aright [those things which are taught], that God certainly gives his grace when a man does only as much as is in him, according to his free will.

From this dogma it follows that they must repent only for actual sins, such as wicked thoughts that are acquiesced in (for wicked emotion [concupiscence, vicious feelings and inclinations], lust and improper dispositions [according to them] are not sins), and for wicked words and deeds, which the free will could readily have omitted. And to such repentance they fix three parts, contrition, confession and satisfaction, with this consolation and promise added: If man truly repent, confess, render satisfaction, he thereby merits forgiveness, and settles for his sins with God. Thus in repentance men were instructed to repose confidence in their own works. Hence the expression originated, which was employed in the pulpit when public absolution was announced to the people: "Prolong, O God, my life, until I shall make satisfaction for my sins and amend my life."

Here neither Christ nor faith was mentioned; but they hoped, by their own works, to overcome and efface sins before God. And with this intention we became priests and monks, that we might array ourselves against sin.

As to contrition, the state of the case was this: Since no one could retain all his sins in memory (especially as committed through an entire year), they inserted this provision, viz. that if the rememberance of a concealed sin should perhaps return, this also should be repented of and confessed, etc. Meanwhile they were commended to the grace of God.

Since also no one could know how great the contrition ought to be which would be sufficient before God, they gave this consolation: He who could not have contrition, at least ought to have attrition, which I may call a half or beginning of contrition. Both these terms every one of them has understood, and now knows, as little as I. Such attrition is reckoned as contrition to those going to confession.

And when any one said that he could not have contrition, or could not lament his sins (as might have occurred in illicit love or the desire for revenge, etc.), they asked whether he did not wish or desire to lament. When one would reply Yes (for who, save the devil himself, would here say No?), they accepted this as contrition, and forgave him his sins on account of this good work of his [which they adorned with the name of contrition]. Here they cite the example of Bernard, etc.

Here we see how blind reason, in matters pertaining to God, gropes about, and, according to its own imagination, seeks for consolation in its own works, and cannot think of Christ and faith. But if it be considered in the light, this contrition is a manufactured and fictitious thought [or imagination], derived from man's own powers, without faith and without the knowledge of Christ. And in it, sometimes the poor sinner, when he reflected upon his own lust and desire for revenge, would have laughed, rather than wept, except one who either has been struck by [the lightning of] the Law, or has been vainly vexed by the devil with a sorrowful spirit. Such contrition is certainly mere hypocrisy, and has not mortified the lust for sins [flames of lust]; for they must grieve, even though, if it had been free to them, they would have preferred to sin.

With confession it stood thus: Every one must enumerate all his sins (which is an impossible thing). This was a great torment. But if any one had forgotten some sins, he would be absolved on the condition that if they would occur to him he must still confess them. Thereby he could never know whether he had confessed sufficiently, or when the confession would ever have an end. Yet they were pointed to their own works, and comforted thus: The more perfectly one confesses, and the more he is ashamed of himself and blames himself to the priest, the sooner and better he renders satisfaction for his sins; for such humility certainly earns grace before God.

Here there was no faith or Christ, and the virtue of the absolution was not declared to him, but upon the enumeration of sins and the shame depended the consolation. What torture, rascality and idolatry such confession has produced cannot be enumerated.

But the satisfaction is most indefinite [involved] of all. For no man could know how much to render for a single sin, to say nothing for all. Here they have resorted to the device of a small satisfaction, which could indeed be rendered, as five Paternosters, a day's fast, etc.; for the rest of the repentance they point to purgatory.

Here also there was extreme misery. For some thought that they would get out of purgatory, because, according to the old canons, seven years' repentance belongs to a single mortal sin. Nevertheless confidence was placed upon our work of satisfaction, and if the satisfaction could have been perfect, confidence would have been placed in it entirely, and neither faith nor Christ would have been of use. But this was impossible. If any one had repented in that way for a hundred years, he would still not have known whether he had repented enough. This is always to repent and never to come to repentance.

Here now the holy See at Rome came to the aid of the poor Church, and invented indulgences, whereby it remitted and waived [expiation or] satisfaction, first, for a single year, for seven years, for a hundred years, and distributed them among the cardinals and bishops, so that one could grant indulgence for a hundred years, and another for a hundred days. But it reserved to itself alone the power to waive all the satisfaction.

Since now this began to yield money, and the traffic in bulls was profitable, it devised a golden jubilee year [a truly gold bearing year], and fixed it at Rome. It called this the remission of all punishment and guilt. Thither the people ran, because every one wished to be freed from a grievous, insupportable burden. This was to find and raise the treasures of the earth.

Immediately the Pope pressed still further, and multiplied the golden years one upon another. But the more he devoured money, the wider did his jaws open. Therefore by his legates these years were published [everywhere] in the countries, until all churches and houses were full of the jubilee. At length he resorted to purgatory among the dead, first by establishing masses and vigils, afterwards by indulgences and a golden year, and finally souls became so cheap that he released one for a farthing.

Nevertheless even this is not half. For although the Pope taught men to depend upon, and trust in, these indulgences for salvation, yet he rendered the whole matter again uncertain. For in his bulls he puts it thus: He who wishes to become participant in the indulgences of a year of jubilee, ought to be contrite, and to have confessed, and to pay money. Moreover we have heard above that this contrition and confession are with them uncertain and hypocrisy. Likewise also no one knew what soul was in purgatory, and if some were therein, no one knew who had repented and confessed aright. Therefore he took the coveted money, and comforted them meanwhile with his power and indulgence, and pointed them again to their uncertain work.

If now there were some who did not regard themselves guilty of such actual sins in thoughts, words and works (as I and my like, in monasteries and chapters, wished to be monks and priests, and by fasting, watching, praying, saying Mass, harsh clothing and hard beds to protect ourselves from evil spirits, and with heart and soul to be holy), yet the hereditary, inborn evil sometimes in sleep did that (as also St. Augustine and Jerome among others confess) which is its nature. Nevertheless each one was regarded by the others as so holy, as we taught, without sin and full of good works, that we could communicate and sell our good works to others, as being superfluous to us for heaven. This is indeed true, and seals, letters and illustrations are at hand.

Such as these did not need repentance. For of what would they repent, as they had not acquiesced in the wicked thoughts? What would they confess [concerning words not uttered], as they had avoided the expression? For what should they render satisfaction, as they were so guiltless of any deed that they could even sell their superfluous righteousness to other poor sinners? Such saints were also the Pharisees and Scribes in the time of Christ.

SMALCALD ARTICLES (1537) (continued)

Here comes the fiery angel, St. John, the true preacher of repentance, and strikes with one bolt all of both classes [those selling and those buying works] in one mass, and says: "Repent" (Matt. 3:2). Thus the former imagine: We nevertheless have repented. The latter: We need no repentance. John says: Repent ye all, for ye are false penitents; so are these false saints, and all of both classes need the forgiveness of sins, because ye all still know not what true sin is, to be silent as to your obligation to repent and escape from it. For no one of you is good; you are full of unbelief, stupidity and ignorance of God and God's will. For here he is present: "Of whose fulness have all we received, and grace for grace" (John 1:16), and without him no man can be just before God. Wherefore if you wish to repent, repent aright; your repentance is nothing. And you hypocrites, who do not need repentance, you generation of vipers, who has warned you to flee from the wrath to come? etc. (Matt. 3:7; Luke 3:7).

In the same way Paul also preaches (Rom. 3:10-12): "There is none righteous, there is none that understandeth, there is none that seeketh after God, there is none that doeth good, no not one; they are all gone out of the way; they are together become unprofitable." And Acts 17:30: "God now commandeth all men everywhere to repent." "All men," he says; no one excepted who is a man. This repentance teaches us to discern sin, viz. that we are altogether lost, and that with us, both within and without, there is nothing good, and that we ought absolutely to become other and new men.

This repentance is not partial and beggarly [incomplete], such as is that for actual sins, nor is it even as uncertain as that. For it does not dispute as to whether there is or is not sin, but it overthrows everything in a mass, and affirms that with respect to us, all is nothing but sin. For why do we wish longer to investigate, to divide or distinguish? Therefore, this contrition also is not uncertain. For nothing remains there by which we can think of any good thing to pay for sin, but we only despair concerning all things that we are, that we think, that we speak and do, etc.

Likewise the confession also cannot be false, uncertain or partial. For he who confesses that all in him is nothing but sin, comprehends all sins, excludes none, forgets none. So also the satisfaction cannot be uncertain, because it is not an uncertain, sinful work of ours, but it is the suffering and blood of the innocent Lamb of God who taketh away the sin of the world.

Of this repentance John preaches; and afterwards Christ in the Gospel, and we also. By this preaching of repentance we dash to the ground the Pope and everything that is built upon our good works. For all are built upon a rotten and vain foundation, which is called a good work or law, even though no good work be there, but only wicked works, and no one does the Law (as Christ, John 7:19, says), but all transgress it. Therefore the building is nothing but falsehood and hypocrisy, even [in the part] where it is most holy and beautiful.

This repentance in Christians continues until death, because, through the entire life, it contends with sin remaining in the flesh, as Paul (Rom. 7:14-25) shows, that he wars with the law in his members, etc.; and this not by his own powers, but by the gift of the Holy Ghost that follows the remission of sins. This gift daily cleanses and purges the remaining sins, and works so as to render man pure and holy. Hereof the Pope, the theologians, the jurists, and every other man know nothing [from their own reason], but it is a doctrine from heaven revealed through the Gospel, and is proclaimed as heresy by the godless saints.

But if certain sectarists would arise, some of whom are perhaps already present, and in the time of the insurrection of the peasants came to my view, holding that all those who have once received the Spirit or the forgiveness of sins, or have become believers, even though they would afterwards sin, would still remain in the faith, and sin would not injure them, and cry thus: "Do whatever you please; if you believe, it is all nothing; faith blots out all sins," etc.—They say, besides, that if any one sins after he has received faith and the Spirit, he never truly had the Spirit and faith. I have seen and heard of many men so insane, and I fear that such a devil is still remaining in some.—

If, therefore, I say, such persons would hereafter also arise, it is necessary to know and teach that if saints who still have and feel original sin, and also daily repent, and strive with it, fall in some way into manifest sins, as David into adultery, murder and blasphemy, faith and the Holy Ghost are then absent from them [they cast out faith and the Holy Ghost]. For the Holy Ghost does not permit sin to have dominion, to gain the upper hand so as to be completed, but represses and restrains it so that it must not do what it wishes. But if it do what it wishes, the Holy Ghost and faith are not there present. For St. John says (1 Ep. 3:9): "Whosoever is born of God doth not commit sin, . . . and he cannot sin." And yet that is also the truth which the same St. John says (1 Ep. 1:8): "If we say that we have no sin, we deceive ourselves and the truth is not in us."

IV. OF THE GOSPEL.

We will now return to the Gospel, which not merely in one way gives us counsel and aid against sin; for God is super-abundantly rich in his grace. First, through the spoken Word by which the forgiveness of sins is preached in the whole world; which is the peculiar office of the Gospel. Secondly, through baptism. Thirdly, through the holy sacrament of the altar. Fourthly, through the power of the keys, and also through the mutual conversation and consolation of brethren, Matt. 18:20: "Where two or three are gathered together," etc.

V. OF BAPTISM.

Baptism is nothing else than the Word of God [with mersion] in the water, commanded by his institution, or as Paul says: "A washing in the Word;" just as Augustine also says: "The Word comes to the element, and it becomes a sacrament." Therefore, we do not hold with Thomas and the monastic preachers or Dominicans, who forget the Word (God's institution) and say that God has imparted to the water a spiritual power, which, through the water, washes away sin. Nor do we agree with Scotus and the Barefooted monks [Minorites or Franciscan monks], who teach that, by the assistance of the divine will, baptism washes away sins, and that this ablution occurs only through the will of God, and by no means through the Word and water.

Of the baptism of children, we hold that children ought to be baptized. For they belong to the promised redemption made through Christ, and the Church should administer it to them.

VI. OF THE SACRAMENT OF THE ALTAR.

Of the sacrament of the altar we hold that bread and wine in the Supper are the true body and blood of Christ, and are given and received not only by the godly, but also by wicked Christians.

And that not only one form is to be given. For we do not need that high art which teaches us that under the one form there is as much as under both, as the sophists and Council of Constance teach.

For although it may perhaps be true that there is as much under one as under both, yet the one form is not the entire ordinance and institution established and commanded by Christ. And we especially condemn, and in God's name execrate, those who not only omit both forms, but also tyrannically prohibit, condemn and blaspheme them as heresy, and so exalt themselves against and above Christ, our Lord and God, etc.

We care nothing about the sophistical subtlety concerning transubstantiation, by which they teach that bread and wine leave or lose their own natural substance, and remain only the appearance and color of bread, and not true bread. For it agrees best with Holy Scripture that the bread be and remain there, as Paul himself calls it (1 Cor. 10:16): "The bread which we break." And (1 Cor. 11:28): "Let him so eat of that bread."

VII. OF THE KEYS.

The keys are an office and power given by Christ to the Church for binding and loosing sins, not only such as are gross and well known, but also such as are subtle, hidden, and known only to God, as it is written in Ps. 19:13: "Who can understand his errors?" And in Rom. 7:25, St. Paul complains that with the flesh he serves the law of sin. For it is not in our power, but belongs to God alone, to judge what, how great and how many are sins, as it is written in Ps. 144 (143:2): "Enter not into judgment with thy servant; for in thy sight shall no man living be justified." And Paul (1 Cor. 4:4) says: "For I know nothing by myself; yet am I not hereby justified?"

VIII. OF CONFESSION.

Since absolution or the power of the keys is also a consolation and aid against sin and a bad conscience, appointed by Christ himself in the Gospel, Confession or absolution ought by no means to be abolished in the Church, especially on account of [tender and] timid consciences and uncultivated youth, in order that they may be heard, and instructed in Christian doctrine.

But the enumeration of sins ought to be free to every one, as to what he wishes to enumerate or not to enumerate. For as long as we are in the flesh, we will not lie when we say: "I am a poor man, full of sins." Rom. 7:23: "I see another law in my members," etc. For since private absolution arises from the office of the keys, it should not be neglected, but must be esteemed of the greatest worth, just as all other offices also of the Christian Church.

And in those things which concern the spoken, outward Word, we must firmly hold that God grants his Spirit or grace to no one, except through or with the preceding outward Word. Thereby we are protected against enthusiasts, *i.e.* spirits who boast that they have the Spirit without and before the Word, and accordingly judge Scripture or the spoken Word, and explain and stretch it at their pleasure, as Münzer did, and many still do at the present day; they wish to be acute judges between the Spirit and the letter, and yet know not what they say or propose. Because the Papacy also is nothing but enthusiasm, by which the Pope boasts that all laws exist in the shrine of his heart, and whatever he decides and commands in his churches is spirit and law, even though it be above and contrary to Scripture and the spoken Word.

All this is the old devil and old serpent, who also converted Adam and Eve into enthusiasts, and led them from the outward Word of God to spiritualism and self-conceit, and nevertheless he effected this through other outward words. Just so our enthusiasts [at the present day] condemn the outward Word, and nevertheless they themselves are not silent, but they fill the world with their pratings and writings, as though indeed the Spirit were unable to come through the writings and spoken word of apostles, but he must come through their writings and words. Why therefore do not they also omit their own sermons and writings, until the Spirit himself come to men, without their writings and before them, as they boast that they have received the Spirit without the preaching of the Scriptures? But of these matters there is not time now to dispute at greater length; we have heretofore paid sufficient attention to this subject.

For even those who believe before baptism, or become believing in baptism, believe through the outward Word that precedes, as the adults, who have come to reason, must first have heard: "He that believeth and is baptized, shall be saved," even though they are at first unbelieving, and receive the Spirit and baptism ten years afterwards. Cornelius (Acts 10:1 sqq.) had heard long before among the Jews of the coming Messiah, through whom he was righteous before God, and in such faith his prayers and alms were acceptable to God (as Luke calls him devout and fearing God), and without such preceding Word and hearing could not believed or been righteous. But St. Peter had to reveal to him that the Messiah (in whom, as one that was to come, he had hitherto believed) had already come, and his faith in the coming Messiah did not hold him captive among the hardened and unbelieving Jews, but he knew that he was now to be saved by a present Messiah, and he neither denied nor persecuted him, as did the Jews.

In a word, enthusiasm inheres in Adam and his children from the beginning to the end of the world; its poison has

SMALCALD ARTICLES (1537) (continued)

been implanted and infused into them by the old dragon, and is the origin, power and strength of all heresy, especially of that of the Papacy and Mahomet. Therefore in regard to this we ought and must constantly maintain that God does not wish to deal with us otherwise than through the spoken Word and the sacraments, and that whatever without the Word and sacraments is extolled as spirit is the devil himself. For God also wished to appear to Moses through the burning bush and spoken Word; and no prophet, neither Elijah nor Elisha, received the Spirit without the Ten Commandments or spoken Word. Neither was John the Baptist conceived without the preceding word of Gabriel, nor did he leap in his mother's womb without the voice of Mary. And Peter says (2 Ep. 1:21): "The prophecy came not by the will of man; but holy men of God spake as they were moved by the Holy Ghost." Without the outward Word they were not holy, neither as unholy did the Holy Ghost move them to speak; but they were holy Peter says, when the Holy Ghost spake through them.

IX. OF EXCOMMUNICATION.

The greater excommunication, as the Pope calls it, we regard only as a civil penalty, and not pertaining to us ministers of the Church. But the less is true Christian excommunication, which prohibits manifest and obstinate sinners from the sacrament and other communion of the Church until they are reformed and avoid sin. And ministers ought not to confound this ecclesiastical punishment or excommunication with civil penalties.

X. OF ORDINATION AND THE CALL.

If the bishops were true bishops, and would devote themselves to the Church and the Gospel, they might be allowed, for the sake of love and unity, and not from necessity, to ordain and confirm us and our preachers; nevertheless, under the condition that all masks and phantoms [deceptions, absurdities and appearances] of unchristian nature and display be laid aside. Yet because they neither are nor wish to be true bishops, but worldly lords and princes, who will neither preach, nor teach, nor baptize, nor administer the Lord's Supper, nor perform any work or office of the Church, but persecute and condemn those who being called discharge this duty; for their sake the Church ought not to remain without ministers.

Therefore, as the ancient examples of the Church and the Fathers teach us, we ourselves will and ought to ordain suitable persons to this office; and (even according to their own laws) they have not the right to forbid or prevent us. For their laws say that those ordained even by heretics should be regarded and remain as ordained, as St. Jerome writes of the Church at Alexandria, that at first it was governed in common by the bishops through the priests and preachers.

XI. OF THE MARRIAGE OF PRIESTS.

In prohibiting marriage, and burdening the divine order of priests with perpetual celibacy, they have neither reason nor right, but have treated it as antichristian, tyrannical, sceptical scoundrels, and have afforded occasion for all kinds of horrible, abominable sins of impurity, in which they still wallow. But just as the power has been given neither to us nor to them to make a woman out of a man, or man out of a woman, or to annihilate both, so also it has not been given them; so also power has not been given them to sunder and separate such creatures of God, or to forbid them from living honorably in marriage with one another. Therefore we are unwilling to assent to their abominable celibacy, nor will we even tolerate it, but we wish to have marriage free as God has instituted and appointed it, and we wish neither to rescind nor hinder his work; for Paul says that this prohibition of marriage is a doctrine of devils (1 Tim. 4:1 sqq.).

XII. OF THE CHURCH.

We do not acknowledge them as the Church, and they are not [because in truth they are not the Church]; we also will not listen to those things which, under the name of Church, they either enjoin or forbid. For, thank God, to-day a child seven years old knows what the Church is, viz. saints, believers and lambs who hear the voice of their Shepherd. For the children repeat: "I believe in one holy [Catholic or] Christian Church." This holiness does not consist in an alb, a tonsure, a long gown and other of their ceremonies devised by them beyond Holy Scripture, but consists in the Word of God and true faith.

XIII. HOW MAN IS JUSTIFIED BEFORE GOD, AND OF GOOD WORKS.

What I have hitherto and constantly taught concerning this I cannot in the least change, viz. that by faith (as St. Peter says) we acquire a new and clean heart, and God accounts, and will account us righteous and holy, for the sake of Christ, our Mediator. And although sin in the flesh has not been altogether removed and become dead, yet he will not punish or regard this.

For good works follow this faith, renewal and forgiveness of sins. And that in them which is still sinful and imperfect is not accounted as sin and defect, even for Christ's sake; but the entire man, both as to his person and his works, is and is called just and holy, from pure grace and mercy, shed upon us [unfolded] and displayed in Christ. Wherefore we cannot boast of our many merits and works, if they be viewed apart from grace and mercy, but as it is written, (1 Cor. 1:31): "He that glorieth, let him glory in the Lord," viz. that he has a gracious God. For thus all is well. We say besides that if good works do not follow, faith is false and not true.

XIV. OF MONASTIC VOWS.

As monastic vows directly conflict with the first chief article, they ought to be absolutely abolished. For it is of them that Christ says (Matt. 24:5, 23 sqq.): "I am Christ," etc. For he who makes a vow to live in a monastery believes that he will enter upon a mode of life holier than the ordinary Christians, and by his own works wishes to earn heaven not only for himself, but also for others; this is to deny Christ. And they boast from their St. Thomas that a monastic vow is on an equality with baptism. This is blasphemy against God.

XV. OF HUMAN TRADITIONS.

The declaration of the Papists that human traditions serve for the remission of sins, or merit salvation, is altogether unchristian and condemned, as Christ says (Matt. 15:9): "In vain they do worship me, teaching for doctrines the commandments of men." And Tit. 1:14: "That turn from the truth." Also their declaration that it is a mortal sin if one do not observe these statutes, is not right.

These are the articles on which I must stand; and if God so will I shall stand even to my death. And I do not know how to change or to concede anything in them. If any one else will concede anything, he will do it at the expense of his conscience.

Lastly, the Pope's bundle of impostures still remains, concerning foolish and childish articles, as the dedication of churches, the baptism of bells, the baptism of the altar-stone, with its godfathers to pray and offer gifts. Such baptism is administered to the reproach and mockery of holy baptism, and should not be tolerated. Afterwards, concerning the consecration of wax tapers, palm-branches, cakes, spices, oats, etc., which nevertheless cannot be called consecrations, but are nothing but mockery and fraud. There are infinite other such deceptions, which we commit to their god, and which may be adored by them, until they are weary of them. We will not be confused by [ought to have nothing to do with] them.

DR. MARTIN LUTHER subscribed.
DR. JUSTUS JONAS, Rector, subscribed.
DR. JOHN BUGENHAGEN, POMERANUS subscribed.
DR. CASPAR CREUTZIGER subscribed.
NICLAS AMSDORF of Magdeburg subscribed.
GEORGE SPALATINE of Altenburg subscribed.
I, PHILIP MELANCHTHON, approve the above articles as right and Christian. But of the Pope, I hold that if he would allow the Gospel, for the sake of the peace and general unity of Christians, who are now under him, and may be under him hereafter, the superiority over bishops which he has in other respects could be allowed to him, according to human right, also by us.
JOHN AGRICOLA of Eisleben subscribed.
GABRIEL DIDYMUS subscribed.
I, DR. URBAN RHEGIUS, Superintendent of the churches in the Duchy of Lüneburg, subscribe my name and the names of my brethren, and of the Church of Hanover.
I, STEPHEN AGRICOLA, Minister at Hof, subscribe.
Also I, JOHN DRACONITES, Professor and Minister at Marburg.
I, CONRAD FIGENBOTZ, for the glory of God subscribe that I have thus believed, and am still preaching and firmly believing as above.
I, ANDREW OSIANDER of Nürnberg, subscribe.
I, M. VEIT DIETERICH, Minister at Nürnberg, subscribe.
I, ERHARD SCHNEPF, Preacher at Stuttgart, subscribe.
CONRAD OETINGER, Preacher of Duke Ulrich at Pforzheim.
SIMON SCHNEEWEIS, Pastor of the Church at Crailsheim.

I, JOHN SCHLAINHAUFFEN, Pastor of the Church at Koethen, subscribe.
M. GEORGE HELT of Forchheim.
M. ADAM of Fulda,
M. ANTHONY CORVINUS, Preachers in Hesse.
I, JOHN BUGENHAGEN, POMERANUS, Doctor, again subscribe in the name of M. JOHN BRENTZ, as on departing from Smalcald he directed me orally and by a letter which I have shown to these breathen who have subscribed.
I, DIONYSIUS MELANDER, subscribe to the Confession, the Apology, and the Concordia on the subject of the Eucharist.
PAUL RHODIUS, Superintendent of Stettin.
GERARD OENIKEN, Superintendent of the Church at Minden.
I, BRIXIUS NORTHANUS, Minister of the Church of Christ which is at Soest, subscribe to the Articles of the reverend Father, Martin Luther, and confess that hitherto I have thus believed and taught, and by the Spirit I will continue thus to believe and teach.
MICHAEL COELIUS, Preacher at Mansfeldt, subscribed.
M. PETER GELTNER, Preacher at Frankfort, subscribed.
WENDAL FABER, Pastor of Seeburg in Mansfeldt.
I, John AEPINUS, subscribe.
Likewise, I, JOHN AMSTERDAM of Bremen.
I, FREDERICK MYCONIUS, Pastor of the Church at Gotha in Thuringia, subscribe in my own name, and in that of JUSTUS MENIUS of Eisenach.
I, JOHN LANG, D., and Preacher of the Church at Erfurt, in my own name, and in that of my other co-workers in the Gospel, viz.:
Licentiate LUDWIG PLATZ of Melsungen.
M. SIGISMUND KIRCHNER.
M. WOLFGANG KISMETTER.
M. MELCHIOR WEITMAN.
M. JOHN TALL.
M. JOHN KILLIAN.
M. NICHOLAS FABER.
M. ANDREW MENSER, I subscribe with my hand.
And I, EGIDIUS MECHLER, have subscribed with my hand.

APPENDIX. OF THE POWER AND PRIMACY OF THE POPE. *(Treatise Written by Theologians assembled at Smalcald, in the year MDXXXVII.)*

The Roman pontiff claims for himself that by divine right he is above all bishops and pastors [in all Christendom].

Secondly, he adds also that by divine right he has both swords, *i.e.* the right of bestowing and transferring kingdoms.

And thirdly, he says that to believe this is necessary for salvation. And for these reasons the Roman bishop calls himself the vicar of Christ on earth.

These three articles we hold to be false, godless, tyrannical and pernicious to the Church.

In order, moreover, that our affirmation may be understood, we will first define what they call to be above all by divine right. For they mean that he is universal, or as they say oecumenical bishop, *i.e.* from whom all bishops and pastors throughout the entire world ought to seek ordination and confirmation, who has the right of electing, ordaining, confirming, deposing all bishops [and pastors]. Besides this, he claims for himself the authority to frame laws concerning services, concerning changing the sacraments and concerning doctrine, and wishes his articles, his decrees, his laws to be regarded equal to the divine laws, *i.e.* he holds that, by the Papal laws, the consciences of men are so bound that those who neglect them, even without public offence, sin mortally [that they cannot be discontinued without sin. For he wishes to found this power upon divine right and the Holy Scriptures; yea, he wishes that they be preferred to the Holy Scriptures and God's commands]. And it is still more horrible that he adds that belief in all these things belongs to the necessity of salvation.

I. OF THE FIRST ARTICLE.

A. FROM THE GOSPEL.

First, therefore, we will show from the Gospel that the Roman bishop is not by divine right above other bishops and pastors.

Luke 22:25. Christ expressly prohibits lordship among the apostles [that any apostle should have the pre-eminence over the rest]. For this was the very question which they were disputing when Christ spake of his passion, viz. who should command, and be as it were the vicar of the absent Christ. There Christ reproves this error of the apostles, and teaches that there shall not be lordship or superiority among them, but that the apostles would be sent forth as equals to the common ministry of the Gospel. Accordingly, he says: "The kings of the Gentiles exercise lordship over them; and they that exercise authority upon them are called benefactors, but ye shall not be so; but he that is greatest among you, let him be as the younger; and he that is chief, as he that doth serve." The antithesis here shows that lordship is disapproved.

The same is taught by the parable when Christ in the same dispute concerning the kingdom (Matt. 18:2) sets a little child in the midst, signifying that among ministers there is not to be sovereignty, just as a child neither takes nor seeks sovereignty for himself.

John 20:21. Christ sends forth his disciples on an equality without any distinction when he says: "As my Father hath sent me, even so send I you." He says that he sends individuals in the same manner as he himself was sent; and hence grants a prerogative or lordship to no one above the rest.

Gal. 2:7 sq. Paul manifestly affirms that he was neither ordained nor confirmed by Peter, nor does he acknowledge Peter to be one from whom confirmation should be sought. And he expressly contends from this circumstance that his call does not depend upon the authority of Peter. But he ought to have acknowledged Peter as a superior if by divine right Peter was superior. Paul accordingly says that he had at once preached the Gospel without consulting Peter. Also: "Of those who seemed to be somewhat (whatsoever they were, it maketh no matter to me; God accepteth no man's person)." And: "They who seemed to be somewhat in conference added nothing to me." Since Paul therefore clearly testifies that he did not even wish to seek for the confirmation of Peter, even when he had come to him, he teaches that the authority of the ministry depends upon the Word of God, and that Peter was not superior to the other apostles, and that ordination or confirmation was not to be sought from Peter alone [that the office of the ministry proceeds from the general call of the apostles, and that it is not necessary for all to have the call or confirmation of this person alone].

In 1 Cor. 3:6, Paul makes ministers equal, and teaches that the Church is above the ministers. Hence superiority or lordship over the Church or the rest of the ministers is not ascribed to Peter. For he says thus: "All things are yours; whether Paul, or Apollos, or Cephas," *i.e.* Let not other ministers or Peter assume for themselves lordship or superiority to the Church; let them not burden the Church with traditions; let not the authority of any avail more than the Word [of God]; let not the authority of Cephas be opposed to the authority of the other apostles, as they reasoned at that time: "Cephas, who is an apostle of higher rank, observes this; therefore, Paul and the rest ought to observe this." Paul removes this pretext from Peter, and denies that his authority is to be preferred to the rest or to the Church.

B. FROM HISTORY.

The Council of Nice resolved that the bishop of Alexandria should administer the churches in the East, and the Roman bishop the suburban, *i.e.* those which were in the Roman provinces in the West. Hence it was first by human law, *i.e.* the resolution of the Council, that the authority of the Roman bishop arose. If already by divine law the Roman bishop would have had the superiority, it would not have been lawful for the Council to have removed any right from him and to have transferred it to the bishop of Alexandria; yea all the bishops of the East ought perpetually to have sought ordination and confirmation from the bishop of Rome. The Council of Nice determined also that bishops should be elected by their own churches, in the presence of a neighboring bishop or of several. The same was observed also in the West and in the Latin churches, as Cyprian and Augustine testify. For Cyprian says in his fourth letter to Cornelius: "For which reason you must diligently observe and keep the divine observance and apostolic practice, as it is also observed among us and in almost all the provinces, that for celebrating properly ordinances all the neighboring bishops of the same province should assemble; and the bishop should be chosen in the presence of the people, who have most fully known the life of each one, which we also see was done among us in the ordination of our colleague, Sabinus; so that by the suffrage of the entire brotherhood, and by the judgment of the bishops who had assembled in their presence, the episcopate was conferred and hands imposed upon him."

Cyprian calls this custom a divine tradition and an apostolic observance, and affirms that it was observed in almost all the provinces. Since therefore neither ordination nor confirmation was sought from a bishop of Rome in the greater part of the world in the Latin and Greek churches, it is sufficiently apparent that the churches did not then ascribe superiority and domination to the bishop of Rome.

Such superiority is impossible. For it is impossible for one bishop to be the inspector of the churches of the whole world, or for churches situated in the most remote lands [all the ministers] to seek ordination from one. For it is manifest that the kingdom of Christ has been dispersed through the whole world; and to-day there are many churches in the East which do not seek ordination or confirmation from the Roman bishop [which have ministers ordained neither by the Pope nor his bishops]. Therefore since such superiority [which the Pope, contrary to all Scripture, arrogates to himself] is impossible, and the churches in the greater part of the world have not acknowledged it, it is sufficiently apparent that it was not established [by Christ, and does not spring from divine law].

Many ancient Synods have been proclaimed and held in which the bishop of Rome did not preside; as that of Nice and very many others. This also testifies that the Church did not then acknowledge the primacy or superiority of the bishop of Rome.

Jerome says: "If authority is sought, the world is greater than the city. Wherever there has been a bishop, whether at Rome, or Eugubium, or Constantinople, or Rhegium, or Alexandria, he is of the same merit and priesthood."

Gregory, writing to the patriarch at Alexandria, forbids himself to be called universal bishop. And in the "Register" he says that in the Council of Chalcedon the primacy was offered to the bishop of Rome, and was not accepted.

Lastly, how can the Pope be by divine right over the entire Church, when the Church has the election, and the custom gradually prevailed that bishops of Rome should be confirmed by emperors?

Also, since there had been for a long time contests concerning the primacy between the bishops of Rome and Constantinople, the emperor Phocas at length determined that the primacy should be assigned to the bishop of Rome. But if the ancient Church had acknowledged the primacy of the Roman pontiff, this contention would not have occurred, neither would there have been need of a decree of the emperor.

C. ARGUMENTS OF THE ADVERSARIES.

But they cite against us certain passages, viz. (Matt. 16:18 sq.): "Thou art Peter, and upon this rock I will build my Church." Also: "I will give unto thee the keys." Also (John 21:15): "Feed my sheep," and some others. But since this entire controversy has been fully and accurately treated of elsewhere in the books of our theologians, and all things cannot be reviewed in this place, we refer to those writings, and wish them to be regarded as repeated. Yet we will briefly reply concerning the interpretation of the passages quoted.

In all these passages Peter is the representative of the entire assembly of apostles, as appears from the text itself. For Christ asks not Peter alone, but says: "Whom do ye say that I am?" And what is here said in the singular number: "I will give unto thee the keys; and whatsoever thou shalt bind," etc., is elsewhere expressed in the plural (Matt. 18:18): "Whatsoever ye shall bind," etc. And in John 20:23: "Whatsoever sins ye remit," etc. These words testify that the keys are given alike to all the apostles, and that all the apostles are alike sent forth.

In addition to this, it is necessary to confess that the keys pertain not to the person of a particular man, but to the Church, as many most clear and firm arguments testify. For Christ, speaking concerning the keys (Matt. 18:19), adds: "If two of you shall agree on earth," etc. Therefore he ascribes the keys to the Church principally and immediately; just as also for this reason the Church has principally the right of calling. [For just as the promise of the Gospel belongs certainly and immediately to the entire Church, so the keys belong immediately to the entire Church, because the keys are nothing else than the office whereby this promise is communicated to every one who desires it, just as it is actually manifest that the Church has the power to ordain ministers of the Church. And Christ speaks in these words: "Whatsoever ye shall bind," etc., and means that to which he has given the keys, namely, the Church: "Where two or three are gathered together in my name" (Matt. 18:20). Likewise Christ gives supreme and final jurisdiction to the Church, when he says: "Tell it to the Church."]

Therefore it is necessary in these passages that Peter be the representative of the entire assembly of the apostles, and for this reason they do not ascribe any prerogative, or superiority, or lordship to Peter.

As to the declaration: "Upon this rock I will build my Church," certainly the Church has not been built upon the authority of man, but upon the ministry of the confession which Peter made, in which he proclaims that Jesus is the Christ, the Son of God. He accordingly addresses him as a minister: "Upon this rock," *i.e.* upon this ministry. [Therefore he addresses him as a minister of such an office as is to be pervaded by this confession and doctrine, and says: "Upon this rock," *i.e.* this declaration and ministry.]

SMALCALD ARTICLES (1537) (continued)

Furthermore, the ministry of the New Testament is not bound to persons and places, as the Levitical ministry, but it is dispersed throughout the whole world, and is there where God gives his gifts, apostles, prophets, pastors, teachers; neither does this ministry avail on account of the authority of any person, but on account of the Word given by Christ.

And in this way most of the holy Fathers, as Origen, Cyprian, Augustine, Hilary and Bede, interpret this passage (Upon this rock). Chrysostom says thus: "'Upon this rock,' not upon Peter. For he built his Church not upon man, but upon the faith of Peter. But what was his faith? 'Thou art the Christ, the Son of the living God.'" And Hilary says: "To Peter the Father revealed that he should say, 'Thou art the Son of the living God.' Therefore the building of the Church is upon this rock of confession; this faith is the foundation of the Church," etc.

And as to that which is said (John 21:15 sqq.): "Feed my sheep," and "Lovest thou me more than these?" it does not as yet follow hence that a peculiar superiority was given Peter. He bids him "feed," i.e. teach the Word, or rule the Church with the Word, which Peter has in common with the other apostles.

II. OF THE SECOND ARTICLE.

The second article is still clearer, because Christ gave to the apostles only spiritual power, i.e. the command to teach the Gospel, to announce the forgiveness of sins, to administer the sacraments, to excommunicate the godless without temporal force; and he did not give the power of the sword or the right to establish, occupy or confer kingdoms of the world. For Christ says (Matt. 28:20): "Go ye, teaching them to observe all things whatsoever I have commanded you." Also (John 20:21): "As my Father hath sent me, even so send I you." But it is manifest that Christ was not sent to bear the sword or possess a worldly kingdom, as he himself says (John 18:36): "My kingdom is not of this world." And Paul says (2 Cor. 1:24): "Not for that we have dominion over your faith." And (2 Cor. 10:4): "The weapons of our warfare are not carnal," etc.

As, therefore, Christ in his passion is crowned with thorns, and led forth to be derided in royal purple, it was thereby signified that his spiritual kingdom being despised, i.e. the Gospel being suppressed, another kingdom of the world would be established with the pretext of ecclesiastical power. Wherefore the constitution of Boniface VIII. and the chapter *Omnes*, Dist. 22, and similar opinions which contend that the Pope is by divine right the ruler of the kingdoms of the world, are false and godless. From this persuasion horrible darkness has overspread the Church, and also great commotions have arisen in Europe. For the ministry of the Gospel was neglected, and the knowledge of faith and a spiritual kingdom became extinct; Christian righteousness was supposed to be that external government which the Pope had established. Then the popes began to seize upon kingdoms for themselves, they transferred kingdoms, they vexed with unjust excommunications and wars the kings of almost all nations in Europe, but especially the German emperors; so that they sometimes occupied the cities of Italy, and at other times reduced to subjection the bishops of Germany, and wrested from the emperors the conferring of episcopates. Yea in the Clementines it is even written: That when the empire is vacant, the Pope is the legitimate successor. Thus the Pope has not only usurped dominion, contrary to Christ's command, but has also tyrannically exalted himself above all kings. Neither in this matter is the deed itself so much to be reprehended as it is to be detested, that he assigns as a pretext the authority of Christ; that he transfers the keys to a worldly government; that he binds salvation to these godless and execrable opinions, when he says that it belongs to necessity for salvation that men believe that this dominion is in accordance with divine right. Since such errors as these obscure faith and the kingdom of Christ, they are in no way to be disguised. For the result shows that they have been great pests to the Church.

III. OF THE THIRD ARTICLE.

In the third place, this must be added: Even though the bishop of Rome would have, by divine right, the primacy and superiority, nevertheless obedience is not due those pontiffs who defend godless services, idolatry and doctrine conflicting with the Gospel; yea such pontiffs and such a government ought to be regarded as a curse, as Paul clearly teaches (Gal. 1:8): "Though an angel from heaven preach any other Gospel unto you than that which we have preached unto you, let him be accursed." And in Acts (5:29): "We ought to obey God, rather than men." Likewise the canons also clearly teach that we should not obey an heretical Pope.

The Levitical priest was high priest by divine right, and yet godless priests were not to be obeyed, as Jeremiah and other prophets dissented from the priests. So the apostles dissented from Caiaphas, and were under no obligations to obey them.

It is, however, manifest that the Roman pontiffs, with their adherents, defend godless doctrines and godless services. And the marks of Antichrist plainly agree with the kingdom of the Pope and his adherents. For Paul (2 Ep. 2:3), in describing to the Thessalonians Antichrist, calls him an adversary of Christ, "who opposeth and exalteth himself above all that is called God, or that is worshipped, so that he as God sitteth in the temple of God." He speaks therefore of one ruling in the Church, not of heathen kings, and he calls this one the adversary of Christ, because he will devise doctrine conflicting with the Gospel, and will assume to himself divine authority.

Moreover, it is manifest, in the first place, that the Pope rules in the Church, and by the pretext of ecclesiastical authority and of the ministry has established for himself this kingdom. For he assigns as a pretext these words: "I will give to thee the keys." Secondly, the doctrine of the Pope conflicts in many ways [in all ways] with the Gospel, and the Pope assumes to himself divine authority in a threefold manner: First, because he takes to himself the right to change the doctrine of Christ and services instituted by God, and wishes his own doctrine and his own services to be observed as divine. Secondly, because he takes to himself the power not only of binding and loosing in this life, but also the right concerning souls after this life. Thirdly, because the Pope does not wish to be judged by the Church or by any one, and prefers his own authority to the decision of Councils and the entire Church. But to be unwilling to be judged by the Church or by any one is to make one's self God. Lastly, these errors so horrible, and this impiety, he defends with the greatest cruelty, and puts to death those dissenting.

This being the case, all Christians ought to beware of becoming partakers of the godless doctrine, blasphemies and unjust cruelties of the Pope. On this account they ought to desert and execrate the Pope with his adherents, as the kingdom of Antichrist; just as Christ has commanded (Matt. 7:15): "Beware of false prophets." And Paul commands that godless teachers should be avoided and execrated as cursed (Gal. 1:8; Tit. 3:10). And (2 Cor. 6:14) says: "Be ye not unequally yoked together with unbelievers; for what communion hath light with darkness?"

To dissent from the agreement of so many nations and to be called schismatics is a serious matter. But divine authority commands all not to be allies and defenders of impiety and unjust cruelty.

On this account our consciences are sufficiently excused; for the errors of the kingdom of the Pope are manifest. And Scripture with its entire voice exclaims that these errors are a doctrine of demons and of Antichrist. The idolatry in the profanation of the masses is manifest, which, besides other faults, are shamelessly applied to most base gain. The doctrine of repentance has been utterly corrupted by the Pope and his adherents. For they teach that sins are remitted because of the worth of our works. Then they bid us doubt whether the remission occur. They nowhere teach that sins are remitted freely for Christ's sake, and that by this faith we obtain remission of sins. Thus they obscure the glory of Christ, and deprive consciences of firm consolation, and abolish true divine services, viz. the exercises of faith struggling with [unbelief and] despair [concerning the promise of the Gospel].

They have obscured the doctrine concerning sin, and have framed a tradition concerning the enumeration of offences, producing many errors and despair. They have devised in addition satisfactions, whereby they have also obscured the benefit of Christ.

From these, indulgences have been born, which are pure falsehoods, fabricated for the sake of gain.

Then how many abuses, and what horrible idolatry, the invocation of saints has produced!

What shameful acts have arisen from the tradition concerning celibacy!

What darkness the doctrine concerning vows has spread over the Gospel! They have there feigned that vows are righteousness before God, and merit the remission of sins. Thus they have transferred the benefit of Christ to human traditions, and have altogether extinguished the doctrine concerning faith. They have feigned that the most trifling traditions are services of God and perfection, and they have preferred these to the works of callings which God requires and has ordained. Neither are these errors to be regarded light; for they detract from the glory of Christ

and bring destruction to souls, neither can they be passed by unnoticed.

Then to these errors two great sins are added: The first, that he defends these errors by unjust cruelty and punishments. The second, that he appropriates the decision of the Church, and does not permit ecclesiastical controversies [such matters of religion] to be judged according to the prescribed mode; yea, he contends that he is above the Council, and that the decrees of Councils can be rescinded, just as the canons sometimes impudently speak. But the examples testify that this was done with much more impudence by the pontiffs.

Quest. 9, canon 3, says: "No one shall judge the first seat; for the judge is judged neither by the emperor, nor by all the clergy, nor by the kings, nor by the people."

The Pope exercises a twofold tyranny; he defends his errors by force and by murders, and forbids judicial examination. The latter does even more injury than any punishments. Because when the true judgment of the Church is removed, godless dogmas and godless services cannot be removed, and for many ages are destroying infinite souls.

Therefore let the godly consider the great errors of the kingdom of the Pope and his tyranny, and let them ponder first that the errors must be rejected and the true doctrine embraced, for the glory of God and to the salvation of souls. Then let them ponder also how great a crime it is to aid unjust cruelty in killing saints, whose blood God will undoubtedly avenge.

But especially the chief members of the Church, kings and princes, ought to guard the interests of the Church, and to see to it that errors be removed and consciences be healed [rightly instructed], as God expressly exhorts kings (Ps. 2:10): "Be wise, now, therefore, O ye kings; be instructed, ye judges of the earth." For it should be the first care of kings [and great lords] to advance the glory of God. Wherefore it is very shameful for them to exercise their influence and power to confirm idolatry and infinite other crimes, and to slaughter saints.

And in case the Pope should hold Synods [a Council], how can the Church be healed if the Pope suffer nothing to be decreed contrary to his will, if he allow no one to express his opinion except his adherents, whom by dreadful oaths and curses he has bound, without any exception concerning God's Word, to the defence of his tyranny and wickedness?

But since the decisions of Synods are the decisions of the Church, and not of the Popes, it is especially incumbent on kings to check the license of the popes [not allow such roguery], and to so act that the power of judging and decreeing from the Word of God be not wrested from the Church. And as other Christians ought to censure the remaining errors of the Pope, so they ought also to rebuke the Pope when he evades and impedes the true knowledge and true decision of the Church.

Therefore even though the bishop of Rome would have the primacy by divine right, yet since he defends godless services and doctrine conflicting with the Gospel, obedience is not due him, yea it is necessary to resist him as

Antichrist. The errors of the Pope are manifest and not trifling.

Manifest also is the cruelty [against godly Christians] which he exercises. And it is clear that it is God's command that we flee from idolatry, godless doctrine and unjust cruelty. On this account all the godly have great, manifest and necessary reasons for not obeying the Pope. And these necessary reasons comfort the godly against all the reproaches which are usually cast against them concerning offences, schism and discord.

But those who agree with the Pope and defend his doctrine and [false] services, defile themselves with idolatry and blasphemous opinions, became guilty of the blood of the godly, whom the Pope [and his adherents] persecutes, detract from the glory of God, and hinder the welfare of the Church, because they strengthen errors and crimes [for injury to all the world and] to all posterity.

PART II. OF THE POWER AND JURISDICTION OF BISHOPS.

[In our Confession and the Apology we have in general narrated what we have had to say concerning ecclesiastical power. For, etc.] The Gospel has assigned to those who preside over churches the command to teach the Gospel, to remit sins, to administer the sacraments, and besides jurisdiction, viz. the command to excommunicate those whose crimes are known, and again of absolving the repenting.

And by the confession of all, even of the adversaries, it is clear that this power by divine right is common to all who preside over churches, whether they be called pastors, or elders, or bishops. And accordingly Jerome openly teaches in the apostolic letters that all who preside over churches are both bishops and elders, and cites from Titus (Tit. 1:5 sq.): "For this cause left I thee in Crete, that thou shouldest ordain elders in every city." Then he adds: "A bishop must be the husband of one wife." Likewise Peter and John call themselves elders (1 Pet. 5:1; 2 John 1). And he then adds: "But that afterwards one was chosen to be placed over the rest," occurred as a remedy for schism, lest each one by attracting to himself might rend the Church of Christ. For at Alexandria, from Mark the evangelist to the bishops Heracles and Dionysius, the elders always elected one from themselves, and placed him in a higher station, whom they called bishop; just as an army would make a commander for itself. The deacons, moreover, may elect from themselves one whom they know to be active, and name him archdeacon. For with the exception of ordination, what does the bishop that the elder does not?

Jerome therefore teaches that it is by human authority that the grades of bishop and elder or pastor are distinct. And the subject itself declares this, because the power [the office and command] is the same, as he has said above. But one matter afterwards made a distinction between bishops and pastors, viz. ordination, because it was so arranged that one bishop might ordain ministers in a number of churches.

But since by divine authority the grades of bishop and pastor are not diverse, it is manifest that ordination by a pastor in his own church has been appointed by divine law [if a pastor in his own church ordain certain suitable persons to the ministry, such ordination is, according to divine law, undoubtedly effective and right].

Therefore when the regular bishops become enemies of the Church, or are unwilling to administer ordination, the churches retain their own right. [Because the regular bishops persecute the Gospel and refuse to ordain suitable persons, every church has in this case full authority to ordain its own ministers.]

For wherever the Church is, there is the authority [command] to administer the Gospel. Wherefore it is necessary for the Church to retain the authority to call, elect and ordain ministers. And this authority is a gift exclusively given to the Church, which no human power can wrest from the Church, as Paul also testifies to the Ephesians (4:8) when he says: "He ascended, he gave gifts to men." And he enumerates among the gifts specially belonging to the Church "pastors and teachers," and adds that such are given "for the ministry, for the edifying the body of Christ." Where there is therefore a true church, the right to elect and ordain ministers necessarily exists. Just as in a case of necessity even a layman absolves, and becomes the minister and pastor of another; as Augustine narrates the story of two Christians in a ship, one of whom baptized the catechumen, who after baptism then absolved the baptizer.

Here belong the words of Christ which testify that the keys have been given to the Church, and not merely to certain persons (Matt. 18:20): "Where two or three are gathered together in my name," etc.

Lastly, the declaration of Peter also confirms this (1 Ep. 2:9): "Ye are a royal priesthood." These words pertain to the true Church, which, since it alone has the priesthood, certainly has the right to elect and ordain ministers.

And this also a most common custom of the Church testifies. For formerly the people elected pastors and bishops. Then a bishop was added, either of that church or a neighboring one, who confirmed the one elected by the laying on of hands; neither was ordination anything else than such a ratification. Afterwards, new ceremonies were added, many of which Dionysius describes. But he is a recent and fictitious author [this book of Dionysius is a new fiction under a false title], just as the writings of Clement also are supposititious. Then the moderns added: "I give thee the power to sacrifice for the living and the dead." But not even this is in Dionysius. From all these things it is clear that the Church retains the right to elect and ordain ministers. And the wickedness and tyranny of bishops afford cause for schism and discord [therefore, if the bishops either are heretics or will not ordain suitable persons, the churches are in duty bound before God, according to divine law, to ordain for themselves pastors and ministers. Even though this be now called an irregularity or schism, it should be known that the godless doctrine and tyranny of the bishops is chargeable with it], because Paul (Gal. 1:7 sq.) enjoins that bishops who teach and defend a godless doctrine and godless services should be regarded accursed.

We have spoken of ordination, which alone, as Jerome says, distinguished bishops from other elders. Therefore there is need of no discussion concerning the other duties of bishops. Nor is it indeed necessary to speak of confirmation, nor of the consecration of bells, which are almost the only things which they have retained. Something must be said concerning jurisdiction.

It is manifest that the common jurisdiction of excommunicating those guilty of manifest crimes belongs to all pastors. This they have tyrannically transferred to themselves alone, and have applied it to the acquisition of gain. For it is manifest that the officials, as they are called, employed a license not to be tolerated, and either on account of avarice or because of other wanton desires tormented men and excommunicated them without any due process of law. But what tyranny is it for the officials in the states to have arbitrary power to condemn and excommunicate men without due process of law! And with respect to what did they abuse this power? Clearly not in punishing true offences, but in regard to the violation of fasts or festivals, or like trifles? Only they sometimes punished adulteries; and in this matter they often vexed [abused and defamed] innocent and honorable men.

Since, therefore, bishops have tyrannically transferred this jurisdiction to themselves alone, and have basely abused it, there is no need, because of this jurisdiction, to obey bishops. But since the reasons why we do not obey are just, it is right also to restore this jurisdiction to godly pastors [to whom, by Christ's command, it belongs], and to see to it that it be legitimately exercised for the reformation of life and the glory of God.

Jurisdiction remains in those cases which, according to canonical law, pertain to the ecclesiastical court, as they say, and especially in cases of matrimony. It is only by human right that the bishops have this also; and indeed the ancient bishops did not have it, as it appears from the *Codex* and *Novelli* of Justinian that decisions concerning marriage at that time belonged to the magistrates. And by divine law worldly magistrates are compelled to make these decisions if the bishops [judge unjustly or] be negligent. The canons also concede the same. Wherefore also on account of this jurisdiction it is not necessary to obey bishops. And indeed since they have framed certain unjust laws concerning marriages, and observe them in their courts, also for this reason there is need to establish other courts. For the traditions concerning spiritual relationship [the prohibition of marriage between sponsors] are unjust. Unjust also is the tradition which forbids an innocent person to marry after divorce. Unjust also is the law which in general approves all clandestine and underhanded betrothals in violation of the right of parents. Unjust also is the law concerning the celibacy of priests. There are also other spares of consciences in their laws, to recite all of which is of no profit. It is sufficient to have recited this, that there are many unjust laws of the Pope concerning matrimonial subjects on account of which the magistrates ought to establish other courts.

Since therefore the bishops, who are devoted to the Pope, defend godless doctrine and godless services, and do not ordain godly teachers, yea aid the cruelty of the Pope, and besides have wrested the jurisdiction from pastors, and exercise this only tyrannically [for their own profit]; and lastly, since in matrimonial cases they observe many unjust laws; the reasons why the churches do not recognize these as bishops are sufficiently numerous and necessary.

But they themselves should remember that riches have been given to bishops as alms for the administration and advantage of the churches [that they may serve the Church, and perform their office the more efficiently], just as the rule says: "The benefice is given because of the office." Wherefore they cannot with a good conscience possess these alms, and meanwhile defraud the Church, which has need of these means for supporting ministers, and aiding studies [educating learned men], and caring for the poor, and establishing courts, especially matrimonial. For so great is the variety and extent of matrimonial controversies, that there is need of a special tribunal for these, and for establishing this there is need of the means of the Church. Peter predicted (2 Ep. 2:13) that there would be godless bishops, who would abuse the alms of the Church for luxury and neglect the ministry. Therefore let those who defraud know that they will pay God the penalty for this crime.

Notes: *These articles, written by Martin Luther primarily for the Holy Roman Emperor, clarified some issues that were a matter of intense controversy between the Reformers and the Roman Catholic Church. The tone is less conciliatory than that of the Augsburg Confession, attacking the pope in the opening paragraphs and presenting a number of Lutheran distinctives in forceful language.*

In 1580, the articles were placed alongside the Augsburg Confession and the Formula of Concord in The Book of Concord, *the main collection of Lutheran doctrinal materials. Today the Smalcald Articles are accepted fully as a doctrinal standard by the Lutheran Church-Missouri Synod and the Wisconsin Evangelical Lutheran Synod, but not accorded an equal status with the Augsburg Confession by either the Lutheran Church in America or the American Lutheran Church.*

* * *

THE FORMULA OF CONCORD (1580)

PART FIRST.

EPITOME. OF THE ARTICLES IN CONTROVERSY AMONG THE THELOGIANS OF THE AUGSBURG CONFESSION, SET FORTH AND RECONCILED IN A CHRISTIAN WAY, ACCORDING TO GOD'S WORD, IN THE FOLLOWING RECAPITULATION.

INTRODUCTION. OF THE COMPREHENSIVE SUMMARY, RULE AND STANDARD ACCORDING TO WHICH ALL DOGMAS SHOULD BE JUDGED, AND THE CONTROVERSIES THAT HAVE OCCURRED SHOULD, IN A CHRISTIAN WAY, BE DECIDED AND SET FORTH.

I.   We believe, teach and confess that the only rule and standard according to which at once all dogmas and teachers should be esteemed and judged are nothing else than the prophetic and apostolic Scriptures of

THE FORMULA OF CONCORD (1580) (continued)

the Old and of the New Testament, as it is written (Ps. 119:105): "Thy Word is a lamp unto my feet, and a light unto my path." And St. Paul (Gal. 1:8): "Though an angel from heaven preach any other Gospel unto you, let him be accursed."

Other writings, of ancient or modern teachers, whatever reputation they may have, should not be regarded as of equal authority with the Holy Scriptures, but should altogether be subordinated to them, and should not be received other or further than as witnesses, in what manner and at what places, since the time of the apostles, the [purer] doctrine of the prophets and apostles was preserved.

II. And because directly after the times of the apostles, and even in their lives, false teachers and heretics arose, and against them, in the early Church, symbols, *i.e.* brief, plain confessions, were composed, which were regarded as the unanimous, universal Christian faith, and confession of the orthodox and true Church, namely, THE APOSTLES' CREED, THE NICENE CREED, and the ATHANASIAN CREED; we confess them as binding upon us, and hereby reject all heresies and dogmas which, contrary to them, have been introduced into the Church of God.

III. Moreover as to the schism in matters of faith which has occurred in our time, we regard the unanimous consensus and declaration of our Christian faith and confession, especially against the Papacy and its false worship, idolatry, superstition, and against other sects, as the symbol of our time, viz. THE FIRST UNALTERED AUGSBURG CONFESSION, delivered to the Emperor Charles V. at Augsburg in the year 1530, in the great Diet, together with its APOLOGY, and the ARTICLES composed at SMALCALD in the year 1537, and subscribed by the chief theologians of that time.

And because such matters pertain also to the laity and the salvation of their souls, we confessionally acknowledge the SMALL and LARGE CATE-CHISMS of Dr. Luther, as they are included in Luther's works, as the Bible of the laity, wherein everything is comprised which is treated at greater length in Holy Scripture, and is necessary that a Christian man know for his salvation.

In accordance with this direction, as above announced, all doctrines should be adjusted, and that which is contrary thereto should be rejected and condemned, as opposed to the unanimous declaration of our faith.

In this way the distinction between the Holy Scriptures of the Old and of the New Testament and all other writings is preserved, and the Holy Scriptures alone remain the only judge, rule, and standard, according to which, as the only test-stone, all dogmas should and must be discerned and judged, as to whether they be good or evil, right or wrong.

But the other symbols and writings cited are not judges, as are the Holy Scriptures, but only a witness and declaration of the faith, as to how at any time the Holy Scriptures have been understood and explained in the articles in controversy in the Church of God by those who then lived, and how the opposite dogma was rejected and condemned [by what arguments the dogmas conflicting with the Holy Scripture were rejected and condemned].

CHAPTER I. OF ORIGINAL SIN.

STATEMENT OF THE CONTROVERSY.

Whether Original Sin be properly and without any distinction man's corrupt nature, substance and essence, or indeed the principal and best part of his essence [substance], namely, the rational soul itself in its highest state and powers? Or whether, even since the fall, there be a distinction between man's substance, nature, essence, body, soul, and Original Sin, so that the nature is one thing, and Original Sin, which inheres in the corrupt nature and corrupts the nature, is another?

AFFIRMATIVE.

The pure doctrine, faith and confession according to the above standard and comprehensive declaration:

1. We believe, teach and confess that there is a distinction between man's nature, not only as he was originally created by God, pure and holy, and without sin, but also as we have it [that nature] now, since the fall, namely, between the nature itself, which ever since the fall is and remains a creature of God, and Original Sin, and that this distinction is as great as the distinction between a work of God and a work of the devil.

2. We believe, teach and confess also that this distinction should be maintained with the greatest care, because the dogma that no distinction is to be made between our corrupt human nature and original sin conflicts with the chief articles of our Christian faith, concerning Creation, Redemption, Sanctification and the resurrection of our body, and cannot coexist therewith.

For God created not only the body and soul of Adam and Eve before the fall, but also our bodies and souls since the fall, notwithstanding that they are corrupt, which God also still acknowledges as his work, as it is written (Job 10:8): "Thine hands have made me and fashioned me together round about." Deut. 32:18; Isa. 45:9 sqq.; 54:5; 64:8; Acts 17:28; Job 10:8; Ps. 100:3; 139:14; Eccl. 12:1.

This human nature, nevertheless without sin, and, therefore, not of other's but our own flesh, the Son of God has assumed into the unity of his person, and according to it become our true brother. Heb. 2:14: "Forasmuch then as the children were partakers of flesh and blood, He also himself likewise took part of the same." Again, v. 16; 4:15: "He took not on him the nature of angels, but he took on him the seed of Abraham. Wherefore in all things it behoved him to be made like unto his brethren," "yet without sin." Therefore Christ has redeemed it, as his work, sanctifies it as his work, raises it from the dead and gloriously adorns it as his work. But Original Sin he has not created, assumed, redeemed, sanctified; he also will not raise it, or with the elect adorn or save it, but in the [blessed] resurrection it will be entirely destroyed.

Hence the distinction between the corrupt nature and the corruption which infects the nature and by which the nature became corrupt, can easily be discerned.

3. But, on the other hand, we believe, teach and confess that Original Sin is not a slight, but so deep a corruption of human nature, that nothing healthy or uncorrupt in man's body or soul, in inner or outward powers, remains, but, as the Church sings:

"Through Adam's fall is all corrupt,
Nature and essence human."

This unspeakable injury cannot be discerned by the reason, but only from God's Word. And [we affirm] that the nature and this corruption of nature no one but God alone can ever separate from one another; and yet this fully comes to pass, through death, in the resurrection, where our nature which we now bear will rise and live eternally, without original sin, and separated and sundered from it, as it is written (Job 19:26): "I shall be compassed again with this my skin, and in my flesh shall I see God, whom I shall see for myself, and mine eyes shall behold."

NEGATIVE. *Rejection of the false opposite dogmas.*

Therefore we reject and condemn the dogma that Original Sin is only a *reatus* or debt, on account of what has been committed by another [diverted to us] without any corruption of our nature.

2. Also that evil lusts are not sin, but concreated, essential properties of the nature, as though the above-mentioned defect and evil were not true sin, because of which man without Christ [not ingrafted into Christ] is to be a child of wrath.

3. We likewise reject the error of the Pelagians, by which it is alleged that man's nature, even since the fall, is incorrupt, and, especially with respect to spiritual things, in *naturalibus, i.e.* in its natural powers, it has remained entirely good and pure.

4. Also that Original Sin is only external, a slight, insignificant spot, sprinkle, or stain dashed upon the nature, beneath which [nevertheless] the nature has retained its powers unimpaired even in spiritual things.

5. Also that Original Sin is only an external impediment to unimpaired spiritual powers, and not a despoliation or want of the same, as when a magnet is smeared with garlic-juice its natural power is not thereby removed, but only impeded; or that this stain can be easily washed away, as a spot from the face or pigment from the wall.

6. Also, that in man the human nature and essence are not entirely corrupt, but that man still has something good in him, even in spiritual things, namely, piety,

skill, aptness or ability in spiritual things to begin to work, or to co-work for something [good].

7. On the other hand, we also reject the false dogma of the Manichaeans, when it is taught that Original Sin, as something essential and self-subsisting, has been infused by Satan into the nature, and intermingled with it, as poison and wine are mixed.

8. Also that not the natural man, but something else and extraneous to man, sins, and, on this account, not the nature, but only Original Sin in the nature, is accused.

9. We reject and condemn also as a Manichaean error the doctrine that Original Sin is properly, and without any distinction, the substance, nature and essence itself of the corrupt man, so that no distinction between the corrupt nature, considered by itself, since the fall, and Original Sin, can be conceived of, nor can they be distinguished from one another even in thought.

10. Moreover this Original Sin is called by Dr. Luther natural sin, personal sin, essential sin (Natursünde, Personsünde, Wesentlichle Sünde); not that the nature, person or essence of the man is, without any distinction, itself Original Sin, but that, by such words, the distinction might be indicated between Original Sin which inheres in human nature, and other sins which are called actual sins.

11. For Original Sin is not a sin which is committed, but it inheres in the nature, substance and essence of man, so that though no wicked thought ever should arise in the heart of corrupt man, nor idle word be spoken, nor wicked deed be done, yet the nature is nevertheless corrupt through Original Sin, which is born in us by reason of the sinful seed, and is a fountain-head of all other actual sins, as wicked thoughts, words and works, as it is written (Matt. 15:19): "Out of the heart proceed evil thoughts." Also (Gen. 6:5; 8:21): "The imagination of man's heart is evil from his youth."

12. Thus it also well to note the diverse signification of the word "nature," whereby the Manichaeans cover their error and lead astray many simple men. For sometimes it means the essence [the very substance] of man, as when it is said: God created human nature. But at other times it means the disposition and the vicious quality [disposition, condition, defect or vice] of a thing, which inheres in the nature or essence, as when it is said: The nature of the serpent is to bite, and the nature and disposition of man is to sin, and is sin; here the word *nature* does not mean the substance of man, but something that inheres in the nature or substance.

13. But as to the Latin terms "substance" and "accident," because they are not words of Holy Scripture, and besides unknown to the ordinary man, they should not be used in sermons before ordinary, uninstructed people, but simple people should be excused from this [in this matter regard should rightly be had to the simple and uneducated]. But in

the schools, among the learned, these words are rightly retained in disputations concerning Original Sin, because they are well known and used without any misunderstanding, to distinguish exactly between the essence of a thing and what is attached to it in an accidental way.

For the distinction between God's work and that of the devil is thereby designated in the clearest way, because the devil can create no substance, but can only, in an accidental way, from God's decree [God permitting] corrupt a substance created by God.

CHAPTER II. OF THE FREE WILL.
STATEMENT OF THE CONTROVERSY.

Since the will of man is found in four dissimilar states, namely: 1. Before the fall; 2. Since the fall; 3. After regeneration; 4. After resurrection of the body, the chief question is only concerning the will and ability of man in the second state, namely, what powers, in spiritual things, he has, from himself, since the fall of our first parents, and before regeneration, and whether, from his own powers, before he has been born again by God's Spirit, he be able to dispose and prepare himself for God's grace, and to accept [and apprehend] or not, the grace offered through the Holy Ghost in the Word and holy [divinely-instituted] sacraments.

AFFIRMATIVE. *The pure doctrine concerning this article, according to God's Word.*

1. Concerning this subject, our doctrine, faith and confession is, that, in spiritual things, the understanding and reason of man are [altogether] blind, and, from their own powers, understand nothing, as it is written (1 Cor. 2:14): "The natural man receiveth not the things of the Spirit of God; for they are foolishness to him; neither can he know them, because he is examined concerning spiritual things."

2. Likewise we believe, teach and confess that the will of unregenerate man is not only turned away from God, but also has become an enemy of God, so that it has inclination and desire for that which is evil and contrary to God, as it is written (Gen. 8:21): "The imagination of man's heart is evil from his youth." Also (Rom. 8:7): "The carnal mind is enmity against God; for it is not subject to the Law of God, neither indeed can be." Yea, as unable as a dead body is to quicken and restore itself to bodily, earthly life, just so unable is man, who by sin is spiritually dead, to raise himself to spiritual life, as it is written (Eph. 2:5): "Even when we were dead in sins, he hath quickened us together with Christ;" (2 Cor. 3:5): "Not that we are sufficient of ourselves to think anything good, as of ourselves, but that we are sufficient is of God."

3. Yet God the Holy Ghost effects conversion, not without means; but uses for this purpose the preaching and hearing of God's Word, as it is written (Rom. 1:16): "The Gospel is the power of God unto salvation to every one that believeth." Also (Rom. 10:17): "Faith cometh by hearing of the Word of God." And it is God's will that his Word should be heard, and that man's ears should not be closed. With this Word the Holy Ghost is present, and opens hearts, so that they, as Lydia, in Acts 16, are attentive to it, and are thus converted through the grace and power of the Holy Ghost, whose work alone the conversion of man is. For, without his grace, and if he do not grant the increase, our willing and running, our planting, sowing and watering, all are nothing, as Christ says (John 15:5): "Without me, ye can do nothing." In these short words he denies to the free will all power, and ascribes everything to God's grace, in order that no one may boast before God: 1 Cor. 1:29 [2 Cor. 12:5; Jer. 9:23].

NEGATIVE. *Contrary false doctrine.*

We therefore reject and condemn all the following errors, as contrary to the standard of God's Word:

1. The host [insane dogma] of philosophers who are called Stoics, as also of the Manichaeans, who taught that everything that happens must have happened so, and could not have happened otherwise, and that everything that man does, even in outward things, he does by necessity, and that he is coerced to evil works and deeds, as inchastity, robbery, murder, theft and the like.

2. We reject also the gross error of the Pelagians, who taught that man by his own powers, without the grace of the Holy Ghost, can turn himself to God, believe the Gospel, be obedient in heart to God's Law, and thus merit the forgiveness of sins and eternal life.

3. We reject also the error of the Semi-Pelagians, who teach that man, by his own powers, can make a beginning of his conversion, but without the grace of the Holy Ghost cannot complete it.

4. Also when it is taught that, although man by his free will before regeneration, is too weak to make a beginning, and, by his own powers, to turn himself to God, and in heart to be obedient to God; yet, if the Holy Ghost, by the preaching of the Word, have made a beginning, and offered therein his grace, then the will of man, from its own natural powers, to a certain extent, although feebly, can add, help and co-operate therewith, can qualify and prepare itself for grace, and embrace and accept it, and believe the Gospel.

5. Also that man, after he has been born again, can perfectly observe and completely fulfil God's Law, and that this fulfilling is our righteousness before God, by which we merit eternal life.

6. Also that we condemn the error of the Enthusiasts,* who imagine that God, without means, without the hearing of God's Word, also without the use of the holy sacraments, draws men to himself, and enlightens, justifies and saves them.

* Enthusiasts are those who expect the illumination of the Spirit [celestial revelation] without the preaching of God's Word.

7. Also that in conversion and regeneration God entirely exterminates the substance and essence of the old Adam, and especially the rational soul, and, in this conversion and regeneration, creates a new soul out of nothing.

8. Also, when the following expressions are employed with out explanation, viz. that the will of man, before, in, and after conversion, resists the Holy Ghost, and that the Holy Ghost is given to those who resist him intentionally and persistently; "for," as Augustine says, "in conversion God changes the unwilling into willing, and dwells in the willing."

As to the expressions of ancient and modern church teachers, when it is said: *Deus trahit, sed volentem trahit, i.e.* "God draws, but he draws the willing," and *Hominis voluntas in conversione non est otiosa sed agit aliquid, i.e.* "In conversion the will of man is not idle, but effects something," we maintain that, inasmuch as these expressions have been introduced for confirming the false opinion concerning the powers of the natural free will in man's conversion, against the doctrine concerning God's grace, they are not in harmony with the form of sound doctrine, and therefore, when we speak of conversion to God, should be avoided.

But, on the other hand, it is correctly said that, in conversion God, through the drawing of the Holy Ghost, changes stubborn and unwilling into willing men, and that after such conversion, in the daily exercise of repentance, the regenerate will of man is not idle, but also co-operates in all the deeds of the Holy Ghost, which he works through us.

9. Also what Dr. Luther has written, viz. that man's will is in his conversion purely passive, *i.e.* it does nothing whatever, is to be understood in respect of divine grace in kindling new motions, i.e. when God's Spirit, through the heard Word or the use of the holy sacrament, lays hold upon man's will, and works [in man] the new birth and conversion. For if [after] the Holy Ghost has wrought and accomplished this, and man's will has been changed and renewed alone by his divine power and working, then the new will of man is an instrument and organ of God the Holy Ghost, so that he not only accepts grace, but also, in the works which follow, co-operates with the Holy Ghost.

Therefore, before the conversion of man, there are only two efficient causes, namely, the Holy Ghost and the Word of God, as the instrument of the Holy Ghost, whereby he works conversion. To this Word man ought to listen, nevertheless it is not from his own powers, but only through the grace and working of the Holy Ghost, that he can believe and accept it.

CHAPTER III. OF THE RIGHTEOUSNESS OF FAITH BEFORE GOD.

STATEMENT OF THE CONTROVERSY.

Since it is unanimously confessed in our churches, upon the authority of God's Word and according to the sense of the Augsburg Confession, that we poor sinners are justified before God, and saved alone by faith in Christ, and thus Christ alone is our righteousness, who is true God and man, because in him the divine and human natures are personally united with one another (Jer. 23:6; 1 Cor. 1:30; 2 Cor. 5:21), the question has arisen: "According to which nature is Christ our righteousness?" and thus two contrary errors have arisen in some churches.

For the one side has held that Christ alone, according to his divinity, is our righteousness, if he dwell in us by faith; contrasted with which divinity, dwelling in men by faith, all the sins of men should be regarded as a drop of water to the great ocean. On the contrary, others have held that Christ is our righteousness before God, alone according to the human nature.

AFFIRMATIVE. *Pure Doctrine of the Christian Churches against both errors just mentioned.*

1. Against both the errors just recounted, we unanimously believe, teach and confess that Christ is our righteousness, neither according to the divine nature alone, nor according to the human nature alone, but the entire Christ according to both natures, alone in his obedience, which as God and man he rendered the Father even to death, and thereby merited for us the forgiveness of sins and eternal life, as it is written: "As by one man's disobedience, many were made sinners, so by the obedience of one, shall many be made righteous" (Rom. 5:19).

2. Therefore we believe, teach and confess that our righteousness before God is, that God forgives us our sins out of pure grace, without any work, merit or worthiness of ours preceding, attending or following, for he presents and imputes to us the righteousness of Christ's obedience, on account of which righteousness we are received into grace by God, and regarded righteous.

3. We believe, teach and confess that faith alone is the means and instrument whereby we lay hold of Christ, and thus in Christ of that righteousness which avails before God, for the sake of which this faith is imputed to us for righteousness (Rom. 4:5).

4. We believe, teach and confess that this faith is not a bare knowledge of the history of Christ, but such a great gift of God that thereby we come to the right knowledge of Christ as our Redeemer in the Word of the Gospel, and trust in him that alone for the sake of his obedience, out of grace, we have the forgiveness of sins, and are regarded holy and righteous before God the Father, and eternally saved.

5. We believe, teach and confess that, according to the usage of Holy Scripture, the word justify means in this article, "to absolve," that is, to declare free from sins. Prov. 17:15: 'He that justifieth the wicked, and he that condemneth the righteous, even they both are abomination to the Lord." Also (Rom. 8:33): "Who shall lay anything to the charge of God's elect? It is God that justifieth."

And when in place of this, the words regeneration and vivification are employed, as in the Apology, this is done in the same sense; for by these terms, in other places, the renewal of man is understood, and [which] is distinguished from justification by faith.

6. We believe, teach and confess also that although many weaknesses and defects cling to the rightly believing and truly regenerate, even to the grave, yet they have reason to doubt neither of the righteousness which is imputed to them by faith, nor of the salvation of their souls, but should regard it certain that for Christ's sake, according to the promise and [immovable] Word of the holy Gospel, they have a gracious God.

7. We believe, teach and confess that, for the maintenance of the pure doctrine concerning the righteousness of faith before God, it is necessary that the exclusive particles, *i.e.*, the following words of the holy apostle Paul, whereby the merit of Christ is entirely separated from our works, and the honor given to Christ alone, be retained with especial care, as when the holy apostle Paul writes: "Of grace," "without merit," "without law," "without works," "not of works." All these words, taken together, mean that "we are justified and saved alone by faith in Christ" (Eph. 2:8; Rom. 1:17; 3:24; 4:3 sqq.; Gal. 3:11; Heb. 11).

8. We believe, teach and confess that although the contrition that precedes, and the good works that follow, do not belong to the article of justification before God, yet such a faith should not be imagined as can coexist with a wicked intention to sin and to act against conscience. But after man is justified by faith, then a true living faith worketh by love (Gal. 5:6). Thus good works always follow justifying faith, and are surely found with it, if it be true and living; for it never is alone, but always has with it love and hope.

ANTITHESIS OR NEGATIVE. *Contrary Doctrine Rejected.*

Therefore we reject and condemn all the following errors:

1. That Christ is our righteousness alone according to his divine nature.

2. That Christ is our righteousness alone according to his human nature.

3. That in the expressions of the prophets and apostles, when the righteousness of faith is spoken of, the words "justify" and "be justified" do not signify to declare or be declared free from sins, and obtain the forgiveness of sins, but actually to be made righteous before God, because of love infused by the Holy Ghost, virtues and the works following them.

4. That faith looks not only to the obedience of Christ, but to his divine nature, as it dwells and works in us, and that by this indwelling our sins are covered.

5. That faith is such a trust in the obedience of Christ as can exist and remain in a man who has no genuine repentance, in whom also no love follows, but he persists in sins against conscience.

6. That not God himself, but only the gifts of God, dwell in the believer.

7. That faith saves, on this account, viz. because by faith the renewal, which consists in love to God and one's neighbor, is begun in us.

8. That faith has the first place in justification, although also renewal and love belong to our righteousness before God, in such a manner that they [renewal and love] are not the chief cause of our righteousness, but, nevertheless, our righteousness before God is, without this love and renewal, not entire or complete.

9. That believers are justified before God, and saved partly by the imputed righteousness of Christ, and by the beginning of new obedience, or in part by the imputation of Christ's righteousness, but in part also by the beginning of new obedience.

10. That the promise of grace is imputed to us by faith in the heart, and by the confession which is made with the mouth, and by other virtues.

11. That faith without good works does not justify, and therefore that good works are necessarily required for righteousness, and without their presence man cannot be justified.

CHAPTER IV. OF GOOD WORKS.

STATEMENT OF THE CONTROVERSY.

Concerning the doctrine of good works two divisions have arisen in some churches:

1. First, some theologians have differed with reference to the following expressions, where the one side wrote: "Good works are necessary for salvation." "It is impossible to be saved without good works." Also: "No one has ever been saved without good works." But the other side, on the contrary, wrote: "Good works are injurious to salvation."

2. Afterwards a schism arose also between some theologians with respect to the two words, "necessary" and "free," since the one side contended that the word "necessary" should not be employed concerning the new obedience, which does not proceed from necessity and coercion, but from the free will. The other side has retained the word "necessary," because this obedience is not at our option, but regenerate men are bound to render this obedience.

From this disputation concerning the terms a controversy concerning the subject itself afterwards occurred. For the one side contended that among Christians the law should not at all be urged, but men should be exhorted to good works alone from the Holy Gospel. The other side contradicted this.

AFFIRMATIVE. *Pure Doctrine of the Christian Churches concerning this Controversy.*

For the thorough statement and decision of this controversy, our doctrine, faith and confession is:

1. That good works certainly and without doubt follow true faith, if it be not a dead, but a living faith, as the fruit of a good tree.

2. We believe, teach and confess also that good works should be entirely excluded, as well when the question at issue is concerning salvation, as in the article of justification before God, as the apostle testifies with clear words, where it is written: "Even as David also describeth the blessedness of the man unto whom God imputeth righteousness without works, saying, . . . Blessed is the man to whom the Lord will not impute sin," etc. (Rom. 4:6 sqq.). And elsewhere: "By grace are ye saved through faith; and that not of yourselves, it is the gift of God; not of works, lest any man should boast" (Eph. 2:8, 9).

3. We believe, teach and confess also that all men, but those especially who are born again and renewed by the Holy Ghost, are bound to do good works.

4. In this sense the words "necessary," "should" and "must" are employed correctly and in a Christian manner, also with respect to the regenerate, and in no way are contrary to the form and language of sound words.

5. Nevertheless by the words mentioned, "necessity" and "necessary," if they be employed concerning the regenerate, not coercion, but only due obedience is understood, which the truly believing, so far as they are regenerate, render not from coercion or the impulse of the Law, but from the free will; because they are no more under the Law, but under grace (Rom. 6:14; 7:6; 8:14).

6. Therefore we also believe, teach and confess that when it is said: The regenerate do good works from the free will; this should not be understood as though it were at the option of the regenerate man to do or to forbear doing good when he wished, and nevertheless could retain faith when he intentionally persevered in sins.

7. Yet this should not be understood otherwise than as the Lord Christ and his apostles themselves declare, namely, that the liberated spirit does not do this from fear of punishment, as a slave, but from love of righteousness, as children (Rom. 8:15).

8. Although this free will in the elect children of God is not complete, but is burdened with great weakness, as St. Paul complains concerning himself (Rom. 7:14-25; Gal. 5:17).

9. Nevertheless, for the sake of the Lord Christ, the Lord does not impute this weakness to his elect, as it is written: "There is therefore now no condemnation to them which are in Christ Jesus" (Rom. 8:1).

10. We believe, teach and confess also, that not works, but alone the Spirit of God, through faith, maintains faith and salvation in us, of whose presence and indwelling good works are evidences.

NEGATIVE. *False Contrary Doctrine.*

1. We reject and condemn the following modes of speaking, viz. when it is taught and written that good works are necessary to salvation. Also, that no one ever has been saved without good works. Also, that it is impossible without good works to be saved.

2. We reject and condemn the unqualified expression: Good works are injurious to salvation, as offensive and detrimental to Christian discipline.

For, especially in these last times, it is no less needful to admonish men to Christian discipline [to the way of living aright and godly] and good works, and instruct them how necessary it is that they exercise themselves in good works as a declaration of their faith and gratitude to God, than that the works be not mingled in the article of justification; because men may be damned by an epicurean delusion concerning faith, as well as by Papistic and Pharisaic confidence in their own works and merits.

3. We also reject and condemn the dogma that faith and the indwelling of the Holy Ghost are not lost by wilful sin, but that the saints and elect retain the Holy Ghost, even though they fall into adultery and other sins, and persist therein.

CHAPTER V. OF THE LAW AND THE GOSPEL.
STATEMENT OF THE CONTROVERSY.

Whether the preaching of the Holy Gospel be properly not only a preaching of grace, which announces the forgiveness of sins, but also a preaching of repentance and censure, rebuking unbelief, which is rebuked not in the Law, but alone through the Gospel.

AFFIRMATIVE. *Pure Doctrine of God's Word.*

1. We believe, teach and confess that the distinction between the Law and the Gospel is to be maintained in the Church as an especially brilliant light, whereby, according to the admonition of St. Paul, the Word of God may be rightly divided.

2. We believe, teach and confess that the Law is properly a divine doctrine, which teaches what is right and pleasing to God, and reproves everything that is sin and contrary to God's will.

3. Therefore everything that reproves sin is and belongs to the preaching of the Law.

4. But the Gospel is properly such a doctrine as teaches what man who has not observed the Law, and therefore is condemned by it, should believe, viz. that Christ has expiated and made satisfaction for all sins, and, without any merit of theirs [no merit of the sinner intervening], has obtained and acquired forgiveness of sins, righteousness that avails before God, and eternal life.

5. But since the term Gospel is not used in one and the same sense in the Holy Scriptures, on account of which this dissension originally arose, we believe, teach and confess that if by the term Gospel the entire doctrine of Christ be understood, which he proposed in his ministry, as also did his apostles (in which sense it is employed, Mark 1:15; Acts 20:21), it is correctly said and written that the Gospel is a preaching of repentance and of the forgiveness of sins.

6. But if the Law and the Gospel be contrasted with one another, as Moses himself is called a teacher of the Law, and Christ a preacher of the Gospel, we

THE FORMULA OF CONCORD (1580) (continued)

believe, teach and confess that the Gospel is not a preaching of repentance or reproof, but properly nothing else than a preaching of consolation, and a joyful message which does not reprove or terrify, but against the terrors of the Law consoles consciences, points alone to the merit of Christ, and again comforts them by the precious preaching of the grace and favor of God, obtained through Christ's merit.

7. As to the revelation of sin, because the veil of Moses hangs before the eyes of all men as long as they hear the bare preaching of the Law, and nothing concerning Christ, and therefore do not learn from the Law to perceive their sins aright, but either become presumptuous hypocrites [who swell with the opinion of their own righteousness] as the Pharisees, or despair as did Judas; Christ takes the Law into his hands, and explains it spiritually (Matt. 5:21 sqq.; Rom. 7:14). And thus the wrath of God is revealed from heaven against all sinners (Rom. 1:18), how great it is; by this means they are instructed in the Law, and then from it first learn to know aright their sins—a knowledge to which Moses never could coerce them.

Therefore, although the preaching of the suffering and death of Christ, the Son of God, is an earnest and terrible proclamation and declaration of God's wrath, whereby men are for the first time led aright to the Law, after the veil of Moses has been removed from them, so that they first know aright how great things God in his Law requires of us, nothing of which we can observe, and therefore should seek all our righteousness in Christ—

8. Yet as long as all this (namely, Christ's suffering and death) proclaims God's wrath and terrifies man, it is still not properly the preaching of the Gospel, but the preaching of Moses and the Law, and therefore a "strange work" of Christ, whereby he attains his proper office, *i.e.* to preach grace, console and quicken, which is properly the preaching of the Gospel.

NEGATIVE. *Contrary Doctrine which is Rejected.*

Therefore we reject and regard incorrect and injurious the dogma that the Gospel is properly a preaching of repentance or reproof, and not alone a preaching of grace. For thereby the Gospel is again converted into a law, the merit of Christ and the Holy Scriptures obscured, Christians robbed of true consolation, and the door opened again to [the errors and superstitions of] the Papacy.

CHAPTER VI. OF THE THIRD USE OF THE LAW.

STATEMENT OF THE CONTROVERSY.

Since the Law was given to men for three reasons: *first,* that thereby outward discipline might be maintained against wild, disobedient men [and that wild and intractable men might be restrained, as though by certain bars]; *secondly,* that men thereby may be led to the knowledge of their sins; *thirdly,* that after they are regenerate and [much of] the flesh notwithstanding cleaves to them, they may

have, on this account, a fixed rule, according to which they should regulate and direct their whole life; a dissension has occurred between some few theologians, concerning the third use of the Law, viz. whether it is to be urged or not upon regenerate Christians. The one side has said, Yea; the other, Nay.

AFFIRMATIVE. *The true Christian Doctrine Concerning this Controversy.*

1. We believe, teach and confess that although men rightly believing [in Christ] and truly converted to God have been freed and exempted from the curse and coercion of the Law, they nevertheless are not on this account without Law, but have been redeemed by the Son of God, in order that they should exercise themselves in it day and night [that they should meditate upon God's Law day and night, and constantly exercise themselves in its observance (Ps. 1:2)], (Ps. 119). For even our first parents before the fall did not live without Law, which Law of God was also written upon their hearts, because they were created in the image of God (Gen. 1:26 sq.; 2:16 sqq.; 3:3).

2. We believe, teach and confess that the preaching of the Law is to be urged with diligence, not only upon the unbelieving and impenitent, but also upon the rightly believing, truly converted, regenerate, and justified by faith.

3. For although they are regenerate and renewed in the spirit of their mind, yet, in the present life, this regeneration and renewal are not complete, but are only begun, and believers are, in the spirit of their mind, in a constant struggle against the flesh, *i.e.* against the corrupt nature and disposition which cleaves to us unto death. On account of this old Adam, which still inheres in the understanding, will and all the powers of man, it is needful that the Law of the Lord always shine upon the way before him, in order that he may do nothing from self-imposed human devotion [that he may frame nothing in a matter of religion from the desire of private devotion, and may not choose divine services not instituted by God's Word]; likewise, that the old Adam also may not employ his own will, but may be subdued against his will, not only by the admonition and threatening of the Law, but also by punishments and blows, so that he may follow and surrender himself captive to the Spirit (1 Cor. 9:27; Rom. 6:12; Gal. 6:14; Ps. 119:1 sqq.; Heb. 13:21 [Heb. 12:1]).

4. Then as to the distinction between the works of the Law and the fruits of the Spirit, we believe, teach and confess that the works which are done according to the Law, as long as they are and are called works of the Law, are only extorted from man by the force of punishment and the threatening of God's wrath.

5. But the fruits of the Spirit are the works which the Spirit of God who dwells in believers works through the regenerate, and are done by believers so far as they are regenerate [spontaneously and freely], as though they knew of no command, threat or reward; for in this manner the children of God live in the

Law and walk according to the Law of God, a manner which St. Paul, in his Epistles, calls the Law of Christ and the Law of the mind [Rom. 7:25; 8:7 [Rom. 8:2; 2; Gal. 6:2]).

6. Thus the Law is and remains both to the penitent and impenitent, both to regenerate and unregenerate men, one and the same Law, namely, the immutable will of God; and the distinction, so far as it concerns obedience, is alone in the men, inasmuch as one who is not yet regenerate does what is required him by the Law out of constraint and unwillingly (as also the regenerate do according to the flesh); but the believer, so far as he is regenerate, without constraint and with a willing spirit, does that which no threatening [however severe] of the Law could ever extort from him.

NEGATIVE. *False Contrary Doctrine.*

Therefore we reject as a dogma and error injurious and conflicting with Christian discipline and true piety that the Law in the above-mentioned way and degree should not be urged upon Christians and those truly believing, but only upon unbelievers and those not Christian, and upon the impenitent.

CHAPTER VII. OF THE LORD'S SUPPER.

Although the Zwinglian teachers are not to be reckoned among the theologians who acknowledge and profess the Augsburg Confession, as they separated from them when this Confession was presented, nevertheless since they are intruding themselves [with their assembly], and are attempting, under the name of this Christian Confession, to introduce their error, we have wished also to make such a report as is needful [we have judged that the Church of Christ should be instructed also] concerning this controversy.

STATEMENT OF THE CONTROVERSY. *Chief Controversy between our Doctrine and that of the Sacramentarians upon this article.*

Whether in the Holy Supper the true body and blood of our Lord Jesus Christ are truly and essentially present, are distributed with the bread and wine, and received with the mouth by all those who use this sacrament, whether they be worthy or unworthy, godly or ungodly, believing or unbelieving; by the believing, for consolation and life; by the unbelieving, for judgment [so that the believing receive from the Lord's Supper consolation and life, but the unbelieving take it for their judgment]? The Sacramentarians say, No; we say, Yea.

For the explanation of this controversy it is to be noted in the beginning that there are two kinds of Sacramentarians. Some are gross Sacramentarians, who declare in clear [deutschen] words what they believe in their hearts, viz. that in the Holy Supper nothing but bread and wine is present, and distributed and received with the mouth. Others, however, are subtle Sacramentarians, and the most injurious of all, who partly speak very speciously in our own words, and assert that they also believe in a true presence of the true, essential, living body and blood of Christ in the Holy Supper, yet that this occurs spiritually through faith. Nevertheless beneath these specious words,

precisely the former gross opinion is contained, viz. that in the Holy Supper nothing is present and received with the mouth except bread and wine. For with them the word *spiritually* means nothing else than the Spirit of Christ, or the power of the absent body of Christ, and his merit, which are present; but the body of Christ is in no mode or way present, except only above in the highest heaven, to which in heaven we should elevate ourselves by the thoughts of our faith, and there, and not at all in the bread and wine of the Holy Supper, should seek this body and blood [of Christ].

AFFIRMATIVE. *Confession of the Pure Doctrine concerning the Holy Supper against the Sacramentarians.*

1. We believe, teach and confess that, in the Holy Supper the body and blood of Christ are truly and essentially present, and are truly distributed and received with the bread and wine.

2. We believe, teach and confess that the words of the testament of Christ are not to be understood otherwise than as they sound, according to the letters; so that the bread does not signify the absent body, and the wine the absent blood of Christ, but that, on account of the sacramental union, they [the bread and wine] are truly the body and blood of Christ.

3. As to the consecration, we believe, teach and confess that no work of man or declaration of the minister [of the church] produces this presence of the body and blood of Christ in the Holy Supper, but that this should be ascribed only and alone to the almighty power of our Lord Jesus Christ.

4. But at the same time we also unanimously believe, teach and confess that in the use of the Holy Supper the words of the institution of Christ should in no way be omitted, but should be publicly recited, as it is written (1 Cor. 10:16): "The cup of blessing, which we bless, is it not the communion of the blood of Christ?" etc. This blessing occurs through the recitation of the Word of Christ.

5. Moreover the foundations upon which we stand against the Sacramentarians in this matter are those which Dr. Luther has laid down in his Large Confession concerning the Lord's Supper.

The first is this article of our Christian faith: Jesus Christ is true, essential, natural, perfect God and man in one person, undivided and inseparable.

The second: That God's right hand is everywhere; at which Christ is in deed and in truth placed according to his human nature, [and therefore] being present rules, and has in his hands and beneath his feet everything that is in heaven and on earth [as Scripture says (Eph. 1:22)]: There [at this right hand of God] no man else, or angel, but only the Son of Mary, is placed; whence he can effect this [those things which we have said].

The third: That God's Word is not false, and does not deceive.

The fourth: That God has and knows of many modes of being in a place, and not only the one [is not

THE FORMULA OF CONCORD (1580) (continued)

bound to the one] which philosophers call local [or circumscribed].

6. We believe, teach and confess that the body and blood of Christ are received with the bread and wine, not only spiritually by faith, but also orally; yet not in a Capernaitic, but in a supernatural, heavenly mode, because of the sacramental union; as the words of Christ clearly show, where Christ directs to take, eat and drink, as was then done by the apostles, for it is written (Mark 14:23): "And they all drank of it." St. Paul likewise says (1 Cor. 10:16): "The bread which we break is it not the communion of the body of Christ?" *i.e.* he who eats this bread, eats the body of Christ, which also the chief ancient teachers of the Church, Chrysostom, Cyprian, Leo I., Gregory, Ambrose, Augustine, unanimously testify.

7. We believe, teach and confess that not only the truly believing [in Christ] and worthy, but also the unworthy and unbelieving, receive the true body and blood of Christ; yet not for life and consolation, but for judgment and condemnation, if they are not converted and do not repent (1 Cor. 11:27,29).

   For although they repel Christ from themselves as a Saviour, yet they must admit him even against their will as a strict Judge, who is present also to exercise and render judgment upon impenitent guests, as well as to work life and consolation in the hearts of the truly believing and worthy.

8. We believe, teach and confess also that there is only one kind of unworthy guests, viz. those who do not believe; concerning whom it is written (John 3:18): "He that believeth not is condemned already." By the unworthy use of the Holy Supper this judgment is augmented, increased, and aggravated (1 Cor. 11:29).

9. We believe, teach and confess that no true believer, as long as he retain living faith, however weak he may be, receives the Holy Supper to his judgment, which was instituted especially for Christians weak in faith, and yet penitent, for the consolation and strengthening of their weak faith (Matt. 9:12; 11:5, 28).

10. We believe, teach and confess that all the worthiness of the guests of this heavenly feast is and consists alone in the most holy obedience and absolute merit of Christ, which we appropriate to ourselves by true faith, and of it [this merit] we are assured by the sacrament. This worthiness does not at all depend upon our virtues or inner and outward preparations.

NEGATIVE. *Contrary condemned Doctrines of the Sacramentarians.*

On the other hand, we unanimously reject and condemn all the following erroneous articles, which are opposed and contrary to the above-presented doctrine, simple [simplicity of] faith, and the [pure] confession concerning the Lord's Supper:

1. The Papistic transubstantiation, where it is taught in the Papacy that in the Holy Supper the bread and wine lose their substance and natural essence, and are thus annihilated; that they are changed into the body of Christ, and the outward form alone remains.

2. The Papistic sacrifice of the mass for the sins of the living and the dead.

3. That [the sacrilege whereby] to laymen only one form of the sacrament is given, and the cup is withheld from them, against the plain words of the testament of Christ, and they are [thus] deprived of his blood.

4. When it is taught that the words of the testament of Christ should not be understood or believed simply as they sound, but that they are obscure expressions, whose meaning must be sought first in other passages of Scripture.

5. That in the Holy Supper the body of Christ is not received orally with the bread; but that with the mouth only bread and wine are received, and the body of Christ only spiritually by faith.

6. That the bread and wine in the Holy Supper are nothing more than [symbols or] tokens, whereby Christians recognize one another.

7. That the bread and wine are only figures, similitudes and representations of the far, absent body of Christ.

8. That the bread and wine are no more than a memorial, seal and pledge, through which we are assured, when faith elevates itself to heaven, that it there becomes participant of the body and blood of Christ as truly as, in the Supper, we eat bread and drink wine.

9. That the assurance and confirmation of our faith [concerning salvation] occur in the Holy Supper alone through the external signs of bread and wine, and not through the truly present true body and blood of Christ.

10. That in the Holy Supper only the power, efficacy and merit of the far absent body and blood of Christ are distributed.

11. That the body of Christ is so enclosed in heaven that it can in no way be at one and the same time in many or all places upon earth where his Holy Supper is celebrated.

12. That Christ has not promised, neither can afford, the essential presence of his body and blood in the Holy Supper, because the nature and property of his assumed human nature cannot suffer or permit it.

13. That God, according to [even by] his omnipotence (which is dreadful to hear), is not able to render his body essentially present in more than one place at one time.

14. That not the omnipotent Word of Christ's testament, but faith, produces and makes [is the cause of] the presence of the body and blood of Christ in the Holy Supper.

15. That believers should not seek the body [and blood] of Christ in the bread and wine of the Holy Supper,

but from the bread should raise their eyes to heaven, and there seek the body of Christ.

16. That unbelieving, impenitent Christians in the Holy Supper do not receive the true body and blood of Christ, but only bread and wine.

17. That the worthiness of the guests in this heavenly meal consists not alone in true faith in Christ, but also in the external preparation of men.

18. That even the truly believing, who have and retain a true, living, pure faith in Christ, can receive this sacrament to their judgment, because they are still imperfect in their outward life.

19. That the external visible elements in the Holy Sacrament should be adored.

20. Likewise, we consign also to the just judgment of God all presumptuous, ironical, blasphemous questions (which out of regard to decency are not to be mentioned), and other expressions, which very blasphemously and with great offence [to the Church] are proposed by the Sacramentarians in a gross, carnal, Capernaitic way concerning the supernatural, heavenly mysteries of this sacrament.

21. As, then, we hereby utterly [reject and] condemn the Capernaitic eating [manducation] of the body of Christ, which the Sacramentarians, against the testimony of their conscience, after all our frequent protests, wilfully force upon us, and in this way make our doctrine odious to their hearers, as though [we taught that] his flesh were rent with the teeth, and digested as other food; on the contrary, we maintain and believe, according to the simple words of the testament of Christ, in the true, yet supernatural eating of the body of Christ, as also in the drinking of his blood, a doctrine which man's sense and reason does not comprehend, but, as in all other articles of faith, our reason is brought into captivity to the obedience of Christ, and this mystery is not embraced otherwise than by faith alone, and is not revealed elsewhere than in the Word alone.

CHAPTER VIII. OF THE PERSON OF CHRIST.

From the controversy concerning the Holy Supper a disagreement has arisen between the pure theologians of the Augsburg Confession and the Calvinists, who also have confused some other theologians, concerning the person of Christ and the two natures in Christ and their properties.

STATEMENT OF THE CONTROVERSY. *Chief Controversy in this Dissension.*

The chief question, however, has been whether, because of the personal union, the divine and human natures, as also their properties, have really, that is, in deed and truth, a communion with one another in the person of Christ, and how far this communion extends?

The Sacramentarians have asserted that the divine and human natures in Christ are united personally in such a way that neither has really, that is, in deed and truth, in common with the other that which is peculiar to either nature, but that they have in common nothing more than the names alone. For "union," they plainly say, "makes common names," *i.e.* the personal union makes nothing more than the names common, namely, that God is called man, and man God, yet in such a way that God has nothing really, that is, in deed and truth, in common with humanity, and humanity nothing in common with divinity, as to its majesty and properties. Dr. Luther, and those who hold with him, have, against the Sacramentarians, contended for the contrary.

AFFIRMATIVE. *Pure Doctrine of the Christian Church concerning the Person of Christ.*

To explain this controversy, and settle it according to the guidance [analogy] of our Christian faith, our doctrine, faith and confession is as follows:

1. That the divine and human natures in Christ are personally united, so that there are not two Christs, one the Son of God, the other the Son of man, but that one and the same is the Son of God and Son of man (Luke 1:35; Rom. 9:5).

2. We believe, teach and confess that the divine and human natures are not mingled into one substance, nor the one changed into the other, but each retains its own essential properties, which can never become the properties of the other nature.

3. The properties of the divine nature are: to be almighty, eternal, infinite, and, according to the property of its nature and its natural essence, to be, of itself, everywhere present, to know everything, etc.; which never become properties of the human nature.

4. The properties of the human nature are: to be a corporeal creature, to be flesh and blood, to be finite and circumscribed, to suffer, to die, to ascend and descend, to move from one place to another, to suffer hunger, thirst, cold, heat, and the like; which never become properties of the divine nature.

5. As the two natures are united personally, *i.e.* in one person, we believe, teach and confess that this union is not such a combination and connection that neither nature should have anything in common with the other, personally, *i.e.* because of the personal union, as when two boards are glued together, where neither gives anything to the other, or takes anything from the other. But here is the highest communion, which God has truly with [assumed] man, from which personal union and the highest and ineffable communion that follows therefrom, all results that is said and believed of the human concerning God, and of the divine concerning the man Christ; as the ancient teachers of the Church explained this union and communion of the natures by the illustration of iron glowing with fire, and also by the union of body and soul in man.

6. Hence we believe, teach and confess that God is man and man is God, which could not be if the divine and human natures had, in deed and truth, absolutely no communion with one another.

For how could a man, the son of Mary, in truth be called or be God, the Son of the Highest, if his humanity were not personally united with the Son of

THE FORMULA OF CONCORD (1580) (continued)

God, and he thus had really, *i.e.* in deed and truth nothing in common with him, except only the name of God?

7. Hence we believe, teach and confess that Mary conceived and bore not a mere man, and no more, but the true Son of God; therefore she is also rightly called and is the mother of God.

8. Hence we also believe, teach and confess that it was not a mere man who, for us, suffered, died, was buried, descended to hell, arose from the dead, ascended into heaven, and was raised to the majesty and almighty power of God, but a man whose human nature has such a profound, ineffable union and communion with the Son of God that it is [was made] one person with him.

9. Therefore the Son of God truly suffered for us, nevertheless according to the property of the human nature, which he assumed into the unity of his divine person, and made it his own, so that he might suffer and be our high priest for our reconciliation with God, as it is written (1 Cor. 2:8): "They have crucified the Lord of glory." And (Acts 20:28): "We are purchased with God's blood."

10. Hence we believe, teach and confess that the Son of man is really, that is, in deed and truth, exalted, according to his human nature, to the right hand of the almighty majesty and power of God, because he [that man] was assumed into God when he was conceived of the Holy Ghost in his mother's womb, and his human nature was personally united with the Son of the Highest.

11. This majesty, according to the personal union, he [Christ] always had, and yet, in the state of his humiliation, he abstained from it, and, on this account, truly grew in all wisdom and favor with God and men; therefore he exercised this majesty, not always, but when [as often as] it pleased him, until, after his resurrection, he entirely laid aside the form of a servant, and not the nature, and was established in the full use, manifestation and declaration of the divine majesty, and thus entered into his glory (Phil. 2:6 sqq.), so that now not only as God, but also as man, he knows all things, can do all things, is present with all creatures, and has, under his feet and in his hands, everything that is in heaven, and on earth, and under the earth, as he himself testifies (Matt. 28:18; John 13:3): "All power is given unto me in heaven and in earth." And St. Paul says (Eph. 4:10): "He ascended up far above all heavens, that he might fill all things." Everywhere present, he can exercise this his power, and to him everything is possible and everything known.

12. Hence, being present, he also is able, and to him it is very easy, to impart his true body and blood in the Holy Supper, not according to the mode or property of the human nature, but according to the mode and property of the right hand of God, as Dr. Luther says in our Christian Faith for Children [according to the analogy of our Christian faith comprised in his Catechism]; which presence [of Christ in the Holy Supper] is not [physical or] earthly, or Capernaitic; nevertheless it is true and substantial, as the words of his testament sound: "This is, *is,* IS my body," etc.

By this our doctrine, faith and confession the person of Christ is not divided, as it was by Nestorius, who denied the *communicatio idiomatum, i.e.* the true communion of the properties of both natures in Christ, and thus separated the person, as Luther has explained in his book concerning the Councils. Neither are the natures, together with their properties, confounded with one another [or mingled] into one essence, as Eutyches erred; neither is the human nature in the person of Christ denied, or extinguished, nor is either creature changed into the other; but Christ is and remains, for all eternity, God and man in one undivided person, which, next to the Holy Trinity, is the highest mystery, as the Apostle testifies (1 Tim. 3:16), upon which our only consolation, life and salvation depend.

NEGATIVE. *Contrary False Doctrines concerning the Person of Christ.*

Therefore we reject and condemn, as contrary to God's Word and our simple [pure] Christian faith, all the following erroneous articles, when it is taught:

1. That God and man in Christ are not one person, but that the one is the Son of God, and the other the Son of man, as Nestorius raved.

2. That the divine and human natures have been mingled with one another into one essence, and the human nature has been changed into Deity, as Eutyches fanatically asserted.

3. That Christ is not true, natural and eternal God, as Arius held [blasphemed].

4. That Christ did not have a true human nature [consisting] of body and soul, as Marcion imagined.

5. That the personal union renders only the names and titles common.

6. That it is only a phrase and mode of speaking when it is said: God is man, man is God; for that the divinity has nothing in common with the humanity, as also the humanity has nothing really, that is, in deed and truth, common with the divinity [Deity].

7. That the communication is only verbal when it is said: "The Son of God died for the sins of the world;" "The Son of man has become almighty."

8. That the human nature in Christ has become an infinite essence in the same manner as the divinity, and from this, essential power and property, imparted and effused upon the human nature, and separated from God, is everywhere present in the same manner as the divine nature.

9. That the human nature has become equal to, and like the divine nature, in its substance and essence, or in its essential properties.

10. That the human nature of Christ is locally extended in all places of heaven and earth, which should not be ascribed even to the divine nature.

11. That, because of the property of his human nature, it is impossible for Christ to be able to be at the same time in more than one place, much less to be everywhere with his body.

12. That only the mere humanity has suffered for us and redeemed us, and that the Son of God in suffering had actually no participation with the humanity, as though it did not pertain to him.

13. That Christ is present with us on earth in the Word, the sacraments and all our troubles, only according to his divinity, and this presence does not at all pertain to his human nature, according to which he has also nothing more whatever to do with us even upon earth, since he redeemed us by his suffering and death.

14. That the Son of God, who assumed human nature, since he has laid aside the form of a servant does not perform all the works of his omnipotence in, through and with his human nature, but only some, and those too only in the place where his human nature is locally.

15. That, according to his human nature, he is not at all capable of omnipotence and other attributes of the divine nature against the express declaration of Christ (Matt. 28:18): "All power is given unto me in heaven and in earth." And [they contradict] St. Paul [who says] (Col. 2:9): "In him dwelleth all the fulness of the Godhead bodily."

16. That to him [to Christ according to his humanity] great power is given in heaven and upon earth, namely, greater and more than to all angels and other creatures, but that he has no participation in the omnipotence of God, and that this also has not been given him. Hence they devise an *intermediate power*, that is, such power between the almighty power of God and the power of other creatures, given to Christ, according to his humanity, by the exaltation, as is less than God's almighty power, and greater than that of other creatures.

17. That Christ, according to his human spirit, has a certain limit as to how much he should know, and that he knows no more than is becoming and needful for him to know for [the execution of] his office as judge.

18. That not even yet does Christ have a perfect knowledge of God and all his works; of whom, nevertheless, it is written (Col. 2:3): "In whom are hid all the treasures of wisdom and knowledge."

19. That it is impossible for Christ, according to his human mind, to know what has been from eternity, what at the present time is everywhere occurring, and will be yet to [all] eternity.

20. When it is taught, and the passage (Matt. 28:18): "All power is given unto me," etc., is thus interpreted and blasphemously perverted, viz. that to Christ according to the divine nature, at the resurrection and his ascension to heaven, was restored, *i.e.* delivered again all power in heaven and on earth; as though, in his state of humiliation, he had also, according to his divinity, divested himself of this and abandoned it. By this doctrine, not only are the words of the testament of Christ perverted, but also the way is prepared for the accursed Arian heresy, so that finally the eternal divinity of Christ is denied, and thus Christ, and with him our salvation, are entirely lost where this false doctrine is not [constantly] contradicted from the firm foundation of God's Word and our simple Christian [Catholic] faith.

CHAPTER IX. OF THE DESCENT OF CHRIST TO HELL.

STATEMENT OF THE CONTROVERSY. *Chief Controversy concerning this Article.*

There has also been a controversy among some theologians, who have subscribed to the Augsburg Confession concerning the following article: When, and in what manner, the Lord Christ, according to our simple Christian faith, descended to hell, whether this was done before or after his death? Also, whether it occurred according to the soul alone, or according to the divinity alone, or in body and soul, spiritually or bodily? Also, whether this article belongs to the passion or to the glorious victory and triumph of Christ?

But since this article, as also the preceding, cannot be comprehended by the senses or by the reason, but must be grasped alone by faith, it is our unanimous advice that there should be no disputation concerning it, but that it should be believed and taught only in the simplest manner; according as Dr. Luther of blessed memory, in his sermon at Torgau in the year 1533, has, in a very Christian manner, explained this article, separated from it all useless, unnecessary questions, and admonished all godly Christians to Christian simplicity of faith.

For it is sufficient that we know that Christ descended to hell, destroyed hell for all believers, and delivered them from the power of death and of the devil, from eternal condemnation [and even] from the jaws of hell. But how this occurred, we should [not curiously investigate, but] reserve until the other world, where not only this point [mystery], but also still others, will be revealed which we here simply believe, and cannot comprehend with our blind reason.

CHAPTER X. OF CHURCH RITES WHICH ARE [COMMONLY] CALLED ADIAPHORA OR MATTERS OF INDIFFERENCE.

Concerning ceremonies or church rites which are neither commanded nor forbidden in God's Word, but have been introduced into the Church for the sake of good order and propriety, a dissension has also occurred among the theologians of the Augsburg Confession.

STATEMENT OF THE CONTROVERSY.

The chief question has been, whether, in time of persecution and in case of confession, even if the enemies of the Gospel do not agree with us in doctrine, yet some abrogated ceremonies, which in themselves are matters of

THE FORMULA OF CONCORD (1580) (continued)

indifference and are neither commanded nor forbidden by God, may without violence to conscience be re-established in compliance with the pressure and demand of the adversaries, and thus in such ceremonies and adiaphora we may [rightly] have conformity with them? The one side says, Yea; the other says, Nay, thereto.

AFFIRMATIVE. *The Pure and True Doctrine and Confession concerning this Article.*

1. For settling also this controversy we unanimously believe, teach and confess that the ceremonics or church rites which are neither commanded nor forbidden in God's Word, but have been instituted alone for the sake of propriety and good order, are in and of themselves no service, nor are even a part of the service of God. Matt. 15:9: "In vain they do worship me, teaching for doctrines the commandments of men."

2. We believe, teach and confess that the Church of God of every place and every time has the power, according to its circumstances, to change such ceremonies, in such manner as may be most useful and edifying to the Church of God.

3. Nevertheless, that herein all inconsiderateness and offence should be avoided, and especial care should be taken to exercise forbearance to the weak in faith (1 Cor. 8:9; Rom. 14:13).

4. We believe, teach and confess that in time of persecution, when a bold [and steadfast] confession is required of us, we should not yield to the enemies in regard to such adiaphora, as the apostle has written (Gal. 5:1): "Stand fast, therefore, in the liberty wherewith Christ hath made us free, and be not entangled again in the yoke of bondage." Also (2 Cor. 6:14): "Be not unequally yoked together with unbelievers," etc. "For what concord hath light with darkness?" Also (Gal. 2:5): "To whom we gave place, no, not for an hour, that the truth of the Gospel might remain with you." For in such a case it is no longer a question concerning adiaphora, but concerning the truth of the Gospel, concerning [preserving] Christian liberty, and concerning sanctioning open idolatry, as also concerning the prevention of offence to the weak in the faith [how care should be taken lest idolatry be openly sanctioned and the weak in faith be offended]; in which we have nothing to concede, but should boldly confess and suffer what God sends, and what he allows the enemies of his Word to inflict upon us.

5. We believe, teach and confess also that no Church should condemn another because one has less or more external ceremonies not commanded by God than the other, if otherwise there is agreement among them in doctrine and all its articles, as also in the right use of the holy sacraments, according to the well-known saying: "Disagreement in fasting does not destroy agreement in faith."

NEGATIVE. *False Doctrines concerning this Article.*

Therefore we reject and condemn as wrong, and contrary to God's Word, when it is taught:

1. That human ordinances and institutions should be regarded in the churches as in themselves a service or part of the service of God.

2. When such ceremonies, ordinances and institutions are violently forced upon the Church of God, contrary to the Christian liberty which it has in external things.

3. Also, that in the time of persecution and public confession [when a clear confession is required] we may comply with the enemies of the Gospel in the observance of such adiaphora and ceremonies, or may come to an agreement with them,—which causes injury to the truth.

4. Also, when these external ceremonies and adiaphora are abrogated in such a manner as though it were not free to the Church of God to employ one or more [this or that] in Christian liberty, according to its circumstances, as may be most useful at any time to the Church [for edification].

CHAPTER XI. OF GOD'S ETERNAL FOREKNOWLEDGE [PREDESTINATION] AND ELECTION.

Concerning this article no public dissension has occurred among the theologians of the Augsburg Confession. But since it is a consolatory article, if treated properly, and by this means the introduction in the future of a controversy likely to cause offence may be avoided, it is also explained in this writing.

AFFIRMATIVE. *The Pure and True Doctrine concerning this Article.*

1. First of all, the distinction between foreknowledge and predestination, that is, between God's foreknowledge and his eternal election, ought to be accurately observed.

2. For the foreknowledge of God is nothing else than that God knows all things before they happen, as it is written (Dan. 2:28): "There is a God in heaven that revealeth secrets and maketh known to the king Nebuchadnezzar what shall be in the latter days."

3. This foreknowledge is occupied alike with the godly and the wicked; but it is not the cause of evil or of sin, so that men do what is wrong (which originally arises from the devil and the wicked, perverse will of man); nor the cause of their ruin [that men perish], for which they themselves are responsible [which they ought to ascribe to themselves]; but only regulates it, and fixes to it a limit [how far it should progress and] how long it should last, and that everything, notwithstanding that in itself it is evil, should serve his elect for their salvation.

4. The predestination or eternal election of God, however, is occupied only with the godly, beloved children of God, and this is a cause of their salvation, which he also provides as well as disposes what belongs thereto. Upon this [predestination of God]

our salvation is founded so firmly that the gates of hell cannot overcome it (John 10:28; Matt. 16:18).

5. This is not to be investigated in the secret counsel of God, but to be sought in the Word of God, where it is also revealed.

6. But the Word of God leads us to Christ, who is the Book of Life, in whom all are written and elected that are to be saved, as it is written (Eph. 1:4): "He hath chosen us in him" [Christ] "before the foundation of the world."

7. Thus Christ calls to himself all sinners, and promises them rest, and he is anxious that all men should come to him and permit him to help them. To them he offers himself in his Word, and wishes them to hear it, and not to stop their ears or [neglect and] despise the Word. He promises besides the power and efficiency of the Holy Ghost, and divine assistance for perseverance and eternal salvation [that we may remain steadfast in the faith and attain eternal salvation].

8. Therefore we should judge concerning this our election to eternal life neither from reason nor from the Law of God, which would lead either into a dissipated, dissolute epicurean life, or into despair, and would excite in the heart of men pernicious thoughts (and such thoughts cannot be effectually guarded against as long as they follow their own reason), so that they think to themselves: "If God has elected me to salvation, I cannot be condemned, although I do whatever I will." And again: "If I am not elected to eternal life, it matters not what good I do; for my efforts are nevertheless all in vain."

9. But the true judgment concerning predestination must be learned alone from the Holy Gospel concerning Christ, in which it is clearly testified that "God hath concluded them all in unbelief, that he might have mercy upon all," and that "he is not willing that any should perish, but that all should come to repentance" (Rom. 11:32; Ez. 18:23; 33:11; 2 Pet. 3:9; 1 John 2:2).

10. To him, therefore, who is really concerned about the revealed will of God, and proceeds according to the order which St. Paul has observed in the Epistle to the Romans, who first directs men to repentance, knowledge of sins, to faith in Christ, to divine obedience, before he speaks of the mystery of the eternal election of God, this doctrine [concerning God's predestination] is useful and consolatory.

11. That, however, "many are called, few are chosen," does not mean that God is unwilling that all should be saved, but the reason is that they either do not at all hear God's Word, but wilfully despise it, close their ears and harden their hearts, and in this manner foreclose the ordinary way to the Holy Ghost, so that he cannot effect his work in them, or, when it is heard, they consider it of no account, and do not heed it. For this [that they perish] not God or his election, but their wickedness, is responsible (2 Pet. 2:1 sqq.; Luke 11:49, 52; Heb. 12:25 sq.).

12. Moreover, a Christian should apply himself [in meditation] to the article concerning the eternal election of God, so far as it has been revealed in God's Word, which presents Christ to us as the Book of Life, which, by the preaching of the holy Gospel, he opens and spreads out to us, as it is written (Rom. 8:30): "Whom he did predestinate, them he also called." In him, therefore, we should seek the eternal election of the Father, who, in his eternal divine counsel, determined that he would save no one except those who acknowledge his Son, Christ, and truly believe on him. Other thoughts are to be entirely banished [from the minds of the godly], as they proceed not from God, but from the suggestion of Satan, whereby he attempts to weaken or to entirely remove from us the glorious consolation which we have in this salutary doctrine, viz. that we know [assuredly] that out of pure grace, without any merit of our own, we have been elected in Christ to eternal life, and that no one can pluck us out of his hand; as he has promised this gracious election not only with mere words, but has also certified it with an oath, and sealed it with the holy sacraments, which we can [ought to] call to mind in our most severe temptations, and from them comfort ourselves, and thereby quench the fiery darts of the devil.

13. Besides, we should endeavor with the greatest pains to live according to the will of God, and, as St. Peter admonishes (2 Ep. 1:10), "make our calling sure," and especially adhere to [not recede a finger's breadth from] the revealed Word, that can and will not fail us.

14. By this brief explanation of the eternal election of God his glory is entirely and fully given to God, that alone, out of pure mercy, without all merit of ours, he saves us, according to the purpose of his will; besides, also, no cause is given any one for despondency or an abandoned, dissolute life [no opportunity is afforded either for those more severe agitations of mind and faintheartedness or for epicureanism].

ANTITHESIS OR NEGATIVE. *False Doctrine concerning this Article.*

Therefore we believe and hold: When the doctrine concerning the gracious election of God to eternal life is so presented that troubled Christians cannot comfort themselves therewith, but thereby despondency or despair is occasioned, or the impenitent are strengthened in their wantonness, that such doctrine is treated [wickedly and erroneously] not according to the Word and will of God, but according to reason and the instigation of Satan. "For," as the apostle testifies (Rom. 15:4), "whatsoever things were written aforetime were written for our learning, that we, through patience and comfort of the Scriptures, might have hope." Therefore we reject the following errors:

1. As when it is taught that God is unwilling that all men repent and believe the Gospel.

2. Also, that when God calls us to himself he is not in earnest that all men should come to him.

3. Also, that God does not wish every one to be saved, but, without regard to their sins, alone from the counsel, purpose and will of God, some are appointed to condemnation, so that they cannot be saved.

4. Also, that not only the mercy of God and the most holy merit of Christ, but also in us is a cause of God's election, on account of which God has elected us to everlasting life.

All these erroneous doctrines are blasphemous and dreadful, whereby there is removed from Christians all the comfort which they have in the holy Gospel and the use of the holy sacraments, and therefore should not be tolerated in the Church of God.

This is a brief and simple explanation of the controverted articles, which for a time have been discussed and taught with conflicting opinions among the theologians of the Augsburg Confession. Hence every simple Christian, according to the guidance of God's Word and his simple Catechism, can distinguish what is right or wrong, where not only the pure doctrine is stated, but also the erroneous contrary doctrine is repudiated and rejected, and thus the controversies, full of causes of offence, that have occurred, are thoroughly settled and decided.

May Almighty God, the Father of our Lord Jesus, grant the grace of his Holy Ghost, that we all may be one in him, and constantly abide in this Christian unity, which is well pleasing to him! Amen.

CHAPTER XII. OF OTHER FACTIONS [HERESIES] AND SECTS, WHICH NEVER EMBRACED THE AUGSBURG CONFESSION.

In order that such [heresies and sects] may not silently be ascribed to us, because, in the preceding explanation, no mention of them has been made, we wish at the end [of this writing] simply to enumerate the mere articles wherein they [the heretics of our time] err and teach what is contrary to our Christian faith and confession above presented.

ERRONEOUS ARTICLES OF THE ANABAPTISTS.

The Anabaptists are divided into many sects, as one contends for more, another for less error; nevertheless, they all in common propound [profess] such doctrine as is neither to be tolerated nor allowed in the Church, the commonwealth and worldly government or domestic life.

ARTICLES THAT CANNOT BE TOLERATED IN THE CHURCH.

1. That Christ did not assume his body and blood of the Virgin Mary, but brought them with him from heaven.

2. That Christ is not true God, but only [is superior to other saints, because he] has more gifts of the Holy Ghost than any other holy man.

3. That our righteousness before God consists not only in the sole merit of Christ, but in renewal, and thus in our own godliness [uprightness] in which we walk. This is based in great part upon one's own special, self-chosen [and humanly-devised] spirituality [holiness], and in fact is nothing else than a new sort of monkery.

4. That children who are not baptized are not sinners before God, but righteous and innocent, who, in their innocency, because they have not yet attained their reason [the use of reason], will be saved without baptism (which, according to their assertion, they do not need). Therefore they reject the entire doctrine concerning original sin, and what belongs to it.

5. That children should not be baptized until they have attained their reason [the use of reason], and can themselves confess their faith.

6. That the children of Christians, because they have been born of Christian and believing parents, are holy and the children of God, even without and before baptism. For this reason also they neither attach much importance to the baptism of children, nor encourage it, contrary to the express words of God's promise, which pertains only to those *who keep God's covenant and do not despise it* (Gen. 17:7 sqq.).

7. That there is no true Christian congregation [church] wherein sinners are still found.

8. That no sermon should be heard or attended in those churches in which the Papal masses have previously been observed and said.

9. That no one [godly man] should have anything to do with those ministers of the Church who preach the Gospel according to the Augsburg Confession, and censure the sermons and errors of the Anabaptists; also, that no one should serve or in any way labor for them, but should flee from and shun them as perverters of God's Word.

ARTICLES THAT CANNOT BE TOLERATED IN THE GOVERNMENT.

1. That, under the New Testament, the magistracy is not an estate pleasing to God.

2. That a Christian cannot, with a good, inviolate conscience, hold or exercise the office of magistrate.

3. That a Christian cannot, without injury to conscience, use the office of the magistracy against the wicked in matters as they occur [matters so requiring], nor may subjects invoke for their protection and screening the power which the magistrates possess and have received from God.

4. That a Christian cannot, with a good conscience, take an oath, neither can he by an oath do homage [promise fidelity] to his prince or sovereign.

5. That, under the New Testament, magistrates cannot, without injury to conscience, inflict capital punishment upon transgressors.

ARTICLES THAT CANNOT BE TOLERATED IN DOMESTIC LIFE.

1. That a Christian cannot [with an inviolate conscience] hold or possess property, but is in duty bound to devote it to the church.

2. That a Christian cannot, with a good conscience, be a landlord, merchant, or cutler [maker of arms].

3. That on account of diverse faith married persons may be divorced and abandon one another, and be married to another person of the same faith.

ERRONEOUS ARTICLES OF THE SCHWENCKFELDIANS.

1. That all who regard Christ according to the flesh as a creature have no true knowledge of Christ as reigning King of heaven.

2. That, by his exaltation, the flesh of Christ has so assumed all divine properties that Christ as man is in might, power, majesty and glory equal to the Father and to the Word, everywhere as to degree and condition of essence, so that now there is only one essence, property, will and glory of both natures in Christ, and that the flesh of Christ belongs to the essence of the Holy Trinity.

3. That the Church service [ministry of the Word], the Word preached and heard, is not a means whereby God the Holy Ghost teaches men, and works in them saving knowledge of Christ, conversion, repentance, faith and new obedience.

4. That the water of baptism is not a means whereby God the Lord seals adoption and works regeneration.

5. That bread and wine in the Holy Supper are not means through and by which Christ distributes his body and blood.

6. That a Christian who is truly regenerated by God's Spirit can, in this life, observe and fulfil the Law of God perfectly.

7. That there is no true Christian congregation [church] where no public excommunication [and some formal mode of excommunication] or no regular process of the ban [as it is commonly called] is observed.

8. That the minister of the church who is not on his part truly renewed, regenerate, righteous and godly cannot teach other men with profit or distribute true sacraments.

ERROR OF THE NEW ARIANS.

That Christ is not true, essential, natural God, of one eternal, divine essence with God the Father and the Holy Ghost, but is only adorned with divine majesty beneath and beside God the Father [is so adorned with divine majesty, with the Father, that he is inferior to the Father].

ERROR OF THE ANTI-TRINITARIANS.

This is an entirely new sect, not heard of before in Christendom, composed of those who believe, teach and confess that there is not only one, eternal, divine essence of the Father, Son and Holy Ghost, but as God the Father, Son and Holy Ghost are three distinct persons, so each person has its essence distinct and separate from the other persons of the Godhead; and nevertheless [some of them think] that all three, just as in another respect three men distinct and separate from one another are of equal power, wisdom, majesty and glory, or [others think that these three persons and essences] are unequal with one another in essence and properties, so that the Father alone is properly and truly God.

These and like errors, one and all, with whatever other errors depend upon and follow from them, we reject and condemn as wrong, false, heretical, contrary to the Word of God, the three Creeds, the Augsburg Confession and Apology, the Smalcald Articles and Luther's Catechisms, against which all godly Christians, of both high and low station, should be on their guard as they love the welfare and salvation of their souls.

That this is the doctrine, faith and confession of us all, for which we will answer, at the last day, before the just Judge, our Lord Jesus Christ, and that against this we will neither secretly nor publicly speak or write, but that we intend, by the grace of God, to persevere therein, we have, after mature deliberation, testified, in the true fear of God and invocation of his name, by signing with our own hands this Epitome.

Bergen, May 29th, 1577.

PART SECOND.

SOLID, PLAIN AND CLEAR REPETITION AND DECLARATION. OF CERTAIN ARTICLES OF THE AUGSBURG CONFESSION, CONCERNING WHICH, FOR SOME TIME, THERE HAS BEEN CONTROVERSY AMONG SOME THEOLOGIANS WHO SUBSCRIBE THERETO, STATED AND SETTLED ACCORDING TO THE ANALOGY OF GOD'S WORD AND THE SUMMARY CONTENTS OF OUR CHRISTIAN DOCTRINE.

PREFACE.

By the inestimable goodness and mercy of the Almighty, the doctrine concerning the chief articles of our Christian religion, which under the Papacy was horribly obscured by human opinions and traditions, has been again explained and corrected, in accordance with God's Word, by Dr. Martin Luther of holy and blessed memory, and the Papistic errors, abuses and idolatry have been rebuked. This pure reformation, however, has been regarded by its opponents as introducing new doctrine; it has been violently and falsely charged with being directly contrary to God's Word and Christian ordinances, and has to bear the burden of numberless other calumnies and accusations. On this account the electors, princes and estates that have embraced the pure doctrine of the Holy Gospel, and have reformed their churches in a Christian manner according to God's Word, at the great Diet of Augsburg in the year 1530 had a Christian Confession prepared from God's Word, which they delivered to the Emperor Charles V. In this they clearly and plainly made a Christian Confession as to what was held and taught in the Christian evangelical churches concerning the chief articles, and those especially in controversy between them and the Papists. This Confession was received by their opponents with disfavor, but, thank God, remains to this day without refutation or invalidation. From our inmost hearts we herewith once again confess this Christian Augsburg Confession, which is so thoroughly grounded in God's Word. We abide by the simple, clear and plain meaning of the same that its words

THE FORMULA OF CONCORD (1580) (continued)

convey, and regard it in all respects as a Christian symbol, which at the present time true Christians should receive next to God's Word; just as in former times, when great controversies arose in the Church of God, symbols and confessions were composed, which pure teachers and hearers confessed with heart and mouth. We intend also, by the grace of the Almighty, to faithfully abide until our end by this Christian Confession, as it was delivered in the year 1530 to the Emperor Charles V.; and it is our purpose, neither in this nor in any other writing, to recede in the least from that Confession or to compose another or new confession.

Although the Christian doctrine of this Confession has, in great part, remained unchallenged, save among the Papists, yet it cannot be denied that some theologians have departed from some of its principal and most important articles, and that they either have not learned the true meaning of these articles, or have not continued steadfastly therein, but that some have even undertaken to attach to it an extraneous meaning, while at the same time professing to adhere to the Augsburg Confession, and availing themselves of this boast as a pretext. From this, grievous and injurious dissensions have arisen in the pure evangelical churches; just as during the lives of the holy apostles, among those who wished to be called Christians and boasted of Christ's doctrine, horrible error arose. For some sought to be justified and saved by the Law (Acts 15: 1-29); others denied the resurrection of the dead (1 Cor. 15:12); and still others did not believe that Christ was true and eternal God. These the holy apostles in their sermons and writings earnestly opposed, although such pernicious errors and severe controversy could not occur without offence, both to believers and to those weak in the faith; just as at present our opponents, the Papists, rejoice at the dissensions among us, in the unchristian and vain hope that these discords will finally cause the suppression of the pure doctrine. Because of them, those that are weak in faith are also greatly offended, and some doubt whether, amid such dissensions, the pure doctrine be with us, while others know not with whom to side with respect to the articles in controversy. For these controversies are not mere misunderstandings or disputes concerning words, as are apt to occur where one side has not sufficiently understood the meaning of the other, and thus the dispute is confined to a few words, whereon nothing of much moment depends. But here the subjects of controversy are great and important, and of such a nature that the opinion of the party in error cannot be tolerated in the Church of God, much less be excused or defended.

Necessity, therefore, requires us to explain these controverted articles according to God's Word and approved writings; so that every one who has Christian understanding can notice what opinion concerning the matters in controversy accords with God's Word, and what disagrees therewith. Thus the errors and corruptions that have arisen may be shunned and avoided by sincere Christians who prize the truth aright.

OF THE COMPREHENSIVE SUMMARY, FOUNDATION, RULE AND STANDARD WHEREBY, ACCORDING TO GOD'S WORD, ALL DOGMAS SHOULD BE JUDGED, AND THE CONTROVERSIES THAT HAVE OCCURRED SHOULD, IN A CHRISTIAN MANNER, BE EXPLAINED AND DECIDED.

Because, for thorough, permanent unity in the Church, it is before all things necessary that we have a comprehensive, unanimously approved summary and form, wherein are brought together from God's Word the common doctrines, reduced to a brief compass, which the churches that are of the true Christian religion acknowledge as confessional (just as the ancient Church always had for this use its fixed symbols); and this authority should not be attached to private writings, but to such books as have been composed, approved and received in the name of the churches which confessionally bind themselves to one doctrine and religion; we have declared to one another, with heart and mouth, that we will neither make nor receive any separate or new confession of our faith, but acknowledge as confessional the public common writings which always and everywhere were received in all the churches of the Augsburg Confession, as such symbols or public confessions, before the dissensions arose among those who accept the Augsburg Confession, and as long as, in all articles, there was, on all sides, a unanimous adherence to, and maintenance and use of, the pure doctrine of God's Word, as the late Dr. Luther explained it.

1. First, we receive and embrace the Prophetic and Apostolic Scriptures of the Old and New Testaments as the pure, clear fountains of Israel, which are the only true standard whereby to judge all teachers and doctrines.

2. And because, of old, the true Christian doctrine, in a pure, sound sense, was collected from God's Word into brief articles or sections against the corruption of heretics, we accept as confessional the three Ecumenical Creeds, namely, the Apostles', the Nicene and the Athanasian, as glorious confessions of the faith, brief, devout and founded upon God's Word, wherein all the heresies which at that time had arisen in the Christian Church are clearly and unanswerably refuted.

3. Thirdly, because, in these last times, God, out of especial grace, from the darkness of the Papacy has brought his truth again to light, through the faithful service of the precious man of God, Dr. Luther, and against the corruptions of the Papacy and also of other sects has collected the same doctrine, from and according to God's Word, into the articles and sections of the Augsburg Confession; we confessionally accept also the first unaltered Augsburg Confession (not because it was composed by our theologians, but because it has been derived from God's Word, and is founded firmly and well therein, precisely in the form in which it was committed to writing in the year 1530, and presented to the Emperor Charles V. by some electors, princes and deputies of the Roman Empire as a common confession of the reformed churches at Augsburg) as

the symbol of our time, whereby our Reformed churches are distinguished from the Papists and other repudiated and condemned sects and heresies, after the custom and usage of the early Church, whereby succeeding councils, Christian bishops and teachers appealed to the Nicene Creed, and confessed it [publicly declared that they embraced it].

4. Fourthly, in order that the proper and true sense of the often-quoted Augsburg Confession might be more fully set forth and guarded against the Papists, and that under the name of the Augsburg Confession condemned errors might not steal into the Church of God after the Confession was delivered, a fuller Apology was composed, and published in the year 1531. We unanimously accept this also as confessional, because in it the said Augsburg Confession is not only sufficiently elucidated and guarded, but also confirmed by clear, irrefutable testimonies of Holy Scripture.

5. Fifthly, the Articles composed, approved and received at Smalcald in the large assembly of theologians in the year 1537 we confessionally accept, in the form in which they were first framed and printed in order to be delivered in the council at Mantua, or wherever it would be held, in the name of the electors, princes and deputies, as an explanation of the above-mentioned Augsburg Confession, wherein by God's grace they determined to abide. In them the doctrine of the Augsburg Confession is repeated, and some articles are stated at greater length from God's Word, and besides the cause and foundation why we have abandoned the papistical errors and idolatries, and can have no fellowship with them, and also why we have not determined or even thought of coming to any agreement with the Pope concerning them, are sufficiently indicated.

6. Lastly, because these highly important matters belong also to the common people and laity, who, for their salvation, must distinguish between pure and false doctrine, we accept as confessional also the Large and the Small Catechisms of Dr. Luther, as they were written by him and incorporated in his works, because they have been unanimously approved and received by all churches adhering to the Augsburg Confession, and publicly used in churches, schools and [privately in] families, and because also in them the Christian doctrine from God's Word is comprised in the most correct and simple way, and, in like manner, is sufficiently explained for simple laymen.

These public common writings have been always regarded in the pure churches and schools as the sum and type of the doctrine which the late Dr. Luther has admirably deduced against the Papacy and other sects from God's Word, and firmly established; to whose full explanations in his doctrinal and polemical writings we appeal in the manner and to the extent indicated by Dr. Luther himself in the necessary and Christian admonition concerning his writings, made in the Latin preface to his published works, wherein he has expressly drawn this distinction, viz. that God's Word alone is and should remain the only standard and rule, to which the writings of no man should be regarded equal, but to it everything should be subordinated.

But hereby other good, useful, pure books, expositions of the Holy Scriptures, refutations of errors, explanations of doctrinal articles (which, as far as consistent with the above-mentioned type of doctrine, are regarded as useful expositions and explanations, and can be used with advantage) are not rejected. But by what has thus far been said concerning the summary of our Christian doctrine we have only meant that we have a unanimously received, definite, common form of doctrine, which our Evangelical churches together and in common confess; from and according to which, because it has been derived from God's Word, all other writings should be judged and adjusted as to how far they are to be approved and accepted.

For that we have embodied the above-mentioned writings, viz. the Augsburg Confession, Apology, Smalcald Articles, Luther's Large and Small Catechisms, as the sum of our Christian doctrine, has occurred for the reason that these have been always and everywhere regarded as containing the common, unanimously received understanding of our churches, since the chief and most enlightened theologians of that time subscribed them, and all evangelical churches and schools have cordially received them. As they also, as before mentioned, were all written and sent forth before the divisions among the theologians of the Augsburg Confession arose, and then because they were held as impartial, and neither can nor should be rejected by any part of those who have entered into controversy, and no one who is true to the Augsburg Confession will complain of these writings, but will cheerfully accept and tolerate them as witnesses [of the truth]; no one, therefore, can blame us that we derive from them an explanation and decision of the articles in controversy, and that, as we lay God's Word, the eternal truth, as the foundation, so also we introduce and quote these writings as a witness of the truth, and a presentation of the unanimously received correct understanding of our predecessors who have steadfastly held to the pure doctrine.

OF THE ARTICLES IN CONTROVERSY WITH RESPECT TO THE ANTITHESIS, OR OPPOSITE DOCTRINE.

For the maintenance of pure doctrine, and for thorough, permanent, godly unity in the Church, it is necessary not only that pure, wholesome doctrine be rightly presented, but also that the opponents who teach otherwise be reproved (1 Tim. 3 [2 Tim. 3:16]; Tit. 1:9). For faithful shepherds, as Luther says, should do both, viz. feed or nourish the lambs and defend from the wolves, so that they may flee from strange voices (John 10:12) and may separate the precious from the vile (Jer. 15:19).

THE FORMULA OF CONCORD (1580) (continued)

Therefore concerning this, we have thoroughly and clearly declared to one another as follows: that a distinction in every way should and must be observed between, on the one hand, unnecessary and useless wrangling, whereby, since it scatters more than it builds up, the Church ought not to be disturbed, and, on the other hand, necessary controversy, as when such a controversy occurs as involves the articles of faith or the chief heads of the Christian doctrine, where for the defence of the truth the false opposite doctrine must be reproved.

Although the aforesaid writings afford the Christian reader, who has pleasure and love for the divine truth, a clear and correct answer concerning each and every controverted article of our Christian religion, as to what, according to God's Word of the Prophetic and Apostolic Scriptures, he should regard and receive as right and true, and what he should reject, shun and avoid as false and wrong; yet, in order that the truth may be preserved the more distinctly and clearly, and be separated from all errors, and be not hidden and concealed under rather general words, we have clearly and expressly made a declaration to one another concerning the chief and highly important articles, taken one by one, which at the present time have come into controversy; so that there might be a public, definite testimony, not only for those now living, but also for our posterity, as to what is and should remain the unanimously received understanding and judgment of our churches in reference to the articles in controversy, namely:

1. First, that we reject and condemn all heresies and errors which, in the primitive, ancient, orthodox Church, were rejected and condemned, upon the true, firm ground of the holy divine Scriptures.

2. Secondly, we reject and condemn all sects and heresies which are rejected in the writings, just mentioned, of the comprehensive summary of the Confession of our churches.

3. Thirdly, because within thirty years, on account of the Interim and otherwise, some divisions arose among some theologians of the Augsburg Confession, we have wished plainly, distinctly and clearly to state and declare our faith and confession concerning each and every one of these taken in thesis and antithesis, *i.e.* the true doctrine and its opposite, for the purpose in all articles of rendering the foundation of divine truth manifest, and censuring all unlawful, doubtful, suspicious and condemned doctrines (wherever and in whatever books they may be found, and whoever may have written them or even now may be disposed to defend them); so that every one may be faithfully warned to avoid the errors, diffused on all sides, in the writings of some theologians, and no one be misled herein by the reputation of any man. If the Christian reader will carefully examine this declaration in every emergency, and compare it with the writings enumerated above, he will find that what was in the beginning confessed concerning every article in the comprehensive summary of our religion and faith, and what was afterward restated

at various times, and is repeated by us in this document, is in no way contradictory, but the simple, immutable, permanent truth, and that we, therefore, do not change from one doctrine to another, as our adversaries falsely assert, but earnestly desire to retain the once-delivered Augsburg Confession, and its unanimously received Christian sense, and through God's grace to abide thereby firmly and constantly, in opposition to all corruptions which have entered.

CHAPTER I. OF ORIGINAL SIN.

First, a controversy concerning Original Sin has occurred among some theologians of the Augsburg Confession with respect to what it properly is. For one side contended that, because, through the fall of Adam, man's nature and essence are entirely corrupt now since the fall, the nature, substance and essence of the corrupt man, or indeed the principal, highest part of his being, namely, the rational soul in its highest state and principal powers, is Original Sin itself. This is called "natural" or "personal sin," for the reason that it is not a thought, word or work, but the nature itself, whence, as from a root, all other sins proceed, and on this account there is now since the fall, because the nature is corrupt through sin, no distinction whatever between the nature and essence of man and Original Sin.

But the other side taught, in opposition, that Original Sin is not properly the nature, substance or essence of man, *i.e.* man's body or soul, which even now since the fall are and remain the creatures and works of God in us, but it is something in the nature, body and soul of man, and in all his powers, namely, a horrible, deep, inexpressible corruption of the same, so that man is destitute of the righteousness wherein he was originally created, and in spiritual things is dead to good and perverted to all evil; and that, because of this corruption and inborn sin, which inheres in the nature, all actual sins flow forth from the heart; and that a distinction must, therefore, be observed between, on the one hand, the nature and essence of the corrupt man, or his body and soul, which as the creatures of God pertain to us even since the fall, and Original Sin, on the other, which is a work of the devil, whereby the nature has become corrupt.

Now this controversy concerning Original Sin is not unnecessary wrangling, but if this doctrine be rightly presented from and according to God's Word, and be separated from all Pelagian and Manichaean errors, then (as the Apology) says, the benefits of Christ and his precious merit, and the gracious efficacy of the Holy Ghost, will be the better known and the more extolled; the honor which belongs to him will also be ascribed to God, if his work and creation in men be rightly distinguished from the work of the devil, whereby the nature has been corrupted. In order, therefore, to explain this controversy in the Christian way and according to God's Word, and to maintain the correct, pure doctrine, we will collect from the above-mentioned writings the thesis and antithesis, that is, the correct doctrine and its opposite, into brief paragraphs:

1. And first it is true that Christians should not only regard and recognize as sins the actual transgression

of God's commands; but also that the horrible, dreadful hereditary malady whereby the entire nature is corrupted, should above all things be regarded and recognized as sin, yea, as the chief sin, which is a root and fountain-head of all actual sins. This is called by Luther a "natural" or "personal sin," in order to declare that even though man would think, speak or do nothing evil (which, nevertheless, since the fall of our first parents, is impossible in this life), yet that his nature and person are sinful, *i.e.* by Original Sin, as a spiritual leprosy, he is thoroughly and utterly infected and corrupted before God; and on account of this corruption, and because of the fall of the first man, the nature or person is accused or condemned by God's Law, so that we are by nature the children of wrath, death and damnation, unless delivered therefrom by the merit of Christ.

2. It is also clear and true, as the Nineteenth Article of the Augsburg Confession teaches, that God is not a creator, author or cause of sin, but from the instigation of the devil, through one man, sin (which is a work of the devil) has entered the world (Rom. 5:12; 1 John 3:7). And even at the present day, in this connection of sin and nature [in this corruption of nature], God does not create and make sin in us, but with the nature which God at the present day still creates and makes in men, Original Sin is propagated from sinful seed, through carnal conception and birth of father and mother.

3. Thirdly, what [and how great] this hereditary evil is, no reason knows and understands, but, as the Smalcald Articles say, it must be learned and believed from the revelation contained in Scripture. And in the Apology this is briefly comprehended in the following paragraphs:

1. That this hereditary evil is the cause of our all being, by reason of the disobedience of Adam and Eve, in God's displeasure, and by nature children of wrath, as the apostle shows (Rom. 5:12 sqq.; Eph. 2:3).

2. Secondly, that there is an entire want or lack of the con-created original righteousness, or of God's image, according to which man was originally created in truth, holiness and righteousness; and likewise an inability and unfitness for all the things of God, or, as the Latin words read: Descriptio peccati originalis detrahit naturae non renovatae, et dona, et vim, seu facultatem et actus inchoandi et efficiendi spiritualia. That is: The definition of original sin takes away from the unrenewed nature the gifts, the power, and all activity for beginning and effecting anything in spiritual things.

3. That Original Sin (in human nature) is not only such an entire absence of all good in spiritual, divine things, but that it is at the same time also, instead of the lost image of God in man, a deep, wicked, horrible, fathomless, inscrutable and unspeakable corruption of the entire nature and all its powers, especially of the highest, principal powers of the soul in understanding, heart and will; that now, since the fall, man receives by inheritance *an inborn wicked disposition, an inward impurity of heart, wicked lusts and propensities;* that we all have by nature inherited from Adam such a heart, feeling and thoughts as, according to their highest powers and the light of reason, are naturally inclined and disposed directly contrary to God and his chief commands, yea, they are at enmity with God, especially as to what concerns divine and spiritual things. For, in other respects, as regards natural, external things which are subject to the reason, man still has, to a certain degree, understanding, power and ability, although very much weakened, all of which, nevertheless, has been so infected and contaminated by Original Sin that before God it is of no use.

4. The penalties of Original Sin, which God has imposed upon the children of Adam and upon Original Sin, are death, eternal damnation, and also other bodily and spiritual, temporal and eternal miseries, and the tyranny and dominion of the devil, so that human nature is subject to the kingdom of the devil, and has been surrendered to the power of the devil, and is held captive under his sway, who stupefies [fascinates] and leads astray many great, learned men in the world by means of dreadful error, heresy and other blindness, and otherwise delivers men to all sorts of crime.

5. Fifthly, this hereditary evil is so great and horrible that it can be covered and forgiven before God only for Christ's sake, and in the baptized and believing. Human nature also, which is deranged and corrupted thereby, must and can be healed only by the regeneration and renewal of the Holy Ghost, which, nevertheless, is only begun in this life, but will at length be fully completed in the life to come.

These points, which have been quoted here only in a summary way, are set forth more fully in the above-mentioned writings of the common confession of our Christian doctrine.

But this doctrine must now be so maintained and guarded that it may not incline either to the Pelagian or the Manichaean side. Therefore the contrary doctrine concerning this article, which is censured and rejected in our churches, should also be briefly reported.

1. And first, in opposition to the old and the new Pelagians, the following false opinions and dogmas are censured and rejected, namely, that Original Sin is only a *reatus* or debt, on account of what has been committed by another without any corruption of our nature.

2. Also that sinful, evil lusts are not sins, but conditions, or concreated and essential properties of the nature.

3. Or as though the above-mentioned defect and evil were not before God properly and truly sin, on

THE FORMULA OF CONCORD (1580) (continued)

account of which man without Christ [unless he be grafted into Christ and be delivered through him] must be a child of wrath and damnation, and also be beneath the power and in the kingdom of Satan.

4. The following Pelagian errors and the like are also censured and rejected, namely: that nature, ever since the fall, is incorrupt, and that especially with respect to spiritual things it is entirely good and pure, and *in naturalibus, i.e.,* in its natural powers, it is perfect.

5. Or that Original Sin is only external, a slight, insignificant spot sprinkled or stain dashed upon the nature of man, or *corruptio tantum accidentium aut qualitatum, i.e.* a corruption only of some accidental things, along with and beneath which the nature, nevertheless, possesses and retains its integrity and power even in spiritual things.

6. Or that Original Sin is not a despoliation or deficiency, but only an external impediment to these spiritual good powers, as when a magnet is smeared with garlic-juice, whereby its natural power is not removed, but only impeded; or that this stain can be easily washed away, as a spot from the face or pigment from the wall.

7. They likewise are rebuked and rejected who teach that the nature has indeed been greatly weakened and corrupted through the fall, but that, nevertheless, it has not entirely lost all good with respect to divine, spiritual things, and that what is sung in our churches, "Through Adam's fall is all corrupt, Nature and essence human," is not true, but from natural birth we still have something good (small, little and inconsiderable though it be), namely: capacity, skill, aptness or ability in spiritual things to begin to work or co-work for something. For concerning external temporal, worldly things and transactions, which are subject to reason, there will be an explanation in the succeeding article.

These and doctrines of like kind, contrary to the truth, are censured and rejected for the reason that God's Word teaches that the corrupt nature, of and by itself, has no power for anything good in spiritual things, not even for the least, as good thoughts, but that, of and by itself, it can do nothing but sin. Gen. 6:5; 8:21.

Therefore [But] this doctrine must also be guarded, on the other side, from Manichaean errors. Accordingly, the following erroneous doctrines and the like are rejected, namely: that now, since the fall, human nature is in the beginning created pure and good, and that afterwards Original Sin from without is infused and mingled by Satan (as something essential) in the nature, as poison is mingled with wine [that in the beginning human nature was created by God pure and good, but that now, since the fall, Original Sin, etc.].

For although in Adam and Eve the nature was originally created pure, good and holy, nevertheless sin has not entered nature through the fall in the way fanatically taught by the Manichaeans, as though Satan had created

or made something essentially evil, and mingled it with their nature. But since, from the seduction of Satan, through the fall, according to God's judgment and sentence, man, as a punishment, has lost his concreated original righteousness, human nature, as has been said above, is perverted and corrupt by this deprivation or deficiency, want and injury, which has been caused by Satan; so that at present the nature of all men, who in a natural way are conceived and born, is transmitted by inheritance with the same want and corruption. For since the fall human nature is not at first created pure and good, and only afterward corrupted by Original Sin, but in the first moment of our conception the seed whence man is formed is sinful and corrupt. Thus also Original Sin is not something existing of itself in or apart from the nature of the corrupt man, as it is also not the peculiar essence, body or soul of the corrupt man, or the man himself.

Original Sin, and the nature of man corrupted thereby, cannot and should not, therefore, be so distinguished, as though the nature before God were pure, good, holy, but Original Sin alone which dwells therein were evil.

Also, as Augustine writes of the Manichaeans, as though it were not the corrupt man himself who sins by reason of inborn Original Sin, but something different and foreign in man, and therefore that God, by the Law, accuses and condemns not the nature as corrupt by sin, but only the Original Sin therein. For, as stated above in the thesis, *i.e.* the explanation of the pure doctrine concerning Original Sin, the entire nature of man, which is born in the natural way of father and mother, is entirely and to the farthest extent corrupted and perverted by Original Sin, in body and soul, in all its powers that pertain and belong to the goodness, truth, holiness and righteousness concreated with it in Paradise. Nevertheless, the nature is not entirely exterminated or changed into another substance [diverse in genus or species], which, according to its essence, is not like our nature, and therefore cannot be one essence with us.

Because of this corruption the entire corrupt nature of man would be accused and condemned by the Law, if sin were not, for Christ's sake, forgiven.

But the Law accuses and condemns nature, not because we have been created men by God, but because we are sinful and wicked; not because and so far as nature and its essence, ever since the fall, is a work and creature of God in us, but because and so far as it has been poisoned and corrupted by sin.

But although Original Sin, like a spiritual poison or leprosy (as Luther says), has poisoned and corrupted all human nature, so that we cannot clearly show and point out the nature apart by itself, and Original Sin apart by itself; nevertheless, *the corrupt nature,* or essence of the corrupt man, body and soul, or the man himself whom God has created (and within whom dwells the Original Sin that also corrupts the nature, essence or the entire man), and *Original Sin,* which dwells in man's nature or essence, and corrupts it, are not one thing; as also in external leprosy the body which is leprous, and the leprosy on or in the body, are not, properly speaking, one thing. A distinction must be observed also between our nature, as created and preserved by God, and Original Sin, which dwells in the nature. These two must and also can be considered, taught and believed with their distinctions according to Holy Scripture.

The chief articles also of our Christian faith urge and compel us to preserve this distinction.

For, *first,* in the article of Creation, Scripture shows that not only has God before the fall created human nature, but also that, since the fall, it is a creature and work of God (Deut 32:6; Isa. 45:11; 54:5; 64:8; Acts 17:25; Rev. 4:11).

"Thine hands," says Job (10:8-12), "have made me and fashioned me together round about; yet thou dost destroy me. Remember, I beseech thee, that thou hast made me as the clay; and wilt thou bring me into dust again? Hast thou not poured me out as milk, and curdled me as cheese? Thou hast clothed me with skin and flesh, and fenced me with bones and sinews. Thou hast granted me life and favor, and thy visitation hath preserved my spirit."

"I will praise thee," says David (Ps. 139:14-16), "for I am fearfully and wonderfully made; marvellous are thy works; and that my soul knoweth right well. My substance was not hid from thee when I was made in secret, and curiously wrought in the lowest parts of the earth. Thine eyes did see my substance yet being unperfect; and in thy book all my members were written, which in continuance were fashioned, when as yet there was none of them."

In the Ecclesiastes of Solomon it is written [12:7]: "Then shall the dust return to the earth as it was, and the spirit to God who gave it."

These passages clearly testify that God ever since the fall is the Creator of man, and creates his body and soul. Therefore the corrupt man cannot be, without any distinction, sin itself, for otherwise God would be a creator of sins; as also our Small Catechism, in the explanation of the First Article, confesses: "I believe that God has created me with all that exists, that he has given and still preserves to me my body and soul, with all my limbs and senses, my reason and all the faculties of my mind." Likewise in the Large Catechism it is thus written: "I believe and mean to say that I am a creature of God, *i.e.* that he has given and constantly preserves to me my body, soul and life, members great and small, and all my senses." Although the same creature and work of God is lamentably corrupted by sin; for the mass (*massa*), from which God now forms and makes man was in Adam corrupted and perverted, and is thus transmitted by inheritance to us.

And here pious Christian hearts ought to consider the unspeakable goodness of God that God did not immediately cast from himself into hell-fire this corrupt, perverted, sinful mass, but from it forms and makes human nature of the present day, which is lamentably corrupted by sin, in order that by his dear Son he may cleanse it from all sin, sanctify and save it.

From this article now the distinction is indisputable and clear. For Original Sin does not originate with God. God is not a creator or author of sin. Original Sin also is not a creature or work of God, but a work of the devil.

If, now, there would be no difference whatever between the nature or essence of our body and soul, which is corrupted by Original Sin, and Original Sin, by which the nature is corrupted, it would follow either that God, because he is the creator of this our nature, also created and made Original Sin, which would also be his work and creature; or, because sin is a work of the devil, that Satan would be the creator of this our nature, soul and body, which must also be a work or creation of Satan if, without any distinction, our corrupt nature should be regarded as sin itself; both of which are contrary to the article of our Christian faith. Wherefore, in order that God's creation and work in man may be distinguished from the work of the devil, we say that it is God's creation that man has body and soul. Also that it is God's work that man can think, speak, do and work anything; for "in him we live, and move, and have our being." But that the nature is corrupt, that its thoughts, words and works are wicked, is originally a work of Satan, who, through sin, thus corrupted God's work in Adam, which from him is transmitted by inheritance to us.

Secondly, in the article of Redemption, the Scriptures testify forcibly that God's Son assumed our human nature without sin, so that he was, in all things, sin excepted, made like us, his brethren, Heb. 2:14. Hence all the old orthodox teachers have maintained that Christ, according to his assumed humanity, is, of one essence with us, his brethren; for he has assumed a human nature, which in all respects (sin alone excepted) is like our human nature in its essence and all essential attributes, and they have condemned the contrary doctrine as manifest heresy.

If, now, there were no distinction between the nature or essence of corrupt man and Original Sin, it must follow that either Christ did not assume our nature, because he did not assume sin; or that because he assumed our nature he also assumed sin; both of which are contrary to the Scriptures. But inasmuch as the Son of God assumed our nature, and not Original Sin, it is hence clear that human nature, ever since the fall, and Original Sin, are not one thing, but must be distinguished.

Thirdly, in the article of Sanctification, Scripture testifies that God cleanses, washes and sanctifies men from sin (1 John 1:7), and that Christ saves his people from their sins (Matt. 1:21). Sin, therefore, cannot be man himself; for God, for Christ's sake, receives man into grace, but he remains hostile to sin to eternity. Wherefore that Original Sin is baptized in the name of the Holy Trinity, sanctified and saved, and other such expressions, whereby we will not offend simple-minded people, that are found in the writings of the recent Manichaeans, are unchristian and dreadful to hear.

Fourthly, in the article of the Resurrection, Scripture testifies that it is precisely the substance of this our flesh, but without sin, which will rise again, and that in eternal life we will have and retain precisely this soul, but without sin.

If, now, there were no difference whatever between our corrupt body and soul, and Original Sin, it would follow, contrary to this article of the Christian faith, that either this our flesh will not rise again at the last day, and that in eternal life we will not have body and soul of the present essence, but another substance (or another soul), because

THE FORMULA OF CONCORD (1580) (continued)

then we will be without sin, or that [at the last day] sin also will rise again, and, in eternal life, will be and remain in the elect.

Hence it is clear that we must reject this doctrine [of the Manichaeans] (with all that depends upon it and follows from it), which asserts and teaches that Original Sin is the nature, substance, essence, body or soul itself or corrupt man, so that between our corrupt nature, substance and essence, and Original Sin, there is no distinction whatever. For the chief articles of our Christian faith forcibly and emphatically testify why a distinction should and must be maintained between man's nature or substance, which is corrupted by sin, and sin, whereby man is corrupted. For a simple statement of the doctrine and its opposite, with respect to the main point involved in this controversy, this is sufficient in this place, where the subject is not argued at length, but only the principal points are treated, article by article.

But with respect to terms and expressions, it is best and surest to use and retain the form of sound words employed concerning this article in the Holy Scriptures and the above-mentioned books.

Also to avoid strife about words, equivocal terms, i.e. words and expressions, which may be understood and used in several senses, should be carefully and distinctly explained, as when it is said: God creates the nature of men, where by the term "nature" the essence, body and soul of men are understood. But often the disposition or vicious quality is called its nature, as: "It is the nature of the serpent to bite and poison." Thus Luther says that sin and to sin are the disposition and nature of the corrupt man.

Therefore Original Sin properly signifies the deep corruption of our nature, as it is described in the Smalcald Articles. But sometimes we thereby understand the concrete or the subject, i.e. man himself with body and soul, wherein sin is and inheres, on account of which man is corrupted, infected with poison and sinful, as when Luther says: "Thy birth, thy nature, thy entire essence is sin", i.e. sinful and unclean.

Luther himself declares that by "natural sin," "personal sin," "essential sin," he means that not only words, thoughts and works are sin, but that the entire nature, person and essence of man is entirely corrupted [and is altogether depraved] by Original Sin.

Moreover, as to the Latin terms "substance" and "accident," we are of the opinion that, in sermons to congregations of plain people, they should be avoided, because such terms are unknown to ordinary men. But when learned men, in treating this subject, employ them among themselves or with others to whom this word is not unknown, as Eusebius, Ambrose and especially Augustine, and also still other eminent church-teachers, from the necessity of explaining this doctrine in opposition to the heretics, they regard them as constituting an "immediate division," i.e. a division between which there is no mean, so that everything which there is must be either "substance," i.e. an independent essence, or "accident," i.e. an incidental

matter which does not exist by itself essentially, but i[n] another independent essence, and can be distinguishe[d] therefrom; which division Cyril and Basil also use.

And because, among others, it is also an indubitable indisputable axiom in theology that every substance o[r] self-existing essence, so far as it is a substance, is eithe[r] God himself or a work and creation of God; Augustine, i[n] many writings against the Manichaeans, in common wit[h] all true teachers, has, after due consideration and wit[h] earnestness, rejected and condemned the expression: *Pec[-] catum originis est substantia vel natura, i.e.* Original Sin i[s] man's nature or substance. In conformity with him, all th[e] learned and intelligent also have always maintained tha[t] what does not exist by itself, neither is a part of anothe[r] self-existing essence, but exists, subject to change, i[n] another thing, is not a substance, i.e. something self existing, but an accident, i.e. something incidental. Thu[s] Augustine is accustomed to speak constantly in this way Original Sin is not the nature itself, but an *accidens vitiun[m] in natura, i.e.* an incidental defect and damage in th[e] nature. In this way also, in our schools and churche[s] previous to this controversy, [learned] men spoke, accord[-] ing to the rules of logic, freely and without any suspicio[n] [of heresy], and, on this account, were never censure[d] either by Dr. Luther or any orthodox teacher of our pure evangelical Church.

For since it is the indisputable truth that everything tha[t] there is, is either a substance or an accident, i.e. either [a] self-existing essence or something incidental in it, as ha[s] been just shown and proved by the testimony of th[e] church-teachers, and no truly intelligent man has eve[r] doubted concerning this; if the question be asked whethe[r] Original Sin be a substance, i.e. such a thing as exists o[f] itself, and not in another, or an accident, i.e. such a thing as does not exist by itself, but in another, and cannot exis[t] or be by itself, necessity constrains us, and no one ca[n] evade it, to confess directly and candidly that Original Si[n] is no substance, but an accident.

Hence also the permanent peace of the Church of Go[d] with respect to this controversy will never be promoted but the dissension will rather be strengthened and maintained, if the ministers of the Church remain in doubt as t[o] whether Original Sin be a substance or accident, an[d] whether it be thus rightly and properly named.

Hence if the churches and schools are to be relieved of thi[s] scandalous and very mischievous controversy, it is necessary that each and every one be properly instructed concerning this matter.

But if it be further asked as to what kind of an acciden[t] Original Sin is, it is another question, and one to which n[o] philosopher, no Papist, no sophist, yea, no human reason, however acute it may be, can give the right explanation, but all understanding and every explanation of it must be derived solely from the Holy Scriptures, which testify tha[t] Original Sin is an unspeakable evil, and such an entire corruption of human nature that in it and all its interna[l] and extenal powers nothing pure or good remains, bu[t] everything is entirely corrupt, so that, on account o[f] Original Sin, man is in God's sight truly, spiritually dead, and, with all his powers, has died to that which is good.

n this way, then, by the word "accident," Original Sin is not extenuated [namely] when it is explained according to the analogy of] God's Word, after the manner in which Dr. Luther, in his Latin exposition of the third chapter of Genesis, has written with great earnestness against the extenuation of Original Sin; but this word is employed only to designate the distinction between the work of God which is our nature, notwithstanding that it is corrupt) and the work of the devil (which is sin), that inheres in God's work, and is a most profound and indescribable corruption of it.

Therefore Luther also has employed in his treatment of his subject the term "accident," as also the term "quality," and has not rejected them; but likewise, with especial earnestness and great zeal, he has taken the greatest pains to explain and to represent to each and every one what a horrible quality and accident it is, whereby human nature is not merely polluted, but is so deeply corrupted that nothing pure or uncorrupt remains in it, as his words on Ps. 90 run: Sive igitur peccatum originis *qualitatem* sive *morbum* vocavermus, profecto extremum malum est non solum pati aeternam iram et mortem, sed ne agnoscere quidem, quae pateris. That is: Whether we call Original Sin a *quality* or a *disease*, it is indeed the utmost evil not only to suffer the eternal wrath of God and eternal death, but also not to understand what we suffer. And again on Gen. 3: Qui isto veneno peccati originis a planta pedis usque ad verticem infecti sumus, siquidem in natura adhuc integra accidere. That is: We are infected by the poison of Original Sin from the sole of the foot to the crown of the head, inasmuch as this happened to us in a nature still perfect.

CHAPTER II. OF THE FREE WILL, OR HUMAN POWERS.

Since a dissent has occurred not only between the Papists and us, but also even among some theologians of the Augsburg Confession, concerning the free will, we will first of all exactly show the points of the controversy.

For since man, with respect to his free will, can be found and considered in four distinct, dissimilar states, the question at present is not concerning his condition with regard to the same *before the fall,* or his ability *since the fall,* and before his conversion, *in external things* which pertain to this temporal life; also not concerning his ability in spiritual things after he has been *regenerated* and is controlled by God's Spirit; or the sort of a free will he will have when he rises *from the dead.* But the principal question is only and alone as to the ability of the understanding and will of the *unregenerate* man in his *conversion* and regeneration from his own *powers surviving* since the fall: Whether when the Word of God is preached, and the grace of God is offered, he can prepare himself for grace, accept the same, and assent thereto? This is the question upon which now for quite a number of years there has been a controversy among some theologians in the churches of the Augsburg Confession.

For the one side has held and taught that although man, from his own powers, cannot fulfil God's command, or truly trust, fear and love God, without the grace of the Holy Ghost; nevertheless, before regeneration sufficient

natural powers survive for him to prepare himself to a certain extent for grace, and to assent, although feebly; yet, if the grace of the Holy Ghost were not added thereto, he could by this accomplish nothing, but must be vanquished in the struggle.

On the other side, the ancient and modern enthusiasts have taught that God, through his Spirit, converts men and leads them to the saving knowledge of Christ, without any means and instrument of the creature, *i.e.* without the external preaching and hearing of God's Word.

Against both these parties the pure teachers of the Augsburg Confession have taught and contended that by the fall of our first parents man was so corrupted that, in divine things pertaining to our conversion and the salvation of our souls, he is by nature blind when the Word of God is preached, and neither does nor can understand it, but regards it foolishness, and also does not of himself draw nigh to God, but is and remains an enemy of God, until by the power of the Holy Ghost, through the preached and heard Word, out of pure grace, without any co-operation of his own, he is converted, made believing [presented with faith], regenerated and renewed.

In order to explain this controversy in a Christian manner, according to the guidance of God's Word, and by his grace to decide it, our doctrine, faith and confession are as follows:

Namely, that in spiritual and divine things the intellect, heart and will of the unregenerate man cannot, in any way, by their own natural powers, understand, believe, accept, think, will, begin, effect, do, work or concur in working anything, but they are entirely dead to good, and corrupt; so that in man's nature, since the fall, there is, before regeneration, not the least spark of spiritual power remaining still present, by which, of himself, he can prepare himself for God's grace, or accept the offered grace, or, for and of himself, be capable of it, or apply or accommodate himself thereto, or, by his own powers, be able of himself, as of himself, to aid, do, work or concur in working anything for his conversion, either entirely, or in half, or in even the least or most inconsiderable part, but he is the servant [and slave] of sin (John 8:34; Eph. 2:2; 2 Tim. 2:26). Hence the natural free will, according to its perverted disposition and nature, is strong and active only with respect to what is displeasing and contrary to God.

This declaration and general reply to the chief question and statement of the controversy presented in the introduction to this article, the following arguments from God's Word confirm and strengthen, and although they are contrary to proud reason and philosophy, yet we know that the wisdom of this perverted world is only foolishness before God, and that articles of faith should be judged only from God's Word.

For, first, although man's reason or natural understanding has still indeed a dim spark of the knowledge that there is a God, as also (Rom. 1:19 sqq.) of the doctrine of the Law; yet it is so ignorant, blind and perverted that when even the most able and learned men upon earth read or hear the Gospel of the Son of God and the promise of eternal salvation, they cannot, from their own powers, perceive, apprehend, understand or believe and regard it true, but

THE FORMULA OF CONCORD (1580) (continued)

the more diligence and earnestness they employ in order to comprehend, with their reason, these spiritual things, the less they understand or believe, and, before they become enlightened or taught of the Holy Ghost, they regard all this only as foolishness or fictions. (1 Cor. 2:14): "The natural man receiveth not the things of the Spirit of God; for they are foolishness to him." (1 Cor. 1:21): "For after that, in the wisdom of God, the world by wisdom knew not God, it pleased God, by the foolishness of preaching, to save them that believe." (Eph. 4:17 sq.): "They" (*i.e.* those not born again of God's Spirit) "walk in the vanity of their mind, having the understanding darkened, being alienated from the life of God, through the ignorance that is in them, because of the blindness of their heart." (Matt. 13:11 sqq. [Luke 8:18]): "They seeing, see not, and hearing, they hear not, neither do they understand; but it is given unto you to know the mysteries of the kingdom of heaven." (Rom. 3:11, 12): "There is none that understandeth, there is none that seeketh after God. They are all gone out of the way, they are all together become unprofitable; there is none that doeth good, no, not one."

So, too, the Scriptures expressly call natural men, in spiritual and divine things, darkness. (Eph. 5:8; Acts 26:18; John 1:5): "The light shineth in darkness" (*i.e.* in the dark, blind world, which does not know or regard God), "and the darkness comprehendeth it not." Also the Scriptures teach that man in sins is not only weak and sick, but also entirely dead (Eph. 2:1, 5; Col. 2:13).

As now a man who is physically dead cannot, of his own powers, prepare or adapt himself to obtain again temporal life; so the man who is spiritually dead in sins cannot, of his own strength, adapt or apply himself to the acquisition of spiritual and heavenly righteousness and life, unless he be delivered and quickened by the Son of God from the death of sin.

Therefore the Scriptures deny to the understanding, heart and will of the natural man all aptness, skill, capacity and ability in spiritual things, to think, to understand, begin, will, undertake, do, work or concur in working anything good and right, as of himself. (2 Cor. 3:5): "Not that we are sufficient of ourselves, to think anything, as of ourselves; but our sufficiency is of God." (Rom. 3:12): "They are altogether unprofitable." (John 8:7): "My Word hath no place in you." (John 1:5): "The darkness comprehendeth" (or receiveth) "not the light." (1 Cor. 2:14): "The natural man perceiveth not" (or, as the Greek word properly signifies, taketh not, comprehendeth not, receiveth not) "the things of the Spirit," *i.e.* he is not capable of spiritual things; "for they are foolishness unto him; neither can he know them." Much less can he truly believe the Gospel, or assent thereto and regard it as truth. (Rom. 8:7): "The carnal mind," or that of the natural man, "is enmity against God; for it is not subject to the Law of God, neither indeed can be." And, in a word, that remains eternally true which the Son of God says (John 15:5): "Without me ye can do nothing." And Paul (Phil. 2:13): "It is God which worketh in you, both to will and to do of his good pleasure." This precious passage is very comforting to all godly Christians, who feel and experience in their

hearts a small spark or earnest longing for divine grace and eternal salvation; for they know that God has kindled in their hearts this beginning of true godliness, and that he will further strengthen and help them in their great weakness to persevere in true faith unto the end.

To this also all the prayers of the saints relate, in which they pray that they may be taught, enlightened and sanctified of God, and thereby declare that those things which they ask of God they cannot have from their own natural powers; as in Ps. 119, alone, David prays more than ten times that God may impart to him understanding, that he may rightly receive and learn the divine doctrine. [Very many] similar prayers are in the writings of Paul (Eph. 1:17; Col. 1:9; Phil. 1:9). These prayers and the testimonies concerning our ignorance and inability have been written, not for the purpose of rendering us idle and remiss in reading, hearing and meditating upon God's Word, but first that from the heart we should thank God that, through his Son, he has delivered us from the darkness of ignorance and the captivity of sin and death, and, through baptism and the Holy Ghost, has regenerated and illumined us.

And after God, through the Holy Ghost in baptism, has kindled and made a beginning of the true knowledge of God and faith, we should pray him without intermission that, through the same Spirit and his grace, by means of the daily exercise of reading, and applying to practice God's Word, he may preserve in us faith and his heavenly gifts, strengthen us from day to day, and support us to the end. For unless God himself be our school-teacher, we can study and learn nothing that is acceptable to him and that is salutary to ourselves and others.

Secondly, God's Word testifies that the understanding, heart and will of the natural, unregenerate man in divine things are not only turned entirely from God, but also turned and perverted against God to every evil. Also, that he is not only weak, feeble, impotent and dead to good, but also through Original Sin is so lamentably perverted, infected and corrupted that, by his disposition and nature, he is entirely evil, perverse and hostile to God, and that, with respect to everything that is displeasing and contrary to God, he is strong, alive and active. (Gen. 8:22): "The imagination of man's heart is evil from his youth." (Jer. 17:9): "The heart of man is defiant and despairing," or perverted and full of misery, "so that it is unfathomable." This passage St. Paul explains (Rom. 8): "The carnal mind is enmity against God." (Gal. 5:17): "The flesh lusteth against the spirit; . . . and these are contrary the one to the other." (Rom. 7:14): "We know that the Law is spiritual; but I am carnal, sold under sin." And soon afterward (18, 23): "I know that in me, that is, in my flesh, dwelleth no good thing. For I delight in the Law of God, after the inward man," which, through the Holy Ghost, is regenerate; "but I see another law in my members, warring against the law of my mind, and bringing me into captivity to the law of sin."

If, now, in St. Paul and in other regenerate men the natural or carnal free will, even after regeneration, strives against God's Law, much more perverse and hostile to God's Law and will, will it be before regeneration. Hence it is manifest as in the article concerning Original Sin it is further declared, to which, for the sake of brevity, we now refer) that the free will, from its own natural powers, not only cannot work or co-work as to anything for its own conversion, righteousness and salvation, or follow, believe or assent to the Holy Ghost, who through the Gospel offers him grace and salvation, but rather from its innate, wicked, perverse nature it hostilely resists God and his will, unless it be enlightened and controlled by God's Spirit.

On this account, also, the Holy Scriptures compare the heart of the unregenerate man to a hard stone, which does not yield to the one who touches it, but resists, and to a rough block, and to a wild, unmanageable beast; not that man, since the fall, is no longer a rational creature, or is converted to God without hearing and meditating upon God's Word, or in external, worldly things cannot understand, or do or abstain from doing, anything of his free will, good or evil.

For, as Doctor Luther says upon Ps. 90: "In worldly and external affairs, which pertain to the livelihood and maintenance of the body, man is intelligent, reasonable and very active, but in spiritual and divine things, which pertain to the salvation of the soul, man is like a pillar of salt, like Lot's wife, yea, like a log and a stone, like a lifeless statue, which uses neither eyes nor mouth, neither sense nor heart. For man neither sees nor perceives the fierce and terrible wrath of God on account of sin and death [resulting from it], but he continues even knowingly and willingly in his security, and thereby falls into a thousand dangers, and finally into eternal death and damnation; and no prayers, no supplications, no admonitions, yea, also no threats, no reprimands are of any avail; yea, all teaching and preaching are lost upon him, until he is enlightened, converted and regenerated by the Holy Ghost. For this [renewal of the Holy Ghost] no stone or block, but man alone, was created. And although God, according to his just, strict sentence, eternally casts away the fallen evil spirits, he has nevertheless, out of pure mercy, willed that poor fallen human nature might again become capable and participant of conversion, the grace of God and eternal life; not from its own natural [active or] effective skill, aptness or capacity (for the nature of man is perverse enmity against God), but from pure grace, through the gracious efficacious working of the Holy Ghost." And this Dr. Luther calls capacity (not active, but passive) which he thus explains: Quando patres liberum arbitrium defendunt, capacitatem libertatis ejus praedicant, quod scilicet verti potest ad bonum per gratiam Dei et fieri revera liberum, ad quod creatum est. That is: When the Fathers defend the free will, they say of it that it is capable of freedom in so far that, through God's grace, it can be turned to good, and become truly free, for which it was created. Tom. 1, p. 236.

Augustine also has written to like effect, lib. 2. *Contra Julianum.* Dr. Luther on Hosea 6; also in the Church-Postils on the Epistle for Good Friday; also on the Gospel for the third Sunday after Epiphany.)

But before man is enlightened, converted, regenerated, renewed and led by the Holy Ghost, he can of himself and of his own natural powers begin, work or co-operate as to anything in spiritual things, and in his own conversion or regeneration, as little as a stone or a block or clay. For although he can control the outward members and hear the Gospel, and to a certain extent meditate upon it and discourse concerning it, as is to be seen in the Pharisees and hypocrites; nevertheless he regards it foolishness, and cannot believe it, and also in this case he is worse than a block, in that he is rebellious and hostile to God's will, if the Holy Ghost be not efficacious in him, and do not kindle and work in him faith and other virtues pleasing to God, and obedience.

Thirdly, for the Holy Scriptures, besides, refer conversion, faith in Christ, regeneration, renewal, and all that belongs to their efficacious beginning and completion, not to the human powers of the natural free will, either entirely, or half, or the least or most inconsiderable part; but ascribe them *in solidum, i.e.* entirely, alone to the divine working and the Holy Ghost, as also the Apology teaches.

The reason and free will have the power, to a certain extent, to live an outwardly decent life; but to be born anew, and to obtain inwardly another heart, sense and disposition, this only the Holy Ghost effects. He opens the understanding and heart to understand the Scriptures and to give heed to the Word, as it is written (Luke 24:45): "Then opened he their understanding, that they might understand the Scriptures." Also (Acts 16:11): "Lydia heard us; whose heart the Lord opened, that she attended unto the things which were spoken of Paul." "He worketh in us, both to will and to do of his own good pleasure" (Phil. 2:13). He gives repentance (Acts 5:31; 2 Tim. 2:25). He works faith (Phil. 1:29): "For unto you it is given, in behalf of Christ, not only to believe on him." (Eph. 2:8): "It is the gift of God." (John 6:29): "This is the work of God, that ye believe on Him whom he hath sent." He gives an understanding heart, seeing eyes, and hearing ears (Deut. 29:4; Matt. 13:15). The Holy Ghost is a spirit of regeneration and renewal (Tit. 3:5, 6). He takes away the hard heart of stone, and gives a new tender heart of flesh, that we may walk in his commands (Ez. 11:19; Deut. 30:6; Ps. 51:10). He creates us in Christ Jesus to good works (Eph 2:10), and makes us new creatures (2 Cor. 5:17; Gal. 6:15). And, in short, every good gift is of God (James 1:17). No one can come to Christ unless the Father draw him (John 6:44). No one knoweth the Father, save him to whom the Son will reveal him (Matt. 11:27). No one can call Christ Lord, but by the Holy Ghost (1 Cor. 12:3). "Without me," says Christ, "ye can do nothing" (John 15:5). All "our sufficiency is of God" (2 Cor. 3:5). "What hast thou which thou didst not receive? Now, if thou didst receive it, why dost thou glory as if thou hadst not received it?" (1 Cor. 4:7). And indeed St. Augustine writes particularly of this passage, that by it he was constrained to lay aside the former erroneous opinion which he had held concerning this subject. *De Proedestinatione,* cap. 3: Gratiam Dei in eo tantum consistere, quod in praeconis veritatis Dei voluntas nobis revelaretur; ut autem praedicato nobis evangelio consentiremus, nostrum esse proprium, et ex nobis esse. Item erravi (inquit), eum dicerem, nostrum esse credere et velle; Dei autem, dare credentibus et volentibus facultatem operandi. That is: "I erred in this,

THE FORMULA OF CONCORD (1580) (continued)

that I held that the grace of God consists alone in that God, in the preaching of the truth, reveals his will; but that we consent to the preached Gospel is our own work, and stands within our own powers." For St. Augustine also writes further: "I erred when I said that it stands within our own power to believe the Gospel and to will; but it is God's work to give to them that believe and will the power of working."

This doctrine is founded upon God's Word, and conformable to the Augsburg Confession and other writings above mentioned, as the following testimonies prove.

In Article XX, the Confession says as follows: "Because through faith the Holy Ghost is given, the heart thus becomes qualified for the doing of good works. For before, because it is without the Holy Ghost, it is too weak, and besides is in the devil's power, who drives poor human nature into many sins." And a little afterward: "For without faith and Christ human nature and ability is much too weak to do good works."

These passages clearly testify that the Augsburg Confession pronounces the will of man in spiritual things as anything else than free, but says that he is the devil's captive; how, then, from his own powers, is he to be able to turn himself to the Gospel or Christ?

The Apology teaches of the free will thus: "We also say that reason has, to a certain extent, a free will; for in the things which are to be comprehended by the reason we have a free will." And a little after: "For such hearts as are without the Holy Ghost are without the fear of God, without faith. Without trust towards God they do not believe that God listens to them, that he forgives their sins, and helps them in necessities; therefore they are godless. Now, 'a corrupt tree cannot bring forth good fruit,' and 'without faith it is impossible to please God.' Therefore, although we concede that it is within our ability to perform such an outward work, nevertheless, we say that, in spiritual things, the free will and reason have no ability," etc. Here it is clearly seen that the Apology ascribes no ability to the will of man, either for beginning good or for itself co-operating.

In the Smalcald Articles the following errors concerning the free will are also rejected: "That man has a free will to do good and omit evil," etc. And shortly afterward the error is also rejected: "That it is not founded upon Scripture, that, for a good work, the Holy Ghost, with his grace, is necessary."

It is further maintained in the Smalcald Articles as follows: "And this repentance, in Christians, continues until death, because through the entire life it contends with sin remaining in the flesh, as Paul (Rom. 7:23) shows that he wars with the Law in his members, etc.; and this, not by his own powers, but by the gift of the Holy Ghost, that follows the remission of sins. This gift daily cleanses and purges the remaining sins, and works so as to render man pure and holy." These words say nothing whatever of our will, or that it also of itself works in regenerate men, but ascribe it to the gift of the Holy Ghost, which cleanses man

and makes him daily more godly and holy, and thus our own powers are entirely excluded therefrom.

In the Large Catechism of Dr. Luther it is written thus "And I also am a part and member of the same, a participant and joint owner of all the good it possesses brought to it and incorporated into it by the Holy Ghost in that I have heard and continue to hear the Word o God, which is the means of entrance. For formerly, befor we had attained to this, we were of the devil, knowing nothing of God and of Christ. Thus, until the last day, the Holy Ghost abides with the holy congregation or Christian people. By means of this congregation he brings us to Christ and teaches, and preaches to us the Word, whereby he works and promotes sanctification, causing [this community] daily to grow and become strong in the faith and the fruits of the Spirit, which he produces."

In these words the Catechism mentions not a word concerning our free will or co-operation, but refer everything to the Holy Ghost, viz. that, through the office of the ministry, he brings us into the Church of God wherein he sanctifies us, and so provides that we daily grow in faith and good works.

And although the regenerate, even in this life, advance so far that they will what is good, and love it, and even do good and grow in it, nevertheless this (as above quoted) is not of our will and ability, but the Holy Ghost, as Paul himself speaks concerning this, works "to will and to do" (Phil. 2:13). As also in Eph. 2:10 he ascribes this work to God alone, when he says: "For we are his workmanship created in Christ Jesus unto good works, which God hath before ordained that we should walk therein."

In the Small Catechism of Dr. Luther it is thus written: ". believe that I cannot by my own reason or strength believe in Jesus Christ, my Lord, or come to him; but the Holy Ghost has called me through the Gospel, enlightened me by his gifts, and sanctified and preserved me in the true faith; in like manner as he calls, gathers, enlightens and sanctifies the whole Christian Church on earth, and preserves it in union with Jesus Christ in the true faith,' etc.

And in the explanation of the second petition of the Lord's Prayer the following words occur: "When is this effected. When our Heavenly Father gives us his Holy Spirit, so that by his grace we believe his holy Word and live a godly life," etc.

These passages declare that, from our own powers, we cannot come to Christ, but God must give us his Holy Ghost, by whom we are enlightened, sanctified, and thus brought to Christ through faith, and upheld in him; and no mention is made of our will or co-operation.

To this we will add a passage in which Dr. Luther expresses himself, together with a solemn declaration added thereto, that he intends to persevere in this doctrine unto the end, in his Large Confession concerning the Holy Supper: "Hereby I reject and condemn, as nothing but error all dogmas which extol our free will; as they directly conflict with this help and grace of our Saviour, Jesus Christ. For since, out of Christ, death and sin are our lords, and the devil our god and prince, there can be no ower or might, no wisdom or understanding, in us, hereby we can qualify ourselves for, or strive after righteousness and life; but we are evidently the blinded and imprisoned ones of sin and the devil, to do and to think that pleases him and is contrary to God and his commandments."

In these words Dr. Luther of godly and holy memory ascribes no power whatever to our free will to qualify itself for righteousness or strive after it, but says that man is blinded and held captive, to do only the devil's will and that which is contrary to God the Lord. Therefore here there is no co-operation of our will in the conversion of man, and man must be drawn and be born anew of God; otherwise the thought of turning one's self to the Holy Gospel for the purpose of accepting it cannot arise in our hearts. Of this matter Dr. Luther also wrote in his book *De servo Arbitrio, i.e.* Of the Captive Will of Man, in opposition to Erasmus, and well and thoroughly elucidated and supported this position, and afterward in his magnificent exposition of the book of Genesis, especially of chapter 26, he repeated and explained it. He has there also in the best and most careful way guarded against all misunderstanding and perversion, his opinion and understanding of some other peculiar disputations introduced incidentally by Erasmus, as Of Absolute Necessity, etc.; to which we also hereby appeal, and we recommend it to others.

On this account the doctrine is incorrect by which it is asserted that the unregenerate man has still sufficient power to desire to receive the Gospel and to be comforted by it, and that thus the natural human will co-operates in a manner in conversion. For such an erroneous opinion is contrary to the holy, divine Scriptures, the Christian Augsburg Confession, its Apology, the Smalcald Articles, the Large and the Small Catechisms of Luther, and other writings of this excellent highly [divinely] illumined theologian.

This doctrine concerning the inability and wickedness of our natural free will, and concerning our conversion and regeneration, viz. that it is a work of God alone and not of our powers, is impiously abused both by enthusiasts and by Epicureans; and by their speeches many persons have become disorderly and irregular, and in all the Christian exercises of prayer, reading and devout meditation have become idle and indolent, as they say that, because from their own natural powers they are unable to convert themselves to God, they will always strive with all their might against god, or wait until God violently convert them against their will; or because they can do nothing in these spiritual things, but everything is of the operation alone of God the Holy Ghost, they will neither hear nor read the Word nor use the sacrament, but wait until God, without means, infuses from heaven his gifts, so that they can truly, in themselves, feel and perceive that God has converted them.

Other desponding hearts [our godly doctrine concerning the free will not being rightly understood] might perhaps fall into hard thoughts and perilous doubt as whether God have elected them, and through the Holy Ghost will work also in them his gifts, especially when they are sensible of no strong, them his gifts, especially when they are sensible of no strong, burning faith and sincere obedience, but only weakness, fear and misery.

For this reason we will now relate still further from God's Word how man is converted to God, how and through what means (namely, through the oral Word and the holy Sacraments) the Holy Ghost is efficacious in us, and is willing to work and bestow, in our hearts, true repentance, faith and new spiritual power and ability for good, and how we should act ourselves towards these means, and [how] use them.

It is not God's will that any one should perish, but that all men should be converted to him and be saved eternally. (Ez. 33:11): "As I live, I have no pleasure in the death of the wicked; but that the wicked turn from his way and live." (John 3:16): "For God so loved the world that he gave his only-begotten Son, that whosoever believeth in him should not perish, but have everlasting life."

Therefore God, out of his immense goodness and mercy, causes his divine eternal Law and his wonderful plan concerning our redemption, namely, the holy, only saving Gospel of his dear Son, our only Saviour and Redeemer, to be publicly proclaimed; and by this [preaching] collects for himself from the human race an eternal Church, and works in the hearts of men true repentance and knowledge of sins, and true faith in the Son of God, Jesus Christ. And by this means, and in no other way, namely, through his holy Word, when it is heard as preached or is read, and the holy Sacraments when they are used according to the Word, God desires to call men to eternal salvation, to draw them to himself, and to convert, regenerate and sanctify them. (1 Cor. 1:21): "For after that, in the wisdom of God, the world by wisdom knew not God, it pleased God, by the foolishness of preaching, to save them that believe." (Acts 10:5, 6): Peter "shall tell thee what thou oughtest to do." (Rom. 10:17): "Faith cometh by hearing, and hearing by the Word of God." (John 17:17, 20): "Sanctify them by thy truth; thy Word is truth," etc. "Neither pray I for these alone; but for them also which shall believe on me through their word." Therefore the eternal Father calls down from heaven, concerning his dear Son, and concerning all who, in his name, preach repentance and forgiveness of sins: "Hear ye him" (Matt. 17:5).

This preaching [of God's Word] all who wish to be saved ought to hear. For the preaching and hearing of God's Word are instruments of the Holy Ghost, by, with and through which he desires to work efficaciously, and to convert men to God, and to work in them both to will and to do.

This Word man can externally hear and read, even though he be not yet converted to God and regenerate; for in these external things, as above said, man, even since the fall, has, to a certain extent, a free will, so that he can go to church and hear or not hear the sermon.

Through this means, namely, the preaching and hearing of his Word, God works, and breaks our hearts, and draws man, so that through the preaching of the Law he sees his sins and God's wrath, and experiences in his heart true terrors, repentance and sorrow [contrition], and, through

THE FORMULA OF CONCORD (1580) (continued)

the preaching and consideration of the holy Gospel concerning the gracious forgiveness of sins in Christ, a spark of faith is kindled in him, which accepts the forgiveness of sins for Christ's sake, and comforts itself with the promise of the Gospel, and thus the Holy Ghost (who works all this) is given to the heart (Gal. 4:6).

Although now both, viz. the planting and watering of the preacher, and the running and willing of the hearer, would be to no purpose, and no conversion would follow, if the power and efficacy of the Holy Ghost were not added thereto, who, through the Word preached and heard, enlightens and converts the hearts, so that men believe this Word, and assent thereto; nevertheless neither preacher nor hearer should doubt this grace and efficacy of the Holy Ghost, but should be certain, if the Word of God is preached purely and clearly, according to the command and will of God, and men listen attentively and earnestly, and meditate upon it, that God is certainly present with his grace, and grants, as has been said, what man can otherwise from his own powers neither accept nor give. For concerning the presence, operation and gifts of the Holy Ghost we should not and cannot always judge from sense, *i.e.* as to how and when they are experienced in the heart; but because they are often covered and occur in great weakness, we should be certain, from and according to the promise, that preaching and hearing the Word of God is [truly] an office and work of the Holy Ghost, whereby he is certainly efficacious and works in our hearts (2 Cor. 2:14 sqq.) [3:5 sqq.].

But if a man will not hear preaching or read God's Word, but despises the Word and Church of God, and thus dies and perishes in his sins, he neither can console himself with God's eternal election nor obtain his mercy; for Christ, in whom we are chosen, offers to all men his grace in Word and holy sacraments, and wishes earnestly that the Word he heard, and has promised that where two or three are gathered together in his name, and are occupied with his holy Word, he will be in their midst.

But where such a man despises the instrument of the Holy Ghost, and will not hear, no injustice befalls him if the Holy Ghost do not enlighten him, but he be allowed to remain in the darkness of his unbelief, and to perish; for of this it is written (Matt. 23:37): "How often would I have gathered thy children together, even as a hen gathereth her chickens under her wings, and ye would not!"

And in this respect it might well be said that man is not a stone or block. For a stone or block does not resist that which moves it, and does not understand and is not sensible of what is being done with it, as a man, as long as he is not converted, with his will resists God the Lord. And it is nevertheless true that a man before his conversion is still a rational creature, having an understanding and will, yet not an understanding with respect to divine things, or a will to will something good and salutary. Yet he can do nothing whatever for his conversion (as has also been said [frequently] above), and is in this respect much worse than a stone and block; for he resists the Word and will of God, until God awakens him from the death of sin, enlightens and renews him.

And although God does not force man to become godl (for those who always resist the Holy Ghost and persis tently oppose the known truth, as Stephen says of th hardened Jews (Acts 7:51), will not be converted), yet Go the Lord draws the man whom he wishes to convert, an draws him, too, in such a way that his understanding, i place of darkened, becomes enlightened, and his will, i place of perverse, becomes obedient. And the Scripture call this "creating a new heart" (Ps. 51:10).

For this reason it cannot be correctly said that man, befor his conversion, has a certain *modus agendi,* namely, a wa of working in divine things something good and salutary For inasmuch as man, before his conversion, is dead in sin (Eph. 2:5), there can be in him no power to work anythin good in divine things, and therefore he has also no *modu agendi,* or way of working in divine things. But when declaration is made concerning this matter as to how Go works in man, God has nevertheless a *modus agendi,* o way of working in a man, as in a rational creature, quit different from his way of working in another creature tha is irrational, or in a stone and block. Nevertheless to man before his conversion, a *modus agendi,* or any way o working something good in spiritual things, cannot b ascribed.

But when man is converted, and is thus enlightened, an his will is renewed, man (so far as he is regenerate or is new man) wills what is good, and "delights in the Law o God after the inward man" (Rom. 7:22), and henceforth does good to such an extent and as long as he is impelle by God's Spirit, as Paul says (Rom. 8:14): "For as many a are led by the Spirit of God, they are the sons of God. And this impulse of the Holy Ghost is not a *coactio* o coercion, but the converted man does good spontaneously as David says (Ps. 110:4): "Thy people shall be willing i the day of thy power." And nevertheless that [the strife o the flesh and spirit] also remains in the regenerate, o which St. Paul wrote (Rom. 7:22 sq.): "For I delight in th Law of God after the inward man: but I see another law i my members, warring against the law of my mind, an bringing me into captivity to the law of sin which is in m members." Also (v. 25): "So then with my mind I mysel serve the Law of God; but with the flesh the law of sin. Also (Gal. 5:17): "For the flesh lusteth against the spirit and the spirit against the flesh; and these are contrary th one to the other; so that ye cannot do the things that y would."

From this, then, it follows that as soon as the Holy Ghost as has been said, through the Word and holy Sacraments has begun in us this his work of regeneration and renewal it is certain that, through the power of the Holy Ghost, w can and should co-operate, although still in grea weakness. But this does not occur from our fleshly natura powers, but from the new powers and gifts which the Hol Ghost has begun in us in conversion, as St. Paul expressl and earnestly exhorts that "as workers together" w "receive not the grace of God in vain" (2 Cor. 6:1). This then, is nothing else, and should thus be understood, tha that the converted man does good to such an extent and s long as God, by his Holy Spirit, rules, guides and lead him, and that as soon as God would withdraw from hir his gracious hand, he could not continue for a moment i obedience to God. But if this would be understood thus [if any one would take the expression of St. Paul in this sense], that the converted man co-works with the Holy Ghost, in the manner that two horses together draw a wagon, this can in no way be conceded without prejudice to the divine truth.

[(2 Cor. 6:1): We who are servants or co-workers with God beseech you who are "God's husbandry" and "God's building" (1 Cor. 3:9) to imitate our example, that the grace of God may not be among you in vain (1 Cor. 15:10), but that ye may be the temple of God, living and dwelling in you (2 Cor. 6:16)].

Therefore there is a great difference between baptized and unbaptized men. For since, according to the doctrine of St. Paul (Gal. 3:27), all who have been baptized have put on Christ, and thus are truly regenerate, they have now a liberated will, *i.e.* as Christ says they have been made free again (John 8:36); for this reason they afterward not only hear the Word, but also, although in great weakness, are able to assent to it and accept it.

For since we, in this life, receive only the first-fruits of the Spirit, and the new birth is not complete, but only begun in us, the combat and struggle of the flesh against the spirit remains even in the elect and truly regenerate man, in which there is a great difference perceptible not only among Christians, in that one is weak and another strong in the spirit, but also every Christian experiences in himself that at one time he is joyful in spirit, and at another fearful and alarmed; at one time ardent in love, strong in faith and hope, and at another cold and weak.

But when the baptized have acted against conscience, allowed sin to prevail in them, and thus have grieved and lost the Holy Ghost in them, they need not be rebaptized, but must again be converted, as has been sufficiently said before.

For it is once for all true that in genuine conversion a change, new emotion [renewal] and movement in understanding, will and heart must occur, namely, that the heart perceive sin, dread God's wrath, turn itself from sin, perceive and accept the promise of grace in Christ, have good spiritual thoughts, a Christian purpose and diligence, and strive against the flesh. For where none of these occurs or is present there is also no true conversion. But since the question is concerning the efficient cause, *i.e.* who works this in us, and whence man has this, and how he attains it, this doctrine is thus stated: Because the natural powers of man cannot act or help thereto (1 Cor. 2:14; 2 Cor. 3:5), God, out of his infinite goodness and mercy, comes first to us, and causes his holy Gospel to be preached, whereby the Holy Ghost desires to work and accomplish in us this conversion and renewal, and through preaching and meditation upon his Word kindles in us faith and other divine virtues, so that they are gifts and operations of the Holy Ghost alone. This doctrine also directs us to the means whereby the Holy Ghost desires to begin and work this [which we have mentioned], instructs us how those gifts are preserved, strengthened and increased, and admonishes us that we should not receive this grace of God in vain, but diligently ponder how grievous a sin it is to hinder and resist such operations of the Holy Ghost.

From this thorough explanation of the entire doctrine concerning the free will we can now judge also with respect to the last of the questions upon which, for quite a number of years, there has been controversy in the churches of the Augsburg Confession: (Whether man before, in or after his conversion resists the Holy Ghost, or does nothing whatever, but only suffers what God works in him [or is purely passive]? Whether in conversion man is like a block? Whether the Holy Ghost is given to those who resist him? Whether conversion occur by coercion, so that God coerces men to conversion against their wills?), and the opposite dogmas and errors are seen, exposed, censured and rejected, namely:

1. First, the folly of the Stoics and Manichaeans, [who asserted] that everything that happens must so happen, and that man does everything from coercion, and that even in outward things the will of man has no freedom or ability to afford to a certain extent external righteousness and respectable deportment, and to avoid external sins and vices, or that the will of man is coerced to external wicked deeds, inchastity, robbery and murder, etc.

2. Secondly, the gross error of the Pelagians, that the free will, from its own natural powers and without the Holy Ghost, can turn itself to God, believe the Gospel, and be obedient in heart to God's Law, and by this, its voluntary obedience, can merit the forgiveness of sins and eternal life.

3. Thirdly, the error of the Papists and scholastics, who have presented it in a somewhat more subtle form, and have taught that man from his own natural powers can make a beginning of doing good and of his own conversion, and that then the Holy Ghost, because man is too weak to bring it to completion, comes to the aid of the good that has been begun from his own natural powers.

4. Fourthly, the doctrine of the Synergists, who pretend that man is not absolutely dead to good in spiritual things, but is badly wounded and half dead. Therefore, although the free will is too weak to make a beginning, and by its own powers to convert itself to God, and to be obedient in heart to God's Law; nevertheless when the Holy Ghost makes a beginning, and calls us through the Gospel, and offers his grace, the forgiveness of sins and eternal salvation, that then the free will, from its own natural powers, meets God, and to a certain extent, although feebly, can act, help and co-operate thereto, can qualify itself for, and apply itself to grace, and embrace and accept it, and believe the Gospel, and also, in the progress and support of this work, it can co-operate, by its own powers, with the Holy Ghost.

   But, on the contrary, it has above been shown at length that such power, namely, the *facultas applicandi se ad gratiam, i.e.* to qualify one's self from nature for grace, does not proceed from our own natural powers, but alone from the operation of the Holy Ghost.

5. Also the following doctrine of the popes and monks, that, since regeneration, man, in this life, can

completely fulfil the Law of God, and through the fulfilment of the Law be righteous before God and merit eternal life.

6. On the other hand, the enthusiasts should be rebuked with great severity and zeal, and should in no way be tolerated in the Church of God, who fabricate that God, without any means, without the hearing of the divine Word, and without the use of the holy Sacraments, draws man to himself, and enlightens, justifies and saves him.

7. Also those who fabricate that in conversion and regeneration God so creates a new heart and new man that the substance and essence of the old Adam, and especially the rational soul, are altogether annihilated, and a new essence of the soul is created out of nothing. This error St. Augustine expressly rebukes on Psalm 25, where he quotes the passage from Paul (Eph. 4:22): "Put off the old man," etc., and explains it in the following words: "That no one may think that some substance is to be laid aside, he has explained what it is to lay aside the old man, and to put on the new, when he says in the succeeding words: 'Putting away lying, speak the truth.' So that is to put off the old man and to put on the new."

8. Also if the following expressions be used without being explained, viz. that the will of man, before, in, and after conversion, resists the Holy Ghost, and that the Holy Ghost is given to those who resist him.

For from the preceding explanation it is manifest that where no change whatever occurs through the Holy Ghost to that which is good in understanding, heart and will, and man does not at all believe the promise, and is not rendered fit by God for grace, but entirely resists the Word, there no conversion has occurred or can exist. For conversion is such a change through the operation of the Holy Ghost, in the understanding, will and heart of man, that, by this operation of the Holy Ghost, man can receive the offered grace. And indeed all those who obstinately and persistently resist the operations and movements of the Holy Ghost, which take place through the Word, do not receive, but grieve and lose the Holy Ghost.

There remains, nevertheless, also in the regenerate a refractoriness of which the Scriptures speak, namely, that "the flesh lusteth against the spirit" (Gal. 5:17), that "fleshly lusts war against the soul" (1 Pet. 2:11), and that "the law in the members wars against the law of the mind" (Rom. 7:23).

Therefore the man who is not regenerate wholly resists God, and is altogether a servant of sin (John 8:34; Rom. 6:16). But the regenerate delights in the Law of God after the inward man, but nevertheless sees in his members the law of sin, which wars against the law of the mind; on this account, with his mind, he serves the Law of God, but, with the flesh, the law of sin (Rom. 7:25). In this way the correct opinion can and should be thoroughly, clearly and discreetly explained and taught.

As to the expressions of Chrysostom and Basil: *Trahit Deus, sed volentem trahit; tantum velis, et Deus praeoccur-*

rit, and also the expression of the scholastics [and Papists], *Hominis voluntas in conversione non est otiosa, sed agit aliquid, i.e.* "God draws, but he draws the willing," and "In conversion the will of man is not idle, but effects something," (expressions which have been introduced for confirming the natural free will in man's conversion, against the doctrine concerning God's grace), from the explanation heretofore presented it is manifest that they are not in harmony with the form of sound doctrine, but are contrary to it, and therefore when we speak of conversion to God should be avoided.

For the conversion of our corrupt will, which is nothing else than a resuscitation of it from spiritual death, is only and alone a work of God, just as also the resuscitation in the resurrection of the body should be ascribed to God alone, as has been above fully set forth and proved by manifest testimonies of Holy Scripture.

But how in conversion, through the drawing of the Holy Ghost, God changes stubborn and unwilling into willing men, and that after such conversion, in the daily exercise of repentance, the regenerate will of man is not idle, but also co-operates in all the deeds of the Holy Ghost, which he works through us, has already been sufficiently explained above.

So also when Luther says that with respect to his conversion man is purely passive, *i.e.* does nothing whatever thereto, but only suffers what God works in him, his meaning is not that conversion occurs without the preaching and hearing of God's Word; his meaning also is not that in conversion no new emotion is awakened in us by the Holy Ghost, and no spiritual operation begun; but he means that man of himself, or from his natural powers, cannot contribute anything or help to his conversion, and that conversion is not only in part, but altogether an operation, gift and present and work of the Holy Ghost alone, who accomplishes and effects it, by his virtue and power, through the Word, in the understanding, will and heart of man, *tanquam in subjecto patiente, i.e.* where man does or works nothing, but only suffers. Not as a statue is cut in a stone or a seal impressed into wax, which knows nothing of it, and also perceives and wills nothing of it, but in the way which is above narrated and explained.

Because also the youth in the schools have been greatly perplexed by the doctrine of the three efficient causes concurring in the conversion to God of the unregenerate man, as to the manner in which they, namely, the Word of God preached and heard, the Holy Ghost and the will of man concur; it is again manifest from the explanation above presented that conversion to God is a work of God the Holy Ghost alone, who is the true master-workman that alone works this in us, for which he uses the preaching and hearing of his Holy Word as his ordinary [and lawful] means and instrument. But the understanding and will of the unregenerate man are nothing else than the *subjectum convertendum, i.e.* that which is to be converted, as the understanding and will of a spiritually dead man, in whom the Holy Ghost works conversion and renewal, for which work the will of the man who is to be converted does nothing, but only lets God work in him, until he is regenerate; and then also by the Holy Ghost he works [co-operates] in other succeeding good works that which is pleasing to God, in the way and to the extent fully set forth above.

CHAPTER III. OF THE RIGHTEOUSNESS OF FAITH BEFORE GOD.

The third dissent has arisen among some theologians of the Augsburg Confession concerning the righteousness of Christ or of faith, which, out of grace, is imputed by God, through faith, to poor sinners for righteousness.

For one side has contended that the righteousness of faith, which the apostle calls the righteousness of God, is God's essential righteousness, which is Christ himself as the true, natural and essential Son of God, who, by faith, dwells in the elect and impels them to do right, and who thus is their righteousness, compared with which righteousness the sins of all men are as a drop of water compared with the great ocean.

On the contrary, others have held and taught that Christ is our righteousness, alone according to his human nature.

In opposition to both these sides, it is unanimously taught by the other teachers of the Augsburg Confession that Christ is our righteousness, not alone according to his divine nature, nor also alone according to his human nature, but according to both natures, who as God and man has, through his complete obedience, redeemed, justified and saved us from our sins; that therefore the righteousness of faith is the forgiveness of sins, reconciliation with God, and our acceptance as God's children on account of the obedience only of Christ, which alone through faith, out of pure grace, is imputed for righteousness to all true believers, and on account of it they are absolved from all their unrighteousness.

Besides this [controversy] there are on account of the Interim [by occasion of the formula of the Interim or of Inter-religion], and otherwise, still other disputes caused and excited concerning the article Of Justification, which will hereafter be explained in the antithesis, *i.e.* in the enumeration of those errors which are contrary to the pure doctrine in this article.

This article concerning Justification by Faith (as the Apology says) is the chief in the entire Christian doctrine, without which no poor conscience has any firm consolation, or can know aright the riches of the grace of Christ, as Dr. Luther also has written: "If only this article remain in view pure, the Christian Church also remains pure, and is harmonious and without all sects; but if it do not remain pure, it is not possible to resist any error or fanatical spirit" (Tom. 5, Jena Ed., p. 159). And concerning this article Paul especially says that "a little leaven leaveneth the whole lump." Therefore, in this article he emphasizes with so much zeal and earnestness the exclusive particles, or the words whereby the works of men are excluded (namely, "without Law," "without works," "out of grace" ["freely," Rom. 3:28; 4:5; Eph. 2:8, 9]), in order to indicate how highly necessary it is that in this article, by the side of the presentation of the pure doctrine, the antithesis, *i.e.* all contrary dogmas, by this means be separated, exposed and rejected.

Therefore, in order that this dissent may be explained in a Christian way according to God's Word, and, by his grace, be settled, our doctrine, faith and confession are as follows:

Concerning the righteousness of faith before God we unanimously believe, teach and confess, according to the comprehensive summary of our faith and confession above presented, viz. that a poor sinful man is justified before God, *i.e.* absolved and declared free and exempt from all his sins, and from the sentence of well-deserved condemnation, and adopted into sonship and heirship of eternal life, without any merit or worth of his own, also without all preceding, present or subsequent works, out of pure grace, alone because of the sole merit, complete obedience, bitter suffering, death and resurrection of our Lord Christ, whose obedience is reckoned to us for righteousness.

These treasures are offered us by the Holy Ghost in the promise of the holy Gospel; and faith alone is the only means whereby we lay hold upon, accept and apply and appropriate them to ourselves. This faith is a gift of God, whereby we apprehend aright Christ our Redeemer in the Word of the Gospel, and trust in him, that for the sake of his obedience alone, out of grace, we have the forgiveness of sins, and before God the Father are regarded godly and righteous, and are eternally saved. Therefore the expressions of Paul, that we are "justified by faith" (Rom. 3:28), or that "faith is counted for righteousness" (Rom. 4:5), and that we are "made righteous by the obedience of one" (Rom. 5:19), or that "by the righteousness of one justification of faith came to all men" (Rom. 5:18), are regarded and received as equivalents. For faith justifies, not because it is so good a work and so fair a virtue, but because, in the promise of the Gospel, it lays hold of and accepts the merit of Christ; for if we are to be justified thereby, this must be applied and appropriated by faith. Therefore the righteousness which, out of pure grace, is imputed to faith or the believer, is the obedience, suffering and resurrection of Christ, by which he has made satisfaction for us to the Law, and paid the price of our sins. For since Christ is not alone man, but God and man in one undivided person, he was as little subject to the Law, because he is the Lord of the Law, as, in his own person, to suffering and death. Therefore his obedience not only in suffering and dying, but also that he in our stead was voluntarily subject to the Law, and fulfilled it by his obedience, is imputed to us for righteousness, so that, on account of this complete obedience, which by deed and by suffering, in life and in death, he rendered his heavenly Father for us, God forgives our sins, regards us godly and righteous, and eternally saves us. This righteousness is offered us by the Holy Ghost through the Gospel and in the sacraments, and is applied, appropriated and received through faith, whence believers have reconciliation with God, forgiveness of sins, the grace of God, sonship and heirship of eternal life.

Accordingly, the word *justify* here means to declare righteous and free from sins, and, for the sake of Christ's righteousness, which is imputed by God to faith (Phil. 3:9), to absolve one from their eternal punishment. For this use and understanding of this word is common in the Holy Scriptures of the Old and the New Testament. (Prov. 17:15): "He that justifieth the wicked, and he that

THE FORMULA OF CONCORD (1580) (continued)

condemneth the just, even they both are abomination to the Lord." (Isa. 5:23): "Woe unto them which justify the wicked for reward, and take away the righteousness of the righteous from him!" (Rom. 8:33): "Who shall lay anything to the charge of God's elect? It is God that justifieth,"*i.e.* absolves from sins, and declares exempt.

But because sometimes the word "regeneration" is employed for the word "justification," it is necessary that this word be properly explained, in order that the renewal which follows the justification of faith may not be confounded with the justification of faith, but they may be properly distinguished from one another.

For, in the first place, the word "regeneration" is employed so as to comprise at the same time the forgiveness of sins alone for Christ's sake, and the succeeding renewal which the Holy Ghost works in those who are justified by faith. Again, it is restricted to the remission of sins and adoption as sons of God. And in this latter sense the word is much and often used in the Apology, where it is written: "Justification is regeneration," although St. Paul has fixed a distinction between these words (Tit. 3:5): "He saved us by the washing of regeneration and renewal of the Holy Ghost." As also the word "vivification" has sometimes been used in a like sense. For if a man is justified through faith (which the Holy Ghost alone works), this is truly a regeneration, because from a child of wrath he becomes a child of God, and thus is transferred from death to life, as it is written (Eph. 2:5): "When we were dead in sins, he hath quickened us together with Christ." Also: "The just shall live by faith" (Rom. 1:17 [Heb. 2:4]). In this sense the word is much and often used in the Apology.

But again, it is often taken for sanctification and renewal, which succeed the righteousness of faith, as Dr. Luther has thus used it in his book concerning the Church and the Councils, and elsewhere.

But when we teach that through the operation of the Holy Ghost we are born anew and justified, the sense is not that after regeneration no unrighteousness clings any more, in being and life, to the justified and regenerate, but that Christ, with his complete obedience, covers all their sins, which still in this life inhere in their nature. But without regard to this, through faith and for the sake of Christ's obedience (which Christ rendered the Father for us from his birth to his most ignominious death upon the cross), they are declared and regarded godly and righteous, although, on account of their corrupt nature, they are still sinners, and so remain to the grave [while they bear about this mortal body]. But, on the other hand, the meaning is not that we dare or should, without repentance, conversion and renewal, obey sins, and remain and continue in them.

For true [and not feigned] contrition must precede; and to those who thus, as has been said, out of pure grace, for the sake of Christ the only Mediator, without all works and merit, are righteous before God, *i.e.* are received into grace, the Holy Ghost is also given, who renews and sanctifies them, and works in them love to God and to their neighbor. But since the incipient renewal is in this life

imperfect, and sins still dwell in the flesh, even in the regenerate, the righteousness of faith before God consists in the gracious imputation of the righteousness of Christ, without the addition of our works, so that our sins are forgiven us, and covered and not imputed (Rom. 4:6 sqq.).

But here with special diligence the greatest attention must afterwards be given, if the article of justification is to remain pure, that not that which precedes faith and that which succeeds it be mingled together or inserted as necessary and belonging to it, because to speak of conversion and to speak of justification are not one and the same thing.

For not everything that belongs to conversion belongs likewise to the article of justification, in and to which only the following belong and are necessary: the grace of God, the merit of Christ, and faith which receives this in the promise of the Gospel, whereby the righteousness of Christ is imputed to us, whence we receive and have forgiveness of sins, reconciliation with God, sonship and heirship of eternal life.

Therefore true, saving faith is not in those who are without contrition and sorrow, and who have a wicked purpose to remain and persevere in sins; but true contrition precedes, and genuine faith is in or with true repentance [justifying faith is in those who repent truly, not feignedly].

Love is also a fruit which surely and necessarily follows true faith. For that one does not love is a sure indication that he is not justified, but is still in death, or has lost again the righteousness of faith, as John says (1 John 3:14). But when Paul says (Rom. 3:28): "We are justified by faith without works," he indicates thereby that neither the contrition that precedes nor the works that follow belong to the article or transaction of justification by faith. For good works do not precede justification, but follow it, and the person must be justified before he can do a good work.

In like manner also, although the renewal or sanctification is also a benefit of Christ the Mediator and a work of the Holy Ghost, it does not belong to the article or transaction of justification before God, but follows the same, since, on account of our corrupt flesh, it is not, in this life, entirely perfect and complete, as Dr. Luther has written well concerning this in his excellent and extended exposition of the Epistle to the Galatians, in which he says as follows: "We concede indeed that instruction should be given also concerning love and good works, yet in such a way that this be done when and where it is necessary, as, namely, when we have to do with works over and beyond this matter of justification. But here the chief point with which we have to do is this, that the question is not whether we should also do and love good works, but by what means we may be justified before God, and saved. And here we answer with St. Paul: that we are justified alone by faith in Christ, and not by the deeds of the Law or love. Not that we hereby entirely reject works and love, as the adversaries falsely defame and accuse us, but that we dare not allow ourselves to be led away, as Satan would desire, from the chief point with which we have here to do, to another and foreign transaction which does not belong whatever to this question. Therefore, whereas, and as long as, we have to do with this article of justification we reject and condemn works, since this article can admit of no disputation or treatment whatever of the subject of works; therefore in this matter we absolutely sever all Law and works of the Law." So far Luther.

In order, therefore, that troubled hearts may have a firm, sure consolation, and also that due honor be accorded the merit of Christ and the grace of God, the Scriptures teach that the righteousness of faith before God consists alone in the gracious [gratuitous] reconciliation or the forgiveness of sins, which is presented to us out of pure grace, for the sake of the merit alone of Christ as Mediator, and is received alone through faith in the promise of the Gospel. Therefore, in justification before God, faith relies neither upon contrition nor upon love or other virtues, but alone upon Christ, and in him upon his complete obedience, whereby for us he has fulfilled the Law, which [obedience] is imputed to believers for righteousness.

It is also neither contrition nor love or any other virtue, but faith alone, which is the sole means and instrument whereby we can receive and accept the grace of God, the merit of Christ, and the forgiveness of sins, which are offered us in the promise of the Gospel.

It is also correctly said that believers who through faith in Christ are justified, in this life have first the imputed righteousness of faith, and afterwards also the incipient righteousness of the new obedience or good works. But these two must not be confounded or inserted at the same time into the article of justification by faith before God. For since this incipient righteousness or renewal is incomplete and imperfect in us in this life because of the flesh, the person cannot stand therewith and thereby before God's tribunal, but before God's tribunal only the righteousness of the obedience, suffering and death of Christ, which is imputed to faith, can stand, namely, that only for the sake of this obedience the person (even after his renewal, when he has already many good works and is in the best life) is pleasing and acceptable to God, and is received into adoption and heirship of eternal life.

Here belongs also what St. Paul writes (Rom. 4:3), that Abraham was justified before God alone through faith, for the sake of the Mediator, without the co-operation of his works, not only when he was first converted from idolatry and had no good works, but also when he was afterwards renewed by the Holy Ghost, and adorned with many excellent good works (Gen. 15:6; Heb. 11:8). And Paul puts the following question (Rom. 4:1 sqq.): In what, then, did the righteousness, for everlasting life, of Abraham before God, whereby God was gracious to him, and he was pleasing and acceptable to God, consist?

Thereupon he answers: "To him who worketh not, but believeth on him that justifieth the ungodly, his faith is counted for righteousness;" as David also (Ps. 32:1) speaks of the blessedness of the man to whom God imputes righteousness without works.

Therefore, even though the converted and believing have incipient renewal, sanctification, love, virtue and good works, yet these neither can nor should be introduced into or confounded with the article of justification before God, in order that that honor which belongs to him may remain with Christ the Redeemer, and since our new obedience is incomplete and imperfect, tempted consciences may have sure consolation.

And this is the intention of the apostle Paul when in this article he so diligently and earnestly emphasizes the exclusive particles, i.e. the words whereby works are excluded from the article of justification: absque operibus, sine lege, gratis, non ex operibus, i.e. "of grace," "without merit," "without works," "not of works." These exclusive particles are all comprised in the expression: "By faith alone in Christ we are justified before God and saved." For thereby works are excluded, not in the sense that a true faith can exist without contrition, or that good works should, must and dare not follow true faith as sure and indubitable fruits, or that believers neither dare nor must do anything good; but that good works are excluded from the article of justification before God, so that in the transaction of the justification of the poor sinner before God they should not be introduced, inserted, or intermingled as necessary or belonging thereto. The true sense of the exclusive particles in the article of justification is this, which should, with all diligence and earnestness, be urged in this article:

1. That thereby [through these particles] all our own works, merit, worth, glory and confidence in all our works in the article of justification be entirely excluded, so that our works be neither constituted nor regarded, either entirely or in half or in the least part, as the cause or merit of justification, upon which God in this article and transaction looks, or we could or should rely.

2. That this office and property abides with faith alone, that it alone, and nothing else whatever, is the means or instrument by and through which God's grace and the merit of Christ are, in the promise of the Gospel, received, apprehended, accepted, applied to us, and appropriated; and that from this office and property of such application or appropriation, love and all other virtues or works are excluded.

3. That neither renewal, sanctification, virtues nor good works be constituted and appointed tanquam forma aut pars aut causa justificationis, i.e. our righteousness before God, or a part or cause of our righteousness, or should otherwise be intermingled under any pretext, title or name whatever in the article of justification as necessary and belonging thereto; but that the righteousness of faith consists alone in the forgiveness of sins out of pure grace, alone for the sake of Christ's merit; which blessings are offered us in the promise of the Gospel, and are received, accepted, applied and appropriated alone by faith.

Therefore the true order between faith and good works, and also between justification and renewal or sanctification, must abide and be maintained.

For good works do not precede faith, neither does sanctification precede justification. But in conversion, first faith is kindled in us by the Holy Ghost from the hearing of the Gospel. It lays hold of God's grace in Christ, whereby the person is justified. Then, when the person is justified, he is renewed and sanctified by the Holy Ghost,

THE FORMULA OF CONCORD (1580) (continued)

from which renewal and sanctification the fruits of good works then follow. This should not be understood as though justification and renewal were sundered from one another, in such a manner that a genuine faith sometimes could exist and continue for a long time, together with a wicked intention, but hereby only the order [of causes and effects, of antecedents and consequents] is indicated, as to how one precedes or succeeds the other. For that nevertheless remains true which Luther has correctly said: "Faith and good works [well] agree and fit [are inseparably connected]; but it is faith alone, without works, which lays hold of the blessing; and yet it is never and at no time alone." This has been set forth above.

Many disputations also are usefully and well explained by means of this true distinction, of which the Apology treats in reference to the passage (James 2:20). For when the subject is concerning how faith justifies, the doctrine of St. Paul is that faith alone, without works, justifies (Rom. 3:28), since, as has been said, it applies and appropriates the merit of Christ. But if the question be: Wherein and whereby a Christian can perceive and distinguish, either in himself or in another, a true living faith from a feigned and dead faith, since many idle, secure Christians imagine for themselves a delusion in place of faith, while they nevertheless have no true faith? the Apology gives this answer: "James calls that dead faith where every kind of good works and fruits of the Spirit do not follow." And to this effect the Latin edition of the Apology says: "James is right in denying that we are justified by such faith as is without works, *i.e.* which is dead."

But James speaks, as the Apology says, concerning the works of those who, through Christ, have already been justified, reconciled with God, and obtained forgiveness of sins. But if the question be asked, Whereby and whence faith has this, and what appertains to its justifying and saving? it is false and incorrect to say: that faith cannot justify without works; or that faith justifies or makes righteous, so far as it has love with it, for the sake of which love this is ascribed to faith [it has love with it, by which it is formed]; or that the presence of works with faith is necessary if man is to be justified thereby before God; or that the presence of good works in the article of justification, or for justification, is needful; likewise that the good works are a cause without which man cannot be justified, and that they are not excluded from the article of justification by the exclusive particles, as when St. Paul says: "Without works," etc. For faith makes righteous alone in that, as a means and instrument, it lays hold of and accepts, in the promise of the Gospel, the grace of God and the merit of Christ.

Let this suffice, according to the plan of this document, as a compendious setting forth of the doctrine of justification by faith, which is treated more at length in the above-mentioned writings. From these, the antitheses also, i.e. the false contrary dogmas, are easily understood, namely, that in addition to the errors recounted above, the following and the like, which conflict with the explanation now published, must be censured, exposed and rejected, as when it is taught:

1. That our love or good works are merit or cause, either entirely or even in part, of justification before God.

2. Or that by good works man must render himself worthy and fit that the merit of Christ be imparted to him.

3. Or that our formal righteousness before God is our inherent newness or love, i.e. that our real righteousness before God is the love or renewal which the Holy Ghost works in us and is in us.

4. Or that the righteousness of faith before God consists of two parts, namely, the gracious forgiveness of sins, and then, secondly, also renewal or sanctification.

5. That faith justifies only initially, or partially, or primarily, and that our newness or love justifies even before God, either completively or secondarily.

6. Also that believers are justified before God, or are righteous before God, at the same time both by imputation and by beginning, or partly by the imputation of Christ's righteousness, and partly by the beginning of new obedience.

7. Also that the application of the promise of grace occurs both by faith of the heart and confession of the mouth, and by other virtues. That is: Faith alone makes righteous, for the reason that righteousness by faith is begun in us, or that in justification faith has the pre-eminence; nevertheless, the renewal and love belong also to our righteousness before God, yet in such a way that it is not the chief cause of our righteousness, but that our righteousness before God is not entire and complete without such love and renewal. Also that believers are justified and righteous before God, at the same time, by the imputed righteousness of Christ and the incipient new obedience, or in part by the imputation of Christ's righteousness and in part by the incipient new obedience. Also that the promise of grace is appropriated by us, by faith in the heart, and confession which is made with the mouth, and by other virtues.

It is also incorrect to teach that man must be saved in some other way, or through something else, than as he is justified before God; so that while we are justified before God by faith alone, without works, yet without works it is impossible to be saved or obtain salvation.

This is false, for the reason that it is directly contrary to the declaration of Paul (Rom. 4:6): "The blessedness of the man unto whom God imputeth righteousness without works." And the basis of Paul's argument is that we obtain salvation just in the same way as righteousness; yea, that precisely by this means, when we are justified by faith, we receive adoption and heirship of eternal life and salvation; and, on this account, Paul employs and emphasizes the exclusive particles, i.e. those words whereby works and our own merits are entirely excluded, namely, "out of grace," "without works," as forcibly in the article concerning salvation as in the article concerning righteousness.

Likewise also the disputation concerning the indwelling in us of the essential righteousness of God must be correctly explained. For although, by faith, in the elect, who are justified by Christ and reconciled with God, God the Father, Son and Holy Ghost, who is eternal and essential righteousness, dwells (for all Christians are temples of God the Father, Son and Holy Ghost, who also impels them to do right); yet this indwelling of God is not the righteousness of faith, of which St. Paul treats and which he calls the righteousness of God, for the sake of which we are declared righteous before God; but it follows the preceding righteousness of faith, which is nothing else than the forgiveness of sins and the gracious acceptance of the poor sinner, alone for the sake of Christ's obedience and merit.

Therefore, since in our churches it is acknowledged [established beyond controversy] among the theologians of the Augsburg Confession that all our righteousness is to be sought outside of ourselves and the merits, works, virtues and worthiness of all men, and rests alone upon Christ the Lord; yet it is well to consider in what respect Christ is called, in this matter of justification, our righteousness, namely, that our righteousness rests not upon one or the other nature, but upon the entire person of Christ, who as God and man is our righteousness in his sole, entire and complete obedience.

For even though Christ had been conceived without sin by the Holy Ghost, and thus been born, and in his human nature alone would have fulfilled all righteousness, and yet would have not been true and eternal God, this obedience and suffering of his human nature could not have been imputed to us for righteousness. As also, if the Son of God had not become man the divine nature alone could not have been our righteousness. Therefore we believe, teach and confess that the entire obedience of the entire person of Christ, which he has rendered the Father for us, even to his most ignominious death upon the cross, is imputed for righteousness. For the human nature alone, without the divine, could neither by obedience nor suffering render satisfaction to eternal almighty God for the sins of all the world; and the divinity alone without the humanity could not mediate between God and us.

But because, as above mentioned, the obedience is [not only of one nature, but] of the entire person, it is a complete satisfaction and expiation for the human race, whereby the eternal, immutable righteousness of God, revealed in the Law, is satisfied, and is thus our righteousness, which avails before God and is revealed in the Gospel, and upon which faith before God relies, which God imputes to faith, as it is written (Rom. 5:19): "For as by one man's disobedience many were made sinners, so by the obedience of one shall many be made righteous." (1 John 1:7): "The blood of Jesus Christ, the Son of God, cleanseth us from all sins." Also: "The just shall live by his faith" (Hab. 2:4 [Rom. 1:17]).

Thus neither the divine nor the human nature of Christ is of itself imputed for righteousness, but only the obedience of the person who is at the same time God and man. And faith thus regards the person of Christ, who was made subject to the Law for us, bore our sins, and in his going to the Father offered to his Heavenly Father for us poor sinners his entire, complete obedience, from his holy birth even unto death, and who has thereby covered all our

disobedience which inheres in our nature, and its thoughts, words and works, so that it is not imputed to us for condemnation, but out of pure grace, alone for Christ's sake, is pardoned and forgiven.

Therefore we reject and unanimously condemn, besides the above-mentioned, also the following and all similar errors, as contrary to God's Word, the doctrine of the prophets and apostles, and our Christian faith:

1. When it is taught that Christ is our righteousness before God, alone according to his divine nature.

2. That Christ is our righteousness, alone according to his human nature.

3. That in the expressions of the prophets and apostles, when the righteousness of faith is spoken of, the words "justify" and "be justified" do not signify to declare free from sins and obtain the forgiveness of sins, but in deed and truth to be made righteous, because of love infused by the Holy Ghost, virtues and the works following thence.

4. That faith looks not only to the obedience of Christ, but to his divine nature, as it dwells and works in us, and that by this indwelling our sins are covered before God.

5. That faith is such a trust in the obedience of Christ as can be and remain in a man who has no genuine repentance, in whom also no love follows, but he persists in sins against conscience.

6. That not God, but only the gifts of God, dwell in the believer.

These errors and the like, one and all, we unanimously reject as contrary to the clear Word of God, and, by God's grace, we abide firmly and constantly in the doctrine of the righteousness of faith before God, as in the Augsburg Confession and the Apology which follows it is presented, developed and proved from God's Word.

Concerning what besides is needful for the real explanation of this sublime and chief article of justification before God, upon which rests the salvation of our souls, we will direct every one to the excellent and magnificent exposition by Dr. Luther of the Epistle of St. Paul to the Galatians, and for the sake of brevity to it we hereby refer.

CHAPTER IV. OF GOOD WORKS.

A disagreement has occurred among the theologians of the Augsburg Confession also concerning good works. For a part are accustomed to speak in the following words and manner: "Good works are necessary for salvation;" "It is impossible to be saved without good works;" "No one can be saved without good works;" because by the rightly believing good works are required as fruits of faith, and faith without love is dead, although such love is no cause of salvation.

But the other side, on the contrary, have contended that good works are indeed necessary; not for salvation, but for other reasons; and that, on this account, the preceding propositions or expressions used (as they are not in accord with the form of sound doctrine and with the Word, and have been always and are still set over against our Christian faith by the Papists, in which we confess "that

THE FORMULA OF CONCORD (1580) (continued)

faith alone justifies and saves") are not to be tolerated in the Church, in order that the merit of Christ our Saviour be not diminished, and the promise of salvation may be and remain firm and certain to believers.

In this controversy also the following controverted proposition or expression was introduced by some few, viz. "that good works are injurious to salvation." It has also been disputed by some that good works are not "necessary," but are "voluntary" [free and spontaneous], because they are not extorted by fear and the penalty of the Law, but are to be done from a voluntary spirit and a joyful heart. On the contrary, the other side contend "that good works are necessary."

This latter controversy was originally introduced with respect to the words "necessity" and "liberty," because especially the word "necessity" signifies not only the eternal, immutable order according to which all men are indebted and obliged to obey God, but also sometimes a coercion, whereby the Law forces men to good works.

But afterwards there was a disputation not alone concerning the words, but, in the most violent manner, the doctrine itself was called into question, and it was contended that the new obedience in the regenerate, in accordance with the above-mentioned divine order, is not necessary.

In order to explain this disagreement in a Christian way and according to the guidance of God's Word, our doctrine, faith and confession are as follows:

First, there is no controversy among our theologians concerning the following points in this article, namely: that it is God's will, regulation and command that believers should walk in good works; and that truly good works are not those which every one, with a good intention, himself contrives, or which are done according to human ordinances, but those which God himself has prescribed and commanded in his Word. Also, that truly good works are done, not from our own natural powers, but when by faith the person is reconciled with God and renewed by the Holy Ghost, or (as Paul says) "created anew in Christ Jesus to good works" (Eph. 2:10).

There is also no controversy as to how and for what reason the good works of believers, although, in this flesh, they are impure and incomplete, please God and are acceptable, namely, for the sake of the Lord Christ, by faith, because the person is acceptable to God. For the works which pertain to the maintenance of external discipline, which are done also by the unbelieving and unconverted, and required of them, although commendable before the world, and besides rewarded by God in this world with temporal possessions; yet, because they do not proceed from true faith, are in God's sight sins, i.e. stained with sin, and are regarded by God as sins and impure on account of the corrupt nature and because the person is not reconciled with God. For "a corrupt tree cannot bring forth good fruit" (Matt. 7:18), as also it is written (Rom. 14:23): "For whatsoever is not of faith is sin." For the person must first be accepted of God, and that alone for the sake of Christ, if the works of that person are to please him.

Therefore, of works that are truly good and well pleasing to God, which God will reward in this world and the world to come, faith must be the mother and source; and on this account they are correctly called by St. Paul "fruits of faith," as also "of the Spirit." For, as Luther writes in the introduction of St. Paul's Epistle to the Romans: "Thus faith is a divine work in us, that changes us, of God regenerates us, and puts to death the old Adam, makes us entirely different men in heart, spirit, mind and all powers, and confers the Holy Ghost. Oh, it is a living, efficacious, active thing that we have in faith, so that it is impossible for it not to do good without intermission. It also does not ask whether good works are to be done; but before the question is asked it has wrought them, and is always busy. But he who does not produce such works is a faithless man, and gropes and looks about after faith and good works, and knows neither what faith nor what good works are, yet meanwhile babbles and prates, in many words, concerning faith and good works. Justifying faith is a living, firm trust in God's grace, so certain that a man would die a thousand times for it [rather than suffer this trust to be wrested from him]. And this trust and knowledge of divine grace renders him joyful, fearless and cheerful with respect to God and all creatures, which joy and cheerfulness the Holy Ghost works though faith; and on account of this, man becomes ready and cheerful to do good to every one and to suffer everything for love and praise to God, who has conferred this grace. Therefore it is impossible to separate works from faith, yea, just as impossible as for heat and light to be separated from fire."

But since there is no controversy on this point among our theologians, we will not treat it here at greater length, but only make a simple and plain statement of the controverted points.

And first as to the necessity or voluntariness of good works, it is manifest that in the Augsburg Confession and its Apology the following expressions are often used and repeated: that good works are necessary, which also should necessarily follow faith and reconciliation, also, that we necessarily should do and must do the good works which God has commanded. Thus also in the Holy Scriptures themselves the words "necessity," "needful" and "necessary," also "should" and "must," are used concerning what we are bound to do, because of God's arrangement, command and will, as Rom. 13:5; 1 Cor. 9:9; Acts 5:29; John 15:12; 1 John 4:21.

Therefore it is wrong to censure and reject the expressions or propositions mentioned in this Christian and proper sense, as has been done by some. For it is right to employ them for the purpose of censuring and rejecting the secure, Epicurean delusion, by which many fabricate for themselves a dead faith or vain persuasion which is without repentance and without good works, as though there could be at the same time in a heart true faith and the wicked intention to persevere and continue in sins—an impossibility; or, as though any one, indeed, could have and retain true faith, righteousness and salvation, even though he be and remain a corrupt and unfruitful tree, whence no good fruits whatever come; yea, even though he persist in sins against conscience, or wilfully relapse into these sins—all of which is incorrect and false.

But here also mention must be made of the following distinction, viz. that necessity of Christ's arrangement, command and will, and of our debt, be understood; but not necessity of coercion. That is: When the word "needful" is employed, it should be understood not of coercion, but alone of the arrangement made by God's immutable will, to which we are debtor; for his commandment also shows that the creature should be obedient to its Creator. For in other places, as 2 Cor. 9:7, and in the Epistle of St. Paul to Philemon (v. 14), also 1 Pet. 5:2, the term "of necessity" is used for that to which any one is forced against his will or otherwise, so that he acts externally for appearance, but nevertheless without and against his will. For such hypocritical works God will not have [does not approve], but wishes the people of the New Testament to be a "willing people" (Ps. 110:3), and "sacrifice freely" (Ps. 54:7), "not grudgingly or of necessity, but to be obedient from the heart" (2 Cor. 9:7; Rom. 6:17). "For God loveth a cheerful giver" (2 Cor. 9:7). In this understanding, and in such sense, it is correctly said and taught that truly good works should be done freely or from a voluntary spirit by those whom the Son of God has liberated; as the disputation concerning the voluntariness of good works has been introduced especially with this intention.

But here, again, it is also well to note the distinction of which St. Paul says (Rom. 7:22 sq.) "I delight in the Law of God" [I am ready to do good] "after the inward man. But I see another law in my members," that is not only unwilling or disinclined, but also "warring against the law of my mind." And concerning the unwilling and rebellious flesh Paul says (1 Cor. 9:27): "I keep under my body, and bring it into subjection," and (Gal. 5:24; Rom. 8:13): "They that are Christ's have crucified," yea, slain, "the flesh with its affections and lusts." But the opinion is false, and must be censured, when it is asserted and taught that good works are so free to believers that it is optional with them to do or to omit them, or that they can act contrary thereto, and none the less are able to retain faith and God's favor and grace.

Secondly, when it is taught that good works are needful, the statement must also be made wherefore and for what reasons they are needful, as these causes are enumerated in the Augsburg Confession and Apology.

But here we must be well on our guard lest into the article of Justification and Salvation works may be introduced, and confused with it. Therefore the propositions are justly rejected, "that to believers good works are needful for salvation, so that it is impossible without good works to be saved." For they are directly contrary to the doctrine concerning the exclusive particles in the article of Justification and Salvation, *i.e.* they directly conflict with the words by which St. Paul entirely excludes our works and merit from the article of Justification and Salvation, and ascribes everything alone to the grace of God and merit of Christ, as explained in the preceding article. Again they [these propositions concerning the necessity of good works for salvation] take from tempted, troubled consciences the comfort of the Gospel, give occasion for doubt, are in many ways dangerous, strengthen presumption in one's own righteousness and confidence in one's own works; besides are accepted by the Papists, and quoted in their interest, against the pure doctrine of salvation by faith alone. Thus they are contrary also to the form of sound words, where it is written that blessedness is only "of the man unto whom God imputeth righteousness without works" (Rom. 4:6). Also in the sixth article of the Augsburg Confession it is written that "we are saved without works, by faith alone." Thus Luther also has rejected and condemned these propositions:

1.   In the false prophets among the Galatians [who led the Galatians into error].

2.   In the Papists, in very many places.

3.   In the Anabaptists, when they presented this interpretation: "We should not indeed rest faith upon the merit of works, but we should nevertheless regard them as things needful to salvation."

4.   Also in some among his contemporaries, who wished to interpret the proposition thus: "Although we require works as needful to salvation, yet we do not teach to place trust in works." On Gen. 22.

Accordingly, and for the reasons now enumerated, it should, in accordance with what is right, be settled in our churches that the aforesaid modes of speech should not be taught, defended or excused, but be rejected from our churches and repudiated as false and incorrect, and as expressions which, being renewed by the Interim, originated in times of persecution, when there was especial need of a clear, correct confession against all sorts of corruptions and adulterations of the article of Justification, and were drawn [again] into disputation.

Thirdly, since also it is disputed whether good works preserve salvation, or whether they be needful for preserving faith, righteousness and salvation, and upon this much that is of great importance depends; for "he that shall endure unto the end, the same shall be saved" (Matt. 24:13); also (Heb. 3:6, 14): "We are made partakers of Christ, if we hold fast the beginning of our confidence steadfast unto the end;" we must declare precisely how righteousness and salvation are to be maintained in us, lest it be again lost.

And therefore the false Epicurean delusion is to be earnestly censured and rejected, by which some imagine that faith and the righteousness and salvation received can be lost through no sins or wicked deeds, even though wilful and intentional, but that even if a Christian without fear and shame indulge his wicked lusts, resist the Holy Ghost, and intentionally acquiesce in sins against conscience, yet that he none the less retains faith, God's grace, righteousness and salvation.

Against this pernicious delusion the following true, immutable, divine threats and severe punishments and admonitions to Christians who are justified by faith should be often repeated and impressed. (1 Cor. 6:9): "Be not deceived: neither fornicators, nor idolaters, nor adulterers, etc., shall inherit the kingdom of God." (Gal. 5:21; Eph. 5:5): "They which do such things shall not inherit the kingdom of God." (Rom. 8:13): "If ye live after the flesh, ye shall die." (Col. 3:6): "For which thing's sake the wrath of God cometh upon the children of disobedience."

THE FORMULA OF CONCORD (1580) (continued)

But when and in what way, from this foundation, the exhortations to good works can be earnestly urged without an obscuration of the doctrine of faith and of the article of Justification, the Apology affords an excellent model, where in Article xx., on the passage (2 Pet. 1:10): "Give diligence to make your calling and election sure," it says as follows: "Peter teaches why good works should be done, viz. that we may make our calling sure, i.e. that we may not fall from our calling if we again sin. 'Do good works,' he says, 'that you may persevere in your heavenly calling, that you may not fall away again, and lose the Spirit and the gifts, which have fallen to you, not on account of works that follow, but of grace, through Christ, and are now retained by faith. But faith does not remain in those who lead a sinful life, lose the Holy Ghost and reject repentance." Thus far the Apology.

But, on the other hand, the sense is not that faith only in the beginning lays hold of righteousness and salvation, and afterwards resigns its office to works that they may in the future sustain faith, the righteousness received and salvation; but in order that the promise, not only of receiving, but also of retaining righteousness and salvation, may be firm and sure to us; St. Paul (Rom. 5:2) ascribes to faith not only the entrance to grace, but also that we stand in grace and boast of future glory, i.e. he ascribes the beginning, middle and end, all to faith alone. Also (Rom. 11:20): "Because of unbelief, they were broken off, and thou standest by faith." (Col. 1:22): "He will present you holy and unblamable and unreprovable in his sight, if ye continue in the faith." (1 Pet. 1:5, 9): "By the power of God we are kept through faith, unto salvation." "Receiving the end of your faith, even the salvation of your souls."

Since, therefore, from God's Word it is manifest that faith is the proper and only means whereby righteousness and salvation are not only received, but also preserved by God, the decree of the Council of Trent, and whatever elsewhere is set forth in the same sense, should by right be rejected, viz. that our good works support salvation, or that the righteousness of faith received, or even faith itself, is either entirely or in part supported and preserved by our works.

For although before this controversy some few pure teachers employed such expressions and the like, in the exposition of the Holy Scriptures, yet thereby it was in no way intended to establish the above-mentioned error of the Papists; nevertheless, because afterwards controversy arose concerning such expressions, from which all sorts of offensive amplifications [debates, offences and dissensions] followed, it is safest of all, according to the admonition of St. Paul (2 Tim. 1:13), to hold fast to the form of sound words, as the pure doctrine itself, whereby much unnecessary wrangling may be avoided and the Church be preserved from many scandals.

Fourthly, as to the proposition that good works are injurious to salvation, we explain ourselves clearly, as follows: If any one should wish to introduce good works into the article of Justification, or rest his righteousness or trust for salvation thereon, in order to merit God's grace and thereby be saved, to this we say nothing, but St. Paul himself declares, and repeats it three times (Phil. 3:7 sqq.),

that to such a man his works are not only useless and a hindrance, but also "injurious." But the fault is not in the good works themselves, but in the false confidence placed upon the works, contrary to the express Word of God.

Nevertheless, it by no means follows thence that we should say simply and barely: "Good works are injurious to believers or to their salvation;" for in believers good works are indications of salvation when they occur from proper causes and for true ends, i.e. as God requires them of the regenerate (Phil. 1:20). Since it is God's will and express command that believers should do good works, which the Holy Ghost works in believers, and with which, for Christ's sake, God is pleased, and to which he promises a glorious reward in this life and the life to come.

For this reason, also, this proposition is censured and rejected in our churches, viz. because it is stated in so absolutely false and offensive a manner, whereby discipline and decency are impaired, and a barbarous, savage, secure, Epicurean life is introduced and strengthened. For what is injurious to his salvation a person should with the greatest diligence avoid.

Since, however, Christians should not be deterred from good works, but should be admonished and urged thereto most diligently, this bare proposition cannot and should not be tolerated, borne or defended in the churches.

CHAPTER V. OF THE LAW AND THE GOSPEL.

As the distinction between the Law and the Gospel is a very brilliant light, which is of service in rightly dividing God's Word, and properly explaining and understanding the Scriptures of the holy prophets and apostles, we must with especial care observe it, in order that these two doctrines may not be mingled with one another, or out of the Gospel a law be made whereby the merit of Christ is obscured and troubled consciences robbed of their comfort, which they otherwise have in the holy Gospel when it is preached in its purity, and by which also they can support themselves in their most grievous temptations against the terrors of the Law.

But here, likewise, there has occurred a dissent among some which rebukes the greatest sin, viz. unbelief. But the other side held and contended that the Gospel is not properly a preaching of repentance or of reproof [preaching of repentance, convicting sin], as it properly belongs to God's Law to reprove all sins, and therefore unbelief also; but that the Gospel is properly a preaching of the grace and favor of God for Christ's sake, through which the unbelief of the converted, which previously inhered in them and which the Law of God reproved, is pardoned and forgiven.

When we now consider aright this dissent, it is especially caused by this, viz. that the term "Gospel" is not always employed and understood in one and the same sense, but in two ways, in the Holy Scriptures, as also by ancient and modern church-teachers. For sometimes it is employed so that thereby is understood the entire doctrine of Christ our Lord, which he inculcated in his ministry upon earth, and commanded to be inculcated in the New Testament, and thus comprised the explanation of the Law and the proclamation of the favor and grace of God, his heavenly

Father, as it is written (Mark 1:1): "The beginning of the Gospel of Jesus Christ, the Son of God." And shortly afterwards the chief heads are stated: "Repentance and forgiveness of sins." Therefore when Christ, after his resurrection, commanded the apostles to preach the Gospel in all the world (Mark 16:15), he compressed the sum of this doctrine into a few words, when he said (Luke 24:46, 47): "Thus it is written, and thus it behoved Christ to suffer, and to rise from the dead the third day; and that repentance and remission of sins should be preached in his name among all nations." So, too, Paul (Acts 20:21) calls his entire doctrine the Gospel, but he embraces the sum of this doctrine under the two heads: "Repentance toward God, and faith toward our Lord Jesus Christ." And in this sense the general definition, *i.e.* the description of the word "Gospel," when employed in a wide sense, and without the peculiar distinction between the Law and the Gospel, is correct, when it is said that the Gospel is a preaching of repentance and remission of sins. For John, Christ and the apostles began their preaching with repentance, and explained and urged not only the gracious promise of the forgiveness of sins, but also the Law of God. Afterwards the term "Gospel" is employed in another, namely, in its peculiar sense, by which it comprises not the preaching of repentance, but only the preaching of the grace of God, as follows directly afterwards (Mark 1:15), where Christ says: "Repent and believe the Gospel."

But also the term "repentance" is not employed in the Holy Scriptures in one and the same sense. For in some passages of Holy Scripture it is employed and understood with reference to the entire conversion of man, as Luke 13:5: "Except ye repent, ye shall all likewise perish." And in chap. 15:7: "Likewise joy shall be in heaven over one sinner that repenteth." But in Mark 1:15, as also elsewhere, where a distinction is made between repentance and faith in Christ (Acts 20:21) or between repentance and remission of sins (Luke 24:46, 47), repentance means to do nothing else than to truly acknowledge sins, from the heart to regret them, and to abstain therefrom. This knowledge proceeds from the Law, but does not suffice for saving conversion to God, if faith in Christ be not added, whose merits the consolatory preaching of the holy Gospel offers to all penitent sinners who are terrified by the preaching of the Law. For the Gospel proclaims the forgiveness of sins, not to coarse and secure hearts, but to the bruised or penitent (Luke 4:18). And that from repentance or the terrors of the Law despair may not result, the preaching of the Gospel must be added, that it may be repentance to salvation (2 Cor. 7:10).

For since the mere preaching of the Law, without Christ, either makes men presumptuous, who imagine that by outward works they can fulfil the Law, or forces them utterly to despair, Christ takes the Law into his hands, and explains it spiritually, from Matt. 5:21 sqq.; Rom. 7:14 and 1:18, and thus reveals his wrath from heaven upon all sinners, and shows how great it is; whereby they are instructed in the Law, and from it first learn aright to know their sins—a knowledge to which Moses never could coerce them. For as the apostle testifies (2 Cor. 3:14 sq.), even though Moses be read, yet nevertheless the veil which hangs before the face always remains unremoved, so that they cannot perceive that the Law is spiritual and how great things it requires of us, and how severely it curses and condemns us because we cannot observe or fulfil it. "Nevertheless, when it shall turn to the Lord, the veil shall be taken away" (2 Cor. 3:16).

Therefore the Spirit of Christ must not only comfort, but also, through the office of the Law, reprove the world of sin, and thus do in the New Testament what the prophet calls "a strange work" (viz. reprove), in order that he may do his own work, which is to comfort and preach of grace. For on this account, through Christ, he was obtained [from the Father] and sent to us, and for this reason also is called the Comforter, as Dr. Luther has explained in his exposition of the Gospel for the Fifth Sunday after Trinity, in the following words:

"That is all a preaching of the Law which holds forth our sins and God's wrath, let it be done how or when it will. Again, the Gospel is such a preaching as shows and gives nothing else than grace and forgiveness in Christ, although it is true and right that the apostles and preachers of the Gospel (as Christ himself also did) sanction the preaching of the Law, and begin it with those who do not yet acknowledge their sins nor are terrified before [by the sense of] God's wrath; as he says (John 16:8): 'The Holy Ghost will reprove the world of sin, because they believe not on me.' Yea, what more forcible and more terrible declaration and preaching of God's wrath against sin is there than the suffering and death of Christ his Son? But as long as this all preaches God's wrath and terrifies men, it is still properly the preaching neither of the Gospel nor of Christ, but of Moses and the Law, against the impenitent. For the Gospel and Christ were never provided and given to us in order to terrify and condemn, but to comfort and cheer those who are terrified and timid." And again, "Christ says (John 16:8): 'The Holy Ghost will reprove the world of sin;' which cannot happen except through the explanation of the Law" (Jena Ed., vol. ii., p. 455).

So, too, the Smalcald Articles say: "The New Testament maintains and urges the office of the Law, which reveals sins and God's wrath; but to this office it immediately adds the promise of grace through the Gospel."

And the Apology says: "To a true and salutary repentance the preaching of the Law is not sufficient, *but the Gospel should be added thereto.*" Therefore the two doctrines belong together, and should also be urged by the side of each other, but in a definite order and with a proper distinction; and the Antinomians or assailants of the Law are justly condemned, who abolish the preaching of the Law from the Church, and wish sins to be reproved, and repentance and sorrow to be taught, not from the Law, but from the Gospel.

But in order that every one may see that in the dissent of which we are treating we conceal nothing, but present the matter to the eyes of the Christian reader plainly and clearly:

We unanimously believe, teach and confess that the Law is properly a divine doctrine, wherein the true, immutable will of God is revealed as to how man ought to be, in his nature, thoughts, words and works, in order to be pleasing and acceptable to God; and it threatens its transgressors

THE FORMULA OF CONCORD (1580) (continued)

with God's wrath and temporal and eternal punishment. For as Luther writes against the Antinomians: "Everything that reproves sin is and belongs to the Law, whose peculiar office it is to reprove sin and to lead to the knowledge of sins (Rom. 3:20; 7:7);" and as unbelief is the root and spring of all reprehensible sins, the Law reproves unbelief also.

But it is likewise true that the Law with its doctrine is illustrated and explained by the Gospel; and nevertheless it remains the peculiar office of the Law to reprove sins and teach concerning good works.

In this manner the Law reproves unbelief if the Word of God be not believed. Since now the Gospel, which alone peculiarly teaches and commands to believe in Christ, is God's Word, the Holy Ghost, through the office of the Law, also reproves unbelief, *i.e.* that sinners do not believe in Christ, although it is the Gospel alone which peculiarly teaches concerning saving faith in Christ.

But the Gospel is properly a doctrine which teaches (as man does not observe the Law of God, but transgresses it, and his corrupt nature, thoughts, words and works conflict therewith, and for this reason he is subject to God's wrath, death, all temporal calamities and the punishment of hell-fire) what man should *believe*, that with God he may obtain forgiveness of sins, viz. that the Son of God, our Lord Christ, has taken upon himself and borne the curse of the Law, has expiated and settled for all our sins, through whom alone we again enter into favor with God, obtain by faith forgiveness of sins, are exempted from death and all the punishments of sins, and are eternally saved.

For everything that comforts, that offers the favor and grace of God to transgressors of the Law, is and is properly said to be the Gospel, a good and joyful message that God does not will to punish sins, but, for Christ's sake, to forgive them.

Therefore every penitent sinner ought to believe, *i.e.* place his confidence alone, in the Lord Christ, that "he was delivered for our offences, and was raised again for our justification" (Rom. 4:25), who was "made sin for us who knew no sin, that we might be made the righteousness of God in him" (2 Cor. 5:21), "who of God is made unto us wisdom and righteousness and sanctification and redemption" (1 Cor. 1:30), whose obedience is reckoned for us before God's strict tribunal as righteousness, so that the *Law*, as above set forth, is a ministration that kills through the letter and preaches condemnation (2 Cor. 3:7), but the Gospel "is the power of God unto salvation to every one that believeth" (Rom. 1:16), that preaches righteousness and gives the Spirit (1 Cor. 1:18; Gal. 3:2). Dr. Luther has urged this distinction with especial diligence in nearly all his writings, and has properly shown that the knowledge of God derived from the Gospel is far different from that which is taught and learned from the Law, because even the heathen had to a certain extent, from the natural law, a knowledge of God, although they neither knew him aright nor glorified him (Rom. 1:20 sq.).

These two proclamations [kinds of doctrines] from the beginning of the world have been always inculcated

alongside of each other in the Church of God, with a proper distinction. For the successors of the venerated patriarchs, as also the patriarchs themselves, not only constantly called to mind how man was in the beginning created by God righteous and holy, and through the fraud of the serpent transgressed God's command, became a sinner, and corrupted and precipitated himself, with all his posterity, into death and eternal condemnation; but also, on the other hand, encouraged and comforted themselves by the preaching concerning the Seed of the woman, who would bruise the serpent's head (Gen. 3:15). Also, concerning the Seed of Abraham, in whom all the nations of the earth shall be blessed (Gen. 22:18). Also, concerning David's Son, who should restore again the kingdom of Israel and be a light to the heathen (Ps. 110:1; Isa. 49:6; Luke 2:32), who "was wounded for our transgressions, and bruised for our iniquities," by whose "stripes we are healed." Isa. 53:5.

These two doctrines we believe and confess, viz. that even to the end of the world they should be diligently inculcated in the Church of God, although with proper distinction, in order that, through the preaching of the *Law* and its threats in the ministry of the New Testament, the hearts of impenitent men may be terrified, and be brought to a knowledge of their sins and to repentance; but not in such a way that they inwardly despair and doubt, but that (since "the Law is a schoolmaster unto Christ, that we might be justified by faith" (Gal. 3:24), and thus points and leads us not from Christ, but to Christ, who "is the end of the Law," Rom. 10:4), they be on the other hand comforted and strengthened by the preaching of the holy *Gospel* concerning Christ our Lord, viz. that to those who believe the Gospel, God, through Christ, forgives all their sins, adopts them for his sake as children, and out of pure grace, without any merit on their part, justifies and saves them, but nevertheless not in such a way that they abuse and sin against the grace of God. Paul (2 Cor. 3:7 sqq.) thoroughly and forcibly shows this distinction between the Law and the Gospel.

Therefore, in order that the two doctrines, viz. that of the Law and that of the Gospel, be not mingled and confounded with one another, and to the one that be ascribed which belongs to the other, whereby the merit and benefits of Christ are obscured and the Gospel made again a doctrine of the Law, as has occurred in the Papacy, and thus Christians be deprived of the true comfort which in the Gospel they have against the terrors of the Law, and the door be again opened in the Church of God to the Papacy; the true and proper distinction between the Law and the Gospel must with all diligence be inculcated and preserved, and whatever gives occasion for confusion between the Law and the Gospel, *i.e.* whereby the two doctrines, Law and Gospel, may be confounded and mingled into one doctrine, should be diligently avoided. It is on this account dangerous and wrong to convert the Gospel, properly so called as distinguished from the Law, into a preaching of repentance or reproof [a preaching of repentance, reproving sin]. For otherwise, if understood in a general sense of the whole doctrine, as the Apology also sometimes says, the Gospel is a preaching of repentance and forgiveness of sins. But close by the Apology also shows that the Gospel is properly the promise of the forgiveness of sins, and of justification through Christ; but that the Law is a doctrine which reproves sins and condemns.

CHAPTER VI. OF THE THIRD USE OF THE DIVINE LAW.

Since the Law of God is useful, not only that thereby, external discipline and decency be maintained against wild, disobedient men; 2, likewise, that through it men be brought to a knowledge of their sins; 3, but even when they have been born anew by the Spirit of God and converted to the Lord, and thus the veil of Moses has been removed from them, they live and walk in the Law; a dissension has occurred between some few theologians concerning this last use of the Law. For the one side taught and maintained that the regenerate should not learn the new obedience, or in what good works they ought to walk, from the Law; neither is this doctrine to be urged thence, because they have been liberated by the Son of God, have become the temples of his Spirit, and therefore are free, so that, just as the sun of itself without any constraint fulfils its course, so also they of themselves, by the prompting and impulse of the Holy Ghost, do what God requires of them. The other side taught, on the contrary: Although the truly believing are really moved by God's Spirit, and thus, according to the inner man, do God's will from a free spirit; yet the Holy Ghost uses with them the written law for instruction, whereby even the truly believing may learn to serve God, not according to their own thoughts, but according to his written Law and Word, which are a sure rule and standard of a godly life and walk, directed according to the eternal and immutable will of God.

For the explanation and final settlement of this dissent we unanimously believe, teach and confess that although the truly believing and truly converted to God and justified Christians are liberated and made free from the curse of the Law; yet that they should daily exercise themselves in the Law of the Lord, as it is written (Ps. 1:2; 119:1): "Blessed is the man whose delight is in the Law of the Lord; and in his Law doth he meditate day and night." For the Law is a mirror, in which the will of God and what pleases him are exactly represented, so that it should be constantly held forth to believers and be diligently urged upon them without intermission.

For although "the Law is not made for a righteous man," as the apostle testifies (1 Tim. 1:9), "but for the unrighteous," yet this is not to be understood so absolutely as that the justified should live without law. For the Law of God is written in their heart, and to the first man immediately after his creation a law also was given, according to which he should have acted. But the meaning of St. Paul is that the Law cannot burden with its curse those who through Christ are reconciled to God, and need not vex with its coercion the regenerate, because, after the inner man, they have pleasure in God's Law.

And indeed, if the believing and elect children of God would be completely renewed by the indwelling Spirit in this life, so that in their nature and all its powers they would be entirely free from sin, they would need no law, and so also no impeller, but what they are in duty bound to do according to God's will they would do of themselves, and altogether voluntarily, without any instruction, admonition, solicitation or urging of the Law; just as the sun, the moon and all the constellations of heaven have of themselves, unobstructed, their regular course, without admonition, solicitation, urging, force or necessity, according to the arrangement of God which God once gave them, yea, just as the holy angels render an entirely voluntary obedience.

But since in this life believers have not been renewed perfectly or completely, *completive vel consummative* [as the ancients say], (for although their sins are covered by the perfect obedience of Christ, so that they are not imputed to believers for condemnation, and also, through the Holy Ghost, the mortification of the old Adam and the renewal in the spirit of their mind is begun), nevertheless the old Adam always clings to them in their nature and all its internal and external powers. Of this the apostle has written (Rom. 7:18 sqq.): "I know that in me [that is, in my flesh] dwelleth no good thing." And again: "For that which I do, I allow not; for what I would, that do I not; but what I hate, that do I." Again: "I see another law in my members, warring against the law of my mind, and bringing me into captivity to the law of sin." Also (Gal. 5:17): "The flesh lusteth against the spirit, and the spirit against the flesh; and these are contrary the one to the other: so that ye cannot do the things that ye would."

Therefore, because of these lusts of the flesh, the truly believing, elect and regenerate children of God require not only the daily instruction and admonition, warning and threatening of the Law, but also frequently reproofs, whereby they are roused [the old man is shaken from them] and follow the Spirit of God, as it is written (Ps. 119:71): "It is good for me that I have been afflicted, that I might learn thy statutes." And again (1 Cor. 9:27): "I keep under my body and bring it into subjection; lest that, by any means, when I have preached to others, I myself should be a castaway." And again (Heb. 12:8): "But if ye be without chastisement, whereof all are partakers, then are ye bastards and not sons;" as Dr. Luther in more words has fully explained in the summer part of the Church Postils, on the Epistle for the Nineteenth Sunday after Trinity.

But we must also separately explain what with respect to the new obedience of believers the Gospel does, affords and works, and what herein, so far as concerns the good works of believers, is the office of the Law.

For the Law says indeed that it is God's will and command that we should walk in a new life, but it does not give the power and faculty so that we can begin and do it; but the Holy Ghost, who is given and received, not through the Law, but through the preaching of the Gospel (Gal. 3:14), renews the heart. Afterwards the Holy Ghost employs the Law, so that from it he teaches the regenerate, and in the Ten Commandments points out and shows them "what is the good and acceptable will of God" (Rom. 12:2), in what good works "God hath before ordained that they should walk" (Eph. 2:10). He exhorts them thereto, and when, because of the flesh in them, they are idle, negligent and rebellious, he reproves them on that account

THE FORMULA OF CONCORD (1580) (continued)

through the Law, so that he carries on both offices together; he slays and makes alive, he leads to hell and brings up again. For his office is not only to *console,* but also to *reprove,* as is written: "When the Holy Ghost is come, he will reprove the world" (under which also is the old Adam) "of sin, and of righteousness and of judgment." But sin is everything that is contrary to God's Law. And St. Paul says: "All Scripture given by inspiration of God is profitable for doctrine, for reproof," etc., and to reprove is the peculiar office of the Law. Therefore as often as believers stumble they are reproved by the Holy Ghost from the Law, and by the same Spirit are again comforted and consoled with the preaching of the Holy Gospel.

But in order that, so far as possible, all misunderstanding may be avoided, and the distinction between the works of the Law and those of the Spirit be properly taught and preserved, it is to be noted with especial diligence that when the subject of good works which are in accordance with God's Law (for otherwise they are not good works) is treated, the word "Law" has only one sense, viz. the immutable will of God, according to which men should conduct themselves in their lives.

But there is a distinction in the works, because of the distinction with respect to the men who strive to live according to this Law and will of God. For as long as man is not regenerate, and conducts himself according to the Law, and does the works because they are thus command- ed, from fear of punishment or desire for reward, he is still under the Law, and his works are properly called by St. Paul works of the Law, for they are extorted by the Law, as those of slaves; and they are saints after the order of Cain [that is, hyprocrites].

But when man is born anew by the Spirit of God, and liberated from the Law, *i.e.* made exempt from this coercion, and is led by the Spirit of Christ, he lives according to the immutable will of God, comprised in the Law, and does everything, so far as he is born anew, out of a free, cheerful spirit; and this is called not properly a work of the Law, but a work and fruit of the Spirit, or as St. Paul names it "the law of the mind" and "the Law of Christ." For such men are no more under the Law, but under grace, as St. Paul says (Rom. 8 [Rom. 7:23; 8:2; 1 Cor. 9:21]).

But since believers are not, in this world, completely renewed, but the old Adam clings to them even to the grave, there also remains in them a struggle between the spirit and the flesh. Therefore they have indeed pleasure in God's Law according to the inner man, but the law in their members struggles against the law in their mind to such an extent that they are never without law, and nevertheless are not under, but in the Law, and live and walk in the Law of the Lord, and yet do nothing from *constraint* of the Law.

But so far as concerns the old Adam, which still clings to them, it must be urged on not only with the Law, but also with punishments; nevertheless it does everything against its will and under coercion, no less than the godless are

urged on and held in obedience by the threats of the Law (1 Cor. 9:27; Rom. 7:18, 19).

So, too, this doctrine of the Law is needful for believers, in order that they may not depend upon their own holiness and devotion, and under the pretext of the Spirit of God establish a self-chosen form of divine worship, without God's Word and command, as it is written (Deut. 12:8, 28, 32): "Ye shall not do . . . every man whatsoever is right in his own eyes" etc., but "observe and hear all these words which I command thee." "Thou shalt not add thereto, nor diminish therefrom."

So, too, the doctrine of the Law, in and with good works of believers, is needful for this reason, for otherwise man can easily imagine that his work and life are entirely pure and perfect. But the Law of God prescribes to believers good works in this way, that, at the same time, it shows and indicates, as in a mirror, that in this life they are still imperfect and impure in us, so that we must say with the apostle (1 Cor. 4:4): "I know nothing by myself; yet am I not hereby justified." Therefore, when Paul exhorts the regenerate to good works, he presents to them expressly the Ten Commandments (Rom. 13:9), and that his good works are imperfect and impure he recognizes from the Law (Rom. 7:7 sqq.); and David declares (Ps. 119:35): "I have run the way of thy commandments," but "enter not into judgment with thy servant; for in thy sight shall no man living be justified" (Ps. 143:2).

But how and why the good works of believers, although in this life, because of sin in the flesh, they are imperfect and impure, nevertheless are acceptable and well pleasing to God, the Law does not teach, as it requires an entire, perfect, pure obedience if it is to please God. But the Gospel teaches that our spiritual offerings are acceptable to God, through faith, for Christ's sake (1 Pet. 2:5; Heb. 11:4 sqq.). In this way Christians are not under the Law, but under grace, because by faith in Christ the persons [of the godly] are freed from the curse and condemnation of the Law; and because their good works, although they are still imperfect and impure, are acceptable, through Christ, to God, because they do, not by coercion of the Law, but by renewing of the Holy Ghost, voluntarily and spontane- ously from their hearts, what is pleasing to God, so far as they have been born anew according to the inner man; although nevertheless they maintain a constant struggle against the old Adam.

For the old Adam, as an intractable, pugnacious ass, is still a part of them, which is to be coerced to the obedience of Christ, not only by the doctrine, admonition, force and threatening of the Law, but also oftentimes by the club of punishments and troubles, until the sinful flesh is entirely put off, and man is perfectly renewed in the resurrection, where he needs no longer either the preaching of the Law or its threatenings and reproofs, as also no longer the Gospel; as these belong to this [mortal and] imperfect life. But as they will behold God face to face, so, through the power of the indwelling Spirit of God, will they do the will of God [the heavenly Father] with unmingled joy, volun- tarily, unconstrained, without any hindrance, with entire purity and perfection, and will eternally rejoice in him.

Accordingly, we reject and condemn as an error pernicious and prejudicial to Christian discipline, as also to true piety, the teaching that the Law, in the above-mentioned way and degree, should not be urged upon Christians and those truly believing, but only upon the unbelieving, not Christian, and impenitent.

CHAPTER VII. OF THE HOLY SUPPER.

Although perhaps, according to the opinion of some, the exposition of this article should not be inserted into this document, wherein it has been our intention to explain the articles which have been drawn into controversy among the theologians of the Augsburg Confession (from which the Sacramentarians almost in the beginning, when the Confession was first composed and presented to the Emperor at Augsburg in 1530, entirely withdrew and separated, and presented their own Confession), yet, alas! as we have still some theologians and others who glory in the Augsburg Confession, who in the last few years no longer secretly, but partly publicly, have given their assent in this article to the Sacramentarians, and against their own conscience have wished violently to cite and pervert the Augsburg Confession as in entire harmony in this article with the doctrine of the Sacramentarians; we neither can nor should forbear in this document to give testimony in accordance with our confession of divine truth, and to repeat the true sense and proper understanding, with reference to this article, of the Word of Christ and of the Augsburg Confession, and [for we recognize it to be our duty] so far as in us lies, by God's help, to preserve it [this pure doctrine] also to posterity, and to faithfully warn our hearers, together with other godly Christians, against this pernicious error, which is entirely contrary to the divine Word and the Augsburg Confession, and has been frequently condemned.

STATEMENT OF THE CONTROVERSY. *The Chief Conflict between our Doctrine and that of the Sacramentarians in this Article.*

Although some Sacramentarians strive to speak and to employ words the very nearest the Augsburg Confession and the form and mode of these churches, and confess that in the Holy Supper the body of Christ is truly received by believers, yet if they be forced to declare their meaning properly, sincerely and clearly, they all unanimously explain themselves thus, viz. that the true essential body and blood of Christ is as far from the consecrated bread and wine in the Holy Supper as the highest heaven is distant from the earth. For their own words run thus: Abesse Christi corpus ct sanguinem a signis tanto intervallo dicimus, quanto abest terra ab altissimis coelis. That is: "We say that the body and blood of Christ are as far from the signs as the earth is distant from the highest heaven." Therefore, they understand this presence of the body of Christ not as here upon earth, but only with respect to faith [when they speak of the presence of the body and blood of Christ in the Supper, they do not mean that they are present upon earth, except with respect to faith], *i.e.* that our faith, reminded and excited by the visible signs, as by the preached Word, elevates itself and rises up above all heavens, and there receives and enjoys the body of Christ, which is present there in heaven, yea, Christ himself,

together with all his benefits, in a true and essential, but nevertheless *only spiritual,* manner. For [they think that] as the bread and wine are here upon earth and not in heaven, so the body of Christ is now in heaven and not upon earth, and on this account nothing else is received by the mouth in the Holy Supper but bread and wine.

In the first place, they have alleged that the Lord's Supper is only an external sign, whereby Christians may be known, and that therein nothing else is offered but mere bread and wine (which are bare signs [symbols] of the absent body of Christ). Since this would not stand the test, they have confessed that the Lord Christ is truly present in his Supper, namely by the *communicatio idiomatum, i.e.* alone according to his divine nature, but not with his body and blood.

Afterwards, when they were forced by Christ's words to confess that the body of Christ is present in the Supper, they still understood and declared it in no other way than spiritually, that is, through faith to partake of his power, efficacy and benefits [than that they believed the presence only spiritual, *i.e.* that Christ only makes us partakers of his power, efficacy and benefits], because [they say] through the Spirit of Christ, who is everywhere, our bodies, in which the Spirit of Christ dwells here upon earth, are united with the body of Christ, which is in heaven.

Thus through these grand, plausible words many great men were deceived when they proclaimed and boasted that they were of no other opinion than that the Lord Christ is present in his Holy Supper truly, essentially, and as one alive; but they understand this alone according to his divine nature, and not of his body and blood, which are now in heaven, and nowhere else [for they think concerning these that they are only in heaven, etc.], and that he gives us with the bread and wine his true body and blood to eat, that we may partake of them spiritually through faith, but not bodily with the mouth.

For they understand the words of the Supper: "Eat, this is my body," not properly, as they sound, according to the letter, but as figurative expressions; thus, that "eating" the body of Christ means nothing else than "believing," and that "body" is equivalent to "symbol," *i.e.* a sign or figure of the body of Christ, which is not in the Supper on earth, but alone in heaven. The word *is* they interpret sacramentally, or in a significative manner, in order that no one may regard the thing so joined with the signs, that the flesh also of Christ is now present on earth in an invisible and incomprehensible manner. That is: "The body of Christ is united with the bread sacramentally, or significatively, so that believing, godly Christians as surely partake spiritually of the body of Christ, which is above in heaven, as with the mouth they eat the bread." But that the body of Christ is present here upon earth in the Supper essentially although invisibly and incomprehensibly, and is received orally, with the consecrated bread, even by hypocrites or those who are Christians only in appearance [by name], this they are accustomed to execrate and condemn as a horrible blasphemy.

On the other hand, it is taught in the Augsburg Confession from God's Word concerning the Lord's Supper, thus:

THE FORMULA OF CONCORD (1580) (continued)

"That the true body and blood of Christ are truly present in the Holy Supper under the form of bread and wine, and are there communicated and received, and the contrary doctrine is rejected" (namely, that of the Sacramentarians, who at the same time at Augsburg presented their own Confession, that the body of Christ, because he has ascended to heaven, is not truly and essentially present here upon earth in the sacrament [which denied the true and substantial presence of the body and blood of Christ in the sacrament of the Supper administered on earth, on this account, viz. because Christ had ascended into heaven]. For this opinion is clearly expressed in Luther's Small Catechism in the following words: "The sacrament of the altar is the true body and blood of our Lord Jesus Christ under the bread and wine, given unto us Christians to eat and to drink, as it was instituted by Christ himself." Still more clearly in the Apology is this not only declared, but also established by the passage from Paul (1 Cor. 10:16), and by the testimony of Cyril, in the following words: "The tenth article has been received [approved], in which we confess that in the Lord's Supper the body and blood of Christ are truly and substantially present, and are truly offered with the visible elements, bread and wine, to those who receive the sacrament. For since Paul says: 'The bread which we break is the communion of the body of Christ,' etc., it would follow, if the body of Christ were not, but only the Holy Ghost were truly present, that the bread is not a communion of the body, but of the Spirit of Christ. Thus we know that not only the Romish, but also the Greek Church, has taught the bodily presence of Christ in the Holy Supper." And testimony is also produced from Cyril that Christ also dwells bodily in us in the Holy Supper by the communication of his flesh.

Afterwards, when those who at Augsburg delivered their Confession concerning this article seemed to be willing to approve the Confession of our churches, the following *Formula Concordia, i.e.* articles of Christian agreement between the Saxon theologians and those of Upper Germany, was composed and signed at Wittenberg in the year 1536, by Dr. Martin Luther and other theologians on both sides:

"We have heard how Mr. Martin Bucer explained his own opinion, and that of other preachers who came with him from the cities, concerning the holy sacrament of the body and blood of Christ, viz. as follows:

"They confess, according to the words of Irenaeus, that in this sacrament there are two things, a heavenly and an earthly. Therefore they hold and teach that, with the bread and wine, the body and blood of Christ are truly and essentially present, offered and received. And although they believe in no trans-substantiation, *i.e.* an essential transformation of the bread and wine into the body and blood of Christ, and also do not hold that the body and blood of Christ are included locally, *i.e.* with respect to space, in the bread, or are otherwise permanently united therewith apart from the use of the sacrament; yet they concede that through the sacramental union the bread is the body of Christ, etc. [that when the bread is offered the body of Christ is at the same time present, and is truly tendered]. For apart from use, if the bread be laid by and preserved in a pyx, or be carried about and exhibited in processions, as occurs in the Papacy, they do not hold that the body of Christ is present.

"Secondly, they hold that the institution of this sacrament made by Christ is efficacious in Christendom [the Church], and that it does not depend upon the worthiness or unworthiness of the minister who offers the sacrament or of the one who receives it. Therefore, as St. Paul says, that even the unworthy partake of the sacrament, they hold that also to the unworthy the body and blood of Christ are truly offered, and the unworthy truly receive them, where the institution and command of the Lord Christ are observed. But such persons receive them to condemnation, as St. Paul says; for they abuse the holy sacrament, because they receive it without true repentance and without faith. For it was instituted for this purpose, viz. that it might testify that to them the grace and benefits of Christ are there applied, and that they are incorporated into Christ and are washed by his blood, who there truly repent and comfort themselves by faith in Christ."

In the following year, when the chief theologians of the Augsburg Confession assembled from all Germany at Smalcald, and deliberated as to what to present in the Council concerning this doctrine of the Church, by common consent the Smalcald Articles were composed by Dr. Luther, and were signed by all the theologians, collectively and individually, in which the true and proper opinion is clearly expressed in short, plain words, which agree most accurately with the words of Christ, and every door and mode of escape for the Sacramentarians was closed. For they had interpreted to their advantage [perverted] the Formula of Concord, *i.e.* the above-mentioned articles of union, framed the preceding year, so that it should be understood that the body of Christ is offered with the bread in no other way than as it is offered, together with all his benefits, by the Word of the Gospel, and that by the sacramental union nothing else than the spiritual presence of the Lord Christ by faith is meant. These articles, therefore, declare: "The bread and wine in the Holy Supper are the true body and blood of Jesus Christ, which are tendered and received, not only by the godly, but also by godless Christians" [those who have nothing Christian except the name].

Dr. Luther has also more amply expounded and confirmed this opinion from God's Word in the Large Catechism, where it is written:

"What is therefore the Sacrament of the Altar? Answer: It is the true body and blood of our Lord Jesus Christ, in and under the bread and wine, which we Christians are commanded by the Word of Christ to eat and to drink." And shortly after: "It is the Word, I say, which makes and distinguishes this sacrament, so that it is not mere bread and wine, but is, and is properly called the body and blood of Christ." Again: "With this Word you can strengthen your conscience and say: If a hundred thousand devils, together with all fanatics, raise the objection, How can bread and wine be the body and blood of Christ? I know that all spirits and scholars together are not as wise as is the Divine Majesty in his little finger. For here stands the

Word of Christ: 'Take, eat; this is my body. Drink ye all of this; this is the new testament in my blood,' etc. Here we abide, and would like to see those who will constitute themselves his masters, and make it different from what he has spoken. It is true, indeed, that if you take away the Word, or regard it without the Word, you have nothing but mere bread and wine. But if the Word be added thereto, as it must be, then in virtue of the same it is truly the body and blood of Christ. For as the lips of Christ have spoken, so it is, as he can never lie or deceive.

"Hence it is easy to reply to all manner of questions about which at the present time men are anxious, as, for instance: Whether a wicked priest can administer and distribute the sacrament? and such like other points. For here conclude and reply: Even though a knave take or distribute the sacrament, he receives the true sacrament, *i.e.* the true body and blood of Christ, just as truly as he who receives or administers it in the most worthy manner. For it is not founded upon the holiness of men, but upon the Word of God. And as no saint upon earth, yea, no angel in heaven, can change bread and wine into the body and blood of Christ, so also can no one change or alter it, even though it be abused.

"For the Word, by which it became a sacrament and was instituted, does not become false because of the person or his unbelief. For he does not say: If you believe or are worthy you will receive my body and blood, but: 'Take, eat and drink; this is my body and blood.' Likewise: 'Do this' (viz. what I now do, institute, give and bid you take). That is as much as to say, No matter whether you be worthy or unworthy, you have here his body and blood, by virtue of these words which are added to the bread and wine. This mark and observe well; for upon these words rest all our foundation, protection and defence against all error and temptation that have ever come or may yet come."

Thus far the Large Catechism, in which the true presence of the body and blood of Christ in the Holy Supper is established from God's Word; and the same is understood not only of the believing and worthy, but also of the unbelieving and unworthy.

But inasmuch as this highly-illumined man [Dr. Luther, the hero illumined with unparalleled and most excellent gifts of the Holy Ghost] foresaw that after his death some would suspect that he had receded from the above-mentioned doctrine and other Christian articles, he has appended the following protest to his Large Confession:

"Because I see the longer the time the greater the number of sects and errors, and that there is no end to the rage and fury of Satan, in order that henceforth during my life, and after my death, some of them may not, in future, support themselves by me, and in order to strengthen their error falsely quote my writings, as the Sacramentarians and Anabaptists begin to do; I will in this writing, before God and all the world, confess my faith, point by point [concerning all the articles of our religion]. In this I intend to abide until my death, and therein (and may God help me as to this!) to depart from this world and to appear before the judgment-seat of Jesus Christ; and if after my death any one will say: If Dr. Luther were now living he would teach and hold this or that article differently, for he

did not sufficiently consider it, against this I say now as then, and then as now, that, by God's grace, I have most diligently considered all these articles by means of the Scriptures [have examined them, not once, but very often, according to the standard of Holy Scripture], and often have gone over them, and will contend as confidently for them as I am now contending for the Sacrament of the Altar. I am not drunk or inconsiderate; I know what I say; I also am sensible of the account which I will render at the coming of the Lord Christ at the final judgment. Therefore no one should interpret this as jest or mere idle talk; to me it is serious; for by God's grace I know Satan in great part; if he can pervert or confuse God's Word, what will he not do with my words or those of another?"

After this protest, Dr. Luther, of holy memory, presents among other articles this also: "In the same manner I also speak and confess" (he says) "concerning the Sacrament of the Altar, that there the body and blood of Christ are in truth orally eaten and drunken in the bread and wine, even though the priests [ministers] who administer it [the Lord's Supper], or those who receive it, do not believe or otherwise abuse it. For it does not depend upon the faith or unbelief of men, but upon God's Word and ordinance, unless they first change God's Word and ordinance and interpret it otherwise, as the enemies of the sacrament do at the present day, who, of course, have nothing but bread and wine; for they also do not have the Word and appointed ordinance of God, but have perverted and changed it according to their own caprice."

Dr. Luther (who certainly, above others, understood the true and proper meaning of the Augsburg Confession, and who constantly, even to his end, remained steadfast thereto, and defended it) shortly before his death, with great zeal, repeated in his last Confession his faith concerning this article, where he writes thus: "I reckon all in one mass as Sacramentarians and fanatics, as they also are who will not believe that the bread in the Lord's Supper is his true natural body, which the godless as Judas himself received with the mouth, as well as did St. Peter, and all [other] saints; he who will not believe this (I say) should let me alone, and not hope for any fellowship with me; there is no alternative [thus my opinion stands, which I am not going to change]."

From these explanations, and especially from that of Dr. Luther as the chief teacher of the Augsburg Confession, every ir 'elligent man, if he be desirous of the truth and of peace, can undoubtedly perceive what has always been the proper sense and understanding of the Augsburg Confession in regard to this article.

For the reason that in addition to the expressions of Christ and St. Paul (viz. that the bread in the Supper "is the body of Christ" or "the communion of the body of Christ"), also the forms: "under the bread," "with the bread," "in the bread" ["the body of Christ is present and offered"], are employed, is that hereby the Papistical transubstantiation may be rejected, and the sacramental union of the unchanged essence of the bread and of the body of Christ may be indicated; just as the expression, "the Word was made flesh" (John 1:14), is repeated and explained by the equivalent expressions: "The Word dwelt among us;" (Col.

THE FORMULA OF CONCORD (1580) (continued)

2:9): "In him dwelleth all the fulness of the Godhead bodily;" also (Acts 10:38): "God was with him;" also (2 Cor. 5:19): "God was in Christ," and the like; namely, that the divine essence is not changed into the human nature, but the two natures unchanged are personally united. [These phrases repeat the expression of John above-mentioned, and declare that, by the incarnation, the divine essence is not changed into the human nature, but that the two natures without confusion are personally united.]

And indeed many eminent ancient teachers, Justin, Cyprian, Augustine, Leo, Gelasius, Chrysostom and others, use this simile concerning the words of Christ's testament: "This is my body," viz. that just as in Christ two distinct, unchanged natures are inseparably united, so in the Holy Supper the two substances, the natural bread and the true natural body of Christ, are present here together upon earth in the appointed administration of the sacrament. Although this union of the body and blood of Christ with the bread and wine is not a personal union, as that of the two natures in Christ, but a sacramental union, as Dr. Luther and our theologians, in the frequently-mentioned Articles of Agreement [Formula of Concord] in the year 1536 and in other places, call it; in order to declare that although they also employ the forms, "in the bread," "under the bread," "with the bread," yet the words of Christ they receive properly and as they sound, and understand the proposition, *i.e.* the words of Christ's testament: "This is my body," not as a figurative, but as an unusual expression. For Justin says: "This we receive not as common bread and common drink, but as Jesus Christ, our Saviour, through the Word of God became flesh, and on account of our salvation also had flesh and blood, so we believe that, by the Word and prayer, the food blessed by him is the body and blood of our Lord Jesus Christ." Dr. Luther also in his Large and especially in his last Confession, concerning the Lord's Supper, with great earnestness and zeal defends the very form of expression which Christ used at the first Supper.

For since Dr. Luther is to be regarded the most distinguished teacher of the churches which confess the Augsburg Confession, whose entire doctrine as to sum and substance was comprised in the articles of the frequently-mentioned Augsburg Confession, and was presented to the Emperor Charles V.; the proper understanding and sense of the said Augsburg Confession can and should be derived from no other source more properly and correctly than from the doctrinal and polemical writings of Dr. Luther.

And indeed this very opinion, just cited, is founded upon the only firm, immovable and indubitable rock of truth, from the words of institution in the holy, divine Word, and was thus understood, taught and propagated by the holy evangelists and apostles and their disciples.

For since our Lord and Saviour, Jesus Christ, concerning whom, as our only Teacher, this solemn command: "Hear ye him," has been given from heaven to all men, who is not a mere man or angel, and also not only true, wise and mighty, but the eternal truth and wisdom itself and Almighty God, who knows very well what and how he should speak, and who also can powerfully effect and execute everything that he speaks and promises, as he says (Luke 21:33): "Heaven and earth shall pass away; but my words shall not pass away;" also (Matt. 28:18): "All power is given unto me in heaven and in earth,"—

Since now this true, almighty Lord, our Creator and Redeemer, Jesus Christ, after the Last Supper, when he is just beginning his bitter suffering and death for our sins, on that last sad time, with great consideration and solemnity, in the institution of this most venerable sacrament (which was to be used until the end of the world with great reverence and obedience [and humility], and was to be an abiding memorial of his bitter suffering and death and all his benefits, a sealing [and confirmation] of the New Testament, a consolation of all distressed hearts and a firm bond and means of union of Christians with Christ their head and with one another), in the founding and institution of the Holy Supper spake these words concerning the bread which he blessed and gave [to his disciples]: "Take, eat; this is my body, which is given for you," and concerning the cup or wine: "This is my blood of the new testament, which is shed for many for the remission of sins;"—

We are in duty bound not to interpret and explain these words of the eternal, true and almighty Son of God, our Lord, Creator and Redeemer, Jesus Christ, as allegorical, metaphorical, tropical expressions, as may appear to be in conformity with our reason, but with simple faith and due obedience to receive the words as they sound, in their proper and plain sense, and allow ourselves to be diverted therefrom [from this express testament of Christ] by no objections or human contradictions spun from human reason, however charming they may appear to the reason.

As when Abraham heard God's Word concerning offering his son, although indeed he had cause enough for disputing as to whether the words should be understood according to the letter or with a moderate or mild interpretation, since they conflicted not only with all reason and with divine and natural law, but also with the chief article of faith concerning the promised Seed, Christ, who was to be born of Isaac; and yet, as before, when the promise of the blessed Seed from Isaac was given him (although it appeared to his reason impossible), he gave God the honor of truth, and most confidently concluded and believed that God could do what he promised; so also here faith understands and believes God's Word and command plainly and simply, as they sound, according to the letter, and resigns the entire matter to the divine omnipotence and wisdom, which it knows has many more modes and ways to fulfil the promise of the Seed from Isaac than man with his blind reason can comprehend.

Thus, with all humility and obedience we too should simply believe the plain, firm, clear and solemn word and command of our Creator and Redeemer, without any doubt and disputation as to how it may agree with our reason or be possible. For these words THE LORD, who is infinite wisdom and truth itself, has spoken, and everything which he promises he also can execute and accomplish.

Now, all the circumstances of the institution of the Holy Supper testify that these words of our Lord and Saviour,

Jesus Christ, which in themselves are simple, plain, clear, firm and indubitable, cannot and should not be understood otherwise than in their usual, proper and common signification. For since Christ gave this command [concerning eating his body, etc.] at his table and at the Supper, there is indeed no doubt that he speaks of real, natural bread and of natural wine, also of oral eating and drinking, so that there can be no metaphor, *i.e.* an alteration of meaning, in the word "bread," as though the body of Christ were a spiritual bread or a spiritual food of souls. So also Christ himself carefully shows that there is no metonymy, *i.e.* that there is no alteration of meaning in the same way, in the word "body," and that he does not speak concerning a sign of his body, or concerning a symbol or figurative body, or concerning the virtue of his body and the benefits which he has earned by the sacrifice of his body [for us], but of his true, essential body, which he delivered for us to death, and of his true, essential blood, which he shed for us on the tree [altar] of the cross, for the remission of sins.

Now, indeed, there is no interpreter of the Word of Jesus Christ so faithful and sure as the Lord Christ himself, who understands best his words and his heart and opinion, and who is the wisest and most knowing in expounding them; who here, as in the making of his last will and testament and of his ever-abiding covenant and union, as elsewhere in [presenting and confirming] all articles of faith, and in the institution of all other signs of the covenant and of grace or sacraments, as [for example] circumcision, the various offerings in the Old Testament and holy baptism, has employed not allegorical, but entirely proper, simple, indubitable and clear words; and in order that no misunderstanding could occur with the words: "given for you," "shed for you," he has made a clear explanation. He also allowed his disciples to rest in the simple, proper sense, and commanded them that they should teach all nations to observe what he had commanded them, the apostles.

Therefore, also, all three evangelists (Matt. 26:26; Mark 14:22; Luke 22:19) and St. Paul, who received it [the institution of the Lord's Supper] after the ascension of Christ [from Christ himself], (1 Cor. 11:24), unanimously and with one and the same words and syllables, concerning the consecrated and distributed bread repeat these distinct, clear, firm and true words of Christ: "This is my body," altogether in one way, without any explanation [trope, figure] and variation. Therefore there is no doubt that also concerning the other part of the sacrament these words of Luke and Paul: "This cup is the new testament in my blood," can have no other meaning than that which St. Matthew and St. Mark give: "This" (namely, that which you orally drink out of the cup) "is my blood of the new testament," whereby I establish, seal and confirm with you men my testament and the new covenant, viz. the forgiveness of sins.

So also that repetition, confirmation and explanation of the Word of Christ which St. Paul makes (1 Cor. 10:16), as an especially clear testimony of the true, essential presence and distribution of the body and blood of Christ in the Supper, is to be considered with all diligence and solemnity [accurately], where he writes as follows: "The cup of blessing which we bless, is it not the communion of the blood of Christ? The bread which we break, is it not the communion of the body of Christ?" From this we clearly learn that not only the cup which Christ consecrated at the first Supper, and not only the bread which Christ broke and distributed, but also that which *we* break and bless, is the communion of the body and blood of Christ, so that all who eat this bread and drink of this cup truly receive and are partakers of the true body and blood of Christ. For if the body of Christ were present and partaken of, not truly and essentially, but only according to its power and efficacy, the bread would not be a communion of the body, but must be called a communion of the Spirit, power and benefits of Christ, as the Apology argues and concludes. And if Paul speaks only of the spiritual communion of the body of Christ through faith, as the Sacramentarians pervert this passage, he would not say that the bread, but that the spirit or faith, was the communion of the body of Christ. But as he says that the bread is the communion of the body of Christ, viz. that all who partake of the consecrated bread also become participants of the body of Christ, he must speak indeed not of a spiritual, but of a sacramental or oral participation of the body of Christ, which is common to godly and godless Christians [Christians only in name].

As also the causes and circumstances of this entire declaration of St. Paul show that he deters and warns those who ate of offerings to idols and had fellowship with heathen demonolatry, and nevertheless went also to the table of the Lord and became partakers of the body and blood of Christ, that they should not receive the body and blood of Christ for judgment and condemnation to themselves. For since all those who were partakers of the consecrated and broken bread in the Supper have communion also with the body of Christ, St. Paul cannot speak indeed of spiritual communion with Christ, which no man can abuse, and from which also no one should be warned.

Therefore, also, our dear fathers and predecessors, as Luther and other pure teachers of the Augsburg Confession, explain this expression of Paul with such words that it accords most fully with the words of Christ when they write thus: The bread which we break is the distributed body of *Christ,* or the common [communicated] body of Christ, distributed to those who receive the broken bread.

By this simple, well-founded exposition of this glorious testimony (1 Cor. 10) we unanimously abide, and we justly are astonished that some are so bold as to venture to cite this passage, which they themselves had previously opposed to the Sacramentarians, as now a foundation for their error, that in the Supper the body of Christ is only spiritually partaken of. [For thus they speak]: "The bread is the communion of the body of Christ, *i.e.* that by which there is fellowship with the body of Christ (which is the Church), or is the means by which we believers are united with Christ, just as the Word of the Gospel is the means, apprehended by faith, through which we are spiritually united to Christ and inserted into the body of Christ, which is the Church."

For that not only the godly, pious and believing Christians, but also unworthy, godless hypocrites, as Judas and his

THE FORMULA OF CONCORD (1580) (continued)

companions, who have no spiritual communion with Christ, and go to the table of the Lord without true repentance and conversion to God, also receive orally in the sacrament the true body and [true] blood of Christ, and by their unworthy eating and drinking grievously sin against the body and blood of Christ, St. Paul teaches expressly. For he says (1 Cor. 11:27): "Whosoever shall eat this bread, and drink this cup of the Lord, unworthily," sins not merely against the bread and wine, not merely against the signs or symbols and representation of the body and blood, but "shall be guilty of the body and blood of the Lord," which, present there [in the Holy Supper], he dishonors, abuses and disgraces, as the Jews who in very deed violated the body of Christ and killed him; just as the ancient Christian Fathers and church-teachers unanimously have understood and explained this passage.

There is, therefore, a twofold eating of the flesh of Christ, one "spiritual," of which Christ especially treats (John 6:54), which occurs in no other way than with the Spirit and faith, in the preaching and consideration of the Gospel, as well as in the Lord's Supper, and by itself is useful and salutary, and necessary at all times for salvation to all Christians; without which spiritual participation also the sacramental or oral eating in the Supper is not only not salutary, but even injurious and a cause of condemnation.

But this spiritual eating is nothing else than *faith,* namely, to hearken to God's Word (wherein Christ, true God and man, is presented, together with all his benefits which he has purchased for us by his flesh given for us to death, and by his blood shed for us, namely, God's grace, the forgiveness of sins, righteousness and eternal life), to receive it with faith and appropriate it to ourselves, and in the consolation that we have a gracious God, and eternal salvation on account of the Lord Jesus Christ, with sure confidence and trust, to firmly rely and abide in all troubles and temptations. [He who hears these things related from the Word of God, and in faith receives and applies them to himself, and relies entirely upon this consolation (that we have God reconciled and life eternal on account of the Mediator, Jesus Christ),—he, I say, who with true confidence rests in the Word of the Gospel in all troubles and temptations, spiritually eats the body of Christ and drinks his blood.]

The other eating of the body of Christ is *oral* or *sacramental,* where, in the Holy Supper, the true, essential body and blood of Christ are received and partaken of by all who eat and drink in the Supper the consecrated bread and wine—by the believing as an infallible pledge and assurance that their sins are surely forgiven them, and Christ dwells and is efficacious in them, but by the unbelieving for their judgment and condemnation. This the words of the institution by Christ expressly teach, when at the table and during the Supper he offers his disciples natural bread and natural wine, which he calls his true body and true blood, and in addition says: "Eat and drink." Such a command, in view of the circumstances, cannot indeed be understood otherwise than of oral eating and drinking, not in a gross, carnal, Capernaitic, yet in a supernatural, incomprehensible way; to which the other command adds still another and spiritual eating, when the Lord Christ says further: "This do in remembrance of me," where he requires faith (which is the spiritual partaking of Christ's body).

Therefore all the ancient Christian teachers expressly, and in full accord with the entire holy Christian Church, teach, according to these words of the institution of Christ and the explanation of St. Paul, that the body of Christ is not only received spiritually by faith, which occurs also without the use of the sacrament, but also orally, not only by believing and godly, but also by unworthy, unbelieving, false and wicked Christians. As this is too long to be narrated here, we will have to refer the Christian reader, for the sake of brevity, to the more ample writings of our theologians.

Hence it is manifest how unjustly and maliciously the Sacramentarian fanatics deride the Lord Christ, St. Paul and the entire Church in calling this oral partaking, and that of the unworthy, *duos pilos caudae equinae et commentum, cujus vel ipsum Satanam pudeat,* as also the doctrine concerning the majesty of Christ, *excrementum Satanae, quo diabolus sibi ipsi et hominibus illudat, i.e.* they speak so dreadfully thereof that a godly Christian man should be ashamed to translate it.

But it must also be carefully stated who are the unworthy guests of this Supper—namely, those who go to this sacrament without true repentance and sorrow for their sins, and without true faith and the good intention to improve their lives, and by their unworthy eating of the body of Christ incur temporal and eternal punishments and are guilty of the body and blood of Christ.

For Christians of weak faith, diffident and troubled, who, because of the greatness and number of their sins, are terrified, and think that, in this their great impurity, they are not worthy of this precious treasure and the benefits of Christ, and who feel and lament their weakness of faith, and from their hearts desire that they may serve God with stronger, more joyful faith and pure obedience, are the truly worthy guests for whom this highly venerable sacrament [and sacred feast] has been especially instituted and appointed; as Christ says (Matt. 11:28): "Come unto me, all ye that labor and are heavy laden, and I will give you rest." Also (Matt. 9:12): "They that be whole need not a physician, but they that be sick." Also (2 Cor. 12:9): "God's strength is made perfect in weakness." Also (Rom. 14:1): "Him that is weak in the faith receive ye" (v.3), "for God hath received him." "For whosoever believeth in the Son of God," be it with a strong or with a weak faith, "has eternal life" (John 3:15 sq.).

And the worthiness does not depend upon great or small weakness or strength of faith, but upon the merit of Christ, which the distressed father of little faith (Mark 9:24) enjoyed as well as Abraham, Paul and others, who had a joyful and strong faith.

Thus far we have spoken of the true presence and two-fold participation of the body and blood of Christ, which occurs either by faith spiritually or also orally, both by worthy and unworthy [which latter is common to worthy and unworthy].

Since also concerning the consecration and the common rule, that "nothing is a sacrament without the appointed use" [or divinely-instituted act], a misunderstanding and dissension has occurred between some teachers of the Augsburg Confession, we have also, concerning this matter, made a fraternal and unanimous declaration to one another to the following purport, viz. that not the word or work of any man produces the true presence of the body and blood of Christ in the Supper, whether it be the merit or declaration of the minister, or the eating and drinking or faith of the communicants; but all this should be ascribed alone to the power of Almighty God and the institution and ordination of our Lord Jesus Christ. [But all that which we have present in the Supper of Christ is to be ascribed absolutely and altogether to the power and Word of Almighty God and the institution, etc.]

For the true and almighty words of Jesus Christ, which he spake at the first institution, were efficacious not only at the first Supper, but they endure, have authority, operate and are still efficacious [their force, power and efficacy endure and avail even to the present]; so that in all places where the Supper is celebrated according to the institution of Christ, and his words are used, from the power and efficacy of the words which Christ spake at the first Supper the body and blood of Christ are truly present, distributed and received. For where his institution is observed and his words concerning the bread and cup [wine] are spoken, and the consecrated bread and cup [wine] are distributed, Christ himself, through the spoken words, is still efficacious *by virtue of the first institution,* through his Word which he wishes to be there repeated. As Chrysostom says in his sermon concerning the passion: "Christ himself prepares this table and blesses it; for no man makes the bread and wine set before us the body and blood of Christ, but Christ himself who was crucified for us. The words are spoken by the mouth of the priest, but, by God's power and grace, the elements presented are consecrated in the Supper by the Word, where he speaks: 'This is my body.' And just as the declaration (Gen. 1:28): 'Be fruitful, and multiply, and replenish the earth,' was spoken only once, but is ever efficacious in nature, so that it is fruitful and multiplies; so also this declaration [This is my body; this is my blood] was once spoken, but even to this day and to his advent it is efficacious, and works so that in the Supper of the churches his true body and blood are present."

Luther also [writes concerning this very subject in the same manner], (vol. vi., Jena Ed., p. 99): "This his command and institution are able and effect it that we administer and receive not mere bread and wine, but his body and blood, as his words run: 'This is my body,' etc.; 'This is my blood,' etc. It is not our work or declaration, but the command and ordination of Christ, that makes the bread the body, and the wine the blood, from the beginning of the first Supper even to the end of the world, and that through our service and office they are daily distributed."

Also (vol. iii., Jena, p. 446): "Thus here also, even though I should pronounce over all bread the words: 'This is Christ's body,' it would of course not follow thence, but if we say, according to his institution and command, in the administration of the Holy Supper: 'This is my body,' it is his body, not on account of our declaration or demonstration [because these words when uttered have this efficacy], but because of his command—that he has commanded us thus to speak and to do, and has united his command and act with our declaration."

And indeed, in the administration of the Holy Supper the words of institution should be publicly [before the church] spoken or sung, distinctly and clearly, and should in no way be omitted [and this for very many and the most important reasons. First,] in order that obedience may be rendered to the command of Christ: "This do" [that therefore should not be omitted which Christ himself did in the Holy Supper], and [secondly] that the faith of the hearers concerning the nature and fruit of this sacrament (concerning the presence of the body and blood of Christ, concerning the forgiveness of sins and all benefits which have been purchased by the death and shedding of blood of Christ, and are bestowed upon us in Christ's testament) may be excited, strengthened and confirmed by Christ's Word, and [besides that the elements of bread and wine may be consecrated or blessed for this holy use], in order that the body and blood of Christ may therewith be administered to be eaten and to be drunk [that with them the body of Christ may be offered us to be eaten and his blood to be drunk], as Paul declares (1 Cor. 10:16): "The cup of blessing which we bless," which indeed occurs in no other way than through the repetition and recitation of the words of institution.

Nevertheless, this blessing, or the narration of the words of institution of Christ, does not alone make a sacrament if the entire action of the Supper, as it was instituted by Christ, be not observed, as [for example] when the consecrated bread is not distributed, received and partaken of, but is enclosed, sacrificed or carried about. But the command of Christ, "This do," which embraces the entire action or transaction in this sacrament, viz. that in an assembly of Christians bread and wine are taken, consecrated, distributed, received, *i.e.* eaten and drunk, and the Lord's death is thereby shown forth, should be observed unseparated and inviolate, as also St. Paul presents before our eyes the entire action of the breaking of bread or of distribution and reception (1 Cor. 10:16).

[Let us now come also to the second point, of which mention was made a little before.] To preserve the true Christian doctrine concerning the Holy Supper, and to avoid and obliterate various idolatrous abuses and perversions of this testament, the following useful rule and standard has been derived from the words of institution: "Nothing has the nature of a sacrament apart from the use instituted by Christ," or "apart from the action divinely instituted." That is: "If the institution of Christ be not observed as he appointed it, there is no sacrament." This is by no means to be rejected, but with profit can and should be urged and maintained in the churches of God. And the use or action here is not chiefly the faith, also not only the oral participation, but the entire, external, visible action of the Lord's Supper instituted by Christ. [To this indeed is required], the *consecration,* or words of institution, and the *distribution* and *reception,* or oral partaking [manducation] of the consecrated bread and wine, likewise the partaking of the body and blood of Christ. And apart from this use,

THE FORMULA OF CONCORD (1580) (continued)

when, in the Papistic mass, the bread is not distributed, but offered up or enclosed and borne about, and presented for adoration, it is to be regarded as no sacrament; just as the water of baptism, if used to consecrate bells or to cure leprosy, or otherwise presented for worship, would be no sacrament or baptism. For from the beginning [of the reviving Gospel] this rule has been opposed to these Papistic abuses, and is explained by Dr. Luther himself (vol. iv., Jena Edition).

But we must besides observe also this, viz. that the Sacramentarians artfully and wickedly pervert this useful and necessary rule, in order to deny the true, essential presence and oral partaking of the body of Christ, which occurs here upon earth alike by the worthy and the unworthy; and who interpret it as referring to the use by faith, *i.e.* the spiritual and inner use of faith, as though with the unworthy there were no sacrament, and the partaking of the body occurred only spiritually through faith, or as though faith made the body of Christ present in the Holy Supper, and therefore unworthy, unbelieving hypocrites do not actually receive the body of Christ.

Now, it is not our faith that makes the sacrament, but only the true word and institution of our Almighty God and Saviour, Jesus Christ, which always is and remains efficacious in the Christian Church, and neither by the worthiness or unworthiness of the minister nor the unbelief of the one who receives it is as anything invalidated or rendered inefficacious. Just as the Gospel, even though godless hearers do not believe it, yet is and remains none the less the true Gospel, but does not work in the unbelieving to salvation; so, whether those who receive the sacrament believe or do not believe, Christ remains none the less true in his words when he says: "Take, eat: this is my body," and effects this [his presence] not by our faith, but by his omnipotence.

But it is a pernicious, shameless error that some from cunning perversion of this familiar rule ascribe more to our faith, which [in their opinion] alone renders present and partakes of the body of Christ, than to the omnipotence of our Lord and Saviour, Jesus Christ.

Concerning what pertains to the various imaginary reasons and futile counter-arguments of the Sacramentarians with respect to the essential and natural attributes of a human body, the ascension of Christ, his departure from this world, etc., inasmuch as these have one and all been considered thoroughly and in detail, from God's Word, by Dr. Luther in his controversial writings: "Against the Heavenly Prophets," "That these words, 'This is my body,' still stand firm;" likewise in his "Large" and his "Small Confession concerning the Holy Supper," [published some years afterwards], and other of his writings, and inasmuch as since his death nothing new has been advanced by the factious spirits, for the sake of brevity we will refer and appeal thereto.

For that we neither will, nor can, nor should allow ourselves to be led away by thoughts of human wisdom, whatever authority or outward appearance they may have, from the simple, distinct and clear sense of the Word and

testament of Christ to a strange opinion, other than the words sound, but that, in accordance with what is above stated, we understand and believe them simply; our reasons upon which we rest in this matter, ever since the controversy concerning this article arose, are those which Dr. Luther himself, in the very beginning, presented against the Sacramentarians in the following words: "The reasons upon which I rest in this matter are the following:

"1.   The first is this article of our faith: Jesus Christ is essential, natural, true, perfect God and man in one person, undivided and inseparable.

"2.   The second, that God's right hand is everywhere.

"3.   The third, that God's Word is not false and does not deceive.

"4.   The fourth, that God has and knows of many modes of being in any place, and not only the single one concerning which fanatics talk flippantly and which philosophers call local."

Also: "The one body of Christ [says Luther] has a three-fold mode or three modes of being anywhere.

"First, the comprehensible, bodily mode, as he went about in the body upon earth, when, according to his size, he made and occupied room [was circumscribed by fixed places]. It is mode he can still use whenever he will, as he did after the resurrection, and will use at the last day, as Paul says (1 Tim. 6:15): "Which in his times He shall show who is the blessed and only Potentate, the King of kings and Lord of lords." And to the Colossians (3:4) he says: "When Christ who is our life shall appear." In this manner he is not in God or with the Father, neither in heaven, as the wild spirits dream; for God is not a bodily space or place. And to this effect are the passages of Scripture which the fanatical spirits cite, how Christ left the world and went to the Father.

"Secondly, the incomprehensible, spiritual mode, according to which he neither occupies nor makes room, but penetrates all creatures according to his [most free] will, as, to make an imperfect comparison, my sight penetrates air, light or water, and does not occupy or make room; as a sound or tone penetrates air or water or board and wall, and is in them, and also does not occupy or make room; likewise, as light and heat penetrate air, water, glass, crystal, and the like, and is in them, and also does not make or occupy room; and much more of the like [many comparisons of this matter could be adduced]. This mode he used when he rose from the closed [and sealed] sepulchre; and passed through the closed door [to his disciples], and in the bread and wine in the Holy Supper, and, as it is believed, when he was born of his mother [the most holy Virgin Mary].

"Thirdly, the divine, heavenly mode, since he is one person with God, according to which, of course, all creatures must be far more penetrable and present to him than they are according to the second mode. For if, according to that second mode, he can be so in and with creatures that they do not feel, touch, circumscribe or comprehend him, how much more wonderfully is he in all creatures according to this sublime third mode, so that they neither circumscribe nor comprehend him, but rather that he has them present before himself, and circumscribes and comprehends them! For you must place this mode of the presence of Christ, as he is one person with God, as far beyond creatures as God is beyond them; and again as deep and near to all creatures as God is in, and near them. For he is one inseparable person with God; where God is there must he also be, or our faith is false. But who will say or think how this occurs? We know indeed that it is so that he is in God beyond all creatures, and is one person with God, but how it occurs we do not know; this [mystery] is above nature and reason, even above the reason of all the angels in heaven; it is understood only by God. Because, therefore, it is unknown to us, and yet is true, we should not deny his words before we know how to prove to a certainty that the body of Christ can by no means be where God is, and that this mode of being [presence] is false. This the fanatics ought to prove; but we challenge them to do so.

"That God indeed has and knows still more modes in which Christ's body is anywhere, I will not herewith deny; but I would indicate what awkward and stupid men our fanatics are, that they concede to the body of Christ no more than the first, comprehensible way; although they can not even prove the same, that it conflicts with our meaning. For I in no way will deny that the power of God is able to effect so much as that a body should at the same time be in a number of places, even in a bodily, comprehensible way. For who will prove that this is impossible with God? Who has seen an end to his power? The fanatics think indeed that God cannot effect it, but who will believe their thoughts? Whereby will they confirm such thoughts?"

From these words of Dr. Luther it is also clear in what sense the word *spiritual* is employed in our churches with reference to this matter. For to the Sacramentarians this word *(spiritual)* means nothing else than the spiritual communion, when through faith those truly believing are in the spirit incorporated into Christ, the Lord, and become true spiritual members of his body.

But when this word *spiritual* is employed in regard to this matter by Dr. Luther or us, we understand thereby the spiritual, supernatural, heavenly mode, according to which Christ is present in the Holy Supper, and not only works trust and life in the believing, but also condemnation in the unbelieving; whereby we reject the Capernaitic thoughts of the gross [and] carnal presence which is ascribed to and forced upon our churches, against our manifold public testimonies, by the Sacramentarians. In this sense we also say [wish the word *spiritually* to be understood when we say] that in the Holy Supper the body and blood of Christ are spiritually received, eaten and drunken; although this participation occurs with the mouth, yet the mode is spiritual.

Therefore our faith in this article, concerning the true presence of the body and blood of Christ in the Holy Supper, is based upon the *truth* and *omnipotence* of the true, almighty God, our Lord and Saviour Jesus Christ. These foundations are sufficiently strong and firm to strengthen and establish our faith in all temptations concerning this article, and to subvert and refute all the counter-arguments and objections of the Sacramentarians,

however agreeable and plausible they may always be to the reason; and upon them a Christian heart also can firmly and securely rest and rely.

Accordingly, with heart and mouth we reject and condemn as false, erroneous and misleading, all errors which are discordant, contrary and opposed to the doctrines above mentioned and founded upon God's Word, as,

1. The Papistic transubstantiation, where it is taught that the consecrated or blessed bread and wine in the Holy Supper lose entirely their substance and essence, and are changed into the substance of the body and blood of Christ, in such a way that only the mere form of bread and wine is left, or the accidents without the object; under which form of the bread, which is no more bread, but according to their assertion has lost its natural essence, the body of Christ is present, even apart from the administration of the Holy Supper, when the bread is enclosed in the pyx or is presented for display and adoration. For nothing can be a sacrament without God's command and the appointed use for which it is instituted in God's Word, as is shown above.

2. We likewise reject and condemn all other Papistic abuses of this sacrament, as the abomination of the sacrifice of the mass for the living and dead.

3. Also, that contrary to the public command and institution of Christ, to the laity only one form of the sacrament is administered; as the same Papistic abuses are thoroughly refuted by means of God's Word and the testimonies of the ancient churches, in the common confession of our churches, and the Apology, the Smalcald Articles, and other writings of our theologians.

But because in this document we have undertaken especially to present our Confession and explanation only concerning the true presence of the body and blood of Christ against the Sacramentarians, some of whom, under the name of the Augsburg Confession, have shamelessly insinuated themselves into our churches; we will also present and enumerate especially here the errors of the Sacramentarians, in order to warn our hearers to [detect and] be on their guard against them.

Accordingly, with heart and mouth we reject and condemn as false, erroneous and misleading all Sacramentarian opinions and doctrines which are discordant, contrary and opposed to the doctrines above presented and founded upon God's Word:

1. As when they assert that the words of institution are not to be understood simply in their proper signification, as they sound, of the true, essential presence of the body and blood of Christ in the Holy Supper, but should be wrested, by means of tropes or figurative interpretations, to another new, strange sense. We hereby reject all such Sacramentarian opinions and self-contradictory notions [of which some even conflict with each other], however various and manifold they may be.

2. Also, that the oral participation of the body and blood of Christ in the Holy Supper is denied [by the

THE FORMULA OF CONCORD (1580) (continued)

Sacramentarians], and it is taught, on the contrary, that the body of Christ in the Holy Supper is partaken of only spiritually by faith, so that in the Holy Supper our mouth receives only bread and wine.

3. Likewise, also, when it is taught that bread and wine in the Lord's Supper should be regarded as nothing more than tokens, whereby Christians are to recognize one another; or,

4. That they are only figures, similitudes and representations [symbols, types] of the far-absent body of Christ, in such a manner that just as bread and wine are the outward food of our body, so also the absent body of Christ, with its merit, is the spiritual food of our souls.

5. Or that they are no more than tokens and memorials of the absent body of Christ, by which signs, as an external pledge, we should be assured that the faith which turns from the Holy Supper and ascends above all heavens becomes there as truly participant of the body and blood of Christ as in the Supper we truly receive with the mouth the external signs; and that thus the assurance and confirmation of our faith occur in the Holy Supper only through the external signs, and not through the true, present body and blood of Christ offered to us.

6. Or that in the Lord's Supper the power, efficacy and merit of the far-*absent* body of Christ are distributed only to *faith*, and we thus become partakers of his absent body; and that, in this just-mentioned way, the sacramental union is to be understood, viz. with respect to the analogy of the sign and that which is signified, *i.e.* as the bread and wine have a resemblance to the body and blood of Christ.

7. Or that the body and blood of Christ cannot be received and partaken otherwise than only spiritually by faith.

8. Likewise, when it is taught that, because of his ascension into heaven with his body, Christ is so enclosed and circumscribed in a definite place in heaven that with the same [his body] he cannot or will not be truly present with us in the Holy Supper, which is celebrated according to the institution of Christ upon earth, but that he is as remote therefrom as heaven and earth are from one another, as some Sacramentarians have wilfully and wickedly falsified the text (Acts 3:21): "Who must occupy heaven," for the confirmation of their error, and instead therefore have rendered it: "Who must be received by heaven" or "in heaven," or be circumscribed and contained, so that in his human nature he could or would be in no way with us upon earth.

9. Likewise, that Christ has not promised the true, essential presence of his body and blood in his Supper, and that he neither can nor will afford it, because the nature and property of his assumed human nature cannot suffer or permit it.

10. Likewise, when it is taught that not only the Word and omnipotence of Christ, but faith, renders the body of Christ present in the Holy Supper; on this account the words of institution in the administration of the Holy Supper are omitted by some. For although the Papistic consecration, in which efficacy is ascribed to the speaking as the work of the priest, as though it constitutes a sacrament, is justly rebuked and rejected, yet the words of institution can or should in no way be omitted, as is shown in the preceding declaration.

11. Likewise, that believers do not seek the body of Christ, according to the words of Christ's institution, with the bread and wine of the Supper, but are sent with their faith from the bread of the Holy Supper to heaven, the place where the Lord Christ is with his body, that they should become partakers of it there.

12. We reject also the doctrine that unbelieving and impenitent, godless Christians, who only bear the name of Christ, but do not have right, true, living and saving faith, receive in the Lord's Supper not the body and blood of Christ, but only bread and wine. And since there are only two kinds of guests found at this heavenly meal, the worthy and the unworthy, we reject also the distinction made [by some] among the unworthy, viz. that the godless Epicureans and deriders of God's Word, who are in the external fellowship of the Church in the use of the Holy Supper, do not receive the body and blood of Christ for condemnation, but only bread and wine.

13. So too the doctrine that worthiness consists not only in true faith, but in man's own preparation.

14. Likewise, the doctrine that even the truly believing, who have and retain a right, true, living faith, and yet are without the above-mentioned sufficient preparation of their own, can, just as the unworthy guests, receive this sacrament to condemnation.

15. Likewise, when it is taught that the elements or the visible form of the consecrated bread and wine ought to be adored. But no one unless he be an Arian heretic can deny that Christ himself, true God and man, who is truly and essentially present in the Supper in the true use of the same, should be adored in spirit and in truth, as also in all other places, especially where his congregation is assembled.

16. We reject and condemn also all presumptuous, derisive, blasphemous questions and expressions which are presented with respect to the supernatural, heavenly mysteries of this Supper in a gross, carnal, Capernaitic way.

Other and additional antitheses, or rejected contrary doctrines, are reproved and rejected in the preceding declaration, which, for the sake of brevity, we will not repeat here. The condemnable or erroneous opinions that still remain, can be easily understood and named from the preceding declaration; for we reject and condemn everything that is discordant, contrary and opposed to the doctrine which is above mentioned and is thoroughly grounded in God's Word.

CHAPTER VIII. OF THE PERSON OF CHRIST.

A controversy has also occurred among the theologians of the Augsburg Confession concerning *the Person of Christ,* which nevertheless did not first arise among them, but was originally introduced by the Sacramentarians.

For since Dr. Luther, in opposition to the Sacramentarians, maintained, with firm foundations from the words of institution, the true, essential presence of the body and blood of Christ in the Holy Supper; the objection was urged against him by the Zwinglians that, if the body of Christ were present at the same time in heaven and on earth in the Holy Supper, it could be no real, true human body; for of such majesty as is peculiar to God, the body of Christ is not capable.

But as Dr. Luther contradicted and effectually refuted this Holy Supper show, which, as well as his doctrinal writings, we hereby publicly confess [approve and wish it to be publicly attested]; some theologians of the Augsburg Confession, since his death, although they have not yet been willing publicly and expressly to confess themselves with the Sacramentarians concerning the Lord's Supper, have introduced and employed precisely the same foundations concerning the person of Christ whereby the Sacramentarians attempted to remove the true, essential presence of the body and blood of Christ from his Supper, viz. that nothing should be ascribed to the human nature in the person of Christ which is above or contrary to its natural, essential property; and in regard to this have burdened the doctrine of Dr. Luther, and all those who have embraced it as in conformity with God's Word, with the charge of almost all the ancient monstrous heresies.

To explain this controversy in a Christian way, in conformity with God's Word, according to the guidance [analogy] of our simple Christian faith, and by God's grace entirely settle it, our unanimous doctrine, faith and confession are as follows:

We believe, teach and confess, although the Son of God has been from eternity a particular, distinct, entire divine person, and thus, with the Father and the Holy Ghost, true, essential, perfect God, nevertheless that, in the fulness of time, he also assumed human nature into the unity of his person, not in such a way that there now are two persons or two Christs, but that Christ Jesus is now in one person, at the same time true, eternal God, born of the Father from eternity, and a true man, born of the blessed Virgin Mary, as it is written (Rom. 9:5): "Of whom, as concerning the flesh, Christ came, who is over all, God blessed for ever."

We believe, teach and confess, that now, in this one undivided person, there are two distinct natures, the divine, which is from eternity, and the human, which in time was assumed into the unity of the person of the Son of God; which two natures in the person of Christ are never either mingled or separated from one another or changed the one into the other, but each abides in its nature and essence in the person of Christ to all eternity.

We believe, teach and confess also, that, as both natures mentioned abide unmingled and destroyed, each retains also its natural, essential properties, and for all eternity

does not lay them aside, neither do the essential properties of the one nature ever become the essential properties of the other nature.

Accordingly we believe, teach and confess, that to be almighty, eternal, infinite, to be of itself everywhere present at the same time naturally, that is, according to the property of its nature and its natural essence, and to know all things, are essential attributes of the divine nature, which never to eternity become essential properties of the human nature.

On the other hand, to be a corporeal creature, to be flesh and blood, to be finite and circumscribed, to suffer, to die, to ascend and descend, to move from one place to another, to suffer hunger, cold, thirst, heat and the like, are properties of the human nature, which never become properties of the divine nature.

We believe, teach and confess also, that now, since the incarnation, each nature in Christ does not so subsist of itself that each is or constitutes a separate person, but that they are so united that they constitute only one person, in which, at the same time, both the divine and the assumed human nature are and subsist, so that now, since the incarnation, to the entire person of Christ belongs not only his divine nature, but also his assumed human nature; and that, as without his divinity, so also without his humanity, the person of Christ or of the incarnate Son of God, *i.e.* the Son of God who has assumed flesh and become man, is not entire. Hence Christ is not two distinct persons, but is only one person, notwithstanding that two distinct natures are found in him, unconfused in their natural essence and properties.

We believe, teach and confess also, that the assumed human nature in Christ not only has and retains its natural, essential properties, but that, besides, through the personal union with divinity, and afterwards through glorification, it has been exalted to the right hand of majesty, power and might, over everything that can be named, not only in this world, but also in that which is to come (Eph. 1:21).

With respect now to this majesty, to which Christ has been exalted according to his humanity, he did not first receive it when he arose from the dead and ascended into heaven, but when, in his mother's womb, he was conceived and became man and the divine and human natures were personally united with one another. Nevertheless, this personal union is not to be understood, as some incorrectly explain it, as though the two natures, the divine and the human, were united with one another, as two boards are glued together, so that they really, *i.e.* in deed and truth, have no communication whatever with one another. For this was the error and heresy of Nestorius and Samosatenus, who, as Suidas and Theodore, presbyter of Raithu, testify, taught and held: δύο ψύσεις ἀχοινωνήτους πρὸς ξαυτὰς παντάπασιν, *i.e.* the two natures have no communication whatever with one another. Thereby the two natures are separated from one another, and thus two Christs are constituted, so that the one is Christ, and the other God the Word, who dwells in Christ.

For thus Theodore the Presbyter wrote: "At the same time in which the heretic Manes lived, one by the name of Paul,

THE FORMULA OF CONCORD (1580) (continued)

who by birth was indeed of Samosata, but was a bishop at Antioch in Syria, wickedly taught that the Lord Christ was nothing but a man in whom God the Word dwelt, just as in each of the prophets; therefore he also held that the divine and human natures are apart and separate, and that in Christ they have no communion whatever with one another, as though the one were Christ, and the other God the Word, who dwells in him."

Against this condemned heresy the Christian Church has always and everywhere simply believed and held that the divine and human natures in the person of Christ are so united that they have a true communion with one another; whereby the natures [do not meet and] are not mingled in one essence, but, as Dr. Luther writes, in one person. Accordingly, on account of this personal union and communion, the ancient teachers of the Church, before and after the Council of Chalcedon, frequently employed the word *mixture* in a good sense and with [true] discrimination. For this purpose [the sake of confirming this matter] many testimonies of the Fathers (if needful) could be adduced, which also are to be found frequently in the writings of our divines, and explain the personal union and communion by the illustration of the soul and body, and of glowing iron. For the body and soul, as also fire and iron, have communion with each other, not by a phrase or mode of speaking, or in mere words, but truly and really, *i.e.* in deed and truth; and, nevertheless, no confusion or equalizing of the natures is thereby introduced, as when from honey and water hydromel is made, which is no more pure water or pure honey, but is a mixed drink. For in the union of the divine and human natures in the person of Christ it is far different. For it is a far different, more sublime, and [altogether] ineffable communion and union between the divine and human natures in the person of Christ, on account of which union and communion God is man and man is God. Nevertheless, thereby neither the natures nor their properties are intermingled, but each nature retains its own essence and properties.

On account of this personal union (without which such a true communion of the natures would not be thought of, neither could exist) not the mere human nature, whose property it is to suffer and die, has suffered for the sins of the world, but the Son of God himself truly suffered (nevertheless, according to the assumed human nature), and in accordance with our simple Christian faith [as our Apostles' Creed testifies] truly died, although the divine nature can neither suffer nor die. This Dr. Luther has fully explained in his Large Confession concerning the Holy Supper in opposition to the blasphemous *alloeosis* of Zwingli, as he taught that one nature should be taken and understood for the other, which Dr. Luther committed, as a mark of the devil, to the abyss of hell.

For this reason the ancient teachers of the Church combined both words, χοινιυνία and ἑνιυσιξ, *i.e.* communion and union, in the explanation of this mystery, and have explained the one by the other. (Irenaeus, Book iv., ch. 37; Athanasius, in the Letter to Epietetus; Hilary, concerning the Trinity, Book 9; Basil and Gregory of Nyssa, in Theodoret; Damascenus, Book 3, ch. 19.)

On account of this personal union and communion of the divine and human natures in Christ we believe, teach and confess also, according to our simple Christian faith, all that is said concerning the majesty of Christ according to his humanity, [by which he sits] at the right hand of the almighty power of God, and what follows therefrom; all of which would not be, and could not occur, if this personal union and communion of the natures in the person of Christ did not exist really, *i.e.* in deed and truth.

On account of this personal union and communion of the natures, Mary, the blessed Virgin, bore not a mere man, but such a man as is truly the Son of the Most High God, as the angel [Gabriel] testifies; who showed his divine majesty even in his mother's womb, that he was born of a virgin, with her virginity uninjured. Therefore she is truly the mother of God, and nevertheless truly remained a virgin.

Because of this he also wrought all his miracles, and manifested this his divine Majesty, according to his pleasure, when and as he willed, and therefore not only after his resurrection and ascension, but also in his state of humiliation. For example, at the wedding at Cana of Galilee; also when he was twelve years old among the learned; also, in the garden, where with a word he cast his enemies to the ground; likewise in death, where he died not merely as any other man, but in and with his death conquered sin, death, hell, and eternal damnation; which his human nature alone would not have been able to do if it had not been thus personally united and did not have communion with the divine nature.

Hence also the human nature had, after the resurrection from the dead, its exaltation above all creatures in heaven and on earth; which is nothing else than that he entirely laid aside the form of a servant, and nevertheless did not lay aside his human nature, but retains it to eternity, and according to his assumed human nature is put in the full possession and use of the divine majesty. This majesty he nevertheless had already in his conception, even in his mother's womb; but as the apostle testifies (Phil. 2:7): "He humbled himself," and, as Dr. Luther explains, in the state of his humiliation he concealed it, and did not employ it except when he wished.

But now, since not merely as any other saint he has ascended to heaven, but, as the apostle testifies (Eph. 4:10), "above all heavens," and also truly fills all things, and is everywhere present not only as God, but also as man [has dominion and] rules from sea to sea and to the ends of the earth; as the prophets predict (Ps. 8:1, 6; 93:1 sq.; Zach. 9:10) and the apostles testify (Mark 16:20) that he everywhere wrought with them and confirmed the word with signs following. Yet this occurred not in an earthly way, but, as Dr. Luther explains, according to the manner of the right hand of God, which is no fixed place in heaven, as the Sacramentarians assert without any ground in the Holy Scriptures, but is nothing else than the almighty power of God, which fills heaven and earth, in [possession of] which Christ is placed according to his humanity, really, *i.e.* in deed and truth, without confusion and equalizing of the two natures in their essence and essential properties. From this communicated [divine] power, according to the words of his testament, he can be and is truly present with his body and blood in the Holy Supper, to which he directs us by his Word. This is possible to no man besides, because no man is in such a way united with the divine nature, and placed in this divine almighty majesty and power through and in the personal union of the two natures in Christ, as Jesus, the Son of Mary. For in him the divine and human natures are personally united with one another, so that in Christ "dwelleth all the fulness of the Godhead bodily" (Col. 2:9), and in this personal union have such a sublime, inner, ineffable communion that even the angels are astonished at it, and, as St. Peter testifies, look into these things with delight and joy (1 Pet. 1:12); all of which will shortly be explained in order and more fully.

From this foundation, of which mention has now been made, and which the personal union declares, *i.e.* from the manner in which the divine and human natures in the person of Christ are united with one another, so that they have not only the names in common, but have communion with one another, without any commingling or equalizing of the same in their essence, proceeds also the doctrine concerning the *Communicatio Idiomatum, i.e.* concerning the true communion of the properties of the natures, of which more will be said hereafter.

For since this is true, viz. that "properties do not leave their subjects," *i.e.* that each nature retains its essential properties, and these are not separated from one nature and transferred to another, as water is poured from one vessel into another; so also no communion of properties could be or subsist if the above-mentioned personal union or communion of the natures in the person of Christ were not true. This, next to the article of the Holy Trinity, is the greatest mystery in heaven and on earth, as Paul says (1 Tim. 3:16): "Without controversy, great is the mystery of godliness, that God was manifest in the flesh." For since the apostle Peter in clear words testifies (2 Ep. 1:4) that we also in whom Christ dwells only by grace, on account of that sublime mystery, are in Christ, "partakers of the divine nature," what then must be the nature of the communion of the divine nature, of which the apostle says that "in Christ dwelt all the fulness of the Godhead bodily," so that God and man are one person?

But since it is highly important that this doctrine of the *Communicatio Idiomatum, i.e.* of the communion of the properties of both natures, be treated and explained with proper discrimination (for the propositions or assertions, *i.e.* expressions, concerning the person of Christ, and his natures and properties, are not all of one kind and mode, and when they are employed without proper discrimination the doctrine becomes erroneous and the simple reader is readily led astray), the following statement should be carefully noted, which, for the purpose of making it plainer and simple, may be presented under three heads:

First, since in Christ two distinct natures exist and remain unchanged and unconfused in their natural essence and properties, and moreover there is only one person of both natures, that which is an attribute of only one nature is ascribed not to that nature apart, as though separate, but to the entire person, which is at the same time God and man, whether called God or man.

But in this genus, *i.e.* this mode of speaking, it does not follow that what is ascribed to the person is at the same time a property of both natures, but a discriminative declaration is made as to what nature it is according to which anything is ascribed to the entire person. Thus the Son of God was "born of the seed of David according to the flesh" (Rom. 1:3). Also: Christ was put to death according to the flesh, and hath suffered according to the flesh (1 Pet. 3:18; 4:1).

But since, when it is said that that is ascribed to the entire person which is peculiar to one nature, beneath the words secret and open Sacramentarians conceal their pernicious error, by naming indeed the entire person, but nevertheless understanding thereby only the one nature, and entirely excluding the other nature—as though merely the human nature had suffered for us—inasmuch as Dr. Luther has written concerning the alloeosis of Zwingli in his Large Confession concerning the Holy Supper, we will here present Luther's own words, in order that the Church of God may be guarded in the best way against this error. His words are as follows:

"Zwingli calls that an *alloeosis* when anything is ascribed to the divinity of Christ which nevertheless belongs to the humanity or the reverse. As Luke 24:26: 'Ought not Christ to have suffered these things, and to enter into his glory?' Here Zwingli triflingly declares that [the word] Christ is understood with respect to the human nature. Beware, beware, I say, of the alloeosis; for it is a mask of the devil, as it at last forms such a Christ after which I certainly would not be a Christian. For its design is that henceforth Christ should be no more, and do no more with his sufferings and life, than another mere saint. For if I believe [permit myself to be persuaded] that only the human nature has suffered for me, Christ is to me a Saviour of little worth, since he indeed himself stands is need of a Saviour. In a word, what the devil seeks by the alloeosis is inexpressible."

And shortly afterwards: "If the old sorceress, Dame Reason, the grandmother of the alloeosis, should say, Yea, divinity can neither suffer nor die; you should reply, That is true; yet, because in Christ divinity and humanity are one person, Scripture, on account of this personal union, ascribes also to divinity everything that occurs to the humanity, and the reverse. And thus, indeed, it is in truth. For this must certainly be said [acknowledged], viz. the person (he refers to Christ) suffers and dies. Now the person is true God; therefore, it is rightly said: The Son of God suffers. For although the one part (so to say), viz. the divinity, does not suffer, yet the person, which is God, suffers in the other part, viz. in his humanity; for in truth God's Son has been crucified for us, *i.e.* the person which is God. For the person, the person, I say, was crucified according to the humanity."

And again shortly afterwards: "If the alloeosis exist, as Zwingli proposes, it will be necessary for Christ to have two persons, one divine and one human, because Zwingli applies the passages concerning suffering, alone to the human nature, and of course diverts them from the

THE FORMULA OF CONCORD (1580) (continued)

divinity. For if the works be parted and disunited, the person must also be divided, since all the works or sufferings, are ascribed not to the natures, but to the person. For it is the person that does and suffers everything, one thing according to one nature, and another according to the other nature, all of which the learned know well. Therefore we consider our Lord Christ as God and man in one person, so that we neither confound the natures nor divide the person."

Dr. Luther says also in his book, "Of the Councils and the Church:" "We Christians must know that if God were not in the [one] balance, and gave it weight, we would sink to the ground with our scale of the balance. By this I mean: If it were not said [if these things were not true], 'God has died for us,' but only a man, we are lost. But if the death of God, and that God died, lie in the scale of the balance, he sinks down, and we rise up as a light, empty scale. But he also can indeed rise again or spring from the scale; yet he could not have descended into the scale unless he had first become a man like us, so that it could be said: 'God died,' 'God's passion,' 'God's blood,' 'God's death.' For in his nature God cannot die; but now God and man are united in one person, so that the expression 'God's death' is correct, when the man dies who is one thing or one person with God." Thus far Luther.

Hence it is manifest that it is incorrect to say or write that the above-mentioned expressions ("God suffered," "God died") are only verbal assertions, that is, mere words, and that it is not so in fact. For our simple Christian faith proves that the Son of God, who became man, suffered for us, died for us, and redeemed us with his blood.

Secondly, as to the execution of the office of Christ, the person does not act and work in, with, through, or according to only one nature, but in, according to, with and through both natures, or, as the Council of Chalcedon declares, one nature operates, with the communion of the other, in that which is a property of either. Therefore Christ is our Mediator, Redeemer, King, High Priest, Head, Shepherd, etc., not only according to one nature, whether it be the divine or the human, but according to both natures, as this doctrine is in other places more fully treated.

Thirdly, but it is still a much different thing when the subject of the question, or declaration, or discussion concerning this is, whether then the natures in the personal union in Christ have nothing else or nothing more than only their natural, essential properties; for that they have and retain these, is mentioned above.

Therefore, as to the divine nature in Christ, since in God there is no change (James 1:17) by the incarnation, his divine nature, in its essence and properties, is not abated or advanced; is thereby, in or by itself, neither diminished nor increased.

But as to the assumed human nature in the person of Christ, there have indeed been some who have wished to contend that this also, in the personal union with divinity, has nothing more than only the natural, essential properties according to which it is in all things like its brethren;

and that, on this account, nothing should or could be ascribed to the human nature in Christ which is beyond or contrary to its natural properties, even though the testimony of Scripture is to this effect. But that this opinion is false and incorrect is so clear from God's Word that even their own comrades censure and reject such error. For the Holy Scriptures, and the ancient Fathers from the Scriptures, very plainly testify that the human nature in Christ, inasmuch as it has been personally united with the divine nature in Christ (because, since the form of a servant and humiliation has been laid aside, it is glorified and exalted to the right hand of the majesty and power of God), has received, over and beyond its natural, essential, permanent properties, also special, high, great, supernatural, inscrutable, ineffable, heavenly prerogatives and excellences in majesty, glory, power and might above everything that can be named, not only in this world, but also in that which is to come (Eph. 1:21). So that the human nature in Christ, in its measure and mode, is employed at the same time in the execution of the office of Christ, and has also its efficacy, *i.e.* power and force, not only from, and according to, its natural, essential attributes, or only so far as its ability extends, but chiefly from and according to the majesty, glory, power and might which it has received through the personal union, glorification and exaltation. And even now the adversaries can or dare scarcely deny this, except that they dispute and contend that those are only created gifts or finite qualities, as in the saints, with which the human nature is endowed and furnished; and that, according to their [artful] thoughts or from their own [silly] argumentations or [fictitious] proofs, they wish to measure and calculate of what the human nature in Christ, without annihilation, is capable or incapable.

But the best, most certain and sure way in this controversy is this, viz. that what Christ has received, according to his assumed nature, through the personal union, glorification or exaltation, and of what his assumed human nature is capable beyond the natural properties, without annihilation, no one can know better or more thoroughly than the Lord Christ himself; and he has revealed in his Word as much thereof as it is needful for us to know. Of this, so far as pertains to the present matter, we have in the Scriptures clear, certain testimonies that we should simply believe, and in no way dispute to the contrary, as though the human nature in Christ were not capable of the same.

Now that is indeed correct and true which has been said concerning the created gifts which have been given and imparted to the human nature in Christ, viz. that it possesses them in or of itself. But these do not sufficiently explain the majesty which the Scriptures, and the ancient Fathers from Scripture, ascribe to the assumed human nature in Christ.

For to quicken, to have all judgment and power in heaven and on earth, to have all things in his hands, to have all things in subjection beneath his feet, to cleanse from sin, etc., are not created gifts, but divine, infinite properties, which, nevertheless, according to the declaration of Scripture, are given and communicated to the man Christ (John 5:27; 6:39; Matt. 28:18; Dan. 7:14; John 3:35; 13:3; Matt. 11:27; Eph. 1:22; Heb. 2:8; 1 Cor. 15:27; John 1:3).

And that this communication is to be understood, not as a phrase or mode of speaking, *i.e.* only in words with respect to the person, and only according to the divine nature, but according to the assumed human nature, the three following strong, irrefutable arguments and reasons show:

. First, there is a unanimously-received rule of the entire ancient orthodox Church that what Holy Scripture testifies that Christ received in time he received not according to the divine nature (according to which he has everything from eternity), but the person has received it in time, by reason of, and with respect to, the assumed human nature.

. Secondly, the Scriptures testify clearly (John 5:21 sq.; 6:39 sq.) that the power to quicken and to exercise judgment has been given to Christ because he is the Son of man and as he has flesh and blood.

. Thirdly, the Scriptures speak not merely in general of the Son of man, but also expressly indicate his assumed human nature (1 John 1:7): "The blood of Jesus Christ, his Son, cleanseth us from all sin," not only according to the merit [of the blood of Christ] which was one attained on the cross; but in this place John speaks thereof, that in the work or act of justification not only the divine nature in Christ, but also his blood, by mode of efficacy, *i.e.* actually, cleanses us from all sins. Therefore, in John 6 [48-58], the flesh of Christ is a quickening food; as the Council of Ephesus also declared that the flesh of Christ has power to quicken; while concerning this article many other glorious testimonies of the ancient orthodox Church are elsewhere cited.

That Christ, therefore, according to his human nature, has received this, and that it has been given and communicated to the assumed human nature in Christ, we should and must believe according to the Scriptures. But, as above said, because the two natures in Christ are so united that they are not mingled with one another or changed one into the other, and each retains its natural, essential property, so that the properties of one nature never become properties of the other nature; this doctrine must also be rightly explained and be diligently preserved against all heresies.

While we, then, invent nothing new from ourselves, but receive and repeat the explanations which the ancient orthodox Church has given hereof from the good foundation of Holy Scripture, viz. that this divine power, light, might, majesty and glory was not given the assumed human nature in Christ it such a way as the Father, from eternity, has communicated to the Son, according to the divine nature, his essence and all divine attributes, whence he is of one nature with the Father and is equal to God. For Christ is only according to the divine nature equal to the Father, but according to the assumed human nature he is beneath God; hence it is manifest that we make no confusion, equalization or abolition of natures in Christ. So, too, the power to quicken is not in the flesh of Christ as in his divine nature, viz. as an essential property.

Moreover, this communication or impartation has not occurred through an essential or natural infusion of the properties of the divine nature into the human, as though the humanity of Christ had these by itself and apart from the divine essence, or as though the human nature in Christ had thereby [by this communication] entirely laid aside its natural, essential properties, and were now either transformed into divinity, or in and by itself, with such communicated properties, had become equal to the same, or that now the natural, essential properties of both natures are of one kind, or indeed equal. For these and similar erroneous doctrines were justly rejected and condemned in ancient approved councils from the foundation of Holy Scripture. "For in no way is either conversion, confusion or equalization of the natures in Christ, or the essential properties, to be either made or admitted."

We indeed never understand the words "*real communication*" or "*communes really*" (*i.e.* the impartation or communion which occurs in deed and truth) of any physical communication or essential transfusion, *i.e.* of any essential, natural communion or effusion, whereby the natures would be confused in their essence, and their essential properties (as, against their own conscience, some have craftily and wickedly made perversions, in order to make the pure doctrine suspected); but only have opposed them to "*verbal communication*," *i.e.* the doctrine when such persons assert that it is only a phrase and mode of speaking, or nothing more than mere words, titles and names, upon which they have also laid so much stress that they are not willing to know of any other communion. Therefore, for the true explanation of the majesty of Christ we have used the terms, "Of the Real Communion," and wish thereby to show that this communion has occurred in deed and truth, nevertheless without any confusion of natures and their essential properties.

Therefore we hold and teach, with the ancient orthodox Church, as it explained this doctrine from the Scriptures, that the human nature in Christ has received this majesty according to the manner of the personal union, viz. because the entire fulness of the divinity dwells in Christ, not as in other holy men or angels, but bodily, as *in its own body*, so that with all its majesty, power, glory and efficacy in the assumed human nature, voluntarily when and as he [Christ] wills, it shines forth, and in, with, and through the same manifests, exercises, and executes its divine power, glory and efficacy, as the sould does in the body and fire in glowing iron. For by this illustration, as is also mentioned above, the entire ancient Church explained this doctrine. At the time of the humiliation this majesty was concealed and withheld [for the greater part]; but now since the form of a servant [or *exinanitio*] has been laid aside, it fully, powerfully and publicly is exercised in heaven and on earth before all saints, and in the life to come we will also behold this his glory face to face (John 17:24).

Therefore in Christ there is and remains only one divine omnipotence, power, majesty and glory, which is peculiar alone to the divine nature; but it shines, manifests and exercises itself fully, yet voluntarily, in, with and through the assumed, exalted human nature in Christ. Just as in glowing iron there are not two kinds of power to shine and burn [(as though the fire had a peculiar, and the iron also a peculiar and separate power of shining and burning)], but the power to shine and to burn is a property of the fire; yet because the fire is united with the iron it manifests and

THE FORMULA OF CONCORD (1580) (continued)

exercises this its power to shine and to burn in, with and through the glowing iron, so that the glowing iron has thence from this union the power to shine and to burn without conversion of the essence and of the natural properties of fire and iron.

On this account we understand such testimonies of Scripture as speak of the majesty to which the human nature in Christ is exalted, not so that the divine majesty which is peculiar to the divine nature of the Son of God should be ascribed in the person of the Son of man [to Christ] only according to his divine nature, or that this majesty in the human nature of Christ should be only of such a kind that his human nature should have only the mere title and name by a phrase and mode of speaking, *i.e.* only in words, but in deed and truth should have no communion whatever with it. For, since God is a spiritual, undivided essence, and therefore is present everywhere and in all creatures, and in whom he is (but he dwells especially in believers and saints), there he has with him his majesty, it might also with truth be said that in all creatures in whom God is, but especially in believers and saints, in whom he dwells, all the fulness of the Godhead dwells bodily, all treasures of wisdom and knowledge are hid, all power in heaven and earth is given, because the Holy Ghost, who has all power, is given them. For in this way there is no distinction made between Christ according to his human nature and other holy men, and thus Christ is deprived of his majesty, which he has received above all creatures, as a man or according to his human nature. For no other creature, neither man nor angel, can or should say: "All power is given unto me in heaven and in earth;" since although God is in the saints with all the fulness of his Godhead, which he has everywhere with himself; yet in them he does not dwell bodily, or with them is not personally united, as in Christ. For from such personal union it follows that Christ says, even according to his human nature (Matt. 28:18): "All power is given unto me in heaven and in earth." Also (John 13:3): "Jesus knowing that the Father had given all things into his hands." Also (Col. 2:9): "In him dwelleth all the fulness of the Godhead bodily." Also: "Thou crownedst him with glory and honor, and didst set him over the works of thy hands; thou hast put all things in subjection under his feet. For in that he put all in subjection under him, he left nothing that is not put under him" (Heb. 2:7 sq.; Ps. 8:6). "He is excepted which did put all things under him" (1 Cor. 15:27).

Moreover we believe, teach and confess that there is in no way such an infusion of the majesty of God, and of all his properties, into the human nature of Christ, whereby the divine nature is weakened [anything of the divine nature departs], or anything of its own is surrendered to another, that [in this manner] it does not retain for itself, or that the human nature has received in its substance and essence, equal majesty separate or diverse from the nature and essence of the Son of God, as when water, wine or oil is poured from one vessel into another. For the human nature, as also no other creature, either in heaven or on earth, is capable of the omnipotence of God in such a manner that it would be in itself an almighty essence, or

have in and by itself almighty properties; for thereby the human nature in Christ would be denied, and would be entirely converted into divinity, which is contrary to our Christian faith, as also to the doctrine of all the apostles and prophets.

But we believe, teach and confess that God the Father has so given his Spirit to Christ his beloved Son, according to the assumed humanity (for on this account he is called also *Messias, i.e.* the Anointed), that he has received the gifts of the Spirit, not, as other saints, in measure. For upon Christ the Lord, according to his assumed human nature (since according to his divinity he is of one essence with the Holy Ghost), there rests "the Spirit of wisdom and understanding, the Spirit of counsel and might, the Spirit of knowledge and of the fear of the Lord" (Col. 2:3; Isa. 11:2; 61:1). This occurs not in such a way that, on this account as a man he knew and had ability only with regard to some things, as other saints know and are able by the grace of God, which works in them only created gifts. But since Christ, according to his divinity, is the second person in the Holy Trinity, and from him, as also from the Father the Holy Ghost proceeds, and is and remains his Spirit and that of the Father for all eternity, not separated from the Son of God; the entire fulness of the Spirit (as the Fathers say) has been communicated by the personal union to Christ according to the flesh, which is personally united with the Son of God. This voluntarily manifests and exercises itself, with all its power therein, therewith and thereby [in, with and through the human nature of Christ] not so that he [Christ according to his human nature] not only knows some things and is ignorant of others, has ability with respect to some and is without ability with respect to others, but [according to the assumed human nature] knows and has ability with respect to all things. For upon him the Father poured without measure the Spirit of wisdom and power, so that, as man in deed and truth, he has received through this personal union all knowledge and all power. And thus all the treasures of wisdom are hidden in him, thus all power is given to him, and he is seated at the right hand of the majesty and power of God. From history it is also manifest that at the time of the Emperor Valens there was among the Arians a peculiar sect which was called the Agnoetae, because they imagined that the Son, the Word of the Father, knew indeed all things, but that his assumed human nature is ignorant of many things; against whom Gregory the Great also wrote.

On account of this personal union, and the communion following therefrom, which the divine and human natures have with one another in deed and truth in the person of Christ, there is ascribed to Christ, according to the flesh, that which his flesh, according to its nature and essence, cannot be of itself, and, apart from this union, cannot have, viz. that his flesh is a true quickening food, and his blood a true quickening blood; as the two hundred Fathers of the Council of Ephesus have testified, that "the flesh of Christ is quickening or a quickener." Hence also this man only, and no man besides, either in heaven or on earth, can say with truth (Matt. 18:20): "Where two or three are gathered together in my name, there am I in the midst of them." Also (Matt. 28:20): "Lo, I am with you always, even unto the end of the world."

These testimonies we also do not understand, as though with us in the Christian Church and congregation only the divinity of Christ were present, and such presence in no way whatever pertained to Christ according to his humanity; for in like manner Peter, Paul and all the saints in heaven would also be with us on earth, since divinity, which is everywhere present, dwells in them. This the Holy Scriptures testify only of Christ, and of no other man besides. But we hold that by these words [the passages of Scripture above] the majesty of the man Christ is declared, which Christ has received, according to his humanity, at the right hand of the majesty and power of God, viz. that he also, according to his assumed human nature and with the same, can be and is present where he will, and especially that in his Church and congregation on earth, as Mediator, Head, King and High Priest, he is not half present or there is only the half [one part of him] present, but the entire person of Christ is present, to which two natures belong, the divine and the human: not only according to his divinity, but also according to and with his assumed human nature, by which he is our brother and we are flesh of his flesh and bone of his bone. For the certain assurance and confirmation of this he has instituted his Holy Supper, that also according to our nature, by which he has flesh and blood, he will be with us, and in us dwell, work and be efficacious.

Upon this firm foundation Dr. Luther, of holy memory, has also written [faithfully and clearly] concerning the majesty of Christ according to his human nature.

In the Large Confession concerning the Lord's Supper he writes thus concerning the person of Christ: "Since Christ is such a man as is supernaturally one person with God, and apart from this man there is no God, it must follow that also, according to the third supernatural mode, he is and can be everywhere that God is, and all things are entirely full of Christ, even according to humanity, not according to the first corporeal, comprehensible mode, but according to the supernatural, divine mode."

'For here you must stand [confess] and say: 'Wherever Christ is according to the divinity, there he is a natural, divine person, and he is also there naturally and personally, as his conception in his mother's womb well shows. For if he were God's Son, he must naturally and personally be in his mother's womb and become man. But if, wherever he is, he is naturally and personally, he must also be in the same place as man. For there are not [in Christ] two separate persons, but only one person. Wherever it is, there the person is only one and undivided; and wherever you can say: 'Here is God,' there you must also say: 'Therefore Christ the man is also there.' And if you would show a place where God would be, and not the man, the person would be already divided, because I could then say with truth: 'Here is God who is not man, and who never as yet has become man.'

'Far be it from me that I should acknowledge or worship such a God. For it would follow hence that space and place separated the two natures from one another, and divided the person, which, nevertheless, death and all devils could not divide or rend from one another. And there would remain to me a poor sort of Christ [a Christ of how much value, pray?], who would be no more than a divine and human person at the same time in only one place, and in all other places he must be only a mere separate God and divine person without humanity. No, friend, wherever you place God for me, there you must also place with him for me humanity; they do not allow themselves to be separated or divided from one another. They became one person, which [as Son of God] does not separate from itself [the assumed humanity]."

In the little book concerning the Last Words of David, which Dr. Luther wrote shortly before his death, he says as follows: "According to the other, the temporal, human birth, the eternal power of God has also been given him, yet in time, and not from eternity. For the humanity of Christ has not been from eternity, as the divinity; but as we reckon and write Jesus, the Son of Mary, is this year 1543 years old. But from the instant when divinity and humanity were united in one person, the man, the Son of Mary, is and is called almighty, eternal God, has eternal might, and has created and sustains, by the *communicatio idiomatum*, all things, because he is one person with divinity, and is also true God. Of this he speaks (Matt. 11:27): 'All things are delivered unto me of my Father;' and (Matt. 28:18): 'All power is given unto me in heaven and in earth.' To what me? To me, Jesus of Nazareth, the Son of Mary, and born man. From eternity I had it of the Father, before I became man. But when I became man I received it in time, according to humanity, and kept it concealed until my resurrection and ascension; then it was to be manifested and declared, as St. Paul says (Rom. 1:4): 'He is declared and proved to be a Son of God with power.' John (17:10) calls it 'glorified.'"

Similar testimonies are found in Dr. Luther's writings, but especially in the book: "That these Words still stand Firm," and in the "Large Confession concerning the Holy Supper;" to which writings, as well-grounded explanations of the majesty of Christ at the right hand of God, and of his testament, we refer, for the sake of brevity, in this article, as well as in the Holy Supper, as has been heretofore mentioned.

Therefore we regard it a pernicious error when to Christ, according to his humanity, such majesty is denied. For thereby there is removed from Christians the very great consolation which they have from the presence and dwelling with them of their Head, King and High Priest, who has promised them that not only his mere divinity should be with them, which to us poor sinners is as a consuming fire to dry stubble, but that very man who has spoken with us, who has experienced all troubles in his assumed human nature, who can therefore have with us, as with men and brethren, sympathy, will be with us in all our troubles also according to the nature in which he is our brother and we are flesh of his flesh.

Therefore we unanimously reject and condemn, with mouth and heart, all errors not in accordance with the doctrine presented, as contrary to the Prophetic and Apostolic Scriptures, the pure [received and approved] symbols, and our Christian Augsburg Confession:

THE FORMULA OF CONCORD (1580) (continued)

1. As when it is believed or taught by any one that, on account of the personal union, the human nature is mingled with the divine or is changed into it.

2. Also, that the human nature in Christ, in the same mode as the divinity, is everywhere present, as an infinite essence, from essential power, likewise from a property of its nature.

3. Also, that the human nature in Christ has become equal to and like the divine nature in its substance and essence or in its essential properties.

4. Also, that the humanity of Christ is locally extended in all places of heaven and earth; which should not be ascribed even to the divinity. But that Christ, by his divine omnipotence, can be present with his body, which he has placed at the right hand of the majesty and power of God, wherever he will; especially where, as in the Holy Supper, he has, in his Word, promised this his presence, this his omnipotence and wisdom can well accomplish without change or abolition of his true human nature.

5. Also, that merely the human nature of Christ has suffered for us and redeemed us, with which the Son of God had no communion whatever in suffering.

6. Also, that Christ is present with us on earth, only according to his divinity, in the preached Word and right use of the sacraments; and this presence of Christ does not in any way pertain to his assumed human nature.

7. Also, that the assumed human nature in Christ has in deed and truth no communion whatever with the divine power, might, wisdom, majesty and glory, but has in common only the mere title and name.

These errors, and all that are contrary and opposed to the [godly and pure] doctrine presented above, we reject and condemn, as contrary to the pure Word of God, the Scriptures of the holy prophets and apostles, and our Christian faith and confession. And we admonish all Christians, since in the Holy Scriptures Christ is called a mystery, upon which all heretics dash their heads, not in a presumptuous manner to indulge in subtile inquiries with their reason concerning such mysteries, but with the venerated apostles simply to believe, to close the eyes of their reason, and bring into captivity their understanding to the obedience of Christ (2 Cor. 10:5), and thence console themselves [seek most delightful and sure consolation]; and thus rejoice without ceasing that our flesh and blood are placed so high at the right hand of the majesty and almighty power of God. Thus will we assuredly find constant consolation in every adversity, and remain well guarded from pernicious error.

CHAPTER IX. OF THE DESCENT OF CHRIST TO HELL.

And because, even in the ancient Christian teachers of the Church, as well as in some among us, dissimilar explanations of the article concerning the Descent to Hell are found, we, in like manner, abide by the simplicity of our Christian faith [comprised in the Creed], to which Dr.

Luther in his sermon in the castle at Torgau in 1533, "Concerning the Descent to Hell," has referred, where we confess: "I believe in Jesus Christ, His only Son, our Lord, . . . dead and buried. He descended into hell." For in this Confession the burial and descent of Christ to hell are distinguished as different articles; and we simply believe that the entire person, God and man, after the burial descended into hell, conquered the devil, destroyed the power of hell, and took from the devil all his might. We should not, however, trouble ourselves with sublime and acute thoughts as to how this occurred; for this article can be comprehended by the reason and the five senses as little as the preceding, as to how Christ is placed at the right hand of the almighty power and majesty of God; but [in such mysteries of faith] we have only to believe and adhere to the Word. Thus we retain the substance [sound doctrine] and [true] consolation that neither hell nor devil can take captive or injure us and all who believe in Christ.

CHAPTER X. OF CHURCH RITES WHICH ARE [COMMONLY] CALLED ADIA PHORA, OR MATTERS OF INDIFFERENCE.

Concerning Ceremonies and Church Rites which are neither commanded nor forbidden in God's Word, but have been introduced into the Church with a good intention, for the sake of good order and propriety, or otherwise to maintain Christian discipline, a dissension has in like manner arisen among some theologians of the Augsburg Confession. Since the one side held that also in time of persecution and in case of confession [when confession of faith is to be made], even though the enemies of the Gospel do not agree with us in doctrine, yet some [long-since] abrogated ceremonies, which in themselves are adiaphora, and neither commanded nor forbidden by God, may, without violence to conscience, be re-established in compliance with the pressure and demand of the adversaries, and thus in such [things of themselves] adiaphora, or matters of indifference, we may indeed have conformity with them. But the other side contended that in case of confession in time of persecution, especially when thereby the adversaries design through force and compulsion, or in an insidious manner, to suppress the pure doctrine, and gradually to introduce again into our churches their false doctrine, this which has been said can in no way occur without violence to conscience and prejudice to the divine truth.

To explain this controversy, and by God's grace at last to settle it, we present to the Christian reader the following simple statement [in conformity with the Word of God]: Namely, when, under the title and pretext of external adiaphora, such things are proposed as (although painted another color) are in fact contrary to God's Word, these are not to be regarded adiaphora, but should be avoided as things prohibited by God. In like manner, also, among the genuine adiaphora such ceremonies should not be reckoned which have the appearance, or to avoid thereby persecution, feign the appearance, as though our religion and that of the Papists were not far apart, or as though the latter were not highly offensive to us; or when such ceremonies are designed for the purpose, and therefore are required and received, as though by and through them two contrary religions were reconciled and became one body;

or, again, when an advance towards the Papacy and a departure from the pure doctrine of the Gospel and true religion should occur or gradually follow therefrom [when there is danger lest we seem to have advanced towards the Papacy, and to have departed, or to be on the point of departing gradually, from the pure doctrine of the Gospel].

For in this case what Paul writes (2 Cor. 6:14, 17) must have weight: "Be ye not unequally yoked together with unbelievers; what communion hath light with darkness? Wherefore, Come out from among them, and be ye separate, saith the Lord."

Likewise, when there are useless, foolish spectacles, that are profitable neither for good order, nor Christian discipline, nor evangelical propriety in the Church, these also are not genuine adiaphora, or matters of indifference.

But concerning those things which are genuine adiaphora, or matters of indifference (as before explained), we believe, teach and confess that such ceremonies, in and of themselves, are no worship of God, also no part of the worship of God, but should be properly distinguished from this, as it stands written: "In vain they do worship me, teaching for doctrines the commandments of men" (Matt. 15:9).

Therefore we believe, teach and confess that the Church of God of every place and every time has, according to its circumstances, the authority, power and right [in matters truly adiaphora] to change, to diminish and to increase them, without thoughtlessness and offence, in an orderly and becoming way, as at any time it may be regarded most profitable, most beneficial and the best for [preserving] good order [maintaining], Christian discipline [and for εὐταξία worthy of the profession of the Gospel], and the edification of the Church. How even to the weak in faith we can yield and give way with a good conscience in such external adiaphora Paul teaches (Rom. 14), and proves it by his example (Acts 16:3; 21:26; 1 Cor. 9:19).

We believe, teach and confess also that at the time [in which a confession of the heavenly truth is required] of confession, when the enemies of God's Word desire to suppress the pure doctrine of the holy Gospel, the entire Church of God, yea, every Christian, but especially the ministers of the Word, as the presidents of the congregation of God [as those whom God has appointed to rule his Church], are bound, according to God's Word, to confess the [godly] doctrine, and what belongs to the whole of [pure] religion, freely and openly, not only in words, but also in works and with deeds; and that then, in this case, even in such [things truly and of themselves] adiaphora, they must not yield to the adversaries, or permit these adiaphora to be forced upon them by their enemies, whether by violence or cunning, to the detriment of the true worship of God and the introduction and sanction of idolatry. For it is written (Gal. 5:1): "Stand fast, therefore, in the liberty wherewith Christ has made us free, and be not again entangled in the yoke of bondage." Also (Gal. 2:4 sq.): "And that because of false brethren unawares brought in, who came in privily to spy out our liberty which we have in Christ Jesus, that they might bring us into bondage; to whom we gave place by subjection, no,

not for an hour; that the truth of the Gospel might continue with you."

And [it is manifest that] Paul speaks in the same place concerning circumcision, which at the time was an adiaphoron (1 Cor. 7:18 sq.), and was used by Paul at other places [nevertheless] with [Christian and] spiritual freedom (Acts 16:3). But when the false apostles demanded and abused circumcision for confirming their false doctrine, as though the works of the Law were needful for righteousness and salvation, Paul says that he would yield not for an hour, in order that the truth of the Gospel might continue [unimpaired].

Thus Paul yields and gives way to the weak in [the observance of] food and times or days (Rom. 14:6). But to the false apostles who wished to impose these upon the conscience as *necessary things* he will yield not even in those things which in themselves are adiaphora (Col. 2:16): "Let no man therefore judge you in meat, or in drink, or in respect of an holy day." And when Peter and Barnabas yielded to a certain extent [more than they ought], Paul openly reproves them as those who have not walked aright, according to the truth of the Gospel (Gal. 2:11 sqq.)

For here it is no longer a question concerning adiaphora, which, in their nature and essence are and remain of themselves free, and accordingly can admit of no command or prohibition that they be employed or be intermitted; but it is a question, in the first place, concerning the sacred article of our Christian faith, as the apostle testifies, "in order that the truth of the Gospel might continue," which is obscured and perverted by such compulsion and command, because such adiaphora are either publicly required for the sanction of false doctrine, superstition and idolatry, and for the suppression of pure doctrine and Christian liberty, or at least are abused for this purpose by the adversaries, and are thus received [or certainly are thus received by them, and are believed to be restored for this abuse and wicked end].

Likewise, the article concerning Christian liberty is also here at stake, to preserve which the Holy Ghost so earnestly charged his Church through the mouth of the holy apostle, as heard above. For as soon as this is weakened and the ordinances of men [human traditions] are urged with compulsion upon the Church, as though they were necessary and their omission were wrong and sinful, the way is already prepared for idolatry, whereby the ordinances of men [human traditions] are gradually multiplied and regarded as a service of God, not only equal to the ordinances of God, but are even placed above them.

So also by such [untimely] yielding and conformity in external things, where there has not been previously Christian union in doctrine, idolaters are confirmed in their idolatry; on the other hand, the truly believing are distressed, offended and weakened in their faith [their faith is grievously shaken, and made to totter as though by a battering-ram]; both of which every Christian for the sake of his soul's welfare and salvation is bound to avoid, as it is written: "Woe unto the world because of offences!" Also: "Whoso shall offend one of these little ones which believe in me, it were better for him that a millstone were hanged

THE FORMULA OF CONCORD (1580) (continued)

about his neck and that he were drowned in the depth of the sea" (Matt. 18:6, 7.)

But especially is that to be remembered which Christ says: "Whosoever therefore shall confess me before men, him will I confess also before my Father which is in heaven."

Moreover, that this has been always and everywhere the faith and confession concerning such adiaphora, of the chief teachers of the Augsburg Confession, into whose footsteps we have entered, and intend by God's grace to persevere, in this their Confession, the following testimonies drawn from the Smalcald Articles, which was composed and subscribed in the year 1537 [most clearly], show:

TESTIMONIES DERIVED FROM THE SMALCALD ARTICLES, WRITTEN IN THE YEAR 1537.

The Smalcald Articles say concerning this as follows: "We do not acknowledge them as the Church, and also they are not; we also will not listen to those things which, under the name of Church, they either enjoin or forbid. For, thank God, today a child seven years old knows what the Church is, namely, saints, believers and lambs, who hear the voice of their Shepherd."

And shortly before: "If the bishops were true bishops, and would devote themselves to the Church and the Gospel, they might be allowed, for the sake of love and unity, and not from necessity, to ordain and confirm us and our preachers; nevertheless, under the condition that all masks and phantoms of an unchristian nature and display be laid aside. Yet because they neither are nor wish to be true bishops, but worldly lords and princes, who will neither preach, nor teach, nor baptize, nor administer the Lord's Supper, nor perform any work or office of the Church, but persecute and condemn those who, being called, discharge their duty; for their sake, the Church ought not to remain without ministers."

And in the article, "Of the Primacy of the Pope," the Smalcald Articles say: "Wherefore, just as we cannot adore the devil himself as Lord and God, so we cannot endure his apostle, the Pope or Antichrist, in his rule as head or lord. For to lie and to kill and to destroy body and soul eternally is a prerogative of the Papal government."

And in the treatise "Concerning the Power and Primacy of the Pope," which is appended to the Smaleald Articles, and was also subscribed by the theologians then present with their own hands, stand these words: "No one should burden the Church with his own traditions, but here it should be enjoined that the power or influence of no one should avail more than the Word of God."

And shortly afterwards: "This being the case, all Christians ought most diligently to beware of becoming partakers of the godless doctrine, blasphemies and unjust cruelties of the Pope; but ought to desert and execrate the Pope with his members as the kingdom of Antichrist, just as Christ has commanded (Matt. 7:15): 'Beware of false prophets.' And Paul commands us to avoid false teachers and execrate them as an abomination. And in (2 Cor. 6:14), he says: 'Be ye not unequally yoked together with unbelievers, for what communion hath light with darkness?'

"It is difficult to separate one's self from so many lands and nations, and to be willing to maintain this doctrine; but here stands God's command, that every one should beware and not agree with those who maintain false doctrine or who think of supporting it by means of cruelty."

So, too, Dr. Luther has amply instructed the Church of God in an especial treatise concerning what should be thought of ceremonies in general, and especially of adiaphora, vol. iii., Jena ed., p. 523; likewise also in 1530, in German, vol. v., Jena ed.

From this explanation every one can understand what it is proper for every Christian congregation and every Christian man, especially in time of confession [when a confession of faith should be made], and most of all preachers, to do or to leave undone, without injury to conscience, with respect to adiaphora, in order that God may not be incensed [provoked to just indignation], love may not be injured, the enemies of God's Word be not strengthened, and the weak in the faith be not offended.

1. Therefore, we reject and condemn as wrong when the ordinances of men in themselves are regarded as a service or part of the service of God.

2. We reject and condemn also as wrong when these ordinances are urged by force upon the congregation of God as necessary.

3. We reject and condemn also as wrong the opinion of those who hold that at a time of persecution we may comply with the enemies of the holy Gospel in [restoring] such adiaphora, or may come to an agreement with them, which causes injury to the truth.

4. We likewise regard it a sin worthy of punishment when, in the time of persecution, on account of the enemies of the Gospel, anything either in adiaphora or in doctrine, and what otherwise pertains to religion, is done in word and act contrary and opposed to the Christian confession.

5. We reject and condemn also when these adiaphora are abrogated [the madness of those who abrogate] in such a manner as though it were not free to the Church of God at any time and place to employ one or more in Christian liberty, according to its circumstances, as may be most useful to the Church.

According to this doctrine the churches will not condemn one another because of dissimilarity of ceremonies when, in Christian liberty, one has less or more of them, provided they otherwise are in unity with one another in doctrine and all its articles, and also in the right use of the holy sacraments, according to the well-known saying; "Disagreement in fasting does not destroy agreement in the faith."

CHAPTER XI. OF GOD'S ETERNAL FOREKNOWLEDGE [PREDESTINATION] AND ELECTION.

Although among the theologians of the Augsburg Confession no public dissension whatever, causing offence, and that is widespread, has as yet occurred concerning the eternal election of the children of God; yet since in other places this article has been brought into very painful controversy, and even among our theologians there was some agitation concerning it, and similar expressions were not always employed concerning it by the theologians; in order by the aid of divine grace to prevent disagreement and separation in the future among our successors, as well as among us, we have desired here also to present an explanation of the same, so that every one may know what is our unanimous doctrine, faith and confession concerning this article also. For the doctrine concerning this article, if presented from and according to the pattern of the divine Word [and analogy of God's Word and of faith], neither can nor should be regarded as useless or unnecessary, much less as causing offence or injury, because the Holy Scriptures not only in but one place and incidentally, but in many places, thoroughly discuss and urge [explain] the same. Therefore, on account of abuse or misunderstanding we should not neglect or reject the doctrine of the divine Word, but precisely on that account, in order to avert all abuse and misunderstanding, the true meaning should and must be explained from the foundation of the Scriptures. According to this the plain sum and substance [of the heavenly doctrine] concerning this article consists in the following points:

First, the distinction between the *eternal foreknowledge of God,* and the *eternal election of his children to eternal salvation*, is to be accurately observed. For foreknowledge or prevision, *i.e.* that God sees and knows everything before it happens, which is called *God's foreknowledge [prescience]*, extends to all creatures, good and bad; namely, that he foresees and foreknows everything that is or will be, that is occurring or will occur, whether it be good or bad, since before God all things, whether they be past or future, are manifest and present. Thus it is written (Matt. 10:29): "Are not two sparrows sold for a farthing, and one of them shall not fall on the ground without your Father." And (Ps. 139:16): "Thine eyes did see my substance, yet being imperfect; and in they book all my members were written, which in continuance were fashioned, when as yet there were none of them." Also (Isa. 37:28): "I know thy abode, and they going out, and thy coming in, and thy rage against me."

But the *eternal election of God*, or predestination, *i.e. God's appointment to salvation*, pertains not at the same time to the godly and the wicked, but only to the children of God, who were elected and appointed to eternal life before the foundation of the world was laid, as Paul says (Eph. 1:4, 5): "He hath chosen us in him, having predestinated us unto the adoption of children by Jesus Christ."

The foreknowledge of God (prescience) foresees and foreknows also that which is evil, but not in such a manner as though it were God's gracious will that evil should happen. But all that the perverse, wicked will of the devil and of men purposes and desires to do, and will do, God sees and knows before; and his prescience, *i.e.* foreknowledge, so observes its order also, even in wicked acts or works, that to the evil which God does not will its limit and measure are fixed by God, how far it should go and how long it should last, when and how he would hinder and punish it; yet all this God the Lord so rules that it must redound to the glory of the divine name and to the salvation of his elect; and the godless, on that account, must be put to confusion.

Moreover, the beginning and cause of the evil is not God's; foreknowledge (for God does not procure and effect or work that which is evil, neither does he help or promote it); but the wicked, perverse will of the devil and of men [is the cause of the evil], as it is written (Hos. 13:9): "O Israel, thou hast destroyed thyself; but in me is thy help." Also (Ps. 5:4): "Thou art not a God that hath pleasure in wickedness."

But the eternal election of God not only foresees and foreknows the salvation of the elect, but is also, from the gracious will and pleasure of God in Christ Jesus, a cause which procures, works, helps and promotes what pertains thereto; upon this [divine predestination] also our salvation is so founded that "the gates of hell cannot prevail against it" (Matt. 16:18). For it is written (John 10:28): "Neither shall any man pluck my sheep out of my hand." And again (Acts 13:48): "And as many as were ordained to eternal life, believed."

This eternal election or appointment of God to eternal life is also not to be considered merely in God's secret, inscrutable counsel in such a manner as though it comprised in itself nothing further, or nothing more belonged thereto, and nothing more were to be considered therein, than that God foresaw who and how many would be saved, and who and how many would be damned, or that he only held a review, and would say thus: "This one shall be saved, that one shall be damned; this one shall remain steadfast [in faith to the end], that one shall not remain steadfast."

For from this many derive and adopt strange, dangerous and pernicious thoughts, which occasion and strengthen either security and impenitence or despondency and despair, so that they fall into troublesome thoughts and [for thus some think, with peril to themselves, nay, even sometimes] speak thus: Since "before the foundation of the world was laid" (Eph. 1:4) "God has foreknown [predestinated] his elect for salvation, and God's foreknowledge cannot err or be injured or changed by any one" (Isa. 14:27; Rom. 9:19), "if I, then, am foreknown [elected] for salvation, nothing can injure me with respect to it, even though, without repentance, I practise all sorts of sin and shame, do not regard the Word and sacraments, concern myself neither with repentance, faith, prayer nor godliness. But I nevertheless will and must be saved; because God's foreknowledge [election] must come to pass. If, however, I am not foreknown [predestinated], it nevertheless helps me nothing, even though I would observe the Word, repent, believe, etc.; for I cannot hinder or change God's foreknowledge [predestination]."

THE FORMULA OF CONCORD (1580) (continued)

And such thoughts occur indeed even to godly hearts, although, by God's grace, they have repentance, faith and a good purpose [of living in a godly manner], so that they think: "If you are not foreknown [predestinated or elected] from eternity for salvation, everything [your every effort and entire labor] is of no avail." This especially occurs when they regard their weakness and the examples of those who have not persevered [in faith to the end], but have fallen away again [from true godliness to ungodliness, and have become apostates].

Against this false delusion and such dangerous thoughts we should establish the following firm foundation, which is sure and cannot fail, namely: Since all Scripture has been given by God, not for [cherishing] security and impenitence, but should serve "for reproof, for correction, for instruction in righteousness" (2 Tim. 3:16); also, since everything in God's Word has been prescribed to us, not that we should thereby be driven to despair, but "that we, through patience and comfort of the Scriptures, might have hope" (Rom. 15:4); it is without doubt in no way the sound sense or right use of the doctrine concerning the eternal foreknowledge of God that thereby either impenitence or despair should be occasioned or strengthened. Therefore the Scriptures present to us this doctrine in no other way than to direct us thereby to the [revealed] Word (Eph. 1:13; 1 Cor. 1:7), exhort to repentance (2 Tim. 3:16), urge to godliness (Eph. 1:14; John 15:3), strengthen faith and assure us of our salvation (Eph. 1:13; John 10:27 sq.; 2 Thess. 2:13 sq.).

Therefore, if we wish to think or speak correctly and profitably concerning eternal election, or the predestination and foreordination of the children of God to eternal life, we should accustom ourselves not to speculate concerning the mere, secret, concealed, inscrutable foreknowledge of God, but how the counsel, purpose and ordination of God in Christ Jesus, who is the true book of life, has been revealed to us through the Word, viz. that the entire doctrine concerning the purpose, counsel, will and ordination of God pertaining to our redemption, call, righteousness and salvation should be taken together; as Paul has treated and explained this article (Rom. 8:29 sq.; Eph. 1:4 sq.), as also Christ in the parable (Matt. 22:1 sqq.), namely, that God in his purpose and counsel decreed:

1. That the human race should be truly redeemed and reconciled with God through Christ, who, by his faultless [innocency] obedience, suffering and death, has merited for us righteousness which avails before God, and eternal life.

2. That such merit and benefits of Christ should be offered, presented and distributed to us through his Word and sacraments.

3. That he would be efficacious and active in us by his Holy Ghost, through the Word, when it is preached, heard and pondered, to convert hearts to true repentance and preserve them in the true faith.

4. That all those who, in true repentance, receive Christ by a true faith he would justify and receive into grace, adoption and inheritance of eternal life.

5. That those also who are thus justified he would sanctify in love, as St. Paul (Eph. 1:4) says.

6. That, in their great weakness, he also would defend them against the devil, the world, and the flesh, and would rule and lead them in his ways, and when they stumble would raise them again [place his hand beneath them], and under the cross and in temptation would comfort and preserve them [for life].

7. That the good work which he has begun in them he would strengthen, increase and support to the end, if they observe God's Word, pray diligently, abide in God's goodness [grace] and faithfully use the gifts received.

8. That those whom he has elected, called and justified, he would eternally save and glorify in life eternal.

And that in his counsel, purpose and ordination he prepared salvation not only in general, but in grace considered and chose to salvation each and every person of the elect, who shall be saved through Christ, and ordained that in the way just mentioned he would by his grace, gifts and efficacy bring them thereto [make them participants of eternal salvation], and aid, promote, strengthen and preserve them.

All this, according to the Scriptures, is comprised in the doctrine concerning the eternal election of God to adoption and eternal salvation, and should be comprised with it, and not omitted, when we speak of God's purpose, predestination, election and ordination to salvation. And when, according to the Scriptures, thoughts concerning this article are thus formed, we can, by God's grace, simply [and correctly] adapt ourselves to it [and advantageously treat of it].

This also belongs to the further explanation and salutary use of the doctrine concerning God's predestination to salvation, viz.: Since only the elect, whose names are written in the book of life, are saved, how can we know whence, and whereby can we decide, who are the elect and those by whom this doctrine can and should be received for comfort?

And of this we should not judge according to our reason, also not according to the Law or from any external appearance. Neither should we attempt to investigate the secret, concealed abyss of divine predestination, but should give heed to the revealed will of God. For he has "made known unto us the mystery of his will," and made it manifest through Christ that it might be preached (Eph. 1:9 sqq; 2 Tim. 1:9 sq.).

But this is revealed to us thus, as St. Paul says (Rom. 8:29 sq.): "Whom God predestinated, elected and foreordained, be also called." Now, God calls not without means, but through the Word, as he has commanded "repentance and remission of sins to be preached in his name" (Luke 24:47). St. Paul also testifies to like effect when he writes (2 Cor. 5:20): "We are ambassadors for Christ, as though God did beseech you by us; we pray you in Christ's stead, Be ye reconciled to God." And the guests whom the King will have at the wedding of his Son he calls through his ministers sent forth (Matt. 22:2 sqq.)—some at the first and some at the second, third, sixth, ninth, and even at the eleventh hour (Matt. 20:3 sqq.).

Therefore, if we wish with profit to consider our eternal election to salvation, we must in every way hold rigidly and firmly to this, viz. that as the preaching of repentance so also the promise of the Gospel is universal, *i.e.* it pertains to all men (Luke 24). Therefore Christ has commanded "that repentance and remission of sins should be preached in his name among all nations." For God loved the world and gave his Son (John 3:16). Christ bore the sins of the world (John 1:29), gave his flesh for the life of the world (John 6:51); his blood is the propitiation for the sins of the whole world (1 John 1:7; 2:2). Christ says: "Come unto me, all ye that labor and are heavy laden, and I will give you rest" (Matt. 11:28). "God hath concluded them all in unbelief, that he might have mercy upon all" (Rom. 11:32). "The Lord is not willing that any should perish, but that all should come to repentance" (2 Pet. 3:9). "The same Lord over all is rich unto all that call upon him." (Rom. 10:12). "The righteousness of God, which is by faith of Jesus Christ, unto all and upon all them that believe" (Rom. 3:22). "This is the will of Him that sent me, that every one that seeth the Son and believeth on him may have everlasting life." Therefore it is Christ's command that to all in common to whom repentance is preached this promise of the Gospel also should be offered (Luke 24:47; Mark 16:15).

And this call of God, which is made through the preaching of the Word, we should regard as no delusion, but know that thereby God reveals his will, viz. that in those whom he thus calls he will work through the World, that they may be enlightened, converted and saved. For the Word, whereby we are called, is "a ministration of the Spirit," that gives the Spirit, or whereby the Spirit is given (2 Cor. 3:8), and "a power of God unto salvation" (Rom. 1:16). And since the Holy Ghost wishes to be efficacious through the Word, and to strengthen and give power and ability, it is God's will that we should receive the Word, believe and obey it.

For this reason the elect are described thus: "My sheep hear my voice, and I know them, and they follow me, and I give unto them eternal life" (John 10:27 sq.) And (Eph. 1:11, 13): Who according to the purpose are predestinated to an inheritance, who hear the Gospel, believe in Christ, pray and give thanks, are sanctified in love, have hope, patience and comfort under the cross (Rom. 8:25); and although in them all this is very weak, yet they hunger and thirst for righteousness (Matt. 5:6).

Thus the Spirit of God gives to the elect the testimony that they are children of God, and when they do not know for what they should pray as they ought, he intercedes with groanings that cannot be uttered (Rom. 8:16, 26).

Thus, also, Holy Scripture shows that God, who has called us, is so faithful when he has begun a good work in us that he also will preserve and continue it to the end, if we do not turn ourselves from him, but retain firmly to the end the work begun, for retaining which he has promised his grace (1 Cor. 1:9; Phil. 1:6; [1 Pet. 5:10]; 2 Pet. 3:9; Heb. 3:2).

With this revealed will of God we should concern ourselves, and should follow and study it, because the Holy Ghost, through the Word whereby he calls us, bestows, to this end, grace, power and ability, and we should not attempt to scrutinize the abyss of God's hidden predestination, as it is written in Luke 13:24, where to one who asks: "Lord, are there few that be saved?" Christ answers: "Strive to enter in at the strait gate." Accordingly, Luther says [in the Preface to the Epistle to the Romans]: "Follow the Epistle to the Romans in its order, concern yourself first with Christ and his Gospel, that you may recognize your sins and his grace. Afterwards contend with sin, as Paul teaches from the first to the eighth chapter. Then when in the eighth chapter you will come into temptation under the cross and afflictions, the ninth, tenth and eleventh chapters will teach you how consolatory is predestination."

But that many are called and few are chosen is not owing to the fact that the meaning of the call of God, made through the Word, is as though God were to say: "Outwardly, through the Word, I indeed call to my kingdom all of you to whom I give my Word, yet in my heart I intend it not for all, but only for a few; for it is my will that the greatest part of those whom I call through the Word should not be enlightened or converted, but be and remain lost, although, through the Word in the call, I declare myself to them otherwise." For this would be to asign to God contradictory wills. That is, in such a manner it would be taught that God, who is, however, eternal truth, would be contrary to himself; and yet God also punishes the fault when one thing is declared, and another is thought and meant in the heart (Ps. 5:9 and 12:2 sq.). Thereby, also, the necessary consolatory foundation is rendered altogether uncertain and of no value, as we are daily reminded and admonished, that only from God's Word, whereby he treats with us and calls us, should we learn and conclude what his will to us is, and that that, to which he gives his Word and which he promises, we should certainly believe and not doubt.

Therefore Christ causes the promise of the Gospel to be offered not only in general, but through the sacraments, which he attaches as seals of the promise, he seals and thereby especially confirms it [the certainty of the promise of the Gospel] to every believer.

For that reason we also retain, as the Ausburg Confession, Art. xi. says, Private Absolution, and teach that it is God's command that we believe such absolution, and regard it as sure, when we believe the word of absolution, that we are as truly reconciled to God as though we had heard a voice from heaven; as the Apology explains this article. This consolation would be entirely taken from us if we are not to infer the will of God towards us from the call which is made through the Word and through the sacraments.

There would also be overthrown and taken from us the foundation that the Holy Ghost wills to be certainly present with the Word preached, heard, considered, and thereby to be efficacious and to work. Therefore the opinion should in no way be entertained of which mention

THE FORMULA OF CONCORD (1580) (continued)

has heretofore been made, that these would be the elect, even though they despise the Word of God, reject, calumniate and persecute it (Matt. 22:6; Acts 13:46), or, when they hear it, harden their hearts (Heb. 4:2, 7), resist the Holy Ghost (Acts 7:51), without repentance persevere in sins (Luke 14:18), do not truly believe in Christ (Mark 16:16), only present [godliness in] an outward appearance (Matt. 7:22; 22:12), or seek other ways for righteousness and holiness apart from Christ (Rom. 9:31). But as God has ordained in his [eternal] counsel that the Holy Ghost should call, enlighten and convert the elect through the Word, and that all those who, through true faith, receive Christ he will justify and save; he has also determined in his counsel that he will harden, reprobate and condemn those who are called through the Word if they reject the Word and resist the Holy Ghost, who wishes to be efficacious and to work in them through the Word. And for this reason "many are called, but few are chosen."

For few receive the Word and follow it; the greatest number despise the Word, and will not come to the wedding (Matt. 22: 3sqq). The cause for this contempt for the Word is not God's knowledge [or predestination], but the perverse will of man, who rejects or perverts the means and instrument of the Holy Ghost, which God offers him through the call, and resists the Holy Ghost, who wishes to be efficacious, and works through the Word, as Christ says (Matt. 23:37): "How often would I have gathered thee together, and ye would not."

Therefore many receive the Word with joy, but afterwards fall away again (Luke 8:13). But the cause is not as though God were unwilling to grant grace for perseverance to those in whom he has begun the good work, for this is contrary to St. Paul (Phil. 1:6); but the cause is that they wilfully turn away again from the holy commandment [of God], grieve and exasperate the Holy Ghost, implicate themselves again in the filth of the world and garnish again the habitation of the heart for the devil; with them the last state is worse than the first (2 Pet. 2:10, 20; Eph. 4:30; Heb. 10:26; Luke 11:25).

Thus far is the mystery of predestination revealed to us in God's Word, and if we abide thereby and cleave thereto, it is a very useful, salutary, consolatory doctrine; for it establishes very effectually the article that we are justified and saved without all works and merits of ours, purely out of grace, alone for Christ's sake. For before the ages of the world, before we were born, yea, before the foundation of the world was laid, when we indeed could do nothing good, we were according to God's purpose chosen out of grace in Christ to salvation (Rom. 9:11; 2 Tim. 1:9). All opinions and erroneous doctrines concerning the powers of our natural will are thereby overthrown, because God in his counsel, before the ages of the world, decided and ordained that he himself, by the power of his Holy Ghost, would produce and work in us, through the Word, everything that pertains to our conversion.

Therefore this doctrine affords also the excellent, glorious consolation that God was so solicitous concerning the conversion, righteousness and salvation of every Christian, and so faithfully provided therefor, that before the foundation of the world was laid he deliberated concerning it, and in his [secret] purpose ordained how he would bring me thereto [call and lead me to salvation] and preserve me therein. Also, that he wished to secure my salvation so well and certainly that since, through the weakness and wickedness of our flesh, it could easily be lost from our hands, or through craft and might of the devil and the world be torn or removed therefrom, in his eternal purpose, which cannot fail or be overthrown, he ordained it, and placed it for preservation in the almighty hand of our Saviour Jesus Christ, from which no one can pluck us (John 10:28). Hence Paul also says (Rom. 8:28, 39): "Because we have been called according to the purpose of God, who will separate us from the love of God in Christ?" [Paul builds the certainty of our blessedness upon the foundation of the divine purpose, when, from our being called according to the purpose of God, he infers that no one can separate us, etc.]

Under the cross also and amid temptations this doctrine affords glorious consolation, namely, that God in his counsel, before the time of the world, determined and decreed that he would assist us in all distresses [anxieties and perplexities], grant patience [under the cross], give consolation, excite [nourish and encourage] hope, and produce such a result as would contribute to our salvation. Also, as Paul in a very consolatory way treats this (Rom. 8:28, 29, 35, 38, 39), that God in his purpose has ordained before the time of the world by what crosses and sufferings he will conform his elect to the image of his Son, and that to every one his cross should and must serve for the best, because called according to the purpose, whence Paul concludes that it is certain and indubitable that "neither tribulation nor distress," "nor death nor life," etc., "shall be able to separate us from the love of God, which is in Christ Jesus our Lord."

This article also affords a glorious testimony that the Church of God will abide against all the gates of hell, and likewise teaches what is the true Church of God, so that we may not be offended by the great authority [and majestic appearance] of the false Church (Rom. 9:24, 25).

From this article also powerful admonitions and warnings are derived, as (Luke 7:30): "They rejected the counsel of God against themselves." (Luke 14:24): "I say unto you that none of those men which were bidden shall taste of my supper." Also (Matt. 20:16): "Many be called, but few chosen." Also (Luke 8:8, 18): "He that hath ears to hear, let him hear," and: "Take heed how ye hear." Thus the doctrine concerning this article can be employed with profit for consolation, and so as to contribute to salvation [and can be transferred in many ways to our use].

But with especial care the distinction must be observed between that which is expressly revealed concerning this in God's Word and what is not revealed. For, in addition to that hitherto mentioned which has been revealed in Christ concerning this, God has still kept secret and concealed much concerning this mystery, and reserved it alone for his wisdom and knowledge. Concerning this we should not investigate, nor indulge our thoughts, nor reach conclusions, nor inquire curiously, but should adhere [entirely] to the revealed Word of God. This admonition is in the highest degree necessary.

For our curiosity has always much more pleasure in concerning itself therewith [with investigating those things which ere hidden and abstruse] than with what God has revealed to us concerning this in his Word, since we cannot harmonize them, which we also have not been commanded to do [since certain things occur in this mystery so intricate and involved that we are not able by the penetration of our natural ability to harmonize them, but this has not been demanded of us by God]:

Thus there is no doubt that God most exactly and certainly saw before the time of the world, and still knows, who of those who are called will believe or will not believe; also who of the converted will persevere [in faith] and who will not; who after a fall [into grievous sins] will return, and who will fall into obduracy [will perish in their sins]. So, too, the number, how many there are of these on both sides, is beyond all doubt perfectly known to God. Yet since God has reserved this mystery for his wisdom, and in his Word revealed nothing to us concerning it, much less commanded us to investigate it with our thoughts, but has earnestly discouraged us therefrom (Rom. 11:33 sqq.), we should not indulge our thoughts, reach conclusions nor inquire curiously therein, but should adhere to his revealed Word, to which he points us.

Thus without any doubt God also knows and has determined for every one the time and hour of his call and conversion [and when he will raise again one who has lapsed]. Yet since this is not revealed, we have the command always to adhere to the Word, but to entrust the time and hour [of conversion] to God (Acts 1:7).

Likewise, when we see that God gives his Word at one place [to one kingdom or realm], but not at another [to another nation]; removes it from one place [people], and allows it to remain at another; also, that one is hardened, blinded, given over to a reprobate mind, while another, who is indeed in the same guilt, is again converted, etc.; in these and similar questions Paul (Rom. 11:22 sqq.) fixes before us a certain limit as to how far we should go, viz. that, in the one part we should recognize God's judgement [for he commands us to consider in those who perish the just judgment of God and the penalties of sins]. For they are richly-deserved penalties of sins when God so punishes a land or nation for despising his Word that the punishment extends also to their posterity, as is to be seen in the Jews. Thereby God shows to those that are his, his severity in some lands and persons, in order to indicate what we all have richly deserved, since we have acted wickedly in opposition to God's Word [are ungrateful for the revealed Word, and live unworthily of the Gospel] and often have sorely grieved the Holy Ghost; so that we may live in God's fear, and acknowledge and praise God's goodness, in and with us, without and contrary to our merit, to whom he gives and grants his Word, and whom he does not harden and reject.

For inasmuch as our nature has been corrupted by sin, and is worthy of, and under obligation to, God's wrath and condemnation, God owes to us neither Word, Spirit, nor grace, and when, out of grace, he bestows these gifts, we often repel them from us, and judge ourselves unworthy of everlasting life (Acts 13:46). Therefore this his righteous, richly-deserved judgment he displays in some countries, nations and persons, in order that when we are considered with respect to them, and compared with them, we may learn the more attentively to recognize and praise God's pure [immense], unmerited grace in the vessels of mercy.

For no injustice is done those who are punished and receive the wages of their sins; but in the rest, to whom God gives and preserves his Word, and thereby enlightens, converts and preserves men, God commends his pure [immense] grace and mercy, without their merit.

When we proceed thus far in this article we remain upon the right [safe and royal] way, as it is written (Hos. 13:9): "O Israel, thou hast destroyed thyself; but in me is thy help."

But with respect to that in this disputation which will proceed too high and beyond these limits, we should, with Paul, place the finger upon our lips, and remember and say (Rom. 9:20): "O man, who art thou that repliest against God?"

For that in this article we neither can nor should inquire after and investigate everything, the great apostle Paul declares [by his own example]. For when, after having argued much concerning this article from the revealed Word of God, he comes to where he points out what, concerning this mystery, God has reserved for his hidden wisdom, he suppresses and cuts off the discussion with the following words (Rom. 11:33 sq.): "Oh the depth of the riches both of the wisdom and knowledge of God! How unsearchable are his judgments, and his ways past finding out! For who hath known the mind of the Lord?" *i.e.* in addition to and beyond that which he has revealed in his Word.

Therefore this eternal election of God is to be considered in Christ, and not beyond or without Christ. For "in Christ," testifies the apostle Paul (Eph. 1:4 sq.), "he hath chosen us before the foundation of the world;" as it is written: "He hath made us accepted in the Beloved." But this election is revealed from heaven through the preached Word when the Father says (Matt. 17:5): "This is my beloved Son, in whom I am well pleased; hear ye him." And Christ says (Matt. 11:28): "Come unto me, all ye that labor and are heavy laden, and I will give you rest." And concerning the Holy Ghost Christ says (John 16:14): "He shall glorify me; for he shall receive of mine, and shall show it unto you." Therefore the entire Holy Trinity, Father, Son and Holy Ghost, direct all men to Christ, as to the Book of Life, in which they should seek the eternal election of the Father. For it has been decided by the Father from eternity that whom he would save he would save through Christ (John 14:6): "No man cometh unto the Father but by me." And again (John 10:9): "I am the door; by me, if any man enter in, he shall be saved."

But Christ as the only-begotten Son of God, who is in the bosom of the Father, has published to us the will of the Father, and thus also our eternal election to eternal life, viz. when he says (Mark 1:15): "Repent ye, and believe the Gospel; the kingdom of God is at hand." He also says (John 6:40): "This is the will of Him that sent me, that

THE FORMULA OF CONCORD (1580) (continued)

every one which seeth the Son and believeth on him may have everlasting life." And again (John 3:16): "God so loved the world that he gave his only-begotten Son, that whosoever believeth in him should not perish, but have everlasting life."

This proclamation the Father wishes that all men should hear, and that they should come to Christ. Those who come Christ does not repel from himself, as it is written (John 6:37): "Him that cometh to me I will in no wise cast out."

And in order that we may come to Christ, the Holy Ghost works, through the hearing of the Word, true faith, as the apostle testifies when he says (Rom. 10:17): "Faith cometh by hearing, and hearing by the Word of God," viz. when it is preached in its purity and without adulteration.

Therefore no one who would be saved should trouble or harass himself with thoughts concerning the secret counsel of God, as to whether he also is elected and ordained to eternal life; for with these miserable Satan is accustomed to attack and annoy godly hearts. But they should hear Christ [and in him look upon the Book of Life in which is written the eternal election], who is the Book of Life and of God's eternal election of all God's children to eternal life; who testifies to all men without distinction that it is God's will that all men who labor and are heavy laden with sin should come to him, in order that he may give them rest and save them (Matt. 11:28).

According to this doctrine of Christ, they should abstain from their sins, repent, believe his promise, and entirely entrust themselves to him; and since this we cannot do by ourselves of our own powers, the Holy Ghost desires to work repentance and faith in us through the Word and sacraments. And in order that we may attain this, and persevere and remain steadfast, we should implore God for his grace, which he promised us in holy baptism, and not doubt he will impart it to us according to his promise, as he has said (Luke 11:11 sqq.); "If a son shall ask bread of any of you that is a father, will he give him a stone? or if he ask a fish, will he for a fish give him a serpent? or if he shall ask an egg, will he offer him a scorpion? If ye then, being evil, know how to give good gifts unto your children, how much more shall your heavenly Father give the Holy Spirit to them that ask him?"

And since the Holy Ghost dwells in the elect, who become believing, as in his temple, and is not inactive in them, but impels the children of God to obedience to God's commands; believers, in like manner, should not be inactive, and much less resist the impulse of God's Spirit, but should exercise themselves in all Christian virtue, in all godliness, modesty, temperance, patience, brotherly love, and give all diligence to make their calling and election sure, in order that the more they experience the power and strength of the Spirit within them they may doubt the less concerning it. For the Spirit bears witness to the elect that they are God's children (Rom. 8:16). And although they sometimes fall into temptation so grievous that they think that they perceive no more power of the indwelling Spirit of God, and say with David (Ps. 31:22): "I said in my

haste, I am cut off from before thine eyes," yet they should again [be encouraged and] say with David, without regard to what they experience in themselves: "Nevertheless thou heardest the voice of my supplications when I cried unto thee."

And since our election to eternal life is founded not upon our godliness or virtue, but alone upon the merit of Christ and the gracious will of his Father, who, because he is unchangeable in will and essence, cannot deny himself; on this account, when his children depart from obedience and stumble, he calls them again through the Word to repentance, and the Holy Ghost will thereby to be efficacious in them for conversion; and when in true repentance by a right faith they turn again to him, he will always manifest his old paternal heart to all those who tremble at his Word and from their heart turn again to him, as it is written (Jer. 3:1): "If a man put away his wife, and she go from him and become another man's, shall he return unto her again? shall not that land be greatly polluted? but thou hast played the harlot with many lovers; yet return again to me, saith the Lord."

Moreover, the declaration (John 6:44) that no one can come to Christ except the Father draw him is right and true. But the Father will not do this without means, and has ordained for this purpose his Word and sacraments as ordinary means and instruments; and it is the will neither of the Father nor of the Son that a man should not hear or should despise the preaching of his Word, and without the Word and sacraments should expect the drawing of the Father. For the Father draws indeed by the power of his Holy Ghost, but, nevertheless, according to his usual order [the order decreed and instituted by himself], by the hearing of his holy, divine Word, as with a net, whereby the elect are delivered from the jaws of the devil. Every poor sinner should therefore repair thereto [to holy preaching], hear it attentively, and should not doubt the drawing of the Father. For the Holy Ghost will be with his Word in his power, and thereby work; and this is the drawing of the Father.

But the reason that not all who hear it believe, and some are therefore condemned the more deeply [eternally to severer punishments], is not that God has not desired their salvation; but it is their own fault, as they have heard the Word in such a manner as not to learn, but only to despise, traduce and disgrace it, and have resisted the Holy Ghost, who through the Word wishes to work in them. There was one form of this at the time of Christ in the Pharisees and their adherents. Therefore the apostle distinguishes with especial care the work of God, who alone makes vessels of honor, and the work of the devil and of man, who by the instigation of the devil, and not of God, has made himself a vessel of dishonor. For thus it is written (Rom. 9:22 sq.): "God endured with much long-suffering the vessels of wrath fitted to destruction, that he might make known the riches of his glory on the vessels of mercy, which he had afore prepared unto glory."

For here the apostle clearly says: "God endured with much long-suffering the vessels of wrath," but does not say that he made them vessels of wrath; for if this had been his will, he would not have required for it any great longsuffering. The fault, however, that they are fitted for destruction belongs to the devil and to men themselves, and not to God.

For all preparation for condemnation is by the devil and man, through sin, and in no respect by God, who does not wish that any man be damned; how then should he prepare any man for condemnation? For as God is not a cause of sins, so too he is no cause of the punishment, *i.e.* the condemnation; but the only cause of the condemnation is sin, for "the wages of sin is death" (Rom. 6:23). And as God does not wish sin, and has no pleasure in sin, he also does not wish the death of the sinner (Ez. 33:11), and has no pleasure in his condemnation. For he is not "willing that any should perish, but that all should come to repentance" (2 Pet. 3:9). So too it is written (in Ez. 18:23; 33:11): "As I live, saith the Lord God, I have no pleasure in the death of the wicked; but that the wicked turn from his way and live." And St. Paul testifies in clear words that from vessels of dishonor vessels of honor may be made by God's power and working, as he writes (2 Tim. 2:21) thus: "If a man, therefore, purge himself from these, he shall be a vessel unto honor, sanctified and meet for the Master's use, and prepared unto every good work." For he who is to purge himself must first have been unclean, and therefore a vessel of dishonor. But concerning the vessels of mercy he says clearly that the Lord himself has prepared them for glory, which he does not say concerning the condemned, who themselves, and not God, have prepared themselves as vessels of condemnation.

It is also to be attentively considered, when God punishes sin with sins, *i.e.* afterwards punishes those who have been converted with obduracy and blindness, because of their subsequent security, impenitence and wilful sins, that it should not be inferred hence that it never was God's good pleasure that such persons should come to the knowledge of the truth and be saved. For it is God's revealed will, both:

First, that God will receive into grace all who repent and believe in Christ.

Secondly, that those who wilfully turn away from the holy commandment, and are again entangled in the pollutions of the world (2 Pet. 2:20), and garnish their hearts for Satan (Luke 11:25 sq.), and do despite unto the Spirit of God (Heb. 10:29), he will punish, and when they persist therein they shall be hardened, blinded and eternally condemned.

Therefore, even Pharaoh (of whom it is written (Ex. 9:16; Rom. 9:17): "In very deed for this cause have I raised thee up, for to show in thee my power; and that my name may be declared throughout all the earth") was lost, not because God did not desire his salvation, or because it was his good pleasure that Pharaoh should be condemned and lost. For God "is not willing that any should perish" (2 Pet. 3:9); he also has "no pleasure in the death of the wicked, but that the wicked turn from his way and live" (Ez. 33:11).

But that God hardened Pharaoh's heart, viz. that Pharaoh still continued to sin, and the more he was admonished the more obdurate he became, were punishments of his preceding sins and horrible tyranny, which, in many and manifold ways, he exercised towards the children of Israel inhumanly and against the accusations of his conscience. And since God caused his Word to be preached and his will to be proclaimed, and Pharaoh wilfully resisted it in direct contradiction of all admonitions and warnings, God withdrew his hand from him, and thus his heart was hardened, and God executed his judgment upon him; for he deserved nothing else than hellfire. And indeed the holy apostle introduces the example of Pharaoh for no other reason than hereby to prove the justice of God, which he exercises towards the impenitent and despisers of his Word. Yet in no way is it there to be thought or understood that God did not desire his salvation, or that there is any man whose salvation he did not desire, but that he was so ordained to eternal damnation in God's secret counsel that he neither should, could, nor might be saved.

Through this doctrine and explanation of the eternal and saving choice of the elect children of God his own glory is entirely and fully given to God, that in Christ he saves us out of pure [and free] mercy, without any merits or good works of ours, according to the purpose of his will, as it is written (Eph. 1:5 sq.): "Having predestinated us unto the adoption of children by Jesus Christ to himself, according to the good pleasure of his will, to the praise of the glory of his grace, wherein he hath made us accepted in the Beloved." Therefore it is false and wrong [conflicts with the Word of God] when it is taught that not alone the mercy of God and the most holy merit of Christ, but also that there is in us a cause of God's election, on account of which God has chosen us to eternal life. For not only before we did anything good, but also before we were born, yea, even before the foundations of the world were laid, he elected us in Christ; and "that the purpose of God according to election might stand, not of works, but of Him that calleth, it was said unto her, The elder shall serve the younger, as it is written, Jacob have I loved, but Esau have I hated" (Rom. 9:11 sqq.; Gen. 25:23; Mal. 1:2 sq.).

Moreover, no occasion is afforded either for despondency or for a shameless, dissolute life by this doctrine, viz. when men are taught that they should seek eternal election in Christ and his holy Gospel, as in the Book of Life, which excludes no penitent sinner, but allures and calls all the poor, heavy-laden, and troubled [with the sense of God's wrath], and promises the Holy Ghost for purification and renewal. This article correctly explained thus gives the most permanent consolation to all troubled, tempted men, viz. that they know that their salvation is not placed in their own hands (for otherwise it would be much more easily lost, as was the case with Adam and Eve in Paradise—ay, it would be lost every hour and moment), but in the gracious election of God, which he has revealed to us in Christ, from whose hand no man shall pluck us (John 10:28; 2 Tim. 2:19).

Wherefore, if any one should so present the doctrine concerning the gracious election of God in such a manner that troubled Christians cannot console themselves therewith, but thereby occasion is afforded for despair, or the impenitent are confirmed in their wickedness; it is undoubtedly sure and true that such a doctrine is put forth, not according to the Word and will of God, but according

THE FORMULA OF CONCORD (1580) (continued)

to [the blind judgment of human] reason and the instigation of the devil.

For, as the apostle testifies (Rom. 15:4): "Whatsoever things were written aforetime were written for our learning, that we through patience and comfort of the Scriptures might have hope." But when by the Scriptures this consolation and hope are weakened or entirely removed, it is certain that they are understood and explained contrary to the will and meaning of the Holy Ghost.

By this simple, correct [clear], useful explanation, which has firm ground in God's revealed will, we abide; we flee from and shun all lofty, acute questions and disputations [useless for edifying]; and reject and condemn that which is contrary to this simple, useful explanation.

So much concerning the controverted articles which have been discussed among the theologians of the Augsburg Confession for many years already, since in reference to them some have erred and severe controversies have arisen.

From this our explanation, friends and enemies, and therefore every one, will clearly infer that we have not thought of yielding aught of the eternal, immutable truth of God for the sake of temporary peace, tranquillity and unity (as to do this is also not in our power). Such peace and unity, since devised against the truth and for its suppression, would have no permanency. Much less are we inclined to adorn and conceal a corruption of the pure doctrine and manifest, condemned errors. But for that unity we entertain heartfelt pleasure and love, and this, on our part, we are sincerely inclined and anxious to advance according to our utmost power, by which his glory remains to God uninjured, nothing of the divine truth of the Holy Gospel is surrendered, no place is admitted for the least error, poor sinners are brought to true, genuine repentance, encouraged by faith, confirmed in new obedience, and thus justified and eternally saved alone through the sole merit of Christ.

CHAPTER XII. OF OTHER FACTIONS [HERETICS] AND SECTS, WHICH NEVER EMBRACED THE AUGSBURG CONFESSION.

The sects and factions [sectarists and heretics] which never embraced the Augsburg Confession, and of which, in this our explanation, express mention has not been made, such as are the Anabaptists, Schwenekfeldians, New Arians and Anti-trinitarians, whose errors are unanimously condemned by all churches of the Augsburg Confession, we have not wished to notice particularly and especially in this explanation; for the reason that at the present time only this has been sought [that we might above all refute the charges of our adversaries the Papists].

Since our opponents, with shameless mouths, alleged and proclaimed, throughout all the world, of our churches and their teachers, that not two preachers are found who in each and every article of the Augsburg Confession agree, but that they are rent asunder and separated from one another to such an extent that not even they themselves any longer know what is the Augsburg Confession and its

proper [true, genuine and germane] sense; we have wished to make a common confession, not only in mere, brief words or names, but to make a clear, luminous, distinct declaration concerning all the articles which have been discussed and controverted only among the theologians of the Augsburg Confession, in order that every one may see that we do not wish in a cunning manner to screen or cover up all this, or to come to an agreement only in appearance; but to remedy the matter thoroughly, and so to set forth our opinion, that even our adversaries themselves must confess that in all this we abide by the true, simple, natural and only sense of the Augsburg Confession, in which we desire, through God's grace, to persevere constantly even to our end, and, so far as it is placed at our service, we will not connive at or be silent, so that anything contrary to the same [the genuine and sacred sense of the Augsburg Confession] be introduced into our churches and schools, in which the Almighty God and Father of our Lord Jesus Christ has appointed us teachers and pastors.

But in order that the condemned errors of the above enumerated factions and sects may not be silently ascribed to us—since for the most part they have secretly stolen into localities, and especially, as is the nature of such spirits, at the time when no place or space was allowed to the pure Word of the holy Gospel, but all its orthodox teachers and confessors were persecuted, and the deep darkness of the Papacy still prevailed, and poor simple men who were compelled to feel the manifest idolatry and false faith of the Papacy embraced, alas! in their simplicity, whatever was said to be according to the Gospel, and was not Papistic—we cannot forbear testifying also against them publicly, before all Christendom, that we have neither part nor fellowship with these errors, but reject and condemn them, one and all, as wrong and heretical, and contrary to the Scriptures of the prophets and apostles, as well as to our well-grounded Augsburg Confession.

ERRONEOUS ARTICLES OF THE ANABAPTISTS.

Namely, the erroneous, heretical doctrines of the Anabaptists, which are to be tolerated and allowed neither in the Church, nor in the commonwealth, nor in domestic life, since they teach:

1. That our righteousness before God consists not only in the sole obedience and merit of Christ, but in our renewal and our own piety, in which we walk before God; which they, for the most part, base upon their own peculiar observances and self-chosen spirituality, as upon a new sort of monkery.

2. That children who are not baptized are not sinners before God, but are righteous and innocent, and thus are saved in their innocency without baptism, which they do not need. And in this way they deny and reject the entire doctrine concerning Original Sin and what belongs to it.

3. That children should not be baptized until they have attained the use of reason and can themselves confess their faith.

4. That the children of Christians, because they have been born of Christian and believing parents, are

holy and the children of God even without and before baptism. For this reason also they neither attach much importance to the baptism of children nor encourage it, contrary to the express words of the promise, which pertains only to those who keep God's covenant and do not despise it (Gen. 17:9).

5. That there is no true Christian assembly or congregation [church] in which sinners are still found.

6. That no sermon should be heard or attended in those churches in which the Papal masses have previously been said.

7. That no one should have anything to do with those ministers of the Church who preach the holy Gospel according to the Augsburg Confession, and censure the errors of the Anabaptists; also that no one should serve or in any way labor for them, but should flee from and shun them as perverters of God's Word.

8. That under the New Testament the magistracy is not a godly estate.

9. That a Christian cannot, with a good, inviolate conscience, hold the office of magistrate.

10. That a Christian cannot, without injury to conscience, use the office of the magistracy in carnal matters against the wicked, neither can subjects appeal to the power of magistrates.

11. That a Christian cannot, with a good conscience, take an oath before a court, neither can he by an oath do homage to his prince or sovereign.

12. That without injury to conscience magistrates cannot inflict upon evil-doers capital punishment.

13. That a Christian cannot, with a good conscience, hold or possess any property, but that he is in duty bound to devote it to the community.

14. That a Christian cannot, with a good conscience, be a landlord, merchant or cutler.

15. That on account of faith [diversity of religion] married persons may be divorced, abandon one another, and be married to another of the same faith.

16. That Christ did not assume his flesh and blood of the Virgin Mary, but brought them with him from heaven.

17. That he also is not true, essential God, but only has more and higher gifts than other men.

And still more articles of like kind; for they are divided into many bands [sects], and one has more and another fewer erros, and thus their entire sect is in reality nothing but a new kind of monkery.

ERRONEOUS ARTICLES OF THE SCHWENCKFELDIANS.

As, when the Schwenckfeldians assert:

1. That all those have no knowledge of Christ as the reigning King of heaven who regard Christ, according to the flesh or his assumed humanity, as a creature; that the flesh of Christ has by exaltation so assumed all divine properties that in might, power, majesty and glory he is everywhere, in degree and place of essence equal to the Father and the eternal Word, so that there is the same essence, properties, will and glory of both natures in Christ, and that the flesh of Christ belongs to the essence of the Holy Trinity.

2. That church service, *i.e.* the Word preached and heard, is not a means whereby God the Holy Ghost teaches men, and works in them saving knowledge of Christ, conversion, repentance, faith and new obedience.

3. That the water of baptism is not a means whereby God the Lord seals adoption and works regeneration.

4. That bread and wine in the Holy Supper are not means whereby Christ distributes his body and blood.

5. That a Christian man who is truly regenerated by God's Spirit can in this life observe and fulfil the Law of God perfectly.

6. That there is no true Christian congregation [church] in which no public excommunication nor regular process of the ban is observed.

7. That the minister of the Church who is not on his part truly renewed, righteous and godly cannot teach other men with profit or administer true sacraments.

ERRONEOUS ARTICLES OF THE NEW ARIANS.

Also, when the New Arians teach that Christ is not a true, essential, natural God, of one eternal divine essence with God the Father, but is only adorned with divine majesty beneath and beside God the Father.

ERRONEOUS ARTICLES OF THE ANTI-TRINITARIANS.

1. Also, when some Anti-trinitarians reject and condemn the ancient approved creeds, the Nicene and Athanasian, both as to their sense and words, and teach that there is not only one eternal divine essence of the Father, Son and Holy Ghost, but as there are three distinct persons, God the Father, Son and Holy Ghost, so each person has also its essence distinct and separate from the other persons; yet that all three, as three men otherwise distinct and separate in their essence, are either [some imagine] of the same power, wisdom, majesty and glory, or [others think] in essence and properties are not equal.

2. That the Father alone is true God.

These and like articles, one and all, with what pertains to them and follows from them, we reject and condemn as wrong, false, heretical, and contrary to the Word of God, the three Creeds, the Augsburg Confession, the Smalcald Articles and the Catechisms of Luther. Of these articles all godly Christians will and should beware, as the welfare and salvation of their souls is dear to them.

Therefore in the sight of God and of all Christendom [the entire Church of Christ], to those now living and those who shall come after us, we wish to testify that the above declaration, concerning all the controverted articles presented and explained, and no other, is our faith, doctrine and confession, in which we also will appear, by God's grace, with unterrified hearts before the judgment-seat of

THE FORMULA OF CONCORD (1580) (continued)

Jesus Christ, and for it will give an account. We also will neither speak nor write, privately or publicly, anything contrary to this declaration, but, by the help of God's grace, intend to abide thereby. After mature deliberation we have, in God's fear and with the invocation of his name, attached our signatures with our own hands.

Notes: *The Formula of Concord was issued on the fiftieth anniversary of the Augsburg Confession. Its purpose was to unite the several factions that had arisen in the Lutheran Church since the death of Martin Luther. While the Augsburg Confession detailed the Lutheran Church's solid standing within the traditional faith of the Christian Church, the Formula of Concord dealt with those issues of most concern to Lutherans and those which distinguished them from both the Roman Catholic Church and the Reformed Church. At the time of its completion, the Formula was placed beside the other Lutheran symbolic books in* The Book of Concord *(1580).*

While the Augsburg Confession finds universal agreement among contemporary Lutherans, the Formula of Concord has not attained that status. Like the Smalcald Articles, the Formula is not accepted as a standard of doctrine to which subscription is required by the American Lutheran Church. The Lutheran Church in America acknowledges the Formula as a valid interpretation of the Augsburg Confession. Both the Lutheran Church-Missouri Synod and the Wisconsin Evangelical Lutheran Synod accept the Formula equally with the Augsburg Confession.

* * *

CONFESSION OF FAITH (AMERICAN LUTHERAN CHURCH)

401. The American Lutheran Church accepts all the canonical books of the Old and New Testaments as a whole and in all their parts as the divinely inspired, revealed, and inerrant Word of God, and submits to this as the only infallible authority in all matters of faith and life.

402. As brief and true statements of the doctrines of the Word of God, the Church accepts and confesses the following Symbols, subscription to which shall be required of all its members, both congregations and individuals:

402.1 The ancient ecumenical Creeds: the Apostolic, the Nicene, and the Athanasian;

402.2 The unaltered Augsburg Confession and Luther's Small Catechism.

403. As further elaboration of and in accord with these Lutheran Symbols, the Church also receives the other documents in the Book of Concord of 1580: the Apology, Luther's Large Catechism, the Smalcald Articles, and the Formula of Concord; and recognizes them as normative for its theology.

404. The American Lutheran Church accepts without reservation the symbolical books of the evangelical Lutheran Church, not insofar as but because they are the presentation and explanation of the pure doctrine of the Word of God and a summary of the faith of the evangelical Lutheran Church.

Notes: *As part of its constitution, the American Lutheran Church has included a brief confessional statement that is the enumeration of both documents to which all members subscribe and those the church accepts as "normative" for its theology. The Lutheran Church-Missouri Synod and the Lutheran Church in America have similar statements.*

* * *

A BRIEF STATEMENT OF THE PRINCIPLES AND DOCTRINE OF THE APOSTOLIC LUTHERAN CHURCH OF AMERICA

There can be found no better or more direct instructions in reference to the principles and doctrine of Christ than the Bible: the Holy Word of God, as is recorded in Hebrews 6:1, and 2:

> "Therefore, leaving the principles of the doctrine of Christ, let us go on unto perfection; not laying again the foundation of repentance from dead works, and of faith toward God. Of the doctrine of baptisms, and of the laying on of hands, and of resurrection of the dead, and of eternal judgment."

CONVERSION AND JUSTIFICATION

An unbeliever is brought to grace through repentance and faith in the Gospel. The baptized person who has fallen from grace has the same condition of heart as an unbeliever, and can be restored to grace only by repentance and faith in the Gospel. Conversion is the work of God in sinful man who in himself is entirely helpless. This person first must be awakened by the righteous and holy Law of God: the Ten Commandments, to see the horror of sin and know that he is condemned under the curse of the Law.

This applies to a careless sinner as well as to a self-righteous person. He is under the curse of the Law and cannot find peace for his soul. Thus, this person is awakened to seek a means of reconciliation. He is now awakened from his dead condition. "And you hath he quickened, who were dead in trespasses and sins." (Ephesians 2:1)

Now the gospel of Christ will lead him to the cross of Calvary where the pains of the newbirth begin, as he beholds that he has nailed the Son of God to the cross with his sins. "My little children, of whom I travail in birth again until Christ be formed in you." (Galatians 4:19)

"And as Moses lifted up the serpent in the wilderness, even so must the Son of man be lifted up: that whosoever believeth in Him should not perish, but have eternal life." (John 3:14, 15)

"A woman when she is in travail hath sorrow, because her hour is come: but as soon as she is delivered of the child, she remembereth no more the anguish, for joy that a man is born into the world. And ye now therefore have sorrow: but I will see you again, and your heart shall rejoice, and your joy no man taketh from you." (John 16:21, 22)

At the cross he will hear the cry of Jesus, "It is finished." The righteous Law has now received all that it demanded by the suffering and death of Jesus.

We believe that the Ten Commandments, or the moral Law, has been given so that unruly men may be governed by it and punishment meted out to those that break it. We also believe that the Law convicts a person of his sins and his corrupt nature, as St. Paul states in Romans 3:20: "For by the law is the knowledge of sin." This Law of God was given "that every mouth may be stopped, and all the world may become guilty before God." (Romans 3:19) But St. Paul also states in 1 Timothy 1:9: "Knowing this, that the law is not made for the righteous man, but for the lawless and disobedient, for the ungodly and for sinners, for unholy and profane," etc. Therefore he concludes: "Wherefore the Law was our schoolmaster to bring us to Christ, that we might be justified by faith. But after that faith is come, we are no longer under a schoolmaster." (Galatians 3:24, 25)

Now the Holy Ghost becomes the Teacher and begins to lead this person into all truth. He takes up his bed of sin and walks; that is, he makes restitution of the wrongs he has done in the past, as Jesus says: "But he that doeth truth cometh to the light, that his deeds may be made manifest, that they are wrought in God." (John 3:21) This person has now come to the narrow road of life and the Holy Spirit is his Guide. He has entered inside the living church of Jesus, Christ being the cornerstone of that building which is not made with hands.

THE DOCTRINE OF THE CHURCH

We believe in the inspired Word of God, as Peter says: "Knowing this first, that no prophecy of the scripture is of private interpretation. For the prophecy came not in old time by the will of man: but holy men of God spake as they were moved by the Holy Ghost." (2 Peter 1:20, 21) And Paul says: "All scripture is given by inspiration of God, and is profitable for doctrine, for reproof, for correction, for instruction in righteousness." (2 Timothy 3:16)

We believe in the unity and trinity of God the Father, the Son and the Holy Ghost. "For there are three that bear record in heaven, the Father, the Word, and the Holy Ghost: and these three are one." (1 John 5:7)

We believe in the forgiveness of sins in Jesus' Name and blood as the means of redemption and reconciliation with God, through repentance and faith, as the Bible records: "The time is fulfilled, and the kingdom of God is at hand: repent ye, and believe the gospel." (Mark 1:15) And in Colossians 1:14: "In whom we have redemption through His blood, even the forgiveness of sins." Then in Hebrews 9:14: "How much more shall the blood of Christ, who through the eternal Spirit offered Himself without spot to God, purge your conscience from dead works to serve the living God?" And in 1 Peter 1:19: "But with the precious blood of Christ, as of a lamb without blemish and without spot." Also in Luke 24:47: "And that repentance and remission of sins should be preached in His name among all nations, beginning at Jerusalem." And in John 20:23: "Whose soever sins ye remit, they are remitted unto them; and whose soever sins ye retain, they are retained."

The fruits of living faith will now appear. "For the kingdom of God is not meat and drink; but righteousness, and peace, and joy in the Holy Ghost." (Romans 14:17) This will lead a person to follow Jesus in doctrine and life and in suffering, as Jesus says: "If any man will come after Me, let him deny himself, and take up his cross, and follow me." (Matthew 16:24) and St. Paul says: "Now thanks be unto God, which always causeth us to triumph in Christ, and maketh manifest the savour of His knowledge by us in every place." (2 Corinthians 2:14)

We believe that a person asks when in need. He seeks when he wants to find and he knocks when he wants to come in, as Jesus says: "Ask, and it shall be given; seek, and ye shall find; knock, and it shall be opened unto you: For every one that asketh receiveth; and he that seeketh findeth; and to him that knocketh it shall be opened." (Matthew 7:7, 8)

BAPTISMS

WATER BAPTISM.   *We believe* in the Doctrine of Baptisms. (Hebrews 6:2)

Water baptism, which was instituted by God, is a means of grace. Even though God changed the outward token of grace from circumcision to baptism, we do not believe that He changed the Covenant. The essence of the Covenant that God made with Abraham of old was this: "And I will establish my covenant between me and thee and thy seed after thee in their generations for an everlasting covenant, to be a God unto thee and to thy seed after thee." (Genesis 17:7)

This Covenant, being everlasting, remains the same even though God Who ended the Old Testament and began the New, in place of circumcision, instituted baptism, and in the place of the Passover Lamb instituted the Lord's Supper. Thus the same wording is needed: "I will be to them a God, and they shall be to me a people." (Hebrews 8:10; Ezekiel 37:27)

The requirement of the Old Covenant commanded those who were circumcised to keep, or fulfill, the Law of God. This they were unable to do, "because they continued not in my covenant, and I regarded them not, saith the Lord." (Hebrews 8:9)

The New Covenant also has its own requirements, for the Lord says: "He that believeth and is baptized shall be saved; but he that believeth not shall be damned." (Mark 16:16) Thus, "Without faith it is impossible to please God" (Hebrews 11:6) no matter what else we may do.

We believe that infants have capacity for faith, for it is God who instills faith in the heart. God-given faith is not a faith of the mind but of the heart. "For with the heart man believeth unto righteousness." (Romans 10:10) They who insist that an infant's mind is not sufficiently developed to believe, ignore the Words of our Saviour Who said: "Except ye be converted, and become as little children, ye shall not enter into the kingdom of heaven. But whoso shall offend one of these little ones *which believe on Me*, it were better for him that a millstone were hanged about his neck, and that he were drowned in the depth of the sea." (Matthew 18:3-6)

If Jesus, the All-Knowing, says they believe on Him, who are we to argue against Him? We believe that Jesus meant infants also, for in Luke 18:15, 16, we read: "And they brought unto Him also infants that He should touch them: but when His disciples saw it, they rebuked them. But Jesus called them unto Him, and said, Suffer little children to come unto me and forbid them not: *for of such* is the kingdom of God."

We believe that God has not instituted a single sacrament for unbelievers, neither has He made a covenant with them. His sacraments and covenants are for believers only. The argument that He made His covenants with adults only does not prove that children were to be excluded, for it is written: "and to thy seed after thee." (Genesis 17:7) "Therefore infants, at the age of eight days were circumcised." (Genesis 17:12)

OF THE HOLY SPIRIT. *We believe* in the baptism of the Holy Ghost and of Fire, as John the Baptist witnesses of Jesus, saying: "He shall baptize you with the Holy Ghost and with fire." (Matthew 3:11)

We believe that Jesus refers to this Baptism as He said: "I am come to send fire on the earth; and what will I, if it be already kindled?" (Luke 12:49) We believe that St. Paul also refers to the Baptism of the Holy Ghost and of fire, as he writes: "And hope maketh not ashamed; because the love of God is shed abroad in our hearts by the Holy Ghost which is given unto us." (Romans 5:5) Likewise St. John writes: "and every one that loveth Him that begat loveth him also that is begotten of Him." (1 John 5:1)

We believe that this divine love binds the children of God together by the Holy Spirit which is in them. This "is the bond of perfectness," (Col. 3:14) and that all who are born of the Holy Spirit are the children of God. "The Spirit itself beareth witness with our spirit that we are the children of God." (Romans 8:16)

THE BAPTISM OF BLOOD. *We believe* this to be the Baptism that Jesus refers to as He states: "But I have a baptism to be baptized with; and how am I straitened till it be accomplished." (Luke 12:50) And again: "Are ye able to drink of the cup that I shall drink of, and to be baptized with the baptism that I am baptized with? (Matt. 20:22)

We believe that those persons who are following Jesus "in the way of regeneration" (Matthew 19:28) are not regenerated until they have experienced this which Jesus states: "Ye shall drink indeed of my cup and be baptized with the baptism that I am baptized with . . . " (Matthew 20:23)

Men who have sinned must taste the bitterness of their sin and the cleansing power of the blood of Jesus in order that they be regenerated. Then they have drunk of the cup that Jesus drank of and are baptized with His baptism. They then have experienced "godly sorrow which worketh repentance to salvation not to be repented of." (2 Corinthians 7:10) And "the blood of sprinkling, that speaketh better things than that of Abel" (Hebrews 12:24) occurs in the spoken words of the forgiveness of sins in the Name of Jesus and His atoning blood.

THE LAYING ON OF HANDS

We believe in the laying on of hands as Ananias did to Paul (Acts 9:12): "And hath seen in a vision a man named Ananias coming in, and putting his hand on him, that he might receive his sight."

And as Peter and John did to the Samaritans, (Acts 8:17): "Then laid they their hands on them, and they received the Holy Ghost."

As Paul did to the disciples at Ephesus, (Acts 19:6): "And when Paul laid his hands upon them, the Holy Ghost came on them; and they spake with tongues, and prophesied."

And as Christ did to the children. Laying on of hands belongs to the principles of the doctrine of Christ.

We also believe that if a Christian falls into sin after he has been blessed with the forgiveness of sins, receiving peace and joy in his heart, the Holy Spirit will guide him, and urge him to put away that sin and ask for the forgiveness of his sin, that the gospel of forgiveness will be extended to him in Jesus' Name and blood. Thus he regains the peace of heart and soul. But if this person continues in sin and does not obey the guidance of the Spirit, the Holy Spirit will flee from him. "And the Lord said, My spirit shall not always strive with man, for that he also is flesh:" (Genesis 6:3) Then he falls again under the condemnation of the Law.

THE DOCTRINE OF CONFESSION

We believe as stated in the Small Catechism that we should confess before God that we are guilty of all kinds of sins, even of those which we do not know. But to the confessor we should confess those sins which we know and feel in our heart, and which burden our consciences. The confession of sins to a trusted Christian brother (confessor) is a good gift of God and a privilege which every Christian should use according to his needs and the demands of his conscience.

Confession should never be taught in an exacting spirit, as if it were a command; neither should it be taught as a condition for salvation, for the only condition for salvation is Scriptural faith in Jesus. Jesus says: "He that believeth on me, as the scripture hath said, out of his belly shall flow rivers of living water." (John 7:38) "Verily, verily, I say unto you, He that believeth on Me hath everlasting life." (John 6:48)

If a believer is burdened in his conscience with some sins which he has committed and which he has never confessed to anybody except God, and these sins are a hindrance to his faith and he feels an inner need and urge to confess them to a trusted Christian brother, this is the voice of the

Holy Spirit to which he should be obedient. Confession of sins to a confessor is no meritorious work and the believer is not justified by that, for he is already righteous in Christ. He confesses his sins in order to restore peace of conscience through absolution, and in order that he may be able to appropriate the Gospel, he is not to think that only those sins which he confessed are forgiven, (for absolution means that all his sins are forgiven, even the sins which he does not know).

If such sins which he already has confessed and which are forgiven, again begin to trouble him, or if doubt assails him as to whether his sins were truly forgiven through the absolution, then that voice is his own corruption and the voice of the devil, which he should reject. He should remember the promise of Christ that his sins which are forgiven by a Christian brother on earth are truly forgiven before God in heaven.

"DEEPENING" IN FAITH, "CIRCUMCISION OF HEART"

Every Christian admits and knows that he has not as yet reached perfection in faith and the knowledge of Christ, or in righteousness, peace, joy, or in sanctification. Therefore, every Christian continues to pray that God will increase in him the grace and light of the Holy Spirit in order that he may know Christ and His redemptive sacrifice better and also grow in love and in the fruits of faith.

"That I may know Him, and the power of his resurrection, and the fellowship of His sufferings, being made conformable unto His death; Not as though I had already attained, either were already perfect: but I follow after, if that I may apprehend that for which also I am apprehended of Christ Jesus." (Philippians 3:10, 12)

Such a deepening and growth do not justify a Christian, for through faith he is already justified before God through Christ and His merits, and is wholly His own without spot or blemish. But he wants to grow in the knowledge of this redemption and justification through the Holy Spirit and the Word of God. This growth and deepening do not, however, mean that the Christian himself feels that he is becoming better and better, but only that he realizes more and more his sinfulness, and at the same time, wholly relies on the grace of God in Christ. Thus he himself decreases, but Christ increases in him.

All this is not an achievement of his own but the work and gift of God, as the Apostle says: "Work out your own salvation with fear and trembling; for it is God which worketh in you both to will and to work, for His good pleasure." (Philippians 2:12, 13)

This is what the Apostle means when he says: "Let us go on to perfection." We are to leave the principles of the doctrine of Christ alone. We are not to change them, to add or to detract from them. Therefore we are warned in Revelation 22:18, 19: "If any man shall add unto these things, God shall add unto him the plagues that are written in this book: And if any man shall take away from the words of the book of this prophecy, God shall take away his part out of the book of life, and out of the holy city, and from the things which are written in this book."

If the repentance or conversion of a person has been only an "outward repentance," that is, if he has confessed his sinfulness and accepted forgiveness, without any real change of heart or comprehension of the redemptive work of Christ within his heart, it is necessary that he experience a real awakening of his conscience and that he comes to know in a personal way, in his heart, the redemptive grace and pardon of God, which is "the circumcision of the heart in the Spirit."

All Christians have received the Holy Spirit to dwell in their hearts when they were converted, and born again, and have become believers. But not all Christians are "filled with the Spirit" in the same measure; that is, not all are fully controlled by the Spirit. A Christian who once was "fervent in Spirit" may grow cold in his faith and spiritual life, losing the living knowledge of Christ and the power to bear witness for Him. Such may and should pray for a new blessing or "filling" of the Holy Spirit (Ephesians 5:18), in order that he may grasp, in a living way, the significance of the redemptive grace of God and the forgiveness of sins, in Jesus' Name and blood, that he may be able to live for Christ with his whole heart and be His witness. It is not the will of God that any of His children should be lukewarm. (Revelation 3:16)

The Apostolic Lutheran Christians, in general, yearn and pray for "new showers of blessings" from God, a new pouring out of His Spirit, a "latter rain." They crave for this in order that they may be refreshed and quickened in their faith and be endued with power from on high. This "latter rain" is also prayed for in order that the children of Christian parents and other unbelievers would again, in multitudes, be awakened, both at home and in foreign lands, and return from the ways of the world to the kingdom of God.

Notes: *Growing out of the institutional expression of an evangelical pietist movement within Finnish Lutheranism, the position of the Apostolic Lutherans is unique in both the content and tone of its doctrinal presentation. It is a much warmer, more personal statement centered upon the Christian's relationship to God. Of all like statements used by American Lutheran bodies, this one alone neglects mention of* The Book of Concord, *though it makes passing reference to Luther's Smaller Catechism. Other Lutherans would possibly have trouble with the doctrines of baptisms and the emphasis upon the "latter rain."*

* * *

DECLARATION OF FAITH (ASSOCIATION OF FREE LUTHERAN CONGREGATIONS)

Having a common purpose and seeking one goal, we join together as free congregations for Christian fellowship, mutual edification, the salvation of souls and whatever work may be necessary that the Kingdom of God may come among us and our fellow men. No bonds of compulsion bind us save those which the Holy Spirit lays upon us.

No man fully understands the times and the situations in which he lives. At best we see through a glass darkly. Nevertheless, each Christian must decide in the light of

DECLARATION OF FAITH (ASSOCIATION OF FREE LUTHERAN CONGREGATIONS) (continued)

God's Word and the evidence which he has what course of action he should take and to what causes his life should be given. It is the same for the Christian congregation. Imperfect as it is, it must decide in what fellowship of other congregations it can best live out its purpose for being. Out of considerable soul-searching and prayer we have come to choose to continue as Lutheran free churches.

As we stand at this particular moment of time we give thanks for the heritage of the past. We recognize and confess our indebtness to many noble souls of the faith, both the relatively unknown who are faithful in their places and the ones on whom God placed the mantle of leadership. Even as it is true that before the Cross of Christ there are no self-made men, so it is true that we have shared in blessings from many and are debtors.

It seems good to us as we join together for common work and fellowship to state our beliefs in regard to the following matters.

I. DOCTRINE

1. We accept and believe in the Holy Bible as the complete written Word of God given and preserved to us by the Holy Spirit for our salvation and instruction.

2. We endorse the statement on the Word as found in the United Testimony on Faith and Life and would quote here the following. "We bear witness that the Bible is our only authentic and infallible source of God's revelation to us and all men, and that it is the only inerrant and completely adequate source and norm of Christian doctrine and life. We hold that the Bible, as a whole and in all its parts, is the Word of God under all circumstances regardless of man's attitude toward it."

3. We accept the ancient ecumenical symbols, namely, the Apostles', the Nicene, and the Athanasian Creeds; Luther's Small Catechism and the Unaltered Augsburg Confession as the true expression of the Christian faith and life.

4. We reject any affiliations or associations which do not accept the Bible alone as definitive for the life and practice of man and the Church.

5. We submit all religious teaching to the test of II John 7-11.

6. We endorse no one version or revision of the Bible to the exclusion of others. We recommend all which are reverent and true translations.

II. CHRISTIAN UNITY

1. He who believes in and accepts the sufficient work of Jesus for his salvation and is baptized is a child of God.

2. The Christian is united by the strongest bonds to those who share this faith with him whether they come from his own denomination or another.

3. We believe that Jesus in His High Priestly Prayer prayed that those who believe in Him might find and accept each other.

4. In some situations and in some times it is possible that unions of groups of congregations may be desirable.

5. We recommend that our congregations cooperate wherever possible with like-minded Lutheran congregations and movements in programs of evangelism and witness.

6. We envision opportunities for our congregations to cooperate with other Protestant churches in the areas of evangelism and witness to their communities. However, care must be taken not to compromise the Lutheran understanding of the Scriptures.

III. CHURCH POLITY

1. We believe that final human authority in the churches is vested in the local congregation, subject to the Word of God and the Holy Spirit.

2. Scripture does not command or forbid any particular organization for fellowship of congregations. In the absence of this we believe it is most safe to operate in a democratic way.

3. Conferences of the congregations of our fellowship do not enact law for the congregations, but simply recommend actions and practices to them.

4. In a free association of congregations such as this, neither its officers or conferences can negotiate the union of any or all of the congregations with another fellowship of congregations. This is an individual matter for the congregation.

5. We accept the Guiding Principles of the Lutheran Free Church as a true statement of our belief in regard to church polity.

6. The Holy Christian Church consists of those who in their hearts truly believe in Jesus Christ as Lord and Saviour.

7. A free congregation selects and calls its own pastor, conducts its own program of worship, fellowship and service, and owns and maintains its own property.

IV. PRACTICAL LIFE

1. The Christian seeks to refrain from those acts, thoughts and words which are against a stated law of God.

2. Where actions and practices are neither forbidden nor encouraged in Scripture by name, the earnest believer will search in the Scriptures for principles to guide his decisions and conduct.

3. He is aware that there is a separation which is necessary between the Christian and the world.

4. Ultimately every Christian makes his own decisions as to life and practice in the presence of His God. But he welcomes the sincere counsel of fellow believers.

5. Every Christian is responsible for his witness by life to others and will govern himself, with the Lord's help, accordingly.

6. The Christian will refrain from belonging to organizations which practice a religion without Christ as the only Saviour. Belonging to such a group places the believer in a hopelessly compromised position and destroys his witness for Christ.

V. CHURCH LIFE

1. We make no recommendation as to the use of liturgy and vestments except that we encourage simplicity in worship.

2. We believe the earliest Christians were extremely simple in their order of service. Whatever is added to the service carries the danger of becoming only form.

3. Even the simple parts of the service may become only form.

4. The preaching of the Word of God must be the central part of the service.

5. True Gospel preaching endeavors to meet the needs of all who hear: the believer who desires to grow in his life with God, the seeking and uncertain souls who want to see Him, the hypocrite who must be awakened from his self-righteousness, and the hardened sinner who must still be called to saving faith.

6. The Sacraments must always be met by the response of faith in the heart of the recipient to be efficacious.

7. Hymn books should be such as will give honor to the Word of God and the Sacraments.

8. Congregations will cherish opportunities for Bible study and prayer fellowship.

9. Congregations are encouraged to have fellowship with one another in various activities.

10. The Lord has given talents and gifts to Christian lay people as well as pastors, and opportunity should be given for the practice of these gifts in the life of the congregations, also in meetings of fellowship outside the congregation, and in service to a needy world.

Notes: *This declaration adopted in 1962 outlines the documents that are accepted as theologically authoritative, but it proceeds to dedicate the body of the text to outlining a position on those issues that occasioned the creation of the association. The separation from those whose doctrinal standards are lax is of prime importance.*

*　　*　　*

CONFESSION (CHURCH OF THE LUTHERAN CONFESSION)

The doctrinal position of this body is defined by the following statements:

A. We accept without reservation the canonical Scriptures of the Old and the New Testaments as the verbally inspired Word of God ("verbally"—I Corinthians 2:13; "inspired"—II Timothy 3:16; cf. also II Peter 1:21) and therefore as the sole and only infallible rule of doctrine and life.

B. We confess the Apostolic, Nicene, and Athanasian Creeds and the Particular Symbols of the Lutheran Church as published in the Book of Concord of 1580,

because they are a true exposition of the Word of God.

C. We also subscribe to the Brief Statement of 1932.

D. Because of differences that have arisen within the Synodical Conference we have found it necessary to define our position in a particular statement entitled *Concerning Church Fellowship* as well as in *Theses on the Relation of Synod and Local Congregation to the Holy Christian Church and Theses on the Ministry of the Keys and the Public Ministry.*

Notes: *Even more conservative than the Wisconsin Synod, the Church of the Lutheran Confession has rejected relations with any church less conservative than itself. Along with adherence to* The Book of Concord, *the church additionally demands adherence to the Brief Statement adopted by the Missouri Synod in 1932. This confession comes from the church's constitution.*

*　　*　　*

CONFESSION (FEDERATION FOR AUTHENTIC LUTHERANISM)

FAL, and every member of FAL, accepts without reservation:

1. The Holy Scripture, both the Old and New Testament, as the very Word of God. His infallible revelation given by inspiration of the Holy Spirit, in all parts and words recorded without error in the original manuscripts by the Prophets, Apostles and Evangelists at the only rule and norm of faith and practice:

2. All the Symbolical Books of the Evangelical Lutheran Church as a true and Unadulterated statement and exposition of the Word of God (and subscribe to these symbols because (*quia*) they are a proper exposition of God's Word), to wit: the three Ecumenical Creeds (the Apostles' Creed, the Nicene Creed, the Athanasian Creed), the Unaltered Augsburg Confession, the Apology of the Augsburg Confession, the Smalcald Articles, the Large Catechism of Luther, the Small Catechism of Luther, and the Formula of Concord:

3. The Brief Statement of the Doctrinal Position of the Missouri Synod adopted in 1932. We recognize the need for the development of additional confessional statements dealing with the theological problems and concerns of each age. Therefore, additional confessional statements may be added to this confessional base as the need arises. All confessional statements which are added must be in total agreement with the existing confessional standard.

Notes: *Withdrawing from the Lutheran Church-Missouri Synod in the 1970s, the Federation for Authentic Lutheranism represented theologically the most conservative wing of the synod, a postion reflected in its confession.*

CONFESSION OF FAITH (LUTHERAN CHURCH IN AMERICA)

Section 1. This church confesses Jesus Christ as Lord of the Church. The Holy Spirit creates and sustains the Church through the Gospel and thereby unites believers with their Lord and with one another in the fellowship of faith.

Section 2. This church holds that the Gospel is the revelation of God's sovereign will and saving grace in Jesus Christ. In Him, the Word Incarnate, God imparts Himself to men.

Section 3. This church acknowledges the Holy Scriptures as the norm for the faith and life of the Church. The Holy Scriptures are the divinely inspired record of God's redemptive act in Christ, for which the Old Testament prepared the way and which the New Testament proclaims. In the continuation of this proclamation in the Church, God still speaks through the Holy Scriptures and realizes His redemptive purpose generation after generation.

Section 4. This church accepts the Apostles', the Nicene, and the Athanasian creeds as true declarations of the faith of the Church.

Section 5. This church accepts the Unaltered Augsburg Confession, and Luther's Small Catechism as true witnesses to the Gospel, and acknowledges as one with it in faith and doctrine all churches that likewise accept the teachings of these symbols.

Section 6. This church accepts the other symbolical books of the evangelical Lutheran church, the Apology of the Augsburg Confession, the Smalcald Articles, Luther's Large Catechism, and the Formula of Concord as further valid interpretations of the confession of the church.

Section 7. This church affirms that the Gospel transmitted by the Holy Scriptures, to which the creeds and confessions bear witness, is the true treasure of the Church, the substance of its proclamation, and the basis of its unity and continuity. The Holy Spirit uses the proclamation of the Gospel and the administration of the Sacraments to create and sustain Christian faith and fellowship. As this occurs, the Church fulfills its divine mission and purpose.

Notes: *This confession is found in the constitution of the church (1962). It is noteworthy because of the manner in which it offers varied reflections upon the Bible and various Lutheran doctrinal documents.*

*　　*　　*

CONFESSION (LUTHERAN CHURCH-MISSOURI SYNOD)

The Synod, and every member of the Synod, accepts without reservation:

1. The Scriptures of the Old and the New Testament as the written Word of God and the only rule and norm of faith and of practice;

2. All the Symbolical Books of the Evangelical Lutheran Church as a true and unadulterated statement and exposition of the Word of God, to wit: the three Ecumenical Creeds (the Apostles' Creed, the Nicene Creed, the Athanasian Creed), the Unaltered Augsburg Confession, the Apology of the Augsburg Confession, the Smalcald Articles, the Large Catechism of Luther, the Small Catechism of Luther, and the Formula of Concord.

Notes: *One of two documents from the Missouri Synod, this brief statement is from the church's constitution. It stands in stark contrast to the like confessions from the constitutions of the American Lutheran Church and the Lutheran Church in America.*

*　　*　　*

BRIEF STATEMENT OF THE DOCTRINAL POSITION OF THE MISSOURI SYNOD [LUTHERAN CHURCH-MISSOURI SYNOD (1932)]

OF THE HOLY SCRIPTURES.

1. We teach that the Holy Scriptures differ from all other books in the world in that they are the Word of God. They are the Word of God because the holy men of God who wrote the Scriptures wrote only that which the Holy Ghost communicated to them by inspiration, 2 Tim. 3, 16; 2 Pet. 1, 21. We teach also that the verbal inspiration of the Scriptures is not a so-called "theological deduction," but that it is taught by direct statements of the Scriptures, 2 Tim. 3, 16; John 10, 35; Rom. 3, 2; 1 Cor. 2, 13. Since the Holy Scriptures are the Word of God, it goes without saying that they contain no errors or contradictions, but that they are in all their parts and words the infallible truth, also in those parts which treat of historical, geographical, and other secular matters, John 10, 35.

2. We furthermore teach regarding the Holy Scriptures that they are given by God to the Christian Church for the foundation of faith, Eph. 2, 20. Hence the Holy Scriptures are the sole source from which all doctrines proclaimed in the Christian Church must be taken and therefore, too, the sole rule and norm by which all teachers and doctrines must be examined and judged.—With the Confessions of our Church we teach also that the "rule of faith" (*analogia fidei*) according to which the Holy Scriptures are to be understood are the clear passages of *Scriptures themselves* which set forth the individual doctrines. (Apologie. *Triglotta*, p. 441, § 60; Mueller, p. 284.) The rule of faith is not the man-made so-called "totality of Scripture" (*"Ganzes der Schrift"*).

3. We reject the doctrine which under the name of science has gained wide popularity in the Church of our day, that Holy Scripture is not in all its parts the Word of God, but in part the Word of God and in part the word of man and hence does, or at least might, contain error. We reject this erroneous doctrine as horrible and blasphemous, since it flatly contradicts Christ and His holy apostles, sets up men as judges over the Word of God, and thus over-

throws the foundation of the Christian Church and its faith.

OF GOD.

4. On the basis of the Holy Scriptures we teach the sublime article of the Holy Trinity; that is, we teach that the one true God, Deut. 6, 4; 1 Cor. 8, 4, is the Father and the Son and the Holy Ghost, three distinct *persons*, but of one and the same divine *essence*, equal in power, equal in eternity, equal in majesty, because each person possesses the one divine essence *entire*, Col. 2, 9; Matt. 28, 19. We hold that all teachers and communions that deny the doctrine of the Holy Trinity are outside the pale of the Christian Church. The Triune God is the God who is *gracious* to man, John 3, 16-18; 1 Cor. 12, 3. Since the Fall no man can believe in the "fatherhood" of God except he believe in the eternal Son of God, who became man and reconciled us to God by His vicarious satisfaction, 1 John 2, 23; John 14, 6. Hence we warn against Unitarianism, which in our country has to a great extent impenetrated the sects and is being spread particularly also through the influence of the lodges.

OF CREATION.

5. We teach that God has created heaven and earth, and that in the manner and in the space of time recorded in the Holy Scriptures, especially Gen. 1 and 2, namely, by His almighty creative word, and in six days. We reject every doctrine which denies or limits the work of creation as taught in Scripture. In our days it is denied or limited by those who assert, ostensibly in deference to science, that the world came into existence through a process of evolution; that is, that it has, in immense periods of time, developed more or less out of itself. Since no man was present when it pleased God to create the world, we must look, for a reliable account of creation, to God's own record, found in God's own book, the Bible. We accept God's own record with full confidence and confess with Luther's Catechism: "I believe that God has made me and all creatures."

OF MAN AND OF SIN.

6. We teach that the first man was not brutelike nor merely capable of intellectual development, but that God created man *in His own image*, Gen. 1, 26. 27; Eph. 4, 24; Col. 3, 10, that is, in true knowledge of God and in true righteousness and holiness and endowed with a truly scientific knowledge of nature, Gen. 2, 19-23.

7. We furthermore teach that sin came into the world by the fall of the first man, as described Gen. 3. By this Fall not only he himself, but also all his natural offspring have lost the original knowledge, righteousness, and holiness, and thus all men are sinners already by birth, dead in sins, inclined to all evil, and subject to the wrath of God, Rom. 5, 12. 18; Eph. 2, 1-3. We teach also that men are unable, through any efforts of their own or by the aid of "culture and science," to reconcile themselves to God and thus to conquer death and damnation.

OF REDEMPTION.

8. We teach that in the fulness of time the eternal Son of God *was made man* by assuming, from the Virgin Mary through the operation of the Holy Ghost, a human nature like unto ours, yet without sin, and receiving it into His divine person. Jesus Christ is therefore "true God, begotten of the Father from eternity, and also true man, born of the Virgin Mary," true God and true man in *one* undivided and indivisible person. The purpose of this miraculous incarnation of the Son of God was that He might become the *Mediator* between God and men, both fulfilling the divine Law and suffering and dying in the place of mankind. In this manner God has reconciled the whole sinful world unto Himself, Gal. 4, 4. 5; 3, 13; 2 Cor. 5, 18. 19.

OF FAITH IN CHRIST.

9. Since God has reconciled the whole world unto Himself through the vicarious life and death of His Son and has commanded that the reconciliation effected by Christ be proclaimed to men in the Gospel, to the end that they may *believe* it, 2 Cor. 5, 18.19; Rom. 1, 5, therefore faith in Christ is the only way for men to obtain personal reconciliation with God, that is, forgiveness of sins, as both the Old and the New Testament Scriptures testify, Acts 10,43; John 3,16—18.36. By this faith in Christ, through which men obtain the forgiveness of sins, is not meant any human effort to fulfil the Law of God after the example of Christ, but faith in the Gospel, that is, in the forgiveness of sins, or justification, which was fully earned for us by Christ and is offered in the Gospel. This faith justifies, not inasmuch as it is a work of man, but inasmuch as it lays hold of the grace offered, the forgiveness of sins, Rom. 4, 16.

OF CONVERSION.

10. We teach that conversion consists in this, that a man, having learned from the Law of God that he is a lost and condemned sinner, *is brought to faith in the Gospel*, which offers him forgiveness of sins and eternal salvation for the sake of Christ's vicarious satisfaction, Acts 11,21; Luke 24,46.47; Acts 26,18.

11. All men, since the Fall, are dead in sins, Eph. 2, 1—3, and inclined only to evil, Gen. 6, 5; 8, 21; Rom. 8, 7. For this reason, and particularly because men regard the Gospel of Christ, crucified for the sins of the world, as foolishness, 1 Cor. 2, 14, faith in the Gospel, or conversion to God, is neither wholly nor in the least part the work of man, but the work of God's grace and almighty power alone, Phil. 1, 29; Eph. 2, 8; 1, 19;—Jer. 31, 18. Hence Scripture calls the faith of man, or his conversion, a raising from the dead, Eph. 1, 20; Col. 2, 12, a being born of God, John 1, 12.13, a new birth by the Gospel, 1 Pet. 1,23—25, a work of God like the creation of light at the creation of the world, 2 Cor. 4, 6.

12. On the basis of these clear statements of the Holy Scriptures we reject every kind of *synergism*, that is, the doctrine that conversion is wrought not by the grace and power of God alone, but in part also by the cooperation of man himself, by man's right conduct, his right attitude, his right self-determination, his lesser guilt or less evil conduct as compared with others, his refraining from wilful resistance, or anything else whereby man's conversion and salvation is taken out of the gracious hands of God and made to depend on what man does or leaves undone. For this refraining from wilful resistance or from any kind of resistance is also solely a work of grace, which "changes unwilling into willing men," Ezek. 36, 26; Phil. 2, 13. We reject also the doctrine that man is able to decide for conversion through "powers imparted by grace," since this doctrine presupposes that *before* conversion man still possesses spiritual powers by which he can make the right use of such "powers imparted by grace."

13. On the other hand, we reject also the *Calvinistic* perversion of the doctrine of conversion, that is, the doctrine that God does not desire to convert and save all hearers of the Word, but only a portion of them. Many hearers of the Word indeed remain unconverted and are not saved, not because God does not earnestly desire their conversion and salvation, but solely because they stubbornly resist the gracious operation of the Holy Ghost, as Scripture teaches, Acts 7, 51; Matt. 23, 37; Acts 13, 46.

14. As to the question why not all men are converted and saved, seeing that God's grace is universal and all men are equally and utterly corrupt, we confess that we cannot answer it. From Scripture we know only this: A man owes his conversion and salvation, not to any lesser guilt or better conduct on his part, but solely to the grace of God. But any man's non-conversion is due to himself alone: it is the result of his obstinate resistance against the converting operation of the Holy Ghost, Hos. 13, 9.

15. Our refusal to go beyond what is revealed in these two Scriptural truths is not "masked Calvinism" ("Cryptocalvinism"), but *precisely* the Scriptural teaching of the Lutheran Church as it is presented in detail in the Formula of Concord (*Triglot*, p. 1081, §§ 57-59. 60 b. 62. 63; M., p. 716 f.): "That one is hardened, blinded, given over to a reprobate mind, while another, who is indeed in the same guilt, is converted again, etc.,—in these and similar questions Paul fixes a certain limit to us how far we should go, namely, that in the one part we should recognize God's *judgment*. For they are well-deserved penalties of sins when God so punishes a land or nation for despising His Word that the punishment extends also to their posterity, as is to be seen in the Jews. And thereby God in some lands and persons exhibits His severity to those that are His in order to indicate what we all would have well deserved and would be worthy and worth, since we act wickedly in opposition to God's Word and often grieve the Holy Ghost sorely; in order that we may live in the fear of God and acknowledge and praise God's *goodness*, to the exclusion of, and contrary to, our merit in and with *us*, to whom He gives His Word and with whom He leaves it and whom He does not harden and reject. . . . And this His righteous, well-deserved judgment He displays in some countries, nations, and persons in order that, when we are placed alongside of them and compared with them (*quam simillimi illis deprehensi, i.e.*, and found to be most similar to them), we may learn the more diligently to recognize and praise God's pure, unmerited grace in the vessels of mercy. . . . When we proceed thus far in this article, we remain on the right way, as it is written, Hos. 13, 9: 'O Israel, thou hast destroyed thyself; but in Me is thy help.' However, as regards these things in this disputation which would soar too high and beyond these limits, we should with Paul place the finger upon our lips and remember and say, Rom. 9, 20: 'O man, who art thou that repliest against God?' " The Formula of Concord describes the mystery which confronts us here not as a mystery in man's heart (a "psychological" mystery), but teaches that, when we try to understand why "one is hardened, blinded, given over to a reprobate mind, while another, who is indeed in the same guilt, is converted again," we enter the domain of the unsearchable judgments of God and ways past finding out, which are not revealed to us in His Word, but which we shall know in eternal life, 1 Cor. 13, 12.

16. Calvinists solve this mystery, which God has not revealed in His Word, by denying the *universality* of grace; synergists, by denying that salvation is by grace *alone*. Both solutions are utterly vicious, since they contradict Scripture and since every poor sinner stands in need of, and must cling to, both the unrestricted *universal grace* and the unrestricted "by grace *alone*," lest he despair and perish.

OF JUSTIFICATION.

17. Holy Scripture sums up all its teachings regarding the love of God to the world of sinners, regarding the salvation wrought by Christ, and regarding faith in Christ as the only way to obtain salvation, in the article of *justification*. Scripture teaches that God has already declared the whole world to be righteous in Christ, Rom. 7, 19; 2 Cor. 5, 18-21; Rom. 4,25; that therefore not for the sake of their good works, but without the works of the Law, by grace, for Christ's sake, He *justifies*, that is, *accounts* as righteous, all those who believe in Christ, that is, believe, accept, and rely on, the fact that for Christ's sake their sins are forgiven. Thus the Holy Ghost testifies through St. Paul: "There is no difference; for all have sinned and come short of the glory of God, being justified freely by His grace, through the redemption that is in Christ Jesus," Rom. 3:23, 24. And again: "Therefore

we conclude that a man is justified by faith, without the deeds of the Law," Rom. 3, 28.

18. Through this doctrine alone Christ is given the *honor* due Him, namely, that through His holy life and innocent suffering and death He is our Savior. And through this doctrine alone can poor sinners have the abiding *comfort* that God is assuredly gracious to them. We reject *as apostasy from the Christian religion* all doctrines whereby man's own works and merit are mingled into the article of justification before God. For the Christian religion is the faith that we have forgiveness of sins and salvation through faith in Christ Jesus, Acts 10, 43.

19. We reject as apostasy from the Christian religion not only the doctrine of the *Unitarians*, who promise the grace of God to men on the basis of their moral efforts; not only the gross work-doctrine of the papists, who expressly teach that good works are necessary to obtain justification; but also the doctrine of the *synergists*, who indeed use the terminology of the Christian Church and say that man is justified "by faith," "by faith alone," but again mix human works into the article of justification by ascribing to man a cooperation with God in the kindling of faith and thus stray into papistic territory.

OF GOOD WORKS.

20. Before God only those works are good which are done for the glory of God and the good of man, according to the rule of the divine Law. Such works, however, no man performs unless he first believes that God has forgiven him his sins and has given him eternal life by grace, for Christ's sake, without any works of his own, John 15, 4. 5. We reject as a great folly the assertion, frequently made in our day, that works must be placed in the fore, and "faith in dogmas"—meaning the Gospel of Christ Crucified for the sins of the world—must be relegated to the rear. Since good works never precede faith, but are always and in every instance the *result* of faith in the Gospel, it is evident that the only means by which we Christians can become rich in good works (and God would have us to be rich in good works, Titus 2, 14) is unceasingly to remember the grace of God which we have received in Christ, Rom. 12, 1; 2 Cor. 8, 9. Hence we reject as unchristian and foolish any attempt to produce good works by the compulsion of the Law or through carnal motives.

OF THE MEANS OF GRACE.

21. Although God is present and operates everywhere throughout all creation and the whole earth is therefore full of the *temporal* bounties and blessings of God, Col. 1, 17; Acts 17, 28; 14, 17, still we hold with Scripture that God offers and communicates to men the *spiritual* blessings purchased by Christ, namely, the forgiveness of sins and the treasures and gifts connected therewith, only through the external means of grace ordained by Him. These means of grace are the Word of the Gospel, in every form in which it is brought to man, and the Sacraments of Holy Baptism and of the Lord's Supper. The Word of the Gospel promises and applies the grace of God, works faith and thus regenerates man, and gives the Holy Ghost, Acts 20, 24; Rom. 10, 17; 1 Pet. 1, 23; Gal. 3, 2. Baptism, too, is applied for the remission of sins and is therefore a washing of regeneration and renewing of the Holy Ghost, Acts 2, 38; 22, 16; Titus 3, 5. Likewise the object of the Lord's Supper, that is, of the ministration of the body and blood of Christ, is none other than the communication and sealing of the forgiveness of sins, as the words declare: "Given for you," and: "Shed for you for the remission of sins," Luke 22, 19. 20; Matt. 26, 28, and: "This cup is the New Testament in My blood," 1 Cor. 11, 23; Jer. 31, 31-34 ("New Covenant").

22. Since it is only through the external means ordained by Him that God has promised to communicate the grace and salvation purchased by Christ, the Christian Church must not remain at home with the means of grace entrusted to it, but go into the whole world with the preaching of the Gospel and the administration of the Sacraments, Matt. 28, 19.20; Mark 16, 15.16. For the same reason also the churches at home should never forget that there is no other way of winning souls for the Church and keeping them with it than the faithful and diligent use of the divinely ordained means of grace. Whatever activities do not either directly apply the Word of God or subserve such application we condemn as "new methods," unchurchly activities, which do not build, but harm, the Church.

23. We reject as a dangerous error the doctrine, which disrupted the Church of the Reformation, that the grace and the Spirit of God are communicated not through the external means ordained by Him, but by an *immediate* operation of grace. This erroneous doctrine bases the forgiveness of sins, or justification, upon a fictitious "infused grace," that is, upon a quality of man, and thus again establishes the work-doctrine of the papists.

OF THE CHURCH.

24. We believe that there is *one* holy Christian Church on earth, the Head of which is Christ and which is gathered, preserved, and governed by Christ through the Gospel.

The members of the Christian Church are the *Christians*, that is, all those who have despaired of their own righteousness before God and believe that God forgives their sins for Christ's sake. The Christian Church, in the proper sense of the term, is composed of believers only, Acts 5, 14; 26, 18; which means that no person in whom the Holy Ghost has wrought faith in the Gospel, or—which is the same thing—in the doctrine of justification, can be divested of his membership in the Christian Church; and, on the other hand, that no person in whose heart this faith does not dwell can be invested with such membership. All unbelievers, though they be in external communion with the Church and even hold the office of teacher or any other office in the Church, are not members of the Church, but, on the

BRIEF STATEMENT OF THE DOCTRINAL POSITION OF THE MISSOURI SYNOD [LUTHERAN CHURCH-MISSOURI SYNOD (1932)] (continued)

contrary, dwelling-places and instruments of Satan, Eph. 2,2. This is also the teaching of our Lutheran Confessions: "It is certain, however, that the wicked are in the power of the devil and members of the kingdom of the devil, as Paul teaches, Eph. 2, 2, when he says that 'the devil now worketh in the children of disobedience,' " etc. (Apology. *Triglot*, p. 231, § 16; M., p. 154.)

25. Since it is by faith in the Gospel alone that men become members of the Christian Church, and since this faith cannot be seen by men, but is known to God alone, 1 Kings 8, 39; Acts 1, 24; 2 Tim. 2, 19, therefore the Christian Church on earth is *invisible*, Luke 17, 20, and will remain invisible till Judgment Day, Col. 3, 3.4. In our day some Lutherans speak of two sides of the Church, taking the means of grace to be its "visible side." It is true, the means of grace are necessarily related to the Church, seeing that the Church is created and preserved through them. But the means of grace are not for that reason a part of the Church; for the Church in the proper sense of the word consists only of *believers*, Eph. 2, 19.20; Acts 5, 14. Lest we abet the notion that the Christian Church in the proper sense of the term is an external institution, we shall continue to call the means of grace the "marks" of the Church. Just as wheat is to be found only where it has been sown, so the Church can be found only where the Word of God is in use.

26. We teach that this Church, which is the invisible communion of all believers, is to be found not only in those external church communions which teach the Word of God purely in every part, but also where, along with error, so much of the Word of God still remains that men may be brought to the knowledge of their sins and to faith in the forgiveness of sins, which Christ has gained for all men, Mark 16, 16; Samaritans: Luke 17, 16; John 4, 25.

27. *Local Churches or Local Congregations.*—Holy Scripture, however, does not speak merely of the *one* Church, which embraces the believers of all places, as in Matt. 16, 18; John 10, 16, but also of churches in the *plural*, that is, of *local churches*, as in 1 Cor. 16, 19; 1, 2; Acts 8, 1: the churches of Asia, the church of God in Corinth, the church in Jerusalem. But this does not mean that there are *two kinds* of churches; for the local churches also, in as far as they are churches, consist solely of believers, as we see clearly from the addresses of the epistles to local churches; for example, "Unto the church which is at Corinth, to *them that are sanctified* in Christ Jesus, called to be *saints*," 1 Cor. 1, 2; Rom. 1, 7, etc. The visible society, containing hypocrites as well as believers, is called a church only in an improper sense, Matt. 13, 47-50. 24-30. 38-43.

28. *On Church-Fellowship.*—Since God ordained that His Word *only*, without the admixture of human doctrine, be taught and believed in the Christian Church, 1 Pet. 4, 11; John 8, 31. 32; 1 Tim. 6, 3. 4, all Christians are required by God to discriminate between orthodox and heterodox church-bodies, Matt. 7, 15, to have church-fellowship only with orthodox church-bodies, and, in case they have strayed into heterodox church-bodies, to leave them, Rom. 16, 17. We repudiate *unionism*, that is, church-fellowship with the adherents of false doctrine, as disobedience to God's command, as causing divisions in the Church, Rom. 16, 17; 2 John 9, 10, and as involving the constant danger of losing the Word of God entirely, 2 Tim. 2, 17-21.

29. The orthodox character of a church is established not by its mere name nor by its outward acceptance of, and subscription to, an orthodox creed, but by the doctrine which is *actually* taught in its pulpits, in its theological seminaries, and in its publications. On the other hand, a church does not forfeit its orthodox character through the casual intrusion of errors, provided these are combated and eventually removed by means of doctrinal discipline, Acts 20, 30; 1 Tim. 1, 3.

30. *The Original and True Possessors of All Christian Rights and Privileges.*—Since the Christians are the Church, it is self-evident that they alone *originally* possess the spiritual gifts and rights which Christ has gained for, and given to, His Church. Thus St. Paul reminds all believers: "All things are yours," 1 Cor. 3, 21.22, and Christ Himself commits to all believers the keys of the kingdom of heaven, Matt. 16, 13-19; 18, 17-20; John 20, 22. 23, and commissions all believers to preach the Gospel and to administer the Sacraments, Matt. 28, 19. 20; 1 Cor. 11, 23-25. Accordingly, we reject all doctrines by which this spiritual power or any part thereof is adjudged as *originally* vested in certain individuals or bodies, such as the Pope, or the bishops, or the order of the ministry, or the secular lords, or councils, or synods, etc. The officers of the Church publicly administer their offices only by virtue of delegated powers, conferred on them by the original possessors of such powers, and such administration remains under the supervision of the latter, Col. 4, 17. Naturally all Christians have also the right and the duty to judge and decide matters of doctrine, not according to their own notions, of course, but according to the Word of God, 1 John 4, 1; 1 Pet. 4, 11.

OF THE PUBLIC MINISTRY.

31. By the public ministry we mean the office by which the Word of God is preached and the Sacraments are administered *by order and in the name* of a Christian congregation. Concerning this office we teach that it is a *divine ordiance*; that is, the Christians of a certain locality must apply the means of grace not only privately and within the circle of their families nor merely in their common intercourse with fellow-Christians, John 5, 39; Eph. 6, 4; Col. 3, 16, but they are also required, by the divine order, to make provision that the Word of God be publicly preached in their midst, and the Sacraments administered

according to the institution of Christ, by persons qualified for such work, whose qualifications and official functions are exactly defined in Scripture, Titus 1,5; Acts 14,23; 20,28; 2 Tim. 2,2.

32. Although the office of the ministry is a divine ordinance, it possesses no other power than the power of the Word of God, 1 Pet. 4,11; that is to say, it is the duty of Christians to yield unconditional obedience to the office of the ministry whenever, and as long as, the minister proclaims to them the Word of God, Heb. 13,17; Luke 10,16. If, however, the minister, in his teachings and injunctions, were to go beyond the Word of God, it would be the duty of Christians not to obey, but to disobey him, so as to remain faithful to Christ, Matt. 23,8. Accordingly, we reject the false doctrine ascribing to the office of the ministry the right to demand obedience and submission in matters which Christ has not commanded.

33. Regarding *ordination* we teach that it is not a divine, but a commendable ecclesiastical ordinance. (Smalcald Articles. *Triglot*, p. 525, § 70; M., p. 342.)

OF CHURCH AND STATE.

34. Although both Church and State are ordinances of God, yet they must not be commingled. Church and State have entirely different aims. By the Church, God would save men, for which reason the Church is called the "mother" of believers, Gal. 4,26. By the State, God would maintain external order among men, "that we may lead a quiet and peaceable life in all godliness and honesty," 1 Tim. 2,2. It follows that the means which Church and State employ to gain their ends are entirely different. The Church may not employ any other means than the preaching of the Word of God, John 18, 11.36; 2 Cor. 10,4. The State, on the other hand, makes laws bearing on civil matters and is empowered to employ for their execution also the sword and other corporal punishments, Rom. 13,4.

Accordingly we condemn the policy of those who would have the power of the State employed "in the interest of the Church" and who thus turn the Church into a secular dominion; as also of those who, aiming to govern the State by the Word of God, seek to turn the State into a Church.

OF THE ELECTION OF GRACE.

35. By election of grace we mean this truth, that all those who by the grace of God alone, for Christ's sake, through the means of grace, are brought to faith, are justified, sanctified, and preserved in faith *here in time*, that all these have already from eternity been endowed by God with faith, justification, sanctification, and preservation in faith, and this *for the same reason*, namely, by grace alone, for Christ's sake, and by way of the means of grace. That this is the doctrine of Holy Scripture is evident from Eph. 1,3-7; 2 Thess. 2,13.14; Acts 13,48; Rom. 8,28-30; 2 Tim 1,9; Matt. 24, 22-24 (cp. Form. of Conc. *Triglot*, p. 1065, §§ 5. 8. 23; M., p. 705).

36. Accordingly we reject as an anti-Scriptural error the doctrine that not alone the grace of God and the merit of Christ are the cause of the election of grace, but that God has, in addition, found or regarded something good *in us* which prompted or caused Him to elect us, this being variously designated as "good works," "right conduct," "proper self-determination," "refraining from wilful resistance," etc. Nor does Holy Scripture know of an election "by foreseen faith," "in view of faith," as though the faith of the elect were to be placed before their election; but according to Scripture the faith which the elect have in time belongs to the spiritual blessings with which God has endowed them by His eternal election. For Scripture teaches, Acts 13,48: "And as many as were ordained unto eternal life believed." Our Lutheran Confession also testifies (*Triglot*, p. 1065, § 8; M., p. 705): "The eternal election of God, however, not only foresees and foreknows the salvation of the elect, but is also, from the gracious will and pleasure of God in Christ Jesus, a cause which procures, works, helps, and promotes our salvation and what pertains thereto; and upon this our salvation is so founded that the gates of hell cannot prevail against it, Matt. 16,18, as is written John 10,28: 'Neither shall any man pluck My sheep out of My hand'; and again, Acts 13,48: 'And as many as were ordained to eternal life believed.'"

37. But as earnestly as we maintain that there is an election of *grace*, or a predestination to salvation, so decidedly do we teach, on the other hand, that there is no election of wrath, or predestination to *damnation*. Scripture plainly reveals the truth that the love of God for the world of lost sinners is universal, that is, that it embraces all men without exception, that Christ has fully reconciled all men unto God, and that God earnestly desires to bring all men to faith, to preserve them therein, and thus to save them, as Scripture testifies, 1 Tim. 2,4: "God will have all men to be saved and to come to the knowledge of the truth." No man is lost because God had predestinated him to eternal damnation.—Eternal election is a cause why the elect are brought to faith in time, Acts 13,48; but election is *not* a cause why men remain unbelievers when they hear the Word of God. The reason assigned by Scripture for this sad fact is that these men judge *themselves* unworthy of everlasting life, putting the Word of God from them and obstinately resisting the Holy Ghost, whose earnest will it is to bring also them to repentance and faith by means of the Word, Acts 13, 46; 7, 51; Matt. 23, 37.

38. To be sure, it is necessary to observe the Scriptural distinction between the election of grace and the universal will of grace. This universal gracious will of God embraces all men; the election of grace, however, does not embrace all, but only a definite number, whom "God hath from the beginning chosen to salvation," 2 Thess. 2, 13, the "remnant," the "seed" which "the Lord left," Rom. 9, 27—29, the "election," Rom. 11, 7; and while the universal

BRIEF STATEMENT OF THE DOCTRINAL POSITION OF THE MISSOURI SYNOD [LUTHERAN CHURCH-MISSOURI SYNOD (1932)] (continued)

will of grace is frustrated in the case of most men, Matt. 22, 14; Luke 7, 30, the election of grace attains its end with all whom it embraces, Rom. 8, 28-30. Scripture, however, while distinguishing between the universal will of grace and the election of grace does not place the two in opposition to each other. On the contrary, it teaches that the grace dealing with those who are lost is altogether earnest and fully efficacious for conversion. Blind reason indeed declares these two truths to be contradictory; but we impose silence on our reason. The seeming disharmony will disappear in the light of heaven, 1 Cor. 13, 12.

39. Furthermore, by election of grace, Scripture does not mean that *one* part of God's counsel of salvation according to which He will receive into heaven those who persevere in faith unto the end, but, on the contrary, Scripture means this, that God, before the foundation of the world, from pure grace, because of the redemption of Christ, has chosen for His own a definite number of persons out of the corrupt mass and has determined to bring them, through Word and Sacrament, to faith and salvation.

40. Christians can and should be assured of their eternal election. This is evident from the fact that Scripture addresses them as the chosen ones and comforts them with their election, Eph. 1, 4; 2 Thess. 2, 13. This assurance of one's personal election, however, springs only from faith in the Gospel, from the assurance that God so loved the world that He gave His only-begotten Son, that whosoever believeth in Him should not perish, but have everlasting life. For God sent not His Son into the world to *condemn* the world; on the contrary, through the life, suffering, and death of His Son He fully *reconciled* the whole world of sinners unto Himself. Faith in this truth leaves no room for the fear that God might still harbor thoughts of wrath and damnation concerning us. Scripture inculcates that in Rom. 8, 32.33: "He that spared not His own Son, but delivered Him up for us all, how shall He not with Him also freely give us all things? Who shall lay anything to the charge of God's elect? It is God that justifieth." Luther's pastoral advice is therefore in accord with Scripture: "Gaze upon the wounds of Christ and the blood shed for you; there predestination will shine forth." (St. Louis Ed., II, 181; on Gen. 26, 9.) That the Christian obtains the personal assurance of his eternal election in this way is taught also by our Lutheran Confessions (Formula of Concord. *Triglot*, p. 1071, § 26; M., p. 709): "Of this we should not judge according to our reason nor according to the Law or from any external appearance. Neither should we attempt to investigate the secret, concealed abyss of divine predestination, but should give heed to the revealed will of God. For He has made known unto us the mystery of His will and made it manifest through *Christ* that it might be preached, Eph. 1, 9 ff.; 2 Tim.

1, 9 f."—In order to insure the proper method of viewing eternal election and the Christian's assurance of it, the Lutheran Confessions set forth at length the principle that election is not to be considered "in a bare manner (*nude*), as though God only held a muster, thus: 'This one shall be saved, that one shall be damned'" (Formula of Concord. *Triglot*, p. 1065, § 9; M., p. 706); but "the Scriptures teach this doctrine in no other way than to direct us thereby to the *Word*, Eph. 1, 13; 1 Cor. 1, 7; exhort to repentance, 2 Tim. 3, 16; urge to godliness, Eph. 1, 14; John 15, 3; strengthen faith and assure us of our salvation, Eph. 1, 13; John 10, 27 f.; 2 Thess. 2, 13 f." (Formula of Concord. *Triglot*, p. 1067, § 12; M., p. 707).—To sum up, just as God in time draws the Christians unto Himself through the Gospel, so He had already in His eternal election endowed them with "sanctification of the Spirit and belief of the truth," 2 Thess. 2, 13. Therefore: If, by the grace of God, you believe in the Gospel of the forgiveness of your sins for Christ's sake, you are to be certain that you also belong to the number of God's elect, even as Scripture, 2 Thess. 2,13, addresses the believing Thessalonians as the chosen of God and gives thanks to God for their election.

OF SUNDAY.

41. We teach that in the New Testament God has abrogated the Sabbath and all the holy-days prescribed for the Church of the Old Covenant, so that neither "the keeping of the Sabbath nor of any other day" nor the observance of at least one specific day of the seven days of the week is ordained or commanded by God, Col. 2, 16; Rom. 14, 5 (Augsburg Confession. *Triglot*, p. 91, §§ 51-60; M., p. 66).

The observance of Sunday and other church festivals is an ordinance of the Church, made by virtue of Christian liberty. (Augsburg Confession; *Triglot*, p. 91, §§ 51-53. 60; M., p. 66. Large Catechism; *Triglot*, p. 603, §§ 83.85.89; M., p. 401.) Hence Christians should not regard such ordinances as ordained by God and binding upon the conscience, Col. 2, 16; Gal. 4, 10. However, for the sake of Christian love and peace they should willingly observe them, Rom. 14, 13; 1 Cor. 14, 40. (Augsburg Confession. *Triglot*, p. 91, §§ 53-56; M., p. 67.)

OF THE MILLENNIUM.

42. With the Augsburg Confession (Art. XVII) we reject every type of Millennialism, or Chiliasm, the opinions that Christ will return visibly to this earth a thousand years before the end of the world and establish a dominion of the Church over the world; or that before the end of the world the Church is to enjoy a season of special prosperity; or that before the general resurrection on Judgment Day a number of departed Christians or martyrs are to be raised again to reign in glory in this world; or that before the end of the world a universal conversion of the Jewish nation (of Israel according to the flesh) will take place.

Over against this, Scripture clearly teaches, and we teach accordingly, that the kingdom of Christ on earth will remain under the cross until the end of the world, Acts 14, 22; John 16, 33; 18, 36; Luke 9, 23; 14, 27; 17, 20-37; 2 Tim. 4, 18; Heb. 12,28; Luke 18,8; that the second visible coming of the Lord will be His final advent, His coming to judge the quick and the dead, Matt. 24, 29.30; 25, 31; 2 Tim. 4, 1; 2 Thess. 2, 8; Heb. 9, 26-28; that there will be but one resurrection of the dead, John 5, 28; 6, 39.40; that the time of the Last Day is, and will remain, unknown, Matt. 24, 42; 25, 13; Mark 13, 32.37; Acts 1, 7, which would not be the case if the Last Day were to come a thousand years after the beginning of a millennium; and that there will be no general conversion, a conversion *en masse*, of the Jewish nation, Rom. 11, 7; 2 Cor. 3, 14; Rom. 11, 25; 1 Thess. 2, 16.

According to these clear passages of Scripture we reject the whole of Millennialism, since it not only contradicts Scripture, but also engenders a false conception of the kingdom of Christ, turns the hope of Christians upon earthly goals, 1 Cor. 15, 19; Col. 3, 2, and leads them to look upon the Bible as an obscure book.

OF THE ANTICHRIST.

43. As to the Antichrist we teach that the prophecies of the Holy Scriptures concerning the Antichrist, 2 Thess. 2, 3-12; 1 John 2, 18, have been fulfilled in the Pope of Rome and his dominion. All the features of the Antichrist as drawn in these prophecies, including the most abominable and horrible ones, for example, that the Antichrist "as God sitteth in the temple of God," 2 Thess. 2,4; that he anathematizes the very heart of the Gospel of Christ, that is, the doctrine of the forgiveness of sins by grace alone, for Christ's sake alone, through faith alone, without any merit or worthiness in man (Rom. 3, 20-28; Gal. 2, 16); that he recognizes only those as members of the Christian Church who bow to his authority; and that, like a deluge, he had inundated the whole Church with his antichristian doctrines till God revealed him through the Reformation,—these very features are the outstanding characterics of the Papacy. (Of. Smalcald Articles. *Triglot*, p. 515, §§ 39-41; p. 401, § 45; M., pp. 336. 258). Hence we subscribe to the statement of our Confessions that the Pope is "the very Antichrist." (Smalcald Articles. *Triglot*, p. 475, § 10; M., p. 308).

OF OPEN QUESTIONS.

44. Those questions in the domain of Christian doctrine may be termed open questions which Scripture answers either not at all or not clearly. Since neither an individual nor the Church as a whole is permitted to develop or augment the Christian doctrine, but are rather ordered and commanded by God to continue in the doctrine of the apostles, 2 Thess. 2, 15; Acts 2, 42, open questions must remain open questions.— Not to be included in the number of open questions are the following: the doctrine of the Church and the Ministry, of Sunday, of Chiliasm, and of Antichrist, these doctrines being clearly defined in Scripture.

OF THE SYMBOLS OF THE LUTHERAN CHURCH.

45. We accept as our confessions all the symbols contained in the Book of Concord of the year 1580.—The symbols of the Lutheran Church are not a rule of faith beyond, and supplementary to, Scripture, but a confession of the doctrines of Scripture over against those who deny these doctrines.

46. Since the Christian Church cannot make doctrines, but can and should simply profess the doctrine revealed in Holy Scripture, the doctrinal decisions of the symbols are binding upon the conscience not because our Church has made them nor because they are the outcome of doctrinal controversies, but only because they are the doctrinal decisions of Holy Scripture itself.

47. Those desiring to be admitted into the public ministry of the Lutheran Church pledge themselves to teach according to the symbols not "in so far as," but "because," the symbols agree with Scripture. He who is unable to accept as Scriptural the doctrines set forth in the Lutheran symbols and their rejection of the corresponding errors must not be admitted into the ministry of the Lutheran Church.

48. The confessional obligation covers all doctrines, not only those that are treated *ex professo*, but also those that are merely introduced in support of other doctrines.

    The obligation does not extend to historical statements, "purely exegetical questions," and other matters not belonging to the doctrinal content of the symbols. All *doctrines* of the symbols are based on clear statements of Scripture.

Notes: *This statement was adopted by the Lutheran Church-Missouri Synod in 1932, at which time the church was considering closer relations with other Lutheran bodies, especially the American Lutheran Church. The statement has become one standard for judging orthodoxy in the synod. Its authority approaches that of the documents mentioned in the constitution, even though in 1962 the synod declared it unconstitutional to bind pastors and college professors to any statement beyond the Bible and The Book of Concord.*

* * *

WE BELIEVE (WISCONSIN EVANGELICAL LUTHERAN SYNOD)

I. GOD AND HIS REVELATION

1. We believe that there is only one true God (John 17:3). He has made Himself known as the Triune God, one God in three persons. This is evident from Jesus' command to His disciples to baptize "in the name of the Father, and of the Son, and of the Holy Ghost" (Matt. 28:19). Whoever does not worship this God worships a false god, a god who does not

exist, for Jesus said: 'He that honoreth not the Son honoreth not the Father which hath sent him" (John 5:23).

2. We believe that God has revealed Himself in nature, for "the heavens declare the glory of God; and the firmament showeth his handiwork" (Ps. 19:1). "For the invisible things of him from the creation of the world are clearly seen, being understood by the things that are made, even his eternal power and Godhead" (Rom. 1:20). So there is no excuse for the atheist. However, we have in nature only a partial revelation of God and one that is wholly insufficient for salvation.

3. We believe that God has given us the full revelation of Himself in His Son, our Lord Jesus Christ. "No man hath seen God at any time; the only-begotten Son, which is in the bosom of the Father, he hath declared him" (John 1:18). Particularly has God revealed Himself in Jesus as the Savior God, who "so loved the world that he gave his only-begotten Son, that whosoever believeth in him should not perish, but have everlasting life" (John 3:16).

4. We believe that God has given the Holy Scriptures to proclaim His grace in Christ to man. In the Old Testament God repeatedly promised His people a divine Deliverer from sin, death, and hell. The New Testament proclaims that this promised Deliverer has come in the person of Jesus of Nazareth. The Scriptures testify of Christ. Jesus Himself says of the Scriptures: "They are they which testify of me" (John 5:39).

5. We believe that God gave us the Scriptures through men whom He chose and used with the language they knew and the style of writing they had. He used Moses and the Prophets to write the Old Testament in Hebrew (some portions in Aramaic) and the Evangelists and Apostles to write the New Testament in Greek.

6. We believe that in a miraculous way that goes beyond all human investigation God the Holy Ghost inspired these men to write His Word. These "holy men of God spoke as they were moved by the Holy Ghost" (II Pet. 1:21). What they said, was spoken "not in the words which man's wisdom teacheth, but which the Holy Ghost teacheth" (I Cor. 2:13). Every thought they expressed, every word they used, was given them by the Holy Spirit by inspiration. St. Paul wrote to Timothy: "All scripture is given by inspiration of God" (II Tim. 3:16). We therefore believe in the verbal inspiration of the Scriptures, not a mechanical dictation, but a word-for-word inspiration.

7. We believe that Scripture is a unified whole, true and without error in everything it says; for our Savior said: "The scripture cannot be broken" (John 10:35). We believe that it, therefore, is the infallible authority and guide for everything we believe and do. We believe that it is fully sufficient, clearly teaching us all we need to know for salvation, making us "wise unto salvation through faith which is in Christ Jesus" (II Tim. 3:15), equipping us for every good work (II Tim. 3:17). No other revelations are to be expected.

8. We believe and accept Scripture on its own terms, accepting as factual history what it presents as history, recognizing a metaphor where Scripture itself indicates one, and reading as poetry what is evident as such. We believe that Scripture must interpret Scripture, clear passages throwing light on those less easily understood. We believe that no authority, be it man's reason, science, or scholarship, may stand in judgment over Scripture. Sound scholarship will faithfully search out the true meaning of Scripture without presuming to pass judgment on it.

9. We believe that the three ecumenical creeds, the Apostles', the Nicene, and the Athanasian, as well as the Lutheran Confessions as contained in the Book of Concord of 1580, give expression to the true doctrine of Scripture. Since the doctrines they confess are drawn from Scripture alone, we feel ourselves bound to them in our faith and life. Therefore all preaching and teaching in our churches and schools must be in harmony with these Confessions.

10. We reject any thought that makes only part of Scripture God's Word, that allows for the possibility of factual error in Scripture, also in so-called nonreligious matters (for example, historical, geographical).

11. We reject all views that fail to acknowledge the Holy Scriptures as God's revelation and Word. We likewise reject all views that see in them merely a human record of God's revelations as He encounters man in history apart from the Scriptures, and so a record subject to human imperfections.

12. We reject the emphasis upon Jesus as the Word of God (John 1:1) to the exclusion of the Scriptures as God's Word.

13. We reject every effort to reduce the Confessions contained in the Book of Concord to historical documents that have little or no confessional significance for the Church today. We likewise reject any claim that the Church is bound only to those doctrines in Scriptures that have found expression in these Confessions.

This is what Scripture teaches about God and His Revelation. This we believe, teach, and confess.

II. CREATION, MAN, AND SIN

1. We believe that the universe, the world, and man came into existence in the beginning when God created heaven and earth and all creatures (Gen. 1,2). Further testimony of this event is found in other passages of the Old and New Testaments (for example, Exod. 20:11; Heb. 11:3). All this happened in the course of six normal days by the power of God's almighty word when He said, "Let there be."

2. We believe that the Bible presents a true and historical account of Creation.

3. We believe that God created man in His own image (Gen. 1:26), that is, holy and righteous. Man's thoughts, desires, and will were in full harmony with God (Col. 3:10; Eph. 4:24), and he was given the capacity to "subdue" God's creation (Gen. 1:28).

4. We believe that man lost this divine image when he yielded to the temptation of Satan and disobeyed God's command. This brought upon him the judgment of God, "Thou shalt surely die" (Gen. 2:17). Since that time mankind is conceived and born in sin (Ps. 51:5), "flesh born of flesh" (John 3:6), and inclined to all evil (Gen. 8:21). Being dead in sin (Eph. 2:1) man is unable to reconcile himself to God by his own efforts and deeds.

5. We reject the theories of evolution as an explanation of the origin of the universe and man, and all attempts to interpret the Scriptural account of Creation so as to harmonize it with such theories.

6. We reject interpretations that reduce the first chapters of Genesis to a narration of symbolical myths and to poetic accounts that are without factual historical content.

7. We reject all views that see inherent goodness in man, that consider his natural bent only a weakness which is not sinful, and that fail to recognize his total spiritual depravity (Rom. 3:9-18).

This is what Scripture teaches about Creation, Man, and Sin. This we believe, teach, and confess.

III. CHRIST AND REDEMPTION

1. We believe that Jesus Christ is the eternal Son of God, who was with the Father from all eternity (John 1:1,2). In the fullness of time He took a true and complete, yet sinless, human nature to Himself (Gal. 4:4) when He was conceived as a holy child in the Virgin Mary through a miracle of the Holy Spirit. The angel testified: "That which is conceived in her is of the Holy Ghost" (Matt. 1:20). Jesus Christ is that unique person in whom the true God and a true human nature are inseparably united in one, the holy God-man, Immanuel.

2. We believe that He at all times possessed the fullness of the Godhead, all divine power, wisdom, and glory (Col. 2:9). This was evident at times when He performed miracles (John 2:11). But while He lived on earth, He took on the form of a servant, humbling Himself by laying aside the continuous and full display and use of His divine characteristics. During this time we see Him living as a man among men, enduring suffering, and humbling Himself to the shameful death on the cross (Phil. 2:7, 8). We believe that He rose again from the grave with a glorified body, ascended, and is exalted on high to rule with power over the world, with grace in His Church, with glory in eternity (Phil. 2:9-11).

3. We believe that Jesus Christ, the God-man, was sent by the Father to humble Himself for the redemption of mankind and that He was exalted as evidence that His mission was accomplished. Jesus came to fulfill the Law perfectly (Matt. 5:17), so that by His perfect obedience all men should be accounted righteous (Rom. 5:19). He came to bear "the iniquity of us all" (Isa. 53:6), ransoming us by His sacrifice for sin on the altar of the cross (Matt. 20:28). We believe that He is the God-appointed Substitute for man in all of this: His righteousness is accepted by the Father as our righteousness; His death for sin, as our death for sin (II Cor. 5:21). We believe that His resurrection gives full assurance that God has accepted this atonement in our behalf (Rom. 4:25).

4. We believe that in Christ, God reconciled the "*world* unto himself" (II Cor. 5:19), that Jesus is "the Lamb of God, which taketh away the sin of the *world*"(John 1:29). The mercy and grace of God are all-embracing; the reconciliation through Christ is universal; the forgiveness of sins has been gained as an accomplished fact for all men. Because of the substitutionary work of Christ, God has justified, that is, declared the verdict of "not guilty" upon all mankind. This forms the firm, objective basis for the sinner's assurance of salvation.

5. We reject any teaching that limits the work of Christ as to either its scope or its completeness, thereby failing to recognize the universality of redemption or the full payment of the ransom.

6. We reject the views which see in the Gospel accounts the early Church's proclamation and interpretation of Jesus Christ rather than a true account of what actually happened in history. We reject the attempts to make the historicity of events in Christ's life, such as His virgin birth, His miracles, or His bodily resurrection, appear unimportant or even doubtful. We reject the attempts to stress a "present encounter with the living Christ" in such a way that Jesus' redemptive work in the fullness of time, as recorded in Scripture, would lose its importance.

This the Scripture teaches about Christ and Redemption. This we believe, teach, and confess.

IV. JUSTIFICATION BY FAITH

1. We believe that God has justified, that is, declared all sinners righteous in His eyes for the sake of Christ. This is the central message of Scripture upon which the very existence of the Church depends. It is a message relevant to men of all times and places, of all races and social strata, for "judgment came upon all men to condemnation" (Rom. 5:18). All need justification before God, and Scripture proclaims that all are justified, for "by the righteousness of one the free gift came upon all men unto justification of life" (Rom. 5:18).

2. We believe that the individual receives this free gift of forgiveness throught Christ, not by works, but only by faith (Eph. 2:8,9). Justifying faith is a firm trust in Christ and His redemptive work. This faith justifies, not because of any inherent virtue, but only because of the salvation prepared by God in Christ, which it embraces (Rom. 3:28; 4:5). On the other

hand, although Jesus died for all, Scripture tells us that "he that believeth not shall be damned" (Mark 16:16). The unbeliever loses the forgiveness won by Christ.

3. We believe that man cannot work this justifying faith, or trust, in his own heart, because "natural man receiveth not the things of the Spirit of God; for they are foolishness unto him" (I Cor. 2:14). In fact, "the carnal mind is enmity against God" (Rom. 8:7). It is the Holy Ghost who moves the heart trustingly to recognize that "Jesus is the Lord" (I Cor. 12:3). This the Holy Spirit works by means of the Gospel (Rom. 10:17). We believe, therefore, that man's conversion is entirely the work of God's grace.

4. We believe that already in eternity God chose those individuals whom He would in time convert through the Gospel of Christ and preserve in the faith to eternal life (Eph. 1:4-6; Rom. 8:29,30). This election to faith and salvation in no way was caused by anything in man, but shows how completely salvation is ours by grace alone (Rom. 11:5,6).

5. We reject every teaching that makes man somehow responsible for his salvation. We reject all efforts to present faith as a condition man must fulfill to complete his justification. We likewise reject any teaching which says that it does not matter what one believes so long as one has faith.

6. We reject any suggestion that the doctrine of justification by faith can no longer be meaningful to "modern man," together with all attempts of man to justify himself or his existence before God.

7. We reject the false and blasphemous conclusion that those who are lost were elected by God to damnation, for God "will have all men to be saved" (I Tim. 2:4).

This is what Scripture teaches about Justification by Faith. This we believe, teach, and confess.

V. GOOD WORKS AND PRAYER

1. We believe that faith in Jesus Christ is a living force within the Christian that must produce works that are pleasing to God. "Faith, if it hath not works, is dead" (Jas. 2:17). A Christian as a branch in Christ the Vine brings forth good fruit (John 15:5).

2. We believe that faith does not set up its own standards to determine what is pleasing to God (Matt. 15:9). True faith, instructed by the Word of God, delights to do only that which conforms to the holy will of God. It recognizes that God's will finds its fulfillment in perfect love, "for love is the fulfilling of the law" (Rom. 13:10).

3. We believe that these works which are the fruits of faith must be distinguished from the works of civic righteousness performed by unbelievers. When unbelievers perform works that outwardly appear as good and upright before men, these works are not good in the sight of God, for "without faith it is impossible to please him" (Heb. 11:6). While we recognize the value of mere civic righteousness for human society, we know that the unbeliever through his works of civic righteousness cannot even begin to do his duty to God.

4. We believe that in this world even the best works of a Christian are still tainted with sin. The flesh, the Old Adam, still afflicts the Christian so that he fails to do the good he would, and does the evil he would not (Rom. 7:19). He must confess that all his righteousnesses are as filthy rags (Isa. 64:6). For the sake of Christ, however, these imperfect efforts of Christians are graciously considered holy and acceptable by our heavenly Father.

5. We believe that also a life of prayer is a fruit of faith. Confidently, through faith in their Savior, Christians address the heavenly Father in petition and praise, presenting their needs and giving thanks. Such prayers are a delight to our God, and He will grant our petitions according to His wisdom.

6. We reject every thought that the good works of Christians contribute toward gaining salvation.

7. We reject every attempt to abolish the unchanging Law of God as an absolute standard by which to measure man's conduct.

8. We reject the "new morality" as a device of Satan to destroy the knowledge of God's holy will and to undermine the consciousness of sin.

9. We reject any view that considers prayer a means of grace or that looks upon it as helpful simply because of its psychological effect upon the one who prays.

10. We reject the view that all prayers are acceptable to God, and we hold the prayers of all who know not Christ to be vain babblings addressed to false gods.

This is what Scripture teaches about Good Works and Prayer. This we believe, teach, and confess.

VI. THE MEANS OF GRACE

1. We believe that God bestows all spiritual blessings upon sinners by special means, ordained by Him. These are the Means of Grace, the Gospel in Word and Sacrament.

2. We believe that through the Gospel of Christ's atoning sacrifice for sinners the Holy Spirit works faith in the heart of man, whose heart by nature is enmity against God. "So then faith cometh by hearing, and hearing by the word of God" (Rom. 10:17). This Spirit-wrought faith, or regeneration, brings about a renewal in man and makes of him an heir of eternal salvation.

3. We believe that also through Baptism the Holy Spirit applies the Gospel to sinful man, regenerating him (Titus 3:5) and cleansing him from all iniquity (Acts 2:38). The Lord points to the blessing of Baptism when He promises: "He that believeth and is baptized shall be saved" (Mark 16:16). We believe that the blessing of Baptism is meant for all people (Matt. 28:19), including infants, who are sinful (John

3:6) and therefore need the regeneration effected through Baptism (John 3:5).

We believe that all who partake of the Sacrament of the Lord's Supper receive the true body and blood of Christ "in, with, and under" the bread and wine. This is true because, when the Lord instituted this Sacrament, He said: "This is my body which is given for you. . . . This cup is the new testament in my blood, which is shed for you" (Luke 22:19, 20). As we partake of His body and blood, given and shed for us, we by faith receive the comfort and assurance that our sins are indeed forgiven and that we are truly His own.

We believe that the Lord gave His Word and the Sacraments to His disciples for a purpose. He commanded them: "Go ye therefore, and teach all nations, baptizing them in the name of the Father, and of the Son, and of the Holy Ghost" (Matt. 28:19). It is by these Means that He preserves and extends the holy Christian Church throughout the world. We should therefore be diligent and faithful in the use of these divinely ordained Means of Grace in our own midst and in our mission efforts. These are the only means through which immortal souls are brought to faith and to salvation.

We reject any views that look for the revelation of the grace of God and salvation apart from the Gospel as found in the Scriptures. We likewise reject the view that the Law is a means of grace.

We reject all teachings that see in the Sacrament of the Altar nothing more than signs and symbols for faith, thereby denying that Christ's true body and blood are received in the Lord's Supper.

We reject the claim that unbelievers and hypocrites do not receive the true body and blood of Jesus in the Sacrament, as well as the view that to eat the body of Christ in the Sacrament is nothing else than to receive Christ spiritually by faith. We reject the view that the body and blood of Christ are present in the Sacrament through the act of consecration as such, apart from the reception of the elements.

We reject the teaching that the real presence of Jesus' body and blood in the Sacrament means merely that the person of Christ is present in His Supper even as He is present in the Gospel.

This is what Scripture teaches about the Means of Grace. This we believe, teach, and confess.

VII. THE CHURCH AND ITS MINISTRY

1. We believe that there is one holy Christian Church, which is the Temple of God (I Cor. 3:16), the Body of Christ (Eph. 1:23; 4:12). The members of this one Church are all those who are "children of God by faith in Christ Jesus" (Gal. 3:26). Whoever believes that Jesus died for his sin and rose again for his justification (Rom. 4:25) belongs to Christ's Church. The Church, then, consists only of believers, or saints, whom God accepts as holy for the sake of Jesus' imputed righteousness (II Cor. 5:21). These saints are scattered throughout the world. Every true believer, regardless of the nation or race or church body to which he belongs, is a member of the holy Christian Church.

2. We believe that the holy Christian Church is a reality, although it is not an external, visible organization. Because "man looketh on the outward appearance, but the Lord looketh on the heart" (I Sam. 16:7), only the Lord knows "them that are his" (II Tim. 2:19). The members of the holy Christian Church are known only to God; we cannot distinguish between true believers and hypocrites. The holy Christian Church is therefore invisible and cannot be identified with any one church body or the sum total of all church bodies.

3. We believe that the presence of the holy Christian Church nevertheless can be recognized. Wherever the Gospel is preached and the Sacraments are administered, the holy Christian Church is present, for through the Means of Grace true faith is produced and preserved (Isa. 55:10,11). Moreover, where these Means are in use, we are confident that the Church is present, for the Lord has entrusted them only to His Church of believers (Matt. 28:19,20). The Means of Grace are therefore called the marks of the Church.

4. We believe that it is the Lord's will that Christians gather together for mutual edification and spiritual growth (Heb. 10:24,25) and for carrying out the whole of the Lord's commission (Mark 16:15). Since these visible gatherings (for example, congregations, synods) confess themselves to the marks of the Church and make use of them, they are called churches. They bear this name, however, only because of the true believers present in them (I Cor. 1:2).

5. We believe that the holy Christian Church is one, united by a common faith, for all true believers have "one Lord, one faith, one baptism, one God and Father of all" (Eph. 4:5,6). Since this is a unity of faith in the heart, it is seen only by God.

6. We believe that God bids us on our part to acknowledge oneness in faith among God's saints on earth only as they by word and deed reveal (confess) the faith of their hearts. Their unity becomes evident when they agree in their confession to the doctrine revealed in Scripture. We believe, furthermore, that the individual through his membership in a church body confesses himself to the doctrine and practice of that body. To assert that unity exists where there is no agreement in confession is to presume to look into man's heart. This only God can do. It is not necessary that all agree on matters of church ritual or organization. About these the New Testament gives no commands.

7. We believe that those who have become evident as united in faith will give recognition to their fellowship in Christ and seek to express it as occasion permits. They may express their fellowship by joint worship, by joint proclamation of the Gospel, by joining in Holy Communion, by joint prayer, by joint

WE BELIEVE (WISCONSIN EVANGELICAL LUTHERAN SYNOD) (continued)

church work. We believe that we cannot practice religious fellowship with those whose confession reveals that error is taught or tolerated, supported or defended. The Lord bids us avoid persistent errorists (Rom. 16:17, 18).

8. We believe that every Christian is a priest and king before God (I Pet. 2:9). All believers have direct and equal access to the throne of grace through Christ, our Mediator (Eph. 2:18). To all believers God has given the Means of Grace to use. All Christians are to show forth the praises of Him who has called us out of darkness into His marvelous light (I Pet. 2:9). In this sense all Christians are ministers of the Gospel.

9. We believe that it is the will of God that the Church in accordance with good order (I Cor. 14:40) call qualified men (I Tim. 3) into the public ministry. They are to preach the Word and administer the Sacraments publicly, that is, not merely as individuals who possess the universal priesthood, but by order and in the name of fellow Christians. These men are the called servants of Christ, ministers of the Gospel, and not lords over God's heritage, His believers (I Pet. 5:3). Through its call the Church in Christian liberty designates the place, form, and scope of service. We believe that when the Church calls men into this public ministry, it is the Lord Himself acting through the Church (Acts 20:28).

10. We reject any attempt to identify the holy Christian Church with an outward organization, and likewise any claim that the Church must function in the world through specific organizational forms.

11. We reject any views that see in the Church, as the Body of Christ, an extension of Christ's incarnation.

12. We reject as false ecumenicity any views that look for the true unity of the Church in some form of external or organizational union, as we oppose all movements toward such union made at the expense of confessional integrity.

13. We reject the contention that religious fellowship may be practiced without confessional agreement.

This is what Scripture teaches about the Church and its Ministry. This we believe, teach, and confess.

VIII. THE CHURCH AND THE STATE

1. We believe that not only the Church, but also the State, that is, all governmental authority, has been instituted by God. "The powers that be are ordained of God" (Rom. 13:1). Christians will, therefore, for conscience's sake be obedient to the government that rules over them (Rom. 13:5) unless the government commands them to disobey God (Acts 5:29).

2. We believe that God has given to each, the Church and the State, responsibilities that do not conflict with one another. To the Church the Lord has assigned the responsibility of calling sinners to repentance, of proclaiming forgiveness through the cross of Christ, of encouraging believers in the Christian living. The purpose is to lead the elect of God through faith in Christ to eternal salvation. To the State the Lord has assigned the keeping of good order and peace, the arranging of all civil matters among men (Rom. 13:3,4). The purpose is "that we may lead a quiet and peaceable life in all godliness and honesty" (I Tim. 2:2).

3. We believe that the only means God has given to the Church to carry out its assigned purpose is His revealed Word in the Holy Scriptures (Mark 16:15). Only by preaching the Law and the Gospel, sin and grace, the wrath of God against sin and the mercy of God in Christ, will men be converted and made wise to salvation. We believe that the means given to the State to fulfill its assignment are civil law and force set up and used according to the light of reason (Rom. 13:4). The light of reason also includes the natural knowledge of God, the inscribed law, and conscience.

4. We believe the proper relation is preserved between the Church and the State and the welfare of all is properly served only when each, the Church and the State, remains within its divinely assigned sphere and uses its divinely entrusted means. The Church is not to exercise civil authority nor to interfere with the State as the State carries out its responsibilities. The State is not to become a messenger of the Gospel nor to interfere with the Church in its preaching mission. The Church is not to attempt to use the civil law and force in leading men to Christ. The State is not to seek to govern by means of the Gospel. On the other hand, the Church and the State may participate in one and the same endeavor as long as each remains within its assigned place and uses its entrusted means.

5. We reject any attempt on the part of the State to restrict the free exercise of religion.

6. We reject any views that look to the Church to guide and influence the State directly in the conduct of its affairs.

7. We reject any attempt on the part of the Church to seek the financial assistance of the State in carrying out its saving purpose.

8. We reject any views that hold that a citizen is free to disobey such laws of the State with which he disagrees on the basis of personal judgment.

This is what Scripture teaches about the Church and the State. This we believe, teach, and confess.

IX. JESUS' RETURN AND THE JUDGMENT

1. We believe that Jesus, true God and true man, who rose from death and ascended to the right hand of the Father, will come again. He will return visibly, in like manner as His Disciples saw Him go into heaven (Acts 1:11).

2. We believe that no one can know the exact time of Jesus' return. This knowledge is hidden even from the angels in heaven (Matt. 24:36). Nevertheless, our Lord has given us signs to keep us in constant

expectation of His return. He has told us to take heed to ourselves and to watch lest that Day come upon us unawares (Luke 21:34).

We believe that at Jesus' return this present world will come to an end. "Nevertheless, we, according to his promise, look for new heavens and a new earth, wherein dwelleth righteousness" (II Pet. 3:13).

We believe that when Jesus returns and His voice is heard throughout the earth, all the dead will rise and together with those still living must appear before His throne of judgment. The unbelievers will be condemned to an eternity in hell. Those who by faith have been cleansed in the blood of Christ will be with Jesus forever in the blessed presence of God in heaven (John 5:28, 29).

We reject every form of millenialism, since it has no valid Scriptural basis and leads Christians to set their hopes upon the kingdom of Christ as an earthly kingdom. We likewise reject as unscriptural any hopes that the Jews will all be converted in those final days, or that all men will ultimately enjoy eternal bliss.

6. We reject any denial of a bodily resurrection and of the reality of hell.

7. We reject as contrary to the clear revelation of Scripture all attempts to interpret eschatological passages in the New Testament (those that speak of the end of the world, Jesus' second coming, and the judgment) symbolically, or to see these eschatological events taking place, not in the end of time, but concurrently with history.

This is what Scripture teaches about Jesus' Return and the Judgment. This we believe, teach, and confess.

Notes: *The most conservative of the major Lutheran bodies, the Wisconsin Synod's statement of faith is noteworthy both for its clear affirmation concerning scripture and scriptural authority (as opposed to liberal-modernist and neo-orthodox interpretations) and for its statements on millennialism in reaction to fundamentalism. It also chastizes those Lutherans who think of* The Book of Concord *as merely an historical statement of relative normative value today.*

Chapter 5
Reformed-Presbyterian Family

Reformed

THE BELGIC CONFESSION

Article I. THERE IS ONLY ONE GOD

We all believe with the heart and confess with the mouth that there is one only simple and spiritual Being, which we call God; and that He is eternal, incomprehensible, invisible, immutable, infinite, almighty, perfectly wise, just, good, and the overflowing fountain of all good.

Article II. BY WHAT MEANS GOD IS MADE KNOWN UNTO US

We know Him by two means: First, by the creation, preservation, and government of the universe; which is before our eyes as a most elegant book, wherein all creatures, great and small, are as so many characters leading us to *see clearly the invisible things of God*, even *his everlasting power and divinity*, as the apostle Paul says (Rom. 1:20). All which things are sufficient to convince men and leave them without excuse. Second, He makes Himself more clearly and fully known to us by His holy and divine Word, that is to say, as far as is necessary for us to know in this life, to His glory and our salvation.

Article III. THE WRITTEN WORD OF GOD

We confess that this Word of God was not sent nor delivered by the will of man, but that *men spake from God, being moved by the Holy Spirit*, as the apostle Peter says; and that afterwards God, from a special care which He has for us and our salvation, commanded His servants, the prophets and apostles, to commit His revealed word to writing; and He Himself wrote with His own finger the two tables of the law. Therefore we call such writings holy and divine Scriptures.

Article IV. CANONICAL BOOKS OF THE HOLY SCRIPTURE

We believe that the Holy Scriptures are contained in two books, namely, the Old and the New Testament, which are canonical, against which nothing can be alleged. These are thus named in the Church of God.

The books of the Old Testament are the five books of Moses, to wit: Genesis, Exodus, Leviticus, Numbers, Deuteronomy; the book of Joshua, Judges, Ruth, the two books of Samuel, the two of the Kings, two books of the Chronicles, commonly called Paralipomenon, the first of Ezra, Nehemiah, Esther; Job, the Psalms of David, the three books of Solomon, namely, the Proverbs, Ecclesiastes, and the Song of Songs; the four great prophets, Isaiah, Jeremiah, Ezekiel, and Daniel; and the twelve lesser prophets, namely, Hosea, Joel, Amos, Obadiah, Jonah, Micah, Nahum, Habakkuk, Zephaniah, Haggai, Zechariah, and Malachi.

Those of the New Testament are the four evangelists, to wit: Matthew, Mark, Luke, and John; the Acts of the Apostles; the fourteen epistles of the apostle Paul, namely, one to the Romans, two to the Corinthians, one to the Galatians, one to the Ephesians, one to the Philippians, one to the Colossians, two to the Thessalonians, two to Timothy, one to Titus, one to Philemon, and one to the Hebrews; the seven epistles of the other apostles, namely, one of James, two of Peter, three of John, one of Jude; and the Revelation of the apostle John.

Article V. WHENCE THE HOLY SCRIPTURES DERIVE THEIR DIGNITY AND AUTHORITY

We receive all these books, and these only, as holy and canonical, for the regulation, foundation, and confirmation of our faith; believing without any doubt all things contained in them, not so much because the Church receives and approves them as such, but more especially because the Holy Spirit witnesses in our hearts that they are from God, and also because they carry the evidence thereof in themselves. For the very blind are able to perceive that the things foretold in them are being fulfilled.

Article VI. THE DIFFERENCE BETWEEN THE CANONICAL AND APOCRYPHAL BOOKS

We distinguish those sacred books from the apocryphal, viz.: the third and fourth books of Esdras, the

THE BELGIC CONFESSION (continued)

books of Tobit, Judith, Wisdom, Jesus Sirach, Baruch, the Appendix to the book of Esther, the Song of the Three Children in the Furnace, the History of Susannah, of Bell and the Dragon, the Prayer of Manasseh, and the two books of the Maccabees. All of which the Church may read and take instruction from, so far as they agree with the canonical books; but they are far from having such power and efficacy that we may from their testimony confirm any point of faith or of the Christian religion; much less may they be used to detract from the authority of the other, that is, the sacred books.

Article VII. THE SUFFICIENCY OF THE HOLY SCRIPTURES TO BE THE ONLY RULE OF FAITH

We believe that those Holy Scriptures fully contain the will of God, and that whatsoever man ought to believe unto salvation is sufficiently taught therein. For since the whole manner of worship which God requires of us is written in them at large, it is unlawful for any one, though an apostle, to teach otherwise than we are now taught in the Holy Scriptures: *nay, though it were an angel from heaven*, as the apostle Paul says. For since it is forbidden to *add unto or take away anything from the Word of God*, it does thereby evidently appear that the doctrine thereof is most perfect and complete in all respects.

Neither may we consider any writings of men, however holy these men may have been, of equal value with those divine Scriptures, nor ought we to consider custom, or the great multitude, or antiquity, or succession of times and persons, or councils, decrees or statutes, as of equal value with the truth of God, since the truth is above all; *for all men are of themselves liars, and more vain than vanity itself.* Therefore we reject with all our hearts whatsoever does not agree with this infallible rule, as the apostles have taught us, saying, *Prove the spirits, whether they are of God.* Likewise: *If any one cometh unto you, and bringeth not this teaching, receive him not into your house.*

Article VIII. GOD IS ONE IN ESSENCE, YET DISTINGUISHED IN THREE PERSONS

According to this truth and this Word of God, we believe in one only God, who is the one single essence, in which are three persons, really, truly, and eternally distinct according to their incommunicable properties; namely, the Father, and the Son, and the Holy Spirit. The Father is the cause, origin, and beginning of all things visible and invisible; the Son is the word, wisdom, and image of the Father; the Holy Spirit is the eternal power and might, proceeding from the Father and the Son. Nevertheless, God is not by this distinction divided into three, since the Holy Scriptures teach us that the Father, and the Son, and the Holy Spirit have each His personality, distinguished by Their properties; but in such wise that these three persons are but one only God.

Hence, then, it is evident that the Father is not the Son, nor the Son the Father, and likewise the Holy Spirit is neither the Father nor the Son. Nevertheless, these persons thus distinguished are not divided, nor intermixed; for the Father has not assumed the flesh, nor has the Holy Spirit, but the Son only. The Father has never been without His Son, or without His Holy Spirit. For They are all three co-eternal and co-essential. There is neither first nor last; for They are all three one, in truth, in power, in goodness, and in mercy.

Article IX. THE PROOF OF THE FOREGOING ARTICLE OF THE TRINITY OF PERSONS IN ONE GOD

All this we know as well from the testimonies of Holy Writ as from their operations, and chiefly by those we feel in ourselves. The testimonies of the Holy Scriptures that teach us to believe this Holy Trinity are written in many places of the Old Testament, which are not so necessary to enumerate as to choose them out with discretion and judgment.

In Genesis, chap. 1:26, 27, God says: *Let us make man in our image, after our likeness*, etc. *And God created man in his own image, male and female created he them.* And Gen. 3:22, *Behold, the man is become as one of us.* From this saying, Let *us* make man in *our* image, it appears that there are more persons than one in the Godhead; and when He says, *God* created, He signifies the unity. It is true, He does not say how many persons there are, but that which appears to us somewhat obscure in the Old Testament is very plain in the New. For when our Lord was baptized in Jordan, the voice of the Father was heard, saying, *This is my beloved Son*; the Son was seen in the water, and the Holy Spirit appeared in the shape of a dove. This form is also instituted by Christ in the baptism of all believers: *Make disciples of all the nations, baptizing them into the name of the Father and of the Son and of the Holy Spirit.* In the Gospel of Luke the angel Gabriel thus addressed Mary, the mother of our Lord: *The Holy Spirit shall come upon thee, and the power of the Most High shall overshadow thee; wherefore also the holy thing which is begotten shall be called the Son of God.* Likewise: *The grace of the Lord Jesus Christ, and the love of God, and the communion of the Holy Spirit, be with you all.* And (A.V.): *There are three that bear record in heaven, the Father, the Word, and the Holy Ghost: and these three are one.*

In all these places we are fully taught that there are three persons in one only divine essence. And although this doctrine far surpasses all human understanding, nevertheless we now believe it by means of the Word of God, but expect hereafter to enjoy the perfect knowledge and benefit thereof in heaven.

Moreover, we must observe the particular offices and operations of these three persons towards us. The

Father is called our Creator, by His power; the Son is our Savior and Redeemer, by His blood; the Holy Spirit is our Sanctifier, by His dwelling in our hearts.

This doctrine of the Holy Trinity has always been affirmed and maintained by the true Church since the time of the apostles to this very day against the Jews, Mohammedans, and some false Christians and heretics, as Marcion, Manes, Praxeas, Sabellius, Samosatenus, Arius, and such like, who have been justly condemned by the orthodox fathers. Therefore, in this point, we do willingly receive the three creeds, namely, that of the Apostles, of Nicea, and of Athanasius; likewise that which, conformable thereunto, is agreed upon by the ancient fathers.

Article X. JESUS CHRIST IS TRUE AND ETERNAL GOD

We believe that Jesus Christ according to His divine nature is the only begotten Son of God, begotten from eternity, not made, nor created (for then He would be a creature), but co-essential and co-eternal with the Father, *the very image of his substance and the effulgence of his glory*, equal unto Him in all things. He is the Son of God, not only from the time that He assumed our nature but from all eternity, as these testimonies, when compared together, teach us. Moses says that God created the world; and St. John says that all things were made by that Word which he calls God. The apostle says that God made the world by His Son; likewise, that God created all things by Jesus Christ. Therefore it must needs follow that He who is called God, the Word, the Son, and Jesus Christ, did exist at that time when all things were created by Him. Therefore the prophet Micah says: *His goings forth are from of old, from everlasting.* And the apostle: *He hath neither beginning of days nor end of life.* He therefore is that true, eternal, and almighty God whom we invoke, worship, and serve.

Article XI. THE HOLY SPIRIT IS TRUE AND ETERNAL GOD

We believe and confess also that the Holy Spirit from eternity proceeds from the Father and the Son; and therefore neither is made, created, nor begotten, but only proceeds from both; who in order is the third person of the Holy Trinity; of one and the same essence, majesty, and glory with the Father and the Son; and therefore is the true and eternal God, as the Holy Scriptures teach us.

Article XII. THE CREATION OF ALL THINGS, ESPECIALLY THE ANGELS

We believe that the Father by the Word, that is, by His Son, has created of nothing the heaven, the earth, and all creatures, when it seemed good unto Him; giving unto every creature its being, shape, form, and several offices to serve its Creator; that He also still upholds and governs them by His eternal providence and infinite power for the service of mankind, to the end that man may serve his God.

He also created the angels good, to be His messengers and to serve His elect; some of whom are fallen from that excellency in which God created them into everlasting perdition, and the others have by the grace of God remained stedfast and continued in their first state. The devils and evil spirits are so depraved that they are enemies of God and every good thing; to the utmost of their power as murderers watching to ruin the Church and every member thereof, and by their wicked stratagems to destroy all; and are, therefore, by their own wickedness adjudged to eternal damnation, daily expecting their horrible torments.

Therefore we reject and abhor the error of the Sadducees, who deny the existence of spirits and angels; and also that of the Manichees, who assert that the devils have their origin of themselves, and that they are wicked of their own nature, without having been corrupted.

Article XIII. THE PROVIDENCE OF GOD AND HIS GOVERNMENT OF ALL THINGS

We believe that the same good God, after He had created all things, did not forsake them or give them up to fortune or chance, but that He rules and governs them according to His holy will, so that nothing happens in this world without His appointment; nevertheless, God neither is the Author of nor can be charged with the sins which are committed. For His power and goodness are so great and incomprehensible that He orders and executes His work in the most excellent and just manner, even then when devils and wicked men act unjustly. And as to what He does surpassing human understanding, we will not curiously inquire into farther than our capacity will admit of; but with the greatest humility and reverence adore the righteous judgments of God, which are hid from us, contenting ourselves that we are pupils of Christ, to learn only those things which He has revealed to us in His Word, without transgressing these limits.

This doctrine affords us unspeakable consolation, since we are taught thereby that nothing can befall us by chance, but by the direction of our most gracious and heavenly Father; who watches over us with a paternal care, keeping all creatures so under His power that *not a hair of our head (for they are all numbered), nor a sparrow can fall to the ground without the will of our Father*, in whom we do entirely trust; being persuaded that He so restrains the devil and all our enemies that without His will and permission they cannot hurt us.

And therefore we reject that damnable error of the Epicureans, who say that God regards nothing but leaves all things to chance.

Article XIV. THE CREATION AND FALL OF MAN, AND HIS INCAPACITY TO PERFORM WHAT IS TRULY GOOD

We believe that God created man out of the dust of the earth, and made and formed him after His own

THE BELGIC CONFESSION (continued)

image and likeness, good, righteous, and holy, capable in all things to will agreeably to the will of God. But *being in honor, he understood it not*, neither knew his excellency, but wilfully subjected himself to sin and consequently to death and the curse, giving ear to the words of the devil. For the commandment of life, which he had received, he transgressed; and by sin separated himself from God, who was his true life; having corrupted his whole nature; whereby he made himself liable to corporal and spiritual death. And being thus become wicked, perverse, and corrupt in all his ways, he has lost all his excellent gifts which he had received from God, and retained only small remains thereof, which, however, are sufficient to leave man without excuse; for all the light which is in us is changed into darkness, as the Scriptures teach us, saying: *The light shineth in the darkness, and the darkness apprehended it not*; where St. John calls men darkness.

Therefore we reject all that is taught repugnant to this concerning the free will of man, since man is but a slave to sin, and *can receive nothing, except it have been given him from heaven*. For who may presume to boast that he of himself can do any good, since Christ says: *No man can come to me, except the Father that sent me draw him*? Who will glory in his own will, who understands that *the mind of the flesh is enmity against God*? Who can speak of his knowledge, since *the natural man receiveth not the things of the Spirit of God*? In short, who dare suggest any thought, since he knows that *we are not sufficient of ourselves to account anything as of ourselves, but that our sufficiency is of God*? And therefore what the apostle says ought justly to be held sure and firm, that *God worketh in us both to will and to work, for his good pleasure*. For there is no understanding nor will conformable to the divine understanding and will but what Christ has wrought in man; which He teaches us, when He says: *Apart from me ye can do nothing.*

Article XV. ORIGINAL SIN

We believe that through the disobedience of Adam original sin is extended to all mankind; which is a corruption of the whole nature and a hereditary disease, wherewith even infants in their mother's womb are infected, and which produces in man all sorts of sin, being in him as a root thereof, and therefore is so vile and abominable in the sight of God that it is sufficient to condemn all mankind. Nor is it altogether abolished or wholly eradicated even by baptism; since sin always issues forth from this woeful source, as water from a fountain; notwithstanding it is not imputed to the children of God unto condemnation, but by His grace and mercy is forgiven them. Not that they should rest securely in sin, but that a sense of this corruption should make believers often to sigh, desiring to be delivered from this body of death.

Wherefore we reject the error of the Pelagians, who assert that sin proceeds only from imitation.

Article XVI. ETERNAL ELECTION

We believe that, all the posterity of Adam being thus fallen into perdition and ruin by the sin of our first parents, God then did manifest Himself such as He is; that is to say, merciful and just: merciful, since He delivers and preserves from this perdition all whom He in His eternal and unchangeable counsel of mere goodness has elected in Christ Jesus our Lord, without any respect to their works; just, in leaving others in the fall and perdition wherein they have involved themselves.

Article XVII. THE RECOVERY OF FALLEN MAN

We believe that our most gracious God, in His admirable wisdom and goodness, seeing that man had thus thrown himself into physical and spiritual death and made himself wholly miserable, was pleased to seek and comfort him, when be trembling fled from His presence, promising him that He would give His Son (who would be *born of a woman)* *to bruise the head of the serpent* and to make him blessed.

Article XVIII. THE INCARNATION OF JESUS CHRIST

We confess, therefore, that God has fulfilled the promise which He made to the fathers by the mouth of His holy prophets, when He sent into the world, at the time appointed by Him, His own only-begotten and eternal Son, who *took upon Him the form of a servant* and *became like unto man*, really assuming the true human nature with all its infirmities, sin excepted; being conceived in the womb of the blessed virgin Mary by the power of the Holy Spirit without the means of man; and did not only assume human nature as to the body, but also a true human soul, that He might be a real man. For since the soul was lost as well as the body, it was necessary that He should take both upon Him, to save both.

Therefore we confess (in opposition to the heresy of the Anabaptists, who deny that Christ assumed human flesh of His mother) that Christ *partook of the flesh and blood of the children*; that He is a *fruit of the loins of David after the flesh; born of the seed of David according to the flesh; a fruit of the womb of Mary; born of a woman; a branch of David; a shoot of the root of Jesse; sprung from the tribe of Judah*; descended from the Jews according to the flesh; of the seed of Abraham, since (A.V.) *he took on him the seed of Abraham*, and *was made like unto his brethren in all things, sin excepted*; so that in truth He is our IMMANUEL, that is to say, *God with us.*

Article XIX. THE UNION AND DISTINCTION OF THE TWO NATURES IN THE PERSON OF CHRIST

We believe that by this conception the person of the Son is inseparably united and connected with the human nature; so that there are not two Sons of God, nor two persons, but two natures united in one single person; yet each nature retains its own distinct properties. As, then, the divine nature has always remained uncreated, without beginning of days or end of life, filling heaven and earth, so also has the human nature not lost its properties but remained a creature, having beginning of days, being a finite nature, and retaining all the properties of a real body. And though He has by His resurrection given immortality to the same, nevertheless He has not changed the reality of His human nature; forasmuch as our salvation and resurrection also depend on the reality of His body.

But these two natures are so closely united in one person that they were not separated even by His death. Therefore that which He, when dying, commended into the hands of His Father, was a real human spirit, departing from His body. But in the meantime the divine nature always remained united with the human, even when He lay in the grave; and the Godhead did not cease to be in Him, any more than it did when He was an infant, though it did not so clearly manifest itself for a while. Wherefore we confess that He is very God and very man: very God by His power to conquer death; and very man that He might die for us according to the infirmity of His flesh.

Article XX. GOD HAS MANIFESTED HIS JUSTICE AND MERCY IN CHRIST

We believe that God, who is perfectly merciful and just, sent His Son to assume that nature in which the disobedience was committed, to make satisfaction in the same, and to bear the punishment of sin by His most bitter passion and death. God therefore manifested His justice against His Son when He laid our iniquities upon Him, and poured forth His mercy and goodness on us, who were guilty and worthy of damnation, out of mere and perfect love, giving His Son unto death for us, and raising Him for our justification, that through Him we might obtain immortality and life eternal.

Article XXI. THE SATISFACTION OF CHRIST, OUR ONLY HIGH PRIEST, FOR US

We believe that Jesus Christ is ordained with an oath to be an everlasting High Priest, after the order of Melchizedek; and that He has presented Himself in our behalf before the Father, to appease His wrath by His full satisfaction, by offering Himself on the tree of the cross, and pouring out His precious blood to purge away our sins, as the prophets had foretold. For it is written: *He was wounded for our transgressions, he was bruised for our iniquities; the chastisement of our peace was upon him; and with his stripes we are healed. He was led as a lamb to the slaughter, and numbered with the transgressors*; and condemned by Pontius Pilate as a malefactor, though he had first declared Him innocent. Therefore, He *restored that which he took not away*, and *suffered, the righteous for the unrighteous*, as well in His body as in His soul, feeling the terrible punishment which our sins

had merited; insomuch that *his sweat became as it were great drops of blood falling down upon the ground*. He called out: *My God, my God, why hast thou forsaken me*? and has suffered all this for the remission of our sins.

Wherefore we justly say with the apostle Paul that we know nothing *save Jesus Christ, and him crucified; we count all things but loss and refuse for the excellency of the knowledge of Christ Jesus our Lord*, in whose wounds we find all manner of consolation. Neither is it necessary to seek or invent any other means of being reconciled to God than this only sacrifice, once offered, by which *he hath perfected forever them that are sanctified*. This is also the reason why He was called by the angel of God, JESUS, that is to say, SAVIOR, because He would *save his people from their sins*.

Article XXII. OUR JUSTIFICATION THROUGH FAITH IN JESUS CHRIST

We believe that, to attain the true knowledge of this great mystery, the Holy Spirit kindles in our hearts an upright faith, which embraces Jesus Christ with all His merits, appropriates Him, and seeks nothing more besides Him. For it must needs follow, either that all things which are requisite to our salvation are not in Jesus Christ, or if all things are in Him, that then those who possess Jesus Christ through faith have complete salvation in Him. Therefore, for any to assert that Christ is not sufficient, but that something more is required besides Him, would be too gross a blasphemy; for hence it would follow that Christ was but half a Savior.

Therefore we justly say with Paul, that we *are justified by faith* alone, or *by faith apart from works*. However, to speak more clearly, we do not mean that faith itself justifies us, for it is only an instrument with which we embrace Christ our righteousness. But Jesus Christ, imputing to us all His merits, and so many holy works which He has done for us and in our stead, is our righteousness. And faith is an instrument that keeps us in communion with Him in all His benefits, which, when they become ours, are more than sufficient to acquit us of our sins.

Article XXIII. WHEREIN OUR JUSTIFICATION BEFORE GOD CONSISTS

We believe that our salvation consists in the remission of our sins for Jesus Christ's sake, and that therein our righteousness before God is implied; as David and Paul teach us, declaring this to be the blessedness of man that *God imputes righteousness to him apart from works*. And the same apostle says that we are *justified freely by his grace, through the redemption that is in Christ Jesus*.

And therefore we always hold fast this foundation, ascribing all the glory to God, humbling ourselves before Him, and acknowledging ourselves to be such as we really are, without presuming to trust in any thing in ourselves, or in any merit of ours, relying and resting upon the obedience of Christ crucified

THE BELGIC CONFESSION (continued)

alone, which becomes ours when we believe in Him. This is sufficient to cover all our iniquities, and to give us confidence in approaching to God; freeing the conscience of fear, terror, and dread, without following the example of our first father, Adam, who, trembling, attempted to cover himself with fig-leaves. And, verily, if we should appear before God, relying on ourselves or on any other creature, though ever so little, we should, alas! be consumed. And therefore every one must pray with David: *O Jehovah, enter not into judgment with thy servant; for in thy sight no man living is righteous.*

Article XXIV. MAN'S SANCTIFICATION AND GOOD WORKS

We believe that this true faith, being wrought in man by the hearing of the Word of God and the operation of the Holy Spirit, regenerates him and makes him a new man, causing him to live a new life, and freeing him from the bondage of sin. Therefore it is so far from being true that this justifying faith makes men remiss in a pious and holy life, that on the contrary without it they would never do anything out of love to God, but only out of self-love or fear of damnation. Therefore it is impossible that this holy faith can be unfruitful in man; for we do not speak of a vain faith, but of such a faith which is called in Scripture a *faith working through love*, which excites man to the practice of those works which God has commanded in His Word.

These works, as they proceed from the good root of faith, are good and acceptable in the sight of God, forasmuch as they are all sanctified by His grace. Nevertheless they are of no account towards our justification, for it is by faith in Christ that we are justified, even before we do good works; otherwise they could not be good works, any more than the fruit of a tree can be good before the tree itself is good.

Therefore we do good works, but not to merit by them (for what can we merit?); nay, we are indebted to God for the good works we do, and not He to us, since it is He who *worketh in us both to will and to work, for his good pleasure.* Let us therefore attend to what is written: *When ye shall have done all the things that are commanded you, say, We are unprofitable servants; we have done that which it was our duty to do.* In the meantime we do not deny that God rewards good works, but it is through His grace that He crowns His gifts.

Moreover, though we do good works, we do not found our salvation upon them; for we can do no work but what is polluted by our flesh, and also punishable; and although we could perform such works, still the remembrance of one sin is sufficient to make God reject them. Thus, then, we would always be in doubt, tossed to and fro without any certainty, and our poor consciences would be contin-

ually vexed if they relied not on the merits of the suffering and death of our Savior.

Article XXV. THE ABOLISHING OF THE CEREMONIAL LAW

We believe that the ceremonies and symbols of the law ceased at the coming of Christ, and that all the shadows are accomplished; so that the use of them must be abolished among Christians; yet the truth and substance of them remain with us in Jesus Christ, in whom they have their completion. In the meantime we still use the testimonies taken out of the law and the prophets to confirm us in the doctrine of the gospel, and to regulate our life in all honorableness to the glory of God, according to His will.

Article XXVI. CHRIST'S INTERCESSION

We believe that we have no access unto God but alone through the only Mediator and Advocate, Jesus Christ the righteous; who therefore became man, having united in one person the divine and human natures, that we men might have access to the divine Majesty, which access would otherwise be barred against us. But this Mediator, whom the Father has appointed between Him and us, ought in no wise to affright us by His majesty, or cause us to seek another according to our fancy. For there is no creature, either in heaven or on earth, who loves us more than Jesus Christ; who, though *existing in the form of God*, yet *emptied himself, being made in the likeness of men and of a servant* for us, and *in all things was made like unto his brethren.* If, then, we should seek for another mediator who would be favorably inclined towards us, whom could we find who loved us more than He who laid down His life for us, even *while we were His enemies*? And if we seek for one who has power and majesty, who is there that has so much of both as He *who sits at the right hand of God* and *to whom hath been given all authority in heaven and on earth*? And who will sooner be heard than the own well beloved Son of God?

Therefore it was only through distrust that this practice of dishonoring, instead of honoring, the saints was introduced, doing that which they never have done nor required, but have on the contrary stedfastly rejected according to their bounden duty, as appears by their writings. Neither must we plead here our unworthiness; for the meaning is not that we should offer our prayers to God on the ground of our own worthiness, but only on the ground of the excellency and worthiness of the Lord Jesus Christ, whose righteousness is become ours by faith.

Therefore the apostle, to remove this foolish fear, or rather distrust, from us, rightly says that Jesus Christ *in all things was made like unto his brethren, that he might become a merciful and faithful high priest, to make propitiation for the sins of the people. For in that he himself hath suffered being tempted, he is able to succor them that are tempted.* And further to encourage us to go to Him, he says: *Having then a great high priest, who hath passed through the heavens, Jesus the Son of God, let us hold fast our confession. For we have not a high priest that cannot be touched with the feeling of our infirmities; but one that hath been in all points tempted like as we are, yet without sin. Let us therefore draw near with boldness unto the throne of grace, that we may receive mercy, and may find grace to help us in time of need.* The same apostle says: *Having boldness to enter into the holy place by the blood of Jesus, let us draw near with a true heart in fulness of faith,* etc. Likewise: *Christ hath his priesthood unchangeable; wherefore also he is able to save to the uttermost them that draw near unto God through him, seeing he ever liveth to make intercession for them.*

What more can be required? since Christ Himself says: *I am the way, and the truth, and the life: no one cometh unto the Father, but by me.* To what purpose should we, then, seek another advocate, since it has pleased God to give us His own Son as an Advocate? Let us not forsake Him to take another, or rather to seek after another, without ever being able to find him; for God well knew, when He gave Him to us, that we were sinners.

Therefore, according to the command of Christ, we call upon the heavenly Father through Jesus Christ our only Mediator, as we are taught in the Lord's Prayer; being assured that whatever we ask of the Father in His Name will be granted us.

Article XXVII. THE CATHOLIC CHRISTIAN CHURCH

We believe and profess one catholic or universal Church, which is a holy congregation of true Christian believers, all expecting their salvation in Jesus Christ, being washed by His blood, sanctified and sealed by the Holy Spirit.

This Church has been from the beginning of the world, and will be to the end thereof; which is evident from this that Christ is an eternal King, which without subjects He cannot be. And this holy Church is preserved or supported by God against the rage of the whole world; though it sometimes for a while appears very small, and in the eyes of men to be reduced to nothing; as during the perilous reign of Ahab the Lord reserved unto Him seven thousand men who had not bowed their knees to Baal.

Furthermore, this holy Church is not confined, boudn, or limited to a certain place or to certain persons, but is spread and dispersed over the whole world; and yet is joined and united with heart and will, by the power of faith, in one and the same Spirit.

Article XXVIII. EVERY ONE IS BOUND TO JOIN HIMSELF TO THE TRUE CHURCH

We believe, since this holy congregation is an assembly of those who are saved, and outside of it there is no salvation, that no person of whatsoever state or condition he may be, ought to withdraw from it, content to be by himself; but that all men are in duty bound to join and unite themselves with it; maintaining the unity of the Church; submitting themselves to the doctrine and discipline thereof; bowing their necks under the yoke of Jesus Christ; and as mutual members of the same body, serving to the edification of the brethren, according to the talents God has given them.

And that this may be the more effectually observed, it is the duty of all believers, according to the Word of God, to separate themselves from all those who do not belong to the Church, and to join themselves to this congregation, wheresoever God has established it, even though the magistrates and edicts of princes were against it, yea, though they should suffer death or any other corporal punishment. Therefore all those who separate themselves from the same or do not join themselves to it act contrary to the ordinance of God.

Article XXIX. THE MARKS OF THE TRUE CHURCH, AND WHEREIN IT DIFFERS FROM THE FALSE CHURCH

We believe that we ought diligently and circumspectly to discern from the Word of God which is the true Church, since all sects which are in the world assume to themselves the name of the Church. But we speak not here of hypocrites, who are mixed in the Church with the good, yet are not of the Church, though externally in it; but we say that the body and communion of the true Church must be distinguished from all sects that call themselves the Church.

The marks by which the true Church is known are these: If the pure doctrine of the gospel is preached therein; if it maintains the pure administration of the sacraments as instituted by Christ; if church discipline is exercised in punishing of sin; in short, if all things are managed according to the pure Word of God, all things contrary thereto rejected, and Jesus Christ acknowledged as the only Head of the Church. Hereby the true Church may certainly be known, from which no man has a right to separate himself.

With respect to those who are members of the Church, they may be known by the marks of Christians; namely, by faith, and when, having received Jesus Christ the only Savior, they avoid sin, follow after righteousness, love the true God and their neighbor, neither turn aside to the right or left, and crucify the flesh with the works thereof. But this is not to be understood as if there did not remain in them great infirmities; but they fight against them through the Spirit all the days of their life, continually taking their refuge in the blood, death, passion, and obedience of our Lord Jesus Christ, in whom they have remission of sins, through faith in Him.

As for the false Church, it ascribes more power and authority to itself and its ordinances than to the Word of God, and will not submit itself to the yoke of Christ. Neither does it administer the sacraments as appointed by Christ in His Word, but adds to and

THE BELGIC CONFESSION (continued)

takes from them, as it thinks proper; it relies more upon men than upon Christ; and persecutes those who live holily according to the Word of God and rebuke it for its errors, covetousness, and idolatry.

These two Churches are easily known and distinguished from each other.

Article XXX. THE GOVERNMENT OF THE CHURCH AND ITS OFFICES

We believe that this true Church must be governed by that spiritual polity which our Lord has taught us in His Word: namely, that there must be ministers or pastors to preach the Word of God and to administer the sacraments; also elders and deacons, who, together with the pastors, form the council of the Church; that by these means the true religion may be preserved, and the true doctrine everywhere propagated, likewise transgressors punished and restrained by spiritual means; also that the poor and distressed may be relieved and comforted, according to their necessities. By these means everything will be carried on in the Church with good order and decency, when faithful men are chosen, according to the rule prescribed by St. Paul in his Epistle to Timothy.

Article XXXI. THE MINISTERS, ELDERS, AND DEACONS

We believe that the ministers of God's Word, the elders, and the deacons ought to be chosen to their respective offices by a lawful election by the Church, with calling upon the name of the Lord, and in that order which the Word of God teaches. Therefore every one must take heed not to intrude himself by improper means, but is bound to wait till it shall please God to call him; that he may have testimony of his calling, and be certain and assured that it is of the Lord.

As for the ministers of God's Word, they have equally the same power and authority wheresoever they are, as they are all ministers of Christ, the only universal Bishop and the only Head of the Church.

Moreover, in order that this holy ordinance of God may not be violated or slighted, we say that every one ought to esteem the ministers of God's Word and the elders of the Church very highly for their work's sake, and be at peace with them without murmuring, strife, or contention, as much as possible.

Article XXXII. THE ORDER AND DISCIPLINE OF THE CHURCH

In the meantime we believe, though it is useful and beneficial that those who are rulers of the Church institute and establish certain ordinances among themselves for maintaining the body of the Church, yet that they ought studiously to take care that they do not depart from those things which Christ, our only Master, has instituted. And therefore we reject all human inventions, and all laws which man would introduce into the worship of God, thereby to bind and compel the conscience in any manner whatever. Therefore we admit only of that which tends to nourish and preserve concord and unity, and to keep all men in obedience to God. For this purpose, excommunication or church discipline is requisite, with all that pertains to it, according to the Word of God.

Article XXXIII. THE SACRAMENTS

We believe that our gracious God, taking account of our weakness and infirmities, has ordained the sacraments for us, thereby to seal unto us His promises, and to be pledges of the good will and grace of God towards us, and also to nourish and strengthen our faith; which He has joined to the Word of the gospel, the better to present to our senses both that which He declares to us by His Word and that which He works inwardly in our hearts, thereby confirming in us the salvation which He imparts to us. For they are visible signs and seals of an inward and invisible thing, by means whereof God works in us by the power of the Holy Spirit. Therefore the signs are not empty or meaningless, so as to deceive us. For Jesus Christ is the true object presented by them, without whom they would be of no moment.

Moreover, we are satisfied with the number of sacraments which Christ our Lord has instituted, which are two only, namely, the sacrament of baptism and the holy supper of our Lord Jesus Christ.

Article XXXIV. HOLY BAPTISM

We believe and confess that Jesus Christ, who is the end of the law, has made an end, by the shedding of His blood, of all other sheddings of blood which men could or would make as a propitiation or satisfaction for sin; and that He, having abolished circumcision, which was done with blood, has instituted the sacrament of baptism instead thereof; by which we are received into the Church of God, and separated from all other people and strange religions, that we may wholly belong to Him whose mark and ensign we bear; and which serves as a testimony to us that He will forever be our gracious God and Father.

Therefore He has commanded all those who are His to be baptized with pure water, *into the name of the Father and of the Son and of the Holy Spirit*, thereby signifying to us, that as water washes away the filth of the body when poured upon it, and is seen on the body of the baptized when sprinkled upon him, so does the blood of Christ by the power of the Holy Spirit internally sprinkle the soul, cleanse it from its sins, and regenerate us from children of wrath unto children of God. Not that this is effected by the external water, but by the sprinkling of the precious blood of the Son of God; who is our Red Sea, through which we must pass to escape the tyranny of Pharaoh, that is, the devil, and to enter into the spiritual land of Canaan.

The ministers, therefore, on their part administer the sacrament and that which is visible, but our Lord gives that which is signified by the sacrament, namely, the gifts and invisible grace; washing, cleansing, and purging our souls of all filth and unrighteousness; renewing our hearts and filling them with all comfort; giving unto us a true assurance of His fatherly goodness; putting on us the new man, and putting off the old man with all his deeds.

We believe, therefore, that every man who is earnestly studious of obtaining life eternal ought to be baptized but once with this only baptism, without ever repeating the same, since we cannot be born twice. Neither does this baptism avail us only at the time when the water is poured upon us and received by us, but also through the whole course of our life.

Therefore we detest the error of the Anabaptists, who are not content with the one only baptism they have once received, and moreover condemn the baptism of the infants of believers, who we believe ought to be baptized and sealed with the sign of the covenant, as the children in Israel formerly were circumcised upon the same promises which are made unto our children. And indeed Christ shed His blood no less for the washing of the children of believers than for adult persons; and therefore they ought to receive the sign and sacrament of that which Christ has done for them; as the Lord commanded in the law that they should be made partakers of the sacrament of Christ's suffering and death shortly after they were born, by offering for them a lamb, which was a sacrament of Jesus Christ. Moreover, what circumcision was to the Jews, baptism is to our children. And for this reason St. Paul calls baptism the *circumcision of Christ*.

Article XXXV. THE HOLY SUPPER OF OUR LORD JESUS CHRIST

We believe and confess that our Savior Jesus Christ did ordain and institute the sacrament of the holy supper to nourish and support those whom He has already regenerated and incorporated into His family, which is His Church.

Now those who are regenerated have in them a twofold life, the one corporal and temporal, which they have from the first birth and is common to all men; the other spiritual and heavenly, which is given them in their second birth, which is effected by the Word of the gospel, in the communion of the body of Christ; and this life is not common, but is peculiar to God's elect. In like manner God has given us, for the support of the bodily and earthly life, earthly and common bread, which is subservient thereto and is common to all men, even as life itself. But for the support of the spiritual and heavenly life which believers have He has sent a living bread, which descended from heaven, namely, Jesus Christ, who nourishes and strengthens the spiritual life of believers when they eat Him, that is to say, when they appropriate and receive Him by faith in the spirit.

In order that He might represent unto us this spiritual and heavenly bread, Christ has instituted an earthly and visible bread as a sacrament of His body, and wine as a sacrament of His blood, to testify by them unto us that, as certainly as we receive and hold this sacrament in our hands and eat and drink the same with our months, by which our life is afterwards nourished, we also do as certainly receive by faith (which is the hand and mouth of our soul) the true body and blood of Christ our only Savior in our souls, for the support of our spiritual life.

Now, as it is certain and beyond all doubt that Jesus Christ has not enjoined to us the use of His sacraments in vain, so He works in us all that He represents to us by these holy signs, though the manner surpasses our understanding and cannot be comprehended by us, as the operations of the Holy Spirit are hidden and incomprehensible. In the meantime we err not when we say that what is eaten and drunk by us is the proper and natural body and the proper blood of Christ. But the manner of our partaking of the same is not by the mouth, but by the spirit through faith. Thus, then, though Christ always sits at the right hand of His Father in the heavens, yet does He not therefore cease to make us partakers of Himself by faith. This feast is a spiritual table, at which Christ communicates Himself with all His benefits to us, and gives us there to enjoy both Himself and the merits of His sufferings and death: nourishing, strengthening, and comforting our poor comfortless souls by the eating of His flesh, quickening and refreshing them by the drinking of His blood.

Further, though the sacraments are connected with the thing signified nevertheless both are not received by all men. The ungodly indeed receives the sacrament to his condemnation, but he does not receive the truth of the sacrament, even as Judas and Simon the sorcerer both indeed received the sacrament but not Christ who was signified by it, of whom believers only are made partakers.

Lastly, we receive this holy sacrament in the assembly of the people of God, with humility and reverence, keeping up among us a holy remembrance of the death of Christ our Savior, with thanksgiving, making there confession of our faith and of the Christian religion. Therefore no one ought to come to this table without having previously rightly examined himself, lest by eating of this bread and drinking of this cup he eat and drink judgment to himself. In a word, we are moved by the use of this holy sacrament to a fervent love towards God and our neighbor.

Therefore we reject all mixtures and damnable inventions which men have added unto and blended with the sacraments, as profanations of them; and affirm that we ought to rest satisfied with the ordinance which Christ and His apostles have taught us, and that we must speak of them in the same manner as they have spoken.

Article XXXVI. THE MAGISTRACY (CIVIL GOVERNMENT)

We believe that our gracious God, because of the depravity of mankind, has appointed kings, princes, and magistrates; willing that the world should be governed by certain laws and policies; to the end that the dissoluteness of men might be restrained, and all things carried on among them with good order and decency. For this purpose He has invested the magistracy with *the sword for the punishment of evildoers and for the protection of them that do well.*

Their office is not only to have regard unto and watch for the welfare of the civil state, but also to protect the sacred ministry, that the kingdom of Christ may thus be promoted. They must therefore countenance the preaching of the Word of the gospel everywhere, that God may be honored and worshipped by every one, as He commands in His Word.

Moreover, it is the bounden duty of every one, of whatever state, quality, or condition he may be, to subject himself to the magistrates; to pay tribute, to show due honor and respect to them, and to obey them in all things which are not repugnant to the Word of God; to supplicate for them in their prayers that God may rule and guide them in all their ways, and *that we may lead a tranquil and quiet life in all godliness and gravity.*

Wherefore we detest the Anabaptists and other seditious people, and in general all those who reject the higher powers and magistrates and would subvert justice, introduce community of goods, and confound that decency and good order which God has established among men.

Article XXXVII. THE LAST JUDGMENT

Finally, we believe, according to the Word of God, when the time appointed by the Lord (which is unknown to all creatures) is come and the number of the elect complete, that our Lord Jesus Christ will come from heaven, corporally and visibly, as He ascended, with great glory and majesty to declare Himself Judge of the living and the dead, burning this old world with fire and flame to cleanse it.

Then all men will personally appear before this great Judge, both men and women and children, that have been from the beginning of the world to the end thereof, being summoned by *the voice of the archangel, and by the sound of the trump of God.* For all the dead shall be raised out of the earth, and their souls joined and united with their proper bodies in which they formerly lived. As for those who shall then be living, they shall not die as the others, but be changed in the twinkling of an eye, and from corruptible become incorruptible. Then *the books* (that is to say, the consciences) *shall be opened, and the dead judged* according to what they shall have done in this world, whether it be good or evil. Nay, all men *shall give account of every idle word they have spoken*, which the world only counts amusement and jest; and then the secrets and hypocrisy of men shall be disclosed and laid open before all.

And therefore the consideration of this judgment is justly terrible and dreadful to the wicked and ungodly, but most desirable and comfortable to the righteous and elect; because then their full deliverance shall be perfected, and there they shall receive the fruits of their labor and trouble which they have borne. Their innocence shall be known to all, and they shall see the terrible vengeance which God shall execute on the wicked, who most cruelly persecuted, oppressed, and tormented them in this world, and who shall be convicted by the testimony of their own consciences, and shall become immortal, but only to be tormented in *the eternal fire which is prepared for the devil and his angels.*

But on the contrary, the faithful and elect shall be crowned with glory and honor; and the Son of God will confess their names before God His Father and His elect angels; all tears shall be wiped from their eyes; and their cause which is now condemned by many judges and magistrates as heretical and impious will then be known to be the cause of the Son of God. And for a gracious reward, the Lord will cause them to possess such a glory as never entered into the heart of man to conceive.

Therefore we expect that great day with a most ardent desire, to the end that we may fully enjoy the promises of God in Christ Jesus our Lord. AMEN.

Amen, come, Lord Jesus.—Rev. 22:20.

Notes: *During the sixteenth century the Reformed Churches, like the Lutherans, found it necessary and expedient to produce statements clarifying their theological affirmations and their continued allegiance to the historic affirmations (as presented in the creeds) of the early church. Unlike the Lutherans, who collected their authoritative creeds into a single volume* (The Book of Concord), *the various Reformed Churches, representing different nations and languages, prepared their own individual statements of faith. English translations of the most important of the sixteenth-century confessions, originally promulgated between 1523 and 1566, were finally compiled into a single volume by Arthur Cochrane,* Reformed Confessions of the 16th Century *(Philadelphia: Westminster Press, 1966).*

In the United States, two of the sixteenth-century confessions stand out because of their acceptance as official doctrinal statements by Reformed churches with members in the United States. The Belgic Confession of 1561, the main product of Dutch Calvinism, is by far the most accepted in America, as many of the Reformed Churches had their beginnings in Holland.

The Belgic Confession was composed by Guido de Bries (1523-1567) in 1561 as part of an unsuccessful effort to convince the Roman Catholic authorities in the Netherlands that the Reformed Church should be released from persecution at the hands of the Spanish-Catholic authorities. The confession was slightly revised in 1566, and in 1619 it was adopted (along with the Heidelberg Catechism and the

Canons of Dort) as the official doctrinal standard of the Dutch Reformed Church.

The Dutch brought the confession to the United States, where it remains the official standard for the Christian Reformed Church and the Reformed Church in America, as well as for the smaller Netherlands Reformed Congregations, Orthodox Christian Reformed Church, and Protestant Reformed Churches of America.

The text of the confession reproduced here was taken from A Treatise of the Compendium by G. H. Kersten (Grand Rapids, MI: Inheritance Publishing Co., 1956).

*   *   *

CANONS OF DORT

FIRST HEAD OF DOCTRINE. DIVINE ELECTION AND REPROBATION

Article 1. As all men have sinned in Adam, lie under the curse, and are deserving of eternal death, God would have done no injustice by leaving them all to perish and delivering them over to condemnation on account of sin, according to the words of the apostle: *That every mouth may be stopped, and all the world may be brought under the judgment of God* (Rom. 3:19). And: *For all have sinned, and fall short of the glory of God* (Rom. 3:23). And: *For the wages of sin is death* (Rom. 6:23).

Article 2. But in this the love of God was manifested, that He *sent his only begotten Son into the world, that whosoever believeth on him should not perish, but have eternal life* (1 John 4:9; John 3:16).

Article 3. And that men may be brought to believe, God mercifully sends the messengers of these most joyful tidings to whom He will and at what time He pleases; by whose ministry men are called to repentance and faith in Christ crucified. *How then shall they call on him in whom they have not believed? And how shall they believe in him whom they have not heard? And how shall they hear without a preacher? And how shall they preach except they be sent?* (Rom. 10:14, 15).

Article 4. The wrath of God abides upon those who believe not this gospel. But such as receive it and embrace Jesus the Savior by a true and living faith are by Him delivered from the wrath of God and from destruction, and have the gift of eternal life conferred upon them.

Article 5. The cause or guilt of this unbelief as well as of all other sins is no wise in God, but in man himself; whereas faith in Jesus Christ and salvation through Him is the free gift of God, as it is written: *By grace have ye been saved through faith; and that not of yourselves*, it is *the gift of God* (Eph. 2:8). Likewise: *To you it hath been granted in the behalf of Christ, not only to believe on him*, etc. (Phil. 1:29).

Article 6. That some receive the gift of faith from God, and others do not receive it, proceeds from God's eternal decree. *For known unto God are all his works from the beginning of the world* (Acts 15:18,

A.V.). *Who worketh all things after the counsel of his will* (Eph. 1:11). According to which decree He graciously softens the hearts of the elect, however obstinate, and inclines them to believe; while He leaves the non-elect in His just judgment to their own wickedness and obduracy. And herein is especially displayed the profound, the merciful, and at the same time the righteous discrimination between men equally involved in ruin; or that decree of election and reprobation, revealed in the Word of God, which, though men of perverse, impure, and unstable minds wrest it to their own destruction, yet to holy and pious souls affords unspeakable consolation.

Article 7. Election is the unchangeable purpose of God, whereby, before the foundation of the world, He has out of mere grace, according to the sovereign good pleasure of His own will, chosen from the whole human race, which had fallen through their own fault from their primitive state of rectitude into sin and destruction, a certain number of persons to redemption in Christ, whom He from eternity appointed the Mediator and Head of the elect and the foundation of salvation. This elect number, though by nature neither better nor more deserving than others, but with them involved in one common misery, God has decreed to give to Christ to be saved by Him, and effectually to call and draw them to His communion by His Word and Spirit; to bestow upon them true faith, justification, and sanctification; and having powerfully preserved them in the fellowship of His Son, finally to glorify them for the demonstration of His mercy, and for the praise of the riches of His glorious grace; as it is written: *Even as he chose us in him before the foundation of the world, that we should be holy and without blemish before him in love: having foreordained us unto adoption as sons through Jesus Christ unto himself, according to the good pleasure of his will, to the praise of the glory of his grace, which he freely bestowed on us in the Beloved* (Eph. 1:4, 5, 6). And elsewhere: *Whom he foreordained, them he also called: and whom he called, them he also justified: and whom he justified, them he also glorified* (Rom. 8:30).

Article 8. There are not various decrees of election, but one and the same decree respecting all those who shall be saved, both under the Old and the New Testament; since the Scripture declares the good pleasure, purpose, and counsel of the divine will to be one, according to which He has chosen us from eternity, both to grace and to glory, to salvation and to the way of salvation, which He has ordained that we should walk therein (Eph. 1:4, 5; 2:10).

Article 9. This election was not founded upon foreseen faith and the obedience of faith, holiness, or any other good quality or disposition in man, as the prerequisite, cause, or condition on which it depended; but men are chosen to faith and to the obedience of faith, holiness, etc. Therefore election is the fountain of every saving good, from which proceed faith, holiness, and the other gifts of salvation, and finally eternal life itself, as its fruits and effects,

CANONS OF DORT (continued)

according to the testimony of the apostle: *He hath chosen us* (not because we were, but) *that we should be holy, and without blemish before him in love* (Eph. 1:4).

Article 10.   The good pleasure of God is the sole cause of this gracious election; which does not consist herein that out of all possible qualities and actions of men God has chosen some as a condition of salvation, but that He was pleased out of the common mass of sinners to adopt some certain persons as a peculiar people to Himself, as it is written: *For* the children *being not yet born, neither having done anything good or bad,* etc., *it was said unto her* (namely, to Rebekah), *The elder shall serve the younger. Even as it is written, Jacob I loved, but Esau I hated* (Rom. 9:11, 12, 13). *And as many as were ordained to eternal life believed* (Acts 13:48).

Article 11.   And as God Himself is most wise, unchangeable, omniscient, and omnipotent, so the election made by Him can neither be interrupted nor changed, recalled, or annulled; neither can the elect be cast away, nor their number diminished.

Article 12.   The elect in due time, though in various degrees and in different measures, attain the assurance of this their eternal and unchangeable election, not by inquisitively prying into the secret and deep things of God, but by observing in themselves with a spiritual joy and holy pleasure the infallible fruits of election pointed out in the Word of God—such as, a true faith in Christ, filial fear, a godly sorrow for sin, a hungering and thirsting after righteousness, etc.

Article 13.   The sense and certainty of this election afford to the children of God additional matter for daily humiliation before Him, for adoring the depth of His mercies, for cleansing themselves, and rendering grateful returns of ardent love to Him who first manifested so great love towards them. The consideration of this doctrine of election is so far from encouraging remissness in the observance of the divine commands or from sinking men in carnal security, that these, in the just judgment of God, are the usual effects of rash presumption or of idle and wanton trifling with the grace of election, in those who refuse to walk in the ways of the elect.

Article 14.   As the doctrine of divine election by the most wise counsel of God was declared by the prophets, by Christ Himself, and by the apostles, and is clearly revealed in the Scriptures both of the Old and the New Testament, so it is still to be published in due time and place in the Church of God, for which it was peculiarly designed, provided it be done with reverence, in the spirit of discretion and piety, for the glory of God's most holy Name, and for enlivening and comforting His people, without vainly attempting to investigate the secret ways of the Most High (Acts 20:27; Rom. 11:33, 34; 12:3; Heb. 6:17, 18).

Article 15.   What peculiarly tends to illustrate and recommend to us the eternal and unmerited grace of election is the express testimony of sacred Scripture that not all, but some only, are elected, while others are passed by in the eternal decree; whom God, out of His sovereign, most just, irreprehensible, and unchangeable good pleasure, has decreed to leave in the common misery into which they have wilfully plunged themselves, and not to bestow upon them saving faith and the grace of conversion; but, permitting them in His just judgment to follow their own ways, at last, for the declaration of His justice, to condemn and punish them forever, not only on account of their unbelief, but also for all their other sins. And this is the decree of reprobation, which by no means makes God the Author of sin (the very thought of which is blasphemy), but declares Him to be an awful, irreprehensible, and righteous Judge and Avenger thereof.

Article 16.   Those in whom a living faith in Christ, an assured confidence of soul, peace of conscience, an earnest endeavor after filial obedience, a glorying in God through Christ, is not as yet strongly felt, and who nevertheless make use of the means which God has appointed for working these graces in us, ought not to be alarmed at the mention of reprobation, nor to rank themselves among the reprobate, but diligently to persevere in the use of means, and with ardent desires devoutly and humbly to wait for a season of richer grace. Much less cause to be terrified by the doctrine of reprobation have they who, though they seriously desire to be turned to God, to please Him only, and to be delivered from the body of death, cannot yet reach that measure of holiness and faith to which they aspire; since a merciful God has promised that He will not quench the smoking flax, nor break the bruised reed. But this doctrine is justly terrible to those who, regardless of God and of the Savior Jesus Christ, have wholly given themselves up to the cares of the world and the pleasures of the flesh, so long as they are not seriously converted to God.

Article 17.   Since we are to judge of the will of God from His Word, which testifies that the children of believers are holy, not by nature, but in virtue of the covenant of grace, in which they together with the parents are comprehended, godly parents ought not to doubt the election and salvation of their children whom it pleases God to call out of this life in their infancy (Gen. 17:7; Acts 2:39; 1 Cor. 7:14).

Article 18.   To those who murmur at the free grace of election and the just severity of reprobation we answer with the apostle: *Nay but, O man, who art thou that repliest against God?* (Rom. 9:20), and quote the language of our Savior: *Is it not lawful for me to do what I will with mine own?* (Matt. 20:15). And therefore, with holy adoration of these mysteries, we exclaim in the words of the apostle: *O the depth of the riches both of the wisdom and the knowledge of God! how unsearchable are his judgments, and his ways past tracing out! For who hath known the mind of the Lord, or who hath been his counsellor? or who hath first given to him, and it shall be recompensed unto him again? For of him, and through him, and unto him are all things. To him be the glory for ever. Amen.* (Rom. 11:33-36).

REJECTION OF ERRORS

The true doctrine concerning election and reprobation having been explained, the Synod rejects the errors of those:

Paragraph 1. Who teach: That the will of God to save those who would believe and would persevere in faith and in the obedience of faith is the whole and entire decree of election unto salvation, and that nothing else concerning this decree has been revealed in God's Word.

For these deceive the simple and plainly contradict the Scriptures, which declare that God will not only save those who will believe, but that He has also from eternity chosen certain particular persons to whom, above others, He will grant, in time, both faith in Christ and perseverance; as it is written: *I manifested thy name unto the men whom thou gavest me out of the world* (John 17:6). *And as many as were ordained to eternal life believed* (Acts 13:48). And: *Even as he chose us in him before the foundation of the world, that we should be holy and without blemish before him in love* (Eph. 1:4).

Paragraph 2. Who teach: That there are various kinds of election of God unto eternal life: the one general and indefinite, the other particular and definite; and that the latter in turn is either incomplete, revocable, non-decisive, and conditional, or complete, irrevocable, decisive, and absolute. Likewise: That there is one election unto faith and another unto salvation, so that election can be unto justifying faith, without being a decisive election unto salvation.

For this is a fancy of men's minds, invented regardless of the Scriptures, whereby the doctrine of election is corrupted, and this golden chain of our salvation is broken: *And whom he foreordained, them he also called: and whom he called, them he also justified: and whom he justified, them he also glorified* (Rom. 8:30).

Paragraph 3. Who teach: That the good pleasure and purpose of God, of which Scripture makes mention in the doctrine of election, does not consist in this, that God chose certain persons rather than others, but in this, that He chose out of all possible conditions (among which are also the works of the law), or out of the whole order of things, the act of faith which from its very nature is undeserving, as well as its incomplete obedience, as a condition of salvation, and that He would graciously consider this in itself as a complete obedience and count it worthy of the reward of eternal life.

For by this injurious error the pleasure of God and the merits of Christ are made of none effect, and men are drawn away by useless questions from the truth of gracious justification and from the simplicity of Scripture, and this declaration of the apostle is charged as untrue: *Who saved us, and called us with a holy calling, not according to our works, but according to his own purpose and grace, which was given us in Christ Jesus before times eternal* (2 Tim. 1:9).

Paragraph 4. Who teach: That in the election unto faith this condition is beforehand demanded that man should use the light of nature aright, be pious, humble, meek, and fit for eternal life, as if on these things election were in any way dependent.

For this savors of the teaching of Pelagius, and is opposed to the doctrine of the apostle when he writes: *Among whom we also all once lived in the lusts of our flesh, doing the desires of the flesh and of the mind, and were by nature children of wrath, even as the rest; but God, being rich in mercy, for his great love wherewith he loved us, even when we were dead through our trespasses, made us alive together with Christ (by grace have ye been saved), and raised us up with him, and made us to sit with him in the heavenly* places, *in Christ Jesus; that in the ages to come he might show the exceeding riches of his grace in kindness towards us in Christ Jesus; for by grace have ye been saved through faith; and that not of yourselves,* it is *the gift of God; not of works, that no man should glory* (Eph. 2:3-9).

Paragraph 5. Who teach: That the incomplete and non-decisive election of particular persons to salvation occurred because of a foreseen faith, conversion, holiness, godliness, which either began or continued for some time; but that the complete and decisive election occurred because of foreseen perseverance unto the end in faith, conversion, holiness, and godliness; and that this is the gracious and evangelical worthiness, for the sake of which he who is chosen is more worthy than he who is not chosen; and that therefore faith, the obedience of faith, holiness, godliness, and perseverance are not fruits of the unchangeable election unto glory, but are conditions which, being required beforehand, were foreseen as being met by those who will be fully elected, and are causes without which the unchangeable election to glory does not occur.

This is repugnant to the entire Scripture, which constantly inculcates this and similar declarations: Election is *not of works, but of him that calleth* (Rom. 9:11). *And as many as were ordained to eternal life believed* (Acts 13:48). *He chose us in him before the foundation of the world, that we should be holy* (Eph. 1:4). *Ye did not choose me, but I chose you* (John 15:16). *But if it is by grace, it is no more of works* (Rom. 11:6). *Herein is love, not that we loved God, but that he loved us, and sent his Son* (1 John 4:10).

Paragraph 6. Who teach: That not every election unto salvation is unchangeable, but that some of the elect, any decree of God notwithstanding, can yet perish and do indeed perish.

175

By this gross error they make God to be changeable, and destroy the comfort which the godly obtain out of the firmness of their election, and contradict the Holy Scripture, which teaches that *the elect can not be led astray* (Matt. 24:24), that Christ *does not lose those whom the Father gave him* (John 6:39), and that *God also glorified those whom he foreordained, called, and justified* (Rom. 8:30).

Paragraph 7. Who teach: That there is in this life no fruit and no consciousness of the unchangeable election to glory, nor any certainty, except that which depends on a changeable and uncertain condition.

For not only is it absurd to speak of an uncertain certainty, but also contrary to the experience of the saints, who by virtue of the consciousness of their election rejoice with the apostle and praise this favor of God (Eph. 1); who according to Christ's admonition rejoice with his disciples that *their names are written in heaven* (Luke 10:20); who also place the consciousness of their election over against the fiery darts of the devil, asking: *Who shall lay anything to the charge of God's elect?* (Rom. 8:33).

Paragraph 8. Who teach: That God, simply by virtue of His righteous will, did not decide either to leave anyone in the fall of Adam and in the common state of sin and condemnation, or to pass anyone by in the communication of grace which is necessary for faith and conversion.

For this is firmly decreed: *He hath mercy on whom he will, and whom he will he hardeneth* (Rom. 9:18). And also this: *Unto you it is given to know the mysteries of the kingdom of heaven, but to them it is not given* (Matt. 13:11). Likewise: *I thank thee, O Father, Lord of heaven and earth, that thou didst hide these things from the wise and understanding, and didst reveal them unto babes; yea, Father, for so it was well-pleasing in thy sight* (Matt. 11:25, 26).

Paragraph 9. Who teach: That the reason why God sends the gospel to one people rather than to another is not merely and solely the good pleasure of God, but rather the fact that one people is better and worthier than another to which the gospel is not communicated.

For this Moses denies, addressing the people of Israel as follows: *Behold unto Jehovah thy God belongeth heaven and the heaven of heavens, the earth, with all that is therein. Only Jehovah had a delight in thy fathers to love them, and he chose their seed after them, even you above all peoples, as at this day* (Deut. 10:14, 15). And Christ said: *Woe unto thee, Chorazin! woe unto thee, Bethsaida! for if the mighty works had been done in Tyre and Sidon which were done in you, they would have repented long ago in sackcloth and ashes* (Matt. 11:21).

SECOND HEAD OF DOCTRINE. THE DEATH OF CHRIST, AND THE REDEMPTION OF MEN THEREBY

Article 1. God is not only supremely merciful, but also supremely just. And His justice requires (as He has revealed Himself in His Word) that our sins committed against His infinite majesty should be punished, not only with temporal but with eternal punishments, both in body and soul; which we cannot escape, unless satisfaction be made to the justice of God.

Article 2. Since, therefore, we are unable to make that satisfaction in our own persons, or to deliver ourselves from the wrath of God, He has been pleased of His infinite mercy to give His only begotten Son for our Surety, who was made sin, and became a curse for us and in our stead, that He might make satisfaction to divine justice on our behalf.

Article 3. The death of the Son of God is the only and most perfect sacrifice and satisfaction for sin, and is of infinite worth and value, abundantly sufficient to expiate the sins of the whole world.

Article 4. This death is of such infinite value and dignity because the person who submitted to it was not only really man and perfectly holy, but also the only begotten Son of God, of the same eternal and infinite essence with the Father and the Holy Spirit, which qualifications were necessary to constitute Him a Savior for us; and, moreover, because it was attended with a sense of the wrath and curse of God due to us for sin.

Article 5. Moreover, the promise of the gospel is that whosoever believes in Christ crucified shall not perish, but have eternal life. This promise, together with the command to repent and believe, ought to be declared and published to all nations, and to all persons promiscuously and without distinction, to whom God out of His good pleasure sends the gospel.

Article 6. And, whereas many who are called by the gospel do not repent nor believe in Christ, but perish in unbelief, this is not owing to any defect or insufficiency in the sacrifice offered by Christ upon the cross, but is wholly to be imputed to themselves.

Article 7. But as many as truly believe, and are delivered and saved from sin and destruction through the death of Christ, are indebted for this benefit solely to the grace of God given them in Christ from everlasting, and not to any merit of their own.

Article 8. For this was the sovereign counsel and most gracious will and purpose of God the Father that the quickening and saving efficacy of the most precious death of His Son should extend to all the elect, for bestowing upon them alone the gift of justifying faith, thereby to bring them infallibly to salvation; that is, it was the will of God that Christ by the blood of the cross, whereby He confirmed the new covenant, should effectually redeem out of every people, tribe, nation, and language, all those, and those only, who were from eternity chosen to salvation and given to Him by the Father; that He should confer upon them faith, which, together with all the other saving gifts of the Holy Spirit, He purchased for them by His death; should purge them from all sin, both original and actual, whether committed before or after believing; and having faithfully preserved them even to the end, should at last bring them, free from every spot and blemish, to the enjoyment of glory in His own presence forever.

Article 9. This purpose, proceeding from everlasting love towards the elect, has from the beginning of the world to this day been powerfully accomplished, and will henceforward still continue to be accomplished, notwithstanding all the ineffectual opposition of the gates of hell; so that the elect in due time may be gathered together into one, and that there never may be wanting a Church composed of believers, the foundation of which is laid in the blood of Christ; which may stedfastly love and faithfully serve Him as its Savior (who, as a bridegroom for his bride, laid down His life for them upon the cross); and which may celebrate His praises here and through all eternity.

REJECTION OF ERRORS

The true doctrine having been explained, the Synod rejects the errors of those:

Paragraph 1. Who teach: That God the Father has ordained His Son to the death of the cross without a certain and definite decree to save any, so that the necessity, profitableness, and worth of what Christ merited by His death might have existed, and might remain in all its parts complete, perfect, and intact, even if the merited redemption had never in fact been applied to any person.

For this doctrine tends to the despising of the wisdom of the Father and of the merits of Jesus Christ, and is contrary to Scripture. For thus says our Savior: *I lay down my life for the sheep, and I know them* (John 10:15, 27). And the prophet Isaiah says concerning the Savior: *When thou shalt make his soul an offering for sin, he shall see* his *seed, he shall prolong his days, and the pleasure of Jehovah shall prosper in his hand* (Is. 53:10). Finally, this contradicts the article of faith according to which we believe the catholic Christian Church.

Paragraph 2. Who teach: That it was not the purpose of the death of Christ that He should confirm the new covenant of grace through His blood, but only that He should acquire for the Father the mere right to establish with man such a covenant as He might please, whether of grace or of works.

For this is repugnant to Scripture which teaches that *Christ hath become the surety and mediator of a better, that is, the new covenant*, and that *a testament is of force where there hath been death* (Heb. 7:22; 9:15, 17).

Paragraph 3. Who teach: That Christ by His satisfaction merited neither salvation itself for anyone, nor faith, whereby this satisfaction of Christ unto salvation is effectually appropriated; but that He merited for the Father only the authority or the perfect will to deal again with man, and to prescribe new conditions as He might desire, obedience to which, however, depended on the free will of man, so that it therefore might have come to pass that either none or all should fulfil these conditions.

For these adjudge too contemptuously of the death of Christ, in no wise acknowledge the most important fruit or benefit thereby gained, and bring again out of hell the Pelagian error.

Paragraph 4. Who teach: That the new covenant of grace, which God the Father, through the mediation of the death of Christ, made with man, does not herein consist that we by faith, in as much as it accepts the merits of Christ, are justified before God and saved, but in the fact that God, having revoked the demand of perfect obedience of faith, regards faith itself and the obedience of faith, although imperfect, as the perfect obedience of the law, and does esteem it worthy of the reward of eternal life through grace.

For these contradict the Scriptures: *Being justified freely by his grace through the redemption that is in Christ Jesus; whom God set forth* to be a *propitiation, through faith, in his blood* (Rom. 3:24, 25). And these proclaim, as did the wicked Socinus, a new and strange justification of man before God, against the consensus of the whole Church.

Paragraph 5. Who teach: That all men have been accepted unto the state of reconciliation and unto the grace of the covenant, so that no one is worthy of condemnation on account of original sin, and that no one shall be condemned because of it, but that all are free from the guilt of original sin.

For this opinion is repugnant to Scripture which teaches that we are *by nature children of wrath* (Eph. 2:3).

Paragraph 6. Who use the difference between meriting and appropriating, to the end that they may instil into the minds of the imprudent and inexperienced this teaching that God, as far as He is concerned, has been minded to apply to all equally the benefits gained by the death of Christ; but that, while some obtain the pardon of sin and eternal life, and others do not, this difference depends on their own free will, which joins itself to the grace that is offered without exception, and that it is not dependent on the special gift of mercy, which powerfully works in them, that they rather than others should appropriate unto themselves this grace.

For these, while they feign that they present this distinction in a sound sense, seek to instil into the people the destructive poison of the Pelagian errors.

Paragraph 7. Who teach: That Christ neither could die, nor needed to die, and also did not die, for those

CANONS OF DORT (continued)

whom God loved in the highest degree and elected to eternal life, since these do not need the death of Christ.

For they contradict the apostle, who declares: *Christ loved me, and gave himself up for me* (Gal. 2:20). Likewise: *Who shall lay anything to the charge of God's elect? It is God that justifieth; who is he that condemneth? It is Christ Jesus that died* (Rom. 8:33, 34), namely, for them; and the Savior who says: *I lay down my life for the sheep* (John 10:15). And: *This is my commandment, that ye love one another, even as I have loved you. Greater love hath no man than this, that a man lay down his life for his friends* (John 15:12, 13).

THIRD AND FOURTH HEADS OF DOCTRINE. THE CORRUPTION OF MAN, HIS CONVERSION TO GOD, AND THE MANNER THEREOF

Article 1. Man was originally formed after the image of God. His understanding was adorned with a true and saving knowledge of his Creator, and of spiritual things; his heart and will were upright, all his affections pure, and the whole man was holy. But, revolting from God by the instigation of the devil and by his own free will, he forfeited these excellent gifts; and in the place thereof became involved in blindness of mind, horrible darkness, vanity, and perverseness of judgment; became wicked, rebellious, and obdurate in heart and will, and impure in his affections.

Article 2. Man after the fall begat children in his own likeness. A corrupt stock produced a corrupt offspring. Hence all the posterity of Adam, Christ only excepted, have derived corruption from their original parent, not by limitation, as the Pelagians of old asserted, but by the propagation of a vicious nature, in consequence of the just judgment of God.

Article 3. Therefore all men are conceived in sin, and are by nature children of wrath, incapable of saving good, prone to evil, dead in sin, and in bondage thereto; and without the regenerating grace of the Holy Spirit, they are neither able nor willing to return to God, to reform the depravity of their nature, or to dispose themselves to reformation.

Article 4. There remain, however, in man since the fall, the glimmerings of natural light, whereby he retains some knowledge of God, of natural things, and of the difference between good and evil, and shows some regard for virtue and for good outward behavior. But so far is this light of nature from being sufficient to bring him to a saving knowledge of God and to true conversion that he is incapable of using it aright even in things natural and civil. Nay further, this light, such as it is, man in various ways renders wholly polluted, and hinders in unrighteousness, by doing which he becomes inexcusable before God.

Article 5. In the same light are we to consider the law of the decalogue, delivered by God to His peculiar people, the Jews, by the hands of Moses. For though it reveals the greatness of sin, and more and more convinces man thereof, yet, as it neither points out a remedy nor imparts strength to extricate him from his misery, but, being weak through the flesh, leaves the transgressor under the curse, man cannot by this law obtain saving grace.

Article 6. What, therefore, neither the light of nature nor the law could do, that God performs by the operation of the Holy Spirit through the word or ministry of reconciliation; which is the glad tidings concerning the Messiah, by means whereof it has pleased God to save such as believe, as well under the Old as under the New Testament.

Article 7. This mystery of His will God revealed to but a small number under the Old Testament; under the New Testament (the distinction between various peoples having been removed) He reveals it to many. The cause of this dispensation is not to be ascribed to the superior worth of one nation above another, nor to their better use of the light of nature, but results wholly from the sovereign good pleasure and unmerited love of God. Hence they to whom so great and so gracious a blessing is communicated, above their desert, or rather notwithstanding their demerits, are bound to acknowledge it with humble and grateful hearts, and with the apostle to adore, but in no wise curiously to pry into, the severity and justice of God's judgments displayed in others to whom this grace is not given.

Article 8. As many as are called by the gospel are unfeignedly called. For God has most earnestly and truly declared in His Word what is acceptable to Him, namely, that those who are called should come unto Him. He also seriously promises rest of soul and eternal life to all who come to Him and believe.

Article 9. It is not the fault of the gospel, nor of Christ offered therein, nor of God, who calls men by the gospel and confers upon them various gifts, that those who are called by the ministry of the Word refuse to come and be converted. The fault lies in themselves; some of whom when called, regardless of their danger, reject the Word of life; others, though they receive it, suffer it not to make a lasting impression on their heart; therefore, their joy, arising only from a temporary faith, soon vanishes, and they fall away; while others choke the seed of the Word by perplexing cares and the pleasures of this world, and produce no fruit. This our Savior teaches in the parable of the sower (Matt. 13).

Article 10. But that others who are called by the gospel obey the call and are converted is not to be ascribed to the proper exercise of free will, whereby one distinguishes himself above others equally furnished with grace sufficient for faith and conversion (as the proud heresy of Pelagius maintains); but it must be wholly ascribed to God, who, as He has chosen His own from eternity in Christ, so He calls them effectually in time, confers upon them faith and repentance, rescues them from the power of darkness, and translates them into the kingdom of

His own Son; that they may show forth the praises of Him who has called them out of darkness into His marvelous light, and may glory not in themselves but in the Lord, according to the testimony of the apostles in various places.

Article 11.   But when God accomplishes His good pleasure in the elect, or works in them true conversion, He not only causes the gospel to be externally preached to them, and powerfully illuminates their minds by His Holy Spirit, that they may rightly understand and discern the things of the Spirit of God; but by the efficacy of the same regenerating Spirit He pervades the inmost recesses of man; He opens the closed and softens the hardened heart, and circumcises that which was uncircumcised; infuses new qualities into the will, which, though heretofore dead, He quickens; from being evil, disobedient, and refractory, He renders it good, obedient, and pliable; actuates and strengthens it, that like a good tree, it may bring forth the fruits of good actions.

Article 12.   And this is that regeneration so highly extolled in Scripture, that renewal, new creation, resurrection from the dead, making alive, which God works in us without our aid. But this is in no wise effected merely by the external preaching of the gospel, by moral suasion, or such a mode of operation that, after God has performed His part, it still remains in the power of man to be regenerated or not, to be converted or to continue unconverted; but it is evidently a supernatural work, most powerful, and at the same time most delightful, astonishing, mysterious, and ineffable; not inferior in efficacy to creation or the resurrection from the dead, as the Scripture inspired by the Author of this work declares; so that all in whose heart God works in this marvelous manner are certainly, infallibly, and effectually regenerated, and do actually believe. Whereupon the will thus renewed is not only actuated and influenced by God, but in consequence of this influence becomes itself active. Wherefore also man himself is rightly said to believe and repent by virtue of that grace received.

Article 13.   The manner of this operation cannot be fully comprehended by believers in this life. Nevertheless, they are satisfied to know and experience that by this grace of God they are enabled to believe with the heart and to love their Savior.

Article 14.   Faith is therefore to be considered as the gift of God, not on account of its being offered by God to man, to be accepted or rejected at his pleasure, but because it is in reality conferred upon him, breathed and infused into him; nor even because God bestows the power or ability to believe, and then expects that man should by the exercise of his own free will consent to the terms of salvation and actually believe in Christ, but because He who works in man both to will and to work, and indeed all things in all, produces both the will to believe and the act of believing also.

Article 15.   God is under no obligation to confer this grace upon any; for how can He be indebted to one who had no previous gifts to bestow as a foundation for such recompense? Nay, how can He be indebted to one who has nothing of his own but sin and falsehood? He, therefore, who becomes the subject of this grace owes eternal gratitude to God, and gives Him thanks forever. Whoever is not made partaker thereof is either altogether regardless of these spiritual gifts and satisfied with his own condition, or is in no apprehension of danger, and vainly boasts the possession of that which he has not. Further, with respect to those who outwardly profess their faith and amend their lives, we are bound, after the example of the apostle, to judge and speak of them in the most favorable manner; for the secret recesses of the heart are unknown to us. And as to others who have not yet been called, it is our duty to pray for them to God, who calls the things that are not as if they were. But we are in no wise to conduct ourselves towards them with haughtiness, as if we had made ourselves to differ.

Article 16.   But as man by the fall did not cease to be a creature endowed with understanding and will, nor did sin which pervaded the whole race of mankind deprive him of the human nature, but brought upon him depravity and spiritual death; so also this grace of regeneration does not treat men as senseless stocks and blocks, nor take away their will and its properties, or do violence thereto; but it spiritually quickens, heals, corrects, and at the same time sweetly and powerfully bends it, that where carnal rebellion and resistance formerly prevailed, a ready and sincere spiritual obedience begins to reign; in which the true and spiritual restoration and freedom of our will consist. Wherefore, unless the admirable Author of every good work so deal with us, man can have no hope of being able to rise from his fall by his own free will, by which, in a state of innocence, he plunged himself into ruin.

Article 17.   As the almighty operation of God whereby He brings forth and supports this our natural life does not exclude but require the use of means by which God, of His infinite mercy and goodness, has chosen to exert His influence, so also the aforementioned supernatural operation of God by which we are regenerated in no wise excludes or subverts the use of the gospel, which the most wise God has ordained to be the seed of regeneration and food of the soul. Wherefore, as the apostles and the teachers who succeeded them piously instructed the people concerning this grace of God, to His glory and to the abasement of all pride, and in the meantime, however, neglected not to keep them, by the holy admonitions of the gospel, under the influence of the Word, the sacraments, and ecclesiastical discipline; so even now it should be far from those who give or receive instruction in the Church to presume to tempt God by separating what He of His good pleasure has most intimately joined together. For grace is conferred by means of admonitions;

and the more readily we perform our duty, the more clearly this favor of God, working in us, usually manifests itself, and the more directly His work is advanced; to whom alone all the glory, both for the means and for their saving fruit and efficacy, is forever due. Amen.

REJECTION OF ERRORS

The true doctrine having been explained, the Synod rejects the errors of those:

Paragraph 1. Who teach: That it cannot properly be said that original sin in itself suffices to condemn the whole human race or to deserve temporal and eternal punishment.

For these contradict the apostle, who declares: *Therefore, as through one man sin entered into the world, and death through sin; and so death passed unto all men, for that all sinned* (Rom. 5:12). And: *The judgment came of one unto condemnation* (Rom. 5:16). And: *The wages of sin is death* (Rom. 6:23).

Paragraph 2. Who teach: That the spiritual gifts or the good qualities and virtues, such as goodness, holiness, righteousness, could not belong to the will of man when he was first created, and that these, therefore, cannot have been separated therefrom in the fall.

For such is contrary to the description of the image of God which the apostle gives in Eph. 4:24, where he declares that it consists in righteousness and holiness, which undoubtedly belong to the will.

Paragraph 3. Who teach: That in spiritual death the spiritual gifts are not separate from the will of man, since the will in itself has never been corrupted, but only hindered through the darkness of the understanding and the irregularity of the affections; and that, these hindrances having been removed, the will can then bring into operation its native powers, that is, that the will of itself is able to will and to choose, or not to will and not to choose, all manner of good which may be presented to it.

This is an innovation and an error, and tends to elevate the powers of the free will, contrary to the declaration of the prophet: *The heart is deceitful above all things, and it is exceedingly corrupt* (Jer. 17:9); and of the apostle: *Among whom* (sons of disobedience) *we also all once lived in the lusts of our flesh, doing the desires of the flesh and of the mind* (Eph. 2:3).

Paragraph 4. Who teach: That the unregenerate man is not really nor utterly dead in sin, nor destitute of all powers unto spiritual good, but that he can yet hunger and thirst after righteousness and life, and offer the sacrifice of a contrite and broken spirit, which is pleasing to God.

For these things are contrary to the express testimony of Scripture: *Ye were dead through your trespasses and sins* (Eph. 2:1, 5). And: *Every imagination of the thoughts of his heart was only evil continually* (Gen.

6:5; 8:21). Moreover, to hunger and thirst after deliverance from misery and after life, and to offer unto God the sacrifice of a broken spirit, is peculiar to the regenerate and those that are called blessed (Ps. 51:17; Matt. 5:6).

Paragraph 5. Who teach: That the corrupt and natural man can so well use the common grace (by which they understand the light of nature), or the gifts still left him after the fall, that he can gradually gain by their good use a greater, that is, the evangelical or saving grace, and salvation itself; and that in this way God on His part shows Himself ready to reveal Christ unto all men, since He applies to all sufficiently and efficiently the means necessary to conversion.

For both the experience of all ages and the Scriptures testify that this is untrue. *He showeth his word unto Jacob, his statutes and his ordances unto Israel. He hath not dealt so with any nation; and as for his ordinances, they have not known them* (Ps. 147:19, 20). *Who in the generations gone by suffered all the nations to walk in their own way* (Acts 14:16). And: *And they* (Paul and his companions) *having been forbidden of the Holy Spirit to speak the word in Asia, when they were come over against Mysia, they assayed to go into Bithynia, and the Spirit of Jesus suffered them not* (Acts 16:6,7).

Paragraph 6. Who teach: That in the true conversion of man no new qualities, powers, or gifts can be infused by God into the will, and that therefore faith, through which we are first converted and because of which we are called believers, is not a quality or gift infused by God but only an act of man, and that it cannot be said to be a gift, except in respect of the power to attain to this faith.

For thereby they contradict the Holy Scriptures, which declare that God infuses new qualities of faith, of obedience, and of the consciousness of His love into our hearts: *I will put my law in their inward parts, and in their heart will I write it* (Jer. 31:33). And: *I will pour water upon him that is thirsty, and streams upon the dry ground; I will pour my Spirit upon thy seed* (Is. 44:3). And: *The love of God hath been shed abroad in our hearts through the Holy Spirit which was given unto us* (Rom. 5:5). This is also repugnant to the constant practice of the Church, which prays by the mouth of the prophet thus: *Turn thou me, and I shall be turned* (Jer. 31:18).

Paragraph 7. Who teach: That the grace whereby we are converted to God is only a gentle advising, or (as others explain it) that this is the noblest manner of working in the conversion of man, and that this manner of working, which consists in advising, is most in harmony with man's nature; and that there is no reason why this advising grace alone should not be sufficient to make the natural man spiritual; indeed, that God does not produce the consent of the will except through this manner of advising; and that the power of the divine working, whereby it surpasses the working of Satan, consists in this that God promises eternal, while Satan promises only temporal goods.

But this is altogether Pelagian and contrary to the whole Scripture, which, besides this, teaches yet another and far more powerful and divine manner of the Holy Spirit's working in the conversion of man, as in Ezekiel: *A new heart also will I give you, and a new spirit will I put within you; and I will take away the stony heart out of your flesh, and I will give you a heart of flesh* (Ezek. 36:26).

Paragraph 8. Who teach: That God in the regeneration of man does not use such powers of His omnipotence as potently and infallibly bend man's will to faith and conversion; but that all the works of grace having been accomplished, which God employs to convert man, man may yet so resist God and the Holy Spirit, when God intends man's regeneration and wills to regenerate him, and indeed that man often does so resist that he prevents entirely his regeneration, and that it therefore remains in man's power to be regenerated or not.

For this is nothing less than the denial of all the efficiency of God's grace in our conversion, and the subjecting of the working of Almighty God to the will of man, which is contrary to the apostles, who teach that *we believe according to the working of the strength of his might* (Eph. 1:19); and that *God fulfils every desire of goodness and every work of faith with power* (2 Thess. 1:11); and that *his divine power hath granted unto us all things that pertain unto life and godliness* (2 Peter 1:3).

Paragraph 9. Who teach: That grace and free will are partial causes which together work the beginning of conversion, and that grace, in order of working, does not precede the working of the will; that is, that God does not efficiently help the will of man unto conversion until the will of man moves and determines to do this.

For the ancient Church has long ago condemned this doctrine of the Pelagians according to the words of the apostle: *So then it is not of him that willeth, nor of him that runneth, but of God that hath mercy* (Rom. 9:16). Likewise: *For who maketh thee to differ? and what hast thou that thou didst not receive?* (I Cor. 4:7). And: *For it is God who worketh in you both to will and to work, for his good pleasure* (Phil. 2:13).

FIFTH HEAD OF DOCTRINE. THE PERSEVERANCE OF THE SAINTS

Article 1. Those whom God, according to His purpose, calls to the communion of His Son, our Lord Jesus Christ, and regenerates by the Holy Spirit, He also delivers from the dominion and slavery of sin, though in this life He does not deliver them altogether from the body of sin and from the infirmities of the flesh.

Article 2. Hence spring forth the daily sins of infirmity, and blemishes cleave even to the best works of the saints. These are to them a perpetual reason to humiliate themselves before God and to flee for refuge to Christ crucified; to mortify the flesh more and more by the spirit of prayer and by holy exercises of piety; and to press forward to the goal of perfection, until at length, delivered from this body of death, they shall reign with the Lamb of God in heaven.

Article 3. By reason of these remains of indwelling sin, and also because the temptations of the world and of Satan, those who are converted could not persevere in that grace if left to their own strength. But God is faithful, who, having conferred grace, mercifully confirms and powerfully preserves them therein, even to the end.

Article 4. Although the weakness of the flesh cannot prevail against the power of God, who confirms and preserves true believers in a state of grace, yet converts are not always so influenced and actuated by the Spirit of God as not in some particular instances sinfully to deviate from the guidance of divine grace, so as to be seduced by and to comply with the lusts of the flesh; they must, therefore, be constant in watching and prayer, that they may not be led into temptation. When these are neglected, they are not only liable to be drawn into great and heinous sins by the flesh, the world, and Satan, but sometimes by the righteous permission of God actually are drawn into these evils. This, the lamentable fall of David, Peter, and other saints described in Holy Scripture, demonstrates.

Article 5. By such enormous sins, however, they very highly offend God, incur a deadly guilt, grieve the Holy Spirit, interrupt the exercise of faith, very grievously wound their consciences, and sometimes for a while lose the sense of God's favor, until, when they change their course by serious repentance, the light of God's fatherly countenance again shines upon them.

Article 6. But God, who is rich in mercy, according to His unchangeable purpose of election, does not wholly withdraw the Holy Spirit from His own people even in their greivous falls; nor suffers them to proceed so far as to lose the grace of adoption and forfeit the state of justification, or to commit the sin unto death or against the Holy Spirit; nor does He permit them to be totally deserted, and to plunge themselves into everlasting destruction.

Article 7. For in the first place, in these falls He preserves in them the incorruptible seed of regeneration from perishing or being totally lost; and again, by His Word and Spirit He certainly and effectually renews them to repentance, to a sincere and godly sorrow for their sins, that they may seek and obtain remission in the blood of the Mediator, may again experience the favor of a reconciled God, through faith adore His mercies, and henceforward more diligently work out their own salvation with fear and trembling.

Article 8. Thus it is not in consequence of their own merits or strength, but of God's free mercy, that they neither totally fall from faith and grace nor continue and perish finally in their backslidings; which, with respect to themselves is not only possible, but would undoubtedly happen; but with respect to God, it is utterly impossible, since His counsel cannot be changed nor His promise fail; neither can the call according to His purpose be revoked, nor the merit, intercession, and preservation of Christ be rendered ineffectual, nor the sealing of the Holy Spirit be frustrated or obliterated.

Article 9. Of this preservation of the elect to salvation and of their preseverance in the faith, true believers themselves may and do obtain assurance according to the measure of their faith, whereby they surely believe that they are and ever will continue true and living members of the Church, and that they have the forgiveness of sins and life eternal.

Article 10. This assurance, however, is not produced by any peculiar revelation contrary to or independent of the Word of God, but springs from faith in God's promises, which He has most abundantly revealed in His Word for our comfort; from the testimony of the Holy Spirit, witnessing with our spirit that we are children and heirs of God (Rom. 8:16); and lastly, from a serious and holy desire to preserve a good conscience and to perform good works. And if the elect of God were deprived of this solid comfort that they shall finally obtain the victory, and of this infallible pledge of eternal glory, they would be of all men the most miserable.

Article 11. The Scripture moreover testifies that believers in this life have to struggle with various carnal doubts, and that under grievous temptations they do not always feel this full assurance of faith and certainty of persevering. But God, who is the Father of all consolation, does not suffer them to be tempted above that they are able, but will with the temptation make also the way of escape, that they may be able to endure it (1 Cor. 10:13), and by the Holy Spirit again inspires them with the comfortable assurance of persevering.

Article 12. This certainty of perseverance, however, is so far from exciting in believers a spirit of pride, or of rendering them carnally secure, that on the contrary it is the real source of humility, filial reverence, true piety, patience in every tribulation, fervent prayers, constancy in suffering and in confessing the truth, and of solid rejoicing in God; so that the consideration of this benefit should serve as an incentive to the serious and constant practice of gratitude and good works, as appears from the testimonies of Scripture and the examples of the saints.

Article 13. Neither does renewed confidence of persevering produce licentiousness or a disregard of piety in those who are recovered from backsliding; but it renders them much more careful and solicitous to continue in the ways of the Lord, which He has ordained, that they who walk therein may keep the assurance of persevering; lest, on account of their abuse of His fatherly kindness, God should turn away His gracious countenance from them (to behold which is to the godly dearer than life, and the withdrawal of which is more bitter than death) and they in consequence thereof should fall into more grievous torments of conscience.

Article 14. And as it has pleased God, by the preaching of the gospel, to begin this work of grace in us, so He preserves, continues, and perfects it by the hearing and reading of His Word, by meditation thereon, and by the exhortations, threatenings, and promises thereof, and by the use of the sacraments.

Article 15. The carnal mind is unable to comprehend this doctrine of the perseverance of the saints and the certainty thereof, which God has most abundantly revealed in His Word, for the glory of His Name and the consolation of pious souls, and which He impresses upon the hearts of the believers. Satan abhors it, the world ridicules it, the ignorant and hypocritical abuse it, and the heretics oppose it. But the bride of Christ has always most tenderly loved and constantly defended it as an inestimable treasure; and God, against whom neither counsel nor strength can prevail, will dispose her so to continue to the end. Now to this one God, Father, Son, and Holy Spirit, be honor and glory forever. Amen.

REJECTION OF ERRORS

The true doctrine having been explained, the Synod rejects the errors of those:

Paragraph 1. Who teach: That the perseverance of the true believers is not a fruit of election, or a gift of God gained by the death of Christ, but a condition of the new covenant, which (as they declare) man before his decisive election and justification must fulfil through his free will.

For the Holy Scripture testifies that this follows out of election, and is given the elect in virtue of the death, the resurrection, and intercession of Christ: *But the election obtained it, and the rest were hardened* (Rom. 11:7). Likewise: *He that spared not his own Son, but delivered him up for us all, how shall he not also with him freely give us all things? Who shall lay anything to the charge of God's elect? It is God that justifieth; who is he that condemneth? It is Christ Jesus that died, yea rather, that was raised from the dead, who is at the right hand of God, who also maketh intercession for us. Who shall separate us from the love of Christ?* (Rom. 8:32-35).

Paragraph 2. Who teach: That God does indeed provide the believer with sufficient powers to persevere, and is ever ready to preserve these in him if he will do his duty; but that, though all things which are necessary to persevere in faith and which God will use to preserve faith are made use of, even then it ever depends on the pleasure of the will whether it will persevere or not.

For this idea contains an outspoken Pelagianism, and while it would make men free, it makes them robbers of God's honor, contrary to the prevailing agreement of the evangelical doctrine, which takes from man all cause of boasting, and ascribes all the praise for this favor to the grace of God alone; and contrary to the apostle, who declares that it is God, *who shall also confirm you unto the end*, that ye be *unreprovable in the day of our Lord Jesus Christ* (1 Cor. 1:8).

Paragraph 3. Who teach: That the true believers and regenerate not only can fall from justifying faith and likewise from grace and salvation wholly and to the end, but indeed often do fall from this and are lost forever.

For this conception makes powerless the grace, justification, regeneration, and continued preservation by Christ, contrary to the expressed words of the apostle Paul: *That, while we were yet sinners, Christ died for us. Much more then, being now justified by his blood, shall we be saved from the wrath* of God *through him* (Rom. 5:8, 9). And contrary to the apostle John: *Whosoever is begotten of God doeth no sin, because his seed abideth in him; and he can not sin, because he is begotten of God* (1 John 3:9). And also contrary to the words of Jesus Christ: *I give unto them eternal life; and they shall never perish, and no one shall snatch them out of my hand. My Father, who hath given* them *to me, is greater than all; and no one is able to snatch* them *out of the Father's hand* (John 10:28, 29).

Paragraph 4. Who teach: That true believers and regenerate can sin the sin unto death or against the Holy Spirit.

Since the same apostle John, after having spoken in the fifth chapter of his first epistle, vs. 16 and 17, of those who sin unto death and having forbidden to pray for them, immediately adds to this in vs. 18: *We know that whosoever is begotten of God sinneth not* (meaning a sin of that character), *but he that was begotten of God keepeth himself, and the evil one toucheth him not* (1 John 5:18).

Paragraph 5. Who teach: That without a special revelation we can have no certainty of future perseverance in this life.

For by this doctrine the sure comfort of the true believers is taken away in this life, and the doubts of the papist are again introduced into the Church, while the Holy Scriptures constantly deduce this assurance, not from a special and extraordinary revelation, but from the marks proper to the children of God and from the very constant promises of God. So especially the apostle Paul: *No creature shall be able to separate us from the love of God, which is in Christ Jesus our Lord* (Rom. 8:39). And John declares: *And he that keepeth his commandments abideth in him, and he in him. And hereby we know that he abideth in us, by the Spirit which he gave us* (1 John 3:24).

Paragraph 6. Who teach: That the doctrine of the certainty of perseverance and of salvation from its own character and nature is a cause of indolence and is injurious to godliness, good morals, prayers, and other holy exercises, but that on the contrary it is praiseworthy to doubt.

For these show that they do not know the power of divine grace and the working of the indwelling Holy Spirit. And they contradict the apostle John, who teaches the opposite with express words in his first epistle: *Beloved, now are we children of God, and it is not yet made manifest what we shall be. We know that, if he shall be manifested, we shall be like him; for we shall see him even as he is. And every one that hath this hope* set *on him purifieth himself, even as he is pure* (1 John 3:2, 3). Furthermore, these are contradicted by the example of the saints, both of the Old and the New Testament, who though they were assured of their perseverance and salvation, were nevertheless constant in prayers and other exercises of godliness.

Paragraph 7. Who teach: That the faith of those who believe for a time does not differ from justifying and saving faith except only in duration.

For Christ Himself, in Matt. 13:20, Luke 8:13, and in other places, evidently notes, besides this duration, a threefold difference between those who believe only for a time and true believers, when He declares that the former receive the seed in stony ground, but the latter in the good ground or heart; that the former are without root, but the latter have a firm root; that the former are without fruit, but that the latter bring forth their fruit in various measure, with constancy and stedfastness.

Paragraph 8. Who teach: That it is not absurd that one having lost his first regeneration is again and even often born anew.

For these deny by this doctrine the incorruptibleness of the seed of God, whereby we are born again; contrary to the testimony of the apostle Peter: *Having been begotten again, not of corruptible seed, but of incorruptible* (Peter 1-23).

Paragraph 9. Who teach: That Christ has in no place prayed that believers should infallibly continue in faith.

For they contradict Christ Himself, who says: *I made supplication for thee* (Simon), *that thy faith fail not* (Luke 22:32), and the evangelist John, who declares that Christ has not prayed for the apostles only, but also for those who through their word would believe: *Holy Father, keep them in thy name*, and: *I pray not that thou shouldest take them from the world, but that thou shouldest keep them from the evil one* (John 17:11, 15, 20).

CONCLUSION

And this is the perspicuous, simple, and ingenuous declaration of the orthodox doctrine respecting the five articles which have been controverted in the Belgic Churches; and the rejection of the errors, with which they have for some time been troubled. This doctrine the Synod judges to be drawn from the Word of God, and to be agreeable to the confession of the Reformed Churches.

CANONS OF DORT (continued)

Whence it clearly appears that some, whom such conduct by no means became, have violated all truth, equity, and charity, in wishing to persuade the public:

'That the doctrine of the Reformed Churches concerning predestination, and the points annexed to it, by its own genius and necessary tendency, leads off the minds of men from all piety and religion; that it is an opiate administered by the flesh and the devil; and the stronghold of Satan, where he lies in wait for all, and from which he wounds multitudes, and mortally strikes through many with the darts both of despair and security; that it makes God the author of sin, unjust, tyrannical, hypocritical; that it is nothing more than an interpolated Stoicism, Manicheism, Libertinism, Turcism; that it renders men carnally secure, since they are persuaded by it that nothing can hinder the salvation of the elect, let them live as they please; and, therefore, that they may safely perpetrate every species of the most atrocious crimes; and that, if the reprobate should even perform truly all the works of the saints, their obedience would not in the least contribute to their salvation; that the same doctrine teaches that God, by a mere arbitrary act of his will, without the least respect or view to any sin, has predestinated the greatest part of the world to eternal damnation, and has created them for this very purpose; that in the same manner in which the election is the fountain and cause of faith and good works, reprobation is the cause of unbelief and impiety; that many children of the faithful are torn, guiltless, from their mothers' breasts, and tyrannically plunged into hell: so that neither baptism nor the prayers of the Church at their baptism can at all profit them;' and many other things of the same kind which the Reformed Churches not only do not acknowledge, but even detest with their whole soul.

Wherefore, this Synod of Dort, in the name of the Lord, conjures as many as piously call upon the name of our Saviour Jesus Christ to judge of the faith of the Reformed Churches, not from the calumnies which on every side are heaped upon it, nor from the private expressions of a few among ancient and modern teachers, often dishonestly quoted, or corrupted and wrested to a meaning quite foreign to their intention; but from the public confessions of the Churches themselves, and from this declaration of the orthodox doctrine, confirmed by the unanimous consent of all and each of the members of the whole Synod. Moreover, the Synod warns calumniators themselves to consider the terrible judgment of God which awaits them, for bearing false witness against the confessions of so many Churches; for distressing the consciences of the weak; and for laboring to render suspected the society of the truly faithful.

Finally, this Synod exhorts all their brethren in the gospel of Christ to conduct themselves piously and religiously in handling this doctrine, both in the universities and churches; to direct it, as well in discourse as in writing, to the glory of the Divine name, to holiness of life, and to the consolation of afflicted souls; to regulate, by the Scripture, according to the analogy of faith, not only their sentiments, but also their language, and to abstain from all those phrases which exceed the limits necessary to be observed in ascertaining the genuine sense of the Holy Scriptures, and may furnish insolent sophists with a just pretext for violently assailing, or even vilifying, the doctrine of the Reformed Churches.

May Jesus Christ, the Son of God, who, seated at the Father's right hand, gives gifts to men, sanctify us in the truth; bring to the truth those who err; shut the mouths of the calumniators of sound doctrine, and endue the faithful ministers of his Word with the spirit of wisdom and discretion, that all their discourses may tend to the glory of God, and the edification of those who hear them. Amen.

Notes: *The Canons of Dort were issued by a synod of the Reformed Church in the Netherlands that met from November 13, 1618, through May 9, 1619. Among the items considered at that synod were the opinions of Jacob Arminius, who had sought to introduce a place for human free-will into the Calvinist theological system. He had proposed these basic ideas: 1) God's foreknowledge as prior to his predestination; 2) partial human depravity; 3) the universality of Christ's atonement; 4) the resistibility of God's grace; and 5) the possibility that a person could fall away from saving grace once received.*

The Synod of Dort (or Dordrecht) responded by declaring faith in 1) God's total and unconditional predestination; 2) complete and utter human depravity; 3) Christ's atonement limited to the saved; 4) the irresistible nature of God's grace; and 5) the guaranteed perseverance of believers. The so-called five points of the synod have frequently been summarized for theological students in a manner appropriate to the Dutch origin of the Canons:

T   Total Depravity

U   Unconditional election (predestination)

L   Limited atonement

I   Irresistible grace

P   Perseverance of the saints

The text of the Canons reproduced here was taken from A Treatise of the Compendium *by G. H. Kersten (Grand Rapids, MI: Inheritance Publishing Co., 1956).*

*   *   *

SECOND HELVETIC CONFESSION (HUNGARIAN REFORMED CHURCH)

CHAPTER 1. OF THE HOLY SCRIPTURE BEING THE TRUE WORD OF GOD

CANONICAL SCRIPTURE. We believe and confess the canonical Scriptures of the holy prophets and apostles of both Testaments to be the true Word of God, and to have sufficient authority of themselves, not of men. For God himself spoke to the fathers, prophets, apostles, and still speaks to us through the Holy Scriptures.

And in this Holy Scripture, the universal Church of Christ has the most complete exposition of all that pertains to a saving faith, and also to the framing of a life acceptable to God; and in this respect it is expressly commanded by God that nothing be either added to or taken from the same.

SCRIPTURE TEACHES FULLY ALL GODLINESS. We judge, therefore, that from these Scriptures are to be derived true wisdom and godliness, the reformation and government of churches; as also instruction in all duties of piety; and, to be short, the confirmation of doctrines, and the rejection of all errors, moreover, all exhortations according to that word of the apostle, "All Scripture is inspired by God and profitable for teaching, for reproof," etc. (II Tim. 3:16-17). Again, "I am writing these instructions to you," says the apostle to Timothy, "so that you may know how one ought to behave in the household of God," etc. (I Tim. 3:14-15). *Scripture Is the Word of God*. Again, the selfsame apostle to the Thessalonians: "When," says he, "you received the Word of God which you heard from us, you accepted it, not as the word of men but as what it really is, the Word of God," etc. (I Thess. 2:13). For the Lord himself has said in the Gospel, "It is not you who speak, but the Spirit of my Father speaking through you"; therefore "he who hears you hears me, and he who rejects me rejects him who sent me" (Matt. 10:20; Luke 10:16; John 13:20).

THE PREACHING OF THE WORD OF GOD IS THE WORD OF GOD. Wherefore when this Word of God is now preached in the church by preachers lawfully called, we believe that the very Word of God is proclaimed, and received by the faithful; and that neither any other Word of God is to be invented nor is to be expected from heaven: and that now the Word itself which is preached is to be regarded, not the minister that preaches; for even if he be evil and a sinner, nevertheless the Word of God remains still true and good.

Neither do we think that therefore the outward preaching is to be thought as fruitless because the instruction in true religion depends on the inward illumination of the Spirit, or because it is written "And no longer shall each man teach his neighbor . . . , for they shall all know me" (Jer. 31:34), and "Neither he who plants nor he who waters is anything, but only God who gives the growth" (I Cor. 3:7). For although "no one can come to Christ unless he be drawn by the Father" (John 6:44), and unless the Holy Spirit inwardly illumines him, yet we know that it is surely the will of God that his Word should be preached outwardly also. God could indeed, by his Holy Spirit, or by the ministry of an angel, without the ministry of St. Peter, have taught Cornelius in the Acts; but, nevertheless, he refers him to Peter, of whom the angel speaking says, "He shall tell you what you ought to do."

INWARD ILLUMINATION DOES NOT ELIMINATE EXTERNAL PREACHING. For he that illuminates inwardly by giving men the Holy Spirit, the same one, by way of commandment, said unto his disciples, "Go into all the world, and preach the Gospel to the whole creation" (Mark 16:15). And so in Philippi, Paul preached the Word outwardly to Lydia, a seller of purple goods; but the Lord inwardly opened the woman's heart (Acts 16:14).

And the same Paul, after a beautiful development of his thought, in Rom. 10:17 at length comes to the conclusion. "So faith comes from hearing, and hearing from the Word of God by the preaching of Christ."

At the same time we recognize that God can illuminate whom and when he will, even without the external ministry, for that is in his power: but we speak of the usual way of instructing men, delivered unto us from God, both by commandment and examples.

HERESIES. We therefore detest all the heresies of Artemon, the Manichaeans, the Valentinians, of Cerdon, and the Marcionites, who denied that the Scriptures proceeded from the Holy Spirit; or did not accept some parts of them, or interpolated and corrupted them.

APOCRYPHA. And yet we do not conceal the fact that certain books of the Old Testament were by the ancient authors called *Apocryphal*, and by others *Ecclesiastical*; inasmuch as some would have them read in the churches, but not advanced as an authority from which the faith is to be established. As Augstine also, in his *De Civitate Dei*, book 18, ch. 38, remarks that "in the books of the Kings, the names and books of certain prophets are cited"; but he adds that "they are not in the canon"; and that "those books which we have suffice unto godliness."

CHAPTER II. OF INTERPRETING THE HOLY SCRIPTURES; AND OF FATHERS, COUNCILS, AND TRADITIONS

THE TRUE INTERPRETATION OF SCRIPTURE. The apostle Peter has said that the Holy Scriptures are not of private interpretation (II Peter 1:20), and thus we do not allow all possible interpretations. Nor consequently do we acknowledge as the true or genuine interpretation of the Scriptures what is called the conception of the Roman Church, that is, what the defenders of the Roman Church plainly maintain should be thrust upon all for acceptance. But we hold that interpretation of the Scripture to be orthodox and genuine which is gleaned from the Scriptures themselves (from the nature of the language in which they were written, likewise according to the circumstances in which they were set down, and expounded in the light of like and unlike passages and of many and clearer passages) and which agree with the rule of faith and love, and contributes much to the glory of God and man's salvation.

INTERPRETATIONS OF THE HOLY FATHERS. Wherefore we do not despise the interpretations of the holy Greek and Latin fathers, nor reject their disputations and treatises concerning sacred matters as far as they agree with the Scriptures; but we modestly dissent from them when they are found to set down things differing from, or altogether contrary to, the Scriptures. Neither do we think that we do them any wrong in this matter; seeing that they all, with one consent, will not have their writings equated with the canonical Scriptures, but command us to prove how far they agree or disagree with them, and to accept what is in agreement and to reject what is in disagreement.

COUNCILS. And in the same order also we place the decrees and canons of councils.

Wherefore we do not permit ourselves, in controversies about religion or matters of faith, to urge our case with only the opinions of the fathers or decrees of councils; much less by received customs, or by the large number of those who share the same opinion, or by the prescription of a long time. *Who is the Judge?* Therefore, we do not admit any other judge than God himself, who proclaims by the Holy Scriptures what is true, what is false, what is to be followed, or what is to be avoided. So we do assent to the judgments of spiritual men which are drawn from the Word of God. Certainly Jeremiah and other prophets vehemently condemned the assemblies of priests which were set up against the law of God; and diligently admonished us that we should not listen to the fathers, or tread in their path who, walking in their own inventions, swerved from the law of God.

TRADITIONS OF MEN. Likewise we reject human traditions, even if they be adorned with high-sounding titles, as though they were divine and apostolical, delivered to the Church by the living voice of the apostles, and, as it were, through the hands of apostolical men to succeeding bishops which, when compared with the Scriptures, disagree with them; and by their disagreement show that they are not apostolic at all. For as the apostles did not contradict themselves in doctrine, so the apostolic men did not set forth things contrary to the apostles. On the contrary, it would be wicked to assert that the apostles by a living voice delivered anything contrary to their writings. Paul affirms expressly that he taught the same things in all churches (I Cor. 4:17). And, again, "For we write you nothing but what you can read and understand" (II Cor. 1:13). Also, in another place, he testifies that he and his disciples— that is, apostolic men—walked in the same way, and jointly by the same Spirit did all things (II Cor. 12:18). Moreover, the Jews in former times had the traditions of their elders; but these traditions were severely rejected by the Lord, indicating that the keeping of them hinders God's law, and that God is worshipped in vain by such traditions (Matt. 15:1 ff.; Mark 7:1 ff.).

CHAPTER III. OF GOD, HIS UNITY AND TRINITY

GOD IS ONE. We believe and teach that God is one in essence or nature, subsisting in himself, all sufficient in himself, invisible, incorporeal, immense, eternal, Creator of all things both visible and invisible, the greatest good, living, quickening and preserving all things, omnipotent and supremely wise, kind and merciful, just and true. Truly we

detest many gods because it is expressly written "The Lord your God is one Lord" (Deut. 6:4). "I am the Lord your God. You shall have no other gods before me" (Ex. 20:2-3). "I am the Lord, and there is no other god besides me. Am I not the Lord, and there is no other God beside me? A righteous God and a Savior; there is none besides me" (Isa. 45:5, 21). "The Lord, the Lord, a God merciful and gracious, slow to anger, and abounding in steadfast love and faithfulness" (Ex. 34:6).

GOD IS THREE. Notwithstanding we believe and teach that the same immense, one and indivisible God is in person inseparably and without confusion distinguished as Father, Son and Holy Spirit so, as the Father has begotten the Son from eternity, the Son is begotten by an ineffable generation, and the Holy Spirit truly proceeds from them both, and the same from eternity and is to be worshipped with both. Thus there are not three gods, but three persons, consubstantial, coeternal, and coequal; distinct with respect to hypostases, and with respect to order, the one preceding the other yet without any inequality. For according to the nature or essence they are so joined together that they are one God, and the divine nature is common to the Father, Son and Holy Spirit.

For Scripture has delivered to us a manifest distinction of persons, the angel saying, among other things, to the Blessed Virgin, "The Holy Spirit will come upon you, and the power of the Most High will overshadow you; therefore the child to be born will be called holy, the Son of God" (Luke 1:35). And also in the baptism of Christ a voice is heard from heaven concerning Christ, saying, "This is my beloved Son" (Matt. 3:17). The Holy Spirit also appeared in the form of a dove. (John 1:32.) And when the Lord himself commanded the apostles to baptize, he commanded them to baptize "in the name of the Father, and the Son, and the Holy Spirit" (Matt. 28:19). Elsewhere in the Gospel he said: "The Father will send the Holy Spirit in my name" (John 14:26), and again he said: "When the Counselor comes, whom I shall send to you from the Father, even the Spirit of truth, who proceeds from the Father, he will bear witness to me," etc. (John 15:26). In short, we receive the Apostles' Creed because it delivers to us the true faith.

HERESIES. Therefore we condemn the Jews and Mohammedans, and all those who blaspheme that sacred and adorable Trinity. We also condemn all heresies and heretics who teach that the Son and Holy Spirit are God in name only, and also that there is something created and subservient, or subordinate to another in the Trinity, and that there is something unequal in it, a greater or a less, something corporeal or corporeally conceived, something different with respect to character or will, something mixed or solitary, as if the Son and Holy Spirit were the affections and properties of one God the Father, as the Monarchians, Novatians, Praxeas, Patripassians, Sabellius, Paul of Samosata, Aëtius,

Macedonius, Anthropomorphites, Arius, and such like, have thought.

CHAPTER IV. OF IDOLS OR IMAGES OF GOD, CHRIST AND THE SAINTS

IMAGES OF GOD. Since God as Spirit is in essence invisible and immense, he cannot really be expressed by any art or image. For this reason we have no fear pronouncing with Scripture that images of God are mere lies. Therefore we reject not only the idols of the Gentiles, but also the images of Christians. *Images of Christ.* Although Christ assumed human nature, yet he did not on that account assume it in order to provide a model for carvers and painters. He denied that he had come "to abolish the law and the prophets" (Matt. 5:17). But images are forbidden by the law and the prophets (Deut. 4:15; Isa. 44:9). He denied that his bodily presence would be profitable for the Church, and promised that he would be near us by his Spirit forever (John 16:7). Who, therefore, would believe that a shadow or likeness of his body would contribute any benefit to the pious? (II Cor. 5:5). Since he abides in us by his Spirit, we are therefore the temple of God (I Cor. 3:16). But "what agreement has the temple of God with idols?" (II Cor. 6:16). *Images of Saints.* And since the blessed spirits and saints in heaven, while they lived here on earth, rejected all worship of themselves (Acts 3:12 f.; 14: 11 ff.; Rev. 14:7; 22:9) and condemned images, shall anyone find it likely that the heavenly saints and angels are pleased with their own images before which men kneel, uncover their heads, and bestow other honors?

But in fact in order to instruct men in religion and to remind them of divine things and of their salvation, the Lord commanded the preaching of the Gospel (Mark 16:15)—not to paint and to teach the laity by means of pictures. Moreover, he instituted sacraments, but nowhere did he set up images. *The Scriptures of the Laity.* Furthermore, wherever we turn our eyes, we see the living and true creatures of God which, if they be observed, as is proper, make a much more vivid impression on the beholders than all the images or vain, motionless, feeble and dead pictures made by men, of which the prophet truly said: "They have eyes, but do not see" (Ps. 115:5).

LACTANTIUS. Therefore we approved the judgment of Lactantius, an ancient writer, who says: "Undoubtedly no religion exists where there is an image." *Epiphanius and Jerome.* We also assert that the blessed bishop Epiphanius did right when, finding on the doors of a church a veil on which was painted a picture supposedly of Christ or some saint, he ripped it down and took it away, because to see a picture of a man hanging in the Church of Christ was contrary to the authority of Scripture. Wherefore he charged that from henceforth no such veils, which were contrary to our religion, should be hung in the Church of Christ, and that rather such questionable things, unworthy of the Church of Christ and the faithful people, should be removed.

Moreover, we approve of this opinion of St. Augustine concerning true religion: "Let not the worship of the works of men be a religion for us. For the artists themselves who make such things are better; yet we ought not to worship them" (*De Vera Religione*, cap. 55).

CHAPTER V. OF THE ADORATION, WORSHIP AND INVOCATION OF GOD THROUGH THE ONLY MEDIATOR JESUS CHRIST

GOD ALONE IS TO BE ADORED AND WORSHIPPED. We teach that the true God alone is to be adored and worshipped. This honor we impart to none other, according to the commandment of the Lord, "You shall worship the Lord your God and him only shall you serve" (Matt. 4:10). Indeed, all the prophets severely inveighed against the people of Israel whenever they adored and worshipped strange gods, and not the only true God. But we teach that God is to be adored and worshipped as he himself has taught us to worship, namely, "in spirit and in truth" (John 4:23 f.), not with any superstition, but with sincerity, according to his Word; lest at any time he should say to us: "Who has required these things from your hands?" (Isa. 1:12; Jer. 6:20). For Paul also says: "God is not served by human hands, as though he needed anything," etc. (Acts 17:25).

GOD ALONE IS TO BE INVOKED THROUGH THE MEDIATION OF CHRIST ALONE. In all crises and trials of our life we call upon him alone, and that by the mediation of our only mediator and intercessor, Jesus Christ. For we have been explicitly commanded: "Call upon me in the day of trouble; I will deliver you, and you shall glorify me" (Ps. 1:15). Moreover, we have a most generous promise from the Lord Who said: "If you ask anything of the Father, he will give it to you" (John 16:23), and: "Come to me, all who labor and are heavy laden, and I will give you rest" (Matt. 11:28). And since it is written: "How are men to call upon him in whom they have not believed?" (Rom. 10:14), and since we do believe in God alone, we assuredly call upon him alone, and we do so through Christ. For as the apostle says, "There is one God and there is one mediator between God and men, the man Christ Jesus" (I Tim. 2:5), and, "If any one does sin, we have an advocate with the Father, Jesus Christ the righteous," etc. (I John 2:1).

THE SAINTS ARE NOT TO BE ADORED, WORSHIPPED OR INVOKED. For this reason we do not adore, worship, or pray to the saints in heaven, or to other gods, and we do not acknowledge them as our intercessors or mediators before the Father in heaven. For God and Christ the Mediator are sufficient for us; neither do we give to others the honor that is due to God alone and to his Son, because he has expressly said: "My glory I give to no other" (Isa. 42:8), and because Peter has said: "There is no other name under heaven given among men by which we must be saved," except the name of Christ

(Acts 4:12). In him, those who give their assent by faith do not seek anything outside Christ.

THE DUE HONOR TO BE RENDERED TO THE SAINTS. At the same time we do not despise the saints or think basely of them. For we acknowledge them to be living members of Christ and friends of God who have gloriously overcome the flesh and the world. Hence we love them as brothers, and also honor them; yet not with any kind of worship but by an honorable opinion of them and just praises of them. We also imitate them. For with ardent longings and supplications we earnestly desire to be imitators of their faith and virtues, to share eternal salvation with them, to dwell eternally with them in the presence of God, and to rejoice with them in Christ. And in this respect we approve of the opinion of St. Augustine in *De Vera Religione*: "Let not our religion be the cult of men who have died. For if they have lived holy lives, they are not to be thought of as seeking such honors; on the contrary, they want us to worship him by whose illumination they rejoice that we are fellow-servants of his merits. They are therefore to be honored by way of imitation, but not to be adored in a religious manner," etc.

RELICS OF THE SAINTS. Much less do we believe that the relics of the saints are to be adored and reverenced. Those ancient saints seemed to have sufficiently honored their dead when they decently committed their remains to the earth after the spirit had ascended on high. And they thought that the most noble relics of their ancestors were their virtues, their doctrine, and their faith. Moreover, as they commend these "relics" when praising the dead, so they strive to copy them during their life on earth.

SWEARING BY GOD'S NAME ALONE. These ancient men did not swear except by the name of the only God, Yahweh, as prescribed by the divine law. Therefore, as it is forbidden to swear by the names of strange gods (Ex. 23:13; Deut. 10:20), so we do not perform oaths to the saints that are demanded of us. We therefore reject in all these matters a doctrine that ascribes much too much to the saints in heaven.

CHAPTER VI. OF THE PROVIDENCE OF GOD

ALL THINGS ARE GOVERNED BY THE PROVIDENCE OF GOD. We believe that all things in heaven and on earth, and in all creatures, are preserved and governed by the providence of this wise, eternal and almighty God. For David testifies and says: "The Lord is high above all nations, and his glory above the heavens! Who is like the Lord our God, who is seated on high, who looks far down upon the heavens and the earth?" (Ps. 113:4 ff.). Again: "Thou searchest out . . . all my ways. Even before a word is on my tongue, lo, O Lord, Thou knowest it altogether" (Ps. 139:3 f.). Paul also testifies and declares: "In him we live and move and have our being" (Acts 17:28), and "from him and through him and to him are all things" (Rom.

11:36). Therefore Augustine most truly and according to Scripture declared in his book *De Agon[e] Christi*, cap. 8, "The Lord said, 'Are not tw[o] sparrows sold for a penny? And not one of them wil[l] fall to the ground without your Father's will'" (Matt. 10:29). By speaking thus, he wanted to sho[w] that what men regard as of least value is governed b[y] God's omnipotence. For he who is the truth says tha[t] the birds of the air are fed by him and the lilies of th[e] field are clothed by him; he also says that the hairs o[f] our head are numbered. (Matt. 6:26 ff.)

THE EPICUREANS. We therefore condemn th[e] Epicureans who deny the providence of God, and al[l] those who blasphemously say that God is busy wit[h] the heavens and neither sees nor cares about us an[d] our affairs. David, the royal prophet, also con[-] demned this when he said: "O Lord, how long sha[ll] the wicked exult? They say, 'The Lord does not see[,] the God of Jacob does not perceive.' Understand, [O] dullest of the people! Fools, when will you be wise[?] He who planted the ear, does he not hear? He wh[o] formed the eye, does he not see?" (Ps. 94:3, 7-9)[.]

MEANS NOT TO BE DESPISED. Nevertheless, w[e] do not spurn as useless the means by which divin[e] providence works, but we teach that we are to adap[t] ourselves to them in so far as they are recommende[d] to us in the Word of God. Wherefore we disapprov[e] of the rash statements of those who say that if al[l] things are managed by the providence of God, the[n] our efforts and endeavors are in vain. It will b[e] sufficient if we leave everything to the governance o[f] divine providence, and we will not have to worr[y] about anything or do anything. For although Pau[l] understood that he sailed under the providence o[f] God who had said to him: "You must bear witnes[s] also at Rome" (Acts 23:11), and in addition ha[d] given him the promise, "There will be no loss of lif[e] among you . . . and not a hair is to perish from th[e] head of any of you" (Acts 27:22, 34), yet when th[e] sailors were nevertheless thinking about abandonin[g] ship the same Paul said to the centurion and th[e] soldiers: "Unless these men stay in the ship, yo[u] cannot be saved" (Acts 27:31). For God, who ha[s] appointed to everything its end, has ordained th[e] beginning and the means by which it reaches its goal[.] The heathen ascribe things to blind fortune an[d] uncertain chance. But St. James does not want us t[o] say: "Today or tomorrow we will go into such an[d] such a town and trade," but adds: "Instead yo[u] ought to say, 'If the Lord wills, we shall live and w[e] shall do this or that'" (James 4:13, 15). An[d] Augustine says: "Everything which to vain me[n] seems to happen in nature by accident, occurs onl[y] by his Word, because it happens only at hi[s] command" (*Enarrationes in Psalmos* 148). Thus i[t] seemed to happen by mere chance when Saul, whil[e] seeking his father's asses, unexpectedly fell in wit[h] the prophet Samuel. But previously the Lord ha[d] said to the prophet: "Tomorrow I will send to you [a] man from the land of Benjamin" (I Sam. 9:16).

CHAPTER VII. OF THE CREATION OF ALL THINGS: OF ANGELS, THE DEVIL, AND MAN

GOD CREATED ALL THINGS. This good and almighty God created all things, both visible and invisible, by his co-eternal Word, and preserves them by his co-eternal Spirit, as David testified when he said: "By the word of the Lord the heavens were made, and all their host by the breath of his mouth" (Ps. 33:6). And, as Scripture says, everything that God had made was very good, and was made for the profit and use of man. Now we assert that all those things proceed from one beginning. *Manichaeans and Marcionites.* Therefore, we condemn the Manichaeans and Marcionites who impiously imagined two substances and natures, one good, the other evil; also two beginnings and two gods contrary to each other, a good and an evil one.

OF ANGELS AND THE DEVIL. Among all creatures, angels and men are most excellent. Concerning angels, Holy Scripture declares: "Who makest the winds thy messengers, fire and flame thy ministers" (Ps. 104:4). Also it says: "Are they not all ministering spirits sent forth to serve, for the sake of those who are to obtain salvation?" (Heb. 1:14). Concerning the devil, the Lord Jesus himself testifies: "He was a murderer from the beginning, and has nothing to do with the truth, because there is no truth in him. When he lies, he speaks according to his own nature, for he is a liar and the father of lies" (John 8:44). Consequently we teach that some angels persisted in obedience and were appointed for faithful service to God and men, but others fell of their own free will and were cast into destruction, becoming enemies of all good and of the faithful, etc.

OF MAN. Now concerning man, Scripture says that in the beginning he was made good according to the image and likeness of God; that God placed him in Paradise and made all things subject to him (Gen., ch. 2). This is what David magnificently sets forth in Psalm 8. Moreover, God gave him a wife and blessed them. We also affirm that man consists of two different substances in one person: an immortal soul which, when separated from the body, neither sleeps nor dies, and a mortal body which will nevertheless be raised up from the dead at the last judgment, in order that then the whole man, either in life or in death, abide forever.

THE SECTS. We condemn all who ridicule or by subtle arguments cast doubt upon the immortality of souls, or who say that the soul sleeps or is a part of God. In short, we condemn all opinions of all men, however many, that depart from what has been delivered unto us by the Holy Scriptures in the apostolic Church of Christ concerning creation, angels, and demons, and man.

CHAPTER VIII. OF MAN'S FALL, SIN AND THE CAUSE OF SIN

THE FALL OF MAN. In the beginning, man was made according to the image of God, in righteousness and true holiness, good and upright. But when at the instigation of the serpent and by his own fault he abandoned goodness and righteousness, he became subject to sin, death and various calamities. And what he became by the fall, that is, subject to sin, death and various calamities, so are all those who have descended from him.

SIN. By sin we understand that innate corruption of man which has been derived or propagated in us all from our first parents, by which we, immersed in perverse desires and averse to all good, are inclined to all evil. Full of all wickedness, distrust, contempt and hatred of God, we are unable to do or even to think anything good of ourselves. Moreover, even as we grow older, so by wicked thoughts, words and deeds committed against God's law, we bring forth corrupt fruit worthy of an evil tree (Matt. 12:33 ff.). For this reason by our own deserts, being subject to the wrath of God, we are liable to just punishment, so that all of us would have been cast away by God if Christ, the Deliverer, had not brought us back.

DEATH. By death we understand not only bodily death, which all of us must once suffer on account of sins, but also eternal punishment due to our sins and corruption. For the apostle says: "We were dead through trespasses and sins . . . and were by nature children of wrath, like the rest of mankind. But God, who is rich in mercy . . . even when we were dead through our trespasses, made us alive together with Christ" (Eph. 2:1 ff.). Also: "As sin came into the world through one man and death through sin, and so death spread to all men because all men sinned" (Rom. 5:12).

ORIGINAL SIN. We therefore acknowledge that there is original sin in all men. *Actual Sins.* We acknowledge that all other sins which arise from it are called and truly are sins, no matter by what name they may be called, whether mortal, venial or that which is said to be the sin against the Holy Spirit which is never forgiven (Mark 3:29; I John 5:16). We also confess that sins are not equal; although they arise from the same fountain of corruption and unbelief, some are more serious than others. As the Lord said, it will be more tolerable for Sodom than for the city that rejects the word of the Gospel (Matt. 10:14 f.; 11:20 ff.).

THE SECTS. We therefore condemn all who have taught contrary to this, especially Pelagius and all Pelagians, together with the Jovinians who, with the Stoics, regard all sins as equal. In this whole matter we agree with St. Augustine who derived and defended his view from Holy Scriptures. Moreover, we condemn Florinus and Blastus, against whom Irenaeus wrote, and all who make God the author of sin.

GOD IS NOT THE AUTHOR OF SIN, AND HOW FAR HE IS SAID TO HARDEN. It is expressly written: "Thou art not a God who delights in wickedness. Thou hatest all evildoers. Thou destroyest those who speak lies" (Ps. 5:4 ff.). And again: "When the devil lies, he speaks according to his own nature, for he is a liar and the father of lies" (John 8:44). Moreover, there is enough sinfulness and corruption in us that it is not necessary for God to infuse into us a new or still greater perversity. When, therefore, it is said in Scripture that God hardens, blinds and delivers up to a reprobate mind, it is to be understood that God does it by a just judgment as a just Judge and Avenger. Finally, as often as God in Scripture is said or seems to do something evil, it is not thereby said that man does not do evil, but that God permits it and does not prevent it, according to his just judgment, who could prevent it if he wished, or because he turns man's evil into good, as he did in the case of the sin of Joseph's brethren, or because he governs sins lest they break out and rage more than is appropriate. St. Augustine writes in his *Enchiridion*: "What happens contrary to his will occurs, in a wonderful and ineffable way, not apart from his will. For it would not happen if he did not allow it. And yet he does not allow it unwillingly but willingly. But he who is good would not permit evil to be done, unless, being omnipotent, he could bring good out of evil." Thus wrote Augustine.

CURIOUS QUESTIONS. Other questions, such as whether God willed Adam to fall, or incited him to fall, or why he did not prevent the fall, and similar questions, we reckon among curious questions (unless perchance the wickedness of heretics or of other churlish men compels us also to explain them out of the Word of God, as the godly teachers of the Church have frequently done), knowing that the Lord forbade man to eat of the forbidden fruit and punished his transgression. We also know that what things are done are not evil with respect to the providence, will, and power of God, but in respect of Satan and our will opposing the will of God.

CHAPTER IX. OF FREE WILL, AND THUS OF HUMAN POWERS

In this matter, which has always produced many conflicts in the Church, we teach that a threefold condition or state of man is to be considered. *What Man Was Before the Fall*. There is the state in which man was in the beginning before the fall, namely, upright and free, so that he could both continue in goodness and decline to evil. However, he declined to evil, and has involved himself and the whole human race in sin and death, as has been said already. *What Man Was After the Fall*. Then we are to consider what man was after the fall. To be sure, his reason was not taken from him, nor was he deprived of will, and he was not entirely changed into a stone or a tree. But they were so altered and weakened that they no longer can do what they could before the fall. For the understanding is darkened, and the will which was free has become an enslaved will. Now it serves sin, not unwillingly but willingly. And indeed, it is called a will, not an unwill (ing).

MAN DOES EVIL BY HIS OWN FREE WILL. Therefore, in regard to evil or sin, man is not forced by God or by the devil but does evil by his own free will, and in this respect he has a most free will. But when we frequently see that the worst crimes and designs of men are prevented by God from reaching their purpose, this does not take away man's freedom in doing evil, but God by his own power prevents what man freely planned otherwise. Thus Joseph's brothers freely determined to get rid of him, but they were unable to do it because something else seemed good to the counsel of God.

MAN IS NOT CAPABLE OF GOOD PER SE. In regard to goodness and virtue man's reason does not judge rightly of itself concerning divine things. For the evangelical and apostolic Scripture requires regeneration of whoever among us wishes to be saved. Hence our first birth from Adam contributes nothing to our salvation. Paul says: "The unspiritual man does not receive the gifts of the Spirit of God," etc. (I Cor. 2:14). And in another place he denies that we of ourselves are capable of thinking anything good (II Cor. 3:5). Now it is known that the mind or intellect is the guide of the will, and when the guide is blind, it is obvious how far the will reaches. Wherefore, man not yet regenerate has no free will for good, no strength to perform what is good. The Lord says in the Gospel: "Truly, truly, I say to you, everyone who commits sin is a slave to sin." (John 8:34.) And the apostle Paul says: "The mind that is set on the flesh is hostile to God; it does not submit to God's law, indeed it cannot." (Rom. 8:7.) Yet in regard to earthly things, fallen man is not entirely lacking in understanding.

UNDERSTANDING OF THE ARTS. For God in his mercy has permitted the powers of the intellect to remain, though differing greatly from what was in man before the fall. God commands us to cultivate our natural talents, and meanwhile adds both gifts and success. And it is obvious that we make no progress in all the arts without God's blessing. In any case, Scripture refers all the arts to God; and indeed, the heathen trace the origin of the arts to the gods who invented them.

OF WHAT KIND ARE THE POWERS OF THE REGENERATE, AND IN WHAT WAY THEIR WILLS ARE FREE. Finally, we must see whether the regenerate have free wills, and to what extent. In regeneration the understanding is illumined by the Holy Spirit in order that it may understand both the mysteries and the will of God. And the will itself is not only changed by the Spirit, but it is also equipped with faculties so that it wills and is able to do the good of its own accord. (Rom. 8:1 ff.) Unless we grant this, we will deny Christian liberty and introduce a legal bondage. But the prophet has God saying: "I will put my law within them, and I will write it upon their hearts" (Jer. 31:33; Ezek. 36:2 f.). The Lord also says in the Gospel: "If the Son makes you free, you will be free indeed" (John 8:36). Paul also writes to the Philippians: "It has been granted to you that for the sake of Christ you should not only believe in him but also suffer for his sake" (Phil. 1:29). Again: "I am sure that he who began a good work in you will bring it to completion at the day of Jesus Christ" (v. 6). Also: "God is at work in you, both to will and to work for his good pleasure" (ch. 2:13).

THE REGENERATE WORK NOT ONLY PASSIVELY BUT ACTIVELY. However, in this connection we teach that there are two things to be observed: First, that the regenerate, in choosing and doing good, work not only passively but actively. For they are moved by God that they may do themselves what they do. For Augustine rightly adduces the saying that "God is said to be our helper. But no one can be helped unless he does something." The Manichaeans robbed man of all activity and made him like a stone or a block of wood.

THE FREE WILL IS WEAK IN THE REGENERATE. Secondly, in the regenerate a weakness remains. For since sin dwells in us, and in the regenerate the flesh struggles against the Spirit till the end of our lives, they do not easily accomplish in all things what they had planned. These things are confirmed by the apostle in Rom., ch. 7, and Gal., ch. 5. Therefore that free will is weak in us on account of the remnants of the old Adam and of innate human corruption remaining in us until the end of our lives. Meanwhile, since the powers of the flesh and the remnants of the old man are not so efficacious that they wholly extinguish the work of the Spirit, for that reason the faithful are said to be free, yet so that they acknowledge their infirmity and do not glory at all in their free will. For believers ought always to keep in mind what St. Augustine so many times inculcated according to the apostle: "What have you that you did not receive? If then you received it, why do you boast as if it were not a gift?" To this he adds that what we have planned does not immediately come to pass. For the issue of things lies in the hand of God. This is the reason Paul prayed to the Lord to prosper his journey (Rom. 1:10). And this also is the reason the free will is weak.

IN EXTERNAL THINGS THERE IS LIBERTY. Moreover, no one denies that in external things both the regenerate and the unregenerate enjoy free will. For man has in common with other living creatures (to which he is not inferior) this nature to will some things and not to will others. Thus he is able to speak or to keep silent, to go out of his house or to remain at home, etc. However, even here God's power is always to be observed, for it was the cause that Balaam could not go as far as he wanted (Num., ch. 24), and Zacharias upon returning from the temple could not speak as he wanted (Luke, ch.1).

HERESIES. In this matter we condemn the Manichaeans who deny that the beginning of evil was for man [created] good, from his free will. We also condemn the Pelagians who assert that an evil man has sufficient free will to do the good that is commanded. Both are refuted by Holy Scripture which says to the former, "God made man upright" and to the latter, "If the Son makes you free, you will be free indeed" (John 8:36).

CHAPTER X. OF THE PREDESTINATION OF GOD AND THE ELECTION OF THE SAINTS

GOD HAS ELECTED US OUT OF GRACE. From eternity God has freely, and of his mere grace, without any respect to men, predestinated or elected the saints whom he wills to save in Christ, according to the saying of the apostle, "God chose us in him before the foundation of the world" (Eph. 1:4). And again: "Who saved us and called us with a holy calling, not in virtue of our works but in virtue of his own purpose and the grace which he gave us in Christ Jesus ages ago, and now has manifested through the appearing of our Saviour Christ Jesus" (II Tim. 1:9 f.).

WE ARE ELECTED OR PREDESTINATED IN CHRIST. Therefore, although not on account of any merit of ours. God has elected us, not directly, but in Christ, and on account of Christ, in order that those who are now ingrafted into Christ by faith might also be elected. But those who were outside Christ were rejected, according to the word of the apostle, "Examine yourselves, to see whether you are holding to your faith. Test yourselves. Do you not realize that Jesus Christ is in you?—unless indeed you fail to meet the test!" (II Cor. 13:5).

WE ARE ELECTED FOR A DEFINITE PURPOSE. Finally, the saints are chosen in Christ by God for a definite purpose, which the apostle himself explains when he says, "He chose us in him for adoption that we should be holy and blameless before him in love. He destined us for adoption to be his sons through Jesus Christ that they should be to the praise of the glory of his grace" (Eph. 1:4 ff.).

WE ARE TO HAVE A GOOD HOPE FOR ALL. And although God knows who are his, and here and there mention is made of the small number of elect, yet we must hope well of all, and not rashly judge any man to be a reprobate. For Paul says to the Philippians, "I thank my God for you all" (now he speaks of the whole Church in Philippi), "because of your fellowship in the Gospel, being persuaded that he who began a good work in you will bring it to completion at the day of Jesus Christ. It is also right that I have this opinion of you all" (Phil. 1:3 ff.).

WHETHER FEW ARE ELECT. And when the Lord was asked whether there were few that should be saved, he does not answer and tell them that few or many should be saved or damned, but rather he exhorts every man to "strive to enter by the narrow door" (Luke 13:24): as if he should say, It is not for you curiously to inquire about these matters, but rather to endeavor that you may enter into heaven by the straight way.

WHAT IN THIS MATTER IS TO BE CONDEMNED. Therefore we do not approve of the

impious speeches of some who say, "Few are chosen,
and since I do not know whether I am among the
number of the few, I will enjoy myself." Others say,
"If I am predestinated and elected by God, nothing
can hinder me from salvation, which is already
certainly appointed for me, no matter what I do. But
if I am in the number of the reprobate, no faith or
repentance will help me, since the decree of God
cannot be changed. Therefore all doctrines and
admonitions are useless." Now the saying of the
apostle contradicts these men: "The Lord's servant
must be ready to teach, instructing those who oppose
him, so that if God should grant that they repent to
know the truth, they may recover from the snare of
the devil, after being held captive by him to do his
will" (II Tim. 2:23 ff.).

ADMONITIONS ARE NOT IN VAIN BECAUSE
SALVATION PROCEEDS FROM ELECTION.
Augustine also shows that both the grace of free
election and predestination, and also salutary admo-
nitions and doctrines, are to be preached (*Lib. de
Dono Perseverantiae*, cap. 14 ff.).

WHETHER WE ARE ELECTED. We therefore
find fault with those who outside of Christ ask
whether they are elected. And what has God decreed
concerning them before all eternity? For the preaching of the Gospel is to be heard, and it is to be
believed; and it is to be held as beyond doubt that if
you believe and are in Christ, you are elected. For
the Father has revealed unto us in Christ the eternal
purpose of his predestination, as I have just now
shown from the apostle in II Tim. 1:9-10. This is
therefore above all to be taught and considered, what
great love of the Father toward us is revealed to us in
Christ. We must hear what the Lord himself daily
preaches to us in the Gospel, how he calls and says:
"Come to me all who labor and are heavy-laden, and
I will give you rest" (Matt. 11:28). "God so loved the
world, that he gave his only Son, that whoever
believes in him should not perish, but have eternal
life." (John 3:16.) Also, "It is not the will of my
Father that one of these little ones should perish."
(Matt. 18:14.)

Let Christ, therefore be the looking glass, in whom
we may contemplate our predestination. We shall
have a sufficiently clear and sure testimony that we
are inscribed in the Book of Life if we have
fellowship with Christ, and he is ours and we are his
in true faith.

TEMPTATION IN REGARD TO PREDESTINA-
TION. In the temptation in regard to predestination,
than which there is scarcely any other more dangerous, we are confronted by the fact that God's
promises apply to all the faithful, for he says: "Ask,
and everyone who seeks, shall receive" (Luke 11:9
f.). This finally we pray, with the whole Church of
God. "Our Father who art in heaven" (Matt. 6:9),
both because by baptism we are ingrafted into the

body of Christ, and we are often fed in his Church
with his flesh and blood unto life eternal. Thereby
being strengthened, we are commanded to work out
our salvation with fear and trembling, according to
the precept of Paul.

CHAPTER XI. OF JESUS CHRIST, TRUE GOD
AND MAN, THE ONLY SAVIOR OF THE
WORLD

CHRIST IS TRUE GOD. We further believe and
teach that the Son of God, our Lord Jesus Christ,
was predestinated or foreordained from eternity by
the Father to be the Savior of the world. And we
believe that he was born, not only when he assumed
flesh of the Virgin Mary, and not only before the
foundation of the world was laid, but by the Father
before all eternity in an inexpressible manner. For
Isaiah said: "Who can tell his generation?" (Ch.
53:8.) And Micah says: "His origin is from of old,
from ancient days" (Micah 5:2.) And John said in
the Gospel: "In the beginning was the Word, and the
Word was with God, and the Word was God," etc.
(Ch. 1:1.) Therefore, with respect to his divinity the
Son is coequal and consubstantial with the Father,
true God (Phil. 2:11), not only in name or by
adoption or by any merit, but in substance and
nature, as the apostle John has often said: "This is
the true God and eternal life" (I John 5:20). Paul
also says: "He appointed the Son the heir of all
things, through whom also he created the world. He
reflects the glory of God and bears the very stamp of
his nature, upholding all things by his word of
power" (Heb. 1:2 f.). For in the Gospel the Lord
himself said: "Father, glorify Thou me in Thy own
presence with the glory which I had with Thee before
the world was made" (John 17:5). And in another
place in the Gospel it is written: "The Jews sought all
the more to kill him because he . . . called God his
Father, making himself equal with God" (John 5:18).

THE SECTS. We therefore abhor the impious
doctrine of Arius and the Arians against the Son of
God, and especially the blasphemies of the Spaniard,
Michael Servetus, and all his followers, which Satan
through them has, as it were, dragged up out of hell
and has most audaciously and impiously spread
abroad in the world.

CHRIST IS TRUE MAN, HAVING REAL
FLESH. We also believe and teach that the eternal
Son of the eternal God was made the Son of man,
from the seed of Abraham and David, not from the
coitus of a man, as the Ebionites said, but was most
chastely conceived by the Holy Spirit and born of the
ever virgin Mary, as the evangelical history carefully
explains to us (Matt., ch. 1). And Paul says: "He
took not on him the nature of angels, but of the seed
of Abraham." Also the apostle John says that
whoever does not believe that Jesus Christ has come
in the flesh, is not of God. Therefore, the flesh of
Christ was neither imaginary nor brought from
heaven, as Valentinus and Marcion wrongly imagined.

A RATIONAL SOUL IN CHRIST. Moreover, our Lord Jesus Christ did not have a soul bereft of sense and reason, as Appollinaris thought, nor flesh without a soul, as Eunomius taught, but a soul with its reason, and flesh with its senses, by which in the time of his passion he sustained real bodily pain, as he himself testified when he said: "My soul is very sorrowful, even to death" (Matt. 26:38). And, "Now is my soul troubled" (John 12:27).

TWO NATURES IN CHRIST. We therefore acknowledge two natures or substances, the divine and the human, in one and the same Jesus Christ our Lord (Heb., ch. 2). And we say that these are bound and united with one another in such a way that they are not absorbed, or confused, or mixed, but are united or joined together in one person—the properties of the natures being unimpaired and permanent.

NOT TWO BUT ONE CHRIST. Thus we worship not two but one Christ the Lord. We repeat: one true God and man. With respect to his divine nature he is consubstantial with the Father, and with respect to the human nature he is consubstantial with us men, and like us in all things, sin excepted (Heb. 4:15).

THE SECTS. And indeed we detest the dogma of the Nestorians who make two of the one Christ and dissolve the unity of the Person. Likewise we thoroughly execrate the madness of Eutyches and of the Monothelites or Monophysites who destroy the property of the human nature.

THE DIVINE NATURE OF CHRIST IS NOT PASSIBLE, AND THE HUMAN NATURE IS NOT EVERYWHERE. Therefore, we do not in any way teach that the divine nature in Christ has suffered or that Christ according to his human nature is still in this world and thus is everywhere. For neither do we think or teach that the body of Christ ceased to be a true body after his glorification, or was deified, and deified in such a way that it laid aside its properties as regards body and soul, and changed entirely into a divine nature and began to be merely one substance.

THE SECTS. Hence we by no means approve of or accept the strained, confused and obscure subtleties of Schwenkfeldt and of similar sophists with their self-contradictory arguments; neither are we Schwenkfeldians.

OUR LORD TRULY SUFFERED. We believe, moreover, that our Lord Jesus Christ truly suffered and died for us in the flesh, as Peter says (I Peter 4:1). We abhor the most impious madness of the Jacobites and all the Turks who execrate the suffering of the Lord. At the same time we do not deny that the Lord of glory was crucified for us, according to Paul's words (I Cor. 2:8).

IMPARTATION OF PROPERTIES. We piously and reverently accept and use the impartation of properties which is derived from Scripture and which has been used by all antiquity in explaining and reconciling apparently contradictory passages.

CHRIST IS TRULY RISEN FROM THE DEAD. We believe and teach that the same Jesus Christ our Lord, in his true flesh in which he was crucified and died, rose again from the dead, and that not another flesh was raised other than the one buried, or that a spirit was taken up instead of the flesh, but that he retained his true body. Therefore, while his disciples thought they saw the spirit of the Lord, he showed them his hands and feet which were marked by the prints of the nails and wounds, and added: "See my hands and my feet, that it is I myself; handle me, and see, for a spirit has not flesh and bones as you see that I have" (Luke 24:39).

CHRIST IS TRULY ASCENDED INTO HEAVEN. We believe that our Lord Jesus Christ, in his same flesh, ascended above all visible heavens into the highest heaven, that is, the dwelling-place of God and the blessed ones, at the right hand of God the Father. Although it signifies an equal participation in glory and majesty, it is also taken to be a certain place about which the Lord, speaking in the Gospel, says: "I go to prepare a place for you" (John 14:2). The apostle Peter also says: "Heaven must receive Christ until the time of restoring all things" (Acts 3:21). And from heaven the same Christ will return in judgment, when wickedness will then be at its greatest in the world and when the Antichrist, having corrupted true religion, will fill up all things with superstition and impiety and will cruelly lay waste the Church with bloodshed and flames (Dan., ch. 11). But Christ will come again to claim his own, and by his coming to destroy the Antichrist, and to judge the living and the dead (Acts 17:31). For the dead will rise again (I Thess. 4:14 ff.), and those who on that day (which is unknown to all creatures [Mark 13:32]) will be alive will be changed "in the twinkling of an eye," and all the faithful will be caught up to meet Christ in the air, so that then they may enter with him into the blessed dwelling-places to live forever (I Cor. 15:51 f.). But the unbelievers and ungodly will descend with the devils into hell to burn forever and never to be redeemed from torments (Matt. 25:46).

THE SECTS. We therefore condemn all who deny a real resurrection of the flesh (II Tim. 2:18), or who with John of Jerusalem, against whom Jerome wrote, do not have a correct view of the glorification of bodies. We also condemn those who thought that the devil and all the ungodly would at some time be saved, and that there would be an end to punishments. For the Lord has plainly declared: "Their fire is not quenched, and their worm does not die" (Mark 9:44). We further condemn Jewish dreams that there will be a golden age on earth before the Day of Judgment, and that the pious, having subdued all their godless enemies, will possess all the kingdoms of the earth. For evangelical truth in Matt., chs. 24 and 25, and Luke, ch. 18, and apostolic teaching in II Thess., ch. 2, and II Tim., chs. 3 and 4, present something quite different.

SECOND HELVETIC CONFESSION (HUNGARIAN REFORMED CHURCH) (continued)

THE FRUIT OF CHRIST'S DEATH AND RESSURRECTION. Further by his passion and death and everything which he did and endured for our sake by his coming in the flesh, our Lord reconciled all the faithful to the heavenly Father, made expiation for sins, disarmed death, overcame damnation and hell, and by his resurrection from the dead brought again and restored life and immortality. For he is our righteousness, life and resurrection, in a word, the fulness and perfection of all the faithful, salvation and all sufficiency. For the apostle says: "In him all the fulness of God was pleased to dwell," and, "You have come to fulness of life in him." (Col., chs. 1 and 2.)

JESUS CHRIST IS THE ONLY SAVIOR OF THE WORLD, AND THE TRUE AWAITED MESSIAH. For we teach and believe that this Jesus Christ our Lord is the unique and eternal Savior of the human race, and thus of the whole world, in whom by faith are saved all who before the law, under the law, and under the Gospel were saved, and however many will be saved at the end of the world. For the Lord himself says in the Gospel: "He who does not enter the sheepfold by the door but climbs in by another way, that man is a thief and a robber. . . . I am the door of the sheep" (John 10:1 and 7). And also in another place in the same Gospel he says: "Abraham saw my day and was glad" (ch. 8:56). The apostle Peter also says: "There is salvation in no one else, for there is no other name under heaven given among men by which we must be saved." We therefore believe that we will be saved through the grace of our Lord Jesus Christ, as our fathers were. (Acts 4:12; 10:43; 15:11.) For Paul also says: "All our fathers ate the same spiritual food, and all drank the same spiritual drink. For they drank from the spiritual Rock which followed them, and the Rock was Christ" (I Cor. 10:3 f.). And thus we read that John says: "Christ was the Lamb which was slain from the foundation of the world" (Rev. 13:8), and John the Baptist testified that Christ is that "Lamb of God, who takes away the sin of the world" (John 1:29). Wherefore, we quite openly profess and preach that Jesus Christ is the sole Redeemer and Savior of the world, the King and High Priest, the true and awaited Messiah, that holy and blessed one whom all the types of the law and predictions of the prophets prefigured and promised; and that God appointed him beforehand and sent him to us, so that we are not now to look for any other. Now there only remains for all of us to give all glory to Christ, believe in him, rest in him alone, despising and rejecting all other aids in life. For however many seek salvation in any other than in Christ alone, have fallen from the grace of God and have rendered Christ null and void for themselves (Gal. 5:4).

THE CREEDS OF FOUR COUNCILS RECEIVED. And, to say many things with a few words, with a sincere heart we believe, and freely confess with open mouth, whatever things are defined from the Holy Scriptures concerning the mystery of the incarnation of our Lord Jesus Christ, and are summed up in the Creeds and decrees of the first four most excellent synods convened at Nicea, Constantinople, Ephesus and Chalcedon—together with the Creed of blessed Athanasius, and all similar symbols; and we condemn everything contrary to these.

THE SECTS. And in this way we retain the Christian, orthodox and catholic faith whole and unimpaired; knowing that nothing is contained in the aforesaid symbols which is not agreeable to the Word of God, and does not altogether make for a sincere exposition of the faith.

CHAPTER XII. OF THE LAW OF GOD

THE WILL OF GOD IS EXPLAINED FOR US IN THE LAW OF GOD. We teach that the will of God is explained for us in the law of God, what he wills or does not will us to do, what is good and just, or what is evil and unjust. Therefore, we confess that the law is good and holy.

THE LAW OF NATURE. And this law was at one time written in the hearts of men by the finger of God (Rom. 2:15), and is called the law of nature (*the law of Moses is in two Tables*), and at another it was inscribed by his finger on the two Tables of Moses, and eloquently expounded in the books of Moses (Ex. 20:1 ff.; Deut. 5:6 ff.). For the sake of clarity we distinguish the moral law which is contained in the Decalogue or two Tables and expounded in the books of Moses, the ceremonial law which determines the ceremonies and worship of God, and the judicial law which is concerned with political and domestic matters.

THE LAW IS COMPLETE AND PERFECT. We believe that the whole will of God and all necessary precepts for every sphere of life are taught in this law. For otherwise the Lord would not have forbidden us to add or to take away anything from this law: neither would he have commanded us to walk in a straight path before this law, and not to turn aside from it by turning to the right or to the left (Deut. 4:2; 12:32).

WHY THE LAW WAS GIVEN. We teach that this law was not given to men that they might be justified by keeping it, but that rather from what it teaches we may know (our) weakness, sin and condemnation, and, despairing of our strength, might be converted to Christ in faith. For the apostle openly declares: "The law brings wrath," and, "Through the law comes knowledge of sin" (Rom. 4:15; 3:20), and, "If a law had been given which could justify or make alive, then righteousness would indeed be by the law. But the Scripture (that is, the law) has concluded all under sin, that the promise which was of the faith of Jesus might be given to those who believe. . . . Therefore, the law was our schoolmaster unto Christ, that we might be justified by faith" (Gal. 3:21 ff.).

THE FLESH DOES NOT FULFIL THE LAW. For no flesh could or can satisfy the law of God and fulfil it, because of the weakness in our flesh which adheres and remains in us until our last breath. For the apostle says again: "God has done what the law, weakened by the flesh, could not do: sending his own Son in the likeness of sinful flesh and for sin" (Rom. 8:3). Therefore, Christ is the perfecting of the law and our fulfilment of it (Rom. 10:4), who, in order to take away the curse of the law, was made a curse for us (Gal. 3:13). Thus he imparts to us through faith his fulfilment of the law, and his righteousness and obedience are imputed to us.

HOW FAR THE LAW IS ABROGATED. The law of God is therefore abrogated to the extent that it no longer condemns us, nor works wrath in us. For we are under grace and not under the law. Moreover, Christ has fulfilled all the figures of the law. Hence, with the coming of the body, the shadows ceased, so that in Christ we now have the truth and all fulness. But yet we do not on that account contemptuously reject the law. For we remember the words of the Lord when he said: "I have not come to abolish the law and the prophets but to fulfil them" (Matt. 5:17). We know that in the law is delivered to us the patterns of virtues and vices. We know that the written law when explained by the Gospel is useful to the Church, and that therefore its reading is not to be banished from the Church. For although Moses' face was covered with a veil, yet the apostle says that the veil has been taken away and abolished by Christ. *The Sects.* We condemn everything that heretics old and new have taught against the law.

CHAPTER XIII. OF THE GOSPEL, OF JESUS CHRIST, OF THE PROMISES, AND OF THE SPIRIT AND LETTER

THE ANCIENTS HAD EVANGELICAL PROMISES. The Gospel is, indeed, opposed to the law. For the law works wrath and announces a curse, whereas the Gospel preaches grace and blessing. John says: "For the law was given through Moses; grace and truth came through Jesus Christ." (John 1:17.) Yet notwithstanding it is most certain that those who were before the law and under the law, were not altogether destitute of the Gospel. For they had extraordinary evangelical promises such as these are: "The seed of the woman shall bruise the serpent's head" (Gen. 3:15). "In thy seed shall all the nations of the earth be blessed" (Gen. 22:18). "The scepter shall not depart from Judah . . . until he comes" (Gen. 49:10). "The Lord will raise up a prophet from among his own brethren" (Deut. 18:15; Acts 3:22), etc.

THE PROMISES TWOFOLD. And we acknowledge that two kinds of promises were revealed to the fathers, as also to us. For some were of present or earthly things, such as the promises of the Land of Canaan and of victories, and as the promise today still of daily bread. Others were then and are still now of heavenly and eternal things, namely, divine grace, remission of sins, and eternal life through faith in Jesus Christ.

THE FATHERS ALSO HAD NOT ONLY CARNAL BUT SPIRITUAL PROMISES. Moreover, the ancients had not only external and earthly but also spiritual and heavenly promises in Christ. Peter says: "The prophets who prophesied of the grace that was to be yours searched and inquired about this salvation." (I Peter 1:10.) Wherefore the apostle Paul also said: "The Gospel of God was promised beforehand through his prophets in the holy scriptures" (Rom. 1:2). Thereby it is clear that the ancients were not entirely destitute of the whole Gospel.

WHAT IS THE GOSPEL PROPERLY SPEAKING? And although our fathers had the Gospel in this way in the writings of the prophets by which they attained salvation in Christ through faith, yet the Gospel is properly called glad and joyous news, in which, first by John the Baptist, then by Christ the Lord himself, and afterwards by the apostles and their successors, is preached to us in the world that God has now performed what he promised from the beginning of the world, and has sent, may more, has given us his only Son and in him reconciliation with the Father, the remission of sins, all fulness and everlasting life. Therefore, the history delineated by the four Evangelists and explaining how these things were done or fulfilled by Christ, what things Christ taught and did, and that those who believe in him have all fulness, is rightly called the Gospel. The preaching and writings of the apostles, in which the apostles explain for us how the Son was given to us by the Father, and in him everything that has to do with life and salvation, is also rightly called evangelical doctrine, so that not even today, if sincerely preached, does it lose its illustrious title.

OF THE SPIRIT AND THE LETTER. That same preaching of the Gospel is also called by the apostle "the spirit" and "the ministry of the spirit" because by faith it becomes effectual and living in the ears, nay more, in the hearts of believers through the illumination of the Holy Spirit (II Cor. 3:6). For the letter, which is opposed to the Spirit, signifies everything external, but especially the doctrine of the law which, without the Spirit and faith, works wrath and provokes sin in the minds of those who do not have a living faith. For this reason the apostle calls it "the ministry of death." In this connection the saying of the apostle is pertinent: "The letter kills, but the Spirit gives life." And false apostles preached a corrupted Gospel, having combined it with the law, as if Christ could not save without the law.

THE SECTS. Such were the Ebionites said to be, who were descended from Ebion the heretic, and the Nazarites who were formerly called Mineans. All these we condemn, while preaching the pure Gospel and teaching that believers are justified by the Spirit alone, and not by the law. A more detailed exposition of this matter will follow presently under the heading of justifiction.

THE TEACHING OF THE GOSPEL IS NOT NEW, BUT MOST ANCIENT DOCTRINE.

And although the teaching of the Gospel, compared with the teaching of the Pharisees concerning the law, seemed to be a new doctrine when first preached by Christ (which Jeremiah also prophesied concerning the New Testament), yet actually it not only was and still is an old doctrine (even if today it is called new by the Papists when compared with the teaching now received among them), but is the most ancient of all in the world. For God predestinated from eternity to save the world through Christ, and he has disclosed to the world through the Gospel this his predestination and eternal counsel (II Tim. 2:9 f.). Hence it is evident that the religion and teaching of the Gospel among all who ever were, are and will be, is the most ancient of all. Wherefore we assert that all who say that the religion and teaching of the Gospel is a faith which has recently arisen, being scarcely thirty years old, err disgracefully and speak shamefully of the eternal counsel of God. To them applies the saying of Isaiah the prophet: "Woe to those who call evil good and good evil, who put darkness for light and light for darkness, who put bitter for sweet and sweet for bitter!" (Isa. 5:20).

CHAPTER XIV. OF REPENTANCE AND THE CONVERSION OF MAN

The doctrine of repentance is joined with the Gospel. For so has the Lord said in the Gospel: "Repentance and forgiveness of sins should be preached in my name to all nations" (Luke 24:47). *What Is Repentance?* By repentance we understand (1) the recovery of a right mind in sinful man awakened by the Word of the Gospel and the Holy Spirit, and received by true faith, by which the sinner immediately acknowledges his innate corruption and all his sins accused by the Word of God; and (2) grieves for them from his heart, and not only bewails and frankly confesses them before God with a feeling of shame, but also (3) with indignation abominates them; and (4) now zealously considers the amendment of his ways and constantly strives for innocence and virtue in which conscientiously to exercise himself all the rest of his life.

TRUE REPENTANCE IS CONVERSION TO GOD.

And this is true repentance, namely, a sincere turning to God and all good, and earnest turning away from the devil and all evil. *1. Repentance is a gift of God.* Now we expressly say that this repentance is a sheer gift of God and not a work of our strength. For the apostle commands a faithful minister diligently to instruct those who oppose the truth, if "God may perhaps grant that they will repent and come to know the truth" (II Tim. 2:25) *2. Laments sins committed.* Now that sinful woman who washed the feet of the Lord with her tears, and Peter who wept bitterly and bewailed his denial of the Lord (Luke 7:38; 22:62) show clearly how the mind of a penitent man ought to be seriously lamenting the sins he has committed. *3. Confesses sins to God.* Moreover, the prodigal son and the publican in the Gospel, when compared with the Pharisee, present us with the most suitable pattern of how our sins are to be confessed to God. The former said: "'Father, I have sinned against heaven and before you: I am no longer worthy to be called your son: treat me as one of your hired servants.'" (Luke 15:8 ff.) And the latter, not daring to raise his eyes to heaven, beat his breast, saying, "God be merciful to me a sinner" (ch. 18:13). And we do not doubt that they were accepted by God into grace. For the apostle John says: "If we confess our sins, he is faithful and just, and will forgive our sins and cleanse us from all unrighteousness. If we say we have not sinned, we make him a liar, and his word is not in us" (I John 1:9 f.).

SACERDOTAL CONFESSION AND ABSOLUTION.

But we believe that this sincere confession which is made to God alone, either privately between God and the sinner, or publicly in the Church where the general confession of sins is said, is sufficient, and that in order to obtain forgiveness of sins it is not necessary for anyone to confess his sins to a priest, murmuring them in his ears, that in turn he might receive absolution from the priest with his laying on of hands, because there is neither a commandment nor an example of this in Holy Scriptures. David testifies and says: "I acknowledged my sin to thee, and did not hide my iniquity: I said, 'I will confess my transgressions to the Lord'; then thou didst forgive the guilt of my sin" (Ps. 32:5). And the Lord who taught us to pray and at the same time to confess our sins said: "Pray then like this: Our Father, who art in heaven. . . . forgive us our debts, as we also forgive our debtors" (Matt. 6:12). Therefore it is necessary that we confess our sins to God our Father, and be reconciled with our neighbor if we have offended him. Concerning this kind of confession, the Apostle James says: "Confess your sins to one another" (James 5:16). If, however, anyone is overwhelmed by the burden of his sins and by perplexing temptations, and will seek counsel, instruction and comfort privately, either from a minister of the Church, or from any other brother who is instructed in God's law, we do not disapprove; just as we also fully approve of that general and public confession of sins which is usually said in Church and in meetings for worship, as we noted above, inasmuch as it is agreeable to Scripture.

OF THE KEYS OF THE KINGDOM OF HEAVEN.

Concerning the keys of the Kingdom of Heaven which the Lord gave to the apostles, many babble many astonishing things, and out of them forge swords, spears, scepters and crowns, and complete power over the greatest kingdoms, indeed, over souls and bodies. Judging simply according to the Word of the Lord, we say that all properly called ministers possess and exercise the keys or the use of them when they proclaim the Gospel; that is, when they teach, exhort, comfort, rebuke, and keep in discipline the people committed to their trust.

OPENING AND SHUTTING (THE KINGDOM). For in this way they open the Kingdom of Heaven to the obedient and shut it to the disobedient. The Lord promised these keys to the apostles in Matt., ch. 16, and gave them in John, ch. 20, Mark, ch. 16, and Luke, ch. 24, when he sent out his disciples and commanded them to preach the Gospel in all the world, and to remit sins.

THE MINISTRY OF RECONCILIATION. In the letter to the Corinthians the apostle says that the Lord gave the ministry of reconciliation to his ministers (II Cor. 5:18 ff.). And what this is he then explains, saying that it is the preaching or teaching of reconciliation. And explaining his words still more clearly he adds that Christ's ministers discharge the office of an ambassador in Christ's name, as if God himself through ministers exhorted the people to be reconciled to God, doubtless by faithful obedience. Therefore, they exercise the keys when they persuade [men] to believe and repent. Thus they reconcile men to God.

MINISTERS REMIT SINS. Thus they remit sins. Thus they open the Kingdom of Heaven, and bring believers into it: very different from those of whom the Lord said in the Gospel. "Woe to you lawyers! for you have taken away the key of knowledge; you did not enter yourselves, and you hindered those who were entering."

HOW MINISTERS ABSOLVE. Ministers, therefore, rightly and effectually absolve when they preach the Gospel of Christ and thereby the remission of sins, which is promised to each one who believes, just as each one is baptized, and when they testify that it pertains to each one peculiarly. Neither do we think that this absolution becomes more effectual by being murmured in the ear of someone or by being murmured singly over someone's head. We are nevertheless of the opinion that the remission of sins in the blood of Christ is to be diligently proclaimed, and that each one is to be admonished that the forgiveness of sins pertains to him.

DILIGENCE IN THE RENEWAL OF LIFE. But the examples in the Gospel teach us how vigilant and diligent the penitent ought to be in striving for newness of life and in mortifying the old man and quickening the new. For the Lord said to the man he healed of palsy: "See, you are well! Sin no more, that nothing worse befall you" (John 5:14). Likewise to the adulteress whom he set free he said: "Go, and sin no more" (ch. 8:11). To be sure, by these words he did not mean that any man, as long as he lived in the flesh, could not sin; he simply recommends diligence and a careful devotion, so that we should strive by all means, and beseech God in prayers lest we fall back into sins from which, as it were, we have been

resurrected, and lest we be overcome by the flesh, the world and the devil. Zacchaeus the publican, whom the Lord had received back into favor, exclaims in the Gospel: "Behold, Lord, the half of my goods I give to the poor; and if I have defrauded any one of anything, I restore it fourfold" (Luke 19:8). Therefore, in the same way we preach that restitution and compassion, and even almsgiving, are necessary for those who truly repent, and we exhort all men everywhere in the words of the apostle: "Let not sin therefore reign in your mortal bodies, to make you obey their passions. Do not yield your members to sin as instruments of wickedness, but yield yourselves to God as men who have been brought from death to life, and your members to God as instruments of righteousness" (Rom. 6:12 f.).

ERRORS. Wherefore we condemn all impious utterances of some who wrongly use the preaching of the Gospel and say that it is easy to return to God. Christ has atoned for all sins. Forgiveness of sins is easy. Therefore, what harm is there in sinning? Nor need we be greatly concerned about repentance, etc. Notwithstanding we always teach that an access to God is open to all sinners, and that he forgives all sinners of all sins except the one sin against the Holy Spirit (Mark 3:29).

THE SECTS. Wherefore we condemn both old and new Novatians and Catharists.

PAPAL INDULGENCES. We especially condemn the lucrative doctrine of the Pope concerning penance, and against his simony and his simoniacal indulgences we avail ourselves of Peter's judgment concerning Simon: "Your silver perish with you, because you thought you could obtain the gift of God with money! You have neither part nor lot in this matter, for your heart is not right before God" (Acts 8:20 f.).

SATISFACTIONS. We also disapprove of those who think that by their own satisfactions they make amends for sins committed. For we teach that Christ alone by his death or passion is the satisfaction, propitiation or expiation of all sins (Isa., ch. 53; I Cor. 1:30). Yet as we have already said, we do not cease to urge the mortification of the flesh. We add, however, that this mortification is not to be proudly obtruded upon God as a satisfaction for sins, but is to be performed humbly, in keeping with the nature of the children of God, as a new obedience out of gratitude for the deliverance and full satisfaction obtained by the death and satisfaction of the Son of God.

CHAPTER XV. OF THE TRUE JUSTIFICATION OF THE FAITHFUL

WHAT IS JUSTIFICATION? According to the apostle in his treatment of justification, to justify means to remit sins, to absolve from guilt and punishment, to receive into favor, and to pronounce a man just. For in his epistle to the Romans the apostle says: "It is God who justifies; who is to condemn?" (Rom. 8:33). To justify and to condemn are opposed. And in The Acts of the Apostles the apostle states: "Through Christ forgiveness of sins is proclaimed to you, and by him everyone that believes is freed from everything from which you could not be freed by the law of Moses" (Acts 13:38 f.). For in the Law and also in the Prophets we read: "If there is a dispute between men, and they come into court . . . the judges decide between them, acquitting the innocent and condemning the guilty" (Deut. 25:1). And in Isa., ch. 5: "Woe to those . . . who acquit the guilty for a bribe."

WE ARE JUSTIFIED ON ACCOUNT OF CHRIST. Now it is most certain that all of us are by nature sinners and godless, and before God's judgment-seat are convicted of godlessness and are guilty of death, but that, solely by the grace of Christ and not from any merit of ours or consideration for us, we are justified, that is, absolved from sin and death by God the Judge. For what is clearer than what Paul said: "Since all have sinned and fall short of the glory of God, they are justified by his grace as a gift, through the redemption which is in Christ Jesus" (Rom. 3:23 f.).

IMPUTED RIGHTEOUSNESS. For Christ took upon himself and bore the sins of the world, and satisfied divine justice. Therefore, solely on account of Christ's sufferings and resurrection God is propitious with respect to our sins and does not impute them to us, but imputes Christ's righteousness to us as our own (II Cor. 5:19 ff.; Rom. 4:25), so that now we are not only cleansed and purged from sins or are holy, but also, granted the righteousness of Christ, and so absolved from sin, death and condemnation, are at last righteous and heirs of eternal life. Properly speaking, therefore, God alone justifies us, and justifies only on account of Christ, not imputing sins to us but imputing his righteousness to us.

WE ARE JUSTIFIED BY FAITH ALONE. But because we receive this justification, not through any works, but through faith in the mercy of God and in Christ, we therefore teach and believe with the apostle that sinful man is justified by faith alone in Christ, not by the law or any works. For the apostle says: "We hold that a man is justified by faith apart from works of law" (Rom. 3:28). Also: "If Abraham was justified by works, he has something to boast about, but not before God. For what does the scripture say? Abraham believed God, and it was reckoned to him as righteousness. . . . And to one who does not work but believes in him who justifies the ungodly, his faith is reckoned as righteousness" (Rom. 4:2 ff.; Gen. 15:6). And again: "By grace you have been saved through faith: and this is not your own doing, it is the gift of God—not because of works, lest any man should boast," etc. (Eph. 2:8 f.). Therefore, because faith receives Christ our righteousness and attributes everything to the grace of God in Christ, on that account justification is

attributed to faith, chiefly because of Christ and not therefore because it is our work. For it is the gift of God.

WE RECEIVE CHRIST BY FAITH. Moreover, the Lord abundantly shows that we receive Christ by faith in John, ch. 6, where he puts eating for believing, and believing for eating. For as we receive food by eating, so we participate in Christ by believing. *Justification Is Not Attributed Partly to Christ or to Faith, Partly to Us.* Therefore, we do not share in the benefit of justification partly because of the grace of God or Christ, and partly because of ourselves, our love, works or merit, but we attribute it wholly to the grace of God in Christ through faith. For our love and our works could not please God if performed by unrighteous men. Therefore, it is necessary for us to be righteous before we may love and do good works. We are made truly righteous, as we have said, by faith in Christ purely by the grace of God, who does not impute to us our sins, but the righteousness of Christ, or rather, he imputes faith in Christ to us for righteousness. Moreover, the apostle very clearly derives love from faith when he says: "The aim of our command is love that issues from a pure heart, a good conscience, and a sincere faith" (I Tim. 1:5).

JAMES COMPARED WITH PAUL. Wherefore, in this matter we are not speaking of a fictitious, empty, lazy and dead faith, but of a living, quickening faith. It is and is called a living faith because it apprehends Christ who is life and makes alive, and shows that it is alive by living works. And so James does not contradict anything in this doctrine of ours. For he speaks of an empty, dead faith of which some boasted but who did not have Christ living in them by faith (James 2:14 ff.). James said that works justify, yet without contradicting the apostle (otherwise he would have to be rejected) but showing that Abraham proved his living and justifying faith by works. This all the pious do, but they trust in Christ alone and not in their own works. For again the apostle said: "It is no longer I who live, but Christ who lives in me; and the life I now live in the flesh I live by faith in the Son of God, who loved me and gave himself for me. I do not reject the grace of God; for if justification were through the law, then Christ died to no purpose," etc. (Gal. 2:20 f.).

CHAPTER XVI. OF FAITH AND GOOD WORKS, AND OF THEIR REWARD, AND OF MAN'S MERIT

WHAT IS FAITH? Christian faith is not an opinion or human conviction, but a most firm trust and a clear and steadfast assent of the mind, and then a most certain apprehension of the truth of God presented in the Scriptures and in the Apostles' Creed, and thus also of God himself, the greatest good, and especially of God's promise and of Christ who is the fulfilment of all promises.

FAITH IS THE GIFT OF GOD. But this faith is a pure gift of God which God alone of his grace gives to his elect according to his measure when, to whom and to the degree he wills. And he does this by the Holy Spirit by means of the preaching of the Gospel and steadfast prayer. *The Increase of Faith.* This faith also has its increase, and unless it were given by God, the apostles would not have said: "Lord, increase our faith" (Luke 17:5). And all these things which up to this point we have said concerning faith, the apostles have taught before us. For Paul said: "For faith is the υποστασις or sure subsistence, of things hoped for, and the ελεγχος, that is, the clear and certain apprehension" (Heb. 11:1). And again he says that all the promises of God are Yes through Christ and through Christ are Amen (II Cor. 1:20). And to the Philippians he said that it has been given to them to believe in Christ (Phil. 1:29). Again, God assigned to each the measure of faith (Rom. 12:3). Again: "Not all have faith" and, "Not all obey the Gospel" (II Thess. 3:2; Rom. 10:16). But Luke also bears witness, saying: "As many as were ordained to life believed" (Acts 13:48). Wherefore Paul also calls faith "the faith of God's elect" (Titus 1:1), and again: "Faith comes from hearing, and hearing comes by the Word of God" (Rom. 10:17). Elsewhere he often commands men to pray for faith.

FAITH EFFICACIOUS AND ACTIVE. The same apostle calls faith efficacious and active through love (Gal. 5:6). It also quiets the conscience and opens a free access to God, so that we may draw near to him with confidence and may obtain from him what is useful and necessary. The same [faith] keeps us in the service we owe to God and our neighbor, strengthens our patience in adversity, fashions and makes a true confession, and in a word, brings forth good fruit of all kinds, and good works.

CONCERNING GOOD WORKS. For we teach that truly good works grow out of a living faith by the Holy Spirit and are done by the faithful according to the will or rule of God's Word. Now the apostle Peter says: "Make every effort to supplement your faith with virtue, and virtue with knowledge, and knowledge with self-control," etc. (II Peter 1:5 ff.) But we have said above that the law of God, which is his will, prescribes for us the pattern of good works. And the apostle says: "This is the will of God, your sanctification, that you abstain from immorality . . . that no man transgress, and wrong his brother in business." (I Thess. 4:3 ff.)

WORKS OF HUMAN CHOICE. And indeed works and worship which we choose arbitrarily are not pleasing to God. These Paul calls εθλεοθρησκειας (Col. 2:23—"self-devised worship"). Of such the Lord says in the Gospel: "In vain do they worship me, teaching as doctrines the precepts of men" (Matt. 15:9). Therefore, we disapprove of such works, and approve and urge those that are of God's will and commission.

THE END OF GOOD WORKS. These same works ought not to be done in order that we may earn eternal life by them, for, as the apostle says, eternal life is the gift of God. Nor are they to be done for ostentation which the Lord rejects in Matt., ch. 6, nor for gain which he also rejects in Matt., ch. 23, but for the glory of God, to adorn our calling, to show gratitude to God, and for the profit of the neighbor. For our Lord says again in the Gospel: "Let your light so shine before men, that they may see your good works and give glory to your Father who is in heaven" (Matt. 5:16). And the apostle Paul says: "Lead a life worthy of the calling to which you have been called." (Eph. 4:1.) Also: "And whatever you do, in word or deed, do everything in the name of the Lord Jesus, giving thanks to God and to the Father through him (Col. 3:17), and. "Let each of you look not to his own interests, but to the interests of others" (Phil. 2:4), and, "Let our people learn to apply themselves to good deeds, so as to help cases of urgent need, and not to be unfruitful" (Titus 3:14).

GOOD WORKS NOT REJECTED. Therefore, although we teach with the apostle that a man is justified by grace through faith in Christ and not through any good works, yet we do not think that good works are of little value and condemn them. We know that man was not created or regenerated through faith in order to be idle, but rather that without ceasing he should do those things which are good and useful. For in the Gospel the Lord says that a good tree brings forth good fruit (Matt. 12:33), and that he who abides in me bears much fruit (John 15:5). The apostle says: "For we are his workmanship, created in Christ Jesus for good works, which God prepared beforehand, that we should walk in them" (Eph. 2:10), and again: "Who gave himself for us to redeem us from all iniquity and to purify for himself a people of his own who are zealous for good deeds" (Titus 2:14). We therefore condemn all who despise good works and who babble that they are useless and that we do not need to pay attention to them.

WE ARE NOT SAVED BY GOOD WORKS. Nevertheless, as was said above, we do not think that we are saved by good works, and that they are so necessary for salvation that no one was ever saved without them. For we are saved by grace and the favor of Christ alone. Works necessarily proceed from faith. And salvation is improperly attributed to them, but is most properly ascribed to grace. The apostle's sentence is well known: "If it is by grace, then it no longer of works; otherwise grace would no longer be grace. But if it is of works, then it is no longer grace, because otherwise work is no longer work" (Rom. 11:6).

GOOD WORKS PLEASE GOD. Now the works which we do by faith are pleasing to God and are approved by him. Because of faith in Christ, those who do good works which, moreover, are done from God's grace through the Holy Spirit, are pleasing to God. For St. Peter said: "In every nation any one who fears God and does what is right is acceptable to him." (Acts 10:35.) And Paul said: "We have not ceased to pray for you . . . that you may walk

SECOND HELVETIC CONFESSION (HUNGARIAN
   REFORMED CHURCH) (continued)

worthily of the Lord, fully pleasing to him, bearing fruit in every good work." (Col. 1:9 f.)

WE TEACH TRUE, NOT FALSE AND PHILOSOPHICAL VIRTUES. And so we diligently teach true, not false and philosophical virtues, truly good works, and the genuine service of a Christian. And as much as we can we diligently and zealously press them upon all men, while censuring the sloth and hypocrisy of all those who praise and profess the Gospel with their lips and dishonor it by their disgraceful lives. In this matter we place before them God's terrible threats and then his rich promises and generous rewards—exhorting, consoling and rebuking.

GOD GIVES A REWARD FOR GOOD WORKS. For we teach that God gives a rich reward to those who do good works, according to that saying of the prophet: "Keep your voice from weeping, . . . from your work shall be rewarded" (Jer. 31:16; Isa., ch. 4). The Lord also said in the Gospel: "Rejoice and be glad, for your reward is great in heaven" (Matt. 5:12), and, "Whoever gives to one of these my little ones a cup of cold water, truly, I say to you, he shall not lose his reward" (ch. 10:42). However, we do not ascribe this reward, which the Lord gives, to the merit of the man who receives it, but to the goodness, generosity and truthfulness of God who promises and gives it, and who, although he owes nothing to anyone, nevertheless promises that he will give a reward to his faithful worshippers; meanwhile he also gives them that they may honor him. Moreover, in the works even of the saints there is much that is unworthy of God and very much that is imperfect. But because God receives into favor and embraces those who do works for Christ's sake, he grants to them the promised reward. For in other respects our righteousnesses are compared to a filthy wrap (Isa. 64:6). And the Lord says in the Gospel: "When you have done all that is commanded you, say, 'We are unworthy servants; we have only done what was our duty.'" (Luke 17:10.)

THERE ARE NO MERITS OF MEN. Therefore, although we teach that God rewards our good deeds, yet at the same time we teach, with Augustine, that God does not crown in us our merits but his gifts. Accordingly we say that whatever reward we receive is also grace, and is more grace than reward, because the good we do, we do more through God than through ourselves, and because Paul says: "What have you that you did not receive? If then you received it, why do you boast as if you had not received it?" (I Cor. 4:7). And this is what the blessed martyr Cyprian concluded from this verse: We are not to glory in anything in us, since nothing is our own. We therefore condemn those who defend the merits of men in such a way that they invalidate the grace of God.

CHAPTER XVII. OF THE CATHOLIC AND HOLY CHURCH OF GOD, AND OF THE ONE ONLY HEAD OF THE CHURCH

THE CHURCH HAS ALWAYS EXISTED AND IT WILL ALWAYS EXIST. But because God from the beginning would have men to be saved, and to come to the knowledge of the truth (I Tim. 2:4), it is altogether necessary that there always should have been, and should be now, and to the end of the world, a Church.

WHAT IS THE CHURCH? The Church is an assembly of the faithful called or gathered out of the world: a communion, I say, of all saints, namely, of those who truly know and rightly worship and serve the true God in Christ the Savior, by the Word and Holy Spirit, and who by faith are partakers of all benefits which are freely offered through Christ. *Citizens of One Commonwealth.* They are all citizens of the one city, living under the same Lord, under the same laws, and in the same fellowship of all good things. For the apostle calls them "fellow citizens with the saints and members of the household of God" (Eph. 2:19), calling the faithful on earth saints (I Cor. 4:1), who are sanctified by the blood of the Son of God. The article of the Creed, "I believe in the holy catholic Church, the communion of saints," is to be understood wholly as concerning these saints.

ONLY ONE CHURCH FOR ALL TIMES. And since there is always but one God, and there is one mediator between God and men, Jesus the Messiah, and one Shepherd of the whole flock, one Head of this body, and, to conclude, one Spirit, one salvation, one faith, one Testament or covenant, it necessarily follows that there is only one Church. *The Catholic Church.* We, therefore, call this Church catholic because it is universal, scattered through all parts of the world, and extended unto all times, and is not limited to any times or places. Therefore, we condemn the Donatists who confined the Church to I know not what corners of Africa. Nor do we approve of the Roman clergy who have recently passed off only the Roman Church as catholic.

PARTS OR FORMS OF THE CHURCH. The Church is divided into different parts or forms; not because it is divided or rent asunder in itself, but rather because it is distinguished by the diversity of the numbers that are in it. *Militant and Triumphant.* For the one is called the Church Militant, the other the Church Triumphant. The former still wages war on earth, and fights against the flesh, the world, and the prince of this world, the devil; against sin and death. But the latter, having been now discharged, triumphs in heaven immediately after having overcome all those things and rejoices before the Lord. Notwithstanding both have fellowship and union one with another.

THE PARTICULAR CHURCH. Moreover, the Church Militant upon the earth has always had many particular churches. Yet all these are to be referred to the unity of the catholic Church. This

[Militant] Church was set up differently before the Law among the patriarchs; otherwise under Moses by the Law; and differently by Christ through the Gospel.

THE TWO PEOPLES. Generally two peoples are usually counted, namely, the Israelites and Gentiles, or those who have been gathered from among Jews and Gentiles into the Church. There are also two Testaments, the Old and the New. *The Same Church for the Old and the New People.* Yet from all these people there was and is one fellowship, one salvation in the one Messiah; in whom, as members of one body under one Head, all united together in the same faith, partaking also of the same spiritual food and drink. Yet here we acknowledge a diversity of times, and a diversity in the signs of the promised and delivered Christ; and that now the ceremonies being abolished, the light shines unto us more clearly, and blessings are given to us more abundantly, and a fuller liberty.

THE CHURCH THE TEMPLE OF THE LIVING GOD. This holy Church of God is called the temple of the living God, built of living and spiritual stones and founded upon a firm rock, upon a foundation which no other can lay, and therefore it is called "the pillar and bulwark of the truth" (I Tim. 3:15). *The Church Does Not Err.* It does not err as long as it rests upon the rock Christ, and upon the foundation of the prophets and apostles. And it is no wonder if it errs, as often as it deserts him who alone is the truth. *The Church as Bride and Virgin.* The Church is also called a virgin and the Bride of Christ, and even the only Beloved. For the apostle says: "I betrothed you to Christ to present you as a pure bride to Christ." (II Cor. 11:2.) *The Church as a Flock of Sheep.* The Church is called a flock of sheep under the one shepherd, Christ, according to Ezek., ch. 34, and John, ch. 10. *The Church as the Body.* It is also called the body of Christ because the faithful are living members of Christ under Christ the Head.

CHRIST THE SOLE HEAD OF THE CHURCH. It is the head which has the preeminence in the body, and from it the whole body receives life; by its spirit the body is governed in all things; from it, also, the body receives increase, that it may grow up. Also, there is one head of the body, and it is suited to the body. Therefore the Church cannot have any other head besides Christ. For as the Church is a spiritual body, so it must also have a spiritual head in harmony with itself. Neither can it be governed by any other spirit than by the Spirit of Christ. Wherefore Paul says: "He is the head of the body, the church; he is the beginning, the firstborn from the dead, that in everything he might be preeminent" (Col. 1:18). And in another place: "Christ is the head of the church, his body, and is himself its Savior" (Eph. 5:23). And again: he is "the head over all things for the church, which is his body, the fulness of him who fills all in all" (Eph. 1:22 f.). Also: "We are to grow up in every way into him who is the head, into Christ, from whom the whole body, joined and knit together, makes bodily growth" (Eph. 4:15 f.). And therefore we do not approve of the doctrine of the Roman clergy, who make their Pope at Rome the universal shepherd and supreme head of the Church Militant here on earth, and so the very vicar of Jesus Christ, who has (as they say) all fulness of power and sovereign authority in the Church. *Christ the Only Pastor of the Church.* For we teach that Christ the Lord is, and remains the only universal pastor, and highest Pontiff before God the Father; and that in the Church he himself performs all the duties of a bishop or pastor, even to the world's end; [*Vicar*] and therefore does not need a substitute for one who is absent. For Christ is present with his Church, and is its life-giving Head. *No Primacy in the Church.* He has strictly forbidden his apostles and their successors to have any primacy and dominion in the Church. Who does not see, therefore, that whoever contradicts and opposes this plain truth is rather to be counted among the number of those of whom Christ's apostles prophesied: Peter in II Peter, ch. 2, and Paul in Acts 20:2; II Cor. 11:2; II Thess., ch. 2, and also in other places?

NO DISORDER IN THE CHURCH. However, by doing away with a Roman head we do not bring any confusion or disorder into the Church, since we teach that the government of the Church which the apostles handed down is sufficient to keep the Church in proper order. In the beginning when the Church was without any such Roman head as is now said to keep it in order, the Church was not disordered or in confusion. The Roman head does indeed preserve his tyranny and the corruption that has been brought into the Church, and meanwhile he hinders, resists, and with all the strength he can muster cuts off the proper reformation of the Church.

DISSENSIONS AND STRIFE IN THE CHURCH. We are reproached because there have been manifold dissensions and strife in our churches since they separated themselves from the Church of Rome, and therefore cannot be true churches. As though there were never in the Church of Rome any sects, nor contentions and quarrels concerning religion, and indeed, carried on not so much in the schools as from pulpits in the midst of the people. We know, to be sure, that the apostle said: "God is not a God of confusion but of peace" (I Cor. 14:33), and, "While there is jealousy and strife among you, are you not of the flesh?" Yet we cannot deny that God was in the apostolic Church and that it was a true Church, even though there were wranglings and dissensions in it. The apostle Paul reprehended Peter, an apostle (Gal. 2:11 ff.), and Barnabas dissented from Paul. Great contention arose in the Church of Antioch between them that preached the one Christ, as Luke records in The Acts of the Apostles, ch. 15. And there have at all times been great contentions in the Church, and the most excellent teachers of the Church have differed among themselves about important matters without meanwhile the Church ceasing to be the

Church because of these contentions. For thus it pleases God to use the dissensions that arise in the Church to the glory of his name, to illustrate the truth, and in order that those who are in the right might be manifest (I Cor. 11:19).

OF THE NOTES OR SIGNS OF THE TRUE CHURCH. Moreover, as we acknowledge no other head of the Church than Christ, so we do not acknowledge every church to be the true Church which vaunts herself to be such; but we teach that the true Church is that in which the signs or marks of the true Church are to be found, especially the lawful and sincere preaching of the Word of God as it was delivered to us in the books of the prophets and the apostles, which all lead us unto Christ, who said in the Gospel: "My sheep hear my voice, and I know them, and they follow me; and I give unto them eternal life. A stranger they do not follow, but they flee from him, for they do not know the voice of strangers" (John 10:5, 27, 28).

And those who are such in the Church have one faith and one spirit; and therefore they worship but one God, and him alone they worship in spirit and in truth, loving him alone with all their hearts and with all their strength, praying unto him alone through Jesus Christ, the only Mediator and Intercessor; and they do not seek righteousness and life outside Christ and faith in him. Because they acknowledge Christ the only head and foundation of the Church, and, resting on him, daily renew themselves by repentance, and patiently bear the cross laid upon them. Moreover, joined together with all the members of Christ by an unfeigned love, they show that they are Christ's disciples by persevering in the bond of peace and holy unity. At the same time they participate in the sacraments instituted by Christ, and delivered unto us by his apostles, using them in no other way than as they received them from the Lord. That saying of the apostle Paul is well known to all: "I received from the Lord what I also delivered to you" (I Cor. 11:23 ff.). Accordingly, we condemn all such churches as strangers from the true Church of Christ, which are not such as we have heard they ought to be, no matter how much they brag of a succession of bishops, of unity, and of antiquity. Moreover, we have a charge from the apostles of Christ "to shun the worship of idols" (I Cor. 10:14: I John 5:21), and "to come out of Babylon," and to have no fellowship with her, unless we want to be partakers with her of all God's plagues (Rev. 18:4; II Cor. 6:17).

OUTSIDE THE CHURCH OF GOD THERE IS NO SALVATION. But we esteem fellowship with the true Church of Christ so highly that we deny that those can live before God who do not stand in fellowship with the true Church of God, but separate themselves from it. For as there was no salvation outside Noah's ark when the world perished in the flood; so we believe that there is no certain salvation outside Christ, who offers himself to be enjoyed by the elect in the Church; and hence we teach that those who wish to live ought not to be separated from the true Church of Christ.

THE CHURCH IS NOT BOUND TO ITS SIGNS. Nevertheless, by the signs [of the true Church] mentioned above, we do not so narrowly restrict the Church as to teach that all those are outside the Church who either do not participate in the sacraments, at least not willingly and through contempt, but rather, being forced by necessity, unwillingly abstain from them or are deprived of them; or in whom faith sometimes fails, though it is not entirely extinguished and does not wholly cease; or in whom imperfections and errors due to weakness are found. For we know that God had some friends in the world outside the commonwealth of Israel. We know what befell the people of God in the captivity of Babylon, where they were deprived of their sacrifices for seventy years. We know what happened to St. Peter, who denied his Master, and what is wont to happen daily to God's elect and faithful people who go astray and are weak. We know, moreover, what kind of churches the churches in Galatia and Corinth were in the apostles' time, in which the apostle found fault with many serious offenses; yet he calls them holy churches of Christ (I Cor. 1:2: Gal. 1:2).

THE CHURCH APPEARS AT TIMES TO BE EXTINCT. Yes, and it sometimes happens that God in his just judgment allows the truth of his Word, and the catholic faith, and the proper worship of God to be so obscured and overthrown that the Church seems almost extinct, and no more to exist, as we see to have happened in the days of Elijah (I Kings 19:10, 14), and at other times. Meanwhile God has in this world and in this darkness his true worshippers, and those not a few, but even seven thousand and more (I Kings 19:18; Rev. 7:3 ff.). For the apostle exclaims: "God's firm foundation stands, bearing this seal, 'The Lord knows those who are his,'" etc. (II Tim. 2:19.) Whence the Church of God may be termed invisible; not because the men from whom the Church is gathered are invisible, but because, being hidden from our eyes and known only to God, it often secretly escapes human judgment.

NOT ALL WHO ARE IN THE CHURCH ARE OF THE CHURCH. Again, not all that are reckoned in the number of the Church are saints, and living and true members of the Church. For there are many hypocrites, who outwardly hear the Word of God, and publicly receive the sacraments, and seem to pray to God through Christ alone, to confess Christ to be their only righteousness, and to worship God, and to exercise the duties of charity, and for a time to endure with patience in misfortune. And yet they are inwardly destitute of true illumination of the Spirit, of faith and sincerity of heart, and of perseverance to the end. But eventually the character of these men, for the most part, will be disclosed. For the apostle John says: "They went out from us, but they were not of us: for if they had been of us, they would indeed have continued with us." (I John 2:19.) And although while they simulate piety they are not of the Church, yet they are considered to be in the Church, just as traitors in a state are numbered among its citizens before they are discovered; and as the tares or darnel and chaff are found among the wheat, and as swellings and tumors are found in a sound body, when they are rather diseases and deformities than true members of the body. And therefore the Church of God is rightly compared to a net which catches fish of all kinds, and to a field, in which both wheat and tares are found (Matt. 13:24 ff., 47 ff.).

WE MUST NOT JUDGE RASHLY OR PREMATURELY. Hence we must be very careful not to judge before the time, nor undertake to exclude, reject or cut off those whom the Lord does not want to have excluded or rejected, and those whom we cannot eliminate without loss to the Church. On the other hand, we must be viligant lest while the pious snore the wicked gain ground and do harm to the Church.

THE UNITY OF THE CHURCH IS NOT IN EXTERNAL RITES. Furthermore, we diligently teach that care is to be taken wherein the truth and unity of the Church chiefly lies, lest we rashly provoke and foster schisms in the Church. Unity consists not in outward rites and ceremonies, but rather in the truth and unity of the catholic faith. This catholic faith is not given to us by human laws, but by Holy Scriptures, of which the Apostles' Creed is a compendium. And, therefore, we read in the ancient writers that there was a manifold diversity of rites, but that they were free, and no one ever thought that the unity of the Church was thereby dissolved. So we teach that the true harmony of the Church consists in doctrines and in the true and harmonious preaching of the Gospel of Christ, and in rites that have been expressly delivered by the Lord. And here we especially urge that saying of the apostle: "Let those of us who are perfect have this mind; and if in any thing you are otherwise minded, God will reveal that also to you. Nevertheless let us walk by the same rule according to what we have attained, and let us be of the same mind" (Phil. 3:15 f.).

CHAPTER XVIII. OF THE MINISTERS OF THE CHURCH, THEIR INSTITUTION AND DUTIES

GOD USES MINISTERS IN THE BUILDING OF THE CHURCH. God has always used ministers for the gathering or establishing of a Church for himself, and for the governing and preservation of the same; and still he does, and always will, use them so long as the Church remains on earth. Therefore, the first beginning, institution, and office of ministers is a most ancient arrangement of God himself, and not a new one of men. *Institution and Origin of Ministers.* It is true that God can, by his power, without any means join to himself a Church from among men; but he preferred to deal with men by the ministry of men. Therefore ministers are to be regarded, not as ministers by themselves alone, but as the ministers of God, inasmuch as God effects the salvation of men through them.

THE MINISTRY IS NOT TO BE DESPISED. Hence we warn men to beware lest we attribute what has to do with our conversion and instruction to the secret power of the Holy Spirit in such a way that we make void the ecclesiastical ministry. For it is fitting that we always have in mind the words of the apostle: "How are they to believe in him of whom they have not heard? And how are they to hear without a preacher? So faith comes from hearing, and hearing comes by the word of God" (Rom. 10:14, 17). And also what the Lord said in the Gospel: "Truly, truly, I say to you, he who receives any one whom I send receives me; and he who receives me receives him who sent me" (John 13:20). Likewise a man of Macedonia, who appeared to Paul in a vision while he was in Asia, secretly admonished him, saying: "Come over to Macedonia and help us" (Acts 16:9). And in another place the same apostle said: "We are fellow workmen for God; you are God's tillage, God's building" (I Cor. 3:9).

Yet, on the other hand, we must beware that we do not attribute too much to ministers and the ministry; remembering here also the words of the Lord in the Gospel: "No one can come to me unless my Father draws him" (John 6:44), and the words of the apostle: "What then is Paul? What is Apollos? Servants through whom you believed, as the Lord assigned to each. I planted, Apollos watered, but only God gives the growth" (I Cor. 3:5 ff.). *God Moves the Hearts of Men.* Therefore, let us believe that God teaches us by his word, outwardly through his ministers, and inwardly moves the hearts of his elect to faith by the Holy Spirit; and that therefore we ought to render all glory unto God for this whole favor. But this matter has been dealt with in the first chapter of this Exposition.

WHO THE MINISTERS ARE AND OF WHAT SORT GOD HAS GIVEN TO THE WORLD. And even from the beginning of the world God has used the most excellent men in the whole world (even if many of them were simple in worldly wisdom or philosophy, but were outstanding in true theology), namely, the patriarchs, with whom he frequently spoke by angels. For the patriarchs were the prophets or teachers of their age whom God for this reason wanted to live for several centuries, in order that they might be, as it were, fathers and lights of the world. They were followed by Moses and the prophets renowned throughout all the world.

CHRIST THE TEACHER. After these the heavenly Father even sent his only-begotten Son, the most perfect teacher of the world: in whom is hidden the wisdom of God, and which has come to us through the most holy, simple, and most perfect doctrine of all. For he chose disciples for himself whom he made apostles. These went out into the whole world, and everywhere gathered together churches by the preaching of the Gospel, and then throughout all the churches in the world they appointed pastors or teachers according to Christ's command; through their successors he has taught and governed the Church unto this day. Therefore, as God gave unto his ancient people the patriarchs, together with Moses and the prophets, so also to his people of the New Testament he sent his only-begotten Son, and, with him, the apostles and teachers of the Church.

MINISTERS OF THE NEW TESTAMENT. Furthermore, the ministers of the new people are called by various names. For they are called apostles, prophets, evangelists, bishops, elders, pastors, and teachers (I Cor. 12:28; Eph. 4:11). *The Apostles.* The apostles did not stay in any particular place, but throughout the world gathered together different churches. When they were once established, there ceased to be apostles, and pastors took their place, each in his church. *Prophets.* In former times the prophets were seers, knowing the future; but they also interpreted the Scriptures. Such men are also found still today. *Evangelists.* The writers of the history of the Gospel were called Evangelists; but they also were heralds of the Gospel of Christ; as Paul also commended Timothy: "Do the work of an evangelist" (II Tim. 4:5). *Bishops.* Bishops are the overseers and watchmen of the Church, who administer the food and needs of the life of the Church. *Presbyters.* The presbyters are the elders and, as it were, senators and fathers of the Church, governing it with wholesome counsel. *Pastors.* The pastors both keep the Lord's sheepfold, and also provide for its needs. *Teachers.* The teachers instruct and teach the true faith and godliness. Therefore, the ministers of the churches may now be called bishops, elders, pastors, and teachers.

PAPAL ORDERS. Then in subsequent times many more names of ministers in the Church were introduced into the Church of God. For some were appointed patriarchs, others archbishops, others suffragans; also, metropolitans, archdeacons, deacons, subdeacons, acolyts, exorcists, cantors, porters, and I know not what others, as cardinals, provosts, and priors; greater and lesser fathers, greater and lesser orders. But we are not troubled about all these, about how they once were and are now. For us the apostolic doctrine concerning ministers is sufficient.

CONCERNING MONKS. Since we assuredly know that monks, and the orders or sects of monks, are instituted neither by Christ nor by the apostles, we teach that they are of no use to the Church of God, nay rather, are pernicious. For, although in former times they were tolerable (when they were hermits, earning their living with their own hands, and were not a burden to anyone, but like the laity were everywhere obedient to the pastors of the churches),

yet now the whole world sees and knows what they are like. They formulate I know not what vows; but they lead a life quite contrary to their vows, so that the best of them deserves to be numbered among those of whom the apostle said: "We hear that some of you are living an irregular life, mere busybodies, not doing any work" etc. (II Thess. 3:11). Therefore, we neither have such in our churches, nor do we teach that they should be in the churches of Christ.

MINISTERS ARE TO BE CALLED AND ELECTED. Furthermore, no man ought to usurp the honor of the ecclesiastical ministry; that is, to seize it for himself by bribery or any deceits, or by his own free choice. But let the ministers of the Church be called and chosen by lawful and ecclesiastical election; that is to say, let them be carefully chosen by the Church or by those delegated from the Church for that purpose in a proper order without any uproar, dissension and rivalry. Not any one may be elected, but capable men distinguished by sufficient consecrated learning, pious eloquence, simple wisdom, lastly, by moderation and an honorable reputation, according to that apostolic rule which is compiled by the apostle in I Tim., ch. 3, and Titus, ch. 1.

ORDINATION. And those who are elected are to be ordained by the elders with public prayer and laying on of hands. Here we condemn all those who go off of their own accord, being neither chosen, sent, nor ordained (Jer., ch. 23). We condemn unfit ministers and those not furnished with the necessary gifts of a pastor.

In the meantime we acknowledge that the harmless simplicity of some pastors in the primitive Church sometimes profited the Church more than the many-sided, refined and fastidious, but a little too esoteric learning of others. For this reason we do not reject even today the honest, yet by no means ignorant, simplicity of some.

PRIESTHOOD OF ALL BELIEVERS. To be sure, Christ's apostles call all who believe in Christ "priests," but not on account of an office, but because, all the faithful having been made kings and priests, we are able to offer up spiritual sacrifices to God through Christ (Ex. 19:6; I Peter 2:9; Rev. 1:6). Therefore, the priesthood and the ministry are very different from one another. For the priesthood, as we have just said, is common to all Christians; not so is the ministry. Nor have we abolished the ministry of the Church because we have repudiated the papal priesthood from the Church of Christ.

PRIESTS AND PRIESTHOOD. Surely in the new covenant of Christ there is no longer any such priesthood as was under the ancient people: which had an external anointing, holy garments, and very many ceremonies which were types of Christ, who abolished them all by his coming and fulfilling them. But he himself remains the only priest forever, and lest we derogate anything from him, we do not impart the name of priest to any minister. For the

Lord himself did not appoint any priests in the Church of the New Testament who, having received authority from the suffragan, may daily offer up the sacrifice, that is, the very flesh and blood of the Lord, for the living and the dead, but ministers who may teach and administer the sacraments.

THE NATURE OF THE MINISTERS OF THE NEW TESTAMENT. Paul explains simply and briefly what we are to think of the ministers of the New Testament or of the Christian Church, and what we are to attribute to them. "This is how one should regard us, as servants of Christ and stewards of the mysteries of God" (I Cor. 4:1). Therefore, the apostle wants us to think of ministers as ministers. Now the apostle calls them ὑπηρετας, rowers, who have their eyes fixed on the coxswain, and so men who do not live for themselves or according to their own will, but for others—namely, their masters, upon whose command they altogether depend. For in all his duties every minister of the Church is commanded to carry out only what he has received in commandment from his Lord, and not to indulge his own free choice. And in this case it is expressly declared who is the Lord, namely, Christ; to whom the ministers are subject in all the affairs of the ministry.

MINISTERS AS STEWARDS OF THE MYSTERIES OF GOD. Moreover, to the end that he might expound the ministry more fully, the apostle adds that ministers of the Church are administrators and stewards of the mysteries of God. Now in many passages, especially in Eph., ch. 3. Paul called the mysteries of God the Gospel of Christ. And the sacraments of Christ are also called mysteries by the ancient writers. Therefore for this purpose are the ministers of the Church called—namely, to preach the Gospel of Christ to the faithful, and to administer the sacraments. We read, also, in another place in the Gospel, of "the faithful and wise steward," whom his master will set over his household, to give them their portion of food at the proper time" (Luke 12:42). Again, elsewhere in the Gospel a man takes a journey in a foreign country and, leaving his house, gives his substance and authority over it to his servants, and to each his work.

THE POWER OF MINISTERS OF THE CHURCH. Now, therefore, it is fitting that we also say something about the power and duty of the ministers of the Church. Concerning this power some have argued industriously, and to it have subjected everything on earth, even the greatest things, and they have done so contrary to the commandment of the Lord who has prohibited dominion for his disciples and has highly commended humility (Luke 22:24 ff.: Matt. 18:3 f.; 20:25 ff.). There is, indeed, another power that is pure and absolute, which is called the power of right. According to this power all things in the whole world are subject to Christ, who is Lord of all, as he himself has testified when he said: "All authority in heaven and on earth has been given to me" (Matt. 28:18),

and again, "I am the first and the last, and behold I am alive for evermore, and I have the keys of Hades and Death" (Rev. 1:18): also, "He has the key of David, which opens and no one shall shut, who shuts and no one opens" (Rev. 3:7).

THE LORD RESERVES TRUE POWER FOR HIMSELF. This power the Lord reserves to himself, and does not transfer it to any other, so that he might stand idly by as a spectator while his ministers work. For Isaiah says, "I will place on his shoulder the key of the house of David" (Isa. 22:22), and again, "The government will be upon his shoulders" (Isa. 9:6). For he does not lay the government on other men's shoulders, but still keeps and uses his own power, governing all things.

THE POWER OF THE OFFICE AND OF THE MINISTER. Then there is another power of an office or of ministry limited by him who has full and absolute power. And this is more like a service than a dominion. *The Keys.* For a lord gives up his power to the steward in his house, and for that cause gives him the keys, that he may admit into or exclude from the house those whom his lord will have admitted or excluded. In virtue of this power the minister, because of his office, does that which the Lord has commanded him to do; and the Lord confirms what he does, and wills that what his servant has done will be so regarded and acknowledged, as if he himself had done it. Undoubtedly, it is to this that these evangelical sentences refer: "I will give you the keys of the kingdom of heaven, and whatever you bind on earth shall be bound in heaven, and whatever you loose on earth shall be loosed in heaven" (Matt. 16:19). Again, "If you forgive the sins of any, they are forgiven; if you retain the sins of any, they are retained" (John 20:23). But if the minister does not carry out everything as the Lord has commanded him, but transgresses the bounds of faith, then the Lord certainly makes void what he has done. Wherefore the ecclesiastical power of the ministers of the Church is that function whereby they indeed govern the Church of God, but yet so do all things in the Church as the Lord has prescribed in his Word. When those things are done, the faithful esteem them as done by the Lord himself. But mention has already been made of the keys above.

THE POWER OF MINISTERS IS ONE AND THE SAME, AND EQUAL. Now the one and an equal power or function is given to all ministers in the Church. Certainly, in the beginning, the bishops or presbyters governed the Church in common; no man lifted up himself above another, none usurped greater power or authority over his fellow-bishops. For remembering the words of the Lord: "Let the leader among you become as one who serves" (Luke 22:26), they kept themselves in humility, and by mutual services they helped one another in the governing and preserving of the Church.

ORDER TO BE PRESERVED. Nevertheless, for the sake of preserving order some one of the ministers called the assembly together, proposed matters to be laid before it, gathered the opinions of the others, in short, to the best of man's ability took precaution lest any confusion should arise. Thus did St. Peter, as we read in The Acts of the Apostles, who nevertheless was not on that account preferred to the others, nor endowed with greater authority than the rest. Rightly then does Cyprian the Martyr say, in his *De Simplicitate Clericorum*: "The other apostles were assuredly what Peter was, endowed with a like fellowship of honor and power; but [his] primacy proceeds from unity in order that the Church may be shown to be one."

WHEN AND HOW ONE WAS PLACED BEFORE THE OTHERS. St. Jerome also in his commentary upon The Epistle of Paul to Titus, says something not unlike this: "Before attachment to persons in religion was begun at the instigation of the devil, the churches were governed by the common consultation of the elders; but after every one thought that those whom he had baptized were his own, and not Christ's, it was decreed that one of the elders should be chosen, and set over the rest, upon whom should fall the care of the whole Church, and all schismatic seeds should be removed." Yet St. Jerome does not recommend this decree as divine; for he immediately adds: "As the elders knew from the custom of the Church that they were subject to him who was set over them, so the bishops knew that they were above the elders, more from custom than from the truth of an arrangement by the Lord, and that they ought to rule the Church in common with them." Thus far St. Jerome. Hence no one can rightly forbid a return to the ancient constitution of the Church of God, and to have recourse to it before human custom.

THE DUTIES OF MINISTERS. The duties of ministers are various; yet for the most part they are restricted to two, in which all the rest are comprehended: to the teaching of the Gospel of Christ, and to the proper administration of the sacraments. For it is the duty of the ministers to gather together an assembly for worship in which to expound God's Word and to apply the whole doctrine to the care and use of the Church, so that what is taught may benefit the hearers and edify the faithful. It falls to ministers, I say, to teach the ignorant, and to exhort; and to urge the idlers and lingerers to make progress in the way of the Lord. Moreover, they are to comfort and to strengthen the fainthearted, and to arm them against the manifold temptations of Satan; to rebuke offenders; to recall the erring into the way; to raise the fallen; to convince the gainsayers to drive the wolf away from the sheepfold of the Lord; to rebuke wickedness and wicked men wisely and severly; not to wink at nor to pass over great wickedness. And, besides, they are to administer the sacraments, and to commend the right use of them,

and to prepare all men by wholesome doctrine to receive them; to preserve the faithful in a holy unity; and to check schisms; to catechize the unlearned, to commend the needs of the poor to the Church, to visit, instruct, and keep in the way of life the sick and those afflicted with various temptations. In addition, they are to attend to public prayers or supplications in times of need, together with common fasting, that is, a holy abstinence; and as diligently as possible to see to everything that pertains to the tranquility, peace and welfare of the churches.

But in order that the minister may perform all these things better and more easily, it is especially required of him that he fear God, be constant in prayer, attend to spiritual reading, and in all things and at all times be watchful, and by a purity of life to let his light to shine before all men.

DISCIPLINE. And since discipline is an absolute necessity in the Church and excommunication was once used in the time of the early fathers, and there were ecclesiastical judgments among the people of God, wherein this discipline was exercised by wise and godly men, it also falls to ministers to regulate this discipline for edification, according to the circumstances of the time, public state, and necessity. At all times and in all places the rule is to be observed that everything is to be done for edification, decently and honorably, without oppression and strife. For the apostle testifies that authority in the Church was given to him by the Lord for building up and not for destroying (II Cor. 10:8). And the Lord himself forbade the weeds to be plucked up in the Lord's field, because there would be danger lest the wheat also be plucked up with it (Matt. 13:29 f).

EVEN EVIL MINISTERS ARE TO BE HEARD. Moreover, we strongly detest the error of the Donatists who esteem the doctrine and administration of the sacraments to be either effectual or not effectual, according to the good or evil life of the ministers. For we know that the voice of Christ is to be heard, though it be out of the mouths of evil ministers; because the Lord himself said: "Practice and observe whatever they tell you, but not what they do" (Matt. 23:3). We know that the sacraments are sanctified by the institution and the word of Christ, and that they are effectual to the godly, although they be administered by unworthy ministers. Concerning this matter, Augustine, the blessed servant of God, many times argued from the Scriptures against the Donatists.

SYNODS. Nevertheless, there ought to be proper discipline among ministers. In synods the doctrine and life of ministers is to be carefully examined. Offenders who can be cured are to be rebuked by the elders and restored to the right way, and if they are incurable, they are to be deposed, and like wolves driven away from the flock of the Lord by the true shepherds. For, if they be false teachers, they are not to be tolerated at all. Neither do we disapprove of ecumenical councils, if they are convened according to the example of the apostles, for the welfare of the Church and not for its destruction.

THE WORKER IS WORTHY OF HIS REWARD. All faithful ministers, as good workmen, are also worthy of their reward, and do not sin when they receive a stipend, and all things that be necessary for themselves and their family. For the apostle shows in I Cor., ch. 9, and in I Tim., ch. 5, and elsewhere that these things may rightly be given by the Church and received by ministers. The Anabaptists, who condemn and defame ministers who live from their ministry are also refuted by the apostolic teaching.

CHAPTER XIX. OF THE SACRAMENTS OF THE CHURCH OF CHRIST

THE SACRAMENTS [ARE] ADDED TO THE WORD AND WHAT THEY ARE. From the beginning, God added to the preaching of his Word in his Church sacraments or sacramental signs. For thus does all Holy Scripture clearly testify. Sacraments are mystical symbols, or holy rites, or sacred actions, instituted by God himself, consisting of his Word, of signs and of things signified, whereby in the Church he keeps in mind and from time to time recalls the great benefits he has shown to men; whereby also he seals his promises, and outwardly represents, and, as it were, offers unto our sight those things which inwardly he performs for us, and so strengthens and increases our faith through the working of God's Spirit in our hearts. Lastly, he thereby distinguishes us from all other people and religions, and consecrates and binds us wholly to himself, and signifies what he requires of us.

SOME ARE SACRAMENTS OF THE OLD, OTHERS OF THE NEW, TESTAMENT. Some sacraments are of the old, others of the new, people. The sacraments of the ancient people were circumcision, and the Paschal Lamb, which was offered up; for that reason it is referred to the sacrifices which were practiced from the beginning of the world.

THE NUMBER OF SACRAMENTS OF THE NEW PEOPLE. The sacraments of the new people are Baptism and the Lord's Supper. There are some who count seven sacraments of the new people. Of these we acknowledge that repentance, the ordination of ministers (not indeed the papal but apostolic ordination), and matrimony are profitable ordinances of God, but not sacraments. Confirmation and extreme unction are human inventions which the Church can dispense with without any loss, and indeed, we do not have them in our churches. For they contain some things of which we can by no means approve. Above all we detest all the trafficking in which the Papists engage in dispensing the sacraments.

THE AUTHOR OF THE SACRAMENTS. The author of all sacraments is not any man, but God alone. Men cannot institute sacraments. For they pertain to the worship of God, and it is not for man to appoint and prescribe a worship of God, but to accept and preserve the one he has received from God. Besides, the symbols have God's promises annexed to them, which require faith. Now faith rests only upon the Word of God; and the Word of God is like papers or letters, and the sacraments are like seals which only God appends to the letters.

CHRIST STILL WORKS IN SACRAMENTS. And as God is the author of the sacraments, so he continually works in the Church in which they are rightly carried out; so that the faithful, when they receive them from the ministers, know that God works in his own ordinance, and therefore they receive them as from the hand of God; and the minister's faults (even if they be very great) cannot affect them, since they acknowledge the integrity of the sacraments to depend upon the institution of the Lord.

THE AUTHOR AND THE MINISTERS OF THE SACRAMENTS TO BE DISTINGUISHED. Hence in the administration of the sacraments they also clearly distinguish between the Lord himself and the ministers of the Lord, confessing that the substance of the sacraments is given them by the Lord, and the outward signs by the ministers of the Lord.

THE SUBSTANCE OR CHIEF THING IN THE SACRAMENTS. But the principal thing which God promises in all sacraments and to which all the godly in all ages direct their attention (some call it the substance and matter of the sacraments) is Christ the Savior—that only sacrifice, and that Lamb of God slain from the foundation of the world; that rock, also, from which all our fathers drank, by whom all the elect are circumcised without hands through the Holy Spirit, and are washed from all their sins, and are nourished with the very body and blood of Christ unto eternal life.

THE SIMILARITY AND DIFFERENCE IN THE SACRAMENTS OF OLD AND NEW PEOPLES. Now, in respect of that which is the principal thing and the matter itself in the sacraments, the sacraments of both peoples are equal. For Christ, the only Mediator and Savior of the faithful, is the chief thing and very substance of the sacraments in both; for the one God is the author of them both. They were given to both peoples as signs and seals of the grace and promises of God, which should call to mind and renew the memory of God's great benefits, and should distinguish the faithful from all the religions in the world; lastly, which should be received spiritually by faith, and should bind the receivers to the Church, and admonish them of their duty. In these and similar respects, I say, the sacraments of both peoples are not dissimilar, although in the outward signs they are different. And, indeed, with respect to the signs we make a great difference. For ours are more firm and lasting, inasmuch as they will never be changed to the end of the world. Moreover, ours testify that both the substance and the promise have been fulfilled or perfected in Christ; the former signified what was to be fulfilled. Ours are also more simple and less laborious, less sumptuous and involved with ceremonies. Moreover, they belong to a more numerous people, one that is dispersed throughout the whole earth. And since they are more excellent, and by the Holy Spirit kindle greater faith, a greater abundance of the Spirit also ensues.

OUR SACRAMENTS SUCCEED THE OLD WHICH ARE ABROGATED. But now since Christ the true Messiah is exhibited unto us, and the abundance of grace is poured forth upon the people of the New Testament, the sacraments of the old people are surely abrogated and have ceased; and in their stead the symbols of the New Testament are placed—Baptism in the place of circumcision, the Lord's Supper in place of the Paschal Lamb and sacrifices.

IN WHAT THE SACRAMENTS CONSIST. And as formerly the sacraments consisted of the word, the sign, and the thing signified; so even now they are composed, as it were, of the same parts. For the Word of God makes them sacraments, which before they were not. *The Consecration of the Sacraments.* For they are consecrated by the Word, and shown to be sanctified by him who instituted them. To sanctify or consecrate anything to God is to dedicate it to holy uses; that is, to take it from the common and ordinary use, and to appoint it to a holy use. For the signs in the sacraments are drawn from common use, things external and visible. For in baptism the sign is the element of water, and that visible washing which is done by the minister; but the thing signified is regeneration and the cleansing from sins. Likewise, in the Lord's Supper, the outward sign is bread and wine, taken from things commonly used for meat and drink; but the thing signified is the body of Christ which was given, and his blood which was shed for us, or the communion of the body and blood of the Lord. Wherefore, the water, bread, and wine, according to their nature and apart from the divine institution and sacred use, are only that which they are called and we experience. But when the Word of God is added to them, together with invocation of the divine name, and the renewing of their first institution and sanctification, then these signs are consecrated, and shown to be sanctified by Christ. For Christ's first institution and consecration of the sacraments remains always effectual in the Church of God, so that those who do not celebrate the sacraments in any other way than the Lord himself instituted from the beginning still today enjoy that first and all-surpassing consecration. And hence in the celebration of the sacraments the very words of Christ are repeated.

SIGNS TAKE NAME OF THINGS SIGNIFIED. And as we learn out of the Word of God that these signs were instituted for another purpose than the usual use, therefore we teach that they now, in their holy use, take upon them the names of things signified, and are no longer called mere water, bread or wine, but also regeneration or the washing of water, and the body and blood of the Lord or symbols and sacraments of the Lord's body and blood. Not that the symbols are changed into the things signified, or cease to be what they are in their own nature. For otherwise they would not be sacraments. If they were only the thing signified, they would not be signs.

THE SACRAMENTAL UNION. Therefore the signs acquire the names of things because they are mystical signs of sacred things, and because the signs and the things signified are sacramentally joined together; joined together, I say, or united by a mystical signification, and by the purpose or will of him who instituted the sacraments. For the water, bread, and wine are not common, but holy signs. And he that instituted water in baptism did not institute it with the will and intention that the faithful should only be sprinkled by the water of baptism; and he who commanded the bread to be eaten and the wine to be drunk in the supper did not want the faithful to receive only bread and wine without any mystery as they eat bread in their homes; but that they should spiritually partake of the things signified, and by faith be truly cleansed from their sins, and partake of Christ.

THE SECTS. And, therefore, we do not at all approve of those who attribute the sanctification of the sacraments to I know not what properties and formula or to the power of words pronounced by one who is consecrated and who has the intention of consecrating, and to other accidental things which neither Christ or the apostles delivered to us by word or example. Neither do we approve of the doctrine of those who speak of the sacraments just as common signs, not sanctified and effectual. Nor do we approve of those who despise the visible aspect of the sacraments because of the invisible, and so believe the signs to be superfluous because they think they already enjoy the things themselves, as the Messalians are said to have held.

THE THING SIGNIFIED IS NEITHER IN-CLUDED IN OR BOUND TO THE SACRA-MENTS. We do not approve of the doctrine of those who teach that grace and the things signified are so bound to and included in the signs that whoever participate outwardly in the signs, no matter what sort of persons they be, also inwardly participate in the grace and things signified.

However, as we do not estimate the value of the sacraments by the worthiness or unworthiness of the ministers, so we do not estimate it by the condition of those who receive them. For we know that the value of the sacraments depends upon faith and upon the truthfulness and pure goodness of God. For as the Word of God remains the true Word of God, in which, when it is preached, not only bare words are repeated, but at the same time the things signified or announced in words are offered by God, even if the ungodly and unbelievers hear and understand the words yet do not enjoy the things signified, because they do not receive them by true faith; so the sacraments, which by the Word consist of signs and the things signified, remain true and inviolate sacraments, signifying not only sacred things, but, by God offering, the things signified, even if unbelievers do not receive the things offered. This is not the fault of God who gives and offers them, but the fault of men who receive them without faith and illegitimately; but whose unbelief does not invalidate the faithfulness of God (Rom. 3:3 f.).

THE PURPOSE FOR WHICH SACRAMENTS WERE INSTITUTED. Since the purpose for which sacraments were instituted was also explained in passing when right at the beginning of our exposition it was shown what sacraments are, there is no need to be tedious by repeating what once has been said. Logically, therefore, we now speak severally of the sacraments of the new people.

CHAPTER XX. OF HOLY BAPTISM

THE INSTITUTION OF BAPTISM. Baptism was instituted and consecrated by God. First John baptized, who dipped Christ in the water in Jordan. From him it came to the apostles, who also baptized with water. The Lord expressly commanded them to preach the Gospel and to baptize "in the name of the Father and of the Son and of the Holy Spirit" (Matt. 28:19). And in The Acts, Peter said to the Jews who inquired what they ought to do: "Be baptized every one of you in the name of Jesus Christ for the forgiveness of your sins; and you shall receive the gift of the Holy Spirit" (Acts 2:37 f.). Hence by some baptism is called a sign of initiation for God's people, since by it the elect of God are consecrated to God.

ONE BAPTISM. There is but one baptism in the Church of God; and it is sufficient to be once baptized or consecrated unto God. For baptism once received continues for all of life, and is a perpetual sealing of our adoption.

WHAT IT MEANS TO BE BAPTIZED. Now to be baptized in the name of Christ is to be enrolled, entered, and received into the covenant and family, and so into the inheritance of the sons of God: yes, and in this life to be called after the name of God; that is to say, to be called a son of God; to be cleansed also from the filthiness of sins, and to be granted the manifold grace of God, in order to lead a new and innocent life. Baptism, therefore, calls to mind and renews the great favor God has shown to the race of mortal men. For we are all born in the pollution of sin and are the children of wrath. But God, who is rich in mercy, freely cleanses us from our sins by the blood of his Son, and in him adopts us to be his sons, and by a holy covenant joins us to himself, and enriches us with various gifts, that we might live a new life. All these things are assured by baptism. For inwardly we are regenerated, purified, and renewed by God through the Holy Spirit; and outwardly we receive the assurance of the greatest gifts in the water, by which also those great benefits are represented, and, as it were, set before our eyes to be beheld.

WE ARE BAPTIZED WITH WATER. And therefore we are baptized, that is, washed or sprinkled with visible water. For the water washes dirt away, and cools and refreshes hot and tired bodies. And the grace of God performs these things for souls, and does so invisibly or spirtually.

THE OBLIGATION OF BAPTISM. Moreover, God also separates us from all strange religions and peoples by the symbol of baptism, and consecrates us to himself as his property. We, therefore, confess our faith when we are baptized, and obligate ourselves to God for obedience, mortification of the flesh, and newness of life. Hence, we are enlisted in the holy military service of Christ that all our life long we should fight against the world, Satan, and our own flesh. Moreover, we are baptized into one body of the Church, that with all members of the Church we might beautifully concur in the one religion and in mutual services.

THE FORM OF BAPTISM. We believe that the most perfect form of baptism is that by which Christ was baptized, and by which the apostles baptized. Those things, therefore, which by man's device were added afterwards and used in the Church we do not consider necessary to the perfection of baptism. Of this kind is exorcism, the use of burning lights, oil, salt, spittle, and such other things as that baptism is to be celebrated twice every year with a multitude of ceremonies. For we believe that one baptism of the Church has been sanctified in God's first institution, and that it is consecrated by the Word and is also effectual today in virtue of God's first blessing.

THE MINISTER OF BAPTISM. We teach that baptism should not be administered in the Church by women or midwives. For Paul deprived women of ecclesiastical duties, and baptism has to do with these.

ANABAPTISTS. We condemn the Anabaptists, who deny that newborn infants of the faithful are to be baptized. For according to evangelical teaching, of such is the Kingdom of God, and they are in the covenant of God. Why, then, should the sign of God's covenant not be given to them? Why should those who belong to God and are in his Church not be initiated by holy baptism? We condemn also the Anabaptists in the rest of their peculiar doctrines which they hold contrary to the Word of God. We therefore are not Anabaptists and have nothing in common with them.

CHAPTER XXI. OF THE HOLY SUPPER OF THE LORD

THE SUPPER OF THE LORD. The Supper of the Lord, (which is called the Lord's Table, and the Eucharist, that is, a Thanksgiving) is, therefore, usually called a supper, because it was instituted by Christ at his last supper, and still represents it, and because in it the faithful are spiritually fed and given drink.

THE AUTHOR AND CONSECRATOR OF THE SUPPER. For the author of the Supper of the Lord is not an angel or any man, but the Son of God himself, our Lord Jesus Christ, who first consecrated it to his Church. And the same consecration or blessing still remains among all those who celebrate no other but that very Supper which the Lord instituted, and at which they repeat the words of the Lord's Supper, and in all things look to the one Christ by a true faith, from whose hands they receive, as it were, what they receive through the ministry of the ministers of the Church.

A MEMORIAL OF GOD'S BENEFITS. By this sacred rite the Lord wishes to keep in fresh remembrance that greatest benefit which he showed to mortal men, namely, that by having given his body and shed his blood he has pardoned all our sins, and redeemed us from eternal death and the power of the devil, and now feeds us with his flesh, and gives us his blood to drink, which, being received spiritually by true faith, nourish us to eternal life. And this so great a benefit is renewed as often as the Lord's Supper is celebrated. For the Lord said: "Do this in remembrance of me." This holy Supper also seals to us that the very body of Christ was truly given for us, and his blood shed for the remission of our sins, lest our faith should in any way waver.

THE SIGN AND THING SIGNIFIED. And this is visibly represented by this sacrament outwardly through the ministers, and, as it were, presented to our eyes to be seen, which is invisibly wrought by the Holy Spirit inwardly in the soul. Bread is outwardly offered by the minister, and the words of the Lord are heard: "Take, eat; this is my body"; and, "Take and divide among you. Drink of it, all of you; this is my blood." Therefore the faithful receive what is given by the ministers of the Lord, and they eat the bread of the Lord and drink of the Lord's cup. At the same time by the work of Christ through the Holy Spirit they also inwardly receive the flesh and blood of the Lord, and are thereby nourished unto life eternal. For the flesh and blood of Christ is the true food and drink unto life eternal; and Christ himself, since he was given for us and is our Savior, is the principal thing in the Supper, and we do not permit anything else to be substituted in his place.

But in order to understand better and more clearly how the flesh and blood of Christ are the food and drink of the faithful, and are received by the faithful unto eternal life, we would add these few things. There is more than one kind of eating. There is corporeal eating whereby food is taken into the mouth, is chewed with the teeth, and swallowed into the stomach. In times past the Capernaites thought that the flesh of the Lord should be eaten in this way, but they are refuted by him in John, ch. 6. For as the flesh of Christ cannot be eaten corporeally without infamy and savagery, so it is not food for the stomach. All men are forced to admit this. We therefore disapprove of that canon in the Pope's decrees, *Ego Berengarius (De Consecrat.*, Dist. 2). For neither did godly antiquity believe, nor do we believe, that the body of Christ is to be eaten corporeally and essentially with a bodily mouth.

SPIRITUAL EATING OF THE LORD. There is also a spiritual eating of Christ's body; not such that we think that thereby the food itself is to be changed into spirit, but whereby the body and blood of the Lord, while remaining in their own essence and property, are spiritually communicated to us, certainly not in a corporeal but in a spiritual way, by the Holy Spirit, who applies and bestows upon us these things which have been prepared for us by the sacrifice of the Lord's body and blood for us, namely, the remission of sins, deliverance, and eternal life; so that Christ lives in us and we live in him, and he causes us to receive him by true faith to this end that he may become for us such spiritual food and drink, that is, our life.

CHRIST AS OUR FOOD SUSTAINS US IN LIFE. For even as bodily food and drink not only refresh and strengthen our bodies, but also keeps them alive, so the flesh of Christ delivered for us, and his blood shed for us, not only refresh and strengthen our souls, but also preserve them alive, not in so far as they are corporeally eaten and drunken, but in so far as they are communicated unto us spiritually by the Spirit of God, as the Lord said: "The bread which I shall give for the life of the world is my flesh" (John 6:51), and "the flesh" (namely what is eaten bodily) "is of no avail; it is the spirit that gives life" (v. 63). And: "The words that I have spoken to you are spirit and life."

CHRIST RECEIVED BY FAITH. And as we must by eating receive food into our bodies in order that it may work in us, and prove its efficacy in us—since it profits us nothing when it remains outside us—so it is necessary that we receive Christ by faith, that he may become ours, and he may live in us and we in him. For he says: "I am the bread of life; he who comes to me shall not hunger, and he who believes in me shall never thirst" (John 6:35); and also, "He who eats me will live because of me . . . he abides in me, I in him" (vs. 57, 56).

SPIRITUAL FOOD. From all this it is clear that by spiritual food we do not mean some imaginary food I know not what, but the very body of the Lord given to us, which nevertheless is received by the faithful not corporeally, but spiritually by faith. In this matter we follow the teaching of the Savior himself, Christ the Lord, according to John, ch.6.

EATING NECESSARY FOR SALVATION. And this eating of the flesh and drinking of the blood of the Lord is so necessary for salvation that without it no man can be saved. But this spiritual eating and drinking also occurs apart from the Supper of the

Lord, and as often and wherever a man believes in Christ. To which that sentence of St. Augustine's perhaps applies: "Why do you provide for your teeth and your stomach? Believe, and you have eaten."

SACRAMENTAL EATING OF THE LORD. Besides the higher spiritual eating there is also a sacramental eating of the body of the Lord by which not only spiritually and internally the believer truly participates in the true body and blood of the Lord, but also, by coming to the Table of the Lord, outwardly receives the visible sacrament of the body and blood of the Lord. To be sure, when the believer believed, he first received the life-giving food, and still enjoys it. But therefore, when he now receives the sacrament, he does not receive nothing. For he progresses in continuing to communicate in the body and blood of the Lord, and so his faith is kindled and grows more and more, and is refreshed by spiritual food. For while we live, faith is continually increased. And he who outwardly receives the sacrament by true faith, not only receives the sign, but also, as we said, enjoys the thing itself. Moreover, he obeys the Lord's institution and commandment, and with a joyful mind gives thanks for his redemption and that of all mankind, and makes a faithful memorial to the Lord's death, and gives a witness before the Church, of whose body he is a member. Assurance is also given to those who receive the sacrament that the body of the Lord was given and his blood shed, not only for men in general, but particularly for every faithful communicant, to whom it is food and drink unto eternal life.

UNBELIEVERS TAKE THE SACRAMENT TO THEIR JUDGMENT. But he who comes to this sacred Table of the Lord without faith, communicates only in the sacrament and does not receive the substance of the sacrament whence comes life and salvation; and such men unworthily eat of the Lord's Table. Whoever eats the bread or drinks the cup of the Lord in an unworthy manner will be guilty of the body and blood of the Lord, and eats and drinks judgment upon himself (I Cor. II:26-29). For when they do not approach with true faith, they dishonor the death of Christ, and therefore eat and drink condemnation to themselves.

THE PRESENCE OF CHRIST IN THE SUPPER. We do not, therefore, so join the body of the Lord and his blood with the bread and wine as to say that the bread itself is the body of Christ except in a sacramental way; or that the body of Christ is hidden corporeally under the bread, so that it ought to be worshipped under the form of bread; or yet that whoever receives the sign, receives also the thing itself. The body of Christ is in heaven at the right hand of the Father; and therefore our hearts are to be lifted up on high, and not to be fixed on the bread, neither is the Lord to be worshipped in the bread. Yet the Lord is not absent from his Church when she celebrates the Supper. The sun, which is absent from us in the heavens, is notwithstanding effectually present among us. How much more is the Sun of

Righteousness, Christ, although in his body he is absent from us in heaven, present with us, not corporeally, but spiritually, by his vivifying operation, and as he himself explained at his Last Supper that he would be present with us (John, chs. 14; 15; and 16). Whence it follows that we do not have the Supper without Christ, and yet at the same time have an unbloody and mystical Supper, as it was universally called by antiquity.

OTHER PURPOSES OF THE LORD'S SUPPER. Moreover, we are admonished in the celebration of the Supper of the Lord to be mindful of whose body we have become members, and that, therefore, we may be of one mind with all the brethren, live a holy life, and not pollute ourselves with wickedness and strange religions; but, persevering in the true faith to the end of our life, strive to excel in holiness of life.

PREPARATION FOR THE SUPPER. It is therefore fitting that when we would come to the Supper, we first examine ourselves according to the commandment of the apostle, especially as to the kind of faith we have, whether we believe that Christ has come to save sinners and to call them to repentance, and whether each man believes that he is in the number of those who have been delivered by Christ and saved; and whether he is determined to change his wicked life, to lead a holy life, and with the Lord's help to persevere in the true religion and in harmony with the brethren, and to give due thanks to God for his deliverance.

THE OBSERVANCE OF THE SUPPER WITH BOTH BREAD AND WINE. We think that rite, manner, or form of the Supper to be the most simple and excellent which comes nearest to the first institution of the Lord and to the apostles' doctrine. It consists in proclaiming the Word of God, in godly prayers, in the action of the Lord himself, and its repetition, in the eating of the Lord's body and drinking of his blood; in a fitting remembrance of the Lord's death, and a faithful thanksgiving; and in a holy fellowship in the union of the body of the Church.

We therefore disapprove of those who have taken from the faithful one species of the sacrament, namely, the Lord's cup. For these seriously offend against the institution of the Lord who says: "Drink ye all of this"; which he did not so expressly say of the bread.

We are now discussing what kind of mass once existed among the fathers, whether it is to be tolerated or not. But this we say freely that the mass which is now used throughout the Roman Church has been abolished in our churches for many and very good reasons which, for brevity's sake, we do not now enumerate in detail. We certainly could not approve of making a wholesome action into a vain spectacle and a means of gaining merit, and of celebrating it for a price. Nor could we approve of saying that in it the priest is said to effect the very body of the Lord, and really to offer it for the

SECOND HELVETIC CONFESSION (HUNGARIAN REFORMED CHURCH) (continued)

remission of the sins of the living and the dead, and in addition, for the honor, veneration and remembrance of the saints in heaven, etc.

CHAPTER XXII. OF RELIGIOUS AND ECCLESIASTICAL MEETINGS

WHAT OUGHT TO BE DONE IN MEETINGS FOR WORSHIP. Although it is permitted all men to read the Holy Scriptures privately at home, and by instruction to edify one another in the true religion, yet in order that the Word of God may be properly preached to the people, and prayers and supplication publicly made, also that the sacraments may be rightly administered, and that collections may be made for the poor and to pay the cost of all the Church's expenses, and in order to maintain social intercourse, it is most necessary that religious or Church gatherings be held. For it is certain that in the apostolic and primitive Church, there were such assemblies frequented by all the godly.

MEETINGS FOR WORSHIP NOT TO BE NEGLECTED. As many as spurn such meetings and stay away from them, despise true religion, and are to be urged by the pastors and godly magistrates to abstain from stubbornly absenting themselves from sacred assemblies.

MEETINGS ARE PUBLIC. But Church meetings are not to be secret and hidden, but public and well attended, unless persecution by the enemies of Christ and the Church does not permit them to be public. For we know how under the tyranny of the Roman emperors the meetings of the primitive Church were held in secret places.

DECENT MEETING PLACES. Moreover, the places where the faithful meet are to be decent, and in all respects fit for God's Church. Therefore, spacious buildings or temples are to be chosen, but they are to be purged of everything that is not fitting for a church. And everything is to be arranged for decorum, necessity, and godly decency, lest anything be lacking that is required for worship and the necessary works of the Church.

MODESTY AND HUMILITY TO BE OBSERVED IN MEETINGS. And as we believe that God does not dwell in temples made with hands, so we know that on account of God's Word and sacred use places dedicated to God and his worship are not profane, but holy, and that those who are present in them are to conduct themselves reverently and modestly, seeing that they are in a sacred place, in the presence of God and his holy angels.

THE TRUE ORNAMENTATION OF SANCTUARIES. Therefore, all luxurious attire, all pride, and everything unbecoming to Christian humility, discipline and modesty, are to be banished from the sanctuaries and places of prayer of Christians. For the true ornamentation of churches does not consist in ivory, gold, and precious stones, but in the frugality, piety, and virtues of those who are in the Church. Let all things be done decently and in order in the church, and finally, let all things be done for edification.

WORSHIP IN THE COMMON LANGUAGE. Therefore, let all strange tongues keep silence in gatherings for worship, and let all things be set forth in a common language which is understood by the people gathered in that place.

CHAPTER XXIII. OF THE PRAYERS OF THE CHURCH, OF SINGING, AND OF CANONICAL HOURS

COMMON LANGUAGE. It is true that a man is permitted to pray privately in any language that he understands, but public prayers in meetings for worship are to be made in the common language known to all. *Prayer.* Let all the prayers of the faithful be poured forth to God alone, through the mediation of Christ only, out of faith and love. The priesthood of Christ the Lord and true religion forbid the invocation of saints in heaven or to use them as intercessors. Prayer is to be made for magistracy, for kings, and all that are placed in authority, for ministers of the Church, and for all needs of churches. In calamities, especially of the Church, unceasing prayer is to be made both privately and publicly.

FREE PRAYER. Moreover, prayer is to be made voluntarily, without constraint or for any reward. Nor is it proper for prayer to be superstitiously restricted to one place, as if it were not permitted to pray anywhere except in a sanctuary. Neither is it necessary for public prayers to be the same in all churches with respect to form and time. Each Church is to exercise its own freedom. Socrates, in his history, says, "In all regions of the world you will not find two churches which wholly agree in prayer." (*Hist. ecclesiast.* V.22, 57.) The authors of this difference, I think, were those who were in charge of the Churches at particular times. Yet if they agree, it is to be highly commended and imitated by others.

THE METHOD TO BE EMPLOYED IN PUBLIC PRAYERS. As in everything, so also in public prayers there is to be a standard lest they be excessively long and irksome. The greater part of meetings for worship is therefore to be given to evangelical teaching, and care is to be taken lest the congregation is wearied by too lengthy prayers and when they are to hear the preaching of the Gospel they either leave the meeting or, having been exhausted, want to do away with it altogether. To such people the sermon seems to be overlong, which otherwise is brief enough. And therefore it is appropriate for preachers to keep to a standard.

SINGING. Likewise moderation is to be exercised where singing is used in a meeting for worship. That song which they call the Gregorian Chant has many foolish things in it; hence it is rightly rejected by many of our churches. If there are churches which have a true and proper sermon but no singing, they ought not to be condemned. For all churches do not have the advantage of singing. And it is well known from testimonies of antiquity that the custom of singing is very old in the Eastern Churches whereas it was late when it was at length accepted in the West.

CANONICAL HOURS. Antiquity knew nothing of canonical hours, that is, prayers arranged for certain hours of the day, and sung or recited by the Papists, as can be proved from their breviaries and by many arguments. But they also have not a few absurdities, of which I say nothing else; accordingly they are rightly omitted by churches which substitute in their place things that are beneficial for the whole Church of God.

CHAPTER XXIV. OF HOLY DAYS, FASTS AND THE CHOICE OF FOODS

THE TIME NECESSARY FOR WORSHIP. Although religion is not bound to time, yet it cannot be cultivated and exercised without a proper distribution and arrangement of time. Every Church, therefore, chooses for itself a certain time for public prayers, and for the preaching of the Gospel, and for the celebration of the sacraments; and no one is permitted to overthrow this appointment of the Church at his own pleasure. For unless some due time and leisure is given for the outward exercise of religion, without doubt men would be drawn away from it by their own affairs.

THE LORD'S DAY. Hence we see that in the ancient churches there were not only certain set hours in the week appointed for meetings, but that also the Lord's Day itself, ever since the apostles' time, was set aside for them and for a holy rest, a practice now rightly preserved by our Churches for the sake of worship and love.

SUPERSTITION. In this connection we do not yield to the Jewish observance and to superstitions. For we do not believe that one day is any holier than another, or think that rest in itself is acceptable to God. Moreover, we celebrate the Lord's Day and not the Sabbath as a free observance.

THE FESTIVALS OF CHRIST AND THE SAINTS. Moreover, if in Christian liberty the churches religiously celebrate the member of the Lord's nativity, circumcision, passion, resurrection, and of his ascension into heaven, and the sending of the Holy Spirit upon his disciples, we approve of it highly. But we do not approve of feasts instituted for men and for saints. Holy days have to do with the first Table of the Law and belong to God alone. Finally, holy days which have been instituted for the saints and which we have abolished, have much that is absurd and useless, and are not to be tolerated. In the meantime, we confess that the remembrance of saints, at a suitable time and place, is to be profitably commended to the people in sermons, and the holy examples of the saints set forth to be imitated by all.

FASTING. Now, the more seriously the Church of Christ condemns surfeiting, drunkenness, and all kinds of lust and intemperance, so much the more strongly does it commend to us Christian fasting. For fasting is nothing else than the abstinence and moderation of the godly, and a discipline, care and chastisement of our flesh undertaken as a necessity for the time being, whereby we are humbled before God, and we deprive the flesh of its fuel so that it may the more willingly and easily obey the Spirit. Therefore, those who pay no attention to such things do not fast, but imagine that they fast if they stuff their stomachs once a day, and at a certain or prescribed time abstain from certain foods, thinking that by having done this work they please God and do something good. Fasting is an aid to the prayers of the saints and for all virtues. But as is seen in the books of the prophets, the fast of the Jews who fasted from food but not from wickedness did not please God.

PUBLIC AND PRIVATE FASTING. Now there is a public and a private fasting. In olden times they celebrated public fasts in calamitous times and in the affliction of the Church. They abstained altogether from food till the evening, and spent all that time in holy prayers, the worship of God, and repentance. These differed little from mourning, and there is frequent mention of them in the Prophets and especially by Joel in ch. 2. Such a fast should be kept at this day, when the Church is in distress. Private fasts are undertaken by each one of us, as he feels himself withdrawn from the Spirit. For in this manner he withdraws the flesh from its fuel.

CHARACTERISTICS OF FASTING. All fasts ought to proceed from a free and willing spirit, and from genuine humility, and not feigned to gain the applause or favor of men, much less that a man should wish to merit righteousness by them. But let every one fast to this end, that he may deprive the flesh of its fuel in order that he may the more zealously serve God.

LENT. The fast of Lent is attested by antiquity but not at all in the writings of the apostles. Therefore it ought not, and cannot, be imposed on the faithful. It is certain that formerly there were various forms and customs of fasting. Hence, Irenaeus, a most ancient writer, says: "Some think that a fast should be observed one day only, others two days, but others more, and some forty days. This diversity in keeping this fast did not first begin in our times, but long before us by those, as I suppose, who did not simply keep to what had been delivered to them from the beginning, but afterwards fell into another custom either through negligence or ignorance" (*Fragm.* 3, ed. Stieren, I. 824 f.). Moreover, Socrates, the historian, says: "Because no ancient text is found concerning this matter, I think the apostles left this to every man's own judgment, that every one might do what is good without fear or constraint" (*Hist. ecclesiast.* V.22, 40).

SECOND HELVETIC CONFESSION (HUNGARIAN REFORMED CHURCH) (continued)

CHOICE OF FOOD. Now concerning the choice of foods, we think that in fasting all things should be denied to the flesh whereby the flesh is made more insolent, and by which it is greatly pleased, and by which it is inflamed with desire whether by fish or meat or spices or delicacies and excellent wines. Moreover, we know that all the creatures of God were made for the use and service of men. All things which God made are good, and without distinction are to be used in the fear of God and with proper moderation (Gen. 2:15 f.). For the apostle says: "To the pure all things are pure" (Titus 1:15), and also: "Eat whatever is sold in the meat market without raising any question on the ground of conscience" (I Cor. 10:25). The same apostle calls the doctrine of those who teach to abstain from meats "the doctrine of demons"; for "God created foods to be received with thanksgiving by those who believe and know this truth that everything created by God is good, and nothing is to be rejected if it is received with thanksgiving" (I Tim. 4:1 ff.). The same apostle, in the epistle to the Colossians, reproves those who want to acquire a reputation for holiness by excessive abstinence (Col. 2:18 ff.).

SECTS. Therefore we entirely disapprove of the Tatians and the Encratites, and all the disciples of Eustathius, against whom the Gangrian Synod was called.

CHAPTER XXV. OF CATECHIZING AND OF COMFORTING AND VISITING THE SICK

YOUTH TO BE INSTRUCTED IN GODLINESS. The Lord enjoined his ancient people to exercise the greatest care that young people, even from infancy, be properly instructed. Moreover, he expressly commanded in his law that they should teach them, and that the mysteries of the sacraments should be explained. Now since it is well known from the writings of the Evangelists and apostles that God has no less concern for the youth of his new people, when he openly testifies and says: "Let the children come to me; for to such belongs the kingdom of heaven" (Mark 10:14), the pastors of the churches act most wisely when they early and carefully catechize the youth, laying the first grounds of faith, and faithfully teaching the rudiments of our religion by expounding the Ten Commandments, the Apostles' Creed, the Lord's Prayer, and the doctrine of the sacraments, with other such principles and chief heads of our religion. Here let the Church show her faith and diligence in bringing the children to be catechized, desirous and glad to have her children well instructed.

THE VISITATION OF THE SICK. Since men are never exposed to more grievous temptations than when they are harassed by infirmities, are sick and are weakened by diseases of both soul and body, surely it is never more fitting for pastors of churches to watch more carefully for the welfare of their flocks than in such diseases and infirmities. Therefore let them visit the sick soon, and let them be called in good time by the sick, if the circumstance itself would have required it. Let them comfort and confirm them in the true faith, and then arm them against the dangerous suggestions of Satan. They should also hold prayer for the sick in the home and, if need be, prayers should also be made for the sick in the public meeting; and they should see that they happily depart this life. We said above that we do not approve of the Popish visitation of the sick with extreme unction because it is absurd and is not approved by canonical Scriptures.

CHAPTER XXVI. OF THE BURIAL OF THE FAITHFUL, AND OF THE CARE TO BE SHOWN FOR THE DEAD; OF PURGATORY, AND THE APPEARING OF SPIRITS

THE BURIAL OF BODIES. As the bodies of the faithful are the temples of the Holy Spirit which we truly believe will rise again at the Last Day, Scriptures command that they be honorably and without superstition committed to the earth, and also that honorable mention be made of those saints who have fallen asleep in the Lord, and that all duties of familial piety be shown to those left behind, their widows and orphans. We do not teach that any other care be taken for the dead. Therefore, we greatly disapprove of the Cynics, who neglected the bodies of the dead or most carelessly and disdainfully cast them into the earth, never saying a good word about the deceased, or caring a bit about those whom they left behind them.

THE CARE FOR THE DEAD. On the other hand, we do not approve of those who are overly and absurdly attentive to the deceased; who, like the heathen, bewail their dead (although we do not blame that moderate mourning which the apostle permits in I Thess. 4:13, judging it to be inhuman not to grieve at all); and who sacrifice for the dead, and mumble certain prayers for pay, in order by such ceremonies to deliver their loved ones from the torments in which they are immersed by death, and then think they are able to liberate them by such incantations.

THE STATE OF THE SOUL DEPARTED FROM THE BODY. For we believe that the faithful, after bodily death, go directly to Christ, and, therefore, do not need the eulogies and prayers of the living for the dead and their services. Likewise we believe that unbelievers are immediately cast into hell from which no exit is opened for the wicked by any services of the living.

PURGATORY. But what some teach concerning the fire of purgatory is opposed to the Christian faith, namely, "I believe in the forgiveness of sins, and the life everlasting," and to the perfect purgation through Christ, and to these words of Christ our Lord: "Truly, truly, I say to you, he who hears my word and believes him who sent me, has eternal life; he shall not come into judgment, but has passed from death to life" (John 5:24). Again: "He who has bathed does not need to wash, except for his feet, but he is clean all over, and you are clean" (John 13:10).

THE APPARITION OF SPIRITS. Now what is related of the spirits or souls of the dead sometimes appearing to those who are alive, and begging certain duties of them whereby they may be set free, we count those apparitions among the laughingstocks, crafts, and deceptions of the devil, who, as he can transform himself into an angel of light, so he strives either to overthrow the true faith or to call it into doubt. In the Old Testament the Lord forbade the seeking of the truth from the dead, and any sort of commerce with spirits. (Deut. 18:11.) Indeed, as evangelical truth declares, the glutton, being in torment, is denied a return to his brethren, as the divine oracle declares in the words: "They have Moses and the prophets; let them hear them. If they hear not Moses and the prophets, neither will they be convinced if some one should rise from the dead" (Luke 16:29 ff.).

CHAPTER XXVII. OF RITES, CEREMONIES AND THINGS INDIFFERENT

CEREMONIES AND RITES. Unto the ancient people were given at one time certain ceremonies, as a kind of instruction for those who were kept under the law, as under a schoolmaster or tutor. But when Christ, the Deliverer, came and the law was abolished, we who believe are no more under the law (Rom. 6:14), and the ceremonies have disappeared; hence the apostles did not want to retain or to restore them in Christ's Church to such a degree that they openly testified that they did not wish to impose any burden upon the Church. Therefore, we would seem to be bringing in and restoring Judaism if we were to increase ceremonies and rites in Christ's Church according to the custom in the ancient Church. Hence, we by no means approve of the opinion of those who think that the Church of Christ must be held in check by many different rites, as if by some kind of training. For if the apostles did not want to impose upon Christian people ceremonies or rites which were appointed by God, who, I pray, in his right mind would obtrude upon them the inventions devised by man? The more the mass of rites is increased in the Church, the more is detracted not only from Christian liberty, but also from Christ, and from faith in him, as long as the people seek those things in ceremonies which they should seek in the only Son of God, Jesus Christ, through faith. Wherefore a few moderate and simple rites, that are not contrary to the Word of God, are sufficient for the godly.

DIVERSITY OF RITES. If different rites are found in churches, no one should think that for this reason the churches disagree. Socrates says: "It would be impossible to put together in writing all the rites of churches throughout cities and countries. No religion observes the same rites, even though it embraces the same doctrine concerning them. For those who are of the same faith disagree among themselves about rites." *(Hist. ecclesiast.* V.22, 30, 62.) This much says Socrates. And we, today, having in our churches different rites in the celebration of the Lord's Supper and in some other things, nevertheless do not disagree in doctrine and faith; nor is the unity and fellowship of our churches thereby rent asunder. For the churches have always used their liberty in such rites, as being things indifferent. We also do the same thing today.

THINGS INDIFFERENT. But at the same time we admonish men to be on guard lest they reckon among things indifferent what are in fact not indifferent, as some are wont to regard the mass and the use of images in places of worship as things indifferent. "Indifferent," wrote Jerome to Augustine, "is that which is neither good nor bad, so that, whether you do it or not, you are neither just nor unjust." Therefore, when things indifferent are wrested to the confession of faith, they cease to be free; as Paul shows that it is lawful for a man to eat flesh if someone does not remind him that it was offered to idols; for then it is unlawful, because he who eats it seems to approve idolatry by eating it (I Cor. 8:9 ff.; 10:25 ff.).

CHAPTER XXVIII. OF THE POSSESSIONS OF THE CHURCH

THE POSSESSIONS OF THE CHURCH AND THEIR PROPER USE. The Church of Christ possesses riches through the munificence of princes and the liberality of the faithful who have given their means to the Church. For the Church has need of such resources and from ancient time has had resources for the maintenance of things necessary for the Church. Now the true use of the Church's wealth was, and is now, to maintain teaching in schools and in religious meetings, along with all the worship, rites, and buildings of the Church; finally, to maintain teachers, scholars, and ministers, with other necessary things, and especially for the succor and relief of the poor. *Management.* Moreover, God-fearing and wise men, noted for the management of domestic affairs, should be chosen to administer properly the Church's possessions.

THE MISUSE OF THE CHURCH'S POSSESSIONS. But if through misfortune or through the audacity, ignorance or avarice of some persons the Church's wealth is abused, it is to be restored to a sacred use by godly and wise men. For neither is an abuse, which is the greatest sacrilege, to be winked at. Therefore, we teach that schools and institutions which have been corrupted in doctrine, worship and morals must be reformed, and that the relief of the poor must be arranged dutifully, wisely, and in good faith.

CHAPTER XXIX. OF CELIBACY, MARRIAGE AND THE MANAGEMENT OF DOMESTIC AFFAIRS

SINGLE PEOPLE. Those who have the gift of celibacy from heaven, so that from the heart or with their whole soul are pure and continent and are not aflame with passion, let them serve the Lord in that calling, as long as they feel endued with that divine gift; and let them not lift up themselves above others, but let them serve the Lord continuously in simplicity and humility (I Cor. 7:7 ff.). For such are more apt to attend to divine things than those who are distracted with the private affairs of a family. But if, again, the gift be taken away, and they feel a continual burning, let them call to mind the words of the apostle: "It is better to marry than to be aflame" (I Cor. 7:9).

MARRIAGE. For marriage (which is the medicine of incontinency, and continency itself) was instituted by the Lord God himself, who blessed it most bountifully, and willed man and woman to cleave one to the other inseparably, and to live together in complete love and concord (Matt. 19:4 ff.). Whereupon we know that the apostle said: "Let marriage be held in honor among all, and let the marriage bed be undefiled." (Heb. 13:4.) And again: "If a girl marries, she does not sin" (I Cor. 7:28). *The sects.* We therefore condemn polygamy, and those who condemn second marriages.

HOW MARRIAGES ARE TO BE CONTRACTED. We teach that marriages are to be lawfully contracted in the fear of the Lord, and not against the laws which forbid certain degrees of consanguinity, lest the marriages should be incestuous. Let marriages be made with consent of the parents, or of those who take the place of parents, and above all for that purpose for which the Lord instituted marriages. Moreover, let them be kept holy with the utmost faithfulness, piety, love and purity of those joined together. Therefore let them guard against quarrels, dissensions, lust and adultery.

MATRIMONIAL FORUM. Let lawful courts be established in the Church, and holy judges who may care for marriages, and may repress all unchastity and shamefulness, and before whom matrimonial disputes may be settled.

THE REARING OF CHILDREN. Children are to be brought up by the parents in the fear of the Lord; and parents are to provide for their children, remembering the saying of the apostle: "If anyone does not provide for his relatives, he has disowned the faith and is worse than an unbeliever" (I Tim. 5:8). But especially they should teach their children honest trades or professions by which they may support themselves. They should keep them from idleness and in all these things instill in them true faith in God, lest through a lack of confidence or too much security or filthy greed they become dissolute and achieve no success.

And it is most certain that those works which are done by parents in true faith by way of domestic duties and the management of their households are in God's sight holy and truly good works. They are no less pleasing to God than prayers, fasting and almsgiving. For thus the apostle has taught in his epistles, especially in those to Timothy and Titus. And with the same apostle we account the doctrine of those who forbid marriage or openly castigate or indirectly discredit it, as if it were not holy and pure, among the doctrine of demons.

We also detest an impure single life, the secret and open lusts and fornications of hypocrites pretending to be continent when they are the most incontinent of all. All these God will judge. We do not disapprove of riches or rich men, if they be godly and use their riches well. But we reject the sect of the Apostolicals, etc.

CHAPTER XXX. OF THE MAGISTRACY

THE MAGISTRACY IS FROM GOD. Magistracy of every kind is instituted by God himself for the peace and tranquillity of the human race, and thus it should have the chief place in the world. If the magistrate is opposed to the Church, he can hinder and disturb it very much; but if he is a friend and even a member of the Church, he is a most useful and excellent member of it, who is able to benefit it greatly, and to assist it best of all.

THE DUTY OF THE MAGISTRATE. The chief duty of the magistrate is to secure and preserve peace and public tranquillity. Doubtless he will never do this more successfully than when he is truly God-fearing and religious; that is to say, when, according to the example of the most holy kings and princes of the people of the Lord, he promotes the preaching of the truth and sincere faith, roots out lies and all superstition, together with all impiety and idolatry, and defends the Church of God. We certainly teach that the care of religion belongs especially to the holy magistrate.

Let him, therefore, hold the Word of God in his hands, and take care lest anything contrary, to it is taught. Likewise let him govern the people entrusted to him by God with good laws made according to the Word of God, and let him keep them in discipline, duty and obedience. Let him exercise judgment by judging uprightly. Let him not respect any man's person or accept bribes. Let him protect widows, orphans and the afflicted. Let him punish and even banish criminals, impostors and barbarians. For he does not bear the sword in vain. (Rom. 13:4.)

Therefore, let him draw this sword of God against all malefactors, seditious persons, thieves, murderers, oppressors, blasphemers, perjured persons, and all those whom God has commanded him to punish and even to execute. Let him suppress stubborn heretics (who are truly heretics), who do not cease to blaspheme the majesty of God and to trouble, and even to destroy the Church of God.

WAR. And if it is necessary to preserve the safety of the people by war, let him wage war in the name of God; provided he has first sought peace by all means possible, and cannot save his people in any other way except by war. And when the magistrate does these things in faith, he serves God by those very works which are truly good, and receives a blessing from the Lord.

We condemn the Anabaptists, who, when they deny that a Christian may hold the office of a magistrate, deny also that a man may be justly put to death by the magistrate, or that the magistrate may wage war, or that oaths are to be rendered to a magistrate, and such like things.

THE DUTY OF SUBJECTS. For as God wants to effect the safety of his people by the magistrate, whom he has given to the world to be, as it were, a father, so all subjects are commanded to acknowledge this favor of God in the magistrate. Therefore let them honor and reverence the magistrate as the minister of God; let them love him, favor him, and pray for him as their father; and let them obey all his just and fair commands. Finally, let them pay all customs and taxes, and all other such dues faithfully and willingly. And if the public safety of the country and justice require it, and the magistrate of necessity wages war, let them even lay down their life and pour out their blood for the public safety and that of the magistrate. And let them do this in the name of God willingly, bravely and cheerfully. For he who opposes the magistrate provokes the severe wrath of God against himself.

SECTS AND SEDITIONS. We, therefore, condemn all who are contemptuous of the magistrate—rebels, enemies of the state, seditious villains, finally, all who openly or craftily refuse to perform whatever duties they owe.

We beseech God, our most merciful Father in heaven, that he will bless the rulers of the people, and us, and his whole people, through Jesus Christ, our only Lord and Savior; to whom be praise and glory and thanksgiving, for all ages. Amen.

Notes: *Of the several Reformed churches in the United States, only the Hungarian Reformed Church, following the lead of the Reformed Church in Hungary, adopted what is possibly the most popular statement of the Reformed faith in Europe, the Second Helvetic Confession, as one of its official doctrinal statements. The confession was originally promulgated in 1566 and was written by Heinrich Bullinger, a reformer in Zurich, Switzerland. First published in Latin and German, it was soon translated in most European languages, including Hungarian, and was officially adopted by the Reformed Church in Hungary in 1642. It should also be noted that the Second Helvetic Confession was placed in* The Book of Confessions *mandated in 1967 by the United Presbyterian Church in the U.S.A. and has continued to appear in subsequent editions.*

Presbyterian

WESTMINSTER CONFESSION

CHAPTER I. OF THE HOLY SCRIPTURE.

I. Although the light of nature, and the works of creation and providence, do so far manifest the goodness, wisdom, and power of God, as to leave men inexcusable; yet are they not sufficient to give that knowledge of God, and of his will, which is necessary unto salvation; therefore it pleased the Lord, at sundry times, and in divers manners, to reveal himself, and to declare that his will unto his Church; and afterwards, for the better preserving and propagating of the truth, and for the more sure establishment and comfort of the Church against the corruption of the flesh, and the malice of Satan and of the world, to commit the same wholly unto writing; which maketh the holy Scripture to be most necessary; those former ways of God's revealing his will unto his people being now ceased.

II. Under the name of the holy Scripture, or the Word of God written, are now contained all the Books of the Old and New Testament, which are these:

OF THE OLD TESTAMENT

Genesis	Ecclesiastes
Exodus	The Song of Songs
Leviticus	Isaiah
Numbers	Jeremiah
Deuteronomy	Lamentations
Joshua	Ezekiel
Judges	Daniel
Ruth	Hosea
I. Samuel	Joel
II. Samuel	Amos
I. Kings	Obadiah
II. Kings	Jonah
I. Chronicles	Micah
II. Chronicles	Nahum
Ezra	Habakkuk
Nehemiah	Zephaniah
Esther	Haggai
Job	Zechariah
Psalms	Malachi
Proverbs	

WESTMINSTER CONFESSION (continued)

OF THE NEW TESTAMENT

The Gospels according to

Matthew	Thessalonians II
Mark	To Timothy I
Luke	To Timothy II
John	To Titus
The Acts of the	To Philemon
Apostles	The Epistle to the Hebrews
Paul's Epistles to	The Epistle of James
the Romans	The First and Second
Corinthians I	Epistles of Peter
Corinthians II	The First, Second, and
Galatians	Third Epistles of John
Ephesians	The Epistle of Jude
Philippians	The Revelation
Colossians	
Thessalonians I	

All which are given by inspiration of God, to be the rule of faith and life.

III. The books commonly called Apocrypha, not being of divine inspiration, are no part of the Canon of the Scripture; and therefore are of no authority in the Church of God, nor to be any otherwise approved, or made use of, than other human writings.

IV. The authority of the holy Scripture, for which it ought to be believed and obeyed, dependeth not upon the testimony of any man or church, but wholly upon God (who is truth itself), the Author thereof; and therefore it is to be received, because it is the Word of God.

V. We may be moved and induced by the testimony of the Church to an high and reverent esteem of the holy Scripture; and the heavenliness of the matter, the efficacy of the doctrine, the majesty of the style, the consent of all the parts, the scope of the whole (which is to give all glory to God), the full discovery it makes of the only way of man's salvation, the many other incomparable excellencies, and the entire perfection thereof, are arguments whereby it doth abundantly evidence itself to be the Word of God; yet, notwithstanding, our full persuasion and assurance of the infallible truth, and divine authority thereof, is from the inward work of the Holy Spirit, bearing witness by and with the Word in our hearts.

VI. The whole counsel of God, concerning all things necessary for his own glory, man's salvation, faith, and life, is either expressly set down in Scripture, or by good and necessary consequence may be deduced from Scripture: unto which nothing at any time is to be added, whether by new revelations of the Spirit, or traditions of men. Nevertheless we acknowledge the inward illumination of the Spirit of God to be necessary for the saving understanding of such things as are revealed in the Word; and that there are some circumstances concerning the worship of God, and government of the Church, common to human actions and societies, which are to be ordered by the light of nature and Christian prudence, according to the general rules of the Word, which are always to be observed.

VII. All things in Scripture are not alike plain in themselves, nor alike clear unto all; yet those things which are necessary to be known, believed, and observed, for salvation, are so clearly propounded and opened in some place of Scripture or other, that not only the learned, but the unlearned, in a due use of the ordinary means, may attain unto a sufficient understanding of them.

VIII. The Old Testament in Hebrew (which was the native language of the people of God of old), and the New Testament in Greek (which at the time of the writing of it was most generally known to the nations), being immediately inspired by God, and by his singular care and providence kept pure in all ages, are therefore authentical; so as in all controversies of religion the Church is finally to appeal unto them. But because these original tongues are not known to all the people of God who have right unto, and interest in the Scriptures, and are commanded, in the fear of God, to read and search them, therefore they are to be translated into the vulgar language of every nation unto which they come, that the Word of God dwelling plentifully in all, they may worship him in an acceptable manner, and, through patience and comfort of the Scriptures, may have hope.

IX. The infallible rule of interpretation of Scripture is the Scripture itself; and therefore, when there is a question about the true and full sense of any Scripture (which is not manifold, but one), it must be searched and known by other places that speak more clearly.

X. The Supreme Judge, by which all controversies of religion are to be determined, and all decrees of councils, opinions of ancient writers, doctrines of men, and private spirits, are to be examined, and in whose sentence we are to rest, can be no other but the Holy Spirit speaking in the Scripture.

CHAPTER II. OF GOD, AND OF THE HOLY TRINITY.

I. There is but one only living and true God, who is infinite in being and perfection, a most pure spirit, invisible, without body, parts, or passions, immutable, immense, eternal, incomprehensible, almighty, most wise, most holy, most free, most absolute, working all things according to the counsel of his own immutable and most righteous will, for his own glory; most loving, gracious, merciful, long-suffering, abundant in goodness and truth, forgiving iniquity, transgression, and sin; the rewarder of them that diligently seek him; and withal most just and terrible in his judgments; hating all sin, and who will by no means clear the guilty.

II. God hath all life, glory, goodness, blessedness, in and of himself; and is alone in and unto himself all-sufficient, not standing in need of any creatures which he hath made, nor deriving any glory from them, but only manifesting his own glory in, by, unto, and upon them: he is the alone foundation of all being, of whom, through whom, and to whom are all things; and hath most sovereign dominion over them, to do by them, for them, or upon them whatsoever himself pleaseth. In his sight all things are open and manifest; his knowledge is infinite, infallible, and independent upon the creature; so as nothing is to him contingent or uncertain. He is most holy in all his counsels, in all his works, and in all his commands. To him is due from angels and men, and every other creature, whatsoever worship, service, or obedience, he is pleased to require of them.

III. In the unity of the Godhead there be three persons, of one substance, power, and eternity: God the Father, God the Son, and God the Holy Ghost. The Father is of none, neither begotten nor proceeding; the Son is eternally begotten of the Father; the Holy Ghost eternally proceeding from the Father and the Son.

CHAPTER III. OF GOD'S ETERNAL DECREE.

I. God from all eternity did, by the most wise and holy counsel of his own will, freely and unchangeably ordain whatsoever comes to pass; yet so as thereby neither is God the author of sin, nor is violence offered to the will of the creatures, nor is the liberty or contingency of second causes taken away, but rather established.

II. Although God knows whatsoever may or can come to pass upon all supposed conditions, yet hath he not decreed any thing because he foresaw it as future, or as that which would come to pass upon such conditions.

III. By the decree of God, for the manifestation of his glory, some men and angels are predestinated unto everlasting life, and others foreordained to everlasting death.

IV. These angels and men, thus predestinated and foreordained, are particularly and unchangeably designed; and their number is so certain and definite that it can not be either increased or diminished.

V. Those of mankind that are predestinated unto life, God, before the foundation of the world was laid, according to his eternal and immutable purpose, and the secret counsel and good pleasure of his will, hath chosen in Christ, unto everlasting glory, out of his mere free grace and love, without any foresight of faith or good works, or perseverance in either of them, or any other thing in the creature, as conditions, or causes moving him thereunto; and all to the praise of his glorious grace.

VI. As God hath appointed the elect unto glory, so hath he, by the eternal and most free purpose of his will, foreordained all the means thereunto. Wherefore they who are elected, being fallen in Adam, are redeemed by Christ, are effectually called unto faith in Christ by his Spirit working in due season; are justified, adopted, sanctified, and kept by his power through faith unto salvation. Neither are any other redeemed by Christ, effectually called, justified, adopted, sanctified, and saved, but the elect only.

VII. The rest of mankind God was pleased, according to the unsearchable counsel of his own will, whereby he extendeth or withholdeth mercy as he pleaseth, for the glory of his sovereign power over his creatures, to pass by, and to ordain them to dishonor and wrath for their sin, to the praise of his glorious justice.

VIII. The doctrine of this high mystery of predestination is to be handled with special prudence and care, that men attending the will of God revealed in his Word, and yielding obedience thereunto, may, from the certainty of their effectual vocation, be assured of their eternal election. So shall this doctrine afford matter of praise, reverence, and admiration of God; and of humility, diligence, and abundant consolation to all that sincerely obey the gospel.

CHAPTER IV. OF CREATION.

I. It pleased God the Father, Son, and Holy Ghost, for the manifestation of the glory of his eternal power, wisdom, and goodness, in the beginning, to create or make of nothing the world, and all things therein, whether visible or invisible, in the space of six days, and all very good.

II. After God had made all other creatures, he created man, male and female, with reasonable and immortal souls, endued with knowledge, righteousness, and true holiness, after his own image, having the law of God written in their hearts, and power to fulfill it; and yet under a possibility of transgressing, being left to the liberty of their own will, which was subject unto change. Beside this law written in their hearts, they received a command not to eat of the tree of the knowledge of good and evil; which while they kept they were happy in their communion with God, and had dominion over the creatures.

CHAPTER V. OF PROVIDENCE.

I. God, the great Creator of all things, doth uphold, direct, dispose, and govern all creatures, actions, and things, from the greatest even to the least, by his most wise and holy providence, according to his infallible foreknowledge and the free and immutable counsel of his own will, to the praise of the glory of his wisdom, power, justice, goodness, and mercy.

II. Although in relation to the foreknowledge and decree of God, the first cause, all things come to pass immutably and infallibly, yet by the same providence he ordereth them to fall out, according to the nature of second causes, either necessarily, freely, or contingently.

III. God, in his ordinary providence, maketh use of means, yet is free to work without, above, and against them, at his pleasure.

IV. The almighty power, unsearchable wisdom, and infinite goodness of God so far manifest themselves in his providence that it extendeth itself even to the first fall, and all other sins of angels and men, and that not by a bare permission, but such as hath joined with it a most wise and powerful bounding, and otherwise ordering and governing of them, in a manifold dispensation, to his own holy ends; yet so as the sinfulness thereof proceedeth only from the creature, and not from God; who, being most holy and righteous, neither is nor can be the author or approver of sin.

V. The most wise, righteous, and gracious God doth oftentimes leave for a season his own children to manifold temptations and the corruption of their own hearts, to chastise them for their former sins, or to discover unto them the hidden strength of corruption and deceitfulness of their hearts, that they may be humbled; and to raise them to a more close and constant dependence for their support unto himself, and to make them more watchful against all future occasions of sin, and for sundry other just and holy ends.

VI. As for those wicked and ungodly men whom God, as a righteous judge, for former sins, doth blind and harden, from them he not only withholdeth his grace, whereby they might have been enlightened in their understandings and wrought upon in their hearts, but sometimes also withdraweth the gifts which they had, and exposeth them to such objects as their corruption makes occasion of sin; and withal, gives them over to their own lusts, the temptations of the world, and the power of Satan; whereby it comes to pass that they harden themselves, even under those means which God useth for the softening of others.

VII. As the providence of God doth, in general, reach to all creatures, so, after a most special manner, it taketh care of his Church, and disposeth all things to the good thereof.

CHAPTER VI. OF THE FALL OF MAN, OF SIN, AND OF THE PUNISHMENT THEREOF.

I. Our first parents, being seduced by the subtilty and temptation of Satan, sinned in eating the forbidden fruit. This their sin God was pleased, according to his wise and holy counsel, to permit, having purposed to order it to his own glory.

II. By this sin they fell from their original righteousness and communion with God, and so became dead in sin, and wholly defiled in all the faculties and parts of soul and body.

III. They being the root of all mankind, the guilt of this sin was imputed, and the same death in sin and corrupted nature conveyed to all their posterity descending from them by ordinary generation.

IV. From this original corruption, whereby we are utterly indisposed, disabled, and made opposite to all good, and wholly inclined to all evil, do proceed all actual transgressions.

V. This corruption of nature, during this life, doth remain in those that are regenerated; and although it be through Christ pardoned and mortified, yet both itself and all the motions thereof are truly and properly sin.

VI. Every sin, both original and actual, being a transgression of the righteous law of God, and contrary thereunto, doth, in its own nature, bring guilt upon the sinner, whereby he is bound over to the wrath of God and curse of the law, and so made subject to death, with all miseries spiritual, temporal, and eternal.

CHAPTER VII. OF GOD'S COVENANT WITH MAN.

I. The distance between God and the creature is so great that although reasonable creatures do owe obedience unto him as their Creator, yet they could never have any fruition of him as their blessedness and reward but by some voluntary condescension on God's part, which he hath been pleased to express by way of covenant.

II. The first covenant made with man was a covenant of works, wherein life was promised to Adam, and in him to his posterity, upon condition of perfect and personal obedience.

III. Man by his fall having made himself incapable of life by that covenant, the Lord was pleased to make a second, commonly called the covenant of grace: wherein he freely offered unto sinners life and salvation by Jesus Christ, requiring of them faith in him that they may be saved, and promising to give unto all those that are ordained unto life his Holy Spirit, to make them willing and able to believe.

IV. This covenant of grace is frequently set forth in the Scripture by the name of a testament, in reference to the death of Jesus Christ the testator, and to the everlasting inheritance, with all things belonging to it, therein bequeathed.

V. This covenant was differently administered in the time of the law and in the time of the gospel: under the law it was administered by promises, prophecies, sacrifices, circumcision, the paschal lamb, and other types and ordinances delivered to the people of the Jews, all foresignifying Christ to come, which were for that time sufficient and efficacious, through the operation of the Spirit, to instruct and build up the elect in faith in the promised Messiah, by whom they had full remission of sins and eternal salvation; and is called the Old Testament.

VI. Under the gospel, when Christ the substance was exhibited, the ordinances in which this covenant is dispensed are the preaching of the word and the administration of the sacraments of Baptism and the Lord's Supper; which, though fewer in number, and administered with more simplicity and less outward glory, yet in them it is held forth in more fullness, evidence, and spiritual efficacy, to all nations, both Jews and Gentiles; and is called the New Testament. There are not, therefore, two covenants of grace differing in substance, but one and the same under various dispensations.

CHAPTER VIII. OF CHRIST THE MEDIATOR.

I. It pleased God, in his eternal purpose, to choose and ordain the Lord Jesus, his only-begotten Son, to be the Mediator between God and man, the Prophet, Priest, and King; the Head and Saviour of his Church, the Heir of all things, and Judge of the world; unto whom he did, from all eternity, give a people to be his seed, and to be by him in time redeemed, called, justified, sanctified, and glorified.

II. The Son of God, the second person in the Trinity, being very and eternal God, of one substance, and equal with the Father, did, when the fullness of time was come, take upon him man's nature, with all the essential properties and common infirmities thereof, yet without sin: being conceived by the power of the Holy Ghost in the womb of the Virgin Mary, of her substance. So that two whole, perfect, and distinct natures, the Godhead and the manhood, were inseparably joined together in one person, without conversion, composition, or confusion. Which person is very God and very man, yet one Christ, the only mediator between God and man.

III. The Lord Jesus, in his human nature thus united to the divine, was sanctified and anointed with the Holy Spirit above measure; having in him all the treasures of wisdom and knowledge, in whom it pleased the Father that all fullness should dwell; to the end that, being holy, harmless, undefiled, and full of grace and truth, he might be thoroughly furnished to execute the office of a mediator and surety. Which office he took not unto himself, but was thereunto called by his Father, who put all power and judgment into his hand, and gave him commandment to execute the same.

IV. This office the Lord Jesus did most willingly undertake, which, that he might discharge, he was made under the law, and did perfectly fulfill it; endured most grievous torments immediately in his soul, and most painful sufferings in his body; was crucified, and died; was buried, and remained under the power of death, yet saw no corruption. On the third day he arose from the dead, with the same body in which he suffered; with which also he ascended into heaven, and there sitteth at the right hand of his Father, making intercession; and

shall return to judge men and angels at the end of the world.

V. The Lord Jesus, by his perfect obedience and sacrifice of himself, which he through the eternal Spirit once offered up unto God, hath fully satisfied the justice of his Father, and purchased not only reconciliation, but an everlasting inheritance in the kingdom of heaven, for all those whom the Father hath given unto him.

VI. Although the work of redemption was not actually wrought by Christ till after his incarnation, yet the virtue, efficacy, and benefits thereof were communicated unto the elect, in all ages successively, from the beginning of the world, in and by those promises, types, and sacrifices, wherein he was revealed, and signified to be the seed of the woman which should bruise the serpent's head, and the lamb slain from the beginning of the world, being yesterday and to-day the same and forever.

VII. Christ, in the work of mediation, acteth according to both natures; by each nature doing that which is proper to itself; yet, by reason of the unity of the person, that which is proper to one nature is sometimes, in Scripture, attributed to the person denominated by the other nature.

VIII. To all those for whom Christ hath purchased redemption he doth certainly and effectually apply and communicate the same; making intercession for them, and revealing unto them, in and by the Word, the mysteries of salvation; effectually persuading them by his Spirit to believe and obey; and governing their hearts by his Word and Spirit; overcoming all their enemies by his almighty power and wisdom, in such manner and ways as are most consonant to his wonderful and unsearchable dispensation.

CHAPTER IX. OF FREE-WILL.

I. God hath endued the will of man with that natural liberty, that is neither forced nor by any absolute necessity of nature determined to good or evil.

II. Man, in his state of innocency, had freedom and power to will and to do that which is good and well-pleasing to God, but yet mutably, so that he might fall from it.

III. Man, by his fall into a state of sin, hath wholly lost all ability of will to any spiritual good accompanying salvation; so as a natural man, being altogether averse from that good, and dead in sin, is not able, by his own strength, to convert himself, or to prepare himself thereunto.

IV. When God converts a sinner, and translates him into the state of grace, he freeth him from his natural bondage under sin, and by his grace alone enables him freely to will and to do that which is spiritually good; yet so as that, by reason of his remaining corruption, he doth not perfectly, nor only, will that which is good, but doth also will that which is evil.

V. The will of man is made perfectly and immutably free to good alone, in the state of glory only.

CHAPTER X. OF EFFECTUAL CALLING.

I. All those whom God hath predestinated unto life, and those only, he is pleased, in his appointed and accepted time, effectually to call, by his Word and Spirit, out of that state of sin and death, in which they are by nature, to grace and salvation by Jesus Christ; enlightening their minds, spiritually and savingly, to understand the things of God; taking away their heart of stone, and giving unto them an heart of flesh; renewing their wills, and by his almighty power determining them to that which is good, and effectually drawing them to Jesus Christ; yet so as they come most freely, being made willing by his grace.

II. This effectual call is of God's free and special grace alone, not from any thing at all foreseen in man; who is altogether passive therein, until, being quickened and renewed by the Holy Spirit, he is thereby enabled to answer this call, and to embrace the grace offered and conveyed in it.

III. Elect infants, dying in infancy, are regenerated and saved by Christ through the Spirit, who worketh when, and where, and how he pleaseth. So also are all other elect persons, who are incapable of being outwardly called by the ministry of the Word.

IV. Others, not elected, although they may be called by the ministry of the Word, and may have some common operations of the Spirit, yet they never truly come unto Christ, and therefore can not be saved: much less can men, not professing the Christian religion, be saved in any other way whatsoever, be they never so diligent to frame their lives according to the light of nature and the law of that religion they do profess; and to assert and maintain that they may is very pernicious, and to be detested.

CHAPTER XI. OF JUSTIFICATION.

I. Those whom God effectually calleth he also freely justifieth; not by infusing righteousness into them, but by pardoning their sins, and by accounting and accepting their persons as righteous: not for any thing wrought in them, or done by them, but for Christ's sake alone; nor by imputing faith itself, the act of believing, or any other evangelical obedience to them, as their righteousness; but by imputing the obedience and satisfaction of Christ unto them, they receiving and resting on him and his righteousness by faith; which faith they have not of themselves, it is the gift of God.

II. Faith, thus receiving and resting on Christ and his righteousness, is the alone instrument of justification; yet is it not alone in the person justified, but is ever accompanied with all other saving graces, and is no dead faith, but worketh by love.

III. Christ, by his obedience and death, did fully discharge the debt of all those that are thus justified, and did make a proper, real, and full satisfaction to his Father's justice in their behalf. Yet inasmuch as he was given by the Father for them, and his obedience and satisfaction accepted in their stead, and both freely, not for anything in them, their justification is only of free grace; that both the exact justice and rich grace of God might be glorified in the justification of sinners.

IV. God did, from all eternity, decree to justify all the elect, and Christ did, in the fullness of time, die for their sins, and rise again for their justification: nevertheless, they are not justified until the Holy Spirit doth, in due time, actually apply Christ unto them.

V. God doth continue to forgive the sins of those that are justified; and although they can never fall from the state of justification, yet they may by their sins fall under God's fatherly displeasure, and not have the light of his countenance restored unto them, until they humble themselves, confess their sins, beg pardon, and renew their faith and repentance.

VI. The justification of believers under the Old Testament was, in all these respects, one and the same with the justification of believers under the New Testament.

CHAPTER XII. OF ADOPTION.

All those that are justified God vouchsafeth, in and for his only Son Jesus Christ, to make partakers of the grace of adoption; by which they are taken into the number, and enjoy the liberties and privileges of the children of God; have his name put upon them; receive the Spirit of adoption; have access to the throne of grace with boldness; are enabled to cry, Abba, Father; are pitied, protected, provided for, and chastened by him as by a father; yet never cast off, but sealed to the day of redemption, and inherit the promises, as heirs of everlasting salvation.

CHAPTER XIII. OF SANCTIFICATION.

I. They who are effectually called and regenerated, having a new heart and a new spirit created in them, are further sanctified, really and personally, through the virtue of Christ's death and resurrection, by his Word and Spirit dwelling in them; the dominion of the whole body of sin is destroyed, and the several lusts thereof are more and more weakened and mortified, and they more and more quickened and strengthened, in all saving graces, to the practice of true holiness, without which no man shall see the Lord.

II. This sanctification is throughout in the whole man, yet imperfect in this life; there abideth still some remnants of corruption in every part, whence ariseth a continual and irreconcilable war, the flesh lusting against the spirit, and the spirit against the flesh.

III. In which war, although the remaining corruption for a time may much prevail, yet, through the continual supply of strength from the sanctifying Spirit of Christ, the regenerate part doth overcome; and so the saints grow in grace, perfecting holiness in the fear of God.

CHAPTER XIV. OF SAVING FAITH.

I. The grace of faith, whereby the elect are enabled to believe to the saving of their souls, is the work of the Spirit of Christ in their hearts, and is ordinarily wrought by the ministry of the Word; by which also, and by the administration of the sacraments and prayer, it is increased and strengthened.

II. By this faith a Christian believeth to be true whatsoever is revealed in the Word, for the authority of God himself speaking therein; and acteth differently upon that which each particular passage thereof containeth; yielding obedience to the commands, trembling at the threatenings, and embracing the promises of God for this life and that which is to come. But the principal acts of saving faith are accepting, receiving, and resting upon Christ alone for justification, sanctification, and eternal life, by virtue of the covenant of grace.

III. This faith is different in degrees, weak or strong; may be often and many ways assailed and weakened, but gets the victory; growing up in many to the attainment of a full assurance through Christ, who is both the author and finisher of our faith.

CHAPTER XV. OF REPENTANCE UNTO LIFE.

I. Repentance unto life is an evangelical grace, the doctrine whereof is to be preached by every minister of the gospel, as well as that of faith in Christ.

II. By it a sinner, out of the sight and sense, not only of the danger, but also of the filthiness and odiousness of his sins, as contrary to the holy nature and righteous law of God, and upon the apprehension of his mercy in Christ to such as are penitent, so grieves for and hates his sins as to turn from them all unto God, purposing and endeavoring to walk with him in all the ways of his commandments.

III. Although repentance be not to be rested in as any satisfaction for sin, or any cause of the pardon thereof, which is the act of God's free grace in Christ; yet is it of such necessity to all sinners that none may expect pardon without it.

IV. As there is no sin so small but it deserves damnation, so there is no sin so great that it can bring damnation upon those who truly repent.

V. Men ought not to content themselves with a general repentance, but it is every man's duty to endeavor to repent of his particular sins particularly.

VI. As every man is bound to make private confession of his sins to God, praying for the pardon thereof, upon which, and the forsaking of them, he shall find mercy; so he that scandalizeth his brother, or the Church of Christ, ought to be willing, by a private or public confession and sorrow for his sin, to declare his repentance to those that are offended, who are thereupon to be reconciled to him, and in love to receive him.

CHAPTER XVI. OF GOOD WORKS.

I. Good works are only such as God hath commanded in his holy Word, and not such as, without the warrant thereof, are devised by men out of blind zeal, or upon any pretense of good intention.

II. These good works, done in obedience to God's commandments, are the fruits and evidences of a true and lively faith; and by them believers manifest their thankfulness, strengthen their assurance, edify their brethren, adorn the profession of the gospel, stop the mouths of the adversaries, and glorify God, whose workmanship they are, created in Christ Jesus thereunto, that, having their fruit unto holiness, they may have the end, eternal life.

III. Their ability to do good works is not at all of themselves, but wholly from the Spirit of Christ. And that they may be enabled thereunto, besides the graces they have already received, there is required an actual influence of the same Holy Spirit to work in them to will and to do of his good pleasure; yet are they not hereupon to grow negligent, as if they were not bound to perform any duty unless upon a special motion of the Spirit; but they ought to be diligent in stirring up the grace of God that is in them.

IV. They who in their obedience attain to the greatest height which is possible in this life, are so far from being able to supererogate and to do more than God requires, as that they fall short of much which in duty they are bound to do.

V. We can not, by our best works, merit pardon of sin, or eternal life at the hand of God, by reason of the great disproportion that is between them and the glory to come, and the infinite distance that is between us and God, whom by them we can neither profit nor satisfy for the debt of our former sins; but when we have done all we can, we have done but our duty, and are unprofitable servants; and because, as they are good, they proceed from his Spirit; and as they are wrought by us, they are defiled and mixed with so much weakness and imperfection that they can not endure the severity of God's judgment.

VI. Yet notwithstanding, the persons of believers being accepted through Christ, their good works also are accepted in him, not as though they were in this life wholly unblamable and unreprovable in God's sight; but that he, looking upon them in his Son, is pleased to accept and reward that which is sincere, although accompanied with many weaknesses and imperfections.

VII. Works done by unregenerate men, although for the matter of them they may be things which God commands, and of good use both to themselves and others; yet because they proceed not from a heart purified by faith, nor are done in a right manner, according to the Word, nor to a right end, the glory of God; they are therefore sinful, and can not please God, or make a man meet to receive grace from God. And yet their neglect of them is more sinful and displeasing unto God.

CHAPTER XVII. OF THE PERSEVERANCE OF THE SAINTS.

I. They whom God hath accepted in his Beloved, effectually called and sanctified by his Spirit, can neither totally nor finally fall away from the state of grace; but shall certainly persevere therein to the end, and be eternally saved.

II. This perseverance of the saints depends, not upon their own free-will, but upon the immutability of the decree of election, flowing from the free and unchangeable love of God the Father; upon the efficacy of the merit and intercession of Jesus Christ; the abiding of the Spirit and of the seed of God within them; and the nature of the covenant of grace: from all which ariseth also the certainty and infallibility thereof.

III. Nevertheless they may, through the temptations of Satan and of the world, the prevalency of corruption remaining in them, and the neglect of the means of their preservation, fall into grievous sins; and for a time continue therein: whereby they incur God's displeasure, and grieve his Holy Spirit; come to be deprived of some measure of their graces and comforts; have their hearts hardened, and their consciences wounded; hurt and scandalize others, and bring temporal judgments upon themselves.

CHAPTER XVIII. OF THE ASSURANCE OF GRACE AND SALVATION.

I. Although hypocrites and other unregenerate men may vainly deceive themselves with false hopes and carnal presumptions of being in the favor of God and estate of salvation, which hope of theirs shall perish: yet such as truly believe in the Lord Jesus, and love him in sincerity, endeavoring to walk in all good conscience before him, may in this life be certainly assured that they are in a state of grace, and may rejoice in the hope of the glory of God, which hope shall never make them ashamed.

II. This certainty is not a bare conjectural and probable persuasion, grounded upon a fallible hope; but an infallible assurance of faith, founded upon the divine truth of the promises of salvation, the inward evidence of those graces unto which these promises are made, the testimony of the Spirit of adoption witnessing with our spirits that we are the children of God: which Spirit is the earnest of our inheritance, whereby we are sealed to the day of redemption.

III. This infallible assurance doth not so belong to the essence of faith, but that a true believer may wait long, and conflict with many difficulties before he be partaker of it: yet, being enabled by the Spirit to know the things which are freely given him of God, he may, without extraordinary revelation, in the right use of ordinary means, attain thereunto. And therefore it is the duty of every one to give all diligence to make his calling and election sure, that thereby his heart may be enlarged in peace and joy in the Holy Ghost, in love and thankfulness to God, and in strength and cheerfulness in the duties of obedience, the proper fruits of this assurance: so far is it from inclining men to looseness.

IV. True believers may have the assurance of their salvation divers ways shaken, diminished, and intermitted; as, by negligence in preserving of it, by falling into some special sin, which woundeth the conscience, and grieveth the Spirit; by some sudden or vehement temptation; by God's withdrawing the light of his countenance, and suffering even such as fear him to walk in darkness and to have no light: yet are they never utterly destitute of that seed of God, and life of faith, that love of Christ and the brethren, that sincerity of heart and conscience of duty, out of which, by the operation of the Spirit, this assurance may in due time be revived, and by the which, in the mean time, they are supported from utter despair.

CHAPTER XIX. OF THE LAW OF GOD.

I. God gave to Adam a law, as a covenant of works, by which he bound him and all his posterity to personal, entire, exact, and perpetual obedience; promised life upon the fulfilling, and threatened death upon the breach of it; and endued him with power and ability to keep it.

II. This law, after his fall, continued to be a perfect rule of righteousness; and, as such, was delivered by God upon mount Sinai in ten commandments, and written in two tables; the first four commandments containing our duty towards God, and the other six our duty to man.

III. Beside this law, commonly called moral, God was pleased to give to the people of Israel, as a Church under age, ceremonial laws, containing several typical ordinances, partly of worship, prefiguring Christ, his graces, actions, sufferings, and benefits; and partly holding forth divers instructions of moral duties. All which ceremonial laws are now abrogated under the New Testament.

IV. To them also, as a body politic, he gave sundry judicial laws, which expired together with the state of that people, not obliging any other, now, further than the general equity thereof may require.

V. The moral law doth forever bind all, as well justified persons as others, to the obedience thereof; and that not only in regard of the matter contained in it, but also in respect of the authority of God the Creator who gave it. Neither doth Christ in the gospel any way dissolve, but much strengthen, this obligation.

VI. Although true believers be not under the law as a covenant of works, to be thereby justified or condemned; yet is it of great use to them, as well as to others; in that, as a rule of life, informing them of the will of God and their duty, it directs and binds them to walk accordingly; discovering also the sinful pollutions of their nature, hearts, and lives; so as, examining themselves thereby, they may come to further conviction of, humiliation for, and hatred against sin; together with a clearer sight of the need they have of Christ, and the perfection of his obedience. It is likewise of use to the regenerate, to restrain their corruptions, in that it forbids sin; and the threatenings of it serve to show what even their sins deserve, and what afflictions in this life they may expect for them, although freed from the curse thereof threatened in the law. The promises of it, in like manner, show them God's approbation of obedience, and what blessings they may expect upon the performance thereof; although not as due to them by the law as a covenant of words: so as a man's doing good, and refraining from evil, because the law encourageth to the one, and deterreth from the other, is no evidence of his being under the law, and not under grace.

VII. Neither are the forementioned uses of the law contrary to the grace of the gospel, but do sweetly comply with it: the Spirit of Christ subduing and enabling the will of man to do that freely and cheerfully which the will of God, revealed in the law, requireth to be done.

CHAPTER XX. OF CHRISTIAN LIBERTY, AND LIBERTY OF CONSCIENCE.

I. The liberty which Christ hath purchased for believers under the gospel consists in their freedom from the guilt of sin, the condemning wrath of God, the curse of the moral law; and in their being delivered from this present evil world, bondage to Satan, and dominion of sin, from the evil of afflictions, the sting of death, the victory of the grave, and everlasting damnation; as also in their free access to God, and their yielding obedience unto him, not out of slavish fear, but a child-like love and willing mind. All which were common also to believers under the law; but under the New Testament the liberty of Christians is further enlarged in their freedom from the yoke of the ceremonial law, to which the Jewish Church was subjected; and in greater boldness of access to the throne of grace, and in fuller communications of the free Spirit of God, than believers under the law did ordinarily partake of.

II. God alone is Lord of the conscience, and hath left it free from the doctrines and commandments of men which are in any thing contrary to his Word, or beside it in matters of faith or worship. So that to believe such doctrines, or to obey such commands out of conscience, is to betray true liberty of conscience; and the requiring of an implicit faith, and an absolute and blind obediene, is to destroy liberty of conscience, and reason also.

III. They who, upon pretense of Christian liberty, do practice any sin, or cherish any lust, do thereby destroy the end of Christian liberty; which is, that, being delivered out of the hands of our enemies, we might serve the Lord without fear, in holiness and righteousness before him, all the days of our life.

IV. And because the power which God hath ordained, and the liberty which Christ hath purchased, are not intended by God to destroy, but mutually to uphold and preserve one another; they who, upon pretense of Christian liberty, shall oppose any lawful power, or the lawful exercise of it, whether it be civil or ecclesiastical, resist the ordinance of God. And for their publishing of such opinions, or maintaining of such practices, as are contrary to the light of nature, or to the known principles of Christianity, whether concerning faith, worship, or conversation; or to the power of godliness; or such erroneous opinions or practices, as, either in their own nature, or in the manner of publishing or maintaining them, are destructive to the external peace and order which Christ hath established in the Church; they may lawfully be called to account, and proceeded against by the censures of the Church, and by the power of the Civil Magistrate.

CHAPTER XXI. OF RELIGION WORSHIP AND THE SABBATH-DAY.

I. The light of nature showeth that there is a God, who hath lordship and sovereignty over all; is good, and doeth good unto all; and is therefore to be feared, loved, praised, called upon, trusted in, and served with all the heart, and with all the soul, and with all the might. But the acceptable way of worshiping the true God is instituted by himself, and so limited to his own revealed will, that he may not be worshiped according to the imaginations and devices of men, or the suggestions of Satan, under any visible representations or any other way not prescribed in the Holy Scripture.

II. Religious worship is to be given to God, the Father, Son, and Holy Ghost; and to him alone: not to angels, saints, or any other creature: and

WESTMINSTER CONFESSION (continued)

since the fall, not without a Mediator; nor in the mediation of any other but of Christ alone.

III. Prayer with thanksgiving, being one special part of religious worship, is by God required of all men; and that it may be accepted, it is to be made in the name of the Son, by the help of his Spirit, according to his will, not with understanding, reverence, humility, fervency, faith, love, and perseverance; and, if vocal, in a known tongue.

IV. Prayer is to be made for things lawful, and for all sorts of men living, or that shall live hereafter; but not for the dead, nor for those of whom it may be known that they have sinned the sin unto death.

V. The reading of the Scriptures with godly fear; the sound preaching; and conscionable hearing of the Word, in obedience unto God with understanding, faith, and reverence; singing of psalms with grace in the heart; as, also, the due administration and worthy receiving of the sacraments instituted by Christ; are all parts of the ordinary religious worship of God: besides religious oaths, vows, solemn fastings, and thanksgivings upon several occasions; which are, in their several times and seasons, to be used in an holy and religious manner.

VI. Neither prayer, nor any other part of religious worship, is now under the gospel, either tied unto or made more acceptable by any place in which it is performed, or towards which it is directed: but God is to be worshiped every where in spirit and truth; as in private families daily, and in secret each one by himself, so more solemnly in the public assemblies, which are not carelessly or willfully to be neglected or foresaken, when God, by his Word or providence, calleth thereunto.

VII. As it is of the law of nature, that, in general, a due proportion of time be set apart for the worship of God; so, in his Word, by a positive, moral, and perpetual commandment, binding all men in all ages, he hath particularly appointed one day in seven for a Sabbath, to be kept holy unto him: which, from the beginning of the world to the resurrection of Christ, was the last day of the week; and, from the resurrection of Christ, was changed into the first day of the week, which in Scripture is called the Lord's day, and is to be continued to the end of the world, as the Christian Sabbath.

VIII. This Sabbath is then kept holy unto the Lord, when men, after a due preparing of their hearts, and ordering of their common affairs beforehand, do not only observe an holy rest all the day from their own works, words, and thoughts, about their worldly employments and recreations; but also are taken up the whole time in the public and private exercises of his worship, and in the duties of necessity and mercy.

CHAPTER XXII. OF LAWFUL OATHS AND VOWS.

I. A lawful oath is a part of religious worship, wherein, upon just occasion, the person swearing solemnly calleth God to witness what he asserteth or promiseth; and to judge him according to the truth or falsehood of what he sweareth.

II. The name of God only is that by which men ought to swear, and therein it is to be used with all holy fear and reverence; therefore to swear vainly or rashly by that glorious and dreadful name, or to swear at all by any other thing, is sinful, and to be abhorred. Yet as, in matters of weight and moment, an oath is warranted by the Word of God, under the New Testament, as well as under the Old, so a lawful oath, being imposed by lawful authority, in such matters ought to be taken.

III. Whosoever taketh an oath ought duly to consider the weightiness of so solemn an act, and therein to avouch nothing but what he is fully persuaded is the truth. Neither may any man bind himself by oath to any thing but what is good and just, and what he believeth so to be, and what he is able and resolved to perform. Yet it is a sin to refuse an oath touching any thing that is good and just, being imposed by lawful authority.

IV. An oath is to be taken in the plain and common sense of the words, without equivocation or mental reservation. It can not oblige to sin; but in any thing not sinful, being taken, it binds to performance, although to a man's own hurt: nor is it to be violated, although made to heretics or infidels.

V. A vow is of the like nature with a promissory oath, and ought to be made with the like religious care, and to be performed with the like faithfulness.

VI. It is not to be made to any creature, but to God alone: and that it may be accepted, it is to be made voluntarily, out of faith and conscience of duty, in way of thankfulness for mercy received, or for the obtaining of what we want; whereby we more strictly bind ourselves to necessary duties, or to other things, so far and so long as they may fitly conduce thereunto.

VII. No man may vow to do any thing forbidden in the Word of God, or what would hinder any duty therein commanded, or which is not in his own power, and for the performance whereof he hath no promise or ability from God. In which respect, popish monastical vows of perpetual single life, professed poverty, and regular obedience, are so far from being degrees of higher perfection, that they are superstitious and sinful snares, in which no Christian may entangle himself.

CHAPTER XXIII. OF THE CIVIL MAGISTRATE.

I. God, the Supreme Lord and King of all the world, hath ordained civil magistrates to be under him, over the people, for his own glory and the public good, and to this end hath armed them with the power of the sword, for the defense and encouragement of them that are good, and for the punishment of evil-doers.

II. It is lawful for Christians to accept and execute the office of a magistrate when called thereunto; in the managing whereof, as they ought especially to maintain piety, justice, and peace, according to the wholesome laws of each commonwealth, so, for that end, they may lawfully, now under the New Testament, wage war upon just and necessary occasion.

III. The civil magistrate may not assume to himself the administration of the Word and Sacraments, or the power of the keys of the kingdom of heaven: yet he hath authority, and it is his duty to take order, that unity and peace be preserved in the Church, that the truth of God be kept pure and entire, that all blasphemies and heresies be suppressed, all corruptions and abuses in worship and discipline prevented or reformed, and all the ordinances of God duly settled, administered, and observed. For the better effecting whereof he hath power to call synods, to be present at them, and to provide that whatsoever is transacted in them be according to the mind of God.

IV. It is the duty of people to pray for magistrates, to honor their persons, to pay them tribute and other dues, to obey their lawful commands, and to be subject to their authority, for conscience's sake. Infidelity or difference in religion doth not make void the magistrate's just and legal authority, nor free the people from their due obedience to him: from which ecclesiastical persons are not exempted; much less hath the Pope any power or jurisdiction over them in their dominions, or over any of their people; and least of all to deprive them of their dominions or lives, if he shall judge them to be heretics, or upon any other pretense whatsoever.

CHAPTER XXIV. OF MARRIAGE AND DIVORCE.

I. Marriage is to be between one man and one woman: neither is it lawful for any man to have more than one wife, nor for any woman to have more than one husband at the same time.

II. Marriage was ordained for the mutual help of husband and wife; for the increase of mankind with a legitimate issue, and of the church with an holy seed; and for preventing of uncleanness.

III. It is lawful for all sorts of people to marry who are able with judgment to give their consent. Yet it is the duty of Christians to marry only in the Lord. And, therefore, such as profess the true reformed religion should not marry with infidels, Papists, or other idolaters: neither should such as are godly be unequally yoked, by marrying with such as are notoriously wicked in their life, or maintain damnable heresies.

IV. Marriage ought not to be within the degrees of consanguinity or affinity forbidden in the Word; nor can such incestuous marriages ever be made lawful by any law of man, or consent of parties, so as those persons may live together, as man and wife. The man may not marry any of his wife's kindred nearer in blood than he may of his own, nor the woman of her husband's kindred nearer in blood than of her own.

V. Adultery or fornication, committed after a contract, being detected before marriage, giveth just occasion to the innocent party to dissolve that contract. In the case of adultery after marriage, it is lawful for the innocent party to sue out a divorce, and after the divorce to marry another, as if the offending party were dead.

VI. Although the corruption of man be such as is apt to study arguments, unduly to put asunder those whom God hath joined together in marriage; yet nothing but adultery, or such willful desertion as can no way be remedied by the Church or civil magistrate, is cause sufficient of dissolving the bond of marriage; wherein a public and orderly course of proceeding is to be observed; and the persons concerned in it, not left to their own wills and discretion in their own case.

CHAPTER XXV. OF THE CHURCH.

I. The catholic or universal Church, which is invisible, consists of the whole number of the elect, that have been, are, or shall be gathered into one, under Christ the head thereof; and is the spouse, the body, the fullness of him that filleth all in all.

II. The visible Church, which is also catholic or universal under the gospel (not confined to one nation as before under the law) consists of all those, throughout the world, that profess the true religion, and of their children; and is the kingdom of the Lord Jesus Christ, the house and family of God, out of which there is no ordinary possibility of salvation.

III. Unto this catholic visible Church Christ hath given the ministry, oracles, and ordinances of God, for the gathering and perfecting of the saints, in this life, to the end of the world: and doth by his own presence and Spirit, according to his promise, make them effectual thereunto.

IV. This catholic Church hath been sometimes more, sometimes less visible. And particular churches, which are members thereof, are more or less pure, according as the doctrine of the gospel is taught and embraced, ordinances administered, and public worship performed more or less purely in them.

V. The purest churches under heaven are subject both to mixture and error; and some have so degenerated as to become no churches of Christ, but synagogues of Satan. Nevertheless, there shall

WESTMINSTER CONFESSION (continued)

be always a Church on earth to worship God according to his will.

VI. There is no other head of the Church but the Lord Jesus Christ: nor can the Pope of Rome, in any sense be head thereof; but is that Antichrist, that man of sin and son of perdition, that exalteth himself in the Church against Christ, and all that is called God.

CHAPTER XXVI. OF THE COMMUNION OF SAINTS.

I. All saints that are united to Jesus Christ their head, by his Spirit and by faith, have fellowship with him in his graces, sufferings, death, resurrection, and glory: and being united to one another in love, they have communion in each other's gifts and graces, and are obliged to the performance of such duties, public and private, as do conduce to their mutual good, both in the inward and outward man.

II. Saints, by profession, are bound to maintain an holy fellowship and communion in the worship of God, and in performing such other spiritual services as tend to their mutual edification; as also in relieving each other in outward things, according to their several abilities and necessities. Which communion, as God offereth opportunity, is to be extended unto all those who, in every place, call upon the name of the Lord Jesus.

III. This communion which the saints have with Christ, doth not make them in anywise partakers of the substance of his Godhead, or to be equal with Christ in any respect: either of which to affirm is impious and blasphemous. Nor doth their communion one with another, as saints, take away or infringe the title or propriety which each man hath in his goods and possessions.

CHAPTER XXVII. OF THE SACRAMENTS.

I. Sacraments are holy signs and seals of the covenant of grace, immediately instituted by God, to represent Christ and his benefits, and to confirm our interest in him: as also to put a visible difference between those that belong unto the Church and the rest of the world; and solemnly to engage them to the service of God in Christ, according to his Word.

II. There is in every sacrament a spiritual relation or sacramental union, between the sign and the thing signified; whence it comes to pass that the names and the effects of the one are attributed to the other.

III. The grace which is exhibited in or by the sacraments, rightly used, is not conferred by any power in them; neither doth the efficacy of a sacrament depend upon the piety or intention of him that doth administer it, but upon the work of the Spirit, and the word of institution, which contains, together with a precept authorizing the use thereof, a promise of benefit to worthy receivers.

IV. There be only two sacraments ordained by Christ our Lord in the gospel, that is to say, Baptism and the Supper of the Lord: neither of which may be dispensed by any but by a minister of the Word lawfully ordained.

V. The sacraments of the Old Testament, in regard of the spiritual things thereby signified and exhibited, were, for substance, the same with those of the New.

CHAPTER XXVIII. OF BAPTISM.

I. Baptism is a sacrament of the New Testament, ordained by Jesus Christ, not only for the solemn admission of the party baptized into the visible Church, but also to be unto him a sign and seal of the covenant of grace, of his ingrafting into Christ, of regeneration, of remission of sins, and of his giving up unto God, through Jesus Christ, to walk in newness of life: which sacrament is, by Christ's own appointment, to be continued in his Church until the end of the world.

II. The outward element to be used in this sacrament is water, wherewith the party is to be baptized in the name of the Father, and of the Son, and of the Holy Ghost, by a minister of the gospel lawfully called thereunto.

III. Dipping of the person into the water is not necessary; but baptism is rightly administered by pouring or sprinkling water upon the person.

IV. Not only those that do actually profess faith in and obedience unto Christ, but also the infants of one or both believing parents are to be baptized.

V. Although it be a great sin to condemn or neglect this ordinance, yet grace and salvation are not so inseparably annexed unto it, as that no person can be regenerated or saved without it, or that all that are baptized are undoubtedly regenerated.

VI. The efficacy of baptism is not tied to that moment of time wherein it is administered; yet, notwithstanding, by the right use of this ordinance the grace promised is not only offered, but really exhibited and conferred by the Holy Ghost, to such (whether of age or infants) as that grace belongeth unto, according to the counsel of God's own will, in his appointed time.

VII. The sacrament of baptism is but once to be administered to any person.

CHAPTER XXIX. OF THE LORD'S SUPPER.

I. Our Lord Jesus, in the night wherein he was betrayed, instituted the sacrament of his body and blood, called the Lord's Supper, to be observed in his Church, unto the end of the world; for the perpetual remembrance of the sacrifice of himself in his death, the sealing all benefits thereof unto true believers, their spiritual nourishment and growth in him, their further engagement in, and to all duties which they owe unto him; and to be a bond and pledge of their communion with him, and with each other, as members of his mystical body.

II. In this sacrament Christ is not offered up to his Father, nor any real sacrifice made at all for remission of sins of the quick or dead, but only a commemoration of that one offering up of himself, by himself, upon the cross, once for all, and a spiritual oblation of all possible praise unto God for the same; so that the Popish sacrifice of the mass, as they call it, is most abominably injurious to Christ's one only sacrifice, the alone propitiation for all the sins of the elect.

III. The Lord Jesus hath, in this ordinance, appointed his ministers to declare his word of institution to the people, to pray, and bless the elements of bread and wine, and thereby to set them apart from a common to an holy use; and to take and break the bread, to take the cup, and (they communicating also themselves) to give both to the communicants; but to none who are not then present in the congregation.

IV. Private masses, or receiving this sacrament by a priest, or any other, alone; as likewise the denial of the cup to the people; worshiping the elements, the lifting them up, or carrying them about for adoration, and the reserving them for any pretended religious use, are all contrary to the nature of this sacrament, and to the institution of Christ.

V. The outward elements in this sacrament, duly set apart to the uses ordained by Christ, have such relation to him crucified, as that truly, yet sacramentally only, they are sometimes called by the name of the things they represent, to wit, the body and blood of Christ; albeit, in substance and nature, they still remain truly, and only, bread and wine, as they were before.

VI. That doctrine which maintains a change of the substance of bread and wine, into the substance of Christ's body and blood (commonly called transubstantiation) by consecration of a priest, or by any other way, is repugnant, not to Scripture alone, but even to common-sense and reason; overthroweth the nature of the sacrament; and hath been, and is the cause of manifold superstitions, yea, of gross idolatries.

VII. Worthy receivers, outwardly partaking of the visible elements in this sacrament, do then also inwardly by faith, really and indeed, yet not carnally and corporally, but spiritually, receive and feed upon Christ crucified, and all benefits of his death: the body and blood of Christ being then not corporally or carnally in, with, or under the bread and wine; yet as really, but spiritually, present to the faith of believers in that ordinance, as the elements themselves are, to their outward senses.

VIII. Although ignorant and wicked men receive the outward elements in this sacrament, yet they receive not the thing signified thereby; but by their unworthy coming thereunto are guilty of the body and blood of the Lord, to their own damnation. Wherefore all ignorant and ungodly persons, as they are unfit to enjoy communion with him, so are they unworthy of the Lord's table, and can not, without great sin against Christ, while they remain such, partake of these holy mysteries, or be admitted thereunto.

CHAPTER XXX. OF CHURCH CENSURES.

I. The Lord Jesus, as king and head of his Church, hath therein appointed a government in the hand of Church officers, distinct from the civil magistrate.

II. To these officers the keys of the kingdom of heaven are committed, by virtue whereof they have power respectively to retain and remit sins, to shut that kingdom against the impenitent, both by the Word and censures; and to open it unto penitent sinners, by the ministry of the gospel, and by absolution from censures, as occasion shall require.

III. Church censures are necessary for the reclaiming and gaining of offending brethren; for deterring of others from the like offenses; for purging out of that leaven which might infect the whole lump; for vindicating the honor of Christ, and the holy profession of the gospel; and for preventing the wrath of God, which might justly fall upon the Church, if they should suffer his covenant, and the seals thereof, to be profaned by notorious and obstinate offenders.

IV. For the better attaining of these ends, the officers of the Church are to proceed by admonition, suspension from the Sacrament of the Lord's Supper for a season, and by excommunication from the Church, according to the nature of the crime and demerit of the person.

CHAPTER XXXI. OF SYNODS AND COUNCILS.

I. For the better government and further edification of the Church, there ought to be such assemblies as are commonly called synods or councils.

II. As magistrates may lawfully call a synod of ministers and other fit persons to consult and advise with about matters of religion; so, if magistrates be open enemies to the Church, the ministers of Christ, of themselves, by virtue of their office, or they, with other fit persons, upon delegation from their churches, may meet together in such assemblies.

III. It belongeth to synods and councils, ministerially, to determine controversies of faith, and cases of conscience; to set down rules and directions for the better ordering of the public worship of God, and government of his Church; to receive complaints in cases of maladministration, and authoritatively to determine the same: which decrees and determinations, if consonant to the Word of God, are to be received with reverence and submission, not only for their agreement with the Word, but also for the power whereby they are made, as being an ordinance of God, appointed thereunto in his Word.

IV. All synods or councils since the apostles' times, whether general or particular, may err, and many have erred; therefore they are not to be made the rule of faith or practice, but to be used as a help in both.

V. Synods and councils are to handle or conclude nothing but that which is ecclesiastical: and are not to intermeddle with civil affairs which concern the commonwealth, unless by way of humble petition in cases extraordinary; or by way of advice for satisfaction of conscience, if they be thereunto required by the civil magistrate.

CHAPTER XXXII. OF THE STATE OF MEN AFTER DEATH, AND OF THE RESURRECTION OF THE DEAD.

I. The bodies of men, after death, return to dust, and see corruption; but their souls (which neither die nor sleep), having an immortal subsistence, immediately return to God who gave them. The souls of the righteous, being then made perfect in holiness, are received into the highest heavens, where they behold the face of God in light and glory, waiting for the full redemption of their bodies: and the souls of the wicked are cast into hell, where they remain in torments and utter darkness, reserved to the judgment of the great day. Besides these two places for souls separated from their bodies, the Scripture acknowledgeth none.

II. At the last day, such as are found alive shall not die, but be changed; and all the dead shall be raised up with the self-same bodies, and none other, although with different qualities, which shall be united again to their souls forever.

III. The bodies of the unjust shall, by the power of Christ, be raised to dishonor; the bodies of the just, by his Spirit, unto honor, and be made conformable to his own glorious body.

CHAPTER XXXIII. OF THE LAST JUDGMENT.

I. God hath appointed a day wherein he will judge the world in righteousness by Jesus Christ, to whom all power and judgment is given of the Father. In which day, not only the apostate angels shall be judged, but likewise all persons, that have lived upon earth, shall appear before the tribunal of Christ, to give an account of their thoughts, words, and deeds; and to receive according to what they have done in the body, whether good or evil.

II. The end of God's appointing this day, is for the manifestation of the glory of his mercy in the eternal salvation of the elect; and of his justice in the damnation of the reprobate, who are wicked and disobedient. For then shall the righteous go into everlasting life, and receive that fullness of joy and refreshing which shall come from the presence of the Lord: but the wicked, who know not God, and obey not the gospel of Jesus Christ, shall be cast into eternal torments, and be punished with everlasting destruction from the presence of the Lord, and from the glory of his power.

III. As Christ would have us to be certainly persuaded that there shall be a day of judgment, both to deter all men from sin, and for the greater consolation of the godly in their adversity: so will he have that day unknown to men, that they may shake off all carnal security, and be always watchful, because they know not at what hour the Lord will come; and may be ever prepared to say, Come, Lord Jesus, come quickly. Amen.

Charles Herle, Prolocutor.
Cornelius Burges, Assessor.
Herbert Palmer, Assessor.
Henry Robroughe, Scriba.
Adoniram Byfield, Scriba.

Notes: *The confession was written in the middle of the seventeenth century by the British and Scottish church leaders gathered at Westminster (1644-49) in the midst of the civil strife that would see the king of England beheaded and the establishment of a Protestant commonwealth. Those gathered produced three major documents: a longer and shorter catechism, and the Westminster Confession. The Westminster Confession soon became the definitive theological standard of the English-speaking Reformed movement, i.e., Presbyterianism.*

Transported to the United States, the confession soon encountered problems on the issues of church and state relations. After the American Revolution, revisions of the several articles on civil magistrates and on synods and councils were required. The Westminster Confession has remained the standard of most Presbyterian church bodies in the United States to the present, though a variety of statements on its use and authority have been issued at various times, usually upon the merger of two churches. In 1967 the United Presbyterian Church in the U.S.A. adopted a new contemporary statement of faith, the Confession of 1967, and at the same time ordered the production of The Book of Confessions. *This action removed the Westminster Confession from the place of honor it had held as the only confession within the church's constitution and set it in the midst of eight other creeds. Many interpreted the church's action as reducing the Westminster Confession's authority to that of a mere historical precedence. The Book of Confessions* has been retained by the new Presbyterian Church (U.S.A.).

The Westminster Confession has been adopted by the Bible Presbyterian Church, the Orthodox Presbyterian Church, the Presbyterian Church in America, and the Reformed Presbyterian Church of North America. Substantive revisions of the Westminster Confession were made prior to its adoption by the Associate Reformed Presbyterian Church and the Cumberland Presbyterian Church. Subsequently, the Cumberland Presbyterian Church completely rewrote its confession.

*　　*　　*

THE CONFESSION OF FAITH (CUMBERLAND PRESBYTERIAN CHURCH)

HOLY SCRIPTURES

1. The Holy Scriptures comprise all the books of the Old and the New Testament which are received as canonical, and which are given by inspiration of God to be the rule of faith and practice, and are these:

OLD TESTAMENT

Genesis	Ecclesiastes
Exodus	Song of Solomon
Leviticus	Isaiah
Numbers	Jeremiah
Deuteronomy	Lamentations
Joshua	Ezekiel
Judges	Daniel
Ruth	Hosea
I. Samuel	Joel
II. Samuel	Amos
I. Kings	Obadiah
II. Kings	Jonah
I. Chronicles	Micah
II. Chronicles	Nahum
Ezra	Habakkuk
Nehemiah	Zephaniah
Esther	Haggai
Job	Zechariah
Psalms	Malachi
Proverbs	

NEW TESTAMENT

Matthew	I. Timothy
Mark	II. Timothy
Luke	Titus
John	Philemon
The Acts	Hebrews
Romans	James
I. Corinthians	I. Peter
II. Corinthians	II. Peter
Galatians	I. John
Ephesians	II. John
Philippians	III. John
Colossians	Jude
I. Thessalonians	Revelation
II. Thessalonians	

2. The authority of the Holy Scriptures depends not upon the testimony of any man or Church, but upon God alone.

3. The whole counsel of God, concerning all things necessary for his own glory—in creation, providence, and man's salvation—is either expressly stated in the Scriptures, or by necessary consequence may be deduced therefrom; unto which nothing at any time is to be added by man, or from the traditions of men; nevertheless, we acknowledge the inward illumination of the Spirit of God to be necessary for the saving understanding of such things as are revealed in the word.

4. The best rule of interpretation of the Scriptures is the comparison of scripture with scripture.

THE HOLY TRINITY

5. There is but one living and true God, a self-existent Spirit, infinite, eternal, and unchangeable in his being, wisdom, power, holiness, justice, goodness, and truth.

6. God has all life, glory, goodness, and blessedness in himself; not standing in need of any creatures which he has made, nor deriving any essential glory from them; and has most sovereign dominion over them to do whatsoever he may please.

7. In the unity of the Godhead there are three persons of one substance, power, and eternity; God the Father, Son, and Holy Spirit.

DECREES OF GOD

8. God, for the manifestation of his glory and goodness, by the most wise and holy counsel of his own will, freely and unchangeably ordained or determined what he himself would do, what he would require his intelligent creatures to do, and what should be the awards, respectively, of the obedient and the disobedient.

9. Though all Divine decrees may not be revealed to men, yet it is certain that God has decreed nothing contrary to his revealed will or written word.

CREATION

10. It pleased God, for the manifestation of the glory of his eternal power, wisdom, and goodness, to create the world and all things therein, whether visible or invisible: and all very good.

11. After God had made all other creatures, he created man in his own image; male and female created he them, enduing them with intelligence, sensibility, and will; they having the law of God written in their hearts, and power to fulfill it, being upright and free from all bias to evil.

PROVIDENCE

12. God the Creator upholds and governs all creatures and things by his most wise and holy providence.

13. God, in his providence, ordinarily works through the instrumentality of laws or means, yet is free to work with and above them, at his pleasure.

14. God never leaves nor forsakes his people; yet when they fall into sin he chastises them in various ways, and makes even their own sin the occasion of discovering unto them their weakness and their need of greater watchfulness and dependence upon him for supporting grace.

15. God's providence over the wicked is not designed to lead them to destruction, but to a knowledge of his goodness, and of his sovereign power over them, and thus to become a means of their repentance and reformation, or to be a warning to others; and if the wicked make it an occasion of hardening their hearts, it is because of their perversity, and not from necessity.

THE CONFESSION OF FAITH (CUMBERLAND PRESBYTERIAN CHURCH) (continued)

16. While the providence of God, in general, embraces all creatures, it does, in a special manner, extend to his Church.

FALL OF MAN

17. Our first parents, being seduced by the subtlety and temptation of Satan, sinned in eating the forbidden fruit; whereupon, God was pleased, for his own glory and the good of mankind, to reveal the Covenant of Grace in Christ, by which a gracious probation was established for all men.

18. By this sin they fell from their original uprightness, lost their communion with God, and so became dead in sin and defiled in all the faculties of their moral being. They being the root of all mankind, sin entered into the world through their act, and death by sin, and so death passed upon all men.

19. From this original corruption also proceeds actual transgression.

20. The remains of this corrupt nature are felt by those who are regenerated, nor will they altogether cease to operate and disturb during the present life.

21. Sin, being a transgression of the law of God, brings guilt upon the transgressor, and subjects him to the wrath of God and to endless torment, unless pardoned through the mediation of Christ.

GOD'S COVENANT WITH MAN

22. The first covenant made with man was a Covenant of Works, wherein life was promised to Adam upon condition of perfect and personal obedience.

23. Man, by his fall, having made himself incapable of life by that covenant, the Lord was pleased to make the second, commonly called the Covenant of Grace, wherein he freely offers unto sinners life and salvation by Jesus Christ, requiring of them faith in him, that they may be saved. This covenant is frequently set forth in the Scriptures by the name of a testament, in reference to the death of Jesus Christ, the testator, and to the everlasting inheritance, with all things belonging to it, therein bequeathed.

24. Under the Old Testament dispensation the Covenant of Grace was administered by promises, prophecies, sacrifices, circumcision, the paschal lamb, and other types and ordinances delivered to the Jews—all foresignifying Christ to come—which were sufficient, through the operation of the Holy Spirit, to instruct them savingly in the knowledge of God, and build them up in the faith of the Messiah.

25. Under the New Testament dispensation, wherein Christ, the substance, is set forth, the ordinances in which the Covenant of Grace is dispensed are the preaching of the Word and the administration of the sacraments of Baptism and the Lord's Supper, which are administered with more simplicity, yet in them it is held forth in more fullness and spiritual efficacy to all nations, Jews and Gentiles.

26. As children were included with their parents in the Covenant of Grace under the Old Testament dispensation, so are they included in it under the New, and should, as under the Old, receive the appropriate sign and seal thereof.

CHRIST THE MEDIATOR

27. Jesus Christ, the only-begotten Son of God, was verily appointed before the foundation of the world to be the Mediator between God and man, the Prophet, Priest, and King, the heir of all things, the propitiation for the sins of all mankind, the Head of his Church, the Judge of the world, and the Savior of all true believers.

28. The Son of God, the second person in the Trinity, did, when the fullness of time was come, take upon himself man's nature, yet without sin, being very God and very man, yet one Christ, the only Mediator between God and man.

29. Jesus Christ, in his human nature, thus united to the Divine, was sanctified and anointed with the Holy Spirit above measure, having in him all the treasures of wisdom and knowledge, in whom it pleased the Father that all fulness should dwell, to the end that, being holy, harmless, undefiled, and full of grace and truth, he might be thoroughly furnished to execute the office of a Mediator and Surety.

30. That he might discharge the office of Mediator Jesus Christ was made under the law, which he perfectly fulfilled, was crucified, died, and was buried, and remained under the power of death for a time, yet saw no corruption. On the third day he arose from the dead, and afterward ascended to heaven, where he sits on the right hand of God, making intercession for transgressors.

31. Jesus Christ, by his perfect obedience and sacrifice of himself, which he, through the Eternal Spirit once offered unto God, became the propitiation for the sins of the whole world, so God can be just in justifying all who believe in Jesus.

32. Although the work of redemption was not actually wrought by Christ until after his incarnation, yet the benefits thereof were communicated unto the believer, in all ages, successively, from the beginning of the world, by the Holy Spirit, and through such instrumentalities as God was pleased to employ.

33. Jesus Christ tasted death for every man, and now makes intercession for transgressors, by virtue of which the Holy Spirit is given to convince of sin and enable man to believe and obey, governing the hearts of believers by his word and Spirit, overcoming all their enemies, by his almighty power and wisdom, in such manner and ways as are most consonant to his wonderful and unsearchable dispensation.

FREE WILL

34. God, in creating man in his own likeness, endued him with intelligence, sensibility, and will, which form the basis of moral character, and render man capable of moral government.

35. The freedom of the will is a fact of human consciousness, and is the sole ground of human accountability. Man, in his state of innocence, was both free and able to keep the Divine law, also to violate it. Without any constraint, from either physical or moral causes, he did violate it.

36. Man, by disobedience, lost his innocence, forfeited the favor of God, became corrupt in heart and inclined to evil. In this state of spiritual death and condemnation, man is still free and responsible; yet, without the illuminating influences of the Holy Spirit, he is unable either to keep the law or lay hold upon the hope set before him in the gospel.

37. When the sinner is born of God, he loves him supremely, and steadfastly purposes to do his will; yet, because of remaining corruption, and of his imperfect knowledge of moral and spiritual things, he often wills what in itself is sinful. This imperfect knowledge and corruption remain, in greater or less force, during the present life; hence the conflict between the flesh and the spirit.

DIVINE INFLUENCE

38. God the Father, having set forth his Son Jesus Christ as a propitiation for the sins of the world, does most graciously vouchsafe a manifestation of the Holy Spirit with the same intent to every man.

39. The Holy Spirit, operating through the written word, and through such other means as God in his wisdom may choose, or directly, without means, so moves upon the hearts of men as to enlighten, reprove, and convince them of sin, of their lost estate, and of their need of salvation; and, by so doing, inclines them to come to Christ.

40. This call of the Holy Spirit is purely of God's free grace alone, and not because of human merit, and is antecedent to all desire, purpose, and intention on the part of the sinner to come to Christ; so that while it is possible for all to be saved with it, none can be saved without it.

41. This call is not irresistible, but is effectual in those only who, in penitence and faith, freely surrender themselves wholly to Christ, the only name whereby men can be saved.

REPENTANCE UNTO LIFE

42. Repentance unto life is a change of mind and feeling toward God, induced by the agency of the Holy Spirit, wherein the sinner resolutely purposes to forsake all sin, to turn unto God, and to walk in all his commandments.

43. There is no merit in repentance, or in any other human exercise; yet God is pleased to require all men to repent.

44. As all men are required to make full and frank confession of sin to God, so he that gives grounds of offense to the Church, or trespasses against his brother, should confess his errors, make amendment and due restitution, so far as is in his power.

SAVING FAITH

45. Saving faith, including assent to the truth of God's holy word, is the act of receiving and resting upon Christ alone for salvation, and is accompanied by contrition for sin and a full purpose of heart to turn from it and to live unto God.

46. While there is no merit in faith, yet it is the condition of salvation. It is not of the nature of good works, from which it must be distinguished.

47. This faith may be tried in many ways, but the believer has the promise of ultimate victory through Christ.

JUSTIFICATION

48. All those who truly repent of their sins, and in faith commit themselves to Christ, God freely justifies; not by infusing righteousness into them, but by pardoning their sins and by counting and accepting their persons as righteous; not for any thing wrought in them or done by them, but for Christ's sake alone; not by imputing faith itself, or any other evangelical obedience, to them as their righteousness, but by imputing the obedience and satisfaction of Christ unto them, they receiving and resting on him and his righteousness by faith.

49. Justification is purely of God's free grace, and is a full pardon for all sins, and exemption from all their penal consequences; but it imparts no moral qualities or merits to the believer, being strictly a legal transaction. Though of free grace alone, it is conditioned upon faith, and is assured to none but penitent and true believers, who, being justified, have peace with God through our Lord Jesus Christ.

50. God continues to forgive the sins of those who are justified, and although he will never permit them to fall from the state of justification, yet they may, by their sins, fall under God's fatherly displeasure, and not have the light of his countenance restored unto them until they humble themselves, confess their sins, and renew their consecration to God.

REGENERATION

51. Those who believe in the Lord Jesus Christ are regenerated, or born from above, renewed in spirit, and made new creatures in Christ.

52. The necessity for this moral purification arises out of the enmity of the human heart against God, its insubordination to his law, and its consequent incapacity to love and glorify God.

53. Regeneration is of God's free grace alone, and is the work of the Holy Spirit, who, by taking of the things which are Christ's and showing them unto the sinner, enables him to lay hold on Christ. This renewal of the heart by the Holy Spirit is not of the nature of a physical but of a moral work—a purification of the heart by faith.

54. All infants dying in infancy, and all persons who have never had the faculty of reason, are regenerated and saved.

ADOPTION

55. All those who are regenerated, and are thus changed into the image of his Son, God the Father is pleased to make partakers of the grace of adoption, by which they are taken into the number, and enjoy the liberties and privileges, of the children of God; have his name put upon them; receive the Spirit of adoption; have access to the throne of grace with boldness; are enabled to cry, Abba, Father; are pitied, protected, provided for, and chastened by him, as by a father, yet never cast off, but sealed to the day of redemption, and inherit the promises as heirs of everlasting salvation.

SANCTIFICATION

56. Sanctification is a doctrine of the Holy Scriptures, and it is the duty and privilege of believers to avail themselves of its inestimable benefits, as taught in the word of God. A state of sinless perfection in this life is not authorized by the Scriptures, and is a dogma of dangerous tendency.

GROWTH IN GRACE

57. Growth in grace is secured by personal consecration to the service of God, regular attention to the means of grace, the reading of the Holy Scriptures, prayer, the ministrations of the sanctuary, and all known Christian duties. By such means the believer's faith is much increased, his tendency to sin weakened, the lusts of the flesh mortified, and he more and more strengthened in all saving graces, and in the practice of holiness, without which no man shall see the Lord.

GOOD WORKS

58. Good works are such only as God has commanded in his word, and not such as may be devised by men out of blind zeal, or any pretense of good intention.

59. Those who, in their obedience and love, attain the greatest height in this life, still fall short of that perfection which the Divine law requires; yet their good works are accepted of God, who, looking upon them in his Son, is pleased to accept and reward that which is sincere, although accompanied with many weaknesses and imperfections.

PRESERVATION OF BELIEVERS

60. Those whom God has justified, he will also glorify; consequently, the truly regenerated soul will not totally fall away from a state of grace, but will be preserved to everlasting life.

61. The preservation of believers depends on the unchangeable love and power of God, the merits, advocacy, and intercession of Jesus Christ, the abiding of the Holy Spirit and seed of God within them, and the nature of the Covenant of Grace. Nevertheless, true believers, through the temptations of Satan, the world, and the flesh, and the neglect of the means of grace, may fall into sin, incur God's displeasure, and grieve the Holy Spirit, and thus be deprived of some measure of their graces and comforts, and have their consciences wounded; but the Christian will never rest satisfied therein.

CHRISTIAN ASSURANCE

62. Those who truly believe in the Lord Jesus Christ, and love him in sincerity, endeavoring to walk in all good conscience before him, may, in this life, be certainly assured that they are in a state of grace, and may rejoice in the hope of the glory of God, which hope shall never make them ashamed.

63. This assurance is founded upon the Divine promises, the consciousness of peace with God, the testimony of the Holy Spirit witnessing with their spirits that they are the children of God, and is the earnest of their inheritance.

64. This comfortable assurance of salvation is not an invariable accompaniment of faith in Christ; hence the believer may have many sore conflicts before he is made a partaker of it; yet he may, by the right use of the means of grace—through the agency of the Holy Spirit—attain thereunto; therefore, it is the duty of every one to give diligence to make his calling and election sure.

65. As this assurance may be very much strengthened by full consecration to God and fidelity in his service, so it may be weakened by worldly-mindedness and negligence in Christian duty, which result in darkness and in doubt; yet true believers have the promise of God that he will never leave nor forsake them.

THE LAW OF GOD

66. The moral law is the rule of duty growing immediately out of the relations of rational creatures to their Creator and to each other. These relations being the product of the Divine purpose, the law has its ultimate source in the will of the Creator.

67. This law is of universal and perpetual obligation, and is written primarily upon the hearts of all accountable beings. It was sufficiently known to Adam to enable him to know and do the will of God, and thus, by the righteousness of works, secure eternal life.

68. After Adam's fall, and that of his posterity through him, a written form of the law became necessary. This was given in the Decalogue, or Ten Commandments, a summary of which is given in these words: Thou shalt love the Lord thy God with all thy heart, and with all thy soul, and with all thy strength, and with all thy mind, and thy neighbor as thyself.

69. This law is not set aside, but rather established, by the gospel, which is the Divine expedient by which sinners are saved, and the end of the law fully met. It accordingly remains in full force as the rule of conduct. It must not, therefore, be confounded with the ceremonial law, which was abolished under the New Testament dispensation.

70. The penalties of this law are the natural and subjective sequences of transgression, and, unless set aside by the provisions of the gospel, must of

necessity be eternal; and such are they declared to be by the Holy Scriptures. These moral retributions must be distinguished from judicial punishments, which are arbitrary, objective, and temporary, and are always inflicted as occasion may require, for administrative purposes.

CHRISTIAN LIBERTY

71. The liberty that Christ has secured to believers under the gospel consists in freedom from the guilt and penal consequences of sin, in their free access to God, and in their yielding obedience to him, not from a slavish fear, but from a cheerful and confiding love.

72. God, who alone is Lord of the conscience, has left it free, in matters of faith and worship, from such opinions and commandments of men as may be contrary to his word.

73. Those who, upon pretense of Christian liberty, practice any sin, or cherish any lust, do thereby destroy the end of Christian liberty, which is, that being delivered from the dominion of sin, we may serve the Lord without fear in righteousness all our days.

74. Those who, upon a similar pretense, shall oppose the proper exercise of any lawful authority, whether civil or ecclesiastical, and thereby resist the ordinance of God, may lawfully be called to account, and be subjected to the censures of the Church.

RELIGIOUS WORSHIP

75. Religious worship is to be rendered to God the Father, Son, and Holy Spirit, and to him alone; not to angels, saints, or any other creature; and, since the fall, this worship is acceptable only through the mediation of the Lord Jesus Christ.

76. Prayer with thanksgiving, being one special part of religious worship, is required of all men; and, by the help of the Holy Spirit, is made efficacious through Christ, when offered according to his will. Prayer is to be made for things lawful, and for the living, but not for the dead.

77. The reading of the Holy Scriptures, attendance upon the ministrations of the word, the use of psalms and sacred songs, the proper observance of the Christian sacraments, visiting the sick, contributing to the relief of the poor, and the support and spread of the gospel, are all proper acts of religious worship. Religious vows, solemn fastings and thanksgivings, are also acts of religious worship, and are of much benefit when properly performed.

78. God is to be worshiped in spirit and in truth, in secret, in private families daily, and in the public assembly.

CHRISTIAN STEWARDSHIP

79. Christian stewardship consists in the recognition that all of life is a trust from God and is to be used for his glory and the advancement of his kingdom. It extends to all gifts which God has bestowed upon man including time, talents, and substance.

80. The motive of Christian stewardship is love toward both God and man and the desire for the propagation of the gospel.

81. Tithing as a principle of stewardship is both a duty and a privilege of every believer. While not expressly commanded in the New Testament, it was endorsed by Christ himself and may be legitimately deduced from the epistles.

82. Tithing is, when rightly practiced, an act of Christian devotion and a means of grace for the believer and is blessed of God in the propagation of the gospel.

83. While tithing is a duty and privilege of every believer, it should be regarded as the minimum basis of Christian giving and not necessarily as the full measure of one's devotion to Christ.

84. Every man must give an account to God of his stewardship.

SABBATH-DAY

85. God has been pleased to appoint one day in seven to be kept holy unto him, which, from the beginning of the world to the resurrection of Christ was the last day of the week; and, after the resurrection of Christ, was changed unto the first day of the week, which in the Scriptures is called the Lord's-day.

86. The Sabbath is kept holy unto the Lord by resting from employments and recreations of a secular character, by the public and private worship of God, and by works of necessity and mercy.

LAWFUL OATHS AND VOWS

87. The name of God only is that by which men ought to swear, and therein it is to be used with all reverence; therefore, to swear vainly or rashly by that glorious and dreadful name, or to swear at all by any other thing, is sinful. Yet, an oath is warranted by the word of God, under the New Testament as well as under the Old, when imposed by lawful authority.

88. Whosoever takes an oath ought duly to consider the weightiness of so solemn an act, and therein to avouch nothing but what he is fully persuaded is the truth. Neither may a man bind himself by oath to any thing but what is good and just, or what he believes so to be, and what he is able and resolved to perform.

89. An oath is to be taken in the plain and common sense of the words, without equivocation or mental reservation. It cannot oblige to sin; but in any thing not sinful, being taken, it binds to performance, although to a man's own hurt.

90. A vow is of a like nature with an oath, and ought to be made with the like religious care, and to be performed with the like faithfulness. No man may vow to do any thing forbidden in the word of God, or what would hinder any duty therein commanded, or which is not in his own power, and for the performance whereof he has no promise or ability from God.

CIVIL GOVERNMENT

91. God, the Supreme Lord and King of all the world, has ordained civil officers to be under him over the people, for his own glory and the public good; and, to this end, has armed them with power for the defense of the innocent and the punishment of evil-doers.

92. It is lawful for Christians to accept civil offices when called thereunto, in the management whereof they ought especially to maintain piety, justice, and peace, according to the wholesome laws of each Common-wealth.

93. Civil officers may not assume to themselves the administration of the word and the sacraments, or in the least interfere in matters of faith; yet it is their duty to protect the Church of our common Lord, without giving preference to any denomination of Christians. And, as Jesus Christ has appointed a government and discipline in his Church, no law of any Commonwealth should interfere therewith, but should provide that all religious and ecclesiastical assemblies shall be held without molestation or disturbance.

94. It is the duty of the people to pray for magistrates, to obey their lawful commands, and to be subject to their authority for conscience's sake.

MARRIAGE AND DIVORCE

95. Marriage is to be between one man and one woman; neither is it lawful for any man to have more than one wife, nor for any woman to have more than one husband, at the same time.

96. Marriage was ordained for the mutual help of husband and wife, and for the benefit of the human race.

97. Marriages ought not to be within the degrees of consanguinity or affinity forbidden in the word of God, nor can such marriages be justified by the human law.

98. The marriage relation should not be dissolved for any cause not justified by the teachings of the word of God, and any immorality in relation to its dissolution is cognizable by the Church-courts.

THE CHURCH

99. The universal Church, which is invisible, consists of all those who have become children of God by faith, and joint-heirs with Christ, who is the head thereof.

100. The visible Church consists of those who hold to the fundamental doctrines of Christianity in respect to matters of faith and morals, and have entered into formal covenant with God and some organized body of Christians for the maintenance of religious worship. The children of such are included in the covenant relations of their parents, and are properly under the special care of the Church.

101. Unto this visible Church Christ has given the ministry, the word, and the ordinances for its edification, and, by his own presence in spirit, makes them effectual thereunto. The Lord Jesus Christ is the only head of his Church on earth.

CHRISTIAN COMMUNION

102. All those united to Christ by faith have fellowship with him, and, being united to one another in love, have communion one with another, and are required to bear one another's burdens, and so fulfill the law of Christ.

103. While it is required of all Christians to live in fellowship, it is the especial duty of those belonging to the same denomination; and also to co-operate in sustaining public worship, and whatever measures are adjudged best for the spiritual interests of the Church and the glory of God.

THE SACRAMENTS

104. As under the Old Testament dispensation two sacraments were ordained, Circumcision and the Passover; so, under the New, there are but two—that is to say, Baptism and the Lord's Supper.

BAPTISM

105. Water-baptism is a sacrament of the New Testament, ordianed by Jesus Christ as a sign or symbol of the baptism of the Holy Spirit, and as the seal of the Covenant of Grace.

106. The outward element to be used in this sacrament is water, wherewith the party is to be baptized in the name of the Father, and of the Son, and of the Holy Spirit, by an ordained minister of the gospel.

107. Baptism is rightly administered by pouring or sprinkling water upon the person, yet the validity of this sacrament does not depend upon any particular mode of administration.

108. The proper subjects of water-baptism are believing adults; also infants, one or both of whose parents or guardians are believers.

109. There is no saving efficacy in water-baptism, yet it is a duty of all believers to confess Christ in this solemn ordinance, and it is also the duty of all believing parents to consecrate their children to God in baptism.

THE LORD'S SUPPER

110. The sacrament, commonly called the Lord's Supper, was instituted by the Lord Jesus Christ at the close of his last passover supper, as a perpetual remem-brance of his passion and death on the cross, by which sacrifice of himself he was made the propitia-tion for the sins of the whole world.

111. In this sacrament no sacrifice of any kind is offered for sin, but the one perfect offering of Christ as a sufficient sacrifice is set forth and commemorated by appropriate symbols. These symbols are bread and wine, which, though figuratively called the body and blood of Christ, nevertheless remain, after consecra-tion, literal bread and wine, and give no countenance

to the doctrines of consubstantiation and transubstantiation.

112. As in this sacrament the communicants have visibly set before them symbols of the Saviour's passion, they should not approach the holy communion without due self-examination, reverence, humility, and gratitude.

113. All who love the Lord Jesus in sincerity and in truth should, on all suitable occasions, express their devotion to him by the use of the symbols of his death. But none who have not faith to discern the Lord's body should partake of his holy communion.

CHURCH AUTHORITY

114. The Lord Jesus, as king and head of his Church, has therein appointed a government intrusted to Church-officers distinct from the civil government.

115. By Divine appointment the officers of the visible church have the power to admit members into its communion, to admonish, suspend, or expel the disorderly and to restore those who, in the judgment of charity, have repented of their sins.

CHURCH COURTS

116. Church-government implies the existence of Church-courts, invested with legislative, judicial, and executive authority; and the Scriptures recognize such institutions, some of subordinate and some of superior authority, each having its own particular sphere of duties and privileges in reference to matters ministerial and ecclesiastical, yet all subordinate to the same general design.

117. It is the prerogative of these courts, ministerially, to determine controversies of faith and questions of morals, to set down rules and directions for the better ordering of the public worship of God and government of his Church, to receive complaints in cases of maladministration, and authoritatively to determine the same, which determinations are to be received with reverence and submission.

DEATH AND THE RESURRECTION

118. The bodies of men, after death, return to dust; but their spirits, being immortal, return to God who gave them. The spirits of the righteous are received into heaven, where they behold the face of God in light and glory, waiting for the full redemption of their bodies; and the spirits of the wicked are cast into hell, where they are reserved to the judgment of the great day. The Scriptures speak of no other place for departed spirits.

119. At the resurrection, those who are alive shall not die, but be changed; and all the dead shall be raised up, spiritual and immortal, and spirits and bodies be reunited forever. There shall be a resurrection both of the just and the unjust: of the unjust to dishonor, and of the just unto honor; the bodies of the latter shall be fashioned like unto Christ's glorious body.

THE JUDGMENT

120. God has appointed a day wherein he will judge the world in righteousness by Jesus Christ—to whom all power and judgment are given by the Father—in which not only the apostate angels shall be judged, but likewise all persons who have lived upon earth shall appear before the tribunal of Christ, and shall receive according to what they have done, whether good or evil.

121. After the judgment, the wicked shall go away into eternal punishment, but the righteous into eternal life.

Notes: *The Cumberland Presbyterian Church emerged on the American frontier at the period usually termed the Second Great Awakening. From the Methodist example, it developed an Arminian theological perspective and followed the practice of formally using untrained ministers, which placed its leaders in conflict with the older Presbyterian authorities on the East Coast. Seeing the need to organize separately, the leaders wished to create a church that was Presbyterian but at the same time did not hold to the strong Calvinist doctrines of limited atonement and predestination.*

In 1814 the new church adopted a confession of faith that was little more than the Westminster Confession modified to eliminate the prime features of what was termed "hyper-Calvinism," i.e., the doctrines of universal foreordination, unconditional election, and rebrobation and limited atonement. [The text of these early revisions can be found in Philip Schaff's The Creeds of Christendom. *(New York: Harper & Brothers, 1877).] However, so integral were these doctrines to the Westminster position that expunging them completely could only be accomplished with a complete rewriting. That rewriting was not done until the 1880s, and the new confession was accepted in 1883. The continuing Cumberland Presbyterian Church has retained the rewritten confession, reproduced here without the Biblical footnotes. This confession is also used by the Second Cumberland Presbyterian Church in the U.S.*

The Arminian emphasis on universal atonement, the free grace of God, and free will had been passed to the Cumberland Presbyterian Church by the Methodists. However, one Methodist emphasis, that on human perfectability, was not accepted by the Presbyterians and is specifically denied by them.

*   *   *

THE CONFESSION OF 1967 [PRESBYTERIAN CHURCH (U.S.A.)]

PREFACE

The Church confesses its faith when it bears a present witness to God's grace in Jesus Christ.

In every age the church has expressed its witness in words and deeds as the need of the time required. The earliest examples of confession are found within the Scriptures. Confessional statements have taken such varied forms as hymns, liturgical formulas, doctrinal definitions, catechisms, theological systems in summary, and declarations of purpose against threatening evil.

Confessions and declarations are subordinate standards in the church, subject to the authority of Jesus Christ, the Word of God, as the Scriptures bear witness to him. No

THE CONFESSION OF 1967 [PRESBYTERIAN CHURCH (U.S.A.)] (continued)

one type of confession is exclusively valid, no one statement is irreformable. Obedience to Jesus Christ alone identifies the one universal church and supplies the continuity of its tradition. This obedience is the ground of the church's duty and freedom to reform itself in life and doctrine as new occasions, in God's Providence, may demand.

The United Presbyterian Church in the United States of America acknowledges itself aided in understanding the gospel by the testimony of the church from earlier ages and from many lands. More especially it is guided by the Nicene and Apostles' Creeds from the time of the early church; the Scots Confession, the Heidelberg Catechism, and the Second Helvetic Confession from the era of the Reformation; the Westminster Confession and Shorter Catechism from the seventeenth century, and the Shorter Catechism from the seventeenth century, and the Theological Declaration of Barmen from the twentieth century.

The purpose of the Confession of 1967 is to call the church to the unity in confession and mission which is required of disciples today. This Confession is not a "system of doctrine," nor does it include all the traditional topics of theology. For example, the Trinity and the Person of Christ are not redefined but are recognized and reaffirmed as forming the basis and determining the structure of the Christian faith.

God's reconciling work in Jesus Christ and the mission of reconciliation to which he has called his church are the heart of the gospel in any age. Our generation stands in peculiar need of reconciliation in Christ. Accordingly this Confession of 1967 is built upon that theme.

THE CONFESSION

In Jesus Christ God was reconciling the world to himself. Jesus Christ is God with man. He is the eternal Son of the Father, who became man and lived among us to fulfill the work of reconciliation. He is present in the church by the power of the Holy Spirit to continue and complete his mission. This work of God, the Father, Son and Holy Spirit, is the foundation of all confessional statements about God, man and the World. Therefore the church calls men to be reconciled to God and to one another.

Part I. GOD'S WORK OF RECONCILIATION

Section A. THE GRACE OF OUR LORD JESUS CHRIST

1. JESUS CHRIST. In Jesus of Nazareth true humanity was realized once for all. Jesus, a Palestinian Jew, lived among his own people and shared their needs, temptations, joys, and sorrows. He expressed the love of God in word and deed and became a brother to all kinds of sinful men. But his complete obedience led him into conflict with his people. His life and teaching judged their goodness, religious aspirations, and national hopes. Many rejected him and demanded his death. In giving himself freely for them He took upon himself the judgment under which all men stand convicted. God raised him from the dead, vindicating him as Messiah and Lord. The victim of sin became victor, and won the victory over sin and death for all men.

God's reconciling act in Jesus Christ is a mystery which the Scriptures describe in various ways. It is called the sacrifice of a lamb, a shepherd's life given for his sheep, atonement by a priest; again it is ransom of a slave, payment of debt, vicarious satisfaction of a legal penalty, and victory over the powers of evil. These are expressions of a truth which remains beyond the reach of all theory in the depths of God's love for man. They reveal the gravity, cost, and sure achievement of God's reconciling work.

The risen Christ is the savior for all men. Those joined to him by faith are set right with God and commissioned to serve as his reconciling community. Christ is head of this community, the church, which began with the apostles and continues through all generations.

The same Jesus Christ is the judge of all men. His judgment discloses the ultimate seriousness of life and gives promise of God's final victory over the power of sin and death. To receive life from the risen Lord is to have life eternal; to refuse life from him is to choose the death which is separation from God. All who put their trust in Christ face divine judgment without fear, for the judge is their redeemer.

2. THE SIN OF MAN. The reconciling act of God in Jesus Christ exposes the evil in men as sin in the sight of God. In sin men claim mastery of their own lives, turn against God and their fellowmen, and become exploiters and despoilers of the world. They lose their humanity in futile striving and are left in rebellion, despair, and isolation.

Wise and virtuous men through the ages have sought the highest good in devotion to freedom, justice, peace, truth and beauty. Yet all human virtue, when seen in the light of God's love in Jesus Christ, is found to be infected by self-interest and hostility. All men, good and bad alike, are in the wrong before God and helpless without his forgiveness. Thus all men fall under God's judgment. No one is more subject to that judgment than the man who assumes that he is guiltless before God or morally superior to others.

God's love never changes. Against all who oppose him, God expresses his love in wrath. In the same love God took on himself judgment and shameful death in Jesus Christ, to bring men to repentance and new life.

Section B. THE LOVE OF GOD

God's sovereign love is a mystery beyond the reach of man's mind. Human thought ascribes to God superlatives of power, widsom, and goodness. But God reveals his love in Jesus Christ by showing power in the form of a servant, wisdom in the folly of the cross, and goodness in receiving sinful men. The power of God's love in Christ to transform the world discloses that the Redeemer is the Lord and Creator who made all things to serve the purpose of his love.

God has created the world of space and time to be the sphere of his dealings with men. In its beauty and vastness, sublimity and awfulness, order and disorder, the world reflects to the eye of faith the majesty and mystery of its Creator.

God has created man in a personal relation with himself that man may respond to the love of the Creator. He has created male and female and given them a life which proceeds from birth to death in a succession of generations and in a wide complex of social relations. He has endowed man with capacities to make the world serve his needs and to enjoy its good things. Life is a gift to be received with gratitude and a task to be pursued with courage. Man is free to seek his life within the purpose of God: to develop and protect the resources of nature for the common welfare, to work for justice and peace in society, and in other ways to use his creative powers for the fulfillment of human life.

God expressed his love for all mankind through Israel, whom he chose to be his covenant people to serve him in love and faithfulness. When Israel was unfaithful, he disciplined the nation with his judgments and maintained his cause through prophets, priests, teachers, and true believers. These witnesses called all Israelites to a destiny in which they would serve God faithfully and become a light to the nations. The same witnesses proclaimed the coming of a new age, and a true servant of God in whom God's purpose for Israel and for mankind would be realized.

Out of Israel God in due time raised up Jesus. His faith and obedience were the response of the perfect child of God. He was the fulfillment of God's promise to Israel, the beginning of the new creation, and the pioneer of the new humanity. He gave history its meaning and direction and called the church to be his servant for the reconciliation of the world.

Section C. THE COMMUNION OF THE HOLY SPIRIT

God the Holy Spirit fulfills the work of reconciliation in man. The Holy Spirit creates and renews the church as the community in which men are reconciled to God and to one another. He enables them to receive forgiveness as they forgive one another and to enjoy the peace of God as they make peace among themselves. In spite of their sin, he gives them power to become representatives of Jesus Christ and his gospel of reconciliation to all men.

1. THE NEW LIFE. The reconciling work of Jesus was the supreme crisis in the life of mankind. His cross and resurrection become personal crisis and present hope for men when the gospel is proclaimed and believed. In this experi-ence the Spirit brings God's forgiveness to men, moves them to respond in faith, repentance, and obedience, and initiates the new life in Christ.

The new life takes shape in a community in which men know that God loves and accepts them in spite of what they are. They therefore accept themselves and love others, knowing that no man has any ground on which to stand except God's grace.

The new life does not release a man from conflict with unbelief, pride, lust, fear. He still has to struggle with disheartening difficulties and problems. Nevertheless, as he matures in love and faithfulness in his life with Christ, he lives in freedom and good cheer, bearing witness on good days and evil days, confident that the new life is pleasing to God and helpful to others.

The new life finds its direction in the life of Jesus, his deeds and words, his struggles against temptation, his compassion, his anger, and his willingness to suffer death. The teaching of apostles and prophets guides men in living this life, and the Christian community nurtures and equips them for their ministries.

The members of the church are emissaries of peace and seek the good of man in cooperation with powers and authorities in politics, culture, and economics. But they have to fight against pretensions and injustices when these same powers endanger human welfare. Their strength is in their confidence that God's purpose rather than man's schemes will finally prevail.

Life in Christ is life eternal. The resurrection of Jesus is God's sign that he will consummate his work of creation and reconciliation beyond death and bring to fulfillment the new life begun in Christ.

2. THE BIBLE. The one sufficient revelation of God is Jesus Christ, the Word of God incarnate, to whom the Holy Spirit bears unique and authoritative witness through the Holy Scriptures, which are received and obeyed as the word of God written. The Scriptures are not a witness among others, but the witness without parallel. The church has received the books of the Old and New Testaments as prophetic and apostolic testimony in which it hears the word of God and by which its faith and obedience are nourished and regulated.

The New Testament is the recorded testimony of apostles to the coming of the Messiah, Jesus of Nazareth, and the sending of the Holy Spirit to the church. The Old Testament bears witness to God's faithfulness in his covenant with Israel and points the way to the fulfillment of his purpose in Christ. The Old Testament is indispensable to understand the New, and is not itself fully understood without the New.

The Bible is to be interpreted in the light of its witness to God's work of reconciliation in Christ. The Scriptures, given under the guidance of the Holy Spirit, are nevertheless the words of men, conditioned by the language, thought forms, and literary fashions of the places and times at which they were written. They reflect views of life, history, and the cosmos which were then current. The church, therefore, has an obligation to approach the Scriptures with literary and historical understanding. As God has spoken his word in diverse cultural situations, the church is confident that he will continue to speak through the Scriptures in a changing world and in every form of human culture.

God's word is spoken to his church today where the Scriptures are faithfully preached and attentively read in dependence on the illumination of the Holy Spirit and with readiness to receive their truth and direction.

Part II. THE MINISTRY OF RECONCILIATION

Section A. THE MISSION OF THE CHURCH

1. DIRECTION. To be reconciled to God is to be sent into the world as his reconciling community. This community, the church universal, is entrusted with God's message of reconciliation and shares his labor of healing the enmities which separate men from God and from each other. Christ has called the church to this mission and given it the gift of the Holy Spirit. The church maintains continuity with the apostles and with Israel by faithful obedience to his call.

   The life, death, resurrection, and promised coming of Jesus Christ has set the pattern for the church's mission. His life as man involves the church in the common life of men. His service to men commits the church to work for every form of human well-being. His suffering makes the church sensitive to all the sufferings of mankind so that it sees the face of Christ in the faces of men in every kind of need. His crucifixion discloses to the church God's judgment on man's inhumanity to man and the awful consequences of its own complicity in injustice. In the power of the risen Christ and the hope of his coming the church sees the promise of God's renewal of man's life in society and of God's victory over all wrong.

   The church follows this pattern in the form of its life and in the method of its action. So to live and serve is to confess Christ as Lord.

2. FORMS AND ORDER. The institutions of the people of God change and vary as their mission requires in different times and places. The unity of the church is compatible with a wide variety of forms, but it is hidden and distorted when variant forms are allowed to harden into sectarian divisions, exclusive denominations, and rival factions.

Wherever the church exists, its members are both gathered in corporate life and dispersed in society for the sake of mission in the world.

The church gathers to praise God, to hear his word for mankind, to baptize and to join the Lord's Supper, to pray for and present the world to him in worship, to enjoy fellowship, to receive instruction, strength, and comfort, to order and organize its own corporate life, to be tested, renewed, and reformed, and to speak and act in the world's affairs as may be appropriate to the needs of the time.

The church disperses to serve God wherever its members are, at work or play, in private or in the life of society. Their prayer and Bible study are part of the church's worship and theological reflection. Their witness is the church's evangelism. Their daily action in the world is the church in mission to the world. The quality of their relation with other persons is the measure of the church's fidelity.

Each member is the church in the world, endowed by the Spirit with some gift of ministry and is responsible for the integrity of his witness in his own particular situation. He is entitled to the guidance and support of the Christian community and is subject to its advice and correction. He in turn, in his own competence, helps to guide the church.

In recognition of special gifts of the Spirit and for the ordering of its life as a community, the church calls, trains, and authorizes certain members for leadership and oversight. The persons qualified for these duties in accordance with the polity of the church are set apart by ordination or other appropriate acts and thus made responsible for their special ministries.

The church thus orders its life as an institution with a constitution, government, officers, finances and administrative rules. These are instruments of mission, not ends in themselves. Different orders have served the gospel, and none can claim exclusive validity. A presbyterian polity recognizes the responsibility of all members for ministry and maintains the organic relation of all congregations in the church. It seeks to protect the church from exploitation by ecclesiastical or secular power and ambition. Every church order must be open to such reformation as may be required to make it a more effective instrument of the mission of reconciliation.

3. REVELATION AND RELIGION. The church in its mission encounters the religions of men and in that encounter becomes conscious of its own human character as a religion. God's revelation to Israel, expressed within Semitic culture, gave rise to the religion of the Hebrew people. God's revelation in Jesus Christ called forth the response of Jews and Greeks and came to expression within Judaism and Hellenism as

the Christian religion. The Christian religion as distinct from God's revelation of himself, has been shaped throughout its history by the cultural forms of its environment.

The Christian finds parallels between other religions and his own and must approach all religions with openness and respect. Repeatedly God has used the insight of non-Christians to challenge the church to renewal. But the reconciling word of the gospel is God's judgment upon all forms of religion, including the Christian. The gift of God in Christ is for all men. The church, therefore, is commissioned to carry the gospel to all men whatever their religion may be and even when they profess none.

4. RECONCILIATION IN SOCIETY. In each time and place there are particular problems and crises through which God calls the church to act. The church, guided by the Spirit, humbled by its own complicity, and instructed by all attainable knowledge, seeks to discern the will of God and learn how to obey in these concrete situations. The following are particularly urgent at the present time.

a. God has created the peoples of the earth to be one universal family. In his reconciling love he overcomes the barriers between brothers and breaks down every form of discrimination based on racial or ethnic difference, real or imaginary. The church is called to bring all men to receive and uphold one another as persons in all relationships of life: in employment, housing, education, leisure, marriage, family, church, and the exercise of political rights. Therefore the church labors for the abolition of all racial discrimination and ministers to those injured by it. Congregations, individuals, or groups of Christians who exclude, dominate, or patronize their fellowmen, however subtly, resist the Spirit of God and bring contempt on the faith which they profess.

b. God's reconciliation in Jesus Christ is the ground of the peace, justice, and freedom among nations which all powers of government are called to serve and defend. The church, in its own life, is called to practice the forgiveness of enemies and to commend to the nations as practical politics the search for cooperation and peace. This requires the pursuit of fresh and responsible relations across every line of conflict, even at risk to national security, to reduce areas of strife and to broaden international understanding. Reconciliation among nations becomes peculiarly urgent as countries develop nuclear, chemical and biological weapons, diverting their manpower and resources from constructive uses and risking the annihilation of mankind. Although nations may serve God's purposes in history, the church which identifies the sovereignty of any one nation or any one way of life with the cause of God denies the Lordship of Christ and betrays its calling.

c. The reconciliation of man through Jesus Christ makes it plain that enslaving poverty in a world of abundance is an intolerable violation of God's good creation. Because Jesus identified himself with the needy and exploited, the cause of the world's poor is the cause of his disciples. The church cannot condone poverty, whether it is the product of unjust social structures, exploitation of the defenseless, lack of national resources, absence of technological understanding, or rapid expansion of populations. The church calls every man to use his abilities, his possessions, and the fruits of technology as gifts entrusted to him by God for the maintenance of his family and the advancement of the common welfare. It encourages those forces in human society that raise men's hopes for better conditions and provide them with opportunity for a decent living. A church that is indifferent to poverty, or evades responsibility in economic affairs, or is open to one social class only, or expects gratitude for its beneficence makes a mockery of reconciliation and offers no acceptable worship to God.

d. The relationship between man and woman exemplifies in a basic way God's ordering of the interpersonal life for which he created mankind. Anarchy in sexual relationships is a symptom of man's alienation from God, his neighbor, and himself. Man's perennial confusion about the meaning of sex has been aggravated in our day by the availability of new means for birth control and the treatment of infection, by the pressures of urbanization, by the exploitation of sexual symbols in mass communication, and by world overpopulation. The church, as the household of God, is called to lead men out of this alienation into the responsible freedom of the new life in Christ. Reconciled to God, each person has joy in and respect for his own humanity and that of other persons; a man and woman are enabled to marry, to commit themselves to a mutually shared life, and to respond to each other in sensitive and lifelong concern; parents receive the grace to care for children in love and to nurture their individuality. The church comes under the judgment of God and invites rejection by man when it fails to lead men and women into the full meaning of life together, or withholds the compassion of Christ from those caught in the moral confusion of our time.

Section B. THE EQUIPMENT OF THE CHURCH

Jesus Christ has given the church preaching and teaching, praise and prayer, and Baptism and the Lord's Supper as means of fulfilling its service of God among men. These gifts remain, but the church is obliged to change the forms of its service in ways appropriate to different generations and cultures.

1. PREACHING AND TEACHING. God instructs his church and equips it for mission through preaching and teaching. By these, when they are carried on in fidelity to the Scriptures and dependence upon the Holy Spirit, the people hear the word of God and accept and follow Christ. The message is addressed to men in particular situations. Therefore effective preaching, teaching, and personal witness require disciplined study of both the Bible and the contemporary world. All acts of public worship should be conducive to men's hearing of the gospel in a particular time and place and responding with fitting obedience.

2. PRAISE AND PRAYER. The church responds to the message of reconciliation in praise and prayer. In that response it commits itself afresh to its mission, experiences a deepening of faith and obedience, and bears open testimony to the gospel. Adoration of God is acknowledgment of the Creator by the creation. Confession of sin is admission of all men's guilt before God and of their need for his forgiveness. Thanksgiving is rejoicing in God's goodness to all men and in giving for the needs of others. Petitions and intercessions are addressed to God for the continuation of his goodness, the healing of men's ills, and their deliverance from every form of oppression. The arts, especially music and architecture, contribute to the praise and prayer of a Christian congregation when they help men to look beyond themselves to God and to the world which is the object of his love.

3. BAPTISM. By humble submission to John's baptism Christ joined himself to men in their need and entered upon his ministry of reconciliation in the power of the Spirit. Christian baptism marks the receiving of the same Spirit by by all his people. Baptism with water represents not only cleansing from sin but a dying with Christ and a joyful rising with him to new life. It commits all Christians to die each day to sin and to live for righteousness. In baptism the church celebrates the renewal of the covenant with which God has bound his people to himself. By baptism individuals are publicly received into the church to share in its life and ministry, and the church becomes responsible for their training and support in Christian discipleship. When those baptized are infants the congregation, as well as the parents, has a special obligation to nuture them in the Christian life, leading them to make, by a public profession, a personal response to the love of God shown forth in their baptism.

4. THE LORD'S SUPPER. The Lord's Supper is a celebration of the reconciliation of men with

God and with one another in which they joyfully eat and drink together at the table of their Savior. Jesus Christ gave his church this remembrance of his dying for sinful men so that by participation in it they have communion with him and with all who shall be gathered to him. Partaking in him as they eat the bread and drink the wine in accordance with Christ's appointment, they receive from the risen and living Lord the benefits of his death and resurrection. They rejoice in the foretaste of the kingdom which he will bring to consummation at his promised coming and go out from the Lord's Table with courage and hope for the service to which he has called them.

PART III. THE FULFILLMENT OF RECONCILIATION

God's redeeming work in Jesus Christ embraces the whole of man's life: social and cultural, economic and political, scientific and technological, individual and corporate. It includes man's natural environment as exploited and despoiled by sin. It is the will of God that his purpose for human life shall be fulfilled under the rule of Christ and all evil be banished from his creation.

Biblical visions and images of the rule of Christ such as a heavenly city, a Father's house, a new Heaven and earth, a marriage feast, and an unending day culminate in the image of the kingdom. The kingdom represents the triumph of God over all that resists his will and disrupts his creation. Already God's reign is present as a ferment in the world, stirring hope in men and preparing the world to receive its ultimate judgment and redemption.

With an urgency born of this hope the church applies itself to present tasks and strives for a better world. It does not justify limited progress with the kingdom of God on earth nor does it despair in the face of disappointment and defeat. In steadfast hope the church looks beyond all partial achievement to the final triumph of God.

"Now to him who by the power at work within us is able to do far more abundantly than all we ask or think, to him be glory in the church and in Christ Jesus to all generations, forever and ever. Amen."

Notes: *In 1967 the United Presbyterian Church in the U.S.A. adopted a new statement of faith. Hailed by the majority as a contemporary statement of the Christian tradition, it was denounced by others as a departure from the standards of the Westminster Confession. While affirming many of the traditional statements of the Westminster Confession, it provided a latitude on a number of theological questions. Contemporaneously with the passing of the confession, the church authorized the publication of* The Book of Confessions, *which included this new confession, the Westminster Confession, six other confessions, and the Heidelberg Catechism. In the act of recognizing the ancient creeds, other Reformed documents, and the twentieth-century Barmen declaration, the church dislodged the Westminster Confession from its unique role as the principal definer of Presbyterian faith to become but one of many acceptable statements. The Book of Confessions continues to be used by the Presbyterian Church (U.S.A.).*

THE SCOTS CONFESSION (1560)

CHAPTER I. GOD

We confess and acknowledge one God alone, to whom alone we must cleave, whom alone we must serve, whom only we must worship, and in whom alone we put our trust. Who is eternal, infinite, immeasurable, incomprehensible, omnipotent, invisible; one in substance and yet distinct in three persons, the Father, the Son, and the Holy Ghost. By whom we confess and believe all things in heaven and earth, visible and invisible, to have been created, to be retained in their being, and to be ruled and guided by his inscrutable providence for such end as his eternal wisdom, goodness, and justice have appointed, and to the manifestation of his own glory.

CHAPTER II. THE CREATION OF MAN

We confess and acknowledge that our God has created man, i.e., our first father, Adam, after his own image and likeness, to whom he gave wisdom, lordship, justice, free will, and self-consciousness, so that in the whole nature of man no imperfection could be found. From this dignity and perfection man and woman both fell; the woman being deceived by the serpent and man obeying the voice of the woman, both conspiring against the sovereign majesty of God, who in clear words had previously threatened death if they presumed to eat of the forbidden tree.

CHAPTER III. ORIGINAL SIN

By this transgression, generally known as original sin, the image of God was utterly defaced in man, and he and his children because by nature hostile to God, slaves to Satan, and the servants to sin. And thus everlasting death has had, and shall have, power and dominion over all who have not been, are not, or shall not be reborn from above. This rebirth is wrought by the power of the Holy Ghost creating in the hearts of God's chosen ones an assured faith in the promise of God revealed to us in his Word; by this faith we grasp Christ Jesus with the graces and blessings promised in him.

CHAPTER IV. THE REVELATION OF THE PROMISE

We constantly believe that God, after the fearful and horrible departure of man from his obedience, did seek Adam again, call upon him, rebuke and convict him of his sin, and in the end made unto him a most joyful promise, that "the seed of the woman should bruise the head of the serpent," that is, that he should destroy the works of the devil. This promise was repeated and made clearer from time to time, it was embraced with joy, and most constantly received by all the faithful from Adam to Noah, from Noah to Abraham, from Abraham to David, and so onwards to the incarnation of Christ Jesus: all (we mean the believing fathers under the law) did see the joyful day of Christ Jesus, and did rejoice.

CHAPTER V. THE CONTINUANCE, INCREASE, AND PRESERVATION OF THE KIRK

We most surely believe that God preserved, instructed, multiplied, honored, adorned, and called from death to life his Kirk in all ages since Adam until the coming of Christ Jesus in the flesh. For he called Abraham from his father's country, instructed him, and multiplied his seed; he marvelously preserved him, and more marvelously delivered his seed from the bondage and tyranny of Pharaoh; to them he gave his laws, constitutions, and ceremonies; to them he gave the land of Canaan; after he had given them judges, and afterwards, Saul, he gave David to be king, to whom he gave promise that of the fruit of his loins should one sit forever upon his royal throne. To this same people from time to time he sent prophets, to recall them to the right way of their God, from which sometimes they strayed by idolatry. And although, because of their stubborn contempt for righteousness he was compelled to give them into the hands of their enemies, as had previously been threatened by the mouth of Moses, so that the holy city was destroyed, the temple burned with fire, and the whole land desolate for seventy years, yet in mercy he restored them again to Jerusalem, where the city and temple were rebuilt, and they endured against all temptations and assaults of Satan till the Messiah came according to the promise.

CHAPTER VI. THE INCARNATION OF CHRIST JESUS

When the fullness of time came God sent his Son, his eternal wisdom, the substance of his own glory, into this world, who took the nature of humanity from the substance of a woman, a virgin, by means of the Holy Ghost. And so was born the "just seed of David," the "Angel of the great counsel of God," the very Messiah promised, whom we confess and acknowledge to be Emmanuel, true God and true man, two perfect natures united and joined in one person. So by our Confession we condemn the damnable and pestilent heresies of Arius, Marcion, Eutyches, Nestorius, and such others as did either deny the eternity of his Godhead, or the truth of his humanity, or confounded them, or else divided them.

CHAPTER VII. WHY THE MEDIATOR HAD TO BE TRUE GOD AND TRUE MAN

We acknowledge and confess that this wonderful union between the Godhead and the humanity in Christ Jesus did arise from the eternal and immutable decree of God from which all our salvation springs and depends.

CHAPTER VIII. ELECTION

That same eternal God and Father, who by grace alone chose us in his Son Christ Jesus before the foundation of the world was laid, appointed him to be our head, our brother, our pastor, and the great bishop of our souls. But since the opposition between the justice of God and our sins was such that no flesh by itself could or might have attained unto God, it behooved the Son of God to descend unto us and take himself a body of our body, flesh of our flesh, and bone of our bone, and so become the Mediator between God and man, giving power to as many as believe in him to be the sons of God; as he himself says, "I ascend to my Father and to your Father, to my God and to your God." By this most holy brotherhood whatever we have lost in Adam is restored to us again. Therefore we are not afraid to call God our Father, not so much because he has created us, which we have in common with the reprobate, as because he has given unto us his only Son to be our brother, and given us grace to acknowledge and embrace him as our only Mediator. Further, it behooved the Messiah and Redeemer to be true God and true man, because he was able to undergo the punishment of our transgressions and to present himself in the presence of his Father's judgment, as in our stead, to suffer for our transgression and disobedience, and by death to overcome him that was the author of death. But because the Godhead alone could not suffer death, and neither could manhood overcome death, he joined both together in one person, that the weakness of one should suffer and be subject to death—which we had deserved—and the infinite and invincible power of the other, that is, of the Godhead, should triumph, and purchase for us life, liberty, and perpetual victory. So we confess, and most undoubtedly believe.

CHAPTER IX. CHRIST'S DEATH, PASSION, AND BURIAL

That our Lord Jesus offered himself a voluntary sacrifice unto his Father for us, that he suffered contradiction of sinners, that he was wounded and plagued for our transgressions, that he, the clean innocent Lamb of God, was condemned in the presence of an earthly judge, that we should be absolved before the judgment seat of our God; that he suffered not only the cruel death of the cross, which was accursed by the sentence of God; but also that he suffered for a season the wrath of his Father which sinners had deserved. But yet we avow that he remained the only, well beloved, and blessed Son of his Father even in the midst of his anguish and torment which he suffered in body and soul to make full atonement for the sins of his people. From this we confess and avow that there remains no other sacrifice for sin; if any affirm so, we do not hesitate to say that they are blasphemers against Christ's death and the everlasting atonement thereby purchased for us.

CHAPTER X. THE RESURRECTION

We undoubtedly believe, since it was impossible that the sorrows of death should retain in bondage the Author of life, that our Lord Jesus crucified, dead, and buried, who descended into hell, did rise again for our justification, and the destruction of him who was the author of death, and brought life again to us who were subject to death and its bondage. We know that his resurrection was confirmed by the testimony of his enemies, and by the resurrection of the dead, whose sepulchres did open, and they did rise and appear to many within the city of Jerusalem. It was also confirmed by the testimony of his angels, and by the senses and judgment of his apostles and of others, who had conversation, and did eat and drink with him after his resurrection.

CHAPTER XI. THE ASCENSION

We do not doubt but that the selfsame body which was born of the virgin, was crucified, dead, and buried, and which did rise again, did ascend into the heavens, for the accomplishment of all things, where in our name and for our comfort he has received all power in heaven and earth, where he sits at the right hand of the Father, having received his kingdom, the only advocate and mediator for

us. Which glory, honor, and prerogative, he alone amongst the brethren shall possess till all his enemies are made his footstool, as we undoubtedly believe they shall be in the Last Judgment. We believe that the same Lord Jesus shall visibly return for this Last Judgment as he was seen to ascend. And then, we firmly believe, the time of refreshing and restitution of all things shall come, so that those who from the beginning have suffered violence, injury, and wrong, for righteousness' sake, shall inherit that blessed immortality promised them from the beginning. But, on the other hand, the stubborn, disobedient, cruel persecutors, filthy persons, idolators, and all sorts of unbelieving, shall be cast into the dungeon of utter darkness, where their worm shall not die, nor their fire be quenched. The rememberance of that day, and of the Judgment to be executed in it, is not only a bridle by which our carnal lusts are restrained but also such inestimable comfort that neither the threatening of worldly princes, nor the fear of present danger or of temporal death, may move us to renounce and forsake that blessed society which we, the members, have with our Head and only Mediator, Christ Jesus: whom we confess and avow to be the promised Messiah, the only Head of his Kirk, our just Lawgiver, our only High Priest, Advocate, and Mediator. To which honors and offices, if man or angel presume to intrude themselves, we utterly detest and abhor them, as blasphemous to our sovereign and supreme Governor, Christ Jesus.

CHAPTER XII. FAITH IN THE HOLY GHOST

Our faith and its assurance do not proceed from flesh and blood, that is to say, from natural powers within us, but are the inspiration of the Holy Ghost; whom we confess to be God, equal with the Father and with his Son, who sanctifies us, and brings us into all truth by his own working, without whom we should remain forever enemies to God and ignorant of his Son, Christ Jesus. For by nature we are so dead, blind, and perverse, that neither can we feel when we are pricked, see the light when it shines, nor assent to the will of God when it is revealed, unless the Spirit of the Lord Jesus quicken that which is dead, remove the darkness from our minds, and bow our stubborn hearts to the obedience of his blessed will. And so, as we confess that God the Father created us when we were not, as his Son our Lord Jesus redeemed us when we were enemies to him, so also do we confess that the Holy Ghost does sanctify and regenerate us, without respect to any merit proceeding from us, be it before or be it after our regeneration. To put this even more plainly: as we willingly disclaim any honor and glory for our own creation and redemption, so do we willingly also for our regeneration and sanctification; for by ourselves we are not capable of thinking one good thought, but he who has begun the work in us alone continues us in it, to the praise and glory of his undeserved grace.

CHAPTER XIII. THE CAUSE OF GOOD WORKS

The cause of good works, we confess, is not our free will, but the Spirit of the Lord Jesus, who dwells in our hearts by true faith, brings forth such works as God has prepared for us to walk in. For we most boldly affirm that it is blasphemy to say that Christ abides in the hearts of those in whom is no spirit of sanctification. Therefore we do not hesitate to affirm that murderers, oppressors, cruel perse-cuters, adulterers, filthy persons, idolators, drunkards, thieves, and all workers of iniquity, have neither true faith nor anything of the Spirit of the Lord Jesus, so long as they obstinately continue in wickedness. For as soon as the Spirit of the Lord Jesus, whom God's chosen children receive by true faith, takes possession of the heart of any man, so soon does he regenerate and renew him, so that he begins to hate what before he loved, and to love what he hated before. Thence comes that continual battle which is between the flesh and the Spirit in God's children, while the flesh and the natural man, being corrupt, lust for things pleasant and delightful to themselves, are envious in adversity and proud in prosperity, and every moment prone and ready to offend the majesty of God. But the Spirit of God, who bears witness to our spirit that we are the sons of God, makes us resist filthy pleasures and groan in God's presence for deliverance from this bondage of corruption, and finally to triumph over sin so that it does not reign in our mortal bodies. Other men do not share this conflict since they do not have God's Spirit, but they readily follow and obey sin and feel no regrets, since they act as the devil and their corrupt nature urge. But the sons of God fight against sin; sob and mourn when they find themselves tempted to do evil; and, if they fall, rise again with earnest and unfeigned repentance. They do these things, not by their own power, but by the power of the Lord Jesus, apart from whom they can do nothing.

CHAPTER XIV. THE WORKS WHICH ARE COUNTED GOOD BEFORE GOD

We confess and acknowledge that God has given to man his holy law, in which not only all such works as displease and offend his godly majesty are forbidden, but also those which please him and which he has promised to reward are commanded. These works are of two kinds. The one is done to the honor of God, the other to the profit of our neighbor, and both have the revealed will of God as their assurance. To have one God, to worship and honor him, to call upon him in all our troubles, to reverence his holy Name, to hear his Word and to believe it, and to share in his holy sacraments, belong to the first kind. To honor father, mother, princes, rulers, and superior powers; to love them, to support them, to obey their orders if they are not contrary to the commands of God, to save the lives of the innocent, to repress tyranny, to defend the oppressed, to keep our bodies clean and holy, to live in soberness and temperance, to deal justly with all men in word and deed, and, finally, to repress any desire to harm our neighbor, are the good works of the second kind, and these are most pleasing and acceptable to God as he has commanded them himself. Acts to the contrary are sins, which always displease him and provoke him to anger, such as, not to call upon him alone when we have need, not to hear his Word with reverence, but to condemn and despise it, to have or worship idols, to maintain and defend idolatry, lightly to esteem the reverend name of God, to profane, abuse, or condemn the sacraments of Christ Jesus, to disobey or resist any whom God has placed in authority, so long as they do not exceed the bounds of their office, to murder, or to consent thereto, to bear hatred, or to let innocent blood be shed if we can prevent it. In conclusion, we confess and affirm that the breach of any other commandment of the first or second kind is sin, by which God's anger and displeasure are kindled against the proud, unthankful world. So that we affirm good works to be those alone which are done in faith and at the command of God who, in his law, has set forth the things that please him. We affirm that evil works are not only those expressly done against God's command, but also, in religious matters and the worship of God, those things which have no other warrant than the invention and opinion of man. From the beginning God has rejected such, as we learn from the words of the prophet Isaiah and of our master. Christ Jesus, "In vain do they worship Me, teaching the doctrines and commandments of men."

CHAPTER XV. THE PERFECTION OF THE LAW AND THE IMPERFECTION OF MAN

We confess and acknowledge that the law of God is most just, equal, holy, and perfect, commanding those things which, when perfectly done, can give life and bring man to eternal felicity; but our nature is so corrupt, weak, and imperfect, that we are never able perfectly to fulfill the works of the law. Even after we are reborn, if we say that we have no sin, we deceive ourselves and the truth of God is not in us. It is therefore essential for us to lay hold on Christ Jesus, in his righteousness and his atonement, since he is the end and consummation of the Law and since it is by him that we are set at liberty so that the curse of God may not fall upon us, even though we do not fulfill the Law in all points. For as God the Father beholds us in the body of his Son Christ Jesus, he accepts our imperfect obedience as if it were perfect, and covers our works, which are defiled with many stains, with the righteousness of his Son. We do not mean that we are so set at liberty that we owe no obedience to the Law—for we have already acknowledged its place—but we affirm that no man on earth, with the sole exception of Christ Jesus, has given, gives, or shall give in action that obedience to the Law which the Law requires. When we have done all things we must fall down and unfeignedly confess that we are unprofitable servants. Therefore, whoever boasts of the merits of his own works or puts his trust in works of supererogation, boasts of what does not exist, and puts his trust in damnable idolatry.

CHAPTER XVI. THE KIRK

As we believe in one God, Father, Son, and Holy Ghost, so we firmly believe that from the beginning there has been, now is, and to the end of the world shall be, one Kirk, that is to say, one company and multitude of men chosen by God, who rightly worship and embrace him by true faith in Christ Jesus, who is the only Head of the Kirk, even as it is the body and spouse of Christ Jesus. This Kirk is catholic, that is, universal, because it contains the chosen of all ages, of all realms, nations and tongues, be they of the Jews or be they of the Gentiles, who have communion and society with God the Father, and with his Son, Christ Jesus, through the sanctification of his Holy Spirit. It is therefore called the communion, not of profane persons, but of saints, who, as citizens of the heavenly Jerusalem, have the fruit of inestimable benefits, one God, one Lord

THE SCOTS CONFESSION (1560) (continued)

Jesus, one faith, and one baptism. Out of this Kirk there is neither life nor eternal felicity. Therefore we utterly abhor the blasphemy of those who hold that men who live according to equity and justice shall be saved, no matter what religion they profess. For since there is neither life nor salvation without Christ Jesus: so shall none have part therein but those whom the Father has given unto his Son Christ Jesus, and those who in time come to him, avow his doctrine, and believe in him. (We include the children with the believing parents.) This Kirk is invisible, known only to God, who alone knows whom he has chosen, and includes both the chosen who are departed, the Kirk triumphant, those who yet live and fight against sin and Satan, and those who shall live hereafter.

CHAPTER XVII. THE IMMORTALITY OF SOULS

The chosen departed are in peace, and rest from their labors; not that they sleep and are lost in oblivion as some fanatics hold, for they are delivered from all fear and torment, and all the temptations to which we and all God's chosen are subject in this life, and because of which we are called the Kirk Militant. On the other hand, the reprobate and unfaithful departed have anguish, torment, and pain which cannot be expressed. Neither the one nor the other is in such sleep that they feel no joy or torment, as is testified by Christ's parable in St. Luke XVI, his words to the thief, and the words of the souls crying under the altar. "O Lord, thou that art righteous and just, how long shalt thou not revenge our blood upon those that dwell in the earth?"

CHAPTER XVIII. THE NOTES BY WHICH THE TRUE KIRK SHALL BE DETERMINED FROM THE FALSE, AND WHO SHALL BE JUDGE OF DOCTRINE

Since Satan has labored from the beginning to adorn his pestilent synagogue with the title of the Kirk of God, and has incited cruel murderers to persecute, trouble, and molest the true Kirk and its members, as Cain did to Abel, Ishmael to Isaac, Esau to Jacob, and the whole priesthood of the Jews to Christ Jesus himself and his apostles after him. So it is essential that the true Kirk be distinguished from the filthy synagogues by clear and perfect notes lest we, being deceived, receive and embrace, to our own condemnation, the one for the other. The notes, signs, and assured tokens whereby the spotless bride of Christ is known from the horrible harlot, the false Kirk, we state, are neither antiquity, usurped title lineal succession, appointed place, nor the numbers of men approving an error. For Cain was before Abel and Seth in age and title; Jerusalem had precedence above all other parts of the earth, for in it were priests lineally descended from Aaron, and greater numbers followed the scribes, pharisees, and priests, than unfeignedly believed and followed Christ Jesus and his doctrine . . . and yet no man of judgment, we suppose, will hold that any of the forenamed were the Kirk of God. The notes of the true Kirk, therefore, we believe, confess, and avow to be first, the true preaching of the Word of God, in which God has revealed himself to us, as the writings of the prophets and apostles declare; secondly, the right administration of the sacraments of Christ Jesus, with which must be associated the Word and promise of God to seal and confirm them in our hearts; and lastly, ecclesiastical discipline uprightly ministered, as God's Word prescribes, whereby vice is repressed and virtue nourished. Then wherever these notes are seen and continue for any time, be the number complete or not, there, beyond any doubt, is the true Kirk of Christ, who, according to his promise, is in its midst. This is not that universal Kirk of which we have spoken before, but particular Kirks, such as were in Corinth, Galatia, Ephesus, and other places where the ministry was planted by Paul and which he himself called Kirks of God. Such Kirks, we the inhabitants of the realm of Scotland confessing Christ Jesus, do claim to have in our cities, towns, and reformed districts because of the doctrine taught in our Kirks, contained in the written Word of God, that is, the Old and New Testaments, in those books which were originally reckoned canonical. We affirm that in these all things necessary to be believed for the salvation of man are sufficiently expressed. The interpretation of Scripture, we confess, does not belong to any private or public person, nor yet to any Kirk for pre-eminence or precedence, personal or local, which it has above others, but pertains to the Spirit of God by whom the Scriptures were written. When controversy arises about the right understanding of any passage or sentence of Scripture, or for the reformation of any abuse within the Kirk of God, we ought not so much to ask what men have said or done before us, as what the Holy Ghost uniformly speaks within the body of the Scriptures and what Christ Jesus himself did and commanded. For it is agreed by all that the Spirit of God, who is the Spirit of unity, cannot contradict himself. So if the interpretation or opinion of any theologian, Kirk, or council, is contrary to the plain Word of God written in any other passage of the Scripture, it is most certain that this is not the true understanding and meaning of the Holy Ghost, although councils, realms, and nations have approved and received it. We dare not receive or admit any interpretation which is contrary to any principal point of our faith, or to any other plain text of Scripture, or to the rule of love.

CHAPTER XIX. THE AUTHORITY OF THE SCRIPTURES

As we believe and confess the Scriptures of God sufficient to instruct and make perfect the man of God, so do we affirm and avow their authority to be from God, and not to depend on men or angels. We affirm, therefore, that those who say the Scriptures have no other authority save that which they have received from the Kirk are blasphemous against God and injurious to the true Kirk, which always hears and obeys the voice of her own Spouse and Paster, but takes not upon her to be mistress over the same.

CHAPTER XX. GENERAL COUNCILS, THEIR POWER, AUTHORITY, AND THE CAUSE OF THEIR SUMMONING

As we do not rashly condemn what good men, assembled together in general councils lawfully gathered, have set before us; so we do not receive uncritically whatever has been declared to men under the name of the general councils, for it is plain that, being human, some of them have manifestly erred, and that in matters of great weight and importance. So far then as the council confirms its decrees by the plain Word of God, so far do we reverence and embrace them. But if men, under the name of a council, pretend to forge for us new articles of faith, or to make decisions contrary to the Word of God, then we must utterly deny them as the doctrine of devils, drawing our souls from the voice of the one God to follow the doctrines and teachings of men. The reason why the general councils met was not to make any permanent law which God had not made before, nor yet to form new articles for our belief, nor to give the Word of God authority; much less to make that to be his Word, or even the true interpretation of it, which was not expressed previously by his holy will in his Word; but the reason for councils, at least of those that deserve that name, was partly to refute heresies, and to give public confession of their faith to the generations following, which they did by the authority of God's written Word, and not by any opinion or prerogative that they could not err by reason of their numbers. This, we judge, was the primary reason for general councils. The second was that good policy and order should be constituted and observed in the Kirk where, as in the house of God, it becomes all things to be done decently and in order. Not that we think any policy or order of ceremonies can be appointed for all ages, times, and places; for as ceremonies which men have devised are but temporal, so they may, and ought to be, changed, when they foster superstition rather than edify the Kirk.

CHAPTER XXI. THE SACRAMENTS

As the fathers under the Law, besides the reality of the sacrifices, had two chief sacraments, that is, circumcision and the passover, and those who rejected these were not reckoned among God's people; so do we acknowledge and confess that now in the time of the gospel we have two chief sacraments, which alone were instituted by the Lord Jesus and commanded to be used by all who will be counted members of his body, that is, Baptism and the Supper or Table of the Lord Jesus, also called the Communion of His Body and Blood. These sacraments, both of the Old Testament and of the New, were instituted by God not only to make a visible distinction between his people and those who were without the Covenant, but also to exercise the faith of his children and, by participation of these sacraments, to seal in their hearts the assurance of his promise, and of that most blessed conjunction, union, and society, which the chosen have with their Head, Christ Jesus. And so we utterly condemn the vanity of those who affirm the sacraments to be nothing else than naked and bare signs. No, we assuredly believe that by Baptism we are engrafted into Christ Jesus, to be made partakers of his righteousness, by which our sins are covered and remitted, and also that in the Supper rightly used, Christ Jesus is so joined with us that he becomes the very nourishment and food of our souls. Not that we imagine any transubstantiation of bread into Christ's body, and of wine into his natural blood, as the Romanists have perniciously taught and wrongly believed: but this union and conjunction which we have with the body and blood of Christ Jesus in the right use of the sacraments is wrought by means of the

Holy Ghost, who by true faith carries us above all things that are visible, carnal, and earthly, and makes us feed upon the body and blood of Christ Jesus, once broken and shed for us but now in heaven, and appearing for us in the presence of his Father. Notwithstanding the distance between his glorified body in heaven and mortal men on earth, yet we must assuredly believe that the bread which we break is the communion of Christ's body and the cup which we bless the communion of his blood. Thus we confess and believe without doubt that the faithful, in the right use of the Lord's Table, do so eat the body and drink the blood of the Lord Jesus that he remains in them and they in him; they are so made flesh of his flesh and bone of his bone that as the eternal Godhood has given to the flesh of Christ Jesus, which by nature was corruptible and mortal, life and immortality, so the eating and drinking of the flesh and blood of Christ Jesus does the like for us. We grant that this is neither given to us merely at the time nor by the power and virtue of the sacrament alone, but we affirm that the faithful, in the right use of the Lord's Table, have such union with Christ Jesus as the natural man cannot apprehend. Further we affirm that although the faithful, hindered by negligence and human weakness, do not profit as much as they ought in the actual moment of the Supper, yet afterwards it shall bring forth fruit, being living seed sown in good ground; for the Holy Spirit, who can never be separated from the right institution of the Lord Jesus, will not deprive the faithful of the fruit of that mystical action. Yet all this, we say again, comes of that true faith which apprehends Christ Jesus, who alone makes the sacrament effective in us. Therefore, if anyone slanders us by saying that we affirm or believe the sacraments to be symbols and nothing more, they are libelous and speak against the plain facts. On the other hand we readily admit that we make a distinction between Christ Jesus in his eternal substance and the elements of the sacramental signs. So we neither worship the elements, in place of that which they signify, nor yet do we despise them or undervalue them, but we use them with great reverence, examining ourselves diligently before we participate, since we are assured by the mouth of the apostle that "whosoever shall eat this bread, and drink this cup of the Lord, unworthily, shall be guilty of the body and blood of the Lord."

CHAPTER XXII. THE RIGHT ADMINISTRATION OF THE SACRAMENTS

Two things are necessary for the right administration of the sacraments. The first is that they should be ministered by lawful ministers, and we declare that these are men appointed to preach the Word, unto whom God has given the power to preach the gospel, and who are lawfully called by some Kirk. The second is that they should be ministered in the elements and manner which God has appointed. Otherwise they cease to be the sacraments of Christ Jesus. This is why we abandon the teaching of the Roman Church and withdraw from its sacraments; firstly, because their ministers are not true ministers of Christ Jesus (indeed they even allow women, whom the Holy Ghost will not permit to preach in the congregation to baptize) and, secondly, because they have so adulterated both the sacraments with their own additions that no part

THE SCOTS CONFESSION (1560) (continued)

of Christ's original act remains in its original simplicity. The addition of oil, salt, spittle, and such like in baptism, are merely human additions. To adore or venerate the sacrament, to carry it through streets and towns in procession, or to reserve it in a special case, is not the proper use of Christ's sacrament but an abuse of it. Christ Jesus said. "Take ye, eat ye," and "Do this in remembrance of Me." By these words and commands he sanctified bread and wine to be the sacrament of his holy body and blood, so that the one should be eaten and that all should drink of the other, and not that they should be reserved for worship or honored as God, as the Romanists do. Further, in withdrawing one part of the sacrament—the blessed cup—from the people, they have committed sacrilege. Moreover, if the sacraments are to be rightly used it is essential that the end and purpose of their institution should be understood, not only by the minister but by the recipients. For if the recipient does not understand what is being done, the sacrament is not being rightly used, as is seen in the case of the Old Testament sacrifices. Similarly, if the teacher teaches false doctrine which is hateful to God, even though the sacraments are his own ordinance, they are not rightly used, since wicked men have used them for another end than what God commanded. We affirm that this has been done to the sacraments in the Roman Church, for there the whole action of the Lord Jesus is adulterated in form, purpose, and meaning. What Christ Jesus did, and commanded to be done, is evident from the Gospels and from St. Paul; what the priest does at the altar we do not need to tell. The end and purpose of Christ's institution, for which it should be used, is set forth in the words. "Do this in rememberance of Me," and "For as often as ye eat this bread and drink this cup ye do show"—that is, extol, preach, magnify, and praise—"the Lord's death, till He come." But let the words of the mass, and their own doctors and teachings witness, what is the purpose and meaning of the mass; it is that, as mediators between Christ and his Kirk, they should offer to God the Father, a sacrifice in propitiation for the sins of the living and of the dead. This doctrine is blasphemous to Christ Jesus and would deprive his unique sacrifice, once offered on the cross for the cleansing of all who are to be sanctified, of its sufficiency; so we detest and renounce it.

CHAPTER XXIII. TO WHOM SACRAMENTS APPERTAIN

We hold that baptism applies as much to the children of the faithful as to those who are of age and discretion, and so we condemn the error of the Anabaptist, who deny that children should be baptized before they have faith and understanding. But we hold that the Supper of the Lord is only for those who are of the household of faith and can try and examine themselves both in their faith and their duty to their neighbors. Those who eat and drink at that holy table without faith, or without peace and goodwill to their brethren, eat unworthily. This is the reason why ministers in our Kirk make public and individual examination of those who are to be admitted to the table of the Lord Jesus.

CHAPTER XXIV. THE CIVIL MAGISTRATE

We confess and acknowledge that empires, kingdoms, dominions, and cites are appointed and ordained by God; the powers and authorities in them, emperors in empires, kings in their realms, dukes and princes in their dominions, and magistrates in cities, are ordained by God's holy ordinance for the manifestation of his own glory and for the good and well being of all men. We hold that any men who conspire to rebel or to overturn the civil powers, as duly established, are not merely enemies to humanity but rebels against God's will. Further, we confess and acknowledge that such persons as are set in authority are to be loved, honored, feared, and held in the highest respect, because they are the lieutenants of God, and in their councils God himself doth sit and judge. They are the judges and princes to whom God has given the sword for the praise and defense of good men and the punishment of all open evil doers. Moreover, we state that the preservation and purification of religion is particularly the duty to kings, princes, rulers, and magistrates. They are not only appointed for civil government but also to maintain true religion and to suppress all idolatry and superstition. This may be seen in David, Jehosaphat. Hezekiah, Josiah, and others highly commended for their zeal in that cause.

Therefore we confess and avow that those who resist the supreme powers, so long as they are acting in their own spheres, are resisting God's ordinance and cannot be held guiltless. We further state that so long as princes and rulers vigilantly fulfill their office, anyone who denies them aid, counsel, or service, denies it to God, who by his lieutenant craves it of them.

CHAPTER XXV. THE GIFTS FREELY GIVEN TO THE KIRK

Although the Word of God truly preached, the sacraments rightly ministered, and discipline executed according to the Word of God, are certain and infallible signs of the true Kirk, we do not mean that every individual person in that company is a chosen member of Christ Jesus. We acknowledge and confess that many weeds and tares are sown among the corn and grow in great abundance in its midst, and that the reprobate may be found in the fellowship of the chosen and may take an outward part with them in the benefits of the Word and sacraments. But since they only confess God for a time with their mouths and not with their hearts, they lapse, and do not continue to the end. Therefore they do not share the fruits of Christ's death, resurrection, and ascension. But such as unfeignedly believe with the heart and boldly confess the Lord Jesus with their mouths shall certainly receive his gifts. Firstly, in this life, they shall receive remission of sins and that by faith in Christ's blood alone; for though sin shall remain and continually abide in our mortal bodies, yet it shall not be counted against us, but be pardoned, and covered with Christ's righteousness. Secondly, in the general judgment, there shall be given to every man and woman resurrection of the flesh. The seas shall give up her dead, and the earth those who are buried within her. Yea, the Eternal, our God, shall stretch out his hand on the dust, and the dead shall arise incorruptible, and in the very substance of the selfsame flesh which every man now bears, to receive according to their works, glory or punishment. Such as now delight in vanity, cruelty, filthiness, superstition, or idolatry, shall be condemned to the fire unquenchable, in which those who now serve the devil in all abominations shall be tormented forever, both in body and in spirit. But such as continue in well doing to the end, boldly confessing the Lord Jesus, shall receive glory, honor, and immortality, we constantly believe, to reign forever in life everlasting with Christ Jesus, to whose glorified body all his chosen shall be made like, when he shall appear again in judgment and shall render up the Kingdom to God his Father, who then shall be and ever shall remain, all in all things, God blessed forever. To whom, with the Son and the Holy Ghost, be all honor and glory, now and ever. Amen.

Arise, O Lord, and let thine enemies be confounded; let them flee from thy presence that hate thy godly Name. Give thy servants strength to speak thy Word with boldness, and let all nations cleave to the true knowledge of thee. Amen.

Notes: *Following the acceptance of the new Confession of 1967, the United Presbyterian Church in the U.S.A., now a constituent part of the Presbyterian Church (U.S.A.), adopted a variety of confessional statements to stand beside the Westminster Confession. These additional statements serve as expressions of the church's full participation in the broad Western Christian tradition as well as the Reformed Church tradition, which the church inherited through sixteenth-century reformers John Calvin (in Geneva) and John Knox (in Scotland). The Scots Confession, originally published in 1560, is a reflection of that Scottish heritage. In several places it deals with issues of grave concern in the sixteenth century, such as the authority of general councils of the Roman Church, one of which had recently met at Trent.*

*   *   *

THE THEOLOGICAL DECLARATION OF BARMEN

I. AN APPEAL TO THE EVANGELICAL CONGREGATIONS AND CHRISTIANS IN GERMANY

The Confessional Synod of the German Evangelical Church met in Barmen, May 29-31, 1934. Here representatives from all the German Confessional Churches met with one accord in a confession of the one Lord of the one, holy, apostolic Church. In fidelity to their Confession of Faith, members of Lutheran. Reformed, and United Churches sought a common message for the need and temptation of the Church in our day. With gratitude to God they are convinced that they have been given a common word to utter. It was not their intention to found a new Church or to form a union. For nothing was farther from their minds than the abolition of the confessional status of our Churches. Their intention was, rather, to withstand in faith and unanimity the destruction of the Confession of Faith, and thus of the Evangelical Church in Germany. In opposition to attempts to establish the unity of the German Evangelical Church by means of false doctrine, by the use of force and insincere practices, the Confessional Synod insists that the unity of the Evangelical Churches in Germany can come only from the Word of God in faith through the Holy Spirit. Thus alone is the Church renewed.

Therefore the Confessional Synod calls upon the congregations to range themselves behind it in prayer, and steadfastly to gather around those pastors and teachers who are loyal to the Confessions.

Be not deceived by loose talk, as if we meant to oppose the unity of the German nation! Do not listen to the seducers who pervert our intentions, as if we wanted to break up the unity of the German Evangelical Church or to forsake the Confessions of the Fathers!

Try the spirits whether they are of God! Prove also the words of the Confessional Synod of the German Evangelical Church to see whether they agree with Holy Scripture and with the Confessions of the Fathers. If you find that we are speaking contrary to Scripture, then do not listen to us! But if you find that we are taking our stand upon Scripture, then let no fear or temptation keep you from treading with us the path of faith and obedience to the Word of God, in order that God's people be of one mind upon earth and that we in faith experience what he himself has said: "I will never leave you, nor forsake you." Therefore, "Fear not, little flock, for it is your Father's good pleasure to give you the kingdom."

II. THEOLOGICAL DECLARATION CONCERNING THE PRESENT SITUATION OF THE GERMAN EVANGELICAL CHURCH

According to the opening words of its constitution of July 11, 1933, the German Evangelical Church is a federation of Confessional Churches that grew out of the Reformation and that enjoy equal rights. The theological basis for the unification of these Churches is laid down in Article 1 and Article 2(1) of the constitution of the German Evangelical Church that was recognized by the Reich Government on July 14, 1933:

> Article 1. The inviolable foundation of the German Evangelical Church is the gospel of Jesus Christ as it is attested for us in Holy Scripture and brought to light again in the Confessions of the Reformation. The full powers that the Church needs for its mission are hereby determined and limited.

> Article 2 (1). The German Evangelical Church is divided into member Churches (*Landeskirchen*).

We, the representatives of Lutheran, Reformed, and United Churches, of free synods, Church assemblies, and parish organizations united in the Confessional Synod of the German Evangelical Church, declare that we stand together on the ground of the German Evangelical Church as a federation of German Confessional Churches. We are bound together by the confession of the one Lord of the one, holy, catholic, and apostolic Church.

We publicly declare before all evangelical Churches in Germany that what they hold in common in this Confession is grievously imperiled, and with it the unity of the German Evangelical Church. It is threatened by the teaching methods and actions of the ruling Church party

THE THEOLOGICAL DECLARATION OF BARMEN (continued)

of the "German Christians" and of the Church administration carried on by them. These have become more and more apparent during the first year of the existence of the German Evangelical Church. This threat consists in the fact that the theological basis, in which the German Evangelical Church is united, has been continually and systematically thwarted and rendered ineffective by alien principles, on the part of the leaders and spokesmen of the "German Christians" as well as on the part of the Church administration. When these principles are held to be valid, then, according to all the Confessions in force among us, the Church ceases to be the Church and the German Evangelical Church, as a federation of Confessional Churches, becomes intrinsically impossible.

As members of Lutheran, Reformed, and United Churches we may and must speak with one voice in this matter today. Precisely because we want to be and to remain faithful to our various Confessions, we may not keep silent, since we believe that we have been given a common message to utter in a time of common need and temptation. We commend to God what this may mean for the interrelations of the Confessional Churches.

In view of the errors of the "German Christians" of the present Reich Church government which are devastating the Church and are also thereby breaking up the unity of the German Evangelical Church, we confess the following evangelical truths:

1. "I am the way, and the truth, and the life; no one comes to the Father, but by me." (John 14:6). "Truly, truly, I say to you, he who does not enter the sheepfold by the door but climbs in by another way, that man is a thief and a robber . . . I am the door; if anyone enters by me, he will be saved." (John 10:1, 9.)

   Jesus Christ, as he is attested for us in Holy Scripture, is the one Word of God which we have to hear and which we have to trust and obey in life and in death.

   We reject the false doctrine, as though the Church could and would have to acknowledge as a source of its proclamation, apart from and besides this one Word of God, still other events and powers, figures and truths, as God's revelation.

2. "Christ Jesus, whom God made our wisdom, our righteousness and sanctification and redemption." (1 Cor. 1:30.)

   As Jesus Christ is God's assurance of the forgiveness of all our sins, so in the same way and with the same seriousness he is also God's mighty claim upon our whole life. Through him befalls us a joyful deliverance from the godless fetters of this world for a free, grateful service to his creatures.

   We reject the false doctrine, as though there were areas of our life in which we would not belong to Jesus Christ, but to other lords—areas in which we would not need justification and sanctification through him.

3. "Rather, speaking the truth in love, we are to grow up in every way into him who is the head, into Christ, from whom the whole body [is] joined and knit together." (Eph. 4:15, 16.)

   The Christian Church is the congregation of the brethren in which Jesus Christ acts presently as the Lord in Word and sacrament through the Holy Spirit. As the Church of pardoned sinners, it has to testify in the midst of a sinful world, with its faith as with its obedience, with its message as with its order, that it is solely his property, and that it lives and wants to live solely from his comfort and from his direction in the expectation of his appearance.

   We reject the false doctrine, as though the Church were permitted to abandon the form of its message and order to its own pleasure or to changes in prevailing ideological and political convictions.

4. "You know that the rules of the Gentiles lord it over them, and their great men exercise authority over them. It shall not be so among you; but whoever would be great among you must be your servant." (Matt. 20:25, 26.)

   The various offices in the Church do not establish a dominion of some over the others; on the contrary, they are for the exercise of the ministry entrusted to and enjoined upon the whole congregation.

   We reject the false doctrine, as though the Church, apart from this ministry, could and were permitted to give to itself, or allow to be given to it, special leaders vested with ruling powers.

5. "Fear God. Honor the emperor." (1 Peter 2:17.) Scripture tells us that, in the as yet unredeemed world in which the Church also exists, the State has by divine appointment the task of providing for justice and peace. [It fulfills this task] by means of the threat and exercise of force, according to the measure of human judgment and human ability. The Church acknowledges the benefit of this divine appointment in gratitude and reverence before him. It calls to mind the Kingdom of God, God's commandment and righteousness, and thereby the responsibility both of rulers and of the ruled. It trusts and obeys the power of the Word by which God upholds all things.

   We reject the false doctrine, as though the State, over and beyond its special commission, should and could become the single and totalitarian order of human life, thus fulfilling the Church's vocation as well.

   We reject the false doctrine, as though the Church, over and beyond its special commission, should and could appropriate the characteristics, the tasks, and the dignity of the State, thus itself becoming an organ of the State.

6. "Lo, I am with you always, to the close of the age." (Matt. 28:20.) "The word of God is not fettered." (II Tim. 2:9.)

   The Church's commission, upon which its freedom is founded, consists in delivering the message of the free grace of God to all people in Christ's stead, and therefore in the ministry of his own Word and work through sermon and sacrament.

We reject the false doctrine, as though the Church in human arrogance could place the Word and work of the Lord in the service of any arbitrarily chosen desires, purposes, and plans.

The Confessional Synod of the German Evangelical Church declares that it sees in the acknowledgment of these truths and in the rejection of these errors the indispensable theological basis of the German Evangelical Church as a federation of Confessional Churches. It invites all who are able to accept its declaration to be mindful of these theological principles in their decisions in Church politics. It entreats all whom it concerns to return to the unity of faith, love, and hope.

Notes: *One of several statements added to* The Book of Confessions *of the United Presbyterian Church in the U.S.A. [now a constituent part of the Presbyterian Church (U.S.A.)], the Barmen declaration was a statement in defiance of Adolf Hitler. It was issued in 1934 by the Confessing Church, a segment of the German Evangelical Church which opposed the attempted co-optation of the church by the new Nazi regime. The Confessing Church, which consisted of elements of the Lutheran, Reformed, and United Churches, opposed the so-called German Christians, that segment of the church supporting Hitler.*

*　　*　　*

Congregationalism

KANSAS CITY STATEMENT OF 1913 (CONGREGATIONAL CHURCHES)

FAITH. "We believe in God the Father, Infinite in wisdom, goodness and love; and in Jesus Christ, His Son, our Lord and Saviour, who for us and our salvation lived and died and rose again and liveth evermore; and in the Holy Spirit, who taketh of the things of Christ and revealeth them to us, renewing, comforting, and inspiring the souls of men. We are united in striving to know the will of God as taught in the Holy Scriptures, and in our purpose to walk in the ways of the Lord, made known or to be made known to us. We hold it to be the mission of the Church of Christ to proclaim the gospel to all mankind, exalting the worship of the one true God, and laboring for the progress of knowledge, the promotion of justice, the reign of peace, and the realization of human brotherhood. Depending, as did our fathers, upon the continued guidance of the Holy Spirit to lead us into all truth, we work and pray for the transformation of the world into the kingdom of God; and we look with faith for the triumph of righteousness and the life everlasting.

POLITY. "We believe in the freedom and responsibility of the individual soul, and the right of private judgment. We hold to the autonomy of the local church and its independence of all ecclesiastical control. We cherish the fellowship of the churches, united in district, state, and national bodies, for counsel and cooperation in matters of common concern.

THE WIDER FELLOWSHIP. "While affirming the liberty of our churches, and the validity of our ministry, we hold to the unity and catholicity of the Church of Christ, and will unite with all its branches in hearty cooperation; and will earnestly seek, so far as in us lies, that the prayer of the Lord for His disciples may be answered, that 'they all may be one'."

Notes: *The Congregational Church tradition underwent a variety of organizational changes during the twentieth century, which added to the confessional heritage passed on by eighteenth-century New England congregationalism and the Reformed Church of Germany. The mergers that ultimately produced the United Church of Christ (UCC) in the middle of the twentieth century clearly reaffirmed the UCC's place in the larger Reformed-Presbyterian family. The mergers also bequeathed to the UCC a present-mindedness symbolized in a new creedal statement that both summarized the previous creeds and assigned them to their historical era. The texts of these Congregational confessions and statements of faith promulgated prior to the twentieth century have been compiled by Williston Walker in* The Creeds and Platforms of Congregationalism *(Philadelphia: Pilgrim Press, 1969).*

The only creedal statement written before the various mergers and schisms of the twentieth century and retaining some visible life in the Congregational churches is the statement passed by the National Council of the Congregational Church in 1913 at Kansas City. It grew out of the increased liberalism (modernism) in theological matters beginning to dominate the Congregational Churches.

The annual meeting of the National Council of Congregational Churches in 1913 adopted a statement of faith reflective of the growing liberal Protestant theological perspective. The statement is noteworthy for what it does not affirm; for example, there is no clear affirmation of either the Trinity or the authority of the Scriptures. The authors left considerable room for theological divergence on most issues. The statement has survived within the liturgy of the United Church of Christ, printed in the hymnal as an alternative along with the Apostles' and Nicene Creeds. It is also widely used by churches of the National Association of Congregational Christian Churches, consisting largely of congregations that refused to enter the United Church of Christ. These churches had an organizational, rather than a theological, complaint with the UCC.

*　　*　　*

BELIEFS OF THE CONSERVATIVE CONGREGATIONAL CHRISTIAN CONFERENCE

We believe in . . .

THE BIBLE

We believe the Bible, consisting of the Old and New Testaments, to be the only inspired, inerrant, infallible, authoritative Word of God written.

BELIEFS OF THE CONSERVATIVE CONGREGATIONAL CHRISTIAN CONFERENCE (continued)

THE TRINITY

We believe that there is one God, eternally existent in three persons: Father, Son, and Holy Spirit.

JESUS CHRIST

We believe in the deity of Christ, in His virgin birth, in His sinless life, in His miracles, in His vicarious and atoning death through His shed blood, in His bodily resurrection, in His ascension to the right hand of the Father, and in His personal return in power and glory.

SALVATION

We believe that for salvation of lost and sinful man regeneration by the Holy Spirit is absolutely essential.

THE HOLY SPIRIT

We believe in the present ministry of the Holy Spirit by Whose indwelling power and fullness the Christian is enabled to live a godly life in this present evil world.

THE RESURRECTION

We believe in the resurrection of both the saved and the lost; they that are saved unto the resurrection of life, and they that are lost unto the resurrection of damnation.

SPIRITUAL UNITY

We believe in the spiritual unity of all believers in Christ.

Notes: *Reacting to the theological liberalism in the main body of congregationalism, the congregations of the Conservative Congregational Christian Church reorganized around a more evangelical theological perspective. Their beliefs specifically affirm many of the beliefs deleted from the Kansas City Statement of 1913, as well as those from the Statement of Faith of the United Church of Christ.*

*　　*　　*

STATEMENT OF FAITH OF THE MIDWEST CONGREGATIONAL CHRISTIAN CHURCH

1. We believe the Bible to be the inspired, the only infallible, authoritative word of God.

2. We believe that there is one God, eternally existent in three persons, Father, Son and Holy Ghost.

3. We believe in the deity of our Lord Jesus Christ, in His virgin birth, in His sinless life, in His miracles in His vicarious and atoning death through His shed blood, in His bodily resurrection, in His ascension to the right hand of the Father, and in His personal return in power and glory.

4. We believe that for the salvation of lost and sinful man regeneration by the Holy Spirit is absolutely essential.

5. We believe in the present ministry of the Holy Spirit by whose indwelling the Christian is enabled to live a Godly life.

6. We believe in the resurrection of both the saved and the lost; they that are saved unto the resurrection of life and they that are lost unto the resurrection of damnation.

7. We believe in the spiritual unity of believers in our Lord Jesus Christ.

Notes: *Like the Conservative Congregational Christian Conference, the Midwest Congregational Christian Church adopted a very conservative theological position, as reflected in its statement of faith.*

*　　*　　*

THE BASIS OF UNION (UNITED CHURCH OF CANADA)

DOCTRINE

We, the representatives of the Presbyterian, the Methodist, and the Congregational branches of the Church of Christ in Canada, do hereby set forth the substance of the Christian faith, as commonly held among us. In doing so, we build upon the foundation laid by the apostles and prophets, Jesus Christ Himself being the chief cornerstone. We affirm our belief in the Scriptures of the Old and New Testaments as the primary source and ultimate standard of Christian faith and life. We acknowledge the teaching of the great creeds of the ancient Church. We further maintain our allegiance to the evangelical doctrines of the Reformation, as set forth in common in the doctrinal standards adopted by the Presbyterian Church in Canada, by the Congregational Union of Ontario and Quebec, and by the Methodist Church. We present the accompanying statement as a brief summary of our common faith and commend it to the studious attention of the members and adherents of the negotiating Churches, as in substance agreeable to the teaching of the Holy Scriptures.

ARTICLE I. OF GOD. We believe in the one only living and true God, a Spirit, infinite, eternal and unchangeable, in His being and perfections; the Lord Almighty, who is love, most just in all His ways, most glorious in holiness, unsearchable in wisdom, plenteous in mercy, full of compassion, and abundant in goodness and truth. We worship Him in the unity of the Godhead and the mystery of the Holy Trinity, the Father, the Son and the Holy Spirit, three persons of the same substance, equal in power and glory.

ARTICLE II. OF REVELATION. We believe that God has revealed Himself in nature, in history, and in the heart of man; that He has been graciously pleased to make clearer revelation of Himself to men of God who spoke as they were moved by the Holy Spirit; and that in the fullness of time He has perfectly revealed Himself in Jesus Christ, the Word made flesh, who is the brightness of the Father's glory and the express image of His person. We receive the Holy Scriptures of the Old and New Testaments, given by inspiration of God, as containing the only infallible rule of faith and life, a faithful record of God's gracious revelations, and as the sure witness to Christ.

ARTICLE III. OF THE DIVINE PURPOSE. We believe that the eternal, wise, holy and loving purpose of God so embraces all events that, while the freedom of man is not taken away, nor is God the author of sin, yet in His providence He makes all things work together in the fulfilment of His sovereign design and the manifestation of His glory.

ARTICLE IV. OF CREATION AND PROVIDENCE. We believe that God is the creator, upholder and governor of all things; that He is above all His works and in them all; and that He made man in His own image, meet for fellowship with Him, free and able to choose between good and evil, and responsible to his Maker and Lord.

ARTICLE V. OF THE SIN OF MAN. We believe that our first parents, being tempted, chose evil, and so fell away from God and came under the power of sin, the penalty of which is eternal death; and that, by reason of this disobedience, all men are born with a sinful nature, that we have broken God's law and that no man can be saved but by His grace.

ARTICLE VI. OF THE GRACE OF GOD. We believe that God, out of His great love for the world, has given His only begotten Son to be the Saviour of sinners, and in the Gospel freely offers His all-sufficient salvation to all men. We believe also that God, in His own good pleasure, gave to His Son a people, an innumerable multitude, chosen in Christ unto holiness, service and salvation.

ARTICLE VII. OF THE LORD JESUS CHRIST. We believe in and confess the Lord Jesus Christ, the only Mediator between God and man, who, being the Eternal Son of God, for us men and for our salvation became truly man, being conceived of the Holy Spirit and born of the Virgin Mary, yet without sin. Unto us He has revealed the Father, by His word and Spirit, making known the perfect will of God. For our redemption He fulfilled all righteousness, offered Himself a perfect sacrifice on the Cross, satisfied Divine justice and made propitiation for the sins of the whole world. He rose from the dead and ascended into Heaven, where He ever intercedes for us. In the hearts of believers He abides for ever as the indwelling Christ; above us and over us all He rules; wherefore, unto Him we render love, obedience and adoration as our Prophet, Priest and King.

ARTICLE VIII. OF THE HOLY SPIRIT. We believe in the Holy Spirit, the Lord and Giver of life, who proceeds from the Father and the Son, who moves upon the hearts of men to restrain them from evil and to incite them unto good, and whom the Father is ever willing to give unto all who ask Him. We believe that He has spoken by holy men of God in making known His truth to men for their salvation; that, through our exalted Saviour, He was sent forth in power to convict the world of sin, to enlighten men's minds in the knowledge of Christ, and to persuade and enable them to obey the call of the Gospel; and that He abides with the Church, dwelling in every believer as the spirit of truth, of power, of holiness, of comfort and of love.

ARTICLE IX. OF REGENERATION. We believe in the necessity of regeneration, whereby we are made new creatures in Christ Jesus by the Spirit of God, who imparts spiritual life by the gracious and mysterious operation of His power, using as the ordinary means the truths of His word and the ordinances of divine appointment in ways agreeable to the nature of man.

ARTICLE X. OF FAITH AND REPENTANCE. We believe that faith in Christ is a saving grace whereby we receive Him, trust in Him and rest upon Him alone for salvation as He is offered to us in the Gospel, and that this saving faith is always accompanied by repentance, wherein we confess and forsake our sins with full purpose of and endeavor after a new obedience to God.

ARTICLE XI. OF JUSTIFICATION AND SONSHIP. We believe that God, on the sole ground of the perfect obedience and sacrifice of Christ, pardons those who by faith receive Him as their Saviour and Lord, accepts them as righteous and bestows upon them the adoption of sons, with a right to all privileges therein implied, including a conscious assurance of their sonship.

ARTICLE XII. OF SANCTIFICATION. We believe that those who are regenerated and justified grow in the likeness of Christ through fellowship with Him, the indwelling of the Holy Spirit, and obedience to the truth; that a holy life is the fruit and evidence of saving faith; and that the believer's hope of continuance in such a life is in the preserving grace of God. And we believe that in this growth in grace Christians may attain that maturity and full assurance of faith whereby the love of God is made perfect in us.

ARTICLE XIII. OF PRAYER. We believe that we are encouraged to draw near to God, our Heavenly Father, in the name of His Son, Jesus Christ, and on our own behalf and that of others to pour out our hearts humbly yet freely before Him, as becomes His beloved children, giving Him the honour and praise due His holy name, asking Him to glorify Himself on earth as in Heaven, confessing unto Him our sins and seeking of Him every gift needful for this life and for our everlasting salvation. We believe also that, inasmuch as all true prayer is prompted by His Spirit, He will in response thereto grant us every blessing according to His unsearchable wisdom and the riches of His grace in Jesus Christ.

ARTICLE XIV. OF THE LAW OF GOD. We believe that the moral law of God, summarized in the Ten Commandments, testified to by the prophets and unfolded in the life and teachings of Jesus Christ, stands for ever in truth and equity, and is not made void by faith, but on the contrary is established thereby. We believe that God requires of every man to do justly, to love mercy, and to walk humbly with God; and that only through this harmony with the will of God shall be fulfilled that brotherhood of man wherein the Kingdom of God is to be made manifest.

ARTICLE XV. OF THE CHURCH. We acknowledge one holy Catholic Church, the innumerable company of saints of every age and nation, who being united by the Holy Spirit to Christ their Head are one body in Him and have communion with their Lord and with one another. Further, we receive it as the will of Christ that His Church on earth should exist as a visible and sacred brotherhood, consisting of those who profess faith in Jesus Christ and obedience to Him, together with their children, and other baptized children, and organized for the confession of His name, for the public worship of God, for the administration of the sacraments, for the upbuilding of the saints, and

THE BASIS OF UNION (UNITED CHURCH OF CANADA) (continued)

for the universal propagation of the Gospel; and we acknowledge as a part, more or less pure, of this universal brotherhood, every particular Church throughout the world which professes this faith in Jesus Christ and obedience to Him as divine Lord and Saviour.

ARTICLE XVI. OF THE SACRAMENTS. We acknowledge two sacraments, Baptism and the Lord's Supper, which were instituted by Christ, to be of perpetual obligation as signs and seals of the covenant ratified in His precious blood, as means of grace, by which, working in us, He doth not only quicken, but also strengthen and comfort our faith in Him, and as ordinances through the observance of which His Church is to confess her Lord and be visibly distinguished from the rest of the world.

(1) Baptism with water into the name of the Father and of the Son and of the Holy Spirit is the sacrament by which are signified and sealed our union to Christ and participation in the blessings of the new covenant. The proper subjects of baptism are believers and infants presented by their parents or guardians in the Christian faith. In the latter case the parents or guardians should train up their children in the nurture and admonition of the Lord and should expect that their children will, by the operation of the Holy Spirit, receive the benefits which the sacrament is designed and fitted to convey. The Church is under the most solemn obligation to provide for their Christian instruction.

(2) The Lord's Supper is the sacrament of communion with Christ and with His people, in which bread and wine are given and received in thankful remembrance of Him and His sacrifice on the Cross; and they who in faith receive the same do, after a spiritual manner, partake of the body and blood of the Lord Jesus Christ to their comfort, nourishment and growth in grace. All may be admitted to the Lord's Supper who make a credible profession of their faith in the Lord Jesus Christ and of obedience to His law.

ARTICLE XVII. OF THE MINISTRY. We believe that Jesus Christ, as the Supreme Head of the Church, has appointed therein a ministry of the word and sacraments, and calls men and women to this ministry; that the Church, under the guidance of the Holy Spirit, recognizes and chooses those whom He calls, and should thereupon duly ordain them to the work of the ministry.

ARTICLE XVIII. OF CHURCH ORDER AND FELLOWSHIP. We believe that the Supreme and only Head of the Church is the Lord Jesus Christ; that its worship, teaching, discipline and government should be administered according to His will by persons chosen for their fitness and duly set apart to their office; and that although the visible Church may contain unworthy members and is liable to err, yet believers ought not lightly to separate themselves from its communion, but are to live in fellowship with their brethen, which fellowship is to be extended, as God gives opportunity, to all who in every place call upon the name of the Lord Jesus.

ARTICLE XIX. OF THE RESURRECTION, THE LAST JUDGMENT AND THE FUTURE LIFE. We believe that there shall be a resurrection of the dead, both of the just and of the unjust, through the power of the Son of God, who shall come to judge the living and the dead; that the finally impenitent shall go away into eternal punishment and the righteous into life eternal.

ARTICLE XX. OF CHRISTIAN SERVICE AND THE FINAL TRIUMPH. We believe that it is our duty as disciples and servants of Christ, to further the extension of His Kingdom, to do good unto all men, to maintain the public and private worship of God, to hallow the Lord's Day, to preserve the inviolability of marriage and the sanctity of the family, to uphold the just authority of the State, and so to live in all honesty, purity and charity, that our lives shall testify of Christ. We joyfully receive the word of Christ, bidding His people go into all the world and make disciples of all nations, declaring unto them that God was in Christ reconciling the world unto Himself, and that He will have all men to be saved, and come to the knowledge of the truth. We confidently believe that by His power and grace all His enemies shall finally be overcome, and the kingdoms of this world be made the Kingdom of our God and of His Christ.

Notes: *Prepared in the first decade of the twentieth century, The Basis of Union formed part of the early agreement of the churches that eventually merged in 1925 to create the United Church of Canada. This statement shows minimal influence from either the Twenty-five Articles of Religion of the Methodists or the Westminster Confession of the Presbyterians. Rather, it draws upon the Brief Statement of the Reformed Faith, issued in 1905 by the Presbyterian Church in the U.S.A., and the Articles of Faith of the Presbyterian Church in England, issued in 1890.*

*   *   *

STATEMENT OF FAITH OF THE UNITED CHURCH OF CHRIST

We believe in God, the Eternal Spirit, Father of our Lord Jesus Christ and our Father, and to his deeds we testify:

He calls the worlds into being, creates man in his own image and sets before him the ways of life and death.

He seeks in holy love to save all people from aimlessness and sin.

He judges men and nations by his righteous will declared through prophets and apostles.

In Jesus Christ, the man of Nazareth, our crucified and risen Lord, he has come to us and shared our common lot, conquering sin and death and reconciling the world to himself.

He bestows upon us his Holy Spirit, creating and renewing the Church of Jesus Christ, binding in covenant faithful people of all ages, tongues, and races.

He calls us into his Church to accept the cost and joy of discipleship, to be his servants in the service of men, to proclaim the gospel to all the world and resist the powers of evil, to share in Christ's baptism and eat at his table, to join him in his passion and victory.

He promises to all who trust him forgiveness of sins and fullness of grace, courage in the struggle for justice and peace, his presence in trial and rejoicing, and eternal life in his kingdom which has no end.

Blessing and honor, glory and power be unto him. Amen

Notes: *Carrying on the liberal Protestant theological tradition that had produced the Kansas City Statement of 1913 and had dominated congregationalism in the twentieth century, the United Church of Christ adopted a new creed in 1960 as part of its basis of union. By doing this the church affirmed the creed's role as a "testimony" to faith rather than a "creed" and pointed out that the statement was never to be used as a test for prospective members or ministers seeking ordination.*

Chapter 6
Pietist-Methodist Family

Scandinavian Pietism

CONFESSION OF THE EVANGELICAL COVENANT CHURCH

The Covenant Church believes in the Holy Scriptures, the Old and the New Testament, as the Word of God and the only perfect rule for faith, doctrine, and conduct.

PREFACE TO THE CHURCH'S CONSTITUTION

The Covenant Church adheres to the affirmations of the Protestant Reformation regarding the Holy Scriptures, the Old and the New Testament, as the Word of God and the only perfect rule for faith, doctrine, and conduct. It has traditionally valued the historic confessions of the Christian church, particularly the Apostles' Creed, while at the same time it has emphasized the sovereignty of the Word over all creedal interpretations. It has especially cherished the pietistic restatement of the doctrine of justification by faith as basic to its dual task of evangelism and Christian nurture, the New Testament emphasis upon personal faith in Jesus Christ as Savior and Lord, the reality of a fellowship of believers which recognizes but transcends theological differences, and the belief in baptism and the Lord's Supper as divinely ordained sacraments of the church. While the denomination has traditionally practiced the baptism of infants, in conformity with its principle of freedom it has given room to divergent views. The principle of personal freedom, so highly esteemed by the Covenant, is to be distinguished from the individualism that disregards the centrality of the Word of God and the mutual responsibilities and disciplines of the spiritual community.

Notes: *The churches of the Pietist-Methodist Family did not have many essential doctrinal disagreements with the Lutheran and Reformed churches out of which they came. Their main emphases were personal religion and the practice of the Christian faith. In creating their doctrinal statements, the Pietist-Methodist churches assumed the existence of the lengthy Reformation confessions, which formed a broad basis of agreement. Their statements moved to affirm, in principle, the perspective of the Reformation,* *without commiting the churches to every particular of the lengthier statements. The emphasis upon precise theological formulas, exemplified in* The Book of Concord *and the* Westminster Confession, *was seen as not productive of piety. The statements also contained controversial opinions about certain issues without threatening the essentials of faith.*

The statement of pietistic churches, therefore, tended to be much shorter than those produced in the sixteenth and seventeenth centuries by the Lutheran and Reformed churches. Possibly the briefest is that of the Evangelical Covenant Church, which has less than thirty words. The preface to the church's constitution gives some content to the brief confession.

* * *

CREED (EVANGELICAL FREE CHURCH OF AMERICA)

The Evangelical Free Church of America believes:

1. The Scriptures, both Old and New Testaments, to be the inspired Word of God, without error in the original writings, the complete revelation of His will for the salvation of men, and the Divine and final authority for all Christian faith and life.

2. In one God, Creator of all things, infinitely perfect and eternally existing in three persons, Father, Son and Holy Spirit.

3. That Jesus Christ is true God and true man, having been conceived of the Holy Ghost and born of the Virgin Mary. He died on the cross a sacrifice for our sins according to the Scriptures. Further, He arose bodily from the dead, ascended into heaven, where at the right hand of the Majesty on High, He now is our High Priest and Advocate.

4. That the ministry of the Holy Spirit is to glorify the Lord Jesus Christ, and during this age to convict men, regenerate the believing sinner, indwell, guide, instruct, and empower the believer for godly living and service.

5. That man was created in the image of God but fell into sin and is therefore lost and only through

CREED (EVANGELICAL FREE CHURCH OF AMERICA) (continued)

regeneration by the Holy Spirit can salvation and spiritual life be obtained.

6. That the shed blood of Jesus Christ and His resurrection provide the only ground for justification and salvation for all who believe, and only such as receive Jesus Christ are born of the Holy Spirit, and thus become children of God.

7. That water baptism and the Lord's Supper are ordinances to be observed by the Church during the present age. They are however, not to be regarded as means of salvation.

8. That the true Church is composed of all such persons who through saving faith in Jesus Christ have been regenerated by the Holy Spirit and are united together in the body of Christ of which He is the head.

9. That only those who are thus members of the true Church shall be eligible for membership in the local church.

10. That Jesus Christ is the Lord and Head of the Church, and that every local church has the right under Christ to decide and govern its own affairs.

11. In the personal and premillennial and imminent coming of our Lord Jesus Christ and that this "Blessed Hope" has a vital bearing on the personal life and service of the believer.

12. In the bodily resurrection of the dead; of the believer to everlasting blessedness and joy with the Lord, of the unbeliever to judgment and everlasting conscious punishment.

Notes: *The statement of beliefs adopted by the Evangelical Free Church grew out of the statements of two bodies that merged to form the church in 1950: the Swedish Evangelical Free Church and the Norwegian-Danish Free Church Association. The statement of the merged church, in its position on scriptural authority, christology, and premillennialism, showed the strong influence of the fundamentalist movement in the early twentieth century.*

* * *

THE MORAVIAN COVENANT FOR CHRISTIAN LIVING (THE MORAVIAN CHURCH)

PREFACE

This Moravian Covenant for Christian Living is an attempt to state in clear arrangement and contemporary form a document which has long served the Moravian Church. The Church today has need of a clear statement of its faith and life through which each member may become aware of the nature of his/her Christian commitment. Such a document can become an invaluable aid in the instruction of both new and present members and a meaningful guide in the expression of the Christian life. That such a revision of the Agreement should have been made is entirely in harmony with the spirit of the early Moravian Church which believed that all forms should be

updated and made relevant to the present life of the Church.

The Moravian Covenant in its original form was adopted by the Moravian Church at Herrnhut, Saxony, as the Brotherly Agreement on May 12 of the year that marked the Church's spiritual renewal, 1727. The Covenant was not intended to be a "discipline" forced on the congregation from above, but rather an "agreement" into which the members entered voluntarily. This spirit pervades the new Covenant which in itself is only a recommended form, to be voluntarily accepted by each of the local congregations before it becomes effective for their congregational life.

Most of the Covenant deals with the Christian life, and since it is in terms of everyday life that the Christian witness is often most effectively borne, the document is subtitled, "Principles by Which We Live and Bear Our Witness." The theme of "witness" is carried out in all the sections. The introductory section, "Ground of Our Witness," deals briefly with the faith and doctrine of the Moravian Church, something that is not explicitly dealt with in older forms of the Covenant. Section I, "The Witness of the Christian Life," describes the "how" of the life in Christ and thus forms a basis for all that follows. The following sections then consider various areas of Christian responsibility. Section II deals largely with Christian responsibility in the local congregation and in relation to Christians of other churches; III, responsibility in the home; IV, one's duties as a citizen; and V, as a Christian in the world.

Variations in the form of the Moravian Covenant recommended by Synod may be adopted only with the approval of the Provincial Elders' Conference.

THE GROUND OF OUR WITNESS

We are called into a Christian fellowship by the Lord Jesus Christ, according to the eternal purpose of God the Father (Eph. 3:11) by the Holy Spirit (Acts 2:18-21), and as members of Christ's Body, the Church, to serve all people by proclaiming the gospel and witnessing to our faith by word and deed.

The Holy Scriptures are and shall remain the only source and rule of our doctrine, faith, and practice.

With the universal Christian Church, we share our faith in the Triune God, who revealed himself in the Lord Jesus Christ as the only Saviour of all people. We particularly declare his living presence and Lordship over the Church, joy in the benefits of his life, sufferings, death and resurrection and emphasize a close bond of fellowship with each other in his name. We believe that Christ is present with us in Word and Sacrament. We decline to determine as binding what the Scriptures have left undetermined, or to argue about mysteries impenetrable to human reason. In this regard, we hold to the principles: "In essentials, unity; in non-essentials, liberty; and in all things, charity."

We thankfully recognize the value of the historic creeds of the Christian Church in calling upon believers in every age to give an obedient and fearless testimony, recognizing Jesus Christ as Lord. A Moravian confession of faith is to be found in the Easter Morning Liturgy.

I. THE WITNESS OF THE CHRISTIAN LIFE

1. We believe that as in baptism we have been united with Christ in his death and resurrection, so we have died to sin and should walk in newness of life. (Romans 6:1-11)

2. When seeking guidance we find that the simplest expression of Christian living is contained in the earliest of Christian confessions, "Jesus Christ is Lord." This implies that obedience is due him as an absolute Ruler and Lord of our lives. Not only his teachings (e.g. Matt. 5-7), but even more, the example of his life (Phil. 2:5; Eph. 4:20) provide an understanding of the obedience that he desires. Although the early Church, guided by the Spirit of Jesus, did not develop a code covering all issues, it offered guidance in various areas of Christian living. (e.g. Col. 3:1-4:6; I Peter 2:11-3:12; Eph. 4:1-6:20)

3. Living the Christian life depends not only on our own effort but upon God our Father, who in Jesus Christ accepts us as heirs of God (Gal. 4:4-7) and strengthens and sustains us. (Phil. 4:13)

4. We realize that our Christian faith must continually be nourished if it is to remain living and vital. Therefore, we desire to grow in our Christian lives through family devotions, personal prayer and study, and the opportunities for spiritual development offered by the church.

II. THE WITNESS OF A LIVING CHURCH

A. THE MORAVIAN UNITY

1. RECOGNITION OF AUTHORITY

   As members of the Moravian Church we will abide by the decisions made by the official boards of our congregation, and agree to be governed, both as individuals and as a congregation, by the enactments of the Unity Synod of the Moravian Church and of the Synods of the Province to which our congregation belongs.

2. STEWARDSHIP

   a. We deem it a sacred responsibility and genuine opportunity to be faithful stewards of all God has entrusted to us: our time, our talents, and our financial resources. We view all of life as a sacred trust to be used wisely.

   b. We will support, according to our ability, the financial needs of the local congregation, the District, the Province, and the Unity. We will consider the support of the benevolent causes of the Moravian Church, both at home and abroad as a privilege, an opportunity, and a responsibility.

   c. We will also recognize the support of worthy causes outside of the Church as part of our stewardship.

3. PERSONAL RELATIONSHIPS

   a. Since disciples of Jesus are to be known by the love they have to one another (John 13:35), we will cherish Christian love as of prime importance.

   b. We will be eager to maintain the unity of the Church, realizing that God has called us from many and varied backgrounds, we recognize the possibility of disagreements or differences. Often these differences enrich the Church, but sometimes they divide. We consider it to be our responsibility to demonstrate within the congregational life the unity and togetherness created by God who made us one. How well we accomplish this will be a witness to our community as to the validity of our faith.

   c. We will endeavor to settle our differences with others in a Christian manner (Gal. 6:1), amicably, and with mediation, and if at all possible avoid resort to a court of law. (Matt. 18:15-17)

4. WORSHIP AND SUNDAY OBSERVANCE

   a. Remembering that worship is one of our proper responses to Almighty God, an experience designed for our benefit, and a part of our Christian witness, we and our children will faithfully attend the worship services of the Church.

   b. We, therefore, will be careful to avoid unnecessary labor on Sunday and plan that the recreations in which we engage on that day do not interfere with our own attendance or that of others at divine worship.

5. HOLY COMMUNION

   In the celebration of this Sacrament we receive the renewed assurance of the forgiveness of our sins, and of our fellowship with Christ; unite with one another as members of his body; and rejoice in the hope of his return in glory. Therefore, we will commune faithfully and thus renew our pledge of allegiance to him.

B. THE UNITY WE SEEK

1. We will have fellowship, in all sincerity, with children of God in other Christian churches, and will carefully avoid all disputes respecting opinions and ceremonies peculiar to one or another church. In this fellowship we will cooperate with other churches in the support of public charities or Christian enterprises, which have a just claim upon us as followers of the Lord Jesus Christ.

2. We realize that it is the Lord's will that the Church of Jesus Christ should give evidence of and seek unity in him with zeal and love. We see how such unity has been promised us and laid upon us as a charge. We recognize that through the grace of Christ the different denominations have received many gifts and that the Church of Christ may be enriched by these many and varied contributions. It is our desire that we may learn from one another and rejoice together in the riches of the love of Christ and the manifold wisdom of God. We welcome every step that brings us nearer the goal of unity in him.

THE MORAVIAN COVENANT FOR CHRISTIAN LIVING
(THE MORAVIAN CHURCH) (continued)

III. THE WITNESS OF THE CHRISTIAN HOME

A. MARRIAGE

1. We regard it as a sacred obligation to hold to the ideal of Christian marriage given by our Lord in his teaching. We consider it essential, therefore, that all persons contemplating marriage should receive premarital counseling and that our young people should be instructed, beginning in adolescence, in the meaning and obligation of true Christian marriage; this instruction to be given through the Church and the home.

2. We regard Christian marriage as an indissoluble union, which requires the lifelong loyalty of the man and the woman towards each other. Because any breaking of the marriage bond involves sin against God and causes human suffering, it is the duty of husband and wife to meet all frictions, offenses, and disagreements with a forgiving spirit that persistently works for reconciliation. Furthermore, if at any time the stability of their marriage is threatened, they are to seek the counsel of their pastor or of other spiritual leaders in the church as soon as possible and before any other action is taken.

B. FAMILY LIFE

1. As parents, remembering that our children are the property of the Lord Jesus Christ, (Acts 20:28; I Peter 1:19) we will bring them up in the nurture and admonition of the Lord (Eph. 6:4) and take all possible care to preserve them from every evil influence. For this reason we will seek to approve ourselves as followers of the Lord Jesus Christ, setting an example for our children. We will give faithful attention to the spiritual development of our children, both in the home and in the church. We will endeavor to conduct regular family devotions.

IV. THE WITNESS OF A CHRISTIAN CITIZEN

A. RECOGNITION OF CIVIL AUTHORITY

We will be subject to the civil authorities as the powers ordained of God, in accordance with the admonitions of Scripture (Rom. 13:1; I Peter 2:13-14) and will in nowise evade the taxes and other obligations which are lawfully required of us (Rom. 13:7).

B. RESPONSIBILITIES

Considering it a special privilege to live in a democratic society, we will faithfully fulfill the responsibilities of our citizenship, among which are intelligent and well-informed voting, a willingness to assume public office, guiding the decisions of government by the expression of our opinions, and supporting good government by our personal efforts.

C. A HIGHER LOYALTY

Though giving our loyalty to the state of which we are citizens, we do recognize a higher loyalty to God and conscience. (Acts 5:29)

D. PEACEMAKERS

For the sake of the peace which we have with God, we earnestly desire to live peaceably with all people and to seek the peace of the places where we dwell.

V. OUR WITNESS IN THE WORLD

A. LOVE TOWARD ALL

We will not hate, despise, slander or otherwise injure anyone. We will ever strive to manifest love towards all people, to treat them in a kind and friendly manner, and in our dealings with them to approve ourselves upright, honest, and conscientious, as becomes children of God. Together with the universal Christian Church, we have a concern for this world, opening our heart and hand to our neighbors with the message of the love of God, and being ever ready to minister of our substance to their necessities. (Matt. 25:40)

B. OUR MANNER OF LIFE

We will at all times be ready cheerfully to witness to our faith (I Peter 3:15, 16) and if need be, to suffer reproach for Christ's sake (Luke 6:22, 23). Being aware that our witness is made both by what we do and what we avoid doing, we will endeavor to let our manner of life "be worthy of the gospel of Christ," (Phil. 1:27) "not being conformed to this world." (Rom. 12:2) But in our yearning for the redemption of the whole creation, we will seek to meet the needs of the world in self-giving love, and as true yokefellows of Jesus Christ, willingly share in the fellowship of his sufferings, walking in his strength, by whom all things "are given us that pertain to life and godliness." (II Peter 1:3)

C. TEMPERANCE IN ALL THINGS

Remembering the admonition of Scripture to be temperate in all things (I Cor. 9:25), we shall endeavor to look upon our bodies as temples of God's spirit (I Cor. 6:19). We must also remember to respect the welfare of others who may be affected by our actions (Rom. 14:20, 21). We are aware of the problems that can be caused by the intemperate use of such things as alcoholic beverages, food, tobacco, drugs, and other things. We consider it the responsibility of every Christian to decide most carefully how they can be used in good conscience. We regard intemperance in any area of living as being inconsistent with the Christian life.

D. UNITY

1. Christian: We recognize no distinction between those who are one in the Lord. We believe that God in Jesus Christ calls his people out of "every race, kindred and tongue," pardons them beneath the Cross, and brings them into a living fellowship with himself. We regard it as a commandment of our Lord to bear public witness to this and to

demonstrate by word and deed that we are one in Christ.

2. Universal: Because we hold that all people are God's creatures (Gen. 1:27) and that he has made of one blood all nations (Acts 17:26) we oppose any discrimination based on color, race, creed or land of origin and declare that we should treat everyone with love and respect.

E. OTHER AREAS

We realize that all areas of Christian life and conduct cannot be covered in this statement of principles by which we live and bear our witness, and we call attention, therefore, to the Christian's responsibility to follow Christ as Lord of all areas of life.

VI. DISCIPLINE

We make it a duty of the Board of Elders, which is charged with the spiritual welfare of the congregation, to see that this "Moravian Covenant" be adhered to and faithfully observed; and we will cooperate with the Board of Elders in its efforts to maintain the discipline of the congregation. As a redemptive community we will be much more concerned in aiding than censuring those who falter, being conscious of our own need for correction and forgiveness.

Notes: *The Moravian Covenant is a revised form of "The Brotherly Agreement," a document originally adopted in 1727. True to its pietist heritage, the Covenant centers on the Christian life and action more than belief. The preface gives some explanation of its history and emphases. The text is the one adopted in 1982 by the Northern Province Synod of the Moravian Church.*

* * *

United Methodism

THE TWENTY-FIVE ARTICLES OF RELIGION (UNITED METHODIST CHURCH)

Article I. OF FAITH IN THE HOLY TRINITY

There is but one living and true God, everlasting, without body or parts, of infinite power, wisdom, and goodness; the maker and preserver of all things, both visible and invisible. And in unity of this Godhead there are three persons, of one substance, power, and eternity—the Father, the Son, and the Holy Ghost.

Article II. OF THE WORD, OR SON OF GOD, WHO WAS MADE VERY MAN

The Son, who is the Word of the Father, the very and eternal God, of one substance with the Father, took man's nature in the womb of the blessed Virgin; so that two whole and perfect natures, that is to say, the Godhead and Manhood, were joined together in one person, never to be divided; whereof is one Christ, very God and very Man, who truly suffered, was crucified, dead, and buried, to reconcile his Father to us, and to be a sacrifice, not only for original guilt, but also for the actual sins of men.

Article III. OF THE RESURRECTION OF CHRIST

Christ did truly rise again from the dead, and took again his body, with all things appertaining to the perfection of man's nature, wherewith he ascended into heaven, and there sitteth until he return to judge all men at the last day.

Article IV. OF THE HOLY GHOST

The Holy Ghost, proceeding from the Father and the Son, is of one substance, majesty, and glory with the Father and the Son, very and eternal God.

Article V. OF THE SUFFICIENCY OF THE HOLY SCRIPTURES FOR SALVATION

The Holy Scripture containeth all things necessary to salvation; so that whatsoever is not read therein, nor may be proved thereby, is not to be required of any man that it should be believed as an article of faith, or be thought requisite or necessary to salvation. In the name of the Holy Scripture we do understand those canonical books of the Old and New Testament of whose authority was never any doubt in the Church. The names of the canonical books are:

Genesis, Exodus, Leviticus, Numbers, Deuteronomy, Joshua, Judges, Ruth, The First Book of Samuel, The Second Book of Samuel, The First Book of Kings, The Second Book of Kings, The First Book of Chronicles, The Second Book of Chronicles, The Book of Ezra, The Book of Nehemiah, The Book of Esther, The Book of Job, The Psalms, The Proverbs, Ecclesiastes or the Preacher, Cantica or Songs of Solomon, Four Prophets the Greater, Twelve Prophets the Less.

All the books of the New Testament, as they are commonly received, we do receive and account canonical.

Article VI. OF THE OLD TESTAMENT

The Old Testament is not contrary to the New; for both in the Old and New Testament everlasting life is offered to mankind by Christ, who is the only Mediator between God and man, being both God and Man. Wherefore they are not to be heard who feign that the old fathers did look only for transitory promises. Although the law given from God by Moses as touching ceremonies and rites doth not bind Christians, nor ought the civil precepts thereof of necessity be received in any commonwealth; yet notwithstanding, no Christian whatsoever is free from the obedience of the commandments which are called moral.

Article VII. OF ORIGINAL OR BIRTH SIN

Original sin standeth not in the following of Adam (as the Pelagians do vainly talk), but it is the corruption of the nature of every man, that naturally is engendered of the offspring of Adam, whereby man is very far gone from original righteousness, and of his own nature inclined to evil, and that continually.

Article VIII. OF FREE WILL

The condition of man after the fall of Adam is such that he cannot turn and prepare himself, by his own natural strength and works, to faith, and calling upon God; wherefore we have no power to do good work, pleasant and acceptable to God, without the grace of God by Christ preventing us, that we may have a good will, and working with us, when we have that good will.

Article IX. OF THE JUSTIFICATION OF MAN

We are accounted righteous before God only for the merit of our Lord and Saviour Jesus Christ, by faith, and not for our own works or deservings. Wherefore, that we are justified by faith, only, is a most wholesome doctrine, and very full of comfort.

Article X. OF GOOD WORKS

Although good works, which are the fruits of faith, and follow after justification, cannot put away our sins, and endure the severity of God's judgment; yet are they pleasing and acceptable to God in Christ, and spring out of a true and lively faith, insomuch that by them a lively faith may be as evidently known as a tree is discerned by its fruit.

Article XI. OF WORKS OF SUPEREROGATION

Voluntary works—besides, over and above God's commandments—which they call works of supererogation, cannot be taught without arrogancy and impiety. For by them men do declare that they do not only render unto God as much as they are bound to do, but that they do more for his sake than the bounden duty is required; whereas Christ saith plainly: When you have done all that is commanded you, say, We are unprofitable servants.

Article XII. OF SIN AFTER JUSTIFICATION

Not every sin willingly committed after justification is the sin against the Holy Ghost, and unpardonable. Wherefore, the grant of repentance is not to be denied to such as fall into sin after justification. After we have received the Holy Ghost, we may depart from grace given, and fall into sin, and, by the grace of God, rise again and amend our lives. And therefore they are to be condemned who say they can no more sin as long as they live here; or deny the place of forgiveness to such as truly repent.

Article XIII. OF THE CHURCH

The visible Church of Christ is a congregation of faithful men in which the pure Word of God is preached, and the Sacraments duly administered according to Christ's ordinance, in all those things that of necessity are requisite to the same.

Article XIV. OF PURGATORY

The Romish doctrine concerning purgatory, pardon, worshiping, and adoration, as well of images as of relics, and also invocation of saints, is a fond thing, vainly invented, and grounded upon no warrant of Scripture, but repugnant to the Word of God.

Article XV. OF SPEAKING IN THE CONGREGATION IN SUCH A TONGUE AS THE PEOPLE UNDERSTAND

It is a thing plainly repugnant to the Word of God, and the custom of the primitive Church, to have public prayer in the church, or to minister the Sacraments, in a tongue not understood by the people.

Article XVI. OF THE SACRAMENTS

Sacraments ordained of Christ are not only badges or tokens of Christian men's profession, but rather they are certain signs of grace, and God's good will toward us, by which he doth work invisibly in us, and doth not only quicken, but also strengthen and confirm, our faith in him.

There are two Sacraments ordained of Christ our Lord in the Gospel; that is to say, Baptism and the Supper of the Lord.

Those five commonly called sacraments, that is to say, confirmation, penance, orders, matrimony, and extreme unction, are not to be counted for Sacraments of the Gospel; being such as have partly grown out of the *corrupt* following of the apostles, and partly are states of life allowed in the Scriptures, but yet have not the like nature of Baptism and the Lord's Supper, because they have not any visible sign or ceremony ordained of God.

The Sacraments were not ordained of Christ to be gazed upon, or to be carried about; but that we should duly use them. And in such only as worthily receive the same, they have a wholesome effect or operation; but they that receive them unworthily, purchase to themselves condemnation, as St. Paul saith.

Article XVII. OF BAPTISM

Baptism is not only a sign of profession and mark of difference whereby Christians are distinguished from others that are not baptized; but it is also a sign of regeneration or the new birth. The baptism of young children is to be retained in the church.

Article XVIII. OF THE LORD'S SUPPER

The Supper of the Lord is not only a sign of the love that Christians ought to have among themselves one to another, but rather is a sacrament of our redemption by Christ's death; insomuch that, to such as rightly, worthily, and with faith receive the same, the bread which we break is a partaking of the body of Christ; and likewise the cup of blessing is a partaking of the blood of Christ.

Transubstantiation, or the change of the substance of bread and wine in the Supper of our Lord, cannot be proved by Holy Writ, but is repugnant to the plain words of Scripture, overthroweth the nature of a sacrament, and hath given occasion to many superstitions.

The body of Christ is given, taken, and eaten in the Supper, only after a heavenly and spiritual manner. And the mean whereby the body of Christ is received and eaten in the Supper is faith.

The Sacrament of the Lord's Supper was not by Christ's ordinance reserved, carried about, lifted up, or worshiped.

Article XIX. OF BOTH KINDS

The cup of the Lord is not to be denied to the lay people; for both the parts of the Lord's Supper, by Christ's ordinance and commandment, ought to be administered to all Christians alike.

Article XX. OF THE ONE OBLATION OF CHRIST, FINISHED UPON THE CROSS

The offering of Christ, once made, is that perfect redemption, propitiation, and satisfaction for all the sins of the whole world, both original and actual; and there is none other satisfaction for sin but that alone. Wherefore the sacrifice of masses, in the which it is commonly said that the priest doth offer Christ for the quick and the dead, to have remission of pain or guilt, is a blasphemous fable and dangerous deceit.

Article XXI. OF THE MARRIAGE OF MINISTERS

The ministers of Christ are not commanded by God's law either to vow the estate of single life, or to abstain from marriage; therefore it is lawful for them, as for all other Christians, to marry at their own discretion, as they shall judge the same to serve best to godliness.

Article XXII. OF THE RITES AND CEREMONIES OF CHURCHES

It is not necessary that rites and ceremonies should in all places be the same, or exactly alike; for they have been always different, and may be changed according to the diversity of countries, times, and men's manners, so that nothing be ordained against God's Word. Whosoever, through his private judgment, willingly and purposely doth openly break the rites and ceremonies of the church to which he belongs, which are not repugnant to the Word of God, and are ordained and approved by common authority, ought to be rebuked openly, that others may fear to do the like, as one that offendeth against the common order of the church, and woundeth the consciences of weak brethren.

Every particular church may ordain, change, or abolish rites and ceremonies, so that all things may be done to edification.

Article XXIII. OF THE RULERS OF THE UNITED STATES OF AMERICA

The President, the Congress, the general assemblies, the governors, and the councils of state, *as the delegates of the people*, are the rulers of the United States of America, according to the division of power made to them by the Constitution of the United States and by the constitutions of their respective states. And the said states are a sovereign and independent nation, and ought not to be subject to any foreign jurisdiction.

Article XXIV. OF CHRISTIAN MEN'S GOODS

The riches and goods of Christians are not common as touching the right, title, and possession of the same, as some do falsely boast. Notwithstanding, every man ought, of such things as he possesseth, liberally to give alms to the poor, according to his ability.

Article XXV. OF A CHRISTIAN MAN'S OATH

As we confess that vain and rash swearing is forbidden Christian men by our Lord Jesus Christ and James his apostle, so we judge that the Christian religion doth not prohibit, but that a man may swear when the magistrate requireth, in a cause of faith and charity, so it be done according to the prophet's teaching, in justice, judgment, and truth.

Notes: *Following the American Revolution, John Wesley prepared doctrinal materials to guide the newly independent Methodists residing in the former British colonies in the New World. Among the items were twenty-five articles of religion. Wesley took them directly from the Thirty-nine Articles of the Church of England (still in use today by most Anglican churches in the United States), deleting what he considered less essential statements, including the more*

controversial articles on eschatology. The Twenty-five Articles were adopted by the Methodist Episcopal Church in 1784 and remain part of the constitution of the United Methodist Church.

The United Methodist Church, in the persona of the General Conference, its highest legislative body, is bound by what are termed the six restrictive rules. The first of these states: "The General Conference shall not revoke, alter, or change our Articles of Religion or establish any new standards or rule of doctrine contrary to our present existing and established standards of doctrine." Deletion of one of these restrictive rules takes almost unanimous consent of the church. These restrictive rules have been retained by most of the churches that have broken away from what is now known as the United Methodist Church. The rules have also helped perpetuate the Twenty-five Articles in the face of periodic attempts to rewrite doctrinal statements.

The Twenty-five Articles of Religion have been among the most influential documents in American religious history. Beyond their service to the multi-million member United Methodist Church and its antecedents, they have served as a base from which many of the holiness and pentecostal churches have begun their doctrinal formulations (though most have now moved considerably beyond the articles).

The articles also are held, in some cases with minor changes or additions, by the Congregational Methodist Church, the Evangelical Methodist Church, the Evangelical Methodist Church of America, the First Congregational Methodist Church of the U.S.A., the Southern Methodist Church, the African Methodist Episcopal Church, the African Methodist Episcopal Zion Church, the African Union First Colored Methodist Protestant Church, the Christian Methodist Episcopal Church, and the Reformed Zion Union Apostolic Church.

*　　*　　*

CHANGES, ADDITIONS, AND FOOTNOTES TO THE *TWENTY-FIVE ARTICLES OF RELIGION* (UNITED METHODIST CHURCH)

OF SANCTIFICATION

Sanctification is that renewal of our fallen nature by the Holy Ghost, received through faith in Jesus Christ, whose blood of atonement cleanseth from all sin; whereby we are not only delivered from the guilt of sin, but are washed from its pollution, saved from its power, and are enabled, through grace, to love God with all our hearts and to walk in his holy commandments blameless.

OF THE DUTY OF CHRISTIANS TO THE CIVIL AUTHORITY

It is the duty of all Christians, and especially of all Christian ministers, to observe and obey the laws and commands of the governing or supreme authority of the country of which they are citizens or subjects or in which they reside, and to use all laudable means to encourage and enjoin obedience to the powers that be.

Notes: *The Methodist Protestant Church (1828-1939), one of the church bodies participating in the series of mergers that led to the formation of United Methodism, added a*

CHANGES, ADDITIONS, AND FOOTNOTES TO THE *TWENTY-FIVE ARTICLES OF RELIGION* **(UNITED METHODIST CHURCH) (continued)**

statement on sanctification to the Articles of Religion. That statement is carried in The Book of Discipline *of the United Methodist Church with a note: "The following Article from the Methodist Protestant Church* Discipline *is placed here by the Uniting Conference (1939). It was not one of the Articles of Religion voted upon by the three churches [which united at that time]."*

A second article was also added in 1939. It grew out of the problems arising from the stated allegiance of the Methodist Church to the government of the United States. A note is appended: "The following provision was adopted by the Uniting Conference. This statement seeks to interpret to our churches in foreign lands Article XXIII of the Articles of Religion. It is a legislative enactment but is not part of the Constitution."

* * *

CONFESSION OF FAITH (UNITED METHODIST CHURCH)

Article I. GOD

1. We believe in the one true, holy and living God, Eternal Spirit, who is Creator, Sovereign and Preserver of all things visible and invisible. He is infinite in power, wisdom, justice, goodness and love, and rules with gracious regard for the well-being and salvation of men, to the glory of his name. We believe the one God reveals himself as the Trinity: Father, Son and Holy Spirit, distinct but inseparable, eternally one in essence and power.

Article II. JESUS CHRIST

2. We believe in Jesus Christ, truly God and truly man, in whom the divine and human natures are perfectly and inseparably united. He is the eternal Word made flesh, the only begotten Son of the Father, born of the Virgin Mary by the power of the Holy Spirit. As ministering Servant he lived, suffered and died on the cross. He was buried, rose from the dead and ascended into heaven to be with the Father, from whence he shall return. He is eternal Savior and Mediator, who intercedes for us, and by him all men will be judged.

Article III. THE HOLY SPIRIT

3. We believe in the Holy Spirit who proceeds from and is one in being with the Father and the Son. He convinces the world of sin, of righteousness and of judgment. He leads men through faithful response to the Gospel into the fellowship of the church. He comforts, sustains and empowers the faithful and guides them into all truth.

Article IV. THE HOLY BIBLE

4. We believe the Holy Bible, Old and New Testaments, reveals the Word of God as far as it is necessary for our salvation. It is to be received through the Holy Spirit as the true rule and guide for faith and practice. Whatever is not revealed in or established by the Holy Scriptures is not to be made an article of faith nor is it to be taught as essential to salvation.

Article V. THE CHURCH

5. We believe the Christian church is the community of all true believers under the Lordship of Christ. We believe it is one, holy, apostolic and catholic. It is the redemptive fellowship in which the Word of God is preached by men divinely called, and the sacraments are duly administered according to Christ's own appointment. Under the discipline of the Holy Spirit the church exists for the maintenance of worship, the edification of believers and the redemption of the world.

Article VI. THE SACRAMENTS

6. We believe the sacraments, ordained by Christ, are symbols and pledges of the Christian's profession and of God's love toward us. They are means of grace by which God works invisibly in us, quickening, strengthening and confirming our faith in him. Two sacraments are ordained by Christ our Lord, namely, Baptism and the Lord's Supper.

We believe Baptism signifies entrance into the household of faith, and is a symbol of repentance and inner cleansing from sin, a representation of the new birth in Christ Jesus and a mark of Christian discipleship.

We believe children are under the atonement of Christ and as heirs of the kingdom of God are acceptable subjects for Christian baptism. Children of believing parents through baptism become the special responsibility of the church. They should be nurtured and led to personal acceptance of Christ, and by profession of faith confirm their baptism.

We believe the Lord's Supper is a representation of our redemption, a memorial of the sufferings and death of Christ, and a token of love and union which Christians have with Christ and with one another. Those who rightly, worthily and in faith eat the broken bread and drink the blessed cup partake of the body and blood of Christ in a spiritual manner until he comes.

Article VII. SIN AND FREE WILL

7. We believe man is fallen from righteousness and, apart from the grace of our Lord Jesus Christ, is destitute of holiness and inclined to evil. Except a man be born again, he cannot see the kingdom of God. In his own strength, without divine grace, man cannot do good works pleasing and acceptable to God. We believe, however, man influenced and empowered by the Holy Spirit is responsible in freedom to exercise his will for good.

Article VIII. RECONCILIATION THROUGH CHRIST

8. We believe God was in Christ reconciling the world to himself. The offering Christ freely made on the cross is the perfect and sufficient sacrifice for the sins

of the whole world, redeeming man from all sin, so that no other satisfaction is required.

Article IX. JUSTIFICATION AND REGENERATION

9. We believe we are never accounted righteous before God through our works or merit, but that penitent sinners are justified or accounted righteous before God only by faith in our Lord Jesus Christ.

We believe regeneration is the renewal of man in righteousness through Jesus Christ, by the power of the Holy Spirit, whereby we are made partakers of the divine nature and experience newness of life. By this new birth the believer becomes reconciled to God and is enabled to serve him with the will and the affections.

We believe, although we have experienced regeneration, it is possible to depart from grace and fall into sin; and we may even then, by the grace of God, be renewed in righteousness.

Article X. GOOD WORKS

10. We believe good works are the necessary fruits of faith and follow regeneration but they do not have the virtue to remove our sins or to avert divine judgment. We believe good works, pleasing and acceptable to God in Christ, spring from a true and living faith, for through and by them faith is made evident.

Article XI. SANCTIFICATION AND CHRISTIAN PERFECTION

11. We believe sanctification is the work of God's grace through the Word and the Spirit, by which those who have been born again are cleansed from sin in their thoughts, words and acts, and are enabled to live in accordance with God's will, and to strive for holiness without which no one will see the Lord.

Entire sanctification is a state of perfect love, righteousness and true holiness which every regenerate believer may obtain by being delivered from the power of sin, by loving God with all the heart, soul, mind and strength, and by loving one's neighbor as one's self. Through faith in Jesus Christ this gracious gift may be received in this life both gradually and instantaneously, and should be sought earnestly by every child of God.

We believe this experience does not deliver us from the infirmities, ignorance and mistakes common to man, nor from the possibilities of further sin. The Christian must continue on guard against spiritual pride and seek to gain victory over every temptation to sin. He must respond wholly to the will of God so that sin will lose its power over him; and the world, the flesh and the devil are put under his feet. Thus he rules over these enemies with watchfulness through the power of the Holy Spirit.

Article XII. THE JUDGMENT AND THE FUTURE STATE

12. We believe all men stand under the righteous judgment of Jesus Christ, both now and in the last day. We believe in the resurrection of the dead; the righteous to life eternal and the wicked to endless condemnation.

Article XIII. PUBLIC WORSHIP

13. We believe divine worship is the duty and privilege of man who, in the presence of God, bows in adoration, humility and dedication. We believe divine worship is essential to the life of the church, and that the assembling of the people of God for such worship is necessary to Christian fellowship and spiritual growth.

We believe the order of public worship need not be the same in all places but may be modified by the church according to circumstances and the needs of men. It should be in a language and form understood by the people, consistent with the Holy Scriptures to the edification of all, and in accordance with the order and DISCIPLINE of the Church.

Article XIV. THE LORD'S DAY

14. We believe the Lord's Day is divinely ordained for private and public worship, for rest from unnecessary work, and should be devoted to spiritual improvement, Christian fellowship and service. It is commemorative of our Lord's resurrection and is an emblem of our eternal rest. It is essential to the permanence and growth of the Christian church, and important to the welfare of the civil community.

Article XV. THE CHRISTIAN AND PROPERTY

15. We believe God is the owner of all things and that the individual holding of property is lawful and is a sacred trust under God. Private property is to be used for the manifestation of Christian love and liberality, and to support the Church's mission in the world. All forms of property, whether private, corporate or public, are to be held in solemn trust and used responsibly for human good under the sovereignty of God.

Article XVI. CIVIL GOVERNMENT

16. We believe civil government derives its just powers from the sovereign God. As Christians we recognize the governments under whose protection we reside and believe such governments should be based on, and be responsible for, the recognition of human rights under God. We believe war and bloodshed are contrary to the gospel and spirit of Christ. We believe it is the duty of Christian citizens to give moral strength and purpose to their respective governments through sober, righteous and godly living.

Notes: *In 1968, the United Methodist Church accepted the Confession of Faith of the Evangelical United Brethren (formed in 1946), originally adopted in 1962, as one of its standards of doctrine. At the same time it added a new restrictive rule to the constitution: "The General Conference shall not revoke, alter, or change our Confession of Faith."*

A MODERN AFFIRMATION (UNITED METHODIST CHURCH)

MINISTER: Where the Spirit of the Lord is, there is the one true Church, apostolic and universal, whose holy faith let us now declare:

MINISTER AND PEOPLE: We believe in God the Father, infinite in wisdom, power and love, whose mercy is over all his works, and whose will is ever directed to his children's good.

We believe in Jesus Christ, Son of God and Son of man, the gift of the Father's unfailing grace, the ground of our hope, and the promise of our deliverance from sin and death.

We believe in the Holy Spirit as the divine presence in our lives, whereby we are kept in perpetual rememberance of the truth of Christ, and find strength and help in time of need.

We believe that this faith should manifest itself in the service of love as set forth in the example of our blessed Lord, to the end that the kingdom of God may come upon the earth. Amen.

Notes: *The United Methodist Church includes a variety of creedal affirmations in its* Hymnal *and* The Book of Worship, *used in the liturgies of its member churches. Among these affirmations are the Apostles' and Nicene Creeds, as well as the Creed of the Church of South Korea. These affirmations do not represent doctrinal standards, like the Twenty-five Articles, and they have never been presented to or voted upon by the General Conference with such intent. They merely appear as additional liturgical resources. However, their inclusion does represent the diversity of opinion that has appeared within the church during this century.*

Added by the Methodist Episcopal Church in the early twentieth century, the creed called "A Modern Affirmation" is similiar to the Congregational Church statement adopted in 1913 in that it does not require ministers and members who repeat it to affirm certain traditional Christian beliefs, especially those debated by theologians in the twentieth century such as the Trinity or the substitutionary atonement of Christ. The affirmation has emerged as a substitute for the Apostles' Creed and is commonly repeated in many United Methodist Church worship services.

* * *

Non-Episcopal Methodism

ADDITIONS TO THE *TWENTY-FIVE ARTICLES OF RELIGION* (ASBURY BIBLE CHURCHES)

OF SEGREGATION

We do not believe that integration, for which so many are clamoring, is the answer to current social problems. In fact, it is our opinion that integration would produce more problems than it would solve. In the light of the present moral and spiritual crisis, and also in the light of Scriptural teaching, we believe in the segregation of the races and practice the principle of segregation in our churches. The practice of this principle, however, does not mean that our churches are not vigorously missionary and evangelistic in their ministries, nor that we would not endeavor to win to Christ and nurture in Christ ANYONE so long as, where differing races are involved, we do so on an INDIVIDU-AL, rather than a SOCIAL, basis.

"[God] hath made of one blood all nations of men for to dwell on all the face of the earth, and hath determined the times before appointed, AND THE BOUNDS OF THEIR HABITATION . . . " (Acts 17:26).

OF SEPARATION

We believe that, in these days of apostasy, the Church should be separated from compromising situations in the world.

Such being the case, no independent Methodist church can consistently hold membership in, or otherwise be connected with, the National Council of Churches (NCC), the World Council of Churches (WCC), or even the National Association of Evangelicals (NAE). In regard to the NCC and the WCC, the apostasy of churches and denominations in those organizations would prohibit an independent Methodist church from being a part thereof. So would the ecumenical world church movement in which the NCC and the WCC are actively engaged. (Such a world church, so-called, would not be a church at all, in the true sense of the word, for every vestige of the fundamentals of the Faith has to be forfeited for the sake of the 'unity' to be effected by this monstrous ecclesiastical-political machine.) In regard to the NAE, this organization is now off-limits to independent Methodist churches, inasmuch as ecumenism and also neo-evangelicalism (modernism disguised as fundamentalism) are characteristics of the NAE as it is presently constituted. The NAE, therefore, is now a compromise organization, and independent Methodist churches are not to compromise. Furthermore, it is now possible for a church or denomination to hold membership in the NAE and also the NCC and the WCC.

We heartily urge that independent Methodist churches seek membership in the American Council of Christian Churches (ACCC). This Council was formed in 1941 to combat the NCC [then the Federal Council of Churches], along with other kindred organizations and enterprises. The ACCC has maintained—and continues to maintain—an aggressive attempt to expose evil wherever it is found, to preserve the integrity of the Scriptures, and to staunchly oppose those who try to destroy such integrity.

Cooperative church and ministerial activities with churches and denominations in the NCC, WCC and NAE are unthinkable for independent Methodist churches, on any level of local church activity or in any kind or degree of participation.

Notes: *The Asbury Bible Churches, the congregations served by the John Wesley Fellowship (a ministerial fellowship), and many otherwise independent Methodist congregations (particularly those in the southeastern United States), have taken their doctrinal statement from* Guidelines for Independent Methodist Church, *compiled by Thomas L. Baird (Colonial Heights, VA: The Author, 1971). This volume, in turn, was taken largely from* The Doctrines and Discipline of the Southern Methodist Church. *The doctrinal section of the* Guidelines *includes the Twenty-five Articles of Religion common to Methodism as well as the additional doctrinal statements made by the Southern Methodist Church (SMC), with two exceptions. The SMC statement on racial segregation have been rewritten and expanded, and a statement on biblical "separation" from apostasy was added.*

* * *

OUR BELIEFS (ASSOCIATION OF INDEPENDENT METHODISTS)

We believe the Bible is the infallible Word of God, inerrant in the originals.

We believe that there is one God, eternally existent in three persons, Father, Son and Holy Spirit.

We believe in the deity of Jesus Christ, His virgin birth, His blood-atoning death, His bodily resurrection, His ascension and His premillennial return.

We believe that Jesus Christ is the only Savior and the only Way to salvation and everlasting life.

We believe that salvation is by grace through faith in the blood atonement of Christ with repentance of sins.

We believe in the Biblical account of creation and all other supernatural acts of God recorded in the Scriptures.

We believe that man was created a free moral agent and remains so all the days of his life, with the God given freedom to choose or reject God throughout one's life.

We believe and practice two ordinances: Baptism (choice of mode) and the Lord's Supper.

We believe in the resurrection of both the saved and the lost; the saved to eternal life and the lost to eternal damnation.

We hold to the traditional twenty-five articles of belief.

We believe in free America. We love and respect our nation, its' leaders, its' laws, its' flag and its' Constitution.

We believe that the believer may be cleansed from all sin through the sanctifying power of the blood of Christ and the work of the Holy Spirit.

Notes: *The Association of Independent Methodists represents a very conservative group who rejected the merger of the Methodist Episcopal Church, South, with what it considered a very liberal (in both doctrine and social policy) Methodist Episcopal Church. The Association's statement of beliefs follows that of nineteenth-century Methodism in general, though its statement on Biblical authority reflects some Protestant fundamentalist influence.*

* * *

DOCTRINAL STATEMENT (BIBLE PROTESTANT CHURCH)

1. We believe the Bible in the original tongues to be the verbally inspired Word of God, and the only infallible rule of faith and Practice, (2 Timothy 3:14-16).

2. We believe that God is Triune; that there are three eternal, co-equal, Divine persons in the Godhead, and these three are one God, (Matthew 28:19).

3. We believe in the Deity of the Lord Jesus Christ; that He was conceived of the Holy Spirit and born of the Virgin Mary, (John 1 and Matthew 1).

4. We believe that the only way to be saved is by faith in the blood sacrifice, death and resurrection of Jesus Christ, the Son of God, and that to those who thus become His sheep He says, "I give unto them eternal life; and they shall never perish, neither shall any man pluck them out of my hand," (John 10:28, Ephesians 2:8,9).

5. We believe that our Lord Jesus Christ ascended into Heaven, and is now seated at the right hand of the Father; that He ever liveth to make intercession for all that come to God by Him, (Acts 1:9-11, Hebrews 4:14, Ephesians 1:20,21).

6. We believe that the Church which is the Body of Christ began with the descent of the Holy Spirit on the Day of Pentecost and that each one who receives the Lord Jesus Christ as his personal Saviour is a member of the Body of Christ, and is indwelled by the Holy Spirit, (I Corinthians 12:12-28, 6:19,20).

7. We believe that the Gospel commission is for the Church; that the Lord's Supper and water Baptism are Divine Institutions and that Christ desires us to practice them in this age, (Matthew 28:18-20, I Corinthians 11:23-29).

8. We believe that Christ may at any moment return in the air to rapture the Saints, and that a tribulation period of approximately seven years shall follow, after which He will come to the earth with His Saints, and rule for a thousand years. After this the wicked will be judged and cast into the lake of fire, (I Thessalonians 4:13-18, I Corinthians 15:51-57, Daniel 9:27, Matthew 24:15-21, 24:27, 25:46, Revelation 19:11, 20:10-15).

9. We believe that Satan is a person, the author of the fall, and that he shall be eternally punished, (Job 1:7, Genesis 3:1-19, Revelation 20:10).

10. We believe in the bodily resurrection of the dead, both of the just and the unjust; and in the eternal conscious punishment of the lost and the eternal joy of the saved, (Revelation 20:11-15, 22:12-14, I Corinthians 15:1-58).

Notes: *The Bible Protestant Church consists of congregations that rejected the merger of the Methodist Protestant Church in 1939. Subsequently, its doctrinal position moved toward Protestant fundamentalism.*

ARTICLES OF FAITH AND PRACTICE (CHURCH OF DANIEL'S BAND)

1. THE HOLY TRINITY

There is but one living and true God, everlasting in infinite power, wisdom and goodness; the maker and preserver of all things, visible and invisible. And in unity of this godhead there are three persons of one substance, power and eternity-the Father, the Son (the Word) and the Holy Ghost. I Cor. viii, 4-6; John xvii, 3, 1; Tim. i, John iv, 24.

2. THE WORD, OR SON OF GOD

The Son, who is the Word of Father, the very and eternal God of one substance with the Father, took man's nature in the womb of the blessed virgin, so that two whole and perface natures, that is to say, the godhead and manhood were joined together one person never to be divided whereof is one Christ God and very man who truly suffered, was crucified, dead and buried to reconcile us to his Father and to be a sacrifice not only for original guilt but also for the actual sins of men. John i, 14-18; chap. iii, 16; Luke i, 27-31, 35; Gal. iv, 4-5; Heb. vii, 27; Rom. v, 10.

3. RESURRECTION OF CHRIST

Christ did truly rise from the dead, taking his body with all things appertained to the perfection of man's nature, wherewith he ascended into heaven, and there sitteth until he return to judge all men at the last day. Acts x, 39-42.

4. THE HOLY GHOST

The Holy Ghost, proceeding from the Father and the Son, is one of substance, majesty and glory, with the Father and the Son, very and eternal God. Acts ii, 2-4.

5. THE SUFFICIENCY OF THE HOLY SCRIPTURES FOR SALVATION

The Holy Scriptures contain all things necessary to salvation, for it is written, "search the scriptures, for in them ye think ye have eternal life, and they are they which testify of me." John v, 39. By the Holy Scriptures we do mean and understand those canonical Books of the Old and New Testament of whose authority there is no doubt in the church. 2 Tim. iii, 15-17.

6. OF THE OLD TESTAMENT

The Old Testament is not contrary to the new; for both in the Old and New Testaments everlasting life is offered to mankind through Christ, who is the only mediator between God and man. Wherefore, they are not to be heard, who feign that the old fathers did look for only transitory promises. 1 Tim. ii, 5; Heb. xi, 39-40.

7. OF ORIGINAL AND ACQUIRED DEPRAVITY

Original depravity is the corruption of the moral nature inherited by every human being, because of Adam's disobedience to the law of God, whereby every man is wholly gone from original righteousness, and without grace, inclined to evil and that continually. Acquired depravity is all the thoughts of our defiled minds resulting from the original depravity of our moral nature. Tit. i, 15; Matt. xv, 19; Rom. iii, 10-18.

8. OF FREE WILL

Man having become so completely ruined, has neither the will nor the power to turn to God, and if left to himself would remain in his wretched and miserable condition forever. But blessed thought, the grace of God that bringeth salvation, hath appeared to all men; hence, God graciously employs the means of enlightening and awakening the mind of the sinner to a sense of his poverty and wretchedness through preaching (1 Cor. 1, 21) it pleased God by the foolishness of preaching to save them that believe. John vi, 44.

9. OF REPENTANCE

This consists of Godly sorrow for sin, and forsaking it by turning to God. 2 Cor. vii, 9, 10.

10. OF CONVERSION

This consists in the forgiveness of actual transgressions of the law, and the regeneration "which is the new birth" of the soul by the Holy Ghost, in which all the corruption of the past sinful life is removed, and the new life implanted. John i, 13.

11. OF ENTIRE SANCTIFICATION

This entire cleansing is the work of the Holy Ghost by which the hereditary body of sin, or inherited depravity, is removed from the flesh. Romans, viii, 21; 2 Cor. iv, 10-11; 1 John iv, 2-3; 2 John i, 7.

12. OF GOOD WORK

Good works are not a condition of salvation, but are the natural fruits of regeneration. Matt. v, 16.

13. OF SIN AFTER CONVERSION

Not every error fallen into after conversion is unpardonable; wherefore repentance is granted to such as fall into error; they may fall therein, and by the grace of God, rise again to obedience. 1 John Chp. 2, verse 1.

14. OF THE RESURRECTION OF THE DEAD

There will be a resurrection of the dead, both of the just and the unjust, at which time the souls and bodies of men will be united to receive together a just retribution for the deeds done in the body in this life. 1 Thess. iv, 14, 15, 17; Rev. xx, 6.

15. FUTURE REWARD AND PUNISHMENT

God has appointed a day in which He will judge the world in righteousness by Jesus Christ according to the Gospel. The righteous shall have in Heaven an inheritance incorruptible, undefiled and that fadeth not away. The wicked shall go away into everlasting punishment, where the worm dieth not, and their fire is not quenched. Matt. xxv, 45-46; Rev. xxi, 6-8.

16. THE CHURCH OF JESUS CHRIST

The Church of Jesus Christ consists of all people that are born again. John iii, 3.

17. SACRAMENTS

Sacraments ordained of Christ are badges and tokens of Christian man's professions, and to them who rightly discern the Lord's body; they are a means used of him to strengthen and confirm our love.. Matt. xxvi, 26, 27, 28; Matt. xxviii, 19; 1 Cor. xi, 26, 26. There are two sacraments ordained of Christ our Lord in the Gospel, that is to say, Baptism, and the Supper of the Lord.

18. OF BAPTISM

Baptism is not only a sign of profession, and mark of difference, whereby Christians are distinguished from others who are not baptised, but is also a sign of regeneration or new birth. Liberty of conscience will be allowed as to the mode of baptism, except in the baptism of young children, the mode shall be left with the preacher. Matt. iii, 11; Acts x, 47-48.

19. OF THE LORD'S SUPPER

The Supper of the Lord is a sign of love that his children have for one another, and when rightly discerned as an emblem of the broken body of Christ, does communicate grace and love to the heart. 1 Cor. x. 16.

20. OF THE RITES AND CEREMONIES OF CHURCHES

It is not necessary that rites and ceremonies should in all places be the same or exactly alike; for they have always been different and may be changed according to the diversities of countries, times and men's manners, so that nothing be ordained against God's word. Each particular church may ordain, change or abolish rites and ceremonies so that all things be done to edification. Roman xiv, 4, 17; Acts xv, 10; Gal. v, 1, 13; 1 Peter ii, 16.

21. OF CHRISTIAN MEN'S GOODS

The goods of Christians are not common as touching the rights, title and possession of the same, as some do falsely boast. But what they have belongs to God, and as his stewards they should use that entrusted to their care with an eye single to his glory. Romans xv, 26; 1 Timothy vi, 17-18; James i, 10; Acts iv, 32.

22. OF DIVINE HEALING

The scriptures plainly declare, "The prayer of faith shall save the sick" All of God's children should be exorted to lay hold upon this promise. James v, 14; Acts iii, 1-9.

23. OF ORDINATION

A minister must set in the class three Consecutive years before Ordination Amendment, if it be necessary we can ordain any minister born in our own organization at any time.

24. OF THE SUPPORT OF THE GOSPEL

The support of the Gospel consists in the offering of ourselves a living sacrific to God, with all that God has instrusted us with as stewards, to be used with an eye single to his glory. Phil. iv, 10-13; Rom. xii, 1-2; 2 Cor. xi, 9; 2 Cor. ix, 5-9.

25. OF MARRIAGE

Holy Matrimony is a sacred institution of divine origin, and no believer should enter into this sacred agreement without positive leadings from God in harmony with His Word which commands his children to marry "only in the Lord". 2 Cor. vi, 14; Duet. xxii, 10.

26. OF DIVORCE

See Matthew, nineteenth chapter, third to twelfth verses inclusive.

27. OF INTEMPERANCE

Intemperance is excess in any kind of action or indulgence; any exertion of body or mind, or any indulgence of appetites or passions which is injurious to the person or contrary to the law of God. 1 Cor. ix, 25.

28. OF CONFORMITY TO THE WORLD

We are as Christians earnestly and lovingly exhorted to be not conformed to this world, but to be transformed by the renewing of our minds, that we may prove what is that good and acceptable and perfect will of God. See Romans xii, 2.

29. OF THE CALL TO THE MINISTRY

There is abundant evidence in the scriptures that God calls whom he will to preach the Gospel, both men and women. And such as he calls and qualifies only can be effective in bringing souls into the Kingdom of God. Consequently the sisters called should have all the privileges given the brethren. Rom. x, 15.

30. LAYING ON OF HANDS

We recognize scriptural authority for the laying on of hands for the gift of the Holy Ghost, for the healing of the sick and in setting apart for the work of the ministry of those called of God. James v, 14; Acts vi, 5-6; Acts xix, 6.

31. OF SALARIED MINISTERS

We believe it to be the duty of the societies to support their ministers, as the laborer is worthy of his hire.

32. OF QUORUM

That when any Annual Conference is called six members present will constitute a quorum.

33. MINISTER SUPPORT

That the classes desiring a minister to serve them should be responsible for the minister getting to the next Annual Conference.

34. PRESIDENT TRANSPORTATION

That the church circuits raise ten dollars or more and send the same to the President to bear his expenses to and from the quarterly conference.

> Amendment to the above resolution: That the amount raised by the church circuit for the President's expenses in case of his absence can be given to the one substituting in his place. Also, if the church circuit cannot raise the ten dollars, but the President is willing to travel for less, the matter can be settled between them.

35. GENERAL FUND

That each and every class of the Church of Daniel's Band take up one offering each and every month for fund and this money be sent to the conference secretary to be used for the building of new classes. Secretary to notify each class who are a month in arrears.

> Amendment to the above resolution: That the head evangelist of the Annual Conference appointed to spend the money sent the order to the President, Secretary, and Treasurer of the Annual Conference.

ARTICLES OF FAITH AND PRACTICE (CHURCH OF DANIEL'S BAND) (continued)

36. CHARGING AN ELDER

That there shall be no charges brought against an Elder only in writing and before calling for reports it should be the duty of the investigating committee to thoroughly investigate both sides of the question separately and also together before any action is taken.

37. OF BANK FAILURE

That any money held by the Church Conference Treasurer belonging to the Church of Daniel's Band shall not be held responsible for money lost in bank failures only to the amount the bank may refund.

Notes: *The statement of the small Church of Daniel's Band, formed in 1893, reflects a desire to make the church's position clear on many matters neglected by the Methodist Articles of Religion, as well as some decisions on financial matters of immediate concern at the time.*

*   *   *

ADDITIONS TO THE *TWENTY-FIVE ARTICLES OF RELIGION* (CONGREGATIONAL METHODIST CHURCH)

As far as respects civil affairs, we believe it the duty of Christians, and especially all Christian ministers, to be subject to the supreme authority of the country where they may reside, and to use all laudable means to enjoin obedience to the powers that be, and therefore it is expected that all our preachers and people, who may be under the British, or any other government, will behave themselves as peaceable and orderly subjects.

Article XXVI. REGENERATION.

"Whereas justification is the judicial act on God's part in that He declares the sinner no longer exposed to the penalty of a broken law because of a new faith relationship to Jesus Christ, regeneration is the instantaneous impartation of spiritual life to the human soul by the Holy Ghost. This experience of grace, sometimes called the (new birth) prepares the human soul for the functions of the new life."

Article XXVII. SANCTIFICATION.

"Entire sanctification is that second definite work of grace, subsequent to regeneration, whereby the heart of a justified person is cleansed from the original or Adamic nature, and is filled with the Holy Ghost."

Article XXVIII. FINANCIAL PLAN FOR THE CHURCH.

The Lord has given the church a financial plan which we believe to be storehouse tithing and free will offerings. (All tithes should go through the church treasury.)

Article XXIX. ETERNAL RETRIBUTION.

The wicked shall have their part in the lake which burneth with fire and brimstone and that everlastingly.

Article XXX. RESURRECTION OF THE DEAD.

There are two resurrections. The first shall be at the pre-millennial second coming of Jesus Christ in which the saved dead shall be resurrected and living saints raptured. The second shall be after the millennium when the unsaved dead will be resurrected at the Great White Throne Judgment.

Notes: *The Congregational Methodist Church, as have most Methodist bodies expanding into foreign lands, experienced difficulties with Article XXIII of the Twenty-five Articles of Religion, which countenanced allegiance to the government of the United States. The church dealt with that problem by placing an addendum to Article XXIII.*

In 1957 the church added five more articles of religion covering, among other matters, sanctification, finances, and eschatology. These additional articles were not accepted by the First Congregational Methodist Church of America, which had left the Congregational Methodist Church in 1941.

*   *   *

ADDITIONS TO THE *TWENTY-FIVE ARTICLES OF RELIGION* (EVANGELICAL METHODIST CHURCH)

XXIII. OF THE DUTY OF CHRISTIANS TO THE CIVIL AUTHORITY.

It is the duty of all Christians, and especially of all Christian ministers, to observe and obey the laws and commands of the governing or supreme authority of the country of which they are citizens or subjects, or in which they reside, and to use all laudable means to encourage and enjoin obedience to the powers that be.

XXVI. PERFECT LOVE.

46.   Perfect love is that renewal of our fallen nature by the Holy Spirit, received through faith in Jesus Christ, whose blood of atonement cleanseth from all sin; whereby we are not only delivered from the guilt of sin, but are washed from its pollution, saved from its power, and are enabled, through grace, to love God with all our hearts and to walk in His holy commandments blameless.

Notes: *The Evangelical Methodist Church adopted the Twenty-five Articles of Religion common to all Methodists, and subsequently prepared a substitute for Article XXIII, "Of the Rulers of the United States of America," for use by member churches in foreign lands. In addition, the church added an article and explanatory footnote on the distinctly Wesleyan doctrine of "Perfect Love."*

*   *   *

ADDITIONS TO THE *TWENTY-FIVE ARTICLES OF RELIGION* (EVANGELICAL METHODIST CHURCH OF AMERICA)

Article XXIII. OF THE DUTY OF CHRISTIANS TO THE CIVIL AUTHORITY.

It is the duty of all Christians, and especially of all Christian ministers, to observe and obey the laws and commands of the governing or supreme authority of the country of which they are citizens or subjects, or in which they reside, so long as they are not contrary to the Word of God. (Acts 5:29)

Notes: *Like many Methodist bodies who adopted the Twenty-five Articles of Religion, a new article for members in foreign lands has been adopted as a substitute for Article XXIII, "Of the Rulers of the United States of America."*

* * *

ARTICLES OF RELIGION (FUNDAMENTAL METHODIST CHURCH)

1. OF FAITH IN THE HOLY TRINITY

There is but one living and true God, everlasting, of infinite power, wisdom and goodness, the maker and preserver of all things, visible and invisible. And in unity of this Godhead, there are three persons of one substance, power and eternity—the Father, the Son, and the Holy Ghost.

2. OF THE WORD, OR THE SON OF GOD, WHO WAS MADE VERY MAN

The Son, who is the Word of the Father, the very and eternal God, of one substance with the Father, took man's nature in the womb of the blessed virgin; so that two whole and perfect natures, that is to say, the Godhead and manhood, were joined together in one person, never to be divided, whereof is one Christ, very God and very man who truly suffered, was crucified, died, and was buried, to reconcile us to God, and to be a sacrifice, not only for original guilt, but also for the actual sins of men.

3. OF THE RESURRECTION OF CHRIST

Christ did truly rise again from the dead, and took again his body, with all things appertaining to the perfection of man's nature, wherewith he ascended into heaven, and there sitteth until he returns to judge all men at the last day.

4. OF THE HOLY GHOST

The Holy Ghost, proceeding from the Father and the Son is of one substance, majesty and glory with the Father and the Son, very and eternal God.

5. THE SUFFICIENCY OF THE HOLY SCRIPTURES FOR SALVATION

The Holy Scriptures contain all things necessary to salvation; so whatsoever is not read therein, nor may be proved thereby, is not to be required of any man that it should be believed as an article of faith, or be thought requisite or necessary to salvation. In the name of the Holy Scriptures, we do understand those canonical books of the Old and New Testament, of whose authority was never any doubt in the church.

The names of the canonical books are: Genesis, Exodus, Leviticus, Numbers, Deuteronomy, Joshua, Judges, Ruth, the First Book of Samuel, the Second Book of Samuel, the First Book of Kings, the Second Book of Kings, the First Book of Chronicles, the Second Book of Chronicles, the Book of Ezra, the Book of Nehemiah, the Book of Esther, the Book of Job, the Psalms, the Proverbs, Ecclesiastes (or the Preacher), Cantica (or Song of Solomon), Four Prophets the Greater, Twelve Prophets the Less; all the books of the New Testament, as they are commonly received, we do receive and account canonical.

6. OF THE OLD TESTAMENT

The Old Testament is not contrary to the New; for in both the Old and New Testament everlasting life is offered to mankind by Christ, who is the only Mediator between God and man, being both God and man. Wherefore they are not to be heard who feign that the old fathers did look for only transitory promises. Although the law given from God by Moses as touching ceremonies and rites doth not bind Christians, nor ought the civil precepts thereof of necessity be received in any commonwealth, yet notwithstanding, no Christian whatsoever is free from obedience of the commandments which are called moral.

7. OF ORIGINAL SIN

Original sin is the corruption of the nature of every man that naturally is engendered of the offspring of Adam, whereby man is very far gone from the original righteousness, and of his own nature inclined to evil, and that continually.

8. OF FREE WILL

The condition of man after the fall of Adam is such that he cannot turn and prepare himself, by his own natural strength and works, to faith and calling upon God; wherefore, we have no power to do good works, pleasant and acceptable to God, without the grace of God by Christ enabling us, that we may have a good will, and working with us, when we have that good will.

9. OF JUSTIFICATION

We are accounted righteous before God, only for the merit of our Lord and Saviour Jesus Christ, by faith, and not for our own works or deservings. Wherefore, that we are justified by faith only is a most wholesome doctrine, and very full of comfort.

10. OF SANCTIFICATION

Sanctification is the setting apart of the regenerated person by the Holy Ghost (or spirit) received through faith in Jesus Christ, whose blood of atonement cleanseth from all sin; whereby we are not only delivered from the guilt of sin, but are washed from its pollution, saved from its power. It is also the continuing of God's grace by which the Christian may constantly grow in grace and in the knowledge of our Lord and Savior Jesus Christ.

11. OF GOOD WORKS

Although good works, which are the fruits of faith, and follow after justification, cannot put away our sins, and endure the severity of God's judgments; yet they are pleasing and acceptable to God in Christ, and spring out of a true and lively faith, insomuch that by them a lively faith may be as evidently known as a tree is discerned by its fruit.

12. OF WORKS OF SUPEREROGATION

Voluntary works—besides, over and above God's commandments—which are called works of supererogation, cannot be taught without arrogancy and impiety. For by them men do declare that they do not only render unto God as much as they are bound to do, but that they do more for his sake than of bounden duty is required;

ARTICLES OF RELIGION (FUNDAMENTAL METHODIST CHURCH) (continued)

whereas, Christ saith plainly, "When ye have done all that is commanded of you, say, 'We are unprofitable servants'."

13. OF SIN AFTER JUSTIFICATION

Not every sin willingly committed after justification is the sin against the Holy Ghost, and unpardonable. Wherefore, the grant of repentance is not to be denied to such as fall into sin after justification. After we have received the Holy Ghost, we may depart from grace given, and fall into sin, and by the grace of God rise again and amend our lives. And therefore they are to be condemned who say they can no more sin as long as they live here; or deny the place of forgiveness to such as truly repent.

14. OF THE CHURCH

The visible Church of Christ is a congregation of faithful men in which the pure Word of God is preached, and the ordinances duly administered according to Christ's command in all those things that of necessity are requisite to the same.

15. OF PURGATORY

The Romish doctrine concerning purgatory, pardon, worshiping and adoration, as well of images, as of relics, and also invocation of saints, is a fond thing vainly invented and grounded upon no warrant of Scripture, but repugnant to the word of God.

16. OF SPEAKING

It is a thing plainly repugnant to the Word of God, and the custom of the primitive church, to have the prayer in the church, or to minister the ordinances, in a tongue not understood by the people.

17. OF THE ORDINANCES

Ordinances of Christ are not only badges or tokens of Christian men's professions: but rather they are certain signs of grace and God's good-will towards us, by which he doth work invisibly in us, and doth not only quicken, but also strengthen and confirm our faith in him.

There are two ordinances of Christ our Lord in the Gospel; that is to say, Baptism and the Supper of the Lord.

18. OF BAPTISM

Baptism by Immersion is not only a sign of profession and mark of difference, whereby Christians are distinguished from others that are not baptized, but it is also a sign of regeneration or the new birth. It is not to be considered the door into the Fundamental Methodist Church. The dedication of young children may be retained in the church, but they are not to be baptized.

19. OF THE LORD'S SUPPER

The Supper of the Lord is not only a sign of the love that Christians ought to have among themselves one to another, but rather is an ordinance of our redemption by Christ's death; insomuch, that to such as rightly, worthily, and with faith receive the same, the bread which we break is a partaking of the body of Christ; and likewise the cup of blessing is the partaking of the blood of Christ.

Transubstantiation, or the change of the substance of bread and wine in the Supper of our Lord, cannot be proved by Holy Writ, but is repugnant to the Plain words of Scripture, overthroweth the nature of the ordinance, and hath given occasion to many superstitions.

The body of Christ is given, taken, and eaten in the Supper, only after a heavenly and spiritual manner. And the means whereby the body of Christ is received and eaten in the Supper is faith.

The Lord's Supper was not by Christ's ordinance reserved, carried about, lifted up, or worshiped.

20. OF BOTH KINDS

The cup of the Lord is not to be denied to the lay people; for both parts of the Lord's Supper by Christ's ordinance and commandment ought to be administered to all Christians alike.

21. OF THE ONE OBLIGATION OF CHRIST FINISHED ON THE CROSS

The offering of Christ, once made, is that perfect redemption, propitiation and satisfaction for all the sins of the whole world, both original and actual; and there is none other satisfaction for sin but that alone. Wherefore the sacrifice of masses, in the which it is commonly said that the priest doth offer Christ for the quick and the dead, to have remission of pain or guilt, is a blasphemous fable and dangerous deceit.

22. OF THE RESURRECTION OF THE DEAD

There shall be two resurrections of the dead, one of the just and the other of the unjust, at which time the souls and bodies will be reunited to receive a just retribution for the deeds done in this life. These resurrections shall be a thousand years apart, according to the Scriptures. (I Thess. 4:16, 17. Rev. 20:5)

23. OF THE JUDGMENTS

There will be a judgment of the saints following the first resurrection at the judgment seat of Christ; then there will be the judgment of the wicked at the great White Throne judgment to adjudge them to everlasting punishment suited to the demerit of their sins. (II Cor. 5:10, Rev. 20:1, 15)

24. OF THE MARRIAGE OF MINISTERS

The ministers of Christ are not commanded by God's law either to vow the state of single life, or to abstain from marriage; therefore, it is lawful for them, as for all Christians, to marry at their own discretion, as they shall judge the same to serve best to godliness.

25. OF THE RITES AND CEREMONIES OF CHURCHES

It is not necessary that rites and ceremonies should in all places be the same, or exactly alike; for they have been always different, and may be changed according to the diversity of countries, times and men's manners, so that nothing be ordained against God's Word. Whosoever, through his private judgment, willingly and purposely doth openly break the rites and ceremonies of the Church to which he belongs, which are not repugnant to the Word of God, and are ordained and approved by common authority, ought to be rebuked openly (that others may fear to do the like), as one that offendeth against the common order of the Church, and woundeth the consciences of weak brethren.

26. OF THE RULERS OF THE UNITED STATES OF AMERICA

The President, the Congress, the General Assemblies, the Governors and the Councils of State, as the delegates of the people, are the rulers of the United States of America, according to the division of power made to them by the Constitution of the United States, and by the Constitution of their respective states. And the said states are a sovereign and independent nation, and ought not to be subject to any foreign jurisdiction.

27. OF CHRISTIAN MEN'S GOODS

The riches and goods of Christians are not common, as touching the right, title and possession of the same, as some do falsely boast. Notwithstanding, every man ought, of such things as he possesseth, liberally to give alms to the poor, according to his ability.

28. OF A CHRISTIAN MAN'S OATH

As we confess that vain and rash swearing is forbidden Christian men by our Lord Jesus Christ, and James his Apostle, so we judge that the Christian religion doth not prohibit, but that a man may swear, or affirm, when the magistrate requireth, in a cause of faith and charity, so it be done according to the prophet's teaching, in justice, judgment and truth.

(Note affixed by the General Conference at Ash Grove, Missouri August 1964)

These articles of religion set forth the doctrinal teachings of the Fundamental Methodist Church, and those who enter the ministry thereof thereby avow their acceptance of the teachings thus formulated; and good faith towards the Church forbids any teaching on their part which is at variance with them.

Notes: *While based upon the Twenty-five Articles of Religion of the United Methodist Church, the Articles of Religion of the Fundamental Methodist Church make enough additions and changes to warrant its inclusion in its entirety. Noteworthy are an article against the practice of speaking in tongues (Pentecostalism) and several on eschatology.*

*   *   *

ADDITIONS TO THE *TWENTY-FIVE ARTICLES OF RELIGION* (SOUTHERN METHODIST CHURCH)

OF PREVENIENT (PRECEDING) GRACE

40. We believe that God must take the initiative if man is to be saved. We believe that since the race fell in Adam and lost all claims to consideration before God, along with the ability in its own strength to return to God, we have in the blessings of life, health, friends, fruitful seasons, prosperity, the delay of punishment, the presence and influence of the Bible, the Holy Spirit, and the church, manifestations of the prevenient grace of God. Prevenient grace is not sufficient for salvation, yet it reveals the goodness of God to all sinful creatures. We believe that the prevenient grace of God constitutes the medium through which the Holy Spirit can operate upon the sinner, and that which makes the soul susceptible to the saving grace of Christ. In other words, we hold that God, in His grace, makes it possible for *all* men to be saved.

Titus 2:11, "For the grace of God that bringeth salvation hath appeared to all men." Gen. 3:8, 9; Isa. 59:15, 16; Rom. 2:4; Prov. 1:23; Isa. 31:6; Eze. 14:6; 18:32; Joel 2:13, 14; Matt. 18:3; Acts 3:19; I Kings 8:47; Matt. 3:2; Mark 1:15; Luke 13:3, 5; Acts 2:38; 17:30; II Chr. 20:20; Isa. 43:10; John 1:9; 6:29; 14:1; Acts 16:31; Phil. 1:29; I John 3:23.

OF REPENTANCE

41. We believe that salvation comes to the individual soul as the free, undeserved gift of God through faith in Christ as a personal Saviour. We do not believe that the sinner is in a proper attitude for the reception of salvation until there is first a change of mind, will, and emotions concerning sin, and this results in a godly sorrow for sin in the heart of the individual.

These changes concerning one's sins constitute the grace of repentance, which grace is wrought in the sinner by the Holy Spirit, and which leads the sinner to forsake his sins and to seek the justifying mercy of God in Christ.

Acts 17:30, "God . . . commandeth all men every where to repent." Rom. 3:20; cf. 1:32; Psm. 51:3,7; Job 42:56; Psm. 51:1,2; II Cor. 7:9, 10; Matt 3:8, 11; Rom. 2:4; II Peter 3:9; Acts 2:38; Rev. 2:5; Acts 11:18; 5:31; II Tim. 2:25; Matt. 11:20, 21; Luke 16:30, 31; Rev. 3:19; John 3:5; Acts 20:21.

OF FAITH

42. We believe that after the Spirit of God has implanted within the human soul the grace of repentance, there remains a condition, on the part of the sinner, namely, belief in the Lord Jesus Christ as personal Saviour.

This belief is infinitely more than a mere mental assent to any doctrine concerning either the person of Christ or of any of His miraculous or atoning works.

Rom. 10:10, "For with the heart man believeth unto righteousness; and with the mouth confession is made unto salvation." Acts 16:31; Eph. 2:8, 9; Rom. 5:1; cf. 9:30, 32; Gal. 3:5, 14; I Peter 1:5; Rom. 11:20; II Cor. 1:24; I John 5:4; Isa. 7:9; II Cor. 5:7; Heb. 11:6; John 16:9; Rom. 14:23; John 7:38; Acts 27:24, 25; Heb. 11:1; Eccl. 1:13; Dan. 2:30; I Kings 3:9; Ex. 35:29; Prov. 4:23; Rom. 10:14; Psm. 9:10; John 2:23. 24; Rom. 10:17; 1:19, 20; 10:14; Psm. 106:12, 13; Matt. 13:20, 21; Mark 12:32-34; John 5:35; Prov. 23:26; Matt. 11:28, 29; Luke 14:26, 33; John 1:12; 4:14; 6:53, 54; Rev. 3:20; II Peter 1:1; John 5:47; Acts 4:4; Heb. 12:2; Judges 6:14; Matt. 25:29; II Thess. 3:2.

ADDITIONS TO THE *TWENTY-FIVE ARTICLES OF RELIGION*
(SOUTHERN METHODIST CHURCH) (continued)

OF REGENERATION

43. When the penitent, believing soul is justified through
the atoning merits of the blood of Christ, simultaneously there takes place within that soul the
washing of regeneration, which work is the act of the
Holy Ghost, and which results in the new creation of
the whole spiritual being.

This definite change in the sinner is referred to in the
Word of God as "the new birth" or "being born
again." Although the believer is truly born of God
and is definitely His child at the time of regeneration,
he is but a babe in Christ, and God desires that His
babes reach maturity. If there is to be maturity, the
seed of holiness that has been sown in the heart in
regeneration must be permitted to germinate and
spring up, and with a prayerful cultivation and
studying of God's Word, under the bountiful showers of God's grace, produce a full harvest of the fruit
of the Spirit.

II Cor. 5:17, "Therefore if any man be in Christ, he
is a new creature; old things are passed away; behold,
all things are become new." John 3:3; James 1:18;
John 3:14-16; I Peter 1:3; I Cor. 4:15; Titus 3:5; I
John 3:9; 5:4, 18; 5:1; Psm. 119:97; Matt. 5:44; 7:11;
Rom. 8:16, 17.

OF THE WITNESS OF THE SPIRIT

44. We believe that a penitent sinner is saved the
moment he believes upon Christ as his personal
Saviour, however; he cannot have full assurance that
he has passed from death unto life until the Holy
Spirit, Himself, gives him this assurance. Our souls
must hear a more authoritative voice and have a
more compelling evidence than that which came
from our own feeble human senses.

Rom. 8:16, "The Spirit itself beareth witness with
our spirit, that we are the children of God." John
3:5, 6; Titus 3:5; I John 1:3; I Cor. 1:9; Gal. 4:6; John
16:12, 13; I Cor. 2:12.

OF CHRISTIAN PERFECTION OR
SANCTIFICATION OR CONSECRATION OR
DEDICATION OR PERFECT LOVE OR TOTAL
YIELDEDNESS

45. Christian perfection is that work of the Holy Spirit
which is subsequent to regeneration, and is wrought
when the believer presents himself a living sacrifice,
holy and acceptable unto God, and is thus enabled
through grace to love God with all his heart.
Methodists have always been very clear and positive
in their teachings that this is not angelic, adamic,
faultless perfection, but rather that Christian perfection where the soul is filled with the love of God and
all its faculties are spiritualized through the fullness
of God's presence within. While in this state, God is
loved with every faculty of one's being, and one's
neighbors are loved as one's self.

I John 1:9, "If we confess our sins, He is faithful and
just to forgive us our sins, and to cleanse us from all
unrighteousness." Gen. 17:1; Duet. 36; Psm. 138;
Ezek. 36:25-29; Matt. 5:48; Luke 1:74, 75; John 17:2-
23; Rom. 8:3, 4; 11:26; I Cor. 6:11; 14:20; Eph. 4:13,
24; 5:25-27; Phil. 2:5, 7; Col. 4:12; I Thess. 3:10;
5:23; II Thess. 2:13; II Tim. 3:17; Titus 2:12; Heb.
9:13, 14; 10:14, 18:22; James 1:27; 4:8; I Peter 1:10;
II Peter 1:4; I John 1:7; 3:8, 9; 4:17, 18; Jude 24.

OF THE UNIVERSALITY OF THE ATONEMENT

46. We believe that God is a mighty God, and that He is
unlimited in greatness, grandeur, and power; that He
is loving and benevolent and is seeking wholeheartedly and continuously for the highest well-being and
the eternal happiness of all His moral creatures. We
believe that in keeping with His benevolent nature,
God has given His only begotten Son, not for a few
favored ones, but for the whole world, that "whosoever believeth in Him should not perish, but have
everlasting life," John 3:16.

We believe that in order to enable His moral
creatures to avail themselves of this salvation in His
Son, God has given to everyone a power of choice—
the ability to choose or reject salvation and spiritual
life in Christ. This power being given to Adam, it
will be possessed by each one of his sons and
daughters throughout all time.

We believe that even though God foreknows all
things, His foreknowledge in no way affects the
destiny of any soul. Even though the Holy Spirit
works upon the will, mind, and emotions of man, He
does not work to the point of absolute compulsion.
Man's will, mind, and emotions, being aroused and
fully awakened by the Holy Spirit, must cooperate
with Him. There must be a full and mutual agreement between the two before the human party can
become the beneficiary of salvation. God works,
while the believing heart of man responds. "For it is
God which worketh in you both to will and to do of
His good pleasure," Phil. 2:13.

Thus, we do not believe in unconditional predestination, but we do believe that when the conditions of
salvation are fully met by the sinner, that sinner is
then elected to be saved.

I Tim. 4:10; John 1:29; I Tim. 2:6; Titus 2:11; II
Peter 2:1; 3:9; Heb. 2:9; I John 2:2; II Cor. 5:18-20.

OF PERSEVERANCE

47. We believe that every true child of God, being a free
moral agent, may, and will be saved eternally, if he
meets the divine conditions of repentance and faith
until the last. Habitual and final failure to meet these
basic conditions will bring eternal loss. We believe
also that although a Christian is now in a state of
salvation, and would be saved eternally if called
before God in his present state, he must be kept
under the saving power of the Holy Ghost until the
last, if he would be saved eternally hereafter. All who
in their obedience to the Holy Spirit faithfully meet

these conditions until death will inherit everlasting life.

Heb. 6:4-6, "For it is impossible for those who were once enlightened . . . if they shall fall away, to renew them again unto repentance . . . " I Chron. 28:9; Ezek. 18:24, 33; 12:13, 18; Matt. 5:13; Luke 9:62; John 15:1-6; Rom. 11:20-22; I Cor. 9:27; 10:12; I Tim. 1:19, 20; 5:12, 15; II Tim. 1:14, 15; Heb. 4:1, 11; 10:26-29, 38, 39; 12:14, 15; II Peter 1:8-10; 2:18-22; Rev. 2:4, 5; 3:10, 11.

OF THE CHURCH

48. The visible church of Christ is a congregation of faithful men, in which the pure Word of God is preached, and the sacraments duly administered according to Christ's ordinance, in all those things that of necessity are requisite to the same.

By the invisible church is understood all those who are known of Christ as belonging to Him, whether they have joined the visible church or not.

I Cor. 12:27, "Now ye are the body of Christ, and members in particular." II Tim. 2:19; Eph. 4:12, 13; 5:26, 27; Heb. 12:22-24; I John 3:2, 3; Rev. 19:7, 8; I Tim. 3:15; Col. 2:16-19.

OF INSPIRATION

49. We believe in the original manuscripts of the Bible as the inerrant Word of God, verbally inspired; by this we mean that inexplicable power which the divine Spirit put forth of old on the authors of Holy Scripture, in order to guide them even in the employment of the words they used, and to preserve them alike from all error and from all omission. We recognize the King James Version of the Bible as a trustworthy translation and we recommend that it be read from the pulpit.

I Peter 1:23, "Being born again . . . by the word of God, which liveth and abideth for ever." Deut. 27:26; II Kings 17:13; Psm. 19:7; 33:4; 119:89; Isa. 8:20; Gal. 3:10; II Peter 3:15, 16; II Tim. 3:16; II Peter 1:20, 21; John 10:34, 35; Luke 24:44; Matt. 5:17; 10:34; 12:34; 15:25; I Cor. 14:21; James 4:5; I John 3:24; Jude 19; Acts 2:4; I Cor. 2:13; 14:37; Gal. 1:12; I Thess. 2:13; 4:2, 8; Rev. 21:5; 22:6, 18, 19.

OF EVANGELIZATION OF THE WORLD

50. We believe in the evangelization of the world, placing emphasis upon the task of reaching the individual with the gospel and its implications, and that no humanitarian and philanthropic schemes may be substituted for the preaching of the Cross.

Mark 16:15, ". . . go ye into all the world, and preach the gospel to every creature." Matt. 28:19; Luke 24:46-48; Acts 1:8; 15:14; Rom. 11:25; Matt. 9:38; Phil. 4:15-18; Rom. 10:15; Matt. 5:13-16; I Cor. 3:9, 10; Eph. 4:11-16; Rev. 22:17.

OF CREATION

51. We believe in the Genesis account of creation, which teaches that all things found their origin in God, Who created by His own fiat instantaneously every living thing after its kind.

Gen. 1:1, 2, "In the beginning God created the heaven and the earth. And the earth was without form, and void . . . " Neh. 9:6; Col. 1:16, 17; Job 38:7; Ezek. 28:12-15; Isa. 14:9-14, 26; 5:18; Psm. 102:18; 139:13-16; Isa. 43:1, 7; 54:16; Ezek. 21:30; John 1:3; Acts 17:24; Rom. 11:36; Eph. 3:9; Rev. 4:11; Psm. 10:30; 148:5.

OF THE SECOND COMING OF CHRIST

52. We believe, according to Scripture, in the sure return of the Lord Jesus Christ; that his second coming will be a literal, bodily, personal, imminent, and premillennial return; that His coming for His bride, the church, constitutes the "blessed hope" set before us, for which we should be constantly looking.

Acts 1:11, ". . . this same Jesus, which is taken up from you into heaven, shall so come in like manner as ye have seen him go into heaven." John 14:1-3; Job 19:25-27; Dan. 12:1-4; Psm. 17:15; Isa. 11:1-12; Zech. 14:1-11; Matt. 24:1-51; 26:64; Mark 13:26-37; Luke 17:26-37; 21:24-36; Acts 1:9-11; I Cor. 1:7, 8; I Thess. 4:13-18; Titus 2:11-14; Heb. 9:27, 28; James 5:7, 8; II Peter 3:1-14; I John 3:2, 3; Jude 14; Rev. 1:7; 19:11-16; 22:6, 7, 12, 20.

OF SATAN, ANGELS, AND DEMONS

53. We believe in the reality of the person of good angels, bad angels, demons, and of Satan, "that old serpent, called the Devil, and Satan, which deceiveth the whole world." Rev. 12:9.

OF TITHING

54. We subscribe heartily to the scriptural command to give the tithe of all our increases to the Lord and the ongoing of His work on earth. Of course, we acknowledge that this law does not bind one saved by grace, but we hasten to say that this would be a poor excuse to do less for One whom we profess to love and One who gave His all for our salvation. We wish to state further that we believe that we are not giving until we have first tithed. We should also remember that God challenges us to try Him and see that He will pour upon those who do more than they can receive. So we conclude that a professed Christian who does not tithe is falling far short of the goal set for us, and thus misses the fullness of the abundant life in Christ.

OF SEGREGATION

55. The Southern Methodist Church is a segregated church. We do not believe that integration, for which so many are clamoring, is the answer to current social problems. In fact, it is our opinion that integration would produce more problems than it would solve.

OF SEPARATION

56. We believe that in these days of apostasy the church should be separated from compromising situations in the world. II Cor. 6:11-18; I Cor. 3:1-3; Rom. 16:17; II Thess. 3:6-9, 14, 15; Eph. 5:11; Titus 3:10, 11; Acts 15:19-29; II John 9-11.

ADDITIONS TO THE *TWENTY-FIVE ARTICLES OF RELIGION* (SOUTHERN METHODIST CHURCH) (continued)

Notes: *Besides the addition of a statement on civic duty for foreign members of the church, the Southern Methodist Church has added a variety of doctrinal statements to the Twenty-five Articles of Religion. These are set apart from the articles in a separate section of* The Doctrine and Discipline of the Southern Methodist Church *under the heading, "Other Southern Methodist Beliefs." Included is a belief in racial segregation.*

* * *

CONFESSIONAL STATEMENT (WESLEY BIBLICAL SEMINARY)

"We hold the following:

"1. The supreme authority of the Word of God which stands written in the sixty-six books of the Holy Bible, all therein being divinely inspired by Almighty God and therefore without error or defect in the autographs. Believing the Bible to be the Word of God written, the only infallible rule of faith and practice, Wesley Biblical Seminary asserts the authority of Scripture alone over the life of the Church and its individual members. We therefore believe that a reverent and loyal approach to the study of the Bible recognizes and affirms its full inspiration and its absolute trustworthiness as the divinely revealed and authoritative Word of God.

"2. The one true God as Creator, Sustainer and Sovereign Ruler of the Universe, eternally existent in the Holy Trinity of Father, Son, and Holy Spirit, each with personality and deity.

"3. The Son of God, our Lord Jesus Christ, as manifested in the flesh through a miraculous conception by the Holy Spirit and virgin birth, who lived a sinless life and then died on Calvary, making a full and satisfactory atonement for the sins of all men, rose bodily the third day, ascended into Heaven and is enthroned at God's right hand as our abiding Intercessor.

"4. The Holy Spirit as the Lord and Giver of life, taking the things of Jesus Christ and applying them to man and to his salvation and service. Assurance of personal salvation and the fruit of the Spirit are clearly distinguished from the gifts of the Spirit which are for the edification of the Church and which carry no guarantee of personal holiness or destiny.

"5. The special original creation of man in God's image and likeness and the willful disobedience through which man became deeply fallen and tragically lost apart from God's redeeming grace.

"6. The privilege and necessity of each person's being made a new creature in Christ by the life-giving Holy Spirit, adopted into God's family, and delivered from the penalty and practice of sinning. In this context

sinning is regarded as known, willful violation of the will of God.

"7. The second definite work of grace subsequent to regeneration, accomplished by the baptism with the Holy Spirit, thereby purifying the heart from original sin and empowering for continuous growth in grace, victorious living and fruitful service. The result of this epochal experience—termed perfect love and/or entire sanctification—is maintained by faith as expressed in continuous obedience to God's revealed will, thus giving perfect cleansing moment by moment (Acts 15:8-9; I Thessalonians 5:23; I John 1:7-9; 4:13-21). Life in the Spirit is dynamically expressed in maturing and enabling grace to progress from glory to glory in personal holiness and Christian mission (II Corinthians 3:18).

"8. The possibility of forfeiting divine grace and being lost since persons are Christians solely by their willing response to the gracious call and enablings of the Holy Spirit. However, backsliders may be restored to their forfeited state of grace if they truly repent and return to the Lord in obedient faith.

"9. The Church as the living body of Christ, constituting all who are united by faith to Him as members of His body and who are under the commandment to love one another with pure and fervent hearts. While in its spiritual essence the Church is an organism created by the Holy Spirit, it is also a divine-human institution functioning visibly on earth. As an institution its divinely assigned mission is the universal proclamation of the Gospel. Application of the Gospel in the political, social, and economic needs of mankind is inherently proper, but secondary and subservient to its primarily spiritual commission.

"10. At the end of this Age, the return of Jesus Christ to gather His Church, to judge the world and to rule over all in righteousness.

"11. The everlasting blessedness of all who die in Christ and the everlasting pain and loss of all others.

"12. The obligation of all who are truly Christ's to live righteously, joyously, and sacrificially, to endeavor to bring salvation to all persons everywhere, and to express compassionate love in ministering to every kind of human need.

"13. No change shall be allowed or made in this Doctrinal Statement of Wesley Biblical Seminary."

Notes: *The Wesley Biblical Seminary is closely associated with the Methodist Protestant Church. Wesley's position is representative of a conservative holiness position held by Methodists in various conservative denominations across the South and to a lesser extent, the United States. Each member of the faculty must ascribe to the statement.*

Black Methodism

ADDITIONS TO THE *TWENTY-FIVE ARTICLES OF RELIGION* (AFRICAN METHODIST EPISCOPAL CHURCH)

FOOTNOTE TO ARTICLE XXIII

Obedience to Civil Government, however, is one of the principal duties of all men, and was honored by our Lord and His Apostles. Though differing in form and policy, all righteous governments rightfully command the obedience, loyalty, support, and defense of all Christian men and women as that they control and protect.

SPECIAL DECLARATION ON APOSTOLIC SUCCESSION

WHEREAS, We have heard with deep regret the dogma of Apostolic Succession and the distinct and separate priesthood of the ministry preached in our pulpit, and

WHEREAS, There are those among us members of this body who are said to be seeking reordination at the hands of the Episcopal Bishops, and Bishops of the Protestant Episcopal Church.

WHEREAS, We have strong reasons for believing that what is thus reported has some foundation in fact, therefore be it

Resolved, By this, Eighteenth General Conference now assembled, that we set forth the following declarations and that any person or persons who are not in harmony with the same or cannot subscribe thereto are hereby declared out of harmony with the standards of Methodism and are liable to impeachment for propagating error and sowing dissension to wit:

We hold and believe that there is no separate priesthood under the Christian symbol set over the Church. That the sacerdotal theory of the Christian ministry is a dishonor to our Lord Jesus and is especially condemned by the tenor of the Epistle to the Hebrews.

Second—That while there is a separate ministry in the New Testament representing the universal priesthood or membership of the Church, yet as has been affirmed above, each and every member is a king and priest under God.

Third—That we recognize the two orders and the one office in our church to be the regularly ordained ministry, and that we are satisfied with the ordinations of the same, holding it to be valid and true in every respect.

Fourth—That the doctrine of Apostolic Succession, according to our belief as Methodists, is erroneous. That there is an uninterrupted succession of ministers which the divine eye can trace up to the Apostolic times, there can be no doubt. But it is utterly impossible to prove that in any part of the world there is a ministry that can trace its orders up through episcopal hands to the Apostles.

Fifth—"That the Apostles had and could have no successors from the fact that their authority, indicated in two ways, was first to teach Christianity by words and writing, for which they had the gift of inspiration in a special sense; and secondly, to found the church, for which they had the power of the keys of binding and loosing, that is, of

uttering unchangeable decrees of ecclesiastical government; that a succession of such men would not have been in harmony with the known will of Christ."

Sixth—That there is an identity between the Bishops and Elders or Presbyters as is evident from Acts 20:17-28; Titus 1:5-7; First Peter 5:1, 2; Phil. 1:1; First Timothy 3:1-8. But as every body must have a head, the Bishops among us are Primus Inter Pares—"Chief among the Elders."

Seventh—That a reordination of any Bishop, Elder, or Deacon by any other ecclesiastical authority cannot and will not be tolerated in the African Methodist Episcopal Church.

Eighth—Any person or persons who shall violate these Declarations by preaching the Dogma of Apostolic Succession shall be guilty of a breach of Discipline and shall be tried and, if found guilty, be suspended or expelled at the discretion of the committee before whom such person or persons shall be tried.

RITUALISM

WHEREAS, We believe that the doctrines, practices, usages, and genius of American Methodism as believed, observed, and conformed to by the founders of African Methodism and their successors to the present day, should in their entirety without modification, restriction, or enlargement, be believed, practiced, and conformed to by us and by those entrusted with the continued preservation and development of African Methodism in its historic and progressive relations, and

WHEREAS, We further believe that in all things essential as touching the doctrines, government, services, order and work of the African Methodist Episcopal Church there should be oneness of purpose, concurrent opinion, continuity of methods and harmony of feeling and relation between the several factors that compose the whole,

Resolved: First—we hold as the result of our best knowledge based upon the facts of history and the teachings of experience, (the same resulting primarily from the origin and development of American Methodism and secondarily from Methodism), that it is highly expedient we set forth the concurrent beliefs, practices, and usages of African Methodism; and in view of this, we do not hesitate to affirm that the Dogma of Apostolic Succession is foreign and repugnant to the concurrent beliefs and teachings of the African Methodist Episcopal Church, and that no Bishop or preacher shall be allowed to publicly proclaim opinions and views favorable thereto.

Second—As touching the usages and practices of the African Methodist Episcopal Church, we are free to aver that while it is desirable to secure uniformity in the order of the public services and to enlist, so far as possible, the thought and spirit of the people in the same, and while we grant that the orderly repetition of the Decalogue, the Apostles' Creed, and the Responsive Reading of the Scriptures may conduce to the attainment therefore, we strenuously deny that the presence and use of heavy and prosy ritualistic service in our public congregations will in any sense increase their spiritual interest and we deprecate any and all efforts that favor the introduction of extreme ritualism in connection with our public services.

ADDITIONS TO THE *TWENTY-FIVE ARTICLES OF RELIGION* **(AFRICAN METHODIST EPISCOPAL CHURCH) (continued)**

Third—That all laws or parts of laws in conflict with the spirit and language of these resolutions be and the same are hereby repealed. General Conference, 1884.

Notes: *As a group, the black Methodist denominations have retained in their constitution the restrictive rule preventing any changes in the Twenty-five Articles of Religion. However, that has not prevented the churches from adopting explanatory footnotes and additional doctrinal statements, even though these may not share the status of the Articles of Religion.*

The African Methodist Church has adopted a footnote to Article XXIII of the Articles of Religion for the benefit of foreign members. In addition, it has adopted statements on apostolic succession and ritualism. These follow the Articles of Religion in the Church's Discipline, but are set apart in a separate section.

*   *   *

ADDITIONS TO THE *TWENTY-FIVE ARTICLES OF RELIGION* **(AFRICAN METHODIST EPISCOPAL ZION CHURCH)**

XXIII. OF THE RULERS OF THE UNITED STATES OF AMERICA

23.   The President, the Congress, the General Assemblies, the Governors and the Councils of State as the Delegates of the People, are the Rulers of the United States of America, according to the division of power made to them by the Constitution of the United States, and by the Constitutions of their respective States. And the said States are a sovereign and independent Nation, and ought not to be subject to any foreign jurisdiction. As far as it respects civil affairs, we believe it the duty of Christians, and especially all Christian Ministers, to be subject to the supreme authority of the country where they may reside and to use all laudable means to enjoin obedience to the powers that be; and, therefore, it is expected that all our Preachers and People who may be under any foreign Government will behave themselves as peaceable and orderly subjects.

Notes: *Though bound by a restrictive rule preventing the alteration of the Articles of Religion, the AMEZ Church added material to Article XXIII.*

*   *   *

ADDITIONS TO THE *TWENTY-FIVE ARTICLES OF RELIGION* **(CHRISTIAN METHODIST EPISCOPAL CHURCH)**

As far as it respects civil affairs we believe it the duty of Christians and especially all Christian ministers, to be subject to the supreme authority of the country where they reside, and to use all laudable means to enjoin obedience to the powers that be and therefore it is expected that all our preachers and people, who may be under any foreign

government, will behave themselves as peaceable and orderly subjects.

Notes: *Like the United Methodist Church and African Methodist Episcopal Church, the Christian Methodist Episcopal Church has added a footnote to Article XXIII for the benefit of foreign members.*

*   *   *

German Methodism

CONFESSION OF FAITH OF THE CHURCH OF THE UNITED BRETHREN

In the name of God we declare and confess before all men, that we believe in the only true God, the Father, the Son, and the Holy Ghost; that these three are one—the Father in the Son, the Son in the Father, and the Holy Ghost equal in essence or being with both; that this triune God created the heavens and the earth and all that in them is, visible as well as invisible, and furthermore sustains, governs, protects and supports the same.

We believe in Jesus Christ; that He is very God and man; that He became incarnate by the power of the Holy Ghost in the Virgin Mary and was born of her; that He is the Savior and Mediator of the whole human race, if they with full faith in Him accept the grace proffered in Jesus; that this Jesus suffered and died on the cross for us, was buried, arose again on the third day, ascended into heaven, and sitteth on the right hand of God to intercede for us; and that He shall come again at the last day to judge the quick and the dead.

We believe in the Holy Ghost; that He is equal in being with the Father and the Son, and that He comforts the faithful, and guides them into all truth.

We believe in a holy Christian church, the communion of saints, the resurrection of the body, and life everlasting.

We believe that the Holy Bible, Old and New Testaments, is the Word of God; that it contains the only true way of our salvation; that every true Christian is bound to acknowledge and receive it with the influence of the Spirit of God as the only rule and guide; and that without faith in Jesus Christ, true repentance, forgiveness of sins and following after Christ, no one can be a true Christian.

We also believe that what is contained in the Holy Scriptures, to-wit; the fall in Adam and redemption through Jesus Christ, shall be preached throughout the world.

We believe that the ordinances, viz: baptism and the remembrance of the sufferings and death of our Lord Jesus Christ, are to be in use and practiced by all Christian societies; and that it is incumbent on all the children of God particularly to practice them; but the manner in which, ought always to be left to the judgment and understanding of every individual. Also the example of washing feet is left to the judgment of every one to practice or not; but it is not becoming of any of our preachers or members to traduce any of their brethren whose judgment and understanding in these respects is different from their own, either in public or in private. Whosoever shall make himself guilty in this respect, shall be considered a traducer of his brethren, and shall be answerable for the same.

Notes: *Methodism spread through the German-American community in the early nineteenth century via two groups, the United Brethren in Christ and the Evangelical Association. Both eventually authored their own doctrinal statements. The association experienced a major schism in 1894. However, the two factions reunited in 1922 to emerge as the Evangelical Church. In 1946 the United Brethren and Evangelical Church merged to become the Evangelical United Brethren. In 1962 that church replaced the prior doctrinal statements of both churches with a new Confession of Faith, which is now a part of the doctrinal standards of the United Methodist Church.*

The United Brethren had originally adopted its Confession of Faith in 1841. In 1885 several changes made in the constitution, including some in the confession, were among the causes of a schism by conservatives who retained the unaltered constitution. The conservative group continues to exist as the Church of the United Brethren.

*　　*　　*

ARTICLES OF RELIGION (EVANGELICAL CONGREGATIONAL CHURCH)

The following Articles contain our confession of Christian Faith:

101. OF GOD

There is but one true and living God, an eternal Being, a Spirit without body, indivisible, of infinite power, wisdom, and goodness, the Creator and Preserver of all things, visible and invisible. In this Godhead there is a Trinity, of one substance and power, and co-eternal, namely, the Father, the Son, and the Holy Ghost.

102. OF JESUS CHRIST

The Lord Jesus Christ, who is the only begotten Son of God, was born of the Virgin Mary, grew into perfect manhood and became acquainted with all the infirmities, temptations, and sorrows of men. In Him dwelt all the fullness of the Godhead, so that, uniting Deity and humanity in one Christ, He is sole Mediator between God and man. He gave His life a ransom for all, and by His death on the cross made a full, perfect and sufficient sacrifice, oblation, and satisfaction for the sins of the whole world. He rose from the dead and ascended into heaven, wherein He abideth, our great High-Priest and King, and must reign until all things are put in subjection under him.

103. OF THE HOLY SPIRIT

The Holy Spirit, proceeding from the Father and the Son, and of the same eternal nature, power, and glory, is everywhere present with men to convict of sin, work newness of life in them that believe, and lead them into all truth.

104. OF THE HOLY SCRIPTURES

By the Holy Scriptures we understand those canonical books of the Old and New Testaments, which the church has at all times received as such. These books in order are as follows:

The Old Testament

Genesis, Exodus, Leviticus, Numbers, Deuteronomy, Joshua, Judges, Ruth, I Samuel, II Samuel, I Kings, II Kings, I Chronicles, II Chronicles, Ezra, Nehemiah, Esther, Job, the Psalms, the Proverbs of Solomon, Ecclesiastes, Song of Solomon, Isaiah, Jeremiah, Lamentations, Ezekiel, Daniel, Hosea, Joel, Amos, Obadiah, Jonah, Micah, Nahum, Habakkuk, Zephaniah, Haggai, Zechariah, Malachi.

The New Testament

Matthew, Mark, Luke, John, The Acts, Epistle to the Romans, I Corinthians, II Corinthians, Galatians, Ephesians, Philippians, Colossians, I Thessalonians, II Thessalonians, I Timothy, II Timothy, Titus, Philemon, Hebrews, Epistle of James, I Peter, II Peter, I John, II John, III John, Jude, Revelation.

These Scriptures, given by Divine inspiration, contain the will of God concerning us in all things necessary to our salvation; so that whatever is not contained therein nor can be proved thereby is not to be enjoined on any as an article of faith.

105. OF HUMAN DEPRAVITY

All men have sinned, and they inherit a depravity of nature which is continually propagated in the entire race of Adam. This corruption of nature so far removes them from the original righteousness of man that of themselves they have no ability to recover from their fallen condition, but are continually inclined to that which is evil.

106. OF SALVATION THROUGH CHRIST

The love of God has made salvation possible to all through the mediation of Jesus Christ, whereby every man is graciously provided with freedom of will to accept or reject the offer of eternal life.

107. OF REPENTANCE

Repentance is sorrow for sin, wrought in the heart by the power of the Holy Spirit. The awakened sinner is thereby made to recognize the holiness of God, the righteousness of His law and the guilt and shame of his own perverse nature. Thus deeply humbled he turns unto God and forsakes his sins.

108. OF JUSTIFICATION

Justification is that act of God by which, when we yield ourselves in full confidence to our Saviour, Jesus Christ, we are freely acquitted from the guilt of sin and accounted righteous in His sight. We are accordingly justified, not by works which we perform, but by faith in Him who died for us.

109. OF REGENERATION

Regeneration is that work of the Holy Spirit wrought in us whereby we are made partakers of the divine nature and experience newness of life in Christ Jesus. By this new birth the believer becomes a child of God, receives the spirit of adoption and is made an heir of the kingdom of heaven.

ARTICLES OF RELIGION (EVANGELICAL CONGREGATIONAL CHURCH) (continued)

110. OF THE WITNESS OF THE SPIRIT

The witness of the Spirit is an inward impression on the soul, whereby the Spirit of God, the heavenly Comforter, immediately convinces the regenerate believer that he has passed from death unto life, that his sins are all forgiven, and that he is a child of God.

111. OF SANCTIFICATION

Entire sanctification, or Christian perfection, is a state of righteousness and true holiness, which every regenerate believer may attain. It consists in being cleansed from all sin, loving God with all the heart, soul, mind, and strength, and loving our neighbor as ourselves. This gracious state of perfect love is attainable in this life by faith, both gradually and instantaneously, and should be earnestly sought by every child of God; but it does not deliver us from the infirmities, ignorance and mistakes which are common to man.

112. OF GOOD WORKS

The Holy Spirit dwelling in man begets within him love, joy, peace, long suffering, gentleness, temperance, and all other ennobling virtues, and these show themselves in numerous outward acts, which become so many evidences of a living faith. Although such good works cannot put away sin, they are ever well-pleasing and acceptable in the sight of God.

113. OF APOSTASY

The gracious help of God is pledged to all those who continue steadfast in faith; but, on account of man's free will, which no power may coerce, apostasy from God is possible so long as we continue in the flesh. Wherefore, constant watchfulness, prayer, and holy living are necessary on the part of man, lest he fall away from the grace of God, grieve and quench the Holy Spirit, and lose his soul at last.

114. OF IMMORTALITY

The soul of man is immortal, and, on its separation from the body at death, continues in a conscious state of existence in the world of spirits. It there either enters into bliss or undergoes torment, according to its character as formed and fixed in the present life.

115. OF THE RESURRECTION

Christ did truly rise from the dead, and took again his own body, and ascended into heaven. Likewise, all the dead shall be raised up by the power of God through Christ, both the just and the unjust; but those who have done good shall come forth unto an eternal life of glory, and those who have wrought wickedness shall be adjudged to everlasting punishment.

116. OF THE FINAL JUDGMENT

God has appointed a day in which He will judge all men by Jesus Christ, to whom is committed the judgment of this world. We must all, accordingly, appear before the judgment-seat of Christ and have our eternal destiny determined according to our works.

117. OF HEAVEN

Our Lord and Saviour Jesus Christ has provided for those who are redeemed by His grace a heavenly and eternal rest, into which He purposes ultimately to gather them and dwell with them in unspeakable glory. There shall be no more sorrow, pain or death, and the glorified saints shall see God and walk in His light forever.

118. OF HELL

The incorrigible sinner, having rejected Christ and all the offers and opportunities of grace, is without God, and without hope in the world, and makes himself a child of Satan. When he dies his soul awakes to the torment of hell, from which there is no promise or hope of deliverance, but the sentence of everlasting punishment prepared for the devil and his angels.

119. OF THE CHURCH

The Holy General Church consists of the great body of believers who confess the Lord Jesus Christ and have life in Him. The individual church is a congregation or society of Christian believers, in which the pure worship of God is maintained, His holy word is preached, and His commandments and ordinances are sacredly observed.

120. OF THE MINISTRY

The ministry of the Gospel is a sacred office and calling, ordained by Christ for the proclamation of His truth in all the world and for the orderly administration of the sacraments, the worship, and the discipline of the Church. No man may assume this office without the conviction of a divine call thereto, and the recognition and ratification of that call by the Church.

121. OF BAPTISM

The sacrament of baptism is the formal application of water to an infant, or to an adult believer, in the name of the Father, and of the Son, and of the Holy Spirit, as a visible sign and seal that the person so consecrated stands in a holy covenant relation to God and His people.

122. OF THE LORD'S SUPPER

The Lord's Supper is not merely a token of love and union that Christians ought to have among themselves, but is a sacrament instituted in memory of the sufferings and death of Christ, whereby those who rightly and worthily receive the same partake of the body and blood of Christ by faith, not in a bodily but in a spiritual manner, in eating the broken bread and in drinking the blessed cup. We thereby also continually show forth our Christian faith and hope.

123. OF CHURCH POLITY

The Lord Jesus Christ ordained no particular form of government for His church, so that whatever polity, rules, regulations, rites, and ceremonies are adopted and approved by common authority, and are not repugnant to the word of God, may be acknowledged as sufficient to constitute a true church of the living God. Such polity, rules, rites, and ceremonies may be lawfully changed from time to time, as the needs of men and the diversity of nations, countries, and manners may require.

124. OF CIVIL GOVERNMENT

Civil government is an ordinance of God, grounded in the necessities of human nature and essential to the maintenance of public order, the security of personal rights, and the punishment of evil-doers. It is the duty of all men to be subject to the supreme authority of the country in which they reside and to respect and honor the civil magistrates.

125. OF THE EVANGELIZATION OF THE WORLD

The Gospel is designed for all nations, its field of operation is the whole world, and the Church and people of God are under solemn obligation to make known its saving truth and power among the heathen. To this great work we are impelled and encouraged by the command of the Lord and the promises and prophecies of the Holy Scriptures.

130. CHAPTER II - CHRISTIAN PERFECTION

131. TAUGHT IN THE WORD OF GOD

We believe that the doctrine of Christian Perfection is clearly taught in the Word of God. For this reason it is accepted as one of the cherished doctrines of the Evangelical Congregational Church. God said to Abram, as recorded in Genesis 17:1: "I am God Almighty; walk before me and be blameless." Our Lord and Saviour expressly said to His disciples, as recorded in Matthew 5:48: "Be perfect, therefore, as your heavenly Father is perfect." Furthermore, to effect this great end was plainly one of the leading purposes of God in instituting the Church and calling laborers into His vineyard. Hear Paul to the Ephesians, "It was he who gave some to be apostles, some to be prophets, some to be evangelists, and some to be pastors and teachers, to prepare God's people for works of service, so that the body of Christ may be built up, until we all reach unity in the faith and in the knowledge of the Son of God and become mature attaining to the whole measure of the fullness of Christ." Ephesians 4:11-13. Paul further taught with much emphasis that the best way to attain to this high standard was to preach the sinless Christ as our pattern of perfection. See Colossians 1:28: "We proclaim him, admonishing and teaching everyone with all wisdom so that we may present everyone perfect in Christ."

131.1. SUMMARY OF JOHN WESLEY'S TEACHING

As to the character of this work of grace, when attainable, and its effect upon its possessor, that most excellent summary given by John Wesley in the year 1764, fully meets our views. This statement was made after the thought and experience of Mr. Wesley had attained their full ripeness, for he was then within a few years of the close of his life. He had given much thought to this doctrine, and finally, after a careful review of the whole subject, wrote the sum of what he had observed in a number of brief propositions, to which we as a body of Christians most heartily subscribe. These propositions are as follows as found in A PLAIN ACCOUNT OF CHRISTIAN PERFECTION, Rev. John Wesley, 1764:

1. "There is such a thing as perfection; for it is again and again mentioned in the Scriptures.

2. It is not so early as justification; for justified persons are to 'go on unto perfection'. (Hebrews 6:1).

3. It is not so late as death; for St. Paul speaks of living men that were perfect. (Phillippians 3:15).

4. It is not absolute. Absolute perfection belongs not to man, nor to angels, but to God alone.

5. It does not make a man infallible; no one is infallible while he remains in the body.

6. Is it sinless? It is not worth while to contend for a term. It is 'salvation from sin.'

7. It is 'perfect love'. (1 John 4:18) This is the essence of it; its properties or inseparable fruits, are, rejoicing evermore, praying without ceasing, and in every thing giving thanks, (1 Thessalonians 5:16, etc.)

8. It is improvable. It is so far from . . . being incapable of increase, that one perfected in love may grow in grace far swifter than he did before.

9. It is losable, capable of being lost; of which we have numerous instances . . .

10. It is constantly both preceded and followed by a gradual work.

11. But is it in itself instantaneous or not? In examining this, let us go on step by step. An instantaneous change has been wrought in some believers; no one can deny this. Since that change, they enjoy perfect love; they feel this and this alone; they 'rejoice evermore, pray without ceasing, and in everything give thanks' . . . But in some this change was not instantaneous. They did not perceive the instant when it was wrought. It is often difficult to perceive the instant when a man dies; yet there is an instant when life ceases. And if even sin ceases, there must be a last moment of its existence, and a first moment of our deliverance from it.

'But if they have this love now they will lose it.' They may; but they need not. And whether they do or no, they have it now; they now experience what we teach. They now are all love; they now rejoice, pray and praise without ceasing.

'However, sin is only suspended in them; it is not destroyed.' Call it which you please; they are all love today; and they take no thought for the morrow.

'But this doctrine has been much abused.' So has that of justification by faith. But that is no reason for giving up either this or any other Scriptural doctrine . . .

'But those who think they are saved from ·sin say they have no need of the merits of Christ.' They say just the contrary. Their language is 'Every moment, Lord, I need the merit of thy death.' They never before had so deep, so unspeakable a conviction of the need of Christ in all His offices as they have now."

Notes: *In 1922 the majority of the United Evangelical Church, which had broken away from the Evangelical Association in 1894, reunited with the Association to form the Evangelical Church. The new church's Articles of Religion were derived from those of the Evangelical*

ARTICLES OF RELIGION (EVANGELICAL CONGREGATIONAL CHURCH) (continued)

Association but rewritten to include additional emphasis on the subjective side of the Christian faith. This new emphasis is detailed in the articles on regeneration, repentance, the witness of the Spirit, sanctification, and the work of the Holy Spirit. Appended to the articles is a lengthy explanation of the doctrine of Christian perfection.

*   *   *

CONFESSION OF FAITH (UNITED CHRISTIAN CHURCH)

1. We believe the Church of God is a community of Saints united together for the worship of God according to Scripture Matt. 18:17; Rom. 16:1; Acts 14:23; 1 Cor. 1:2. We believe no church to be scripturally organized without a competent number of elders, Tit. 1:5 and deacons, Acts 6:1-5; 20:17, 28. We believe the Bible, the Old and New Testament, to be the Word of God, a revelation from God to man and the only authoritative rule of faith and practice. Luke 16:29; 2 Tim. 3:16; 2 Pet. 1:19.

2. She believes in one supreme God consisting of Father, Son, and Holy Spirit and that these three are one. Matt. 28:19; 1 John 5:7.

3. She believes in the Fall and Depravity of man. Rom. 3:10, 23; 5:10; 8:7.

4. She believes in the redemption of man through the atonement of Jesus Christ. Rom. 3:25; 5:6; 2 Cor. 5:19.

5. She believes in the gifts and office work of the Holy Spirit to enlighten, regenerate, and sanctify the believers, body, soul, and spirit. John 17:17.

6. She believes that man is justified by faith in Christ and not by the works of the law. Rom. 3:28; 4:4.

7. She believes in the new birth without which no man can see the kingdom of God. John 3:5.

8. She believes in three ordinances in the church of God; baptism, the Lord's supper, and feet-washing. Acts 2:38; 1 Cor. 11:23; John 13:1-14.

9. She believes that faith is essential to baptism, and that it should be done in the water if possible. 1 Pet. 3:21; Acts 8:37, 38.

10. She believes that the Lord's supper should be administered to believers only, 1 Cor. 11:23; and if it could be done, always in the evening.

11. She believes that the church, if she can, ought to relieve and take care of her own poor. Acts 6:1; 11:29.

12. She believes that all wars are sinful and unholy and in which the saints of God ought never participate. Matt. 5:39; 26:52; 2 Cor. 10:4.

13. She believes that the saints of God should not sue and go to law with each other. Matt. 5:40; 1 Cor. 6:1.

14. She believes that all governments are ordained of God and that Christians ought to be subject to the same in all things, except what is manifestly unscriptural; and that appeals to the law—for rights, liberty, and life are not inconsistent with the Christian religion. Rom. 13:1; Acts 25:11-31.

15. She believes in the resurrection of the dead, both of the just and the unjust. John 5:28, 29; Acts 24:15.

16. She believes in the immortality of the soul, in a universal and eternal judgment and in future and everlasting rewards and punishments. Matt. 25:3-46; Mark 8:36; Luke 16:19-31.

Notes: *Breaking away from the United Brethren in 1877, the United Christian Church adopted its own distinct confession. It espoused the unique (for Methodism) beliefs in pacifism, foot washing, and the exclusivity of the Lord's Supper (closed communion for believers only), which was to be held only in the evening.*

*   *   *

British Methodism

REVISION OF THE *TWENTY-FIVE ARTICLES OF RELIGION* (METHODIST CHURCH, CANADA; METHODIST CHURCH OF CANADA)

XXIII. OF THE CIVIL GOVERNMENT

21. We believe it is the duty of all Christians to be subject to the powers that be; for we are commanded by the Word of God to respect and obey the Civil Government: we should therefore not only fear God, but honour the King.

Notes: *Canadian Methodists adopted the Twenty-five Articles of Religion common to Methodism in North America, but as with all Methodist churches outside of the United States, had to revise the twenty-third article, which in the statement adopted by the Methodist Episcopal Church (now the United Methodist church) professed loyalty to the government of the United States of America.*

Chapter 7

Holiness Family

STATEMENT OF FAITH (NATIONAL HOLINESS ASSOCIATION)

We believe:

1. That both Old and New Testaments constitute the divinely-inspired word of God, inerrant in the originals, and the final authority for life and truth;

2. That there is one God, eternally existent in the Holy Trinity of Father, Son, and Holy Spirit, each with personality and deity;

3. That the Son, our Lord Jesus Christ, manifested in the flesh through the virgin birth, died on Calvary for the redemption of the human family, all of whom may be saved from sin through faith in Him;

4. That men, although created by God in His own image and likeness, fell into sin through disobedience and "so death passed upon all men, for that all have sinned" (Romans 5:12);

5. In the salvation of the human soul, including the new birth; and in a subsequent work of God in the soul, a crisis, wrought by faith, whereby the heart is cleansed from all sin and filled with the Holy Spirit; this gracious experience is retained by faith as expressed in a constant obedience to God's revealed will, thus giving us perfect cleansing moment by moment (1 John 1:7-9). We stand for the Wesleyan position;

6. That the church is the body of Christ, that all who are united by faith to Christ are members of the same, and that, having thus become members one of another, it is our solemn and covenant duty to fellowship with one another in peace, and to love one another with pure and fervent hearts;

7. That our Lord Jesus Christ in His literal resurrection from the dead is the living guarantee of the resurrection of all human beings, the believing saved to conscious eternal joy, and the unbelieving lost to conscious eternal punishment;

8. That our Lord Jesus Christ, in fulfillment of His own promise, both angelically and apostolically attested, will personally return in power and great glory.

Notes: *Emerging out of the holiness revival that spread through Methodism after the Civil War, the holiness churches developed a special emphasis upon the doctrine of sanctification. Succinctly stated, they teach that after a person is justified (born again), God's Holy Spirit continues to work in the believer. The believer is said to grow in grace. Held out as a possibility toward which Christians strive, sanctification is experienced as a second definite act of grace in the Christian's life through the action of the Holy Spirit. This second blessing, as it is frequently termed, makes the person perfect in love.*

In the late nineteenth century, Methodist leaders attacked several basic assumptions underlying the holiness system. Most importantly, they emphasized the process of conversion, as opposed to the instantaneous conversion often precipitated around a personal crisis. While believing in the possibility of the Christian's process of growth through grace, they shied away from any affirmation of the possibility of perfection in this life. Finally, they talked of numerous "blessings" given as part of the Christian life, as opposed to a special "second blessing."

The trend of Methodist theology to deny holiness emphases, and the growing opposition of bishops and presiding elders to holiness advocates, led to the establishment of distinctly holiness churches in the late nineteenth century. Joining the holiness movement were some of the previously existing independent Methodist denominations (i.e., the Free Methodist Church and the Wesleyan Methodist Church) which had strong holiness leanings and had been drawn into the revival.

Among the earliest structures of the holiness revival was the National Camp Meeting Association for the Promotion of Holiness, popularly called the National Holiness Association, founded in 1867. In the early years it promoted camp meetings across the United States. By the beginning of the twentieth century it had become the common meeting ground between holiness denominations and individuals who held a holiness doctrine but remained in "non-holiness" churches.

STATEMENT OF FAITH (CHRISTIAN HOLINESS ASSOCIATION)

The Christian Holiness Association is a body of churches, organizations, and individuals who accept the inspiration and infallibility of sacred Scripture and evangelical doctrine that pertains to divine revelation, the incarnation, the resurrection, the second coming of Christ, the Holy Spirit, and the Church as affirmed in the historic Christian creeds. The particular concern of this fellowship is the biblical doctrine of sanctification identified historically in what is known as the Wesleyan position.

The Association believes that personal salvation includes both the new birth and entire sanctification wrought by God in the heart by faith. Entire sanctification is a crisis experience subsequent to conversion which results in a heart cleansed from all sin and filled with the Holy Spirit. This grace is witnessed to by the Holy Spirit. It is maintained by that faith which expresses itself in constant obedience to God's revealed will and results in a moment by moment cleansing.

Notes: *In 1970 the National Holiness Association, following the entry of several groups from outside the United States, changed its name to the Christian Holiness Association. At that time, it also adopted a new brief statement of faith.*

* * *

Nineteenth-Century Holiness

ARTICLES OF RELIGION (AMERICAN RESCUE WORKERS)

1. We believe in one Supreme God, who is "from everlasting to everlasting," who is infinitely perfect, benevolent and wise, who is omnipotent, omnipresent, and omnicient, and who is the Creator and Ruler of heaven and earth.

2. We believe in a Triune God—the Father, the Son and the Holy Ghost. We believe these three Persons are one, and while separate in office, are undivided in essence, co-equal in power and glory, and that all men everywhere ought to worship and serve this Triune God.

3. We believe the contents of the Bible to have been given by inspiration of God, and the Scriptures form the divine rule of all true, godly faith and Christian practice.

4. We believe that Jesus Christ, when upon earth, was truly man and yet was as truly God, the Divine and human being blended in the one being, hence His ability to feel and suffer as a man and yet supremely love and triumph as the Godhead.

5. We believe that our first parents were created without sin, but by listening to the tempter and obeying his voice fell from grace and lost their purity and peace; and that in consequences of their disobedience and fall all men have become sinful by propensity and are consequently exposed to the wrath of God.

6. We believe that Jesus Christ, the only begotten Son of God, by the sacrifice of His life, made an atonement for all men, and that whosoever will call upon Him and accept His overtures of grace may be saved.

7. We believe that in order to be saved it is necessary (a) to repent toward God, (b) to believe with the heart in Jesus Christ, and (c) to become regenerated through the operation of the Holy Spirit.

8. We believe that the Holy Ghost gives to each person thus saved the inward witness of acceptance by God.

9. We believe that the Scriptures teach and urge all Christians to be cleansed in heart from inbred sin, so that they may walk uprightly and "serve Him without fear in holiness, and righteousness before Him all the days of our lives."

10. We believe the soul shall never die; and that we shall be raised again; that the world shall be judged by God, and that the punishment of the wicked will be eternal and the joy and reward of the righteous will be everlasting before the throne of God.

The American Rescue Workers, Inc., believe in two sacraments —Baptism and the Lord's Supper.

Baptism may be administered by sprinkling, pouring or immersion according: as the Candidate may elect.

Notes: *Most of the large holiness bodies have their roots in groups which emerged in the nineteenth century. One of these groups, The American Rescue Workers, was founded by former members of the Salvation Army. While retaining the Army's military bearing, it has rejected the Army's peculiar stance in regard to the sacraments.*

* * *

SUMMARY OF DOCTRINE (BIBLE HOLINESS MOVEMENT)

We believe there is One God—the Father, Son and Holy Spirit;

That the Bible is the inspired and authoritative Word of God;

That man is born spiritually and morally depraved;

That the atonement provided by the sufferings and death of our Lord Jesus Christ is universal;

That all men may be saved who repent and believe the Gospel;

That it is the privilege of every believer to be sanctified wholly;

That it is the privilege of the entirely sanctified to be anointed with the Holy Spirit and made effective witnesses;

That all true Christians should lead godly lives in conformity with the Holy Scriptures;

And that Jesus Christ will come again in the end of the world to raise the dead and judge all mankind.

Notes: *The Bible Holiness Movement has roots in the Salvation Army. Its brief statement affirms the central affirmations of the holiness tradition while avoiding any mention of the Army's controversial position on the sacraments.*

* * *

DOCTRINAL STATEMENT (CHRISTIAN AND MISSIONARY ALLIANCE)

Qualifications for membership shall consist of:

1. Satisfactory evidence of regeneration;

2. Belief in God the Father, Son and Holy Spirit; in the verbal inspiration of the Holy Scriptures as originally given; in the vicarious atonement of the Lord Jesus Christ; in the eternal salvation of all who believe in Him and the eternal punishment of all who reject Him;

3. Acceptance of the doctrines of the Lord Jesus Christ as Saviour, Sanctifier, Healer and Coming King.

The following doctrinal statement shall be adopted in all of our home and foreign Bible schools:

1. The Scriptures of the Old and New Testaments are the inspired Word of God. They contain a complete revelation of His will for the salvation of men, and constitute the Divine and only rule of Christian faith and practice.—2 Timothy 3:16-17; 2 Peter 1:21.

2. There is one God, Who is infinitely perfect, existing eternally in three persons: Father, Son and Holy Spirit.

3. Jesus Christ is true God and true man. He was conceived by the Holy Ghost and born of the Virgin Mary. He died upon the cross, the just for the unjust, as a substitutionary sacrifice, and all who believe in Him are justified on the ground of His shed blood. He arose from the dead according to the Scriptures. He is now at the right hand of the Majesty on high as our great High Priest, and He will return again to establish His Kingdom of righteousness and justice.

4. The Holy Spirit is a Divine Person, the Executive of the Godhead, the Comforter sent by the Lord Jesus Christ to indwell, to guide, and to teach the believer, and to convince the world of sin, of righteousness, and of judgment.

5. Man was originally created in the likeness and image of God; he fell through disobedience, incurring thereby both physical and spiritual death. All men are born with a sinful nature, are separated from the life of God, and can be saved only through the atoning work of the Lord Jesus Christ. The portion of the impenitent and unbelieving is existence forever in conscious torment; and that of the believer, in everlasting joy and bliss.

6. Salvation has been provided through Jesus Christ for all men; and those who receive Him are born again of the Holy Spirit, obtain the gift of eternal life, and become the children of God.

7. There shall be a bodily resurrection of the just and of the unjust; for the former, a resurrection unto life; for the latter, a resurrection unto judgment.

8. The Church consists of all those who have believed on the Lord Jesus Christ, are washed in His blood, and have been born again of the Holy Spirit. It has been commissioned of the Lord to witness in His name, to comfort and build up its members in the holy faith, and especially to fulfill the terms of the Great Commission to go forth into all the world as a witness, preaching the Gospel to all nations.

9. It is the will of God that each believer should be filled with the Holy Spirit and thus be sanctified wholly, being separated from sin and the world and fully consecrated to the will of God, thereby receiving power for holy living and effective service. This is recognized as an experience wrought in the life subsequent to conversion.

10. Provision is made in the redemption of the Lord Jesus Christ for the healing of the mortal body in accordance with His Word. The anointing with oil, as set forth in the fifth chapter of James, is to be practiced by the Church in this present age.

11. The premillennial coming of the Lord Jesus Christ is a practical truth which should be preached, showing its relation to the personal life and the service of the believer.

Notes: *The Christian and Missionary Alliance was founded by Albert Benjamin Simpson, a former Presbyterian minister who had been healed at a holiness camp meeting. He is rightfully credited as being one of the major spokespersons for the revival of the healing ministry in twentieth-century Christianity. In conjunction with his mature ministry, he developed a theology centering on the work of Christ as Saviour, Sanctifier, Healer, and Coming King. This theology was known as the four-fold gospel and became the distinguishing feature of the alliance's holiness doctrine. The constitution of the alliance spells out the minimal doctrinal essentials in its statement on membership. However, the more complete presentation of the alliance's position is found in the doctrinal statement mandated for adoption for all Bible schools associated with the alliance.*

* * *

ARTICLES OF FAITH (CHRIST'S SANCTIFIED HOLY CHURCH)

That there is but one uncreated, unoriginated, infinite and eternal Being, the Creator, Preserver and Governor of all things. That there is in this infinite essence a plurality of what is commonly called persons, not separately subsisting but essentially belonging to the Godhead, which persons are commonly termed the Father, Son and Holy Ghost, and are generally named the Trinity. That the sacred Scriptures or Holy Books which form the Old and New Testaments, contain a full revelation of the will of God in relation to man, and alone sufficient for everything relative to the faith and practice of the Christian, and were given by the inspiration of God. That man was created in

ARTICLES OF FAITH (CHRIST'S SANCTIFIED HOLY CHURCH) (continued)

righteousness and true holiness, without any moral imperfection or any kind of propensity to sin, but free to stand or fall, but he fell from this state, became morally corrupt in his nature, and transmitted his moral defilment to all his posterity. That to counteract the evil principle and bring man into a saveable state, God, from his infinite love, formed the purpose of redeeming man from his lost estate by Jesus Christ and in the interim sent His holy spirit to enlighten, strive with and convince men of sin, righteousness and judgment. That in due time Jesus, the Christ, the Son of God, the Savior of the world, became incarnated and sojourned among men, teaching the purest truth and working the most stupendous, beneficent miracles. That this divine person, foretold by the prophets and described by the evangelists and apostles, is really and properly God, having by the inspired writers assigned to Him every attribute essential to the Deity, being one with Him who is called God, Jehovah, etc. That He is also a perfect man in consequence of his incarnation, and in that man or manhood dwelt all the fullness of the Godhead bodily; so His nature is twofold—divine and human, or God manifested in the flesh. That His human nature is derived from the blessed Virgin Mary through the creative energy of the Holy Ghost, but His divine nature, because God is infinite and eternal, uncreated, underived, and unbegotten, which, were it otherwise, He could not be God in any proper sense of the word. That, as He took upon Himself the nature of man, He died for the whole human race without respect of person equally for all and every person. That, on the third day after His crucifixion and burial He arose from the dead, and after showing Himself many days to His disciples and others, He ascended to heaven, where as God manifest in the flesh, He continues and shall continue to be mediator for the human race till the consummation of all things. That there is no salvation but through Him, and that throughout the Scriptures His passion and death are obtained by the shedding of His blood. That no human being since the fall either has or can have merit or worthiness of or by himself, and therefore has nothing to claim from God, but in the way of His mercy through Christ, therefore pardon and holiness and every other blessing promised in the Gospel have been purchased by His sacrificial death, and are given to man, not on account of anything he has done, or suffered, or can do, but for His sake or through His merit alone. That these blessings are received by faith, because not of works, nor of sufferings, that the power to believe or grace of faith is the free gift of God, without which none can believe, but that the act of faith or actual believing is the act of the soul under the influence of that power, but this power to believe, like all other gifts of God, may be slighted, not used or misused, in consequence of which is that declaration, He that believeth and is baptized shall be saved, but he that believeth not shall be damned (Mark xvi, 16). That justification or the pardon of all actual sin is an instantaneous act of God's infinite mercy in behalf of a penitent soul, trusting only in the merits of Jesus Christ. That this act is absolute in respect of all past actual sins, all being forgiven where any are forgiven. That the souls of all

believers or justified persons must be purified and cleansed from all inbred sin. That moral corruption of the natural human heart, by the precious blood of Jesus Christ, here in this life without which none are prepared for heaven, and that we must live under the continual influence of the grace of Christ, without sinning against God, all evil tempers and sinful propensities being destroyed and the heart being filled with pure love of God; and man being sanctified by the Holy Ghost and received instantaneously as justification. That unless a person live and walk in the spirit of perfect obedience to God's Holy Law, he will fall from the grace of God and forfeit all his Christian privileges and rights, which state of backsliding he may pursue, and if so, perish everlastingly. That the whole period of human life is a state of probation, in every part of which a sinner may repent and turn to God, and in every part of it a believer may, if he wills, give way to sin and fall from the grace attained, and that this possibility of attainments in grace or falling from them are essential to a state of trial or probation. That all the promises and threatenings of the Word of God are conditional as they regard man in reference to his being here and hereafter, and on this ground alone the Sacred Writings can be consistently interpreted or rightly judged. That man is a free agent, never being impelled by any necessitating influence, either to do evil or good, but has it continually in his power to choose the life or death that is set before him, on which ground he is an accountable being and answerable for his own actions, and on this ground also he is alone capable of being rewarded or punished. That his free will is a necessary constituent of his rational soul, without which man must be a mere machine, either the sport of blind chance or a mere patient of an irresistible necessity, and consequently not accountable for any acts to which he was irresistibly impelled. That every human being has this freedom of will with a sufficiency of light and power to direct its operations, and that this powerful light is not inherent in any man's nature, but is graciously bestowed by Him who is a true light, that lighteth every man that cometh into the world. That Jesus Christ has made by His once offering Himself upon the cross as a sufficient sacrifice, oblation and satisfaction for the sins of the whole world, and that His gracious Spirit strives with and enlightens all men, thus putting them in a saveable state; therefore every human soul may be saved. If they are not it is their own fault.

Q.—What is conversion?
Ans.—It is pardon of all past willful sins.

Q.—What are the fruits of conversion?
Ans.—It gives a hungering and thirsting for holiness; the power to become the sons of God.

Q.—Does sin still remain in the heart at conversion?
Ans.—It does, yea, the seed of all sin until they are entirely sanctified.

Q.—Is any soul born of God at conversion?
Ans.—No! Whosoever is born of God doth not commit sin, neither willful nor through error. Unless they are converted from the error of their way, they will go to hell.

Q.—Why are not the people converted from the error of their way, which is inbred sin?

Ans.—Because they have been taught by professing ministers that they are saved at conversion.

Q.—Why is it that the whole world is not saved?

Ans.—The word of God teaches, If they had stood in My counsel, and had caused My people to hear My words, then they should have turned them from the evil of their way.

Q.—Who is the Father of them that say they are saved, and say they sin every day?

Ans.—He that commiteth sin is of the devil.

Q.—Was any soul ever saved at any moment until it was entirely sanctified?

Ans.—No. Without holiness no man shall see the Lord. And again, He that abideth not in Me is cast forth as a branch, and is withered, and men gather them and they are cast into the fire and are burned.

Q.—What is the one Lord, one Faith, one Baptism?

Ans.—It is to be baptized in Jesus Christ by being sanctified and made holy.

Q.—Can any soul be saved without keeping the commandments?

Ans.—No. They that offend in the least are guilty of the whole. So everyone that is forgiven and not sanctified is lost.

Q.—Can anyone be saved without loving God?

Ans.—No. The Scriptures teach that if ye love Me ye will keep My word, which is the commandments, and every one that keepeth the commandments is sanctified and made holy.

Q.—Do persons still have the carnal mind in them after they are converted?

Ans.—Yes, and they are still the enemy of God, for His Word says the carnal mind is enmity to God. It is not subject to God, neither indeed can be. Then to be carnal-minded is death, but to be spiritual-minded is life and peace.

Q.—Can anyone be Christ's disciple without forsaking all that he hath?

Ans.—No.

Q.—When do persons forsake all?

Ans.—Not until they are sanctified.

Q.—Can a person be holy without being sanctified?

Ans.—No. The Word of God teaches us to abstain from all appearance of evil, and the very God of peace sanctify you wholly. So no one is holy unless he is sanctified.

Q.—Are people taught of God who have to study all the week to get up a sermon for Sunday?

Ans.—No, for God has said, Settle it in your hearts not to premeditate before what ye shall say, for I will give you a mouth and wisdom which all your adversaries may not be able to gainsay nor resist. And again—Open your mouth wide and I will fill it.

Q.—What kind of a discipline will be used at the millennial year?

Ans.—This very one, for the millennial year has already come with all Sanctified Holy people.

Q.—Does anyone know God at conversion?

Ans.—No. He that sinneth hath neither seen Him, neither known Him.

Q.—What is sanctification?

Ans.—It is to love the Lord thy God with all thy heart, with all thy soul, and with all thy mind, and with all thy strength, and thy neighbor as thyself.

Notes: *Two groups share the name "Christ's Sanctified Holy Church." The older one, founded in 1887, has its headquarters in South Carolina and is predominantly composed of whites. The other, organized in 1904, is headquartered in Louisiana and predominantly composed of blacks. The statement reproduced here is taken from the South Carolina group. It is not known whether or not the Louisiana group uses the same statement.*

*   *   *

ARTICLES OF FAITH [CHURCH OF GOD (HOLINESS)]

ARTICLE I

There is one God over all, the same yesterday, today, and forever; the Creator of all things, and in whom all things consist. (Deut. 6:4; Heb. 11:3).

ARTICLE II

There is one Savior, Jesus Christ, the only begotten Son of God, who is the Supreme Head of the Church, which He redeemed unto God by His own blood. (Matt. 3:16, 17).

ARTICLE III

There is one Holy Spirit, the third person of the Holy Trinity, who is now the representative of the Godhead on earth, who came from the Father and the Son, to convict the world of sin, of righteousness, and of judgment. (John 14:16, 17, 26; 15:26).

God the Father, God the Son, and God the Holy Spirit are three persons, united and inseparable, of one substance and eternal. (Matt. 28:19; II Cor. 13:14).

ARTICLE IV

We emphatically affirm the divine inspiration of the Holy Scriptures, both Old and New Testaments, infallibly true as originally inspired, constituting our only divinely authorized rule of faith and practice. (II Tim. 3:16; II Pet. 1:21).

ARTICLES OF FAITH [CHURCH OF GOD (HOLINESS)] (continued)

ARTICLE V

Man, in his natural state, is sinful, apart from saving grace, and consequently is in need of salvation. (Gen. 6:5; Psa. 14:2, 3; Matt. 15:19; Rom. 3:9-23).

ARTICLE VI

The Scriptures declare the necessity of repentance, implying a previous conviction for sins, followed by a hearty sorrow for them and immediate abandonment thereof, together with suitable confession to God and men, and prompt and honest restitution of all that is due to others, according to his ability; and all such gracious states and experiences, constituting scriptural repentance, etc., must be inwrought by the efficient grace of the Holy Ghost. (Isaiah 55:6, 7; Matt. 9:13; Luke 13:3, 5; Acts 17:30, 31; II Cor. 7:10; Ezek. 33:15).

ARTICLE VII

Justification is a legal act on the part of God, including the forgiveness of sins and the impartation of personal righteousness, through faith in the Lord Jesus Christ. (Jer. 36:3; Psalm 130:4; Acts 13:38, 39; Rom. 5:1; I John 3:7; Rev. 19:8; Rom. 8:16).

ARTICLE VIII

Regeneration is the quickening to spiritual life by the Holy Ghost, of the sinner who is dead in trespasses and sins, which gracious act of the Divine Spirit accompanies justification. (Isa. 55:3; John 3:3, 5; Eph. 2:1; Col. 2:13; Titus 3:15).

ARTICLE IX

The Scriptures affirm the necessity of entire sanctification, or deliverance from inbred sin, implying the complete purification of the nature from depravity, or inherited sin, and the complete renewal of the nature in holiness, whereby the child of God is enabled to love God perfectly, and to serve Him in righteousness and true holiness. This gracious act of purification, or entire sanctification, is accomplished instantaneously for the believer by the Holy Spirit, and is distinct from, and takes place subsequent to, the believer's regeneration, being preceded by a definite conviction of remaining inbred sin, an entire and unreserved consecration of the whole being to God, and a definite faith in the Lord Jesus Christ for the entire sanctification of the nature. (Lev. 11:44, 45; Luke 1:73-75; John 17:17; I Thess. 4:3; 5:23, 24; Heb. 10:14, 15).

This work of entire sanctification attended by the infilling of the Holy Spirit, is witnessed to directly by the Holy Spirit, and not by any special manifestations or gifts, such as speaking in unknown tongues.

ARTICLE X

The New Testament Scriptures teach that there is one true Church, which is composed only of those who have savingly believed in the Lord Jesus Christ, and who willingly submit themselves to His divine order concerning the ministries of the Church through the instrumentalities of God-chosen elders and deacons, ordained in the Church by laying on of the hands of the presbytery. The attributes of the Church are unity, spirituality, visibility, and catholicity. (Matt. 16:18; Eph. 4:4; Col. 1:18; I Tim. 3:1-7; Titus 1:5).

ARTICLE XI

The second advent of our Savior, Jesus Christ, is premillennial and visible. The children of God are admonished to look for the personal coming of Christ with confident hope, and with the assurance that at His appearing they will become the happy partakers of His glory in the Kingdom prepared for them from the foundation of the world. (Dan. 7:13, 14; Matt. 24:30, 31; Acts 1:11; I Thess. 4:15-17; 22:20).

ARTICLE XII

The Scriptures affirm the resurrection of the body, the judgment of all mankind, the everlasting punishment of the wicked, and the eternal happiness of the righteous, (John 5:28, 29; I Cor. 15:52-55; Rom. 14:10; II Cor. 5:10; Rev. 20:12, 13; John 14:1-3; Psa. 9:17; Matt. 25:46; Rev. 21:8).

ARTICLE XIII

We urge our people to embrace the Bible doctrine of Divine healing and to offer the prayer of faith for the healing of the sick, according to James 5:14-16; Acts 4:10, 14; Luke 9:2; 10:9.

ARTICLE XIV

Recognizing the fact that water baptism is an outward sign of an inward work of grace wrought in the heart by the Holy Ghost, we recommend that this ordinance be observed by all born-again children of God.

ARTICLE XV

Believing that the sacrament of the Lord's Supper represents our redemption through Christ, we recommend that this ordinance be reverently observed.

Notes: *The Church of God (Holiness) was among the first of the holiness churches to emerge after the Civil War and a leading exponent of what became known as the "come out" [of denominations] movement. The church has adopted a premillennial eschatology indicative of the influence of Protestant fundamentalism.*

* * *

ARTICLES OF FAITH (CHURCH OF THE NAZARENE)

I. THE TRIUNE GOD

We believe in one eternally existent, infinite God, Sovereign of the universe; that He only is God, creative and administrative, holy in nature, attributes, and purpose; that He, as God, is Triune in essential being, revealed as Father, Son, and Holy Spirit.

II. JESUS CHRIST

We believe in Jesus Christ, the Second Person of the Triune Godhead; that He was eternally one with the Father; that He became incarnate by the Holy Spirit and was born of the Virgin Mary, so that two whole and perfect natures, that is to say the Godhead and manhood, are thus united in one person very God and very man, the God-man.

We believe that Jesus Christ died for our sins, and that He truly arose from the dead and took again His body, together with all things appertaining to the perfection of man's nature, wherewith He ascended into heaven and is there engaged in intercession for us.

III. THE HOLY SPIRIT

We believe in the Holy Spirit, the Third Person of the Triune Godhead, that He is ever present and efficiently active in and with the Church of Christ, convincing the world of sin, regenerating those who repent and believe, sanctifying believers, and guiding into all truth as it is in Jesus.

IV. THE HOLY SCRIPTURES

We believe in the plenary inspiration of the Holy Scriptures, by which we understand the sixty-six books of the Old and New Testaments given by divine inspiration, inerrantly revealing the will of God concerning us in all things necessary to our salvation, so that whatever is not contained therein is not to be enjoined as an article of faith.

V. ORIGINAL SIN, OR DEPRAVITY

We believe that original sin, or depravity, is that corruption of the nature of all the offspring of Adam by reason of which every one is very far gone from original righteousness or the pure state of our first parents at the time of their creation, is averse to God, is without spiritual life, and inclined to evil, and that continually. We further believe that original sin continues to exist with the new life of the regenerate, until eradicated by the baptism with the Holy Spirit.

VI. ATONEMENT

We believe that Jesus Christ, by His sufferings, by the shedding of His own blood, and by His meritorious death on the Cross, made a full atonement for all human sin, and that this atonement is the only ground of salvation, and that it is sufficient for every individual of Adam's race. The atonement is graciously efficacious for the salvation of the irresponsible and for the children in innocency, but is efficacious for the salvation of those who reach the age of responsibility only when they repent and believe.

VII. FREE AGENCY

We believe that man's creation in Godlikeness included ability to choose between right and wrong, and that thus he was made morally responsible; that through the fall of Adam he became depraved so that he cannot now turn and prepare himself by his own natural strength and works to faith and calling upon God. But we also believe that the grace of God through Jesus Christ is freely bestowed upon all men, enabling all who will to turn from sin to righteousness, believe on Jesus Christ for pardon and cleansing from sin, and follow good works pleasing and acceptable in His sight.

We believe that man, though in the possession of the experience of regeneration and entire sanctification, may fall from grace and apostatize and, unless he repent of his sin, be hopelessly and eternally lost.

VIII. REPENTANCE

We believe that repentance, which is a sincere and thorough change of the mind in regard to sin, involving a sense of personal guilt and a voluntary turning away from sin, is the demand of all who have by act or purpose become sinners against God. The Spirit of God gives to all who will repent the gracious help of penitence of heart and hope of mercy, that they may believe unto pardon and spiritual life.

IX. JUSTIFICATION, REGENERATION, AND ADOPTION

We believe that justification is the gracious and judicial act of God by which He grants full pardon of all guilt and complete release from the penalty of sins committed, and acceptance as righteous, to all who believe on Jesus Christ and receive Him as Lord and Saviour.

We believe that regeneration, or the new birth, is that gracious work of God whereby the moral nature of the repentant believer is spiritually quickened and given a distinctively spiritual life, capable of faith, love, and obedience.

We believe that adoption is that gracious act of God by which the justified and regenerated believer is constituted a son of God.

We believe that justification, regeneration, and adoption are simultaneous in the experience of seekers after God and are obtained upon the condition of faith, preceded by repentance; and that to this work and state of grace the Holy Spirit bears witness.

X. ENTIRE SANCTIFICATION

We believe that entire sanctification is that act of God, subsequent to regeneration, by which believers are made free from original sin, or depravity, and brought into a state of entire devotement to God, and the holy obedience of love made perfect.

It is wrought by the baptism with the Holy Spirit, and comprehends in one experience the cleansing of the heart from sin and the abiding indwelling presence of the Holy Spirit, empowering the believer for life and service.

Entire sanctification is provided by the blood of Jesus, is wrought instantaneously by faith, preceded by entire consecration; and to this work and state of grace the Holy Spirit bears witness.

This experience is also known by various terms representing its different phases, such as "Christian perfection," "perfect love," "heart purity," "the baptism with the Holy Spirit," "the fullness of the blessing," and "Christian holiness."

XI. SECOND COMING OF CHRIST

We believe that the Lord Jesus Christ will come again; that we who are alive at His coming shall not precede them that are asleep in Christ Jesus; but that, if we are abiding in Him, we shall be caught up with the risen saints to meet the Lord in the air, so that we shall ever be with the Lord.

XII. RESURRECTION, JUDGMENT, AND DESTINY

We believe in the resurrection of the dead, that the bodies both of the just and of the unjust shall be raised to life and united with their spirits—"they that have done good, unto the resurrection of life; and they that have done evil, unto the resurrection of damnation."

ARTICLES OF FAITH (CHURCH OF THE NAZARENE) (continued)

We believe in future judgment in which every man shall appear before God to be judged according to his deeds in this life.

We believe that glorious and everlasting life is assured to all who savingly believe in, and obediently follow, Jesus Christ our Lord; and that the finally impenitent shall suffer eternally in hell.

XIII. BAPTISM

We believe that Christian baptism is a sacrament signifying acceptance of the benefits of the atonement of Jesus Christ, to be administered to believers as declarative of their faith in Jesus Christ as their Saviour, and full purpose of obedience in holiness and righteousness.

Baptism being the symbol of the New Testament, young children may be baptized, upon request of parents or guardians who shall give assurance for them of necessary Christian training.

Baptism may be administered by sprinkling, pouring, or immersion, according to the choice of the applicant.

XIV. THE LORD'S SUPPER

We believe that the Memorial and Communion Supper instituted by our Lord and Saviour Jesus Christ is essentially a New Testament sacrament, declarative of His sacrificial death, through the merits of which believers have life and salvation and promise of all spiritual blessings in Christ. It is distinctively for those who are prepared for reverent appreciation of its significance and by it they show forth the Lord's death till He come again. It being the Communion feast, only those who have faith in Christ and love for the saints should be called to participate therein.

XV. DIVINE HEALING

We believe in the Bible doctrine of divine healing and urge our people to seek to offer the prayer of faith for the healing of the sick. Providential means and agencies when deemed necessary should not be refused.

Notes: *Beginning as a single mission in Los Angeles pastored by a man who had already finished a lengthy and distinguished career as a Methodist minister [Phineas F. Bresee], the Church of the Nazarene has become one of the largest of the holiness denominations. The statements on "Entire Sanctification" and "Healing" reflect, in part, the church's attempt to distinguish itself from Pentecostalism.*

* * *

STATEMENT OF DOCTRINE [CHURCHES OF GOD (INDEPENDENT HOLINESS PEOPLE)]

1. The scriptural truth concerning the naturally sinful condition of all men, apart from saving grace, and their consequent need of salvation.—Gen. 6:5; Psa. 14:2, 3; Matt. 15:19; Rom 3:9-18.

2. The atonement, in that Jesus Christ has made full and complete satisfaction for all. He "tasted death for every man", so that all may be saved who will, upon scriptural conditions, accept Him as their Saviour.—John 3:16; Rom. 5:18; 1 Tim. 2:6; 2 Pet. 3:9.

3. The necessity of repentance, implying a previous conviction for sins, followed by hearty sorrow for and immediate abandonment thereof, together with suitable confession to God and men, and a prompt and honest restitution of all that is due unto others, according to ability; all which gracious states and experiences, as containing true scriptural repentance, must be inwrought by the efficient grace of the Holy Ghost.—Isa. 55:6, 7; Ezek. 33:15; Matt. 9: 13; Luke 13:3-5; Acts 17:30, 31; 2 Cor. 7: 10,11.

4. Justification, implying forgiveness, through faith in the Lord Jesus Christ.—Jer. 36:3; Psa. 130:4; Acts 13:38, 39; Rom. 5:1, 8:16; 1 John 4:7; Rev. 19:8.

5. Regeneration, being the quickening into spiritual life, by the Holy Ghost, of the sinner who is dead in trespasses and sins, which gracious work of the Divine Spirit accompanies justification.—Isa. 55:3; John 3:3-5; Eph. 2:1; Col. 2:13; Titus 3:15.

6. Entire sanctification, being deliverance from inborn sin, implying the complete purification of the nature from depravity, or inherited sin, and the complete renewal of the nature in holiness, whereby the child of God is enabled perfectly to love God, and to serve Him in righteousness and true holiness. This gracious work of purification, or entire sanctification, is accomplished instantaneouly, for the believer, by the Holy Spirit, and is distinct from, and takes place subsequent to, the believer's justification, being preceded by a definite conviction of remaining inward sin, an entire and unreserved consecration of the whole being to God, and a definite faith in the Lord Jesus Christ for the entire sanctification of the nature, and is witnessed to by the Holy Ghost.—Lev. 11:44, 45; Luke 1:73-75; Heb. 10:14, 15.

The work of entire sanctification thus inwrought by the Holy Ghost, through the believer's faith in the Lord Jesus Christ, includes all possibilities of gracious experience in the present life, and neither do the Scriptures teach that said holy estate is to be followed in this world by other super-added and distinctive experiences, as of special divine enlightenment independent of, and superior to, the written Word of God; present immortality or deathlessness; the experience of a present physical resurrection; the consequent glorification of the body and spirit, or other kindred hallucinations which have no warrant from Scripture, but are superinduced by neglect of, or disobedience to, the plainly written truths of God's Word, and imply a willing or wilful following of satanic delusion. Nor does the experience of entire sanctification involve an impossibility of falling away.

7. The institution of the holy Sabbath, or Lord's Day; its sanctity and perpetuity, implying obligation of due and proper observance on the part of all men, according to God's holy commandment. The Convention would express utter disapproval of public

teaching or private conduct, whether under the name of holiness or otherwise, that has a tendency to secularize the holy Sabbath, to weaken or destroy the sense of its sanctity and its perpetual obligation as ordained of God, or to impair either the sacred or civil sanction of the holy day whose proper observance has ever been attended with the evident blessing of God and with national and individual prosperity.—Ex. 20:8-11; Mark 2:27, 28; Luke 6:5; Acts 20:7; 1 Cor. 16:1, 2.

8. The ordinances of the church are but two—baptism of water and the Lord's Supper, which are heartily received and conscientiously observed, as instituted by the head of the church, our Lord and Saviour Jesus Christ.—Matt. 28:19. 20; 1 Cor. 11: 23, 24.

9. The second literal personal advent of our Saviour, Jesus Christ, who will come actually and visibly in like manner as He ascended, for whose personal coming the children of God are admonished to look with confident hope, and with the blessed assurance that when He shall come to be glorified in His saints, and admired by all them that believe, they will become the happy partakers of His glory in the Kingdom prepared for them from the foundation of the world.—Dan. 7:13, 14; Matt. 24:30, 31; Acts 1:11; 1 Thess. 4:15-17; Rev. 1:7, 22:20.

10. The resurrection of the body, according to the Scriptures, which declare that all who die shall live again; that the saints who are alive at the coming of the Lord shall be changed in a moment, in the twinkling of an eye, and shall be glorified, and that all who are dead shall hear the voice of the Son of God, and shall rise again.—Isa. 26:19; Dan. 12:2; John 5:28, 29; 1 Cor. 15:52-55; Job 14:14, 15.

11. The future and final judgment, in which all who have lived shall be summoned into the presence of the Lord, there to be judged for the deeds done in the body.—Rom. 14:10; 2 Cor. 5:10; Rev. 20:12, 13; 22:11; Acts 17:30, 31; Heb. 9:27.

12. The final glorification of the saints, at the coming of our Lord Jesus Christ, which is yet future, and can only be realized when Christ shall come, in the glory of the Father, to end the dispensation and to receive His saints to Himself, that where He is, there they may be also, according to His own blessed promise.—Matt. 13:43; John 14:13; 17:24; Rev. 21:1-4.

13. The final rejection, condemnation and eternal punishment of all impenitent and unsaved persons.—Psa. 9:17; Prov. 14:32; Matt. 25:26; 2 Thess. 1:7-9; Rev. 20:14, 15.

Notes: *Closely related to the Church of God (Holiness), the Independent Holiness People differ primarily on matters of organization. However, unlike the Church of God (Holiness), their statement makes no reference to premillennialism or the nature of Biblical authority.*

PRINCIPLES OF FAITH (EMMANUEL ASSOCIATION)

GOD THE FATHER

There is but one living and true God (Isa. 45:21, 22; Deut. 6:4), everlasting (Psalm 90:2), of infinite power, wisdom, and goodness—the Maker and Preserver of all things visible and invisible. And in the unity of this Godhead there are three Persons (I John 5:7; II Cor. 13:14) equal in power and eternity—the Father, the Son, and the Holy Ghost (John 1:1; 15:26).

GOD THE SON

The Son of God is the Word, the eternal and true God, one with the Father (John 1:1-3), who took man's nature upon Him by being conceived of the Holy Ghost and born of the Virgin Mary; so that both natures—divine and human—were perfectly and inseparably joined in Him (John 1:14; Phil. 2:6-8). Therefore He is Christ the Anointed, very God and very Man, who suffered, was crucified, died, and was buried, and rose again (He "is risen again, who is even at the right hand of God, who also maketh intercession for us" [Rom. 8:34]), and thus presented Himself a sacrifice for both our original sin (Rom. 6:6; Heb. 10:10) and actual sins (Gal. 1:4; Eph. 1:7; I Peter 3:18), in order to reconcile us to the Eternal Father (II Cor. 5:19).

GOD THE HOLY GHOST

The Holy Ghost proceeds from the Father and the Son (John 15:26), and is one with Them, ever present and efficiently active in and with the Church of Christ. As the Executive of the God-head He convinces the world of sin (John 16:8), regenerates those who repent (John 3:5), sanctifies believers (Acts 15:8, 9), and guides all into the truth as the truth is in Jesus (John 16:13).

THE HOLY SCRIPTURES

We understand the sixty-six canonical books of the Old and New Testaments to be the Word of God, given by divine inspiration (II Tim. 3:16; II Peter 1:20), revealing the will of God concerning us in all things necessary to our salvation (John 5:39; II John 10); so that whatever is not contained therein is not to be enjoined as an article of faith (Isa. 8:20).

ORIGINAL SIN

Original sin, or total depravity, is that corruption of the nature of all the offspring of Adam by reason of which everyone is destitute of original righteousness (I Cor. 15:22; Rom. 5:12, 18; 3:12), and is inclined to evil and that continually (Gen. 6:5; 8:2). In the Scriptures it is designated as "the carnal mind" (Rom. 8:7), "our old man" (Rom. 6:6), "the flesh" (Rom. 8:5, 8), "sin that dwelleth in me" (Rom. 7:17), and similar expressions. It continues to exist after regeneration, though subdued, until eradicated and destroyed (I John 3:8) by the mighty baptism of the Holy Ghost and Fire.

The condition of man since the fall of Adam is such that he cannot turn and prepare himself by his own natural strength and works to faith and calling upon God; wherefore, we have no power to do good works pleasant and acceptable unto God, without the grace of God, which is freely given by Christ to all men without respect of

PRINCIPLES OF FAITH (EMMANUEL ASSOCIATION) (continued)

persons (Titus 2:11, 12), assisting us. "For it is God which worketh in you both to will and to do of his good pleasure."

FAITH

Living faith is the gift of God (Eph. 2:8) imparted to the obedient heart through the Word of God (Rom. 10:17) and the ministry of the Holy Ghost (Eph. 2:18). This faith becomes effective as it is exercised by man with the aid of the Spirit, which aid is always assured when the heart has met the divine condition (Heb. 5:9). Living faith is to be distinguished from intellectual confidence which may be in the possession of any unawakened soul (Rom. 10:1-4).

JUSTIFICATION AND REGENERATION

Though these two phases of the New Birth occur simultaneously, they are, in fact, two separate and distinct acts. Justification is that gracious and judicial act of God whereby a soul is granted complete absolvence from all guilt and a full release from the penalty of sin (Rom. 3:23-25). This act of divine grace is wrought by faith in the merits of our Lord and Saviour Jesus Christ (Rom. 5:1). Regeneration is the impartation of divine life which is manifested in that radical change in the moral character of man from the love and life of sin to the love of God and the life of righteousness (II Cor. 5:17; I Peter 1:23).

CONSECRATION

Consecration necessary for entire sanctification is the total abandonment of the redeemed soul to the whole will of God (Rom. 12:1; 6:11, 13, 22). As such it takes place after the work of regeneration and must be completed before the soul is sanctified. While the act of consecration depends wholly upon the individual, the scope of consecration must be dictated by the Holy Spirit (Acts 5:32). In saying that consecration is the act of the creature, it must be understood that every step in grace is undertaken through the assistance of the Holy Spirit (I Peter 1:22). This consecration becomes so deep that it includes perfect submission to the crucifixion of the body of sin (Rom. 6:6; Gal. 2:20; 5:24).

ENTIRE SANCTIFICATION OR THE BAPTISM WITH THE HOLY GHOST

Entire sanctification is that second definite, instantaneous work of grace subsequent to regeneration (John 17:9; Eph. 1:12, 13) wrought in the heart of the justified person through faith by the baptism of the Holy Ghost fire, whereby the heart of the believer is cleansed from all original sin, and purified by the filling of the Holy Ghost (Acts 15:8, 9; Rom. 15:16).

THE WITNESS OF THE SPIRIT

The witness of the Spirit is that inward impression wrought on the soul whereby the Spirit of God immediately and directly assures our spirit that Bible conditions are met for salvation and that the work of grace is complete in the soul (Rom. 8:15, 16). Therefore none should think they are either saved or sanctified until the Spirit of God has added His testimony (I John 5:10). And if we take care to walk with God and not grieve the Holy Spirit, we shall have an abiding testimony (Eph. 4:30).

SIN AFTER JUSTIFICATION

Not every sin wilfully committed after justification is blasphemy against the Holy Ghost, and is unpardonable. Therefore the grant of repentance is not to be denied to such as fall into sin after justification (James 5:19, 20).

SIN AFTER ENTIRE SANCTIFICATION

After we have received the Holy Ghost, any careless attitude toward the covenant that we entered when we were sanctified shall cause us to depart from grace given, and to fall into sin. Only through deep repentance, which God may permit, shall we then turn to God and receive forgiveness of our sins.

WATER BAPTISM

As revealed in the Gospel, water baptism bore a twofold testimony. First, that the candidate had been a partaker of divine grace, which qualified him to enter into fellowship with the children of God. Second, that his testimony was accepted by the one who baptized him (Matt. 3:7; Acts 8:35-38; 10:47, 48).

It is not to be held as being essential in bringing either justifying or sanctifying grace to one's heart, for the apostle administered it to Cornelius, who had previously received the baptism of the Holy Ghost.

The individual conscience should be satisfied as to the mode.

THE LORD'S SUPPER

The Lord's Supper was instituted by our Saviour with bread and the fruit of the vine on the night of His betrayal (Luke 22:19, 20). In observing it, we commemorate the fact that His body was broken and His blood was shed upon the cross, to redeem us from the curse of sin and death (I Cor. 11:23-29).

The elements used are representative, and the means whereby the body of Christ is received and eaten in the supper is faith. God has directed that each one examine himself before partaking, and so let him eat of that bread and drink of that cup (Matt. 26:26-29; I Cor. 10:16; 11:20-29).

HEALING

We believe and embrace the scriptural doctrine of healing for the body, and maintain that it is the privilege of every child of God to be healed in answer to the prayer of faith, according to James 5:14, 15. Yet we are not to sever fellowship from, or pass judgment on, those who use other providential means for the restoration of health (James 5:16; Acts 4:14; Matt. 10:8; Luke 9:2; II Cor. 12:9; John 9:1-34).

THE CHRISTIAN SABBATH

We believe the Christian Sabbath to be of divine origin. The Jewish Sabbath was obligatory upon those living under the law of Moses until the time of its consummation. We recognize the first day of the week as being the Christian Sabbath under the present dispensation (Rev. 1:10; I Cor. 16:2), the observance of which we hold obligatory and sacredly binding upon the followers of the

Lord Jesus, in commemoration of the glorious victory achieved through His resurrection from the dead on that eventful day. It was also duly and persistently observed by the Apostolic Church (Acts 20:7; I Cor. 16:2), and was the day upon which the Holy Ghost was poured out on the disciples.

THE SECOND COMING OF THE LORD

We believe that the coming of our Lord is to be personal and premillennial, also that it is imminent (Acts 1:9-11; I Thess. 4:14-17; Matt. 25:13; Rev. 22:12). We must distinguish between the Rapture—His coming in the air to receive His saints, which may occur at any moment—and the Revelation—His coming down to earth with His saints (II Thess. 1:7-10; Matt. 24:27; 26:29; Rev. 20:4), which latter will not occur until after the gathering of Israel, the manifestation of Antichrist, and other prophesied events (II Thess. 2:8-10; Rev. 19:20).

Notes: *The principles of the association are based upon, but differ from many points contained in, the statement of belief of its parent, the Pilgrim Holiness Church. The differences are not so much in doctrine as in standards of conduct (the association being more strict). The principles deleted some articles (such as the one on "Eternal Security") and added others (such as the one on the "Christian Sabbath"). The Pilgrim Holiness Church merged with the Wesleyan Methodist Church in 1968 to form the Wesleyan Church. At that time, the Pilgrim Holiness Church's statement of belief was replaced by that of the Wesleyan Church.*

* * *

ARTICLES OF RELIGION [FREE METHODIST CHURCH (PRIOR TO 1974)]

I. OF FAITH IN THE HOLY TRINITY

21.   There is but one living and true God, everlasting, without body or parts, of infinite power, wisdom, and goodness the maker and preserver of all things, visible and invisible. And in unity of this Godhead there are three persons of one substance, power, and eternity—the Father, the Son, and the Holy Ghost.

II. OF THE WORD, OR SON OF GOD, WHO WAS MADE VERY MAN

22.   The Son, who is the Word of the Father, the very and eternal God, of one substance with the Father, took man's nature in the womb of the blessed virgin so that the two whole and perfect natures, that is to say, the Godhead and manhood, were joined together in one person, never to be divided, whereof is one Christ, very God and very man, who truly suffered, was crucified, dead, and buried, to be the one mediator between God and man, by the sacrifice of Himself both for original sin and for the actual transgressions of men.

III. OF THE RESURRECTION OF CHRIST

23.   Christ did truly rise again from the dead, and took again His body, with all things appertaining to the perfection of man's nature, wherewith He ascended into heaven, and there sitteth until He returns to judge all men at the last day.

IV. OF THE HOLY GHOST

24.   The Holy Ghost, proceeding from the Father and the Son, is of one substance, majesty, and glory with the Father and the Son, very and eternal God.

V. THE SUFFICIENCY OF THE HOLY SCRIPTURES FOR SALVATION

25.   The Holy Scriptures contain all things necessary to salvation; so that whatsoever is not read therein, nor may be proved thereby, is not to be required of any man, that it should be believed as an article of faith, or be thought requisite or necessary to salvation. By the term Holy Scriptures we understand those canonical books of the Old and New Testaments of whose authority there was never any doubt in the Church.

The names of the canonical books are: Genesis, Exodus, Leviticus, Numbers, Deuteronomy, Joshua, Judges, Ruth, I and II Samuel, I and II Kings, I and II Chronicles, Ezra, Nehemiah, Esther, Job, Psalms, Proverbs, Ecclesiastes, Song of Solomon, Isaiah, Jeremiah, Lamentations, Ezekiel, Daniel, Hosea, Joel, Amos, Obadiah, Jonah, Micah, Nahum, Habakkuk, Zephaniah, Haggai, Zechariah, Malachi.

All the books of the New Testament, as they are commonly received, we do receive and account canonical: Matthew, Mark, Luke, John, Acts, Romans, I and II Corinthians, Galatians, Ephesians, Philippians, Colossians, I and II Thessalonians, I and II Timothy, Titus, Philemon, Hebrews, James, I and II Peter, I, II, and III John, Jude, Revelation.

VI. OF THE OLD TESTAMENT

26.   The Old Testament is not contrary to the New; for in both the Old and New Testaments everlasting life is offered to mankind by Christ, who is the only mediator between God and man. Wherefore they are not to be heard who feign that the old fathers did look only for transitory promises. Although the law given from God by Moses, as touching ceremonies and rites, doth not bind Christians, nor ought the civil precepts thereof, of necessity to be received in any commonwealth; yet, notwithstanding, no Christian whatsoever is free from obedience to the commandments which are called moral.

VII. OF ORIGINAL OR BIRTH SIN

27.   Original sin standeth not in the following of Adam, as the Pelagians do vainly talk, but it is the corruption of the nature of every man that naturally is engendered of the offspring of Adam, whereby man is very far gone from original righteousness, and of his own nature inclined to evil and that continually.

VIII. OF FREE WILL

28.   The condition of man after the fall of Adam is such that he cannot turn and prepare himself by his own natural strength and works to faith and calling upon God, wherefore we have no power to do good works, pleasing and acceptable to God, without the grace of God by Christ enabling us, that we may have a good

will, and working with us, when we have that good will.

IX. OF THE JUSTIFICATION AND REGENERATION OF MAN

29. We are accounted righteous before God only for the merit of our Lord and Saviour Jesus Christ by faith, and not for our own works or deservings; wherefore, that we are justified by faith only, is a most wholesome doctrine, and very full of comfort. Concurrently with justification we are regenerated by the Holy Spirit, who imparts spiritual life and renews us after the image of Him who created us.

X. OF GOOD WORKS

30. Although good works, which are the fruits of faith and follow after justification, cannot put away our sins and endure the severity of God's judgments, yet they are pleasing and acceptable to God in Christ, and spring out of a true and lively faith, insomuch that by them a lively faith may be as evidently known as a tree is discerned by its fruit.

XI. OF WORKS OF SUPEREROGATION

31. Voluntary works—besides, over and above God's commandments—which are called works of supererogation, cannot be taught without arrogancy and impiety. For by them men do declare that they do not only render unto God as much as they are bound to do, but that they do more for His sake than of bounden duty is required; whereas Christ saith plainly, "When ye have done all that is commanded you, say, We are unprofitable servants."

XII. OF SIN AFTER JUSTIFICATION

32. Not every sin willingly committed after justification is the sin against the Holy Ghost, and unpardonable. Wherefore the grant of repentance is not to be denied to such as fall into sin after justification. After we have received the Holy Ghost, we may depart from grace given, and fall into sin, and by the grace of God rise again and amend our lives. Therefore, they are to be condemned who say they can no more sin as long as they live here, or who deny the place of forgiveness to such as truly repent.

XIII. OF ENTIRE SANCTIFICATION

33. Entire sanctification is that work of the Holy Spirit, subsequent to regeneration, by which the fully consecrated believer, upon exercise of faith in the atoning blood of Christ, is cleansed in that moment from all inward sin and empowered for service. The resulting relationship is attested by the witness of the Holy Spirit and is maintained by obedience and faith. Entire sanctification enables the believer to love God with all his heart, soul, strength, and mind, and his neighbor as himself, and prepares him for greater growth in grace.

XIV. FUTURE REWARD AND PUNISHMENT

34. God has appointed a day in which He will judge the world in righteousness by Jesus Christ, according to the gospel. The righteous shall have in heaven an inheritance incorruptible, undefiled, and that fadeth not away. The wicked shall go away into everlasting punishment, where their worm dieth not, and the fire is not quenched.

XV. OF SPEAKING IN THE CONGREGATION IN SUCH A TONGUE AS THE PEOPLE UNDERSTAND

35. It is a thing plainly repugnant to the Word of God and the custom of the primitive Church to have public prayer in the church or to minister the sacrament in a tongue not understood by the people.

XVI. OF THE CHURCH

36. The visible Church of Christ is a congregation of faithful men, in which the pure Word of God is preached, and the sacraments are duly administered, according to Christ's ordinance, in all those things that of necessity are requisite to the same.

XVII. OF THE SACRAMENTS

37. Sacraments ordained of Christ are not only badges or tokens of Christian men's profession, but they are also certain signs of grace, and of God's good will toward us, by the which He doth work invisibly in us, and doth not only quicken but also strengthen and confirm our faith in Him.

XVIII. OF BAPTISM

38. Baptism is not only a sign of profession and mark of difference, whereby Christians are distinguished from others who are not baptized, but it is also a sign of regeneration or the new birth. The baptism of young children is to be retained in the church.

XIX. OF THE LORD'S SUPPER

39. The Supper of the Lord is not merely a sign of the love that Christians ought to have among themselves one to another, but rather is a sacrament of our redemption by Christ's death, insomuch that, to such as rightly, worthily, and with faith receive the same, the bread which we break is a partaking of the body of Christ; and likewise the cup of blessing is a partaking of the blood of Christ.

Transubstantiation, or the change of the substance of bread and wine in the Supper of our Lord, cannot be proved by Holy Writ, but is repugnant to the plain word of the Scripture, overthroweth the nature of a sacrament, and hath given occasion to many superstitions.

The body of Christ is given, taken, and eaten in the Supper only after a heavenly and spiritual manner; and the means whereby the body of Christ is received and eaten in the Supper, is faith. The sacrament of the Lord's Supper was not by Christ's ordinance reserved, carried about, lifted up, or worshipped.

XX. OF THE ONE OBLATION OF CHRIST, FINISHED UPON THE CROSS

40. The offering of Christ, once made, is a perfect redemption, propitiation, and satisfaction for all the sins of the whole world, both original and actual; and there is none other satisfaction for sin but that alone.

Wherefore the sacrifice of the masses, in the which it is said that the priest doth offer Christ for the quick and the dead, to have remission of pain or guilt, is a blasphemous and dangerous deceit.

XXI. OF THE RITES AND CEREMONIES OF CHURCHES

41. It is not necessary that rites and ceremonies should in all places be the same, or exactly alike; for they have been always different, and may be changed according to the diversity of countries, times, and men's manners, so that nothing be ordained against God's Word. Whosoever through his private judgment, willingly and purposely doth openly break the rites and ceremonies of the church to which he belongs, which are not repugnant to the Word of God, and are ordained and approved by common authority, ought to be rebuked openly, that others may fear to do the like, as one that offendeth against the common order of the church, and woundeth the conscience of the weak brethren. We recognize the right of every denomination to ordain, change, or abolish rites and ceremonies so that all things may be done to edification.

XXII. OF CHRISTIAN MEN'S GOODS

42. The riches and goods of Christians are not common, as touching the right, title, and possession of the same, as some do falsely boast. Notwithstanding, every man ought, of such things as he possesseth, liberally to give alms to the poor according to his ability.

XXIII. OF A CHRISTIAN MAN'S OATH

43. As we confess that vain and rash swearing is forbidden Christian men by our Lord Jesus Christ, and James the apostle; so we hold that the Christian religion doth not prohibit, but that a man may take oath when the magistrate requireth in a case of faith and charity, so it be done according to the prophet's teaching, in justice, judgment, and truth.

Notes: *In 1974 the Free Methodist Church adopted a newly-written set of Articles of Religion. Prior to that time, it had adopted a modified version of the Twenty-five Articles of Religion common to Methodism. The Free Methodist revisions included additions to several articles (Of Justification and Regeneration of Man), deletions from some (Of the Sacraments), the addition of two articles (Of Entire Sanctification, Future Reward and Punishment), and the deletion of four articles (Of Purgatory, Of Both Kinds, Of the Marriage of Ministers, and Of the Rulers of the United States). A footnote to the article "Of a Christian Man's Oath" upholds the rights of members who have a conscientious objection to oath-taking.*

These articles became the basis for the articles of religion of the Evangelical Wesleyan Church whose original members left the Free Methodist Church in the early 1960s.

ARTICLES OF RELIGION [FREE METHODIST CHURCH (1974)]

GOD

I. THE HOLY TRINITY

101. We believe in the one living and true God, the maker and preserver of all things. And in the unity of this Godhead there are three persons: the Father, the Son, and the Holy Spirit. These three are one in eternity, deity, and purpose; everlasting, of infinite power, wisdom, and goodness.

II. THE FATHER

102. We believe the Father is the cause of all that exists whether of matter or spirit. He with the Son and the Holy Spirit made man to bear his image. By intention he relates to man as Father, thereby forever declaring his goodwill toward man. He is, according to the New Testament, the one who both seeks and receives penitent sinners.

III. THE SON

HIS INCARNATION

103. We believe God was himself in Jesus Christ to reconcile man to God. Conceived by the Holy Spirit, born of the Virgin Mary, he joined together the deity of God and the humanity of man. Jesus of Nazareth was God in human flesh, truly God and truly man. He came to save us. For us the Son of God suffered, was crucified, dead and buried. He poured out his life as a blameless sacrifice for our sin and transgressions. We gratefully acknowledge that he is our Savior, the one perfect mediator between God and man.

HIS RESURRECTION AND EXALTATION

104. We believe Jesus Christ is risen victorious from the dead. His resurrected body became more glorious, not hindered by ordinary human limitations. Thus he ascended into heaven. There he sits as our exalted Lord at the right hand of God the Father, where he intercedes for us until all his enemies shall be brought into complete subjection. He will return to judge all men. Every knee will bow and every tongue confess Jesus Christ is Lord, to the glory of God the Father.

IV. THE HOLY SPIRIT

HIS PERSON

105. We believe the Holy Spirit is the third person of the Trinity. Proceeding from the Father and the Son, he is one with them, the eternal Godhead; equal in deity, majesty, and power. He is God effective in creation, in life, and in the church. The incarnation and ministry of Jesus Christ were accomplished by the Holy Spirit. He continues to reveal, interpret, and glorify the Son.

HIS WORK IN SALVATION

106. We believe the Holy Spirit is the administrator of the salvation planned by the Father and provided by the Son's death, resurrection, and ascension. He is the effective agent in our conviction, regeneration, sanc-

ARTICLES OF RELIGION [FREE METHODIST CHURCH (1974)] (continued)

tification, and glorification. He is our Lord's ever-present self, indwelling, assuring, and enabling the believer.

HIS RELATION TO THE CHURCH

107. We believe the Holy Spirit is poured out upon the church by the Father and the Son. He is the church's life and witnessing power. He bestows the love of God and makes real the lordship of Jesus Christ in the believer so that both his gifts of words and service may achieve the common good and build and increase the church. In relation to the world he is the Spirit of truth, and his instrument is the Word of God.

THE SCRIPTURES

V. SUFFICIENCY

108. We believe the Holy Scriptures are God's record, uniquely inspired by the Holy Spirit. They have been given without error faithfully recorded by holy men of God as moved by the Holy Spirit, and subsequently transmitted without corruption of any essential doctrine. They are the authoritative record of the revelation of God's acts in creation, in history, in our salvation, and especially in his Son, Jesus Christ.

We believe this written Word fully reveals the will of God concerning man in all things necessary to salvation and Christian living; so that whatever is not found therein, nor can be proved thereby, is not to be required of one as an article of faith or as necessary to salvation.

VI. AUTHORITY OF THE OLD TESTAMENT

109. We believe the Old Testament is not contrary to the New. Both Testaments bear witness to God's salvation in Christ; both speak of God's will for his people. The ancient laws for ceremonies and rites, and the civil precepts for the nation Israel are not necessarily binding on Christians today. But, on the example of Jesus we are obligated to obey the moral commandments of the Old Testament.

The books of the Old Testament are: Genesis, Exodus, Leviticus, Numbers, Deuteronomy, Joshua, Judges, Ruth, I Samuel, II Samuel, I Kings, II Kings, I Chronicles, II Chronicles, Ezra, Nehemiah, Esther, Job, Psalms, Proverbs, Ecclesiastes, The Song of Solomon, Isaiah, Jeremiah, Lamentations, Ezekiel, Daniel, Hosea, Joel, Amos, Obadiah, Jonah, Micah, Nahum, Habakkuk, Zephaniah, Haggai, Zechariah, Malachi.

VII. NEW TESTAMENT

110. We believe the New Testament fulfills and interprets the Old Testament. It is the record of the revelation of God in Jesus Christ and the Holy Spirit. It is God's final word regarding man, his sin, and his salvation, the world, and destiny.

The books of the New Testament are: Matthew, Mark, Luke, John, Acts, Romans, I Corinthians, II Corinthians, Galatians, Ephesians, Philipians, Colos-

sians, I Thessalonians, II Thessalonians, I Timothy, II Timothy, Titus, Philemon, Hebrews, James, I Peter, II Peter, I John, II John, III John, Jude, Revelation.

MAN

VIII. A FREE MORAL PERSON

111. We believe God created man in his own image, innocent, morally free and responsible to choose between good and evil, right and wrong. By the sin of Adam, man as the offspring of Adam is corrupted in his very nature so that from birth he is inclined to sin. He is unable by his own strength and work to restore himself in right relationship with God and to merit eternal salvation. God, the Omnipotent, provides all the resources of the Trinity to make it possible for man to respond to his grace through faith in Jesus Christ as Savior and Lord. By God's grace and help man is enabled to do good works with a free will.

IX. LAW OF LIFE AND LOVE

112. We believe God's law for all human life, personal and social, is expressed in two divine commands: Love the Lord God with all your heart, and love your neighbor as yourself. These commands reveal what is best for man in his relationship with God, persons, and society. They set forth the principles of human duty in both individual and social action. They recognize God as the only Sovereign. All men as created by him and in his image have the same inherent rights regardless of sex, race, or color. Men should therefore give God absolute obedience in their individual, social, and political acts. They should strive to secure to everyone respect for his person, his rights, and his greatest happiness in the possession and exercise of the right within the moral law.

X. GOOD WORKS

113. We believe good works are the fruit of faith in Jesus Christ, but works cannot save us from our sins nor from God's judgment. As expressions of Christian faith and love, our good works performed with reverence and humility are both acceptable and pleasing to God. However, good works do not earn God's grace.

SALVATION

XI. CHRIST'S SACRIFICE

114. We believe Christ offered once and for all the one perfect sacrifice for the sins of the whole world. No other satisfaction for sin is necessary; none other can atone.

XII. THE NEW LIFE IN CHRIST

115. We believe a new life and a right relationship with God are made possible through the redemptive acts of God in Jesus Christ, God, by his Spirit, acts to impart new life and put us into a relationship with himself as we repent and our faith responds to his grace. Justification, regeneration, and adoption speak significantly to entrance into and continuance in the new life.

JUSTIFICATION

116. Justification is a legal term that emphasizes that by our new relationship in Jesus Christ we are in fact accounted righteous, being freed from both the guilt and the penalty of our sins.

REGENERATION

117. Regeneration is a biological term which illustrates that by our new relationship in Christ we do in fact have a new life and a new spiritual nature capable of faith, love, and obedience to Christ Jesus as Lord. The believer is born again. He is a new creation. The old life is past; a new life is begun.

ADOPTION

118. Adoption is a filial term full of warmth, love, and acceptance. It denotes that by our new relationship in Christ we have become his wanted children freed from the mastery of both sin and Satan. The believer has the witness of the Spirit that he is a child of God.

XIII. ENTIRE SANCTIFICATION

119. We believe entire sanctification to be that work of the Holy Spirit, subsequent to regeneration, by which the fully consecrated believer, upon exercise of faith in the atoning blood of Christ, is cleansed in that moment from all inward sin and empowered for service. The resulting relationship is attested by the witness of the Holy Spirit and is maintained by faith and obedience. Entire sanctification enables the believer to love God with all his heart, soul, strength, and mind, and his neighbor as himself, and it prepares him for greater growth in grace.

XIV. RESTORATION

120. We believe the Christian may be sustained in a growing relationship with Jesus as Savior and Lord. However, he may grieve the Holy Spirit in the relationships of life without returning to the dominion of sin. When he does, he must humbly accept the correction of the Holy Spirit, trust in the advocacy of Jesus, and mend his relationships.

The Christian can sin willfully and sever his relationship with Christ. Even so by repentance before God, forgiveness is granted and the relationship with Christ restored, for not every sin is the sin against the Holy Spirit and unpardonable. God's grace is sufficient for those who truly repent and, by his enabling, amend their lives. However, forgiveness does not give the believer liberty to sin and escape the consequences of sinning.

God has given responsibility and power to the church to restore a penitent believer through loving reproof, counsel, and acceptance.

THE CHURCH

XV. THE CHURCH

121. We believe the church is created by God; it is the people of God. Christ Jesus is its Lord and Head; the Holy Spirit is its life and power. It is both divine and human, heavenly and earthly, ideal and imperfect. It is an organism, not an unchanging institution. It exists to fulfill the purposes of God in Christ. It redemptively ministers to persons. Christ loved the church and gave himself for it that it should be holy and without blemish. The church is a fellowship of the redeemed and the redeeming, preaching the Word of God and administering the sacraments according to Christ's instruction. The Free Methodist Church purposes to be representative of what the church of Jesus Christ should be on earth. It therefore requires specific commitment regarding the faith and life of its members. In its requirements it seeks to honor Christ and obey the written Word of God.

XVI. THE LANGUAGE OF WORSHIP

122. We believe that according to the Word of God and the custom of the early church, public worship and prayer and the administration of the sacraments should be in a language understood by the people. The Reformation applied this principle to provide for the use of the common language of the people. It is likewise clear that the Apostle Paul places the strongest emphasis upon rational and intelligible utterance in worship. We cannot endorse practices which plainly violate these scriptural principles.

XVII. THE HOLY SACRAMENTS

123. We believe water baptism and the Lord's Supper are the sacraments of the church commanded by Christ. They are means of grace through faith, tokens of our profession of Christian faith, and signs of God's gracious ministry toward us. By them, he works within us to quicken, strengthen, and confirm our faith.

BAPTISM

124. We believe water baptism is a sacrament of the church, commanded by our Lord, signifying acceptance of the benefits of the atonement of Jesus Christ to be administered to believers, as declaration of their faith in Jesus Christ as Savior.

Baptism is a symbol of the new covenant of grace as circumcision was the symbol of the old covenant; and, since infants are recognized as being included in the atonement, we hold that they may be baptized upon the request of parents or guardians who shall give assurance for them of necessary Christian training. They shall be required to affirm the vow for themselves before being accepted into church membership.

THE LORD'S SUPPER

125. We believe the Lord's Supper is a sacrament of our redemption by Christ's death. To those who rightly, worthily, and with faith receive it, the bread which we break is a partaking of the body of Christ; and likewise the cup of blessing is a partaking of the blood of Christ. The supper is also a sign of the love and unity that Christians have among themselves.

Christ, according to his promise, is really present in the sacrament. But his body is given, taken, and eaten only after a heavenly and spiritual manner. No change is effected in the element; the bread and wine are not literally the body and blood of Christ. Nor is the body and blood of Christ literally present with the elements. The elements are never to be considered objects of worship. The body of Christ is received and eaten in faith.

LAST THINGS

XVIII. THE KINGDOM OF GOD

126. We believe that the kingdom of God is a prominent Bible theme providing the Christian with both his task and hope. Jesus announced its presence. The kingdom is realized now as God's reign is established in the hearts and lives of believers.

The church, by its prayers, example, and proclamation of the gospel, is the appointed and appropriate instrument of God in building his kingdom.

But the kingdom is also future and is related to the return of Christ when judgment will fall upon the present order. The enemies of Christ will be subdued; the reign of God will be established; a total cosmic renewal which is both material and moral shall occur; and the hope of the redeemed will be fully realized.

XIX. THE RETURN OF CHRIST

127. We believe the return of Christ is certain and may occur at any moment. It is not given us to know the hour. At his return he will fulfill all prophecies concerning his final triumph over all evil. The believer's response is joyous expectation, watchfulness, readiness, and diligence.

XX. RESURRECTION

128. We believe in the bodily resurrection from the dead of both the just and the unjust, they that have done good unto the resurrection of life; they that have done evil unto the resurrection of damnation. The resurrected body will be a spiritual body, but the person will be whole and identifiable. The resurrection of Christ is the guarantee of resurrection unto life to those who are in him.

XXI. JUDGMENT

129. We believe God has appointed a day in which he will judge the world in righteousness in accordance with the gospel and men's deeds in this life.

XXII. FINAL DESTINY

130. We believe the eternal destiny of man is determined by God's grace and man's response, not by arbitrary decrees of God. For those who trust him and obediently follow Jesus as Savior and Lord, there is a heaven of eternal glory and the blessedness of Christ's presence. But for the finally impenitent there is a hell of eternal suffering and of separation from God.

131. The doctrines of the Free Methodist Church are based upon the Holy Scriptures and are derived from their total biblical context. The references below are appropriate passages related to the given articles. They are listed in their biblical sequence and are not intended to be exhaustive.

GOD

I. HOLY TRINITY

Genesis 1:1-2; Exodus 3:13-15; Deuteronomy 6:4; Matthew 28:19; John 1:1-3; 5:19-23; 8:58; 14:9-11; 15:26; 16:13-15; II Corinthians 13:14.

II. FATHER

Genesis 1:26-27; Psalm 103:13-14; Isaiah 40:28-29; 64:8; Matthew 6:8; 18:14; Luke 15:11-32; John 4:23; I John 1:3.

III. SON - HIS INCARNATION

Matthew 1:21; 20:28; 26:27-28; Luke 1:35; 19:10; John 1:1, 10, 14; II Corinthians 5:18-19; Philippians 2:5-8; Hebrews 2:17; 9:14-15.

SON - HIS RESURRECTION AND EXALTATION

Matthew 25:31-32; Luke 24:1-7; 24:39; John 20:19; Acts 1:9-11; 2:24; Romans 8:33-34; II Corinthians 5:10; Philippians 2:9-11; Hebrews 1:1-4.

IV. HOLY SPIRIT - HIS PERSON

Matthew 28:19; John 4:24; 14:16-17, 26; 15:26; 16:13-15

HOLY SPIRIT - HIS WORK IN SALVATION

John 16:7-8; Acts 15:8-9; Romans 8:9, 14-16; I Corinthians 3:16; II Corinthians 3:17-18; Galatians 4:6.

HOLY SPIRIT - HIS RELATION TO THE CHURCH

Acts 5:3-4; Romans 8:14; I Corinthians 12:4-7; II Peter 1:21.

THE SCRIPTURES

V. SUFFICIENCY

Deuteronomy 4:2; 28:9; Psalm 19:7-11; John 14:26; 17:17; Romans 15:4; II Timothy 3:14-17; Hebrews 4:12; James 1:21.

VI. AUTHORITY OF THE OLD TESTAMENT

Matthew 5:17-18; Luke 10:25-28; John 5:39, 46-47; Acts 10:43; Galatians 5:3-4; I Peter 1:10-12.

VII. NEW TESTAMENT

Matthew 24:35; Mark 8:38; John 14:24; Hebrews 2:1-4; II Peter 1:16-21; I John 2:2-6; Revelation 21:5; 22:19.

MAN

VIII. MAN: A FREE MORAL PERSON

Genesis 1:27; Psalm 51:5; 130:3; Romans 5:17-19; Ephesians 2:8-10.

IX. LAW OF LIFE AND LOVE

Matthew 22:35-40; John 15:17; Galatians 3:28; I John 4:19-21.

X. GOOD WORKS

Matthew 5:16; 7:16-20; Romans 3:27-28; Ephesians 2:10; II Timothy 1:8-9; Titus 3:5.

SALVATION

XI. CHRIST'S SACRIFICE

Luke 24:46-48; John 3:16; Acts 4:12; Romans 5:8-11; Galatians 2:16; 3:2-3; Ephesians 1:7-8; 2:13; Hebrews 9:11-14, 25-26; 10:8-14.

XII. THE NEW LIFE IN CHRIST

John 1:12-13; 3:3-8; Acts 13:38-39; Romans 8:15-17; Ephesians 2:8-9; Colossians 3:9-10.

JUSTIFICATION

Psalm 32:1-2; Acts 10:43; Romans 3:21-26, 28; 4:2-5; 5:8-9; I Corinthians 6:11; Philippians 3:9.

REGENERATION

Ezekiel 36:26-27; John 5:24; Romans 6:4; II Corinthians 5:17; Ephesians 4:22-24; Colossians 3:9-10; Titus 3:4-5; I Peter 1:23.

ADOPTION

Romans 8:15-17; Galatians 4:4-7; Ephesians 1:5-6; I John 3:1-3.

XIII. ENTIRE SANCTIFICATION

Leviticus 20:7-8; John 14:16-17; 17:19; Acts 1:8; 2:4; 15:8-9; Romans 5:3-5; 8:12-17; 12:1-2; I Corinthians 6:11; 12:4-11; Galatians 5:22-25; Ephesians 4:22-24; I Thessalonians 4:7; 5:23-24; II Thessalonians 2:13; Hebrews 10:14.

XIV. RESTORATION

Matthew 12:31-32; 18:21-22; Romans 6:1-2; Galatians 6:1; I John 1:9; 2:1-2; 5:16-17; Revelation 2:5; 3:19-20.

THE CHURCH

XV. THE CHURCH

Matthew 16:15-18; 18:17; Acts 2:41-47; 9:31; 12:5; 14:23-26; 15:22; 20:28; I Corinthians 1:2; 11:23; 12:28; 16:1; Ephesians 1:22-23; 2:19-22; 3:9-10; 5:22-23; Colossians 1:18; I Timothy 3:14-15.

XVI. THE LANGUAGE OF WORSHIP

Nehemiah 8:5, 6, 8; Matthew 6:7; I Corinthians 14:6-9; I Corinthians 14:23-25.

XVII. THE HOLY SACRAMENTS

Matthew 26:26-29; 28:19; Acts 22:16; Romans 4:11; I Corinthians 10:16-17; 11:23-26; Galatians 3:27.

BAPTISM

Acts 2:38, 41; 8:12-17; 9:18; 16:33; 18:8; 19:5; John 3:5; I Corinthians 12:13; Galatians 3:27-29; Colossians 2:11-12; Titus 3:5.

THE LORD'S SUPPER

Mark 14:22-24; John 6:53-58; Acts 2:46; I Corinthians 5:7-8; 10:16; 11:20, 23-29.

LAST THINGS

XVIII. THE KINGDOM OF GOD.

Matthew 6:10, 19-20; 24:14; Acts 1:8; Romans 8:19-23; I Corinthians 15:20-25; Philippians 2:9-10; I Thessalonians 4:15-17; II Thessalonians 1:5-12; II Peter 3:3-10; Revelation 14:6; 21:3-8; 22:1-5, 17.

XIX. THE RETURN OF CHRIST

Matthew 24:1-51; 26:64; Mark 13:26-27; Luke 17:26-37; John 14:1-3; Acts 1:9-11; I Thessalonians 4:13-18; Titus 2:11-14; Hebrews 9:27-28; Revelation 1:7; 19:11-16; 22:6-7, 12, 20.

XX. RESURRECTION

John 5:28-29; I Corinthians 15:20, 51-57; II Corinthians 4:13-14.

XXI. JUDGMENT

Matthew 25:31-46; Luke 11:31-32; Acts 10:42; 17:31; Romans 2:15-16; 14:10-11; II Corinthians 5:6-10; Hebrews 9:27-28; 10:26-31; II Peter 3:7.

XXII. DESTINY

Mark 9:42-48; John 14:3; Hebrews 2:1-3; Revelation 20:11-15; 21:22-27.

Notes: *The new articles, rewritten in a more confessional style, were adopted by the Free Methodist Church in 1974. They reflect the twentieth-century debate over the nature of biblical authority and expand the statements on eschatological issues. They also added a lengthy set of scriptural references as a grounding for the new articles.*

* * *

WE BELIEVE (HOLINESS CHRISTIAN CHURCH)

1. In one God, the Creator of all things and man; eternally existing in three Persons, in a threefold relationship, that of the Father, Son and Holy Spirit.

2. That Jesus Christ was begotten by the Holy Spirit, born of the Virgin Mary, and became God in the flesh.

3. That man was created in the image of God, that he sinned and thereby incurred not only physical death, but also the spiritual death which is separation from God. That Adam's sin is imputed to the whole race of mankind, and that all human beings are born with a sinful nature and in the case of those who reach the state of moral responsibility, become sinners before God in thought, word and deed.

4. That Jesus Christ died for our sins (the sins of all men) according to the Scriptures as a substitutionary sacrifice, and that all who believe in Him are freely justified and stand before God accepted in the character and merit of Jesus Christ, with a transformation of life and conduct.

5. That God has provided through the Lord Jesus Christ for a complete cleansing from the sin nature and that this work is subsequent to the new birth, wherein the believer is filled with the Holy Spirit.

6. In the bodily resurrection of Jesus Christ, in His ascension into heaven, and in His present life He is the Head of the Church, the Lord of the individual believer, the High Priest over the house of God, and the Advocate of the family of God.

7. In the personal imminent and premillennial second coming of Christ; first, to receive His own unto Himself, and later to set up His earthly kingdom and

to reign over redeemed Israel and all nations of the world; that is, to bring peace and blessing to the whole world.

8. In the bodily resurrection of the just and the unjust, the everlasting blessedness of the saved, and the everlasting punishment of the unsaved.

9. In the Scriptures of the Old and New Testaments as verbally inspired of God and inerrant in the original writings, and that they are the Word of God and the final authority for faith and conduct.

* * *

ARTICLES OF FAITH (METROPOLITAN CHURCH ASSOCIATION)

I. THE APOSTLES' CREED

I believe in God the Father Almighty, Maker of Heaven and earth; and in Jesus Christ His only Son our Lord, who was conceived by the Holy Ghost; born of the virgin Mary; suffered under Pontius Pilate; was crucified, dead and buried; the third day He rose from the dead; He ascended into Heaven, and sitteth at the right hand of God the Father Almighty; from thence He shall come to judge the quick and the dead.

I believe in the Holy Ghost, the holy catholic church, the communion of saints, the forgiveness of sins, the resurrection of the body and the life everlasting. Amen.

II. THE HOLY TRINITY

There is but one living and true God, existing from eternity, of infinite power, wisdom and goodness, the Maker and Preserver of all things visible and invisible. The Godhead consists of three persons, of one substance and power and eternity—the Father, the Son and the Holy Ghost.

III. JESUS CHRIST THE SON

The Son, who is the Word of the Father, the very and eternal God of one substance with the Father, took man's nature in the womb of the blessed virgin, so that the two whole and perfect natures, that is to say, the Godhead and manhood, were joined together in one Person, never to be divided, whereof is one Christ, very God and very man.

IV. RESURRECTION OF CHRIST

Christ did truly rise from the dead and took again His body, with all things pertaining to the completeness of man's nature, wherewith He ascended into Heaven, and there sitteth on the right hand of God until He shall return to judge all men at the last day.

V. THE HOLY GHOST

The Holy Ghost, proceeding from the Father and the Son, is of one substance, majesty and glory with the Father and the Son, very and eternal God.

VI. THE HOLY SCRIPTURES

The Holy Scriptures contain all things necessary to salvation; so that whatsoever is not read therein, nor may be proved thereby, is not to be required of any man, that it should be believed as an article of faith or be thought requisite or necessary to salvation. By the term "the Holy Scriptures" we understand those canonical books of the Old and New Testament given in the King James version, of whose authority there never was any doubt in the church.

VII. MANKIND

Man, in the person of Adam, was made in the image of God, created a holy being. By transgressing God's law, his nature became depraved, and this condition has been transmitted to all mankind; so that man is very far gone from original righteousness and of his own nature inclined to evil, and that continually.

VIII. OF FREE WILL

The condition of man after the fall is such that, unassisted by divine grace, he cannot find his way back to God and holiness. The office of the Holy Ghost is to draw mankind to God and to work God's grace in the soul. All men can, if they will, yield to the Holy Spirit and turn from sin to God and holiness.

IX. OF THE ATONEMENT

The atonement is the satisfaction made to God for the sins of all mankind, original and actual, by the mediation of Christ, and especially by His passion and death; so that pardon might be granted to all, while the divine perfections are kept in harmony, the authority of the Sovereign is upheld, and the strongest motives are brought to bear upon sinners to lead them to repentance and to faith in Christ, the necessary conditions of pardon, and to a life of obedience, by the gracious aid of the Holy Spirit.

X. JUSTIFICATION

We are justified by faith only, through the merit of our Lord and Savior Jesus Christ, and are accounted righteous before God, not by our own works and deservings but by virtue of the shed blood of Christ.

XI. OF GOOD WORKS

Although good works, which are the fruits of faith and follow after justification, cannot put away our sins or endure the severity of God's judgments, yet they are pleasing and acceptable to God in Christ, and spring out of a true and lively faith; insomuch that by them a lively faith is evidently known, as a tree is discerned by its fruits.

XII. SIN AFTER JUSTIFICATION

Not every sin willingly committed after justification is the sin against the Holy Ghost and unpardonable. While it is possible for a person never to fall into sin after being justified, yet is is possible to fall, and by the grace of God to be restored again. After we have received the Holy Ghost in the grace of entire sanctification, we may depart from grace given and fall into sin, and by the grace of God be restored to justification and holiness. This is not intended in any way to countenance the teaching commonly known as the doctrine of the final perseverance of the saints, and again, as the doctrine of eternal security, which teaches that once having received grace it is impossible so to fall away from God as to be finally lost.

XIII. ENTIRE SANCTIFICATION

Justified persons, while they do not outwardly commit sin, are nevertheless conscious of sin still remaining in the heart. They feel a natural tendency to evil, a proneness to depart from God and to cleave to the things of earth. Those who are sanctified wholly are saved from all inward sin, from evil thoughts and evil tempers. No wrong temper, none contrary to pure love, remains in the soul. All their thoughts, words and actions are governed by pure love.

Entire sanctification takes place subsequently to justification, and is the work of God wrought instantaneously in the soul through faith in the shed blood of Christ.

XIV. FUTURE REWARDS AND PUNISHMENTS

God hath appointed a day in which He will judge the world in righteousness by Jesus Christ, according to the Gospel. The righteous shall have in Heaven an inheritance incorruptible and that fadeth not away. The wicked shall go away into everlasting punishment, where the worm dieth not and the fire is not quenched.

XV. THE CHURCH

The church is the body of Christ. It is not a material structure but is composed of those who are born of the Spirit and washed in the blood of Christ. The visible church of Christ is a congregation of godly men in which the pure Word of God is preached and the sacraments are duly administered, according to Christ's ordinance.

XVI. OF BAPTISM

Baptism is a sign of profession and mark of difference whereby Christians are distinguished from others. It is not essential to salvation, but it serves as the outward sign of an inward work of regeneration wrought by the Holy Ghost, and is to be administered to all that require it. We hereby repudiate the doctrine known as baptismal regeneration, teaching that saving grace is communicated only in the act of baptism.

XVII. OF THE LORD'S SUPPER

The supper of the Lord is a sacrament of our redemption by Christ's death, and its observance shows forth His death till He come. It is a sign, too, of the love that Christians ought to have among themselves, one to another. It is a certain means of grace, by the which He doth work invisibly in us, and doth not only quicken but also strengthens and confirms our faith in Him.

XVIII. OF CHRIST'S SECOND COMING

Of this glorious event, commonly spoken of as the second coming of Christ, Jesus often spoke, and His apostles. It will be premillennial, and the world will be found in a state of sin and rebellion. It will be sudden and visible. It will close the day of grace, thus shutting off all hope of any second probation for those in sin. We repudiate any view of Christ's second coming that militates against the Scripture commands for present holiness of heart and life.

Notes: *After the initial restatement of the Apostles' Creed, these articles are condensed from the Twenty-five Articles of Religion common to Methodism. Two articles on eschatology have been added, including the statement on "Future Rewards and Punishments," borrowed from the Free*

Methodist Church. The statement on scripture has been altered to affirm the exclusive use of the King James Version of the Bible.

*   *   *

THE STATEMENTS OF FAITH OF THE MISSIONARY CHURCH

GOD. There is but one eternal, all powerful, all knowing, and everywhere present triune God—Father, Son and Holy Spirit—who is the Creator and Sustainer of all things. (Deuteronomy 6:4, 5; I Timothy 2:5)

JESUS CHRIST. He is God Incarnate, yet human, lived a sinless life, died to make atonement for the sins of all mankind, was bodily resurrected and is now Mediator at the right hand of the Father, is assuredly coming in power and glory for His believing followers, and is the only Savior of men. (John 1:1,14; Titus 2:11-14)

HOLY SPIRIT. He convicts the world of sin, righteousness and judgment; regenerates all who repent of their sins and believe on the Lord Jesus Christ; and sanctifies, empowers, teaches, guides, and comforts the believers. (John 16:7,8,12-15)

BIBLE. To us, the Bible is the divinely inspired Word of God and thus authoritative in all matters of Christian faith and practice. (II Timothy 3:16; II Peter 1:20,21)

SALVATION. Salvation is genuine repentance of sin and faith in the atoning work of Christ. It brings forgiveness to the penitent, makes him a partaker of the divine nature and gives peace with God. We call this new birth. (Titus 3:5; I Peter 1:3-5)

CHURCH. We believe in the invisible and universal Church as an organism, composed of all believers in the Lord Jesus Christ who have been vitally united by faith to Christ, its living Head and sovereign Lord. (Matthew 16:18; Hebrews 12:22-24)

ORDINANCES. We also believe that the Christian ordinances are two, baptism and the Lord's Supper, and that they are outward rites appointed by Christ to be administered in each church, not as a means of salvation, but as a visible sign and seal of its reality. (Acts 2:36; I Corinthians 11:23-34)

SERVICE. Service includes witnessing to one's faith in Christ and meeting social physical needs in the name of Christ. (I Peter 3:8; Matthew 25:40)

Notes: *The Missionary Church is a holiness church with roots in the Mennonite Church. It sees itself as sound and pure in Biblical interpretation, avoiding extremes while maintaining a balance of teaching that encourages holy living and service.*

*   *   *

CREED (MISSIONARY METHODIST CHURCH)

1. That the Holy Scriptures are of Divine origin, and are given to us by Inspiration for our instruction, edification and final sanctification.

CREED (MISSIONARY METHODIST CHURCH) (continued)

2. That Christ is the Head of the Church, and the Holy Scriptures the only guide to our faith.

3. That all who believe in the Scriptures and follow Christ are entitled to membership in the Missionary Methodist Church.

4. That God having made man to choose between good and evil, it is his right and duty, acting upon his judgment, based upon the Word of God to choose that society or church, which accords with his judgment and the Holy Scriptures.

5. That no member of these societies shall be tried for any cause or deprived of the benefits of the church, except for those things forbidden in the Holy Scriptures.

6. That ministers, deacons, elders and stewards in the church are of Divine origin, and all elders in the church are equal in rank.

7. That the church has only the right to enforce such rules and regulations as are plainly taught in the Holy Scriptures.

8. That all inherent power to make laws and regulations for the government of the church, is vested in the ministers and members; this power, however, may be delegated to representatives, for the purpose of better organization.

9. That it is the duty of both members and ministers, of these societies, to stand for the right and oppose the wrong at all times.

10. That it is the solemn duty of all ministers to be faithful to their trust, and the duty of the members to regard the ministers as those sent of God, to minister in Holy things.

11. That all ministers and members are to be temperate in all things, and do none of those things that would cause a weaker brother to fall, or bring reproach upon the cause for which we stand, and bring His name into disrepute among men.

12. That we believe in a missionary movement upon the world, for that all mankind are brethren, and our duty to our brother must needs be that we go or send the Gospel to every nation.

Notes: *The Missionary Methodist Church has two doctrinal documents. Its articles of faith derive from the Articles of Religion of the Wesleyan Methodist Church, from whence the Missionary Methodist Church came. The creed deals with issues not covered in the articles.*

*　　*　　*

ARTICLES OF FAITH (MISSIONARY METHODIST CHURCH)

1. FAITH IN THE HOLY TRINITY.

We believe that there is but one GOD, infinitely and eternally the Maker and Preserver of all mankind. And of this Godhead, there are three persons, of one power and eternity—God, the Father; God, the Son (or Word); and God, the Holy Ghost. Genesis, 1:1; John, 1:1; John 3:16; Acts, 5:3-4.

2. THE SON OF GOD.

We believe that Jesus Christ is the only begotten Son of God, and was conceived by the Holy Ghost, born of the Virgin Mary, suffered and was crucified at the hands of the Jews and Gentiles—was dead and buried—to be a sacrifice for original and actual sins of all mankind, and to reconcile us to God. Luke, 1 and 2; Mark, 15; and 2 Corinthians, 5:17-19.

3. THE RESURRECTION OF CHRIST.

Now if Christ be preached that He rose from the dead how say some among you that there is no resurrection of the dead? But if there be no resurrection of the dead, then is Christ not risen: And if Christ be not risen, then is our preaching vain, and your faith is also vain . . . But now is Christ risen from the dead and become the first fruits of them that slept. 1 Corinthians, 15:12-14; 20. He then ascended into heaven and there sitteth on the right hand of God, until he shall so come in like manner as he went into heaven, to judge all men on the final day. Psalms, 16; 8:10; Matthew, 28:5-7; Psalms, 24:7-10; Ephesians, 4:8-10.

4. THE HOLY GHOST. (OR SPIRIT).

The Holy Ghost (or Spirit) is the third Person in the Divine Trinity, the Spirit of God proceeding from the Father. Genesis, 1:2; Job, 33:4; John 4:24-26; 16, 17, 26.

5. SUFFICIENCY OF HOLY SCRIPTURES.

All things necessary to salvation, are contained in the Holy Scriptures. Nothing is required of man as an article of faith if it is not found in the Holy Scriptures, or may not be proved thereby. We understand the names of the Old and New Testament Books to be those whose authority is no doubt in the Church, as being and containing the Holy Scriptures.

The Books of the Old Testament are: Genesis, Exodus, Leviticus, Numbers, Deuteronomy, Joshua, Judges, Ruth, 1 Samuel, 2 Samuel, 1 Kings, 2 Kings, 1 Chronicles, 2 Chronicles, Ezra, Nehemiah, Esther, Job, Psalms, Proverbs, Ecclesiastes, The Song of Solomon, Isaiah, Jeremiah, Lamentations, Ezekiel, Daniel, Hosea, Joel, Amos, Obadiah, Jonah, Micah, Nahum, Habakkuk, Zephaniah, Haggai, Zechariah, Malachi.

The books of the New Testament are: Matthew, Mark, Luke, John, The Acts, Romans, I Corinthians, 2 Corinthians, Galatians, Ephesians, Philippians, Colossians, I Thessalonians, 2 Thessalonians, I Timothy, 2 Timothy, Titus, Philemon, Hebrews, James, I Peter, 2 Peter, I John, 2 John, 3 John, Jude, Revelation. Psalms, 19:7-8; also 119; Luke, 24:27; 2 Timothy, 3-16; Revelation 22:14 and 19; Hebrews, 4:12.

6. THE OLD TESTAMENT.

Some would do away with the Old Testament, but without the Old Testament, we could not interpret some things in the New Testament. The New Testament in the Old Testament is concealed, the Old Testament in the New Testament is revealed. As touching some of the civil, ceremonial, and sacrificial rites, given in the law, they are not binding upon Christians now, notwithstanding, no

Christian may ignore or disregard the moral and ethical commandments.

7. RELATIVE DUTIES.

Under the Old Covenant, God commanded, saying, Thou shalt not avenge, nor bear any grudge against the children of thy people, but thou shalt love thy neighbor as thyself: I am the Lord. Leviticus 19:18. Under the New Covenant, His Son Jesus said "Love your enemies, bless them that curse you, do good to them that hate you, and pray for them which despitefully use you and persecute you." Matthew, 5:44. We are to do no wrong toward the stranger, the fatherless, nor the widow; but we are to show love, peace and friendship toward all our neighbors. Psalms 15; Luke, 10:25-37.

8. THE CORRUPT NATURE.

The Scriptures plainly teach that the natural man is corrupt, that he was born in that state, and is continually inclined to sin, and needs the grace of God to elevate and lift him to a higher plane. Genesis, 8:21; Psalms, 51:5; Jeremiah, 17:9; Romans, 3:10-12; Ephesians, 2:1-3.

9. THE WILL AND CHOICE.

God has mercifully endowed all his created intelligence with the power of will and choice, or free moral agency, called the "King of man"—that which chooses and shapes destiny. Deut. 30:19; Joshua, 24:15; John, 5:40; Revelation, 22:17. However this will is always subservient to the will of God; for we do not have power to do acceptable works before God, except by the grace of God; working in us through His Son, and our Saviour, Jesus Christ. Prov. 16:1; Jeremiah, 10:23; Matthew, 16:17; John 6:44.

10. MAN JUSTIFIED.

All have sinned and come short of the glory of God, says the Scriptures. Therefore we can stand before God, in a state of justification, only by faith, in the meritorious and vicarious blood of His Son, Jesus Christ. Romans, 3:23; 5:1; Ephesians, 2:8-9; Hebrews, 11.

11. GOOD WORKS.

Although good works are not altogether religion, they have a part in revealing our prosperity and fruitfulness in the Gospel, for we are created in Christ Jesus unto good works, and if professing Godliness, God is able to make all grace abound toward you; that ye always having all sufficiency in all things may abound to every good work. 2 Corinthians, 9:8; Colossians, 1:10; 2 Timothy, 2:21; Titus, 3:8.

12. SIN AFTER JUSTIFICATION.

For thus saith the Lord: "when the righteous turneth away from his righteousness, and committeth iniquity; in his trespass that he hath trespassed, and in his sin that he hath sinned, in them shall he die." Ezekial, 18:24. Now this is to be understood of as eternal death, appears when a righteous man turneth away from his righteousness, and committeth iniquity and dieth in them. (Here is temporal or physical death.) For his iniquity that he hath done he shall die. (Here is eternal death.) Now justification is an act of God's free grace, wherein he pardoned all our sins, and accepted us as righteous in his sight, only for the righteousness of Christ imputed to us and received by faith alone. Justification is to make righteous. Scripturally, however, this belongs to the field of regeneration, rather than to that of justification. According to the Bible usage, justification is the act of counting, declaring or pronouncing one righteous, or free from guilt and exposure to punishment. Romans, 4:25; 5:16-18.

13. REGENERATION OR THE NEW BIRTH.

Regeneration is an act of the Holy Spirit, by which we obtain the new birth or salvation through faith in Jesus Christ. The word means "begetting again," and the result is that "old things are passed away; behold, all things are become new."—John, 3:1-13; Titus, 3:5.

14. HOLINESS AND ENTIRE SANCTIFICATION.

We believe and teach entire sanctification to be synonymous with the Baptism with the Holy Ghost, Heart Purity, Christian Perfection and Holiness. 1 Thessalonians, 5:23; Joel, 2:28-29; Acts, 2; Psalms, 24:4; Matthew, 5:8; Genesis, 17:1; Matthew, 5:48; Leviticus, 20:7; Hebrews, 12:14. It is that work of grace wrought in the heart of man, by the Holy Ghost, subsequent to regeneration, when the believer presents himself a living sacrifice, holy, and acceptable to God; thus enabling him to love the Lord with all the heart, soul, mind and strength, and to walk in all his holy commandments, blameless. Titus, 2:11-12; John, 17:1-23; Romans, 12:1-2; Ephesians, 5:25-27.

15. SACRAMENTS OF THE CHURCH.

Baptism, the Supper of the Lord, and the Washing of the Brethren's feet, are recognized by our Church, as sacraments ordained of our Lord, as a token of Christian profession. Not merely an outward form, but to vivify and ratify our faith in Him. For Scriptural proof, see: Matthew, 26:26-28; Matthew 28:19; Mark, 14:22; 24; John, 13; 1 Corinthians, 10:16; 11:23-26; 1 Timothy 5:10.

16. BAPTISM.

Baptism, is the sacrament, ordinance or rite, commanded by Christ, in which water is used to initiate the recipient into the Christian faith. Christ himself, did not baptize, but His disciples. John baptized with water, Christ with the Holy Ghost and with fire. Jesus was baptized by John. The word "baptism" means, dipping, bathing, therefore we grant the candidate the choice of immersion, or sprinkling. Matt. 18:19; John, 4:2; Matt. 3:1-12; Luke, 3:16.

17. THE SUPPER OF THE LORD.

The Supper of the Lord is practiced by Christians to show their love to each other and their love and faith to God for the redemption provided through Jesus Christ's atoning death. It is a medium of grace communicated to the heart of all who rightly and worthily receive it. And He took bread and gave thanks and brake it, and gave unto them saying, "This is my body which is given for you; this do in remembrance of me." Likewise also the cup after supper saying, "This cup is the new Testament in my blood, which is shed for you." Luke, 22:19-20. See also 1 Corinthians, 11:23-29.

18. THE OFFERING OF CHRIST ON THE CROSS.

Jesus Christ made the perfect and supreme sacrifice on the cross for the salvation of all people of all time. He finished the plan of salvation. Therefore being justified by faith, we have peace through our Lord Jesus Christ. Romans 5:1. For when we were yet without strength, in due time Christ died for the ungodly. Romans, 5:6. For as by one man's disobedience many were made sinners, so by the obedience of one shall many be made righteous. Romans, 5:19. For the wages of sin is death, but the gift of God is eternal life through Jesus Christ our Lord. Romans, 6:23. For with the heart man believeth unto righteousness; and with the mouth confession is made unto salvation. Romans, 10:10. This is the stone which was set at naught of you builders, which is become the head of the corner. Neither is there salvation in any other; for there is none other name under heaven given among men, whereby we must be saved. Acts, 4:11-12.

19. CHURCH RITES AND CEREMONIES.

Our rites and ceremonies may be different from others in some respects. But we know as the customs of men change it may require the changing of rites and ceremonies in the churches, for so it has been down through the ages of time, so long as it does not contravene the Word of God. Acts, 15:10, 28, 29; Romans, 14:1-6; Galatians, 5:13.

20. RESURRECTION OF THE DEAD.

There will be a resurrection of the dead; the just unto the resurrection of life, and the unjust unto the resurrection of damnation. At this time the soul and body of every man will be reunited, and shall appear before the Judgment seat of Christ; that every one may receive the things done in the body, according to that he hath done, whether it be good or bad. Dan. 12:2; 2 Cor. 5:10; Rev. 20:4-6; vs. 12 and 13.

21. THE GENERAL OR FINAL JUDGMENT.

At the end of time there is to be a final or general judgment, at which time the dead shall be judged and rewarded according to their works in this life. Jesus Christ is to be the Judge, and the righteous will receive a crown of life for their righteous works, and be received into heaven to be forever, with Christ. The wicked shall be judged for their evil deeds and rewarded with eternal punishment in hell. 2 Cor. 5:10; Heb. 9:27; Rev. 20:11-12.

Notes: *These articles derive from those of the Wesleyan Methodist Church, though the wording has been altered in almost every item. The church practices foot washing as a third ordinance.*

* * *

DOCTRINES OF THE SALVATION ARMY

We believe that the Scriptures of the Old and New Testaments were given by inspiration of God and that they only constitute the divine rule of Christian faith and practice.

We believe there is only one God who is infinitely perfect the Creator Preserver and Governor of all things and who is the only proper object of religious worship.

We believe that there are three persons in the Godhead the Father the Son and the Holy Ghost undivided in essence and co-equal in power and glory.

We believe that in the person of Jesus Christ the divine and human natures are united so that He is truly and properly God and truly and properly man.

We believe that our first parents were created in a state of innocency but by their disobedience they lost their purity and happiness and that in consequence of their fall all men have become sinners totally depraved and as such are justly exposed to the wrath of God.

We believe that the Lord Jesus Christ has by His suffering and death made an atonement for the whole world so that whosoever will may be saved.

We believe that repentance toward God faith in our Lord Jesus Christ and regeneration by the Holy Spirit are necessary to salvation.

We believe that we are justified by grace through faith in our Lord Jesus Christ and that he that believeth hath the witness in himself.

We believe that continuance in a state of salvation depends upon continued obedient faith in Christ.

We believe that it is the privilege of all believers to be 'wholly sanctified' and that their 'whole spirit and soul and body' may 'be preserved blameless unto the coming of our Lord Jesus Christ' (1 Thess. 5:23).

We believe in the immortality of the soul in the resurrection of the body in the general judgment at the end of the world in the eternal happiness of the righteous and in the endless punishment of the wicked.

Notes: *Known publicly for modelling its organization on the military, within holiness circles the Salvation Army is known for not observing any sacraments. The Army does not mention sacraments in its statement of beliefs.*

* * *

DOCTRINES OF THE VOLUNTEERS OF AMERICA

1. We believe in one supreme God, who is "from everlasting to everlasting," who is infinitely perfect, benevolent and wise, who is omnipotent and omnipresent, and who is creator and ruler of heaven and earth.

2. We believe in a Triune God,—The Father, Son and the Holy Ghost. We believe these three Persons are one, and while separate in office, are undivided in essence, co-equal in power and glory, and that all men everywhere ought to worship and serve this Triune God.

3. We believe the contents of the Bible to have been given by inspiration of God, and the Scriptures form the Divine rule of all true, Godly faith and Christian practice.

4. We believe that Jesus Christ, when upon earth, was truly man and yet was as truly God—The Divine and human being blended in the one Being, hence

His ability to feel and suffer as a man and yet supremely love and triumph as the Godhead.

5. We believe that our first parents were created without sin, but by listening to the tempter and obeying his voice fell from grace and lost their purity and peace; and that in consequence of their disobedience and fall all men have become sinful by propensity and are consequently exposed to the wrath of God.

6. We believe that Jesus Christ, the only begotten Son of God, by the sacrifice of His life, made an atonement for all men, and that whosoever will call upon Him and accept His overtures of grace shall be saved.

7. We believe that in order to be saved it is necessary (a) to repent toward God; (b) to believe with the heart in Jesus Christ; and (c) to become regenerated through the operation of the Holy Spirit.

8. We believe that the Spirit beareth witness with our spirit, that we are the children of God, thus giving the inward witness of acceptance by God.

9. We believe that the Scriptures teach and urge all Christians to be cleansed in heart from inbred sin, so that they may walk uprightly and serve Him without fear in holiness and righteousness all the days of their lives.

10. We believe the soul shall never die; that we shall be raised again; that the world shall be judged by God; and that the punishment of the wicked shall be eternal, and the joy and reward of the righteous will be everlasting before the throne of God.

Notes: *Organized by former members of the Salvation Army, the Volunteers of America rejected the Army's position on the sacraments and adopted the observation of both baptism and the Lord's Supper. Like the Army, the sacramental issue is not dealt with in the Volunteers' doctrinal statement.*

*   *   *

ARTICLES OF RELIGION (WESLEYAN CHURCH)

I. FAITH IN THE HOLY TRINITY

8. There is but one living and true God, everlasting, of infinite power, wisdom and goodness; the Maker and Preserver of all things, visible and invisible. And in unity of this Godhead there are three persons of one substance, power and eternity—the Father, the Son (the Word), and the Holy Ghost.

   Gen. 1:1; 17:1; Ex. 3:13-15; 33:20; Deut. 6:4; Psalms 90:2; 104:24; Isa. 9:6; Jer. 10:10; John 1:1, 2; 4:24; 5:18; 10:30; 16:13; 17:3; Acts 5:3, 4; Rom. 16:27; I Cor. 8:4, 6; 2 Cor. 13:14; Eph. 2:18; Phil. 2:6; Col. 1:16; I Tim. 1:17; I John 5:7, 20, Rev. 19:13.

II. THE SON OF GOD

9. The only begotten Son of God was conceived by the Holy Ghost, born of the Virgin Mary, suffered under Pontius Pilate, was crucified, dead and buried—to be a sacrifice, not only for original guilt, but also for the actual sins of men, and to reconcile us to God.

   Mark 15; Luke 1:27, 31, 35; John 1:14, 18; 3:16, 17; Acts 4:12; Rom. 5:10, 18; I Cor. 15:3; 2 Cor. 5:18, 19; Gal. 1:4; 2:20; 4:4, 5; Eph. 5:2; I Tim. 1:15; Heb. 2:17; 7:27; 9:28; 10:12; I Peter 2:24; I John 2:2; 4:14.

III. THE RESURRECTION OF CHRIST

10. Christ did truly rise again from the dead, taking His body with all things appertaining to the perfection of man's nature, wherewith He ascended into heaven, and there sitteth until He returns to judge all men at the last day.

    Psalms 16:8-10; Matt. 27:62-66; 28:5-9, 16, 17; Mark 16:6, 7, 12; Luke 24:4-8, 23; John 20:26-29; 21; Acts 1:2; 2:24-31; 10:40; Rom. 8:34; 14:9, 10; 1 Cor. 15:6, 14; Heb. 13:20.

IV. THE HOLY GHOST

11. The Holy Ghost proceeding from the Father and the Son is of one substance, majesty and glory with the Father and the Son, very and eternal God.

    Job 33:4; Matt. 28:19; John 4:24-26; Acts 5:3; 4; Rom. 8:9; 2 Cor. 3:17; Gal. 4:6.

V. THE SUFFICIENCY AND FULL AUTHORITY OF THE HOLY SCRIPTURES FOR SALVATION

12. The Holy Scriptures contain all things necessary to salvation; so that whatsoever is not read therein, nor may be proved thereby, is not to be required of any man, that it should be believed as an article of faith, or be thought requisite or necessary to salvation. In the name of the Holy Scriptures, we do understand the books of the Old and New Testaments. These Scriptures we do hold to be the inspired and infallibly written Word of God, fully inerrant in their original manuscript and superior to all human authority.

The canonical books of the Old Testament are:

Genesis, Exodus, Leviticus, Numbers, Deuteronomy, Joshua, Judges, Ruth, 1 Samuel, 2 Samuel, 1 Kings, 2 Kings, 1 Chronicles, 2 Chronicles, Ezra, Nehemiah, esther, Job, Psalms, Proverbs, Ecclesiastes, The Song of Solomon, Isaiah, Jeremiah, Lamentations, Ezekiel, Daniel, Hosea, Joel, Amos, Obadiah, Jonah, Micah, Nahum, Habakkuk, Zephaniah, Haggai, Zechariah and Malachi.

The canonical books of the New Testament are:

Matthew, Mark, Luke, John, The Acts, The Epistle to the Romans, 1 Corinthians, 2 Corinthians, Galatians, Ephesians, Philippians, Colossians, 1 Thessalonians, 2 Thessalonians, I Timothy, 2 Timothy, Titus, Philemon, Hebrews, James, 1 Peter, 2 Peter, 1 John, 2 John, 3 John, Jude and Revelation.

Psalms 19:7; Luke 24:27; John 17:17; Acts 17:2, 11; Rom. 1:2; 15:4; 16:26; Gal. 1:8; I Thess. 2:13; 2 Tim. 3:15-17; Heb. 4:12; James 1:21; 1 Peter 1:23; 2 Peter 1:19-21; Rev. 22:14, 19.

VI. THE OLD TESTAMENT

13. The Old Testament is not contrary to the New; for both in the Old and New Testaments everlasting life is offered to mankind through Christ, Who is the only Mediator between God and man. Wherefore they are not to be heard, who feign that the old fathers did look only for transitory promises. Although the law given from God by Moses, as touching ceremonies and rites, doth not bind Christians, nor ought the civil precepts thereof of necessity be received in any commonwealth, yet not withstanding no Christian whatsoever is free from the obedience of the commandments which are called moral.

Matt. 5:17-19; 22:37-40; Luke 24:27, 44; John 1:45; 5:46; Rom. 15:8; 2 Cor. 1:20; Eph. 2:15, 16; 1 Tim. 2:5; Heb. 10:1; 11:39; I John 2:3-7.

VII. RELATIVE DUTIES

14. Those two great commandments which require us to love the Lord our God with all the heart, and our neighbors as ourselves, contain the sum of the divine law as it is revealed in the Scriptures: they are the measure and perfect rule of human duty, as well for the ordering and directing of families and nations, and all other social bodies, as for individual acts, by which we are required to acknowledge God as our only Supreme Ruler, and all men as created by Him, equal in all natural rights. Wherefore all men are bound so to order all their individual and social and political acts as to render to God entire and absolute obedience, and to secure to all men the enjoyment of every natural right, as well as to promote the greatest happiness of each in the possession and exercise of such rights.

Lev. 19:18, 34; Deut. 1:15, 17; 2 Sam. 23:3; Job 29:16; 31:13, 14; Jer. 21:12; 22:3; Matt. 5:44-47; 7:12; Luke 6:27-29, 35; John 13:34, 35; Acts 10:34, 35; 17:26; Rom. 12:9; 13:1, 7, 8, 10; Gal. 5:14; 6:10; Titus 3:1; James 2:8; 1 Peter 2:17; 1 John 2:5; 4:12, 13; 2 John 6.

VIII. ORIGINAL OR BIRTH SIN

15. Original sin standeth not in the following of Adam (as the Pelagians do vainly talk), but it is the corruption of the nature of every man, that naturally is engendered of the offspring of Adam, whereby man is wholly gone from original righteousness, and of his own nature inclined to evil, and that continually.

Gen. 8:21; Psalms 51:5; Jer. 17:9; Mark 7:21-23; Rom. 3:10-12; 5:12, 18, 19; Eph. 2:1-3.

IX. FREE WILL

16. The condition of man after the fall of Adam is such that he cannot turn and prepare himself, by his own natural strength and work, in faith and calling upon God; wherefore we have no power to do good works, pleasant and acceptable to God, without the grace of God by Christ working in us, that we may have a good will, and working with us when we have that good will.

Prov. 16:1; 20:24; Jer. 10:23; Matt. 16:17; John 6:44, 65; 15:5; Rom. 5:6, 7, 8; Eph. 2:5-9; Phil. 2:13; 4:13.

X. JUSTIFICATION OF MAN

17. We are accounted righteous before God only for the merit of our Lord and Saviour Jesus Christ, by faith, and not our own works or deservings. Wherefore, that we are justified by faith only is a most wholesome doctrine, and very full of comfort.

Acts 13:38, 39; 15:11; 16:31; Rom. 3:28; 4:2-5; 5:1, 2, 9; Eph. 2:6, 9; Phil. 3:9; Heb. 11.

XI. GOOD WORKS

18. Although good works, which are the fruit of faith and follow after justification, cannot put away our sins and endure the severity of God's judgment, yet they are pleasing and acceptable to God in Christ, and spring out of a true and lively faith, insomuch that by them a lively faith may be as evidently known as a tree is discerned by its fruit.

Matt. 5:16; 7:16-20; John 15:8; Rom. 3:20; 4:2, 4, 6; Gal. 2:16; Phil. 1:11; Titus 3:5; James 2:18, 22; 1 Peter 2:9, 12.

XII. SIN AFTER JUSTIFICATION

19. Not every sin willingly committed after justification is the sin against the Holy Ghost, and unpardonable. Wherefore repentance is not denied to such as fall into sin after justification; after we have received the Holy Ghost we may depart from grace given and fall into sin, and by the grace of God rise again to amend our lives. And therefore, they are to be condemned who say they can no more sin as long as they live here, or deny the place of forgiveness to such as truly repent.

Psa. 32:5; 95:7, 11; Eccl. 7:20; Jer. 3:13-15; Matt. 24:12; John 5:14; Gal. 5:4, 7; Eph. 5:14; Heb. 3:7-13, 15; James 3:2, 8; I John 1:8, 9; 2:12; Rev. 2:5.

XIII. REGENERATION

20. Regeneration is that work of the Holy Spirit by which the pardoned sinner becomes a child of God; this work is received through faith in Jesus Christ, whereby the regenerate are delivered from the power of sin which reigns over all the unregenerate, so that they love God and through grace serve Him with the will and affections of the heart-receiving the Spirit of adoption whereby we cry, Abba Father.

John 1:12, 13; 3:3, 5; Rom. 8:15, 17; Gal. 3:26; 4:5, 7; Eph. 1:5; 2:5, 19; 4:24; Col. 3:10; Titus 3:5; James 1:18; I Peter 1:3, 4; 2 Peter 1:4; I John 3:1.

XIV. ENTIRE SANCTIFICATION

21. Entire sanctification is that work of the Holy Spirit by which the child of God is cleansed from all inbred sin through faith in Jesus Christ. It is subsequent to regeneration, and is wrought when the believer presents himself a living sacrifice, holy and acceptable unto God, and is thus enabled through grace to

love God with all the heart and to walk in His holy commandments blameless.

Gen. 17:1; Deut. 30:6; Psa. 130:8; Ezek. 36:25-29; Matt. 5:48; Luke 1:74, 75; John 17:2-23; Rom. 8:3, 4; 11:26; 1 Cor. 6:11; 14:20; Eph. 4:13, 24; 5:25-27; Phil. 2:5, 7; Col. 4:12; I Thess. 3:10; 5:23; 2 Thess. 2:13; 2 Tim. 3:17; Titus 2:12; Heb. 9:13, 14; 10:14, 18-22; James 1:27; 4:8; I Peter 1: 10; 2 Peter 1:4; 1 John, 1:7, 9; 3:8, 9; 4:17, 18; Jude 24.

XV. THE SACRAMENTS

22. Sacraments ordained of Christ are not only tokens of Christian profession, but they are certain signs of grace and God's good will toward us, by which He doth work invisibly in us, and doth not only quicken but also strengthen and confirm our faith in Him.

There are two sacraments ordained of Christ our Lord in the Gospel: that is to say, Baptism, and the Supper of the Lord.

Matt. 26:26-28; 28:19; Mark 14:22-24; Rom. 2:28, 29; 4:11; 1 Cor. 10:16; 11:23-26; Gal. 3:27.

XVI. BAPTISM

23. Baptism is not only a sign of profession and mark of difference whereby Christians are distinguished from others who are not baptized, but it is also a sign of regeneration or new birth. The baptism of young children is to be retained in the Church.

Num. 8:7; Isa. 52:15; Ezek. 36:25; Matt. 3:13-17; Mark 1:10; 16:16; John 3:22, 26; 4:1, 2; Acts 2:38, 41; 8:12, 13-17; 9:18; 16:33; 18:8; 19:5; 22:16; I Cor. 12:13; Gal. 3:27-29; Col. 2:11, 12; Titus 3:5.

XVII. THE LORD'S SUPPER

24. The Supper of the Lord is not only a sign of love that Christians ought to have among themselves one to another, but rather it is a Sacrament of our redemption by Christ's death; insomuch that to such as rightly, worthily and with faith receive the same, it is made a medium through which God doth communicate grace to the heart.

Luke 22:19, 20; John 6:53, 56; 1 Cor. 5:7, 8; 10:3, 4, 16; 11:28.

XVIII. THE ONE OBLATION OF CHRIST FINISHED UPON THE CROSS

25. The offering of Christ, once made, is that perfect redemption and propitiation for all the sins of the whole world, both original and actual; and there is none other satisfaction for sin but that alone. Wherefore, to expect salvation on the ground of our own works, or by suffering the pains our sins deserve, either in the present or future state, is derogatory to Christ's offering for us, and a dangerous deceit.

Acts 4:12; Rom. 5:8; 8:34; Gal. 2:16; 3:2, 3, 11; 1 Tim. 2:5, 6; Heb. 7:23-27; 9:11-15, 24-28; 10:14.

XIX. THE RITES AND CEREMONIES OF CHURCHES

26. It is not necessary that rites and ceremonies should in all places be the same or exactly alike, for they have always been different and may be changed according to the diversities of countries, times, and men's manners, so that nothing be ordained against God's Word.

Every particular church may ordain, change or abolish rites and ceremonies, so that all things may be done to edification.

Acts 15:10, 28, 29; Rom. 14:2-6, 15, 17, 21; 1 Cor. 1:10; 12:25; 14:26; 2 Cor. 13:11; Gal. 5:1, 13; Col. 2:16, 17; 2 Thess. 3:6, 14; I Tim. 1:4, 6; I Peter 2:16.

XX. THE SECOND COMING OF CHRIST

27. The doctrine of the second coming of Christ is a very precious truth, and this good hope is a powerful inspiration to holy living and godly effort for the evangelization of the world. We believe the Scriptures teach the coming of Christ to be a bodily return to the earth and that He will cause the fulfillment of all prophecies made concerning His final and complete triumph over all evil. Faith in the imminence of Christ's return is a rational and inspiring hope to the people of God.

Job 19:25-27; Daniel 12:1-4; Psalm 17:15; Isaiah 11:1-12; Zech. 14:1-11; Matt. 24:1-51; Matt. 26:64; Mark 13:26-37; Luke 17:26-37; Luke 21:24-36; John 14:1-3; Acts 1:9-11; 1 Cor. 1:7, 8; 1 Thess. 4:13-18; Titus 2:11-14; Hebrews 9:27, 28; James 5:7, 8; 2 Pet. 3:1-14; 1 John 3:2, 3; Jude 14; Revelation 1:7; Revelation 19:11-16; Revelation 22:6, 7, 12, 20.

XXI. THE RESURRECTION OF THE DEAD

28. We hold the scriptural statements concerning the resurrection of the dead to be true and worthy of universal acceptance. We believe the bodily resurrection of Jesus Christ was a fact of history and a miracle of supreme importance. We understand the manner of the resurrection of mankind to be the resurrection of the righteous dead, at Christ's second coming, and the resurrection of the wicked at a later time, as stated in Revelation 20:4-6. Resurrection will be the reuniting of soul and body preparatory to final reward or punishment.

Job 19:25-27; Psalms 17:15; Daniel 12:2; Matthew 22:30-32; Matthew 28:1-20; Luke 14:14; John 5:28, 29; Acts 23:6-8; Romans 8:11; 1 Corinthians 6:14; 1 Corinthians 15; 2 Corinthians 4:14; 2 Corinthians 5:1-11; 1 Thessalonians 4:14-17; Revelation 20:4-6.

XXII. THE JUDGMENT OF MANKIND

29. The Scriptures reveal God as the Judge of all mankind and the acts of His judgment to be based on His omniscience and eternal justice. His administration of judgment will culminate in the final meeting of mankind before His throne of great majesty and power, where records will be examined and final rewards and punishments will be administered.

Ecclesiastes 12:14; Romans 14:10, 11; 2 Corinthians 5:10; Acts 17:31; Romans 2:16; Matthew 10:15; Luke 11:31, 32; Acts 10:42; 2 Timothy 4:1; Hebrews 9:27; Matthew 25:31-46; Revelation 20:11, 12, 13; 2 Peter 3:7.

It is not to be understood that a dissenting understanding on the subject of the millennium shall be held to break or hinder either church fellowship or membership.

APPENDIX A

THE REAFFIRMATION OF THE DOCTRINES OF OUR FAITH

30. Be It Resolved, That the General Conference of the Wesleyan Methodist Connection (or Church) of America, now in its twenty-first quadrennial session, do hereby declare and reaffirm our faith and adherence to those Doctrines that have been held as fundamental.

   1st. We reaffirm our faith in the Bible, as the inerrant and inspired Word of God, containing a sufficient revelation of God's will to man in order to secure his eternal salvation and perfect in its system of religion and moral teachings and precepts.

   2nd. We reaffirm our faith in the Deity of Jesus Christ, Who was supernaturally conceived by the Holy Ghost, and born of the virgin Mary, free from moral taint of nature, and perfect in His life and conduct.

   3rd. We reaffirm our faith in the expiatory death, and vicarious atonement of Christ, which adjusted matters in the government of God so that mercy and grace could be extended to the sinner.

   4th. We reaffirm our faith in the resurrection of Jesus Christ from the dead; that He arose with the same body that was placed in the tomb, supernaturally transformed from its physical properties to that of spiritual.

   5th. We reaffirm our faith in His ascension to the right hand of the Father, and that He now occupies the throne of His mediation.

   6th. We reaffirm our faith in the doctrine and promise of His second coming "in like manner" as He went away.

   7th. We reaffirm our faith in the creation of man by the immediate creative act of God, according to the Bible narrative, and not by the process of evolutionary transition from a lower order of animalism to his present physical and intellectual condition.

   8th. We reaffirm our faith in the doctrine of the fall of man from that holy state in which he was created, to his present sinful and depraved state, "and of his own nature is inclined to evil and that continually."

   9th. We reaffirm our faith in the doctrine of regeneration, or the "new birth," by which the sinner becomes a child of God through faith in Jesus Christ, by which the sinner is delivered from the power of sin, and is enabled through grace to love and serve God.

   10th. We reaffirm our faith in the doctrine of entire sanctification, by which work of grace the heart is cleansed by the Holy Spirit from all inbred sin through faith in Jesus Christ when the believer presents himself a living sacrifice, holy and acceptable unto God, and is enabled through grace to love God with all his heart and to walk in His holy commandments blameless. By the act of cleansing it is to be interpreted and taught by the ministry and teachers that it is not a "suppression" or a "counteraction" of "inbred sin" so as to "make it inoperative"; but "to destroy" or "to eradicate" from the heart so that the believer not only has a right to heaven, but is so conformed to God's nature that he will enjoy God and heaven forever. These terms are what we hold that cleansing from all sin implies.

[Adopted by the General Conference held at Fairmount, Indiana, in 1923.]

Notes: *These articles replace the statements of both the Pilgrim Holiness Church and the Wesleyan Methodist Church, which merged in 1968 to form the Wesleyan Church. Of particular interest is the detailed statement on sanctification.*

*   *   *

ARTICLES OF RELIGION [WESLEYAN METHODIST CHURCH (1968)]

I. OF FAITH IN THE HOLY TRINITY.

There is but one living and true God, everlasting, of infinite power, wisdom, and goodness; the maker and preserver of all things, visible and invisible. And in unity of this Godhead there are three persons of one substance, power, and eternity;—the Father, the Son, [the Word] and the Holy Ghost.

II. OF THE SON OF GOD.

The only begotten Son of God was conceived by the Holy Ghost, born of the Virgin Mary, suffered under Pontius Pilate, was crucified, dead, and buried, to be a sacrifice, not only for original guilt, but also for the actual sins of men, and to reconcile us to God.

III. OF THE RESURRECTION OF CHRIST.

Christ did truly rise again from the dead, taking his body, with all things appertaining to the perfection of man's nature, wherewith he ascended into heaven, and there sitteth until he return to judge all men at the last day.

IV. OF THE HOLY GHOST.

The Holy Ghost proceeding from the Father and the Son, is of one substance, majesty, and glory, with the Father and the Son, very and eternal God.

V. THE SUFFICIENCY OF THE HOLY SCRIPTURES FOR SALVATION.

The Holy Scriptures contain all things necessary to salvation: so that whatsoever is not read therein, nor may be proved thereby, is not to be required of any man, that it should be believed as an article of faith, or be thought requisite or necessary to salvation. In the name of the Holy Scriptures, we do understand these canonical books of the

Old and New Testament, of whose authority there is no doubt in the Church.

The canonical books of the Old Testament are—

Genesis	Proverbs
Exodus	Ecclesiastes
Leviticus	The Song of Solomon
Numbers	Isaiah
Deuteronomy	Jeremiah
Joshua	Lamentations
Judges	Ezekiel
Ruth	Daniel
I. Samuel	Hosea
II. Samuel	Joel
1. Kings	Amos
II. Kings	Obadiah
I. Chronicles	Jonah
II. Chronicles	Micah
Ezra	Nahum
Nehemiah	Habakkuk
Esther	Zephaniah
Job	Haggai
Psalms	Zachariah
	Malachi

The canonical books of the New Testament are—

Matthew	II. Thessalonians
Mark	I. Timothy
Luke	II. Timothy
John	Titus
The Acts	Philemon
The Epistles to the	Hebrews
Romans	James
I. Corinthians	I. Peter
II. Corinthians	II. Peter
Galatians	I. John
Ephesians	II. John
Philippians	III. John
Colossians	Jude
I. Thessalonians	Revelation

VI. OF THE OLD TESTAMENT.

The Old Testament is not contrary to the New; for both in the Old and New Testament, everlasting life is offered to mankind through Christ, who is the only Mediator between God and man. Wherefore they are not to be heard, who feign that the old fathers did look only for transitory promises. Although the law given from God by Moses, as touching ceremonies and rites, doth not bind Christians, nor ought the civil precepts thereof of necessity be received in any commonwealth; yet, notwithstanding, no Christian, whatsoever is free from the obedience of the commandments which are called moral.

VII. OF RELATIVE DUTIES.

Those two great commandments which require us to love the Lord our God with all our hearts, and our neighbor as ourselves, contain the sum of the divine law as it is revealed in the Scriptures, and are the measure and perfect rule of human duty, as well for the ordering and directing of families and nations, and all other social bodies, as for individual acts; by which we are required to acknowledge God as our only supreme ruler, and all men as created by him, equal in all natural rights. Wherefore all men are bound so to order all their individual and social acts, as to render to God entire and absolute obedience, and to secure to all men the enjoyment of every natural right, as well as to promote the greatest happiness of each in the possession and exercise of such rights.

VIII. OF ORIGINAL OR BIRTH SIN.

Original sin standeth not in the following of Adam, (as the Pelagians do vainly talk,) but it is the corruption of the nature of every man, that naturally is engendered of the offspring of Adam, whereby man is wholly gone from original righteousness, and of his own nature inclined to evil, and that continually.

IX. OF FREE WILL.

The condition of man after the fall of Adam is such, that he cannot turn and prepare himself, by his own natural strength and works, to faith, and calling upon God; wherefore we have no power to do good works, pleasant and acceptable to God, without the grace of God by Christ working in us, that we may have a good will, and working with us, when we have that good will.

X. OF THE JUSTIFICATION OF MAN.

We are accounted righteous before God, only for the merit of our Lord and Saviour Jesus Christ by faith, and not for our own works or deservings:—Wherefore, that we are justified by faith, only, is a most wholesome doctrine, and very full of comfort.

XI. OF GOOD WORKS.

Although good works, which are the fruit of faith, and follow after justification, cannot put away our sins, and endure the severity of God's judgments; yet are they pleasing and acceptable to God in Christ, and spring out of a true and lively faith, insomuch that by them a lively faith may be as evidently known as a tree is discerned by its fruit.

XII. OF SIN AFTER JUSTIFICATION.

Not every sin willingly committed after justification is the sin against the Holy Ghost, and unpardonable. Wherefore, repentance is not denied to such as fall into sin after justification; after we have received the Holy Ghost, we may depart from grace given, and fall into sin, and, by the grace of God, rise again to amend our lives. And therefore they are to be condemned, who say they can no more sin as long as they live here; or deny the place of forgiveness to such as truly repent.

XIII. OF SANCTIFICATION.

Sanctification is that renewal of our fallen natures by the Holy Ghost, received through faith in Jesus Christ, whose blood of atonement cleanseth from all sin; whereby we are not only delivered from the guilt of sin, but are washed from its pollution, saved from its power, and are enabled, through grace, to love God with all our hearts, and to walk in his holy commandments blameless.

XIV. OF THE SACRAMENTS.

Sacraments ordained of Christ, are not only badges or tokens of Christian men's profession, but they are certain signs of grace, and God's good will toward us, by which he doth work invisibly in us, and doth not only quicken, but also strengthen and confirm our faith in him.

ARTICLES OF RELIGION [WESLEYAN METHODIST CHURCH (1968)] (continued)

There are two sacraments ordained of Christ our Lord, in the Gospel; that is to say, Baptism and the Supper of the Lord.

XV. OF BAPTISM.

Baptism is not only a sign of profession, and mark of difference, whereby Christians are distinguished from others that are not baptized, but it is also a sign of regeneration or the new birth. The baptism of young children is to be retained in the Church.

XVI. OF THE LORD'S SUPPER.

The supper of the Lord is not only a sign of the love that Christians ought to have among themselves one to another, but rather it is a sacrament of our redemption by Christ's death: insomuch that, to such as rightly, worthily, and with faith receive the same, it is made a medium through which God doth communicate grace to the heart.

XVII. OF THE ONE OBLATION OF CHRIST FINISHED UPON THE CROSS.

The offering of Christ, once made, is that perfect redemption and propitiation for all the sins of the whole world, both original and actual: and there is none other satisfaction for sin but that alone. Wherefore to expect salvation on the ground of our own works, or by suffering the pains our sins deserve, either in the present or future state, is derogatory to Christ's offering for us, and a dangerous deceit.

XVIII. OF THE RITES AND CEREMONIES OF CHURCHES.

It is not necessary that rites and ceremonies should in all places be the same, or exactly alike: for they have always been different, and may be changed according to the diversity of countries, times, and men's manners, so that nothing be ordained against God's word.

Every particular Church may ordain, change, or abolish rites and ceremonies, so that all things may be done to edification.

XIX. OF THE RESURRECTION OF THE DEAD.

There will be a general resurrection of the dead, both of the just and the unjust, at which time the souls and bodies of men will be re-united to receive together a just retribution for the deeds done in the body in this life.

XX. OF THE GENERAL JUDGMENT.

There will be a general judgment at the end of the world, when God will judge all men by Jesus Christ, and receive the righteous into his heavenly kingdom, where they shall be forever secure and happy; and adjudge the wicked to everlasting punishment suited to the demerit of their sins.

Notes: *At the time of its formation in the 1840s, the Wesleyan Methodist Church adopted a set of articles taken from the Twenty-five Articles of Religion of what was then the Methodist Episcopal Church. Although the Wesleyan Methodist Church adopted a restrictive rule concerning the revision of the Articles of Religion, the procedures were more lax than those of the Methodist Episcopal Church. Over the years the original twenty articles of the Wesleyan Methodist*

Church (including articles on sanctification and relative duties, added at the original general conference) were increased by the addition of an article on the second coming of Christ. These additions, plus numerous wording changes, produced the version of the articles taken into the church's 1968 merger with the Pilgrim Holiness Church that resulted in the formation of the Wesleyan Church. At the time of merger, both the Articles of Religion of the Wesleyan Methodist Church and the Statement of Faith of the Pilgrim Holiness Church were replaced by the Articles of Religion of the Wesleyan Church.

The Articles of Religion of the Wesleyan Methodist Church were adopted by the Allegheny Wesleyan Methodist Connection, formed in 1968 by members of the Wesleyan Methodist Church who did not wish to participate in the merger with the Pilgrim Holiness Church. The connection considers itself a continuing Wesleyan Methodist Church.

*   *   *

Twentieth-Century Holiness

ARTICLES OF FAITH (EVANGELICAL CHURCH OF NORTH AMERICA)

ARTICLE I. OF THE HOLY TRINITY

1. There is but one true and living God, an eternal Being, a Spirit without body, indivisible, of infinite power, wisdom, and goodness; the Creator and Preserver of all things visible and invisible. And in this Godhead there is a Trinity, of one substance and power, and co-eternal; namely, the Father, the Son, and the Holy Spirit.

ARTICLE II. OF THE SON OF GOD

2. Jesus Christ is truly God and truly man, in Whom the divine and human natures are perfectly and inseparably united. He is the eternal Word made flesh, the only begotten Son of the Father, born of the Virgin Mary by the power of the Holy Spirit. As ministering Servant, He lived, suffered and died on the cross. He was buried, rose from the dead and ascended into heaven to be with the Father, from whence He shall return. He is eternal Savior and Mediator, who intercedes for us, and by Him all men will be judged.

ARTICLE III. OF THE RESURRECTION OF CHRIST

3. Christ did truly rise from the dead, and took again His body, with all things appertaining to the perfection of Man's nature; and with the same body He ascended into heaven, and is seated there until He returns, at the last day, to judge all men.

ARTICLE IV. OF THE HOLY SPIRIT

4. The Holy Spirit proceeds from the Father and the Son, as the true and eternal God, of one substance, majesty, and glory with the Father and the Son; He convinces the world of sin, of righteousness, and of

judgment and comforts the faithful and guides them into all truth.

ARTICLE V. OF THE HOLY SCRIPTURES

5. The Holy Scriptures are the divinely inspired Word of God, written; they contain the will of God so far as it is necessary for us to know for our salvation, so that whatsoever is not contained therein, nor can be proved thereby, is not to be enjoined on any as an article of faith, or as a doctrine essential to salvation. By the Holy Scriptures we understand those canonical books of the Old and New Testament, which the church has at all times received as follows:

THE NAMES OF THE CANONICAL BOOKS

The Old Testament

Genesis	The First Book of Kings
Exodus	The Second Book of Kings
Leviticus	The First Book of
Numbers	Chronicles
Deuteronomy	The Second Book of
Joshua	Chronicles
Judges	The Book of Ezra
Ruth	Amos
The First Book of	The Book of Nehemiah
Samuel	The Book of Esther
The Second Book	The Book of Job
of Samuel	The Psalms
Ecclesiastes	The Proverbs of Solomon
The Song of	Obadiah
Solomon	Jonah
Isaiah	Micah
Jeremiah	Nahum
Lamentations	Habakkuk
Ezekiel	Zephaniah
Daniel	Haggai
Hosea	Zechariah
Joel	Malachi

The New Testament

Matthew	1 Timothy
Mark	2 Timothy
Luke	Titus
John	Philemon
The Acts	Hebrews
Romans	James
1 Corinthians	1 Peter
2 Corinthians	2 Peter
Galatians	1 John
Ephesians	2 John
Philippians	3 John
Colossians	Jude
1 Thessalonians	Revelation
2 Thessalonians	

ARTICLE VI. OF THE OLD TESTAMENT

6. The Old Testament is not contrary to the New. In both the Old as well as the New Testament, everlasting life is offered to mankind by Christ, who being both God and man, is the only Mediator between God and man.

We are, therefore, not to listen to those who teach that the fathers of the ancient covenant grounded their expectations only on the temporal promises. Though the law given from God by Moses, as touching ceremonies and rites, does not bind Christians, nor ought the civil precepts thereof necessarily be received in any commonwealth; yet no Christian is exempt from obeying the ten commandments, which are also called the moral law.

ARTICLE VII. OF DEPRAVITY

7. Man is fallen from original righteousness, and, apart from the grace of our Lord Jesus Christ, is not only entirely destitute of holiness, but is inclined to evil, and that continually; and except a man be born again, he cannot see the Kingdom of God.

ARTICLE VIII. OF PREVENIENT GRACE AND FREE WILL

8. The condition of man since the fall of Adam is so wretched that he cannot turn to God by the mere powers of his nature; and hence we cannot, by our own natural strength, do any good works pleasing and acceptable in the sight of God, without the grace of God by Christ assisting us and influencing us, that we may have a good will, and working with us, when we have that good will.

ARTICLE IX. OF JUSTIFICATION BY FAITH

9. We are never accounted righteous before God on account of our works or merits, but only for the merit of our Lord and Savior, Jesus Christ, and by faith in His name. Wherefore, it is a most wholesome doctrine, and full of comfort, that we are justified by faith only.

ARTICLE X. OF REGENERATION AND ADOPTION

10. Regeneration is the renewal of the heart of man after the image of God, through the Word, by the act of the Holy Spirit, by which the believer receives the Spirit of adoption, and is enabled to serve God with the will and the affections. The witness of the Spirit is an inward impression on the soul, whereby the Spirit of God, the heavenly Comforter, immediately convinces the regenerate believer that he has passed from death unto life, that his sins are all forgiven, and that he is a child of God.

ARTICLE XI. OF GOOD WORKS

11. Although good works are the fruits of faith and follow justification, they have not the virtue to put away our sins, or to avert the judgment, or endure the severity of God's justice; yet they are pleasing and acceptable to God in Christ, spring from a true and living faith, for through and by them a living faith may be as evidently known, as a tree is discerned by its fruits.

ARTICLE XII. OF SIN AFTER JUSTIFICATION

12. Not every sin willingly committed after justification is therefore the sin against the Holy Spirit, which is unpardonable. They cannot all be precluded from repentance who fall into sin after justification, nor can reacceptance straightway be denied them. After we have received the Holy Spirit, it may happen that we depart from grace, and fall into sin; and we may even then, by the grace of God, rise again and amend

our lives. Therefore, the doctrine of those is to be rejected, who say that they can no more fall into sin so long as they live here, or who deny forgiveness to such as truly repent.

ARTICLE XIII. OF ENTIRE SANCTIFICATION

13. Entire sanctification is that work of the Holy Spirit by which the child of God is cleansed from all inbred sin through faith in Jesus Christ. It is subsequent to regeneration and is wrought instantaneously by faith when the believer consecrates himself a living sacrifice, holy and acceptable unto God. The evidence of this gracious work is love out of a pure heart thus enabling us to love God with all of the heart, soul, mind and strength, and our neighbor as ourselves, and to walk in God's holy commandments blameless.

   There is a clear distinction that must be made between consecration and entire sanctification. Consecration is that more or less gradual process of devoting oneself to God, by the help of the Holy Spirit, that comes to a completion at a point in time. Total consecration of necessity precedes and prepares the way for that act of faith which brings God's instantaneous sanctifying work to the soul.

   We believe this gracious work does not deliver us from the infirmities, ignorance and mistakes common to man, nor from the possibilities of further sin. The Christian must continue to guard against the temptation to spiritual pride and seek to gain victory over this and every temptation to sin.

ARTICLE XIV. OF THE CHURCH

14. The visible Church of Christ is the community of true believers, among whom the Word of God is preached in its purity, and the means of grace are duly administered, according to Christ's own appointment.

ARTICLE XV. OF THE CHRISTIAN SABBATH

15. We believe that the Christian Sabbath is divinely appointed; that it is commemorative of our Lord's resurrection from the grave and is an emblem of our eternal rest; that it is essential to the welfare of the civil community, and to the permanence and growth of the Christian Church, and that it should be reverently observed as a day of holy rest and of social and public worship.

ARTICLE XVI. OF THE LANGUAGE TO BE USED IN PUBLIC WORSHIP

16. The use of any language in any public service which is not understood by the people is plainly repugnant to the Word of God and the customs of the early Church.

ARTICLE XVII. OF THE SACRAMENTS

17. Baptism and the Lord's Supper are the only sacraments ordained by Christ. They were ordained by Christ that we should duly use, but not abuse them. And in such persons only as properly receive the same, they produce a wholesome effect; while such as

receive them improperly they bring upon themselves condemnation, as Paul writes in reference to the Lord's Supper. (I Corinthians 11:29).

(a) Holy Baptism. Baptism is a token of the Christian profession, whereby Christians are distinguished from others, and whereby they obligate themselves to observe every Christian duty; it is also a sign of internal cleansing, or the new birth.

(b) The Lord's Supper. The Supper of the Lord is a token of love and union that Christians ought to have among themselves; it is also a mystery or a representation of our redemption by the sufferings and death of Christ; insomuch that such as rightly, properly and faithfully receive the same, partake of the body and blood of Christ by faith, not in a bodily, but in a spiritual manner, in eating the broken bread, and in drinking the cup. The changing of the bread and wine into the body and blood of Christ, cannot be supported by Holy Writ, but is contrary to the plain words of Scriptures.

ARTICLE XVIII. OF THE ONE SACRIFICE OF CHRIST

18. The offering which was once made by Christ on the Cross is the perfect redemption, propitiation, and satisfaction for the sins of the whole world, both original and actual; so that there is no other satisfaction required but that alone.

ARTICLE XIX. OF THE RITES AND CEREMONIES OF THE CHURCH

19. It is by no means necessary that ceremonies and rites should in all places be the same; for they have always been different, and may be changed according to the diversity of countries, times, and national customs, provided that nothing be introduced contrary to God's ordinances. Whosoever, through his private judgment, willingly and purposely breaks the ordinances, ceremonies and rites of the church to which he belongs (if they are not contrary to the Word of God, and are ordained by proper authority), ought to be rebuked openly, as one that offends against the order of the Church and wounds the consciences of the weaker brethren, in order that others may be deterred from similar audacity.

ARTICLE XX. OF CIVIL GOVERNMENT

20. We recognize the sovereign governments under whose protection our members reside. The sovereignty of these governments should be respected. Generally speaking, war and bloodshed are not in keeping with the Gospel and Spirit of Christ, nevertheless, at times, in order to preserve orderly governments in the world, war is the unpleasant alternative. As Christian citizens it is our duty to give moral strength and purpose to our respective nations through sober, righteous and godly living.

ARTICLE XXI. OF CHRISTIANS' PROPERTY

21. The property of Christians is not to be considered as common, in regard to the right, title, and possession of the same, as some do erroneously pretend, but as

lawful possessions. Notwithstanding, everyone ought, of the things he possesses to give to the poor and needy and manifest Christian love and liberality toward them.

ARTICLE XXII. OF THE SECOND COMING OF CHRIST

22. The Scriptures teach the coming of Christ to be a bodily return to the earth and that He will cause the fulfillment of all prophecies made concerning His final and complete triumph over all evil. Faith in the imminence of Christ's return is a rational and inspiring hope to the people of God.

ARTICLE XXIII. OF THE LAST JUDGMENT

23. Jesus Christ will come in the last day to judge all mankind by a righteous judgment; God will give unto the believers eternal life and happiness, and rest, peace, and joy without end. But God will bid the impenitent and ungodly depart to the devil and his angels, to endure everlasting damnation, punishment, and pain, torment and misery. We are, therefore, not to agree to the doctrine of those who maintain that devils and ungodly men will not have to suffer eternal punishment.

Notes: *In 1968 when the Methodist Church and the Evangelical United Brethren merged to become the United Methodist Church, some former members of the Brethren declined to join the merger. They established the Evangelical Church of North America. For their statement of belief they returned to the articles of religion of the Evangelical Church, one of the bodies that had merged in 1946 to found the Evangelical United Brethren. To those articles, they added statements concerning the sabbath and the second coming of Christ and made some minor changes in wording. The article on sanctification was condensed from a lengthy statement that the Evangelical Church had appended to its articles.*

*   *   *

BIBLICAL DOCTRINES (GOSPEL MISSION CORPS)

INTRODUCTION

We believe in the fundamental doctrines of evangelical, orthodox Christianity. We shall not lay great stress on the study of dogma and theorizing, but will preach and teach sound, wholesome doctrine, upholding our "common salvation," earnestly contending "for the faith once delivered unto the saints" (Jude 3), and guarding against liberalism, modernism, and other heresies. We will emphasize the necessity of the New Birth (John 3:3) and a transformed life through Christ (II Corinthians 5:17).

However, doctrine is important, and neither the Church of Christ nor its ministry can be effective without it. No doubt there will be, and already are, numerous ones in the area who, as men did in the time of Christ, "question among themselves, saying: 'What thing is this? What new doctrine is this?'" (Mark 1:27; see also Acts 17:19). Let us assure them as far as we possibly can, by the grace of God in our lives and in our testimony, both as individual

members of the Body of Christ (I Corinthians 12:27), and as a fellowship in the Gospel (Phillippians 1:5-6 & 27), that we accept the teachings of the Bible as our way of life. We are a part of the Holy Christian Church, and therefore we are "ambassadors" in bonds to the Truth (John 14:6); our message is: "Be ye reconciled to God" (II Corinthians 5:20).

Yet within the unity of the Spirit there must be the principles of the Faith, and thus we are reminded of St. Paul's admonition to the young pastor-evangelist, Timothy: "Take heed unto thyself (discipline), and unto the doctrine; continue in them: for in doing this thou shalt both save thyself, and them that hear thee" (I Timothy 4:16).

Following we shall state briefly the fundamental Biblical Doctrines of The Gospel Mission Corps:

1. We believe that the Scriptures of the Old and New Testaments have been given to man by the divine inspiration of God, and that they are the only sufficient revelation and rule of faith and practice.

2. We believe in the unity and trinity of the one, only, and true Lord God Jehovah, eternally existent in three Divine Personalities: the Father Almighty, Creator of the universe and all therein; Jesus Christ, His only begotten Son, our Saviour and Messiah; and the Holy Spirit, our Comforter and Sanctifier.

3. We believe the Son of God, Jesus Christ, took upon Himself by the instrumentality of the Holy Spirit, man's true human nature, but remained sinless, and that without losing His divinity He was born of the Virgin Mary, and came among men "not to condemn the world, but that the world through Him might be saved."

4. We believe in repentance toward God and faith toward our Lord Jesus Christ, and in regeneration by the Holy Spirit, thus bringing to personal experience the new birth, or justification "by grace through faith" for the salvation and eternal welfare of the soul.

5. We believe that "Jesus Christ died for our sins and rose again for our justification," and that personal faith in His shed blood brings complete cleansing and deliverence from the guilt and power of all confessed and forsaken sin.

6. We believe in the "deeper life"—a victorious Christian experience through sanctification, or the baptism of the Holy Spirit, for all who are fully consecrated to the Lord, and in growing in grace experienced by complete surrender and obedience to God and continued faith and fellowship with Christ; this is both the duty and privilege of every believer to be filled with the Holy Ghost, be kept by the power of God, and to do His will.

7. We believe in the immortality of the soul and the resurrection of the body.

8. We believe in the present intercessory ministry of Christ, His spiritual presence within and among His followers, and in His pre-millenial, visible, literal, and glorious return to earth, otherwise known as the

Secong Coming of Christ, which event may be at any moment and will climax this age or dispensation of grace.

9. We believe in the future judgment of mankind and the world, and in the eternal conscious destiny of each individual; Heaven is the prepared Home for the righteous (those who are saved from sin), and Hell is the place of punishment for the unsaved (those who remain in sin by either rejecting or neglecting Christ).

10. We believe that the message of the Gospel is being spread throughout the world in preparation for the end of the age, that God is gathering out a people for His name and preparing His Church to be the Bride of Christ, and also that the national and spiritual restoration of the Jews is a fulfillment of prophecy and a principal sign of the last times in which we are now living.

11. We believe in the spiritual unity of all born-again, Bible-believing Christians, and that the true Church is the body of believers, a militant and united fellowship of all men, women, and children—whether they be Jews or Gentiles—who have been brought "from darkness to light, from the power of Satan unto God, that they may receive forgiveness of sins, and inheritance among them who are sanctified by faith" in Christ; it is the brotherhood of saints, disciples of Jesus by belief in and obedience to His Word, regardless of race, nationality, or denominational affiliation.

12. We believe in water baptism as the believer's testimony and as the act of obedience to Christ's command, although not necessary for regeneration; the candidate is given preference as to the mode of pouring, immersion, or sprinkling, but the required form is "in the name of the Father, and of the Son, and of the Holy Ghost."

13. We believe in the sacrament, or ordinance of the Lord's Supper, as the holy communion of the body and blood of Jesus Christ, Who commanded: "This do in remembrance of Me;" as a memorial of His death and passion until He comes again in glory, the bread (unleavened) and the cup (unfermented wine) are to be partaken of only by believers, and then after careful self-examination and prayer.

14. We believe marriage is a divinely ordained institution, the bonds of which are sacred and not to be broken in this life; the wedded life of believers is to be within the fellowship of Christ.

15. We believe that infants and children of Christians should be dedicated to the Lord by their parents or guardians, and be trained and nourished in the ways of God; "Forbid them not," said Jesus, to come unto Him early in life.

16. We believe Christ is the Great Physician, and He provides deliverance and divine healing according to His will for the physical and the mental afflictions of mankind; His Word tells us to lay hands on the sick, anoint them with oil in the name of the Lord, and pray in faith for their well-being. Some cases are cured instantaneously, some gradually, and others are like Paul's "thorn in the flesh". . . . "My grace is sufficient."

17. We believe that concerning family relationships, upright business dealings, proper employment, civic affairs, and other worthy responsibilities, it is the duty of Christians to be subject to the appropriate authorities, first as faithful and obedient followers of Jesus Christ, and then as good citizens of our Country. We stress loyalty to our nation, respectful obedience to sound legislation, responsible participation and co-operation in legitimate community, social and educational activities, and in Christ-honoring personal, family, and group living, work, and service. However, we feel that being required to swear by oath to a statement of truth, and also the taking up of arms or weapons for the intent purpose of destroying human life, are both contrary to what Christ allows of His disciples.

18. We believe in the efficacy of prayer, the necessity of private and public worship, the enjoyment of praise to God, the privilege of Christian fellowship, the importance of Bible study, teaching, preaching, witnessing, and service as all a part of God's plan for His people. We gladly acknowledge that in the midst of these changing times in which we live, we can trust "Jesus Christ the same yesterday, and today, and for ever," and while human ideas and ideologies come and go, we can learn that "these three" "now abide—faith, hope, and divine love. . . . but the greatest of these is divine love."

CONCLUSION

"The preaching of these and kindred truths has been instrumental in the salvation of souls down the ages. It is not theory, not new philosophies of religion that are needed, but the old truths faithfully preached and reinforced by holy living. True religion consists in one's personal relationship with Christ. He is our Priest, making expiation for our sins and purging away defilement. He is our Prophet, instructing us in the way of life. He is our King, ruling over us."

(From the pen of Bishop Alma White, in the book—*The New Testament Church,* ch. III p. 46.)

REPENT ye, and BELIEVE the Gospel. (Mark 1:15)

Notes: *The doctrines of the Gospel Mission Corps are based upon those of the Pillar of Fire, the founder having been a member of that organization at one time.*

*   *   *

DOCTRINAL STATEMENT (GRACE AND HOPE MISSION)

WE BELIEVE:

1. "All scripture is given by inspiration of God, and is profitable for doctrine, for reproof, for correction, for instruction in righteousness." 2 Tim. 3:16.

2. There is one living and true God, the Creator and Preserver of all things, who is infinite in being and perfection, almighty, all-wise, all-holy, working all things according to the counsel of His most holy will, and for His own eternal glory and praise.

3. In the unity of the Godhead there are three persons: God the Father, God the Son and God the Holy Spirit, equal in power and divine perfection.

4. Our first parents being seduced by the subtilty and temptation of Satan fell from their sinless state, and as a consequence the sentence of death was placed upon the entire human race. Ps. 14:3.

5. Man's salvation is all through God's grace and mercy. He was willing to sacrifice His only begotten Son, the spotless Lamb of God as a sin-offering, that He might make full atonement for all sin. On the cross He shed His blood and tasted death for every man and all who believe in Him are fully justified. Isa. 53:5, 6.

6. Conversion or regeneration implies a new birth, a new man in Christ Jesus, it is nothing short of a miracle of grace. The Holy Spirit convicts and leads sinners to repentance and faith in the Lord Jesus Christ; by simply believing on the Lord Jesus Christ they are saved.

7. Sanctification is the work of the Holy Spirit, the third Person of the Trinity, whereby the believer is separated from ungodliness, unto a life of holiness. The divine injunction is—"Walk in the Spirit and ye shall not fulfill the desires of the flesh." Gal. 5:16.

8. The Word of God faithfully warns us against backsliding, as we find recorded in Heb. 10:26-29, Rom. 11:22 and Eze. 18:26-29. The Bible assures the backslider of forgiveness and cleansing from sin according to 1 John 2:1 and 1 John 1:9.

9. The return of the Lord Jesus Christ is the comforting hope of the church. "Unto them that look for him shall he appear the second time, without sin unto salvation." Heb. 9:28.

10. As to the resurrection of the just and the unjust: "The hour is coming, in which all that are in the graves shall hear his voice, and shall come forth; they that have done good, unto the resurrection of life; and they that have done evil unto the resurrection of damnation." John 5:28, 29.

* * *

STATEMENT OF DOCTRINE (KENTUCKY MOUNTAIN HOLINESS ASSOCIATION)

Kentucky Mountain Bible Institute is definitely committed to the Wesleyan interpretation of Christian doctrine including the following positions:

* the divine, plenary inspiration of the Holy Scriptures, inerrant in the original.

* the deity of Jesus Christ, His virgin birth, vicarious atonement, bodily resurrection, and personal pre-millenial return.

* the deity of the Holy Spirit.

* the fall of man.

* the universal inheritance of the carnal nature.

* justification by faith.

* sanctification as an instantaneous work of grace wrought in the believer through faith subsequent to regeneration and witnessed to by the Holy Spirit. The heart is cleansed from all sin and filled with the pure love of God. This excludes all speaking in unknown tongues either in private or in public.

* the resurrection and glorification of the saints and the eternal punishment of the wicked.

Notes: *This statement is derived from that of the Association's school.*

* * *

THE STATEMENT OF BELIEFS OF THE MEGIDDO MISSION

Megiddo means

"a place of troops" (Gesenius' Hebrew Lexicon); "a place of God" (Young's Analytical Concordance). Megiddo was and is a town in Palestine, strategically located, and the scene of frequent warfare. In the spiritual parallel, it is a place where soldiers engaged in spiritual warfare gather to renew their strength and courage (II Cor. 10:4-5).

WE BELIEVE

—in God the Creator of all things, all men, and all life.

WE BELIEVE

—in the Bible as containing the genuine revelation of God and His purposes for men, and as being our only source of divine knowledge today.

WE BELIEVE

—in Christ the Son of God and our Perfect Example, who was born of a Virgin, ministered among men, was crucified, resurrected, and taken to heaven, and who shall shortly return to be king of the whole earth.

WE BELIEVE

—in life as the gift of God, and in our sacred responsibility to use it for God and His coming Kingdom.

WE BELIEVE

—in all mankind as providing the nucleus from which a superior, God-honoring people shall be chosen to receive the blessings of immortal life.

WE BELIEVE

—in ourselves as capable of fulfilling the demands and disciplines given us in the law of God, thus perfecting that high quality of character which God has promised to reward with life everlasting in His heavenly Kingdom on earth.

WE BELIEVE

—in the promise of God, that a new age is coming—is near—when the earth will be filled with His glory, His people, and His will be done here as it is now done in heaven.

* * *

STATEMENT OF FAITH (ORIENTAL MISSIONARY SOCIETY HOLINESS CONFERENCE OF NORTH AMERICA)

We believe that:

1. THE GODHEAD

The Godhead eternally exists in three persons—the Father, the Son, and the Holy Spirit. These three are one God; of precisely identical nature, attributes and perfection.

A. GOD THE FATHER

God the Father Almighty, creator, preserver, and ruler of the universe, in His essential nature, is Spirit, and to His essential attribute is absolutely holy, and to His essential character, is love.

B. GOD THE SON, JESUS CHRIST

Jesus Christ, the eternal Son, was conceived by the Holy Spirit and born of the Virgin Mary, thereby having a truly divine nature in one person, and is the only mediator between God and man.

To accomplish salvation, He lived a sinless life, completely fulfilling righteousness and offered Himself a substitutionary sacrifice for the sin of the world, satisfying divine justice.

He was crucified under Pontius Pilate, died, and was buried. On the third day, He arose bodily from the dead. He ascended into heaven where in His glorified state, He intercedes for believers. He shall come again personally and visibly to judge the world in righteousness and to establish His kingdom.

C. GOD THE HOLY SPIRIT

The Holy Spirit is the third person of the Godhead. His ministry is to reveal Christ through the Word of God; to fulfill salvation in the regeneration and sanctification of the believers; to direct and empower the church in fulfillment of the Great Commission; and to convict the world of sin, of righteousness and of judgment.

II. THE BIBLE

The Bible, both the Old and New Testaments, the Word of God, is a divinely inspired revelation. It is the supreme and final authority in matters pertaining to faith and practice.

III. MAN

Man was created in the image of God, and he disobeyed God, thereby incurring spiritual death which is separation from God. Man is saved from the condition of spiritual death only by the grace of God through faith in Christ and His redemptive act, and by the ministry of the Holy Spirit. His spiritual growth and maturity is initiated by God's Spirit and by a conscious act of dedication on the part of the believer, and is effected by the indwelling of the Holy Spirit.

IV. THE CHURCH

The Church consists of all who have been regenerated through faith in Christ and have been united into one body under Christ, the Head thereof. It is called to worship God; to preach the Gospel; to administer baptism and holy communion by its duly appointed ministers; to care for and nurture the believers.

Notes: *Over the years of its existence, the Oriental Missionary Society Holiness Conference of North America has moved away from its unique holiness beginning to an emphasis on the common affirmations of evangelical Christianity. Its statement deals with only the most essential issues.*

* * *

APOSTOLIC DOCTRINES (PILLAR OF FIRE CHURCH)

We believe in the fundamental doctrines of the orthodox denominations. We do not lay great stress on the study of systematic theology, but preach wholesome, practical doctrine, guarding against liberalism and latter-day heresies. We are contending for the faith once delivered to the saints (Jude 3). We emphasize the necessity of a vital Christian experience and a transformed life. But doctrine is important, and neither the Church nor the ministry will be effective without it.

1. We believe that the Scriptures are given by inspiration of God, and that they are "the only sufficient rule of faith and practise." The tendency is to eliminate the supernatural from the Bible. It is our business to preach the Word and not to criticize it.

2. We believe in "repentance toward God and faith toward our Lord Jesus Christ." Repentance is giving up a wrong way and taking up a right way; that is, ceasing from sin. Repentance, like the pain of a physical malady, leads the patient to the great Physician. John the Baptist, the forerunner of Christ, said, "Repent ye," and this implied renunciation of all sin.

3. We believe in justification by faith. How is a man justified before God? is the old question ever recurring. Faith is the one condition, for by the deeds of the law shall no man be justified. Faith must be preceded by an absolute surrender to the will of God. Then, when one stands on believing ground, one beholds Christ as the bleeding sacrifice to take away sin, and divine life is imparted. Holy living then becomes an evidence of the change.

Justification by faith is the doctrine that sent the thunders of the Reformation around the world. A justified person lives without knowingly committing sin. He may ignorantly transgress the law, but in this case sin is not imputed. "Whosoever is born of God doth not commit sin." "Whosoever abideth in him sinneth not" (1 John 3:6, 9).

4. We believe in Christian perfection, or entire sanctification, which is the cleansing of the believer's heart from inbred sin, or spiritual defilement, so that the whole spirit, soul and body may be preserved blameless unto the coming of our Lord Jesus Christ. This is the second work of grace, called by Mr. Wesley the second blessing. Sanctification is preceded by perfect consecration, and is an act of faith, and therefore instantaneous (Acts 26:18; 1 Thess. 5:23). We do not preach absolute perfection in the sense that one is free from mistakes and infirmities, but Christian perfection, which is purity of heart and life. This is the fundamental doctrine of the New Testament. It is that "holiness, without which no man shall see the Lord" (Heb. 12:14). It is the doctrine of the old-time Methodists, and for the propagation of it, John Wesley said God had raised them up. This experience is identical with the baptism of the Holy Ghost.

5. We believe in the immortality of the soul and the resurrection of the body. Soul-sleep, annihilation, no-hellism, and the denial of a literal resurrection are latter-day heresies and are soul-destroying. The Scriptures teach that there are to be at least two resurrections. There is to be a resurrection unto life, and a resurrection unto damnation (John 5:29). At Christ's coming the sanctified dead and the living saints are to be caught up to meet Him in the air (1 Cor. 15:22-23; 1 Thess 4:16-17). Paul speaks of "the resurrection out of the dead ones," or, as another has translated it, "the out-resurrection." It must be this "better resurrection" that he wished to obtain (Phil. 3:11; Heb. 11:35; Rev. 20:5-6).

6. We believe in the Judgments as taught in the Scriptures. The time is coming when all the wrongs of earth must be righted; the uneven scales of Justice will find their balance, and man will be dealt with according to the deeds done in the body. Christ paid the debt on Calvary for all who will accept (John 19:17-18). Those who repent and continue to the end do not come into judgment, except it be to receive their reward (John 5:24, R.V.). The soul undergoes a deep heart searching in seeking the experience of holiness. Jacob had his judgment day, in a sense, at the brookside when he wrestled all night in prayer (Gen. 32:24). There is next the judgment of the Church, or Bride of Christ, which takes place when she is caught up in the clouds to meet the Lord. This may be called a judgment of works. Paul says, "For we shall all stand before the judgment seat of Christ" (Rom. 14:10). When Christ shall come again, faithful Christians will be rewarded according to their works (Luke 14:14; Rev. 22:12). The next is the judgment of nations, which takes place when Christ returns with His Bride. This will be at Jerusalem. The last judgment is that of the great white throne (Rev. 20:12-15). The saints will be associated with Christ in this judgment and hence will not be a part of it. It will be for the wicked dead who will be raised after the Millennium and be brought before the Judge to receive their final sentence, prior to their banishment to the lake of fire (Acts 17:31). That will be a momentous hour, when the secrets of all ages will be unfolded before men, angels, and devils.

7. We believe in water baptism; not that it is essential to salvation, but that it is an outward sign of regeneration, or of divine life that is imparted to the soul in the new birth. We believe that either pouring or sprinkling is scriptural, and will immerse those who prefer that mode.

8. We believe in the sacrament of the Lord's Supper, and administer the same to those who have knowledge of sins forgiven or are earnestly seeking to be delivered from their sins. It is a means of grace, inasmuch as Jesus said, "This do in remembrance of me."

9. We believe that marriage is a divine institution and should not be entered into indiscreetly. Those who wish to give their lives up to the service of the Master should not enter into such relationship unless in so doing they can better glorify His name.

10. We believe in divine healing for the body, a doctrine very much abused, and yet clearly taught in the Scriptures. While there are many false teachers and many false movements, such as Christian Science, Mormonism, Spiritualism, Russellism, Seventh Day-ism, and the so-called Pentecostal Tongues, or Latter Rain—Four-square Gospel—working miracles through demoniacal power, there are those who are divinely healed in answer to prayer (James 5:14-16). As a Church we have great reason to rejoice for the physical deliverances we have witnessed through the power of the great Physician.

11. We believe in the premillennial coming of the Lord and the Restoration of the Jews. More than three hundred times, Christ's second coming is mentioned in the New Testament. It is the polar star of the Church and the hope of every believer. By His return we mean His visible appearing on earth at the close of the Gentile Age to reign a thousand years. This is the kingdom symbolized by Daniel's stone cut out of the mountain, and which is to fall upon the feet of the image and grind it to powder. The figure implies a sudden catastrophe, which harmonizes with the tribulation spoken of in the gospels. We are now nearing the time of the end, when the Jews will be restored and the overthrow of the Gentile dominion is to take place.

12. We believe the wicked will go into eternal punishment and the righteous into life everlasting (Matt. 25:46). Heaven is a prepared place for a prepared people. "Blessed are the pure in heart: for they shall see God." The natural heart would fain believe there is no future punishment, but between the holy and the unholy in the other world there is an impassable gulf (Luke 16:26). And it is written also, "He which is filthy, let him be filthy still. . . . Without are dogs, and sorcerers, and whoremongers, and murderers, and idolaters, and whosoever loveth and maketh a lie" (Rev. 22:11, 15). There is to be a place of punishment for the incorrigible somewhere in the

universe. God calls it the place of outer darkness where there is weeping and wailing and gnashing of teeth.

The preaching of these and kindred truths has been instrumental in the salvation of souls down the ages. It is not theory, not new philosophies of religion that are needed, but the old truths faithfully preached and reinforced by holy living. True religion consists in one's personal relationship with Christ. He is our Priest, making expiation for our sins and purging away defilement. He is our Prophet, instructing us in the way of life. He is our King, ruling over us.

The New Testament Church is built on Christ. It is a regenerated Church, a Spirit-baptized Church, a joyful, witnessing Church, going forth with girded loins and burning lamp, carrying the salvation of a lost world upon its heart, and looking forward to the blessed hope and glorious appearing of our Lord and Savior Jesus Christ (Titus 2:13). It is as fair as the moon, clear as the sun, and terrible as an army with banners (Cant. 6:10).

Notes: *This statement of belief is taken from* The New Testament Church *by Bishop Alma White, founder of the Pillar of Fire Church. The Pillar of Fire had originally adopted a set of articles of religion based upon the Twenty-five Articles of Religion of the Methodist Episcopal Church. The present statement reflects that religious heritage as well as the debates that led to the founding of an independent church. There is also an affirmation of premillennialism.*

*   *   *

ARTICLES OF FAITH (SANCTIFIED CHURCH OF CHRIST)

I. THE HOLY TRINITY

1. God the Father: We believe there is but one true God everlasting and eternal, of infinite power, wisdom and goodness; the Maker and Preserver of all things visible and invisible. In unity of and in this Godhead there are three persons, of one substance and power,—the Father, the Son and the Holy Ghost.

2. God the Son: We believe that in due time, Jesus the Christ, the Son of God, the Saviour of the world became incarnated and sojourned among men, teaching the purest of truth and working the most amazing and beneficient miracles. That this divine person, foretold by the prophets and described by the Evangelists and Apostles is really and properly God, having assigned to Him by the inspired writers every attribute essential to the Deity, being one with Him who is called God, Jehovah, etc.

    That He is also a perfect man in consequence of His incarnation and in that man, or manhood, dwelt all the fulness of the Godhead bodily; so His nature is two-fold—divine and human, or God manifest in the flesh.

We believe that His human nature is derived from the Blessed Virgin Mary through the creative energy of the Holy Ghost, so that two whole or perfect natures, that is to say, the Godhead and manhood are united in one person, never to be divided, whereof is one Christ very God and very man who truly suffered, was crucified and buried to reconcile His Father to us and to be a vicarious sacrifice, not only for sins of commission but also for the original or inherent sin.

We further believe that on the third day after His crucifixion and burial, Jesus Christ arose from the dead and took again His body with all things appertaining to the perfection of man's nature, wherewith He ascended into Heaven and there sitteth at the right hand of God, as the mediator until the consummation of all things (Luke 1:27; 35; John 3:16; Acts 4:12).

3. God the Holy Ghost: We believe in the Holy Ghost, the Third Person of the Triune Godhead, proceeding from the Father and the Son as the true and eternal God, of one substance, majesty and glory with the Father and the Son. He is ever present and efficiently active in and with the church or Christ, convincing the world of sin, of righteousness and of judgment and guiding into all truth as it is in Jesus (John 16:8; 3:5-9; Acts 15:8-9).

II. THE SACRED SCRIPTURES

4. We believe that the sacred scriptures or Holy Books which constitute the old and new testament are the inerrant and inspired word of God (II Tim. 3:16) and that they contain a full revelation of the will of God in relation to man concerning us in all things necessary to our salvation, so that whatever is not contained therein nor may be proved thereby, is not to be enjoined as an article of faith (II Peter 1:20-21).

III. FREE MORAL AGENCY

5. We believe in the beginning man was created in righteousness and true holiness without any moral imperfection or any kind of propensity to sin but with the divine right of choice, free to stand or fall and thus was made morally responsible, that man fell from this state, became corrupt in His nature and transmitted his defilement to all his posterity.

6. We further believe that man, though in the possession of the experience of forgiveness and sanctification, may fall from grace; and unless he repent of his sins and be cleansed from the nature of sin, be hopelessly and eternally lost.

IV. ORIGINAL OR INHERENT SIN

7. We believe that original sin or depravity is that corruption of every man's nature that is naturally engendered of the off-spring of Adam. Man is inclined to evil and that continually. (Gen. 6:5; Rom. 5:12-18) The scripture hath concluded all under sin (I John 1:8, Rom. 5:12) that the promise by faith of Jesus Christ might be given to all that believe (Rev. 22:17; John 3:16). God does not forgive original sin in us and it continues to exist, though suppressed,

after we have been forgiven of sins of commission and will remain within the nature of man until eradicated or destroyed by the Baptism with the Holy Ghost (I John 1:9; 3:8; Acts 15:8-9).

V. THE ATONEMENT

8. We believe that Jesus Christ, by the sacrificial shedding of His blood through an expiatory death on the cross made a full atonement for all sin (Rom. 5:8-11), and that this atonement is the only ground for salvation, it being sufficient for every individual of Adam's race. The atonement is graciously efficacious for the salvation of the irresponsible from birth, or for the righteous who have become irresponsible (Rom. 4:15) and to children in innocency (Mark 10:14) but is efficacious for the salvation of those who reach the age of responsibility only when they repent and believe (Luke 24:47; Acts 17:30).

VI. FAITH

9. We believe that there is no salvation except through faith in Jesus Christ and that this faith is a gift from God and without it, it is impossible to please God (Eph. 2:8; Heb. 11:6). No human since the fall of Adam has or ever can, through his own righteousness or works merit salvation (Eph. 2:9; Titus 3:5), but is saved by a living faith that becomes effective when it is exercised by man with the aid of the Spirit, which aid is assured, when the heart has met the divine condition (Heb. 5:9).

VII. REPENTANCE

10. We believe that genuine repentance toward God consists in a knowledge of, a sorrow for, and a voluntary confession and forsaking of sin. This is brought about by the knowledge of the goodness and severity of God, through the medium of the truth and the convincing power of the Holy Spirit. It is demanded of all who have by act or purpose become sinners against God. The Spirit of God gives to all who will repent the gracious help of penitence of heart and hope of mercy, that they may believe unto pardon and spiritual life (Matt. 3:2; Rom. 3:23; II Cor. 7:10; John 16:7-11; Luke 13:5; Acts 11:18).

VIII. JUSTIFICATION

11. We believe that justification is that gracious and judicial act of God in which He grants full pardon from the penalty of sins committed in behalf of a pentitent soul, trusting only in the merits of the shed blood of Jesus Christ (Rom. 5:1). That this act is absolute in respect of all past sins of commission, all being forgiven where any are forgiven.

IX. SANCTIFICATION

12. We believe that the souls of justified persons must be purified and cleansed from all inbred sin or the corruption of the natural human heart, which cleansing we term Sanctification or being made holy as truly, sanctification is that act of God, subsequent to forgiveness, by which believers are made free from original sin, or depravity, and brought in to a state of entire devotement to God, and the holy obedience of love made perfect. This is not a suppression or counteraction of inbred sin as to make it inoperative, but its destruction or eradication so that the believer not only has a right to heaven but is so conformed to God's nature that he will enjoy heaven forever (I Thess. 3:13; 5:23; Rom. 6:6, 18, 22).

13. We believe also that sanctification is provided through the shed blood of Jesus (Heb. 10:10; 13:12; I Pet. 1:2; I John 1:9) and is wrought instantaneously by the believer's faith in the blood, preceded by entire consecration (Rom. 12:1) and to this work of grace the Holy Spirit bears witness (Rom. 6:6; Gal. 2:20; II Cor. 1:22; Heb. 10:14-15).

14. We further believe that this experience is wrought by the baptism with the Holy Ghost, and is that essential "holiness without which no man shall see the Lord" (Heb. 12:14); and that it is a two-fold act of cleansing the heart from sin and filling the believer with the indwelling presence of the Holy Ghost, empowering him for life and service (Acts 2:1-4; John 7:39; 14:16; 17, 26; 16:13, 14; Acts 15:8, 9).

X. WITNESS OF THE SPIRIT

15. The witness of the Spirit is that inward impression wrought in the soul, whereby the Spirit of God immediately and directly assures our spirit that Bible conditions are met for salvation, and the work of grace is complete in the soul (Rom. 15:16). Therefore the Spirit bears witness to both the justification of the sinner and the sanctification of the believer (I John 5:10; Heb. 10:14-15).

XI. THE SECOND COMING OF CHRIST

16. We believe that the Lord Jesus Christ will come again and that his personal return will be "in like manner" as he ascended (Acts 1:11; Phil. 3:20; I Thess. 4:14-18).

FOOTNOTE: It is to be understood that a dissenting understanding on the subject of the second coming of Christ shall not be held to break or hinder either church fellowship or membership.

XII. RESURRECTION, JUDGMENT, AND DESTINY

17. We believe in the resurrection of the dead, "They that have done good, unto the resurrection of life; and they that have done evil, unto the resurrection of damnation" (I Cor. 15:52; John 5:28, 29; Phil. 3:21). We believe also in the future judgment in which every man shall appear before God to be judged according to his deeds in this life (II Cor. 5:10; Heb. 9:27). We believe that glorious and everlasting life is assured to all who savingly believe in, and obediently follow Jesus Christ our Lord; and that the finally impenitent shall suffer eternally in Hell (Matt. 25:41; II Peter 3:7; Jude 15).

ARTICLES OF FAITH (WESLEYAN TABERNACLE ASSOCIATION)

ARTICLE I

There is one God over all, the same yesterday, today and forever; the Creator of all things, and in Whom all things consist.

ARTICLE II

There is one Saviour, Jesus Christ, the only begotten Son of God, Who is the Supreme head of the Church, which He redeemed unto God by His own blood.

ARTICLE III

There is one Holy Spirit, the third person in the Trinity, Who is now the representative of the God-head on earth, Who came from the Father and the Son, to convict the world of sin, of righteousness and of judgment.

God the Father, God the Son and God the Holy Spirit are three persons, united and inseparable, of one substance and eternal.

ARTICLE IV. THE HOLY SCRIPTURES

We emphatically affirm our unwavering faith in the Holy Scriptures of the Old and New Testaments, as divinely and supernaturally inspired, infalibly true as originally given and our only divinely authorized rule of faith and practice.

ARTICLE V. THE PLAN OF REDEMPTION

True repentance toward God and faith in the shed blood of our Lord Jesus Christ bring the forgiveness of all our sins and the experience of the New Birth, whereby we become children of God.

The unconditional abandonment of all we are and have to God forever and unwavering faith in the promise of the Father, bring the Baptism with the Holy Spirit by Whom we are sanctified wholly. This baptism is always subsequent to regeneration. It is an instantaneous experience received by faith, cleansing the heart of the recipient from all sin and endowing him with power for service.

Regeneration and sanctification thus wrought by God's free grace are witnessed to by the Holy Spirit.

ARTICLE VI

We believe in the resurrection of the body, the judgment of all mankind, the everlasting punishment of the wicked and the eternal happiness of the righteous.

RECOMMENDATIONS

DIVINE HEALING

We urge our people to embrace the Bible doctrine of Divine Healing and to offer the prayer of faith for the healing of the sick, according to James 5:14-16; Acts 4:10, 14; and Luke 9:2, 10:9.

THE ORDINANCES

(A)   BAPTISM. Recognizing the fact that water baptism is an outward sign of an inward work wrought in the heart by the Holy Spirit, we recommend that this ordinance be observed by the members of this Association.

(B)   THE LORD'S SUPPER. Believing the sacrament of the Lord's Supper represents our redemption through Christ, we recommend that this ordinance be reverently observed.

THE RETURN OF OUR LORD

We believe that the Holy Scriptures teach the personal and premillennial return of the Lord, and that we are commanded to be ready and daily watching for His glorious appearing. We therefore recommend that our preachers proclaim this truth from time to time.

Notes: *The brevity of the statement of the Wesleyan Tabernacle Association, with significant items placed under the heading of "recommendations," reflects the looseness of its congregations' affiliation with the association.*

* * *

Black Holiness

ARTICLES OF FAITH [CHURCH OF CHRIST (HOLINESS)]

I. GOD

We believe in one God, and that He only is God, and that as God, He is Triune, being revealed as Father, Son and Holy Spirit.

II. THE SON OF GOD

We believe that the Son of God is the Second Person of The Holy Trinity, and as The Son of God, He became incarnate by the Holy Spirit, and being born of The Virgin Mary, united with Himself the divinely begotten Son of Man, called Jesus, thus uniting in one person, God and man.

III. THE HOLY SPIRIT

We believe that the Holy Spirit is the Third Person of the Godhead, and is ever present, and active in and with the Church of Christ, convicting, and regenerating those who believe and sanctifying believers, and guiding into all truth as it is in Jesus.

IV. THE HOLY BIBLE

We believe that the Holy Bible is composed of sixty-six books, commonly known as the Old and New Testaments, and that they are the revealed words of God written by Holy men as they were moved by The Holy Ghost.

V. ORIGINAL SIN

We believe that original sin is that corruption of the nature of all offsprings of Adam, by which we all are separated from original righteousness; and that in the Scriptures it is described as "the carnal mind," "the flesh," "sin that dwelleth in me," and such like. It continues to exist until eradicated or destroyed by The Holy Ghost, through the blood of Christ, I John 1: 6-10; Rom. 7; Heb. 9: 11-14; 10 29; 13: 12.

VI. ATONEMENT

We believe that the atonement made by Jesus Christ through the shedding of His blood for the remission of sins, is for the whole human race; and that whosoever repents and believes on the Lord Jesus Christ is justified and regenerated and saved from the dominion of sin. Rom. 3: 22-26; 5:9, Heb. 2:9.

VII. REPENTANCE

We believe that a repentance is a sincere change of the mind, involving a sense of personal guilt of sin, and a turning away from the same. And that the pentinent heart is graciously helped by the Spirit of God. Acts 2: 38; 26: 18; 3: 19.

VIII. JUSTIFICATION

We believe that justification is God's word done for us, by which full pardon is granted to all who believe and receive Jesus Christ as Savior and Lord. Rom. 3: 24; Acts 10: 43.

IX. REGENERATION

We believe that regeneration is the new birth, that is, God's work done in us, by which the believer is given a Spiritual life, and rectifying the attitude of the will toward God and Holy things. John 3: 6; Titus 3: 5.

X. SANCTIFICATION

We believe that sanctification is that act of Divine grace whereby we are made holy. In justification, the guilt of sin is removed; in sanctification, the inclination to sin is removed. Sanctification must be definitely experienced to fit us to see the Lord. I Thes. 5: 23; Heb. 10: 14; John 17: 17; Heb. 12: 1-14.

XI. RESURRECTION

We believe that Christ truly rose from the dead, and ascended into heaven, and is now sitting at the right hand of God The Father making intercession for us. I Cor. 15: 14-20.

XII. THE SECOND COMING

We believe that The Lord Jesus Christ will return to judge the quick and the dead; and that we who are alive at His coming shall not precede them that are asleep in Christ Jesus. I Thes. 4: 13-18.

XIII. BAPTISM

We believe that baptism is commanded of Our Lord and that it belongs to the believer of the Gospel, "not infants who cannot believe," and that the Bible way of administering it is by immersion. Matt. 28: 19-20; Mark 16: 14-16; Rom. 6: 1-7.

XIV. THE LORD'S SUPPER

We believe that The Lord's Supper is a New Testament Ordinance, and that it was instituted when our Lord celebrated His last Passover with His disciples, and that it consists of bread and wine, and that as often as we take it we show forth the Lord's death till He comes again. Matt. 26: 26-29; Mark 14: 22-25; Luke 22: 19-20; I Cor. 5: 11: 23-24.

XV. THE GIFT OF THE HOLY GHOST

(a) We believe that every true believer is heir to the gift of the Holy Ghost. Gal. 4: 6-7.

(b) We believe that He is the gift of God in Christ Jesus to the Children of God, sanctifying, quickening, guiding into all truth, and giving power to obey and witness God's Word. John 14: 16-26; Acts 1:8.

(c) We believe that the receiving of The Holy Ghost is subsequent to conversion. Acts 8: 14-16; 19: 1-4.

(d) We believe that a backslider must be reclaimed before he or she can receive the Holy Ghost.

(e) We believe that The Holy Ghost baptized the whole church on the day of Pentecost because of the Jewish nation, and the whole Church in Cornelius' house because of the gentile nation; and that always thereafter, He is referred to as a gift, Acts 2: 38-39; a receiving, Acts 19: 1-2, a filling, Eph. 5: 18; an annointing, John 2-27; II Cor. 1: 21. He is never again referred to as a baptism for there is but one baptism. Eph. 4: 1-5.

XVI. FOOTWASHING

We believe in foot washing as an act of obedience in following the example given by our Lord Jesus Christ.

XVII. SPIRITUAL GIFTS

We believe that spiritual gifts are set forth in the 12th, 13th, and 14th chapters of First Corinthians.

1. That no one gift is the specific sign or evidence of the Holy Spirit's presence, but faith (Heb. 11: 1) and Love (I Cor. 13; John 13: 35) are the evidences; not even power alone is the evidence for that may be as Satan.

2. That these gifts, though they may be of use to edification, may be counterfeited and are not to be trusted as evidence. II Thes. 2: 7-12; II Tim. 3: 8.

3. That there are three essential evidences of true religion. Faith, Hope, and Love. I Cor. 13: 13.

4. That the Bible endorses speaking in tongues, or a gift of tongues, but that no one really speaks in tongues unless he speaks a language understood by men, as in Acts 2.

5. That though one speak with tongues, it is no evidence of the Holy Ghost at all, but merely a sign.

XVIII. DIVINE HEALING

1. We do not condemn physicians and medicines because the Bible does not. Prov. 17: 22; Ezek. 47: 12; Col. 4: 44; Matt. 9:12.

2. We believe and teach Divine Healing according to the Scriptures. Isa. 8: 20.

3. We believe that it is a gift set in the Church and that the prayer of faith will save the sick and The Lord will raise them up. James 5: 15.

Notes: *The holiness movement, which drew much of its strength from the South, very quickly segregated along racial lines. Although the racial question determined the outward life of these groups, it is not reflected in their statements of doctrine, which follow similar patterns.*

The Church of Christ (Holiness) is the oldest of the predominantly black holiness bodies. Its statement of faith was derived from that of the Church of the Nazarene. The statement was also adopted by the Associated Churches of Christ (Holiness).

DOCTRINAL ELEMENTS OF THE CHURCH, GENERALLY [CHURCH OF GOD (SANCTIFIED CHURCH)]

The doctrinal elements of the Original Church of God or Sanctified Church consists of: Hearing, Repentance, Faith, Confession, Baptism.

On the merits of the sinner putting these elements into actions or, other words, obeying from the heart this form of doctrine he is then JUSTIFIED by the blood and he is a Regenerated child; and he is received into fellowship with God through Jesus Christ. He is made a partaker of His divine life and an heir to the Holy Spirit. The Holy Spirit imparts entire Sanctification to or in the believer. "Not by works of righteousness which we have done, but according to his mercy he saved us, by the washing of REGENERATION, and renewing of the HOLY GHOST; which he shed on us abundantly through Jesus Christ our Lord and Saviour; that being justified by his grace, we should be made heirs according to the hope of eternal life." Titus 3:5-7.

This is called by some, the Second Blessing or a Second Work of Grace, or Entire Sanctification. It is so called because man, in his unregenerated state, is a two fold sinner. A sinner by nature, also a sinner by practice. When he believes on the Lord Jesus Christ, the atoning blood of the cross cleanses him from all sin. And the stain of guilt washed away leaving him with a clean heart or a clear conscience. "For if the blood of bulls and of goats, and the ashes of an heifer sprinkling the unclean, sanctifieth to the purifying of the flesh; How much more shall the blood of Christ, who through the eternal Spirit offered himself without spot to God, purge your conscience from dead works to serve the living God? Heb. 9:13-14.

In this it will clearly be seen, that the believer is clean when he is converted to Christ, because the New life from God to us through Christ makes us new Creatures. That act places us in a New State which is a Justified State, clean. But this converted one must be filled with the Holy Ghost. To be clean is one thing, and to be filled with the Holy Ghost is another. The following scriptures will surely convince anyone who has any knowledge or respect for what the Bible teaches. Luke 24:49-The Holy Ghost was given to the disciples after they were believers. It was promised to those who believed on Christ through John the Baptist's preaching. Matt. 3:11-12.

READ CAREFULLY

Luke 3:16-17	Acts 1:8-9
John 1:33	Eph 1:13
Rom. 5:1-5	Acts 19:1-6
Acts 8:14	Acts 1:5
Mark 1:8	I. Cor 6:9
Rom. 15:16	

The scriptures referred to will show that all of the primitive disciples or christians received the Holy Ghost as a second blessing after they were regenerated. The doctrine of Holiness gets its foundation on regeneration of the sinner. This places him in a Justified state. The person then receiving the proper teaching, has right to believe that the same God who has the power to regenerate him through Christ, has the power to fill him with the Holy Ghost, which is Sanctification.

Because Sanctification is the work of the Holy Spirit in the believer subsequent to Regeneration, or Born again. "But we are bound to give thanks to God for you brethren beloved of the Lord, because God hath from the beginning chosen you to salvation through sanctification of the Spirit and belief of the truth." 2 Thes. 2:13.

When the doctrine ceased to be preached the results were, carnal ministers, carnal Churches and worldly profess christians. The doctrine of Holiness, coupled with a holy life is the only remedy. Heb. 12:14; I Pet. 1:1-4.

ARTICLE 26. MARRIAGE AND DIVORCE

Is it lawful for a Christian to put away their husbands or wives and marry while the other lives?

The law on the "second marriage" was clearly set forth by Christ, the law giver of the New Testament. Hear His words: "The Pharisees also came unto him, tempting him, and saying unto him, Is it lawful for a man to put away his wife for every cause? And he answered and said unto them, Have ye not read, that he which made them at the beginning made them male and female, And said, for this cause shall a man leave father and mother, and shall cleave to his wife; and they two shall be one flesh. Wherefore they are no more twain, but one flesh. What therefore God hath joined together, let not man put asunder. They say unto him, Why did Moses then command to give a writing of divorcement, to and to put her away? He saith unto them, Moses because of the hardness of your hearts suffered you to put away your wives: but from the beginning it was not so. And I say unto you, Whosoever shall put away his wife, except it be for fornication, and shall marry another, committeth adultery; and whose marrieth her which is put away doth commit adultery. Matt. 19:3. Mark 10:2-12; Luke 16:18; Rom. 7:1-4; I Cor. 7:10-15. These references should serve to convince us that Christ, the Law Giver of the New Testament Church makes only one exception. Matt. 5:32; Matt. 19:9.

ARTICLE 27

Should a Holy man marry people to the Second Husband or wife if he knows that their husband or wife is living?

We have no direct scriptures forbidding it. But if it is wrong for them to marry, it surely would be wrong for a saved Minister to encourage it. I Tim. 5:21-22.

ARTICLE 28. PAYING TITHES

There is no special command given in the New Testament to pay tithes and there is none directly against it. If any one makes a vow to that effect, God would hold them responsible if they deferred to pay. Tithes were paid under the old Covenant because it was a law to that effect. There must be something about it that merited God's approval because He encouraged it before the law was given. Gen. 14:18; Gen. 28:18-22.

God renewed the command to Israel through Malachi 3:8-12; Matt. 23:23. In this you can see that it had Christ's attention. Yet He gave no special command to pay them. The saints paid a slight tribute to paying tithes under the law, but only to show that the libidical priesthood which was made so by the law, changed when Christ came. Therefore the law that supported it was changed. If you will read carefully the seventh chapter of Hebrews, you will see that Paul labored to show the converted Jews that they were not under the same compulsory law to pay tithes as did the fathers under the law, verse 19. For the law made nothing perfect, but the bringing in of a better hope did; by which we draw nigh to God. Heb. 7:19.

*   *   *

Glenn Griffith Movement

ARTICLES OF RELIGION (BIBLE MISSIONARY CHURCH)

ARTICLES OF RELIGION (1955)

I. THE TRIUNE GOD

1. We believe in one eternally existent, infinite God, Sovereign of the universe; that He only is God, creative and administrative, holy in nature, attributes, and purpose; that He, as God, is Triune in essential being, revealed as Father, Son, and Holy Ghost. (I John 5:7; John 1:1; Matt. 3:16-17; John 14:16-17, 26)

II. GOD THE FATHER

2. The Father is the supreme Person in the Godhead, to Whom the Son and the Holy Ghost, though of equal essence, are subordinate in office. The Father sent the Son into the world; He also sends the Holy Ghost. To the Father the Son reconciles the penitent sinner; and to the Father pertains the worship of every believer.

ARTICLES OF RELIGION (CURRENT)

I. GOD THE FATHER

1. We believe there is but one living and true God; everlasting, of infinite power, wisdom and goodness; the Maker and Preserver of all things, visible and invisible; that in unity of the Godhead there are three persons, of one substance, power and eternity—the Father, the Son and the Holy Ghost.

II. GOD THE SON

2. We believe in Jesus Christ, the only begotten Son of God, the Second Person of the Triune God-head; that He was eternally one with the Father, that He was conceived by the Holy Ghost, was born of the Virgin Mary and became incarnate, so that two whole and perfect natures, that is to say, the Godhead and manhood, are thus united in one person, very God and very man, the God-man.

We believe that Jesus Christ died for our sins, and not only for actual sins, but also for original sin, that He might reconcile us to God. He arose from the dead and took again His body, together with all things appertaining to the perfection of man's nature, wherewith He ascended into heaven and is there engaged in intercession for us (Luke 1:27-35; John 1:14; John 3:16; Acts 4:12; Rom. 5:10; Heb. 7:25).

III. GOD THE HOLY GHOST

3. We believe in the Holy Ghost, the Third Person of the Triune Godhead; that He proceeds from the Father and the Son as the true and eternal God, of one substance, majesty and glory with the Father and Son. (Matt. 28:19; Acts 5:32; Rom. 8:9-11). He is ever present and efficiently active in and with the Church of Christ, convincing the world of sin, regenerating those who repent and believe, sanctifying believers, and guiding into all truth as it is in Jesus (John 16:18; John 3:5-9); Acts 15:8-9; John 16:13).

IV. THE HOLY SCRIPTURES

4. We believe that the sixty-six canonical books of the Old and New Testaments were given by divine inspiration (2 Tim. 3:16), and are the Word of God. We believe the Holy Scriptures inerrantly reveal the will of God concerning all things necessary to our salvation, so that whatever is not contained therein nor may be proved thereby, is not to be enjoined as an article of faith (2 Pet. 1:20-21).

V. ORIGINAL SIN, OR DEPRAVITY

5. We believe that original sin, or depravity, is that corruption of the nature of all the offspring of Adam by reason of which every one is very far gone from original righteousness or the pure state of our first parents at the time of their creation, is averse to God, without spiritual life, and inclined to evil, and that continually (Gen. 6:5; Rom. 3:12; 5:12-18; 1 Cor. 15:22). In the Scriptures, it is spoken of as the carnal mind, the old man and the flesh (Rom. 6:6; Rom. 7:7; Rom. 8:5-8). We further believe that original sin continues to exist after regeneration, though suppressed, until crucified (eradicated) and destroyed by the baptism with the Holy Ghost (Acts 15:8-9; 1 John 3:8).

VI. THE ATONEMENT

6. We believe that Jesus Christ, by His suffering (Acts 3:18), by the shedding of His own blood (Rom. 5:8-10; Heb. 9:12), and by His meritorious death on the cross (Eph. 2:13-16), made full atonement (Rom. 5:11) for all sin, and that this atonement is the only ground for salvation (Acts 4:12; Eph. 1-7), it being sufficient for every individual of Adam's race (John 3:16; 1 John 2:2). The atonement is graciously efficacious for the salvation of the irresponsible, the righteous who have become irresponsible (Rom. 4:5) and children in innocency (Mark 10:14), but is efficacious for the salvation of those who reach the age of responsibility only when they repent and believe (Luke 24:47; Acts 16:30-31; 17:30).

VII. FREE WILL

7. We believe that man was created with ability to choose between right and wrong and thus was made morally responsible. The condition of man since the fall is such that he cannot prepare himself by his own natural strength and works, to faith and calling upon

God. But the grace of God through Jesus Christ is freely bestowed upon all men, enabling all who will to turn from sin to righteousness, believe on Jesus Christ for pardon and cleansing from sin and follow good works pleasing and acceptable in His sight. "Whosoever will, let him take of the water of life freely" (Rev. 22:17; John 4:14, 15).

8. We further believe that man, though in the possession of the experience of regeneration and entire sanctification, may fall from grace and apostatize, and unless he repents of his sin, be hopelessly and eternally lost.

VIII. FAITH

9. We believe that living faith is the gift of God, and without it, it is impossible to please God (Heb. 11:6). Faith becomes effective as it is exercised by man, with the aid of the Spirit, which aid is assured when the heart has met the divine condition (Heb. 5:9).

IX. REPENTANCE

10. We believe that genuine repentance toward God consists in a knowledge of, a godly sorrow for, and a voluntary confession and forsaking of sin. This is brought about by the knowledge of the goodness and severity of God, through the medium of the truth and the convincing power of the Holy Spirit. It is demanded of all who have by act or purpose become sinners against God. The Spirit of God gives to all who will repent, the gracious help of penitence of heart and hope of mercy, that they may believe unto pardon and spiritual life (Matt. 3:2; Rom. 3:23; 2 Cor. 7:10; John 16:7-11; Luke 13:5).

X. JUSTIFICATION, REGENERATION AND ADOPTION

11. We believe that justification is that gracious and judicial act of God, by which He grants full pardon of all guilt and complete release from the penalty of sins committed, and acceptance as righteous to all who believe on Jesus Christ and receive Him as Lord and Saviour (Rom. 3:23-25; Rom. 5:1).

12. We believe that regeneration, or the new birth, is that gracious work of God whereby the moral nature of the repentant believer is spiritually quickened and given a distinctly spiritual life, capable of faith, love, and obedience (2 Cor. 5:17; 1 Pet. 1:23).

13. We believe that adoption is that gracious act of God by which the justified and regenerated believer is constituted a son of God.

14. We believe that justification, regeneration and adoption are simultaneous in the experience of seekers after God and are obtained upon the condition of faith in the merits of the shed blood of Jesus Christ, preceded by repentance; and that to this work and state of grace the Holy Spirit bears witness.

XI. ENTIRE SANCTIFICATION

15. We believe that entire sanctification is that act of God, subsequent to regeneration, by which believers are made free from original sin, or depravity, and brought into a state of entire devotement to God and the holy obedience of love made perfect.

16. It is wrought by the baptism with the Holy Ghost and comprehends in one experience the cleansing of the heart from sin and the abiding, indwelling presence of the Holy Ghost, empowering the believer for life and service.

17. Entire Sanctification is provided through the blood of Jesus; is wrought instantaneously by faith, preceded by entire consecration; and to this work and state of grace the Holy Spirit bears witness (Rom. 12:1; Rom. 6:11, 13, 22; Rom. 6:6; Gal. 2:20; Rom. 15:16; Heb. 13:12-13; Heb. 10:14-15).

18. This experience is also known by various terms representing its different phases, such as "Christian Perfection," "Perfect Love," "Heart Purity," "The Baptism with the Holy Ghost," "The Fullness of the Blessing," and "Christian Holiness."

XII. THE WITNESS OF THE SPIRIT

19. The Witness of the Spirit is that inward impression wrought on the soul, whereby the Spirit of God immediately and directly assures our spirit that Bible conditions are met for salvation and the work of grace is complete in the soul (Rom. 8:16). Therefore, the Spirit bears witness to both the salvation of the sinner and the sanctification of the believer (1 John 5:10; Heb. 10:14-15).

XIII. GROWTH IN GRACE

20. We believe that growth in grace is possible and necessary to maintain a right relationship with God, both before and after sanctification (Eph. 4:15-16; 2 Peter 3:18).

XIV. THE SECOND COMING OF CHRIST

21. We believe that the Lord Jesus Christ will come again. We believe that His coming will be literal and bodily and that we who are alive at His coming shall not precede them that are asleep in Christ Jesus; but that, if we are abiding in Him, we shall be caught up with the risen saints to meet the Lord in the air, so that we shall ever be with the Lord. We believe that the coming of Christ will be premillennial and that we should distinguish between His coming for His saints (1 Thess. 4:4-18) and with His saints (Jude 1:14). The latter will not occur until after the manifestation of the Antichrist and the Great Tribulation (Rev. 19:20; 2 Thess. 2:7-11). The one hope of the church is the premillennial coming of Jesus (Acts 15:13-17; Titus 2:13).

XV. RESURRECTION, JUDGMENT AND DESTINY

22. We believe in the resurrection of the dead, that the bodies both of the just and of the unjust shall be raised to live and unite with their spirits. "They that have done good, unto the resurrection of life; and they that have done evil, unto the resurrection of damnation" (John 5:29) (1 Cor. 15:52; 2 Cor. 5:10; 1 Thess. 4:15-16; Phil. 3:21).

We believe in future judgment in which every man shall appear before God to be judged according to his deeds in this life.

We believe that glorious and everlasting life is assured to all who savingly believe in and obediently follow Jesus Christ our Lord; and that the finally impenitent shall suffer eternally in hell (John 6:38; Matt. 6:20; Matt. 5:29; Matt. 10:28; Matt. 23:33; Matt. 25:41; Luke 16:23).

XVI. BAPTISM

23. We believe that Christian Baptism is a sacrament signifying acceptance of the benefits of the atonement of Jesus Christ. It is to be administered to believers as declarative of their faith in Jesus Christ as their Saviour, and full purpose of obedience in holiness and righteousness.

Baptism may be administered by sprinkling, pouring or immersion, according to the choice of the applicant.

XVII. THE LORD'S SUPPER

24. We believe that the Memorial and Communion Supper instituted by our Lord and Saviour Jesus Christ is essentially a New Testament sacrament, declarative of His sacrificial death, through the merits of which believers have life and salvation and promise of all spiritual blessings in Christ. It is distinctively for those who are prepared for reverent appreciation of its significance and by it they show forth the Lord's death till He comes again. Being the Communion feast, only those who have faith in Christ and love for the saints should be called to participate therein (Luke 22:19-20; 1 Cor. 11:23-29; Matt. 26:26-29).

XVIII. THE CHRISTIAN SABBATH

25. We recognize the first day of the week as being the Christian Sabbath under the present dispensation. It was the custom of the New Testament churches to meet for worship on the first day of the week. It was also selected and held sacred because the Lord Himself was resurrected on that day and He further emphasized it by pouring out the Holy Spirit on the day of Pentecost (1 Cor. 16:2; Matt. 28:1; Mark 16:2; Luke 24:1; John 20:1-19).

XIX. DIVINE HEALING

26. We believe in the Bible doctrine of divine healing and urge our people to seek to offer the prayer of faith for healing of the sick. Providential means and agencies, when deemed necessary, should not be refused (James 5:16; Matt. 10:8; Luke 9:2).

XX. THE CHURCH

27. The invisible church of God is composed of all spiritually regenerated persons whose names are written in heaven.

Notes: *The most conservative and strict wing of the holiness movement, the Glenn Griffith Movement emerged in the 1950s as a reaction to what its leaders considered a loss of holiness standards among the older holiness churches. The issues of contention were not doctrinal, but behavioral;*

therefore, the movement's doctrinal statements closely follow those of the parent bodies.

The Bible Missionary Church was organized by former members of the Church of the Nazarene. At the time of its formation, it accepted the articles of religion of the Nazarenes, with two changes. The first article on the Trinity was slightly rewritten, scriptural references were appended, and a second article on God the Father was added.

More recently, the Bible Missionary Church completely rewrote its Articles of Religion. The first article is taken from the Twenty-five Articles of Religion common to Methodism.

* * *

CREEDAL STATEMENTS (CHURCH OF THE BIBLE COVENANT)

1. THE HOLY TRINITY. We believe there is but one living and true God, everlasting, of infinite power, wisdom, and goodness; the Maker and Preserver of all things, visible and invisible. And in unity of this God-head there are three persons of one substance, power, and eternity—the Father, the Son (the Word), and the Holy Spirit. The Father is specially related to God's work in creation; the Son by incarnation is specially related to God's work in redemption; and the Holy Spirit by His indwelling is specially related to God's work in sanctification.

5. JESUS CHRIST. We believe the only begotten Son of God was conceived by the Holy Spirit, born of the Virgin Mary, suffered under Pontius Pilate, was crucified, dead and buried—to be a sacrifice, not only for original sin, but also for the actual sins of men, and to reconcile us to God. In resurrection He came forth from the dead, took again His body, together with all things appertaining to the perfection of man's nature, wherewith He ascended into heaven and is there engaged in intercession for us.

10. THE HOLY SPIRIT. We believe the Holy Spirit, proceeding from the Father and the Son, is of one substance, majesty and glory with the Father and the Son, very and eternal God. He is ever present and efficiently active in and with the Church of Christ, convincing the world of sin, righteousness and judgment, regenerating those who repent and believe, sanctifying belivers and guiding into all truth.

15. THE HOLY SCRIPTURES. We believe in the plenary inspiration of the Holy Scriptures, by which we mean the sixty-six books of the Old and New Testaments to be given by divine inspiration. These Scriptures we hold to be the infallible written Word of God, superior to all human authority, containing all things necessary to our salvation, so that whatever is not contained therein is not to be considered an article of faith.

20. ORIGINAL SIN. We believe original sin is the corruption of the nature of every man and is naturally engendered of the offspring of Adam, whereby man is wholly gone from original righ-

teousness, and of his own nature inclined to evil and that continually. We believe that original sin continues to exist in the life of the regenerate until eradicated by the baptism with the Holy Spirit.

25. THE ATONEMENT—GROUND OF SALVATION. We believe that Jesus Christ, by the shedding of His own blood, and by His meritorious death on the Cross, made a full atonement for all human sin, and that this atonement is the only ground of salvation, and that it is sufficient for every individual. The atonement is graciously efficacious for the salvation of the irresponsible and those not having reached the age of accountability, but is efficacious for the salvation of all others only when they repent and believe. Wherefore, to expect salvation on the ground of good works, or by the suffering the pains our sins deserve, either in the present or future state, is derogatory of Christ's sacrifice for us, and is a dangerous deceit.

30. FREE WILL. We believe the condition of man after the fall of Adam is such that he cannot turn and prepare himself, by his own natural strength and work, to faith and calling upon God. But being created in God-likeness we believe all have been granted the ability to choose between right and wrong, and that they are made morally responsible. Thus, grace is freely bestowed upon all men, enabling them to turn from sin to righteousness, believe on Jesus Christ, for pardon and cleansing from sin, and follow good works pleasing and acceptable in His sight. Despite this, man after receiving the experience of regeneration and entire sanctification, is free to elect the way of sin again and may thus apostatize and be eternally lost except he repent of his sin and be restored to Divine favor.

35. REPENTANCE. We believe that genuine repentance toward God consists in a knowledge of, a sorrow for, and a voluntary confession and forsaking of sin. This is brought about by the knowledge of both the goodness and severity of God, through the medium of the truth and the convincing and convicting power of the Holy Spirit. It is required of all who have by act or purpose become sinners before God. The Spirit of God gives to all who repent, the gracious help of penitence of heart and hope of mercy, that they may believe unto pardon and spiritual life.

40. JUSTIFICATION, REGENERATION AND ADOPTION. We believe that *justification* is that gracious and judicial act of God, by which He grants full pardon of all guilt and complete release from the penalty of sins committed, and acceptance as righteous, to all who believe on Jesus Christ and receive Him as Lord and Saviour. We believe *regeneration* is that work of the Holy Spirit by which the pardoned sinner enters spiritual life. This work is received through faith in Jesus Christ, whereby the regenerate are delivered from the power of sin which reigns over all the unregenerate, so that they love God and through grace serve Him with the will and affections of the heart. We believe that *adoption* is that gracious act of God whereby the justified and regenerated believer is made a son of God, receiving even the Spirit of adoption whereby he cries, Abba Father.

We further believe that justification, regeneration and adoption are simultaneous in the experience of seekers after God and are obtained upon the condition of faith in the merits of the shed blood of Jesus Christ, preceded by repentance; and that to this work and state of grace the Holy Spirit bears witness.

45. ENTIRE SANCTIFICATION. We believe entire sanctification to be that work of the Holy Spirit by which the child of God is cleansed from all inbred sin through faith in Jesus Christ. It is subsequent to regeneration, and is wrought when the believer presents himself a living sacrifice, holy and acceptable unto God, and is thus enabled through grace to love God with all the heart and to walk in His holy commandments blameless. Entire sanctification is provided by the blood of Jesus, is wrought instantaneously by faith, is preceded by entire consecration and is attested to by the direct witness of the Spirit as well as by the fruit of the Spirit. It is wrought by the baptism with the Holy Spirit and comprehends in one experience the cleansing of the heart from sin and the abiding indwelling presence of the Holy Spirit empowering the believer for life and service. We believe that this experience admits of expansion both in this life and the next, but that it is, by the Scriptures, the end of the commandment.

50. THE SECOND COMING OF CHRIST. We believe in the second coming of Christ and that this precious truth and good hope is an inspiration to holy living and godly effort. We believe the Scriptures to teach the coming of Christ in bodily return to the earth and that He will cause the fulfillment of all prophecies made concerning His final and complete triumph over all evil. Faith in the imminence of Christ's return is a rational and inspiring hope to the people of God. We further believe that those who are abiding in Him when He so comes will be caught up with the risen saints to meet the Lord in the air, so that they shall ever be with the Lord.

55. RESURRECTION, JUDGMENT AND DESTINY. We believe in the resurrection of the dead, both of the just and the unjust. We further believe that God is the Judge of all mankind and that His administration of judgment will culminate the final meeting of mankind before His throne of great majesty and power where records will be examined and final awards and punishments administered. In this light, everlasting life is assured to all who savingly believe in, and obediently follow, Jesus Christ our Lord, and the finally impenitent shall suffer eternally in hell.

60. THE SACRAMENTS. We believe the sacraments ordained by Christ are not only tokens of Christian profession, but they are certain signs of grace and

God's good will toward us, by which He works in us the strengthening of our faith in Him. There are two sacraments, namely, Baptism and the Lord's Supper. *Baptism* is not only a sign of profession and mark of difference whereby Christians are distinguished from others who are not so walking, but it is a sign of regeneration or new birth. The *Lord's Supper* is not only a sign of love and a memorial feast, but it is a sacrament of our redemption by Christ's death, and a token of His coming again; insomuch to such as rightly, worthily and with faith receive the same, it is made a medium through which God communicates blessing and strength to the heart.

65. DIVINE HEALING. We believe in the Bible doctrine of divine healing and urge our people to seek to offer the prayer of faith for the healing of the sick. Providential means and agencies when deemed necessary are not to be refused.

70. RELATIVE DUTIES. We believe those two great commandments which require us to love the Lord our God with all the heart and our neighbors as ourselves, contain the sum of the Divine law as it is revealed in the Scriptures. They are the measure and perfect rule of human duty and are for the ordering and directing of families and nations, and all other social bodies. By them we are required to acknowledge God as our only Supreme Ruler and all men as created by Him, equal in all natural rights. Wherefore, all men are bound so to order all their individual and social and political acts as to render to God entire and absolute obedience, and to secure to all men the enjoyment of every natural right as well as to promote the greatest happiness of each in the possession and exercise of such rights.

CONDENSED STATEMENT OF BELIEF

75. Following is a summary of our doctrinal position:

a. We believe that the Bible, both Old and New Testaments, is the inspired Word of God, and that it is the final authority governing the faith and practice of His people.

b. We believe in the Triune God; that is, the existence of one God manifested in three persons: Father, Son and Holy Spirit.

c. We believe that Jesus Christ was verily conceived of the virgin, and that He is the God-Man. We believe that He alone is mediator between God and man.

d. We believe in the personality of the third person of the Trinity, and that He is presently engaged in the great work of making Christ known to human hearts.

e. We believe that man was created in the image and likeness of God and that, through his disobedience, he sinned and brought upon himself spiritual death.

f. We believe in the vicarious death of Jesus Christ and that His shed blood is the meritorious means of our redemption.

g. We believe our salvation rests upon our attitude toward God's Son, and that repentance and contrition are necessary to the appropriation of saving faith.

h. We believe that entire sanctification is a second, definite work of grace wrought in the heart of the believer by the Holy Spirit when conditions for such a work are properly met.

i. We believe in the second coming of Jesus Christ and His subsequent reign upon the earth.

j. We believe in the resurrection of Jesus Christ from the dead and the resurrection of the just and unjust. We believe in the eternal happiness of the just and the everlasting punishment of the unjust.

Notes: *The Church of the Bible Covenant has printed two statements in its* Manual: *a longer set of articles of faith and a condensed statement of belief. The longer statement is derived in large part from that of the Church of the Nazarene, but has been extensively edited. Also, a final article on relative duties, taken from the Wesleyan Methodists, has been added.*

*　　*　　*

SUMMARY STATEMENT OF BELIEF (NATIONAL ASSOCIATION OF HOLINESS CHURCHES)

God the Father, God the Son, and God the Holy Spirit are three persons, united and inseparable, of one substance, and eternal.

The Holy Scriptures are divinely inspired and are infallibly true as originally given. They constitute our only divinely authorized rule of faith and practice.

Man in his natural state is sinful apart from saving grace. Repentance is the attitude toward sin which stems from conviction and godly sorrow, involving abandonment of the practice of sin, suitable confession to God and men, and restitution of all that is due to others, according to one's ability.

Justification is a legal act on the part of God whereby sins are forgiven through faith in the Lord Jesus Christ on the part of guilty sinners.

Regeneration is the quickening to spiritual life by the Holy Ghost through faith in the Lord Jesus Christ.

Entire sanctification is the complete purification of the nature from inherited sin and the complete renewal of the nature in Holiness, whereby the Child of God is enabled to love God with all his soul, mind, and strength, and to serve Him in righteousness and true Holiness. This experience is attended by the infilling of the Holy Spirit. This gracious work of God is wrought instantaneously in answer to faith.

There is one true Church which is composed only of those who have savingly believed in the Lord Jesus Christ.

The second coming of Christ is personal and visible.

The Scriptures affirm the resurrection of the body, both of the just and the unjust, the judgment of all mankind, the everlasting punishment of the wicked, and the eternal happiness of the righteous.

*   *   *

DOCTRINE (WESLEYAN TABERNACLE ASSOCIATION OF CHURCHES)

ARTICLE I. GOD

We believe in one eternal, infinite God, Sovereign of the universe; that He only is God, creative and administrative, holy in nature, attributes, and purpose; that He, as God, is triune in essential being, revealed as Father, Son, and Holy Ghost. (Matt. 3:16-17; John 1:1; John 14:16, 17, 26; I John 5:7)

A.   FATHER. The Father is the supreme person in the Godhead, to whom the Son and the Holy Ghost, though of equal essence, are subordinate in office. The Father sent the Son into the world. He also sends the Holy Ghost. To the Father the Son reconciles the penitent sinner, and to the Father belongs the worship of every believer.

B.   SON. We believe in Jesus Christ, the only begotten Son of God, the second person of the triune Godhead; that He is eternally one with the Father; was born of the Virgin Mary and became incarnate, so that two whole perfect natures, that is to say the Godhead and manhood, are thus united in one person, very God and very man, the Godman.

We believe that Jesus Christ died for our sins and not only for committed sins but also for original sin that He might reconcile us to God. He truly arose from the dead and took again his body, together with all things appertaining to the perfection of man's nature, wherewith He ascended into Heaven and is there engaged in intercession for us. (Luke 1:27-35; John 1: 14; John 3:16; Acts 4:12; Rom. 5:10; Heb. 7:25.)

C.   HOLY GHOST. We believe in the Holy Ghost, the third person of the triune Godhead, that He proceeds from the Father and the Son as the true and eternal God, of one substance, majesty and glory with the Father and Son. (Matt. 28:19; Acts 5:3-4; Rom. 8:9-11.) He is ever present and efficiently active in and with the church of Christ, convincing the world of sin, regenerating those who repent and believe, sanctifying believers, and guiding into all truth as it is in Jesus. (John 3:5-9; John 16:8, 13; Acts 15:8-9.)

ARTICLE II. BIBLE

We believe that the sixty-six canonical books of the Old and New Testaments are the Holy Scriptures, were given by divine inspiration and are the invincible Word of God. We believe that it unerringly reveals the will of God concerning us in all things necessary to our salvation, so that whatever is not contained therein nor may be proved thereby, is not to be enjoined as an article of faith. We definitely take our stand against the Revised Standard Version as not being acceptable. (II Tim. 3:15-17; II Peter 1:20-21.)

ARTICLE III. SIN

A.   ORIGINAL SIN. We believe that original sin, or depravity, is the corruption of the nature of all the offspring of Adam, and that man is born a fallen and depraved creature, far removed from the righteousness and pure state of our first parents at the time of creation. We believe that this sin, spoken of in the Bible as the carnal mind, the old man and the flesh is averse to God, is without spiritual life, and though it be suppressed, is continually inclined to evil and war against God, even after regeneration. We believe that only by complete surrender and consecration on the part of the believer can the Holy Ghost eradicate and destroy this sin nature. (Gen. 6:5; Acts 15:8-9; Rom. 3:12, 5:12-18; I Cor. 15:22; I John 3:8.)

B.   COMMITTED SINS. We believe that sin is the willful transgression of the known law of God, and that such sin condemns a soul to eternal punishment unless pardoned by God through repentance, confession, restitution, and believing in Jesus Christ as his personal Savior. This includes all men "For all have sinned and come short of the glory of God," Rom. 3:23. (Prov. 28:13; John 6:47; Acts 16:31; Rom. 6:23; I John 1:9; I John 3:4.)

ARTICLE IV. GOD'S PLAN OF REDEMPTION

"For God so loved the world, that he gave His only begotten Son, that whosoever believeth in Him should not perish, but have everlasting life." (John 3:16.)

A.   ATONEMENT. We believe that Jesus Christ, by His suffering, by the shedding of His own blood, and by His meritorious death on the cross, made full atonement for all sin.

This atonement is the only source of salvation and is sufficient for every individual of Adam's race. The atonement is graciously efficacious for the salvation of the irresponsible from birth, for the righteous who have become irresponsible and for children in innocency, but is efficacious for the salvation of those who reach the age of responsibility, only when they repent and believe. (Mark 10:14; Luke 24:47; John 3:3, 3:16; Acts 3:18, 4:12, 16:30, 31, 17:30; Rom. 4:15, 5:8, 11; Eph. 2:13-16; Heb. 9:12.)

B.   FREE WILL. We believe that man was created with ability to choose between right and wrong and thus was made morally responsible. The condition of man since the fall is such that he cannot prepare himself, by his own natural strength and works, to faith and calling upon God. But the grace of God through Jesus Christ is freely bestowed upon all men, enabling all who will, to turn from sin to righteousness, believe on Jesus Christ for pardon and cleansing from sin, and follow good works, pleasing and acceptable in His sight. "And whosoever will, let him take the water of life freely." Rev. 22:17. (John 4:14-15.)

We also believe that man through the transgression of God's law by using his free will to choose wrong, will fall from that state of regeneration and entire sanctification and be eternally lost, unless he repents of his sin.

C. FAITH. We believe that living faith is the gift of God and without faith it is impossible to please God. Faith becomes effective as it is exercised by man, with the aid of the Spirit. This aid is assured when the heart has met the divine condition. (Eph. 2:8; Heb. 11:6; Heb. 5:9.)

D. REPENTANCE. We believe that genuine repentance toward God consists in a knowledge of, sorrow for, and voluntary confession and forsaking of sin. This is brought about by the knowledge of the goodness and severity of God, through the medium of the truth and the convincing power of the Holy Spirit. Repentance is demanded of all who have by act or purpose become sinners against God. The Spirit of God gives to all who will repent, the gracious help of penitence of heart and hope of mercy, that they may believe unto pardon and spiritual life. (Matt. 3:2; Luke 13:5; John 16:7-11; Rom. 3:23; II Cor. 7:10.)

E. JUSTIFICATION. We believe that justification is the gracious and judicial act of God, by which He grants full pardon of sins committed and acceptance as righteous, to all who repent, believe on Jesus Christ and receive Him as Lord and Savior. (Romans 3:23-25; Romans 5:1.)

We believe that regeneration, or the new birth, is that gracious work of God whereby the moral nature of the repentant believer is spiritually quickened and given a distinct spiritual life, capable of faith, love and obedience. (II Cor. 5:17; I Peter 1:23.)

We believe that adoption is that gracious act of God by which the justified and regenerated believer is constituted a son of God.

We believe that justification, regeneration, and adoption are simultaneous in the experience of seekers after God and are obtained upon the conditions of repentance and faith in the merits of the shed blood of Jesus Christ. To this work and state of grace the Holy Spirit bears witness.

F. SANCTIFICATION. We believe that entire sanctification is that act of God, subsequent to regeneration, by which a believer is made free from original sin or depravity and brought into a state of entire devotement to God and the holy obedience of love made perfect.

It is wrought by the baptism with the Holy Ghost, and includes in one experience the cleansing of the heart from sin and the abiding, indwelling presence of the Holy Ghost, empowering the believer for life and service.

Entire Sanctification is provided by the blood of Jesus, is wrought instantaneously by faith, preceded by entire consecration, and to this work and state of grace the Holy Spirit bears witness. (Rom. 6:6; Rom. 6:11, 13, 22; Rom. 12:1; Rom. 15:16; Gal. 2:20; Heb. 10:14-15; Heb. 13:12-13.)

This experience is also known by various terms representing its different phases such as "Christian Perfection," "Perfect Love," "Heart Purity," "The Baptism with the Holy Ghost," "The fullness of the Blessing," and "Holiness of Heart."

G. WITNESS OF THE SPIRIT. The witness of the Spirit is that inward impression wrought on the soul whereby the Spirit of God immediately and directly assures our spirits that Bible conditions are met for salvation, and the work of grace is complete in the soul. In this way the Spirit bears witness to both the salvation of the sinner and the sanctification of the believer. (Heb. 10:14-15; I John 5:10.)

H. GROWTH IN GRACE. We believe that growth in grace is possible and necessary to maintain a right relationship with God, both before and after sanctification, and that only he that endureth to the end shall be saved.

ARTICLE V. ETERNAL DESTINY

We believe that man is born an eternal living soul, who will exist forever from birth throughout the endless ages of eternity. The short span appearing on the horizon of eternity is called time, the period of probation which God has allotted man to make his choice and preparation of where he will spend eternity. Either death or the return of Jesus will end this period, and the destiny of the soul will have been fixed. Then only the judgment and eternal life or eternal death remain.

A. SECOND COMING. We believe that the Lord Jesus Christ shall bodily come to earth again. This second coming will be premillennial and shall be distinguished between His coming for His saints and with His saints. The latter will occur after the great Tribulation, while the former will occur before the great Tribulation and is the "blessed hope" of the saints.

We believe at this time the righteous dead shall be resurrected and their glorified bodies shall be united with their spirits. The just who are alive shall be caught up with the risen saints to meet the Lord in the air and taken to the Marriage Supper of the Lamb, where they shall receive their rewards and will reign with Christ forever. The unjust shall be left behind on earth to endure the agonies of the great Tribulation, and at the end of the millennium, the unjust dead shall be resurrected. (Phil. 3:21; I Thess. 4:14-18; Jude 1:14; Rev. 19:20.)

B. JUDGMENT. We believe that following the Tribulation and Millennium comes the great and final Judgment Day of God in which every member of Adam's race shall appear before God to give an account and to be judged according to his deeds done in the body. (Dan. 12:2; Matt. 25:31-41; Rev. 20:12-13.)

C. HELL. We believe that after the Judgment, the impenitent sinner is banished forever from the presence of God and cast into a place of eternal

DOCTRINE (WESLEYAN TABERNACLE ASSOCIATION OF CHURCHES) (continued)

punishment and outerdarkness prepared for the devil and his angels, which is the Lake of Fire, called Hell. Here the damned and doomed shall die an eternal death of suffering, torment and endless agony forevermore. (Matt. 10:28; Matt. 25:41-46; Mark 9:44-48; Luke 16:23; John 8:21.)

D. HEAVEN. We believe, and humbly thank God that, through His mercies, the Christian has the glorious hope of eternal life with Christ, our Savior and Redeemer, in a place of everlasting joy, contentment and bliss, called Heaven. This place of eternal peace is being prepared by Jesus for those who have been washed in Jesus's blood and cleansed from all sin. (Matt. 25:34; Luke 23:39-43.)

ARTICLE VI. STATEMENTS OF RELIGIOUS FAITH

A. BAPTISM. We believe that the sacrament of Baptism is an outward sign which signifies the inward acceptance of the benefits of the Atonement of Jesus. It is to be administered to each believer as a testimony of his faith in Jesus as his personal Savior and showing intention to obey in following the paths of righteousness. Baptism may be administered by sprinkling or pouring, but preferably by immersion. (Matt. 28:19; Acts 2:38; Acts 8:36-38; I Peter 3:21.)

B. THE LORD'S SUPPER. We believe that the Memorial and Communion Supper instituted by our Lord and Savior Jesus Christ is essentially a New Testament sacrament, declarative of His sacrificial death. Through the merits of His death believers have life and salvation and promise of all spiritual blessings in Christ. It is distinctively for those who are prepared for reverent appreciation of its significance. By it they show forth the Lord's death till he come again. Being the Communion Feast, only those who have faith in Christ and love for the saints should be called

to participate. (Matt. 26:26-29; Luke 22:19-20; I Cor. 11:23-29; Matt. 26:26-29.)

C. THE CHRISTIAN SABBATH. We recognize the first day of the week as being the Christian Sabbath under the present dispensation. It was the custom of the New Testament churches to meet for worship on the first day of the week. It was selected and held sacred because the Lord Himself was resurrected on that day and He further emphasized it by pouring out the Holy Spirit on the day of Pentecost. (Matt. 28:1; Mark 16:2; Luke 24:1; John 20:1-19; Acts 20:7; I Cor. 16:2; Rev. 1:10.)

D. DIVINE HEALING. We believe in the Bible doctrine of divine healing for the body through Jesus, the Great Physician, Who is touched by our infirmities and by His stripes are the sick healed. It is the privilege of every child of God to call upon the elders to anoint him with oil in the name of the Lord, and pray the prayer of faith for healing. We realize that there is no particular virtue in the human agency but through faith in Jesus is the work done. (Isa. 53:5; John 9:1-34; James 5:14-16.)

E. THE CHURCH. We believe that God's church is composed of all spiritually regenerated persons who have separated themselves from the world, have a living faith in Christ as their personal Savior, and have their names written in the Lamb's Book of Life in Heaven. (Luke 10:20; Acts 2:46-47; II Cor. 6:17-18; Phil. 4:3-4; Rev. 3:5, 13:8.)

Notes: *The Wesleyan Tabernacle Association of Churches was formed by former members of the Bible Missionary Church. The association's doctrinal statement was derived from the original articles of religion of that church, which were in turn derived from those of the Church of the Nazarene. The articles have, however, been extensively edited to include an article on God's Plan of Redemption, a statement opposing the Revised Standard Version of the Bible, and an expanded presentation of eschatological beliefs.*

Chapter 8
Pentecostal Family

White Trinitarian Holiness Pentecostal

DOCTRINAL TEACHINGS [APOSTOLIC FAITH (KANSAS)]

TRINITY OF THE GOD-HEAD

(God the Father, Jesus Christ the Son, the Holy Ghost) "For there are THREE that bear record in heaven, the Father, the Word (Jesus) and the Holy Ghost: . . . " 1 John 5-7

REPENTANCE

(Act of Man) "Now after that John was put in prison, Jesus came into Galilee, preaching the gospel of the kingdom of God, And saying, The time is fulfilled, and the kingdom of God is at hand: REPENT YE, and believe the gospel." Mark 1:14-15

"The Lord is not slack concerning His promise, as some men count slackness; but is longsuffering to us-ward, not willing that any should perish, but that ALL SHOULD COME TO REPENTANCE." 2 Pet. 3:9

"REPENT YE therefore, and BE CONVERTED, that your sins may be blotted out, when the times of refreshing shall come from the presence of the Lord." Acts 3:19

CONVERSION

(Justification) (Act of God) ". . . Verily I say unto you, EXCEPT YE BE CONVERTED, and become as little children ye shall not enter into the kingdom of heaven." Matt. 18:3

"Be it known unto you therefore, men and brethren, that through this man (Jesus) is preached unto you the FORGIVENESS OF SINS: And by Him all that believe are JUSTIFIED from all things, from which we could not be justified by the law of Moses." Acts 13:38-39

"Therefore if any man be in Christ, he is a NEW CREATURE: old things are passed away, behold, all things are become new." 2 Cor. 5:17

CONSECRATION

(Act of Man) "I beseech you therefore, brethern, by the mercies of God, that YE PRESENT YOUR BODIES a living sacrifice, holy acceptable unto God, which is your reasonable service. And be not conformed to this world, but be ye transformed by the renewing of your mind, that ye may prove what is that good, and acceptable, and perfect will of God." Rom. 12:1-2

SANCTIFICATION

(Act of God) (a second, definite work of grace) "Wherefore Jesus also, that He might SANCTIFY the people with His own blood, suffered without the gate. Let us go forth therefore unto Him without the camp, bearing His reproach." Heb. 13:12-13

"Husbands, love your wives, even as Christ also loved the CHURCH, and gave Himself for it; That He might SANCTIFY and CLEANSE it with washing of the water by the word, that He might present it unto HIMSELF a glorious church, not having spot or wrinkle, or any such thing; but that it should be HOLY and without blemish. Eph. 5:25-27

"And the very God of peace SANCTIFY YOU WHOLLY; and I pray God, your WHOLE SPIRIT AND SOUL AND BODY be preserved blameless unto the coming of our Lord Jesus Christ." 1 Thes. 5:23

BAPTISM OF HOLY GHOST

"John answered, saying unto them all, I indeed baptize you with water; but one mightier than I cometh, the latchet of whose shoes I am not worthy to unloose: He shall BAPTIZE YOU WITH THE HOLY GHOST and with fire." Luke 3:16

"For John truly baptized with water; but ye shall be baptized with the Holy Ghost not many days hence." Acts 1:5

The EVIDENCE of the baptism of the Holy Ghost is the speaking with other tongues. (No fanaticism)

"And they were all filled with the Holy Ghost and began to speak with other tongues, as the spirit gave them utterance." Acts 2:4

"And they of the circumcision which believed were astonished, as many as came with Peter, because that on the Gentiles also was poured out the gift of the Holy

DOCTRINAL TEACHINGS [APOSTOLIC FAITH (KANSAS)] (continued)

Ghost. For they heard them speak with tongues, and magnify God." Acts 10:45-46

DIVINE HEALING

"And Jesus went about all Galilee, teaching in their synagogues, and preaching the gospel of the kingdom, and HEALING ALL MANNER OF SICKNESS AND ALL MANNER OF DISEASES among the people." Matt. 4:23

"Who His own self (Jesus) bare our sins in His own body on the tree, that we, being dead to sins, should live unto righteousness: by whose stripes YE ARE HEALED." 1 Peter 2:24

"Is any sick among you? let him call for the elders of the church; and let them pray over him, annointing him with oil in the name of the Lord: And the prayer of faith shall save the sick and the Lord shall raise him up; and if he have committed sins, they shall be forgiven him. Confess your faults one to another, and pray one for another, that ye may be healed. The effectual fervent prayer of a righteous man availeth much." James 5:14-16

ORDINANCES

WATER BAPTISM (by immersion). "Go ye therefore, and teach all nations, baptizing them in the name of the Father, and of the Son, and of the Holy Ghost." Matt. 28:19

"Know ye not, that so many of us as were baptized into Jesus Christ were baptized into His death? Therefore we are buried with Him by baptism into death: that like as Christ was raised up from the dead by the glory of the Father, even so we also should walk in newness of life." Rom. 6:3-4

THE LORD'S SUPPER. "And as they were eating, Jesus took bread, and blessed it, and brake it, and gave it to the disciples, and said, Take, eat; this is my body. And He took the cup, and gave thanks, and gave it to them, saying, Drink ye all of it. For this is my blood of the new testament, which is shed for many for the remission of sins." Matt 26:26-28 (Read 1 Cor. 11:23-30)

FEET WASHING. "He (Jesus) riseth from supper, and laid aside His garments; and took a towel, and girded Himself, After that He poured water into a basin, and began to wash the disciples feet, and to wipe them with the towel wherewith He was girded . . . " "If I then, your Lord and Master, have washed your feet; ye also ought to wash one another's feet." John 13:4-5, 14

NO DIVORCE AND REMARRIAGE

"Whosoever putteth away his wife, and marrieth another, committeth adultery: and whosoever marrieth her that is put away from her husband committeth adultery." Luke 16-18

"The wife is bound by the law as long as her husband liveth; but if her husband be dead, she is at liberty to be married to whom she will; only in the Lord." 1 Cor. 7:39

SECOND COMING OF CHRIST

"And if I go and prepare a place for you, I WILL COME AGAIN, and receive you unto Myself; that where I am, there ye may be also." John 14:3

". . . Ye men of Galilee, why stand ye gazing into heaven? this same Jesus which is taken up from you into heaven, SHALL SO COME in like manner as ye have seen Him go into heaven." Acts 2:11

"And then shall appear the sign of the Son of man in heaven: and then shall all the tribes of the earth mourn, and they shall see the SON OF MAN COMING IN THE CLOUDS OF HEAVEN with power and great glory." Matt. 24:30

THOUSAND YEAR REIGN OF CHRIST

"And I saw thrones, and they sat upon them, and judgment was given unto them: and I saw the souls of them that were beheaded for the witness of Jesus — and they lived and REIGNED WITH CHRIST A THOUSAND YEARS." Rev. 20:4

"Blessed and holy is he that hath part in the first resurrection: on such the second death hath no power, but they shall be priests of God and of Christ and shall REIGN WITH HIM A THOUSAND YEARS." Rev. 20-6

CONDITIONAL IMMORTALITY

(Life through Christ) ". . . I am come that they might have LIFE, and that they might have it more abundantly." John 10:10

"And this is the record, that God has given to us ETERNAL LIFE, and this life IS IN HIS SON. HE THAT HATH THE SON HATH LIFE, and he that hath not the Son of God hath not life." 1 John 5:11-12

"To them who by patient continuance in well doing SEEK FOR glory and honor and IMMORTALITY, eternal life." Rom. 2:7

(Immortality is yet future. Read 1 Cor. 15:51-54)

DESTRUCTION OF THE WICKED

"Enter ye in at the strait gate: for wide is the gate, and broad is the way that leadeth to DESTRUCTION, and many there be which go in thereat: . . . " Matt. 7:13

. . . In flaming fire taking vengeance on them that know not God, and that obey not the gospel of our Lord Jesus Christ: who shall BE PUNISHED WITH EVERLASTING DESTRUCTION from the presence of the Lord, and from the glory of His power." 2 Thes. 1:7-9

"For the wages of sin is DEATH; but the gift of God is ETERNAL LIFE through Jesus Christ our Lord." Rom. 6:23

"For, behold, the day cometh, that shall burn as an oven; and all the proud, yea, all that do wickedly, shall be stubble: and the day that cometh shall BURN THEM UP, saith the Lord of hosts, that it shall LEAVE THEM NEITHER ROOT NOR BRANCH." Mal. 4:1

TITHES AND OFFERINGS

"Will a man rob God? Yet ye have robbed me. But ye say, Wherein have we robbed thee? In TITHES AND OFFER-

INGS. — Bring ye all the tithes into the storehouse, that there may be meat in mine house, and prove me herewith, saith the Lord of hosts, if I will not open you the windows of heaven, and pour you out a blessing, that there be not room enough to receive it." Mal. 3:8, 10.

"But woe unto you, Pharisees! for ye tithe mint and rue and all manner of herbs, and pass over judgment and the love of God: THESE OUGHT YE TO HAVE DONE, and not to leave the other undone." Luke 11:42.

Notes: *The Pentecostal Movement arose in the early twentieth century simultaneously with fundamentalism. However, while the movement participated in the general conservative evangelical Christian world view, fundamentalists rejected pentecostals because of their holiness leanings and their doctrine of the baptism of the Holy Spirit. Pentecostals derived their beliefs directly and literally from the Bible, with little reference to the authority of Christian tradition. Hence the authority of the Bible became crucial to their theological position. Any doctrinal statements are considered, at best, summaries of the major Biblical teachings, and churches have consistently prefaced such statements with some affirmation of the authority of the Bible.*

The crucial item found throughout the pentecostal statements is a belief in the baptism of the Holy Spirit. Most modern pentecostals believe that the believer's experience of baptism, like that which occurred at the first Christian Pentecost, is initially accompanied by the gift of speaking-in-tongues and followed by the emergence of other gifts (such as healing or prophecy).

The Holiness-Pentecostal Churches share a belief in three major experiences in the pilgrimage of the Christian life, each initiated by the action of the Holy Spirit in the individual's life. First, the sinner, by repentence of sin and faith in Christ, can be justified. Second, the Christian can be cleansed of inbred sin and made perfect in love, an experience termed santification. Third, the sanctified believer can be baptized in the Holy Spirit and begin to manifest the gifts of the spirit.

The Apostolic Faith derives from the original pentecostal work in Topeka, Kansas in 1901. Its doctrinal statement is primarily a compilation of texts from the Bible.

* * *

DOCTRINE (APOSTOLIC FAITH BIBLE COLLEGE)

It is recognized that the true church of Jesus Christ consists of all believers in the saving grace of our Lord and Saviour Jesus Christ who have accepted him as their personal Saviour. It is recognized and agreed that no organization or man has been granted authority by the Lord to exclude from or accept anyone into the Kingdom of Heaven, as this is done by Jesus Christ only. It is further recognized and agreed that we as Christians are to love all members of the Body of Christ (Christians), and this love and fellowship derives from the unity instilled by the Holy Spirit. Although differences in doctrinal beliefs and interpretations should not influence our love for one another,

adherence to similar doctrinal beliefs and modes of worship have bonded together those of the Apostolic Faith Movement as founded by Charles F. Parham in the early 1900's. The scripture teaches us to adhere to the truth and proper doctrine.

These common doctrinal beliefs are essentially as follows:

Triune God; Father, Son and Holy Spirit.

Creation and Formation.

Man is basically sinful and in need of Salvation.

Salvation by Grace upon repentance toward God and acceptance of Jesus Christ as one's personal Saviour, which is the conception of Spiritual Life.

Sanctification of the Spirit, Soul and Body. A second definite work of Grace by the Lord Jesus Christ.

Baptism of the Holy Spirit; evidenced by speaking in other languages.

Water Baptism (of all believers) by immersion in water in the name of the Father, and of the Son, and of the Holy Spirit.

Sacrament of the Lord's Supper.

Washing of Feet.

Divine Healing through Jesus Christ for all believers.

Do not condone divorce and remarriage. Matthew 19:8-9

Destruction of the Wicked.

Conditional Immortality.

Rapture of the Man Child Class.

Return of Jesus Christ to earth again; bodily and visibly.

A Ministry supported by tithes and offerings.

These basic doctrines shall be adhered to in the teaching of the Apostolic Faith Bible College, which in addition to other doctrinal teachings approved by the Board from time to time if they are not inconsistent with the above listed basic doctrines.

Notes: *This oldest school in the pentecostal movement has a statement in agreement with its sponsoring body, the Apostolic Faith (Kansas).*

* * *

BIBLE DOCTRINES (APOSTOLIC FAITH CHURCH)

THE DIVINE TRINITY. The Godhead consists of three Persons in one: the Father, the Son, and the Holy Ghost. These are separate and distinct Persons not merely three names for one Person. "For there are three that bear record in heaven, the Father, the Word, and the Holy Ghost: and these three are one" (I John 5:7). (See Matthew 3:16,17.)

REPENTANCE TOWARD GOD. Repentance is a godly sorrow for sin with a renunciation of sin. Isaiah 55:7; Mark 1:15; Acts 3:19; 20:21; II Corinthians 7:10

RESTITUTION. Restitution includes restoring where you have defrauded, stolen, or slandered; paying back debts,

BIBLE DOCTRINES (APOSTOLIC FAITH CHURCH) (continued)

and making confession. Leviticus 6:4; Ezekiel 33:15; Matthew 5:23, 24; Luke 19:8,9

JUSTIFICATION AND REGENERATION. Justification is the act of God's grace whereby we receive remission of sins and stand before God as though we had never sinned. John 1:12,13; 3:3,16; II Corinthians 5:17

ENTIRE SANCTIFICATION (Holiness). Entire sanctification is the act of God's grace by which we are made holy. It is the second, definite work wrought by the Blood of Jesus through faith, and subsequent to salvation and regeneration. Luke 1:74,75; John 17:15-17; II Corinthians 7:1; Ephesians 5:25-27

THE BAPTISM OF THE HOLY GHOST. The baptism of the Holy Ghost is the enduement of power from on High upon the clean, sanctified life. Matthew 3:11; Luke 24:49; John 7:38,39; 14:16,17,26; Acts 1:5-8

When we receive the gift of the Holy Ghost, it is accompanied by the same sign as the disciples had on the Day of Pentecost, viz., speaking with tongues as the Spirit gives utterance. Mark 16:17; Acts 2:4; 10:45,46; 19:6; I Corinthians 14:21,22

DIVINE HEALING. The healing of sickness and disease is provided for God's people in the Atonement. "With his stripes we are healed" (Isaiah 53:5). Matthew 8:17; Mark 16:18; Luke 13:16; Acts 10:38; James 5:14-16

THE SECOND COMING OF JESUS. The return of Jesus will be just as literal and visible as His going away. John 14:3; Acts 1:9-11

There will be two appearances under one coming: first, to catch away His waiting Bride. Matthew 24:40-44; I Thessalonians 4:15-17; second, to execute judgment upon the ungodly. Zechariah 14:3,4; II Thessalonians 1:7-10; Jude 14,15

THE TRIBULATION. During the interim between Christ's coming for His Bride and His return in judgment, there is to be the Great Tribulation, or the time of Jacob's trouble. Isaiah 26:20,21; Jeremiah 30:7; Daniel 12:1; Matthew 24:21,22,29; Mark 13:19; Revelation 9 and 16

CHRIST'S MILLENNIAL REIGN. Christ's Millennial Reign is the 1000 years' literal reign of Jesus on earth, which will be ushered in by the coming of Jesus back to earth with ten thousands of His saints. At this time He will judge the nations that dwell upon the face of the earth. II Thessalonians 1:7-10; Jude 14, 15

During this time the devil will be bound. Revelation 20:2-6

THE GREAT WHITE THRONE JUDGMENT. God will finally judge the quick and the dead according to their works. Daniel 12:2; Acts 10:42; Revelation 20:11-15

THE NEW HEAVEN AND THE NEW EARTH. The Word teaches that this earth which has been polluted by sin shall pass away after the White Throne Judgment, and God will create a new heaven and a new earth in which righteousness shall dwell. Isaiah 65:17; 66:22; II Peter 3:12,13; Revelation 21:1-3

ETERNAL HEAVEN AND ETERNAL HELL. The Bible teaches that hell is as eternal as Heaven. Matthew 25:41-46. The wicked shall be cast into a burning hell, a lake of fire burning with brimstone forever and ever. Mark 9:43,44; Luke 16:24; Revelations 14:10,11

NO DIVORCE AND REMARRIAGE. The Word teaches that marriage is binding for life. Under the New Testament law, the law of Christ, there is but one cause for separation—fornication; and no right to marry again while the first companion lives. Matthew 5:31,32; 19:3-9; Mark 10:11,12; Luke 16:18; Romans 7:2,3

WATER BAPTISM. One immersion (not three) "in the name of the Father, and of the Son, and of the Holy Ghost," as Jesus commanded. Matthew 28:19. Examples: Matthew 3:16; Acts 8:38,39. Types: Romans 6:4,5; Colossians 2:12

THE LORD'S SUPPER. Jesus instituted the Lord's Supper that we might "shew the Lord's death till he come." I Corinthians 11:23-26; Matthew 26:26-29

WASHING THE DISCIPLES' FEET. Jesus said, "If I then, your Lord and Master, have washed your feet; ye also ought to wash one another's feet. For I have given you an example, that ye should do as I have done to you." John 13:14,15

Notes: *The doctrinal statement of the Apostolic Faith Church is an expansion of that of the Apostolic Faith (Kansas), the original pentecostal organization. The statement commits the church to belief in divine healing, premillennialism, and foot washing, and contains a specific denial of triune immersion.*

* * *

DECLARATION OF FAITH (AND RELATED DOCUMENTS) [CHURCH OF GOD (CLEVELAND, TENNESSEE)]

DECLARATION OF FAITH

We believe:

1. In the verbal inspiration of the Bible.

2. In one God eternally existing in three persons; namely, the Father, Son, and Holy Ghost.

3. That Jesus Christ is the only begotten Son of the Father, conceived of the Holy Ghost, and born of the Virgin Mary. That Jesus was crucified, buried, and raised from the dead. That He ascended to heaven and is today at the right hand of the Father as the Intercessor.

4. That all have sinned and come short of the glory of God and that repentance is commanded of God for all and necessary for forgiveness of sins.

5. That justification, regeneration, and the new birth are wrought by faith in the blood of Jesus Christ.

6. In sanctification subsequent to the new birth, through faith in the blood of Christ; through the Word, and by the Holy Ghost.

7. Holiness to be God's standard of living for His people.

8. In the baptism with the Holy Ghost subsequent to a clean heart.

9. In speaking with other tongues as the Spirit gives utterance and that it is the initial evidence of the baptism of the Holy Ghost.

10. In water baptism by immersion and all who repent should be baptized in the name of the Father, and of the Son, and of the Holy Ghost.

11. Divine healing is provided for all in the atonement.

12. In the Lord's Supper and washing of the saints' feet.

13. In the premillennial second coming of Jesus. First, to resurrect the righteous dead and to catch away the living saints to Him in the air. Second, to reign on the earth a thousand years.

14. In the bodily resurrection; eternal life for the righteous, and eternal punishment for the wicked.

CHURCH OF GOD TEACHINGS

The Church of God stands for the whole Bible rightly divided. The New Testament is the only rule for government and discipline. Below are given some of the teachings that are made prominent:

1. Repentance. Mark 1:15; Luke 13:3; Acts 3:19.

2. Justification. Rom. 5:1; Titus 3:7.

3. Regeneration. Titus 3:5.

4. New birth. John 3:3; 1 Peter 1:23; 1 John 3:9.

5. Sanctification subsequent to justification. Rom. 5:2; 1 Cor. 1:30; 1 Thess. 4:3; Heb. 13:12.

6. Holiness. Luke 1:75; 1 Thess. 4:7; Heb. 12:14.

7. Water baptism. Matt. 28:19; Mark 1:9, 10; John 3:22, 23; Acts 8:36, 38.

8. Baptism with the Holy Ghost subsequent to cleansing; the enduement of power for service. Matt. 3:11; Luke 24:49, 53; Acts 1:4-8.

9. The speaking in tongues as the Spirit gives utterance as the initial evidence of the baptism of the Holy Ghost. John 15:26; Acts 2:4; 10:44-46; 19:1-7.

10. Spiritual gifts. 1 Cor. 12:1, 7, 10, 28, 31; 1 Cor. 14:1.

11. Signs following believers. Mark 16:17-20; Rom. 15:18, 19; Heb. 2:4.

12. Fruits of the Spirit. Rom. 6:22; Gal. 5:22, 23; Eph. 5:9; Phil. 1:11.

13. Divine healing provided for all in the atonement. Psa. 103:3; Isa. 53:4, 5; Matt. 8:17; Jas. 5:14-16; 1 Pet. 2:24.

14. The Lord's Supper. Luke 22:17-20; 1 Cor. 11:23-26.

15. Washing the saints' feet. John 13:4-17; 1 Tim. 5:9, 10.

16. Tithing and giving. Gen. 14:18-20; 28:20-22; Mal. 3:10; Luke 11:42; 1 Cor. 9:6-9; 16:2; Heb. 7:1-21.

17. Restitution where possible. Matt. 3:8; Luke 19:8.

18. Premillennial second coming of Jesus. First, to resurrect the dead saints and to catch away the living saints to Him in the air. 1 Cor. 15:52; 1 Thess. 4:15-17; 2 Thess. 2:1. Second, to reign on the earth a thousand years. Zech. 14:4; 1 Thess. 4:14; 2 Thess. 1:7-10; Jude 14, 15; Rev. 5:10; 10:11-21; 20:4-6.

19. Resurrection. John 5:28, 29; Acts 24:15; Rev. 20:5, 6.

20. Eternal life for the righteous. Matt. 25:46; Luke 18:30; John 10:28; Rom. 6:22; 1 John 5:11-13.

21. Eternal punishment for the wicked. No liberation nor annihilation. Matt. 25:41-46; Mark 3:29; 2 Thess. 1:8, 9; Rev. 20:10-15; Rev. 21:8.

22. Total abstinence from all liquor or strong drinks. Prov. 20:1; 23:29-32; Isa. 28:7; 1 Cor. 5:11; 6:10; Gal. 5:21.

23. Against the use of tobacco in any form, opium, morphine, etc. Isa. 55:2; 1 Cor. 10:31, 32; 2 Cor. 7:1; Eph. 5:3-8; Jas. 1:21.

24. Meats and drinks. Rom. 14:2, 3, 17; 1 Cor. 8:8; 1 Tim. 4:1-5.

25. The Sabbath. Rom. 14:5, 6; Col. 2:16, 17; Rom. 13:1, 2.

26. Against members wearing jewelry for ornament or decoration, such as finger rings (this does not apply to wedding bands), bracelets, earrings, lockets, etc. 1 Tim. 2:9; 1 Pet. 3:3.—31st A., 1936, p. 34; Amended 47th A., 1958, p. 31.

27. Against members belonging to lodges. John 18:20; 2 Cor. 6:14-17.

28. Against members swearing. Matt. 5:34; Jas. 5:12.

29. Divorce and remarriage. Mat. 19:7-9; Mark 10:11, 12; Luke 16:18; 1 Cor. 7:2, 10, 11.—45th A., 1954, p. 29.

RESOLUTION RELATIVE TO PRINCIPLES OF HOLINESS OF CHURCH OF GOD

The foundation of the Church of God is laid upon the principles of Biblical holiness. Even before the Church experienced the outpouring of the Holy Ghost, its roots were set in the holiness revival of the past century. It was, and is, a holiness church—holiness in fact and holiness in name.

The passing of three-quarters of a century has not diminished our holiness position or convictions. The years have, instead, strengthened our knowledge that without holiness it is impossible to please God.

We, hereby, remind ourselves that the Scriptures enjoin us at all times to examine our own hearts. The continuing and consistent life of holiness require this. Conditions of our day desperately require it. The subtle encroachment of worldliness is a very real and unrelenting threat to the Church. We must therefore beware lest *we* become conformed to the world, or lest a love for the world take root in *our* hearts and manifest itself as lust of the flesh, lust of the eye, or the pride of life.

For these reasons, we present the following:

Whereas, the Church of God is historically a holiness church, and

Whereas, we are enjoined by the Scriptures to be so and

DECLARATION OF FAITH (AND RELATED DOCUMENTS)
[CHURCH OF GOD (CLEVELAND,
TENNESSEE)] (continued)

Whereas, a tide of worldliness threatens the spirituality of the Church,

Be it resolved that we, the Church of God, reaffirm our standard of holiness, in stated doctrine, in principles of conduct, and as a living reality in our hearts.

Be it further resolved that we, as ministers, maintain this standard in our own lives, in our homes, and in our pulpits

Be it further resolved that we, as ministers and members, rededicate ourselves to this purpose, and guard our lives against conformity to the world in appearance, in selfish ambition, in carnal attitudes, and in evil associations

Be it further resolved that we, as ministers and members, seek to conform to the positive virtues of love, mercy, and forgiveness as taught by Jesus Christ.

Notes: *The Church of God (Cleveland, Tennessee) is one of the older pentecostal bodies, having existed as a holiness church for several decades before the message of pentecost was brought from California to the mountains of Tennessee. The basic doctrinal statement is the church's Declaration of Faith. It is expanded upon by a second doctrinal item, Church of God Teachings, which offers scriptural references to the prominent teachings of the church. The Teachings also refer to specific matters not covered in the Declaration such as prohibitions on secret lodges, alcohol, tobacco, drugs, and jewelry (apart from wedding rings). A slightly modified form of this statement is also used by the Church of God (World Headquarters). A third item, the Holiness Resolution, expands the church's stance on holiness.*

* * *

DOCTRINE (CHURCH OF GOD, HOUSE OF PRAYER)

DOCTRINE

The apostles who preached Christ—not creed—gave the body of Christ its doctrine as they were inspired by the Holy Ghost, therefore, it shall be our purpose to continue in the apostles' doctrine and fellowship, "for we preach not ourselves, but Christ Jesus the Lord." Acts 2:42; 2 Cor. 4:5.

We believe the body of Christ should have unity on essentials, liberty on non-essentials, and charity toward all men.

We believe the Bible sets forth the following as being essential in our day. Acts 15:28.

THE BIBLE

We accept both divisions of the Bible as the inspired Word of God, but rely on the New Testament for church government and rule of Christian conduct. We believe the New Testament is God's last message spoken by His Son for the day and age in which we live, revealing the church with its gifts, graces, and government; therefore, the New Testament shall be our all-sufficient rule of faith and practice. Heb. 1:1, 2.

"Therefore leaving the principles of the doctrine of Christ, let us go on to perfection; not laying again the foundation of repentance from dead works, and of faith toward God, of the doctrine of baptisms, and of laying on of hands, and of resurrection of the dead, and of eternal judgment. And this will we do, if God permit." Heb. 6:1-3.

REPENTANCE

Repentance is impelled by godly sorrow and followed by restitution and conversion. It is the entrance into the way of salvation and there must be repentance before sins can be remitted. Mark 1:4; Luke 3:8; Acts 2:38; 3:19; 17:30; 26:20; 2 Cor. 7:10.

FAITH TOWARD GOD

REGENERATION. The Spiritual or new birth is made possible by the vicarious atonement and where there is no spiritual birth, there is no spiritual life.

We accept the teaching of Christ in His discourse to Nicodemus as fundamental, and rely on the fact that when a man is regenerated he is born of God, and made a new creature in Christ. St. John 3:1-8; Eph. 2:8; Gal. 6:15.

JUSTIFICATION. The Bible teaches that those who are born (Gr. begotten) of God doth not commit sin, therefore they are justified by faith in the blood of Jesus Who was "delivered for our offences, and was raised again for our justification." Acts 13:38, 39; Rom. 4:25, 5:9; 1 John 3:9.

SANCTIFICATION. All who have been born of God, and are justified by faith in the blood, may also be sanctified with the blood. Heb. 13:12. Regeneration or the "new birth" is the impartation of divine life; justification is the accounting of one just in the sight of God; sanctification is cleansing.

DIVINE HEALING BY FAITH. The atonement provides healing for the body and complete deliverance for those who are possessed with evil spirits. The gifts of healing and power over demons is transmitted to the church through Christ by the power of the Holy Ghost. Isaiah 53:4, 5; Matt. 8:17; Mark 16:18; James 5:14-16; 1 Peter 2:24.

LAYING ON OF HANDS

DIVINE HEALING BY LAYING ON OF HANDS. Concerning the believers, Jesus said: "They shall lay hands on the sick, and they shall recover." Mark 16:18; Acts 9:12.

BAPTISM WITH THE HOLY GHOST BY LAYING ON OF HANDS. In the great revival at Samaria the apostles, Peter and John, layed their hands on the believers and prayed for them to receive the Holy Ghost. Acts 8:17, 18. The apostle Paul did likewise on finding certain believers at Ephesus. Acts 19:6.

ORDINATION TO CHRISTIAN SERVICE BY LAYING ON OF HANDS. The apostles layed their hands on and prayed for the seven men who had been chosen to look after the church business in the early church. Acts 6:1-6.

Paul and Barnabas were ordained to go forth into the work to which the Holy Ghost had specifically called them. Acts 13:1-3.

Timothy's calling and work was recognized by the laying on of the hands of the presbytery. 1 Timothy 4:14.

RESURRECTION

There are two resurrections mentioned in the New Testament, the first, being the resurrection of life and the second, the resurrection of damnation. Saint Paul speaks of the resurrection from the dead which is proof that some will be raised from among the dead at the first resurrection, while others will remain in their graves until the second resurrection, which takes place at the close of the thousand years reign with Christ. John 5:28, 29; Acts 4:2; 24:15; Rom. 1:4; 1 Cor. 15:12-55; Rev. 20:5, 6, 13.

DOCTRINE OF BAPTISMS

BAPTISM WITH WATER. We accept immersion in the name of the Father, and of the Son, and of the Holy Ghost, as the scriptural mode of water baptism. Matt. 28:19; Mark 1:9, 10; Acts 8:36-39; 1 Peter 3:21.

BAPTISM WITH THE SPIRIT. Those who are sanctified may tarry for and receive the baptism of the Holy Ghost, which is the gift of power for service upon a sanctified life. Luke 24:49; Acts 1:8.

On the day of Pentecost when the first disciples were baptized with the Holy Ghost, God gave the sign of speaking with other tongues as the initial evidence. This sign also followed when the Holy Ghost fell on the Gentiles at the house of Cornelius, and is positive proof that the same spiritual baptism and the same evidence of said baptism is for both Jews and Gentiles. Matt. 3:11; Mark 16:17; Acts 1:5-8; 2:4; 10:44-46; 19:6.

CHRIST'S SECOND ADVENT. The Bible specifically announces the return of our Lord to this earth. John 14:1-3; Acts 1:11; Heb. 9:28. He will first descend into the air, where the saints will meet Him and be kept during the great tribulation period. 1 Thes. 4:14-17; Rev. 3:10; 4:1-5; 5:5-10. When the tribulation is past, He will come to earth with all the saints who meet Him in the air, and will reign with His people for one thousand years upon the earth. 2 Thes. 1:7-10; Rev. 1:7; 19:11-16; 20:6.

SACRAMENT. Jesus instituted the sacrament or Lord's Supper the same night in which He was betrayed of Judas Iscariot. Its purpose is to show the Lord's death until He comes again; therefore, all true believers should participate in the communion of the body and blood of Christ, the elements consisting of bread and the unfermented fruit of the vine. Unbelievers should not partake. The Communion should not be neglected, but should be observed often. We encourage believers to observe this ordinance quarterly, and especially the night preceding Good Friday of every year and as often as the churches

decide to do so. Matt. 26:17-29; Luke 22:19, 20; 1 Cor. 10:16; 11:23-29.

FEET WASHING. Following the supper, Jesus poured water into a basin and washed the disciples' feet saying, "I have given you an example that ye should do as I have done unto you." This ordinance is also for believers and only believers should be invited to be present when it is observed. John 13:2-17; 1 Tim. 5:10.

ETERNAL JUDGMENT

The Bible plainly teaches that every man must stand before God to be judged. The righteous on that day shall go into life eternal and the unrighteous shall go away into everlasting punishment.

"For we must all appear before the judgment seat of Christ; that every one may receive the things done in his body, according to that he hath done, whether it be good or bad." 2 Cor. 5:10. See also Romans 2:2-11; Matt. 25:46; Rev. 20:11-15; 21:7, 8.

Approved this 18th day of August, 1963, at Markleysburg, Pennsylvania, U.S.A., by the General Assembly of the Church of God House of Prayer.

Notes: *This statement was adopted in 1963.*

* * *

ARTICLES OF FAITH [CHURCH OF GOD (JERUSALEM ACRES)]

1. WE BELIEVE in the eternal existence of one God in three Persons—namely, God the Father (Yahweh), God the Son (Yahshua or Jesus), and God the Spirit (Ruach Hachodesh).

2. WE BELIEVE in the eternal pre-existence of the Son of God as the Lamb slain from the foundation of the world and as the Creator of all things, both visible and invisible.

3. WE BELIEVE that Jesus Christ was miraculously conceived of the Holy Spirit by the Virgin Mary and that He was both God and man—God in the sense of the ever-inherent divinity shown by His resurrection from the dead, and man in the sense that He voluntarily made Himself lower than the angels that He might suffer and taste death for every man.

4. WE BELIEVE that Jesus Christ lived a sinless life, overcoming every temptation that is common to man; that He died on the cross to atone for the sins of all men; that He was buried on the day of Passover; that He was in the heart of the earth for three days and three nights; that at the end of the Sabbath He arose again; and that He ascended into heaven, to sit at the right hand of God as the only Mediator between God and man.

5. WE BELIEVE that on the Day of Pentecost Jesus confirmed His High Priest ministry by filling the Church with the Holy Spirit, thereby giving them power for service.

6. WE BELIEVE that the whole Bible is the inspired Word of God and that true doctrine for faith,

practice, government, and discipline must be determined from the New Testament, witnessed by the law and the prophets.

7. WE BELIEVE that God is the Author of one eternal religion set forth and systematized at Sinai by Moses, reformed and perfected at Calvary by Jesus Christ, believed and practiced by the New Testament Church, and restored and observed among the Gentiles by the last days' Church.

8. WE BELIEVE in the total brotherhood of the Christian community and in the higher calling of the Church which distinguishes it within the Kingdom of God.

9. WE BELIEVE that Jesus Christ came into the earth not only to die for man's sins but also to establish the Church of God according to the divine pattern.

10. WE BELIEVE that the Church was and is an organism for the fulfillment of prophecy and that prophecy is the primary witness and identification of the Church.

11. WE BELIEVE that Jesus established the theocratic order of government for the Church with one Anointed Leader, Twelve Apostles, Seventy Prophets, and Seven Men of Wisdom, and that this order is to be restored in the last days.

12. WE BELIEVE that all matters of doctrine and polity of the Church (called Apostles' Doctrine) have been and must be settled in the Council of Apostles and Elders, in which the Anointed Leader is the moderator and final authority.

13. WE BELIEVE that all men err and that Jesus Christ alone proved to be infallible; therefore, we do not equate verbal utterances (prophesying) with the written Word of God.

14. WE BELIEVE that both the Old and New Testaments predicted the apostasy of the early Church and that although the Kingdom of God continued through the Dark Ages, the Church as an organism ceased to exist in 325 A.D. with the uniting of Church and State.

15. WE BELIEVE that following the restoration of the fundamental doctrines of faith through the Protestant Reformation, The Church of God was resurrected from the Dark Ages according to prophecy in 1903, by A.J. Tomlinson.

16. WE BELIEVE in water baptism by immersion and in the seven spiritual baptisms—namely, the baptism of repentance (born again), the baptism of the blood (sanctification), the baptism of the Holy Spirit (speaking with tongues), the baptism of fire (zeal), the baptism into the Body of Christ (the covenant of church membership), the baptism of suffering, and the baptism of death.

17. WE BELIEVE in the full restoration of the gifts to individuals, both the nine gifts of the Spirit and the five gifts of the ministry.

18. WE BELIEVE in the New Testament observance of the seventh-day Sabbath and of the principal Feasts of the Lord, Passover (the Lord's Supper and washing the saints' feet), Pentecost, and Tabernacles.

19. WE BELIEVE that marriage is an institution of God and that no one has the right to divorce his companion and be remarried except for the cause of fornication (the act of adultery); however, we believe converts should remain in the state in which they are called.

20. WE BELIEVE that Israel will be fully restored, that their land (or inheritance) will be given to them as a nation, and that the remnant of Israel will be saved with an everlasting salvation.

21. WE BELIEVE that the Church will be supernaturally protected during the period of Great Tribulation (Indignation).

22. WE BELIEVE in the pre-millennial second-coming of Christ to establish His Kingdom in Jerusalem, Israel, where the resurrected and living saints will reign with Him for one thousand years.

23. WE BELIEVE in eternal life for the righteous and eternal punishment for the wicked.

24. WE BELIEVE that there will be a new heaven and a new earth after the Millennial Kingdom and that the righteous will inhabit the new earth forever.

Notes: *The Church of God headquartered at Jerusalem Acres (Cleveland, Tennessee) is one of a number of groups deriving from the Church of God (Cleveland, Tennessee). Its beliefs, however, differ in a number of respects from the other churches of that lineage. The influence of the Sacred Name Movement is evident in the use of the Hebrew transliterations of God's name (Yahweh) and Jesus's (Yahshua), in the church's sabbatarianism, and in the adoption of the Old Testament feasts. Among the church's unique beliefs is that of the seven spiritual baptisms.*

* * *

TWENTY-NINE IMPORTANT BIBLE TRUTHS (CHURCH OF GOD OF PROPHECY)

These twenty-nine vital points of New Testament doctrine are some of the prominent teachings of the Church of God of Prophecy. These teachings are all based on the Scripture; they were taught and practiced by the early Church; and they have been searched out in these last days by Godly men not concerned with their own opinions. However, the Church does not make a "hobby horse" of any one teaching or group of teachings, but accepts the whole Bible rightly divided with the New Testament as the only rule for government and discipline.

REPENTANCE. Repentance is both a condition and an act; it is the state of being in Godly sorrow for sins committed and the act of turning from and forsaking those sins. "For godly sorrow worketh repentance to salvation not to be repented of: but the sorrow of the world worketh death." 2 Corinthians 7:10. Also, read Mark 1:15; Luke 13:3; Acts 3:19. Repentance is a prerequisite for justification.

JUSTIFICATION. Justification is both a state and an act; it is the state of being void of offense toward God brought about by the act of God in forgiving actual transgressions for which one has repented. It is the result of repentance and faith. "Therefore being justified by faith, we have peace with God through our Lord Jesus Christ." Romans 5:1. Also, read Romans 5:2-9; Titus 3:7. Justification precedes regeneration.

REGENERATION. Regeneration is an act of God performed in the justified heart whereby new, spiritual life is generated. Man is dead in trespasses and sin through Adam; he must be quickened or regenerated through Christ. It is a vital part of the plan of salvation by faith. "Not by works of righteousness which we have done, but according to his mercy he saved us, by the washing of regeneration, and renewing of the Holy Ghost." Titus 3:5. Other Scriptures are Matthew 19:28; Ephesians 2:1, 4, 5. Regeneration is simultaneous with the new birth.

BORN AGAIN. To be born again is to become a new creature in Christ and a child of God. This new birth is the result of repentance, justification and regeneration. It is a definite and instantaneous experience wrought in the heart accompanied by a definite inner witness. There is no other way to enter the kingdom of God. (However, the new birth does not make one a member of the Church of God.) "Marvel not that I said unto thee, Ye must be born again." John 3:7. Read John 3:3-8; 1 Peter 1:23; 1 John 3:9; Romans 8:16; 1 John 3:14. The new birth is a prerequisite for the experience of sanctification.

SANCTIFICATION. Sanctification is the second definite work of grace, an instantaneous work wrought in the regenerated heart by the Holy Ghost with the blood of Christ. Whereas in regeneration actual transgressions are blotted out, in sanctification the Adamic nature, or inbred sin, is eradicated. "Wherefore Jesus also, that he might sanctify the people with his own blood, suffered without the gate. Let us go forth therefore unto him without the camp, bearing his reproach." Hebrews 13:12, 13. Read Romans 5:2; 1 Corinthians 1:30; 1 Thessalonians 4:3; 1 John 1:9. Sanctification restores man to the holy estate of Adam before the fall gives him the grace to live a life of holiness, and makes him eligible for the indwelling of the Holy Ghost.

HOLINESS. Holiness is the state of being free from sin, a condition made possible by the experience of sanctification. God requires man to live without sin in this present world and provided the means through the shed blood of Christ. "For the grace of God that bringeth salvation hath appeared to all men, Teaching us that, denying ungodliness and worldly lusts, we should live soberly, righteously, and godly, in this present world." Titus 2:11, 12. "Follow peace with all men, and holiness, without which no man shall see the Lord." Hebrews 12:14. Read Luke 1:74, 75; 1 Thessalonians 4:7; Ephesians 4:24; 1 Peter 1:15, 16. Holiness is a necessity not only for the individual but also for the Church, the body of Christ. Read Ephesians 1:4; 5:27; 2 Corinthians 7:1; Psalm 93:5.

WATER BAPTISM. Water baptism is the act of being immersed in water according to the commandment and instructions of Christ. This ordinance has no power to wash away sin but is the answer of a good conscience toward God, representing the death, burial and resurrection of Christ through which one has obtained new life. Only those who have already been born again are eligible for water baptism. "The like figure whereunto even baptism doth also now save us (not the putting away of the filth of the flesh, but the answer of a good conscience toward God,) by the resurrection of Jesus Christ." 1 Peter 3:21. Water baptism has divine approval only when it is done "in the name of the Father, and of the Son, and of the Holy Ghost." Read Matthew 28:19; Mark 1:8-10; John 3:22, 23; Acts 10:47, 48.

BAPTISM WITH THE HOLY GHOST. When a person is sanctified wholly he is eligible for the indwelling of the Holy Ghost. This indwelling is a definite and instantaneous experience described in the Scripture by the word "baptism," and always accompanied by the evidence of speaking in other tongues as the Spirit gives the utterance. It has no reference to water baptism, regeneration or sanctification. It is the filling of the temple already made clean by sanctification. It is not a work of grace but a gift of God in answer to the prayer of Christ. The baptism of the Holy Ghost is an enduement of power for service. "But ye shall receive power, after that the Holy Ghost is come upon you: and ye shall be witnesses unto me both in Jerusalem, and in all Judaea, and in Samaria, and unto the uttermost part of the earth." Acts 1:8. Read 1 Corinthians 3:16, 17.

SPEAKING IN TONGUES. Speaking in tongues as the Spirit gives utterance is the initial, physical evidence of the baptism of the Holy Ghost. No one ever receives the Holy Ghost without speaking in tongues. This is separate and distinct from the gift of tongues which is one of the nine gifts of the Spirit. "And they were ALL filled with the Holy Ghost, and began to speak with other tongues, as the Spirit gave them utterance." Acts 2:4. Also read John 15:26; Acts 10:44-46 and 19:6.

FULL RESTORATION OF THE GIFTS TO THE CHURCH. The nine gifts of the Spirit were set in the Church and are operated through individuals by the prompting of the Spirit. Since these gifts were given to the Church, they are subject to its government and cannot be taken away by any individual who leaves the Church. Although these gifts were lost when the Church went into the dark ages, they were fully restored to the Church when it arose out of darkness. 1 Corinthians 12:28, "And God hath set some in the church, first apostles, secondarily prophets, thirdly teachers, after that miracles, then gifts of healings, helps, governments, diversities of tongues." Read 1 Corinthians 12:1, 4-11; 1 Corinthians 14:1.

SIGNS FOLLOWING BELIEVERS. Miraculous signs and wonders will accompany the work and ministry of true believers. These signs are recorded in Mark 16:17-20, "And these signs shall follow them that believe; In my name shall they cast out devils; they shall speak with new tongues; They shall take up serpents; and if they drink any deadly thing, it shall not hurt them; they shall lay hands on the sick, and they shall recover . . . And they went forth, and preached everywhere, the Lord working with

TWENTY-NINE IMPORTANT BIBLE TRUTHS (CHURCH OF GOD OF PROPHECY) (continued)

them, and confirming the word with signs following. Amen." Also read Romans 15:18, 19; Hebrews 2:4.

FRUIT OF THE SPIRIT. The Spirit-filled life will manifest the fruit of the Spirit. Galatians 5:22, 23, "But the fruit of the Spirit is love, joy, peace, longsuffering, gentleness, goodness, faith, Meekness, temperance: against such there is no law." These virtues cannot be manifested by the flesh or by human nature. They are divine in origin and must spring from a Spirit-filled heart. Read Romans 6:22; Ephesians 5:9; Philippians 1:11.

DIVINE HEALING. Christ's atoning sacrifice on the cross provided not only for the salvation of the souls of men but also for the healing of man's physical ailments. Psalm 103:2, 3, "Bless the Lord, O my soul, and forget not all his benefits: Who forgiveth all thine iniquities; who healeth all thy diseases." Divine healing is healing accomplished by the power of God without the aid of medicine or surgical skills. This healing virtue is available to all who believe, the same as salvation. Read also Isaiah 53:4, 5; Matthew 8:17; James 5:14-16; 1 Peter 2:24.

THE LORD'S SUPPER. The Lord's Supper was instituted by Christ and is a sacred ordinance which we are commanded to observe. The Supper consists of unleavened bread, which represents His body broken on the cross for our sins, and the wine (unfermented grape juice), which represents the blood of Christ shed for our sanctification. This ordinance is observed in commemoration of Christ and His death. Only sinless and consecrated Christians are eligible to partake of this Supper. Read Luke 22:17-20; 1 Corinthians 11:23-33.

WASHING THE SAINTS' FEET. Feet washing was instituted by Jesus on the night of the Last Supper and is a New Testament ordinance we are enjoined to observe—as much so as communion. Its observance was taught by the apostles and practiced by the early Church. Charity and good works do not fulfill this obligation. "If I then, your Lord and Master, have washed your feet; ye also ought to wash one another's feet." John 13:14. Read John 13:4-17; 1 Timothy 5:10.

TITHING AND GIVING. Tithing is the paying of one tenth of our increase into the treasury of the Church. It began with Abraham, continued under the law and received Christ's approval. "Woe unto you, scribes and Pharisees, hypocrites! for ye pay tithe of mint and anise and cummin, and have omitted the weightier matters of the law, judgment, mercy, and faith: these ought ye to have done, and not to leave the other undone." Matthew 23:23. The obligation for tithing is not fulfilled by giving ten percent to the poor or to some good cause but only by paying it into the Church treasury.

Giving differs from and is in addition to tithing. Both are parts of God's plan to finance His work on earth. Read Genesis 14:18-20; Malachi 3:10; Luke 11:42; 1 Corinthians 16:2; 2 Corinthians 9:6-9; Hebrews 7:1-21.

RESTITUTION WHERE POSSIBLE. Restitution is the act of restoring something wrongfully taken or the satisfying of one who has been wronged. God requires those who become converted to perform such tasks if at all possible. "And Zacchaeus stood, and said unto the Lord; Behold, Lord, the half of my goods I give to the poor; and if I have taken any thing from any man by false accusation, I restore him fourfold. And Jesus said unto him, This day is salvation come to this house, forsomuch as he also is a son of Abraham." Luke 19:8, 9. Read Matthew 3:8; Romans 13:8.

PRE-MILLENNIAL SECOND COMING OF JESUS. Christ is coming back to earth again. First, to resurrect the dead saints and to catch away the living saints to meet Him in the air, where they will attend the marriage supper of the Lamb. "For the Lord himself shall descend from heaven with a shout, with the voice of the archangel, and with the trump of God: and the dead in Christ shall rise first: Then we which are alive and remain shall be caught up together with them in the clouds, to meet the Lord in the air: and so shall we ever be with the Lord." 1 Thessalonians 4:16, 17. Read Matthew 24:27, 28; 1 Corinthians 15:51, 52.

Second, to return with the saints to reign on earth a thousand years. ". . . And they lived and reigned with Christ a thousand years. But the rest of the dead lived not again until the thousand years were finished. This is the first resurrection." Revelation 20:4, 5. Read Zechariah 14:4, 5; Luke 1:32; 1 Thessalonians 4:14; 2 Thessalonians 1:7-10; Jude 14, 15; Revelation 5:10; 19:11-21.

RESURRECTION. All the dead, both righteous and wicked, will be resurrected. The righteous dead will be raised in the first resurrection which is at Christ's appearing. The resurrection of the wicked dead will occur after the thousand years reign of Christ on earth. "And have hope toward God, which they themselves also allow, that there shall be a resurrection of the dead, both of the just and unjust." Acts 24:15. Read Daniel 12:2; John 5:28, 29; 1 Corinthians 15:12-23; 41-58; Revelation 20:5, 6.

ETERNAL LIFE FOR THE RIGHTEOUS. Those who die in the Lord and those who are serving Him when He returns will receive a reward of eternal life—eternal happiness in the presence of the Lord. "And these shall go away into everlasting punishment: but the righteous into life eternal." Matthew 25:46. Read Luke 18:30; John 10:28; Romans 6:22; 1 John 5:11-13.

ETERNAL PUNISHMENT FOR THE WICKED. Our life in this present world determines our eternal reward. The unconverted and the wicked are doomed to eternal punishment, from which there is no escape—no liberation or annihilation. "And these shall go away into everlasting punishment: but the righteous into life eternal." Matthew 25:46. Read Mark 3:29; 2 Thessalonians 1:8, 9; Revelation 20:10-15; 21:8.

TOTAL ABSTINENCE FROM LIQUOR OR STRONG DRINK. The Bible expressly forbids the use of intoxicating beverages. Even slight indulgence is sinful and not in keeping with Scriptural standards of holiness. "Wine is a mocker, strong drink is raging: and whosoever is deceived thereby is not wise." Proverbs 20:1. Read also Isaiah 28:7; 1 Corinthians 5:11; 6:10; Galatians 5:21.

AGAINST USE OF TOBACCO, OPIUM, MORPHINE, ETC. The use of tobacco in any form is forbidden as well as the habitual use of narcotics. These sinful practices defile the body, the temple of the Holy Ghost, and are outward evidence of an impure heart. "Having therefore these promises, dearly beloved, let us cleanse ourselves from all filthiness of the flesh and spirit, perfecting holiness in the fear of God." 2 Corinthians 7:1. Read Isaiah 55:2; 1 Corinthians 10:31, 32; Ephesians 5:3-8; James 1:21.

ON MEATS AND DRINKS. The New Testament makes no rigid rule concerning what the Christian shall eat or drink (with the exception of strong drink). Thus, we have no right to judge what our brother eats or what he drinks. The legal restrictions of Jewish law concerning these were not extended into the Grace Dispensation. "For the kingdom of God is not meat and drink; but righteousness, and peace, and joy in the Holy Ghost." Romans 14:17. Read Romans 14:2, 3; 1 Corinthians 8:8; 1 Timothy 4:1-5.

ON THE SABBATH. The observance of the Sabbath was a requirement of Jewish law and as such was not carried over into the Grace Dispensation. Sunday is not the Sabbath but is merely a day set aside to give special attention to the worship of God. Instead of keeping only the Sabbath day holy, we are required in this dispensation to keep every day holy. The Jewish Sabbath is a type of Christ, who is our rest, rather than the day. "Let no man therefore judge you in meat, or in drink, or in respect of an holyday, or of the new moon, or of the sabbath days: Which are a shadow of things to come; but the body is of Christ." Colossians 2:16, 17. Read Hosea 2:11; Romans 13:1, 2; Romans 14:5, 6; Hebrews 4:1-11.

AGAINST WEARING GOLD FOR ORNAMENT. Ornaments of gold or other precious metals are a useless and frivolous waste of money, for they do not benefit the wearer either physically or spiritually. For this reason, and because they are evidences of a prideful heart, they are unbecoming to a child of God. Isaiah 55:2, "Wherefore do ye spend money for that which is not bread? and your labour for that which satisfieth not? hearken diligently unto me, and eat ye that which is good, and let your soul delight itself in fatness." Read 1 Timothy 2:9; 1 Peter 3:3; 1 John 2:16.

AGAINST BELONGING TO LODGES. The Bible is opposed to the people of God being unequally yoked together with unbelievers; it is opposed to deeds done in secret; and it demands the complete and undivided loyalty of God's children. John 18:20, "Jesus answered him, I spake openly to the world; I ever taught in the synagogue, and in the temple, whither the Jews always resort; and in secret have I said nothing." Read 2 Corinthians 6:14-17; Ephesians 5:12, 13; 2 Corinthians 11:2. Also many secret societies require the taking of an oath which is expressly forbidden by Scripture. (See next paragraph.)

AGAINST SWEARING. The taking of an oath is a vain thing and condemned by the Scripture. An affirmation to the truth of anything is sufficient. Matthew 5:34, "But I say unto you, Swear not at all; neither by heaven; for it is God's throne." Also, the use of profanity is forbidden. Read Exodus 20:7; James 5:12.

AGAINST DIVORCE AND REMARRIAGE EVIL. Divorce and remarriage constitute the sin of adultery. Matthew 5:32, "But I say unto you, That whosoever shall put away his wife, saving for the cause of fornication, causeth her to commit adultery: and whosoever shall marry her that is divorced commiteth adultery." The only allowable causes for remarriage are fornication and death. However, fornication is not unfaithfulness or simple adultery, but is a state of being married to another's wife or husband. 1 Corinthians 7:2, "Nevertheless, to avoid fornication, let every man have his own wife, and let every woman have her own husband." Read Romans 7:2, 3; 1 Corinthians 5:1-5, 13; 1 Corinthians 6:16-18; Revelation 2:22.

Notes: *The Church of God of Prophecy continues in the lineage of the Church of God as established in Cleveland, Tennessee by A.J. Tomlinson, who split with the group now referred to as the Church of God (Cleveland, Tennessee). There is no difference of doctrinal position between the two bodies. However, the Church of God of Prophecy has prepared its own presentation of the prime teachings. In summarizing its teachings, the Church of God of Prophecy emphasizes that it accepts the whole Bible as the Word of God. New members assume an obligation by affirmatively answering a question: "Will you sincerely promise in the presence of God and these witnesses that you will accept the Bible as the Word of God—believe and practice its teachings rightly divided—the New Testament as your rule of faith and practice, government and discipline, and walk in the light to the best of your knowledge and ability?" Thus, this statement of twenty-nine items is considered not a creed, but a presentation of prominent Biblical teachings.*

As with the Church of God (Cleveland, Tennessee), there is an acceptance of divine healing, premillennialism, and foot washing, and a rejection of secret lodges, intoxicating drinks, tobacco, narcotics, and jewelry (the exception clause for wedding rings does not appear).

* * *

TEACHINGS (CHURCH OF GOD OF THE MOUNTAIN ASSEMBLY)

Regeneration—St. John 3:3-8.

Water Baptism—By immersion in the name of the Father, and of the Son, and of the Holy Ghost.—St. Matt. 28:19; Rom. 6:4.

Sanctification—Following regeneration—St. John 17:17; I Cor. 1:30 I Cor. 5:11; Eph. 5:26; Heb. 10:20, 13:12.

Baptism of the Holy Ghost—Following sanctification, with the Bible evidence of speaking in tongues. St. John 15:26: Acts 2:4; 10:44-47.

Holiness—St. Luke 1:74-75; Heb. 12:14.

Fruit of the Spirit—Gal. 5:22-23.

Spiritual Gifts of the Church—I Cor. 12:8-10.

Signs following the Believers—St. Mark 16:17-18.

Divine Healing—St. Mark 16:18; I Cor. 12:9; James 5:14.

The Lord's Supper—I Cor. 11:23-24.

TEACHINGS (CHURCH OF GOD OF THE MOUNTAIN ASSEMBLY) (continued)

Washing the Saints' Feet—St. John 13:4-17.

Tithing and Giving—Gen. 14:20, 28:22; Mal. 3:10; I Cor. 16:2; II Cor. 8:11-15; Gal. 6:6.

Restitution When Possible—St. Luke 19-8.

Thousand Year Reign with Christ—Rev. 20:4.

Resurrection of the Dead—St. John 5:28-29; I Cor. 15.

Eternal Life for the Righteous—St. Matt. 25-46; Rom 6:22.

Eternal Punishment for the Wicked—St. Matt. 25:41; Rev. 14:10-11.

Total Abstinence from Strong Drink—Pr. 20:1; Gal. 5:21.

Keeping the Sabbath Day Holy—Ex. 20:8.

Against Pride—Wearing of gold for decoration, such as finger rings, bracelets, lockets, etc.—Pr. 16:18; I Pet. 3:3; I John 2:15-16.

Against Uncleanness—(This includes the use of tobacco in any form.)—II Cor. 7:1; James 1:21.

Against Women Members Cutting Their Hair—I Cor. 11:5-15.

Against Swearing—St. Matt. 5:34; James 5:12.

Modesty Is Required of the Sisters of the Church—I Tim. 2:9-10; I Pet. 3:3-5.

Against Going to War and Killing—Ex. 20-13; St. Luke 3:14; St. John 18:36; St. Luke 18-20.

Against Infants Being Taken into the Church—All children under twelve years of age are under question by the Church.

The New Testament Is Our Creed and Teachings—And we further believe all scripture as being given by inspiration of God, is profitable for doctrine, for reproof, for correction, and for instruction in righteousness.—2 Tim. 3:16.

We Prefer the King James Version of the Bible—and therefore advise our members to use this version.

Notes: *These teachings derive directly from the Church of God Teachings of the Church of God (Cleveland, Tennessee); however, there have been a number of additions and deletions. Additions include statements on pacifism, women cutting their hair, and the preference for the King James Version of the Bible. Deletions include the prohibition on secret lodges.*

* * *

COVENANT AND BIBLE DOCTRINE (CHURCH OF GOD OF THE UNION ASSEMBLY)

FIRST—REPENTANCE. For you to repent you must be sorry enough to quit the things that are wrong. II Cor. 7 ch., 9 and 10 verses; Jonah 3 ch., 8-10 verses; Matt. 3 ch., 2 verse; Mark 1 ch., 15 verse; Luke 24 ch., 47 verse; Acts 2 ch., 38 verse. Goodness of God leadeth to repentance—Rom. 2 ch., 4 verse. Repentance toward God, Acts 20 ch., 21 verse.

SECOND—WATER BAPTISM BY IMMERSION. Matt. 3 ch., 13 through 17 verses; Mark 16 ch., 16 verse; Rom. 6 ch., 4 and 5 verses; Col. 2 ch., 11 thru 13 verses.

THIRD—JUSTIFICATION BY FAITH IN JESUS CHRIST. Rom. 5 ch., 1 and 9 verses; Titus 3 ch., 7 verse; Rom. 3 ch., 25 and 26 verses; Acts 13 ch., 39 verse.

FOURTH—SANCTIFICATION THROUGH THE BLOOD. St. John 17 ch., 17 and 19 verses; Eph. 5 ch., 25 and 26 verses; I Thess. 4 ch., 3 verses; Heb. 2 ch., 11 verse; Heb. 13 ch., 12 verse.

FIFTH—BAPTISM OF THE HOLY GHOST. Matt. 3 ch., verse 11; Luke 24 ch., 49 verse; St. John 7 ch., 37 thru 39 verses; St. John 14 ch., 16 and 26 verses.

SIXTH—EVIDENCE THAT YOU HAVE RECEIVED THE HOLY GHOST IS STAMMERING LIPS AND OTHER TONGUES. FRUIT OF THE SPIRIT. Gal. 5 ch., 22 to 24 verses; Isaiah 28 ch., 11 and 12 verses; I Cor. 14 ch., 21 verse; Acts 2 ch., 4 verse; Acts 10 ch., 46 and 47 verses; Acts 19 ch., 6 verse.

SEVENTH—LORD'S SUPPER. Matt. 26 ch., 26 thru 30 verses; Luke 22 ch., 17 and 20 verses; I Cor. 11 ch., 23 thru 26 verses; I Cor. 5 ch., 7 and 8 verses.

EIGHTH—FEET WASHING. St. John 13 ch., 4 thru 17 verse; I Tim. 5 ch., 9 and 10 verses; I Peter 2 ch., 21 verse.

NINTH—HEALING OF THE BODY. Mark 6 ch., 13 verse; Mark 16 ch., 18 verse; James 5 ch., 14 and 15 verses.

FOR MEMBERS WHO ARE SOLDIERS

All members are forbidden to take up arms and go to war.

The nature of our belief is as follows:

The Word of God said "Thou Shalt Not Kill." Mark 10 ch., 17 thru 19 verses reads "And when he was gone forth into the way, there came one running, and kneeled to him, and asked him, Good Master, what shall I do that I may inherit eternal life?

"And Jesus said unto him, Why callest thou me good? There is none good but one, that is, God.

"Thou knowest the commandments, Do not commit adultery, Do not kill, Do not steal, Do not bear false witness, Defraud not, Honor they father and mother."

WHY WE DON'T BELIEVE IN KILLING. Mark 3 ch., 4 verse reads "And he saith unto them, Is it lawful to do good on the sabbath days, or to do evil? to save life or to kill? But they held their peace."

James 2 ch., 11 thru 13 verses reads "For he that said, Do not commit adultery, said also, Do not kill. Now if thou commit no adultery, yet if thou kill, thou art become a transgressor of the law."

"So speak ye, and so do, as they that shall be judged by the law of liberty."

"For he shall have judgment without mercy, that hath shewed no mercy, and mercy rejoiceth against judgment."

Matthew 26 ch., 51 and 52 verses reads "And, behold, one of them which were with Jesus stretched out his hand, and drew his sword, and struck a servant of the high priest's and smote off his ear.

"Then said Jesus unto him, Put up again thy sword into his place: for all they that take the sword shall perish with the sword."

II Cor. 10 ch., 3 and 4 verses reads "For though we walk in the flesh, we do not war after the flesh:

"For the weapons of our warfare are not carnal, but mighty through God to the pulling down of strong holds."

Romans 12 ch., 17 thru 21 verses reads "Recompence to no man evil for evil. Provide things honest in the sight of all men.

"If it be possible, as much as lieth in you, live peaceably with all men.

"Dearly beloved, avenge not yourselves, but rather give place unto wrath: for it is written, Vengeance is mine; I will repay, saith the Lord.

"Therefore if thine enemy hunger, feed him; if he thirst, give him drink: for in so doing thou shalt heap coals of fire on his head.

"Be not overcome of evil, but overcome evil with good."

I Thess. 5 ch., verse 15 reads, "See that none render evil for evil unto any man; but ever follow that which is good both among yourselves, and to all men."

HOW WE WILL SERVE AS A SOLDIER FOR OUR COUNTRY. We will proudly serve our country in any way we can except doing violence to any man. We don't believe in being forced to do anything contrary to our God and our conscience. Some of our boys have been manhandled, held by Sergeants and others, and forced to take shots, vaccinations and medicine contrary to Rule 23 set forth in the Minutes of this Church and Assembly.

We are not trying to change the Army. We ask them not to try to change us. We ask no special favor but to be treated as other Americans. We are proud to go to the battle fronts and help the wounded and be of service in any other way that is not contrary to our conscience and belief as set forth in the above.

Luke 3 ch.—13 and 14 verses reads "And he said unto them, Exact no more than that which is appointed you.

"And the soldiers likewise demanded of him saying, And what shall we do. And he said unto them, Do violence to no man, neither accuse any falsely; and be content with your wages."

If we can be a soldier under these conditions, we will proudly do so.

Rule 23 of the General Rules of this Minute

All members of the Church are forbidden to use medicine, vaccinations or shots of any kind but are taught by the Church to live by faith. However, new members who have recently taken up fellowship with the Church or future members will be given time to grow in the faith until they attain to the teaching of the Church of God of the Union Assembly as found in James 5 ch.—13 thru 15 verses. "Is any among you afflicted? let him pray. Is any merry? let him sing psalms.

"Is any sick among you? let him call for the elders of the church; and let them pray over him, annointing him with oil in the name of the Lord:

"And the prayer of faith shall save the sick, and the Lord shall raise him up; and if he have committed sins, they shall be forgiven him."

Romans 14 ch., 1 verse reads "Him that is weak in faith receive ye, but not to doubtful disputations."

Notes: *The Covenant of the Church of God of the Union Assembly is a statement binding upon all pastoral leaders (ministers and evangelists) of the church. The brief summary of nine important biblical teachings introduces a more complete exposition of the church's teachings on a wide variety of matters. In general, the church follows the teachings of the Church of God of the Mountain Assembly and has produced a lengthy statement against war and killing. It has also added a statement on its controversial position against the use of medicine.*

* * *

ADDITION TO THE TWENTY-NINE IMPORTANT BIBLE TRUTHS [CHURCH OF GOD (WORLD HEADQUARTERS)]

30. The Kingdom of God on Earth as it is in Heaven—Matt. 6:10; Matt. 6:28-34; Mark 1:14-15; Luke 4:43; Luke 12-31-32; Luke 16:16; Luke 22:29; Matt. 13th Chapter; Daniel 2:44; Daniel 7:27; Rev. 11:15; Matt. 21:43.

Notes: *This branch of the Church of God movement follows the Church of God Teachings adopted by the Church of God (Cleveland, Tennessee). To these teachings, however, it has added a thirtieth statement on the Kingdom of God, which is reproduced here. For a more complete exposition of this branch's unique emphases, see* The Book of Doctrines, 1903-1970 *(Huntsville, AL: Church of God Publishing House, 1970).*

* * *

WE BELIEVE (CONGREGATIONAL HOLINESS CHURCH)

There is but one living and true God, the great Creator, and there are three persons in the Godhead: the Father, the Son and the Holy Ghost. Genesis 1:1-27; Matthew 28:19; I John 5:7.

The Holy Bible to be the inspired Word of God. 2 Timothy 3:16; 2 Peter 1:20, 21.

We are justified when we repent of our sins and believe in Jesus Christ. Mark 1:5; Acts 13:38, 39; Romans 5:1.

Sanctification to be a definite work of grace subsequent to salvation. St. John 15:2; 17:16, 17; Ephesians 5:25-27; 1 John 1:9.

In the baptism with the Holy Ghost, and speaking with other tongues as the Spirit gives utterance to be the initiatory evidence of this experience. Acts 2:4; 19:6; 10:44-46.

In divine healing for the body. Acts 3:2-12; 9:32-43; 5:15, 16; James 5:14. We do not condemn medical science.

Every blessing we receive from God, including divine healing, comes through the merits of the atonement. Romans 5:11; James 1:16, 17.

WE BELIEVE (CONGREGATIONAL HOLINESS CHURCH) (continued)

In the operation of the nine Gifts of the Spirit and encourage our people to so live that these gifts may be manifest in their lives. 1 Corinthians 12:1-12.

Notes: *These brief statements of belief are derived from the Articles of Faith of the International Pentecostal Holiness Church, from which the Congregational Holiness Church derived.*

* * *

COVENANT, BASIS OF UNION, AND ARTICLES OF FAITH (EMMANUEL HOLINESS CHURCH)

COVENANT

We, having been called out of the world by the blessed spirit of God, and accepted the Lord Jesus Christ as our Saviour and Preserver, and become acquainted with the articles of faith and policy of the Emmanuel Holiness Church, and believing it to be of God, we do solemnly, but cheerfully and with joy and gladness enter into this covenant with you. We will watch over each other and walk together in brotherly love and kindness, sharing each other's joys and sorrows, praying for ourselves and others. Not forsake the assembling of ourselves together as the manner of some is. Endeavoring to bring up those under our care in the nurture and admonition of the Lord.

We will minister to each other in sickness and affliction, in distress and imprisonment, in poverty and want.

Never speak of anyone as we would not have them speak of us. Defend one another in things that are right. Bearing one anothers burdens, prefer one another in honor, affiliate with no party nor faction in the measures of evil. Strive in all things to exemplify our profession by corresponding practice.

We will abstain from all sinful conformity to the world and be just in all our dealings, and endeavor to pay all our debts, be exemplary in all deportment, having family worship in our homes, and offering thanks for our daily food.

We will contribute cheerfully, according to our ability to the support of the ministry, the expense of the church, the relief of the poor, and the general spread of the gospel. And will sustain the worship, ordinance, discipline, and the doctrines of this church. In keeping this solemn covenant may we ever enjoy the blessings and presence of the Lord and the fellowship of the saints.

CHAPTER II. BASIS OF UNION

Art. 1. We believe that Jesus Christ shed His blood for the remission of sins that are past; and for the regeneration of penitent sinners, and for salvation from sin, and from sinning. (Rom. 3:25, I John 3:5-10, Eph. 2:1-10.)

Art. 2. We believe, teach and firmly maintain the scriptural doctrine of justification by faith alone. (Rom. 5:1.)

Art. 3. We believe also that Jesus Christ shed His blood for the complete cleansing of the justified believer from all indwelling sin and from its pollution. Subsequent to regeneration. (I John 1:7-9.)

Art. 4. We believe also that entire sanctification is an instantaneous, definite, second work of grace, obtainable by faith on the part of the fully justified believer. (John 15:2, Acts 26:18, II Cor. 1:15, Luke 24:30-33, 50-53, John 17, I Thes. 5:16-23.)

Art. 5. We believe also that the Pentecostal Baptism of the Holy Ghost and fire is obtainable by a definite act of appropriating faith on the part of the fully cleansed believer, and that the initial evidence of the reception of this experience is speaking with other tongues as the spirit gives utterance. (Luke 11:13, Acts 1-5, Acts 2:1-4, Acts 8:17, Acts 10:44-46, Acts 19:6).

Art. 6. We believe also in divine healing as in the atonement. (Isaiah 53:4-5, Matt. 8:16-17, Mark 16:14-18, Jas. 5:14-16, I Peter 2:24.)

Art. 7. We believe in the imminent, personal, premillennial second coming of our Lord Jesus Christ. (I Thes. 4:15-18, Titus 2:13, II Peter 3:1-4, Matt. 24:29-44) and we love and wait for His appearing. (II Tim. 4:8.)

Art. 8. We forbid that our members participate in actual combat service, in taking of arms in war, if their conviction is objective.

Art. 9. The Emmanuel Holiness Church is utterly opposed to the teachings of the so-called Christian Scientists, Spiritualists, Unitarians, Universalists and Mormons. We deny as false and unscriptural Seventh Day Adventism, Annihilation of the wicked, conditional immortality, and antinomianism, absolute perfection, so-called comeoutism, the so-called resurrection in this life, the redemption or glorification of the body in this life, the doctrine of the restitution of all things (as set forth in the millennial-dawnism), and the teaching that we are not born of God until we are sanctified wholly.

Art. 10. No subsequent General Assembly shall have the authority to change the Basis of Union without a full representation of the General officers, elder body and its ministerial members and one lay delegate from each local church present at its General Assembly.

CHAPTER III. ARTICLES OF FAITH

Art. 1. We believe there is but one living and true God, everlasting, of infinite power, wisdom and goodness; Maker and preserver of all things, both visible and invisible. And in the unity of this Godhead, there are three persons of one substance, of eternal beings, and equal in holiness, justice, wisdom, power and dignity; the Father, the Son, and the Holy Ghost.

Art. 2. We believe that the Son, who is the word of the Father, the very and eternal God, of one substance with the Father, took Man's nature in the womb of the blessed Virgin; so that two whole and perfect natures, that is to say, the Godhead and the Manhood, were joined together in one Person, never to be divided, whereof is one Christ, very God and perfect Man, who actually suffered, was crucified, dead and buried, to reconcile the Father to us and to make atonement, not only for our actual guilt, but also for original sin.

Art. 3. We believe that Christ did truly rise again from the dead, and took again His body, with all things appertaining to the perfections of man's nature. And ascending into heaven and there sitteth until He shall return to judge all men at the last day.

Art. 4. We believe the Holy Ghost, proceeding from the Father and the Son, is of one substance, majesty and glory with the Father and the Son, Very and Eternal God.

Art. 5. We believe that eternal life with God in heaven is a portion of the reward of the finally righteous; and that everlasting banishment from the presence of the Lord, and unending torture in hell, the wages of the persistently wicked. (Matt. 25:46, Psalm 9:17, Rev. 21:7,8.)

Notes: *There have been four basic doctrinal documents adopted by the Emmanuel Holiness Church. The creed of the church is the Apostles' Creed. The covenant is identical to the one used by the (Original) Church of God. The basis of union was taken from that of the Pentecostal Fire-Baptized Holiness Church, from which the Emmanuel Holiness Church came. The articles of faith are identical to those of the International Pentecostal Holiness Church, from which the Pentecostal Fire-Baptized Holiness Church came.*

The three doctrinal statements of the Emmanuel Holiness Church, along with the Apostles' Creed, are found at the beginning of the church's book of Discipline and Doctrine. *Besides these statements, an additional set of general rules advocate the exclusive use of the King James Version of the Bible and prescribe a lengthy set of behavioral norms. In the basis of union, pacifism is advocated.*

*   *   *

FAITH (FREE WILL BAPTIST CHURCH OF THE PENTECOSTAL FAITH)

1. THE HOLY SCRIPTURES

These are the Old and New Testaments. They were written by men divinely inspired, and contain God's will as revealed to man. They are a sufficient and infallible guide in religious faith and practice, and the supreme standard by which all human conduct, creeds and opinions should be tried. II Timothy 3:16-19

2. THE TRUE GOD

The Scriptures teach that there is only one true and living God (Deut. 6:4; 1 Cor. 8:4; Jer. 10:10; John 7:28; II Cor. 1:18; I John 5:20; I Tim. 6:17), who is a Spirit (John 4: 24; II Cor. 3:17), self-existent (Ex. 3:14; Psalm 83:18; John 5:26; Rev. 1:4), eternal (Psalm 90:2; Deut. 33:27; Isa. 57:15; Rom. 1:20; I Tim. 1:17), Immutable (Mal. 3:6; Num. 23:19; James 1:17), omnipresent (I Kings 8:27; Jer. 23:24; Psalm 139:7-10; Isa. 57:15; Acts 17:24), omniscient (Acts 15:18; I Chron. 28:9; Psalm 94:9, 10; Acts 1:24), Omnipotent (Rev. 19:6; Job 42:2; Psalm 135:6; Matt. 19:26; Mark 14:36; Luke 18:27), independent (Eph. 4:6; Job 9:12; Isa. 14:13, 14; Daniel 4: 35; Rom. 11:33-36), good (Psalm 119:68; 25: 8; 106:1; 145:9; Matt. 19:17), wise (Rom. 16: 27; Daniel 2:20; I Tim. 1:17; Jude 25), holy (Lev. 19:2 Job 6:10); just (Deut. 32:4; Psalm 92:15; 119:137; Zeph. 3:5), and merciful (Eph. 2:4; Ex. 34:6; Neh.

9:17; Psalm 100:5), the Creator (Gen. 1:1; Ex. 20:11; Psalm 33:6, 9; Col. 1:16; Heb. 11:3), Preserver (Neh. 9:6; Job 7:20; Col. 1:17; Heb. 13) and Governor (Psalm 47:7; II Chron. 20:6; Psalm 95:3) of the Universe; the Redeemer (Isa. 47:4; Psalm 73: 35; Prov. 23:11; Isa. 41:14; 59:20; Jer. 50:34), Saviour (Isa. 45:21; 43:3, 11; 49:26), Sanctifier (Ex. 31:13; I Thess. 5:23; Jude 1), and Judge (Heb. 12:23; Gen. 18:25; Psalm 50:6; II Tim. 4:8) of men; and the only proper object of divine worship (Ex. 34:14; 20:4, 5; Matt. 4:10; Rev. 19:10).

The mode of His existence, however, is a subject far above the understanding of man (Job 11:7; Isa. 40:28; finite beings can not comprehend Him (Rom. 11:33; Job 26:14). There is nothing in the universe that can justly represent Him for there is none like Him (Ex. 9:14; 8:10; I Chron. 17:20). He is the foundation of all perfection and happiness. He is glorified by the whole inanimate creation, and is worthy to be loved and served by all intelligences (Psalm 19:1, 2; 145:10; 150:6).

3. DIVINE GOVERNMENT AND PROVIDENCES

God exercises a providential care and superintendence over all His creatures (Acts 17:28; Matt. 10:20; Psalm 104:13, 14; Job 14:5, Eph. 1:11), and governs the world in wisdom and mercy, according to the testimony of His Word (Psalm 22:28; 97:2; Isa. 33:22; Ex. 34:6; Job 36:5). God has endowed man with power of free choice, and governs him by moral laws and motives; and the power of free choice is the exact measure of his responsibility (Deut. 30:19; Isa. 1:18-20; John 5:40; Rom. 2:14, 15; Prov. 1:24-28).

All events are present with God from everlasting to everlasting, but His knowledge of them does not in any way cause them, nor does He decree all events which He knows will occur (Ezek. 33:11; Acts 15:11; I Sam. 2:30; Ezek. 18:20, 25, 31; Jer. 44:4).

4. CREATION, PRIMITIVE STATE OF MAN AND HIS FALL

God created the world and all things that it contains, for His own pleasure and glory, and for the enjoyment of His creatures (Rev. 4:11; Isa. 43:7; I Tim. 6:17). The angels were created by God (Col. 1:16), to glorify Him (Rev. 7:11), and obey His commandments (Psalm 103:20).

Those who have kept their first estate, He employs in ministering blessings to the heirs of salvation (Heb. 1:14; Jude 6), and in executing His judgments upon the world (II Sam. 24:16; Rev. 16:1).

God created man, consisting of a material body and a thinking, rational soul (Gen. 2:7). He was made in the image of God to glorify his Maker (Gen. 1:26, 27; I Cor. 6:20).

Our first parents, in their original state of probation, were upright; they naturally preferred and desired to obey their Creator, and had no preference or desire to transgress His will (Eccl. 7:29; Eph. 4:24; Col. 3:10), till they were influenced and inclined by the tempter to disobey God's commands. Previously to this, the only tendency of their nature was to do righteousness. In consequence of the first transgression, the state under which the posterity of Adam came into the world is so far different from that of Adam,

FAITH (FREE WILL BAPTIST CHURCH OF THE PENTECOSTAL FAITH) (continued)

that they have not that righteousness and purity which Adam had before the fall; they are not naturally willing to obey God, but are inclined to evil (Psalm 51:5; Rom. 8:7; Eph. 2:4; Psalm 58:3; Gen. 8:21; John 3:6; Gal. 5:19-21; Rom. 5:12).

Hence, none by virtue of any natural goodness and mere work of their own, can become the children of God (John 6:44; I Cor. 2:14); but all are dependent for salvation upon the redemption effected through the blood of Christ, and upon being created anew unto obedience through the operation of the Spirit (John 3:25; 1:13; Heb. 12:14; Col. 1:14; Titus 3:5), both of which are freely provided for every descendant of Adam.

5. CHRIST

Jesus Christ, the Son of God, possesses all Divine perfections. As He and the Father are one, He in His Divine nature filled all the offices and performed the works of God to His creatures that have been the subject of revelation to us. As man, He performed all the duties toward God that we are required to perform, repentance of sin excepted.

His divinity is proved from His titles, His attributes and His works. The Bible ascribes to Christ the title of Saviour (Isa. 45:25; 43:10; 11; John 4:42; Phil. 3:20; II Tim. 1:10; Titus 2:13), Jehovah (Psalm 83:18; Isa. 40: 3; Luke 1:76), Lord of Hosts (Isa. 8:13, 14; I Peter 2:4-6; Isa. 6:5; John 12:41), the first and the last (Rev. 21:13; 1:1, 11; Isa. 44:6), God (I Tim. 3:16; I John 3:16; John 1:1; Heb. 1:8; John 20:28, 29) true God (I John 5:20), great God (Titus 2:13), God over all (Rom. 9:5), Mighty God, and the everlasting Father (Isa. 9:6).

He is eternal (Col. 1:17; Micah 5:2; Heb. 1:8), unchangeable (Heb. 13:8; 1:12), omnipresent (John 3:13; Matt. 18:20; 28:20; Eph. 1:23), omniscient (John 16:30; 2:25, 26; 21:17; Rev. 2:23), omnipotent (Col. 2:8, 10; Matt. 28:18; Heb. 1:3; Rev. 1:8), holy (Acts 3:14; Luke 1:35; Heb. 7:26; Rev. 3:7), and is entitled to Divine worship (Heb. 1:6; John 5:23; Phil. 2:10, 11; Matt. 28:9; Luke 24:52).

By Christ the world was created (Heb. 1:8, 10; John 1:3, 10; Col. 1:16), He preserves (Heb. 1:3; Col. 1:17), and governs it (Isa. 9:6; I Peter 3:22; Eph. 1:21); He has provided redemption for all men (Eph. 1:7; Heb. 9:12; Gal. 3:13; Isa. 44:6; I Peter 1:18, 19; Rev. 5:9), and He will be their final Judge (II Tim. 4:1; Matt. 25:31-46; John 5:22).

The Word, which in the beginning was with God, and which was God, by whom all things were made, condescended to a state of humiliation in becoming like us, pollution and sin excepted (John 1:14; Phil. 2:6, 7; II Cor. 8:9; Heb. 4:15). In this state, as a subject of the law, He was liable to the infirmities of our nature (Heb. 2:17; Matt. 8:17; 4:2; 8:24; John 11:33, 35; 19:28; Isa. 53:3; Luke 22:44); was tempted as we are (Heb. 4:15; Matt. 4:1-11); but He lived our example, and rendered perfect obedience to the Divine requirements (I Peter 2:21; John 13:15; I John 2:6). As Christ was made of the seed of David according to the flesh, He is called The Son of Man (Isa. 42:21; Matt. 5:17; 3:15; Gal. 4:4); and as the Divine

existence is the fountain from which He proceeded, and was the only agency by which He was begotten (Luke 19:10), He is called the Son of God (John 16:27; Matt. 1:18, 20), being the only begotten of the Father (Luke 1:35; Mark 1:1; John 1:34; 20:31), and the only incarnation of the Divine Being (John 3:16; 1:18).

6. THE HOLY SPIRIT

The Scriptures ascribe to the Holy Spirit the acts of an intelligent being. He is said to guide (John 16:13), to know (I Cor. 2:11), to move (Gen. 1:2; Acts 8:39), to give information (Acts 10:19; I Cor. 2:13; Acts 21:11; John 14:26), to command (Acts 13:2), to forbid (Acts 16:6), to send forth (Acts 13:4), to reprove (John 16:8; Gen. 6:3), and to be sinned against (Mark 3:29; Isa. 63:10; Acts 7:51; Eph. 4:30). The attributes of God are ascribed to the Holy Spirit; such as eternity (Heb. 9:14), omnipresence (Psalm 139:7), omniscience (I Cor. 2:10), goodness (Neh. 9:20; Psalm 143:10), and truth (John 14:17). The works of God are ascribed to the Holy Spirit; creation (Job 33:4; 26:13; Psalm 104:30), inspiration (II Peter 1:21), giving of life (I Peter 3:18; Rom. 8:11), and sanctification (I Cor. 6:11).

The same acts which in one part of the Bible are attributed to the Holy Spirit are in other parts said to be performed by God (Isa. 6:8, 9; Acts 28:25, 26; John 3:16; Matt. 1:18). The apostles assert that the Holy Spirit is Lord and God (II Cor. 3:17; Acts 5:3, 4). From the foregoing the conclusion is, that the Holy Spirit is in reality God, and one with the Father in all Divine perfections. It has also been shown that Jesus Christ is God, one with the Father. Then these three, the Father, Son, and Holy Spirit, are one God.

The truth of this doctrine is also proved from the fact that the Father, the Son, and the Holy Ghost are united in the authority by which believers are baptized, and in the benedictions pronounced by the apostles (Matt. 28:19; II Cor. 13:14; I Peter 1:2), which are acts of the highest religious worship.

7. THE ATONEMENT AND MEDIATION OF CHRIST

As sin cannot be pardoned without a sacrifice, and the blood of beasts could never wash away sin, Christ gave Himself a sacrifice for the sins of the world (I John 2:2; Isa. 53:5; 10:11; Rom. 4:25; Matt. 20:28; I Peter 3:18; John 1:29; Heb. 9:26; Rom. 5:6-8), and thus made salvation possible for all men (Titus 2:11; Heb. 2:9; I Tim. 2:6; Isa. 45:22; II Peter 3:9; II Cor. 5:14, 15; I Tim. 4:10).

He died for us, suffering in our stead, to make known the righteousness of God, that He might be just in justifying sinners who believe in His Son (Rom. 3:25, 26; 5:9, 18; Matt. 26:28; Eph. 1:7; Rev. 1:9; I Peter 2:24). Through the redemption effected by Christ, salvation is actually enjoyed in this world, and will be enjoyed in the next, by all who do not in this life refuse obedience to the known requirements of God (Rom. 5:18; 8:1; Mark 16:15; Rom. 2:14, 15). The atonement for sin was necessary (Heb. 9:22; Eph. 1:7; Rom. 5:19). For present and future obedience can no more blot out past sins than past obedience can remove the guilt of present and future sins. Had God pardoned the sins of men without satisfaction for the violation of His law, it would follow that transgressions might go on with impunity, government would be abrogated and the obligation of obedience to God would be, in effect, removed. Our Lord not only died for our sins, but He arose for our justification (Rom. 4:25; I Cor. 15:17), and ascended to heaven (Acts 1:11; Mark 16:19), where as Mediator between God and man He will make intercession for men until the final judgment (Heb. 7:25; Rom. 8:34; Heb. 9:24; I Tim. 2:5; I Cor. 15:24).

8. THE GOSPEL CALL

The call of the Gospel is coextensive with the atonement of all men (Mark 16:15; Isa. 45:22; Prov. 8:4; Isa. 55:1; Rev. 22:17), both by the Word and the Striving of the Spirit (Joel 2:28; John 16:18; 1:9; Isa. 55:11; Luke 2:10; so that salvation is rendered equally possible to all (I Tim. 2:4; Acts 10:34; Ezek. 33:11; II Peter 3:9), and if any fail of eternal life, the fault is wholly their own (Hosea 13:9; Prov. 1:24-31; Isa. 65; 12; Jer. 7:13, 14; Zech. 7:11, 13; John 5:40; Matt. 23:37).

9. REPENTANCE

The repentance which the Gospel requires includes a deep conviction, a penitential sorrow, an open confession, a decided hatred, and an entire forsaking of all sin (II Cor. 7:10; Psalm 51:17; Prov. 28:13; Psalm 32:3, 5; Ezek. 36:31; Psalm 51:3, 4; Ezek. 18:30). This repentance God has enjoined on all men; and without it in this life, the sinner must perish eternally (Acts 17:30; Luke 13:5; Acts 3:19).

10. FAITH

Saving faith is an assent of the mind to the fundamental truths of revelation (Heb. 11:1, 6; John 5:46, 47; Rom. 10:9), an acceptance of the Gospel through the influence of the Holy Spirit (Rom. 10:10; Gal. 5:22; I Cor. 12:8, 9); and a firm confidence and trust in Christ (Acts 16:31; John 3:16; Rom. 4:20, 22; Eph. 3:12). The fruit of faith is obedience to the Gospel (James 2:17; Gal. 5:6; I Tim. 1:5). The power to believe is the gift of God (Phil. 1:29; II Peter 1:1; Eph. 2:8); but believing is an act of the creature which is required as a condition for pardon, and without which the sinner can not obtain salvation (John 3:36; Mark 16:16; John 18:21, 24; Heb. 11:6). All men are required to believe in Christ; and those who yield obedience to His requirements become the children of God by faith (John 1:7; Gal. 3:26; Acts 10:43; Rom. 5:1; John 3:15).

11. REGENERATION

As man is a fallen and sinful being, he must be regenerated in order to obtain salvation (John 3:3; Heb. 12:14; Rev. 21:27; Gal. 5:19-21). This change is an instantaneous renewal of the heart by the Holy Spirit (John 3:5; 1:13; Ezek. 36:26, 27; Titus 3:5; Eph. 2:10), whereby the penitent sinner receives new life, becomes a child of God (Rom. 8:16; John 1:12; 5:25; James 1:18; II Cor. 5:17), and disposed to serve Him (Ezek. 11:19, 20; I Peter 2:5). This is called in Scripture being born again, born of the Spirit (John 3:5, 6, 8; I John 4:7; 5:1), being quickened (Eph. 2:1; Psalm 119:50, 93; Eph. 2:5; Col. 2:13), passing from death unto life (John 5:24; I John 3:14), and a partaking of Divine nature (II Peter 1:4; Heb. 3:14).

12. JUSTIFICATION

Personal justification implies that the person justified has been guilty before God; and in consideration of the atonement of Christ, accepted by faith, the sinner is pardoned and absolved from the guilt of sin, and restored to the Divine favor (Rom. 5:1, 16; Acts 13:39; Isa. 53:11). Though Christ's atonement is the foundation of the sinner's redemption, yet without repentance and faith it can never give him justification and peace with God (Acts 13:19; Heb. 4:2; 11:6; Rom. 9:31, 32; Acts 13:38, 39).

13. SANCTIFICATION

MAN'S SIDE. A complete consecration of himself and all his to God and His service (Rom. 12:1; I Cor. 6:19, 20; Lev. 20:7; II Cor. 7:1; I Cor. 10:31; Mal. 3:10; Luke 12:22, 23; 14:25-33).

GOD'S SIDE. Is an instantaneous work of God's grace in a believer's heart whereby the heart is cleansed from all sin and made pure by the blood of Christ; it is obtained by faith and is subsequent to regeneration. The Christian can and should abide in this state unto the end of life, constantly growing in grace and in the knowledge of our Lord Jesus Christ (I Thess. 4:3; John 17:17; I Thess. 5:23; Heb. 13:12; Eph. 5:26; I John 1:7; Lev. 20:8; Heb. 9:13, 14; II Tim. 2:20, 21; Heb. 2:11; 10:1-22; Luke 24:49; Acts 2:1-4; 15:8, 9; 26:16-18; I Cor. 1:30; I John 4:16-18).

14. BAPTISM OF THE HOLY GHOST

We believe that the baptism of the Holy Ghost may be obtained by a definite act of appropriating faith on the part of the fully cleansed believer, and that the first evidence of the reception of this experience is the speaking with other tongues as the Spirit gives utterance (Luke 11:13; Acts 1:5; 2:1-4; 8:17).

15. GIFTS OF THE SPIRIT

We believe that it is the privilege of the Spirit-baptized believer to enjoy the benefits of spiritual gifts—wisdom, knowledge, faith, gifts of healing, working of miracles, prophecy, discerning of spirits, divers kinds of tongues, and the interpretation of tongues (I Cor. 12:1-14), and that these gifts are separate and apart from the baptism.

16. PERSEVERANCE OF THE SAINTS

There are strong grounds to hope that the truly regenerate will persevere unto the end and be saved through the power of Divine grace which is pledged for their support (Rom. 8:38, 39; I Cor. 10:13; II Cor. 12:9; Job 17:9; Matt. 16:18; John 10:27, 28; Phil. 1:6), but their future obedience and final salvation are neither determined nor certain, since through infirmity and manifold temptations, they are in danger of falling; they ought therefore to watch and pray lest they make shipwreck of their faith and be lost (II Chron. 15:2; II Peter 1:10; Ezek. 33:18; John 15:6; I Cor. 10:12; Heb. 6:6; 12:15; I Chron. 28:9; Rev. 2:4; I Tim. 1:19; II Peter 2:20, 21; I Cor. 9:27; Matt. 24:13).

17. THE LORD'S DAY

Before the death and resurrection of Christ, under the old dispensation, the seventh day of the week, as commemorative of the work of creation, was set apart for the Sabbath (Ex. 20:8-11). Under the Gospel, the first day of the week, in commemoration of the resurrection of Christ, and by authority of the apostles, is observed as the Christian Sabbath or The Lord's Day. (Luke 24:1-7; 33:36; John 20:19-26; Acts 2:1; 20:7; I Cor. 16:2; Rev. 1:10).

In these days when The Lord's Day is being desecrated by so many, we as a church feel it our duty to take a stand against the practice of buying and selling on Sunday, attending meetings for worldly amusement, visiting pleasure resorts, promiscuous and questionable, joy-riding, etc., on The Lord's Day.

18. WORLDLY AND SINFUL AMUSEMENTS

We believe that it is decidedly against the Christian character and influence of all people to engage in dancing, card playing, attend fairs, shows, carnivals, etc.; going to swimming lakes and pools and bathing with mixed crowds.

19. TEMPERANCE

To be temperate is to abstain from the use of all intoxicating liquors, be moderate in eating, avoiding immodest styles and fashions of the world; leaving off those things that will make us conform to the ways of the world. "Abstain from all appearance of evil" is a good motto.

Members of the Free-Will Baptist Church who persist in the use of intoxicating liquors, after they have been admonished, are to be excluded.

We believe that the use of tobacco in any form is in direct opposition to the principles of gospel temperance. Our churches and Sunday schools should discourage every form of intemperance, and do what they can to encourage the enforcement of the prohibition laws and regulations.

20. TITHING

While the individual member of the church is left free to decide for himself the amount he should give to God's cause, we believe that one-tenth of our net income belongs to God. While this was practiced under the law, instead of repealing, as some would have us believe, Jesus endorsed it (Matt. 23:23). For other Scriptures on tithing, see Gen. 28:22; Lev. 27:30; Mal. 3:8-10.

21. DIVORCE

We believe that there is only one Scriptural reason for divorce, and that is, fornication on the part of the person from whom the divorce is desired. We do not believe that there is any Scripture that sets either the husband or wife free to marry again so long as both parties live (Matt. 5:32; 19:9; Luke 16:18; Rom. 7:3; I Cor. 7:10).

22. THE CHURCH

The Church is an organized body of believers in Christ, who statedly assemble to worship God, and who sustain the ordinances of the Gospel agreeably to His Word (I Cor. 1:2; Acts 2:41, 47; 20:7; I Cor. 16:1, 2; Rev. 1:4). In a more general sense it is the whole body of Christians throughout the world, and none but the regenerate are its real members (Eph. 5:25, 27; 1:22, 23; I Cor. 12:27, 28; Col. 1:18, 24; I Peter 2:5; John 18:36; 15:2, 6). Believers are admitted to a particular Church on their giving

evidence of faith, being baptized and receiving the hand of fellowship (Acts 2:41; 8:12; Gal. 3:27).

23. THE GOSPEL MINISTRY

QUALIFICATIONS OF MINISTERS. They must possess good natural and acquired abilities (II Tim. 2:15; I Tim. 4:13-16; Titus 1:9; 2:7, 8; II Tim. 1:7; 2:2; I Tim. 3:2-7, deep and ardent piety (Psalm 50:16; II Tim. 1:8-11, 14; 2:22; 3:5; Titus 1:5-9; I Cor. 2:12-16), be specially called by God to the work (Acts 20:28; Heb. 5:4; I Cor. 9:16; Acts 13:2), and ordained by the laying on of hands (I Tim. 4:14; II Tim. 1:6; Acts 13:3).

DUTIES OF MINISTERS. They are to preach the Word (Mark 16:15; II Tim. 4:2; II Cor. 4:5; Ezek. 33:7;), administer the ordinances of the Gospel (Matt. 28:19; Luke 22:19, 20; Acts 20:11; 27:35; I Cor. 11:23-28; 10:16), visit their people, and otherwise perform the work of faithful pastors (Heb. 13:17; I Peter 5:2; Acts 20:28, 31; Jer. 3:15). (See "The Pastor" under Government.)

24. ORDINANCES OF THE GOSPEL

CHRISTIAN BAPTISM. This is the immersion of believers in water in the name of the Father, the Son, and the Holy Ghost (Matt. 28:19; Col. 2:12; Acts 8:36-39; Matt. 3:16; Mark 1:5; John 3:23; Acts 16:32-34; 2:41), in which are represented the burial and resurrection of Christ, the death of Christians to the world, the washing of their souls from the pollution of sin, their rising of newness of life, their engagement to serve God, and their resurrection at the last day (Rom. 6:4; Col. 3:3; 2:12; Titus 3:5; Gal. 3:27; I Cor. 15:29).

THE LORD'S SUPPER. This is a commemoration of the death of Christ for our sins, in the use of bread, which He made the emblem of His broken body; and the cup, the emblem of His shed blood (I Cor. 11:23-26; Matt. 26:26-28; Luke 22:19, 20). And by it the believer expresses his love for Christ, his faith and hope in Him, and pledges to Him perpetual fidelity (I Cor. 10:16, 21; 11:27-29). It is the privilege and duty of all who have spiritual union with Christ thus to commemorate His death; and no man has a right to forbid these tokens to the least of His disciples (I Cor. 10:17; Matt. 26:27; Rom. 14:1, 10; I Cor. 12:12-27; Acts 2:42; 20:7).

FEET-WASHING. This is a sacred ordinance of humility, instituted by our Lord Jesus Christ and enjoined upon His disciples as a duty to be observed by them. In this He set the example (Matt. 28:19, 20; John 13:1-17).

LAYING ON OF HANDS. In this the believer is taught to receive the gift of the Holy Ghost (Acts 8:14-17; 19:6).

25. DEATH AND THE INTERMEDIATE STATE

DEATH. As the result of sin, all mankind are subject to the death of the body (Rom. 5:12; Heb. 9:27; I Cor. 15:22; Psalm 89:48; Eccl. 8:8).

INTERMEDIATE STATE. The soul does not die with the body; but immediately after death, it enters into a conscious state of happiness or misery, according to the moral character here possessed (Eccl. 12:7; Phil. 1:23; Luke 23:43; Matt. 17:3; 22:31, 32; Acts 7:59; Matt. 10:28; II Cor. 5:8; Luke 16:22-26; Rev. 6:9).

26. SECOND COMING OF CHRIST

The Lord Jesus, who ascended on high and sits at the right hand of God, will come again to close the gospel dispensation, glorify His saints, and judge the world (Acts 1:11; Matt. 25:31; I Cor. 15:24-28; I Thess. 4:15-17; II Thess. 1:7, 10; II Peter 3:3-13; Matt. 24:12-14).

27. THE RESURRECTION

The Scriptures teach the resurrection of the bodies of all men at the last day, each in its own order; they that have done good will come forth to the resurrection of life, and they that have done evil, unto the resurrection of damnation (John 5:28, 29; Acts 24:15; I Cor. 15:22, 23; II Tim. 2:18; Phil. 3:21; I Cor. 15:35-44; Daniel 12:2).

28. THE GENERAL JUDGMENT AND FUTURE RETRIBUTION

There will be a general judgment, when time and man's probation will close forever (Acts 17:31; I Cor. 15:24; Rev. 10:6; 22:11; II Peter 3:11, 12; Eccl. 9:10). Then all men will be judged according to their works (II Cor. 5:10; Eccl. 12:14; Matt. 12:36; Rev. 20:12; Rom. 2:16). Immediately after the general judgment the righteous will enter into eternal life, and the wicked go into a state of endless punishment (Matt. 25:40; II Thess 1:8-10; Rom. 6:23; II Peter 1:11; Mark 3:29; 9:43, 44; Jude 7; Rev. 14:11; 21:7, 8; Matt. 13:41-43; Rom. 2:6-10).

CHURCH COVENANT

Having been brought, as we believe, by Divine grace to accept the Lord Jesus as our Savior and Preserver, we do now solemnly and joyfully covenant and agree, by God's help, to walk together in brotherly love.

We, therefore, enter into covenant as members of this Church and as Christians, that we will watch over each other in love, sharing together each other's joys and sorrows; that we will not forsake the assembling of ourselves together, nor omit the great duty of prayer for ourselves and others; that by Divine assistance we will endeavor to bring up those under our care in the nurture and admonition of the Lord; that in all things we will strive to exemplify our profession by a corresponding practice; to abstain from all sinful conformity to the world; to be just in our dealings, faithful in our engagements, and exemplary in all our deportment; that we will abstain from the sale and use of intoxicating liquors; that we will abstain from remarriage as long as a former husband or wife lives; that we will sustain the worship, ordinances, discipline and doctrines of this Church; that we will contribute cheerfully, according to our ability, to the support of the ministry, the expense of the church, the relief of the poor and the general spread of the Gospel.

In keeping this solemn Covenant, may we ever enjoy the blessings and presence of the Great Head of the Church.

Notes: *This statement is closely related to the Faith of Free Will Baptists of the National Association of Free Will Baptists, even though it differs on a number of significant points. Most importantly, the section on sanctification has been rewritten, and statements on the baptism of the Holy Spirit and the gifts of the Spirit have been added. Quite apart from these central doctrinal issues, statements have also been added on worldly and sinful amusements, temperance, and divorce. There is an important addition in the item on ordinances where beside baptism, the Lord's Supper, and foot washing, the laying-on-of-hands is accepted as a fourth ordinance. The Free Will Baptist Church of the Pentecostal Faith has not seen the necessity of adding the statement on the inerrancy of scripture, which has been placed at the beginning of the statement by the National Association of the Free Will Baptists.*

* * *

STATEMENT OF FAITH OF THE GENERAL CONFERENCE OF THE EVANGELICAL BAPTIST CHURCH

THE BIBLE INSPIRED. The Bible is the Word of God, verbally inspired and inerrable in the original writings. 2 Timothy 3:16-17; 2 Peter 1:21.

THE HOLY TRINITY. God, the Father, God, the Son, and God, the Holy Spirit; co-existent, eternal, omniscient, all powerful. Deuteronomy 6:4-5; Matthew 28:19; 2 Corinthians 13:14; Luke 1:35; John 1:14.

JUSTIFICATION. Through the fall we all become "dead in trespasses and sins." Through Christ we are "made alive," "born again," and "justified by faith through the atonement." Acts 2:38; John 3:3-8; Romans 5:1-12; Psalms 51:5; Ephesians 2:1-3.

SANCTIFICATION. A work of grace subsequent to justification. "Wherefore Jesus also, that He might sanctify the people with His own blood, suffered without the gate," Hebrews 13:12. "For He hath made Him to be sin for us, who knew no sin; that we might be made the righteousness of God in Him." 2 Corinthians 5:21. "Knowing this, that our old man is crucified with Him, that the body of sin might be destroyed, that henceforth we should not serve sin." Romans 6:6. There is therefore a holy and victorious life for the believer, as we fully consecrate ourselves to Him, and "reckon ourselves to be dead unto sin, but alive unto God." Romans 6:11; Ephesians 4:22-24.

BAPTISM OF THE HOLY SPIRIT. There is for every believer whose heart has been cleansed, an enduement of "power from on high" according to Acts 2:1-4; Acts 1:4-8; Acts 15-8; Acts 19:1-6; I Corinthians 14:22.

SPIRITUAL GIFTS. If "we abide in Him" and "follow on to know the Lord" it is possible to have the "signs" that are promised to follow believers in Mark 16:17-20, and the spiritual gifts spoken of in the 12 chapter of I Corinthians in operation in our assemblies. "For the perfecting of the saints, for the work of the ministry, for the edifying of the body of Christ." Ephesians 4:12.

HEALING IN THE ATONEMENT. "Himself took our infirmities and bare our sicknesses," Matthew 8:17; and

STATEMENT OF FAITH OF THE GENERAL CONFERENCE OF THE EVANGELICAL BAPTIST CHURCH (continued)

"with His stripes we are healed," Isaiah 53:5. It is our blessed privilege to "lay hands on the sick and to anoint them with oil in the Name of the Lord," and "the prayer of faith shall save the sick." Matthew 16:18; James 5:14-16.

THE PRE-MILLENNIAL RETURN OF OUR LORD. The rapture of the prepared and waiting saints, the great tribulation, the return of our Lord with His saints and the Holy angels in power and great glory to reign on earth a thousand years. I Thessalonians 4:14-17; Matthew 25:31; Acts 1:11; Revelation 20:4; Jude 1:14-15.

THE RESURRECTION. The resurrection of the crucified body of our Lord and the bodily resurrection of the just before the thousand years and of the unjust after the thousand years. Acts 2:22-24; I Corinthians 15:4-8; Romans 8:34; Daniel 12:2-3; John 5:25-29; Revelation 20:4-5.

HEAVEN AND HELL. The everlasting blessedness and reward of the righteous and the everlasting punishment of the wicked. Matthew 25:46; Revelation 21:8; Luke 16:19-25.

A PERSONAL DEVIL. Called Satan, who accomplished the fall of man, and who is now the prince of the power of the air, the accuser of the brethren, and the tempter of all mankind. I Peter 5:8; Revelation 12:9-10; 2 Thessalonians 3:5; Ephesians 2:1-2.

SUNDAY. We accept and observe Sunday as the Lord's rest day under the new covenant. Revelation 1:10; Acts 20:7.

ORDINANCES

We observe the Lord's Supper, Luke 22:19-20; I Corinthians 11:23-26; and Water Baptism by immersion "in the Name of the Father, the Son, and the Holy Spirit," Matthew 28:19; Matthew 3:15-17; Acts 2:38; Romans 6:3-4; Colossians 2:12.

HOLY COMMUNION. As instructed by the Holy Scriptures the Holy Communion shall be an ordinance of this Church and all Evangelical Baptist churches. The Holy Communion shall be small particles of bread representing the body of Christ; and wine (grapejuice) representing the Blood of Christ, which shall be blest by a prayer offered by the minister of the church, or the officiating minister. This service shall be held as often as the pastor of the church might feel disposed, and the service shall be in remembrance of Jesus Christ, the Son of God, Who was crucified on the middle cross. Luke 22:19-20; I Corinthians 11:23-26; All Christians, irrespective to their church affiliation, or whether they belong to any church or not, shall be invited by the officiating minister to participate in this service. The minister having the right to officiate shall be an ordained minister. The custom in which the participants shall follow shall be either about the altar or served in the pews by members of the board of deacons and deaconess. As to the number of times the Lord's Supper shall be observed during a church year shall be left entirely to the discretion of the pastor of the church.

WATER BAPTISM. This Church, and all Evangelical Baptist churches, has adopted the mode of baptism as immersion, and every person uniting with the church for the first time shall be baptized by immersion within six months following their reception into the church. If they do not, they are automatically regarded as persons not in good and regular standing of the church, and do not have any right to vote on any issue that might be brought before the church until they meet all requirements of the church.

If a person comes to this Church by letter or profession of faith and has been baptized by any ordained minister and is satisfied with their baptism, they are received into full fellowship of the church. Matthew 3:1-17; Mark 1:8; Matthew 28:18-20; Acts 2:38-42; Acts 10:44-48; Romans 6:3-4; Acts 16:13-15; Acts 16:25-34; Colossians 2:12; Galatians 3:27. The baptismal service shall be a public service, and all candidates shall be immersed in the Name of the Father, the Son and the Holy Ghost. Only ordained ministers shall have the authority to perform this Gospel rite.

DEDICATION OF CHILDREN. It is the belief of this Church, and all Evangelical Baptist churches, that children should be publicly dedicated to God, in which an ordained minister officiates. In this service parents promise to bring up their children in the "nurture and admonition of the Lord," Ephesians 6:4. This custom was adopted when they learned that men and women of old dedicated their children to Almighty God. Instead of using water, as is generally done in the christening of a child, the Evangelical Baptists use flowers in the dedicatory service, in which a child is dedicated to Almighty God. Every parent belonging to this Church, and any other Evangelical Baptist church, is urged to dedicate their children publicly to God, and the service can be arranged by negotiating with the pastor of the church.

TITHING. It shall be expected that all members of the church shall give one-tenth of their income to the support of the church as instructed in Malachi 3:10, "bring ye all the tithes into the storehouse (church) that there may be meat (funds) in mine house and prove me now herewith, saith the Lord of hosts, if I will not open you the windows of heaven, and pour you out a blessing that there shall not be room enough to receive it." Genesis 14:20; Malachi 3:8; Hebrows 7:5; 2 Chronicles 31:5. The time instructed by the Word of God to bring the tithe is on the first day of the week, which is the Lord's Day, I Corinthians 16:2.

* * *

STATEMENT OF FAITH (INTERNATIONAL PENTECOSTAL CHURCH OF CHRIST)

1. THE SCRIPTURES INSPIRED

The Bible is the revealed Word of God to man: The New Testament is our sole rule for discipline and government (II Timothy 3:15-17; II Peter 1:21).

2. THE ONE TRUE GOD

The triune Godhead consists of one true God the Father, Jesus Christ His Son, and the Holy Ghost the third person of the Godhead (John 10:36; 14:26; 20:21).

3. THE FALL OF MAN

Man was created good and upright: for God said, "Let us make man in our image, after our likeness!" However, man by voluntary transgression fell and thereby incurred not only physical death but also spiritual death, which is separation from God (Genesis 1:26, 27; 2:17; 3:6; Romans 5:12-19).

4. THE SALVATION OF MAN

Man's only hope of redemption is through the shed blood of Jesus Christ the Son of God.

(a) Conditions to Salvation. Salvation is received through repentance toward God and faith toward the Lord Jesus Christ. By the washing of regeneration and renewing of the Holy Ghost, being justified by grace through faith, man becomes an heir of God according to the hope of eternal life (Luke 24:47; John 3:3; Romans 10:13-15; Ephesians 2:8; Titus 2:11; 3:5-7).

(b) The Evidences of Salvation. The inward evidence of salvation is the direct witness of the Spirit (Romans 8:16). The outward evidence to all men is a life of righteousness and true holiness (Ephesians 4:24; Titus 2:12).

5. SANCTIFICATION

Sanctification is an act of separation from that which is evil, and of dedication unto God (Romans 12:1,2; I Thessalonians 5:23; Hebrews 13:12).

Sanctification is obtainable as a second definite work of grace, received by faith in the blood of Christ.

Sanctification is realized in the believer by recognizing his identification with Christ in His death and resurrection, and by faith reckoning daily upon the fact of that union, and by offering every faculty continually to the dominion of the Holy Spirit (Romans 6:1-11, 13; 8:1, 2, 13; Galatians 2:20; Philippians 2:12, 13; I Peter 1:5).

6. THE BAPTISM IN THE HOLY GHOST

All believers are entitled to, should ardently expect and earnestly seek the promise of the Father, the baptism in the Holy Ghost and fire, according to the command of our Lord Jesus Christ. The Bible evidence of the Baptism in the Holy Ghost is witnessed by the physical sign of speaking with other tongues as the Spirit of God gives utterance. (Acts 2:4; 10:46; 19:6). This was the normal experience of all in the early Christian Church. With it comes the enduement of power for life and service, the bestowment of the gifts and their uses in the work of the ministry (Luke 24:49; Acts 1:4; I Corinthians 12:1-31). With the baptism in the Holy Ghost comes such experiences as an overflowing fullness of the Spirit (John 7:37-39; Acts 4:8), a deepened reverence for God (Acts 2:42), and a more active love for Christ, for His Word, and for the lost (Mark 16:20).

7. THE ORDINANCES OF THE CHURCH

(a) Baptism in Water. The ordinance of baptism by immersion in the name of the Father, and of the Son and of the Holy Ghost is commanded in the Scriptures. All who repent and believe on Christ as Saviour and Lord are to be baptized. Thus they declare to the world that they died with Christ and that they also have been raised with Him to walk in newness of life (Matthew 28:19; Mark 16:16; Acts 10:47, 48: Romans 6:4).

(b) Holy Communion. The Lord's Supper, consisting of the elements—bread and fruit of the vine—is the symbol expressing our sharing the divine nature of our Lord Jesus Christ (II Peter 1:4); a memorial of His suffering and death (I Corinthians 11:26); and a prophecy of His second coming (I Corinthians 11:26); and is enjoined on all believers "till He comes!"

(c) Foot Washing. The ordinance of washing the saints feet is scripturally sound, and its practice in the local assembly is left optional. (John 13:4-17).

(d) Child Dedication. Since water baptism is an outward expression of an inward work of grace, we do not practice infant baptism. However, we do encourage presenting our children to the Lord in child dedication and blessing until they are old enough to make their own choice and decision (Luke 2:27; Mark 10:13-16).

8. THE CHURCH AND ITS MISSION

The Church is the Body of Christ, the habitation of God through the Spirit, with divine appointments for the fulfillment of her great commission. Each believer, born of the Spirit, is an integral part of the General Assembly and Church of the Firstborn, which are written in heaven (Ephesians 1:22, 23; 2:22; Hebrews 12:23).

Since God's purpose concerning man is to seek and to save that which is lost, to be worshipped by man, and to build a body of believers in the image of His Son, the priority reason-for-being of the International Pentecostal Church of Christ as part of the Church is:

(a) To be an agency of God for evangelizing the world (Acts 1:8; Matthew 28:19, 20; Mark 16:15, 16).

(b) To be a corporate body in which man may worship God (I Corinthians 12:13).

(c) To be a channel of God's purpose to build a body of saints being perfected in the image of His Son (Ephesians 4:11-16; I Corinthians 12:28; I Corinthians 14:12).

The International Pentecostal Church of Christ exists expressly to give continuing emphasis to this reason-for-being in the New Testament apostolic pattern by teaching and encouraging believers to be baptized in the Holy Spirit. This experience:

(a) Enables them to evangelize in the power of the Spirit with accompanying supernatural signs (Mark 16:15-20; Acts 4:29-31; Hebrews 2:3, 4).

(b) Adds a necessary dimension to worshipful relationship with God (I Corinthians 2:10-16; I Corinthians 12, 13, and 14).

(c) Enables them to respond to the full working of the Holy Spirit in expression of fruit and gifts and ministries as in New Testament times for the edifying of the body of Christ (Galatians 5:22-26; I Corinthians 14:12; Ephesians 4:11, 12; I Corinthians 28; Colossians 1:29).

9. THE MINISTRY

A divinely called and scripturally ordained ministry has been provided by our Lord for the threefold purpose of leading the Church in: (1) Evangelization of the world (Mark 16:15-20); (2) Worship of God (John 4:23, 24); (3) Building a body of saints being perfected in the image of His Son (Ephesians 4:11-16).

10. DIVINE HEALING

Divine healing is an integral part of the gospel. Deliverance from sickness is provided for in the atonement, and is the privilege of all believers (Isaiah 53:4, 5; Matthew 8:16, 17; James 5:14-16).

11. THE BLESSED HOPE

The resurrection of those who have fallen asleep in Christ and their translation together with those who are alive and remain unto the coming of the Lord is the imminent and blessed hope of the church (I Thessalonians 4:16, 17; Romans 8:23; Titus 2:13; I Corinthians 15:51, 52).

12. THE MILLENNIAL REIGN OF CHRIST

The Word of God promises the catching away of the prepared and waiting saints. Followed by the great tribulation, and then the return of our Lord with His saints and holy angels in power and great glory to reign on earth a thousand years. This millennial reign will bring the salvation of national Israel (Ezekiel 37:21, 22; Zephaniah 3:19, 20; Romans 11:26, 27) and the establishment of universal peace (Isaiah 11:6-9; Psalm 72:3-8; Micah 4:3, 4).

13. THE FINAL JUDGMENT

There will be a final judgment in which the wicked dead will be raised and judged according to their works. Whosoever is not found written in the Book of Life, together with the devil and his angels, and the beast and false prophet, will be consigned to everlasting punishment in the lake which burneth with fire and brimstone, which is the second death (Matthew 25:46; Mark 9:43-48; Revelation 19:20; 20:11-15; 21:8).

14. THE NEW HEAVENS AND THE NEW EARTH

"We, according to His promise, look for new heavens and a new earth wherein dwelleth righteousness" (II Peter 3:13; Revelation 21:22).

15. TITHES AND OFFERINGS

The needs of the New Testament Church, its varied ministries along with its God ordained leadership are to be met by the tithes and offerings of the believers (Matthew 23:23; I Corinthians 16:1, II Corinthians 9:6, 7).

Notes: *This statement replaces the Basis of Fellowship of the former International Pentecostal Assemblies and the Statement of Faith of the former Pentecostal Church of Christ. It is unique for its position on child dedication, a fourth ordinance beside baptism, holy communion, and foot washing. Not included from the International Pentecostal Assemblies statement is the item against war.*

ARTICLES OF FAITH (INTERNATIONAL PENTECOSTAL HOLINESS CHURCH)

1. We believe there is but one living and true God, everlasting, of infinite power, wisdom and goodness; Maker and Preserver of all things, both visible and invisible. And in the unity of this Godhead, there are three Persons of one substance, of eternal being, and equal in holiness, justice, wisdom, power, and dignity: the Father, the Son, and the Holy Ghost.

2. We believe that the Son, who is the Word of the Father, the very and eternal God, of one substance with the Father, took man's nature in the womb of the blessed Virgin; so that two whole and perfect natures, that is to say, the Godhead and manhood, were joined together in one person, never to be divided, whereof is one Christ, very God and perfect man, who actually suffered, was crucified, dead, and buried, to reconcile the Father to us, and to make atonement, not only for our actual guilt, but also for original sin.

3. We believe that Christ did truly rise again from the dead, and took again His body, with all things appertaining to the perfections of man's nature, and ascended into heaven and there sitteth until He shall return to judge all men at the last day.

4. We believe the Holy Ghost proceeding from the Father and the Son, is of one substance, majesty and glory, with the Father and the Son, very and eternal God.

5. We believe in the verbal and plenary inspiration of the Holy Scriptures, known as the Bible, composed of sixty-six books and divided into two departments, Old and New Testaments. We believe the Bible is the Word of God, the full and complete revelation of the plan and history of redemption.

6. We believe that eternal life with God in heaven is a portion of the reward of the finally righteous; and that everlasting banishment from the presence of the Lord, and unending torture in hell, the wages of the persistently wicked (Matt. 25:46; Psalm 9:17; Rev. 21:7, 8).

7. We believe that Jesus Christ shed His blood for the remission of sins that are past; and for the regeneration of penitent sinners, and for salvation from sin and from sinning (Rom. 3:25; I Jno. 3:5-10; Eph. 2:1-10).

8. We believe, teach and firmly maintain the scriptural doctrine of justification by faith alone (Rom. 5:1).

9. We believe that Jesus Christ shed His blood for the complete cleansing of the justified believer from all indwelling sin and from its pollution, subsequent to regeneration (I John 1:7-9).

10. We believe that entire sanctification is an instantaneous, definite second work of grace, obtainable by faith on the part of the fully justified believer (John 15:2; Acts 26:18).

11. We believe that the Pentecostal baptism of the Holy Ghost and fire is obtainable by a definite act of

appropriating faith on the part of the fully cleansed believer, and the initial evidence of the reception of this experience is speaking with other tongues as the Spirit gives utterance (Luke 11:13; Acts 1:5; 2:1-4; 8:17; 10:44-46; 19:6).

12. We believe in divine healing as in the atonement (Isa. 53:4, 5; Matt. 8:16, 17; Mark 16:14-18; Jas. 5:14-16; Ex. 15:26).

13. We believe in the imminent, personal, premillennial second coming of our Lord Jesus Christ (I Thess. 4:15-18; Titus 2:13; II Peter 3:1-4; Matt. 24:29-44), and we love and wait for His appearing (II Timothy 4:8).

CHANGES IN ARTICLES OF FAITH

No subsequent General Conference shall have authority to change the Articles of Faith until the proposed change has been submitted to each local church, the majority voting favorable to the change.

Notes: *One of the oldest of the pentecostal church bodies, the International Pentecostal Holiness Church (formerly the Pentecostal Holiness Church) has adopted a variety of doctrinal statements. The church's creed is the Apostles' Creed. The Articles of Faith have been adopted by the Emmanuel Holiness Church and used by the Congregational Holiness Church as a basis for its statement of doctrine. The first four of these articles were taken verbatim from the Twenty-five Articles of Religion of the Methodist Episcopal Church. The remaining statements incorporate the church's particular doctrinal emphases such as the baptism of the Holy Ghost, divine healing, and premillennialism. The present statement was derived from two others, the Articles of Faith and the Basis of Union, which dated to the 1911 union of the Fire-Baptized Holiness Church and the Pentecostal Holiness Church.*

In addition to the Articles of Faith, the International Pentecostal Holiness Church has added two lengthy statements which offer elaboration on the church's beliefs and the history of the articles' development. Only the articles are reproduced here.

*   *   *

CHURCH COVENANT AND BASIS OF FELLOWSHIP [(ORIGINAL) CHURCH OF GOD]

CREED AND COVENANT

"We believe in God the Father Almighty, maker of heaven and earth; and in Jesus Christ, His only Son, our Lord: which was conceived by the Holy Ghost, born of the virgin Mary, suffered under Pontius Pilate, was crucified, dead and buried: the third day He arose from the dead; He ascended into heaven and sitteth on the right hand of God the Father Almighty: from thence He shall come to judge the quick and dead. We believe in the Holy Ghost, The Church of God, the Communion of the saints, the forgiveness of sins, Sanctification by the Blood of Jesus Christ, the filling of the Holy Ghost, the resurrection of the body, and life everlasting" Amen.

CHURCH COVENANT

We, having been called out from the world by the blessed Spirit of God, and being acquainted with the articles of faith and pality of "The (Original) Church of God," and believing it to be *The "True" Church of God*, and having given our names, and thereby become members of the same, do solemnly, but cheerfully, and with joy and gladness enter into this covenant:

We will watch over one another with brotherly love and kindness, that we may with meekness assist in sustaining each other to the extent of our ability.

We will abstain (refrain) from frivolous conversations, foolish talking and jesting, from backbiting, tattling, taking up a reproach against any one, especially of our union. We will endeavor to walk worthy of the vocation wherewith we are called, with meekness and long-suffering, forbearing one another in love, doing all in our power to keep the unity of the Spirit in the bonds of peace.

We will share one another's burdens, and "so fulfill the law of Christ." We will also heed 1 Thes. 5:12, "And we beseech you, brethren, to know them which labor among you, and are over you in the Lord, and admonish. . . . And be at peace among yourselves." "We exhort you, brethren, warn them that are unruly, comfort the feebleminded, support the weak, be patient toward all men. See that none render evil for evil unto any man." Read Romans 12:17, also Ephesians 4:32.

We will endeavor to engage in some kind of Christian work, visiting the sick and distressed, and to all who will accept our deed of charity, so far as in our power lies, avoiding all sin. Eph. 5:11; 1 Peter 4:5; James 1:27; and all this we do, the Lord helping us. We will pay our Tithes, and give offerings, as the Lord has prospered us.

We accept this obligation of this Covenant in the name of the Father, and of the Son, and of the Holy Ghost.

DOCTRINE—BASIS OF FELLOWSHIP

The Following is a Summary of the Teachings, Precepts and Examples of our Lord, which The (Original) Church of God stands for and practices.

We stand for the whole Bible, rightly divided as set forth by the prophets, Jesus Christ and the Apostles, accepting nothing but the plainly written Word of God on all subjects.

1. REPENTANCE TOWARD GOD. A godly sorrow which arises from love to God and is accompanied with a hatred of sin, a love for holiness, and a fixed resolution to forsake sin, and an expectation of favor and forgiveness through the words of Christ. This is evangelistic or Gospel Repentance. Matt. 3: 2-8; 2 Cor. 7:10; Acts 20:21; Luke 13:3; Acts 3:19.

2. RESTITUTION. The blood of Jesus will never blot out any sin that we can make right: We must have a conscience void of offence toward God and man. Restitution includes restoring where one has defrauded, paying back debts, and confessing when necessary. Luke 19:8, 9; Psalms 69:4; Exodus 22:3; Luke 3:14.

CHURCH COVENANT AND BASIS OF FELLOWSHIP
[(ORIGINAL) CHURCH OF GOD] (continued)

3. REGENERATION. A change and renovation of the soul by the Spirit and grace of God. Matt. 19:28; Titus 3:4, 5. Born again, or from above, to receive spiritual life in the soul, enabling us to perform spiritual actions and live to God. To be Regenerated, renewed, to receive spiritual life, John 3:3, 5; 6:1; 1 Peter 1:23.

4. JUSTIFICATION. A state of being justified before God at any time in the Christian experience. It is that act of God's free grace by which we receive remission of sins. James 2:24; Rom. 5:1; 2 Cor. 5:21; Phil. 3:9; Romans 3:24-26; St. John 1:12.

5. SANCTIFICATION. Sanctification is subsequent to regeneration. Romans 5:2; 1 Cor. 1:30. Sanctification is that act of God's free grace, by which He makes us holy: and is the *Second Definite Work of Grace*, wrought with the blood of Christ through faith in Him. Heb. 10:10; therefore believers are saints. Heb. 13:12; 1 John 1:9; 1 Thes. 4:3; Heb. 2:11. Holiness, a life hid with Christ in God. Col. 3:3; Gal. 5:24; Luke 1:74-76; 1 Thes. 4:7; Heb. 12:14. Sanctification and holiness, with their equivalents are mentioned in the Word of God over five hundred times.

6. ENTIRE SANCTIFICATION. Entire Sanctification is by the work of the Holy Ghost through the knowledge of the Scriptures. St. John 17:17; 1 Thes. 5:23, 24. This is obtained by knowledge of the Scriptures and perfect obedience to them, and retained by the same method. The redemption of the body in the First Resurrection, and the uniting of redeemed soul and spirit into a redeemed body: then both soul and body is redeemed, made like unto the glorious body of Christ. 1 John 3:2, and we shall see Him and be like Him.

7. BAPTISM, OR FILLING WITH THE SPIRIT. Baptism with the Holy Ghost is subsequent to cleansing: the enduement of power for service and holy living which comes upon Sanctified believers only, and is Jesus Christ's baptism (Matt. 3:11), and is received through faith in the Word of God, and obtained through perfect obedience with a full surrender and complete sacrifice. John 20:22; Luke 24:49; John 7:38, 39; 14:16, 17, 26; Acts 1:5-8; 2:1-4; 10:44-46; 19:1-6.

8. SPEAKING WITH OTHER TONGUES. As the initiating evidence of the filling of the Holy Ghost to an overflowing: you will have the same sign or evidence that the disciples had on the day of Pentecost at Jerusalem (Acts 2:4), and the Gentiles had at the home of Cornelius (Acts 10:44-49), and at Ephesus (Acts 19:1-8). It is one of the signs that shall follow believers (Mark 16:17), and is one of the gifts of the Spirit to "The Church of God," for the day of grace until the return of the Bridegroom (1 Cor. 12:10). And, it was "other tongues" for it had to be interpreted.

The above Scriptures correctly read and prayerfully studied should convince every honest seeker of the truth that when one is filled with the Holy Ghost to overflowing, as were the saints at Jerusalem, he will "speak with other tongues as the Spirit gives the utterance." Every man, woman or child who is filled with the Holy Ghost *WILL Speak With Other Tongues.*

9. DIVINE HEALING. Jesus not only made provision for the salvation of the soul in His suffering on earth, but for the healing of the body as well. Isaiah 53:4, 5; Matt. 8:16-17; Mark 16:14-18; James 5:14-16; Exodus 15:26. Divine healing is obtained by faith, laying on of hands, the anointing of oil, and by special gift (1 Cor. 12:9).

The (Original) Church of God considers it not as a test of fellowship, but as an individual matter between themselves and God. It can clearly be seen through the Scriptures, that provision was made for body afflictions. This is a great blessing to those who can exercise the faith. 1 Peter 2:24; Heb. 12:12, 13.

10. GIFTS ACCOMPANYING GOD'S CHURCH. The full working of ALL the gifts in the Church. 1 Cor. 12:1-12; 28:32; 14:1.

11. SIGNS FOLLOWING BELIEVERS. We believe this exactly as the 16th chapter of Mark sets forth, and we believe every one of them will follow the ministry of God's Word. Mark 16:17-20; Heb. 2:4; Romans 15:18-19.

12. FRUITS OF THE SPIRIT. John 15:1-11. By our fruits all will know and judge whether we have what we profess. Romans 6:22; Gal. 5:22-23; Eph. 5:9; Phil. 1:11. May all take heed that the Spirit we manifest is a stronger evidence of the kind of spirit we possess than is our testimony or profession in words. It is a reflection on the plan of salvation to manifest one kind of spirit and profess another (1 Thes. 4:4).

13. WORKS OF THE FLESH. The (Original) Church of God stands against ALL the works of the flesh as in Gal. 5:19-21. By these are the unsaved dominated and controlled, and they can be seen on the surface by expressions and acts (2 Cor. 12:20.)

14. PRE-MILLENNIAL SECOND COMING OF CHRIST. The return of Jesus is just as literal as His going away (Acts 1:11; John 14:3). There will be two appearances under one coming: first, to resurrect the sleeping saints, and to catch away His waiting Bride (both the living and the dead) to meet Him in the air (Matt. 24:40-44; 1 Thes. 4:16-17).

In the First Resurrection every soul shall come out of Paradise, and shall enter their immortal bodies to live forever with Christ (Rev. 20:4). Verse 6 tells us who will have a part in the first resurrection. Second. Christ's coming on down to earth at the close of the great tribulation.

The Millineum will be a reign of peace and blessing with Jesus Christ our King and Ruler, and takes place between the resurrection of the saints and the resurrection of the wicked.

15. ETERNAL LIFE FOR THE RIGHTEOUS. Matt. 25:46; Luke 18:29-30; John 10:28; Romans 6:22; 1 John 5:11-13; Matt. 25:34-46.

16. THE WHITE THRONE JUDGEMENT. At the end of the Millineum or the one thousand years have expired, the ungodly and sinner will be called into judgement (Rev. 20:7, 10; 2 Thes. 1:7-9; Rev. 20:13-15). This is the resurrection of the wicked dead only, the second death.

17. ETERNAL PUNISHMENT FOR THE WICKED. Concerning the punishment for the wicked we read the following Scriptures and let the Word of God decide the question. On one thing we can be assured, that God will do right and give justice to every one, Matt. 25:41-46; Mark 3:29; Rev. 20:10-15; 21:18-19.

The foregoing Scriptures teach that the lake of fire is just as eternal as heaven. The wicked shall be cast into the lake of fire where the beast and false prophet are. Read the above Scriptures and flee the wrath to come on all them that know not God and who obey not His commandments.

18. TOTAL ABSTINENCE FROM ALL LIQUORS AND STRONG DRINKS. Christian people should be "temperate in all things" lawful; they should abstain from the use of intoxicants, tobacco and kindred carnal habits; they should not seek popularity, worldly power, nor offices, nor desire any of the follies of this world; "Wherefore come ye out from among them, and be ye separate, saith the Lord, and touch not the unclean thing; and I will receive you." 2 Cor. 6:17; Rev. 18:4; 1 Cor. 9:25; Gal. 5:25; 1 Thes. 5:22; Judges 13:4; Hab. 2:15; Prov. 23:29-32.

19. AGAINST ALL UNCLEANNESS AND FILTHINESS OF THE FLESH. God's people should be pure, holy, devout, reverent, with "Chaste Conversation coupled with fear" not yeilding to the lust of the flesh; therefore vulgar conversation, secret vice, and other improper and sinful conduct which give rise to social evils are entirely outside of the realms of Christian living (1 Peter 1:15; 2:12; 3:1; 2 Peter 3:11-14; 2 Cor. 7:1; Gal. 5:19-25; 1 John 3:3; Heb. 12:14; 1 Cor. 10:21; 2 Cor. 6:17-18; 1 Thes. 4:7). We, The (Original) Church of God, are *against and Forbid* the use of tobacco in any form either by ministers or laymen, and No One should be taken into the church until they have cleansed themselves from this and other sinful habits!

20. AGAINST MEMBERS GOING TO WAR. The Letter and the Spirit of the Gospel are emphatically against strife, contention, and carnal warfare, and therefore, no Christian should have part in carnal strife, whether among individuals, in suits of law, or in conflicts among nations. The nonresistant doctrine was taught and exemplified by Christ and the apostles and adhered to by true Christians until the present time. Matt. 5:38-45; 26:52; John 18:36; 1 Cor. 6:1-8; Romans 12:17-21; 2 Cor. 10:4; Luke 22:49-52; 3:10-14.

We believe it to be wrong for Christians to take up arms and go to war, as Jesus said: "Thou shalt not kill"; therefore, we would rather our members not engage in war.

21. SABBATH. The Sabbath (cessation) appears in the Scriptures as a day of God's rest in the finishing work of creation (Genesis 2:2, 3). For the next 2500 years of human life, there is absolutely no mention made of it in the Scripture. At Sinai the Sabbath was revealed (see Neh. 9:13, 14). This important passage fixes beyond all cavil the time when the Sabbath, God's rest (Gen. 2:1-3) was given to man. The seventh day Sabbath was never made a day of sacrificial worship, or any manner of religious service: it was simply and only a day of complete rest for man and beast—a humane provision for man's needs. In Christ's words, "The Sabbath was made for man, and not man for the Sabbath" (Mark 2:27). Christ, Himself, was held to be a Sabbath-breaker by the religious authorities of that day.

The Christians' first day perpetuates in the dispensation of Grace the principles that one-seventh of the time is especially sacred, but in all other respects is in contrast with the Sabbath: one is the seventh day, the other the first. The Sabbath commemorates God's Creation Rest; the First Day, Christ's Resurrection from the dead. On the seventh day God rested: on the first day Christ was busy all day. Jesus appeared to His disciples eight times that day. The Sabbath was a day of legal obligation, the first day one of voluntary worship service.

22. AGAINST MEMBERS SWEARING. Matt. 5:34; James 5:12.

23. MARRIAGE AND DIVORCE. Marriage was divinely instituted for the propagation, purity and happiness of the human race; it receives divine sanction between one man and one woman; the bond is dissoluable only by death or fornication, and there should be no marriage between a believer and an unbeliever, nor between members of The Church of God and other denominations (1 Cor. 7:39). "She is at liberty to be married to whom she will: only in the Lord" (Gen. 2:18; Mark 10:2-12; Rom. 7:2; Matt. 5:32; 19: 3-12).

We, The (Original) Church of God, accept as a Bible reason only one cause for divorce and remarriage as given in Matthew 5:32; but this is solely to God's children, having no reference to sinners or unbelievers. We do not go back of one's conversion, nor hold anything against them, inasmuch as the Word says "Old things have passed away, and, behold, all things are become new." Isaiah 43:18; 2 Cor. 5:17; Rev. 21:5. We accept both men and women where God accepts them, and hold them responsible from that time forward, as does God's Holy Word, and not from that time backward. God's law does not govern sinners. Jesus told the Samaritan woman (John 4: 10, 14, 39) that she had had five husbands, and she admitted it, and the man she was now living with was not her husband. Jesus offered her salvation: told her she could have it by asking, as all the past was done in sin.

A Hint to the Wise is Sufficient!

Deacons and Bishops are not to have more than one living wife under any circumstances.

24. THE TRIBULATION. Jesus prophesied a great tribulation, such as was not since the beginning of the world (Matt. 24: 21, 29; Rev. 9th and 16th chapters). This will come under the ten-toe government of Daniel just ahead.

25. CHRIST'S MILLENNIAL REIGN. One thousand years of a literal reign of Jesus on earth. It will be ushered in by the coming of Jesus back to earth with ten thousands of His saints (Jude 14, 15; 2 Thes. 1:5-10). During this time the devil will be bound (Rev. 20: 2, 3). This will be a reign of peace and blessing. Read the prophesy which shows the quality of the kingdom during this time (Isaiah 11: 6-9; 65:25; Hosea 2:18; Isaiah 2: 2-4; Micah 4:3).

26. DOOM OF THE UNBELIEVING DEAD. The last judgement of the Great White Throne. God will judge the quick and dead according to their works (Rev. 20: 11-15; Acts 10:42; Daniel 12:2.)

27. A NEW HEAVEN AND A NEW EARTH. The Word teaches that this earth, which has been polluted by sin, shall pass away, or be regenerated, cleansed, purified and made holy, after the Great White Throne Judgement, and God will make a new heaven and a new earth in which dwelleth righteousness. This will be a glorious scene. The heaven and the earth like as they were before there was any sin (Matt. 24: 35; 2 Peter 3: 12-13; Rev. 21:3).

28. AGAINST MEMBERS WEARING GOLD FOR DECORATION. Such as finger rings, ear rings, bracelets, lockets, etc. (1 Peter 3:3: 1 John 2: 15-16).

29. CHRISTIANS TO BE CLOTHED IN MODEST APPAREL. Christian people should be clothed in modest apparel: the wearing of jewelry, costly array, fashionable attire, gaudy dress, and bodily ornamentation should be strictly avoided by all believers; "Be not conformed to this world; but be ye transformed, by the renewing of your mind" (Romans 12.1, 2; Isaiah 3:16-24; 1 Tim. 2:9, 10; 1 Peter 3:3-5; 1 John 2:15-17).

Under no consideration should Christian women be guilty of putting on men's apparel, or dressing like men, as this is strictly forbidden in God's Word, and it is unthinkable that a Christian woman would put on shorts, etc. Man is not to put on a woman's garment under any circumstance (Deut. 22:5): "The woman shall not wear that which pertaineth unto a man (pants, shorts, shirts, etc.), neither shall a man put on a woman's garment: for all that do so ARE ABOMINATION unto the Lord thy God."

30. PRIDE GOETH BEFORE DESTRUCTION. We believe that pride is an abomination in the sight of God; that humility and contrition characterize God's people in whom is not found an haughty, overbearing spirit. "For whosoever exalteth himself shall be abased; and he that humbleth himself shall be exalted." (Luke 14:11; Prov. 6:16, 17;) "Pride goeth before destruction" (1 John 2:15-17; Prov. 16:18; James 4:6).

31. COMPLETE SEPARATION OF CHURCH AND STATE. We believe that there should be a complete separation of Church and State; that though "Strangers and Pilgrims on the earth," we should be subject unto the higher powers. "Submit yourselves to every ordinance of man for the Lord's sake." Nevertheless we owe our first allegiance to God. John 18:36; Acts 5:29; Rom. 13:1-5; Heb. 11:13.

Notes: *The (Original) Church of God has three doctrinal statements. The Basis of Union (not reproduced here) is derived from the Church of God Teachings and the Twenty-nine Important Bible Truths used by other branches of the Church of God. The Church Covenant has been adopted by the Emmanuel Holiness Church.*

* * *

BASIS OF UNION (PENTECOSTAL FIRE-BAPTIZED HOLINESS CHURCH)

1. We believe that Jesus Christ shed His blood for the remission of sins that are past (Rom. 3:25), and for the regeneration of penitent sinners, and for salvation from sin and sinning (1 John 3:5-10; Eph. 2:1-10).

2. We believe, teach and firmly maintain the Scriptural doctrine of justification by faith (Rom. 5:1).

3. We believe also that Jesus Christ shed His blood for the complete cleansing of the justified believer from all indwelling sin, and from its pollution subsequent to regeneration (1 John 1:7-9).

4. We believe also that entire sanctification is an instantaneous, definite, second work of grace, obtainable by faith on the part of the justified believer (John 15:2; Acts 26:18; 2 Cor. 13:15; Luke 24:30-33, 50-54; John 17).

5. We believe also that the Pentecostal baptism of the Holy Ghost and fire is obtainable by a definite act of appropriating faith on the part of the fully cleansed believer, and that the initial evidence of the reception of this experience is speaking with other tongues as the Spirit gives utterance (Luke 11:13; Acts 1:5; 2:1-4; 8:17; 10:44-46; 19:6; St. John 15:26).

6. We also believe in divine healing as in the atonement (Isa. 53:4-5; Matt. 8:16-17; Mark 16:14-18; James 5:14-16; Ex. 15:26).

7. We believe in the imminent, personal, premillenial second coming of our Lord Jesus Christ (1 Thess. 4:15-18; Titus 2:13; 2 Peter 3:1-14; Matt. 24:29-44), and we love and wait for His appearing (2 Tim. 4:8).

8. The Pentecostal Fire-Baptized Holiness Church is utterly opposed to the teaching of the so-called Christian Scientists, Spiritualists, Unitarians, Universalists and Mormons. We deny as false and unscriptural, Seventh-Day Adventism, annihilation of the wicked, conditional immortality anti-nomianism; absolute perfection, so-called come-outism, the so-called resurrection life, the so-called redemption or glorification of the body in life, the doctrine of the restitution of all things (as set forth in millenial-dawnism), and the teaching that we are not born of God until we are sanctified wholly.

9. No subsequent General Council shall have authority to change the Basis of Union without a full representation from the local churches.

Notes: *This statement is derived from the Basis of Union of the Pentecostal Holiness Church prior to the rewriting of its Articles of Faith in 1941. The Pentecostal Holiness Church had merged with the Fire-Baptized Holiness Church in 1911, and the Pentecostal Fire-Baptized Holiness Church broke away in 1918.*

* * *

THIS WE BELIEVE (PENTECOSTAL FREE WILL BAPTIST CHURCH)

We believe the BIBLE to be the inspired Word of God.

We believe that there is ONE GOD, eternally existing in three persons: Father, Son, and Holy Ghost.

We believe in the DEITY OF JESUS CHRIST; that Christ is the only begotten Son of God, and born of the Virgin Mary. That Christ died for our sins, was buried, and raised from the dead. That He ascended to heaven and is today at the right hand of the Father as our intercessor.

We believe that "ALL HAVE SINNED and come short of the glory of God," and that repentance is necessary for the forgiveness of sins.

We believe that JUSTIFICATION IS BY FAITH ALONE, and that regeneration or the new-birth through faith in the blood of Christ is absolutely essential.

We believe that SANCTIFICATION IS SUBSEQUENT TO REGENERATION AND IS A SECOND DEFINITE, INSTANTANEOUS WORK OF GRACE; obtained by faith on the part of the fully justified believer.

We believe that the PENTECOSTAL BAPTISM OF THE HOLY GHOST IS AN ENDUEMENT OF POWER FOR THOSE WHO HAVE CLEAN HEARTS, and the initial evidence of the reception of this experience is speaking with other tongues as the Spirit gives utterance.

We believe that the SAVED SHOULD RECEIVE WATER BAPTISM, in the name of the Father, and the Son, and the Holy Ghost, as a testimony to the world that he has accepted Christ as Saviour and Lord.

WE BELIEVE IN DIVINE HEALING as provided in the Atonement.

WE BELIEVE IN THE SACRAMENT of the LORD'S SUPPER as commemorating Christ's death and anticipating His Second Coming, and feet washing.

WE BELIEVE IN THE PERSONAL, PREMILLENNIAL, SECOND COMING OF JESUS; First, to resurrect the righteous dead and to catch away the living saints to meet Him in the air; second, to reign with His saints on earth a thousand years.

We believe in the bodily resurrection OF BOTH THE SAVED AND THE LOST; the saved to life eternal and the lost to everlasting punishment.

* * *

White Trinitarian Pentecostal

STATEMENT OF FUNDAMENTAL TRUTHS [(GENERAL COUNCIL OF THE) ASSEMBLIES OF GOD]

The Bible is our all-sufficient rule for faith and practice. This Statement of Fundamental Truths is intended simply as a basis of fellowship among us (i. e., that we all speak the same thing, 1 Cor. 1:10; Acts 2:42). The phraseology employed in this Statement is not inspired or contended for, but the truth set forth is held to be essential to a full Gospel ministry. No claim is made that it contains all Biblical truth, only that it covers our need as to these fundamental doctrines.

1. THE SCRIPTURES INSPIRED

    The Scriptures, both the Old and New Testaments, are verbally inspired of God and are the revelation of God to man, the infallible, authoritative rule of faith and conduct (2 Tim. 3:15-17; 1 Thess. 2:13; 2 Peter 1:21).

2. THE ONE TRUE GOD

    The one true God has revealed Himself as the eternally self-existent "I AM," the Creator of heaven and earth and the Redeemer of mankind. He has further revealed Himself as embodying the principles of relationship and association as Father, Son and Holy Ghost (Deut. 6:4; Isaiah 43:10,11; Matthew 28:19; Luke 3:22).

    THE ADORABLE GODHEAD

    (a) TERMS DEFINED

    The terms "Trinity" and "persons," as related to the Godhead, while not found in the Scriptures, are words in harmony with Scripture, whereby we may convey to others our immediate understanding of the doctrine of Christ respecting the Being of God, as distinguished from "gods many and lords many." We therefore may speak with propriety of the Lord our God, who is One Lord, as a trinity or as one Being of three persons, and still be absolutely scriptural (examples, Matt. 28:19; 2 Cor. 13:14; John 14:16, 17).

    (b) DISTINCTION AND RELATIONSHIP IN THE GODHEAD

    Christ taught a distinction of Persons in the Godhead which He expressed in specific terms of relationship, as Father, Son, and Holy Ghost, but that this distinction and relationship, as to its mode is *inscrutable* and *incomprehensible*, because *unexplained*. Luke 1:35; 1 Cor. 1:24; Matt. 11:25-27; 28:19; 2 Cor. 13:14; 1 John 1:3,4.

(c) UNITY OF THE ONE BEING OF FATHER, SON AND HOLY GHOST

Accordingly, therefore, there is *that* in the Son which constitutes Him *the Son* and not the Father; and there is *that* in the Holy Ghost which constitutes Him *the Holy Ghost* and not either the Father or the Son. Wherefore the Father is the Begetter, the Son is the Begotten; and the Holy Ghost is the one proceeding from the Father and the Son. Therefore, because these three persons in the Godhead are in a state of unity, there is but one Lord God Almighty and His name one. John 1:18; 15:26; 17:11,21; Zech. 14:9.

(d) IDENTITY AND CO-OPERATION IN THE GODHEAD

The Father, the Son and the Holy Ghost are never *identical* as to *Person*; nor *confused* as to *relation*; nor *divided* in respect to the Godhead; nor *opposed* as to *co-operation*. The Son is *in* the Father and the Father is *in* the Son, as to relationship. The Son is *with* the Father and the Father is *with* the Son, as to fellowship. The Father is not *from the Son, but the Son is from* the Father, as to authority. The Holy Ghost is *from* the Father and the Son proceeding, as to nature, relationship, co-operation and authority. Hence, neither Person in the Godhead either exists or works separately or independently of the others. John 5:17-30, 32, 37; John 8:17, 18.

(c) THE TITLE, LORD JESUS CHRIST

The appellation, "Lord Jesus Christ," is a proper name. It is never applied, in the New Testament, either to the Father or to the Holy Ghost. It therefore belongs exclusively to the *Son of God*. Rom. 1:1-3,7; 2 John 3.

(f) THE LORD JESUS CHRIST, GOD WITH US

The Lord Jesus Christ, as to His divine and eternal nature, is the proper and only Begotten of the Father, but as to His human nature, He is the proper Son of Man. He is, therefore, acknowledged to be both God and man; who because He is God and man, is "Immanuel," God with us. Matt. 1:23; 1 John 4:2, 10, 14; Rev. 1:13, 17.

(g) THE TITLE, SON OF GOD

Since the name "Immanuel" enbraces both God and man in the one Person, our Lord Jesus Christ, it follows that the title, Son of God, describes His proper deity, and the title Son of Man, His proper humanity. Therefore, the title, Son of God, belongs to the *order of eternity*, and the title, Son of Man, to the *order of time*. Matt. 1:21-23; 2 John 3; 1 John 3:8; Heb. 7:3; 1:1-13.

(h) TRANSGRESSION OF THE DOCTRINE OF CHRIST

Wherefore, it is a transgression of the Doctrine of Christ to say that Jesus Christ derived the title, Son of God, solely from the fact of the incarnation, or because of His relation to the economy of redemption. Therefore, to deny that the Father is a real and eternal Father, and that the Son is a real and eternal Son, is a denial of the distinction and relationship in the Being of God; a denial of the Father and the Son; and a displacement of the truth that Jesus Christ is come in the flesh. 2 John 9; John 1:1, 2, 14, 18, 29, 49; 1 John 2:22, 23; 4:1-5; Heb. 12:2.

(i) EXALTATION OF JESUS CHRIST AS LORD

The Son of God, our Lord Jesus Christ, having by Himself purged our sins, sat down on the right hand of the Majesty on high; angels and principalities and powers having been made subject unto Him. And having been made both Lord and Christ, He sent the Holy Ghost that we, in the name of Jesus, might bow our knees and confess that Jesus Christ is Lord to the glory of God the Father until the end, when the Son shall become subject to the Father that God may be all in all. Heb. 1:3; 1 Peter 3:22; Acts 2:32-36; Rom. 14:11; 1 Cor. 15:24-28.

(j) EQUAL HONOR TO THE FATHER AND TO THE SON

Wherefore, since the Father has delivered all judgment unto the Son, it is not only the *express duty* of all in heaven and on earth to bow the knee, but it is an *unspeakable* joy in the Holy Ghost to ascribe unto the Son all the attributes of Deity, and to give Him all the honor and the glory contained in all the names and titles of the Godhead (except those which express relationship. See paragraphs b, c, and d), and thus honor the Son even as we honor the Father. John 5:22, 23; 1 Peter 1:8; Rev. 5:6-14; Phil. 2:8, 9; Rev. 7:9, 10; 4:8-11.

3. THE DEITY OF THE LORD JESUS CHRIST

The Lord Jesus Christ is the eternal Son of God. The Scriptures declare:

(a) His virgin birth (Matthew 1:23; Luke 1:31, 35).

(b) His sinless life (Hebrews 7:26; 1 Peter 2:22).

(c) His miracles (Acts 2:22; 10:38).

(d) His substitutionary work on the cross (1 Cor. 15:3; 2 Cor. 5:21).

(e) His bodily resurrection from the dead (Matthew 28:6; Luke 24:39; 1 Cor. 15:4).

(f) His exaltation to the right hand of God (Acts 1:9, 11; 2:33; Philippians 2:9-11; Hebrews 1-3).

4. THE FALL OF MAN

Man was created good and upright; for God said, "Let us make man in our image, after our likeness." However, man by voluntary transgression fell and thereby incurred not only physical death but also spiritual death, which is separation from God (Genesis 1:26, 27; 2:17; 3:6; Romans 5:12-19).

5. THE SALVATION OF MAN

Man's only hope of redemption is through the shed blood of Jesus Christ the Son of God.

(a) CONDITIONS TO SALVATION

Salvation is received through repentance toward God and faith toward the Lord Jesus Christ. By the washing of regeneration and renewing of the Holy Ghost, being justified by grace through faith, man becomes an heir of God according to the hope of eternal life (Luke 24:47; John 3:3; Romans 10:13-15; Ephesians 2:8; Titus 2:11; 3:5-7).

(b) THE EVIDENCES OF SALVATION

The inward evidence of salvation is the direct witness of the Spirit (Romans 8:16). The outward evidence to all men is a life of righteousness and true holiness (Eph. 4:24; Titus 2:12).

6. THE ORDINANCES OF THE CHURCH

(a) BAPTISM IN WATER

The ordinance of baptism by immersion is commanded in the Scriptures. All who repent and believe on Christ as Saviour and Lord are to be baptized. Thus they declare to the world that they have died with Christ and that they also have been raised with Him to walk in newness of life (Matthew 28:19; Mark 16:16; Acts 10:47, 48; Romans 6:4).

(b) HOLY COMMUNION

The Lord's Supper, consisting of the elements—bread and the fruit of the vine—is the symbol expressing our sharing the divine nature of our Lord Jesus Christ (2 Peter 1:4); a memorial of His suffering and death (1 Cor. 11:26); and a prophecy of His second coming (1 Cor. 11:26); and is enjoined on all believers "till He come!"

7. THE BAPTISM IN THE HOLY GHOST

All believers are entitled to and should ardently expect and earnestly seek the promise of the Father, the baptism in the Holy Ghost and fire, according to the command of our Lord Jesus Christ. This was the normal experience of all in the early Christian Church. With it comes the enduement of power for life and service, the bestowment of the gifts and their uses in the work of the ministry (Luke 24:49; Acts 1:4,8; 1 Cor. 12:1-31). This experience is distinct from and subsequent to the experience of the new birth (Acts 8:12-17; 10:44-46; 11:14-16; 15:7-9). With the baptism in the Holy Ghost come such experiences as an overflowing fullness of the Spirit (John 7:37-39; Acts 4:8), a deepened reverence for God (Acts 2:43; Heb. 12:28), an intensified consecration to God and dedication to His work (Acts 2:42), and a more active love for Christ, for His Word and for the lost (Mark 16:20).

8. THE EVIDENCE OF THE BAPTISM IN THE HOLY GHOST

The Baptism of believers in the Holy Ghost is witnessed by the initial physical sign of speaking with other tongues as the Spirit of God gives them utterance (Acts 2:4). The speaking in tongues in this instance is the same in essence as the gift of tongues (1 Cor. 12:4-10, 28), but different in purpose and use.

9. SANCTIFICATION

Sanctification is an act of separation from that which is evil, and of dedication unto God (Rom. 12:1, 2; 1 Thess. 5:23; Heb. 13:12). The Scriptures teach a life of "holiness without which no man shall see the Lord" (Heb. 12:14). By the power of the Holy Ghost we are able to obey the command: "Be ye holy, for I am holy" (1 Pet. 1:15, 16).

Sanctification is realized in the believer by recognizing his identification with Christ in His death and resurrection, and by faith reckoning daily upon the fact of that union, and by offering every faculty continually to the dominion of the Holy Spirit (Rom. 6:1-11, 13; 8:1,2,13; Gal. 2:20; Phil. 2:12,13; 1 Pet. 1:5).

10. THE CHURCH

The Church is the Body of Christ, the habitation of God through the Spirit, with divine appointments for the fulfillment of her great commission. Each believer, born of the Spirit, is an integral part of the General Assembly and Church of the First-born, which are written in heaven (Ephesians 1:22,23; 2:22; Hebrews 12:23).

11. THE MINISTRY

A divinely called and scripturally ordained ministry has been provided by our Lord for a twofold purpose: 1) The evangelization of the world, and 2) The edifying of the Body of Christ (Mark 16:15-20; Ephesians 4:11-13).

12. DIVINE HEALING

Divine healing is an integral part of the gospel. Deliverance from sickness is provided for in the atonement, and is the privilege of all believers (Isaiah 53:4,5; Matt. 8:16,17; James 5:14-16).

13. THE BLESSED HOPE

The resurrection of those who have fallen asleep in Christ and their translation together with those who are alive and remain unto the coming of the Lord is the imminent and blessed hope of the Church (1 Thess. 4:16,17; Romans 8:23; Titus 2:13; 1 Cor. 15:51,52).

14. THE MILLENNIAL REIGN OF CHRIST

The second coming of Christ includes the rapture of the saints, which is our blessed hope, followed by the visible return of Christ with His saints to reign on the earth for one thousand years (Zech. 14:5; Matt. 24:27, 30; Revelation 1:7; 19:11-14; 20:1-6). This millennial reign will bring the salvation of national Israel (Ezekiel 37:21, 22; Zephaniah 3:19-20; Romans 11:26,27) and the establishment of universal peace (Isaiah 11:6-9; Psalm 72:3-8; Micah 4:3, 4).

15. THE FINAL JUDGMENT

There will be a final judgment in which the wicked dead will be raised and judged according to their works. Whosoever is not found written in the Book of Life, together with the devil and his angels, the beast and the false prophet, will be consigned to everlasting punishment in the lake which burneth with fire and brimstone, which is the second death (Matt. 25:46; Mark 9:43-48; Revelation 19:20; 20:11-15; 21:8).

16. THE NEW HEAVENS AND THE NEW EARTH

"We, according to His promise, look for new heavens and a new earth, wherein dwelleth righteousness" (2 Peter 3:13; Revelation 21:22).

(At the 33rd General Council of the Assemblies of God (1969) the following paragraphs were adopted to replace paragraphs 10 and 11 of the *Statement* of Fundamental Truths. The change incorporates the statement of mission, which was also adopted at that time.)

10. THE CHURCH AND ITS MISSION

The Church is the Body of Christ, the habitation of God through the Spirit, with divine appointments for the fulfillment of her great commission. Each believer, born of the Spirit, is an integral part of the General Assembly and Church of the Firstborn, which are written in heaven (Ephesians 1:22, 23; 2:22; Hebrews 12:23).

Since God's purpose concerning man is to seek and to save that which is lost, to be worshiped by man, and to build a body of believers in the image of His Son, the priority reason-for-being of the Assemblies of God as part of the Church is:

a. To be an agency of God for evangelizing the world (Acts 1:8; Matthew 28:19,20; Mark 16:15,16).

b. To be a corporate body in which man may worship God (1 Corinthians 12:13).

c. To be a channel of God's purpose to build a body of saints being perfected in the image of His Son (Ephesians 4:11-16; 1 Corinthians 12:28; 1 Corinthians 14:12).

The Assemblies of God exists expressly to give continuing emphasis to this reason-for-being in the New Testament apostolic pattern by teaching and encouraging believers to be baptized in the Holy Spirit. This experience:

a. Enables them to evangelize in the power of the Spirit with accompanying supernatural signs (Mark 16:15-20; Acts 4:29-31; Hebrews 2:3,4).

b. Adds a necessary dimension to worshipful relationship with God (1 Corinthians 2:10-16; 1 Corinthians 12, 13, and 14).

c. Enables them to respond to the full working of the Holy Spirit in expression of fruit and gifts and ministries as in New Testament times for the edifying of the body of Christ (Galatians 5:22-26; 1 Corinthians 14:12; Ephesians 4:11, 12; 1 Corinthians 12:28; Colossians 1:29).

11. THE MINISTRY

A divinely called and scripturally ordained ministry has been provided by our Lord for the threefold purpose of leading the Church in: (1) Evangelization of the world (Mark 16:15-20), (2) Worship of God (John 4:23, 24), (3) Building a body of saints being perfected in the image of His Son (Ephesians 4:11-16).

Notes: *The earliest doctrinal division in the Pentecostal Movement became manifest in Los Angeles during the midst of the revival taking place at the Azusa Street Mission. The pastor, William Seymour, was firmly committed to the holiness pentecostal position that one must be saved and sanctified before receiving the baptism of the Holy Spirit. He was opposed by William Durham, a Chicago Baptist minister who had received the baptism at Azusa but believed that baptism was the immediate prospect of all Christians.*

Durham's position was termed the "finished work," referring to the Reformation theological position that sanctification and justification were included in Christ's finished work on the cross. To all who had faith in Christ, his atonement imputed justification (freedom from the divine wrath of sin) and sanctification (holiness in God's eyes). Believers considered to be both justified and sanctified faced the task of ending their participation in sin of thought and action and becoming holy; a lifelong process to be completed only after death. The "finished work" appealed especially to those who had come into the pentecostal experience from non-Methodist backgrounds. It had been adopted by those who came together in 1914 to organize the General Council of the Assemblies of God, the first prominent group to formally align itself with Durham's understanding.

The Statement of Fundamental Truths by the (General Council of the) Assemblies of God was hammered out in such a way as to distinguish the Assemblies of God from both the holiness-pentecostal groups and the non-Trinitarian pentecostal bodies. Particular note should be made of the statements on the baptism of the Holy Ghost and sanctification (7 and 9), as well as the detailed statements on the Trinity (2). In 1969 new statements on the church and the ministry (10 and 11) were adopted.

* * *

TENETS OF FAITH (CALIFORNIA EVANGELISTIC ASSOCIATION)

TENETS OF FAITH

This corporation shall accept the Holy Scriptures as the revealed will of God, the all-sufficient rule for faith and practice, and for the purpose of maintaining general unity, adopts the statement of Fundamental Truths approved by the Board of Trustees.

FUNDAMENTAL TRUTHS

The human phraseology employed in this statement is not inspired or contended for, but the truth set forth is held to be essential to a full gospel ministry. No claims are made that it contains all truth in the Bible, only that it covers our present needs as to those fundamental matters.

1. **THE SCRIPTURES INSPIRED.**

   The Bible is the inspired Word of God, a revelation from God to man, the infallible rule of faith and conduct, and is superior to conscience and reason. II. Tim. 3:16; II. Pet. 1:21; Heb. 4:12.

2. **THE ONE TRUE GOD.**

   The one true God has revealed Himself as the eternally self-existent, self-revealed creator of the universe and is the Father of our Lord Jesus Christ. Deut. 6:4; Mark 12:29; Isa. 43:10; Matt. 28:19.

3. **MAN, HIS FALL AND REDEMPTION.**

   Man was created good and upright, for God said, "Let us make man in our image, after our likeness." But man, by voluntary transgression fell, and his only hope of redemption is in Jesus Christ the Son of God. Gen. 1:26, 31; 3:1-7, Rom. 5:12,21.

4. **THE SALVATION OF MAN.**

   (a) Conditions to salvation: The grace of God, which bringeth salvation hath appeared to all man through the preaching of repentance toward God and faith toward the Lord Jesus Christ; man is saved by the washing of regeneration and renewing of the Holy Ghost, and being justified by grace through faith, he becomes an heir of God according to the hope of eternal life. Titus 2:11; Rom. 8:16,15; Luke 24:47; Titus 3:5,7.

   (b) The Evidences of Salvation: The inward evidence to the believer of his salvation is the direct witness of the Spirit. Rom. 8:16. The outward evidence to all men is a life of righteousness and true holiness.

5. **BAPTISM IN WATER.**

   The ordinance of baptism by burial with Christ should be observed as commanded in the Scriptures, by all who have really repented and in their hearts have truly believed on Christ as Savior and Lord. In so doing, they declare to the world that they have been buried with Jesus Christ and that they have also been raised with Him to walk in newness of life. Mat. 28:19; Acts 10:47,48; Rom. 6:4.

6. **THE LORD'S SUPPER.**

   The Lord's Supper, consisting of the elements, bread and the fruit of the vine, is the symbol expressing our sharing the divine nature of our Lord Jesus Christ, a memorial of His suffering and death and a prophecy of His second coming, and is enjoined on all believers, "until He comes." John 6:48, 51-58; Luke 22:19, 20; II. Pet. 1:4; I. Cor. 11:26.

7. **THE PROMISE OF THE FATHER.**

   All believers are entitled to and should ardently expect and earnestly seek, the promise of the Father, the Baptism of the Holy Ghost according to the Command of our Lord Jesus Christ. This was the normal experience of all in the early Christian Church. With it comes the enduement of power for life and service, the bestowment of the gifts and their uses in the work of the ministry. Luke 24:49; Acts 1:4,8; I. Cor. 12:1,31. This wonderful experience is distinct from and subsequent to the experience of the new birth. Acts 2:38; 10:44,46; 15:7-9.

8. **THE EVIDENCE OF THE BAPTISM IN THE HOLY GHOST.**

   The Full consummation of the Baptism of believers in the Holy Ghost is evidenced by the initial physical sign of speaking with other tongues as the Spirit gives utterance, and by subsequent manifestation of spiritual power in public testimony and service. Acts 2:4; 10:44,46; 1:8; 2:42, 43.

9. **ENTIRE SANCTIFICATION.**

   The Scriptures teach a life of holiness, without which no man shall see the Lord. By the power of the Holy Ghost we are able to obey the command, "Be ye holy, for I am holy." Entire Sanctification is the will of God for all believers, and should be earnestly pursued by walking in obedience to God's word. Heb. 12:14; I. Pet. 1:15; I. Thess. 5:23,24; I. John 2:6; Rom. 8:3,4.

10. **THE CHURCH.**

    The Church is the body of Christ, the habitation of God through the Spirit, with divine appointments for the fulfillment of her great commission. Each believer, born of the Spirit, is an integral part of the general Assembly and Church of the First-born, which are written in Heaven. Eph. 1:22; Heb. 12:23; Eph. 2:19,22.

11. **THE MINISTRY AND EVANGELISM.**

    A divinely called and scripturally ordained ministry has been provided by our Lord for a two-fold purpose: (1) the evangelism of the world, and (2) the edifying of the body of Christ. Mark 16:15, 20; Eph. 4:11,13.

12. **DIVINE HEALING.**

    Deliverance from sickness is provided for in the Word of God and is the privilege of the believers. Mark 16:18; John 5:14; Matt. 8:16, 17.

13. **THE BLESSED HOPE.**

    The resurrection of those who have fallen asleep in Christ and their translation, together with those who are alive and remain unto the coming of the Lord, we believe, is imminent and is the blessed hope of the Church. I. Thess. 4:16-18; Rom. 8:23; Titus 2:13; I. Cor. 15:41-52.

14. **THE EVERLASTING REIGN OF JESUS.**

    The revelation of the Lord Jesus Christ from Heaven, the salvation of spiritual Israel, and the everlasting reign of Christ on the earth is the scriptural promise and the only hope of the church. II. Thess. 1:7; Rev. 19:11-16; Rom. 11:25-27: Rev. 21:1-7.

TENETS OF FAITH (CALIFORNIA EVANGELISTIC ASSOCIATION) (continued)

15. THE LAKE OF FIRE.

The Devil and his angels, and whosoever is not found written in the Book of Life shall be punished with everlasting destruction from the presence of the Lord, which is the second death. II. Thess. 1:9; Rev. 20:10.

16. THE NEW HEAVENS AND NEW EARTH.

We, "according to His promise look for new heavens and a new earth wherein dwelleth righteousness." II. Pet. 3:13; Rev. 21:1.

Notes: *These tenets are derived from the Fundamental Truths of the Assemblies of God. The items on the church and on the ministry and evangelism were part of the Assemblies's statement until 1969. The Assemblies are premillennial in their eschatology.*

*　　*　　*

WE BELIEVE (CALVARY CHAPEL CHURCH)

The Calvary Chapel Church has been formed as a fellowship of believers in the Lordship of Jesus Christ.

Our supreme desire is to know Christ and to be conformed into His image by the power of the Holy Spirit.

We are not a denominational church, nor are we opposed to denominations as such, only their over-emphasis of the doctrinal differences that have led to the division of the Body of Christ.

We believe that the only true basis of Christian fellowship is His (Agape) love, which is greater than any differences we possess and without which we have no right to claim ourselves Christians.

WE BELIEVE worship of God should be Spiritual.

Therefore: We remain flexible and yielded to the leading of the Holy Spirit to direct our worship.

WE BELIEVE worship of God should be Inspirational.

Therefore: We give a great place to music in our worship.

WE BELIEVE worship of God should be Intelligent.

Therefore: Our services are designed with great emphasis upon teaching the Word of God that He might instruct us how He should be worshipped.

WE BELIEVE worship of God is Fruitful.

Therefore: We look for His love in our lives as the supreme manifestation that we have truly been worshipping Him.

Notes: *As with many of the newer churches, the statement of Calvary Chapel is brief, dealing with only a few essential issues. Rather than emphasize doctrine, the statement centers on the Christian fellowship of love as a uniting force above denominational barriers.*

STATEMENT OF FUNDAMENTAL TRUTHS (CALVARY MINISTRIES, INC.)

1. THE SCRIPTURES INSPIRED

The Scriptures, both the Old and New Testaments, are verbally inspired of God and are the revelation of God to man, the infallible, authoritative rule of faith and conduct (2 Timothy 3:15-17; 1 Thessalonians 2:13: 2 Peter 1:21).

2. THE ONE TRUE GOD

The one true God has revealed Himself as the eternally self-existent "I AM," the Creator of heaven and earth and the Redeemer of mankind. He has further revealed Himself as embodying the principles of relationship and association as Father, Son and Holy Ghost (Deuteronomy 6:4; Isaiah 43:10, 11; Matthew 28:19; Luke 3:22).

THE ADORABLE GODHEAD

(a) TERMS DEFINED. The terms "Trinity" and "persons," as related to the Godhead, while not found in the Scriptures, are words in harmony with Scripture, whereby we may convey to others our immediate understanding of the doctrine of Christ respecting the Being of God, as distinguished from "gods many and lords many." We therefore may speak with propriety of the Lord our God, who is One Lord, as a trinity or as one Being of three persons, and still be absolutely scriptural (examples, Matthew 28:19; 2 Corinthians 13:14; John 14:16, 17).

(b) DISTINCTION AND RELATIONSHIP IN THE GODHEAD. Christ taught a distinction of Persons in the Godhead which He expressed in specific terms of relationship, as Father, Son, and Holy Ghost, but that this distinction and relationship, as to its mode is *inscrutable* and *incomprehensible,* because *unexplained.* (Luke 1:35; 1 Corinthians 1:24; Matthew 11:25-27; 28:19; 2 Corinthians 13:14; 1 John 1:3, 4.)

(c) UNITY OF THE ONE BEING OF FATHER, SON AND HOLY GHOST. Accordingly, therefore, there is *that* in the Son which constitutes Him *the* Son and not the Father, and there is *that* in the Holy Ghost which constitutes him *the Holy Ghost* and not either the Father or the Son. Wherefore the Father is the Begetter, the Son is the Begotten; and the Holy Ghost is the one proceeding from the Father and the Son. Therefore, because these three persons in the Godhead are instate of unity, there is but one Lord God Almighty and His name one. (John 1:18; 15:26; 17:11, 21; Zechariah 14:9.)

(d) IDENTITY AND CO-OPERATION IN THE GODHEAD. The Father, the Son and the Holy Ghost are never *identical* as to *Person;* nor *confused* as to *relation;* nor *divided* in respect to the Godhead; nor *opposed* as to *co-operation.* The Son is *in* the Father and the Father is *in* the Son as to relationship. The Son is *with* the Father and the Father is *with* the Son, as to fellowship. The Father is not *from* the Son, but the Son is *from* the Father, as to authority. The Holy Ghost is *from* the Father and the Son proceeding, as to nature, relationship, co-operation and authority. Hence, neither Person in the Godhead either exists or works separately or independently of the others. (John 5:17-30, 32, 37; 8:17, 18.)

(e) THE TITLE, LORD JESUS CHRIST. The appellation, "Lord Jesus Christ," is a proper name. It is never applied, in the New Testament, either to the Father or to the Holy Ghost. It therefore belongs exclusively to the *Son of God.* (Romans 1:1-3, 7; 2 John 3.)

(f) THE LORD JESUS CHRIST, GOD WITH US. The Lord Jesus Christ, as to His Divine and eternal nature, is the proper and only Begotten of the Father, but as to His human nature. He is the proper Son of Man. He is, therefore, acknowledged to be both God and man: who because He is God, and man, "Immanuel," God with us. (Matthew 1:23; 1 John 4:2, 10, 14; Revelation 1:13, 17.)

(g) THE TITLE, SON OF GOD. Since the name, "Immanuel" embraces both God and man in the one Person, our Lord Jesus Christ, it follows that the title, Son of God, describes His proper deity, and the title Son of Man, His proper humanity. Therefore, the title, Son of God, belongs to the *order of eternity,* and the title, Son of Man, to the *order of time.* (Matthew 1:21-23; 2 John 3; 1 John 3:8; Hebrews 7:3; 1:1-13.)

(h) TRANSGRESSION OF THE DOCTRINE OF CHRIST. Wherefore, it is a transgression of the doctrine of Christ to say that Jesus Christ derived the title, Son of God, solely from the fact of the incarnation, or because of His relation to the economy of redemption. Therefore, to deny that the Father is a real and eternal Father, and that the Son is a real and eternal Son, is a denial of the distinction and relationship in the Being of God; a denial of the Father and the Son; and a displacement of the truth that Jesus Christ is come in the flesh. (2 John 9; John 1:1, 2, 14, 18, 29, 49; 1 John 2:22, 23; 4:1-5; Hebrews 12:2.)

(i) EXALTATION OF JESUS CHRIST AS LORD. The Son of God, our Lord Jesus Christ, having by Himself purged our sins, sat down on the right hand of the Majesty on high; angels and principalities and powers having been made subject unto Him. And having been made both Lord and Christ, He sent the Holy Ghost that we, in the name of Jesus, might bow our knees and confess that Jesus Christ is Lord to the glory of God the Father until the end, when the Son shall become subject to the Father that God may be all in all. (Hebrews 1:3; 1 Peter 3:22; Acts 2:32-36; Romans 14:11; 1 Corinthians 15:24-28.)

(j) EQUAL HONOR TO THE FATHER AND TO THE SON. Wherefore, since the Father has delivered all judgment unto the *Son,* it is not only the *express duty* of all in heaven and on earth to bow the knee, but it is an *unspeakable* joy in the Holy Ghost to ascribe unto the Son all the attributes of Deity, and to give Him all the honor and the glory contained in all the names and titles of the Godhead except those which express relationship (see paragraphs b, c, and d), and thus honor the Son even as we honor the Father. (John 5:22, 23; 1 Peter 1:8; Revelation 5:6-14; Philippians 2:8, 9; Revelation 7:9, 10; 4:8-11.)

3. THE DEITY OF THE LORD JESUS CHRIST

The Lord Jesus Christ is the eternal Son of God. The Scriptures declare:

(a) His virgin birth (Matthew 1:23; Luke 1:31, 35).

(b) His sinless life (Hebrews 7:26; 1 Peter 2:22).

(c) His miracles (Acts 2:22; 10:38).

(d) His substitutionary work on the cross (1 Corinthians 15:3; 2 Corinthians 5:21).

(e) His bodily resurrection from the dead (Matthew 28:6; Luke 24:39; 1 Corinthians 15:4).

(f) His exaltation to the right hand of God (Acts 1:9, 11; 2:33; Philippians 2:9-11; Hebrews 1-3).

4. THE FALL OF MAN

Man was created good and upright; for God said, "Let us make man in our image, after our likeness." However, man by voluntary transgression fell and thereby incurred not only physical death but also spiritual death, which is separation from God (Genesis 1:26, 27; 2:17; 3:6; Romans 5:12-19).

5. THE SALVATION OF MAN

Man's only hope of redemption is through the shed blood of Jesus Christ the Son of God.

(a) CONDITIONS TO SALVATION. Salvation is received through repentance toward God and faith toward the Lord Jesus Christ. By the washing of regeneration and renewing of the Holy Ghost, being justified by grace through faith, man becomes an heir of God according to the hope of eternal life (Luke 24:47; John 3:3; Romans 10:13-15; Ephesians 2:8; Titus 2:11; 3:5-7).

(b) THE EVIDENCES OF SALVATION. The inward evidence of salvation is the direct witness of the Spirit (Romans 8:16). The outward evidence to all men is a life of righteousness and true holiness (Ephesians 4:24; Titus 2:12).

6. THE ORDINANCES OF THE CHURCH

(a) BAPTISM IN WATER. The ordinance of baptism, by immersion is commanded in the Scriptures. All who repent and believe in Christ as Saviour and Lord are to be baptized. Thus they declare to the world that they have died with Christ and that they also have been raised with Him to walk in newness of life. (Matthew 28:19; Mark 16:16; Acts 10:47, 48; Romans 6:4).

(b) HOLY COMMUNION. The Lord's Supper, consisting of the elements—bread and the fruit of the vine—is the symbol expressing our sharing the divine nature of our Lord Jesus Christ (2 Peter 1:4); a memorial of His suffering and death (1 Corinthians 11:26); and a prophecy of His second coming (1 Corinthians 11:26); and is enjoined on all believers "till He come!"

STATEMENT OF FUNDAMENTAL TRUTHS (CALVARY MINISTRIES, INC.) (continued)

7. THE BAPTISM IN THE HOLY GHOST

All believers are entitled to and should ardently expect and earnestly seek the promise of the Father, the baptism in the Holy Ghost and fire, according to the command of our Lord Jesus Christ. This was the normal experience of all in the early Christian Church. With it comes the enduement of power for life and service, the bestowment of the gifts and their uses in the work of the ministry (Luke 24:49; Acts 1:4-8; 1 Corinthians 12:1-31). This experience is distinct from and subsequent to the experience of the new birth (Acts 8:12-17; 10:44-46; 11:14-16; 15:7-9). With the baptism in the Holy Ghost come such experiences as an overflowing fullness of the Spirit (John 7:37-39; Acts 4:8), a deepened reverence for God (Acts 2:43; Hebrews 12:28), an intensified consecration to God and dedication to His work (Acts 2:42), and a more active love for Christ, for His Word, and for the lost (Mark 16:20).

8. THE EVIDENCE OF THE BAPTISM IN THE HOLY GHOST

The Baptism of believers in the Holy Ghost is witnessed by the initial physical sign of speaking with other tongues as the Spirit of God gives them utterance (Acts 2:4). The speaking in tongues in this instance is the same in essence as the gift of tongues (1 Corinthians 12:4-10, 28), but different in purpose and use.

9. SANCTIFICATION

Sanctification is an act of separation from that which is evil, and of dedication unto God (Romans 12:1, 2; 1 Thessalonians 5:23; Hebrews 13:12). The Scriptures teach a life of "holiness without which no man shall see the Lord" (Hebrews 12:14). By the power of the Holy Ghost we are able to obey the command: "Be ye holy, for I am holy" (1 Peter 1:15, 16).

Sanctification is realized in the believer by recognizing his identification with Christ in His death and resurrection, and by faith reckoning daily upon the fact of that union, and by offering every faculty continually to the dominion of the Holy Spirit (Romans 6:1-13; Romans 8:1, 2, 13; Galatians 2:20; Philippians 2:12, 13; 1 Peter 1:5).

10. THE CHURCH

The Church is the Body of Christ, the habitation of God through the Spirit, with divine appointments for the fulfillment of her great commission. Each believer, born of the Spirit, is an integral part of the General Assembly and Church of the First-born, which are written in heaven (Ephesians 1:22, 23; 2:22; Hebrews 12:23).

11. THE MINISTRY

A divinely called and scripturally ordained ministry has been provided by our Lord for a twofold purpose: (1) The evangelization of the world, and (2) The edifying of the Body of Christ (Mark 16:15-20; Ephesians 4:11-13).

12. DIVINE HEALING

Divine healing is an integral part of the gospel. Deliverance from sickness is provided for in the atonement, and is the privilege of all believers (Isaiah 53:4, 5; Matthew 8:16, 17; James 5:14-16).

13. THE BLESSED HOPE

The resurrection of those who have fallen asleep in Christ and their translation together with those who are alive and remain unto the coming of the Lord is the imminent and blessed hope of the Church (1 Thessalonians 4:16, 17; Romans 8:23; Titus 2:13; 1 Corinthians 15:51, 52).

14. THE MILLENNIAL REIGN OF CHRIST

The second coming of Christ includes the rapture of the saints, which is our blessed hope, followed by the visible return of Christ with His saints to reign on the earth for one thousand years (Zechariah 14:5; Matthew 24:27, 30; Revelation 1:7; 19:11-14; 20:1-6). This millennial reign will bring the salvation of national Israel (Ezekiel 37:21, 22; Zephaniah 3:19-20; Romans 11:26, 27) and the establishment of universal peace (Isaiah 11:6-9; Psalm 72:3-8; Micah 4:3, 4).

15. THE FINAL JUDGMENT

There will be a final judgment in which the wicked dead will be raised and judged according to their works. Whosoever is not found written in the Book of Life, together with the devil and his angels, the beast and the false prophet, will be consigned to everlasting punishment in the lake which burneth with fire and brimstone, which is the second death (Matthew 25:46; Mark 9:43-48; Revelation 19:20; 20:11-15; 21:8).

16. THE NEW HEAVENS AND THE NEW EARTH

"We, according to his promise, look for new heavens and a new earth, wherein dwelleth righteousness" (2 Peter 3:13; Revelation 21:22).

Notes: *This statement is based upon that of the General Council of the Assemblies of God, differing only in its omission of the most recent revisions of, and additions to, the Assemblies' statement.*

* * *

WHAT WE BELIEVE (CHRISTIAN CHURCH OF NORTH AMERICA)

We believe and accept the entire Bible as the infallible Word of God, inspired by the Holy Ghost; the only and perfect order of our faith; and manner of living; to which nothing can be added or taken away, which is the power of God unto salvation to believers. 2 Pet. 1:21; 2 Tim. 3:16-17; Rom. 1:16.

We believe there is only one living and true God, eternal with unlimited power, Creator of all things; and in the one God are three distinct persons: The Father, the Son, and the Holy Ghost. Eph. 4:6; Matt. 28:19; 1 John 5:7.

We believe that the Son of God is the Word, made flesh, who assumed the human body through the virgin Mary, and so is true God and true man, two natures in one person, the divine and human; and, therefore, is the only Saviour, who in reality suffered death, not only for the primitive transgressions, but also for the actual sins of man. John 1:14; Lk. 1:27-35; 1 Pet. 3:18.

We believe in the existence of a personal devil, who, with all evil spirits, will be eternally punished in the Lake of Fire. Matt. 25:41.

We believe that regeneration or the new birth is received only through faith in Christ Jesus; who was raised for our justification. They who are in Christ Jesus (cleansed through His blood) are new creatures, and have Him for wisdom and righteousness and sanctification and redemption. Rom. 3:24, 25; 2 Cor. 5:17; 1 Cor. 1:30.

We believe in water baptismal by single immersion, in the name of the Father and of the Son and the Holy Ghost according to Christ's commission. Matt. 28:18,19.

We believe in the baptism in the Holy Ghost as an experience received subsequent to salvation, with the sign of speaking in tongues as the Holy Ghost gives utterance. Acts 2:4; 10:45-47; 19:6.

We believe in the Lord's Supper, when Christ, then, taking bread—"He gave thanks, and brake it and gave unto them Saying: 'This is my body which is given for you: this do in rememberance of me.' Likewise also the cup after supper, saying 'This cup is the new testament in my blood, which is shed for you.'" Luke 22;19,20; I Cor. 11:24.

We believe it is necessary to abstain from things offered to idols, from blood, from things strangled and from fornication, as decreed by the Holy Ghost in the General Assembly held at Jerusalem according to Acts 15:28,29; 16:4; 21.25.

We believe that Jesus Christ, Himself, bore all our infirmities and, therefore, we obey the following commandment: "Is any sick among you? Let him call for the elders of the church: and let them pray over him, anointing him with oil in the name of the Lord; and the prayer of faith shall save the sick, and the Lord shall raise him up; and if he has committed sins, they shall be forgiven him." James 5:14; Matt. 8:17.

We believe that the Lord, Himself, (before the millenium) "shall descend from heaven with a great shout, with the trump of God, and the dead in Christ shall rise first; then we that are left, shall together with them be caught up in the clouds to meet the Lord in the air; and so shall we ever be with the Lord." 1 Thess. 4:16, 17; Rev. 20:6.

We believe there shall be a bodily resurrection of all dead, just and unjust, and these shall go away into everlasting punishment but the righteous into life eternal. Acts 24:16; Matt. 25:46.

*　　*　　*

DOCTRINAL STATEMENT (ELIM BIBLE INSTITUTE)

1. We believe the Bible to be the only inspired, infallible Word of God. II Peter 1:21.

2. We believe the Godhead consists of the Father, the Son, and the Holy Spirit. II Cor. 13:14. Three in One and One in Three.

3. We believe in the Deity of Jesus Christ, in His virgin birth, in His atoning death, in His bodily resurrec-tion, in His ascension to the right hand of the Father. I Timothy 3:16.

4. We believe in evangelistic and missionary fervor and endeavor. Acts 1:18; Mark 16:15-18.

5. We believe in salvation through the redeeming blood of Christ. Hebrews 9:22.

6. We believe in sanctification and holiness of heart and the overcoming life as Scriptural requirements for the Bride of Christ. Eph. 5:25-27.

7. We believe in sanctification and the Holy Spirit according to Acts 2:4, 10:46, 19:6, and the present ministry of the Spirit in and through the believer as manifest in the five ministries as they are being restored in end-time revival (Eph. 4:11), the gifts of the Spirit (I Cor. 12:8-11), and the fruit of the Spirit (Gal. 5:22,23).

8. We believe that divine healing is obtained on the basis of the Atonement. I Peter 2:24.

9. We believe in Christ's imminent personal return in power and great glory, in His millennial reign and in His everlasting dominion. Acts 1:11; Rev. 20:4; Dan. 7:14.

10. We believe in the resurrection of both the saved and the lost; they that are saved unto the resurrection of eternal life and they that are lost unto the resurrection of eternal punishment. John 5:28,29; Rev. 20:15.

Notes: *The Elim Bible Institute is the school affiliated with the Elim Fellowship.*

*　　*　　*

ARTICLES OF FAITH (GENERAL ASSEMBLY AND CHURCH OF THE FIRST BORN)

We believe in God, the Eternal Father, and his Son, Jesus Christ, and in the Holy Ghost.

We believe that man will be punished for their own sins, and not for Adam's transgression.

We believe that through the Atonement of Christ, all mankind may be saved, by obedience to the laws and ordinances of the Gospel.

We believe that the first principles and ordinances of the Gospel are: first, Faith in the Lord Jesus Christ; second, Repentance; third, Baptism by immerson for the remission of sins; fourth, Laying on of hands for the gift of the Holy Ghost.

We believe in the same organization that existed in the Primitive Church, viz: apostles, prophets, pastors, teach-ers, evangelists, etc.

We believe in the gift of tongues, prophecy, revelation, visions, healing, interpretation of tongues, etc.

We believe in being honest, true, chaste, benevolent, virtuous, and in doing good to all men; indeed we may say that we follow the admonition of Paul—We believe all things, we hope all things, we have endured many things, and hope to be able to endure all things. If there is anything virtuous, lovely, or of good report or praisewor-thy, we seek after these things.

ARTICLES OF FAITH (GENERAL ASSEMBLY AND CHURCH OF THE FIRST BORN) (continued)

Notes: *This group is noteworthy for its position on the ordinances. It has four, but the Lord's Supper is not among them.*

* * *

STATEMENT OF FAITH [GOSPEL ASSEMBLIES (SOWDER)]

We believe that the Bible, both the Old and New Testaments, was given by inspiration of God, and is our only rule in matters of faith, doctrine and practice. We believe in creation; that man was created by the direct act of God and in the image of God. We believe that Adam and Eve, in yielding to the temptation of Satan, became fallen creatures. We believe that all men are born in sin, and thus the necessity for repentance. We believe in the Incarnation, the Virgin Birth, and the Deity of our Lord and Saviour, Jesus Christ, the Son of the Living God. We believe in His vicarious and substitutional death on the cross as (the) Atonement for the sins of mankind by the shedding of His own blood at Calvary. We believe that the Atonement also provides deliverance and healing for those who believe in His name. We believe in justification by faith, and sanctification to be the way of holiness. We believe that grace and works as recorded in James, chapter two, are compatible. We believe that justification must be sustained by obedience to God's Word. We believe in the resurrection of His body from the tomb, His ascension to Heaven, and that He is now our Advocate. We believe the church to be a direct result of the first advent and that men are to be actively drawn into it. We believe water baptism to be scriptural when administered to believers only. We believe in the necessity of the New Birth, and that this New Birth is through the regeneration by the Holy Spirit as recorded in the second chapter of Acts. We believe in the restoration of Israel. We believe that He is personally coming again at His glorious premillennial second advent to judge the wicked, to resurrect the righteous dead, and to establish the Kingdom of God upon this earth.

We believe that this statement of faith is a sufficient basis for Christian fellowship and that all born-again men and women who sincerely accept this, can, and should, live together in peace, and that it is their Christian duty to promote harmony among the members of the Body of Christ, and also to work together to get the Gospel to as many people as possible in the shortest period of time.

* * *

DECLARATION OF FAITH (INDEPENDENT ASSEMBLIES OF GOD INTERNATIONAL)

We Believe:

In the God Head manifested in the Father, Son and the Holy Ghost.

In the virgin birth of Jesus Christ.

In the deity of the Lord Jesus Christ.

Repentance is necessary unto salvation.

In water baptism for the believer after salvation.

In the verbal inspiration of the Holy Scriptures.

In the baptism of the Holy Ghost with the evidence of speaking in other tongues.

In eternal life for the believer in Jesus Christ and the eternal damnation for the lost (wicked).

In the literal return of the Lord Jesus Christ.

Notes: *This brief statement is derived from that of the Assemblies of God.*

* * *

DECLARATION OF FAITH (INTERNATIONAL CHURCH OF THE FOURSQUARE GOSPEL)

1. THE HOLY SCRIPTURES

We believe that the Holy Bible is the Word of the living God; true, immutable, steadfast, unchangeable, as its author, the Lord Jehovah; that it was written by holy men of old as they were moved upon and inspired by the Holy Spirit; that it is a lighted lamp to guide the feet of a lost world from the depths of sin and sorrow to the heights of righteousness and glory; an unclouded mirror that reveals the face of a crucified Saviour; a plumbline to make straight the life of each individual and community; a sharp two-edged sword to convict of sin and evil doing; a strong cord of love and tenderness to draw the penitent to Christ Jesus; a balm of Gilead, inbreathed by the Holy Spirit, that can heal and quicken each drooping heart; the only true ground of Christian fellowship and unity; the loving call of an infinitely loving God; the solemn warning, the distant thunder of the storm of wrath and retribution that shall overtake the unheeding; a sign post that points to Heaven; a danger signal that warns from Hell; the divine, supreme, and eternal tribunal by whose standards all men, nations, creeds, and motives shall be tried.

Scripture References Where Taught:

Heaven and earth shall pass away, but my words shall not pass away. Matt. 24:35. Forever, O Lord, Thy Word is settled in Heaven. Ps. 119:89.

All Scripture is given by inspiration of God, and is profitable for doctrine, for reproof, for correction, for instruction in righteousness: that the man of God may be perfect, thoroughly furnished unto all good works. II Tim. 3:16, 17.

Thy Word is a lamp unto my feet, and a light unto my path. Ps. 119:105.

We have also a more sure word of prophecy; whereunto ye do well that ye take heed, as unto a light that shineth in a dark place, until the day dawn, and the day star arise in your hearts: knowing this first, that no prophecy of the scripture is of any private interpretation. For the prophecy came not in old time by the will of men: but holy men of God spake as they were moved by the Holy Ghost. II Peter 1:19-21.

Search the scriptures; for in them ye think ye have eternal life: and they are they which testify of me. John 5:39.

Study to show thyself approved unto God, a workman that needeth not to be ashamed, rightly dividing the Word of truth. II Tim. 2:15. . . . Let us walk by the same rule, let us mind the same thing. Phil. 3:16. (Also I John 4:1; Isa. 8:20; I Thess. 5:21; Acts 17:11; I John 4:6; Jude 3; Eph. 6:17; Ps. 119:59, 60; Phil. 1:9-11.)

II. THE ETERNAL GODHEAD

We believe that there is but one true and living God; maker of heaven and earth and all that in them is; the Alpha and Omega, who ever was, and is and shall be time without end, Amen; that He is infinitely holy, mighty, tender, loving and glorious; worthy of all possible love and honor, confidence and obedience, majesty, dominion and might, both now and forever; and that in the unity of the Godhead there are three, equal in every divine perfection executing distinct but harmonious offices in the great work of redemption:

THE FATHER. Whose glory is so exceeding bright that mortal man cannot look upon His face and live, but whose heart was so filled with love and pity for His lost and sin-benighted children that He freely gave His only begotten Son to redeem and reconcile them unto Himself.

THE SON. Co-existent and co-eternal with the Father, who, conceived by the Holy Spirit and born of the Virgin Mary took upon Himself the form of man, bore our sins, carried our sorrows, and by the shedding of His precious blood upon the cross of Calvary purchased redemption for all that would believe upon Him: then, bursting the bonds of death and hell rose from the grave and ascended on high leading captivity captive, that as the great Mediator betwixt God and man, He might stand at the right hand of the Father making intercession for those for whom He laid down His life.

THE HOLY SPIRIT. The third person of the Godhead, the Spirit of the Father shed abroad, omnipotent, omnipresent, performing an inexpressibly important mission upon earth, convicting of sin, of righteousness and of judgment, drawing sinners to the Saviour, rebuking, pleading, searching, comforting, guiding, quickening, teaching, glorifying, baptizing and enduing with power from on high, them who yield to His tender ministrations, preparing them for the great day of the Lord's appearing.

Scripture References Where Taught:

. . . Before me there was no God formed, neither shall there be after me. Isa. 43:10. . . . Is there a God beside me? yea, there is no God; I know not any. Isa. 44:8.

Thou canst not see my face: for there shall no man see me, and live. Ex. 33:20.

For God so loved the world, that He gave His only begotten Son, that whosoever believeth in Him should not perish, but have everlasting life. John 3:16.

In the beginning was the Word, and the Word was with God, and the Word was God. The same was in the beginning with God. All things were made by Him, and without Him was not anything made that was made. John 1:1-3. (Also Job 38:4-7.)

Behold, a virgin shall be with child, and shall bring forth a Son and they shall call his name Emmanuel. Matt. 1:23.

I, even I, am the Lord; and beside me there is no saviour. Isa. 43:11. For there is one God, and one Mediator between God and men, the man Christ Jesus; who gave Himself a ransom for all. I Tim. 2:5. For through Him we both have access by one Spirit unto the Father. Eph. 2:18.

For there are three that bear record in Heaven, the Father, the Word, and the Holy Ghost: and these three are one. I John 5:7.

But when the Comforter is come, whom I will send unto you from the Father, even the Spirit of truth, which proceedeth from the Father, He shall testify of me. John 15:26. (Also II Cor. 13:14; Matt. 28:19; Rom. 8:11; John 16:7-14.)

III. THE FALL OF MAN

We believe that man was created in the image of God, before whom he walked in holiness and purity, but that by voluntary disobedience and transgression, he fell from the Eden of purity and innocence to the depths of sin and iniquity, and that in consequence of this, all mankind are sinners sold unto Satan, sinners not by constraint but by choice, shapen in iniquity and utterly void by nature of that holiness required by the law of God, positively inclined to evil, guilty and without excuse, justly deserving the condemnation of a just and holy God.

Scripture References Where Taught:

God created man in His own image. Gen. 1:27.

Wherefore as by one man sin entered into the world and death by sin; and so death passed upon all men, for all have sinned. Rom. 5:12. By one man's disobedience many were made sinners. Rom. 5:19. (Also John 3:6; Ps. 51:5; Rom. 5:15-19; 8:7.)

We have turned every one to his own way. Isa. 53:6. (Also Gen. 6:12; 3:9-18.)

Among whom also we had our conversation in times past in the lusts of our flesh, fulfilling the desires of the flesh and of the mind; and were by nature the children of wrath, even as others. Eph. 2:3. (See Rom. 1:18, 32; 2:1-16; Matt. 20:15; Gal. 3:10; Ezek. 18:19, 20.)

. . . So that they are without excuse. Rom 1:20. That every mouth may be stopped, and all the world may become guilty before God. Rom. 3:19. (Also Gal. 3:22.)

IV. THE PLAN OF REDEMPTION

We believe that while we were yet sinners Christ died for us, the Just for the unjust; freely, and by divine appointment of the Father taking the sinner's place, bearing his sins, receiving his condemnation, dying his death, fully paying his penalty, and signing with His life's blood, the pardon of every one who should believe upon Him; that upon simple faith and acceptance of the atonement purchased on Mount Calvary, the vilest sinner may be cleansed of his iniquities and made whiter than the driven snow.

DECLARATION OF FAITH (INTERNATIONAL CHURCH OF THE FOURSQUARE GOSPEL) (continued)

Scripture References Where Taught:

He was wounded for our transgressions. He was bruised for our iniquities: the chastisement of our peace was upon Him; and with His stripes we are healed. Isa. 53:5.

Who gave Himself for us, that He might redeem us from all iniquity, and purify unto Himself a peculiar people, zealous of good works. Titus 2:14.

Let the wicked forsake his way, and the unrighteous man his thoughts: and let him return unto the Lord, and He will have mercy upon him; and to our God, for He will abundantly pardon. Isa. 55:7.

Wherefore He is able also to save them to the uttermost that come unto God by Him, seeing He ever liveth to make intercession for them. Heb. 7:25.

Come now, and let us reason together, saith the Lord: though your sins be as scarlet, they shall be white as snow; though they be red like crimson, they shall be as wool. Isa 1:18.

V. SALVATION THROUGH GRACE

We believe that the salvation of sinners is wholly through grace; that we have no righteousness or goodness of our own wherewith to seek divine favor, and must come, therefore, throwing ourselves upon the unfailing mercy and love of Him who bought us and washed us in His own blood, pleading the merits and the righteousness of Christ the Saviour, standing upon His word and accepting the free gift of His love and pardon.

Scripture References Where Taught:

By grace are ye saved. Eph. 2:8.

. . . There is none righteous, no, not one. Rom. 3:10.

All have sinned, and come short of the glory of God. Rom. 3:23.

We are all as an unclean thing, for all our righteousnesses are as filthy rags, and we all do fade as a leaf; and our iniquities, like the wind, have taken us away. Isa. 64:6.

Verily, verily, I say unto you, He that believeth on me hath everlasting life. John 6:47.

But now in Christ Jesus ye who sometimes were far off are made nigh by the blood of Christ. Eph. 2:13.

For the wages of sin is death; but the gift of God is eternal life through Jesus Christ our Lord. Rom. 6:23.

VI. REPENTANCE AND ACCEPTANCE

We believe that upon sincere repentance, godly sorrow for sin, and a whole-hearted acceptance of the Lord Jesus Christ, they who call upon Him may be justified by faith, through His precious blood and that in place of condemnation they may have the most blessed peace, assurance and favor with God; that with open arms of mercy and pardon the Saviour waits to receive each penitent who will in unfeigned contrition and supplication for mercy, open the door of his heart and accept Him as Lord and King.

Scripture References Where Taught:

If we confess our sins, He is faithful and just to forgive us our sins, and to cleanse us from all unrighteousness. I John 1:9.

Being justified by faith, we have peace with God through our Lord Jesus Christ; by whom also we have access, by faith, into this grace wherein we stand, and rejoice in hope of the glory of God. Rom. 5:1, 2.

There is, therefore, now no condemnation to them which are in Christ Jesus, who walk not after the flesh, but after the spirit. Rom. 8:1.

To give knowledge of salvation unto His people by the remission of their sins, through the tender mercy of our God; whereby the day-spring from on high hath visited us, to give light to them that sit in darkness and in the shadow of death, to guide our feet into the way of peace. Luke 1:77-79.

. . . Him that cometh to me, I will in no wise cast out. John 6:37.

VII. THE NEW BIRTH

We believe that the change which takes place in the heart and life at conversion is a very real one; that the sinner is then born again in such a glorious and transforming manner that old things are passed away and all things are become new; insomuch that the things once most desired are now abhorred, Whilst the things once abhorred are now held most sacred and dear; and that now having had imputed to him the righteousness of the Redeemer and having received of the Spirit of Christ, new desires, new aspirations, new interests, and a new perspective of life, time, and eternity, fills the blood-washed heart so that his desire is now to openly confess and serve the Master, seeking ever those things which are above.

Scripture References Where Taught:

. . . Except a man be born again, he cannot see the kingdom of God. John 3:3.

Therefore, if any man be in Christ, he is a new creature: old things are passed away; behold all things are become new. II Cor. 5:17.

If ye were of the world, the world would love its own; but because ye are not of the world, but I have chosen you out of the world, therefore the world hateth you. John 15:19.

I am crucified with Christ: nevertheless I live; yet not I, but Christ liveth in me; and the life which I now live in the flesh I live by the faith of the Son of God, who loved me, and gave Himself for me. Gal 2:20. Being justified freely by His grace, through the redemption that is in Christ Jesus, whom God hath sent forth to be a propitiation through faith in His blood, to declare His righteousness for the remission of sins that are past, through the forbearance of God. Rom. 3:24, 25.

Blessed is the man that walketh not in the counsel of the ungodly, nor standeth in the way of sinners, nor sitteth in the seat of the scornful. But his delight is in the law of the Lord; and in His law doth he meditate day and night. Ps. 1:1, 2.

VIII. DAILY CHRISTIAN LIFE

We believe that having been cleansed by the precious blood of Jesus Christ and having received the witness of the Holy Spirit at conversion, it is the will of God that we be sanctified daily and become partakers of His holiness; growing constantly stronger in faith, power, prayer, love and service, first as babies desiring the sincere milk of the Word; then as dear children walking humbly, seeking diligently the hidden life, where self decreases and Christ increases; then as strong men having on the whole armour of God marching forth to new conquests in His name beneath His blood-stained banner, ever living a patient, sober, unselfish, godly life that will be a true reflection of the Christ within.

Scripture References Where Taught:

For this is the will of God, even your sanctification. I Thess. 4:3. And the very God of peace sanctify you wholly; and I pray God your whole spirit and soul and body be preserved blameless unto the coming of our Lord Jesus Christ. I Thess. 5:23.

Having therefore these promises, dearly beloved, let us cleanse ourselves from all filthiness of the flesh and spirit, perfecting holiness in the fear of God. II Cor. 7:1.

The path of the just is as the shining light that shineth more and more unto the perfect day. Prov. 4:18.

Therefore, leaving the principles of the doctrine of Christ, let us go on unto perfection. Heb. 6:1.

For they that are after the flesh do mind the things of the flesh; but they that are after the Spirit, the things of the Spirit. Rom. 8:5.

A highway shall be there, and a way, and it shall be called the way of holiness; the unclean shall not pass over it; but it shall be for those: the wayfaring men, though fools, shall not err therein. Isa. 35:8. (Also I Peter 2:2.)

IX. BAPTISM AND THE LORD'S SUPPER

We believe that water baptism in the name of the Father and of the Son and of the Holy Ghost, according to the command of our Lord, is a blessed outward sign of an inward work; a beautiful and solemn emblem reminding us that even as our Lord died upon the cross of Calvary so we reckon ourselves now dead indeed unto sin, and the old nature nailed to the tree with Him; and that even as He was taken down from the tree and buried, so we are buried with Him by baptism into death: that like as Christ was raised up from the dead by the glory of the Father, even so we should walk in newness of life.

We believe in the commemoration and observing of the Lord's supper by the sacred use of the broken bread, a precious type of the Bread of Life even Jesus Christ, whose body was broken for us; and by the juice of the vine, a blessed type which should ever remind the participant of the shed blood of the Saviour who is the true Vine of which His children are the branches; that this ordinance is as a glorious rainbow that spans the gulf of the years between Calvary and the coming of the Lord, when in the Father's kingdom, He will partake anew with His children; and that the serving and receiving of this blessed sacrament should be ever preceded by the most solemn heart-searching, self-examination, forgiveness and love toward all men, that none partake unworthily and drink condemnation to his own soul.

Scripture References Where Taught:

Go ye therefore, and teach all nations, baptizing them in the name of the Father, and of the Son, and of the Holy Ghost. Matt. 28:19. (Also Acts 1:47, 48; Gal. 3:27, 28.)

Therefore, we are buried with Him by baptism into death: that like as Christ was raised up from the dead by the glory of the Father, even so we also should walk in newness of life. Rom. 6:4. (Also Col. 2:12; I Peter 3:20, 21; Acts 22:16.)

Then they that gladly heard His Word were baptized: and the same day there were added unto them about three thousand souls. Acts 2:41. (Also Matt. 28:19, 20.)

For as often as ye eat this bread, and drink this cup, ye do show the Lord's death till He come. I Cor. 11:26. But let a man examine himself, and so let him eat of that bread, and drink of that cup. I Cor. 11:28.

Examine yourselves, whether ye be in the faith; prove your own selves. II Cor. 13:5.

X. THE BAPTISM OF THE HOLY SPIRIT

We believe that the baptism of the Holy Spirit is the incoming of the promised Comforter in mighty and glorious fulness to endure the believer with power from on high; to glorify and exalt the Lord Jesus; to give inspired utterance in witnessing of Him; to foster the spirit of prayer, holiness, sobriety; to equip the individual and the church for practical, efficient, joyous, Spirit-filled soul-winning in the fields of life; and that this being still the dispensation of the Holy Spirit, the believer may have every reason to expect His oncoming to be after the same manner as that in which He came upon Jew and Gentile alike in Bible days, and as recorded in the Word, that it may be truly said of us as of the house of Cornelius: the Holy Ghost fell on them as on us at the beginning.

Scripture References Where Taught:

I will pray the Father, and He shall give you another Comforter, that He may abide with you forever; even the Spirit of truth; whom the world cannot receive, because it seeth Him not, neither knoweth Him; for He dwelleth with you, and shall be in you. John 14:16, 17.

For John truly baptized with water, but ye shall be baptized with the Holy Ghost. . . . Ye shall receive power, after that the Holy Ghost is come upon you: and ye shall be witnesses unto me, both in Jerusalem, and in all Judea, and in Samaria, and unto the uttermost part of the earth. Acts 1:5, 8.

And they were all filled with the Holy Ghost, and began to speak with other tongues, as the Spirit gave them utterance. Acts 2:4.

Then they laid their hands on them, and they received the Holy Ghost. Acts 8:17.

While Peter yet spake these words, the Holy Ghost fell on all them which heard the word. And they of the circumcision which believed were astonished, as many as came with Peter because that on the Gentiles also was poured out the gift of the Holy Ghost. For they heard

DECLARATION OF FAITH (INTERNATIONAL CHURCH OF THE FOURSQUARE GOSPEL) (continued)

them speak with tongues, and magnify God. Acts 10:44-46.

And when Paul had laid his hands upon them, the Holy Ghost came on them; and they spake with tongues, and prophesied. Acts 19:6. Know ye not that ye are the temple of God, and that the Spirit of God dwelleth in you? I Cor. 3:16.

XI. THE SPIRIT-FILLED LIFE

We believe that while the Holy Spirit is as a mighty rushing wind and as tongues of living flame that can shake and set ablaze whole communities for God, He is also as a gentle dove, easily grieved and wounded by impiety, coldness, idle conversation, boastfulness, a judging or criticizing spirit and by thoughts and actions dishonoring to the Lord Jesus; that it is therefore, the will of God that we live and walk in the Spirit, moment by moment, under the precious blood of the Lamb; treading softly as with unshod feet in the presence of the King; being patient, loving, truthful, sincere, prayerful, unmurmuring, instant in season, out of season serving the Lord.

Scripture References Where Taught:

And grieve not the Holy Spirit of God, whereby ye are sealed unto the day of redemption. Let all bitterness, and wrath, and anger, and clamor, and evil speaking, be put away from you, with all malice: and be ye kind one to another, tender-hearted, forgiving one another, even as God for Christ's sake hath forgiven you. Eph. 4:30-32. Praying always with all prayer and supplication in the Spirit and watching thereunto with all perseverance and supplication for all saints. Eph. 6:18.

I beseech you, therefore, brethren, by the mercies of God, that ye present your bodies a living sacrifice, holy, acceptable unto God, which is your reasonable service. And be not conformed to this world: but be ye transformed by the renewing of your mind, that ye may prove what is that good, and acceptable, and perfect, will of God. Rom. 12:1, 2.

He that saith he abideth in Him ought himself also to walk, even as He walked. I John 2:6.

Walk in the Spirit, and ye shall not fulfill the lust of the flesh. If we live in the Spirit, let us also walk in the Spirit. Gal. 5:16, 25.

If any man defile the temple of God, him shall God destroy; for the temple of God is holy, which temple ye are. I Cor. 3:17.

XII. THE GIFTS AND FRUITS OF THE SPIRIT

We believe that the Holy Spirit has the following gifts to bestow upon the believing church of the Lord Jesus Christ: wisdom, knowledge, faith, healing, miracles, prophecy, discernment, tongues, interpretation; that, according to the degree of grace and faith possessed by the recipient, these gifts are divided to every man severally, as He, the Holy Spirit, will; that they are to be most earnestly desired and coveted, in the order and proportion wherein they prove most edifying and beneficial to the church; and that the fruit of the Spirit: love, joy, peace, long-suffering, gent-

leness, goodness, faith, meekness, temperance, should be put forth, cultivated, and diligently guarded as the resultant adornment, the constant, eloquent, and irrefutable evidence of a Spirit-filled life.

Scripture References Where Taught:

Concerning spiritual gifts, brethren, I would not have you ignorant. . . . Covet earnestly the best gifts. I Cor. 12:1, 31. But all these worketh that one and the selfsame Spirit, dividing to every man severally as He will. I Cor. 12:11.

Even so ye, forasmuch as ye are zealous of spiritual gifts, seek that ye may excel to the edifying of the church. I Cor. 14:12. The gifts and calling of God are without repentance. Rom. 11:29.

Having then gifts according to the grace that is given to us, whether prophecy, let us prophesy according to the proportion of faith; or ministry, let us wait upon our ministering: or he that teacheth, on teaching; or he that exhorteth on exhortation; he that giveth, let him do it with simplicity; he that ruleth, with diligence; he that showeth mercy, with cheerfulness. Rom. 12:6-8.

Herein is My Father glorified, that ye bear much fruit; so shall ye be My disciples. John 15:8.

And now also the axe is laid upon the root of the trees: every tree, therefore, which bringeth not forth good fruit is hewn down, and cast into the fire. Luke 3:9.

XIII. MODERATION

We believe that the moderation of the believer should be known of all men; that his experience and daily walk should never lead him into extremes, fanaticisms, unseemly manifestations, back-bitings, murmurings; but that his sober, thoughtful, balanced, mellow, forgiving, and zealous Christian experience should be one of steadfast uprightness, equilibrium, humility, self-sacrifice and Christ-likeness.

Scripture References Where Taught:

Let your moderation be known unto all men. The Lord is at hand. Phil. 4:5.

That we, henceforth, be no more children, tossed to and fro, and carried about with every wind of doctrine. . . . But speaking the truth in love, may grow up into Him in all things, which is the head, even Christ. Eph. 4:14, 15.

Charity doth not behave itself unseemly. I Cor. 13:5.

Put on therefore, as the elect of God, holy and beloved, bowels of mercies, kindness, humbleness of mind, meekness, longsuffering: forbearing one another, and forgiving one another, if any man have a quarrel against any: even as Christ forgave you, so also do ye. Col. 3:12, 13.

XIV. DIVINE HEALING

We believe that divine healing is the power of the Lord Jesus Christ to heal the sick and the afflicted in answer to believing prayer; that He who is the same yesterday, today and forever has never changed but is still an all-sufficient help in the time of trouble, able to meet the needs of, and quicken into newness of life the body, as well as the soul and spirit in answer to the faith of them who ever pray with submission to His divine and sovereign will.

Scripture References Where Taught:

Himself took our infirmities, and bare our sicknesses. Matt. 8:17.

Whether is easier, to say, Thy sins be forgiven thee; or to say, Arise, and walk? Matt. 9:5.

These signs shall follow them that believe; in my name shall they cast out devils; they shall speak with new tongues; they shall take up serpents; and if they drink any deadly thing, it shall not hurt them; they shall lay hands on the sick, and they shall recover. Mark 16:17, 18.

And now, Lord, behold their threatenings; and grant unto Thy servants, that with all boldness they shall speak Thy Word, by stretching forth Thine hand to heal; that signs and wonders may be done by the name of Thy holy child Jesus. Acts 4:29, 30.

Is any sick among you? Let him call for the elders of the church: and let them pray over him, anointing him with oil in the name of the Lord and the prayer of faith shall save the sick, and the Lord shall raise him up; and if he have committed sins, they shall be forgiven him. Confess your faults one to another, and pray one for another, that ye may be healed. James 5:14-16.

XV. THE SECOND COMING OF CHRIST

We believe that the second coming of Christ is personal and imminent; that He will descend from Heaven in the clouds of glory with the voice of the archangel and with the trump of God; and that at this hour, which no man knoweth beforehand, the dead in Christ shall rise, then the redeemed that are alive and remain shall be caught up together with them in the clouds, to meet the Lord in the air, and that so shall they ever be with the Lord; that also seeing that a thousand years is as a day with the Lord, and that no man knoweth the hour of His appearance, which we believe to be near at hand, each day should be lived as though He were expected to appear at even, yet that in obedience to His explicit command, "Occupy till I come," the work of spreading the gospel, the sending forth of missionaries, and the general duties for the upbuilding of the church should be carried on as diligently, and thoroughly, as though neither ours nor the next generation should live in the flesh to see that glorious day.

Scripture References Where Taught:

For the Lord Himself shall descend from heaven with a shout, with the voice of the archangel, and with the trump of God: and the dead in Christ shall rise first: then we which are alive and remain shall be caught up together with them in the clouds, to meet the Lord in the air: and so shall we ever be with the Lord. I Thess. 4:16, 17.

. . . Denying ungodliness and worldly lusts we should live soberly, righteously, and godly, in this present world; looking for that blessed hope, and the glorious appearing of the great God and our Saviour Jesus Christ. Titus 2:12, 13.

But of that day and hour knoweth no man, no, not the angels of heaven, but my Father only. Watch, therefore: for ye know not what hour your Lord doth come.

Therefore, be ye also ready: for in such an hour as ye think not, the Son of man cometh. Matt. 24:36, 42, 44.

Christ was once offered to bear the sins of many; and unto them that look for Him shall He appear the second time without sin unto salvation. Heb. 9:28.

. . . Occupy till I come. Luke 19:13.

Let your loins be girded about, and your lights burning, and ye yourselves like unto men that wait for their Lord . . . that when He cometh and knocketh, they may open unto Him immediately. Blessed are those servants, whom the Lord when He cometh shall find watching: verily, I say unto you, that He shall gird Himself, and make them to sit down to meat, and will come forth and serve them. Luke 12:35-37.

XVI. CHURCH RELATIONSHIP

We believe that having accepted the Lord Jesus Christ as personal Saviour and King, and having thus been born into the family and invisible body or church of the Lord, it is the sacred duty of the believer, whenever this lieth within his power, to identify himself with, and labor most earnestly for the upbuilding of God's kingdom with the visible church of Christ upon earth; and that such visible church is a congregation of believers, who have associated themselves together in Christian fellowship and in the unity of the Spirit, observing the ordinances of Christ, worshipping Him in the beauty of holiness, speaking to each other in psalms, and hymns and spiritual songs, reading and proclaiming His Word, laboring for the salvation of souls, giving of their temporal means to carry on His work, edifying, encouraging, establishing one another in the most holy faith, and working harmoniously together as dear children who are many members but one body of which Christ is the head.

Scripture References Where Taught:

I will praise the Lord with my whole heart, in the assembly of the upright, and in the congregation. Ps. 111:1.

Let us consider one another to provoke unto love and to good works: not forsaking the assembling of ourselves together, as the manner of some is; but exhorting one another: and so much the more, as ye see the day approaching. Heb. 10:24, 25.

. . . And the Lord added to the church daily such as should be saved. Acts 2:47. And so were the churches established in the faith, and increased in numbers daily. Acts 16:5.

So we, being many, are one body in Christ, and every one members one of another. Rom. 12:5. (Also see Rom. 12:6, 7, 8.)

Then they that feared the Lord spake often one to another; and the Lord hearkened, and heard it, and a book of remembrance was written before him for them that feared the Lord, and that thought upon His name. And they shall be mine, saith the Lord of hosts, in that day when I shall make up my jewels; and I shall spare them, as a man spareth his own son that serveth him. Mal. 3:16, 17.

XVII. CIVIL GOVERNMENT

We believe that civil government is of divine appointment, for the interest and good order of human society; and that

DECLARATION OF FAITH (INTERNATIONAL CHURCH OF THE FOURSQUARE GOSPEL) (continued)

governors and rulers should be prayed for, obeyed, and upheld, at all times except only in things opposed to the will of our Lord Jesus Christ, who is the ruler of conscience of His people, the King of Kings, and the Lord of Lords.

Scripture References Where Taught:

. . . The powers that be are ordained of God. . . . For rulers are not a terror to good works, but to the evil. Rom. 13:1, 3. (Also Deut. 16:18; II Sam. 23:3; Ex. 18:21-23; Jer. 30:21.)

. . . We ought to obey God rather than man. Acts 5:29. Fear not them which kill the body, but are not able to kill the soul. Matt. 10:28. (Also Dan. 3:15-18; 6:7-10; Acts 4:18-20.)

. . . One is your Master, even Christ. Matt. 23:10.

And He hath on His vesture and on His thigh a name written, KING OF KINGS, AND LORD OF LORDS. Rev. 19:16. (Also Ps. 72:11; Rom. 14:9-13.)

XVIII. THE FINAL JUDGMENT

We believe that the death both small and great shall be raised up and stand with the living before the judgment seat of God; and that when a solemn and awful separation shall take place wherein the wicked shall be adjudged to everlasting punishment and the righteous to life eternal; and that this judgment will fix forever the final state of men in heaven or in hell on principles of righteousness as set forth in his holy Word.

Scripture References Where Taught:

For we must all appear before the judgment seat of Christ; that every one may receive the things done in his body, according to that he hath done, whether it be good or bad. II Cor. 5:10.

The Son of man shall send forth His angels, and they shall gather out of His kingdom all things that offend, and them which do iniquity; and shall cast them into a furnace of fire: there shall be wailing and gnashing of teeth. Then shall the righteous shine forth as the sun in the kingdom of their Father. Who hath ears to hear, let him hear. Matt. 13:41-43.

XIX. HEAVEN

We believe that Heaven is the indescribably glorious habitation of the living God; and that thither the Lord has gone to prepare a place for His children; that unto this four-square city, whose builder and maker is God, the earnest believers who have washed their robes in the blood of the Lamb and have overcome by the word of their testimony will be carried; that the Lord Jesus Christ will present them to the Father without spot or wrinkle; and that there in unutterable joy they will ever behold His wonderful face, in an everlasting kingdom whereunto comes no darkness nor light, neither sorrow, tears, pain nor death, and wherein hosts of attending angels sweep their harps, sing the praise of our King, and bowing down before the throne, cry: "Holy, holy, holy."

Scripture References Where Taught:

Eye hath not seen nor ear heard, neither have entered into the heart of man, the things which God hath prepared for them that love Him. I Cor. 2:9.

In My Father's house are many mansions; if it were not so I would have told you. I go to prepare a place for you. John 14:2.

And there shall be no night there; and they need no candle, neither light of the sun; for the Lord God giveth them light: and they shall reign forever and ever. Rev. 22:5.

And God shall wipe away all tears from their eyes; and there shall be no more death, neither sorrow, nor crying, neither shall there be any more pain; for the former things are passed away. Rev. 21:4.

Therefore are they before the throne of God, and serve Him day and night in His temple: and He that sitteth on the throne shall dwell among them. They shall hunger no more; neither thirst any more; neither shall the sun light upon them, nor any heat. For the Lamb, which is in the midst of the throne, shall feed them, and shall lead them unto living fountains of water. Rev. 7:15-17.

XX. HELL

We believe that hell is a place of outer darkness and deepest sorrow, where the worm dieth not and the fire is not quenched; a place prepared for the devil and his angels where there shall be weeping and wailing and gnashing of teeth, a place of grief and eternal regret on the part of them who have rejected the mercy, love and tenderness of the crucified Saviour, choosing death rather than life; and that there into a lake that burns with fire and brimstone shall be cast the unbelieving, the abominable, the murderers, sorcerers, idolaters, all liars, and they who have rejected and spurned the love and sacrifice of a bleeding Redeemer,—passing the cross to their doom, in spite of every entreaty and warning of the Holy Spirit.

Scripture References Where Taught:

The Son of man shall send forth His angels, and they shall gather out of His kingdom all things that offend, and them which do iniquity; and shall cast them into a furnace of fire: there shall be wailing and gnashing of teeth. Matt. 13:41, 42.

And the devil that deceived them was cast into the lake of fire and brimstone, where the beast and the false prophet are, and shall be tormented day and night forever and ever. And whosoever was not found written in the book of life was cast into the lake of fire. Rev. 20:10, 15.

The same shall drink of the wrath of God, which is poured out without mixture into the cup of his indignation; and he shall be tormented with fire and brimstone in the presence of the holy angels, and in the presence of the Lamb; and the smoke of their torment ascendeth up forever and ever. Rev. 14:10, 11.

Then shall He say unto them . . . Depart from me, ye cursed, into everlasting fire, prepared for the devil and his angels. Matt. 25:41. And if thy hand offend thee, cut it off: it is better for thee to enter into life maimed, than having two hands to go into hell, into the fire that never shall be quenched: where their worm dieth not and the fire is not quenched. Mark 9:43, 44.

. . . As I live, saith the Lord God, I have no pleasure in the death of the wicked; but that the wicked turn from his way and live; turn ye, turn ye from your evil ways; for why will ye die, O house of Israel? Ezek. 33:11.

XXI. EVANGELISM

We believe that seeing then that all these things shall be dissolved, and that the end of all things is at hand, the redeemed children of the Lord Jehovah should rise and shine forth as a light that cannot be hid, a city set upon a hill, speeding forth the gospel to the ends of the earth, girding the globe with the message of salvation, declaring with burning zeal and earnestness the whole council of God; that when the Lord of Glory shall appear, they shall be found standing, with their loins girded about with truth, their activities and ministry laden down with the wealth of jewels they have won and guarded for Him, the precious souls, whom, by their faithful testimony they have been instrumental in leading from darkness into light; that soul winning is the one big business of the church upon earth; and that therefore every weight and hindrance which would tend to quench the flame or hamper the efficiency of world-wide evangelism should be cut off and cast away as unworthy of the church, detrimental to the most sacred cause of Christ and contrary to the great commission by our Lord.

Scripture References Where Taught:

I charge thee therefore before God, and the Lord Jesus Christ, who shall judge the quick and the dead at His appearing and His kingdom; preach the word; be instant in season, out of season; reprove, rebuke, exhort with all longsuffering and doctrine. II Tim. 4:1, 2.

Redeeming the time, because the days are evil. Eph. 5:16.

. . . He that winneth souls is wise. Prov. 11:30.

Let him know, that he which converteth the sinner from the error of his way shall save a soul from death, and shall hide a multitude of sins. James 5:20.

Son of man I have made thee a watchman unto the house of Israel; therefore hear the word at my mouth, and give them warning from me. When I say unto the wicked, Thou shalt surely die; and thou givest him not warning, nor speakest to warn the wicked from his wicked way, to save his life; the same wicked man shall die in his iniquity; but his blood will I require at thine hand. Ezek. 3:17, 18.

. . . Lift up your eyes, and look on the fields; for they are white, already to harvest. And he that reapeth receiveth wages, and gathereth fruit unto life eternal; that both he that soweth and he that reapeth may rejoice together. And herein is that saying true, One soweth and another reapeth. John 4:35-37.

Pray ye therefore the Lord of the harvest, that he will send forth labourers into His harvest. Matt. 9:38.

. . . Go ye into all the world, and preach the Gospel to every creature. Mark 16:15.

XXII. TITHING AND OFFERINGS

We believe that the method ordained of God to sustain His ministry and the spread of the gospel after His command is "Tithing" and is generally accepted throughout all Foursquare Churches, not only as God's method to take care of the material and financial needs of His church, but to raise the spiritual morale of His people to the extent that God must bless them. We are commanded in Malachi 3:10 to "Bring ye all the tithes into the storehouse, that there may be meat in mine house, and prove me now herewith, saith the Lord of hosts, if I will not open you the windows of heaven, and pour you out a blessing that there shall not be room enough to receive it."

In the matter of "giving" and "free-will offerings," they are ordered of the Lord and practiced in all Foursquare Churches as part of God's plan for the church's material needs and the spirituality of His people. We are admonished in Luke 6:38, "Give, and it shall be given unto you; good measure, pressed down, and shaken together, and running over, shall men give into your bosom, for with the same measure that ye mete withal it shall be measured to you again."

Being "joint heirs" with Him we know that giving unto His kingdom which is also ours is an enjoyable thing, it being more blessed to give than to receive, for we are commanded in II Corinthians 9:7, "Every man according as he purposeth in his heart, so let him give; not grudgingly, or of a necessity: for the Lord loveth a cheerful giver."

Notes: *This lengthy statement (one of the most detailed by any pentecostal church) was compiled by Aimee Semple McPherson, the founder of the church. It roughly follows the outline of the statement of the Assemblies of God, but covers a variety of additional issues. The church is not specifically premillennial in its eschatology.*

*　　　*　　　*

ARTICLES OF FAITH (OPEN BIBLE STANDARD CHURCHES, INC.)

A. THE BIBLE. We believe the Bible to be the inspired word of God, and accept the same as the only infallible guide and rule of our faith and practice.

Scripture References: Matt. 24:35; Psa. 119:89; II Tim. 3:16-17; II Tim. 2:15; II Pet. 1:19-21.

B. GOD. We believe in the eternal omnipotent, omniscient, omnipresent, and immutable triune God; maker of heaven and earth, and all that in them is; and in the unity of the Godhead there are three persons, equal in every divine perfection and attribute, executing distinct, but harmonious offices, in the great work of redemption.

Scripture References: I John 5:7; II Cor. 13:14; Gen. 1:26; I Tim. 1:17.

GOD THE FATHER. Isa. 43:10; Isa. 44:8; John 3:16.

GOD THE SON. Coexistent and coeternal with the Father, who, conceived by the Holy Spirit, and born of the Virgin Mary, took upon himself the form of man: and by His becoming obedient unto death, bearing the curse of sin, sickness and sorrow, redeemed us back to God. He arose the

ARTICLES OF FAITH (OPEN BIBLE STANDARD CHURCHES, INC.) (continued)

third day and ascended unto heaven, where He sits on the right hand of God, the father, where He lives to make intercession for us.

Scripture References: John 1:1-3; Matt. 1:23; I Tim. 2:5; Eph. 2:18; Phil. 2:6-11.

GOD THE HOLY SPIRIT. The third person of the Godhead, coexistent and equal with the Father. Sent by the Father, through the Son, to reprove the world of sin and prepare the bride of Christ.

Scripture References: John 14:26; John 15:26; John 16:8.

C. THE FALL OF MAN. Scripture References: Gen. 1:27; Rom. 5:12; Rom. 5:19; Isa. 53:6; Rom. 3:10; Rom. 3:23.

D. THE PLAN OF REDEMPTION. We believe that Christ was the Lamb of God, foreordained from the foundation of the world, and by the shedding of His blood, on the cross, made provision for salvation for ALL men.

Scripture References: I Pet 1:19-20; Isa. 53:5; Titus 2:14; Heb. 7:25.

E. THE NEW BIRTH. We believe that because of man's total inability to save himself, salvation is by God's grace alone; is received through sincere godly repentance, and a wholehearted acceptance of Jesus Christ as his personal Saviour; through being born again, he becomes a new creature in Christ Jesus. Old things have passed away, behold all things have become new.

Scripture References: John 3:3; II Cor. 5:17; Gal. 2:20; I Pet. 2:24.

F. DAILY CHRISTIAN LIFE. We believe that having been cleansed by the blood, and quickened by the Spirit, it is God's will that we should be sanctified daily, and be made partakers of His holiness; walking not after the flesh but after the Spirit; forsaking the very appearance of evil, such as wordly dress, worldly amusements, worldly conversation, worldly habits, etc.

Scripture References: Rom. 8:1; Rom. 8:5; Rom. 12:1-2; II Cor. 7:1; I Pet. 1:15; I Thess. 5:22.

G. MARRIAGE AND DIVORCE. Knowing that marriage was instituted by God; sanctioned by the Lord Jesus Christ, and was commended of Saint Paul to be honorable among all men, we believe that a Christian man or woman should not marry an unsaved person. Having been united by God in holy matrimony, neither person, as long as both shall live, shall be free to remarry, "Except it be for fornication" (Matt. 19:9).

Scripture References: II Cor. 6:15; Matt. 19:5-6; Luke 16:18; Heb. 13:4.

H. WATER BAPTISM. We believe that water baptism by immersion, in the name of the Father, Son and the Holy Ghost, is commanded by God; that it is subsequent to conversion, that it is not a saving ordinance, but an outward sign of an inward work.

Scripture References: Matt. 28:19; Rom. 6:4; Acts 2:38.

1. THE LORD'S SUPPER. We believe in the commemoration of the Lord's Supper as a type of the broken body and shed blood of our Lord Jesus Christ, and as an ordinance showing forth the death, burial and resurrection of our Lord, and a looking forward to the marriage supper of the Lamb. We believe that all Christian believers, regardless of church affiliation, may partake of the Lord's Supper.

Scripture References: I Cor. 11:23-28; II Cor. 13:5; Luke 22:7-22.

J. BAPTISM OF THE HOLY SPIRIT. We believe the baptism of the Holy Spirit is a definite experience, not identical with conversion. The initial evidence of this experience is the speaking in other tongues as the Spirit gives utterance. The baptism of the Holy Spirit is given to endue the believer with power from on high; to give inspired utterance in witnessing for Christ; to lead the believer into holiness and sobriety; to equip him for a practical, efficient, spiritfilled soul winning ministry and service; that inasmuch as this is the dispensation of the Holy Spirit, every believer has a right to expect His incoming to be after the same manner as recorded by the Word of God in Bible days.

Scripture References: John 14:16; Acts 1:8, 2:4, 2:38-39, 19:6; I Cor. 3:16.

K. SPIRIT FILLED LIFE. We believe that having received the initial filling, the baptism of the Holy Spirit, the believer should experience a continual renewing of the power from on high; that the Holy Spirit is as a gentle dove, easily grieved and wounded by coldness, prayerlessness, idle conversation, worldliness, and a judging and criticizing spirit; therefore, it is the will of God that we walk and abide in the Spirit.

Scripture References: Eph. 5:18; Acts 4:31; Eph. 4:30-32; I Cor. 3:17; Gal. 5:16-25; I John 2:6.

L. GIFTS AND FRUIT OF THE SPIRIT. We believe that for the edification of the saints and the upbuilding of the church of Jesus Christ, the Holy Spirit has the following gifts to bestow upon the individual believer: the word of wisdom, the word of knowledge, faith, gifts of healing, working of miracles, prophecy, discerning of spirits, and divers kinds of tongues, and the interpretation of tongues, dividing to every man severally as He will; that they should be coveted earnestly by all spiritual believers and exercised in the spirit of love. We believe that the fruit of the Spirit is love, joy, peace, longsuffering, gentleness, goodness, faith, meekness, temperance; against such there is no law. These should be cultivated in the life of every believer.

Scripture References: I Cor. 12:7-11; I Cor. 12:31; Gal. 5:22-23; John 15:4; John 15:8.

M. MODERATION. We believe that our moderation should be known to all men. The Christian should be sober, well balanced, and seasoned with love. His zeal should be governed by godly wisdom.

Scripture References: Phil. 4:5; Eph. 4:14-15; I Cor. 13:5; Col. 3:12-13.

N. DIVINE HEALING. We believe that divine healing is the power of God to heal the sick and afflicted in answer to believing prayer, and is provided for in the atonement. We believe that God is willing to, and does, heal the sick today.

Scripture References: Isa. 53:4-5; Matt. 8:16-17; James 5:14-16; Acts 3:16.

O. SECOND COMING OF CHRIST.

(1) RAPTURE. We believe that the second coming of Christ is personal, imminent and premillennial; that the Lord Himself will descend from heaven with a shout, with the voice of the archangel, with the trump of God, and the dead in Christ shall rise first. Then the redeemed which are alive and remain, shall be caught up together with them in the clouds to meet the Lord in the air, and so shall they ever be with the Lord: that we should, therefore, be ready, for in such an hour as we think not, the Son of Man will come.

Scripture References: I Thess. 4:16-17; Titus 2:12-13; Matt. 24:36; 24:44; Acts 1:11.

(2) REVELATION. We believe that the coming of Jesus Christ with His saints will end the great tribulation, and establish the millennial kingdom on earth, when Christ shall rule and reign as King of kings and Lord of lords.

Scripture References: Rev. 1:7; Zech. 14:4; II Thess. 1:7-10, 2:8.

P. CHURCH RELATIONSHIP. We believe that every born again child of God should identify himself with the visible church of Jesus Christ, and should labor diligently, and contribute his temporal means toward the spreading of the gospel here on earth. We believe that all the tithes should be given into the storehouse of the Lord, which is the local church.

Scripture References: Heb. 10:24-25; Ps. 111:1; Acts 2:47, 16:5; Rom. 12:5; Mal. 3:8-10; II Cor. 9:6-7; I Cor. 16:2.

Q. CIVIL GOVERNMENT. We believe that government is ordained of God, and all Christians should be subject to the laws of the land, except those contrary to the revealed will of God. We pledge allegiance and moral and spiritual support of the United States of America. In times of war the individual's participation in actual combat and taking of life shall be governed by his own conscience.

Scripture References: Rom. 13:1-7; Acts 5:29; Matt. 5:39-48; Heb. 12:14.

R. FINAL JUDGMENT. We believe in the final judgment of the wicked at the great white throne, when the dead, both small and great, shall be resurrected to stand before God to receive the reward of their deeds done in the flesh.

Scripture References: Matt. 13:41-43; Rev. 20:11-15.

S. HELL. We believe hell is a literal place of outer darkness, bitter sorrow, remorse, and woe, prepared by God for the devil and his angels and that there, into a lake that burns with fire and brimstone, shall be cast the unbelieving, the abominable, the murderers, sorcerers, idolators, and all liars, and those who have rejected the love of Jesus Christ, whose names are not written in the Lamb's book of life.

Scripture References: Rev. 20:10, 14-15; Rev. 21:7-8; Rev. 14:10-11; Matt. 25:41; Mark 9:43-44.

T. HEAVEN. We believe that heaven is the habitation of the living God, where Christ has gone to prepare a place for all His children, where they shall dwell eternally in happiness and security with Him.

Scripture References: I Cor. 2:9; John 14:2; Rev. 21:4; Rev. 22:5; Rev. 7:15-17.

U. EVANGELISM. We believe that as long as conditions indicate that the coming of Jesus Christ draws near, we, His redeemed children, should put forth our utmost efforts to the promulgation of the gospel to every kindred, tribe, and tongue; that soul winning is the chief mission of the church upon the earth, and that therefore every hindrance and hairsplitting doctrine, which would tend to quench or dampen the flame of worldwide evangelism, should be cut off and cast away as falling short of the church's great commission.

Scripture References: II Tim. 4:1-2; Eph. 5:16; Prov. 11:30; Ezek. 3:17-18; John 4:35-37.

V. MISSIONS. We believe that the great commission of our Lord Jesus Christ to carry the gospel message to the entire world is literal, imperative, and binding today; and that it is the supreme privilege and duty of the church of Jesus Christ to stress the cause of worldwide missions. Furthermore, we believe that the very life and strength of the home church depends on its wholehearted sacrifice for, and support of, the world missions program.

Scripture References: Matt. 9:38; Mark 16:15; Rev. 5:9; Rom. 10:13-15; James 5:20; Ps. 2:8.

Notes: *These articles to a large extent follow the text of the Declaration of Faith of the International Church of the Foursquare Gospel. They differ in being specifically premillennial in eschatology and deleting any statement on tithing.*

* * *

STATEMENT OF FAITH (PENTECOSTAL CHURCH OF GOD)

WE BELIEVE . . .

1. In the verbal inspiration of the Scriptures, both the Old and New Testaments.

2. Our God is a trinity in unity, manifested in three persons: the Father, the Son, and the Holy Ghost.

3. In the deity of our Lord Jesus Christ, in His virgin birth, in His sinless life, in His miracles, in His vicarious and atoning death on the cross, in His bodily resurrection, in His ascension to the right hand of the Father, and in His personal return in power and glory.

4. That regeneration by the Holy Ghost for the salvation of lost and sinful man, through faith in the shed blood of Jesus Christ, is absolutely essential.

5. In a life of holiness, without which no man can see the Lord, through sanctification as a definite, yet progressive, work of grace.

6. In the Baptism of the Holy Ghost, received subsequent to the new birth, with the speaking in other tongues, as the Spirit gives utterance, as the initial physical sign and evidence.

7. In water baptism by immersion for believers only, which is a direct commandment of our Lord, in the Name of the Father, and of the Son, and of the Holy Ghost.

8. In the Lord's supper and washing of the saints' feet.

9. That divine healing is provided for in the atonement, and is available to all who truly believe.

10. In the premillennial second coming of Jesus: first, to resurrect the righteous dead and to catch away the living saints to meet Him in the air; and, second, to reign on the earth a thousand years.

11. In the bodily resurrection of both the saved and the lost: they that are saved unto the resurrection of life, and they that are lost unto the resurrection of damnation.

Notes: *The Penecostal Church of God teaches a premillennial eschatology and practices foot washing.*

*   *   *

ARTICLES OF RELIGION (PENTECOSTAL CHURCH OF ZION)

ARTICLE 1. THE BIBLE

The Holy Bible, including the divisions commonly known as the Old and New Testament, is the divinely inspired Word of God. No other writing is so inspired. The Bible is infallible in teaching and containeth all things necessary to salvation: so that whatsoever is not read therein, nor may be proved thereby, is not required of any man, that it should be believed as an article of faith, or thought requisite or necessary to salvation. The Bible thus contains the complete will and revelation of God to man.

II Peter 1:20, 21. Knowing this first, that no prophesy of the scripture is of any private interpretation. For the prophesy of the scripture came not in old time by the will of man; but holy men of God spake as they were moved by the Holy Ghost.

II Timothy 3:16, 17. All scripture is given by inspiration of God, and is profitable for doctrine, for reproof for correction, for instruction in righteousness: That the man of God may be perfect, thoroughly furnished unto all good works.

Isaiah 45:23; Hebrews 4:12; Matthew 24:35.

ARTICLE 2. GOD

The supreme Deity of the universe is God. He is the Almighty Creator and Sustainer of the heaven, the earth, and all things therein. The doctrine of evolution is not scriptural.

Genesis 1:1. In the beginning God created the heaven and the earth. Acts 17:24-28, Acts 14:15, Psalms 124:8; Revelation 14:7.

ARTICLE 3. JESUS

Jesus of Nazareth is the only begotten Son of God, conceived of the Holy Ghost and born of the Holy Virgin Mary. He is the Christ, Messiah, Saviour and Redeemer. He was God manifested in the flesh. Outside of Jesus Christ, God has no body.

I Timothy 3:16. And without controversy great is the mystery of godliness: God was manifested in the flesh, justified in the Spirit, seen of angels, preached unto the Gentiles, believed on in the world, received up into glory.

Col. 2:9. For in him dwelleth all the fullness of the Godhead bodily. Matthew 1:18-25; Isaiah 9:6; 7:14; John 10:30.

ARTICLE 4. HOLY GHOST

The Holy Ghost (Holy Spirit) is the Comforter promised by our Lord, who will abide in the hearts of those who diligently seek Him. He will guide us into all Godly truths and give us power. Speaking in other tongues as the spirit of God giveth utterance is the initial evidence of the presence of the Holy Ghost, however the Holy Ghost must also be manifest both in word and by the "Fruits of the Spirit" and keeping the commandments of God.

Acts 2:4. And they were all filled with the Holy Ghost and began to speak with other tongues, as the Spirit gave them utterance. Acts 1:8; John 14:15-19, 26; Romans 5:5; John 16:13; I Cor. 12:7-11; Gal. 5: 22-26.

ARTICLE 5. THE BLOOD OF CHRIST

The condition of man after the fall of Adam is such that he cannot turn and prepare himself by his own natural strength and works, for eternal life. The blood of Christ was shed on the cross to redeem man from sin. I John 1:7. But if we walk in the light, as He is in the light, we have fellowship one with another, and the blood of Jesus Christ his Son cleanseth us from all sin. I Peter 1:18-19; Matthew 26:28; Rev. 5:9.

ARTICLE 6. ACCEPTING CHRIST

To secure the benefits of the Plan of Salvation, each individual must believe on the Lord Jesus Christ, repent and turn from sin, and accept Him as his personal Saviour; be baptised in the name of the Lord Jesus Christ; by immersion in water; and receive the Holy Ghost with the evidence of speaking in other tongues as did the early church on the day of pentecost.

Romans 10:9-10. That if thou shalt confess with thy mouth the Lord Jesus, and shalt believe in thine heart that God hath raised Him from the dead, thou shall be saved. For with the heart man believeth unto righteousness; and with the mouth confession is made unto salvation.

Acts 4:12. Neither is there salvation in any other; for there is none other name under heaven given among men whereby we must be saved.

Acts 2:38. Then Peter said unto them, Repent, and be baptised every one of you in the name of Jesus Christ for remission of sins, and ye shall receive the gift of the Holy Ghost.

Romans 6:4. Therefore we are buried with him by baptism into death: that like as Christ was raised up from the dead by the Glory of the Father, even so we also should walk in newness of life.

John 3:5. Jesus answered, Verily, verily, I say unto thee, except a man be born of water and of the Spirit, he cannot enter into the Kingdom of God. I John 3:4; Matthew 3:13-17; Acts 10:43-48.

ARTICLE 7. CONCERNING BACKSLIDING

It is possible for a man to sin and lose his status with God in any phase of his experience. If this should happen and said person repent and confess such sin and make restitution where possible and necessary, the Lord will forgive them and so will the church.

Jeremiah 3:14. Turn, O backsliding children, saith the Lord; for I am married unto you: and I will take you one of a city, and two of a family, and I will bring you to Zion.

Galatians 6:1. Brethren, if a man be overtaken in a fault, ye which are spiritual, restore such an one in the spirit of meekness; considering thyself, lest thou also be tempted. Matthew 18:12; Jer. 50:6.

ARTICLE 8. THE TEN COMMANDMENTS

1. "Thou shalt have no other Gods before me."

   This commandment teaches we should give all our love and honor to God and worship only Him.

2. "Thou shalt not make unto thee any graven image, or any likeness of anything that is in heaven above, or that is in the earth beneath, or that is in the water under the earth; thou shalt not bow down thyself to them, nor serve them; for I the Lord thy God am a jealous God, visiting the iniquity of the fathers upon the children unto the third and fourth generation of them that hate me; and showing mercy unto thousands of them that love me and keep my commandments."

   This commandment teaches us that if we worship graven images and idols, not only we, but our descendents will have to pay for it.

3. "Thou shalt not take the name of the Lord thy God in vain; for the Lord will not hold him guiltless that taketh his name in vain."

   This commandment teaches us that we should not take the name of God upon our lips lightly, or in blasphemy or profanity; or in vain oaths and curses; but only in reverence are we to name God.

4. "Remember the Sabbath day, to keep it holy. Six days shalt thou labor and do all thy work; but the seventh day is the sabbath of the Lord thy God; in it thou shalt not do any work, thou, nor thy son, nor thy daughter, thy manservant, nor thy maidservant, nor thy cattle, nor thy stranger that is within thy gates; for in six days the Lord made heaven and earth, the sea, and all that in them is, and rested the seventh day: wherefore the Lord blessed the sabbath day, and hallowed it."

   This commandment teaches us to do our earthly and natural work in the first six days of the week, and to refrain from all labor on the seventh day (Saturday) and set this day aside for rest and worship to God. Christ taught that it is lawful to do good such as healing the sick, or helping the ox out of the ditch on the Sabbath. The Sabbath begins on Friday at sunset and ends at Saturday at sunset. We should impose no labor on those in our employment or under our control on the Sabbath.

5. "Honor thy father and mother, that thy days may be long upon the land which the Lord thy God giveth thee."

   This commandment teaches us that a child is to respect and obey their parents, and that God regards the reverent and dutiful child with special favor.

6. "Thou shalt not kill."

   This commandment teaches us that we should regard human life as sacred and that we should refrain from every act that needlessly endangers the life or physical well being of ourself and our fellowmen. Jesus taught that hating anyone violates this commandment also.

7. "Thou shalt not commit adultery."

   This commandment teaches us to respect the divine institution of marriage; to maintain the sanctity of the home; and to be chaste, pure, and modest in all our behavior and speech. Jesus also stated, "But I say unto you that whosoever looketh upon a woman to lust after her hath committed adultery with her already in his heart." Matthew 5:27-28.

   Concerning divorce Jesus said, "It hath been said Whosoever shall put away his wife, let him give her a writing of divorcement. But I say unto you that whosoever shall put away his wife, saving for the cause of fornication, causeth her to commit adultery: and whosoever shall marry her that is divorced committeth adultery." Matthew 5:31-32.

8. "Thou shalt not steal."

   This commandment teaches us never to take anything that belongs to another; to be honest in all things; and never to deprive anyone of his property or of his rights therein by force or fraud.

9. "Thou shalt not bear false witness against thy neighbor."

   This commandment teaches us to avoid deceit, slander, or falsehood and to rule our tongues always by law of truth and love.

10. "Thou shalt not covet thy neighbor's house, thou shalt not covet thy neighbor's wife, nor his manser-

vant, nor his maidservant, nor his ox, nor his ass, nor anything that is thy neighbors."

This commandment teaches us that we should not envy our neighbor, his property, or his possessions, or desire to deprive him of that which is rightfully his.

ARTICLE 9. CHURCH ORGANIZATION

Salvation is through faith in Christ, but for the purpose of cooperation in the proclamation of the Gospel, and the upholding of true Bible standards and doctrines, and for the fellowship of the saints, the church should be organized in accordance with the Bible plan. Acts 6:1-8, Acts 1:23-26, I Cor. 12:27-30, Eph. 2:19-20, Eph. 4:10-17, I Tim. 5:17, I Tim. 3:1-5, Heb. 13:7-17.

ARTICLE 10. TITHES AND OFFERINGS

The Bible plan of financial support for the Gospel work is the paying of the tithes and offering by the members of the church. The tithe is one-tenth part of the increase, and should be paid as a part of the Christian obligation. Offerings are also a part of the Christian obligation to the Lord, and should be given liberally as one is prospered of Him.

Mal. 3:8-10. Will a man rob God? Yet ye have robbed me. But they say, wherein have we robbed thee? In tithes and offering. Ye are cursed with a curse: for ye have robbed me, even this whole nation. Bring ye all the tithes into the storehouse, that there may be meat in mine house, and prove me now herewith, saith the Lord of hosts, if I will not open you the windows of heaven, and pour you out a blessing, that there shall not be room enough to receive it. Matt 23:23, I Cor. 9:13-14, Lev. 27:30.

ARTICLE 11. LAW OF CLEAN AND UNCLEAN

The people of God and the followers of Christ in this age are to use for food those things which were given by God for that purpose, as distinguished from those things designated as unclean for human use.

Lev. 11:1-46. And the Lord spoke unto Moses and to Aaron, saying unto them, Speak unto the children of Israel, saying these are the beasts which ye shall eat among all the beasts that are on the earth. Whatsoever parteth the hoof, and is clovenfooted, and cheweth the cud, among the beasts, that shall ye eat.

Nevertheless these shall ye not eat of them that chew the cud, or of them that divide the hoof: as the camel, because he cheweth the cud, but divideth not the hoof; he is unclean to you. And the coney, because he cheweth the cud, but divideth not the hoof; he is unclean to you. And the hare, because he cheweth the cud, but divideth not the hoof; he is unclean to you.

And the swine, though he divide the hoof, and be clovenfooted, yet he cheweth not the cud; he is unclean to you. Of their flesh shall ye not eat; and their carcase shall ye not touch; they are unclean to you.

These shall ye eat of all that are in the waters; whatsoever hath fins and scales in the waters, in the seas, and in the rivers, them shall ye eat. And all that have not fins and scales in the seas, and in the rivers, of all that move in the waters, and of any living thing which is in the waters, they shall be an abomination unto you:

They shall be even an abomination unto you; ye shall not eat of their flesh, but ye shall have their carcases in abomination. Whatsoever hath no fins nor scales in the waters, that shall be an abomination unto you.

And these are they which ye shall have in abomination among the fowls; they shall not be eaten, they are an abomination: the eagle, and the ossifrage, and the ospray, and the vulture, and the kite after his kind; Every raven after his kind, and the owl, and the night hawk, and the cuckow, and the hawk after his kind, and the little owl, and the cormat, and the great owl, and the swan, and the pelican, and the gier eagle, and the stork, and heron after her kind, and the lapwing, and the bat. All fowls that creep, going upon all four, shall be an abomination unto you. (Read the next verses of the chapter paying special attention to the last five verses.) I Tim. 4:5, Isa. 65:15-17, Deut. 3:21.

ARTICLE 12. UNCLEAN HABITS

The body is the temple of the Holy Ghost, and God's people should be clean, refraining from any practice which would defile their bodies physically or spiritually. Therefore, the smoking, chewing or snuffing of tobacco; the drinking of intoxicating (alcoholic) liquors, and the habitual use of narcotic drugs, are not to be practiced by the members of the Pentecostal Church of Zion.

I Cor. 3:16-17. Know ye not that ye are the temple of God, and that the Spirit of God dwelleth in you? If any man defile the temple of God, him shall God destroy; for the temple of God is holy, which temple ye are. II Cor. 6:16-18; I John 2:15-18; James 1: 14-15; Gal. 5:19-21; Prov. 23:21-23; Prov. 23:29-32; Eph. 5:18; I Tim. 3:3.

ARTICLE 13. PRAYER FOR THE SICK

The Bible teaches both individual and collective prayer for the healing of the sick, and also the calling for the Elders of the church to anoint and pray for the sick, and that God hears and answers the prayer of faith.

James 5:13-16. Is any among you afflicted? Let him pray. Is any merry? Let him sing psalms. Is any sick among you? Let him call for the elders of the church; and let them pray over him, anointing him with oil in the name of the Lord: and the prayer of faith shall save the sick, and the Lord shall raise him up; and if he have committed sins, they shall be forgiven him. Confess your faults one to another, and pray one for another, that ye may be healed. The effectual fervent prayer of a righteous man availeth much. James 1:6, John 5:14-15, Psalms 103:1-3.

ARTICLE 14. PUNISHMENT OF THE WICKED

The wicked dead will be resurrected at the end of the thousand year reign of Christ, to receive final judgment and to be cast into the lake of fire which is the second death.

Rev. 20:11-15. And I saw a great white throne, and him that sat on it, from whose face the earth and the heaven fled away; and there was found no place for them. And I saw the dead, small and great, stand before God; and the books were opened; and another book was opened, which is the book of life: and the dead were judged out of those things which were written in the books, according to their works. And the sea gave up the dead which were in it; and death and hell delivered up the dead which were in them; and they were judged every man according to their works. And death and hell were cast into the lake of fire. This is the second death. And whosoever was not found written in the book of life was cast into the lake of fire. Matt. 5:22, Matt. 13:41, 42. Matt. 25:41, Mark 9:43-48, Luke 16:22-24.

ARTICLE 15. WORLDLINESS AND WORDLY PLEASURES

The scriptures condemn worldliness, and worldly pleasures, which include the lust of the flesh, the lust of the eye, and the pride of life. We should separate ourselves from the world and come out from among them. Attendance at movie theatres, pool halls, dances, and certain other public so-called recreation centers where there are wicked people, drinking or using profane language should be avoided when possible.

The excessive wearing of jewelry, and make-up, playing cards, mixed swimming (men and women together) is also considered worldly and should not be practiced.

Eph. 5:11, And have no fellowship with the unfruitful works of darkness, but rather reprove them. 2 Thes. 3:6. Now we command you brethren, in the name of our Lord Jesus Christ, that ye withdraw yourselves from every brother that walketh disorderly, and not after the tradition which he received of us. Matt. 13:22, Ex. 23:2, 2 Kings 17:15, Mark 6:22, I John 2:15-17, I Peter 3:3-4.

The following articles of religion are accepted and practiced by most of the members and clergy in the Pentecostal Church of Zion; however some have different opinions on some of the articles.

ARTICLE 16. CONCERNING CHILDREN

Children when born in the natural are under the grace of God until they reach an undetermined age when they are able to understand the way of Salvation. At any age that a child feels the need to come to the altar and repent he should be allowed to do so, and will be accepted as a member of the church when complying with the membership rules.

ARTICLE 17. CONCERNING THE KEEPING OF THE PASSOVER (OR SO CALLED LORD'S SUPPER)

The last passover to be observed was kept by Jesus and the Apostles the night before his death. We believe that his body was the "Bread from Heaven" and his blood was the "Fruit of the Vine." The passover is now celebrated through communion of the Holy Ghost daily and is not to be kept through the symbols literally.

John 13:14. If I then, your master, have washed your feet; ye also ought to wash one another's feet. 1 Tim. 5:9-10, 1 Peter 2:21.

ARTICLE 18. CRUCIFIXION OF JESUS

The Bible teaches that Jesus was crucified on the day of the week commonly known to us as Wednesday (midst of the week), and He was in the tomb three days and three nights, arising in the end of the Sabbath, thus fulfilling the prophesy of His sign as recorded in Matt. 12:39,40. But He answered and said unto them, An evil and adulterous generation seeketh after a sign; and there shall no sign be given to it, but the sign of the prophet Jonas: For as Jonas was three days and three nights in the whale's belly; so shall the Son of Man be three days and three nights in the heart of the earth. Matt. 28:1-8, Dan. 9:27, 1 Cor. 15:3-4, Mark 16:1-6, Mark 15:42, John 20:1-10, John 19:14, Luke 24:1-8, Luke 23:54-56.

ARTICLE 19. SIGNS OF THE TIMES

The regathering of literal Israel to the land of Palestine, as portrayed in the prophesies began to be fulfilled in 1948 when Israel became a state. The fulfillment of the signs in the political, religious, physical and social world lead us to believe that we are living in the time of the end, and that the second coming of Christ is very near.

Ezekiel 37:21-22. And say unto them, Thus saith the Lord God; Behold, I will take the children of Israel from among the heathen, whither they be gone, and will gather them on every side, and bring them into their own land: And I will make them one nation in the land upon the mountains of Israel; and one king shall be king to them all: and they shall be no more two nations, neither shall they be divided into two kingdoms any more at all. Jer. 31:9-11, Isa. 61:4.

Luke 21:24-26. And they shall fall by the edge of the sword, and shall be led away captive into all nations: and Jerusalem shall be trodden down of the Gentiles, until the times of the Gentiles be fulfilled. And there shall be signs in the sun, and in the moon, and in the stars; and upon the earth distress of nations, with perplexity; the sea and the waves roaring, Men's hearts failing them for fear, and for looking after those things which are coming on the earth: for the powers of heaven shall be shaken. Ezek. 21:25-27; Luke 17:26-31, Rev. 11-18, Matt. 24, 2 Tim. 4:3-4, 2 Tim. 3:1-13.

ARTICLE 20. KINGDOM OF HEAVEN

The Kingdom of Heaven is divided into three phases.

(1) The church, built by Christ (and established on the day of Pentecost) (Acts 2) in Matt. 16:18, 19. And I say also unto thee, Thou art Peter, and upon this rock I will build my church; and the gates of hell shall not prevail against it. And I will give unto thee the keys of the kingdom of heaven: and whatsoever thou shalt bind on earth shall be bound in heaven; and whatsoever thou lasht loose on earth shall be loose heaven.

(2) The second phase of the kingdom of heaven will begin at the second coming of Christ, when the dead in Christ is raised and the living saints are changed from mortal to immortality and rise to meet Him in the air, and so shall they ever be with the Lord. The saints will live and reign with him a thousand years.

Rev. 20:4. And I saw thrones, and they sat upon them, and judgment was given unto them: and I saw the souls of them that were beheaded for the witness of Jesus, and for the word of God, and which had not worshipped the beast, neither his image, neither had

ARTICLES OF RELIGION (PENTECOSTAL CHURCH OF ZION) (continued)

received his mark upon their foreheads, or in their hands; and they lived and reigned with Christ a thousand years.

(3) The third and final phase of the kingdom will begin after the thousand year reign of Jesus Christ and the resurrection of the wicked dead. There will be a new heaven and a new earth upon which Christ will set up his everlasting Kingdom and will reign with His saints forever.

2 Peter 1:11. For so an entrance shall be ministered unto you abundantly into the everlasting kingdom of our Lord and Saviour Jesus Christ. Rev. 22:14.

ARTICLE 21. STATE OF THE DEAD

When man dies, he is unconscious and in the grave awaits the resurrection. There will be no chance to repent and make restitution for sin after the natural death of a man.

Ecclesiastes 9:5. For the living know that they shall die: but the dead know not anything, neither have they any more reward; for the memory of them is forgotten. Psalms 146:4, I Cor. 15:42-56, Job 17: 13, Rev. 20:11-15, Job 14:13-14.

ARTICLE 22. CONCERNING WEARING APPAREL

Men and ladies alike should dress at all times in modest apparel. They should not dress so laviously that they are conspicuous, nor so odd that they are a public spectacle. The wearing of dresses with no sleeves, or the wearing of shorts by either sex is not considered modest street apparel.

I Tim. 2:9-10. In like manner also that women adorn themselves in modest apparel, with shamefacedness and sobriety; not with braided hair, or gold, or pearls or costly array: But (which becometh women professing Godliness) with good works. Mark 12:38, James 2:3, I Peter 3:3.

Notes: *These articles are unusual for their division following Article 15 into those beliefs held by the whole church and those about which there is some difference of opinion. Among the teachings are those concerning the annual observance of the Lord's Supper at Passover, the dating of Christ's crucifixion on Wednesday instead of Friday, and soul sleep.*

*   *   *

Deliverance Pentecostal

STATEMENT OF FAITH [ABUNDANT LIVING CHRISTIAN FELLOWSHIP (KINGSPORT, TENNESSEE)]

The church accepts the holy scriptures as the revealed will of God, the all-sufficient rule for faith and practice; and for the purpose of maintaining general unity adopts the following statement of fundamental truths:

1. We believe the Bible to be the inspired and only infallible and authoritative Word of God. II Tim 3:16; Heb 4:12

2. We believe that there is one God, eternally existent in three personalities: God the Father, God the Son, and God the Holy Ghost. II Cor 13:14; Mat 3:16, 17

3. We believe in the deity of our Lord Jesus Christ in His virgin birth, in His bodily resurrection, in His ascension to the right hand of the Father, and in the blessed hope of His personal visible future return to the earth to receive to Himself, His blood-bought church, that it may be with Him forever. Rom 10:9, 10; I Peter 1:18-21

4. We believe that the only means of being cleansed from sin is through repentance and faith in the precious blood of Christ. Eph 1:3-7; Rom 5:9

5. We believe that regeneration by the Holy Spirit is absolutely essential for personal salvation. John 3:5-6; Titus 3:5

6. We believe in baptism by immersion in water (Acts 8:14-16; Acts 19:1-5) to be administered to all those who have repented of their sins and who have believed on the Lord Jesus Christ to the saving of their souls and who give clear evidence of their salvation. Romans 6:3-5; Colossians 2:12

7. We believe that the redemptive work of Christ on the cross provides healing of the human body in answer to believing prayer. I Peter 2:24; Is 53:4, 5

8. We believe that the baptism in the Holy Spirit, according to Acts 2:4, is given to believers who ask for Him. Acts 19:2-6

9. We believe in the sanctifying power of the Holy Spirit by whose indwelling the Christian is enabled to live a holy life. Rom 8:1,2; Acts 13:2-4

10. We believe in the Lord's Supper to be observed regularly as enjoined by the scriptures. Luke 22:19-20; I Corinthians 11:23-26

11. We believe in the resurrection of both the saved and the lost, the one to everlasting life and the other to everlasting damnation. Matt 25:31-46; I Thess 4:15-18

12. We believe that God becomes the Heavenly Father of every person who accepts Jesus Christ as Savior and Lord and that because He is a good Father, He meets all our needs and gives us the desires of our hearts. Phil 4:19; Mark 11:24

Notes: *As a whole, the deliverance churches do not have formal statements of faith or, as is true in most cases, do not make an issue of them. Most of these churches try to work in an interdenominational atmosphere, where too much emphasis upon doctrine leads to unnecessary doctrinal controversy. In spite of a diligent search, only one statement of a local congregation was located.*

The Statement of Faith of the Abundant Living Christian Fellowship, a congregation founded by a student of Kenneth Hagin, summarizes the position presented at greater length in the writings of Hagin and other ministers (such as Fred Price) in the International Convention of Faith Churches.

This statement is typical of, and similar to, those adopted by churches associated with the convention, though it is merely the statement of a single congregation.

* * *

Apostolic Pentecostal

CHURCH DOCTRINES [APOSTOLIC FAITH (HAWAII)]

We preach Christ, His birth, His baptism, His works, His teachings, His crucifixion, His resurrection, His ascension, His second coming, His millennial reign, His white throne judgement, and the new heavens and new earth when He shall have put all enemies under His feet, and shall reign eternally, and we shall abide with Him forever and ever.

REPENTENCE TOWARD GOD—Acts 20:21. Repentance is Godly sorrow for sin. II Cor. 7:10. Mark 1:15.

RESTITUTION—The Blood of Jesus will never blot out any sin that we can make right. We must have a conscience void of offense toward God and man. Restitution includes restoring where you have defrauded or stolen, paying back debts and confession. Luke 19:8, 9. Ezekiel 33:15.

THE BAPTISM OF THE HOLY GHOST is the gift of power upon the sanctified. Luke 24:49. Matt. 3:11. John 7:38, 39. John 14:16, 17, 26. Acts 1:5-8.

And when we receive it, we have the same sign or Bible evidence as the disciples had on the day of Pentecost, speaking with tongues, as the Spirit gives utterance. Mark 16:17. I Cor. 14:21, 22. Examples—Acts 2:4. Acts 10:45, 46. Acts 19:6.

HEALING OF THE BODY—Sickness and disease are destroyed through the atonement of Jesus. Isa. 53:4, 5. Matt. 8:17. Mark 16:18. Jas. 5:14-16. All sickness is the work of the devil, which Jesus came to destroy. I John 3:8. Luke 13:16. Acts 10:38. Jesus cast out devils and commissioned His disciples to do the same. Mark 16:17. Luke 10:19. Mark 9:25, 26.

THE SECOND COMING OF JESUS—The return of Jesus is just as literal as His going away. Acts 1:9-11. John 14:3. There will be two appearances under one coming; first, to catch away His waiting bride (Matt. 24:40, 44 and I Thess. 4:15-17), (second), to execute judgment upon the ungodly. II Thess. 1:7-10. Jude 14 and 15. Zech. 14:3, 4.

ORDINANCES.

1st. WATER BAPTISM BY IMMERSION (SINGLE)—Jesus went down into the water and came up out of the water, giving us an example that we should follow. Matt. 3:16. Acts 8:38, 39. Acts 2:38. Rom. 6:4, 5. Col. 2:12.

2nd. THE LORD'S SUPPER—Jesus instituted the Lord's Supper that we might "show His death till He come." I Cor. 11:23, 26. Luke 22:17-20. Matt. 26:26-29.

It brings healing to our bodies if we discern the Lord's body. I Cor. 11:29, 30.

Why we take the Lord's Supper at night, and in the evening he cometh with the twelve. Mark 14:17.

THE TRIBULATION—Jesus prophesied a great tribulation such as was not from the beginning of the world. Matt. 24:21, 22, 29. Rev. 9. Rev. 16. Isa. 26:20, 21. Mal: 4:1.

CHRIST'S MILLENNIAL REIGN is the 1000 years of the literal reign of Jesus on this earth. It will be ushered in by the coming of Jesus back to earth with ten thousands of His saints. Jude 14, 15. II Thess. 1:7-10. During this time the devil will be bound. Rev. 20:2, 3. It will be a reign of peace and blessing. Isa. 11:6-9. Isa. 65:25. Hos. 2:18. Zech. 14:9-20. Isa. 2:2-4.

THE GREAT WHITE THRONE JUDGMENT—God will judge the quick and dead according to their works. Rev. 20:11-14. Dan. 12:2. Acts 10:42.

ETERNAL HEAVEN AND ETERNAL HELL—The Bible teaches that hell is as eternal as heaven. Matt. 25:41-46. The wicked shall be cast into a burning hell, a lake of fire burning with brimstone forever and ever. Rev. 14:10, 11. Luke 16:24. Mark 9:43, 44.

SANCTIFICATION is that act of God's grace by which He makes us holy. It is a second definite work wrought by the Blood of Jesus through faith. John 17:15-17. I Thess. 4:3. Heb. 13:12. Heb. 2:11. Heb. 12:14. I John 1:7.

JUSTIFICATION is that act of God's free grace by which we receive remission of sins. Acts 10:43. Rom. 5:1. Rom. 3:25. Acts 13:38, 39. John 1:12. John 3:3.

NEW HEAVENS AND NEW EARTH—The Word teaches that this earth, which has been polluted by sin, shall pass away after the White Throne Judgment, and God will make a new heaven and new earth in which righteousness shall dwell. Matt. 24:35. II Peter 3:12, 13. Rev. 21:1-3. Isa. 65:17.

CLUBS, SECRET SOCIETIES, ETC.—We firmly believe and hold that God's people should have no connection whatsoever with clubs, secret societies or any organization or body wherein there is fellowship with unbelievers, bound by an oath. Eph. 5:12. II Tim. 2:4. II Cor. 6:14-18. James 4:4.

HUMAN GOVERNMENT—We recognize the institution of human government as being ordained of God. Therefore, we should be loyal to our government and stand ready to fulfill our obligations as loyal citizens. The Word of God commands us to pray for the rulers of our country. There is a growing number of conscientious objectors in our country today who claim that they do so in obedience to the Bible, yet they brazenly defy the law and constituted authority. It is outright disloyalty to established government. In fact that stand is in sympathy with the enemy. Such conduct is based upon a false impression and the true Christian church verily does not condone their action. We, therefore, strongly exhort our members to freely and willingly respond to the call of our government for military service in time of peace and in time of war. I Peter 2:13. Rom. 13:1-3. I Tim. 2:1-3. II Cor. 4:2.

MARRIAGE AND DIVORCE—Marriage is a divine institution, established and sanctified by God. Marriage is honorable in all. Only death dissolves the marriage bond.

CHURCH DOCTRINES [APOSTOLIC FAITH (HAWAII)] (continued)

Divorce is only a privilege permitted by Moses because of the hardness of the human heart. Deut. 24:1-4. Matt. 5:31-32. Matt. 19:7-9. I Cor. 7:1-16 & 39. Rom. 7:1-3.

TITHING & FREE-WILL OFFERING—We believe and teach that tithing and free-will offerings is God's financial plan to provide for this work upon earth. It is a voluntary matter between every believer and God. Matt. 22:21. Malachi. 3:7-11. Heb. 7:1-10. II Cor. 9:6-7.

Notes: *The Non-Trinitarian, Apostolic, or "Jesus Only" Pentecostal churches are defined by their denial of the Trinity. Though the Trinity has been recognized as a central affirmation of Christianity for many centuries, the apostolic churches claim that it is not taught in the Bible and is a later doctrinal accretion. Most of the Apostolic churches have some roots in the Assemblies of God, within which the "Jesus only" issue was raised and discussed most vigorously.*

The church doctrines of the Apostolic Faith are derived from those of the (Original) Church of God, which in turn are derived from the Church of God Teachings of the Church of God (Cleveland, Tennessee). Unlike most apostolic churches, the Apostolic Faith believes in sanctification as a second work of grace. The Apostolic Faith continues the (Original) Church of God's position on secret societies, but has taken an opposite stance on the issue of participation in war.

*   *   *

WHAT WE BELIEVE (APOSTOLIC FAITH MISSION CHURCH OF GOD)

WHAT WE BELIEVE. We believe in the resurrection of the dead and the second coming of Christ.

No one shall hold an office in this church who is a member of another church.

No man, woman, boy or girl is a member of this church who uses intoxicants, or uses snuff, tobacco, morphine or any habit forming drugs.

Even foolish talking, jesting or using any slang language is discouraged. We command all members to abstain from all appearances of evil. II Cor. 7:1; I Thes. 5:23; I Cor. 6:1.

DIVINE HEALING. We believe that this is a divine instruction built upon the foundation of the Apostles and Prophets. Jesus Christ the Chief Cornerstone and it is the Christian's right and privilege to trust God for their healing when they are sick and afflicted. James 1:14; Mark 11:22; Mark 9:23; Heb. 11:6; Acts 3:6-16.

We do not condemn those who are weak in the faith for using medicine, but exhort and nourish and cherish them until they become strong: for the Bible says: Him that is weak in the faith receive ye, but not to doubtful disputations. Rom. 14:1 also said, that some would use herbs, but not to judge them. Rom. 14:2.

COMMUNION AND FEET WASHING. On the night of our Lord's betrayal He ate the Passover supper with His Apostles after which He instituted the sacrament.

"And He took bread and gave unto them, saying, This is my body which is given for you: This do in remembrance of me. Likewise also the cup after supper, saying, This cup is the new testament in my blood, which is shed for you." (Luke 22:19-20.)

Paul instructed the church how to observe it. (I Cor. 11:23-34).

Thus was instituted the use of literal bread and the fruit of the vine, which are partaken of, literally as emblems of His broken body and shed blood. There is also a spiritual significance and blessing in partaking of the sacrament.

When the Passover was ended, we read in John 13:4-5, "He riseth from supper and laid aside His garments; and took a towel and girded himself. After that he poureth water into a basin and began to wash the disciples feet, and to wipe them with the towel wherewith he was girded."

Jesus said, "If I then, your Lord and Master washed your feet; ye also ought to wash one another's feet. For I have given you an example that ye should do as I have done to you" (John 13:14-15).

WOMEN PREACHERS. This church believes that a woman has a right to teach or preach. God said He would pour out His spirit upon all flesh. Your sons and daughters shall prophesy. The word prophesy means to utter predictions, to make declarations of events to come, to instruct in religious doctrine. Read Acts 2:17; Joel 2:28; Acts 21:9; Rom. 16:1-2; Phil. 4:3, when God made man he also made a woman to help man. (Gen. 2:19-23).

ARTICLE OF FAITH

> SECTION 1. We believe in justification by faith according to Romans 5:1 and that no man is justified with God as long as he is doing what God says not to do.

> SECTION 2. We believe that Jesus Christ shed His blood to sanctify the people according to Heb. 13:12; I John 1:7-9; Rom. 6:6; I Thes. 5:23; St. John 17:17; Acts 26:18.

> SECTION 3. We believe that sanctification does affect the innermost being according to Matt. 23:26; I Thes. 5:23; and that is instantaneous and is carried on into Holiness, Lev. 11:44.

LAWS OF THE LAND. We believe the magistrates are ordered for peace, safety, welfare of all people. Therefore, under this condition our duty is to be in obedience to all of the laws of the land so long as they are not contrary to the word of God. We do not believe in war, nor going to war, for God is not the author of confusion, but of peace.

THE COMING OF JESUS. That Jesus is coming again in person is a doctrine clearly set forth in apostolic times. Jesus taught it, the Apostles preached it, and the saints expected it. (I Thes. 4:14-17; Titus 2:13-14.)

TRANSLATION OF THE SAINTS. We believe that the time draweth near for the coming of the Lord to make a change in the present order of things. At that time, all the righteous dead shall arise from their graves, and they that are living righteous before God shall be translated or "caught up to meet the Lord in the air." (Matt. 24:36-42;

Luke 17:20-37; I Cor. 15:51-54; Philippians 3:20-21; I Thes. 5:1-10).

FINAL JUDGMENT. When the thousand years shall have passed, there shall be a resurrection of the dead who shall be summoned before the Great White Throne for their final judgment. All those whose names are not found written in the Book of Life shall be cast into the Lake of Fire and brimstone which God has prepared for the Devil and his angels. (Rev. 20:10-15).

SANCTIFICATION. We believe that Sanctification is a work of grace, and it begins in regeneration by the application of the blood of Jesus. I John 1:7; Heb. 12:2; Acts 20:28; Rom. 5:6; Heb. 9:14; I Peter 1:8-19; Rev. 7:14.

We understand the word Sanctified or Sanctification means Separation and Consecration, St. John 17:17; I Cor. 1:30; Eph. 5:25-26; II Tim. 2:21; I Peter 1:2.

We believe that God's church in the early dispensation was Sanctified, Duet. 14:2; Duet. 7:6; Ezek. 36:23; St. John 17:19; Acts 20:32; I Cor. 1:2; I Cor. 6:11; Heb. 2:11; Jer. 1:5; Dan. 7:27.

THE GOD HEAD. We believe that Jesus is God, and there is no other beside Him. (Duet. 4:35; 6:4; II Sam. 7:22; I Chron. 17:20: Psa. 83:18; Isa. 43:10; 44:6; 45:8; Mark 12:29; I Cor. 8:4; Eph. 4:5; I Tim. 2:5; Acts 9:5; Rev. 1:13).

We believe that there are three (3) that bear record in Heaven, Viz: The Father, The Word, The Holy Ghost. These three are one manifested in the person of Jesus Christ and Jesus Christ is image of the Invisible God, the Creator of all things, the Alpha and Omega, the beginning and the ending. Isaiah 9:6; John 14:8-11; Rev. 1:8: John 10:30-38.

WATER BAPTISM. Water Baptism is an essential part of the New Testament Salvation: and not, as some teach. "Just an outward form of an inward cleansing. Without proper baptism it is impossible to enter into the kingdom of God (God's true Church, the Bride of Christ), and therefore, is not merely a part of local church membership.

MANNER OF BAPTISM. Water Baptism can only be administered by immersion (Col. 2:12). Note the following: Jesus said "Born (to bring forth) of the water," (John 3:5); Paul said, "We are buried with Him (Lord Jesus Christ) by baptism," (Rom. 6:4); Jesus "Came up out of the water," (Mark 1:10); Phillip and the eunuch "Went down into the water," and "Came up out of the water" (Acts 8:38-39).

Jesus' death, burial and resurrection was a type of our salvation. "Repent (death to sin), and he baptized (burial) everyone of you in the name of Jesus Christ for the remissions of sins, and ye shall receive the gift of the Holy Ghost" (resurrection).

FORMULA FOR WATER BAPTISM. The Name in which baptism is administered is as important as immersion. This name is Lord Jesus Christ.

Jesus' last command to His disciples was, "Go ye therefore and teach all nations, baptizing them (all nations) in the name of the Father and the Son and of the Holy Ghost." (Matt. 28:19).

You will notice He said name, not names. As we have previously explained, Father, Son, and Holy Ghost are not names but titles of positions held by God. We see quickly that this is true as we hear the angel announce "She shall bring forth a SON, and thou shalt call His name Jesus." (Matt. 1:21).

This name the Apostles understood to be Lord Jesus Christ, and from the first day that the Church of God was established on the day of Pentecost (Act 2:36-41). Until the end of their ministry, they baptized in the name of the Lord Jesus Christ.

"Thou shalt call His name Jesus: for he shall save his people from their sins." (Matt. 1:21).

Are you looking for Salvation? "Neither is there Salvation in any other, for there is none other name under Heaven given among men, whereby we must be saved." (Acts 4:12).

Without this name, water baptism is void.

HOLINESS. Godly living should characterize the life of every child of the Lord, and we should live according to the pattern and example given in the Word of God. "For the grace of God that bringeth salvation hath appeared to all men, teaching us that, denying ungodliness and worldly lusts, we should live soberly, righteously, and Godly, in this present world" (Titus 2:11-12). "For even hereunto were ye called: because Christ also suffered for us, leaving us an example that ye should follow His steps: who did no sin, neither was guile found in His mouth; who, when He was reviled, reviled not again; when He suffered He threatened not; but committed Himself to Him that judgeth righteously" (I Peter 2:21-23).

"Follow peace with all men and holiness, without which no man shall see the Lord" (Heb. 12:14).

But as He which hath called you is holy, so be ye holy in all manner of conversation; because it is written, be ye holy: for I am holy. And if ye call on the Father, who without respect of persons judgeth according to every man's work, pass the time of your sojourning here in fear: forasmuch as ye know that ye were not redeemed with corruptible things, as silver and gold, from your vain conversation received by tradition from your fathers; but with the precious blood of Christ as of a lamb without blemish and without spot" (I Peter 1:15-19).

Notes: *One of the earliest apostolic churches, the Apostolic Faith Mission Church of God teaches sanctification as a second definite work of grace, the necessity of baptism for salvation, and pacifism. It practices foot washing.*

* * *

ARTICLES OF FAITH (ASSEMBLIES OF THE LORD JESUS CHRIST)

INTRODUCTION

We believe the Bible to be the direct and absolute word of God, (II Tim. 3:16) given to us by the inspiration of the Holy Ghost as it moved upon the tongues and pens of men who had received special anointing of God for this express purpose. (II Peter 1:21) "For the prophecy came not in old

ARTICLES OF FAITH (ASSEMBLIES OF THE LORD JESUS CHRIST) (continued)

time by the will of man: But Holy men of God spoke as they were moved by the Holy Ghost." We believe the Bible to be God's means of doctrine, instruction, and comfort to the church today, infallible in its authority, singular in interpretation, and man's only avenue of access to God.

ARTICLES OF FAITH

"THE ONE TRUE GOD"

We believe in the one everliving, eternal God; infinite in power. Holy in nature, attributes and purpose; and possessing absolute, indivisible deity. This one true God has revealed Himself as Father in creation; through His Son in redemption; and as the Holy Spirit, by animation. (I Cor. 8:6; Eph. 4:6; II Cor. 5:19; Joel 2:28).

The scripture does more than attempt to prove the existence of God; it asserts, assumes and declares that the knowledge of God is universal. (Romans 1, 19, 21, 28, 32, 2:15) God is invisible, incorporeal, without parts, without body and therefore free from all limitations. He is Spirit (John 4:24), and "a spirit hath not flesh and bones. . . . " (Luke 24:39).

. . . "The first of all the commandments is, Hear, O Israel; the Lord our God is one Lord" (Mark 12:29; Deut. 6:4). "One God and Father of All, who is above all, and through all, and in you all" (Eph. 4:6).

This one true God manifested Himself in the Old Testament in divers ways; in the Son while He walked among men; as the Holy Spirit after the ascension.

THE SON OF GOD

The one true God, the Jehovah of the Old Testament, took upon Himself the form of man, and as the son of man, was born of the virgin Mary. As Paul says, "And without controversy great is the mystery of godliness; God was manifest in the flesh, justified in the spirit, seen of angels, preached unto the Gentiles believed on in the world, received up into Glory" (I Timothy 3:16; John 1:10).

"He came unto His own, and His own received Him not" (John 1:11). This one true God was manifest in the flesh, that is, in His Son Jesus Christ.

". . . God was in Christ, reconciling the world unto Himself, not imputing their trespasses unto them . . . " (II Cor. 5:19).

We believe that, ". . . in Him (Jesus) dwelleth all the fullness of the Godhead bodily" (Col. 2:9).

THE NAME

". . . unto us a child is born, unto us a son is given; . . . and His name shall be called Wonderful, counselor, The Mighty God, The Everlasting Father, The Prince of Peace" (Isaiah 9:6). This prophecy of Isaiah was fulfilled when the Son of God was named, "And she shall bring forth a son, and thou shalt call His name Jesus: For He shall save His people from their sins" (Matthew 1:21).

Neither is there salvation in any other; for there is none other name under heaven given among men, whereby we must be saved (Acts 4:12).

MAN AND HIS FALL

God created man in His own image (Gen. 1:26,27), innocent, pure and holy. By transgression man lost his standing. (Rom. 5:11; Eph. 2:3). Man needed a redeemer which has been supplied in the seed of the woman, which seed bruised the serpent's head (Gen 3:15; Luke 2:10, 11); that is: Our Lord and Saviour Jesus Christ in whom we have redemption, through his blood, even the forgiveness of sins. (Eph. 1:7; Rev. 1:5).

THE GRACE OF GOD

"For the grace of God that bringeth salvation hath appeared to all men, teaching us that denying ungodliness and worldly lusts, we should live soberly, righteously, and godly in this present world." (Titus 2:11,12).

"For the law was given by Moses, but grace and truth came by Jesus Christ" (John 1:17).

A Christian, to keep saved, must walk with God and keep himself in the love of God (Jude 21) and in the grace of God. The word "grace" means "favor." When a person transgresses and sins against God, He loses His favor. If he continues to commit sin and does not repent, he will eventually be lost and cast into the lake of fire. (Read John 15:2, 6:2; II Peter 2:20, 21, 22). Jude speaks of the backsliders of his day and their reward. (And read Hebrews 6:4-6).

"For by grace are ye saved through faith; and that not of yourselves; it is the Gift of God." (Eph. 2:8)

THE COMMUNION

Melchizedek, the Priest of the Most High God, gave the first Communion to our Father Abraham, consisting of bread and wine. (Gen. 14:18) Christ, being "made a High Priest forever after the order of Melchizedek" evidently administered the same. (Heb. 7:21; Matthew 26:26-29; I Cor. 11:23-32).

On the night of our Lord's betrayal, He ate the Passover Supper with His Apostles, after which He instituted the sacrament. "And He took bread, and gave thanks, and brake it, and gave unto them, saying, this is my body which is given for you: This do in remembrance of me. Likewise also the cup after supper, saying, this cup is the new testament in my blood, which is shed for you." (Luke 22:19, 20)

Paul instructed the church how to observe it: (I Cor. 11:23-24).

THE WASHING OF FEET

This ordinance is as much a divine command as any other New Testament ordinance. Jesus gave us an example that we do even as He had done. He said that we ought to wash one another's feet. And again, "If ye know these things, happy are ye if you do them." (John 13:4-17) There is scriptural evidence that this was practiced by the Church in the days of the Apostle Paul. (I Tim. 5:10)

DIVINE HEALING

The physical suffering of the Lord Jesus Christ purchased healing for our bodies, as His death, burial and resurrection provided for the salvation of our souls, for: . . . "with His stripes we are healed" (Isaiah 53:5). Matthew

8:17 read, ". . . Himself took our infirmities, and bore our sicknesses." (See also I Peter 2:24).

We see from this that healing for the body is in the atonement. That being true, then it is for all who believe. Jesus said of believers, ". . . they shall lay hands on the sick, and they shall recover." Later James wrote in his Epistle to all the churches: "Is any sick among you? Let him call for the elders of the church; and let them pray over him, anointing him with oil in the name of the Lord: and the prayer of faith shall save the sick, and the Lord shall raise him up; and if he have committed sins, they shall be forgiven him. Confess your faults one to another, and pray one for another, that ye may be healed. The effectual fervent prayer of a righteous man availeth much." (James 5:14-16)

REPENTANCE AND REMISSION OF SIN

The only grounds upon which God will accept a sinner is repentance, from the heart, for the sins that he has committed. A broken and contrite heart, He will not despise. (Psa. 51:17) John preached repentance, Jesus proclaimed it, and before His ascension commanded that repentance and remission of sins should be preached in His name, beginning at Jerusalem (Luke 24:47). Peter fulfilled this command on the Day of Pentecost. (Acts 2:38).

WATER BAPTISM

The scriptural mode of baptism is immersion, and is only for those who have fully repented, having turned from their sins and a love of the world. It should be administered by a duly authorized minister of the Gospel in obedience to the Word of God, and in the name of Jesus Christ, according to the Acts of the Apostles 2:38; 8:16; 10:48; 19:5; thus obeying and fulfilling Matthew 28:19.

HOLY SPIRIT BAPTISM

John the Baptist, in Matthew 3:11, said, ". . . He shall baptize you with the Holy Ghost, and with fire."

Jesus, in Acts 1:5, said, ". . . ye shall be baptized with the Holy Ghost not many days hence."

Luke tells us in Acts 2:4, ". . . they were all filled with the Holy Ghost, and began to speak with other tongues (languages) as the Spirit gave them utterance."

The terms "Baptize with the Holy Ghost and fire," "Filled with the Holy Ghost," and the "Gift of the Holy Ghost" are synonymous terms used interchangeably in the Bible.

APOSTOLIC DOCTRINE OF NEW BIRTH

The basic and fundamental doctrine of this Organization shall be the Bible standard of full salvation, which is repentance, baptism in water by immersion in the name of Jesus Christ for the remission of sins, and the baptism of the Holy Ghost with the evidence of speaking with other tongues as the Spirit gives utterance. (Acts 2:4 and 2:38; John 3:5)

HOLINESS

We believe that godly living should characterize the life and walk of all saints according to the sign and example found in (I Peter 2:21; Titus 2:11; Gal. 2:20; Heb. 12:14; I Peter 1:15-17).

We believe we are to cleanse ourselves from all filthiness of the flesh and spirit perfecting holiness in the fear of God (II Cor. 7-1), and to abstain from ALL appearance of EVIL, (I Thes. 5:22) and to turn away from those who have a form of godliness but deny the power thereof. (II Tim. 3:5; I Cor. 11:6; I Tim. 2:9, 10; I Peter 2:3,4)

TITHING

We believe tithing is God's financial plan to provide for His work, and has been since the days of Abraham. Tithing came with faith under Abraham; Moses' law enjoined it, and Israel practiced it when she was right with God; Jesus endorsed it (Matt. 23:23); and Paul said to lay by in store as God has prospered you. Do not rob God of His portion, that is tithes and offerings. (Read Mal. 3).

MARRIAGE AND DIVORCE

"Whosoever shall put away his wife, except it be for fornication, and shall marry another, committeth adultery." (Mat. 5:32 and 19:9)

In order to lift a higher standard in the ministry, no minister, shall be accepted in this organization who has married for the second time, after his conversion, unless the first marriage was terminated by a death.

SECRET SOCIETIES, ETC.

According to the word of God we firmly believe and hold that the people of God should have no connection whatever with secret societies, or any other organization or body wherein is a fellowship of unbelievers bound by an oath.

(James 5:3-7; II Cor. 6:14-18) We are exhorted by the Word of God to "be content with such things as we have," and "be content with our wages." (I Tim. 6:8; Heb. 13:5; Luke 3:14).

THE RETURN OF THE LORD JESUS CHRIST

That the Lord Jesus Christ is to come to earth in person is a doctrine clearly set forth in apostolic times. Jesus taught it; the apostles preached it; the saints expect it. (See Matt. 24:1 etc.; Acts 1:11; 3:19-21; I Cor. 1:7-8; 11:26; Phil. 3:20-21; Titus 2:13).

TRANSLATION OF SAINTS

We believe the catching away of the church draweth nigh, and at that time all the dead in Christ shall arise from their graves, and we that are alive and, remain shall be translated or "caught up" to meet the Lord in the air. (Matt. 24:36-42; Luke 17:20-37; I Cor. 15:51; Phil. 3:20-21; I Thes. 4:13-17)

Whereas, the Word of God teaches the imminent second coming of our Lord Jesus Christ; and that there will be first an appearing or catching away of the church (I Thes. 4:13) preceding His second coming back to earth; and said first appearing we believe to be at hand and likely to occur at any moment.

TRIBULATION

Moreover, we believe that the distress upon the earth is the "beginning of sorrows" and will become more intense until there "shall be a time of trouble such as never was since there was a nation even to that same time" (Matt. 24:1; Hab. 2:14; Rom. 11:25-27).

ARTICLES OF FAITH (ASSEMBLIES OF THE LORD JESUS CHRIST) (continued)

MILLENNIUM

We believe that the period of "Tribulation" will be followed by the dawn of a better day on earth, and that for one thousand years there shall be "peace on earth and good will toward men." (Rev. 20:1-5; Isa. 65:17-25; Matt. 5:5; Dan. 7:27; Mic. 4:1; Hab. 2:14; Rom. 11:25-27).

FINAL JUDGMENT

When the thousand years are finished, there shall be a resurrection of the dead, who shall be summoned before the Great White Throne for their final judgment; and all whose names are not found written in the Book of Life shall be cast into the Lake of Fire, burning with brimstone, which God has prepared for the devil and his angels. Satan being cast in first. (Rev. 20:5-15; Matt. 25:41-46; Rev. 21:8).

CIVIL GOVERNMENT

All civil magistrates are ordained of God for peace, safety and the welfare of all people (Rom. 13:1-10; Titus 3:1-2; I Peter 2:13-14;) therefore, it is our duty to be in obedience to all requirements of the laws that are not contrary to the Word of God, and that do not force one to the violation of the sixth commandment, by bearing arms. Is is our duty to honor them, pay tribute, or such taxation as may be required without murmuring (Matt. 17:24-27; 22:17-21), and show respect to them in all lawful requirements of the civil government.

CONSCIENTIOUS SCRUPLES

We propose to fulfill all the obligations of loyal citizens, but are constrained to declare against participation in combatant service in war, armed insurrection, property destruction, aiding or abetting in or the actual destruction of human life.

Furthermore, we cannot conscientiously affiliate with any union boycott, or organization which will force or bind any of its members, to perform any duties contrary to our conscience, or receive any mark, without our right to affirm or reject same.

However, we regret the false impression created by some groups, or so-called "conscientious objectors," that to obey the Bible is to have a contempt for law or magistrates, to be disloyal to our government and in sympathy with our enemies, or to be unwilling to sacrifice for the preservation of our commonwealth. This attitude would be as contemptible to us as to any patriot. The Word of God commands us to do violence to no man. It also commands us that first of all we are to pray for rulers of our country. We, therefore, exhort our members to freely and willingly respond to the call of our Government, except in the matter of bearing arms. When we say service—we mean service—no matter how hard or dangerous. The true church has no more place for cowards than has the nation. First of all, however, let us earnestly pray that we will with honor be kept out of war.

We believe that we can be consistent in service to our Government in certain noncombatant capacities, but not in the bearing of arms.

PUBLIC SCHOOL ACTIVITIES

We disapprove of school students attending shows, dances, dancing classes, theaters, engaging in school activities against their religious scruples and wearing gymnasium clothes which immodestly expose the body.

Notes: *The Assemblies of the Lord Jesus Christ's articles are derived in part from those of the United Pentecostal Church. Like that body, the Assemblies practice foot washing and disavow participation in secret societies, war, and public school activities considered frivolous (dances) or immodest (gymnasium activities).*

*　　　*　　　*

ARTICLES OF FAITH (ASSOCIATED BROTHERHOOD OF CHRISTIANS)

PREFACE

Be it understood that this is a Christian Association, based upon brotherly love and Christian principles. Its intentions are to promote Christian fellowship and to encourage unity of the Spirit among all Christians everywhere; not making controversial issues and doctrinal convictions a test of fellowship. We recognize, acknowledge, and appreciate the fact that there are convictions, revelations, and doctrinal truths revealed to some Christians which are not revealed to; nor understood by others. In such cases the A. B. of C. recommends that both parties be considerate of each other, recognizing the fallibility of man; endeavoring to keep the unity of the Spirit in the bonds of peace—until we all come to the unity of the faith. This being, in effect, the general principles of this Association, we, therefore, will follow in our Articles of Faith with only the fundamental truths we deem necessary for our general good.

ARTICLES OF FAITH

A. THE SCRIPTURES. We believe the Bible to be the inspired Word of God, infallible in its original writings. II Tim. 3:16; II Peter 1:21.

B. THE GODHEAD. We believe in the one everliving, eternal God, infinite in power, holy in nature, attributes, and purpose; in His absolute diety. That this one true God has revealed Himself as Father, in creation; as Son in redemption; and as the Holy Ghost in this church age. That God was manifest in the flesh (Jesus Christ), justified in the Spirit, seen of angels, preached unto the Gentiles, believed on in the world, received up into glory. I Tim. 3:16. That the fullness of diety was revealed and manifest in the Lord Jesus Christ; and that Jesus is the name of God for this dispensation. I Cor. 8:6; II Cor. 5:19; Matt. 1:21; and Eph. 4:6.

C. FALLIBILITY OF MAN. We believe in the fallibility of all mankind. Thru the transgression and fall of Adam in the Garden of Eden, all men are declared to be sinners, therefore, in order to be restored to favor with God all must be born again. Jn. 3:3-5.

D. SUFFERING OF CHRIST. We believe in the vicarious suffering of Jesus Christ the Son of God; that thru His shed blood, atonement for sin has been made for all mankind. Isa. 53:1-12; Matt. 26:28; and Heb. 9:11-28.

E. THE CRUCIFIXION AND RESURRECTION. We believe that Jesus Christ was rejected by the world, especially His own nation; was tried and suffered under the hands of Pilate; died on the cross by crucifixion, was buried, rose again the third day; His resurrection being confirmed by many definite proofs. He was seen by many witnesses for about forty days after His resurrection, after which He ascended up on high, and is now seated at the right hand of the throne of God, there to intercede and advocate for all believers. Heb. 12:2.

F. GRACE. We believe that our present dispensation is a time of grace, that we are saved by grace thru faith, not of works lest any man should boast. Eph. 2:4-10.

G. NEW COVENANT. We believe that God took away the first (covenant) that He might establish the second (Heb. 8:6-10; 10:9) and that under this new covenant in this dispensation none of the statutes of the Mosaic Law are binding. "But now we are delivered from the law, that being dead wherein we were held: that we should serve in newness of Spirit, and not in oldness of the letter" (Rom. 7:6). "For Christ is the end of the law for righteousness to everyone that believeth" (Rom. 10:4). "The law and the prophets were until John: since that time the Kingdom of God is preached" (Luke 16:16).

H. THE CHURCH. Jesus said: "Upon this Rock I will build My church." We believe that it is a Spiritual house (church) to offer up Spiritual Sacrifices. (I Peter 2:5). See John 4:23; & Heb. 13:15-16.

I. CHURCH MEMBERSHIP.

   a. REPENTANCE. We believe in and teach Repentance and faith toward God as the first step for the sinner, as there is but one true entrance into the great Spiritual Church which is the body of Christ (Eph. 1:22-23). God accepts a sinner only when he repents; therefore Repentance and Remission of sins should be preached in Jesus' Name (Luke 24:45-47; Acts 2:37-38).

   b. BAPTISM. We believe in Water Baptism by immersion, and that it should be administered in the name of the Lord Jesus, Jesus Christ, or Lord Jesus Christ as practised by the Apostles. See Acts 2:38; 8:16; 10:48; 1 Cor. 1:13; Col. 3:17.

   c. BAPTISM OF THE HOLY GHOST. We believe in and teach the baptism of the Holy Ghost for believers, witnessed by the physical sign of speaking in other tongues as the Spirit gives utterance. Acts 2:4; 10:46; 19:6. This procedure is recognized as being the teaching of the Apostles regarding the New Birth and as placing us as members of the New Testament Church. Acts 2:41, 47; 1 Cor. 12:13, 18.

J. HOLINESS. Dearly beloved, let us cleanse ourselves from all filthiness of the flesh and spirit perfecting holiness in the fear of God, for God hath not called us unto uncleanliness; but unto holiness. Follow peace with all men and holiness without which no man shall see the Lord. (II Cor. 7:1; I Thes. 4:7; Heb. 12:14; I Pet. 1:15-16).

K. DIVINE HEALING. Deliverance from sickness is provided for in the atonement and is a privilege for believers. As the Lord made our bodies it is not incredible that He should heal them. (Isa. 53:5; Mark 16:15-18; James 5:14).

L. SPIRITUAL GIFTS. We believe the nine gifts of the Spirit should be manifested in the church today, and that all Spirit-filled believers should earnestly covet the best gifts for the edification and up-building of the church. (I Cor. 12:8-11; 14:1).

M. FRUITS OF THE SPIRIT. We believe the Spirit-filled believers will produce the fruit of the Spirit in their lives and their walk will be according to godliness and holy living. (Gal. 5:22-23; I John 2:6; I Pet. 1:16; Tit. 2:11-13; II Cor. 7:1).

N. COMMUNION. Whereas the word Communion expresses Fellowship; we believe in Communion with God through the Spirit as typified in the Shadows of the Old Testament and taught by Jesus and the Apostles in the New Testament. In order to have this Fellowship with God we must be a partaker of the Flesh and Blood of Jesus through the Spirit, as there is no Spiritual Life outside of Him. We believe that the literal emblems of bread and fruit of the vine used at the Passover were shadows of good things to come, and as they were partaking of these emblems Jesus said, This is my body which is broken for you, and This is my blood which is shed for the remission of sins. Matt. 26:17-29; Mark 14:12-25; Luke 22:1-20; I Cor. 11:23-27. That, since Christ, our Passover, is sacrificed for us (I Cor. 5:7), the Passover instituted at the time of the exodus of Israel from Egypt (Ex. 12th chapter) is fulfilled in the Kingdom of God. "The Kingdom of God is not meat and drink; but righteousness, peace and joy in the Holy Ghost." (Rom. 14:17). When we are all baptised into the one body by the Holy Ghost we are made to drink of the one Spirit. (I Cor. 12:13). So then, the cup of Blessing which we bless is the Communion (fellowship) of the Blood of Christ and the bread which we break is the Communion (fellowship) of the Body of Christ. (I Cor. 10:16). For we being many, are one bread, and one body; for we are all partakers of that one bread. (I Cor. 10:17). Hence, we believe in partaking of the flesh and blood of the Lord through the spirit as referred to by the scripture, (Jn. 6:48-63). We hold then, that partaking of natural, or literal elements is not essential to our Salvation, and therefore, refrain from partaking thereof; but with due Christian courtesy we respect those who may hold an opposite view.

O. FOOT WASHING. Since Jesus did not wash the disciples' feet in public, in the Temple or Synagogue, and since there is no Scriptural reference to it other than as a common custom, we believe He was giving us an example of Love and Humility. (Luke 22:24-27; John 13:12-15; I Tim. 5:10). Hence: we do not

ARTICLES OF FAITH (ASSOCIATED BROTHERHOOD OF CHRISTIANS) (continued)

support the practice of washing feet in public as a church ordinance.

P.   SECOND COMING OF CHRIST. We believe in the second personal coming of the Lord as taught by the Scriptures. (Acts 1:11; I Thes. 4:16; Heb. 9:28).

Q.   RESURRECTION. We believe in the Resurrection of the dead (Job 19:26; Isa. 26:19; Dan. 12:2; Rev. 20:11-15).

R.   JUDGEMENT. We believe that all will appear before the judgement Seat of Christ to be judged according to the deeds done in the body (Eccl. 12:14; II Cor. 5:10; Rev. 20:11-15).

S.   THE SABBATH. We do not hold that our Salvation is contingent upon keeping of certain days, or times. See Romans 14:5-6; Gal. 5:1; Col. 2:16.

T.   MARRIAGE AND DIVORCE. We believe that divorce and remarriage is unscriptural and forbidden, except where fornication (as defined by the Scripture) is proven to be the cause of separation. See Matt. 19:3-17; I Cor. 5:1.

U.   MORAL STANDARD. We believe in the highest possible standard of moral living, therefore we do not tolerate the Doctrine of Free Love, Spiritual Companionship, Social Purity, or any other kindred teachings that might lead to immoral conduct.

V.   BELIEVERS SECURITY. We believe that it is possible for those who have been enlightened, and have tasted of the good Word of God to fall from their steadfastness in Christ (Heb. 3:12-19; II Pet. 3:17). Therefore, the believer is secure from the judgements of God only as he maintains his fellowship with Christ.

W.   MEATS AND DRINKS. We believe in total abstinence from all alcoholic drinks. We believe that the eating of meats referred to by Moses under the Law and the drinking of Tea, or Coffee is not obligatory to our Christian experience. However, anyone may refrain from these things at his or her own discretion but must not try to impose such personal opinions upon others.

X.   REDEMPTION OF THE BODY. We believe we shall receive our Redeemed Bodies at the Second Appearing of our Lord. (Rom. 8:22-23; I Cor. 5:1-5; 15:43-55; I Thes. 4:16-17).

Y.   WAR. We believe that war comes from the enemy of mankind and that it is condemned by the Word of God: That if smitten on one cheek, we as Christians should "turn the other also" (Matt. 5:39; Luke 6:29). Thou shalt not kill (Matt. 5:21). We therefore, desire to be loyal to our Government and above all loyal to God, and since the Scriptures forbids us to kill we recommend that our members accept the provision offered them by the Laws of our Government which gives them the privilege to register as a conscientious objector to War in Any Form, or to register as an objector to Combat Duty where the bearing of Arms is required.

Z.   FINALLY. We believe in the seven principles of the doctrine of Christ (Heb. 6:1-2), with all their connections throughout the New Testament as revealed by the Holy Spirit from time to time.

* * *

WHAT WE BELIEVE (BETHEL MINISTERIAL ASSOCIATION)

PREAMBLE

The purpose of the Bethel Temple is to proclaim the gospel of the Lord Jesus Christ as it was taught by the Apostles in the beginning of the Church Age, which we believe to be as follows:

DIVINE INSPIRATION OF THE SCRIPTURE

"For the prophecy came not in old time by the will of man; but holy men of God spake as they were moved by the Holy Ghost" (2 Peter 1:21).

The Bible, being a revelation of the supernatural God, is a supernatural Book—a Book of miracles—not understood by the natural mind (1 Cor. 2:14).

The Bible gives the only plausible explanation of life. The wisest of men, so called, who do not believe the Bible must admit: "Concerning the origin of life, we know little." The Bible reveals God as the source of all life.

The Divine Authorship of the Bible is further proved by the scientific and biological fact that God made all creation with seed in itself able to reproduce after its kind, according to the record in Genesis 1:11, 21, 24, 28. And the Genesis account that man was made from dust (chemical substances in the ground) is corroborated by the fact that man must subsist from that which the ground produces (same chemical substances).

The prophecies of the Bible prove conclusively that the Bible is Divinely inspired. No man could predict 4,000 years ahead concerning future events and describe those events in minute detail, as does the Bible.

Jesus Christ sanctioned all the Writings of the prophets (Matt. 24:37-39; Luke 17:28-32). He sanctioned all the Old Testament Scriptures (Luke 24:27). He sanctioned the Genesis account of the creation of man (Matt. 19:14).

Jesus Christ proved that He was Divine by His resurrection from the dead.

Since Jesus Christ was Divine, and He sanctioned the Scriptures, we must conclude that the Bible is the Divinely inspired Word of God, and the true revelation of God to man.

CHURCH MEMBERSHIP

Bethel's Articles of Incorporation, dated February 17, 1944, state: "This Church will welcome into its membership all who desire to unite in a common effort toward the achievement of its aims and purposes."

We believe God's people are ONE because of Calvary. It is our love and loyalty to Christ which bind us together. Briefly, our position is this:

In things non-essential . . . LIBERTY

In things essential . . . UNITY

In all things . . . CHARITY

CHURCH GOVERNMENT

The Church is governed by the pastor, a Church Board consisting of five members or more, a Board of Trustees consisting of three members or more, a secretary and treasurer, which may be one person or two persons, and any other officers which may be considered necessary. Any business of major importance shall be brought before the entire Church for decision.

The officers of the Church shall be appointed by the pastor, approved by the Church and shall serve until their successors are appointed (a copy of all appointed and elected officers of the church may be obtained by telephoning the church office).

CIVIL GOVERNMENT

Bethel Temple hereby declares its loyalty to our government and to its Chief Executive, and hereby states its fixed purpose to assist our government in every way morally possible, consistent with our faith (Romans 13:1-7).

Bethel Temple believes that nations can and should whenever possible, settle their differences without going to war; however, in the event of war, if a member engages in combatant service, it will not affect his status with the Church. In case a member is called into military service who has conscientious objections to combatant service, Bethel Temple and the Ministers of the Bethel Baptist Assembly will support him in his constitutional rights.

MAN

Man was created in the image and likeness of God (Gen. 1:26). Adam's sin was passed on to the human family (Rom. 5:12-14). For all have sinned and come short of the glory of God (Rom. 3:23). In the last man Adam (1 Cor. 15:45), all are made alive (Rom. 5:15-21).

SALVATION

Salvation is obtained through obedience to the gospel which is the death, burial and resurrection of Jesus Christ (1 Cor. 15:1-4). God's plan of obedience is faith, repentance and baptism in order to receive the Holy Ghost, which is the Spirit of Christ (Acts 2:38, Acts 16:31-33, Acts 10:44-48).

WATER BAPTISM

Baptism is burial with Christ by immersion in water in the Name of the Lord Jesus Christ, and should be administered immediately after one has thoroughly repented of sins and turned from the world (Acts 2:38, Rom. 6:4,5, Acts 16:33).

SPIRIT BAPTISM

Baptism in the Spirit is the new birth which places one in the Body of Christ, which is the Church (1 Cor. 12:13, Gal. 3:27, Col. 1:4). The evidence of the new birth or baptism in the Spirit is the love of God (1 John 3:14). On the day of Pentecost there was a two-fold operation of the Spirit. They were first baptized into the Spirit which formed the Church, the Body of Christ, and they were also immediately filled with the Spirit (Acts 1:5, Acts 2:4).

THE FILLING OF THE SPIRIT

We teach that every Christian who has received the Spirit through the new birth, or baptism into Christ, should yield to the Spirit to be possessed or filled with the Spirit for the operation of all the gifts of the Spirit according to 1 Cor. 12:7-11, Acts 2:4, Acts 10:46, Acts 19:6. To receive the Spirit, and be possessed by or filled with the Spirit are two different experiences in a believer's life. This is the same Spirit but greater possession.

To illustrate: Every sinner has the spirit of the devil but not every sinner is demon possessed, so every Christian has the Spirit of Christ but not every Christian is filled with the Spirit.

THE GODHEAD

There is one God in three manifestations, Father, Son and Holy Spirit. God is an invisible Spirit (John 4:24, Col. 1:15). Jesus Christ is God, the invisible Spirit, manifest in the flesh (1 Tim. 3:16, John 1:14).

THE VIRGIN BIRTH

Jesus was born of a virgin (Matt. 1:23).

TITHING

Tithing is God's financial plan to provide for His work, and has been His only plan since the days of Abraham. It was practiced under Moses' law and Jesus endorsed it (Matt. 23:23). If a Christian gives less than one-tenth of his increase to the work of God, he is robbing God (Mal. 3:10.

THE CHRISTIAN'S CONDUCT

Christians should dress in modest apparel and not follow the extreme, immodest fashions of the world (1 Tim. 2:9, 10). His speech should be as becometh a Christian (Col. 4:6).

TOBACCO AND ALCOHOLIC BEVERAGES

We urge our members to refrain from the use of tobacco and alcoholic beverages in any form (Gal. 5:24, 1 Pet. 2:11, 2 Cor. 7:1).

THE SECOND COMING OF CHRIST

The second coming of Christ is in two stages, the rapture and revelation. In the rapture Jesus will come for His saints before the great tribulation period starts (1 Thess. 4:13-18). In the revelation Jesus will come with His saints (Rev. 19:11-16) to smite the Anti-Christ and set up the millennial kingdom.

ETERNAL SECURITY

The eternal security of the believer depends on his obedience to God's Word (2 John 1:9, 1 John 3:24). God is able to keep us from falling and will keep us if we obey Him (2 Pet. 1:10). When a Christian sins or fails God he should repent, but if he fails to repent and persists in willful disobedience, the ultimate result will be spiritual death and eventually the lake of fire (1 John 5:16, Heb. 10:26, 27, 39).

RESTORATION OF ALL THINGS

The Scriptures teach the restoration of all things that were spoken of by the mouth of the prophets, but the prophets did not include the devil and his angels, nor sinners who reject the Lord Jesus Christ (Acts 3:21).

WHAT WE BELIEVE (BETHEL MINISTERIAL ASSOCIATION) (continued)

MARRIAGE AND DIVORCE

It is impossible to deal with the complicated marriage and divorce problems here. Suffice it to say that we advise Christians to marry Christians. To those who are divorced and remarried, and afterwards become saved, it is advisable to live with the companion to whom they are legally married at the time of their conversion.

THE LORD'S SUPPER

The Lord Jesus instituted the Lord's Supper (Matt. 26:26-29). This is an ordinance of the Church and as such is to be taken literally. Self-examination should precede partaking of the Lord's Supper. The Lord's Supper is a memorial service to shew the Lord's death till He comes (1 Cor. 11:26). The order and meaning of the Lord's table is set forth in 1 Cor. 11:23-34.

HEAVEN AND HELL

There is a literal hell for those who reject the Lord Jesus Christ as their personal Saviour (Matt. 10:28, Rev. 20:15). There is a literal heaven for those who accept the Lord Jesus Christ as their personal Saviour and live a life of obedience unto Him (John 14:1, 2, Rev. 7:9).

DIVINE HEALING

God heals in many ways; through medical science, the processes of nature and in answer to prayer. It is the privilege of the Christian today to go to the Lord for the healing of his body (James 5:14, 15).

During the earthly ministry of Jesus, He went about healing all manner of sickness and all manner of disease among the people (Matt. 4:23).

THE CHURCH

The Church had its beginning on the day of Pentecost and consists of all who are truly born of the Spirit, wherever they may be found (Acts 1:5, Gal. 3:27, 1 Cor. 12:13, Eph. 1:22, 23).

DENOMINATIONAL AFFILIATION

Though all the Bethel Churches are sovereign within themselves and emphasize a NON-SECTARIAN POSITION, they are affiliated with the Bethel Baptist Assembly and their ministers are licensed or ordained by the Bethel Baptist Assembly.

The Bethel Temple is incorporated as a non-profit corporation under the laws of the state of Indiana as Bethel Temple of Evansville, Incorporated.

Notes: *The Bethel Ministerial Association holds to several positions not found in the statements of other apostolic pentecostals. While not pacifist, it will support individual conscientious objectors. It teaches that those who have divorced and remarried should stay with their legal marriage partner at the time of their becoming Christians. There is no statement on foot washing.*

ARTICLES OF FAITH (NEW BETHEL CHURCH OF GOD IN CHRIST)

THE ONE TRUE GOD

We believe in the one everliving, eternal God: infinite in power, Holy in nature, attributes and purpose; and possessing absolute, indivisible deity. This one true God has revealed Himself as Father, through His Son, in redemption; and as the Holy Spirit, by emanation. (1 Cor. 8:6; Eph. 4:6; 2 Cor. 5:19; Joel 2:28).

The Scripture does more than attempt to prove the existence of God; it asserts, assumes and declares that the knowledge of God is universal. (Romans 1:19, 21, 28, 32; 2:15). God is invisible, incorporeal, without parts, without body, and therefore free from all limitations. He is Spirit (John 4:24), and ". . . a spirit hath not flesh and bones . . . " (Luke 24:39).

". . . The first of all the commandments is, hear, O Israel; the Lord our God is one Lord" (Mark 12:39; Deut. 6:4). "One God and Father of all, who is above all, and through all, and in you all" (Eph. 4:6).

This one true God manifested Himself in the Old Testament in divers ways; in the Son while He walked among men; as the Holy Spirit after the ascension.

THE SON OF GOD

The one true God, the Jehovah of the Old Testament, took upon Himself the form of man, and as the Son of man, was born of the virgin Mary. As Paul says, "and without controversy great is the mystery of Godliness: God was manifest in the flesh, justified in the Spirit, seen of angels, preached unto the Gentiles, believed on in the world, received up into glory" (I Timothy 3:16).

"He came unto His own, and His own received Him not (John 1:11). This one true God was manifest in the flesh, that is, in His Son Jesus Christ. ". . . God was in Christ, reconciling the world unto Himself, not imputing their trespasses unto them. . ." (2 Cor. 5:19).

We believe that, ". . . in Him (Jesus) dwelleth all the fulness of the Godhead bodily" (Col. 2:9). "For it pleased the Father that in Him should all fulness dwell" (Col. 1:19). Therefore, Jesus in His humanity was and is man; in his diety was and is God. His flesh was the lamb, or the sacrifice of God. He is the only mediator between God and man. "For there is one God, and one mediator between God and men, the man Christ Jesus" (1 Timothy 2:5).

Jesus on His Father's side was divine, on His mother's side, human; Thus, He was known as the Son of God and also the Son of man, or the God-man.

"For He hath put all things under His feet. But when He saith all things are put under Him, it is manifest that He is excepted, which did put all things under Him" (1 Cor. 15:27). "And when all things shall be subdued unto Him, then shall the Son also Himself be subject unto Him that put all things under Him, that God may be all in all" (1 Cor. 15:28).

"I am Alpha and Omega, the beginning and the ending, saith the Lord, which is, and which was, and which is to come, the Almighty" (Rev. 1:8).

THE NAME

God used different titles, such as "God Elohim," "God Almighty," "El Shaddai," Jehovah," and especially "Jehovah Lord," the redemptive name in the Old Testament.

". . . unto us a child is born, unto us a son is given; . . . and His name shall be called Wonderful, Counsellor, The Mighty God, The Everlasting Father, The Prince of Peace" (Isaiah 9:6). This prophecy of Isaiah was fulfilled when the Son of God was named, "And she shall bring forth a son, and thou shalt call His name Jesus: for He shall save His people from their sins" (Matt. 1:21).

"Neither is there salvation in any other: for there is none other name under heaven given among men, whereby we must be saved" (Acts 4:12).

CREATION OF MAN AND HIS FALL

In the beginning God created man innocent, pure and holy; but through the sin of disobedience, Adam and Eve, the first of the human race, fell from their holy state, and God banished them from Eden. Hence by one man's disobedience, sin entered into the world. (Gen. 1:27; Rom. 3:23, 5:12).

REPENTANCE AND CONVERSION

Pardon and forgiveness of sins is obtained by genuine repentance, a confessing and forsaking of sins. We are justified by faith in the Lord Jesus Christ (Romans 5:1). John the Baptist preached repentance, Jesus proclaimed it, and the Apostles emphasized it to both Jews and Gentiles. (Acts 2:38; 11:18; 17:30).

The word "repentance" comes from several Greek words which mean, change of views and purpose, change of heart, change of mind, change of life, to transform, etc.

Jesus said, ". . . except ye repent, ye shall all likewise perish" (Luke 13:3).

Luke 24:47 says, "And that repentance and remission of sins should be preached in His name among all nations, beginning at Jerusalem."

WATER BAPTISM

The scripture mode of baptism is immersion, and is only for those who have fully repented, having turned from their sins and a love of the world. It should be administered by a duly authorized minister of the Gospel, in obedience to the word of God, and in the name of our Lord Jesus Christ, according to the Acts of the Apostles 2:38; 8:16; 10:48; 19:5; thus obeying and fulfilling Matthew 28:19.

THE BAPTISM OF THE HOLY SPIRIT

John the Baptist, in Matthew 3:11, said, ". . . He shall baptize you with the Holy Ghost, and with fire."

Jesus, in Acts 1:5, said ". . . ye shall be baptized with the Holy Ghost not many days hence."

Luke tells us in Acts 2:4, ". . . they were all filled with the Holy Ghost, and began to speak with other tongues (languages), as the Spirit gave them utterance."

The terms "baptize with the Holy Ghost and fire," "filled with the Holy Spirit," and the "gift of the Holy Ghost" are synonymous terms used interchangeably in the Bible.

It is scriptural to expect all who receive the gift, filling, or baptism of the Holy Spirit to receive the same physical, initial sign of speaking with other tongues.

The speaking with other tongues, as recorded in Acts 2:4; 10:46, and 19:6, and the gift of tongues, as explained in 1 Corinthians, chapters 12 and 14, are the same in essence but different in use and purpose.

The Lord, through the Prophet Joel, said, ". . . I will pour out my Spirit upon all flesh; . . . (Joel 2:28).

Peter, in explaining this phenomenal experience, said, ". . . having received of the Father the promise of the Holy Ghost, He (Jesus) hath shed forth this which ye now see and hear." (Acts 2:33).

Further, ". . . the promise is unto you, and to your children, and to all that are afar off, even as many as the Lord our God shall call." (Acts 2:39).

FUNDAMENTAL DOCTRINE

The basic and fundamental doctrine of this organization shall be the Bible standard of full salvation, which is repentance, baptism in water by immersion in the name of the Lord Jesus Christ, and the baptism of the Holy Ghost with the initial sign of speaking with other tongues as the Spirit gives utterance.

We shall endeavor to keep the unity of the Spirit until we all come into the unity of the faith, at the same time admonishing all brethren that they shall not contend for their different views to the disunity of the body.

DIVINE HEALING

The first covenant that the Lord (Jehovah) made with the children of Israel after they were brought out of Egypt was a covenant of healing. The Lord said, ". . . if thou wilt diligently hearken to the voice of the Lord (Jehovah-Rapha, the Lord that healeth) thy God, and wilt do that which is right in His sight, and wilt give ear to His commandments, and keep all His statutes, I will put none of these diseases upon thee, which I have brought upon the Egyptians; for I am the Lord that healeth thee." (Exodus 15:26).

Some translations read: "For I am Jehovah, thy physician." He being our physician or doctor, we have the most capable in the whole world. Our Lord Jesus went about Galilee, preaching the Gospel of the Kingdom, and healing all manner of sickness and disease among the people. Matthew 4:23, 24).

"Jesus Christ the same yesterday, and today, and forever." (Hebrews 13:8).

The vicarious suffering of the Lord Jesus Christ paid for the healing of our bodies, the same as for the salvation of our souls, for ". . . with His stripes we are healed" (Isaiah 35:5). Matthew 8:17 reads, ". . . Himself took infirmities, and bare our sickness." (See also 1 Peter 2:24).

We see from this that divine healing for the body is in the atonement. That being true, then it is for all who believe. Jesus said of believers, ". . . they shall lay hands on the sick, and they shall recover." Later, James wrote in his Epistle to all the churches: "Is any sick among you? Let him call for the elders of the church; and let them pray over him, anointing him with oil in the name of the Lord:

and the prayer of faith shall save the sick, and the Lord shall raise him up; and if he have committed sins, they shall be forgiven him. Confess your faults one to another, and pray one for another, that ye may be healed. The effectual fervent prayer of a righteous man availeth much." (James 5:14-16).

All of these promises are for the church today.

SACRAMENT OR COMMUNION

On the night of our Lord's betrayal, He ate the Passover supper with His Apostles, after which He instituted the sacrament. "And He took bread, and gave thanks, and brake it, and gave unto them, saying, this is my body which is given for you: This do in remembrance of me. Likewise also the cup after supper, saying, this cup is the New Testament in my blood, which is shed for you." (Luke 22:19-20).

Paul instructed the church how to observe it (1 Cor. 11:23-34).

Thus was instituted the use of literal bread and the fruit of the vine, which are partaken of, literally, as emblems of His broken body and shed blood. There is also a spiritual significance and blessing in partaking of the sacrament.

FEET-WASHING

When the Passover supper was ended, we read in John 13:4; "He riseth from supper, and laid aside His garments; and took a towel, and girded Himself. After that He poureth water into a basin, and began to wash the disciples' feet, and to wipe them with the towel wherewith He was girded."

Jesus said, "If I then, your Lord and Master, have washed your feet; ye also ought to wash one another's feet. For I have given you an example, that ye should do as I have done to you" (John 13:14-15).

This first example was given by our Lord, and it is a divine institution. It is well to follow His example and wash one another's feet; thus manifesting the spirit of humility.

HOLINESS

Godly living should characterize the life of every child of the Lord, and we should live according to the pattern and example given in the Word of God. "For the grace of God that bringeth salvation hath appeared to all men, teaching us that, denying ungodliness and worldly lusts, we should live soberly, righteously, and Godly, in this present world" (Titus 2:11, 12). "For even hereunto were ye called: because Christ also suffered for us, leaving us an example, that ye should follow His steps: who did no sin, neither was guile found in His mouth: who, when He was reviled, reviled not again; when He suffered, He threatened not; but committed Himself to Him that judgeth righteously" (1 Peter 2:21-23).

"Follow peace with all men, and holiness, without which no man shall see the Lord" (Heb. 12:14).

"But as He which hath called you is holy, so be ye holy in all manner of conversation; because it is written, be ye holy; for I am holy. And if ye call on the Father, who without respect of persons judgeth according to every man's work, pass the time of your sojourning here in fear: forasmuch as ye know that ye were not redeemed with corruptible things, as silver and gold, from your vain conversation received by tradition from your fathers; but with the precious blood of Christ, as of a lamb without blemish and without spot" (1 Peter 1:15-19).

THE GRACE OF GOD

"For the grace of God that bringeth salvation hath appeared to all men, teaching us that, denying ungodliness and worldly lusts, we should live soberly, righteously, and Godly, in this present world" (Titus 2:11, 12).

"For the law was given by Moses, but grace and truth came by Jesus Christ" (John 1:17).

A Christian, to keep saved, must walk with God and keep himself in the love of God (Jude 21) and in the grace of God. The word "grace" means "favor." When a person transgresses and sins against God, he loses his favor. If he continues to commit sin and does not repent, he will eventually be lost and cast into the lake of fire. (Read John 15:2, 6; 2 Peter 2:20-22). Jude speaks of the backsliders of his day, and their reward. (Also, read Hebrews 6:4-6).

"For by grace are ye saved through faith; and that not of yourselves; it is the gift of God" (Eph. 2:8).

RESTITUTION OF ALL THINGS

We understand the scripture to teach the restitution of all things, which God hath spoken by the mouth of all His holy prophets since the world began. (Acts 3:21). But we cannot find where the devil, his angels, and all sinners are included. (See Rev. 20:10).

CONSCIENTIOUS SCRUPLES

We recognize the institution of human government as being of divine ordination, and, in so doing, affirm unswerving loyalty to our government; however, we take a definite position regarding the bearing of arms or the taking of human life.

As followers of the Lord Jesus Christ, the Prince of Peace, we believe in implicit obedience to His commandments and precepts, which instruct us as follows: ". . . that ye resist not evil. . ." (Matt. 5:39): "Follow peace with all men. . ." (Heb. 12:14). (See also Matt. 26:52; Rom. 12:19; James 5:6; Revelation 13:10). These we believe and interpret to mean Christians shall not shed blood nor take human life.

Therefore, we propose to fulfill all obligations of loyal citizens, but are constrained to declare against participating in combat service in war, armed insurrection, property destruction, aiding or abetting in or the actual destruction of human life.

Furthermore, we cannot conscientiously affiliate with any union, boycott, or organization which will force or bind any of its members to belong to any organization, perform any duties contrary to our conscience or receive any mark, without our right to affirm or reject same. (1930).

However, we regret the false impression created by some groups or so-called "conscientious objectors" that to obey the Bible is to have a contempt for law or magistrates, to be disloyal to our government and in sympathy with our enemies, or to be willing to sacrifice for the preservation of our commonwealth. This attitude would be as contemptible to us as to any patriot. The Word of God commands us to do violence to no man. It also commands us that first of all we are to pray for rulers of our country. We, therefore, exhort our members to freely and willingly respond to the call of our Government except in the matter of bearing arms. When we say service, we mean service—no matter how hard or dangerous. The true church has no more place for cowards than has the nations. First of all, however, let us earnestly pray that we will with honor be kept out of war.

We believe that we can be consistent in serving our Government in certain noncombatant capacities, but not in the bearing of arms. (1940).

SECRET SOCIETIES, ETC.

According to the Word of God, we firmly believe and hold that the people of God should have no connection whatever with secret societies, or any other organization or body wherein there is a fellowship with unbelievers, bound by an oath. (James 5:3-7; 2 Cor. 6:14-18).

TRANSLATION OF SAINTS

We believe that the time is drawing near when our Lord shall appear; then the death in Christ shall arise, and we who are alive and remain shall be caught up with them to meet our Lord in the air. (1 Thess. 4:13-17; 1 Cor. 15:51-54; Phil. 3:20-21).

MARRIAGE AND DIVORCE

"Whosoever shall put away his wife, except it be for fornication, and shall marry another, committeth adultery: (Matt. 19:9), Matt. 5:32). When this sin has been committed, the innocent party may be free to remarry only in the Lord. Our desire being to raise a higher standard for the ministry. We recommend that ministers do not marry again.

Judgment begins at the House of God. See instructions for the ministry under Article VI, Section 6.

TITHING

We believe tithing is God's financial plan to provide for His work, and has been since the days of Abraham. Tithing came with faith under Abraham; Moses' law enjoined it, and Israel practiced it when she was right with God; Jesus endorsed it (Matt. 23:23); and Paul said to lay by in store as God has prospered you. Do not rob God of His portion, viz., tithes and offerings. (Read Mal. 3.)

SECOND COMING OF JESUS

That Jesus is coming again the second time in person, just as He went away, is clearly set forth by the Lord Jesus Himself, and was preached and taught in the early Christian church by the apostles; hence, the children of God today are earnestly, hopefully, looking forward to the glorious event. (Matt. 24; Acts 1:11, 3:19-21; 1 Cor. 11:26; Phil. 3:20-21; 1 Thess. 4:14-17; Titus 2:13, 14.)

THE MILLENNIUM

Moreover, we believe that the distress upon the earth is the "beginning of sorrows" and will become more intense until there "shall be a time of trouble such as there never was since there was a nation even to that same time" (Matt. 24:3-8; Dan. 12:1), and that period of "tribulation" will be followed by the dawn of a better day on earth and that for a thousand years there shall be "peace on earth and good will toward men." (Rev. 20:1-5; Isa. 65:17-25; Matt. 5:5; Dan. 7:27; Mic. 4:1, 2; Heb. 2:14; Rom. 11:25-27.)

FINAL JUDGMENT

When the thousand years are finished, there shall be a resurrection of all the dead, who will be summoned before the great white throne for their final judgment, and all whose names are not found written in the Book of Life shall be cast into the lake of fire, burning with brimstone, which God hath prepared for the Devil and his angels, Satan himself being cast in first. (Matt. 25:41; Rev. 20:7-15; 21:8).

PUBLIC SCHOOL ACTIVITIES

We disapprove of school students attending shows, dancing classes, theatres, engaging in school activities against their religious scruples and wearing gymnasium clothes which immodestly expose the body.

Notes: *Although the New Bethel Church of God in Christ was formed by former members of the Church of God in Christ, its doctrinal statement follows the text and format of the United Pentecostal Church's articles.*

* * *

CREED (PENTECOSTAL ASSEMBLIES OF THE WORLD)

PREAMBLE

In order to foster better cooperation among all churches and saints of the P. A. of W. Inc., and to advance the kingdom of God among ministers and saints of the said churches, we do set forth the following legislation as our Constitution, Fundamental Rules, and Articles of Religion, Organization and Government.

ARTICLE I

Apostolic Doctrine and Fellowship According to the Bible. Our Creed, Discipline, Rules of Order, and Doctrine is the Word of God as taught and revealed by the Holy Ghost. (John 14:26; I Corinthians 2:9-13.)

"All scripture is given by inspiration of God, and is profitable for doctrine, for reproof, for correction, for instruction in righteousness, that the man of God may be perfect, thoroughly furnished unto all good works." (II Timothy 3:16, 17).

ARTICLE II. THE GODHEAD

We fully believe in the mystery of the Godhead. We believe that God has been pleased to manifest Himself as a Father, the Source of all life, as a Son, the Channel and Redeemer of all life, and as the Holy Ghost, the Revealer and Energizer of all life. The Father is the invisible God who is made visible in Jesus, and the Holy Ghost is the invisible counterpart of God. The Father is God in creation, the Son is God in redemption, and the Holy Ghost is God in inspiration. When one manifestation of the Godhead is patent, that is, can be seen, the other two are latent, that is, they can only be seen through the one that is patent. (John 14:6-12). Jesus was both human and

CREED (PENTECOSTAL ASSEMBLIES OF THE WORLD) (continued)

divine; Mary's son and Mary's God; Creator and Creature; God manifest in the flesh and Eternal Father made visible apart from whom there is no God. We believe that at the final consummation of all things, the one visible God will be our Lord Jesus Christ.

ARTICLE III. NAME OF GOD

We believe that God has changed His name to suit the dispensational needs of His people. His present dispensational name is the Lord Jesus Christ.

ARTICLE IV. MEMBERSHIP—HOW OBTAINED

As members of the Body of Christ, which is the true Church, (Ephesians 1:22, 23,) the Word of God declares but one way of entrance therein and that is, "By one Spirit are we all baptized into one body." This is a baptism of "water and spirit." (I Corinthians 12:12-27; Gal. 3:26-28; Rom. 6:3, 4; John 3:5; Acts 2:38.)

ARTICLE V. REPENTANCE AND REMISSION OF SINS

The only condition on which God will accept a sinner is repentance from the heart for the sins which he has committed—a broken and contrite heart He will not despise. (Psalm 51:17.) John preached repentance, Jesus proclaimed it, and before His Ascension, commanded that repentance and remission of sins should be preached in His Name, beginning at Jerusalem. (Luke 24:47.) Peter fulfilled this command on the Day of Pentecost. (Acts 2:38.)

ARTICLE VI. BAPTISM

We believe that baptism by immersion should be administered "in the name of the Lord Jesus Christ for the remission of sins" only to persons who have reached the age of understanding, and under no condition, do we approve of the baptism of infants. We believe that the initial sign of the Holy Ghost is speaking in tongues. (Acts 2:4; 10:46; 19:6.)

As this rite of baptism is only effectual when one repents of one's sins and believes the Gospel with his heart, prior to its administration, the officiating minister should be careful to examine each candidate as to his belief in the Gospel of Grace which concerns the Person, death, burial, and resurrection of the Lord Jesus Christ for the remission of sins" to persons who have reached the age of understanding and not to infants, under any condition.

FORM OF BAPTISM

The Candidate having entered the water with the Baptizer, shall surrender (himself or herself) to the Baptizer who shall cross the hands of the Candidate. Then a short prayer shall be offered and the following said:

My dearly beloved _____ upon the confession of your faith in the Death, Burial and Resurrection of the Lord Jesus Christ and in the confidence which we have in the Blessed Word of God, I now baptize thee in the name of the Lord Jesus Christ, for the Remission of Sins and ye shall receive the gift of the Holy Ghost. Amen.

ARTICLE VII. RECORD OF MEMBERSHIP

The names of the members are kept on record in heaven. (Luke 10:20.) For it is written, "The Lord shall count, when He writeth up the people, that this man was born there." (Psalms 87:6.) All in this dispensation must be born of "water and spirit," if they desire their names to be written in heaven. (See Hebrews 12:22-23.)

Nevertheless, each church should keep a record of its membership in order to know for whom it is responsible.

ARTICLE VIII. SECOND BIRTH

We believe the second birth to be limited to the human family only, and to be born again is to be born of the water and of the spirit. (John 3:5.)

ARTICLE IX. HOW NAMES ARE BLOTTED OUT

We have nothing whatever to do with the blotting out of names, for thus saith the Lord. "Whosoever hath sinned against me, him will I blot out of my book." (Exodus 32:33.) "He that overcometh—I will not blot out his name out of the book of life." (Rev. 3:5.)

ARTICLE X. GOD'S STANDARD OF SALVATION

We earnestly contend for God's standard of salvation. In the Word of God, we can find nothing short of a holy spirit-filled life with signs following as on the Day of Pentecost. (Mark 16:17-18; Acts 2:4; 8:14-17; 9:17-18; 10:44-48; 19:1-16; Rom. 12:1-21; Heb. 12:14; Matt. 5:48; I Peter 1:15-16.)

ARTICLE XI. THE WHOLLY SANCTIFIED LIFE

We believe that in order to escape the judgment of God and to have the hope of enjoying the glory of life eternal, one must be thoroughly saved from his sins, wholly sanctified unto God, and filled with the Holy Ghost. A wholly sanctified life is the only true standard of a Christian life. (Heb. 12:14; I Peter 1:15-17.)

ARTICLE XII. THE LORD'S SUPPER

Melchisedec, "Priest of the Most High God," gave the first communion consisting of bread and wine to our father Abraham. (Gen. 14:18.) Christ being our "High Priest after the order of Melchisedec," (Heb. 6:20) evidently administered the same. Water and grape juice are modern substitutes that have been introduced by the formal churches of today in which there are many who have never been regenerated and born of the Spirit. (Matt. 26:26-29; I Cor. 11:23-34.)

ARTICLE XIII. FEET WASHING

This ordinance is as much a divine command as any other New Testament ordinance. Jesus gave us an example in order that we should do even as He did. He said that we ought to wash one another's feet. There is scriptural evidence in I Timothy 5:10 that this was practised by the Church in the day of the Apostle Paul. "If ye know these things, happy are ye if ye do them." (See John 13:14-17.)

ARTICLE XIV. HEALING BY FAITH

The Lord is our Healer. (Ex. 15:26; Psalms 103:2-3.) Since the Lord made our bodies, should it be thought incredible that He should be able to heal them? "With his stripes we are healed." (Isa. 53:4-5; Matt. 8:14-17; John 14:12; Mark 16-17-18; James 5:14.)

ARTICLE XV. THE COMING OF JESUS

That Jesus is coming again in person is a doctrine clearly set forth in apostolic times. Jesus taught it, the Apostles preached it, and the saints expected it. (I Thess. 4:14-17. Titus 2:13-14.)

ARTICLE XVI. TRANSLATION OF THE SAINTS

We believe that the time draweth near for the coming of the Lord to make a change in the present order of things. At that time, all the righteous dead shall arise from their graves, and they that are living righteous before God shall be translated or "caught up to meet the Lord in the air." (Matt. 24:36-42; Luke 17:20-37; I Cor. 15:51-54; Phillippians 3:20-21; I Thess. 5:1-10.)

ARTICLE XVII. THE MILLENIUM

Moreover, we believe that the distress upon the earth is the beginning of sorrows and will become more intense until "there shall be a time of trouble such as never was since there was a nation even to that same time." (Matt. 24:3-12; Dan. 12:1.) That period of tribulation will be followed by the dawn of a better day on earth, and for one thousand years thereafter, there shall be peace on earth and good will toward men. (Matt. 5:5; Isa. 65:17-25; Dan. 7:27; Micah 4:1-2; Heb. 2:14; Rom. 11:25-27.)

ARTICLE XVIII. FINAL JUDGMENT

When the thousand years shall have passed, there shall be a resurrection of the dead who shall be summoned before the Great White Throne for their final judgment. All those whose names are not found written in the Book of Life shall be cast into the Lake of Fire, burning with brimstone, which God has prepared for the Devil and his angels. (Rev. 20:10-15.)

ARTICLE XIX. RELATIONSHIP TO CIVIL GOVERNMENT

All civil rulers are ordained of God for peace, safety, and for the welfare of the people. (Rom. 13:1-17.) Therefore, it is our duty to be in obedience to all requirements of the law which are not contrary to the Word of God, or do not force us to the violation of the Sixth Commandment by bearing arms and taking life. It is our duty to honor our rulers, to show respect to them in all requirements of the civil law, and to pay tribute or such taxation as may be required without murmuring. (Matt. 17:24-27; 22:17-21.)

ARTICLE XX. MALTREATMENT

In times of persecution or ill-treatment at the hands of an enemy, we should not avenge ourselves, "but rather give place unto wrath: for it is written, Vengeance is mine; I will repay, saith the Lord." (Rom. 12:19; Deut. 32:33.) Neither should we take up any weapon of destruction to slay another, whether in our own defense or in the defense of others, for it is also written, "Do violence to no man." (Luke 3:14; Matt. 26:52; John 18:10-11, 36.) We should rather suffer wrong than do wrong.

ARTICLE XXI. SECRET SOCIETIES

According to the Word of God, we firmly believe and hold that the people of God should have no connection whatsoever with Secret Societies or any other organization or body wherein there is a fellowship of unbelievers bound by an oath (James 4:4). Members of the Pentecostal Assemblies of the World and its auxiliaries shall not work as pickets or by any other measure bar the way of others to or from their work. This does not abridge their rights to pay dues to the union and work for their families.

Notes: *One of the oldest of pentecostal churches, the Pentecostal Assemblies of the World was also one of the first to adopt the apostolic position. The church practices foot washing.*

* * *

APOSTOLIC DOCTRINE AND FELLOWSHIP ACCORDING TO THE BIBLE [UNITED CHURCH OF JESUS CHRIST (APOSTOLIC)]

The United Church of Jesus Christ (Apostolic) accepts as its Creed, Discipline, Rules of Order and Doctrine the Word of God as taught and revealed by the Holy Ghost. John 14:26; I. Cor. 2:9-13.

"All scriptures are given by the inspiration of God, and is profitable for doctrine, for reproof, for correction, for instruction in righteousness; that the man of God may be perfect, thoroughly furnished unto all good works." II Timothy 3:16-17.

We stand for all Scripture when rightly divided.

THE UNITY OF THE DIVINE BEING

"God is Spirit, and those who worship Him must worship Him in Spirit and truth." John 4:24 RSV. There is but one God, in essence and in person, from whom and in whom there is a divine threefold manifestation and relationship made known as the Father, Son and Holy Ghost. As Father, God is Creator, Source, Origin, and progenitor of all that is, things and souls. He is the self-existent, omniscient, omnipresent, and omnipotent one. As Son, God becomes the perfect Man that He intends all men to be like. Thus, as Son He redeems man from sin, coming into the world and assuming personality through the miracle and mystery of the virgin birth. "In His own body He bore our sins" and wrought redemption through death for all mankind. "For all have sinned and fallen short of the glory of God." As Holy Ghost, God is regenerator and perfector of those who believe, the organizer and baptizer and sustainer of the church, the divine executor of the world. God as Father is Creator and first cause of all existence; as Son He is the Redeemer in time, and as the Holy Spirit He is Regenerator—The Lord Jesus Christ our Saviour, and "this is the true God and eternal life." "And we know that the Son of God has come and has given us understanding, to know Him who is true; and we are in Him who is true, in His son Jesus Christ. This is the true God and eternal life." I John 5:20. Thus we believe that Jesus was both human and divine; God manifest in the flesh, the Eternal Father made visible, apart from whom there is no God.

MEMBERSHIP—HOW OBTAINED

As members of the Body of Christ, which is the true church (Eph. 1:22-23), the Word of God declares that there is one way of entrance therein—"By one spirit are we

APOSTOLIC DOCTRINE AND FELLOWSHIP ACCORDING TO THE BIBLE [UNITED CHURCH OF JESUS CHRIST (APOSTOLIC)] (continued)

all baptized into one body." Believers are added to the church and believers accept His Spirit, His Name and His Nature. Thus they are born of "water and the spirit." I Cor. 12:12-27; Gal. 3:26-28; Romans 6:3-8; John 3:5; Acts 2:38.

GOD'S STANDARD OF SALVATION

We believe in and earnestly contend for God's Standard of Salvation. The Word of God reveals nothing short of a Holy Spirit filled life with signs following as on the day of Pentecost. (Mark 16:16-17; Acts 2:4; 8:14-17; 9:17-18; 10:44-48; 19:1-6; Rom. 12:1-2; Heb. 12:14; Matt. 5:48; I Peter 1:15).

Those admitted to membership must subscribe to God's standard of salvation in full accord with the teaching of the same as set forth in the Bible.

(1) All members shall take as their rule of conduct the Word of God and shall conform outwardly and inwardly in their daily walk and conversation to its teachings.—Gal. 6:16.

(2) God's word commands that we not be unequally yoked together with unbelievers and that we should not have communion or fellowship with the unfruitful works of darkness, such as oath-bound social clubs, etc. (II Cor. 6:14; Eph. 5:11); that we should not conform to this world or the spirit of the age (Rom. 12:2); that we come out from among them, be separate, and turn away from those who have a form of godliness but deny the power thereof. (II Cor. 6:16; II Tim. 3:5); that we should cleanse ourselves from all filthiness of the flesh and Spirit, perfecting holiness in the fear of God (II Cor.7:1), thus we should refrain from the use, growth, or sale of tobacco in any form, and the use of "dope," or intoxicants. We should not use filthy speech, indulge in foolish talking or jesting, and so abstain from all appearance of evil (I Thes. 5:22). As members of the church and of His Body we should not become involved in activities which do not deepen our own spirituality and promote God's glory.

THE LORD'S SUPPER

The Lord's Supper is a sacramental rite instituted by our Lord. It was an act first instituted by the Lord to show forth an example of commemorating His suffering and death. The twelve disciples were witnesses as narrated in Matthew, Mark, and Luke. When Paul wrote the Corinthians concerning it, he said that it was given him by revelation. The Lord's Supper, therefore, is a sacred rite to be carried out by the Christian Church. It cannot be neglected without suffering serious harm and incurring the gravest responsibility.

We believe the "fruit of the vine" and unleavened bread to be the proper elements for this ordinance. As to time, place, and frequency of observation, we have no direct scriptural teaching. Our custom is to observe it once each month, at an evening service. (I Cor. 11:23-32; Luke 22:18; Matt. 26:26-29).

FEET WASHING

We believe that this ordinance is as much a divine command as any other New Testament ordinance. Jesus gave us an example that we should do even as He had done. He said that we ought to wash one another's feet. Again, "If ye know these things, happy are ye if you do them." (John 13:4-17). There is scriptural evidence that feet washing was practiced by the church in the days of Apostle Paul. (I Tim. 5:10).

MALTREATMENT

In times of persecution or ill-treatment at the hands of an enemy, we should not "avenge ourselves," but rather give place to wrath; for it is written, "Vengeance is mine; I will repay, saith the Lord," (Rom. 12:18; Deut. 32:35). Neither shall we take up any weapons to stay another, whether in our own defense or in the defense of others, for it is written, "Do violence to no man." (Luke 3:14; Matt. 26:52; John 18:36; 15:18, 19). We should rather suffer wrong than do wrong. We subscribe to the principle of non-violence. We believe that the shedding of human blood or the taking of human life to be contrary to the teaching of our Lord and Saviour, and as a body we are averse to war in all of its forms. We herewith offer our services to the President for any service that will not conflict with our conscientious scruples in this respect; with love to all, malice toward none, and due respect to all who differ with us in our interpretation of the scriptures.

CIVIL GOVERNMENT

All civil magistrates are ordained of God for peace, safety, and the well-being of all people (Rom. 13:1-10), therefore, it is our duty to be in obedience to all requirements of the laws that are not contrary to the Word of God. It is our duty to honor them, pay tribute, or such taxation as may be required without murmuring (Matt. 17:24-27; 22:17-21), and show respect to them in all lawful requirements of civil government.

BAPTISM

We baptize in the Name of Jesus Christ because it is Apostolic in origin and practice. (Acts 2:38; 8:12-17; 10:47, 48; 19:1-6). Bible students agree that the apostles founded and gave direction to the Church of God, Jesus Christ Himself being the chief cornerstone. Their teachings and doctrines are the fundamental principles upon which the church is built. In the days of His flesh Jesus taught His disciples the plan of salvation. Following His resurrection they saw Him alive and Jesus opened their understanding. The two men en route to Emmaus had their understanding opened up as Jesus said unto them, "Thus it behooved Christ to suffer and to rise from the dead the third day; and that repentance and remission of sins should be preached IN HIS NAME among all nations, beginning at Jerusalem. And ye are witnesses of these things." (Luke 24:46, 47).

According to Acts 2:38, the apostles obeyed the command of Jesus Christ in Luke 24:46, 47. In their obedience to the command of Jesus the apostles became first in the long line of believers to baptize in the Name of Jesus Christ.

Thus baptizing in the Name of Jesus Christ is not only Apostolic in origin, but in practice as well. No other mode of baptism is to be found in the New Testament. For more than one hundred years after Pentecost believers were baptized only in the Name—Jesus Christ, for the remission of sins.

We are exhorted to believe, to obey and follow the teaching of the apostles. (Heb. 2:1-4; Acts 2:38-43; Col. 2:3-9). To reject the teaching of the Apostles is to reject even Jesus Christ. In St. John 17:20 Jesus prayed that we should believe on Him through (the apostles') words.

We do not believe that there is a contradiction between Matt. 28:19, Luke 24:45-48, Mark 16:15-19, and Acts 2:38. We believe that the NAME of the Father and of the Son and of the Holy Ghost in Matt. 28:19, and MY NAME in Mark 16:15-18, and HIS NAME in Luke 24:47, all mean the same name—Jesus Christ. In Matt. 28:19, we have a commission or a command *given*; in Acts 2:38, we have the command *executed*. In the former, the apostles were told *what* to do; in the latter, they *did* it.

We do not baptize infants. We *bless* them or *dedicate* them to the Lord as early as possible after birth. It is the duty and privilege of parents to dedicate their children to God, thereby claiming God's covenant promises to parents and children.

Baptism is administered to all adult persons who show genuine repentance from the heart for sins. Indeed, genuine repentance is the only grounds upon which God will accept a sinner. "A broken and a contrite heart He will not despise." (Psalms 51:17). The time when children and young people come of years of discretion cannot be precisely fixed. A prudent minister should know when the Spirit is moving and when baptism is in order. In questionable cases involving children who appear to be too young, it is better to give an explanation of baptism in childlike language and go on with the baptism.

It should be kept in mind that not only is baptism for remission of sins, it is also an outward and visible sign of the grace of the Lord Jesus Christ. Through it we are initiated into the fellowship of His Holy Church, and become partakers of His righteousness and heirs of His life. In baptism, we "put on Christ," confessing that we believe in His life, His death, His burial, and His resurrection. As St. Paul writes to the Romans, "Know ye not, that so many of us as were baptized into Jesus Christ were baptized into His death? Therefore we are buried with Him by baptism into death: that like as Christ was raised up from the dead by the glory of the Father, even so we also should walk in newness of life." (Rom. 6:3-4).

(At the time of baptism, the candidate, having been examined as to his readiness for the rite, shall be led into the water, and the minister or the baptizer shall say:)

"Beloved Brother or Sister _____ , according to the confession of your faith in the life, death, burial and resurrection of our Lord Jesus Christ from the dead, and by the authority granted to me as minister of the Church of Jesus Christ, I now baptize thee in the Name—Lord Jesus Christ for the remission of sins, and God grant that you shall receive the gift of the Holy Ghost. Amen."

(Then shall the minister or the baptizer immerse the candidate into the water and immediately lift him up again.)

Notes: *While several of the items of the United Church's doctrine derive from the Pentecostal Assemblies of the World (foot washing, civil government), most of it is original to this body.*

* * *

ARTICLES OF FAITH (UNITED PENTECOSTAL CHURCH)

PREAMBLE

We believe the Bible to be inspired of God; the infallible Word of God. "All scripture is given by inspiration of God, and is profitable for doctrine, for reproof, for correction, for instruction in righteousness" (2 Timothy 3:16).

The Bible is the only God-given authority which man possesses; therefore, all doctrine, faith, hope, and all instruction for the church must be based upon, and harmonize with, the Bible. It is to be read and studied by all men everywhere, and can only be clearly understood by those who are anointed by the Holy Spirit (1 John 2:27). ". . . no prophecy of the scripture is of any private interpretation. For the prophecy came not in old time by the will of man: but Holy men of God spake as they were moved by the Holy Ghost" (2 Peter 1:20-21).

THE ONE TRUE GOD

We believe in the one everliving, eternal God: infinite in power, Holy in nature, attributes and purpose; and possessing absolute, indivisible deity. This one true God has revealed Himself as Father, through His Son, in redemption; and as the Holy Spirit, by emanation. (1 Cor. 8:6; Eph. 4:6; 2 Cor. 5:19; Joel 2:28).

The Scripture does more than attempt to prove the existence of God; it asserts, assumes and declares that the knowledge of God is universal. (Romans 1:19, 21, 28, 32; 2:15). God is invisible, incorporeal, without parts, without body, and therefore free from all limitations. He is Spirit (John 4:24), and ". . . a spirit hath not flesh and bones. . ." (Luke 24:39).

". . . The first of all the commandments is, hear, O Israel; the Lord our God is one Lord" (Mark 12:29; Deut. 6:4). "One God and Father of all, who is above all, and through all, and in you all" (Eph. 4:6).

This one true God manifested Himself in the Old Testament in divers ways; in the Son while He walked among men; as the Holy Spirit after the ascension.

THE SON OF GOD

The one true God, the Jehovah of the Old Testament, took upon Himself the form of man, and as the Son of man, was born of the virgin Mary. As Paul says, "and without controversy great is the mystery of Godliness: God was manifest in the flesh, justified in the Spirit, seen of angels, preached unto the Gentiles, believed on in the world, received up into glory" (1 Timothy 3:16).

"He came unto His own, and His own received Him not" (John 1:11). This one true God was manifest in the flesh, that is, in His Son Jesus Christ. ". . . God was in Christ, reconciling the world unto Himself, not imputing their trespasses unto them . . . " (2 Cor. 5:19).

We believe that, ". . . in Him (Jesus) dwelleth all the fulness of the Godhead bodily" (Col. 2:9). "For it pleased the Father that in Him should all fulness dwell" (Col. 1:19). Therefore, Jesus in His humanity was man; in His deity was and is God. His flesh was the lamb, or the sacrifice of God. He is the only mediator between God and man. "For there is one God, and one mediator between God and men, the man Christ Jesus" (1 Timothy 2:5).

Jesus on His Father's side was divine, on His mother's side, human; Thus, He was known as the Son of God and also the Son of man, or the God-man.

"For He hath put all things under His feet. But when He saith all things are put under Him, it is manifest that He is excepted, which did put all things under Him" (1 Cor. 15:27). "And when all things shall be subdued unto Him, then shall the Son also Himself be subject unto Him that put all things under Him, that God may be all in all" (1 Cor. 15:28).

"I am Alpha and Omega, the beginning and the ending, saith the Lord, which is, and which was, and which is to come, the Almighty" (Rev. 1:8).

THE NAME

God used different titles, such as "God Elohim," "God Almighty," "El Shaddai," "Jehovah," and especially "Jehovah Lord," the redemptive name in the Old Testament.

". . . unto us a child is born, unto us a son is given: . . . and His name shall be called Wonderful Counsellor, The Mighty God, The Everlasting Father, The Prince of Peace" (Isaiah 9:6). This prophecy of Isaiah was fulfilled when the Son of God was named, "And she shall bring forth a son, and thou shalt call His name Jesus: for He shall save His people from their sins" (Matt. 1:21).

"Neither is there salvation in any other: for there is none other name under heaven given among men, whereby we must be saved" (Acts 4:12).

CREATION OF MAN AND HIS FALL

In the beginning God created man innocent, pure and holy; but through the sin of disobedience, Adam and Eve, the first of the human race fell from their holy state, and God banished them from Eden. Hence by one man's disobedience, sin entered into the world. (Gen. 1:27; Rom. 3:23; 5:12).

REPENTANCE AND CONVERSION

Pardon and forgiveness of sins is obtained by genuine repentance, a confessing and forsaking of sins. We are justified by faith in the Lord Jesus Christ (Romans 5:1). John the Baptist preached repentance, Jesus proclaimed it, and the Apostles emphasized it to both Jews and Gentiles. (Acts 2:38; 11:18; 17:30).

The word "repentance" comes from several Greek words which mean, change of views and purpose, change of heart, change of mind, change of life, to transform, etc.

Jesus said, ". . . except ye repent, ye shall all likewise perish" (Luke 13:3).

Luke 24:47 says, "And that repentance and remission of sins should be preached in His name among all nations, beginning at Jerusalem."

WATER BAPTISM

The scriptural mode of baptism is immersion, and is only for those who have fully repented, having turned from their sins and a love of the world. It should be administered by a duly authorized minister of the Gospel, in obedience to the Word of God, and in the name of our Lord Jesus Christ, according to the Acts of the Apostles 2:38; 8:16; 10:48; 19:5; thus obeying and fulfilling Matthew 28:19.

THE BAPTISM OF THE HOLY SPIRIT

John the Baptist, in Matthew 3:11, said, ". . . He shall baptize you with the Holy Ghost, and with fire."

Jesus, in Acts 1:5, said, ". . . ye shall be baptized with the Holy Ghost not many days hence."

Luke tells us in Acts 2:4, ". . . they were all filled with the Holy Ghost, and began to speak with other tongues (languages), as the Spirit gave them utterance."

The terms "baptize with the Holy Ghost and fire," "filled with the Holy Spirit," and the "gift of the Holy Ghost" are synonymous terms used interchangeably in the Bible.

It is scriptural to expect all who receive the gift, filling, or baptism of the Holy Spirit to receive the same physical, initial sign of speaking with other tongues.

The speaking with other tongues, as recorded in Acts 2:4; 10:46, and 19:6, and the gift of tongues, as explained in 1 Corinthians, chapters 12 and 14, are the same in essence, but different in use and purpose.

The Lord, through the Prophet Joel, said, ". . . I will pour out my Spirit upon all flesh; . . . " (Joel 2:28).

Peter, in explaining this phenomenal experience, said, ". . . having received of the Father the promise of the Holy Ghost, He (Jesus) hath shed forth this which ye now see and hear." (Acts 2:33).

Further, ". . . the promise is unto you, and to your children, and to all that are afar off, even as many as the Lord our God shall call." (Acts 2:39).

FUNDAMENTAL DOCTRINE

The basic and fundamental doctrine of this organization shall be the Bible standard of full salvation, which is repentance, baptism in water by immersion in the name of the Lord Jesus Christ, and the baptism of the Holy Ghost with the initial sign of speaking with other tongues as the Spirit gives utterance.

We shall endeavor to keep the unity of the Spirit until we all come into the unity of the faith, at the same time admonishing all brethren that they shall not contend for their different views to the disunity of the body.

DIVINE HEALING

The first covenant that the Lord (Jehovah) made with the children of Israel after they were brought out of Egypt was a covenant of healing. The Lord said, ". . . if thou wilt diligently hearken to the voice of the Lord (Jehovah-Rapha, the Lord that healeth) thy God, and wilt do that which is right in His sight, and wilt give ear to His commandments, and keep all His statutes, I will put none of these diseases upon thee, which I have brought upon the Egyptians; for I am the Lord that healeth thee." (Exodus 15:26).

Some translations read: "For I am Jehovah, thy physician." He being our physician or doctor, we have the most capable in the whole world. Our Lord Jesus Christ went about Galilee, preaching the Gospel of the Kingdom, and healing all manner of sickness and disease among the people. (Matthew 4:23, 24).

"Jesus Christ the same yesterday, and today, and forever." (Hebrews 13:8).

The vicarious suffering of the Lord Jesus Christ paid for the healing of our bodies, the same as for the salvation of our souls, for ". . . with His stripes we are healed" (Isaiah 53:5). Matthew 8:17 reads, ". . . Himself took our infirmities, and bare our sicknesses." (See also 1 Peter 2:24.)

We see from this that divine healing for the body is in the atonement. That being true, then it is for all who believe. Jesus said of believers, ". . . they shall lay hands on the sick, and they shall recover." Later, James wrote in his Epistle to all the churches: "Is any sick among you? Let him call for the elders of the church; and let them pray over him, anointing him with oil in the name of the Lord: and the prayer of faith shall save the sick, and the Lord shall raise him up; and if he have committed sins, they shall be forgiven him. Confess your faults one to another, and pray one for another, that ye may be healed. The effectual fervent prayer of a righteous man availeth much." (James 5:14-16).

All of these promises are for the church today.

SACRAMENT OR COMMUNION

On the night of our Lord's betrayal, He ate the Passover supper with His Apostles, after which He instituted the sacrament. "And He took bread, and gave thanks, and brake it, and gave unto them, saying, this is my body which is given for you: This do in remembrance of me. Likewise also the cup after supper, saying, this cup is the New Testament in my blood, which is shed for you." (Luke 22:19-20).

Paul instructed the church how to observe it (1 Cor. 11:23-34).

Thus was instituted the use of literal bread and the fruit of the vine, which are partaken of, literally, as emblems of His broken body and shed blood. There is also a spiritual significance and blessing in partaking of the sacrament.

FOOT-WASHING

When the Passover supper was ended, we read in John 13:4-5, "He riseth from supper, and laid aside His garments; and took a towel, and girded Himself. After that He poureth water into a basin, and began to wash the disciples' feet, and to wipe them with the towel wherewith He was girded."

Jesus said, "If I then, your Lord and Master, have washed your feet; ye also ought to wash one another's feet. For I have given you an example, that ye should do as I have done to you" (John 13:14-15).

This first example was given by our Lord, and it is a divine institution. It is well to follow His example and wash one another's feet; thus manifesting the spirit of humility.

HOLINESS

Godly living should characterize the life of every child of the Lord, and we should live according to the pattern and example given in the Word of God. "For the grace of God that bringeth salvation hath appeared to all men, teaching us that, denying ungodliness and worldly lusts, we should live soberly, righteously, and Godly, in this present world" (Titus 2:11, 12). "For even hereunto were ye called: because Christ also suffered for us, leaving us an example, that ye should follow His steps: who did no sin, neither was guile found in His mouth: who, when He was reviled, reviled not again; when He suffered, He threatened not; but committed Himself to Him that judgeth righteously" (1 Peter 2:21-23).

"Follow peace with all men, and holiness, without which no man shall see the Lord" (Heb. 12:14).

"But as He which hath called you is holy, so be ye holy in all manner of conversation; because it is written, be ye holy; for I am holy. And if ye call on the Father, who without respect of persons judgeth according to every man's work, pass the time of your sojourning here in fear: forasmuch as ye know that ye were not redeemed with corruptible things, as silver and gold, from your vain conversation received by tradition from your fathers; but with the precious blood of Christ, as of a lamb without blemish and without spot" (1 Peter 1:15-19).

We wholeheartedly disapprove of our people indulging in any activities which are not conducive to good Christianity and Godly living, such as theatres, dances, mixed bathing, women cutting their hair, make-up, any apparel that immodestly exposes the body, all worldly sports and amusements, and unwholesome radio programs and music. Furthermore, because of the display of all of these evils on television, we disapprove of any of our people having television sets in their homes. We admonish all of our people to refrain from any of these practices in the interest of spiritual progress and the soon coming of the Lord for His church.

THE GRACE OF GOD

"For the grace of God that bringeth salvation hath appeared to all men, teaching us that, denying ungodliness and worldly lusts, we should live soberly, righteously, and Godly, in this present world" (Titus 2:11, 12).

"For the law was given by Moses, but grace and truth came by Jesus Christ" (John 1:17).

A Christian, to keep saved, must walk with God and keep himself in the love of God (Jude 21) and in the grace of God. The word "grace" means "favor." When a person

ARTICLES OF FAITH (UNITED PENTECOSTAL CHURCH) (continued)

transgresses and sins against God, he loses his favor. If he continues to commit sin and does not repent, he will eventually be lost and cast into the lake of fire. (Read John 15:2, 6; 2 Peter 2:20-22.) Jude speaks of the backsliders of his day, and their reward. (Also, read Hebrews 6:4-6).

"For by grace are ye saved through faith; and that not of yourselves; it is the gift of God" (Eph. 2:8).

RESTITUTION OF ALL THINGS

We understand the scripture to teach the restitution of all things, which God hath spoken by the mouth of all His holy prophets since the world began. (Acts 3:21). But we cannot find where the devil, his angels, and all sinners are included. (See Rev. 20:10).

CONSCIENTIOUS SCRUPLES

We recognize the institution of human government as being of divine ordination, and, in so doing, affirm unswerving loyalty to our Government; however, we take a definite position regarding the bearing of arms or the taking of human life.

As followers of the Lord Jesus Christ, the Prince of Peace, we believe in implicit obedience to His commandments and precepts, which instruct us as follows: ". . . that ye resist not evil . . . " (Matt. 5:39): "Follow peace with all men . . . " (Heb. 12:14). (See also Matt. 26:52; Rom. 12:19; James 5:6; Revelation 13:10). These we believe and interpret to mean Christians shall not shed blood nor take human life.

Therefore, we propose to fulfill all the obligations of loyal citizens, but are constrained to declare against participating in combatant service in war, armed insurrection, property destruction, aiding or abetting in or the actual destruction of human life.

Furthermore, we cannot conscientiously affiliate with any union, boycott, or organization which will force or bind any of its members to belong to any organization, perform any duties contrary to our conscience, or receive any mark, without our right to affirm or reject same. (1930).

However, we regret the false impression created by some groups or so-called "conscientious objectors" that to obey the Bible is to have a contempt for law or magistrates, to be disloyal to our Government and in sympathy with our enemies, or to be unwilling to sacrifice for the preservation of our commonwealth. This attitude would be as contemptible to us as to any patriot. The Word of God commands us to do violence to no man. It also commands us that first of all we are to pray for rulers of our country. We, therefore, exhort our members to freely and willingly respond to the call of our Government except in the matter of bearing arms. When we say service, we mean service—no matter how hard or dangerous. The true church has no more place for cowards than has the nation. First of all, however, let us earnestly pray that we will with honor be kept out of war.

We believe that we can be consistent in serving our Government in certain noncombatant capacities, but not in the bearing of arms. (1940).

SECRET SOCIETIES, ETC.

According to the Word of God, we firmly believe and hold that the people of God should have no connection whatever with secret societies, or any other organization or body wherein there is a fellowship with unbelievers, bound by an oath. (James 5:3-7; 2 Cor. 6:14-18).

TRANSLATION OF SAINTS

We believe that the time is drawing near when our Lord shall appear; then the dead in Christ shall arise, and we who are alive and remain shall be caught up with them to meet our Lord in the air. (1 Thess. 4:13-17; 1 Cor. 15:51-54; Phil. 3:20-21).

MARRIAGE AND DIVORCE

"Whosoever shall put away his wife, except it be for fornication, and shall marry another, committeth adultery:" (Matt. 19:9), (Matt. 5:32). When this sin has been committed, the innocent party may be free to remarry only in the Lord. Our desire being to raise a higher standard for the ministry, we recommend that ministers do not marry again.

Judgment begins at the House of God. See instructions for the ministry under Article VI, Section 6.

TITHING

We believe tithing is God's financial plan to provide for His work, and has been since the days of Abraham. Tithing came with faith under Abraham; Moses' law enjoined it, and Israel practiced it when she was right with God; Jesus indorsed it (Matt. 23:23); and Paul said to lay by in store as God has prospered you. Do not rob God of His portion, viz., tithes and offerings. (Read Mal. 3.)

SECOND COMING OF JESUS

That Jesus is coming again the second time in person, just as He went away, is clearly set forth by the Lord Jesus Himself, and was preached and taught in the early Christian church by the apostles; hence, the children of God today are earnestly, hopefully, looking forward to the glorious event. (Matt. 24; Acts 1:11; 3:19-21; 1 Cor. 11:26; Phil. 3:20-21; 1 Thess. 4:14-17; Titus 2:13, 14.)

THE MILLENNIUM

Moreover, we believe that the distress upon the earth is the "beginning of sorrows" and will become more intense until there "shall be a time of trouble such as there never was since there was a nation even to that same time" (Matt. 24:3-8; Dan. 12:1), and that period of "tribulation" will be followed by the dawn of a better day on earth and that for a thousand years there shall be "peace on earth and good will toward men." (Rev. 20:1-5; Isa. 65:17-25; Matt. 5:5; Dan. 7:27; Mic. 4:1-2; Heb. 2:14; Rom. 11:25-27.)

FINAL JUDGMENT

When the thousand years are finished, there shall be a resurrection of all the dead, who will be summoned before the great white throne for their final judgment, and all whose names are not found written in the Book of Life shall be cast into the lake of fire, burning with brimstone, which God hath prepared for the Devil and his angels, Satan himself being cast in first. (Matt. 25:41; Rev. 20:7-15; 21:8.)

PUBLIC SCHOOL ACTIVITIES

We disapprove of school students attending shows, dances, dancing classes, theaters, engaging in school activities against their religious scruples, and wearing gymnasium clothes which immodestly expose the body.

RELIGIOUS HOLIDAY

The annual Conference is declared to be an International Religious Holiday for all members and all members are urged to attend.

Notes: *The articles are related to those of the Pentecostal Assemblies of the World, of which the United Pentecostal Church was once a part. These articles in turn have become the source of statements by the Assemblies of the Lord Jesus Christ and the New Bethel Church of God in Christ.*

*   *   *

Black Trinitarian Pentecostal

BASIS OF UNION (AFRICAN UNIVERSAL CHURCH)

SECTION 1. We believe that Jesus Christ shed His blood for the remission of sins. (Romans 3:25) and for the regeneration of penitent sinners, and for salvation from sin and from sinning (1 John 3:5-10: Eph. 2:1-10).

SECTION 2. We believe also that Jesus Christ shed His blood for the complete cleansing of the justified believer from all indwelling sin, and from its pollution subsequent to regeneration.

SECTION 3. We believe, Teach and firmly maintain the scriptural doctrine of justification of faith alone, as taught in Rom. 5:1.

SECTION 4. We believe also that entire sanctification destroys and eradicates sin (Rom. 6:6; Heb. 13:12; 1 John 1:7-9; 1 Thess. 5:23; St. John 17:17; Acts 26:18).

SECTION 5. We believe that entire sanctification is an instantaneous, definite, second work of grace obtainable by faith on the part of the fully consecrated believer.

SECTION 6. We believe that the baptism of the Holy Ghost is obtainable by a definite appropriation of faith on the part of the fully cleansed believer. Acts 1:5; 2:1; 4:38; Luke 11:13; Acts 19).

SECTION 7. We believe also that the baptism with fire is a definite, scriptural experience, obtainable by faith on the part of the spirit filled believer (Matt. 3:11; Luke 3:16; Rev. 15:2; Psa. 104:4; Acts 2:1-4; Heb. 12:29; Ezek. 1:4-14, 10:2-7; Isa. 33:14, 6:1-8.

SECTION 8. We believe also in the divine healing of both soul and body as the atonement (Isa. 5:3; Matt. 8:16-17; Mark 16:14-18; James 5:14-16; Exo. 15:26.)

SECTION 9. We believe in the second coming of Christ according to the revealed light of the scripture (John 3:1-2; Rom. 8:29; 2 Peter 1:4; Psa. 16:11; Matt. 5; John 4:24; John 1:1-10).

SECTION 10. We do not believe that the baptism with fire is an experience independent or disassociated from the Holy Ghost, but we do believe that the divine baptism of Jesus is two fold; Christ Baptism is with the Holy Ghost and with fire. We believe that it is He, the Comforter abiding in the heart of the purified believed who creates an intense longing for the experience of the Baptism of fire and as the executive of the God Head Baptizes those in whom He dwells with fire, and that none can receive the experience of the baptism of fire except those in whom the personal Holy Ghost already abides.

SECTION 11. African Universal Church and Commercial League Corporation do opposed to [sic] all doctrines that are contrary to God's revealed word.

Notes: *Churches serving a predominantly black constituency have played an important part in the whole pentecostal movement. William Seymour, a black holiness preacher, became pastor of a small group of former Baptists at what became the first pentecostal center in Los Angeles, where the famous Azusa Street revival occurred. Early attempts at racial inclusiveness failed within a few years, and black churches were segregated, pushed to the edge of the movement as a whole. The Pentecostal Assemblies of the World, a non-Trinitarian apostolic group, has been the most successful at keeping a limited degree of racial inclusiveness over the years.*

Black churches follow the same division as those whose membership is predominantly white—holiness and two-experience denominations—though most tend to favor the holiness position. The Black Pentecostal churches are treated together because of the very real consequences of racial factors in molding their life and their relationship to the larger Pentecostal movement.

The African Universal Church is a holiness-pentecostal church which has accepted an extreme definition of sanctification as the destruction and eradication of sin.

*   *   *

CONFESSION OF FAITH (CHURCH OF GOD IN CHRIST)

1. TRINITY

We believe in the Trinity of the Father, Son and Holy Spirit.

2. THE SON

We believe that Jesus Christ was and is the Son of God, co-equal in wisdom and power and holiness with the Father, and that through His atonement the world is saved from sin and reconciled to God.

3. THE HOLY SPIRIT

We believe in the personality of the Holy Spirit. That He proceedeth from the Father and the Son, and that He is co-equal with the Father and the Son, and that He is the Executive of the Trinity, through which the plan of salvation is carried on in the earth.

4. FALLEN NATURE

We believe that man, by nature is sinful and unholy. Being born in sin he needs to be born again, sanctified and cleansed from all sins by the blood of Jesus.

CONFESSION OF FAITH (CHURCH OF GOD IN CHRIST) (continued)

We believe that man is saved by confessing and forsaking his sins, and believing on the Lord Jesus Christ, and that having become a child of God, by being born again and adopted into the family of God, he may, and should, claim the inheritance of the sons of God, namely, the baptism of the Holy Spirit.

5. BAPTISM OF THE HOLY SPIRIT

We believe in the baptism of the Holy Ghost with the sign and seal of speaking in tongues, as recorded in Acts 2:4; 19:6; 10:46.

We do not believe that we are baptized with the Spirit in order to be saved and become the sons of God, but that we are baptized with the Holy Ghost because we are saved and are the sons of God. (We hold that we are saved by being born of the Spirit, not by being baptized with the Spirit.)

6. THE FATHER

We believe in God, the Father, Almighty, the Author and Creator of all things.

While we do not presume to teach that no one has the Spirit that does not speak in tongues, or that one is not saved that does not speak in tongues, yet we believe that a full baptism of the Holy Ghost as poured out on the day of Pentecost is accompanied by the speaking in tongues. And that the baptism of the Holy Ghost has the same effects and results upon every child of God that receives it the same as the new birth has the same effects and results on every one that is born of the Spirit. And we do not consider anyone Pentecostal who teaches contrary to this doctrine.

7. WATER BAPTISM

We believe that the instructions given us by the Saviour, as recorded in Mt. 28:19, 29 are sufficient for our guide and rule as to the formula of water baptism, namely in the name of the Father and the Son, and of the Holy Ghost.

8. THE SECOND COMING OF CHRIST

We believe in the second coming of our Lord and Saviour Jesus Christ, and that He will reign on the earth in millennial power and glory, and in the rapture of the bride of Christ, when she shall be caught up to meet her bridegroom in the air. We admonish all who have this in them to purify themselves as He is pure.

9. THE SABBATH

We recognize the first day of the week as the Christian Sabbath.

10. GENERAL CHURCH OFFICERS

The Chief Apostle, General Superintendent and State Overseers shall compose the official heads of the church. Said officers are to be elected from among the ordained Elders of the church by the General Assembly, and shall have the care of the work at large. They are empowered to organize and reorganize churches and missions and to ordain Elders and commission Evangelists.

11. ELIGIBILITY OF ELDERS

The certificate of credentials of an Elder are valid only as long as his life adorns the Gospel of Christ, and his teaching are in harmony with the Church of God in Christ. Any Elder, Evangelist or member acting as Pastor of a church, who teaches contrary doctrines, or causes dissensions or in any way proves his inability as a Pastor, may be removed by a State Overseer, or a General Superintendent, and another appointed in his place.

12. CHURCH PROPERTY

All church property must be held in trust for the Church of God in Christ by a legally elected board of trustees, which trustees must be members of said church are subject to removal (sic).

No individual church can change any of the doctrines of the Church of God in Christ. The Chief Apostle, a General Superintendent, or State Overseer, may disorganize a church whose members accept or promulgate doctrine contrary to the Church of God in Christ, and confiscate the property for the general church purpose.

Members of any Church of God in Christ disorganizing or dissolving cannot use or take any property with them, but church property will revert to the State Assembly, for church purposes only, under the supervision of the General Superintendent or State Overseer.

13. POLITICAL GOVERNMENTS

We believe that governments are God-given institutions for the benefit of mankind. We admonish and exhort our members to honor magistrates and the powers that be, to respect and obey civil laws.

We hereby and herewith declare our loyalty to the president and the constitution of the United States, and pledge fidelity to the flag for which the republic stands. But as a God-fearing, peace-loving and law-abiding people, we only claim our inheritance as American citizens, namely: To worship God according to the dictates of our mind.

We believe the shedding of human blood or taking of human life to be contrary to the teaching of our Lord and Saviour, and as a body, we are adverse to war in all its various forms.

We herewith offer our services to the president for any services that will not conflict with our conscientious scruples in this respect, with love to all, with malice toward none, and with due respect to all who differ from us in our interpretation of the Scriptures.

Notes: *Among the oldest of the Pentecostal bodies, the Church of God in Christ began among former Baptists who had accepted holiness doctrines. Its doctrinal position was forged in a split among holiness people who did not follow founder C. H. Mason into the pentecostal movement and in reaction against the Apostolic non-Trinitarian movement. Notice the sophisticated treatment of the relation of salvation, the baptism of the Holy Spirit, and the experience of speaking-in-tongues. The church is also pacifist.*

WHAT WE BELIEVE [CHURCH OF THE LIVING GOD (CHRISTIAN WORKERS FOR FELLOWSHIP)]

What We Believe:

I. ABOUT THE CHURCH:

A. The C.W.F.F. meaning "Christian Workers for Fellowship" is not a part of the name of the Church, but it is only the adopted motto of the Church, which is used in connection with the name "Church of the Living God."

1. For one to become a member of the Church, he does not join the church, except in the sense that he unites with a local church. To gain entrance into the church one must follow the Plan of Salvation, which will be mentioned later in this writing.

B. We Believe the Church is

1. The Church is that company of believers called out from the world by the gospel of Jesus Christ and indwelled with the Holy Spirit. These believers are called by His Father's name.

C. We Believe the true scriptural name of the Church is

1. Church of God or Church of the Living God. Act 20:28; I Cor. 1:1, 2; 10:32; 11:16; 11:22; 15:9; II Cor. 1:1; I Thess. 2:14; II Thess. 1:4; I Tim. 3:5; 3:15

D. The Mission and the purpose of the Church

1. According to the Scriptures.

   a. The immediate purpose of the Church. Our present concern "Preach the Gospel." Mark 16:15

   b. Make disciples or converts. Matt. 28:19

   c. Teach them to observe all things.

   d. Commit the word to faithful men.

2. The ultimate purpose.

   a. To gather together in Christ, to praise of His Name.

   b. To perfect the saints; to bring all to the fullness of Christ. Eph. 4:12

   c. To prepare for Christ a glorious Church, without spot or anything. Eph. 5:27

II. ABOUT JESUS CHRIST

A. We believe that Jesus was a man, not a myth, not a phantom, not a mere creation of some fruitful imagination, but a man—a real person, having a human body and soul, and endowed with all the faculties, powers, and susceptibilities of human nature in its primitive state.

We further believe that He was born of a Virgin, lived a holy life, and was crucified, buried, resurrected, and ascended back to His Father with glory and honor. He was both human and divine.

1. Facts about the Virgin Birth

   a. Matthew and Luke are the only gospel writers who were witness to the Virgin Birth of Christ.

   b. These birth accounts are genuine parts of the gospel narrative which belong to the Apostolic Age.

   c. The virgin birth is never contradicted by other New Testaments writers. Many statements by Mark, John, Paul and Peter are very meaningful in light of the virgin birth.

   d. Isaiah 7:14 is rightly applied to the virgin birth.

2. Scriptural evidence of a bodily resurrection

   a. The post-resurrection appearances

   (1.) To certain women as they returned from the tomb after seeing an angel. Matt. 28:1-10

   (2.) To Mary Magdalene. Jn. 20:1-18; Mk. 16:12, 13

   (3.) To Peter before the evening of the first day. Lk. 24:13; I Cor. 15:5

   (4.) To two disciples on the way to Emmaeus late the first day. Mk. 16:12, 13; Luke 24

   (5.) To ten apostles and others in the evening. Mk. 16:14-18; Lk. 24:36-40; Jn. 20:19-23

   (6.) To Saul. I Cor. 9:ff; 15:8

   (7.) To John on Patmos. Rev. 1:13

3. We Believe Jesus Christ to be the eternal Son of God, eternal Word, Creator and Preserver of all things.

III. ABOUT THE BIBLE

A. We Believe the Bible is the inspired Word of God. We accept the revelation of God in the person of Jesus Christ and our only reliable source of information about him is the Bible and Jesus Christ is the central theme in the Holy Scripture.

1. The Word meets every requirement.

   a. The Bible offers an unchangeable standard as a revelation from God to man. It is ultimate and final.

   b. It provides the power by which man can be led to live up to its high standard. The love of God planted in the Bible is the prime source of power.

   c. It is universally applicable to mankind. It demands that you love and serve your neighbor.

1. The Unity of the Bible.

   This factor is one of the greatest marvels of the Bible. Sixty-six books produced by forty writers in different languages, under many governments and over a period of around fifteen hundred years, yet all brought together to form the Book.

   a. Unity of the Theme

   The theme is the plan of redemption. This plan begins in the book of Genesis with the promise concerning woman's seed and continues in the shed blood of the animals whose skin furnished covering for Adam and Eve. It is perpetuated through the Messianic prophecies of the Old

Testament and is typified in animal sacrifices and other types and shadows. John the Baptist pointed that He had come to give His life as a ransom. The Acts and the Epistles further continue the theme, until the last song of the heavenly choir, which is also the song of redemption . . . The Book of Revelation. We take a fundamental view of God's word, that we must live by every word that proceeds out of the mouth of God. We believe that the Bible is perfect from cover to cover. It is our belief that the Scripture is profitable for doctrine, for reproof, or correction and for instruction in righteousness. II Tim. 3:16; II Peter 1:19-21.

IV. ABOUT THE HOLY SPIRIT

We Believe in the Holy Spirit or Holy Ghost. We believe Him to be a person. We believe Him to be the third person in the Godhead. We believe the Holy Spirit is the creative, living, loving and lasting presence of God in the world. There is only one God, but He has three basic roles: Creator, Redeemer and Friend. So we say Father, Son and Holy Spirit.

A. Holy Spirit is like Jesus.

1. He is accessible to all men; as accessible as was Jesus who invited all men to come to him for rest and commanded his disciples to go into all the world and make disciples of all nations. Everybody in the world is included and no one is excluded except he excludes himself.

B. Holy Spirit is understandable like Jesus.

1. The work of the Spirit is full of mystery, but it is not magical. The Holy Spirit makes as much sense as Jesus made. The gift of the Holy Spirit is bestowed upon the repentant and obedient. Luke records in Acts 5:32 "And we are his witnesses in these things and so is also Holy Spirit whom God hath given to them that obey Him." God gives His Spirit to everyone that has fulfilled the steps to salvation.

C. The Holy Spirit is not necessarily an emotional outburst.

1. Speaking in tongues in this age is not an evidence of the Holy Spirit. It is not necessary to go into trance to receive the Spirit but merely obey. We believe that the tongues on Pentecost were languages and not unintelligible utterance. The basic evidence of the Holy Spirit in our lives is the fruit we bear. Gal. 5:22

D. The Holy Spirit has a purpose.

1. The purpose of the Holy Spirit in the life of the Christian is to lead, to guide, sanctify, comfort. We believe the Holy Spirit of God is alive, real and present. He is willing to do exceedingly abundantly above all that we can ask or think. Eph. 3:20-21.

V. ABOUT THE PLAN OF SALVATION

We believe for one to be saved he has to take certain steps to salvation. The commands to be obeyed are: hear, understand, believe, repent, confess, be baptized, partake in the Lord's Supper, and participate in Foot Washing. The commands to be obeyed constitute the Plan of Salvation.

A. Hearing and Understanding

Understanding through preaching by which the facts of the gospel are brought to one's conscious mind for his consideration and action upon them. Hearing consists in giving heed or attention to things presented with the intention of accepting the facts and being obedient to the commands enjoined. Rom. 10:11.

B. Believing (Faith) Heb. 11:6 (acting upon word of another)

1. Means to faith presentation of adequate confirmed evidence. Rom. 10:17

2. Elements of Faith

Faith affects the intellect, fills the heart with powerful emotion, emotion moves the will to act. Hence, we can say that faith is marked by:

a. A change in views and sentiments

b. A change of heart

c. Change of will when faith has its complete work in the life it embraces.

d. A strong conviction of the truth of the gospel as being God's power unto salvation to everyone that believeth.

e. A firm and abiding trust in Christ as the way, the Truth, and the Life. To believe is to be persuaded of an historical fact, but to believe in Christ is not only to assent to His historicity but to place confidence in Him for salvation and justification.

C. Repentance (a change of mind which leads to a change of life)

1. Elements which lead to repentance.

a. Sinner obtains new views of Christ, of sin, and of holiness.

b. He obtains a new view of his condition before God.

c. He feels Godly sorrow for sin and determination to be free.

2. Elements involved in repentance.

a. Intellectual change caused by truth presented.

b. Emotional change caused by truth presented.

c. Change of life resulting from change of will.

3. Results of repentance.

a. Death to sin. Rom. 6:1, 2

b. Hatred for sin. Heb. 1:9; Jude 23

c. Moral impossibility to live longer in sin. Rom. 6:2

d. Position to receive blessings of God which follow repentance. II Corinthians 7:10

D. Confession of Faith (an oral proclamation with the mouth, of the faith within the heart).

1. The importance of the Good Confession

a. To be saved. Rom. 10, 9:10

b. To bear testimony of Christ. I Tim. 6:12

c. Commits us to Christ

d. Signifies to others our own belief

E. Ordinances of the Church

We believe that there are three Sacraments or Rites that are ordained of Christ in the New Convenant namely: Baptism, The Lord's Supper, and the Washing of Feet.

A. Baptism

1. We believe the first Rite of the Church is Baptism. Baptism comes from the Greek word Baptizo—immerse, dip, plunge, submerge. We believe this is the only valid way to be baptized.

2. What Baptism is

(a.) Act of submission and obedience

(b.) An act performed in the manner of a burial, portraying and witnessing to the burial and resurrection.

3. Importance of Baptism

(a.) First public act of Jesus preparatory to beginning of ministry. St. Matt. 3:13-15

(b.) The last public command to his apostles

(c.) The first command given to inquiring sinners

(d.) Mentioned in New Testament at least 117 times

4. Subjects for Christian Baptism

(a.) Those capable of and guilty of committing sin

(b.) Those capable of knowing, reasoning and obeying by their own will the plan of salvation

5. Special consideration showing that infants are not subject to Christian Baptism

(a.) Infants cannot fulfill all or any of the above qualifications

(b.) Not capable of being taught the plan of salvation

(c.) Cannot fulfill the purpose of I Peter 3:21. "Answer of a good conscience."

(d.) Historically infant baptism was not introduced until after the apostles.

B. Lord's Supper

We believe the Lord's Supper or Communion, points backward to the death of Christ and forward to His return.

1. According to the Bible.

(a.) It is a memorial. Luke 22:19; I Cor. 11:28

(b.) It is atonement for sin. Matt. 28:26; Mk. 14:26

(c.) It is communion of the Saint. 1 Cor. 10:16, 17

(d.) The bread is His body. Lk. 22:19. Mk. 14:22. Matt. 26:28

(e.) The cup is His blood. Lk. 22:20. Mk. 14:24. Matt. 26:28

2. Jesus declared Himself to be the Vine.

(a.) Not a grape vine or some other kind

(b.) Old Testament and New. Ps. 80:8; Matt. 2:13; Jn. 15:1

3. Water to be used for the Lord's Supper.

Water is a pure drink.

(a.) Old Testament Scriptures. Gen. 1:2; Ps. 73:10

4. New Testament Scriptures

Matt. 10:42; Mk. 9:41; Lk. 22:20; Jn. 19:34; Rev. 22:1; Rev. 21:6

5. Wine and strong Drinks

We believe that wine and strong drink should not be used by Christians.

(a.) Old Testament Scripture

Gen. 19:38; Lev. 10:8-10; Ps. 75:10; Prov. 20:1; 23:29-30; 23:32; Isa. 5:11; 5:22; 23; Isa. 28:7; Hos. 4:11; 5:22, 23; Isa. 28:7, 8; Hos. 4:11

(b.) New Testament Scriptures. Mk. 15:23; Lk. 1:11-16; 1 Cor. 6:9-10; 9:9.

C. Foot Washing

We Believe if one is to become a member of the Church of the Living God, he must have his feet washed. After he has obtained membership, he must wash the feet of others. The specific purpose of foot washing as an ordinance is closely bound up with the basic reasons underlying the other ordinances of the Church. But why ordinances at all, one might ask? We ought to be willing to obey plain commandments of our Lord, just because He is Lord, whether or not we can discern the reason for such commands.

1. Expressly Commanded

Jesus said, "If I then, your Lord and Master, have washed your feet, Ye also ought to wash one another's feet. For I have given you an example, that ye should do as I have done to you. If ye know these things happy are ye if ye do them" Jn 13:14-15, 17. Some say that this part of the Word does not assert that we must do it but merely that we should or ought. Now the New Testament law of liberty does not consist of "thou shalt" as did the Mosaic law, but is, instead, a law of love, Jesus said, "If a man love me, he will keep my words." (Jn. 14:23) The words ought and should are the strongest words in our language expressing moral obligation or duty.

2. What it symbolizes

As a Rite, foot washing symbolizes the sacredness and holiness of that blessed relationship of God's redeemed saints with each other. Having fellowship with each other.

(a.) Practiced by the Early Church

Paul, writing to Timothy relative to certain conditions under which a widow should be taken under consideration of financial care of the church says "She should be well reported of for good works; if she has brought up children; if she has lodged strangers, if she has washed the Saints feet; if she has relieved the afflicted, if she has diligently followed every good work." I Tim. 5:9-10.

VI. ABOUT PRAYER

We Believe the prayer that Jesus gave to His disciples in the Sermon on the Mount is the prayer to be prayed by all Christians. Matt. 6:9-13; Lk. 11:1-2. This is commonly known as the Lord's Prayer, but it is not the Lord's Prayer but the disciples Prayer. This prayer sustains all of our needs and it contains seven petitions.

Notes: *This statement is reflective of a number of debates within the black religious community, such as the relation of the baptism of the Holy Spirit to trance. It is unique for its position on the Lord's Supper, directing the use of water instead of wine. Foot washing is also practiced.*

* * *

THE FAITH OF THE CHURCH OUTLINED (CHURCH OF THE LIVING GOD, THE PILLAR AND GROUND OF TRUTH)

We believe and really know, according to the word of Christ, that it is necessary to observe and keep the commandment of Christ by washing one another's feet as was His example to do as he did.

We believe it is right and necessary to observe the Lord's supper or passover as He did with His disciples before He was crucified by using unleavened bread as a token of His body and by using pure unadulterated water as a token and agreement of His blood, as nothing except water will agree with His blood.

Read on this subject, the following scripture: Wine forbidden by the word of God: Lev. 10-8, 9, 10; Hosea 4-11; Hosea 9-4; Luke 1:15; Mark 15:23. Water approved of by the word of God: I Cor. 10:1, 2, 3, 4; Exodus 17:6; Matt. 10:42; Mark 9:41; Rev. 22:16-17.

We believe in praying; we believe in fasting; we believe in keeping the Sabbath with the covenant which is God, Christ and the Holy Ghost, instead of with types and shadows which was fulfilled by the coming of Christ. We believe that to cease from our own works is to cease from sin.

We believe that Christ hath given us rest from sin evil and confusion in our bodies instead of rest from carnal labor which is necessary for the sustenance of our temporal bodies. We believe there is a place of inheritance and joy and happiness beyond expression for those that long for the appearing of the Lord to those that keep His sayings and do His will; and that this place is not a place of carnal rest, for they rest neither day nor night there, but continually give glory to God; and we believe that eyes have not seen, neither have ears heard, what is in store in that city for those that love the Lord, do His will and keep His commandments. We believe that flesh and blood cannot enter there, that sorrow and sighing are not there and that nothing that sin or worketh iniquity, nor any sin has ever been or can ever enter there. This place we believe is eternal into Heaven and is the Heaven of heavens.

We believe also that there is a final Judgment Day in store for all, both the good and for the bad. In it we believe that sinners will be justly judged, condemned and separated from the righteous and turned into the place called the Lake of Fire and Brimstone, prepared for those that do evil for the wicked and for the devil and his angels.

In the Judgment we believe that the righteous shall be changed from this corruptible body and given a body fashioned like the glorious body of the Son of God. For we shall be like Him.

We believe the Church of the Living God, the Pillar and Ground of the Truth is the waiting or preparing bride of Christ and that when she is sufficiently prepared and made glorious without spot or wrinkle Christ will catch His bride away to the marriage supper of the Lamb to live and reign with Him for a period of a thousand years and that in this all the dead in Christ will rise first at the sounding of the first trumpet.

Notes: *This statement covers only those issues above and beyond the basic beliefs on God, Christ, and salvation. Like the Church of the Living God (Christian Workers for Fellowship), the Church of the Living God, the Pillar and Ground of Truth uses water instead of wine for the Lord's Supper.*

* * *

WHAT WE BELIEVE AND TEACH (DELIVERANCE EVANGELICAL CENTERS)

ARTICLE 1. THE BIBLE

The BIBLE is our all-sufficient rule for faith and practice. It is the inspired Word of God, a revelation from GOD to man the INFALLIBLE guide of conduct and faith, the BIBLE is SUPERIOR to conscience and reason, but not contrary to wisdom. 2 Tim. 3:15, 16; I Pet. 2:2; 2 Pet. 1:21. THE WHOLE BIBLE, both the OLD and NEW TESTAMENTS, is the pure Word of God that cannot be changed, added to, nor taken away from its words, without terrific consequences. Rev. 22:18, 19.

ARTICLE 2. GOD

GOD is ONE eternal, omni-present, omniscient, all-powerful God in three persons: namely, the FATHER, the SON, and the HOLY GHOST. God created the whole universe out of nothing in the beginning. Gen. 1:1.

ARTICLE 3. JESUS CHRIST

Jesus Christ, the Son of the Living God, came in the flesh, born of the virgin Mary, begotten by the Holy Spirit and took on Himself the form of man to be able to redeem us from our sins and deliver us from the powers of Satan Matt. 1:18-21; Luke 1:31; John 1:2-14.

For the salvation of man from sin, Jesus Christ suffered under Pontius Pilate, was crucified, died and was buried and rose triumphantly the third day from the dead, ascended into heaven from Mt. Olivet in the presence of many witnesses, and today is sitting on the right hand of the Throne of God interceding for us, from whence He shall come again to raise the dead and judge the world, Matt. 27:6, 28:1-7; Mark 16:19; Luke 24:51; Acts 7:55; Heb. 12:2; John 5:26-29, 11:25; Matt. 25:31-46; I Thess. 4:13-17; I Cor. 15:15-58; Rev. 19:1-10, 20:11-15, 27; Matt. 25:1-13.

There is an eternal punishment for the wicked, and eternal bliss for the righteous. Luke 16:19-31; Matt. 25:41, 46; Rev. 20:11-15, 21:8, 27.

ARTICLE 4. THE HOLY SPIRIT

The Holy Spirit is the third person of the Trinity, sent from the Father to "guide us into all truth", "convict the world of sin, of righteousness and of judgment to come", "to comfort, lead and teach the believers in Jesus Christ . . . to anoint, inspire and empower believers to continue the work Jesus began both to do and teach." Acts 1:1, 8; 2:38, 39; John 14:16, 17, 26; 16:7-15.

The HOLY SPIRIT is the "PROMISE OF THE FATHER"—all believers in Jesus Christ are entitled to receive, and should earnestly seek the Baptism of the HOLY GHOST and fire, according to the command of our Lord. Acts 1:4, 5, 8. THIS is the normal experience of all the early church. With this experience comes power to preach and bestowment of the GIFTS OF THE SPIRIT. Luke 24:19; Acts 1:4, 8; I Cor. 12:1-31. THIS wonderful experience is distinct from and subsequent to the experience of the "NEW BIRTH", Acts 10:44-46; 11:14-16; 15:7-9; Acts 2:38, 39.

THE EVIDENCE OF THE BAPTISM IN THE HOLY SPIRIT

When the believer is filled with the Holy Spirit, there is a physical sign of "speaking in other tongues as the Spirit of God gives the utterance." Acts 2:4. This is accompanied and followed by a burning desire and supernatural power to witness to others of God's salvation and power! Acts 10:44-47.

ARTICLE 5. THE CREATION

1) In the beginning GOD created the heavens and the earth and all things therein by His mighty WORD. Gen. 1:1; John 1.

2) GOD made man in His own image: pure, holy and free from sin—but gave man the free choice of life or death, obedience or disobedience to God's eternal commands and will. Gen. 1:26, 27; 2:17.

ARTICLE 6. THE FALL OF MAN

1) Satan tempted Adam and Eve, who believed his lies, and fell into sin, thus bringing death upon the whole human race. Gen. 2:17, 3:19.

2) Through the fall of Adam and Eve, all children of men are born with sinful natures, and the wages of sin is death—they will be lost throughout eternity if not redeemed from their sins by the grace of God, through Jesus Christ. Romans 5:12; John 3:16.

ARTICLE 7. REDEMPTION OF MAN

In the fulness of time, GOD sent His only begotten Son, Jesus Christ, into this world to pay the penalty for our sins, and redeem us from the power of Satan, sin, sickness, death and hell . . . all of which are the results of Adam's sin and the fall. Matt. 1:21; Luke 1:35.

Man can be saved if he hears the Gospel, believes the provision Christ has made for his salvation, accepts Jesus Christ as the Son of God, to wash away all his sins, and is ready to follow the teachings of Jesus Christ! Romans 10:9-17; Mark 16:15-18.

ARTICLE 8. SALVATION—ETERNAL LIFE

WHAT ONE MUST DO TO RECEIVE SALVATION:

1) REPENT:—this is a genuine sorrow for past sins committed and complete decision and turning FROM all forms of known sin in the life, and from all the appearance of sin. Repentance is accompanied by confession of our personal sins to GOD ALONE, who only can forgive sinners and change their hearts and lives! God is ready to forgive all who confess, and will never remember their sins against them anymore forever. I John 1:9 TRUE repentance makes a man make things right with those he has done wrong to, as far as possible. Luke 3:8; 19:9.

2) When man repents . . . then GOD GIVES SALVATION as a FREE GIFT—we could not earn it by any merits or good works we have done . . . good works cannot cover over the sins of the past . . . it takes GOD to wash away a man's sins and change his sinful nature to one that loves and follows holiness. John 3:16-18; Ephes. 1:13; I John 1:9.

3) EVIDENCES of Salvation: The inward evidence to the believer of his salvation is the direct witness of the SPIRIT of God to one's own spirit. Rom. 8:16. The outward evidence to all men, is a life of righteousness and true holiness. Matt. 5:16.

ARTICLE 9. SANCTIFICATION

Is purification of the nature from sin and filthiness of the flesh. This starts at the moment we are saved and should be a daily experience of "washing by the WORD"—complete dedication daily to God's Will. MAN CAN LIVE ABOVE SIN because our sinful natures have been changed by the "new birth" (John 3:7) and Christ lives in our hearts: I Pet. 1:15, 16; Matt. 5:48; 2 Cor. 7:7.

WHAT WE BELIEVE AND TEACH (DELIVERANCE EVANGELICAL CENTERS) (continued)

ARTICLE 10. WATER BAPTISM

Water baptism is administered to those who hear and believe the Gospel and accept Jesus Christ with all their heart. Infants are not baptized, but dedicated to God in prayer, for until a child comes to the age when he knows right from wrong and chooses wrong . . . he is under God's protection—if they die they go to heaven. Water baptism by immersion (in the Name of the FATHER, the SON, and the HOLY GHOST) is an outward testimony that we are as dead to our old sins, but rise to walk in newness of life with Jesus Christ. Water Baptism by immersion is a direct command of Christ to all who are "saved". Matt. 28:19; Mark 16:16; Rom. 6:4, 6: John 3:22, 23; John 4:1.

Notes: *The position of the Deliverance Evangelical Centers is close to that of the Assemblies of God. Baptism is by immersion and is reserved for adult believers.*

* * *

BASIS OF UNION (FIRE-BAPTIZED HOLINESS CHURCH OF GOD OF THE AMERICAS)

Section 1. We believe Jesus Christ shed His blood for the remission of sins that are past (Rom. 3:25) and for the regeneration of penitent sinners and for the salvation from sin and from sinning. (I John 3:5-10; Eph. 2:1-10).

Section 2. We believe, teach and firmly maintain the scriptural doctrine of Justification by faith alone through the blood. (Rom. 5:6-9; Eph. 1:7; Rom. 3:24-25; Col. 1:14).

Section 3. We believe also that Jesus Christ shed His blood for complete cleansing of the justified believer from all indwelling sin and from its pollution subsequent to regeneration. (Rom. 6:6; Heb. 13:12; I John 1:7-9; I Thess. 5:23; John 17:17; Acts. 26:18).

Section 4. We believe also that sanctification is an instantaneous, definite, second work of grace obtainable by faith on the part of the fully justified believer. (Heb. 10:9-14; Exodus 31:13).

Section 5. We believe also that the pentecostal baptism of the Holy Ghost and fire is obtainable by a definite act of appropriating faith on the part of the wholly sanctified believer, and that the initial evidence of the reception of this experience is speaking with other tongues as the spirit gives utterance. (Acts 8:14-17; Acts 1:5; Acts 8:7; Acts 10:44-46 and 19:6).

Section 6. We believe also in divine healing as in the atonement (Isa. 53:4-5; Matt. 8:16-17; Mark 16:14-15; James 5:14-15; Exodus 15:26; Psalms 103:3; Acts 8-7).

Section 7. We believe in the imminent personal premillennial second coming of our Lord Jesus Christ (I Thess. 4:15-18; Titus 2:13; II Peter 3:1-14; Matt. 24:20-44) and we love and wait for His appearing. (II Tim. 4:8).

Section 8. The F.B.H.C. of God of the Americas is utterly opposed to the teachings of the so-called Christian Scientists, Spiritualists, Unitarians, Universalists and Mormons. We deny as false un-Scriptural Seventh Day Adventism, (Col. 2:16-17; Gal. 3:11) annihilation of the wicked, conditional immortality, and antinomianism, absolute perfection, so-called comeoutism, the so-called resurrection life, the so-called redemption or glorification of the body in this life, and the doctrine of the restitution of all things as set forth in millennial dawnism and the false teaching that we are not born of God until we are sanctified wholly. (Matt. 25:26; Rev. 20:10-14; Mark 9:44).

Section 9. The Lord says marriage is honorable in all and the bed undefiled, and the Fire Baptized Holiness Church of God of the Americas FIRMLY HOLDS THAT THERE ARE CERTAIN RELATIONS BETWEEN HUSBAND AND WIFE which are strictly private, according to the word of God, and into this sacred privacy no one has any right to inquire. (Heb. 13:4, I Cor. 7:15).

Section 10. No subsequent General Council shall have authority to change the Basis of Union of the Fire Baptized Holiness Church of God of the Americas without a full representation from the local Churches.

Notes: *The Fire-Baptized Holiness Church of God of the Americas resulted from a division along racial lines of the Fire-Baptized Holiness Church (now a constituent part of the International Pentecostal Holiness Church). This Basis of Union is almost identical with that of the other church sharing similar roots, the Pentecostal Fire-Baptized Church.*

* * *

ARTICLES OF FAITH (UNITED HOLY CHURCH OF AMERICA)

1. We believe in one God, the Father Almighty, Maker of heaven and earth, and all things visible. I Timothy 2:5. And in Jesus Christ, His only Son, our Lord, who is of one substance with the Father, by whom all things were made. Col. 1:15-18. And in the Holy Spirit, the Comforter, who is sent from the Father and Son and who together with the Father and Son is worshipped and glorified. John 14:15-17; Acts 2:4.

2. We believe that man was made in the image of God that he might know, love and obey God, and enjoy Him forever; that our first parents by disobedience fell under the righteous condemnation of God; and that all men are so alienated from God that there is no salvation from the guilt and power of sin, except through God's redeeming grace. Titus 2:11, 12.

3. We believe that God would have all men return to Him; that to this end He has made Himself known, not only through the works of nature, the course of His providence, and the consciences of men, but also through supernatural revelations made especially to a chosen people, and above all when the fulness of time was come, through Jesus Christ, His Son. Gal. 4:4; I Peter 3:9.

4. We believe that the scriptures of the Old and New Testaments are the records of God's revelation of Himself in the work of redemption; that they were written by men under the special guidance of the Holy Spirit; that they are able to make wise unto salvation, and that they constitute the authoritative

standard by which religious teaching and human conduct are to be regulated and judged. II Tim. 3:15; II Peter 1:19-21.

5. We believe that the love of God to sinful men has found its highest expression in the redemptive work of His Son; who became man, uniting His divine nature with our human nature in one person; who was tempted like other men, yet without sin; who by His humiliation, His Holy obedience, His suffering, His death on the cross, and His resurrection, became a perfect Redeemer whose sacrifice of Himself for the sins of the world declares the righteousness of God, and is the sole and sufficient ground of forgiveness, and of reconciliation with Him. Gal. 3:13; Heb. 2:16, 4:15; Phil. 2:8.

6. We believe that Jesus Christ, after He had risen from the dead, ascended into heaven, where, as the one mediator between God and man, He carries forward His work of saving men; that He sends the Holy Spirit to convict them of their sin and to lead them to repentance, and faith; and that those, who through renewing grace turn to righteousness, and trust in Jesus Christ as their Redeemer, receive for His sake the forgiveness of their sins, and are made the children of God. I Tim. 2:5; Eph. 1:7; Gal. 1:14; Heb. 9:24.

7. We believe that justification is an act of God whereby all the sins of past life are forgiven through faith in our Lord Jesus Christ, and comes immediately in connection with true repentance and includes regeneration or being born again. Rom. 5; Titus 3:5; Rom. 3:24, 25.

8. We believe that sanctification is the second act of grace whereby the believer is separated, dedicated and consecrated unto God; body, soul, and spirit. This act of sanctification may be viewed in three aspects: instantaneous, progressive, and entire—

  A. Instantaneous sanctification is an act wrought in connection with regeneration. St. John 17:17; Rom. 6:22, 12:1; Heb. 13:12, 13.

  B. Progressive sanctification is the process in which the believer continues to grow in grace. II Cor. 3:18; II Peter 3:18; I Peter 1:15, 16; Heb. 2:11, 12:14.

  C. Entire sanctification denotes a state of being wholly sanctified, body, soul and spirit. I Thes. 5:23; Heb. 12:14; Jude 24.

9. We believe in the baptism of the Holy Ghost, as the gift of power on the sanctified life. Luke 24:49; Matt. 3:11; John 7:38-39, 14-16, 17-26; Acts 1:5-8, 2:4.

10. We believe in divine healing of the body, through the precious atonement of Jesus, by which sickness and disease are destroyed. Isa. 53:4, 5; Matt. 8:17; Mark 16:18; James 5:14-16.

11. We believe in the observance of Sunday, the first day of the week as a day of holy rest and worship in the ministry of the word.

12. We believe in the ultimate prevalence of the kingdom of Christ over the earth; in the glorious appearing of the Great God and our Saviour Jesus Christ in the resurrection of the dead; and in a final judgment, the issues of which are everlasting life and everlasting punishment. Matt. 25:31-46; Acts 1:11, 17:31; Matt. 13:49; Rev. 1:7.

Notes: *Like the International Pentecostal Holiness Church, the United Holy Church of America accepts the Apostles' Creed as its creed, and has a similarly-worded church covenant. Its articles of faith are unique and include phrases from the Nicene Creed and the Westminster Catechism.*

* * *

THE ORTHODOX HOLY CHRISTIAN SPIRITUAL CREED OF CHRISTIAN SPIRITUAL CHURCH AND BELIEVERS [UNIVERSAL CHRISTIAN SPIRITUAL FAITH AND CHURCHES FOR ALL NATIONS (NATIONAL DAVID SPIRITUAL TEMPLE)]

I BELIEVE:

In God the Holy Father Eloheim Almighty, the Father of Spirits and Creator of heaven and earth; and in Jesus Christ the Holy Word and Emmanuel and only begotten Son of God, our Saviour; Who was conceived by the Holy Ghost, born of the Holy Virgin Saint Mary; He taught and demonstrated spiritual knowledge of His kingdom and church by sermons, teachings, healings, prophesying, mind reading and mastery of mind and matter, flesh and blood, life and death, natural and spiritual forces to the glory of God; He was reviled and persecuted because of His spiritual faith, works and power, as an evil doer; He suffered under the rule and by the hands of Pontius Pilate and spiritually blind sinners; He was tried on false charges by Pontius Pilate, condemned by the Jews, crucified, giving up His life according to the Scriptures of Prophecies for the salvation of sinners, and the sins of the People; He was buried in Saint Joseph's new sepulchre under guard and seal; He descended into Hell (prison of the disembodied souls), and preached to the spirits in prison who perished out of their natural bodies, before, during and after the antediluvian flood; the third day He arose from among the disembodied dead; He was seen forty days upon the earth by His holy Apostles and disciples by personal communion, and by over five hundred spectators at one time; He finally ascended into heaven and sitteth at the right hand of God the Father Almighty; He has become the everlasting spiritual High Priest of His Christian spiritual saints and church; after His ascension His disembodied Spirit (Holy Ghost) has come and set (9) spiritual gifts (spirits) in His New Testament spiritual church (Body) by the Holy Ghost, for the edifying of the spiritual saints in the church (Body), and the spreading of the Gospel of spiritual salvation of souls, and the demonstration of the spiritual mysteries of His Kingdom; that He will return in like manner to gather His elects to himself forever; He is the justifier, sanctifier, and spiritual magnifier of all orthodox Christian spiritual believers in Him; I believe in the Holy Ghost, the Spirit of Promise and

THE ORTHODOX HOLY CHRISTIAN SPIRITUAL CREED OF CHRISTIAN SPIRITUAL CHURCH AND BELIEVERS [UNIVERSAL CHRISTIAN SPIRITUAL FAITH AND CHURCHES FOR ALL NATIONS (NATIONAL DAVID SPIRITUAL TEMPLE)] (continued)

Divine Guide into all the ways of Truth, the Third Person (Power) in the Holy Trinity; I believe in the baptism of the Holy Ghost and the Nine Gifts (Spirits) as demonstrated by the Holy Ghost spirits through the gifted Saints in the orthodox Christian spiritual church of Christ; I believe in the communion of spirits which make known secret mysteries of the past, present and future to the gifted people of all generations, nations and tongues who live in corporeal (natural) bodies upon the earth; I believe that all nations, kindred and tongues should worship God the Holy Father Almighty in spirit and in truth, together in one Lord, one spiritual Faith, and one Baptism, in the body of Christ through the Holy Ghost in the oneness of the Trinity inseparable, whether they be Jews or Gentiles, bond or free, white, red, brown, black or yellow, as saints of our Lord and Saviour Jesus Christ; I believe in the New Testament Scripture's spiritual church doctrines, teachings and practices as examples to be followed by the followers of the Holy Ghost in all genuine churches of the orthodox Christian spiritual faith; I believe in the forgiveness of sin; the resurrection of the quickened body, and life everlasting through the Grace of our Lord and Saviour Jesus Christ. A-men! A-men! A-men Selah!"

Notes: *In 1952 the National David Spiritual Temple merged to become a constituent part of the Universal Christian Spiritual Faith and Churches for All Nations. The statement affirms many orthodox Christian beliefs, the Pentecostal emphases on the gifts of the spirit, and some Spiritualist tenents (in the belief in the communion of spirits). The statement also mentions many items believed by some Christians but almost never included in creedal statements, such as Jesus' trial on "false charges," "Saint Joseph's [of Arimathea] new sepulchre," and the "demonstration of the spiritual mysteries."*

*   *   *

Spanish-Speaking Pentecostal

WE TEACH (DEFENDERS OF THE FAITH)

WE TEACH: The Bible as the inspired Word of God, the revelation of His divine scheme of redemption.

Jesus Christ as God's divinely and only begotten Son.

The gospel as the only power of God unto salvation through the atoning blood of Jesus Christ.

The need of holy living through the power of the Holy Spirit, bringing into the Christian's life the fruits of the Spirit.

Prayer as a power for the unfolding, empowering, and guidance of Christian life, and as a ministry of intercession.

The imminent personal return of Jesus Christ for His saints, and to the earth to set up His kingdom over the nations.

The duty and privilege of all Christians to have some part in the evangelization of the world.

The fact of eternal life through Jesus Christ, and the just punishment of all evil.

Notes: *This statement, not specifically pentecostal, is from the parent organization (a non-church-forming, non-pentecostal organization) of the Defenders of the Faith congregations which emerged in Puerto Rico. In Puerto Rico, members of the Defenders of the Faith became pentecostal, and subsequently migrated to the United States.*

*   *   *

WHAT WE BELIEVE (SOLDIERS OF THE CROSS OF CHRIST)

WE BELIEVE: In the direct calling of the believer to dedicate himself for the cause of God. Jn. 6:65; Jn. 17:2,12; Jn. 18:9; Acts 2:47.

WE BELIEVE: In the complete renunciation of material things to serve the Lord, Lu. 14:33; 1 Kings 19:20,21; Mt. 4:18-22.

WE BELIEVE: In baptism by inmersion as the first step to salvation. Mt. 28:19; Col. 2:12; Ga. 3:27; Acts 22:16.

WE BELIEVE: In the observance, of the commandments of God and Jesus the Son and the Holy Spirit. Ex. 20:1-17; Lu. 4:46; Ga. 3:21; Mt. 5:17.

WE BELIEVE: That the *Sabath*, the seventh day, is the day of rest blessed by God. He. 4: 1-11; Ex. 20:10; Mt. 5:17,18.

WE BELIEVE: In the resurrection of the dead, when Christ will appear in glory; Jn. 5:28; Lu. 14:15; Mr. 12:24; Da. 12:2.

WE BELIEVE: That the ministers ought to practice their life through faith. Jn. 6:27; He. 10:38,39; Ro. 1:17.

WE BELIEVE: In divine healing by means of prayer and anointing. Mt. 10:8; Mk. 6:13; 16: 18.

WE BELIEVE: That all men are equal with the same responsibilities and the same privileges before God. Ga. 3:28; Acts 2:39; 10:34,35; 17:26.

WE BELIEVE: In the baptism of the Holy Spirit. Jl. 2:27,28; Acts 1:5,8; 2:1;14; 1 Co. 14 9-28.

WE BELIEVE: In the prophecy and divine revelation by means of dreams or visions and manifestations of the Holy Spirit. Job 33:14, 15; Jo. 2:28; Nu. 12:6; Mt. 2:12.

WE BELIEVE: In the glory or eternal life for the faithful. Ro. 6:23; 2 Ti. 2:10; He. 11:14-16; Mt. 13:43; 2 Co. 5:1.

WE BELIEVE: In hell, or place of punishment for the unfaithful and unbelievers. Lu. 17:29; Mt. 13:50; Pr. 15:11,24; Ps. 55:15.

WE BELIEVE: That the Bible's healthfulness should be observed by the children of God. That there are clean as well as unclean foods. Ge. 7:2; Le. 11; Acts 10:14; 1 Co. 6:17.

WE BELIEVE: That Christ is the Saviour of mankind and that there is no eternal life by any other means. Acts 4:12; Jn. 10:28,29. 1 Ti. 2:5; Jn. 17:2,3.

WE BELIEVE: In the Bible, as eternal truth and the holy word of God. Jn. 5:39; 20:31; 1 Pe. 1:25.

WE BELIEVE: That the minister should not involve himself in politics. 2 Ti. 2:4; 1 Pe. 4:15; Jn. 18:36.

WE BELIEVE: In the universal message proclaimed by the Lord's church. Mk. 16:15; Mt. 24:14; Mt. 10:7.

WE BELIEVE: In the holy communion, or the Lord's supper, to commemorate his death, not His resurrection. 1 Co. 11:23-32; Jn. 6:48-58.

WE BELIEVE: In the washing of feet as a sign of humility. Lu. 7:44; Jn. 13:2-9.

WE BELIEVE: That we are saved by grace: by faith. Acts 15:11; Ep. 2:5,8; Ro. 4:16.

WE BELIEVE: That fasting and prayer are factors that strengthen the believer. Est. 4:16; Jn. 3:7,8; Mt. 17:21; Mt. 9:15.

WE BELIEVE: In the second coming of Jesus Christ personally that he will descend in clouds of glory and that no one knows the day nor the hour. S. Mt. 25:31; 1 Th. 4:16,17. 2 Pe. 3:10.

Notes: *Formerly known as the Iglesia Bando Evangelico Gedeon/Gilgal Evangelistic International Church, the Soldiers of the Cross of Christ is a two-experience church which also practices sabbatarianism.*

*　　*　　*

Miscellaneous Pentecostal

STATEMENT OF BELIEF OF THE ALPHA AND OMEGA CHRISTIAN CHURCH AND BIBLE SCHOOL

1. We believe the Bible to be the only inspired, infallible Word of God. II Peter 1:21.

2. We believe the Godhead consists of the Father, the Son, and the Holy Spirit. II Cor. 13:14. Three in One and One in Three.

3. We believe in the Deity of Jesus Christ, in His Virgin birth, in His atoning death, in His bodily resurrection, in His ascension to the right hand of the Father. I Timothy 3:16.

4. We believe in evangelistic and missionary fervor and endeavor. Acts 1:8; Mark 16:15-18.

5. We believe in salvation through the redeeming blood of Christ. Hebrews 9:22.

6. We believe in the keeping power of God. Jude 24.

7. We believe in sanctification and holiness of heart and the overcoming life as Scriptural requirements for the Bride of Christ. Eph. 5:25-27.

8. We believe in the Baptism of the Holy Spirit according to Acts 2:4, 10:46, 19:6, and the present ministry of the Spirit in and through the believer as manifest in the five ministries as they are being restored in end-time revival (Eph. 4:11), the gifts of the Spirit (I Cor. 12:8-11), and the fruit of the Spirit (Gal. 5:22, 23).

9. We believe that divine healing is obtained on the basis of the Atonement. I Peter 2:24.

10. We believe in Christ's imminent personal return in power and great glory, in His millennial reign and in His everlasting dominion. Acts 1:11; Rev. 20:4; Dan. 7:14.

11. We believe in the resurrection of both the saved and the lost; they that are saved unto the resurrection of eternal life and they that are lost unto the resurrection of eternal punishment. John 5:28, 29; Rev. 20:15.

*　　*　　*

WE BELIEVE (ASSOCIATION OF SEVENTH DAY PENTECOSTAL ASSEMBLIES)

WE BELIEVE:

In the blood of Jesus for the remission of sins, Heb. 9:22; Lev. 17:11.

In Baptism by immersion in water, Rom. 6:4; Col. 2:12; I Peter 2:21; Matt. 28:19; Acts 2:38.

In sanctification by the blood, I John 1:7; Heb. 13:12.

In santification by the Spirit, I Pet. 1:2; II Thess. 2:13; Rom. 15:16.

In sanctification by the Word, John 17:17, 19.

That the Spirit leads us to the Truth, John 16:13, and the Truth makes us free, John 8:31, 32; 6:44, 45.

In the Baptism of the Holy Spirit as rest for the soul, Acts 2:4; Heb. 4:1; Is. 28:12, and endowment of power for service, Acts 1:8.

In keeping the Sabbath as rest for the body, Ex. 20:8-11, Heb. 4:1, 4, 10.

In the millennium as rest for both soul and body.

In the healing of all sickness and disease, Is. 53:5; I Pet. 2:24; Mark 16:18; James 5:14.

That each of the Ten Commandments are equal, and that no one commandment is subordinate of the other, James 2:10; Rom. 7:6.

That Christ has a church which represents His Body, and to have fellowship in said church we must endeavour to keep the unity of the Spirit in the bond of peace, Eph. 4:3.

That we should and will have this unity by obeying God's order of lifting our voices together, and singing together, Is. 52:8, and that we will see eye to eye when He (Christ) brings again Zion, and . . .

That His second coming is personal, imminent, and is the blessed hope of the church, I Thess. 4:16-17.

We believe that Christ is the only one who can help everyone. We preach the whole gospel for the whole man. I Thess. 5:23.

Notes: *As the name implies, this organization is sabbatarian in practice.*

THE FUNDAMENTAL DOCTRINE OF THE CHURCH (CHURCH OF GOD BY FAITH)

I. We believe in supporting and observing civil laws that are supported by and in harmony with righteous principles. Rom. 13:1-4.

II. We do not believe in becoming actively involved in armed combat in any capacity. We absolutely do not believe in anyway that the destruction of life is in accord with God's law.

III. We do not believe that a Christian should swear or falsify any statement of any kind, regardless to the situation or condition.

IV. We believe in a total self-committal to one God, who is the sovereign ruler of the universe.

V. We believe in and support the idea of peace for all men; for God has made all men equal, regardless of race, creed, or color.

VI. We believe in obedience to God as supreme. We believe and support the fact that God is, and should be, recognized as the sovereign ruler of all things.

VII. We believe in obeying God.

We believe that God created the heaven and the earth. Gen. 1:1.

We believe that "God created man." Gen. 1:26-27; Gen. 2:7; Isa. 42:5-6.

Christ has forewarned His people to "fear God." St. Matt. 10:28: Eccl. 12:1; 12-13.

"For I am the Lord and I change not." Mal. 3:6.

Notes: *The Church of God by Faith's brief statement reveals the church to be a holiness-pentecostal body, which is pacifist in practice and believes in racial equality.*

*　　*　　*

STATEMENT OF FAITH (COMMUNITY CHAPEL AND BIBLE TRAINING CENTER)

We believe in the absolute inspiration of the Bible and hold it to be the inerrant and final authority in all matters of Christian faith and practice (2 Tim. 3:16; Mtt. 5:17-19).

We believe in God the Father, almighty and eternal, Creator of the heavens and the earth and all that dwell therein, contrary to all evolutionary theory (1 Cor. 8:6; 2 Cor. 6:18; 1 Tim. 1:17; Gen. 1:1ff).

We believe in the Lord Jesus Christ, the Son of God, fully God and fully man, who was born of the virgin Mary, suffered and died for our sins on the cross, was buried, rose bodily from the dead on the third day, appeared unto men, ascended into heaven in the sight of many witnesses, and who is coming again with power and great glory (1 Cor. 8:6; Mtt. 16:16; John 20:28; 1 Tim. 2:5; Mtt. 1:23; 1 Cor. 15:3-7; Acts 1:9-11; Mtt. 24:30).

We believe in the Holy Spirit, the Comforter, who inspired the holy apostles and prophets of old; who indwells believers with His presence today as He did in the early church, giving them the ability to speak in languages they have never learned; and who convicts the world concerning sin, righteousness, and judgment (John 14:26; 2 Pe. 1:21; Acts 2:4; John 16:8).

We believe that no one can be saved from sin and judgment and have eternal life without repenting of his sins and personally accepting Jesus Christ as his Lord and Savior, receiving forgiveness through the shed blood of Jesus, the sinless Lamb of God. All who have been born again according to John 3:3-8, we accept as members of the body of Christ, sharing fellowship with them based on our common salvation, not on doctrine, as important as it is (Rom. 6:23; 10:9,10; Luke 13:3; John 1:12; Eph. 1:7; 1 Pe. 1:19; 1 Cor. 12:12; 1 Jn. 1:3).

We believe that water baptism is for the remission of sins (Acts 2:38; 22:16) and should be administered to believers by immersion in keeping with the commission of Jesus in Matthew 28:19 and apostolic practice (Acts 2:38; 19:5).

We believe in participating in the New Covenant communion of the Lord's body, partaking of the emblems which typify the body and blood of Jesus Christ, remembering His death until He comes again. We examine ourselves, confessing our faults and sins, always discerning those in the Lord's body—both locally and universally (1 Cor. 10:16,17; 11:23-33).

We believe that Christians must live in obedience to God's Word, and that those who remain in the faith unto the end shall be saved (2 Tim. 2:19; Luke 8:13; 1 Cor. 15:2; Heb. 3:14; Mtt. 24:13).

We believe that God is a God of order who has established a specific structure of authority within both the church and the family. He has established offices in the church (pastors, elders, and deacons) through which the affairs of the local assembly are to be governed. Members of the assembly are enjoined to obey those who have the rule over them in spiritual matters. God has also ordained that children are to obey their parents, wives are to submit to their husbands, and citizens are to obey their civil governmental authorities. In all the aforementioned cases of submission, exception must be made if obedience would cause one to violate his conscience before God (Rom. 13:1-7; 1 Cor. 12:28; Eph. 4:11-13; 1 Tim. 3:1-13; Heb. 13:17; Eph. 6:1; 5:22; 1 Pe. 2:13, 14; Acts 4:19).

We believe that all New Testament believers should purpose in their hearts to financially support the ministry of their church with at least as much liberality as the tithe and offering which was required to be given to the Lord under the Old Covenant (Lev. 27:30-32; Mal. 3:10; 2 Cor. 9:6,7).

We believe that bodily healing continues to be available to believers today, having been provided by the atonement of Christ on the cross and promised to all who will put their trust in Him (Mark 16:18; Jas. 5:14, 15; 1 Pe. 2:24).

We believe in the exercise of the gifts and ministries of the Holy Spirit within the church body, as described in Romans 12:3-8 and in 1 Corinthians 12 through 14.

We believe that Christians are to endeavor to keep the unity of the Spirit in the bond of peace, so that God may bring the willing and obedient, who truly love Him, unto the unity of the faith before Jesus Christ returns (Eph. 4:1-6, 13-16).

We believe in the out-translation of the bride of Christ, followed by the great tribulation in which the antichrist shall rule over the earth through a world government, world church, and false prophet. Those Christians who fail to make the bride of Christ will, if they are faithful, be martyred in the great tribulation and come into the great wedding feast as guests of the Groom. God will pour out plagues on the earth; the devil will gather all nations against Jerusalem to battle; Christ will return to rule over the earth in the Millennium; all shall stand before God at the great judgment (1 Th. 4:17; Luke 21:27, 28, 36; Rev. 7:14; 2 Th. 2:1-8; Rev. 13:1-18; 17:1-18; 8:7-9:19; 11:15,19; 16:12-14,16; Zec. 14:2-5,9; Rev. 1:7; 20:11-15).

We believe in everlasting life for the believer and everlasting judgment for the unbeliever (John 3:16; Mtt. 25:46; Rev. 20:11-15).

Notes: *This statement strongly affirms the authority of the Bible, adult baptism by immersion, a structure of church authority and government, tithing, divine healing, the gifts of the Spirit, and a pre-millennial eschatology. Though the statement asserts a belief in God the Father; Jesus Christ as the Son of God; and the Holy Spirit, there is no affirmation of the Trinity.*

* * *

DOCTRINE (FULL GOSPEL MINISTER ASSOCIATION)

1. The Bible is the inspired Word of God, and is infallible as to any and all other writings, messages, or man's teachings, II Pet. 1:19-21, and II Tim. 3:16-17.

2. God. There are three persons united and equal in attributes, in the one true and living God, Father, Son and Holy Ghost, I Tim. 2:5, II Cor. 13:14, John 14:26.

3. Man and his fall. Man is a created being, made in the likeness and image of God, Gen. 1:27. Through Adam's disobedience, Gen. 3:1-7 man fell and sin has come into the world, Rom. 5:12, so under the curse of Adam, all men have sinned and have come short of the Glory of God, Rom. 3:23, and Rom. 3:10 none righteous.

4. Man's Redemption is in Jesus Christ, who was God manifested in the flesh, to undo the work of the devil, and He gave His life, shed His Blood, to redeem man back to God, I John 3:8.

5. Born-again is essential to all men in order to enter the Kingdom of God, John 3:3-5.

6. Holy Living is required of man, a life separated from the world, I John 2:15-16.

7. Heaven, the eternal abode of the righteous, I Thess. 1:7-10, Rev. 19:11-16.

8. Hell, the abode of the unrighteous until the day of judgment, Rev. 20:13, and shall be cast into the Lake of Fire together with the unrighteous, Rev. 20:14-15.

9. Ministry, a two-fold purpose is provided and ordained of God in the Bible. The evangelism of the world, and the edifying of the body of Christ, which is the Church, Mark 16:15-20, Eph. 4:11-13, with the confirming of the Word, with signs following and evidence of the power of God, Matt. 11:5.

10. Conscientious Statement, We believe that civil Government is ordained of God, Rom. 3:1-2, and we are thankful for this Government under which we live, for freedom of Worship in spirit and in truth, and that the Bible teaches that man shall not wilfully kill, Exodus 20:13, Romans 13:9, Matt. 5:21. But in time of war or other crisis, we will serve our Government in any capacity consistent with non-combative services.

Notes: *The association has a pacifist orientation.*

* * *

DOCTRINAL STATEMENT (INTERNATIONAL EVANGELISM CRUSADES)

We accept the entire Bible as Truth. There is but ONE GOD, maker and Creater of all things. Jesus Christ as the Son of God who was one with the Father before the foundations of the World. There is personal Salvation through faith in the Son of God, Jesus Christ. There is Divine Healing through Faith in the Bible and in Jesus Christ. The Baptism of the Holy Ghost is for believers (Acts 2:4). There are 9 gifts of the Spirit. The hope of all Christians is the personal return of Jesus Christ. Worldwide Evangelism, Christian Education and Study of the Word, Christian literature and publications, radio and TV, shall be instituted to spread the Truth of the Living God, to fulfill the great God-given Commission (Mark 16:9-20).

Notes: *Designed as a fellowship across traditional denominational lines, the International Evangelism Crusades has a very minimal statement, which allows room for almost the entire doctrinal spectrum within pentecostalism.*

* * *

STATEMENT OF THE BASIC DOCTRINE (JESUS PEOPLE CHURCH)

We believe . . .

The Bible is the inspired and only infallible and authoritative Word of God.

There is one God; God the Father, God the Son, and God the Holy Spirit.

In the Diety of our Lord Jesus Christ, in His virgin birth, in His sinless life, in His miracles, in His atoning death, in His bodily resurrection, in His ascension to the right hand of the Father, and His personal future return to this earth in power and glory to rule for 1,000 years.

In the Blessed Hope, the rapture of the Church, when we shall meet Him in the air.

The only means of being cleansed from sin is through repentance and faith in the blood of Jesus.

Regeneration by the Holy Spirit is essential for personal salvation.

STATEMENT OF THE BASIC DOCTRINE (JESUS PEOPLE CHURCH) (continued)

The redemptive work of Jesus Christ on the cross provides healing of the human body in answer to believing prayer.

The baptism of the Holy Spirit, according to Acts 2:4, is given to believers who ask for it.

In the sanctifying power of the Holy Spirit by whose indwelling the Christian is enabled to live a holy life.

In the resurrection of both the saved and the lost, the one to everlasting life, and the other to everlasting damnation.

Notes: *The doctrine of the Jesus People Church is close to the essential position of the Assemblies of God and includes an affirmation of a premillennial eschatology.*

* * *

THESE THINGS WE BELIEVE (LIBERTY FELLOWSHIP)

INSPIRATION OF THE SCRIPTURES

We believe in the verbal inspiration of the Bible, both the Old and New Testaments (II Timothy 3:16; Hebrews 4:12; I Peter 1:23-25; II Peter 1:19-21).

GOD

We believe in one God revealed in three Persons: The Father, the Son, and the Holy Ghost (Matthew 3:16,17;28:29; John 17).

MAN

We believe that man, in his natural state, is a sinner, lost, undone, without hope, and without God (Romans 3:19-23; Galatians 3:22; Ephesians 2:1,2,12).

DIVINITY AND HUMANITY OF CHRIST JESUS

We believe that Jesus is God come in the flesh and that He is both divine and human (Luke 1:26-38; John 14:1-3; Acts 2:36; 3:14,15; Philippians 2:5-12; Hebrews 2:9-18).

BLOOD ATONEMENT

We believe in the saving power of the Blood of Jesus and His *imputed righteousness* (Acts 4:12; Romans 4:1-9; 5:1-11; Ephesians 1:3-15).

BODILY RESURRECTION

We believe in the bodily resurrection of Jesus Christ (Luke 24:39-43; John 20:24-29).

ASCENSION

We believe that Christ Jesus ascended to the Father and is presently engaged in building Heaven and interceding for the saints (John 14:1-6; Romans 8:34).

SECOND COMING

We believe in the visible, bodily return of Christ Jesus to this earth to rapture His Church (Bride) and judge the world (Acts 1:10,11; I Thessalonians 4:13-18; II Thessalonians 1:7-10; James 5:8; Revelation 1:7). (It is not necessary that we all believe alike concerning whether He is coming before, during, or after the Great Tribulation.)

SALVATION

We believe that the terms of salvation are repentance toward God for sin, and a personal, heartfelt faith in the Lord Jesus Christ, which results in regeneration of the person. This salvation is entirely by grace of our Lord and not of works. Works are excluded except as FRUIT of salvation (Acts 3:19,20; Romans 4:1-5; 5:1; Ephesians 2:8-10).

LOCAL CHURCH

We believe the Church of the Lord Jesus Christ is a Body of believers who have been baptized in the Name of the Father, Son, and Holy Ghost; who are under recognized, delegated authorities; and who assemble to worship, carry forth the Great Commission, and minister as the Holy Ghost leads (Matthew 16:18; 28:19,20; Acts 2:40-47; 20:28; Ephesians 5:22-32; I Timothy 3:15).

ORDINANCES

We believe that the two ordinances of the Church are Water Baptism and the Lord's Supper.

WATER BAPTISM: Immersion in water in the Name of the Father, Son, and Holy Ghost (Matthew 3:15,16; 28:19,20; Acts 8:38; Romans 6:1-4). A symbol of identification with Jesus Christ in His death, burial, and resurrection.

LORD'S SUPPER: A memorial of the death, resurrection, and Second Coming of our Lord Jesus Christ (Luke 22:13-20).

SEPARATED LIFE

We believe that believers should seek, as the early disciples did, to practice the separated life from the world and unto Christ and to set standards of conduct which shall exalt our Lord and His Church (Romans 12:1-3; II Corinthians 6:17; Galatians 6:14; Ephesians 5:11; Colossians 3:17).

HEAVEN AND HELL

We believe the Scriptures clearly set forth the doctrines of eternal punishment for the lost and eternal bliss and service for the saved—Hell for the unsaved and Heaven for the saved (Matthew 25:34, 41, 46; Luke 16:19-31; John 14:1-3; Revelation 20:11-15).

HOLY SPIRIT

We believe the Holy Spirit to be the third Person of the Trinity whose purpose in the redemption of man is to convict men of sin, regenerate the repentant believer, guide the believer into ALL truth, indwell and give gifts to believers as He wills, that they may minister as Christ would to men. We believe that the manifestations of the Holy Spirit recorded in I Corinthians 12:8-11 shall operate in present-day churches which yield to the Lord Jesus Christ (Luke 11:13; John 7:37-39; 14:16,17; 16:7-14: Acts 2:39-48). We believe that the Baptism in the Holy Spirit, with the evidence of speaking with other tongues as the Spirit gives utterance, is for all believers as promised by John the Baptist (Matthew 3:11) and Jesus (Acts 1:4,5, 8) and Peter (Acts 2:38-41), was witnessed by the early disciples of Christ (Acts 2:4; 10:44-47; 19:1-6), and is evidenced by many present-day disciples of the Lord Jesus Christ.

DIVINE HEALING

We believe that God has used doctors, medicines, and other material means for healing; but divine healing was also provided for in the Atonement (Isaiah 53:5) and may be appropriated by laying on of hands by elders (James 5:14-16), laying on of hands by the believers (Mark 16:18), by the prayer of an anointed person gifted for healing the sick (I Corinthians 12:9), or by a direct act of receiving this provision by faith (Mark 11:23).

PRIESTHOOD OF BELIEVERS

We believe that each believer is a priest of the Lord (Revelation 1:6) and has direct access to the Father through the Lord Jesus Christ. Each person must believe for himself, be baptized for himself, obey for himself, and answer to his Creator for himself.

GOVERNMENT OF THE CHURCH

We believe that the New Testament Church should be apostolic in nature and is governed by delegated authorities. These authorities at Liberty Church are set forth in Article VI of the Liberty Church Charter. When it is deemed best for the life of the church and testimony of the Lord, these authorities may discipline, in the spirit of love, any member who departs from the doctrines set forth in the articles of the Liberty Church Charter or whose conduct is contrary to the spirit and practice of this body.

ORDAINED OFFICERS

The ordained officers of the Church are apostle, prophet, evangelist, pastor, teacher, local (counseling) elders and deacons (Ephesians 4:11; I Timothy 3; Titus 1:5-9). Apostles, prophets, evangelists, pastors, and teachers shall not necessarily all function in one local church. However, it is believed that all of these officers shall function under the covering of a local church and all local (counseling) elders are under the supervision of the five-fold ministry listed in Ephesians 4:11 (Acts 15; I Timothy 5:17-21; Titus 1:5-9).

(All churches in Liberty Fellowship of Churches and Ministers must adopt the same Articles of Faith, but each church sets its own by-laws for local church membership.)

In conclusion, though we believe that the doctrines of the Bible were written by God's men and that they are verbally inspired, it is entirely possible for a person to believe a doctrine and never experience the life set forth in the doctrine. For example, one could believe the new birth without experiencing it; he could believe the Baptism in the Holy Spirit and never experience it; he could give mental assent about the work of the Lord Jesus and never personally know Him. Jesus is not a doctrine—He is a Person. He is not a plan of salvation—He is the Man of salvation. Therefore, it is our desire that those reading these doctrines not only mentally agree with them, but have a witness within themselves that these doctrines are true.

We do not judge those who do not believe as we do, and we have no desire to debate doctrines. It is our commission to proclaim the gospel, not to defend it.

Notes: *The Liberty Fellowship shares the basic Pentecostal affirmations. Its unique feature is the attention given to a hierarchy of authority in the hands of apostles and other church leaders.*

STATEMENT OF FAITH (MARANATHA CHRISTIAN CHURCHES)

We Believe . . .

The Bible to be the inspired, the only infallible, authoritative Word of God.

We believe . . .

There is one eternal, almighty and perfect God; Father, Son and Holy Spirit.

We believe . . .

In the deity of our Lord Jesus Christ, in His virgin birth, in His sinless life, in His miracles, in His vicarious and atoning death through His shed blood, in His bodily resurrection, in His ascension to the right hand of the Father, and in His personal return in power and glory.

We believe . . .

That for the salvation of lost and sinful man regeneration by the Holy Spirit is absolutely essential.

We believe . . .

In the present ministry of the Holy Spirit by whose indwelling the Christian is enabled to live a godly life.

We believe . . .

In the resurrection of both the saved and the lost; they that are saved unto the resurrection of life and they that are lost unto the resurrection of damnation.

We believe . . .

In the spiritual unity of believers in our Lord Jesus Christ.

Notes: *This minimal statement mentions the more controversial aspect of Maranatha's belief and practice (the present ministry of the Holy Spirit) only in the most abstract manner.*

*　　*　　*

STATEMENT OF FAITH (UNITED EVANGELICAL CHURCHES)

ONE IN FAITH

Spiritual unity within U. E. C. rests upon a solid biblical statement of faith.

1. We believe the Bible to be the inspired, infallible, ultimately authoritative Word of God.

2. We believe that there is one God, eternally existent in three Personalities, Father, Son and Holy Spirit.

3. We believe that the Lord Jesus Christ is The Deity, that He was born of a virgin, that He lived a sinless life, performed miracles, that we are redeemed by His atoning death through His shed blood, that He bodily resurrected and ascended to the right hand of the Father, that He will personally return in power and glory.

4. We believe in the total depravity of man.

5. We believe that men are saved through a personal encounter with the Lord Jesus Christ and regeneration by the Holy Spirit.

STATEMENT OF FAITH (UNITED EVANGELICAL CHURCHES) (continued)

6. We believe in the present ministry of the Holy Spirit by Whose indwelling the Christian is enabled to live a victorious life, and the Spirit unites all believers in our Lord Jesus Christ.

7. We believe that every man shall stand before God to give an account of his stewardship of his earthly life.

WE BELIEVE in God the Father, Almighty Creator of the heavens and the earth, and ruler of us all.

WE BELIEVE in Jesus Christ the only begotten Son of God; conceived by the Holy Ghost and born of the virgin Mary, who lived upon this earth and suffered stripes unto Pontius Pilate for our healing.

WE BELIEVE Jesus was crucified, dead and buried; rose again the third day from the dead, ascended unto the heavens and is now sitting on the right hand of God the Father Almighty.

WE BELIEVE that this same Jesus will return to this earth to reign as King of Kings and Lord of Lords.

WE BELIEVE in the Holy Spirit that was given at Pentecost as promised by the Lord Jesus Christ as evidence by miracles, signs and wonders.

WE BELIEVE on the Holy Word of God that gives the highest hope for this world and world to come.

WE BELIEVE the Bible is the inspired Word of God.

WE BELIEVE in the hereafter for all people.

WE BELIEVE in the ultimate triumph of righteousness, resurrection from the dead and life everlasting for the faithful.

WE BELIEVE in being born again by God's Spirit and regeneration into a new life.

WE BELIEVE in forgiveness of sins, sanctification, and baptism of the Holy Spirit. We stand against that which is evil in the sight of God. We stand against drunkeness, brawling, and riotous living.

WE BELIEVE the basic plan of God for man toward others is the golden rule: "Therefore all things whatsoever ye would that men should do to you, do even so to them, for this is the law and the prophets." Matt. 7:12

WE BELIEVE and adhere to the Ten Commandments as given to Moses.

WE BELIEVE in God Eternal, Infinite and unchangeable.

WE BELIEVE both the Old and New Testament to be the Word of God.

WE BELIEVE that the eternal purpose of God is in all things to them that love Him.

WE BELIEVE that God created the Heavens and the earth by his own will.

WE BELIEVE sin violates God's laws whether it be omission or commission and those that break God's law shall be out of favor with Him.

WE BELIEVE that salvation is for all that believe on the name of Jesus.

WE BELIEVE in election, ordination and predestination to God's Word.

WE BELIEVE that the Lord Jesus Christ is the Only redeemer able to forgive sin.

WE BELIEVE in the Holy Ghost and its abode in the hearts of the redeemed.

WE BELIEVE in the justification as given by faith; as received by one upon accepting Christ Jesus as his personal saviour.

WE BELIEVE in all spiritual life imparted by the Holy Ghost, thus helping one to live Christ-like.

WE ACKNOWLEDGE the Church to be the Bride of Christ all born again and baptized believers.

WE BELIEVE in the sacraments; baptism, feet washing and the Lord's Supper.

WE BELIEVE in two states of future existence; heaven the final home of the redeemed; and hell, the final abode of the sinful.

WE BELIEVE that the Lord adds to the church daily such as should be saved.

Notes: *This organization is unique in pentecostalism for its affirmation of belief in total depravity and predestination. The statement is in two parts, a formal statement of faith and a number of additional affirmations.*

Chapter 9

European Free-Church Family

SCHLEITHEIM CONFESSION (1527)

BROTHERLY UNION OF A NUMBER OF CHILDREN OF GOD CONCERNING SEVEN ARTICLES

May joy, peace and mercy from our Father through the atonement of the blood of Christ Jesus, together with the gifts of the Spirit—Who is sent from the Father to all believers for their strength and comfort and for their perseverance in all tribulation until the end, Amen—be to all those who love God, who are the children of light, and who are scattered everywhere as it has been ordained of God our Father, where they are with one mind assembled together in one God and Father of us all: Grace and peace of heart be with you all, Amen.

Beloved brethren and sisters in the Lord: First and supremely we are always concerned for your consolation and the assurance of your conscience (which was previously misled) so that you may not always remain foreigners to us and by right almost completely excluded, but that you may turn again to the true implanted members of Christ, who have been armed through patience and knowledge of themselves, and have therefore again been united with us in the strength of a godly Christian spirit and zeal for God.

It is also apparent with what cunning the devil has turned us aside, so that he might destroy and bring to an end the work of God which in mercy and grace has been partly begun in us. But Christ, the true Shepherd of our souls, Who has begun this in us, will certainly direct the same and teach [us] to His honor and our salvation, Amen.

Dear brethren and sisters, we who have been assembled in the Lord at Schleitheim on the Border, make known in points and articles to all who love God that as concerns us we are of one mind to abide in the Lord as God's obedient children, [His] sons and daughters, we who have been and shall be separated from the world in everything, [and] completely at peace. To God alone be praise and glory without the contradiction of any brethren. In this we have perceived the oneness of the Spirit of our Father and of our common Christ with us. For the Lord is the Lord of peace and not of quarreling, as Paul points out. That you may

understand in what article this has been formulated you should observe and note [the following].

A very great offense has been introduced by certain false brethren among us, so that some have turned aside from the faith, in the way they intend to practice and observe the freedom of the Spirit and of Christ. But such have missed the truth, and to their condemnation are given over to the lasciviousness and self-indulgence of the flesh. They think faith and love may do and permit everything, and nothing will harm them nor condemn them, since they are believers.

Observe, you who are God's members in Christ Jesus, that faith in the Heavenly Father through Jesus Christ does not take such form. It does not produce and result in such things as these false brethren and sisters do and teach. Guard yourselves and be warned of such people, for they do not serve our Father, but their father, the devil.

But you are not that way. For they that are Christ's have crucified the flesh with its passions and lusts. You understand me well and [know] the brethren whom we mean. Separate yourselves from them for they are perverted. Petition the Lord that they may have the knowledge which leads to repentance, and [pray] for us that we may have constancy to persevere in the way which we have espoused, for the honor of God and of Christ, His Son, Amen.

The articles which we discussed and on which we were of one mind are these 1. Baptism; 2. The Ban [excommunication]; 3. Breaking of Bread; 4. Separation from the Abomination; 5. Pastors in the Church; 6. The Sword; and 7. The Oath.

First. Observe concerning baptism: Baptism shall be given to all those who have learned repentance and amendment of life, and who believe truly that their sins are taken away by Christ, and to all those who walk in the resurrection of Jesus Christ, and wish to be buried with Him in death, so that they may be resurrected with him, and to all those who with this significance request it [baptism] of us and demand it for themselves. This excludes all infant baptism, the highest and chief abominations of the pope. In this you have the foundation and testimony of the apostles. Mt. 28,

SCHLEITHEIM CONFESSION (1527) (continued)

Mk. 16, Acts 2, 8, 16, 19. This we wish to hold simply, yet firmly and with assurance.

Second. We agree as follows on the ban: The ban shall be employed with all those who have given themselves to the Lord, to walk in His commandments, and with all those who have been baptized into the one body of Christ and who are called brethren and sisters, and yet who slip sometimes and fall into error and sin, being inadvertently overtaken. The same shall be admonished twice in secret and the third time openly disciplined or banned according to the command of Christ. Mt. 18. But this shall be done according to the regulation of the Spirit (Mt. 5) before the breaking of bread, so that we may break and eat one bread, with one mind and in one love, and may drink of one cup.

Third. In the breaking of bread we are of one mind and are agreed [as follows]: All those who wish to break one bread in remembrance of the broken body of Christ, and all who wish to drink of one drink as a remembrance of the shed blood of Christ, shall be united beforehand by baptism in one body of Christ which is the church of God and whose Head is Christ. For as Paul points out we cannot at the same time be partakers of the Lord's table and the table of devils; we cannot at the same time drink the cup of the Lord and the cup of the devil. That is, all those who have fellowship with the dead works of darkness have no part in the light. Therefore all who follow the devil and the world have no part with those who are called unto God out of the world. All who lie in the evil have no part in the good.

Therefore it is and must be [thus]: Whoever has not been called by one God to one faith, to one baptism, to one Spirit, to one body, with all the children of God's church, cannot be made [into] one bread with them, as indeed must be done if one is truly to break bread according to the command of Christ.

Fourth. We agreed [as follows] on separation: A separation shall be made from the evil and from the wickedness which the devil planted in the world; in this manner, simply that we shall not have fellowship with them [the wicked] and not run with them in the multitude of their abominations. This is the way it is: Since all who do not walk in the obedience of faith, and have not united themselves with God so that they wish to do His will, are a great abomination before God, it is not possible for anything to grow or issue from them except abominable things. For truly all creatures are in but two classes, good and bad, believing and unbelieving, darkness and light, the world and those who [have come] out of the world, God's temple and idols, Christ and Belial; and none can have part with the other.

To us then the command of the Lord is clear when He calls upon us to be separate from the evil and thus He will be our God and we shall be His sons and daughters.

He further admonishes us to withdraw from Babylon and the earthly Egypt that we may not be partakers of the pain and suffering which the Lord will bring upon them.

From all this we should learn that everything which is not united with our God and Christ cannot be other than an abomination which we should shun and flee from. By this is meant all popish and antipopish works and church services, meetings and church attendance, drinking houses, civic affairs, the commitments [made in] unbelief and other things of that kind, which are highly regarded by the world and yet are carried on in flat contradiction to the command of God, in accordance with all the unrighteousness which is in the world. From all these things we shall be separated and have no part with them for they are nothing but an abomination, and they are the cause of our being hated before our Christ Jesus, Who has set us free from the slavery of th flesh and fitted us for the service of God throught the Spirit Whom He has given us.

Therefore there will also unquestionably fall from us the unchristian, devilish weapons of force—such as sword, armor and the like, and all their use [either] for friends or against one's enemies—by virtue of the word of Christ, Resist not [him that is] evil.

Fifth. We are agreed as follows on pastors in the church of God: The pastor in the church of God shall, as Paul has prescribed, be one who out-and-out has a good report of thsoe who are outside the faith. This office shall be to read, to admonish and teach, to warn, to discipline, to ban in the church, to lead out in prayer for the advancement of all the brethren and sister, to lift up the bread when it is to be broken, and in all things to see to the care of the body of Christ, in order that it may be built up and developed, and the mouth of the slanderer be stopped.

This one moreover shall be supported of the church which has chosen him, wherein he may be in need, so that he who serves the Gospel may live of the Gospel as the Lord has ordained. But if a pastor should do something requiring discipline, he shall not be dealt with except [on the testimony of] two or three witnesses. And when they sin they shall be disciplined before all in order that the others may fear.

But should it happen that through the cross this pastor should be banished or led to the Lord [through martyrdom] another shall be ordained in his place in the same hour so that God's little flock and people may not be destroyed.

Sixth. We are agreed as follows concerning the sword: The sword is ordained of God outside the perfection of Christ. It punishes and puts to death the wicked, and guards and protects the good. In the Law the sword was ordained for the punishment of the wicked and for their death, and the same [word] is [now] ordained to be used by the wordly magistrates.

In the perfection of Christ, however, only the ban is used for a warning and for the excommunication of the one who has sinned, without putting the flesh to death,—simply the warning and the command to sin no more.

Now it will be asked by many who do not recognize [this as] the will of Christ for us, whether a Christian may or should employ the sword against the wicked for the defense and protection of the good, or for the sake of love.

Our reply is unanimously as follows: Christ teaches and commands us to learn of Him, for He is meek and lowly in heart and so shall we find rest to our souls. Also Christ says to the heathenish woman who was taken in adultery, not that one should stone her according to the law of His Father (and yet He say, As the Father has commanded me, thus I do), but in mercy and forgiveness and warning, to sin no more, Such [an attitude] we also ought to take completely according to the rule of the ban.

Secondly, it will be asked concerning the sword, whether a Chrisian shall pass sentence in worldly dispute and strife such as unbelievers have with one another. This is our united answer: Christ did not wish to decide or pass judgment between brother and brother in the case of the inheritance, but refused to do so. Therefore we should do likewise.

Thirdly, it will be asked concerning the sword, Shall one be a magistrate if one should be chosen as such? The answer is as follows: They wished to make Christ king, but He fled and did not view it as the arrangement of His Father. Thus shall we do as He did, and follow Him, and so shall we not walk in darkness. For He Himself says, He who wishes to come after me, let him deny himself and take up his cross and follow me. Also, He Himself forbids [the employment of] the force of the sword saying, The worldly princes lord it over them, etc., but not so shall it be with you. Further, Paul says, Whom God did foreknow He also did predestinate to be conformed to the image of His son, etc. Also Peter says, Christ has suffered (not ruled) and left us an example, that ye should follow His steps.

Finally, it will be observed that it is not appropriate for a Christian to serve as a magistrate because of these points: The government magistracy is according to the flesh, but the Christians' is according to the Spirit; their houses and dwelling remain in this world, but the Christians' citizenship is in heaven; the weapons of their conflict and war are carnal and against the flesh only, but the Christians' weapons are spiritual, against the fornication of the devil. The worldlings are armed with steel and iron, but the Christians are armed with the armor of God, with truth, righteousness, peace, faith, salvation and the Word of God. In brief, as is the mind of Christ toward us, so shall the mind of the members of the body of Christ be through Him in all things, that there may be no schism in the body through which it would be destroyed. For every kingdom divided against itself will be destroyed. Now since Christ is as it is written of Him, His members must also be the same, that His body may remain complete and united to its own advancement and upbuilding.

Seventh. We are agreed as follows concerning the oath: The oath is a confirmation among those who are quarreling or making promises. In the Law it is commanded to be performed in God's Name, but only in truth, not falsely. Christ, who teaches the perfection of the Law, prohibits all swearing to His [followers], whether true or false,—neither by heaven, nor by the earth, nor by Jerusalem, nor by our head,—and that for the reason which He shortly thereafter gives, For you are not able to make one hair white or black. So you see it is for this reason that all swearing is forbidden: we cannot fulfill that which we promise when we swear, for we cannot change [even] the very least thing on us.

Now there are some who do not give credence to the simple command of God, but object with this question: Well now, did not God swear to Abraham by Himself (since He was God) when He promised him that He would be with him and that He would be his God if he would keep His commandments,—why then should I not also swear when I promise to someone? Answer: Hear what the Scripture says: God, since He wished more abundantly to show unto the heirs the immutability of His counsel, inserted an oath, that by two immutable things (in which it is impossible for God to lie) we might have a strong consolation. Observe the meaning of this Scripture: What God forbids you to do, He has power to do, for everything is possible for Him. God swore an oath to Abraham, says the Scripture, so that He might show that His counsel is immutable. That is, no one can withstand nor thwart His will; therefore He can keep His oath. But we can do nothing, as is said above by Christ, to keep or perform [our oaths]: therefore we shall not swear at all [nichts schweren].

Then others further say as follows: It is not forbidden of God to swear in the New Testament, when it is actually commanded in the Old, but it is forbidden to swear by heaven, earth, Jerusalem and our head. Answer: Hear the Scripture, He who swears by heaven swears by God's throne and by Him who sitteth thereon. Observe: It is forbidden to swear by heaven, which is only the throne of God: how much more is it forbidden [to swear] by God Himself! Ye fools and blind, which is greater, the throne or Him that sitteth thereon?

Further some say, Because evil is now [in the world, and] because man needs God for [the establishment of] the truth, so did the apostles Peter and Paul also swear. Answer: Peter and Paul only testify of that which God promised to Abraham with the oath. They themselves promise nothing, as the example indicates clearly. Testifying and swearing are two different things. For when a person swears he is in the first place promising future things, as Christ was promised to Abraham Whom we a long time afterwards received. But when a person bears testimony he is testifying about the present, whether it is good or evil, as Simeon spoke to Mary about Christ and testified, Behold this (child) is set for the fall and rising of man in Israel, and for a sign which shall be spoken against.

Christ also taught us along the same line when He said, Let your communication be Yea, yea; Nay, nay; for whatsoever is more than these cometh of evil. He says, Your speech or word shall be yea and nay. (However) when one does not wish to understand, he remains closed to the meaning. Christ is simply Yea and Nay, and all those who seek Him simply will understand His word. Amen.

Dear brethren and sisters in the Lord: These are the articles of certain brethren who had heretofore been in error and who had failed to agree in the true understanding, so that many weaker consciences were perplexed, causing the Name of God to be greatly slandered. Therefore there has been a great need for us to become of one mind in the Lord, which has come to pass. To God be praise and glory!

Now since you have so well understood the will of God which has been made known by us, it will be necessary for you to achieve perseveringly, without interruption, the known will of God. For you know well what the servant who sinned knowingly heard as his recompense.

Everything which you have unwittingly done and confessed as evil doing is forgiven you through the believing prayer which is offered by us in our meeting for all our shortcomings and guilt. [This state is yours] through the gracious forgiveness of God and through the blood of Jesus Christ. Amen.

Keep watch on all who do not walk according to the simplicity of the divine truth which is stated in this letter from [the decisions of] our meeting, so that everyone among us will be governed by the rule of the ban and henceforth the entry of false brethren and sisters among us may be prevented.

Eliminate from you that which is evil and the Lord will be your God and you will be His sons and daughters.

Dear brethren, keep in mind what Paul admonishes Timothy when he says, The grace of God that bringeth salvation hath appeared to all men, teaching us that, denying ungodliness and worldly lusts, we should live soberly, righteously, and godly, in this present world; looking for that blessed hope, and the glorious appearing of the great God and our Saviour Jesus Christ; Who gave Himself for us, that He might redeem us from all iniquity, and purify unto Himself a people of His own, zealous of good works. Think on this and exercise yourselves therein and the God of peace will be with you.

May the Name of God be hallowed eternally and highly praised, Amen. May the Lord give you His peace, Amen.

The Acts of Schleitheim on the Border [Canton Schaffhausen, Switzerland], on Matthias' [day], Anno MDXXVII.

Notes: *The European Free-Church tradition, especially as it has become manifest in the United States, finds its roots in the Swiss Brethren. The brethren took the Reformation in a much more radical direction than that envisioned by Luther in Germany, or John Calvin or Helmut Zwingli in Switzerland. In 1527, a number of the brethren gathered at Schleitheim to prepare a confession of their faith. Unfortunately, the document served to focus persecution against them, and eventually the movement was destroyed. It survived only through the Mennonite Church. The Schleitheim Confession is no longer used as an official document by any church (in North America), but its historic value as a pioneering statement of free-church faith has earned it a place of respect among free churchmen, and it provided a source for the major Mennonite confession. The text reproduced here is from the translation of J. C. Wenger which appeared in the* Mennonite Quarterly Review *XIX (1974) 247-53.*

German Mennonites/Amish

THE DORDRECHT CONFESSION (1632)

Ariticle I. OF GOD AND THE CREATION OF ALL THINGS

Whereas it is declared, that "without faith it is impossible to please God" (Heb. 11:6), and that "he that cometh to God must believe that He is, and that He is a rewarder of them that diligently seek Him," therefore we confess with the mouth and believe with the heart, together with all the pious, according to the Holy Scriptures, that there is one eternal, almighty, and incomprehensible God, Father, Son, and the Holy Ghost, and none more and none other, before whom no God existed, neither will exist after Him. For from Him, through Him, and in Him are all things. To Him be blessing, praise, and honor, for ever and ever. Gen. 17:1; Deut. 6:4; Isaiah 46:9; I John 5:7.

In this one God, who "worketh all in all," we believe. Him we confess as the Creator of all things, visible and invisible; who in six days created and prepared "heaven and earth, and the sea, and all things that are therein." And we further believe, that this God still governs and preserves the same, together with all His works, through His wisdom, His might, and the "word of His power." Gen. 5:1, 2; Acts 14:15; I Cor. 12:6; Heb. 1:3.

When He had finished His works and, according to His good pleasure, had ordained and prepared each of them, so that they were right and good according to their nature, being, and quality, He created the first man, Adam, the father of all of us, gave him a body formed "of the dust of the ground, and breathed into his nostrils the breath of life," so that he "became a living soul," created by God "in His own image and likeness," in "righteousness and true holiness" unto eternal life. He also gave him a place above all other creatures and endowed him with many high and excellent gifts, put him into the garden of Eden, and gave him a commandment and an interdiction. Thereupon He took a rib from the said Adam, made a woman out of it, brought her to him, and gave her to him as a helpmate and housewife. Consequently He has caused, that from this first man, Adam, all men who "dwell on the face of the earth," have been begotten and have descended. Gen. 1:27; 2:7, 15-17, 22; 5:1; Acts 17:26.

ARTICLE II. OF THE FALL OF MAN

We believe and confess, that, according to the purport of the Holy Scriptures, our first parents, Adam and Eve, did not long remain in the happy state in which they were created; but did, after being seduced by the deceit and subtilty of the serpent, and envy of the devil, violate the high command of God, and became disobedient to their Creator; through which disobedience "sin entered into the world, and death by sin;" so that "death passed upon all men, for that all have sinned," and thereby incurred the wrath of God and condemnation. For which reason our first parents were, by God, driven out of Paradise, to cultivate the earth, to maintain themselves thereon in sorrow, and to "eat their bread in the sweat of their face," until they "returned to the ground, from which they were taken." And that they did, therefore, through this one sin, so far apostatize, depart, and estrange themselves from God, that they could neither help themselves, nor be helped by any of their descendants, nor by angels, nor by any other creature in heaven or on earth, nor be redeemed, or reconciled to God; but would have had to be lost forever, had not God, who pitied His creatures, in mercy, interposed in their behalf and made provision for their restoration. Gen. 3:6, 23; Rom. 5:12-19; Ps. 47:8, 9; Rev. 5:3; John 3:16.

ARTICLE III. OF THE RESTORATION OF MAN THROUGH THE PROMISE OF THE COMING OF CHRIST

Regarding the Restoration of our first parents and their descendants, we believe and confess: That God, not withstanding their fall, transgression and sin, and although they had no power to help themselves, He was nevertheless not willing that they should be cast off entirely, or be eternally lost; but again called them unto Him, comforted them, and showed them that there were yet means with Him for their reconciliation; namely, the immaculate Lamb, the Son of God; who "was fore-ordained" to this purpose "before the foundation of the world," and who was promised to them and all their descendants, while they (our first parents) were yet in paradise, for their comfort, redemption, and salvation; yea, who was given to them thenceforward, through faith, as their own; after which all the pious patriarchs, to whom this promise was often renewed, longed and searched, beholding it through faith at a distance, and expecting its fulfillment—expecting that He (the Son of God), would, at His coming, again redeem and deliver the fallen race of man from their sins, their guilt, and unrighteousness. John 1:29; 11:27; I Pet. 1:18, 19; Gen. 3:15; I John 2:1, 2; 3:8; Gal. 4:4, 5.

ARTICLE IV. OF THE ADVENT OF CHRIST INTO THIS WORLD, AND THE REASON OF HIS COMING

We believe and confess further: That "when the fulness of the time was come," after which all the pious patriarchs so ardently longed, and which they so anxiously awaited—the previously promised Messiah, Redeemer, and Saviour, proceeded from God, being sent by Him, and according to the prediction of the prophets and the testimony of the evangelists, came into the world, yea, into the flesh—, so that the Word itself thus became flesh and man; and that He was conceived by the Virgin Mary (who was espoused to a man named Joseph, of the house of David), and that she bare Him as her first-born son at Bethlehem, "wrapped Him in swaddling clothes, and laid Him in a manger." John 4:25; 16:28; I Tim. 3:16; Matt. 1:21; John 1:14; Luke 2:7.

Further we believe and confess, that this is the same One, "whose goings forth have been from of old, from everlasting;" who has "neither beginning of days, nor end of life." Of whom it is testified, that He is "Alpha and Omega, the beginning and the end, the first and the last." That this is also He—and none other—who was chosen, promised, and sent; who came into the world; and who is God's only, first, and proper Son; who was before John the Baptist, before Abraham, before the world; yea, who euas David's

Lord, and who was God of the "whole earth," "the first-born of every creature;" who was sent into the world, and Himself delivered up the body prepared for Him, as "an offering and a sacrifice to God for a sweet smelling savour;" yea, for the comfort, redemption, and salvation of all—of the human race. Micah 5:2; Heb. 7:3; Rev. 1:8; John 3:16; Rom. 8:32; Col. 1:15; Heb. 10:5.

But how, or in what manner, this worthy body was prepared, or how the Word became flesh, and He Himself man, we content ourselves with the declaration which the worthy evangelists have given and left in their description thereof; according to which we confess with all the saints, that He is the Son of the living God, in whom exist all our hope, comfort, redemption, and salvation, and which we are to seek in no one else. Luke 1:31-35; John 20:31.

Further, we believe and confess by authority of scripture, that when He had ended His course, and "finished" the work for which He was sent into the world, He was, by the providence of God, delivered into the hands of the unrighteous; suffered under the judge, Pontius Pilate, was crucified, died, was buried, rose again from the dead on the third day, and ascended into heaven, where He now sits at the right hand of the Majesty of God on high; from whence He will come again to judge the living and dead. Luke 23:1, 52, 53; 24:5, 6, 51.

Thus we believe the Son of God died—"tasted death for every man," shed His precious blood, and thereby bruised the head of the serpent, destroyed the works of the devil, "blotted out the hand-writing," and purchased redemption for the whole human race; and thus He became the source of eternal salvation to all who from the time of Adam to the end of the world, shall have believed in Him, and obeyed Him. Gen. 3:15; I John 3:8; Col. 2:14; Rom. 5:18.

Article V. OF THE LAW OF CHRIST, WHICH IS THE HOLY GOSPEL, OR THE NEW TESTAMENT

We also believe and confess, that Christ, before His ascension, established and instituted His New Testament and left it to His followers, to be and remain an everlasting testament, which He confirmed and sealed with His own precious blood; and which He has so highly commended to them, that neither men or angels may change it, neither take therefrom nor add thereto. Jer. 31:31; Heb. 9:15-17; Matt. 26:28; Gal. 1:8; 1 Tim. 6:3-5; Rev. 22:18, 19; Matt. 5:18; Luke 21:33.

And that He has caused this Testament (in which the whole counsel and will of His heavenly Father, so far as these are necessary to the salvation of man, are comprehended), to be proclaimed, in His name, through His beloved apostles, messengers, and servants (whom He chose and sent into all the world for this purpose)—to all nations, people and tongues; these apostles preaching repentance and remission of sins; and that He, in said Testament, caused it to be declared, that all men without distinction, if they are obedient, through faith, follow, fulfill and live according to the precepts of the same, are His children and rightful heirs; having thus excluded none from the precious inheritance of eternal salvation, except the unbelieving and disobedient, the headstrong and unconverted; who despise such salvation; and thus by their

THE DORDRECHT CONFESSION (1632) (continued)

own actions incur guilt by refusing the same, and "judge themselves unworthy of everlasting life." Mark 16:15; Luke 24:46, 47; Rom. 8:17; Acts 13:46.

Article VI. OF REPENTANCE AND AMENDMENT OF LIFE

We believe and confess, that, as the "imagination of man's heart is evil from his youth," and consequently inclined to all unrighteousness, sin, and wickedness, that, therefore, the first doctrine of the precious New Testament of the Son of God is, Repentance and amendment of life. Gen. 8:21; Mark 1:15.

Therefore those who have ears to hear, and hearts to understand, must "bring forth fruits meet for repentance," amend their lives, believe the Gospel, "depart from evil and do good," desist from wrong and cease from sinning, "put off the old man with his deeds and put on the new man," which after God is created in "righteousness and true holiness." For neither *Baptism, Supper, nor church-fellowship*, nor any other external ceremony, can, without faith, the new birth, and a change or renewal of life, help, or qualify us, that we may please God, or receive any consolation or promise of salvation from Him. Luke 3:8; Eph. 4:22-24; Col. 3:9, 10.

But on the contrary, we must go to God "with a sincere heart in full assurance of faith," and believe in Jesus Christ, as the Scriptures speak and testify of Him. Through which faith we obtain the pardon of our sins, become sanctified, justified, and children of God; yea, partakers of His mind, nature and image, as we are born again of God through His incorruptible seed from above. Heb. 10:21, 22; John 7:38; II Pet. 1:4.

Article VII. OF HOLY BAPTISM

Regarding baptism, we confess that all penitent believers, who through faith, the new birth and renewal of the Holy Ghost, have become united with God, and whose names are recorded in heaven, must, on such Scriptural confession of their faith, and renewal of life, according to the command and doctrine of Christ, and the example and custom of the apostles, be baptized with water in the ever adorable name of the Father, and of the Son, and of the Holy Ghost, to the burying of their sins, and thus to become incorporated into the communion of the saints; whereupon they must learn to observe all things whatsoever the Son of God taught, left on record, and commanded His followers to do. Matt. 3:15; 28:19, 20; Mark 16:15, 16; Acts 2:38; 8:12, 38; 9:18; 10:47; 16:33; Rom. 6:3, 4; Col. 2:12.

Article VIII. OF THE CHURCH OF CHRIST

We believe in and confess a visible Church of God, consisting of those, who, as before remarked, have truly repented, and rightly believed; who are rightly baptized, united with God in heaven, and incorporated into the communion of the saints on earth. I Cor. 12:13.

And these, we confess, are a "chosen generation, a royal priesthood, an holy nation," who have the testimony that they are the "bride" of Christ; yea, that they are children and heirs of eternal life—a "habitation of God through the Spirit," built on the foundation of the apostles and prophets, of which "Christ Himself is the chief corner-stone"—the foundation on which His church is built. John 3:29; Matt. 16:18; Eph. 2:19-21; Tit. 3:7; I Pet. 1:18, 19; 2:9.

This church of the living God, which He has purchased and redeemed through His own precious blood, and with which He will be—according to His own promise—for her comfort and protection, "always, even unto the end of the world;" yea, will dwell and walk with her, and preserve her, that no "winds" nor "floods," yea, not even the "gates of hell shall prevail against her"—may be known by her evangelical faith, doctrine, love, and godly conversation; also by her pure walk and practice, and her observance of the true ordinances of Christ, which He has strictly enjoined on His followers. Matt. 7:25; 16:18; 28:20; II Cor. 6:16.

Article IX. OF THE ELECTION, AND OFFICES OF TEACHERS, DEACONS, AND DEACONSESSES, IN THE CHURCH

Regarding the offices, and election of persons to the same, in the church, we believe and confess: That, as the church cannot exist and prosper, nor continue in its structure, without offices and regulations, that therefore the Lord Jesus has Himself (as a father in his house), appointed and prescribed His offices and ordinances, and has given commandments concerning the same, as to how each one should walk therein, give heed to His own work and calling, and do it as it becomes Him to do. Eph. 4:11, 12.

For He Himself, as the faithful and great Shepherd, and Bishop of our souls, was sent into the world, not to wound, to break, or destroy the souls of men, but to heal them; to seek that which is lost, and to pull down the hedges and partition wall, so as to make out of many one; thus collecting out of Jews and heathen, yea, out of all nations, a church in His name; for which (so that no one might go astray or be lost) He laid down His own life, and thus procured for them salvation, made them free and redeemed them, to which blessing no one could help them, or be of service in obtaining it. I Pet. 2:25; Matt. 18:11; Eph. 2:13, 14; John 10:9, 11, 15.

And that He, besides this, left His church before His departure, provided with faithful ministers, apostles, evangelists, pastors, and teachers, whom He had chosen by prayer and supplication through the Holy Spirit, so that they might govern the church, feed His flock, watch over, maintain, and care for the same: yea, do all things as He left them an example, taught them, and commanded them to do; and likewise to teach the church to observe all things whatsoever He commanded them. Eph. 4:11, 12; Luke 6:12, 13; 10:1; Matt. 28:20.

Also that the apostles were afterwards, as faithful followers of Christ and leaders of the church, diligent in these matters, namely, in choosing through prayer and supplication to God, brethren who were to provide all the churches in the cities and circuits, with bishops, pastors, and leaders, and to ordain to these offices such men as took "heed unto themselves and unto the doctrine," and also unto the flock; who were sound in the faith, pious in their life and conversation, and who had—as well within the church as "without"—a good reputation and a good report; so that they might be a light and example in all godliness and good works; might worthily administer the Lord's ordinances—baptism and supper—and that they (the brethren sent by the apostles) might also, at all places, where such were to be had, appoint faithful men as elders, who were able to teach others, confirm them in the name of the Lord "with the laying on of hands," and who (the elders) were to take care of all things of which the church stood in need; so that they, as faithful servants, might well "occupy" their Lord's money, gain thereby, and thus "save themselves and those who hear them." I Tim. 3:1; 4:14-16; Acts 1:23, 24; Tit. 1:5; Luke 19:13.

That they should also take good care (particularly each one of the charge over which he had the oversight), that all the circuits should be well provided with deacons, who should have the care and oversight of the poor, and who were to receive gifts and alms, and again faithfully to distribute them among the poor saints who were in need, and this is in all honesty, as is becoming. Acts 6:3-6.

Also that honorable old widows should be chosen as deaconesses, who, besides the deacons are to visit, comfort, and take care of the poor, the weak, afflicted, and the needy, as also to visit, comfort and take care of widows and orphans; and further to assist in taking care of any matters in the church that properly come within their sphere, according to their ability. I Tim. 5:9, 10; Rom. 16:1, 2.

And as it further regards the deacons, that they (particularly if they are fit persons, and chosen and ordained thereto by the church), may also in aid and relief of the bishops, exhort the church (being, as already remarked, chosen thereto), and thus assist in word and doctrine; so that each one may serve the other from love, with the gift which he has received from the Lord; so that through the common service and assistance of each member, according to his ability, the body of Christ may be edified, and the Lord's vineyard and church be preserved in its growth and structure. II Tim. 2:2.

Article X. OF THE LORD'S SUPPER

We also believe in and observe the breaking of bread, or the Lord's Supper, as the Lord Jesus instituted the same (with bread and wine) before His sufferings, and also observed and ate it with the apostles, and also commanded it to be observed to His remembrance, as also the apostles subsequently taught and observed the same in the church, and commmanded it to be observed by believers in commemoration of the death and sufferings of the Lord—the breaking of His worthy body and the shedding of His precious blood—for the whole human race. So is the observance of this sacrament also to remind us of the benefit of the said death and sufferings of Christ, namely, the redemption and eternal salvation which He purchased thereby, and the great love thus shown to sinful man; whereby we are earnestly exhorted also to love one another—to love our neighbor—to forgive and absolve him—even as Christ has done unto us—and also to endeavor to maintain and keep alive the union and communion which we have with God, and amongst one another; which is thus shown and represented to us by the

aforesaid breaking of bread. Matt. 26:26; Mark 14:22; Luke 22:19, 20; Acts 2:42, 46; I Cor. 10:16; 11:23-26.

Article XI. OF THE WASHING OF THE SAINTS' FEET

We also confess a washing of the feet of the saints, as the Lord Jesus did not only institute and command the same, but did also Himself wash the feet of the apostles, although He was their Lord and Master; thereby giving an example that they also should wash one another's feet, and thus do to one another as He did to them; which they also afterwards taught believers to observe, and all this is a sign of true humiliation; but yet more particularly as a sign to remind us of the true washing—the washing and purification of the soul in the blood of Christ. John 13:4-17; I Tim. 5:9, 10.

Article XII. OF MATRIMONY

We also confess that there is in the church of God an "honorable" state of matrimony between two believers of the different sexes, as God first instituted the same in paradise between Adam and Eve, and as the Lord Jesus reformed it by removing all abuses which had crept into it, and restoring it to its first order. Gen. 1:27; 2:18, 21-24.

In this manner the Apostle Paul also taught and permitted matrimony in the church, leaving it to each one's own choice to enter into matrimony with any person who would unite with him in such state, provided that it was done "in the Lord," according to the primitive order; the words "in the Lord," to be understood, according to our opinion, that just as the patriarchs had to marry amongst their own kindred or generation, so there is also no other liberty allowed to believers under the New Testament dispensation, than to marry among the "chosen generation," or the spiritual kindred of Christ; that is, to such—and none others—as are already, previous to their marriage, united to the church in heart and soul, have received the same baptism, belong to the same church, are of the same faith and doctrine, and lead the same course of life, with themselves. I Cor. 7:39; 9:5; Gen. 24:4; 28:6, 7; Num. 36:6-9.

Such are then, as already remarked, united by God and the church according to the primitive order, and this is then called, "Marrying in the Lord." I Cor. 7:39.

Article XIII. OF THE OFFICE OF CIVIL GOVERNMENT

We also believe and confess, that God has instituted civil government, for the punishment of the wicked and the protection of the pious; and also further, for the purpose of governing the world, countries and cities; and also to preserve its subjects in good order and under good regulations. Wherefore we are not permitted to despise, revile, or resist the same, but are to acknowledge it as a minister of God and be subject and obedient to it, in all things that do not militate against the law, will, and commandments of God; yea, "to be ready to every good work;" also faithfully to pay it custom, tax, and tribute; thus giving it what is its due; as Jesus Christ taught, did Himself, and commanded His followers to do. That we are also to pray to the Lord earnestly for the government and its welfare, and in behalf of our country, so that we may

THE DORDRECHT CONFESSION (1632) (continued)

live under its protection, maintain ourselves, and "lead a quiet and peaceable life in all godliness and honesty." And further, that the Lord would recompense them (our rulers), here and in eternity, for all the benefits, liberties, and favors which we enjoy under their laudable administration. Rom. 13:1-7; Titus 3:1, 2; I Pet. 2:17; Matt. 17:27; 22:20, 21; I Tim. 2:1, 2.

Article XIV. OF DEFENSE BY FORCE

Regarding revenge, whereby we resist our enemies with the sword, we believe and confess that the Lord Jesus has forbidden His disciples and followers all revenge and resistance, and has thereby commanded them not to "return evil for evil, nor railing for railing;" but to "put up the sword into the sheath," or, as the prophet foretold, "beat them into ploughshares." Matt. 5:39, 44; Rom. 12:14; I Pet. 3:9; Isa. 2:4; Micah 4:3.

From this we see, that, according to the example, life, and doctrine of Christ, we are not to do wrong, or cause offense or vexation to anyone; but to seek the welfare and salvation of all men; also, if necessity should require it, to flee, for the Lord's sake, from one city or country to another, and suffer the "spoiling of our goods," rather than give occasion of offense to anyone; and if we are struck in our "right cheek, rather to turn the other also," than revenge ourselves, or return the blow. Matt. 5:39; 10:23; Rom. 12:19.

And that we are, besides this, also to pray for our enemies, comfort and feed them, when they are hungry or thirsty, and thus by well-doing convince them and overcome the evil with good. Rom. 12:20, 21.

Finally, that we are to do good in all respects, "commending ourselves to every man's conscience in the sight of God," and according to the law of Christ, do nothing to others that we would not wish them to do unto us. II Cor. 4:2; Matt. 7:12; Luke 6:31.

Article XV. OF THE SWEARING OF OATHS

Regarding the swearing of oaths, we believe and confess that the Lord Jesus has dissuaded His followers from and forbidden them the same; that is, that He commanded them to "swear not at all;" but that their "Yea" should be "yea," and their "Nay, nay." From which we understand that all oaths, high and low, are forbidden; and that instead of them we are to confirm all our promises and covenants, declarations and testimonies of all matters, merely with "Yea that is yea," and "Nay that is nay;" and that we are to perform and fulfill at all times, and in all things, to every one, every promise and obligation to which we thus affirm, as faithfully as if we had confirmed it by the most solemn oath. And if we thus do, we have the confidence that no one—not even government itself—will have just cause to require more of us. Matt. 5:34-37; Jas. 5:12; II Cor. 1:17.

Article XVI. OF THE ECCLESIASTICAL BAN OR EXCOMMUNICATION FROM THE CHURCH

We also believe in and acknowledge the ban, or excommunication, a separation or spiritual correction by the church, for the amendment, and not for the destruction, of offenders; so that what is pure may be separated from that which is impure. That is, if a person, after having been enlightened, and received the knowledge of the truth, and has been received into the communion of the saints, does willfully, or out of presumption, sin against God, or commit some other "sin unto death," thereby falling into such unfruitful works of darkness, that he becomes separated from God, and is debarred from His Kingdom—that such an one—when his works are become manifest, and sufficiently known to the church—cannot remain in the "congregation of the righteous;" but must, as an offensive member and open sinner, be excluded from the church, "rebuked before all," and "purged out as a leaven," and thus remain until his amendment, as an example and warning to others, and also that the church may be kept pure from such "spots" and "blemishes;" so that not for the want of this, the name of the Lord be blasphemed, the church dishonored, and a stumblingblock thrown in the way of those "without," and finally, that the offender may not be condemned with the world, but that he may again be convinced of the error of his ways, and brought to repentance and amendment of life. Isa. 59:2; I Cor. 5:5, 6, 12; I Tim. 5:20; II Cor. 13:10.

Regarding the brotherly admonition, as also the instruction of the erring, we are to "give all diligence" to watch over them, and exhort them in all meekness to the amendment of their ways (Jas. 5:19, 20); and in case any should remain obstinate and unconverted, to reprove them as the case may require. In short, the church must "put away from among herself him that is wicked," whether it be in doctrine or life.

Article XVII. OF THE SHUNNING OF THOSE WHO ARE EXPELLED

As regards the withdrawing from, or the shunning of, those who are expelled, we believe and confess, that if any one, whether it be through a wicked life or perverse doctrine—is so far fallen as to be separated from God, and consequently rebuked by, and expelled from, the church, he must also, according to the doctrine of Christ and His apostles, be shunned and avoided by all the members of the church (particularly by those to whom his misdeeds are known), whether it be in eating or drinking, or other such like social matters. In short, that we are to have nothing to do with him; so that we may not become defiled by intercourse with him, and partakers of his sins; but that he may be made ashamed, be affected in his mind, convinced in his conscience, and thereby induced to amend his ways. I Cor. 5:9-11; Rom. 16:17; II Thess. 3:14; Tit. 3:10, 11.

That nevertheless, as well in shunning as in reproving such offender, such moderation and Christian discretion be used, that such shunning and reproof may not be conducive to his ruin, but be serviceable to his amendment. For should he be in need, hungry, thirsty, naked, sick or visited by some other affliction, we are in duty bound, according to the doctrine and practice of Christ and His apostles, to render him aid and assistance, as necessity may require; otherwise the shunning of him might be rather conducive to his ruin than to his amendment. I Thess. 5:14.

Therefore we must not treat such offenders as enemies, but exhort them as brethren, in order thereby to bring them to a knowledge of their sins and to repentance; so that they may again become reconciled to God and the church, and be received and admitted into the same—thus exercising love towards them, as is becoming. II Thess. 3:15.

Article XVIII. OF THE RESURRECTION OF THE DEAD AND THE LAST JUDGMENT

Regarding the resurrection of the dead, we confess with the mouth, and believe with the heart, that according to the Scriptures all men who shall have died or "fallen asleep," will, through the incomprehensible power of God, at the day of judgment, be "raised up" and made alive; and that these, together with all those who then remain alive, and who shall be "changed in a moment, in the twinkling of an eye, at the last trump," shall "appear before the judgment seat of Christ," where the good shall be separated from the evil, and where "every one shall receive the things done in his body, according to that he hath done, whether it be good or bad"; and that the good or pious shall then further, as the blessed of their Father, be received by Christ into eternal life, where they shall receive that joy which "eye hath not seen, nor ear heard, nor hath entered into the heart of man." Yea, where they shall reign and triumph with Christ for ever and ever. Matt. 22:30-32; 25:31; Dan. 12:2; Job 19:25, 26; John 5:28, 29; I Cor. 15:51, 52; I Thess. 4:13.

And that, on the contrary, the wicked or impious, shall, as the accursed of God, be cast into "outer darkness;" yea, into eternal, hellish torments; "where their worm dieth not, and the fire is not quenched;" and where—according to Holy Scripture—they can expect no comfort nor redemption throughout eternity. Isa. 66:24; Matt. 25:46; Mark 9:46; Rev. 14:10. 11.

May the Lord through His grace make us all fit and worthy, that no such calamity may befall any of us; but that we may be diligent, and so take heed to ourselves, that we may be found of Him in peace, without spot, and blameless. Amen.

Notes: *Mennonites in the United States are of two basic varieties—German and Russian. The German Mennonites came to the United States in the seventeenth century at the invitation of William Penn and settled in Pennsylvania. From there they spread south and west. The Russian Mennonites arrived in the late nineteenth century. The Dordrecht Confession predates the division of the Mennonite community.*

Deriving from the radical reformers of the previous century, the Mennonites found haven in relatively tolerant Holland. Gathering at Dordrecht in 1632, they adopted a confession that is still used by the Mennonite Church and has some authority among all Mennonite bodies. It affirms the practices of foot washing, shunning, and pacifism.

In the late seventeenth century, the Amish also adopted the Dordrecht Confession, and it is still accepted by the several Amish bodies currently existing in America.

STATEMENT OF FAITH (CONGREGATIONAL BIBLE CHURCH)

1. We believe in THE HOLY SCRIPTURES: Accepting fully the writings of the Old and New Testaments as the very Word of God, verbally inspired in all parts and therefore wholly without error as originally given of God, altogether sufficient in themselves as our only infallible authority of faith and practice. Psa. 119:89; Matt. 24:35; John 17:17; II Tim. 3:16,17; II Pet. 1:21.

2. We believe in THE ONE TRIUNE GOD: who is personal spirit, and sovereign (Mark 12:29; John 4:24; 14:9; Psa. 135:6); perfect, infinite, and eternal in his being, holiness, love, wisdom, and power (Psa. 18:30; 147:5; Deut. 33:27); absolutely separate and above the world as its Creator, yet everywhere present in the world as the Upholder of all things (Gen. 1:1; Psa. 104); self-existent and self-revealing in three distinct Persons—The Father, the Son, and the Holy Spirit (John 5:26; Matt. 28:19; II Cor. 13:14); each of whom is to be honored and worshipped equally as true God (John 5:23; Acts 5:3,4).

3. We believe in THE LORD JESUS CHRIST: who is the second Person of the Triune God, the Eternal Word and Only Begotten Son, our Great God and Saviour (John 1:1, 3:15; Titus 2:13; Rom. 9:5); that, without any essential change in His divine Person (Heb. 13:8) He became man by the miracle of the virgin birth (John 1:14; Matt. 1:23), thus to continue forever as both true God and true man, one Person with two natures (Col. 2:9; Rev. 22:16); that as man He was in all points tempted like as we are, yet without sin (Heb. 4:15; John 8:46); that as the perfect Lamb of God He gave Himself in death upon the cross, bearing there the sin of the world, and suffering its full penalty of divine wrath in our stead (Isa. 53:5,6; Matt. 20:28; Gal. 3:13; John 1:29); that He rose again from the dead and was glorified in the same body in which He suffered and died (Luke 24:36-43, John 20: 25-28); that as our great High Priest He ascended into heaven there to appear before the face of God as our Advocate and Intercessor (Heb. 4:14; I John 2:1).

4. We believe in THE HOLY SPIRIT: who is the third Person of the Triune God (Matt. 28:19; Acts 5:3,4), the divine Agent in nature, revelation, and redemption (Gen. 1:2; Psa. 104:30; I Cor. 2:10; II Cor. 3:18); that He convicts the world of righteousness, and judgment (John 16:8-11), regenerates those who believe (John 3:5), and baptizes, indwells, seals, empowers, guides, teaches, and sanctifies all who become children of God through Christ (I Cor. 12:13; 6:19; Eph. 4:30; 3:16; Acts 1:8; Rom. 8:14; John 16:13-15; I Cor. 6:11).

5. We believe in THE CREATION AND FALL OF MAN: that he was the direct creation of God, spirit, and soul and body, not in any sense the product of an animal ancestry, but made in the divine image (Gen. 1:26-28; 2:7; 18:24, Matt. 19:4; I Thess. 5:23); that by personal disobedience to the revealed will of God

man became a sinful creature and the progenitor of a fallen race (Gen. 3:1-24; 5:3), all of whom are universally sinful in both nature and practice (Eph. 2:3; Rom. 3:23; 5:12); alienated from the life and family of God (Eph. 4:18; John 8:42-44); under the righteous judgment and wrath of God (Rom. 1:8; 3:19); and has within himself no possible means of recovery or salvation (Mark 7:21-23; Matt. 19:25,26; Rom. 7:18).

6. We believe in SALVATION BY GRACE THROUGH FAITH: that salvation is the free gift of God (Rom. 3:24; 6:23), neither merited nor secured in part or in whole by any virtue or work of man (Titus 3:5; Rom. 4:4,5), but received only by personal faith in the Lord Jesus Christ because of the merit of His shed blood (John 3:16; 6:28,29; Acts 16:30, 31; I Cor. 15:1-4; Heb. 9:22; Eph 2:8,9), in whom all true believers have as a present possession the gift of eternal life, a perfect righteousness, a sonship in the family of God, in which family believers are dealt with as sons, God the Father disciplining and chastening every son whom He receives and are assured deliverance and security from all condemnation, every spiritual resource needed for life and godliness, and divine assurance that they shall never perish (I John 5:13; Rom. 3:22; Gal. 3:26; Heb. 12:5-11; John 5:24; Eph. 1:3; II Pet. 1:3; John 10:27-30); that this salvation includes the whole man, spirit and soul and body (I Thess. 5: 23, 24); and that apart from Christ there is no possible salvation (John 14:6; Acts 4:12).

7. We believe in HOLY LIVING AND GOOD WORKS: not as the procuring cause of salvation in any sense, but as the proper evidence and fruit (I John 3:9-11; 4:19; 5:4; Eph. 2:8-10; Titus 2:14; Matt. 7:16-18; I Cor. 15:10); and therefore as Christians we should keep the Word of our Lord (John 14:23); seek the things which are above (Col. 3:1), walk as He walked (I John 2:6), be careful to maintain good works (Titus 3:8), and ESPECIALLY ACCEPT AS OUR SOLEMN RESPONSIBILITY THE DUTY AND PRIVILEGE OF BEARING THE GOSPEL TO A LOST WORLD IN ORDER THAT WE MAY BEAR MUCH FRUIT (Acts 1:8; II Cor. 5:19; John 15:16); remembering that a victorious and fruitful Christian life is possible only for those who have learned that they are not under law but under grace (Rom. 6:14), and who in gratitude for the infinite and undeserved mercies of God have presented themselves wholly to Him for His service (Rom. 12:1,2).

8. We believe in THE EXISTENCE OF SATAN: who originally was created a holy and perfect being, but through pride and unlawful ambition rebelled against God (Ezek. 28:13-17; Isa. 14:13,14; I Tim. 3:7), thus becoming utterly depraved in character (John 8:44), the great adversary of God and His people (Matt. 4:1-11; Rev. 12:10), leader of all other evil angels and spirits (Matt. 12:24-26, 25:41), the deceiver and god of this present world (Rev. 12:9; II Cor. 4:4), that his powers are supernaturally great, but strictly limited by the permissive will of God who overrules all his wicked devices for good (Job 1:1-22; Luke 22:31,32); that he was defeated and judged at the cross, and therefore his final doom is certain (John 12:31, 32; 16:11; Rev. 20:10); that we are able to resist and overcome him only in the armor of God and by the blood of the lamb (Eph. 6:12-18; Rev. 12:11).

9. We believe in THE SECOND COMING OF CHRIST: that His return from heaven will be personal, visible, and glorious—the blessed hope for which we should constantly watch and pray, the time being unrevealed but always imminent (Acts 1:11; Rev. 1:7; Mark 13:33-37; Titus 2:11-13; Rev. 22:20); that when He comes He will first by resurrection and translation remove from the earth His waiting church (I Thess. 4:16-18), and then pour out the righteous judgments of God upon the unbelieving world (Rev. 6:1-18,24).

10. We believe in FUTURE LIFE, BODILY RESURRECTION, AND ETERNAL JUDGMENT: that the spirits of the saved at death go immediately to be with Christ in heaven (Phil. 1:21-23; II Cor. 5:8), where they abide in joyful fellowship with Him until His second coming, when their bodies shall be raised from the grave and changed into the likeness of His own glorious body (Phil. 3:20,21; I Cor. 15:35-58; I John 3:2), at which time their works shall be brought before the judgment seat of Christ for the determination of rewards, a judgment which may issue in the loss of rewards, but not the loss of the soul (I Cor. 3:8-15; II Cor. 5:10); that the spirits of the unsaved at death descend immediately into Hades where they are kept under punishment until the final day of judgment (Luke 16:19-31; II Pet. 2:9, ARV), at which time their bodies shall be raised from the grave, and they themselves shall be judged according to their works, and cast into the place of final and everlasting punishment (Rev. 20:11-15; 21:8; Mark 9:43-48; Jude 1:13).

11. We believe in THE ONE TRUE CHURCH: the mystical body and bride of the Lord Jesus (Eph. 4:4; 5:25-32), that He began to build on the day of Pentecost (Matt. 16:18; Acts 2:47), and will complete at His second coming (I Thess. 4:16, 17), and into which all true believers of the present age are baptized immediately by the Holy Spirit (I Cor. 12:12-18 with 1:2); that the supreme task of the church is the evangelization of the world (Matt. 28:10,20; Mark 16:15,16; II Cor. 5:18-20); that all the various members of this one spiritual body should gather together in local assemblies for worship, prayer, fellowship, teaching, united testimony, and observance of the ordinances of our Lord (Heb. 10:25; Acts 2:41-47); among which are the following: the baptism of believers upon their confession of faith in the Lord Jesus Christ as their Saviour (Acts 8:35-38; 10:47,48; I Pet. 3:21), the communion of the

bread and cup as a memorial of the broken body and shed blood of our Lord Jesus Christ, thereby proclaiming the Lord's death until He comes (I Cor. 11:23-26); and in prayer for, and anointing of the sick. (James 5:13-18).

12. We believe in SEPARATION FROM THE WORLD UNTO GOD: that since our Christian citizenship is in heaven, as the children of God we should walk in separation from this present world, having no fellowship with its evil ways (Phil. 3:20, ARV; II Cor. 6:14-18; Rom. 12:2; Eph. 5:11), abstaining from all worldly amusements and unclean habits which defile mind and body (Luke 8:14; I Thess. 5:22; I Tim. 5:6; I Pet. 2:11; Eph. 5:3-11, 18; Col. 3:17; I Cor. 6:19,20), from the sin of divorce and remarriage as forbidden by our Lord (Matt. 19:9, Mark 10:11,12; Luke 16:18), from swearing of any oath (Jas. 5:12), from the use of civil courts for the settlement of disputes between Christians (I Cor. 6:1-8). We believe further that the way of life as lived and taught by Christ implies the fullest exercise of love toward mankind: (Rom. 12:18-21). We believe further that the Christian life will of necessity express itself in conformity to Christ in life and conduct (Col. 3).

We understand that the above articles do not by any means exhaust the content of the believer's creed, which is the whole Word of God, and they are not intended to set a limit beyond which faith cannot go within this Word: but we do believe that in so far as these articles extend they are a true presentation of the sound doctrine taught in the Scriptures, and therefore enjoined upon us as Christian believers.

Notes: *The Congregational Bible Church is a small Mennonite body centered on a single congregation in Pennsylvania.*

*   *   *

WE BELIEVE (MENNONITE CHURCH)

We Believe . . .

In a Triune God—Father, Son, and Holy Ghost (I John 5:7), Creator of all things.—Colossians 1:16.

In Jesus Christ as the Son of God, conceived of the Holy Ghost, born of a virgin.—Matthew 1:20-25.

In the personality and deity of the Holy Spirit.—Acts 1:8, 5:3, 4.

In the plenary and verbal inspiration of the Bible as the Word of God.—Psalm 119:160; II Timothy 3:16.

That man was created pure (Genesis 1:27); that he, by transgression, fell (Genesis 2:17); and that sin, sorrow, and death (natural and spiritual) are results of the Fall.—Romans 5:12.

That the blood of Jesus Christ so atoned for all as to make their salvation possible.—John 3:16.

That innocent children will be saved.—Mark 10:14.

That to be saved, all accountable persons must believe, repent, be "born again," "walk in newness of life."—John 3:3-5; Romans 6:1-7.

That those thus born again are obedient to God and constitute the true Church, of which Christ is the Head.—Romans 6:17; Colossians 1:18.

That self-denial and humility are essential to Christian discipleship.—Luke 9:23; I Peter 5:5, 6.

That Christian baptism is commanded and that pouring is the Scriptural mode.—Matthew 28:19, 20; Acts 1:5, 2:2, 16-18, 41; 10:44-48.

That the bread and cup in communion are symbols of the body and blood of Christ, and show a common union of members.—I Corinthians 10:16-21.

That feet washing as a religious ceremony should be observed literally.—John 13:1-17.

That Christian women should wear the veiling.—I Corinthians 11:2-16.

That the "kiss of charity" should be practiced among believers.—Romans 16:16; I Peter 5:14.

That anointing with oil is for physical restoration of the believer who, in sickness, calls in faith for such anointing.—James 5:14, 15.

That mixed marriages between believers and unbelievers are unscriptural, and marriage with divorced persons with former companions living constitutes adultery.—Nehemiah 13:23-26; Mark 10:2-12.

That it is unscriptural for Christian people to follow wordly fashions, engage in carnal warfare, swear oaths, or hold membership in secret societies.—Romans 12:2; Matthew 5:33-48; II Corinthians 6:14-18; I Peter 3:3, 4; Ephesians 5:11, 12; Jeremiah 49:11.

That obstinate sinners within the Church should be expelled.—I Corinthians 5:13.

That the Church is commanded to evangelize the world.—Matthew 28:19, 20.

In the personal and imminent coming of our Lord Jesus Christ as the blessed hope of the believers.—Acts 1:11; John 14:2, 3; Matthew 24:44; I Thessalonians 4:13-18.

That there will be a bodily resurrection both of the just and of the unjust.—John 5:28, 29.

That the final judgment will be followed by eternal rewards and punishments.—Matthew 25:46; II Corinthians 5:10.

Notes: *This statement is a brief summary of present-day Mennonite faith. Note the affirmation of the "plenary and verbal inspiration of the Bible," a reflection of twentieth-century debates within the North American conservative evangelical community.*

Russian Mennonites

CHURCH COVENANT AND ARTICLES OF FAITH (EVANGELICAL MENNONITE BRETHREN CHURCH)

CHURCH COVENANT

Having been led by the Spirit of God to receive Jesus Christ as my Saviour and Lord and on profession of my faith, having been baptized in the name of the Father, of the Son, and of the Holy Spirit, and accepting the Holy Scriptures as my rule of faith and practice, and recognizing the privilege and duty of uniting myself for Christian fellowship, the enjoyment of Christian ordinances, the public worship of God and this assembly, most solemnly and joyfully enter into covenant and agree to associate myself as a member of this assembly of believers.

I engage, and promise therefore, by the aid of the Holy Spirit to forsake the paths of sin, to walk together in Christian love, to strive for unity and spiritual welfare of this church, to sustain its doctrines, ordinances, worship and discipline; to contribute cheerfully and regularly to its charities, institutions, its local expenses and to the advancement of the Gospel of Christ to all nations.

I also engage and agree to maintain a prayer-life; to seek the salvation of the lost; to walk circumspectly in the world; to be just in my dealings, faithful in my engagements, exemplary in my deportment.

I further engage and promise to watch over another in brotherly love; to pray for another; to aid in sickness and distress; to cultivate Christian sympathy, to be slow to take offense, but always ready for reconciliation; and I shall endeavor at all times and in all places to carry out the spirit of this covenant and the principles of God's Word.

ARTICLES OF FAITH

I.   HOLY SCRIPTURE. We believe that all Scripture, the Old and New Testament, is the only inerrant inspired Word of God, written by holy men of God as they were moved by the Holy Spirit (II Tim. 3:16-17; II Peter 1:21). It reveals the will of God to man (I Cor. 2:9-12). It is the truth (John 17:17; I Thess. 2:13; II Tim. 2:15). The Gospel is the power of God unto salvation to every one that believeth (Rom. 1:16; II Tim. 3:15), and all Scripture is profitable for doctrine, for reproof, for correction, and for instruction in righteousness: that the man of God may be prefect, throughly furnished unto all good works (II Tim. 3:16-17). It is the guide to eternal bliss (Titus 3:4-7; Gal. 4:7).

II. GOD. We believe in only one living and true God as the infinite, perfect, and eternal Spirit, in whom all things have their source, support, and end (Isa. 45:21; Eph. 4:6; Gen 1:1; Acts 17:28; Heb. 11:3; Luke 24:39; Col. 1:15; Ps. 90:2; I Tim. 6:16).

We believe in God as omniscient (Heb. 4:13; Acts 15:18); omnipresent (Ps. 139:7; Jer. 23:24; Amos 9:2-3); omnipotent (Jer. 10:12-13; Gen. 35:11; Gen. 1:1, 26); Creator (Gen. 1:1, 26; Jn. 1:1-3); Sustainer (Col.

1:15-17; Ps. 104:27-30; Ps. 75:6-7; Heb. 1:3; Matt. 10:29-30; Gen. 39:21; Gen. 50:20; Dan. 1:9); immutable in His being, holiness, justice, love, and truth (Mal. 3:6; Isa. 6:3; I Jn. 4:8; James 1:17); eternal (Ps. 90:2; Ps. 102:24-27; Heb. 1:12).

Though God is a Spirit (Jn. 4:24), yet Scripture very definitely teaches God as a personality (Ex. 3:14; Gen. 22:13-14; Ps. 23:1; Jn. 17; Acts 14:15; Job 1:12; Gen. 3:8-9, 11, 13, 14; I Thess. 1:9; Ps. 94:9-10; Gen. 6:6; Jn. 3:16; Rev. 3:19f; Gen. 1:1, 26).

III. JESUS CHRIST. We believe in Jesus Christ as the eternal Son of God. The Son is from eternity the only begotten of the Father. Being conceived of the Holy Spirit He was born man of the virgin Mary (Jn. 3:16; Heb. 1:5-10; Luke 1:35; Matt. 1:18-25), in order to fulfill the purpose of God from the foundation of the world to redeem us from eternal curse and bring about our eternal salvation by making full atonement for our sins through His vicarious suffering and death on the cross of Calvary (Jn. 1:14, 29; Mark 10:45; Heb. 10:10-14; I Peter 1:18-29; Isa. 53: 4-6). He took upon Himself the likeness of sinful flesh (Heb. 2:14), thus being true God and also perfect man (I Jn. 3:5; I Tim. 2:5), being made in all things like as we are, yet without sin (Heb. 4:15).

He rose triumphantly from the grave the third day and ascended into heaven, and is now at the right hand of God interceding in our behalf: from whence He shall come again in visible form to judge the living and the dead and to establish His rule as Lord of lords and King of kings (John chapters 20 and 21; Acts 1:9-11; II Tim. 4:1; I Tim. 6:15; John 5:22-29; Matthew 25:31ff).

IV. THE HOLY SPIRIT. We believe that the Holy Spirit is the third person in the Godhead and proceedeth from the Father through the Son, (John 15:26). He took part in the creation of the universe (Gen. 1:2; Job 33:4; Ps. 33:6). He directed God's servants in revealing the will of God to mankind (I Peter 1:10-11). He is the author of the Scriptures, (II Peter 1:20-21; Rev. Ch. 2 and 3). At Pentecost He was poured out upon all man (Acts 2:17-18). In this age of grace He reproves the world of sin, of righteousness, and of judgment (John 16:8-11). He restrains the progress of evil until God's purposes are accomplished (II Thess. 2:7). He regenerates the penitent soul (John 3:3, 5), lives in the body of the believer, which is the temple of the Holy Spirit (I Cor. 3:16; I Cor. 6:19), gives the believer the assurance of salvation (Rom. 8:16), comforts, (John 14:16-17), teaches, and brings to his remembrance the proper Scripture verses in witnessing (John 14:26); and guides the believer into all truth (John 16:13). He will sanctify the believer (II Thess. 2:13), and empower him for life and service (Eph. 3:16; I Cor. 2:1-4), and will quicken his mortal body (Rom. 8:11).

V.   TRINITY. We believe, though inscrutable yet not self-contradictory, in the unity of the Godhead, commonly known as the Trinity. This Trinity is made up of three distinct persons; namely, God the Father (Rom. 1:7); God the Son (Heb. 1:18); God the Holy Spirit (Acts 5:3-4). These three, though one in essence, i.e. equal in their divine perfection, yet individual in personality, perform different but harmonious offices in the great plan of redemption (Matt. 28:19; II Cor. 13:14; Eph. 2:18; Jn. 15:26; Jn. 10:30; Jn. 16:14).

God, who is one with respect to His essence, is three with respect to the modes or distinctions of His being.

"The Father is all the fulness of the Godhead invisible (John 1:18); the Son is all the fulness of the Godhead manifested (John 1:14-18); the Spirit is all the fulness of the Godhead acting immediately upon the creature" (I Cor. 2:9-10). Broadman.

VI. SATAN. We believe that Satan is a real supernatural personality, a fallen angel of great power, cunning, and wicked, the enemy of God and of all good, seeking the destruction of Christ and the eternal ruin of every soul (Mark 1:13; John 13:2; Matt. 13:19, 39); but is limited in the scope of his power by God (Job 1:12; Job 2:1-6; Luke 22:31f; I Cor. 10:13).

Satan introduced sin into this world, when he by his subtlety brought about the transgression and fall of our first parents (Gen. 3:1-15). Since then he and the host of fallen angels and evil spirits under his control dominate the present world system deceiving mankind, obstructing the course of the Gospel, blinding the minds of the unbelieving (Eph. 6:11-12; Eph. 2:2; II Cor. 4:4; I John 5:19 R.V.).

Scripture describes his work and character by names such as: "a murderer from the beginning", "a liar and the father of lies", "the accuser of our brethren", "the devil", "the adversary", "the evil one", "the prince of the power of the air", "the god of this world".

His present abode is "in the air", "in the heavenly places" (Eph. 6:12 R.V.); yet the earth is the special field of his awful activity, where he works disguised as an angel of light or roams about as a roaring lion (II Cor. 11:14f; I Peter 5:8).

Christ by His death on the cross defeated and judged Satan and stripped him of his power over death (Col. 2:15; John 12:31; John 16:11; Heb. 2:14; I Cor. 15:54-56) and secured victory for the believer over all the wiles of the devil (I John 4:4; Eph. 6:11-13; I John 5:4-5; I Cor. 15:57; James 4:7).

He is doomed first to be cast from his present abode, then at Christ's second coming to be bound a thousand years, and finally to be cast into the lake of fire where he and his angels shall be tormented forever and ever (Matt. 25:41; Rev. 20:10).

VII. ANGELS. We believe in the existence of a higher order of created, yet spiritual beings between God and man frequently known as ministering spirits, or messengers of God, but more frequently known as angels. These are superior to man but inferior to God (Matt. 18:10; Mark 13:32; Matt. 13:41; I Pet. 3:22; Heb. 12:22; Col. 1:16; Ps. 104:4; Jn. 5:4; I Cor. 4:9).

Though "spirits", yet they have appeared in visible form as ministers through whom God's power was manifested (Judges 6:11-22; Luke 1:26; John 20:12; Isa. 37:36; Rev. 20:2-10; Gen. 19:1-26; Heb. 1:14).

Angels announced the birth of Jesus (Luke 1:28-35); an angel appeared to the shepherds (Luke 2:9-13); legions of angels were ready to help Jesus (Matt. 26:53); angels ministered to Jesus after His temptation (Matt. 4:11); an angel strengthened Him after the agony in Gethsemane (Luke 22:43); angels were associated with His resurrection (Matt. 28:2-7); attended His ascension (Acts 1:10-11); and will also be associated with His return (I Thess. 4:16; II Thess. 1:7).

Angels assist God in executing judgments upon the earth (Isa. 37:36; Rev. 9:1-5; II Sam. 24:16-17; Gen. 19:13-15; Rev. 19:17).

They are ministering spirits sent forth to minister for them who shall be heirs of salvation (Heb. 1:14); they guard, defend, and deliver God's people (Acts 5:19; II Kings 6:17; Acts 12:7-11; Ps. 34:7); cheer and strengthen them (Acts 5:19, 20); guide the worker to the sinner (Acts 10:3); guard the children, beholding the face of the Father for them (Mt. 18:10); they are eyewitnesses of the church and the believer (I Tim. 5:21; I Cor. 4:9); and receive the departing saints (Luke 16:22).

VIII. ANTHROPOLOGY - MAN

A. HIS CREATION. We believe that by an immediate act of God, man was created in His image (Gen. 1:26-27); possessing righteousness, holiness, and wisdom (Eph. 4:24; Col. 3:10), for the purpose that man should be the object of His love, to praise and glorify Him (Eph. 1:4-6), to replenish the earth with God-fearing people, and to subdue and have dominion over the earth and all animate creatures upon it (Gen. 1:26-28; Gen. 9:1, 2).

B. HIS FALL. We believe that man was subjected to trial in the garden of Eden (Gen. 2:15-17), and voluntarily and consciously transgressed God's command (Gen. 3:1-3, 6), and so fell from his holy estate (Gen. 3:16-19; Gen. 2:16, 17). Thus man became alienated from God (Gen. 3:7-13; Eph. 4:18; Col. 1:21), and became physically, morally, and spiritually depraved (Rom. 1:19-32). As a result of the fall sin was imputed upon the entire human race (Romans 5:12; I Cor. 2:14). Man's heart, being desperately wicked (Jer. 17:9-10), leads to acts of sin in his life and finally to just condemnation (Rom. 5:18).

C. HIS REDEMPTION. We believe that God as the Sovereign Ruler must punish sin (Rom. 6:23). Christ, the Son of God, voluntarily (John 10:17-18) offered Himself on the cross as the perfect sacrifice for sin, the just suffering for the unjust, bearing sin's curse, and tasting death for every man (John 1:29; Heb. 9:11-12; I Tim. 2:5-6; II Cor. 5:21; Gal. 3:13). Nothing prevents the salvation of the greatest sinner on earth but his own stubborn will, his voluntary rejection of Jesus Christ as substitute for penalty (John 3:14-16; John 3:36; Acts 16:31).

D. HIS RESURRECTION. Every person will be raised up. The saved unto life everlasting; the unsaved to eternal condemnation (John 5:28, 29).

IX. SOTERIOLOGY—SALVATION

A. REPENTANCE. We believe that repentance is a prerequisite to regeneration (Acts 17:30; II Peter 3:9). It manifests itself in the godly sorrow for sin, i.e., in the forsaking of sin and in turning to God (Isa. 55:7; I Thess. 1:9). It is wrought by the convicting power of the Holy Spirit. An illustration of pure repentance is found in the prodigal son (Luke 15:11-24). True repentance, coupled with faith, will result in forgiveness of sins (Acts 3:19).

B. FAITH. Faith is fundamental to salvation and Christian conduct (Gen. 15:6). "Faith is the substance of things hoped for, the evidence of things not seen" (Heb. 11:1). Jesus Christ is the author and finisher of our faith (Heb. 12:2). Only faith in Jesus Christ and his work of atonement on the cross saves from eternal condemnation (John 1:12; John 3:16). Faith being both the gift of God and act of man (Eph. 2:8), is based on the Word of God (John 20:30-31), giving assent to the truth, embracing and appropriating Christ as his Lord and Saviour (John 20:25-29), and then worshipping Him (John 4:20-24).

C. REGENERATION. Regeneration is the impartation of a new and divine life, a new creation; not the old nature altered or re-invigorated, but a new birth from above (John 3:3-8; Eph. 2:10; II Cor. 5:17). We are made partakers of the divine nature (II Peter 1:4). A new governing power comes into the regenerated man's life, by which he is enabled to become holy in character and conduct: "Old things are passed away; behold, all things are become new", (II Cor. 5:17; I Jn. 5:11-12, 20).

D. JUSTIFICATION. As regeneration has to do with the change of the believer's nature, so justification has to do with the change from guilt and condemnation to acquittal and acceptance. We have become justified through the redemption that is in Christ Jesus (Rom. 3:24), and by the faith of Jesus Christ (Gal. 2:16; Rom. 5:1). Therefore, being justified by faith, forgiveness of sin (Eph. 1:7) is imparted to the believer, and he is fully restored to God's favor and receives access to all of God's graces (Rom. 5:1-2).

E. ADOPTION. Regeneration begins a new life in the soul; justification deals with the new relation-ship of that soul to God; and adoption admits that soul into the family of God with filial joy. Adoption deals with the position the soul holds as a child of God. It is the present position of the believer (I John 3:2; Gal. 3:26). The complete revelation of our position as a child of God is future (I John 3:1-3; Col. 3:3-4).

F. SANCTIFICATION. Sanctification has to do with our character and conduct in our Christian life. Justification is what God does for us, while sanctification is what God does in us. Sanctification exhibits the fruit of our relationship to God and manifests itself in a cordial love to the brethren and fellowmen (Gal. 5:22-23). Sanctification may be viewed as instantaneous, progressive, and complete. The believer is sanctified at the time of regeneration, that is, he is set aside for the service of God (I Cor. 6:11; Heb. 10:10,14). Then the believer will mortify the deeds of the body (Rom. 8:13; Col. 3:1-9) and "put on the new man which is renewed in the knowledge after the image of Him that created him" (Col. 3:10-17; Eph 4:22-24), and God will sanctify him wholly unto the coming of our Lord Jesus Christ (I Thess. 5:23,24).

G. PRAYER. Prayer is the Christian's vital breath. It is the pouring out of the heart to God (Psa. 42:4; Psa. 62:8). It is God's appointed method for man to obtain what He has to bestow (Mt. 7:7-11). It is but the natural way of a child to commune with his father. The possibility to communicate with God, our heavenly Father, was brought about through the sacrificial death of Jesus Christ (Heb. 10:19-22), and with the help of the Holy Spirit (Rom. 8:26) prayer is the means of appropriating the promises of the Bible.

X. ECCLESIOLOGY—THE CHURCH

1. The Church as an organism includes all regenerate believers gathered out of the world between the first and second advents of Christ, while as an organization it includes believers united for the service of Christ in any given assembly.

2. The local visible church is an institution of divine appointment and is composed of professed, baptized believers in Christ: voluntarily joined together and meeting at stated times to worship, to fellowship, to observe ordinances, and when necessary to administer and accept discipline.

XI. ESCHATOLOGY—THE LAST THINGS

A. SECOND COMING OF CHRIST. We believe in the personal, visible, imminent, premillenial return of Christ (Acts 1:11; Rev. 1:7; John 14:3; Titus 2:13; Rev. 5:9-10; Rev. 20:4-6). As the first coming covers a period of events, so also His second coming covers a period of events, such as the rapture (I Thess. 4:13-17; I Cor. 15:50-52), the great tribulation (Mt. 24:21; II Thess. 2:3-10), the revelation of Christ at the end of the great tribulation period (Mt. 24:29-31), the Millenium

Age (Rev. 20:1-9), and The Great White Throne judgment (Rev. 20:10-15). The day nor the hour of the beginning of Christ's second coming no one knows (Mt. 24:36-42), but we can know when it is near at hand (I Tim. 4:1-3; II Tim. 3:1-5; James 5:1-9; Mt. 24:24,32; Mt. 24:32-34). This hope of the Second Coming of Christ to receive His own (I Thess. 4:13-17) is a purifying element in the life of the believer (I John 3:3), and a warning to the unbeliever (Matt. 24:42; II Pet. 3:10).

B. THE RESURRECTION. We believe in the bodily resurrection of the just and the unjust (John 5:28-29; I Cor. 15:22) to receive the things done in the body (II Cor. 5:10; Rev. 20:12). The believer's body shall be fashioned like unto His glorious body (Phil. 3:21), but there is no description of the body of the unbeliever.

C. RECOMPENCE OF THE JUST AND THE UNJUST

1. The believer's works will be judged according to his deeds here upon earth (I Cor. 3:11-15; II Cor. 5:10; Rev. 22:12). He will receive rewards or crowns for his service (James 1:12; I Peter 5:4; II Tim. 4:8; I Thess. 2:19; Rev. 4:4; I Cor. 9:25; Rev. 3:11).

2. The unbeliever's wage for sin is death (Rom. 6:23), and in the end will be judged according to his works (Rev. 20:11-15).

D. THE FINAL STATE

1. The wicked after death will be in torment (Luke 16:23) until the final judgment at the Great White Throne when he will be eternally separated from God and cast into the lake of fire or more commonly known as everlasting hell (Matt. 25:41; John 3:36; Rev. 20:14-15).

2. The final state of the believer is far better than this present life in the body (Phil. 1:23; I John 3:2; Rev. 14:13); his final and eternal home is in heaven, the New Jerusalem (Rev. 21-22:5).

ORDINANCES

1. ORDINANCE DEFINED: An ordinance is a symbolic observance which by the specific command of Christ is to be ministered in the church, thereby setting forth the central truths of the Christian faith. It is of a universal and perpetual obligation.

2. BAPTISM:

a. Water baptism expresses the experience of regeneration and union with Christ (Acts 8:36-39); it is a public testimony of the inner experience preceding church membership (Acts 2:38, 41,47; Mark 16:16); it is to be administered to believers only. (Acts 8:37; 16:30-34; 18:8)

b. Water baptism has no saving or cleansing merits, but is rather an act of obedience demonstrating the new relationship with Christ. Infant baptism cannot be recognized as valid according to Scripture. (Mark 16:16; Acts 8:12; Acts 18:8)

c. While the Evangelical Mennonite Brethren churches practice the immersion mode of baptism, other modes are recognized as valid providing salvation preceeded baptism.

3. LORD'S SUPPER:

a. The Lord's Supper is an ordinance, instituted by Christ in the night of betrayal, to be observed frequently (in our Conference at least four times a year) by believers until he returns.

b. The consecrated emblems consist of bread symbolizing Christ's broken body, and the fruit of the vine as a symbol of His shed blood (I Cor. 11:23-29). The observance of this ordinance is to be preceeded by honest self-examination.

c. There is no salvation element in this ordinance; it rather serves as a reminder of Christ's vicarious atonement (I Peter 3:18), and our continued dependence upon Him.

d. The communion table is open to all believers who practice consistent Christian living.

CHURCH PRACTICES

1. HOME AND FAMILY: The Christian home is recognized as the bulwark of the nation in upholding the social, political and spiritual integrity of the country. It behooves the Christian family to observe closely the Biblical teaching regarding the home. Grace at every table, daily family altar, hospitality to friends and strangers, profitable leisure time and reasonable working hours, and regular church attendance should be the unfluctuating standard of every Christian home.

2. MARRIAGE:

a. We believe that marriage is a sacred institution, ordained of God, and is an indissoluble union of one husband and one wife to be entered into with an attitude of godly reverence and wisdom, love and purity. (Gen. 1:27; 2:18, 24; Prov. 18:22; Matt. 19:4-6)

b. We believe that it is unscriptural for a believer to unite with an unbeliever in the bond of matrimony (Deut. 7:2-4; Neh. 13:25-27). Consequently, social friendships with unbelievers inclined to lead toward courtship and marriage should be discouraged.

c. Ministers are forbidden to officiate at the marriage of a believer with an unbeliever, and cautioned against officiating at marriages of questionable social, moral or mixed relationships.

d. Weddings, and all activities connected therewith, shall be planned and proceed in a demonstration of simplicity and dignity without ceremonial display or worldly formality.

3. DIVORCE AND REMARRIAGE:

a. Since we believe in the indissoluble union of husband and wife, a divorce should not as much as be anticipated among believers (Gen. 2:18, 21-23; Matt. 19:3-9); neither divorced party should marry another as long as both live. (Mark 10:11-

CHURCH COVENANT AND ARTICLES OF FAITH (EVANGELICAL MENNONITE BRETHREN CHURCH) (continued)

12; 5:32; I Cor. 6:16) Note: Evangelical Christianity is not united on the question of divorce and remarriage. There are those who would grant a divorce on the ground of fornication or adultery as based upon Matthew 5:31-32; 19:9, and would not stand in the way of remarriage while both divorcees live. Our Conference has not found liberty to yield to this interpretation.

b. Separation without divorce is recognized but deprecated in Scriptures. (I Cor. 7:10-16)

c. Remarriage after death of either husband or wife has Biblical sanction. (I Cor. 7:30; Rom. 7:2-3)

4. THE LORD'S DAY: We believe that the first day of the week is of divine origin, commonly called the Lord's Day, and is to be held sacred in commemoration of Christ's resurrection from the dead (Acts 20:7; John 20:19; Mark 2:27-28; I Cor. 16:1-2), as a day of worship, Christian service, and rest from all secular labor and abstinence from active participation in organized sport.

5. GENERAL CHRISTIAN WALK: We believe that man is created in the image and similitude of God (James 3:9; Eph. 2:24; Gen. 1:26). A Christian, therefore, should be willing to walk in all simplicity and humility, love and unity, honesty and purity. Discretion should be used in regards to appearance and dress. Believers should glorify God in all things. (Rom. 12:1-2; I Tim. 2:8-10; I Peter 3:1-16; I Tim. 4:12; Col. 3:1-14; Eph. 4:1-7; Rom. 12:9-12; I Cor. 11:1-16; Deut. 22:5)

6. CHRISTIAN STEWARDSHIP: We believe and teach that God is the possessor and sustainer of everything (Hag. 2:8; Ps. 24:1; Col. 1:16-17). The Bible clearly teaches systematic and proportionate giving (I Cor. 16:1-2; II Cor. 9:7-8). To give the tithe and beyond the tithe has the promise of God's blessing (Mal. 3:10; Luke 6:38; II Cor. 9:6, 10). The Christian is also steward over that which he retains as well as his time and talents (Matt. 35:14-30; Eph. 5:16; Col. 4:5).

7. DEDICATION OF CHILDREN: We believe that it is scriptural to dedicate children to the Lord (I Sam. 1:28; Matt. 19:13-16; Luke 18:15-17) by the setting apart and prayer at a public meeting where parents make voluntary declaration of their willingness to submit their children to the Lord for whatever ministry He would choose for them.

8. DIVINE HEALING: We believe that divine healing of the body can be realized by God's children on conditions as set forth in Scripture (James 5:13-16). The Believer is admonished to preserve life and health. (Ex. 20:13; Phil. 4:5,11; I Cor. 9:27; 10:31; I John 4:1-6; II Cor. 11:13-15) In light of these passages we caution against the obvious abuse of the spectacular in the modern day phenomena of mass "faith healing".

9. TONGUES: We believe the New Testament use of "tongues" was an Apostolic sign gift to proclaim the "mighty works of God to Jews out of every nation under heaven" in their own language. (I Cor. 14:20-22; Acts 2:5-21; Joel 2:26-32) The Holy Spirit's purpose in causing tongues was to authenticate those specially appointed representatives of Christ, that is, the Apostles. Tongues speaking was a sign of His presence and ministry for the purpose of validating the Apostolic message before it was inscripturated. The purpose of Biblical tongues limits them to the Apostolic age. In light of historical and grammatical interpretation of Scripture, we believe the gift of tongues as emphasized by the present day charismatic movement is not a valid gift for the church today and should not be tolerated in the church. (I Cor. 13:8-10; Eph. 2:19-20)

10. CIVIL GOVERNMENT: We believe that civil government is ordained of God for the punishment of evil doers, for the protection of the good, and to justly direct the interaction of society. (Rom. 13:1-7; Ex. 18:21-23) We, therefore, consider it our duty to pray for our rulers and magistrates (I Tim. 2:1-3), and to be submissive and obedient to their authority except in things which militate against the supreme law and will of our Lord Jesus Christ. (Titus 3:1; I Peter 3:13-14; Acts 4:19; 5:29; Matt. 23:10; Rev. 19:16; Rom. 14:9-13)

11. EDUCATION: Educational provision is recommended in the Bible. Throughout the years educational opportunities have advanced through improved facilities and teaching qualities. While Christianity has enjoyed its freedom in the separation of church and state, there are increasingly strong indication that the school will become grafted wholly in the state trunk. Our children and youth are a God-given heritage which must be preserved at any cost. The quality of our school rests largely upon the parents and teachers. As long as these will remain true to Scriptural principles and are willing to stand on guard for our rights and privileges, we need not fear the future.

12. OATHS AND PROFANITY: We believe that the Scriptures strictly forbid the swearing of oaths (Matt. 5:33-37, James 5:12), and that everything beyond an affirmation which is as binding as though we confirmed it by an oath, is violating the command of our Lord Jesus Christ. The Scripture also teaches that it is a sin to use the name of the Lord irreverently. (Ex. 21:7)

13. SECRET SOCIETIES: We believe that all secret orders are contrary to the teaching of the Scriptures. There is nothing belonging to Christianity of which the followers of Christ need to be ashamed or want to conceal to men. Therefore, under no circumstances should members be allowed to hold membership in any secret organization. (John 3:18-20; Eph. 5:11-12; II Cor. 6:14-18), neither shall any such person be received into church membership.

14. GOING TO LAW: The Scriptures teach to "Follow peace with all men" (Heb. 12:14), to be inoffensive (Eph. 4:3; Rom. 12:8), not to seek revenge or recompense evil for evil of those who do us evil (Rom. 12:17-21), and particularly forbids going to law with a believer before unbelievers. (I Cor. 6:1-8; Matt. 5:25)

15. CARNAL WARFARE:

a. We believe that God has called us to live peaceably with all men, to overcome evil with good, and to walk worthy of our vocation. (II Cor. 10:3-4; I Thess. 5:15; I Peter 2:21-23; John 15:12; Gal. 5:3-15; I Peter 3:8-9; I John 3:15,23)

b. The Historic position of the Evangelical Mennonite Brethren Church has been to oppose the bearing of arms in warfare and the development of strife between nations, classes, groups, or individuals.

c. Our churches, however, respect the right of individual conviction and recognize that various positions will be taken on war and military service. Our churches support our Christian youth who because of faith and conscience accept the exemptions or alternatives to combat service. In any event, our churches give spiritual aid to all of our youth in service by encouraging them to exert a positive testimony for Christ.

d. We believe that the proper expression of Christian love and discipleship is by a daily manifestation of a meek spirit. We believe that it is necessary in daily living to return evil with good and not evil for evil. The position of non-resistance is as important in daily contacts with people as it is in any national or international crisis.

e. We also believe that the taking of a non-resistant position, and the registering of the same with our government, shall be a matter of personal conscience and conviction.

Notes: *These documents are taken from the church's constitution. The Articles of Faith are unique primarily for their affirmations concerning angels. The constitution covers the ordinances (baptism and the Lord's Supper) and a variety of practices in a separate section.*

*　　　*　　　*

ARTICLES OF FAITH (EVANGELICAL MENNONITE CHURCH)

I. THE SCRIPTURES

We believe that the Old and New Testament Scriptures were given by holy men of God, who were divinely inspired, who wrote in obedience to the divine command, and were kept from error whether the truths were familiar or unknown. God is the author, salvation the objective, and by its principles all will be judged. (II Tim. 3:16-17, II Pet. 1:21, Acts 3:21, Rom. 2:1-16). The scripture is not to be broken. (Jno. 10:35). It is the supreme standard by which all human conduct, creeds, and opinions shall be tried. (Psa. 119:105, Acts 17:2, II Tim. 3:16-17). It is the revelation of God Himself, speaking to man, revealing man's state by nature, and presenting the only means of his salvation. (Rom. 3:10-12, Acts 4:12).

II. GOD

We believe there is only one living and true God, Perfect, Infinite and Eternal. (Isa. 45:21-22, Eph. 4:6, I Cor. 8:6, I Kings 8:27, Psa. 90:2, 102:24-27, I Tim. 6:16). God is omniscient, (Heb. 4:13, Acts 15:18), omnipresent, (Psa. 139:7-10, Jer. 23:24, Amos 9:2-3,) omnipotent, (Jer. 10:12-13, Gen. 35:11) and is unchangeable in His being, holiness, justice, love and truth. (Mal. 3:6, Isa. 6:3, Psa. 19:9, Jas. 1:17). He is the Creator, Preserver and Ruler of the Universe. (Gen. 1:1, Heb. 11:3, Psa. 103:19, Acts 17:28). He exists in three persons, namely: Father, Son and Holy Spirit, who are equal in their divine perfection though distinct in personality and execute distinct but harmonious offices in the great work of redemption. (Matt. 28:19, Jno. 15:26, I Cor. 2:10, Jno. 10:30, Eph. 2:18, II Cor. 13:14).

III. JESUS CHRIST

We believe the Son was made in the likeness of men, being born of the Virgin Mary, thus uniting organically and indissolubly the divine and human natures in their completeness in the one unique person of Jesus Christ. (Phil. 2:6-11, Matt. 1:18-25, Jno. 1:14, I Tim. 3:16, Heb. 2:14). The purpose of the incarnation was redemption. He took upon Himself the likeness of sinful flesh (Phil. 2:6-7, II Cor. 5:21) and by His death made full atonement for our sins. (Isa. 53:4-5, Matt. 20:28. Heb. 10:9-10, I Jno. 4:10). And having risen from the dead He ascended into heaven, and is now at the right hand of God (I Pet. 3:22, Heb. 8:1, Col. 3:1) interceding in our behalf. (I Jno. 2:1, Rom. 8:34).

IV. THE HOLY SPIRIT

We believe the Holy Spirit, the third person of the Trinity, proceedeth from the Father and the Son. (Jno. 15:26). His principal ministry, since His advent at Pentecost is to reprove or convict the world of sin, of righteousness, and of judgment, (Jno. 16:8-11 see R.V.) to restrain the progress of evil until God's purposes are accomplished, (II Thess. 2:7) to bear witness to the truth preached, (Jno. 15:26, Acts 5:30-32) to regenerate those who repent of their sins and exercise faith in Christ, (Jno. 3:5-8, Titus 3:5) to instruct, comfort and guide God's children, (Jno. 14:16-18, Jno. 16-13, Rom. 8:26) to sanctify them, (II Thess. 2:13, I Pet. 1:2) to empower them for life and service, (Acts 1:8, Eph. 3:16, I Cor. 2:1-4, I Thess. 1:5) and to quicken their mortal bodies. (Rom. 8:11).

V. MAN

A. HIS CREATION. We believe that man was created by an immediate act of God, that he was created in the image and likeness of God, possessing personality and holiness and that the purpose of his creation was to glorify God. (Gen. 2:7, Gen. 1:27, Eph. 4:24, Col. 3:10, Eph. 1:5-6, 12).

B. HIS FALL. We believe that man was subjected to trial in the Garden of Eden in order to test his loyalty to his Creator. (Gen. 2:15-17). By voluntarily transgressing God's positive command and yielding to the enticement of Satan, man lost his holy state, was alienated from God, and became physically,

ARTICLES OF FAITH (EVANGELICAL MENNONITE CHURCH) (continued)

morally, and spiritually depraved. In consequence of this act of disobedience, the entire human race became involved in sin so that in every heart there is by nature that evil disposition which eventually leads to responsible acts of sin and just condemnation. (Gen. 3:1-6, Rom. 5:12, 18, Rom. 3:10-12, Rom. 1:19-32, I Jno. 1:8-10, I Cor. 2:14, Isa. 53:6, Jer. 17:9).

C. HIS REDEMPTION. We believe that God as the Sovereign Ruler must punish sin. Christ, the son of God, voluntarily offered Himself on the cross as the perfect sacrifice for sin, the just suffering for the unjust, bearing sin's curse, and tasting death for every man. Nothing prevents the salvation of the greatest sinner on earth, but his own stubborn will, and voluntary rejection of Jesus Christ as substitute for penalty. (Matt. 20:28, Heb. 9:11, 12, I Pet. 3:18, I Pet. 1:18-21, Gal. 3:13, Heb. 2:9, Titus 3:4-7, I Tim. 2:5-6, II Cor. 5:21).

VI. SALVATION

A. REPENTANCE. We believe that the scriptures teach that repentance precedes regeneration, and is manifested in genuine Godly sorrow for sin, and a consequent turning therefrom unto God, that it involves a heart confession wrought by the convicting power of the Holy Spirit. (Isa. 55:7, Mk. 1:15, Acts 11:18, Acts 3:19).

FAITH. We believe that faith is essential to salvation. It is that persuasion by which the Word of God is received as true (Heb. 11:1). It is both the gift of God and the act of the creature (Rom. 10:9, 10, 17; Eph. 2:8; Col. 2:12). It is a reasonable confidence based upon good evidence (John 20:30, 31; 10: 37, 38). Salvation by faith supersedes mental assent by laying hold of moral powers and relying upon them (Rom. 10:10; 3:25). It not only believes that the death of Christ is the sacrifice for sin but is a trust in its efficacy.

B. REGENERATION AND JUSTIFICATION. We believe that salvation is wholly of grace and free to all, (Isa. 55:1, Rev. 22:17, Eph. 2:8) but is conditioned solely on repentance toward God and acceptance of Christ by faith. (Eph. 2:8-9, Titus 3:5, Acts 4:12, 16:31, 20:21, II Cor. 7:10). When the sinner has met these requirements, God justifies and regenerates him. Justification is a judicial declaration absolving from punishment and restoring to divine favor. (Rom. 5:1-9, Gal. 3:11, Acts 13:39). Regeneration is the impartation of Divine life. By the operation of the Holy Spirit through the word he is given a disposition to obey God (Jno. 3:3-5, 1:12-13, II Cor. 5:17, I Pet. 1:23, Phil. 2:13). This experience is witnessed to by the Holy Spirit. Proper evidence appears in the holy fruits of repentance and faith, and a personal knowledge of forgiveness of sin, perfect peace to the soul and newness of life. (Gal. 5:22-23, I Jno. 5:4, Eph. 5:9).

C. SANCTIFICATION AND BAPTISM OF THE SPIRIT. We believe that the Scriptures teach that sanctification is both instantaneous and progressive and is made possible by the vicarious death of Jesus Christ. (Heb. 10:10, I Cor. 1:30). It is a work of the Holy Spirit, separating and keeping the believer separated from sin unto God. (Psa. 4:3). This He does by indwelling, filling and controlling. It involves a voluntary separation from sin, a yielding to God, and a putting off of the old man by the power of the Holy Spirit. (Rom. 6:13, 19, Eph. 4:22-24, Col. 3:9-10). It is the call of God. (I Thess. 4:7). It is the will and work of God. (Jno. 17:17, I Thess. 4:3). It is provided for in the atonement. (Heb. 13:11-12). It is experienced by the individual through faith and dedication. (Acts 15:9, 26:18, Gal. 2:20, Rom. 12:1). The word and the blood are the means used to accomplish it. (Jno. 17:17, Eph. 5:25-27, Heb. 9:14).

We believe that the baptism with the Holy Spirit is a distinct experience of the believer subsequent to regeneration. (Luke 11:13, Jno. 14:16, 17, Acts 1:4-5, 8:12-18, 19:1-6, Gal. 4:6). It is variously designated and referred to in the scriptures. (Luke 24:49, Acts 1:4, 5, 8, 2:4, 8:15-17, 10:44, 11:15-16, Eph. 1:13). It is necessary for holiness and fruitfulness of life and enduement with power for service, (I Cor. 12:4-13, Gal. 5:22-23, Luke 24:49, Acts 1:8, 4:31), and is experienced on conditions of complete obedience to God. (Acts 5:32). It involves separation, sacrifice, self denial and death to self, (Rom. 6:11-13, 12:1, Matt. 16:24), is received by prayer, (Luke 11:13) and appropriating faith. (Gal. 3:2). We must trust the Holy Spirit's leadership unreservedly and let him work unhindered. (Eph. 4:30-32, Rom. 8:13-14, Gal. 5:16, Isa. 59:19).

VII. THE CHURCH

We believe that the church, invisible and universal, is composed of all true regenerated believers of whatever name, race or nation, who are separated from sin and vitally united by faith to Christ, the living Head and Ruler. (Jno. 10:1-5, 15:1-8, I Pet. 2:9-10, Eph. 1:22-23, 4:15-16, I Cor. 12:12-27). Jesus Christ Himself being the chief cornerstone. (Eph. 2:19-22). The church local and visible is an organization made up of a company of professed believers in Christ, voluntarily joined together and meeting at stated times to worship and fellowship, to observe ordinances and when necessary to administer discipline. (Acts 2:46-47, 20:7, I Cor. 16:2, Matt. 18:15-17, I Cor. 5:1-4, Acts 6:1-6, 14:23). It is the duty of the church to give the Gospel as a witness to all men, (Matt. 28:18-20, Acts 1:8) to build itself up in the most holy faith, (Jude 20-21, Eph. 4:11-16, Acts 20:32, II Pet. 3:18) and to glorify God. (Eph. 1. 1:5-6, 3:21, I Pet. 4:11).

VIII. THE LORD'S DAY

We believe that the first day of the week is of Divine origin commonly called the Lord's Day or Christian Sabbath, (Acts 20:7, Jno. 20:19, Mark 2:27-28, I Cor. 16:1-2) and is to be kept sacred for religious purposes (Exod. 20:8, Rev. 1:10, Psa. 118:24) in commemoration of the resurrection of our Lord from the dead (Jno. 20:19, 26), by resting from all secular labor except works of mercy and necessity.

IX. ORDINANCES

A. BAPTISM. We believe that water baptism symbolizes the experience of regeneration and union with Christ, (Acts 8:36-39) is a public confession of the same and initiates the believer into the visible church, (Acts 2:38, 41, 47, Mark 16:16) is to be administered to believers only, (Acts 8:37, 16:30-34) in the name of the Father and of the Son and of the Holy Ghost. (Matt. 28:19). Water baptism has no saving or cleansing efficacy. (Rom. 10:9-10, Jno. 1:12). We cannot recognize infant baptism as valid according to Scripture.

B. FEET WASHING. The washing of the saint's feet was instituted by our Lord who also Himself washed the disciple's feet. (Jno. 13:4-17). This practice is encouraged in our churches where it can be used effectively as a means of growth in Grace.

C. LORD'S SUPPER. The Lord's supper is an ordinance, instituted by Christ in the night of betrayal, to be observed by His children until He returns. It consists in partaking of the consecrated emblems of bread and the fruit of the vine which symbolizes the death of Christ for the remission of our sins and our continual dependence upon Him for our sustenance. Its observance is to be preceded by faithful self-examination. The communion table shall be open to all believers who are living consistent Christian lives, regardless of denomination. (Matt. 26:26-30, Luke 22:19-20, I Cor. 10:16, 11:23-29).

D. DEDICATION OF CHILDREN. The Scriptures give instances where children were publicly dedicated. (I Sam. 1:28, Luke 2:22-24, Matt. 19:13-16, Luke 18:15-17). We therefore encourage parents to dedicate their children to the Lord by prayer and the laying on of hands of the ministers.

X. ESCHATOLOGY

A. SECOND ADVENT OF CHRIST. We believe in the personal, visible, pre-millenial and imminent return of Christ. (Jno. 14:1-3, Acts 1:10-11, Mark 13:22-37). This will be accomplished in two stages. First Christ will descend into mid-air to catch away His waiting bride the church. (I Thess. 4:16-17). Then after the tribulation judgments are visited upon the apostate and rebellious world. (I Tim. 4:1-3, II Tim. 4:1-4, Matt. 24:21, II Thess. 1:3-10). He will descend with His saints (Jude 14, Rom. 8:16-19, Col. 3:4, Rev. 19:7, 8, 19) to establish the long promised kingdom and to reign upon the earth for a thousand years. (Dan. 7:13-14, Luke 1:32-33, Rev. 5:9, 10, 20:4-6).

B. JUDGMENTS. We believe that the believer's works will be judged for rewards at the judgment seat of Christ at the time of His coming. (I Cor. 3:8-15, 4:5, 5:10, II Tim. 4:8). We believe that the impenitent wicked will appear before God for judgment at the Great White Throne after the millenium, and that they will be consigned to the lake of fire, there to suffer torment forever and ever together with the devil and his angels according as their works deserve. (Eccl. 12:14, Mark 9:43-48, Rom. 2:8-9, Heb. 9:27, Rev. 20:10-15).

C. ETERNAL STATE. We believe that after all God's enemies are consigned to their place of punishment, the present order of things will be dissolved and the new heaven and the new earth, wherein dwelleth righteousness, shall be brought in as the final state in which the righteous shall dwell forever. (Isa. 65:17, 66:22, II Pet. 3:13, Rev. 21:1-7, 22:3-7).

XI. DIVINE HEALING

We believe that healing for the body has been provided in the atonement of Christ, (Isa. 53:4-5, Matt. 8:16-17) and it can be realized by God's children on conditions as set forth in Mark 6:13, Jas. 5:13-16.

XII. GENERAL PRINCIPLES

A. MARRIAGE. We believe that marriage is a sacred institution, ordained of God, and is an indissoluble union of one husband and one wife, to be entered into in the fear of God and according to the teachings of the Holy Scriptures. (Gen. 1:27, 2:18, 24, Matt. 19:4-6, I Cor. 7:39).

We believe that it is unscriptural for believers to unite with unbelievers in the bond of matrimony, (Duet. 7:2-4, Neh. 13:25-27, II Cor. 6:14-15) and therefore such unions should be discouraged by our churches and our ministers are forbidden to officiate at the marriage of an unbeliever with a believer. We definitely discourage a Protestant-Catholic courtship or courtship with a follower of any of the various cults.

B. DIVORCE. We believe that the Scriptures forbid divorce except on the grounds of adultery, and that neither divorced party should marry another as long as both live. (Matt. 5:31-32, 19:3-12, I Cor. 6:16, Mark 10:11-12). If the offender fully repents and both agree, there may be a remarriage except in a case described in Duet. 24:1-4. Separation without divorce is recognized but deprecated in the Scriptures. In the case of an unbeliever who is dissatisfied to live with a believer, the former shall not be forbidden to depart. (I Cor. 7:12-15).

C. CIVIL GOVERNMENT. We believe that civil government is ordained of God for the punishment of evil doers, for the protection of the good, and to justly direct the interaction of society. (Rom. 13:1-7, Exod. 18:21-23). We, therefore consider it our duty to pray for our rulers and magistrates (I Tim. 2:1-3) and to be submissive and obedient to their authority except in things which militate against the supreme law and will of our Lord Jesus Christ. (Titus 3:1, I Pet. 2:13, 14, Acts 4:19, 5:29, Matt. 23:10, Rev. 19:16, Rom. 14:9-13).

D. OATHS. We believe that the Scriptures strictly forbid the swearing of oaths, (Matt. 5:33-37, Jas. 5:12) and that everything beyond an affirmation which is as binding as though we confirmed it by an

oath, is violating the command of our Lord Jesus
Christ.

E.　NON-RESISTANCE.

1.　GOING TO LAW. The Scriptures teach to
"Follow peace with all men," (Heb. 12:14), to be
inoffensive (Eph. 4:3, Rom. 12:8), and it is
forbidden for a disciple of Christ to seek revenge,
or recompense evil for evil, of those who do us evil
(Rom. 12:17-21) and particularly is it forbidden to
go to law with a believer before unbelievers (I Cor.
6:1-8, Matt. 5:25).

2.　CARNAL WARFARE. We believe it is contrary
to the teachings of Christ and the New Testament
for Christians to take up arms in wars of
aggression, revenge, and self defense. (Matt. 5:44,
26:51-52, Rom. 12:17-21, II Cor. 10:3-4, I Thess.
5:15, I Pet. 2:21-23, Jno. 15:12, Gal. 5:13-15, I
Pet. 3:8-9, I Jno. 3:15, 23).

F.　SECRET SOCIETIES. We believe that all secret
orders are contrary to the teaching of the Scriptures.
There is nothing belonging to Christianity of which
the followers of Christ need to be ashamed or to
conceal from men. Therefore, under no circumstances should members be allowed to hold membership in any secret organization (Jno. 3:19, 18:20,
Eph. 5:11-12, II Cor. 6:14-18), neither shall any such
person be received into church membership.

G.　TITHING. God is the owner of everything. (Hag.
2:8; Psa. 24:1). He has a system whereby the
Christian ministry is financed. Abraham practiced it
(Gen. 14:18-20); Jacob continued it (Gen. 28:20-22);
Moses confirmed it (Lev. 27:30; Malachi commanded it (Mal. 3:10); and the Lord Jesus Christ
commended it (Mt. 23:23). The Scriptures teach
systematic giving. (I. Cor. 16:2). A blessing is
promised to the liberal giver. (Lu. 6:38; Mal. 3:10-
12).

Notes: *The Evangelical Mennonite Church has adopted the
major belief of the Holiness movement, which identifies the
baptism of the Holy Spirit with sanctification. Sanctification
is seen as a second work of the Holy Spirit in the believer,
separating the believer from sin. Otherwise, Mennonite
distinctives such as pacifism are maintained, and foot
washing is practiced.*

*　　*　　*

OUR COMMON CONFESSION (GENERAL CONFERENCE MENNONITE CHURCH)

A.　BASIC FAITH. The General Conference believes in
the divine inspiration and the infallibility of the Bible
as the Word of God and the only trustworthy guide
of faith and life; in Jesus Christ as the only Savior
and Lord. For no other foundation can any one lay
than that which is laid, which is Jesus Christ" (1
Cor. 3:11).

In the matter of faith it is, therefore, required of the
congregations which unite with the conference that,
accepting the above confession, they hold fast to the
doctrine of salvation by grace through faith in the
Lord Jesus Christ (Eph. 2:8, 9; Tit. 3:5), baptism on
confession of faith (Mk. 16:16; Acts 2:38), the
avoidance of oaths (Mt. 5:34-37; Jas. 5:12), the
biblical doctrine of nonresistance (Mt. 5:39-48; Rom.
12:9-21), nonconformity to the world (Rom. 12:1, 2;
Eph. 4:22-24), and the practice of a scriptural church
discipline (Mt. 18:15-17; Gal. 6:1).

At no time shall any rules be made or resolutions
adopted which in any way contradict the historical
principles of faith as laid down in this Constitution.

B.　SEPARATED LIFE.

1.　The General Conference believes that membership
in oathbound secret societies, military organization, or other groups which tend to compromise
the loyalty of the Christian to the Lord and to the
church is contrary to such apostolic admonitions
as: "Do not be mismated with unbelievers" (2
Cor. 6:14, 15, and that the church "should be holy
and without blemish" (Eph. 5:27).

2.　Further, regarding "the works of the flesh" (Gal.
5:19-21), the conference believes "that those who
do such things shall not inherit the kingdom of
God."

Therefore, every congregation should seriously
strive to remain free from these evils.

Much rather, "If we live by the Spirit, let us also
walk by the Spirit" (Gal. 5:25).

(ADOPTED IN 1941)

Accepting the full Bible and the Apostolic Creed:

1.　We believe in one God, eternally existing and
manifest as Father, Son and Holy Spirit.

2.　We believe in the deity of Jesus Christ, the only
begotten of the Father, full of grace and truth, born
of the virgin Mary, in His perfect humanity, His
atoning death, His bodily resurrection from the dead,
and His personal triumphant return.

3.　We believe in the immortality of the soul, the
resurrection of the dead, and a future state determined by divine judgment.

4.　We believe in the divine inspiration and the infallibility of the Bible as the Word of God and the only
trustworthy guide of faith and life.

5.　We believe a Christian is one saved by grace, whose
life is transformed into the likeness of Christ by His
atoning death and the power of His resurrection.

6.　We believe that Christ lived and taught the way of
life as recorded in the Scriptures, which is God's plan
for individuals and the race; and that it becomes
disciples of Christ to live in this way, thus manifesting in their personal and social life and relationship
the love and holiness of God. And we believe that
this way of life also implies nonresistance to evil by
carnal means, the fullest exercise of love, and the
resolute abandonment of the use of violence, includ-

ing warfare. We believe further that the Christian life will of necessity express itself in nonconformity to the world in life and conduct.

7. We believe in prayer as fellowship with God, a desire to be in His will, and in its divine power.

8. We believe that the Christian Church consists of believers who have repented from their sins, have accepted Christ by faith and are born again, and sincerely endeavor by the grace of God to live the Christian life.

9. We believe in the brotherhood of the redeemed under the fatherhood of God in Christ.

Notes: *The first brief statement, taken from the church's constitution, covers only the most essential beliefs. A lengthier statement of doctrine was adopted at the General Conference session in 1941.*

* * *

Brethren

WE BELIEVE (ASSOCIATION OF FUNDAMENTAL GOSPEL CHURCHES)

WE BELIEVE:

1. In the Diety-God in Trinity—Father, Son, and Holy Ghost.

2. In the Virgin Birth, Crucifixion, Death and Resurrection; Ascension and Second Coming of Christ.

3. The Blood of Jesus Christ was shed for the remission of sins.

4. In the Resurrection of the dead.

5. In the return of Jesus Christ for His Bride (The Church).

6. In a literal Heaven as the future abode for the righteous.

7. In a literal Hell as the future abode for the wicked.

8. It is the responsibility of every individual to work out his own soul's salvation.

9. The Church (The Body of Christ) to be the accepted believer of all ages.

WE BELIEVE, PRACTICE, AND TEACH:

1. Faith in our Lord Jesus Christ.

2. Repentence.

3. Baptism by immersion and the application of the Blood of Jesus Christ for the remission of sins.

4. Laying on of Hands for the Gift of the Holy Ghost.

5. The new Birth, a life dedicated and consecrated to God.

6. Feet washing.

7. Lord's Supper.

8. Holy Communion.

9. Kiss of Charity.

10. Anointing with oil of the sick.

11. The Sisters cover, the Brethren uncover their heads in worship.

12. Going to war, taking an oath, divorce, going to law, ornamental adorning to be unscriptural.

OUR PURPOSE:

Believing salvation is the responsibility of each individual, our purpose is to:

Establish a church where man can worship God, find access to God, and be taught of God. Lay claim to every attribute of God available to us. Use every means at our command to bring lost and dying humanity to a saving knowledge of our Lord and Saviour Jesus Christ.

Notes: *Originating as an independent fellowship in Germany, the Brethren came to America and settled in Lancaster County, Pennsylvania, from whence they spread across the United States. Like the Amish they wore plain clothes until recent decades when they experienced splinters along a conservative-liberal spectrum concerning such issues as wearing apparel, behavior, and doctrine. Brethren have traditionally practiced foot washing. Also, the Lord's Supper among the Brethren refers to a meal (love feast) which is eaten concurrently with the taking of the traditional communion elements, bread and wine.*

The Association of Fundamental Gospel Churches is one of the more conservative bodies in the Brethren tradition.

* * *

AFFIRMATION OF FAITH [ASHLAND THEOLOGICAL SEMINARY—BRETHREN CHURCH (ASHLAND, OHIO)]

Acknowledging the absolute supremacy and Lordship of Jesus Christ, and believing that His Word and Will must be final in all matters to those who claim to be Christian, on His authority we affirm the following truths as the basic faith and teaching of this institution.

1. The Holy Scriptures of the Old and New Testaments, as originally given of God, are the infallible record of the perfect, final and authoritative revelation of His work and will, together sufficient in themselves as the rule of faith and practice.

2. The One True God, perfect and infinite in His being, holiness, love, wisdom and power; transcendent above the world as its Creator, yet immanent in the world as the Preserver of all things; self-existent and self-revealing in three divine Persons, the Father, the Son, and the Holy Spirit, who are equal in power and glory.

3. Jesus Christ the Eternal Son, Revealer of the invisible God, Who became incarnate by virgin birth, lived the perfect human life upon earth, gave Himself in death upon the Cross as the Lamb of God bearing sin and its penalty in our stead, was raised and glorified in the body in which He suffered and died, ascended as our only Saviour and Lord into Heaven, from whence He will come again personally and visibly to raise and translate His waiting Church,

establish His Kingdom fully over all the nations, and at last be the Raiser and Judge of the Dead.

4. The Holy Spirit, third person of the Godhead, the divine Lifegiver and Artist in creation, history and redemption; Who indwells, seals, empowers, guides, teaches and perfects all them who become children of God through Christ.

5. That Man was the direct creation of God, made in the divine image, not in any sense the offspring of an animal ancestry; and that by transgression man became a fallen creature, alienated from the life of God, universally sinful by nature and practice, and having within himself no means of recovery.

6. That Salvation is the free gift of God's grace, received through personal faith in the Lord Jesus Christ, in Whom all those who believe have eternal life, a perfect righteousness, sonship in the family of God, and even spiritual blessing needed for life and godliness; but those who reject the gift of grace in Christ shall be forever under the abiding wrath of God.

7. That Christian Character and Conduct are the outgrowth and evidence of salvation in Christ; and therefore the Christian is bound to honor His Word, to walk as He walked, to keep His commandments and ordinances, and thus bear the fruit of the Spirit which is love, joy, peace, long-suffering, kindness, goodness, faithfulness, meekness, and self-control, against which there is no law; and that the teachings of the Bible on such matters as marriage, divorce and the family are of permanent value and obligation to the Church and society.

Notes: *The Brethren Church, a liberal church on issues of dress and behavior in the nineteenth century, absorbed a theological perspective in the twentieth century close to that of conservative evangelicalism. The church is a member of the National Association of Evangelicals. It has refused, as a body, to adopt any statement of faith or creed, taking the whole Bible as its standard of faith and teaching. The seminary of the church has, however, published a statement which generally represents the church's beliefs. It has also published the "Message of the Brethren Ministry," a statement adopted in 1921 by the National Brethren Ministry Association.*

The church has remained open on the question of premillenialism in its eschatology.

* * *

DOCTRINAL STATEMENT OF THE BRETHREN IN CHRIST CHURCH

ARTICLE I. THE HOLY SCRIPTURES

The Holy Bible, Old and New Testaments, is the Word of God. This Word, given by divine inspiration, completes the revelation of God partially disclosed through nature, providence and the voice of conscience. The Holy Scriptures are necessary for the understanding of God and His character, attributes and purposes for men.

The Bible as the written Word of God reaches its climax in revelation in the incarnation of Jesus Christ as the living Word of God. Through Christ, the living Word, and the Bible, the written Word, are unfolded God's purpose, provision and plan for the salvation of men.

The Holy Scriptures as the revelation of God and His will constitute an authoritative standard of truth, a basis for faith and the supreme guide for life and conduct. The illumination of the Holy Spirit is necessary to the proper understanding of the Scriptures. The best source of interpretation of the Scripture is the Scriptures themselves.

II Timothy 3:16; Psalms 19:14; Romans 2:14, 15; John 1:1, 14; John 6:45; I Corinthians 2:9, 10, 12; Matthew 22:29, 31.

ARTICLE II. GOD—THE HOLY TRINITY

There is but one living and true God, infinite, eternal, almighty, omniscient, omnipresent, righteous, loving and merciful. The Scriptures reveal that the God-head is a Trinity of three eternal, divine persons: God the Father, God the Son, and God the Holy Spirit. These three are one.

Intimations of the Trinity are found in the Old Testament, where God is revealed as the Creator and Sustainer of the universe, as providing the standard for man's holiness, and the sole object of his worship. The Spirit of God is revealed as associated in the work of creation, and as representing the God-head in personal relationships with men. The Son and His work as the world's Redeemer are prophetically revealed.

In the New Testament the work of the three Persons of the Trinity and Their oneness in the God-head are more fully brought into view. Here is revealed the active participation of the Son with the Father in the work of creation. Here the functions of the Trinity find their highest expression in relation to the plan of redemption. This plan was conceived through the love of God, the Father; it was provided through the death of God, the Son; and it becomes operative through the work of God, the Holy Spirit.

Thus from eternity to eternity the three Persons of the Trinity through Their separate yet complementary functions accomplish the divine purposes of the triune God-head.

Jno. 14:26; I Pet. 1:2; Jno. 1:1, 2; I Jno. 5:7; Gen. 1; Neh. 9:6; Lev. 11:45; 20:26; Ex. 20:3; Deut. 6:4, 5; Gen. 1:2; Gen. 6:3; Ex. 31:3; Isa. 9:6, 7; Isa. 63; Matt. 3:16, 17; II Cor. 13:14; Jno. 1:3; Heb. 1; Jno. 3:16; I Cor. 15:3; Jno. 14:16, 17; 16:8.

ARTICLE III. SIN

The Holy Scriptures teach that man was created by God, in His own image and likeness. He was righteous and holy in character and enjoyed fellowship with God.

The Word also teaches that by sin, through the transgression of our first parents, man's original righteousness and communion with God were lost and the image of God marred and defaced. Thus the human family became dead in sin, unholy, and incapable of doing right according to the divine standard. By this original sin man by nature is inclined to evil, and actual transgressions of the law of God inevitably result.

Controlled by Satan through the inherited depravity of man's fallen nature, guilty by sins both of commission and omission, man by nature stands condemned under the dominion of spiritual, physical, and eternal death. Moreover, man by his own effort cannot change his inherent preference for sin to love for God, nor even make an approach to such a change without the aid of the Holy Spirit.

Gen. 2:17; Rom. 5:12; Eph. 4:18; Rom. 6:23a; II Thess. 1:9; Jno. 1:13; 6:44.

ARTICLE IV. REDEMPTION

Scripture reveals the fact that the plan of redemption was included in the eternal counsel of God. Its purpose is to deliver all men from the dominion of Satan and restore them to divine favor and fellowship with God. To accomplish this, God, in infinite love and grace, gave His only begotten Son to be Mediator between God and men.

When the fulness of time was come, Christ as the Son of God was born of the Virgin Mary. Thus, He took upon Himself the likeness of men, yet without sin.

This divine-human Saviour, anointed by the Spirit, revealed God and taught by His life how man should live. He atoned for the sins of man by shedding His blood on Calvary's cross. His resurrection witnessed to His glorious triumph over death and Satan. He ascended to the Father by Whom the Holy Spirit was poured out upon His Church. Christ now sits at the right hand of God to make intercession for us.

Eph. 1:4; II Thess. 2:13; II Pet. 3:9; I Tim. 2:5, 6; Phil. 2:7; Gal. 4:4; Heb. 10:5, 7; 9:26; II Tim. 1:10; Heb. 7:25; I Jno. 2:1.

ARTICLE V. FREE WILL

God created man in His own image, a moral being with free will, obligated to exercise personal choice and responsibility to his Creator with respect to his conduct relative to right and wrong.

Through the fall of Adam, man became so depraved that he cannot prepare himself by his own works to merit or receive God's favor. However, God through Jesus Christ, freely extends His grace by mercy to all men, enabling all who will to turn from sin to righteousness, thus preparing them to do works pleasing unto Him.

The believer's relationship of life in Christ remains secure as he exercises his own voluntary will unto yieldedness and obedience to the known will of God. To willfully disregard God's will and commandments will result in his being eternally lost.

Gen. 2:16, 17; Eph. 2:8, 9; Jno. 1:11, 12; Phil. 2:13; Rom. 12:1, 2; Rom. 6:16; II Pet. 1:10; II Pet. 2:20-22; Rev. 3:5.

ARTICLE VI. JUSTIFICATION

Justification and condemnation are the only two possibilities existing in man's relationship to God. A man is either condemned to pay the penalty of his wickedness, or he is justified (acquitted) of all guilt and set free.

Universal guilt has been charged against every member of the human race. God, the Judge, holds all men to be sinners and He must deal with mankind as such, unless some provision for his salvation is found. Such provision has been made through the redemptive work of Christ on the cross of Calvary, where He became the substitute for all men. He assumes all man's guilt, bears all his penalty and he is adjudged free from all his sins. This is the glorious realization of all repentant sinners who appropriate the offer of redemptive love and atoning blood.

Judicially, justification accounts man as guiltless with regard to all his past sins and as the recipient of the imputed righteousness of Christ. Experientially, justification implies a spiritual birth and a new life. The Holy Spirit witnesses to this divine relationship and gives peace with God. The believer maintains this vital relationship with God, even unto eternal life, subject to his obedience to the revealed will of God.

Rom. 5:12; Rom. 3:23; 3:10; II Cor. 5:21; I Pet. 2:24; Rom. 3:25; II Cor. 5:21; Jno. 3:3; II Cor. 5:17; Rom. 8:16; Rom. 5:1; I Jno. 2:24, 25.

ARTICLE VII. SANCTIFICATION

Sanctification throughout the Word of God is used with various meanings: to declare holy, to set apart, and to cleanse.

As a Christian experience, sanctification embodies the setting apart of the believer in entire consecration, and the cleansing of the believer's heart from carnality, accompanied by the baptism of the Holy Spirit.

The sanctification of the believer is required by God, provided for by Christ in His atonement, and divinely wrought by the Holy Spirit.

When the believer led by the Spirit becomes aware of an inner conflict of flesh and Spirit, loathes his condition, confesses his state and need; makes an unreserved consecration, and exercises a living faith in the work of Christ on Calvary, he is definitely cleansed from the carnal mind. Thus the work of holiness which was begun in regeneration is perfected, and the believer is "sanctified wholly."

This experience for believers is obtained instantaneously and subsequent to the new birth. The scriptural terms used to describe the cleansing of the believer's heart imply the same: purifying the heart; crucifixion of the old man; body of sin destroyed; circumcision of the heart; deliverance; creation.

Even though it is possible for a sanctified believer to fall into sin, the Scriptures reveal that by giving heed to the Word, being devoted in prayer, and by rendering loving and obedient service to Christ he is kept from willful transgression by the power of God.

Although sanctification perfects the motives and desires of the heart, the expression of these in terms of accomplishment is a progressive growth in grace until the close of this life.

Gen. 2:3; Ex. 29:43, 44; Ex. 13:2; Jno. 17:19; Ex. 19:10; Eph. 5:26, 27; Rom. 12:1, 2; Jno. 17:17; Acts 15:8, 9; Eph.

DOCTRINAL STATEMENT OF THE BRETHREN IN CHRIST CHURCH (continued)

5:26; Matt. 3:11; Acts 2:1-10; Rom. 8:5-8; Heb. 12:14; Heb. 10:10; Heb. 13:12; Heb. 10:14, 15; Acts 15:8, 9; Gal. 5:17; Rom. 7:14-24; Rom. 6:13-16; Rom. 12:1; II Cor. 7:1; I Thess. 5:23; Acts 8:14-17; Jas. 4:8; Acts 15:8, 9; Rom. 6:6; Rom. 6:6; Col. 2:11; Rom. 7:24; Psa. 51:10; Jno. 15:6; II Pet. 2:20-22; I Tim. 4:15, 16; Heb. 4:15, 16; Rom. 6:16; Jude 20-24; II Tim. 3:16, 17; II Pet. 3:18.

ARTICLE VIII. THE CHURCH

The Church is composed of all those of every nation who through saving faith in Christ have entered into spiritual union with Him.

This body of believers is characterized by having been cleansed from sin, possessing the Holy Spirit, having the hope of glory, holding joint heirship with Christ and having fellowship with one another. Her eternal foundation is secured in the sonship, atonement, and resurrection of her living Head, the Christ.

The Church came into being through the operation of the Holy Spirit on the day of Pentecost. Through election of grace she stands actively performing the functions of ambassador and evangel, light of the world, and salt of the earth.

Her perfection is attained through the mediums of her experiences, gifts, growth, fruitage, doctrine, and ordinances. Ultimately as the bride of Christ she will become the glorious church triumphant.

Acts 10:34, 35; Rom. 1:14-16; Eph. 5:26; Eph. 1:13; Col. 1:27; Rom. 8:17; Acts 2:42; Jno. 3:16; Eph. 1:4; Rom. 5:10; Acts 2; Eph. 2:8; Matt. 28:19, 20; II Cor. 5:20; Matt. 5:14; Phil. 2:15; Matt. 5:13; Eph. 4:11-16; I Cor. 11:2; Rev. 19:7-9; Eph. 5:27.

ARTICLE IX. WATER BAPTISM

Water baptism, an inclusion in the Great Commission, is a rite of public profession, indicating that one has now come into the family of God the Father, into the mystical body of Christ, the Son, and into the communion of the Holy Spirit, which relationships are symbolized in the observance of this ordinance by triune immersion. Baptism is to be accompanied by a teaching ministry that guides the believer into the observance of all things, "whatsoever I have commanded you."

The necessity of water baptism is established by the command and example of Jesus and the practice of the New Testament Church. Those who have sincerely repented of sin, who have by the exercise of their own personal faith received the Lord Jesus Christ as Saviour and have been "born again" by the Holy Spirit, are eligible for the observance of this ordinance.

Baptism has no saving merit in and of itself. It is an outward sign or symbol by which the believer testifies to the inner change of heart and redirection of life. Christian experience is illustrated by the figure of a spiritual baptism which suggests the death and burial of the old life and the resurrection to a new life in Christ. Baptism by immersion typifies and witnesses to such a burial and the coming forth to walk in newness of life.

Matt. 28:19; Matt. 28:20; Jno. 15:12-17; Matt. 3:13-17; Acts 2:38-41; I Pet. 3:21; Rom. 6:4; Col. 2:12.

ARTICLE X. THE LORD'S SUPPER

In connection with His last observance of the Passover feast Jesus instituted the sacred ordinance of the Lord's Supper, through the use of the broken bread and the cup. On this occasion He consecrated the bread, which represents His broken body; and the fruit of the vine, which represents His shed blood, as symbols of His redemptive sacrifice.

The Lord's Supper thus commemorates with renewed and tender meaning the sufferings and death of our crucified Lord; it beautifully portrays through the sharing of the sacred emblems the unity of the body of Christ; and it also points forward with hope and expectancy to the time when, according to His promise, Christ will again fellowship in person with His followers.

This ordinance is observed by those, who having been saved by faith in Christ, and who having examined themselves as to their present fellowship with Him, esteem it a blessed privilege to partake of the sacred emblems in remembrance of their Lord.

As often as the church observes the Lord's Supper, she witnesses to the world concerning the death of Christ, and the promise of His coming again.

I Cor. 11:24; Jno. 6:48-51; Lu. 22:20; I Cor. 11:25; Heb. 10:12; Jno. 19; Phil. 2:7, 8; Rom. 12:5; I Cor. 10:17; Matt. 26:29; Lu. 22:19; I Cor. 11:28; I Cor. 11:26.

Notes: *This statement of belief is noteworthy for its position on sanctification, which shows the influence of the Holiness movement. The church is a member of the Christian Holiness Association. The statement on the Lord's Supper differentiates the Brethren in Christ from many other Brethren churches which partake of a full meal at the time of receiving the communion; however, triune immersion is practiced as a baptismal form.*

The Brethren in Christ also use the Apostles' Creed. The Lutheran text, which includes both the phrase "He descended into hell" and the affirmation of the "holy Christian Church," has been adopted.

*　　　*　　　*

A DECLARATION OF FAITH (CHURCH OF THE BRETHREN)

1. We believe that the Holy Scriptures of the Old and the New Testament have their authority from God and are a sufficient standard of faith and practice.

2. We believe there is one true and living God, infinite, self-existent, omnipresent, omniscient, omnipotent, good, wise, just, and merciful; that he is the Creator, Preserver, and Sovereign of the universe; that in the Godhead there are three persons—the Father, the Son, and the Holy Ghost.

3. We believe in Jesus Christ, the Son of God, the Redeemer and Savior of men.

4. We believe in the Holy Spirit, one with the Father and the Son in will and purpose.

5. We believe that man was created in holiness, but through temptation and voluntary transgression fell under condemnation and needs salvation.

6. We believe that the salvation of sinners can be obtained alone through the merits of the Son of God, who by his death made a full atonement for our sins.

7. We believe that in his death he conquered, rose triumphant from the grave, and ascended to the right hand of the Father; that he will come again to judge the world in righteousness.

8. We believe that repentance and faith are absolutely essential, enabling us to receive holy baptism, confessing the Lord Jesus Christ as an all-sufficient Savior.

9. We believe that Christian baptism is the immersion in water of a believer by a triune immersion.

10. We believe that justification is an act of God, on the condition of faith in and obedience to the truth as revealed in the Scriptures.

11. We believe that the visible church of Christ is a body of baptized believers, associated by covenant in faith and fellowship of the gospel, observing all the ordinances of Christ governed by all his laws, and exercising the gifts, rights, and privileges invested in them by his Word.

12. We believe that it is our duty to keep all the ordinances "as they were delivered to us by our Lord Jesus Christ":

    a. That feet-washing is an ordinance, instituted by our Lord.

    b. That the Lord's Supper is a sacred meal, in connection with the communion.

    c. That the communion is the partaking of bread and wine as emblems of the broken body and the shed blood of our Lord and Savior Jesus Christ, a memorial of his suffering and death.

    d. That the anointing of the sick for healing is appointed by the Lord, to be perpetuated in his church.

13. We believe that the first day of the week is the true Christian Sabbath.

14. We believe that civil government is ordained of God for the care and protection of the good and for the punishment of those who do evil.

15. We believe that the principle of nonresistance is clearly taught in the Scriptures and therefore has been accepted as a doctrine of the church.

16. We believe it wrong to swear or to take the civil oath.

17. We believe temperance to be a moderate use of the things that are essential and useful, and total abstinence from such things as are harmful or lead to evil.

18. We believe it to be wrong to conform to the vain fashions, maxims, and customs of the world.

Notes: *There is no official statement of faith for the Church of the Brethren. However, several attempts at statements have been made and published by the church in its* Manual. *The statement reproduced here was written by H. B. Brumbaugh and first published in 1916.*

*   *   *

A STATEMENT OF BELIEF AND PURPOSE (CHURCH OF THE BRETHREN)

I. We believe that Jesus Christ is the expression of God's love for all men.

   Therefore, we pledge our loyalty to him and his way of life.

II. We accept the New Testament as the guidebook to abundant Christian living.

   Therefore, we pledge ourselves to study its message for our day and to follow the light we discover.

III. We believe that communion with God and fellowship with Christ are essential to daily living and spiritual growth.

   Therefore, we will devote time regularly to private devotions, family worship, and group meditation.

IV. We believe that God is our Father and all men are our brothers.

   Therefore, as we attempt to live Christ's way of reconciling love, we can consider no man our enemy, we dare not hate, we cannot kill.

V. We believe that spiritual values are more important than material possessions.

   Therefore, we will live modestly, dress simply, and eat temperately in order to place God's kingdom first.

Notes: *This statement was written and adopted by the National Youth Cabinet of the Church of the Brethren in 1948. It is much more confessional than the church's declaration of faith.*

*   *   *

BIBLE TEACHINGS (DUNKARD BRETHREN)

From a careful study of God's Word we conclude:

1. That there is only one true, almighty, everliving God, the Creator and Sustainer of all things visible and invisible, the Ruler of heaven and earth.—Gen. 1:1; 2:7; Psa. 97:9; Isa. 45:5-7; 64:8; 66:1,2.

2. That Jesus Christ is the Son of the living God; that He was born of Virgin Mary, lived in the flesh, and died on the cross, the Redeemer and Saviour of man; that He was buried, rose from the dead the third day, ascended to heaven the fortieth day, where He now "liveth to make intercession"—Matt. 3:17; Luke 2:7; John 3:16; 19:40-42; Acts 1:9-11; Heb. 4:15; 7:25.

3. That the Holy Ghost is the Spirit of the living God, sent forth by the Father and the Son; that He is the Reprover of the wicked, and the Guide and abiding Comforter of God's elect.—John 14:16, 26; 16:7-11, 13; Acts 2:4.

BIBLE TEACHINGS (DUNKARD BRETHREN) (continued)

4. That man was created pure and spotless, in the image of his Maker.—Gen. 1:26, 27, 31; Eccl. 7:29.

5. That the human family became alienated from God as a result of the transgression of our first parents in the Garden of Eden; that sin, sorrow, depravity and death (natural and spiritual) are results of the fall.—Gen. 3:22-24; Rom. 3:10, 23; 5:12; Eph. 2:12.

6. That man was again reconciled through the atonement of Christ on the cross.—Rom. 5:11, 19; Heb. 10:14.

7. That there is no salvation but by Jesus Christ.—John 14:6; Acts 4:12.

8. That salvation is offered as a free gift to all them that believe.—Rom. 5:18; 6:23; Eph. 2:8.

9. That a faith which does not take hold of the individual and bind him to a life of obedience, made manifest in works, has no Bible recognition.—Jas. 2:14-20.

10. That every one who is converted to God will manifest by a holy life that he has been saved from his sins.—Jas. 2:14-20; Tit. 3:3-8.

11. That a sinful, disobedient life is an evidence that the soul is not converted, and that the heart is not right with God.—Matt. 7:16; I John 3:8.

12. That self-denial is an essential feature in Christian living and the gratification of carnal lusts is an abomination in the sight of God.—Matt. 10:38; Luke 9:23; Eccl. 11:9; Gal. 5:19-24; Tit. 2:12.

13. That every child of God should be sober, serious, industrious, spiritually-minded and obedient to the will of God as revealed in His Word.—Tit. 2:12; I Tim. 5:8; I John 2:3-5; Col. 1:8.

14. That the Word of God and the Spirit of God never conflict; that there is no such thing, therefore, as the Spirit leading any one to do differently from what the Bible teaches; and that all our impressions of right and wrong should be diligently compared with God's Word.—John 14:26; 16:13, 14; I John 4:1.

15. That God has on earth a church, instituted by Himself, designed as the earthly home of His people, in which they may labor together for the edification and spiritual growth of the saved and the salvation of the unsaved.—Eph. 4:11-24.

16. That the visible church should be composed of converted souls; that applicants should give evidence of conversion before being received into the church; that the church should exercise a vigilant care over the spiritual welfare of its individual members; and that whenever it becomes clearly apparent that any of them are wedded to sin rather than righteousness (and all available means to effect a reformation have proved fruitless) they should be no longer fellowshipped as members.—Matt. 3:7,8; 18:15-18; Luke 13:6-9; I Cor. 5:7-13; 10:20; II Cor. 6:14, 15.

17. That all believers are to be baptized for the remission of sins. Acts 2:38. Baptism in mode, is immersion. In form it is triune, and consists of an immersion into the name of the Father, and of the Son, and of the Holy Ghost. Matt. 28:19; Mark 1:8; Matt. 3:6; Acts 8:38, 39; Baptism a necessity. John 3:3-5; Mark 16:16. The door to the church. Rom. 6:3; I Cor. 12:13. A new birth. John 3:3-5; I Peter 1:23.

18. That the washing of the saints' feet as an ordinance instituted by our Saviour, and enjoined upon His disciples, should be literally observed by all believers. John 13:1-17; I Tim. 5:10.

19. That the Lord's Supper as instituted by Christ in the night of His betrayal is a full meal to be kept among His people until His return. Matt. 26:20-23; Luke 22:20; John 13:1-17, 30.

20. That the Communion as instituted by Christ consists in partaking of the bread and the cup in a worthy manner at the close of the day, in connection with, but following feet washing and the Lord's Supper. (1) The bread and the cup representing the broken body and the shed blood of Jesus; (2) a common union of communicants. Mark 14:22-24; I Cor. 10:16; 11:21-26.

21. That the believing woman should wear a modest, appropriate head-covering in time of prayer, gospel teaching or other seasons of devotion.—I Cor. 11:2-16.

22. That the salutation of the kiss of brotherhood, "holy kiss," or "kiss of charity," should be practiced by believers.—Rom. 16:16; I Pet. 5:14.

23. That the anointing with oil for the sick is divinely recommended.—Jas. 5:14.

24. That marriage is an institution ordained of God for the purity of humanity and the perpetuation of the race; that believers should marry "only in the Lord"; that man and wife once united remain so until death separates them.—Matt. 19:3-9; I Cor. 7:1-11, 39; II Cor. 6:14.

25. That the Bible specifies a line of demarcation between the Church and the world in every department of life, which if adhered to by the church, so completely separates the two bodies that no one need ever mistake a child of God for a worldling if we know their "manner of life."—Rom. 12:2; Eph. 2:3; 4:16; Tit. 2:14; Jas. 1:27.

26. That it is wrong for Christians to dress according to the fashion of the world; that they should adorn themselves as men and women professing godliness, in modest apparel; that costly array and jewelry and superfluities of all kinds should be scrupulously avoided.—Rom. 12:2; Isa 3:16-24; I Tim. 2:9, 10; I Pet. 3:3,4.

27. That no Christian should ever engage in any business, occupation, recreation or amusement in which he cannot conscientiously ask God to bless him in what he is doing.—I Cor. 10:31; Col. 3:17, 23; Tit. 2:12; I Pet. 3:3,4.

28. That carnal warfare is contrary to the spirit of the Gospel; that it is inconsistent, therefore, for Chris-

tians to manifest a quarrelsome disposition in the home, in the church, in society, or in business; that it is unscriptural to take vegeance upon enemies, or to grasp carnal weapons to inflict injury upon or take the life of our fellow men on the field of battle, or under any circumstances whatsoever.—Matt. 5:38-40; Luke 2:14; John 18:36; Rom. 12:17-21; II Cor. 10:4.

29. That Christians should at all times be law-abiding citizens, subject to the powers that be, obedient to all laws which do not conflict with the higher laws of God, in which case "we ought to obey God rather than men."—Rom. 13:1, 2; Luke 20:25; Acts 4:19; 5:29; Tit. 3:1.

30. That swearing of oaths, both profane and judicial, under any and all circumstances, is wrong.—Matt. 5:33-37; Jas. 5:12.

31. That law-suits are contrary to the spirit of the Gospel, and should be avoided,—Matt. 5:40; Acts 4:19; I Cor. 6:1-8.

32. That it is contrary to the teaching of the Gospel to hold membership in secret organizations.—Matt. 5:15; John 3:19; 18:20; II Cor. 6:14-17; Eph. 5:11-13.

33. That the Christian, as a child of God, put his entire trust in his heavenly Father for support and keeping in this life; as well as glorification in the life to come; that he must therefore consider life-insurance contrary to the spirit of the Gospel.—Jer. 49:11; Psa. 37:25; 118:8; Matt. 6:19, 20, 27-34; Heb. 13:5.

34. That obedience to God's commandments is one of the foremost requirements of God's Word, and that the truly converted child of God has only to know the will of God in any matter and he is ready to obey.—I Sam. 15:22,23; Eccl. 12:13; John 14:15; 15:14.

35. That the Christian's aim should be to get all the light that he can, and live up to all the light that he has.—John 5:39; Acts 17:11; II Tim. 2:15.

36. That God hears and answers prayer; that in answer to prayer He lightens life's burdens, arms us against the power of temptation, gives us His Holy Spirit and whatsoever things we need.—Luke 11:9, 10, 13; 22:42, 43, 46; I John 5:14, 15; Jas. 1:5.

37. That the great mission of the Christian Church is to teach "all nations" to observe "all things" which our Saviour taught His disciples to keep; that it is the duty of the church to Christianize the world.—Matt. 10:8; 28:19, 20; Luke 24: 47.

38. That Christ will come again with power and great glory to gather to Himself the elect of the earth and to bring the world to judgment; that there will be a coming forth of all the dead, who shall appear before the judgment bar of God to be rewarded according to their deeds done in the body.—Matt. 24:30, 31; 25:31-46; John 5:28, 29; II Cor. 5:10; Rev. 1:7; 20: 12, 13.

39. That the eternal abode of the wicked is the place prepared for the devil and his angels—the horrible, bottomless pit, where the smoke of their torment ascendeth for ever and for ever.—Psa. 9:17; Matt. 25:41; Rev. 14:9-11; 21:8.

40. That the righteous, saved and redeemed through Christ, will be received into glory, where in the presence of God they will sing the new song and enjoy the loveliness, holiness and bliss of heaven in eternity.—Matt. 25:34; II Tim. 4:8; Rev. 21:3, 4; 22:3-5.

Notes: *This statement of teachings identifies the Dunkard Brethren as the strict and conservative group within the Brethren tradition. It includes strong statements on baptism by triune immersion, foot washing, the Lord's Supper, communion, and the holy kiss.*

* * *

STATEMENT OF BELIEF (EMMANUEL'S FELLOWSHIP)

We believe that the Bible teaches authority and discipline in the church, and to be exercised by the church, to help to maintain order and unity of purpose among the members. Titus 2:15, 1 Tim. 5:20, 2nd Thessalonians 3:6-15, 1 Cor. 11:1, 1 Tim. 4:12.

We believe in one God, the Father, Almighty Creator of heaven and earth. And in Jesus Christ, His only begotten son, our Lord. Who was conceived of the Holy Ghost, and born of the virgin Mary. Who suffered under Pontius Pilate, was crucified, died and was buried. Rose again from the dead on the third day, ascended into heaven, and sitteth at the right hand of God, the Almighty Father. From whence He will come to judge the quick and the dead. We believe in the Holy Ghost, in the holy general Christian Church, the communion of saints. We believe in forgiveness of sins, resurrection of the body, and in eternal life.

1. We believe the law of Christ is the supreme law of love. Teaching us to love one another as He has loved us. His love was to seek and to save that which was lost. Luke 19:10, John 13:34, 35.

2. We believe that all men are guilty before God, need to repent, confess and forsake their sin, and to believe and obey God's word. Rom. 3:23, Acts 2:38, Rom. 10:9.

3. We believe in water baptism (as a sign that we have received the Spirit baptism, which gives a regenerated mind to walk in newness of life) upon confession of faith in Christ. One must meet this requirement in order to be baptized. Rom. 6:3-4; Acts 10:47, 1 Peter 3:21, Matt. 3:15, 17.

4. Those admitted to membership are to show evidence of the new birth by their way of life and personal testimony, and are to agree with and be willing to uphold these regulations to the glory of God and for a testimony to the world, living victoriously over sin, walking by faith in the son of God, rightly dividing the word of the truth. Eph. 7:19, 21, 1 Cor. 15:57, 1 John 4:4.

5. We believe that new applicants for membership should serve 6 mo. probationary period in order to become better acquainted with the brotherhood and to prove their testimony.

6. We believe that if one has been taken into the church and fallen away from the truth; and when the church has prayed, fasted, admonished, and exhorted such a person, without acknowledgement, that such a person should be excommunicated from the church. Matt. 18:17 to 19, 1 Cor. 5:11, 2nd Thes. 3:14, 15, Titus 3:10.

7. We believe in the practice of nonresistance in life, in words, and in whatsoever things we do. Whether in Church matters, school problems, paying taxes, occupations or taking up arms, etc. Jer. 17:5, Matt. 5:44, 22:21.

8. We believe in nonconformity, in not being conformed to the things of this world. Members shall not be unequally yoked with unbelievers in business and in other phases of life. They shall abstain from politics, secret societies, labor unions, life insurance, etc. We disapprove of accepting unearned government handouts. 2 Cor. 6:14, 1 John 2:15.

9. We believe in the Lord's Supper as a memorial of His suffering instituted with bread and fruit of the vine for those of like faith and Christian Standards. All who partake must have (a) peace with God, (b) victory over lusts of the flesh, (c) as much as possible peace with their fellow man. Luke 22:19, 1 Cor. 10:21, 11:28, Gal. 5:19.

10. We believe in the Christian ordinances, such as baptism, communion, feet washing, marriage, women's head covering, holy kiss, annointing with oil, etc. 1 Cor. 11:2.

11. We believe that we are called with an high and holy calling to live lives of victory, obedience, and holiness. 1 Pet. 1:15, 16, Acts 5:32, 1 Cor. 16:57.

PRACTICES OF THE CHURCH

1. Our bodies are the temples of God and all that we do or say should be done to His honor and glory. Worldly practices and fleshly lusts, such as strong drink, tobacco, dope, card playing, radios, television, movies, musical instruments, carnivals, circuses, fairs, auto and horse races, public ball games, skating rinks, foolish talk and filthy jokes, games that steal precious time from the Lord, all gatherings that are not edifying, membership in lodges, boys' clubs, etc. are not permitted. Rom. 32, 6:16, 13:13, 1 Cor. 3:16, 6:16-17, Eph. 2:3, 5:3-11, 2nd Tim. 3:4.

2. We believe in the Christian home, the standards of which include regular family worship, and in bringing children up in nurture and admonition of the Lord. Unclean literature is not permitted. Gen. 18:19, Eph. 6:4, 1 John 2:15.

3. Good Stewardship of earthly possessions is encouraged so we can help the poor and extend the kingdom of God with our means. We believe in mission work. Expect each member to participate.

4. Automobiles are to be plain models and black in color, and moderately priced. White sidewalls tires, radio aerials and all unnecessary equipment such as extra chrome etc. are not acceptable.

5. The Bible teaches that the Lord's Day is set aside for special worship, and testimony, and that we must not desecrate it in unnecessary labor, pleasure seeking, joy riding and other unnecessary driving.

6. We believe in purity in courtship. Courtship not recommended before age of 18, and not permitted before age of 17. Also not to be practiced too frequently. Courtship with non-Christians, in dark rooms, autos, on beaches, petting, late hours, and other impure actions are not permitted. Weddings to be simple, with spiritual emphasis.

7. Sisters are to wear the devotional covering made with opaque material corners and strings, we encourage a plain bonnet, consistent in size; not to be mistaken for a hat. Sisters also to wear a cape dress with sufficient length halfway between knee and sole, sleeves to be full length in public, necklines to be full height at all times. No flashy or loud colors, no thin or transparent materials are allowed. No anklets. Black hose not less than service weight and shoes with low heel to be worn. 1 Pet. 3:3, 1 Tim. 2:9, 1 John 2:15-17.

8. Brethern to wear plain suits. Short and rolled up sleeves not permitted in church services. Dress hats are to be plain and black except straw hats. Hair to be parted in middle, not shingled or combed straight back, and to have definite hair line in back. Brethern to wear full beard.

9. Wrist watches not permitted except where duty calls, such as nurses, etc. Jewelery of all descriptions not permitted, including wedding bands.

10. Guidelines for childrens dress, girls hair should not be cut or curled, modestly dressed skirt length below the knees, no anklets. No jewelery permitted. Boys no flat tops, crew cuts or any sort of ridiculous hair cuts. No neckties permitted.

11. These regulations are of a general nature and any member who feels to go beyond these requirements should feel free to do so.

Notes: *Emmanuel's Fellowship is a small conservative Brethren group.*

* * *

THE MESSAGE OF THE BRETHREN MINISTRY (FELLOWSHIP OF GRACE BRETHREN CHURCHES)

THE MESSAGE

The message which Brethren ministers accept as a Divine Entrustment to be heralded to a lost world, finds its sole source and authority in the Bible. This message is one of hope for a lost world and speaks with finality and authority. Fidelity to the apostolic injunction to preach the Word demands our utmost endeavor of mind and heart. We, the members of the National Ministerial Association of the Brethren Church, hold that the essential and constituent elements of our message shall continue to be the following declarations:

1. Our Motto: The Bible, the whole Bible and nothing but the Bible.

2. The Authority and Integrity of the Holy Scriptures. The ministry of the Brethren Church desires to bear testimony to the belief that God's supreme revelation has been made through Jesus Christ, a complete and authentic record of which revelation is the New Testament; and, to the belief that the Holy Scripture of the Old and New Testaments, as originally given, is the infallible record of the perfect, final and authoritative revelation of God's will, altogether sufficient in themselves as a rule of faith and practice.

3. We understand the Basic Content of our Doctrinal Preaching and Teaching to Be:

(1) The Pre-existence, Deity and Incarnation by Virgin Birth of Jesus Christ, the Son of God;

(2) The Fall of Man, his consequent spiritual death and utter sinfulness, and the necessity of his New Birth;

(3) The Vicarious Atonement of the Lord Jesus Christ through the shedding of His own Blood;

(4) The Resurrection of the Lord Jesus Christ in the body in which He suffered and died and His subsequent Glorification at the Right Hand of God;

(5) Justification by personal faith in the Lord Jesus Christ, of which obedience to the will of God and works of righteousness are the evidence and result; the resurrection of the dead; the judgment of the world, and the life everlasting of the just;

(6) The Personality and Deity of the Holy Spirit Who indwells the Christian and is his Comforter and Guide;

(7) The Personal and Visible Return of our Lord Jesus Christ from Heaven as King of Kings and Lord of Lords; the glorious goal for which we are taught to watch, wait and pray;

(8) The Christian should "be not conformed to this world, but be transformed by the renewing of the mind," should not engage in carnal strife and should "swear not at all";

(9) The Christian should observe, as his duty and privilege, the ordinances of our Lord Jesus Christ, among which are (a) baptism of believers by Triune Immersion; (b) confirmation; (c) The Lord's Supper; (d) The Communion of the Bread and Wine; (e) the washing of the saints' feet; and (f) the anointing of the sick with oil.

STATEMENT OF BIBLICAL TRUTHS

The National Fellowship of Brethren Churches, standing firmly on the historic slogan of The Brethren Church,

"The Bible, the whole Bible, and nothing but the Bible," and feeling our responsibility to make known its divine truths, hereby presents the following articles as a Statement in part of those Biblical truths essential to our Christian faith and practice:

1. The verbal inspiration and infallibility of the Bible as the written Word of God.

2. The One Triune God; existing eternally in three persons—the Father, the Son, and the Holy Spirit.

3. The Lord Jesus Christ: His deity, incarnation, virgin birth, sinless life, substitutionary death, bodily resurrection, and heavenly ascension.

4. The Holy Spirit: His personality, deity, and work in creation, preservation, revelation, and redemption.

5. The divine creation of man as a holy being, his subsequent fall into sin, and the hopeless condition of all men apart from Jesus Christ.

6. A complete and eternal salvation by God's grace alone, apart from works of law, received through personal faith in the Lord Jesus Christ and His finished work.

7. The existence and personality of Satan, the great adversary of God: his judgment and final doom.

8. The personal, visible, and premillennial second coming of our Lord Jesus Christ; the time being unrevealed but always imminent.

9. The conscious existence of the dead, the resurrection of the body, final judgment, eternal life of the saved, and everlasting punishment of the lost.

10. The one true Church which is the body and bride of Christ, composed of all true believers of the present age; and the organization of its members in local churches, self-supporting and self-governing, each supreme in its own affairs, but cooperating in fellowship and work.

11. A Christian life of righteousness, good works, and separation unto God from the world and its ways, such as unclean amusements and habits, divorce and remarriage, the swearing of oaths, the use of civil courts to settle disputes between members of our churches, and the taking of human life in carnal strife.

12. The solemn obligations of a worldwide gospel witness; the baptism of believers by triune immersion with the laying on of hands; the training of an evangelistic and Bible-teaching ministry; sacrificial proportionate giving by every believer; a family altar in every home; and prayer with anointing for the sick.

13. The Threefold Communion Service, symbolical of the threefold ministry of our Lord Jesus Christ; consisting of the Washing of the Saints' Feet as a symbol of His present ministry of cleansing, the Lord's Supper as a symbol of His future ministry at His coming, and the Bread and Cup as a symbol of His past ministry.

We want all to know that we take the Bible literally from Genesis to Revelation. The National Fellowship of Breth-

**THE MESSAGE OF THE BRETHREN MINISTRY
(FELLOWSHIP OF GRACE BRETHREN
CHURCHES) (continued)**

ren Churches is strictly a Bible church. The Word of God as the Holy Spirit reveals it is our *supreme rule and authority for faith and practice.*

We believe that these are days of apostasy. Churchmen and whole denominations are departing from the truth of God's Word (Jude 3-4). As a result the church has become largely powerless. Often it has degenerated into a purely social agency.

Therefore, it is supremely important that we understand at the outset the uncompromising position of the NFBC on the whole Word of God (II Tim. 4:1-5), and that continued membership in the church is dependent upon the pastors and churches maintaining this Biblical doctrinal position.

Notes: *The refusal of the Brethren Church (Ashland, Ohio) to adopt The Message of the Brethren Ministry (originally adopted by the National Brethren Ministerial Association in 1921) was one of several factors leading to the formation of the Fellowship of Grace Brethren Churches. In more recent years, the fellowship adopted an additional expanded statement that is specifically premillennial in its eschatology.*

* * *

DOCTRINAL STATEMENT OF THE OLD GERMAN BAPTIST BRETHREN

The Dunkers accept the ancient belief in:

JEHOVAH the God of Abraham, Isaac, and Jacob, and in the Messiah, Jehovah's only Son,

JESUS CHRIST, miraculously born of the Virgin, who saved us from the penalty of sin by willingly shedding His blood as an atonement for sins, and who is now our Resurrected Lord and Master; who strengthens us by His Spirit, the Spirit of Truth, the

HOLY SPIRIT who enables us to overcome the world, the flesh and Satan. We believe that the

BIBLE is the verbally inspired Word of God, and that the

CHURCH is built by Christ; He is her only head, therefore she cannot be overthrown. She stands as a refuge or haven from the sin-engulfing storms of Satan. Her duties involve the faithful preaching of the Gospel, practical obedience to the commands of our Lord, the administration of God's means of grace, and the application of Christian principles in the life and conduct of her membership, thereby presenting an unfailing witness to the world.

We believe

FAITH is simply nothing else but believing the Word of God, taking God at His word, believing without seeing, or even to obey without fully understanding. Faith, without which it is impossible to please God, follows the hearing of the Gospel, is the product of the Word of God in the heart, and prompts to action. The Faith endorsed by the Word of God is never "belief alone," being invariably accompanied by the duties for which faith calls, taking in all that has been enjoined by Christ and the Apostles. With Faith as the "conception" of the "new life,"

REPENTANCE is the heart's response to the divinely wrought sense of conviction in the soul, the result of the Holy Spirit's work condemning the conscience or heart of the guilt of sin, and is the first step fallen humanity can take back toward the bosom of the Father. This is a work each must do for himself, and unless this "first work" is done, everything else seemingly good is useless and worthless. True repentance reclines on the mercy of God for help, cannot do one thing in overcoming the flesh without it. The sinner now sees that through the work of saving grace, he may turn from the desire to sin and be filled with the love for holiness. With Faith as the "conception" and with Repentance as the "prenatal growth" of the new life,

CONFESSION makes known the desire for birth; but neither of these can be said to be birth itself. Not until the body is brought forth has birth transpired; therefore water

BAPTISM is the initatory rite into the church, is for believers only, and is a covenant between God and man. On the part of man it is a seal of faith in Christ and His Word, a renunciation of Satan and sin, and a dedication or complete surrender to the holy life of Christ; on the part of God it is the seal to man of the remission of sins and of the gift of the Holy Ghost. It signifies the burial of the carnal nature and the birth of the new creature by putting on of Christ by being baptized into Him. Children, dying in innocence without baptism, are saved by the virtue of Christ's atonement "for of such is the kingdom of God."

After confessing before God and many witnesses that Jesus is indeed the Christ, the Son of God, and that He brought the Gospel of Salvation from Heaven; and after promising to live a faithful Christian life devoted to Jesus till death or until His coming; after willingly renouncing Satan with all his pernicious ways and all the sinful pleasures of this world; we are then, upon this confession, thrice dipped forward, submersed once into each name of the Godhead, "into the name of the Father, and of the Son, and of the Holy Ghost." This, we believe, is the pattern of the first Christians.

These are the first principles that lead to right standing with God, and they are binding upon all who know them and have it within their power to observe them.

The sinner has his heart changed by faith, his conduct by repentance, and his relation by baptism, but the pardoning act itself takes place in heaven. In "going on unto perfection" we find that true

CONVERSION involves a change of mind, a change of heart, and a change of life and service from selfish and worldly goals to serve the living God. The appearance is changed; speech, conduct, associates—all combine to make manifest the new creature in Christ. He will bear criticism, rebuke, and persecution for Christ's sake and do it without wavering or complaint. He will show love and kindness toward all. If there be any lasting or eternal benefit,

OBEDIENCE must spring from a willing heart. Jesus makes it plain that love of the truth is the only motive which makes obedience acceptable. True obedience is the measure of our faith, and alone can be used as the basis for

SELF EXAMINATION which judgment of self is a lifetime work and not just of passing moment. Especially important before partaking of the communion emblems of His body and blood that we enter not into condemnation, "self judgment" precedes the literal observance of

FEET-WASHING, a command and ordinance in which is exemplified the virtues of faith, love, obedience, humility, service, and sacrifice. As we are "washed" in baptism, so feet-washing symbolizes our need of an additional "washing" or "after cleansing" by the Lord. The

LORD'S SUPPER is a common meal taken at night as did the early Christians and beautifully shows forth the mutual fellowship of love and union that should characterize the people of God in this world of strife and division. Also, the Supper, being a "type," looks forward in anticipation to the "marriage supper of the Lamb," which is the "Lord's Supper" being "fulfilled in the Kingdom of God." After supper we take the

COMMUNION, unleavened bread and fermented wine, which are set apart as emblematical of the broken body and the shed blood of our Lord and Saviour, Jesus Christ. There can be no real communion (a common union) without unity, and fellowship, and purpose. We believe in

CLOSE COMMUNION because there is "common union" only where there exists sufficient union, harmony, and oneness to worship, work, and keep the rest of the ordinances together. We believe in the mystery of the

TRINITY, the Father, Son, and Holy Spirit being equally divine, and also personally distinct from each other. The spiritual baptism of the

HOLY SPIRIT wherein the Spirit dwells within and directs the life of the believer is plainly revealed in God's Word. In this the Spirit comforts the saints and reproves the world of sin. We preach both Faith and

WORKS, believing that man cannot adopt the promises of God without heeding the requirements of Grace. The witness of God's Spirit with man's spirit establishes a reciprocatory relation between the Father and His children. Our simple

WORSHIP consists of reading the Scriptures, preaching, praying, and singing. Musical instruments are not used in worship and the singing is congregational, thus encouraging worship appealing to the understanding and avoiding purely emotional methods. Our favorite position in

PRAYER is kneeling, and as commanded through the Apostle Paul, the sisters always have their heads veiled when praying or prophesying, and the brethren's heads are uncovered in worship. We advocate closet religion in the home; also prayer, singing, family worship and the parental duties of training the children to reverence and love God. The love of God shed abroad in the hearts of His adopted children overflows, and they delight to give expression to that holy love by observing the

HOLY KISS, as oft commanded in the Scriptures, not only on various special occasions, but when greeting one another privately. Thus, the brethren greet the brethren and the sisters the sisters, and between the sexes we greet with a handclasp. Brethren labor for

NONCONFORMITY to the world in all its vain and wicked customs. The church is a light and a life-saving station to men dwelling in darkness and sin. The Scriptures and the spirit of the life of Christ are the guide, "bringing into captivity every thought to the obedience of Christ." Dunkers are willingly subject to every

CIVIL LAW wherein that law does not conflict with the spirit of Christ and demand of us those "things belonging to God." Since God has "made of one blood all nations" we hold that all human life is equally sacred, and therefore we do not join in

WARFARE. Consistency demands that we refrain from supporting the cause of war in any way, also refusing to join or support any peacetime organization which may use violent means. As did our Lord Jesus, we choose to suffer, rather than retaliate, and we refuse all violent methods of self-defense. In short, we believe that the Sermon on the Mount can be lived today, and that it has always been the rule of His Church. True Christians are "peace makers" not "peace breakers." True

CONSCIENTIOUS OBJECTION to war is not found only in literally obeying a few Scriptures but springs from a life in which the Spirit of Jesus has subdued those passions that make violence possible, a "new life" lived on a plane above the causes and occasions of war.

CHURCH DISCIPLINE has for its object, restoration through the principle of correction administered in love. That the Church as a body is held responsible for the condition of the body is clearly defined in the book of Revelation. Dunkers follow "democratic" form of church

GOVERNMENT, for to be scriptural it must be applied with equal respect to every member of the body. Matters of general import for which an answer is not clearly defined in the Scriptures are brought up at an Annual Meeting and those decisions based upon the Spirit and tenor of the Scriptures we consider no less binding than did those Gentiles who received the decision of the Jerusalem council. The sick receive the

ANOINTING with oil (at their request) for the forgiveness of sins and the restoring of health according to the will of God. Brethren generally regard the advances of medical science as an aid to natural healing. This is doing what man has been enjoined to do in taking care of the body, as the temple of the Holy Spirit. All healing, whether in nature or by a special act of His will, is by the power of God. We do not give

OATHS but simply affirm or deny. Oath-taking implies a double standard of honesty, but a follower of Jesus desires to be consistently truthful. Brethren believe that the marriage covenant is irrevocable, that the Scriptures permit separation only on the grounds of fornication, but forbid

DIVORCE. We believe that mixed marriages between believers and unbelievers is unscriptural, and marriage with divorced persons with former companions living constitutes adultery. Thus, it is imperative that in this we maintain a standard above reproach, seeing that no

DOCTRINAL STATEMENT OF THE OLD GERMAN BAPTIST BRETHREN (continued)

institution in nature can be more holy, and none should be more highly respected than that which "God hath joined together." We firmly believe in the imminent, literal

SECOND COMING of Jesus, and that we should each be in a constant state of readiness to meet our Lord should He make His appearance at any hour to receive His Bride, the Church. The way of natural death, for the saints, leads to life. The truth of the

RESURRECTION assures us that death is but the portal to eternity. The Scriptures intimately and inseparably connect the fact of the resurrection of Christ, and that of the resurrection of the saints. The hour of death and the call to

JUDGMENT are universally given to all mankind. "For if we would judge ourselves, we should not be judged." If we repent, confess our sins, and are baptized, we are promised forgiveness for all our sins. The additional Gospel means of self-judgment are given to separate the faithful from a life of sin for the rest of life's journey.

Notes: *The separatism of the Old German Baptist Brethren is best shown in its position on the Lord's Supper, communion, and closed communion.*

* * *

Quakers (Friends)

STATEMENT OF FAITH (EVANGELICAL FRIENDS ALLIANCE)

The Holy Bible:

We believe that the Holy Scriptures were given by the inspiration of God; that there can be no appeal from them to any other authority whatsoever; that they are fully sufficient to make one wise unto salvation through faith which is in Jesus Christ; that the Holy Spirit who inspired the scriptures must ever be its true interpreter as He works through the disciplined and dedicated minds of those within His Church; that any professed guidance which is contrary to these scriptures must be counted as a delusion.

God:

We believe in one God, revealed through the Holy Bible in the person of Jesus Christ; that He is both the Creator and Preserver of all things visible and invisible; that He alone is worthy of worship—honor, glory, dominion, praise, and thanksgiving—both now and forevermore; and that in the unity of the Godhead there exists three persons, Father, Son, and Holy Spirit, inseparable in divinity, power, glory, and eternity.

Jesus Christ:

We believe Jesus Christ to be the only begotton Son of God; that He was conceived by the Holy Spirit and born of the virgin Mary; that He is the express image of the invisible God; and that He combines within Himself both the nature of God and the nature of man in one perfect indivisible personality—the God-man.

We believe that He was crucified as an atonement for the sins of the whole world, making provision whereby man could find the forgiveness of sins, the power for a new life, and be brought back into a perfect relationship with the Father.

We believe that He arose from the dead, ascended to the right hand of God, making intercession for us, and that He will come to earth again to receive His Church unto Himself and to judge the world in righteousness.

Holy Spirit:

We believe the Holy Spirit to be the third person of the Godhead, proceeding from both Father and Son, but equal with them in authority, power, and glory; that He convicts the world of sin, imparts life to the penitent believer, sanctifies the child of God, and enables one by His indwelling presence to love God supremely.

Man:

We believe that God created man in His own image; that he enjoyed unbroken fellowship with his maker; and that his whole life centered in the person of God. We believe that man fell from this original state by an act of transgression; that in this fall man suffered the immediate loss of his perfect relationship to God, making self the center of his life; and that in this act he suffered immediate spiritual death. In this disposition to sin all men are born. We own no principle inherent naturally in man by which he may be saved, except by the grace of our Lord Jesus Christ as a provision for all mankind.

Salvation:

We believe that by the grace of our Lord Jesus Christ, and by the direct and immediate agency of the Holy Spirit, man may be recovered from his fallen state through divine enlightenment, forgiveness of sin, regeneration and sanctification of his affections, and the final glorification of his body; that in this life man may love God with all his heart, soul, mind, and strength; that he may live in victory over sin, and enjoy unbroken fellowship with his Father; and that once more his whole life may center in and revolve around his Creator and Father.

We believe that the experience of sanctification is the work of God's grace by which the affections of men are purified and exalted to a supreme love to God; and the believer is empowered to witness to the living Christ. This is accomplished by the baptism with the Holy Spirit in the life of a dedicated and believing child of God; that this is both an act in which the heart is cleansed from an imperfect relationship and state, and a process in which the life is continuously disciplined into paths of holiness.

The Church:

We believe that all those persons who repent of their sins, and believe in Jesus Christ as their Savior are born again into His kingdom by the Holy Spirit, and that these constitute the church universal of Jesus Christ. This church we believe to be spiritual in nature, universal in scope, holy in character, and redemptive in her life and purpose.

We believe that wherever two or three are gathered together in the name of Christ, He is truly present in the person of the Holy Spirit, and that such an assembly is a local church, the visible expression of His body, and the church universal.

We believe that every believer must relate himself to the local and visible body of Christ being fitly framed together with others into a holy temple in the Lord and builded together for a habitation of His Spirit.

Spiritual Realities:

We believe that both Christian baptism and communion are spiritual realities beyond the mere physical and outward ordinances; that baptism is an inward receiving of the Holy Spirit in which He becomes Lord over all—guiding, cleansing, empowering, and in general representing God to us in immediate experience; that communion is the daily receiving and realization of Jesus Christ as Savior and Lord; that this communion is dependent not only upon the condition of the believer walking daily in the light of Christ, but in the historic act of Christ on Calvary as His body was broken and blood shed once and for all for us; that Christ thus becomes a daily personal spiritual reality known immediately in Christian experience; and that through Him and His baptism God and divine realities are known experientially and immediately.

Christian Work:

We believe that in the church, the believer is committed to both the worship and the work of God; that this work involves not only personal righteousness as the fruit of a new life, but the ministry of evangelism and teaching; that in this commission of Christ every believer is involved in the stewardship of the Kingdom, and that it is fulfilled only by faithful service in and through the fellowship of His Church; and that this work is continuous until Christ comes again calling the Church unto Himself. We believe that all Christians are called upon to witness by word and by deed within a sinful world, not returning evil for evil, but in Christlikeness demonstrating love, forgiveness, and the way of peace.

We believe that in the fellowship of His body, the Holy Spirit gives to every member a gift to be exercised for the mutual advantage of every member in the body, and for the influence of the church upon those outside; that the ministry is such a gift given to certain ones whom God calls and ordains for a special service of leadership in His church; that this service may be that of pastoring, teaching, evangelizing, or administration.

Liberty:

We believe in the doctrine of Christian liberty, and that this liberty is to be granted in all areas that are not essential to one's final salvation. While we recognize that among God's children there are differences of faith and practice, due to our imperfection, we must look forward to the time when we shall all come into a greater unity of the faith. Until then we believe that in essentials there must be unity, that in non-essentials there must be liberty, but in all things there must be charity.

Resurrection and Judgment:

We believe in the second coming of Christ: that at His coming the dead shall be resurrected some to everlasting glory and others to everlasting shame; that we shall all stand before the judgment seat of Christ to receive recompense for the things done in the flesh; that the judgment of the blessed shall be unto heaven, and the judgment of the lost unto hell; that the punishment of the wicked and the blessedness of the righteous shall be everlasting; that this judgment is in the hands of our compassionate Redeemer, who doeth all things after the counsel of His wisdom, love and holiness.

Notes: *The Friends, usually thought of as a noncreedal fellowship, have nevertheless produced a number of statements of belief, especially among those groups in America which were most influenced by Wesleyan evangelicalism in the nineteenth century.*

The basic organizational unit for Friends is the annual meeting, composed of congregations in a given area (in the United States, often a state). Each yearly meeting usually publishes a manual containing doctrinal statements or documents. Yearly meetings may combine nationally into loosely organized associations. The Evangelical Friends Alliance has several conservative evangelical yearly meetings as members, including the Evangelical Friends Church, Eastern Division, the Mid-America Yearly Meeting, and the Rocky Mountain Yearly Meeting.

The Evangelical Friends Alliance is a member of the National Association of Evangelicals. Although the alliance is also a member of the Christian Holiness Association, its statements of belief (and those of its member yearly meetings) do not contain a specific statement of the distinctive holiness doctrine of sanctification as a second definite work of grace in the life of the Christian.

*　　　*　　　*

STATEMENT OF FAITH (EVANGELICAL FRIENDS CHURCH, EASTERN REGION)

GOD

We believe in one eternal, omnipresent, unchanging, personal God; perfect in holiness, wisdom, love, power and justice; without preceding cause or beginning; creator and preserver of all things, visible and invisible.

He exists as one divine being and yet as a trinity of three distinct persons, identical, inseparable, and equal in divinity, power and eternity: God the Father, God the Son, and God the Holy Spirit.

God revealed Himself in the past in many and various ways, though supremely in the person of Jesus Christ. He continues to reveal Himself today through His creation, the Holy Scriptures and the workings of the Holy Spirit in the hearts of men.

He alone is worthy of our worship, honor, praise and thanksgiving, now and forevermore.

JESUS CHRIST

We believe that Jesus Christ, the Word who was with God and was God, is the only begotten Son of God. He was conceived by the Holy Spirit and born of the virgin Mary; and is the express image of the invisible God. He combines within Himself both the nature of God and the nature of man in one perfect indivisible personality—the God-man.

He lived and suffered in the world to show the Way of Life. He was crucified and died as the atonement for the sin of the whole world, making the only provision whereby man can find forgiveness of sins and cleansing from all unrighteousness.

He died in our place and rose again the third day for our justification; He ascended into heaven and sits at the right hand of God, ever living as our only mediator and High Priest making intercession for us, and from there will return again to receive His church unto Himself and to judge the world in righteousness.

THE HOLY SPIRIT

We believe in the Holy Spirit, not as an impersonal principle or influence, but as a divine person, and though distinct from the Father and Son, proceeding from both, with whom He is equal in authority, power, glory, and titles.

He is the divine agent in conviction of sin, regeneration, sanctification and the believers' assurance.

He is given as an indwelling Presence to every believer to be a teacher, guide, and source of comfort. He purifies the heart of the believer and imparts at His own choosing spiritual gifts for service and the building up of the Body of Christ. He produces in believers the fruit of the Spirit so that they may conform to the image of Christ.

HOLY SCRIPTURE

With early Friends, we believe that all Scripture both of the Old and New Testaments is given by inspiration of God, without error in all that it affirms and is the only infallible rule of faith and practice. It is fully authoritative and trustworthy, fully sufficient to all believers now and always, and profitable for teaching, reproof, correction, and training in righteousness.

Thus, the declarations contained in it rest on the authority of God Himself, and there can be no appeal from them to any other authority whatever. They are the only divinely authorized record of the doctrines which we are bound as Christians to believe, and of the moral principles which are to regulate our behavior. Only such doctrines as are contained in the Scripture can be regarded as Articles of Faith. The Holy Spirit, who inspired the Scripture, must ever be its true interpreter. Whatsoever any man says or does which is contrary to the Scripture, though under profession of the guidance of the Spirit, must be reckoned and accounted a delusion.

The Scripture demands of believers complete obedience and is made increasingly open to those who study and obey it.

CREATION

We believe creation to be that free act of the triune God, the Father, Son, and Holy Spirit, by which in the beginning and for His own glory God made, without the use of pre-existing material, the whole visible and invisible universe.

SATAN

We believe in the existence of the Evil One, "that old serpent which is the Devil, and Satan", the old deceiver who by his own choice rebelled against God and became evil, who tempted our first parents to sin, and who through their disobedience brought about the fall of the human race; with all its attendant degeneracy, unhappiness and misery.

Satan has demonstrated his evil character and purpose in his perpetual opposition to Christ by the temptation in the wilderness, and to His people and to His kingdom. But his power is limited, and in God's own time he will be chained and finally cast into the lake of fire.

While Satan is active in this world the Christian, through the power of the Holy Spirit dwelling in him, is able to resist Satan's temptation and have victory over him.

MAN

HIS CREATION: We believe that by a definite act God created man in His own image, holy and capable of knowing and obeying God's will, so that he might glorify God and enjoy His fellowship forever.

HIS FALL: We believe that man fell from this original state by a voluntary act of disobedience. In this fall man suffered the immediate loss of his perfect relationship to God, making self the center of his life. By this act, he suffered spiritual death, and sin entered the world and death by sin, so that death passed upon all.

We further believe that as a consequence of the fall mankind are all born with a nature which is thoroughly sinful and not subject to the law of God, so that only through the operation of the grace of God can they repent and call upon Him. However, by God's grace infants are not under condemnation but are heirs of salvation.

SALVATION

We believe that by the grace of our Lord Jesus Christ through the direct and immediate agency of the Holy Spirit, man may be reconciled to God and recovered from his fallen state through justification, regeneration, sanctification and ultimately the resurrection of his body.

JUSTIFICATION: In response to sinners' repentance, surrender of themselves, and sincere faith in the power and sufficiency of Jesus' atoning death and shed blood, God pardons them from past sins and declares them righteous, not for anything they have done but because of the obedience and atoning death of Christ.

REGENERATION: In response to sinners' repentance, surrender of themselves, and sincere faith in the power and sufficiency of Jesus' atoning death and shed blood, God also by His gracious power makes them new creatures. By the Holy Spirit they are born again into the family of God to a new life of love to God and to men. Their minds are enlightened to understand His truth, and their wills are renewed to do His will, as He begins to conform them to His image. The evidence of this regeneration of the believer is the fruit of the Spirit.

SANCTIFICATION: We believe that children of God at the moment of their conversion do receive the Holy Spirit. As they trust in Him and obey His will, they manifest more and more of the fruit of the Spirit and conform more and more to the likeness of God and thus are being continously sanctified.

It is also the will of God that believers receive the fullness of the Spirit which He will graciously grant in response to their full consecration to His will and their faith in Christ's promises and in His atoning death. Sanctification is thus a process in which the Holy Spirit continuously disciplines the believer into paths of holiness and an act in which He cleanses the heart from an imperfect relationship and state.

We further believe that the fullness of the Holy Spirit does not make believers incapable of choosing to sin, nor even from completely falling away from God, yet it so cleanses and empowers them as to enable them to have victory over sin, to endeavor fully to love God and man, and to witness to the living Christ.

THE CHURCH

We believe that the church is made up of all those from the apostles until now, both the triumphant dead and the living, who through response to God's gracious offer of salvation by repentance of their sins and faith in the Lord Jesus Christ as their Saviour have been born again as new creatures in Christ. This church is spiritual in nature, universal in scope, holy in character, and redemptive in its life and purpose.

Its purposes are to make disciples of all nations by its witness to the grace and love of God and to live as a loving brotherhood who build up one another in the grace and knowledge of God.

The church accomplishes these purposes by its existence as particular local congregations gathered out of the world and as associations of congregations in larger organizations under the leadership and service of those called and gifted to such service. It worships in prayer, thanksgiving and song; diligently studies the Word of God; witnesses to and proclaims the gospel of God's Son; exercises the gifts of the Spirit; administers discipline; and performs works of blessing and service both physical and spiritual to its members and to all men in need.

LAST THINGS

We believe that upon death the bodies of men will return to the dust from which they came. The spirits of the righteous will experience joy and life in the presence of God, but the unrighteous will be separated from His presence in the darkness and torment of their evil.

We believe in the literal and personal return of the Lord Jesus Christ to this earth at a time not revealed. At His return the righteous dead will be raised and the righteous living will be changed to their glorification in bodies like their Lord's glorious resurrected body—bodies which they possessed in earthly life but now with glorified, heavenly qualities. The unrighteous will also be resurrected for the final judgment.

We believe that Christ will consummate His kingdom over men and nations by His final triumph over Satan.

We believe that the Lord Jesus Christ will finally judge all mankind for their belief in Him as demonstrated by commitment of their lives to the way of the cross, the lost to everlasting punishment, the redeemed to eternal blessing and life.

Notes: *The Evangelical Friends Church, Eastern Region is a member of the Evangelical Friends Alliance, which in turn is a member of the National Association of Evangelicals as well as the Christian Holiness Association. In the original text of the church's statement of faith, each sentence is footnoted with Biblical references. These references have been deleted here.*

* * *

DECLARATION OF FAITH [FRIENDS UNITED MEETING—WESTERN YEARLY MEETING (1881)]

We believe in God, the Father Almighty, (I Cor. viii. 6.) Maker of Heaven and earth, (Gen.i.I.) and of all things visible and invisible; and in Jesus Christ, His only son, (John iii. 16.) our Lord, by whom he created all things; (Heb. I. 2.) and in the Holy Spirit, who proceedeth from the Father and the Son; (John XV. 26.) and that these three, the Father, and the Son, and the Holy Spirit, are one in the Eternal Godhead. (John x. 30; Acts v. 3, 4.)

OUR LORD JESUS CHRIST

We believe that Jesus of Nazareth was conceived of the Holy Spirit, (Luke i. 35.) and born of the Virgin Mary, (Matt. i. 18, 25.) and that He is the beloved and only begotten Son of God, in whom the Father is well pleased. (Matt. xvii. 5.) We believe that the eternal Word, who was with God, and was God, was made flesh and dwelt among men in the person of Him, our Lord and Saviour Jesus Christ. (John i. 14,) "In Him dwelleth all the fullness of the Godhead bodily." (Colos. ii. 9.) He is the one perfect man, who hath fulfilled all righteousness, and who was in all points tempted like as we are, yet without sin. (Heb. iv. 15.)

We believe that He died for our sins, (I Cor. xv. 3.) that He was buried, and rose again the third day, (I Cor. xv. 4) that He ascended into Heaven, (Luke xxiv. 51.) and is on the right hand of God, angels and authorities and powers being made subject unto Him. (I Peter iii. 22.) He is the one Mediator between God and man, (I Tim. ii. 5.) our Advocate with the Father, (I John ii. I.) our High-Priest forever, (Heb. vi. 20.) who is able to save them to the uttermost that come unto God by Him, seeing He ever liveth to make intercession for them. (Heb. vii. 25.) He baptizes with the Holy Spirit. (Matt. iii. II.) He is the Shepherd and Bishop of souls, (I Peter ii. 25.) the Head over all things to the Church, (Ephes. i. 22.) the King who reigns in righteousness, the Prince of Peace. (Isaiah ix. 6, 7.) By Him the world shall be judged in righteousness, for the Father judgeth no man, but hath committed all judgment unto the Son, that all men should honor the Son, even as they honor the Father. [John v. 22, 23.] We believe

DECLARATION OF FAITH [FRIENDS UNITED MEETING— WESTERN YEARLY MEETING (1881)] (continued)

in the Deity and manhood of our Lord Jesus Christ, [Heb. i. 8; ii. 16, 17.] and that His willing sacrifice [John x. 17, 18.] upon the cross was the one propitiation and atonement for the sins of the whole world, wherein God hath declared his righteousness, that He might be just, and the justifier of him that believeth in Jesus. [Rom. iii. 24, 25, 26.] He is the Lamb of God, without blemish and without spot, with whose precious blood we are redeemed. [I Peter i. 18, 19.] The remission of sins which any partake of is only in and by virtue of that most satisfactory sacrifice. [Acts iv. 12; Heb. ix. 22.] We sincerely confess and believe in Jesus Christ, both as He is the true God and perfect man. We confess that Divine Honor and worship are due to Him, and that He is in true faith to be prayed unto, and the name of the Lord Jesus Christ be called upon, as the primitive Christians did, because of the glorious union, or oneness, of the Father and the Son, and that we can not acceptably offer up prayers or praises to God, nor receive a gracious answer or blessing from Him, but in and through his dear Son, Christ. 1693.

THE HOLY SPIRIT

We believe that the Holy Spirit is, in the unity of the Eternal Godhead, one with the Father and the Son; [Acts v. 3, 4.] that He is the promise of the Father [Acts i. 4, 5.] whom Christ declared He would send in His name: [John xiv. 26.] that He is come and convicts the world of sin; that he leads to repentance towards God, [Rom. ii. 4.] and, as the Gospel is known, to faith in the Lord Jesus Christ. Coming in the name [John xiv. 26.] and in the authority of the risen and ascended Saviour, the Holy Spirit is the most precious pledge of his continued love and care. He glorifies the Saviour and takes of the things of Christ and gives them as a realized possession to the believing soul. He dwells in the hearts of believers according to the promise of the Saviour; "I will pray the Father, and He shall give you another Comforter, [John xvi. 7-15.] that He may abide with you forever." He opens to them the truths of the Gospel as set forth in Holy Scripture, and as they exercise faith, guides, sanctifies, comforts and supports them. [John xiv. 16, 17.]

His light must ever be distinguished, both from the conscience he illumines, and from the natural faculty of reason, which, when unsubjected to His holy influences, is, in the things of God, very foolishness. [I Cor. ii. 14.]

We believe that the qualification for the Lord's service in the enduement of power for His work is bestowed on His children through the reception and baptism of the Holy Ghost. [Acts ii. 16-18.]

The Holy Spirit is the seal of reconciliation to the humble believer in Jesus, the earnest and the foretaste of the full communion and perfect joy which are reserved for them that endure unto the end. [Ephes. i, 13, 14.]

THE HOLY SCRIPTURES

It is the belief of the Society of Friends, that the Holy Scriptures of the Old and New Testament were given by inspiration of God; [2 Tim. iii. 15-17.] that, therefore, the declarations contained in them rest on the authority of God Himself, and that there can be no appeal from them to any other authority whatsoever; that they are able to make wise unto salvation, through faith which is in Christ Jesus. "These are written that ye might believe that Jesus is the Christ, the Son of God; and that believing ye might have life through his name." [John xx. 31.] The Scriptures are the only divinely authorized record of the doctrines which we are bound as Christians to accept, and of the moral principles which are to regulate our actions. No one can be required to believe as an article of faith any doctrine which is not contained in them; [Isaiah viii. 20.] and whatsoever any one says or does contrary to the Scriptures, though under profession of the immediate guidance of the Holy Spirit, must be reckoned and accounted a delusion of the Devil. [Rev. xxii. 18, 19; Gal. i. 8-12.]

MAN'S CREATION AND FALL

It pleased God in His wisdom and goodness, to create man out of the dust of the earth, and to breathe into his nostrils the breath of life, so that man became a "living soul," [Gen. ii. 7.] formed after the image and likeness of God, capable of fulfilling the divine law, and of holding communion with his Maker. Being free to obey or to disobey, under the temptation of Satan, through unbelief he fell into transgression, [Gen. iii. 6.] and thereby lost that spiritual life of righteousness in which he was created; and so death passed upon him as the inevitable consequence of his sin. [Rom. v. 12.] As the children of fallen Adam, all mankind bear his image, [Gen. v. 3.] and partake of his nature: and until created anew in Christ Jesus by the regenerating power of the Holy Spirit they are fallen, degenerated, and dead to the divine life. [I Cor. xv. 21, 22.]

But while we hold these views of the lost condition of man in the fall, we rejoice to believe that sin is not imputed to any until they transgress the divine law after sufficient capacity has been given to understand it, and that infants, though inheriting this fallen nature, are saved, in the infinite mercy of God, through the redemption, which is in Christ Jesus. [Mark x. 14.]

JUSTIFICATION AND SANCTIFICATION

"God so loved the world that He gave His only begotten Son, that whosoever believeth in Him should not perish but have everlasting life." [John iii. 16.]

We believe that justification is of God's free grace [Rom iii. 24, 25.] through which, upon repentance and faith, He pardons our sins and accepts us as righteous in His sight for the sake of the Lord Jesus Christ; [Rom. v. I.] that it is received, not because of our works, but of our acceptance of God's mercy in Christ Jesus; [Titus. iii. 5.] that through faith in Him and His atoning blood, the guilt of sin is taken away, and we stand reconciled to God. [Colos. i. 19, 20.]

We believe that in connection with Justification is Regeneration; that being reconciled to God by the death of His Son, we are saved by His life, [Rom. v. 10.] a new heart is given and new desires, old things are passed away, and we become children of God through faith in Christ Jesus. [Ezek. xxxvi. 25-27.] Sanctification, or being made holy, is experienced in connection with justification, in so far that every pardoned sinner, on account of faith in Christ, is clothed with a measure of His righteousness and receives the promised Holy Spirit. [I Cor. vi. II.] The provisions of God's grace are sufficient to deliver from the power of evil, John xvii. 15,] as well as from the guilt of sin, and to enable His believing children always to triumph in Christ. [2 Cor. ii. 14.] This is to be experienced by faith: "according to your faith be it unto you." [Matt. ix. 29.] Whoever submits himself wholly to God, believing His promises, and exercises faith in Christ Jesus, will have his heart continually cleansed from all sin by His precious blood, [I John i.-7.] and through the renewing, refining power of the Holy Spirit be brought into perfect conformity to the will of God, [Rom. xii. 2.] love him with all his heart, mind, soul and strength, and be able to say with the Apostle Paul: "The law of the spirit of life in Christ Jesus hath made me free from the law of sin and death." [Rom. viii. 2.] "This is the will of God, even your sanctification," and if any fall short of this experience, it is because they frustrate the grace of God. [Ephes. v. 25-27.]

RESURRECTION OF THE DEAD AND THE FINAL JUDGMENT

Concerning the resurrection of the dead, and the great day of judgment yet to come, beyond the grave, or after death, and Christ's coming without us, to judge the quick and the dead: (as divers questions are put in such terms,) what the Holy Scriptures plainly declare and testify in these matters, we have been always ready to embrace.

1. For the doctrine of the resurrection; if, in this life only, we have hope in Christ, we are of all men most miserable. [I Cor. x. v. 19.] We sincerely believe, not only a resurrection in Christ from the fallen sinful state here, but a rising and ascending into glory with him hereafter: that when he at last appears, we may appear with him in glory. [Col. iii. 4; I John iii. 2.]

But that all the wicked who live in rebellion against the light of grace, and die finally impenitent, shall come forth to the resurrection of condemnation.

"For our conversation is in heaven, from whence also we look for the Savior, the Lord Jesus Christ, who shall change our vile body, that it may be fashioned like unto his glorious body according to the working whereby he is able even to subdue all things unto himself." [Phill. iii. 20-21.]

And that the soul or spirit of every man and woman shall be reserved in its own distinct and proper being, and every seed (yea every soul) shall have its proper body, as God is pleased to give it. [I Cor. xv.]

It is sown a natural body; it is raised a spiritual body. There is a natural body, and there is a spiritual body. That being first which is natural, and afterward that which is spiritual. And though it is said, this corruptible shall put on incorruption, and this mortal shall put on immortality; the change shall be such as flesh and blood cannot inherit the kingdom of God, neither doth corruption inherit incorruption. (I Cor. xv.) We shall be raised out of all corruption and corruptibility, out of all mortality; and the children of God and of the resurrection shall be equal to the Angels of God in heaven. And as the celestial bodies do far excel terrestrial, so we expect our spiritual bodies in the resurrection shall far excel what our bodies now are.

2. For the doctrine of eternal judgment; God hath committed all judgment unto his Son Jesus Christ; and he is Judge both of quick and dead, and of the states and ends of all mankind. [John v. 22, 27; Acts x, 42; 2 Timothy iv, I; I Peter iv, 5.]

That there shall be hereafter a greater harvest, which is the end of the world, a great day of judgment, and concerning the judgment of that great day, the Holy Scripture is clear. [Matt. xiii. 39, 40, 41; ch. x. 15, and xi. 24; Jude. 6.]"When the Son of Man cometh in His glory, and all the holy angels with him, then shall he sit upon the throne of his glory, and before him shall be gathered all nations," &c. [Matt. xxv. 31, 32, to the end, compared with ch. xxii, 31; Mark viii, 38, Luke ix, 26, and I Cor. xv, 52; 2 Thess, i, 7, 8, to the end, and I Thess. iv, 16; Rev. xx, 12, 13, 14, 15: John v, 24-29.]

THE EVIL SPIRIT

We believe in the existence of an evil being, distinct from man, who tempted our first parents to sin, and through their disobedience wrought the fall of our race, whom the Saviour met and resisted when tempted in the wilderness.

In the degeneracy of man, and all its consequent woes; in the crucifixion of the Son of God; and in all his mighty opposition to the Messiah's reign in all ages, Satan has developed, and still continues to develop, the malignity of his character and purposes. His power is limited, and in God's own time he will be chained, and finally "cast into the lake of fire." [John xii. 31; Eph. ii, 2; 2 Cor. iv. 4; Rev. xx. 2; I John v. 18; I Peter v. 8; John viii, 44; Matt. xii, 24; 2 Cor. vi. 15; Rev. xii. 10, &c.]

CONCERNING THE SABBATH,

which, since the time of Christ, is observed on the First day of the week.

The observance of a day of worship and rest is traced back to the time of the creation, when, it is said, "And on the seventh day God ended His work, which He had made; and He rested on the seventh day from all His works which He had made; And God blessed the seventh day, and sanctified it." We feel ourselves religiously bound to observe the spirit of the Fourth Commandment, and to regard one day in seven, as a day of rest and devotion. And since, in accordance with the practice of the apostles and early church, Christians by common consent, have set apart for religious services the day of the week upon which our Saviour rose from the dead, it is the judgment of the Yearly Meeting that Friends, and others in their employ, should lay aside all avocations of a temporal nature in which they are engaged, and devote the time to the important duties of the day, in accordance with its sacred associations. This observance is of so much importance to the preservation of piety and virtue, and the neglect of it so evidently marked with irreligion, and frequently with immorality, that every reasonable consideration recommends a faithful maintenance of this duty, as affording an opportunity which many could not otherwise obtain of receiving religious instruction and improvement, and of publicly worshiping our Heavenly Father. We therefore earnestly advise all our members to avoid unprofitably passing their time on this day of the week, either in listless idleness, or in indulging in mere social pastime, but rather devoting themselves to such reading, conversation and meditation, as will most advance their spiritual welfare.

BAPTISM

"One Lord, one Faith, one Baptism." (Ephes. iv. 5.) "John answered, saying unto them all, I indeed baptize you with water; but one mightier than I cometh, the latchet of whose shoes I am not worthy to unloose; he shall baptize you with the Holy Ghost, and with fire." (Luke iii. 16.)

We believe the one and saving baptism of the Gospel dispensation is that of Christ, who baptizes his people with the Holy Ghost. The ordinances instituted by God under the law were typical. When Christ the great antitype came and fulfilled the law, he took away the handwriting of ordinances, "nailing it to His cross," (Col. ii. 14,) and since He opened the new and living way, which He hath consecrated for us, through the Vail, that is to say, His flesh, we have access by faith, and enter into the holiest by the blood of Jesus, without the intervention of priest, or ordinance, or any mediation, but that of Him, the one Mediator. (Heb. x. 19, 22.)

We believe that he established no new rite or ordinance, and that the "one baptism," which now saveth, and which is essential to living membership in His church, is that which He himself administers as the glorious Minister of the sanctuary—the baptism of the Holy Spirit—as saith the apostle, "by one spirit are ye all baptized into one body." (I Cor. xii. 13.)

THE SUPPER OF THE LORD

We believe that the true supper of the Lord is the Communion which His believeing children are enabled to hold with Him, through the realization of the presence of the Lord Jesus Christ in their hearts, who has cleansed them from all sin, through the offering of His body, and the shedding of His blood upon the cross.

This communion is described by Him in the words: "Behold, I stand at the door and knock; if any man hear my voice, and open the door, I will come into him, and sup with him, and he with me." [Rev. iii. 20.]

We believe this experience to be essential to the life of the Christian. It is only in the strength of this communion that he can pursue his heavenward journey, or bring forth fruit unto holiness; for, saith our blessed Lord, "Except ye eat the flesh of the son of man and drink His blood, ye have no life in you." [John vi. 53-63.]

PUBLIC WORSHIP

God is a Spirit, and they that worship Him, must worship Him in Spirit, and in truth. [John iv. 24.] We recognize worship as the adoring response of the heart and mind to the influence of the Spirit of God, whether in silent or vocal prayer, preaching the word, reading the Holy Scriptures, or in singing His praise. The preparation of the heart and the answer of the tongue are of the Lord.

Having become His children through faith in the Lord Jesus Christ, it is our privilege to meet together and unite in the worship of Almighty God; to wait upon Him for the renewal of our strength, [Isaiah x. 31,] for communion with Him and with one another, for the edification of believers in the exercise of spiritual gifts, and for the declaration of the glad tidings of salvation to the unconverted who may gather with us. [I Cor. xiv. 26.]

By the immediate operations of the Holy Spirit, the Head of the Church alone selects and qualifies those who are to present His messages, or to engage in other service for Him, and hence we cannot admit of a formal arrangement of exercises, or commit them to any individual. [I Cor. xii. 3-6.]

The worship of any heart or assembly most glorifies God, which most perfectly responds to the promptings of His Spirit, whether it be in vocal service or in silent adoration.

THE MINISTRY

We believe the preaching of the Gospel is one of the means divinely appointed for the spreading of glad tidings of life and salvation through our crucified Redeemer, for the awakening and conversion of sinners, and for the comfort and edification of believers. [Matt. xxviii. 19,20.]

As it is prerogative of the great Head of the Church alone, to select and call the ministers of his Gospel, so we believe both the gift and the qualification to exercise it must be derived immediately from Him, and that, as in the primitive church, so now also, he confers them on women as well as men, agreeably to the prophecy recited by the Apostle Peter: "It shall come to pass in the last days, saith God, I will pour out of my Spirit upon all flesh; and your sons and your daughters shall prophesy;" [Acts ii. 16, 18,] respecting which the apostle declares, "the promises is unto you and to your children, and to all that are afar off, even as many as the Lord our God shall call." As this gift is freely received, so it is to be freely exercised, in simple obedience to the will of God.

The Apostle Paul in speaking of his ministry declares, "I neither received it of man, neither was I taught it, but by the revelation of Jesus Christ; [Gal. i. 12,] that the exercise of it was not in the words which man's wisdom teacheth, but which the Holy Ghost teacheth; and that his speech and his preaching was not with enticing words of man's wisdom, but in demonstration of the Spirit and of power; that the faith of his hearers might not stand in the wisdom of men, but in the power of God. [I Cor. ii. 4, 5.] Nothing but power from on high, renewedly furnished, can enable men to preach the Gospel. A clear apprehension of Scripture doctrine, or a heart enlarged in love to others, is not sufficient for this work. Whatever may be the talents or Scriptural knowledge of any, unless there be a distinct call to the ministry our Society cannot acknowledge it.

While the Church cannot confer Spiritual gifts, it is its duty to recognize and foster them, and to promote their efficiency by all the means in its power. And while on the one hand the Gospel should never be preached for money, [Matt. x. 8,] on the other it is the duty of the Church to make such provision that it shall never be hindered for want of it. [I Cor. ix. 13, 14.]

PRAYER

We have ever believed in the obligation of prayer, both silent and vocal. We should cultivate the habit of frequently turning the mind to God in prayer and praise, breathing our secret desires and aspirations unto Him. This should be done, not only when we are apart from others, but also in the midst of our ordinary engagements. Prayer is the result of a feeling of need and dependence upon God. The condition of heart and mind which cries, in substance, "God be merciful to me a sinner," [Luke xviii. 13,] must precede pardon and remission of sins. At every stage, prayer is essential to Christian life. [Phil. iv. 6.]

Prayer and praise are indispensable to a growth in grace, and for a qualification for those duties which devolve upon every Christian; that without these, any religious experience which may have been gained will finally be lost.

Without prayer there can be no acceptable worship. It is therefore incumbent upon all Christians, in their meetings especially, to seek after Divine help to offer spiritual sacrifices, acceptable to God by Jesus Christ. [I Peter ii. 5.] Vocal prayer, uttered in response to the promptings of the Holy Spirit, is an important part of public worship; and whenever God's people meet together in his name, they should reverently seek unto Him in united prayer. [I Tim. ii. I—3.]

We would encourage parents and heads of families to be faithful in the exercise of this privilege before their children or households, and instruct and admonish them to faithfulness in this exercise. The qualification for such services may differ in degree from that which should be looked for on more public occasions. The sense of need, of parental responsibility, of the priceless value of the souls entrusted to our care, not only warrant, but require, such acts of dedication, whilst our countless blessings claim the tribute of praise from thankful hearts.

The spirit of prayer and thanksgiving will be bestowed upon us if we duly ask for it; and thus to ask is a prayer which may be safely regarded as always in accordance with the Divine will. "If ye, then, being evil, know how to give good gifts unto your children, how much more shall your Heavenly Father give the Holy Spirit to them that ask Him." [Luke xi. 13.]

"I will therefore that men pray everywhere, lifting up holy hands, without wrath and doubting." [I Tim. ii. 8.]

WAR

"From whence come wars and fightings among you? Come they not hence even of your lusts that war in your members?" [James iv. I.]

War, and keeping about our persons weapons for self-defense, conflict with and are a violation of the principles, precepts, and injunctions of the Gospel, which brings peace on earth and good will toward men. War is entirely incompatible with the commands of our holy Redeemer, "I say unto you that ye resist not evil," "Love your enemies, bless them that curse you, do good to them that hate you, and pray for them which despitefully use you and persecute you; that ye may be the children of your Father which is in Heaven; for He maketh His sun to rise on the evil and the good, and sendeth rain on the just and on the unjust. [Matt. v. 39. 44. 45.]

The emphatic prayer of our Lord, "Forgive us our debts, as we forgive our debtors," [Matt. vi. 12,] and His declaration, "If ye forgive not men their trespasses, neither will your Father forgive your trespasses," [Matt. vi. 15.] continue of binding force. No Divine injunction or command that is binding upon individuals, under the Christian dispensation, can be rendered void by any number of individuals in a collective capacity, as nations or otherwise. The prophecy which foretold the coming of the Messiah declared him to be the Prince of Peace; [Isaiah ix. 6,] and his birth was announced by the Heavenly anthem, "Glory to God in the highest, and on earth peace, goodwill toward men." [Luke ii. 14.]

CAPITAL PUNISHMENT

The fundamental moral law has ever been, "Thou shalt not kill." We accept that Christ, in the New Testament, has abrogated the law of retribution in the Old Testament, requiring men to inflict by Divine authority the death penalty; and now, "Vengeance is mine; I will repay," saith the Lord. To neither men as citizens, or as rulers, is given the right to inflict the death penalty upon their fellow-men.

OATHS

Our Lord evidently forbade a kind of swearing which had been allowed before: "Ye have heard that it hath been said by them of old time, thou shalt not forswear thyself, but shalt perform unto the Lord thine oaths; but I say unto you, swear not at all, neither by Heaven, for it is God's throne, nor the earth, for it is His footstool; neither by Jerusalem, for it is the city of the Great King; neither shalt thou swear by thy head, because thou canst not make one hair white or black; but let your communication be yea, yea, nay, nay; for whatsoever is more than these cometh of evil." [Matt. v. 33-37.] And the Apostle James declared, "But above all things, my brethren, swear not, neither by heaven, neither by the earth, neither by any other oath; but let your yea be yea, your nay, nay, lest ye fall into condemnation." [James v. 12.]

We therefore consider the prohibition to include judicial oaths, and refuse, for conscience sake, either to administer or take an oath. In courts of law and in the authentication of documents, instead of taking an oath we make affirmation to the truth of that which we assert.

DECLARATION OF FAITH, AS STATED IN THE EPISTLE OF GEORGE FOX, TO THE GOVERNOR OF BARBADOS, 1671

We own and believe in the only wise, omnipotent, and everlasting God, the Creator of all things in Heaven and in Earth, and the Preserver of all that He hath made; who is God over all, blessed forever; to whom be all honor, glory, dominion, praise, and thanksgiving, both now and forevermore! And we own and believe in Jesus Christ, His beloved and only begotten Son, in whom He is well pleased; who was conceived by the Holy Ghost and born of the Virgin Mary; in whom we have redemption through His blood, even the forgiveness of sins; who is the express image of the invisible God, the first born of every creature, by whom were all things created that are in heaven and in earth, visible and invisible, whether they be thrones, dominions, principalities or powers; all things were created by Him. And we own and believe that He was made a sacrifice for sin, who knew no sin, neither was guile found in His mouth; that He was crucified for us in the flesh without the gates of Jerusalem; and that he was buried and rose again the third day by the power of His Father for our justification; and that He ascended up into heaven, and now sitteth at the right hand of God. This Jesus, who was the foundation of the holy prophets and apostles, is our foundation, and we believe there is no other foundation to be laid but that which is laid, even Christ Jesus; who tasted death for every man, shed His blood for all men, is the propitiation for our sins, and not for ours only, but also for the sins of the whole world; according as John the Baptist testified of Him, when he said: "Behold the Lamb of God which taketh away the sin of the world," [John i. 29.] We believe that He alone is our Redeemer and Saviour, the Captain of our salvation (who saves us from sin, as well as from hell and from the wrath to come, and destroys the devil and his works). He is the seed of the woman that bruiseth the serpent's head, to wit, Christ Jesus, the Alpha and Omega, the First and the Last; He is, as the Scriptures of truth say of Him, our wisdom, righteousness, sanctification, and redemption; neither is there salvation in any other, for there is no other name under heaven given among men, whereby we must be saved. He alone is the Shepherd and Bishop of our souls; He is our Prophet whom Moses long since testified of, saying, "A Prophet shall the Lord your God raise up unto you of your brethren, like unto me; Him shall ye hear in all things, whatsoever He shall say unto you: and it shall come to pass, that every soul which will not hear that Prophet shall be destroyed from among the people." [Acts ii. 22, 23.] He it is that has now come, "and hath given us an understanding, that we know Him that is true." He rules in our hearts by His law of love and of life, and makes us free from the law of sin and death. We have no life but by Him, for He is the quickening Spirit, the second Adam, the Lord from heaven by whose blood we are cleansed, and our consciences sprinkled from dead works to serve the living God. He is our Mediator that makes peace and reconciliation between God offended and us offending; He being the Oath of God, the new covenant of light, life, grace, and peace, the author and finisher of our faith. This Lord Jesus Christ, the heavenly man, the Emmanuel, God with us, we all own and believe in; He whom the high-priest raged against, and said he had spoken blasphemy; whom the priests and elders of the Jews took counsel together against, and put to death; the same whom Judas betrayed for thirty pieces of silver, which the priests gave him as a reward for his treason; who also gave large money to the soldiers to broach an horrible lie, namely, "That His disciples came and stole Him away by night whilst they slept." After He was risen from the dead, the history of the Acts of the Apostles sets forth how the chief priests and elders persecuted the disciples of this Jesus for preaching Christ and His resurrection. This, we say, is that Lord Jesus Christ, whom we own to be our life and salvation.

Concerning the Holy Scriptures, we believe that they were given forth by the Holy Spirit of God, through the holy men of God, who, as the Scripture itself declares (2 Peter i. 21), spake as they were moved by the Holy Ghost. We believe they are to be read, believed, and fulfilled—he that fulfills them is Christ—and they are "profitable for doctrine, for reproof, for correction, for instruction in righteousness, that the man of God may be perfect, thoroughly furnished unto all good works," (2 Tim. iii. 16, 17); and are able to make wise unto salvation, "through faith which is in Christ Jesus."

We believe the Holy Scriptures are the words of God, for it is said in Exodus xx. I; "God spake all these words, saying," etc., meaning the ten commandments given forth upon Mount Sinai; and in Revelation xxii. 18, 19, saith John, "I testify unto every man that heareth the words of the prophecy of this book. If any man shall add unto these things." "And if any man shall take away from the words of the book of this prophecy" (not the word). So in Luke i, 20: "Because thou believest not my words;" and in John v. 47; xv. 7; xiv. 23; xii. 47. So that we call the Holy Scriptures, as Christ, the Apostles, and holy men of God called them—the words of God.

We declare that we esteem it a duty incumbent on us to pray with and for, to teach, instruct, and admonish those in and belonging to our families. This being a command of the Lord, disobedience thereunto will provoke His displeasure, as may be seen in Jeremiah x. 25: "Pour out Thy fury upon the heathen that know Thee not, and upon the families that call not upon Thy name." Now Negroes, Tawnies, and Indians make up a very great part of the families in this island, for whom an account will be required by Him who comes to judge both quick and dead, at the great day of judgment, when every one shall be rewarded according to the deeds done in the body, whether they be evil—at that day, we say, of the resurrection both of the good and of the bad, of the just and of the unjust, "when the Lord Jesus shall be revealed from heaven with His mighty angels in flaming fire, taking vengeance on them that know not God and obey not the Gospel of our Lord Jesus Christ; who shall be punished with everlasting destruction from the presence of the Lord, and from the glory of His power; when He shall come to be glorified in His Saints, and to be admired in all them that believe, in that day." (2 Thess, i. 7, 10; 2 Peter iii. 3, 7.)

Notes: *This older statement of the Western Yearly Meeting is typical of those nineteenth-century meetings which eventually combined to create the Friends' Five Years Meeting (now the Friends United Meeting). This statement was in effect until 1887, when a new statement was written at the first of the conferences held to pursue union with other yearly meetings. It includes a letter from George Fox, founder of the Quakers, to the Governor of Barbados.*

ESSENTIAL TRUTHS AND GENERAL DOCTRINAL STATEMENTS (FRIENDS UNITED MEETING—WESTERN YEARLY MEETING)

ESSENTIAL TRUTHS

The vital principle of the Christian faith is the truth that man's salvation and higher life are personal matters between the individual soul and God.

Salvation is deliverance from sin and possession of spiritual life. This comes through a personal faith in Jesus Christ as the Saviour, Who, through His love and sacrifice draws us to Him.

Conviction for sin is awakened by the operation of the Holy Spirit causing the soul to feel its need of reconciliation with God. When Christ is seen as the only hope of salvation, and a man yields to Him, he is brought into newness of life, and realizes that his sonship to God has become an actual reality. This transformation is wrought without the necessary agency of any human priest, or ordinance, or ceremony whatsoever. A changed nature and life bear witness to this new relation to Him.

The whole spiritual life grows out of the soul's relation to God and its co-operation with Him, not from any outward or traditional observances.

Christ Himself baptizes the surrendered soul with the Holy Spirit, enduing it with power, bestowing gifts for service. This is an efficient baptism, a direct incoming of divine power for the transformation and control of the whole man. Christ Himself is the Spiritual bread which nourishes the soul, and He thus enters into and becomes a part of the being of those who partake of Him. This participation with Christ and apprehension of Him become the goal of life for the Christian. Those who thus enter into oneness with Him become also joined in living union with each other as members of one body.

Both worship and Christian fellowship spring out of this immediate relation of believing souls with their Lord.

The Holy Scriptures were given by inspiration of God and are the divinely authorized record of the doctrines which Christians are bound to accept, and of the moral principles which are to regulate their lives and actions. In them, as interpreted and unfolded by the Holy Spirit, is an ever fresh and unfailing source of spiritual truth for the proper guidance of life and practice.

The doctrines of the apostolic days are held by the Friends as essentials of Christianity. The Fatherhood of God, the Deity and humanity of the Son; the gift of the Holy Spirit; the atonement through Jesus Christ by which men are reconciled to God; the Resurrection; the High-priesthood of Christ, and the individual priesthood of believers, are most precious truths, to be held not as traditional dogmas, but as vital, life giving realities.

The sinful condition of man and his proneness to yield to temptation, the world's absolute need of a Saviour, and the cleansing from sin in forgiveness and sanctification through the blood of Jesus Christ, are unceasing incentives to all who believe to become laborers together with God in extending His kingdom. By this high calling the Friends

are pledged to the proclamation of the truth wherever the Spirit leads, both in home and in foreign fields.

The indwelling Spirit guides and controls the surrendered life, and the Christian's constant and supreme business is obedience to Him. But while the importance of individual guidance and obedience is thus emphasized this fact gives no ground for license; the sanctified conclusions of the Church are above the judgment of a single individual.

The Friends find no scriptural evidence or authority for any form or degree of sacerdotalism in the Christian Church, or for the establishment of any ordinance or ceremonial rite for perpetual observance. The teachings of Jesus Christ concerning the spiritual nature of religion, the impossibility of promoting the spiritual life by the ceremonial application of material things, the fact that faith in Jesus Christ Himself is all-sufficient, the purpose of His life, death, resurrection and ascension, and His presence in the believer's heart, virtually destroys every ceremonial system and points the soul to the only satisfying source of spiritual life and power.

With faith in the wisdom of Almighty God, the Father, the Son and the Holy Spirit, and believing that it is His purpose to make His Church on earth a power for righteousness and truth, the Friends labor for the alleviation of human suffering; for the intellectual, moral and spiritual elevation of mankind; and for purified and exalted citizenship. The Friends believe war to be incompatible with Christianity, and seek to promote peaceful methods for the settlement of all the differences between nations and between men.

It is an essential part of the faith that a man should be in truth what he professes in word, and the underlying principle of life and action for individuals, and also for society, is transformation through the power of God, and implicit obedience to His revealed will.

For more explicit and extended statements of belief, reference is made to those officially put forth at various times, especially to the letter of George Fox to the Governor of Barbados in 1671, and to the Declaration of Faith issued by the Richmond Conference in 1887.

GENERAL DOCTRINAL STATEMENTS

EXTRACT FROM GEORGE FOX'S LETTER TO THE GOVERNOR OF BARBADOS, 1671

We do own and believe in God, the only wise, omnipotent, and evelasting God, the Creator of all things both in heaven and in earth, and the Preserver of all that He hath made; who is God over all, blessed forever; to whom be all honor and glory, dominion, praise and thanksgiving, both now and forevermore.

And we own and believe in Jesus Christ, His beloved and only-begotten Son, in whom He is well pleased; who was conceived by the Holy Ghost, and born of the Virgin Mary; in whom we have redemption through His blood, even the forgiveness of sins; who is the express image of the invisible God, the first-born of every creature, by whom were all things created that are in heaven and that are in earth, visible and invisible, whether they be thrones

ESSENTIAL TRUTHS AND GENERAL DOCTRINAL STATEMENTS [FRIENDS UNITED MEETING—WESTERN YEARLY MEETING] (continued)

or dominions, principalities, or powers; all things were created by Him. And we do own and believe that He was made a sacrifice for sin, who knew no sin, neither was guile found in His mouth; that He was crucified for us in the flesh, without the gates of Jerusalem; and that He was buried, and rose again the third day by the power of His Father, for our justification; and that He ascended up into heaven, and now sitteth at the right hand of God. This Jesus, who was the foundation of the holy prophets and apostles, is our foundation; and we believe that there is no other foundation to be laid than that which is laid, even Christ Jesus; who tasted death for every man, shed His blood for all men and is the propitiation for our sins, and not for ours only, but also for the sins of the whole world according as John the Baptist testified of Him, when he said, "Behold the Lamb of God, that taketh away the sin of the world!" (John 1:29.) We believe that He alone is our Redeemer and Saviour, even the captain of our salvation, who saves us from sin, as well as from hell and the wrath to come, and destroys the devil and his works. He is the Seed of the woman that bruises the serpent's head, to wit, Jesus Christ, the Alpha and Omega, the First and the Last. He is (as the Scriptures of truth say of Him) our wisdom and righteousness, justification, and redemption; neither is there salvation in any other, for there is no other name under heaven given among men, whereby we may be saved. It is He alone who is the Shepherd and Bishop of our souls: He is our Prophet, whom Moses long since testified of, saying, "A prophet shall the Lord your God raise up unto you of your brethren, like unto me; him shall ye hear in all things whatsoever he shall say unto you; and it shall come to pass, that every soul that will not hear that prophet shall be destroyed from among the people." (Acts 3:22, 23.)

He it is that is now come, "and hath given us an understanding, that we may know him that is true." He rules in our hearts by His law of love and of life, and makes us free from the law of sin and death. We have no life, but of Him; for He is the quickening Spirit, the second Adam, the Lord from heaven, by whose blood we are cleansed, and our consciences sprinkled from dead works, to serve the living God. He is our Mediator, that makes peace and reconciliation between God offended and us offending; He being the Oath of God, the new covenant of light, life, grace and peace; the author and finisher of our faith. This Lord Jesus Christ, the heavenly man, the Emmanuel, God with us, we all own and believe in; He whom the high-priest raged against and said, He had spoken blasphemy; whom the priests and elders of the Jews took counsel together against and put to death; the same whom Judas betrayed for thirty pieces of silver, which the priests gave him as a reward for his treason; who also gave large money to the soldiers to broach a horrible lie, namely, "That his disciples came and stole him away by night whilst they slept." After He was arisen from the dead, the history of the acts of the apostles sets forth how the chief priests and elders persecuted the disciples of this Jesus, for preaching Christ and His resurrection. This, we

say, is that Lord Jesus Christ, Whom we own to be our life and salvation.

Concerning the Holy Scriptures, we do believe that they were given forth by the Holy Spirit of God, through the holy men of God, who, as the Scripture itself declares, (2 Pet. 1:21) spake as they were moved by the Holy Ghost. We believe they are to be read, believed, and fulfilled; (He that fulfills them is Christ), and they are "profitable for doctrine, for reproof, for correction, and for instruction in righteousness, that the man of God may be perfect, throughly furnished unto all good works," (2 Tim. 3:16, 17); and are able to make wise unto salvation. "through faith in Christ Jesus."

DECLARATION OF FAITH ISSUED BY THE RICHMOND CONFERENCE IN 1887

(N. B. It should be understood that the quotations from Scripture are made from the Authorized Version unless stated to be from the Revised Version.)

It is under a deep sense of what we owe to Him who has loved us that we feel called upon to offer a declaration of those fundamental doctrines of Christian truth that have always been professed by our branch of the Church of Christ.

OF GOD

We believe in one holy, (Isa. 6:3, 57:15.) almighty, (Gen. 17:1.) all-wise, (Rom. 11:33, 16:27.) and everlasting (Ps. 90:1, 2.) God, the Father, (Matt. 11:25-27.) the Creator (Gen. 1:1.) and Preserver (Job 7:20.) of all things; and in Jesus Christ, His only Son, our Lord, by whom all things were made, (John 1:3.) and by whom all things consist; (Col. 1:17.) and in one Holy Spirit, proceeding from the Father and the Son, (John 15:26, 16:7.) the Reprover (John 16:8.) of the world, the Witness for Christ, (John 15:26.) and the Teacher, (John 14:26.) Guide, (John 16:13.) and Sanctifier (2 Thes. 2:13.) of the people of God; and that these three are one in the eternal Godhead; (Matt. 28:19, John 10:30, 17:21) to whom be honor, praise, and thanksgiving, now and forever. Amen.

THE LORD JESUS CHRIST

It is with reverence and thanksgiving that we profess our unwavering allegiance to our Lord and Saviour, Jesus Christ. No man hath seen God at any time; the only begotten Son, who is in the bosom of the Father, He hath declared Him (John 1:18.). In Him was life; and the life was the light of men (John 1:4.). He is the true Light which lighteth every man that cometh into the world (John 1:9.); through whom the light of truth in all ages has proceeded from the Father of lights (James 1:17.). He is the eternal Word (John 1:1.) who was with God and was God, revealing Himself in infinite wisdom and love, both as man's Creator and Redeemer; for by Him were all things created that are in heaven and that are on earth, visible and invisible (Col. 1:13-16). Conceived of the Holy Ghost (Matt. 1:20.) born of the virgin Mary, (Matt. 1:23-25, Luke 1:35.) the word was made flesh, and dwelt amongst men (John 1:14.). He came in the fullness (Gal. 4:4.) of the appointed time, being verily foreordained before the foundation of the world (I Peter 1:20.) that He might fulfill (Isa. 11:1-5, Isa. 52:13-15.) the eternal counsel of the righteousness and love of God for the redemption of man (Isa. 53.). In Him dwelleth all the fullness of the Godhead bodily (Col. 2:9.). Though He was rich, yet, for our sakes, He became poor, veiling in the form of a servant (Phil. 2:7.) the brightness of His glory, that, through Him the kindness and love of God (Titus 3:4.) toward man might appear in a manner every way suited to our wants and finite capacities. He went about doing good (Acts 10:38.); for us He endured (Isa. 53:4, Luke 12:50, Luke 19:41, 22:44.) sorrow, hunger, thirst, weariness, (John 4:6.) pain, unutterable anguish (Luke 22:43, 44.) of body and of soul, being in all points tempted like as we are, yet without sin (Heb. 4:15.). Thus humbling Himself that we might be exalted, He emphatically recognized the duties and the sufferings of humanity as among the means whereby, through the obedience of faith, we are to be disciplined for heaven, sanctifying them to us, by Himself performing and enduring them, leaving us the one perfect example (1 Peter 2:21.) of all righteousness (Matt. 3:15.) in self-sacrificing love.

But not only in these blessed relations must the Lord Jesus be ever precious to His people. In Him is revealed as true God and perfect man, (Eph. 4:13.) a Redeemer, at once able to suffer and almighty to save. He became obedient (Phil. 2:8.) unto death, even the death of the cross, and is the propitiation for our sins, and not for ours only, but also for the sins of the whole world (1 John 2:2.); in whom we have redemption through His blood, (Eph. 1:7.) the forgiveness of sins according to the riches of His grace. It is our joy to confess that the remission of sins which any partake of is only in and by virtue of His most satisfactory sacrifice and not otherwise. (Barclay's Apology, Propos. v. and vi. par. 15, p. 141.) He was buried and rose again the third day (1 Cor. 15:4.) according to the Scriptures, becoming the first fruits (1 Cor. 15:23.) of them that sleep, and having shown Himself alive after His passion, by many infallible proofs (Acts 1:3.), He ascended into heaven, and hath sat down at the right hand of the Majesty on high, now to appear in the presence of God for us (Heb. 1:3, 9:24.). With the apostles who beheld His ascension, we rest in the assurance of the angelic messengers, "This same Jesus, which is taken up from you into heaven shall so come in like manner as ye have seen him go into heaven." (Acts 1:11, and see v. 7.). With the Apostle John, we would desire to unite in the words "Amen; even so, come, Lord Jesus." (Rev. 22:20.). And now, whilst thus watching and waiting, we rejoice to believe that He is our King and Saviour. He is the one Mediator of the new and everlasting covenant, (1 Tim. 2:5, Heb. 9:15.); Who makes peace and reconciliation between God offended and man offending (George Fox's Epistle to the Governor of Barbados.); the great High Priest whose priesthood is unchangeable (Heb. 4:14, 7:24.). He is able to save them to the uttermost that come unto God by Him, seeing He ever liveth to make intercession for them (Heb. 7:25.). All power is given unto Him in heaven and in earth (Matt. 28:18.). By Him the world shall be judged in righteousness (Acts 17:31.); for the Father judgeth no man, but hath committed all judgment unto the Son, that all men should honor the Son even as they honor the Father (John 5:22, 23.). All that are in the graves shall hear His voice, and shall come forth, they that have done good unto the resurrection of judgment (John 5:28, 29 R. V.).

We reverently confess and believe that divine honor and worship are due to the Son of God, and that He is in true faith to be prayed unto, and His name to be called upon, as the Primitive Christians did because of the glorious oneness of the Father and the Son; and that we cannot acceptably offer prayers and praises to God, nor receive from Him a gracious answer or blessing, but in and through His dear Son (Declaration of 1693, in Sewell's Hist., vol. II, 379.).

We would, with humble thanksgiving, bear an especial testimony to our Lord's perpetual dominion and power in His church. Through Him the redeemed in all generations have derived their light, their forgiveness, and their joy. All are members of this church, by whatsoever name they may be called among men, who have been baptized by the one Spirit into the one body; who are builded as living stones upon Christ, the Eternal Foundation, and are united in faith and love in that fellowship which is with the Father and with the Son. Of this church the Lord Jesus Christ is the alone Head (Eph. 1:22.). All its true members are made one in Him. They have washed their robes and made them white in His precious blood (Rev. 7:14.), and He has made them priests unto God and His Father (Rev. 1:6.). He dwells in their hearts by faith, and gives them of His peace. His will is their law, and in Him they enjoy the true liberty, a freedom from the bondage of sin.

THE HOLY SPIRIT

We believe that the Holy Spirit is, in the unity of the eternal Godhead, one with the Father and with the Son (Matt. 28:19; 2 Cor. 13:14.). He is the Comforter "Whom," saith Christ, "the Father will send in my name" (John 14:26.). He convinces the world of sin, of righteousness, and of judgment (John 16:8.). He testifies of and glorifies Jesus (John 16:14.). It is the Holy Spirit Who makes the evil manifest. He quickens them that are dead in trespasses and sins, and opens the inward eye to behold the Lamb of God that taketh away the sin of the world (Eph. 2:1.). Coming in the name and with the authority of the risen and ascended Saviour, He is the precious pledge of the continued love and care of our exalted King. He takes of the things of Christ and shows them, as a realized possession, to the believing soul (John 16:14.). Dwelling in the hearts of believers (John 16:17.), He opens their understandings that they may understand the Scriptures, and becomes, to the humbled and surrendered heart, the Guide, Comforter, Support, and Sanctifier.

We believe that the essential qualifications for the Lord's service is bestowed upon His children through the reception and baptism of the Holy Ghost. This Holy Spirit is the seal of reconciliation to the believer in Jesus (Eph. 1: 13, 14), the witness to His adoption into the family of the redeemed (Rom. 8:15, 16.); the earnest and the foretaste of the full communion and perfect joy which are reserved for them that endure unto the end.

We own no principle of spiritual light, life of holiness, inherent by nature in the mind or heart of man. We believe in no principle of spiritual light, life or holiness, but the influence of the Holy Spirit of God, bestowed on mankind, in various measures and degrees, through Jesus Christ our Lord. It is the capacity to recieve this blessed influence, which, in an especial manner, gives man preeminence above the beasts that perish; which distinguishes him, in every nation and in every clime, as an object of the redeeming love of God; as a being not only intelligent but responsible; for whom the message of salvation through our crucified Redeemer is, under all possible circumstances, designed to be a joyful sound. The Holy Spirit must ever be distinguished, both from the conscience which He enlightens, and from the natural faculty of reason, which when unsubjected to His Holy influence, is, in the things of God, very foolishness. As the eye is to the body, so is the conscience to our inner being, the organ by which we see; and, as both light and life are essential to the eye, so conscience, as the inward eye, cannot see aright, without the quickening and illumination of the Spirit of God. One with the Father and the Son, the Holy Spirit can never disown or dishonor our once crucified and now risen and glorified Redeemer. We disavow all professed illumination or spirituality that is divorced from faith in Jesus Christ of Nazareth, crucified for us without the gates of Jerusalem.

THE HOLY SCRIPTURES

It has ever been, and still is, the belief of the Society of Friends that the Holy Scriptures of the Old and New Testaments were given by inspiration of God; that, therefore, there can be no appeal from them to any other authority whatsoever; that they are able to make wise unto salvation, through faith which is in Jesus Christ. "These are written that ye might believe that Jesus is the Christ the Son of God; and that believing ye might have life through His name" (John 20:31.) The Scriptures are the only divinely authorized record of the doctrines which we are bound, as Christians, to accept, and of the moral principles which are to regulate our actions. No one can be required to believe, as an article of faith, any doctrine which is not contained in them; and whatsoever any one says or does, contrary to the Scriptures, though under profession of the immediate guidance of the Holy Spirit, must be reckoned and accounted a mere delusion. To the Christian, the Old Testament comes with the solemn and repeated attestation of his Lord. It is to be read in the light and completeness of the New; thus will its meaning be unveiled, and the humble disciple will be taught to discern the unity and mutual adaptation of the whole, and the many-sidedness and harmony of its testimony to Christ. The great Inspirer of Scripture is ever its true Interpreter. He performs this office in condescending love, not by superseding our understandings, but by renewing and enlightening them. Where Christ presides, idle speculation is hushed; His doctrine is learned in the doing of His will, and all knowledge ripens into a deeper and richer experience of His truth and love.

MAN'S CREATION AND FALL

It pleased God, in His wisdom and goodness, to create man out of the dust of the earth, and to breathe into his nostrils the breath of life, so that man became a living soul; formed after the image and likeness of God, capable of fulfilling the divine law, and of holding communion with his Maker (Gen. 2:7; 1:26, 27.). Being free to obey, or to disobey, he fell into transgression, through unbelief, under the temptation of Satan (Gen. 3:1-7.), and, thereby, lost that spiritual life of righteousness, in which he was created; and, so, death passed upon him, as the inevitable consequence of his sin (Rom. 5:12.). As the children of fallen Adam, all mankind bear his image. They partake of his nature, and are involved in the consequences of his fall. To every member of every successive generation, the words of the Redeemer are alike applicable, "Ye must be born again" (John 3:7.). But while we hold these views of the lost condition of man in the fall, we rejoice to believe that sin is not imputed to any, until they transgress the divine law, after sufficient capacity has been given to understand it; and that infants, though inheriting this fallen nature, are saved in the infinite mercy of God through the redemption which is in Christ Jesus.

JUSTIFICATION AND SANCTIFICATION

"God so loved the world that He gave His only begotten Son, that whosoever believeth in Him should not perish, but have everlasting life" (John 3:16.). We believe that justification is of God's free grace, through which, upon repentance and faith, He pardons our sins, and imparts to us a new life. It is received, not for any works of righteousness that we have done (Titus 3:5.), but in the unmerited mercy of God in Christ Jesus. Through faith in Him, and the shedding of His precious blood, the guilt of sin is taken away, and we stand reconciled to God. The offering up of Christ as the propitiation for the sins of the whole world, is the appointed manifestation both of the righteousness and of the love of God. In this propitiation the pardon of sin involves no abrogation or relaxation of the law of holiness. It is the vindication and establishment of that law (Rom. 3:31.), in virtue of the free and righteous submission of the Son of God Himself to all its requirements. He, the unchangeably just, proclaims Himself the justifier of him that believeth in Jesus (Rom. 3:26.). From age to age, the sufferings and death of Christ have been a hidden mystery, and a rock of offense to the unbelief and pride of man's fallen nature; yet, to the humble penitent whose heart is broken under the convicting power of the Spirit, life is revealed in that death. As he looks upon Him who was wounded for our transgressions (Isa. 53:5.), and upon whom the Lord was pleased to lay the iniquity of us all (Isa. 53:6.), his eye is more and more opened to see, and his heart to understand, the exceeding sinfulness of sin for which the Saviour died; whilst, in the sense of pardoning grace, he will joy in God through our Lord Jesus Christ, by whom we have now received the atonement (Rom. 5:11.).

We believe that in connection with Justification is Regeneration: that they who come to this experience know that they are not their own (1 Cor. 6:19.), that being reconciled to God by the death of His Son, we are saved by His life

(Rom. 5:10.); a new heart is given and new desires; old things are passed away, and we become new creatures (2 Cor. 5:17.), through faith in Christ Jesus; our wills being surrendered to His holy will, grace reigns through righteousness, unto eternal life, by Jesus Christ our Lord (Rom. 5:21.).

Sanctification is experienced in the acceptance of Christ in living faith for justification, in so far as the pardoned sinner, through faith in Christ, is clothed with a measure of His righteousness and receives the Spirit of promise; for, as saith the Apostle, "Ye are washed, ye are sanctified, ye are justified, in the name of the Lord Jesus, and by the Spirit of our God" (1 Cor. 6:11.). We rejoice to believe that the provisions of God's grace are sufficient to deliver from the power, as well as from the guilt, of sin, and to enable His believing children always to triumph in Christ (2 Cor. 2:14.). How full of encouragement is the declaration, "According to your faith be it unto you" (Matt. 9:29.). Whosoever submits himself wholly to God, believing and appropriating His promises, and exercising faith in Christ Jesus, will have his heart continually cleansed from all sin, by His precious blood, and, through the renewing, refining power of the Holy Spirit, be kept in conformity to the will of God, will love Him with all his heart, mind, soul and strength, and be able to say, with the Apostle Paul, "The law of the Spirit of life in Christ Jesus hath made me free from the law of sin and death" (Rom. 8:2.). Thus, in its full experience, Sanctification is deliverance from the pollution, nature, and love of sin. To this we are every one called, that we may serve the Lord without fear, in holiness and righteousness before Him, all the days of our life (Luke 1:74, 75.). It was the prayer of the apostle for the believers, "The very God of peace sanctify you wholly; and I pray God your whole spirit and soul and body be preserved blameless unto the coming of our Lord Jesus Christ. Faithful is He that calleth you who also will do it" (1 Thes. 5:23, 24). Yet the most holy Christian is still liable to temptation, is exposed to the subtle assaults of Satan, and can only continue to follow holiness as he humbly watches unto prayer, and is kept in constant dependence upon his Saviour, walking in the light (1 John 1:7), in the loving obedience of faith.

THE RESURRECTION AND FINAL JUDGMENT

We believe, according to the Scriptures, that there shall be a resurrection from the dead, both of the just and of the unjust (Acts 24:15.), and that God hath appointed a day in which He will judge the world in righteousness, by Jesus Christ whom He hath ordained (Acts 17:31.). For, as saith the apostle, "We must all appear before the judgment seat of Christ, that every one may receive the things done in his body, according to that he hath done, whether it be good or bad" (2 Cor. 5:10.).

We sincerely believe, not only a resurrection in Christ from the fallen and sinful state here, but a rising and ascending into glory with Him hereafter; that when He at last appears we may appear with Him in glory. But that all the wicked, who live in rebellion against the light of grace, and die finally impenitent, shall come forth to the resurrection of condemnation. And that the soul of every man and woman shall be reserved, in its own distinct and proper being, and shall have its proper body as God is pleased to give it. It is sown a natural body, it is raised a spiritual body (1 Cor. 15:44.); that being first which is natural, and afterward that which is spiritual. And though it is said, "this corruptible shall put on incorruption, and this mortal shall put on immortality" (1 Cor. 15:53.), the change shall be such as will accord with the declaration, "Flesh and blood cannot inherit the Kingdom of God, neither doth corruption inherit incorruption" (1 Cor. 15:50.). We shall be raised out of all corruption and corruptibility, out of all mortality, and shall be the children of God, being the children of resurrection (Luke 20:36.). (See also Declaration of 1693, Sewell's History, vol. II, 383-384.)

"Our citizenship is in heaven" (R. V.), from whence also we look for the Saviour the Lord Jesus Christ, who shall change our vile body that it may be fashioned like unto His glorious body, according to the working whereby He is able even to subdue all things unto Himself (Phil. 3:20, 21.).

We believe that the punishment of the wicked and the blessedness of the righteous shall be everlasting; according to the declaration of our compassionate Redeemer, to whom the judgment is committed, "These shall go away into eternal punishment, but the righteous into eternal life" (R. V., Matt. 25:46.).

BAPTISM

We would express our continued conviction that our Lord appointed no outward rite or ceremony for observance in His church. We accept every command of our Lord in what we believe to be its genuine import, as absolutely conclusive. The question of the use of outward ordinances is with us a question, not as to the authority of Christ, but as to His real meaning. We reverently believe that, as there is one Lord and one faith, so there is, under the Christian dispensation, but one baptism (Eph. 4:4, 5.), even that whereby all believers are baptized in the one Spirit into the one body (1 Cor. 12:13, R.V.). This is not an outward baptism with water, but a spiritual experience; not the putting away of the filth of the flesh (1 Pet. 3:21.), but that inward work which, by transforming the heart and settling the soul upon Christ, brings forth the answer of a good conscience towards God, by the resurrection of Jesus Christ, in the experience of His love and power, as the risen and ascended Saviour. No baptism in outward water can satisfy the description of the apostle, of being buried with Christ by baptism unto death (Rom. 6:4). It is with the Spirit alone that any can thus be baptized. In this experience the announcement of the Forerunner of our Lord is fulfilled, "He shall baptize you with the Holy Ghost and with fire" (Matt. 3:11.). In this view we accept the commission of our blessed Lord as given in Matthew 28:18, 19 and 20th verses: "And Jesus came to them and spake unto them saying. All authority hath been given unto me in heaven and on earth. Go ye, therefore, and make disciples of all the nations, baptizing them into the name of the Father and of the Son and of the Holy Ghost; teaching them to observe all things whatsoever I commanded you, and, lo, I am with you always, even unto the end of the world" (R. V.). This commission, as we believe, was not designed to set up a new ritual under the new covenant, or to connect the initiation into a membership, in its nature essentially spiritual, with a mere ceremony of a typical character. Otherwise it was not possible for the Apostle Paul, who was not a whit behind the very chiefest apostle (2 Cor. 11:5.), to have disclaimed that which would, in that case, have been of the essence of his commission when he wrote, "Christ sent me not to baptize, but to preach the Gospel" (1 Cor. 1:17.). Whenever an external ceremony is commanded, the particulars, the mode and incidents of that ceremony, become of its essence. There is an utter absence of these particulars in the text before us, which confirms our persuasion that the commission must be construed in connection with the spiritual power which the risen Lord promised should attend the witness of His apostles and of the church to Him, and which, after Pentecost, so mightily accompanied their ministry of the word and prayer, that those to whom they were sent were introduced into an experience wherein they had a saving knowledge of, and living fellowship with, the Father and the Son and the Holy Spirit.

THE SUPPER OF THE LORD

Intimately connected with the conviction already expressed is the view that we have ever maintained as to the true supper of the Lord. We are well aware that our Lord was pleased to make use of a variety of symbolical utterances, but He often gently upbraided His disciples for accepting literally what He had intended only in its spiritual meaning. His teaching, as in His parables or in the command to wash one another's feet, was often in symbols, and ought ever to be received in the light of His own emphatic declaration, "The words that I speak unto you they are spirit and they are life" (John 6:63.). The old covenant was full of ceremonial symbols; the new covenant, to which our Saviour alluded at the last supper, is expressly declared by the prophet to be "not according to the old" (Jer. 31:32; Heb. 8:9.). We cannot believe that in setting up this new covenant the Lord Jesus intended an institution out of harmony with the spirit of this prophecy. The eating of His body and the drinking of His blood cannot be an outward act. They truly partake of them who habitually rest upon the sufferings and death of their Lord as their only hope, and to whom the indwelling Spirit gives to drink of the fullness that is in Christ. It is this inward and spiritual partaking that is the true supper of the Lord.

The presence of Christ with His church is not designed to be by symbol or representation, but in the real communication of His own Spirit. "I will pray the Father and He shall give you another Comforter, who shall abide with you forever" (John 14:16.) convincing of sin, testifying of Jesus, taking of the things of Christ, this blessed Comforter communicates to the believer and to the church, in a gracious, abiding manifestation, the REAL PRESENCE of the Lord. As the great remembrancer, through whom the promise is fulfilled, He needs no ritual or priestly intervention in bringing to the experience of the true

commemoration and communion. "Behold," saith the risen Redeemer, "I stand at the door and knock. If any man hear my voice and open the door, I will come in and sup with him and he with me" (Rev. 3:20.). In an especial manner, when assembled for congregational worship, are believers invited to the festival of the Saviour's peace, and, in a united act of faith and love, unfettered by any outward rite or ceremonial, to partake together of the body that was broken and of the blood that was shed for them, without the gates of Jerusalem. In such a worship they are enabled to understand the words of the apostle as expressive of a sweet and most real experience: "The cup of blessing which we bless, is it not the communion of the blood of Christ? The bread that we break, is it not the communion of the body of Christ? For we being many are one bread, and one body; for we are all partakers of that one bread" (1 Cor. 10:16, 17.).

PUBLIC WORSHIP

Worship is the adoring response of the heart and mind to the influence of the Spirit of God. It stands neither in forms nor in the formal disuse of forms: it may be without words as well as with them, but it must be in spirit and in truth (John 4:24.). We recognize the value of silence, not as an end, but as a means toward the attainment of the end; a silence, not of listlessness or of vacant musing, but of holy expectation before the Lord. Having become His adopted children through faith in the Lord Jesus Christ, it is our privilege to meet together and unite in the worship of Almighty God, to wait upon Him for the renewal of our strength, for communion one with another, for the edification of believers in the exercise of various spiritual gifts, and for the declaration of glad tidings of salvation to the unconverted who may gather with us. This worship depends not upon numbers. Where two or three are gathered together in the name of Christ there is a church, and Christ, the living Head, in the midst of them. Through His mediation without the necessity for any inferior instrumentality, is the Father to be approached and reverently worshiped. The Lord Jesus has forever fulfilled and ended the typical and sacrificial worship under the law, by the offering up of Himself upon the cross for us, once for all. He has opened the door of access into the inner sanctuary, and graciously provided spiritual offerings for the service of His temple, suited to the several conditions of all who worship in spirit and in truth. The broken and the contrite heart, the confession of the soul prostrate before God, the prayer of the afflicted when he is overwhelmed, the earnest wrestling of the spirit, the outpouring of humble thanksgiving, the spiritual song and melody of the heart (Eph. 5:19.), the simple exercise of faith, the self denying service of love, these are among the sacrifices which He, our merciful and faithful High Priest, is pleased to prepare, by His Spirit, in the hearts of them that receive Him, and to present with acceptance unto God.

By the immediate operations of the Holy Spirit, He as the Head of the church, alone selects and qualifies those who are to present His messages or engage in other service for Him; and, hence, we cannot commit any formal arrangement to any one in our regular meetings for worship. We are well aware that the Lord has provided a diversity of gifts (1 Cor. 12:4-6.) for the needs both of the church and of the world, and we desire that the church may feel her responsibility, under the government of her Great Head, in doing her part to foster these gifts, and in making arrangements for their proper exercise.

It is not for individual exaltation, but for mutual profit, that the gifts are bestowed (1 Cor. 12:7.); and every living church, abiding under the government of Christ is humbly and thankfully to receive and exercise them, in subjection to her Holy Head. The church that quenches the Spirit and lives to itself alone must die.

We believe the preaching of the Gospel to be one of the chief means, divinely appointed, for the spreading of the glad tidings of life and salvation through our crucified Redeemer, for the awakening and conversion of sinners, and for the comfort and edification of believers. As it is the prerogative of the Great Head of the church alone to select and call the ministers of His Gospel, so we believe that both the gift and the qualification to exercise it must be derived immediately from Him; and that, as in the primitive church, so now also, He confers spiritual gifts upon women as well as upon men, agreeably to the prophecy recited by the Apostle Peter, "It shall come to pass in the last days, saith God, I will pour out my Spirit upon all flesh; and your sons and your daughters shall prophesy" (Acts 2:17.). Respecting which the apostle declares, "the promise is unto you, and to your children, and to all that are afar off, even as many as the Lord our God shall call" (Acts 2:39.). As the gift is freely received so it is to be freely exercised (Matt. 10:8. See also Acts 20:33-35.), in simple obedience to the will of God.

Spiritual gifts, precious as they are, must not be mistaken for grace; they add to our responsibility, but do not raise the minister above his brethren or sisters. They must be exercised in continued dependence upon our Lord and blessed is that ministry in which man is humbled, and Christ and His grace exalted. "He that is greatest among you," said our Lord and Master, "let him be as the younger; and he that is chief as he that doth serve. I am among you as he that serveth" (Luke 22:26, 27.).

While the church cannot confer spiritual gifts, it is its duty to recognize and foster them, and to promote their efficiency by all the means in its power. And while, on the one hand, the Gospel should never be preached for money (Acts 8:20; 20:33-35.), on the other, it is the duty of the church to make such provisions that it shall never be hindered for want of it.

The church, if true to her allegiance, cannot forget her part in the command, "Go ye into all the world, and preach the Gospel to every creature" (Mark 16:15.). Knowing that it is the Spirit of God that can alone prepare and qualify the instruments who fulfill this command, the true disciple will be found still sitting at the feet of Jesus, listening that he may learn, and learning that he may obey. He humbly places himself at his Lord's disposal, and, when he hears the call, "Whom shall I send, and who will go for us?" is prepared to respond, in childlike reverence and love, "Here am I, send me" (Isaiah 6:8.).

PRAYER AND PRAISE

Prayer is the outcome of our sense of need, and of our continual dependence upon God. He who uttered the invitation, "Ask and it shall be given you" (Matt. 7:7.), is Himself the Mediator and High Priest who, by His Spirit, prompts the petition, and who presents it with the acceptance before God. With such an invitation, prayer becomes the duty and the privilege of all who are called by His name. Prayer is, in the awakened soul, the utterance of the cry, "God be merciful to me a sinner" (Luke 18:13.), and, at every stage of the believer's course, prayer is essential to his spiritual life. A life without prayer is a life practically without God. The Christian's life is a continual asking. The thirst that prompts the petition produces, as it is satisfied, still deeper longings, which prepare for yet more bounteous supplies, from Him who delights to bless. Prayer is not confined to the closet. When uttered in response to the promptings of the Holy Spirit, it becomes an important part of public worship, and, whenever the Lord's people meet together in His name, it is their privilege to wait upon Him for the spirit of grace and supplications (Zech. 12:10.). A life of prayer cannot be other than a life of praise. As the peace of Christ reigns in the church, her living members accept all that they receive, as from His pure bounty, and each day brings them fresh pledges of their Father's love. Satisfied with the goodness of His house, whether as individuals, in families, or in congregations, they will be still praising Him (Psalm 84:4.), heart answering to heart, "Bless the Lord, O my soul: and all that is within me, bless His holy name" (Ps. 103:1.).

LIBERTY OF CONSCIENCE IN ITS RELATION TO CIVIL GOVERNMENT

That conscience should be free, and that in matters of religious doctrine and worship man is accountable only to God, are truths which are plainly declared in the New Testament; and which are confirmed by the whole scope of the Gospel, and by the example of our Lord and His disciples. To rule over the conscience, and to command the spiritual allegiance of his creature man, is the high and sacred prerogative of God alone. In religion every act ought to be free. A forced worship is plainly a contradiction in terms, under that dispensation in which the worship of the Father must be in spirit and in truth (John 4:24.).

We have ever maintained that it is the duty of Christians to obey the enactments of civil government, except those which interfere with our allegiance to God. We owe much to its blessings. Through it we enjoy liberty and protection, in connection with law and order. Civil government is a divine ordinance (Rom. 13:1; I Pet. 2:13-16.), instituted to promote the best welfare of man, hence magistrates are to be regarded as God's ministers who should be a terror to evil doers and a praise to them that do well. Therefore, it is with us a matter of conscience to render them respect and obedience in the exercise of their proper functions.

MARRIAGE

Marriage is an institution graciously ordained by the Creator Himself, for the help and continuance of the human family. It is not a mere civil contract, and ought never to be entered upon without a reference to the sanction and blessing of Him who ordained it. It is a solemn engagement for the term of life (Matt. 19:5, 6.), designed for the mutual assistance and comfort of both sexes, that they may be helpmeets to each other in things temporal and spiritual. To this end it should imply concurrence in spiritual as well as temporal concerns, and should be entered upon discreetly, soberly, and in the fear of the Lord.

PEACE

We feel bound explicitly to avow our unshaken persuasion that all war is utterly incompatible with the plain precepts of our divine Lord and Law-giver, and the whole spirit of His Gospel, and that no plea of necessity or policy, however urgent or peculiar, can avail to release either individuals or nations from the paramount allegiance which they owe to Him who hath said, "Love your enemies" (Matt. 5:44; Luke 6:27). In enjoining this love, and the forgiveness of injuries, He who has bought us to Himself has not prescribed for man precepts which are incapable of being carried into practice, or of which the practice is to be postponed until all shall be persuaded to act upon them. We cannot doubt that they are incumbent now, and that we have in the prophetic Scriptures the distinct intimation of their direct application not only to individuals, but to nations also (Isaiah 2:4; Micah 4:1.). When nations conform their laws to this divine teaching, wars must necessarily cease.

We would, in humility, but in faithfulness to our Lord, express our firm persuasion that all the exigencies of civil government and social order may be met under the banner of the Prince of Peace, in strict conformity with His commands.

OATHS

We hold it to be the inalienable privilege of the disciple of the Lord Jesus that his statements concerning matters of fact within his knowledge should be accepted, under all circumstances, as expressing his belief as to the fact asserted. We rest upon the plain command of our Lord and Master, "Swear not at all" (Matt. 5:34.); and we believe any departure from this standard to be prejudicial to the cause of truth and to that confidence between man and man, the maintenance of which is indispensable to our mutual well being. This command, in our persuasion, applies not to profane swearing only, but to judicial oaths also. It abrogates any previous permission to the contrary, and is, for the Christian, absolutely conclusive.

THE FIRST DAY OF THE WEEK

Whilst the remembrance of our Creator ought to be at all times present with the Christian, we would express our thankfulness to our Heavenly Father that He has been pleased to honor the setting apart of one day in seven for the purposes of holy rest, religious duties, and public worship; and we desire that all under our name may avail themselves of this great privilege as those who are called to be risen with Christ, and to seek those things that are

above where He sitteth at the right hand of God (Coloss. 3:1.). May the release thus granted from other occupations be diligently improved. On this day of the week especially ought the households of Friends to be assembled for the reading of the Scriptures and for waiting upon the Lord; and we trust that, in a Christianly wise economy of our time and strength, the engagements of the day may be so ordered as not to frustrate the gracious provision thus made for us by our Heavenly Father, or to shut out the opportunity either for public worship or for private retirement and devotional reading.

In presenting this declaration of our Christian faith, we desire that all our members may be afresh encouraged, in humility and devotedness, to renewed faithfulness in fulfilling their part in the great mission of the Church, and through the Church to the world around us, in the name of our Crucified Redeemer. Life from Christ, life in Christ, must ever be the basis of life for Christ. For this we have been created and redeemed, and, by this alone, can the longings of our immortal souls be satisfied.

THE EXPANDING APPRECIATION OF TRUTH

Human understanding of truth is always subject to growth. This basic principle also underlies the development of the organizations and institutions through which the spirit of Christianity is made operative in life. While fundamental principles are eternal, expressions of truth and methods of Christian activity should develop in harmony with the needs of the times. God, who spoke through the prophets, and supremely in Jesus Christ, still speaks through men and women who have become new creatures in Christ, being transformed by the renewing of their minds and, therefore, able and willing to receive fresh revelations of truth.

Frequently, however, men see "through a glass darkly," and may misinterpret or make incorrect applications. Therefore, as the stream of life flows on, bringing new conceptions, insights, and situations, it is necessary to strive constantly for a clearer comprehension of divine truth that will enter vitally into personal experience and become a creative factor for the redemption of human character and the remolding of society on the Christian pattern. "A religion based on truth must be progressive. Truth being so much greater than our conception of it, we should ever be making fresh discoveries."

ORIGIN AND DEVELOPMENT OF THE DISCIPLINE

The term "discipline" is used by Friends to designate those arrangements which they have instituted for their civil and religious nurture and guidance as a Christian group. For almost a decade following the beginning of the ministry of George Fox, the founder of the Society of Friends, his followers were without organization, but as they grew in unity and in numbers there arose responsibilities to admonish, encourage, and help one another both in spiritual and in temporal affairs. They found it necessary to make certain provisions for the preservation of order in their fellowship and for the care of the poor and those who suffered for conscience sake.

There was also need for the supervision of the exercise of spiritual gifts and of the work of publishing truth. The rules and advices pertaining to such ministrations were finally incorporated in the discipline. The earliest Quaker advice on Christian practice was issued by the famous gathering of Friends at Balby in Yorkshire in 1656, a statement that well describes the spirit which should characterize all books of discipline: "Dearly beloved friends, these things we do not lay upon you as a rule or form to walk by, but that all with the measure of light which is pure and holy may be guided, and so in the light walking and abiding these may be fulfilled in the spirit, not from the letter; for the letter killeth, but the spirit giveth life."

An important step in the development of the discipline was the drafting by George Fox in 1668 of a body of advices and regulations to which his opponents gave the name of "Canons and Institutions." This served for a long time as the discpline of the Society, although the name was formally disclaimed by Friends in 1675. It formed the basis for the Discipline of London Yearly Meeting and for all later books of discipline. As the various Yearly meetings were established in America, each prepared and adopted its own book of discipline, but there was much similarity because of the common use of material from older editions. These disciplines were revised from time to time as the rules and advices which they contained became inadequate and inappropriate. Thus, as the conscience of Friends became aware of the evils involved in human slavery or in the use of intoxicating drinks, these convictions were expressed in their disciplines.

ADOPTION OF THE UNIFORM DISCIPLINE

Many diverse factors during the latter half of the nineteenth century had affected the outlook, activities, and relationships of members of the Society of Friends. As these cross currents were faced in the conferences of Yearly Meetings held in 1887, 1892, and 1897, sentiment developed for a closer union of the Yearly Meetings to be accomplished partly by a general representative meeting and partly by the adoption of a uniform discipline. A committee of two representatives from each of the Yearly Meetings taking part in the conferences of 1897 was appointed to formulate a plan of union and to prepare the proposed discipline. "The Constitution and Discipline for the American Yearly Meetings of Friends," was the official name of the discipline which was written to serve the needs of the new organization, to be known as the Five Years Meeting of Friends in America. It was adopted by the Yearly Meetings of New England, Wilmington, Indiana, and Kansas in 1900; California, New York, Western, and Baltimore in 1901; Oregon, North Carolina, and Iowa in 1902; Nebraska, when it was established in 1908. Canada Yearly Meeting, when received into the Five Years Meeting in 1907, was given the privilege of adapting the Discipline to its own needs.

THE BOOK OF FAITH AND PRACTICE

The Uniform Discipline met quite acceptable the needs of the Yearly Meetings which adopted it. But the revolutionary changes in life and thought experienced in the twentieth century brought to Friends the realization that the statements of faith and practice as set forth by the Discipline should be re-examined and revised that they might more adequately meet the needs of the Yearly Meetings. This concern found expression in numerous proposals by Yearly Meetings for amendments to the Discipline. Eventually in 1940, the Executive Committee of the Five Years Meeting recommended to that body that steps be taken for a revision. The Five Years Meeting of 1940, acting upon a recommendation of its Executive Committee that steps be taken for a revision, adopted a method of procedure providing for the appointment of a committee which was instructed to prepare a revised draft of the Discipline for the consideration of the Five Years Meeting and its constituent Yearly Meetings.

Notes: *The largest of the Quaker bodies in North America can be traced to a meeting at Richmond, Indiana in 1887. It was officially formed as the Five Years Meeting in 1902, and later adopted its present name. The Western Yearly Meeting includes in its statement of faith the confession agreed upon in 1887 and a shortened version of a letter from George Fox, founder of the Quakers, to the Governor of Barbados.*

* * *

THE CHURCH AND ITS ESSENTIAL DOCTRINES [MID-AMERICA (FORMERLY KANSAS) YEARLY MEETING]

CHAPTER I. THE CHURCH AS A DENOMINATION

Section 1. *Christ's Members.* The Church of Jesus Christ is composed of those persons who, through repentance of their sins and faith in the Lord Jesus Christ as their Saviour, have been born into His kingdom by the Holy Spirit. By the revelation of the Holy Spirit they look to Christ as their Prophet, Priest, and King; and, by the baptism with the Holy Spirit they are enabled to resist temptation and to live in obedience to God's Holy will.

Section 2. *Friends as a Denomination.* A Christian denomination is an organization composed of those who hold similar views of the teachings of the Holy Scriptures, maintain certain practices based upon these teachings, and voluntarily associate themselves for joint participation in worship, for fellowship and mutual help, and for united effort in the promotion of truth and righteousness. The denomination of Friends is such a Christian body.

Each denominational body has its own system of government and rules for the transaction of its business and for individual observance by its members.

CHAPTER II. ESSENTIAL TRUTHS

Section 1. *God's Dealings with Man.* The vital principle of the Christian faith is the truth that man's salvation and higher life are personal matters between the individual soul and God. Salvation is deliverance from sin and the possession of spiritual life. This comes through a personal faith in Jesus Christ as the Saviour, who through His love and sacrifice draws us to Him.

The whole spiritual life grows out of the soul's relation to God and its co-operation with Him, not from any outward or traditional observances.

Christ Himself baptizes the surrendered soul with the Holy Spirit, enduing it with power, bestowing gifts for service. This is an efficient baptism, a direct incoming of divine power for the transformation and control of the whole man. Christ Himself is the Spiritual bread which nourishes the soul, and He thus enters into and becomes a part of the being of those who partake of Him. This participation with Christ and apprehension of Him become the goal of life for the Christian. Those who thus enter into oneness with Him become also joined in living union with each other as members of one body. Both worship and Christian fellowship spring out of this immediate relation of believing souls with their Lord.

Section 2. *The Scriptures.* The Holy Scriptures were given by inspiration of God and are the divinely authorized record of the doctrines which Christians are bound to accept, and of the moral principles which are to regulate their lives and actions. In them, as interpreted and unfolded by the Holy Spirit, is an ever fresh and unfailing source of spiritual truth for the proper guidance of life and practice.

Section 3. *Fundamental Doctrines.* The doctrines of the apostolic days are held by the Friends as essentials of Christianity. The Fatherhood of God, the deity and humanity of the Son, the gift of the Holy Spirit, the atonement through Jesus Christ by which men are reconciled to God, the resurrection of our Lord which gives us assurance of the resurrection of of all true believers, the high-priesthood of Christ, by whom we have access to the Father in the forgiveness of our sins, the individual priesthood of believers—these are all most precious truths, to be held as vital, life-giving realities.

Section 4. *The Spirituality of Religious Experience.* The sinful condition of man, his proneness to yield to temptation, the world's absolute need of a Saviour, and the cleansing from sin in the work of forgiveness and sanctification through the blood of Jesus are clearly set forth in the gospel of salvation. The possession of spiritual life is thus assured man through a personal faith in Jesus Christ as the Saviour who through His love and sacrifice draws us to Him. The teachings of Jesus Christ concerning the spiritual nature of religion, the impossibility of promoting the spiritual life by the ceremonial application of material things, the fact that faith in Jesus Christ Himself is all-sufficient, and His presence in the believer's heart—these virtually make unnecessary every priestly system and point the soul to the only satisfying source of spiritual life and power. Friends accord to every man the right of equality with every other.

Section 5. *The Work of the Holy Spirit.* The indwelling Spirit guides and controls the surrendered life, and the Christian's constant and supreme business is obedience to Him. But while the importance of individual guidance and obedience is thus emphasized, this fact gives no ground for license; the sanctified conclusions of the church are above the judgment of a single individual. Conviction for sin is awakened by the operation of the Holy Spirit, Who causes the soul to feel its need of reconciliation with God. The Holy Spirit testifies of Christ as the only hope of salvation; as man yields to Him, he is brought into newness of life through the regenerating power of the Spirit, and has a true realization of citizenship in the kingdom of God. The Holy Spirit witnesses further to the fact of a saved man's adoption into the family of God and of a consequent sonship through Christ. A changed nature and life give evidence of this new relation. Thus established in grace, man is able to bring forth the fruit of the Spirit, which gives further confirmation of a renewed state in grace.

Section 6. *The Baptism with the Holy Spirit.* The newly converted child of God soon realizes that, although his Christian experience is well begun, he is not yet been met. As he seeks for further light, he is but a babe in Christ. He senses a soul need that has a longing for a greater triumph over the sin in his nature that so constantly besets him. At this point Friends call his attention to the purifying and empowering baptism with the Holy Spirit with which Christ baptizes the earnest believer. Through it the Spirit is poured out upon him, and a complete separation takes place in his life, in that sin and holiness are clearly seen as antipodes which cannot coexist if complete victory is to be experienced. The soul is thus sanctified wholly, or made pure from the defilement of sin within. Thus a complete triumph over sin in the nature is provided for and growth in grace is greatly accelerated.

Section 7. *The Bestowment of Gifts.* The spiritual gifts are bestowed by the Holy Spirit, and by His incoming in cleansing baptism the essential power for their most efficient employment is given. It is thus that the Head of the Church has been pleased to make use of human instrumentalities in the accomplishment of His purposes. To this end He bestows special gifts upon certain members of the body for the propagation of the Gospel, for the perfecting of believers, and for the edifying and strengthening of the whole body in faith and life and power. The exercise of these gifts is a potent means by which the Church brings the truth to the individual consciousness, interprets and proclaims its message, and reveals its scope and purpose. There are varieties of gifts in the ministry, and in a properly organized body provision is made for the exercise and development of them all. It is not easy to draw a sharp distinction between the different types of ministry; frequently they are united in one person, who is thus peculiarly qualified for helpful service.

There is a gift for the ministry of instruction and of exposition, or of teaching the truth. Those who possess this gift are enabled to contribute in different degrees to the establishment of the membership, and to the expansion of the conception of divine things. This ministry of teaching requires a balanced, trained and well-stored mind, and the consecration of that mind to the service of Him who is the Truth.

There is a gift of speaking to states and needs of individuals, and of congregations. This prophetic ministry is characterized by the spiritual vision, the self-evidence of its message, and its fitness for the situation. It is a gift of seeing truth immediately and of effectively teaching it to others.

There is a gift for exhortation, which is an ability for making an appeal to the hearts of men, and for stirring them to a sense of God's love and of His purposes for men—the power of moving and convincing souls. Those who possess this gift are peculiarly fitted for evangelistic work.

There is also the pastoral gift, which consists especially in ability to do personal work with individuals or with families. This gift fits the possessor of it to comfort those who mourn, to lead the members into a closer religious life, to arouse in the young an interest in the things of the Spirit, and to impress others with a sense of the scope and reality of the spiritual life. It is the gift of shepherding and feeding the flock.

A gift of the Spirit is given to "every man to profit withal." There are many gifts set forth in the Scriptures in addition to those for the ministry of the Word. All should prayerfully await and receive the divine leading, to be open to the movings of the Spirit on any line that He may bring as a concern for special service. He who calls will empower, will equip, and will lead into avenues of blessed usefulness.

Section 8. *Worship.* The counsel of Hebrews 10:25 is timely: "Not forsaking the assembling of ourselves together, as the manner of some is; but exhorting one another; and so much the more, as ye see the day approaching." It is the duty and the privilege of believers to meet together for the public worship of God. In doing this they each time make a public profession to the world of their faith in Christ, and avail themselves of opportunities for spiritual blessings and mutual helpfulness not otherwise offered.

Worship is the highest act of which the human faculties are capable, and it can be truly performed only as it is in response to the influence of the Spirit of God. Public worship in the Christian church is in accordance with the declaration of our Lord, that "where two or three are met together in My name, there am I in the midst of them." The congregation is thus "the congregation of the Lord," and the meeting is primarily with Him. He touches the spiritual consciousness of believers, and thus, through Him, their High Priest and Intercessor, they are enabled to worship the Father in spirit and in truth. Worship stands neither in forms nor in the formal disuse of forms; it may be without words as well as with them. Both silence and vocal exercises are recognized and valued, not as ends but as means toward the attainment of an end, which is the divine blessing upon the individual and the congregation.

As Master of the Assembly, the Lord directs and leads the profitable exercises of His congregation. He calls and qualifies whom He will to be the bearer of His message, and the individual believer should hold himself in obedient submission to His will. The occasions of public worship are divinely appointed for the edification of believers in the truth and for the proclamation of fresh and vital messages of salvation to the world.

Section 9. *Christianity in Action.* With faith in the wisdom of Almighty God, the Father, the Son, and the Holy Spirit, and believing that it is His purpose to make His Church on earth a power for righteousness and truth, the Friends labor for the alleviation of human suffering; for the intellectual, moral, and spiritual elevation of mankind; and for purified and exalted citizenship. The Friends believe war to be incompatible with Christianity, and seek to promote peaceful methods for the settlement of all the differences between men and between nations.

It is an essential part of the faith that a man should be in truth what he professes in word; and the underlying principle of life and action for individuals, and also for society, is transformation through the power of God and implicit obedience to His revealed will.

Section 10. *The Lord's Return.* The grand consummation of the divine purpose in regard to His people is seen in the prophetic utterances found in the Scriptures concerning the return of the Lord. He will come as King of kings and Lords of lords to reign over all His universe and thus bring to an end the operations of Satan and his minions. The saints are comforted, as they view the devastations caused by sin in the world, in the assurance that the Lord will come in power and great glory for the punishment of evil doers and the eternal deliverance of His people from the evils of the world. The Lord declares in Revelation 22:20, "Surely I come quickly": and the church responds. "Even so, come, Lord Jesus." Friends should ever keep this great truth in mind, and thus not be misled by the arguments and reasoning of unbelievers.

For explicit and more extended statement of belief, the reader is referred to those officially put forth at various times by the Friends, especially to the letter of George Fox to the Governor of Barbados in 1671, and to the Declaration of Faith issued by the Richmond Conference in 1887. See pages 17-45.

CHAPTER III. EXTRACT FROM GEORGE FOX'S LETTER TO THE GOVERNOR OF BARBADOS, 1671

We do own and believe in God, the only wise, omnipotent, and everlasting God, the Creator of all things both in heaven and in earth, and the Preserver of all that He hath made; who is God over all, blessed forever; to whom be all honor and glory, dominion, praise, and thanksgiving, both now and forevermore.

And we own and believe in Jesus Christ, His beloved and only-begotten Son, in whom He is well pleased; who was conceived by the Holy Ghost and born of the Virgin Mary; in whom we have redemption through His blood, even the forgiveness of sins; who is the express image of the invisible God, the first-born of every creature, by whom were all things created that are in heaven and that are in earth, visible and invisible, whether they be thrones or dominions, principalities, or powers; all things were created by Him. And we do own and believe that He was made a sacrifice for sin, who knew no sin, neither was guile found in His mouth; that He was crucified for us in the flesh, without the gates of Jerusalem; and that He was buried, and rose again the third day by the power of His Father, for our justification; and that He ascended up into heaven,

THE CHURCH AND ITS ESSENTIAL DOCTRINES [MID-AMERICA (FORMERLY KANSAS) YEARLY MEETING] (continued)

and now sitteth at the right hand of God. This Jesus, who was the foundation of the holy prophets and apostles, is our foundation; and we believe that there is no other foundation to be laid than that which is laid, even Christ Jesus; who tasted death for every man, shed His blood for all men and is the propitiation for our sins, and not for ours only, but also for the sins of the whole world according as John the Baptist testified of Him, when he said, "Behold the Lamb of God, that taketh away the sin of the world!" (John 1:29). We believe that He alone is our Redeemer and Saviour, even the captain of our salvation, who saves us from sin, as well as from hell and the wrath to come, and destroys the devil and his works; he is the Seed of the woman that bruises the serpent's head, to wit, Jesus Christ, the Alpha and Omega, the First and the Last. He is (as the Scriptures of truth say of Him) our wisdom and righteousness, justification, and redemption; neither is there salvation in any other, for there is no other name under heaven given among men whereby we may be saved. It is He alone who is the Shepherd and Bishop of our souls. He is our Prophet, whom Moses long since testified of saying, "A prophet shall the Lord your God raise up unto you of your brethren, like unto me; him shall ye hear in all things whatsoever he shall say unto you; and it shall come to pass, that every soul that will not hear that prophet shall be destroyed from among the people." (Acts 3:22, 23.)

He it is that is now come, "and hath given us an understanding, that we may know him that is true." He rules in our hearts by His law of love and of life, and makes us free from the law of sin and death. We have no life, but of Him; for He is the quickening Spirit, the second Adam, the Lord from heaven, by whose blood we are cleansed, and our consciences sprinkled from dead works, to serve the living God. He is our Mediator, that makes peace and reconciliation between God offended and us offending; He being the Oath of God, the new covenant of light, life, grace, and peace; the author and finisher of our faith. This Lord Jesus Christ, the heavenly man, the Emmanuel, God with us, we all own and believe in; He whom the high-priest raged against and said, He had spoken blasphemy; whom the priests and elders of the Jews took counsel together against and put to death; the same whom Judas betrayed for thirty pieces of silver, which the priests gave him as a reward for his treason; who also gave large money to the soldiers to broach a horrible lie, namely, "That his disciples came and stole him away by night whilst they slept." After He was arisen from the dead, the history of the acts of the apostles sets forth how the chief priests and elders persecuted the disciples of this Jesus, for preaching Christ and His resurrection. This, we say, is that Lord Jesus Christ, whom we own to be our life and salvation.

Concerning the Holy Scriptures we do believe that they were given forth by the Holy Spirit of God, through the holy men of God, who, as the Scripture itself declares, spake as they were moved by the Holy Ghost. (II Peter 1:21) We believe they are to be read, believed, and fulfilled

(He that fulfills them is Christ); and they are "profitable for doctrine, for reproof, for correction, and for instruction in righteousness that the man of God may be perfect, throughly furnished unto all good works," (II Tim. 3:15); and are able to make wise unto salvation, "through faith in Christ Jesus."

CHAPTER IV. DECLARATION OF FAITH ISSUED BY THE RICHMOND CONFERENCE IN 1887

(N.B. It should be understood that the quotations from Scripture are made from the Authorized Version unless stated to be from the American Standard Version—R.V.)

It is under a deep sense of what we owe to Him who has loved us that we feel called upon to offer a declaration of those fundamental doctrines of Christian truth that have always been professed by our branch of the Church of Christ.

OF GOD

We believe in one holy, almighty, all-wise, and everlasting God the Father, the Creator and Preserver of all things; and in Jesus Christ, His only Son, our Lord, by whom all things are made, and by whom all things consist; and in one Holy Spirit, proceeding from the Father and the Son, the Reprover of the world, the Witness for Christ, and the Teacher, Guide, and Sanctifier of the people of God; and that these three are one in the eternal Godhead; to whom be honor, praise, and thanksgiving, now and forever. Amen.

(Taken from these verses: Isa. 6:3; Isa. 57:15; Gen. 17:1; Rom. 11:33; Rom. 16:27; Psa. 90:1, 2; Matt. 11:25-27; Gen. 1:1; Job 7:20; John 1:3; Col. 1:17; John 15:26; John 16:7; John 16:8; John 15:26; John 14:26; John 16:13; II Thess. 2:13; Matt. 28:19; John 10:30; John 17:21.)

THE LORD JESUS CHRIST

It is with reverence and thanksgiving that we profess our unwavering allegiance to our Lord and Saviour, Jesus Christ. No man hath seen God at any time; the only begotten Son, who is in the bosom of the Father, He hath declared Him. In Him was life, and the life was the light of men. He is the true Light which lighteth every man that cometh into the world; through whom the light of truth in all ages has proceeded from the Father of lights. He is the eternal Word who was with God and was God, revealing Himself in infinite wisdom and love, both as man's Creator and Redeemer; for by Him were all things created that are in heaven and that are on earth, visible and invisible. Conceived of the Holy Ghost, born of the virgin Mary, the Word was made flesh and dwelt amongst men. He came in the fulness of the appointed time, being verily foreordained before the foundation of the world, that He might fulfill the eternal counsel of the righteousness and love of God for the redemption of man. In Him dwelleth all the fullness of the Godhead bodily. Though He was rich, yet for our sakes He became poor, veiling in the form of a servant the brightness of His glory, that through Him the kindness and love of God toward man might appear in a manner every way suited to our wants and finite capacities. He went about doing good; for us He endured sorrow, hunger, thirst, weariness, pain, unutterable anguish of body and of soul, being in all points tempted like as we are, yet without sin. Thus humbling Himself that we might be exalted, He emphatically recognized the duties and the sufferings of humanity as among the means whereby, through the obedience of faith, we are to be disciplined for heaven, sanctifying them to us, by Himself performing and enduring them, leaving us the one perfect example of all righteousness in self-sacrificing love.

But not only in these blessed relations must the Lord Jesus be ever precious to His people. In Him is revealed, as true God and perfect man, a Redeemer, at once able to suffer and almighty to save. He became obedient unto death, even the death of the cross, and is the propitiation for our sins, and not for ours only, but also for the sins of the whole world; in whom we have redemption through His blood for the forgiveness of sins according to the riches of His grace. It is our joy to confess that the remission of sins which any partake of is only in and by virtue of His most satisfactory sacrifice and not otherwise. He was buried and rose again the third day according to the Scriptures, becoming the first fruits of them that sleep, and having shown Himself alive after His passion, by many infallible proofs. He ascended into heaven, and hath sat down at the right hand of the Majesty on high, now to appear in the presence of God for us. With the apostles who beheld His ascension, we rest in the assurance of the angelic messengers, "This same Jesus, which is taken up from you into heaven shall so come in like manner as ye have seen him go into heaven." With the apostle John, we would desire to unite in the words "Amen; even so, come, Lord Jesus."

And now, whilst thus watching and waiting, we rejoice to believe that He is our King and Saviour. He is the one Mediator of the new and everlasting covenant, who makes peace and reconciliation between God offended and man offending; the great High Priest whose priesthood is unchangeable. He is able to save them to the uttermost that come unto God by Him, seeing He ever liveth to make intercession for them. All power is given unto Him in heaven and in earth. By Him the world shall be judged in righteousness; for the Father judgeth no man, but hath committed all judgment unto the Son, that all men should honor the Son even as they honor the Father. All that are in the tombs shall hear his voice, and shall come forth, they that have done good unto the resurrection of life, and they that have done evil unto the resurrection of judgment. (John 5:28, 29 R.V.)

We reverently confess and believe that divine honor and worship are due to the Son of God, and that He is in true faith to be prayed unto, and His name to be called upon, as the primitive Christians did, because of the glorious oneness of the Father and the Son; and that we cannot acceptably offer prayers and praises to God, nor receive from Him a gracious answer or blessing, but in and through his dear Son.

We would, with humble thanksgiving, bear an especial testimony to our Lord's perpetual dominion and power in His church. Through Him the redeemed in all generations have derived their light, their forgiveness, and their joy. All are members of this church, by whatsoever name they may be called among men, who have been baptized by the one Spirit into the one body; who are builded as living stones upon Christ, the Eternal Foundation, and are united in faith and love in that fellowship which is with the Father and with the Son. Of this church the Lord Jesus Christ is the alone Head. All its true members are made one in Him. They have washed their robes and made them white in His precious blood, and He has made them priests unto God and His Father. He dwells in their hearts by faith, and gives them of his peace. His will is their law, and in Him they enjoy the true liberty, a freedom from the bondage of sin.

(Taken from these verses: Paragraph 1—John 1:18; John 1:4, 9; James 1:17; John 1:1; Col. 1:13-16; Matt. 1:20, 23-25; Luke 1:35; John 1:14; Gal. 4:4; I Peter 1:20; Isa. 11:1-5; Isa. 52:13-15; Isa. 53; Col. 2:9; Phil. 2:7; Titus 3:4; Acts 10:38; Isa. 53:4; Luke 12:50; 19:41; 22:44; John 4:6; Luke 22:43, 44; Heb. 4:15; I Peter 2:21; Matt. 3:15. Paragraph 2—Eph. 4:13; Phil. 2:8; I John 2:2; Eph. 1:7; I Cor. 15:4, 23; Acts 1:3; Heb. 1:3; 9:24; Acts 1:11, 7; Rev. 22:20; I Tim. 2:5; Heb. 9:15; 4:14; 7:24, 25; Matt. 28:18; Acts 17:31; John 5:22, 23. Paragraph 4—Eph. 1:22; Rev. 7:14; 1:6.)

THE HOLY SPIRIT

We believe that the Holy Spirit is, in the unity of the eternal Godhead, one with the Father and with the Son. He is the Comforter "Whom," saith Christ, "the Father will send in my name." He convinces the world of sin, of righteousness, and of judgment. He testifies of and glorifies Jesus. It is the Holy Spirit who makes the evil manifest. He quickens them that are dead in trespasses and sins, and opens the inward eye to behold the Lamb of God that taketh away the sin of the world. Coming in the name and with the authority of the risen and ascended Saviour, He is the precious pledge of the continued love and care of our exalted King. He takes of the things of Christ and shows them, as a realized possession, to the believing soul. Dwelling in the hearts of believers, He opens their understandings that they may understand the Scriptures, and becomes, to the humbled and surrendered heart, the Guide, Comforter, Support, and Sanctifier.

We believe that the essential qualification for the Lord's service is bestowed upon His children through the reception and baptism of the Holy Ghost. This Holy Spirit is the seal of reconciliation to the believer in Jesus, the witness to his adoption into the family of the redeemed; the earnest and the foretaste of the full communion and perfect joy which are reserved for them that endure unto the end.

We own no principle of spiritual light, life, or holiness inherent by nature in the mind or heart of man. We believe in no principle of spiritual light, life, or holiness but the influence of the Holy Spirit of God bestowed on mankind in various measures and degrees, through Jesus Christ our Lord. It is the capacity to receive this blessed influence, which, in an especial manner, gives man pre-eminence above the beasts that perish; which distinguishes him, in every nation and in every clime, as an object of the redeeming love of God, as a being not only intelligent but responsible, for whom the message of salvation through our crucified Redeemer is, under all possible circumstances, designed to be a joyful sound. The Holy Spirit must ever be distinguished both from the conscience which

He enlightens and from the natural faculty of reason, which when unsubjected to His holy influence, is, in the things of God, very foolishness. As the eye is to the body, so is the conscience to our inner being, the organ by which we see; and as both light and life are essential to the eye, so conscience, as the inward eye, cannot see aright without the quickening and illumination of the Spirit of God. One with the Father and the Son, the Holy Spirit can never disown or dishonor our once crucified and now risen and glorified Redeemer. We disavow all professed illumination or spirituality that is divorced from faith in Jesus Christ of Nazareth, crucified for us without the gates of Jerusalem.

(Taken from these verses: Matt. 28:19; II Cor. 13:14; John 16:26, 8, 14; John 14:17; Eph. 2:1; 1:13, 14; Rom. 8:15, 16.)

THE HOLY SCRIPTURES

It has ever been, and still is, the belief of the Society of Friends that the Holy Scriptures of the Old and New Testament were given by inspiration of God; that, therefore, there can be no appeal from them to any other authority whatsoever; that they are able to make wise unto salvation, through faith which is in Jesus Christ. "These are written that ye might believe that Jesus is the Christ, the Son of God; and that believing ye might have life through His name." (John 20:31.) The Scriptures are the only divinely authorized record of the doctrines which we are bound as Christians to accept and of the moral principles which are to regulate our actions. No one can be required to believe, as an article of faith, any doctrine which is not contained in them; and whatsoever any one says or does, contrary to the Scriptures, though under profession of the immediate guidance of the Holy Spirit, must be reckoned and accounted a mere delusion. To the Christian the Old Testament comes with the solemn and repeated attestation of his Lord. It is to be read in the light and completeness of the New; thus will its meaning be unveiled, and the humble disciple will be taught to discern the unity and mutual adaptation of the whole and the many-sidedness and harmony of its testimony to Christ. The great Inspirer of Scripture is ever its true Interpreter. He performs this office in condescending love, not by superseding our understandings, but by renewing and enlightening them. Where Christ presides, idle speculation is hushed; His doctrine is learned in the doing of His will, and all knowledge ripens into a deeper and richer experience of His truth and love.

MAN'S CREATION AND FALL

It pleased God, in His wisdom and goodness, to create man out of the dust of the earth, and to breathe into his nostrils the breath of life, so that man became a living soul; formed after the image and likeness of God, capable of fulfilling the divine law, and of holding communion with his Maker. Being free to obey or to disobey, he fell into transgression, through unbelief, under the temptation of Satan and thereby lost that spiritual life of righteousness in which he was created; and so death passed upon him as the inevitable consequence of his sin. As the children of fallen Adam, all mankind bear his image. They partake of his

nature and are involved in the consequences of his fall. To every member of every successive generation, the words of the Redeemer are alike applicable, "Ye must be born again." But while we hold these views of the lost condition of man in the fall, we rejoice to believe that sin is not imputed to any until they transgress the divine law after sufficient capacity has been given to understand it; and that infants, though inheriting this fallen nature, are saved in the infinite mercy of God through the redemption which is in Christ Jesus.

(Scripture verses quoted are Gen. 2:7; 1:26, 27; 3:1-7; Rom. 5:12; John 3:7.)

JUSTIFICATION AND SANCTIFICATION

"God so loved the world that He gave His only begotten Son, that whosoever believeth in Him should not perish, but have everlasting life." We believe that justification is of God's free grace, through which, upon repentance and faith, He pardons our sins and imparts to us a new life. It is received, not for any works of righteousness that we have done, but in the unmerited mercy of God in Christ Jesus. Through faith in Him and the shedding of His precious blood, the guilt of sin is taken away, and we stand reconciled to God. The offering up of Christ as the propitiation for the sins of the whole world is the appointed manifestation both of the righteousness and of the love of God. In this propitiation the pardon of sin involves no abrogation or relaxation of the law of holiness. It is the vindication and establishment of that law, in virtue of the free and righteous submission of the Son of God Himself to all its requirements. He, the unchangeably just, proclaims Himself the justifier of him that believeth in Jesus. From age to age, the sufferings and death of Christ have been a hidden mystery and a rock of offense to the unbelief and pride of man's fallen nature; yet, to the humble penitent whose heart is broken under the convicting power of the Spirit, life is revealed in that death. As he looks upon Him who was wounded for our transgressions, and upon whom the Lord was pleased to lay the iniquity of us all, his eye is more and more opened to see, and his heart to understand, the exceeding sinfulness of sin for which the Saviour died; whilst, in the sense of pardoning grace, he will joy in God through our Lord Jesus Christ, by Whom we have now received the atonement.

We believe that in connection with justification is regeneration: that they who come to this experience know that they are not their own; that being reconciled to God by the death of His Son, we are saved by His life; a new heart is given and new desires; old things are passed away, and we become new creatures through faith in Christ Jesus. Our wills being surrendered to His holy will, grace reigns through righteousness unto eternal life by Jesus Christ our Lord.

Sanctification is experienced in the acceptance of Christ in living faith for justification, in so far as the pardoned sinner, through faith in Christ, is clothed with a measure of His righteousness and receives the Spirit of promise; for, as saith the Apostle, "Ye are washed, ye are sanctified, ye are justified, in the name of the Lord Jesus, and by the Spirit of our God." We rejoice to believe that the provisions of God's grace are sufficient to deliver from the power, as well as from the guilt, of sin and to enable His believing children always to triumph in Christ. How full of encouragement is the declaration, "According to your faith be it unto you." Whosoever submits himself wholly to God, believing and appropriating His promises and exercising faith in Christ Jesus, will have his heart continually cleansed from all sin by His precious blood and, through the renewing, refining power of the Holy Spirit, be kept in conformity to the will of God, will love Him with all his heart, mind, soul, and strength, and be able to say with the Apostle Paul, "The law of the Spirit of life in Christ Jesus hath made me free from the law of sin and death." Thus, in its full experience sanctification is deliverance from the pollution, nature, and love of sin. To this we are every one called that we may serve the Lord without fear, in holiness and righteousness before Him all the days of our life. It was the prayer of the apostle for the believers, "The very God of peace sanctify you wholly; and I pray God your whole spirit and soul and body be preserved blameless unto the coming of our Lord Jesus Christ. Faithful is he that calleth you who also will do it." Yet the most holy Christian is still liable to temptation, is exposed to the subtle assaults of Satan, and can only continue to follow holiness as he humbly watches unto prayer and is kept in constant dependence upon his Saviour, walking in the light in the loving obedience of faith.

(Taken from these verses: Paragraph 1—John 3:16; Titus 3:5; I John 2:2; Rom. 3:31, 26; Isa. 53:5, 6; Rom. 5:11. Paragraph 2—I Cor. 6:19; Rom. 5:10; II Cor. 5:17; Rom. 5:21. Paragraph 3—I Cor. 6:11; II Cor. 2:14; Matt. 9:29; Rom. 8:2; Luke 1:74, 75; I Thess. 5:23, 24; I John 1:7.)

THE RESURRECTION AND FINAL JUDGMENT

We believe, according to the Scriptures, that there shall be a resurrection from the dead, both of the just and of the unjust, and that God hath appointed a day in which He will judge the world in righteousness, by Jesus Christ whom he hath ordained. For, as saith the apostle, "We must all appear before the judgment seat of Christ, that every one may receive the things done in his body according to that he hath done, whether it be good or bad."

We sincerely believe not only a resurrection in Christ from the fallen and sinful state here but a rising and ascending into glory with Him hereafter; that when He at last appears we may appear with Him in glory, but that all the wicked, who live in rebellion against the light of grace and die finally impenitent, shall come forth to the resurrection of condemnation. The soul of every man and woman shall be reserved in its own distinct and proper being and shall have its proper body as God is pleased to give it. It is sown a natural body, it is raised a spiritual body; that being first which is natural, and afterward that which is spiritual. And though it is said, "this corruptible shall put on incorruption, and this mortal shall put on immortality," the change shall be such as will accord with the declaration, "Flesh and blood cannot inherit the Kingdom of God, neither doth corruption inherit incorruption." We shall be raised out of all corruption and corruptibility, out of all mortality, and shall be the children of God, being the children of resurrection.

"Our citizenship is in heaven" (R.V.), from whence also we look for the Savior the Lord Jesus Christ, who shall change our vile body that it may be fashioned like unto His glorious body, according to the working whereby He is able even to subdue all things unto Himself.

We believe that the punishment of the wicked and the blessedness of the righteous shall be everlasting; according to the declaration of our compassionate Redeemer, to whom the judgment is committed, "These shall go away into eternal punishment but the righteous into eternal life." (R. V., Matt. 25:46.)

(Verses quoted are: Paragraph 1—Acts 24:15; 17:31; II Cor. 5:10. Paragraph 2—I Cor. 15:44, 53, 50; Luke 20:36. Paragraph 3—Phil. 3:20, 21.)

BAPTISM

We would express our continued conviction that our Lord appointed no outward rite or ceremony for observance in His church. We accept every command of our Lord, in what we believe to be its genuine import, as absolutely conclusive. The question of the use of outward ordinances is with us a question, not as to the authority of Christ but as to his real meaning. We reverently believe that, as there is one Lord and one faith, so there is under the Christian dispensation but one baptism, even that whereby all believers are baptized in one Spirit into one body. (I Cor. 12;13. R. V.) This is not an outward baptism with water, but a spiritual experience; not the putting away of the filth of the flesh, but that inward work which, by transforming the heart and settling the soul upon Christ, brings forth the answer of a good conscience towards God by the resurrection of Jesus Christ in the experience of His love and power as the risen and ascended Saviour. No baptism in outward water can satisfy the description of the apostle of being buried with Christ by baptism unto death. It is with the Spirit alone that any can thus be baptized. In this experience the announcement of the forerunner of our Lord is fulfilled, "He shall baptize you with the Holy Ghost and with fire." In this view we accept the commission of our blessed Lord as given in Matthew 28:18-20 R.V.: "And Jesus came to them and spake unto them saying, All authority hath been given unto me in heaven and on earth. Go ye, therefore, and make disciples of all the nations, baptizing them into the name of the Father and of the Son and of the Holy Spirit: teaching them to observe all things whatsoever I commanded you; and lo, I am with you always, even unto the end of the world." This commission, as we believe, was not designed to set up a new ritual under the new covenant, or to connect the initiation into a membership—in its nature essentially spiritual—with a mere ceremony of a typical character. Otherwise it was not possible for the Apostle Paul, who was not a whit behind the very chiefest apostle, to have disclaimed that which would in that case have been of the essence of his commission when he wrote, "Christ sent me not to baptize, but to preach the Gospel." Whenever an external ceremony is commanded, the particulars, the mode, and incidents of that ceremony become of its essence. There is an utter absence of these particulars in the text before us which confirms our persuasion that the commission must be construed in connection with the spiritual power which the risen Lord promised should attend the witness of his apostles and of the church to Him and which, after Pentecost, so mightily accompanied their ministry of the word and prayer, that those to whom they were sent were introduced into an experience wherein they had a saving knowledge of, and living fellowship with, the Father and the Son and the Holy Spirit.

(Taken from these verses: Eph. 4:4, 5; I Peter 3:21; Romans 6:4; Matt. 3:11; II Cor. 11:5; I Cor. 1:17.)

THE SUPPER OF THE LORD

Intimately connected with the conviction already expressed is the view that we have ever maintained as to the true supper of the Lord. We are well aware that our Lord was pleased to make use of a variety of symbolical utterances, but He often gently upbraided His disciples for accepting literally what He had intended only in its spiritual meaning. His teaching, as in His parables or in the command to wash one another's feet, was often in symbols, and ought ever to be received in the light of His own emphatic declaration, "The words that I speak unto you, they are spirit and they are life." The old covenant was full of ceremonial symbols; the new covenant, to which our Saviour alluded at the last supper, is expressly declared by the prophet to be "not according to the old." We cannot believe that in setting up this new covenant the Lord Jesus intended an institution out of harmony with the spirit of this prophecy. The eating of His body and the drinking of His blood cannot be an outward act. They truly partake of them who habitually rest upon the sufferings and death of their Lord as their only hope, and to whom the indwelling Spirit gives to drink of the fullness that is in Christ. It is this inward and spiritual partaking that is the true supper of the Lord.

The presence of Christ with His church is not designed to be by symbol or representation, but in the real communication of His own Spirit. "I will pray the Father, and He shall give you another Comforter, that he may abide with you forever." Convincing of sin, testifying of Jesus, taking of the things of Christ, this blessed Comforter communicates to the believer and to the church in a gracious, abiding manifestation the REAL PRESENCE of the Lord. As the great remembrancer through whom the promise is fulfilled, He needs no ritual or priestly intervention in bringing to the experience of the true commemoration and communion. "Behold," saith the risen Redeemer, "I stand at the door and knock. If any man hear my voice and open the door, I will come in and sup with him and he with me." In an especial manner, when assembled for congregational worship, are believers invited to the festival of the Saviour's peace and, in a united act of faith and love, unfettered by any outward rite or ceremonial, to partake together of the body that was broken and of the blood that was shed for them without the gates of Jerusalem. In such a worship they are enabled to understand the words of the apostle as expressive of a sweet and most real experience: "The cup of blessing which we bless, is it not the communion of the blood of Christ? The bread that we break, is it not the communion of the body of Christ? For we being many are one bread and one body; for we are all partakers of that one bread."

(Taken from these verses: John 6:63; Jer. 31:32; Heb. 8:9; John 14:16; Rev. 3:20; I Cor. 10:16, 17.)

PUBLIC WORSHIP

Worship is the adoring response of the heart and mind to the influence of the Spirit of God. It stands neither in forms nor in the formal disuse of forms: it may be without words as well as with them, but it must be in spirit and in truth. We recognize the value of silence, not as an end but as a means toward the attainment of the end; a silence, not of listlessness or of vacant musing but of holy expectation before the Lord. Having become His adopted children through faith in the Lord Jesus Christ, it is our privilege to meet together and unite in the worship of Almighty God and to wait upon Him for the renewal of our strength, for communion one with another, for the edification of believers in the exercise of various spiritual gifts, and for the declaration of the glad tidings of salvation to the unconverted who may gather with us. This worship depends not upon numbers. Where two or three are gathered together in the name of Christ there is a church, and Christ, the living Head, in the midst of them. Through His mediation, without the necessity for any inferior instrumentality, is the Father to be approached and reverently worshipped. The Lord Jesus has forever fulfilled and ended the typical and sacrificial worship under the law by offering up of Himself upon the cross for us, once for all. He has opened the door of access into the inner sanctuary and graciously provided spiritual offerings for the service of His temple, suited to the several conditions of all who worship in spirit and in truth. The broken and the contrite heart, the confession of the soul prostrate before God, the prayer of the afflicted when he is overwhelmed, the earnest wrestling of the spirit, the outpouring of humble thanksgiving, the spiritual song and melody of the heart, the simple exercise of faith, the self-denying service of love—these are among the sacrifices which He, our merciful and faithful High Priest, is pleased to prepare by His Spirit in the hearts of them that receive Him and to present with acceptance unto God.

By the immediate operations of the Holy Spirit, He, as the Head of the church, alone selects and qualifies those who are to present His messages or engage in other service for Him; and hence, we cannot commit any formal arrangement to any one in our regular meetings for worship. We are well aware that the Lord has provided a diversity of gifts for the needs both of the church and of the world, and we desire that the church may feel her responsibility, under the government of her Great Head, in doing her part to foster these gifts and in making arrangements for their proper exercise.

It is not for individual exaltation, but for mutual profit, that the gifts are bestowed; and every living church, abiding under the government of Christ, is humbly and thankfully to receive and exercise them in subjection to her Holy Head. The church that quenches the Spirit and lives to itself alone must die.

We believe the preaching of the Gospel to be one of the chief means, divinely appointed, for the spreading of the glad tidings of life and salvation through our crucified Redeemer, for the awakening and conversion of sinners, and for the comfort and edification of believers. As it is the prerogative of the Great Head of the church alone to select and call the ministers of His Gospel, so we believe that both the gift and the qualification to exercise it must be derived immediately from Him; and that, as in the primitive church so now also, He confers spiritual gifts upon women as well as upon men, agreeably to the prophecy recited by the apostle Peter, "It shall come to pass in that the last days saith God, I will pour out of my Spirit upon all flesh; and your sons and your daughters shall prophesy." Respecting which the apostle declares, "The promise is unto you, and to your children, and to all that are afar off, even as many as the Lord our God shall call." As the gift is freely received, so it is to be freely exercised in simple obedience to the will of God.

Spiritual gifts, precious as they are, must not be mistaken for grace; they add to our responsibility, but do not raise the minister above his brethren or sisters. They must be exercised in continued dependence upon our Lord, and blessed is that ministry in which man is humbled, and Christ and His grace exalted. "He that is greatest among you," said our Lord and Master, "let him be as the younger; and he that is chief as he that doth serve. I am among you as he that serveth."

While the church cannot confer spiritual gifts, it is its duty to recognize and foster them and to promote their efficiency by all means in its power. And while, on the one hand, the Gospel should never be preached for money, on the other, it is the duty of the church to make such provision that it shall never be hindered for want of it.

The church, if true to her allegiance, cannot forget her part in the command, "Go ye into all the world, and preach the Gospel to every creature." Knowing that it is the Spirit of God that can alone prepare and qualify the instruments who fulfill this command, the true disciple will be found still sitting at the feet of Jesus, listening that he may learn and learning that he may obey. He humbly places himself at his Lord's disposal, and when he hears the call, "Whom shall I send, and who will go for us?" is prepared to respond, in childlike reverence and love. "Here am I, send me."

(Taken from these verses: Paragraph 1—John 4:24; Eph. 5:19; Paragraph 2—I Cor. 12:4-6. Paragraph 3—I Cor. 12:7. Paragraph 4—Acts 2:17, 39; Matt. 10:8; Acts 20:33-35. Paragraph 5—Luke 22:26, 27. Paragraph 6—Acts 8:20; 20:33-35. Paragraph 7—Mark 16:15; Isa. 6:8.)

PRAYER AND PRAISE

Prayer is the outcome of our sense of need and of our continual dependence upon God. He who uttered the invitation, "Ask and it shall be given you," is Himself the Mediator and High Priest who, by His Spirit, prompts the petition and presents it with acceptance before God. With such an invitation, prayer becomes the duty and the privilege of all who are called by His name. Prayer is, in the awakened soul, the utterance of the cry, "God be merciful to me a sinner," and at every stage of the believer's course prayer is essential to his spiritual life. A life without prayer is a life practically without God. The Christian's life is a continual asking. The thirst that prompts the petition produces, as it is satisfied, still deeper longings, which prepare for yet more bounteous supplies from Him who delights to bless. Prayer is not confined to the closet. When uttered in response to the promptings of the Holy Spirit, it becomes an important part of public worship, and whenever the Lord's people meet together in His name, it is their privilege to wait upon Him for the spirit of grace and supplications. A life of prayer cannot be other than a life of praise. As the peace of Christ reigns in the church, her living members accept all that they receive as from His pure bounty, and each day brings them fresh pledges of their Father's love. Satisfied with the goodness of His house, whether as individuals, in families, or in congregations, they will be still praising Him, heart answering to heart, "Bless the Lord, O my soul: and all that is within me, bless His holy name."

(Scripture verses quoted are: Matt. 7:7; Luke 18:13; Zech. 12:10; Psa. 84:4; 103:1.)

LIBERTY OF CONSCIENCE IN ITS RELATION TO CIVIL GOVERNMENT

That conscience should be free and that in matters of religious doctrine and worship man is accountable only to God are truths which are plainly declared in the New Testament, and which are confirmed by the whole scope of the Gospel and by the example of our Lord and His disciples. To rule over the conscience and to command the spiritual allegiance of his creature man are the high and sacred prerogatives of God alone. In religion every act ought to be free. A forced worship is plainly a contradiction in terms, under that dispensation in which the worship of the Father must be in spirit and in truth.

We have ever maintained that it is the duty of Christians to obey the enactments of civil government, except those which interfere with our allegiance to God. We owe much to its blessings. Through it we enjoy liberty and protection in connection with law and order. Civil government is a divine ordinance, instituted to promote the best welfare of man; hence magistrates are to be regarded as God's ministers who should be a terror to evil doers and a praise to them that do well. Therefore, it is with us a matter of conscience to render them respect and obedience in the exercise of their proper functions.

(Taken from these verses: John 4:24; Rom. 13:1; I Peter 2:13-16.)

MARRIAGE

Marriage is an institution graciously ordained by the Creator Himself for the help and continuance of the human family. It is not a mere civil contract and ought never to be entered upon without a reference to the sanction and blessing of Him who ordained it. It is a solemn engagement for the term of life, (Matt. 19:5, 6), designed for the mutual assistance and comfort of both sexes, that they may be helpmates to each other in things temporal and spiritual. To this end it should imply concurrence in spiritual as well as temporal concerns and

THE CHURCH AND ITS ESSENTIAL DOCTRINES [MID-AMERICA (FORMERLY KANSAS) YEARLY MEETING] (continued)

should be entered upon discreetly, soberly, and in the fear of the Lord.

(Scripture verses quoted are: Matt. 5:44; Luke 6:27; Isaiah 2:4; Micah 4:1.)

PEACE

We feel bound explicitly to avow our unshaken persuasion that all war is utterly incompatible with the plain percepts of our divine Lord and Law-giver and the whole spirit of His Gospel, and that no plea of necessity or policy, however urgent or peculiar, can avail to release either individuals or nations from the paramount allegiance which they owe to Him who hath said, "Love your enemies." In enjoining this love and the forgiveness of injuries, He who has bought us to Himself has not prescribed for man precepts which are incapable of being carried into practice, or of which the practice is to be postponed until all shall be persuaded to act upon them. We cannot doubt that they are incumbent now, and that we have in the prophetic Scriptures the distinct intimation of their direct application not only to individuals, but to nations also. When nations conform their laws to this divine teaching, wars must necessarily cease.

We would, in humility but in faithfulness to our Lord, express our firm persuasion that all the exigencies of civil government and social order may be met under the banner of the Prince of Peace in strict conformity with His command.

OATHS

We hold it to be the inalienable privilege of the disciple of the Lord Jesus that his statements concerning matters of fact within his knowledge should be accepted, under all circumstances, as expressing his belief as to the fact asserted. We rest upon the plain command of our Lord and Master, "Swear not at all" (Matt. 5:34); and we believe any departure from this standard to be prejudicial to the cause of truth and to that confidence between man and man, the maintenance of which is indispensable to our mutual well being. This command, in our persuasion, applies not to profane swearing only but to judicial oaths also. It abrogates any previous permission to the contrary, and is, for the Christian, absolutely conclusive.

THE FIRST DAY OF THE WEEK

Whilst the remembrance of our Creator ought to be at all times present with the Christian, we would express our thankfulness to our Heavenly Father that He has been pleased to honor the setting apart of one day in seven for the purpose of holy rest, religious duties, and public worship; and we desire that all under our name may avail themselves of this great privilege as those who are called to be risen with Christ and to seek those things that are above where He sitteth at the right hand of God. (Coloss. 3:1.) May the release thus granted from other occupations be diligently improved. On this day of the week especially ought the households of Friends to be assembled for the reading of the Scriptures and for waiting upon the Lord; and we trust that, in a Christianly wise economy of our

time and strength, the engagements of the day may be so ordered as not to frustrate the gracious provision thus made for us by our Heavenly Father, or to shut out the opportunity either for public worship or for private retirement and devotional reading.

In presenting this declaration of our Christian faith, we desire that all our members may be afresh encouraged, in humility and devotedness, to renewed faithfulness in fulfiling their part in the great mission of the Church, and through the Church to the world around us in the name of our Crucified Redeemer. Life *from* Christ, life *in* Christ, must ever be the basis of life *for* Christ. For this we have been created and redeemed, and by this alone can the longings of our immortal souls be satisfied.

Notes: *The Kansas Yearly Meeting has recently changed its name to the Mid-America Yearly Meeting. It is a member of the Evangelical Friends Alliance, which is a member of the National Association of Evangelicals as well as the Christian Holines Association.*

*　　*　　*

QUAKER FAITH AND PRACTICE (PACIFIC YEARLY MEETING)

Friends from the first have stressed the interdependence of faith and practice. They refrain from fixing their faith in a formal set of words because they feel the divine lies deeper than words: it must be lived and demonstrated throughout the whole of life. They value greatly the record of God's dealing with men in the Judeo-Christian scriptures and feel these are to be interpreted in the Spirit which inspired them and which continues to reveal Truth to men. Friends have used various expressions—the Light Within, the Light or Spirit of Christ, living God, Word, that of God, Truth, Power, Seed, and many more—in trying to describe their experience of the divine Life at the heart of the universe. They have emphasized that by living and walking in this Light, which was revealed in the life of Jesus on earth and which enlightens every man, they may answer to the same Light, or that of God, in other persons. Friends thus approach faith less as a matter of profession than of experience. The Quaker interpretation of Christianity keeps in creative tension its particular and universal character, its Christ-centered and God-centered orientation, its mystical and practical demands.

The religious practices of Friends follow from the conviction that the divine Light is accessible to all; yet it is one Light; therefore men are to wait in the Light for agreement in their common affairs. This is the key to the Quaker Meeting, whether for worship or for business. Quaker worship has been described as "group mysticism." Meetings for business and for action on social concerns are thought of as worship translated into action. Through agreement in a "sense of the Meeting," Quaker practice seeks to reconcile the demands both of freedom and order, individual inspiration and corporate wisdom. (In its early days, the Quaker movement specifically rejected so-called "Ranterism," the view that religious activities ought to be left entirely to individual inspiration, with no accepted common order of any kind.) The Quaker movement has found coherence and continuity in a system of Monthly, Quarterly, and Yearly Meetings, with certain more general gatherings for larger associations of Friends.

Notes: *The Pacific Yearly Meeting includes congregations stretched from Canada to Mexico. It emphasizes the experience of the inner light and the freedom of belief of its members.*

* * *

BASIC BELIEFS (ROCKY MOUNTAIN YEARLY MEETING)

Friends believe that apostolic (New Testament) doctrines are essentials of Christianity. Fundamental truths considered as vital and life-giving are: the Fatherhood of God; the deity and humanity of Jesus the Son, the ministry of the Holy Spirit; Christ's atonement which reconciles men to God; the resurrection of Jesus Christ which assures true believers of life after death; the high priesthood of Christ who gives access to the Father by forgiving men's sins; and the individual priesthood of believers who may approach God directly without human intervention.

While Friends do not stress a formal written creed, they do state the primary principles of their faith in order to make their doctrinal position clear. Not wishing to be dogmatic, they record certain beliefs which are held as basic to their faith. The statement of faith of Friends may be summarized as follows:

> The Bible is the inspired rule of faith and subject to the Holy Spirit's interpretation.
>
> God is sovereign.
>
> Jesus Christ offers vicarious atonement through His death and resurrection.
>
> The Holy Spirit brings men to experience salvation.
>
> Man is sinful, but redeemable.
>
> Salvation comprises both forgiveness and sanctification.
>
> The Church is the visible expression of Christ; it will be fulfilled in the final resurrection and judgment.
>
> Inner communion and the baptism with the Holy Spirit are spiritual realities beyond outward symbols.
>
> Christian witness is given through word and deed both in general and specific ministries.

The following pages amplify the subjects mentioned above; for more complete statements on fundamental doctrines, refer to the historical documents which appear in the Appendix.

1. THE BIBLE. The Holy Bible was given to men by the direct inspiration of God. It is sufficient to inform men of salvation through faith in Jesus Christ. God's Holy Spirit, who inspired the Scriptures, also interprets them, working through those yielded to Him within His Church. The Bible is the final authority by which all guidance should be measured for truth. Genuine guidance from God is in accord with the Holy Scriptures.

2. GOD. There is one sovereign God who is revealed through the Bible in the person of His Son, Jesus Christ. God is the Maker and Preserver of all things; He alone is worthy of worship. In the unity of the Godhead exist three equal and distinct, yet inseparable, persons: the Father, the Son Jesus Christ, and the Holy Spirit.

3. JESUS CHRIST. Jesus Christ, the only begotten Son of God, is God's revelation of Himself to man. He was divine and yet human, being conceived by God's Spirit and born of a virgin. Through the blood He shed dying on the cross, Jesus Christ became the atonement for man's sin, thus providing direct access to God by His priesthood. Upon His resurrection from the dead, He ascended again to the right hand of His Father, assuming the role of Intercessor and drawing men to God by His Spirit. When Jesus Christ returns to earth, He will receive His Church and judge the world.

4. THE HOLY SPIRIT. The Holy Spirit proceeds from the Father and the Son and is equal with them. He convinces men of their sin, gives life to penitent believers, and sanctifies the child of God. He enables one to love God supremely and to give evidence of the Spirit's presence in his life. The Holy Spirit works through individual lives as well as in corporate groups of the church, enabling men to serve in various ways as He chooses.

5. MAN. Created in the image of God, at first man enjoyed unbroken fellowship with His Maker. By his disobedience, he incurred the displeasure of God and the penalty of spiritual death. Consequently, since Adam sinned, all men are born in a sinful state; there is no inherent principle which naturally leads man to salvation outside the atoning provision of Jesus Christ for all mankind. While man is sinful by nature, he can be redeemed from sin's penalty, which is eternal death, because Christ paid this penalty in full.

Through His sacrificial death, Jesus Christ destroyed the wall separating man from God. By the individual priesthood of believers, all men stand equal before God and may approach Him directly.

6. SALVATION. Salvation is a personal matter between man and his Maker. It consists of forgiveness for sin as well as sanctification or the cleansing of man's sinful nature. Man can be redeemed because of the atoning death of Jesus Christ and the direct work of the Spirit. The Holy Spirit restores man to fellowship with God the Father and enables man to love Him wholeheartedly. Salvation does not depend on outward ceremonies or symbols.

Sanctification is the work of God which is accomplished through baptism with the Holy Spirit in the life of a believer who yields himself totally to God. He is thus empowered to witness to the living Christ. Sanctification is both an act in which one's heart is cleansed and a process in which life is continuously disciplined to God's holy standards.

7. BAPTISM AND COMMUNION. Both Christian baptism and communion are spiritual realities beyond the mere physical, outward ordinances. Therefore Friends believe so strongly in these spiritual realities that most do not practice the ceremonies. True baptism is the inward receiving of God's Spirit by asking in faith for Him to become the Lord of one's life. Communion is the continuing fellowship with Jesus Christ as Saviour and Lord; it is often practiced in worship and may be exercised in a period of quiet waiting before the Lord, in verbal witness, through prayer, sharing of the Holy Spirit's witness in one's life, or in the expression of needs or concerns. Although it is rooted in the historical act of Christ's body being broken and His blood shed, communion depends upon obedience to Him.

8. THE CHURCH. Those who repent of their sins and trust in Jesus Christ as their personal Saviour are born again into His kingdom by His Spirit. These persons make up the true Church of Jesus Christ which is spiritual in nature and universal in scope. By His Spirit, Christ is present wherever two or three meet together in His name. Such a meeting is a local church which is a visible manifestation of the Church universal. Every believer should be related to a local visible part of Christ's universal body in order to worship, witness and work more effectively for the glory of God. Every believer is committed to be involved in the stewardship of God's Kingdom through the Church until the Lord returns.

9. CHRISTIAN WORSHIP AND WORK. Christians should meet together for public worship; it is both a duty and a privilege. By doing so, they testify to others of their faith in Christ and also receive mutual benefit. Worship may be silent or vocal, taking various forms; it does not depend on certain ceremonies or traditions. Worship is a natural outgrowth of union with Christ and should be directed by His Spirit. Friends emphasize that Christ may be known experientially through His Holy Spirit and hold that He is present to lead His people Himself. Though Friends worship has been noted for its silence, in reality it is not a worship of silence but a worship on the basis of obedience to God.

The emphasis is on the ministry of each individual in the body of Christ and the importance of each one ministering to the spiritual needs of others according to the direction of the Holy Spirit.

It is extremely important that as one attends meetings among Friends that he come not as an observer but as a participator in an exciting adventure which is unpredictable for the precise reason that we are seeking to do God's will rather than our own. He should come not primarily to hear a sermon or to repeat ready made phrases but with fellow Christians to sense the presence of the living Christ and to be led by Him.

Every meeting should be an adventure in which God speaks to individuals through His Spirit. In addition to public worship, Friends encourage daily private and family worship.

Believers are committed to the work of God, not only to manifest personal righteousness as the fruit of a new life, but also to share their faith. All Christians are called upon to witness by word and deed, in Christlikeness demonstrating love, forgiveness, and the way of peace. Certain ones are called and ordained by God for a special service of leadership in His Church; this service may be that of teaching, evangelizing, pastoring or administration. The church should recognize such special gifts among its members and encourage their use.

10. FRUIT AND GIFTS OF THE SPIRIT. The Holy Spirit is the indwelling agent of leadership for each Christian. He always leads in harmony with Holy Scriptures. Growth and maturity come as the Spirit is allowed to control the individual life, producing love, joy, peace, patience, kindness, goodness, faithfulness, gentleness, and self-control. Gifts, or abilities, are also given by the Spirit to be used to encourage and strengthen each other. While each gift is Spirit-given, Friends prefer to emphasize seeking the Giver more than the gifts.

As believers receive gifts, love will provide the motivation for the best use of each one. Speaking in other tongues does not constitute the essential sign of the baptism with the Holy Spirit. The evidence of the fullness of the Holy Spirit is the fruit of the Spirit, and especially *agape* love emanating from a truly transformed life.

11. THE LORD'S RETURN. At His second coming, Jesus Christ will return in power as King of kings to consummate His rule over men and nations by the final triumph over Satan. The dead shall be resurrected, some to eternal life, others to everlasting punishment. All shall be judged by God and receive just recompence for their deeds. The blessed ones shall live forever in heaven, but the lost suffer eternally in hell.

12. LIBERTY. Christian liberty is to be granted in all areas not essential to one's final salvation. Due to human imperfection, there are differences of faith and practice among God's children, but we anticipate a time of greater unity in the faith. Until that time, there must be unity in essentials but liberty in nonessentials, with love in all things.

Notes: *The Rocky Mountain Yearly Meeting is a member of the Evangelical Friends Alliance, which is a member of the National Association of Evangelicals as well as the Christian Holiness Association.*

Miscellaneous European Free

THE COMMON VIEWS [CHRISTIAN COMMUNITY OF UNIVERSAL BROTHERHOOD (DOUKHOBORS)]

1. The members of the Community honour and love God, as the source of all being.

2. They respect the merit and worth of mankind, both of themselves, and likewise of other [persons].

3. The members of the Community regard all that is, lovingly and with delight. They try to inspire their growing ones with this line [of thought].

4. By the word 'God', the members of the Community understand the power of love, the power of life, which is the source of all being.

5. The world is based upon going forward; all things strive for perfection, and through this process seek to rejoin their source, as seeds yield ripe fruit.

6. In all that is in our world we see changing steps toward perfection, as, for example, beginning with stones, it passes on to plants, then beasts, of which the very last one can count is man—in the sense of life, in the sense of a thinking creature.

7. To do away with, to destroy, that which lives, the members of the Community count blameworthy. In every single being there is life, hence [there is] God, and above all in man. To rob the life from a person is not, in whatever case, [to be] allowed.

8. The members of the Community in their beliefs allow utter freedom to all that is, including the life of man. Every organization, founded upon violence, is counted unlawful.

9. The chief base of the life of man—thought, reason serves as [that]. For material food this serves: air, water, fruits and vegetables.

10. It is held that the life of mankind is communal, upheld through the strength of moral law, for which [this] rule serves: 'Whatever I do not want for myself, that I should not wish for others.'

Notes: *This statement, originally written in Russian, dates to December 1896, appearing in a letter written by Doukhobor leader Peter Vasilievich Verigin. It served as the ideological manifesto of the community until it was replaced in 1934 by the Declaration of the Society of Named Doukhobors (now the Union of Spiritual Communities of Christ).*

* * *

FUNDAMENTAL PRINCIPLES (SCHWENKFELDER CHURCH)

1. Every person desiring to be a member of this Church should concern himself about a proper and approved ideal upon which the members are to be established in all things, and in accordance with which they are to form their union.

2. All those who would be in this religious association should place this foundation and ideal before their eyes as an aim set before them for which they are to strive with becoming zeal and energy.

3. In God's nature one beholds love primarily as that excellent outflowing virtue which binds together God and man. All those who wish to take sure steps for the realization of said ideal must, first of all, form and maintain their unity by this bond of perfection among themselves.

4. Built on this fundamental principle of the divine nature—namely, love—their single, immovable aim must and will be to glorify God and promote the general welfare of each member.

5. In compliance with such object, their first care in their common affairs must be directed to a proper arrangement of public worship flowing from said foundation and agreeing with said ideal.

6. The gospel or word of God is the treasure which the Lord Jesus gave his apostles, and by which, as He commanded, the nations were to be called to faith and gathered, to be nurtured and ruled. It is the chief element in public worship and the rule of all its exercises.

7. It follows that they not only ought to possess this treasure, but they must also, with care, see to it that the gospel and the word of God are preserved and practiced by them in purity and simplicity, without which they cannot be nor remain a Christian people.

8. It follows, also, that they must have persons among themselves who know, live and teach the doctrine: otherwise it would be a dead letter, and could not bring about the good referred to in 6; hence proper plans must be devised in this respect.

9. There follow also the unceasing effort and care for the instruction of youth, both in what may be learned in schools as also in what should be taught in the study of the word of God or Christian doctrine, without which their aim referred to in 4 cannot be maintained nor the doctrine be upheld.

10. The repeated voluntary gathering for public worship with appointment of time and place for the same belongs also to the common care and concern.

11. Besides the appointment of public worship and the practice of God's word, a religious society, if it would at all attain its object, must strive to uphold a proper discipline among themselves, in order that through the same a guard and restraint may be set against the attacks and hindrances of the evil one, and that his work may be destroyed where it has taken root; that a good and useful deportment may be maintained in intercourse and conduct; that the hand of mutual help may be offered under all occurrences, and that virtue and good morals may be promoted.

12. They must have fixed rules and regulations among themselves by which they may know who belong to their society or not; they must also use diligence to keep correct records of all that is enacted by them

and upon which they have mutually agreed in matters relating to discipline, in order that no one may take ignorance as an excuse, but that all may conform thereto.

13. Since good rules are necessary in the exercise of commendable discipline, the revealed will of God contained in the Ten Commandments in their full and perfect sense will be to them the best and most adequate rule for the promotion of good conduct or morals, for defense against the evil, for discriminating between the good and the evil.

14. In conformity to their aim and rules, they will, besides this, also consider useful and proper regulations, so that commendable decorum may be preserved under the diverse circumstances, as marriage, training of children, family life, death, burials and the like.

15. The practice and maintenance of such discipline and regulations will always have their temptations, since we all carry these by nature in our own bosoms; it will, therefore, likewise be necessary to have faithful persons who will see to it that discipline and good order are not neglected, but maintained and promoted by each member.

16. In order, however, that such service may not be made too difficult, but be possible and endurable for such persons, each and every member, by proper regulations, must take part in said exercises and supervision, whereby at the first notice of the outbreak of an offence its progress may at once be checked, and the deacon not be troubled by it.

17. Certain conferences should also be appointed as time may occasion or the circumstances of the general welfare may demand, at which the condition of the Church, for weal or woe, may be considered, doubtful or questionable matters decided, and the general welfare and useful arrangements and institutions in general may be cared for.

Notes: *The Schwenkfelder Church has grown out of the mystical Christianity of its founder, Casper Schwenkfeld. The Fundamental Principles were adopted in 1782.*

* * *

DECLARATION! (UNION OF SPIRITUAL COMMUNITIES OF CHRIST)

1. We, "The Union of Spiritual Communities of Christ," have been, are and will be members of Christ's Church, confirmed by the Lord and Saviour Jesus Christ Himself and assembled by His Apostles.

2. Members of "The Union of Spiritual Communities of Christ" essentially are of the law of God and of the faith of Jesus. The law of God is expounded in the Ten Commandments and the faith is professed thus: We believe in and profess—Jesus Christ the Son of God—Who came in the flesh and was crucified. He is our sole—Leader, Saviour and only Hope. There is none and could not be any other name under the heavens—through which man ought to be saved. We have faith and hope through His name to attain the highest blessings. There is no higher blessing than "eternal life in unutterable joy." This is the hope and reward in Christ Jesus and the principle aim of "The Union of Spiritual Communities of Christ." Following in the footsteps of our Divine Teacher, we, "The Union of Spiritual Communities of Christ" proclaim as did He: we have come into this world not to transgress the law of God, but to fulfill it, and therefore all idolatry and desecration we strongly renounce and acknowledge only the law and supreme authority of God. We, "The Union of Spiritual Communities of Christ," having acknowledged and submitted ourselves to the law and authority of God by this have liberated ourselves from the guardianship and power established by men, because: "we cannot serve two masters" and members of "The Union of Spiritual Communities of Christ" cannot be slaves of men–having been redeemed by the precious blood of Jesus Christ. Members of "The Union of Spiritual Communities of Christ" are not slaves of corruption, but are Sons of the Free Spirit of Christ and declare: we ought to submit more to God than to man. We triumphantly declare that we do not allow any force whatever by man over man and even more so the allowance of killing of man or of men by a man or men under no circumstances, causes or arguments whatsoever. Every individual, group of individuals, parties or governments of men, and anyone whoever they may be proclaiming their struggle against war and its non-allowance but at the same time agreeing and allowing to kill every one individual for the sake of any interests whatsoever.— is a lie and a hypocrisy and nothing but a "leaven of the Pharisees." The life of one individual is of equal value to the lives of many individuals. The commandment of God states: "Thou shalt not kill." Christ explains and warns: "No murderer shall inherit Eternal Life." War—mass slaughter is an item compiled, where the killing of one individual is allowed there the allowance of mass murder is inevitably admitted—which is war.

3. The modern world—mankind, has scattered and divided itself into countless numbers of groups— following the watch-words and programmes of the various political parties. Every political party struggles against each other not for the good and benefit of the people but for dominance over them—with all the consequences as a "diabolical incitement." Members of "The Union of Spiritual Communities of Christ" have never recognized and do not recognize any political party. They have never entered nor will they ever enter into the ranks of any political party. They have never given nor will they ever give their votes during elections, thereby, are free from any responsibility before God or man for the acts of any government established of men. Members of "The Union of Spiritual Communities of Christ" essential-

ly are above party politics—they not only gave their votes but their bodies, blood and souls to the One and Unreplaceable—Guardian of the hearts and souls of men—the Lord and Saviour Jesus Christ, thereby we have attained perfect freedom by egressing from the slavery of corruption into the freedom of glory to the children of God. We emphatically declare unto all: KNOW THE TRUTH AND THE TRUTH SHALL SET YOU FREE.

4. Members of "The Union of Spiritual Communities of Christ accepted and are fulfilling the command of Jesus Christ: 'Render therefore unto Caesar the things which are Caesar's (meaning the governments of men); and unto God the things that are God's.'" Residing in whatever state or country in this world, we triumphantly declare: going under of the banner of "Toil and Peaceful Life"—everything demanded of us which is not contradictory to the law of God and to the faith of Jesus, we will accept, fulfill and execute, not through fear but by conscientious guidance.

Notes: *This declaration, originally issued by the Society of Named Doukhobors, still serves as the ideological manifesto of the largest segment of the Doukhobor community. The statement covers many of the Christian beliefs neglected in the earlier and briefer statement by leader Peter Verigin, The Common Views. While the declaration affirms many common Christian doctrines, its emphasis is upon the free life under Christ. Submission to human authority ultimately leads to war and killing. Taking a pacifist stance, the Doukhobors affirm the ultimate worth of each life.*

Chapter 10
Baptist Family

NEW HAMPSHIRE CONFESSION OF FAITH (1830)

I. THE SCRIPTURES.

We believe that the Holy Bible was written by men divinely inspired, and is a perfect treasure of heavenly instruction; that it has God for its author, salvation for its end, and truth without any mixture of error for its matter; that it reveals the principles by which God will judge us, and therefore is, and shall remain to the end of the world, the true center of Christian union, and the supreme standard by which all human conduct, creeds, and opinions shall be tried.

2 Timothy 3:16, 17; Romans 1:16; Proverbs 30:5; Romans 2:12; Philippians 3:16.

II. THE TRUE GOD.

We believe the Scriptures teach that there is one, and only one, living and true God, an infinite, intelligent Spirit, whose name is Jehovah, the Maker and Supreme Ruler of heaven and earth; inexpressibly glorious in holiness, and worthy of all possible honor, confidence and love; that in the unity of the Godhead there are three persons, the Father, the Son, and the Holy Ghost; equal in every divine perfection, and executing distinct but harmonious offices in the great work of redemption.

John 4:24; 10:30; Psalm 147:5; Exodus 15:11; Mark 12:30.

III. THE FALL OF MAN.

We believe the Scriptures teach that Man was created in holiness, under the law of his Maker; but by voluntary transgressions fell from that holy and happy state; in consequence of which all mankind are now sinners, not by constraint but choice; being by nature utterly void of that holiness required by the law of God, positively inclined to evil; and therefore under just condemnation to eternal ruin, without defense or excuse.

Genesis 1:27; Romans 5:12, 19; Ephesians 2:1-3.

IV. THE WAY OF SALVATION.

We believe that the Scriptures teach that the salvation of sinners is wholly of grace; through the mediatorial offices of the Son of God; who by the appointment of the Father, freely took upon him our nature, yet without sin; honored the divine law by his personal obedience, and by his death made a full atonement for our sins; that having risen from the dead, he is now enthroned in heaven; and uniting in his wonderful person the tenderest sympathies with divine perfections, he is in every way qualified to be a suitable, a compassionate, and an all-sufficient Saviour.

Ephesians 2:8; John 3:16; Philippians 2:6, 7; Isaiah 42:21; 53:4, 5; Hebrews 7:25.

V. JUSTIFICATION.

We believe the Scriptures teach that the great Gospel blessing which Christ secures to such as believe in him is justification; that justification includes the pardon of sin, and the promise of eternal life on principles of righteousness; that it is bestowed, not in consideration of any works of righteousness which we have done, but solely through faith in the Redeemer's blood; by virtue of which faith his perfect righteousness is freely imputed to us of God; that it brings us into a state of most blessed peace and favor with God, and secures every other blessing needful for time and eternity.

John 1:16; Acts 13:39; Romans 5:17; 4:4, 5.

VI. THE FREENESS OF SALVATION.

We believe that the Scriptures teach that the blessings of salvation are made free to all by the Gospel; that it is the immediate duty of all to accept them by cordial, penitent and obedient faith; and that nothing prevents the salvation of the greatest sinner on earth, but his own determined depravity and voluntary rejection of the Gospel; which rejection involves him in an aggravated condemnation.

Isaiah 55:1; Revelation 22:17; Romans 16:25, 26; John 5:40; John 3:16, 19.

VII. REGENERATION.

We believe that the Scriptures teach that in order to be saved, sinners must be regenerated, or born again; that regeneration consists in giving a holy disposition to the mind that it is effected in a manner above our comprehension by the power of the Holy Spirit in connection with divine truth, so as to secure our voluntary obedience to the Gospel; and that its proper evidence appears in the holy fruits of repentance and faith, and newness of life.

NEW HAMPSHIRE CONFESSION OF FAITH (1830) (continued)

John 3:3; 2 Corinthians 5:17; John 3:8; 1 Peter 1:22-25; Ephesians 5:9.

VIII. REPENTANCE AND FAITH.

We believe the Scriptures teach that repentance and faith are sacred duties, and also inseparable graces, wrought in our souls by the regenerating Spirit of God; whereby being deeply convinced of our guilt, danger and helplessness and of the way of salvation by Christ, we turn to God with unfeigned contrition, confession, and supplication for mercy; at the same time heartily receiving the Lord Jesus Christ as our prophet, priest and king, and relying on him alone as the only and all-sufficient Saviour.

Mark 1:15; Romans 10:9; John 16:8; Luke 18:13.

IX. GOD'S PURPOSE OF GRACE.

We believe the Scriptures teach that election is the eternal purpose of God, according to which he graciously regenerates, sanctifies and saves sinners; that being perfectly consistent with the free agency of man, it comprehends all the means in connection with the end; that it is a most glorious display of God's sovereign goodness, being infinitely free, wise, holy and unchangeable; that it utterly excludes boasting and promotes humility, love, prayer, praise, trust in God, and active imitation of his free mercy; that it encourages the use of means in the highest degree; that it may be ascertained by its effects in all who truly believe the Gospel; that it is the foundation of Christian assurance; and that to ascertain it with regard to ourselves demands and deserves the utmost diligence.

2 Timothy 1:8; Exodus 33:18, 19; 1 Corinthians 4:7; 2 Timothy 2:10; 2 Thessalonians 2:13-14.

X. SANCTIFICATION.

We believe the Scriptures teach that Sanctification is the process by which, according to the will of God, we are made partakers of his holiness; that it is a progressive work; that it is begun in regeneration; and that it is carried on in the hearts of believers by the presence and power of the Holy Spirit, the Sealer and Comforter, in the continual use of the appointed means especially the word of God, self-examination, self-denial, watchfulness, and prayer.

1 Thessalonians 4:3; 1 John 2:29; Philippians 2:12, 13.

XI. PERSERVERANCE OF SAINTS.

We believe the Scriptures teach that such only are real believers as endure to the end; that their persevering attachment to Christ is the grand mark which distinguishes them from superficial professors; that a special Providence watches over their welfare; and they are kept by the power of God through faith unto salvation.

John 8:31; 1 John 2:19; Romans 8:28; Philippians 1:6.

XII. THE LAW AND GOSPEL.

We believe the Scriptures teach that the Law of God is the eternal and unchangeable rule of his moral government; that it is holy, just and good; and that the inability which the Scriptures ascribe to fallen men to fulfill its precepts, arise entirely from their love of sin; to deliver them from which, and to restore them through a Mediator to unfeigned obedience to the Holy Law, it is one great end of the Gospel, and of the Means of Grace connected with the establishment of the visible church.

Romans 3:31; 7:12; 8:7, 8; 8:2-4.

XIII. A GOSPEL CHURCH.

We believe the Scriptures teach that a visible church of Christ is a congregation of baptized believers, associated by covenant in the faith and fellowship of the Gospel; observing the ordinances of Christ; governed by his laws; and exercising the gifts, rights, and privileges invested in them by His Word; that its only scriptural officers are Bishops or Pastors, and Deacons whose Qualifications, claims and duties are defined in the Epistles to Timothy and Titus.

1 Corinthians 1:1-13; Acts 2:41, 42; 1 Corinthians 11:2; Matthew 28:20.

XIV. BAPTISM AND THE LORD'S SUPPER.

We believe the Scriptures teach that Christian baptism is the immersion in water of a believer, in the name of the Father, and Son, and Holy Ghost; to show forth in a solemn and beautiful emblem, our faith in the crucified, buried, and risen Saviour, with its effect, in our death to sin and resurrection to a new life; that it is prerequisite to the privileges of a church relation; and to the Lord's Supper, in which the members of the church, by the sacred use of bread and wine, are to commemorate together the dying love of Christ; preceded always by solemn self-examination.

Acts 8:36-39; Matthew 28:20; Acts 2:41, 42; 1 Corinthians 11:26, 28.

XV. THE CHRISTIAN SABBATH.

We believe the Scriptures teach that the first day of the week is the Lord's Day, or Christian Sabbath, and is to be kept sacred to religious purposes, by abstaining from all secular labor and sinful recreations, by the devout observance of all the means of grace, both private and public, and by preparation for that rest that remaineth for the people of God.

Acts 20:7; Exodus 20:8; Isaiah 58:13, 14; Hebrew 10:24, 25.

XVI. CIVIL GOVERNMENT.

We believe the Scriptures teach that civil government is of divine appointment, for the interest and good order of human society; and that magistrates are to be prayed for, conscientiously honored and obeyed; except only in things opposed to the will of our Lord Jesus Christ, who is the only Lord of the conscience, and the Prince of the Kings of the earth.

Romans 13:1-7; Matthew 22:21; Acts 5:29; Matthew 23:10.

XVII. RIGHTEOUS AND WICKED.

We believe the Scriptures teach that there is a radical and essential difference between the righteous and the wicked; that such only as through faith are justified in the name of the Lord Jesus, and sanctified by the Spirit of our God, are truly righteous in his esteem; while all such as continue in impenitence and unbelief are in his sight wicked, and under the curse; and this distinction holds among men both in and after death.

Malachi 3:18; Romans 1:17; 1 John 5:19; Proverbs 14:32.

XVIII. THE WORLD TO COME.

We believe the Scriptures teach that the end of the world is approaching; that at the last day, Christ will descend from heaven, and raise the dead from the grave for final retribution; that a solemn separation will then take place; that the wicked will be adjudged to endless punishment, and the righteous to endless joy; and that this judgment will fix forever the final state of men in heaven or hell, on principles of righteousness.

1 Peter 4:7; Acts 1:11, 24:15; Matthew 25:31-46; 13:49.

Notes: *Baptist confessions of faith really begin with the London Confession of 1644, though some authors see precursors in the prior Continental Free Church confessions such as Schleitheim or Dordrecht, or in those of the British Separatists. The Second London Confession (1677), based upon the Westminster Confession, became the basis of the first American confessions, especially the Philadelphia Confession of Faith (1742). The most influential confession of faith for American Baptists, however, has been the New Hampshire Confession. It is still used by the great majority of Baptists, in spite of numerous twentieth-century doctrinal statements.*

During the first decades of the nineteenth century, the growing Baptist community was torn between old line Calvinists, who followed the perspective of the Westminster Confession on such issues as predestination, and Free Will Baptists, who followed a more Arminian position which emphasized free will and free grace. The mainstream of the Baptist movement gravitated toward a more moderate Calvinist position, which was articulated in the New Hampshire Confession. This position is most clearly presented in Article VI, "The Freeness of Salvation."

The New Hampshire Confession remains the accepted doctrine of the several National Baptist Conventions and the American Baptist Association, among others. It was the basis of the Articles of Faith of the General Association of Regular Baptist Churches, and of new statements issued in 1925 and 1960 by the Southern Baptist Convention. The Black Baptist conventions have either formally adopted or informally adhere to the New Hampshire Confession. The text presented here is the version published by the National Baptist Convention of America to which scriptural references (not in the original) have been added.

*　　　*　　　*

Calvinist Missionary Baptist

DOCTRINAL STATEMENT (AMERICAN BAPTIST ASSOCIATION)

DOCTRINAL STATUS

This Association shall recognize the freedom of speech as essential to the highest achievements in its work. It shall stand or fall upon its own conformity of truth. It shall exercise no ecclesiastical authority but it shall by every precaution recognize the sovereignty of every individual church. It shall encourage on the part of the churches and messengers that greatest possible freedom of expression in discussing matters pertaining to its work, and in the pre-eminence of missions and evangelism in the work of the churches.

DOCTRINAL STATEMENT

1. We believe in the infallible verbal inspiration of the whole Bible, II Tim. 3:16.

2. The Triune God, Matt. 28:19.

3. The Genesis Account of Creation.

4. The Virgin Birth of Jesus Christ, Matt. 1:20.

5. The Deity of Jesus Christ.

6. His crucifixion and suffering as vicarious substitutionary.

7. The bodily resurrection and ascension of Christ and the bodily resurrection of His saints, I Cor. 15th chapter.

8. The second coming of Christ, personal and bodily as the crowning event of this Gentile age, Acts 1:11.

9. The Bible doctrine of eternal punishment of the finally impenitent, Matt. 25:48.

10. We also hold in common what real Baptists have ever held: That the great commission was given to the churches only. That in kingdom activities the church is the unit and only unit that the churches have, and should exercise equal authority, and responsibility should be met by them according to their several abilities.

11. That all co-operating bodies, such as Association, Conventions and the Board of Committees, etc., are and properly should be the servants of the churches.

12. We believe that the great commission teaches that there has been a succession of Missionary Baptist Churches from the days of Christ to this day.

13. We believe that Baptism, to be valid, must be administered by a Scriptural Baptist Church.

Notes: *The New Hampshire Confession does not address the great debates which split the Baptists in the early nineteenth century—the organization of missionary societies, Sunday schools, and national associations and conventions which seemed to claim powers and authority rightfully belonging to the local church. It also could not predict the heated debate about the Bible and the nature of its authority, and the premillennial dispensational theology that would arrive from England and become so popular among Baptists in the early twentieth century. Since 1830, newer Baptist bodies have thus felt the need to define their position on local church autonomy, the nature of scripture, and eschatology.*

The American Baptist Association (ABA) grew out of the "Old Landmarks" controversy in the Southern Baptist Convention (SBC). Adherents to the Old Landmark position believed in the sovereignty of the local church and opposed the growing centralization of authority in the SBC. Forming as a separate association of churches in 1905, the ABA adopted the New Hampshire Confession, to which it added a number of statements, including those on scriptural authority and the local church.

* * *

ARTICLES OF FAITH (BAPTIST BIBLE FELLOWSHIP)

A Bible Baptist is one who believes in a supernatural Bible, which tells of a supernatural Christ, Who had a supernatural birth, Who spoke supernatural words, Who performed supernatural miracles, Who lived a supernatural life, Who died a supernatural death, Who rose in supernatural splendor, Who intercedes as a supernatural priest and Who will one day return in supernatural glory to establish a supernatural kingdom on the earth.

I. OF THE SCRIPTURES

We believe that the Holy Bible was written by men supernaturally inspired; that it has truth without any admixture of error for its matter; and therefore is, and shall remain to the end of the age, the only complete and final revelation of the will of God to man; the true center of Christian union and the supreme standard by which all human conduct, creeds, and opinions should be tried.

1. By "The Holy Bible" we mean that collection of sixty-six books, from Genesis to Revelation, which as orignally written does not only contain and convey the Word of God, but IS the very Word of God.

2. By "inspiration" we mean that the books of the Bible were written by holy men of old, as they were moved by the Holy Spirit, in such a definite way that their writings were supernaturally and verbally inspired and free from error, as no other writings have ever been or ever will be inspired.

II Tim. 3:16-17; II Pet. 1:19-21; Acts 1:16; Acts 28:25; Psa. 119:160; Psa. 119:105; Psa. 119: 130; Luke 24:25-27; John 17:17; Luke 24:44-45; Psa. 119:89; Prov. 30:5-6; Rom. 3:4; I Pet. 1: 23; Rev. 22:19; John 12:48; Isa. 8:20; Eph. 6:17; Rom. 15:4; Luke 16:31; Psa. 19:7-11; John 5: 45-47; John 5:39.

II. OF THE TRUE GOD

We believe that there is one, and only one, living and true God, and infinite, intelligent Spirit, the maker and supreme ruler of heaven and earth; inexpressibly glorious in holiness and worthy of all possible honor, confidence and love; that in the unity of the Godhead there are three persons, the Father, the Son and the Holy Ghost, equal in every divine perfection, and executing distinct but harmonious offices in the great work of redemption.

Ex. 20:2-3; Gen. 17:1; I Cor. 8:6; Eph. 4:6; John 4:24; Psa. 147:5; Psa. 83:18; Psa. 90:2; Jer. 10:10; Ex. 15:11; Rev. 4:11; I Tim. 1:17; Rom. 11:33; Mark 12:30; Matt. 28:19; John 15: 26; I Cor. 12:4-6; I John 5:7; John 10:30; John 17:5; Acts 5:3-4; I Cor. 2:10-11; Phil. 2:5-6; Eph. 2:18; II Cor. 13:14.

III. OF THE HOLY SPIRIT

That the Holy Spirit is a divine person; equal with God the Father and God the Son and of the same nature; that He was active in the creation; that in His relation to the unbelieving world He restrains the Evil one until God's purpose is fulfilled; that He convicts of sin, of judgment and of righteousness; that He bears witness to the Truth of the Gospel in preaching and testimony; that He is the agent in the New Birth: that He seals, endues, guides, teaches, witnesses, sanctifies and helps the believer.

John 14:16-17; Matt. 28:19; Heb. 9:14; John 14: 26; Luke 1:35; Gen. 1:1-3; II Thess. 2:7; John 16: 8-11; John 15:26-27; Acts 5:30-32; John 3:5-6; Eph. 1:13-14; Matt. 3:11; Mark 1:8; Luke 3:16; John 1:33; Acts 11:16; Luke 24:49; John 16:13; John 14:26; Rom. 8:14; Rom. 8:16; II Thess. 2: 13; I Pet. 1:2; Rom. 8:26-27.

IV. OF THE DEVIL, OR SATAN

We believe that Satan was once holy, and enjoyed heavenly honors; but through pride and ambition to be as the Almighty, fell and drew after him a host of angels; that he is now the malignant prince of the power of the air, and the unholy god of this world. We hold him to be man's great tempter, the enemy of God and His Christ, the accuser of the saints, the author of all false religions, the chief power back of the present apostasy; the lord of the antichrist, and the author of all the powers of darkness— destined however to final defeat at the hands of God's own Son, and to the judgment of an eternal justice in hell, a place prepared for him and his angels.

Isa. 14:12-15; Ezek. 28:14-17; Rev. 12:9; Jude 6; II Pet. 2:4; Eph. 2:2; John 14:30; I Thess. 3:5; Matt. 4:1-3; I Pet. 5:8; I John 3:8; Matt. 13:25; 37:39; Luke 22:3-4; Rev. 12:10; II Cor. 11:13-15; Mark 13:21-22; I John 4:3; II John 7; I John 2:22; Rev. 13:13-14; II Thess. 2:8-11; Rev. 19:11, 16, 20; Rev. 12:7-9; Rev. 20:1-3; Rev. 20:10; Matt. 25:41.

V. OF CREATION

We believe in the Genesis account of creation, and that it is to be accepted literally, and not allegorically or figuratively; that man was created directly in God's own image and after His own likeness; that man's creation was not a matter of evolution or evolutionary change of species, or development through interminable periods of time from lower to higher forms; that all animal and vegetable life was made directly and God's established law was that they should bring forth only "after their kind."

Gen. 1:1; Ex. 20:11; Acts 4:24; Col. 1:16-17; Heb. 11:3; John 1:3; Rev. 10:6; Rom. 1:20; Acts 17:23-26; Jer. 10:12; Neh. 9:6; Gen. 1:26-27; Gen. 2:21-23; Gen. 1:11; Gen. 1:24.

VI. OF THE FALL OF MAN

We believe that man was created in innocence under the law of his Maker, but by voluntary transgression fell from his sinless and happy state, in consequence of which all mankind are now sinners, not by constraint, but of choice; and therefore under just condemnation without defense or excuse.

Gen. 3:1-6, 24; Rom. 5:12; Rom. 5:19; Rom. 3: 10-19; Eph. 2:1, 3; Rom. 1:18; Ezek. 18:19-20; Rom. 1:32; Rom. 1:20; Rom. 1:28; Gal. 3:22.

VII. OF THE VIRGIN BIRTH

We believe that Jesus Christ was begotten of the Holy Ghost, in a miraculous manner; born of Mary, a virgin, as no other man was ever born or can ever be born of woman, and that He is both the Son of God, and God, the Son.

Gen. 3:15; Isa. 7:14; Matt. 1:18-25; Luke 1:35; Mark 1:1; John 1:14; Psa. 2:7; Gal. 4:4; I John 5:20; I Cor. 15:47.

VIII. OF THE ATONEMENT FOR SIN

We believe that the salvation of sinners is wholly of grace; through the mediatorial offices of the Son of God, who by appointment of the Father, freely took upon Him our nature, yet without sin, honored the divine law by His personal obedience, and by His death made a full and vicarious atonement for our sins; that His atonement consisted not in setting us an example by His death as a martyr, but was the voluntary substitution of Himself in the sinner's place, the Just dying for the unjust, Christ, the Lord, bearing our sins in His own body on the tree; that, having risen from the dead, He is now enthroned in heaven and uniting in His wonderful person the tenderest sympathies with divine perfection, He is every way qualified to be a suitable, a compassionate and an all-sufficient Saviour.

Eph. 2:8; Acts 15:11; Rom. 3:24; John 3:16; Matt. 18:11; Phil. 2:7; Heb. 2:14; Isa. 53:4-7; Rom. 3:25; I John 4:10; I Cor. 15:3; II Cor. 5:21; John 10:18; Phil. 2:8; Gal. 1:4; I Pet. 2:24; I Pet. 3:18; Isa. 53:11; Heb. 12:2; I Cor. 15:20; Isa. 53:12; Heb. 9:12-15; Heb. 7:25; I John 2:2.

IX. OF GRACE IN THE NEW CREATION

We believe that in order to be saved, sinners must be born again; that the new birth is a new creation in Christ Jesus; that it is instantaneous and not a process; that in the new birth the one dead in trespasses and in sins is made a partaker of the divine nature and receives eternal life, the free gift of God; that the new creation is brought about in a manner above our comprehension, not by culture, not by character, nor by the will of man, but wholly and solely by the power of the Holy Spirit in connection with divine truth, so as to secure our voluntary obedience to the gospel; that its proper evidence appears in the holy fruits of repentance and faith and newness of life.

John 3:3; II Cor. 5:17; Luke 5:27; I John 5:1; John 3:6-7; Acts 2:41; II Pet. 1:4; Rom. 6:23; Eph. 2:1; II Cor. 5:19; Col. 2:13; John 1:12-13; Gal. 5:22; Eph. 5:9.

X. OF THE FREENESS OF SALVATION

We believe in God's electing grace; that the blessings of salvation are made free to all by the gospel; that it is the immediate duty of all to accept them by a cordial, penitent and an obedient faith; and nothing prevents the salvation of the greatest sinner on earth but his own inherent depravity and voluntary rejection of the gospel; which rejection involves him in an aggravated condemnation.

I Thess. 1:4; Col. 3:12; I Pet. 1:2; Titus 1:1; Rom. 8:29-30; Matt. 11:28; Isa. 55:1; Rev. 22:17; Rom. 10:13; John 6:37; Isa. 55:6; Acts 2:38; Isa. 55:7; John 3:15-16; I Tim. 1:15; I Cor. 15:10; Eph. 2:4-5; John 5:40; John 3:18; John 3:36.

XI. OF JUSTIFICATION

We believe that the great gospel blessing which Christ secures to such as believe in Him is Justification; that Justification includes the pardon of sin, and the gift of eternal life on principles of righteousness; that it is bestowed not in consideration of any works of righteousness which we have done; but solely through faith in the Redeemer's blood, His righteousness is imputed unto us.

Acts 13:39; Isa. 53:11; Zech. 13:1; Rom. 8:1; Rom. 5:9; Rom. 5:1; Tit. 3:5-7; Rom. 1:17; Hab. 2:4; Gal. 3:11; Rom. 4:1-8; Heb. 10:38.

XII. OF REPENTANCE AND FAITH

We believe that Repentance and Faith are solemn obligations, and also inseparable graces, wrought in our souls by the quickening Spirit of God; thereby, being deeply convicted of our guilt, danger and helplessness, and of the way of salvation by Christ, we turn to God with unfeigned contrition, confession and supplication for mercy; at the same time heartily receiving the Lord Jesus Christ and openly confessing Him as our only and all-sufficient Saviour.

Acts 20:21; Mark 1:15; Acts 2:37-38; Luke 18:13; Rom. 10:13; Psa. 51:1-4; Psa. 51:7; Isa. 55: 6-7; Luke 12:8; Rom. 10:9-11.

XIII. OF THE CHURCH

We believe that a Baptist Church is a congregation of baptized believers associated by a covenant of faith and fellowship of the gospel, said church being understood to be the citadel and propagator of the Divine and Eternal Grace; observing the ordinances of Christ; governed by His laws; exercising the gifts, rights, and privileges invested in them by His Word; that its officers of ordination are pastors or elders whose qualifications, claims, and duties are clearly defined in the scriptures; we believe the true mission of the church is found in the Great Commission: First, to make individual disciples; Second, to build up the church; Third, to teach and instruct as He has commanded. We do not believe in the reversal of this order; we hold that the local church has the absolute right of self government, free from the interference of any hierarchy of individuals or organizations; and that the one and only superintendent is Christ through the Holy Spirit; that it is scriptural for true churches to cooperate with each other in contending for the faith and for the furtherance of the Gospel; that every church is the sole and only judge of the measure and method of its cooperation; on all matters of membership, of policy, of government, of discipline, of benevolence, the will of the local church is final.

Acts 2:41; Acts 2:42; I Cor. 11:2; Eph. 1:22-23; Eph. 4:11; I Cor. 12:4, 8-11; Acts 14:23; Acts 6:5-6; Acts 15:23; Acts 20:17-28; I Tim. 3:1-13; Matt. 28:19-20; Col. 1:18; Eph. 5:23-24; I Pet. 5:1-4; Acts 15:22; Jude 3,4; II Cor. 8:23-24; I Cor. 16:1; Mal. 3:10; Lev. 27:32; I Cor. 16:2; I Cor. 6:1-3; I Cor. 5:11-13.

XIV. OF BAPTISM AND THE LORD'S SUPPER

We believe that Christian baptism is the immersion in water of a believer; in the name of the Father, of the Son,

ARTICLES OF FAITH (BAPTIST BIBLE FELLOWSHIP) (continued)

and of the Holy Ghost, with the authority of the local church, to show forth in a solemn and beautiful emblem our faith in the crucified, buried and risen Saviour, with its effect in our death to sin and resurrection to a new life; that it is pre-requisite to the privileges of a church relation and to the Lord's supper; in which the members of the church, by the sacred use of bread and the fruit of the vine are to commemorate together the dying love of Christ; preceded always by solemn self-examination.

Acts 8:36-39; Matt. 3:6; John 3:23, Rom. 6:4-5; Matt. 3:16; Matt. 28:19; Rom. 6:3-5; Col. 2:12; Acts 2:41-42; Matt. 28:1, 9-20; I Cor. 11:23-28.

XV. OF THE PERSEVERANCE OF THE SAINTS

We believe that such only are real believers as endure unto the end; that their persevering attachment to Christ is the grand mark which distinguishes them from superficial professors; that a special Providence watches over their welfare; and that they are kept by the power of God through faith unto eternal salvation.

John 8:31-32; Col. 1:21-23; I John 2:19; Matt. 13:19-21; Rom. 8:28; Matt. 6:20; Psa. 121:3; Heb. 1:14; I Pet. 1:5; Phil. 1:6; John 10:28, 29; John 16:8; Rom. 8:35-39.

XVI. OF THE RIGHTEOUS AND THE WICKED

We believe that there is a radical and essential difference between the righteous and the wicked; that such only as through faith are justified in the name of the Lord Jesus, and sanctified by the Spirit of our God, are truly righteous in His esteem; while all such as continue in impenitence and unbelief are in His sight wicked, and under the curse, and this distinction holds among men both in and after death, in the everlasting felicity of the saved and the everlasting conscious suffering of the lost.

Mal. 3:18; Gen. 18:23; Rom. 6:17-18; Prov. 11:31; I Pet. 1:18; Rom. 1:17; I Cor. 15:22; Acts 10: 34-35; I John 2:29; I John 2:7; Rom. 6:16; I John 5:19; Gal. 3:10; Rom. 7:6; Rom. 6:23; Prov. 14: 32; Luke 16:25; Matt. 25:34, 41; John 8:21; Luke 9:26; John 12:25; Matt. 7:13-14.

XVII. OF CIVIL GOVERNMENT

We believe that civil government is of divine appointment, for the interests and good order of human society; that magistrates are to be prayed for, conscientiously honored and obeyed; except only in things opposed to the will of our Lord Jesus Christ; who is the only Lord of the conscience, and the coming Prince of the kings of the earth.

Rom. 13:7; II Sam. 23:3; Ex. 18:21-22; Acts 23:5; Matt. 22:21; Tit. 3:1; I Pet. 2:13, 14; I Pet. 2:17; Acts 4:19-20; Dan. 3:17-18; Matt. 10:28; Matt. 23:10; Phil. 2:10-11; Psa. 72:11.

XVIII. OF THE RESURRECTION AND RETURN OF CHRIST AND RELATED EVENTS

We believe in and accept the sacred Scriptures upon these subjects at their face and full value. Of the Resurrection, we believe that Christ rose bodily "the third day according to the Scriptures;" that He alone is our "merciful and faithful high priest in things pertaining to God;" "that this same Jesus which is taken up from you into heaven shall so come in like manner as ye have seen Him go into heaven"—bodily, personally and visible; that the "dead in Christ shall rise first," that the living saints "shall all be changed in a moment, in the twinkling of an eye, at the last trump;" "that the Lord God shall give unto Him the throne of His Father David;" and that "Christ shall reign a thousand years in righteousness until He hath put all enemies under His feet."

Matt. 28:6-7; Luke 24:39; John 20:27; I Cor. 15: 4; Mark 16:6; Luke 24:2, 4-6; Acts 1:9, 11; Luke 24:51; Mark 16:19; Rev. 3:21; Heb. 8:1; Heb. 12: 2; Heb. 8:6; I Tim. 2:5; I John 2:1; Heb. 2:17; Heb. 5:9-10; John 14:3; I Thess. 4:16; Matt. 24: 27; Matt. 24:42; Heb. 9:28; I Cor. 15:42-44, 51-53; I Thess. 4:17; Phil. 4:20-21; Luke 1:32; I Cor. 15:25; Isa. 11:4-5; Psa. 72:8; Rev. 20:1-4; Rev. 20:6.

XIX. OF MISSIONS

The command to give the gospel to the world is clear and unmistakable and this Commission was given to the churches.

Matt. 28:18-20, "And Jesus came and spake unto them saying, All power is given unto me in heaven and in earth. Go ye therefore, and teach all nations, baptizing them in the name of the Father, and of the Son, and of the Holy Ghost: Teaching them to observe all things whatsoever I have commanded you and, lo I am with you alway, even unto the end of the world. Amen."

Mark 16:15, "And he said unto them, Go ye into all the world, and preach the gospel to every creature."

John 20:21, "Then said Jesus to them again, Peace be unto you: as my Father hath sent me, even so send I you."

Rom. 10:13-15, "For whosoever shall call upon the name of the Lord shall be saved. How then shall they call on him in whom they have not believed? And how shall they believe in him of whom they have not heard? And how shall they hear without a preacher? And how shall they preach except they be sent? As it is written, How beautiful are the feet of them that preach the gospel of peace, and bring glad tidings of good things!"

XX. OF THE GRACE OF GIVING

Scriptural giving is one of the fundamentals of the faith.

II Cor. 8:7, "Therefore as ye abound in everything, in faith, and utterance, and knowledge, and in all diligence, and in your love to us, see that ye abound in this grace also."

We are commanded to bring our gifts into the storehouse (common treasury of the church) upon the first day of the week.

I Cor. 16:2, "Upon the first day of the week let every one of you lay by him in store, as God hath prospered him, that there be no gatherings when I come."

Under Grace we give, and do not pay, the tithe—"Abraham GAVE the tenth of the spoils"—Hebrews 7:2, 4—and this was four hundred years before the law, and is confirmed in the New Testament; Jesus said concerning the tithe, "These ye ought to have done"—Matt. 23:23.

We are commanded to bring the tithe into the common treasury of the church.

Lev. 27:30, "The tithe . . . is the Lord's."

Mal. 3:10, "Bring ye all the tithes into the storehouse, that there may be meat in mine house, and prove me now herewith, saith the Lord of hosts, if I will not open you the windows of heaven, and pour you out a blessing, that there shall not be room enough to receive it."

In the New Testament it was the common treasury of the church.

Acts 4:34, 35, 37, "And brought the prices of the things that were sold and laid them down at the apostles' feet . . . Having land, sold it, and brought the money, and laid it AT THE APOSTLES' FEET."

Notes: *The statement of the Baptist Bible Fellowship, one of the largest of the contemporary fundamentalist churches, is the epitome of the fundamentalist position. Notice its affirmation of supernaturalism, biblical authority, creation, and the virgin birth. Otherwise, it follows the mild Calvinism of the New Hampshire Confession.*

*   *   *

A CONFESSION (BAPTIST CONVENTION OF ONTARIO AND QUEBEC)

The regular Baptist Denomination, whereby is intended Regular Baptist churches exclusively composed of persons who have been baptised in a personal profession of their faith in Christ holding and maintaining *substantially* the following doctrines that is to say

The Divine Inspiration of the Scriptures of the Old and New Testaments and their absolute supremacy and sufficiency in matters of faith and practice,

The existence of one living and true God sustaining the personal relations of Father, Son and Holy Spirit, the same in essence and equal in attributes

The total and universal depravity of mankind

The election and effectual calling of all God's people

The atoning efficacy of the death of Christ

The free justification of believers in Him by His imputed righteousness

The preservation unto eternal life of the Saints

The necessity and efficacy of the Spirit in regeneration and sanctification

The resurrection of the dead both just and unjust

The general judgment

The everlasting happiness of the righteous and the everlasting misery of the wicked

Immersion in the name of the Father, the Son and the Holy Spirit, *the only* gospel baptism

That parties so baptised are alone entitled to communion at the Lord's Table

and that a Gospel Church is a Body of baptised believers voluntarily associated together for the service of God.

Notes: *The loosely constructed Canadian Baptist Federation is a noncreedal body, as are the several conventions of which it is composed. However, one of these conventions, the Baptist Convention of Ontario and Quebec, did adopt a*

confessional statement in 1925 during the height of the fundamentalist controversy. The statement was not published as a binding document of the convention's member churches; rather it appeared as a statement of those who were supporting McMaster University in Toronto. The school had become an issue when fundamentalists accused it of deviations in doctrine. In this document, the convention affirmed its allegiance to those traditional Baptist beliefs under question and asserted that its member churches substantially hold and teach these beliefs.

*   *   *

DOCTRINAL STATEMENT (BAPTIST MISSIONARY ASSOCIATION)

1. The Trinity of God.

2. The infallible and plenary verbal inspiration of the Scriptures.

3. The Biblical account of creation.

4. The personality of Satan.

5. Hereditary and total depravity of man in his natural state involving his fall in Adam.

6. The virgin birth and deity of Jesus Christ.

7. Christ's blood atonement for fallen man.

8. His bodily resurrection and ascension back to His Father.

9. The person and work of the Holy Spirit.

10. Justification before God by faith without any admixture of works.

11. Separation of God's children from the world.

12. Water baptism (immersion) to be administered to believers only and by Divine authority as given to Missionary Baptist churches.

13. The Lord's Supper, a church ordinance to be administered to baptized believers only and in Scriptural church capacity.

14. Eternal security of the believer.

15. The establishment of a visible church by Christ himself during His personal ministry on earth.

16. World-wide missions according to the Great Commission which Christ gave His Church. (Matthew 28:19, 20.)

17. The perpetuity of Missionary Baptist churches from Christ's day on earth until His second coming.

18. The right of scriptural churches to be held as equal units in their associated capacities, with equal right and privileges for all.

19. The subjection of all scriptural associational assemblies and their committees to the will of the churches, so that they shall forever remain as servants of the churches originating them.

20. The separation of the Lord's Church from all so-called churches or church alliances which advocate, practice, or uphold heresies and other human innovations which are not in harmony with the word of God. Open communion, alien baptism, pulpit affilia-

DOCTRINAL STATEMENT (BAPTIST MISSIONARY ASSOCIATION) (continued)

tion with heretical churches, Modernism, and all kindred evils arising from these practices are unscriptural.

21. The only valid baptism is that administered by the authority of a scriptural Missionary Baptist Church. Any so-called Baptist Church which knowingly receives alien baptism, habitually practices this or other evils as those listed in statement 20 cannot be a scriptural Baptist Church, nor can its ordinances remain valid.

22. The personal, bodily and imminent return of Christ to earth.

23. The bodily resurrection of the dead.

24. The reality of heaven, involving Divine assurance of eternal happiness for the redeemed of God.

25. The reality of Hell, involving everlasting punishment of the incorrigible wicked.

26. We believe in absolute separation of church and state.

NOTE: The following statements are not binding upon the churches already affiliated with this association nor require adoption by churches petitioning this body for privileges of cooperation, nor are to be a test of fellowship between brethren or churches. However, they do express the preponderance of opinion among the churches of the Baptist Missionary Association of America:

1. We believe in the premillennial return of Christ to earth after which He shall literally reign in peace upon the earth for a thousand years. (Rev. 20:4-6.)

2. We believe the Scriptures to teach two resurrections: the first of the righteous at Christ's coming; the second of the wicked dead at the close of the thousand-year reign. (I Thes. 4:13-17; Rev. 20:4-6, 12-15.)

It is easy for the fellowshipping churches of one Baptist group to think of themselves as being sound in the faith and of all others as being unsound or loose in their principles and practices. However, the real test is that of how well a church or denominational group measures up to the Bible requirements for a New Testament church.

Churches of the B.M.A. of America have the assurance from the Holy Scriptures that their doctrinal beliefs and practices are the same as those taught by the Lord Jesus, believed and preached by the Apostles, and practiced by the first century churches.

(With a few alterations the following is a summary of things believed, of things not believed, of the characteristics of truly New Testament Baptist churches, and of the composition of associations as prepared by W. J. Burgess, who for eighteen years served as General Secretary of Missions for the B.M.A. of America—J.W.D.).

SOME THINGS WE BELIEVE

1. We believe in salvation solely by grace through faith.

2. We believe in the doctrines and Scriptural order of repentance and faith.

3. We believe one must be born again to enter Heaven.

4. We believe in "heartfelt" salvation that can be known.

5. We believe in absolute equality among local churches.

6. We believe that churches may cooperate together without losing their sovereignty or independency.

7. We believe that women have a place in public worship and service, but not as ordained Ministers.

8. We believe that the Gospel is the power of God unto salvation to believers only.

9. We believe that true worship is worship in Spirit and in truth.

10. We believe that all of our preaching and teaching should be Christ-Centered.

11. We believe in living a separate life from the world.

12. We believe that church associations must ever be the servants of the churches composing them.

SOME THINGS WE DO NOT BELIEVE

1. We do not believe in being Modernists (Liberals) in any sense of the word.

2. We do not believe in pulpit affiliation with heretical groups.

3. We do not believe in alien (non-Baptist) immersion.

4. We do not believe in the invisible, universal church theory.

5. We do not believe in pastor dictatorship.

6. We do not believe in deacon dictatorship.

7. We do not believe in one church dictatorship over other churches.

8. We do not believe in dictatorship (overlordship) of any kind.

9. We do not believe in showing respect of persons, a "Big I and little you" sort of philosophy.

10. We do not believe that the Gospel is merely a social formula.

11. We do not believe in the now-popular "Universal Fatherhood of God—Brotherhood of Men" idea, except in the sense of creation.

12. We do not believe in the modern ecumenical church movement.

Notes: *Formed in 1950, the Baptist Missionary Association grew out of the American Baptist Association. Its statement is based upon, but enlarges, that of its parent body. New articles, such as those on alien baptism and the reality of heaven and hell, were added. Notice the final declaration concerning the relation of the Doctrinal Statement to churches and members affiliated with the association.*

CONSERVATIVE BAPTIST MANIFESTO AND DECLARATION OF FAITH (CONSERVATIVE BAPTIST ASSOCIATION OF AMERICA)

CONSERVATIVE BAPTIST MANIFESTO

Whereas, on this happy and historic celebration of Conservative Baptist advance, which gives us occasion to reflect upon God's gracious blessing in the formation and ongoing of various Conservative Baptist agencies, we desire to give a real assurance to Bible-believing Baptists everywhere of our position and direction:

Therefore, be it resolved, that we re-affirm our unchanging confidence in the trustworthiness of the Scriptures and in those foundational truths as expressed in the Confession of Faith and Constitution of our various Conservative Baptist organizations; and

Be it further resolved, that we re-affirm our unswerving opposition to the practice of the Inclusive Policy, that policy which is inclusive of belief and unbelief alike, and results in division and conflicting testimony at home and abroad, and that we acknowledge that the Conservative Board movement logically thereby continues to be separatist in spirit and objective; and

Be it further resolved, that it is our conviction that Conservative Baptist board members and officers be men who have openly declared themselves to stand with Conservative Baptists on the principles set forth in this declaration, to be in sympathy with the purposes of the Conservative Baptist movement, and to be in opposition to the Inclusive Policy as shown by their personal non-cooperation with the inclusive program.

Finally, that a committee be authorized to study the problems inherent in our growing Conservative Baptist movement, the interrelations of the Boards, the role of the Regional and National Conferences, and other related problems; that this committee be composed of two representatives from each of the four Boards, one representative from each of the two Seminaries, plus two members elected from each of the Regional Conferences; and that this committee report at the 1954 Annual Meeting.

THE REPORT OF THE MANIFESTO COMMITTEE

The Manifesto Committee, authorized at the annual meeting in Portland in 1953, held two meetings in the city of Chicago. Attendance on the part of many members of the committee entailed very heavy expenses, borne either by the individuals, or their churches, or the institutions they represented. The Committee meetings were irenical and amicable in spirit. We present our report with great optimism for the future of our Conservative Baptist movement and our societies and organizations.

We have sought to more clearly define and delineate our ideology and objectives. We have sought to deal thoroughly and faithfully with all points of difference or of potential difference. Our report consists of three parts: (1) our findings relative to the intent and purpose of the Manifesto, (2) a statement of the ideology of our movement, and (3) recommendations for the consideration of the boards of the organizations concerned.

THE INTENT AND PURPOSE OF THE MANIFESTO

The Intent and Nature of the Manifesto:

A. It is only an expressional instrument from messengers of churches and from Board members of our four Societies assembled in Annual Meeting in Portland, Oregon, in June, 1953.

B. The Manifesto is not binding upon any church or any Society represented in this expression.

C. The Manifesto is a purely voluntary, democratic and positive expression of a working and workable ideal to serve as a common denominator for each of our four organizations in particular and for the whole Conservative Baptist Movement in general.

D. The Manifesto as a working and workable ideal, in its very language in at least two places, makes this Manifesto self-interpreting:

  1. "Unswerving opposition to the practice of the inclusive policy;"

    a. Theological form of the inclusive policy which is an admixture of belief and unbelief.

    b. Ecclesiastical form of inclusive policy which is churches and individuals being associated with unsound bodies.

    c. Financial form of inclusive policy which is giving financial support to unsound bodies, individuals, or objectives and enterprises.

    d. Practical form of the inclusive policy which is giving one's vote, voice or volitional influence to unsoundness as expressed in the inclusive policy in its theological, ecclesiastical or financial form, without protest.

  2. "Separatist in spirit and objective"

    a. Separatist in spirit means: the sincere heart attitudes, motives, impulses, desires, expressions, prayers and actions of the individual, or individuals comprising a church or organization to give with protest the least possible cooperation to all forms of the inclusive policy as named above which will be determined in degree of cooperation by the particular circumstances that prevail.

    b. Separatist in objective means: the individual, church, or organization desires as soon as possible to arrive at the place where

      (1) All disbelief can be disfellowshipped.

      (2) All unsound associations can be disassociated.

      (3) All unsound objectives can be met with nonsupport.

      (4) All participation with unbelief, unsound organizations, and financial objectives can be discontinued.

CONSERVATIVE BAPTIST MANIFESTO AND DECLARATION OF FAITH (CONSERVATIVE BAPTIST ASSOCIATION OF AMERICA) (continued)

IDEOLOGY OF THE CONSERVATIVE BAPTIST MOVEMENT

AS CONSERVATIVE BAPTISTS:

1. We hold the New Testament pattern of the inter-dependence of autonomous local churches in which messengers gather from local churches in association meetings for the purpose of inspiration and business, rejecting the concept of a convention as we have come to know it in the form of an ecclesiastical hierarchy with delegates, a convention and an incorporation.

2. We hold that severance resolutions from other bodies are not to be regarded as a pre-requisite to affiliation with our Conservative Baptist agencies. We hold that the ethical problem of affiliations, and severance resolutions is the problem of the local autonomous Baptist church.

    While it is not our province to regulate affiliations, we do declare that cooperation with inclusivism in any form does militate against the best interests of both the local churches and their agencies.

3. We hold that no form of coercion on local churches should be employed by any of our agencies in order to enlist them in fellowship and cooperation.

4. Recognizing that the relationship of our C. B. movement to outside groups must be guided by our own need of preserving our distinctives as Conservative Baptists, let us agree that in these relationships we:

    > Will not support affiliations with apostate ecumenical organizations (that is, organizations that would combine the professed Christian communions of the world into one universal church) knowing that God's blessing in such affiliations would not be upon us.

DECLARATION OF FAITH

ONE. We believe that the Bible is God's Word, that it was written by men Divinely inspired and that it is the supreme infallible authority in all matters of faith and conduct.

TWO. We believe in God the Father, perfect in holiness, infinite in wisdom, measureless in power. We rejoice that He concerns Himself mercifully in the affairs of men, that He hears and answers prayer, and that He saves from sin and death all that come to Him through Jesus Christ.

THREE. We believe in Jesus Christ, the eternal and only begotten Son of God, conceived of the Holy Spirit, of virgin birth, sinless in His life, making atonement for the sins of the world by His death. We believe in His bodily resurrection, His ascension and visible, pre-millennial return to the world according to His promise.

FOUR. We believe in the Holy Spirit who came forth from God to convince the world of sin, or righteousness and of judgment, and to regenerate, sanctify and comfort those who believe in Jesus Christ.

FIVE. We believe that all men by nature and by choice are sinners but that "God so loved the world that He gave His only begotten Son that whosoever believeth in Him should not perish but have everlasting life;" we believe, therefore, that those who accept Christ as Lord and Saviour will rejoice forever in God's presence and those who refuse to accept Christ as Lord and Saviour will be forever separated from God.

SIX. We believe in the Church—a living spiritual body of which Christ is the head and of which all regenerated people are members. We believe that a local church is a company of believers in Jesus Christ, immersed on a credible confession of faith, and associated for worship, work and fellowship. We believe that to these local churches were committed, for perpetual observance, the ordinances of baptism and the Lord's supper, and that God has laid upon these churches the task of proclaiming to a lost world the acceptance of Jesus Christ as Saviour, and the enthroning of Him as Lord and Master. We believe that all human betterment and social improvements are the inevitable by-products of such a Gospel.

SEVEN. We believe that every human being is responsible to God alone in all matters of faith; that each church is independent and autonomous and must be free from interference by any ecclesiastical or political authority; that therefore Church and State must be kept separate as having different functions, each fulfilling its duties free from the dictation or patronage of the other.

Notes: *The Conservative Baptist Manifesto was adopted in 1953 and provides an overall perspective on the conservative Baptist position.*

The Declaration of Faith is taken from the constitution of the Conservative Baptist Association. It is derived from the original statement of the Fundamental Fellowship, but differs in wording. Most importantly, it adds specific references to the virgin birth and premillennialism.

* * *

ARTICLES OF FAITH (DUCK RIVER AND KINDRED ASSOCIATIONS OF BAPTISTS)

1. We believe in only one true and living God. Father, Word and Holy Ghost and these three are one.

2. We believe that by one man sin entered into the world, and death by sin, and so death passed upon all men, for that all have sinned and are by nature the children of wrath.

3. We believe that the scriptures of the Old and New Testaments are *the words of God,* and the only rules of faith and practice.

4. We believe that Jesus Christ, by the grace of God, tasted death for every man, and through his meritorious death, the way of salvation is made possible for God to have mercy upon all who come unto him upon Gospel terms.

5. We believe that sinners are justified in the sight of God only by the righteousness of God imputed unto them through faith in the Lord Jesus Christ.

6. We believe that the saints will persevere in grace, and that not one of them will be finally lost.

7. We believe that there will be a resurrection of the dead, both of the just and of the unjust, and a general judgment, and that the happiness of the righteous and the punishment of the wicked will be eternal.

8. We believe that the visible church of Christ is a congregation of faithful men and women, who have given themselves to the Lord, and have obtained fellowship with each other, and have agreed to keep a godly discipline according to the rules of the Gospel.

9. We believe in revealed religion by the operation of the Spirit, agreeable to the word of God, and that Jesus Christ is the great head of the Church, and that the government thereof is with the body.

10. We believe that water baptism, the Lord's supper and the washing of the saints' feet are ordinances of the Gospel, to be continued until the second coming of the Lord Jesus Christ, and that true believers are the only fit subjects for baptism and immersion the only true Gospel mode.

11. We believe that none but the regularly baptized members have a right to commune at the Lord's table, and that no person has the right to administer the ordinance of the Gospel, except that he is legally called and qualified.

12. We believe that the Lord's day ought to be observed and set apart for the worship of God, and that no work or worldly business should be transacted thereon—works of piety and mercy and necessity excepted.

Notes: *Several of the issues which led to the formation of both the Duck River and Kindred Associations of Baptists (such as support for missions) are not mentioned in the Articles of Faith, but others (such as general atonement) are. Association members also practice foot washing.*

* * *

DOCTRINAL STATEMENT (FUNDAMENTAL BAPTIST FELLOWSHIP)

1. We believe that the Bible is God's Word, that it was written by men divinely inspired, and that it has supreme authority in all matters of faith and conduct.

2. We believe in God the Father, perfect in holiness, infinite in wisdom, measureless in power. We rejoice that He concerns Himself mercifully in the affairs of men, that He hears and answers prayer, and that He saves from sin and death all who come to Him through Jesus Christ.

3. We believe in Jesus Christ, God's only begotten Son, miraculous in His birth, sinless in His life, making atonement for the sins of the world by His death. We believe in His bodily resurrection, His ascension into Heaven, His perpetual intercession for His people and His personal visible return to the world according to His promise.

4. We believe in the Holy Spirit who came forth from God to convince the world of sin, of righteousness, and of judgment, and to regenerate, sanctify and comfort those who believe in Jesus Christ.

5. We believe that all men by nature and by choice are sinners, but that "God so loved the world that He gave His only begotten Son that whosoever believeth in Him should not perish but have everlasting life;" we believe therefore that those who accept Christ as Lord and Saviour will rejoice forever in God's presence, and those who refuse to accept Christ as Lord and Saviour will be forever separated from God.

6. We believe in the Church—a living spiritual body of which Christ is the head and of which all regenerated people are members. We believe that a visible church is a company of believers in Jesus Christ, baptized on a credible confession of faith, and associated for worship, work and fellowship. We believe that to these visible churches were committed, for perpetual observance, the ordinances of baptism and the Lord's Supper, and that God has laid upon these churches the task of persuading a lost world to accept Jesus Christ as Saviour, and to enthrone Him as the Lord and Master. We believe that all human betterment and social improvements are the inevitable byproduct of such a Gospel.

7. We believe that every human being has direct relations with God, and is responsible to God alone in all matters of faith; that each church is independent and autonomous and must be free from interference by any ecclesiastical or political authority; that therefore Church and State must be kept separate as having different functions, each fulfilling its duties free from the dictation or patronage of the other.

8. We believe in our Lord's return—a personal, visible, imminent, pre-tribulation rapture, and subsequent millennial enthronement, in fulfillment of His promise.

Notes: *The doctrinal statement of the Fundamental Baptist Fellowship is derived from the original statement of the Fundamental Fellowship, differing in its addition of a new statement on premillennial eschatology which commits the fellowship to specific refinement within the larger premillennial eschatological picture. The fellowship believes that those who have saving faith in Christ will be "raptured," or taken from earth to be with Jesus, prior to the time of tribulation preceeding His second coming and the millennium.*

* * *

A CONFESSION OF FAITH (FUNDAMENTAL FELLOWSHIP)

1. We believe that the Bible is God's Word, that it was written by men divinely and uniquely inspired, that it is absolutely trustworthy and has supreme authority in all matters of faith and conduct.

A CONFESSION OF FAITH (FUNDAMENTAL FELLOWSHIP) (continued)

2. We believe in God the Father, creator of heaven and earth, perfect in holiness, infinite in wisdom, measureless in power. We rejoice that He concerns Himself mercifully in the affairs of men, that He hears and answers prayer and that He saves from sin and death all who comes to Him through Jesus Christ.

3. We believe in Jesus Christ, God's only begotten Son, conceived of the Holy Spirit, born of the Virgin Mary, sinless in His life, making atonement for the sin of the world by His death on the cross. We believe in His bodily resurrection, His Ascension into heaven, His high priestly intercession for His people and His personal, visible return to the world according to His promise.

4. We believe in the Holy Spirit, who came forth from God to convince the world of sin, of righteousness and of judgment, and to regenerate, sanctify and comfort those who believe in Jesus Christ.

5. We believe that all men by nature and by choice are sinners, but that "God so loved the world that He gave His only begotten Son, that whosoever believeth in Him should not perish, but have everlasting life." We believe, therefore, that those who accept Christ as their Lord and Saviour will rejoice forever in God's presence and those who refuse to accept Christ as Lord and Saviour will be forever separated from God.

6. We believe in the Church—a living, spiritual body of which Christ is the Head and of which all regenerated people are members. We believe that a visible church is a company of believers in Jesus Christ, buried with Him in baptism and associated for worship, work and fellowship. We believe that to these visible churches were committed for observance "till He come," the ordinances of baptism and the Lord's Supper; and that God has laid upon these churches the task of persuading a lost world to accept Jesus Christ as Saviour and to enthrone Him as Lord and Master. We believe that human betterment and social improvement are essential products of the Gospel.

7. We believe that every human being is responsible to God alone in all matters of faith.

8. We believe that each church is independent and autonomous, and must be free from interference by any ecclesiastical or political authority; that, therefore, Church and State must be kept separate as having different functions, each fulfilling its duties free from the dictation or patronage of the other.

Notes: *The Fundamental Fellowship was the original organization formed by conservative members of the Northern Baptist Convention (now the American Baptist Churches in the U.S.A.). This confession, written by Frank M. Goodchild, was adopted by the fellowship at a meeting preceeding the 1921 gathering of the Northern Baptist Convention. Members of the fellowship tried, unsuccessfully, to get the entire convention to adopt it. The confession became the basis of the present statements of the Conservative Baptist Association of America and the Fundamental Baptist Fellowship.*

* * *

ARTICLES OF FAITH (GENERAL ASSOCIATION OF REGULAR BAPTIST CHURCHES)

I. OF THE SCRIPTURES

We believe that the Holy Bible as originally written was verbally inspired and the product of Spirit-controlled men, and therefore, has truth without any admixture of error for its matter. We believe the Bible to be the true center of Christian union and the supreme standard by which all human conduct, creeds, and opinions shall be tried.

2 Tim. 3:16, 17; 2 Pet. 1:19-21.

II. OF THE TRUE GOD

We believe there is one and only one living and true God, an infinite Spirit, the Maker and supreme Ruler of heaven and earth; inexpressibly glorious in holiness, and worthy of all possible honor, confidence and love; that in the unity of the Godhead there are three persons, the Father, the Son and the Holy Ghost, equal in every divine perfection, and executing distinct but harmonious offices in the great work of redemption.

Exod. 20:2, 3: I Cor. 8:6; Rev. 4:11.

III. OF THE HOLY SPIRIT

We believe that the Holy Spirit is a divine person, equal with God the Father and God the Son and of the same nature; that He was active in the creation; that in His relation to the unbelieving world He restrains the evil one until God's purpose is fulfilled; that He convicts of sin, of righteousness and of judgment; that He bears witness to the truth of the Gospel in preaching and testimony; that He is the Agent in the new birth; that He seals, endues, guides, teaches, witnesses, sanctifies and helps the believer.

John 14;16, 17; Matt. 28:19; Heb. 9:14; John 14:26; Luke 1:35; Gen. 1:1-3; John 16:8-11; Acts 5:30-32; John 3:5,6; Eph. 1:13, 14; Mark 1:8; John 1:33; Act 11:16; Luke 24:49; Rom. 8:14, 16, 26, 27.

IV. OF THE DEVIL, OR SATAN

We believe in the personality of Satan, that he is the unholy god of this age, and the author of all the powers of darkness, and is destined to the judgment of an eternal justice in the lake of fire.

Matt. 4:1-3; 2 Cor. 4:4; Rev. 20:10.

V. OF CREATION

We accept the Genesis account of creation and believe that man came by direct creation of God and not by evolution.

Gen. 1 and 2; Col. 1:16, 17; John 1:3.

VI. OF THE FALL OF MAN

We believe that man was created in innocence under the law of his Maker, but by voluntary transgression fell from his sinless and happy state in consequence of which all mankind are now sinners, not only by constraint, but of choice; and therefore under just condemnation without defense or excuse.

Gen 3:1-6, 24; Rom. 3:10-19; Rom. 1:18, 32.

VII. OF THE VIRGIN BIRTH

We believe that Jesus was begotten of the Holy Ghost in a miraculous manner, born of Mary, a virgin, as no other man was ever born or can be born of woman, and that He is both the Son of God and God, the Son.

Gen. 3:15; Isa. 7:14; Matt. 1:18-25; Luke 1:35; John 1:14.

VIII. OF THE ATONEMENT FOR SIN

We believe that the salvation of sinners is wholly of grace; through the mediatorial offices of the Son of God, Who by the appointment of the Father, freely took upon Him our nature, yet without sin, honored the divine law by His personal obedience, and by His death made a full and vicarious atonement for our sins; that His atonement consisted not in setting us an example by His death as a martyr, but was a voluntary substitution of Himself in the sinner's place, the Just dying for the unjust; Christ, the Lord, bearing our sin in His own body on the tree; that having risen from the dead, He is now enthroned in Heaven, and uniting in His wonderful person the tenderest sympathies with divine perfection, He is in every way qualified to be a suitable, a compassionate and an all-sufficient Savior.

Eph. 2:8; Acts 15:11; Rom. 3:24; John 3:16; Matt. 18:11; Phil. 2:7; Heb. 2:14; Isa. 53:4-7; Rom 3:25; I John 4:10; I Cor. 15:3; 2 Cor. 5:21.

IX. OF GRACE IN THE NEW CREATION

We believe that in order to be saved, sinners must be born again; that the new birth is a new creation in Christ Jesus; that it is instantaneous and not a process; that in the new birth the one dead in trespasses and in sins is made a partaker of the divine nature and receives eternal life, the free gift of God; that the new creation is brought about in a manner above our comprehension, solely by the power of the Holy Spirit in connection with divine truth, so as to secure our voluntary obedience to the gospel; that its proper evidence appears in the holy fruits of repentance and faith and newness of life.

John 3:3; 2 Cor. 5:17; I John 5:1; John 3:6, 7; Acts 16:30-33; 2 Pet. 1:4; Rom. 6:23; Eph. 2:1, 5; 2 Cor. 5:19; Col. 2:13; John 3:8.

X. OF JUSTIFICATION

We believe that the great gospel blessing which Christ secures to such as believe in Him is Justification;

(a) That Justification includes the pardon of sin, and the gift of eternal life, on principles of righteousness;

(b) That it is bestowed not in consideration of any works of righteousness which we have done; but solely through faith in the Redeemer's blood, His righteousness is imputed to us.

Acts 13:39; Isa. 53:11; Zech. 13:1; Rom. 8:1; Rom. 5:1, 9.

XI. OF FAITH AND SALVATION

We believe that faith in the Lord Jesus Christ is the only condition of salvation.

Acts 16:31.

XII. OF THE LOCAL CHURCH

We believe that a local church is a congregation of immersed believers, associated by covenant of faith and fellowship of the Gospel; observing the ordinances of Christ; governed by His laws; and exercising the gifts, rights, and privileges invested in them by His Word; that its officers are pastors and deacons, whose qualifications, claims, and duties are clearly defined in the Scriptures. We believe the true mission of the church is the faithful witnessing of Christ to all men as we have opportunity. We hold that the local church has the absolute right of self-government free from the interference of any hierarchy of individuals or organizations; and that the one and only Superintendent is Christ through the Holy Spirit; that it is scriptural for true churches to cooperate with each other in contending for the faith and for the furtherance of the Gospel; that each local church is the sole judge of the measure and method of its cooperation; on all matters of membership, of polity, of government, of discipline, of benevolence, the will of the local church is final.

Acts 2:41, 42; 1 Cor. 11:2; Eph. 1:22, 23; Eph. 4:11; Acts 20:17-28; 1 Tim. 3:1-7; Col. 1:18; Eph. 5:23, 24; Acts 15:13-18.

XIII. OF BAPTISM AND THE LORD'S SUPPER

We believe that Christian baptism is the immersion of a believer in water to show forth in a solemn and beautiful emblem our faith in the crucified, buried and risen Savior, with its effect in our death to sin and resurrection to a new life; that it is prerequisite to the privileges of a church relation. We believe that the Lord's Supper is the commemoration of His death until He come, and should be preceded always by solemn self-examination.

Acts 8:36, 38, 39; John 3:23; Rom. 6:3-5; Matt. 3:16; Col. 2:12; 1 Cor. 11:23-28.

XIV. OF THE SECURITY OF THE SAINTS

We believe that all who are truly born again are kept by God the Father for Jesus Christ.

Phil. 1:6; John 10:28, 29; Rom. 8:35-39; Jude 1 (A.S.V.).

XV. OF THE RIGHTEOUS AND THE WICKED

We believe that there is a radical and essential difference between the righteous and the wicked; that such only as though faith are justified in the name of the Lord Jesus Christ, and sanctified by the Spirit of our God, are truly righteous in His esteem; while all such as continue in impenitence and unbelief are in His sight wicked, and under the curse; and this distinction holds among men both in and after death, in the everlasting felicity of the saved and the everlasting conscious suffering of the lost.

Mal. 3:18; Gen. 18:23; Rom. 6:17, 18; 1 John 5:19; Rom. 7:6; Rom. 6:23; Prov. 14:32; Luke 16:25; Matt. 25:34-41; John 8:21.

XVI. OF CIVIL GOVERNMENT

We believe that civil government is of divine appointment for the interests and good order of human society; that magistrates are to be prayed for, conscientiously honored, and obeyed; except in things opposed to the will of our

ARTICLES OF FAITH (GENERAL ASSOCIATION OF REGULAR BAPTIST CHURCHES) (continued)

Lord Jesus Christ Who is the only Lord of the conscience, and the coming Prince of the kings of the earth.

Rom. 13:1-7; 2 Sam. 23:3; Exod. 18:21, 22; Acts 23:5; Matt. 22:21; Acts 5:29; Acts 4:19, 20; Dan. 3:17, 18.

XVII. OF THE RESURRECTION, PERSONAL, VISIBLE, PREMILLENNIAL RETURN OF CHRIST, AND RELATED EVENTS

(a) We believe in the Bodily Resurrection.

Matt. 28:6, 7; Luke 24:39; John 20:27; I Cor. 15:4; Mark 16:6; Luke 24:2-6.

(b) The Ascension.

Acts 1:19-11; Luke 24:51; Rev. 3:21; Heb. 12:2.

(c) The High Priesthood.

Heb. 8:6; I Tim. 2:5; I John 2:1; Heb. 2:17; Heb. 5:9, 10.

(d) The Second Coming.

John 14:3; Acts 1:11; I Thess. 4:16; James 5:8; Heb. 9:28.

(e) The Resurrection of the Righteous Dead.

I Thess. 4:13-18; I Cor. 15:42-44, 51-54.

(f) The Change of the Living in Christ.

I Cor. 15:51-53; I Thess. 4:13-18; Phil. 3:20, 21.

(g) The Throne of David.

Luke 1:32; Isa. 9:6, 7; Acts 2:29, 30.

(h) The Millennial Reign.

I Cor. 15:25; Isa. 32:1; Isa. 11:4, 5; Psa. 72:8; Rev. 20:1-4, 6.

Notes: *Using the New Hampshire Confession as a basis, the General Association of Regular Baptist Churches has added references to the verbal inspiration of scripture, the personality of Satan, the virgin birth, and premillennialism.*

* * *

CONFESSION OF FAITH (MINNESOTA BAPTIST ASSOCIATION)

CONCERNING THE SCRIPTURES

We believe that the Holy Bible was written inerrant in its original languages by men divinely inspired, and is a perfect treasure of heavenly instruction;[1] that is has God for its Author, salvation for its end,[2] and truth without any mixture of error, for its matter;[3] that it reveals the principles by which God will judge us;[4] and therefore is, and shall remain to the end of the age, the true center of Christian union,[5] and the supreme standard by which all human conduct, creeds, and opinions should be tried.[6]

Places in the Bible Where Taught. [1]2 Tim. 3:16, 17. (Also 2 Peter 1:21; 2 Sam. 23:2; Acts 1:16; 3:21; John 10:35; Luke 16:29, 31; Ps. 119:111; Rom. 3:1, 2). [2]2 Tim. 3:15. (Also I Peter 1:10-12; Acts 11:14; Rom. 1:16; Mark 16:16; John 5:38, 39). [3]Prov. 30:5, 6. (Also John 17:17; Rev. 22:18, 19; Rom. 3:4). [4]Rom. 2:12. (Also I Cor. 4:3, 4; Luke 10:10-16; 12:47, 48). [5]Phil. 3:16. (Also Eph. 4:3-6; Phil. 2:1, 2; I Cor.

1:10; I Peter 4:11). [6]I John 4:1, (Also Acts 17:11; I John 4:6; Jude 3; Eph. 6:17; Ps. 119:59, 60; Phil. 1:9-11).

CONCERNING THE TRUE GOD

We believe that there is one, and only one, living and true God, an infinite, intelligent, perfect Spirit and personal Being, the Creator, Preserver, and Supreme Ruler of the universe,[1] inexpressibly glorious in holiness[2] and all other perfections, and worthy of all possible honor, confidence and love;[3] that in the unity of the Godhead there are three persons, the Father, the Son, and the Holy Ghost;[4] equal in every divine perfection,[5] and executing distinct but harmonious offices in the great work of redemption.[6]

Places in the Bible Where Taught. [1]I John 4:24. (Also Heb. 3:4; Rom. 1:20; Jer. 10:10). [2]Exod. 15:11. (Isa. 6:3; I Peter 1:15, 16; Rev. 4:6-8). [3]Mark 12:30. (Matt. 10:37; Jer. 2:12, 13). [4]Matt. 28:19. (I Cor. 12:4-6; I John 5:7). [5]John 10:30. (John 5:17; 14:23; 17:5, 10; Acts 5:3, 4; I Cor. 2:10, 11; Phil. 2:5, 6). [6]Eph. 2:18. (Rev. 1:4, 5; comp. ch, 2:7).

CONCERNING THE FALL OF MAN

We believe that man was created by the special act of God, as recorded in Genesis. "So God created man in His own image, in the image of God created He him; male and female created He them" (Gen. 1:27).[1]"And the Lord God formed man of the dust of the ground, and breathed into his nostrils the breath of life; and man became a living soul" (Gen. 2:7).[2]

We believe that man was created in a state of holiness, under the law of his Maker,[3] but through the temptation of Satan he voluntarily transgressed and fell from this holy state;[4] in consequence of which all mankind are now sinners,[5] not by constraint, but choice,[6] being by nature utterly void of that holiness required by law of God, positively inclined to evil, and therefore under just condemnation to eternal ruin,[7] without defense or excuse.[8]

Places in the Bible Where Taught. [1]Gen. 1:27. [2]Gen. 2:7. [3]Gen. 1:27. (Eccl. 7:29; Acts 17:26-29; Gen. 2:16, 17). [4]Gen. 3:6-24. (Rom. 5:12). [5]Rom. 5:19. (John 3:6; Ps. 51:5; Rom. 5:15-19; 8:7). [6]Isa. 53:6. (Gen. 6:12; Rom. 3:9-18). [7]Eph. 2:13. (Rom. 1:32; 2:1-16; Gal. 3:10; Matt. 20:15). [8]Ezek. 18:19, 20. (Gal.3:22).

CONCERNING THE WAY OF SALVATION

We believe that the salvation of sinners is wholly of grace;[1] through the mediatorial offices of the Son of God;[2] Who pre-existed,[3]and Who by the appointment of the Father, and Who by the Holy Spirit was conceived, and born of the virgin Mary, freely took upon Him man's nature, yet without sin;[4] honored the divine law by His perfect obedience,[5] and after a miraculous ministry, by His death made a full atonement for our sins;[6] that having risen from the dead bodily He is now enthroned in heaven[7] to reign in eternal sovereignty and uniting in His wonderful person the tenderest sympathies with divine perfections, He is in every way qualified to be a suitable, a compassionate and all-sufficient Savior and Lord.[8]

Places in the Bible Where Taught. [1]Eph. 2:8. (Matt. 18:11; I John 4:10; I Cor. 3:5, 7; Acts 15:11). [2]John 3:16. (John 1:1-14; Heb. 4-14; 12:24). [3]John 8:58. [4]Phil. 2:6, 7. (Heb. 2:9, 14; 2 Cor. 5:21). [5]Heb. 5:8, 9. (Phil. 2:8; Gal. 4:4, 5; Rom. 3:21). [6]Isa. 53:4, 5. (Matt. 20:28; Rom. 4:25; 3:21-26;

1 John 4:10; 2:2; 1 Cor. 15:1-3; Heb. 9:13-15). [7]Heb. 1:8. (Heb. 1:3; 8:1; Col. 3:1-4). [8]Heb. 7:25. (Heb. 7:26; Ps. 89:19; Ps. 34).

CONCERNING JUSTIFICATION

We believe that the great Gospel blessing which Christ[1] secures to such as believe in Him is Justification;[2] that Justification includes the pardon of sin,[3] and the promise of eternal life on principles of righteousness;[4] that it is bestowed, not in consideration of any works of righteousness which we have done, but solely through faith in the Redeemer's blood;[5] by virtue of which faith His perfect righteousness is freely imputed to us of God;[6] that it brings us into a state of most blessed peace and favor with God, and secures every other blessing needful for time and eternity.[7]

Places in the Bible Where Taught. [1]John 1:16. (Eph. 3:8). [2]Acts 13:39. (Isa. 53:11, 12; Rom. 8:1). [3]Rom. 5:9. (Zech. 13:1; Matt. 9:6; Acts 10:43). [4]Rom. 5:17. (Titus 3:5-7; 1 Peter 3:7; 1 John 2:25; Rom. 5:21). [5]Rom. 4:4, 5. (Rom. 5:21; 6:23; Phil. 3:7-9). [6]Rom. 5:19. (Rom. 3:24-26; 4:23-25; 1 John 2:12). [7]Rom. 5:1, 2. (I Cor. 1:30, 31; Matt, 6:33; I Tim. 4:8).

CONCERNING THE FREENESS OF SALVATION

We believe that the blessings of salvation are made free to all by the Gospel;[1] that it is the immediate duty of all to accept them by a cordial, penitent, and obedient faith;[2] and that nothing prevents the salvation of the greatest sinner on earth but his own inherent depravity and voluntary rejection of the Gospel;[3] which rejection involves him in an aggravated condemnation.[4]

Places in the Bible Where Taught. [1]Isa. 55:1. (Luke 14:17). [2]Rom. 16:25, 26. (Mark 1:15; Rom. 1:15-17). [3]John 5:40. (Matt. 23:37; Rom. 9:32; Prov. 1:24; Acts 13:46). [4]John 3:19. (Matt. 11:20; Luke 19:27; 2 Thess. 1:8).

CONCERNING GRACE IN REGENERATION

We believe that, in order to be saved, sinners must be regenerated or born again,[1] that regeneration consists in giving a holy disposition to the soul;[2] that it is effected, in a manner above our comprehension, by the power of the Holy Spirit in connection with divine truth,[3] so as to secure our voluntary obedience to the Gospel;[4] and that its proper evidence appears in the holy fruits of repentance and faith and newness of life.[5]

Places in the Bible Where Taught. [1]John 3:3. (John 3:6, 7; 1 Cor. 2:14; Rev. 14:3; 21:27). [2]Cor. 5:17. (Ezek. 36:26; Deut. 30:6; Rom. 2:28, 29; 5:5; 1 John 4:7). [3]John 3:8. (1 Cor. 1:30; Phil. 2:13). [4]1 Peter 1:22-25. (Eph. 4:20-24; Col. 3:9-11). [5]Eph. 5:9. (Rom. 8:9; Gal. 5:16-23; Eph. 2:14-21; Matt. 3:8-10; 7:20; 1 John 5:4, 18).

CONCERNING REPENTANCE AND FAITH

We believe that Repentance and Faith are sacred duties, and also inseparable graces, wrought in our souls by the regenerating Spirit of God;[1] whereby, being deeply convinced of our guilt, danger, and helplessness, and of the way of salvation by Christ,[2] we turn to God with unfeigned contrition, confession, and supplication for mercy;[3] at the same time heartily receiving the Lord Jesus Christ as the only and all-sufficient Savior.[4]

Places in the Bible Where Taught. [1]Mark 1:15. [2]John 16:8. (Acts 16:30, 31). [3]Luke 18:13. (Luke 15:18-21; James 4:7-10; 2 Cor. 7:11; Rom. 10:12, 13; Psalm 51). [4]Rom. 10:9-11. (Acts 3:22, 23; Heb. 4:14; Ps. 2:6; Heb. 1:8; 7:25; 2 Tim. 1:12).

CONCERNING GOD'S PURPOSE OF GRACE

We believe that Election is the eternal purpose of God, according to which He graciously regenerates, sanctifies, and saves sinners;[1] that being perfectly consistent with the free agency of man, it comprehends as wells as embraces all the means in connection with the end;[2] that it is a most glorious display of God's soverign goodness, being infinitely free, wise, holy and unchangeable;[3] that it utterly excludes boasting, and promotes humility, love, prayer, praise, trust in God, and active imitation of His free mercy;[4] that it encourages the use of means in the highest degree;[5] that it may be ascertained by its effects in all who truly believe the Gospel;[6] that it is the foundation of Christian assurance;[7] and that to ascertain it with regard to ourselves demands and deserves the utmost diligence.[8]

Places in the Bible Where Taught. [1]Tim. 1:8, 9. (Eph. 1:3-14; 1 Peter 1:1, 2; Rom. 11:5, 6; John 15:16; 1 John 4:19). [2]2 Thess. 2:13, 14. (Acts 13:48; John 10:16; Matt. 20:16; Acts 15:14). [3]Exod. 33:18, 19. (Eph. 1:11; Rom. 9:23, 24; Jer. 31:3; Rom. 11:28, 29; James 1:17, 18; 2 Tim. 1:9; Rom. 11:32-36). [4]1 Cor. 4:7. (1 Cor. 1:26-31; Rom. 3:27; 4-16; Col. 3:12; 1 Cor. 15:10; 1 Peter 5:10; 1 Thess. 2:12, 13; 1 Peter 2:9; Luke 18:7). [5]Tim. 2:10. (John 6:37-40; 2 Peter 1:10). [6]1 Thess. 1:4-10. [7]Rom. 8:28-31. (Isa. 42:16; Rom. 11:29). [8]2 Peter 1:10, 11. (Phil. 3:12; Heb. 6:11).

CONCERNING SANCTIFICATION

We believe that Sanctification is the process by which, according to the will of God, we are made partakers of His holiness;[1] that it is a progressive work;[2] that it is begun in regeneration;[3] and that it it is carried on in the hearts of believers through out their earthly life, by the presence and power of the Holy Spirit, the Sealer and Comforter, in the continual use of the appointed means, especially the Word of God, self-examination, self-denial, watchfulness, and prayer.[4]

Places in the Bible Where Taught. [1]Thess. 4:3. (2 Cor. 7:1; 13:9; Eph. 1:4). [2]Prov. 4:18. (Heb. 6:1; 2 Peter 1:5-8; Phil. 3:12-16). [3]1 John 2:29. (John 3:6; Phil. 1:9-11). [4]Phil. 2:12, 13. (Eph. 4:11, 12, 30; 6:18; 1 Peter 2:2; 2 Peter 3:18; 2 Cor. 13:5; Luke 9:23; 11:35; Matt. 26:41).

CONCERNING THE PERSEVERANCE OF THE SAINTS

We believe that all real believers endure unto the end,[1] that their persevering attachment to Christ is the grand mark which distinguishes them from superficial professors;[2] that a special Providence watches over their welfare;[3] and they are kept by the power of God through faith unto salvation.[4]

Places in the Bible Where Taught. [1]John 8:31. (1 John 2:27, 28; 3:9; 5:18). [2]I John 2:19. (John 13:18; Matt. 13:20, 21; John 6:66-69). [3]Rom. 8:28. (Matt. 6:30-33; Jer. 32:40; Ps. 121:2; 91:11, 12). [4]Phil. 1:6. (Phil 2:12, 13; Jude 24, 25; Heb. 1:14; 13:5; 1 John 4:4).

CONERNING THE HARMONY OF THE LAW AND THE GOSPEL

We believe that the Law of God is the eternal and unchangeable rule of His moral government;[1] that it is holy, just and good;[2] and that the inability which the Scriptures ascribe to fallen men to fulfil its precepts arises entirely from their love of sin;[3] to deliver them from which, and to restore them through a Mediator to unfeigned obedience to the holy Law, is one great end of the Gospel, and of the means of grace connected with the establishment of the visible church.[4]

Places in the Bible Where Taught. [1]Rom. 3:31. (Matt. 5:17; Luke 16:17; Rom. 3:20; 4:15). [2]Rom. 7:12. (Rom. 7:7, 14, 22; Gal. 3:21; Ps. 119). [3]Rom. 8:7, 8. (Josh. 24:19; Jer. 13:23; John 6:44; 5:44). [4] Rom. 8:2-4. (Rom. 10:4; Heb. 8:10; 12:14; Jude 20, 21).

CONCERNING A GOSPEL CHURCH

We believe that a visible church of Christ is a congregation of baptized believers,[1] associated by convenant in the faith and fellowship of the Gospel;[2] observing the ordinances of Christ;[3] governed by His Laws;[4] and exercising the gifts, rights, and privileges invested in them by His Word;[5] seeking to extend the Gospel to the ends of the earth;[6] that its only Scriptural officers are Bishops, or Pastors, and Deacons,[7] whose qualifications, claims, and duties are defined in the epistles to Timothy and Titus.

Places in the Bible Where Taught. [1]1 Cor. 1:1-13 (Matt. 18:17; Acts. 5:11; 8:1; 11:21-23; 1 Cor. 4:17; 14:23; 3 John 9). [2]Acts 2:41, 42. (Acts 2:47; 1 Cor. 5:12; 13). [3]1 Cor. 11:2. (2 Thess. 3:6; Rom. 16:17-20; 1 Cor. 4:17). [4]Matt. 28:20. (John 14:15; 15:12; 1 John 4:21; John 14:21; 1 Thess. 4:2; 2 John 6; Gal. 6:2; all the Epistles). [5]Eph. 4:7. [6]Matt. 28:20. [7]Phil. 1:1. (Acts 14:23; 15:22; 1 Tim. 3; Titus 1).

CONCERNING A GOSPEL CHURCH IN ITS INDEPENDENCE AND RELATIONSHIPS

We believe that the local visible church of Christ is a voluntary and independent autonomous group of baptized believers;[1] that it is a pure democracy, which organically can join nothing;[2] and that it has the power and right within itself to confess its own faith in accordance with the New Testament;[3] and that each congregation recognizes its own democratic self-containing government as its highest authority for carrying out the will of the Lord Jesus Christ.[4]

Places in the Bible Where Taught. [1]Matt. 18:15-18. (Matt. 23:8-10; 1 Peter 5:3). [2]Rom. 12:16. (1 Cor. 1:10; Eph. 4:3; Phil. 1:27). [3] Tim. 3:15. (Jude 3; Rev. 2 and 3). [4]Matt. 18:15-18. (Acts 1:23-26; 6:3-5; 1 Cor. 5:4, 5, 13).

CONCERNING BAPTISM AND THE LORD'S SUPPER

We believe that both Christian baptism and the Lord's Supper are each a memorial, a symbol and a prophecy.[1] We believe that Christian baptism is the immersion in water of a believer;[2] into the name of the Father, the Son, and the Holy Ghost;[3] to show forth, in a solemn and beautiful emblem, our faith in the crucified, buried, and risen Savior, with its effect in our death to sin and resurrection to a new life;[4] that it is prerequisite to the privileges of a church relation; and a commendable prerequisite to the Lord's Supper;[5] in which the members of the Church, by the sacred use of bread and fruit of the vine to commemorate together the dying love of Christ;[6] preceded always by solemn self-examination.[7]

Places in the Bible Where Taught. [1]Rom. 6:3. (Mark 10:38; Rom. 6:4; Gal. 3:27; 1 Peter 3:21; Eph. 4:5; 1 Cor. 12:13; 1 Cor. 15:12, 22). [2]Acts 8:36-39. (Matt. 3:5, 6; John 3:22, 23; 4:1, 2; Matt. 28:19; Mark 16:16; Acts 2:38; 8:12; 16:32-34; 18:8). [3]Matt. 28:19. (Acts 10:47, 48; Gal. 3:27, 28). [4]Rom. 6:4. (Col. 2:12; 1 Peter 3:20, 21; Acts 22:16). [5]Acts 2:41, 42. (Matt. 28:19, 20; Acts and Epistles). [6]1 Cor. 11:26. (Matt. 26:26-29; Mark 14:22-25; Luke 22:14-20). [7]1 Cor. 11:28. (1 Cor. 5:1, 8; 10:3-32; 11:17-32; John 6:26-71).

CONCERNING THE LORD'S DAY

We believe that the first day of the week is the Lord's Day, and is a Christian institution,[1] it is to be kept sacred to spiritual purposes,[2] by abstaining from all unnecessary secular labor and sinful recreations,[3] for it commemorates the resurrection of the Lord Jesus Christ from the dead;[4] by the devout observance of all the means of grace, both private,[5] and public,[6] and by preparation for the rest that remaineth for the people of God.[7]

Places in the Bible Where Taught. [1]Acts 20:7. (Gen. 2:3; Col. 2:16, 17; Mark 2:27; John 20:19; 1 Cor. 16:1, 2). [2]Exod. 20:8. [3]Isa. 58.13, 14. [4]Acts 20:7. (Mark 16:9; John 20:19). [5]Ps. 118:15. [6]Heb. 10:24, 25. [7]Heb. 4:3-11.

CONCERNING CIVIL GOVERNMENT AND RELIGIOUS LIBERTY

We believe that civil government is of divine appointment, for the interests and good order of human society;[1] and that magistrates are to be prayed for, conscientiously honored and obeyed;[2] except only in things opposed to the will of our Lord Jesus Christ,[3] Who, is the only Lord of the conscience, and the Prince of the kings of the earth;[4] and that church and state should be separated, the state owing the church protection and full freedom;[5] no ecclesiastical group or denomination should be preferred above another by the state;[6] the state should not impose taxes for the support of any form of religion; a free church in a free state is the Christian ideal.[7]

Places in the Bible Where Taught. [1]Rom. 13:1-7. (Deut. 16:18; 2 Sam. 23:3; Exod. 18:21-23; Jer. 30-21). [2]Matt. 22:21. (Titus 3:1; 1 Peter 2:13; 1 Tim. 2:1-3). [3]Acts 5:29. (Dan. 3:15-18: 6:7-10; Acts 4:18-20). [4]Matt. 23:10. (Ps. 72:11; Ps. 2; Rom. 14:9-13). [5]1 Tim. 2:1, 2. (2 Pet. 2:18-21). [6]James 4:12. [7]1 Cor. 3:5. (Matt. 22:21; Mark 12:17).

CONCERNING THE STATE OF THE RIGHTEOUS AND THE WICKED

We believe that there is a radical and essential difference between the righteous and the wicked,[1] that such only as through faith are justified in the name of the Lord Jesus, and sanctified by the Spirit of our God, are truly righteous in His sight;[2] while all such as continue in impenitence and unbelief are in His sight wicked, and under the curse,[3] and this distinction holds among men both in and after death.[4]

Places in the Bible Where Taught. [1]Mal. 3:18. (Prov. 12:26; Isa. 5:20; Gen. 18:23; Acts 10:34, 35; Rom. 6:16). [2]Rom. 1:17. (1 John 3:7; Rom. 6:18, 22; 1 Cor. 11:32; Prov. 11:31; 1 Peter 4:17, 18). [3]1 John 5:19. (John 3:36; Isa. 57:21; Ps. 10:4; Isa. 55:6, 7). [4]Prov. 14:32. (John 8:21-24; Luke 12:4, 5; 9:23-26; John 12:25, 26; Eccl. 3:17; Matt. 7:13, 14).

CONCERNING THE RESURRECTION

We believe the Scriptures clearly teach that Jesus rose from the dead bodily, His grave was emptied of its contents;[1] that He appeared to the disciples after His resurrection in many convincing manifestations;[2] that He now exists in His glorified body at God's right hand;[3] and that there will be a resurrection of the righteous and a resurrection, of the wicked, separated in time;[4] that the bodies of the righteous will conform to the glorious spiritual body of the Lord Jesus Christ.[5]

Places in the Bible Where Taught. [1]Matt. 28:1-8. (1 Cor. 15:1-58; 2 Cor. 5:1-8). [2]Matt. 28:6. (John 20:9, 20; Acts 1:3; 10:39-41). [3]Peter 3:22; Heb. 4:14. [4]John 5:28, 29; Acts 24:15. [5]Phil. 3.21.

CONCERNING THE RETURN OF THE LORD

We believe that the end of the age is approaching;[1] "For the Lord Himself shall descend from heaven with a shout, with the voice of the archangel, and with the trump of God: and the dead in Christ shall rise first: Then we which are alive and remain shall be caught up together with them in the clouds, to meet the Lord in the air; and so shall we ever be with the Lord. Wherefore comfort one another with these words."[2] "Marvel not at this: for the hour is coming, in the which all that are in the graves shall hear His voice, And shall come forth; they that have done good, unto the resurrection of life; and they that have done evil, unto the resurrection of damnation."[3] "But the rest of the dead lived not again until the thousand years were finished, This is the first resurrection. Blessed and holy is he that hath part in the first resurrection; on such the second death hath no power, but they shall be priests of God and of Christ, and shall reign with Him a thousand years. And when the thousand years are expired, Satan shall be loosed out of his prison . . .";[4] that a solemn separation will then take place;[5] that the wicked will be adjudged to endless punishment, and the righteous to endless joy;[6] and that this judgment will fix forever the final state of men in heaven and hell, on principles of righteousness.

Places in the Bible Where Taught. [1]Peter 4:7. (1 Cor. 7:29-31; Heb. 1:10, 12; Matt. 25:31; 28:20; 13:39-43; 1 John 2:17; 2 Peter 3:3-13; Acts 1:11). [2]1 Thess. 4:16-18. [3]John 5:28, 29. [4]Rev. 20:5-7. [5]Matt. 13:49. (Matt. 13:37-43; 24:30, 31; 25:31-33). [6]Matt. 25:31-46. (1 Cor. 6:9, 10; Mark 9:43-48; 2 Peter 2:9; Jude 7; Phil. 3:19; Romans 6:23; 2 Cor. 5:10, 11; John 4:36; 2 Cor. 4:18). [7]Rom. 3:5, 6. (Heb. 6:1, 2; 1 Cor. 4:5; Acts 17:31; Rom. 2:2-16; Rev. 20:11, 12; 1 John 2:28, 4:17).

CONCERNING CHRISTIAN EDUCATION

We believe that Christianity is the religion of enlightenment and intelligence; that in Jesus Christ are hidden all the treasures of wisdom and knowledge;[1] and that all sound learning is therefore a part of our Christian heritage;[2] that the new birth opens all human faculties and creates a thirst for knowledge; that an adequate system of school is necessary to a complete spiritual program for Christ's church; and that the cause of education among New Testament churches is coordinate with the causes of evangelism, missions and general benevolence, and should receive along with these the liberal support of the churches.[3]

Places in the Bible Where Taught. [1]Matt. 28:20; Col. 2:3. [2]Deut. 4:1, 5, 9, 13, 14; 6:1, 7-10; Ps. 19:7, 8; Prov. 8:1-7; 4:1-10; Neh 8:1-4. [3]Matt. 28:20.

CONCERNING SOCIAL SERVICE

We believe that every Christian is under obligation to seek to make the will of Christ regnant in his own life and in human society;[1] to oppose in the spirit of Christ every form of greed, selfishness, and vice; to provide for the orphaned, the aged, the helpless, and the sick; to support everything that is good and righteous in industry, government and society as a whole for the benefit of men so that all men may live spiritually and righteously before God;[2] and that all means and methods used in social service for the amelioration of society and the establishment of righteousness among men must finally depend on the regeneration of the individual by the saving grace of God in Christ Jesus.[3]

Places in the Bible Where Taught. [1]Luke 10:25-27; Ex. 22:10, 14. [2]Lev. 6:2, Deut. 20:10; 4:42; Deut. 15:2; 27:17; Ps. 101:5. [3]Heb. 2:15; Zech. 8:16; Ex. 20:16; James 2:8; Rom. 12:14; Col. 3:12-17.

Notes: *In 1951, at the direction of the Minnesota Baptist Convention (now the Minnesota Baptist Association), George J. Carlson, Richard V. Clearwaters, and William H. Murk were appointed to prepare a statement of faith. Beginning with the New Hampshire Confession and the Baptist Faith and Message (adopted by the Southern Baptist Convention in 1925), they added items which drew from contemporary fundamentalist concerns. The result of their efforts was unanimously adopted in 1952. The confession includes an item which commits the association to a belief in a pretribulation rapture of the saints and a premillennial return of Christ.*

*   *   *

CONFESSION OF FAITH (NEW TESTAMENT ASSOCIATION OF INDEPENDENT BAPTIST CHURCHES)

I. CONCERNING THE SCRIPTURES

We believe that the Bible, sixty-six books in the Old and New Testaments, is without error in its original writing;[1] its author was God[2] using Spirit-guided men,[3] being thereby verbally and plenarily inspired;[4] it is the sole authority for faith and practice.[5]

Some places where taught: [1]Prov. 30:5, 6; John 17:17; Rev, 22:18, 19. [2]II Pet. 1:19-21; Acts 3:21; Jude 3; Heb. 1:1-3. [3]II Pet. 1:19-21; II Sam. 23:2; Acts 1:16; I Cor. 2:13, 14. [4]II Tim. 3:16; Matt. 5:18; Gal. 3:16. [5]II Tim. 3:15; Rom. 1:16; I Cor. 10:6-12; Eph. 6:17; I Tim 5:18; II Tim 3:17; II Pet. 3:15, 16; John 10:35; Acts 17:11; I John 4:1.

CONFESSION OF FAITH (NEW TESTAMENT ASSOCIATION OF INDEPENDENT BAPTIST CHURCHES) (continued)

II. CONCERNING THE TRUE GOD

We believe that there is one, and only one living and true God,[1] an infinite, eternal, self-existing, perfect Spirit;[2] He is a personal Being, the creator and upholder of the universe;[3] in the unity of the Godhead there are three persons, the Father, and Son, and the Holy Spirit,[4] equal in essence and in every divine perfection[5] but having distinct work.[6]

Some places where taught: [1]Deut. 6:4, 5; Jer. 10:10. [2]John 4:24; James 1:17; Hab. 1:12. [3]Heb. 3:4; Ps. 139:1-16. [4]Matt. 28:19; Matt. 3:16, 17; II Cor. 13:14; Ps. 2:2; Isa. 48:16 (ASV); Isa. 63:10. [5]John 10:30; John 17:5; Phil. 2:5, 6; I Cor. 8:6. [6]John 3:16; John 15:26.

III. CONCERNING CREATION

We believe in the Genesis account of Creation and that it is to be accepted literally and not figuratively;[1] that the six days of creation in Genesis chapter one were solar, that is twenty-four hour, days;[2] that all animal and vegetable life was made directly and God's established law is that they bring forth only "after their kind",[3] that man was created directly in God's own image and after His own likeness and did not evolve from any lower form of life.[4]

Some places where taught: [1]Gen. 1:1-2:25; Heb. 11:3; John 1:3: Col. 1:16-17: Ps. 33:6-9; Neh. 9:6; Rev. 4:11. [2]Ex. 20:11; 31:17. [3]Gen. 1:11, 12, 21, 24, 25. [4]Gen. 1:26.

VIII. CONCERNING THE LOCAL CHURCH

We believe that a local, visible church[1] is a congregation of baptized believers[2] associated together by a common faith and fellowship in the Gospel; observing the ordinances of Christ[3] and governed by His Word;[4] seeking to extend the Gospel to the ends of the earth; that its only Scriptural officers are bishops (or pastors) and deacons, whose qualifications, claims and duties are defined in the Epistles to Timothy and Titus.[5]

Some places where taught: [1]Matt. 18:17; Acts 5:11; Acts 8:1. [2]Acts 2:41, 42. [3]Matt. 28:19, 20; I Cor. 11:23, 24; Heb. 10:25. [4]II Tim. 3:15, 16. [5]I Tim. 3:1-16; Titus 1:5-9.

IX. CONCERNING A GOSPEL CHURCH IN ITS INDEPENDENCE AND RELATIONSHIPS

We believe that the local visible church of Christ is a voluntary and independent autonomous group of baptized believers;[1] that it is a pure democracy, which organically can join nothing, and that it has the power and right within itself to confess its own faith in accordance with the New Testament;[2] and that each congregation recognizes its own democratic self-containing government as its highest authority for carrying out the will of the Lord Jesus Christ.[3]

Some places where taught: [1]Matt. 18:15-18; I Cor. 5:4, 5, 13. [2]I Tim. 3:15; Jude 3; Rev. 2 and 3. [3]Matt. 18:15-18; Acts 6:3-5; I Cor. 5:4, 5, 13; I Tim. 3:15.

X. CONCERNING BAPTISM AND THE LORD'S SUPPER

We believe that both Christian baptism and the Lord's Supper are each a memorial, a symbol and a prophecy.[1] We believe that Christian baptism is the immersion in water of a believer,[2] in the name of the Father, the Son, and the Holy Ghost;[3] to show forth, in a solemn and beautiful figure, our faith in the crucified, buried, and risen Savior, with its effect in our death to sin and resurrection to a new life;[4] that it is prerequisite to the privileges of church membership; and a prerequisite to the Lord's Supper;[5] in which the members of the Church by the use of bread and fruit of the vine commemorate together the death of Christ;[6] preceded always by solemn self-examination.[7]

Some places where taught: [1]Rom 6:3, 4; I Pet. 3:21. [2]Acts 8:36-39; John 3:22, 23; 4:1, Matt 28:19; Mark 16:16; Acts 2:38; 8:12; 16:32-34; 18:8. [3]Matt. 28:19. [4]Rom. 6:4; Col. 2:12; I Pet. 3:20, 21; Acts 22:16. [5]Acts 2:41, 42; Matt. 28:19, 20. [6]I Cor. 11:26; Matt. 26:26-29. [7]I Cor. 11:28; 5:1, 8; 11:17-32.

XI. CONCERNING THE LORD'S DAY

We believe that the first day of the week in the Lord's Day, and is a Christian institution;[1] it is to be kept sacred to spiritual purposes by abstaining from all unnecessary secular labor and recreation, for it commemorates the resurrection of the Lord Jesus Christ from the dead;[2] by the devout, observance of all the means of growing in grace, both private and public[3] and by predicting the rest that remaineth for the people of God.[4]

Some places where taught: [1]Acts 20:7; Col. 2:16, 17; John 20:19; I Cor. 16:1, 2. [2]Acts 20:7; Mark 16:9; John 20:19. [3]Heb. 10:24, 25. [4]Heb. 4:3-11.

XII. CONCERNING CIVIL GOVERNMENT AND RELIGIOUS LIBERTY

We believe that civil government is of divine appointment, for the interests and good order of human society;[1] and that civil authorities are to be prayed for, conscientiously honored and obeyed;[2] except only in the things opposed by the Word of God, which reveals the will of our Lord Jesus Christ,[3] Who is the only Lord of the conscience, and the Prince of the kings of the earth;[4] and that church and state should be separate, the state owing the church protection and full freedom; no ecclesiastical group or denomination should be preferred above another by the state;[6] the state should not impose taxes for the support of any form of religion; a free church in a free state is the Christian ideal.[7]

Some places where taught: [1]Rom. 13:1-7. [2]Matt. 22:21; Titus 3:1; I Pet. 2:13, 14; I Tim. 2:1-3. [3]Acts 5:29; Acts 4:18-20. [4]Matt. 23:10; Ps. 72:11; Ps. 2; Rom. 14:9-13. [5]I Tim. 2:1.2. [6]James 4:12. [7]Matt 22:21.

XIII. CONCERNING THE STATE OF THE RIGHTEOUS AND THE WICKED

We believe that there is a radical and essential difference between the righteous and the wicked;[1] that such only as through faith are justified in the name of the Lord Jesus, and sanctified by the Spirit of our God, are truly righteous in His sight;[2] while all such as continue in impenitence and unbelief are in His sight wicked,[3] and under condemnation, and that there will be a resurrection of the righteous and a resurrection of the unrighteous.

Some places where taught: [1]Mal. 3:18. [2]Rom. 1:17. [3]John 3:18. [4]Dan. 12:2; Matt. 7:13, 14; Luke 9:23-26.

XIV. CONCERNING FUTURE EVENTS

We believe the Scriptures teach that at death the spirit and soul of the believer pass instantly into the presence of Christ and remain in conscious joy until the resurrection of the body when Christ[1] comes for His own[2] the blessed hope of the believer is the imminent, personal, pre-tribulational, premillennial appearance of Christ to rapture the church,[3] His bride; His righteous judgments will then be poured out on an unbelieving world during the Tribulation (the seventieth week of Daniel), the last half of which is the Great Tribulation;[4] the climax of this fearful era will be the physical return of Jesus Christ to the earth in great glory to introduce the Davidic kingdom;[5] Israel will be saved and restored as a nation;[6] Satan will be bound and the curse will be lifted from the physical creation;[7] following the Millennium, the Great White Throne judgment will occur, at which time the bodies and souls of the wicked shall be reunited and cast into the Lake of Fire.[8]

Some places where taught: [1]II Cor. 5:8. [2]I Cor. 15:51-57. [3]Titus 2:13; I Thess. 4:14-17. [4]Matt 24:21. [5]Rev. 19:11-16. [6]Rom. 11:26, 27. [7]Rev. 20:2, 3. [8]Rev. 20:11-15.

XV. CONCERNING HERESY AND APOSTASY

We believe in total and complete separation as taught in the Word of God from all forms of heresy and ecclesiastical apostasy. We believe the Scripture teaches that we are to: 1. Try them.[1] 2. Mark them.[2] 3. Rebuke them.[3] 4. Have no fellowship.[4] 5. Withdraw ourselves.[5] 6. Receive them not.[6] 7. Have no company with him.[7] 8. Reject them.[8] 9. Separate ourselves.[9]

Some places where taught: [1]I John 4:1. [2]Rom. 16:17. [3]Titus 1:13. [4]Eph. 5:11. [5]II Thess. 3:6. [6]II John 10, 11. [7]II Thess. 3:14. [8]Titus 3:10. [9]II Cor. 6:17.

Notes: *Adopted in 1966 as part of the association's constitution, this confession emphasizes the verbal plenary inspiration of scripture, the literalism of the creation account in the book of Genesis, the pretribulation rapture of the saints, premillennialism, and separation from those considered apostate Christians.*

* * *

PREAMBLE (TO THE CONSTITUTION OF THE NORTH AMERICAN BAPTIST CONFERENCE)

We, as New Testament Baptists, affirm our faith in the Lord Jesus Christ for our salvation and believe in those great distinctive principles for which Baptists have lived and died, such as:

1. Soul liberty;
2. The inspired authority of the Scriptures in matters of faith and conduct;
3. The separation of Church and State;
4. The Revelation of God through Jesus Christ as only Savior and Lord;
5. Regenerated church membership;
6. Believer's baptism by immersion;
7. The congregational form of church government; and
8. The proclamation of the Gospel throughout all the world, and we do hereby set forth and declare the following as our Constitution and By-Laws.

Notes: *This brief statement emphasizes a few Baptist distinctives.*

* * *

ARTICLES OF FAITH (UNION ASSOCIATION OF REGULAR BAPTIST CHURCHES)

1. We believe in one true and living God, Father, Son, and Holy Ghost and these three are one.
2. We believe that the Old and New Testaments Scriptures are the written word of God, and the only rule of faith and practice.
3. We believe in the doctrine of election by grace.
4. We believe in the doctrine of original sin, and man's impotency to rescue himself from the fallen state he is in by nature by his own free will ability.
5. We believe that sinners are called, converted, regenerated and sanctified by the Holy Spirit and all are so regenerated and born again by the Spirit of God shall never fall finally away.
6. We believe sinners are justified in the sight of God only by the imputed righteousness of Jesus Christ.
7. We believe that baptism, the Lord's Supper and feet washing are ordinances of Jesus Christ and that true believers are the only proper subjects of these ordinances and we believe the only true mode of baptism is by immersion.
8. We believe in the resurrection of the dead and a general judgment and that the joys of the righteous and the punishment of the wicked will be eternal.
9. We believe no minister has the right to administer the ordinances of the Gospel, except such as are regularly called, and come under the imposition of hands by a presbytery of the church.

Notes: *Regular Baptists follow a Calvinist doctrine of election and perseverance of the saints. They practice foot washing.*

* * *

BAPTIST FAITH AND MESSAGE (1925) (SOUTHERN BAPTIST CONVENTION)

REPORT OF COMMITTEE ON BAPTIST FAITH AND MESSAGE

Your committee beg leave to report as follows:

Your committee recognize that they were appointed "to consider the advisability of issuing another statement of the Baptist Faith and Message, and to report at the next Convention."

In pursuance of the instructions of the Convention, and in consideration of the general denominational situation, your committee have decided to recommend the New Hampshire Confession of Faith, revised at certain points, and with some additional articles growing out of present

BAPTIST FAITH AND MESSAGE (1925) (SOUTHERN BAPTIST CONVENTION) (continued)

needs, for approval by the Convention, in the event a statement of the Baptist faith and message is deemed necessary at this time.

The present occasion for a reaffirmation of Christian fundamentals is the prevalence of naturalism in the modern teaching and preaching of religion. Christianity is supernatural in its origin and history. We repudiate every theory of religion which denies the supernatural elements in our faith.

As introductory to the doctrinal articles, we recommend the adoption by the Convention of the following statement of the historic Baptist conception of the nature and function of confessions of faith in our religious and denominational life, believing that some such statement will clarify the atmosphere and remove some causes of misunderstanding, friction, and apprehension. Baptists approve and circulate confessions of faith with the following understandings, namely:

(1) That they constitute a consensus of opinion of some Baptist body, large or small, for the general instruction and guidance of our own people and others concerning those articles of the Christian faith which are most surely held among us. They are not intended to add anything to the simple conditions of salvation revealed in the New Testament, viz., repentance towards God and faith in Jesus Christ as Saviour and Lord.

(2) That we do not regard them as complete statements of our faith, having any quality of finality or infallibility. As in the past so in the future Baptists should hold themselves free to revise their statements of faith as may seem to them wise and expedient at any time.

(3) That any group of Baptists, large or small, have the inherent right to draw up for themselves and publish to the world a confession of their faith whenever they may think it advisable to do so.

(4) That the sole authority for faith and practice among Baptists is the Scriptures of the Old and New Testaments. Confessions are only guides in interpretation, having no authority over the conscience.

(5) That they are statements of religious convictions, drawn from the Scriptures, and are not to be used to hamper freedom of thought or investigation in other realms of life.

THE SCRIPTURES

1. We believe that the Holy Bible was written by men divinely inspired, and is a perfect treasure of heavenly instruction; that it has God for its author, salvation for its end, and truth, without any mixture of error, for its matter; that it reveals the principles by which God will judge us; and therefore is, and will remain to the end of the world, the true center of Christian union, and the supreme standard by which all human conduct, creeds and religious opinions should be tried.

GOD

2. There is one and only one living and true God, an intelligent, spiritual and personal Being, the Creator, Preserver and Ruler of the universe, infinite in holiness and all other perfections, to whom we owe the highest love, reverence and obedience. He is revealed to us as Father, Son and Holy Spirit, each with distinct personal attributes, but without division of nature, essence or being.

THE FALL OF MAN

3. Man was created by the special act of God, as recorded in Genesis. "So God created man in his own image, in the image of God created he him; male and female created he them." (Gen. 1:27). "And the Lord God formed man of the dust of the ground, and breathed into his nostrils the breath of life; and man became a living soul." (Gen. 2:7.) He was created in a state of holiness under the law of his maker, but, through the temptation of Satan he transgressed the command of God and fell from his original holiness and righteousnss; whereby his posterity inherit a nature corrupt and in bondage to sin, are under condemnation, and as soon as they are capable of moral action, become actual transgressors.

THE WAY OF SALVATION

4. The salvation of sinners is wholly of grace, through the mediatorial office of the Son of God, who by the Holy Spirit was born of the Virgin Mary and took upon him our nature, yet without sin; honored the divine law by his personal obedience, and made atonement for our sins by his death. Being risen from the dead, he is now enthroned in heaven, and, uniting in his person the tenderest sympathies with divine perfections, he is in every way qualified to be a compassionate and all-sufficient Saviour.

JUSTIFICATION

5. Justification is God's gracious and full acquittal upon principles of righteousness of all sinners who believe in Christ. This blessing is bestowed, not in consideration of any works of righteousness which we have done, but through the redemption that is and through Jesus Christ. It brings us into a state of most blessed peace and favor with God, and secures every other needed blessing.

THE FREENESS OF SALVATION

6. The blessings of salvation are made free to all by the Gospel. It is the duty of all to accept them by penitent and obedient faith. Nothing prevents the salvation of the greatest sinner except his own voluntary refusal to accept Jesus Christ as teacher, Saviour and Lord.

REGENERATION

7. Regeneration or the new birth is a change of heart wrought by the Holy Spirit, whereby we become partakers of the divine nature and a holy disposition is given, leading to the love and practice of righteousness. It is a work of God's free grace condi-

tioned upon faith in Christ and made manifest by the fruit which we bring forth to the glory of God.

REPENTANCE OF FAITH

8. We believe that repentance and faith are sacred duties, and also inseparable graces, wrought in our souls by the regenerating Spirit of God; whereby being deeply convinced of our guilt, danger, and helplessness, and of the way of salvation by Christ, we turn to God with unfeigned contrition, confession, and supplication for mercy; at the same time heartily receiving the Lord Jesus Christ as our Prophet, Priest and King, and relying on him alone as the only and all-sufficient Saviour.

GOD'S PURPOSE OF GRACE

9. Election is the gracious purpose of God, according to which he regenerates, sanctifies and saves sinners. It is perfectly consistent with the free agency of man, and comprehends all the means in connection with the end. It is a most glorious display of God's sovereign goodness, and is infinitely wise, holy and unchangeable. It excludes boasting and promotes humility. It encourages the use of means in the highest degree.

SANCTIFICATION

10. Sanctification is the process by which the regenerate gradually attain to moral and spiritual perfection through the presence and power of the Holy Spirit dwelling in their hearts. It continues throughout the earthly life, and is accomplished by the use of all the ordinary means of grace, and particularly by the Word of God.

PERSEVERANCE

11. All real believers endure to the end. Their continuance in well-doing is the mark which distinguishes them from mere professors. A special Providence cares for them, and they are kept by the power of God through faith unto salvation.

A GOSPEL CHURCH

12. A church of Christ is a congregation of baptized believers, associated by covenant in the faith and fellowship of the gospel; observing the ordinances of Christ, governed by his law, and exercising the gifts, rights and privileges invested in them by his word, and seeking to extend the Gospel to the ends of the earth. Its Scriptural officers are bishops or elders and deacons.

BAPTISM AND THE LORD'S SUPPER

13. Christian baptism is the immersion of a believer in water in the name of the Father, the Son and the Holy Spirit. The act is a symbol of our faith in a crucified, buried and risen Saviour. It is prerequisite to the privileges of a church relation and to the Lord's Supper, in which the members of the church, by the use of bread and wine, commemorate the dying love of Christ.

THE LORD'S DAY

14. The first day of the week is the Lord's day. It is a Christian institution for regular observance. It com-
memorates the resurrection of Christ from the dead, and should be employed in exercises of worship and spiritual devotion, both public and private, and by refraining from worldly amusements, and resting from secular employments, works of necessity and mercy only excepted.

THE RIGHTEOUS AND THE WICKED

15. There is a radical and essential difference between the righteous and wicked. Those only who are justified through the name of the Lord Jesus Christ and sanctified by the Holy Spirit are truly righteous in his sight. Those who continue in impenitence and unbelief are in his sight wicked and are under condemnation. This distinction between the righteous and the wicked holds in and after death, and will be made manifest at the judgment when final and everlasting awards are made to all men.

THE RESURRECTION

16. The Scriptures clearly teach that Jesus rose from the dead. His grave was emptied of its contents. He appeared to the disciples after his resurrection in many convincing manifestations. He now exists in his glorified body at God's right hand. There will be a resurrection of the righteous and the wicked. The bodies of the righteous will conform to the glorious spiritual body of Jesus.

THE RETURN OF THE LORD

17. The New Testament teaches in many places the visible and personal return of Jesus to this earth. "This same Jesus which is taken up from you into Heaven, shall so come in like manner as ye have seen him go into Heaven." The time of his coming is not revealed. "Of that day and hour knoweth no one, no, not the angels in heaven, but my Father only." (Matt. 24:36). It is the duty of all believers to live in readiness for his coming and by diligence in good works to make manifest to all men the reality and power of their hope in Christ.

RELIGIOUS LIBERTY

18. God alone is Lord of the conscience, and he has left it free from the doctrines and commandments of men which are contrary to his word or not contained in it. Church and state should be separate. The state owes to the church protection and full freedom in the pursuit of its spiritual ends. In providing for such freedom no ecclesiastical group or denomination should be favored by the state more than others. Civil government being ordained of God, it is the duty of Christians to render loyal obedience thereto in all things not contrary to the revealed will of God. The church should not resort to the civil power to carry on its work. The Gospel of Christ contemplates spiritual means alone for the pursuit of its ends. The state has no right to impose penalties for religious opinions of any kind. The state has no right to impose taxes for the support of any form of religion. A free church in a free state is the Christian ideal, and this implies the right of free and unhindered access to God on the part of all men, and the right to

form and propagate opinions in the sphere of religion without interference by the civil power.

PEACE AND WAR

19. It is the duty of Christians to seek peace with all men on principles of righteousness. In accordance with the spirit and teachings of Christ they should do all in their power to put an end to war.

The true remedy for the war spirit is the pure gospel of our Lord. The supreme need of the world is the acceptance of his teachings in all the affairs of men and nations, and the practical application of his law of love.

We urge Christian people throughout the world to pray for the reign of the Prince of Peace, and to oppose everything to provoke war.

EDUCATION

20. Christianity is the religion of enlightenment and intelligence. In Jesus Christ are hidden all the treasures of wisdom and knowledge. All sound learning is therefore a part of our Christian heritage. The new birth opens all human faculties and creates a thirst for knowledge. An adequate system of schools is necessary to a complete spiritual program for Christ's people. The cause of education in the Kingdom of Christ is co-ordinate with the causes of missions and general benevolence, and should receive along with these the liberal support of the churches.

SOCIAL SERVICE

21. Every Christian is under obligation to seek to make the will of Christ regnant in his own life and in human society; to oppose in the spirit of Christ every form of greed, selfishness and vice; to provide for the orphaned, the aged, the helpless, and the sick; to seek to bring industry, government and society as a whole under the sway of the principles of righteousness, truth and brotherly love; to promote these ends Christians should be ready to work with all men of good will in any good cause, always being careful to act in the spirit of love without compromising their loyalty to Christ and his truth. All means and methods used in social service for the amelioration of society and the establishment of righteousness among men must finally depend on the regeneration of the individual by the saving grace of God in Christ Jesus.

CO-OPERATION

22. Christ's people should, as occasion requires, organize such associations and conventions as may best secure co-operation for the great objects of the Kingdom of God. Such organizations have no authority over each other or over the churches. They are voluntary and advisory bodies designed to elicit, combine and direct the energies of our people in the most effective manner. Individual members of New Testament churches should co-operate with each other, and the churches themselves should co-operate with each

other, in carrying forward the missionary, educational and benevolent program for the extension of Christ's Kingdom. Christian unity in the New Testament sense is spiritual harmony and voluntary co-operation for common ends by various Christian denominations, when the end to be attained is itself justified, and when such co-operation involves no violation by conscience or compromise of loyalty to Christ and his Word as revealed in the New Testament.

EVANGELISM AND MISSIONS

23. It is the duty of every Christian man and woman, and the duty of every church of Christ, to seek to extend the gospel to the ends of the earth. The new birth of man's spirit of God's Holy Spirit means the birth of love for others. Missionary effort on the part of all rests thus upon a spiritual necessity of the regenerate life. It is also expressly and repeatedly commanded in the teachings of Christ. It is the duty of every child of God to seek constantly to win the lost to Christ by personal effort and by all other methods sanctioned by the Gospel of Christ.

STEWARDSHIP

24. God is the source of all blessings, temporal and spiritual; all that we have and are we owe to him. We have a spiritual debtorship to the whole world, a holy trusteeship in the Gospel, and a binding stewardship in our possessions. We are therefore under obligation to serve him with our time, talents and material possessions; and should recognize all these as entrusted to us to use for the glory of God and helping others. Christians should cheerfully, regularly, systematically, proportionately, and liberally contribute of their means to advancing the Redeemer's cause on earth.

THE KINGDOM

25. The Kingdom of God is the reign of God in the heart and life of the individual in every human relationship, and in every form and institution of organized human society. The chief means for promoting the Kingdom of God on earth are preaching the Gospel of Christ, and teaching the principles of righteousness contained therein. The Kingdom of God will be complete when every thought and will of man shall be brought into captivity to the will of Christ. And it is the duty of all Christ's people to pray and labor continually that his Kingdom may come and his will be done on earth as it is in heaven.

Since matters of science have no proper place in a religious confession of faith, and since it is desirable that our attitude towards science be clearly understood, your committee deem it proper to submit the following statement on the relation between science and religion, adopted in 1923 by this Convention at Kansas City, and request that it be published in the minutes of the Convention.

SCIENCE AND RELIGION

1. We recognize the greatness and value of the service which modern science is rendering to the cause of truth in uncovering the facts of the natural and the

Christian religion. We have no interest or desire in covering up any fact in any realm of research. But we do protest against certain unwarranted procedures on the part of some so-called scientists. First, in making discoveries, or alleged discoveries, in physical nature, a convenient weapon of attack upon the facts of religion; second, using the particular sciences, such as psychology, biology, geology, and various others, as if they necessarily contained knowledge pertaining to the realm of the Christian religion, setting aside the supernatural; third, teaching as facts what are merely hypotheses. The evolution doctrine has long been a working hypothesis of science, and will probably continue to be, because of its apparent simplicity in explaining the universe. But its best exponents freely admit that the causes of the origin of species have not been traced, nor has any proof been forthcoming that man is not the direct creation of God as recorded in Genesis. We protest against the imposition of this theory upon the minds of our children in denominational, or public schools, as if it were a definite and established truth of science. We insist that this and all other theories be dealt with in a truly scientific way, that is, in careful conformity to establish facts.

2. We record again our unwavering adherence to the supernatural elements in the Christian religion. The Bible is God's revelation of himself through men moved by the Holy Spirit, and is our sufficient, certain and authoritative guide in religion. Jesus Christ was born of the Virgin Mary, through the power of the Holy Spirit. He was the divine and eternal Son of God. He wrought miracles, healing the sick, casting out demons, raising the dead. He died as the vicarious, atoning Saviour of the world, and was buried. He arose again from the dead. The tomb was emptied of its contents. In his risen body he appeared many times to his disciples. He ascended to the right hand of the Father. He will come again in person, the same Jesus who ascended from the Mount of Olives.

3. We believe that adherence to the above truths and facts is a necessary condition of service of teachers in our Baptist schools. These facts of Christianity in no way conflict with any fact of science. We do not sit in judgment upon the scientific views of teachers of science. We grant them the same freedom of research in their realm that we claim for ourselves in the religious realm. But we do insist upon a positive content of faith in accordance with the preceding statement as a qualification for acceptable service in Baptist schools. The supreme issue today is between naturalism and super-naturalism. We stand unalterably for the supernatural in Christianity. Teachers in our schools should be careful to free themselves from any suspicion of disloyalty on this point. In the present period of agitation and unrest they are obligated to make their position clear. We pledge our support to all schools and teachers who are thus loyal to the facts of Christianity as revealed in the Scriptures.

Signed by the Committee,

E. Y. MULLINS, Chairman;

S. M. BROWN,

W. J. McGLOTHLIN,

E. C. DARGAN,

L. R. SCARBOROUGH.

Notes: *The preamble of this statement, derived in part from the New Hampshire Confession, establishes the limited context for the statement's use. The statement should be compared with its revision adopted in 1963. The paragraphs on science are of particular importance. They constitute a significant appraisal of the creation-evolution controversy of the 1920s and were adopted by the convention meeting in Memphis, Tennessee, during the height of the debate on the Bible's account of the natural world.*

* * *

BAPTIST FAITH AND MESSAGE (1963) (SOUTHERN BAPTIST CONVENTION)

COMMITTEE ON BAPTIST FAITH AND MESSAGE

The 1962 session of the Southern Baptist Convention, meeting in San Francisco, California, adopted the following motion:

"Since the report of the Committee on Statement of Baptist Faith and Message was adopted in 1925, there have been various statements from time to time which have been made, but no overall statement which might be helpful at this time as suggested in Section 2 of that report, or introductory statement which might be used as an interpretation of the 1925 Statement.

"We recommend, therefore, that the president of this Convention be requested to call a meeting of the men now serving as presidents of the various state conventions that would qualify as a member of the Southern Baptist Convention committee under Bylaw 18 to present to the Convention in Kansas City some similar statement which shall serve as information to the churches, and which may serve as guidelines to the various agencies of the Southern Baptist Conventions. It is understood that any group or individual may approach this committee to be of service. The expenses of this committee shall be borne by the Convention Operating Budget."

Your committee thus constituted begs leave to present its report as follows:

Throughout its work your committee has been conscious of the contribution made by the statement of "The Baptist Faith and Message" adopted by the Southern Baptist Convention in 1925. It quotes with approval its affirmation that "Christianity is supernatural in its origin and history. We repudiate every theory of religion which denies the supernatural elements in our faith."

Furthermore, it concurs in the introductory "statement of the historic Baptist conception of the nature and function of confessions of faith in our religious and denominational

BAPTIST FAITH AND MESSAGE (1963) (SOUTHERN BAPTIST CONVENTION) (continued)

life. . . . " It is, therefore, quoted in full as a part of this report to the Convention:

"(1) That they constitute a consensus of opinion of some Baptist body, large or small, for the general instruction and guidance of our own people and others concerning those articles of the Christian faith, which are most surely held among us. They are not intended to add anything to the simple conditions of salvation revealed in the New Testament, viz., repentance towards God and faith in Jesus Christ as Saviour and Lord.

"(2) That we do not regard them as complete statements of our faith, having any quality of finality or infallibility. As in the past so in the future, Baptists should hold themselves free to revise their statements of faith as may seem to them wise and expedient at any time.

"(3) That any group of Baptists, large or small, have the inherent right to draw up for themselves and publish to the world a confession of their faith whenever they may think it advisable to do so.

"(4) That the sole authority for faith and practice among Baptists is the Scriptures of the Old and New Testaments. Confessions are only guides in interpretation, having no authority over the conscience.

"(5) That they are statements of religious convictions, drawn from the Scriptures, and are not to be used to hamper freedom of thought or investigation in the other realms of life."

The 1925 Statement recommended "the New Hampshire Confession of Faith, revised at certain points, and with some additional articles growing out of certain needs . . . " Your present committee has adopted the same pattern. It has sought to build upon the structure of the 1925 Statement, keeping in mind the "certain needs" of our generation. At times it has reproduced sections of that statement without change. In other instances it has substituted words for clarity or added sentences for emphasis. At certain points it has combined articles, with minor changes in wording, to endeavor to relate certain doctrines to each other. In still others—e.g., "God" and "Salvation"—it has sought to bring together certain truths contained throughout the 1925 Statement in order to relate them more clearly and concisely. In no case has it sought to delete from or to add to the basic contents of the 1925 Statement.

Baptists are a people who profess a living faith. This faith is rooted and grounded in Jesus Christ who is "the same yesterday, and to-day, and for ever." Therefore, the sole authority for faith and practice among Baptists is Jesus Christ whose will is revealed in the Holy Scriptures.

A living faith must experience a growing understanding of truth and must be continually interpreted and related to the needs of each new generation. Throughout their history Baptist bodies, both large and small, have issued statements of faith which comprise a consensus of their beliefs. Such statements have never been regarded as complete, infallible statements of faith, nor as official creeds carrying mandatory authority. Thus this generation of Southern Baptists is in historic succession of intent and purpose as it endeavors to state for its time and theological climate those articles of the Christian faith which are most surely held among us.

Baptists emphasize the soul's competency before God, freedom of religion, and the priesthood of the believer. However, this emphasis should not be interpreted to mean that there is an absence of certain definite doctrines that Baptists believe, cherish, and with which they have been and are now closely identified.

It is the purpose of this statement of faith and message to set forth certain teachings which we believe.

I. THE SCRIPTURES

The Holy Bible was written by men divinely inspired and is the record of God's revelation of Himself to man. It is a perfect treasure of divine instruction. It has God for its author, salvation for its end, and truth, without any mixture of error, for its matter. It reveals the principles by which God judges us; and therefore is, and will remain to the end of the world, the true center of Christian union, and the supreme standard by which all human conduct, creeds, and religious opinions should be tried. The criterion by which the Bible is to be interpreted is Jesus Christ.

II. GOD

There is one and only one living and true God. He is an intelligent, spiritual, and personal Being, the Creator, Redeemer, Preserver, and Ruler of the universe. God is infinite in holiness and all other perfections. To him we owe the highest love, reverence, and obedience. The eternal God reveals Himself to us as Father, Son, and Holy Spirit, with distinct personal attributes, but without division of nature, essence, or being.

1. GOD THE FATHER. God as Father reigns with providential care over His universe, His creatures, and the flow of the stream of human history according to the purpose of His grace. He is all powerful, all loving, and all wise. God is Father in truth to those who become children of God through faith in Jesus Christ. He is fatherly in his attitude toward all men.

2. GOD THE SON. Christ is the eternal Son of God. In His incarnation as Jesus Christ He was conceived of the Holy Spirit and born of the virgin Mary. Jesus perfectly revealed and did the will of God, taking upon Himself the demands and necessities of human nature and identifying Himself completely with mankind yet without sin. He honored the divine law by His personal obedience, and in His death on the cross He made provision for the redemption of men from sin. He was raised from the dead with a glorified body and appeared to His disciples as the person who was with them before His crucifixion. He ascended into heaven and is now exalted at the right hand of God where He is the One Mediator, partaking of the nature of God and of man, and in whose Person is effected the reconciliation between

God and man. He will return in power and glory to judge the world and to consummate His redemptive mission. He now dwells in all believers as the living and ever present Lord.

3. GOD THE HOLY SPIRIT. The Holy Spirit is the Spirit of God. He inspired holy men of old to write the Scriptures. Through illumination He enables men to understand truth. He exalts Christ. He convicts of sin, of righteousness and of judgment. He calls men to the Saviour, and effects regeneration. He cultivates Christian character, comforts believers and bestows the spiritual gifts by which they serve God through His church. He seals the believer unto the day of final redemption. His presence in the Christian is the assurance of God to bring the believer into the fulness of the stature of Christ. He enlightens and empowers the believer and the church in worship, evangelism, and service.

III. MAN

Man was created by the special act of God, in His own image, and is the crowning work of His creation. In the beginning man was innocent of sin and was endowed by His Creator with freedom of choice. By his free choice man sinned against God and brought sin into the human race. Through the temptation of Satan man transgressed the command of God, and fell from his original innocence; whereby his posterity inherit a nature and an environment inclined toward sin, and as they are capable of moral action become transgressors and are under condemnation. Only the grace of God can bring man into His holy fellowship and enable man to fulfil the creative purpose of God. The sacredness of human personality is evident in that God created man in His own image, and in that Christ died for man; therefore every man possesses dignity and is worthy of respect and Christian love.

IV. SALVATION

Salvation involves the redemption of the whole man, and is offered freely to all who accept Jesus Christ as Lord and Saviour, who by His own blood obtained eternal redemption for the believer. In its broadest sense salvation includes regeneration, sanctification, and glorification.

1. Regeneration, or the new birth, is a work of God's grace whereby believers become new creatures in Christ Jesus. It is a change of heart wrought by the Holy Spirit through conviction of sin, to which the sinner responds in repentance toward God and faith in the Lord Jesus Christ.

   Repentance and faith are inseparable experiences of grace. Repentance is a genuine turning from sin toward God. Faith is the acceptance of Jesus Christ and commitment of the entire personality to Him as Lord and Saviour. Justification is God's gracious and full acquittal upon principles of his righteousness of all sinners who repent and believe in Christ. Justification brings the believer into a relationship of peace and favor with God.

2. Sanctification is the experience, beginning in regeneration, by which the believer is set apart to God's purposes, and is enabled to progress toward moral and spiritual perfection through the presence and power of the Holy Spirit dwelling in him. Growth in grace should continue throughout the regenerate person's life.

3. Glorification is the culmination of salvation and is the final blessed and abiding state of the redeemed.

V. GOD'S PURPOSE OF GRACE

Election is the gracious purpose of God, according to which He regenerates, sanctifies, and glorifies sinners. It is consistent with the free agency of man and comprehends all the means in connection with the end. It is a glorious display of God's sovereign goodness, and is infinitely wise, holy, and unchangeable. It excludes boasting and promotes humility.

All true believers endure to the end. Those whom God has accepted in Christ, and sanctified by His Spirit, will never fall away from the state of grace, but shall persevere to the end. Believers may fall into sin through neglect and temptation, where by they grieve the Spirit, impair their graces and comforts, bring reproach on the cause of Christ, and temporal judgments on themselves, yet they shall be kept by the power of God through faith unto salvation.

VI. THE CHURCH

A New Testament church of the Lord Jesus Christ is a local body of baptized believers who are associated by covenant in the faith and fellowship of the gospel, observing the two ordinances of Christ, committed to His teachings, exercising the gifts, rights, and privileges invested in them by His Word, and seeking to extend the gospel to the ends of the earth.

The church is an autonomous body, operating through democratic processes under the Lordship of Jesus Christ. In such a congregation, members are equally responsible. Its Scriptural officers are pastors and deacons.

The New Testament speaks also of the church as the body of Christ which includes all the redeemed of all the ages.

VII. BAPTISM AND THE LORD'S SUPPER

Christian baptism is the immersion of a believer in water in the name of the Father, the Son, and the Holy Spirit. It is an act of obedience symbolizing the believer's faith in a crucified, buried, and risen Saviour, the believer's death to sin, the burial of the old life, and the resurrection to walk in newness of life in Christ Jesus. It is a testimony to his faith in the final resurrection of the dead. Being a church ordinance, it is prerequisite to the privileges of church membership and to the Lord's Supper.

The Lord's Supper is a symbolic act of obedience whereby members of the church, through partaking of the bread and the fruit of the vine, memorialize the death of the Redeemer and anticipate His second coming.

VIII. THE LORD'S DAY

The first day of the week is the Lord's Day. It is a Christian institution for regular observance. It commemorates the resurrection of Christ from the dead and should be employed in exercises of worship and spiritual devotion, both public and private, and by refraining from worldly amusements, and resting from secular employments, work of necessity and mercy only being excepted.

IX. THE KINGDOM

The kingdom of God includes both His general sovereignty over the universe and His particular kingship over men who willfully acknowledge Him as King. Particularly the kingdom is the realm of salvation into which men enter by trustful, childlike commitment to Jesus Christ. Christians ought to pray and to labor that the kingdom may come and God's will be done on earth. The full consummation of the kingdom awaits the return of Jesus Christ and the end of this age.

X. LAST THINGS

God, in His own time and in His own way, will bring the world to its appropriate end. Acording to His promise, Jesus Christ will return personally and visibly in glory to the earth; the dead will be raised; and Christ will judge all men in righteousness. The unrighteous will be consigned to hell, the place of everlasting punishment. The righteous in their resurrected and glorified bodies will receive their reward and will dwell forever in heaven with the Lord.

XI. EVANGELISM AND MISSIONS

It is the duty and privilege of every follower of Christ and of every church of the Lord Jesus Christ to endeavor to make disciples of all nations. The new birth of man's spirit by God's Holy Spirit means the birth of love for others. Missionary effort on the part of all rests thus upon a spiritual necessity of the regenerate life, and is expressly and repeatedly commanded in the teachings of Christ. It is the duty of every child of God to seek constantly to win the lost of God to Christ by personal effort and by all other methods in harmony with the gospel of Christ.

XII. EDUCATION

The cause of education in the kingdom of Christ is co-ordinate with the causes of missions and general benevolence and should receive along with these the liberal support of the churches. An adequate system of Christian schools is necessary to a complete spiritual program for Christ's people.

In Christian education there should be a proper balance between academic freedom and academic responsibility. Freedom in any orderly relationship of human life is always limited and never absolute. The freedom of a teacher in a Christian school, college, or seminary is limited by the preeminence of Jesus Christ, by the authoritative nature of the Scriptures, and by the distinct purpose for which the school exists.

XIII. STEWARDSHIP

God is the source of all blessings, temporal and spiritual; all that we have and are we owe to Him. Christians have a spiritual debtorship to the whole world, a holy trusteeship in the gospel, and a binding stewardship in their possessions. They are therefore under obligation to serve Him with their time, talents, and material possessions; and should recognize all these as entrusted to them to use for the glory of God and for helping others. According to the

Scriptures, Christians should contribute of their means cheerfully, regularly, systematically, proportionately, and liberally for the advancement of the Redeemer's cause on earth.

XIV. CO-OPERATION

Christ's people should, as occasion requires, organize such associations and conventions as may best secure co-operation for the great objects of the kingdom of God. Such organizations have no authority over one another or over the churches. They are voluntary and advisory bodies designed to elicit, combine, and direct the energies of our people in the most effective manner. Members of New Testament churches should co-operate with one another in carrying forward the missionary, educational, and benevolent ministries for the extension of Christ's kingdom. Christian unity in the New Testament sense is spiritual harmony and voluntary co-operation for common ends by various groups of Christ's people. Co-operation is desirable between the various Christian denominations, when the end to be attained is itself justified, and when such co-operation involves no violation of conscience or compromise of loyalty to Christ and his Word as revealed in the New Testament.

XV. THE CHRISTIAN AND THE SOCIAL ORDER

Every Christian is under obligation to make the will of Christ supreme in his own life and human society. Means and methods used for the improvement of society and the establishment of righteousness among men can be truly and permanently helpful only when they are rooted in the regeneration of the individual by the saving grace of God in Christ Jesus. The Christian should oppose in the spirit of Christ every form of greed, selfishness, and vice. He should work to provide for the orphaned, the needy, the aged, the helpless, and the sick. Every Christian should seek to bring industry, government, and society as a whole under the sway of the principles of righteousness, truth, and brotherly love. In order to promote these ends Christians should be ready to work with all men of good will in any good cause, always being careful to act in the spirit of love without compromising their loyalty to Christ and his truth.

XVI. PEACE AND WAR

It is the duty of Christians to seek peace with all men on principles of righteousness. In accordance with the spirit and teachings of Christ they should do all in their power to put an end to war.

The true remedy for the war spirit is the gospel of our Lord. The supreme need of the world is the acceptance of His teachings in all the affairs of man and nations, and the practical application of His law of love.

XVII. RELIGIOUS LIBERTY

God alone is Lord of the conscience, and He has left it free from the doctrines and commandments of men which are contrary to His Word or not contained in it. Church and state should be separate. The state owes to every church protection and full freedom in the pursuit of its spiritual ends. In providing for such freedom no ecclesiastical group or denomination should be favored by the state more than others. Civil government being ordained of God, it is the duty of Christians to render loyal obedience thereto in all things not contrary to the revealed will of God. The church should not resort to the civil power to carry on its work. The gospel of Christ contemplates spiritual means alone for the pursuit of its ends. The state has no right to impose penalties for religious opinions of any kind. The state has no right to impose taxes for the support of any form of religion. A free church in a free state is the Christian ideal, and this implies the right of free and unhindered access to God on the part of all men and the right to form and propagate opinions in the sphere of religion without interference by the civil power.

Notes: *In 1963 the Southern Baptist Convention adopted a revised form of the statement originally adopted in 1925. The lengthy item on science was dropped, and a more positive item on "The Christian and the Social Order" replaced the item "Social Service."*

* * *

STATEMENT OF FAITH (SOUTHWIDE BAPTIST FELLOWSHIP)

We believe in the verbal inspiration of the 66 books of the Bible in its original writings and that it is without error and is the sole authority in all matters of faith and practice.

We believe there is only one true God, existing in three Persons, Father, Son and Holy Spirit. These three are co-eternal and co-equal from all eternity, each with distinct personalities but of one essence.

We believe that Adam was created without sin but fell by disobedience and thus the whole race fell and is by nature spiritually dead and lost.

We believe that Jesus Christ is the Son of God, co-existent with the Father and the Holy Spirit, and that He came to the world, born of a virgin, shed His blood on Calvary as a vicarious substitute for all sin, that He was buried and rose again bodily and ascended to the right hand of the Father.

We believe in the Person work of the Holy Spirit which includes conviction of sin, regeneration of sinners, and indwelling believers.

We believe that a soul is saved when Christ is accepted as personal Saviour and Lord and the Holy Spirit imparts eternal life.

We believe that it is the plan of God for each believer to walk after the spirit and not fulfill the lusts of the flesh.

We believe in the eternal preservation and therefore the eternal perseverance of the saints.

We believe in the immersion of the believer in water to signify His death, burial, and resurrection and the believer's identification with Him.

We believe that a New Testament Church is a local group of baptized believers united for His purpose and the knowledge and spread of the Word including worldwide missions. We believe that it is completely self-determining and responsible only to Christ, the Head of the church. We believe it to be completely independent with no other

person, group, or body having any authority, right or intervention, or control in any form whatsoever over or within a local church. The Lord's Supper constitutes the other of the only two ordinances of the church.

We believe in the Premillennial Second Coming of the Lord, in the bodily resurrection of the righteous dead at His coming, and in an endless Heaven for all the redeemed and an endless punishment for the lost.

We believe the Revised Standard Version of the Bible is a perverted translation of the original languages, and that collaboration or participation with all forms of modernism, whether in the Nation Council of Churches or otherwise is wrong, and demands separation on our part.

Notes: *The Southwide Baptist Fellowship is among the most theologically conservative of Baptist bodies. It is premillennial in its eschatology and opposes the use of the Revised Standard Version of the Bible.*

* * *

Primitive Baptist

ABSTRACTS OF PRINCIPLES [*BANNER HERALD* (PROGRESSIVE)]

The editors of the Banner Herald subscribe to the following scriptural principles which have identified the cause of Bible truth in every generation, and pledge the purpose of this publication to be to the upholding and declaration of these Bible truths.

We believe in the only true and living God, and that there are three persons in the Godhead, Father, Son, and Holy Ghost, and that these agree in one, are co-equal, co-eternal, and co-existent.

We believe in the total depravity of the entire human family, and that man is unable to recover himself from his lost and ruined estate.

We believe Jesus Christ to be the Son of God, the only Saviour and Redeemer, and that salvation is by His grace and that alone.

We believe in particular, eternal and unconditional election, the effectual calling of the elect, and the final preservation of the saints.

We believe the scriptures of the Old and New Testaments to be the word of God, inspired and inerrant, and only rule of faith and practice.

We believe that Baptism and the Lord's Supper are ordinances of the Church of Jesus Christ, and that washing of the Saint's feet is an example to be kept, and that true believers, born of the Holy Spirit, are the only fit subjects of these ordinances. And that the only water baptism taught and recognized in the Bible is immersion or dipping.

We believe that no minister has the right to administer the ordinances of Baptism and the Lord's Supper but such as are regularly called by the God of Heaven and come under the imposition of hands by a presbytery.

**ABSTRACTS OF PRINCIPLES [*BANNER HERALD*
(PROGRESSIVE)]** (continued)

We believe in the resurrection of the just and the unjust, that the just shall be raised, changed and fashioned like unto the glorious body of the Son of God, and dwell in heaven forever, soul and body reunited, and that the unjust shall be raised and consigned to eternal punishment.

Notes: *Doctrinally, the Primitive Baptists represent the assertion of a Calvinist theological perspective against both the general (Arminian) or free-will theological position and the mild Calvinism of the early Philadelphia and New Hampshire Confessions. Primitive Baptists emerged in the 1830s as a distinctive set of Baptist associations who rejected the new missionary societies, which did not have their base in the local church.*

Progressive Primitive Baptists are those associations which, in recent decades, have been most open to innovation in organization activities (and in particular, cooperative endeavors). Their theology remains very close to that of the "regulars," those Primitive Baptists holding a more lax position on predestination. This theology is evident in the statement of the Banner Herald, *the most prominent Progressive periodical.*

* * *

ARTICLES OF FAITH (COVENANTED BAPTIST CHURCH OF CANADA)

We believe that there is but one only true God, and that there is none other than He.—John xvii. 3; Deuteronomy vi. 4.

We believe that this God is Almighty, Eternal, Invisible, Incomprehensible.—1 Timothy i. 17.

We believe that this God is unspeakably perfect in all His attributes of Power, Wisdom, Truth, Holiness, Justice, Mercy and Love.

We believe that in the Godhead there are three Persons, the Father, the Word and the Holy Ghost, and these three are one.—1 John i. 5, 7.

We believe there will be a resurrection of the dead, both of the Just and of the Unjust.—John v. 25, 29.

We believe that because God in His own nature is holy and just, even so He is good and merciful; therefore all having sinned, none can be saved without the means of a Redeemer.—Job xxxiii. 24; Hebrews ix. 15.

We believe that Jesus Christ Himself is Lord and Redeemer.—1 Peter i. 18, 19.

We believe the great reason why the Lord did clothe Himself with our flesh and blood was that He might be capable of obtaining the Redemption, which before the world was ordained for us.—Hebrews ii. 15, 16; ix. 15; Ephesians ii. 10.

We believe that the time when He clothed Himself with our flesh was in the days of the reign of Caesar Augustus. Then, and not till then, was the Word made flesh.—Luke ii. 1, 2.

We believe therefore that this very child, as afore is testified, is both God and man, the Christ of the living God.—Luke i. 26-34.

We believe therefore the righteousness and redemption by which we that believe stand just before God, as saved from the curse of the law, is the righteousness and redemption that consists in the permanent acts and performances of this child Jesus, this God-man, the Lord's Christ; it consists in fulfilling the law for us to the utmost requirements of the justice of God.—Matthew i. 21; Daniel ix. 24; 1 Corinthians i. 30.

We believe that for the completing of this work He was always sinless, did always the things that pleased God's justice; that every one of His acts, both of doing and suffering and rising again from the dead, was really and infinitely perfect, being done by Him as God-man; the Godhead, which gave virtue to all the acts of the human nature, was then in perfect union with it when He hanged upon the cross for the sins of His people.—Romans iii. 22; Hebrews x. 14.

We believe that the righteousness that saveth the sinner from the wrath to come is properly and personally Christ's, and ours but as we have union with Him, God by grace imputing it to us.—1 Corinthians i. 30; Philippians iii. 8. 9.

HOW CHRIST IS MADE OURS.

We believe that being sinful creatures in ourselves, no good thing done by us can procure of God the imputation of the righteousness of Jesus Christ, but that the imputation thereof is an act of grace, a free gift, without our deserving.—Romans iii. 24-27; 2 Timothy i. 9.

We believe also that the power of imputing righteousness resteth in God only by Jesus Christ.—Romans iv. 6-8.

PREDESTINATION AND ELECTION.

We believe that God has freely ordained all things that come to pass, which doctrine is called Absolute Predestination.—Isaiah xlvi. 9, 10; Acts iv. 27, 28; ii. 22, 23.

We believe that election is free and permanent, being founded in grace and the unchangeable will of God.—Romans ix. 11; xi, 5, 7; Ephesians i, 4, 5.

We believe that the decree of election is so far from making works in us foreseen the ground or cause of the choice, that it containeth in the bowels of it not only the persons, but also the graces that accompany salvation.—Ephesians ii. 5, 10; 2 Timothy i. 10.

We believe that Christ is He in whom the elect are always considered, and that without Him there is neither election, grace nor salvation.—Ephesians i. 5-10; Acts iv. 12.

We believe there is not any impediment attending the elect of God that can hinder their conversion of eternal salvation.—Romans viii. 30-33; xi. 7.

We believe no man can know his election but by his calling.—Romans ix. 21-23; 2 Peter i. 10.

OF THE SCRIPTURES.

We believe that the Holy Scriptures of themselves, without the addition of human inventions, are able to make the man of God perfect in all things, and thoroughly to furnish him unto all good works.—2 Timothy iii. 16, 17.

We believe that they cannot be broken, but will certainly be fulfilled in all the prophecies, threatenings, promises, either to the salvation or damnation of men.—Acts xiii. 41; Matthew v. 17; Psalm ix. 8.

We believe that God made the world and all things that are therein.—Genesis i. 31; ii. 2; Colossians i. 16.

OF PREACHING.

We do not believe that sinners dead in trespasses and sins should be urged to believe savingly in the Lord Jesus Christ; but we hold it right to preach to such their lost and ruined condition, and point out the only way of escape from the wrath of God, which is through the finished work of the Savior.

We do not therefore believe that the general call or use of general invitations and exhortations is preaching the gospel.

OF BAPTISM.

We believe that believers are the only fit subjects of baptism.—Mark xvi. 16; Acts ii. 41; viii. 37.

We believe that immersion is the only scriptural mode of administering the holy ordinance of baptism.—Matthew iii. 15, 16; Acts viii. 37-40.

We believe that baptism and the Lord's Supper are to be administered by lawfully ordained Elders only.—1 Corinthians xi. 23, 26; Titus i. 5; Acts xiv. 23.

We believe that baptized believers only are fit communicants.—Acts ii. 42, 43.

We believe that converts ought to relate their religious experience before the church only.—Psalm lxvi. 16; Matthew vii. 6.

We believe in close communion.—Song iv. 12; Acts vi. 14-16.

We believe that all matters of importance ought to be settled, conducted, transacted, only before the church.—1 Corinthians vi. 1-8; Acts vi. 6; xv. 6, 7, 12, 19, 22, 23.

We believe that the children of God ought not to frequent meetings, nor associate with any sect professing religion, who maintains error either in doctrine or principle.—2 John 10.

We believe that the first day of the week is proper to be observed as a day of worship, and that no work or worldly business ought to be transacted thereon.

We believe that brethren ought not to go to law with each other before the unbelievers.—1 Corinthians vi. 1-7.

Notes: *The Covenanted Baptist Church of Canada is a small absolute predestinarian Primitive Baptist church that fellowships with the various predestinarian Baptist associations in the United States. Soon after its formation, it adopted a lengthy statement of its belief. These articles of faith are important for their statements of beliefs commonly held among predestinarians but rarely stated, concerning preaching and personal witnessing to non-Christians.*

ARTICLES OF FAITH [FORKED DEER ASSOCIATION (REGULAR)]

1. We believe in one true and living God, the Father, Son and Holy Spirit, and that these three are one.

2. We believe that the Scriptures of the Old and New Testaments are the inspired word of God, and they furnish us all we ought to know, or practice religiously.

3. We believe in the doctrine of unconditional election, that is upon the sinner's part, but according to the foreknowledge and predestation of God.

4. We believe in the doctrine of original or inherited sin.

5. We believe that man is wholly unable to expedite himself from the fallen state he is in by reason of sin and transgression.

6. We believe poor sinners are justified by the imputed righteousness of Jesus Christ.

7. We believe in the final security or surety of all the heirs of promise.

8. We believe that baptism, and the Lord's Supper, and washing the saints' feet are ordinances of the church, given by Jesus Christ, its head and lawgiver, and that true believers are the only subjects for baptism: that immersion the only true mode of baptism.

9. We believe that regular ordained ministers of the gospel, having been baptized by the authority of the church, and having come under the hands of a presbytery, are the only ones authorized to administer the ordinances of baptism.

10. We believe Christ, while suffering on the cross, made a complete atonement for the elect only.

11. We believe in the resurrection of the dead bodies; and that the joys of the righteous will be eternal and the punishment of the wicked everlasting.

Notes: *Those Primitive Baptists holding the less strict position on predestination or "single-edged" predestination, are designated "Regulars." Each association has its own individual articles of faith, but those of the Forked Deer (Tennessee) Association are typical. Items 3 and 10 are the crucial and central statements representative of the association's theological stance.*

* * *

ARTICLES OF FAITH [KEHUKEE (NORTH CAROLINA) ASSOCIATION (PREDESTINARIAN)]

1. We believe in the being of God as almighty, eternal, unchangeable, of infinite wisdom, power, justice, holiness, goodness, mercy, and truth; and that this God has revealed Himself in His word under the characteristics of Father, Son and Holy Ghost.

2. We believe that Almighty God has made known His mind and will to the children of men in His word which word we believe to be of divine authority, and contains all things necessary to be known for the salvation of men and women. The same is compre-

hended or contained in the Books of the Old and New Testaments as are commonly received.

3. We believe that God, before the foundation of the world, for a purpose of His own glory, did elect a certain number of men and angels to eternal life and that His election is particular, eternal and unconditional on the creature's part.

4. We believe that, when God made man first, he was perfect, holy and upright, able to keep the law, but liable to fall and that he stood as a federal head, or representative, of all his natural offspring or exposed to the misery which sprang from his disobedience.

5. We believe that Adam fell from his state of moral rectitude, and that he involved himself and all his natural offspring in a state of death; and, for that original transgression, we are both guilty and filthy in the sight of our holy God.

6. We believe that it is utterly out of the power of men, as fallen creatures, to keep the law of God perfectly, repent of their sins truly, or believe in Jesus Christ, except they be drawn by the Holy Ghost.

7. We believe that in God's appointed time and way (by means which He has ordained) the elect shall be called, justified, pardoned and sanctified, and that it is impossible they can utterly refuse the call, but shall be made willing by divine grace to receive the offers of mercy.

8. We believe that justification in the sight of God is only by the imputed righteousness of Jesus Christ, received and applied by faith alone.

9. We believe, in like manner, that God's elect shall not only be called, and justified, but that they shall be converted, born again, and changed by the effectual workings of God's holy spirit.

10. We believe that such as are converted, justified and called by His grace, shall persevere in holiness, and never fall finally away.

11. We believe it to be duty incumbent on all God's people to walk religiously in good works; not in the Old Covenant way of seeking life and favor of the Lord by it, but only as a duty from a principle of love.

12. We believe baptism and the Lord's Supper are gospel ordinances, both belonging to the converted or true believers: and that persons who are sprinkled or dipped while in unbelief were not regularly baptised according to God's word, and that such ought to be baptised after they are savingly converted into the faith of Christ.

13. We believe that every church is independent in matters of discipline; and that Associations, Councils and Conferences of several ministers, or churches, are not to impose on the churches the keeping, holding or maintaining of any principle or practice.

14. We believe in the resurrection of the dead, both of the just and unjust and a general judgment.

15. We believe the punishment of the wicked is everlasting and the joys of the righteous are eternal.

16. We believe that no minister has a right to administration of the ordinances, only such as are regularly called and come under the imposition of hands by the presbytery.

17. Lastly, we believe that, for the mutual comfort, union and satisfaction of the several churches of the aforesaid faith and order, we ought to meet in an Association way, wherein each church ought to represent their case by their delegates and attend as often as is necessary to advise with the several churches in conference and that the decision of matters in such associations are not to be imposed, or in any wise binding, on the churches, without their consent, but only to sit and act as an advisory council.

Notes: *Many Primitive Baptists look to the Kehukee as the first of the Baptist associations to formally adopt the Old School, or Primitive, position in the face of rising support for missionary societies. The association legislated against such support in 1927. However, its position on missionary societies was not addressed in its doctrinal statement. The association would later become identified with the absolute predestinarian stance about which Primitive Baptist disagree among themselves. As with missionary societies, the association's opinion on predestination was not added to its statement of faith.*

*   *   *

ARTICLES OF FAITH [KETOCTON (NORTH CAROLINA) ASSOCIATION (REGULARS)]

1. We believe there is one living and true God; that He is self-existent and independent, in whom all power, wisdom, holiness, justice, godliness and truth center; who is omniscient and omnipotent—the almighty Creator of all things that do exist, visible and invisible, who upholds and governs all things by His providential hand, according to the council of His own will.

2. That in the divine essence there are (according to the scripture) three persons or subsistences, distinguished by the relative names of Father, Son, and Holy Ghost; and that each subsistence possesses proper Deity; that the work of creation is ascribed to them; divine worhip is addressed to each of them; each one of them is called by divine names and in the name of Three in One, the New Testament ordinances are to be administered.

3. That the Holy Scriptures of the Old and New Testaments are the word of God; that they were given by divine inspiration, and that this system of revelation comprehends everything necessary for us to know concerning God, and the direction of our obedience to Him. By this divine book, God hath made revelation of His gracious design in saving poor sinners, and pointing out the way through the mediation of the Lord Jesus; that the instrumentality

of this sacred word, stubborn and obstinate sinners are brought into the ordinances of faith, and the incorrigible left without excuse; and that by this word of the Lord all men shall be judged in the last day.

4. That man was created upright, free from sin, and possessed with holiness of nature; that he fell from that innocent state in which he was created, by transgressing God's command, by which he became morally dead, and subjected himself to bodily and eternal death, and as a public head involved his unborn progeny in like ruin, for all descending from him by ordinary generation are born in a state of pollution, and under the dominion of sin, and guilty before God.

5. That in eternity, God, out of His own good pleasure, chose a certain number of Adams's progeny to eternal life, and that He did not leave the accomplishment of His decrees to accident or chance; but decreed all the means to bring about the event; therefore they are chosen to salvation, through sanctification of the Spirit unto obedience and sprinkling of the blood of Jesus Christ. Their calling was decreed to the purpose of election. It is said, when called, they are called according to His purpose and grace given us in Christ Jesus before the world began; and all in order to manifest the glory of His grace.

6. That the covenant of redemption was between the Father and the Son, that the elect were given by the Father to the Son, to be by Him redeemed and finally saved; and that the Son, as Head and representative of His people, engaged to perform everything necessary or requisite to carry their complete salvation into effect. It is called in scripture, a well ordered covenant in all things, and sure.

7. That in the fulness of time, the Son of God was manifested, by taking human nature into union with His divine person, in which capacity He wrought out a righteousness for the justification of His people, yielding a perfect and spotless obedience to all the requirements of the divine law, and submitted Himself to the shameful and ignominious death on the cross, as an atonement for their sins, and reconciliation of their souls to God.

8. That those that are redeemed by Christ, are in due time called to a saving knowledge of the Lord Jesus—embracing Him as the only way to God and Savior of poor sinners. This effectual calling is accomplished by the agency of the Holy Ghost operating in a free, irresistible and unfrustrable manner, by which the understanding is enlightened and the will subjected to Christ. Hence the scriptures testify that they are made willing in the day of His power. This eternal change or new birth in the souls is wholly ascribed to the power of God; for it is said of the regenerate, they are begotten of God, quickened of God, born of God—all expressive that it is the Lord's work, and He is entitled to the praise.

9. All that are effectually called by efficacious grace, are fully justified of God. This perfect obedience, or in other words, the righteousness of Christ being imputed to them, their sins are pardoned, and their persons accepted in God's beloved Son. Such are taken under the care of the great Shepherd of souls, and rest on the infallible promises and power of God, which has engaged to protect them under all their trials; to succor them when tempted; to supply all their wants, and withhold no good thing from them; to continue the good work of grace begun in them, and crown the end of their faith in the complete salvation of their souls.

10. That being bought with the precious blood of Christ, and called by rich grace, it becomes a bounden duty to walk in all the commandments and ordinances of the Lord; although justified by grace, to which our works can add nothing, yet by good works the declarative glory of God is manifested, and the genuineness of faith proved, which while others behold, they may be led to glorify God who is in heaven.

11. And lastly, that God will judge men and angels in the last day, by Jesus Christ. That when Christ appears in the clouds of heaven with the sound of the trumpet, the dead saints shall be raised incorruptible and reunited to their soul; then shall they, together with the living saints, be caught up to meet the Lord in the air; and so shall they be forever with the Lord. The wicked will be raised likewise in that sinful state in which they died; and never having been regenerated and qualified by grace for the kingdom of heaven, will be sentenced to unspeakable torments, for ever and ever, form which there will be no recovery, to endless duration.

These Articles, or Principles of Faith, were supported and defended by such ministers as Elders Jeremiah Moore, James Ireland, William and Daniel Fristoe, David Thomas, John Alderson; and more recently by Elders John Clark, W. S. Athey, Dr. C. Waters, T. N. Alderton, T. S. Dalton, Thomas W. Alderton, J. E. L. Alderton, and many others.

Notes: *The Ketocton Association was formed in 1766, making it one of the oldest Baptist associations in the United States. Its articles of faith were adopted at its organizational session and formally reaffirmed in 1927 in the midst of the missionary society controversy.*

* * *

ARTICLES OF FAITH (NATIONAL PRIMITIVE BAPTIST CONVENTION)

ARTICLE I—WE BELIEVE in only one true and living God and the trinity of persons in the God-head, Father, Son, and Holy Ghost, and yet there are not three, but one God. Reference: Deuteronomy 6:4, Matthew 3:16, 17; 28:19; John 1:1, 14, 16; II Corinthians 13:14; I Peter 1:2; I John 5:7.

ARTICLE II—WE BELIEVE the Scriptures of the Old and New Testaments are the Word of God, and the only rule of faith and practice. Reference: Isaiah 8:20; II Peter 1:21; II Timothy 3:16-17; Romans 1:19-21.

ARTICLE III—WE BELIEVE in the doctrine of eternal and particular election of a definite number of the human race and chosen in Christ before the foundation of the world, that they should be holy and without blame before Him in love. Reference: John 6:7; 13:18-19; Acts 13:48; Romans 11:5; I Thessalonians 5:9; II Timothy 1:9; I Corinthians 7:9; Ephesians 1:1-4; Revelations 20:15.

ARTICLE IV—WE BELIEVE in a covenant redemption between God the Father, and God the Son. Reference: Genesis 3:15; Psalms 51:5; Romans 5:12; I Corinthians 15:22.

ARTICLE V—WE BELIEVE in the fall of man and the communication of Adam's sinful nature to his posterity by ordinary generation and their impotency to recover themselves from the fallen state they are in by nature by their own free will and ability. Reference: Jeremiah 13:23; John 6:44; Ephesians 2:8; Romans 3:23; I Thessalonians 1:10.

ARTICLE VI—WE BELIEVE that all chosen in Christ shall hear the voice of the Son of God, and be effectually called, regenerated and born again. Reference: Psalms 37:28; John 10:28; Acts 2:39; Colossians 3:3; Jude 1; II Timothy 1:8, 9; Romans 8:29, 30.

ARTICLE VII—WE BELIEVE that those born again are justified in the sight of God alone by the righteousness of Jesus Christ imputed to them by faith. Reference: Jeremiah 33:6; II Corinthians 5:21.

ARTICLE VIII—WE BELIEVE that faith is the gift of God, and good works the fruit of faith, and justify us in the sight of men and angels as evidences of our gracious state. Reference: Acts 13:37; Romans 3:20-24; 5:1; 8:1; James 2:18, 19, 22; Hebrews 13:20, 21; I John 2:3, 5.

ARTICLE IX—WE BELIEVE that all the Saints of God justified by the righteousness of Christ shall preserve in grace, and none of them finally fall away so as to be lost. Reference: Deuteronomy 32:6; Psalms 12:5; John 10:27-29; Romans 3:24-25; I Peter 1:5; Phil. 1:6 II Timothy 2:19; I John 2:19.

ARTICLE X—WE BELIEVE in the general judgment, both of the just and the unjust, and that joys of the righteous shall be eternal and the punishment of the wicked shall be everlasting. Reference: Ecclesiastes 12:14; Psalms 16:9; Isaiah 26:19; John 5:28 and Revelations 20:12.

ARTICLE XI—WE BELIEVE that the visible Church of Christ is a congregation of Baptized Believers in Christ adhering to a special covenant, which recognizes Christ as their only lawgiver and ruler, and His word their exclusive guide in all religious matters. It is complete in itself and independent under Christ of every other church organization. It is alone a religious assembly, selected and called out of the world by the doctrine of the Gospel to worship the true God according to His Word. Reference: Acts 2:41, 42; I Corinthians 1:13; Ephesians 4:7; 5:23, 27, 32; Colossians 1:18; Revelations 2:7.

ARTICLE XII—WE BELIEVE that the Scriptural officers of the church are: Pastor and Deacon, whose, qualifications and duties are defined in the Epistles of 1st Timothy 3rd chapter and Titus 1st chapter. Reference: Phil. 1:1; Acts 20:17, 21; Hebrews 13:17.

ARTICLE XIII—WE BELIEVE that Baptism is the immersion of a believer in water by a proper administrator in the name of the Father, Son, and Holy Ghost. Reference: Matthew 28:19; Mark 16:12-16; Acts 8:36; Acts 8:36, 39; Romans 6:3, 4; Colossians 2:12.

ARTICLE XIV—WE BELIEVE that no Minister has a right to administer the ordinances of the gospel only such as have been regularly baptized, called and come under the imposition of a Presbytery by the majority of the Church of Christ. Reference: Matthew 28:18; Ephesians 4:11-14; Acts 9:15; 13:1, 2; Titus; Acts 14:23.

ARTICLE XV—WE BELIEVE that none but regularly baptized and orderly Church Members have a right to communion at the Lord's Table. Reference: Matthew 26; Mark 14; Luke 22; I Corinthians 14:24, 25, 26.

ARTICLE XVI—WE BELIEVE in washing the Saints' Feet in a Church capacity immediately after the Lord's Supper. Reference: John 13.

THE NAMES OF THE CANONICAL BOOKS OF THE BIBLE

Genesis, Exodus, Leviticus, Numbers, Deuteronomy, Joshua, Judges, Ruth, The 1st Book of Samuel, 2nd Book of Samuel, The 1st Book of Kings, 2nd Book of Kings, The 1st Book of Chronicles, 2nd Book of Chronicles, The Book of Ezra, The Book of Nehemiah, The Book of Esther, The Book of Job, The Psalms, The Proverbs, Ecclesiastes or the Preacher, Canticle or Songs of Solomon, Four Prophets the Greater, Twelve Prophets the Lesser. All the books of the New Testament, as they are commonly received, we do receive and account canonical.

Notes: *Some Primitive Baptist associations composed predominantly of black members have organized into a national convention, which has in turn adopted a statement of faith for the participating associations. The statement reflects the Regular (less strict) position on predestination.*

* * *

ARTICLES OF FAITH [SUCARNOCHEE RIVER (MISSISSIPPI) ASSOCIATION (BLACK)]

1. We believe in one true and living God the Father, the Word and the Holy Ghost—St. John 1:1; 1 Tim. 2:5.

2. We believe that the scriptures of the Old and New Testaments are the word of God, and the only rule of faith and practice—2 Tim. 8:16; St. John 5:39.

3. We believe in the doctrine of election by grace and that God chose His people in Christ before the foundation of the world—Eph. 1:4; 2 Thess. 2:13.

4. We believe in the doctrine of originalism—Psa. 58:3, 1 Jn. 5:16.

5. We believe in man's impotency to recover himself from the fallen state he is in by nature, by his own will and ability—Eph. 2:1-5; Prov. 20:9; Eccl. 8:8.

6. We believe that sinners are justified in the sight of God only by imputed righteousness of Christ—Rom. 3:4; 5:16.

7. We believe that the saints shall persevere in grace and never fall finally away—1 Pet. 1:5; Psa. 7:10.

8. We believe that baptism and the Lord's Supper and the washing of the saint's feet are ordinances of Jesus Christ and that true believers are the only subjects and the only mode of baptism is by burial in water—Matt. 3:13-17; St. John 13:14, 15.

9. We believe in the resurrection of the dead and that the joys of the righteous and the punishment of the wicked will be eternal—I Cor. 15:12-23: Matt. 25:46.

10. We believe that no minister has the right to administer the ordinances of the gospel only such as are baptised, called and come under the imposition of hands by a presbytery.—Rom. 10:15; 1 Tim. 3:17.

11. We believe that none but regularly baptised members have a right to commune at the Lord's table—2 Epistle of Jn. 1:10; Acts 19:1-5.

Notes: *Those Primitive Baptists in predominantly black associations who did not affiliate with the national convention continued a more loosely affiliated fellowship. There are no significant doctrinal differences between the two groups.*

* * *

ARTICLES OF FAITH AND EXPOSITION OF THE DOCTRINE [UPPER COUNTRY LINE (NORTH CAROLINA) ASSOCIATION (PREDESTINARIAN)]

ARTICLES OF FAITH

We, the messengers of the several churches composing the Upper Country Line Association, agree, for the satisfaction of our brethren and friends, to publish an abstract of principles upon which we unite and will endeavor with the help of the Lord to maintain.

1. We believe in the being of God, as Almighty, eternal, unchangeable, of infinite wisdom, power, justice, holiness, goodness, mercy and truth, and that this God has revealed Himself in His word under the character of Father, Son and Holy Ghost.

2. We believe Almighty God has made known His mind and will to the children of men in His word, which word we believe to be divine authority, and contains all things necessary to be known for the salvation of men. The same is comprehended or contained in the books of the Old and New Testaments.

3. We believe that God before the foundation of the world, for a purpose of His own glory, did elect a certain number of men and angels to eternal life, and that this election is particular, eternal and unconditional on the creature's part.

4. We believe that when God made man he was good and upright, but by his own transgression he fell from that good and upright state, and being the head representative of the whole human race, they being his natural offspring, he involved all of them in the same ruined state with himself, and they were partakers of, the exposed to the miseries which sprang from his disobedience.

5. We believe that it is utterly out of the power of man as a fallen creature to keep the law of God perfectly, or to truly repent of his sins, or believe in Christ, except, he be drawn by the Holy Spirit.

6. We believe in God's own appointed time and way the elect will be called, justified, pardoned, and sanctified, and that it is impossible that they can utterly refuse the call; but shall be willing by divine grace to receive mercy.

7. We believe that justification to the sight of God is only by the imputed righteousness of Jesus Christ received and applied by faith.

8. We believe that God's elect will be converted and born again by the effectual work of the Holy Spirit.

9. We believe that those who are called by grace and born again shall persevere in holiness and never fall finally away.

10. We believe it to be a duty incumbent on all God's people to walk religiously in all good works, not in the old covenant way of seeking life and favor of the Lord by it, but only as a duty from a principle of love.

11. We believe baptism by immersion and the Lord's Supper are gospel ordinances, both belonging to the converted or true believer.

12. We believe that every church is independent in matters of discipline, and that Associations, councils and conferences of ministers or churches, are not to impose on the church the keeping, holding or maintaining of any principle or practice contrary to the church's judgment.

13. We believe in the general resurrection of the dead, both of the just and the unjust, and final judgment.

14. We believe the punishment of the wicked is everlasting and the joys of the righteous eternal.

15. We believe that no minister has a right to administer the ordinances unless called and comes under the imposition of hands by the Presbytery.

EXPOSITION OF THE DOCTRINE

An exposition of the doctrine relating to God's Decree, His Purpose, Predestination, Providence, Good Works, and Obedience, as approved by a majority of our churches in the Upper Country Line Association in their conferences in 1932, and now authorized, forms or constitutes a part of the Articles of Faith of this Association, as follows, to-wit:

Our position and contention on certain controverted questions of doctrine disturbing our people at this time is as follows: London Confession, Chapter III, of God's Decree, Section 1: God hath (Isa. 46:10; Eph. 1:11; Heb.

ARTICLES OF FAITH AND EXPOSITION OF THE
DOCTRINE [UPPER COUNTRY LINE (NORTH
CAROLINA) ASSOCIATION
(PREDESTINARIAN)] (continued)

6:17; Rom. 9:15, 18) decreed in Himself from all eternity,
by the most wise and holy counsel of His will freely and
unchangeably all things whatsoever come to pass; yet so as
thereby is God neither the author of sin (Jas. 1:15; 1 Jn.
1:5), nor hath fellowship with any therein; nor is violence
offered to the will of the creature, nor is the liberty or
contingency of second causes taken away, but rather (Acts
4:27, 28; Jn. 19:11) established, in which appears His
wisdom in disposing all things and power and faithfulness
(Num. 23:19; Eph. 1:3-5) in accomplishing His decree; Sec.
2: Although God knoweth whatsoever may or can come to
pass upon all (Acts 15:18) supposed conditions, yet hath
He not decreed anything (Rom. 9:11, 13, 16, 18) because
He foresaw it as future, or as that which would come to
pass upon such conditions;" Chapter V: Divine Providence, Sec. 1: God, the Creator of all things, in His infinite
power and wisdom, doth (Heb. 1:3; Job 38:11; Isa. 46:10,
11; Psa. 13:5, 6) uphold, direct, dispose and govern all
creatures and things, from the greatest event to the (Matt.
10:26, 30, 31) least, by His most holy providence, to the
end for which they were created, according unto His
infallible foreknowledge and the free and immutable
counsel of His (Eph. 1:11) own will; to the praise of the
glory of His wisdom, power, justice, infinite goodness and
mercy; 2nd. Although in relation to the foreknowledge and
decree of God, the first cause, all things come to pass (Acts
2:28) immutably, and infallibly, so that there is not
anything befalls any (Prov. 16:23) by chance or without
His providence; yet by the same providence He ordereth
them to fall out according to the nature of second causes,
either (Gen. 8:22) necessarily, freely or contingently;
thirdly, God in His ordinary providence (Acts 27:31, 44;
Isa. 55:10, 11) maketh use of means; yet is free (Hosea 1:7)
to work without (Rom. 4:19, 21), above the (Dan. 3:27)
against them at His pleasure; fourthly, The Almighty
power, unsearchable wisdom and infinite goodness of God
so far manifest themselves in His providence, that His
determinate counsel (Rom. 11:32-34; 2 Sam. 24:1; 1
Chron. 2:11) extendeth itself even to the first fall, and all
other sinful actions both of angels and men (and that not
by a bare permission); which also He most wisely and
powerfully (2 Kings 19:28; Psa. 76:10) boundeth, and
otherwise ordereth and governeth, in a manifold dispensation to His most holy (Gen. 1:20; Isa. 10:6, 7:12) ends; yet
so as the sinfulness of their acts proceedeth only from the
creatures, and not from God, who being most holy and
righteous, neither is, nor can be the author or (Psa. 11:21;
Jn. 2:16) approver of sin . . . Of Good Works, Chapter
16, Sec. 1: Good works are only such as God hath (Micah
6:8; Heb. 13:21) commanded in His holy word, and not
such as without the warrant thereof are devised by man,
out of blind zeal (Matt. 15:9; Isa. 19:13), or upon any
pretense of good intentions.

N. B. We believe that God has wrought all the works of
His children in them (Isa. 26:12), and they as His
workmanship, are created in Christ Jesus unto good
works, which God hath before ordained that they should
walk in them (Eph. 2:10), and that their ability to do good
works is not of themselves, but wholly of the Spirit, and
according as God works in them both to will and to do of
His own good pleasure (Phil 2:13), and that as the
branches are in the vine, so are His children in Him, and
have their fruits unto holiness and the end everlasting life
(Rom. 6:22); and that it is of God that His children are in
Christ, who, of God are made unto them, wisdom,
righteousness, sanctification and redemption, and hence
God not only puts them in this Way, which is Christ, but
they are kept by the power of God through faith unto
salvation ready to be revealed in the last time (1 Pet. 1:5),
and that the preservation of the saints depends not upon
their own free will, but upon the immutability of the
decree of (Rom. 8:30; 9:11, 16) election, flowing from the
free and unchangeable love of God the Father, upon the
efficacy of the merit and intercession of Jesus Christ (Rom.
5:9, 19; Jn. 14:19) and union with Him, the (Heb. 6:17, 18)
oath of God, the abiding of His spirit and the (1 Jn. 3:9)
seed of God within them and the nature of the (Jer. 22:40)
covenant of grace, from all which ariseth also the certainty
and infallibility thereof;" and in our conclusion, join with
Elder Hassell in saying that "While the sinner has
destroyed himself, all his salvation, from first to last, is of
the pure, unmerited, almighty grace of God." (Hassell's
History, page 942).

Now upon the subject of obedience, our faith lays hold on
Christ Jesus, the Savior of sinners—the Obedient One, for
strength and every necessary help in time of need,
confessing that of myself I can do nothing, but all things
through Christ that strengtheth me. When God works the
will, He also works the strength, and, obedience always
follows. David said unto the Lord, When thou saidst, Seek
ye My face, my heart said unto thee, Thy face, Lord will I
seek (Psa. 27:8), and again, Paul declares, having received
grace and apostleship, for obedience to the faith among all
nations (Rom. 1:5) his obedience, saying, "So as much as
in me is, I am ready to preach the gospel to you that are at
Rome also (Rom. 1:15), and we believe as God has said,
My word shall not return unto me void, but it shall
accomplish that which I please, and it shall prosper in the
thing whereunto I send it (Isa. 55:11); and when Jesus was
exceeding sorrowful, even unto death, we hear His words,
O My Father, if it be possible, let this cup pass from me:
nevertheless, not as I will, but as thou wilt (Matt. 26:39);
hence, concerning His people (the children of obedience)
He says, Thy people shall be willing in the day of thy
power (Psa. 110:3), and all the promises of God in Him are
yea, and in Him Amen, unto the glory of God by us (2
Cor. 1:26). All obedience is based on love—God's love
toward us, which causes our love toward Him, and with
His mind in us, His will and pleasure becomes our will and
pleasure—acquiescence—obedience.

Submitted by Elder J. W. Gilliam

N. B.—The above expression of the doctrine was adopted
by the churches of our Association in 1982, and ordered
inserted as part of our Articles of Faith.

Notes: *Predestinarian Primitive Baptists are generally
differentiated from the Regulars by their acceptance of what
is termed "double-edged," or absolute, predestination.*

Associations' positions on predestination are rarely spelled out in their statements of faith, most having been composed before the issue between Absolute Predestinarians and the Regulars arose. The Upper Country Line Association, however, has adopted an additional statement to its Articles of Religion which spelled out the predestinarian position in some detail.

* * *

General Baptist

AN AFFIRMATION OF OUR FAITH (BAPTIST GENERAL CONFERENCE)

1. THE WORD OF GOD

We believe that the Bible is the Word of God, fully inspired and without error in the original manuscript, written under the inspiration of the Holy Spirit, and that it has supreme authority in all matters of faith and conduct.

2. THE TRINITY

We believe that there is one living and true God, eternally existing in three persons; that these are equal in every divine perfection, and that they execute distinct, but harmonious offices in the work of creation, providence and redemption.

3. GOD THE FATHER

We believe in God, the Father, an infinite, personal spirit, perfect in holiness, wisdom, power and love. We believe that He concerns Himself mercifully in the affairs of men, that He hears and answers prayer, and that He saves from sin and death all who come to Him through Jesus Christ.

4. JESUS CHRIST

We believe in Jesus Christ, God's only begotten Son, conceived by the Holy Spirit. We believe in His virgin birth, sinless life, miracles and teachings. We believe in His substitutionary atoning death, bodily resurrection, ascension into heaven, perpetual intercession for His people, and personal visible return to earth.

5. THE HOLY SPIRIT

We believe in the Holy Spirit who came forth from the Father and Son to convict the world of sin, righteousness, and judgment, and to regenerate, sanctify, and empower all who believe in Jesus Christ. We believe that the Holy Spirit indwells every believer in Christ, and that He is an abiding helper, teacher and guide.

6. REGENERATION

We believe that all men are sinners by nature and by choice and are, therefore, under condemnation. We believe that those who repent of their sins and trust in Jesus Christ as Savior are regenerated by the Holy Spirit.

7. THE CHURCH

We believe in the universal church, a living spiritual body of which Christ is the head and all regenerated persons are members. We believe in the local church, consisting of a company of believers in Jesus Christ, baptized on a credible profession of faith, and associated for worship, work and fellowship. We believe that God has laid upon the members of the local church the primary task of giving the Gospel of Jesus Christ to a lost world.

8. CHRISTIAN CONDUCT

We believe that a Christian should live for the glory of God and the well being of his fellowmen; that his conduct should be blameless before the world; that he should be a faithful steward of his possessions; and that he should seek to realize for himself and others the full statute of maturity in Christ.

9. THE ORDINANCES

We believe that the Lord Jesus Christ has committed two ordinances to the local church, baptism and the Lord's Supper. We believe that Christian baptism is the immersion of a believer in water into the name of the triune God. We believe that the Lord's Supper was instituted by Christ for commemoration of His death. We believe that these two ordinances should be observed and administered until the return of the Lord Jesus Christ.

10. RELIGIOUS LIBERTY

We believe that every human being has direct relations with God, and is responsible to God alone in all matters of faith; that each church is independent and must be free from interference by an ecclesiastical or political authority; that therefore Church and State must be kept separate as having different functions, each fulfilling its duties free from dictation or patronage of the other.

11. CHURCH COOPERATION

We believe that local churches can best promote the cause of Jesus Christ by cooperating with one another in a denominational organization. Such an organization, whether a regional or district conference, exists and functions by the will of the churches. Cooperation in a conference is voluntary and may be terminated at any time. Churches may likewise cooperate with inter-denominational fellowships on a voluntary independent basis.

12. THE LAST THINGS

We believe in the personal and visible return of the Lord Jesus Christ to earth and the establishment of His kingdom. We believe in the resurrection of the body, the final judgment, the eternal felicity of the righteous, and the endless suffering of the wicked.

Notes: *The General Baptists differ from the Calvinist Baptists in their adoption of an Arminian theological position, which emphasizes God's free grace and humanity's free will (as opposed to predestination). The differences represented by the general Baptist perspective are but another example of the controversy which led to the production of the Canons of Dort in response to Arminianism. Among items about which General (free-will) Baptists disagree is the inclusion of foot washing as a third ordinance.*

The affirmation reflects the larger concerns of conservative evangelical controversy concerning scriptural authority. There is no mention of foot washing. The statement on "Church Cooperation" is rare among Baptists, but not incompatible with the usual statements on the authority of the local church.

STATEMENT OF FAITH (GENERAL ASSOCIATION OF GENERAL BAPTISTS)

I. GOD

We believe that there is only one true, living, and eternal God and that the Godhead is revealed as Father, Son, and Holy Spirit.

A. One true and eternal God: Deut. 6:4; 33:27; Jer. 10:10; Matt. 3:15-16; 28:19; Mk. 12:29; Jn. 14:9-11; 10:30; Rom. 8:9-11; I Cor. 8:4-6; II Cor. 3:17; I Thess. 1:9; I Timothy 1:17; 2:5; 6:17; Hebrews 1:1-13; 3:12

B. The Godhead:

1. God as Father: Gen. 1:1; Matt. 6:9; Eph. 4:6

2. God as Son: Isa. 9:6; Matt. 16:16; Jn. 1:1; 3:14, 16; 14:28; I Cor. 15:28; Heb. 1:8

    Virgin Birth of Jesus: Matt. 1:18-25; Luke 1:26-38

3. God as Holy Spirit: Jn. 14:16, 26; Acts 1:5, 8; 2:1-4; Rom. 8:16

II. THE BIBLE

We believe that the Holy Scriptures are the Old and New Testaments; the inspired and infallible Word of God and therein is found the only reliable guide of Christian faith and conduct.

A. The Inspired Revelation: Lk. 24:44-46; Rom. 16: 25-26; II Tim. 3:15-17; Heb. 1:1-2; II Pet. 1:20-21

B. The Infallible Word: Isa. 40:8; Lk. 21:33; Jn. 17: 17; Titus 1:2; I Pet. 1:25

C. The Reliable Guide: Deut. 6:6-9; Ps. 19:7-10; 119:105, 140; Jn. 5:39; Acts 17:11-12; Rom. 10:14-15; 15:4; II Tim. 3:16-17

III. MAN

We believe that God created man in his own image to bring Him honor through obedience, and that when man disobeyed, he became a fallen and sinful creature, unable to save himself. We believe that infants are in the covenant of God's grace and that all all persons become accountable to God when they reach a state of moral responsibility.

A. Man's Origin: Gen. 1:26-27; 2:7; Ps. 8:5

B. Man's Purpose: Gen. 1:28-31; 2:15-25; Isa. 43:7

C. Man's Sin: Gen. 3:1-24; Ps. 51:5; Jer. 13:23; Rom. 1:18—3:23; 5:12-21; 7:1-25

D. Man's Accountability: Matt. 19:13-15; Rom. 4:15; 5:13; 6:16; Heb. 11:24-26.

IV. SALVATION

We believe that Salvation (regeneration, sanctification, justification and redemption) has been provided for all mankind through the redemptive work (life, death, resurrection, ascension, and intercession) of Jesus Christ, and that this Salvation can be received only through repentance toward God and faith toward our Lord Jesus Christ.

Salvation: Heb. 5:9; I Thess. 5:9; I Pet. 1:9; Heb. 7:25

Regeneration: Jn. 3:3-8; 1:11-13; I Pet. 1:23; Eph. 2:1-10; II Cor. 5:17; II Pet. 1:4; Titus 3:5

Sanctification: I Cor. 1:30; Eph. 5:26; Heb. 10:9-10, 29; II Tim. 2:21; Heb. 13:12; Rom. 12:1-2; I Pet. 1:2

Justification: Rom. 3:20-24; 5:1-2, 18; 8:30-33; Acts 13:38-39; I Cor 6:11; II Cor. 5:21

Redemption: Matt. 20:28; Isa. 53:6; Col. 1:14; Titus 2:14; I Pet. 1:18-19; Rev. 5:9

Christ's Redemptive Work: Jn. 3:16; Rom. 5:8; Heb. 2:9; Rev. 22:17; II Pet. 3:9; Jn. 14:6; Acts 4:12; Rom. 6:23; Eph. 2:8-9

Life and Death: Rom. 5:10; Heb. 9:12-15; Jn. 10:11; Jn. 3:16

Resurrection: Rom. 4:25; I Pet. 1:3; I Cor. 15:14, 17

Ascension: Heb. 4:14-16, 19-20; 9:24; 10:11-12

Intercession: Rom. 8:34; Heb. 9:15; Isa. 53:12; I Tim. 2:5

Repentance: Isa. 55:6-7; Luke 24:47; Luke 13:3-5; Acts 2:38; I Thess. 1:9-10

Faith: Jn 3:16-18; Heb. 11:1, 6; I Pet. 1:5

V. ASSURANCE AND ENDURANCE

We believe that those who abide in Christ have the assurance of salvation. However, we believe that the Christian retains his freedom of choice; therefore, it is possible for him to turn away from God and be finally lost.

A. Assurance: Matt. 28:20; I Cor. 10:13; Heb. 5:9

B. Endurance: Matt. 10:22; Lk. 9:62; Col. 1:23; Rev. 2:10-11; 3:3-5

C. Warnings: Jn. 15:6; Rom. 11:20-23; Gal. 5:4; Heb. 3:12; 10:26-29; II Pet. 2:20-21

D. Finally lost: Jn. 15:6; I Cor. 9:27; Heb. 6:4-6

VI. CHRISTIAN DUTIES

We believe that Christians should live faithfully by serving in and through the local church, praying diligently, witnessing earnestly, practicing tolerance, showing loving kindness, giving as God prospers, and conducting themselves in such a way as to bring glory to God.

A. Faithful service: I Chron. 16:11; Ps. 101:6; Matt. 28:18-20; Jn. 15:7-14; Rom. 12:14; I Cor. 13; II Cor. 8, 9; Eph. 4, 6; Heb. 12:1

B. Prayer: II Chron. 7:14; Dan. 6:10; Matt. 6:1-13; 26:41; Lk. 18:1; I Thess. 5:17

C. Witnessing: Matt. 28:19-20; Acts 1:8

D. Tolerance: Matt. 18:15-17; Lk. 10:27; Gal. 5:22-23; II Pet. 1:5-9

E. Loving Kindness: Jn. 13:35; I Jn. 3:11; 4:7, 11-12

F. Financial Stewardship: Matt. 23:23; I Cor. 16:2; II Cor. 9:6-7

VII. THE CHURCH

We believe that the Church Universal is the body of Christ, the fellowship of all believers, and that its members have been called out from the world to come under the dominion and authority of Christ, its head. We believe that a local church is a fellowship of Christians, a part of the Body of Christ, voluntarily banded together for worship, nurture, and service.

A. The Church Universal: Matt. 16:18; Jn. 10:10; I Cor. 3:16; 12:12-14, 27; Eph. 1:22-23; Col. 1:18, 24; Heb. 12:23

B. The Local Church: Matt. 18:17; Acts 2:38-47; 11: 19-30; Rev. 1:4; 3:22

1. Worship and Service: Rom. 12:1; I Cor. 14:12, 23:25; Heb. 10:25; Ja. 1:26-27

2. Nurture: Eph. 4; II Pet. 1:2-8; 3:18

VIII. ORDINANCES

We believe that baptism and the Lord's Supper are ordinances instituted by Christ to be observed by Christians only. We also believe that the Biblical mode of baptism is immersion and that participation in the Lord's Supper should be open to all Christians.

(NOTE: Several associations and local churches recognize foot washing as an ordinance. We believe that this should be left to the individual, and that neither the practice nor the non-practice of it should be any bar to fellowship, either in the church, the local association, the Presbytery, or the General Association. Jn. 13; I Tim. 5:10.)

A. Baptism

1. Instituted: Matt. 3:13-15; 28:19

2. Subjects: Acts 2:41; 8:12, 37-38; 10:47-48; 16:30-33; 19:5

3. Biblical Mode: Rom. 6:3-5; Col. 2:12

4. Purpose: Matt. 3:14; I Pet. 3:21

B. Communion

1. Instituted: Matt. 26:26-29; Mk. 14:22-25; Lk. 22:19-20; I Cor. 11:23-25

2. Subjects: I Cor. 11:27-29

3. Purpose: I Cor. 11:26

IX. THE LORD'S DAY

We believe in the Sanctify of the Lord's Day, the first day of the week, and that this day ought to be observed by worshipping God, witnessing for Christ, and ministering to the needs of humanity. We believe that secular work on Sunday should be limited to cases of necessity or mercy.

A. Sanctity: Ex. 20:8; Isa. 58:13-14

B. Observance: Mk. 2:27-28; Lk. 4:16; 14:1-6; Acts 20:7; I Cor. 16:2; Rev. 1:10

X. LAST THINGS

We believe in the personal return of Jesus Christ, and in the bodily resurrection of the dead. We believe that God will judge all mankind by Jesus Christ; that He will reward the righteous with eternal life in heaven, and that He will banish the unrighteous to everlasting punishment in hell.

A. Return: Matt. 24, 25; Lk. 12:40; Jn. 14:3; Acts 1: 11; I Jn. 3:2; Rev. 1:7

B. Resurrection: Jn. 5:25, 28-29; 6:40; 11:24-25; Rom. 8:11; I Cor. 15; Phil. 3:21; I Thess. 4:16-17; Rev. 20:4-6

C. Judgment and Reward: Matt. 25:21; Mk. 9:43- 48; Jn. 5:27; Acts 17:31; Rom. 2:16; 14:12; II Cor. 5:1, 10; Col. 3:24; II Thess. 1:7-10; Heb. 9: 27; II Pet. 3:8-13; Jude 21; Rev. 2:7; 14:13; 20: 10-15; 22:12

Notes: *This brief statement is in contrast to the very detailed statement of the National Association of Free-Will Baptists.*

* * *

THE FAITH OF FREE-WILL BAPTISTS (NATIONAL ASSOCIATION OF FREE-WILL BAPTISTS)

CHAPTER I. THE HOLY SCRIPTURES

These are the Old and the New Testaments: they were written by holy men, inspired by the Holy spirit, and are God's revealed word to man. They are a sufficient and infallible rule and guide to salvation and all Christian worship and service.

Since the Bible is the Word of God, it is without error in all matters upon which it speaks, whether history, geography, matters relating to science or any other subject.

CHAPTER II. BEING AND ATTRIBUTES OF GOD

The Scriptures teach that there is only one true and living God, who is Spirit, self-existent, eternal, immutable, omnipresent, omniscient, omnipotent, independent, good, wise, holy, just, and merciful, the . . . Creator, Preserver, and Governor of the Universe; the Redeemer, Saviour, Sanctifier, and Judge of men; and the only proper object of worship.

The mode of His existence, however, is a subject far above the understanding of man—finite beings cannot comprehend Him. There is nothing in the universe that can justly represent Him, for there is none like Him. He is the fountain of all perfection and happiness. He is glorified by the whole creation, and is worthy to be loved and served by all intelligence.

CHAPTER III. DIVINE GOVERNMENT AND PROVIDENCE

1. God exercises a providential care and superintendence over all His creatures, and governs the world in wisdom and mercy, according to the testimony of His Word.

2. God has endowed man with power of free choice, and governs him by moral laws and motives; and this power of free choice is the exact measure of man's responsibility.

3. All events are present with God from everlasting to everlasting; but His knowledge of them does not in any sense cause them, nor does He decree all events which He knows will occur.

CHAPTER IV. CREATION, PRIMITIVE STATE OF MAN, AND HIS FALL

SECTION I. CREATION

1. OF THE WORLD. God created the world, and all things that it contains, for His own pleasure and glory and the enjoyment of His creatures.

2. OF THE ANGELS. The angels were created by God to glorify Him and obey His commandments. Those who have kept their first estate He employs

in ministering blessings to the heirs of salvation and in executing His judgements upon the world.

3. OF MAN. God created man, consisting of a material body and a thinking, rational soul. He was made in the image of God, to glorify his Maker.

SECTION II. PRIMITIVE MAN, AND HIS FALL

Our first parents, in their original state, were upright. They naturally preferred and desired to obey their Creator, and had no preference or desire to transgress His will until they were influenced and inclined by the tempter to disobey God's commands. Previous to this, the only tendency of their nature was to do righteousness. In consequence of the first trangression, the state under which the posterity of Adam came into the world is so different from that of Adam that they have not that righteousness and purity which Adam had before the fall; they are not willing to obey God, but are inclined to evil. Hence, none, by virtue of any natural goodness and mere work of their own, can become the children of God, but they are all dependent for salvation upon the redemption effected through the blood of Christ, and upon being created anew unto obedience through the operation of the Spirit; both of which are freely provided for every descendant of Adam.

CHAPTER V. OF CHRIST

SECTION I. HIS DIVINITY

Jesus Christ, the Son of God, possesses all divine perfections. As He and the Father are one, He in His divine nature, filled all the offices and performed the works of God to His creatures that have been the subjects of revelation to us. As man, He performed all the duties toward God that we are required to perform, repentance of sin excepted.

His divinity is proved from His titles, His attributes, and His works.

A. HIS TITLES. The Bible ascribes to Christ the titles of Saviour, Jehovah, Lord of hosts, the first and the last, God, true God, great God, God over all, mighty God, and the everlasting Father.

B. HIS ATTRIBUTES. He is eternal, unchangeable, omnipresent, omniscient, omnipotent, holy, and to be worshipped.

C. HIS WORKS. By Christ the world was created. He preserves and governs it; He has provided redemption for all men and He will be their final Judge.

SECTION II. THE INCARNATION OF CHRIST

The Word, which in the beginning was with God and which was God, by whom all things were made, condescended to a state of humiliation in being united with human nature and becoming like us, pollution and sin excepted. In this state, as a subject of the law, He was liable to the infirmities of our nature, was tempted as we are, but lived our example, perfect obedience to the divine requirements. As Christ was made of the seed of David, according to the flesh, He is "Son of man," and as the divine existence is the fountain from which He proceeded, and was the only agency by which He was begotten, He is "the Son of God," being the only begotten of the Father, and the only incarnation of the Divine Being.

CHAPTER VI. THE ATONEMENT AND MEDIATION OF CHRIST

1. THE ATONEMENT. As sin cannot be pardoned without a sacrifice, and the blood of beasts could never wash away sin, Christ gave Himself a sacrifice for the sins of the world, and thus made salvation possible for all men. He did for us, suffering in our stead, to make known the righteousness of God, that he might be just in justifying sinners who believe in His Son. Through the redemption effected by Christ, salvation is actually enjoyed in his world, and will be enjoyed in the next by all who do not in this life refuse obedience to the known requirements of God. The atonement for sin was necessary. For present and future obedience can no more blot out our past sins than past obedience can remove the guilt of present and future sins. If God pardoned the sins of men without satisfaction for the violation of His law, it would follow that transgression might go on with impunity; government would be abrogated, and the obligation of obedience to God would be, in effect, removed.

2. MEDIATION OF CHRIST. Our Lord not only died for our sins, but He arose for our justification, and ascended up to heaven, where, as the only mediator between God and man, He makes intercession for us until He comes again.

3. We believe that all children dying in infancy, having not actually transgressed against the law of God in their own persons, are only subject to the first death, which was brought on by the fall of the first Adam, and not that any one of them dying in that state shall suffer punishment in hell by the guilt of Adam's sin for of such is the Kingdom of God.

CHAPTER VII. THE HOLY SPIRIT

1. The Scriptures ascribe to the Holy Spirit the acts and attributes of an intelligent being. He guides, knows, moves, gives information, commands, forbids, sends forth, reproves, and can be sinned against.

2. The attributes of God are ascribed to the Holy Spirit.

3. The works of God are ascribed to the Holy Spirit: creation, inspiration, giving of life, and sanctification.

4. The apostles assert that the Holy Spirit is Lord of God.

From the foregoing the conclusion is that the Holy Spirit is in reality God and one with the Father in all divine perfections. It has also been shown that Jesus Christ is God—one with the Father. Then these three—the Father, Son, and Holy Spirit—are one God.

The truth of this doctrine is also proved from the fact that the Father, the Son and the Holy Ghost are united in the authority by which believers are baptized; and in the benedictions pronounced by the apostles, which are acts of the highest religious worship.

CHAPTER VIII. THE GOSPEL CALL

The call of the Gospel is co-extensive with the atonement to all men, both by the word and strivings of the Spirit, so that salvation is rendered equally possible to all; and if any fail of eternal life, the fault is wholly his own.

CHAPTER IX. REPENTANCE

The repentance which the Gospel requires includes a deep conviction, a penitential sorrow, an open confession, a decided hatred, and an entire forsaking of all sin. This repentance God has enjoined on all men; and without it in this life the sinner must perish eternally.

CHAPTER X. FAITH

Saving faith is an assent of the mind to the fundamental truths of revelation, an acceptance of the Gospel, through the influence of the Holy Spirit, and a firm confidence and trust in Christ. The fruit of faith is obedience to the Gospel. The power to believe is the gift of God, but believing is an act of the creature, which is required as a condition of pardon, and without which the sinner cannot obtain salvation. All men are required to believe in Christ, and those who yield obedience to this requirement become the children of God by faith.

CHAPTER XI. REGENERATION

As man is a fallen and sinful being, he must be regenerated in order to obtain salvation. This change is an instantaneous renewal of the heart by the Holy Spirit, whereby the penitent sinner receives new life, becomes a child of God, and is disposed to serve him. This is called in Scripture being born again, born of the Spirit, being quickened, passing from death unto life, and a partaking of the divine nature.

CHAPTER XII. JUSTIFICATION AND SANCTIFICATION

1. JUSTIFICATION. Personal justification implies that the person justified has been guilty before God; and, in consideration of the atonement of Christ, accepted by faith, the sinner is pardoned and obsolved from the guilt of sin, and restored to the divine favor. Christ's atonement is the foundation of the sinner's redemption, yet, without repentance and faith, it can never give him justification and peace with God.

2. SANCTIFICATION is the continuing of God's grace by which the Christian may constantly grow in grace and in the knowledge of our Lord Jesus Christ.

CHAPTER XIII. PERSEVERANCE OF THE SAINTS

There are strong grounds to hope that the truly regenerate will persevere unto the end, and be saved, through the power of divine grace which is pledged for their support;

but their future obedience *and final salvation are neither determined nor certain,* since through infirmity and manifold temptations they are in *danger of falling;* and they ought, therefore, to watch and pray lest they make *shipwreck* of their faith and be lost.

CHAPTER XIV. THE LORD'S DAY

This is one day in seven, which from the creation of the world God has set apart for sacred rest and holy service. Under the former dispensation, the seventh day of the week, as commemorative of the work of creation, was set apart for the Lord's Day. Under the Gospel, the first day of the week, in commemoration of the resurrection of Christ, and by authority of Christ and the Apostles, is observed as the Christian Sabbath. On this day all men are required to refrain from secular labor and devote themselves to the worship and service of God.

CHAPTER XV. THE CHURCH

A *Christian Church* is an organized body of believers in Christ who stately assemble to worship God, and who sustain the ordinances of the Gospel according to the Scriptures. Believers in Christ are admitted to this church on giving evidence of faith in Christ, obtaining consent of the body, being baptized, and receiving the right hand of fellowship.

The church of God, or members of the body of Christ, is the whole body of Christians throughout the whole world, and none but the regenerate are its members.

CHAPTER XVI. TITHING

Both the Old and New Scriptures teach tithing as God's financial plan for the support of His work.

CHAPTER XVII. THE GOSPEL MINISTRY

1. QUALIFICATION OF MINISTERS. They must possess good, natural and acquired abilities, deep and ardent piety, be especially called of God to the work, and ordained by prayer and the laying on of hands.

2. DUTIES OF MINISTERS. These are to preach the Word, administer the ordinances of the Gospel, visit their people, and otherwise perform the work of faithful ministers.

CHAPTER XVIII. ORDINANCES OF THE GOSPEL

1. CHRISTIAN BAPTISM. This is the immersion of believers in water, in the name of the Father, the Son, and the Holy Spirit, in which are represented the burial and resurrection of Christ, the death of Christians to the world, the washing of their souls from the pollution of sin, their rising to newness of life, their engagement to serve God, and their resurrection at the last day.

2. THE LORD'S SUPPER. This is a commemoration of the death of Christ for our sins in the use of *bread* which He made the emblem of His broken body, and the *cup,* the emblem of His shed blood, and by it the believer expresses his love for Christ, his faith and hope in Him, and pledges to Him perpetual fidelity.

    It is the privilege and duty of all who have spiritual union with Christ to commemorate His death, and no man has a right to forbid these tokens to the least of His disciples.

3. WASHING THE SAINTS' FEET. This is a sacred ordinance, which teaches humility and reminds the believer of the necessity of a daily cleansing from all sin. It was instituted by the Lord Jesus Christ, and called an "example" on the night of His betrayal, and in connection with the institution of the Lord's Supper. It is the duty and happy prerogative of every believer to observe this sacred ordinance.

CHAPTER XIX. DEATH

As a result of sin, all mankind is subject to the death of the body. The soul does not die with the body, but immediately after death enters into a conscious state of happiness or misery, according to the character here possessed.

CHAPTER XX. SECOND COMING OF CHRIST

The Lord Jesus, who ascended on high and sits at the right hand of God, will come again to close the Gospel dispensation, glorify His saints, and judge the world.

CHAPTER XXI. THE RESURRECTION

The Scriptures teach the resurrection of the bodies of all men, each in its own order; they that have done good will come forth to the resurrection of life, and they that have done evil to the resurrection of damnation.

CHAPTER XXII. THE JUDGMENT AND RETRIBUTION

1. THE JUDGMENT. There will be a judgment, when time and man's probation will close forever. Then all men will be judged according to their works.

2. RETRIBUTION. Immediately after the judgment, the righteous will enter into eternal life, and the wicked will go into a state of endless punishment.

APPENDIX TO CHAPTER XIII. ADOPTED JULY, 1969

1. We believe that salvation is a present possession by faith in the Lord Jesus Christ as Savior and that a person's eternal destiny depends on whether he has this possession. This we hold in distinction from those who teach that salvation depends on human works or merit.

2. We believe that a saved individual may, in freedom of will, cease to trust in Christ for salvation and once again be lost. This we hold in distinction from those who teach that a believer may not again be lost.

3. We believe that any individual living in the practice of sin (whether he be called "backslider" or "sinner") must be judged by that evidence to be lost should he so die in his sins. This we hold in distinction from those who suggest that pernicious doctrine that a man may live in sin as he pleases and still claim Heaven as his eternal home.

4. We believe that any regenerate person who has sinned (again, whether he be called "backslider" or "sinner") and in whose heart a desire arises to repent may do so and be restored to favor and fellowship with God. This we hold in distinction from those who teach that when a Christian sins he can not repent and be restored to favor and fellowship with God.

APPENDIX TO CHAPTER I. ADOPTED JULY, 1979

Free Will Baptist believe in the plenary, verbal inspiration of the Bible. By *plenary* we mean "full and complete." We hold that all parts of the Bible are inspired and that inspiration extends to all its subjects. By verbal we mean that inspiration extends to the very words of the Scriptures, not just to the thoughts and ideas expressed by human authors.

We believe the Scriptures are infallible and inerrant. The Bible is without error and trustworthy in all its teachings, including cosmogony, geology, astronomy, anthropology, history, chronology, etc. as well as in matters of faith and practice. Being the very word of God, it is God's final revelation and our absolute authority.

APPENDIX TO CHAPTER VII. ADOPTED JULY, 1979

Free Will Baptists understand the Bible teaches the following facts: On the Day of Pentecost believers spoke in distinct foreign languages which were readily understood by the nationalities present.

Tongues were given as a special gift to the early church as only one sign which confirms the witness of the Gospel to unbelievers.

While tongues were bestowed by the sovereign will of God on some believers, all did not speak with tongues. When this gift was abused, it became a source of disturbance in the congregational meetings. To eliminate confusion and correct the error, Paul set particular guidelines for the Christian church to follow. The gift of tongues was neither an evidence of the baptism of the Holy Spirit, nor does it bring about sanctification.

We believe that speaking in tongues as a visible sign of the baptism of the Holy Spirit is an erroneous doctrine to be rejected. Any implication of a "second work of grace" has never been tolerated in our fellowship of churches, and will not be permitted.

We teach and preach the fulness of the Holy Spirit and heed the scriptural admonition. "Be filled with the Spirit; Speaking to yourselves in psalms and hymns and spiritual songs, singing and making melody in your heart to the Lord; Giving thanks always for all things unto God and the Father in the name of our Lord Jesus Christ."

Notes: *Approaching the length and thoroughness of the reformation confessions, this document is the most definitive statement of the General Baptist position. The text has undergone periodic revision, the latest in 1981. In 1979, the statement on biblical authority (chapter 1) was modified to make explicit the church's position on matters in the forefront of contemporary evangelical theological debate. An appendix to chapter 1 was also adopted. The church practices foot washing. A pentecostal variant of this document was adopted by the Free Will Baptist Church of the Pentecostal Faith.*

ARTICLES OF FAITH (NATIONAL ASSOCIATION OF FREE-WILL BAPTISTS)

1. THE BIBLE. The Scriptures of the Old and New Testaments were given by inspiration of God, and are our infallible rule of faith and practice.

2. GOD. There is one living and true God, revealed in nature as the Creator, Preserver, and Righteous Governor of the universe; and in the Scriptures as Father, Son, and Holy Ghost; yet as one God, infintely wise and good, whom all intelligent creatures are supremely to love, adore, and obey.

3. CHRIST. Christ is God manifest in the flesh; in His divine nature truly God, in His human nature truly man. The mediator between God and man, once crucified, He is now risen and glorified, and is our ever present Saviour and Lord.

4. THE HOLY SPIRIT. The Scriptures assign to the Holy Spirit all the attributes of God.

5. THE GOVERNMENT OF GOD. God exercises a wise and benevolent providence over all beings and all things by maintaining the constitution and laws of nature. He also performs special acts, not otherwise provided for, as the highest welfare of men requires.

6. THE SINFULNESS OF MAN. Man was created innocent, but by disobedience fell into a state of sin and condemnation. His posterity, therefore, inherit a fallen nature of such tendencies that all who come to years of accountability, sin and become guilty before God.

7. THE WORK OF CHRIST. The Son of God by His incarnation, life, sufferings, death, and resurrection effected for all a redemption from sin that is full and free, and is the ground of salvation by faith.

8. THE TERMS OF SALVATION. The conditions of salvation are: 1. Repentance or sincere sorrow for sin and hearty renunciation of it. 2. Faith or the unreserved committal of one's self to Christ as Saviour and Lord with purpose to love and obey Him in all things. In the exercise of saving faith, the soul is renewed by the Holy Spirit, freed from the dominion of sin, and becomes a child of God. 3. Continuance in faith and obedience until death.

9. ELECTION. God determined from the beginning to save all who should comply with the conditions of Salvation. Hence by faith in Christ men become His elect.

10. FREEDOM OF THE WILL. The human will is free and self-controlled, having power to yield to the influence of the truth and the Spirit, or to resist them and perish.

11. SALVATION FREE. God desires the salvation of all, the Gospel invites all, the Holy Spirit strives with all, and whosoever will may come and take of the water of life freely.

12. PERSEVERANCE. All believers in Christ, who through grace persevere in holiness to the end of life, have promise of eternal salvation.

13. GOSPEL ORDINANCES. BAPTISM, or the immersion of believers in water, and the LORD'S SUPPER, are ordinances to be perpetuated under the Gospel. FEET WASHING, an ordinance teaching humility, is of universal obligation, and is to be ministered to all true believers.

14. TITHING. God commanded tithes and offerings in the Old Testament; Jesus Christ endorsed it in the Gospel (Matt. 23:23), and the apostle Paul said, "Upon the first day of the week let every one of you lay by him in store, as God hath prospered him" (I Cor. 16:2a).

15. THE CHRISTIAN SABBATH. The divine law requires that one day in seven be set apart from secular employments and amusements, for rest, worship, holy works, and activities, and for personal communion with God.

16. RESURRECTION, JUDGMENT, AND FINAL RETRIBUTION. The Scriptures teach the resurrection of all men at the last day. They that have done good will come forth to the resurrection of life, and they that have done evil unto the resurrection of damnation; then the wicked will "go away into eternal punishment, but the righteous into eternal life."

Notes: *This document is a very condensed summary of The Faith of Free Will Baptists.*

* * *

AGREED UPON BELIEFS OF THE GREEN RIVER (KENTUCKY) ASSOCIATION OF UNITED BAPTISTS

1. The scriptures of the old and new Testaments are the infallible word of God, and the only true rule of faith and practice.

2. There is only one true God, and in the Godhead or divine essence, there are the Father, the Son and the Holy Ghost.

3. By nature we are depraved and fallen creatures.

4. Salvation, regeneration, santification and justification are by the life, death, resurrection and ascension of Jesus Christ.

5. The saints will finally persevere through grace to glory.

6. Believer's baptism by immersion are necessary to receive the Lord's Supper.

7. The salvation of the righteous and the punishment of the wicked will be eternal.

8. It is our duty to tender affection to each other, and study the happiness of the children of God; in general, to to be engaged singly to promote the honor of God.

9. The preaching, "Christ tasted death for every man, shall be no bar to communion."

Notes: *One of several associations formed by the union of Regular and Separate Baptists in the 1790s, the Green River*

Association of United Baptists, like other United Baptists, embraces beliefs that are Arminian in perspective. However, the association's unnamed statement is mildly Calvinist in its affirmation of human depravity (item 3) and the perseverance of the saints (item 5). There is no mention of election or predestination, and the last item allows some freedom on the issue of limited (Christ died for the elect) versus unlimited (Christ died for every person) atonement.

* * *

Seventh-Day Baptist

STATEMENT OF BELIEF OF SEVENTH-DAY BAPTISTS (SEVENTH-DAY BAPTIST GENERAL CONFERENCE)

1. GENERAL STATEMENT

Seventh Day Baptists cherish liberty of thought as an essential condition for the guidance of the Holy Spirit. Therefore they have no binding creed to which members must subscribe. They hold however, that certain beliefs and practices, having the support of Scripture and adhered to by followers of Christ through the centuries, are binding upon all Christians. Among these are the following which they hold to be fundamental.

These statements approved by Conference are passed on to the churches for such action as the Holy Spirit shall lead them to take. It is believed they will be helpful in training the children in religion, in establishing the young people in the fundamentals of Christian faith, in deepening the work of God's grace in all our people, and in making these essential Christian truths known to others.

2. POLITY

The Seventh Day Baptist denomination is historically, like other Baptists, congregational in polity, and desires that its churches and its members shall continue to enjoy freedom of conscience in all matters of religion. Therefore, the Statement of Belief here set forth is simply an exhibition of the views generally held by Seventh Day Baptists and is not adopted as having binding force in itself.

3. ARTICLES OF BELIEF

I. GOD. We believe in God, the one personal, perfect, and eternal Spirit, Creator, and Sustainer of the universe, our Father, who manifests a holy, redeeming love toward all men.

II. JESUS CHRIST. We believe in Jesus Christ, God manifest in the flesh, our Saviour, Teacher, and Guide, who draws to himself all men who will come to him in love and trustful obedience.

III. THE HOLY SPIRIT. We believe in the Holy Spirit, the indwelling God, the Inspirer of Scripture, the Comforter, active in the hearts and minds and lives of men, who reproves of sin, instructs in righteousness, and empowers for witnessing and service.

IV. THE BIBLE. We believe that the Bible is the inspired record of God's will for man, of which Jesus Christ is the supreme interpreter; and that it is our final authority in matters of faith and conduct.

V. MAN. We believe that man was made in the image of God in his spiritual nature and personality, and is therefore the noblest work of creation; that he has moral responsibility, and was created for divine sonship and human fellowship, but because of disobedience he is in need of a Savior.

VI. SIN AND SALVATION. We believe that sin is any want of conformity to the character and will of God, and that salvation from sin and death, through repentance and faith in Christ our Savior, is the gift of God by redeeming love, centered in the atoning death of Christ on the cross.

VII. ETERNAL LIFE. We believe that Jesus rose from the dead and lives eternally with the Father, and that he will come in heavenly glory; and that because he lives, eternal life with spiritual and glorified bodies, is the gift of God to the redeemed.

VIII. THE CHURCH. We believe that the Church of god is the whole company of redeemed people gathered by the Holy Spirit into one body of which Christ is the head: and that the local church is a community of Christ's followers organized for fellowship and service, practicing and proclaiming common convictions.

IX. THE SACRAMENTS. We believe that baptism of believers by immersion is a witness to the acceptance of Jesus Christ as Savior and Lord, and is a symbol of death to sin, a pledge to a new life in Christ. We believe that the Lord's Supper commemorates the suffering and death of the world's Redeemer, "Til he come," and is a symbol of Christian fellowship and a pledge of renewed allegiance to our risen Lord.

X. THE SABBATH. We believe that the Sabbath of the Bible, the seventh day of the week, is sacred time, antedating Moses and having the sanction of Jesus; that it should be faithfully kept by all Christians as a day of rest and worship, a symbol of God's presence in time, a pledge of eternal Sabbath rest.

XI. EVANGELISM. We believe that Jesus Christ by his life and ministry and his final command to the disciples, commissions us to promote evangelism, missions, and religious education, and that it is through these agencies that the church must promote Christianity throughout the whole world and in all human relationships.

SOME SCRIPTURE REFERENCES

POLITY

Matthew 18: 15-20; 23: 8-10; Luke 22: 24-27; Acts 6: 1-6; 2: 44, 45; Colossians 3: 15-17; I Peter 5: 1-5.

I. GOD

Genesis 1: 1; Isaiah 25: 1-9; Psalms 90: 1, 2; 91: 2; John 4: 24; I Timothy 1: 17; John 3: 16; I John 3: 1; Ephesians 4: 6.

II. JESUS CHRIST

John 1: 14-18; 12: 32; Romans 1: 3-5; Galatians 4: 4-6; Ephesians 1: 18-23; I John 3: 16; 2: 2.

III. THE HOLY SPIRIT

John 14: 26; 16: 7-14; Acts 1: 8; Romans 5: 5; II Peter 1: 21.

IV. THE BIBLE

II Timothy 3: 14-17; Hebrews 1: 1, 2; II Peter 1: 19, 20; John 20: 30, 31.

V. MAN

Genesis 1: 26, 27; Micah 6: 8; Psalms 8: 4, 5; II Corinthians 4: 15, 16; Ephesians 2: 4-10.

VI. SIN AND SALVATION

John 1: 29; 3: 5; I John 3: 4; Romans 3: 23-27; Acts 2: 37-39; I Peter 2: 21-25; Ephesians 2:8.

VII. ETERNAL LIFE

John 3: 14, 15; 17: 1-3; I Corinthians 15: 20-22, 42-44; I John 5: 11, 12; Matthew 25: 31-34; Colossians 3: 1-4.

VIII. THE CHURCH

Matthew 16: 16-19; Colossians 1: 18; I Corinthians 12: 13, 14; Ephesians 1: 22, 23; 2: 19-22; Acts 14: 23.

IX. THE SACRAMENTS

Matthew 3: 13-17; Acts 2: 37-39; Romans 6: 3, 4; Mark 16: 16; Matthew 26: 26-28; I Corinthians 10: 16, 17; 11: 23-29.

X. THE SABBATH

Genesis 2: 2, 3; Exodus 20: 8-11; Isaiah 58: 13, 14; Ezekiel 20: 20; Luke 4: 16; Mark 2: 27, 28; Acts 13: 42-44; Matthew 5: 17-19.

XI. EVANGELISM

Deuteronomy 6: 6, 7; Matthew 28: 18-20; 4: 19, 23; Acts 5: 42; 20: 28-32; I Corinthians 4: 17; I Thessalonians 5: 12-22.

Notes: *The sabbatarian Baptists differ primarily on their keeping of Saturday, rather than Sunday, as a day of rest and worship. The statement follows a General Baptist theological perspective.*

*   *   *

Christian Church

A DECLARATION OF THE TRUTH REVEALED IN THE BIBLE AS DISTINGUISHABLE FROM THE THEOLOGY OF CHRISTENDOM (AMENDED CHRISTADELPHIANS)

THE BIBLE

1. The Bible is a revelation of God's purpose given through chosen men who were guided by His Spirit. It is therefore an infallible and authoritative expression of His will for man.

God, who at sundry times and in divers manners spake in time past unto the fathers by the prophets, hath in these last days spoken unto us by his Son, whom he hath appointed heir of all things, by whom also he made the worlds (Heb.1:1,2).

Now these be the last words of David. David the son of Jesse said, and the man who was raised up on high, the annointed of the God of Jacob, and the sweet psalmist of Israel, said, The Spirit of the Lord spake by me, and his word was in my tongue. The God of Israel said, the Rock of Israel spake to me. He that ruleth over men must be just, ruling in the fear of God (2 Sam. 23:1-3).

Yet many years didst thou forbear them, and testifiedst against them by thy spirit in thy prophets : yet would they not give ear : therefore gavest thou them into the hand of the people of the lands (Neb. 9:30).

For David himself said by the Holy Spirit, The Lord said to my Lord, Sit thou on my right hand, till I make thine enemies thy footstool (Mark 12:36).

All scripture is given by inspiration of God, and is profitable for doctrine, for reproof, for correction, for instruction in righteousness : that the man of God may be perfect, thoroughly furnished unto all good works (2 Tim. 3:16,17).

I will raise them up a Prophet from among their brethren, like unto thee, and will put my words in his mouth ; and he shall speak unto them all that I shall command him (Deut. 18:18,19).

For the prophecy came not in old time by the will of man : but holy men of God spake as they were moved by the Holy Spirit (2 Peter 1:21.)

See also Ezek. 1:3; Micah 1:1; Zeph. 1:1; Jer. 1:1-9.

GOD

2. The Bible reveals God to be the Creator and Sustainer of all things. He dwells in the heavens in unapproachable light. He is all powerful, all wise, a God of love, mercy, holiness, righteousness and truth. God is a unity.

In the beginning God created the heaven and the earth (Gen. 1:1).

The blessed and only potentate, the King of kings, and Lord of lords, who only hath immortality, dwelling in the light which no man can approach unto (1 Tim. 6:15).

And this is life eternal, that they might know thee, the only true God, and Jesus Christ, whom thou hast sent (John 17:3).

He made known his ways unto Moses, his acts unto the children of Israel. The Lord is merciful and gracious, slow to anger, and plenteous in mercy. He will not always chide: neither will he keep his anger for ever. He hath not dealt with us after our sins: nor rewarded us according to our iniquities. For as the heaven is high above the earth, so great is his mercy toward them that fear him (Psa. 103:8-11).

Hear, O Israel, the Lord our God is one lord (Deut. 6:4).

But to us there is but one God, the Father, of whom are all things, and we in him; and one Lord Jesus Christ, by whom are all things, and we by him (1 Cor. 8:6).

For there is one God, and one mediator between God and men, the man Christ Jesus (1 Tim. 2:5).

A DECLARATION OF THE TRUTH REVEALED IN THE BIBLE AS DISTINGUISHABLE FROM THE THEOLOGY OF CHRISTENDOM (AMENDED CHRISTADELPHIANS) (continued)

See also Isa. 45:12; Psa. 11:4; Psa. 33: 104:30; Mark 12:29; Eph. 4:6.

THE SPIRIT OF GOD

3. The Spirit of God is His power by which He sustains creation, is everywhere present, and reveals and fulfils His will.

And the Spirit of God moved upon the face of the waters (Gen. 1:2).

Thou knowest my downsitting and mine uprising; thou understandest my thoughts afar off. Thou compassest my path and my lying down, and art acquainted with all my ways. For there is not a word on my tongue, but lo, Lord, thou knowest it altogether. Thou hast beset me behind and before, and laid thine hand upon me. Such knowledge is too wonderful for me; it is high, I cannot attain unto it. Whither shall I go from thy Spirit, or whither, shall I flee from thy presence? If I ascend up into heaven thou art there: if I make my bed in hell (*sheol,* the grave), behold, thou art there . . . The darkness hideth not from thee, but the night shineth as the day: the darkness and the light are both alike to thee (Psa. 139:2-12).

The Spirit of God hath made me, and the breath of the Almighty hath given me life (Job 26:13).

Yet many years didst thou forbear them, and testifiedst against them by thy Spirit in thy prophets (Neh. 9:30).

See also Psa. 10:30; Micah 3:8.

4. The Holy Spirit is the same power of God directed to fulfil any special purpose, as in His redeeming work. Thus by the Holy Spirit God's revelation was made through the prophets: by the Holy Spirit Jesus was begotten and enabled to do his mighty works and speak the Father's words: by it the apostles were guided into all truth and were able to attest their message by wonderful works. Special gifts of the Holy Spirit were granted in the early church, and by the Holy Spirit God dwelt among the believers.

For the prophecy came not in old time by the will of man: but holy men of God spake as they were moved by the Holy Spirit (2 Peter 1:21).

And the angel answered and said unto her, The Holy Spirit shall come upon thee, and the power of the Highest shall overshadow thee; therefore also that holy thing that shall be born of thee shall be called the Son of God (Luke 1:35).

And John bare record, saying, I saw the Spirit descending from heaven like a dove, and it abode upon him. And I knew him not: but he that sent me to baptize with water, the same said unto me, Upon whom thou shalt see the Spirit descending, and remaining on him, the same is he which baptizeth with the Holy Spirit (John 1:32, 33).

God anointed Jesus of Nazareth with the Holy Spirit and with power; who went about doing good, and healing all that were oppressed of the devil, for God was with him (Acts 10:38).

The Spirit of the Lord is upon me, because he hath anointed me to preach the gospel to the poor; he hath sent me to heal the brokenhearted, to preach deliverance to the captives, and recovering of sight to the blind, to set at liberty them that are bruised, to preach the acceptable year of the Lord. And he closed the book, and he gave it again to the minister, and sat down. And the eyes of all them that were in the synagogue were fastened on him. And he began to say unto them. This day is this scripture fulfilled in your ears (Luke 4:18-21).

The Comforter, which is the Holy Spirit whom the Father will send in my name, he shall teach you all things, and bring all things to your remembrance, whatsoever I have said unto you (John 14:26).

John truly baptized with water, but ye shall be baptized with the Holy Spirit not many days hence . . . Ye shall receive power after the Holy Spirit is come upon you (Acts 1:5-8).

And suddenly there came a sound from heaven as of a rushing mighty wind, and it filled all the house where they were sitting, and they were all filled with the Holy Spirit (Acts 2:2-4).

And as I began to speak, the Holy Spirit fell on them as on us at the beginning. Then remembered I the word of the Lord how that he said, John indeed baptized with water, but ye shall be baptized with the Holy Spirit (Acts 11:15-16).

Then laid they their hands on them, and they received the Holy Spirit; and when Simon saw that through the laying on of the apostles' hands the Holy Spirit was given, he offered them money, saying, Give me also this power (Acts 8:17-19).

Now there are diversities of gifts, but the same Spirit. And there are differences of administrations, but the same Lord. And there are diversities of operations, but it is the same God which worketh all in all. But the manifestation of the Spirit is given to every man to profit withal. For to one is given by the Spirit the word of wisdom; to another the word of knowledge by the same Spirit; to another faith by the same Spirit; to another the gifts of healing by the same Spirit; to another the working of miracles; to another prophecy; to another discerning of spirits; to another divers kinds of tongues; to another the interpretation of tongues; but all these worketh that one and the selfsame Spirit, dividing to every man severally as he will (1 Cor. 12:4-11).

Know ye not that your body is the temple of the Holy Spirit, which is in you, which ye have of God, and ye are not your own? (1 Cor. 6:19).

JESUS CHRIST

5. Jesus Christ, the only begotten Son of God, was born of the virgin Mary. He was raised up a last Adam, born of our nature, tempted as we are, yet without sin, to remove by his obedience, death and resurrection, all the evils resulting from the disobedience of the first Adam.

But while he thought on these things, behold, the angel of the Lord appeared unto him in a dream, saying, Joseph, thou son of David, fear not to take unto thee Mary thy wife: for that which is conceived in her is of the Holy Spirit. And she shall bring forth a son, and thou shalt call his name JESUS: for he shall save his people from their sins (Matt. 1:20, 21).

And the angel answered and said unto her, The Holy Spirit shall come upon thee, and the power of the Highest shall overshadow thee: therefore also that holy thing which shall be born of thee shall be called the Son of God (Luke 1:35).

But when the fulness of the time was come, God sent forth his Son, made of a woman, made under the law (Gal. 4:4).

Who in the days of his flesh, when he had offered up prayers and supplications with strong crying and tears upon him that was able to save him from death, and was heard in that he feared: though he were a Son, yet learned he obedience by the things which he suffered (Heb. 5:7, 8).

For verily he took not on him the nature of angels; but he took on him the seed of Abraham. Wherefore in all things it behoved him to be made like unto his brethren, that he might be a merciful and faithful high priest in things pertaining to God, to make reconciliation for the sins of the people. For in that he himself hath suffered being tempted, he is able to succour them that are tempted (Heb. 2:16-18).

For since by man came death, by man came also the resurrection of the dead. For as in Adam all die, even so in Christ shall all be made alive . . . And so it is written, The first man Adam was made a living soul; the last Adam was made a quickening spirit. Howbeit that was not first which is spiritual, but that which is natural; and afterward that which is spiritual. The first man is of the earth, earthy: the second man is the Lord from heaven. As is the earthy, such are they also that are earthy: and as is the heavenly, such are they also that are heavenly. And as we have borne the image of the earthy, we shall also bear the image of the heavenly (1 Cor. 15:21, 22, 45, 49).

For there is one God, and one mediator between God and men, the man Christ Jesus (1 Tim. 2:5).

6. Death which sin brought into the world could only be conquered by the conquest of sin itself. This, man himself could not achieve. The death of Jesus was an act of loving obedience to God by which we may have forgiveness of our sins and be reconciled to God, the sinless life of Jesus making him conqueror over sin, an effective offering for sin, and ensuring his triumph over death by resurrection. God revealed His love is providing him as a saviour.

For God so loved the world, that he gave his only begotten Son, that whosoever believeth in him should not perish, but have everlasting life (John 3:16).

The next day John seeth Jesus coming unto him, and saith, Behold the Lamb of God, which taketh away the sin of the world (John 1:29).

Whom God hath set forth to be a propitiation through faith in his blood, to declare his righteousness for the remission of sincs that are past, through the forbearance of God (Rom. 3:25).

But God commendeth his love toward us, in that, while we were yet sinners, Christ died for us (Rom. 5:8).

In whom we have redemption through his blood, the forgiveness of sins, according to the riches of his grace (Eph. 1:7).

Who hath delivered us from the power of darkness, and hath translated us into the kingdom of his dear Son: in whom we have redemption through his blood, even the forgiveness of sins (Col. 1:13, 14).

Who gave himself for our sins, that he might deliver us from the present evil world, according to the will of God and our Father (Gal. 1:4).

Who gave himself for us, that he might redeem us from all iniquity, and purify unto himself a peculiar people, zealous of good works (Titus 2:14).

For he hath made him to be sin for us, who knew no sin; that we might be made the righteouness of God in him (2 Cor. 5:21).

But he was wounded for our transgressions, he was bruised for our iniquities: the chastisement of our peace was upon him; and with his stripes we are healed . . . He shall see of the travail of his soul, and shall be satisfed: by his knowledge shall my righteous servant justify many; for he shall bear their iniquities (Isa. 53:5 and 11).

7. Jesus was raised from death on the third day, bringing life and immortality to light. Exalted to his Father's right hand he is alive for evermore, and pleads the cause of his people as their High Priest and Mediator.

Whom God hath raised up, having loosed the pains of death: because it was not possible that he should be holden of it (Acts 2:24).

Him God raised up the third day, and shewed him openly (Acts 10:40).

Concerning his Son Jesus Christ our Lord, which was made of the seed of David according to the flesh; and declared to be the Son of God with power, according to the spirit of holiness, by the resurrection from the dead (Rom. 1:3, 4).

Knowing that Christ being raised from the dead dieth no more; death hath no more dominion over him (Rom. 6:9).

Which he wrought in Christ, when he raised him from the dead, and set him at his own right hand in the heavenly places, far above all principality, and power, and might, and dominion, and every name that is named, not only in this world, but also in that which is to come (Eph. 1:20, 21).

Wherefore, holy brethren, partakers of the heavenly calling, consider the Apostle and High Priest of our profession, Christ Jesus (Heb. 3:1).

Wherefore he is able to save them to the uttermost that come unto God by him, seeing he ever liveth to make intercession for them (Heb. 7:25).

For there is one God, and one mediator between God and men, the man Christ Jesus (1 Tim. 2:5).

8. At the time appointed God is to send His Son to the earth again in power and great glory, to judge the living and the dead, and to establish upon earth a universal and abiding Kingdom.

A DECLARATION OF THE TRUTH REVEALED IN THE
BIBLE AS DISTINGUISHABLE FROM THE THEOLOGY
OF CHRISTENDOM (AMENDED
CHRISTADELPHIANS) (continued)

And when he had spoken these things, while they beheld, he was taken up; and a cloud received him out of their sight. And while they looked stedfastly toward heaven as he went up, behold, two men stood by them in white apparel; which also said, Ye men of Galilee, why stand ye gazing up into heaven? this same Jesus, which is taken up from you into heaven, shall so come in like manner as ye have seen him go into heaven (Acts 1:9-11).

And he shall send Jesus Christ, which before was preached unto you: whom the heaven must receive until the times of restitution of all things, which God hath spoken by the mouth of all his holy prophets since the world began (Acts 3:20, 21).

For the Son of man shall come in the glory of his Father with his angels; and then shall he reward every man according to his works (Matt. 16:27).

For this we say unto you by the word of the Lord, that we which are alive and remain unto the coming of the Lord shall not prevent them which are asleep. For the Lord himself shall descend from heaven with a shout, with the voice of the archangel, and with the trump of God: and the dead in Christ shall rise first: then we which are alive and remain shall be caught up together with them in the clouds to meet the Lord in the air: and so shall we ever be with the Lord (1 Thess. 4:15-17).

For our conversation is in heaven; from whence also we look for the Saviour, the Lord Jesus Christ (Phil. 3:21).

I charge thee therefore before God, and the Lord Jesus Christ, who shall judge the quick and the dead at his appearing and his kingdom (2 Tim. 4:1).

And the seventh angel sounded; and there were great voices in heaven, saying, The kingdoms of this world are become the kingdoms of our Lord, and of his Christ; and he shall reign for ever and ever (Rev. 11:15).

For he must reign, till he hath put all enemies under his feet (1 Cor. 15:25).

MAN

9. A creature of dust, man is mortal: that is, subject to death or dissolution of being, in consequence of the disobedience of Adam which brought death as the penalty of sin. In the death state a man is a body deprived of life, and is as utterly unconscious as if he had never existed. His dead body corruption will presently destroy.

And the Lord God formed man of the dust of the ground, and breathed into his nostrils the breath of life; and man became a living soul (Gen. 2:7).

In the sweat of thy face shalt thou eat bread, till thou return unto the ground; for out of it wast thou taken: for dust thou art, and unto dust shalt thou return (Gen. 3:19).

For he knoweth our frame; he remembereth that we are dust (Psa. 103:14).

Wherefore, as by one man sin entered into the world, and death by sin; and so death passed upon all men, for that all have sinned (Rom. 5:12).

For in death there is no remembrance of thee: in the grave who shall give thee thanks? (Psa. 6:5).

Thou hidest thy face, they are troubled: thou takest away their breath, they die, and return to their dust (Psa. 104:29).

Put not your trust in princes, nor in the son of man, in whom there is no help. His breath goeth forth, he returneth to his earth; in that very day his thoughts perish (Psa. 146:3, 4).

For the living know that they shall die: but the dead know not anything, neither have they any more a reward; for the memory of them is forgotten. Also their love, and their hatred, and their envy, is now perished: neither have they any more a portion for ever in any thing that is done under the sun . . . Whatsoever thy hand findeth to do, do it with thy might; for there is no work nor device, nor knowledge, nor wisdom, in the grave, whither thou goest (Eccl. 9:5, 6 and 10).

For the grave cannot praise thee, death cannot celebrate thee: they that go down into the pit cannot hope for thy truth. The living, the living, he shall praise thee, as I do this day: the father to the children shall make known thy truth (Isa. 38:18, 19).

10. "Soul" in the Bible means, primarily, creature; but it is also used of the various aspects in which a living creature—man or beast—can be contemplated, such as person, body, life, breath, mind. It never expresses the idea of immortality.

And God said, Let the waters bring forth abundantly the moving creature that hath life, (margin-soul) and fowl that may fly above the earth in the open firmament of heaven . . . And God said, Let the earth bring forth the living creature afater his kind, cattle, and creeping thing, and beast of the earth after his kind (Gen. 1:20, 24).

It shall even be as when an hungry man dreameth, and, behold, he eateth; but he awaketh, and his soul is empty: or as when a thirsty man dreameth, and, behold, he drinketh; but he awaketh, and, behold he is faint, and his soul hath appepite: so shall the multitude of all nations be, that fight against mount Zion (Isa. 29:8).

And in the first day there shall be an holy convocation, and in the seventh day there shall be an holy convocation to you: no manner of work shall be done in them, save that which every man (margin—soul) must eat (Exod. 12:16).

Men do not despise a thief, if he steal to satisfy his soul when he is hungry (Prov. 6:30).

Behold, for peace I had great bitterness: but thou hast in love to my soul delivered it from the pit of corruption: for thou hast cast all my sins behind thy back (Isa. 38:17).

And levy a tribute unto the Lord of the men of war which went out to battle: one soul of five hundred, both of the persons, and of the beeves, and of the asses, and of the sheep (Num. 31:28).

And Samson said, Let me (margin—my soul) die with the Philistines. And he bowed himself with all his might; and the house fell upon the lords, and upon all the people that were therein. So the dead which he slew at his death were more than they which he slew in his life (Judges 16:30).

Behold, all souls are mine; as the soul of the father, so also the soul of the son is mine: the soul that sinneth, it shall die . . . The soul that sinneth, it shall die (Ezek. 18:4, 20).

Yea, a sword shall pierce through thy own soul also (Luke 2:35).

And it shall come to pass that every soul, which will not hear that prophet, shall be destroyed from among the people (Acts 3:23).

Let every soul be subject unto the higher powers. For there is no power but of God: the powers that be are ordained of God (Rome 13:1).

And the second angel poured out his vial upon the sea; and it became as the blood of a dead man: and every living soul died in the sea (Rev. 16:3).

11. "Spirit" in the Scripture, as applied to man, is no more expressive of the notion of an immortal soul than is "soul", but signifies breath, life, energy, disposition, mind, conscience, as attributes of man while alive.

And it came to pass in the morning that his spirit was troubled; and he sent and called for all the magicians of Egypt, and all the wise men thereof: and Pharaoh told them his dream; but there was none that could interpret them unto Pharaoh (Gen. 41:8).

And they told him all the words of Joseph, which he had said unto them: and when he saw the wagons which Joseph had sent to carry them, the spirit of Jacob their father received (Gen. 45:27).

And Moses spake so unto the children of Israel: but they hearkened not unto Moses for anguish of spirit, and for cruel bondage (Exod. 6:9).

And Hannah answered and said, No, my lord, I am a woman of sorrowful spirit: I have drunk neither wine nor strong drink, but have poured out my soul before the Lord (1 Sam. 1:15).

And when the queen of Sheba had seen the wisdom of Solomon . . . and the attendance of his ministers, and their apparel; his cup bearers also, and their apparel; and his ascent by which he went up into the house of the Lord; there was no more spirit in her (2 Chron. 9:4).

I remembered God, and was troubled: I complained, and my spirit was overwhelmed . . . I call to remembrance my song in the night: I commune with mine own heart: and my spirit made diligent search (Psa. 77:3 and 6).

A merry heart maketh a cheerful countenance: but by sorrow of the heart the spirit is broken (Prov. 15:13).

Blessed are the poor in spirit: for theirs is the kingdom of heaven (Matt. 5:3).

When Jesus had thus said, he was troubled in spirit, and testified, and said, Verify, verify, I say unto you, that one of you shall betray me (John 13:21).

Now while Paul waited for them at Athens, his spirit was stirred in him, when he saw the city wholly given to idolatry (Acts 17:16).

Not slothful in business; fervent in spirit; serving the Lord (Rom. 12:11).

And he renewed in the spirit of your mind (Eph. 4:23).

12. Immortality is not inherent in man, but is the gift of God, made available through the work of Jesus Christ His Son, to all who truly believe and follow his example.

For God so loved the world, that he gave his only begotten Son, that whosoever believeth in him should not perish, but have everlasting life (John 3:16).

And I give unto them eternal life; and they shall never perish, neither shall any man pluck them out of my hand (John 10:28).

As thou hast given him power over all flesh, that he should give eternal life to as many as thou hast given him (John 17:2).

For the wages of sin is death; but the gift of God is eternal life through Jesus Christ our Lord (Rom. 6:23).

But is now made manifest by the appearing of our Saviour Jesus Christ, who hath abolished death, and hath brought life and immortality to light through the gospel (2 Tim. 1:10).

And this is the record, that God hath given to us eternal life, and this life is in his Son. He that hath the Son hath life; and he that hath not the Son of God hath not life (1 John 5:11, 12).

And Jesus answered and said, Verify, I say unto you. There is no man that hath left house, or brethren, or sisters, or father, or mother, or wife, or children, or lands, for my sake, and the gospel's, but he shall receive an hundredfold now in this time, houses, and brethren, and sisters, and mothers, and children, and lands, with persecutions; and in the world to come eternal life (Mark 10:29, 30).

13. Immortality is not possessed now but will be bestowed at the resurrection and judgment at the advent of the Lord Jesus.

For I know that my redeemer liveth, and that he shall stand at the latter day upon the earth: and though after my skin worms destroy this body, yet in my flesh shall I see God: whom I shall see for myself, and mine eyes shall behold, and not another: though my reins be consumed within me (Job 19:25-27).

And many of them that sleep in the dust of the earth shall awake, some to everlasting life, and some to shame and everlasting contempt (Dan. 12:2).

And this is the Father's will which hath sent me, that of all which he hath given me I should lose nothing, but should raise it up again at the last day. And this is the will of him that sent me, that every one which seeth the Son, and believeth on him, may have everlasting life: and I will raise him up at the last day . . . No man can come to me, except the Father which hath sent me draw him: and I will raise him up at the last day (John 6:39, 40 and 44).

A DECLARATION OF THE TRUTH REVEALED IN THE BIBLE AS DISTINGUISHABLE FROM THE THEOLOGY OF CHRISTENDOM (AMENDED CHRISTADELPHIANS) (continued)

But I would not have you to be ignorant, brethren, concerning them which are asleep, that ye sorrow not even as others which have no hope. For if we believe that Jesus died and rose again, even so them also which sleep in Jesus will God bring with him. For this we say unto you by the word of the Lord, that we which are alive and remain unto the coming of the Lord shall not prevent them which are asleep. For the Lord himself shall descent from heaven with a shout, with the voice of the archangel, and with the trump of God: and the dead in Christ shall rise first: then we which are alive and remain shall be caught up together with them in the clouds, to meet the Lord in the air; and so shall we ever be with the Lord. Wherefore comfort one another with these words (1 Thess. 4:13-18).

But if there be no resurrection of the dead, then is Christ not risen: and if Christ be not risen, then is our preaching vain, and your faith is also vain (1 Cor. 15:13, 14).

Now this I say, brethren, that flesh and blood cannot inherit the kingdom of God; neither doth corruption inherit incorruption. Behold, I shew you a mystery: we shall not all sleep, but we shall all be changed, in a moment, in the twinkling of an eye, at the last trump: for the trumpet shall sound, and the dead shall be raised incorruptible, and we shall be changed. For this corruptible must put on incorruption, and this mortal must put on immortality. So when this corruptible shall have put on incorruption, and this mortal shall have put on immortality, then shall be brought to pass the saying that is written, Death is swallowed up in victory (1 Cor. 15:50-54).

But they which shall be accounted worthy to obtain that world, and the resurrection from the dead, neither marry nor are given in marriage: neither can they die any more: for they are equal unto the angels, and are children of God, being the children of the resurrection (Luke 20:35, 36).

14.   The earth is the destined sphere of the activity of God's people, when made immortal.

For evildoers shall be cut off: but those that wait upon the Lord, they shall inherit the earth. For yet a little while, and the wicked shall not be: yea, thou shalt diligently consider his place, and it shall not be. But the meek shall inherit the earth; and shall delight themselves in the abundance of peace . . . For such as be blessed of him shall inherit the earth: and they that be cursed of him shall be cut off (Psa. 37:9-11 and 22).

And the kingdom and dominion, and the greatness of the kingdom under the whole heaven, shall be given to the people of the saints of the most High, whose kingdom is an everlasting kingdom, and all dominions shall serve and obey him (Dan. 7:27).

Blessed are the meek: for they shall inherit the earth (Matt. 5:5).

And Jesus said unto them, Verily I say unto you, That ye which have followed me, in the regeneration when the Son of Man shall sit in the throne of his glory, ye also shall sit upon twelve thrones, judging the twelve tribes of Israel (Matt. 19:28).

For the promise, that he should be the heir of the world, was not to Abraham, or to his seed, through the law, but through the righteousness of faith (Rom. 4:13).

And he that overcometh, and keepeth my works unto the end, to him will I give power over the nations: and he shall rule them with a rod of iron; as the vessels of the potter shall they be broken to shivers: even as I received of my Father (Rev. 2:26, 27).

And they sung a new song, saying, Thou art worthy to take the book, and to open the seals thereof: for thou wast slain, and hast redeemed us to God by thy blood, out of every kindred, and tongue, and people, and nation; and hast made us unto our God kings and priests: and we shall reign on the earth (Rev. 5:9, 10).

15.   It follows also of necessity that the once popular theory of hell as a place of eternal torments, is untrue. The original, unspoilt meaning of "hell" was an unseen or covered place. "Hell" in the Bible often means the grave. (In the Old Testament, the original Hebrew word SHEOL occurs 65 times, being translated 31 times "hell", 31 times "the grave" and three times "pit". In the New Testament the original Greek word HADES occurs 11 times, being translated 10 times "hell" and once "the grave".)

Let me not be ashamed, O Lord: for I have called upon thee: let the wicked be ashamed, and let them be silent in the grave (Psa. 31:17).

For great is thy mercy toward me: and thou hast delivered my soul from the lowest hell (Psa. 86:13).

Then Jonah prayed unto the Lord his God out of the fish's belly, and said, I cried by reason of mine affliction unto the Lord, and he heard me; out of the belly of hell cried I, and thou heardest my voice. For thou hadst cast me into the deep, in the midst of the seas; and the floods compassed me about: all thy billows and thy waves passed over me (Jonah 2:1-3).

And if ye take this also from me, and mischief befall him, ye shall bring down my gray hairs with sorrow to the grave. Now therefore when I come to thy servant my father, and the lad be not with us; seeing that his life is bound up in the lad's life; it shall come to pass, when he seeth that the lad is not with us, that he will die: and thy servants shall bring down the gray hairs of thy servant our father with sorrow to the grave (Gen. 44:29-31).

For in death there is no remembrance of thee: in the grave who shall give thee thanks? (Psa. 6:5).

Whatsoever thy hand findeth to do, do with thy might: for there is no work, nor device, nor knowledge, nor wisdom, in the grave, whither thou goest (Eccl. 9:10).

I said in the cutting of my days, I shall go to the gates of the grave: I am deprived of the residue of my years . . . For the grave cannot praise thee, death cannot celebrate thee: they that go down into the pit cannot hope for thy truth (Isa. 38:10 and 18).

I will ransom them from the power of the grave; I will redeem them from death: O death, I will be thy plagues: O grave, I will by thy destruction: repentance shall be hid from mine eyes (Hosea 13:14).

And thou, Capernaum, which art exalted unto heaven, shalt be brought down to hell: for if the mighty works, which have been done in thee, had been done in Sodom, it would have remained until this day (Matt. 11:23).

Because thou wilt not leave my soul in hell, neither wilt thou suffer thine Holy One to see corruption. Thou hast made known to me the ways of life: thou shalt make me full of joy with thy countenance. Men and brethren, let me freely speak unto you of the patriach David, that he is both dead and buried, and his sepulchre is with us unto this day. Therefore being a prophet, and knowing that God had sworn with an oath to him, that of the fruit of his loins, according to the flesh, he would raise up Christ to sit on his throne; he seeing this before spake of the resurrection of Christ, that his soul was not left in hell, neither his flesh did see corruption (Acts 2:27-31).

I am he that liveth, and was dead: and, behold, I am alive for evermore, Amen; and have the keys of hell and of death (Rev. 1:18).

O death, where is thy sting? O grave, where is thy victory? (1 Cor. 15:55).

16. Sometimes in the New Testament the original word for hell is GETHENNA, a term associated with the valley of Hinnom, a place near Jerusalem once the scene of idolatrous burnings and consequently so abhorred by the Jews of later Bible times that it was used as a place for the destruction of refuse and the dead bodies of animals and criminals, fires being continually kept burning for this purpose. It is therefore fittingly used to describe the future judgment.

And if thy hand offend thee, cut it off: it is better for thee to enter into life maimed, than having two hands to go into hell, into the fire that never shall be quenched (Mark 9:43).

But I say unto you, That whosoever is angry with his brother without a cause shall be in danger of the judgment: and whosoever shall say to his brother, Raca, shall be in danger of the council: but whosoever shall say, Thou fool, shall be in danger of hell fire (Matt. 5:22).

And fear not them which kill the body, but are not able to kill the soul; but rather fear him which is able to destroy both soul and body in hell (Matt. 10:28).

17. The true Bible doctrine of reward and punishment is that at his return in power and glory Jesus Christ will judge all those who are made responsible to him by knowledge of God's will; these will include some living at the time, and those whom he will raise from the dead, both righteous and unrighteous. He will invest the righteous with immortality in his kingdom, but will commit the wicked to destruction.

And at that time shall Michael stand up, the great prince which standeth for the children of thy people: and there shall be a time of trouble, such as never was since there was a nation even to that same time: and at that time thy people shall be delivered, every one that shall be found written in the book. And many of them that sleep in the dust of the earth shall awake, some to everlasting life, and some to shame and everlasting contempt (Dan. 12:1, 2).

For God so loved the world, that he gave his only begotten Son, that whosoever believeth in him should not perish, but have everlasting life. For God sent not his Son into the world to condemn the world; but that the world through him might be saved. He that believeth on him is not condemned: but he that believeth not is condemned already, because he hath not believed in the name of the only begotten Son of god. And that is the condemnation, that light is come into the world, and men loved darkness rather than light, because their deeds were evil (John 3:16-19).

Marvel not at this: for the hour is coming, in the which all that are in the graves shall hear his voice, and shall come forth; they that have done good, unto the resurrection of life; and they that have done evil unto the resurrection of damnation (John 5:28.29).

He that rejecteth me, and receiveth not my words, hath on that judgeth him: the word that I have spoken, the same shall judge him in the last day (John 12:48).

Who then is a faithful and wise servant, whom his lord hath made ruler over his household, to give them meat in due season? Blessed is that servant, whom his lord when he cometh shall find so doing. Verily I say unto you, That he shall make him ruler over all his goods. But and if that evil servant shall say in his heart, My lord delayeth his coming; and shall begin to smite his fellowservants, and to eat and drink with the drunken: the lord of that servant shall come in a day when he looketh not for him, and in an hour that he is not aware of, and shall cut him asunder, and appoint him his portion with the hypocrites: there shall be weeping and gnashing of teeth (Matt. 24:44-51).

And he commanded us to preach unto the people, and to testify that it is he which was ordained of God to be the Judge of quick and dead. To him give all the prophets witness, that through his name whosoever believeth in him shall receive remission of sins (Acts 10:42, 43).

And have hope toward God, which they themselves also allow, that there shall be a resurrection of the dead, both of the just and unjust (Acts 24:15).

For we must all appear before the judgment seat of Christ; that every one may receive the things done in his body, according to that he hath done, whether it be good or bad (2 Cor. 5:10).

The Lord Jesus shall be revealed from heaven, in flaming fire taking vengeance on them that know not God, and that obey not the gospel of our Lord Jesus Christ: who shall be punished with everlasting destruction from the presence of the Lord, and from the glory of his power (2 Thess. 1:8, 9).

I charge thee therefore before God and the Lord Jesus Christ, who shall judge the quick and the dead at his appearing and his kingdom (2 Tim. 4:1).

And the nations were angry, and thy wrath is come, and the time of the dead, that they should be judged, and that thou shouldest give reward unto thy servants the prophets, and to the saints, and them that fear thy name, small and great; and shouldest destroy them which destroy the earth (Rev. 11:18).

See also Matt. 25:31, 46; Luke 13:24-30; Rom. 2:1-16.

18. Without the knowledge of the saving gospel men have no hope of life; but neither are they responsible to judgment; their death will be an endless sleep.

For God so loved the world, that he gave his only begotten Son, that whosoever believeth in him should not perish, but have everlasting life (John 3:16).

Wherefore remember, that ye being in time past Gentiles in the flesh, . . . that at that time ye were without Christ, being aliens from the commonwealth of Israel, and strangers from the covenants of promise, having no hope, and without God in the world (Eph. 2:11, 12).

This I say therefore, and testify in the Lord, that ye henceforth walk not as other Gentiles walk, in the vanity of their mind, having the understanding darkened, being alienated from the life of God through the ignorance that is in them, because of the blindness of their heart (Eph. 4:17, 18).

But I would not have you to be ignorant, brethren, concerning them which are asleep, that ye sorrow not, even as others which have no hope (1 Thess. 4:13).

He that hath the Son hath life; and he that hath not the Son of God hath not life (1 John 5:12).

Man that is in honour, and understandeth not, is like the beasts that perish (Psa. 49:20).

O Lord our god, other lords beside thee have had dominion over us: but by thee only will we make mention of thy name. They are dead, they shall not live; they are deceased, they shall not rise; therefore hast thou visited and destroyed them, and made all their memory to perish (Isa. 26:13, 14).

They shall . . . sleep a perpetual sleep, and not wake, saith the Lord (Jer. 51:39).

The man that wandereth out of the way of understanding shall remain in the congregation of the dead (Prov. 21:16).

THE DEVIL

19. Since Jesus was manifested expressly for the purpose of destroying the Devil and his works (1 John 3:8; Heb. 2:14) the Lord's mission is imperfectly understood when the nature of the Bible Devil is not comprehended. The Devil is not a supernatural person but a personification of sin in its various manifestations—individual, social and political.

Jesus answered them, Have not I chosen you twelve, and one of you is a devil? (John 6:70).

Ye are of your father the devil, and the lusts of your father ye will do. He was a murderer from the beginning, and abode not in the truth, because there is not truth in him. When he speaketh a lie, he speaketh of his own: for he is a liar, and the father of it (John 8:44).

God anointed Jesus of Nazareth with the Holy Spirit and with power: who went about doing good and healing all that were oppressed of the devil; for God was with him (Acts 10:38).

Be sober, be vigilant; because your adversary the devil, as a roaring lion, walketh about, seeking whom he may devour (1 Peter 5:8).

Fear none of those things which thou shalt suffer: behold, the devil shall cast some of you into prison, that ye may be tried; and ye shall have tribulation ten days: be thou faithful unto death, and I will give thee a crown of life (Rev. 2:10).

The following parallels illustrate Scripture usage of the word "devil":

Sin bringeth forth death (Jas. 1:15). Parallel with the devil hath the power of death (Heb. 2:14).

He put away sin by the sacrifice of himself (Heb. 9:26). Parallel with That through death he might destroy the devil (Heb. 2:14).

Why hast thou conceived this in thine heart? (Acts 5:4). Parallel with Why hath Satan filled thine heart? (Acts 5:3).

According to the course of this world (Eph. 2:2). Parallel with According to the prince of the power of the air (Eph. 2:2).

The desires of the flesh and of the mind (Eph. 2:3). Parallel with The spirit that now worketh in the children of disobedience (Eph. 2:2).

Every man tempted is drawn away of his own lust, and enticed (Jas. 1:14). Parallel with Taken captive by the devil at his will (2 Tim. 2:26).

The children of disobedience (Eph. 2:2). Parallel with The children of the devil (1 John 3:10).

Put off the old man, which is corrupt according to the deceitful lusts (Eph. 4:22). Parallel with Stand against the wiles of the devil (Eph. 6:11).

Loved this present world (2 Tim. 4:10). Parallel with The god of this world hath blinded their minds (2 Cor. 4:4).

Deliver us from this present evil world (Gal. 1:4). Parallel with Deliver us from the evil one (Revised Version) (Matt. 6:13).

The children of this world (Luke 20:34). Parallel with The children of the wicked one (Matt. 13:38).

Overcome the world (1 John 5:5). Parallel with Overcome the wicked one (1 John 2:14).

Keep himself unspotted from the world (Jas. 1:27). Parallel with Keep them from the evil one (Revised Version) (John 17:15).

The lamb shall overcome them (the ten kings) (rev. 17:14). Parallel with He laid hold on the dragon, that old serpent, which is the Devil, and Satan (Rev. 20:2).

20. The Bible term Satan means simply "adversary" and is used of human beings.

And the princes of the Philistines were wroth with him; and the princes of the Philistines said unto him, Make this fellow return, that he may go again to his place which thou hast appointed him, and let him not go down with us to battle, lest in the battle he be an adversary to us (1 Sam. 29:4).

And the Lord stirred up an adversary unto Solomon, Hadad the Edomite: he was of the king's seed in Edom . . . And God stirred him up another adversary, Rezon the son of Eliadah . . . And he was an adversary to Israel all the days of Solomon, beside the mischief that Hadad did: and he abhorred Israel, and reigned over Syria (1 Kings 11:14, 23, 25).

For my love they are my adversaries: but I give myself unto prayer . . . Let this be the reward of mine adversaries from the Lord, and of them that speak evil against my soul . . . Let mine adversaries be clothed with shame, and let them cover themselves with their own confusion, as with a mantle (Psa. 109: 4, 20 and 29).

But he turned, and said unto Peter, Get thee behind me, Satan: thou art an offence unto me: for thou savourest not the things that be of God, but those that be of men (Matt. 16:23).

Later it came to mean much the same as Devil, *i.e.* a personification of the influence of sin or evil, individual or political.

And ought not this woman, being a daughter of Abraham, whom Satan hath bound, lo, these eighteeen years, be loosed from this bond on the sabbath day? (Luke 13:16).

Then entered Satan into Judas surnamed Iscariot, being of the number of the twelve (Luke 22:3). And the Lord said, Simon, Simon, behold, Satan hath desired to have you, that he may sift you as wheat (Luke 22:31).

To open their eyes, and to turn them from darkness to light, and from the power of Satan unto God, that they may receive forgiveness of sins, and inheritance among them which are sanctified by faith that is in me (Acts 26:18).

And the God of peace shall bruise Satan under your feet shortly (Rom. 16:20).

Defraud ye not one the other, except it be with consent for a time, that ye may give yourselves to fasting and prayer; and come together again, that Satan tempt you not for your incontinency (1 Cor. 7:5).

Fear none of those things which thou shalt suffer: behold, the devil shall cast some of you into prison, that ye may be tried; and ye shall have tribulation ten days: be thou faithful unto death, and I will give thee a crown of life . . . I know thy works, and where thou dwellest, even where Satan's seat is: and thou holdest fast my name, and hast not denied my faith, even in those days wherein Antipas was my faithful martyr, who was slain among you, where Satan dwelleth (Rev. 2:10, 13).

Sometimes the personification of the Devil or Satan is on a dramatic scale.

Job 1 and 2; Matt. 4; Luke 4; Luke 10:18; Jude 9.

THE PURPOSE AND PROMISES OF GOD

21. God has unfolded His purpose in the past by promises made at certain stages in human history. Peter calls them "exceeding great and precious promises" by which we might become partakers of the divine nature.

According as his divine power hath given unto us all things that pertain unto life and godliness, through the knowledge of him that hat called us to glory and virtue: whereby are given unto us exceeding great and precious promises: that by these ye might be partakers of the divine nature, having escaped the corruption that is in the world through lust (2 Peter 1:3, 4).

(a) The first promise was made when Adam had transgressed God's law in Eden, and revealed that one would be born in whom sin would be overcome and through whom all the evil that resulted from sin would be abolished.

And I will put enmity between thee and the woman, and between thy seed and her seed: it shall bruise thy head, and thou shalt bruise his heel (Gen. 3:15).

(b) An important unfolding of God's purpose arose when He called Abram to leave Ur of the Chaldees and to go to Palestine. It was revealed to Abram that his descendants should be God's people, that Abram and his seed should have the land for an eternal inheritance, and that all nations should be blessed in him. This great promise is called the Gospel in the New Testament, for it involves Abraham's greatest seed, Jesus Christ, the resurrection fro the dead of Abraham and all in his faithful line, and the eternal blessing of the world when Jesus establishes the Kingdom of Heaven upon earth.

Now the Lord had said unto Abram, Get thee out of thy country, and from thy kindred, and from thy father's house, unto a land that I will show thee: and I will make of thee a great nation, and I will bless thee, and make thy name great; and thou shalt be a blessing: and I will bless them that bless thee, and curse him that curseth thee: and in thee shall all families of the earth be blessed (Gen. 12:1-3).

And the Lord said unto Abram, after that Lot was separated from him, Lift up now thine eyes, and look from the place where thou art northward and southward, and eastward, and westward: for all the land which thou seest, to thee will I give it, and to thy seed for ever. And I will make thy seed as the dust of the earth: so that if a man can number the dust of the earth, then shall thy seed also be numbered. Arise, walk through the land in the length of it and in the breadth of it; for I will give it unto thee (Gen. 13:14-17).

And the scripture, foreseeing that God would justify the heathen through faith, preached before the gospel unto Abraham saying, In thee shall all nations be blessed . . . Now to Abraham and his seed were the promises made. He saith not, And to seeds as of many; but as of one, And to thy seed, which is Christ . . . And if ye be Christ's, then are ye Abraham's seed, and heirs according to the promise (Gal. 3:8, 16, 29).

Your father Abraham rejoiced to see my day: and he saw it, and was glad (John 8:56).

And Jesus answering said unto them. The children of this world marry, and are given in marriage: but they which shall be accounted worthy to obtain that world, and the resurrection from the dead, neither marry, nor are given in marriage: neither can they die any more: for they are equal unto the angels; and are the children of God, being the children of the resurrection. Now that the dead are raised, even Moses showed at the bush, when he calleth the Lord the God of Abraham and the God of Isaac, and the God of Jacob. For he is not a God of the dead but of the living: for all live unto him (Luke 20:34-38).

And I say unto you, That many shall come from the east and west, and shall sit down with Abraham, and Isaac, and Jacob, in the kingdom of heaven (Matt. 8:11).

Ye are the children of the prophets, and of the covenant which God made with our fathers, saying unto Abraham. And in thy seed shall all the kindreds of the earth be blessed (Acts 3:25).

The word that Isaiah the son of Amoz saw concerning Judah and Jerusalem. And it shall come to pass in the last days, that the mountain of the Lord's house shall be established in the top of the mountains, and shall be exalted above the hills; and all nations shall flow unto it. And many people shall go and say, Come ye, and let us go up to the mountain of the Lord, to the house of the god of Jacob; and he will teach us of his ways, and we will walk in his paths: for out of Zion shall go forth the law, and the word of the Lord from Jerusalem. And he shall judge among the nations, and shall rebuke many people: and they shall beat their swords into plowshares, and their spears into pruninghooks: nation shall not lift up sword against nation, neither shall they learn war any more (Isa. 2:1-4).

Say to them that are of a fearful heart. Be strong, fear not: behold, your God will come with vengeance, even God with a recompence; he will come and save you. Then the eyes of the blind shall be opened, and the ears of the deaf shall be unstopped. Then shall the lame man leap as an hart, and the tongue of the dumb sing: for in the wilderness shall waters break out, and streams in the desert . . . And the ransomed of the Lord shall return and come to Zion with songs and everlasting joy upon their heads: they shall obtain joy and gladness, and sorrow and sighing shall flee away (Isa. 35:4-10).

Rejoice greatly, O daughter of Zion: shout, O daughter of Jerusalem: behold thy King cometh unto thee: he is just, and having salvation: lowly, and riding upon an ass, and upon a colt the foal of an ass. And I will cut off the chariot from Ephraim, and the horse from Jerusalem, and the battle bow shall be cut off: and he shall speak peace unto the heathen: and his dominion shall be from sea even to sea, and from the river even to the ends of the earth (Zech. 9:9, 10).

And the Lord shall be king over all the earth: in that day shall there be one Lord, and his name one (Zech. 14:9).

See also Heb. 11:8-16.

(c)   The promises were renewed to Isaac and Jacob, who are henceforth associated with Abraham in Scriptures of promise.

And the Lord appeared unto him, and said, Go not down into Egypt; dwell in the land which I shall tell thee of: sojourn in this land, and I will be with thee, and will bless thee: for unto thee, and unto thy seed, I will give all these countries, and I will perform the oath which I sware unto Abraham thy father: and I will make thy seed to multiply as the stars of heaven, and will give unto thy seed all these countries; and in thy seed shall all nations of the earth be blessed . . . And the man waxed great, and went forward, and grew until he became very great: for he had possession of flocks, and possession of herds, and great store of servants, and the Philistines envied him (Gen. 26:3-4, 13, 14).

Thou wilt perform the truth to Jacob, and the mercy to Abraham, which thou hast sworn into our fathers from the days of old (Miah 7:20).

There shall be weeping and gnashing of teeth, when ye shall see Abraham, and Isaac, and Jacob, and all the prophets, in the kingdom of God, and you yourselves thrust out (Luke 13:28).

(d)   The promises received a partial fulfilment in Israel's occupation of Palestine (Neh. 9:7, 8), but their ultimate, perfect and lasting fulfilment, especially in their personal application to Abraham and all his faithful line, is associated with Christ and his Kingdom.

And he gave him none inheritance in it (the land), no, not so much as to set his foot on: yet he promised that he would give it to him for a possession, and to his seed after him, when as yet he had no child (Acts 7:5).

These all died in faith, not having received the promises, but having seen them afar off, and were persuaded of them, and embraced them, and confessed that they were strangers and pilgrims on the earth . . . And these all, having obtained a good report through faith, received not the promise: God having provided some better thing for us, that they without us should not be made perfect (Heb. 11:13, 39, 40).

Blessed be the Lord God of Israel; for he hath visited and redeemed his people, and hath raised up an horn of salvation for us in the house of his servant David: as he spake by the mouth of his holy prophets, which have been since the world began: that we should be saved from our enemies, and from the hand of all that hate us; to perform the mercy promised to our fathers, and to remember his holy covenant; the oath which he sware to our father Abraham (Luke 1:68-73).

And I say unto you, That many shall come from the east and west, and shall sit down with Abraham, and Isaac, and Jacob, in the kingdom of heaven (Matt. 8:11).

Now I say that Jesus Christ was a minister of the circumcision for the truth of God, to confirm the promises made unto the fathers; and that the Gentiles might glorify God for his mercy; as it is written, For this cause I will confess to thee among the Gentiles, and sing unto thy name. And again he saith, Rejoice, ye Gentiles, with his people. And again, Praise the Lord, all ye Gentiles; and laud him, all ye people. And again, Esaias saith, There shall be a root of Jesse, and he that shall rise to reign over the Gentiles; in him shall the Gentiles trust (Rom. 15:8-12).

(e)   When Abraham's descendants had become fully established as God's Kingdom in the land of Palestine and David ruled over them, God revealed His purpose concerning the future of mankind. A descendant of David who would also be the Son of God should reign on David's restored and glorified throne forever.

The heir to David's throne is Jesus Christ.

(The significance of the first verse of the New Testament should be noted in connection with God's promises to Abraham and David.)

And when thy days be fulfilled, and thou shalt sleep with thy fathers, I will set up they seed after thee, which shall proceed out of thy bowels, and I will establish his kingdom. He shall build an house for my name, and I will establish the throne of his kingdom forever. I will be his father, and he shall be my son. If he commit iniquity, I will chasten him with the rod of men, and with the stripes of the children of men: but my mercy shall not depart away from him, as I took it from Saul, whom I put away before thee. And thine house and thy kingdom shall be established for ever before thee: thy throne shall be established for ever (2 Sam. 7:12-16).

The Lord hath sworn in truth unto David; he will not turn from it; Of the fruit of thy body will I set upon thy throne (Psa. 132:11).

And the angel said unto her, Fear not, Mary: for thou has found favour with God. And behold, thou shalt conceive in thy womb, and bring forth a son, and shalt call his name JESUS. He shall be great, and shall be called the Son of the Highest: and the Lord God shall give unto him the throne of his father David: and he shall reign over the house of Jacob for ever; and of his kingdom there shall be no end (Luke 1:30-33).

God had sworn with an oath to him (David) that of the fruit of his loins, according to the flesh, he would raise up Christ to sit on his throne (Acts 2:30).

Now these be the last words of David. David the son of Jesse said, and the man who was raised up on high, the anointed of the God of Jacob, and the sweet psalmist of Israel, said, The Spirit of the Lord spake by me, and his word was in my tongue. The God of Israel said, the Rock of Israel spake to me, He that ruleth over men must be just, ruling in the fear of God . . . Although my house be not so with God; yet he hath made with me an everlasting covenant, ordered in all things, and sure: for this is all my salvation, and all my desire, although he make it not to grow (2 Sam. 23:1-3,5).

For unto us a child is born, unto us a son is given: and the government shall be upon his shoulder: and his name shall be called Wonderful, Counsellor, The mighty God, The everlasting Father, The Prince of Peace. Of the increase of his government and peace there shall be no end, upon the throne of David, and upon his kingdom, to order it, and to establish it with judgment and with justice from henceforth even for ever. The zeal of the Lord of hosts will perform this (Isa. 9:6, 7).

See also Isaiah 11:1-10

(f)   The unique character of the Kingdom of God was further revealed through the ministry of the prophets.

The word that Isaiah to son of Amoz saw concerning Judah and Jerusalem. And it shall come to pass in the last days, that the mountain of the Lord's house shall be established in the top of the mountains, and shall be exalted above the hills; and all nations shall flow unto it. And many people shall go and say, Come ye, and let us go up to the mountain of the Lord, to the house of the God of Jacob; and he will teach us of his ways, and we will walk in his paths: for out of Zion shall go forth the law, and the word of the Lord from Jerusalem. And he shall judge among the nations, and shall rebuke many people: and they shall beat their swords into plowshares, and their spears into pruning hooks: nation shall not lift up sword against nation, neither shall they learn war any more (Isa. 2:1-4).

And in this mountain shall the Lord of hosts make unto all people a feast of fat things, a feast of wines on the lees, of fat things full of marrow, of wines on the lees well refined. And he will destroy in this mountain the face of the covering cast over all people, and the vail that is spread over all nations. He will swallow up death in victory; and the Lord God will wipe away tears from off all faces; and the rebuke of his people shall he take away from off all the earth; for the Lord hath spoken it. And it shall be said in that day, Lo, this is our God; we have waited for him, and he will save us: this is the Lord; we have waited for him, we will be glad and rejoice in his salvation (Isa. 25:6-9).

Then the eyes of the blind shall be opened, and the ears of the deaf shall be unstopped. Then shall the lame man leap as an hart, and the tongue of the dumb sing: for in the wilderness shall waters break out, and streams in the desert . . . And an highway shall be there, and a way, and it shall be called

The way of holiness; the unclean shall not pass over
it; but it shall be for those: the wayfaring men,
though fools, shall not err therein . . . And the
ransomed of the Lord shall return, and come to Zion
with songs and everlasting joy upon their heads: they
shall obtain joy and gladness, and sorrow and sighing
shall flee away (Isa. 35:5, 6, 8, 10).

For the nation and kingdom that will not serve thee
shall perish; yea, those nations shall be utterly
wasted . . . Violence shall no more be heard in thy
land, wasting nor destruction within thy borders; but
thou shalt call thy walls Salvation, and thy gates
Praise . . . Thy people also shall be all righteous:
they shall inherit the land for ever, the branch of my
planting, the work of my hands, that I may be
glorified (Isa. 60:12, 18, 21).

For, behold, I create new heavens and a new earth:
and the former shall not be remembered, nor come
into mind. But be ye glad and rejoice for ever in that
which I create: for, behold, I create Jerusalem a
rejoicing, and her people a joy. And I will rejoice in
Jerusalem, and joy in my people: and the voice of
weeping shall be no more heard in her, nor the voice
of crying. There shall be no more thence an infant of
days, nor an old man that hath not filled his days: for
the child shall die an hundred years old; but the
sinner being an hundred years old shall be accursed
(Isa. 65:17-20).

Behold, the days come, saith the Lord, that I will
perform that good thing which I have promised unto
the house of Israel and to the house of Judah. In
those days, and at that time, will I cause the Branch
of righteousness to grow up into David; and he shall
execute judgment and righteousness in the land. In
those days shall Judah be saved, and Jerusalem shall
dwell safely: and this is the name wherewith she shall
be called. The Lord our righteousness (Jer. 33:14-
16).

Thus speaketh the Lord of hosts, saying, Behold the
man whose name is The BRANCH; and he shall
grow up out of his place, and he shall build the
temple of the Lord: even he shall build the temple of
the Lord; and he shall bear the glory, and shall sit
and rule upon his throne; and he shall be a priest
upon his throne: and the counsel of peace shall be
between them both (Zech. 6:12, 13).

And the Lord shall be king over all the earth: in that
day shall there be one Lord, and his name one . . .
And it shall come to pass, that every one that is left
of all the nations which came against Jerusalem shall
even go up from year to year to worship the King,
the Lord of hosts, and to keep the feast of tabernacles . . . In that day shall there be upon the bells of
the horses, HOLINESS UNTO THE LORD; and
the pots in the Lord's house shall be like the bowls
before the alter. Yea, every pot in Jerusalem and in

Judah shall be holiness unto the Lord of hosts; and
all they that sacrifice shall come and take of them,
and seethe therein: and in that day there shall be no
more the Canaanite in the house of the Lord of hosts
(Zech. 14:9, 16, 20, 21).

Behold, I will send my messenger, and he shall
prepare the way before me: and the Lord, whom ye
seek, shall suddenly come to his temple, even the
messenger of the covenant, whom ye delight in:
behold, he shall come, saith the Lord of hosts. But
who may abide the day of his coming? and who shall
stand when he appeareth? for he is like a refiner's
fire, and like fullers' soap: and he shall sit as a refiner
and purifier of silver: and he shall purify the sons of
Levi, and purge them as gold and silver, that they
may offer unto the Lord an offering in righteousness.
Then shall the offering of Judah and Jerusalem be
pleasant unto the Lord, as in the days of old, and as
in former years (Mal. 3:1-4).

And he shall send Jesus Christ, which before was
preached unto you: whom the heaven must receive
until the times of restitution of all things, which God
hath spoken by the mouth of all his holy prophets
since the world began (Acts 3:20, 21).

THE KINGDOM OF ISRAEL

22. "Salvation is of the Jews", Jesus said. The Kingdom
to be established is so far rooted in God's dealings
with the Jews in the past that it is described as the
Kingdom of Israel restored, enlarged and perfected.

(a) The kingdom of Israel, as divinely constituted at
Sinai and established in the land of Palestine was
the kingdom of God.

And of all my sons (for the Lord hath given me
many sons), he hath chosen Solomon my son to sit
upon the throne of the kingdom of the Lord over
Israel (1 Chron. 28:5).

Then Solomon sat on the throne of the Lord as king
instead of David his father, and prospered; and all
Israel obeyed him (1 Chron. 29:23).

And now ye think to withstand the kingdom of the
Lord in the hand of the sons of David (2 chron.
13:8).

(b) It was divinely overturned on account of the
iniquity of its rulers and people.

For he rent Israel from the house of David; and they
made Jeroboam the son of Nebat king: and Jeroboam
drave Israel from following the Lord, and made
them sin a great sin. For the children of Israel
walked in all the sins of Jeroboam which he did; they
departed not from them; until the Lord removed
Israel out of his sight, as he had said by all his
servants the prophets. So was Israel carried away out
of their own land to Assyria unto this day (2 Kings
17:21-23).

And thou, profane wicked prince of Israel, whose
day is come, when iniquity shall have an end, Thus,
saith the Lord God; Remove the diadem, and take
off the crown: this shall not be the same: exalt him

that is low, and abase him that is high. I will overturn, overturn, overturn, it: and it shall be no more, until he come whose right it is: and I will give it him (Ezek. 21:25-27).

For the children of Israel shall abide many days without a king, and without a prince, and without a sacrifice, and without an image, and without an ephod, and without teraphim (Hosea 3:4).

And they shall fall by the edge of the sword, and shall be led away captive into all nations: and Jerusalem shall be trodden down of the Gentiles, until the times of the Gentiles be fulfilled (Luke 21:24).

I have sent also unto you all my servants the prophets, rising up early and sending them, saying, Return ye now every man from his evil way, and amend your doing, and go not after other gods to serve them, and ye shall dwell in the land which I have given to you and to your fathers: but ye have not inclined your ear, nor hearkened unto me . . . Therefore thus saith the Lord God of hosts, the God of Israel; Behold I will bring upon Judah and upon all the inhabitants of Jerusalem all the evil that I have pronounced against them: because I have spoken unto them, but they have not heard; and I have called unto them, but they have not answered (Jer. 35:15 and 17).

(c) It is to be re-established in glory.

In that day will I raise up the tabernacle of David that is fallen, and close up the breaches thereof; and I will raise up his ruins, and I will build it as in the days of old (Amos 9:11).

Lift up thine eyes round about, and see: all they gather themselves together, they come to thee: thy sons shall come from far, and thy daughters shall be nursed at thy side (Isa. 60:4).

And the Lord shall inherit Judah his portion in the holy land, and shall choose Jerusalem again (Zech. 2:12).

But upon mount Zion shall be deliverance, and there shall be holiness; and the house of Jacob shall possess their possessions . . . And the captivity of this host of the children of Israel shall possess that of the Canaanites . . . And saviours shall come up on mount Zion to judge the mount of Esau; and the kingdom shall be the Lord's (Obadiah 17, 20, 21).

But in the last days it shall come to pass that the mountain of the house of the Lord shall be established in the top of the mountains, and it shall be exalted above the hills; and people shall flow unto it. And many nations shall come, and say. Come, and let us go up to the mountain of the Lord, and to the house of the God of Jacob; and he will teach us of his ways, and we will walk in his paths: for the law shall go forth of Zion, and the word of the Lord from Jerusalem. And he shall judge among many people, and rebuke strong nations afar off; and they shall beat their swords into plowshares, and their spears into pruninghooks: nation shall not lift up a sword against nation, neither shall they learn war any more. But they shall sit every man under his vine and under his fig tree; and none shall make them afraid: for the mouth of the Lord of hosts hath spoken it. For all people will walk every one in the name of his god, and we will walk in the name of the Lord our God for ever and ever. In that day, saith the Lord, will I assemble her that halteth, and I will gather her that is driven out, and her that I have afflicted; and I will make her that halted a remnant, and her that was cast far off a strong nation: and the Lord shall reign over them in mount Zion from henceforth, even for ever. And thou, O tower of the flock, the strong hold of the daughter of Zion, unto thee shall it come, even the first dominion: the kingdom shall come to the daughter of Jerusalem (Micah 4:1-8).

When they therefore were come together, they asked of him, saying, Lord, wilt thou at this time restore again the kingdom to Israel? And he said unto them, It is not for you to know the times or the seasons, which the Father hath put in his own power (Acts 1:6, 7).

23. The establishment of the Kingdom of God will thus involve the regathering of the Jews to the land of Palestine which will be restored to its former fertility, and made wondrously beautiful.

And it shall come to pass in that day, that the Lord shall set his hand again the second time to recover the remnant of his people, which shall be left, from Assyria, and from Egypt, and from Pathros, and from Cush, and from Elam, and from Shinar, and from Hamath, and from the islands of the sea. And he shall set up an ensign for the nations, and shall assemble the outcasts of Israel, and gather together the dispersed of Judah from the four corners of the earth (Isa. 11:11, 12).

For the Lord shall comfort Zion: he will comfort all her waste places; and he will make her wilderness like Eden, and her desert like the garden of the Lord; joy and gladness shall be found therein, thanksgiving and the voice of melody (Isa. 51:3).

Whereas thou hast been forsaken and hated, so that no man went through thee, I will make thee an eternal excellency, a joy of many generations (Isa. 60:15).

Hear the word of the Lord, O ye nations, and declare it in the isles afar off, and say, He that scattered Israel will gather him, and keep him, as a shepherd doth his flock . . . Behold, the days come, said the Lord, that I will sow the house of Israel and the house of Judah with the seed of man, and with the seed of beast. And it shall come to pass, that like as I have watched over them, to pluck up, and to break down, and to throw down, and to destroy, and to afflict; so will I watch over them, to build, and to plant, saith the Lord (Jer. 31:10, 27, 28).

And all the nations shall call you blessed: for ye shall be a delightsome land, said the Lord of hosts (Mal. 3:12).

Therefore say unto the house of Israel, Thus saith the Lord God; I do not this for your sakes, O house of Israel, but for mine holy name's sake, which ye have profaned among the heathen, whither ye went. And I will sanctify my great name, which was profaned among the heathen, which ye have profaned in the midst of them; and the heathen shall know that I am the Lord, saith the Lord God, when I shall be sanctified in you before their eyes. For I will take you from among the heathen, and gather you out of all countries, and will bring you into your own land (Ezek. 36:22-24).

And the desolate land shall be tilled, whereas it lay desolate in the sight of all that passed by. And they shall say, This land that was desolate is become like the garden of Eden; and the waste and desolate and ruined cities are become fenced, and are inhabited (Ezek. 37:34-36).

Thus saith the Lord God; Behold, I will take the children of Israel from among the heathen, whither they be gone, and will gather them on every side, and bring them into their own land: and I will make them one nation in the land upon the mountains of Israel: and one king shall be king to them all: and they shall be no more two nations, neither shall they be divided into two kingdoms any more at all (Ezek. 37:218 22).

Thus saith the Lord of hosts; Behold, I will save my people from the east country, and from the west country. And I will bring them, and they shall dwell in the midst of Jerusalem: and they shall be my people, and I will be their God, in truth and in righteousness (Zech. 8:7, 8).

And all the nations shall call you blessed: for ye shall be a delightsome land, saith the Lord of hosts (Mal. 3:12).

24. Jerusalem, rebuilt and glorified, will become the metropolis of God's Kingdom which will embrace all nations.

Beautiful for situation, the joy of the whole earth, is Mount Zion, on the sides of the north, the city of the great King (Psa. 48:2).

Then the moon shall be confounded, and the sun ashamed, when the Lord of hosts shall reign in mount Zion, and in Jerusalem, and before his ancients gloriously (Isa. 25:23).

Awake, awake; put on thy strength, O Zion; put on thy beautiful garments, O Jerusalem, the holy city; for henceforth there shall no more come into thee the uncircumcised and the unclean (Isa. 52:1).

The sons also of them that afflicted thee shall come bending unto thee; and all they that despised thee shall bow themselves down at the soles of thy feet; and they shall call thee, The city of the Lord, The Zion of the Holy One of Israel (Isa. 60:14).

At that time they shall call Jerusalem the throne of the Lord; and all the nations shall be gathered unto it, to the name of the Lord, to Jerusalem: neither shall they walk any more after the imagination of their evil heart (Jer. 3:17).

And many nations shall come, and say, Come, and let us go up to the mountain of the Lord, and to the house of the God of Jacob; and he will teach us of his ways, and we will walk in his paths: for the law shall go forth of Zion, and the word of the Lord from Jerusalem . . . And I will make her that halted a remnant, and her that was cast far off a strong nation: and the Lord shall reign over them in mount Zion from henceforth, even for ever. And thou, O tower of the flock, the strong hold of the daughter of Zion, unto thee shall it come, even the first dominion; the kingdom shall come to the daughter of Jerusalem (Micah 4:2, 7, 8).

And it shall come to pass, that every one that is left of all the nations which came against Jerusalem shall even go up from year to year to worship the King, the Lord of Hosts, and to keep the feast of tabernacles (Zech. 14:16).

But I say unto you, Swear not at all; neither by heaven; for it is God's throne; nor by the earth; for it is his footstool: neither by Jerusalem: for it is the city of the great King (Matt. 5:34, 35).

25. The Kingdom of God will be a visible, irresistible and everlasting dominion to be established on earth in the place of all existing kingdoms for the purpose of subjecting, blessing and perfecting the world.

And in the days of these kings shall the God of heaven set up a kingdom, which shall never be destroyed: and the kingdom shall not be left for other people, but it shall break in pieces and consume all these kingdoms, and it shall stand forever (Dan. 2:44).

I saw in the night visions, and, behold, one like the Son of Man came with the clouds of heaven, and came to the Ancient of days, and they brought him near before him. And there was given him dominion, and glory, and a kingdom, that all people, nations and languages, should serve him: his dominion is an everlasting dominion, which shall not pass away, and his kingdom that which shall not be destroyed . . . And the kingdom and dominion, and the greatness of the kingdom under the whole heaven, shall be given to the people of the saints of the most High, whose kingdom is an everlasting kingdom, and all dominions shall serve and obey him (Dan. 7:13, 14, 27).

And the Lord shall be king over all the earth: in that day shall there be one Lord, and his name one (Zech. 14:9).

Ask of me, and I shall give thee for heathen for thine inheritance, and the uttermost parts of the earth for thy possession. Thou shalt break them with a rod of iron; thou shalt dash them in pieces like a potter's vessel (Psa. 2:8, 9).

And the seventh angel sounded: and there were great voices in heaven, saying. The kingdoms of this world are become the kingdoms of our Lord, and of his Christ: and he shall reign for ever and ever (Rev. 11:15).

And I saw heaven opened, and behold a white horse; and he that sat upon him was called Faithful and True, and in righteousness he doth judge and make war. His eyes were as a flame of fire, and on his head were many crowns; and he had a name written, that no man knew, but he himself. And he was clothed with a vesture dipped in blood: and his name is called The Word of God. And the armies which were in heaven followed him upon white horses, clothed in fine linen, white and clean. And out of his mouth goeth a sharp sword, that with it he should smite the nations: and he shall rule them with a rod of iron: and he treadeth the winepress of the fierceness and wrath of Almighty God (Rev. 19:11-16).

26. Christ and his saints will reign a thousand years, until all that is evil, including finally death itself, is abolished.

And I saw an angel come down from heaven, having the key of the bottomless pit and a great chain in his hand. And he laid hold on the dragon, that old serpent, which is the Devil, and Satan, and bound him a thousand years, and cast him into the bottomless pit, and shut him up, and set a seal upon him, that he should deceive the nations no more till the thousand years should be fulfilled: and after that he must be loosed a little season. And I saw thrones, and they sat upon them, and judgment was given unto them: and I saw the souls of them that were beheaded for the witness of Jesus, and for the word of God, and which had not worshipped the beast, neither his image, neither had received his mark upon their foreheads, or in their hands; and they lived and reigned with Christ a thousand years. But the rest of the dead lived not again until the thousand years were finished. This is the first resurrection. Blessed and holy is he that hath part in the first resurrection: on such the second death hath no power, but they shall be priests of God and of Christ, and shall reign with him a thousand years. And when the thousand years are expired, Satan shall be loosed out of his prison, and shall go out to deceive the nations which are in the four quarters of the earth, Gog and Magog, to gather them together to battle: the number of whom is as the sand of the sea. And they went up on the breadth of the earth, and compassed the camp of the saints about, and the beloved city: and fire came down from God out of heaven, and devoured them . . . And I saw the dead, small and great, stand before God, and the books were opened: and another book was opened, which is the book of life: and the dead were judged out of those things which were written in the books, according to their works. And the sea gave up the dead which were in it; and death and hell delivered up the dead which were in them: and they were judged every man according to their works. And death and hell were cast into the lake of fire. This is the second death. And whosoever was not found written in the book of life was cast into the lake of fire (Rev. 20:1-9, 12-15).

There shall be no more thence an infant of days, nor an old man that hath not filled his days: for the child shall die an hundred years old; but the sinner being an hundred years old shall be accursed (Isa. 65:20).

Then cometh the end, when he shall have delivered up the kingdom to God, even the Father; when he shall have put down all rule and all authority and power. For he must reign, till he hath put all enemies under his feet. The last enemy that shall be destroyed is death. For he hath put all things are put under him, it is manifest that he is excepted, which did put all things under him. And when all things shall be subdued unto him, then shall the Son also himself be subject unto him that put all things under him, that God may be all in all (1 Cor. 15:24-28).

27. The Gospel preached by Jesus and the apostles concerns the Kingdom of God.

And Jesus went about all Galilee, teaching in the synagogues, and preaching the gospel of the kingdom, and healing all manner of sickness and all manner of disease among the people (Matt. 4:23).

Now after that John was put in prison, Jesus came into Galilee, preaching the gospel of the kingdom of God (Mark 1:14).

And it came to pass afterward, that he went throughout every city and village, preaching and showing the glad tidings of the kingdom of God (Luke 8:1).

But when they believed Philip preaching the things concerning the kingdom of God, and the name of Jesus Christ, they were baptized, both men and women (Acts 8:12).

And he went into the synagogue, and spake boldly for the space of three months, disputing and persuading the things concerning the kingdom of God (Acts 19:8).

And now, behold, I know that ye all among whom I have gone preaching the kingdom of God, shall see my face no more (Acts 20:25).

Preaching the kingdom of God and teaching those things which concern the Lord Jesus Christ, with all confidence, no man forbidding him (Acts 28:31).

God by the Gospel invites men to participate in this Kingdom and share with Christ in the glory.

Then shall the King say unto them on his right hand, Come, ye blessed of my Father, inherit the kingdom prepared for you from the foundation of the world (Matt. 25:34).

Fear not, little flock; for it is your Father's good pleasure to give you the kingdom (Luke 12:32).

That ye would walk worthy of God, who hath called you unto his kingdom and glory (1 Thess. 2:12).

Hath not God chosen the poor of this world, rich in faith, and heirs of the kingdom which he hath promised to them that love him? (James 2:5).

Wherefore the rather, brethren, give diligence to make your calling and election sure: for if ye do these things, ye shall never fall: for so an entrance shall be ministered unto you abundantly into the everlasting kingdom of our Lord and Saviour Jesus Christ (2 Peter 1:10, 11).

And he that overcometh, and keepeth my works unto the end, to him will I give power over the nations: and he shall rule them with a rod of iron; as the vessels of a potter shall they be broken to shivers: even as I received of my Father (Rev. 2:26, 27).

I charge thee therefore before God, and the Lord Jesus Christ, who shall judge the quick and the dead at his appearing and his kingdom . . . Henceforth there is laid up for me a crown of righteousness, which the Lord, the righteous judge, shall give me at that day: and not to me only, but unto all them also that love his appearing (2 Tim. 4:1 and 8).

28. The Way to God's Kingdom and eternal life is by accepting God's gracious invitation, believing His word, and obeying His will. This involves;

A DECLARATION OF THE TRUTH REVEALED IN THE BIBLE AS DISTINGUISHABLE FROM THE THEOLOGY OF CHRISTENDOM (AMENDED CHRISTADELPHIANS) (continued)

(a)   Belief in His Son as Saviour and Lord.

For God so loved the world, that he gave his only begotten Son, that whosoever believeth in him should not perish, but have everlasting life . . . He that believeth on the Son hath everlasting life: and he that believeth not the Son shall not see life; but the wrath of God abideth on him (John 3:16, 36).

And this is the will of him that sent me, that every one which seeth the Son, and believeth on him, may have everlasting life: and I will raise him up at the last day (John 6:40).

Jesus saith unto him, Thomas, because thou hast seen me, thou hast believed: blessed are they that have not seen, and yet have believed . . . But these are written, that ye might believe that Jesus is the Christ, the Son of God; and that believing ye might have life through his name (John 20:29, 31).

And they said, Believe on the Lord Jesus Christ, and thou shalt be saved, and thy house (Acts 16:31).

If thou shalt confess with thy mouth the Lord Jesus, and shalt believe in thine heart that God hath raised him from the dead, thou shalt be saved (Rom. 10:9).

(b)   Repentance from past sin, error or indifference.

From that time Jesus began to preach, and to say, Repent: for the kingdom of heaven is at hand (Matt. 4:17).

The time is fulfilled, and the kingdom of God is at hand: repent ye: and believe the gospel (Mark 1:15).

There were present at that season some that told him of the Galilaeans, whose blood Pilate had mingled with their sacrifices. And Jesus answering said unto them, Suppose ye that these Galilaeans were sinners above all the Galilaeans, because they suffered such things? I tell you, Nay: but, except ye repent, ye shall all likewise perish. Or those eighteen, upon whom the tower in Siloam fell, and slew them, think ye that they were sinners above all men that dwelt in Jerusalem? I tell you. Nay: but, except ye repent ye shall all likewise perish (Luke 13:1-5).

Repent ye therefore, and be converted, that your sins may be blotted out, when the times of refreshing shall come from the presence of the Lord (Acts 3:19).

And the times of this ignorance God winked at; but now commandeth all men every where to repent (Acts 17:30).

The Lord is not slack concerning his promise, as some men count slackness; but is longsuffering to us-ward, not willing that any should perish, but that all should come to repentance (2 Peter 3:9).

(c)   Baptism for the remission of sins.

Go ye therefore, and teach all nations, baptizing them in the name of the Father, and of the Son, and of the Holy Spirit: teaching them to observe all things whatsoever I have commanded you: and lo, I am with you alway, even unto the end of the world (Matt. 28:19, 20).

He that believeth and is baptized shall be saved; but he that believeth not shall be damned (Mark 16:16).

Jesus answered, Verily, verily, I say unto thee, Except a man be born of water and of the Spirit, he cannot enter into the kingdom of God (John 3:5).

The Peter said unto them, Repent, and be baptized every one of you in the name of Jesus Christ for the remission of sins, and ye shall receive the gift of the Holy Spirit (Acts 2:38).

But when they believed Philip preaching the things concerning the kingdom of God, and the name of Jesus Christ, they were batized, both men and women. Then Simon himself believed also: and when he was baptized, he continued with Philip, and wondered, beholding the miracles and signs which were done . . . And as they went on their way, they came upon a certain water: and the eunuch said, See, here is water; what doth hinder me to be baptized. And Philip said, If thou believest with all thine heart, thou mayest. And he answered and said, I believe that Jesus Christ is the Son of God. And he commanded the chariot to stand still: and they went down both into the water, both Philip and the eunuch; and he baptized him. And when they were come up out of the water, the Spirit of the Lord caught away Philip, that the eunuch saw him no more: and he went on his way rejoicing (Acts 8:12, 13, 36-39).

And immediately there fell from his eyes as it had been scales: and he received sight forthwith, and arose, and was baptized (Acts 9:18).

For they heard them speak with tongues, and magnify God. Then answered Peter, Can any man forbid water, that these should not be baptized, which have received the Holy Spirit as well as we? And he commanded them to be baptized in the name of the Lord. Then prayed they him to tarry certain days (Acts 10:46-48).

And when she was baptized, and her household, she besought us, saying, If ye have judged me to be faithful to the Lord, come into my house, and abide there . . . And he took them the same hour of the night, and washed their stripes and was baptized, he and all his, straightway (Acts 16:15, 35).

The like figure whereunto even baptism doth also now save us (not the putting away of the filth of the flesh, but the answer of a good conscience toward God) by the resurrection of Jesus Christ (1 Peter 3:21).

(d)   This baptism as an act of faith unites the believer with Jesus Christ, the Saviour. Through a symbolic burial by immersion in water he is identified with Christ's death and resurrection. Baptism marks the end of the old undedicated life. It indicates, with the forgiveness of past sins, the

538

rising to a new life in Christ, with the privilege of being a son or daughter of God: and confers heirship to eternal life in the Lord's Kingdom at his advent.

What shall we say then? Shall we continue in sin, that grace may abound? God forbid. How shall we, that are dead to sin, live any longer therein? Know ye not, that so many of us as were baptized into Jesus Christ were baptized into his death? Therefore we are buried with him by baptism into death: that like as Christ was raised up from the dead by the glory of the Father, even so we also should walk in newness of life. For if we have been planted together in the likeness of his death, we shall be also in the likeness of his resurrection: knowing this, that our old man is crucified with him, that the body of sin might be destroyed, that henceforth we should not serve sin. For he that is dead is freed from sin. Now if we be dead with Christ, we believe that we shall also live with him (Rom. 6:1-8).

And such were some of you: but ye are washed, but ye are sanctified, but ye are justified in the name of the Lord Jesus, and by the Spirit of our God (1 Cor. 6:11).

That he might sanctify and cleanse it with the washing of water by the word (Eph. 5:26).

Jesus answered and said unto him, Verily, verily, I say unto thee, Except a man be born again, he cannot see the kingdom of God (John 3:5).

For ye are all the children of God by faith in Christ Jesus. For as many of you as have been baptized into Christ have put on Christ. There is neither Jew nor Greek, there is neither bond nor free, there is neither male nor female: for ye are all one in Christ Jesus. And if ye be Christ's, then are ye Abraham's seed, and heirs according to the promise (Gal. 3:26-29).

Not by works of righteousness which we have done, but according to his mercy he saved us, by the washing of regeneration, and renewing of the Holy Spirit (Titus 3:5).

(e)   Union with Christ involves a life devoted to God's service in love to Him and to one's neighbour, characterized by the regular, thoughtful reading of God's Word, prayer to God through Jesus for forgiveness, strength and guidance; the first-day remembrance of the Lord's saving death and resurrection in the breaking of bread with those of like precious fatih; the letting of the light of the Gospel shine in word and deed; the patient waiting for the Lord's advent; the forsaking of sin, the separation from all that is evil in the world, and the doing of good to all, especially to the household of faith.

Jesus said unto him, Thou shalt love the Lord thy God with all thy heart, and with all thy soul, and with all thy mind. This is the first and great commandment. And the second is like unto it, Thou shalt love thy neighbour as thyself. On these two commandments hang all the law and the prophets (Matt. 22:37-40).

If we say that we have fellowship with him, and walk in darkness, we lie, and do not the truth: but if we walk in the light, as he is in the light, we have fellowship one with another, and the blood of Jesus Christ his Son cleanseth us from all sin. If we say that we have no sin, we deceive ourselves, and the truth is not in us. If we confess our sins, he is faithful and just to forgive us our sins, and to cleanse us from all unrighteousness (1 John 1:6-9).

But continue thou in the things which thou hast learned and hast been assured of, knowing of whom thou hast learned them; and that from a child thou hast known the holy scriptures, which are able to make thee wise unto salvation through faith which is in Christ Jesus. All scripture is given by inspiration of God, and is profitable for doctrine, for reproof, for correction, for doctrine, for reproof, for correction, for instruction in righteousness: that the man of God may be perfect, thoroughly furnished unto all good works (2 Tim. 3:14-17).

Pray without ceasing (1 Thess. 5:17).

And it came to pass, that, as he was praying in a certain place, when he ceased, one of his disciples said unto him, Lord, teach us to pray, as John also taught his disciples. And he said unto them, when ye pray, say, Our Father which art in heaven, hollowed by thy name. They kingdom come. Thy will be done, as in heaven, so in earth. Give us day by day our daily bread. And forgive us our sins; for we also forgive every one that is indebted to us. And lead us not into temptation: but deliver us from evil (Luke 11:1-4).

But of that day and that hour knoweth no man, no, not the angels which are in heaven, neither the Son, but the Father. Take ye heed, watch and pray: for ye know not when the time is. For the Son of man is as a man taking a far journey, who left his house, and gave authority to his servants, and to every man his work, and commanded the porter to watch. Watch ye therefore: for ye know not when the master of the house cometh, at even, or at midnight, or at the cockcrowing, or in the morning: lest coming suddenly he find you sleeping. And what I say unto you I say unto all, Watch (Mark 13:32-37).

And as they did eat, Jesus took bread, and blessed, and brake it, and gave to them, and said, Take, eat: this is my body. And he took the cup, and when he had given thanks, he gave it to them: and they all drank of it. And he said unto them, This is my blood of the new testament, which is shed for many. Verily I say unto you, I will drink no more of the fruit of the vine, until that day that I drink it new in the kingdom of God (Mark 14:22-25).

And he took bread, and gave thanks, and brake it, and gave unto them, saying This is my body, which is given for you: this do in remembrance of me. Likewise also the cup after supper, saying, This cup is the new testament in my blood, which is shed for you (Luke 22:19, 20).

For I have received of the Lord that which also I delivered unto you, That the Lord Jesus the same night in which he was betrayed took bread: and when he had given thanks, he brake it, and said, Take, eat: this is my body, which is broken for you: this do in remembrance of me. After the same manner also he took the cup, when he had supped, saying, This cup is the new testament in my blood: this do ye, as oft as ye drink it, in remembrance of me. For as often as ye eat this bread, and drink this cup, ye do show the Lord's death till he come. Wherefore whosoever shall eat this bread, and drink this cup of the Lord, unworthily, shall be guilty of the body and blood of the Lord. But let a man examine himself, and so let him eat of that bread, and drink of that cup (1 Cor. 11:23-28).

Not forsaking the assembling of ourselves together, as the manner of some is; but exhorting one another: and so much the more, as ye see the day approaching (Heb. 10:25).

Preach the word; be instant in season, out of season, reprove, rebuke, exhort with all longsuffering and doctrine (2 Tim. 4:2).

Blessed are they which do hunger and thirst after righteousness: for they shall be filled. Blessed are the merciful: for they shall obtain mercy (Matt. 5:6, 7).

And to wait for his Son from heaven, whom he raised from the dead, even Jesus which delivered us from the wrath to come (1 Thess. 1:10).

Love not the world, neither the things that are in the world. If any man love the world, the love of the Father is not in him. For all that is in the world, the lust of the flesh, and the lust of the eyes, and the pride of life, is not of the Father, but is of the world. And the world passeth away, and the lust thereof; but he that doeth the will of God abideth forever (1 John 2; 15-17).

I beseech you therefore, brethren, by the mercies of God, that ye present your bodies a living sacrifice, holy, acceptable unto God, which is your reasonable service. And be not conformed to this world: but be ye transformed by the renewing of your mind, that ye may prove what is that good, and acceptable, and perfect, will of God (Rom. 12:1, 2).

As we have therefore opportunity, let us do good unto all men, especially unto them who are of the household of faith (Gal. 6:10).

Be careful for nothing; but in every thing by prayer and supplication with thanksgiving let your requests be made known unto God. And the peace of God, which passeth all understanding, shall keep your hearts and minds through Christ Jesus. Finally, brethren, whatsoever things are true, whatsoever things are honest, whatsoever things are just, whatsoever things are pure, whatsoever things are of good report; if there be any virtue, and if there by any praise, think on these things (Phil. 4:6-8).

Read also Psa. 119; Col. 3; Eph. 4:17-32 and very many other Scriptures.

AN APPENDIX

THE CALL TO SEPARATION. Some are at first disturbed to find that the true teaching of Scripture is very different from much popular religious belief, and wonder how so many can be wrong. The answer is that from the earliest times men were drawn away by false philosophy and eventually the apostles' forecasts of apostasy were fulfilled. The proof is fourfold:

1. The contrast between Scripture truth as set out in the preceding pages and current views, which may be briefly indicated as follows:

BIBLE TEACHING	CURRENT RELIGIOUS VIEWS
THE BIBLE	
A fully authoritative expression of God's unfolding purpose with the earth and His will for men.	Though unique, not thoroughly reliable.
GOD	
Is One.	Is three Persons in unity, often involving tritheism.
JESUS	
Son of God, subordinate to the Father: born of the virgin Mary, raised from the dead.	God the Son, co-equal with the Father. Some leading churchmen reject his virgin birth and resurrection.
MAN	
Mortal because of sin.	Possesses an immortal soul.
FINAL RECOMPENSE	
On earth, after resurrection, in the Kingdom of God to be established at Christ's return.	In heaven at death.
BAPTISM	
The act of faith and obedience ordained by God's grace for entry in a new life in Christ. A "burial" by immersion in water.	Baptism by immersion is unnecessary.

2. The witness of Scripture, foretelling departure from the truth, and calling men and women who believe to be separate, "in the world" but "not of the world".

There shall come in the last days scoffers, walking after their own lust, and saying, Where is the promise of his coming? For since the fathers fell asleep, all things continue as they were from the beginning of the creation (2 Peter 3:3, 4).

The time will come when they will not endure sound doctrine; but after their own lusts shall they heap to themselves teachers, having itching ears. And they shall turn away their ears from the truth, and shall be turned unto fables (2 Tim. 4:3, 4).

For I know this, that after my departing shall grievous wolves enter in among you not sparing the flock. Also of your own selves shall men arise, speaking perverse things, to draw away disciples after them (Acts 20:29, 30).

For, behold, the darkness shall cover the earth, and gross darkness the people (Isa. 60:2).

As the days of Noah were, so also shall the coming of the Son of Man be. For as in the days that were before the flood they were eating and drinking, marrying, and giving in marriage, until the day Noah entered into the ark, and knew not until the flood came and took them all away; so shall also the coming of the Son of Man be (Matt. 24:27-39).

Wherefore come out from among them, and be ye separate, saith the Lord, and touch not the unclean *thing*; and I will receive you, and will be a Father unto you, and ye shall be my sons and daughteres, saith the Lord Almighty (2 Cor. 6:17-18).

3. The Scriptures reveal that it is God's purpose at the present time to take out a people for His Name, and not to convert the world. Relatively few respond today.

Notes: *The Christadelphians originated with John Thomas, an early close associate of Alexander Campbell, one of the founders of the Christian Church (Disciples of Christ). Thomas left the Christian Church over a number of doctrinal points. Christadelphians do not believe in the Trinity (see item 2), humanity's natural immortality (see items 9, 10, and 13), and hell as a place of eternal torment (see items 15-17). They do believe in the necessity of baptism by immersion for salvation (see item 28c). In the 1890s the Christadelphians were split, at least in part, over a disagreement on eschatology. One group affirmed that only those who die "in Christ" (i.e., Christians) will be resurrected to face the judgment of Christ. The group amended the beliefs of the Christadelphians in accordance with those teachings and thus became know as Amended Christadelphians. This crucial doctrine, which continues to divide Christadelphians after almost a century, is presented in item 17. The statement reproduced here is circulated by the office of* The Christadelphian, *the leading Amended Christadelphian periodical, which is published in Birmingham, England.*

* * *

PREAMBLE TO A DESIGN FOR THE CHRISTIAN CHURCH (DISCIPLES OF CHRIST)

As members of the Christian Church,
We confess that Jesus is the Christ,
   the Son of the living God,
   and proclaim him Lord and Savior of the world.
In Christ's name and by his grace

we accept our mission of witness
   and service to all people.
We rejoice in God,
   maker of heaven and earth,
   and in the covenant of love
   which binds us to God and one another.
Through baptism into Christ
   we enter into newness of life
   and are made one with the whole people of God.
In the communion of the Holy Spirit
   we are joined together in discipleship
   and in obedience to Christ.
At the table of the Lord
   we celebrate with thanksgiving
   the saving acts and presence of Christ.
Within the universal church
   we receive the gift of ministry
   and the light of scripture.
In the bonds of Christian faith
   we yield ourselves to God
   that we may serve the One
   whose kingdom has no end.
Blessing, glory and honor
   be to God forever. Amen.

Notes: *The church bodies that have grown out of the work of such men as Alexander Campbell, Barton Stone, and James O'Kelley generally follow the theology and practice of the Baptists, out of which many of the early leaders and members of the Christian Churches had come. Baptism by immersion is almost universally accepted. An extreme congregational polity is followed, an outgrowth of the original committment to a "nondenominational" approach to church life.*

The Christian Churches as a whole are noncreedal and take the Bible as their standard of faith and practice. They have been reluctant to codify doctrinal affirmations into summary articles of belief and highly critical of individuals making the attempt. The Disciples of Christ has only recently produced a confessional statement.

During the 1960s the Christian Church (Disciples of Christ) involved itself in an intensive self-study which culminated in a denominational restructuring. A Design for the Christian Church (Disciples of Christ) has served as the constituting document for the restructured body. Adopted in 1968, it contains a preamble offering a broad doctrinal perspective, which allows a wide variety of theological opinions.

* * *

A DECLARATION OF THE TRUTH REVEALED IN THE BIBLE, THE SUBLIME AND SIMPLE THEOLOGY OF THE PRIMITIVE CHRISTIANS (UNAMENDED CHRISTADELPHIANS)

THE THINGS CONCERNING THE KINGDOM OF GOD

I. The gospel preached by Jesus when upon the earth had reference to THE KINGDOM OF GOD.

A DECLARATION OF THE TRUTH REVEALED IN THE BIBLE, THE SUBLIME AND SIMPLE THEOLOGY OF THE PRIMITIVE CHRISTIANS (UNAMENDED CHRISTADELPHIANS) (continued)

Now after that John was put in prison, Jesus came into Galilee preaching the gospel of the KINGDOM OF GOD (Mark 1:14).

And Jesus went about all Galilee teaching in their synagogues, and preaching the gosepl of THE KINGDOM (Matt. 4:17, 23).

And he said unto them, I must preach the KINGDOM OF GOD to other cities also; for therefore am I sent (Luke 4:43).

And it came to pass afterwards that he went throughout every city and village, preaching and shewing the glad tidings of THE KINGDOM OF GOD, and the twelve were with him (Luke 8:1).

ADDITIONAL TESTIMONIES (Matt. 9:35; 6:33; 13:19; Luke 9:11; 13:28).

II. The gospel preached by the Apostles had reference to the same thing—that is, THE KINGDOM OF GOD.

When they believed Philip, preaching THE THINGS CONCERNING THE KINGDOM OF GOD and the name of Jesus Christ they were baptized, both men and women (Acts 8: 12, 25).

And he (Paul) went into the synagogue and spake boldly for the space of three months, disputing and persuading THE THINGS CONCERNING THE KINGDOM OF GOD (Acts 19:8).

And now, behold, I know that ye all, among whom I (Paul) have gone preaching THE KINGDOM OF GOD, shall see my face no more (Acts 20:25).

Paul dwelt in his own hired house . . . preaching THE KINGDOM OF GOD, and teaching those things which concern the Lord Jesus Christ with all confidence, no man forbidding him (Acts 28:30, 31).

III. What is this Kingdom? It is a DIVINE POLITICAL DOMINION to be *established* on the earth, on the ruins of all existing governments, for the purpose of blessing and bringing the world into subjection of God.

And in the days of these kings shall the God of heaven SET UP A KINGDOM which shall never be destroyed, and the kingdom shall not be left to other people, but it *shall break in pieces and consume all these* kingdoms, and it shall stand for ever (Dan. 2:44; see also Dan. 7:13, 14, 18, 22, 27).

And *I will overthrow* the throne of kingdoms, and *I will destroy* the strength of the kingdoms of the heathen (Heb. nations).—(Hag. 2:22).

And the seventh angel sounded: and there were great voices in heaven, saying, THE KINGDOMS OF THIS WORLD ARE BECOME THE KINGDOMS OF OUR LORD AND OF HIS CHRIST, and he shall reign for ever and ever (Rev. 11:15).

And the Lord *shall be king* OVER ALL THE EARTH; *in that day* shall there be one Lord, and his name one (Zech. 14:9).

Ask of me, and I shall give thee the heathen (*i.e. nations*) for thine inheritance and the UTTERMOST PARTS OF THE EARTH *for* thy possession. Thou shalt break them with a rod of iron; thou shalt dash them in pieces like a potter's vessel (Psalm 2: 8, 9).

And I saw heaven opened, and behold, a white horse; and he that sat upon him was called Faithful and True, and in righteousness he doth *judge* and make *war* . . . Out of his mouth goeth a sharp sword, that with it he should *smite the nations;* and *he shall rule them* with a rod of iron and he treadeth the winepress of the fierceness and wrath of Almighty God. And he hath on his vesture and on his thigh a name written KING OF KINGS and LORD OF LORDS (Rev. 19:11, 13, 15, 16).

For he *must reign* till he hath put ALL ENEMIES under his feet (I Cor. 15:25).

IV. This purpose of God to establish a universal kingdom on earth, with Christ at its head, *has a connection with God's past dealings with the nation of Israel.* This connection must be perceived before the bearing of God's purpose can be clearly understood. To assist in the attainment of this understanding, consider the following facts:

a. The kingdom of Israel, as divinely constituted under the hand of Moses, and existent in the land of Palestine 3,000 years ago, was the kingdom of God.

And of all my sons (for the Lord hath given me many sons), he hath chosen Solomon my son to sit upon the throne of THE KINGDOM OF THE LORD over Israel (1 Chron. 28:5; see also 29:23).

And now ye think to withstand the KINGDOM OF THE LORD in the hand of the sons of David (2 Chron. 13:8).

b. It was divinely overturned and scattered to the winds on account of iniquity.

Return for thy servant's sake, the tribes of thine inheritance. The people of thy holiness have possessed it but a little while: our adversaries have trodden down thy sanctuary. We are thine: thou never barest rule over them (the nations); they were not called by thy name (Isa. 63:17-19).

And thou, profane wicked prince of Israel, whose day is come, when iniquity shall have an end, thus saith the Lord God: Remove the diadem and take off the crown; this shall not be the same: exalt him that is low, and abase him that is high. *I will overturn, overturn, overturn* it: and *it shall be no more,* UNTIL HE COME WHOSE RIGHT IT IS; AND I WILL GIVE IT HIM (Ezek. 21: 25-27).

For the children of Israel shall abide many days without a king, and without a prince, and without a sacrifice, and without an image, and without an ephod, and without teraphim. Afterwards shall the children of Israel return and seek the Lord their

God, and David (HEB. "beloved") their king; and shall fear the Lord and his goodness *in the latter days* (Hos. 3:4-5).

And they shall fall by the edge of the sword, and *shall be led away captive into all nations:* and Jerusalem shall be trodden down of the Gentiles, UNTIL the times of the Gentiles *be fulfilled* (Luke 21: 24; Matt. 23: 36-39).

c.   It is to be re-established.

Thou shalt arise, and have mercy upon Zion: FOR THE TIME to favour her, yea, THE SET TIME is come (Psa. 102;13).

And they shall BUILD the old wastes, they shall RAISE UP the former desolations, and they shall REPAIR *the waste cities, the desolation of* MANY GENERATIONS (Isa. 61: 4; 33: 20, 21).

In that day will I *raise up the Tabernacle of David that is fallen,* and close up the breaches thereof; and I will raise up his ruins, and I WILL BUILD IT AS IN THE DAYS OF OLD (Amos 9:11).

Cry yet, saying, Thus saith the Lord of Hosts: My cities through prosperity shall yet be spread abroad; *and the Lord shall* YET *comfort Zion, and shall* YET *choose Jerusalem* (Zech. 1: 16, 17).

The Lord shall inherit Judah, his portion in the holy land, and *shall choose Jerusalem* AGAIN (Zech. 2:12).

The Lord God shall give unto him (Jesus) *the throne of his father David,* and he shall reign over the house of Jacob for ever and of his KINGDOM there shall be no end (Luke 1:32, 33).

Lord, wilt thou at this time *restore again* THE KINGDOM *to Israel?* (Acts 1:6).

And to this agree the words of the prophets; as it is written. After this I will return, and will build again *the tabernacle of David, which is fallen down;* and I *will build again* the ruins thereof, and I will set it up (Acts 14:16; see also Amos 9:11, above).

V.   The Kindgom of God to be set up on the earth will be the ancient Kingdom of Israel restored.

In that day, saith the Lord, *will I assemble her* that halteth, and *I will gather her* that is driven out and her that I have afflicted. And I will make her that halted a remnant, and her that was cast far off *a strong nation;* and the LORD SHALL REIGN over them in Mount Zion from henceforth even for ever. And thou, O tower of the flock, the stronghold of the daughter of Zion, *unto thee shall it come, even* THE FIRST DOMINION; THE KINGDOM *shall come to the daughter of Jerusalem* (Micah 4:6-8).

But upon Mount Zion shall be deliverance, and there shall be holiness; and the house of Jacob shall possess their possessions . . .   And the captivity of this host of the children of Israel shall possess that of the Canaanites, even unto Zarephath; and the captivity of Jerusalem, which *is in Sepharad, shall possess the cities of the* south. And saviours shall come up on Mount Zion to judge the mount of Esau; AND THE KINGDOM SHALL BE THE LORD'S (Obad. 17, 20, 21).

VI.   The establishment of the Kingdom of God by the restoration of the Kingdom of Israel, will involve the gathering of the Jews from their present dispersion among the nations of the earth.

He shall *assemble the outcasts of Israel, and gather together the dispersed of Judah,* from the four corners of the earth (Isa. 11:12).

Hear the word of the Lord, O ye nations, and declare it in the isles afar off, and say, *He that scattered Israel* WILL GATHER HIM, *and keep him as a* shepherd doth his flock (Jer. 31:10).

Behold, I will *save my people from the east country, and from the west country:* and I will bring them, *and they shall dwell in the midst of Jerusalem;* and they shall be my people, and I will be their God in truth and in righteousness (Zech. 8:7, 8).

Behold the days come, saith the LORD, that I will sow *the house of Israel, and the house of Judah* with the seed of man, and with the seed of beast. And it shall come to pass, that like as I have watched over them, to pluck up, and to break down, and to throw down, and to destroy, and to afflict: *so will I watch over them, to build and to plant,* saith the Lord (Jer. 31:27, 28).

Behold the days come, saith the LORD, that *I will perform* THAT GOOD THING WHICH I HAVE PROMISED UNTO THE HOUSE OF ISRAEL, AND TO THE HOUSE OF JUDAH. *In those days, and at that time, will I cause the Branch of Righteousness to grow up unto David,* and he shall execute judgment and righteousness.—*In those days shall Judah be saved, and Jerusalem shall dwell safely,* and this is the name whereby she shall be called, THE LORD OUR RIGHTEOUSNESS (Jer. 33: 14-16).

I do not this for your sakes, O house of Israel, but for mine holy name's sake, which ye have profaned among the heathen, whither ye went. *For I will take you from among the heathen, and gather you out of all countries, and will bring you into your own land (Ezek. 36: 22-24).*

And say unto them, Thus saith the Lord God: Behold, *I will take the children of Israel from among the heathen,* whither they be gone, and will gather them on every side, and bring them into their own land: AND I WILL MAKE THEM ONE NATION *in the land upon the mountains of Israel;* and ONE KING SHALL be king to them all: and they shall be *no more* two nations, neither shall they be divided into two kingdoms *any more* at all (Ezek. 37: 21, 22).

And I will make her that halted a remnant, and *her that was cast far off a* strong nation; and the LORD shall reign *over them* in MOUNT ZION from henceforth, even for ever (Micah 4:7).

Thus saith the Lord of hosts; In those days shall it come to pass, that ten men shall take hold, out of all languages of the nations, even shall take hold of the skirt of him that is a Jew, saying, We will go with you; for we have heard that God is with you (Zech. 8:23).

And all nations shall call you blessed: for ye shall be a delightsome land, saith the Lord of hosts (Mal. 3:12).

A DECLARATION OF THE TRUTH REVEALED IN THE BIBLE, THE SUBLIME AND SIMPLE THEOLOGY OF THE PRIMITIVE CHRISTIANS (UNAMENDED CHRISTADELPHIANS) (continued)

VII. The city Jerusalem will then become the residence of the Lord Jesus, the headquarters and metropolis of the Kingdom of God, whose dominion will stretch to the utmost bounds of the earth.

Then the moon shall be confounded, and the sun ashamed, when the *Lord of Hosts shall reign* IN MOUNT ZION, *and* IN JERUSALEM, and before his ancients gloriously (Isa. 24:23).

Awake, awake, put on thy strength, O Zion; put on thy beautiful garments, O Jerusalem, THE HOLY CITY: for henceforth there shall *no more* come into thee the uncircumcised and the unclean (Isa. 52:1).

And they shall call thee, THE CITY OF THE LORD, THE ZION OF THE HOLY ONE OF ISRAEL (Isa. 60:14).

For behold, I create new heavens and a new earth; and the former shall not be remembered, nor come into mind. But be ye glad and rejoice for ever in that which I create: for behold, *I create Jerusalem a rejoicing, and her people a joy* (Isa. 65: 17, 18).

At that time they shall call *Jerusalem* THE THRONE OF THE LORD; and all the nations shall be gathered unto it, to the name of the LORD to *Jerusalem;* neither shall they walk any more after the imagination of their evil heart (Jer. 3:17).

Thus saith the Lord of hosts, the God of Israel: As yet they shall use this speech in the land of Judah and in the cities thereof when I shall bring agaign their captivity; The Lord bless, O HABITATION OF JUSTICE, *and* MOUNTAIN OF HOLINESS (Jer. 31:23).

Beautiful for situation, *the joy of the whole earth,* is Mount Zion, on the sides of the north, *the city of the great King* (Psa. 48:2).

The Lord shall reign over them in MOUNT ZION . . . THE KINGDOM SHALL COME TO THE DAUGHTER OF JERUSALEM (Micah 4:7, 8).

So shall ye know that I *am* the Lord your God, *dwelling in Zion, my holy mountain;* THEN SHALL JERUSALEM BE HOLY, *and there shall no strangers pass through her any more* (Joel 3:17).

And it shall come to pass, that every one that is left of all the nations which came against Jerusalem shall even *go up from year to year to worship the King,* the Lord of hosts, and to keep the feast of tabernacles (Zech. 14:16).

But I say unto you, Swear not at all . . . neither by Jerusalem, *for it is the city of the great King* (Matt. 5:34, 35).

VIII. The Supreme Ruler in this glorious order of things will be Jesus of Nazareth. It is important to put this in a more specific form, by calling attention to THE COVENANT MADE WITH DAVID, in which God promised him a SON, under whom his kingdom should be established for ever.

And when thy days be fulfilled, and thou shalt sleep with thy fathers, I will set up thy seed after thee, which shall proceed out of thy bowels, and I will establish his kingdom. He shall build a house for my name, and *I will establish the throne of his kingdom for ever.* If he commit iniquity, I will chasten him with the rod of men, and with the stripes of the children of men (2 Sam. 7:12-14).

The Lord HATH SWORN IN TRUTH UNTO DAVID; He will not turn from it; *Of the fruit of thy body will I set upon thy throne* (Psa. 132:11).

These be the last words of David . . . He that ruleth over men must be just, ruling in the fear of God. And HE SHALL BE AS THE LIGHT OF THE MORNING, when the sun riseth, even a morning without clouds; as the tender grass springing out of the earth by clear shining after rain. Although my house be not so with God: yet HE HATH MADE WITH ME AN EVERLASTING COVENANT, ordered in all things and sure: for this is all my salvation, and all my desire, although he make it not to grow. (2 Sam. 23:1, 3-5).

IX. The Son promised to David is Jesus Christ, who will sit on David's throne, when it is restored in the era of his re-appearing on the earth.

(David) being a prophet and knowing that God had sworn with an oath to him that of the fruit of his loins, according to the flesh, he would RAISE UP CHRIST TO SIT ON HIS THRONE (Acts 2:30).

And, behold, thou shalt conceive in thy womb, and bring forth a son, and shalt call his name JESUS. He shall be great, and shall be called the Son of the Highest; *and the Lord God shall give unto him* THE THRONE OF HIS FATHER DAVID. And he shall reign over the House of Jacob for ever; And of HIS KINGDOM there shall be no end (Luke 1:30-33).

And Pilate asked him, Art thou the King of the Jews? and he answering said unto him, Thou sayest it (Mark 15:2).

And Jesus said unto them, Verily I say unto you, That ye which have followed me, in the regeneration when THE SON OF MAN SHALL SIT IN THE THRONE OF HIS GLORY, ye also shall sit upon twelve thrones, judging the twelve tribes of Israel (Matt. 19:28).

Of the increase of his government and peace there shall be no end, UPON THE THRONE OF DAVID, AND UPON HIS KINGDOM, to order it, and to establish it with judgment and with justice from henceforth even for ever. The zeal of the Lord of hosts will perform this (Isa 9:7).

In those days, and at that time, will I cause the BRANCH OF RIGHTEOUSNESS to *grow up unto David:* and he shall execute judgment and righteousness in the land (Jer 33:15). Behold the man whose name is the Branch; and he shall grow up out of his place, and he *shall build the temple* of the Lord. Even he shall build the temple of the Lord . . . HE SHALL SIT AND RULE UPON HIS THRONE; and he shall be a priest upon his throne, and the counsel of peace shall be between them both (Zech. 6 12, 13).

X. The reward in store for those whom Christ shall acknowledge in the day of his glory, is A PARTICI-

PATION IN THE "GLORY, HONOUR, AND POWER" OF THE KINGDOM in the sense of being his associates and coadjutors (as kings and priests) in the work of ruling the world in righteousness.

THY KINGDOM COME. *Thy will be done on earth as it is in heaven* (Matt. 6:10).

Blessed are the meek: for they shall inherit the earth (Matt. 5:5; Psa. 37:11).

Therefore I say unto you, THE KINGDOM OF GOD shall be taken from you (Scribes and Pharisees) and given to a nation bringing forth the fruits thereof (viz., the saints, see 1 Peter 2:9).—Matt. 21:43).

Fear not, little flock, for it is your Father's good pleasure to GIVE YOU THE KINGDOM . . . and be yourselves like unto men that wait for their Lord, when he will return from the wedding (Luke 12:32, 36).

And I appoint unto you a KINGDOM, as my Father hath appointed unto me; that ye may eat and drink at my table in my kingdom, and *sit on thrones judging the twelves tribes of Israel* (Luke 22:29, 30).

I charge thee therefore before God, and the Lord Jesus Christ, who shall judge the quick and the dead at his appearing and HIS KINGDOM (2 Tim. 4:1).

Henceforth there is laid up for me a crown of righteousness, which the Lord, the righteous judge, shall give me at that day: *and not to me only,* BUT UNTO ALL THEM ALSO THAT LOVE HIS APPEARING (2 Tim. 4:8).

There shall be weeping and gnashing of teeth, when ye shall see Abraham, and Isaac, and Jacob, and all the prophets in the KINDGOM OF GOD, and ye yourselves thrust out. And they shall come from the east, and from the west, and from the north, and from the south, and SHALL SIT DOWN IN THE KINGDOM OF GOD (Luke 13:28, 29).

If we suffer, we shall also REIGN WITH HIM; if we deny him, he also will deny us (2 Tim. 2:12).

And hast made us unto our God KINGS AND PRIESTS; *and we shall reign* ON THE EARTH (Rev. 5:10).

But the saints of the Most High shall take THE KINGDOM, and possess the kingdom for ever, even for ever and ever . . . And the kingdom and dominion, and the greatness of the kingdom UNDER THE WHOLE HEAVEN, shall be given to the people of the saints of the Most High, whose kingdom is an everlasting kingdom, and all dominions shall serve and obey him (Dan. 7:18, 27).

And he that overcometh, and keepeth my works unto the end, to him will I give POWER OVER THE NATIONS: *and he shall rule them with a rod of iron,* as the vessels of a potter shall they be broken to shivers: even as I received of my father (Rev. 2:26, 27).

To him that overcometh will I grant to SIT WITH ME IN MY THRONE, even as I also overcame, and am set down with my Father in his throne (Rev. 3:21).

XI. The state of blessedness developed among the nations of the earth when they are thus ruled by Jesus and his brethren, has been the subject of promise from the earliest dealings of Jehovah with mankind, and will be the realization of the purpose enunciated from the beginning. The reader will perceive this in the consideration of THE COVENANT MADE WITH ABRAHAM, and its bearing upon the future development of the divine purpose. This covenant guaranteed:

FIRST. The ultimate blessing of all nations through him and his seed.

Now the Lord had said unto Abram, Get thee out of thy country, and from thy kindred, and from thy father's house, unto a land that I will show thee. And I will make of thee a great nation, and make thy name great; and thou shalt be a blessing. And I will bless them that bless thee, and curse him that curseth thee; AND IN THEE SHALL ALL FAMILIES *of the earth be blessed* (Gen. 12:1-3).

And the Scripture, foreseeing that God would justify the heathen through faith, preached before THE GOSPEL unto Abraham saying, *In thee shall all nations be blessed* (Gal. 3:8).

> SECOND. The everlasting, personal possession of the territory lying between the Euphrates and the Nile, known in the terms of modern geography as Syria and Israel, and Biblically as Canaan.

And the Lord said unto Abraham, after that Lot was separated from him, Lift up now thine eyes and look from the place where thou art, northward, and southward, and eastward, and westward: for *all the land which thou seest, to thee will I give it, and to thy seed for ever.* Arise, walk through the land in the length of it and in the breadth of it; FOR I WILL GIVE IT UNTO THEE (Gen. 13: 14-17; see also 12:7; 15: 8-18; 17:8).

XII. The promises made were renewed to Isaac and Jacob.

And the Lord appeared unto him (Isaac) and said, Sojourn in this land, and I will be with thee, and will bless thee; *for unto thee and unto thy seed I will* GIVE ALL THESE COUNTRIES, and I will perform the oath which I sware unto Abraham thy father (Gen. 26:2, 3, 4).

And God Almighty bless thee (Jacob), and give thee the blessing of Abraham, to thee and to *thy seed* with thee; *that thou mayest inherit the land wherein thou art a stranger,* which God gave unto Abraham (Gen. 28: 3, 4).

I am the Lord God of Abraham, thy father, and the God of Isaac; THE LAND WHEREON THOU LIEST, TO THEE WILL I GIVE IT, AND TO THY SEED, and in thee and in thy seed shall all the families of the earth be blessed. (Gen. 28: 13, 14).

XIII. These promises were not fulfilled in the experience of Abraham, Isaac, and Jacob, nor have they been fulfilled at any time since.

And he (God) gave him (Abraham) *none inheritance in it, no, not so much as to set his foot on,* YET HE PROMISED THAT HE WOULD GIVE IT TO HIM FOR A POSSESSION (Acts 7:5).

By faith Abraham, when he was called to go out into a place which he should after receive for an inheritance, obeyed; and he went out, not knowing whither he went. By

A DECLARATION OF THE TRUTH REVEALED IN THE BIBLE, THE SUBLIME AND SIMPLE THEOLOGY OF THE PRIMITIVE CHRISTIANS (UNAMENDED CHRISTADELPHIANS) (continued)

faith HE SOJOURNED IN THE LAND OF PROMISE *as in a strange country,* dwelling in tabernacles with Isaac and Jacob, *the heirs with him of the same promise* (Heb. 11:8-9).

These all died in faith, *not having received the promises,* but having SEEN THEM AFAR OFF, and were persuaded of them and embraced them, and confessed that they were strangers and pilgrims on the earth (Heb. 11: 13-35, 39, 40).

Now to Abraham and his seed were the promises made. He saith not, And to seeds as of many; but as of one, And to thy seed, which is Christ . . . And if ye be Christ's then are ye Abraham's seed, and heirs according to the promise (Gal. 3:16, 29).

Now, I Paul, say that Jesus Christ was a minister of the circumcision for the truth of God, to *confirm* the promises made unto the fathers (Rom. 15:8).

Blessed be the Lord God of Israel: for he hath visited and redeemed his people, and hath raised up a horn of salvation for us (that is Jesus—see context) in the house of his servant David; as he spake by the mouth of his holy prophets, which have been since the world began; that we should be saved from our enemies, and from the hand of all that hate us: *to perform the mercy promised to* OUR FATHERS, *and to remember his holy covenant,* THE OATH WHICH HE SWARE TO OUR FATHER ABRAHAM (Luke 1: 68-73).

XIV. These promises will be fulfilled in the establishment of THE KINGDOM OF DAVID UNDER CHRIST (that is, in the setting up of the kingdom of God on Earth) as the centre of a universal empire.

FIRST, as to THE BLESSING OF ALL NATIONS:

THE EARTH SHALL BE FULL OF THE KNOWLEDGE OF THE LORD as the waters cover the sea (Isa. 11:9).

And he shall judge among the nations, and shall rebuke many people: and they shall beat their swords into ploughshares, and their spears into pruning hooks: *nation shall not lift up sword against nation, neither shall they learn war any more* (Isa. 2:4).

He shall judge the poor of the people, he shall save the children of the needy, and shall break in pieces the oppressor . . . His name shall endure for ever: his name shall be continued as long as the sun: *and men shall be blessed in him: all nations shall call him blessed* (Psa. 72:4, 17).

Behold, a king shall reign in righteousness, and princes shall rule in judgment; and a man shall be *as an hiding place from the wind, and a covert from the tempest; as rivers of water in a dry place, as the shadow of a great rock in a weary land. And the eyes of them that see shall not be dim, and the ears of them that hear shall hearken. The heart also of the rash shall understand knowledge, and the tongue of*

the stammerers shall be ready to speak plainly (Isa. 32:1-4; Jer. 3:17).

The battle bow shall be cut off, *and he shall speak peace unto the heathen (nations),* and his dominion shall be from sea even to sea, and from the river even to the ends of the earth (Zech. 9:10).

The Lord is exalted: . . . and wisdom and knowledge *shall be the stability of thy times, and strength of salvation* (Isa. 33: 5, 6).

O, let the nations be glad and sing for joy, for thou shalt judge the people righteously, and govern the nations upon earth (Psa. 67:4).

SECOND, as to the INHERITANCE OF THE LAND OF PROMISE:

Then will I remember my covenant with Jacob, and also my covenant with Isaac, and also my covenant with Abraham will I remember; AND I WILL REMEMBER THE LAND (Lev. 26:42).

Then will the Lord be *jealous for his* land, and pity his people . . . *Fear not, O land;* be glad and rejoice: for the Lord will do great things (Joel 2: 18, 21).

And *the desolate land shall be tilled,* whereas it lay desolate in the sight of all that passed by; and they shall say, *This land that was desolate is become* LIKE THE GARDEN OF EDEN, and the waste and desolate and ruined cities are become fenced, and are inhabited. Then the heathen that are left round about you shall know that I the Lord build the ruined places, and plant that that was desolate: *I the Lord have spoken it and I will do it* (Ezek. 36: 34-36).

For the Lord shall comfort Zion: he will comfort all her waste places; and he will *make her wilderness* LIKE EDEN, and *her desert* LIKE THE GARDEN OF THE LORD; joy and gladness shall be found therein, thanksgiving and the voice of melody (Isa. 51:3).

Thou shalt no more be termed forsaken; neither shall THY LAND *any more be termed desolate;* but thou shalt be called Hephzibah (i.e. *my delight is in her*) and thy land Beulah (i.e. *married*): for the Lord delighteth in thee, and thy land shall be married (Isa. 62:4).

Whereas thou hast been forsaken and hated, so that no man went through thee, I will make thee *an eternal excellency, a joy of many generations* (Isa. 60:15).

And I say unto you, that many shall come from the east and west, *and shall sit down* WITH ABRAHAM, AND ISAAC, AND JACOB, *in the kingdom of heaven* (Matt. 8:11; see also Luke 13:28).

THOU WILT PERFORM THE TRUTH TO JACOB, AND THE MERCY TO ABRAHAM, WHICH THOU HAST SWORN UNTO OUR FATHERS FROM THE DAYS OF OLD (Micah 7:20).

XV. Jesus Christ will return from Heaven, AND VISIBLY APPEAR AND TAKE UP HIS RESIDENCE ON EARTH A SECOND TIME, for the purpose of bringing about the accomplishment of all these things. The second coming of Christ is therefore the true hope of the believer.

This same Jesus, which is taken up from you into heaven, *shall so come in like manner as ye have seen him go into heaven* (Acts 1:9-11).

Jesus Christ, who shall judge the quick and the dead, *at his appearing and his kingdom* (2 Tim. 4:1).

For the Son of man SHALL COME in the glory of his Father with his angels, and then he shall reward every man according to his works (Matt. 16:27).

HE SHALL SEND JESUS CHRIST, which before was preached unto you: whom the heaven must receive until the times of restitution of all things, *which God hath spoken by the mouth of all his holy prophets* since the world began (Acts 3: 20, 21).

Unto them that look for him *shall he* APPEAR THE SECOND TIME without sin unto salvation (Heb. 9:28).

The Lord himself shall descend from heaven with a shout, with the voice of the archangel, and the trump of God; and the dead in Christ shall rise first (1 Thess. 4:16).

Wherefore gird up the loins of your mind, be sober, and hope to the end for the grace that is to be brought unto you *at the revelation of Jesus Christ* (1 Pet. 1:13).

Our conversation is in heaven; *from whence* also we look for the Saviour, the Lord Jesus Christ (Phil. 3:20).

So that ye come behind in no gift; *waiting for* THE COMING OF OUR LORD JESUS CHRIST (1. Cor. 1:7).

That when he shall appear we may have confidence, and not be ashamed before him AT HIS COMING (1 John 2:28).

XVI. The Kingdom of God is the inheritance to which men are called by the gospel, and the thing presented as *the object of hope:* a proposition which destroys the popular Gospel of "Kingdoms beyond the skies."

God hath called you UNTO HIS KINGDOM and glory (1 Thess. 2:12).

Fear not, little flock, for it is your father's good pleasure to give you THE KINGDOM (Luke 12:32).

Hearken, my beloved brethren, hath not God chosen the poor of this world, rich in faith, and heirs of THE KINGDOM WHICH HE HATH PROMISED TO THEM THAT LOVE HIM? (Jas. 2:5).

Then shall the king say unto them on his right hand, Come, ye blessed of my Father, INHERIT THE KING-DOM prepared for you from the foundation of the world (Matt. 25:34).

For so an entrance shall be ministered unto you abundantly into THE EVERLASTING KINGDOM OF OUR LORD AND SAVIOUR JESUS CHRIST (2 Pet. 1:11).

And they shall come from the east, and from the west, and from the north, and from the south, and shall sit down IN THE KINGDOM OF GOD (Luke 13:29).

Jesus answered, Verily, verily, I say unto thee, except a man be born of water and of the Spirit, he cannot enter into THE KINGDOM OF GOD (John 3:5).

Now this I say, brethren, that flesh and blood cannot inherit THE KINGDOM OF GOD; neither doth corruption inherit incorruption (1 Cor. 15:50).

Know ye not that the unrighteous shall not inherit THE KINGDOM OF GOD? (1 Cor. 6:9).

XVII. The Kingdom of God will last a Thousand Years, during which Christ and his brethren will rule the mortal nations of the earth; sin and death continuing among mankind, but in a milder degree than now. At the end of that period, an entire change will take place. Christ will surrender his position of supremacy, and become subject to the Father, Who will then manifest Himself as the FATHER, STRENGTH, GOVERNOR AND FRIEND OF ALL. As a preparation for this sublime manifestation, sin and death will be abolished, but not before and extensive revolt of nations at the close of the Millennium. This revolt will succeed to the last point, and will be suppressed by a summary outburst of judgment; after which will occur a resurrection and judgment of those who shall have died during the thousand years and a judging of those who are alive at the end of that period; resulting in the immortalization of the approved and the consignment of the rejected to destruction. None will remain but a generation of righteous, redeemed, immortal persons, who shall *inhabit the earth for ever.* Christ's work will be finished, and the Father will reveal Himself without mediation.

And I saw an angel come down from heaven having the key of the bottomless pit, and a great chain in his hand. And he laid hold on the dragon, that old serpent, the Devil and Satan and bound him *a thousand years,* and cast him into the bottomless pit, and shut him up, and set a seal upon him that he should deceive the nations no more till the *thousand years* should be fulfilled, and after that to be loosed a little season. And I saw thrones, and they sat upon them, and judgment was given unto them: and I saw the souls of them that were beheaded for the witness of Jesus and for the word of God, and which had not worshipped the beast, neither his image, neither had received his mark upon their foreheads, or in their hands; and *they lived and reigned with Christ* A THOUSAND YEARS. Blessed and holy is he that hath part in the first resurrection; on such the second death hath no power, but they shall be priests of God and of Christ, *and shall reign with him a* THOUSAND YEARS. But the rest of the dead lived not again until the thousand years were finished. This is the first resurrection. *And when the thousand years are expired,* Satan shall be loosed out of his prison and shall go out to deceive the nations which are in the four quarters of the earth, Gog and Magog, to gather them together to battle: the number of whom is as the sand of the sea. And they went up on the breadth of the earth and encompassed the camp of the saints about, and the beloved city; and fire came down from God out of heaven and devoured them. And I saw the dead, small and great, stand before God; and the books were opened: and another book was opened which is the book of life; and the dead were judged out of those things which were written in the books, according to their works. And the sea gave up the dead which were in

A DECLARATION OF THE TRUTH REVEALED IN THE BIBLE, THE SUBLIME AND SIMPLE THEOLOGY OF THE PRIMITIVE CHRISTIANS (UNAMENDED CHRISTADELPHIANS) (continued)

it; and death and hell (the grave) delivered up the dead which were in them: *and they were judged every man according to their works,* and death and hell (the grave) were cast into the lake of fire. *This is the second death.* And *whosoever was not written in the book of life was cast into* THE LAKE OF FIRE (Rev. 20:1-9, 12-15).

And there was given him dominion, and glory, and A KINGDOM, *that all people, nations, and languages should serve him:* his dominion is an everlasting dominion which shall not pass away, and HIS KINGDOM that which shall not be destroyed (Dan. 7:14).

There shall be no more thence an infant of days, nor an old man that hath not filled his days; for *the child shall* DIE *an hundred years old:* but the sinner being an hundred years old shall be accursed (Isa. 65:20).

Then cometh the end *when he shall have delivered up the* KINGDOM TO GOD, even the Father; when he shall have put down all rule, and all authority and power. For he must reign, till he hath put all enemies under his feet. *The last enemy that shall be destroyed* IS DEATH. And when all things shall be subdued unto him, *then shall the Son also himself be subject unto him that put all things under him,* THAT GOD MAY BE ALL IN ALL (1 Cor. 15: 24-28).

THE THINGS CONCERNING THE NAME OF JESUS CHRIST

XVIII. That there is but ONE GOD by Whom and out of Whom all things have been created, and in Whose immensity-filling Spirit all things subsist; that He Who is thus the FATHER OF ALL dwells in UNAPPROACHABLE LIGHT styled in the Scriptures, "heaven, *his dwelling place*". He and the Spirit are one, but only in the sense in which the sun in the heavens and the light of day are one. Jesus is His manifestation by the Spirit. This proposition strikes at the root of the popular doctrine of the Trinity, which confuses the revealed relations of the Father, the Son and the Holy Spirit.

Hear, O Israel, the Lord our God is ONE *Lord* (Deut. 6:4).

I am the Lord, and *there is none else,* THERE IS NO GOD BESIDE ME (Isa. 45:5).

And Jesus answered him, The first of all the commandments is, Hear, O Israel, the Lord our God is ONE LORD (Mark 12:29).

And this is life eternal, that they might know thee, THE ONLY TRUE GOD, and Jesus Christ, whom thou hast sent (John 17:3).

But to us there is but ONE GOD, the Father, of whom are all things, and we in him; and one Lord Jesus Christ, by whom are all things, and we by him (1 Cor. 8: 6; Eph. 4:6).

For there is ONE GOD, and one mediator between God and men, the man Christ Jesus (1 Tim. 2:5).

The blessed and ONLY POTENTATE, the King of Kings, and Lord of Lords, who only hath immortality, *dwelling in the light which no man can approach unto* (1 Tim. 6:16).

Hear thou in HEAVEN THY DWELLING PLACE (1 Kings 8:30, 34, 39).

Our Father who art in HEAVEN (Matt. 6:9).

Unto thee lift I up mine eyes, O THOU THAT DWELLEST IN THE HEAVENS (Psa. 123:1).

XIX. That the Spirit is not a personal God distinct from the Father, but the radiant invisible power or energy of the Father; the distinction between the Father and the Spirit being not that they are two persons, but that the Spirit is the Father's power, in space-filling diffusion, forming with the Father, a unity in the stupendous scheme of creation, which is in revolution around the Supreme Source of all Power.

And the spirit of God moved upon the face of the waters (Gen. 1:2).

Thou knowest my downsitting and mine uprising; thou understandest my thought afar off. Thou compassest my path and my lying down, and art acquainted with all my ways. There is not a word in my tongue, but lo, O Lord, thou knowest it altogether. Thou has beset me behind and before, and laid thine hand upon me. Such knowledge is too wonderful for me; it is high, I cannot attain unto it. WHITHER SHALL I GO FROM THY SPIRIT, OR WHITHER SHALL I FLEE FROM THY PRESENCE? If I ascend up into heaven thou art there: if I make my bed in hell (*sheol,* the grave) behold thou art there . . . The darkness hideth not from thee, but the night shineth as the day. The darkness and the light are both alike to thee (Psa. 139:2-12).

The SPIRIT OF GOD *hath made me,* and the breath of the Almighty hath given me life (Job 33:4).

BY HIS SPIRIT *he hath garnished the heavens* (Job 26:13).

Thou sendeth forth THY SPIRIT, *they are created:* and thou renewest the face of the earth (Psa. 104:30).

And the Spirit of the Lord came mightily upon him, and he rent him (the lion) as he would have rent a kid (Judges 14:6).

And the Lord said unto Moses, Take thee Joshua the son of Nun, *a man in whom is* THE SPIRIT, and lay thine hand upon him (Num. 27:18).

Yet many years didst thou forbear them, and testifiedst against them BY THY SPIRIT IN THE PROPHETS (Neh. 9:30).

For the prohecy came not in old time by the will of man; *but holy men of God spake* AS THEY WERE MOVED BY THE HOLY GHOST (2 Pet. 1:21).

XIXA. The Holy Spirit is the Spirit of God in official manifestation. This is a mode of description almost peculiar to the New Testament. The Holy Spirit is the same Spirit mentioned in the testimonies quoted from the Old Testament, but styled Holy Spirit by way of distinction from Spirit in its free, spontaneous, universal form in nature. It is the same Spirit, gathered up, as it were, under the focalizing power of the divine will, for the bestowal of divine gifts and the accomplishment of divine results.

And the angel answered and said unto her, The Holy Ghost shall come upon thee, and the power of the Highest shall over-shadow thee; therefore also that holy thing that shall be born of thee shall be called the Son of God (Luke 1:35).

God anointed Jesus of Nazareth *with the Holy Ghost and with power;* who went about doing good, and healing all that were oppressed of the devil, for God was with him (Acts 10:38).

The Comforter, which is *the Holy Ghost* whom the Father will send in my name, he shall teach you all the things and bring all things to your remembrance whatsoever I have said unto you (John 14:26).

He shall baptize you with the Holy Ghost and with fire (Mat. 3:11).

John truly baptized with water, but ye shall be baptized with the Holy Spirit not many days hence . . . Ye shall receive *power after that the Holy Spirit is come upon you* (Acts 1:5-8).

And suddenly there came a sound from heaven *as of a rushing might wind,* and it *filled all the house* where they were sitting, and they were all filled with the Holy Spirit (Acts 2:2-4).

And as I began to speak, the Holy Spirit fell on them as on us at the beginning. Then remembered I the word of the Lord how that he said, John indeed baptized with water, but ye shall be baptized with the Holy Spirit (Acts 11:15-16).

Then laid they their hands on them, and they received the Holy Ghost; and when Simon saw that through the laying on of the apostles' hands the Holy Spirit was given, he offered them money, saying, *Give me also this power* (Acts 8:17-19).

The foregoing testimonies make plain the New Testament meaning of being baptized with the Holy Spirit, which is a very different meaning from that attached to it by professors of popular theology. It means an immersion or enswathement in spirit power, conferring miraculous gifts. No baptism of the Holy Spirit now takes place. All that can now be done is to preach the Word, and this having been given through the agency of the Spirit, working in ancient prophets and apostles, is the Spirit's instrument— the Spirit's sword, by which the Spirit makes war on the natural mind, and hews it into the similitude of the mind of the Spirit.

XX. Jesus Christ, the Son of God, is not the "second person" of an eternal Trinity, but the manifestation of the ONE ETERNAL CREATOR, who is "above all and through all" (Eph. 4:6), and "out of whom are all things" (Rom. 11:36). This Creator, is Spirit, dwelling personally in heaven yet, in His Spirit effluence filling immensity. By this Spirit-effluence, He begot Jesus, who was therefore HIS SON: by the same power He anointed him and dwelt in him, and spoke to Israel through him (Heb. 1:1). Jesus Christ, therefore, in the days of his weakness, must be considered from two points of view, one DEITY, the other MAN. The man was the son, whose existence dates from the birth of Jesus; the Deity dwelling in him was the Father, who, without beginning of days, is alone eternally pre-existent. God's relation to the Son was afterwards exemplified in the event related in Luke 1:35, by which was established what Paul styles the "mystery of godliness": "God manifest in the flesh, justified in the spirit, seen of angels, preached unto the Gentiles, believed on in the world, received up into glory" (1 Tim. 3:16).

And the angel said unto her (Mary), The Holy Spirit shall come upon thee, and the power of the Highest shall over-shadow thee; THEREFORE *also that holy thing that shall be born of thee shall be called* THE SON OF GOD (Luke 1:35).

The angel of the Lord appeared unto Joseph in a dream, saying, Joseph, thou son of David, fear not to take unto thee Mary, they wife, *for that which is conceived in her is of the Holy Spirit* (Matt. 1:20).

Unto us a child is born, unto us a son is given, and the government shall be upon his shoulder; and his name shall be called Wonderful, Counsellor, the Mighty God, the Everlasting Father, the Prince of Peace (Isa. 9:6).

And Jesus when he was baptized, went up straightway out of the water; and lo the heavens were opened unto him; and he saw the Spirit of God descending like a dove, and lighting upon him, and lo, a voice from heaven, saying, This is my beloved Son, in whom I am well pleased (Matt. 3:16-17).

The Spirit of the Lord is upon me, because he hath anointed me to preach the gospel to the poor; he hath sent me to heal the broken-hearted, to preach deliverance to the captives (Luke 4:18).

For he whom God hath sent speaketh the words of God: for God giveth not the Spirit by measure unto him. The Father loveth the Son, and *hath given all things into his hands* (John 3:34-35).

I can of mine own self do nothing: I seek not mine own will, but the will of the Father which hath sent me (John 5:30).

Jesus answered them, and said, *My doctrine is not mine,* but his that sent me (John 7:16).

I am in the Father, and the Father in me. The words that I speak unto you, I speak not of myself: but the Father that dwelleth in me, he doeth the works (John 14:10).

I go unto the Father; for my Father is greater than I (John 14:28).

Jesus of Nazareth, a MAN approved of God among you by miracles, and wonders, and signs, *which God did by him* in the midst of you, as ye yourselves also know (Acts 2:22).

God anointed Jesus of Nazareth with the Holy Spirit and with power; who went about doing good, and healing all that were oppressed of the devil, for God was with him (Acts 10:38).

XXI. That Jesus was of our nature, notwithstanding the mode of his conception and his anointing with the Holy Spirit. He was raised up as a SECOND ADAM (constituted of flesh and blood as we are, and

A DECLARATION OF THE TRUTH REVEALED IN THE BIBLE, THE SUBLIME AND SIMPLE THEOLOGY OF THE PRIMITIVE CHRISTIANS (UNAMENDED CHRISTADELPHIANS) (continued)

tempted in all points like unto us, yet without sin), to remove (by his obedience, death, and resurrection) the evil consequences resulting from the disobedience of the first Adam.

THE MAN CHRIST JESUS (1 Tim. 2:5).

God sending his own Son in THE LIKENESS OF SINFUL FLESH, *and for sin, condemned* sin in the flesh (Rom. 8:3).

Forasmuch then as the children are partakers of *flesh and blood,* he also himself likewise TOOK PART OF THE SAME (Heb. 2:14).

God sent forth his Son MADE OF A WOMAN (Gal. 4:4).

He was MADE SIN for us, who knew no sin (2 Cor. 5:21).

By man came death, BY MAN CAME *also the resurrection of the dead* . . . The first man, Adam, was made a living soul; the LAST ADAM was made a quickening spirit (1 Cor. 15:21, 45).

The gift by grace (or favour), which is by ONE MAN, *Jesus Christ,* hath abounded unto many . . . For as by one man's disobedience many were made sinners, so by the obedience of one shall many be made righteous (Rom. 5:15, 19).

He was heard in that he feared: though he were a Son, *yet learned he obedience by the things which he suffered* (Heb. 5:7, 8).

In all things it behoved him to be made LIKE UNTO HIS BRETHREN, that he might be a merciful and faithful high priest in things pertaining to God . . . *He was in all points tempted like as we are, yet without sin (Heb. 2:17; 4:15).*

XXII. The Death of Christ was not to appease the wrath of an offended God but to express the love of the Father in a necessary sacrifice for sin that the law of sin and death which came into force by the first Adam might be nullified in the second in a full discharge of its claims through a temporary surrender to its power; after which immortality by resurrection might be acquired, in harmony with the law of obedience. Thus sin is taken away, and righteousness established.

God *so loved the world* that he gave his only begotten Son, that whosoever believeth on him might not perish, but have everlasting life (John 3:16).

Behold the Lamb of God that *taketh away the sin of the world* (John 1:29).

To him give all the prophets witness, that through his name whosoever believeth in him *shall receive remission of sins* (Acts 10:43).

Neither is there salvation in ANY OTHER: FOR THERE IS NONE OTHER NAME UNDER HEAVEN *given among men,* whereby we must be saved (Acts 4:12).

Whom God hath set forth to be a propitiation through faith in his blood, to declare his righteousness for the remission of sins that are past, through the forbearance of God (Rom. 3:25).

He putteth away sin *by the sacrifice of himself* (Heb. 9:26).

Who *gave himself for our sins,* that he might deliver us from this present evil world, according to the will of God and our Father (Gal. 1:4).

Who *gave himself for us* that he might redeem us from all inquity, and purify unto himself a peculiar people, zealous of good works (Titus 2:14).

For he hath made him to be sin for us, who knew no sin; *that we might be made the righteousness of God in him* (2 Cor. 5:21).

XXIIA. God raised Jesus from the dead and exalted him to a glorified, incorruptible, immortal (because spiritual) state of existence, in which he at the present time acts as priestly mediator between the Father and those who come unto God by him.

Whom God hath raised up, having loosed the pains of death: because it was not possible that he should be holden of it (Acts 2:24).

The God of our fathers RAISED UP JESUS, whom ye slew and hanged on a tree (Acts 5:30).

Him God raised up the third day, and showed him openly; not to all the people, but unto witnesses chosen before of God, even to us, who did eat and drink with him after he rose from the dead (Acts 10:40).

God hath appointed a day in which he will judge the world in righteousness by that man whom he hath ordained; whereof he hath given assurance unto all men IN THAT HE HATH RAISED HIM FROM THE DEAD (Acts 17:31).

Jesus Christ our Lord, who was made of the seed of David according to the flesh; *and declared to be the son of God,* with power, according to the spirit of holiness, BY THE RESURRECTION FROM THE DEAD (Rom. 1:3-4).

Though he was *crucified through weakness,* YET HE LIVETH BY THE POWER OF GOD (2 Cor. 13:4).

Christ being raised from the dead *dieth no more;* DEATH HATH NO MORE DOMINION OVER HIM (Rom. 6:9).

God hath glorified his son Jesus (Acts 3:13).

GOD HATH RAISED HIM FROM THE DEAD and set him at his own right hand in the heavenly places, far above all principality, and power, and might, and dominion, and every name that is named not only in this world, but also in that which is to come (Eph. 1:20-21).

The apostle and *High Priest of our* profession, Christ Jesus (Heb. 3:1).

We have a *great High Priest* that is passed into the heavens, Jesus the Son of God. We have not an High Priest who cannot be touched with the feeling of our infirmities, but was in all points tempted like as we are, yet without sin (Heb. 4: 14-15).

We have such *an High Priest,* who is set on the right hand of the throne of the Majesty in the heavens (Heb. 8:1).

XXIII. THE DEVIL—Who is he? It is of great importance to understand this question, because the Son of God was manifested *expressly for the purpose of destroying the Devil and his works* (1 John 3:8; Heb. 2:14). The mission of Christ is, therefore, imperfectly understood when the nature of the Bible Devil is not comprehended. It will be found upon examination that the Devil is not (as is commonly supposed) a personal supernatural agent of evil, and, that in fact, *there is no such BEING in existence.* The Devil is a *Scriptural personification of sin in the flesh,* in its several phases of manifestation—subjective, individual, aggregate, social, and political, in history, current experience, and prophecy; after the style of metaphor which speaks of wisdom as a woman, riches as MAMMOM and *the god of this world,* sin as a master, etc.

Forasmuch then as the children are partakers of flesh and blood, he (Christ) also himself likewise took part of the same: *that THROUGH DEATH he might destroy him that had the power of death,* THAT IS, THE DEVIL *(diabolos)* (Heb. 2:14).

The wages of SIN *is death* (Rom. 6:23).

He put away SIN *by the sacrifice of himself* (Heb. 9:26).

Resist THE DEVIL and he will flee from you (Jas. 4:7).

Ye have not yet resisted unto blood, striving against SIN (Heb. 12:4). The DEVIL *having now put it into the heart of Judas Iscariot* (John 13:2).

[The betrayal of Christ was the result of Judas's thievish propensities; therefore, says Jesus, "It were good for that *man* that he had not been born."] Have I not chosen you twelve, and *one of you (Judas)* IS A DEVIL? (John 6:70).

Why hath *Satan filled thine heart* to lie to the Holy Spirit? . . . How is it that YE HAVE AGREED TOGETHER to tempt the Spirit of the Lord? (Acts 5:3, 9).

Every man is tempted *when he is drawn away* OF HIS OWN LUST, and enticed. Then when lust hath conceived, it bringeth forth sin; and sin, when it is finished, bringeth forth death (Jas. 1:14-15).

Wherein in time past ye walked according to the course of this world, according to *the price of the power of the air,* THE SPIRIT THAT NOW WORKETH IN THE CHILDREN OF DISOBEDIENCE (Eph. 2:2).

Give none occasion to the adversary to speak reproachfully, *for some are already turned aside* AFTER SATAN (1 Tim. 5:14-15).

Whom *I have delivered unto* SATAN, that they may learn not to blaspheme (1 Tim. 1:20).

But he turned, and said unto PETER, *Get thee behind me,* SATAN: thou art an offence unto me; for thou savourest not the things that be of God, but those that be of men (Matt. 16:23; Mark 8:33; Luke 4:8).

SATAN hindered us (1 Thess. 2:18).

And to the angel of the church in *Pergamos* write: I know thy works, and where thou dwellest, even WHERE SATAN'S SEAT IS: and thou holdest fast my name, and hast not denied my faith, even in those days wherein

Antipas was my faithful martyr, who was slain among you, WHERE SATAN DWELLETH (Rev. 2:12-13).

Be sober, be vigilant, because your adversary, *the Devil,* as a roaring lion, walketh about, seeking whom he may devour (1 Pet. 5:8).

THE DEVIL *shall cast some of you into prison* (Rev. 2:10).

And the God of peace *shall bruise* SATAN *under your feet shortly* (Rom. 16:20).

And I will put enmity between thee (the serpent) and the woman, and between thy seed and her seed; IT SHALL BRUISE THY HEAD, *and thou shalt bruise his heel* (Gen. 3:15).

But God shall wound *the head of* HIS ENEMIES (Psa. 68:21).

Thou (Israel) art my battle axe and weapons of war; for with thee will I *break in pieces* THE NATIONS, *and with thee will I destroy* KINGDOMS (Jer. 51:20).

And there appeared another wonder in heaven; and behold a GREAT RED DRAGON, having *seven heads and ten horns,* and seven crowns upon his heads . . . And the dragon was wroth with the woman, and *went to make war with the remnant of her seed,* which keep the commandments of God, and have the testimony of Jesus Christ (Rev. 12:3-17).

And he laid hold on the dragon, that old serpent, WHICH IS THE DEVIL AND SATAN, and bound him a thousand years (Rev. 20:2).

(The symbolism of the verses immediately foregoing is explained in the following.)

He shall judge among the heathen, he shall fill the places with the dead bodies; *he shall wound the heads over many countries (Psa. 110:6).*

And in the days of these kings shall the God of heaven set up a kingdom . . . *it shall break in pieces and consume all these kingdoms,* and it shall stand for ever (Dan. 2:44).

XXIIIA. Demons, devils, or so-called evil Spirits were the fanciful creation of the pagan mind. They were supposed to be a kind of demi-god inhabiting the air, and producing disease in human being by taking possession of them. The following passages show that in the Bible, the word is not used to express this idea.

They sacrifice unto *devils,* not *to* God: TO GODS *whom they knew not,* to NEW GODS that came newly up, whom your fathers feared not (Deut. 32:17; Psa. 106:37).

And he ordained him priests for the high places, and *for the devils,* and for the calves which he had made (2 Chron. 11:15: Levs. 17:7).

The things which the Gentiles sacrifice they sacrifice to *devils* (that is, to the idols in the temples) and not to God (1 Cor. 10:20).

Lord, have mercy on my son, for he is LUNATIC and sore vexed, for oftimes he falleth into the fire, and oft into the water, and they brought him to thy disciples and they could not *cure* him . . . And Jesus rebuked *the devil,* and he departed out of him, and the child was whole from that very hour (Matt. 17: 15-18).

A DECLARATION OF THE TRUTH REVEALED IN THE BIBLE, THE SUBLIME AND SIMPLE THEOLOGY OF THE PRIMITIVE CHRISTIANS (UNAMENDED CHRISTADELPHIANS) (continued)

(From this, the identity of lunacy with supposed diabolical possession is apparent. The expulsion of the evil which deranged the child's faculties is the casting out of the demon).

Then was brought unto him one possessed with a devil, blind and dumb: and he healed him, insomuch that the *blind and dumb both spake and saw* (Matt. 12: 22).

And one of the multitude answered and said, Master, I have brought unto thee my son, which hath a dumb spirit (Mark 9:17).

XXIV. HUMAN NATURE—What is it? Philosophy and orthodox religion say it is a thing made up of two parts—*body* and *soul* (and some add, spirit); that the soul is the real, conscious, thinking part of man, in its nature indestructible and immortal; that when the body is destroyed in death, the soul is liberated and departs to another sphere of existence, there to undergo endless happiness or misery, according to the life developed in the body. This doctrine is known in theology as THE IMMORTALITY OF THE SOUL. This is a PAGAN FICTION *subversive of every principle of eternal truth,* as will be discovered by a consideration of the evidence, which proves:

A. That Man is a creature of dust formation, whose individuality and faculties are the attributes of his bodily *organization.*

And the Lord God formed man of the dust of the ground, and breathed into his nostrils the breath of life, and man became a living soul (Heb. *nephesh chaiyah,* living creature)—(Gen. 2:7).

In the sweat of thy face shalt thou eat bread, till thou return unto the ground; for out of it wast thou taken: for DUST THOU ART, AND UNTO DUST SHALT THOU RETURN (Gen. 3:19).

The Lord God sent him forth from the *garden of Eden to till* THE GROUND *from whence he was taken* (Gen. 3:23).

He knoweth our frame, he remembereth that WE ARE DUST (Psa. 103:14).

And Abraham answered and said, Behold now, I have taken upon me to speak unto the Lord, WHICH AM BUT DUST AND ASHES (Gen. 18:27).

Remember, I beseech thee, that *thou hast made me* AS THE CLAY; and wilt thou bring me into *dust* AGAIN? (Job. 10: 9).

For *all flesh is as grass, and all the glory of man as the flower of grass.* The grass withereth, and the flower thereof falleth away (1 Pet. 1:24; Jas. 1:10-11).

For that which befalleth the sons of men befalleth beasts; even one thing befalleth them; *as the one dieth,* SO DIETH THE OTHER; yea, they have all one breath; *so that a man hath no pre-eminence above a beast;* for all is vanity; all go unto one place; ALL ARE OF THE DUST; *and all turn to dust again* (Eccles. 3:19-20).

Then shall *the dust return to the earth* AS IT WAS: *and the spirit (ruach,* spirit or breath, which in Eccles. 3:19, above quoted, Solomon says the beasts have as well as man) shall return unto God who gave it (Eccles. 12:7).

Thou hidest thy face, they are troubled: *thou takest away their breath,* THEY DIE, *and return to their dust* (Psa. 104:29).

Shall the clay say to him who fashioned it, What makest thou? (Isa 45:9).

We are the clay and Thou our potter (Isa. 64:8).

He that is of the earth is EARTHLY (John 3:31).

The first man is of the earth, EARTHY . . . as is the earthy, such are they also WHO ARE EARTHY . . . we have borne the image of the EARTHY (1 Cor. 15:47-49).

B. That Man is mortal (that is subject to death or *dissolution of being* in consequence of the disobedience of Adam, which brought death as the penalty of sin.

For in the day that thou (Adam) eatest thereof, thou shalt surely die (see margin, Heb. *dying thou shalt die)*—Gen. 2:17). Because thou has eaten of the tree . . . *dust thou art, and* UNTO DUST SHALT THOU RETURN (Gen. 3:19).

And now, *lest he put forth his hand and take also of the tree of life,* AND EAT AND LIVE FOR EVER (Gen. 3:22-23).

By one man sin entered into the world and DEATH BY SIN; *and so death passed upon all men, for that all have sinned* (Rom. 5:12).

In Adam all DIE (1 Cor. 15:22).

What man is he that liveth and shall not see death? *Shall he deliver* HIS SOUL *from the hand of* THE GRAVE (Psa. 89: 48; 30:3; 86:13; Job. 33:22).

All (cattle, beast and creeping thing, and EVERY MAN) *in whose nostrils was the breath of life,* of all that was in the dry land, DIED (at the flood) (Gen. 7:22).

Shall MORTAL MAN be more just than God? Shall a man be more pure than his maker? (Job 4:17).

Cease ye from man whose BREATH (n'shamah) IS IN HIS NOSTRILS: *for wherein is he to be accounted of?* (Isa. 2:22).

C. That in the Death State, a man, instead of having "gone to another world" is simply *a body deprived of life,* and as utterly unconscious as if he had never existed. Corruption will destroy his dead body, and he will pass away like a dream. Hence the necessity for "resurrection".

IN DEATH *there is no remembrance of thee;* in the grave, who shall give thee thanks? (Psa. 6:5).

552

For the living know that they shall die: but THE DEAD KNOW NOT ANYTHING, neither have they any more a reward; for the memory of them is forgotten. Also their *love,* and their *hatred,* and their *envy* is now perished; neither have they any more a portion for ever in anything that is done under the sun (Eccles. 9:5-6).

Whatsoever thy hand findeth to do, do it with thy might; *for there is no work, nor device, nor knowledge, nor wisdom,* IN THE GRAVE, *whither thou goest* (Eccles. 9:10).

Put not your trust in princes, nor in the son of man, in whom there is no help. *His* breath goeth forth, HE *returneth to his earth;* IN THAT VERY DAY HIS THOUGHTS PERISH (Psa. 146:3-4).

THE GRAVE CANNOT PRAISE THEE, *death cannot celebrate thee; they that go down into the pit* CANNOT HOPE FOR THY TRUTH. The living, the living, he shall praise thee, as I do this day (Isa. 38:18-19).

Hear my prayer, O Lord, and give ear unto my cry . . . O spare me (David) that I may receive strength *before I go hence and* BE NO MORE (Psa. 39:12-13).

For David after he had served his own generation by the will of God, *fell on sleep, and was laid unto his fathers, and saw,* CORRUPTION; but he whom God raised again saw no corruption (Acts 13:36; also 2:29-34).

D.   "Soul" in the Bible means creatures in its primary use, but is also employed to express the variety of aspects in which a living creature can be contemplated, such as person, body, life, individuality, mind, disposition, breath, etc. *It never expresses the idea of immortality.*

And God said, Let the earth bring forth the living creature (the same original word translated "soul" as applied to Adam) after his kind, cattle, and creeping thing, and beast of the earth after his kind (Gen. 1:24).

And God said, Let the waters bring forth abundantly the moving creature that hath life (in the margin "*soul*"—Heb. *nephesh,*) and fowl that may fly above the earth in the open firmament of heaven (Gen. 1:20).

In whose hands is the SOUL OF *every living thing,* and the breadth of all mankind (Job 12:10).

And he stretched himself upon the child three times, and cried unto the Lord and said, O Lord my God, I pray thee let this child's soul (*nephesh*) come into him again. And the Lord heard the voice of Elijah; and the SOUL (*nephesh*) of the child came into him again, and he revived (1 Kings 17:21-22).

And it came to pass that her soul (*nephesh,* life), was in departing (for she died)—(Gen. 35:18).

It shall be even as when an hungry man dreameth, and behold, he eateth; but he awaketh, and his

SOUL is empty: behold, he is faint, and his soul hath appetite (Isa. 29:8; Exod. 12:16; see margin).

Men do not despise a thief, if he steal to satisfy his SOUL when he is hungry (Prov. 6:30; cp. Lev. 17:10-12).

And levy a tribute unto the Lord of the men of war which went out to battle: ONE SOUL of five hundred, both of the *persons,* and of the beeves, and of the *asses,* and of the *sheep* (Num 31:28).

But if the priest buy any SOUL with his money, he shall eat of it, and he that is born in his house: they shall eat of his meat (Lev. 22:11).

And they smote all the SOULS that were therein with the edge of the sword, utterly destroying them: there was not any left to breathe: and he burnt Hazor with fire (Jos. 11:11; 10:32; Jer. 4:10; Job. 36:14; see margin).

Also in thy skirt is found *the blood of the souls* of the poor inocents (Jer. 2:34; Ezek. 13:18-19; 22:25-27).

So that my SOUL chooseth strangling, and death rather than my life (Job. 7-15; Psa. 105:18, see margin).

And Samson said, Let me (in the margin, Heb. *my soul*) die with the Philistines (Judges 16:30).

And it shall come to pass, that every soul which will not hear that prophet shall be destroyed from among the people (Acts 3:23).

Thou hast in love to *my soul* (that is, to me) delivered it from the pit of corruption (Isa. 38:17).

Behold, all souls are mine: as the soul of the father, so also the soul of the son is mine: the soul that sinneth, it shall die (Ezek. 18:4, 20).

For whosoever will save *his life (psuche)* shall lose it: and whosoever will lose *his life* for my sake shall find it. For what is a man profited if he shall gain the whole world and lose his own soul? (*psuche,* same word translated "life" in the previous verse; comp. also Revised Version which gives "life" in both verses): or what shall a man give in exchange for his soul *(psuche)?* (Matt. 16:25-26).

And I will say to my soul *(psuche),* Soul *(psuche),* thou hast much goods laid up for many years: take thine ease, eat, drink, and be merry. But God said unto him, Thou fool, this night thy soul *(psuche)* shall be required of thee (Luke 12:19-20).

And fear not them which kill the body but are not able to kill the soul *(psuche);* but rather fear him which is able to destroy both soul *(psuche)* and body in hell *(gehenna)—(Matt.* 10:28).

E.   "Spirit" in the Scriptures, as applied to man, is no more expressive of the philosophical conception of an immortal soul than "soul", but signifies breath, life, vital energy, mind, disposition, etc., as attributes of human nature while alive.

And behold, I even I do bring a flood of waters upon the earth to destroy *all flesh wherein is the breath*

(ruach) of life, from under heaven; and everything
that is in the earth shall die (Gen. 6:17).

For as the body without the spirit *(pneuma,* in the
margin, *breath*), is dead, so faith without works is
dead (Jas. 2:26).

And they stoned Stephen, calling upon God, and
saying, Lord Jesus, receive my spirit *(pneuma)* (Acts
7:59).

And Hannah answered and said, No, my lord, I am a
woman of a sorrowful *spirit (ruach)* (1 Sam. 1:15).

Who knoweth the spirit *(ruach)* of man that goeth
upward, and the spirit *(ruach)* of the beast that goeth
downward to the earth? (Eccles. 3:21).

And it came to pass, when all the kings of the
Amorites, which were on the side of Jordan westward, and all the kings of the Canaanites, which
were by the sea, heard that the Lord had dried up the
waters of Jordan from before the children of Israel,
until we were passed over, that their heart melted,
neither was there SPIRIT *(ruach) in them any more,*
because of the children of Israel (Josh. 5:1).

And they heard the voice of the Lord God walking
in the garden in the cool *(ruach,* in the margin
"wind") of the day: and Adam and his wife hid
themselves from the presence of the Lord God,
amongst the trees of the garden (Gen. 3:8).

And God made a wind *(ruach)* to pass over the
earth, and the waters assuaged (Gen. 8:1).

There is no man that hath power over the spirit
(ruach) to retain the spirit *(ruach):* neither hath he
power in the day of death: and there is no discharge
in that war: neither shall wickedness deliver those
that are given to it (Eccles. 8:8).

To the general assembly and church of the firstborn,
which are written in heaven, and to God the Judge of
all, and to the spirits of just men made perfect (Heb.
12:23).

Are they not all ministering spirits, sent forth to
minister for them who shall be heirs of salvation?
(Heb. 1:14).

Beloved, believe not every spirit *(pneuma),* but try
the spirits whether they are of God; because many
false prophets are gone out into the world. Hereby
know ye the Spirit of God; every *spirit* that confes-
seth that Jesus Christ is come in the flesh is of God
(1 John 4:1-2).

But when they saw him walking upon the sea, they
supposed it had been a spirit (in the original,
phantasma), and cried out (Mark 6:49).

XXV.   The doctrine of the immortality of the soul not
being in the Bible, the question is, where has it come
from? It has been borrowed by Christendom from
pagan teaching. We direct attention to the following
quotations:

Herodotus, the oldest historian, writes as follows: "The
Egyptians say that Ceres (the goddess of corn), and
Bacchus (the god of wine), hold the chief sway in the
infernal regions; and the *Egyptians* also *were the first who
asserted the doctrine that the soul of man is immortal"*
(Herod. Book ii.; Sec. 123).

Mosheim says, "Its first promoters argued from that
known doctrine of the Platonic School, which was *also
adopted by Origen and his disciples,* that the divine nature
was diffused through all human souls; or in other words,
that the faculty of reason, from which proceed the health
and vigour of the mind, was an emanation from God into
the human soul, and comprehended it in the principles and
elements of all truth, human and *divine"* (*Ecclesiastical
History,* vol. i., p. 86).

Justin Martyr (A.D. 150) said, "For if you have conversed
with some that are indeed called Christians, and do not
maintain these opinions, but even dare to blaspheme the
God of Abraham, and the God of Isaac, and the God of
Jacob, and say that there is no resurrection of the dead,
that the souls, as soon as they leave the body, are received
up into heaven, *take care that you do not look upon these.*
But I and all those Christians, that are really orthodox in
every respect, do know that there will be a resurrection of
the body and a thousand years in Jerusalem, when it is
built again, and adorned, and enlarged, as Ezekiel, and
Esaias, and the rest of the prophets declare" (*Dialogue with
Trypho the Jew,* section 80).

An extract from a canon which was passed under Leo X.,
by the Lateran Council, shows that the doctrine of an
"immortal soul" that lives when the man is dead was
supported in those days, as it generally has been since, *by
the authority of creeds,* rather than the word of God:
"Some have dared to assert, concerning the nature of the
reasonable soul, that it is mortal; we, with the approbation
of the sacred councils, do condemn and rebrobate all such,
seeing according to the canon of Pope Clement the Fifth,
the soul is immortal; and we strictly inhibit all from
dogmatizing otherwise; and we decree that all who adhere
to the like erroneous assertions shall be shunned and
punished as heretics" (*Caranza,* p. 412, 1681).

Martin Luther ironically responded to the decree of the
Lateran Council held during the Pontificate of Pope Leo:
"I permit the Pope to make articles of faith for himself and
his faithful—such as the soul is the substantial form of the
human body,—the soul is immortal,—*with all those
monstrous opinions to be found in the Roman dunghill of
decretals;* that such as his faith is, such may be his gospel,
such his disciples, and such his Church, that the mouth
may have meat suitable for it, and the dish a cover worthy
of it" (*Luther's Works,* vol ii., folio 107, Wittenburg,
1562).

"And ye in putting them in heaven, hell and purgatory,
destroy the arguments wherewyth Christ and Paul prove
the resurrection. What God doth with them, that shall we
know when we come to them. The true faith putteth the
resurrection, which we be warned to looke for every houre.
The heathen philosophers denying that, did put that the
soules did ever lyve. And the pope joyneth the spirituall
doctrine of Christ and the fleshly doctrine of philosophers

together, things so contrary that they can not agree, no more than the Spirite and the flesh do in a Christian man. And because the fleshly mynded pope consenteth unto the healthen doctrine, therefore he corrupteth the Scripture to stablish it." William Tyndall, the translator of the Scriptures into English, who suffered martydom in 1536.

Gibbon declares that "The doctrine of the immortality of the soul is omitted in the law of Moses". (*Gibbon,* chap. xv).

Richard Watson remarks, "That the soul is naturally immortal, *is contradicted by Scripture,* which makes our immortality a gift dependent, on the will of the Giver" (*Institutes,* vol. ii., p. 250).

The authentic Christian doctrine has three special characteristics:

(a) It is a doctrine, not of Immortality, but of Resurrection.

(b) It regards this Resurrection as an act and gift of God, not an inherent right of the human soul as such.

(c) It is not so much a doctrine of rewards and punishments, as the proclamation of the inherent joy of love and the inherent misery of selfishness.

Nature, Man and God, by Wm. Temple.

Another consideration of the highest importance is that the natural immortality of the soul is a doctrine wholly unknown to the Holy Scriptures, and standing on no higher plane than that of an ingeniously sustained, but gravely and formidably contested, philosophical opinion. And surely there is nothing, as to which we ought to be more on our grand, than the entrance into the precinct of Christian doctrine, either without authority or by an abuse of authority, of philosophical speculations disguised as truths of Divine Revelation. They bring with them a grave restraint on mental liberty; but what is worse is, that their basis is a pretension essentially false, and productive by rational retribution of other falsehoods. Under these two heads, we may perhaps find that we have ample warrant for declining to accept the tenet of natural immortality as a truth of Divine Revelation. *Studies Subsidiary to the Works of Bishop Butler,* by W. E. Gladstone.

Careful attention to the origin of the doctrine of the necessary immortality or indestructibility of each human soul, as stated for instance by Augustine and Aquinas, will probably convince us that it was no part of the original Christian message, or of early catholic doctrine. It was rather a speculation of Platonism taking possession of the Church. *The Epistle to the Romans,* by Charles Gore.

XXVI. The true doctrine of immortality. There is a doctrine of immortality in the Bible: but it differs from the popular doctrine in every particular.

FIRST. Instead of immortality being inherent and natural, the Bible teaches it is a quality brought within reach by Christ in the Gospel, and will only be attained on condition of believing the Gospel and obeying the divine commandments.

Jesus Christ hath abolished death, *and brought life and immortality to light* THROUGH THE GOSPEL (2 Tim. 1:10).

I am the Resurrection and the Life; *he that believeth on me,* though he were *dead* YET SHALL HE LIVE (that is, by resurrection: see foregoing context) (John 6:40: John 11:25).

For the wages of sin is *death;* but the gift of God is ETERNAL LIFE *through Jesus Christ our Lord* (Rom. 6:23).

And *this is the promise that he hath promised us,* EVEN ETERNAL LIFE (1 John 2:25).

Paul, an Apostle of Jesus Christ, by the will of God, according to THE PROMISE OF LIFE, *which is in Christ Jesus* (2 Tim. 1:1).

IN HOPE OF ETERNAL LIFE, which God, that cannot lie, *promised* before the world began (Titus 1:2).

That being justified by his grace, we should be made heirs *accordings to* THE HOPE OF ETERNAL LIFE (Titus 3:7).

For we are saved *by hope;* but HOPE THAT IS SEEN IS NOT HOPE: for what a man seeth why doth he yet hope for? But if we hope for that we see not then do we with patience WAIT FOR IT (Rom. 8:24-25).

He that soweth to the Spirit shall of the Spirit reap LIFE EVERLASTING (Gal. 6:8).

God so loved the world that he gave his only begotten son, that *whosoever believeth on him* should not perish, but have EVERLASTING LIFE (John 3:16).

And this is the record, that God hath given to us ETERNAL LIFE, and this life is in his Son. He that hath the Son hath life; and he that hath not the Son of God hath not life (1 John 5:11-12).

Blessed are they that do his commandments, that they may have right to *the tree of life* (Rev. 22:14).

He that believeth on the Son HATH EVERLASTING LIFE: and he that believeth not the Son shall not see life; but the wrath of God abideth on him (John 3:36).

He that hateth his life in this world SHALL KEEP IT UNTIL LIFE ETERNAL (John 12:25).

He shall receive . . . in the world to come, ETERNAL LIFE (Mark 10:30).

To them, who by patient continuance in well doing *seek for glory* and honour and immortality (God will render: see verse 6), eternal life (Rom. 2:7).

They which shall be accounted worthy to obtain that world, and the resurrection from the dead, neither marry, nor are given in marriage; NEITHER CAN THEY DIE ANY MORE: for they are equal unto the angels; and are the children of God, *being the children of the resurrection* (Luke 20:35-36).

And I will give unto them *(my sheep) eternal life;* and THEY SHALL NEVER PERISH, neither shall any man pluck them out of my hand (John 10:28).

A DECLARATION OF THE TRUTH REVEALED IN THE BIBLE, THE SUBLIME AND SIMPLE THEOLOGY OF THE PRIMITIVE CHRISTIANS (UNAMENDED CHRISTADELPHIANS) (continued)

As thou hast given him power over all flesh, *that he should give* ETERNAL LIFE *to as many as thou hast given him* (John 17:2).

Blessed is *the man that endureth temptation; for when he is tried,* he shall receive THE CROWN OF LIFE, which the Lord hath promised to them that love him (Jas. 1:12).

And the world passeth away and the lust thereof: BUT HE THAT DOETH THE WILL OF GOD ABIDETH FOR EVER (1 John 2:17).

For in this we groan, earnestly desiring to be clothed upon with our house which is from heaven. For we that are in this tabernacle do groan, being burdened: not for that we would be unclothed, but clothed upon, *that mortality might be* SWALLOWED UP OF LIFE (2 Cor. 5:1-4).

So when THIS CORRUPTIBLE *shall have put on incorruption,* and THIS MORTAL *shall have put on immortality,* then shall be brought to pass the saying that is written, Death is swallowed up in victory. O death, where is thy sting? O grave, where is thy victory? (1 Cor. 15:54-55).

And God shall wipe away all tears from their eyes; and there shall be NO MORE DEATH, neither sorrow, nor crying, neither shall there be any more pain; for the former things are passed away (Rev. 21:4).

He that overcometh shall not be hurt of the second death. *To him that overcometh* will I give to eat of THE TREE OF LIFE, which is in the midst of the paradise of God (Rev. 2:11, 7).

> SECOND. The immortality of the Bible, unlike the inherent immortality of popular belief, is to be manifested *in connection with, and as the result of, the resurrection or change of* THE BODY. (The reason is evident: *immortality is life manifested through* AN UNDECAYING BODY). This proposition is established in many of the testimonies cited under the last heading; it obtains further support from the following:

And many of them that sleep in the dust of the earth *shall awake,* SOME TO EVERLASTING LIFE, *and some to shame and everlasting contempt* (Dan. 12:2).

And shall come forth; they that have done good, unto the RESURRECTION OF *(resulting in)* LIFE; and they that have done evil unto the resurrection of *(resulting in)* damnation (John 5:29).

And thou shalt be blessed; for they cannot recompense thee: for *thou shalt be recompensed* AT THE RESURRECTION OF THE JUST (Luke 14:14).

And this is the Father's will which hath sent me, that of all which he hath given me I should lose nothing, BUT SHOULD RAISE IT UP AGAIN AT THE LAST DAY (John 6:39, 40, 44).

Matha said unto him, I know that he shall rise again IN THE RESURRECTION at the last day (John 11:24).

For the Lord himself shall descend from heaven with a shout, with the voice of the archangel, and with the trump of God: AND THE DEAD IN CHRIST SHALL RISE FIRST (1 Thess. 4:16).

Awake and sing, *ye that dwell in dust;* for thy dew is as the dew of herbs, and the earth shall cast out the dead (Isa. 26:19).

There shall be *a resurrection of the dead,* both of the just and unjust (Acts 24:15).

So also is the resurrection of the dead. It is sown in corruption, it is raised in incorruption (1 Cor. 15:42-44).

Behold I shew you a mystery: We shall not all sleep, but WE (the awakened dead and those who do not sleep) SHALL ALL BE CHANGED (after judgment) . . . For the trumpet shall sound, and THE DEAD SHALL BE RAISED INCORRUPTIBLE, and we shall be changed: *for this corruptible must put on incorruption, and this mortal must put on immortality* (1 Cor. 15:51-53).

If there be no resurrection of the dead, then is Christ not risen: and if Christ be not risen, then is our preaching vain, and your faith is also vain (1 Cor. 15:13-14).

For I know that my redeemer liveth, and that he shall stand *at the latter day upon the earth;* and though after my skin worms destroy this body, yet IN MY FLESH shall I see God, whom *mine eyes shall behold,* and not another (Job. 19: 25-27).

What advantageth it me (Paul) *if the dead rise not?* (1 Cor. 15:32).

I (Paul) have suffered the loss of all things . . . *if by any means I might attain* unto THE RESURRECTION OF THE DEAD (Phil. 3:8, 11).

Now that the dead are raised, even Moses shewed at the bush, when he calleth the Lord the God of Abraham, and the God of Isaac, and the God of Jacob. For he is not a God of the dead, but of the living, for all live unto him (Luke 20:37-38).

> THIRD. The immortality of the Bible, in addition to depending upon "the resurrection of the body", is a thing to be manifested and enjoyed ON THE EARTH, instead of something to which a man ascends in starry regions after death.

Behold, the righteous shall be recompensed IN THE EARTH: much more the wicked and the sinner (Prov. 11:31).

Blessed are the meek: FOR THEY SHALL INHERIT THE EARTH (Matt. 5:5).

The earth which he hath established for ever (Psa. 78:69; Eccles. 1:4).

For the evil-doers *shall be cut off;* but those that wait upon the Lord, THEY SHALL INHERIT THE EARTH (Psa. 37:9).

But the meek shall INHERIT THE EARTH, and shall delight themselves in the abundance of peace (Psa. 37:11).

For such as he blessed of him SHALL INHERIT THE EARTH: and they that be cursed of him shall be cut off (Psa. 37:22).

The righteous SHALL INHERIT THE LAND and dwell therein, *for ever* (Psa. 37:29).

Wait on the Lord, and keep his way, and he shall exalt thee to INHERIT THE LAND: when the wicked are cut off, thou shalt see it (Psa. 37:34).

The righteous *shall never be removed;* but the wicked *shall not inhabit* THE EARTH (Prov. 10:30).

For the promise, that he should be the HEIR OF THE WORLD, was not to Abraham, or to his seed, through the law, *but through the righteousness of faith* (Rom. 4:13).

By faith Abraham, when he was called to go out into A PLACE (the land of Canaan-Acts 7:4) *which he should afterwards receive for an inheritance,* obeyed (Heb. 11:8).

And they sung a new song, saying, Thou art worthy to take the book, and to open the seals thereof; for thou wast slain, and hast redeemed us to God by thy blood out of every kindred, and tongue, and people, and nation; and hast made us unto our God kings and priests: and we SHALL REIGN ON THE EARTH (Rev. 5:9).

And the kingdom, and dominion, and the greatness of the kingdom UNDER THE WHOLE HEAVEN *shall be given to the people of the saints* of the Most High, whose kingdom is an everlasting kingdom, and all dominions shall serve and obey him (Dan. 7:27).

XXVII. The Earth the destined Inheritance of the Righteousness—It follows that THE EARTH and not "heaven above the skies", is the inheritance of the saints, and the scene of God's work with the human race.

For thus saith the Lord that created the heavens; God himself that formed the earth and made it; *he hath established it, he created it not in vain,* HE FORMED IT TO BE INHABITED (Isa. 45:18).

The heavens, even the heavens, are the Lord's; but THE EARTH HE HATH GIVEN *to the children of men* (Psa. 115:16).

And NO MAN HATH ASCENDED UP TO HEAVEN (John 3:13).

Men and brethren, let me freely speak unto you of the patriach David, that *he is both dead and buried, and his sepulchre is with us unto this day* . . . For DAVID IS NOT ASCENDED INTO THE HEAVENS: but he saith himself, The Lord said unto my Lord, Sit thou on my right hand (Acts 2:29, 34).

Little children, yet a little while I am with you. Ye shall seek me; and as I said unto the Jews, *Whither I go* YE CANNOT COME; so now I say to you (John 13:33).

In my Father's House are many mansions: if it were not so I would have told you. I go to prepare a place for you. And if I go and prepare a place for you, *I will come again and receive you unto myself;* that where I am, there ye may be also (John 14:2-3).

XXVIII. HELL.—It follows also, of necessity, that the popular theory of hell and "eternal torments" is a fiction. The word "hell" occurs in the English Bible, but a comparison of the texts quoted below will show that its significance is totally different from that which ignorance and supersition have come to

attach to it; that, in fact, it, almost without exception, means the grave.

O, that thou wouldst hide me in the *grave (sheol),* that thou wouldst keep me secret, until thy wrath be passed, that thou wouldst appoint me a set time, and remember me (Job 14:13).

And they shall not lie with the mighty that are fallen of the uncircumcised, which are *gone down to hell (sheol, grave),* WITH THEIR WEAPONS OF WAR: and *they have laid their swords under their heads,* but their iniquities shall be upon their bones, though they were the terror of the mighty in the land of the living (Ezek. 32:27, compare with Ezek. 31:14-17).

The wicked shall be turned into hell *(sheol, grave),* and all nations that forget God (Psa. 9:17).

Let the wicked be ashamed, and let them be silent in the grave *(sheol)* (Psa. 31:17).

For thou wilt not leave my soul in hell *(sheol, grave;* see Peter's application of this to the resurrection of Christ—Acts 2:27, 30-32); neither wilt thou suffer thine Holy One to see corruption (Psa. 16:10).

The sorrows of death compassed me, and the pains of hell *(sheol, grave)* got hold upon me: I found trouble and sorrow (Psa. 116:3).

Then Jonah prayed unto the Lord his God out of the fish's belly, and said, I cried by reason of my affliction unto the Lord, and he heard me; out of the belly of hell (margin, *the grave*), cried I, and thou heardest my voice (Jonha 2:1-3).

For great is thy mercy towards me: and thou has delivered my soul from the lowest hell [*sheol* (see margin) *grave*] (Psa. 86:13).

But those that seek my soul, to destroy it, shall go into the lower parts of the earth *(grave)* (Psa. 63:9).

And thou, Capernaum, which art exalted unto heaven, shall be brought down to hell *(hades, grave):* for if the mighty works which have been done in thee had been done in Sodom, it would have remained until this day (Matt. 11:23).

And I say also unto thee, that thou art Peter, and upon this rock I will build my church; and the gates of hell *(hades, grave)* shall not prevail against it (Matt. 16:18).

He (David) seeing this before, spake of the resurrection of Christ, that his soul was not left in hell *(hades, grave),* neither his flesh did see corruption (Acts 2:31).

I am he that liveth and was dead; and behold I am alive for evermore. Amen; and have the keys of hell *(hades, grave),* and of death (Rev. 1:18).

O death, where is thy sting? O grave *(hades),* where is thy victory? (1 Cor. 15:55; see Hosea 13:14).

And death and hell *(hades, grave)* delivered up the *dead* which were in them; and they were judged according to their works. And death and hell *(hades, grave)* were cast into the lake of fire (Rev. 20:13-14).

XXVIII. Gehenna—There is another class of texts in which the word "hell" occurs, which have to be differently understood from those quoted in the foregoing section: in this the original is *Gehenna.* A reference to the passages and notes below will, however, show that they give as little countenance to the hell of popular theology as those in which the word "hell" simply means grave. They refer to a locality in the land of Israel, which was, in past times, the scene of judicial inflictions, and which is again to become so on a larger scale.

And if thy hand offend thee, cut it off; it is better for thee to enter into life maimed than having two hands to go into hell (*Gehenna, valley of Hinnom*), into the fire that never shall be quenched: where their worm dieth not, and the fire is not quenched (Mark 9:43).

And fear not them which kill the body but are not able to kill the soul (*psuche,* life), but rather fear him which is able to destroy both soul (*psuche,* life) and body in hell (*Gehenna*) (Matt. 10:28).

For it is the day of the Lord's vengeance, and the year of recompences for the controversy of Zion. And the streams thereof shall be turned into pitch, and the dust thereof into brimstone, and the land thereof shall become burning pitch. It shall not be quenched night nor day; the smoke thereof shall go up for ever; from generation to generation it shall lie waste; none *shall pass* through it for ever and ever (Isa. 34:8-10; see Jer. 7:17-20; 17:27; 2 Chron. 34:25).

Whose fan is in his hand, and he will thoroughly purge his floor, and gather his wheat into the garner:; but *he will burn up the chaff with unquenchable fire* (Matt. 3:12).

The sinners in Zion are afraid; fearfulness hath surprised the hypocrites. Who among us shall dwell with the devouring fire? Who among us shall dwell with everlasting burnings? (Isa. 33:14).

For our God is a consuming fire. (Heb. 12:29).

Behold the day cometh that shall *burn as an oven,* and all the proud, yea, and all that do wickedly shall be stubble, and the day that cometh shall *burn them up,* THAT IT SHALL LEAVE THEM NEITHER ROOT NOR BRANCH. But unto you that fear my name shall the sun of righteousness arise with healing in his wings. And ye shall go forth and grow up as calves of the stall, and *ye shall tread down the wicked,* FOR THEY SHALL BE ASHES UNDER THE SOLES OF YOUR FEET in the day that I shall do this, saith the Lord of Hosts (Mal. 4:1-3).

XXIX. The Destiny of the Wicked. If the hell of popular belief is a mere figment of the imagination it will be asked, What then is the destiny of the wicked according to the Scripture? The answer justified by the foregoing and subjoined testimonies is that they will be put out of existence by divine judgment, with attendant circumstances of shame and suffering.

But *the wicked shall perish,* and the enemies of the Lord shall be as the fat of lambs; they shall consume; INTO SMOKE SHALL THEY CONSUME AWAY (Psa. 37:20).

For the day of the Lord is near upon all the heathen. For as ye have drunk upon my holy mountain, so shall the heathen drink continually, yea, they shall drink, and they shall swallow down, and they shall be AS THOUGH THEY HAD NOT BEEN (Obad. 15-16).

For yet a little while, and the wicked *shall not be:* yea, thou shalt diligently consider his place, and *it shall not be* (Psa. 37:10).

Wait on the Lord, and keep his way, and he shall exalt thee to inherit the land: when the wicked are cut off, thou shalt see it. But *the transgressors shall be destroyed together:* the end of the wicked shall be cut off (Psa. 37:34, 38).

Who shall be punished with EVERLASTING DESTRUCTION from the presence of the Lord, and from the glory of His power, when he shall come to be glorified in his saints, and to be admired in all them that believe (2 Thess. 1:9-10).

The Lord preserveth all them that love him; but ALL THE WICKED WILL HE DESTROY (Psa. 145:20).

Let the sinners be CONSUMED OUT OF THE EARTH, and let the wicked be no more (Psa. 104:35).

For we are unto God a sweet savour of Christ, in them that are saved, and in them that perish; to the one we are the savour of DEATH UNTO DEATH; and to the other the savour of life unto life (2 Cor. 2:15-16).

Whoso despiseth the word SHALL BE DESTROYED: but he that feareth the commandment shall be rewarded (Prov. 13:13).

And these shall go away into *everlasting punishment:* but the righteous into life eternal (Matt. 25:46).

XXX. The irresponsible of Mankind—There is a class, forming by far the largest part of mankind, who have never heard the Gospel, and are in the darkness of complete barbarism. What is to be done with them? Popular theology says (sometimes), They will go to hell; and at other times, They will be admitted to heaven. The first assumption *outrages justice;* the second *violates every divine principle.* We submit, on the strength of the following passages, that they are exempted from responsibility, and will pass away in death, as though they had never existed. THEY WILL NEVER SEE THE LIGHT OF RESURRECTION.

O Lord, our God, other lords besides thee have had dominion over us . . . They are dead, *they shall not live:* they are deceased, THEY SHALL NOT RISE; therefore thou hast visited and DESTROYED them, *and made all their memory to perish* (Isa. 26:13-14).

In their heat I will make their feasts, and I will make them drunken, that they may rejoice, and *sleep a perpetual sleep, and not awake, saith the Lord* (Jer. 51:39).

The man that wandereth out *of the way of understanding* SHALL REMAIN IN THE CONGREGATION OF THE DEAD (Prov. 21:16; Jer. 51:57).

By one man *sin* entered into the world, and *death* by sin, and so *death passed* upon ALL MEN, for that all have sinned (Rom. 5:12).

That ye henceforth walk not as other Gentiles walk, having the *understanding darkened,* being ALIENATED FROM THE LIFE OF GOD *through the ignorance that is in them* because of the blindness of their heart (Eph. 4:17-18).

If our Gospel be hid, IT IS HID *to them that are lost* (2 Cor. 4:3).

Man that is in honour and UNDERSTANDETH NOT, *is like the beasts* THAT PERISH (Psa. 49:20).

There shall be a resurrection of the dead, both of the just and unjust (at Christ's coming) (Acts 24:15).

The Lord Jesus Christ, who shall judge the quick and the dead AT HIS APPEARING and *his kingdom* (2 Tim. 4:1).

For we must *all appear before the judgment seat of Christ,* that every one may receive the things done in his body according to that he hath done, whether it be good or bad (2 Cor. 5:10).

We shall all *stand before the judgment seat* of Christ . . . So then every one of US SHALL GIVE *account of himself* to God (Rom. 14:10-12).

XXXI. The Judgment-Seat of Christ—That at the return of Jesus Christ from heaven, to establish his kingdom on earth, he will, first of all, summon before him for judgment the whole of those who are responsible to his judgment. Those that are dead he will cause to come forth from the dust, and assemble them with the living to his presence. Faithful and unfaithful will be mustered together before his judgment-seat, for the purpose of having it declared, after account rendered, who is worthy of being *invested with immortality* and promoted to the kingdom, and who is deserving of rejection, and *re-consignment to corruption after punishment.* (This precludes the idea created by a superficial reading of the apostolic testimony, that there are no judgments for the saints, and that the resurrection at the coming of Christ will be confined to the accepted, who according to this theory, awake to instantaneous incorruption and immortality).

Every idle word that men shall speak, they SHALL GIVE ACCOUNT thereof in the day of judgment. For by thy words thou shalt be justified, and by thy words thou shalt be condemned (Matt. 12:36-37).

All that are in the graves shall hear his voice, and *shall come forth:* they that have done good unto the resurrection of (*to receive*) life, and they that have done evil unto the resurrection of (*to receive*) damnation (John 5:28-29).

For he that soweth to his flesh shall of the flesh REAP (after judgment) *corruption,* but he that soweth to the Spirit shall of the Spirit REAP (after judgment) life *everlasting* (Gal. 6:8).

Little children, abide in him; that when he shall appear, we may have confidence, and *not be ashamed* before him AT HIS COMING (1 John 2:28).

If that evil servant shall say in his heart, My lord delayeth his coming . . . the lord of that servant SHALL COME in a day when he looketh not for him . . . and shall cut him asunder (Matt. 24:48-51). Of him also shall the Son of Man be ashamed WHEN HE COMETH in the glory of his Father with the holy angels (Mark 8:38).

For the Son of Man *shall come* in the glory of his Father, with his angels, and THEN he shall reward EVERY (good and evil servants) man according to his works (Matt. 16:27).

He shall set the sheep on his right hand, but the goats on the left. Then shall the king say unto them on his right hand, Come ye blessed my Father inherit the kingdom prepared for you from the foundation of the world . . . Then shall he say also unto them on the left hand, Depart from me, ye cursed, into everlasting (aionian) fire . . . And these shall go away into everlasting punishment, but the righteous into (shall have) life eternal (Matt. 25:31-46; Dan 12:2).

And it came to pass that when HE was returned, having received THE KINGDOM then he commanded these servants to be called to him, to whom he had given the money, that *he might know how much every man had gained* by trading (Luke 19:15).

There shall be weeping and gnashing of teeth, when ye shall see Abraham, Isaac, and Jacob, and all the prophets in the kingdom of God, and you yourselves *thrust out* (Luke 13:25-30).

It is appointed unto men once to die, but after this (that is, when the deathstate ends in resurrection) the judgment (Heb. 9:27; Rev. 22:11-12). Who SHALL *give account* to him that is ready to judge both the quick and the dead (1 Pet. 4:5; 1:17; 1 Cor. 3:13; Rev. 11:18; John 12:48).

Therefore, judge nothing before the time, *until the Lord come,* who will both bring to light the hidden things of darkness, and will make manifest the counsels of the hearts (1 Cor. 4:5).

XXXII. BAPTISM is an act of obedience required of all who believe the Gospel. It is a bodily immersion in, and not a face-sprinkling or headpouring with water. Its administration to infants, in any form, is unauthorized and useless: it is only enjoined on those who have intelligence enough to believe the glad tidings of the kingdom of God and the things concerning the name of Jesus Christ. To such it is the means of that present union with Christ which is preparatory to perfect assimilation at the resurrection. It is, therefore, necessary to salvation.

Go ye into all the world and preach the gospel to every creature. He that believeth and is baptized shall be saved: but he that believeth not shall be damned (Mark 16:15-16).

Jesus answered, Verily, verily, I say unto you, Except a man be *born of water* and of the Spirit, he cannot enter into the kingdom of God (John 3:5).

Then Peter said unto them, Repent and *be baptized* every one of you, in the name of Jesus Christ . . . Then they that gladly receive his word *were baptized* (Acts 2:38-41).

And when they (the people of Samaria believed Philip preaching the things concerning the kingdom of God and the name of Jesus Christ, *they were baptized,* both MEN AND WOMEN (Acts 8:12).

A DECLARATION OF THE TRUTH REVEALED IN THE BIBLE, THE SUBLIME AND SIMPLE THEOLOGY OF THE PRIMITIVE CHRISTIANS (UNAMENDED CHRISTADELPHIANS) (continued)

And he commanded the chariot to stand still; and they went down *into the water,* both Philip and the eunuch: and HE BAPTIZED HIM (Acts 8:38).

Paul (after his conversion) arose and WAS BAPTIZED (Acts 9:18).

Lydia was BAPTIZED, and her household (Acts 16:15).

The keeper of the prison (at Philippi) . . . *was BAPTIZED, he and all his straightway . . . believing in God with all his house* (Acts 16:27, 33, 34).

When they (twelve men at Ephesus) *heard this,* they were baptized in the name of the Lord Jesus (Acts 19:5).

The like figure whereunto even BAPTISM DOTH ALSO NOW SAVE us (not the putting away of the filth of the flesh, but the answer of a good conscience toward God) by the resurrection of Jesus Christ (1 Pet. 3:21).

Know ye not that so many of us as were baptized into Jesus Christ were BAPTIZED INTO HIS DEATH? Therefore, WE ARE BURIED WITH HIM BY BAPTISM into death: that like as Christ was raised up from the dead by the glory of the Father even so we also should walk in newness of life. For if we have been planted together in the likenss of his death, we shall be also in the likeness of his resurrection (Rom. 6:3-5).

For as many of you as have been BAPTIZED INTO Christ have put on Christ . . . and if ye be Christ's then are ye Abrahams's seed, and heirs according to the promise (Gal. 3:27-29).

XXXIII. How can so many be wrong? It is usual to rely on numbers in deciding questions of religious belief. This disposition takes the form of the question: "Can so many hundreds of thousands of people, including thousands of clergymen and ministers, be in the wrong?" As a general answer to this, attention is invited to the following testimonies, which declare the fewness of those who receive the truth.

Enter ye in at the strait gate; for wide is the gate and broad is the way that leadeth to destruction, and *many there be that go in thereat* (Matt. 7:13).

Strait is the gate and narrow is the way which leadeth unto life, and FEW THERE BE THAT FIND IT (Matt. 7:14).

Many are called, but FEW ARE CHOSEN (Matt. 22:14).

Hearken, my beloved brethren, Hath not God chosen *the poor of this world, rich in faith,* and heirs of the kingdom which he hath promised to them that love him? (Jas. 2:5).

For ye see your calling, brethren, how that *not many wise men after the flesh,* not many mighty, nor many noble, are called (1 Cor. 1:26-27).

For the WISDOM OF THIS WORLD is foolishness with God (1 Cor. 3:19).

God hath chosen *the foolish things* of the world to confound the wise; and God hath chosen *the weak things* of the world to confound the things which are mighty; and *base things of the world,* and *things which are despised,* hath

God chosen, yea, and things which are not, to bring to nought things that are (1 Cor. 1:27-28).

I pray for them: *I pray not for the world,* but FOR THEM WHICH THOU HAST GIVEN ME; for they are thine. Neither pray I for these alone, but for them also which shall believe on me through their word (John 17:9, 20).

As concerning THIS SECT, we know that *everywhere it is spoken against* (Acts 28:22).

Blessed are ye when men shall hate you, and when they shall separate you from their company, and shall reproach you, and cast out your name as evil, for the Son of Man's sake (Luke 6:22).

If *ye be reproached for the name of Christ* happy are ye; . . . Yet, if any man suffer as a Christian, let him not be ashamed (1 Pet. 4:14-16).

I have given them thy word, and the world hath hated them because they are not of the world, as I am not of the world (John 17:14).

XXXIV. Popular Error and Divine Truth in Contrast— The true test to apply in the determination of religious truth is the one given by Isaiah (8:20): "TO THE LAW AND TO THE TESTIMONY; if they speak not according to this word, *it is because there is* NO LIGHT *in them.*" This principle is extensively applied in the classification of Scripture testimony contained in this pamphlet as a whole. To bring the matter to a focus, the following tabularized contrast of popular tradition with the word of God is here presented:

POPULAR TRADITION	THE WORD OF GOD
"I can imagine that when a man dies *suddenly,* one of the first emotions he experiences in the next world will be surprise . . . He looks about him, 'Oh, that glory, how resplendent yon throne!' He listens to harps of glory, and he can scarce believe it is true. I, the chief of sinners, and yet *in heaven;* and then, when he is conscious that he is *really in heaven,* 'Oh! what everlasting joy'." *C. H. Spurgeon,* Sermon No. 349, p. 311.	And *no man hath ascended up to heaven* (John 3:13). For David *is not ascended* into the heavens (Acts 2:34). As for me, I will behold thy face in righteousness: I shall be satisfied, *when I awake, with thy likeness (Psa. 17:15).*
"I'll praise my Maker with my breath, And when my voice *is fast in death,* Praise shall my nobler powers employ." *Dr. Watts*	For the living know that they shall die: but the dead *know not anything,* neither have they any more a reward; for the memory of them is forgotten. Also their love and their hatred, and their envy, *is now perished;* neither have they any more a portion for

ever in anything that is done under the sun (Eccl. 9:5-6).

His breath goeth forth, he returneth to his earth, *in that very day* HIS THOUGHTS PERISH (Psa. 146:4).

The *dead praise not* the Lord, neither any that go down into silence (Psa. 115:17).

For *in death there* is no remembrance of thee: *in the grave,* who shall give thee thanks? (Psa. 6:5).

"The souls of believers a death do *immediately* pass into glory." *Meth. and Presby. Cathechism.*

God will redeem my soul *from the power of* THE GRAVE (Psa. 49:15).

And this is the Father's will which hath sent me, that of all which he hath given me I should lose nothing , but should *raise it up* again at THE LAST DAY (John 6:39; 11:24; I Thess. 4:13-16).

"With Thee we'll *reign,*
With Thee we'll rise,
And kingdoms gain,
Beyond the skies."

But go thou (Daniel) thy way till the end be, for *thou shalt rest,* and stand in thy lot *at the end of the days* (Dan. 12:13; Job 19:25).

"Beyond the bounds of
time and space,
The saints' secure abode."
Dr. Watts

Blessed are the meek, for they shall inherit the earth (Matt. 5:5).

Thou hast made us unto our God kings and priests, and we shall *reign on the earth* (Rev. 5:10).

"A never dying soul to
save,
And fit it for the sky."
Chas. Wesley

And the kingdom and dominion and the greatness of the kingdom UNDER THE WHOLE HEAVEN shall be given to the people of the saints of the Most High (Dan. 7:27).

"Up to the courts here
angels dwell
It *mounts* triumphant
there;

The soul that sinneth, it shall die (Ezek. 18:4, 20).

He casteth the wicked

Or devils plunge it *down to hell,*
In infinite despair."
Dr. Watts

"When the poor soul shall find itself in the hands of angry fiends, it shall seem in that first moment as though it had been athirst for a thousand years. What will be his surprise. 'And am I,' he will say, 'really here? I was in the streets of *London* but *a moment ago;* I was singing a song but an *instant ago;* and here am I *in hell.*' "—*Chas. H. Spurgeon,* Sermon No. 369, p. 312.

down to the ground (Psa. 147:6).

The wicked is *reserved to the day of* destruction; they shall be *brought forth* to the *day of wrath* (Job. 21:30).

As smoke is driven away, so drive them away; as wax melteth before the fire, so let the *wicked perish* AT THE PRESENCE OF GOD (Psa. 68:2). But the wicked *shall perish,* and the enemies of the Lord shall be as the *fat of lambs;* they shall consume; *into smoke they shall consume away* (Psa. 37:20).

IN VAIN DO THEY WORSHIP ME, TEACHING FOR DOCTRINES THE COMMANDMENTS OF MEN (Matt. 15:9).

IF ANY MAN SPEAK, LET HIM SPEAK AS THE ORACLES OF GOD (1. Pet. 4:11).

XXXV. Departure from the truth foretold—The thoughtful mind, on which the testimony cited in the foregoing thirty-four sections may have made an impression, will enquire, How comes the religious world, with the Bible circulated so freely, and honored so universally, to be so much astray? Without attempting in this limited work to indicate the process by which the result has been arrived at, we call attention to the fact apparent on the face of the subjoined Scriptural quotations, that the truth of apostolic prophecy requires that *the world at the present time should be in a state of complete and universal apostasy.*

There shall come in the last days scoffers, walking after their own lust, and saying, WHERE IS THE PROMISE OF HIS COMING? For since the fathers fell asleep, all things continue as they were from the beginning of the creation (2 Pet. 3:3-4).

A DECLARATION OF THE TRUTH REVEALED IN THE BIBLE, THE SUBLIME AND SIMPLE THEOLOGY OF THE PRIMITIVE CHRISTIANS (UNAMENDED CHRISTADELPHIANS) (continued)

The time will come when *they will not endure sound doctrine;* but after their own lusts shall they HEAP TO THEMSELVES TEACHERS, having itching ears. And *they shall turn away their ears* FROM THE TRUTH, AND SHALL BE TURNED UNTO FABLES (2 Tim. 4:3-4).

When the Son of Man cometh, shall he find faith on the earth? (Luke 18:8).

Now the Spirit speaketh expressly that in the *latter days some shall depart from the faith (tes pistios),* giving heed to seducing spirits and doctrines of devils; speaking lies in hypocrisy; having their conscience seared with a hot iron; FORBIDDEN TO MARRY, and commanding to abstain from meats, which God hath created to be received with thanksgiving of them which BELIEVE and KNOW THE TRUTH (1 Tim. 4:1-3).

For I know this, that after my departing, shall grievous wolves enter in among you, not sparing the flock. Also of your own selves shall men arise, *speaking perverse things,* to draw away disciples after them (Acts 20:29-30).

And for this cause God shall send them *strong delusions,* that they should believe A LIE (2 Thess. 2:11).

For the mystery of iniquity *doth already work* (in Paul's day); only he who now letteth (that is, hindereth), will let (or hinder), until he *(paganism)* be taken out of the way. And then shall that wicked *(the Papacy)* be revealed, whom the Lord shall consume with the spirit of his mouth, and shall destroy with the brightness of His coming (2 Thess. 2:7-8).

And upon her forehead (the forehead of the woman representing Papal Rome—see Rev. 17:18) was a name written, Mystery, Babylon the Great *(Papacy),* The Mother of Harlots *(that is, of State Religions),* and Abominations *(the innumerable sects) of the Earth* (Rev. 17:5).

For behold, the darkness shall cover the earth, and gross darkness the people (Isa. 60:2).

As the days of Noah were, so also shall the coming of the Son of Man be. For as in the days that were before the flood they were eating and drinking, marrying, and giving in marriage, until the day Noah entered into the ark, and knew not until the flood came and took them all away; so shall also the coming of the Son of Man be (Matt. 24:37-39).

XXXVI. Coming Deliverance—It is a common belief that the world's deliverance from the state of things portrayed in the foregoing testimonies is to be effected by the preaching of the gospel. The erroneousness of this view will be apparent from the following testimonies, which teach that it is to result from divine intervention:

Gentiles shall come UNTO THEE from the ends of the earth, and shall say, Surely *our fathers have inherited* lies, vanity and things wherein there is no profit. Therefore, behold, I will *this once* cause them to know, I will cause them to know mine hand and my might; and they shall know that my name is the Lord (Jer. 16:19-21).

For *when thy judgments are in the earth* THE INHABITANTS OF THE WORLD SHALL LEARN RIGHTOUSNESS (Isa. 26:9).

And in this mountain shall the Lord of Hosts make unto all people a feast of fat things . . . And he will destroy in this mountain the face of the covering cast over all people, and the veil that is spread over all nations (Isa. 25:6-7).

Thus saith the Lord of Hosts: In those days it shall come to pass that ten men shall take hold out of *all languages of the nations,* even shall take hold of the skirt of him that is a Jew, saying, We will go with you: for we have heard that God is with you. Yea, many people and strong nations *shall come to seek* the Lord of Hosts in Jerusalem, and to pray before the Lord (Zech 8:23, 22; Mic. 5:2; Isa. 2:3).

And it shall come to pass, that *every one that is left of all the nations* which came against Jerusalem shall even go up from year to year to worship the King, the Lord of Hosts, and to keep the feast of tabernacles (Zech. 14:16).

For the earth *shall be filled* with the knowledge of the glory of the Lord, as the waters cover the sea (Hab. 2:14).

In conclusion, the time is near for the occurrence of the great events outlined in the Scriptures of Truth, and set forth in this pamphlet. The reader is referred to works advertised herewith, for the evidence that *we are now nearing the time of the advent.* May the reader be induced to accept THE TRUTH herein defined, and be found worthy of the inheritance then to be manifested.

AMEN.

"PROVE ALL THINGS: HOLD FAST THAT WHICH IS GOOD" (1. Thess. 5:21).

Notes: *Unamended Christadelphians follow Christadelphian belief on most points. They do not, however, accept the perspective on resurrectional responsibility. They teach instead that all humans will be resurrected to be judged by Christ at the end of time. See items 29-31 of the declaration. This statement is circulated in North America by the Brethren of Messiah, an Unamended organization in Canada.*

* * *

DOCTRINES CHRISTADELPHIANS BELIEVE AND TEACH (UNAMENDED CHRISTADELPHIANS)

That the Bible is the only source now extant of Knowledge concerning God and His purposes, and it was given wholly by the unerring inspiration of God in the writers, and that such errors as have since crept in are due to transcription or translation.

That there is but ONE God, the Father, dwelling in heaven, who, out of His own underived energy created heaven and earth, and all that in them is.

That Jesus Christ is the Son of God (not "God the Son", a phrase not found in Scriptures), begotten of the Virgin Mary by the power of the Holy Spirit.

That God is omnipresent by means of His spirit flowing out from His personal presence. This spirit power is universal in upholding all things in the natural world. For the performance of work that is supernatural and sacred the same spirit by special concentration of the Divine Will becomes Holy Spirit for the holy or sacred work determined to be done.

That man is mortal; a creature of the dust. Immortality is not a present possession, but will be bestowed upon the worthy at the resurrection.

That man in death is unconscious, and depends upon a resurrection for a future life.

That death came into the world through the disobedience of one man. "Wherefore, as by one man sin entered into the world, and death by sin; and so death passed upon all men, in whom all have sinned." (Rom. 5-12).

That as death came into the world through sin, it can only be abolished through the righteousness of One who was raised up of the condemned race of Adam, in the line of Abraham and David, who though wearing the condemned nature was to obtain a title to resurrection by perfect obedience, and by dying abrogate the law of condemnation for HIMSELF, and all who should believe and obey Him.

That at the appearing of Christ prior to the establishment of the Kingdom, the responsible (faithful and unfaithful), dead and living of both classes, will be summoned before His judgment seat "to be judged according to their works"; "and receive in body according to what they have done, whether it be good or bad."

That the gospel concerns the "Kingdom of God" (for the establishment of which Christ taught his disciples to pray, and of which the prophet Daniel says, "the God of Heaven shall set up"), and the "Things Concerning the Name of Jesus Christ," a knowledge and adherence to which are necessary for salvation.

That the kingdom when established will be the kingdom of Israel restored, in the territory it formerly occupied, viz., the land bequeathed to Abraham and his seed (the Christ), by covenant.

That baptism into the name of the Lord Jesus Christ, after knowledge of God's plan, and a faithful walk therein, is essential to salvation.

Notes: *This statement is a much briefer form of the essentials of the belief of Unamended Christadelphians. It is published periodically in* The Christadelphian Advocate, *a leading Unamended journal published in Richmond, Virginia.*

Chapter 11

Independent Fundamentalist Family

Fundamentalism/Evangelicalism

STATEMENT OF FAITH (NATIONAL ASSOCIATION OF EVANGELICALS)

1. We believe the Bible to be the inspired, the only infallible, authoritative Word of God.

2. We believe that there is one God, eternally existent in three persons: Father, Son and Holy Spirit.

3. We believe in the deity of our Lord Jesus Christ, in His virgin birth, in His sinless life, in His miracles, in His vicarious and atoning death through his shed blood, in His bodily resurrection, in His ascension to glory.

4. We believe that for the salvation of lost and sinful man, regeneration by the Holy Spirit is absolutely essential.

5. We believe in the present ministry of the Holy Spirit by whose indwelling the Christian is enabled to live a godly life.

6. We believe in the resurrection of both the saved and the lost; they that are saved unto the resurrection of life and they that are lost unto the resurrection of damnation.

7. We believe in the spiritual unity of believers in our Lord Jesus Christ.

Notes: *Growing out of Plymouth Brethren perspectives, Fundamentalism has adopted as its focus the authority of scripture and the dispensational approach to its interpretation. That dispensation is highlighted by a particular view of eschatology termed "premillennialism." According to premillennialists, Jesus' second coming is imminent and will be followed by the millennium, a thousand years of peace on earth under Christ's personal reign. This will be followed by the final judgment of humankind. The millennium is mentioned prominently in the Book of Revelation, the last book of the Bible.*

Premillennialism is contrasted with other popular eschatologies. According to amillennialism, there will be no millennium. Postmillennialism teaches that the human race will grow into the millennium, and Christ will return only after such a period. Both amillennialism and postmillennialism tend to place less emphasis upon eschatology in their overall presentation of the Christian faith.

During the twentieth century, fundamentalists have spent much of their time defining the nature of scriptural authority. A major difference has centered around two technical terms, "inerrancy" and "infallibility." All fundamentalists affirm the infallibility of scripture (i.e., the Bible is sufficient, complete and trustworthy in matters of humanity's relationship to God). The Bible contains all that God intended to communicate to his human children. The affirmation of the Bible as the Word of God is usually equated with an affirmation of infallibility.

Inerrancy, on the other hand, deals with Biblical statements concerning scientific, historical, poetic, or prophetic matters. To believe in inerrancy is to affirm the Bible is without error on such matters, even in the face of scientific evidence or historical data to the contrary. Statements of faith from fundamentalist churches will often affirm both infallibility and inerrancy. The absence of such statements may merely indicate that the statements predate the development of the terminology and no effort has been made to update them, or may indicate a willingness to tolerate a range of opinion on the subject, especially of inerrancy. Those who believe in inerrancy are generally considered fundamentalists, and those who do not (or tolerate those who do not) are considered conservative evangelicals. The National Association of Evangelicals is the most prominent of several conservative evangelical ecumenical organizations.

Fundamentalists are also concerned with the nature of the Bible's inspiration. They commonly affirm plenary (or verbal) inspiration; that is, the very words, not just thoughts and concepts, were inspired and hence bear the authority of God's revelation. In this regard, fundamentalists have taken into account the problems of textual scholarship. Only the original manuscripts of the Biblical books are held to be ultimately infallible and inerrant. However, none of these original manuscripts are known to be in existence today. The earliest manuscripts available are much later copies of the originals. It is the fundamentalists' belief that these later copies have faithfully retained all matters of importance.

STATEMENT OF FAITH (NATIONAL ASSOCIATION OF EVANGELICALS) (continued)

Quite apart from its statements on scripture, Fundamentalism manifests a continuation of the Reformed theological tradition in the constant affirmation of the total depravity of man and the eternal security of the believer. Because of these affirmations, many from a Methodist tradition (including Holiness and Pentecostal churches), while affirming the infallibility, inerrancy, and/or plenary inspiration of the Bible, have refused to be identified with the fundamentalist movement as a whole and will not attend fundamentalist conferences.

Statements issued by fundamentalist bodies are generally quite brief. Inheriting the Plymouth Brethren reluctance to write "creeds," the fundamentalists have done so only to refute "modernist" theologies, which they believe deny essentials (fundamentals) of the faith. Thus their statements will, on occasion, deal only with crucial matters considered to be under attack.

* * *

DOCTRINAL STATEMENT (AMERICAN COUNCIL OF CHRISTIAN CHURCHES)

Among other equally biblical truths, we believe and maintain the following:

a. The plenary divine inspiration of the Scriptures in the original languages, their consequent inerrancy and infallibility, and, as the Word of God, the supreme and final authority in faith and life;

b. The Triune God: Father, Son, and Holy Spirit;

c. The essential, absolute, eternal deity, and the real and proper, but sinless, humanity of our Lord Jesus Christ;

d. His birth of the Virgin Mary;

e. His substitutionary, expiatory death, in that He gave His life "a ransom for many";

f. His resurrection from among the dead in the same body in which He was crucified, and the second coming of this same Jesus in power and great glory;

g. The total depravity of man through the fall;

h. Salvation, the effect of regeneration by the Spirit and the Word, not by works but by grace through faith;

i. The everlasting bliss of the saved, and the everlasting suffering of the lost;

j. The real spiritual unity in Christ of all redeemed by His precious blood;

k. The necessity of maintaining, according to the Word of God, the purity of the Church in doctrine and life.

Notes: *Conservative even by Fundamentalist standards, the American Council of Christian Churches affirms plenary inspiration, infallibility, and inerrancy.*

THE CONFERENCE TESTIMONY (PROPHETIC BIBLE CONFERENCE OF 1914)

The brethren gathered for the International Conference on the Prophetic Scriptures heartily endorse the declarations made by the previous prophetic conferences; but also feel it their solemn duty, in view of existing conditions in the professing church, to restate and reaffirm their unswerving belief in the following fundamental truths of our holy faith:

1. We believe that the Bible is the Word and Revelation of God and therefore our only authority.

2. We believe in the Deity of our Lord Jesus Christ, that He is very God by whom and for whom "all things were created."

3. We believe in His virgin birth, that He was conceived by the Holy Spirit and is therefore God manifested in the flesh.

4. We believe in salvation by divine sacrifice, that the Son of God gave "His life a ransom for many" and bore "our sins in His own body on the tree."

5. We believe in His physical resurrection from the dead and in His bodily presence at the right hand of God as our Priest and Advocate.

6. We believe in the universality and heinousness of sin, and in salvation by Grace, "not of works lest any man should boast"; that Sonship with God is attained only by regeneration through the Holy Spirit and faith in Jesus Christ.

7. We believe in the Personality and Deity of the Holy Spirit, who came down upon earth on the day of Pentecost to indwell believers and to be the administrator in the church of the Lord Jesus Christ; Who is also here to "reprove the world of sin, and of righteousness, and of judgment."

8. We believe in the great commission which our Lord has given to His church to evangelize the world, and that this evangelization is the great mission of the church.

9. We believe in the second, visible and imminent coming of our Lord and Saviour Jesus Christ to establish His world-wide Kingdom on the earth.

10. We believe in a Heaven of eternal bliss for the righteous and in the conscious and eternal punishment of the wicked.

Furthermore, we exhort the people of God in all denominations to stand by these great truths, so much rejected in our days, and to contend earnestly for the faith which our God has, in His Holy Word, delivered unto the saints.

Notes: *Fundamentalist forces were rallied through a series of conferences held in the late nineteenth and early twentieth centuries which focused upon biblical and prophetic themes. Many of these conferences passed statements [see George W. Dollar's* A History of Fundamentalism in America *(Greenville, SC: Bob Jones University Press, 1973), pp. 27-66, for some sample texts]. The statement reproduced here follows the trend of previous statements, but was distinguished in 1915 by its insertion in the catalog of*

Moody Biblical Institute at the direction of the trustees. A more formal statement was adopted by Moody in 1928.

* * *

DOCTRINAL STATEMENT [DALLAS (TEXAS) THEOLOGICAL SEMINARY]

Article I. THE SCRIPTURES

We believe that "all Scripture is given by inspiration of God," by which we understand the whole Bible is inspired in the sense that holy men of God "were moved by the Holy spirit" to write the very words of Scripture. We believe that this divine inspiration extends equally and fully to all parts of the writings—historical, poetical, doctrinal, and prophetical—as appeared in the original manuscripts. We believe that the whole Bible in the originals is therefore without error. We believe that all the Scriptures center about the Lord Jesus Christ in His person and work in His first and second coming, and hence that no portion, even of the Old Testament, is properly read, or understood until it leads to Him. We also believe that all the Scriptures were designed for our practical instruction. (Mark 12: 26, 36; 13:11; Luke 24:27, 44; John 5:39; Acts 1:16; 17:2-3; 18:28; 26:22-23; 28:23; Rom. 15:4; 1 Cor. 2:13; 10:11; 2 Tim. 3:16; 2 Peter 1:21.)

Article II. THE GODHEAD

We believe that the Godhead eternally exists in three persons—the Father, the Son, and the Holy Spirit—and that these three are one God having precisely the same nature, attributes, and perfections, and worthy of precisely the same homage, confidence, and obedience. (Matt. 28:18-19; Mark 12:29; John 1:14; Acts 5:3-4; 2 Cor. 13:14; Heb. 1:1-3; Rev. 1:4-6.)

Article III. ANGELS, FALLEN AND UNFALLEN

We believe that God created an innumerable company of sinless, spiritual beings, known as angels; that one, "Lucifer, son of the morning"—the highest in rank—sinned through pride, thereby becoming Satan; that a great company of the angels followed him in his moral fall, some of whom became demons and are active as his agents and associates in the prosecution of his unholy purposes, while others who fell are "reserved in everlasting chains under darkness unto the judgment of the great day." (Isa. 14:12-17; Ezek. 28:11-19; 1 Tim. 3:6; 2 Peter 2:4; Jude 1:6.)

We believe that Satan is the originator of sin, and that, under the permission of God, he, through subtlety, led our first parents into transgression, thereby accomplishing their moral fall and subjecting them and their posterity to his own power; that he is the enemy of God and the people of God, opposing and exalting himself above all that is called god or that is worshipped; and that he who in the beginning said, "I will be like the most High," in his warfare appears as an angel of light, even counterfeiting the works of God by fostering religious movements and systems of doctrine, which systems in every case are characterized by a denial of the efficacy of the blood of Christ and of salvation by grace alone. (Gen. 3:1-19; Rom. 5:12-14; 2 Cor. 4:3-4; 11:13-15; Eph. 6:10-12; 2 Thess. 2:4; 1 Tim. 4:1-3.)

We believe that Satan was judged at the cross though not then executed, and that he, a usurper, now rules as the "god of this world;" that, at the second coming of Christ, Satan will be bound and cast into the abyss for a thousand years, and after the thousand years he will be loosed for a little season and then "cast into the lake of fire and brimstone," where he "shall be tormented day and night for ever and ever." (Col. 2:15; Rev. 20:1-3, 10.)

We believe that a great company of angels kept their holy estate and are before the throne of God, from whence they are sent forth as ministering spirits to minister for them who shall be heirs of salvation. (Luke 15:10; Eph. 1:21; Heb. 1:14; Rev. 7:12.)

We believe that man was made lower than the angels; and that, in His incarnation, Christ took for a little time this lower place that he might lift the believer to His own sphere above the angels. (Heb. 2:6-10.)

Article IV. MAN CREATED AND FALLEN

We believe that man was originally created in the image and after the likeness of God, and that he fell through sin, and, as a consequence of his sin, lost his spiritual life, becoming dead in trespasses and sins, and that he became subject to the power of the devil. We also believe that this spiritual death, or total depravity of human nature, has been transmitted to the entire human race of man, the Man Christ Jesus alone being excepted; and hence that every child of Adam is born into the world with a nature which not only possesses no spark of divine life, but is essentially and unchangeably bad apart from divine grace. (Gen. 1:26; 2:17; 6:5; Ps. 14:1-3; 51:5; Jer. 17:9; John 3:6; 5:40; 6:53; Rom. 3:10-19; 8:6-7; Eph. 2:1-3; 1 Tim. 5:6; 1 John 3:8.)

Article V. THE DISPENSATIONS

We believe that the dispensations are stewardships by which God administers His purpose on the earth through man under varying responsibilities. We believe that the changes in the dispensational dealings of God with man depend on changed conditions or situations in which man is successively found with relation to God, and that these changes are the result of the failures of man and the judgments of God. We believe that different administrative responsibilities of this character are manifest in the biblical record, that they span the entire history of mankind, and that each ends in the failure of man under the respective test and in an ensuing judgment from God. We believe that three of these dispensations or rules of life are the subject of the Mosaic Law, the present dispensation of grace, and the future dispensation of the millennial kingdom. We believe that these are distinct and are not to be intermingled or confused, as they are chronologically successive.

We believe that the dispensations are not ways of salvation nor different methods of administering the so-called Covenant of Grace. They are not in themselves dependent on covenant relationships but are ways of life and responsibility to God which test the submission of man to His revealed will during a particular time. We believe, that, if man does trust in his own efforts to gain the favor of God or salvation under any dispensational test, because of inherent sin his failure to satisfy fully the just requirements of God is inevitable and his condemnation sure.

We believe that according to the "eternal purpose" of God (Eph. 3:11) salvation in the divine reckoning is always "by grace, through faith," and rests upon the basis of the shed blood of Christ. We believe that God has always been gracious, regardless of the ruling dispensation, but that man has not at all times been under an administration or stewardship of grace as is true in the present dispensation. (1 Cor. 9:17; Eph. 3:2; 3:9, A.S.V.; Col. 1:25; 1 Tim. 1:4, A.S.V.)

We believe that it has always been true that "without faith it is impossible to please" God (Heb. 11:6), and that the principle of faith was prevalent in the lives of all the Old Testament saints. However, we believe that it was historically impossible that they should have had as the conscious object of their faith the incarnate, crucified Son, the Lamb of God (John 1:29), and that it is evident that they did not comprehend as we do that the sacrifices depicted the person and work of Christ. We believe also that they did not understand the redemptive significance of the prophecies or types concerning the sufferings of Christ (1 Peter 1:10-12): therefore, we believe that their faith toward God was manifested in other ways as is shown by the long record in Hebrews 11:1-40. We believe further that their faith thus manifested was counted unto them for righteousness (cf. Rom. 4:3 with Gen. 15:6; Rom. 4:5-8; Heb. 11:7).

Article VI. THE FIRST ADVENT

We believe that, as provided and proposed by God and as preannounced in the prophecies of the Scriptures, the eternal Son of God came into this world that He might manifest God to men, fulfill prophecy, and become the Redeemer of a lost world. To this end He was born of the virgin, and received a human body and a sinless human nature. (Luke 1:30-35; John 1:18; 3:16; Heb. 4:15.)

We believe that, on the human side, He became and remained a perfect man, but sinless throughout His life; yet He retained His absolute deity, being at the same time very God and very man, and that His earth-life sometimes functioned within the sphere of that which was human and sometimes within the sphere of that which was divine. (Luke 2:40; John 1:1-2; Phil. 2:5-8.)

We believe that in fulfillment of prophecy He came first to Israel as her Messiah-King, and that, being rejected of that nation, He, according to the eternal counsels of God, gave His life as a ransom for all. (John 1:11; Acts 2:22-24; 1 Tim. 2:6.)

We believe that, in infinite love for the lost, He voluntarily accepted His Father's will and became the divinely provided sacrificial Lamb and took away the sin of the world; bearing the holy judgments against sin which the righteousness of God must impose. His death was, therefore, substitutionary in the most absolute sense—the just for the unjust—and by His death He became the Savior of the lost. (John 1:29; Rom. 3:25-26; 2 Cor. 5:14; Heb. 10:5-14; 1 Peter 3:18.)

We believe that, according to the Scriptures, He arose from the dead in the same body, though glorified, in which He had lived and died, and that His resurrection body is the pattern of that body which ultimately will be given to all believers. (John 20:20; Phil. 3:20.)

We believe that, on departing from the earth, He was accepted of His Father and that His acceptance is a final assurance to us that His redeeming work was perfectly accomplished. (Heb. 1:3.)

We believe that He became Head over all things to the church which is His body, and in this ministry He ceases not to intercede and advocate for the saved. (Eph. 1:22-23; Heb. 7:25; 1 John 2:1.)

Article VII. SALVATION ONLY THROUGH CHRIST

We believe that, owing to universal death through sin, no one can enter the kingdom of God unless born again; and that no degree of reformation however great, no attainments in morality however high, no culture however attractive, no baptism or other ordinance however administered, can help the sinner to take even one step toward heaven: but a new nature imparted from above, a new life implanted by the Holy Spirit through the Word, is absolutely essential to salvation, and only those thus saved are sons of God. We believe, also, that our redemption has been accomplished solely by the blood of our Lord Jesus Christ, who was made to be sin and was made a curse for us, dying in our room and stead; and that no repentance, no feeling, no faith, no good resolutions, no sincere efforts, no submission to the rules and regulations of any church, nor all the churches that have existed since the days of the Apostles can add in the very least degree to the value of the blood, or to the merit of the finished work wrought for us by Him who united in His person true and proper deity with perfect and sinless humanity. (Lev. 17:11; Isa. 64:6; Matt. 26:28; John 3:7-18; Rom. 5:6-9; 2 Cor. 5:21; Gal. 3:13; 6:15; Eph. 1:7; Phil. 3:4-9; Titus 3:5; James 1:18; 1 Peter 1:18-19, 23.)

We believe that the new birth of the believer comes only through faith in Christ and that repentance is a vital part of believing, and is in no way, in itself, a separate and independent condition of salvation; nor are any other acts, such as confession, baptism, prayer, or faithful service, to be added to believing as a condition of salvation. (John 1:12; 3:16, 18, 36; 5:24; 6:29; Acts 13:39: 16:31; Rom. 1:16-17; 3:22, 26; 4:5; 10:4; Gal. 3:22.)

Article VIII. THE EXTENT OF SALVATION

We believe that when an unregenerate person exercises that faith in Christ which is illustrated and described as such in the New Testament, he passes immediately out of spiritual death into spiritual life, and from the old creation into the new; being justified from all things, accepted before the Father according as Christ His Son is accepted, loved as Christ is loved, having his place and portion as linked to Him and one with Him forever. Though the saved one may have occasion to grow in the realization of his blessings and to know a fuller measure of divine power through the yielding of his life more fully to God, he is, as soon as he is saved, in possession of every spiritual blessing and absolutely complete in Christ, and is, therefore, in no way required by God to seek a so-called "second blessing," or a "second work of grace." (John 5:24; 17:23; Acts 13:39; Rom. 5:1; 1 Cor. 3:21-23; Eph. 1:3; Col. 2:10; 1 John 4:17; 5:11-12.)

Article IX. SANTIFICATION

We believe that sanctification, which is a setting apart unto God, is three-fold: It is already complete for every saved person because his position toward God is the same as Christ's position. Since the believer is in Christ, he is set apart unto God in the measure in which Christ is set apart unto God. We believe, however, that he retains his sin nature, which cannot be eradicated in this life. Therefore, while the standing of the Christian in Christ is perfect, his present state is no more perfect than his experience in daily life. There is, therefore a progressive sanctification wherein the Christian is to "grow in grace" and to "be changed" by the unhindered power of the Spirit. We believe, also, that the child of God will yet be fully sanctified in his state as he is now sanctified in his standing in Christ when he shall see his Lord and shall be "like Him." (John 17:17; 2 Cor. 3:18, 7:1; Eph. 4:24; 5:25-27; 1 Thess. 5:23; Heb. 10:10, 14; 12:10.)

Article X. ETERNAL SECURITY

We believe that, because of the eternal purpose of God toward the objects of His love, because of His freedom to exercise grace toward the meritless on the ground of the propitiatory blood of Christ, because of the very nature of the divine gift of eternal life, because of the present and unending intercession and advocacy of Christ in heaven, because of the immutability of the unchangeable covenants of God, because of the regenerating, abiding presence of the Holy Spirit in the hearts of all who are saved, we and all true believers everywhere, once saved shall be kept saved forever. We believe, however, that God is a holy and righteous Father and that, since He cannot overlook the sin of His children, He will when they persistently sin chasten them and correct them in infinite love; but having undertaken to save them and keep them forever, apart from all human merit, He, who cannot fail, will in the end present every one of them faultless before the presence of His glory and conformed to the image of His Son. (John 5:24; 10:28; 13:1; 14:16-17; 17:11; Rom. 8:29; 1 Cor. 6:19; Heb. 7:25; 1 John 2:1-2; 5:13; Jude 1:24.)

Article XI. ASSURANCE

We believe it is the privilege, not only of some, but of all who are born again by the Spirit through faith in Christ as revealed in the Scriptures, to be assured of their salvation from the very day they take Him to be their Savior and that this assurance is not founded upon any fancied discovery of their own worthiness or fitness, but wholly upon the testimony of God in His written Word, exciting within His children filial love, gratitude, and obedience. (Luke 10:20; 22:32; 2 Cor. 5:1; 6-8; 2 Tim. 1:12; Heb. 10:22; 1 John 5:13.)

Article XII. THE HOLY SPIRIT

We believe that the Holy Spirit, the Third Person of the blessed Trinity, though omnipresent from all eternity, took up His abode in the world in a special sense on the day of Pentecost according to the divine promise, dwells in every believer, and by His baptism unites all to Christ in one body, and that He, as the Indwelling One, is the source of all power and all acceptable worship and service. We believe that He never takes His departure from the church, nor from the feeblest of the saints, but is ever present to testify of Christ; seeking to occupy believers with Him and not with themselves nor with their experiences. We believe that His abode in the world in this special sense will cease when Christ comes to receive His own at the completion of the church. (John 14:16-17; 16:7-15; 1 Cor. 6:19; Eph. 2:22; 2 Thess. 2:7.)

We believe that, in this age, certain well-defined ministries are committed to the Holy Spirit, and that it is the duty of every Christian to understand them and to be adjusted to them in his own life and experience. These ministries are: The restraining of evil in the world to the measure of the divine will; the convicting of the world respecting sin, righteousness, and judgment; the regenerating of all believers; the indwelling and anointing of all who are saved, thereby sealing them unto the day of redemption; the baptizing into the one body of Christ of all who are saved; and the continued filling for power, teaching, and service of those among the saved who are yielded to Him and who are subject to His will. (John 3:6; 16:7-11; Rom. 8:9; 1 Cor. 12:13; Eph. 4:30; 5:18; 2 Thess. 2:7; 1 John 2:20-27.)

We believe that some gifts of the Holy Spirit such as speaking in tongues and miraculous healings were temporary. We believe that speaking in tongues was never the common or necessary sign of the baptism nor of the filling of the Spirit, and that the deliverance of the body from sickness or death awaits the consummation of our salvation in the resurrection. (Acts 4:8, 31: Rom. 8:23; 1 Cor. 13:8.)

Article XIII. THE CHURCH A UNITY OF BELIEVERS

We believe that all who are united to the risen and ascended Son of God are members of the church which is the body and bride of Christ, which began at Pentecost and is completely distinct from Israel. Its members are constituted as such regardless of membership or nonmembership in the organized churches of earth. We believe that by the same Spirit all believers in this age are baptized into, and thus become, one body that is Christ's, whether Jews or Gentiles, and having become members one of another, are under solemn duty to keep the unity of the Spirit in the bond of peace, rising above all sectarian differences, and loving one another with a pure heart fervently. (Matt. 16:16-18; Acts 2:42-47; Rom. 12:5; 1 Cor. 12:12-27; Eph. 1:20-23; 4:3-10; Col. 3:14-15.)

Article XIV. THE SACRAMENTS OR ORDINANCES

We believe that water baptism and the Lord's Supper are the only sacraments and ordinances of the church and that they are a scriptural means of testimony for the church in this age. (Matt. 28:19; Luke 22:19-20; Acts 10:47-48; 16:32-33; 18:7-8; 1 Cor. 11:26.)

Article XV. THE CHRISTIAN'S WALK

We believe that we are called with a holy calling, to walk not after the flesh, but after the Spirit, and so to live in the power of the indwelling Spirit that we will not fulfill the lust of the flesh. But the flesh with its fallen, Adamic nature, which in this life is never eradicated, being with us to the end of our earthly pilgrimage, needs to be kept by the Spirit constantly in subjection to Christ, or it will surely manifest its presence in our lives to the dishonor of our Lord. (Rom. 6:11; 8:2, 4, 12-13; Gal. 5:16; Eph. 4:22-24; Col. 2:1-10; 1 Peter 1:14-16; 1 John 1:4-7; 3:5-9.)

Article XVI. THE CHRISTIAN'S SERVICE

We believe that divine, enabling gifts for service are bestowed by the Spirit upon all who are saved. While there is a diversity of gifts, each believer is energized by the same Spirit, and each is called to his own divinely appointed service as the Spirit may will. In the apostolic church there were certain gifted men-apostles, prophets, evangelists, pastors, and teachers—who were appointed by God for the perfecting of the saints unto their work of the ministry. We believe also that today some men are especially called of God to be evangelists, pastors and teachers, and that it is to the fulfilling of His will and to His eternal glory that these shall be sustained and encouraged in their service for God. (Rom. 12:6; 1 Cor. 12:4-11; Eph. 4:11.)

We believe that, wholly apart from salvation benefits which are bestowed equally upon all who believe, rewards are promised according to the faithfulness of each believer in his service for his Lord, and that these rewards will be bestowed at the judgment seat of Christ after He comes to receive His own to Himself. (1 Cor. 3:9-15; 9:18-27; 2 Cor. 5:10.)

Article XVII. THE GREAT COMMISSION

We believe that it is the explicit message of our Lord Jesus Christ to those whom He has saved that they are sent forth by him into the world even as He was sent forth of His Father into the world. We believe that, after they are saved, they are divinely reckoned to be related to this world as strangers and pilgrims, ambassadors and witnesses, and that their primary purpose in life should be to make Christ known to the whole world. (Matt. 28:18-19; Mark 16:15; John 17:18; Acts 1:8; 2 Cor. 5:18-20; 1 Peter 1:17; 2:11.)

Article XVIII. THE BLESSED HOPE

We believe that, according to the Word of God, the next great event in the fulfillment of prophecy will be the coming of the Lord in the air to receive to Himself into heaven both His own who are alive and remain unto His coming, and also all who have fallen asleep in Jesus, and that this event is the blessed hope set before us in the Scripture, and for this we should be constantly looking. (John 14:1-3; 1 Cor. 15:51-52; Phil. 3:20; 1 Thess. 4:13-18; Titus 2:11-14.)

Article XIX. THE TRIBULATION

We believe that the translation of the church will be followed by the fulfillment of Israel's seventieth week (Dan. 9:27; Rev. 6:1; 19:21) during which the church, the body of Christ, will be in heaven. The whole period of Israel's seventieth week will be a time of judgment on the whole earth, at the end of which the times of the Gentiles will be brought to a close. The latter half of this period will be the time of Jacob's trouble (Jer. 30:7), which our Lord called the great tribulation (Matt. 24:15-21). We believe that universal righteousness will not be realized previous to the second coming of Christ, but that the world is day by day ripening for judgment and that the age will end with a fearful apostasy.

Article XX. THE SECOND COMING OF CHRIST

We believe that the period of great tribulation in the earth will be climaxed by the return of the Lord Jesus Christ to the earth as He went, in person on the clouds of heaven, and with power and great glory to introduce the millennial age, to bind Satan and place him in the abyss, to lift the curse which now rests upon the whole creation, to restore Israel to her own land and to give her the realization of God's covenant promises, and to bring the whole world to the knowledge of God. (Deut. 30:1-10; Isa. 11:9; Ezek. 37:21-28; Matt. 24:15-25; 46; Acts 15:16-17; Rom. 8:19-23; 11:25-27; 1 Tim. 4:1-3; 2 Tim. 3:105; Rev. 20:1-3.)

Article XXI. THE ETERNAL STATE

We believe that at death the spirits and souls of those who have trusted in the Lord Jesus Christ for salvation pass immediately into His presence and there remain in conscious bliss until the resurrection of the glorified body when Christ comes for His own, whereupon souls and body reunited shall be associated with Him forever in glory; but the spirits and souls of the unbelieving remain after death conscious of condemnation and in misery until the final judgment of the great white throne at the close of the millennium, when soul and body reunited shall be cast into the lake of fire, not to be annihilated, but to be punished with everlasting destruction from the presence of the Lord, and from the glory of His power. (Luke 16:19-26; 23:42; 2 Cor. 5:8; Phil. 1:23; 2 Thess. 1:7-9; Jude 1 6-7; Rev. 20:11-15.)

Notes: *The Dallas Theological Seminary is among the most prominent schools serving the Independent Fundamentalist community. Several church bodies, such as the Independent Bible Church Movement, have grown directly out of the Seminary through the bonding together of alumni. The Seminary's lengthy statement gives substance to the many brief documents published by fundamentalist churches on their doctrine. The article on sanctification places the statement squarely in the Reformed theological position (of the Westminster Confession) as opposed to the Wesleyan-Methodist tradition. The eschatological statements (articles 18-21) provide a concise presentation of premillennial doctrine. The statement also includes the idea of Christ's appearance prior to the seventh dispensational period known as the tribulation and His true second coming to establish the millennium following that tribulation period. This position is frequently termed "pretribulation" (or simply "pretrib") premillennialism.*

ARTICLES OF FAITH (AMERICAN EVANGELICAL CHRISTIAN CHURCHES)

The A.E.C.C. was founded as an inter-doctrinal ecclesiastical body. Inter-doctrinal because we feel that its Seven Articles of Faith to which each member must subscribe are the first and foremost doctrines of the Bible and are found in both Calvinistic and Arminian teachings.

The Seven Articles of Faith are set forth as follows:

1. The Bible as the written word of God.
2. The Virgin Birth.
3. The Deity of Jesus the Christ.
4. Salvation through the Atonement.
5. The guidance of our life through prayer.
6. The return of the Saviour.
7. The establishment of the kingdom of God on earth.

We call the above seven points "The Essentials" and beyond these the A.E.C.C. does not stress any denominational doctrines. Anyone who can subscribe thereto may become a member of the organization and is welcome to fellowship with us. If the individual holds to certain views, not in conflict to these, in dress, observance of holy days, the eating of or abstinence of certain foods, etc., we feel that he or she should be allowed the liberty to do so.

Notes: *This short statement provides significant room for different opinions on a variety of controversial issues among evangelicals.*

*   *   *

WHAT WE BELIEVE (AMERICAN MISSION FOR OPENING CHURCHES)

1. We believe that all Scripture is the infallible, divinely inspired Word of God; inerrant in the original autographs; and is the guide for Christian faith and practice. II Tim. 3:16,17

2. We believe in one God eternally existing in three Persons: Father, Son, and Holy Spirit. Matt. 28:18,19; Mark 12:29

3. We believe that Jesus Christ was begotten by the Holy Spirit, born of the Virgin Mary, and is true God and true man. Matt. 1:16,18,21,25

4. We believe that the Holy Spirit, the Third Person of the Godhead, dwells in every believer, sealing them unto the day of redemption, and by His baptism unites all to Christ in one body. John 16:8-11; 1 Cor. 12:12-14, Eph. 1:13,14

5. We believe that man, who was created in the image of God, sinned and thereby incurred physical death as well as that spiritual death which is separation from God and that all human beings are born with a sinful nature. Gen. 1:26,27; 3:1-13; Psalm 51:5

6. We believe that Jesus Christ died for our sins according to the Scriptures as a representative and substitutionary sacrifice; and all who believe in Him are justified by faith and regenerated by the Holy Spirit, becoming children of God. 1 Tim. 1:15; Acts 4:12; John 1:12,13

7. We believe in the literal, physical resurrection of our Lord, His ascension into Heaven, and His present life there for us as High Priest and Advocate. John 20:11-18, 19-24; Acts 1:10; Heb. 8:1

8. We believe in the personal, imminent, pretribulational and premillennial coming of the Lord Jesus Christ for His redeemed ones. I Thess. 4:13-17

9. We believe in the bodily resurrection of the just and unjust, the everlasting blessedness of the saved and everlasting punishment of the lost. Acts 24:15; Rev. 20:5,6

Notes: *The statement of the American Mission is similar to those of both the Independent Fundamental Churches of America and the Bethany Bible Church.*

*   *   *

DOCTRINE AND TENETS (BERACHAH CHURCH)

The following basic doctrines contained in the Holy Scriptures are adopted:

1. THE HOLY SCRIPTURES

We believe the Holy Scriptures to be the inspired Word of God, authoritative, inerrant, and God-breathed (II Timothy 3:16-17; II Peter 1:20-21; Matthew 5:18; John 16:12-13).

2. THE GODHEAD

We believe in one Triune God, existing in three persons, Father, Son and Holy Spirit, eternal in being, identical in nature, equal in power and glory and having the same attributes and perfections. (Deuteronomy 6:4; II Corinthians 13:14).

3. THE TOTAL DEPRAVITY OF MAN

We believe that man was created in the image and likeness of God but that in Adam's sin the race fell, inherited a sinful nature, became alienated from God, and is totally unable to retrieve his lost condition (Genesis 1:26-27; Romans 3:22-23; 5:12; Ephesians 2:12).

4. THE PERSON AND WORK OF CHRIST

We believe that the Lord Jesus Christ, the eternal Son of God, became man, without ceasing to be God, having been conceived of the Holy Spirit and born of the virgin Mary, in order that He might reveal God and redeem sinful man; that He accomplished our redemption through His spiritual death on the cross as a substitutionary sacrifice; that our redemption is made sure to us by his literal physical resurrection from the dead (John 1:1-2, 14; Luke 1:35; Romans 3:24-25; 4:25; I Peter: 3-5); that the Lord Jesus Christ is now in Heaven, exalted at the right hand of God, where as the High Priest for His people, He fulfills the ministry of Representative, Intercessor and Advocate (Hebrews 9:24; 7:25; Romans 8:34; I John 2:1-2).

DOCTRINE AND TENETS (BERACHAH CHURCH) (continued)

5. THE PERSONALITY AND WORK OF THE HOLY SPIRIT

We believe that the Holy Spirit is a person who convicts the world of sin, indwells all believers in the present age, baptizes them into the body of Christ, seals them unto the day of redemption, and that it is the duty of every believer to be filled with the Holy Spirit (Romans 8:9; I Corinthians 12:12-14; Ephesians 1:13-14; 5:18).

6. SALVATION

We believe that salvation in every dispensation is the gift of God brought to man by grace and received by personal faith in the Lord Jesus Christ, whose efficatious death on the cross provided man's reconciliation to God. (Ephesians 2:8-20; John 1:12; Ephesians 1:7).

7. THE ETERNAL SECURITY OF BELIEVERS

We believe that all believers are kept secure forever (Romans 8:1, 38-39; John 10:27-30; I Corinthians 1:4-8).

8. THE CHURCH

We believe that the Church, which is now the body and shall be the bride of Christ, is a spiritual organism made up of all born-again persons of this age irrespective of their affiliation with Christian organizations (Ephesians 1:22-23; 5:25-27; I Corinthians 12:12-14).

9. THE PERSONALITY OF SATAN

We believe in the personality of Satan, who is the open and declared enemy of God and man (Job 1:6-7; Matthew 4:2-11; Isaiah 14:12-17).

10. THE BLESSED HOPE

We believe that the next great event in the fulfillment of prophecy will be the coming of the Lord Jesus in the air to receive to Himself the dead in Christ and believers who are alive at His coming, otherwise known as the Rapture and Translation of the Church (I Corinthians 15:51-57; I Thessalonians 4:13-18; Titus 2:11-14).

11. THE TRIBULATION

We believe that the Rapture of the Church will be followed by the fulfillment of Israel's seventieth week, the latter half of which is the time of Jacob's trouble, the great tribulation (Daniel 9:27; Jeremiah 30:7; Matthew 24:15-21; Revelation 6:1-19; 21).

12. THE SECOND COMING OF CHRIST

We believe that the great tribulation will be climaxed by the (premillennial) return of the Lord Jesus Christ to earth to set up his kingdom (Zechariah 14:4-11; Matthew 24:15-25; 46; II Thessalonians 1:7-10; Revelation 20:6).

13. THE ETERNAL STATE

We believe that the soul and human spirit of those who have believed in the Lord Jesus Christ for salvation do at death immediately pass into His presence, and there remain in the conscious bliss until the resurrection of the body at His coming, when soul, human spirit and body reunited shall be associated with Him forever in the glory; but the souls of unbelievers remain after death in conscious misery until the final judgement of the Great White Throne at the close of the millennium, when soul and body reunited shall be cast into the lake of fire, not to be annihilated, but to be punished with everlasting destruction from the presence of the Lord and from the glory of His power (Luke 16:19-26; 23:43; II Corinthians 5:8; Philippians 1:23; II Thessalonians 1:7-9; Jude, verses 6-7; Revelation 20:11-15).

14. THE RESPONSIBILITY OF BELIEVERS

To "Grow in grace and knowledge of the Lord Jesus Christ," to the end that His life is consistent with the Lord's plan thus bringing both blessing to the believer and honor to the Lord.

15. CHURCH ORDINANCES

We believe that the Lord Jesus Christ instituted the Lord's Supper to be observed until His return (Matthew 28:19-20: I Corinthians 11:23-26).

16. SOVEREIGNTY

We believe that God, existing as Father, Son and Holy Spirit, is sovereign, and exercises supreme and absolute rule over all creation as a part of and consistent with the essence and attributes of deity. (I Chronicles 29:11, 12; Daniel 4:35; Psalms 24:1; Ephesians 1:11; I Timothy 6:15).

17. SPIRITUALITY

We believe that spirituality is an absolute condition in the life of a believer in this dispensation wherein he is filled or controlled by the Holy Spirit, walking in love and fellowship with the Lord Jesus Christ.

We believe that spirituality is distinct from maturity, that a believer becomes carnal through any act of mental, verbal or overt sin and that spirituality or fellowship with Christ is restored solely by personal confession of that sin to God the Father. (John 15:7, 8; II Corinthians 5:6; Galatians 5:16; Ephesians 5:18; Romans 6:11-13; I John 1:9, I John 1:5; 2:2; I Corinthians 11:30, 31).

18. SPIRITUAL GIFTS

We believe that God the Holy Spirit in grace and apart from human merit sovereignly bestows spiritual gifts to believers in this dispensation. Some of the permanent spiritual gifts which exist today are pastor-teacher, evangelist, administrator. We further believe that the temporary spiritual gifts ceased with the completion of the Canon of Scripture and these were: Apostleship, Prophecy, Speaking in Tongues, Interpreting Tongues, Healing and Working of Miracles. (I Corinthians 12, 13; Ephesians 4:7-12; Romans 12:4-8). Any member practicing these temporary gifts shall be subject to immediate dismissal.

B. TENETS

1. This Church shall not at any time become a member, sanction, or support any denomination, association of Churches or religious organization of any kind.

2. This Church shall not solicit anyone to become a member. Those who desire to affiliate with this Church may do so by complying with the provision of Article V.

3. This Church shall not knowingly accept gifts from unbelievers nor make individual solicitation of funds or pledges among believers.

Notes: *The Berachah Church was formed by a graduate of Dallas Theological Seminary, and the church's statement in large part is derived from the one published by the school.*

*   *   *

STATEMENT OF FAITH (BETHANY BIBLE CHURCH)

1. We believe in the Scriptures of the Old and New Testaments as being verbally inspired and completely inerrant in the original writings and of supreme and final authority in faith and life.

2. We believe in one God, eternally existing in three persons: Father, Son and Holy Spirit.

3. We believe that Jesus Christ was begotten of the Holy Spirit and born of the Virgin Mary and is true God and true man.

4. We believe that man was created in the image of God; that he sinned and thereby incurred not only physical death but also that spiritual death which is separation from God; and that all human beings are born with a sinful nature and in the case of those who reach moral responsibility, become sinners in thought, word and deed.

5. We believe that the Lord Jesus Christ died for our sins according to the scriptures as a representative and substitutionary sacrifice, and that all who believe in Him are justified on the ground of His shed blood.

6. We believe in the resurrection of the crucified body of our Lord, in His ascension into Heaven, and His present life for us as High Priest and Advocate.

7. We believe in "that blessed hope," the personal, premillennial and imminent return of our Lord and Saviour, Jesus Christ.

8. We believe that all who receive by faith the Lord Jesus Christ are born of the Holy Spirit and thereby become children of God, a relationship in which they are eternally secure.

9. We believe in the bodily resurrection of the just and of the unjust; the everlasting blessedness of the saved and the everlasting conscious punishment of the lost.

Notes: *The Bethany Bible Church congregation and its associated churches have a close relationship with Dallas Theological Seminary, where most of the ministers graduated.*

*   *   *

STATEMENT OF FAITH (CHURCH OF CHRISTIAN LIBERTY)

We believe in and earnestly contend for the verbal, plenary inspiration and consequent inerrancy of the Scriptures; the Trinity of the Godhead; the Deity and Virgin Birth of Christ; the Person and work of the Holy Spirit; the Genesis account of creation; the fall and resulting total depravity of man by nature; the sovereign unconditional election of God; the particular redemption wrought by the death of Jesus Christ; the irresistible grace of God; the perseverance and preservation of the saints; salvation by grace through faith apart from works; the maintenance of good works by believers as evidence of their faith; the independence of the local church; the Bible as its only rule of faith and practice; a regenerated church membership; the baptism of believers; the Lord's Table as a memorial of His once-for-all death; the priesthood of believers; the bodily resurrection, ascension, and personal, visible, return of Christ; the personality of the Devil; the resurrection of the just and the unjust; and the everlasting happiness of the just in Heaven and the everlasting conscious suffering of the unjust in the lake of fire.

Notes: *The founder of the Church of Christian Liberty graduated from Trinity Theological Seminary, the school sponsored by the Evangelical Free Church.*

*   *   *

STATEMENT OF FUNDAMENTAL TRUTHS (INDEPENDENT CHRISTIAN CHURCHES INTERNATIONAL)

We believe in the complete and entire Divine inspiration of the Bible (both the Old and New Testaments); the creation of many by the direct act of Jehovah God; the incarnation and virgin birth of our blessed Lord and Saviour, Jesus Christ: the Son of God; His vicarious atonement for the sins of mankind by the shedding of His blood on the cross; His literal physical death and His bodily resurrection from the tomb; His power to save men from sin; the adoption into the family of God through the regeneration by the Holy Spirit; and the gift of eternal life by the grace of God.

We accept the Bible as our all-sufficient rule of faith and practice. Therefore, this STATEMENT OF FUNDAMENTAL BELIEFS is intended only as a basis of fellowship among us in order that we might all "speak the same thing" (I Corinthians 1:10 and Acts 2:42). The human phraseology which is employed in this statement is not inspired, but the truths set forth in it are held to be essential to a fundamental ministry. No claim is made that it contains all truths in the Bible, but that it covers our present needs regarding these fundamental matters.

1. THE SCRIPTURES INSPIRED

The Bible is the inspired Word of God, a revelation from God to man. It is the infallible rule of faith and conduct, and is superior to conscience and reason, while not being contrary to reason. (II Timothy 3:15-16; II Peter 1:21; I Peter 1:23-25 and Hebrews 4:12).

2. THE ONE TRUE GOD

The one true God has revealed Himself as the eternally self-existent, self-revealed "I AM"; and has further revealed Himself as embodying the principles of relationship and association, ie., as the Father, Son and Holy Spirit. (Deuteronomy 6:4; Mark 12:29; Isaiah 43:10; Matthew 28:19 and Luke 3:22).

3. MAN, HIS FALL AND REDEMPTION

Man was created good and perfect; for God said: "Let us make man in our image, after our likeness." But man, by voluntary transgression, fell, and his only hope of redemp-

tion is in Jesus Christ. (Genesis 1:26-31; 3:1-17 and
Romans 5:12-21).

4. THE SALVATION OF MAN

(a) CONDITIONS OF SALVATION: The grace of
God, which brings salvation, has appeared to all
men, through the preaching of repentance toward
God and faith toward the Lord Jesus Christ. Man is
therefore saved by the washing of regeneration and
the renewing of the Holy Spirit, and being justified
by the grace through faith of both God and man, he
becomes an heir of God according to the hope of
eternal life. (Titus 2:11; 3:5-7; Romans 10:8-15 and
Luke 24:47).

(b) THE EVIDENCE OF SALVATION: The inward
evidence to the believer of his salvation is the direct
witness of the Spirit (Romans 8:16). The outward
evidence to all men is a life of righteousness and true
holiness.

5. BAPTISM IN WATER

The ordinance of Baptism by a burial with Christ should
be observed as commanded in the Holy Writ by all who
have truly repented and in their hearts have really believed
in Christ as Saviour and Lord. In so doing, they have the
body washed in pure water as an outward sign or symbol
of cleansing, while their hearts have already been sprinkled
with the blood of Christ as an inner cleansing. Thus, they
proclaim to the world that they have died with Christ to
sin, and that they have also been raised with Him to live
and walk in newness of life. (Matthew 28:19; Acts 10:47-
48; Romans 6:4 and Hebrews 10:22).

6. THE LORD'S SUPPER

The Lord's Supper, consisting of the elements, is the
symbol expressing our sharing the divine nature of our
Lord Jesus Christ (II Peter 1:4); a memorial of His
suffering and death (I Corinthians 11:26) and a prophecy
of His second advent (I Corinthians 11:26); and is
commended to all believers as such a sign until He returns.

7. ENTIRE SANCTIFICATION

The Scriptures teach a life of holiness without which no
man can see the Lord. By the power of the Holy Spirit we
are able to obey the command, "be ye holy, for I am holy."
Entire sanctification is the will of God for all believers, and
should earnestly be pursued by walking in obedience to
God's word. (Hebrews 12:14; I Peter 1:15-16; I Thessalonians 5:23-24 and I John 2:6).

8. THE CHURCH

The Church is the body of Christ, the habitation of God
through the Spirit, with Divine appointments for the
fulfillment of her great commission. Each believer is an
integral part of that General Assembly and the Church of
the First-born, which are written in Heaven. (Ephesians
1:22-23; 2:19-22 and Hebrews 1:23).

9. THE MINISTRY AND EVANGELISM

A divinely called and Scripturally appointed and ordained
ministry has been provided for by our Lord for a two-fold

purpose: (1) The evangelization of the world, and (2) the
edifying of the Body of Christ. (Mark 16:15-20 and
Ephesians 4:11-13).

10. DIVINE HEALING

Deliverance from sickness is provided for in the atonement, just as is salvation from sin. (Isaiah 53:4-5; Matthew
8:16-17 and James 5:14-16).

11. THE BLESSED HOPE

The resurrection of those who have fallen asleep in Christ
and their translation together with those who are alive and
remaining unto the day of the coming of the Lord is the
imminent and blessed hope of the Church. (I Thessalonians 4:16-17; Romans 8:2; Titus 2:13 and I Corinthians
15:51-52).

12. THE MILLENNIAL REIGN OF JESUS

The revelation of the Lord Jesus from Heaven, the
salvation of mankind then completed, and the millennial
reign of Christ is the Scriptural promise of the world's
hope. (II Thessalonians 1:7; Revelation 19:11-14 and 20:1-
7).

13. THE LAKE OF FIRE

The devil and his angels, the beast and the false prophet,
and whosoever is not found written in the Book of Life,
shall be sentenced to everlasting punishment in the lake
which burns with fire and brimstone, which is the second
death. (Revelation 19:20 and 20:10-15).

14. THE NEW HEAVENS AND NEW EARTH

We, according to His promise, look for new heavens and a
new earth, wherein dwelleth righteousness. (II Peter 3:13
and Revelation 21 and 22).

Notes: *The beliefs of the loosely affiliated churches belonging to the Independent Christian Churches International
are held as fallible summaries which set forth their attempts
briefly to specify essential Biblical Truth. The statement
reproduced here, less detailed than those of many fundamentalist churches, differs in that it does not affirm either
the inerrancy of the Bible or dispensationalism. The Trinity,
baptism by immersion, and a premillennial eschatology are
affirmed.*

* * *

FAITH AND DOCTRINE (INDEPENDENT FUNDAMENTAL CHURCHES OF AMERICA)

Each person, church, or organization, in order to become
or remain a member of the IFCA, shall be required to
subscribe to the following articles of faith:

1. THE HOLY SCRIPTURES

We believe the Holy Scriptures of the Old and New
Testaments to be the verbally inspired Word of God, the
final authority for faith and life, inerrant in the original
writings, infallible and God-breathed (II Tim. 3:16, 17; II
Peter 1:20, 21; Matt. 5:18; John 16:12, 13).

2. THE GODHEAD

We believe in one triune God, eternally existing in three
persons—Father, Son, and Holy Spirit—coeternal in
being, co-identical in nature, co-equal in power and glory,

and having the same attributes and perfections (Deut. 6:4; II Cor. 13:14).

3. THE PERSON AND WORK OF CHRIST

a. We believe that the Lord Jesus Christ, the eternal Son of God, became man, without ceasing to be God, having been conceived by the Holy Spirit and born of the Virgin Mary, in order that He might reveal God and redeem sinful men (John 1:1, 2, 14; Luke 1:35).

b. We believe that the Lord Jesus Christ accomplished our redemption through His death on the cross as a representative, vicarious, substitutionary sacrifice; and, that our justification is made sure by His literal, physical resurrection from the dead (Rom. 3:24, 25; I Peter 2:24; Eph. 1:7; I Peter 1:3-5).

c. We believe that the Lord Jesus Christ ascended to heaven, and is now exalted at the right hand of God, where, as our High Priest, He fulfills the ministry of Representative, Intercessor, and Advocate (Acts 1:9, 10; Heb. 9:24; 7:25; Rom. 8:34; I John 2:1, 2).

4. THE PERSON AND WORK OF THE HOLY SPIRIT

a. We believe that the Holy Spirit is a person who convicts the world of sin, of righteousness, and of judgment; and, that He is the supernatural agent in regeneration, baptizing all believers into the body of Christ, indwelling and sealing them unto the day of redemption (John 16:8-11; II Cor. 3:6; I Cor. 12:12-14; Rom. 8:9; Eph. 1:13, 14).

b. We believe that He is the divine Teacher who guides believers into all truth; and, that it is the privilege and duty of all the saved to be filled with the Spirit (John 16:13; I John 2:20, 27; Eph. 5:18).

5. THE TOTAL DEPRAVITY OF MAN

We believe that man was created in the image and likeness of God, but that in Adam's sin the race fell, inherited a sinful nature, and became alienated from God; and, that man is totally depraved, and, of himself, utterly unable to remedy his lost condition (Gen. 1:26, 27; Rom. 3:22, 23; 5:12; Eph. 2:1-3, 12).

6. SALVATION

We believe that salvation is the gift of God brought to man by grace and received by personal faith in the Lord Jesus Christ, whose precious blood was shed on Calvary for the forgiveness of our sins (Eph. 2:8-10; John 1:12; Eph. 1:7; I Peter 1:18, 19).

7. THE ETERNAL SECURITY AND ASSURANCE OF BELIEVERS

a. We believe that all the redeemed, once saved, are kept by God's power and are thus secure in Christ forever (John 6:37-40; 10:27-30; Rom. 8:1, 38, 39; I Cor. 1:4-8; I Peter 1:5).

b. We believe that it is the privilege of believers to rejoice in the assurance of their salvation through the testimony of God's Word; which, however, clearly forbids the use of Christian liberty as an occasion to the flesh (Rom. 13:13, 14; Gal. 5:13; Titus 2:11-15).

8. THE TWO NATURES OF THE BELIEVER

We believe that every saved person possesses two natures, with provision made for victory of the new nature over the old nature through the power of the indwelling Holy Spirit; and, that all claims to the eradication of the old nature in this life are unscriptural (Rom. 6:13; 8:12, 13; Gal. 5:16-25; Eph. 4:22-24; Col. 3:10; I Peter 1:14-16; I John 3:5-9).

9. SEPARATION

We believe that all the saved should live in such a manner as not to bring reproach upon their Saviour and Lord; and, that separation from all religious apostasy, all worldly and sinful pleasures, practices and associations is commanded of God (II Tim. 3:1-5; Rom. 12:1, 2; 14:13; I John 2:15-17; II John vss. 9-11; II Cor. 6:14-7:1).

10. MISSIONS

We believe that it is the obligation of the saved to witness by life and by word to the truths of Holy Scripture and to seek to proclaim the Gospel to all mankind (Mark 16:15; Acts 1:8; II Cor. 5:19, 20).

11. THE MINISTRY AND SPIRITUAL GIFTS

a. We believe that God is sovereign in the bestowment of all His gifts; and, that the gifts of evangelists, pastors, and teachers are sufficient for the perfecting of the saints today; and, that speaking in tongues and the working of sign miracles gradually ceased as the New Testament Scriptures were completed and their authority became established (I Cor. 12:4-11; II Cor. 12:12; Eph. 4:7-12).

b. We believe that God does hear and answer the prayer of faith, in accord with His own will, for the sick and afflicted (John 15:7; I John 5:14, 15).

12. THE CHURCH

a. We believe that the Church, which is the body and the espoused bride of Christ, is a spiritual organism made up of all born-again persons of this present age (Eph. 1:22, 23; 5:25-27; I Cor. 12:12-14; II Cor. 11:2).

b. We believe that the establishment and continuance of local churches is clearly taught and defined in the New Testament Scriptures (Acts 14:27; 20:17, 28-32; I Tim. 3:1-13; Titus 1:5-11).

13. DISPENSATIONALISM

We believe in the dispensational view of Bible interpretation but reject the extreme teaching known as "hyper dispensationalism" such as that teaching which opposes either the Lord's table or water baptism as a Scriptural means of testimony for the church in this age (Matt. 28:19, 20; Acts 2:41, 42; 18:8; I Cor. 11:23-26).

14. THE PERSONALITY OF SATAN

We believe that Satan is a person, the author of sin and the cause of the fall; that he is the open and declared enemy of God and man; and, that he shall be eternally punished in the lake of fire (Job 1:6, 7; Isa. 14:12-17; Matt. 4:2-11; 25:41; Rev. 20:10).

FAITH AND DOCTRINE (INDEPENDENT FUNDAMENTAL CHURCHES OF AMERICA) (continued)

15. THE SECOND ADVENT OF CHRIST

We believe in that "blessed hope," the personal, imminent, pre-tribulation and premillennial coming of the Lord Jesus Christ for His redeemed ones; and in His subsequent return to earth, with His saints, to establish His millennial kingdom (I Thess. 4:13-18; Zech. 14:4-11; Rev. 19:11-16; 20:1-6; I Thess. 1:10; 5:9; Rev. 3:10).

16. THE ETERNAL STATE

a. We believe in the bodily resurrection of all men, the saved to eternal life, and the unsaved to judgment and everlasting punishment (Matt. 25:46; John 5:28, 29; 11:25, 26; Rev. 20:5, 6, 12, 13).

b. We believe that the souls of the redeemed are, at death, absent from the body and present with the Lord, where in conscious bliss they await the first resurrection, when spirit, soul and body are reunited to be glorified forever with the Lord (Luke 23:43; Rev. 20:4-6; II Cor. 5:8; Phil. 1:23; 3:21; I Thess. 4:16, 17).

c. We believe that the souls of unbelievers remain after death, in conscious misery until the second resurrection, when with soul and body reunited they shall appear at the great white throne judgment, and shall be cast into the lake of fire, not to be annihilated, but to suffer everlasting conscious punishment (Luke 16:19-26; Matt. 25:4-46; II Thess. 1:7-9; Jude vss. 6,7; Mark 9:43-48; Rev. 20:11-15).

SECTION 2. FELLOWSHIP COVENANT

In subscribing to these articles of faith, we by no means set aside, or undervalue, any of the Scriptures of the Old and New Testaments; but we deem the knowledge, belief and acceptance of the truth as set forth in our doctrinal statement, to be essential to sound faith and fruitful practice, and therefore requisite for Christian fellowship in the IFCA.

Notes: *The Independent Fundamental Churches of America (IFCA) is among the most influential of fundamentalist bodies. It draws many of its pastors from Dallas Theological Seminary and Moody Biblical Institute graduates.*

* * *

STATEMENT OF FAITH (INTERNATIONAL MINISTERIAL FELLOWSHIP)

The International Ministerial Fellowship accepts the Holy Scriptures as the revealed will of God, the all-sufficient rule for faith and practice; and for the purpose of maintaining general unity adopts the following Statement of Fundamental Truths:

1. We believe the Bible to be the inspired, the only infallible, authoritative Word of God.

2. We believe that there is one God eternally existent in three persons: Father, Son and Holy Spirit.

3. We believe in the deity of our Lord Jesus Christ, in His virgin birth, in His sinless life, in His miracles, in His vicarious and atoning death through His shed blood, in His bodily resurrection, in His ascension to the right hand of the Father, and in his personal return in power and glory.

4. We believe that for the salvation of lost and sinful man, regeneration by the Holy Spirit is absolutely essential.

5. We believe in the present ministry of the Holy Spirit by whose indwelling the Christian is enabled to live a godly life.

6. We believe that the baptism of the Holy Spirit, according to Acts 2:4, is given to believers who ask for it.

7. We believe in the sanctifying power of the Holy Spirit by Whose indwelling the Christian is enabled to live a holy life.

8. We believe in the resurrection of both the saved and the lost: they that are saved unto the resurrection of life and they that are lost unto the resurrection of damnation.

9. We believe in the spiritual unity of believers in our Lord Jesus Christ.

Notes: *This brief statement was adopted in 1984.*

* * *

DOCTRINAL STATEMENT (MOODY BIBLICAL INSTITUTE)

In view of the present unrest concerning doctrinal questions within the sphere of evangelical Christianity, and to answer inquiries regarding the position of the Moody Bible Institute thereupon, be it *Resolved*, That this Board of Trustees places on record the following statement of faith as that to which its members severally subscribe, and to which it requires the subscription of the members of the faculty of the Educational Branch and all the official heads of the Institute, to wit:

ARTICLE I. God is a Person who has revealed Himself as a Trinity in unity, Father, Son and Holy Spirit—three Persons and yet but one God (Deut. 6:4; Matt. 28:19; I Cor. 8:6).

ARTICLE II. The Bible, including both the Old and the New Testaments, is a divine revelation, the original autographs of which were verbally inspired by the Holy Spirit (II Tim. 3:16; II Pet. 1:21).

ARTICLE III. Jesus Christ is the image of the invisible God, which is to say, He is Himself very God; He took upon Him our nature, being conceived by the Holy Ghost and born of the Virgin Mary; He died upon the cross as a substitutionary sacrifice for the sin of the world; He arose from the dead in the body in which He was crucified; He ascended into heaven in that body glorified, where He is now, our interceding High Priest; He will come again personally and visibly to set up His kingdom and to judge the quick and the dead (Col. 1:15; Phil. 2:5-8; Matt. 1:18-25; I Pet. 2:24, 25; Luke 24; Heb. 4:14-16; Acts 1:9-11; I Thess. 4:16-18; Matt. 25:31-46; Rev. 11:15-17; 20:4-6, 11-15).

ARTICLE IV. Man was created in the image of God but fell into sin, and, in that sense, is lost; this is true of all men, and except a man be born again he cannot see the kingdom of God; salvation is by grace through faith in Christ who His own self bare our sins in His own body on the tree; the retribution of the wicked and unbelieving and the reward of the righteous are everlasting, and as the reward is conscious, so is the retribution (Gen. 1:26, 27; Rom. 3:10, 23; John 3:3; Acts 13:38, 39; 4:12; John 3:16; Matt. 25:46; II Cor. 5:1; II Thess. 1:7-10.)

ARTICLE V. The Church is an elect company of believers baptized by the Holy Spirit into one body; its mission is to witness concerning its Head, Jesus Christ, preaching the gospel among all nations; it will be caught up to meet the Lord in the air ere He appears to set up His kingdom (Acts 2:41; 15:13-17; Eph. 1:3-6; I Cor. 12:12, 13; Matt. 28:19, 20; Acts 1:6-8; I Thess. 4:16-18).

Notes: *This statement was adopted in 1928 by the trustees of Moody Biblical Institute. It superseded an earlier statement placed in the institute's catalog in 1915.*

*   *   *

DOCTRINAL STATEMENT (MOODY MEMORIAL CHURCH)

1. We believe the Holy Scriptures to be the inspired Word of God absolutely authoritative and infallible.

2. We believe in one God existing in three persons, Father, Son, and Holy Spirit, co-equal and eternal.

3. We believe that man was created in innocence but fell in Adam and is now totally unable to retrieve his lost condition.

4. We believe that salvation has been provided through our Lord Jesus Christ who was born of the virgin Mary, suffered and died for our sins upon the Cross, rose from the dead, ascended to God's right hand, and is coming again in power and great glory.

5. We believe that the Church is the Body of Christ formed by the baptism of the Holy Spirit, and that all believers are members thereof and are a holy and royal priesthood.

6. We believe in the eternal security and everlasting blessedness of the saved and the eternal judgment of all who reject our Lord Jesus Christ.

7. We believe that Christ instituted the ordinances of baptism and the Lord's Supper to be observed until He come.

8. We believe that it is the responsibility of all who are saved to seek to win others to Christ.

Notes: *Though closely related to Moody Biblical Institute, Moody Church is completely autonomous and has adopted its own statement of doctrine.*

FAITH AND DOCTRINE (OHIO BIBLE CHURCH)

13. BAPTISM

A. We believe immersion to be the New Testament mode of baptism to be administered upon personal acceptance and public confession of Christ as Saviour. We believe Christ Himself established and commanded the ordinance to symbolize the believer's death to the old life of sin and his spiritual resurrection to the new life in Christ (Acts 2:41; 8:12; 9:18; 10:47, 48; Romans 6:3-6).

B. Since baptism is not essential to salvation we recognize the sovereign right of any local church to accept for membership those who have not yet been baptized or who have been baptized by other modes if it so desires.

Notes: *The statement of the Ohio Bible Church is identical to that of the Independent Fundamental Churches of America except in its addition of an article on baptism, reproduced here.*

*   *   *

Grace Gospel Movement

DOCTRINAL STATEMENT (BEREAN BIBLE SOCIETY)

We hold the following doctrinal beliefs:

The verbal inspiration and plenary authority of the BIBLE in its original writings.

The eternal trinity of the GODHEAD.

The eternal deity, the virgin birth, the spotless humanity and the vicarious death of THE LORD JESUS CHRIST.

The personality and deity of the HOLY SPIRIT.

The total depravity of MAN by nature.

SALVATION by grace, through faith in the crucified, risen and glorified Christ.

The essential unity of all believers of the present dispensation as members of the ONE TRUE CHURCH, the Body of Christ.

The GIFTS enumerated in EPHESIANS 4:7-16, and that these alone are necessary for the building up of the Body of Christ.

The privilege and duty of all the saved to WALK as children of light.

The communion of the LORD'S SUPPER as revealed through Paul for the members of the Body of Christ "till He come."

One divine BAPTISM, the operation of the Holy Spirit, by which all true believers are made members of the Body of Christ, being identified with Him in His death, burial and resurrection. In the light of I COR. 1:17, EPH. 4:5 and COL. 2:12 we affirm that water baptism has no place in God's spiritual program for the Body of Christ in the present dispensation of grace.

DOCTRINAL STATEMENT (BEREAN BIBLE SOCIETY) (continued)

The RESURRECTION of the body.

The pre-tribulation RAPTURE of the Church.

The personal, pre-millennial RETURN OF CHRIST to reign on earth.

The ETERNAL PUNISHMENT of the unsaved dead.

The GOSPEL which Paul called "my gospel," and "the gospel of the grace of God," as God's specific message for the world today.

Notes: *The Grace Gospel Movement, often called ultra-dispensationalism, resembles fundamentalism, out of which it came. The movement developed some unique views, however. Among the most important views is that only a few of Paul's epistles, especially the Epistle to the Ephesians, were meant for this present church age or dispensation. Among other peculiarities, their unique position has led them to abandon water baptism, though the Lord's Supper is retained as an ordinance.*

One of the two most prominent Grace Gospel organizations, the Berean Bible Society does not differ from the older Grace Gospel Fellowship on essential doctrinal points. Notice the citation of Ephesians concerning spiritual gifts (an anti-pentecostal statement) and the item on baptism (apart from which any fundamentalist could accept this statement).

*　　*　　*

DOCTRINAL STATEMENT (GRACE GOSPEL FELLOWSHIP)

"I therefore, the prisoner of the Lord, beseech you that ye walk worthy of the vocation wherewith ye are called, with all lowliness and meekness, with long-suffering, forbearing one another in love; endeavoring to keep the unity of the Spirit in the bond of peace. There is one body, and one Spirit, even as ye are called in one hope of your calling; one Lord, one faith, one baptism, one God and Father of all, who is above all, and through all, and in you all. But unto every one of us is given grace according to the measure of the gift of Christ" (Eph. 4:1-7).

We affirm that the seven-fold unity expressed in this passage is the Holy Spirit's doctrinal statement for the Church, which is the Body of Christ. We believe that all the expressions of doctrinal position and requirements for this Dispensation of the Grace of God must be in full accord with the Holy Spirit's outline. We recognize other doctrinal unities for other dispensations, but we affirm that Ephesians 4:4-6 stands alone as the doctrinal unity for this dispensation.

Desiring to be in full accord with the Mind of the Spirit, we hold and require the following doctrinal beliefs:

THE BIBLE

The entire Bible in its original writings is verbally inspired of God and is of plenary authority (2 Tim. 3:16, 17; 2 Pet. 1:21).

THE GODHEAD

There is one God, eternally existing in three Persons: Father, Son, and Holy Spirit (Deut. 6:4; I Tim. 2:5; Eph. 4:4-6; Matt. 28:19; 2 Cor. 13:14).

THE PERSON OF CHRIST

Jesus Christ was begotten by the Holy Spirit and born of the Virgin Mary and is true God and true man (Lk. 1:35; Phil. 2:6-9; Rom. 1:3, 4).

TOTAL DEPRAVITY

All men by nature are dead in trespasses and sins and are, therefore, totally unable to do anything pleasing to God (Eph. 2:1-3; Rom. 3:9-12).

REDEMPTION

God justifies ungodly sinners by His grace upon the ground of the blood of Christ through the means of faith. This complete salvation is bestowed as the free gift of God apart from man's works (Rom. 3:24-28; 5:1, 9; Eph. 2:8, 9).

ETERNAL SECURITY

All of the saved are eternally secure in Christ (Col. 3:1-4; Phil. 1:6; Rom. 8:1; 8:29-34; Rom. 8:38, 39; John 10:27-29; Eph 1:13-14).

PERSONALITY AND WORK OF THE HOLY SPIRIT

The Holy Spirit is a Person, Who convicts the world of sin and Who regenerates, baptizes, indwells, enlightens, and empowers (John 16:8; Tit. 3:5; 1 Cor. 12:13; Eph. 1:13, 17, 18; 3:16).

THE CHURCH

In the present dispensation there is only one true Church, which is called the Body of Christ (I Cor. 12:13; Eph. 1:22, 23; 3:6). The historical manifestation of the Body of Christ began with the Apostle Paul before he wrote his first epistle (I Thess. 2:14-16 cf. Acts 13:45, 46; Phil. 1:5, 6 cf. Acts 16; I Cor. 12:13, 27 cf. Acts 18).

GIFTS

The only gifts necessary for the ministry of the Body of Christ are those enumerated in Ephesians 4:7-16. Of these, only the gifts of Evangelists, Pastors, and Teachers are in operation today. All of the sign gifts of the Acts period, such as tongues, prophecy, and healing (I Cor. 12:1-31), being temporary in character, have ceased (I Cor. 13:8-11).

WALK

By reason of Christ's victory over sin and of His indwelling Spirit, all of the saved may and should experience deliverance from the power of sin by obedience to Romans 6:11; but we deny that man's nature of sin is ever eradicated during this life (Rom. 6:6-14; Gal. 5:16-25; Rom. 8:37; II Cor. 2:14; 10:2-5).

LORD'S SUPPER

The communion of the Lord's Supper as revealed through the Apostle Paul in I Corinthians 11:23-26 is for members of the Body of Christ to observe "until He comes."

There is no place in Scripture where the Lord's supper and water baptism are linked together either as ordinances or as sacraments for the Church.

BAPTISM

All saved persons have been made members of the Body of Christ by one divine baptism (I Cor. 12:13). By that one baptism every member of the Body of Christ is identified with Christ in His death, burial, and resurrection. In the light of the statement concerning the one baptism in Ephesians 4:5, the statements concerning baptism in Colossians 2:12 and Romans 6:3, 4, and Paul's statement in I Corinthians 1:17 that "Christ sent me not to baptize, but to preach the gospel," we conclude that water baptism has no place in God's spiritual program for the Body of Christ in this Day of Grace.

RESURRECTION

Jesus Christ was resurrected bodily from the dead (Luke 24:39-43). Therefore (I Cor. 15:21), all men will have a bodily resurrection (Acts 24:15): the saved to everlasting glory and the unsaved to everlasting punishment (John 5:29; Rev. 20:11-15).

SECOND COMING OF CHRIST

The rapture of the Church and the second coming of Christ will be pre-millennial. He will come first to receive the Church unto Himself (I Thess. 4:13-18; Phil. 3:20, 21) and then come to receive His Millennial Kingdom, over which He will reign (Zech. 14:4, 9; Acts 1:10, 11; Rev. 19:11-16; 20:4-6). Because of the nature of the Body of Christ, the resurrection and rapture of the Church, which is His Body, will take place before the Great Tribulation (Jer. 30:7; Matt. 24:15-31) at His appearing in the air (I Thess. 4:13-18; Phil. 3:20, 21; Titus 2:13, 14; I Cor. 15:51-53). The resurrection of the other saved dead will occur after the Tribulation (Rev. 20:4-6).

STATE OF THE DEAD

Nowhere does Scripture extend the hope of salvation to the unsaved dead but instead reveals that they will ever continue to exist in a state of conscious suffering (Luke 16:23-28; Rev. 14:11; 20:14, 15; Col. 3:6; Rom. 1:21-32; John 3:36; Phil. 3:19; II Thess. 1:9). The teachings of Universalism, of probation after death, of annihilation of the unsaved dead, and of the unconscious state of the dead, saved or unsaved (Luke 16:23-28; Phil. 1:23; II Cor. 5:6-8), are opposed by us as being thoroughly unscriptural and dangerous doctrines.

MISSION

The mission and commission of the Church, which is His Body, is to proclaim the message of reconciliation (II Cor. 5:14-21) and endeavor to make all men see what is the Dispensation of the Mystery (Eph. 3:8, 9). In this, we should follow the Apostle Paul (I Cor. 4:16; 11:1; Phil. 3:17; I Tim. 1:11-16). That distinctive message which the Apostle of the Gentiles (Rom. 11:13, 15:16) calls "my gospel" (Rom. 2:16; 16:25) is also called the "gospel of the grace of God" (Acts 20:24). We, like Paul, must preach the entire Word of God in the light of *this* Gospel (II Tim. 4:2; Gal. 1:8, 9) and strive to reach those in the regions beyond where Christ is not yet named (Rom. 15:20; II Cor. 10:16).

Notes: *This statement most clearly spells out the essential position concerning the Epistle to the Ephesians among Grace Gospel churches. Also note the statement of "Gifts" and "Baptism."*

*   *   *

WE BELIEVE IN . . . (LAST DAY MESSENGER ASSEMBLIES)

We believe in:

1. The verbal inspiration of the Word of God (2 Tim. 3:16).
2. The deity of Jesus Christ, and the trinity of the Godhead (Titus 2:13, 2 Cor. 13:14).
3. The total depravity of man, and everlasting punishment of the rejecters of Christ (Romans 3, John 3:36, Rev. 20:15).
4. Redemption by the blood of Christ, by grace, not of works (Titus 3:5, Eph. 2:8-9).
5. Everlasting life and security of the believer (John 10:28).
6. The personality and punishment of Satan (Job 1, Rev. 20).
7. The imminent rapture of the church, followed by the Great Tribulation and the millennial reign of Christ on earth (1 Thess. 4:16-17, Matt. 24, Rev. 20).

Notes: *This statement has been regularly printed in the* Last Day Messenger, *the periodical which unofficially ties together the assemblies.*

*   *   *

STATEMENT OF BELIEFS (THE WAY INTERNATIONAL)

1. We believe the scriptures of the Old and New Testaments were *Theopneustos*, "God-breathed," and perfect as originally given; that the Scriptures, or the Word of God, are of supreme, absolute and final authority for believing and godliness.
2. We believe in one God, the creator of the heavens and earth; in Jesus Christ, God's only begotten Son our lord and savior, whom God raised from the dead; and we believe in the workings of the Holy Spirit.
3. We believe that the virgin Mary conceived Jesus Christ by the Holy Spirit; that God was in Christ, and that Jesus Christ is the "mediator between God and men," and is "the man Christ Jesus."
4. We believe that Adam was created in the image of God, spiritually; that he sinned and thereby brought upon himself immediate spiritual death, which is separation from God, and physical death later, which is the consequence of sin; and that all human beings are born with a sinful nature.
5. We believe that Jesus Christ died for our sins according to the Scriptures, as a representative and substitute for us, and that all who believe that God raised him from the dead are justified and made righteous, born again by the Spirit of God, receiving

eternal life on the grounds of His eternal redemption, and thereby are the sons of God.

6. We believe in the resurrection of the crucified body of our Lord Jesus Christ, his ascension into heaven and his seating at the right hand of God.

7. We believe in the blessed hope of Christ's return, the personal return of our living lord and savior Jesus Christ and our gathering together unto him.

8. We believe in the bodily resurrection of the just and the unjust.

9. We believe in the receiving of the fullness of the holy spirit, the power from on high, plus the corresponding nine manifestations of the holy spirit, for all born-again believers.

10. We believe it is available to receive all that God promises us in His Word according to our believing faith. We believe we are free in Christ Jesus to receive all that he accomplished for us by his substitution.

11. We believe the early Church flourished rapidly because they operated within a Root, Trunk, Limb, Branch and Twig setup, decently and in order.

Notes: *The Way International departs from other Grace Gospel groups on several major points, especially in its denial of the Trinity and its acceptance of the charismatic gifts of I Corinthians 12. Compare item 9 with the item on gifts in the Grace Gospel Fellowship's statement.*

*　　*　　*

Miscellaneous Bible Students

THE BELIEFS AND PRACTICES (THE LOCAL CHURCH)

OUR BELIEF

1. We believe that the Holy Bible is the complete divine revelation verbally inspired by the Holy Spirit.

2. We believe that God is the only one Triune God—the Father, the Son, and the Spirit—co-existing equally from eternity to eternity.

3. We believe that the Son of God, even God Himself, became incarnated to be a man by the name of Jesus, born of the virgin Mary, that He might be our Redeemer and Savior.

4. We believe that Jesus, a genuine man, lived on this earth for thirty-three and a half years to make God the Father known to men.

5. We believe that Jesus, the Christ anointed by God with His Holy Spirit, died on the cross for our sins and shed His blood for the accomplishment of our redemption.

6. We believe that Jesus Christ, after being buried for three days, resurrected from the dead physically and spiritually and that, in resurrection, He has become the life-giving Spirit to impart Himself into us as our life and our everything.

7. We believe that after His resurrection Christ ascended to the heavens and that God has made Him the Lord of all.

8. We believe that after His ascension Christ poured down the Spirit of God to baptize His chosen members into one Body and that the Spirit of God, who is also the Spirit of Christ, is moving on this earth today to convict sinners, to regenerate God's chosen people, to dwell in the members of Christ for their growth in life, and to build up the Body of Christ for His full expression.

9. We believe that at the end of this age Christ will come back to take up His members, to judge the world, to take possession of the earth, and to establish His eternal kingdom.

10. We believe that the overcoming saints will reign with Christ in the millennium and that all the believers in Christ will participate in the divine blessings in the New Jerusalem in the new heaven and new earth for eternity.

OUR STANDING

1. We stand on the Holy Scriptures, not according to any traditional interpretation, but according to the pure Word of God.

2. We stand on Christ, the living rock, the foundation stone, the Head of the Body, and the life and reality of the church.

3. We stand on the genuine unity of the Body of Christ. We are not sectarian, nor denominational, nor nondenominational, nor interdenominational.

4. We stand on the ground of the oneness of all believers in each locality; we recognize all the blood-redeemed and Spirit-regenerated believers in Christ as members of the one church in each city.

OUR MISSION

1. To preach the gospel of grace and of the kingdom to sinners that they may be saved.

2. To minister the life supply to believers that they may grow in Christ.

3. To establish the church in each city that the believers may become a local corporate expression of Christ in practicality.

4. To release the living and rich word of God from the Holy Scriptures that the believers may be nourished to grow and mature.

5. To build up the Body of Christ so that the Bride may be prepared for the coming back of Christ as the Bridegroom.

OUR HOPE

1. We hope that as many as are ordained by God to eternal life will believe in the Lord Jesus.

2. We hope that all regenerated Christians will seek the growth in life, not the mere increase of knowledge.

3. We hope that all seeking Christians will see the vision of the church and come into the practical church life in their locality.

4. We hope that the Lord will have a remnant of overcomers that His Bride may be prepared.

5. We hope that the coming back of the Lord will be hastened by our growth and that we may participate in the blessed rapture and in His coming kingdom.

CONCERNING THE RECOVERY

We in the local churches are for God's recovery. A basic definition of what we mean by recovery is necessary for an accurate understanding of our testimony.

1. The word "recover" means to obtain again something that has been lost, or to return something to a normal condition. "Recovery" means the restoration or return to a normal condition after a damage or a loss has been incurred. To say that God is recovering certain matters means that in the course of church history they have been lost, misused, or corrupted and that God is restoring them to their original state or condition.

2. Because the church has become degraded through the many centuries of its history, it needs to be restored according to God's original intention. Concerning the church, our vision is governed not by the present situation nor by traditional practice, but by God's original intention and by His unchanging standard as revealed in His Word. We regard the New Testament revelation of the church not merely as a historical antecedent, but as the norm for church practice in the present day.

3. God's recovery did not begin in the twentieth century. Although it is difficult to fix an exact date for its beginning, it is convenient to set it at the time of the Reformation. The recovery has gone through several stages since the Reformation, passing through the partial recovery of the church life in Bohemia under the leadership of Zinzendorf, moving on to the unveiling of the many precious Bible truths through the Plymouth Brethren, and then going on to the genuine experience of the inner life. Now it has reached its present stage with the establishment of genuine local churches as the expression of the Body of Christ.

4. In His recovery today the Lord is doing two things. He is recovering the experience of the riches of Christ—that is, the enjoyment of Christ as our life and our everything—and He is recovering the practice of the church life. These two matters go hand in hand, for the practical church life is the issue of the enjoyment of the riches of Christ. We in the Lord's recovery today testify that Christ is unsearchably rich, that He is the all-inclusive One for our enjoyment. Furthermore, we testify that the Lord has burdened us for the practice of the church life according to the revelation of the pure Word of God.

CONCERNING SALVATION

1. In Christ God has provided for man a full and complete salvation. This full salvation includes our whole being: spirit, soul, and body. In God's salvation, man's spirit is regenerated, his soul is being transformed, and his body will be transfigured.

2. In order to be saved, one must have a living faith in the Person and work of Jesus Christ, the Son of God. Every genuinely saved one has what the Bible calls the "common faith" (Titus 1:4), which includes what we must believe in order to be saved: we must believe that the Bible is the complete divine revelation wholly inspired by God; that there is a unique Triune God, the Father, the Son, and the Spirit; that Jesus Christ is the Son of God incarnated to be a man; that Christ died on the cross for our sins, shedding His blood for our redemption; that on the third day He was bodily raised from the dead; that He had been exalted to the right hand of God and made the Lord of all; and that He is coming again for His own and to set up His kingdom on earth.

3. Eternal salvation is by grace through faith, not by our works.

4. In order to be saved, one must have a living contact with Jesus Christ. Therefore, in bringing unbelievers to salvation, we emphasize prayer and calling on the name of the Lord. According to Romans 10:9 and 10, if a man is to be saved, he must believe in his heart and confess with his mouth.

5. Once a person has been saved, he may have both the assurance of salvation and the security of salvation. Once we are saved, we are saved forever.

CONCERNING THE CHRISTIAN LIFE

1. REGENERATION. The Christian life begins with regeneration. To be regenerated is to be born of the Spirit in our spirit (John 3:6) through the redemption of Christ and thereby to have the life and nature of God imparted into our spirit. This makes our spirit alive with the very life of God.

2. SEPARATION. The true Christian life requires a proper separation from this corrupt and evil world. This separation is not according to legalistic, man-made rules; it is according to the life and nature of the holy One who dwells within us. We are separated unto God by the redeeming blood of Christ, by the Holy Spirit, and in the name of the Lord Jesus. In order to live a proper Christian life, we must maintain such a separated position. Although we are not of the world, we nevertheless live a godly life in the world.

3. CONSECRATION. The Christian life is a life of consecration. To be consecrated to the Lord means that we are utterly given to the Lord, not to do something for Him nor to become something, but to make ourselves available to Him as a living sacrifice so that He may work on us and in us according to His good pleasure. We consecrate to the Lord because we love Him and delight to belong to Him. We also recognize that we already belong to Him because He has purchased us with His precious blood. We in the local churches are living not for

ourselves, but for God and for the fulfillment of His eternal purpose.

4. LOVING THE LORD. In our Christian life we emphasize loving the Lord. Above all else, God desires that we love Him. We testify that our Lord Jesus Christ is the altogether lovely One, that He has won our hearts, and that we love Him, not with a love of our own, but with the very love with which He first loved us.

5. THE WORD OF GOD. The Bible occupies a very important place in our Christian life. All those in the local churches are encouraged to read the Word in a regular way, even to read it through once a year. We read the Word, we study the Word, and we take the Word by prayer as spiritual food. All teachings, inspirations, and guidance which claim the Holy Spirit as their source must be checked by God's revelation in His Word. Although the Bible reveals the mind of God concerning so many matters, to us the Bible is not primarily a book of doctrine; instead, it is mainly a book of life. We come to the Word not merely for knowledge, but, through a prayerful reading of the Scripture, to contact the Lord Jesus, who is Himself the living Word.

6. PRAYER. The Christian life is also a life of prayer. In prayer we enjoy sweet, intimate personal communion with the Lord. By prayer we declare our dependence on God, our submission to Him, and our desire to cooperate with Him in the fulfillment of His purpose. All those in the local churches are encouraged to have a time of personal prayer every day.

7. THE EXPERIENCE OF CHRIST. We have seen from God's revelation in the Bible that the Christian life is actually Christ Himself living in us. For this reason, we lay great emphasis on the experience of Christ. According to the New Testament Epistles, Christ is revealed in us, is living in us, is being formed in us, is making His home in us, is being magnified in us, and is becoming all in all to us. Instead of imitating Christ according to an outward pattern, we seek to live out Christ and to live by Christ by allowing the indwelling Christ to occupy our whole inward being and to express Himself through us in our daily living.

8. A CRUCIFIED LIFE. As genuine Christians, we are to live a crucified life. We are not ashamed of the cross of Christ, and we do not shrink back from following the Lord along the narrow pathway of the cross. If we would truly experience Christ and live by Him, we need to experience daily the subjective work of the cross in our lives. We have seen something of the ugliness of man's fallen flesh in the eyes of God, and we agree with God's judgment upon it. Moreover, we have seen that both the self and the natural man are opposed to God. Therefore, we welcome the inward working of the death of Christ so that we may experience Christ and live by Him in the riches of His resurrection life.

9. NOURISHMENT. If we would live a normal Christian life, we need to be nourished daily with spiritual food and spiritual drink. For this reason, we emphasize the partaking of Christ as our spiritual food and drink. In the Spirit and through the Word, we enjoy Him as our life supply. As He Himself said, "He that eateth me, even he shall live by me" (John 6:57). The Lord is the living bread, the bread of life, and the bread of God who came down from heaven to give life to the world (John 6:33, 35, 51), and we are nourished by Him day by day.

10. THE GROWTH IN LIFE. In the local churches we emphasize the fact that in the Christian life we should grow normally in life. We are not content to remain spiritual infants. The divine life, like the human life, must have a normal development leading to maturity. Therefore, as seekers of the Lord, we pursue the growth in life. We desire to be a full-grown man to express the Lord, to represent Him with His authority, and to engage in spiritual warfare to defeat His enemy.

11. HUMAN LIVING. As Christians, we also live a normal human life, free from extremes and balanced in every way. We desire that our entire being, spirit, soul, and body, be maintained for the glory of God. We seek to express the humanity of Jesus in all our relationships and bear a worthy testimony of Him in all walks of human life: at home, at school, in our neighborhoods, and at our places of employment. To us, the Christian life cannot be divorced from our daily human life. We find that the more we grow in Christ, the more truly human we become, and the more we enjoy in a practical way the uplifted, transformed humanity of Jesus.

12. THE SPIRIT. The Christian life is a life of walking according to the Spirit. To walk in the Spirit is to have our living and our being according to the Spirit. Therefore, we need to set our mind on the Spirit and put to death the practices of the body (Rom. 8:6, 13). When we walk according to the Spirit, all the righteous requirements of God are fulfilled in us spontaneously. Only by living in the Spirit and walking according to the Spirit will the divine things revealed in the Scriptures become real to us. Hence, to be a normal Christian we must know the Spirit, live in the Spirit, and walk according to the Spirit.

13. TRANSFORMATION. Many Christians know of the regeneration of the spirit and the transfiguration of the body, but they neglect the crucial matter of the transformation of the soul. Nevertheless the Bible says, "Be ye transformed by the renewing of your mind" (Rom. 12:2). Therefore, we recognize the need to be dispositionally transformed in our souls by the inward working of the Spirit of life. As we are transformed, an inward change takes place in our very being. As our soul is permeated with the element of God, it is purified and sanctified. It can thereby fulfill its God-created function to express the Lord who dwells in our regenerated spirit. This transformation of the soul is intimately related to our

readiness to meet the Lord at His coming. Those who would dwell in His holy and glorious presence must not merely be positionally sanctified, but be dispositionally transformed. This transformation requires the operation of the cross negatively and the working of the Spirit of life positively.

14. TRANSFIGURATION. Finally, at the culmination of the Christian experience in life, our body will be transfigured and made like the Lord's glorious body (Phil. 3:21). In the Bible this is called the redemption of the body, the fullness of sonship. Therefore, the Christian life begins with regeneration, passes through transformation, and consummates with the transfiguration of the body.

CONCERNING THE CHURCH LIFE

1. A CORPORATE LIFE. By its very nature the Christian life, which is the living out of Christ as life from within us, is a corporate life. Many expressions in the New Testament confirm this: we are sheep in God's flock, we are living stones in God's building, we are branches in the vine, we are members of the Body of Christ. Although we remain individuals, as Christians we should no longer live individualistically, that is, caring only for our own interests, activities, and goals. On the contrary, God desires that we live a corporate life, conscious of the Body of Christ, mindful of the things of others, and concerned for the building up of the church. Therefore, we are experiencing a recovery not only of the normal Christian life, but also of the normal church life.

2. THE HEADSHIP OF CHRIST. In the church life we all need to honor the headship of Christ. We are the Body, and He is the unique Head of the Body. No one and nothing can presume to usurp Christ's headship. We cannot tolerate any system, organization, or leadership that insults the headship of Christ. Among us there is no permanent, official, organized leadership. Furthermore, there is no hierarchy. Rather, all the members of the Body are encouraged to have direct fellowship with the Head and receive from Him all directions concerning their life and movements. We recognize no subheads, no intermediaries between Christ and the members of His Body.

3. FELLOWSHIP. Even as we honor the headship of Christ, we also enjoy the fellowship of the Body of Christ. We recognize that, in Christ, we should no longer live in an individualistic way. On the contrary, we greatly value the fellowship among the members of the Body. How we enjoy the flow of life that circulates through the Body of Christ! We testify that this flow, this fellowship, is a blessed reality.

4. ONENESS. Another vital concern in the church life is the keeping of the oneness. Before He was crucified, the Lord prayed that those who believe in Him would be one even as He and the Father are one. Therefore, we must diligently maintain the unique oneness of the Body of Christ, which is expressed in local churches established on the ground of oneness with all believers in a locality. We must care for the oneness; therefore, we must repudiate all division and abhor it. What a shame and a reproach to the testimony of the Lord is the divisive state of today's Christians! In the church life, we stand for the unique oneness of Christ's Body. In order to maintain this oneness, we meet as believers on the ground of oneness, we receive all believers according to the common faith, and we seek to grow in Christ so that we may be with Him in the Father and in the Father's glory, where we are perfected into one. We believe that the Lord's prayer in John 17 will be answered on earth and that as we are perfected into one, the world will believe and know that the Father has sent the Son.

5. MUTUAL CARE FOR ONE ANOTHER. In the practice of the church life, we care for the saints, the believers in Christ, in a practical way. We delight to bear one another's burdens, to extend hospitality to visitors, to open our homes for fellowship, and to meet the practical needs of the brothers and sisters through loving service in the name of Christ. We encourage one another, refresh one another, minister Christ as life to one another, and build up one another. Our church life is not limited to meetings in our place of meeting; it goes on all the time.

6. THE CONSCIENCE. In the church life we also honor the conscience of others. This means that all the believers in Christ have the liberty to follow the Lord according to their conscience and in the light they have received from God through His Word. There is no external control molding and manipulating our daily lives, and there is no authoritarian disregard of our conscience. There is no coercion nor compulsion. Rather, all are encouraged to deal thoroughly with their conscience in the sight of God and to maintain a conscience void of offense toward God and toward man. Thus, we care for our conscience and for the conscience of others.

7. MEETINGS. Because the church life is a meeting life, we usually have meetings several times a week. To us, meetings are not a drudgery; they are an enjoyment. In the church meetings we are supplied, instructed, strengthened, encouraged, enlightened, inspired, equipped, built up, and commissioned by the Lord. In the proper church life there is a balance between the personal Christian life and the corporate meeting life. The personal time with the Lord cannot replace the meetings, and the meetings cannot replace the personal time. We delight to meet with Him individually, and we enjoy even more the meeting with Him corporately. We testify that in the church meetings the resurrected Christ truly is with us as we are gathered into His name.

8. THE FUNCTION OF ALL THE MEMBERS. In the church life every member of the Body can function. Although we do not all have the same function, we all have a function, and the function of every member is appreciated. We absolutely repudiate the clergy-laity system as a strategy of Satan to

THE BELIEFS AND PRACTICES (THE LOCAL CHURCH) (continued)

frustrate the function of the members of the Body of Christ. In the local churches we have no clergy and we have no laity; rather, we are members of the Body, all of whom have the right to function according to their measure. Furthermore, we have no pastor and no janitor. All the saints may share in the meetings, and all may also partake of the cleaning service.

Notes: *Of several groups growing out of the Plymouth Brethren tradition, The Local Church alone has produced a lengthy doctrinal statement, in part to refute charges that the church was doctrinally unsound. The statement affirms most of the traditional Christian beliefs in the authority of scripture, the Trinity, the incarnation, the virgin birth, the substitutionary atonement, and so on. It also systematically details some of the church's peculiar beliefs such as its ecclesiology, i.e., its doctrine of the church (from which its name derives) and its idea of God's present work of recovery.*

Chapter 12
Adventist Family

Sunday Adventist

DECLARATION OF PRINCIPLES (ADVENT CHRISTIAN CHURCH)

I. We believe that the Bible is the inspired Word of God, being in its entirety a revelation given to man under Divine inspiration and providence; that its historic statements are correct, and that it is the only Divine and infallible standard of faith and practice. (*Romans 15:4; II Timothy 3:15, 16; John 17:17*)

II. We believe, as revealed in the Bible:

(a) In one God, our Father, eternal, and infinite in His wisdom, love and power, the Creator of all things, "in whom we live, and move, and have our being." (*Genesis 1:1; Isaiah 40:28; Matthew 6:6*)

(b) And in Jesus Christ, our Lord, the only begotten Son of God, conceived of the Holy Spirit, born of the Virgin Mary; who came into our world to seek and to save that which was lost; who died for our sins, who was raised bodily from the dead for our justification; who ascended into heaven as our High Priest and Mediator, and who will come again in the end of this age, to judge the living and the dead, and to reign forever and ever. (*I Timothy 3:16*)

(c) And in the Holy Spirit, the Comforter, sent from God to convince the world of sin, of righteousness and of judgment, whereby we are sanctified and sealed unto the day of redemption. (*John 14:16, 26; 16:7-11; Ephesians 1:13*)

III. We believe that man was created for immortality, but that through sin he forfeited his Divine birthright; that because of sin, death entered into the world, and passed upon all men; and that only through faith in Jesus Christ, the divinely ordained Life-giver, can men become "partakers of the divine nature," and live forever. (*II Timothy 1:10; Romans 2:7; I Corinthians 15:22, 51-54*)

IV. We believe that death is a condition of unconsciousness to all persons, righteous and wicked; a condition which will remain unchanged until the resurrection at Christ's second coming, at which time the righteous will receive everlasting life while the wicked will be "punished with everlasting destruction"; suffering complete *extinction of being*. (*Ecclesiastes 9:5; Job 14:14; John 5:28, 29; Matthew 10:28*)

V. We believe that salvation is free to all those who, in this life and in this age, accept it on the conditions imposed, which conditions are simple and inflexible; namely, turning from sin, repentance toward God, faith in the Lord Jesus Christ, and a life of consecration to the service of God; thus excluding all hope of a future probation, or of universal salvation. (*John 3:16; II Corinthians 6:2; Luke 13:25-28*)

VI. We believe that Jesus Christ, according to His promise, will come again to this earth, even "in like manner" as He went into heaven—personally, visibly and gloriously—to reign here forever; and that this coming is the hope of the Church, inasmuch as upon that coming depend the resurrection and the reward of the righteous, the abolition of sin and its consequences, and the renewal of the earth—now marred by sin—to become the eternal home of the redeemed, after which event the earth will be forever free from sin and death. (*Acts 1:11; I Thessalonians 4:16, 17; Revelation 22:12, 20*)

VII. We believe that Bible prophecy has indicated the approximate time of Christ's return; and comparing its testimony with the signs of our times, we are confident that He is near, "even at the doors," and we believe that the great duty of the hour is the proclamation of this soon-coming redemption, the defense of Bible authority, inspiration and truth, and the salvation of lost men. (*II Peter 1:19-21; Matthew 24:42-45; Revelation 22:17*)

VIII. We believe the Church of Christ is an institution of Divine origin, which includes all true Christians of whatever name; but that local church organizations should be independent of outside control, congregational in government, and subject to no dictation of priest, bishop or pope—although true fellowship and

DECLARATION OF PRINCIPLES (ADVENT CHRISTIAN CHURCH) (continued)

unity of action should exist between all such organizations. (*Matthew 16:18; Ephesians 5:25; Ephesians 4:15*)

IX. We believe that the only ordinances of the Church of Christ are Baptism and the Lord's Supper; immersion being the only true baptism. (*Matthew 28:19; Romans 6:3-5; I Corinthians 11:23-26*)

X. We believe that the first day of the week, as the day set apart by the early Church in commemoration of Christ's resurrection, should be observed as the Christian Sabbath, and used as a day of rest and religious worship. (*Psalms 118:22-24; Luke 24:1-12; I Corinthians 16:2*)

XI. We believe that war is contrary to the spirit and teachings of our Lord and Master, Jesus Christ; that it is contrary to the spirit of true brotherhood, and inimical to the welfare of humanity. We believe that Christ's followers are under obligation to use their influence against war; that they are justified in refusing to bear arms for conscience' sake in loyalty to their divine Master.

Notes: *Historically, Adventists have a relationship to the Baptists and their beliefs have followed a Baptist pattern. Baptism by immersion is practiced and affirmed in most statements. However, most statements lack clear affirmation of the doctrine of the Trinity.*

The declaration of the Advent Christian Church highlights distinguishing doctrines of the church: conditional immortality (item 3) and soul sleep (item 4). The doctrine of God (item 2) is so stated that both Trinitarian and non-Trinitarian views could be included. While affirming God the Father, Son, and Holy Spirit, neither the Trinity nor the personhood of the Holy Spirit are specifically mentioned. The church also continues the pacifism of the first generation of Adventists.

* * *

A SIMPLE STATEMENT OF FAITH [CHURCH OF GOD GENERAL CONFERENCE (ABRAHAMIC FAITH)]

This simplified Statement of Faith is included in the Constitution and By-Laws of the Church of God General Conference. While it is not a creed, it is a summary of the truths commonly believed and taught in the Church of God.

A. GOD. We believe that only one person is God, and that He is a literal (corporeal) being—almighty, eternal, immortal, and the Creator of all things. (Deut. 6:4; Isa. 45:18; 1 Tim. 2:5.)

B. JESUS CHRIST. We believe that Jesus Christ, born of the virgin Mary, is the sinless and only begotten Son of God. He did not personally pre-exist. (Luke 1:32, 33; 3:22; 1 Pet. 1:18, 19.)

C. THE HOLY SPIRIT. We believe that the Holy Spirit is not a person, but is God's divine power and influence manifest in God's mighty works and in the lives of His people. (Gen. 1:2; Rom. 8:1.)

D. THE BIBLE. We believe that the Bible is the Word of God, given by divine inspiration, and that it is the only authoritative source of doctrine and practice for Christians. (2 Tim. 2:15; Heb. 4:12; 2 Pet. 1:3.)

E. MAN. We believe that man was created innocent, but through disobedience to God fell under condemnation of death—the cessation of all life and consciousness. All men, being both sinful and mortal, are in need of salvation. (Gen. 2:7, 17; 3:4, 19; 5:5; Eccl. 9:4, 10; Rom. 3:9-11; 6:23.)

F. SALVATION. We believe that salvation is by the grace of God, through the atoning blood of Christ, and that it consists of God's forgiveness of sin, the imparting of His Spirit to the believer, and finally the gift of immortality at the resurrection when Christ returns. The steps in the gospel plan of salvation are:

1) Belief of the gospel of the Kingdom and the things concerning Jesus Christ (Acts 8:12; Rom. 1:16);

2) Sincere repentance for sin, which may be evidenced by confession and restitution (Acts 2:38);

3) Baptism—which is immersion—in the name of Jesus Christ for the remission of sins (Mark 16:15, 16; Rom. 6:1-6; Acts 22:16);

4) Growth in grace and in the knowledge of our Lord Jesus Christ (1 Pet. 2:1-3).

G. THE CHURCH OF GOD. We believe that the Church of God is the Scriptural name for that body of people who have been called out from among all nations through obedience to the gospel plan of salvation. Christ is the Head of the Church; and the nature, work, and government of the Church are set forth in the New Testament. (2 Cor. 1:1; Eph. 5:23-25.)

H. THE CHRISTIAN LIFE. We believe that the Christian life is primarily a life of consecrated discipleship to Jesus Christ as Lord, Saviour, and Teacher. It will be based on the standards which He taught and exemplified. Thus, it will be characterized by prayerful dependence on God, study of His Word, and faithful stewardship of time and possessions—with tithing as a practical expression of such stewardship. The Church of God will recognize those members who, because of their religious convictions, claim exemption from military service. (1 Tim. 4:11-16; Titus 2:11-14; Mal. 3:10.)

I. ISRAEL. We believe that "Israel" is the name of the literal descendants of Abraham through Jacob. As God's chosen nation, Israel was given the land of Palestine, but because of disobedience they were scattered throughout the world. In accordance with God's covenant with them, they will be restored to Palestine as the head of the nations in the Kingdom of God. (Ezek. 36:21-32.)

J. THE KINGDOM OF GOD. We believe that the Kingdom of God will be established on earth when Christ returns personally and visibly to reign as King in Jerusalem over the whole earth, with the Church as joint-heirs with Him. His Millennial reign will be followed by the final judgment and destruction of the wicked, after which will be established "New Heavens and a New Earth" wherein there will be no more death and God will be all in all. (Acts 1:11; 1 Thess. 4:16, 17; Rev. 5:9, 10; 20:4, 5; 21:1-4, 7, 8; 2 Pet. 2:12-14.)

Notes: *The Church of God General Conference specifically denies the Trinity (in its affirmation of one God), the preexistence of Jesus Christ, and the personhood of the Holy Spirit.*

* * *

DECLARATION OF FAITH (PRIMITIVE ADVENT CHRISTIAN CHURCH)

SECTION ONE

We believe in God, the Father Almighty, creator of heaven and earth, and in His Son, the Lord Jesus Christ, our Saviour from sin and death, and in the Holy Spirit our ever present sanctifier, comforter and guide.

SECTION TWO

We believe the Bible is the inspired Word of God, containing a revelation given to man by Divine inspiration, that its historic statements are true, that it is the only Divine standard of faith and practice.

SECTION THREE

We believe the teachings of our Lord Jesus Christ and his holy apostles are a full and sufficient statement of the duties and the faith of the church, and we reject all modern visions and revelations, so-called.

SECTION FOUR

We believe in conditional immortality. That man was created for immortality, but through sin he forfeited his divine birthright; that because of sin death entered into the world and was passed upon all men, and that only through faith in the Lord Jesus Christ can man become "partakers of the divine nature" and live forever. See Matt. 25:46, John 3:16, Rom. 6:23, 11:5-9, 1st Tim. 6:14.

SECTION FIVE

We believe that Jesus Christ died for our sins, that he was buried, that he arose from the dead the third day immortal; that he ascended bodily from earth to heaven, where he sitteth at the right hand of God the Father, there to make intercession for us; and from thence he shall come again personally to judge the living and the dead, and to establish his everlasting kingdom under the whole heavens, that his glorious coming is near and is daily to be watched for.

SECTION SIX

We believe that death is a condition of unconsciousness to all persons, righteous or wicked: a condition which will remain unchanged until the resurrection at the coming of Christ, at which time the righteous will receive everlasting life and the wicked will be punished with everlasting destruction, suffering extinction of being.

SECTION SEVEN

We believe in a change of heart at conversion. That salvation is free to all who in this life accept it on the conditions imposed, namely, repentance toward God, and faith in Jesus Christ with a life of consecration to the service of God; thus excluding all hope of a universal salvation or future probation. Acts 2:38, 3:19, 16:31, Hebrews 12:14.

SECTION EIGHT

We believe in the second coming of Jesus Christ, personally, visibly, and gloriously, to reign forever. At which time the dead will be raised, the world judged in righteousness, sin and its consequences abolished, and the everlasting kingdom, the eternal home of the redeemed set up on the new earth forever free from sin and death. That the earth made new will be inhabited by the righteous forever, and their reward will be eternal life with glory, honor, peace and fullness of joy forever.

SECTION NINE

We believe that the second coming of Christ will be the day of final judgment to all men, both saint and sinner. That all men will receive their final reward at that day, according as their works have been.

SECTION TEN

We believe the Bible sets forth three ordinances to be observed by the Christian Church, namely:

1. Baptism by immersion.

2. The Lord's Supper, by partaking of unleavened bread and wine.

3. Feet washing, to be observed by the saints washing one anothers feet.

We further believe that there is no substitute set forth in the scriptures to take the place of either of the above named ordinances.

SECTION ELEVEN

We believe that backsliders lose their covenant favor with God and that before they can be renewed in his favor they must again do the first works, including repentance toward God, faith in the Lord Jesus Christ and baptism.

SECTION TWELVE

We do not believe in opposing other denominations, but we believe in fighting the good fight of faith in Christian fellowship, love, peace and unity in the spirit of God.

Notes: *This statement is derived from that of the Advent Christian Church. The section on pacifism has been dropped, and a statement on foot washing as an ordinance has been added.*

Seventh-Day Adventist

FUNDAMENTAL BELIEFS (SEVENTH-DAY ADVENTIST CHURCH)

Seventh-day Adventists accept the Bible as their only creed and hold certain fundamental beliefs to be the teaching of the Holy Scriptures. These beliefs, as set forth here, constitute the church's understanding and expression of the teaching of Scripture. Revision of these statements may be expected at a General Conference session when the church is led by the Holy Spirit to a fuller understanding of Bible truth or finds better language in which to express the teachings of God's Holy Word.

1. THE HOLY SCRIPTURES

The Holy Scriptures, Old and New Testaments, are the written Word of God, given by divine inspiration through holy men of God who spoke and wrote as they were moved by the Holy Spirit. In this Word, God has committed to man the knowledge necessary for salvation. The Holy Scriptures are the infallible revelation of His will. They are the standard of character, the test of experience, the authoritative revealer of doctrines, and the trustworthy record of God's acts in history. (2 Peter 1:20, 21; 2 Tim. 3:16, 17; Ps. 119:105; Prov. 30:5, 6; Isa. 8:20; John 17:17; 1 Thess. 2:13; Heb. 4:12.)

2. THE TRINITY

There is one God: Father, Son, and Holy Spirit, a unity of three co-eternal Persons. God is immortal, all-powerful, all-knowing, above all, and ever present. He is infinite and beyond human comprehension, yet known through His self-revelation. He is forever worthy of worship, adoration, and service by the whole creation. (Deut. 6:4; Matt. 28:19; 2 Cor. 13:14; Eph. 4:4-6; 1 Peter 1:2; 1 Tim. 1:17; Rev. 14:7.)

3. THE FATHER

God the eternal Father is the Creator, Source, Sustainer, and Sovereign of all creation. He is just and holy, merciful and gracious, slow to anger, and abounding in steadfast love and faithfulness. The qualities and powers exhibited in the Son and the Holy Spirit are also revelations of the Father. (Gen. 1:1; Rev. 4:11; 1 Cor. 15:28; John 3:16; 1 John 4:8; 1 Tim. 1:17; Ex. 34:6, 7; John 14:9.)

4. THE SON

God the eternal Son became incarnate in Jesus Christ. Through Him all things were created, the character of God is revealed, the salvation of humanity is accomplished, and the world is judged. Forever truly God, He became also truly man, Jesus the Christ. He was conceived of the Holy Spirit and born of the virgin Mary. He lived and experienced temptation as a human being, but perfectly exemplified the righteousness and love of God. By His miracles He manifested God's power and was attested as God's promised Messiah. He suffered and died voluntarily on the cross for our sins and in our place, was raised from the dead, and ascended to minister in the heavenly sanctuary in our behalf. He will come again in glory for the final deliverance of His people and the restoration of all things. (John 1:1-3, 14; Col. 1:15-19; John 10:30; 14:9; Rom. 6:23; 2 Cor. 5:17-19; John 5:22; Luke 1:35; Phil. 2:5-11; Heb. 2:9-18; 1 Cor. 15:3, 4; Heb. 8:1, 2; John 14:1-3.)

5. THE HOLY SPIRIT

God the eternal Spirit was active with the Father and the Son in Creation, incarnation, and redemption. He inspired the writers of Scripture. He filled Christ's life with power. He draws and convicts human beings; and those who respond He renews and transforms into the image of God. Sent by the Father and the Son to be always with His children, He extends spiritual gifts to the church, empowers it to bear witness to Christ, and in harmony with the Scriptures leads it into all truth. (Gen. 1:1, 2; Luke 1:35; 4:18; Acts 10:38; 2 Peter 1:21; 2 Cor. 3:18; Eph. 4:11, 12; Acts 1:8; John 14:16-18, 26; 15:26, 27; 16:7-13.)

6. CREATION

God is Creator of all things, and has revealed in Scripture the authentic account of His creative activity. In six days the Lord made "the heaven and the earth" and all living things upon the earth, and rested on the seventh day of that first week. Thus He established the Sabbath as a perpetual memorial of His completed creative work. The first man and woman were made in the image of God as the crowning work of Creation, given dominion over the world, and charged with responsibility to care for it. When the world was finished it was "very good," declaring the glory of God. (Gen. 1; 2; Ex. 20:8-11; Ps. 19:1-6; 33:6, 9; 104; Heb. 11:3.)

7. THE NATURE OF MAN

Man and woman were made in the image of God with individuality, the power and freedom to think and to do. Though created free beings, each is an indivisible unity of body, mind, and soul, dependent upon God for life and breath and all else. When our first parents disobeyed God, they denied their dependence upon Him and fell from their high position under God. The image of God in them was marred and they became subject to death. Their descendants share this fallen nature and its consequences. They are born with weaknesses and tendencies to evil. But God in Christ reconciled the world to Himself and by His Spirit restores in penitent mortals the image of their Maker. Created for the glory of God, they are called to love Him and one another, and to care for their environment. (Gen. 1:26-28; 2:7; Ps. 8:4-8; Acts 17:24-28; Gen. 3; Ps. 51:5; Rom. 5:12-17; 2 Cor. 5:19, 20; Ps. 51:10; 1 John 4:7, 8, 11, 20; Gen. 2:15.)

8. THE GREAT CONTROVERSY

All humanity is now involved in a great controversy between Christ and Satan regarding the character of God, His law, and His sovereignty over the universe. This conflict originated in heaven when a created being, endowed with freedom of choice, in self-exaltation became Satan, God's adversary, and led into rebellion a portion of the angels. He introduced the spirit of rebellion into this world when he led Adam and Eve into sin. This human sin resulted in the distortion of the image of God in humanity, the disordering of the created world, and its eventual devastation at the time of the worldwide flood. Observed by the whole creation, this world became the arena of the universal conflict, out of which the God of love will ultimately be vindicated. To assist His people in this controversy, Christ sends the Holy Spirit and the loyal angels to guide, protect, and sustain them in the way of salvation. (Rev. 12:4-9; Isa. 14:12-14; Eze. 28:12-18; Gen. 3; Rom. 1:19-32; 5:12-21; 8:19-22; Gen. 6-8; 2 Peter 3:6; 1 Cor. 4:9; Heb. 1:14.)

9. THE LIFE, DEATH, AND RESURRECTION OF CHRIST

In Christ's life of perfect obedience to God's will, His suffering, death, and resurrection, God provided the only means of atonement for human sin, so that those who by faith accept this atonement may have eternal life, and the whole creation may better understand the infinite and holy love of the Creator. This perfect atonement vindicates the righteousness of God's law and the graciousness of His character; for it both condemns our sin and provides for our forgiveness. The death of Christ is substitutionary and expiatory, reconciling and transforming. The resurrection of Christ proclaims God's triumph over the forces of evil, and for those who accept the atonement assures their final victory over sin and death. It declares the Lordship of Jesus Christ, before whom every knee in heaven and on earth will bow. (John 3:16; Isa. 53; 1 Peter 2:21, 22; 1 Cor. 15:3, 4, 20-22; 2 Cor. 5:14, 15, 19-21; Rom. 1:4; 3:25; 4:25; 8:3, 4; 1 John 2:2; 4:10; Col. 2:15; Phil. 2:6-11.)

10. THE EXPERIENCE OF SALVATION

In infinite love and mercy God made Christ, who knew no sin, to be sin for us, so that in Him we might be made the righteousness of God. Led by the Holy Spirit we sense our need, acknowledge our sinfulness, repent of our transgressions, and exercise faith in Jesus as Lord and Christ, as Substitute and Example. This faith which receives salvation comes through the divine power of the Word and is the gift of God's grace. Through Christ we are justified, adopted as God's sons and daughters, and delivered from the lordship of sin. Through the Spirit we are born again and sanctified; the Spirit renews our minds, writes God's law of love in our hearts, and we are given the power to live a holy life. Abiding in Him we become partakers of the divine nature and have the assurance of salvation now and in the judgment. (2 Cor. 5:17-21; John 3:16; Gal. 1:4; 4:4-7; Titus 3:3-7; John 16:8; Gal. 3:13, 14; 1 Peter 2:21, 22; Rom. 10:17; Luke 17:5; Mark 9:23, 24; Eph. 2:5-10; Rom. 3:21-26; Col. 1:13, 14; Rom. 8:14-17; Gal. 3:26; John 3:3-8; 1 Peter 1:23; Rom. 12:2; Heb. 8:7-12; Eze. 36:25-27; 2 Peter 1:3, 4; Rom. 8:1-4; 5:6-10.)

11. THE CHURCH

The church is the community of believers who confess Jesus Christ as Lord and Saviour. In continuity with the people of God in Old Testament times, we are called out from the world; and we join together for worship, for fellowship, for instruction in the Word, for the celebration of the Lord's Supper, for service to all mankind, and for the worldwide proclamation of the gospel. The church derives its authority from Christ, who is the incarnate Word, and from the Scriptures, which are the written Word. The church is God's family; adopted by Him as children, its members live on the basis of the new covenant. The church is the body of Christ, a community of faith of which Christ Himself is the Head. The church is the bride for whom Christ died that He might sanctify and cleanse her. At His return in triumph, He will present her to Himself a glorious church, the faithful of all the ages, the purchase of His blood, not having spot or wrinkle, but holy and without blemish. (Gen. 12:3; Acts 7:38; Eph. 4:11-15; 3:8-11; Matt. 28:19, 20; 16:13-20; 18:18; Eph. 2:19-22; 1:22, 23; 5:23-27; Col. 1:17, 18.)

12. THE REMNANT AND ITS MISSION

The universal church is composed of all who truly believe in Christ, but in the last days, a time of widespread apostasy, a remnant has been called out to keep the commandments of God and the faith of Jesus. This remnant announces the arrival of the judgment hour, proclaims salvation through Christ, and heralds the approach of His second advent. This proclamation is symbolized by the three angels of Revelation 14; it coincides with the work of judgment in heaven and results in a work of repentance and reform on earth. Every believer is called to have a personal part in this worldwide witness. (Rev. 12:17; 14:6-12; 18:1-4; 2 Cor. 5:10; Jude 3, 14; 1 Peter 1:16-19; 2 Peter 3:10-14; Rev. 21:1-14.)

13. UNITY IN THE BODY OF CHRIST

The church is one body with many members, called from every nation, kindred, tongue, and people. In Christ we are a new creation: distinctions of race, culture, learning, and nationality, and differences between high and low, rich and poor, male and female, must not be divisive among us. We are all equal in Christ, who by one Spirit has bonded us into one fellowship with Him and with one another; we are to serve and be served without partiality or reservation. Through the revelation of Jesus Christ in the Scriptures we share the same faith and hope, and reach out in one witness to all. This unity has its source in the oneness of the triune God, who has adopted us as His children. (Rom. 12:4, 5; 1 Cor. 12:12-14; Matt. 28:19, 20; Ps. 133:1; 2 Cor. 5:16, 17; Acts 17:26, 27; Gal. 3:27, 29; Col. 3:10-15; Eph. 4:14-16; 4:1-6; John 17:20-23.)

14. BAPTISM

By baptism we confess our faith in the death and resurrection of Jesus Christ, and testify of our death to sin and of our purpose to walk in newness of life. Thus we acknowledge Christ as Lord and Saviour, become His people, and are received as members by His church. Baptism is a symbol of our union with Christ, the forgiveness of our sins, and our reception of the Holy Spirit. It is by immersion in water and is contingent on an affirmation of faith in Jesus and evidence of repentance of sin. It follows instruction in the Holy Scriptures and acceptance of their teachings. (Rom. 6:1-6; Col. 2:12, 13; Acts 16:30-33; 22:16; 2:38; Matt. 28:19, 20.)

15. THE LORD'S SUPPER

The Lord's Supper is a participation in the emblems of the body and blood of Jesus as an expression of faith in Him, our Lord and Saviour. In this experience of communion Christ is present to meet and strengthen His people. As we partake, we joyfully proclaim the Lord's death until He comes again. Preparation for the Supper includes self-examination, repentance, and confession. The Master ordained the service of foot washing to signify renewed cleansing, to express a willingness to serve one another in Christlike humility, and to unite our hearts in love. The communion service is open to all believing Christians. (1 Cor. 10:16, 17; 11:23-30; Matt. 26:17-30; Rev. 3:20; John 6:48-63; 13:1-17.)

16. SPIRITUAL GIFTS AND MINISTRIES

God bestows upon all members of His church in every age spiritual gifts which each member is to employ in loving ministry for the common good of the church and of humanity. Given by the agency of the Holy Spirit, who apportions to each member as He wills, the gifts provide all abilities and ministries needed by the church to fulfill its divinely ordained functions. According to the Scriptures, these gifts include such ministries as faith, healing, prophecy, proclamation, teaching, administration, reconciliation, compassion, and self-sacrificing service and charity for the help and encouragement of people. Some members are called of God and endowed by the Spirit for functions recognized by the church in pastoral, evangelistic, apostolic, and teaching ministries particularly needed to equip the members for service, to build up the church to spiritual maturity, and to foster unity of the faith and knowledge of God. When members employ these spiritual gifts as faithful stewards of God's varied grace, the church is protected from the destructive influence of false doctrine, grows with a growth that is from God, and is built up in faith and love. (Rom. 12:4-8; 1 Cor. 12:9-11, 27, 28; Eph. 4:8, 11-16; Acts 6:1-7; 1 Tim. 2:1-3; 1 Peter 4:10, 11.)

17. THE GIFT OF PROPHECY

One of the gifts of the Holy Spirit is prophecy. This gift is an identifying mark of the remnant church and was manifested in the ministry of Ellen G. White. As the Lord's messenger, her writings are a continuing and authoritative source of truth which provide for the church comfort, guidance, instruction, and correction. They also make clear that the Bible is the standard by which all teaching and experience must be tested. (Joel 2:28, 29; Acts 2:14-21; Heb. 1:1-3; Rev. 12:17; 19:10.)

18. THE LAW OF GOD

The great principles of God's law are embodied in the Ten Commandments and exemplified in the life of Christ. They express God's love, will, and purposes concerning human conduct and relationships and are binding upon all people in every age. These precepts are the basis of God's covenant with His people and the standard in God's judgment. Through the agency of the Holy Spirit they point out sin and awaken a sense of need for a Saviour. Salvation is all of grace and not of works, but its fruitage is obedience to the Commandments. This obedience develops Christian character and results in a sense of well-being. It is an evidence of our love for the Lord and our concern for our fellow men. The obedience of faith demonstrates the power of Christ to transform lives, and therefore strengthens Christian witness. (Ex. 20:1-17; Ps. 40:7, 8; Matt.

22:36-40; Deut. 28:1-14; Matt. 5:17-20; Heb. 8:8-10; John 16:7-10; Eph. 2:8-10; 1 John 5:3; Rom. 8:3, 4; Ps. 19:7-14.)

19. THE SABBATH

The beneficent Creator, after the six days of Creation, rested on the seventh day and instituted the Sabbath for all people as a memorial of Creation. The fourth commandment of God's unchangeable law requires the observance of this seventh-day Sabbath as the day of rest, worship, and ministry in harmony with the teaching and practice of Jesus, the Lord of the Sabbath. The Sabbath is a day of delightful communion with God and one another. It is a symbol of our redemption in Christ, a sign of our sanctification, a token of our allegiance, and a foretaste of our eternal future in God's kingdom. The Sabbath is God's perpetual sign of His eternal covenant between Him and His people. Joyful observance of his holy time from evening to evening, sunset to sunset, is a celebration of God's creative and redemptive acts. (Gen. 2:1-3; Ex. 20:8-11; Luke 4:16; Isa. 56:5, 6; 58:13, 14; Matt. 12:1-12; Ex. 31:13-17; Eze. 20:12, 20; Deut. 5:12-15; Heb. 4:1-11; Lev. 23:32; Mark 1:32.)

20. STEWARDSHIP

We are God's stewards, entrusted by Him with time and opportunities, abilities and possessions, and the blessings of the earth and its resources. We are responsible to Him for their proper use. We acknowledge God's ownership by faithful service to Him and our fellow men, and by returning tithes and giving offerings for the proclamation of His gospel and the support and growth of His church. Stewardship is a privilege given to us by God for nurture in love and the victory over selfishness and covetousness. The steward rejoices in the blessings that come to others as a result of his faithfulness. (Gen. 1:26-28; 2:15; 1 Chron. 29:14; Haggai 1:3-11; Mal. 3:8-12; 1 Cor. 9:9-14; Matt. 23:23; Rom. 15:26, 27.)

21. CHRISTIAN BEHAVIOR

We are called to be a godly people who think, feel, and act in harmony with the principles of heaven. For the Spirit to recreate in us the character of our Lord we involve ourselves only in those things which will produce Christlike purity, health, and joy in our lives. This means that our amusement and entertainment should meet the highest standards of Christian taste and beauty. While recognizing cultural differences, our dress is to be simple, modest, and neat, befitting those whose true beauty does not consist of outward adornment but in the imperishable ornament of a gentle and quiet spirit. It also means that because our bodies are the temples of the Holy Spirit, we are to care for them intelligently. Along with adequate exercise and rest, we are to adopt the most healthful diet possible and abstain from the unclean foods identified in the Scriptures. Since alcoholic beverages, tobacco, and the irresponsible use of drugs and narcotics are harmful to our bodies, we are to abstain from them as well. Instead, we are to engage in whatever brings our thoughts and bodies into the discipline of Christ, who desires our wholesomeness, joy, and goodness. (Rom. 12:1, 2; 1 John 2:6; Eph. 5:1-21; Phil. 4:8; 2 Cor. 10:5; 6:14-7:1; 1 Peter 3:1-4; 1 Cor. 6:19, 20; 10:31; Lev. 11:1-47; 3 John 2.)

22. MARRIAGE AND THE FAMILY

Marriage was divinely established in Eden and affirmed by Jesus to be a lifelong union between a man and a woman in loving companionship. For the Christian a marriage commitment is to God as well as to the spouse, and should be entered into only between partners who share a common faith. Mutual love, honor, respect, and responsibility are the fabric of this relationship, which is to reflect the love, sanctity, closeness, and permanence of the relationship between Christ and His church. Regarding divorce, Jesus taught that the person who divorces a spouse, except for fornication, and marries another, commits adultery. Although some family relationships may fall short of the ideal, marriage partners who fully commit themselves to each other in Christ may achieve loving unity through the guidance of the Spirit and the nurture of the church. God blesses the family and intends that its members shall assist each other toward complete maturity. Parents are to bring up their children to love and obey the Lord. By their example and their words they are to teach them that Christ is a loving disciplinarian, ever tender and caring, who wants them to become members of His body, the family of God. Increasing family closeness is one of the earmarks of the final gospel message. (Gen. 2:18-25; Matt. 19:3-9; John 2:1-11; 2 Cor. 6:14; Eph. 5:21-33; Matt. 5:31, 32; Mark 10:11, 12; Luke 16:18; 1 Cor. 7:10, 11; Ex. 20:12; Eph. 6:1-4; Deut. 6:5-9; Prov. 22:6; Mal. 4:5, 6.)

23. CHRIST'S MINISTRY IN THE HEAVENLY SANCTUARY

There is a sanctuary in heaven, the true tabernacle which the Lord set up and not man. In it Christ ministers on our behalf, making available to believers the benefits of His atoning sacrifice offered once for all on the cross. He was inaugurated as our great High Priest and began His intercessory ministry at the time of His ascension. In 1844, at the end of the prophetic period of 2300 days, He entered the second and last phase of His atoning ministry. It is a work of investigative judgment which is part of the ultimate disposition of all sin, typified by the cleansing of the ancient Hebrew sanctuary on the Day of Atonement. In that typical service the sanctuary was cleansed with the blood of animal sacrifices, but the heavenly things are purified with the perfect sacrifice of the blood of Jesus. The investigative judgment reveals to heavenly intelligences who among the dead are asleep in Christ and therefore, in Him, are deemed worthy to have part in the first resurrection. It also makes manifest who among the living are abiding in Christ, keeping the commandments of God and the faith of Jesus, and in Him, therefore, are ready for translation into His everlasting kingdom. This judgment vindicates the justice of God in saving those who believe in Jesus. It declares that those who have remained loyal to God shall receive the kingdom. The completion of this ministry of Christ will mark the close of human probation before the Second Advent. (Heb. 8:1-5; 4:14-16; 9:11-28; 10:19-22; 1:3; 2:16, 17; Dan. 7:9-27; 8:13, 14; 9:24-27; Num. 14:34; Eze. 4:6; Lev. 16; Rev. 14:6, 7; 20:12; 14:12; 22:12.)

24. THE SECOND COMING OF CHRIST

The second coming of Christ is the blessed hope of the church, the grand climax of the gospel. The Saviour's coming will be literal, personal, visible, and worldwide. When He returns, the righteous dead will be resurrected, and together with the righteous living will be glorified and taken to heaven, but the unrighteous will die. The almost complete fulfillment of most lines of prophecy, together with the present condition of the world, indicates that Christ's coming is imminent. The time of that event has not been revealed, and we are therefore exhorted to be ready at all times. (Titus 2:13; Heb. 9:28; John 14:1-3; Acts 1:9-11; Matt. 24:14; Rev. 1:7; Matt. 26:43, 44; 1 Thess. 4:13-18; 1 Cor. 15:51-54; 2 Thess. 1:7-10; 2:8; Rev. 14:14-20; 19:11-21; Matt. 24; Mark 13; Luke 21; 2 Tim. 3:1-5; 1 Thess. 5:1-6.)

25. DEATH AND RESURRECTION

The wages of sin is death. But God, who alone is immortal, will grant eternal life to His redeemed. Until that day death is an unconscious state for all people. When Christ, who is our life, appears, the resurrected righteous and the living righteous will be glorified and caught up to meet their Lord. The second resurrection, the resurrection of the unrighteous, will take place a thousand years later. (Rom. 6:23; 1 Tim. 6:15, 16; Eccl. 9:5, 6; Ps. 146:3, 4; John 11:11-14; Col. 3:4; 1 Cor. 15:51-54; 1 Thess. 4:13-17; John 5:28, 29; Rev. 20:1-10.)

26. THE MILLENNIUM AND THE END OF SIN

The millennium is the thousand-year reign of Christ with His saints in heaven between the first and second resurrections. During this time the wicked dead will be judged; the earth will be utterly desolate, without living human inhabitants, but occupied by Satan and his angels. At its close Christ with His saints and the Holy City will descend from heaven to earth. The unrighteous dead will then be resurrected, and with Satan and his angels will surround the city; but fire from God will consume them and cleanse the earth. The universe will thus be freed of sin and sinners forever. (Rev. 20; 1 Cor. 6:2, 3; Jer. 4:23-26; Rev. 21:1-5; Mal. 4:1; Eze. 28:18, 19.)

27. THE NEW EARTH

On the new earth, in which righteousness dwells, God will provide an eternal home for the redeemed and a perfect environment for everlasting life, love, joy, and learning in His presence. For here God Himself will dwell with His people, and suffering and death will have passed away. The great controversy will be ended, and sin will be no more. All things, animate and inanimate, will declare that God is love; and He shall reign forever. Amen. (2 Peter 3:13; Isa. 35; 65:17-25; Matt. 5:5; Rev. 21:1-7; 22:1-5; 11:15.)

Notes: *The Seventh-Day Adventist Church is Trinitarian in belief. Besides its sabbatarianism, it is distinguished most by its particular beliefs concerning spiritual gifts and the prophetic ministry of founder Ellen G. White (items 16 and 17). A number of the items in this statement concern eschatology.*

BELIEFS (SEVENTH-DAY ADVENTIST REFORM MOVEMENT)

"In the mouth of two or three witnesses shall every word be established." *2 Corinthians 13:1.*

1. There is an intelligent Supreme Being called God, whose activities are visible throughout nature. He created the universe, this earth, and every living organism. *Acts 17:23-28; Genesis 1:1; Colossians 1:16.*

2. Jesus Christ is His Son who existed in heaven before being born on earth. Together with His Father He created this world. *John 20:31; 17:5; 1:1-3, 14.*

3. The Holy Spirit is the third person in the divine family. *1 John 5:5, 6; John 16:7, 8, 13.*

4. God's will for man was recorded by select men who were inspired by the Holy Spirit. Those writings were gathered into one volume called "The Bible." *2 Peter 1:21; 2 Timothy 3:16, 17.*

5. God created human beings to be happy, content, and immortal. *Proverbs 8:30, 31; Genesis 1:29; 2:9.*

6. The whole universe, including our world and its creatures, is controlled by divine laws. *Job 38, 39.*

7. There is clear evidence of other, invisible beings, called angels, who were created before man. *1 Corinthians 15:39, 40; Job 38:4, 7; Genesis 3:24.*

8. One of the angels, called Lucifer, or Satan, perverted his liberty and began to counterwork and disrupt the existing harmony. For this reason he was cast out of heaven. *Isaiah 14:12-17; Ezekiel 28:12-19; Luke 10:18; Revelation 12:9.*

9. He confused and deceived the first human pair into trying a new experience by stepping outside God's order into forbidden territory. *Genesis 3.*

10. Trespassing against God's law is called "sin." Man's nature became sinful and degenerated through continued sinful practices. *1 John 3:4; Ephesians 2:3; Psalm 51:5.*

11. God's character is love, as seen in the beauty of nature. *1 John 4:8, 16; Philippians 4:7-9.*

12. He is the source of all higher intelligence. With His Son He devised a plan to counteract the degeneration of transgression by creating a unique plan for restoration, called "The Plan of Redemption." *Colossians 2:2, 3; Matthew 20:28; 1 Timothy 2:5, 6.*

13. The sure result of transgression and sin is eternal death unless the redemption of Christ is accepted. *Romans 6:23; 5:12; Colossians 1:13, 14; John 3:16.*

14. So that justice may be carried out, God requires the life of very sinner, which means the shedding of his blood. *Ezekiel 18:19, 20; Hebrews 9:22; Exodus 12:13.*

15. The Plan of Redemption provided for Christ to become the sinner's substitute, paying for our guilt with His own blood. *Hebrews 2:9; Romans 5:6, 8; Hebrews 9:11, 12.*

16. The sinner must accept this substitute ransom payment by faith in order to receive forgiveness. *Romans 3:22-25, 28, 31; Isaiah 1:18.*

17. The sinner must accept Christ as his personal Saviour and Redeemer. *John 20:31; 3:15, 16, 36.*

18. The Holy Spirit convinces the sinner that all things earthly are transitory and not worth living for. His outlook on life will be drawn to eternal subjects, and his affections and longings will completely change. This is the experience of the "new birth," or "conversion." *James 4:14; Ecclesiastes 2:11; Psalm 144:3, 4; John 3:3-8.*

19. This change of heart is attested to publicly by being baptized by immersion, representing the death of the old man and the birth of the new. *Romans 6:3-11; 1 Peter 3:21.*

20. In the Old Testament, animals that were slain for the guilty sinner symbolized Christ, the true Sin Bearer and sacrificial Lamb. *Exodus 12:5, 6, 13; Hebrews 8:5; John 1:29.*

21. When Christ died, the symbolic laws connected with the temple service ended. *Matthew 27:51; Colossians 2:14-17.*

22. Christ's blood does not cover premeditated, willful sins but only weakness and ignorance. *Hebrews 10:26, 27; 4:15; Acts 17:30.*

23. Salvation cannot be earned by good works, for man is saved by unmerited grace alone. *Romans 3:24; Ephesians 2:8; Romans 9:16.*

24. God's law consisting of ten commandments checks human behavior, shows sins when committed, and therefore must be obeyed. *Matthew 19:17-19; Romans 7:7, 8; Matthew 5:19.*

25. Obedience to God's law, motivated by love, shows that the person's faith is genuine. *1 John 5:2, 3; James 2:14, 18, 24, 26.*

26. God rested on the seventh day of the creation week and commanded mankind to rest also. This obedience shows that we recognize and worship Him as our Creator. The Lord's day is not the pagan day of sun worship, Sunday, but the seventh day of the week, Saturday. *Genesis 2:1-3; Exodus 20:8-11; Romans 1:25; Mark 2:28.*

27. This lifespan is an education for the afterlife. The change in a Christian's life is effected by the working of the Holy Spirit. A new, divine nature eventually replaces the old, sinful nature. This is called sanctification. At death, all opportunities for perfecting character cease. *Colossians 3:1-3; 2 Peter 1:4-8; 1 Thessalonians 4:3; Hebrews 9:27.*

28. Death is an unconscious sleep of body and soul, but it will not last forever. Through a miraculous resurrection, human beings will one day become alive again. *Ecclesiastes 9:5, 6; John 5:25-29.*

29. Those who accepted Christ as their Saviour before they died will be raised at His second coming to receive a new body that will never die. *1 Thessalonians 4:16; 1 Corinthians 15:53, 54.*

30. Christ's second coming is imminent and will be an actual happening visible to all people on earth. *Matthew 24:42; Acts 1:10, 11; Revelation 1:7.*

31. In Noah and Lot's times all unbelievers were destroyed by physical elements (water and fire). Likewise, in the last days literal fire will destroy the wicked, making this earth a desolate wilderness. *2 Peter 3:5-7; 2:4-6; Malachi 4:1; Joel 2:3.*

32. The destruction of the unbelievers will bind Satan for a thousand years, because he will have no one to deceive, for all people are then dead. *Revelation 20:1, 2; 2 Peter 2:4.*

33. During the 1,000 years (millennium), judgment is held in heaven to determine the degree of the unbelievers' guilt. *Revelation 20:4, 12; 1 Corinthians 6:2, 3.*

34. At the millennium's end, the unbelievers will be resurrected to hear their sentence of doom and receive their punishment. *John 5:29; Revelation 20:5, 9, 14, 15.*

35. The earth will be renovated and made new like Eden, and God's kingdom will be established forever. *Revelation 21:1, 5, 3; Daniel 2:44.*

36. A large part of the Bible is prophetic, and the historic fulfillment of these predictions proves that the Bible is inspired. *2 Peter 1:19; Luke 24:44-46; Acts 8:30-35.*

37. The books Daniel and The Revelation of the Bible predict the rise and fall of the empires of antiquity and their characteristics, as well as the religious developments up to our own time. These prophecies help the Christian understand present-day events. *Daniel 7:3-8, 17; Revelation 13; Matthew 24:15; Revelation 1:3.*

38. Since Daniel 7 and 8 use symbols throughout, the 2,300-day period of Daniel 8:14 is also symbolic and represents 2,300 literal years. Since the period's beginning is historically set at 457 B.C., it extends to 1844, at which time an investigative judgment of all Christians began in the heavenly sanctuary. *Numbers 14:34; Ezekiel 4:6; Ezra 7:12-26; Daniel 7:9, 10.*

39. The gift of the Spirit of prophecy is given to the remnant church of the last days to warn and guide them. *Revelation 12:17; 19:10; 2 Chronicles 20:20.*

40. Earthly governments are ordained by God and should be obeyed within their rightful sphere. *Romans 13:1-7; Titus 3:1.*

41. All governments are under God and therefore under obligation to obey Him. *Daniel 2:21; 4:17; Psalm 2:10, 11.*

42. If governments command the Christian to destroy the life of any fellow human being in peace or war, he is obliged to obey God's superior law first. The Christian cannot support warfare. *Luke 3:14; Matthew 26:52; Acts 4:19; 5:29.*

43. Marriage is a lifelong partnership. Divorce and remarriage are contrary to God's will. *Romans 7:2, 3; Matthew 19:6-9.*

44. Since Christ sacrificed everything for us and everything belongs to Him, it is a blessing to return to Him that portion of our income which He claims as His. *Matthew 23:23; Hebrews 7:8; Malachi 3:8-11.*

45. The physical body belongs to God, and we must keep it in good, healthy condition with proper food, rest, cleanliness, exercise, etc. *1 Corinthians 3:16, 17; 6:19, 20.*

46. Narcotics, stimulants, drugs, etc. are unnatural and destroy the body and mind. *Proverbs 20:1; 23:29-32; Luke 1:15.*

47. In His original plan, God never intended the living creatures to be man's food. *Genesis 1:29; Exodus 16:3, 4; Numbers 11:18-20, 33.*

48. Extreme fashions, dictated by modern society, are unhealthful, immoral, and contrary to Christian ethics. *1 Timothy 2:9, 10; 1 Peter 3:1-5.*

49. God recognizes only one true church, whether small or large—the one which keeps His commandments, has the Spirit of prophecy, and is separate from the world. It is His agency on earth, and He works through it to accomplish His purpose. *Ephesians 4:5; Solomon's Song 6:8-10; Matthew 28:19, 20; Revelation 12:17.*

50. God's church carries the responsibility of proclaiming the last warning preparatory to Christ's second coming. *Revelation 14:6-12; Matthew 24:14; Revelation 18:1-4.*

Notes: *The Seventh-Day Adventist Reform Movement departs from traditional Christian belief primarily in its position on Christ's atonement. Christ's atonement does not apply to willful sin, only ignorance and weakness (item 22). Pacifism is affirmed (item 42).*

* * *

Church of God Adventist

FUNDAMENTAL BELIEFS (ASSOCIATED CHURCHES OF GOD)

1. GOD

We believe that one God, the heavenly Father, is the supreme Deity of the universe (Eph. 4:6; I Cor. 8:4-6; 15:24-28). He is composed of spirit and is eternal (John 4:24; I Tim. 1:17). He is a personal Being of supreme love, wisdom, knowledge, judgment, mercy and power; He possesses every attribute of perfect character (Matt. 5:48; I John 4:8; Prov. 2:6-8; Isa. 40:12-31). He is Creator of the heavens and the earth and all that is in them and the source of life (Gen. 1; Acts 17:24-29; John 5:26).

2. JESUS CHRIST

We believe that Jesus of Nazareth is the Son of God, conceived of the Holy Spirit and born in the human flesh of the virgin Mary (Matt. 1:18-25; Luke 1:34-35). Before His human birth, Christ existed eternally with God and as God (John 1:1-2, 14; Rev. 1:8). God created everything in the universe by and through Jesus Christ (Col. 1:16; John

FUNDAMENTAL BELIEFS (ASSOCIATED CHURCHES OF GOD) (continued)

1:3). Jesus is the Christ, or Messiah, sent from God to be our Saviour and Redeemer (John 1:29; 3:15-17; Acts 4:12).

3. HOLY SPIRIT

We believe that the Holy Spirit is the spirit of God the Father and of Jesus Christ. The Holy Spirit is not a person but rather it is the power of God by which all things were made (Gen. 1:2; Psalm 104:30). Through the Holy Spirit God is omnipresent (Psalm 139:7-11). Through the Holy Spirit God the Father imparts His life, power, mind, and attributes, and Jesus Christ abides and lives in true Christians (Luke 24:49; Acts 1:8; 2:38; 5:32; John 1:12; 14:16-17, 23; 15:4-5; I John 3:24; 4:13; 5:12; Rom. 5:5; 8:9; II Tim. 1:7; Gal. 5:22-23).

4. THE BIBLE

We believe that the Scriptures of the Old and New Testaments are God's revelation to man. The original writings were divinely inspired (II Tim. 3:16; II Pet. 1:21). The Bible is the source of divine truth and wisdom (John 17:17; Prov. 2:6) and all doctrines and philosophies contrary to the Bible are false (Rom. 3:4). The Bible reveals God's will and plan of salvation and contains God's instruction for man (II Tim. 3:15-17; Prov. 1:2-7; Matt. 4:4).

5. SATAN

We believe that Satan, the Devil, is a literal spirit being. He is the adversary of God and His people and is the deceiver of mankind (Rev. 12:9; II Cor. 4:4; I Pet. 5:8; Matt. 4:1,3; John 8:44; Eph. 6:11-12). Demons are those angels who sinned against God (Rev. 12:9,4; II Pet. 2:4).

6. MAN

We believe that man is a physical, mortal being created in the image of God from the elements and given the breath of life by God (Gen. 1:26-27; 2:7). Man is subject to corruption and death and does not have eternal life inherent in himself prior to receiving the gift of God's Holy Spirit (Gen. 2:17; 3:3-4, 19, 22; Eccl. 3:19-20; Ezek. 18:4, 20; I Cor. 15:45, 47, 50-54; Rom. 5:12; 6:23; I John 3:14-15; 5:11-12). Though there is a spirit in man (Job 32:8; I Cor. 2:11), we believe that spirit is not the conscious being apart from the body; death is the cessation of both life and consciousness (Rom. 6:23; Psa. 6:5; 115:17; 146:4; Eccl. 9:4-6, 10; Acts 2:29, 34; John 3:13; I Cor. 15:20-23, 52-54).

7. GOD'S PURPOSE FOR MAN

We believe that God's purpose for each human being is that he ultimately become a member of His divine Family, composed of spirit and possessing eternal life and the attributes of Godly character (John 1:12-13; Rom. 8:14-19, 28-29; I Cor. 15:39-54; Heb. 2:5-10). It is God's desire that all men be saved and come to the knowledge of the truth; He has a step-by-step plan by which He is fulfilling His purpose and bringing all men to the full knowledge and stature of Jesus Christ (Acts 4:12; John 6:44; 17:2-8, 17-21; 15:16; Matt. 28:18-20; Acts 1:7-8; 2:22-39; 3:17-26; Eph. 4:11-15; Rom. 1:16; 11:22-26; II Pet. 3:9; I Tim. 2:4-6).

8. SIN

We believe that all men have sinned and come short of the glory of God (Rom. 3:10, 23; 5:12). Sin is the transgression of God's law (I John 3:4). By the law is the knowledge of sin (Rom. 3:20; 7:7); to him who knows to do good and does it not, to him it is sin (James 4:17); whatever is not of faith is sin (Rom. 14:23). The penalty for sin is death (Rom. 6:23).

9. SACRIFICE OF CHRIST

We believe that God sent Jesus Christ to this earth to die for the sins of the world. Though tempted in all points as we are, Christ lived without sin and gave His life as the full atonement for the sins of all mankind (John 3:16-17; I John 2:1-2; Rom. 5:6-11; 6:23; Heb. 4:15). He was crucified, died, was buried, and was resurrected after three days and three nights in the grave (I Cor. 15:3-4; Matt. 12:40). He ascended to heaven where He now sits at the right hand of the Father as our High Priest and Advocate (Heb. 1:2-3; 4:14-16; 7:25-27; 12:2).

10. FORGIVENESS OF SINS

We believe that all who repent of their sins, believe the gospel of Jesus Christ, accept Him as their personal Saviour and, following the example of Christ, are baptized by immersion, are forgiven their sins by God's grace, through faith in Christ's blood (Mark 1:15; 16:15-16; Matt. 3:2,6,8,13-17; Acts 2:38-39; 4:12; Rom. 1:16; 3:23-25; 5:1-2; 6:3-6; Eph. 1:7).

11. GIFT OF THE HOLY SPIRIT

We believe that all who repent and are forgiven of past sins through Christ can receive the gift of God's Holy Spirit through the laying on of hands (Acts 2:38; 8:15-17; 19:1-6; Heb. 6:1-2). God's Holy Spirit literally comes and abides in them, bearing the fruits of God's Spirit in the individual's life (John 14:16-17, 23; 15:1-8; Gal. 5:16-25; Rom. 6:4-6, 12-22). Those who have God's Holy Spirit in this life, and are led by it, shall be changed from mortal to immortal at the return of Jesus Christ (Rom. 5:8-10; 8:1-18; I Cor. 15:50-58).

12. THE TEN COMMANDMENTS

We believe that God's way of life is expressed in His Ten Commandments (Ex. 20, Deut. 5) as magnified by Christ in explaining their full spiritual intent (Matt. 5, 6, 7) and summarized by Him in the two great spiritual principles of love toward God and love toward neighbor (Matt. 22:36-40). We believe God's Commandments are spiritual precepts (Rom. 7:12-14) that were in effect prior to the Old Covenant (Rom. 4:15; I John 3:4; Gen. 4:7; Rom. 5:12-14; Gen. 26:5) and were taught by Christ and the Apostles as a fundamental part of the New Covenant (Matt. 5:17-48; 7:12-29; 19:16-19; Rom. 6:4-6, 12-22; I Cor. 7:19; Heb. 8:6-10; 10:16; James 2:8-12; I John 2:3-5; 3:24; 5:2-3; Rev. 21:8; 22:14).

13. OBEDIENCE

We believe that Jesus Christ lived without sin as an example for us (John 15:9-12; I Pet. 2:21-25; I John 2:6; Eph. 5:1-2; I Cor. 11:1). Though justification and salvation are a gift of God through faith in Christ's blood (Rom. 3:23-25; 5:1-2; 6:23) and are not earned by obedience

(Rom. 3:20, 23; Gal. 2:16; Eph. 2:8-10), those who abide in Christ should live as He lived (I John 2:3-6). Christ and the love of God dwelling in them will be keeping God's Commandments (John 14:15-24; I John 3:24; 5:2-3; Rom. 5:8-10; Gal. 5:16-25). ". . . to whom ye yield yourselves servants to obey, his servants ye are to whom ye obey; whether of sin unto death, or of obedience unto righteousness" (Rom. 6:16-23; 2:5-11; I Cor. 6:9-10; Gal. 5:19-23; II Pet. 1:5-11).

14. SPIRITUAL CHRISTIANITY

We believe that the emphasis in true Christianity is on the spiritual more than on the physical (II Cor. 3:6, 16-18; Matt. 5:20; Gal. 5:13-25; Rom. 8:1-9). God is spirit and they who worship Him must worship in spirit and in truth (John 4:23-24). God is primarily concerned with the heart, mind, attitude, spirit and character of man (Acts 10:34-35; 15:8; Phil. 2:2-8; Rom. 2:23-29). The kingdom of God is not meat and drink, but righteousness, peace, and joy in the Holy Spirit (Rom. 14:17). Christianity is not established on human teachings regarding ". . . touch not; taste not; handle not; which all are to perish with the using . . . " (Col. 2:20-22).

Christ explained true Christianity by amplifying God's Commandments to reveal their positive spiritual intent (Matt. 5,6,7). The New Covenant involves internalizing those spiritual laws and having them written in our hearts and minds (Heb. 10:16; II Cor. 3:3). Spiritual Christianity leads to a positive orientation with an outward expression of the fruits of God's Spirit—love, joy, peace, judgment, mercy, and faith (Matt. 23:23; Gal. 5:22-23).

15. CHRISTIAN INDIVIDUALITY & RESPONSIBILITY

We believe that each person is a unique individual and personality. He has the responsibility in this life not only of growing in Christian character and Godliness but also of fully developing his mind, personality, talents and abilities (Rom. 12:3-8; I Cor. 12:4-11; 3:10-14; 6:19-20; Eph. 4:7, 15-16; Luke 19:11-26; Matt. 25:15). Each human being has the God-given right to maintain his individuality, self-respect, and human dignity, and is personally responsible before God for his own mind, conscience, and convictions.

16. THE CHURCH

We believe that God's Church, the body of Christ, is a spiritual organism composed of all people who have God's Holy Spirit (I Cor. 12:12-14; Rom. 8:9; I John 4:13). It has only one Head, which is Christ (Eph. 1:22-23; Col. 1:18). The spiritual body of Christ is not limited to any one organization on earth; membership in that body is not determined by adherence to the teachings of any one man or group of men; members of Christ's body are those who live in Christ and in whom Christ dwells (John 14:23; 15:4-5; I Cor. 1:12-13; 3:1-11; Eph. 4:4-6; Matt. 7:16-23; I John 2:3-5; 3:23-24).

17. CHURCH ORGANIZATION AND GOVERNMENT

We believe that Christians should be organized in order to effectively serve God, each other, and mankind (I Cor. 12:7, 15-27; 14:33; 1:10; Eph. 4:3-7, 11-13). Such an organization should have proper order and government to facilitate coordination of effort and the effectual working of God's Spirit through all the members (I Cor. 12:4-11; 14:40; Eph. 4:11-16; Rom. 12:3-8). But that government should not restrict or impede the individual's spiritual growth, subvert his personal conscience or convictions, or interfere with the working of God's Spirit in his mind and life. The government of God in a Christian's life is not the human authority within an organization; rather, it is the direct authority of Jesus Christ and the Word of God that is accepted personally and voluntarily by each member of the body of Christ (Eph. 1:22; I Tim. 2:5; Matt. 23:10; Rom. 14:4; Acts 5:27-29).

18. COMMISSION TO THE CHURCH

We believe that Christ's commission to His Church is set forth in Mark 16:15-16, Luke 24:47, and Matthew 28:19-20: "Go ye therefore, and teach [make disciples of] all nations, baptizing them in the name of the Father, and of the Son, and of the Holy Spirit: Teaching them to observe all things whatsoever I have commanded you. . . . " This work of the Church involves preaching the good news of Jesus Christ and the Kingdom of God to the world; it involves being a light and example of God's way (Matt. 5:16; John 15:8, 16; Phil 2:15-16); it involves baptizing and teaching those who repent; and it involves edifying the body of Christ, feeding the flock of God, and perfecting the saints (Matt. 5:48; Eph. 4:12-13; John 21:15-17; I Pet. 5:2). God has placed every member in the body of Christ in order to fulfill the various facets of this commission (I Cor. 12:7-11, 18-20, 27-30: Eph. 4:4,7,11-16).

19. FINANCING THE COMMISSION TO THE CHURCH

We believe that Christ's commission to the Church should be financed through the freewill offerings of the Church (Matt. 6:19-33; I Cor. 9:1-14; II Cor. 11:8-9; 12:13; Phil. 4:14-19; Gal. 6:6-8; I Tim. 5:17-18), not by having to charge the public for the gospel (Matt. 10:7-8; III John 5-8), nor by prescribing a specific amount or percentage that the Church members must give as was done under the Old Testament tithing laws. It is the responsibility of every Christian to give generously to support the various facets of the work of the Church and of the ministry of Jesus Christ; ". . . He which soweth sparingly shall reap also sparingly; and he which soweth bountifully shall reap also bountifully" (II Cor. 9:6-11; Prov. 3:9-10; I Tim. 6:17-19; Mark 12:41-44; Luke 6:38).

20. NEW TESTAMENT PASSOVER

We believe that we should annually, each Passover, observe the anniversary of Christ's death by partaking of the bread and the wine that symbolize His broken body and shed blood (Matt. 26:26-29; I Cor. 11:23-30).

21. NEW TESTAMENT SABBATH

We believe that the seventh day of the week, from Friday sunset to Saturday sunset, is God's Sabbath (Gen. 2:2-3; 1:5; Lev. 23:32). We are to rest from our labors on this day following the example of God (Gen. 2:1-3; Ex. 20:11). We are to observe the Sabbath according to the teachings and example of Jesus Christ in the New Testament (Mark 2:23-28; 3:1-4; Matt. 12:7-12; Luke 4:16; Mark 6:2) and following the practice of the Apostles and the New Testament Church (Acts 13:42-44; 17:2; 18:4).

22. RETURN OF CHRIST

We believe that Jesus Christ will return to this earth, personally and visibly, in power and glory, before His one thousand year reign on earth (Acts 1:11; 3:19-21; I Thess. 4:16; Rev. 1:7; 11:15; 19:11-16; 20:4,6; Matt. 24:23-30; 25:31; Dan. 2:44; Zech. 14:3-4, 9). He will reign with love and justice over all nations as King of kings and Lord of lords (Isa. 11:1-10; Rev. 19:16).

23. RESURRECTION OF SAINTS

We believe that the dead in Christ will be resurrected to eternal life at Christ's return, and that those Christians who are alive at that time will be changed from mortal to immortal (I Thess. 4:13-17; I Cor. 15:50-54; Phil. 3:20-21). They will be composed of spirit and have eternal life as immortal members of God's divine Family (Rev. 2:11; 20:6; 21:7; I John 3:2; Rom. 8:11, 16-17). They will rule with Christ over the nations for the one-thousand-year reign of God's Kingdom on earth (Rev. 20:4-6; 1:5-6; 2:25-27; 5:10; Dan. 7:18,22,27; Luke 1:31-33; 22:29-30; Matt. 19:28; Ezek. 37:23-25).

24. GENERAL RESURRECTION

We believe that God will resurrect to physical life again all who have not had a full, complete opportunity to know God and Christ, to understand God's purpose and truth, and to develop Godly character through the experiences of life (Acts 4:12; John 17:2-3; I John 5:11-12, 19-20; Heb. 8:8-12; Rev. 20:5; Matt. 12:41-42; Ezek. 37; Rom. 11:25-32; John 5:21-30).

It is God's desire that all men be saved and come to the knowledge of the truth (I Tim. 2:4-6; II Pet. 3:9). God will judge people according to their works after they receive knowledge and understanding and have had opportunity to use God's Holy Spirit to live God's way of life; God will not eternally condemn people because of sins committed in ignorance of the true God and His way (Acts 17:23-31; James 4:17; Rom. 7:7; John 6:37-40, 44-45; Acts 10:34-35; Rev. 20:5, 11-12; Ezek. 37:13-14; I Tim. 2:6; Heb. 9:25-28; John 3:16-17).

Notes: *The Church of God Adventist churches are sabbatarian, but did not follow the revelations given to Ellen G. White, founder of the Seventh-Day Adventist Church. Many not only worship on Saturday, but keep the Old Testament (Jewish) holy days.*

The Associated Churches of God follows the non-Trinitarian perspective of its parent organization, the Worldwide Church of God. Statements on church government (item 17) and church finances (item 19) reflect issues that led to the founding of the church.

FUNDAMENTAL BELIEFS (CHURCH OF GOD EVANGELISTIC ASSOCIATION)

FOREWORD

The fundamental beliefs of the Church of God Evangelistic Association are based on the careful study of the Holy Scriptures. We adhere to these precepts and are dedicated to teach and live by them. THEY DO NOT, HOWEVER, FORM A CLOSED CREED. Individually and collectively we recognize the need for continual study, growth, and change. We seek to grow in knowledge and understanding "Till we all come in the unity of the faith, and of the knowledge of the Son of God, unto a perfect man, unto the measure of the stature of the fullness of Christ" (Eph. 4:13).

We do not believe that compliance with all of our fundamental beliefs is required of each individual for salvation. On the other hand, the Bible does set specific standards and outlines definite requirements for salvation. Our beliefs concerning those basic requisites are essentially explained in sections 10 through 13, with some elaboration in other sections.

The Church of God Evangelistic Association is committed to teach the Word of God, not to legislate its present understanding on others. We believe Christians should not judge one another in matters of individual conscience and understanding (Matt. 7:1-2; Rom. 14:4, 12-13, 17-23; 15:1-2; James 4:11-12).

For further explanation on any of these subjects or for information on scriptural teachings not covered in this statement of belief, write to the Church of God Evangelistic Association, 11824 Beaverton, Bridgeton, Missouri 63044. Phone (314) 739-4490.

1. GOD

We believe that one God, the heavenly Father, is the supreme Diety of the universe (Eph. 4:6; I Cor. 8:4-6; 15:24-28). He is composed of spirit and is eternal (John 4:24; I Tim. 1:17). He is a personal Being of supreme love, wisdom, knowledge, judgement, mercy and power. He possesses every attribute of perfect character (Matt. 5:48; I John 4:8; Prov. 2:6-8; Isa. 40:12-31). He is Creator of the heavens and the earth and all that is in them and the source of life (Gen. 1; Acts 17:24-29; John 5:26).

2. JESUS CHRIST

We believe that Jesus of Nazareth is the Son of God, conceived of the Holy Spirit and born in the human flesh of the virgin Mary (Matt. 1:18-25; Luke 1:34-35). Before His human birth, Christ existed eternally with God and as God (John 1:1-2, 14; Rev. 1:8). God created everything in the universe by and through Jesus Christ (Col. 1:16; John 1:3). Jesus is the Christ, or Messiah, sent from God to be our Saviour and Redeemer (John 1:29; 3:15-17; Acts 4:12).

3. HOLY SPIRIT

We believe that the Holy Spirit is the spirit of God the Father and of Jesus Christ. The Holy Spirit is not a person but rather it is the power of God by which all things were made (Gen. 1:2; Psalm 104:30). Through the Holy Spirit God is omnipresent (Psalm 139:7-11). Through the Holy Spirit God the Father imparts His life, power, mind, and attributes, and Jesus Christ abides and lives in true Christians (Luke 24:49; Acts 1:8; 2:38; 5:32; John 1:12; 14:16-17, 23; 15:4-5; I John 3:24; 4:13; 5:12; Rom. 5:5; 8:9; II Tim. 1:7; Gal. 5:22-23).

4. THE BIBLE

We believe that the Scriptures of the Old and New Testaments are God's revelation to man. The original writings were divinely inspired (II Tim. 3:16; II Pet. 1:21). The Bible is the source of divine truth and wisdom (John 17:17; Prov. 2:6) and all doctrines and philosophies contrary to the Bible are false (Rom. 3:4). The Bible reveals God's will and plan of salvation and contains God's instruction for man (II Tim. 3:15-17; Prov. 1:2-7; Matt. 4:4).

5. SATAN

We believe that Satan, the Devil, is a literal spirit being. He is the adversary of God and His people and is the deceiver of mankind (Rev. 12:9; II Cor. 4:4; I Pet. 5:8; Matt. 4:1, 3; John 8:44; Eph. 6:11-12). Demons are those angels who sinned against God (Rev. 12:9, 4; II Pet. 2:4).

6. MAN

We believe that man is a physical, mortal being created in the image of God from the elements and given the breath of life by God (Gen. 1:26-27; 2:7). Man is subject to corruption and death and does not have eternal life inherent in himself prior to receiving the gift of God's Holy Spirit (Gen. 2:17; 3:3-4, 19, 22; Eccl. 3:19-20; Ezek. 18:4, 20; I Cor. 15:45, 47, 50-54; Rom. 5:12; 6:23; I John 3:14-15; 5:11-12). Though there is a spirit in man (Job 32:8; I Cor. 2:11), we believe that spirit is not the conscious being apart from the body; death is the cessation of both life and consciousness (Rom. 6:23; Psa. 6:5; 115:17; 146:4; Eccl. 9:4-6, 10; Acts 2:29, 34; John 3:13; I Cor. 15:20-23, 52-54).

7. GOD'S PURPOSE FOR MAN

We believe that God's purpose for each human being is that he ultimately become a member of His divine Family, composed of spirit and possessing eternal life and the attributes of Godly character (John 1:12-13; Rom. 8:14-19, 28-29; I Cor. 15:39-54; Heb. 2:5-10). It is God's desire that all men be saved and come to the knowledge of the truth; He has a step-by-step plan by which He is fulfilling His purpose and bringing all men to the full knowledge and stature of Jesus Christ (Acts 4:12; John 6:44; 17:2-8, 17-21; 15:16; Matt. 28:18-20; Acts 1:7-8; 2:22-39; 3:17-26; Eph. 4:11-15; Rom. 1:16; 11:22-26; II Pet. 3:9; I Tim. 2:4-6).

8. SIN

We believe that all men have sinned and come short of the glory of God (Rom. 3:10, 23; 5:12). Sin is the transgression of God's law (I John 3:4). By the law is the knowledge of sin (Rom. 3:20; 7:7); to him who knows to do good and does it not, to him it is sin (James 4:17); whatever is not of faith is sin (Rom. 14:23). The penalty for sin is death (Rom. 6:23).

9. SACRIFICE OF CHRIST

We believe that God sent Jesus Christ to this earth to die for the sins of the world. Though tempted in all points as we are, Christ lived without sin and gave His life as the full atonement for the sins of all mankind (John 3:16-17; I John 2:1-2; Rom. 5:6-11; 6:23; Heb. 4:15). He was crucified, died, was buried, and was resurrected after three days and three nights in the grave (I Cor. 15:3-4; Matt. 12:40). He ascended to heaven where He now sits at the right hand of the Father as our High Priest and Advocate (Heb. 1:2-3; 4:14-16; 7:25-27; 12:2).

10. FORGIVENESS OF SINS

We believe that all who repent of their sins, believe the gospel of Jesus Christ, accept Him as their personal Saviour and, following the example of Christ, are baptized by immersion, are forgiven their sins by God's grace, through faith in Christ's blood (Mark 1:15; 16:15-16; Matt. 3:2, 6, 8, 13-17; Acts 2:38-39; 4:12; Rom. 1:16; 3:23-25; 5:1-2; 6:3-6; Eph. 1:7).

11. GIFT OF THE HOLY SPIRIT

We believe that all who repent and are forgiven of past sins through Christ can receive the gift of God's Holy Spirit through the laying on of hands (Acts 2:38; 8:15-17; 19:1-6; Heb. 6:1-2). God's Holy Spirit literally comes and abides in them, bearing the fruits of God's Spirit in the individual's life (John 14:16-17, 23; 15:1-8; Gal. 5:16-25; Rom. 6:4-6, 12-22). Those who have God's Holy Spirit in this life, and are led by it, shall be changed from mortal to immortal at the return of Jesus Christ (Rom. 5:8-10; 8:1-18; I Cor. 15:50-58).

12. THE TEN COMMANDMENTS

We believe that God's way of life is expressed in His Ten Commandments (Ex. 20, Deut. 5) as magnified by Christ in explaining their full spiritual intent (Matt. 5, 6, 7) and summarized by Him in the two great spiritual principles of love toward God and love toward neighbor (Matt. 22:36-40). We believe God's Commandments are spiritual precepts (Rom. 7:12-14) that were in effect prior to the Old Covenant (Rom. 4:15; I John 3:4; Gen. 4:7; Rom. 5:12-14; Gen. 26:5) and were taught by Christ and the Apostles as a fundamental part of the New Covenant (Matt. 5:17-48; 7:12-29; 19:16-19; Rom. 6:4-6, 12-22; I Cor. 7:19; Heb. 8:6-10; 10:16; James 2:8-12; I John 2:3-5; 3:24; 5:2-3; Rev. 21:8; 22:14).

13. OBEDIENCE

We believe that Jesus Christ lived without sin as an example for us (John 15:9-12; I Pet. 2:21-25; I John 2:6; Eph. 5:1-2; I Cor. 11:1). Though justification and salvation are a gift of God through faith in Christ's blood (Rom. 3:23-25; 5:1-2; 6:23) and are not earned by obedience (Rom. 3:20, 23; Gal. 2:16; Eph. 2:8-10), those who abide in Christ should live as He lived (I John 2:3-6). Christ and the love of God dwelling in them will be keeping God's Commandments (John 14:15-24; I John 3:24; 5:2-3; Rom. 5:8-10; Gal. 5:16-25). ". . . to whom ye yield yourselves servants to obey, his servants ye are to whom ye obey; whether of sin unto death, or of obedience unto righteousness" (Rom. 6:16-23; 2:5-11; I Cor. 6:9-10; Gal. 5:19-23; II Pet. 1:5-11).

14. SPIRITUAL CHRISTIANITY

We believe that the emphasis in true Christianity is on the spiritual more than on the physical (II Cor. 3:6, 16-18; Matt. 5:20; Gal. 5:13-25; Rom. 8:1-9). God is spirit and they who worship Him must worship in spirit and in truth (John 4:23-24). God is primarily concerned with the heart, mind, attitude, spirit and character of man (Acts 10:34-35; 15:8; Phil. 2:2-8; Rom. 2:23-29). The kingdom of God is not meat and drink, but righteousness, peace, and joy in the Holy Spirit (Rom. 14:17). Christianity is not established on human teachings regarding ". . . touch not; taste not; handle not; which all are to perish with the using . . . " (Col. 2:20-22).

Christ explained true Christianity by amplifying God's Commandments to reveal their positive spiritual intent (Matt. 5, 6, 7). The New Covenant involves internalizing those spiritual laws and having them written in our hearts and minds (Heb. 10:16; II Cor. 3:3). Spiritual Christianity leads to a positive orientation with an outward expression of the fruits of God's Spirit—love joy, peace, judgment, mercy, and faith (Matt. 23:23; Gal. 5:22-23).

15. CHRISTIAN INDIVIDUALITY & RESPONSIBILITY

We believe that each person is a unique individual and personality. He has the responsibility in this life not only of growing in Christian character and Godliness but also of fully developing his mind, personality, talents and abilities (Rom. 12:3-8; I Cor. 12:4-11; 3:10-14; 6:19-20; Eph. 4:7, 15-16; Luke 19:11-26; Matt. 25:15). Each human being has the God-given right to maintain his individuality, self-respect, and human dignity, and is personally responsible before God for his own mind, conscience, and convictions.

16. THE CHURCH

We believe that God's Church, the body of Christ, is a spiritual organism composed of all people who have God's Holy Spirit (I Cor. 12:12-14; Rom. 8:9; I John 4:13). It has only one Head, which is Christ (Eph. 1:22-23; Col. 1:18). The spiritual body of Christ is not limited to any one organization on earth; membership in that body is not determined by adherence to the teachings of any one man or group of men; members of Christ's body are those who live in Christ and in whom Christ dwells (John 14:23; 15:4-5; I Cor. 1:12-13; 3:1-11; Eph. 4:4-6; Matt. 7:16-23; I John 2:3-5; 3:23-24).

17. CHURCH ORGANIZATION AND GOVERNMENT

We believe that Christians should be organized in order to effectively serve God, each other, and mankind (I Cor. 12:7, 15-27; 14:33; 1:10; Eph. 4:3-7, 11-13). Such an organization should have proper order and government to facilitate coordination of effort and the effectual working of God's Spirit through all the members (I Cor. 12:4-11; 14:40; Eph. 4:11-16; Rom. 12:3-8). But that government should not restrict or impede the individual's spiritual growth, subvert his personal conscience or convictions, or interfere with the working of God's Spirit in his mind and life. The government of God in a Christian's life is not the human authority within an organization; rather, it is the direct authority of Jesus Christ and the Word of God that is accepted personally and voluntarily by each member of

the body of Christ (Eph. 1:22; I Tim. 2:5; Matt. 23:10; Rom. 14:4; Acts 5:27-29).

18. COMMISSION TO THE CHURCH

We believe that Christ's commission to His Church is set forth in Mark 16:15-16, Luke 24:47, and Matthew 28:19-20: "Go ye therefore, and teach (make disciples of) all nations, baptizing them in the name of the Father, and of the Son, and of the Holy Spirit: Teaching them to observe all things whatsoever I have commanded you . . . " This work of the Church involves preaching the good news of Jesus Christ and the Kingdom of God to the world; it involves being a light and example of God's way (Matt. 5:16; John 15:8, 16; Phil. 2:15-16); it involves baptizing and teaching those who repent; and it involves edifying the body of Christ, feeding the flock of God, and perfecting the saints (Matt. 5:48; Eph. 4:12-13; John 21:15-17; I Pet. 5:2). God has placed every member in the body of Christ in order to fulfill the various facets of this commission (I Cor. 12:7-11, 18-20, 27-30; Eph. 4:4, 7, 11-16).

19. FINANCING THE COMMISSION TO THE CHURCH

We believe that Christ's commission to the Church should be financed through the freewill offerings of the Church (Matt. 6:19-33; I Cor. 9:1-14; II Cor. 11:8-9; 12:13; Phil. 4:14-19; Gal. 6:6-8; I Tim. 5:17-18), not by having to charge the public for the gospel (Matt. 10:7-8; III John 5:8). It is the responsibility of every Christian to give generously to support the various facets of the work of the Church and of the ministry of Jesus Christ; ". . . He which soweth sparingly shall reap also sparingly; and he which soweth bountifully shall reap also bountifully" (II Cor. 9:6-11; Prov. 3:9-10; I Tim. 6:17-19; Mark 12:41-44; Luke 6:38).

20. NEW TESTAMENT PASSOVER

We believe that we should annually, each Passover, observe the anniversary of Christ's death by partaking of the bread and the wine that symbolize His broken body and shed blood (Matt. 26:26-29: I Cor. 11:23-30).

21. NEW TESTAMENT SABBATH

We believe that the seventh day of the week, from Friday sunset to Saturday sunset, is God's Sabbath (Gen. 2:2-3; 1:5; Lev. 23:32). We are to rest from our labors on this day following the example of God (Gen. 2:1-3; Ex. 20:11). We are to observe the Sabbath according to the teachings and example of Jesus Christ in the New Testament (Mark 2:23-28; 3:1-4; Matt. 12:7-12; Luke 4:16; Mark 6:2) and following the practice of the Apostles and the New Testament Church (Acts 13:42-44; 17:2; 18:4).

22. RETURN OF CHRIST

We believe that Jesus Christ will return to this earth, personally and visibly, in power and glory, before His one thousand year reign on earth (Acts 1:11; 3:19-21; I Thess. 4:16; Rev. 1:7; 11:15; 19:11-16; 20:4, 6; Matt. 24:23-30; 25:31; Dan. 2:44; Zech. 14:3-4, 9). He will reign with love and justice over all nations as King of kings and Lord of lords (Isa. 11:1-10; Rev. 19:16).

23. RESURRECTION OF SAINTS

We believe that the dead in Christ will be resurrected to eternal life at Christ's return, and that those Christians who are alive at that time will be changed from mortal to immortal (I Thess. 4:13-17; I Cor. 15:50-54; Phil. 3:20-21). They will be composed of spirit and have eternal life as immortal members of God's divine Family (Rev. 2:11; 20:6; 21:7; I John 3:2; Rom. 8:11, 16-17). They will rule with Christ over the nations for the one-thousand-year reign of God's Kingdom on earth (Rev. 20:4-6; 1:5-6; 2:25-27; 5:10; Dan. 7:18, 22, 27; Luke 1:31-33; 22:29-30; Matt. 19:28; Ezek. 37:23-25).

24. GENERAL RESURRECTION

We believe that God will resurrect to physical life again all who have not had a full, complete opportunity to know God and Christ, to understand God's purpose and truth, and to develop Godly character through the experiences of life (Acts. 4:12; John 17:2-3; I John 5:11-12, 19-20; Heb. 8:8-12; Rev. 20:5; Matt. 12:41-42; Ezek. 37; Rom. 11:25-32; John 5:21-30).

It is God's desire that all men be saved and come to the knowledge of the truth (I Tim. 2:4-6; II Pet. 3:9). God will judge people according to their works after they receive knowledge and understanding and have had opportunity to use God's Holy Spirit to live God's way of life; God will not eternally condemn people because of sins committed in ignorance of the true God and His way (Acts 17:23-31; James 4:17; Rom. 7:7; John 6:37-40, 44-45; Acts 10:34-35; Rev. 20:5, 11-12; Ezek. 37:13-14; I Tim. 2:6; Heb. 9:25-28; John 3:16-17).

25. HOLY DAYS

We believe the Holy Days are for Christians today to understand the unfolding plan of God for all mankind. We believe they ARE shadows of good things to come as well (Col. 2:16-17). The Feasts are Festivals of the Lord (Jesus Christ) (Lev. 23:1-2). They are statutes forever (Lev. 23:14,21,31,41). Feasts of Christ are times of great rejoicing (Lev. 23:40; Deut. 16:11,14,15; Neh. 8:10-12, 17). Jesus, our example of pleasing the heavenly Father, kept them (Jn. 5:30; 8:29; Lk. 2:41-42; Jn. 2:13; 7:2,8,10,14, 37). The original Apostles kept them (Acts 2; 18:21; 20:16; 1 Cor. 5:7-8). If anyone will observe the Holy Days of God, that person will KNOW the doctrine is of God (Jn. 7:17).

Notes: *A Bible-oriented church, the association explains the nature of its statement in its prefatory remarks. Compare this statement to that of the Associated Church of God which, like the association, was also formed by former members of the Worldwide Church of God.*

* * *

DOCTRINES (CHURCH OF GOD INTERNATIONAL)

The Church of God, International, claims for its basic and entire doctrines, the most ancient and purest examples of Holy Writ: the Bible in its entirety as originally inspired. We believe in Jesus Christ, born of woman, become man in the flesh, crucified and buried, resurrected the third day according to the scriptures, ascended to heaven to become High Priest and Author of our Salvation, and who awaits His Father's time to return to this earth as conquering King, and Divine Ruler of the world for one thousand years. We believe in the Ten Commandments of God as magnified by the teachings and life's examples of Jesus Christ of Nazareth, and believe that Jesus Christ has given, as He promised, that "other comforter," through whose indwelling presence the Church is being led, through the ages, into "all truth."

Notes: *Only a brief statement was adopted for the constitution of the Church of God International, and it does not deal with most of the particular beliefs to which church members adhere.*

* * *

WHAT THE "CHURCH OF GOD" BELIEVES, AND WHY [CHURCH OF GOD (SEVENTH-DAY, SALEM, WEST VIRGINIA)]

1. We believe the Bible is the book through which God has revealed His will to man, and that all contrary teachings are false and spurious.

   REASON: "All scripture is given by inspiration of God."—2 Tim. 3:16.

2. We believe in examining everything in the light of the Bible, weighing everything in the balance of the Bible and if it will not stand the test, reject it, but if it will stand the test, accept it.

   We believe in granting liberty of thought, and speech, and we stand for an open forum where advanced light can be given, thus stimulating a growth in knowledge.

   REASON: 1 Thess. 5:21, "Prove all things; hold fast that which is good." "Grow in grace . . . and knowledge."—2 Peter 3:18.

3. We believe in God the Father, the Creator of heaven and earth.

   REASON: "In the beginning God created the heaven and the earth."—Gen. 1:1.

4. We believe that Christ is the Son of God, that after His death, burial, and resurrection, He ascended to heaven and is now at the right hand of the throne of God.

   REASON: ". . . This is my beloved Son, in whom I am well pleased."—Matt. 3:17. "He was received up into heaven, and sat on the right hand of God."—Mark 16:19.

5. We believe that Christ was in the grave just three days and three nights, that He was resurrected in the end of the Sabbath, and placed in the tomb just three days and three nights previous.

   REASON: He said He would be in the heart of the earth three days and three nights. Matt. 12:40. It was in the end of the Sabbath when the earthquake occurred, when the angel descended, when the stone was rolled away and when the resurrection occurred. Matt. 28:1-6.

WHAT THE "CHURCH OF GOD" BELIEVES, AND WHY [CHURCH OF GOD (SEVENTH-DAY, SALEM, WEST VIRGINIA)] (continued)

6. We believe that the Commandments of God and the Faith of Jesus are the standards of righteousness by which the future destiny of man will be determined in the day of judgment.

   REASON: In Rev. 14:9-11, an account of the destruction of the wicked is given, and in verse 12 we are told that the saints or the ones saved are those who keep the commandments of God and the Faith of Jesus. See also Rev. 12:17; Rev. 22:14; 1 John 5:3; and James 2:10-12.

7. We believe in the literal, personal, visible return of Christ to the earth at the end of this age.

   REASON: The inspired apostles Peter and Paul say He will come personally and literally. Acts 3:20, 21; 1 Thess. 4:16, 17; 2 Thess. 1:7, 8. John and James also testify the same. The angel from heaven said in Acts 1:11, "This same Jesus which is taken up from you into heaven, shall so come in like manner as ye have seen him go into heaven." Jesus Himself said He would come again and the event would be as the lightning flashing from the sky. Matt. 24:27.

8. We believe God's people will be posted regarding this event and will therefore be looking for His return.

   REASON: "But ye, brethren, are not in darkness, that that day should overtake you as a thief. Ye are all the children of light. . . . "—1 Thess. 5:4, 5. ". . . If therefore thou shall not watch, I will come on thee as a thief."—Rev. 3:3.

   Speaking of His coming and giving a series of events which will transpire before He returns, Christ says, "So likewise ye, when ye shall see all these things, know that it is near, even at the doors."—Matt. 24:33.

9. We believe that when people die they become unconscious and remain in the grave in this condition until the judgment. We believe that their thoughts perish, and all hatred, love, and envy ceases.

   REASON: "For the living know that they shall die: but the dead know not anything . . . "—Eccl. 9:5. "Also their love, and their hatred, and their envy, is now perished . . . "—Verse 6. Psa. 146:6, "His breath goeth forth, he returneth to his earth; in that very day his thoughts perish."

10. We believe the righteous dead will be resurrected at the coming of Christ.

    REASON: 1 Thess. 4:16, ". . . The Lord himself shall descend from heaven with a shout, with the voice of the archangel, and with the trump of God: and the dead in Christ shall rise first."

    1 Cor. 15:52, "In a moment, in the twinkling of an eye at the last trump; for the trumpet shall sound and the dead shall be raised incorruptible, and we shall be changed."

    1 Cor. 15:22, 23, "For as in Adam all die, even so in Christ shall all be made alive. But every man in his own order: Christ the firstfruits; afterward they that are Christ's at his coming."

11. We believe that the signs of the times indicate the nearness of Christ's return.

    REASON: "This know also, that in the last days perilous times shall come."—2 Tim. 3:1. This is a time of worldliness and pleasure, covetousness and ungodliness. It is a time when knowledge is increased as never before. Dan. 12:4 says, ". . . Seal the book, even to the time of the end: many shall run to and fro, and knowledge shall be increased." The prophecies of God have nearly all been fulfilled: Dan. 2; Matt. 24; Luke 21; Dan. 7, and many others.

12. We believe that the living and the dead will be judged and receive their reward at the coming of Christ at the end of this age.

    REASON: "I charge thee therefore before God, and the Lord Jesus Christ, who shall judge the quick and the dead at his appearing and his kingdom."—2 Tim. 4:1. As this was spoken in 66 A.D., it was a future event at that time and as no occurrence of this nature has ever transpired since, it is yet future.

    It would be absurd to think of the dead receiving their reward before they were judged. This would be an impossibility. They are judged when Christ comes, therefore, they could not receive their reward before that time. This is the exact teaching of Christ. In Rev. 22:12, He says, ". . . Behold, I come quickly; and my reward is with me, to give every man according as his work shall be." This does away with the belief that people are now in heaven receiving their reward, which would place the judgment in the past. To believe that the judgment was in the past would necessitate our denying the plain statements of our Savior.

13. We believe in the inspired church name, "Church of God."

    REASON: It is the only church name found in the Bible. There are over six hundred different church denominations, but not one of them is mentioned in the Bible as pertaining to the name of a church. In one place the statement, "The churches of Christ," is made, but in every other place (twelve in all) the name "Church of God" is given. It was the Church of God that Christ purchased with His own blood (Acts 20:28); it was the Church of God which Paul persecuted before his conversion (1 Cor. 15:9; Gal. 1:13); it was the Church of God of which he afterwards became a member (1 Cor. 12:12, 13).

14. We believe that among the different instruments of law given by God the Father, the Ten Commandments were far superior to any other, that they constitute the fundamental organic code of all law and the constitution of the supreme court of heaven.

    REASON: They were thundered from Sinai's quaking summit, with a voice that shook the earth. See Ex. 19:16-18. They were written with the finger of

God on tables of stone. See Ex. 31:18; 32:15, 16. No other code of law in the Bible was written with the finger of God on tables of stone, but the other documents were written by Moses in a book. However, this was not true of the Ten Commandments. God did this work Himself, writing with His own finger on tables of stone. By this very act we see that He magnified them above all else, that they were exalted by the Almighty and considered superior to all other documents or codes.

15. We believe that the wages of sin is death, and that all sinners will be destroyed out of the earth.

REASON: "The wages of sin is death."—Rom. 6:23. "Behold, the day of the Lord cometh, cruel both with wrath and fierce anger, to lay the land desolate: and he shall destroy the sinners thereof out of it."—Isa. 13:9.

16. We believe that sin is the transgression of the law.

REASON: "Whosoever committeth sin transgresseth also the law: for sin is the transgression of the law."—1 John 3:4.

17. We believe that one becomes a sinner in the sight of God just as soon as he breaks any one of the commandments of this eternal code of law. To break any one of them makes him a transgressor of the law, and therefore a sinner.

REASON: "For whosoever shall keep the whole law, and yet offend in one point, he is guilty of all. For he that said, Do not commit adultery, said also, Do not kill. Now if thou commit no adultery, yet if thou kill, thou art become a transgressor of the law."—James 2:10, 11.

NOTE: This eternal document of ten commandments contains the two above named precepts. Therefore, beyond any question of doubt, this was the law to which the apostle referred. This was twenty-seven years after Christ's ascension.

James informed the people of that day that if they kept all the commandments and yet violated just one, they were guilty of all. That is, as "sin is the transgression of the law," to transgress in only one point would make the guilty party a sinner, showing that this code of law which God wrote on tables of stone is still in force.

18. We believe that as the fourth precept, or article of the constitution of high heaven forbids labor on the seventh day of the week, and commands that this day be kept holy, it would be a violation of the law to desecrate it, the same as to break any one of the other ten, and thereby make the guilty party a sinner in the eyes of God.

REASON: "For whosoever shall keep the whole law, and yet offend in one point, he is guilty of all."—James 2:10. "For this is the love of God, that we keep his commandments: and his commandments are not grievous."—1 John 5:3.

Those who are saved in the end of the world are the ones who have kept the commandments of God, and the faith of Jesus. See Rev. 14:12.

19. We believe that the life which Christ lived while on earth is the life that will save, and that all Christians should accept Him as their example, and follow in His footsteps. If they will do this they will not be in darkness, but will have the light of life.

REASON: "In him was life; and the life was the light of men."—John 1:4. ". . . He that followeth me shall not walk in darkness, but shall have the light of life."—John 8:12.

20. We believe that all professed Christians who keep Sunday for the Sabbath are not living in accordance with their name, as they do not follow Christ in this practice.

REASON: We have no record that Christ, in all His life, mentioned the first day of the week, neither did He keep it as a sacred or holy day, but to the contrary He kept the seventh day Sabbath all His life. "And he came to Nazareth, where he had been brought up: and as his custom was, he went into the synagogue on the Sabbath day, and stood up for to read."—Luke 4:16. The following verses tell of the sermon He preached. Christ's mother and the holy women kept the Sabbath day according to the commandment. Luke 23:56.

21. We believe that the commandments which were nailed to the cross included only the code of commandments contained in the sacrifical ordinance, that is, the atonement for sin by animal sacrifices, the yearly sabbath days, governed by the day of the month or moon, the feasts and holy days included in the same code of law. We believe that Christ's death on the cross did not in any way effect the Ten Commandment Law of God which is, and will forever be, the constitution for the supreme court of heaven and earth.

Reason: "Having abolished in his flesh the enmity, even the law of commandments contained in ordinances."—Eph. 2:15. (Not the Ten Commandments.) In speaking of the sacrificial commandments Paul says, "Which stood only in meats and drinks, and divers washings, and carnal ordinances, imposed on them until the time of reformation. But Christ being come an high priest of good things . . . by his own blood he entered in once into the holy place, having obtained eternal redemption for us."—Heb. 9:10-15.

The ten commandments did not cease at the cross, for 57 years afterward, John tells us that "this is the love of God, that we keep his commandments: and his commandments are not grievous."—1 John 5:3. Sixty-three years after the cross, he told the people that the ones who are saved in the end of the world are those who keep the commandments of God and the faith of Jesus. See Rev. 14:12. The seventh day Sabbath was also sacred and holy 31 years after the cross, as Paul mentions the seventh day, and tells the people to enter into that rest as God did, and that there remained a rest (i.e., "the keeping of a Sabbath") to the people of God. See Heb. 4:4-11.

22. We believe that the foreknowledge of God is portrayed in the scriptures of truth by divine prophecy, and that God purposed the authenticity of His word to be proven by the response of history to the call of prophecy.

Reason: Isa. 41:22,23, "Let them bring them forth, and shew us what shall happen: let them shew the former things, what they be, that we may consider them, and know the latter end of them; or declare us things for to come. Shew the things that are to come hereafter, that we may know that ye are gods. . . . "

Deut. 18:22, "When a prophet speaketh in the name of the Lord, if the thing follow not, nor come to pass, that is the thing which the Lord hath not spoken. . . . "

23. We believe that there is but one faith of which God is the Author, and that there is only one form of baptism acceptable to Him.

REASON: "One Lord, one faith, one baptism."—Eph. 4:5.

24. We believe this one faith is the one revealed to us in His Word through the life and teachings of Christ and the gospel of the apostles, and that any other gospel foreign to such teachings, regardless of the claim of divinity, is not genuine but counterfeit.

REASON: John 1:4 says, "In him was life; and the life was the light of men." Paul says, "But though we, or an angel from heaven, preach any other gospel unto you than that which we have preached unto you, let him be accursed."—Gal. 1:8.

25. We believe the one form of baptism acceptable to God is immersion, being buried in the watery grave, which is typical of the burial and resurrection of Christ.

REASON: "Know ye not, that so many of us as were baptized into Jesus Christ were baptized into his death? Therefore we are buried with him by baptism into death: that like as Christ was raised up from the dead by the glory of the Father, even so we also should walk in newness of life. For if we have been planted together in the likeness of his death, we shall be also in the likeness of his resurrection."—Rom. 6:3-5.

Matt. 3:16, "And Jesus, when he was baptized, went up straightway out of the water." We read in John 8:12, ". . . I am the light of the world: he that followeth me shall not walk in darkness, but shall have the light of life."

We read in Col. 2:12, "Buried with him in baptism, wherein also ye are risen with him through the faith of the operation of God, who hath raised him from the dead."

NOTE: This is the gospel of the apostles, and Paul says as follows, "But though . . . an angel from heaven, preach any other gospel . . . let him be accursed." Is there a different gospel being preached today, and can we discern the genuine from the counterfeit?

26. We believe that faith is the essential quality through which soul salvation is gained, and not through dead works.

REASON: Gal. 2:16, "Knowing that a man is not justified by the works of the law (sacrificial code), but by the faith of Jesus Christ. . . . that we might be justified by the faith of Christ."

Gal. 3:26,27, "For ye are all the children of God by faith in Christ Jesus. For as many of you as have been baptized into Christ have put on Christ."

NOTE: After Christ, the great sacrificial Lamb, had been slain, redemption and remission of sins could only be received through faith in Him, and not by the works of the law which commanded the killing of lambs for a sin offering. This law ceased at the cross but those who rejected Christ continued the works of the law and the killing of animal sacrifices.

Speaking of the Ten Commandment Law, written on stone by the finger of God, Paul says, "For not the hearers of the law are just before God, but the doers of the law shall be justified."—Rom. 2:13.

27. We believe that the individual having faith, will be prompted to higher ideals, and will conform his life to the requirements of God, and his faith will be manifested by works.

REASON: ". . . Shew me thy faith without thy works, and I will shew thee my faith by my works."—James 2:18. "Even so faith, if it hath not works, is dead, being alone."—James 2:17.

"Not every one that saith unto me, Lord, Lord, shall enter into the kingdom of heaven: but he that doeth the will of my Father which is in heaven." Matt. 7:21.

28. We believe that in the day of judgment many will be disappointed and rejected who have believed in Christ and performed works in His name. Therefore, we admonish every one to carefully consider the following:

REASON: "There is a way which seemeth right unto a man, but the end thereof are the ways of death."—Prov. 14:12. "Many will say to me in that day. Lord, Lord, have we not prophesied in thy name? and in thy name have cast out devils? and in thy name done many wonderful works? And then will I profess unto them, I never knew you: depart from me, ye that work iniquity."—Matt. 7:21, 22. ". . . . The devils also believe, and tremble."—Jas. 2:19. "Wherefore let him that thinketh he standeth take heed lest he fall."—1 Cor. 10:12.

29. We believe that the benefits of God's plan of salvation will be realized only by those who, through faith, accept it as divine, make use of it in accordance with God's purpose, and conform their lives to His requirements, to do His will continually.

REASON: "Here is the patience of the saints: here are they that keep the commandments of God, and the faith of Jesus."—Rev. 14:12. "Blessed are they that do his commandments, that they may have right to the tree of life, and may enter in through the gates into the city."—Rev. 22:14. "Not every one that saith unto me, Lord, Lord, shall enter into the kingdom of heaven; but he that doeth the will of my Father which is in heaven."—Matt. 7:21.

30. We believe that man is mortal and therefore, is subject to death.

REASON: "Shall mortal man be more just than God? . . . "—Job 4:17.

31. We believe that man will put on immortality at the resurrection rather than at death.

REASON: 1 Cor. 15:51-53, "Behold, I shew you a mystery; we shall not all sleep, but we shall all be changed, In a moment, in the twinkling of an eye, at the last trump: for the trumpet shall sound, and the dead shall be raised incorruptible, and we shall be changed. For this corruptible must put on incorruption, and this mortal must put on immortality."

32. We believe that God only hath immortality.

REASON: 1 Tim. 6:16, "Who only hath immortality, dwelling in the light which no man can approach unto; whom no man hath seen, nor can see: to whom be honour and power everlasting. Amen.

33. We believe that the dead are unconscious between death and the resurrection.

REASON: Eccl. 9:5, "For the living know that they shall die: but the dead know not any thing. . . . "

Psalms 146:4, "His breath goeth forth, he returneth to his earth; in that very day his thoughts perish."

34. We believe that the soul of man, which is in many places translated "person" means the essentials of life; the real person dies.

REASON: "The soul that sinneth, it shall die."—Ezek. 18:4,20.

35. We believe that the wicked will be totally destroyed, that they will be consumed as stubble fully dry.

REASON: Nahum 1:10, ". . . they shall be devoured as stubble fully dry."

Mal. 4:1, "For, behold, the day cometh, that shall burn as an oven; and all the proud, yea, and all that do wickedly, shall be stubble: and the day that cometh shall burn them up, saith the Lord of hosts, that it shall leave them neither root nor branch." 2 Thess. 1:9, "Who shall be punished with everlasting destruction from the presence of the Lord, and from the glory of his power."

36. We believe that the righteous will be rewarded and recompensed in the earth and that they will never be permanently removed.

REASON: Prov. 10:30, "The righteous shall never be removed: but the wicked shall not inhabit the earth."

Prov. 11:31, "Behold, the righteous shall be recompensed in the earth: much more the wicked and the sinner."

Matt. 5:5, "Blessed are the meek, for they shall inherit the earth . . . "

37. We believe that the kingdom of God will be established on the earth, and is a future event.

REASON: "And the kingdom and dominion, and the greatness of the kingdom under the whole heaven, shall be given to the people of the saints of the most High, whose kingdom is an everlasting kingdom, and all dominions shall serve and obey him."—Dan. 7:27.

Paul says in 2 Tim. 4:1, "I charge thee therefore before God, and the Lord Jesus Christ, who shall judge the quick and the dead at his appearing and his kingdom." In verse eight he says, "Henceforth there is laid up for me a crown of righteousness, which the Lord, the righteous judge, shall give me at that day. . . . "

Acts 14:22, "Confirming the souls of the disciples, and exhorting them to continue in the faith, and that we must through much tribulation enter into the kingdom of God."

NOTE: The kingdom at this time was recognized by the apostles as future. We have no history to prove that it has ever been established and surrounding conditions indicate plainly that it is not present with us today, so we may conclude that it is yet future. "When the Son of man shall come in his glory, and all the holy angels with him, then shall he sit upon the throne of his glory."—Matt. 25:31.

38. We believe there have been four universal kingdoms to rule the world, Babylon, Medo-Persia, Greece, and Rome, and that the dream of Nebuchadnezzar, as interpreted by Daniel, was consequently true. The fifth universal kingdom yet to be established, represented by the stone cut out of the mountain without hands, will be the kingdom of God.

REASON: Daniel, speaking to Nebuchadnezzar, said, "Thou art this head of gold. And after thee shall arise another kingdom inferior to thee, and another third kingdom of brass, which shall bear rule over all the earth. And the fourth kingdom shall be strong as iron."—Dan. 2:38-40. After stating that the kingdoms of earth would be divided in their last stages of existence, he said, "And in the days of these kings shall the God of heaven set up a kingdom, which shall never be destroyed: and the kingdom shall not be left to other people, but it shall break in pieces and consume all these kingdoms, and it shall stand for ever."—verse 44.

39. We believe that Christ's return to the earth will be at a time of war, bloodshed and strife—a time when nations, in their divided state, are angry, and there is a time of trouble such as was never before witnessed.

REASON: Rev. 16:14,15, "For they are the spirits of devils, working miracles, which go forth unto the kings of the earth and of the whole world, to gather them to the battle of that great day of God Almighty. Behold, I come as a thief. Blessed is he that watcheth, and keepeth his garments, lest he walk naked, and they see his shame."

Dan. 12:1,2, "And at that time shall Michael stand up, the great prince which standeth for the children of thy people: and there shall be a time of trouble, such as never was since there was a nation even to that same time: and at that time thy people shall be delivered, every one that shall be found written in the book. And many of them that sleep in the dust of the earth shall awake, some to everlasting life, and some to shame and everlasting contempt."

Rev. 11:18, "And the nations were angry, and thy wrath is come, and the time of the dead, that they should be judged, and that thou shouldest give reward unto thy servants the prophets, and to the saints, and them that fear thy name, small and great; and shouldest destroy them which destroy the earth."

40. We believe that the ordinance of the Lord's Supper, as Christ instituted it, should be observed yearly. We believe that the wine and bread are typical of His shed blood, and broken body.

REASON: "And he took the cup, and gave thanks, and said, Take this, and divide it among yourselves: For I say unto you, I will not drink of the fruit of the vine, until the kingdom of God shall come. And he took bread, and gave thanks, and brake it, and gave unto them, saying, This is my body which is given for you: this do in remembrance of me. Likewise also the cup after supper, saying, This cup is the new testament in my blood, which is shed for you."— Luke 22:17-20.

This was the passover supper, and was to be a perpetual ordinance. We read the words of the Savior in verse 16, "For I say unto you, I will not any more eat thereof, until it be fulfilled in the kingdom of God." He repeats the same in verse 18, making it all the more emphatic that this ordinance would reach even into the kingdom of God.

As God is a God of order, He has set a time for this ordinance which we find to be once a year. "Thou shalt therefore keep this ordinance in his season from year to year."—Exod. 13:10. ". . . Behold, there is a feast of the Lord in Shiloh yearly. . . . "—Judges 21:19.

This feast of the Lord, commonly called the passover, was instituted by God on the 14th day of the first month and was kept by His chosen people for many centuries on that day. The sacrificial lamb, which for hundreds of years was slain on this day, pointed forward to Christ. The bread and wine which Christ instituted on the same day points backward to Him.

The foregoing forty principles, which the Church of God accepts, are Bible facts and we believe these truths should be sounded to the world. Let us with one voice send out the message for our day. The warning cry and message of salvation must go to earth's remotest bounds.

Notes: *This statement is derived from, and closely resembles, older Church of God statements. A number of notes supporting the individual affirmations have been added.*

* * *

WHAT THE CHURCH OF GOD BELIEVES AND WHY (GENERAL CONFERENCE OF THE CHURCH OF GOD)

THE BIBLE

1. The Holy Bible, including the divisions commonly known as the Old Testament and the New Testament, is the divinely inspired Word of God. No other writing is so inspired. The Bible is infallible in teaching, and contains the complete will and revelation of God to man. 2 Peter 1:19-21; Isa. 45:23; Heb. 4:12; Matt. 24:35; 2 Tim. 3:16, 17.

GOD, THE CREATOR

2. The Supreme Deity of the universe is God. He is the Almighty Creator and Sustainer of the heaven, the earth, and all things therein. Acts 17:24-28; Acts 14:15; Gen. 1:1; Rev. 14:7; Psa. 124:8; Neh. 9:6; Isa. 40:28; Isa. 44:24; Psa. 55:22.

JESUS, THE SON OF GOD

3. Jesus of Nazareth is the only begotten Son of God, conceived of the Holy Spirit and born of the Virgin Mary. He is the Christ, or Messiah, sent from God to be our Saviour and Redeemer. John 3:16; 1 John 4:9; Matt. 16:16; Isa. 7:14; John 1:18; John 6:65; John 4:25, 26; Matt. 1:18-25; Matt. 14:33; Luke 1:26-36; Luke 2:6-32; Luke 4:14-21; Acts 4:12; Titus 2:14.

THE HOLY SPIRIT

4. The Holy Spirit (also called the Holy Ghost) is the Comforter promised by our Lord, who will abide in the hearts of those who diligently seek Him; and who will guide us into all godly truths, and give us power to witness for Him; evidence of whose presence is manifest both in word and in "fruit of the Spirit," and in keeping the commandments of God. John 14:15-19, 26; John 16:13; Luke 11:9-13; Acts 1:8; Romans 5:5; Gal. 5:22-26; 1 Cor. 12:7-11.

SATAN

5. Satan is "that old serpent, which is called the Devil"; he is the adversary of God and His people. Rev. 20:2; 1 Peter 5:8; 2 Cor. 11:14; Matt. 13:39; Eph. 6:10-12;

Luke 10:18; John 8:44; Rev. 12:9; 2 Cor. 11:15; Rev. 20:10.

THE FALL OF MAN

6. Man was created a perfect being, but through disobedience fell, bringing imperfection, death, and God's curse upon all mankind. Gen. 1:26-31; Gen. 3:8-20; 1 Cor. 15:21, 22; Romans 5:12.

THE PLAN OF SALVATION

7. The Plan of Salvation was made by God the Father as the way of escape for man from the results of the fall. In this plan God gave His Son, Jesus, who paid the penalty for mankind, and made possible our salvation and redemption to eternal life. 2 Peter 3:9; 2 Thess. 2:13; John 3:16; John 10:1, 7; Acts 4:12; Romans 5:11; 1 Peter 1:18, 19; 1 Peter 2:24; 1 John 2:2-4; Heb. 9:13, 14, 28.

THE BLOOD OF CHRIST

8. The blood of Christ was shed for the remission of sins, and the atonement was made on the Cross. Matt. 26:28; Matt. 20:28; Romans 5:6-13; Romans 3:25; Luke 24:47; Acts 10:43; Phil. 2:8-12; Col. 1:19-23; Titus 2:13, 14; 1 Cor. 15:1-5.

ACCEPTING CHRIST

9. To secure the benefits of the Plan of Salvation, each individual must believe on the Lord Jesus Christ and accept Him as his personal Saviour, obey the terms of the gospel, and pattern his life after the example of Christ. Acts 4:12; Luke 24:47; Rom. 10:6-10; 1 John 5:10-14; Romans 6:16-18; 1 Peter 2:21; John 13:15.

THE TERMS OF THE GOSPEL

10. The terms of the gospel include faith in God, and in His Son, Jesus Christ, repentance and confession of sin, including restitution where possible, baptism by immersion in water, signifying the burial of the old life of sin and the arising to a new life of obedience to God. Heb. 11:6; Rom. 10:9, 10, 17; Rom. 6:1; 1 John 5:10-14; 1 John 5:1-9; Gal. 3:26, 27; Luke 13:3; Luke 24:47; Luke 19:8; Acts 2:38; Acts 3:19; Eph. 4:21-25; Col. 2:12.

THE TEN COMMANDMENTS

11. The Ten Commandments are the eternal, constitutional Law of God, and are to be observed by the people of God in this age. Ex. 20:2-17; James 2:9, 10; 1 Cor. 7:19; Matt. 5:18; Matt. 19:16-23; 1 John 2:4; 1 John 3:4; John 12:50; 2 Kings 17:37.

THE SABBATH

12. The fourth commandment enjoins the observance of the Sabbath, the seventh day of the week, commonly called Saturday. It is to be kept as sacred and holy time, from sunset Friday until sunset Saturday. It is given to all the people of God as a memorial of His creation. Gen. 2:2, 3; Ex. 20:8-11; Isa. 58:13; Heb. 4:4-11; Luke 4:16; Luke 23:56; Matt. 28:1; Acts 13:14, 42, 44; Acts 16:13; Mark 2:27, 28; Lev. 23:32; Mark 1:32.

THE LORD'S SUPPER

13. The Lord's Supper is an ordinance given to the Church as a memorial of the death of Christ, and it should be observed annually (on the beginning of the fourteenth of the Hebrew month Nisan). Unleavened bread and unfermented grape juice should be used in this service as emblems of the broken body and the shed blood of Christ. Lev. 23:5, 27, 32; Matt. 26:26-29; Luke 22:7-21, 29, 30; 1 Cor. 11:1, 2, 18-31; 1 Cor. 5:7; John 19:14, 15, 31.

FEET WASHING

14. The ordinance of feet washing was given by Jesus as an example for us, to teach humility, and is to be practiced in connection with the observance of the Lord's Supper. John 13; Luke 14:11; James 4:10; 1 Peter 2:21; 1 Tim. 5:9, 10.

CHURCH ORGANIZATION

15. Salvation is through faith in Christ, but for the purpose of co-operation in the proclamation of the gospel, and the upholding of true Bible standards and doctrines, and for the fellowship of the believers, the Church should be organized in accordance with the Bible plan. Acts 6:1-8; Acts 1:23-26; 1 Cor. 12:27-30; Eph. 2:19, 20; Eph. 4:10-17; 1 Tim. 5:17; 1 Tim. 3:1-5; Heb. 13:17; Titus 1:5-7.

CHURCH NAME

16. The organization of the people of God should be known by the Bible name—The Church of God. Acts 20:28; Eph. 3:14, 15; John 17:11, 12; Dan. 9:19; Jer. 15:16; 1 Cor. 15:9; 1 Cor. 1:2; 1 Cor. 11:22; 1 Tim. 3:15; Deut. 28:10.

TITHES AND OFFERINGS

17. The Bible plan of financial support for the gospel work is the paying of the tithes and offerings, by the members of the church. The tithe is one-tenth part of the increase, and should be paid as a part of the Christian obligation. Offerings are also a part of the Christian obligation to the Lord, and should be given liberally as one is prospered of Him. Matt. 23:23; 1 Cor. 9:13, 14; Lev. 27:30; Mal. 3:8-10.

LAW OF CLEAN AND UNCLEAN

18. The people of God and the followers of Christ in this age are to use for food those things which were given by God for that purpose, as distinguished from those things designated as unclean for human use. Gen. 7:1, 2, 20; Lev. 11:4-20; 1 Tim. 4:5; Isa. 66:15-17.

UNCLEAN HABITS

19. The body is the temple of the Holy Ghost, and God's people should be clean, refraining from any practice which would defile their bodies. Therefore, the smoking, chewing or snuffing of tobacco; the drinking of intoxicating liquors, and the habitual use of narcotic drugs, are not to be practiced by the members of the Church of God. 1 Cor. 3:16, 17; 2 Cor. 6:16-18; 2 Cor. 7:1; 1 John 2:15-17; James 1:14, 15; Gal. 5:19-21; Prov. 23:21-23, 29-32; Eph. 5:18; 1 Tim. 3:3.

20. Since Christians are to love their enemies and work for the salvation of mankind, we stand opposed to carnal warfare. Ex. 20:13; Matt. 5:44; Romans 12:17-21; 2 Cor. 10:4; Eph. 6:12.

PRAYER

21. God's people are to pray to Him, through and in the name of Jesus, their Mediator and High Priest at the right hand of God in heaven. We believe in the efficacy of prayer in the name of Jesus for all our needs, and that answer will be given in accordance with God's will for us. 1 Tim. 2:8; Phil. 4:6; John 14:13, 14; Heb. 7:25; Heb. 12:2; Heb. 4:14-16; Romans 8:34; 1 Tim. 2:5; 1 John 5:14; Luke 18:1; Matt. 7:7, 8; Matt. 6:5-9; James 1:6.

PRAYER FOR THE SICK

22. The Bible teaches both individual and collective prayer for the healing of the sick, and also the calling for the elders of the Church to anoint and pray for the sick, and that God hears and answers the prayer of faith. James 5:13-16; James 1:6; John 5:14, 15; Psalm 103:1-3.

23. We believe that Jesus Christ, the Son of God, was in the plan of salvation before the foundation of the world. He was the Word spoken of in John 1:1, 2, and His birth of the virgin Mary was in fulfillment of, "And the Word was made flesh, and dwelt among us. . . . " John 1:1, 2, 14; John 8:57, 58; Gen. 11:7; John 17:5; Col. 1:16-18.

CRUCIFIXION OF JESUS

24. The Bible teaches that Jesus was crucified on the day of the week commonly known as Wednesday, and He was in the tomb three days and three nights, arising therefrom in the end of the Sabbath, thus fulfilling the prophecy of His sign as recorded in Matt. 12:39, 40; Matt. 28:1-8; Dan. 9:27; 1 Cor. 15:3, 4; Mark 16:1-6; Mark 15:42; John 20:1-10; John 19:14; Luke 24:1-8; Luke 23:54-56.

MILLENNIAL REIGN

25. At the second advent of Christ, He will establish His kingdom on the earth, and the redeemed will reign with Him on the earth for a period of one thousand years. This is the "regeneration" (Matt. 19:28), and also the "times of restitution" (Acts 3:21). At the close of the millennium, Christ will have "put all enemies under His feet," and will deliver up the kingdom to God that God may be all in all. 1 Cor. 15:24, 25, 28; Zech. 14:4-9; Rev. 11:15; Rev. 20:4-6; Rev. 21:1-5; Rev. 19:16; Matt. 25:34; Matt. 5:5; Psalm 37:11; Rev. 5:10; Dan. 7:27; Isa. 2:2-4; Micah 4:1-5.

NEW EARTH

26. At the close of the millennium, the restitution will be complete, and the earth will have been made new; the New Earth will be the eternal home of the saved. Rev. 21:1-8; Prov. 10:30; Isa. 45:8, 9.

THE KINGDOM

27. The Kingdom is divided into three phases: (1) The Spiritual Kingdom of Grace, (2) The Millennial Reign of Christ, (3) The Eternal Kingdom of God. We are now in the Kingdom of Grace during which Christ reigns in the hearts of the believers, through the Holy Spirit. During the millennium, Christ will reign on the throne of His glory, literally, and jointly, with the redeemed for one thousand years. Following the millennium will be the third phase, The Eternal Kingdom of God, in which God will be all in all. Heb. 4:16; Matt. 25:31; Rev. 20:6; 1 Cor. 15:24-28; Romans 12:2; Col. 1:12-14; 1 Peter 2:5-9; Acts 26:18.

Please see Scriptures under Articles 25 and 26.

REGATHERING OF ISRAEL

28. The regathering of literal Israel to the land of Palestine, as portrayed in the prophecies, is in process of fulfillment, and is the sign of the soon coming of Christ. Jer. 31:9; Isa. 61:4; Luke 21:24; Ezek. 21:25-27; Ezek. 37:21-28.

SECOND COMING OF CHRIST

29. The personal and visible return of Christ to this earth will be to establish His kingdom. He will come in the clouds of heaven in the same manner as was His departure into heaven. Acts 1:10, 11; John 14:1-3; Rev. 1:7; Acts 3:20; Job 19:25-27.

PROPHECY

30. "Prophecy came not in old time by the will of man: but holy men of God spake as they were moved by the Holy Ghost," and it is given to us to study that we might watch, as we travel the highway of time, for the prophetic signboards, showing us where we are living in respect to the second coming of Christ. 2 Peter 1:19-21; Romans 15:4; Matthew 24; Psa. 119:105.

SIGNS OF THE TIMES

31. Considering the fulfillment of the signs in the political, religious, physical, and social world, we believe that we are living in the time of the end, and that the second advent of Christ is very near. Luke 21:25; Luke 17:26-31; Rev. 11:18; Matt. 24:6, 7, 36-40; 2 Tim. 4:3, 4; 2 Tim. 3:1-7, 13.

STATE OF THE DEAD

32. When man dies, he is unconscious, and in the grave awaits the resurrection, at which time the righteous will receive immortality, and the wicked, eternal death. Psa. 146:4; Eccl. 9:5, 6; 1 Cor. 15:42-56; Job 17:13; Rev. 20:11-15; Job 14:13, 14.

PUNISHMENT OF THE WICKED

33. The wicked dead will be resurrected at the end of the thousand-year reign of Christ, to receive final judgment, be cast into the Lake of Fire, which is the second death, and will be completely destroyed. Rev. 20:5, 11-15; Mal. 4:1.

WORLDLINESS

34. The Scriptures condemn worldliness, which includes the lust of the flesh, the lust of the eye, and the pride

of life. Attendance at the movie theaters, pool halls, and dances, and the excessive use of jewelry are of the world, and should be eradicated from the lives of the people of God. 1 John 2:15, 16; John 17:16; Romans 12:2; Gal. 5:17-26; 1 Peter 3:3, 4; 1 Tim. 2:9; Romans 8:12-14; Col. 3:1-10.

PAGAN DAYS

35. The days commonly known as Christmas, Lent, Easter, Good Friday, and Sunday are of pagan origin, and are not Biblical; therefore, they should not be observed by members of the Church of God. (In addition to the Scriptures, please see profane history and other reference books for origins of the above-mentioned days.)

THE PLAGUES

36. We believe that the wrath of God against sin and sinners reaches its fullness before and at the time of the second advent of Christ in the seven last plagues described in Rev. 16. These plagues represent events in the world which cause great trouble and distress. It is a part of the message of the Church to warn the world against the troubles and distress to come as the result of sin.

THIRD ANGEL'S MESSAGE

37. An evil power known as the beast exists prior to and at the time of the second advent of Christ. A message known as the Third Angel's Message should be, and is being given by the Church of God as a warning against that evil power. This is a part of the gospel by the acceptance of which people may escape the wrath of God. Rev. 13:1-10; Rev. 14:9-11; Rev. 17:7-14; Rev. 15:1.

MARRIAGE AND DIVORCE

38. We believe marriage to be a sacred ordinance of God, and that as such it belongs to the Church. Because of this fact our people should secure the services of one of our ministers to perform the marriage ceremony.

We believe that any marriage contract entered into between husband and wife at a time prior to the conversion of either party to the marriage, should be recognized as acceptable to the Church if recognized by civil law at the time either party is converted.

We believe that after one has been converted and is in fellowship in the Church, divorce is not to be tolerated, except for Bible reason. Matt. 5:32.

Notes: *This oldest branch of the Church of God perpetuates a peculiar set of beliefs held by most branches of the "Adventist" Church of God bodies. These include the annual practice of the Lord's Supper, foot washing, adherence to the Old Testament dietary laws, condemnation of popular holidays such as Christmas and Easter, and the understanding that annihilation, not eternal torment, is the result of sin.*

FUNDAMENTAL ARTICLES OF FAITH (GENERAL COUNCIL OF THE CHURCHES OF GOD)

"Forasmuch as many have taken in hand to set forth in order a declaration of those things most commonly believed among us" (Luke 1:1).

A. GENERAL STATEMENT

The Churches of God (7th Day) cherish liberty of thought as an essential condition for the guidance of the Holy Spirit. Therefore we have no binding creed to which members must subscribe. However, there are certain fundamental truths which have been binding upon Christians through all ages. Therefore, these are the historic doctrines taught by the Church of God, which we reaffirm as the fundamental principles of the faith.

These statements of faith approved by the General Council are passed on to the churches of God for such action as the Spirit of God may direct. It is believed that they will be helpful in giving Christian training to our children, in establishing our people in the faith, and making known our essential doctrines to others.

B. POLITY

The Church of God (7th Day) is, historically, congregational in polity. We desire that our churches and their members continue to enjoy this blessed freedom of local autonomy. Therefore, the statements set forth here are simply an exhibition of the things most commonly believed among us and is not adopted as having binding force in itself, nor is the inspiration of the phraseology contended for.

THE FUNDAMENTAL ARTICLES OF FAITH

1. THE BIBLE

We believe the Bible (both Old and New Testament) to be the inspired Word of God, containing the revelation of God given to man under Divine supervision and providence; that its historic statements are correct and that it is the only rule for faith and practice (Romans 15:4; 2 Timothy 3:15, 16; John 17:17).

2. THE GODHEAD

We believe, as revealed in the Bible—

a. In the one true God the Father who is the eternal and supreme Deity. He is infinite in His wisdom, love and power, the Creator and Sustainer of all things, "in whom we live, and move, and have our being" (Genesis 1:1; Isaiah 40:28; Matthew 6:6).

b. In Jesus Christ, our Lord and Savior, the only begotten Son of God; who came into the world to seek and to save that which was lost. We believe in His deity, in His virgin birth, in His sinless life, in His miracles, in His vicarious and atoning death on Calvary, in His bodily resurrection late on the Sabbath day, in His ascension to the right hand of God in heaven, in His ministry as our High Priest and Mediator, in His personal return to the earth at the end of this age to establish His kingdom and rule this earth in great power and glory, judging the living and the dead (1 Timothy 3:16).

FUNDAMENTAL ARTICLES OF FAITH (GENERAL COUNCIL OF THE CHURCHES OF GOD) (continued)

c. And in the Holy Spirit, the promised Comforter, which is the agency of the Father and the Son to convince the world of sin, of righteousness and of judgment to come. But this same Spirit of God we are sanctified and sealed unto the day of redemption. For those who diligently seek Him, He will lead and guide into all truth and empower the believer for witnessing and service (John 14:16, 26; 16:7-11; Ephesians 1:13).

3. CRUCIFIXION AND RESURRECTION OF CHRIST

We believe the Scriptures plainly teach that Jesus Christ was crucified in the middle of the week, on the day we call Wednesday, and He was in the tomb three days and three nights. He arose towards the end of the Sabbath day (Saturday) and thus fulfilled the sign given by Jesus in Matthew 12:39-40.

4. MAN'S CONDITION

We believe man was created for immortality, but through sin he forfeited his Divine birthright; that because of sin, death entered into the world, and passed upon all men; and that only through faith in Jesus Christ can depraved man become "partakers of the divine nature," and live forever (2 Timothy 1:10; Romans 2:7; 1 Corinthians 15:22, 51-54).

5. STATE OF THE DEAD

We believe that death is a condition of unconsciousness (sleep) to all persons, both the just and the unjust, a condition which shall remain unchanged until the great resurrection at Christ's second advent, at which time the righteous will receive eternal life, while at their appointed time the wicked will be "punished with everlasting destruction," suffering the complete extinction of being, this is the second death (Ecclesiastes 9:5; Job 14:14; John 5:28-29; Matthew 10:28).

6. MAN'S SALVATION

We believe that man in his state of depravity cannot extricate himself and, therefore, God provided salvation free to all those who, in this life and this age, accept it on the conditions imposed, which conditions are simple; namely, turning from sin, repenting before God, exercising faith in our Lord Jesus Christ and His precious blood, making restitution where possible, and obeying the command to be baptized in the name of the Lord Jesus and receive the gift of the Holy Spirit. A life of consecration to Christ and obedience to His commandments must follow in order to obtain eternal life (John 3:16; 2 Corinthians 6:2; Luke 13:25-28; Acts 2:38).

7. A HOLY LIFE AND SANCTIFICATION

We believe that God is holy and requires that His children be holy and sanctified. Sanctification means a cleansing from sin, separation from the world, and consecration to God. The sanctification of a Christian is attained through faith in the Word, faith in the blood of Jesus and the work of the Holy Spirit in the believer's life. Sanctification is effected instantaneously at the time of conversion, and continuously, each day as the believer walks with God (1 Peter 3:15; 1 Corinthians 1:2; 1 Corinthians 6:11).

8. THE CHURCH

We believe "The Church of God" to be the common Bible name for God's Church and that the church is of divine origin, established upon the foundation of the prophets and apostles with Jesus Christ being the chief cornerstone. This spiritual body includes all true Christians who have been "called out" of the world and gathered into it. Jesus Christ is the Head of the church of God, which is His body; and all the local churches should be independent of outside control, congregational in government, under the spiritual oversight of the godly elders and under the direction of the Holy Spirit, and subject to no priest, bishop or overseer—although true Christian fellowship and unity of action should exist between all local churches of God (Matthew 16:18; Ephesians 5:25, 4:15, 2:19-22; Acts 20:28).

9. ORDINANCES OF THE CHURCH

We believe Christ has placed in His church certain ordinances that all of the children of God should participate in. We believe they are:

a. Christian baptism of believers by immersion as the only true water baptism. After repentance of sin the believer is to be baptized into Christ for the remission of sin and as a public witness to his acceptance of Christ as Lord and Savior, a symbol of death to sin, and a pledge to walk in "newness of life" in Christ Jesus.

b. The Lord's Supper, which commemorates the suffering and death of our Lord Jesus Christ, "Till He comes," and is a memorial that should be observed yearly at the beginning of the 14th of Nisan (Abib) with unleavened bread and "fruit of the vine," which represent the broken body and shed blood of Christ. It is also a loving symbol of Christian fellowship, and a pledge of renewed allegiance to our risen Lord and Savior.

c. The observance of the act of humility, the washing of the saints' feet, should be held in connection with the Lord's Supper. Jesus said, "If I then, your Lord and Master have washed your feet, ye also ought to wash one another's feet" (Acts 2:38; 1 Corinthians 11:23-26; Matthew 28:19; Romans 6:3-5; John 13:4-17).

10. THE TEN COMMANDMENT LAW AND THE SABBATH DAY

We believe the Ten Commandments are the eternal law of God and this law is still binding upon all Christians. Christ did not come to destroy it but, instead, to magnify it. Therefore, the Scriptures enjoin the observance of the fourth commandment, which declares the observance of the 7th day of the week as the Christian Sabbath (which is commonly called Saturday). It should be observed from sunset on Friday until sunset on Saturday and is to be observed as a day of rest and religious worship. However, the handwriting of ordinances that was against us was blotted out and taken out of the way, by Christ nailing it to His cross (Exodus 20:2-17; Deuteronomy 9:10; Matthew 5:17; 19:16-22; 5:18; James 2:8-12; 1 Corinthians 7:19

Romans 3:20; Genesis 2:3; Matthew 28:1; Leviticus 23:32; Mark 2:27-28; Colossians 2:14).

1. PRAYER AND DIVINE HEALING

We believe prayer is the privilege and duty of every Christian, and it is a drawing near to God in spiritual communion, in order to worship Him and praise Him for His mercies and to bring our requests to Him and to intercede on behalf of others. Prayer should be made to God in the name of Jesus Christ, in the power of the Holy Spirit, and with understanding. We believe in the "laying on of hands" of the elders and the prayer of faith for divine healing (Acts 5:15-16; 28:9; James 5:14-16; 1 Timothy 2:8; Luke 4:6; John 14:13; Romans 3:34; Philippians 4:6).

2. THE SECOND COMING AND THE KINGDOM OF GOD

We believe that Jesus Christ, according to His promise, will come again to this earth, even "in like manner" as He went into heaven—personally, visibly and gloriously—to reign here on earth with His holy saints for a thousand years; and that this coming is the blessed hope of the church, inasmuch as upon that coming depend the resurrection of the dead and the reward of the righteous, the abolition of sin and its fruits, and the renewal of the earth now marred by sin, which will become the eternal home of the redeemed, after which event the earth will forever be free from sin and the curse of death (Acts 1:11; 1 Thessalonians 4:16-17; Revelation 22:12-20; Matthew 25:31-32; 1 Corinthians 15:24-28; Acts 3:21; Revelation 19:11-16; Daniel 7:27; 2 Peter 3:13; Proverbs 10:30; Matthew 5:5).

3. SIGNS OF THE TIMES

We believe that Bible prophecy has indicated the approximate time or season of Christ's return; comparing testimony with the signs of the times (such as the regathering of Israel). We are confident that He is near, "even at the doors," and we believe that the great duty of the hour is the proclamation of this soon coming redemption, the defense of the Bible truth and authority, warning the nations to flee the wrath to come and following the last command of our Savior to His disciples to preach (teach) his message to all of the world, and to remember His promise that He would be with us even till the end of the age (2 Peter 1:19-21; Matthew 24:42-45; Revelation 22:17; 1:18; 2 Timothy 3:1-7; Romans 15:4).

—Even So, Come Lord Jesus—Amen

STANDING RESOLUTIONS

Realizing the need for higher standards in the church of today, we recommend that the following resolutions be presented to the General Council. In no way are they designed to be "high church dictation or religious legislation," but resolutions formulated as guides for our churches and a testimony to the world of our determination to hold fast to that which is good in the face of the present moral and spiritual decline in the United States and elsewhere.

BE IT RESOLVED that we accept the Bible plan for financing the general ministry of the church. We believe the paying of tithes and giving freewill offerings the duty and obligation of all Christians. By dedicated Christian stewardship the work of the church can be greatly blessed.

BE IT RESOLVED that the General Council go on record as being opposed to worldliness. The Scriptures condemn worldliness and it involves our manner of speech, actions, patronizing of certain places of amusement, immodesty of dress and the participation in certain things that a Christian should not participate in or be a part of.

BE IT RESOLVED that we maintain the following position concerning defiling habits, since our bodies are the temples of the Holy Spirit. Each child of God should refrain from all fleshly lusts, and this would include tobacco, narcotic drugs, and intoxicating liquors.

BE IT RESOLVED that we reaffirm our position on marriage. We believe it is a sacred ordinance instituted by God, and thus it belongs to the church. Divorce is a present day evil and since it breaks the law of God and weakens the homes of our nation, we therefore encourage our members to avoid this evil, except for the Bible reason.

BE IT RESOLVED that we now reaffirm our faith in the commandments of God and the faith of Jesus. Therefore, as we near the second advent of our Savior, let us boldly declare the traditional faith of our fathers with new zeal and devotion that all men might hear the Gospel and escape the wrath to come. May we use every means at our disposal to spread the Gospel of Jesus Christ.

STATEMENT ON CARNAL WARFARE

Whereas the General Council of the Churches of God (7th Day) recognizes that the young people who refuse military service for reasons of religious conscience have taken a position that is upright, honest, and above reproach; therefore,

BE IT RESOLVED, that we as Christians stand opposed to carnal warfare, and whereas there is a sincere difference of opinion as to the duty of a Christian concerning military service, some of the members of our churches being conscientiously opposed to any participation in war on the ground that war is contrary to the teaching of Christ, and others believing that they can conscientiously serve the cause of righteousness through such participation, therefore,

BE IT RESOLVED, that we recognize the need of maintaining fellowship in spite of these differences of opinion, pledging our moral support and protection to those who follow the voice of conscience.

We invite the conscientious objectors among our people to register their conviction in writing with the corresponding secretary of the General Council with respect to their status.

Notes: *The council is in general agreement with the General Conference of the Church of God but has added an item on pacifism to its statement.*

DOCTRINAL POINTS OF THE FAITH (SEVENTH DAY CHURCH OF GOD)

Inasmuch as the Church, as an organized body of believers, accepts and upholds certain tenets of faith, and as the licensed, and ordained ministers, and officers of the Church have accepted these articles of faith without reservations, and such are the faith of the body at large, the same are published as follows, that each member may acquaint themselves better with the Faith of The Church of God. II Tim. 3:15; 1 Tim. 4:6, 16; John 7:16, 17; II Tim. 3:16, 17; Matt. 4:4.

DOCTRINE

Doctrine shall in all cases be according to the Holy Bible as it is summed up in the Saviour, and inasmuch as the Scriptures clearly teach the following points of doctrine, the same are listed as essential parts of "the Whole Armour" of our faith; Eph. 6:11.

1. THAT the Bible, the Old and New Testaments, is inspired as no other writings is, and is complete, infallible, and expresses God's complete will for man.—II Tim. 3:16; Rom. 15:4; II Peter 1:20; Rev. 22:18, 19; Deut. 4:2; Deut. 12:32.

2. THAT Jehovah alone is God, the Creator of the heaven, the earth, the sea, and all that is therein.—Gen. 1:1; Jer. 10:10, 12; Eph. 3:9; Heb. 1:10; Rev. 10:6.

3. THAT Jesus of Nazareth is the only begotten Son of God, conceived of the Holy Spirit, born of the virgin Mary, and is our Lord, Saviour, and Redeemer.—Matt. 1:18-21; 3:17; Luke 1:28-35; John 3:16.

4. THAT Jesus proved His Messiahship by remaining in the tomb exactly three days and three nights, rising in the end of the Sabbath.—Matt. 12:40; Dan. 9:26, 27; Crucified in the midst of the week, Wednesday.—Matt. 28:1-6 (Rose on Sabbath).

5. THAT the Holy Spirit is "the Comforter," which abides in the believer and He is manifested by the power, and the fruits of the Spirit, as in Acts 2nd Chapter, John 16:7-14, and Gal. 5:22-26. Manifestations regulated according to I Corinthians 14th chapter.

6. THAT Satan is a personality, and as "the devil," he is an adversary of God and the children of God.—Isaiah 14:12-20; Ezek. 28:13-19; Rev. 12:7-9; John 8:44.

7. THAT man was created perfect originally, but through disobedience fell, bringing imperfection, death, and God's wrath upon mankind.—Gen. 3:17-19; Matt. 19:8; Romans 5:12, 17; I Cor. 15:21, 22; Gen. 1:26-28.

8. THAT the Christian's life must be patterned after the example of the perfect man—Christ Jesus, who shall have pre-eminence in all things.—II Cor. 5:17; I Peter 2:21-25; I John 2:6; I John 3:5; Col. 1:18.

9. THAT an inspired Bible name for God's called out assembly is the "Church of God." These saints will faithfully uphold all the principles of the Kingdom of God.—Acts 20:28; I Cor. 15:9; Gal. 1:13; I Cor. 1:2; I Tim. 3:15; Ex. 19:5, 6.

10. THAT the apostolic organization and government of God's Kingdom is the only one taught in the Bible for the Church of God.—Isa. 9:6; I Cor. 12:28; Eph. 4:11-16.

11. THAT "Pure Religion," personally experienced by the one regenerated by its power, is the only safe one to trust in.—John 3:1-12; Romans 6:1-12; Romans 13:14; Gal. 3:26, 27; Matt. 19:28; James, 1:27.

12. THAT repentance must be preached.—Matt. 4:17; Mark 6:7, 12; Luke 13:3; Luke 24:47; Acts 2:38; Acts 17:30, 31.

13. THAT conversion is essential to salvation.—Luke 22:32; Acts 3:19; Psalms 19:7.

14. THAT the sanctification of holy living is commanded for the people of God.—John 17:17; Acts 26:18; I Cor. 1:2; I Cor. 6:11; II Tim. 2:21; Heb. 13:12; I Peter 3:15; I Peter 1:15.

15. THAT baptism by immersion for the remission of sins is vital and typical of the burial and resurrection of Christ.—Romans 6:3-6; Matt. 3:16; Col. 2:11, 12.

16. THAT there is efficacy in the fervent prayer of the righteous.—Prov. 15:8; John 14:13; Matt. 21:22; James 5:16; I John 3:22; I John 5:14.

17. THAT the prayer of faith and anointing will save the sick.—James 5:14-16; Mark 6:13; Acts 5:15, 16; Acts 9:17; Acts 28:8.

18. THAT the laying on of hands is to be practiced.—see above references and Acts 8:14-18; Acts 19:6; II Tim. 1:6.

19. THAT the Passover is to be observed annually on the beginning of the 14th of Abib, and after the example of Jesus.—Ex. 12:6; Ex. 13:10; Lev. 23:5; Luke 22:8-17. The Lord's Supper is a perpetual ordinance until it is fulfilled in the Kingdom of God. (Verses 16, 18).

20. THAT we ought to wash one another's feet.—John 13:1-17.

21. THAT we should observe the seventh day of the week, from even to even, as "the Sabbath of the Lord".—Gen. 2:2, 3; Eccl. 3:14; Ex. 20:8-11; Ex. 31:14-17; Ezek. 20:12; Isa. 58:13; Isa. 56:2, 7; Luke 4:16; Mark 2:27, 28; Matt. 12:10, 12. Evening is at sunset, when the day ends and another begins.—Gen. 1:5, 8, 13, 14: Deut. 16:6; Mark 1:32; Lev. 23:32 (last part); II Chron. 18:34; Neh. 13:19; Heb. 4:3-12.

22. THAT we recognize the Bible calendar, and "observe" the Seven Annual Holy Days of God as "The Way" to fulfill: "Come to the Marriage Feast" of Matt. 22—Lev. 23rd chapter; Ex. 23:14-17; Matt. 23:1-3; Matt. 28:18-20.

23. THAT the paying of "the tithe" of all "increase" is a continued obligation.—Gen. 14:18-20; Heb. 6:20; Heb. 7:1, 2; Lev. 27:32; Num. 18:21; Deut. 8:18; Prov. 3:9; Psa. 24:1, Mal. 3:8, 10; Matt. 23:23; I Cor. 9:11-14; Romans 15:27; Phil. 4:17, 18.

24. THAT all carnal warfare, and the participation therein is condemned, as declared by the Master and our earliest belief.—Ex. 20:13; Matt. 5:21, 22; Romans 13:8-10; Matt. 26:52; John 18:36; Rev. 13:10.

25. THAT the law of the clean and unclean is still to be observed in this age.—Lev. 11th chapter; Eccl. 3:14; Mal. 3:6; James 1:17; Acts 15:20, 29; II Cor. 6:16-18; Rev. 16:13; Isa. 65:4; Isa. 66:11-17.

26. THAT the use of intoxicating liquors, alcoholic stimulants, narcotics, tobacco, and any habit-forming drugs, is condemned.—I Cor. 9:25; Prov. 23:29, 30; Dan. 1:8, 12; Gal. 5:19-21; I Cor. 3:16, 17; I Cor. 5:11; I Cor. 6:10.

27. THAT our perfecting thru the continuation in the observance of "the Law of God," should be taught as Jesus directed. This is "The Law of Life in Christ."—Isa. 42:21; Matt. 5:17-32; Matt. 19:17; Matt. 22:34-40; Romans 8:1, 2; I Cor. 9:21; James 2:10, 11; I John 5:3; Rev. 14:12; Rev. 22:14.

28. THAT sin is the transgression of "the Law" as Jesus demonstrated it.—Romans 6:23; I John 3:4; John 8:1-11; John 16:9.

29. THAT justification from sins is through Christ alone.—John 1:29; Romans 3:24-31; Romans 4:24, 25; Romans 5:1.

30. THAT the return of Jesus Christ will be literal, visible, personal, and is imminent.—Acts 1:11; Acts 3:20, 21; I Thess. 4:16, 17; II Thess. 1:7, 8; Matt. 24:15-31; Rev. 1:7.

31. THAT the throne of David will be established at Jerusalem by the person of Jesus Christ.—Zech. 14:4; Dan. 2:44, 45; Dan. 7:13, 14, 27; Rev. 5:9, 10; Micah 4:8; Luke 1:23, 33; Isa. 24:20-23.

32. THAT the institution of the millennial reign of the kingdom of heaven is at the return of Jesus.—See above; also Rev. 20:4.

33. THAT judgment is upon the house of God during the gospel age.—I Peter 4:17; John 3:18-21.

34. THAT the righteous are resurrected and rewarded at the coming of Jesus.—I Thess. 4:16, 17; I Cor. 15:22, 23, 52; Rev. 20:6; Matt. 25:31-46.

35. THAT the meek shall inherit the earth.—Matt. 5:5; Psalms 37:11, 34; Prov. 10:30; Rev. 5:9, 10; Rev. 21:2, 3.

36. THAT there shall be a final regathering of the dispersed nation of Israel.—Ezek. 37:21, 22; Joel 3:1; Jer. 31:8, 9; Isa. 61:4.

37. THAT the wicked dead are resurrected to final judgment, and not to probation.—Eccl. 3:17; Eccl. 12:14; Acts 17:31; II Cor. 5:10; II Peter 2:9; Rev. 20:7, 8, 12, 15.

38. THAT the wicked are destroyed.—Ezek. 18:4; Romans 6:23; Nahum 1:10; Mal. 4:1-3; Psalms 37:10, 20, 38; Rev. 20:10, 15; Rev. 21:8; Rev. 22:10.

39. THAT the Third Angel's Message is a present day message, and will continue to the advent of Jesus.—Rev. 14:9.

40. THAT the seven last plagues are literal, and fall at the termination of this Gospel age.—Rev. 14:9, 10.

41. THAT we shall practice fellowship in the brotherhood of Christ according to:—Prov. 4:18; I John 1:7; I John 5:1; Eph. 4:11-16; I Cor. 1:1-3.

Notes: *The doctrinal points were adopted as revised in 1965. No member is allowed to teach any doctrine contrary to these statements.*

* * *

DOCTRINE, AND BASIS FOR FELLOWSHIP (WORLDWIDE CHURCH OF GOD)

Section 1. Basic Doctrine: The doctrine of this Church shall be that of a plain and literal understanding of the Holy Bible, believing it means exactly what it says; —of the Bible alone, and not as interpreted by any other book or person, but it is a point of basic doctrine in this Church that we understand the Bible to reveal a divine Creator, the Almighty God, a divine Saviour, the Son of God, Jesus Christ, who came in the human flesh, proclaimed the Gospel of the coming world-ruling Kingdom of God, which it is obligatory for all Christians to believe; who died to pay the penalty of our sins in our stead; who was raised from the dead after three days and three nights in the grave by God the Father; who ascended to the right hand of the Father in heaven; who is soon coming again literally and in Person to earth to set up the Kingdom of God, and as King of kings and Lord of lords, to rule all nations by this world-ruling Kingdom for one thousand years; we believe in the Commandments of God and the faith of Jesus Christ our Lord.

Section 2. Belief on Bearing Arms: It is the conviction and firm belief of this Church and its membership that Christian disciples of Christ are forbidden by Him and the Commandments of God to kill, or in any manner directly or indirectly to take human life, by whatsoever means; and we believe that bearing arms is directly contrary to this fundamental doctrine of our belief; and we therefore conscientiously refuse to bear arms or to come under the military authority.

Section 3. Basis for Fellowship: The basis for fellowship in this Church or any of its local congregations shall be LOVE alone, plus the adherence to and belief in the general basic doctrine stated in Section 1 above, and the requirement of repentance of sin (the transgression of God's law), and the acceptance of Jesus Christ as personal Saviour, and the receiving of the Holy Spirit of God evidenced by the fruits of the Spirit (Gal. 5) in the member's life.

Notes: *This brief statement is taken from the constitution of the church. It emphasizes the church's belief in the soon-coming kingdom of God and its refusal to participate in war. A number of church bodies, such as the Church of God International and the Associated Churches of God, have*

DOCTRINE, AND BASIS FOR FELLOWSHIP (WORLDWIDE CHURCH OF GOD) (continued)

arisen from the Worldwide Church of God and continue these emphases.

* * *

Sacred Name Groups

MAJOR POINTS OF DOCTRINE (ASSEMBLIES OF THE CALLED OUT ONES OF YAH)

1. "Yah" name we know.
2. "Yah's" name we are called by.
3. "Yah's" name and word we publish.
4. "Yah's" voice through "Yeshuah" we know and hear.
5. "Yah" has called us out.
6. "Yah" through "Yeshuah" is our salvation and joy.
7. "Yah's" Son, "Yeshuah," is our Saviour.
8. "Yah's" repentance, baptisms, commandments, laws and statutes we obey and the testimony of "Yeshuah."
9. "Yah's" gifts of the Holy Spirit we recognize and cherish.
10. "Yah's" prophecies we see and believe.
11. "Yah's" signs and seals we know and keep.
12. "Yah's" great power is the living power of the Holy Spirit, making us the "Called Out Ones" of "Yah" all in one accord through the Son, "Yeshuah," with the Heavenly Father, "Yah."
13. "Yah" is not a liar, but all men are.

Notes: *The Sacred Name groups are distinguished by their use of Hebrew transliterations as the actual name of the Creator (Yah, Yahweh, Yahvah, etc.) and his Son (Yeshuah, Yahshua, etc.) in place of the more common designations, God and Jesus. On other points they are very close to other Church of God Adventists.*

The Assemblies of the Called Out Ones of Yah uses "Yah" and "Yeshuah" for the names of the Creator and His Son. Members practice the charismatic gifts of the Holy Spirit usually associated with pentecostal churches.

* * *

BELIEFS [ASSEMBLY OF YAHVAH (ALABAMA)]

The Assembly of Yahvah teaches that "according to the Holy Spirit inspired scriptures, "Yahvah is the oldest and most correct rendering of the four sacred consonants from the Hebrew scriptures into the English scriptures, and the true and correct abbreviated form Yahshua, is the Saviour's name, as transferred from the language (Hebrew) in which the Saviour himself revealed it." "The keeping of all ten commandments including the observance of the seventh day Sabbath as taught in the fourth commandment." "That Yahshua is the only begotton Son of Yahvah, formed by the Holy Spirit, born of the virgin Mary (Miriam)." "That Salvation is only through the blood of Yahshua the Messiah and repentance, conversion, sanctification, the immersion (in water) must be preached." "That the baptism of the Holy Spirit and the nine gifts of the spirit are for the followers of Yahvahshua today, and all must live a clean, humble, Holy Spirit filled life." "A decent dress code for both sexes according to the Holy inspired Word and the abstaining from the habitual use of intoxicating liquors and drugs."

Notes: *The Alabama branch of the assembly is specifically charismatic and believes in the nine gifts of the spirit. The Creator and His Son's names are Yahvah and Yahshua.*

* * *

DOCTRINE [ASSEMBLY OF YAHVAH (OREGON)]

1. That "All scripture is given by inspiration of Yahvah, and is profitable for doctrine, for reproof, for correction, for instruction in righteousness: That the man of Yahvah may be perfect, thoroughly furnished unto all good works."

2. According to the Holy Spirit inspired Scriptures, "Yahvah" is the oldest and most correct rendering of the four Sacred Consonants from the Hebrew Scriptures into the English Scriptures; therefore "Yahvah" is the correct Name of the Creator, and Yahshua is the true and correct abbreviated form to use in English for the Saviour's Name, as transferred from the language (Hebrew) in which the Saviour Himself revealed it.

3. THAT Yahvah in six days made heaven and earth, the sea, and all that in them is, and rested the seventh day.

4. THAT Yahshua is the only begotten Son of Yahvah, formed by the Holy Spirit, born of the Virgin Miriam (Mary).

5. THAT Yahshua prove His Messiahship by remaining in the tomb exactly 3 days and 3 nights, rising in the end of, or late on the Sabbath.

6. THAT the baptism of the Holy Spirit and the nine gifts of the Spirit are for the followers of Yahshua today, and each follower of Yahshua must live a clean, humble, Holy Spirit-filled life; manifestations of the Spirit regulated according to 1 Corinthians 12th and 14th chapters.

7. THAT the inspired scriptural name for Yahvah's children is "The Assembly of Yahvah."

8. THAT Adam who was created perfect originally, through disobedience to Yahvah fell, bringing death, and the wrath of Yahvah upon mankind.

9. THAT experimental salvation, or salvation personally experienced by the one regenerated by the power of the Holy Spirit, is the only safe one to trust in.

10. THAT repentance, conversion, sanctification, and immersion (in water) must be preached.

11. THAT prayer and anointing will heal the sick.

12. THAT the passover, which consists of unleavened bread and the fruit of the vine (grape juice), is to be observed annually in honor of our Saviour's death, in the beginning (dark part) of the 14th of Abib.

13. THAT, according to the example of our Saviour, we ought to wash one another's feet.

14. THAT the seventh day of the week shall be observed from evening to evening as Yahvah's Sabbath.

15. THAT the paying of tithe should be practiced by Yahvah's children.

16. THAT all carnal warfare is condemned.

17. THAT the law of clean and unclean is still to be observed and taught.

18. THAT the habitual use of intoxicating liquors, alcoholic stimulants, narcotics, tobacco and any habit-forming drug, is condemned.

19. THAT the perfection and continuity of the law of Yahvah, the Ten Commandments, should be taught.

20. THAT the return of Yahshua will be literal, perceivable to the eye, personal and is impending.

21. THAT the Kingdom of Yahvah will be established under the leadership and in the person of Yahshua the Messiah on the throne of David at Jerusalem during the restitution of all things or during the one thousand year reign of the Saviour on earth, beginning at the second coming of Yahshua.

22. THAT the righteous are resurrected and rewarded at the second coming of Yahshua.

23. THAT the saints shall inherit the earth and will reign with the Saviour on earth during the millennium and throughout eternity.

24. THAT the dead are unconscious.

25. THAT the wicked dead are resurrected to final judgment, and not to a second trial or chance.

26. THAT the wicked will be eternally destroyed.

27. THAT the seven last plagues are literal, and will fall at the conclusion of this age.

In addition to the Statements or Belief and our Stand on Israel, here is how we stand on other scriptural points:

WATER BAPTISM CEREMONY. We believe that "Yahvah-shua the Messiah" is the correct form to use in the ceremony of water baptism, and that this is a complete fulfillment of the command given by our Saviour in Matt. 28:19, "Go ye therefore, and teach all nations, baptizing them in the name (not names) of the Father, and of the Son, and of the Holy Spirit." "Yahvah" (pronounced Yah Vah, Yahvah) is the Father's NAME, "Yahvah" is His Son's NAME, and it was in the Son's NAME that the Holy Spirit came, and please remember that the Son came in His Father's NAME, "Yahvah." "Shua" is the official title or term applied to the Son which shows what His Father does through Him, that is, "save or redeem." So when the ONE full correct form of the Son's NAME, "Yahvah-Shua the Messiah" is used in baptizing, this fulfills Matt. 28:19.

PASSOVER CALCULATION. We believe the Passover should be observed exactly 14 days from the time the first New Moon nearest the true Spring Equinox first becomes visible after the conjunction of the sun and moon, which is marked new moon on our calendars.

THE NEW COVENANT AND THE HUNDRED AND FORTY-FOUR THOUSAND. We believe just what the Scriptures state concerning this number and that is, that twelve thousand were sealed from each of the 12 fleshly tribes of (a man named) Israel. We believe that this work was accomplished under the personal ministry of our Saviour and the apostles and the early assembly. In other words, we believe the hundred and forty-four thousand were the FIRST to hear and accept the kingdom message, the FIRST to be sealed in the beginning of this great harvest age, "being the first fruits unto Yahvah and the lamb." (Rev. 14:4). We are living in the END of the harvest and for that reason, no sect, organization, association or individuals can constitute the "hundred and forty-four thousand."

We believe that Yahvah-Shua (Yahshua), was and is the mediator and testator of the New Testament, and He sealed it with His own blood. And according to Heb. 8:6-13; 9:15-17; 10:15-22; 1 Cor. 11:25, we believe that Yahvah-shua made the New Testament with the "house of Israel (10 tribes) and the house of Judah (2 tribes, Benjamin and Judah)" when He was there the first time.

After the hundred and forty-four thousand were sealed, we see that the work of the "great multitude" (Rev. 7:9) began, which meant spreading the "kingdom news" to any and all nations, therefore the "great multitude" is composed of believers redeemed from all nations, regardless of race or color. This work evidently started at the house of Cornelius and will continue unto the second coming of our Saviour or thereabout. Rev. 7:9; Acts 10:28-35; 13:46; Rom. 1:16.

THE MILLENNIUM. We do not believe that the Saviour will reinstate any part of the Mosaic or sacrificial system, in the millennium, which He died to abolish, but instead He will restore the entire earth to its original Edenic state and beauty, and will give to the saints of the Most High the dominion promised to Adam, that is, the whole earth. Dan. 7:18,27; 2 Pet. 3:13; Micah 4:8; Gen. 1:26-29.

WOMEN PREACHERS. We do not find one single text of Scripture that "women" ever received the titles evangelist, apostle, bishop, pastor or overseer. We do find that "women" were among those who were called "fellow-laborers" (Phil. 4:3), together with some men "helpers" (Rom. 16:3), "prophetess" (Luke 2:36), and "teachers" according to Titus 2:3-5.

Under these tithes we believe that "women" (the sisters) can fulfill any obligation put on them through the spirit toward Yahvah and His service. They can pray, sing prophesy under divine inspiration as a prophetess, be a personal witness for the Saviour and teach according to Titus 2:3-5. But all must be in harmony with 1 Tim. 2:11, 12; 1 Cor. 14:34, 35.

PENTECOST AND FEAST OF TABERNACLES. While we do not consider Pentecost and Feast of Taberna-

DOCTRINE [ASSEMBLY OF YAHVAH (OREGON)] (continued)

cles as binding on the saints of this age as we do the Passover and Ten Commandments, yet we have no objection to holding Campmeetings at these seasons. And it is the privilege of the individual or assemblies who so desired to observe these feasts. But we do not feel it best to open the Eliyah Messenger and the tracts we put out for advocating the observance of Pentecost and Tabernacles to the extent that some have, and are advocating.

Notes: *The Oregon branch of the assembly is non-Pentecostal. Yahvah and Yahshua are the names used for the Creator and His Son.*

*   *   *

STATEMENT OF DOCTRINE (ASSEMBLIES OF YAHWEH)

THE BASIS OF OUR FAITH

1. We affirm that in order to interpret the inspired Scriptures correctly, we must use the Old Testament as a basis for our faith. We must therefore interpret the New Testament through the teachings of the Old, recognizing complete harmony in the Word, thereby achieving sound doctrine, John 10:35. In the New Testament we find that repeated reference is made to the law, the Psalms, and the prophets: in other words, the Word of Almighty Yahweh, Matt. 4:4; John 5:39; Luke 24:44-46; 2 Timothy 3:14-17; Isaiah 8:16, 20; Acts 17:11. The Old Testament Scriptures saw partial fulfillment in the accounts that are recorded in the New, while they will find complete fulfillment in the years that will follow the Second Coming of our Savior.

2. We affirm that there is one Almighty Heavenly Father who is above all, and to whom we owe our reverence and worship, Deut. 6:4, 13; Matt. 4:10; 1 Cor. 8:4-6.

3. We affirm that the Messiah has come in human form as the man recognized as the Savior in the New Testament Scriptures, that He pre-existed with the Father, John 16:28-30; Psalm 2; Micah 5:2; John 17:5; Phil. 2:5-8; that He was born of a virgin, Matt. 1:18, 23; Luke 1:26-38; that He lived a sinless life, 1 Peter 2:22; that through His death upon the tree of Calvary we may have atonement for our sins, Isaiah 53; Hebrews 9; and that He rose again the third day, Matt. 12:40; 1 Cor. 15:1-8; to give us a hope of a resurrection also, Romans 5:6-12; 1 John 5:9-13.

4. We affirm that it is necessary and most important to our salvation that we accept the revealed, personal Name of our Heavenly Father YAHWEH and the Name of His Son, our Savior YAHSHUA the MESSIAH. We affirm also that the most accurate transliteration of these Names from the Hebrew into the English is by the spellings employed above, Exodus 3:14-15; Psalm 68:4; Psalm 83:18; Isaiah 42:8; Isaiah 52:6; Acts 4:12.

5. We affirm that the Holy Spirit is the mighty power from the Heavenly Father and the Messiah dwelling within us so that we may have the ability and strength to bring our lives into a state of perfection pleasing to our Heavenly Father, John 14:15-27. We find the trinitarian doctrine to be foreign to the inspired Scriptures. The Holy Spirit is imparted to the obedient believers by the laying on of hands of the elders of the Assemblies of Yahweh after baptism, Acts 19:1-6; Acts 8:14-24; 1 Timothy 4:14; Acts 2:38; Acts 5:32.

6. We affirm that as obedient children it is necessary to keep all the commandments, statutes, and judgments (except the ritual and animal sacrifice laws) which the Heavenly Father gave to Israel to make them a separate people, Lev. 20:7-8; Deut. 6:6-9, 25; Deut. 7:6-11; Matt. 5:17-20; Romans 7:12. It is now possible through the Holy Spirit to keep these commandments by faith for our salvation, Eph. 2:8-10; James 2:17-20. We now keep a spiritual sacrifice rather than animal sacrifices, meal, and drink offerings, Hebrews 13:15-16; 1 Peter 2:5; Romans 12:1; Phil. 4:18.

7. We affirm that sin is the transgression of the law of Yahweh, Lev. 4:2, 13, 27; 1 John 3:4.

8. We affirm that in order to be free from sin, a person must accept the shed blood of Yahshua the Messiah as his atonement and live in submission to the will of our Heavenly Father by keeping His laws, Micah 6:6-8; 1 John 1:7; 1 John 2:2; Hebrews 10:26-31; Eph. 1:6-7. Yahweh has extended grace (unmerited kindness or mercy) to all who keep His law, Rom. 3:24. Grace is not license to do as you please, Jude 4.

9. We affirm that water baptism is a necessary act following repentance, Acts 2:38; Matt. 3:13-17; that this baptism is immersion in water, backward, one time, into the Name of Yahshua the Messiah; Rom. 6:3-6; John 5:43; John 14:26; that this baptism symbolically indicates an inner cleansing, Romans 6:7-23; 1 Cor. 10:1-10. We also affirm that baptism, except in rare instances, is a necessary step in receiving the Holy Spirit, 1 Pet. 3:21.

10. We affirm that obedience to the commandments of Almighty Yahweh includes observing and keeping holy His commanded observances of Leviticus 23 and Numbers 28-29.

11. We affirm that the weekly seventh-day Sabbath (commonly called Saturday) is upheld in both Old and New Testament Scriptures, Exodus 20:8-11; Mark 2:27-28; Luke 4:16; Hebrews 4:4, 9. The Sabbath is a sign between Yahweh and His people, Ex. 31:12-17.

12. We affirm that the scriptural months are determined by the visible new moons, Deut. 16:1. The first day of each month is delineated by the appearance of the crescent. We find that the Scriptures indicate further that the law will go forth from Zion in the Millennium, Isaiah 2:3; the holy days will then be set from Jerusalem, Isaiah 66:23. The scriptural day begins and ends with sunset, Lev. 23:32; Mark 1:32.

13. We affirm that the Passover Memorial Supper in this New Testament era is the annual observance of our Savior's death. The Passover Memorial is to be observed on the evening of the 14th day of the scriptural month of Abib, soon after sundown, at the commencement of the day, Exodus 12:3-14; Numbers 28:16; 1 Cor. 5:7-8; 1 Cor. 11:23.

14. The Passover observance utilizes the emblems that are to be partaken in this New Testament era. The unleavened bread (matzoth) is the symbol of the broken body of our Savior, 1 Cor. 10:16; Exodus 23:18. The symbol of our Savior's shed blood is understood to be the fruit of the vine (Heb. tirosh, 'asis—grape juice), Matt. 26:27-29; Isaiah 65:8-9; Deut. 32:14. We find the Passover day to necessitate the use of unleavened bread, but it is not a Sabbath of rest, Deut. 16:3-4. It is the preparation for the feast, the day before the annual Sabbath, Mark 15:42; Luke 23:54; John 19:31, 42; Exodus 12:18; Exodus 34:25. Foot washing precedes the taking of the emblems, John 13.

15. We affirm that the Feast of Unleavened Bread is observed from the 15th to the 21st (inclusive) of the month of Abib; during this period we eat unleavened bread with our meals, Lev. 23:6, while symbolically cleansing ourselves of everything that corrupts, meaning false doctrine (teaching) which leads to sin, 1 Cor. 5:6-8; Matt. 16:12; Mark 8:14-15; Luke 12:1. The first and last days of this observance are to be kept as holy Sabbaths and convocations for the worship and praise of our Heavenly Father, Exodus 12:15-20; Numbers 28:17-25; Acts 20:6-7.

16. We affirm that the Feast of Shavuoth (Pentecost) is to be observed seven weeks after Passover, beginning our count with the day following the weekly Sabbath falling on Passover or during the week of Unleavened Bread, Joshua 5:10-12, NEB. Shavuoth (Feast of Weeks) is always observed on the first day of the week, Lev. 23:9-21; Acts 2. We find that it was the day of the outpouring of the Holy Spirit upon the New Testament assembly and was also the time when Israel ratified the convenant law with Yahweh given to Israel at Mt. Sinai.

17. We affirm that we shall observe the Feast of Trumpets in anticipation of our Savior's return from heaven for His bride, the assembly, Lev. 23:24-25; Numbers 10:1-10; Numbers 29:1; 1 Thess. 4:16.

18. We affirm that the fast of Atonement (Yom Kippur) is to be observed as a memorial of our Savior's atonement for us on the tree of Calvary. This day is to be observed as a strict Sabbath and fast day, Lev. 23:27-32; Acts 27:9.

19. We affirm that the Feast of Tabernacles is to be observed in this New Testament era as a preview of the Kingdom of Yahweh and the Millennium, Lev. 23:34-39; John 7:1-39; Zech. 14:16-21. The Feast of Tabernacles is a feast of seven days, the first day being a holy convocation, while the eighth day, called the Last Great Day, is to be observed as a holy convocation also, John 7:37.

20. We affirm that our Savior Yahshua the Messiah will establish the Kingdom of Yahweh, the Kingdom of the Heavens, on this earth, Ps. 115:16; Prov. 11:31; Matt. 5:5; Rev. 5:10. This Millennial Kingdom will prevail for 1,000 years and will be set up by Yahshua the Messiah at His Second Coming. At that time righteousness will be established as the order of the day, and this earth will be rebuilt into an Edenic paradise which man lost originally through sin, Isaiah 11:1-10; Matt. 6:10. After the Millennium, a new heaven and earth will be brought forth, Isaiah 66:22; Rev. 21:1.

21. We affirm that the Scriptures teach eternal punishment for the wicked, that this punishment is complete destruction in the lake of fire (Gehenna), and we disavow an eternal torment in an ever-burning hell, 2 Thess. 1:7-10; Mal. 4:1-3; Psalm 37:20-22; Isaiah 33:12; Matt. 25:46; Jude 7. We affirm that the Bible teaches the existence of a literal devil (Satan), Genesis 3:1-15, Isaiah 14:12-20, Zech. 3:1-2, Matt. 4:1-11, 1 Peter 5:8, Rev. 12:9. Satan will be destroyed at the end of the Millennium, Ezek. 28:18-19, Romans 16:20, Rev. 20:7-10.

22. We affirm that adherence to the law of clean meats in Lev. 11 and Deut. 14 remains in effect and binding in our era, and that it is important to our physical health, 2 Cor. 6:16-18.

23. We affirm that the Scriptures teach anointing with oil in the Name of Yahweh and in the Name of Yahshua the Messiah for healing of illness. This anointing service should be done by at least two elders if possible, James 5:13-20; Ex. 15:26.

24. We affirm that in order to preach this true doctrine of salvation around the world, every member of the body of the Messiah is obligated by scriptural law to tithe (10 percent of his increase) to the Assemblies of Yahweh, Prov. 3:9. These tithes are to be paid to the headquarters treasury so that no duplication of the ministry shall occur, Mal. 3:8-12; Lev. 27:30-33; Matt. 23:23. The Assemblies of Yahweh teaches also the second (feast day) tithe, Deut. 14:22-26, and the third (third year poor fund) tithe, Deut. 14:27-29; Deut. 26:12-17.

Notes: *This statement of the largest of the Sacred Name bodies was issued to bring unity to the movement. It is the most complete and systematic of the statements from the various Sacred Name organizations. Yahweh is the accepted name of the Creator.*

*   *   *

STATEMENT OF THE ASSEMBLIES OF YAHWEH (MICHIGAN)

This magazine is published for the glory of our Heavenly Father and His only begotten Son, our Saviour. It upholds the original inspired Scriptures—". . . the whole counsel of Yahweh." (Acts 20:27). Its aim is to remove the names substituted by man for the Memorial Name of the Creator and his Son, the Saviour of the world. Therefore, the

STATEMENT OF THE ASSEMBLIES OF YAHWEH (MICHIGAN) (continued)

originally inspired name Yahweh, the title Elohim (Mighty One) and the name Yahshua, the Messiah will be found on its pages. It upholds the Ten Commandments: restoring the Sacred Name in the third and the observing of the 7th Day Sabbath (Saturday) in the fourth. It stands for baptism by immersion in the Name of Yahshua the Messiah according to Acts 2:38 and Matthew 28:19; the ordinance of feet washing and the commemoration of Messiah's death at the Passover Season; the Feasts of Unleavened, Weeks, and Tabernacles, and the annual Sabbaths in Leviticus 23. It advocates tithing and the observance of all Yahweh's health laws including clean foods. It teaches justification by faith in the blood of Yahshua and advocates healing of the whole man—physically and spiritually. It stresses the importance of the sanctified life and the power of the Holy Spirit by which Yahweh works in us—". . . to will and do of His good pleasure." Philippians 2:13. It is supported entirely by the "Called Out Ones of Yahweh," which is the meaning of "The Assembly of Yahweh." It is of His People and for His People: all those who have heard and heeded the call of Revelation 18:4.

Notes: *Possibly the oldest Sacred Name congregations are associated with* The Faith, *a periodical begun in the mid-1930s. Each issue carries a declaration of basic affirmations which distinguish the Sacred Name cause from the Church of God Adventists as a whole.*

*   *   *

Jehovah's Witnesses Groups

WE BELIEVE (CHRISTIAN MILLENNIAL CHURCH)

GOD

We believe in ONE GOD; and that in the beginning He created Heaven and earth. That He is immortal, Divine and self-existing; having no beginning and will have no end.

That He is the Father of our Lord Jesus Christ. God is perfect in His four attributes of power, justice, wisdom and love. And that such attributes lie plain before the eyes of men; revealed to them in nature. In its universal order and beauty. To all who obey Him; through accepting and belief in His Son Jesus Christ; by recognizing His sovereignty; will receive eternal life.

For further reading: Genesis 1:1; Psalms 90:2; 83:18; 103:19; Deut. 32:4; I Chron. 29:10-13; Isa. 40:12-15; 42:9; 44:68; 46:8-11; 48:3; Rom. 1:19; I Tim. 1:17; I Tim. 6:16; John 3:36; 5:24; Titus 1:2.

JESUS CHRIST

Jesus Christ is the very first and only creation of God; the only begotten Son of God. As such He was known as the *Logos* or the Word. A most glorious Spirit Being in Heaven, who created all things under the guidance and direction of His Heavenly Father. In God's due time, Jesus willingly gave up His Heavenly glory, to be born to a virgin Mary; and was a perfect human being.

Jesus became the Savior and Redeemer of the human race, by giving His perfect life on the cross of Calvary, a ransom for Adam's life; thus satisfying Divine Justice. He was therefore rewarded by God His Father for His "faithfulness unto death"; by being raised from the dead, and given all power in Heaven and on earth; along with glory, honor and immortality; to be seated on His Father's right hand in the highest Heaven.

For further reading: John 1:1, 2; 3:16; Matt. 26:42; Luke 1:26-38; 19:10; Acts 1:6-11; 2:24; Col. 1:16; I Tim. 2:3-6; Heb. 8:1; Rev. 3:14.

THE HOLY BIBLE

The Bible is a collection of sixty-six books; written by the prophets, apostles and other men of God, who wrote under God's inspiration and direction, given them through God's Holy Spirit. From Genesis to Revelation, the Bible is God's message to men, revealing His will for mankind, and His wonderful plan for the redemption and salvation of the world. It tells of our legacy of eternal life—a reward for obedience to His just laws.

For further reading: John 17:3, 17; Ps. 119:1-5; 2 Tim. 3:16 & 17.

GOD'S PLAN OF THE AGES

God's Plan, as revealed in the Holy Bible, encompasses a period of about 7,000 years. From the creation of Adam to the end of Christ's (thousand-year) reign. Redemption through the blood of Jesus, is woven like a golden thread throughout the Bible; from Genesis to Revelation.

Genesis reveals the fall of man into sin and death, as well as the promise of the "seed"; Jesus; to expiate and atone for that sin of disobedience in the Garden of Eden. Then throughout the Old Testament the 'thread' is picked up, and extended to the actual giving of Christ's life on the cross. It further predicts the return of Christ to this earth, when He will set up God's Kingdom with His elected Church. During this first thousand years, God's purpose will be accomplished: A resurrection of all the dead; the just AND unjust. The just to reign with Christ; the unjust to have their trial or decision period; which includes every person who ever lived. Including the restoration of the earth and its order of things. Thus, at the end of His reign, Christ will turn over this perfected, sinless world to God, so God can be all in all.

For further reading: Genesis 3:1-19; Matt. 1:21; John 3:17; John 5:28; 14:1-3; I Cor. 15:20-28; I Tim. 2:3-6; I John 4:14; Rev. 11:15-18; Rev. 20:11, 12.

SATAN

Originally, Satan was created by God as a beautiful, powerful and wise cherub whose name was Lucifer. He was placed by God in the Garden of Eden to care for our first parents, Adam and Eve. However, Lucifer's heart was full of pride, ambition and a desire to be like the Most High, and desired to be worshipped as He is worshipped. So Lucifer lied to Eve, which led to her disobeying God. Adam soon followed, thus plunging all mankind into sin and death. Satan also seduced or influenced a great multitude of angels to follow him, and do his bidding, before the great Flood. Afterwards they were placed in everlasting chains until the Judgment Day.

But Satan and other of his demoniacal associates are still very active in the world today: influencing and causing fear and confusion among people of all nations. He has very cleverly learned to use all means of communications: Television, movies, radio, stage plays, books, pornographic magazines, etc.

At the very beginning of Christ's Kingdom on earth, Satan will be imprisoned in a "bottomless abyss," so as not to deceive the nations. At the end of the Millennium, Satan will be destroyed.

For further reading: Genesis 3:1-6; Isa. 14:1-15; Ezek. 28:11-19; Matt. 4:1-11; II Cor. 4:4; John 14: 30; Jude 6; Ephes. 2:2; Rev. 20:7-10.

SIN

The Bible declares that sin is disobedience to the expressed will of God. And that the penalty for sin is DEATH: not eternal torment. For God warned Adam he would die if he disobeyed Him. But Adam willfully disobeyed His Creator, and with Eve was sentenced to death.

So by heredity, all Adam's children, all mankind, have been born under his condemnation. Therefore, no matter how they live, where they live, what race or nationality they are, all mankind is appointed to die.

For further reading: Genesis 3:17-19; Psa. 51:5; Rom. 2:23; 6:23; 5:12; Heb. 9:27; James 1:15; I Tim. 2:6; Rev. 1:5.

Man can be freed from slavery to sin by accepting the Lord Jesus Christ as His Lord or Master, and Savior; which is indicated by repentance and true conversion which leads to baptism; thus indicating he is a "new creature" in Christ Jesus. As redeemed by the Lord, they will; upon His return to earth; be resurrected and rewarded with eternal life. Then, by the end of Christ's reign, sin and death will have been completely eradicated from the face of the earth.

For further reading: I Peter 2:24, Acts 2:38, I John 2:12 and I Corinthians 15:26, 27.

ADAMIC DEATH

Adamic death is the result of sin. It has engulfed all of mankind because "all have sinned." So all mankind is under this sentence of death, as pronounced on father Adam: "Thou wast made of dust, and unto dust shalt thou return." Genesis 3:19. This is called Adamic death.

Death is a cessation of life; not a continuation of life somewhere else. The Bible reveals that when a man dies he loses all consciousness, knowledge, feeling, wisdom, etc. Man is placed into the grave (*sheol* in Hebrew; *hades* in Greek) where he sleeps until Christ's return, and the resurrection of the dead. Eccles. 9:5 and 10; John 5:28 & 29; I Cor. 15:22; Rom. 3:23; I Tim. 2:14; Ezek. 18:2-23; Isaiah 35:10.

SECOND DEATH

The second death is different from the first, or Adamic death, in that it means total destruction of the sinner; with no hope of a second resurrection.

Second death is vividly illustrated by the Valley of Hinnom, south of Jerusalem; the valley at the time of Christ, which was used as a garbage dump and incinerator for the city of Jerusalem. Its Greek name was *gehenna*. The fires in the Valley of Hinnom were always kept alive to burn and completely destroy all the trash, garbage and carcasses that were thrown or dumped there. No living thing was ever thrown into the fires; only the bodies of animals and of executed criminals. And what the fire did not destroy, worms did. Thus showing the complete annihilation of whatever was put into it. At the end of the Millennium, Adamic death and hell (the grave) will be thrown into Gehenna (destroyed). This is also pictured as "the lake burning with fire and brimstone"; where also Satan and his unrepentant fallen angels (demons) and obstinate sinners will be thrown. Forever more destroyed; thus ending all death. For further reading: Psalms 145:20; Matt. 10:28; Rev. 20:7-10; 20:14; 21:8.

ISRAEL

From Moses to Jesus, the people of Israel as a nation were God's chosen people. To them the Law was given; the prophets sent; the promises made. But the nation continually failed to obey God and His Law, which culminated in their rejection and crucifixion of Jesus. As a result of this rejection, Israel was destroyed as a nation, and dispersed throughout the Roman Empire. In God's Plan, favor came instead, to the Gentile (non-Jew) converts, who accepted Christ.

Nevertheless, prophecies declare that God is going to restore a relationship with the nation of Israel; restoring them as a nation and allowing His full favor to be theirs again when they accept Christ as their Messiah. The present state of Israel and events in the Middle East verify the fulfilling of these prophecies.

For further reading: Exodus 19:5,6; Zech. 12:10; Isa. 51:1-3; Mal. 2:1-9; Matt. 23:39; Luke 23:18-25; Acts 7:51-53; Rom. 11:26; Ezek. 37:1-14.

GRACE

Grace is a gift of God to us. It is His gracious favor shown unto us. None of us are deserving of such but God in His mercy provides grace through our faith in Christ Jesus. It is through His favor or Grace that we are accepted into His family as His children.

For further reading: Psa. 84:11; Acts 15:11; Romans 5:15-17; Ephes. 2:8; II Tim. 2:1; II Peter 3:18 and Romans 6:23.

SALVATION

Salvation of the human race was accomplished by the death of Christ Jesus on the cross. Since all men are under the condemnation of sin and death (see SIN and ADAMIC DEATH), to be saved one must repent of his sins and accept Jesus as Lord and Savior of his life. The Lord promised that anyone taking this step will be forgiven their sins, and if obedient unto death, will receive eternal life at the resurrection.

For further reading: Luke 9:10; Acts 2:37, 38; Rom. 5:6; I Cor. 15:3; II Cor. 6:2; Hebrews 5:9 and John 3:36.

WE BELIEVE (CHRISTIAN MILLENNIAL CHURCH) (continued)

CONSECRATION

The next logical step for the converted or saved Christian is to consecrate or dedicate his life to Christ. His life is then devoted to the service of the Lord, and learning obedience in all things of God. The exterior manifestation of this important step is baptism by water immersion. This baptism symbolizes the Christian's death to self and the world, and a rebirth or resurrection to a new life in Christ. As a new creature, the Christian should present his body a "living sacrifice"; leading a God-directed life, and thus establishing a close and intimate relationship with God as a son or daughter.

For further reading: Ephes. 5:26; I Thess. 4:3; 5:23; Heb. 2:11; 10:10; 13:12; I Pet. 3:11 and Romans 12:1 and 2.

BAPTISM

Baptism by immersion was ordered by Christ, so is considered mandatory. The immersion into water signifies the believer's death to self-will; the coming up out of the water, his intention to live "in Christ," or for Him. This then considers him to be a "new creature" in Christ; a member of God's New Creation. To which He has promised glory, honor and immortality; the Divine Nature, provided he or she remains faithful unto death.

For further reading: Rom. 6:1-11; 12:1,2; I Cor. 12:13; Gal. 3:27, Col. 3:1-4; Rev. 2:10.

GOD'S HOLY SPIRIT

God's Holy Spirit was shed on the gathered disciples at Pentecost. Ever since, it has been shed upon His disciples in varied measure, right to this day. And will be poured out upon all flesh; for His Spirit will work on the hearts of man in the next age also.

The Holy Spirit is a wondrous gift of God. It is like energy generating from Him. It is His power, His influence, which gives Christians guidance, enlightenment, comfort, wisdom, strength and joy. Without it, life for the Christian would be impossible, and he or she would miss many of the promised blessings of God.

For further reading: Luke 11:13; John 14:26; Acts 2:1-12; Joel 2:28,29; Rom. 5:5; 15:13; I Cor. 6:19; Ephes. 1:13; I Thess. 4:8; and I Pet. 1:12.

THE END OF THE WORLD

The Bible tells us that "this present evil world," dominated by Satan, is going to pass away during "the Great Day of the Wrath of the Lord God Almighty." On that day will be seen the "death" of this present evil world, as prophetically described in Daniel 2:35, and Malachi 4:1. Then follows the "birth" of God's new world of tomorrow, wherein "dwelleth righteousness." Everything on earth that is based on greed, selfishness, dishonesty, lust, violence, evil principles and wickedness will be destroyed forever. This destruction and purification will influence many to turn to God, and be in a condition to welcome the Kingdom then established on the earth.

For further reading: Matt. 4:8,9; II Cor. 4:4; John 13:31; 14:30; 16:11; Rev. 21:5; II Pet. 3:8-13; Mal. 4:1; James 5:1-6; Ezek. 7:19; Isa. 2:7-19; Rev. 6:15-17; Jer. 25:30-33; Isa. 34:1-4; Zech. 14:1-5; Rev. 19:11-21.

THE KINGDOM

God's Kingdom is seen in the New Testament as being made up of two phases—the spiritual Kingdom of God in Heaven, which has ever existed and will ever exist; and the earthly Kingdom of God, which will come into existence following the return of our Lord and Savior, Jesus Christ.

Now, during this Gospel Age, Christians who have dedicated their lives to God, and been baptized in obedience to the doing of His will, are said to be delivered from the power of darkness, (Satan's), and delivered unto the Kingdom of Christ. (Coloss. 1:13). They are said to be living (in Spirit) in the "heavenlies" with Christ Jesus. What is true now in spirit, will, at the return of Jesus, be an accomplished fact. For with Jesus, God's Kingdom reign will commence, and continue until God's plan of salvation and restoration is fulfilled through and by them.

For further reading: Col. 1:13 & 14; Ps. 2:7-9; Ps. 145:13; Isa. 9:7; Dan. 2:35,44; Dan. 7:13,14; Matt. 6:10, 33; 25:34; Luke 1:33; Luke 12:32; Eph. 5:4; I Thes. 2:12; Heb. 12:28; Rev. 11:15.

THE MILLENNIUM AND RESTORATION

The term "millennium" means one thousand years. It is applied to Christ's Kingdom on earth; which is to be established following His return from Heaven. During this period, Satan will be bound in a bottomless pit, so as not to deceive the people who will be resurrected on earth at that time. Christ and His Church will be the absolute, worldwide rulers of this Kingdom. The resurrection and judgment period of the "unjust" will then commence. Each person will have an individual trial or decision period, in which to decide as to whether or not they will accept God's righteous ways and live on forever, or reject His ways and thus die the Second Death. But each will have a full opportunity for instruction and rehabilitation, by coming to a full knowledge of Truth. For further reading: Acts 3:19-24; Rev. 20:3,4; John 5:28,29; Isa. 2:4; John 12:48. A final judgment will take place at the end of the Millennium, when Satan is loosed for a short period of time, for the testing of mankind; and will make one final attempt to deceive the people. Those who side with him will be destroyed along with Satan and his evil forces. This destruction is called the Second Death, from which there is no return.

The then proved faithful ones will continue to live on forever, completely restored to perfection, in a completely restored earth, as God always intended it to be, but thwarted in the Garden of Eden through Adam's disobedience.

Wars, violence, sorrow, sickness, suffering and death will no longer exist. They will be nothing more than memories of a painful past, and a remembrance of God's loving mercy provided through their Savior's sacrifice.

For further reading: Isa. 9:6,7; 11:1-10; 25:6-9; 26:9; 33:24; 35:1-10; 65:17-25; Acts 24:15; John 5:28, 29; Rev. 29:1-3; 11-14; I Cor. 15:24-28.

A NEW HEAVEN AND A NEW EARTH

In several places the Bible speaks of a "new heaven and a new earth," as opposed to the present heaven and present earth. We understand the old "heaven" is not God's Heaven, for it is eternal and will never pass away. But rather is Satan's lower abode of existence from which he presently rules; influencing mankind to do evil. Paul reveals to us this "heaven" is made up of "principalities, powers, rulers of darkness, and of spiritual wickedness in high places." (Ephes. 6:12). See also Ephes. 2:2; Col. 2:15. Satan is called the "god (mighty one) of this world" in II Cor. 4:4, and was called by Jesus "the prince of this world." (John 14:30). And Satan boasted to Jesus that he would give all the kingdoms of this world to Him, if He would bow down and worship him. Of course Jesus did not contest this boast. (Matt. 4:8-10). With the Lord's return this present dispensation or civilization will pass away. Just as the first dispensation was destroyed at the time of Noah by the Great Flood, so will this dispensation pass away; though not by a flood. The New English Bible explains it as "The heavens will disappear with a great rushing sound; the elements will disintegrate in flames, and the earth with all that is in it, will be laid bare." II Peter 3:10. But the earth will not be destroyed. God's plan is to make it glorious. (Num. 14:21). His footstool (Isa. 66:1). Eccles. 1:4 reminds us it will last forever.

Thus purified and renewed, this will be a beautiful "new earth, where righteousness shall abide." (Isa. 65:7; II Peter 3:12; Rev. 21:1-4).

THE RESURRECTION AND THE SOUL

The whole world has been led to believe that man has within himself something called an "immortal soul," which at death of the body goes off somewhere into space, be it heaven, hell, purgatory, nirvana, Valhalla, happy hunting ground, etc. This belief is NOT taught in the Bible, for nowhere in the Bible do we find the term "immortal soul," or that the soul is immortal. Rather we find that man IS a soul; not *has* one, for Genesis 2:7 states: "God breathed into man the breath of life and he BECAME a living soul." And Ezekiel 18:4, 20 tells us: "the soul that sinneth, it shall die." In sentencing Adam God made no mention of Adam's soul going anywhere after Adam's death. Rather, He plainly said: "for thou art dust, and unto dust shalt thou return." Period. (Gen. 3:19).

This means then, that man *IS* a soul: A conscious being, capable of thinking and feeling, and when dead he is incapable of thinking and feeling. (Eccles. 9:5 & 10). Therefore we conclude that according to the Scriptures, the grave awaits us all, good and bad, and there is no eternal torment awaiting the wicked dead, but instead the resurrection from the grave. (John 5:28 & 29).

If man had an immortal soul, there would be no need of a resurrection, for immortality means being imperishable; therefore in no need for a resurrection. God has designed the resurrection because man, the living soul, ceases to exist at the time of death. Paul clearly states that "if there is no resurrection, they also which have fallen asleep (died) are perished." Thus we see the dead are truly dead in the grave; not in Heaven or a place of torment, and without the resurrection would remain dead—perished forever. (I Corinthians 15:18).

So we must make a choice. We can either believe in the immortality of the soul (a doctrine taught by men) or in the resurrection of the dead; as taught by God and the Lord Jesus Christ, in the Bible. We cannot believe in both. We choose to believe God and His Word. How about you?

For further reading: Psa. 115:17; Isa. 26:19; John 5:26-28; I. Cor. 15:21, 22, 35-57; John 11:25; Rev. 12, 13.

SHEOL, HADES, HELL AND THE GRAVE

As noted in our discussion of Adamic death, hell is a translation of the Hebrew word *sheol*; and of the Greek word *hades*. The original meaning of these words was hole, pit, grave, tomb, a place of silence where the living placed their dead. However, centuries after the Apostles fell asleep a new meaning of heathen origin was introduced, and believed and adopted by the clergy.

The place called "hell" was described as a place of boiling and burning with fire and brimstone, where the immortal souls of sinners would be sent upon the death of their bodies. There, the devil with pitchfork, was said to inflict pain and everlasting torture upon them. But never consumed. (A question: since a soul is not made of matter, in this human theory, how then can it be roasted and burned?)

This Satanic doctrine, borrowed from heathen religions, has caused fear in the hearts of the people, thus keeping them in absolute subjection to the clergy. No such place of punishment is mentioned in the Bible, for sinners. Though in Revelation they have taken the symbolic language used in chapters 20:14 & 15, and 21:8, to indicate such a place of torment does exist. However note carefully in 20:14 that *death* and *hell* were cast into the lake of fire. How then can hell, if it be the lake of fire, be cast into hell? Notice the rest of this verse as well as 21:8 gives the proper explanation as to what the lake of fire really is: "This is the second death."

What then is the lake of fire, since it is not a literal lake? Revel. 21:8 further confirms the lake of fire to be the second death, or total destruction. Thus we can truly believe what is stated in Romans 6:23: "For the wages of sin is DEATH," but the gift of God is Eternal LIFE through Jesus Christ our Lord." Thank God for He is love and would never torture man, no matter how evil they may be, just as you or I would never think of torturing an animal or child. And thank Him for promising that in due time the grave itself will be defeated and abolished, for "the last enemy to be destroyed is death." (I Corin. 15:26). Praise God for this.

THE TRINITY

One doctrine which is believed by almost all of mainstream Christianity, is the doctrine of "The Trinity." This doctrine has led a great many people to believe that God did not send His Son Jesus into the world to become the Savior of mankind, but rather that God Himself (though the scriptures state Him to be immortal, therefore death-proof) incarnated Himself into Mary's womb, and was born half man and half God. A demi-god. Interestingly enough, the word "Trinity" is never used in the Bible.

WE BELIEVE (CHRISTIAN MILLENNIAL CHURCH) (continued)

Furthermore, history tells us that it was at the Council of Nice, in 325 A.D. that the majority of the 318 bishops officially adopted the doctrine of the Trinity as most now know it—a doctrine of which the Apostles knew nothing.

The Bible records God as the Father, the Giver of life. That He created Jesus as His only begotten Son, sending Jesus to earth through a woman, Mary. (Luke 1:26-28; John 1:14; 3:16); to be the Savior of the world. Which was accomplished by His death on the cross, thus ransoming Adam, and providing redemption for the whole human race. Both the living and the dead. (Matthew 20:28; I. Tim. 2:6).

It was God who awoke Jesus from His three-day sleep in death. Forty days later God received Him back into Heaven, and rewarded Him by making Him head of *all* things, including the Church. He is now seated on the right hand of God, a Divine immortal being, so "Christ dieth no more." (Ephes. 1:2-22; Rom. 6:9; Rev. 1:18). We see then, that it is evident that there are here but two separate entities—God the Father, and Jesus, His Son.

As for the Holy Spirit being a third entity or third person of a Triune God, the Bible tells us rather, that the Holy Spirit is used in reference to God Himself, when speaking of His power, wisdom and understanding which accomplishes His mighty words, in both the material and spiritual worlds.

We who are His sons and daughters in Christ, are the blessed recipients of this power or Spirit. This same Holy Spirit which was given to Jesus when He was baptized by John in the Jordan. (Matthew 3:13-17; Acts 2:38, John 14:26).

Many use I John 5:6 to prove the Father, Son and Holy Spirit are one. However, in reading other translations than the King James, we find it properly reads: "For there are three witnesses: the Spirit, the water, and the blood, and these three are in agreement." We therefore affirm there is ONE GOD, and we say with the Apostle Peter: "To Him be glory and dominion for ever and ever . . . Amen."

—written by Gaetano Boccaccio

—edited by Dawn Kersula

Notes: *Though many groups derive from what is today known as Jehovah's Witnesses, most became independent organizations prior to the Witnesses' acceptance of "Jehovah" as God's name; hence they do not call God "Jehovah." These groups are non-Trinitarian, believing that Jesus is not God but the first creation of God. Most of the groups have not published doctrinal statements.*

The Christian Millennial Church broke with the Jehovah's Witnesses (then known as the Millennial Dawn Bible Students) over the doctrine of the ransom atonement (item 2).

BELIEFS (DAWN BIBLE STUDENTS ASSOCIATION)

THE BELIEFS. The Bible is accepted as the inspired Word of God, and the only infallible authority to guide a Christian in his life and belief.

CREATION AND FALL. Man was created in the image of God, and given the opportunity to live in an earthly paradise forever, on conditions of obedience. He disobeyed, and was driven out of his garden home to die.—Gen. 1:26-31; 3:16-19

SIN'S PENALTY. "In the day that thou eatest thereof thou shalt surely die." (Gen. 2:17) "The wages of sin is death." (Rom. 6:23) "The soul that sinneth it shall die." (Ezek. 18:4, 20) "Fear not them which kill the body, but are not able to kill the soul: but rather fear him which is able to destroy [not torment] both soul and body in hell."—Matt. 10:28

REDEMPTION. Jesus took the sinner's place in death. Thus he became the satisfaction, the "propitiation for our sins: and not for ours only, but also for the sins of the whole world." (I John 2:2) To accomplish this redemption Jesus "poured out his soul unto death." (Isa. 53:12) Jesus gave himself a "ransom for all." (I Tim. 2:3-6) Having died for the world, Jesus was raised from the dead by the power and glory of his Heavenly Father. (Acts 2:24; Eph. 1:19, 20) His soul was not left in death, the Bible hell. (Ps. 16:10) Now he "ever liveth to make intercession" for us.—Heb. 7:25

SALVATION. "The gift of God is eternal life through Jesus Christ our Lord." (Rom. 6:23) Salvation from death, through Christ, is made possible through a resurrection of the dead, Jesus himself being the "firstfruits" of the resurrection. If Christ had not been raised from the dead, then there would have been no hope of a resurrection for others, and "they also which are fallen asleep in Christ are perished."—I Cor. 15:17-19

The church of Christ comes forth in the "first resurrection," to "live and reign with Christ a thousand years." (Rev. 20:4, 6) Then there will be the general resurrection, when the "dead, small and great, stand before God," the "books" of divine revelation are opened and they are judged upon the basis of the will of God thereby revealed to them. Those whose works conform to the will of God will live forever.—Rev. 20:11-15

The followers of Jesus in this age partake of a "heavenly calling." (Heb. 3:1) They will be with Jesus in the "place" he prepares for them. (John 14:2, 3) They are joint-heirs with Jesus, and will sit with him on his throne. (Rom. 8:17; Rev. 3:21) In the resurrection they partake of the "divine nature," of "glory and honor and immortality."—II Pet. 1:4; Rom. 2:7

Those awakened from death in the general resurrection will have the opportunity of being restored to perfection of human life here on earth as enjoyed by our first parents before they transgressed the law of God. These are the "sheep" class of Matthew 25:34, to whom it will be said, "Come, ye blessed of my Father, inherit the kingdom prepared for you from the foundation of the world." Peter describes this general restoration of all the willing and obedient of mankind as the "restitution of all things," adding that it had been foretold by the mouth of all God's holy prophets since the world began. In the "times of restitution," those who do not accept Christ and obey the laws of his kingdom will "be destroyed from among the people."—Acts 3:19-23

THE SECOND ADVENT. Christ came at his first advent to give his life a "ransom for all." For this purpose he was made flesh, and he gave his flesh, his humanity, "for the the life of the world." (John 6:51) He was raised from the dead in the "express image" of his Father's person, "whom no man hath seen, nor can see." (Heb. 1:1-3; I Tim. 6:15, 16) It is the divine Christ who returns and establishes his authority in the earth, and, for a thousand years, is both Ruler and Judge, his church being associated with him.—Isa. 9:6; II Tim. 4:1; I Pet. 4:5; I Cor. 6:2, 3; Rev. 2:26, 27; 3:21

PROPHECY. Prophecies descriptive of world conditions at the time of Christ's return are in process of fulfilment. These prophecies describe the destruction of "this present evil world," the social order over which Satan is prince, but "the earth abideth forever." (Gal. 1:4; Eccl. 1:4) God created the earth, "not in vain, he formed it to be inhabited."—Isa. 45:18

CHRISTIAN WORK. The present work of the church is to disseminate the Gospel for the perfecting of the saints for the future work of service; to develop in herself every grace; and to bear testimony to the world concerning the love of God through Christ, and the imminence of his long-promised kingdom.—Matt. 24:14

Notes: *This statement is in general agreement with that of the Pastoral Bible Institute from which the association is derived.*

*   *   *

TO US THE SCRIPTURES CLEARLY TEACH (PASTORAL BIBLE INSTITUTE)

Chartered in 1918, the Pastoral Bible Institute, Inc., was formed for the promotion of Christian knowledge. Its journal, *The Herald of Christ's Kingdom,* stands firmly for the defense of the only true foundation of the Christian's hope now being so generally repudiated—Redemption through the precious blood of "the man Christ Jesus, who gave himself a ransom [a corresponding price, a substitute] for all" (1 Pet. 1:19; 1 Tim. 2:6). Building upon this sure foundation the gold, silver, and precious stones (1 Cor. 3:11-15; 2 Pet. 1:5-11) of the Word of God, its further mission is to—"make all see what is the fellowship of the mystery which . . . has been hid in God . . . to the intent that now might be made known by the Church the manifold wisdom of God"—"which in other ages was not made known unto the sons of men as it is now revealed."—Eph. 3:5-10.

It stands free from all parties, sects, and creeds of men, while it seeks more and more to bring its every utterance into fullest subjection to the will of God in Christ, as expressed in the Holy Scriptures. It is thus free to declare

boldly whatsoever the Lord hath spoken—according to the Divine wisdom granted unto us, to understand. Its attitude is not dogmatic, but confident; for we know whereof we affirm, treading with implicit faith upon the sure promises of God. It is held as a trust, to be used only in his service; hence our decisions relative to what may and may not appear in its columns must be according to our judgment of his good pleasure, the teaching of his Word, for the upbuilding of his people in grace and knowledge. And we not only invite but urge our readers to prove all its utterances by the infallible Word, to which reference is constantly made, to facilitate such testing.

TO US THE SCRIPTURES CLEARLY TEACH

THAT the Church is the "Temple of the Living God"—peculiarly "his workmanship"; that its construction has been in progress throughout the Gospel Age—ever since Christ became the world's Redeemer and the Chief Corner Stone of this Temple, through which when finished, God's blessing shall come to "all people" and they find access to him.—1 Cor. 3:16, 17; Eph. 2:20-22; Gen. 28:14, Gal. 3:29.

THAT meantime the chiseling, the shaping, and polishing of consecrated believers in Christ's atonement for sin, progresses; and when the last of these "living stones," "elect and precious," shall have been made ready, the Great Master Workman will bring all together in the First Resurrection; and the Temple shall be filled with his glory, and be the meeting place between God and men throughout the Millennium.—1 Pet. 2:4-9; Rev. 20:4, 6.

THAT the basis of hope for the Church and the world lies in the fact that "Jesus Christ by the grace of God, tasted death for every man," "a ransom for all," and will be "the true light which lighteth every man that cometh into the world," "in due time."—Heb. 2:9; John 1:9; 1 Tim. 2:5, 6.

THAT the hope of the Church is that she may be like her Lord, "see him as he is," be "partaker of the divine nature," and share his glory as his joint-heir.—1 John 3:2; John 17:24; Rom. 8:17; 2 Pet. 1:4.

THAT the present mission of the Church is the perfecting of the saints for the future work of service; to develop in herself every grace; to be God's witness to the world; and to prepare to be kings and priests in the next Age.—Eph. 4:12; Matt. 24:14; Rev. 1:6; 20:6.

THAT the hope for the world lies in the blessings of knowledge and opportunity to be brought to all by Christ's Millennial Kingdom—the restitution of all that was lost in Adam, to all the willing and obedient, at the hands of their Redeemer and his glorified Church—when all the willfully wicked will be destroyed.—Acts 3:19-23; Isa. 35.

Notes: *This statement is printed in each issue of* The Herald of Christ's Kingdom, *the periodical of the Pastoral Bible Institute, one of the earliest rivals of what is now known as Jehovah's Witnesses.*

Southcottites

SOME OF THE TRUTHS FOR WHICH THE CHRISTIAN ISRAELITE CHURCH STANDS

We believe the Holy Bible to be the Word of God. We believe in the Fall of man from an immortal life by the Spirit of God (in the image of God) to a mortal life of blood with an evil heart—which became the image of fallen man (Gen. 5: 3)—resulting from the disobedience of Adam and Eve, our first parents (Gen. 2:17). Death of the physical body was thus introduced because of the evil contamination. The Fall of man was permitted (Rom. 8:20), foreseen and provided for in God's plan of Salvation (Acts 15:18) to work out for mankind a greater weight of glory (2 Cor. 4:17).

By faith "we trust in the living God who is the Saviour of All men, specially of those that believe" (1 Tim. 4:10). Hence, the souls of all who die will rise again at God's appointed times, with spiritual (celestial) bodies; their physical bodies having returned to dust will be no more (Gen. 3:19). The dead in Christ (who have accepted Him as their personal Saviour) will enter upon their reward at the First Resurrection, they being "children of the Resurrection" equal unto the angels (Luke 20:36). The Unrepentant also will rise and be judged, but will be returned to their graves; this is the "Second death." They will remain there until the Second Resurrection, 1,000 years later (at the end of the Millenium), when they also will come forth and acknowledge Jesus Christ as their Saviour. For at the Name of Jesus, every knee shall bow, "of things in heaven and things in earth, and things under the earth" (Phill. 2:10). This great consummation has been made possible by the Obedience and Sacrifice of God's Son, Jesus Christ; for God required the shedding of the blood of a pure and sinless man for man's transgressions—and He alone could provide that requirement. He having died for the ungodly, and tasted death for every man (Rom. 5:6; Heb. 2:9), hence, "as in Adam all die, even so in Christ, shall ALL be made alive; but every man in his own order" (1 Cor. 15:22-23).

But we believe that besides celestial bodies there also are bodies terrestrial; "the glory of the celestial is one, and the glory of the terrestrial is another" (1 Cor. 15:40). God has an Elect number, whom He foreknew, and pre-destinated to be conformed to the image of His Son (Rom. 11:2 and 8:29). They will NOT DIE, for their physical bodies will be Cleansed of all evil, and changed like unto the glorified terrestrial body of "flesh and bone," as manifested by Jesus Christ (Phill. 3:21; Luke 24:39); blood not being their life, but living by the Abiding Presence of the Spirit of God.

We believe that in the year 1822 the Lord selected a "Messenger" to revive and preach the "Gospel of the Kingdom" embracing the abolition of death, overthrow of Satan, and the establishment of the Kingdom of God upon earth.

The Elect number (Rev. 7:4; Matt. 24: 22-24, 31) will be descendants of the Twelve sons of Jacob, whose name God changed to Israel; Two tribes of whom are the people known as Jews, and the other Ten tribes being at present in Christian churches—ignorant of the great destiny which is their inheritance. Hitherto they have been content with the assurance of the Salvation of the Soul alone (1 Peter 1:9), but when they hear the Gospel of the salvation of the whole being (spirit, and Soul and Physical Body, 1 Thess 5:23) and of Israel's Ingathering (Isa. 11:11-12) in these "latter days," they will come forth and surname themselves by the name of Israel, as foretold in Isaiah 44:5 and thereafter will be known as Christian Israelites. As the distinction implies, they will observe the dual obligation of both Gospel and Law as did Jesus Christ (Matt. 23: 2-3; Luke 10: 25-27; John 5: 46-47), who left us an example that we should follow in His steps (1 Peter 2:21). HE is the foundation upon whom we build; "for other foundation can no man lay than that is laid, which is Jesus Christ" (1 Cor. 3:11). This glorious manifestation of Faith in Action will be reinforced by God's Holy Spirit descending upon His "Chosen Remnant." The evil within their physical bodies will pass away, and their whole being will be preserved Alive unto the Second Coming of Jesus Christ, when they will be Purified (Dan. 12:10) and Glorified by their mortal bodies putting on PHYSICAL IMMORTALITY. In them will be fulfilled those words of Jesus in John 14: 12, "He that believeth on Me, the works that I do shall he do also." "They shall be known among the Gentiles, and all that see them shall acknowledge them that they are the seed which the Lord hath blessed" (Isa 61:9). When "Born again" by God's Holy Spirit being grafted "within" them, they then will possess the Kingdom of God within them; the Law of the Spirit of Life in Christ Jesus making them free from the law of sin and death (Rom. 8:2).

Notes: *Understanding the statement of the Christian Israelite Church requires some background of the movement begun by Joanna Southcott. The "messenger" mentioned in the text is John Wroe, a follower of Southcott. Following her failure to bear a child in 1814 as predicted, Southcott died, leaving her movement in disarray. She was succeeded in leadership by George Turner, who predicted the appearance of the child, Shiloh, in 1820, and then in 1821. John Wroe had stepped forward to denounce Turner's prophecies as false. He rose to leadership when Turner's predictions failed, and in 1822 reorganized the Southcott following.*

*　　　*　　　*

British Israelism

THE ANGLO-SAXON-CELTIC-ISRAEL BELIEF (ANGLO-SAXON FEDERATION OF AMERICA)

We believe in God—the God of the Bible (*Ex. 3: 6, 14*).

We believe in Jesus Christ, the only begotten Son of God (*John 1:14*).

We believe in the atoning sacrifice of Jesus Christ on Calvary (*Matt. 26:28; Rom. 5*).

We believe Christ died for us (*Rom. 5:8*); also that He was raised up from the dead (*Rom. 6:4*).

We believe He ascended into Heaven (*Mk. 16:19*).

We believe John 3:16—"For God so loved the world that He gave His only begotten Son, that whosoever believeth in Him should not perish, but have everlasting life."

We believe in the Holy Ghost and His mission (*John 14:26; Acts 2*).

We believe the whole Bible, both the Old Testament and the New Testament; that it is the inerrant Word of God (*II Pet. 1:19-21*). We believe its history; its covenants; its prophecies.

We believe in its Gospel of Grace (*Acts 20:24; Eph. 2:1-8*), which is the Gospel of Salvation for all men; that *personal* salvation by faith in the atonement of Jesus Christ is necessary for *all*, Israelite, Jew, Gentile (*Rom. 3:22-25*).

We also believe in the Gospel of the Kingdom (*Matt. 4:23, 24:14*).

We believe in the bodily return of Christ (*Acts 1:9-11*), who will take the Throne of David (*Isa. 9:6-7; Lk. 1:32*), and rule on this earth for a thousand years (*Rev. 20:1-6*).

We believe the Bible contains God's plan for the remedy of all human ills, and we believe that plan is working out through the Bible people, called Israel (*II Sam. 7*).

We believe this people Israel, consisting of twelve tribes (*Ex. 28:21; Rev. 21:12*), the descendants of the twelve sons of Jacob (*Gen. 49*), were chosen of God to be His servant people (*Ex. 19:5; Deut. 7:6-8*), through whom all nations are to be blessed (*Gen. 22:18*).

We find that through Israel God has revealed Himself ever since the days of Moses (*Ex. 19; Matt. 15:24*). To them He gave the law (*Ex. 20*). Through their prophets came the inspired Scriptures. Our Lord was of that race (*Matt. 1*), and is Prophet, Priest and King. His Apostles also were of Israel, and we believe the Divine plan is still working through that appointed race.

Bible history shows that twelve-tribed Israel, after a checkered career covering some five centuries, came to its greatest historic development in Palestine under Kings David and Solomon (*II Sam. 7; I Kings 10*). Upon the death of King Solomon there was civil war among the tribes of Israel. Ten tribes revolted and set up the "House" or "Kingdom" of Israel, known as the Northern Kingdom, having its capital in Semaria. The remaining tribes became the "House" or "Kingdom" of Judah and were known as the Southern Kingdom (*I Kings 12*). The Royal line of the House of David remained for a time with the Southern Kingdom and its kings reigned from the throne in Jerusalem.

This divided condition continued for about two hundred and fifty years. Then, because of wicked conduct and defiance of God, the Northern Kingdom, or "House of Israel," was overthrown as the result of several military invasions by the Assyrian Empire and the people were driven into captivity in northern Assyria. Following that, as time went on, they disappeared from history (*II Kings 17*).

The Southern Kingdom, or "House of Judah," kept itself intact for approximately another hundred and thirty years. Then, because of national decadence and rebellion against God, it was repeatedly attacked by the armies of the Babylonian Empire and eventually conquered. Its people were taken into captivity by the Babylonians where they were destined to remain for a period of seventy years (*II Chron, 36:21; Jer. 25:9-11*). It was at the time of the captivity of the Southern Kingdom that the term "Jew" began to be used and it applied only to the remnant of Judah (*II Kings 18:26; Jer. 41:3*).

At the close of this exile period, a "remnant" of these Babylonian captives of the House of Judah were permitted to return to Jerusalem and establish themselves therein (*Ezra and Nehemiah*). During this resettlement of the land of Palestine the Nation of the Jews came into being. These returned captives were thereafter generally known as Jews (*Ezra 4:12*) and their descendants were the Jews of the time of Jesus (*Matt. 2:2*).

It will thus be seen that it is wholly erroneous to say that the Jews constitute all of Israel when they actually came only from the Southern Kingdom. Jews who can trace their ancestry through Judah to Abraham are of Israel, just as Georgia is a part of the United States. But just as it is absurd to say that all in the United States are Georgians, it is equally absurd to say that all Israelites are Jews.

The differentiation made in the Scriptures between "Israel" and "Judah" must not be overlooked or ignored (*see I Kings 12; Jer. 3:6-11; Ps. 114:1-2; Ex. 37; Zech. 11:7-14; II Chron. 10, 11, etc.*). They are by no means interchangeable terms. *To realize this is to possess the key to the identity of the true Israel of God in the world today.*

Diligent research into the Bible and historical records has disclosed the fact that the Anglo-Saxon-Celtic peoples are the lineal descendants of the House of Israel. Supporting proof is found in the records of heraldry, the findings of archaeology and in a study of ethnology and philology.

When the people of the Northern Kingdom went into Assyrian captivity, they did not remain there. During the subsequent dissolution of the Assyrian power through its involvement in foreign wars, the people of Israel escaped in successive independent waves, leaving the land of their captors when the opportunity came to do so. Under different names (*Scutai, Sak-Geloths, Massagetae, Khumri, Cimmerians, Goths, Ostrogoths, Visigoths, etc.*), they moved westward into the wilderness, across Asia Minor, then into Europe and eventually into the Scandinavian countries and the British Isles. From the "Isles of the Sea" they went further westward to the "desolate heritages" of the North American continent and to Australia, New Zealand, etc.

In the prophetic Scriptures many references are made to this Great Trek of the House of Israel. The records of medieval history reveal the emergence from time to time of bands of virile people of mysterious origin, who left their mark upon the course of empire wherever they appeared. These were the trekking tribes of Israel, whose identity had been lost to themselves but not to God (*Amos 9:9*).

The Gentile kingdoms are being broken, and heathen powers coming to judgment, while the time of Israel's punishment is terminating. The old Gentile social order is disintegrating, to be replaced by the restoration of the Kingdom of God on the earth. The world is being prepared for the coming and reign of our Lord upon the Throne of David and the institution of the Age of Righteousness when "out of Zion shall go forth the law, and the word of the Lord from Jerusalem" (Isa. 2:2-5).

We believe the Israel peoples must and will, under God, lead the world out of the chaos which now afflicts mankind (Isa. 2:1-4). After much chastisement for their sins, the favor of God will again be upon them for the blessing of the world. "I do not this for your sakes, O house of Israel, but for mine holy name's sake" (Ez. 36:22-32).

We do not constitute a new sect or a new religion. We are Christians of many denominations who have formed a nonprofit educational center with the single purpose of getting the Bibles of America opened to permit them to present their entire revelation. We stress particularly the neglected fact of the modern identity of the Israel of God and the necessity to restore in our nation the administration of the Law of the Lord, for this is the Gospel of the Kingdom. We encourage a more complete grasp of the Biblical message of personal salvation and national redemption, for a consideration of the whole story the Bible tells will open to one's understanding the vast hemisphere of national and prophetic truths which we must all soon take into account.

Notes: *The British Israelite groups are distinguished by their belief in the identity of modern Anglo-Saxon people (especially those of the United States and Great Britain) as the literal descendents of the Ten Lost Tribes of ancient Israel, and thus heirs to all of the Old Testament prophecies given about Israel. Most groups have not committed their beliefs to a summary format.*

The statement of the Anglo-Saxon Federation of America details the understanding of the history of Israel and the Anglo-Saxon people held by most British Israelites.

* * *

WE BELIEVE (BRITISH ISRAEL WORLD FEDERATION)

AS ORTHODOX CHRISTIANS—OF ALL DENOMINATIONS—WE BELIEVE:

That our Lord Jesus Christ is the Son of God: that He spoke with the authority of Almighty God and that He meant what He said.

That our civilisation is approaching the Crisis so precisely foreseen and described by Him and that the End-of-the-Age sequence of events indicated by Him, revealing a tremendous upsurge of evil, has been reflected in the crescendo of visitations which have scourged mankind since the early days of the present century. We emphasize our positive conviction that the world at this moment stands on the threshold of a New Age and that this will be heralded by the promised Personal return of the King of kings. As a non-sectarian, interdenominational Movement, we urge Christians who truly accept the whole Gospel of

Christ to prepare themselves for His Imminent Second Coming.

That we—the English-speaking Nations—with our kinsfolk among the peoples of the North Sea fringe, embody the bulk of the present-day descendants of God's ancient people of Israel. As responsible servants He has commissioned us to form the core of His Kingdom on earth, bearing the Gospel of Jesus as our watchword, under the guidance of the Church of Christ.

We assert, therefore, that our associated peoples are none other than God's promised Company of Nations—the Commonwealth of Israel—which the Scriptures declare will be the nucleus of His earthly Kingdom, now open to all who will accept Jesus as Lord and Saviour, whatever may be their race or color.

We are able to adduce secular evidence to prove that the forebears of our kindred Celto-Saxon peoples originated in Bible lands. The Jewish folk of today contain only a residue of the people of Israel.

Notes: *This brief statement summarizes the British-Israel position.*

* * *

DOCTRINAL STATEMENT OF BELIEFS (CHRISTIAN IDENTITY CHURCH)

The following is a brief statement of our major doctrinal beliefs as taught by the Holy Scriptures. This list is not exhaustive, but a basic digest defining the true faith once delivered to the saints. For a further explanation of our beliefs and the implications of these truths, please contact us.

We believe in YHVH the one and only true and living eternal God (Isa. 44:6); the God of our fathers Abraham, Isaac and Jacob (Exo. 3:14-16), the Creator of all things (1 Cor. 8:6) who is omnipotent, omnipresent, unchangeable and all-knowing; the Great I Am who is manifested in three beings: God the Father, God the Son, and God the Holy Spirit, all one God (Deut. 6:4).

We believe the entire Bible, both Old and New Testaments, as originally inspired, to be the inerrant, supreme, revealed Word of God. The history, covenants, and prophecy of this Holy Book were written for and about a specific elect family of people who are children of YHVH God (Luke 3:38; Psalm 82:6) through the seedling of Adam (Gen. 5:1). All scripture is written as a doctrinal standard for our exhortation, admonition, correction, instruction and example; the whole counsel to be believed, taught and followed (II Tim. 3:16, Act. 20:27).

We believe Yahshua the Messiah (Jesus the Christ) to be the only incarnate begotten son of God, the Word made flesh (John 1:14), born of the Virgin Mary in fulfillment of divine prophecy (Isa. 7:14; Luke 1:27) at the appointed time, having had His eternal existence as one with the Father before the world was (John 17:5, 21-22).

We believe in the personally revealed being of God the Holy Spirit, the Comforter (John 15:26, 16:7), who was sent by God the Son to glorify Him (John 16:14) and teach us all truth (John 14:26, 16:13; I Cor. 2:10-12) according to promise (Ezek. 36:25-27; Acts 2:33; Eph. 1:13-14). The Holy Spirit is sent to dwell in (I Cor. 3:16; John 14:17) the members of the body of Christ, giving unto each different gifts (1 Cor. 12) empowering them to witness (Acts 1:8) of sin, of righteousness, and of judgement (John 16:8-11). Natural man cannot know the things of the Spirit (John 14:17; I Cor. 2:14), which God sent forth to His sons (Gal. 4:6), thus identifying the children of Israel (Isa. 44:1-3, 59:20-21; Haggai 2:5; Rom. 8:16) in this world.

We believe that God the Son, Yahshua the Messiah (Jesus Christ), became man in order to redeem His people Israel (Luke 1:68) as a kinsman of the flesh (Heb. 2:14-16; Rom. 9:3-5); died as the Passover Lamb of God on the Cross of Calvary finishing His perfect atoning sacrifice for the remission of our sins (Matt. 26:28); He arose from the grave on the third day (1 Cor. 15:4) triumphing over death; and ascended into Heaven where He is now reigning at the right hand of God (Mark 16:19).

We believe in the literal return to this Earth of Yahshua the Messiah (Jesus Christ) in like manner as He departed (Acts 1:11), to take the Throne of David (Isa. 9:7; Luke 1:32) and establish His everlasting Kingdom (Dan. 2:44; Luke 1:33; Rev. 11:15). Every knee shall bow and every tongue shall confess that He is King of kings and Lord of lords (Phil. 2:10-11; 1 Tim. 6:14-15).

We believe Salvation is by grace through faith, not of works (Eph. 2:8-9). Eternal life is the gift of God through the redemption that is in our Saviour Yahshua (Jesus Christ) (Rom. 6:23) who will reward every man according to his works (Rev. 22:12).

We believe membership in the church of Yahshua our Messiah (Jesus Christ) is by Divine election (John 6:44, 65, 15:16; Acts 2:39, 13:48; Rom. 9:11, 11:7; II Thes. 2:13). God foreknew, chose and predestined the Elect from before the foundation of the world (Psalm 139:16; Jer. 1:5; Matt. 25:34; Rom. 8:28-30; Eph. 1:4-5; II Tim. 1:9; Rev. 13:8) according to His perfect purpose and sovereign will (Rom. 9:19-23). Only the called children of God can come to the Savior to hear His words and believe; those who are not of God, cannot hear his voice (John 8:47, 10:26-27).

We believe Yahshua the Messiah (Jesus the Christ) came to redeem (a word meaning purchase back according to the law of kinship) only His people Israel (Psalm 130:7-8; Isa. 54:5; Matt. 10:5-6, 15:24; Gal. 4:4-5) who are His portion and inheritance (Deut. 32:9).

We believe individual Israelites are destined for judgement (II Cor. 5:10; Heb. 9:27) and must believe on the only begotten Son of God, Yahshua the Messiah (Jesus Christ), in whom only there is salvation (Acts 4:12), that they be not condemned (John 3:18; Mark 16:16). Each individual Israelite must repent, putting off the old corrupt man and become a new creature (Eph. 4:22-24; II Cor. 5:17) walking in the newness of life (Rom. 6:4). This spiritual rebirth (John 3:3-6; I Peter 1:23) being necessary for a personal relationship with our Savior.

We believe in water baptism by immersion according to the Scriptures for all true believers; being buried into the death of Yahshua the Messiah (Jesus Christ) for the remission of our sins and in the likeness of His resurrection being raised up into the newness of life (Rom. 6:3-6). Baptism being ordained of God a testimony to the New Covenant as circumcision was under the Old Covenant (Col. 2:11-13).

We believe Yahshua the Messiah (Jesus Christ) to be our only High Priest (1 Tim. 2:5; Heb. 3:1, 6:20, 7:17, 24-25) and head over His body of called-out saints, the Church (Rom. 12:5; 1 Cor. 12:12, 27; Eph. 1:22-23, 4:12, 5:23, 30; Col. 1:18, 24). His bride, the wife of the Lamb, is the twelve tribes of the children of Israel (Isa. 54:5; Jer. 3:14; Hosea 2:19-20; Rev. 21:9-12).

We believe God chose unto Himself a special race of people that are above all people upon the face of the earth (Deut. 7:6; Amos 3:2). These children of Abraham through the called-out seedline of Isaac and Jacob (Psalm 105:6; Rom. 9:7) were to be a blessing to all the families of the earth who bless them and a cursing to those that curse them (Gen. 12:3). The descendants of the twelve sons of Jacob, called "Israel," were married to God (Isa. 54:5), have not been cast away (Rom. 11:1-2), have been given the adoption, glory, covenants, law, service of God, and promises; are the ones to whom the Messiah came (Rom. 9:4-5) electing out of all twelve tribes those who inherit the Kingdom of God (Rev. 7:4, 21:12).

We believe that the New Covenant was made with the Children of Israel, the same people the Old Covenant was made with (Jer. 31:31-33; Heb. 8:8-10) in fulfillment of the mercy promised our forefathers (Luke 1:72).

We believe the White, Anglo-Saxon, Germanic and kindred people to be God's true, literal Children of Israel. Only this race fulfills every detail of Biblical Prophecy and World History concerning Israel and continues in these latter days to be heirs and possessors of the Covenants, Prophecies, Promises and Blessings YHVH God made to Israel. This chosen seedline making up the "Christian Nations" (Gen. 35:11; Isa. 62:2; Acts 11:26) of the earth stands far superior to all other peoples in their call as God's servant race (Isa. 41:8, 44:21; Luke 1:54). Only these descendants of the 12 tribes of Israel scattered abroad (James 1:1; Deut. 4:27; Jer. 31:10; John 11:52) have carried God's Word, the Bible, throughout the world (Gen. 28:14; Isa. 43:10-12, 59:21), have used His Laws in the establishment of their civil governments and are the "Christians" opposed by the Satanic Anti-Christ forces of this world who do not recognize the true and living God (John 5:23, 8:19, 16:2-3).

We believe in an existing being known as the Devil or Satan and called the Serpent (Gen. 3:1; Rev. 12:9), who has a literal "seed" or posterity in the earth (Gen. 3:15) commonly called Jews today (Rev. 2:9; 3:9; Isa. 65:15). These children of Satan (John 8:44-47; Matt. 13:38; John 8:23) through Cain (1 John 3:12) are a race of vipers (Matt. 23:31-33), anti-Christs (1 John 2:22, 4:3) who have throughout history always been a curse to true Israel, the Children of God, because of a natural enmity between the two races (Gen. 3:15), because they do the works of their father the Devil (John 8:38-44), and because they please not God, and are contrary to all men (1 Thes. 2:14-15), though they often pose as ministers of righteousness (II Cor. 11: 13:15). The ultimate end of this evil race whose hands bear the blood of our Savior (Matt. 27:25) and all the righteous slain upon the earth (Matt. 23:35), is Divine judgement (Matt. 13:38-42, 15:13; Zech. 14:21).

We believe that the Man Adam (a Hebrew word meaning: ruddy, to show blood, flush, turn rosy) is father of the White Race only. As a son of God (Luke 3:38), made in His likeness (Gen. 5:1), Adam and his descendants, who are also the children of God (Psalm 82:6; Hos. 1:10; Rom. 8:16; Gal. 4:6; 1 John 3:1-2), can know YHVH God as their Father, not merely as their creator. Adamic man is made trichotomous, that is, not only of body and soul, but having an implanted spirit (Gen. 2:7; I Thes. 5:23; Heb. 4:12) giving him a higher form of consciousness and distinguishing him from all the other races of the earth (Deut. 7:6, 10:15; Amos 3:2).

We believe that as a chosen race, elected by God (Deut. 7:6, 10:15; I Peter 2:9), we are not to be partakers of the wickedness of this world system (I John 2:15; James 4:4; John 17:9, 15, 16), but are called to come out and be a separated people (II Cor. 6:17; Rev. 18:4; Jer. 51:6; Exodus 33:16; Lev. 20:24). This includes segregation from all non-white races, who are prohibited in God's natural divine order from ruling over Israel (Deut. 17:15, 28:13; 32:8; Joel 2:17; Isa. 13:14; Gen. 1:25-26; Rom. 9:21). Race-mixing is an abomination in the sight of Almighty God, a satanic attempt meant to destroy the chosen seedline, and is strictly forbidden by His commandments (Exo. 34:14-16; Num. 25:1-13; I Cor. 10:8; Rev. 2:14; Deut. 7:3-4; Joshua 23:12-13; I Kings 11:1-3; Ezra 9:2, 10-12; 10:10-14; Neh. 10:28-30, 13:3, 27; Hosea 5:7; Mal. 2:11-12).

We believe sin is transgression of God's Law (I John 3:4; Rom. 3:31, 7:7) and that all have sinned (Rom. 3:23). Only through knowledge of God's Law as given in His Commandments, Statutes and Judgments, can we define and know what sin is. We are to keep and teach the laws of God (Matt. 5:17-19) on both a personal and national basis.

We believe God gave Israel His Laws for their own good (Deut. 5:33). Theocracy being the only perfect form of government, and God's divine Law for governing a nation being far superior to man's laws, we are not to add to or diminish from His commandments (Deut. 4:1-2). All present world problems are a result of disobedience to the Laws of God, which if kept will bring blessings and if disregarded will bring cursings (Deut. 28).

We believe men and women should conduct themselves according to the role of their gender in the traditional Christian sense that God intended. Homosexuality is an abomination before God and should be punished by death (Lev. 18:22, 20:13; Rom. 1:24-28, 32; I Cor. 6:9).

We believe that the United States of America fulfills the prophesied (II Sam. 7:10, Isa. 11:12; Ezek. 36:24) place where Christians from all the tribes of Israel would be regathered. It is here in this blessed land (Deut. 15:6, 28:11, 33:13-17) that God made a small one a strong nation (Isa. 60:22), feeding His people with knowledge and understanding through Christian pastors (Jer. 3:14-15) who have carried the light of truth and blessings unto the nations of the earth (Isa. 49:6, 2:2-3; Gen. 12:3). North America is the wilderness (Hosea 2:14) to which God brought the dispersed seed of Israel, the land between two seas (Zech. 9:10), surveyed and divided by rivers (Isa. 18:1-2,7), where springs of water and streams break out and the desert blossoms as the rose (Isa. 35:1,6-7).

We believe the ultimate destiny of all history will be the establishment of the Kingdom of God upon this earth (Psalm 37:9, 11, 22; Isa. 11:9; Matt. 5:5, 6:10; Rev. 21:2-3) with Yahshua our Messiah (Jesus Christ) reigning as King of kings over the house of Jacob forever, of this kingdom and dominion there shall be no end (Luke 1:32-33; Dan. 2:44, 7:14; Zech. 14:9). When our Savior returns to restore righteous government on the earth, there will be a day of reckoning when the kingdoms of this world become His (Rev. 11:15; Isa. 9:6-7) and all evil shall be destroyed (Isa. 13:9; Mal. 4:3; Matt. 13:30, 41:42; II Thes. 2:8). His elect Saints will be raised immortal at His return (I Cor. 15:52-53; I Thes. 4:16; Rev. 20:6) to rule and reign with Him as kings and priests (Rom. 8:17; II Tim. 2:12; Rev. 5:10; Exodus 19:6; Dan. 7:18, 27).

Notes: *In its use of the names "YHWH" and "Yahshua" as the proper designations for God and Christ, this statement shows the influence of the Sacred Name Movement which has affected the theology of many modern British-Israel organizations. However, unlike most Sacred Name and British-Israel groups, the Christian Identity Church is trinitarian; its doctrinal statement contains a strong affirmation of the personality of the Holy Spirit. Baptism is by immersion. The statement highlights the beliefs of many modern British-Israel groups such as the church's position on the white race, the identity of present-day Israel, and the place of the United States in God's plan.*

* * *

ARTICLES OF FAITH AND DOCTRINE (CHURCH OF ISRAEL)

THE CHURCHES OF ISRAEL. Diocese of Manasseh, United States of America, issue the ARTICLES OF FAITH AND DOCTRINE which set forth the tenets of religious belief and conviction for the Covenant People, who combine and covenant themselves together under authority of Jesus Christ in pursuant to His Word in the historic Christian Faith and Birthright of our Fathers, under the protection of the United States Constitution and of the various State Constitutions under which religious freedom and association is guaranteed. These Articles of Faith and Doctrine provide the ground and foundation for the CHURCHES OF ISRAEL in the establishment of religious belief and conscience. These principles and tenets of faith will govern all Christian Israel people who covenant and combine themselves together under the name THE CHURCH OF ISRAEL.

RELIGIOUS LIBERTY

The Churches of Israel humbly acknowledge before Jesus Christ our appreciation of the inalienable rights of freemen to assemble before Almighty God and to read and interpret the Holy Scriptures in free religious association together. For the protection of these rights under the

United States Constitution, and the various State Constitutions where the Churches of Israel are organized, we give special and prayerful acknowledgement to Jesus Christ, and to the Christian Fathers, who bled and died that the Faith once delivered to the Saints would not perish from the earth. Moreover, we give thanks to Jesus Christ, that through him and pursuant to His Word, we have the right to organize a Church, and that such Churches receive their Christian Common Law Charter from the Holy Bible which is the ground and foundation of the Christian State.

CHRISTIAN PRESUPPOSITIONS

The Articles of Faith and Doctrine are set forth in terms of presuppositional statements. These presuppositions become the cornerstones of the religious tenets of faith espoused by Christian Israelites who seek to stand under the Blood of Jesus Christ, who seek to walk by His immutable Law Word, and who seek to walk in communion with the Holy Spirit. These presuppositions are intended to build a valid, consistent and systematic theology, a House of Faith, that will be built upon Jesus Christ the Rock and upon His Word in all of the Churches of Israel throughout the Diocese of Manasseh, the United States of America.

EPISTEMOLOGY

WE BELIEVE that all members of the CHURCH OF ISRAEL are required to have a valid Christian Epistemology (valid theory of knowledge). Yahweh must be the reference point for the beginning of all thought. The Christian presupposes God as the premise of knowledge. God, who alone created all factuality, and revealed it to His children (Deut. 29:29) must alone give the meaning for all revealed knowledge through His Holy Scripture. Apart from God, man can know nothing. The source of all truth is God. Only in His light can we see light. (Psm. 36.9) Only by thinking God's thoughts after Him (Holy Scripture) can we know truth. Scripture: Genesis 1.1-3, 3.1-5, Deut. 6.1-9, 30.15-20, Job 32.8, 42.1-3, Psa. 19.1-14, 33.11, 78.1-7, Provl. 1.1-7, 3.1-20, 4.1-5, 23.23, Eccl. 3.14, 12.13-14, Isa. 28.9-10, 55.8-11, Matt. 5.6, 16, 18, 6.22, 33, 7.24-29, Luke 4.4, John 14.26-27, John 16.13, 17.17, Acts 15.18, 17.28, Rom. 1. 18-20, I Cor. 2.6-16, 3. 11-13, I Cor. 12.5-11, Phil. 2.5, James 1.5-8, II Tim 3.7, Heb. 11.1-7, and I John 2.27.

DOCTRINAL IMPLICATIONS OF EPISTEMOLOGY: The Doctrine of Knowledge, The Doctrine of the Law of Faith, and the Doctrine of Conceptual Thinking.

BIBLIOLOGY

WE BELIEVE that the ultimate authority for Adam Man and the creation is the Revealed, Transcendent, Mediated Word of Yahweh, i.e., His Law Command Word as contained in the Holy Scriptures. The Holy Bible contains the infallible, inherent Word of God. The sufficiency of the Holy Scriptures for the Elect is certain; the sixty-six books of the historic canon are all that is necessary for building Christian Doctrine. The Books of the Apocrypha and the Pseudipigrapha are good for instruction and amplification and should, next to the Bible, be the chief source of all truth for the Christian. Scripture: Gen. 5.1, Deut. 4.2, 6.6-9, 8.3, 19.15, 29.29, Psalms 12.6, 119.89, 105, 142, 160,

Proverbs 30.5, Jer. 23.18, 29, Isa. 55.11, 59.21, Matt. 7.24-27, 18.16, Mark 14.49, Luke 21.33, John 1.1-14, 5.39, 10.35, 12.48, 17.17, Acts 17.11, Rom. 10.17, 15.4, Matt. 4.4, Eph. 6.17, Heb. 4.12, I Tim. 5.19, II Cor. 10.11, 13.1, John 20.31, I John 5.13, II Tim. 3.15-16, II Tim. 2.15.

DOCTRINAL IMPLICATIONS OF BIBLIOLOGY: The Doctrine of Scripture, The Doctrine of the Undivided Word, The Doctrine of Bible Numerics, The Study of Bible Hermeneutics, The Doctrine of Transcendance, and the History and Transmission of the Holy Scriptures. The Churches of Israel in the English-speaking world stand upon the Authorized King James Version of the Bible. This position is defended in a series of sermon lessons entitled "Defending the King James Version of the Bible," available on cassette tape.

COSMOLOGY

WE BELIEVE as the Elect in Christ that there exist two different kinds of being, i.e., the Uncreated and the Created, Yahweh is one kind, the UNCREATED. All the Created Universe (including the Angelic hosts) is the other Kind, the CREATED. The Universe and all that therein is was created and spoken into existence. The created cannot transcend into the Being of God. The line between the Uncreated and the Created cannot be transcended by the created. Scripture: Genesis 1.1-31, Genesis 2.1-7, Psalm 33.1-9, 95.5, Isaiah 45.12, 48.13, Jer. 51.15-16, and Hebrews 11.3.

DOCTRINAL IMPLICATIONS OF COSMOLOGY: The Doctrine of Creation, The Doctrine of Kind after His Kind, The Doctrine of Seed in Itself, The Law of the Sabbath, and The Divine Biblical Calendar.

THE BEING OF GOD

WE BELIEVE that Yahweh is one God, one God in three subsistences, God the Father, Son, and Holy Ghost. ALL ONE GOD! His relationship to Himself is ontological, and His relationship to His creation is transcendent, providential, and economical. The belief in the One, Holy, Triune God of Scripture is summarized in the words of the Schell City creedal statement, which reads, "I Believe in one true and everliving, self-existing and uncreated God, whose Name is YAHWEH, and in the Unity of His Being, there exist three subsistences of one essence, substance, power and eternity, God the Father, Son, and Holy Ghost, all one God, world without end." This One, Holy, and True God created the world, sustains the world, governs the world, and will one day judge His children in righteousness. The "unity" and the "triunity" of the one true God is of profound significance in building a House of Faith. Scripture: Genesis 1.1, 1.26, Es. 20.3, Deut. 6.4, Isa. 43.15, Isa. 6.3, Isa. 44.6-8, Mark 12.29-30, I Cor. 8.4-6, I Tim. 2.5, James 2.19, Matt. 3.16-17, Matt. 28.19, Mark 1.9-11, John 1.1-14, II Cor. 4.4, I Pet. 1.2, Num. 6.22-27, Isa. 6.9, Micah 5.2, Psa. 86.10, Isa. 45.6, John 17.3, II Cor. 13.14, John 2.28-29, 8. 17-18, 42, 58, 10.30, 10.38, 12.45, 14.9-10, 16.27-38, I John 5.7, Num. 6.24-26, I Pet. 1.2, Mark 1.9-11, Heb. 1.3, and Col. 1.15.

DOCTRINAL IMPLICATIONS OF THE BEING OF GOD: The Doctrine of the Triune God, The Doctrine of the Unity of Yahweh, The Doctrine of the Triunity of

ARTICLES OF FAITH AND DOCTRINE (CHURCH OF ISRAEL) (continued)

Yahweh, The Doctrine of the One and the Many, and The Doctrine of the Divine Name & Titles for the Unity and the Triunity of Yahweh.

ANGELOLOGY

WE BELIEVE that Angels are created beings, one step above Adam Man, who were all created to dwell in immortal, celestial bodies. Angels are subject to all of the Laws of God and were all created good. A portion of those Angels participated in a rebellion against God in the government of heaven (Rev. 12.4-9), were cast out into the earth (Rev. 12.9), and then went after strange flesh (Jude 6-7, II Peter 2.4, Heb. 2.2, Gen. 6.1-4). The offspring of the sinful Angels who cohabited with the daughters of Adam were the giants or Nephilim (fallen ones). The spirits of these out of kind beings are the demons or devils which Jesus Christ cast out. Mark 5.1-20, Mark 1.23-34, 3.14-15, 3.22, 5.1-20, 6.7-13, 9.14-29, 16.9-17, Luke 8.2, Luke 4.3-4, 9.1, 10.17, 13.16, 32.

The angels are classified in the government of God according to a rank or hierarchy. one order of Angels is assigned to minister to those who are the heirs of salvation. (Heb. 1.14, Psa. 34.7). Satan was, before his fall (Isa. 14.12-21, Rev. 12.7-9) the anointed cherub, standing at the head of all the realm of Angels (Ezek. 28.13-19). Satan has been defeated by the incarnation, atonement, and resurrection of Jesus Christ, and now holds dominion only when Christians will it to so be. Scripture: Genesis 2.1, Psa. 8.3-5, Job 1.6-7, 2.1, 38.7, Heb. 1.1-14, Rev. 12.7-9, Jude 6-13, II Pet. 2.4, Heb. 2.1-9, Rev. 12.1-4, Gen. 6.1-4, Rev. 20.1-2, Rev. Ch. 8, Rev. Ch. 16, I Cor. 6.2-3, Matt. 12.43-45, Mark 5.1-13.

DOCTRINAL IMPLICATIONS OF ANGELOLOGY: The Doctrine of Angels, The Government of Angels, The Ministry of Angels, The Doctrine of Satanology, The Doctrine of the Angels That Sinned, and the Doctrine of Demonology.

ANTHROPOLOGY

The man, Adam, was made (asah) trichotomous. His being was made from a created soul (Gen. 1.26-27), barah, a formed body (yatsar), and an implanted spirit. (Gen. 2.7). Adam was the particular of the Creation who was made in the image and after the likeness of Yahweh, the Ontological Triune God (Isa. 43.7), I Thess. 5.23, Heb. 4.12, Luke 1.46-47 Matt. 10.28, Eph. 4.23, and Psa. 35.9. The man, Adam, (Gen. 1.26) was made in the image and after the likeness of ELOHIYM (God), was told to be fruitful, multiply and replenish the earth, and was given the dominion mandate to subdue the earth and rule over all the creation. Scripture: Carefully study all of the following scriptures to see that Genesis 1.26-28 and Genesis 2.7 have reference to only Adam Kind Man. Genesis 5.1-3, 9.1-2, Psalm 8.1-9, St. Matthew 19.4-6, St. Mark 10.6-9. The Hebrew root word for the English word "man" is identical in both Genesis 1.26 and Genesis 2.7. Only the "souls" of Adam Kind Man were created in Genesis 1.27. The created soul (Gen. 1.27) was placed into a formed body (Genesis 2.7) and given an implanted spirit, that is, the breath of life.

Adam was the father of only one race on this earth, that is the caucasion race. The Hebrew root meaning for the English man is #119, 120, and 121. These numbers are catalogued in Strong's Exhaustive Concordance to the Holy Bible. #119 Aw-Dam—To show blood in the face, flush or turn rosey. Be dyed, made red (ruddy); #120 Aw-Dawm—Ruddy, i.e., a human being (an individual or the species, mankind, etc.) man, person; #121 Aw-dawm— The same as #120 . . . Adam, the name of the first man, also of a place in Palestine. All of the other races preceded Adam in this earth. All of the non-Caucasion races were on the earth before Adam was created. (Genesis 1.24-25). They were all created after the law of Kind after His Kind, and were pronounced by ELOHIYM to be very good. (Genesis 1.31). All races were created according to the Law of Kind after His Kind, and were to remain segregated in the habitat given each of them by the Eternal God.

THE DOCTRINAL IMPLICATIONS OF ANTHROPOLOGY: The Doctrine of Adam Man, The Study of Creationism, Traducianism and Pre-existence, The Examination of the Spirit, the Soul and the Body of Adam Man, The Terrestrial-Celestial Hypostatic Union of Adam Man before the Fall, The Doctrine of Adam Man and the Dominion Mandate, and The Study of Anthropoidology.

HARMARTIOLOGY

WE BELIEVE that the man, Adam, by the act of Original Sin, (Gen. 3.1-16) an act which follows a particular pathology (I John 2.15-17), transgressed God's Law, and by this act of disobedience, Adam lost his conditional immortality and came under the *Dominion of Death*. (Genesis 2.17, 3.22-24, Romans 5.12). By Adam's transgression he lost his hypostatic union of celestial-terrestrial existence (I Cor. 15.40, Gen. 2.25, 3.7-11) and all men came under the *Sentence of Death*. (Roman 3.9-23, 5.12, Gal. 3.22, Psa. 51.5 and Psa. 58.3). The malignity of Sin infected all the seed from Adam's loins (Romans 5.12, 17). By the Act of Original Sin, Adam lost the dominion to death and death reigned from Adam to Jesus Christ. (Col. 1.18, I Cor. 15.20, II Tim. 1.10, Rev. 1.18, Rom. 6.8-9, Heb. 2.14).

The Fall of Adam from dominion into death resulted in the fall of all the creation. (Rom. 8.19-23). Satan, being created immortal (Ezek. 28.15) and not subject to the organic laws of death, exercised the power of dominion by his own progeny or offspring which he placed in this earth, beginning with Cain. The serpent of Genesis 3.15 is Satan (Rev. 12.9 and 20.2) and Satan appeared as an angel of light in the Garden of Eden (Ezek. 28.13 and II Cor. 11.14). The two seeds of Genesis 3.15 are literal progeny or offspring (Hebrew zera) and the same Hebrew root word for the English word "seed" is used in the remainder of the Old Testament. You cannot spiritualize the two seeds of Genesis 3.15! To spiritualize the two seeds of Genesis 3.15 would do away with the existence of physical Israel coming from the same Hebrew root word (zera) "seed" as in Genesis 3.15. Cain was the progeny of the wicked one. I John 3.11-12, St. Matthew 13.38, 23.29-35, St. Luke 11.51

and John 8.44. Adam was not the father of Cain. (Genesis 5.1-32). For additional scripture read: I John 3.4, Romans 7.7, Romans 3.20, Gen. 6.5, 8.21, Isa. 58.1, Isa. 59.1-2, Isa. 64.6-12, Jer. 17.9-10, II Cor. 5.14-15, Psa. 52.2-3, Rom. 8.5-8, I Cor. 2.14.

THE DOCTRINAL IMPLICATIONS OF HARMARTIOLOGY: The Doctrine of Original Sin, The Doctrine of the Pathology of Sin, The Doctrine of the Two Seedlines, Satan's Family Tree, Adam's Family Tree, The Rights of the Firstborn as a Consequence of Original Sin, The Doctrine of Blood Sacrifice and Atonement for Sin, and The Doctrine of Kinsman Redemption.

CHRISTOLOGY

WE BELIEVE that the second subsistence of the Godhead, Jesus Christ, is very God of very God and became very man of very man, in order to Redeem His people Israel and to deliver His creation. Scripture: Isa. 7.14, John 1.1-14, Jer. 31.22. Heb. 10.5, I Cor. 15.38, Matt. 1.18-25, Luke 1.26-35, Luke 2.21, Isa. 66.7, Matt. 12.46, Heb. 2.16, Heb. 7.3, John 7.42, Isa. 11.1, Rev. 5.5, Rev. 22.16, II Tim. 2.8, Acts 13.23, Psa. 132.11, Acts 2.30. Rom. 9.5.

We believe that Jesus Christ was born of the virgin Mary without taint or spot of sin (I Pet. 1.19-20 and Heb. 9.14). We believe in one Jesus Christ, eternally begotten of the Father, very God and very man, perfect God, perfect man, and in this one Jesus Christ there exist two perfect natures, inseparably united, without division, change, confusion or comingling. We believe that Jesus Christ made an all sufficient and perfect sacrifice for sin and that by His atonement upon the cross he fulfilled and made perfect the Law of Blood Sacrifice, making a sufficient payment for the ransom and redemption of those He came to save.

We believe that justification to salvation is by the blood of Jesus Christ. We believe that Jesus Christ is the paschal lamb who came to redeem His people from the bondage of sin. We believe that Jesus Christ descended into Sheol and that He led the Elect in Christ (Old Testament Saints) from the prison of Sheol-Hades. We believe that the souls of the righteous are now in Paradise, expectant and awaiting the redemption of their body. We believe that Jesus Christ rose for the dead on the third day as the firstborn from the dead and the firstfruits of them that slept. We believe in the Doctrine of Eternal Life. We believe that Jesus Christ is both the first and the last Adam. We believe that Jesus Christ is the only mediator between God and man, and that He stands as Prophet, Priest and King, making daily intercession for His saints.

THE DOCTRINAL IMPLICATIONS OF CHRISTOLOGY: The Doctrine of the Incarnation (Virgin Birth), The Doctrine of the Two Perfect Natures of the One Jesus Christ, The Doctrine of the Atonement (Justification), The Doctrine of Christ the Passover Lamb, The Doctrine of Christ into Sheol, The Doctrine of paradise, The Doctrine of the Resurrection, The Doctrine of Eternal Life, The Doctrine of the First and the Last Adam, The Doctrine of Mediatorial Intercession, The Doctrine of Christ as Prophet, Priest and King, and The Feast of Passover and Unleavened Bread.

PNEUMATOLOGY

WE BELIEVE that God the Holy Spirit is the third subsistence of the one true and everliving Triune God. God the Holy Ghost visited and empowered the Church on the day of Pentecost and He gave them the power, the authority, and the modus operandi to bring forth the government of God into the earth and this Body became the Church Militant. The Head, Jesus Christ, came forth to create a new Adamic Body, the Redeemed Israel, the Church Militant, to whom was given power and authority in the creation and in time to take Dominion of the whole earth and to establish the Kingdom for Jesus Christ, the King, and to defend His Crown Rights. God the Holy Ghost is the Comforter, Teacher, Counselor, and Sustainer of the Church and from Him come all the Spiritual Gifts and Fruits of the Spirit. Scripture: Num. 6.27, Lam. 1.16, Psa. 51.11, Isa. 6.3, Deut. 30.6, Ezek. 36.24-27, Jer. 31.31-34, Isa. 59.21, Joel 2.28-32, John 14.15-27, John 15.26, John 16.7-14, Acts Ch. 2, I Cor. Ch. 12, Gal. 5.22-23.

DOCTRINAL IMPLICATIONS OF PNEUMATOLOGY: The Doctrine of the Holy Spirit, The Doctrine of the Empowering at Pentecost, The Doctrine of Sanctification, The spiritual Gifts of the Holy Spirit, The Fruits of the Holy Spirit, The Apostolic Doctrine of Tongues (Languages), and the Feast of Pentecost or Feast of Weeks.

SOTERIOLOGY

WE BELIEVE that Yahweh, in the council of His own will, elected and chose (John 15.16 and Rom. 9.11, 11.7) as His vice regents before the foundation of the world (Eph. 1.4, II Tim. 1.90, Matt. 24.34) Priests and Kings on the earth and in His creation, a seed of a race by His Grace. (Gen. 12.1-3, 17.1-7, Psa. 22.30, Amos. 3.2, Psa. 135.4, Exod. 19.5-6, Jer. 31.1). The Elect in Christ from the Seed of Abraham (Gen. 17.7, 21.12, Rom. 9.7) were chosen by God the Father, (I Pet. 1.2). Redeemed by God the Son, (Gal. 4.4-5), and Sanctified and called by God the Holy Spirit, all one and holy triune God. (I Pet. 12). The elect in Christ are His workmanship (Eph. 2.8-10) and are passive in the matter of their salvation. They are made willing and repentent vessels of His mercy by the Grace of Jesus Christ, and are made holy by the atoning blood of Jesus Christ. (Psa. 65.4, 110.3, Rom. 2.4, I Cor. 1.29-31, II Cor. 4.6, Rom. 3.25, and Rev. 1.5).

The Elect were chosen in Christ and their names were written in the Lamb's Book of Life before the foundation of the world, to be born in the fulness of time, according to the perfect and sovereign will of God. (Rom. 9.6-7, Gal. 3.16, Rev. 13.8, 17.8, Phil. 4.3, Luke 10.20, John 10.3, Psa. 139.14-16, Dan. 12.1, Rev. 20.12-15, Rev. 21.27, and 22.19. We believe that the Election of God in the matter of salvation is unconditional, that the Atonement was definite with a people in view, that the Grace to effect this election is irresistible, and that the Elect in Christ will persevere and will be powerfully preserved. We believe that the Messianic Covenant of Grace was made from the foundation of the world (I Pet. 1.19-20). We believe that the Abrahamic Covenant of Promise was necessary to bring to pass the terms of the Messianic Covenant of Grace.

We believe that the Mosaic Covenant of Law was given that Israel might have a mirror from God to expose their sin nature and see that salvation is not by law, not by any work of man, but by atoning blood and righteousness of Jesus Christ. We believe that the Israelites of the Scripture, Old and New Testaments, are identified in the Caucasion Nations of Europe, America, Canada, the British Isles, Scandinavia, Australia, So. Africa, New Zealand and wherever the seed of these people has been dispersed throughout the whole earth. We believe that the everlasting Birthright walks with Joseph, that the everlasting Sceptre belongs to Judah, and that the Everlasting Priesthood is in the possession of Levi. We believe that the Birthright, the Sceptre, and the Priesthood are all present on the world stage today as confirmation of the existence of true Biblical Israel in this earth.

THE DOCTRINAL IMPLICATIONS OF SOTERIOLOGY: The Doctrine of Original Sin, The Doctrinal of Unconditional Election, The Doctrine of Definite Atonement, The Doctrine of Irresistible Grace, The Doctrine of the Preservation of the Saints, The Doctrine of the Messianic Covenant of Grace, The Abrahamic Covenant of Promise and the Mosaic Covenant of Law, The Doctrine of the Children of Promise, The Doctrine of Law and Grace, The History of Israel in the Bible beginning with the call of Abraham, and ending with the divorce, exile, captivity and dispersion into Asia Minor, Western Asia, Europe, Scandinavia and the British Isles, The Study of the Birthright, The Priesthood and the Sceptre, and The Implication of These Promises upon Modern Israel.

ECCLESIOLOGY

WE BELIEVE that the Apostolic Church Militant is the body of Jesus Christ in the creation and in time. The Church Triumphant is those who have fought the fight, won the victory, and are now expectant. The ecclesia describes both the Church Militant on earth, and the Church Triumphant, those who have conquered and gained the victory. (Heb. Ch. 11). The doctrinal presuppositions of the Apostolic Faith of Christ's Church Militant are articulated in the three historic creeds of the Apostolic, i.e., The Apostles Creed, the Nicene Creed, and the Athanasian Creed. In the Church Militant all worship must be lawful and hallow His Name. Worship must serve to exalt Jesus Christ (the One) and bring the Body (the many) into a communion with the Head, thus effecting a verticle communion with Jesus Christ (the Head), and a horizontal communion of the saints (the body).

The Tree of Life containing the Holy Sacraments of the Church enables the Elect in Christ (ecclesia) to walk in hypostatic union with Jesus Christ, the Head, and walk forth in Christian Dominion. From the Pulpit the Law and the Doctrine of Jesus Christ is to be taught, and from the Altar the Blood and Body of Jesus Christ (The Holy Eucharist) serves to bring the Body into union with Christ the Head.

We believe in the Doctrine of the Hypostatic Union of Christ and His Church. We believe in an everlasting Priesthood, in a Divine Pattern of Worship, and in the fact that the Sacraments of the Church continue to be a vital union of Christ with His Church. The seven historic

Sacraments of the Church include Holy Baptism, Holy Communion, Holy Confirmation, Holy Matrimony, Holy Ordination, Holy Repentance (penance), and Holy Unction (healing). We believe in the three historic creeds of the Christian Faith, i.e., the Apostles Creed, the Nicene Creed, and the Athanasian Creed. We believe in the doctrinal work of the first Seven Councils of the Church: Jerusalem A.D. 52 (waged a war against Judiasm), Nicea A. D. 325 (waged a war against Arianism), I Constantinople A. D. 381 (waged a war against semi-Arianism), Ephesus A. D. 431 (waged a war against Nestorianism), Chalcedon A. D. 451 (waged a war against humanism by setting forth the truth of the two natures of Christ), II Constantinople A. D. 553 (waged a war against the Monophysites), and III Constantinople A. D. 680-681 (waged a war against the introduction of humanity into the Deity of Jesus Christ). We do not subscribe to much of the work accomplished at the Councils after the date of 680-681, but do believe that they should be studied for an evaluation of history from A. D. 700 to the time of the Reformation.

We believe that the Christian Family is the basic unit of all government, both for the Church and the State. It is the duty of the parents in the home and the Clergy to teach and practice those laws that will build strong Christian family units of Government out of which the Church and the Nation will be built.

DOCTRINAL IMPLICATIONS OF ECCLESIOLOGY: The Doctrine of the Church, The Doctrine of the Hypostatic Union of Christ and His Church, The Doctrine of an Everlasting Priesthood, The Pulpit and the Altar, The Doctrine of the Divine Pattern of Worship, The Doctrine of Church Government, The Doctrine of the Great Commission, The Doctrine of the Tree of Life & the Holy Sacraments, The History of the Three Historic Creeds of Christianity, The History of the Apostolic and Church Fathers, The History of the First Seven Church Councils, The Doctrine of the Christian Church and the Dominion Mandate, and The Doctrine of the Christian Family. The Writings of the Church Fathers should be studied for the historical and doctrinal value to be gained from these important writings.

THEOCRACY

WE BELIEVE that the Kingdom of God is the final goal of all history, the event toward which the Elect in Christ structure their lives and the event by which all priorities by Jesus Christ (The Head) to His Apostles (the Body) must be established in time and the creation. Scripture: Matt. 4.23, Matt. 10.7. Mark 1.14, Luke 8.1, Matt. 24.14, Isa. 9.6-7, Isa. 65.17-25, Micah 4.1-5. Micah 5.2, Luke 1.31-33, Zach. 14.9, Rev. 11.15, and Rev. 21 and 22 (all). We believe that the Church and the State represent the undivided government of God and that they are equal aspects of created reality. There is no separation between Church and State in God's Word. Both the Church and the State are under God and must be subject to Christ and His Law as contained in the Holy Scriptures.

We believe that the law of God is immutable and without change. (St. Matt. 5.17-20, Rom. 3.32, I Jn. 3.4, Mal. 3.6 and Heb. 13.8). We believe that the Commandments, the Statutes, the Judgments and the Ordinances are all immutable and eternal aspects of God's created reality. We believe that it is the moral responsibility of the Covenant Family, called into the saving knowledge of Jesus Christ, to make their lives relevant to the Law of God. We believe that parents, teachers, and all Ministers are under severe obligation to teach and practice the commandments and other vital personal and family areas of the law, and to demand that Civil Leaders make these laws relevant to all activities of government.

We believe in the Doctrine of the Tithe, and we believe in the Holy Feast Days of Yahweh, established in Holy Scripture. We believe that the Religious Festivals of Passover, Pentecost, The Feast of Trumpets, The Day of Atonement and Feast of Tabernacles are all vital to the Christian Dominion of this earth for Jesus Christ. We believe in the Holy Sabbath, and we believe that all aspects of God's Law must be honored by the Covenant people called into the saving knowledge of Jesus Christ. We believe in the Dietary Laws and all else that is in the Law that pertains to living life in terms of God's Law.

We believe that Jesus Christ will rule upon a literal throne, David's Throne, as the greater David of Prophecy, and that He will establish a theocratic government over all the earth at His Second Coming. (Ezekial 37.21-28, St. Matthew 19.28, 25.31-32, St. Luke 1.31-33, Rev. 11.15). We believe that there will be a literal regathering of Israel at the Second Coming of Jesus Christ, and that all of the Elect will be regathered, both of the Church Triumphant and of the Church Militant. (Matt. 24.31, Mark 13.27, Luke 13.29, Jer. 30.3, 33.7, Amos 9.13-15). We believe that a literal Kingdom will be restored to Israel at the Second Coming of Jesus Christ. Luke 1.31-33, Acts 1.6, I Cor. 15.24, Luke 12.32, Luke 19.11-13, Isa. 9.6-7, Dan. 2.44-45, Isa. 2.1-5, and Micah 4.1-7.

DOCTRINAL IMPLICATIONS OF THE STUDY OF THEOCRACY: The Doctrine of the Kingdom of God, The Doctrine of the Undivided Church and State, The Doctrine of an Everlasting Throne (Sceptre), The Doctrine of the Threefold Government of God, the Family, Church and State, The Doctrine of God's Immutable Law as Contained in the Commandments, Statutes, Judgments and Ordinances, The Doctrine of the Tithe, Tithe of the Firstborn and Firstfruits, The Poor Tithe, and The Festival Tithe, The Doctrine of Holy Feast Days, The Doctrine of Clean and Unclean, and all else that pertains to living in Sanctification before Yahweh, The Covenant God of Israel.

ESCHATOLOGY

WE BELIEVE that the consummation of history is to witness a time of great increasing world wide tribulation wherein the Living Church must occupy until Jesus Christ comes to establish His Kingdom upon this earth. (Luke 19.13 and Mark 13.34). The Second Coming of Jesus Christ will be climaxed by a time of great tribulation and judgment upon the wicked and the establishment of His Kingdom into the earth. (Matthew 24, Mark 13, Luke 21, and all of the Book of Revelation, I and II Chapters of Thess.). We believe that the white western Christian culture, the ninth culture to exist upon this earth, is now in the final stages of the Organic Culture Curve of history.

As this age comes to a close we believe that a time of increasing trouble and tribulation for all the Tribes of Israel, in all the countries of their dispersion, will take place. (Jer. 30.7-11, Ezek. 34.12, Dan. 12.1) We believe that the ending of this age will witness the Second Coming of Jesus Christ to rule upon a literal throne of David in this earth, that there will be a resurrection of the Elect in Christ (Rev. 20.6, I Thess. 4.16) and a regathering of all the Tribes of Israel to the land of their fathers, the promised land, and that the Kingdom will be "restored" again (Acts 1.6) to Israel. Since all the earth will be filled with the government of God, the Tribes of Israel will be apportioned throughout much of the globe with the capitol city the New Jerusalem, being the land deeded to Abraham, Isaac and Jacob-Israel by Covenant forever.

We believe that Hades or Sheol is the place of the departed souls of the wicked Adamites where they are taken following the death of the body, and that they will remain there until the resurrection of the body to stand in judgment at the Great White Throne Judgment. We believe that the souls of the righteous Elect go to be with Christ and are at rest with Christ, until the Second Coming. (I Thess. 3.13, 4.14, II Cor. 5.6-9, Phil. 1.23-24, John 14.3, John 17.24, John 12.26, Col. 3.4). We believe that the Elect in Christ, throughout all ages, will be resurrected at the first resurrection (Rev. 20.6) and that the rest of the dead will be resurrected following the thousand year millenium and little season. (Rev. Ch. 20). Following the Great White Throne Judgment we believe that the wicked will be cast into Gehenna, which is the second death. (Rev. 20.12-15). We believe that as the time of tribulation grows more severe (St. Matt. 24.21-22, John 16.1-4), all true Christians must stand firm in their religious conviction of faith and doctrine. We believe that Christians are absolutely prohibited from receiving any kind of mark, visible or invisible, of any kind or description, into the hand, forehead, of any part of the body. We believe that it is against the Word of God for Christians to be numbered or identified by government marking systems of any kind.

We believe that as we approach the ending of this age the counterfeit Kingdom of Satan and the reign of the antiChrist will seek to ensnare all Christian people into a false pseudo, and counterfeit Kingdom. As the Elect in Christ seek to make their lives relevant to Jesus Christ and His Word, they will be bound by their religious convictions to stand true to their conscience and not forfeit their spiritual inheritance in Jesus Christ. Where public policy affords Christian people no option to follow their religious convictions as established upon the Word of God, Christians will have no other choice but to obey God rather than men. (Acts. 5.29) It is the desire of all members of the Church of Israel to be the sons of God in the midst of a crooked and perverse world order (Phil. 2.15) and to be at peace with all men. When it is no longer possible to live by the terms of God's Word because of "public policy," Christians must be willing to cast their fate upon the mercy of God, and suffer whatever may come; they cannot forfeit their spiritual and moral convictions as established upon God's Word. (See Daniel 3.12-27, Daniel 6.4-23).

ARTICLES OF FAITH AND DOCTRINE (CHURCH OF ISRAEL) (continued)

As a body of Christian people, bound to Jesus Christ and the Holy Scriptures, there is already a number of public policies which are offensive to God and to the Holy Scriptures. A listing of those "public policies" would be beyond the scope of this work. For the benefit of those Covenant Christian people who walk in the religious conviction of these tenets of Faith, the following specified areas of concern are clearly spelled out:

1.) We believe that it is a violation of God's Word to be marked or numbered in any way by a government agency at any level of operation. If, for example, the Social Security Number in the United States becomes the universal number of identification, then Christians have a moral responsibility to refuse or deny such a number as a matter of religious conscience. (See Revelation Chapters 7, 13, 14 and 15 and Ezekiel Chapter 9).

2.) We believe that it is a violation of God's Law to accept inoculations or vaccines into the body. Parents cannot allow their children to be made the subjects of vaccines and inoculations, and all parents living under these tenets of faith have a moral responsibility to oppose such inoculations as a violation of their religious conscience. (Leviticus 19.28, I Cor. 6.15, and I Thess. 5.23).

3.) We believe that Christians should abstain from harmful drugs of any kind or description and that the body must be kept holy for the indwelling of the Holy Spirit. (Romans 12.1-2, I Cor. 6.19-20).

4.) We believe that God's Law demands segregation of the races and that all races will be more happy living in the state which God assigned to them. Christians are thereby duty bound to practice segregation in their family life, dating and marriage relationships, pursuit of education, and wherever the safety and welfare of the family and Church are in question.

5.) The Church of Israel *DOES NOT* teach white supremacy. We do teach that the white people are the Israelites of the Bible and are called to be the *Servant People of God*. In this capacity they have built the churches, translated the Bible, clothed the world and provided food for the world. We do teach white separtism, black separtism, brown separtism and yellow separtism. We *Do Not* teach hatred toward non-white races. We as a Covenant people seek as per the Holy Scriptures to live and dwell, work and play, worship and educate our children separated and segregated as much as is humanly possible to do so in a multi-racial society. We likewise seek the same options for all races.

6.) We believe that Marriage is a Holy Sacrament of the Church, and that only the Church, acting in accordance with the requirements of Scripture, can establish two people, a man and woman, together in the State of Marriage. To seek a license from the State is to allow the state to license the Holy Sacrament of Matrimony. This would be a violation of the reli-gious conscience of all who stand under the tenets of these religious and moral teachings of Jesus Christ and the Holy Bible.

7.) We believe that healing is a Sacrament of the Church, and that people who are sick in mind or body should look to the Church for the divine healing that comes from Yahweh, through prayer, anointing with oil by the Elders of the Church, by following the Dietary Laws of Scripture, and through natural means of healing as outlined in the Holy Scriptures of truth.

8.) We believe that it is Biblically wrong for women to serve in the military service of the United States or any other country where Israelites may live. (Deut. Ch. 20). We believe that boys should be a minimum of 20 years of age before serving in the Military Service of the United States. We further believe that where war is being waged in violation of Bible Law (Deut. Ch. 20) they should register with the government as a conscientious objector.

9.) We *do not* advocate, nor do we believe in the use of violence for any cause. *We deplore all acts of terror* and believe that they that live by the sword will die by the sword. (St. Matthew 26.52). The weapons of our warfare are not carnal. (II Cor. 10.3-5 and Rev. 13.10). Christians do have a moral and Biblical right to keep and bear arms in defense of their lives and property. (St. Luke 22.36 and St. Matthew 12.29.).

10.) We believe that Abortion is murder of the unborn and innocent children of God. Life begins at conception and to destroy that life through any type of abortion amounts to an act of murder. Since abortion is an act of overt violence and terror of the unborn we oppose abortion and believe it is the duty of the family and the Church to oppose the murder of the unborn. (Exodus 21.22-25, Exodus 20.13, Deut. 5.17)

11.) We believe that it is the reponsibility of the parents to give their children a Christian Education as a fulfillment of the Baptismal vows and as required by the Word of God. Parents are responsible before God to see that their children are not offered to Molech in the form of brainwashing them and leading them away from Jesus Christ into humanism. Parents can fulfill their responsibility before God in the education of their children by providing home schooling or private Christian Education. (Deut. 6.7.20, Deut. 4.10, Deut. 11.19, Deut. 31.13, Prov. 22.6, Isa. 28.9, John 21.15, Lev. 18.21)

12.) We believe that Christians are called in Jesus Christ to take dominion of the earth to the glory of God. As Christians we stand as redeemed men under Jesus Christ and walk forth as Covenant Children of God, called into Christian Service in all areas of life. We stand under God as Covenant Men, called to walk in obedience to His Law Command Word. We are commissioned to Occupy till He comes. (St. Luke 19.13) The example of living for this age is established in the life and mission of Noah, who walked in fear before God, perfect in his generations and living in obedience to God. (Genesis 6:8-9, Heb. 11.7). Like Noah we seek to build an *Ark of Safety* in this time of national and world travail. We seek only to live in obedience to the Law of Yahweh, the Covenant God of Israel. We do not seek to impose our religious beliefs upon anyone and seek to cultivate peace and good will among all of God's people, and to walk as Covenant men, under Jesus Christ, and in obedience to His Laws throughout all our days.

13.) We do believe in the Constitution of the United States of America! We do believe in the Flag of the United States of America and we pledge our allegiance to the Republic for which it stands. We believe that this is a *Nation under God*, and that it is a great and wonderful privilege to live in these United States of America. We look with great pride upon the men who bled and died for this nation and we gratefully acknowledge the following documentation as proof of our Christian status as One Nation Under Jesus Christ.

In 1799, Justice Chase stated, "By our form of government, the Christian religion is the established religion; and all sects and denominations of Christians are placed upon the same equal footing, and are equally entitled to protection in their religious liberty." (Runkel v. Winemiller, 4 Harris & McHenry (MD) 429, I AD 311, 417).

In the 1892 Supreme Court case entitled "Church of the Holy Trinity v. United States," the Court found, "it is impossible that it should be otherwise: and in this sense and to this extent our civilization and our institutions are emphatically Christian . . . this is a religious people. This is historically true. From the discovery of this continent to the present hour, there is a single voice making this affirmation . . . we find everywhere a clear recognition of the same truth . . . this is a Christian Nation."

In the 1952 case of Zorach v. Clauson the liberal U.S. Supreme Court Justice William O. Douglas admitted, "The first amendment . . . does not say that in every and all respects there shall be a separation of Church and State . . . Otherwise, the state and religion would be aliens to each other—hostile, suspicious, and even unfriendly."

WE THE CHRISTIAN ISRAELITE PEOPLE OF THE CHURCHES OF ISRAEL DO COVENANT AND COMBINE OURSELVES TOGETHER IN SUPPORT OF THESE ARTICLES OF FAITH AND DOCTRINE, AND FOR AUTHORITY AND SUPPORT OF THESE TENETS WE DO LOOK TO JESUS CHRIST AND THE HOLY SCRIPTURES. FOR THE PROTECTION OF THESE TENETS OF RELIGIOUS LIBERTY WE GRATEFULLY ACKNOWLEDGE BEFORE ALMIGHTY YAHWEH, THE COVENANT GOD OF ISRAEL, OUR THANKSGIVING FOR THE UNITED STATES CONSTITUTION, AMENDMENT NO. 1. AND THE RELIGIOUS LIBERTIES GUARANTEED BY THE STATE CONSTITUTIONS OF THE MANY STATES WHICH COMBINED MAKE UP THE UNITED STATES OF AMERICA.

These Articles of Faith and Doctrine adopted and approved by The Board of Trustees, acting for and on behalf of the CHURCH OF ISRAEL at Schell City, Missouri, January 10, 1982.

Notes: *The Church of Israel began as a splinter of a Latter-Day Saint group, the Church of Christ (Temple Lot), and has moved into an acceptance of the British-Israel position, which is spelled out in detail in the church's statement of beliefs. The major remnant of Latter-Day Saint belief is evident in the discussion of priesthood in the section on ecclesiology. The church is also trinitarian. The discussion of racial issues is one of many public policy statements included at the end of this document. The church opposes abortion.*

* * *

FIRST PRINCIPLES (HOUSE OF PRAYER FOR ALL PEOPLE)

WE FOLLOW THE BIBLE IN ALL THINGS. Study your Bible and see if we are right. Name of Building—"HOUSE OF PRAYER FOR ALL PEOPLE" (Isa. 56:7, Matt. 21:13). A follower of Christ is—"A CHRISTIAN" (I Peter 4:16, Acts 26:28). All followers of Christ are—"CHRISTIANS" (Isa. 56:5, Isa. 62:2, Acts 11:26). All congregations of Christians are—"THE CHURCHES OF CHRIST" (Rom. 16:16). The officers of a local congregation are—ELDERS (Titus 1:5), DEACONS (I Tim. 3:1-5, Acts 6:1-6).

THE PLAN OF SALVATION—The true Bible way to be saved:

First: HEAR THE WORD OF YAHVEH PREACHED. (Rev. 2:7, Rom. 10:14). Second BELIEVE—have faith in Yahveh (Heb. 11:6). Third: REPENT OF YOUR SINS (Matt. 3:2, Matt. 4:17, Acts 2:38, Acts 17:30). Fourth: CONFESS FAITH IN YAHSHUA THE MESSIAH (Matt. 10:32, Rom. 10:9-10). Fifth: BE BAPTIZED IN WATER (Acts 2:28, Acts 22:16, I Peter 3:21). Hearing, Faith, Repentance, Confession and Baptism is the one and only complete plan of Salvation in the Bible.

HAVING OBEYED THE GOSPEL. THEN—YAHSHUA THE MESSIAH ADDS YOU TO HIS CHURCH (Acts 2:47, Eph. 2:19-22). And that is all there is to Church membership in the Church, which is His Body. (Eph. 5:30).

HOW TO WORSHIP ON SUNDAY—All believers in Yahshua the Messiah are to assemble for worship (Heb. 10:22-25). The services of a local congregation on every first day of the week (Sunday) consist of five parts.

THE KINGDOM MEAL (Gen. 14:18, Matt. 26:26, Lev. 24:5-9, I Chron. 9:32, Acts 20:7, I Cor. 10:2-4, John 6:53-56). 2. THE TITHE—Ten per cent of gross earnings (Gen. 14:20, Heb. 7:1-8, Mal. 3:10, I Cor. 16:2). 3. PREACHING THE GOSPEL (Matt. 28:18-20, Rom. 10:14-15, II Tim. 4:1-2). 4. SINGING HYMNS WITH INSTRUMENTAL MUSIC (Eph. 5:19, Col. 3:16, Psalm, 150:3-5, Psalm 87:7). 5. PRAYERS (I Thes. 5:17, James 5:13-16). The Kingdom Meal, Tithing, Preaching, Singing and Praying are the five parts that make a complete worship

FIRST PRINCIPLES (HOUSE OF PRAYER FOR ALL PEOPLE) (continued)

service on the first day of every week. By following this complete Bible program you will help to answer the prayer of Yahshua the Messiah for the unity of his people (John 17:11, 20-22, I Cor. 1:10-13).

Ephraim and Manasseh, the sons of Joseph, were exalted over all Israel (I Chron. 5:1). The names of Abraham, Isaac and Israel were called upon them. (Gen. 48:16, Gen. 49:22-26). Ephraim was to become a company of nations and Manasseh a Great Nation. (Gen. 48:19). This is fulfilled in Great Britain and the United States of America—the latter day Israel of Yahveh. We rule over the earth and no weapon that is formed against us shall prosper (Isa. 54:17). Read carefully all of Isaiah 54th chapter and Gal. 4:27-31, Deut. 28:1-44, Ezek. 34:25-31, Isa. 56:7, Matt. 21:13, Isa. 56:5, Isa. 62:2, Acts 11:26:26.

THE TRUE NAME of our Heavenly Father is YAHVEH and the name of His wife and our Heavenly Mother is KHAVEH the Holy Ghost. The name of their Son and our Saviour is YAHSHUA THE MESSIAH—We and all the sons of Yahveh are the ELOHIM (Gods) in ONENESS. The redemptive names are as follows: For your prosperity pray to YAHVEH—YIRETH (Gen. 22:14). For the healing of your body call upon YAHVEH - RAPHA (Ex. 15:26). For the restoration of the Kingdom on earth pray to YAHVEH - TSIDKENU (Jer. 23:6). For your protection the name is YAHVEH - NISSI (Ex. 17:8-15). For divine guidance the name is YAHVEH - RAAH (Ps. 23). For peace on earth use the name YAHVEH - SHALOM (Judges 6:24). For all present nearness and future hope call upon YAHVEH - SHAMMAH (Esek. 48:35). These are the true redemptive names of our Father. There is a contact and a power in these names.

Then realize that YAHVEH'S only true order is "The order of MELCHIZEDECK" (Gen. 14:18-20, Ps. 110:1-7, Heb. 6:13-20, Heb. 7:1-28). I have now revealed to you the true names of "OUR FATHER." Be very careful how you use them. The power of life and death is in those names.

We are Anglo - Saxon, Cymric, and Scandinavian Israelites and we are definitely interested in establishing the Kingdom politically and economically as the dominion of YAHVEH on earth as much as we are in establishing the Church as the temple of YAHVEH in the heart of Israel. With the Church and Israel restored, then will begin the gradual resurrection and restoration of all nations in their allotted places on earth and ultimately the reconciliation of all men and angels in ONENESS with YAHVEH.

Notes: *This statement, printed in most issues of the church's magazine, shows the House of Prayer to be one of the British Israel groups directly influenced by the Sacred Name movement (in accepting "Yahveh" and "Yahshua" as the names of the Creator and His Son). It is different in its designation of "Khaveh," the Holy Ghost, as our "Heavenly Mother."*

* * *

STATEMENT FROM THE PROPHETIC HERALD MINISTRY

The PROPHETIC HERALD proclaims Jesus Christ pre-eminent in all things (Col. 1:12-20). He is the only Saviour, Redeemer, Healer, Baptizer with the Holy Spirit (Acts 2), and only Mediator between God and man (1 Tim. 2:5). Atonement is possible only through His shed blood (Heb. 9:19-23).

The PROPHETIC HERALD advocates: the near return of Christ (Acts 1:11), and life only through Him (Col. 3:3); the literal resurrection of the dead (John 5:28); the immortalization of those in Christ (1 Cor. 15:53-54); the judgment of the wicked (Rev. 21:8); the final restoration of true Israel (Rom. 9:6, 11:7; Gal. 3:16) and true Judah (Rom. 2:28-29), as the *terrestrial* kingdom of God under the Kingship of Christ (Luke 1:32) and His *celestial* body (the "little flock" of overcomers) who will be *joint heirs* with Him (Rom. 8:17); restored true Israel and Judah (Ezek. 37 and Jer. 50:4-6; Gal. 3:26-29); to be *heirs* and head of nations over unrepentant Gentiles and heathen nations (Rev. 22:8-21); the "restitution of all things which God hath spoken by the mouth of all his holy prophets since the world began" ("Acts 3:21). It also firmly advocates repentance and immersion in the name of the Lord Jesus Christ for the remission of sins (Acts 2:38), and a consecrated life as essential to celestial glorification (1 Cor. 15:22-23).

Notes: *Though no longer in existence, this statement carried in most issues of the ministry's magazine would find approval among British Israelites. It carries some hint of the particular presentation of the International Church of the Foursquare Gospel in its affirmation of Christ as Saviour, Redeemer, Healer, and Baptizer with the Holy Spirit.*

Chapter 13
Liberal Family

Liberal

PRINCIPLES [DEISTICAL SOCIETY OF NEW YORK (1790s)]

Proposals for forming a society for the promotion of moral science and the religion of nature—having in view the destruction of superstition and fanaticism—tending to the development of the principles of a genuine natural morality—the practice of a pure and uncorrupted virtue—the cultivation of science and philosophy—the resurrection of reason, and the renovation of the intelligent world.

At a time when the political despotism of the earth is disappearing, and man is about to reclaim and enjoy the liberties of which for ages he has been deprived, it would be unpardonable to neglect the important concerns of intellectual and moral nature. The slavery of the mind has been the most destructive of all slavery; and the baneful effects of a dark and gloomy superstition have suppressed all the dignified efforts of the human understanding, and essentially circumscribed the sphere of intellectual energy. It is only by returning to the laws of nature, which man has so frequently abandoned, that happiness is to be acquired. And, although the efforts of a few individuals will be inadequate to the sudden establishment of moral and mental felicity; yet, they may lay the foundation on which a superstructure may be reared incalculably valuable to the welfare of future generations. To contribute to the accomplishment of an object so important, the members of this association do approve of the following fundamental principles:—

1. That the universe proclaims the existence of one supreme Deity, worthy the adoration of intelligent beings.

2. That man is possessed of moral and intellectual faculties sufficient for the improvement of his nature, and the acquisition of happiness.

3. That the religion of nature is the only universal religion; that it grows out of the moral relations of intelligent beings, and that it stands connected with the progressive improvement and common welfare of the human race.

4. That it is essential to the true interest of man, that he love truth and practise virtue.

5. That vice is every where ruinous and destructive to the happiness of the individual and of society.

6. That a benevolent disposition, and beneficent actions, are fundamental duties of rational beings.

7. That a religion mingled with persecution and malice cannot be of divine origin.

8. That education and science are essential to the happiness of man.

9. That civil and religious liberty is equally essential to his true interests.

10. That there can be no human authority to which man ought to be amenable for his religious opinions.

11. That science and truth, virtue and happiness, are the great objects to which the activity and energy of the human faculties ought to be directed.

Every member admitted into this association shall deem it his duty, by every suitable method in his power, to promote the cause of nature and moral truth, in opposition to all schemes of superstition and fanaticism, claiming divine origin.

Notes: *Among the first of the radical religious groups of the United States, the Deistical Society of New York was founded by Elihu Palmer. The society espoused the religion of nature, which contrasted sharply with orthodox Christianity. It affirmed one God, adherence to the laws of nature, and the necessity of virtue and benevolence. Persecution in the name of religion was decried.*

*   *   *

STATEMENTS BY AMERICAN ATHEISTS, INC.

DEFINITIONS

1. Atheism is the life philosophy (Weltanschauung) of persons who are free from theism. It is predicated on the ancient Greek philosophy of Materialism.

2. American Atheism may be defined as the mental attitude which unreservedly accepts the supremacy of reason and aims at establishing a system of philosophy and ethics verifiable by experience, independent of all arbitrary assumptions of authority or creeds.

3. The Materialist philosophy declares that the cosmos is devoid of immanent conscious purpose; that it is governed by its own inherent, immutable and impersonal law; that there is no supernatural interference in human life; that man—finding his resources within himself—can and must create his own destiny; and that his potential for good and higher development is for all practical purposes unlimited.

ATHEISM TEACHES THAT:

There is no heavenly father. Man must protect the orphans and foundlings, or they will not be protected.

There is no god to answer prayer. Man must hear and help man.

There is no hell. We have no vindictive god or devil to fear or imitate.

There is no atonement or salvation by faith. We must face the consequence of our acts.

There is no beneficent or malevolent intent in nature. Life is a struggle against preventable and unpreventable evils. The cooperation of man is the only hope of the world.

There is no chance after death to "do our bit." We must do it now or never.

There is no divine guardian of truth, goodness, beauty and liberty. These are attributes of man. Man must defend them or they will perish from the earth.

Notes: *Among the most militant of atheist organizations is American Atheists, Inc., founded by Madelyn Murray O'Hair. Reproduced here are three basic definitions used by the organization as well as a brief statement on what Atheism teaches. Despite the popular claim that atheism is a positive world view in which God plays no role, these statements seem overwhelmingly to be denials of Christian and/or theistic positions.*

*   *   *

STATEMENT OF PRINCIPLES AND AFFIRMATIONS OF THE ETHICAL MOVEMENT (AMERICAN ETHICAL UNION)

STATEMENT OF PRINCIPLES

(1) We believe that morality is independent of theology. We hold that the moral law is imposed upon us by our own rational nature and that its authority is absolute. We maintain that the moral life should be brought to the foreground in religion.

(2) We affirm the need of a new statement of the ethical code of mankind. The formulations of duty which were given by the greatest religious teachers of the past are not sufficient for the changed conditions of modern society. We believe that moral problems have arisen in this industrial, democratic, scientific age, which require new and larger formulations of duty. Hence a new interest in ethical problems and a profounder study and discussion of them are demanded.

(3) We regard it our duty as a Society for Ethical Culture, to engage in works of philanthropy on as large a scale as our means will allow. The ultimate purpose of such philanthrophy should be the advancement of morality. When we contemplate the low moral condition of society and its indifference to moral aims, we feel called upon to do what we can to raise our fellow men to a higher plane of life and to awaken within them a deeper moral purpose.

(4) We hold that the task of self-reform should go hand in hand with efforts to reform society. The mere fact of membership in an Ethical Society must be regarded as a tacit avowal of the desire to lead a wholly upright life and to aid in developing a higher type of manhood and womanhood than has been known in the past.

(5) We believe that organization is indispensable to carrying out the aims of ethical culture and that this organization should be republican rather than monarchical. While we recognize the need of a public lecturer for the Society, we believe that the work of ethical culture in its broadest sense—the study, discussion, and the application of its principles, should be carried on as far as possible by the members themselves.

(6) We agree that the greatest stress should be laid on the moral instruction of the young, to the end that in the pure hearts of children may be sown the seeds of a higher moral order, that early in life they may be impressed with the work and dignity of human existence, and that the work of social and individual perfection may be carried on with larger and nobler results from generation to generation.

AFFIRMATIONS OF THE ETHICAL MOVEMENT
CENTRALITY OF ETHICS

We believe that ethical aspirations should be central in religion and in life, and that ethical conduct need not be dependent on theological belief. For too long men have been divided by their creeds. We do not ask that men put aside their religious beliefs, but rather that they recognize that no one world-view has a monopoly of wisdom or virtue. We ask that men reach across the theological lines which have divided them and seek unity in their common ethical concerns.

ETHICS AND MORALITY

We hold that the morality of an action is not determined by its conformity to any rigid moral code, but by the application of certain general ethical principles to the particular circumstances surrounding the action. Among these general principles are the following:

We affirm the dignity and worth of all human beings, however different their abilities or backgrounds. We do not consider a person's worth to be dependent on his usefulness or his conduct towards others, though we are by no means indifferent to his conduct. We hold that it is the task of ethics to encourage him to base his conduct on a respect for the worth of others.

Recognizing the principle of reciprocity in human relations we affirm that any action which brings out the distinctive worth in others brings out the distinctive worth in one's self. By the same token any action which demeans others demeans one's self.

Increasing one's capacity for bringing out the distinctive worth in others and one's self is what we mean by ethical growth. This process begins in the family and extends into friendships and civic endeavor, culminating in a sense of loyalty and relatedness to the total community of man. Through such relationships we believe a person can find his greatest personal fulfillment and meaning in life.

RELIGION

We are a movement committed to man's quest for values worthy of his supreme allegiance. Many of our members identify this quest as religious. Others designate it as philosophical.

We see the various conceptions of "God," "Divine Revelation," and "Immortality" as expressions of man's attempt to find meaning in the universe and guidance in life. We are profoundly sympathetic with this endeavor, and we believe that a study of traditional doctrine can often yield valuable ethical insight. Hence, we acknowledge the traditional religions as being among the sources of our own ethical and religious concerns.

At the same time, the traditional theological conceptions contain much that is inadequate and misleading, and we deny any moral responsibility to adhere to doctrines if reason and experience belie them. Moreover, though many believers have found great inspiration in such doctrines, the acceptance of dogmatic assumptions is tantamount, in our view, to accepting restraints on man's ethical and religious development. This we find objectionable, for we see the essence of religion in a commitment to growth: growth in passion for truth, growth in appreciation of beauty, and growth in dedication to good.

Truth, beauty, and good are in themselves abstractions, which must continually be made real in the lives and efforts of human beings. For us religion is essentially an ethical process, not an act of subscribing to beliefs. We believe that the religious is to be the most fully realized within the ethical life, rather than beyond it.

HUMANISM

Our Humanism is a faith that there is in human beings something worthy of ethical or religious commitment: a capacity for growth and creativity, for sensitivity and responsiveness to other people, and for being responsibility-carrying members of a human community. We think this capacity can best be cultivated if we assume it to be present in people even when not immediately manifest. Our humanist faith as Ethical Culturists can be justified only by the quality of human relationships resulting from the attempt to live by it.

This faith is grounded in a respect for the human accomplishments of the past. We find inspiration for this faith in the humanist tradition of the past—in the humanism of ancient Greece, in the humanism of the Renaissance, in the scientific, philosophical and religious humanisms of later centuries.

Our humanism is a commitment to humanity-as-a-whole and to the humanity in those we meet; and it is also a commitment to a vision of humanity as it yet may be and to the responsibility for helping achieve this vision. This commitment gains strength in the knowledge that humanity has the capacity for surviving the individual and carrying on the values for which he lived.

MAN AND NATURE

Unlike many traditional religions ethical culture does not regard man as the being for whom the world was created. We maintain not that man is the objective center of nature, but rather that he should be treated as central in any attempt to find human meaning in nature.

We do not share the confidence of some that man can formulate doctrines which give a final and over-all explanation of the universe in which we find ourselves.

Though some things which were once in the realm of mystery have already been explained, and others will yet be successfully probed, we see no reason for believing that man will ever completely penetrate the unknown. Our confidence in man's abilities is mingled with a sense of humility in the face of a vast universe beyond man's experience.

SCIENCE

We look upon scientific method as man's greatest ally in his attempt to discover truths about the universe. Many of us see Ethical Culture as an attempt to apply the insights of science to religion and human relations. While we do not expect the exactitude of the physical sciences, we hold that some sort of empirical verification is required for religious and ethical hypotheses. This does not rule out certain kinds of intuition, which can be useful even in science.

Our commitment is to the scientific spirit—not to any particular school of opinion or conceptual scheme, but rather to the methods of free and honest inquiry.

We are keenly aware that science has not always been used for the good of man. When, in the name of science, human beings are treated merely as statistics and human values are trampled upon, science is misused. Science is made for man, not man for science. It is the task of ethics to determine the human use of scientifically acquired knowledge.

DEMOCRACY

We believe in the democratic process—not alone in government, but also in the family and in all other day-to-day interpersonal relations, for it is only through participation in decisions affecting their lives that people will develop their own inner resources.

Democracy means that people have the right to determine their own destiny and that decisions should be made in such a way that people will grow through the process, not

STATEMENT OF PRINCIPLES AND AFFIRMATIONS OF THE ETHICAL MOVEMENT (AMERICAN ETHICAL UNION) (continued)

become more dependent. It requires the formulation of social policy through free and open dialogue and the removal of barriers between races, classes, and religions. It entails the widespread development of critical intelligence and creative ability, not the concentration of these qualities in any elite group.

Democracy is a process of growth, and a concern for growth is central to our ethic.

SOCIAL RESPONSIBILITY

We hold that ethics involves a responsibility to the society in which we live, including a responsibility for the conditions which prevail within that society. Though we do not agree on any one concept of the ideal society, we do agree that societies are subject to judgment by certain ethical standards, such as those expressed in the Universal Declaration of Human Rights. We have an ethical responsibility to study the social issues of our time and lend our support to efforts to secure for all people the political, economic, social and cultural rights to which they are entitled.

WORLD COMMUNITY

Social responsibility and the possibilities for friendship and cooperation do not end at national borders. A humanist ethic demands a concern for the well-being of all peoples. Hence, we accept the responsibility for fostering loyalty to the emerging world community and to seeking practical expressions of this loyalty.

Man stands today on the threshold of nuclear destruction and also on the threshold of a new era in which science can provide for the material needs of all people and maintain the proper balance between human population and natural resources. Which threshold is crossed will probably depend upon whether man succeeds in broadening group loyalty to embrace the community of man.

ETHICAL UNIVERSALISM

We believe there is a universality to our ethical message and that where men are divided in their creeds they may yet unite in certain fundamental ethical concerns. At the same time we recognize that for many human beings an ethical faith without a theology may be inadequate. We claim universalism for our ethical message, not for our Movement. We would in fact question the desirability of all men belonging to the same religious movement, for we believe that religious freedom can best be fostered by the cooperative co-existence of numerous religious traditions, each respecting the right of the individual to choose the tradition most meaningful to him.

FREEDOM OF BELIEF

Because we cherish the freedom of the individual to work out his own answers to the great questions of life, we reject any creedal or dogmatic statement of our beliefs. A scientific and democratic ethic demands full intellectual freedom as an essential condition for the advancement of truth.

Notes: *The Statement of Principles was originally adopted by the American Ethical Union in the 1870s and reflects the Union's early concern for ethics and social reform. The Affirmations of the Ethical Movement, circulated by the Union almost a century later, reflects the Union's broadening concerns during the twentieth century. The statement was written by a special commission of the Fraternity of Leaders of the Union. Central to the Union's position is the autonomy of ethical concerns from religious or world view decisions, though the Union is decidedly Humanist in outlook.*

* * *

HUMANIST MANIFESTO I (AMERICAN HUMANIST ASSOCIATION)

The time has come for widespread recognition of the radical changes in religious beliefs throughout the modern world. The time is past for mere revision of traditional attitudes. Science and economic change have disrupted the old beliefs. Religions the world over are under the necessity of coming to terms with new conditions created by a vastly increased knowledge and experience. In every field of human activity, the vital movement is now in the direction of a candid and explicit humanism. In order that religious humanism may be better understood we, the undersigned, desire to make certain affirmations which we believe the facts of our contemporary life demonstrate.

There is great danger of a final, and we believe fatal, identification of the word *religion* with doctrines and methods which have lost their significance and which are powerless to solve the problem of human living in the Twentieth Century. Religions have always been means for realizing the highest values of life. Their end has been accomplished through the interpretation of the total environing situation (theology or world view), the sense of values resulting therefrom (goal or ideal), and the technique (cult) established for realizing the satisfactory life. A change in any of these factors results in alteration of the outward forms of religion. This fact explains the changefulness of religions through the centuries. But through all changes religion itself remains constant in its quest for abiding values, an inseparable feature of human life.

Today man's larger understanding of the universe, his scientific achievements, and his deeper appreciation of brotherhood, have created a situation which requires a new statement of the means and purposes of religion. Such a vital, fearless, and frank religion capable of furnishing adequate social goals and personal satisfactions may appear to many people as a complete break with the past. While this age does owe a vast debt to traditional religions, it is none the less obvious that any religion that can hope to be a synthesizing and dynamic force for today must be shaped for the needs of this age. To establish such a religion is a major necessity of the present. It is a responsibility which rests upon this generation. We therefore affirm the following.

FIRST: Religious humanists regard the universe as self-existing and not created.

SECOND: Humanism believes that man is a part of nature and that he has emerged as the result of a continuous process.

THIRD: Holding an organic view of life, humanists find that the traditional dualism of mind and body must be rejected.

FOURTH: Humanism recognizes that man's religious culture and civilization, as clearly depicted by anthropology and history, are the product of a gradual development due to his interaction with his natural environment and with his social heritage. The individual born into a particular culture is largely molded to that culture.

FIFTH: Humanism asserts that the nature of the universe depicted by modern science makes unacceptable any supernatural or cosmic guarantees of human values. Obviously humanism does not deny the possibility of realities as yet undiscovered, but it does insist that the way to determine the existence and value of any and all realities is by means of intelligent inquiry and by the assessment of their relation to human needs. Religion must formulate its hopes and plans in the light of the scientific spirit and method.

SIXTH: We are convinced that the time has passed for theism, deism, modernism, and the several varieties of "new thought."

SEVENTH: Religion consists of those actions, purposes, and experiences which are humanly significant. Nothing human is alien to the religious. It includes labor, art, science, philosophy, love, friendship, recreation—all that is in its degree expressive of intelligently satisfying human living. The distinction between the sacred and the secular can no longer be maintained.

EIGHTH: Religious humanism considers the complete realization of human personality to be the end of man's life and seeks its development and fulfillment in the here and now. This is the explanation of the humanist's social passion.

NINTH: In place of the old attitudes involved in worship and prayer the humanist finds his religious emotions expressed in a heightened sense of personal life and in a cooperative effort to promote social well-being.

TENTH: It follows that there will be no uniquely religious emotions and attitudes of the kind hitherto associated with belief in the supernatural.

ELEVENTH: Man will learn to face the crises of life in terms of his knowledge of their naturalness and probability. Reasonable and manly attitudes will be fostered by education and supported by custom. We assume that humanism will take the path of social and mental hygiene and discourage sentimental and unreal hopes and wishful thinking.

TWELFTH: Believing that religion must work increasingly for joy in living, religious humanists aim to foster the creative in man and to encourage achievements that add to the satisfactions of life.

THIRTEENTH: Religious humanism maintains that all associations and institutions exist for the fulfillment of human life. The intelligent evaluation, transformation, control, and direction of such associations and institutions with a view to the enhancement of human life is the purpose and program of humanism. Certainly religious institutions, their ritualistic forms, ecclesiastical methods, and communal activities must be reconstituted as rapidly as experience allows, in order to function effectively in the modern world.

FOURTEENTH: The humanists are firmly convinced that existing acquisitive and profit-motivated society has shown itself to be inadequate and that a radical change in methods, controls, and motives must be instituted. A socialized and cooperative economic order must be established to the end that the equitable distribution of the means of life be possible. The goal of humanism is a free and universal society in which people voluntarily and intelligently cooperate for the common good. Humanists demand a shared life in a shared world.

FIFTEENTH AND LAST: We assert that humanism will: (a) affirm life rather than deny it; (b) seek to elicit the possibilities of life, not flee from it; and (c) endeavor to establish the conditions of a satisfactory life for all, not merely for the few. By this positive morale and intention humanism will be guided, and from this perspective and alignment the techniques and efforts of humanism will flow.

So stand the theses of religious humanism. Though we consider the religious forms and ideas of our fathers no longer adequate, the quest for the good life is still the central task for mankind. Man is at last becoming aware that he alone is responsible for the realization of the world of his dreams, that he has within himself the power for its achievement. He must set intelligence and will to the task.

J.A.C. Fagginer Auer
E. Burdette Backus
Harry Elmer Barnes
L.M. Birkhead
Raymond B. Bragg
Edwin Arthur Burtt
Ernest Caldecott
A.J. Carlson
John Dewey
Albert C. Dieffenbach
John H. Dietrich
Bernard Fantus
William Floyd
F.H. Hankins
A. Eustace Haydon
Llewellyn Jones
Robert Morss Lovett
Harold P. Marley
R. Lester Mondale
Charles Francis Potter
John Herman Randall, Jr.
Curtis W. Reese
Oliver L. Reiser
Roy Wood Sellars
Clinton Lee Scott
Maynard Shipley
W. Frank Swift
V.T. Thayer
Eldred C. Vanderlaan

HUMANIST MANIFESTO I (AMERICAN HUMANIST ASSOCIATION) (continued)

Joseph Walker
Jacob J. Weinstein
Frank S. C. Wicks
David Rhys Williams
Edwin H. Wilson

Notes: *One of two statements generally accepted as reflective of the Humanist position, the original Humanist Manifesto was issued in 1933 and signed by a number of prominent early Humanist thinkers. True to the Humanist perspective, the statement not only clarifies a position on cosmological (or theological) issues, but makes pronouncements on a variety of social (i.e., human) problems. The position on a collective society has separated Humanists from others who share their cosmological views (see item 14).*

*   *   *

HUMANIST MANIFESTO II (AMERICAN HUMANIST ASSOCIATION)

PREFACE

It is forty years since *Humanist Manifesto I* (1933) appeared. Events since then make that earlier statement seem far too optimistic. Nazism has shown the depths of brutality of which humanity is capable. Other totalitarian regimes have suppressed human rights without ending poverty. Science has sometimes brought evil as well as good. Recent decades have shown that inhuman wars can be made in the name of peace. The beginnings of police states, even in democratic societies, widespread government espionage, and other abuses of power by military, political, and industrial elites, and the continuance of unyielding racism, all present a different and difficult social outlook. In various societies, the demands of women and minority groups for equal rights effectively challenge our generation.

As we approach the twenty-first century, however, an affirmative and hopeful vision is needed. Faith, commensurate with advancing knowledge, is also necessary. In the choice between despair and hope, humanists respond in this *Humanist Manifesto II* with a positive declaration for times of uncertainty.

As in 1933, humanists still believe that traditional theism, especially faith in the prayer-hearing God, assumed to love and care for persons, to hear and understand their prayers, and to be able to do something about them, is an unproved and outmoded faith. Salvationism, based on mere affirmation, still appears as harmful, diverting people with false hopes of heaven hereafter. Reasonable minds look to other means for survival.

Those who sign *Humanist Manifesto II* disclaim that they are setting forth a binding credo; their individual views would be stated in widely varying ways. The statement is, however, reaching for vision in a time that needs direction. It is social analysis in an effort at consensus. New statements should be developed to supersede this, but for today it is our conviction that humanism offers an alternative that can serve present-day needs and guide humankind toward the future.

Paul Kurtz
Edwin H. Wilson

The next century can be and should be the humanistic century. Dramatic scientific, technological, and ever-accelerating social and political changes crowd our awareness. We have virtually conquered the planet, explored the moon, overcome the natural limits of travel and communication; we stand at the dawn of a new age, ready to move farther into space and perhaps inhabit other planets. Using technology wisely, we can control our environment, conquer poverty, markedly reduce disease, extend our lifespan, significantly modify our behavior, alter the course of human evolution and cultural development, unlock vast new powers, and provide humankind with unparalleled opportunity for achieving an abundant and meaningful life.

The future is, however, filled with dangers. In learning to apply the scientific method to nature and human life, we have opened the door to ecological damage, overpopulation, dehumanizing institutions, totalitarian repression, and nuclear and biochemical disaster. Faced with apocalyptic prophesies and doomsday scenarios, many flee in despair from reason and embrace irrational cults and theologies of withdrawal and retreat.

Traditional moral codes and newer irrational cults both fail to meet the pressing needs of today and tomorrow. False "theologies of hope" and messianic ideologies, substituting new dogmas for old, cannot cope with existing world realities. They separate rather than unite peoples.

Humanity, to survive, requires bold and daring measures. We need to extend the uses of scientific method, not renounce them, to fuse reason with compassion in order to build constructive social and moral values. Confronted by many possible futures, we must decide which to pursue. The ultimate goal should be the fulfillment of the potential for growth in each human personality—not for the favored few, but for all of humankind. Only a shared world and global measures will suffice.

A humanist outlook will tap the creativity of each human being and provide the vision and courage for us to work together. This outlook emphasizes the role human beings can play in their own spheres of action. The decades ahead call for dedicated, clear-minded men and women able to marshal the will, intelligence, and cooperative skills for shaping a desirable future. Humanism can provide the purpose and inspiration that so many seek; it can give personal meaning and significance to human life.

Many kinds of humanism exist in the contemporary world. The varieties and emphases of naturalistic humanism include "scientific," "ethical," "democratic," "religious," and "Marxist" humanism. Free thought, atheism, agnosticism, skepticism, deism, rationalism, ethical culture, and liberal religion all claim to be heir to the humanist tradition. Humanism traces its roots from ancient China, classical Greece and Rome, through the Renaissance and the Enlightenment, to the scientific revolution of the modern world. But views that merely reject theism are not equivalent to humanism. They lack commitment to the positive belief in the possibilities of human progress and to the values central to it. Many within religious groups, believing in the future of humanism, now claim humanist credentials. Humanism is an ethical process through which we all can move, above and beyond the divisive particulars, heroic personalities, dogmatic creeds, and ritual customs of past religions or their mere negation.

We affirm a set of common principles that can serve as a basis for united action—positive principles relevant to the present human condition. They are a design for a secular society on a planetary scale.

For these reasons, we submit this new *Humanist Manifesto* for the future of humankind; for us, it is a vision of hope, a direction for satisfying survival.

RELIGION

FIRST: In the best sense, religion may inspire dedication to the highest ethical ideals. The cultivation of moral devotion and creative imagination is an expression of genuine "spiritual" experience and aspiration.

We believe, however, that traditional dogmatic or authoritarian religions that place revelation, God, ritual, or creed above human needs and experience do a disservice to the human species. Any account of nature should pass the tests of scientific evidence; in our judgment, the dogmas and myths of traditional religions do not do so. Even at this late date in human history, certain elementary facts based upon the critical use of scientific reason have to be restated. We find insufficient evidence for belief in the existence of a supernatural; it is either meaningless or irrelevant to the question of the survival and fulfillment of the human race. As nontheists, we begin with humans not God, nature not deity. Nature may indeed be broader and deeper than we now know; any new discoveries, however, will but enlarge our knowledge of the natural.

Some humanists believe we should reinterpret traditional religions and reinvest them with meanings appropriate to the current situation. Such redefinitions, however, often perpetuate old dependencies and escapisms; they easily become obscurantist, impeding the free use of the intellect. We need, instead, radically new human purposes and goals.

We appreciate the need to preserve the best ethical teachings in the religious traditions of humankind, many of which we share in common. But we reject those features of traditional religious morality that deny humans a full appreciation of their own potentialities and responsibilities. Traditional religions often offer solace to humans, but, as often, they inhibit humans from helping themselves or experiencing their full potentialities. Such institutions, creeds, and rituals often impede the will to serve others. Too often traditional faiths encourage dependence rather than independence, obedience rather than affirmation, fear rather than courage. More recently they have generated concerned social action, with many signs of relevance appearing in the wake of the "God Is Dead" theologies. But we can discover no divine purpose or providence for the human species. While there is much that we do not know, humans are responsible for what we are or will become. No deity will save us; we must save ourselves.

SECOND: Promises of immortal salvation or fear of eternal damnation are both illusory and harmful. They distract humans from present concerns, from self-actualization, and from rectifying social injustices. Modern science discredits such historic concepts as the "ghost in the machine" and the "separable soul." Rather, science affirms that the human species is an emergence from natural evolutionary forces. As far as we know, the total personality is a function of the biological organism transacting in a social and cultural context. There is no credible evidence that life survives the death of the body. We continue to exist in our progeny and in the way that our lives have influenced others in our culture.

Traditional religions are surely not the only obstacles to human progress. Other ideologies also impede human advance. Some forms of political doctrine, for instance, function religiously, reflecting the worst features of orthodoxy and authoritarianism, especially when they sacrifice individuals on the altar of Utopian promises. Purely economic and political viewpoints, whether capitalist or communist, often function as religious and ideological dogma. Although humans undoubtedly need economic and political goals, they also need creative values by which to live.

ETHICS

THIRD: We affirm that moral values derive their source from human experience. Ethics is *autonomous* and *situational*, needing no theological or ideological sanction. Ethics stems from human need and interest. To deny this distorts the whole basis of life. Human life has meaning because we create and develop our futures. Happiness and the creative realization of human needs and desires, individually and in shared enjoyment, are continuous themes of humanism. We strive for the good life, here and now. The goal is to pursue life's enrichment despite debasing forces of vulgarization, commercialization, bureaucratization, and dehumanization.

FOURTH: *Reason* and *intelligence* are the most effective instruments that humankind possesses. There is no substitute: neither faith nor passion suffices in itself. The controlled use of scientific methods, which have transformed the natural and social sciences since the Renaissance, must be extended further in the solution of human problems. But reason must be tempered by humility, since no group has a monopoly of wisdom or virtue. Nor is there any guarantee that all problems can be solved or all questions answered. Yet critical intelligence, infused by a sense of human caring, is the best method that humanity has for resolving problems. Reason should be balanced with compassion and empathy and the whole person fulfilled. Thus, we are not advocating the use of scientific intelligence independent of or in opposition to emotion, for we believe in the cultivation of feeling and love. As science pushes back the boundary of the known, one's sense of wonder is continually renewed, and art, poetry, and music find their places, along with religion and ethics.

THE INDIVIDUAL

FIFTH: *The preciousness and dignity of the individual person* is a central humanist value. Individuals should be encouraged to realize their own creative talents and

HUMANIST MANIFESTO II (AMERICAN HUMANIST ASSOCIATION) (continued)

desires. We reject all religious, ideological, or moral codes that denigrate the individual, suppress freedom, dull intellect, dehumanize personality. We believe in maximum individual autonomy consonant with social responsibility. Although science can account for the causes of behavior, the possibilities of individual *freedom of choice* exist in human life and should be increased.

SIXTH: In the area of sexuality, we believe that intolerant attitudes, often cultivated by orthodox religions and puritanical cultures, unduly repress sexual conduct. The right to birth control, abortion, and divorce should be recognized. While we do not approve of exploitive, denigrating forms of sexual expression, neither do we wish to prohibit, by law or social sanction, sexual behavior between consenting adults. The many varieties of sexual exploration should not in themselves be considered "evil." Without countenancing mindless permissiveness or unbridled promiscuity, a civilized society should be a *tolerant* one. Short of harming others or compelling them to do likewise, individuals should be permitted to express their sexual proclivities and pursue their life-styles as they desire. We wish to cultivate the development of a responsible attitude toward sexuality, in which humans are not exploited as sexual objects, and in which intimacy, sensitivity, respect, and honesty in interpersonal relations are encouraged. Moral education for children and adults is an important way of developing awareness and sexual maturity.

DEMOCRATIC SOCIETY

SEVENTH: To enhance freedom and dignity the individual must experience a full range of *civil liberties* in all societies. This includes freedom of speech and the press, political democracy, the legal right of opposition to governmental policies, fair judicial process, religious liberty, freedom of association, and artistic, scientific, and cultural freedom. It also includes a recognition of an individual's right to die with dignity, euthanasia, and the right to suicide. We oppose the increasing invasion of privacy, by whatever means, in both totalitarian and democratic societies. We would safeguard, extend, and implement the principles of human freedom evolved from the *Magna Carta* to the *Bill of Rights*, the *Rights of Man*, and the *Universal Declaration of Human Rights*.

EIGHTH: We are committed to an open and democratic society. We must extend *participatory democracy* in its true sense to the economy, the school, the family, the workplace, and voluntary associations. Decision-making must be decentralized to include widespread involvement of people at all levels—social, political, and economic. All persons should have a voice in developing the values and goals that determine their lives. Institutions should be responsive to expressed desires and needs. The conditions of work, education, devotion, and play should be humanized. Alienating forces should be modified or eradicated and bureaucratic structures should be held to a minimum. People are more important than decalogues, rules, proscriptions, or regulations.

NINTH: *The separation of church and state and the separation of ideology and state are imperatives*. The state should encourage maximum freedom for different moral, political, religious, and social values in society. It should not favor any particular religious bodies through the use of public monies, nor espouse a single ideology and function thereby as an instrument of propaganda or oppression, particularly against dissenters.

TENTH: Humane societies should evaluate economic systems not by rhetoric or ideology, but by whether or not they *increase economic well-being* for all individuals and groups, minimize poverty and hardship, increase the sum of human satisfaction, and enhance the quality of life. Hence the door is open to alternative economic systems. We need to democratize the economy and judge it by its responsiveness to human needs, testing results in terms of the common good.

ELEVENTH: *The principle of moral equality* must be furthered through elimination of all discrimination based upon race, religion, sex, age, or national origin. This means equality of opportunity and recognition of talent and merit. Individuals should be encouraged to contribute to their own betterment. If unable, then society should provide means to satisfy their basic economic, health, and cultural needs, including, wherever resources make possible, a minimum guaranteed annual income. We are concerned for the welfare of the aged, the infirm, the disadvantaged, and also for the outcasts—the mentally retarded, abandoned or abused children, the handicapped, prisoners, and addicts—for all who are neglected or ignored by society. Practicing humanists should make it their vocation to humanize personal relations.

We believe in the *right to universal education*. Everyone has a right to the cultural opportunity to fulfill his or her unique capacities and talents. The schools should foster satisfying and productive living. They should be open at all levels to any and all; the achievement of excellence should be encouraged. Innovative and experimental forms of education are to be welcomed. The energy and idealism of the young deserve to be appreciated and channeled to constructive purposes.

We deplore racial, religious, ethnic, or class antagonisms. Although we believe in cultural diversity and encourage racial and ethnic pride, we reject separations which promote alienation and set people and groups against each other; we envision an *integrated* community where people have a maximum opportunity for free and voluntary association.

We are *critical of sexism or sexual chauvinism*—male or female. We believe in equal rights for both women and men to fulfill their unique careers and potentialities as they see fit, free of invidious discrimination.

WORLD COMMUNITY

TWELFTH: We deplore the division of humankind on nationalistic grounds. We have reached a turning point in human history where the best option is to *transcend the limits of national sovereignty* and to move toward the building of a world community in which all sectors of the human family can participate. Thus we look to the development of a system of world law and a world order based upon transnational federal government. This would appreciate cultural pluralism and diversity. It would not exclude pride in national origins and accomplishments nor the handling of regional problems on a regional basis. Human progress, however, can no longer be achieved by focusing on one section of the world, Western or Eastern, developed or underdeveloped. For the first time in human history, no part of humankind can be isolated from any other. Each person's future is in some way linked to all. We thus reaffirm a commitment to the building of world community, at the same time recognizing that this commits us to some hard choices.

THIRTEENTH: This world community must *renounce the resort to violence and force* as a method of solving international disputes. We believe in the peaceful adjudication of differences by international courts and by the development of the arts of negotiation and compromise. War is obsolete. So is the use of nuclear, biological, and chemical weapons. It is a planetary imperative to reduce the level of military expenditures and turn these savings to peaceful and people-oriented uses.

FOURTEENTH: The world community must engage in *cooperative planning* concerning the use of rapidly depleting resources. The planet earth must be considered a single ecosystem. Ecological damage, resource depletion, and excessive population growth must be checked by international concord. The cultivation and conservation of nature is a moral value; we should perceive ourselves as integral to the sources of our being in nature. We must free our world from needless pollution and waste, responsibly guarding and creating wealth, both natural and human. Exploitation of natural resources, uncurbed by social conscience, must end.

FIFTEENTH: The problems of *economic growth and development* can no longer be resolved by one nation alone; they are worldwide in scope. It is the moral obligation of the developed nations to provide—through an international authority that safeguards human rights—massive technical, agricultural, medical, and economic assistance, including birth control techniques, to the developing portions of the globe. World poverty must cease. Hence extreme disproportions in wealth, income, and economic growth should be reduced on a worldwide basis.

SIXTEENTH: *Technology is a vital key* to human progress and development. We deplore any neo-romantic efforts to condemn indiscriminately all technology and science or to counsel retreat from its further extension and use for the good of humankind. We would resist any moves to censor basic scientific research on moral, political, or social grounds. Technology must, however, be carefully judged by the consequences of its use; harmful and destructive changes should be avoided. We are particularly disturbed when technology and bureaucracy control, manipulate, or modify human beings without their consent. Technological feasibility does not imply social or cultural desirability.

SEVENTEENTH: We must expand communication and transportation across frontiers. Travel restrictions must cease. The world must be open to diverse political, ideological, and moral viewpoints and evolve a worldwide system of television and radio for information and education. We thus call for full international cooperation in culture, science, the arts, and technology *across ideological borders*. We must learn to live openly together or we shall perish together.

HUMANITY AS A WHOLE

IN CLOSING: The world cannot wait for a reconciliation of competing political or economic systems to solve its problems. These are the times for men and women of good will to further the building of a peaceful and prosperous world. We urge that parochial loyalties and inflexible moral and religious ideologies be transcended. We urge recognition of the common humanity of all people. We further urge the use of reason and compassion to produce the kind of world we want—a world in which peace, prosperity, freedom, and happiness are widely shared. Let us not abandon that vision in despair or cowardice. We are responsible for what we are or will be. Let us work together for a humane world by means commensurate with humane ends. Destructive ideological differences among communism, capitalism, socialism, conservatism, liberalism, and radicalism should be overcome. Let us call for an end to terror and hatred. We will survive and prosper only in a world of shared humane values. We can initiate new directions for humankind; ancient rivalries can be superseded by broad-based cooperative efforts. The commitment to tolerance, understanding, and peaceful negotiation does not necessitate acquiescence to the status quo nor the damming up of dynamic and revolutionary forces. The true revolution is occurring and can continue in countless non-violent adjustments. But this entails the willingness to step forward onto new and expanding plateaus. At the present juncture of history, commitment to all humankind is the highest commitment of which we are capable; it transcends the narrow allegiances of church, state, party, class, or race in moving toward a wider vision of human potentiality. What more daring a goal for humankind than for each person to become, in ideal as well as practice, a citizen of a world community. It is a classical vision; we can now give it new vitality. Humanism thus interpreted is a moral force that has time on its side. We believe that humankind has the potential intelligence, good will, and cooperative skill to implement this commitment in the decades ahead.

We, the undersigned, while not necessarily endorsing every detail of the above, pledge our general support to *Humanist Manifesto II* for the future of humankind. These affirmations are not a final credo or dogma but an expression of a living and growing faith. We invite others in all lands to join us in further developing and working for these goals.

Lionel Abel, *Prof. of English, State Univ. of New York at Buffalo*
Khoren Arisian, *Board of Leaders, NY Soc. for Ethical Culture*
Isaac Asimov, *author*
George Axtelle, *Prof. Emeritus, Southern Illinois Univ.*
Archie J. Bahm, *Prof. of Philosophy Emeritus, Univ. of N.M.*
Paul H. Beattie, *Pres., Fellowship of Religious Humanists*

HUMANIST MANIFESTO II (AMERICAN HUMANIST ASSOCIATION) (continued)

Keith Beggs, *Exec. Dir., American Humanist Association*

Malcolm Bissell, *Prof. Emeritus, Univ. of Southern California*

H.J. Blackham, *Chm., Social Morality Council, Great Britain*

Brand Blanshard, *Prof. Emeritus, Yale University*

Paul Blanshard, *author*

Joseph L. Blau, *Prof. of Religion, Columbia University*

Sir Hermann Bondi, *Prof. of Math., King's Coll., Univ. of London*

Howard Box, *Leader, Brooklyn Society for Ethical Culture*

Raymond B. Bragg, *Minister Emer., Unitarian Ch., Kansas City*

Theodore Brameld, *Visiting Prof., C.U.N.Y.*

Lester R. Brown, *Senior Fellow, Overseas Development Council*

Bette Chambers, *Pres., American Humanist Association*

John Ciardi, *poet*

Francis Crick, *M.D., Great Britain*

Arthur Danto, *Prof. of Philosophy, Columbia University*

Lucien de Coninck, *Prof., University of Gand, Belgium*

Miriam Allen deFord, *author*

Edd Doerr, *Americans United for Separation of Church and State*

Peter Draper, *M.D., Guy's Hospital Medical School, London*

Paul Edwards, *Prof. of Philosophy, Brooklyn College*

Albert Ellis, *Exec. Dir., Inst. Adv. Study Rational Psychotherapy*

Edward L. Ericson, *Board of Leaders, NY Soc. for Ethical Culture*

H.J. Eysenck, *Prof. of Psychology, Univ. of London*

Roy P. Fairfield, *Coordinator, Union Graduate School*

Herbert Feigl, *Prof. Emeritus, Univ. of Minnesota*

Raymond Firth, *Prof. Emeritus of Anthropology, Univ. of London*

Antony Flew, *Prof. of Philosophy, The Univ., Reading, England*

Kenneth Furness, *Exec. Secy., British Humanist Association*

Erwin Gaede, *Minister, Unitarian Church, Ann Arbor, Mich.*

Richard S. Gilbert, *Minister, First Unitarian Ch., Rochester, N.Y.*

Charles Wesley Grady, *Minister, Unit. Univ. Ch., Arlington, Ma.*

Maxine Green, *Prof., Teachers College, Columbia University*

Thomas C. Greening, *Editor, Journal of Humanistic Psychology*

Alan F. Guttmacher, *Pres., Planned Parenthood Fed. of America*

J. Harold Hadley, *Min., Unit. Univ. Ch., Pt. Washington, N.Y.*

Hector Hawton, *Editor, Question, Great Britain*

A. Eustace Haydon, *Prof. Emeritus of History of Religions*

James Hemming, *Psychologist, Great Britain*

Palmer A. Hilty, *Adm. Secy., Fellowship of Religious Humanists*

Hudson Hoagland, *Pres. Emeritus, Worcester Fdn. for Exper. Bio.*

Robert S. Hoagland, *Editor, Religious Humanism*

Sidney Hook, *Prof. Emeritus of Philosophy, New York University*

James F. Hornback, *Leader, Ethical Society of St. Louis*

James M. Hutchinson, *Minister Emer., First Unit. Ch., Cincinnati*

Mordecai M. Kaplan, *Rabbi, Fndr. of Jewish Reconstr. Movement*

John C. Kidneigh, *Prof. of Social Work., Univ. of Minnesota*

Lester A. Kirkendall, *Prof. Emeritus, Oregon State Univ.*

Margaret Knight, *Univ. of Aberdeen, Scotland*

Jean Kotkin, *Exec. Secy., American Ethical Union*

Richard Kostelanetz, *poet*

Paul Kurtz, *Editor, The Humanist*

Lawrence Lader, *Chm., Natl. Assn. for Repeal of Abortion Laws*

Edward Lamb, *Pres., Lamb Communications, Inc.*

Corliss Lamont, *Chm., Natl. Emergency Civil Liberties Comm.*

Chauncey D. Leake, *Prof., Univ. of California, San Francisco*

Alfred McC. Lee, *Prof. Emeritus, Soc.-Anthropology, C.U.N.Y.*

Elizabeth Briant Lee, *author*

Christopher Macy, *Dir., Rationalist Press Assn., Great Britain*

Clorinda Margolis, *Jefferson Comm. Mental Health Cen., Phila.*

Joseph Margolis, *Prof. of Philosophy, Temple Univ.*

Harold P. Marley, *Ret. Unitarian Minister*

Floyd W. Matson, *Prof. of American Studies, Univ. of Hawaii*

Lester Mondale, *former Pres., Fellowship of Religious Humanists*

Lloyd Morain, *Pres., Illinois Gas Company*

Mary Morain, *Editorial Bd., Intl. Soc. for General Semantics*

Charles Morris, *Prof. Emeritus, Univ. of Florida*

Henry Morgentaler, *M.D., Past Pres., Humanist Assn. of Canada*

Mary Mothersill, *Prof. of Philosophy, Barnard College*

Jerome Nathanson, *Chm. Bd. of Leaders, NY Soc. Ethical Culture*

Billy Joe Nichols, *Minister, Richardson Unitarian Church, Texas*

Kai Nielsen, *Prof. of Philosophy, Univ. of Calgary, Canada*

P. H. Nowell-Smith, *Prof. of Philosophy, York Univ., Canada*

Chaim Perelman, *Prof. of Philosophy, Univ. of Brussels, Belgium*

James W. Prescott, *Natl. Inst. of Child Health and Human Dev.*

Harold J. Quigley, *Leader, Ethical Humanist Society of Chicago*

Howard Radest, *Prof. of Philosophy, Ramapo College*

John Herman Randall, Jr., *Prof. Emeritus, Columbia Univ.*

Oliver L. Reiser, *Prof. Emeritus, Univ. of Pittsburgh*

Robert G. Risk, *Pres., Leadville Corp.*

Lord Ritchie-Calder, *formerly Univ. of Edinburgh, Scotland*

B. T. Rocca, Jr., *Consultant, Intl. Trade and Commodities*

Andre D. Sakharov, *Academy of Sciences, Moscow, U.S.S.R.*

Sidney H. Scheuer, *Chm., Natl. Comm. for an Effective Congress*

Herbert W. Schneider, *Prof. Emeritus, Claremont Grad. School*

Clinton Lee Scott, *Universalist Minister, St. Petersburgh, Fla.*

Roy Wood Sellars, *Prof. Emeritus, Univ. of Michigan*

A. B. Shah, *Pres., Indian Secular Society*

B. F. Skinner, *Prof. of Psychology, Harvard Univ.*

Kenneth J. Smith, *Leader, Philadelphia Ethical Society*

Matthew Ies Spetter, *Chm., Dept. Ethics, Ethical Culture Schools*

Mark Starr, *Chm., Esperanto Info. Center*

Svetozar Stojanovic, *Prof. of Philosophy, Univ. Belgrade, Yugoslavia*

Harold Taylor, *Project Director, World University Student Project*

V.T. Thayer, *author*

Herbert A. Tonne, *Ed. Board, Journal of Business Education*

Jack Tourin, *Pres., American Ethical Union*

E.C. Vanderlaan, *lecturer*

J.P. van Praag, *Chm., Intl. Humanist and Ethical Union, Utrecht*

Maurice B. Visscher, *M.D. Prof. Emeritus, Univ. of Minnesota*

Goodwin Watson, *Assn. Coordinator, Union Graduate School*

Gerald Wendt, *author*

Henry N. Weiman, *Prof. Emeritus, Univ. of Chicago*

Sherwin Wine, *Rabbi, Soc. for Humanistic Judaism*

Edwin H. Wilson, *Ex. Dir. Emeritus, American Humanist Assn.*

Bertram D. Wolfe, *Hoover Institution*

Alexander S. Yesenin-Volpin, *mathematician*

Marvin Zimmerman, *Prof. of Philosophy, State Univ. NY at Bflo.*

ADDITIONAL SIGNERS

Gina Allen, *author*

John C. Anderson, *Humanist Counselor*

Peter O. Anderson, *Assistant Professor, Ohio State University*

William F. Anderson, *Humanist Counselor*

John Anton, *Professor, Emory University*

Sir Alfred Ayer, *Professor, Oxford, Great Britain*

Celia Baker

Ernest Baker, *Associate Professor, University of the Pacific*

Marjorie S. Baker, *Ph.D., Pres., Humanist Community of San Francisco*

Henry S. Basayne, *Assoc. Exec. Off., Assn. for Humanistic Psych.*

Walter Behrendt, *Vice Pres., European Parliament, W. Germany*

Mildred H. Blum, *Secy., American Ethical Union*

W. Bonness, *Pres., Bund Freirelgioser Gemeinden, West Germany*

Robert O. Boothe, *Prof. Emer. Cal. Polytechnic*

Clement A. Bosch

Madeline L. Bosch

Bruni Boyd, *Vice Pres., American Ethical Union*

J. Lloyd Brereton, *ed.,* Humanist in Canada

Nancy Brewer, *Humanist Counselor*

D. Bronder, *Bund Freirelgioser Gemeinden, West Germany*

Charles Brownfield, *Asst. Prof., Queensborough Community College, CUNY*

Costantia Brownfield, *R.N.*

Margaret Brown, *Assoc. Prof., Oneonta State Univ. College*

Beulah L. Bullard, *Humanist Counselor*

Joseph Chuman, *Leader, Ethical Soc. of Essex Co.*

Gordon Clanton, *Asst. Prof., Trenton State College*

Daniel S. Collins, *Leader, Unitarian Fellowship of Jonesboro, Ark.*

Wm. Creque, *Pres., Fellowship of Humanity, Oakland, Ca.*

M. Benjamin Dell, *Dir., Amer. Humanist Assn.*

James Durant IV, *Prof., Polk Comm. College, Winter Haven, Fla*

Gerald A. Ehrenreich, *Assoc. Prof., Univ. of Kansas School of Medicine*

Marie Erdmann, *Teacher, Campbell Elementary School*

Robert L. Erdmann, *Ph.D., IBM*

Hans S. Falck, *Disting, Professor, Menninger Foundation*

James Farmer, *Director, Public Policy Training Institute*

Ed Farrar

Joe Felmet, *Humanist Counselor*

Thomas Ferrick, *Leader, Ethical Society of Boston*

Norman Fleishman, *Exec. Vice Pres., Planned Parenthood World Population, Los Angeles*

Joseph Fletcher, *Visiting Prof., Sch. of Medicine, Univ. of Virginia*

Douglas Frazier, *Leader, American Ethical Union*

Betty Friedan, *Founder, N.O.W.*

Harry M. Geduld, *Professor, Indiana University*

Roland Gibson, *President, Art Foundation of Potsdam, N.Y.*

Aron S. Gilmartin, *Minister, Mt. Diablo Unitarian Church, Walnut Creek, Ca.*

Annabelle Glasser, *Director, American Ethical Union*

Rebecca Goldblum, *Director, American Ethical Union*

Louis R. Gomberg, *Humanist Counselor*

Harold N. Gordon, *Vice President, American Ethical Union*

Sol Gordon, *Professor, Syracuse University*

Theresa Gould, *American Ethical Union*

Gregory O. Grant, *Captain, USAF*

Ronald Green, *Asst. Professor, New York University*

LeRue Grim, *Secretary, American Humanist Association*

S. Spencer Grin, *Publisher,* Saturday Review/World

Josephine R. Gurbarg, *Secy., Humanist Society of Greater Philadelphia*

Samuel J. Gurbarg

Lewis M. Gubrud, *Executive Director, Mediator Fellowship, Providence, R.I.*

Frank A. Hall, *Minister, Murray Univ. Church, Attleboro, Mass.*

Harold Hansen, *President, Space Coast Chapter, AHA*

Abul Hasanat, *Secretary, Bangladesh Humanist Society*

HUMANIST MANIFESTO II (AMERICAN HUMANIST
ASSOCIATION) (continued)

Ethelbert Haskins, *Director, American Humanist Association*

Lester H. Hayes, *Public Relations Director, American Income Life Insurance Company*

Donald E. Henshaw, *Humanist Counselor*

Alex Hershaft, *Principal Scientist, Booz Allen Applied Research*

Ronald E. Hestand, *author and columnist*

Irving Louis Horowitz, *editor,* Society

Warren S. Hoskins, *Humanist Counselor*

Mark W. Huber, *Director, American Ethical Union*

Harold J. Hutchison, *Humanist Counselor*

Sir Julian Huxley, *former head, UNESCO, Great Britain*

Arthur M. Jackson, *Exec. Dir., Humanist Community of San Jose; Treasurer, American Humanist Association*

Linda R. Jackson, *Director, American Humanist Association*

Steven Jacobs, *former President, American Ethical Union*

Thomas B. Johnson, Jr., *consulting psychologist*

Robert Edward Jones, *Exec. Dir., Joint Washington Office for Social Concern*

Marion Kahn, *Pres., Humanist Society of Metropolitan New York*

Alec E. Kelley, *Professor, University of Arizona*

Marvin Kohl, *Professor, SUNY at Fredonia*

Frederick C. Kramer, *Humanist Counselor*

Eugene Kreves, *Minister, DuPage Unit. Church, Naperville, Ill.*

Pierre Lamarque, *France*

Helen B. Lamb, *economist*

Jerome D. Lang, *Pres., Humanist Assoc. of Greater Miami, Fla.*

Harvey Lebrun, *Chairman, Chapter Assembly, AHA*

Helen Leibson, *President, Philadelphia Ethical Society*

John F. MacEnulty, Jr., *Pres., Humanist Soc. of Jacksonville, Fla.*

James T. McCollum, *Humanist Counselor*

Vashti McCollum, *former President of AHA*

Russell L. McKnight, *Pres., Humanist Association of Los Angeles*

Ludlow P. Mahan, Jr., *Pres., Humanist Chapter of Rhode Island*

Andrew Malleson, *M.D., psychiatrist*

Clem Martin, *M.D.*

James R. Martin, *Humanist Counselor*

Stanley E. Mayabb, *Co-Fndr.: Humanist Group of Vacaville and Men's Colony, San Luis Obispo*

Zhores Medvedev, *scientist, U.S.S.R.*

Abelardo Mena, *M.D., senior psychiatrist, V.A. Hospital, Miami, Fla.*

Jacques Monod, *Institut Pasteur, France*

Herbert J. Muller, *Professor, University of Indiana*

Robert J. Myler, *Title Officer, Title Insurance & Trust Company*

Gunnar Myrdal, *Professor, University of Stockholm, Sweden*

H. Kyle Nagel, *Minister, Unit. Univ. Church of Kinston, N.C.*

Dorothy N. Naiman, *Professor Emerita, Lehman College, CUNY*

Muriel Neufeld, *Executive Committee, American Ethical Union*

Walter B. Neumann, *Treasurer, American Ethical Union*

G.D. Parikh, *Indian Radical Humanist Association, India*

Eleanor Wright Pelrine, *author, Canada*

Bernard Porter, *President, Toronto Humanist Association*

William Earl Proctor, Jr., *President, Philadelphia area, AHA*

Gonzalo Quiogue, *Vice Pres., Humanist Assn. of the Philippines*

James A. Rafferty, *Lecturer, USIU School of Human Behavior*

Anthony F. Rand, *President, Humanist Society of Greater Detroit*

A. Philip Randolph, *President, A. Philip Randolph Institute*

Ruth Dickinson Reams, *President, Humanist Association National Capital Area*

Jean-Francois Revel, *journalist, France*

Bernard L. Riback, *Humanist Counselor*

B. T. Rocca, Sr., *President, United Secularists of America*

M. L. Rosenthal, *Professor, New York University*

Jack C. Rubenstein, *Executive Committee, AEU*

Joseph R. Sanders, *Professor, University of West Florida*

William Schulz, *Ph.D. cand., Meadville/Lombard, Univ. of Chicago*

Walter G. Schwartz, *Dir., Humanist Comm. of San Francisco*

John W. Sears, *clinical psychologist*

Naomi Shaw, *Pres., National Women's Conference, AEU*

R. L. Shuford, III, *Instructor, Charlotte Country Day School*

Sidney Siller, *Chm. Comm. for Fair Divorce and Alimony Laws*

Joell Silverman, *Chm., Religious Education Committee, AEU*

Warren A. Smith, *Pres., Variety Sound Corp.*

A. Solomon, *coordinator, Indian Secular Society*

Robert Sone

Robert M. Stein, *Co-Chairman, Public Affairs Committee, AEU*

Stuart Stein, *Director, American Ethical Union*

Arnold E. Sylvester

Emerson Symonds, *Director, Sensory Awareness Center*

Carolyn Symonds, *marriage counselor*

Ward Tabler, *Visiting Professor, Starr King School*

Barbara M. Tabler

V. M. Tarkunde, *Pres., All Indian Radical Humanist Assn., India*

Erwin Theobold, *Instructor, Pasadena City College*

Ernest N. Ukpaby, *Dean, University of Nigeria*

Renate Vambery, *Ethical Soc. of St. Louis, President, AHA St. Louis Chapter*

Nick D. Vasileff, *St. Louis Ethical Society*

Robert J. Wellman, *Humanist Chaplain, C.W. Post Center, Long Island University*

May H. Weis, *UN Representative for IHEU*

Paul D. Weston, *Leader, Ethical Culture Society of Bergen County*

Georgia H. Wilson, *retired, Political Sc. Dept., Brooklyn College*

H. Van Rensselaer Wilson, *Prof., Emer., Brooklyn College*

James E. Woodrow, *Exec. Dir., Asgard Enterprises, Inc.*

Notes: *This second Humanist Manifesto was issued in 1973, forty years after the first, with the intention of updating the original on a number of points, and venturing observations on a broader range of issues. In light of events taking place since the first statement appeared (World War II, the Holocaust), its tone was thought to be overly optimistic. Widely circulated prior to its formal publication, the Humanist Manifesto II appeared with the signatures of a number of prominent academics. In the years since its publication, many more prominent individuals, primarily from the United States and England, have also signed it.*

The Humanist Manifesto II was also an attempt to expand upon the agreement of the Amsterdam Declaration, the somewhat hastily written statement of the International and Ethical Union issued in 1952.

*   *   *

AMSTERDAM DECLARATION [INTERNATIONAL HUMANIST AND ETHICAL UNION (AMERICAN HUMANIST ASSOCIATION AND THE AMERICAN ETHICAL UNION)]

This congress is a response to the widespread demand for an alternative to the religions which claim to be based on revelation on the one hand and totalitarian systems on the other. The alternative offered as a third way out of the present crisis of civilization is Humanism, which is not a sect, but the outcome of a long tradition that has inspired many of the world's thinkers and creative artists, and given rise to science. Ethical Humanism unites all those who cannot any longer believe the various creeds and are willing to base their convictions on respect for man as a spiritual and moral being. The fundamentals of modern ethical Humanism are as follows:

1. *It is democratic.* It aims at the fullest possible development of every human being. It holds that this is a matter of right. The democratic principle can be applied to all human relationships and is not restricted to methods of government.

2. *It seeks to use science creatively, not destructively.* It advocates a worldwide application of scientific method to problems of human welfare. Humanists believe that the tremendous problems with which mankind is faced in this age of transition can be solved. Science gives the means but science itself does not propose ends.

3. *Humanism is ethical.* It affirms the dignity of man and the right of the individual to the greatest possible freedom of development compatible with the rights of others. There is a danger that in seeking to utilise scientific knowledge in a complex society individual freedom may be threatened by the very impersonal machine that has been created to save it. Ethical Humanism, therefore, rejects totalitarian attempts to perfect the machine in order to obtain immediate gains at the cost of human values.

4. *It insists that personal liberty is an end that must be combined with social responsibility* in order that it shall not be sacrificed to the improvement of material conditions. Without intellectual liberty, fundamental research, on which progress must in the long run depend, would not be possible. Humanism ventures to build a world on the free person responsible to society. On behalf of individual freedom humanism is undogmatic, imposing no creed upon its adherents. It is thus committed to education free from indoctrination.

5. *It is a way of life,* aiming at the maximum possible fulfillment, through the cultivation of ethical and creative living. It can be a way of life for everyone everywhere if the individual is capable of the response required by the changing social order. The primary task of humanism to-day is to make men aware in the simplest terms of what it can mean to them and what it commits them to. By utilizing in this context, and for purposes of peace, the new power which science has given us, humanists have confidence that the present crisis can be surmounted. Liberated from fear the energies of man will be available for a self-realisation to which it is impossible to foresee the limit.

Ethical Humanism is thus a faith that answers the challenge of our times. We call upon men who share this conviction to associate themselves with us.

Notes: *Both the American Humanist Association and the American Ethical Union participated in the formation of the International Humanist and Ethical Union, which brought together like minded individuals and organizations from a number of countries in Europe and North America. At the original meeting in the Netherlands in 1952, a declaration was drafted. The statement reflected the broad concensus, but, proving unsatisfactory to many, later spurred the production of the Humanist Manifesto II.*

*   *   *

THE SIXTEEN COMMANDMENTS (CHURCH OF THE CREATOR)

Basic to our Religion. To emphasize that the Sixteen Commandments as set forth in NATURE'S ETERNAL RELIGION are still and forever the Basic Commandments of CREATIVITY we spell them out again in this, the White Man's Bible. Since I have already expanded on the commandments in NATURE'S ETERNAL RELIGION, I will not repeat it here, and let the record stand.

1. It is the avowed duty and holy responsibility of each generation to assure and secure for all time the existence of the White Race upon the face of this planet.

2. Be fruitful and multiply. Do your part in helping to populate the world with your own kind. It is our sacred goal to populate the lands of this earth with White people exclusively.

3. Remember that the inferior colored races are our deadly enemies, and the most dangerous of all is the Jewish race. It is our immediate objective to relentlessly expand the White Race, and keep shrinking our enemies.

4. The guiding principle of all your actions shall be: What is best for the White Race?

5. You shall keep your race pure. Pollution of the White Race is a heinous crime against Nature and against your own race.

6. Your first loyalty belongs to the White Race.

7. Show preferential treatment in business dealings with members of your own race. Phase out all dealings with Jews as soon as possible. Do not employ niggers or other coloreds. Have social contacts only with members of your own racial family.

8. Destroy and banish all Jewish thought and influence from society. Work hard to bring about a White world as soon as possible.

9. Work and creativity are our genius. We regard work as a noble pursuit and our willingness to work a blessing to our race.

10. Decide in early youth that during your lifetime you will make at least one major lasting contribution to the White Race.

11. Uphold the honor of your race at all times.

12. It is our duty and our privilege to further Nature's plan by striving towards the advancement and improvement of our future generations.

13. You shall honor, protect and venerate the sanctity of the family unit, and hold it sacred. It is the present link in the long golden chain of our White Race.

14. Throughout your life you shall faithfully uphold our pivotal creed of Blood, Soil and Honor. Practice it diligently, for it is the heart of our faith.

15. As a proud member of the White Race, think and act positively, Be courageous, confident and aggressive. Utilize constructively your creative ability.

16. We, the Racial Comrades of the White Race, are determined to regain complete and unconditional control of our own destiny.

Notes: *The Church of the Creator has issued a number of statements as manifestos, but these sixteen guiding commandments are the most authoritative document accepted by church members. The commandments delineate quite clearly the church's racial attitudes and the actions appropriate for anyone who accepts them.*

THE HUMANITARIAN CREED (CHURCH OF THE HUMANITARIAN GOD)

I am alive today to help in some way a fellow man. May my daily service to humanity be a credit for this proving ground that is Earth.

Let no man, or no country, or any allegiance deter me from observing the natural law of sustaining life.

I pledge myself to rebuke injustice openly and to aid my fellow man as best I can.

May I injure or kill no other human, except in a moral case of self-defense. I pledge never to serve in the armed forces of any nation at a time when that nation is engaged in immoral combat.

Above all, may I forever seek and accept truth, and the reason for my being.

Notes: *This creed defines humanitarianism as taught by the Church of the Humanitarian God.*

* * *

THE CREED (CONFRATERNITY OF DEISTS)

I BELIEVE in ONE GOD—THE SUPREME INTELLIGENCE.

I BELIEVE that constructive exercise of human intelligence contributes to the glorification of THE SUPREME.

I BELIEVE that ALL man-written scriptures are literary works, having no value as religious, historical or chronological records.

I BELIEVE that the church of the Deist should constitute the FREE UNIVERSITY, disseminating SCIENTIFIC knowledge and nurturing the arts.

I BELIEVE that it is my social duty to work mutually for the Spiritual and Temporal elevation of the people.

Notes: *Deism, as promulgated by the confraternity, is the religion of the free and carries few of the connotations of classical Deism. The creed allows a wide variation of opinion on even the most basic issues.*

* * *

SOME BASIC STATEMENTS ASSUMED BY THE SOCIETY OF EVANGELICAL AGNOSTICS

One should approach all questions and issues with an open mind.

One should consider it to be immoral to advocate conclusions without adequate or satisfactory evidence.

One should accept not knowing as a fundamental reality in one's life

Notes: *The three statements around which the society is organized constitute a definition of agnosticism.*

WHAT DO UNITARIANS BELIEVE?
[UNITARIAN-UNIVERSALIST ASSOCIATION (AMERICAN UNITARIAN ASSOCIATION)]

For the purpose of rendering, if I may, some little assistance to the large number of persons all about us, who are asking the above question, as well as with the hope, possibly, of stirring up others still, who have not yet done so, to inquire, I have prepared the following brief summary of information regarding the principles and positions of Unitarians.

FREEDOM OF INQUIRY IN RELIGION. We believe that the same God who is the author of religion is also the author of reason; that there is no other way in which truth can possibly be separated from error in religion except by investigation and the use of reason; and therefore, that it is of the highest importance that there should be everywhere the freest and fullest inquiry with reference to religious things,—in this inquiry every man being permitted to stand upon his own feet, and to judge for himself, subject to no dictation or pressure from councils, synods, conferences, presbyteries, creeds, catechisms, fathers of the church, doctors of the church, or preachers.

NO CREED. We have no creed, that is, no authoritative statement of beliefs which persons are required to subscribe to; first, because we believe to the fullest extent in liberty of thought, and would do nothing to check it; secondly, because, in the very nature of the case, it is impossible for any two persons to see all truth exactly alike, and therefore a creed made by one man for another must be more or less inadequate if not false; thirdly, because if we had a creed fitted to our wants to-day, we should either have to stop growing in knowledge and insight or else get a new one to-morrow; fourthly, because neither Jesus nor the Apostles taught any, nor did the early church possess any; fifthly, because history gives unmistakable proof that creeds and authoritative statements of doctrine have always tended to tear the Christian Church to pieces, to multiply sects, to suggest and foster persecutions, and to hinder progress.

SOMETHING BETTER. But while we have no creed or fixed statements of doctrine which we prescribe as a condition of Christian fellowship, we *do* have a *great, central principle*, and a *few great, simple, central faiths*. Our central principle is this: the necessary harmony of true religion with reason, or the supreme authority of reason and moral consciousness in the search after religious truth. From this fundamental principle, everywhere held to among us, has resulted as essential agreement as to the general, fundamental faiths upon which our movement builds—an agreement probably quite as great as can be found in churches which have authoritative creeds.

GOD. We believe God to be one, not three or more; an intelligent First Cause, not an ultimate blind force; beyond our utmost thought powerful, wise, holy, just, good, not malignant, or indifferent, or in any way imperfect: the embodiment of all, and more than all, that we can possibly mean by that name which Jesus taught us to call him, "our Father," and hence one who can never cease to love and care for all his children, in this world or any other.

INSPIRATION. We believe that inspiration is not something which can be locked up in writing, or confined to any age or people; but that now, to-day, and here with us, just as truly as 2,000 or 8,000 years ago and in Palestine, the Infinite Spirit of Wisdom, Truth, Beauty and Love, waits to come with its inspiration into every receptive mind.

REVELATION. We believe that revelation is progressive, not stationary; that it is of all times, countries and races, not of the remote past or of a single people only; that it comes through many channels, including nature, history and the mind of man, not through any single channel alone, or in any miraculous way; that, so far from revelation being confined to one book, all moral and spiritual truth known to man belongs to it; that as a race we are now standing only in the morning dawn of revelation, not in its evening twilight.

THE BIBLE. We believe that the Bible is the greatest, the most influential, the most important, the noblest depository of this revelation that has come down to us from the past, and is therefore to be prized by us as the most precious and sacred of books; though not as the only sacred book of the world, nor by any means an infallible book.

JESUS. Accepting the Bible teaching that all men are "sons of God," we yet believe that Jesus, by reason of the exceptional purity and perfectness of his character, was pre-eminently what the New Testament in a number of places calls him, *the* son of God. We believe him to have been divine, but not Deity,—as we believe that humanity, in the degree of its perfection, is everywhere divine. We teach tender love and earnest reverence toward him, but we do not worship him, because, among other reasons, he himself, both by word and example, taught us to worship only God—his Father and ours.

COMING TO JESUS. While we believe that no words in our day are more often used among certain large classes of religious people, in a sense which has in it *no sense*, but is mere sentimentalism and cant, we at the same time most sincerely believe in a real coming to Jesus:—that is, a coming (through study and reflection and effort) to a constantly more and more perfect conformity to his pure and exalted spirit and life.

BELIEVING IN JESUS. Believing in Jesus we do not understand to consist in believing any speculative theological doctrines *about* him,—as his incarnation, his deity, his atonement, his relation to a trinity. True believing in Jesus we understand to consist in believing in *him*,—in what he was and did, in the kind of life he lived and character he exhibited; in such love to God and man, such devotion to truth and duty, such beautiful self-sacrifice, such patience and gentleness, such bravery and fidelity as he everywhere taught and exemplified.

FOLLOWING CHRIST. We believe that the truest following of Christ is to go about doing good.

CONVERSION. The word "convert" means "to turn," or "to turn about." Inasmuch, therefore as all men, being imperfect, are liable to commit errors, and fall to walking in ways that are not right, we believe that all men have need to be converted, not once but again and again.

THE NEW BIRTH. We believe that to be born again, and to continue to be born again, into new and perpetually new, into finer and higher and forevermore finer and higher spiritual life, is what Jesus taught to be the law of our being, and the design of the Creator for all men.

SALVATION. We believe in salvation by character, not salvation by purchase or transfer; and that Jesus saves men solely by helping them to become better, not by vicariously atoning for their sins.

The whole idea, in all its forms, that God, before he can or will pardon men's sins, must have some third party to make him willing, or some sort of "plan" or "scheme," whereby he becomes able to pardon, we utterly reject. We believe that God's paternity is real, and not a mere pretense of paternity, and therefore that the moment any human child of his manifests sincere penitence and seeks forgiveness of his sin, God freely and joyfully forgives—without any thought, ever, of requiring first the suffering of an innocent person in the place of the guilty. In our reading of the Parable of the Prodigal Son—that part of the teaching of Jesus in which he illustrates most fully God's dealing with his erring children—we find the father represented as running to meet the penitent son "while he was yet a great way off": and we do not find even a hint that the elder brother, who had not sinned, was required first to make an "atonement" for the younger, or to "intercede" for him, or to "satisfy justice," or to "propitiate" the father, or do anything in any way to promote the father's willingness or ability to forgive.

THE GUILT OF THE RACE FOR ADAM'S TRANS-GRESSION. We believe that nobody can be guilty for anybody's sin but his own.

GOOD AND EVIL. We believe that the world is not fallen, but incomplete: and that, in the nature of things, evil is transient and good eternal.

HUMAN NATURE. We believe that human nature is imperfect but not inherently bad; that it has been wisely appointed to man to rise by slow degrees and long and even painful effort out of low conditions into conditions even higher and better, and not that we are the degenerate descendants of pure and perfect ancestors in some remote past. We believe that the race as a whole occupies a higher plane to-day than ever before, and that this progress of the past gives us ground for faith in a greatly increased progress in the future.

RETRIBUTION. We believe that no wrong-doing will go unpunished, and no right-doing unrewarded; that all punishment for sin is natural, not arbitrary, reformatory in its aim, not vindictive, and therefore cannot, in the nature of things, be everlasting.

HEAVEN AND HELL. The doctrine of an eternal hell we unqualifiedly reject, as the foulest imputation upon the character of God possible to be conceived, and as something which would render happiness in heaven itself impossible, since no beings whose hearts were not stone, could be happy anywhere knowing that half the human family, including many of their own loved ones, were in torments. Instead of such a dark and God-dishonoring doctrine, we believe that the future existence will be one ruled by Eternal Justice and Love, that he whom in this world we call "our Father," will be no less a Father to all his human children in the world to come, and that that world will be so planned as not only to bring eternal good to all who have done well here, but also to offer eternal hope to such as have done ill here.

FAITH AND WORKS. We believe in faith:—faith in God, faith in man, faith in truth, faith in duty; and that all these faiths are "saving faiths." We believe in works:—that the more good works a man does, so that his motives be good, the better pleasing to heaven is his life; and that no salvation of any worth ever comes to any human being except through faithful and earnest work.

WORSHIP, LOVE AND SERVICE OF GOD. We believe that man is as much made to worship as to think; but that perfect worship of God includes reverence for everything high and pure in humanity; that perfect love of God includes love to all God's children; that he best serves God who is most useful, and who obeys best every law of his being—physical, intellectual, moral, spiritual.

CHURCH MEMBERSHIP. We believe that the true basis of church membership and all Christian fellowship is not an intellectual belief of formulated creeds or articles of faith, but a sincere desire to unite for a common purpose of Christian worship, moral culture and human helpfulness.

SCIENCE AND RELIGION. We believe that science and religion, having the same author, can never, by any possibility be antagonistic; but that true religion is scientific and true science is religious. We cheerfully acknowledge that science has already been of incalculable service to religion, in helping to rid it of many degrading and hurtful superstitions and errors; and we bid all scientific investigators a most sincere god-speed in any and every investigation which can throw light upon any of the great religious questions of the time.

FELLOWSHIP OF RELIGIONS. While we believe that Christianity is the highest and best religion of the world, we believe also that the other great religions of mankind have in them much that is true and of God; and that God, instead of having arbitrarily chosen out one single people and made it the sole channel of his communication with the race, leaving the rest in midnight darkness, "has not left himself without witness" among any people, and that "in every nation he that feareth God and worketh righteousness (according to the best light he has) is accepted with God."

THE ABOVE. The above, while not a creed, or authoritative statement, or one binding upon any but the writer, is yet believed to be in essential harmony with what is commonly held and taught as fundamental among Unitarians: as it is also believed to be in essential harmony with reason, science, the best scholarship and thought of the age, and the teachings of Jesus.

SOME LEADING POINTS OF UNITARIAN BELIEF, WITH SCRIPTURE REFERENCES

1. One God, and only one, the Father, a Spirit, the only proper object of worship: in contradistinction from a trinity, and worship of Jesus or of the Virgin Mary. Matt. vi. 9; Mark xii. 29; Jno. iv. 24; xvii. 3; xx. 17; Eph. iv. 6; 1 Tim. ii. 5.

2. Jesus not God the Son, but the son of God his sonship consisting in moral god-likeness, many others besides him being called in Scripture "sons of God"); not Deity but divine (all humanity being the "offspring of God," and therefore, in the degree of its perfection, divine). Matt. xvi. 16; Acts ix. 20; Acts xvii. 29; 1 Jno. iii. 1,2; Hosea i. 10; Matt. v. 9; Gen. i. 37; James iii. 9.

3. Human nature not inherently evil (or, as the creeds of at least two of our great Christian denominations say, "dead in sin, wholly defiled in all the faculties and parts of soul and body, and therefore bound over to the wrath of God"), but, created "in the image of God," and even in its lowest estate containing much that is beautiful, noble and well-pleasing to God. Gen. i. 26,27; Rom. ii. 14,15; Mark x. 14, 15; Luke vii. 1-9 and 36-48.

4. God's love universal and everlasting, extending as much to the next world as to this; all punishment remedial and disciplinary; all men finally to be saved. Is. xlix. 15; Jer. xxxi. 3; Ps. cxxxvi. 1; Matt. xviii. 14; Col. i. 20; Heb. xii. 5-10: 1 Cor. xv. 22-28; Luke xv. 20-24.

5. The Bible the most important and sacred of books, but not to be accepted as infallible, because in some of its parts opposed to the teachings of science, the best conscience and reason of our time and the teachings of Jesus. Matt. v. 33-44. Compare Matt. v. 44 with Ps. cix., with Deut. xix. 13-21, with Josh. xi. 6-23, and with 1 Sam. xv. 2-11. Joshua x. 12-13; Jonah i. 17, and ii. 10.

6. Conscience sacred: inquiry to be full and free. Luke xii. 54-57; Rom. xiv. 1-5; 1 Cor. x. 15; 1 Thess. v. 21.

7. Man's whole duty included in love to God and love to man. Mark xii. 29-33; Rom. xiii. 8-10.

Notes: *Unitarians have been reluctant to issue any official "creeds" or "affirmations of belief." However, individuals have periodically attempted such statements. This treatise written by prominent Unitarian minister Jabez T. Sutherland was issued by the American Unitarian Association in 1906 and frequently reprinted throughout the first half of the twentieth century (prior to the Unitarian-Universalist merger).*

THE WINCHESTER PROFESSION, THE ESSENTIAL PRINCIPLES OF THE UNIVERSALIST FAITH, AND THE BOND OF FELLOWSHIP AND STATEMENT OF FAITH [UNITARIAN-UNIVERSALIST ASSOCIATION (UNIVERSALIST CHURCH IN AMERICA)]

THE WINCHESTER PROFESSION

Article I. We believe that the Holy Scriptures of the Old and New Testament contain a revelation of the character of God, and of the duty, interest and final destination of mankind.

Article II. We believe that there is one God, whose nature is Love, revealed in one Lord Jesus Christ, by one Holy Spirit of Grace, who will finally restore the whole family of mankind to holiness and happiness.

Article III. We believe that holiness and true happiness are inseparably connected, and that believers ought to be careful to maintain order and practice good works; for these things are good and profitable unto men.

THE ESSENTIAL PRINCIPLES OF THE UNIVERSALIST FAITH

The Universal Fatherhood of God.

The Spiritual Authority and Leadership of His Son, Jesus Christ.

The trustworthiness of the Bible as containing a revelation from God.

The certainty of just retribution for sin.

The final harmony of all souls with God.

BOND OF FELLOWSHIP AND STATEMENT OF FAITH

The bond of fellowship in this church shall be a common purpose to do the will of God as Jesus revealed it and to co-operate in establishing the Kingdom for which he lived and died.
To that end we avow our faith in
God as Eternal and All-conquering Love,
The spiritual leadership of Jesus,
The supreme worth of every human personality,
The authority of truth known or to be known,
And in the power of men of good will and sacrificial spirit to overcome all evil and progressively to establish the Kingdom of God.

Notes: *On at least three occasions the Universalist Church in America (prior to its merger into the Unitarian-Universalist Association) passed statements representative of its positions on those issues most important in the formation of the church. The Winchester Profession was adopted in 1803 with a "liberty clause," making explicit the understanding that it was not binding upon any member or congregation. In 1870 it was adopted by the church's general convention without the liberty clause. The Principles statement replaced the Profession in 1899, with the liberty clause added. The Bond of Fellowship was adopted in 1935.*

STATEMENT OF BELIEFS AND DOCTRINES (UNITED LIBERTARIAN FELLOWSHIP)

STATEMENT OF BELIEFS

God is the supreme universal reality; all that has ever existed or will ever exist; the fundamental force of the universe.

Human beings have the capacity to think and act. It is our rational functioning mind which differentiates us from the rest of existence.

It is our duty to use our minds and bodies to search for the truth, as we are capable of understanding it, and to act in accordance with that truth.

All individuals are capable of influencing their own destinies, and must accept the accompanying responsibility for their own actions and their consequences. We are each responsible for governing our own affairs and being the guardian of our own physical and spiritual well being.

The basic principle of human conduct derived from the religious principles of the Fellowship is that no one may initiate the use of force or fraud on another. Every individual must grant to others the freedom of body and spirit which is required for the development and manifestation of their religious nature.

DOCTRINES

The worldly manifestation of the beliefs of the Fellowship is a doctrine of maximum individual freedom and autonomy, consistent with the right of each person of life, liberty, and the fruits of their labor. Each member of the Fellowship is bound by the beliefs to refrain from, and refuse to contribute to, any aggressive action which forcibly deprives another of their property or their right to pursue life in their own chosen manner.

In particular, a member of the Fellowship may not:

> force others to use their money, lives, or property, in ways inconsistent with their own beliefs;

> accept money or property obtained by wrongfully taking it from others;

> accept money from public insurance against physical harm, property damage, death, disability, old age, retirement, or medical care;

> prevent or punish others who ingest substances into their own bodies for religious, medical, or any other purpose;

> prevent or punish others who engage in private voluntary actions together for commercial, intellectual, spiritual, or any other reason.

Notes: *This statement describes a method of approaching religious truth and the religious life much more than it asserts a set of mutually held beliefs.*

STATEMENT OF THE UNITED SECULARISTS OF AMERICA

OUR POLICY

We uphold the right of every person to freedom of thought, of inquiry, and of expression, and we oppose every form of tyranny over the mind of man.

We look to advancing science rather than to religious tradition in formulating our concepts of man and the universe.

We are committed to the intellectual, ethical, and cultural growth of all peoples and their advancement toward a more rational, humane and civilized world order.

Politically, our organization is non-partisan, and it stands for the full Constitutional and civil rights of all citizens.

WE ADVOCATE

Complete separation of church and state.

Taxation of all church property.

The exclusion of all religious indoctrination from the public schools.

No public tax funds to be used for any kind of aid to any private or church-connected institution.

More adequate government support of public education, recreational facilities, and cultural opportunities for all the people.

Effective enforcement of the Constitutional rights, privileges, and obligations of all citizens.

Notes: *This brief statement appeared in each issue of the United Secularists' magazine,* Progressive World.

* * *

Mail Order Churches

WE BELIEVE (MISSIONARIES OF THE NEW TRUTH)

We believe in man as a seeker of Truth, an inquirer, thirsting to know himself, his fellows in life and the Universe about him.

We believe that the nobility of man lies in the *seeking* of these Truths. If a man is to live a meaningful, happy life, he must seek the Truth.

We believe that there are many areas in life within which a man should seek the Truth, spiritual, emotional, political and many others.

We believe that our members should actively seek these Truths by all just means available to us.

We believe that certain Truths will differ for each man as each man is different. Subjective Truths of a man's spiritual and emotional life must relate to his uniqueness of structure, experience, capabilities and environment. For this reason we place no restrictions on a man's search for Truth except that he follow his best convictions with honesty and integrity. We thus exhort all our members to seek the Truth by all just means, in any place and in any way that they see fit.

We believe that since we accept all devout seekers of Truth, we should welcome all believers in established faiths as well as those who have not yet embraced any form of religion. Many men have found a wealth of meaningful Truth in the Bible. We recognize the great wisdom of the Bible but recognize that wisdom may also derive from many other sources.

We pledge to ourselves and to all mankind that we will honor, respect and love all men as fellow seekers of Truth. We pledge to keep our faith as free as possible from encumbering dogma and stultifying moral and social strictures.

Finally, we pledge to actively propagate our faith and to follow and promote those Truths revealed to us in our holy search.

Notes: *The Missionaries of the New Truth is now defunct, its leaders having sought Truth in psychedelic drugs until arrested and convicted.*

*　　*　　*

THIS IS MY CREED (OMNIUNE CHURCH)

Believe what ye will, so long as ye do good to thy fellow man: For verily, he that doeth Godly deeds is a Godly man: And he that hath loving-kindness in his heart hath God in his soul.

Notes: *The Omniune Church, like other churches organized basically to grant ministerial licenses, has followed the tendency to make broad, vague affirmations which allow the widest possible potential membership.*

Chapter 14
Latter-Day Saints Family

Utah Mormons

BASIC BELIEFS (AARONIC ORDER)

1. We believe in the triune godhead of the Bible, namely—God, the Father; Jesus Christ, the Son; and the Holy Spirit.

2. We worship Jesus Christ as the literal Son of God. He is also the Jehovah of the Old Testament, the Saviour and Redeemer of this world, and the only name under heaven whereby man must be saved.

3. We believe that men generally are in a fallen state and thereby estranged from God, and will remain so unless they repent and become obedient to His commandments.

4. We believe that salvation is available to all men if they (1) exercise faith in the Lord, Jesus Christ, and accept His atoning sacrifice, (2) sincerely repent of their sins, (3) undergo baptism by immersion for the remission of sins, and (4) receive the Holy Spirit.

5. We believe that full acceptance of the Gospel of Christ must lead to discipleship, which requires literal consecration of all things to Him. No one can serve in a leadership capacity, nor can any man officiate in the Priesthood in the True Church of God, unless he first qualifies as a disciple.

6. We accept the Bible as the Word of God and the ultimate basis of our doctrine. We also believe that God has revealed and does yet reveal many other truths to men in the flesh.

7. We believe in the literal restoration of lineal Israel in these last days as spoken in the Bible, which restoration has already begun with the re-establishment through the angel Elias of the House of Levi and Aaron.

8. We believe that God ordained the Levites and Aaronites to be priests and teachers for Israel for all time. The present-day Aaronic Order is the continuation and promised restoration of that original priesthood body.

9. We believe that Christian communal living is essential to the purification and restoration of the Levites, and that it is part of the divine plan to separate us from the world to become a peculiar people for the Lord.

10. We honor the seventh day of the week as the Sabbath of the Lord.

11. We believe in the literal second coming of the Lord, Jesus Christ, and that His return is imminent.

Notes: *The Aaronic Order is a sabbatarian communal group.*

*   *   *

THE ARTICLES OF FAITH (CHURCH OF JESUS CHRIST OF LATTER-DAY SAINTS)

1. We believe in God, the Eternal Father, and in His Son, Jesus Christ, and in the Holy Ghost.

2. We believe that men will be punished for their own sins, and not for Adam's transgression.

3. We believe that through the Atonement of Christ, all mankind may be saved, by obedience to the laws and ordinances of the Gospel.

4. We believe that the first principles and ordinances of the Gospel are: first, Faith in the Lord Jesus Christ; second, Repentance; third, Baptism by immersion for the remission of sins; fourth, Laying on of hands for the gift of the Holy Ghost.

5. We believe that a man must be called of God, by prophecy, and by the laying on of hands, by those who are in authority to preach the Gospel and administer in the ordinances thereof.

6. We believe in the same organization that existed in the Primitive Church, viz., apostles, prophets, pastors, teachers, evangelists, etc.

7. We believe in the gift of tongues, prophecy, revelation, visions, healing, interpretation of tongues, etc.

8. We believe the Bible to be the word of God as far as it is translated correctly; we also believe the Book of Mormon to be the word of God.

THE ARTICLES OF FAITH (CHURCH OF JESUS CHRIST OF LATTER-DAY SAINTS) (continued)

9. We believe all that God has revealed, all that He does now reveal, and we believe that He will yet reveal many great and important things pertaining to the Kingdom of God.

10. We believe in the literal gathering of Israel and in the restoration of the Ten Tribes; that Zion will be built upon this [the American] continent; that Christ will reign personally upon the earth; and, that the earth will be renewed and receive its paradisiacal glory.

11. We claim the privilege of worshiping Almighty God according to the dictates of our own conscience, and allow all men the same privilege, let them worship how, where, or what they may.

12. We believe in being subject to kings, presidents, rulers, and magistrates, in obeying, honoring, and sustaining the law.

13. We believe in being honest, true, chaste, benevolent, virtuous, and in doing good to all men; indeed, we may say that we follow the admonition of Paul—We believe all things, we hope all things, we have endured many things, and hope to be able to endure all things. If there is anything virtuous, lovely, or of good report or praiseworthy, we seek after these things.—*Joseph Smith.*

Notes: *The Latter-Day Saints, especially the older groups, retained enough Protestantism (from which most of the early members came) to put together statements of faith in a similar fashion, usually following a similar format. While appearing to affirm the traditional Christian doctrine of the Trinity as spelled out in the Nicene Creed (i.e., one God manifest in three persons: Father, Son, and Holy Ghost), the Latter-Day Saints statements actually affirm the three persons of the Godhead as three separate deities, not one.*

Joseph Smith, Jr., the prophet and founder of the Church of Jesus Christ of Latter-Day Saints, wrote the articles of faith prior to his death in the 1840s. In its first generations, the church was a charismatic body in which the manifestation of the gifts of the spirit were evident (item 7). Mormons believe that Christ, by His atonement, established a situation by which individuals could be saved if they followed the church's laws and ordinances (i.e., if they have faith, repent their sins, are properly baptized, and have a minister of the church lay hands upon them). The emphasis upon immersion is similar to that of the Baptist church.

*　　*　　*

DECLARATION OF ESSENTIAL BELIEFS (ZION'S ORDER OF THE SONS OF LEVI)

I believe in being just, fair and charitable towards all men, and claim the right to be treated likewise. Matthew 5:1 through 18; 1st Cor. 13; Romans 14 and first three verses of chapter 15 are the basis for such beliefs and essential to promotion and maintenance of this united order work.

I believe in kindness and pure holy love towards all humanity regardless of nationality, race, color, or politics, and liberty to all according to their obedience to eternal laws and tenable laws of our land.

I believe in equal rights to all humanity according to their abilities and adaptabilities, efficiency and cooperation with the management, and necessary tenacious qualities that must be in whatever business or other any seeks employment, and that all adults should have a right to vote except they that are mentally deranged, incompetent, or criminals, or aliens.

I believe in looking for the good in all persons. Good thoughts make good, joyous feelings. We all have evil as well as good in our makeup, or at least what some thinks of as evil. The proclaimed Savior of perfection was found fault with so much that they crucified him. Thinking of evil in others makes us feel evil or bad, thus let us look for, and think good.

I believe if we claim freedom in a nation for ourselves, to keep that freedom we must zealously allow and maintain and foster just as much freedom for every other human dwelling in that nation, else we lose our freedom.

I believe in accepting truth no matter where it is found and rejecting error likewise. Though rejecting such errors, I do not condemn the maker of such, but seek a way if possible to help that one in an orderly and unoffensive way to see their error and correct such to their joy.

I believe in eternal and divine Creators and worship them. I feel that all peoples that believe in such are worshipping the same creators, whether they call them by the same names as I do or not. And also that all will be rewarded for the good they do regardless of what religion they claim or do not claim, and that we must all suffer for evils or broken laws according to our understanding or lack thereof. Thus degrees of glory. (Ref. 1st Cor. 15:40-42; and Mark 4:20)

I believe that Christ Jesus will return, at which time the willful wicked shall be destroyed for a period of time until they learn their lesson and return or are resurrected to a repentant life in a degree of glory.

I believe the Savior shall also at His return redeem the righteous and they shall dwell with Him a thousand years in progressive joy and the devil and his chief followers shall be bound for a thousand years. During that time all of the inventions of marvel will be put to good usage of purity and holiness: television and radio programs then will be all good.

I believe in the ultimate end of the thousand years reign of the Savior that the leader of evils shall be loosed again for a short time, and great multitudes of followers will make their great stand against the righteous and their defeat shall be such that nearly all will return to the Lord and reject the great deceivers. And only a terrible end shall be for the devil and they with beastly natures and false prophets. (Ref. Rev. 7:9)

I believe all methods of doctoring and healing arts hold a worthy place, and what is good and an aid for one is not so for another. And that all should be used judiciously without prejudice. My choice is Physical Culture methods.

I believe from years of experience in dealing with uncounted thousands seeking help physically, mentally, and spiritually that happiness, success, and joy only can be obtained by a balancing of the three above mentioned, plus a balanced education, free from racial, religious, cultural, color, nationality, tribal, personal, continental, or family bias or prejudice whether one is religious or not so. Yet moral decency must prevail always with an inner responsibility of fairness felt towards all our fellow men. This takes faith coupled with works of love. (Ref. Ephes. 2:5 thru 10.)

I believe last but not least in the redemptive powers of Jesus Christ through the Law of Grace, and that Faith, Repentance, Baptism by immersion for the remission of sins, and the laying on of hands of the gift of the Holy Ghost was essential for me because of my convictions.

Notes: *This statement was composed by founder Marl V. Kilgore.*

*   *   *

Polygamy-Practicing Mormons

ARTICLES OF FAITH (CHRIST'S CHURCH)

1. We believe in God the Eternal Father—as Michael-Adam-God, the Creator; and in His Son, Jesus Christ, the Savior of the World; and in the Holy Ghost, Joseph Smith, Jr., the Witness and Testator and third member of the Godhead that rules the Earth!

2. We believe the first principles and ordinances of the Gospel of Jesus Christ, are:

   (1) Faith in the Lord Jesus Christ, His saving blood, that He atoned for our sins if we accept Him and keep His commandments.

   (2) That in order to receive effective Baptism and the other ordinances and blessings of the Gospel, all men and women must and shall offer the sacrifice of a broken heart (repentance) and a contrite (teachable) spirit.

   (3) Every candidate for receiving the Holy Ghost must be baptised, by immersion in water, by one having authority of Jesus Christ, who himself holds the Priesthood of the Living God and who personally has the Holy Ghost!

   (4) The laying on of hands of those who have the Holy Priesthood and the Holy Ghost, for the conferring of the Holy Ghost.

3. We believe that no one shall be confirmed, or accepted as a member of Christ's Church, until they have shown by a righteous walk of life, and have been voted upon by the members of the body of the Church. They are then to be confirmed a member of the Church by the laying on of hands.

4. We believe that men will be punished for their own sins and not for Adam's transgression.

5. We believe that through the Atonement of Christ all mankind may be saved by obedience to the laws and ordinances of the Gospel.

6. We believe that a man must be called of God, by prophecy, and by the laying on of hands by those who are in authority to preach the Gospel and administer in the ordinances thereof.

7. We believe in the Gifts of the Spirit, namely, the gift of tongues, prophecy, revelation, visions, healings, interpretations of tongues, etc.

8. We believe the Holy Bible to be the word of God as far as it is translated correctly, we also believe the Book of Mormon, the Doctrine and Covenants and the Pearl of Great Price to be the word of the Lord.

9. We believe all that God has revealed, all that He does now reveal, and we believe He will yet reveal many great and important things pertaining to the Kingdom of God!

10. We believe in the literal gathering of Israel and in the restoration of the Ten Tribes; that Zion will be built upon this the American continent; that Christ will reign personally upon the earth; and that the earth will be renewed and receive its paradisiacal glory.

11. We claim the privilege of worshipping the Almighty God according to the dictates of our own conscience and allow all men the same privilege, let them worship how, when, or what they may.

12. We believe in being subject to Almighty God and those kings, presidents, rulers and magistrates who honor and sustain the divine laws of God.

13. We believe in being honest, true, chaste, benevolent, virtuous, and in doing good to all men; indeed we may say that we follow the admonition of Paul—we believe all things, we have endured many things, and hope to be able to endure all things. If there is anything virtuous, lovely, or of good report or praiseworthy, we seek after these things. (*The Branch Magazine*, Volume 1, Number 3, Provo, Utah: Christ's Church, 1979, pp. 2-3)

Notes: *Christ's Church follows the Mormon Fundamentalist position concerning the practice of polygamy, but its statement of faith deals with the more basic beliefs concerning God, the gospel ordinances, atonement, the gifts of the Spirit, and progressive revelation.*

*   *   *

ALEXANDER'S CREED (CHURCH OF JESUS CHRIST IN SOLEMN ASSEMBLY)

We believe in POSTERITY: that the glory of God is intelligence and that intelligence is the right use of knowledge.

We believe in REALITY: that all truth is self-evident and can be and should be demonstrated by those who profess a love for the truth.

We believe in FREEDOM: that all men should worship diety according to the dictates of their own consciences.

We believe in RESPONSIBILITY: that the supreme law makes all men free and that everyone is therefore responsible for his own acts.

ALEXANDER'S CREED (CHURCH OF JESUS CHRIST IN SOLEMN ASSEMBLY) (continued)

We believe in JUSTICE: that all men are at all times immediately surrounded by the best opportunity to win the greatest exaltation they are capable of.

We believe in GRACE: that the law of God is written in the hearts and minds of those elected to the redemption of Israel.

We believe in PATRIARCHAL GOVERNMENT: that the brotherhood of man does not and cannot exist independent of the Fatherhood.

Notes: *Polygamy-practicing groups dissent from the Church of Jesus Christ of Latter-Day Saints primarily by their adherence to the practice of polygamy, rather than in any matter of belief. Thus many of the groups would accept the articles of that church, believing that they had not departed from the faith and practice of the church from the time of its founding. They have no need to write an additional statement of faith.*

The brief statement of the Church of Jesus Christ in Solemn Assembly does little to illuminate the beliefs of this church without some detailed knowledge of the church's doctrine otherwise.

* * *

ARTICLES OF FAITH (CHURCH OF THE FIRST BORN)

1. We believe in Michael, the Eternal Father, and in His Son, Jesus Christ, and in Joseph Smith, the Witness and Testator.

2. We believe that men will be punished for their own sins, and not for Adam's transgression; for He partook of mortality, that He might bring forth mortal bodies for His spiritual offspring.

3. We believe that through the Atonement of Christ, all mankind may be saved, by obedience to the laws and ordinances of the Gospel of the First-born.

4. We believe that the first principles and ordinances of the Gospel are; first, Faith in Michael the Archangel, and in His Son Jesus Christ, and in Joseph the Testator; second, Repentance; third, Baptism by immersion for the remission of sins; fourth, Laying on of hands for the gift of the Holy Ghost.

5. We believe that man must be called of God, by prophecy, and by the laying on of hands, by those who are in authority to preach the gospel and administer in the ordinances thereof.

6. We believe in the same organization that Adam first established-upon this earth, viz: the Right of the First-born, Patriarchs, Prophets, Priests, etc; and that the Church of Jesus Christ is an appendage thereto, that the Gentiles might be heirs of salvation.

7. We believe in the Holy Spirit of Promise, the gift of tongues, prophecy, revelation, visions, healing, interpretation of tongues etc.

8. We believe the Bible to be the word of God as far as it is translated correctly; We also believe that the Fullness of the Everlasting Gospel was restored by the Prophet Joseph Smith, and that any departure therefrom is apostasy.

9. We believe all that God has revealed, all that He does now reveal, and we believe that He will yet reveal many great and important things pertaining to the Church and Kingdom of the First-born.

10. We believe that the literal descendants of Israel are legal heirs of the Church and Kingdom of the First-born; and that the Patriarchal Reign shall be re-established upon this continent, as in Adam's day.

11. We claim the privilege of worshiping Almighty God according to the dictates of our own conscience, and allow all men the same privilege, let them worship how, where, or what they may.

12. We believe in being subject to kings, presidents, rulers, and magistrates, in obeying, honoring, and sustaining the law - as declared in the 98th sec. of the Doctrine and Covenants.

13. We believe that this is the dispensation of the Fullness of Times, when all things shall be revealed, and that men are required to obey all the laws and ordinances; we also believe that the Lord will send One Mighty and Strong, to set in order the House of God.

Notes: *These articles are based directly upon those of the Church of Jesus Christ of Latter-Day Saints. The statement differs primarily in the identification of the angel Michael with God the Father (item 1) and in its focus on the prophesied "One Mighty and Strong" (item 13).*

* * *

S.A.I. BELIEFS (SONS AHMAN ISRAEL)

1. We believe in an all-powerful, all-loving Heavenly Father and Heavenly Mother, in their son Jesus Christ, in their Holy Spirit pervading all things, in innumerable choirs of archangels, angels, ministers of flame, just men made perfect, etc.

2. We believe we are the literal offspring of these parents, that we have come down to this earth to experience the mystery of mortality preparatory to becoming one with the Messiah, thru whom we have hope of eventual maturity into his very image, becoming Heavenly Progenitors ourselves in the eternities.

3. We believe man has been created to experience joy, not only in this life, but in the life to come; and that thru observance of celestial law upon which all blessings are predicated, man may indeed come to experience perpetual peace and never ending happiness.

4. We believe most of mankind to be in a state of darkness and division from divinity, slaves to their lower passions, tossed to and fro by their love of materialism and by conspiring and self seeking men;

and that only thru gaining a true knowledge of the plan and pattern of the Gospel and by applying such, can man place himself in a position to be purified thru the grace of Jesus Christ.

5. We believe that redemption from this fall can come only thru surrendering our lives to Yeheshuah the Christ, and thru developing a close and intimate relationship to Him thru His Holy Ordinances, and only in this manner is it possible to be quickened by His Spirit and thus become heir to all things.

6. We believe that a religion that does not require the sacrifice of all things never has power sufficient to produce the faith necessary unto life and salvation; and that the mocking finger of the Spiritual Sluggard will ever be pointed at those embarking on the sublime Spiritual quest toward perfection.

7. We believe it possible to learn the dynamics of the creation of worlds even in this life, and that a fully restored priesthood program must include instruction in developing the seeds of Godliness latent within, and in the various methods of controlling the elements and situations in which we dwell.

8. We believe that eternal happiness and everlasting life is obtainable only inasmuch as we take upon ourselves the nature and name of the Messiah, and in enduring to the end of our trial by faith; and that despite the depth of depravity to which we have lowered ourselves, the everenduring mercy of God is ever ready to restore us to his Holy presence.

9. We believe this miraculous cleansing from all sin by the Messiah is effected thru his infinite mercy which can only be received in its fulness thru the temple ordinances and ritualistic ceremonies, without which we have little if any hope of salvation, for in their mystery is hidden the mystery which is Christ who is our only sure road to eternal felicity, peace, and purity.

10. We believe these Holy Ordinances can and will cause tremendous transformation and change within those that receive such in a proper manner and by qualified servants of God, and that it is the Spiritual Counterpart and not the physical rite that effects this metamorphosis.

11. We believe the Law of Moses is dead in Christ, nevertheless we feel that much which is considered such, including many of the more ancient and patriarchal portions and many of the feasts and Holy Days, are yet applicable and advantageous for the Spiritual growth of modern man; and that from the ashes of the Old Law shall arise Phoenix like, a new covenant wherein Israel may be renewed in their relationship to God.

12. We believe that aspiring men, seeking self-honor and glory, have ever been the plague of religious leadership; and that self-righteous gossip and condemnation of others has ever been the folly of their followers; and only thru total tolerance concerning the weakness of others, and thru the ascension of humble and unassuming men to positions of influ-

ence, may Zion be rebuilt and the Kingdom of God restored.

13. We believe in the perfect equality of the sexes, that the ultimate destiny of righteous women is to follow in the footsteps of their heavenly mother on high, becoming Queens and Goddesses in the eternities above. To do this we feel it imperative that women share with men the burden of priesthood on earth, that they might reign with them in heaven.

14. We believe that an actual transformation into a new creature in Christ must occur for man to inherit perfect peace, and that the temple ceremonies known to most are insufficient and devoid of the necessary power needed to effect this metamorphosis, and are but an introduction and preparation for deeper and more holy endowments reserved for the more valiant and elect.

15. We believe pearls of great truth can be gleaned from even the most unlikely sources, that some have fallen into the defiling hands of the adversary and are reclaimable; and that there is truth in all religions and that they exist in the will of God for the benefit of all incapable of accepting the fulness of God's higher law.

16. We believe that continual angelic visitations, revelations, and visions must and will prevail in the lives of all that magnify their priesthood properly, and that an increased influx of the Holy Spirit is a direct result of daily inflaming oneself with love for both God and man.

17. We believe it man's prerogative to live only a few of the laws of God, following leaders that encourage such; but feel it more pleasing in the eyes of God to break away from such stagnation, seeking whole heartedly avenues where one may more quickly progress on the road to godhood.

18. We believe in a secret oral tradition of the gospel as revealed by Moses to seventy select elders on Mount Sinai, and perpetuated thru an ancient institution known as the school of the prophets; being a tradition taught by Elijah, Essenes, Jesus, Valentinus, Joseph Smith, etc. and presently preserved in such ancient texts as the Sephir Yetzira, Sephir Zohar, Pistis Sophia, etc.

19. We believe in what is scriptually known as the times of Jacob's trouble, a time of nuclear holocaust survivable thru construction of underground communities of refuge made impregnable to the destroyer; and that thru such communities the elect will preserve all that is virtuous, lovely, and true in anticipation of a dawning of a new age of peace and light after man has learned not to wage war anymore.

20. We believe in the literal gathering of Israel, that the times of the gentiles has come to an end, that the earth and man will be renewed after the tribulation to come; that we can recreate The Garden of Eden once again thru equal sharing of possessions, by purging our minds and bodies of all corruption, and

S.A.I. BELIEFS (SONS AHMAN ISRAEL) (continued)

by learning to live in harmony with natural law and with one another.

21. We believe that thru observance of celestial law, and thru applying principles of perfection, fallen man is redeemed from his alienation from God and brought back into the presence of the Elohiem; that the shekinah glory will return once again to Israel, and a fulness of God's Holy Spirit be enjoyed by all the faithful.

22. We believe that those that endure to the end and who rise up above all things thru their perseverance and fortitude, and who have perfected themselves thru charity, devotion, and ordinance work, will return home into the presence of God and the Lamb, being crowned with eternal glory and celestial splendor, seeing as they are seen, and knowing as they are known, being heir to all the grandeur of godliness.

Notes: *This esoteric organization (see items 14, 16, and 18) departs at numerous points from traditional Mormon belief and practice.*

* * *

Missouri Mormons

ARTICLES OF FAITH [CHURCH OF CHRIST (TEMPLE LOT)]

1. We believe in God the Eternal Father, who only is Supreme; Creator of the universe; Ruler and Judge of all; unchangeable and without respect of persons.

2. We believe in Jesus Christ, the Only Begotten Son of God, the manifestation of God in flesh, who lived, suffered, and died for all mankind; whom we own as our only Leader, Witness and Commander.

3. We believe in the Holy Ghost, the Spirit of Truth, the Comforter, which searcheth the deep things of God, brings to our minds things which are past, reveals things to come, and is the medium by which we receive the revelation of Jesus Christ.

4. We believe that men will be punished for their own sins and not for Adam's transgression, and that as a consequence of the atonement of Christ "all little children are alive in Christ, and also all they that are without the law. For the power of redemption cometh on all they that have no law; wherefore, he that is not condemned, or he that is under no condemnation, can not repent; and unto such, baptism availeth nothing." (Moroni 8:25, 26)

5. We believe that through the atonement of Christ all men may be saved by obedience to the laws and ordinances of the Gospel; viz.: Faith in God and in the Lord Jesus Christ; Repentance and Baptism by immersion for the remission of sins; Laying on of Hands for: (a) Ordination; (b) Blessing of Children; (c) Confirmation and the Gift of the Holy Ghost; (d) Healing of the Sick.

6. We believe in the literal second coming and millennial reign of Jesus Christ; in the resurrection of the Dead, and in Eternal Judgment; that men will be rewarded or punished according to the good or evil they may have done.

7. We believe in the powers and gifts of the everlasting Gospel; viz.: The word of wisdom; the word of knowledge; the gift of faith; the gift of healing; working of miracles; prophecy; discerning of spirits; divers kinds of tongues; interpretation of tongues.

8. We believe the fruits of the spirit to be love, joy, peace, long suffering, gentleness, goodness, faith, meekness and temperance.

9. We believe that in the Bible is contained the word of God, that the Book of Mormon is an added witness for Christ, and that these contain the "fullness of the gospel."

10. We believe in the principle of continuous revelation; that the canon of scripture is not full, that God inspires men in every age and among all people, and that He speaks when, where, and through whom He may choose.

11. We believe that where there are six or more regularly baptized members, one of whom is an elder, there the Church exists with full power of church extension when acting in harmony with the law of God.

12. We believe that a man must be called of God by revelation, and ordained by those having authority, to enable him to preach the gospel and administer the ordinances thereof.

13. We believe in the same church organization as existed in the time of Christ and His Apostles. The highest office in the church is that of an apostle, of whom there are twelve, who constitute special witnesses for Jesus Christ. They have the missionary supervision and the general watchcare of all of the churches.

14. The primary function of the general church, of which each local church is a component part, is missionary and the building up and extension of the Kingdom of God in all the world.

15. We believe that local churches should govern their own affairs, and that general church officials should not dominate or interfere therewith. On invitation such general officers may, with propriety, give counsel and assistance. Local congregations are subject to the Articles of Faith and Practice and must be governed thereby.

16. We believe the Church of Christ comprehends the true brotherhood of man where each esteems his brother as himself and wherein the divine command to "love your neighbor as yourself" is demonstrated by the prevalence of social equality.

17. We believe that all men are stewards under God and answerable to Him not only for the distribution of accumulated wealth, but for the manner in which such wealth is secured. The primary purpose of stewardship is not the increase of church revenue or

the mere contribution of money by those who have to those who have not, but to bring men to a realization of the common fatherhood of God, and the universal brotherhood of man in all the affairs and expressions of life, and to maintain such social adjustment that each may enjoy the bounty and gifts of God, and be free to exercise his talents and ability to enrich the life of all.

18. We believe that men should labor for their own support and that of their dependents. Ministers of the gospel are not absolved from this responsibility, but when chosen or appointed by the church to devote their entire time to missionary work, their families are to be provided for out of the general church funds. The admonition of Christ that the ministry should not provide purse or scrip for their journey, but go trusting in God and the people is applicable.

19. We believe that the temporal affairs of the general church are to be administered by the general bishopric under the direction of the general conferences of the church and under the supervision of the Council of Twelve. The temporal affairs of the local churches shall be administered by local bishops under the supervision and direction of the local congregations.

20. We believe that marriage is ordained of God, and that the law of God provides for but one companion in wedlock for either man or woman. In case of a breach of this covenant by adultery, the innocent one may remarry.

21. We are opposed to war. Men are not justified in taking up arms against their fellows except as a last resort in defense of their lives and to preserve their liberty.

22. We believe in the literal gathering of Israel, and in the restoration of the ten lost tribes.

23. We believe a temple will be built in this generation, in Independence, Missouri, wherein Christ will reveal himself and endow his servants whom he chooses with power to preach the gospel in all the world to every kindred, tongue, and people, that the promise of God to Israel may be fulfilled.

24. We believe that a New Jerusalem shall be built upon this land "unto the remnant of the seed of Joseph." (Ether 6:6-8; III Nephi 10:1-4), "which city shall be built, beginning at the Temple Lot." (Doc. and Cov. 83:1)

25. We believe that ministry and membership should abstain from the use of tobacco, intoxicating liquors and narcotics, and should not affiliate with any society which administers oaths or covenants in conflict with the law of God, or which interferes with their duties as freemen and citizens.

Notes: *The Latter-Day Saints groups remaining in the midwest after the death of Joseph Smith, Jr., never accepted polygamy or many other doctrines that became prominent during the period under Brigham Young's leadership. The*

Missouri Mormons have tended to follow a montheism, believing that Jesus Christ was not God, but God's Son.

Compare the articles of the Church of Christ (Temple Lot) with those of the Church of Jesus Christ of Latter-Day Saints. There is no assertion of three deities. The number of ordinances (item 5) has increased. Pacifism is advocated. Tobacco, alcohol and drugs are opposed. Most distinctively, the church owns property in Independence, Missouri, which it believes will be the site of a future kingdom of God (item 24). These identical articles are followed by the Church of Christ with the Elijah Messenger, formed by former members of the Church of Christ (Temple Lot).

* * *

FAITH AND DOCTRINE (CHURCH OF JESUS CHRIST RESTORED)

"We believe in God, the Creator of all things, our Father, who is unchangeable, from everlasting to everlasting, without beginning of days or end of years, the source of all righteous inspiration, whose capacity for love and wrath are beyond man's ability to know or find out. We believe He has given His Son the task of judging each man according to the works and faith they have practiced while on this earth. Therefore, there is no condemnation for the man who lives and dies ignorant of God's laws. Men choosing to ignore God's laws, however, live under the threat of condemnation from day to day and their just judgment is sure, except they repent and live according to all the principles of the gospel of Christ.

"We believe that just as God spoke to man in days past, so he speaks today. We expect it. We experience it. We are grateful because it delivers man's mind from unstability, confusion and anxiety.

"We believe that Jesus of Nazareth was and is the Only Begotten Son of God; that with God He presided in the beginning over the creation of all things and that it was by Jesus Christ that God created all things that are.

"We believe God directs, comforts, teaches, chastizes and/or reproves men by the ministry of His Holy Spirit, either directly or through divinely called ministers.

"We believe that as man 'feels after God' by diligent study and constant prayer, he is practicing faith and that by willfully enduring and gradually overcoming all things, under the protection and guidance of divinely called ministers, his faith will become knowledge.

"We believe that Jesus built His own church for the purpose of making men perfect in this life. Anything less than this, is not of Jesus Christ. The church that preaches the fullness of His gospel, accordingly promises the perfection of the soul in this life on condition of total obedience to godly principles.

"We believe repentance from doing sin and living an unproductive life (dead works), is essential for any man, woman or youth who by reason of intelligence (knowing right from wrong) are accountable before God and therefore as often as may be necessary, must conscientiously practice sincere repentance.

"Baptism by immersion in water, as performed by the Son of God in the river Jordan by an authoritative minister of God, for the remission of sins, is absolutely necessary to man's salvation. Without it there is no membership in the church and kingdom of Christ.

"We believe the Eucharist or Sacrament of the Lord's Supper, properly observed by authoritative ministers of God, provides for those who are members of Jesus' church and them alone, the opportunity to consider the blessed sacrifice of the Lamb, Jesus, to give thanks for that atonement His death made possible, and to confess to God publicly or privately the sins that separate man from his Maker and the Holy Ghost.

"The physical body and the spirit (or intelligence) in every man born into this world constitutes the soul of man and because God so loved the world (the souls of men), He allowed His Only Begotten Son to come in the meridian of time, to offer the only acceptable sacrifice for the sins of the world—His death on a cross and by so doing He gave His Father (and our Father) an acceptable offering and a complete and effectual reconciliation and mediation for mankind. Men may lay claim to this atonement only in the church that bears His name and teaches all He taught.

"We believe the fullness of the doctrine of Christ Jesus, is the only way by which man may be saved, and that giving support to any church which does not preach the fullness of the doctrine of Jesus is supporting that which may be well-intentioned perhaps but nevertheless, a counterfeit and therefore, her promises are vain.

"Man is required (if he desires the salvation of his soul) to live by every word that proceedeth forth out of the mouth of God. We believe those words as they are found recorded in the Inspired Correction of the Scriptures (Bible)—even though all biblical references in this tract are to the King James Version—plus the Book of Mormon, the Doctrine and Covenants, and the latest revelations (called Supplements), received by our present prophet, Elder Stanley King and sanctioned by the saints.

"We believe that just as the original Church of Christ as organized by Jesus himself, apostacized, so also the Reorganized Church of Jesus Christ of Latter Day Saints—lawful successor to the church restored by Joseph Smith, Jr. in 1830—has also apostacized administratively. There are many good honorable people within that denomination as there are in many other denominations of the world today but this fact does not negate the evidences of her unfortunate apostasy.

"We believe Joseph Smith, Jr. was and is the great Prophet of this last dispensation and that as a man he may possibly have erred from time to time but as God's servant, ordained from before the foundation of the world, to speak forth His Word, He did not err.

"We believe Sanctification must be attained by the honest in heart. It is the process of perfection. Attaining perfection while living in a system of houses, stores, streets and divisive devilish influences of this present age is impossible. We believe the only way to effectively live in the world but

not be part of it, is in the stake; the stake as revealed by God through Joseph Smith, Jr., not those promoted by the RLDS or Utah churches. The Stakes divinely organized always start with the building of the House of the Lord (temple) first. This church has prepared for five years to do this and at this writing (1975) are very near to commencing such a work in obedience to His word and to His glory.

"The obligation upon the saint (member of the church) is to become independent above every other creature or system beneath the Celestial world. Practicing daily the attributes of God is a way of life in the Stake. The Law of Preference is taught and lived.

"We believe in being good stewards over all God gives us. Sacrifice is expected and desired by members in this church so that God's final glorious chapter of His strange act might be completed. There is no perfection without sacrifice and where there is no perfection there is no church. Man must not fail to please God. Jesus willingly sacrificed all for His Father. So must we.

"We believe heaven is a place of varied glories. There is the Celestial, Terrestrial and Telestial glory that man may attain. We believe that when this earth has fulfilled itself in the present system of things that it will be changed and provide for the righteous the greatest glory of all—Celestial glory.

"We believe there are no authoritative High Priests on the earth today (1975) but that very soon this ministry will be restored to the salvation of man, the redemption of Zion and the everlasting glory of God.

"There is historical support for Presidencies in the Church of Christ. We do believe they are acceptable to God and necessary for the church to function orderly.

"There are other tenets of faith that make up the fullness of the doctrine of Jesus such as Ministerial Authority (who really are the servants of God?), the gifts and fruits of God's Holy Spirit, Baptism for the dead (by revelation through a prophet), Endowments, and other temple ordinances, Celestial Priesthood Education (School of the Prophets), equality, the gathering of scattered Israel, plus many many more."

Notes: *The Church of Jesus Christ Restored, a recent splinter from the Reorganized Church of Jesus Christ of Latter-Day Saints, has based its statement upon that of the parent body.*

*   *   *

A BRIEF STATEMENT OF FAITH (REORGANIZED CHURCH OF JESUS CHRIST OF LATTER-DAY SAINTS)

There is no official creed endorsed as such by the Church of Jesus Christ. It has been well stated that the creed of the church is "all Truth." We believe fundamentals leading to all truth are stated in the Bible, Book of Mormon, and Doctrine and Covenants.

Certain of the basic truths, however, have stood out in bold relief because of their very nature and have been gathered together in a statement or Epitome of Faith. This basic list is worthy of study and understanding which, of course, can only come as a member searches diligently in the Scriptures just mentioned and in the standard literary works of representative church writers.

We Believe:

In God the Eternal Father, creator of the heavens and the earth.

In the divine Sonship of Jesus Christ the Savior of all men who obey his gospel;

In the Holy Ghost whose function it is to guide all men unto the truth.

In the Gospel of Jesus Christ which is the power of God unto salvation.

In the six fundamental doctrinal principles of the gospel: Faith; Repentance; Baptism by immersion in water; the Baptism of the Holy Ghost; Laying on of the Hands for the healing of the sick, for conferring of the Holy Ghost, ordination, blessing of children, and other special blessings; Resurrection of the dead, and the Eternal Judgment.

In the justice of God who will reward or punish all men according to their works, and not solely according to their profession.

In the same kind of organization that existed in the primitive church: apostles, prophets, evangelists, pastors, teachers, elders, bishops, seventies, etc.

In the word of God contained in the Bible, as far as it is correctly translated.

In the word of God contained in the Book of Mormon, being a record of divine dealings with men in the new world as in the old.

In the word of God revealed today and recorded in the Doctrine and Covenants of the church.

In the willingness and ability of God to continue his revelation of his will to men to the end of time.

In the powers and gifts of the gospel: faith, discernment of spirits, prophecy, revelation, healing, visions, tongues, and their interpretation, wisdom, charity, temperance, brotherly love, etc.

In marriage as instituted and ordained of God whose law provides for but one companion in wedlock, for either man or woman, excepting in case of death. When the marriage contract is broken by trangression, the innocent party is free to remarry.

In the Book of Mormon declaration: "There shall not any man among you have save it be one wife; and concubines he shall have none."

In the Doctrine of Stewardships; that is, that every man is accountable to God for the conduct of his life and the use of his material blessings.

In the Divine Commission to the church to establish a Christian Community called Zion built upon the basis of stewardship and the principle of equality of opportunity, and where each member shall give according to his capacity and receive according to his needs.

Notes: *The statement of the Reorganized Church of Latter-Day Saints, the second largest of the Mormon groups, is much closer to that of the other Missouri groups than to that of the Church of Jesus Christ of Latter-Day Saints. The ordinances, here considered as "fundamental doctrinal principles," differ in number. There is no statement on pacifism, and polygamy is explicitly opposed.*

* * *

STATEMENT OF FAITH AND BELIEF (REORGANIZED CHURCH OF JESUS CHRIST OF LATTER-DAY SAINTS)

We believe in God the eternal Father, source and center of all love and life and truth, who is almighty, infinite, and unchanging, in whom and through whom all things exist and have their being.

We believe in Jesus Christ, the Only Begotten Son of God, who is from everlasting to everlasting; through whom all things were made, who is God in the flesh, being incarnate by the Holy Spirit for man's salvation; who was crucified, died and rose again; who is mediator between God and man, and the judge of both the living and the dead, whose dominion has no end.

We believe in the Holy Spirit, the living presence of the Father and the Son, who in power, intelligence, and love works in the minds and hearts of men to free them from sin, uniting them with God as his sons, and with each other as brethren. The Spirit bears record of the Father and of the Son, which Father, Son, and Holy Ghost are one God.

We believe that the Holy Spirit empowers men committed to Christ with gifts of worship and ministry. Such gifts, in their richness and diversity, are divided severally as God wills, edifying the body of Christ, empowering men to encounter victoriously the circumstances of their discipleship, and confirming the new creation into which men are called as sons of God.

We believe that the Holy Spirit creates, quickens, and renews in men such graces as love, joy, peace, mercy, gentleness, meekness, forbearance, temperance, purity of heart, brotherly kindness, patience in tribulation, and faithfulness before God in seeking to build up his kingdom.

We believe that man is endowed with freedom and created to know God, to love and serve him, and enjoy his fellowship. In following the dictates of pride and in declaring his independence from God, man loses the power to fulfill the purpose of his creation and becomes the servant of sin, whereby he is divided within himself and estranged from God, and his fellows. This condition, experienced by our ancestors who first came to a knowledge of good and evil, is shared by all who are granted the gift of accountability.

We believe that man cannot be saved in the kingdom of God except by the grace of the Lord Jesus Christ, who loves us while we are yet in our sins, and who gave his life to reconcile us unto God. Through this atonement of the Lord Jesus Christ and by the gift of the Holy Spirit, men receive power to choose God and to commit their lives to him; thus are they turned from rebellion, healed from sin,

**STATEMENT OF FAITH AND BELIEF (REORGANIZED
CHURCH OF JESUS CHRIST OF LATTER-DAY
SAINTS) (continued)**

renewed in spirit, and transformed after the image of God in righteousness and holiness.

We believe that all men are called to have faith in God and to follow Jesus Christ as Lord, worshipping the Father in his name. In this life those who hear the gospel and repent should commit their lives to Christ in baptism by immersion in water and the laying on of hands. Through living by these principles they participate in God's promise of forgiveness, reconciliation, and eternal life.

We believe that the church was established by Jesus Christ. In its larger sense it encompasses those both living and dead, who, moved by the Spirit of God, acknowledge Jesus as Lord. In its corporate sense, it is the community of those who have covenanted with Christ. As the body of Christ through which the Word of God is tangibly expressed among men, the church seeks to discern the will of God and to surrender itself to him in worship and service. It is enlightened, sustained, and renewed by the Holy Spirit. It is to bring the good news of God's love to all people, reconciling them to God through faith in Jesus Christ. The church administers the ordinances through which the covenant is established, cares for all within its fellowship, ministers to the needy, wages war on evil, and strives for the kingdom of God.

We believe that all men are called to be stewards under God. They are accountable to him, in the measure of their perception of the divine purpose in creation and redemption, for managing all gifts and resources given their care. In the exercise of stewardship, men embody the divine will and grow in spiritual maturity through developing native powers and skills achieving dominion over the physical order and perfecting human relationships in the Spirit of Christ.

We believe that the kingdom of God sustains men as the stable and enduring reality of history, signifying the total Lordship of God over all human life and endeavor. The kingdom is always at hand in judgment and promise, confronting all men with the joyful proclamation of God's rule and laying claim upon them as they acknowledge the new Creation in Christ. The full revelation of the kingdom awaits the final victory over evil, when the will of God shall prevail and his rule shall extend over all human relations to establish the dominion of peace, justice, and truth. To this end the church proclaims the gospel of the kingdom both as present reality and future hope in the midst of a faithless world.

We believe that Zion is the means by which the prophetic church participates in the world to embody the divine intent for all personal and social relations. Zion is the implementation of those principles, processes, and relationships which give concrete expression to the power of the kingdom of God in the world. It affirms the concern of the gospel with the structures of our common life together and promotes the expression of God's reconciling love in the world, thus bringing forth the divine life in human society. The church is called to gather her covenant people into signal communities where they live out the will of God in the total life of society. While this concrete expression of the kingdom of God must have a central point of beginning it reaches out to every part of the world where the prophetic church is in mission.

We believe that all are called according to the gifts of God unto them to accept the commission and cost of discipleship. Some are chosen through the spirit of wisdom and revelation and ordained by those who are in authority in the church to serve in specialized ministries. These include ministry to persons, families, and community, as well as preaching, teaching, administering the ordinances, and directing the affairs of the church. The authority of every member of the body in this respective calling emerges out of divine endowment to him and his faithfulness in servanthood with Christ.

We believe that the ordinances witness the continuing life of Christ in the church, providing the experiences in which God and man meet in the sealing of covenant. In the ordinances God uses common things, even the nature of man, to express the transcendent and sacramental meaning of creation. God thereby provides the continuing means of investing his grace in human life for its renewal and redemption.

We believe that God reveals himself to man. He enters into the minds of men through the Holy Spirit to disclose himself to them and to open their understanding to the inner meaning of his revelation in history and in the physical order. Revelation centers in Jesus Christ, the incarnate word, who is the ultimate disclosure of truth and the standard by which all other claims to truth are measured.

We believe that the Scriptures witness to God's redemptive action in history and to man's response to that action. When studied through the light of the Holy Spirit they illumine men's minds and hearts and empower them to understand in greater depth the revelation in Christ. Such disclosure is experienced in the hearts of men rather than in the words by which the revelation is interpreted and communicated. The Scriptures are open because God's redemptive work is eternal, and our discernment of it is never complete.

We believe in the resurrection. This principle encompasses the divine purpose to conserve and renew life. It guarantees that righteousness will prevail and that, by the power of God, men move from death into life. In resurrection God quickens and transforms the soul, i.e. the body and spirit, bringing man into fellowship with his Son.

We believe in eternal judgment. It is the wisdom of God bringing the whole creation under divine judgment for good. This judgment is exercised through men as they are quickened by the Holy Spirit to comprehend the eternal implications of divine truth. Through the judgment of God the eternal destiny of men is determined according to divine wisdom and love and according to their response to God's call to them. The principle of eternal judgment acknowledges that Christ is the judge of all human aspiration and achievement and that he summons men to express truth in decision until all things are reconciled under God.

We believe that the inner meaning and end toward which all history moves is revealed in Christ. He is at work in the midst of history, reconciling all things unto God in order, beauty, and peace. This reconciliation brings to fulfillment the kingdom of God upon earth. Christ's presence guarantees the victory of righteousness and peace over the injustice, suffering, and sin of our world. The tension between our assurance that the victory has been won in Christ and our continuing experience in this world where God's sovereignty is largely hidden is resolved in the conviction that Christ will come again. The affirmation of his coming redeems us from futility and declares the seriousness of all life under the unfailing and ultimate sovereignty of God.

Notes: *This statement, one of several circulated by the church, is taken from a volume published by the church's publishing concern,* Exploring the Faith *(Independence, MO: Herald House, 1970).*

* * *

Miscellaneous Mormons

ARTICLES OF FAITH [CHURCH OF JESUS CHRIST (BICKERTONITE)]

1. We believe in God, the Eternal Father, and in His Son, Jesus Christ, and in the Holy Ghost.

2. We believe that man will be punished for his own transgressions, and not for Adam's.

3. We believe that through the Atonement of Jesus Christ, all people may be saved, through obedience to the ordinances of the Gospel.

4. We believe in the principles of the Gospel as taught by the Saviour, Faith in Jesus Christ; Repentance and then baptism by immersion for the remission of sins, and the Laying on of hands for the gift of the Holy Ghost.

5. We believe in Feet Washing. John 13:5.

6. We believe the angel has flown. Rev. 14:6,7.

7. We believe that a man must be called by God, by His Holy Spirit and by the laying on of hands, by those in authority to preach the Gospel and administer in the Holy Ordinances thereof.

8. We believe in the same organization as was instituted by Jesus Christ, namely apostles, prophets, pastors, teachers, evangelists, etc.

9. We believe in the various gifts of the Gospel such as the gifts of tongues, prophecy, revelation, visions, healing, interpretation of tongues, etc.

10. We believe the Bible to be the word of God as far as it is correctly translated, and we also believe the Book of Mormon to be the word of God.

11. We believe what God has revealed, and what He may yet reveal. We believe that He will reveal much pertaining to the building up of His Kingdom upon the earth.

12. We believe in the literal gathering of Israel, including the Ten lost Tribes, also the Seed of Joseph (American Indians) on this land of America; and that Christ will eventually come, and reign on the earth one thousand years, between the First and Second Resurrections. See Rev. 20-1 & 6 inclusive.

13. We believe in, and claim the privilege of worshipping God according to the dictates of our own conscience. We concede and allow all others the same right.

14. We believe in being subject to Kings, Queens, Presidents, Rulers and Magistrates; in obeying, honoring and sustaining the Laws.

15. In conclusion, we say "whatever things are true, and honest, and just, and pure, and lovely, and of good report," we seek to uphold and maintain: for the fruits of the Spirit are love, joy, peace, long suffering, gentleness, goodness, faith, meekness, and temperance; "against such there is no law." The apostle Paul says to "prove all things, and hold fast to that which is good," Amen.

Notes: *These articles are derived directly from those of the Church of Jesus Christ of Latter-Day Saints. The church has added several articles on foot washing (item 5) and the angel of Revelation 14:6-7 (item 6), and has made several minor changes in wording.*

* * *

STATEMENT OF BELIEF [RESTORED CHURCH OF JESUS CHRIST (WALTON)]

1. We believe in the Godhead there are two personages, God the Father and Christ the Son. They both dwell in Celestial glory. Man was created, male and female, in the image (likeness) of both the Father and the Son, by whom were all things created. (Genesis 1:2, 29; John 1:1, 10, 16 I.V.; 3 Nephi 4:44-48; D & C 17:4-5)

2. We believe there is a Devil-Satan and that he is also from the beginning and that he is a fallen angel spirit and that he has legions of fallen spirits with him, and their stated purpose is to destroy man both body and soul and our disobedience to God gives the Devil power over us. (Genesis 3:1, 4-5; Rev. 12:8 I.V.; 2 Nephi 1:101-103, 120-125; D & C 1:6, 28:10-11; 2 Cor. 4:4)

3. We believe in the Holy Ghost, the Spirit of Truth, which is the life and power of God, to lead men into all truth, and back into the likeness and image of God, even a life of holiness, which is eternal life with God and the Christ. (Genesis 6:59-65, 67-71 I.V.; John 16:13-15; 3 Nephi 5:32-38; D & C 32:3, 34:5b)

4. We believe that men will be punished for their own sins and not for Adam's transgression, and that as a consequence of the atonement of Christ "all little children are alive in Christ, and also all they that are without the law." (Moroni 8:25-26). We believe that through Christ's Law and His Ordinances of the Gospel administered by Priesthood called of God by Revelation.

5. All of His Commandments must be kept! We believe that the Doctrine of Jesus Christ consists of the following laws and ordinances: 1. Faith toward God and in the Lord Jesus Christ; 2. Repentance from all sin; 3. Baptism by immersion, both men and women, and children after 8 years of age, for the remission of sins; 4. Laying on of hands for the gift of the Holy Ghost, according to the scriptures (Acts 2:38, 8:14-19, 19:2-6 and Hebrews 6:1-3); 5. Resurrection of the dead; 6. Eternal judgement.

6. We believe that the "Kingdom Order" can exist without the church, but the church cannot be without the "Keys of the Kingdom" and through priesthood ordained of God. (Matthew 16:19-20 I.V.; D & C 65 and 87:1-3)

7. We believe Jesus Christ is the same today as He was yesterday, and we believe in the principle of continuous revelation; that the canon of scripture is not full, that God raises up Prophets and inspires them in every age and among all people, and that He speaks when, where and through whom He may choose. (Isaiah 28:10, 13; Hebrews 13:8; Amos 3:7)

8. We believe in the "Holy Order of Enoch" and in sharing all things equal in order to establish Zion. (D & C 51, 77:1). We Believe Zion will be established before Christ returns (D & C 49:4-5) and that only those who keep all of His commandments will be authorized of God. (D & C 81:3b)

9. We believe in the same kind of organization that existed in the primitive church, viz. apostles, evangelists, pastors, teachers, and all other officers provided for in the scriptures. (Ephesians 4:11-15). We believe in the powers and gifts of the everlasting gospel, viz: wisdom, knowledge, faith, healing, and miracles, prophecy, tongues and interpretation of tongues, etc.

10. We believe that a man must be called of God by prophecy and by the laying on of hands, by those in authority to do so, to entitle him to preach the gospel and administer in the ordinances thereof. And that men only are to be ordained to preach the gospel and function in the priesthood ordinances. (Exodus 40:15, John 15:16, Galatians 1:11-12, Hebrews 5:1-6)

11. We believe that in all matters of controversy upon the duty of man toward God, and in reference to preparation and fitness for the world to come, the word of God should be decisive and the end of dispute; and that when God directs, man should obey. We believe in the doctrine of the resurrection of the body, that man will be judged and rewarded or punished according to his works; according to the good or degree of evil he shall have done. (Matthew 7:18-29, 1 Cor. 15:34-42, Rev. 20:12-13)

12. We believe in the Inspired Version of the Bible, and in the Stick of Joseph commonly known as the Nephite Record and in the 1835 first edition of the Doctrine and Covenants containing the Lectures on Faith accepted by the Church in General Assembly at Kirtland, Ohio.

13. We believe a temple will be built in Independence, Missouri, wherein Christ will reveal himself and endow his servants whom He chooses with power to preach the gospel in all the world to every kindred, tongue and people, that the promises of God may be fulfilled and the tribes of Israel gathered. This temple will be recognized as God's temple by a celestial cloud over it. (D & C 83:2)

14. We believe that marriage is ordained of God; and that the law of God provides for but one companion in wedlock for either man or woman. In cases where the contract of marriage is broken by death the remaining one is free to marry again, and in case of breach of the marriage covenant the innocent one is free to remarry. We believe that the doctrine of a plurality and a community of wives are heresies, and are opposed to the Law of God. (Mark 10:2-12, Jacob 2:36, D & C 49:3a-c)

15. We believe that men should worship God in spirit and in truth; and we claim the privilege for ourselves and all men of worshipping Almighty God according to the dictates of their conscience providing that such worship does not require a violation of the constitutional law of the land. (John 4:23-24) (From an undated tract published by the church.)

SETTING THE CHURCH IN ORDER

The underlying theme and mission of the church is to bring about a reunited restoraton movement. The church teaches that this disunity has been allowed by God in order for believers to see that things must be done God's way and that a recognition of errors must take place in order to reunite and build Zion together on these points:

1. Taking as our standard of faith the Inspired Version of the Holy Scriptures, the Nephite Record, and the divine revelations given to Joseph Smith, Jr.

2. Affirming that the Nephite Record is a divine record written by men inspired of God, delivered by an angel of God and interpreted by Joseph Smith, Jr., by command of God with the use of ancient instruments of interpretation called the Urim and Thummim.

3. That God has designated Independence, Missouri, as the center place of Zion. That the honest in heart, the saints of God, will begin their gathering here.

4. That Israel shall be gathered and God shall restore the ten lost tribes.

5. That the Law of Consecration is necessary to the establishment of Zion, with God's Bishop, directing a people pure in heart, by sacrifice and covenant.

6. That God is unchangeable and speaks His divine will yesterday, today and forever to an obedient people, and that Christ will reign personally upon the earth, and that the earth will be restored to its paradisiacal glory.

7. That in order to accomplish the work of the Lord committed to his people, it is necessary for them to

unite in "one" organization, in harmony with the Holy and Sacred Law of God. (*Let's Together Set the Church in Order*, published by the church, nd)

Notes: *This statement is unique among Mormon groups for its assertion of a bipartite Godhead (rather than a tripartite one). As in the state of the Church of Christ (Temple Lot), the temple lot in Independence is affirmed as the center of a coming kingdom. Like the Reorganized Church of Jesus Christ of Latter-Day Saints, the Restored Church of Jesus Christ uses the Inspired Version of the Bible, produced by Joseph Smith, Jr. The "Record of the Nephites" is what is commonly known as the Book of Mormon.*

* * *

BELIEFS OF THE TRUE CHURCH OF CHRIST, RESTORED (ROBERTS)

1. We believe in God the eternal father, and his son Jesus Christ, and in the Holy Ghost, which is the glory and power of God. It is neither a person nor a personage in the Godhead.

2. We believe that men and women will be punished for their own sins, and not for Adam's transgressions.

3. We believe that through the atonement of Jesus Christ all of the human race is saved by obedience to the laws and ordinances of the true gospel of Jesus Christ.

4. We believe and practice these ordinances of the true gospel of Jesus Christ are: 1st, faith in the Lord Jesus Christ; 2nd, Repentance: 3rd, water baptism for the remission of sins by immersion: 4th, laying on of hands for the true gift of the Holy Ghost, with the physical evidence of speaking in other tongues and the baptism of fire with the evidence of gloven tongues of fire coming upon our physical body in order to receive divine health: 5th, the Lord's supper by the miracle of consubstantiation, communion and washing of the saints' feet during the new moon sabbaths and the seven annual feasts of the Lord our God.

5. We believe that men and women must be called of God by inspiration and ordained by laying on of hands by those who are duly commissioned to preach the true gospel of Jesus Christ and administer in the ordinances thereof.

6. We believe in the same organization that existed in the primitive church of Jesus Christ, viz., apostles, prophets, evangelists, pastors, teachers, etc.

7. We believe and practice the powers and gifts of the everlasting gospel, viz., the word of wisdom, the word of knowledge, the gift of great faith, the gifts the healing, the gift of mighty miracles, the gift of prophesy, the gift of beholding of angels and ministering spirits, the gift of all kinds of tongues, the gift of the interpretation of languages and of divers kinds of tongues, dreams, visions, the gift of revelation, and the fruit of spirit is love, joy, peace, longsuffering, gentleness, goodness, faith, meekness and temperance.

8. We believe in the word of God recorded in the Holy Bible and the word of God recorded in the book of Mormon (The Nephite Record), and in the revelations of the prophets Joseph Smith, Jr., and James J. Strang.

9. We believe all that God has revealed; all that he does now reveal; and all that God will yet reveal many more great and important things pertaining to the theocratic kingdom of God, and the second coming of Jesus Christ.

10. We believe in the literal gathering of Israel, and in the restoration of the ten tribes, that Zion (New Jerusalem) will be established upon the western continent; that Jesus Christ will reign personally upon the earth a thousand years; and that the earth will be renewed, and receive its paradisiacal glory.

11. We believe in the literal resurrection of the body, and that the dead in Jesus Christ will rise first, and that the rest of the dead live not again until the thousand years are expired.

12. We claim the privilege of worshipping almighty God according to the dictates of our conscience unmolested, and allow all men and women the same privilege, let them worship how or where they may.

13. We believe in being subject to Kings, Queens, Presidents, Rulers, and Magistrates, in obeying, honoring, and sustaining the law according to the word of God.

14. We believe in being honest, true, chaste, temperate, benevolent, virtuous, and upright, and in doing good to all; indeed, we may say that we follow the admonition of Paul, we believe all things, we hope all things, we have endured very many things, and hope to be able to endure all things. Everything virtuous, lovely, praiseworthy, and of good report, we seek after, looking forward to the recompense of reward.

15. We believe that the seventh day is the true sabbath of the Lord our God and the seventh day sabbath begins at sunset Friday to sunset Saturday and all believers in Christ Jesus must keep this day as the true sabbath day and no other day ever.

16. We believe that the new moon sabbaths, the seven annual feasts, the seventh year sabbath, and the jubilee year sabbath of the Lord our God must be observed and kept by all believers in Christ Jesus forever.

17. We believe that the law of clean and unclean meats and all other laws of health must be observed and kept by all believers in Christ Jesus forever.

18. We believe in salvation for the living and the dead and in building temples and in performing temple ordinances for both the living and the dead, such as, the baptism for the dead, washings, anointings, sealings and marriage for time and for all eternity, etc.

19. We believe in the virgin birth of Jesus Christ. We believe that he was conceived by the power of the Holy Spirit and that neither the seed of Mary nor the

BELIEFS OF THE TRUE CHURCH OF CHRIST, RESTORED (ROBERTS) (continued)

seed of Joseph was used in the virgin birth. Also that the Virgin Mary only encompasseth the child Jesus. Read St. Matt. 1:18-25: St. Luke 1:26-38; Isaiah 66:7 and Jeremiah 31:22.

20. We believe and practice all things common, even the united firm of Zion in all our stakes of Zion, according to the Holy Scriptures.

21. We believe in the translation of the Saints, such as Enoch, Elijah, John the beloved and the three Nephite disciples; also that the faithful Saints on earth will obtain complete Christ-like righteousness and be caught up in the air to meet our Lord Jesus Christ at his second coming.

Notes: *This statement is derived from that of the Church of Jesus Christ of Latter-Day Saints, but contains numerous additions such as the reference to James J. Strang, who claimed to be the successor to Joseph Smith, Jr., founder of the Mormon movement. The church is sabbatarian and keeps the Old Testament holy days and dietary practices.*

Chapter 15
Communal Family

Communal—Before 1960

TWENTY-FOUR RULES (AMANA CHURCH SOCIETY)

Buedingen, July 4, 1716

A most important revelation of the Spirit of the Lord through Johann Adam Gruber in accordance with which the new communities were established and received into "the gracious covenant of the Lord." These rules remain the basis of the faith of the community and are, indeed, the foundation on which the whole edifice of the community is erected.

Hear yea, Hear yea, the word of the Lord, you who are still here and profess to be members of the community! So speaketh the Lord: You have seen what I have begun among you and how my servants have, to some extent, prepared the ground to lay the foundation stones on which the whole structure shall be founded.

But do you consider this sufficient? That would be far from my justice. I have only, to some extent, revealed your motives as far as you were able to bear it. I, who have stepped in your midst, have heard all your words, all your promises, which you have given me although I find amongst you only a very few who have a heart as I wish to find it. These, and all of you, shall know, however, that all your words have been recorded in my book, and in accordance with this and your innermost thoughts you shall be judged.

You shall then once more avow openly before My holy face and the presence of My holy angels and of the members of your community with hand and mouth to My servant, the Elder given unto you, what I shall speak unto you and also what you have promised with words in your heart. And if you break this vow then this and all your words shall stand against you as a quick witness and all my promises will become, instead of a blessing, a fiery and heavy burden.

Is there still anybody among you who is still fearful and lacks courage and is afraid not to be able to live up to my commandments which may seem to him difficult at this time in spite of the grace given by me? Such a one may still step aside, for I know that there are still some whose hearts are hard and unbroken and who consider my wonders and my ways too lightly but of whom I expect that they hold them in fitting respect.

(Here followed a brief pause.)

Are they all willing?

Hear then what I say unto you. I, the Lord your God am holy! And therefore you, too, shall be and become a holy community, if I am to abide in your midst as you desire. And therefore you shall henceforth resolve:

I. To tear all crude and all subtle idols out of your hearts, that they may no longer befool you and mislead you further to idolatry against your God, so that His name be not defamed and He not suddenly go forth and avenge and save the glory of His name.

II. I desire that you shall have naught in common with the fruitless work of darkness; neither with grave sins and sinners, nor with the subtle within and without you. For what relationship and likeness has My holy temple with the temples of pride, unchasteness, ambition, seeking for power; and of the useless superfluous, condemning prattling, which steals the time away from Me. How could the light unite with the darkness? How can you as children of the light unite with the ungodly, the liars and their works, the scoffers and blasphemers, who are nothing but darkness?

III. You shall henceforth in your external life conduct yourself so that those standing without find no longer cause for ill reports and for defaming My name. Suffer rather the wrong if you are abused. But above all flee from associations which hinder you from growing in godliness. All mockers and scoffers and those who recommend you unto vanity, you shall shun and have no dealings with them.

IV. You shall also perform your earthly task the longer the more according to the dictates of your conscience; and gladly desist from that which My spirit shows you to be sinful—not heeding your own loss, for I am the Lord, who can and will care and provide

for the needs of your body—that through this you
may not give cause for censure to the scoffer. The
time which I still grant you here is very short;
therefore, see to it well that My hand may bring
forth and create within you a real harvest.

V. Let, I warn you, be far from you all falseness, lying,
and hypocrisy. For I say unto you that I will give the
spirit of discernment and will lay open unto you
through the Spirit of Prophecy such vices. For to
what end shall clay and metal be together? Would it
not make for Me a useless vessel, which I could not
use and should have to cast away with the rest.
Behold, My children, I have chosen before many,
many, many, and have promised to be unto you a
fiery entrenchment against the defiance of your inner
and outer enemies. Verily! Verily! I shall keep my
promises, if only you endeavor to fulfill what you
have promised and are promising.

VI. You shall therefore, none of you, strive for particular
gifts and envy the one or the other to whom I give
perchance the gift of prayer or maybe of wisdom.
For such the enemy of My glory seeks ever to instill
into you, especially into the passionate and fickle
souls, to impart to you thereby a poison destructive
to the soul. You shall, all, all, all of you be filled with
My pure and holy spirit when the time will come to
pass, if you will let yourself be prepared in humility
and patience according to My will. Then you too
shall speak with tongues different from the tongues
you now speak with. Then I shall be able to
communicate with you most intimately.

VII. Put aside henceforth all slander, and all malice of the
heart toward each other, which you have harbored
hitherto! None of you are free from it!

Behold I shall command the Spirit of my Love that
He as often as you assemble in true simplicity of
heart and in humility for prayer be in your very
midst with His influence and may flow through the
channels of His Love into the hearts He finds empty.

VIII. You must make yourself willing for all outer and
inner suffering. For Belial will not cease to show
unto you his rancor through his servants and
through his invisible power. It is also pleasing to Me
and absolutely necessary for you that you be tried
through continuous sorrow, suffering, and cross, and
to be made firm and precious in My crucible. And he
who does not dare (but none must be indolent
himself in this) to exert all his physical and spiritual
powers through My strength, let him depart that he
may not be later a blemishing spot upon My glory.

IX. Do not lend in future your ears to suspicion and
prejudice and take, because of your lack of self-
knowledge, offense at each other where there is none.
But each one among you shall become the mirror for
the other. You shall, moreover, also endeavor to
stand every day and hour before the Lord as a

oneness, as a city or a light on a high mountain,
which near and far shines bright and pure.

X. At the same time practice the longer the more outer
and inner quiet. Seek ever, though it will be for the
natural man which is inexperienced in this a hard
death, to hide yourself, in humility in the inner and
undermost chamber of your nothingness, that I may
bring in this soil to a befitting growth My seed which
I have concealed therein.

XI. Behold, my people! I make with you this day a
covenant which I bid you to keep faithfully and
sacredly. I will daily wander amongst you and visit
your place of rest, that I may see how you are
disposed toward Me.

XII. Guard yourself. I, the Lord, warn you against
indifference towards this covenant of grace and
against negligence, indolence, and laziness which
thus far have been for the most part your ruler and
have controlled your heart. I shall not depart from
your side nor from your midst, but shall Myself on
the contrary reveal Myself ever more powerfully,
holier, and more glorious through the light of My
face in and among you, as long as you will bring
forth to meet Me the honest and sincere powers of
your will. This shall be the tie with which you can
bind and hold Me. Behold I accept you this day as
slaves of My will, as free-borns of My kingdom, as
possessors, of My heart! Therefore let yourself gladly
and willingly be bound with the ties of My love, and
the power of love shall never be wanting unto you.

XIII. And you who are the heads and fathers of
households hear what I say unto you: The Lord has
now chosen you as members of His Community with
whom He desires to associate and dwell day by day.
See, therefore, to this that you prove truly heads and
lights of your households, which, however, always
stand under their faithful head, your King; see that
you may bring your helpmates to true conduct and
fear of God through your own way of living, which
you shall strive to make ever more faultless, more
earnest and manly.

XIV. Your children, you who have any, you shall endeav-
or with all your power to sacrifice to Me and to lead
to Me. I shall give you in abundance, if you only
inwardly keep close to Me, wisdom, courage, understanding, bravery, and earnestness mingled with
love, that you yourself may be able to live before
them in the fear of God and that your training may
be blessed—that is, in those who want to submit to
My hand in and through Me. But those who scorn
you and do not heed my voice in and through you
and otherwise, shall have their blood come upon
their own heads. But you shall never abandon hope
but wrestle for them with earnest prayer, struggle,
and toil, which are the pangs of spiritual birth. But if
you neglect them through indifference, negligence,
half-heartedness, and laziness, then every such soul
shall verily be demanded of such a father.

XV. Do now your part as I command you from without
and frequently inwardly through My Spirit; do not

desist, just as I never cease to work on you my disobedient children; then you will abide in my grace and save your souls. And such women and children shall bear the fruits of their sins as do not want to bow themselves under you and Me. I will henceforth no longer tolerate those grave offenses among you and in your houses about which the world and the children of wrath and disbelief have so much to say; but I have commanded the Spirit of My living breath, that He pass through all your houses and breathe upon every soul which does not wantonly close itself to Him. The dew of blessing shall flow from the blessed head of your high priest and prince of peace upon every male head among you, and through them it shall flow upon and into your helpmates, and through both man and wife into the offspring and children, so that all your seed shall be acceptable, pure, and holy before the Lord, since He has nourished and will nourish the same among you.

XVI. And none of your grown up children shall be permitted to attend your meetings, who have not previously received from their parents a good testimony according to the truth, not appearance, and without self-deception, as also from the Elders and leaders especially from the one who with his fellow workers has to watch over the training of the children, which is to be carried on with earnestness and love, but without all severity and harshness. This training is to be watched over with all earnestness; and should the parents be negligent and the case require it, so shall the latter be temporarily excluded (from the prayer-meetings) for their humiliation.

XVII. Prove yourselves as the people whom I have established for an eternal monument to Me, and whom I shall impress upon My heart as an eternal seal, so that the Spirit of My love may dwell upon you and within you, and work according to His desire.

XVIII. And this is the word which the Lord speaks of these strangers who so often visit you and cause so much disturbance: None, whom you find to be a scoffer, hypocrite, mocker, sneerer, derider, and unrepenting sinner, shall you admit to your Community and prayer-meetings. Once for all they are to be excluded that My refreshing dew and the shadow of My Love be never prevented from manifesting themselves among you. But if some should come to you with honest intentions who are not knowingly scoffers, hypocrites, and deriders, though it be one of those whom you call of the world, if he to your knowledge does not come with deceitful intentions, then you may well admit him. I shall give you My faithful servants and witnesses especially the spirit of discrimination and give you an exact feeling, whether they are sincere and come with honest intentions or otherwise.

XIX. If they then desire to visit you more frequently, you shall first acquaint them with your rules and ask them whether they will submit to these rules and to the test of the Elders. And then you shall read to them My laws and commands, which I give unto you; and if you see that they are earnestly concerned about their souls, then you shall gladly receive the weak, and become weak with them for a while, that is, you shall with them and for them repent and make their repentance your own. But if a scoffer or mocker declares that he repents, him you should only admit after considerable time and close scrutiny and examination of his conduct, if you find the latter to be righteous. For Satan will not cease to try to launch at you his fatal arrows through such people. Be therefore on your guard and watch that not the wolf come among you and scatter or even devour the sheep.

XX. And those who pledge themselves with hand and mouth after the aforesaid manner to you shall make public profession before the Community and also make an open confession of their resolve, and I shall indeed show you if this latter comes from their hearts; the conduct of those you shall watch closely, whether they live according to their profession and promise or not, lest the dragon defile your garments with his drivel.

XXI. (To the Elders.) Thus My Elder and his fellow-workers shall frequently visit the members of the Community and see how things are in their homes and how it stands about their hearts. I shall give to you my servant (E.L. Gruber) and to your Brothers keen eyes, if you only pray for it. And if you find that one is in uncalled sadness, or lives in negligence, impudence, boisterousness, or the like, then you shall admonish him in love. If he repents you shall rejoice. But if after repeated admonition he does not mend his ways, then you shall put him to shame openly before the Community; and if even this does not help then you shall exclude him for a while. Yet I shall ever seek my sheep, those who are already excluded and those who in the future because of their own guilt must be excluded, and I shall ever try to lead them in their nothingness into my pasture.

XXII. And to all of you I still give this warning: Let none of you reject brotherly admonition and punishment, so that secret pride grows not like a poisonous thorn in such a member and torment and poison his whole heart.

XXIII. You shall not form a habit of anything of the external exercises (forms of worship) and the duties committed to you, or I shall be compelled to forbid them again; on the contrary, you shall make your meetings ever more fervent, more earnest, more zealous, in the true simple love towards each other, fervent and united in Me, the true Prince of Peace.

XXIV. This the members and brethren of the Community shall sincerely and honestly pledge with hand and mouth to my Elders, openly in the assembly, after they have carefully considered it, and it shall be kept sacred ever after.

Notes: *These rules, which still govern the religious life of the Amana community, originated with Johann A. Gruber, the prophet who led the group during the eighteenth century.*

*They were revealed during a session in which he spoke as
one inspired by a spirit of prophecy. The entire text of that
session is reproduced here.*

* * *

ACCOUNT OF OUR RELIGION, DOCTRINE AND FAITH (HUTTERITE BRETHREN)

I. DOCTRINE OF THE CHURCH AND OF THE SPIRIT

An assembly of children of God who have separated
themselves from all unclean things is the church. It is
gathered together, has being, and is kept by the Holy
Spirit. Sinners may not be members unless and until they
have repented of their sins. The essence of the church is its
bearing of the Light; it is a lantern of righteousness in a
world of unbelief, darkness, and blindness. It is a pillar and
ground of the truth, which is confirmed, ratified, and
brought to pass in her by the Holy Spirit. The "power and
key" to forgive sins which was received by Christ from the
Father is given to the church as a whole and not to
individual persons. In its nature the church is spiritual, but
concretely it is known as the pure sacred community.
Church assembly and community are equated together.

II. DOCTRINE OF REDEMPTION AND ENTRANCE INTO THE CHURCH

Redemption means the working of the Spirit in the
individual and his preparation for entrance into the
church. It is the Spirit of Christ that leads into the church.
("The Christ of Ridemann is the inwardly experienced and
fought-for Christ.") The work of Christ in man means a
complete conversion and rebirth. Salvation and redemption consists in the liberation from the dominion of sin.
Apart from Christ there is no goodness. Salvation also is a
new covenant. God has cast out from our heart evil, sin,
and the lust to sin, and we are to seek, love, hear, and keep
His Word.

III. DOCTRINE OF FAITH

Faith is a real divine power which renews man and makes
him like God in nature, ardent in love and in keeping His
commandments.

IV. DOCTRINE OF BAPTISM

Baptism means the entrance into the covenant of grace of
God and the incorporation into the Church of Christ. The
"right and necessary" sequence is preaching, faith, rebirth,
and baptism. Children cannot be baptized in the right way
because they are not reborn through preaching, faith, and
the Spirit.

V. DOCTRINE OF THE FELLOWSHIP OF THE LORD'S TABLE

The Supper is a sign of the community of Christ's body, in
that each member thereby declares himself to be of the one
mind, heart, and Spirit of Christ. It is an act of
remembrance at which God's children become aware again
of the grace which they have received. Only a true member
of Christ may participate. The unity of the fellowship of
the Lord's Table must already exist prior to the celebrating.

VI. DOCTRINE OF ORIGINAL SIN

The inheritance that we have from our Father Adam is
inclination to sin. Original sin means that all of us have by
nature a tendency toward evil and have pleasure in sin.
This inheritance removes, devours, and consumes all that
is good and of God in man; so that none may attain it
again except to be born again.

VII. THE FORMULA FOR BAPTISM

The baptizer first testifies to the baptizand and asks if he
believes in God, the Father, the Son, and the Holy Spirit.
The baptizand confesses. He then is asked if he desires to
yield himself to God to live for Him and His church. If so,
he is told to kneel before God and the church, and water is
poured upon him. If baptism cannot be performed before
the entire church, the baptizer may perform the ordinance
alone.

Notes: *Long before the Hutterite Brethren divided into
three distinct groups in North America in the twentieth
century, a confession of faith accepted by all was written by
Peter Riederman in 1540 and published in 1565. It is a
lengthy document of over 200 pages, and hence, is not
reproduced here. Theologically the document, still accepted
as authoritative by contemporary Hutterites, follows the
Anabaptist-Mennonite tradition (see the Schleitheim and
Dordrecht Confessions). It covers all of the major Christian
doctrinal emphases, and in traditional fashion advocates
adult baptism, separation from the world, and the use of the
ban. It forbids participation in war and war industries (the
manufacture of swords), litigation, swearing, and any
association with strong drink (selling and/or consuming).*

*An English translation by Kathleen Hasenburg was pub-
lished in 1950 (London: Hodder and Stoughton; Rifton,
NY: Plough Publishing House). Commentaries summarizing the content have been published in several Mennonite
sources. See, for example, Robert Friedman,* Hutterite
Studies *(Goshen, IN: Mennonite Historical Society, 1961).*

*The summary of the Riederman Account reproduced here
was originally published in* Baptist Confessions of Faith *by
William L. Lumpkin (Chicago: Judson Press, 1959). It
covers seven major points of the group's doctrine.*

* * *

SYNOPTICAL OUTLINE OF KORESHAN THEOLOGY (KORESHAN UNITY)

KORESHANITY DIFFERENTIATED FROM THE FALLACIOUS PANTHEISM OF MODERN TIMES

First, Pantheism is the all-God, the God of the Shepherds.
The Lord Jesus Christ is Jehovah, the Shepherd of the
sheep, and the Father-Mother of the Shepherds who stand
on Mount Zion and sing the song of Moses and the Lamb.
Jesus the Shepherd, the God Jehovah of the Shepherds,
when coming again, comes not in sacrifice as the Lamb of
God, for He must have a new name. He comes to sacrifice
for the cleansing of the sanctuary, and is the goat
Shepherd. It is the goat that is sacrificed for the cleansing
of the sanctuary. Pan was the god of the "hollow earth."

The word "pan" signifies "a concavity or depression," and as all life develops in the shell, or from within the shell, the common order of development will not be violated in the development of the life proceeding toward the maturity of the Sons of God.

Second. Pantheism, as accepted today by the superficial thinker, supposes that the universe is, as it were, a body, and that its soul is Deity. The universe, conceived as circumference and center, furnishes the idea of a pivot or central point, which in Koreshanity is regarded as the Astral or Stellar Center. This, being the pivot and focal point of all influx from the pediment, rind or periphery, provides a demonstration or astronomical proof of a localized conscious point, affectional and intellectual, of the system of integralism. It furnishes such a demonstration because the physical universe, being center and circumference, and necessarily the expression of mind or cause, must be correspondentially like it. It will be noticed that the Deity of the Koreshan syntheticism is not a universal Deity, but, as the nucleus of the alchemico-organic cosmos, is a comparatively minute focal point, so the Astral Center of the anthropostic cosmos is the personal, individual and microcosmic Man. Such a Man was the Lord Jesus, who was and is Jehovah.

Third. It will be seen that there is a divine and a diabolic pantheism; and that while God (Elohi) is all and in all, the Lord, the Son of God, the Bridegroom in whom was the Bride, is the personal Deity, and, therefore, that the personal Deity of the Koreshan syntheticism is the God-Man and Man-God. When the process of regeneration is complete, in which the Sons of God (of the Lord Jesus) are manifest, these Sons also will be like the parent, namely, Father-Mother, and they each will be also Bride and Bridegroom, for they will be male and female—not dual, but biune in the image and likeness of God. "It doth not yet appear what we shall be: but we know that, when he shall appear, we shall be like him" (I John 3:2). "But as many as received him, to them gave he power to become the sons of God, even to them that believe on his name" (John 1:12).

Fourth. When this development is complete it will necessarily be the production of a new genus. This genus we denominate Theo-Anthropos—the God-Man genus.

CONTRAST BETWEEN MORTAL AND IMMORTAL LIFE

First. Man, as now existing, is mortal. He is mortal because the male and female are in two parts; and because of this, life does not form a cycle or wheel of perpetual being. Man is ignorant of the law of life; therefore he dies or goes to corruption. Whatsoever his profession, "Christian" and "pagan" alike, he passes to a corruptible decay.

Second. Man cannot become immortal but by obedience to the law of immortality.

Third. The science of immortal life is involved in the ten precepts of the Decalogue. These comprise the ten categories of natural immortality. The Lord Jesus kept these laws, and overcame the tendency to corruption. When He departed this existence, or life in the natural, He became spiritual; He dematerialized and passed out alive. This is the new and living way.

Fourth. No man can be saved but by the process that saved the Lord Jesus.

Fifth. Natural immortality does not mean that man will live in this earth eternally. Man, then, becomes immortal as the fruit of the Tree of Life, passes out of the natural into the invisible, but leaves behind a lower and subsequent form of human life in which the Seed of the Sons of God is planted for another fruitage at the end of another Grand Cycle.

Sixth. Time is divided into long and shorter cycles, consisting of solar, lunar, planetary and stellar cycles or periods. We are now terminating a lunar period of about twenty-four thousand years. In it we are reaching the greatest crisis of the world's history. From it will unfold the Kingdom of Righteousness. In a lunar period of twenty-four thousand years there are four ages of six thousand years each, designated: Gold, Silver, Brass, and Iron Ages. Each age is also divided into four periods or dispensations. gold, silver, brass, and iron. We are now in the iron portion of the last or Iron Age.

The world enjoyed a period of greatest light and goodness for six thousand years, beginning twenty-four thousand years ago, and ending with the beginning of the Silver Age, eighteen thousand years ago. The world then entered into its grand Silver Age, and remained there for six thousand years. It then entered the Brass Age, and at the end of that, the Iron Age. The last six thousand, the Iron Age, has been the degenerate and degenerating period of the world's history. We are just now emerging from the darkest period of the most benighted age of all the ages, and about to enter, again, the Golden Age.

THE NEW KORESHAN DISPENSATION

The Koreshan system is inaugurated for the purpose of restoring normal states and relations, and insuring their permanency through their scientific regulation of all the functions of life. The want of equilibrium in the social fabric has its inception in the radical and willful violation of organic law, actuated either through the conscious disregard of religious, moral, political, social and physiological obligations, or through ignorance of the science of law, and lack of application because of such ignorance. The attainment and maintenance of a state of equibalance can accrue only as the result of a thorough comprehension of the principles of both life and death; and these may be resolved to a simple and unitary radix, whose quality may be stated in a brief but inclusive formulary.

Love is the fulfilling of the law. Is argument required for the demonstration of the distinctive virtue of love to God and the neighbor, as differentiated from the love of self, which now comprises the basis of nearly every impulse to human enterprise and activity? Life and death are two antithetical states involving properties of diametric force, whose "energies" are so at variance as to insure a perpetual opposition and struggle for supremacy and perpetuity. We mean by life and death, the two states properly denominated "immortality" and "mortality."

SYNOPTICAL OUTLINE OF KORESHAN THEOLOGY
(KORESHAN UNITY) (continued)

The ultimate of man's natural destiny is in reaching such a degree of development and control of the functions of his physical organism, as to insure to him a passage from the natural to the spiritual or heavenly domain without the death of the body. The Lord Jesus in His earthly career—fraught with a succession of triumphal combats against the hells and final achievement of victory over the grave—conquered death in His own organism, and became the promise of a corresponding victory for all such as will obey the same law with the same fidelity, overcoming in themselves the power of corruptible dissolution as He overcame and entered through theocrasis into Glory.

Mortality is man's birthright through propagation from his sensual and lower origin. Immortality is the birthright of man through regeneration from God, by virtue of the divine planting or impregnation by the operation of the Holy Spirit. "I am from above," said Jesus; and this annunciation was proclaimed pursuantly to the central law of His conception by the divine overshadowing or spiritual impregnation. "Ye are from beneath," was uttered upon the basis of human origin through sensuous propagation, a propagation which involves inevitably a final corruptible dissolution through decay. (See John 8:23.)

The present system of religious, political and social activity has its momentuations in the central potency and force of self love. It is opposed to the law of God, as theoretically stated and practically applied by the Lord; and its career and termination are essentially mortal. In the presentation of two diametrically opposite determinations of human purpose as the two rival potencies of being, namely, love to the neighbor and self love, we have denoted the foundation stones of both life and death, or of immortality and mortality.

Love to God, manifest in love to the neighbor, is the keynote to the concord of harmonies soon to vibrate the octaves of terrestrial resonance, as the Deific respiration fills the body with God's eternal, vital Presence. "And the Lord God . . . breathed into his nostrils the breath of life; and man became a living soul" (Gen. 2:7), was true when, in the first Eden, the Sons of God awoke to the consciousness of divine origin, inception, birth, and destiny. Again God is about to breathe into man's nostrils the breath of life, through the coming theocrasis; and Eden restored will confirm the testimony of the sacred witnesses of God's humanity and humanity's Godhood and celestial origin.

The Kingdom of God established in the earth will fulfill the hope of consummate aspiration. This Kingdom established will verify God's promises, and also human expectation as predicated upon, and resting in, His purpose to reclaim the earth (man's body), and His power to achieve the victory over death, and make His triumphal entry into a domain hitherto under the jurisdiction of His Satanic Majesty. Nothing less than God's own Kingdom, inaugurated with men, will satisfy the longings of the chosen race; nothing less than this will fulfill the expectations of humanity as built upon the verity of the Word of God's annunciation. Nothing less than this can verify man's predication of the omnipotence, omniscience, and omnipresence of Deity, and the immortal destiny of the race—the hope of which is fixed in his confidence in the promised purpose of the Eternal.

If the Kingdom of Righteousness, involving the immortality of man, and with it his resurrection or restoration to his Edenic state, must exist by virtue of the dominance of love to the neighbor as originating in supreme love to God, then with the building of such a Kingdom must depart the system of competitive activity originating in self love, and concomitant with the evils of unwholesome agitation. If the promises of God are of any import, there is coming an adjustment of human affairs, the basis of which will be the plenary adjudication of the righteous claims and prerogatives of the downtrodden.

The wail of human degradation has reached the ears of the God of Sabaoth; the cry for bread, fuel, and shelter from those who are ground into the dust of despair by the unrelenting heel of affluent and imperialistic despotism, under the cloak of a democracy prostituted to the interests of an illegitimate aggrandizement and supremacy, has ascended, until, responsive to its pleadings, the God of Justice hurls back the thunderbolts of retributive wrath, the keen-edged sword of a divine vengeance and prosecuting force of a holy equation.

We behold with prophetic prescience the coming retribution, and therefore list the note of warning, both to the oppressor and the oppressed, who, in the struggle for supremacy, constitute Gog and Magog; that is, the roof and floor of a conflict, the inevitable culmination of which will be the overthrow of both parties to the contest. There is but a single remedy to the evils now afflicting society—the eradication of selfishness; and this can be insured only through the fulfillment of the divine purpose to inaugurate the Everlasting Kingdom, to be ushered in through the coming overshadowing and outpouring of the divine fire.

Notes: *Not a creed, this statement is one of the most recent attempts to restate the Koreshan religious perspective without mentioning the more controversial aspects of the cellular cosmology for which founder Cyrus Teed is best remembered.*

*   *   *

A CONCISE STATEMENT OF THE PRINCIPLES OF THE ONLY TRUE CHURCH, ACCORDING TO THE PRESENT APPEARANCE OF CHRIST [UNITED SOCIETY OF BELIEVERS IN CHRIST'S SECOND APPEARANCE (THE SHAKERS)]

We believe that the first light of salvation was given or made known to the patriarchs by promise; and they that believed in the promise of Christ, and were obedient to the command of God made known unto them, were the people of God and were accepted of God as righteous, or perfect in their generations; according to the measure of light and truth manifested unto them; which was as waters to the ankles signified by Ezekiel's vision of the holy waters (chapter 47). And altho' they could not receive regeneration or the fulness of salvation, from the fleshly or fallen nature in this life; because the fulness of time was not yet come, that they should receive the baptism of the Holy Ghost and fire; for the destruction of the body of sin, and purification of the soul; but Abram being [4] called, and chosen of God as the father of the faithful; was received into covenant relation with God by promise; that in him (and his seed which was Christ) all the families of the earth should be blessed, and these earthly blessings, which were promised to Abram, were a shadow of gospel or spiritual blessings to come: and circumcision, though it was a seal of Abram's faith, yet it was but a sign of the mortification and destruction of the flesh by the gospel in a future day. Observe, circumcision, or outward cutting of the foreskin of the flesh, did not cleanse the man from sin; but was a sign of the baptism of the Holy Ghost and fire: which is by the power of God manifested in divers operations and gifts of the spirit, as in the days of the apostles; which does indeed destroy the body of sin, or fleshly nature, and purify the man from all sin both soul and body. So that Abram, though in the [5] full faith of the promise; yet, as he did not receive the substance of the thing promised, his hope of eternal salvation was in Christ, by the Gospel to be attained in the resurrection from the dead.

The second dispensation was the law that was given of God to Israel, by the hand of Moses; which was a further manifestation of that salvation which was promised through Christ by the gospel, both in the order and ordinances which was instituted and given to Israel, as the church and people of God according to that dispensation; which was as waters to the ankles, Ezekiel XLVII. by which they were distinguished from all the families of the earth. For, while they were strictly obedient to all the commands, ordinances, and statutes, that God gave them, they were approbated of God according to the promise for life; and blessing was promised [6] unto them in the line of obedience: Cursing and death, in disobedience: for God, who is ever jealous for the honor and glory of his own great name, always dealt with them according to his word; for while they were obedient to the command of God, and purged out sin from amongst them, God was with them, according to his promise. But when they disobeyed the command of God, and committed sin, and became like other people, the hand of the Lord was turned against them; and those evils came upon them which God had threatened; so we see that they were wholly obedient to the will of God made known in that dispensation, were accepted as just, or righteous: yet, as the dispensation was short, they did not attain that salvation which was promised in the gospel; so that as it respected the new-birth, or real purification of the man from all sin; the law made nothing perfect, but was a [7] shadow of good things to come; their only hope of eternal redemption was in the promise of Christ, by the gospel to be attained in the resurrection from the dead. Acts of the Apostles XXVI. 6, 7.

The third dispensation was the gospel of Christ's first appearance, in the flesh: and that salvation which took place in consequence of his life, death, resurrection, and ascension at the right hand of the father being accepted in his obedience, as the first born among many brethren; he received power and authority to administer the power of the resurrection and eternal judgment to all the children of men: so that he has become the author of eternal salvation to all that obey him; and as Christ has this power in himself, he did administer power and authority to his church at the day of Pentecost, as his body: with all the gifts that he had promised them, which was the first [8] gift of the Holy Ghost, as an in-dwelling comforter to abide with them forever: and by which they were baptised into Christ's death; death to all sin; and were in the hope of the resurrection from the dead, through the operation of the power of God, which wrought in them. And as they had received the substance of the promise of Christ come in the flesh, by the gift and power of the Holy Ghost; they had power to preach the gospel in Christ's name to every creature;—and to administer the power of God to as many as believed, and were obedient to the gospel which they preached; and also to remit and retain sin in the name and authority of Christ on earth: so that they that believed in the gospel, and were obedient to that form of doctrine which was taught them; by denying all ungodliness and worldly lusts; and became entirely dead to the law by the body of Christ, [9] or power of the Holy Ghost, were in the travel of the resurrection from the dead; or the redemption of the body. So that they who took up a full cross against the world, flesh, and devil; and who forsook all for Christ's sake; and followed him in the regeneration, by preserving in that line of obedience to the end; found the resurrection from the dead, and eternal salvation in that dispensation was only as water to the loins; the mystery of God not finished; but there was another day prophesied of, called the second appearance of Christ, or final and last display of God's grace to a lost world: in which the mystery of God should be finished as he has spoken by his prophets since the world began: which day could not come, except there was a falling away from that faith and power that the church then stood in; in which time anti-christ was to have [10] his reign, whom Christ should destroy with the spirit of his mouth and brightness of his appearance: which falling away began soon after the apostles, and gradually increased in the church, until about four hundred and fifty seven years from Christ's birth (or thereabouts) at which time the power of the Holy People, or church of Christ, was scattered or lost by reason of transgression: and anti-christ, or false religion, got to be established. Since that time the witnesses of Christ have prophesied in sackcloth or under darkness; and altho' many have been faithful to testify against sin; even to the laying down of their lives for the testimony which they held; so that God accepted them in their obedience; while they were faithful and just to live or walk up to the measure of light and truth of God, revealed or made known unto them, but as it is written, that all they that will live godly in Christ [11] Jesus, shall suffer persecution: and so it has been, and those faithful witnesses lost their lives, by those falsely called the church of Christ: which is anti-christ; for the true church of Christ never persecuted any; but were inoffensive, harmless, separate from sin, living in obedience to God they earnestly contend for the fame. Therefore it may be plainly seen and known, where the true church of Christ is: but as it is writen anti-christ or false churches should prevail against the saints and overcome them, before Christ's

A CONCISE STATEMENT OF THE PRINCIPLES OF THE ONLY TRUE CHURCH, ACCORDING TO THE PRESENT APPEARANCE OF CHRIST [UNITED SOCIETY OF BELIEVERS IN CHRIST'S SECOND APPEARANCE (THE SHAKERS)] (continued)

second appearance, 2 Thess. II. 3. Let no man deceive you by any means for that day shall not come except there come a falling away first; and that man of sin be revealed, the son of perdition, Rev. XIII. 7. And it was given unto him to overcome them, and power was given him [12] over all kindreds, tongues, and nations; and this is the state Christ prophesied the world of mankind should be in, at his second appearance, Luke XVII. 26. And as it was in the day of Noe, so shall it be in the days of the son of man, verse 30. Even so shall be in the day when the son of man is revealed; plainly referring to his second appearance to consume or destroy anti-christ, and make a final end of sin; and establish his kingdom upon earth: but as the revelation of Christ must be in his people, whom he had chosen to be his body, to give testimony of him and to preach his gospel to a lost world.

The fourth dispensation or day is the second appearance of Christ, or final, or last display of God's grace to a lost world, in which the mystery of God will be finished and a decisive work, to the final salvation, or damnation of all the children [13] of men. (Which according to the prophecies rightly calculated, and truly understood, began in the year of our Saviour Jesus Christ, 1747.) See Daniel and the Revelations. In the manner following, 1st. To a number, in the manifestation of great light—and mighty trembling by the invisible power of God, and visions, and revelations, and prophecies; which has progressively increased, with administration of all those spiritual gifts, that was administered to the apostles at the day of Pentecost: which is the comforter that has led us into all truth: which was promised to abide with the true church of Christ unto the end of the world, and by which we find baptism into Christ's death; death to all sin, become alive to God, by the power of Christ's resurrection, which worketh in us mightily; by which a dispensation of the gospel is committed unto us; and woe be unto us if we [14] preach not the gospel of Christ. (For in finding so great a salvation and deliverance from the law of sin and death in believing and obeying this gospel which is the gospel of Christ, in confessing and forsaking all sin, and denying ourselves and bearing the cross of Christ, against the world, flesh, and devil.) We have found repentance of all our sins; and are made partakers of the grace of God wherein we now stand: which all others in believing and obeying, have acceptance with God, and find salvation from their sins as well as we; God being no respecter of persons but willing that all should come to the knowledge of the truth, and be saved. Thus we have given a short information of what we believe of the dispensations of God's grace to mankind, both past and present: and in what manner the people of God have found justification, or acceptance of God, which was and is still in believing [15] and obeying the light and truth of God, revealed or made known, in the day or dispensation in which it is revealed: for as the wrath of God is revealed from heaven against all ungodliness, and unrighteousness of men, who

hold the truth in unrighteousness or live in any known sin against him; so his mercy and grace is towards all them that truly fear him, and turn from all their sins, by confessing, and forsaking, and repenting, which is the way and manner in which all must find the forgiveness of their sins, and acceptance with God through our Lord Jesus Christ, or finally fail of the grace of God; and that salvation which is brought to light by the gospel. But to conclude, in short, as we believe, and do testify, that the present gospel of God's grace unto us is the day which in the scripture, is spoken or prophesied of, as the second appearing of Christ to consume [16] or destroy anti-christ, or false religion, and to make an end of the reigning power of sin (for he that committeth sin is the servant of sin and satan) over the children of men: and to establish his kingdom, and that righteousness that will stand forever: and that the present display of the work and power of God, will increase until it is manifest to all; which it must be in due time: for every eye shall see him; and he will reward every man according to his deeds: and none can stand in sin or unrighteousness; but in that righteousness which is pure and holy: even without fault before the throne of God which is obtained by grace, through faith in obedience to the truth of the everlasting gospel of our Lord Jesus Christ, in denying all ungodliness and worldly lusts; by confessing all sin, and taking up the cross of Christ, against the world, flesh, and devil: we desire therefore, that the children [17] of men would believe the testimony of truth, and turn from their sins by repentance, that they might obtain the mercy of God, and salvation from sin before it be too late.

Notes: *This statement written by Joseph Meacham appeared in 1790. It centers upon the understanding of history's successive dispensations as seen by the Shaker community. As a full statement of Shaker belief, it assumes an understanding of older Protestant confessions, elements of which are hastily affirmed in the closing section.*

*　　*　　*

TENETS (UNIVERSAL PEACE MISSION MOVEMENT)

POLITICALLY

We greet all mankind with Peace. We are Americans. We believe in the Declaration of Independence and the Constitution with its Bill of Rights and Amendments.

We respect and revere the American flag.

We are interracial, interdenominal, nonsectarian and nonpartisan.

We believe that all men and nations should be independent, pay all just debts and return all stolen goods or the equivalent.

This includes:

> Restitution by individual nations for all territories taken by force.

> Restitution by all individuals of mobs for all damage, injury or looting by the mob, and if murder is committed, payment of the full penalty of the law.

Also the county wherein the crime is committed should justly pay the heirs of the deceased.

SOCIALLY

We are all equal to and independent of each other in the sight of GOD. We believe that all men are entitled to not only equal but the same inalienable rights to Life, Liberty and the Reality of Happiness.

We believe that self control is birth control.

We believe that every man has the responsibility to protect his fellowman from being denied any right or freedom guaranteed by the Constitution.

We believe that nothing good will be restrained from man when all live together in the unity of Spirit, Mind, Aim and Purpose and that all men who are worthy to live shall live well.

We live FATHER DIVINE's International Modest Code:

No Smoking. No Drinking. No Obscenity. No Vulgarity. No Profanity. No Undue Mixing of Sexes. No Receiving of Gifts, Presents, Tips or Bribes.

EDUCATIONALLY

We believe in the Public School System.

We believe that the doors of all educational institutions should be open and free for universal education, with the same rights for all to higher education and professional training, according to ability.

We believe in English as the Universal Language and that it should be taught in the educational institutions of all nations.

We believe that a man is a man and not a so-called color, creed or race.

Therefore, we have deleted from all books in the Peace Mission Free Schools and recommend abolishing in all educational institutions every qualifying adjective that tends to low-rate or produce inequality between man and man. We do not use expressions such as N-people, B-people, C-people or W-people.

ECONOMICALLY

We believe in individual independence. We believe in serving the Cause of humanity through the Cooperative System, individually cooperating to purchase, own and manage hotels, apartment houses and businesses.

We believe in full employment for all able-bodied persons.

No true follower of FATHER DIVINE is on relief.

Social Security and compulsory insurance are not only unconstitutional but unnecessary when men express their individual independence as true Americans.

We pay our way as we go, pay cash on the spot and refuse to purchase on credit or on the instalment plan.

We believe in mass production as the best means of eliminating poverty and want universally.

We believe that all men have the right to be safe and secure in any possession permitted under the Constitution.

RELIGIOUSLY

We believe that the Scripture is being fulfilled as recorded in the King James Version of the Old and the New Testaments of the Holy Bible.

We believe that FATHER DIVINE fulfils the Scriptural Prophecy of the Second Coming of CHRIST for the Christian world and the Coming of the Messiah for the Jewish world.

We have ONE FATHER and ONE MOTHER — GOD Personified in FATHER DIVINE and HIS SPOTLESS VIRGIN BRIDE, MOTHER DIVINE.

We live in the Brotherhood of man under the FATHERHOOD of GOD, therefore, we are one family indivisible.

We believe that the Principles of all true religion are synonymous.

True religion is faith in ONE INDIVISIBLE GOD.

We have the Ten Commandments and the precepts given in Jesus' Sermon on the Mount.

We believe that Heaven is a State of Consciousness to be universally established in fulfillment of Jesus' prayer: "Let Thy Kingdom come and Thy Will be done on earth . . . "

We believe that America is the Birthplace of the Kingdom of GOD on earth and IT shall be fully realized when all men live the synonymous Principles of true Americanism, Brotherhood, Democracy, Christianity, Judaism and all true religion.

We believe that GOD is Eternally Present with or without a Body.

True followers of FATHER DIVINE refuse to fight their fellowman for any cause whatsoever. However, if any individual will fight physically for himself in self-defense, then he has a right to fight physically in the defense of his country.

Under The Peace Mission Movement there are six incorporated Churches with branches in the U.S.A. and throughout the world of which FATHER DIVINE is the Bishop, Founder and Pastor.

The Church Services are without ritual and the general public is welcome to attend and participate harmoniously.

We believe in the serving of Communion daily after the manner of the Lord's Supper, as practical service for the sustenance of the body and benefit of the soul.

Neither FATHER DIVINE or MOTHER DIVINE, nor Officers and Co-workers in the Churches receive salary, compensation or remuneration.

No collections are ever taken for any Spiritual Service rendered, but all are requested to donate for material services received, such as for meals, lodging and other services provided.

We do not proselyte because the Life of CHRIST, when lived, is magnetic.

We believe that WOODMONT fulfils the prophecy of the Mount of the House of the Lord from which shall go forth

the Law to all nations, spoken of in Isaiah 2:2, 3 and
Micah 4:1, 2.

Notes: *Father Divine, founder of the Universal Peace
Mission, is popularly remembered as a flamboyant, uncon-
ventional black religious figure of the Depression years. In
more recent years, however, he has been recognized for his
efforts to respond positively to a number of important issues
for the black community. In light of recent historical
reevaluation, Father Divine, divorced from exclusive focus
upon his claims of divine status, has emerged as a leader
articulating a meaningful approach to interracial harmony.
The Tenets of the mission he founded outline the program
still being followed by members today.*

*   *   *

Communal—After 1960

ARTICLES OF FAITH (JESUS PEOPLE U.S.A.)

(1) The undersigned believe in one eternal existent
     infinite God, Sovereign of the Universe; that He only
     is God, creative and administrative, Holy in Nature,
     attributes and purpose.

(2) The undersigned believe in the one true God who has
     revealed Himself as the externally self-existent, self-
     revealed "I AM," and has further revealed Himself
     as embodying the principles of relationship and
     association, i.e., Father, Son, and Holy Ghost,
     Deuteronomy 6:4; Mark 12:29; Isaiah 43:10, 11;
     Matthew 28:19; Luke 3:22.

(3) The undersigned believe the Bible is the inspired
     Word of God, a revelation from God to men, the
     infallible rule of faith and conduct, and is superior to
     conscience and reason, but not contrary to reason. 2
     Timothy 3:15, 16; 1 Peter 2:2.

(4) The undersigned believe in the Holy Spirit, ever
     present and active in convicting souls of their sins
     and regenerating those who repent and believe on the
     Lord Jesus Christ; and that he also sanctified all
     believers who consecrate themselves unto God; that
     the Holy Scriptures are truly inspired Words of God,
     revealing God's will concerning us in all things
     necessary to our salvation and Holy living; and
     whatsoever is not contained therein is not to be
     enjoined as essential to salvation. We also believe
     that inasmuch that we do unto others, we do unto
     Christ, and will be rewarded accordingly.

Notes: *These brief articles are taken from those of the Full
Gospel Church in Christ, a Pentecostal church which
originally chartered the Jesus People U.S.A.*

THE SEVEN IMMUTABLE LAWS OF THE UNIVERSE (RENAISSANCE CHURCH OF BEAUTY)

1. The order of mind, the expansion of deepening of
    mind, to attain an even balance of mind that is not
    swayed by the devils of scorn and judgment, for
    where there is not order in the universe, there is
    chaos of the atomic law.

2. The balance of mind positive, and the balance of the
    brain negative. Through thought force you bring a
    discipline within the brain and mind so that there
    will be a constant flow of balance to all that your life
    touches upon. To express a true understanding that
    encompasses all progressions of life, this is the
    attainment of balance.

3. Harmony means a direct alignment with all vibration
    of electrical energy. It is harmony that flows over the
    earth and through it. It is what changes the layers of
    the universe into different patterns, that forces a
    change in all vibrational structures, and thus, as
    mankind enters into a new condition, this new
    condition is only brought about by the consistency of
    the thoughts which connect the mind of man and the
    mind of eternity.

4. Growth is needed from the carnal to the celestial.
    And it is the will of a person that decides what that
    growth will be. And this is the free will of true
    expression, where man assumes a spiritual attitude
    toward his material body, and looks ever deeper into
    the spirit to find the order and balance of which we
    have spoken.

5. The fifth law of the universe is god-perception. That
    is to perceive the shape of a cloud or of a tree, or of
    how many legs can be found upon the little ant that
    travels over the vast surface of the earth. It is to
    perceive the full vibration, to give a fuller interpreta-
    tion to the various rooms within the mansion of the
    soul. The word "perception" means to look ahead
    into that which does operate, but does not control
    the free will of an individual spirit.

6. Love is that substance, that electrical force, that
    want, that gives to people the restlessness, the
    uncertainties, and the desire for a higher expression.
    It is truly found that that love must be given in
    accordance with the celestial law of full giving. It
    must be a total love, not limited by conditions of a
    material nature, but given to each person in a
    constant consideration of what each life expresses.
    And it is through the giving of the fullness of your
    all-in-all being that you come into the growth that
    gives you the fullness of life.

7. Man must now realize the true structure of the
    universe, the true energy that animates his physical
    structure, that gives him the precious flow of life,
    and allows him the very understanding of his full
    expression upon this earth. Life is simplicity, com-
    pounded by this great word, compassion. And wise is
    the man who not only sits in meditation, but also
    gives full realization, a true definition, to his life.

Compassion holds a true theme, through all his previous lives, his present, and aye, even his future.

Notes: *This document was received as a revelation by Michael Metelica, founder of the church.*

* * *

THE SYNANON PHILOSOPHY (SYNANON CHURCH)

The Synanon Philosophy is based on the belief that there comes a time in everyone's life when he arrives at the conviction that envy is ignorance; that imitation is suicide; that he must accept himself for better or for worse as is his portion; that though the wide universe is full of good, no kernel of nourishing corn can come to him but through his toil bestowed on that plot of ground which is given to him to till. The power which resides in him is new in nature, and none but he knows what it is that he can do, nor does he know until he has tried. Bravely let him speak the utmost syllable of his conviction. God will not have his work made manifest by cowards.

A man is relieved and gay when he has put his heart into his work and done his best; but what he has said or done otherwise shall give him no peace. As long as he willingly accepts himself, he will continue to grow and develop his potentialities. As long as he does not accept himself, much of his energies will be used to defend rather than to explore and actualize himself.

No one can force a person towards permanent and creative learning. He will learn only if he wills to. Any other type of learning is temporary and inconsistent with the self and will disappear as soon as the threat is removed. Learning is possible in an environment that provides information, the setting, materials, resources, and by his being there. God helps those who help themselves.

THE NEW COVENANT, THE WORLD BILL OF RIGHTS [UNIVERSAL INDUSTRIAL CHURCH OF THE NEW WORLD COMFORTER (ONE WORLD COMMUNE)]

Let each of us share all the world—the kingdom of God—and call one place of our choosing our own and be free to come and go in the world and stay at any dwelling place accommodating travelers.

Let each of us give of ourselves to the extent of our abilities to the One World Company, and in return all things shall be added unto us.

Let each person be judged only by his conscience in God and let no one judge his fellow beings, but rather judge himself.

Let no person or group hold any authority over another except that person be willingly led by wisdom and true personality.

Let the government be of the people, where the people are self-governed; by the people, where the people enjoy perfect freedom; for the people, where the people give themselves abundant living.

Let the Government seat be only the storehouse and inventory of the people's products.

Let all things be done unto edification, for God is not the author of confusion.

Notes: *This document was promulgated by Allan Noonan, founder of the One World Commune. It is illustrative of their planetary vision.*

Chapter 16

Christian Science-Metaphysical Family

Christian Science

THE TENETS OF CHRISTIAN SCIENCE (CHURCH OF CHRIST, SCIENTIST)

1. As adherents of Truth, we take the inspired Word of the Bible as our sufficient guide to eternal Life.

2. We acknowledge and adore one supreme and infinite God. We acknowledge His Son, one Christ; the Holy Ghost or divine Comforter; and man in God's image and likeness.

3. We acknowledge God's forgiveness of sin in the destruction of sin and the spiritual understanding that casts out evil as unreal. But the belief in sin is punished so long as the belief lasts.

4. We acknowledge Jesus' atonement as the evidence of divine, efficacious Love, unfolding man's unity with God through Christ Jesus the Way-shower; and we acknowledge that man is saved through Christ, through Truth, Life, and Love as demonstrated by the Galilean Prophet in healing the sick and overcoming sin and death.

5. We acknowledge that the crucifixion of Jesus and his resurrection served to uplift faith to understand eternal Life, even the allness of Soul, Spirit, and the nothingness of matter.

6. And we solemnly promise to watch, and pray for that Mind to be in us which was also in Christ Jesus; to do unto others as we would have them do unto us; and to be merciful, just, and pure.

Notes: *The tenets of the Church of Christ, Scientist, are found on p. 497 of the authorized edition of Mary Baker Eddy's Science and Health with Key to the Scriptures. This statement highlights the essential Christian element in Christian Science. It affirms several of the major ideas for which the church is well known: the unreality of evil, the nothingness of matter, and the allness of Soul or Spirit.*

New Thought

DECLARATION OF PRINCIPLES (INTERNATIONAL NEW THOUGHT ALLIANCE)

DECLARATION OF PRINCIPLES, 1917

We affirm the freedom of each soul as to choice and as to belief, and would not, by the adoption of any declaration of principles, limit such freedom. The essence of the New Thought is Truth, and each individual must be loyal to the Truth he sees. The windows of his soul must be kept open at each moment for the higher light, and his mind must be always hospitable to each new inspiration.

We affirm the Good. This is supreme, universal and everlasting. Man is made in the image of the Good, and evil and pain are but the tests and correctives that appear when his thought does not reflect the full glory of this image.

We affirm health, which is man's divine inheritance. Man's body is his holy temple. Every function of it, every call of it, is intelligent, and is shaped, ruled, repaired, and controlled by mind. He whose body is full of light is full of health. Spiritual healing has existed among all races in all times. It has now become a part of the higher science and art of living the life more abundant.

We affirm the divine supply. He who serves God and man in the full understanding of the law of compensation shall not lack. Within us are unused resources of energy and power. He who lives with his whole being, and thus expresses fullness, shall reap fullness in return. He who gives himself, he who knows and acts in his highest knowledge, he who trusts in the divine return, has learned the law of success.

We affirm the teachings of Christ that the Kingdom of Heaven is within us, that we are one with the Father, that we should not judge, that we should love one another, that we should heal the sick, that we should return good for evil, that we should minister to others, and that we should be perfect even as our Father in Heaven is perfect. These are not only ideals, but practical, everyday working principles.

DECLARATION OF PRINCIPLES (INTERNATIONAL NEW THOUGHT ALLIANCE) (continued)

We affirm the new thought of God as Universal Love, Life, Truth and Joy, in whom we live, move, and have our being, and by whom we are held together; that His mind is our mind now, that realizing our oneness with Him means love, truth, peace, health and plenty, not only in our own lives but in the giving out of these fruits of the Spirit to others.

We affirm these things, not as a profession, but practice, not on one day of the week, but in every hour and minute of every day, sleeping and waking, not in the ministry of a few, but in the service that includes the democracy of all, not in words alone, but in the innermost thoughts of the heart expressed in living the life. "By their fruits ye shall know them."

We affirm Heaven here and now, the life everlasting that becomes conscious immortality, the communion of mind with mind throughout the universe of thoughts, the nothingness of all error and negation, including death, the varity in unity that produces the individual expressions of the One-Life, and the quickened realization of the indwelling God in each soul that is making a new heaven and a new earth.

We affirm that the universe is spiritual and we are spiritual beings. This is the Christ message to the twentieth century, and it is a message not so much of words as of works. To attain this, however, we must be clean, honest and trustworthy and uphold the Jesus Christ standards as taught in the Four Gospels. We now have the golden opportunity to form a real Christ movement. Let us build our house upon this rock, and nothing can prevail against it. This is the vision and mission of the ALLIANCE.

These principles were adopted and made unanimous at the Congress held in St. Louis, in 1917.

DECLARATION OF PRINCIPLES, 1957

What We Believe . . .

We affirm the inseparable oneness of God and man, the realization of which comes through spiritual intuition, the implications of which are that man can reproduce the Divine perfection in his body, emotions, and in all his external affairs.

We affirm the freedom of each person in matters of belief.

We affirm the Good to be supreme, universal, and eternal.

We affirm that the Kingdom of Heaven is within us, that we are one with the Father, that we should love one another, and return good for evil.

We affirm that we should heal the sick through prayer, and that we should endeavor to manifest perfection "even as our Father in Heaven is perfect."

We affirm our belief in God as the Universal Wisdom, Love, Life, Truth, Power, Peace, Beauty, and Joy, "in whom we live, move, and have our being."

We affirm that man's mental states are carried forward into manifestation and become his experience through the Creative Law of Cause and Effect.

We affirm that the Divine Nature expressing Itself through man manifests Itself as health, supply, wisdom, love, life, truth, power, peace, beauty, and joy.

We affirm that man is an invisible spiritual dweller within a human body, continuing and unfolding as a spiritual being beyond the change called physical death.

We affirm that the universe is the body of God, spiritual in essence, governed by God through laws which are spiritual in reality even when material in appearance.

(Adopted by 42nd Congress, July 25, 1957)

Notes: *The International New Thought Alliance (INTA) is an ecumenical group to which many New Thought groups belong. It adopted two statements, one in 1917 and another in 1957. The older statement is longer and makes specific reference to the teachings of Christ, identifying New Thought with "the Christ message to the twentieth century." In the second version, all specific mention of Christ and/or Christianity have been deleted. In both statements an impersonal God, prosperity, and life after death are affirmed. In 1916 a committee was appointed by INTA to prepare a declaration of principles. A number of people submitted proposed statements, among them Alliance president James A. Edgerton. His proposed statement was largely adapted without change, although a paragraph was added identifying New Thought as a Christ movement in order to answer criticisms of the INTA from the Unity School of Christianity. In spite of these references, Unity soon withdrew from the Alliance. When a revised declaration was adopted in 1957, no references to Christianity were made.*

*　　*　　*

A NEW THOUGHT CREED (ELIZABETH TOWNE)

We affirm that God, the All Wise, All Powerful, All Present Spirit, is the Life, Wisdom, and Power of every human being.

We affirm that all humans are "members one of another," that in and through each God "works to will and to do of his good pleasure," which is the Good and the Pleasure of each and all.

We affirm that the Desire for Good, and the Desire to Do Good, found in every human soul, is God's Will working in him.

We affirm that by constant recognition of God in all and through all, man co-operates with God to fulfill his destiny, his individual desires for Being Good, Doing Good and Having the Good Things of the world.

We affirm that God's nature is Love and His Universe One Living Organism, all its individual members made to function in Freedom and Loving kindness, each after its own pattern.

We affirm that through constant recognition of man as One with God, man comes to realize and manifest God, or Love, in increasing measure, each after his own soul's pattern.

We affirm that in truth all soul patterns are equally indispensable to the working out of God's Good Pleasure for all; that all souls are equally valuable to the world, equally entitled to the world's Opportunities and Good Things.

We affirm that man's nature is Love, and that Self-Expression in Lovingkindness is the Way of Enjoyment of Peace and Prosperity of mind, body and conditions.

We affirm that, as God is the Infinite One, so mankind is Infinite, and One, able through recognition, realization and manifestation of God within, and by co-operation with all men to think out and work out on this earth heavenly conditions such as are beyond those dreamed of in the imaginations of seers and prophets.

Notes: *Elizabeth Towne, as editor of the* Nautilus *and head of her own publishing company, was one of the most powerful figures in early New Thought. She was elected president of the International New Thought Alliance (INTA) in 1924. She was also one of four persons appointed on the committee to draft a Declaration of Principles for the INTA in 1916. She was one of several who wrote personal statements on New Thought for use by the committee. While not adopted by the INTA, A New Thought Creed summarizes the meaning of New Thought for one who was a significant leader in the movement for over half a century.*

*   *   *

WHAT THE NEW THOUGHT STANDS FOR (HORATIO DRESSER)

The New Thought is a practical philosophy of the inner life in relation to health, happiness, social welfare and success.

It stands for the inner life first of all because the life within is found to be the source of power, the basis of health and happiness, the clue to success, individuality and freedom.

It stands for an affirmative attitude in contrast with older types of thought, for optimism instead of pessimism, and for the unity of life instead of any teaching which separates the forces of the universe into hostile powers. To understand its practical values and its sphere of activity one needs to consider both its essential principles and its special methods.

As a philosophy the New Thought starts with the principle that all power is essentially one—the Universal Life or Infinite Spirit.

The world is regarded as an expression or manifestation of this Life, disclosed in the orderly processes of creation. The world exists for spiritual ends.

Man as a spiritual being is living an essentially spiritual life, for the sake of the soul His life proceeds from within outward, and makes for harmony, health, freedom, efficiency, service.

Health and freedom, individuality and success are his birthright privileges.

It is natural and right to be well and prosperous. What man needs, in his ignorance and bondage is THE TRUTH

concerning this, his spiritual being and birthright. He needs to learn that he is a soul or spirit possessing the physical body as an instrument of experience and expression. He needs to REALIZE this, the spiritual truth of his being, that he may rise above all ills and all obstacles into fullness of power. Every resource he could ask for is at hand, in the omnipresent divine wisdom. Every individual can learn to draw upon the divine resources.

The special methods of the New Thought grow out of this central spiritual principle. Much stress is put upon inner or spiritual meditation, through the practice of silence, concentration and inner control, because each of us needs to become still to learn how to be affirmative, optimistic.

Great emphasis is also put upon the subconscious mind as the agency for the realization of ideals, the execution of affirmations. Suggestion or affirmation is employed to banish ills and errors and establish spiritual truth in their place. Silent or mental treatment is employed to overcome disease and secure freedom and success.

The New Thought teaches that every individual can use its method of spiritual meditation and mental healing. What is required is that one shall gain the inner point of view, get the impetus, become aware that the spirit is supreme. To some this comes as a sense of the newness and freshness of life, in contrast with the old idea that the world is a field of warfare between good and evil. To others it comes as an awakening that man is a spirit, not a body; that he can acquire inner self-mastery and control the flesh. It comes to many as a theory and method of mental healing at first, and when illness is banished as a theory of the whole of life. Whatever the starting point the end is the same. The important point is to learn to apply here and now the best that has been lived and taught concerning the things of the spirit.

The New Thought then is not a substitute for Christianity, but an inspired return to the original teaching and practice of the gospels. It is not opposed to the churches, but aims to make religion immediately serviceable and practical. It is not hostile to science, but wishes to spiritualize all facts and laws. It encourages each man to begin wherever he is, however conditioned, whatever he may find to occupy his hands; and to learn the great spiritual lessons taught by this present experience. Thus apparent failure may be turned into success, weakness to strength and an apparent curse into a blessing.

Notes: *This statement was one of many submitted to the International New Thought Alliance committee appointed in 1916 to draft a Declaration of Principles. Although Dresser was not a member of the committee that prepared the final statement presented to the Alliance in 1917, he was an intellectual leader in the movement for many years. He never identified with any of the several New Thought churches (he eventually joined the Swedenborgian Church of the New Jerusalem).*

THE NEW THOUGHT RELIGION AND PHILOSOPHY (ABEL L. ALLEN)

New Thought has been defined as the latest product of growing mind; also as an attitude of mind and not a cult. Neither definition is complete.

New Thought is a search for light and understanding of man's relations with the Infinite, and hence is not susceptible of definition in terms.

New Thought is old thought stated in modern terms of expression, adapted to man's spiritual development and welfare.

It is a philosophy and Religion of Life. It is a quest for truth and inner peace.

Its supreme purpose is to awaken the highest aspirations of the soul and lead man into conscious unity with God.

Its teachings are positive, constructive and optimistic.

It deals with life and reveals inner sources of power for man's essential needs.

It does not deny the existence of matter, but asserts the dominion of mind over matter.

It propounds no fixed creeds or ecclesiastical dogmas, because it sets no limitation to man's progress, and man is limited by the creeds and dogmas for which he stands.

It does not depend on a particular book or books for spiritual light or look outward for revelation, but to the soul within.

It recognizes no spiritual authority save the light of the individual soul.

It endeavors to keep pace with the progress of science and modern psychology.

It recognizes no conflict between true religion and real science, since truth is the ultimate goal of each.

A conception of God is the basis of every religion and philosophy.

The orthodox Christian Religions rest on the quality of God and man; New Thought on the unity of God and man.

New Thought is founded on primary, eternal and immutable principles. Thought may change, but principles are changeless.

These fundamental principles, boundless as infinity, may support a religion or philosophy that may expand to the full circle of truth—that may keep pace with man's development, as he reaches out towards the infinite.

PRINCIPLES OF NEW THOUGHT:

1. God is Unity, Universal Love, Life, Intelligence and Power, pervading and animating the Universe, existing with equal power at every point, manifesting in every created entity, reaching its highest expression in man, revealing to him his own individuality and the consciousness of his own Divine Soul.

2. The individual soul is an inlet to the Great Divine Soul. As man becomes conscious of his contact with Universal Life, Intelligence and Power, he realizes the unlimited potentialities within himself and that he may draw from his Infinite Source at will, for health, wisdom, life abundant and prosperity. The consciousness of this truth removes all limitations to man's possibilities.

3. The reign of universal law uniform in the mental and spiritual worlds as in the physical universe. Because of the unity of all things, whatsoever affects one part, affects all parts. The law of cause and effect enters into every thought, act and relationship in human life. Thought is the maker and molder of man's destiny. Thought is expressed in the life and personality of the individual. The consciousness of individual responsibility is necessary to man's development. Man is punished by every sin and rewarded by every virtue. Whatsoever he sows, that shall he also reap.

4. Nature is man's teacher and the revelation of the purposes of the Infinite Supreme wisdom. Power and Intelligence are in all entities from atoms to planes. Within man are the hidden meanings of creation. Through Nature and the voices of Intuition alone, God speaks to man. Man's life can be peaceful and harmonious only as he obeys Nature's laws.

5. Man is the result of the processes of evolution. He is an evolved and an evolving being. Evolution springs from within; it is a law of inner progress. Its trend is towards perfection. The ascent is the invisible spirit. The fruit of evolution is the unfolding and development of consciousness. Through the steps of evolution the soul of man is reaching up to a conscious union with the great Divine Soul.

6. Truth is the one reality. Every enduring religion must conform to the standard of truth. Truth is the only basis for right living. Truth alone sets man free. The only slavery is self-imposed through ignorance of man's Divine Inheritance. Truth dispels fear, man's greatest enemy. Truth alone brings Peace, Power and satisfaction to man.

7. The conscious identity of the soul after the event called death. This conclusion is written in man's nature; he feels and knows this voiceless message of truth. The soul persists in expression and life knows no diminution.

8. That Jesus, the Christ, is the most illumined Prophet and Teacher of the ages and has given man the true message of life.

9. The brotherhood of man as the true foundation of every human relationship.

10. Man's highest duty to God is to live a constructive life, in harmony with the laws of nature and serve his fellowmen.

11. The good, the true and the beautiful as the highest ideals of right living.

12. The purpose of New Thought is to point the way to truth and not to limit or circumscribe it.

13. New Thought is unalterably opposed to all practices of Hypnotism.

14. It does not recognize the hypotheses of what are popularly known as Spiritualism, Astrology or Rein-

carnation as a part of the Philosophy and Religion of New Thought.

Notes: *Abel L. Allen, a judge, was one of four people appointed to the committee to draft a Declaration of Principles for the International New Thought Alliance in 1916. He used his legal mind to draft one of the longest statements dealt with by the committee. Notice his denunciation of hypnotism, spiritualism, astrology, and reincarnation.*

* * *

DECLARATION OF PRINCIPLES PROPOSED FOR THE INTERNATIONAL NEW THOUGHT ALLIANCE (CHARLES GILBERT DAVIS)

Eternal progress marks the destiny of the human race. Up through the ages of the misty past, man has been seeking for his God. Step by step through the phenomena of nature, through every branch of science and philosophy and the various expressions of religion he has been searching for eternal truth. The journey has been long, wearisome and full of pain. Often at different periods of the world's history and in different localities, the cry has gone forth that the great mystery had been revealed. These have only been stages of development revealing slight glimpses of truth along the evolutionary path. Now in the dawn of the twentieth century, the windows of the soul are again opened and a new revelation is given to mankind. It is a new life, a new birth, a new step toward infinite perfection. We are just beginning to realize that the evolutionary progress has arrived at the transition stage that marks the boundary between the physical and the spiritual in human development. It is like awakening from a troubled dream and the world is not yet adjusted to the new impulses that are throbbing through the hearts of man. Some have caught glimpses of the light and have felt the glorified radiance of the new environment. But the great multitudes are yet in ignorance, wandering through the dark forest where the haunting ghosts of fear and other depressing emotions fill the soul with terror and drive men to the madness of despair. In vain each nation, tribe and tongue reaches out with pleading, uplifted hands to the unknown God on his distant throne, claiming him as their very own according to each dogmatic, theological belief, and demanding his special effort in their deliverance.

Through the centuries and millenniums, man has been following an unreality. He has imagined his God far off in an imaginary heaven sitting in majesty on a kingly throne. But he has wakened from this nightmare. He has dismissed the unreal and at last embraced the real. He has looked into his own soul and found God. In a flood of joy, the truth has burst upon his vision and he is awakened to the realization that he is an emanation from the Divine, that he and the Father are one. The joy of the discovery of this divine inheritance has renewed the life currents and lifted man up and sent him rejoicing on his journey to carry the glad tidings to all the world. In this new enlightenment, man has discovered God immanent in His world. We who have grasped the full significance of this new revelation and being desirous that all the earth should understand

and join with us in this great evolutionary advance toward infinite life and love, make the following declaration of principles:

1. We believe in the existence of an Infinite power of Life and Love and Beauty behind all the physical universe, which now and forevermore is working through evolutionary law for the betterment of all things.

2. The soul of man is immortal and co-existent with Divine Spirit.

3. A full recognition of the brotherhood of mankind is essential to all progress, all development and all unity of purpose.

4. Science is the handwriting of the Infinite Spirit on the walls of time. Hence all verified and classified wisdom must be recognized as the footprints of the Almighty and be followed and utilized for the betterment of the world.

5. God is imminent in humanity and every living soul is not only a reservoir of Divine Energy but also a distributing center from whence emanates the creative power that makes manifest the evolutionary law.

6. Our bodies are the instruments of the soul, hence it devolves upon us to keep them clean and undefiled.

7. Divine Spirit is creative, and when manifested through the individual may be utilized for the uplift of man physically, mentally and spiritually.

8. The subjective mind or soul of man is dynamic, and while directed along the currents of evolutionary progress, it may send forth and distribute the universal energy for the healing of humanity: physically, mentally and spiritually. Neither time nor distance can interpose against the working of this law.

9. All life is existent on a progressive plane. The materializations of the Divine Spirit are evidence of eternal progress. No creed of philosophy or religion that aims at truth can be forever stationary. As the light is thrown upon the pathway of the soul, new facts are revealed and a new door is opened for a greater revelation.

10. Christ is the manifestation of the fulfillment of the law. He and the Father are one-God manifest in the flesh. He points the way to life, truth and evolution. Let us follow Him.

Darkness shadows the earth and through the violation of law man has wandered far from the highway that leads to the perfection of the soul. It is time for a new revelation There must be a new adjustment of human vision. God and his world are inseparable. Science and religion must join hands to rescue mankind.

Notes: *Charles Gilbert Davis was a member of the committee to draft a Declaration of Principles for the International New Thought Alliance in 1916. As part of his work for the committee, he wrote and submitted a personally written article.*

ARTICLES OF FAITH AND ALTRURIAN BELIEF (ALTRURIAN SOCIETY)

ARTICLES OF FAITH

I accept as a working hypothesis, "The Spirit of God dwelleth in me," therefore I covenant to love and serve God in and through inner consciousness.

I accept universal brotherhood as a means to God attainment.

I promise to pay debts, be moral, adjust difficulties, back up when wrong and do all things necessary to God attainment.

I promise to introspect my daily acts, and to follow the outline in "The Four Keys" as a means to Health, Happiness and Prosperity.

I promise to make the laws, acts and experiences of Jesus Christ, my guide and to live them to the best of my ability.

ALTRURIAN BELIEF

We believe in Jesus Christ as the way to Salvation all can follow, and His way as law and not "Blood Atonement." Nothing left out,—no creed or dogma put in. We believe that man must control his body, and therefore "Penances and Restraints" consisting of Prayer, Love, Fasting and Service are the principles of attainment.

We believe in the Corruptible and the Incorruptible body, one temporary and the other everlasting. As we control the one, the other becomes free,—and freedom of the Incorruptible means everlasting life. The means of control is in strict morality, probity, truth, freedom from evil and devotion to the inner consciousness of God.

We believe the Love gift at the Altar is necessary before prayer, and prayer to be effective must be silent in introspection; consisting of paying debts and freedom from evil, in which the body and mind becomes purged and clean. Then the asking will result in an answer,—the petitioner getting what is needed.

We believe in a Brotherhood without caste, and in one God, Omnipotent, Omniscient and Omni-present and we as individuals can by strict obedience to law, become conscious of God within. We believe Jesus Christ as the Son of God, and potentially every man a "Son of God."

We believe Jesus Christ healed the Sick, cast out Devils and performed mighty works as a demonstration of His work and the means of salvation. We believe the same works and the same plan is applicable now, and the means of salvation. What He did we can do, and must do, if there is realization.

We believe in the Ordinances of God, the First of which must be Belief, Second—Faith, Third—Surrender or Repentance, Fourth—Baptism, Fifth—Remission of Sin through confession and work, Sixth—Divine consciousness and the descent of the "Holy Ghost," Seventh—Transmission from one to another of the power of the "Holy Ghost" by "laying on of hands."

We believe in Prophecy, Divine inspiration. Gifts and the power to demonstrate them. We believe in Vision and Divine direction. We believe in law and order of things, and man must experience Religious fervor in order to be true to his Vision. We believe it is through Vision and Prophecy given to Master men that have given and is giving man an understanding of Divine law. We believe these laws are given to mankind through revelation,—the spoken word—or laying on of hands, through which sickness, sin and death are banished.

We believe Healing the Sick,—creating Abundance and Happiness are ordinances of God and should be a part of Christian inheritance. We believe the Signs of "The Christian" are those given in the last Chapter of St. Mark, and include them in our ordinance.

We believe that Christians should be Healthy, Happy and Prosperous: debt payers, giving no offense, save in a cause righteous. We believe in obedience to law, all law whether Divine or man made. We believe all church organizations are seeking correct principles of living and so ask for humble privilege to demonstrate our plans.

We believe "The Kingdom of God" is here and everywhere, when man is ready to comply with the law of God understanding. This is in belief, Acceptance, Faith, Intention, Contemplation, Meditation and Conviction that mellow objective intelligence into abeyance while arousing the "Hidden and latent" within belonging to God into control of body function.

We believe in being honest, sober, true, moral, clean in our dealings, just in account, loving, generous, forgiving, kind, and obedient to our vision of usefulness. We accept the new Testament as the direct revelation of the later dispensation, the Four Gospels as Christ's direction and all other writing of an inspired nature as collateral.

Notes: *New members of the Altrurian Society were asked to sign a card subscribing to the brief Articles of Faith. The longer statement of belief provides a fuller understanding of the society's broad perspective.*

*   *   *

FUNDAMENTAL PRINCIPLES (CHRISTIAN ASSEMBLY)

The fundamental principles of the teaching of the Christ form the basis of all the teaching presented. Some of these are as follows:

1. God is Spirit, Whose nature is love and wisdom. As Spirit, God is One: Omnipotent, Omniscient, and Omnipresent.

2. The kingdom of God is within the soul of every one. The real creation of God is spiritual humanity. As God did not create man a carnal being, it is necessary for him to regenerate in order to enter the kingdom. The kingdom of heaven is for the living, for the Christ said: "He is not God of the dead, but of the living; for all are alive to him" (Luke 20:38 lit.).

3. Jesus is the Christ, the Son of the living God, the Saviour of the world. As the Son of God He is divine; and as the Son of man He is human. In Him the divine and human are a perfect unit. Jesus Christ, the

risen Lord, abides in His kingdom within the hearts and souls of His disciples.

4. True faith comes from God and makes all things possible to them that believe. Divine faith is, therefore, a mighty power which one may use in prayer and in all good works into which the Holy Spirit leads him with most gratifying results.

5. Evil has no power from God; the power it seems to have, unregenerate man through ignorance and fear has given it.

6. Divine love is the fulfillment of the law which is constitutional with man. It is the only sovereign power in time, as well as in eternity. The power of love works for the good of man, and when he believes and trusts in it, he is helped in his every need.

7. Christian healing is properly part of the gospel.

8. Through works of faith and love, and the renunciation of the false selfhood, regenerate man comes to know that the kingdom of heaven is within. He also realizes that as he does the will of God he becomes one with him, and joint heir with the Christ in all the Father has.

Notes: *This small body centered in San Jose, California, is a specifically Christian branch of the New Thought movement. Its position, as distinct within New Thought, is found in item 3.*

*　　*　　*

BASIC TENETS OF THEOLOGIA 21 [CHURCH OF THE TRINITY (INVISIBLE MINISTRY)]

We believe that . . .

The Presence of God, as Father, Son and Holy Spirit, fills all space and time. There is no spot where God is not. (Psa. 90:2; 139:7-12)

The nature of God is forever perfect in every way, for in him there is no darkness at all. (Mat. 5:48; 1 John 1:5)

Christ-Jesus, the only begotten Son, shares the divine Nature of The Father, and is therefore indestructible, omniscient, omnipotent, immutable and eternal. (Mal. 3:6; Mat. 28:18; Heb. 13:8; Jas. 1:17; 1 John 4:9)

By divine Grace, The Christ-Jesus Consciousness indwells every man in potentia, and that potential may be cultivated and developed in unlimited degree. (Eph. 2:5; Phi. 2:5; Col. 1:27)

Man's awareness and acceptance of the gift of Grace fulfills God's will. It is The Father's good pleasure to give us the kingdom, and our spiritual destiny to be perfect, as he is perfect. (Luke 12:32; Eph. 2:8)

The power of God flows outward, radiating from the secret place of the most High at the center of every man. (Zep. 3:17; Luke 17:21; 1 John 4:4)

This power is therefore available to all, and is always available now. (Psa. 46:1; Mark 11:24; Acts 10:34; 2 Cor. 6:2)

Faith in this power, through Christ-Jesus, sets man free from the law of sin and death, and aligns him with the royal Law of eternal Life. Amen. (Mat. 14:13-14; John 1:12; John 3:15; Rom 8:2; Jas. 2:8)

Notes: *Theologia 21 is the name given to the Church of the Trinity's theological teachings. It is aligned to the common New Thought perspective.*

*　　*　　*

STATEMENTS BY THE CHURCH OF THE TRUTH

THE CHURCH OF THE TRUTH BELIEVES

That always there is perfect guidance for each one in any and every time of uncertainty.

That always there is healing power greater than the seeming power of disease.

That always conditions and events are working toward a great and ultimate good surpassing the most extravagant hopes of man.

That always there is a way out.

That always the attitude of alert calmness and of steadfast expectation makes easy the demonstration of needed good.

That always we may think new thoughts about old conditions, and thereby set new forces into action.

That always the TRUE MAN is good and beautiful and kind and just and loving and strong and divine.

That always God is available to man for wisdom, supply, good will, strength, self-confidence, health, efficiency and happiness.

THE STATEMENT OF THE TRUTH

To outline the vision of the Truth as it is revealed to us, but not as a finality, we utter this statement of the Truth:

God is all and God is Spirit.

Man is the child of God, inheriting His nature.

Jesus, the Christ, entered into the fullness of his God-heritage.

God's world and man's world are thought created.

To think in harmony with God is to enter God's Good.

The Kingdom of Heaven is within the soul.

What faith shapes in the within God manifests in the without.

When man thinks God's thought, God's power is with his thought.

To know this Divine Omnipresence and realize its power is eternal life.

The essence of Divine Omnipresence is love.

And Love is Heaven in every realm.

THE CHURCH OF THE CHURCH

Our universal mission is to make this Church so great and so beautiful and so filled with transforming and healing power, to make it such a demonstration of what the life

STATEMENTS BY THE CHURCH OF THE TRUTH (continued)

lived in God may mean, that all mankind will hasten to establish just such places as this throughout the hungry, sin-sick, suffering world.

Each church is feeding a certain state of consciousness in man, and so we can bless, without one thought of condemnation, every organization, every religious movement in the world. But if we did not believe, if we did not know that there is a line of Truth, a hair-breadth line, which no other church has ever followed, there would be no excuse for this new denomination, the Church of the Truth. If I did not believe with my whole soul that it gives expression in fuller and truer outline to the vision of Jesus the Christ, I should not have dared to assist you in its organization. I am so cognizant of the fact that a peculiar and absolutely divine mission has been placed in our hands, that nothing can shake that conviction in my soul. And it is because I see this, that I say these words, and because many of you also realize it, you will understand me.

I want to tell you now that the ultimate goal of the Church of the Truth of this ministry, is the discovering and establishing for the future of mankind that platform, broad enough so that no one who may ever come to it will be crowded off.

I am seeking a kind of healing power a kind of philosophy big enough to last mankind for all time; and if not one of you follows me, if not one of you believes as I do, I can go alone. I see that which is a thousand years from the present time, and I am speaking the word not only for you, but every man who comes into the world for all future generations.

This Church is the biggest thing on earth. If anyone asks me the question: "What is the ultimate work of your organization?" I want to bear testimony to this thing, that its purpose, regardless of present opinions of man, is to build a church so big and so broad, so universal and so absolutely true, that no evolution of man, no progress of the souls of man, no discovery of the mind of man shall be so vast that it cannot stand upon this platform which we are uncovering—for we are uncovering the Truth of Almighty God. We are trying to get at the secret of God, to find the very kernel of the thought of Jesus, to get hold of the lines of power of Infinite Intelligence, and we are striving to make them so clear that a little child can understand them. Is not that a great work to do? Oh, the glory of a church that brings up its children to the knowledge of the mighty program of the Father!

To this Church, in addition to all its potency in the way of healing men's bodies, in the way of healing the circumstances of their lives, in the way of giving them a power through which they may make life's pathway smooth and ascend to the heights of God to this Church has been given the shaping of a religion so broad, so universal, so absolutely true that all the discoveries of all future times shall not find one flaw or one break in its structure. We are to state for men and women, today, the ultimate and absolute and perfect Truth of the Christ, so that wounds shall be healed, hearts shall be made whole, tears shall be

wiped from all faces; we are to place in the hand of man the power of the God-life, and in addition to that, we are to state, for all time that Truth of God on which the hope of the future of humanity rests. I am endeavoring, in the silence and in all the work which I do, to let the Holy Spirit of Truth speak to me the word that shall live throughout the ages, as the word of Christ has lived since Jesus spoke upon this earth. And I pray that God will give me wisdom and power and fineness of spirit to discern, that I may lead you to the uncovering of this marvelous platform on which by and by, at the great white throne of God, shall be gathered all the nations of the earth, all of the children of our Father.

Notes: *Growing out of the mystical vision of founder Albert Grier, the Church of the Truth has a variety of guiding and confessional statements. H. Edward Mills wrote The Church of the Truth Believes, while Grier wrote the church's Statement of the Truth and the missional statement, The Church of the Church. The Statement of the Truth describes Christ as a person who entered into the "fullness of his God-heritage," a possibility for each person.*

* * *

STATEMENT OF BEING (DIVINE SCIENCE FEDERATION INTERNATIONAL)

God is all, both invisible and visible.

One Presence, One Mind, One Power is all.

This One that is all is perfect life, perfect love, and perfect substance.

Man is the individualized expression of God and is ever one with this perfect life, perfect love, and perfect substance.

* * *

PRINCIPLES OF MIRACLES (MIRACLES EXPERIENCES, INC.)

1. There is no order of difficulty in miracles. One is not "harder" or "bigger" than another. They are all the same. All expressions of love are maximal.

2. Miracles as such do not matter. The only thing that matters is their Source, Which is far beyond evaluation.

3. Miracles occur naturally as expressions of love. The real miracle is the love that inspires them. In this sense everything that comes from love is a miracle.

4. All miracles mean life, and God is the Giver of life. His Voice will direct you very specifically. You will be told all you need to know.

5. Miracles are habits, and should be involuntary. They should not be under conscious control. Consciously selected miracles can be misguided.

6. Miracles are natural. When they do not occur something has gone wrong.

7. Miracles are everyone's right, but purification is necessary first.

8. Miracles are healing because they supply a lack; they are performed by those who temporarily have more for those who temporarily have less.

9. Miracles are a kind of exchange. Like all expressions of love, which are always miraculous in the true sense, the exchange reverses the physical laws. They bring more love both to the giver and the receiver.

10. The use of miracles as spectacles to induce belief is a misunderstanding of their purpose.

11. Prayer is the medium of miracles. It is a means of communication of the created with the Creator. Through prayer love is received, and through miracles love is expressed.

12. Miracles are thoughts. Thoughts can represent the lower or bodily level of experience, or the higher or spiritual level of experience. One makes the physical, and the other creates the spiritual.

13. Miracles are both beginnings and endings, and so they alter the temporal order. They are always affirmations of rebirth, which seem to go back but really go forward. They undo the past in the present, and thus release the future.

14. Miracles bear witness to truth. They are convincing because they arise from conviction. Without conviction they deteriorate into magic, which is mindless and therefore destructive; or rather, the uncreative use of mind.

15. Each day should be devoted to miracles. The purpose of time is to enable you to learn how to use time constructively. It is thus a teaching device and a means to an end. Time will cease when it is no longer useful in facilitating learning.

16. Miracles are teaching devices for demonstrating it is as blessed to give as to receive. They simultaneously increase the strength of the giver and supply strength to the receiver.

17. Miracles transcend the body. They are sudden shifts into invisibility, away from the bodily level. That is why they heal.

18. A miracle is a service. It is the maximal service you can render to another. It is a way of loving your neighbor as yourself. You recognize your own and your neighbor's worth simultaneously.

19. Miracles make minds one in God. They depend on cooperation because the Sonship is the sum of all that God created. Miracles therefore reflect the laws of eternity, not of time.

20. Miracles reawaken the awareness that the spirit, not the body, is the altar of truth. This is the recognition that leads to the healing power of the miracle.

21. Miracles are natural signs of forgiveness. Through miracles you accept God's forgiveness by extending it to others.

22. Miracles are associated with fear only because of the belief that darkness can hide. You believe that what your physical eyes cannot see does not exist. This leads to a denial of spiritual sight.

23. Miracles rearrange perception and place all levels in true perspective. This is healing because sickness comes from confusing the levels.

24. Miracles enable you to heal the sick and raise the dead because you made sickness and death yourself, and can therefore abolish both. *You* are a miracle, capable of creating in the likeness of your Creator. Everything else is your own nightmare, and does not exist. Only the creations of light are real.

25. Miracles are part of an interlocking chain of forgiveness which, when completed, is the Atonement. Atonement works all the time and in all the dimensions of time.

26. Miracles represent freedom from fear. "Atoning" means "undoing." The undoing of fear is an essential part of the Atonement value of miracles.

27. A miracle is a universal blessing from God through me to all my brothers. It is the privilege of the forgiven to forgive.

28. Miracles are a way of earning release from fear. Revelation induces a state in which fear has already been abolished. Miracles are thus a means and revelation is an end.

29. Miracles praise God through you. They praise Him by honoring His creations, affirming their perfection. They heal because they deny body-identification and affirm spirit-identification.

30. By recognizing spirit, miracles adjust the levels of perception and show them in proper alignment. This places spirit at the center, where it can communicate directly.

31. Miracles should inspire gratitude, not awe. You should thank God for what you really are. The children of God are holy and the miracle honors their holiness, which can be hidden but never lost.

32. I inspire all miracles, which are really intercessions. They intercede for your holiness and make your perceptions holy. By placing you beyond the physical laws they raise you into the sphere of celestial order. In this order you *are* perfect.

33. Miracles honor you because you are lovable. They dispel illusions about yourself and perceive the light in you. They thus atone for your errors by freeing you from your nightmares. By releasing your mind from the imprisonment of your illusions, they restore your sanity.

34. Miracles restore the mind to its fullness. By atoning for lack they establish perfect protection. The spirit's strength leaves no room for intrusions.

35. Miracles are expressions of love, but they may not always have observable effects.

36. Miracles are examples of right thinking, aligning your perceptions with truth as God created it.

37. A miracle is a correction introduced into false thinking by me. It acts as a catalyst, breaking up erroneous perception and reorganizing it properly. This places you under the Atonement principle,

where perception is healed. Until this has occurred, knowledge of the Divine Order is impossible.

38. The Holy Spirit is the mechanism of miracles. He perceives both God's creations and your illusions. He separates the true from the false by His ability to perceive totally rather than selectively.

39. The miracle dissolves error because the Holy Spirit identifies error as false or unreal. This is the same as saying that by perceiving light, darkness automatically disappears.

40. The miracle acknowledges everyone as your brother and mine. It is a way of perceiving the universal mark of God.

41. Wholeness is the perceptual content of miracles. They thus correct, or atone for, the faulty perception of lack.

42. A major contribution of miracles is their strength in releasing you from your false sense of isolation, deprivation and lack.

43. Miracles arise from a miraculous state of mind, or a state of miracle-readiness.

44. The miracle is an expression of an inner awareness of Christ and the acceptance of His Atonement.

45. A miracle is never lost. It may touch many people you have not even met, and produce undreamed of changes in situations of which you are not even aware.

46. The Holy Spirit is the highest communication medium. Miracles do not involve this type of communication, because they are *temporary* communication devices. When you return to your original form of communication with God by direct revelation, the need for miracles is over.

47. The miracle is a learning device that lessens the need for time. It establishes an out-of-pattern time interval not under the usual laws of time. In this sense it is timeless.

48. The miracle is the only device at your immediate disposal for controlling time. Only revelation transcends it, having nothing to do with time at all.

49. The miracle makes no distinction among degrees of misperception. It is a device for perception-correction, effective quite apart from either the degree or the direction of the error. This is its true indiscriminateness.

50. The miracle compares what you have made with creation, accepting what is in accord with it as true, and rejecting what is out of accord as false.

Notes: *These statements from the first pages of* A Course in Miracles *summarize the content of the book around which the organization is built. See:* A Course in Miracles *(New York: Foundation for Inner Peace, 1975).*

STATEMENT OF BELIEF [PHOENIX INSTITUTE (CHURCH OF MAN)]

The Church of Man is established because we believe:

There is only One Presence: God;

That God and man cannot be separated;

That every man is hungering for the experience of Oneness with the Self of his own being;

That this One acts in only one way;

That this way is a reciprocal action according to man's belief;

That man is the evidence of this action of the One;

That there is a way for man to experience this satisfaction of finding HimSelf;

That this occurs within man and then outer man is at peace with himself, his world, and his God;

That every man is the church;

That the teaching "Ye are gods" is verified by esoteric as well as exoteric knowledge synthesizing the principles of Science, Art, and Religion.

* * *

BASIC TENETS OF THE TRUTH OF LIFE MOVEMENT, SUMMARY OF TEACHINGS, AND THE SEVEN PROMULGATIONS OF LIGHT (SEICHO-NO-IE)

BASIC TENETS

WE ARE ALL CHILDREN OF GOD

The Truth of Life philosophy teaches that mankind is created in the image of God, and that we already possess the perfection of divine nature within us, whether we recognize it or not. As children of God, we are heirs to all of God's power and abundance. We are in reality without sin, disease, poverty, pain, or suffering. This is one of the most important points of the teachings.

Man is a spiritual being. Once we come to this realization, all negative delusions disappear and we naturally manifest perfect health, love, harmony, and abundance.

We believe that we can live God-like, profound lives now, and achieve a heavenly existence while still living in this world. We need only awaken to that which we already possess.

POWER OF THE WORD

Word is the creator of our spiritual universe. What we think and say has a profound effect on our lives and on others. We believe that prayer, words of love, and praise nourish our souls and provide the means to bring out the indwelling divinity within ourselves and others.

ONENESS OF ALL RELIGIONS

The Truth of Life philosophy embraces all religions, races, and creeds. It incorporates the teachings of Christianity, Buddhism, and Shintoism and emphasizes the truth that all major religions emanate from one universal God.

We encourage members to maintain their original beliefs and affiliations and do not seek to replace any religion or one's own image of God. The Truth of Life philosophy is intended to enhance what one has already learned and to shed additional light upon the path so that the individual may progress more rapidly.

THE SOUL OF EACH INDIVIDUAL IS IMMORTAL

Each of us comes to this school of life for our soul's development. We are given opportunities to learn to overcome obstacles, to develop our character, and to increase our ability to love, thereby gaining spiritual growth. It is our purpose to awaken to our true identities as divine beings, and to unfold the inner perfection, love, spirituality, and God-given potential which are inherent within each of us.

DELIVERANCE FROM SIN CONSCIOUSNESS

The Truth of Life philosophy teaches that in reality there is no sin; that we do not have to be redeemed because we do not carry the burden of "original sin." A sense of guilt has concealed the divinity of the human race for a long, long time. The mission of the Truth of Life Movement is to awaken mankind to the truth that we are in reality children of God, and, as such, perfect in nature.

THE PHENOMENAL WORLD DULY REFLECTS OUR OWN THOUGHTS

The physical world is a reflection of the mind. Our environment will appear according to our thoughts—dark or bright. To be healthy, we must have healthy thoughts and harmonious feelings. Here the law, "Like attracts like," works precisely; once we change our attitudes, the world around us changes.

RECONCILIATION AND PERFECT HARMONY

Since our environment is a reflection of our thoughts, as long as we possess a deep-rooted discordant feeling, our inner perfection will never be able to manifest in this world. Therefore, it is essential that we become reconciled with everyone and everything in the universe in order to be able to manifest genuine peace and happiness. We are not truly reconciled until we are grateful; therefore, we are taught to be grateful to all people and all things.

SUMMARY OF TEACHINGS

The teachings of SEICHO-NO-IE are summarized as follows:

1. Man is a child of God. This is one of the most important points of the teaching. Man is really created in the image of God in the world of Truth, and already has the divine quality within himself, whether he recognizes it or not. All we have to do is to manifest this perfect quality in this phenomenal world, then we can enjoy genuine happiness.

2. The power of Word is applied as a means of manifesting this indwelling infinite quality. For Word is the Creator of *the Spiritual Universe*. (Here Word implies Divine thought or Spiritual vibration at the same time.) Prayer or the recitation of Holy Sutra—these are another example of the power of Word.

3. The phenomenal world duly reflects our own thoughts (mind). If you wish to be really happy, therefore, you have to change your mind. According to your thoughts (mind), dark or bright, your environment will appear so, often concealing the real phase of the Spiritual Universe. In order to be healthy, you must have a healthy thought and harmonious feeling. Here the law, "Like attracts like" works precisely.

4. In Absolute Truth, all religions are basically one and same. This One Truth has appeared in the different forms such as Christianity, Buddhism, Shintoism and others according to the difference of time, race and place. We have to know the oneness of Truth. Through this understanding, people will be united regardless of the difference of their religions. One of the *raison d'etre* of Seicho-No-Ie lies here.

5. Deliverance from the Sense of Guilt. Sense of Guilt has concealed the Divinity of human race for a long, long time. With deep-rooted feeling of sin, man can never be saved forever. The mission of Seicho-No-Ie is to deliver humanity by letting them know that man is, in Reality, a child of God and already immaculate and redeemed.

6. Reconciliation, Perfect Harmony. Since our environment is the reflection of our thoughts (mind) as long as we possess a deep-rooted discordant feeling, the inner perfectness will never be made manifest in this world. Therefore, it is essential to reconcile with everyone and all things in the universe in order to manifest genuine peace and happiness. It is revealed in the Divine Revelation, "Spiritual Teachings Written on the Seven Golden Candlesticks to Light the Path of life." (See the Truth of Life, vol. I, p. 4-6)

7. Shinsokan (Prayerful Meditation). In order to realize oneness with God, Seicho-No-Ie teaches this unique meditation called "Shinsokan." This is also spiritually initiated through Dr. MASAHARU TANIGUCHI. Those who clearly realize their own divinity through this meditation can manifest their inner perfectness upon him. Numerous healings through Shinsokan are reported.

THE SEVEN PROMULGATIONS OF LIGHT

1. We resolve to transcend religious and sectarian differences, to worship Life, and to live in accordance with the laws of Life.

2. We believe that the laws governing the manifestation of Life constitute the path to infinite spiritual growth and that the Life dwelling within the individual is also immortal.

3. We study and make known to others the creative laws of Life so that humanity may tread the true path, which leads to infinite spiritual growth.

4. We believe that the proper nourishment for Life is love, and that prayer, words of love, and praise express the creative power of the Word necessary for the realization of love.

BASIC TENETS OF THE TRUTH OF LIFE MOVEMENT, SUMMARY OF TEACHINGS, AND THE SEVEN PROMULGATIONS OF LIGHT (SEICHO-NO-IE) (continued)

5. We believe that we as children of God, harbor within us infinite potentiality and that we can reach a state of magnificent freedom through the correct utilization of the creative power inherent in words.

6. We shall propagate our doctrines by writing and publishing good words, holding classes and lectures, broadcasting on radio and television, and by utilizing other cultural facilities, so that we may improve the destiny of mankind through the creative power of good words.

7. We shall organize an actual movement to conquer diseases and other afflictions of life through a proper outlook on life, a proper way of living and proper education and thereby establish a heaven, here on earth, that is based on spiritual fellowship.

Notes: *The Seicho-No-Ie is a Japanese version of Religious Science. It has published three "creedal" documents which summarize its beliefs.*

* * *

DECLARATION OF PRINCIPLES (UNITED CHURCH OF RELIGIOUS SCIENCE)

LEADER: We believe in God, the Living Spirit Almighty; one, indestructible, absolute, and self-existent Cause.

CONGREGATION: This One manifests Itself in and through all creation but is not absorbed by Its creation.

LEADER: The manifest universe is the body of God; it is the logical and necessary outcome of the infinite self-knowingness of God.

CONGREGATION: We believe in the incarnation of the Spirit in man and that all men are incarnations of the One Spirit.

LEADER: We believe in the eternality, the immortality, and the continuity of the individual soul, forever and ever expanding.

CONGREGATION: We believe that the Kingdom of Heaven is within man and that we experience this Kingdom to the degree that we become conscious of it.

LEADER: We believe the ultimate goal of life to be a complete emancipation from all discord of every nature, and that this goal is sure to be attained by all.

CONGREGATION: We believe in the unity of all life, and that the highest God and the innermost God is one God.

LEADER: We believe that God is personal to all who feel this Indwelling Presence.

CONGREGATION: We believe in the direct revelation of Truth through the intuitive and spiritual nature of man, and that any man may become a revealer of Truth who lives in close contact with the Indwelling God.

LEADER: We believe that the Universal Spirit, which is God, operates through a Universal Mind, which is the Law of God.

CONGREGATION: We are surrounded by this Creative Mind, which receives the direct impress of our thoughts and acts upon it.

LEADER: We believe in the healing of the sick through the Power of this Mind. We believe in the control of conditions through the Power of this Mind.

CONGREGATION: We believe in the eternal Goodness, the eternal Loving-kindness, and the eternal Givingness of Life to all.

LEADER: We believe in our own soul, our own spirit, and our own destiny.

CONGREGATION: We understand that the life of man is God.

WHAT I BELIEVE (1965)

This topic naturally divides itself into three parts: What I believe about God, what I believe about man, and what I believe about the relationship between God and man.

First, I believe that God is Universal Spirit, and by Spirit I mean the Life-Essence of all that is, that subtle Intelligence which permeates all things and which, in man, is self-conscious mind. I believe that God is present in every place, conscious in every part, the Intelligence or Mind of all that is.

I believe that man is the direct representative of this Divine Presence on this plane of existence. Man is the most highly evolved intelligence of which we have any knowledge. Man, being the highest representation of God here, is more nearly like God than any other manifestation on earth.

I believe that the relationship between God and man, between the Infinite and the finite, is a direct one; and that the avenue through which the Mind of God expresses to the mind of man is through the mind of man himself. We have the ability to think, to know, to perceive, to receive, and to act. What are these attributes other than a direct channel through which the Universal Spirit flows to us?

I do not feel that we approach God through any formula, sacred prayer, or intermediary, but rather that the Spirit of God, the eternal Mind, is the Power by which we think and know. It is self-evident that the only God whom we can know is the only God whom we do know, and that this knowing is an interior process of our own belief and perception. We can know no God other than the God whom our consciousness perceives.

But, some will say, while it is true that we cannot think outside of ourselves, we can know that which is outside of ourselves, because we do know things that are not within us. This is true, as it is true that we have a city hall; but to me that city hall would have no existence unless I were first aware of the fact. It has no existence to those who never heard of it. This is true of everything; and, while the possibility of knowledge may and must expand, we cannot know that which we do not perceive.

Therefore, I feel that God is to each one what each is to God. The Divine nature must be, and is, infinite; but we can know only as much of this nature as we permit to flow through us. In no other way can God be known to us. I believe the relationship between God and man is hidden within, and that when we discover a new truth, or find out something further about an old truth, it is really more of this infinite Mind revealing Itself through us.

I believe, then, in a direct communication between the Spirit of God and man—God personifying Himself through each and all. This is a beautiful as well as a logical concept, and an unavoidable conclusion. This makes of the human being a Divine being, a personification of the Infinite.

But if we are Divine beings, why is it that we appear to be so limited, so forlorn, so poor; so miserable, sick, and unhappy? The answer is that we are ignorant of our own nature, and also ignorant of the Law of God which governs all things.

I believe that all things are governed by immutable and exact laws; these laws cannot be changed or violated. Our ignorance of any law will offer no excuse for its infringement and we are made to suffer; not because God wills it, but because we are ignorant of the truth. We are individuals and have free will and self-choice. We shall learn by experience about things mental and spiritual just as we do about things physical and material. There is no other way to learn, and God Himself could not provide any other way without contradicting His own nature.

But if everything is governed by Law, is there any spontaneous Mind in the universe? Yes, but this spontaneous Mind, which is God, never contradicts Its own nature; It never violates Its own Law. We shall cease to misuse the Law as we learn more about ourselves and our relationship to the Whole. Experience alone will do this for us. We are made free, and because we are made free we shall have to abide by our nature and gradually wake up to the truth of our being.

Since I believe that everything is governed by exact laws, I believe all that the scientific world teaches, provided it is true in theory and principle. But should anyone in the scientific world, realizing that all is governed by law, thereby exclude the necessity of a spontaneous Spirit pervading all things, I would ask him this question: By what power of intelligence do you recognize that all things are governed by exact laws? And he would be compelled to answer that he knew by the power of a spontaneous intelligence welling up within him.

We are living in a universe governed by mechanical laws which have no conscious intelligence or personal volition. Of this we are sure. But the very fact that we can make this declaration proves that we are not governed by mechanical law alone, for mechanical law cannot, by reason of its very nature, recognize itself. When we come to self-recognition we have already arrived at spontaneous self-knowingness.

We are subject to the Law of our being, but this Law is not a Law of bondage, but one of liberty—liberty under Law.

I can conceive of a spontaneous Spirit and an immutable Law, the Spirit, and the way It works. This position has been accepted by deep thinkers of every age. It is self-evident. Spirit can never contradict Itself. Neither can It violate Its creative action through Its own Law.

God works through what we call the principle of evolution or unfoldment and we are subject to the laws involved. It is not a limitation, but is the only way through which our freedom and individuality can be guaranteed to us. There is an unfolding principle within us which is ever carrying us forward to greater and greater expressions of life, in freedom, love, and joy.

Each one of us is, I feel, at a certain level of evolution, and on the pathway of an endless expression of Life, Truth, and Beauty. Behind us is the All, before us is the All, and within, or expressing through us, is as much of this All as we are ready to receive. I believe absolutely in the immortality and the continuity of the individual stream of consciousness, which is what we mean by the individual life-stream. Humanity is an ascending principle of life, individuality, and expression through experience and unfoldment.

I do not believe in hell, the devil, damnation, or in any future state of punishment; or any other of the fantastic ideas which have been conceived in the minds of those who are either morbid, or who have felt the need of a future state of damnation to which to consign the immortal souls of those who have not agreed with their absurd doctrines. God does not punish people. There is, however, a Law of Cause and Effect which governs all and which will automatically punish, impartially and impersonally, if we conflict with the fundamental Harmony. This is bad enough, but it seems to me to be necessary, else we could not learn. It is one thing to believe in hell and damnation and quite another proposition to believe in a Law of just retribution.

The Law of retribution is the Law of balance, compensation, and equilibrium which is necessary to the universe. As we sow we shall, no doubt, reap. But I am sure that full and complete salvation will come alike to all. Heaven and hell are states of consciousness in which we now live according to our own state of understanding. We need not worry about either reward or punishment, for both are certain. In the long run, all will be saved from themselves through their own discovery of their Divine nature, and this is the only salvation necessary and the only one that could really be.

I believe in every man's religion for it is the avenue through which he worships God. I believe in my own religion more than in that of anyone else because this is the avenue through which I worship God.

I do not believe that there is anything in the Universe which is against us but ourselves. Everything is and must be for us. The only God who exists, the "Ancient of Days," wishes us well, knows us only as being perfect and complete. When we shall learn to know as God knows, we shall be saved from all mistakes and all troubles. This is heaven.

The apparent imperfection is but a temporary experience of the soul on the pathway of unfoldment. Man is a creature of time and of the night, but the day will break and the dawn of an everlasting morning of pure joy is in store for all. Meantime, God is with us and we need have no fear for He doeth all things well. I feel that we have reason to rejoice in what truth we now have; and that we

DECLARATION OF PRINCIPLES (UNITED CHURCH OF RELIGIOUS SCIENCE) (continued)

may look toward the future in confident expectancy, with gratitude and certainty that as we gain greater understanding we shall receive greater illumination.

I believe that we are surrounded by a mental or spiritual law—the Law of Mind—which receives the impress of our thought and acts upon it. This is the Law of all life and we may consciously use It for definite purposes. I am not superstitious about this Law anymore than I would be about the law of electricity or any other natural law, for nature is always natural.

I believe in a religion of happiness and joy. There is too much depression and sorrow in the world; these things were never meant to be and have no real place in God's world of Love. Religion should be like the morning sun, sending forth its glorious rays of light; it should be like the gently falling dew covering all, like the cool of the evening and the repose of the night. It should be a spontaneous song of joy and not a funeral dirge. From the fullness of the heart the mouth should speak.

I believe in the brotherhood of man, the Fatherhood of God, and the bond of Unity that binds all together in One Perfect Whole. I believe that God speaks to us in the wind and the wave and proclaims His Presence to us through all nature, but most completely through our own minds and in our hearts which proclaim His Life and Love.

Notes: *In 1927 Ernest Holmes, founder of United Church of Religious Science, published a statement entitled "What I Believe" in the first issue of* Science of Mind Magazine *(October 1927). This statement has been frequently republished as a summary of the church's belief (as well as that of Religious Science International). In January 1965, a lengthier statement with the same title was published in* Science of Mind Magazine. *This statement has been reprinted as a leaflet by the church. In 1954, the original statement was adapted with only slight modifications as the "Declaration of Principles" of the International Association of Religious Science Churches. It was printed in the* Religious Science Hymnal *in the format of a responsive reading. The declaration from the* Hymnal *and the statement published in 1965 are reproduced here.*

Chapter 17

Spiritualist, Psychic, and New Age Family

Swedenborgian Groups

THE NEW JERUSALEM AND ITS HEAVENLY DOCTRINE

OF THE NEW HEAVEN AND NEW EARTH, AND WHAT IS MEANT BY THE NEW JERUSALEM.

1. It is written in the Apocalypse, "I saw a new heaven and a new earth; for the first heaven and the first earth had passed away. And I saw the holy city, New Jerusalem, coming down from God out of heaven, prepared as a bride adorned for her husband. The city had a wall great and high, which had twelve gates, and at the gates twelve angels, and names written thereon, which are the names of the twelve tribes of the children of Israel. And the wall of the city had twelve foundations, and in them the names of the twelve apostles of the Lamb. And the city lieth four square, and the length is as large as the breadth. And he measured the city with the reed twelve thousand furlongs; and the length, and the breadth, and the height of it were equal. And he measured the wall thereof, a hundred and forty and four cubits, the measure of a man, that is, of an angel. And the wall of it was of jasper; but the city itself was pure gold, like unto pure glass; and the foundations of the wall of the city were of every precious stone. And the twelve gates were twelve pearls; and the street of the city was pure gold, as it were transparent glass. The glory of God enlightened it, and its lamp was the Lamb. And the nations of them which are saved shall walk in the light of it, and the kings of the earth shall bring their glory and honor into it." Ch. xxi. ver. 1, 2, 12 to 24. When man reads these words, he does not understand them otherwise than according to the sense of the letter, thus, that the visible heaven and earth will be dissolved, and a new heaven be created, and that the holy city Jerusalem will descend upon the new earth, and that it will be, as to its measures, according to the description. But the angels understand these things very differently; that

is, what man understands naturally, they understand spiritually. And as the angels understand them, such is their signification; and this is the internal or spiritual sense of the Word. According to this internal or spiritual sense, in which the angels are, by a new heaven and a new earth is meant a new church, both in the heavens and the earths, which shall be spoken of hereafter; by the city Jerusalem descending from God out of heaven, is signified its heavenly doctrine; by the length, breadth, and height, which are equal, are signified all the goods and truths of that doctrine, in the complex; by its wall are meant the truths which protect it; by the measure of the wall, which is a hundred and forty-four cubits, which is the measure of a man, that is, of an angel, are meant all those defending truths in the complex, and their quality; by the twelve gates which are of pearls, are meant introductive truths; which are likewise signified by the twelve angels at the gates; by the foundations of the wall, which are of every precious stone, are meant the knowledges whereupon that doctrine is founded; by the twelve tribes of Israel, and also by the twelve apostles, are meant all things of the church in general and in particular; by gold like unto pure glass, whereof the city and its streets were built, is signified the good of love, from which the doctrine and its truths are made transparent; by the nations who are saved, and the kings of the earth who bring glory and honor into the city, are meant all from the church who are in goods and truths; by God and the Lamb is meant the Lord, as to the essential Divine and the Divine Human. Such is the spiritual sense of the Word, to which the natural sense, which is that of the letter, serves as a basis; nevertheless these two senses, the spiritual and the natural, make one by correspondences. It is not, however, the design of the present work to prove, that such a spiritual meaning is involved in the fore-mentioned passages, but it may be seen proved at large in the ARCANA CŒLESTIA, in the following places. That by EARTH, in the Word, is meant the church, particularly when it is applied to signify the land of Canaan, n. 662, 1066, 1067, 1262,

THE NEW JERUSALEM AND ITS HEAVENLY DOCTRINE (continued)

1413, 1607, 2928, 3355, 4447, 4535, 5577, 8011, 9325, 9643. Because by earth, in the spiritual sense, is signified the nation inhabiting it, and its worship, n. 1262. That the people of the land signify those who belong to the spiritual church, n. 2928. That a new heaven and new earth signify something new in the heavens and the earths, with respect to goods and truths, thus with respect to those things that relate to the church in each, n. 1733, 1850, 2117, 2118, 3355, 4535, 10373. What is meant by the first heaven and the first earth, which passed away, may be seen in the small Treatise on the last Judgment and the Destruction of Babylon, throughout, but particularly from n. 65 to 72. That by JERUSALEM is signified the church with regard to doctrine, n. 402, 3654, 9166. That by cities [*urbes*] and cities [*civitates*] are signified the doctrines which belong to the church and religion, n. 402, 2450, 2712, 2943, 3216, 4492, 4493. That by the WALL of a city is signified the defensive truth of doctrine, n. 6419. That by the GATES of a city are signified such truths as are introductory to doctrine, and thereby to the church, n. 2943, 4478, 4492, 4493. That by the twelve TRIBES OF ISRAEL were represented and thence signified all the truths and goods of the church, in general and in particular, thus all things of faith and love, n. 3858, 3926, 4060, 6335. That the same is signified by the Lord's TWELVE APOSTLES, n. 2129, 2329, 3354, 3488, 3858, 6397. That when it is said of the apostles, *that they shall sit upon twelve thrones, and judge the twelve tribes of Israel*, it is signified that all are to be judged according to the goods and truths of the church, and of consequence by the Lord, from whom those truths and goods proceed, n. 2129, 6397. That by TWELVE are signified all things in their complex, n. 577, 2089, 2129, 2130, 3272, 3858, 3913. The same is also signified by a hundred and forty-four, inasmuch as that number is the product of twelve multiplied by twelve, n. 7973. That twelve thousand has likewise the same signification, n. 7973. That all numbers in the Word signify things, n. 482, 487, 647, 648, 755, 813, 1963, 1988, 2075, 2252, 3252, 4264, 6175, 9488, 9659, 10217, 10253. That the products arising from numbers multiplied into each other have the same signification with the simple numbers so multiplied, n. 5291, 5335, 5708, 7973. That by MEASURE is signified the quality of a thing with respect to truth and good, n. 3104, 9603, 10262. That by the FOUNDATIONS of a wall are signified the knowledges of truth whereupon doctrinals are founded, n. 9642. That by a QUADRANGULAR figure, or SQUARE, is signified what is perfect, n. 9717, 9861. That by LENGTH is signified good and its extension, and by BREADTH is signified truth and its extension, n. 1613, 9487. That by PRECIOUS STONES are signified truths from good, n. 114, 9863, 9865. What is signified, both in general and particular, by the precious stones in the URIM and THUMMIM, may be seen, n. 3862, 9864, 9866, 9905, 9891, 9895. What is signified by the JASPER, of which the wall was built, may be seen, n. 9872. That by the STREET of the city is signified the truth of doctrine from good, n. 2336. That by GOLD is signified the good of love, n. 113, 1551, 1552, 5658, 6914, 6917, 9510, 9874, 9881. That by GLORY is signified divine truth, such as it is in heaven, with the intelligence and wisdom thence derived, n. 4809, 5292, 5922, 8267, 8427, 9429, 10574. That by NATIONS are signified those in the church who are in good, and in an abstract sense the goods of the church, n. 1059, 1159, 1258, 1260, 1288, 1416, 1849, 4574, 7830, 9255, 9256. That by KINGS are signified those in the church who are in truths, and in an abstract sense the truths of the church, n. 1672, 2015, 2069, 4575, 5044. That the rites at the coronations of kings involve such things as are of divine truth, but that the knowledge of them at this day is lost, n. 4581, 4966.

2. Before the new Jerusalem and its doctrine are treated of, some account shall be given of the new heaven and new earth. It was shown in the small Treatise concerning the last Judgment and the Destruction of Babylon, what is meant by the first heaven, and the first earth, which have passed away. After this event, that is, when the last judgment was finished, a new heaven was created or formed by the Lord; which heaven was formed of all those who, from the advent of the Lord even to this time, had lived a life of faith and charity; as these alone are forms of heaven. For the form of heaven, according to which all consociations and communications there exist, is the form of divine truth from divine good, proceeding from the Lord; and man puts on this form, as to his spirit, by a life according to divine truth. That the form of heaven is thence derived, may be seen in the Treatise concerning Heaven and Hell, n. 200 to 212, and that all the angels are forms of heaven, n. 51 to 58, and 73 to 77. Hence it may be known of whom the new heaven is formed, and thereby what is its quality, viz. that it is altogether unanimous. For he that lives a life of faith and charity loves another as himself, and by love conjoins him with himself, and this reciprocally and mutually; for love is conjunction in the spiritual world. Wherefore when all act in like manner, then from many, yea, from innumerable individuals consociated according to the form of heaven, unanimity exists, and they become as one; for there is then nothing which separates and divides, but every thing conjoins and unites.

3. Inasmuch as this heaven was formed of all those who had been of such a quality from the coming of the Lord until the present time, it is plain that it is composed as well of Christians as of Gentiles, but chiefly of infants, from all parts of the world, who have died since the Lord's coming; for all these were received by the Lord, and educated in heaven, and instructed by the angels, and then reserved, that they, together with the others, might constitute a new heaven; whence it may be concluded how great

that heaven is. That all who die infants are educated in heaven, and become angels, may be seen in the Treatise concerning Heaven and Hell, n. 329 to 345. And that heaven is formed as well of Gentiles as of Christians, n. 318 to 328.

4. Moreover, with respect to this new heaven, it is to be observed, that it is distinct from the ancient heavens which were formed before the coming of the Lord; and yet there is such an orderly connection established between them, that they form together but one heaven. The reason why this new heaven is distinct from the ancient heaven is, because in the ancient churches there was no other doctrine than the doctrine of love and charity, and at that time they were unacquainted with any doctrine of faith separated from those principles. Hence also it is that the ancient heavens constitute superior expanses, whilst the new heaven constitutes an expanse below them; for the heavens are expanses one above another. In the highest expanses are they who are called celestial angels, many of whom were of the most ancient church; they are called celestial angels from celestial love, which is love towards the Lord; in the expanses below them are they who are called spiritual angels, many of whom were of the ancient church; they are called spiritual angels, from spiritual love, which is charity towards the neighbor: below these are the angels who are in the good of faith, who are they that have lived a life of faith; to live a life of faith, is to live each according to the doctrine of his particular church; and to live is to will and to do. All these heavens, however, make one by a mediate and immediate influx from the Lord. But a more full idea concerning these heavens may be obtained from what is shown in the Treatise concerning Heaven and Hell, and particularly in the article which treats of the two kingdoms into which the heavens in general are divided, n. 20 to 28; and in the article concerning the three heavens, n. 29 to 40; concerning mediate and immediate influx in the extracts from the ARCANA CŒLESTIA, after n. 603; and concerning the ancient and most ancient churches in a small Treatise on the last Judgment and the Destruction of Babylon, n. 46.

5. This may suffice concerning the new heaven; now something shall be said concerning the new earth. By the new earth is understood a new church upon earth: for when a former church ceases to be, then a new one is established by the Lord. For it is provided by the Lord that there should always be a church on earth, as by means of the church there is a conjunction of the Lord with mankind, and of heaven with the world; there the Lord is known, and therein are divine truths, by which man is conjoined to him. That a new church is at this time establishing, may be seen in the small Treatise concerning the last Judgment, n. 74. That a new church is signified by a new earth, is from the spiritual sense of the Word; for in that sense no particular earth is understood by earth, but the nation therein, and its divine worship; this being the spiritual thing whereof

earth is representative. Moreover by earth in the Word, without the name of any particular country affixed, is signified the land of Canaan; and in the land of Canaan a church has existed from the earliest ages, which was the reason why all the places therein, and in the adjacent countries, with their mountains and rivers, which are mentioned in the Word, are made representative and significative of those things which are the internals of the church, which are what are called its spiritual things; hence it is, as was observed, that by earth in the Word, inasmuch as the land of Canaan is understood, is signified the church, and in like manner here by a new earth. It is therefore usual in the church to speak of the heavenly Canaan, and by it to understand heaven. That by the land of Canaan, in the spiritual sense of the Word, is understood the church, was shown in the ARCANA CŒLESTIA in various places, of which the following shall be adduced: That the most ancient church which was before the flood, and the ancient church which was after the flood, were in the land of Canaan, n. 567, 3686, 4447, 4454, 4516, 4517, 5136, 6516, 9327. That then all places therein became representative of such things as are in the kingdom of the Lord and in the church, n. 1505, 3686, 4447, 5136. That therefore Abraham was commanded to go thither, to the intent that among his posterity, for Jacob, a representative church might be established, and the Word might be written whose ultimate should consist of representatives and significatives existing in that land, n. 3686, 4447, 5136, 6516. Hence it is that by earth and the land of Canaan, in the Word, is signified the church, n. 3038, 3481, 3705, 4447, 4517, 5757, 10658.

6. What is understood by Jerusalem in the Word, in its spiritual sense, shall also be briefly declared. By Jerusalem is understood the church with respect to doctrine, inasmuch as at Jerusalem in the land of Canaan, and in no other place, there were the temple, the altar, the sacrifices, and of consequence all divine worship; wherefore also three festivals were celebrated there every year, to which every male throughout the whole land was commanded to go: this, then, is the reason why by Jerusalem in its spiritual sense is signified the church with respect to worship, or, what is the same thing, with respect to doctrine; for worship is prescribed in doctrine, and is performed according to it. The reason why it is said *the holy city, new Jerusalem, descending from God out of heaven,* is, because, in the spiritual sense of the Word, by a city [*civitas*] and a city [*urbs*] is signified doctrine, and by a holy city the doctrine of divine truth, inasmuch as divine truth is what is called holy in the Word. It is called the New Jerusalem for the same reason that the earth is called new, because, as was observed above, by earth is signified the church, and by Jerusalem the church with respect to doctrine; and it is said to descend from God out of heaven, because all divine truth, from whence doctrine is, descends out of heaven from the Lord.

THE NEW JERUSALEM AND ITS HEAVENLY DOCTRINE (continued)

That by Jerusalem is not understood a city, although it was seen as a city, appears manifestly from hence, that it is said that *its height was* as its length and breadth, 12000 *furlongs,* ver. 16; *and that the measure of its wall, which was 144 cubits, was the measure of a man, that is, of an angel,* ver. 17; and also from its being said to be *prepared as a bride before her husband,* ver. 2; and afterwards, *the angel said, Come hither, I will shew thee the bride, the Lamb's wife,* and he shewed me the holy city, that Jerusalem, ver. 9. The church is what is called in the Word the bride and the wife of the Lord; the bride before conjunction, and the wife after conjunction, as may be seen in the ARCANA CŒLESTIA, n. 3103, 3105, 3164, 3165, 3207, 7022, 9182.

7. As to what particularly concerns the following doctrine, that also is from heaven, inasmuch as it is from the spiritual sense of the Word; and the spiritual sense of the Word is the same with the doctrine which is in heaven. For there is a church in heaven as well as on earth; for in heaven there is the Word, and doctrine from the Word; there are temples there and preaching in them; there are also both ecclesiastical and civil governments there: in short, there is no other difference between the things which are in heaven, and the things which are on earth, except that all things in the heavens are in a more perfect state; inasmuch as all who dwell there are spiritual, and things that are spiritual immensely exceed in perfection those that are natural. That such things exist in heaven may be seen in the work concerning Heaven and Hell throughout, particularly in the article concerning governments in heaven, n. 213 to 220, and also in the article on divine worship in heaven, n. 221 to 227. Hence it may plainly be seen what is meant by the holy city, New Jerusalem, being seen to descend from God out of heaven. But I proceed to the doctrine itself, which is for the new church, and which is called HEAVENLY DOCTRINE, because it was revealed to me out of heaven; for to deliver this doctrine is the design of this work.

INTRODUCTION TO THE DOCTRINE.

8. That the end of the church takes place when there is no faith because there is no charity, was shown in the little work concerning the last Judgment and the Destruction of Babylon, n. 33 to 39. Now forasmuch as the churches throughout Christendom have distinguished themselves solely by such things as relate to faith, and yet there is no faith where there is no charity, therefore I will here premise something concerning the doctrine of charity among the ancients, before I proceed to deliver the doctrine of the New Jerusalem. It is said THE CHURCHES IN CHRISTENDOM, and by them are understood the reformed or evangelical Churches, but not the popish or Roman Catholic church, inasmuch as that is no part of the Christian church; because wherever the church is, there the Lord is worshipped, and the Word is read; whereas, among the Roman Catholics, they worship themselves instead of the Lord, forbid the Word to be read by the people, and affirm the pope's decree to be equal, yea, superior to it.

9. The doctrine of charity, which is the doctrine of life, was the essential doctrine in the ancient churches; concerning which churches the reader may see more in the ARCANA CŒLESTIA, n. 1238, 2385; and that doctrine conjoined all churches, and thereby formed one church out of many. For they acknowledged all those to be members of the church, who lived in the good of charity, and called them brothers, howsoever they might differ in truths, which at this day are called matters of faith. In these they instructed one another which was among their works of charity; nor were they angry if one did not accede to another's opinion, knowing that every one receives truth in such proportion as he is in good. Forasmuch as the ancient churches were of such a quality, therefore the members of them were interior men, and forasmuch as they were interior men, they were wiser men. For they who are in the good of love and charity, are, with respect to the internal man, in heaven, and in an angelic society there which is in similar good; whence there is an elevation of their mind to interior things, and consequently they are in wisdom: for wisdom cannot come from any other source than from heaven, that is, through heaven from the Lord; and in heaven there is wisdom because those who are there are in good: wisdom consists in seeing truth from the light of truth, and the light of truth is the light which is in heaven. But in process of time that ancient wisdom decreased; for so far as mankind removed themselves from the good of love to the Lord, and the good of love towards the neighbor, which love is called charity, so far also they removed themselves from wisdom, because they so far removed themselves from heaven. Hence it was that man from internal became external, and this successively; and when man became external, he also became worldly and corporeal; and when this is his quality, he little cares for the things which are of heaven; for the delights of earthly loves, and the evils which are delightful to man from those loves, then occupy him entirely; and the things which he hears concerning a life after death, concerning heaven and hell, and concerning spiritual subjects in general, are then as it were without him and not within him, as nevertheless they ought to be. Hence it is that the doctrine of charity, which was of such estimation among the ancients, is at this day among the things which are lost; for who at this day knows what charity is, in a genuine sense, and what our neighbor is, in a genuine sense? when nevertheless that doctrine not only teaches this, but innumerable things beside, of which not a thousandth part is known at this day. The whole sacred scripture is nothing else than the doctrine of love and charity, which the Lord also teaches, saying. "Thou shalt love the Lord thy God from thy whole heart, and in

thy whole soul, and in thy whole mind; this is the primary and great commandment; the second is like unto it; thou shalt love they neighbor as thyself: on these two commandments hang all the law and the prophets." Matt. xxii. verses 37, 38, 39. The law and the prophets are the Word in general and in particular.

OF GOOD AND TRUTH.

11. All things in the universe, which are according to divine order, have relation to good and truth. Nothing exists in heaven, and nothing in the world, which does not relate to these two. The reason is, because both, as well good as truth, proceed from the Divine, from whom are all things.

12. Hence it appears, that nothing is more necessary for man than to know what good and truth are, and how each regards the other, and in what manner they are mutually conjoined. But it is most necessary for the man of the church; for as all things of heaven have relation to good and truth, so also have all things of the church, inasmuch as the good and truth of heaven are also the good and truth of the church. It is on this account that good and truth are first treated of.

13. It is according to divine order that good and truth should be conjoined, and not separated; thus that they should be one and not two: for they proceed in conjunction from the Divine, and they are in conjunction in heaven, and therefore they should be in conjunction in the church. The conjunction of good and truth is called in heaven celestial marriage, for all therein are in this marriage. Hence it is, that, in the Word, heaven is compared to marriage, and the Lord is called Bridegroom and Husband, but heaven bride and wife; in like manner the church. That heaven and the church are so called, is because they who are therein receive divine good in truths.

14. All the intelligence and wisdom which angels possess is from that marriage, and not any of it from good separate from truth, nor from truth separate from good. It is the same with men of the church.

15. Inasmuch as the conjunction of good and truth bears resemblance to marriage, it is plain that good loves truth, and that truth, in its turn, loves good, and that each desires to be conjoined with the other. The man of the church, who has not such love and such desire, is not in celestial marriage, consequently the church as yet is not in him; for the conjunction of good and truth constitutes the church.

16. Goods are manifold; in general there is spiritual good and natural good, and both conjoined in genuine moral good. As goods are manifold, so also are truths, inasmuch as truths are of good, and are the forms of good.

17. As is the case with good and truth, so it is in the opposite with evil and the false; for as all things in the universe, which are according to divine order, have relation to good and truth, so all things which are contrary to divine order have relation to evil and the false. Again, as good loves to be conjoined to truth, and *vice versa,* so evil loves to be conjoined to the false, and *vice versa.* And again, as all intelligence and wisdom are born of the conjunction of good and truth, so all insanity and folly are born of the conjunction of evil and the false. This conjunction of evil and the false is called infernal marriage.

18. From the circumstance that evil and the false are opposite to good and truth, it is plain that truth cannot be conjoined to evil, nor good to the false of evil; if truth be adjoined to evil, it becomes truth no longer, but the false, inasmuch as it is falsified; and if good be adjoined to the false of evil, it becomes good no longer, but evil, inasmuch as it is adulterated. Nevertheless the false which is not of evil may be conjoined to good.

19. No one who is in evil, and thence in the false from confirmation and life, can know what good and truth is, for he believes his own evil to be good, and thence he believes his own false to be truth; but every one who is in good and thence in truth may know what evil and the false is. The reason of this is, because all good and its truth is, in its essence, celestial, and what is not celestial in its essence is still from a celestial origin; but evil and its false is in its essence infernal, and what is not infernal in its essence has nevertheless its origin from thence; and every thing celestial is in light, but every thing infernal is in darkness.

OF WILL AND UNDERSTANDING.

28. Man has two faculties which constitute his life: one is called WILL, and the other UNDERSTANDING: they are distinct from each other, but so created that they may be one; and when they are one, they are called MIND: wherefore of these consists the human mind, and all the life of man is in them.

29. As all things in the universe; which are according to divine order, have relation to good and truth, so all things with man have relation to will and understanding; for good with man is of his will, and truth with him is of his understanding. These two faculties, or these two lives of man, are their receptacles and subjects; the will being the receptacle and subject of all things of good, and the understanding the receptacle and subject of all things of truth. Goods and truths have no other residence with man: and forasmuch as goods and truths have no other residence with man, so neither have love and faith; for love is of good, and good is of love; and faith is of truth, and truth is of faith.

30. Now forasmuch as all things in the universe have relation to good and truth, and all things of the church to the good of love and the truth of faith; and forasmuch as man is man from these two faculties; therefore they also are treated of in this doctrine; otherwise man could have no distinct idea concerning them, whereon to found his thought.

31. The will and understanding likewise constitute the spirit of man, for his wisdom and intelligence, and

his life in general, reside in them, the body being only obedience.

32. Nothing is more important to be known, than in what manner will and understanding make one mind. They make one mind as good and truth make one; for there is a similar marriage between will and understanding as there is between good and truth. What is the quality of that marriage may appear from what has been said above, concerning good and truth. As good is the very esse of a thing, and truth the existere of a thing thence derived, so the will with man is the very esse of his life, and the understanding the existere of life thence; for good, which is of the will, assumes a form, and renders itself visible, in the understanding.

33. They who are in good and truth have will and understanding, but they who are in evil and the false have not will and understanding; but, instead of will, they have cupidity, and, instead of understanding, they have science. For the truly human will is the receptacle of good, and the understanding the receptacle of truth; wherefore will cannot be predicated of evil, nor understanding of the false, because they are opposite, and opposites destroy each other. Hence it is that the man who is in evil, and thence in the false, cannot be called rational, wise, and intelligent. With the evil, also, the interiors which are of the mind, wherein the will and the understanding principally reside, are closed up. It is supposed that the evil also have will and understanding, because they say that they will and that they understand; but their will is mere lust, and their understanding is mere science.

OF THE INTERNAL AND EXTERNAL MAN.

36. Man is so created as to be, at one and the same time, in the spiritual world and in the natural world. The spiritual world is that in which angels are, and the natural world is that in which men are. And because man is so created, therefore he is endowed with an internal and an external; an internal by which he may be in the spiritual world, and an external by which he may be in the natural world. His internal is what is called the internal man, and his external is what is called the external man.

37. Every man has an internal and an external; but there is a difference in this respect between the good and the evil. The internal with the good is in heaven and its light, and the external is in the world and its light, which light with them is illuminated by the light of heaven, so that with them the internal and the external act in unity, as the efficient cause and the effect, or as what is prior and what is posterior. But with the evil the internal is in the world and its light, as is also the external; wherefore they see nothing from the light of heaven, but only from the light of the world, which light they call the light of nature. Hence it is that the things of heaven are to them in darkness, and the things of the world in light. It is

therefore manifest that the good have an internal man and an external man, but that the evil have no internal man, but only an external.

38. The internal man is what is called the SPIRITUAL MAN, because it is in the light of heaven, which light is spiritual; and the external man is what is called the NATURAL MAN, because it is in the light of the world, which light is natural. The man whose internal is in the light of heaven, and his external in the light of the world, is a spiritual man as to each; but the man whose internal is not in the light of heaven, but only in the light of the world, in which is also his external, is a natural man as to each. The spiritual man is he who is called in the Word ALIVE, but the natural man is he who is called DEAD.

39. The man whose internal is in the light of heaven, and his external in the light of the world, thinks both spiritually and naturally; but then his spiritual thought flows in into the natural, and is there perceived. But the man whose internal, together with his external, is in the light of the world, does not think spiritually, but materially; for he thinks from such things as are in the nature of the world, all which are material. To think spiritually is to think of things as they essentially are in themselves, to see truths from the light of truth, and to perceive goods from the love of good; also to see the qualities of things, and to perceive their affections, abstractedly from what is material: but to think materially is to think, see, and perceive them together with matter, and in matter, thus respectively in a gross and obscure manner.

40. The internal spiritual man, regarded in himself, is an angel of heaven; and, also, during his life in the body, notwithstanding his ignorance of it, is in society with angels; and after his separation from the body, he comes among them. But the merely natural internal man, regarded in himself, is a spirit, and not an angel; and, also, during his life in the body, is in society with spirits, but with those who are in hell, among whom he also comes after his separation from the body.

41. The interiors, with those who are spiritual men, are also actually elevated towards heaven, for that is what they primarily regard; but the interiors which are of the mind with those who are merely natural, are turned to the world, because that is what they primarily regard. The interiors, which are of the mind [mens], are turned with every one to that which he loves above all things; and the exteriors which are of the mind [animus], are turned the same way as the interiors.

42. They who have only a common [or general] idea concerning the internal and external man, believe that to be the internal man which thinks and wills, and that to be the external which speaks and acts; because to think and to will is internal, and to speak and to act thence is external. But it is to be observed, that when man thinks intelligently, and wills wisely,

he then thinks and wills from a spiritual internal; but when man does not think intelligently, and will wisely, he thinks and wills from a natural internal. Of consequence, when man thinks well concerning the Lord and those things which are of the Lord, and well concerning the neighbor, and those things which are of the neighbor, and wills well to them, he then thinks and wills from a spiritual internal, because he then thinks from the faith of truth and from the love of good, thus from heaven. But when man thinks ill concerning them, and wills ill to them, he then thinks and wills from a natural internal, because he thinks and wills from the faith of what is false and from the love of what is evil, thus from hell. In short, so far as man is in love to the Lord, and in love towards his neighbor, so far he is in a spiritual internal, from which he thinks and wills, and from which also he speaks and acts: but so far as man is in the love of self, and in the love of the world, so far he is in a natural internal, from which he thinks and wills, and from which also he speaks and acts.

43. It is so provided and ordered by the Lord, that so far as man thinks and wills from heaven, so far the internal spiritual man is opened and formed. It is opened into heaven even to the Lord, and it is formed according to those things which are of heaven. But, on the contrary, so far as man does not think and will from heaven, but from the world, so far his internal spiritual man is closed, and his external is opened; it is opened into the world, and it is formed according to those things which are of the world.

44. They, with whom the internal spiritual man is opened into heaven to the Lord, are in the light of heaven, and in illumination from the Lord, and thence in intelligence and wisdom; these see truth because it is truth, and perceive good because it is good. But they with whom the internal spiritual man is closed, do not know that there is an internal man, and much less what the internal man is; neither do they believe that there is a Divine, nor that there is a life after death; consequently they do not believe the things which are of heaven and the church. And forasmuch as they are only in light of the world and in illumination thence, they believe in nature as the Divine, they see the false as truth, and they perceive evil as good.

45. He whose internal is so far external, that he believes nothing but what he can see with his eyes and touch with his hands, is called a sensual man: this is the lowest natural man, and is in fallacies concerning all the things which are of faith and the church.

46. The internal and external, which have been treated of, are the internal and external of the spirit of man; his body is only an additional external, within which they exist; for the body does nothing from itself, but from its spirit which is in it. It is to be observed that the spirit of man, after its separation from the body, thinks and wills, speaks and acts, the same as before; to think and to will is its internal, and to speak and

to act is its external; concerning which, see the Treatise on Heaven, n. 234 to 245, 265 to 275, 432 to 444, 453 to 484.

OF LOVE IN GENERAL.

54. The very life of man is his love, and such as the love is, such is the life, yea, such is the whole man. But it is the governing or ruling love which constitutes the man. That love has many other loves subordinate to it, which are derivations from it. These appear under another form, but still they are all present in the ruling love, and constitute, with it, one kingdom. The ruling love is as their king and head; it directs them, and, by them, as mediate ends, it regards and intends its own end, which is the primary and ultimate end of them all; and this it does both directly and indirectly. The object of the ruling love is what is loved above all things.

55. That which man loves above all things is continually present in his thought, and also in his will, and constitutes his most essential life. As, for example, he who loves riches above all things, whether in money or possessions, is continually revolving in his mind how he may obtain them. He rejoices exceedingly when he acquires them, and is equally grieved at their loss; his heart is in them. He who loves himself above all things regards himself in every thing: he thinks of himself, he speaks of himself, he acts for the sake of himself, for his life is the life of self.

56. Man regards that which he loves above all things as an end; he is governed by it in all and every particular of his conduct. It is in his will like the latent current of a river, which draws and bears him away, even when he is doing something else; for it is this which animates him. It is of such a quality, that one man explores and also discovers it in another, and either leads him, or regulates his dealings with him, according to it.

57. Man is altogether of such a quality as the ruling principle of his life is: by this he is distinguished from others; according to this is his heaven if he be good, and his hell if he be evil. It is his will itself, his proprium, and his nature, for it is the very esse of his life: this cannot be changed after death, because it is the man himself.

58. Every one enjoys delight, pleasure and happiness from his ruling love, and according to it; for man calls that delightful which he loves, because he perceives it; but that which he thinks and does not love, he may also call delightful, but it is not the delight of his life. That which is delightful to his love is what man esteems good, and that which is undelightful is what he esteems evil.

59. There are two loves, from which, as from their fountains, all goods and truths exist; and there are two loves, from which all evils and falses exist. The two loves, from which all goods and truths exist, are love to the Lord, and love towards the neighbor; and the two loves, from which all evils and falses exist,

are the love of self and the love of the world. These two loves are in direct opposition to the former.

60. The two loves from which are all goods and truths, which are, as was said, love to the Lord and love towards the neighbor, constitute heaven with man, wherefore also they reign in heaven; and forasmuch as they constitute heaven with man, they also constitute the church with him. The two loves from which are all evils and falses, which are, as was said, the love of self and the love of the world, constitute hell with man, wherefore also they reign in hell.

61. The two loves from which all goods and truths are, which as was said, are the loves of heaven, open and form the internal spiritual man, because they reside therein. But the two loves from which all evils and falses are derived, when they have the dominion, shut up and destroy the internal spiritual man, and render man natural and sensual, according to the extent and quality of their dominion.

OF THE LOVES OF SELF AND OF THE WORLD.

65. The love of self consists in willing well to ourselves alone, and not to others except for the sake of ourselves, not even to the church, to our country, to any human society, or to a fellow-citizen; and also in doing good to them only for the sake of our own fame, honor and glory; for unless it sees that these will be promoted by the goods which it does to others, it says in its heart, What matters it? why should I do this? and what advantage will it be to me? and so it passes them over. Whence it is plain that he who is in the love of self does not love the church, nor his country, nor society, nor his fellow-citizen, nor anything good, but himself alone.

66. Man is in the love of self, when, in those things which he thinks and does, he has no respect to his neighbor, nor to the public, much less to the Lord, but only to himself and his own connections; consequently when every thing which he does is for the sake of himself and his own connections, and when, if he does any thing for the public and his neighbor it is only for the sake of appearance.

67. It is said for the sake of himself and his own connections, because he who loves himself also loves his own connections, who are, in particular, his children and relations, and in general, all who make one with him, and whom he calls his own. To love these is still to love himself, for he regards them as it were in himself, and himself in them:—among those whom he calls his own, are also all they who praise, honor, and pay their court to him.

68. That man is in the love of self, who despises his neighbor in comparison with himself, who esteems him his enemy if he does not favor him, and if he does not respect and pay his court to him: he is still more in the love of self who for such reasons hates his neighbor and persecutes him; and he is still more

so who for such reasons burns with revenge against him, and desires his destruction: such persons at length delight in cruelty.

69. From a comparison with celestial love, it may plainly appear what is the quality of the love of self. Celestial love consists in loving uses for the sake of uses, or goods for the sake of goods such as man should perform to the church, to his country, to human society, and to his fellow-citizens. But he who loves them for the sake of self, loves them no otherwise than he loves his domestics because they are serviceable to him. Hence it follows that he who is in the love of self, would that the church, his country, human societies, and his fellow-citizens, should serve him, and not that he should serve them. He places himself above them, and them below himself.

70. Moreover, so far as any one is in celestial love, which consists in loving uses and goods, and in being affected with delight of heart when he performs them, so far he is led by the Lord, because that is the love in which the Lord is, and which is from Him. But so far as any one is in the love of self, so far he is led by himself; and so far as he is led by himself, so far he is led by his own proprium; and the proprium of man is nothing but evil; for it is his hereditary evil, which consists in loving self more than God, and the world more than heaven.

71. The love of self is also of such a quality, that so far as the reins are given to it, that is, so far as external restraints are removed, which are fears on account of the law and its penalties, and on account of the loss of fame, of honor, of gain, of office, and of life, it rushes on till it would not only extend its empire over the universal globe, but also over heaven, and over the Divine itself; it has no bound nor end. This propensity lurks in every one who is in the love of self, although it does not appear before the world, on account of the checks and restraints before mentioned. Besides, every one who is of such a quality, when he meets with an insuperable obstacle in his way, waits till it is removed; hence it is that the man who is in such love does not know that such a mad, unbounded cupidity is latent within him. Nevertheless, any one may see that this is the case, who observes the conduct of potentates and kings, who are not withheld by such checks, restraints, and insuperable obstacles; who rush on and subjugate provinces and kingdoms as long as success attends them, and aspire after power and glory without bounds. And it may be seen still more clearly from the case of those who extend their dominion into heaven, and transfer to themselves all the divine power of the Lord, and are continually lusting after more.

72. There are two kinds of dominion, that of love towards our neighbor, and that of the love of self. These two kinds of dominion are in their essence entirely opposite to each other. He who rules from love towards his neighbor, wills good to all, and loves nothing more than to perform uses, consequently to

serve others; (to serve others consists in doing them good from good will, and in performing uses;) this is his love, and this is the delight of his heart. He is also rejoiced in proportion as he is exalted to dignities, not for the sake of the dignities, but for the sake of uses, which he is thereby enabled to perform in more abundance and in a greater degree; such is the quality of dominion in the heavens. But he who rules from the love of self, wills good to none except to himself and his own connections: the uses which he performs are for the sake of his own honor and glory, which he esteems the only uses: when he serves others, it is in order that he may be served, honored and exalted: he seeks dignities, not for the sake of the goods which he might perform, but that he may be in eminence and glory, and thence in the delight of his heart.

73. The love of dominion also remains with every one after the termination of his life in the world. They who have ruled from love towards their neighbor, are then intrusted with dominion in the heavens; but then it is not they that rule, but the uses and goods which they love; and when uses and goods rule, the Lord rules. But they who have ruled in the world from the love of self, are after the termination of their life in the world, in hell, where they are vile slaves.

74. Hence it may be known who they are that are in the love of self. It is of no importance how they appear externally, whether elate or submissive; for such things reside in the interior man, and the interior man is concealed by many, whilst the exterior is instructed to assume the contrary appearance of love for the public and the neighbor. And this is also done for the sake of self: for they know that the love of the public and the neighbor has a power of interiorly affecting all men, and that they shall be loved and esteemed in proportion. The reason why that love has such a power is, because heaven flows in into it.

75. The evils which belong to those who are in the love of self, are, in general, contempt of others, envy, enmity against those who do not favor them, hostility on that account, hatreds of various kinds, revenge, cunning, deceit, unmercifulness, and cruelty; and where such evils exist, there is also contempt of the Divine, and of divine things, which are the truths and goods of the church: if these are honored by such persons, it is only with the mouth, and not with the heart. And because such evils are thence, so there are similar falses, for falses proceed from evils.

76. But the love of the world consists in wishing to appropriate the wealth of others to ourselves by any artifice, in placing the heart in riches, and in suffering the world to draw us back, and lead us away from spiritual love, which is love towards the neighbor, consequently, from heaven. They are in the love of the world who desire to appropriate the goods of others to themselves by various artifices, particularly they who do so by means of cunning and deceit, esteeming their neighbor's good as of no importance.

They who are in that love covet the goods of others, and so far as they do not fear the laws and the loss of reputation, which they regard for the sake of gain, they deprive others of their property, and even commit depredations.

77. But the love of the world is not opposite to celestial love in the same degree that the love of self is, inasmuch as such great evils are not concealed in it. This love is manifold: there is the love of riches as the means of obtaining honors; there is the love of honors and dignities as the means of obtaining riches; there is the love of riches for the sake of various uses with which people are delighted in the world; there is the love of riches for the sake of riches alone, which is avarice, and so on. The end for the sake of which riches are desired, is called their use, and it is the end or use from which the love derives its quality; for the quality of the love is the same as that of the end which it has in view, to which other things only serve as means.

78. In a word, the love of self and the love of the world are altogether opposite to love to the Lord and love towards the neighbor; wherefore the love of self and the love of the world are infernal loves, for they reign in hell, and also constitute hell with man; but love to the Lord and love towards the neighbor are heavenly loves, for they reign in heaven, and also constitute heaven with man.

79. From what has been now said, it may be seen that all evils are in and from those two loves; for the evils which were enumerated at n. 75 are common; the others, which were not enumerated, because they are specific, originate in and flow from them. Hence it may appear, that man, forasmuch as he is born into these two loves, is born into evils of every kind.

80. In order that man may know what evils are, he ought to know their origin; and unless he knows what evils are, he cannot know what goods are, consequently he cannot know of what quality he himself is: this is the reason that these two origins of evils are treated of here.

OF LOVE TOWARDS THE NEIGHBOR, OR CHARITY.

84. It shall first be shown what the neighbor is, as it is the neighbor who is to be loved, and towards whom charity is to be exercised. For unless it be known what our neighbor is, charity may be exercised in a similar manner, without distinction, towards the evil as well as towards the good, whence charity ceases to be charity: for the evil, from the benefactions conferred on them, do evil to their neighbor, but the good do good.

85. It is a common opinion at this day, that every man is equally a neighbor, and that benefits are to be conferred on every one who needs assistance; but it is the business of Christian prudence to examine well the quality of a man's life, and to exercise charity to him accordingly. The man of the internal church exercises his charity with discrimination, conse-

quently with intelligence; but the man of the external church, forasmuch as he is not able thus to discern things, does it indiscriminately.

86. The distinctions of neighbor, which the man of the church ought well to know, depend upon the good which is with every one; and forasmuch as all goods proceed from the Lord, therefore the Lord is our neighbor in a supreme sense and in a supereminent degree, and the origin is from Him. Hence it follows that so far as any one is receptive of the Lord, in that degree he is our neighbor; and forasmuch as no one receives the Lord, that is, good from Him, in the same manner as another, therefore no one is our neighbor in the same manner as another. For all who are in the heavens, and all the good who are on the earths, differ in good; no two ever received a good that is altogether one and the same; it must be various, that each may subsist by itself. But all these varieties, consequently all the distinctions of neighbor, which depend on the reception of the Lord, that is, on the reception of good from Him, can never be known by any man, nor indeed by any angel, except in a general manner, or with respect to their kinds and species: neither does the Lord require any more of the man of the church, than to live according to what he knows.

87. Forasmuch as good is different with every one, it follows, that the quality of his good determines in what degree and in what proportion any one is our neighbor. That this is the case is plain from the Lord's parable concerning him that fell among robbers, whom, when half dead, the priest passed by, and also the Levite; but the Samaritan, after he had bound up his wounds, and poured in oil and wine, took him up on his own breast, and led him to an inn, and ordered that care should be taken of him: he, forasmuch as he exercised the good of charity, is called neighbor, Luke x. 29 to 37; whence it may be known that they are our neighbor who are in good: oil and wine, which the Samaritan poured into the wounds, also signify good and its truth.

88. It is plain, from what has now been said, that, in a universal sense, good is the neighbor, forasmuch as a man is neighbor according to the quality of the good that is with him from the Lord; and forasmuch as good is the neighbor, so is love, for all good is of love; consequently every man is our neighbor according to the quality of the love which he receives from the Lord.

89. That love is what causes any one to be a neighbor, and that every one is a neighbor according to the quality of his love, appears manifestly from the case of those who are in the love of self, who acknowledge for their neighbor those who love them most; that is, so far as they belong to themselves they embrace them, they treat them with kindness, they confer benefits on them and call them brothers; yea, forasmuch as they are evil, they say, that these are

their neighbor more than others: they esteem others as their neighbor in proportion as they love them, thus according to the quality and quantity of their love. Such persons derive the origin of neighbor from self, by reason that love constitutes and determines it. But they who do not love themselves more than others, as is the case with all who belong to the kingdom of the Lord, will derive the origin of neighbor from Him whom they ought to love above all things, consequently, from the Lord; and they will esteem every one as neighbor according to the quality of his love to Him and from Him. Hence it appears from whence the origin of neighbor is to be drawn by the man of the church; and that every one is neighbor according to the good which he possesses from the Lord, consequently that good itself is the neighbor.

90. That this is the case, the Lord also teaches in Matthew, "for he said to those who were in good that they had given him to eat, that they had given him to drink, that they had gathered him, had clothed him, had visited him, and had come to him in prison; and afterwards that, so far as they had done it to one of the least of their brethren, they had done it unto him," xxv. 34 to 40; in these six kinds of good, when understood in the spiritual sense, are comprehended all the kinds of neighbor. Hence, likewise, it is evident, that when good is loved the Lord is loved, for it is the Lord from Whom good is, Who is in good, and Who is good itself.

91. But the neighbor is not only man singly, but also man collectively, as a less or greater society, our country, the church, the Lord's kingdom, and, above all, the Lord Himself; these are the neighbor to whom good is to be done from love. These are also the ascending degrees of neighbor, for a society consisting of many is neighbor in a higher degree than a single man is; in a still superior degree is our country; in a still superior degree is the church; and in a still superior degree is the Lord's kingdom; but in the supreme degree is the Lord: these ascending degrees are as the steps of a ladder, at the top of which is the Lord.

92. A society is our neighbor more than a single man, because it consists of many. Charity is to be exercised towards it in a like manner as towards a man singly, that is, according to the quality of the good that is with it; consequently in a manner totally different towards a society of well-disposed persons, than towards a society of ill-disposed persons; the society is loved when its good is provided for from the love of good.

93. Our country is our neighbor more than a society, because it is like a parent; for a man is born therein, and is thereby nourished and protected from injuries. Good is to be done to our country from a principle of love according to its necessities, which principally regard its sustenance, and the civil and spiritual life of those therein. He who loves his country, and does good to it from good will, in the other life loves the

Lord's kingdom, for there the Lord's kingdom is his country, and he who loves the Lord's kingdom loves the Lord, because the Lord is all in all in His kingdom.

94. The church is our neighbor more than our country, for he who provides for the church, provides for the souls and eternal life of the men who dwell in his country; wherefore he who provides for the church from love, loves his neighbor in a superior degree, for he wishes and wills heaven and happiness of life to eternity to others.

95. The Lord's kingdom is our neighbor in a still superior degree, for the Lord's kingdom consists of all who are in good, as well those on the earths as those in the heavens; thus the Lord's kingdom is good with all its quality in the complex: when this is loved, the individuals are loved who are in good.

96. These are the degrees of neighbor, and love ascends, with those who are principled in love towards their neighbor, according to these degrees. But these degrees are degrees in successive order, in which what is prior or superior is to be preferred to what is posterior or inferior; and forasmuch as the Lord is in the supreme degree, and He is to be regarded in each degree as the end to which it tends, consequently He is to be loved above all persons and things. Hence, now, it may appear in what manner love to the Lord conjoins itself with love towards the neighbor.

97. It is a common saying, that every one is his own neighbor; that is, that every one should first consider himself; but the doctrine of charity teaches how this is to be understood. Every one should provide for himself the necessaries of life, such as food, raiment, habitation, and other things which the state of civil life, in which he is, necessarily requires, and this not only for himself, but also for his family, and not only for the present time, but also for the future; for, unless a man procures himself the necessaries of life, he cannot be in a state to exercise charity, for he is in want of all things.

98. But in what manner every one ought to be his own neighbor may appear from this comparison: every one ought to provide food and raiment for his body; this must be the first object, but it should be done to the end that he may have a sound mind in a sound body. And every one ought to provide food for his mind, viz. such things as are of intelligence and wisdom, to the end that it may thence be in a state to serve his fellow-citizens, human society, his country, and the church, thus the Lord. He who does this provides for his own good to eternity; whence it is plain that the first thing is to discover the end in view, for all other things look to this. The case is like that of a man who builds a house: he first lays the foundation; but the foundation is for the house, and the house is for habitation, he who believes that he is his own neighbor in the first place, is like him who regards the foundation as the end, not the house and habitation: when yet the habitation is the very first

and ultimate end, and the house with the foundation is only a medium to this end.

99. The end declares in what manner every one should be his own neighbor, and provide for himself first. If the end be to grow richer than others only for the sake of riches, or for the sake of pleasure, or for the sake of eminence, and the like, it is an evil end, and that man does not love his neighbor, but himself: but if the end be to procure himself riches, that he may be in a state of providing for the good of his fellow-citizens, of human society, of his country, and of the church, in like manner if he procure himself offices for the same end, he loves his neighbor. The end itself, for the sake of which he acts, constitutes the man; for the end is his love, forasmuch as every one has for a first and ultimate end, that which he loves above all things.

What has hitherto been said is concerning the neighbor; love towards him, or CHARITY, shall now be treated of.

100. It is believed by many, that love towards the neighbor consists in giving to the poor, in assisting the indigent, and in doing good to every one; but charity consists in acting prudently, and to the end that good may result. He who assists a poor or indigent villain does evil to his neighbor through him, for, through the assistance which he renders, he confirms him in evil, and supplies him with the means of doing evil to others: it is otherwise with him who gives support to the good.

101. But charity extends itself much more widely than to the poor and indigent; for charity consists in doing what is right in every work, and our duty in every office. If a judge does justice for the sake of justice, he exercises charity; if he punishes the guilty and absolves the innocent, he exercises charity, for thus he consults the welfare of his fellow-citizens, and of his country. The priest who teaches truth, and leads to good, for the sake of truth and good, exercises charity. But he who does such things for the sake of self and the world, does not exercise charity, because he does not love his neighbor, but himself.

102. The case is the same in all other instances, whether a man be in any office or not; as with children towards their parents, and with parents towards their children; with servants towards their masters, and with masters towards their servants; with subjects towards their king, and with a king towards his subjects: whoever of these does his duty from a principle of duty, and what is just from a principle of justice, exercises charity.

103. The reason why such things belong to the love towards the neighbor, or charity, is, because, as was said above, every man is our neighbor, but in a different manner. A less and greater society is more our neighbor; our country is still more our neighbor; the Lord's kingdom still more; and the Lord above all; and in a universal sense, good, which proceeds from the Lord, is our neighbor; consequently sincerity and justice are so too. Wherefore he who does any

good for the sake of good, and he who acts sincerely and justly for the sake of sincerity and justice, loves his neighbor and exercises charity; for he does so from the love of what is good, sincere, and just, and consequently from the love of those in whom good, sincerity, and justice are.

104. Charity therefore is an internal affection, from which man wills to do good, and this without remuneration; the delight of his life consists in doing it. With them who do good from internal affection, there is charity in every thing which they think and speak, and which they will and do: it may be said that a man or angel, as to his interiors, is charity, when good is his neighbor. So widely does charity extend itself.

105. They who have the love of self and of the world for an end, cannot in any wise be in charity; they do not even know what charity is, and cannot at all comprehend that to will and do good to the neighbor without reward as an end, is heaven in man, and that there is in that affection a happiness as great as that of the angels of heaven, which is ineffable; for they believe, if they are deprived of the joy proceeding from the glory of honors and riches, that nothing of joy can be experienced any longer; when yet it is then that heavenly joy first begins, which infinitely transcends the other.

OF FAITH.

108. No man can know what faith is in its essence, unless he know what charity is, because where there is no charity there is no faith, forasmuch as charity makes one with faith as good does with truth. For what man loves or holds dear, this he esteems good, and what man believes, this he esteems truth; whence it is plain that there is a like union of charity and faith, as there is of good and truth; the quality of which union may appear from what has been said above concerning GOOD and TRUTH.

109. The union of charity and faith is also like that of will and understanding with man; for these are the two faculties which receive good and truth, the will receiving good and the understanding truth; thus, also, these two faculties receive charity and faith, forasmuch as good is of charity and truth is of faith. No one is ignorant that charity and faith reside with man, and in him, and forasmuch as they are with him and in him, they must be in his will and understanding, for all the life of man is therein, and from thence. Man has also memory, but this is only the outer court, where those things are collected together which are to enter into the understanding and the will: whence it is plain that there is a like union of charity and faith, as there is of will and understanding; the quality of which union may appear from what has been said above concerning WILL and UNDERSTANDING.

110. Charity conjoins itself with faith with man, when man wills that which he knows and perceives; to will is of charity, but to know and perceive is of faith. Faith enters into man, and becomes his, when he wills and loves that which he knows and perceives; otherwise it is without him.

111. Faith does not become faith with man, unless it become spiritual, and it does not become spiritual, unless it become of the love, and it then becomes of the love, when man loves to live truth and good, that is, to live according to those things which are commanded in the Word.

112. Faith is the affection of truth originating from willing truth because it is truth; and to will truth because it is truth is the very spiritual principle of man; for it is abstracted from the natural principle, which consists in willing truth not for the sake of truth, but for the sake of one's own glory, reputation or gain. Truth abstractedly from such things is spiritual, because it is from the Divine: that which proceeds from the Divine is spiritual, and this is conjoined to man by love, for love is spiritual conjunction.

113. Man may know, think, and understand much, but when he is left to himself alone, and meditates, he rejects from himself those things which do not agree with his love; and thus he rejects them also after the life of the body, when he is in the spirit, for that only remains in the spirit of man which has entered into his love: other things after death are regarded as foreign, and because they are not of his love he casts them out. It is said in the spirit of man, because man lives a spirit after death.

114. An idea concerning the good which is of charity, and concerning the truth which is of faith, may be formed from the light and heat of the sun. When the light which proceeds from the sun is conjoined to heat, as is the case in the time of spring and summer, then all the productions of the earth germinate and flourish; but when there is no heat in the light, as in the time of winter, then all the productions of the earth become torpid and die: the truth of faith is also spiritual light, and love is spiritual heat. Hence an idea may be formed concerning the man of the church, what his quality is when faith with him is conjoined to charity—that he is indeed as a garden and paradise; and what his quality is when faith with him is not conjoined to charity—that he is as a desert and earth covered with snow.

115. The confidence or trust, which is said to be of faith, and is called indeed saving faith, is not spiritual confidence or trust, but natural, when it is of faith alone. Spiritual confidence or trust has its essence and life from the good of love, but not from the truth of faith separate. The confidence of faith separate is dead; wherefore true confidence cannot be given with those, who lead an evil life: the confidence also of obtaining salvation on account of the Lord's merit with the Father, whatever a man's life may have been, is likewise not from truth. All those who are in

spiritual faith have confidence that they are saved by the Lord, for they believe that the Lord came into the world to give eternal life to those who believe, and live according to the precepts which He taught, and that He regenerates them, and renders them fit for heaven, and that He alone does this from pure mercy, without the aid of man.

116. To believe those things which the Word teaches, or which the doctrine of the church teaches, and not to live according to them, appears as if it were faith, and some also fancy that they are saved by it, but by this alone no one is saved, for it is persuasive faith, the quality of which shall now be declared.

117. Faith is persuasive, when the Word and the doctrine of the church are believed and loved, not for the sake of truth and of a life according to it, but for the sake of gain, honor, and the fame of erudition, as ends; wherefore they who are in that faith, do not look to the Lord and to heaven, but to themselves and the world. They who aspire after great things in the world, and covet many things, are in a stronger persuasive principle that what the doctrine of the church teaches is true, than they who do not aspire after great things and covet many things: the reason is, because the doctrine of the church is to the former only a medium to their own ends, and so far as the ends are coveted, so far the means are loved, and are also believed. But the case in itself is this: so far as any persons are in the fire of the loves of self and of the world, and from that fire speak, preach, and act, so far they are in the above persuasive principle, and then they know no other than that it is so: but when they are not in the fire of those loves, then they believe but little, and many not at all; whence it is evident, that persuasive faith is a faith of the mouth and not of the heart, and that in itself it is not faith.

118. They who are in persuasive faith do not know, from any internal illustration, whether the things which they teach be true or false; yea, neither do they care, provided they be believed by the vulgar; for they are in no affection of truth for the sake of truth. Wherefore they recede from faith, if they are deprived of honors and gains, provided their reputation be not endangered. For persuasive faith is not inwardly with man, but stands without, in the memory only, out of which it is taken when it is taught. Wherefore that faith with its truths vanishes after death; for then there remains only that faith which is inwardly in man, that is, which is rooted in good, thus which has become of the life.

119. They who are in persuasive faith are understood by these persons in Matthew: "Many will say to me in that day, Lord, Lord, have we not prophesied by Thy name, and by Thy name cast out demons, and in Thy name done many virtues? but then I will confess to them, I have not known you, ye workers of iniquity." vii. 22, 23. Also in Luke: "Then will ye begin to say, We have eaten before Thee, and have drunk, and Thou hast taught in our streets; but He will say, I say to you, I have not known you whence you are; depart from Me, all ye workers of iniquity." xiii. 26,27. They are understood also by the five foolish virgins who had no oil in their lamps, in Matthew: "At length came those virgins, saying, Lord, Lord, open to us; but He answering will say, Verily I say unto you, I have not known you." xxv. 11, 12: oil in lamps is the good of love in faith.

OF PIETY.

123. It is believed by many, that spiritual life, or the life which leads to heaven, consists in *piety,* in *external sanctity,* and in the *renunciation of the world:* but piety without charity, and external sanctity without internal sanctity, and a renunciation of the world without a life in the world, do not constitute spiritual life: but piety from charity, external sanctity from internal sanctity, and a renunciation of the world with a life in the world, constitute it.

124. Piety consists in thinking and speaking piously, in spending much time in prayer, in behaving humbly at that time, in frequenting temples and attending devoutly to the preaching there, in frequently every year receiving the sacrament of the supper, and in performing the other parts of worship according to the ordinances of the church. But the life of charity consists in willing well and doing well to our neighbor, in acting in all our works from justice and equity, and from good and truth, and in like manner in every office; in a word, the life of charity consists in performing uses. Divine worship primarily consists in this life, but secondarily in the former; wherefore he who separates one from the other, that is, who lives the life of piety, and not that of charity at the same time, does not worship God. He thinks indeed of God, but not from God, but from himself; for he thinks of himself continually, and not at all of his neighbor; and if he does think of his neighbor, he regards him as vile, if he be not of such a quality also. He likewise thinks of heaven as a reward, whence his mind entertains the idea of merit, and also the love of self, together with a contempt or neglect of uses, and thus of his neighbor; and at the same time he cherishes a belief that he is blameless. Hence it may appear that the life of piety, separate from the life of charity, is not the spiritual life which should be in divine worship. Compare Matt. vi. 7,8.

125. External sanctity is like such piety, and is not holy with man unless his internal be holy; for such as man is as to his internal, such he also is as to his external, as this proceeds from the former as action does from its spirit; wherefore external sanctity without internal sanctity is natural and not spiritual. Hence it is that external sanctity is found with the evil as well as with the good; and they who place the whole of worship therein are for the most part void; that is, without knowledges of good and truth. And yet goods and truths are the real sanctities which are to be known, believed and loved, because they are from the Divine, and thus the Divine is in them. Internal sanctity, therefore, consists in loving good and truth for the sake of good and truth, and justice and

sincerity for the sake of justice and sincerity. So far also as man thus loves them, so far he is spiritual, and his worship too, for so far also he is willing to know them and to do them; but so far as man does not thus love them, so far he is natural, and his worship too, and so far also he is not willing to know them and do them. External worship without internal may be compared with the life of the respiration without the life of the heart; but external worship from internal may be compared with the life of the respiration conjoined to the life of the heart.

126. But to proceed to what relates to the renunciation of the world. It is believed by many, that to renounce the world, and to live in the spirit and not in the flesh, is to reject worldly things, which are chiefly riches and honors; to be continually engaged in pious meditation concerning God, concerning salvation, and concerning eternal life; to spend one's life in prayer, in the reading of the Word and pious books; and also to afflict one's self: but this is not renouncing the world; but to renounce the world is to love God and to love the neighbor; and God is loved when man lives according to His commandments, and the neighbor is loved when man performs uses. In order, therefore, that man may receive the life of heaven, it is necessary that he should live in the world, and in offices and business there. A life abstracted from worldly things is a life of thought and faith separate from the life of love and charity, in which life the principle of willing good and doing good to the neighbor perishes. And when this perishes, spiritual life is as a house without a foundation, which either sinks down successively into the ground, or becomes full of chinks and openings, or totters till it falls.

127. That to do good is to worship the Lord, appears from the Lord's words. "Every one who heareth my words and doeth them, I will liken to a prudent man who built a house upon a rock; but he who heareth my words and doeth them not, I will liken to a foolish man who built a house upon the sand, or upon the ground without a foundation," Matt. vii. 24 to 27; Luke vi. 47, 48, 49.

128. Hence now it is manifest, that a life of piety is of value, and is acceptable to the Lord, so far as a life of charity is conjoined to it; for this is the primary, and such as the quality of this is, such is that of the former. Also, that external sanctity is of value, and is acceptable to the Lord, so far as it proceeds from internal sanctity; for such as the quality of this is, such is that of the former. And also, that the renunciation of the world is of value, and is acceptable to the Lord, so far as it is practised in the world; for they renounce the world who remove the love of self and the world, and act justly and sincerely in every office, in every business, and in every work, from an interior, thus from a celestial origin; which origin dwells in that life when man acts

well, sincerely, and justly, because it is according to the divine laws.

OF CONSCIENCE.

130. Conscience is formed with man from the religious principle in which he is, according to its reception inwardly in himself.

131. Conscience, with the man of the church, is formed by the truths of faith from the Word, or from doctrine out of the Word, according to their reception in the heart; for when man knows the truths of faith, and apprehends them in his own manner, and then wills them and does them, he acquires conscience. Reception in the heart is reception in the will, for the will of man is what is called the heart. Hence it is that they who have conscience, speak from the heart the things which they speak, and do from the heart the things which they do: their mind also is undivided, for according to that which they understand and believe to be true and good they do.

132. A more perfect conscience can be given with those who are enlightened in the truths of faith more than others, and who are in a clear perception above others, than with those who are less enlightened, and who are in obscure perception.

133. The real spiritual life of man resides in a true conscience, for his faith, conjoined to his charity, is therein; wherefore, with those who are possessed of it, to act from conscience is to act from their own spiritual life, and to act contrary to conscience is, with them, to act contrary to their own spiritual life. Hence it is that they are in the tranquility of peace, and in internal blessedness, when they act according to conscience, and in intranquility and pain, when they act contrary to it: this pain is what is called remorse of conscience.

134. Man has a conscience of what is good, and a conscience of what is just: the conscience of what is good is the conscience of the internal man, and the conscience of what is just is the conscience of the external man. The conscience of what is good consists in acting according to the precepts of faith from internal affection, but the conscience of what is just consists in acting according to civil and moral laws from external affection. They who have the conscience of what is good, have also the conscience of what is just; and they who have only the conscience of what is just, are in a faculty of receiving the conscience of what is good; and they also do receive it when they are instructed.

135. Conscience, with those who are in charity towards the neighbor, is the conscience of truth, because it is formed by the faith of truth; but with those who are in love to the Lord, it is the conscience of good, because it is formed by the love of truth. The conscience of these is a superior conscience, and is called the perception of truth from good. They who have the conscience of truth, are of the Lord's spiritual kingdom; but they who have the superior

conscience, which is called perception, are of the Lord's celestial kingdom.

136. But let examples illustrate what conscience is. If a man be in possession of another man's goods, whilst the other is ignorant of it, and thus can retain them without fear of the law, or of the loss of honor and reputation, and he still restores them to the other, because they are not his own, he has conscience, for he does what is good for the sake of what is good, and what is just for the sake of what is just. Again, if a person has it in his power to obtain an office, but knows that another, who also desires it, would be more useful to his country, and gives way to him, for the sake of the good of his country, he has a good conscience. So in other cases.

137. From these instances it may be concluded, what quality they are of who have not conscience; they are known from the opposite. Thus, they who for the sake of any gain make what is unjust appear as just, and what is evil appear as good, and *vice versa,* have not conscience. Neither do they know what conscience is, and if they are instructed what it is, they do not believe; and some are not willing to know. Such is the quality of those, who, in all their actions, have respect only to themselves and the world.

138. They who have not received conscience in the world, cannot receive it in the other life; thus they cannot be saved. The reason is, because they have no plane into which heaven, that is, the Lord through heaven, may flow in, and by which He may operate, and lead them to Himself. For conscience is the plane and receptacle of the influx of heaven.

OF FREEDOM.

141. All freedom is of love, for what man loves, this he does freely; hence also all freedom is of the will, for what man loves, this he also wills; and forasmuch as love and the will constitute the life of man, so also does freedom. From these considerations it may appear what freedom is, namely, that it is that which is of the love and the will, and thence of the life of man: hence it is, that what a man does from freedom, appears to him as if he did it from his own proprium.

142. To do evil from freedom, appears as if it were freedom, but it is bondage, because that freedom is from the love of self and from the love of the world, and these loves are from hell. Such freedom is actually turned into bondage after death, for the man who has been in such freedom then becomes a vile servant in hell. But to do good from freedom is freedom itself, because it proceeds from love to the Lord and from love towards the neighbor, and these loves are from heaven. This freedom also remains after death, and then becomes freedom indeed, for the man who has been in such freedom, becomes in heaven like a son of the house. This the Lord thus teaches: "Every one that doeth sin is the servant of sin; the servant abideth not in the house forever: the son abideth forever; if the Son shall have made you free, you shall be truly free," John viii. 34, 35, 36. Now, forasmuch as all good is from the Lord, and all

evil from hell, it follows, that freedom consists in being led by the Lord, and slavery in being led by hell.

143. That man has the liberty of thinking what is evil and false, and also of doing it, so far as the laws do not withhold him, is in order that he may be capable of being reformed; for goods and truths are to be implanted in his love and will, so that they may become of his life, and this cannot be done unless he have the liberty of thinking what is evil and false as well as what is good and true. This liberty is given to every man by the Lord, and so far as he does not love evil and the false, so far, when he thinks what is good and true, the Lord implants them in his love and will, consequently in his life, and thus reforms him. What is inseminated in freedom, this also remains, but what is inseminated in a state of compulsion, this does not remain, because what is from compulsion is not from the will of the man, but from the will of him who compels. Hence also it is, that worship from freedom is pleasing to the Lord, but not worship from compulsion; for worship from freedom is worship from love, but worship from compulsion is not so.

144. The liberty of doing good, and the liberty of doing evil, though they appear alike in the external form, are as different and distant from each other as heaven and hell are: the liberty of doing good also is from heaven, and is called heavenly liberty; but the liberty of doing evil is from hell, and is called infernal liberty; so far, likewise, as man is in the one, so far he is not in the other, for no man can serve two lords, Matt. vi. 24; which also appears from hence, that they who are in infernal liberty believe that it is slavery and compulsion not to be allowed to will evil and think what is false at their pleasure, whereas they who are in heavenly liberty abhor willing evil and thinking what is false, and would be tormented if they were compelled to do so.

145. Forasmuch as acting from freedom appears to man like acting from his own proprium, therefore heavenly freedom may also be called the heavenly proprium, and infernal freedom may be called the infernal proprium. The infernal proprium is that into which man is born, and this is evil; but the heavenly proprium is that into which man is reformed, and this is good.

146. Hence it may appear what *Free-will* is; that it consists in doing good from choice or will, and that they are in that freedom who are led by the Lord; and they are led by the Lord who love good and truth for the sake of good and truth.

147. Man may know what is the quality of the liberty in which he is, from the delight which he feels when he thinks, speaks, acts, hears, and sees; for all delight is of love.

OF MERIT.

150. They who do good with a view to merit, do not do good from the love of good, but from the love of

reward, for he who wills to have merit, wills to be rewarded; they who do thus, regard and place their delight in the reward, and not in good; wherefore they are not spiritual, but natural.

151. To do good, which is good, must be from the love of good, thus for the sake of good. They who are in that love are not willing to hear of merit, for they love to do, and perceive satisfaction therein, and, on the other hand, they are sorrowful if it be believed that what they do is for the sake of any thing of themselves. The case herein is nearly the same as with those who do good to their friends for the sake of friendship; to a brother for the sake of brother-hood, to wife and children for the sake of wife and children, to their country for the sake of their country, thus from friendship and love. They who think well, also say and insist, that they do not do good for the sake of themselves, but for the sake of them to whom the good is done.

152. They who do good for the sake of reward do not do good from the Lord, but from themselves, for they regard themselves in the first place, inasmuch as they regard their own good; and the good of their neighbor, which is the good of their fellow-citizens, of human society, of their country, and of the church, they regard no otherwise than as means to this end. Hence it is, that the good of the love of self and of the world lies concealed in the good of merit and that good is from man and not from the Lord, and all good which is from man is not good; yea, so far as self and the world lies concealed in it, it is evil.

153. Genuine charity and genuine faith disclaim all merit, for good itself is the delight of charity, and truth itself is the delight of faith; wherefore they who are in that charity and faith know what good not meritorious is, but not they who are not in charity and faith.

154. That good is not to be done for the sake of reward, the Lord himself teaches in Luke: "If ye love those who love you what grace have ye, for sinners do the same: rather love your enemies, and do good, and lend, hoping for nothing; then shall your reward be great, and ye shall be the sons of the Most High," vi. 32, 33, 34, 35. That man cannot do good that is good from himself, the Lord also teaches in John: "A man cannot take any thing, unless it be given him from heaven," iii. 27; and in another place, "Jesus said, I am the vine, ye are the branches: as the branch cannot bear fruit from itself, unless it shall abide in the vine, so neither can ye unless ye shall abide in Me: He who abideth in Me and I in him, he beareth much fruit, for except from Me ye cannot do any thing," xv. 4 to 8.

155. Forasmuch as all good and truth is from the Lord, and nothing of them from man, and forasmuch as good from man is not good, it follows that merit belongs to no man, but to the Lord alone; the merit of the Lord consists in this, that from His own proper power He has saved the human race, and also, that He saves those who do good from Him. Hence it is that in the Word, he is called just to whom the merit and justice of the Lord are ascribed, and he is called unjust to whom are ascribed his own justice and the merit of self.

156. The delight itself, which is in the love of doing good without regard to reward, is a reward which remains to eternity, for heaven and eternal happiness are insinuated into that good by the Lord.

157. To think and believe that they who do good will come into heaven, and also that good is to be done in order that they may come into heaven, is not to regard reward as an end, nor yet to place merit in words; for even they who do good from the Lord think and believe so, but they who thus think, believe and do, and are not in the love of good for the sake of good, have regard to reward as an end, and place merit in works.

OF REPENTANCE AND THE REMISSION OF SINS.

159. He who would be saved must confess his sins, and do the work of repentance.

160. To *confess sins*, is to know evils, to see them in ourselves, to acknowledge them, to make ourselves guilty, and to condemn ourselves on account of them. This, when it is done before God, is the confession of sins.

161. *To do the work of repentance*, is to desist from sins after a man has thus confessed them, and from an humble heart has made supplication for remission, and to live a new life according to the precepts of charity and faith.

162. He who only acknowledges generally that he is a sinner, and makes himself guilty of all evils, and yet does not explore himself, that is, see his own evils, makes confession indeed, but not the confession of repentance; he, forasmuch as he does not know his own evils, lives afterwards as he did before.

163. He who lives the life of charity and faith does the work of repentance daily; he reflects upon the evils which are with him, he acknowledges them, he guards against them, he supplicates the Lord for help. For man of himself continually lapses towards evil, but he is continually raised by the Lord, and led to good. Such is the state of those who are in good; but they who are in evil lapse continually, and are also continually elevated by the Lord, but are only withdrawn from falling into the most grievous evils, to which of themselves they tend with all their power.

164. The man who explores himself in order to do the work of repentance, must explore his thoughts and the intentions of his will, and must there examine what he would do if it were permitted him, that is, if he were not afraid of the laws, and of the loss of reputation, honor and gain. There the evils of man reside, and the evils which he does in the body are all from thence. They who do not explore the evils of

their thought and will, cannot do the work of repentance, for they think and will afterwards as they did before, and yet to will evils is to do them. This is self-examination.

165. Repentance of the mouth and not of the life is not repentance, and sins are not remitted by means of repentance of the mouth, but by repentance of the life. Sins are indeed continually remitted to man by the Lord, for He is mercy itself, but still they adhere to man, however he may suppose that they are remitted; nor are they removed from him but by a life according to the precepts of true faith. So far as he lives according to those precepts, so far sins are removed; and so far as they are removed, so far they are remitted.

166. It is supposed that sins are wiped away, or are washed off, as filth is by water, when they are remitted; but sins are not wiped away, but they are removed; that is, man is withheld from them when he is kept in good by the Lord; and when he is kept in good, it appears as if he were without them, thus as if they were wiped away; and so far as man is reformed, so far he is capable of being kept in good. How man is reformed will be shown in the following doctrinal on regeneration. He who supposes that sins are in any other manner remitted, is much deceived.

167. The signs that sins are remitted, that is, removed, are these which follow. They whose sins are remitted, perceive a delight in worshiping God for the sake of God, and in serving their neighbor for the sake of their neighbor, thus in doing good for the sake of good, and in speaking truth for the sake of truth; they are unwilling to claim merit by any thing of charity and faith; they shun and are averse to evils, as enmities, hatreds, revenges, adulteries, and the very thoughts of such things with intention. But the signs that sins are not remitted, that is, removed, are these which follow. They whose sins are not remitted, worship God not for the sake of God, but serve their neighbor not for the sake of their neighbor, thus they do not do good and speak truth for the sake of good and truth, but for the sake of themselves and the world; they wish to claim merit by their deeds; they perceive nothing undelightful in evils, as in enmity, in hatred, in revenge, in adulteries; and from these evils they think of them in all licentiousness.

168. The repentance which takes place in a free state is of avail, but that which takes place in a state of compulsion is of no avail. States of compulsion are states of sickness, states of dejection of mind in consequence of misfortune, states of imminent death, as also every state of fear which takes away the use of reason. He who is evil, and in a state of compulsion promises repentance, and also does good, when he comes into a free state returns to his former life of evil; the case is otherwise with one who is good.

169. After a man has explored himself, and acknowledged his sins, and done the work of repentance, he must remain constant in good even to the end of life. For if he afterwards relapses into his former evil life, and

embraces it, he commits profanation, for he then conjoins evil with good; whence his latter state becomes worse than his former, according to the words of the Lord: "When the unclean spirit goes out from a man, he walks through dry places, seeking rest, but doth not find; then he says, I will return into my house whence I went out; and when he comes and finds it void, and swept, and adorned for him, then he goes away, and adjoins to himself seven other spirits worse than himself, and, entering in, they dwell there, *and the latter things of the man become worse than the first*," Matt. xii. 43, 44, 45.

OF REGENERATION.

173. He who doth not receive spiritual life, that is, who is not begotten anew by the Lord, cannot come into heaven; which the Lord teaches in John, "Verily, verily, I say unto thee, except any one be begotten again, he cannot see the kingdom of God," iii. 3.

174. Man is not born of his parents into spiritual life, but into natural life. Spiritual life consists in loving God above all things, and in loving his neighbor as himself, and this according to the precepts of faith, which the Lord taught in the Word. But natural life consists in loving ourselves and the world more than our neighbor, yea, more than God Himself.

175. Every man is born of his parents into the evils of the love of self and of the world; for every evil, which by habit has acquired as it were a nature, is derived into the offspring; thus it descends successively from parents, from grand-fathers, and from great-grandfathers, in a long series backwards; whence the derivation of evil at length becomes so great, that the whole of man's proper life is nothing else but evil. This continual derivation of evil is not broken and altered, except by the life of faith and charity from the Lord.

176. Man continually inclines to, and lapses into, what he derives from his hereditary principle: hence he confirms with himself that evil, and also superadds more of himself. These evils are altogether contrary to spiritual life, and destroy it; wherefore, unless man receives new life, which is spiritual life, from the Lord, thus unless he is conceived anew, is born anew, is educated anew, that is, is created anew, he is damned, for he wills nothing else, and thence thinks nothing else, but what is of self and the world, in like manner as they do who are in hell.

177. No man can be regenerated unless he knows such things as belong to the new life, that is, to spiritual life; and the things which belong to the new life, which is the spiritual life, are truths which are to be believed and goods which are to be done; the former are of faith, the latter of charity. These things no one can know from himself, for man apprehends only those things which are obvious to the senses, from which he procures to himself a light which is called natural light, by virtue of which he sees nothing else than what relates to the world and to self, but not the things which relate to heaven and to God. These he must learn from revelation; as that the Lord, who is

God from eternity, came into the world to save the human race; that He has all power in heaven and in earth; that the all of faith and the all of charity, thus all truth and good, is from Him; that there is a heaven, and that there is a hell; and that man is to live to eternity in heaven if he have done well, in hell if he have done evil.

178. These and many other things belong to faith, and ought to be known by the man who is to be regenerated, for he who knows them, may think them, afterwards will them, and lastly do them, and so have new life, whilst he who does not know that the Lord is the Saviour of the human race, cannot have faith in Him, love Him, and thus do good for the sake of Him. He who does not know that all good is from Him, cannot think that his own salvation is from Him, still less can he will it to be so, thus he cannot live from Him. He who does not know that there is a hell and that there is a heaven, nor that there is eternal life, cannot even think about the life of heaven, nor apply himself to receive it, and so in other cases.

179. Every one has an internal man and an external man; the internal is what is called the spiritual man, and the external is what is called the natural man, and each is to be regenerated, that the man may be regenerated. With the man who is not regenerated, the external or natural man rules, and the internal serves; but with the man who is regenerated, the internal or spiritual man rules, and the external serves. Whence it is manifest that the order of life is inverted with man from his birth, namely, that that principle serves which ought to rule, and that that principle rules which ought to serve. In order that man may be saved, this order must be inverted; and this inversion can by no means exist, but by regeneration from the Lord.

180. What it is for the internal man to rule and the external to serve, and *vice versa*, may be illustrated thus:—If a man places all his good in voluptuousness, in gain, and in pride, and has delight in hatred and revenge, and inwardly in himself seeks for reasons which confirm such evils, then the external man rules and the internal serves. But when a man perceives good and delight in thinking and willing well, sincerely, and justly, and in outwardly speaking and doing in like manner, then the internal man rules and the external serves.

181. The internal man is first regenerated by the Lord, and afterwards the external, and the latter by means of the former. For the internal man is regenerated by thinking those things which are of faith and charity, but the external by a life according to them. This is understood by the words of the Lord, "Unless any one be begotten of water and the spirit, he cannot enter into the kingdom of God," John iii. 5. Water, in the spiritual sense, is the truth of faith, and the spirit is a life according to it.

182. The man who is regenerated, is, as to his internal man, in heaven, and is an angel there with the angels, among whom he also comes after death; he is then able to live the life of heaven, to love the Lord, to love his neighbor, to understand truth, to relish good, and to perceive the blessedness thence derived.

OF TEMPTATION.

187. They alone who are regenerated undergo spiritual temptations; for spiritual temptations are pains of the mind, induced by evil spirits, with those who are in goods and truths. Whilst these spirits excite the evils which are with such persons, there arises an anxiety which is that of temptation; man knows not whence it comes, because he is unacquainted with this its origin.

188. For there are evil spirits and good spirits attendant on every man; the evil spirits are in his evils, and the good spirits are in his goods. When the evil spirits approach, they draw forth his evils, and the good spirits, on the contrary, draw forth his goods, whence collision and combat take place, from which the man perceives an interior anxiety, which is temptation. Hence it is plain that temptations are not from heaven, but are induced by hell, which is also according to the faith of the church, which teaches that God tempts no one.

189. Interior anxieties also take place with those who are not in goods and truths, but these are natural anxieties, not spiritual ones; they are distinguished by this, that natural anxieties have worldly things for their objects, but spiritual anxieties have heavenly things for their objects.

190. In temptations, the dominion of good over evil, or of evil over good, is what is contended for. The evil which desires to have the dominion, is in the natural or external man, and the good is in the spiritual or internal; if evil conquers, then the natural man has dominion, but if good conquers, then the spiritual man has dominion.

191. Those combats are fought by means of the truths of faith, which are from the Word. It is from these that man must fight against evils and falses; for if he combats from any other principles than these, he does not conquer, because the Lord is not in any other principles. Forasmuch as the combat is fought by means of the truths of faith, therefore man is not admitted into that combat before he is in the knowledges of good and truth, and has thence obtained some spiritual life; wherefore those combats do not take place with man until he has arrived at years of maturity.

192. If man falls in temptation, his state after it becomes worse than his state before it, inasmuch as evil has thereby acquired power over good, and the false over truth.

193. Inasmuch as at this day faith is rare because there is no charity, the church being at its end, therefore few at this day are admitted into any spiritual tempta-

tions; hence it is that it is scarcely known what they are and to what end they conduce.

194. Temptations conduce to acquire for good, dominion over evil, and for the truth, dominion over the false; also to confirm truths, and to conjoin them to goods, and at the same time to disperse evils and the falses thence derived. They conduce likewise to open the internal spiritual man, and to subject the natural thereto, as also to break the loves of self and the world, and to subdue the concupiscences which proceed from them. When these things are effected, man acquires illustration and perception respecting what truth and good are, and what the false and evil are; whence man obtains intelligence and wisdom, which afterwards continually increase.

195. The Lord alone combats for man in temptations; if man does not believe that the Lord alone combats and conquers for him, he then only undergoes an external temptation, which does not conduce to his salvation.

OF BAPTISM.

202. Baptism was instituted for a sign that the man belongs to the church, and for a memorial that he is to be regenerated; for the washing of baptism signifies nothing else than spiritual washing, which is regeneration.

203. All regeneration is effected by the Lord, by means of the truths of faith and of a life according to them; therefore baptism testifies that the man is of the church, and that he is capable of being regenerated; for in the church, the Lord, who regenerates, is acknowledged, and therein is the Word, which contains the truths of faith, by means of which regeneration is effected.

204. This the Lord teaches in John, "Except a man be begotten of water and the spirit, he cannot enter into the kingdom of God," iii.5; water, in the spiritual sense, is the truth of faith from the Word: the spirit is a life according to it, and to be begotten is to be regenerated thereby.

205. Forasmuch as every one who is regenerated also undergoes temptations, which are spiritual combats against evils and falses, therefore by the waters of baptism those temptations are also signified.

206. Since baptism is for a sign and for a memorial of those things, therefore a man may be baptized when an infant, and if he be not baptized then, he may be baptized when he is an adult.

207. Let it be known therefore to those who are baptized, that baptism itself gives neither faith nor salvation, but that it testifies that they will receive faith, and that they will be saved, if they are regenerated.

208. Hence it may appear what is understood by the Lord's words in Mark, "He who shall believe and be baptized shall be saved, but he who shall not believe shall be condemned," xvi. 16; he who shall believe is he who acknowledges the Lord, and receives divine truths from Him by means of the Word; he who shall

be baptized is he who by means of those truths is regenerated by the Lord.

OF THE HOLY SUPPER.

210. The Holy Supper was instituted by the Lord, that by means thereof there may be a conjunction of the church with heaven, thus with the Lord; it is therefore the most holy thing of worship.

211. But in what manner conjunction is effected by it is not apprehended by those who do not know any thing concerning the internal or spiritual sense of the Word, for they do not think beyond the external sense, which is the sense of the letter. From the internal or spiritual sense of the Word it is known what is signified by body and blood, and what by bread and wine, also what is signified by eating.

212. In that sense, the body or flesh of the Lord is the good of love, as is the bread likewise; and the blood of the Lord is the good of faith, as is the wine likewise; and eating is appropriation and conjunction. The angels, who are attendant on man when he receives the sacrament of the supper, understand those things in no other manner; for they perceive all things spiritually. Hence it is that a holy principle of love and a holy principle of faith then flows in with man from the angels, thus through heaven from the Lord; hence there is conjunction.

213. From these considerations it is evident, that when man takes the bread, which is the body, he is conjoined to the Lord by means of the good of love to Him from Him; and when he takes the wine, which is the blood, he is conjoined to the Lord by means of the good of faith in Him from Him. But it is to be noted, that conjunction with the Lord by means of the sacrament of the supper is effected solely with those who are in the good of love to, and faith in, the Lord from the Lord; with these there is conjunction by means of the holy supper; with others there is presence, but not conjunction.

214. Besides, the holy supper includes and comprehends all the divine worship instituted in the Israelitish church; for the burnt-offerings and sacrifices, in which the worship of that church principally consisted, were called, in a single word, bread; hence also the holy supper is its completion.

OF THE RESURRECTION.

223. Man is so created, that as to his internal he cannot die, for he is capable of believing in God, and also of loving God, and thus of being conjoined to God by faith and love; and to be conjoined to God is to live to eternity.

224. This internal is with every man who is born; his external is that by means of which he brings into effect the things which are of faith and love. The internal is what is called the spirit, and the external is what is called the body. The external, which is called the body, is accommodated to uses in the natural world; this is rejected when man dies; but the internal, which is called the spirit, is accommodated to uses in the spiritual world; this does not die. This

internal is then a good spirit and an angel, if the man had been good when in the world, but an evil spirit, if the man had been evil when in the world.

225. The spirit of man, after the death of the body, appears in the spiritual world in a human form, altogether as in the world; he enjoys also the faculty of seeing, of hearing, of speaking, of feeling, as in the world; and he is endowed with every faculty of thinking, of willing, and of acting as in the world. In a word, he is a man as to all things and every particular, except that he is not encompassed with that gross body which he had in the world; he leaves that when he dies, nor does he ever re-assume it.

226. This continuation of life is what is understood by the resurrection. The reason why men believe that they are not to rise again before the last judgment, when also every visible object of the world is to perish, is because they have not understood the Word; and because sensual men place their life in the body, and believe that unless this were to live again, it would be all over with the man.

227. The life of man after death is the life of his love and the life of his faith, hence such as his love and such as his faith had been, when he lived in the world, such his life remains to eternity. It is the life of hell with those who have loved themselves and the world above all things, and the life of heaven with those who have loved God above all things and their neighbors as themselves. The latter are they that have faith, but the former are they that have not faith. The life of heaven is what is called eternal life, and the life of hell is what is called spiritual death.

228. That man lives after death, the Word teaches, as that God is not the God of the dead, but of the living, Matt. xxii. 31; that Lazarus after death was taken up into heaven, but the rich man cast into hell, Luke xvi. 22, 23, and the following verses; that Abraham, Isaac, and Jacob are there, Matt. viii. 11; chap. xxii. 31, 32; Luke xx. 37, 38; that Jesus said to the thief, To-day shalt thou be with me in Paradise, Luke xxiii. 43.

OF HEAVEN AND HELL.

230. There are two things which constitute the life of man's spirit, love and faith; love constituting the life of his will, and faith the life of his understanding. The love of good, and the faith of truth thence derived, constitute the life of heaven; and the love of evil, and the faith of what is false thence derived, constitute the life of hell.

231. Love to the Lord and love towards the neighbor constitute heaven, and so does faith, so far as it has life from those loves; and forasmuch as each of those loves and the faith thence derived is from the Lord, it is evident from hence that the Lord constitutes heaven.

232. Heaven is with every one according to his reception of love and faith from the Lord; and they who receive heaven from the Lord whilst they live in the world, come into heaven after death.

233. They who receive heaven from the Lord are they who have heaven in themselves; for heaven is in man, as the Lord also teaches: "They shall not say, The kingdom of God, lo it is here! or lo there! for behold the kingdom of God is in you," Luke xvii. 21.

234. Heaven with man resides in his internal, thus in willing and thinking from love and faith, and thence in his external, which consists in acting and speaking from love and faith. But it does not reside in the external without being in the internal; for all hypocrites are capable of acting and speaking well, but not of willing well and thinking well.

235. When man comes into the other life, which takes place immediately after death, it is then manifest whether heaven is in him, but not whilst he lives in the world. For in the world the external appears, and not the internal; but in the other life the internal is made manifest, because man then lives as to his spirit.

236. Eternal happiness, which is also called heavenly joy, is imparted to those who are in love and faith to the Lord, from the Lord; that love and that faith have in them that joy, into which the man who has heaven in himself comes after death; in the mean time it lies stored up in his internal. In the heavens there is a communion of all goods; the peace, the intelligence, the wisdom, and the happiness of all, are communicated to every one therein, yet to every one according to his reception of love and faith from the Lord. Hence it appears how great peace, intelligence, wisdom and happiness are in heaven.

237. As love to the Lord, and love towards our neighbor, constitute the life of heaven with man, so the love of self and the love of the world, when they reign, constitute the life of hell with him, for these latter loves are opposite to the former. Wherefore they with whom the loves of self and of the world reign, are incapable of receiving any thing from heaven; but the things which they receive are from hell; for whatever a man loves, and whatever he believes, is either from heaven or from hell.

238. They with whom the loves of self and of the world reign, do not know what heaven and the happiness of heaven are; and it appears incredible to them that happiness should be given in any other loves than in those, when yet the happiness of heaven only enters, so far as those loves, as ends, are removed. The happiness which succeeds on their removal is so great, that it exceeds all human comprehension.

239. The life of man cannot be changed after death, but remains then such as it had been in the world; for the whole spirit of man is such as his love is, and infernal love cannot be transcribed into heavenly love, because they are opposite: this is understood by the words of Abraham to the rich man in hell: "There is a great gulf between us and you, so that they who would pass to you cannot, neither can they pass from

thence to us." Luke xvi. 26. Hence it is plain that they who come into hell remain there to eternity, and that they who come into heaven remain there to eternity.

OF THE CHURCH.

241. That which constitutes heaven with man, also constitutes the church; for as love and faith constitute heaven, so also love and faith constitute the church. Hence, from what has been said before concerning heaven, it is evident what the church is.

242. Where the Lord is acknowledged, and where the Word is, the church is said to be; for the essentials of the church are love to, and faith in, the Lord from the Lord; and the Word teaches how man is to live, in order that he may receive love and faith from the Lord.

243. In order that there may be a church, there must be doctrine from the Word, since without doctrine the Word is not understood. But doctrine alone does not constitute the church with man, but a life according to it; whence it follows that faith alone does not constitute the church, but the life of faith, which is charity. Genuine doctrine is the doctrine of charity and of faith together, and not the doctrine of faith without that of charity; for the doctrine of charity and of faith together, is the doctrine of life, but not the doctrine of faith without the doctrine of charity.

244. They who are without the church, and still acknowledge one God, and live according to their religious principles in a certain charity towards their neighbor, are in communion with those who are of the church, for no one, who believes in God and lives well, is damned. Hence it is evident that the church of the Lord is every where in the universal globe, although it is specifically where the Lord is acknowledged, and where there is the Word.

245. Every one with whom the church is, is saved, but every one with whom the church is not, is condemned.

OF THE SACRED SCRIPTURE, OR THE WORD.

249. Without a revelation from the Divine, man cannot know any thing concerning eternal life, nor even any thing concerning God, and still less any thing concerning love to, and faith in Him: for man is born into mere ignorance, and must therefore learn every thing from worldly things, from which he must form his understanding. He is also born hereditarily into every evil which proceeds from the love of self and of the world; the delights from thence prevail continually, and suggest such things as are diametrically contrary to the Divine. Hence it is that man knows nothing concerning eternal life; wherefore there must necessarily be a revelation to communicate such knowledge.

250. That the evils of the love of self and of the world induce such ignorance concerning the things which are of eternal life, appears manifestly from those within the church, who, although they know from revelation that there is a God, that there is a heaven and a hell, that there is eternal life, and that that life is to be acquired by means of the good of love and faith, still lapse into denial concerning those subjects, as well the learned as the unlearned. Hence it is further evident how great ignorance would prevail, if there were no revelation.

251. Since therefore man lives after death, and then lives to eternity, and a life awaits him according to his love and faith, it follows that the Divine, out of love towards the human race, has revealed such things as may lead to that life, and conduce to man's salvation. What the Divine has revealed, is with us the Word.

252. The Word, forasmuch as it is a revelation from the Divine, is divine in all and every particular part; for what is from the Divine cannot be otherwise. What is from the Divine descends through the heavens even to man; wherefore in the heavens it is accommodated to the wisdom of the angels who are there, and on earth it is accommodated to the apprehension of the men who are there. Wherefore in the Word there is an internal sense, which is spiritual, for the angels, and an external sense, which is natural, for men; hence it is that the conjunction of heaven with man, is effected by means of the Word.

253. No others understand the genuine sense of the Word but they who are enlightened; and they only are enlightened who are in love to, and faith in, the Lord; for their interiors are elevated by the Lord into the light of heaven.

254. The Word in the letter cannot be understood, but by means of doctrine drawn from the Word by one who is enlightened; for the literal sense thereof is accommodated to the apprehension even of simple men, wherefore doctrine drawn from the Word must serve them for a lamp.

OF PROVIDENCE.

267. The government of the Lord in the heavens and in the earths is called Providence; and forasmuch as all the good of love and all the truth of faith, which give salvation, are from Him, and nothing at all of them from man, it is evident that the Divine Providence of the Lord is in all and singular the things which conduce to the salvation of the human race. This the Lord thus teaches in John: "I am the way, the truth, and the life," xiv. 6; and in another place, "As the branch cannot bear fruit of itself, unless it shall abide in the vine, so neither can ye, unless ye shall abide in Me; except from Me ye cannot do any thing," xv. 4, 5.

268. The Divine Providence of the Lord extends to the most singular things of the life of man; for there is only one fountain of life, which is the Lord, from whom we are, live, and act.

269. They who think from worldly things concerning the Divine Providence, conclude from them that it is only universal, and that singulars appertain to man. But such persons do not know the arcana of heaven, for they form their conclusions only from the loves of self and of the world, and their pleasures; wherefore,

THE NEW JERUSALEM AND ITS HEAVENLY DOCTRINE (continued)

when they see the evil exalted to honors, and acquire wealth more than the good, and that success attends them according to their artifices, they say in their hearts, that this would not be the case if the Divine Providence were in all things and singulars; not considering that the Divine Providence does not regard that which briefly passes away, and ends with the life of man, in the world, but that it regards that which remains to eternity, thus which has no end. What has no end, that Is; but what has an end, that respectively Is not. Let him who is capable consider, whether a hundred thousand years be any thing to eternity, and he will perceive that they are not; what then are some years of life in the world?

270. Every one who rightly considers it, may know, that eminence and opulence in the world are not real divine blessings, notwithstanding man, from the pleasure he finds in them, calls them so; for they pass away, and also seduce many, and turn them away from heaven; but that eternal life, and its happiness, are real blessings, which are from the Divine: this the Lord also teaches in Luke: "Make to yourselves a treasure that faileth not in the heavens, where the thief cometh not, nor the moth corrupteth; for where your treasure is, there will your heart be also."

271. The reason why success attends the evil according to their arts is, because it is according to divine order that every one should act what he acts from reason, and also from freedom; wherefore, unless man were left to act from freedom according to his reason, and thus unless the arts which are thence derived were to succeed, man could by no means be disposed to receive eternal life, for this is insinuated when man is in freedom, and his reason is enlightened. For no one can be forced to good, forasmuch as nothing that is forced inheres with him, for it is not his own; that becomes a man's own, which is done from freedom according to his reason, and that is done from freedom which is done from the will or love, and the will or love is the man himself. If a man were forced to that which he does not will, his mind would continually incline to that which he does will; and besides, every one strives after what is forbidden, and this from a latent cause, because every one strives to be in freedom. Whence it is plain, that, unless man were kept in freedom, good could not be provided for him.

272. To leave man from his own freedom also to think, to will, and, so far as the laws do not restrain him, to do evil, is called permission.

273. To be led to felicities in the world by means of arts, appears to man as if it were from his own proper prudence, but still the Divine Providence incessantly accompanies by permitting and continually withdrawing from evil. But to be led to felicities in heaven is known and perceived to be not from man's own proper prudence, because it is from the Lord,

and is effected of his Divine Providence by disposing and continually leading to good.

274. That this is the case, man cannot comprehend from the light of nature, for from that light he does not know the laws of divine order.

275. It is to be noted that there is providence, and prævidence; good is what is provided by the Lord, but evil is what is prævided. The one must accompany the other, for what comes from man is nothing but evil, but what comes from the Lord is nothing but good.

OF THE LORD.

280. There is one God, who is the Creator and Conservator of the universe; thus, who is the God of heaven and the God of the earth.

281. There are two things which constitute the life of heaven with man, the good of love and the truth of faith. Man has this life from God, and nothing at all of it is from man; wherefore the primary principle of the church is, to acknowledge God, to believe in God, and to love Him.

282. They who are born within the church ought to acknowledge the Lord, His Divine, and His Human, and to believe in Him, and to love Him; for from the Lord is all salvation. This the Lord teaches in John: "He who believeth in the Son hath eternal life, but he who believeth not the Son shall not see life, but the anger of God abideth with him," iii. 36. Again, "This is the will of him who sent me, that every one who seeth the Son, and believeth in Him, should have eternal life, and I will resuscitate Him in the last day," vi. 40. Again, "Jesus said, I am the resurrection and the life; he who believeth in Me, although he dies, shall live; but every one who liveth and believeth in Me, shall not die to eternity," xi. 21, 23.

283. Wherefore they within the church who do not acknowledge the Lord, and His divine, cannot be conjoined to God, and thus cannot have any lot with the angels in heaven, for no one can be conjoined to God but from the Lord and in the Lord. That no one can be conjoined to God but from the Lord, the Lord teaches in John, "No one hath ever seen God; the only-begotten Son, who is in the bosom of the Father, He hath shown Him," i.20. Again, "Ye have never heard the voice of the Father, nor seen His shape," v. 37. Again, "No one knoweth the Father but the Son, and to whom the Son shall be willing to reveal Him," xi. 27. And again, "I am the way, the truth, and the life; no one cometh to the Father but by Me," xiv. 6. The reason why no one can be conjoined to God but in the Lord, is because the Father is in Him, and they are one, as He also teaches in John: "If ye know Me, ye know my Father also; he who seeth Me seeth the Father; Philip, believest thou not that I am in the Father and the Father in Me? believe Me that I am in the Father and the Father in Me," xiv. 7 to 11. And again, "The Father and I are One; that ye may know and believe

that I am in the Father and the Father in Me," x. 30, 38.

284. Forasmuch as the Father is in the Lord and the Father and the Lord are One; and forasmuch as He ought to be believed in, and he that believes in Him has eternal life, it is evident that the Lord is God. That the Lord is God, the Word also teaches, as in John: "In the beginning was the Word, and the Word was with God, and GOD WAS THE WORD: all things were made by Him, and without Him was not any thing made which was made; and THE WORD WAS MADE FLESH, and dwelt among us, and we saw His glory, the glory as of the only-begotten of the Father," i. 1, 3, 14. In Isaiah, "A child is born to us, a Son is given to us, on whose shoulder is the government, and His name shall be called GOD, HERO, THE FATHER OF ETERNI-TY, the Prince of Peace," ix. 5. Again, "A virgin shall conceive and bring forth, and His name shall be called GOD WITH US," vii. 14; Matthew i. 23. And in Jeremiah, "Behold the days shall come when I will raise up to David a just branch, who shall reign a king, and shall prosper; and this is His name which they shall call Him, JEHOVAH OUR JUSTICE," xxiii. 5, 6; chap. xxxiii. 15, 16.

285. All they who are of the church, and in light from heaven, see the Divine in the Lord; but they who are not in light from heaven, see nothing but the Human in the Lord; when yet the Divine and Human are in Him so united, that they are one; as the Lord also taught in another place, in John: "Father, all Mine are Thine, and all Thine Mine," xvii. 10.

286. That the Lord was conceived from Jehovah the Father, and was thus God from conception, is known in the church; and also that He rose again with His whole body, for He left nothing in the sepulchre; of which he also afterwards confirmed the disciples, saying, "See My hands and My feet, that it is I Myself; feel Me and see; for a spirit hath not flesh and bones as ye see Me have," Luke xxiv. 39. And although He was a man as to the flesh and bones, still He entered through the closed doors, and, after He had manifested himself, became invisible, John xx. 19, 26; Luke xxiv. 3. The case is otherwise with every man, for man only rises again, as to the spirit, and not as to the body, wherefore when He said, "that He is not as a spirit," He said that He is not as another man. Hence it is evident that the Human in the Lord is also Divine.

287. Every man has his esse of life, which is called his soul, from his father; the existere of life thence derived is what is called the body; hence the body is the effigy of its soul, for the soul, by means of the body, exercises its life at pleasure. Hence it is that men are born into the likeness of their parents, and that families are distinguished from each other; from this circumstance it is evident what was the quality of the body or Human of the Lord, viz. that it was as the Divine Itself, which was the esse of His life, or

the soul from the Father; wherefore he said, "He that seeth Me, seeth the Father," John xiv. 9.

288. That the Divine and Human of the Lord is one person, is agreeable to the faith received in the whole Christian world, which is to this effect: "Although Christ is God and man, still He is not two, but one Christ; yea, He is altogether one and a single person; because as body and soul are one man, so God and man are one Christ." This is from the Athanasian creed.

289. They who, respecting the Divinity, have an idea of three persons, cannot have an idea of one God; if with the mouth they say one, still they think three; but they who, respecting the Divinity, have an idea of three principles in one person, can have an idea of one God, and can say one God, and also think one God.

290. An idea of three principles in one person is attained, when it is thought that the Father is in the Lord, and that the Holy Spirit proceeds from Him; there is then a trine in the Lord, the Divine itself which is called the Father, the Divine Human which is called the Son, and the Divine Proceeding which is called the Holy Spirit.

291. Forasmuch as all the Divine is in the Lord, therefore He has all power in the heavens and in the earths; which he also says in John: "The Father hath given all things into the hands of the Son," ii.35. Again, "The Father hath given to the Son power over all flesh," xvii. 2. In Matthew, "All things are delivered to Me by the Father," xi. 27. Again, "All power is given to Me in heaven and in earth," xxviii. 16. Such power is divine.

292. They who make the Human of the Lord like the human of another man, do not think of His conception from the Divine Itself, nor do they consider that the body of every thing is the effigy of its soul. Neither do they reflect on His resurrection with the whole body, nor of His appearance at His transformation, when His face shone as the sun. Neither do they think, respecting those things which the Lord said concerning faith in Him, concerning His unity with the Father, concerning His glorification, and concerning His power over heaven and earth, that these are divine, and were mentioned in relation to His Human. Neither do they remember that the Lord is omnipresent also as to His human, Matthew xxviii. 20, although the faith of His omnipresence in the sacred supper is derived from this consideration: omnipresence is divine. Yea, perhaps they do not think that the Divine principle which is called the Holy Spirit, proceeds from His Human; when yet it proceeds from His glorified Human, for it is said, "The Holy Spirit was not yet, because Jesus was not yet glorified," John vii. 39.

293. The Lord came into the world that He might save the human race, who would otherwise have perished in eternal death; and He saved them by this, that He subjugated the hells, which infested every man coming into the world and going out of the world;

**THE NEW JERUSALEM AND ITS HEAVENLY
DOCTRINE** (continued)

and at the same time by this, that he glorified His Human: for thus He can keep the hells in subjugation to eternity. The subjugation of the hells, and the glorification of His Human at the same time, were effected by means of temptations admitted into the human which He had from the mother, and by continual victories therein. His passion on the cross was the last temptation and full victory.

294. That the Lord subjugated the hells, He Himself teaches in John: when the passion of the cross was at hand, then Jesus said, "Now is the judgment of this world; *now the prince of this world shall be cast out* ," xii. 27, 28, 31; again, "Have confidence, *I have overcome the world* ," xvi. 33. And in Isaiah, "Who is this that cometh from Edom, going on in the multitude of His strength, great to save? My own arm brought salvation to Me; so He became to them for a Saviour," lxiii, 1 to 20; chap. lix. 16 to 21. That He glorified His Human, and that the passion of the cross was the last temptation and full victory, by means of which He glorified it, He teaches also in John: "After Judas went out, Jesus said, Now is the Son of Man glorified, and God will glorify Him in Himself, and will immediately glorify Him," xiii. 31, 32. Again, "Father, the hour has come; glorify Thy Son, that Thy Son also may glorify Thee," xvii. 1, 5. Again, "Now is My soul troubled; Father, glorify Thy Name; and a voice came out from heaven, saying, I have both glorified it, and will glorify it again," xii. 27, 28. And in Luke, "Ought not Christ to suffer these things, and to enter into His glory," xxiv. 30. These words were said in relation to His passion: to glorify is to make Divine. Hence, now, it is manifest, that, unless the Lord had come into the world, and been made a man, and in this manner had liberated from hell all those who believe in Him and love Him, no mortal could have been saved; this is understood by the saying, that without the Lord there is no salvation.

295. When the Lord fully glorified His Human, He then put off the human from the mother, and put on the human from the Father, which is the Divine Human, wherefore he was then no longer the son of Mary.

296. The first and primary principle of the church is, to know and acknowledge its God; for without that knowledge and acknowledgment there is no conjunction; thus, in the church, without the acknowledgment of the Lord. This the Lord teaches in John: "He who believeth in the Son hath eternal life, but he who believeth not the Son shall not see life, but the anger of God abideth with him," iii. 36. And in another place, "Except ye believe that I am, ye shall die in your sins," viii. 24.

297. That there is a trine in the Lord, viz. the Divine Itself, the Divine Human, and the Divine Proceeding, is an arcanum from heaven, and is for those who shall be in the Holy Jerusalem.

OF ECCLESIASTICAL AND CIVIL GOVERNMENT.

311. There are two things which ought to be in order among men, viz. the things which are of heaven, and the things which are of the world: the things which are of heaven are called ecclesiastical things, and those which are of the world are called civil things.

312. Order cannot be maintained in the world without governors, who are to observe all things which are done according to order, and which are done contrary to order; and are to reward those who live according to order, and to punish those who live contrary to order. If this be not done, the human race must perish; for the will to command others, and to possess the goods of others, is hereditarily connate with every one, whence proceed enmities, envyings, hatreds, revenges, deceits, cruelties, and many other evils: wherefore, unless men were kept under restraint by the laws, and by rewards suited to their loves, which are honors and gains for those who do good things; and by punishments contrary to those loves, which are the loss of honor, of possessions, and of life, for those who do evil things; the human race would perish.

313. There must therefore be governors to keep the assemblages of men in order, who should be persons skilled in the laws, wise, and men who fear God. There must also be order among the governors, lest any one, from caprice or inadvertence, should permit evils which are against order, and thereby destroy it: which is guarded against when there are superior and inferior governors, among whom there is subordination.

314. Governors over those things among men which relate to heaven, or over ecclesiastical matters, are called priests, and their office is called the priesthood. But governors over those things among men which relate to the world, or over civil concerns, are called magistrates, and their chief, where such a form of government prevails, is called king.

315. With respect to the priests, they ought to teach men the way to heaven, and also to lead them; they ought to teach them according to the doctrine of their church derived from the Word, and they ought to lead them to live according to it. Priests who teach truths, and thereby lead to the good of life, and so to the Lord, are the good shepherds of the sheep; but they who only teach, and do not lead to the good of life, and so to the Lord, are the evil shepherds.

316. Priests ought not to claim to themselves any power over the souls of men, inasmuch as they do not know in what state the interiors of a man are; still less ought they to claim the power of opening and shutting heaven, since that power belongs to the Lord alone.

317. Dignity and honor ought to be paid to priests on account of the sanctity of their office; but they who are wise give the honor to the Lord, from whom all sanctity is derived, and not to themselves, whilst they

who are not wise attribute the honor to themselves, whereby they take it from the Lord. They who attribute honor to themselves, on account of the sanctity of their office, prefer honor and gain to the salvation of souls, which they ought to provide for; but they who give the honor to the Lord, and not to themselves, prefer the salvation of souls to honor and gain. The honor of any employment is not in the person, but is adjoined to him according to the dignity of the thing which he administers; and what is adjoined does not belong to the person himself, and is also separated from him with the employment. All personal honor is the honor of wisdom and the fear of the Lord.

318. Priests ought to teach the people, and to lead them by means of truths to the good of life, but still they ought to force no one, since no one can be forced to believe contrary to what he thinks from his heart to be truth. He who believes otherwise than the priest, and makes no disturbance, ought to be left in peace; but he who makes disturbance ought to be separated; for this also is agreeable to order, for the sake of which the priesthood is established.

319. As priests are appointed to administer those things which relate to the divine law and worship, so kings and magistrates are appointed to administer those things which relate to civil law and judgment.

320. Forasmuch as the king alone cannot administer all things, therefore there are governors under him, to each of whom a province is given to administer, where the administration of the king cannot be extended. These governors, taken collectively, constitute the royal function, but the king himself is the chief.

321. Royalty itself is not in the person, but is adjoined to the person. The king who believes that royalty is in his own person, and the governor who believes that the dignity of government is in his own person, is not wise.

322. Royalty consists in administering according to the laws of the realm, and in judging according thereto, from justice. The king who regards the laws as above himself, is wise, and he who regards himself as above the laws, is not wise. The king who regards the laws as above himself, places royalty in the law, and the law has dominion over him, for he knows that the law is justice, and that all justice which is justice, is divine. But he who regards himself as above the laws, places royalty in himself, and either believes himself to be the law, or the law, which is justice, to be derived from himself; hence he arrogates to himself that which is divine, to which nevertheless he ought to be in subjection.

323. The law, which is justice, ought to be enacted in the realm by persons skilled in the law, wise, and men who fear God; and the king and his subjects ought afterwards to live according to it. The king who lives according to the law so enacted, and therein sets an example to his subjects, is truly a king.

324. A king who has absolute power, and believes that his subjects are such slaves that he has a right to their possessions and lives, and exercises such a right, is not a king, but a tryant.

325. The king ought to be obeyed according to the laws of the realm, and by no means to be injured either by word or deed; for on this the public security depends.

Notes: *Emanuel Swedenborg, whose voluminous writings fill several shelves, prepared a condensation of his teachings into a small volume which was published in English in a paperback volume. It summarizes the teachings of this religious teacher, now largely forgotten, whose role in the development of nineteenth-century American thought was vast. This document also serves as a creedal statement for the several Swedenborgian churches.*

* * *

CONFESSIONS OF THE GENERAL CHURCH OF THE NEW JERUSALEM

1

I believe in the Lord Jesus Christ, the almighty and everlasting God, the Maker of heaven and earth, the Redeemer and Savior of the world.

I believe in the Sacred Scripture, the Word of God, the Fountain of wisdom, the Source of life, and the Way to heaven.

I believe in the Second Coming of the Lord, in the Spiritual Sense of the Word, and in the Heavenly Doctrine of the New Jerusalem.

I believe in the New Angelic Heaven, in the New Christian Church, in the communion of angels and men, in repentance from sin, in the life of charity, in the resurrection of man, in the judgment after death, and in the life everlasting.

2

I believe that the Lord from eternity, who is Jehovah, came into the world to subdue the hells, and to glorify His Human; and that without this no mortal could have been saved; and they are saved who believe in Him. (F 34)

3

I believe that God is One in person and in essence, in whom is the Trinity, and that the Lord is that God.

I believe that no mortal could have been saved unless the Lord had come into the world.

I believe that the Lord came into the world in order to remove hell from man, and He removed it by combats against it and by victories over it; thus He subdued it, and reduced it into order and under obedience to Himself.

I believe that the Lord came into the world to glorify the Human which He took upon Him in the world, that is, in order to unite it to the all-originating Divine (the Divine itself).

I believe that in this way the Lord to eternity holds the hells in order and under obedience to Himself.

CONFESSIONS OF THE GENERAL CHURCH OF THE NEW JERUSALEM (continued)

I believe that these mighty works could not have been accomplished except by means of temptations even to the uttermost, which was the passion of the cross; and that is why the Lord underwent that most grievous temptation. (F 35)

4

I believe that the Lord came into the world to reduce into order all things in heaven and on the earth.

I believe that this was accomplished by means of combats against the hells, which were then infesting every man that came into the world and that went out of the world.

I believe that thereby the Lord became righteousness, and saved men, who otherwise could not have been saved. (Lord 14)

5

I believe that the Lord from eternity, who is Jehovah, came into the world to subdue the hells and to glorify His Human; and that without this no flesh could have been saved, and those are saved who believe in Him.

I believe that man is conjoined with the Lord by faith in Him, and through conjunction with the Lord he is saved.

I believe that to have faith in the Lord is to have confidence that He will save; and because none can have such confidence except he who leads a good life, therefore this also is understood by having faith in the Lord.

I believe that Jehovah God is love itself and wisdom itself, or good itself and truth itself.

I believe that as the Divine truth, which is the Word, and which was God with God, He came down and took on the Human for the purpose of reducing to order all things that were in heaven, and all things in hell, and all things in the church.

I believe that Jehovah God did this because at that time the power of hell prevailed over the power of heaven, and upon the earth the power of evil over the power of good, and in consequence a total damnation stood threatening at the door.

I believe that Jehovah God removed this threat by means of His Human which was Divine truth, and thus He redeemed angels and men; for He united in His Human, Divine truth with Divine good, or Divine wisdom with Divine love; and so, with and in His glorified Human, He returned into His Divine in which He was from eternity.

6

I believe that the Lord came into the world, and assumed a Human, in order to put Himself into the power of subjugating the hells, and of reducing all things to order both in the heavens and on the earths.

I believe that He superinduced this Human over His former Human, and that that which was superinduced was like the human of a man in the world.

I believe that both these Humans are Divine, and therefore infinitely transcend the finite humans of angels and men.

I believe that because the Lord fully glorified the natural Human even to its ultimates, therefore He rose again with the whole body, therein differing from any man.

I believe that by the assumption of this Human the Lord put on Divine omnipotence, not only for subjugating the hells and reducing the heavens to order, but also for holding the hells in subjection to eternity, and thus saving mankind.

7

I believe that without the coming of the Lord into the world no mortal could have been saved, and they are saved who believe in Him, and who live well.

8

I believe that Jehovah God Himself came into the world to deliver men and angels from the assault and violence of hell, and thus from damnation.

I believe that He did this by means of combats against hell and by victories over it, whereby He subjugated it, reduced it to order, and brought it under obedience to Himself.

I believe that He also formed a new heaven, and through this instaurated a new church.

By this means Jehovah God put Himself in the power of saving all who believe in Him and who do His precepts. Thus He redeemed all in the whole world, and all in the whole heaven. (Can. Redemption VI)

Notes: *A contemporary branch of the Swedenborg churches, the General Church of the New Jerusalem has published seven brief confessions of faith in addition to the lengthy creedal-confessional statement written by Emanuel Swedenborg, which summarizes the creeds of the church he founded. All eight confessions are used primarily for liturgical purposes and are reproduced here from the church's hymnal.*

* * *

Spiritualism

WHAT AQUARIANS BELIEVE (AQUARIAN FOUNDATION)

THE AQUARIAN FOUNDATION does not hold to any specific creeds or dogmas, for Aquarians themselves do not believe in "belief" so much as in knowledge. How and where such knowledge has been gained, they feel is not as important as how it is applied in one's life. Any fixed creed or statement of belief, therefore, might tend more to "crystallize" philosophy and thought than to allow "room for growth."

There can be no single word or descriptive phrase which fully categorizes the Aquarian teachings; for human language itself is, at best, a conveyor of "half-truths." Some of the terms often applied to various phases of our study can be considered appropriate, however, so long as no one of them—nor all of them together—are ever considered all-encompassing.

Some *AQUARIANS* consider themselves to be *CHRISTIANS*; some consider themselves *BUDDHISTS*; and others, good members of certain other great religious faiths. Yet, all or nearly all Aquarians are aware of the values and truths, as well as the distortions and half-truths brought to the group-consciousness by EACH of these movements. Aquarians are aware, too, of the many similarities which may be found in the spiritual and moral precepts of Jesus, Gautama Buddha, Krishna, Babaji and many other teachers.

AQUARIANS are SPIRITUALISTS, to the extent that they believe in and practice communication with the so-called dead, some of whom serve as "guides" or "guardian angels," through human instruments called "mediums." This would seem to presuppose a belief in the continuity of life beyond the grave, and in other planes of life than this physical plane. Aquarians are not content, however, with presupposing alone, but tend to investigate thoroughly the field of psychic phenomena and mediumship until absolute proof is found to the satisfaction of each one of them.

On the other hand, Aquarians do not allow the belief and practice of contacting loved ones and guides in spirit to become the main focal point of their religion. Neither do they seek psychic phenomena for the sake of phenomena alone; for they know that when such a thing is sought after as an end in itself, it becomes injurious rather than beneficial. Only when psychic phenomena is used as a means to a greater benefit, such as the giving of helpful service or the stimulation of needed truths, is it worthwhile.

AQUARIANS are THEOSOPHISTS to the extent that they continue the studying and sharing with those on earth ready to receive such knowledge, the teachings of the Masters of the Great Brotherhood of Cosmic Light, as was received in the West nearly a century ago by Madame H.P. Blavatsky and her successors. These include teachings on soul evolution, reincarnation, the law of cause and effect, or "Karma," the attainment of personal Mastership, or mastery over life and death, and a great many not-so-obvious facets of nature.

Aquarians also, continuing the Theosophical principle, embrace the idea of continuous service to humanity and of striving to establish world brotherhood, without regard to race, creed or nationality. On the other hand, Aquarians, like many other students of the occult, are aware that no book or library or lecture course can ever contain the "last word" on any subject, and that any such materials which are general enough to be given to the public may be prone to man-made error and distortion.

AQUARIANS are YOGA PHILOSOPHERS in a sense, inasmuch as they recognize the "yoke" to God, or pathway to Divine Realization, in its various forms. They have been taught in the Eastern Yoga schools throughout the ages, and the Aquarian recognizes the validity and worth of each of these pathways, be it one of advanced exercises and postures, special meditations, mental development through meditations, mental development through

concentration and study, or of some related type of activity. Aquarians are not inclined to follow any one of the others, however, unless it is so indicated by their development and by advice from their spiritual Gurus, or Master Teachers.

AQUARIANS are FREE-THINKERS in their approach to life and morals, knowing the truth of cause-and-effect, the need for personal independent action, the merit of the Golden Rule: "Do unto others as you would have others do unto you" and the worth of the Aquarian New Age Commandment: "You shall love and respect yourself."

AQUARIANS are TRANSCENDENTALISTS, continuing the line of thought advanced by Ralph Waldo Emerson, who was surely inspired in turn by numerous others who had gone before him. Transcendentalists, like Emerson, affirm the truth, not only that the higher meanings of life are to be perceived by means other than the five physical senses, but also that the Divine Life exists in all things. They note with interest the fact that one of the means of perception developed and used AFTER one's transition into the spirit world is called the "organs of transcendence"; also that the great universities in that plane of life are called "Schools of Transcendentalism."

AQUARIANS are UNIVERSALISTS in the original meaning of that term, Universal in that they acknowledge a kinship with everything that exists, and a *SURETY OF ULTIMATE UNIVERSAL SALVATION*, for all members of the human race.

Notes: *Rooted in Spiritualism, the Aquarian Foundation has become extremely eclectic, as its statement of belief amply demonstrates. The foundation is gnostic, with an emphasis upon the member's acquisition of cosmic knowledge over any communal agreement upon a set of specific beliefs. Nevertheless, the foundation has reached a unique perspective that sets it apart from similar organizations.*

* * *

WHAT DOES THE OLD CHRISTIAN INITIATE TEACH? AS TAUGHT BY THE CHURCH OF REVELATION

1. The Old Christian Initiate as taught by the Master Jesus, is the Messenger from the inner soul to humanity, linking earth and heaven, bringing the only proof of immortality. It is the broad Educator, the great Revealer, the Comforter.

2. It teaches that death is not the cessation of life, but a mere change of conditions.

3. It teaches a personal responsibility.

4. It removes all fear of death, which is really the portal of the spirit world.

5. It teaches not only that a man has a soul, but that man is spirit with a soul which is the spiritual house in which the spirit dwells.

6. That a man is a spiritual being now, even while incased in the flesh.

7. That as man sows on the earth he reaps in the life to come.

WHAT DOES THE OLD CHRISTIAN INITIATE TEACH? AS TAUGHT BY THE CHURCH OF REVELATION (continued)

8. That those who have passed on are conscious—not asleep.

9. The Old Christian initiate is the world religion, non-sectarian Philosophy based upon Scientific Truth, shows how to find spirit, understand the "Natural Law" and have life everlasting without death.

10. That communion between the living and the so-called dead, is scientifically proven.

11. The Old Christian Initiate is based upon the full teaching of the Master Jesus consisting of three facts; the spirit ability after the physical death to communicate with mortals.

12. The Old Christian Initiate is the Science, Philosophy and Religion of continuous life, based upon the demonstrated fact of communication by means of mediumship, with those who live in the Spirit World.

13. It brings to the surface man's spiritual powers, gifts such as inspiration, clairvoyance, clairaudience and healing powers.

14. It teaches that the spark of divinity dwells in all.

15. That as a flower gradually unfolds in beauty, so the spirit of man unfolds and develops in the spirit Phores.

16. The Old Christian Initiate is God's message to mortals, declaring that there is no death. That all who have passed on still live. That there is hope in the life beyond for the most sinful. Jesus said "Why marvel at the things I do, Ye shall do these things and even greater things, because I go to my Father to prepare a place for you and if I go I will come again."

17. That every soul will progress through thes to heights, sublime and glorious, where God is Love and Love is God.

18. The Old Christian Initiate is both a religion and a rule of life, based upon fundamental truth, explained and amplified by revelation from the wiser ones who have passed through death.

19. The Old Christian Initiate is the only science, religion and philosophy, which furnishes positive proof (by oft-repeated mental and Physical Phenomena through mediumship) of the knowledge of spirit life, spirit return and imortality.

20. It demonstrates the many spiritual gifts which mankind is endowed but which through want of knowledge have been allowed to lay dormant, or through prejudice have been violently and unjustly suppressed.

21. The Old Christian Initiate does not create truth, but is a living witness of the truth of a future existence. It reveals, it demonstrates it, describing its inhabitants, their occupations and characteristics.

22. The Old Christian Initiate, the teaching of spirit and those who worship in spirit are some times called Spiritualist or a teacher of Spiritualism. The "Ist" and "Ism" is merely a phrase or expression. It is used in the same manner as we use the Word "Americanism."

23. The Old Christian Initiate is not spiritism, that is talking to the dead for curiosity, for fleshly gratification, for selfish gain, for ambitious end, or for unworthy amusing and irreligious purposes. If this was the witch-spiritism that Moses condemned or disapproved of he did well. It should be discouraged, condemned today as unworthy of rational, royal-souled men and women.

24. The Old Christian Initiate as taught by Jesus, brings a sweet reward for welldoing and certain punishment for every wrong action, and that the good and divine that is attained here will be retained when entering the spiritual world: that we are building now, by our conduct and characters, our homes in the future state of immortality.

25. The teaching of spirit does not say "Goodnight" in the hour of death but rather gives the glad assurance of a most welcome "Good morning" just across the crystal river. It does not drape the mourners home in gloom, but lifts the grim curtain, permitting us to hear responsive words of undying affection from those we love. The future life is a social life, a constructive life, a progressive life, where the soul sweeps onward and upward, in glory transcending glory, through ages into eternal progression.

26. The Old Christian Initiate brings comfort to all who know the law. It aims at the unfoldment and upliftment of the race. It is the best key with which to unlock the store house of spiritual knowledge. It brings all realms of nature under the law and asserts that Man's whole duty in life is to find out the laws of Nature and conform to them.

27. War is regarded with Horror by all true believers of spirit. All whom believe in peace and brotherhood between man and man, and world wide peace among nations.

28. All aggressive wars, wars of conquest, wars of extension, of territory or commercial privilege or trade or colonization, are absolutely condemned by the ethics of spirit truth or teaching of the Old Christian Initiate.

29. Wars of self defense, wars of liberation for the oppressed, wars for the privilege vital to human life and happiness are justified reluctantly on the ground that a nation has the same right to fight in defense of its national life and in defense of human liberty as an individual has to fight in defense of his life and liberty under attack.

30. The Old Christian Initiate brings through the development of the moral consciousness in man, and through the ministry of Unseen angels and Spirits; the touch of a vanished hand, the sound of a voice that is still. That is why out of all the churches today, members are going in Secret like Nicodemeus, to the Medium for comfort.

The organized seekers of truth recognize the good the churches are doing in various ways and the student of truth is taught the great lesson continually to grant freely to others the same right of independent thinking and judging which they claim for themselves.

Ministers of the Old Christian Initiate do not employ speakers to tour the country in order to preach against anybody's religion.

They do not get money under false pretenses, by instilling into human minds, fear of Hell and perdition. The old deceptions of Hell have fallen out of the minds of all reasonable people of modern thinking.

Notes: *This statement combines Spiritualist, Christian, and esoteric traditions.*

* * *

ARTICLES OF OUR FAITH (INTERNATIONAL CHURCH OF AGELESS WISDOM)

1. WE BELIEVE that God is our Father and the Creator of all that is. That because He is our Father, all men everywhere are our Brothers and therefore no discrimination can be tolerated, for we are all His offspring. We acknowledge our relationship with all Kingdoms: mineral, vegetable, animal and that of man.

2. WE BELIEVE that we must depend on God for all things, but we must do our part in making our desires manifested.

3. WE BELIEVE that all souls are immortal; that no soul can ever be lost, for the opportunity for reformation is always open.

4. WE BELIEVE in the progression of the soul through successive incarnations whereby man eventually learns the meaning of "As you sow, so shall ye reap," thereby leading every soul to ultimate perfection.

5. WE BELIEVE this earthly life is the effect of the cause we have set into motion, either in this or in previous live Earth acts as a school where we learn the qualities of Godliness.

6. WE BELIEVE that we are all children of God, created in His spiritual image for the body contains within it replicas of the Universe and the steps in the life of Christ as taught through the spiritual anatomy of man. We do not believe in an anthropomorphic God.

7. WE BELIEVE that we must spiritually progress to the point where we will be able to follow the commandment of the Master Teacher Jesus, "The things I do must ye do and even greater things must ye do." We will be given the Christ Power to do these things when we have raised ourselves, through study, meditation and Service to mankind to the Christ Consciousness.

8. WE BELIEVE in the Power of Love to conquer all so-called evil. We believe in the Power of Prayer to save the human race and our beloved planet Earth.

9. WE BELIEVE that if we conscientiously practice the Golden Rule, we can be instrumental in uplifting mankind from their material bondage. We believe in teaching by example.

10. WE BELIEVE that it is possible and necessary to communicate with Spiritual Beings on the Higher Planes of life and that communion of the Saints, as said in the Apostle's Creed means communion with those who have left the world of flesh and entered the Heaven or Spirit worlds. The early Church taught this and Jesus exemplified this teaching, for He communed with the Saints on the mountain top and in the garden.

Notes: *This church believes in reincarnation. It also lives with the tension of affirming God as Father while denying a belief in an anthropomorphic deity.*

* * *

PRINCIPLES OF SPIRITUALISM (INTERNATIONAL SPIRITUALIST ALLIANCE)

1. The Fatherhood of God

2. The Brotherhood of Man

3. The immortality of the soul and its personal characteristics

4. Communion between departed human spirits and mortals

5. Personal responsibility

6. Compensation and retribution for all the good and evil deeds done here

7. A path of eternal progress open to every soul

WE BELIEVE IN ONE GOD WHO IS LOVE, Father of all souls, of the just and of the unjust; creator and sustainer of all worlds, visible and invisible; manifest in the holy breath, supreme emanation of truth and power, whereby we and all creation move forward unto perfection.

AND IN JESUS, OUR SPIRITUAL LORD, who was incarnated for the salvation of men, and in simplicity and with supreme courage, in obedience to His Heavenly Father, was perfected after much suffering, and is become unto us both Lord and Christ.

WE ACKNOWLEDGE the guardianship of the Holy Angels; the ministry of just men made perfect.

WE REJOICE in the fellowship and communion with our loved departed, and

WE LOOK for full reunion with them in the joy of life everlasting.

Notes: *These brief documents present a mildly Christian-Spiritualist perspective.*

* * *

BELIEFS OF THE LOTUS ASHRAM

Our beliefs have proven themselves to be true to many thousands of persons. They are wide, undogmatic and universal in principle. The old adage, "there is no teaching,

BELIEFS OF THE LOTUS ASHRAM (continued)

only learning," plays an important part in our lives. In other words, knowledge may be imparted but unless the self is out of the way, it falls on stoney ground.

The teachings have a kinship with the world religions, although they are basically Christian. To us God is dual, both male and female, a creative as well as a sustaining power. The link between our spirits and God's spirit is made through the ability to meditate perfectly. We believe in developing the Fruits and Gifts of the Spirit as St. Paul writes in the Bible.

FRUITS OF THE SPIRIT: Love, joy, peace, longsuffering, gentleness, goodness, faith, meekness, temperance. Corinthians 1, v 8-10

GIFTS OF THE SPIRIT: Wisdom, knowledge, faith, healing, working of miracles, prophecy, discerning of spirits, speaking in tongues, interpretation of tongues. Galatians 5, v 22-23

A part of the Lotus philosophy is that one's spirit returns to earth and other planets again and again in order to learn the necessary experiences in life and so attain perfection. You will find it explained in Revelations, Chapter 3, v 12, "Him that overcometh will I make a pillar in the temple of God, and he shall go no more out."

Another important belief is that cleanliness is next to Godliness. Our bodies must be kept clean and healthy through exercise, especially yoga, and natural eating habits. Several Lotus publications are directed towards this area. The body, after all is the temple of the soul.

Notes: *This small group presents a popular Spiritualist notion of the dual sexual nature of God.*

* * *

DECLARATION OF FAITH (NATIONAL FEDERATION OF SPIRITUAL SCIENCE CHURCHES)

ARTICLE I.

We believe in GOD ALMIGHTY, whose existence, power and wisdom nature proclaims; and the human soul recognizes His Love and Goodness.

ARTICLE II.

We declare that the foundation of our Science and Philosophy is based on the teachings of the Master, JESUS the Christ.

ARTICLE III.

The Bible contains inspirational truths, worthy of careful study, all of which are to be tested by reason and the Laws of GOD, which are in the human soul.

ARTICLE IV.

JESUS announced the great truth about human salvation when He said: "Ye shall know the truth and the truth shall make you free." Salvation is not a gift but a reward of living in accord with truth and Divine Law.

ARTICLE V.

We declare that the Spiritual and Divine Healing practiced in churches of the Federation is accomplished with prayer and faith in the power and love of GOD.

ARTICLE VI.

History proves that religion is inherent in the human soul, is normal and beneficial, when practiced in harmony with reason and natural Law.

ARTICLE VII.

Spiritual Science teaches the immortality of the soul, and that the spiritual life is abundantly demonstrated by the reappearance of the departed in their communication with Mortals.

ARTICLE VIII.

Man is a Creation of GOD and an inheritor of all His Divine Attributes; and is destined to eternal progression and ultimate happiness.

ARTICLE IX.

The great purpose of Spiritual Science is to demonstrate that Life's manifestations are continuous, and teach man the Harmonial Philosophy; and help him to spiritualize his human character.

Notes: *This federation was one of the more Christian of the Spiritualist organizations.*

* * *

SPIRITUAL SCIENCE GUIDELINES (NATIONAL SPIRITUAL SCIENCE CENTER)

1. God, the Universal Creative Energy, the creator and sustainer of the universe, permeates all within it.

2. The universe is a whole in a dynamic state of constant growth.

3. The life drive of every entity aims at complete unification with the Universal Creative Power.

4. Man, as an immortal spirit and a co-creator, is the master of his own destiny, completely responsible for his every thought, word and deed.

5. Individual free will embodies a relationship to Universe Will. Growth of awareness and spirituality is directly coupled to the increase of role of Universal Will.

6. Wisdom, the secret of all religion, the power of the mysteries, and the essence of all philosophy, lies latent in man awaiting the discovery and realization of the light and power of God within.

7. Communication at spirit levels is a fact and everyone is psychic. The path of wisdom however, is seeking first the kingdom of God and his righteousness. All things are added to man as he grows.

8. Soul unfoldment is the purpose of life. Fraternal service is the way of life.

9. The God Force is just, impersonal and totally accepting, drawing all the perfection.

Notes: *The Christian Science roots of the center have almost completely disappeared, as can be seen in this thoroughly Spiritualist affirmation.*

* * *

DECLARATION OF PRINCIPLES (NATIONAL SPIRITUALIST ASSOCIATION OF CHURCHES)

1. We believe in Infinite Intelligence.

2. We believe that the phenomena of nature, both physical and spiritual, are the expression of Infinite Intelligence.

3. We affirm that a correct understanding of such expression and living in accordance therewith constitute true religion.

4. We affirm that the existence and personal identity of the individual continue after the change called death.

5. We affirm that communication with the so-called dead is a fact, scientifically proven by the phenomena of Spiritualism.

6. We believe that the highest morality is contained in the Golden Rule: "Whatsoever ye would that others should do unto you, do ye also unto them."

7. We affirm the moral responsibility of the individual, and that he makes his own happiness or unhappiness as he obeys or disobeys Nature's physical and spiritual laws.

8. We affirm that the doorway to reformation is never closed against any human soul here or hereafter.

9. We affirm that the precept of Prophecy contained in the Bible is a divine attribute proven through Mediumship.

DEFINITIONS (Adopted by the National Spiritualist Association of Churches: Adopted October, 1914, 1919, 1930, 1951.)

1. Spiritualism is the Science, Philosophy and Religion of continuous life, based upon the demonstrated fact of communication, by means of mediumship, with those who live in the Spirit World.

2. A Spiritualist is one who believes, as the basis of his or her religion, in the communication between this and the spirit world by means of mediumship, and who endeavors to mould his or her character and conduct in accordance with the highest teachings derived from such communion.

3. A Medium is one whose organism is sensitive to vibrations from the spirit world and through whose instrumentality intelligences in that world are able to convey messages and produce the phenomena of Spiritualism.

4. A Spiritualist Healer is one who, either through his own inherent powers or through his mediumship, is able to impart vital, curative force to pathologic conditions.

5. The Phenomena of Spiritualism consist of Prophecy, Clairvoyance, Clairaudience, Gift of Tongues, Laying on of Hands, Healing, Visions, Trance, Apports, Revelation, Levitation, Raps, Automatic and Independent Writing and Paintings, Photography, Materialization, Psychometry, Voice and any other manifestation proving the continuity of life as demonstrated through the physical and Spiritual Senses and faculties of Man.

"Spiritualism Is a Science" because it investigates, analyzes and classifies facts and manifestations demonstrated from the spirit side of life.

"Spiritualism Is a Philosophy" because it studies the laws of nature both on the seen and unseen sides of life and bases its conclusions upon present observed facts. It accepts statements of observed facts of past ages and conclusions drawn therefrom, when sustained by reason and by results of observed facts of the present day.

"Spiritualism Is a Religion" because it strives to understand and to comply with the Physical, Mental and Spiritual Laws of Nature, "which are the laws of God."

Notes: *The National Spiritualist Association of Churches is the oldest and largest of the Spiritualist churches. The association's statement has been adopted in a modified form by several other Spiritualist associations and has exerted great influence throughout the movement. The association has also adopted a set of basic definitions which explain the terms used in the declaration.*

The International General Assembly of Spiritualists has adopted the association's declaration, using the first eight items as its Tenets. The Universal Church of the Master has rewritten the association's declaration to form its Basic Principles.

* * *

CONFESSION OF FAITH (PROGRESSIVE SPIRITUAL CHURCH)

We believe in the communion of Spirits; man's restoration to an everlasting life; the resurrection of the soul, not flesh: acknowledging God as Absolute Divine Spirit, whose voice and presence is always with us, and that of the Angels who are departed spirits who communicate and materialize with the living by means of mediums; manifesting by demonstration in origin and in phenomena all Biblical phases or reading, and the relation between God and soul and between the soul and the body, and bridging the hitherto "impassable gulf" between the dead and the living.

We believe that Jesus Christ was a medium, controlled by the Spirit of Elias and the Spirit of Moses and the Spirit of John the Baptist * * *, who after His death and resurrection materialized before His disciples * * *. That Moses communicated with the Divine Spirit, God. That the celebrated Nun of Kent received communications direct from God.

We believe that all these Spirits have desires; that the Spiritual body and the material body can commune together through the mouthpiece of another in harmony with the Spiritual; that through this channel we can receive the desires of the Spirit forces, concerning all

CONFESSION OF FAITH (PROGRESSIVE SPIRITUAL CHURCH) (continued)

human affairs; that we are obligated to these desires, and their fulfillment is pleasing to God.

We believe that the fingers of the hand of a medium under control can write and deliver divine messages and visions * * *. That a divine understanding of dreams can be had * * *. That God revealeth secrets that should be made known * * *. That the stars divine the pathway of life of every character * * *. That the rewards of divinations are in the hand of every character * * *. That the length of our days, riches, and honor are shown in the hands * * *.

We believe that Divine Metaphysics are designed by God, guiding the mind of the medium from the visible to the invisible, and that it is only through this channel that the cause of disease can be detected and over-powered. That God has a fixed law for the preservation of the Spiritual body until death itself shall die, and that a departed spirit can be relieved from this death through prayer to a higher state or sphere of Spirituality.

We acknowledge the Holy Bible to be the inspired word of God, a guide to Spirit life, and all phases of Spiritualism such as prophecies, spiritual palmistry, spiritual automatic writing, spiritual suggestions and radiations, spiritual materialization, spiritual trumpet speaking, spiritual healing by magnetized articles, spiritual levitation and spiritual tests * * *, and as so practiced was and is a real science. That it is present with us now and does not belong to a dispensation now ended. That when a person does not possess the necessary understanding of either of the above, a Teacher or Reader may be employed for compensation to explain and teach the Truth relating to these mental and spiritual thought forms as revealed to him or her through the Divine Spirit.

We believe that heaven and hell are conditions, not locations. That it is necessary that we hold personal communication with the spirits of the departed and their forces, to confess to them the renunciation of our material wills and intelligence that we may be properly guided in our daily life by messages received from the Spiritual realm according to the strength of our harmony with the spirits of the departed and their Spiritual love and desires. That it is necessary for us in consulting Spiritual mediums to place ourselves in harmony with such belief.

We believe that the change called death should be met without fear; that our sins stay with us forever; provided, that we have not lived in obedience to the law of spiritual harmony. That man is perfection, the image and likeness of God. That he exists independent of human will, controlled by the Spirit forces free from malicious magnetic elements.

Notes: *The doctrine of the Progressive Spiritual Church was conceived to be that of conventional Christianity, modified by the revelations of spiritualist mediums in the late-nineteenth century. These revelations affirmed the immortality of the soul, the existence of angels, and a spiritual hierarchy including the angels and Christ.*

OUR SPIRITUAL DOCTRINE (ROOSEVELT SPIRITUAL MEMORIAL BENEVOLENT ASSOCIATION)

This organization is the association of its Members as a Religious, Non-profit, Self-supporting, Educational, Civic, Fraternal, Charitable and Benevolent Corporation, dedicated to the Glory of God and the reality of His Truth, and for the Spiritual emancipation and Salvation of all Humanity.

To help those in need, to visit the sick and afflicted, those in the prisons, care of the dying, to comfort those who mourn, defend the helpless, to awaken to realization those who are Spiritually unconscious of The Truth, Love and Power of God.

To spread, broadcast, among all Mankind, the everlasting gospel of Christ Jesus and the Truth from the Holy Bible as He taught it and in accordance with the proved and demonstrated knowledge of Reason, Science and Spirituality.

To teach, preach, and practice the Religion, Philosophy and Science of Truth as found in the Holy Bible (which is the Truth of all Religion) including the provable and demonstrable knowledge of the Continuity of Life in the Spiritual World after the Change (called death).

To communicate with persons (so-called dead) in the Spiritual World as Jesus did through Spiritual Gifts of God and harmoniously with the statements of such Communications, which are contained both in the Old and New Testaments of the Holy Bible.

To teach, practice and conduct investigations in Psychic Research, Extrasensory Perception, Clairvoyance, Clairaudience, prognosis and other constructive and helpful forms of Spiritual, Mental, Psychic phenomena, as manifestations in such light and upon such conditions that anyone present may see or hear, for themselves, whatever physical phenomena and manifestations may occur.

To teach and practice Spiritual Healings through the Almighty Power of Prayer and the Spiritual Gifts of God in accordance with, and not against, the Laws of the State of Florida or other states or countries in which this association and churches may operate.

To teach, train, ordain and issue charters for Churches, Clubs, Associations, Seminaries, organizers, etc.; to issue Certificates to Doctors of Divinity. Teachers, Ministers, Healers, Class Leaders and all others found worthy according to their duties and their teachings of Truth and of the Religion as taught by Our Saviour, Jesus the Christ. Provided such persons are qualified (by the Board of Directors) to receive said diplomas, degrees (etc.) either because of having successfully completed the study of prescribed Scholastic, Theological or Ecclesiastical subjects, or courses, of instruction and training, or because of the excellence of their knowledge or because of their accomplishments in the Service of God.

The membership of this organization shall consist of any and all persons, regardless of nationality, race or creed, or membership in any other churches, who shall conform to the Charter, Constitution and By-Laws of this organization, and who have been accepted by its Board of Directors.

Notes: *This statement is more a program for action than a statement of belief. However, it does manifest a Christian Spiritualist perspective while remaining silent on most controversial subjects.*

*　　*　　*

THIS WE BELIEVE (TEMPLE OF UNIVERSAL LAW)

"There is one body and one Spirit; just as you were called to the one hope there belongs to your call; one Lord, one faith, one baptism, one God and Father of us all, who is above all and through all and in all." (Eph. 4:4-6)

"One Lord, one faith, one God." This is the foundation of Universal Law. There is only one Lord, the indwelling Christ Spirit that seeks to guide and inspire our every action, word and thought. There is only one faith and the many religions in the world today are but different manifestations of that faith. There is only one Eternal Spirit who lives, moves and has His Being within all of the universe.

We believe that Deity expresses as a Trinity, which we call God the Father, God the Son and God the Holy Spirit. God the Father is Spirit. God the Son is the manifested creative expression of Spirit. God the Holy Spirit is the action of Spirit through created manifestation.

We believe that God the Father is the infinite Universal Law of life which creates and sustains all manifestation, both large and small, through evolution of progression to eternal life.

We believe that God the Son is the Christ Principle, the perfect demonstration of Divine Mind. We believe that this Christ has come to earth many times in human form. We believe that Jesus, the Son of God, most perfectly manifested this Principle and that by following his example, we awaken the Christ power that dwells within us. Thus we are able to become a great light to mankind, as he was and is.

We believe that God the Holy Spirit is the action of Divine Mind which leads us to expression of the God Power within us.

We believe in the worship of God, no matter what name he may be given by man, and regardless of the kind of ritual performed by the different religions. We can worship God in the quiet of a sanctuary or in the hustle of our busy, daily life. We can worship God in communion with many others, or in the silent secret place of our soul. Man has devised many and varied forms to express his worship of the Divine, and all are good insofar as they lead men to find their innate oneness with all of life.

We seek to interpret the teachings of the Bible and the utterances of all prophets and spiritual teachers, for it is only through study and understanding that the glowing words and ideas of the religious scriptures of the world can be made to apply to each person as an individual.

We strive to guide and help our fellow man in understanding his relationship to God and to the universe around him. By awakening our soul consciousness to a complete awareness of the unity of all life, we lift our minds to the higher spiritual realms of thought and realize our oneness with God.

We believe that all life is immortal and there is no death. That which is called death is merely a change from a material body to a spiritual body. That which God has created cannot be destroyed. The outer form may change and decay but that which is the real you, the divine Spirit within, is eternal. Life is a school in which we advance from one grade to the next, evolving upward and onward.

We believe that man is the highest evolved creature on the earth, made after the spiritual image of God, gifted with creative reasoning power and the ability to worship Deity. We believe man is an immortal soul clothed in a physical form; a spark of infinite Divine Spirit.

We recognize Universal Law in all faiths for we believe that God is universal. He manifests to different peoples in different ways at different times. All faiths have their deep wells of spiritual truth which shine forth in the lives and teachings of the great prophets and leaders of those religions.

In our worship, we use the Christian Bible as a record of man's search for God and an attempt to explain our life on the earth. We believe that the basic teachings of the Christ are to be found in the Sermon on the Mount.

We are aware that in order to survive in this world of ours, man must begin to practice universal brotherhood. We must learn to see our fellow man as our brother, regardless of race, creed or color. We must cast out all forms of discrimination and strive to love our fellow man without judging according to his nationality, his belief or the color of his skin. All are created by one Spirit, instilled with the same Divine Life Force.

We believe the way to accomplish these goals is by studying the operations of nature around us and by looking deep within our own being to awaken the Christ Spirit which dwells in each and every one. Only by realizing those goals and by manifesting the Spirit within us will we attain health, strength, wisdom, understanding, peace, prosperity and happiness now and forever. Only by learning and understanding the Universal Law which rules our lives can we consciously come into complete oneness with God.

We present no new religion or new ideals to strive to attain. These are the oldest truths known to man. We seek only to inspire those we contact to begin now to travel on the pathway of wisdom and understanding of the Law of God, the Universal Law of life.

We cannot erase the thought habits of centuries that have led man to his present state of existence. Further, we would not, for we believe that all of life is an evolution of progression to eternal life. We are all on the path that leads to eventual oneness with Spirit. If we could realize it, we are one in Spirit right now.

The path of life we offer is not an easy one. It requires study and concentration. It hold many pitfalls for those

THIS WE BELIEVE (TEMPLE OF UNIVERSAL LAW) (continued)

whose aims are selfish and shallow. Many scoff at those who seek to improve and elevate their soul consciousness. But the reward is well worth the effort involved. The peace of mind, the silent joy, the overflowing love for all of life are, in themselves, reward enough. But the greatest reward is the sure knowledge that we are one with God, and that His Spirit dwells within us, guiding and inspiring us along life's pathway.

Your faith, your belief, can blend with the teachings of Universal Law, for we believe there is truly one Lord, one faith and one God, now and forever.

Notes: *This church teaches reincarnation.*

* * *

BASIC PRINCIPLES (UNIVERSAL CHURCH OF THE MASTER)

1. We believe in the Fatherhood of God and the Brotherhood of man.

2. All Phenomena that occur within the realms of nature, both physical and spiritual, are manifestations of Infinite Intelligence.

3. True religion is discovered by understanding correctly the Laws of Nature and of God, and by living in harmony therewith.

4. Individual existence, personal identity and memory continue after the transitional experience called death.

5. Communication with the "Living Dead" is a scientific fact, fully proven under test conditions by the phenomena of psychical research.

6. The Golden Rule, "Whatsoever ye would that others should do unto you, do ye also unto them," is the essence of morality.

7. Every individual is morally self-responsible. Happiness flows from consonance with the Laws of Nature and God.

8. The genuine improvement and reformation of the human soul are always possible in this world and the next.

9. Prophecy exists in our times as in Biblical Days, and is proven scientifically through mediumistic powers of divination.

10. The Universe, as a spiritual system expressing Divine Wisdom, makes possible the eternal progress of the aspiring soul who loves truth and goodness.

Notes: *Although derived from the Declaration of Principles of the National Spiritualist Association of Churches, these principles were heavily edited and revised. The last item is a reference to reincarnation.*

SEVEN AFFIRMATIONS OF THE LIVING SPIRIT (UNIVERSAL HARMONY FOUNDATION)

The Universal Harmony Foundation is a Religious Non-Profit Organization. Its Philosophy, a union of Religion-and-Science, promulgates the following Seven Affirmatives of the Living Spirit.

1. I AFFIRM the Fatherhood of God and the Brotherhood of Man.

2. I AFFIRM the Eternality of Life-and-Living.

3. I AFFIRM the Power of Prayer.

4. I AFFIRM the Practice of Spiritual Healing.

5. I AFFIRM the Reality of the Psychic Principle.

6. I AFFIRM Soul Growth—as the Purpose of Life.

7. I AFFIRM Fraternal Service—as the Way of Life.

Notes: *These affirmations present only the most basic statement of belief.*

* * *

PRACTICE AND FAITH (UNIVERSAL SPIRITUALIST ASSOCIATION)

SECTION 1. The Universal Spiritualist Association is an organization of believers in and practitioners of the religion of Spiritualism as understood in the following:

A. Spiritualism is the Science, Philosophy and Religion of continuous life, based upon the demonstrated fact of communication, by means of mediumship, with those who live in the spirit world.

B. A Spiritualist is one who believes, as the basis of his or her religion, in the communication between this and the spirit world by means of mediumship, and who endeavors to mould his or her character and conduct in accordance with the highest teachings derived from such communion.

C. A medium is one whose organism is sensitive to vibrations from the spirit world, and through whose instrumentality intelligences in that world are able to convey messages and produce the psychic phenomena of Spiritualism.

D. A Healer is one who, through his own inherent power, or through his mediumship, is able to impart vital curative force to pathologic conditions.

E. The psychic phenomena on which Spiritualism is based are of two types. Mental and Physical. Mental phenomena are subjective experiences in which mental energy is expended and include those phases of mediumship known as Impressional Mediumship, Prophecy, Inspirational Mediumship, Psychometry, Clairvoyance, Clairaudience, Clairsentience, Clairgustience, Trance Speaking, and Xenoglossis or Polyglot Mediumship. Physical phenomena are objective phenomena in which physical energy is expended and include those phases of mediumship known as Concussion or Rapping, Parakinesis, Telekinesis, Precipitation, Direct Writing and/or Drawing, Direct Voice including Independent Voice and Trumpet, Transfiguration, Materialization including Etherealization, Apport, Skotograph, and Spirit Photography.

F. The Precepts, Confession and Acts of Faith to be acceptable and binding upon the associates forming this organization shall be:

(a) The Precepts of Faith.

1. The Lord is Almighty God.

2. Thou shalt worship the Lord thy God.

3. There is a natural world and there is a spiritual world.

4. Divine Law is holy, and just, and good.

5. The gift of God to all men is eternal life.

6. Man in the natural world and man in the spiritual world can communicate, one with the other.

7. All men shall turn to righteousness and dwell in the house of the Lord forever.

(b) The Confession of Faith

We believe in the Fatherhood of God, the brotherhood of all life everywhere, the leadership of Christ, salvation by character, and the progression of man upward and onward forever.

(c) The Acts of Faith

1. We believe that God is Love, and Power, and Truth, and Light; that perfect justice rules the worlds; that all His sons shall one day reach His feet, however far they stray. We hold the Fatherhood of God, the brotherhood of man; we know that we do serve Him best when best we serve our brother man. So shall His blessings rest on us and peace for evermore. Amen.

2. We place our trust in God, the holy and all-glorious Trinity, who dwelleth in the Spirit of man. We place our trust in Christ, the Lord of love and wisdom, first among many brethren, who leadeth us to the glory of the Father, and is Himself the Way, the Truth, and the Life. We place our trust in the Law of Good which rules the worlds; we strive towards the ancient narrow path that leads to life eternal; we know that we do serve our Master best when best we serve our brother man. So shall His blessing rest on us and peace for evermore. Amen.

G. Spiritualists accept, practice and promulgate spiritual truths; as recorded in the Holy Bible, as revealed in the life and teachings of Jesus the Christ, and as manifested in modern times through mental and physical mediumship.

Notes: *The Universal Spiritualists have expressed their faith through a series of documents grouped together in their association's constitution.*

THE PRINCIPLES OF THE CHURCH OF THE WHITE EAGLE LODGE

The White Eagle Lodge teaches:

1. That God, the Eternal Spirit, is both Father and Mother.

2. That the Son—the Cosmic Christ—is also the light which shines in the human heart. By reason of this divine sonship, all are brothers and sisters in spirit, a brotherhood which embraces all life visible and invisible, including the fairy and angelic kingdom.

3. The expression of these principles in daily life, through service.

4. The awareness of the invisible world, which bridges separation and death and reveals the eternal unity of life.

5. That life is governed by five cosmic laws: Reincarnation : Cause and Effect : Opportunity : Correspondences : Compensation (Equilibrium and Balance).

6. The ultimate goal of mankind is that the inner light should become so strong and radiant that even the cells of the physical body are transmuted into finer substances which can overcome mortality. This is known as the Christing of Man, or in the words of the Ancient Brotherhood, the blooming of the Rose upon the Cross of matter.

Notes: *The Principles of the Church of the White Eagle Lodge tie the lodge broadly to both popular Spiritualism and the more exclusive occult orders, especially Rosicrucianism and Theosophy. Of particular notice is the lodge's belief in ascension, the idea that the body's cells can be transformed into a fine immortal substance.*

*   *   *

Teaching Spiritualism (Channeling)

THE LAWS AND PRECEPTS (COSMIC AWARENESS COMMUNICATIONS)

THE UNIVERSAL LAW is that knowledge that awareness, that all living things, all life has within it that vitality, that strength to gather into it all things necessary for its growth and its fruition.

THE LAW OF LOVE is that law which places the welfare and the concern and the feeling for others above self. The Law of Love is that close affinity with all forces that you associate with as good. The Law of Love is that force which denies the existence of evil in the world, that resists not evil.

THE LAW OF MERCY is that law which allows one to forgive all error, to forgive equally those who err against you as you err against them. This is to be merciful. To be merciful is akin to the Law of Love, and if one obeys the Law of Mercy, there can be no error in the world.

THE LAW OF GRATITUDE is that sense of satisfaction where energy which has been given receives a certain reward.

THE LAWS AND PRECEPTS (COSMIC AWARENESS COMMUNICATIONS) (continued)

JUDGE NOT. BE HUMBLE. DENY SELF. NEVER DO ANYTHING CONTRARY TO THE LAW OF LOVE. RESIST NOT EVIL. DO NOTHING WHICH IS CONTRARY TO THE LAW OF MERCY.

Notes: *This brief statement is not only used by Cosmic Awareness Communications, but has been assumed by the splinter groups that emerged after the death of William Ralph Duby (d. 1967), the original channel for the spiritual entity, Cosmic Awareness. These groups include the Anthropological Research Foundation and the several branches of the Organization of Awareness.*

* * *

CREDO (FELLOWSHIP OF THE INNER LIGHT)

JOHN 1:1-5

In the beginning God expressed Himself, and the expression of God is Love and Love is God expressing Himself.

The Love that is God expressing Himself was with God when all things were made. Love made all things and all things were made of Love.

In Love is Life and without Love there is no Life. It is Love that gives Light and consciousness to all who are born. Love shines out in the darkness as the Source of Life and awareness though there are some who do not know it.

A gift of those who become aware that it is Love that gives Life and Light is the ability to know themselves to be Sons and Daughters of God.

We believe that at least once, in the life of Jesus the Christ, man has so perfectly expressed God as to be Love personified and God incarnate.

We believe that Love has an opposite and the opposite of Love is fear. Just as Life is the expression of Love, so death is the expression of fear. Without Love there is no Life and without fear there is no death.

While it is true that all things were made by God and nothing exists that is not made of Love, yet God did not make fear or death. For death is no more than the absence of what is and fear is a fantasy entertained in minds of those who do not believe in and depend upon Love for life and security.

Fear is nothing more than an expression of faith in evil and evil is loss of Life. Just as faith in good and faith in God will increase life and vitality, so faith or believing in lack, limitation and evil will take away life, love and vitality, so bringing about death.

We believe that Love heals and can repair both mind and body. Love is the key to communication with both God and mankind.

It is our ideal to become the perfect Love which casts out fear.

We believe it is not necessary to consider others wrong to make ourselves right. It is likely that every prophet throughout time had something valuable to share. It is likely that every religion has a gift to give to those who have ears to hear. We shall therefore, welcome all who wish to worship with us in Love and we will love those who choose not to worship with us. Amen.

Notes: *This statement begins with a metaphysical paraphrase of the opening verses of the biblical Gospel of John. It emphasizes the popular metaphysical affirmation of the unreality of fear and death.*

* * *

TENETS (INNER CIRCLE KETHRA E'DA FOUNDATION)

"The tenets of our organization are: That man is born in love and is a free agent: that knowledge is cosmic honey and man should not only be permitted to gather this honey, but should be aided and abetted in doing so."

—Yada di Shi'ite

* * *

OUR CREED (LIGHT OF THE UNIVERSE)

Man is lost amid a myriad of stars which feign their glory and engulf Man's soul, and the One Star, which is the brightest, is shunned because its brilliance and glorious radiance cannot be borne by the weak, cowardly heart of Man. The Light of this Star shines so brilliantly that only those with a soul as Powerful and as brilliant as the Light of this single Star can face it and receive its well-hidden secrets. This Star rules all the Universe including Man, who so conceitedly states that he is the ruler of the Universe.

What then, is this Glorious Star, which has the Power to engulf Man, body and soul into this zone?

The Star is Man, not Man as we know him with his dictatorial spirit, but Man's True Self.

"Man's Soul, the True Divine Soul of Man, rules the Universe. The True Divine Soul of every wisp of the breeze, the True Divine Soul in every blade of grass and every leaf of every tree. This Divine Soul, which is within all, animate and inanimate, organic and inorganic, rules the Universe. This Divine Soul, this Omniscient, Omnipotent, Omnipresent Being, which is within all, rules the Universe.

"This Divine Soul is the maker and Creator of us all. This Soul, this Divine Presence, which has created all, every race, every religion, black and white, rich and poor, this Divine Soul has created everything, everyone, every Being. This Divine Soul is All."

"DEUS OMNIS EST"

Notes: *This creed affirms the single metaphysical reality of God. The true self of individuals participates in the divine and could even be thought of as God.*

STATEMENT OF THE RADIANT SCHOOL OF SEEKERS AND SERVERS

I believe, God has a Divine Plan for all to follow. This Plan is never separated from anyone and each can be "conscious" of this Plan.

I believe, this Plan is wrapped into the folds of every Life Pattern and is permanent, perfect and indestructible. If you relax yourself in the presence of this Divine Plan, it will work to manifest all good, so that you may recognize it in action, leaving you filled with Joyful Thoughts and that Inner Peace—all is well with the Soul.

I believe, as each seeks to unfold their Divine Plan, co-operating with the urge to receive Truth, they will learn to serve their fellowman, helping them to find the way to unfold their Divine Plan.

I believe, that all Divine Life Patterns are connected, and they are interwoven in a Great Universal Pattern, so that each Pattern depends upon another to find complete success (as you give, so shall you receive), thus unfolding together, God's Great Universal Plan for all mankind.

I believe, God expects each to unfold his own Divine Plan in full, not choosing only those parts which pleases or appeals to the mental mind.

I believe, God has given to each the opportunity to meet all other Divine Plans in which we have interfered, by creating against the Law of Truth, leaving sin or Karma—instead of Perfection. This is the opportunity to learn perfection. When each realizes that none are the select or chosen by God, but that the Laws of God help each to select that part of their Pattern which they alone must work out on their Path of Perfection.

I believe, that each Divine Plan includes three Divine Rights. These Divine Rights are: Health, Happiness and prosperity. These Divine Rights reflect upon man (as he thinketh, so he will be), so his Divine Plan will be made.

I believe, each should realize that the Physical Body is the "Temple" and through it all contacts are made manifest to our Higher Self.

I believe, that all should remember these words, found in the 91st Psalm: "I shall give my Angels charge over thee, and they shall keep thee in all thy ways." When realization comes, that no man is ever alone, then each will strive to perfect his own Life Pattern.

I believe, Happiness is the KEY of attraction and all who come in contact with this reflection will receive Faith overcoming fear, Love overcoming hate, Strength that overcomes weariness and Understanding that will overcome doubt.

I believe, that the act of Praying, should be the expression of desires, and by longing to know "The Great Love of God" will bring about abundance. Prayers should be the Soul expressing from the God Mind to the physical mental mind. When this is the way of Praying, the door to Peace and Understanding will open and Praying will become a daily practice.

I believe, to be patient, forgiving, willing and enduring, through the effort of seeking, is the KEY to perfection.

TEACHINGS OF THE SCHOOL OF NATURAL SCIENCE

The School of Natural Science Teaches:

That there exists a Universal Intelligence which is revealed in Nature by the establishment of an intelligent order governed by certain inexorable, immutable Laws;

That all life is endowed with the same potential of growth and refinement. Nature is absolutely and unconditionally just and is engaged in the evolvement of individual intelligences;

That man's Essential Self or Soul is an immortal, evolving entity possessing, simultaneously, a body of physical material and a body of spiritual material;

That there is a principle in Nature that impels the individual to attain higher and higher levels of consciousness;

That man is invested with Free Will and Choice and is held personally responsible and morally accountable for his deeds within the scope of his knowledge, The Law of Compensation is acknowledged and the standard of values is personal effort;

That prayer is a means of communication with other individuals from whom response may be expected if the need is genuine, the attitude unselfish and the motives worthy;

That knowledge of and willing conformity to the Laws of Nature are rewarded by the attainment of Self Mastery, Poise and Happiness;

That by persistent application of intelligent effort to the "living of a life" in conformity to the laws of Nature, an individual may personally demonstrate that there is a spiritual existence and a continuity of Life.

Notes: *These affirmations of the underlying Universal Intelligence, human free will under the reign of Law, the necessary progress of the soul, and the soul's accountability to the Law of Compensation (generally called "karma"), are common to occult philosophies.*

* * *

CREDO OF AMBER/CRYSTAL LIGHT BEARERS (SISTERS OF AMBER)

CREDO: He who abuses power, loses power; and he who loves and serves his fellow-man with all his compassionate understanding—as well as all his strength so loves and serves his God. For God is in all—and for all—and the reason for all . . . be it high or low or here or there or coming or going . . . in the eyes of those who, as yet, can see the Whole only in fragmentary bits. PEACE! BE STILL AND KNOW THAT I AM GOD! And that I shall forever reign supreme over the Universal Scheme and teach My children Life and Growth and Love and Laughter . . . and the darkness shall disappear in the Light of Truth!

THE DECLARATION (UNIVERSAL BROTHERHOOD OF FAITHISTS)

I declare unto Thee, JEHOVIH, in the presence of the Faithists here assembled, that henceforth I will worship none but Thee, Thou All Highest Creator. Who art variously named by mortals, Jehovih, The Great Spirit, The Almighty, The Eternal Father, The I Am, The All Light, Eolin, Ormazd. The Architect of the Universe, Ever Present in all and yet above all, unto Whom none can attain for ever.

I declare that I will henceforth turn from evil and strive to do good, that I may come into at-one-ment with Thee, Thou All Father, Life of all life, and Soul of all souls, Who art to the understanding of all the living even as the sun is to the light of day.

I promise to abnegate self and dwell in harmony with my brother and sister Faithists, also to respect the authority of the Chief of the Community.

I promise to put aside the uncharitable tongue, and not to perceive evil in any man, woman, or child, but only the limitations of their birth and surroundings. In Thee, O Jehovih, is my trust. Amen.

Notes: *The Declaration is taken from the* Kosmon Church Service Book, *where it is an important liturgical element. It is frequently repeated in the various church rituals.*

* * *

Flying Saucer Groups

THE SPIRITUAL AIMS (AETHERIUS SOCIETY)

1. To spread the teachings of the Master Aetherius, Jesus and other Cosmic Masters.

2. To administer Spiritual Healing.

3. To prepare the way for the coming of the next Master.

4. To organize the Society so as to create favourable conditions for closer contact with and ultimately meetings with people from the other Planets.

5. To tune in and radiate the Power transmitted during a Holy time or Spiritual Push, in order to enhance all Spiritual practices, irrespective of one's religious beliefs.

6. To form a Brotherhood based on the teachings and knowledge of the Cosmic Masters.

7. To spread the Spiritual Operation known as Operation Starlight throughout the World, as directed by the Space People.

* * *

SPIRITUAL CREED FOR LIGHT WORKERS (MARK-AGE)

We all are of the one Spirit.
Spirit is Divine Mind.

We all think (send and receive thoughts) through the one Mind, therefore what you think about others is received by them through one Mind Source.

What you wish for them or believe of them is received and returned (re-acted) to you by the same Energy Source, Mind.

As you think, so it is manifested in your life now or later.

What you think about, you form.

As thought is energy and mind is force, so you create your own life, relationships, supply, services, love.

As you think, so you are, bad or good, ugly or beautiful, ill or healthy, hated or loved.

This is divine law in action.

Notes: *Not a statement of Mark-Age belief, this creed is a liturgical affirmation representative of a general New Age perspective. It nevertheless affirms some basic opinions about the supremacy of Mind and Spirit, common to New Age groups.*

* * *

DECALOG, THE TWELVE BIDS FROM PETALE (SEMJASE SILVER STAR CENTER)

1. You ought have no other powers and no gods, idols and saints besides The Creation.

2. You ought keep holy the Name of The Creation and not misuse it.

3. You ought make every day a holiday and keep it holy (control it).

4. You ought not be in violation to your bond with The Creation; contained therein: you ought not commit adultery.

5. Honor The Creation as you honor, respect and love your father and mother.

6. You ought not kill by degeneration.

7. You ought not be depriving or expropriating.

8. You ought not bear false witness against The Creation and the Life.

9. You ought never ever speak an untruth.

10. You ought not desire with greediness material treasures and the possessions of your fellow creatures.

11. You ought not swear at the truth.

12. Never ever place The Creation's Laws and The Creations Bids into unworthy cults.

Notes: *With an obvious reliance upon the traditional Ten Commandments, the Twelve Bids [or Commandments] were given to Edmund "Billy Meier" by the space brothers (spiritual teachers believed to have come from outer space). Ultimate reality is named the Creation, which has both a male and female aspect. "Bid" is a translation of the German word "Gebote," meaning to command or to bid.*

PRINCIPLES (SOLAR LIGHT CENTER)

1. Belief in an Infinite Creator (the All-Knowing One. Our Radiant One, of the Space beings) and in the Cosmic Christ, the Spiritual Hierarchy, and the Great White Brotherhood.

2. Belief in the expression of universal love, compassion and understanding as the true basis for world peace and the healing of all mankind's ills. This embodies reverence for all life and non-violence toward man and animals.

3. Acceptance of the eternal truths given by World Avatars (Jesus, Buddha, Krishna) and spiritual Masters as taught in most esoteric schools of thought. These include Man's spiritual evolution through many embodiments on an ever-ascending spiral path of consciousness under the Laws of Cause and Effect (Karma) and Rebirth. They outline methods whereby the individual may speed up spiritual unfoldment by attunement with the higher self, the "god-self" within, and by the transmutation of old Karma utilizing the higher frequencies.

4. Belief that other planets are inhabited by advanced beings who have attained mastery over space travel, hence they are called Space Beings. (Their civilization is far superior to any found on Earth. They have ended war, disease, poverty, taxes, and famine; they control the weather and gravity and provide free energy.)

5. Belief in communication with advanced Space Beings by such means as direct physical contact, tele-thought, telepathy, tensor beam, light beam, and other means. Recognition that such communications provide information of vital importance to Earth man and should be given out to all New Age souls who are ready to accept such teachings.

6. Belief that a spiritual Light is being sent to uplift Earth and raise the frequency level of all cells, all atoms, in preparation for the coming change, and this Light can be focused through certain Light Centers in Vortex areas. Space Beings are assisting at this time of change in many ways. They are concerned for Earth-man's welfare and are prepared to prevent complete destruction of the planet through a nuclear holocaust or gigantic geological change.

7. Belief that our Freedom of Attitude toward: (1) the Infinite Creator, (2) Self (ego), (3) Other beings, are the deciding factors on the path to the All Highest, and service in the Universal Program is the key to this.

8. Belief that as the end of a Great Cycle of approximately 26,000 years approaches, a "cleansing" is taking place due to Light energies received, and the planet is being prepared for a density level transition into a higher frequency. Such a change heralds the Second Coming of Christ and the beginning of a Golden Age.

WHAT IS UNDERSTANDING (UNDERSTANDING, INC.)

Begin with this: to know yourself is to begin to understand others, who thereby increase their understanding of you.

To communicate is to understand. Communicate.

To truly desire to understand is to begin to understand the person, matter, condition or situation desired.

To pray to understand is to approach understanding; but prayer must have wings or feet provided by you to be increasingly efficient.

To understand another, listen to his words with the true desire to understand them and him/her. If you don't begin to understand you're not listening or being heard.

Love Understanding is the law of magnetic attraction in the Universe which maintains its parts in their Divine-Law relation to one another. If you're not thus related to your environment and its inhabitants, you are imbalancing or contributing to imbalance. If your environment is sick you cannot be wholly well.

Understanding begins with you, me, our families, our political sub-divisions, extending gradually from you and me, endlessly in *all* directions. Not to seek beyond ourselves is to ourselves remain lost.

Understanding is love, graduated through acquaintance, friendship, cooperation, collaboration *wherever indicated*, listening and being heard, talking with intent to contribute and clearly transmit sincere motive, mutual understanding being the intent and desire.

Understanding balances you/he/him/it/they, exalting all.

Understanding is a sincere attempt to expand consciousness, never wholly by yourself alone.

"Understanding" is the best definition of "love."

"The love that passeth (or seeth through) understanding," is the love-understanding which Understanding, Inc., Understanding Magazine, Understanding Units and individual members, seek to awaken in all men.

Nations are no more different from one another than any two individuals. To understand the individual is to approach understanding of the nation, any nation. Each nation is an aggregate individual composed of its people.

Understanding units are forums for discussion. Discussion, even heated if positive, leads to understanding.

Individual members of Units and members-at-large are volunteer counsellors. They will listen to individual misunderstanding to the nearest member of Understanding, Inc., who will listen and comment as inspired.

Notes: *According to Understanding, Inc., its philosophy is best expressed in the belief that there are more areas of agreement than disagreement between all men and that finding those areas will bring about understanding, cooperation, and peace to all. A more substantive statement, What Is Understanding, was written by Arthur J. Burks and published in the organization's periodical.*

THE CREED OF FAHSZ (UNIVERSE SOCIETY CHURCH)

I am Fahsz. I am the servant of the Father and Brsgv and the Master of Anahsz who permeates, the universe on the physical plain of existence. On my right hand there are seven stars and on my left hand seven golden pyramids. The seven pyramids are the seven steps to Fahsz through Anahsz, and the seven stars the seven Inner teachers. Write of the things I have told you and the Things you have seen in the Kingdom or marveled at during the Shel. There are two great forces in the universe of which only my deserving acceptors can be aware. These are HAL and SHEL; the Force of Light and The Creative Force. You are to create a temple of many pyramids which is ordered to be opened unto all who receive Anahsz and the one who is at the right hand of Anahsz. These two have received Shel; no others have. Follow my teachings and you shall live, obey my acceptors and you shall permeate the universe. The one who sits at the right hand of Anahsz is his opposite number; each of these has an opposite number who acts as a mirror.

Notes: *Fahsz is the extraterrestial contacted by Hal Wilcox, founder of the Universe Society Church. His creed is a cryptic document that requires some deciphering as it uses jargon and symbols peculiar to the church.*

* * *

Drug-Related Groups

AFFIRMATIONS (CHURCH OF THE AWAKENING)

1. WE AFFIRM the unity of all mankind, of whatever nation, race or religion.

2. WE AFFIRM the reality of man's spiritual nature, called Christ, Light, Life, Atman or Buddha, and the importance of our recognition of this Light or Christ as our real Being, rather than the physical or intellectual form.

3. WE AFFIRM the importance of achieving a personal experience of this Reality and its oneness with Universal Reality, through the Unitive Experience.

4. WE AFFIRM the importance of a properly directed psychedelic sacrament (through the use of peyote or other sacramental substance approved by the Board of Directors) as a means toward the achievement of the Unitive Experience.

5. WE AFFIRM the importance of the practical application of the Unitive Experience in our daily lives, through the loving acceptance of each person, and the recognition of the Being of each as this Reality or Christ.

6. WE AFFIRM the importance of extending the awareness of the reality of man's spiritual Being, both in ourselves and in others, as a major factor in the solution of both personal and world problems.

Notes: *This statement simply explains the church's mystical approach to life through the ingestion of psychedelic sacramental substances.*

* * *

PRINCIPLES OF THE NEO-AMERICAN CHURCH

Members of the NEO-AMERICAN CHURCH subscribe to the following principles:

(1). Everyone has the right to expand his consciousness and stimulate visionary experience by whatever means he considers desirable and proper without interference from anyone.

(2). The psychedelic substances, such as LSD, are the True Host of the Church, not "drugs". They are sacramental foods, manifestations of the "the Grace of God", of the infinite imagination of the Self, and therefore belong to everyone.

(3). We do not encourage the ingestion of psychedelics by those who are unprepared.

Notes: *The principles of the church are much more a manifesto for the religious use of psychedelic substances than a full statement of the church's teaching.*

* * *

Miscellaneous Psychic New Age Groups

CREED (CHURCH OF DIVINE MAN)

We the church believe in: limitless space, timeless endurance, neverending acceptance, everlasting patience, and continuous comprehension. "What if a man gain the whole world and lose his own soul?" asks Jesus. To a mystic, with eyes turned inward to infinity and cosmic consciousness, His words have great meaning. Psychic freedom creates no ideologies, no isms, no dissenting philosophies which divide, corrupt and destroy communication between human souls. No governments are upturned, no faiths cut down by the sword, no sects or types eliminated: only a one to one contact between the cosmic and a living soul, which flames quietly, bringing a lifetime of contentment and a realization that nothing in this world is worth exchanging for that attainment.

Notes: *This creed is not so much a statement of beliefs (it denies the need of ideologies and isms) as an assertion of the freedom necessary for a psychically atuned person to develop. The church strives not for agreement of opinion, but the provision of a context in which personal contact with the divine can be most easily realized.*

* * *

THE CREED (CHURCH OF EDUCTIVISM)

WE, the members of the Church of Spiritual Freedom, have joined ourselves together in order to proclaim and promulgate these considerations of the human spirit which we embrace and endorse.

WE BELIEVE that men and women are born with the rights of the human spirit and that these rights are not to be suspended by any agency whatever.

WE BELIEVE that men and women have the right to seek God however He may be found and perceived.

WE BELIEVE that men and women have the right to create alternatives in accordance with their ability and to select freely those alternatives which they perceive will provide them with the highest standards of survival possible to them.

We believe that men and women have the right to their lives, the right to their thoughts and opinions and to their sanity, and the right to defend these blessed rights from those who would coerce or defraud them thereof.

WE BELIEVE that men and women have the right to freely communicate with one another by the spoken or written word and to concur with, augment or offer rebuttal to whichever ideas they may care to consider, or not, as they choose.

WE BELIEVE that men and women have the right to freely join together in organizations, churches or governments for their mutual betterment and to support these institutions so long as they keep the faith reposed in them.

WE BELIEVE that it is wicked to coerce and/or defraud one's fellow man and that those who sanction coercion or fraud, publicly or secretly, thereby eschews such activity whereas virtue is manifested by him that knoweth to do good and doeth it.

WE BELIEVE that the human spirit is fundamentally well disposed and we believe that the occlusions which mar and blemish the human spirit can be removed by the application of spiritual technology and that the psychic upliftment which accompanies these spiritual activities is frequently manifested in physical improvement as well.

WE BELIEVE that in order to responsibly implement these rights, the spirit of man must be free to create and exercise the power of choices, and, to this end,

WE DEDICATE OURSELVES AND OUR CHURCH, and we invite those who find themselves in accord, to consider uniting with us in this endeavor.

Notes: *This church, founded by Jack Horner, a former member of the Church of Scientology, promulgated its creed in 1970, at which time the church was known as the Church of Spiritual Freedoms.*

* * *

DOCTRINE (CHURCH OF MERCAVAH)

1. Man is a spiritual being with a physical classification. All forms of life are spiritual; all of life itself is spiritual. If life is born of action and action born of abstract ideas, then all of existence is abstract. That factor which moves life, which moves it beyond the abstract into application, is spiritual.

2. Since man is a spiritual being, those paths we each walk, our individual lives, must be defined and refined spiritually. "The search to know is a spiritual path, whether it be science or religion." (R. O. M.)

3. Each individual is a light within the universe. Each is a star.

4. Each individual must find both within and without himself the path to self-knowledge.

5. This path will ultimately lead to harmony. Discord is a part of the balance within the equilibrium of all. We can not achieve harmony until we see the harmony within the discord. Discord is nothing but imperfect harmony.

6. Our responsibility is first to that flame within each of us. Our responsibility is then to let our light shine before all men.

7. When we limit the truth of others we cast shadows on our own path.

8. To allow others the freedom of search and the freedom of error is to increase the light on our own way.

9. Within everything is Truth, and within Truth is born responsibility.

10. Life IS. Life is the plane of spirit and the plane of reality.

Notes: *Like the Church of Divine Man, the statement of the Church of Mercavah does not strive to present a whole perspective but to argue for the freedom of individuals to find a path to self-knowledge within the context of spiritual attainment.*

* * *

CREED (CHURCH OF SCIENTOLOGY)

We of the Church believe:

That all men of whatever race, color or creed were created with equal rights.

That all men have inalienable rights to their own religious practices and their performance.

That all men have inalienable rights to their own lives.

That all men have inalienable rights to their sanity.

That all men have inalienable rights to their own defence.

That all men have inalienable rights to conceive, choose, assist and support their own organizations, churches and governments.

That all men have inalienable rights to think freely, to talk freely, to write freely their own opinions and to counter or utter or write upon the opinions of others.

That all men have inalienable rights to the creation of their own kind.

That the souls of men have the rights of men.

That the study of the mind and the healing of mentally caused ills should not be alienated from religion or condoned in non-religious fields.

CREED (CHURCH OF SCIENTOLOGY) (continued)

And that no agency less than God has the power to suspend or set aside these rights, overtly or covertly.

And we of the Church believe:

That man is basically good.

That he is seeking to survive.

That his survival depends upon himself and upon his fellows, and his attainment of brotherhood with the Universe.

And we of the Church believe that the laws of God forbid Man:

To destroy his own kind.

To destroy the sanity of another.

To destroy or enslave another's soul.

To destroy or reduce the survival of one's companions or one's group.

And we of the Church believe:

That the spirit can be saved *and*

That the spirit alone may save or heal the body.

Notes: *The Creed of the Church of Scientology is not so much a statement of beliefs as of human rights. While a few basic church beliefs are affirmed (man is good and seeking to survive), few of the church's essential teachings are even mentioned.*

*   *   *

STATEMENT OF BELIEFS (CONGREGATIONAL CHURCH OF PRACTICAL THEOLOGY)

PREAMBLE

You will notice in number 14 of the following statement of beliefs that it is our contention that a person should not be restricted to a specific creed or set of beliefs. Our minds should be like an "open book" through which we are constantly seeking to find God's truth in all of life, and therefore, we should be growing spiritually each day. If we try to restrict ourselves to a certain creed or a specific set of beliefs, we may at the same time be restricting our spiritual growth.

The following statement of beliefs has been written by the Administrative Committee, approved by the Executive Committee and the General Assembly of The Congregational Church of Practical Theology, however, we emphasize the fact that they are not, and will not be adopted as final, for we are still seeking spiritual enlightenment, and as we learn new truths, those which are presented here may be changed or completely disregarded.

1. We believe that God is our loving Father, and the loving Father of all mankind.

2. We believe that God is the power and energy which brought the worlds into being, has made man and has given man that part of Himself which we call life, and has set before man the way which will enable him to walk free and secure.

3. We believe that God is Spirit. God is not a being separate and far away, but is a Spirit within us. God is part of us and we are part of Him. God is right where we are at all times. We have constant access to Him.

4. We believe that God made man as a manifestation of His love, for part of love is sharing, and God wanted to share even a part of Himself, therefore, man was made through the love of God, thus all men are equal in God's sight.

    NOTE! We emphasize the dignity and love of all mankind, people of all races, colors, religions, social backgrounds, and economic levels. Therefore, we are dedicated to living service to all individuals, society and the world at large, with no restrictions or prejudice based on race, color, religion, social background or economic level.

5. We believe that God is love, God's will is good for all mankind; Joy, not pain or sorrow; Life, not death or destruction; wholeness, not imperfection; plenty, no lack; peace, not fear and anxiety.

6. We believe that God will supply everything we need for a full, happy life, if we trust His love and let ourselves be used by His wisdom. When we let ourselves be used by the wisdom of God, we believe that every adversity, every failure, every disappointment, every error of judgment, and every defeat can be used as stepping stones of priceless value.

7. We believe that God's will for all persons is good, and that behind all appearances the goodness of God stands, that through every change His good is unchanging, that through every experience His power is present to help and to bless. God kindles anew the dead hope of all who tune themselves to Him and draw upon the great reservoir of His unlimited intelligence.

8. We believe that whatever man needs will come to him through the love of God. When we are willing to give our efforts to make a worthwhile contribution to live, our prosperity will be supplied by our loving Father.

9. We believe that God has provided us with the power to shape our own thoughts, and the privilege of fitting them to the pattern of our choice.

    In other words, God has placed before us the possibility of attaining the riches of life. The riches of true friendship; the riches of achievement; the riches of harmony in home relationships; the riches of sound physical health; the riches of freedom from fear; the riches of enthusiasm; the riches of song and laughter; the riches of self-discipline; the riches of play; the riches of discovery; the riches of faith; the riches of meditation; the riches of understanding and the riches of economic security.

    Buddha taught "all that we are is the result of what we have thought." The Bible says, "As a man thinketh in his heart, so is he."

    We believe this means we have the power to form our own character and to create our own happiness.

This is the reason it is so important to be careful about the thoughts we permit to permeate our minds.

"Whatsoever things are true, whatsoever things are honest, whatsoever things are just, whatsoever things are pure, whatsoever things are lively, whatsoever things are of good report . . . think on these things." Philippians 4:8.

We are literally what we think. Our character is the sum of all our thoughts. A noble character is not a thing of favor or chance, but the natural result of continued effort in right thinking, the effect of long-cherished association with noble thoughts.

0. We believe that we become spiritually rich when we discover the reality of God within; when we are conscious of the oneness of all life; when we know the power of meditation, and when we experience kinship with nature.

1. We believe that life is an eternal unfoldment; an existence which has no end. In other words, we do not believe that God made man just for the purpose of living in a body for a few minutes or a few years, then to die and cease to exist. Nor do we believe that, if man fails to fulfill his life now he is everlastingly damned. The life which God put into man is a part of God Himself, and is for eternity. We are constantly growing, learning, unfolding—failing, perhaps many times—but eventually attaining the stature of the fullness of God.

NOTE! We suggest reincarnation as a possible explanation concerning the way in which this unfoldment may take place, but, we by no means insist that this idea be accepted. In fact, we believe the present is more important to us now than the past or the future. The important thing is what we are making of the present moment.

8. We believe in the divinity of Jesus Christ, but we also believe that, like Jesus, each of us is a child of God and therefore, we are all divine in nature.

9. We believe that Jesus Christ came to earth and shared the common lot of man. In doing this, he lived an outstanding life of love, which revealed to us an example of the true Spirit of God, and He calls for us to follow His example of love.

0. We believe that love is the most important characteristic we can possess. We accept the definition of love as it has been recorded in I Corinthians the 13th chapter, believing that love does not pass away. Nor does it fail those who live by it.

1. We believe that God calls us to be His Church, to accept the cost and joy of discipleship, as it is revealed through us when we show true love to all mankind.

2. We believe that God calls us to be His servants in the service of men, and that we are to be channels through which God's will is done.

3. We believe there can be no richer man than he who is devoted to a labor of love and who keeps himself busy serving others, for this type of labor is the highest form of human expression which reveals the God-part of man.

24. We believe that every person we meet in our daily life, regardless of his race, color, religion, social background or economic level, is a child of God and we, therefore, should look to him as one worthy of our love, understanding and consideration.

25. We believe that love is the part of man which reveals God's image. Love is an outward expression of the spiritual nature of man. True love clears out selfishness, greed, jealousy, envy and prejudice. True greatness will not be found where love does not abide.

26. We believe that every change which comes into our life and world provides us with an opportunity to learn and grow. And whatever comes to us, we know that God can help us to meet it courageously, working through us to accomplish good.

27. We accept the Bible as a textbook of truth, and we believe it represents much of the truth which has been revealed to men in ages past, however, we believe Truth is never final and that it is still being revealed. Therefore, we accept statements of truth from all souces, secular and religious.

28. We believe it is our privilege and duty to praise and honor God whom we recognize as that creative Force, behind and in the universe, who reveals Himself as energy, as life, as order, as beauty, as thought as conscience, and as love.

Blessing and honor, glory and power be unto Him. Amen.

SUBMITTED AND APPROVED BY THE BOARD OF DIRECTORS OF THE CONGREGATIONAL CHURCH OF PRACTICAL THEOLOGY, OCTOBER 17, 1970.

E. Arthur Winkler, Ph.D., Th.D., President, The Congregational Church of Practical Theology.

Notes: *This statement was written to be as inclusive of different opinions as possible.*

* * *

COPTIC BELIEFS (COPTIC FELLOWSHIP OF AMERICA)

1. That revelations of truth are ever present to all men and are understood as capacities are developed.

2. That these truths as they were perceived and passed on to the White Brotherhood, the Essenes and the Coptic Order are the foundation of our teachings.

3. That God's love, made evident by and through natural law, is universal and everlasting.

4. That life, creation, progress and evolution emanate from this God Love Expression—that it has ever been and ever will be.

5. That love, will and wisdom are natural attributes that guide individual and social destinies to perfection.

COPTIC BELIEFS (COPTIC FELLOWSHIP OF
    AMERICA) (continued)

6.   That each individual soul lives in eternal continuity, wherein the threshold of reformation can be crossed at any time in the here or hereafter by those who will it so. That continuity of life is an essential part of this belief.

7.   That the law of Karma (cause and effect) is Nature's unavoidable mode of refinement of Man, his expressions and his environment.

8.   That ignorance and misdirection obscure these realities from the majority of mankind.

9.   That joy and happiness and health are the natural state of those who have achieved a harmonious God-Nature-Man relationship.

*   *   *

STATEMENT OF FAITH (FOUNDATION FAITH OF GOD)

GOD. THERE IS ONE GOD OVER ALL, WHO IS THE GOD OF LOVE. WE ARE HIS CHILDREN, AND HE IS OUR FATHER.

GOD created all things. He created matter, the universe, the world, and all that is in the world.

> *And he is before all things, and by him all things consist.* Colossians 1:17

We can know GOD through His Works, the stars, the sky, the planets, the earth, the creatures, the seasons, the elements.

We can know GOD through His Word, the Scriptures of the Bible.

We can know GOD through Jesus Christ GOD the Son, through His life and the gift of the Holy Ghost.

> *Great is our Lord, and of great power: his understanding is infinite.* Psalm 147:5

It is our duty to love and obey GOD.

> *Fear GOD, and keep his commandments: for this is the whole duty of man.* Ecclesiastes 12:13

GOD AND THE SIN OF MAN.

Man is ashamed of his own sin. He is ashamed that he so freely lets Satan fill his heart with wickedness. The sin is Satan's, but man adopts it.

GOD is merciful and filled with compassion. He does not want man to suffer at the hand of Satan.

> *For I have no pleasure in the death of him that dieth, saith the Lord GOD.* Ezekiel 18:32

But GOD's Love is a Love of Justice; justice requires that sin be accounted for.

> *But I say unto you, that every idle word that men shall speak, they shall give account thereof in the day of judgment.* Matthew 12:36

JESUS CHRIST.

Jesus Christ is the Son of GOD — GOD the Son. GOD, in His great mercy, sent into the world Jesus Christ, offering true salvation to man.

Jesus is the one link between GOD and fallen man. He is the only being who, as man, overcame the works of Satan. This He did in His life and in His triumph over death through His resurrection.

> *For there is one GOD, and one mediator between GOD and men, the man Christ Jesus.* Timothy 2:5
>
> *For GOD so loved the world, that he gave his only begotten Son, that whosoever believeth in him should not perish.* John 3:16

JESUS AND THE SINS OF MAN.

Jesus Christ, the Son of GOD, became man and took on the nature of man, facing and overcoming the temptations of Satan. By thus taking on man's sinful state to His death and in triumph overcoming death (Satan) through His Resurrection, He made possible the redemption of man.

> *But GOD commendeth his love toward us, in that, while we were yet sinners, Christ died for us.* Romans 5:8
>
> *For GOD sent not his Son into the world to condemn the world; but that the world through him might be saved.* John 3:17

SALVATION FOR MAN.

Salvation for man, through the redemptive spirit of Jesus Christ, is a gift from GOD. Man alone, separated from GOD, cannot free himself from the wiles of Satan, nor can he alone make true recompense for the sins which he thereby assumes.

Jesus took on man's sins, and paid sufficient sacrifice for them.

Salvation is a gift from GOD, granted to those who confess Jesus as their only Savior, humbly, and in repentance, for their sin — for the sin of having let Satan rule their thoughts and actions.

> *Repent: for the kingdom of heaven is at hand.* Matthew 4:17
>
> *And this is the will of him that sent me, that every one which seeth the Son, and believeth on him, may have everlasting life: and I will raise him up at the last day.* John 6:40

THE HOLY GHOST.

Jesus, after His Ascension, gave His followers the gift of the Holy Ghost (Holy Spirit) — the lasting presence of GOD — to be our Comforter.

The Holy Ghost is the third person of the Trinity (Father, Son and Holy Ghost) and is available to all who believe in Jesus as Savior.

> *But the Comforter, which is the Holy Ghost whom the Father will send in my name, he shall teach you all things, and bring all things to your remembrance, whatsoever I have said unto you.* John 14:26

BAPTISM.

The Baptism of a believer (in the Name of the Father, Son and Holy Ghost) is a symbol of his rebirth in Christ — his repentance and acceptance of Jesus as Savior.

> *He that believeth and is baptized, shall be saved; but he that believeth not shall be damned.* Mark 16:16

DUTIES OF THE BELIEVER.

Rebirth in Jesus, being "born again," is a gift of GOD's Grace. For this we are thankful and resolve to work, in Jesus's Name, to cast out Satan, both as a tempter to ourselves and to the lives of others. Jesus has given us the strength to do this and made it possible by His atonement for our former sin.

JESUS LIVES.

Jesus was raised from the dead, a miracle and a demonstration of His ascent over Satan — who would that all men come to death.

In the Resurrection He appeared to men, and in particular His Disciples, granting them the gift of the Holy Ghost, that GOD's work might continue in the world.

Jesus ascended into Heaven, returning to GOD the Father.

> *Who is gone into heaven, and is on the right hand of GOD; angels and authorities and powers being made subject unto him.* I Peter 3:22

JESUS WILL COME AGAIN.

There will be trials and hardships in the world, for Satan still lives. Satan is conquered by Jesus and may be overcome by Christians, but he still has much to work with.

> *And ye shall hear of wars and rumours of war: see that ye be not troubled; for all these things must come to pass, but the end is not yet. For nation shall rise against nation, and kingdom against kingdom: . . .* Matthew 24:6-7

But Jesus will come again to earth to judge all men in justice and to rule in peace. He will honor those who have acknowledged Him as Savior and have truly served Him. He will come in GODly righteousness, and works of iniquity will be to no avail. This will be His true hour of glory, when the cycle of this world will be ended, and the people of GOD will return to GOD whence they came.

> *. . . this same Jesus, which is taken up from you into heaven, shall so come in like manner as ye have seen him go into heaven.* Acts 1:11

> *And if I go and prepare a place for you, I will come again, and receive you unto myself; that where I am, there ye may be also.* John 14:3

SATAN CAST OUT.

At the end time, when Jesus will rule on earth in righteousness, the devil, Satan, will be cast out, and have no more influence, seen or unseen, upon GOD's people.

> *Now is the judgement of this world: now shall the price of this world* be cast out.* *Satan John 12:31

> *And the devil that deceived them was cast into the lake of fire and brimstone . . . and shall be*

tormented day and night for ever and ever. Revelation 20:10

THE GLORY OF GOD.

The Glory of GOD's Kingdom will be seen, both on earth and in Heaven. For that which is of GOD in the world must return to Him.

The works of man, however inspired, are small when compared to the immensity of the universe and the Greatness of the Creator.

Man's struggles for existence and attempts at an understanding of the great mysteries are of little avail when compared to the Will of the Lord.

GOD is to be praised, for the highest hope of man is to walk in peace with his GOD. In Jesus Christ we have this opportunity and have only to reach out in true repentance and trust to be received in Grace.

It is right that man should praise the Lord, and spend his days in worship and thanksgiving.

> *Praise ye the LORD. Praise GOD in his sanctuary: praise him in the firmament of his power.*

> *Let every thing that hath breath praise the LORD. Praise ye the LORD.* Psalm 150:1, 6

Notes: *The Foundation Faith of God was founded in the mid-1970s by a group of individuals, many of whom had been members and/or leaders of the Church of the Final Judgment. Since its founding, the church has moved consistently toward an orthodox Christian position.*

*   *   *

THIRTEEN PURPOSES (WORLD CATALYST CHURCH)

1. To be a Light unto the feet of all men.

2. To lead mankind to the truth that all wisdom, all the Kingdom, is within HIMSELF.

3. To point the way to that inner door where man may find himself.

4. To open the way to that inner wisdom of the soul through meditation and self-searching . . . without any false bait to appease sensual cravings or desires for idle amusements.

5. To be a church of the road, with no expensive buildings but an earnest response to wherever the need may be.

6. To give spiritual enlightenment or counselling to all who truly seek, regardless of race, color or creed.

7. A church that condemns no other religion or church but one that is willing to work with all toward the one goal.

8. To be a church that recognizes all things are evolving, including truth and the need to work harmoniously with both spiritual and scientific efforts.

9. To be a church that exerts no pressure or persuasion but one that grants free choice to all as to whether they wish to follow us or not.

THIRTEEN PURPOSES (WORLD CATALYST CHURCH) (continued)

10. A church that relies entirely upon the freewill effort and financial assistance of all men.

11. To gain an understanding of the fixed laws of the universe and how to conform to them in joy and harmony, and *not* to flatter, coax or cajole God to grant our impossible whims.

12. To awaken all men to the only enemy that obstructs and darkens our doorway to glory . . . the greatest of all deceivers, MAN'S SELF!

13. To abolish anger, self-desire and ignorance.

Chapter 18
Ancient Wisdom Family

Rosicrucianism

OBJECTIVES OF THE ROSICRUCIAN ANTHROPOMORPHIC LEAGUE

To investigate the occult laws of nature and the super physical powers of man;

To promote the principles which will eventually lead to recognition of the truth of the universal brotherhood of man, without distinction as to sex, creed, race or color;

To acquire, disseminate, and exemplify a knowledge of spiritual truth as given to the world by the Elder Brothers of the White Lodge;

To study and teach ancient religion, philosophy and astrology in the light of modern needs;

To encourage the study of science and art in the hope that religion, art and science—which are a veritable trinity, the equilateral triangle which has always been used as a symbol of the Divine—may again be recognized as portals through which egos must pass in attaining to the mastery of self;

And, finally, to attain to self-conscious immortality, which is the crowning feat of evolution.

The Path is not strewn with roses, but thereon only can self-conscious immortality be won—THERE IS NO OTHER WAY.

Notes: *Rosicrucian groups are part of a secret occult tradition and, as a whole, have refrained from making any public statements concerning their position. The principles of the Rosicrucian Anthropomorphic League were published occasionally in the League's periodical.*

* * *

Occult Orders

TENETS (HOLY ORDER OF MANS)

1. The Holy Order of MANS is a non-denominational, non-sectarian group of people, banded together for the purpose of a more thorough understanding of the Universal Laws of the Creator, so they might better manifest His Creation, and thus, promote Peace and Harmony among men.

2. We accept the basic law of the Triangle and the spoken word, as tools given to us by the Creator to fulfill our needs in this life and the one to come.

3. We accept that there is both a seen and unseen plane of the Life Force as set down by the Creator when It created us.

4. We accept that Life is continuous, uninterrupted, and ever evolving at the point of Being.

5. We accept that Man has the ability as an instrument of healing, as given by the Creator, to heal the sick, the lame and the halt, as well as the mentally ill, of the spirit, as vouched for by the Master Man, Jesus.

6. We accept the giving of Communion, both materially and spiritually.

7. We accept Baptism of the child, the adult, as the baptism of the Holy Spirit, as the lifting of consciousness.

8. We accept the confession of sins, through the confessional, if it is so desired by the individual, by and through the Word given as a divine edict to every truly ordained Priest.

9. We accept the unity of the Great Creator in God, Mind and matter, throughout this solar system.

10. We accept that all men and women be accepted on an equal basis in the eyes of the Creator and the Holy Order of MANS.

11. We accept that, above all things, man must be free to choose the things in this life, both spiritual and material, which are one.

12. We accept man as an Evolving Being of unlimited resources and unlimited expansion, with a God of Infinite Wisdom.

Notes: *The Holy Order accepts the Nicene Creed as a full statement of the community's faith. It has also published a set of tenets which cover matters not mentioned in the creed.*

Theosophy

THE THREE OBJECTS OF THE THEOSOPHICAL SOCIETY

FIRST. To form a nucleus of the Universal Brotherhood of Humanity, without distinction of race, creed, sex, caste or color.

SECOND. To encourage the study of Comparative Religion, Philosophy and Science.

THIRD. To investigate the unexplained laws of Nature and the powers latent in man.

Notes: *Common to all branches of theosophy are the three objectives which gave direction to its early program.*

* * *

THE TEMPLE AS A WORLD MOVEMENT (TEMPLE OF THE PEOPLE)

In order to do anything well we must have a plan, a program. Therefore, it is well to outline what the Temple program for the world consists of. This can be summed up in five definite objectives:

FIRST: To formulate the truths of religion as the fundamental factor in human evolution. This does not mean the formulation of a creed, but rather the recognition of the religious instinct in human beings. Every religion that the world has ever known has been an attempt to interpret this primary impulse in human nature. To the extent that we are able to interpret wisely this impulse, are we able to undersand what true religion is.

SECOND: To set forth a philosophy of life that is in accord with natural and Divine Law.

THIRD: To promote the study of the sciences and the fundamental facts and laws on which the sciences are based. This will permit us to extend our belief and knowledge from what is known to the unknown, from the physical to the super-physical. When accomplished, such will corroborate those spiritual teachings which have been given to mankind from time to time by the Masters of Light.

FOURTH: To promote the study and practice of the Arts on Fundamental lines, showing that the Arts are in reality the application of knowledge to human good and welfare. The Christos can speak to humanity through art as well as through any other fundamental line of manifestation.

FIFTH: The promotion of knowledge of a true social science based on immutable law, the law showing the relationship between man and man, man and God, and man and nature. When these relationships are once understood, we will instinctively formulate and follow the Law of true Brotherhood. It is ignorance that perpetuates separateness, and once humanity can spiritually see the relation of all things, the Law of Unity begins to operate instantaneously.

Remember, the Temple as a principle includes the whole world. We become a mighty power for good as we keep attuned to the ideal of unselfish service, and with minds open and receptive to truth from every angle.

Notes: *Within this statement are references to theosophical basics such as reliance on natural and Divine law and the teachings of the masters.*

* * *

SOME PRINCIPLES OF THEOSOPHY (THEOSOPHICAL SOCIETY OF AMERICA)

1. One Life pervades the universe and keeps it in being.

2. The phenomenal universe is the manifestation of an eternal, boundless and Immutable Principle beyond the range of human understanding.

3. Spirit (or consciousness) and matter are the two polar aspects of the ultimate Reality. These two with the interplay between them comprise a trinity from which proceed innumerable universes, which come and go in an endless cycle of manifestation and dissolution, all being expressions of the Reality.

4. Every solar system is an orderly scheme governed by laws of nature that reflect transcendental intelligence. 'Deity is Law,' said H.P. Blavatsky. The visible planets of the solar system are its densest parts; it also contains invisible worlds of exceedingly tenuous matter interpenetrating the physical. The entire system is the scene of a great scheme of evolution.

5. The spirit of man (often called the soul) is in essence identical with the one supreme Spirit, 'that Unity (as Emerson put it), that Oversoul, within which every man's particular being is contained and made one with all other.' The gradual unfolding of this latent divinity takes place by means of a process of reincarnation, in accordance with the Cyclic Law, seen everywhere in Nature, of periods of activity alternating with periods of rest and assimilation.

6. 'Whatsoever a man soweth, that shall he also reap.' This is the Law of Karma under which men weave their own destiny through the ages. This is the great hope for humanity, for man can indeed become the master of his future fate by what he does in the present.

7. Man's pilgrimmage takes him from his source in the One through his experience of the many back to union with the One Divine Source. The goal for man is thus to complete the cosmic cycle of manifestation in full conscious realization of his self, no longer as polarized between consciousness and matter—self and other—but as both all and one with the Source of all. This realization constitutes Enlightenment.

Notes: *This unofficial statement published by the Theosophical Society of America attempts to summarize the society's teachings. These teachings identify the human and divine very closely and are centered upon progress through reincarnation.*

DECLARATION (UNITED LODGE OF THEOSOPHISTS)

The policy of this Lodge is independent devotion to the cause of Theosophy without professing attachment to any Theosophical organization. It is loyal to the great Founders of the Theosophical Movement, but does not concern itself with dissensions or differences of individual opinion.

The work it has on hand and the end it keeps in view are too absorbing and too lofty to leave it the time or inclination to take part in side issues. That work and that end is the dissemination of the Fundamental Principles of the philosophy of Theosophy, and the exemplification in practice of those principles, through a truer realization of the SELF; a profounder conviction of Universal Brotherhood.

It holds that the unassailable *Basis for Union* among Theosophists, wherever and however situated, is "similarity of aim, purpose and teaching," and therefore has neither Constitution, Bye-Laws nor Officers, the sole bond between its Associates being that basis. And it aims to disseminate this idea among Theosophists in the furtherance of Unity.

It regards as Theosophists all who are engaged in the true service of Humanity, without distinction of race, creed, sex, condition or organization, and

It welcomes to its association all those who are in accord with its declared purposes and who desire to fit themselves, by study and otherwise, to be the better able to help and teach others.

"The true Theosophist belongs to no cult or sect, yet belongs to each and all."

The following is the form signed by Associates of the United Lodge of Theosophists:

Being in sympathy with the purposes of this Lodge as set forth in its "Declaration," I hereby record my desire to be enrolled as an Associate, it being understood that such association calls for no obligation on my part other than that which I, myself, determine.

Notes: *Members of the United Lodge are required to sign a statement of "sympathy" with the Declaration at the time of their becoming an "associate" (member) of the United Lodge.*

* * *

Alice Bailey Groups

THE GREAT INVOCATION

From the point of Light within the Mind of God Let light stream forth into the minds of men. Let Light descend on Earth.

From the point of Love within the Heart of God Let love stream forth into the hearts of men. May Christ return to Earth.

From the centre where the Will of God is known Let purpose guide the little wills of men—The purpose which the Masters know and serve.

From the centre which we call the race of men Let the Plan of Love and Light work out. And may it seal the door where evil dwells.

Let Light and Love and Power restore the Plan on Earth.

Notes: *The Alice Bailey groups are non-creedal, but common to all the groups which have formed around Bailey's books is The Great Invocation. It is frequently repeated, and copies are widely disseminated. The invocation is similiar in intent to the Spiritual Creed for Light Workers.*

* * *

Liberal Catholic Churches

THE TEACHINGS OF THE AMERICAN CATHOLIC CHURCH

THE TEACHING OF AMERICAN CATHOLIC CHURCH is Catholic in scope. There are three immutable and fundamental truths of Christian Theosophy (1st Cor. Ch. 2, v. 6 and 7).

1. That our ignorance of God and Nature is the result of the want of the Spirit and Life of God in us.

2. The only way to the Divine Knowledge is the way of the Gospel, which calls and leads us to a new birth of the Divine Nature brought forth in us.

3. The Way of the New Birth lies wholly in man's will to it, and every step of it consists in a continual dying to the selfish, corrupt will, which man has in flesh and blood.

This teaching of the Church can be summarised as follows: First—The Words of Christ. Second—The Words of the Apostles. Third—The teaching of the Catholic Church. Any teaching that is contrary to the first two cannot be deemed to be the teaching of the True and Catholic Church.

All of this teaching can be summarised in the *Beatitudes*. (There are twelve. Matt. 5, v. 3-11; 11, v. 6; 13, v. 16 and 25, v. 34.)

Notes: *The American Catholic Church uses the Apostles' and Nicene creeds, but has also published a less formal statement which is more indicative of its theosophical teachings.*

* * *

STATEMENT OF PRINCIPLES (CHURCH OF ANTIOCH)

PREAMBLE: At the heart of our faith stands the conviction: That the universe is the visible body of God and that, therefore, in God all things live, and move, and have their being;

STATEMENT OF PRINCIPLES (CHURCH OF
   ANTIOCH) (continued)

That man is, in essence, a Divine being and was created to achieve a consciousness of oneness with the Creative Intelligence;

That man will realize this exalted achievement by a gradual unfolding of the powers that are latent within him and about him, through growth in understanding, through mastery of himself, and through the implementation of currents of Divine Grace operating in and about him;

That the purpose of the CHURCH OF ANTIOCH is to provide a priestly ministry of mature spiritual guidance for all who seek this ultimate goal of human perfection (Matthew 5:48).

ARTICLE I: Inasmuch as this our faith rests on universal principles observable in Nature, we have banded ourselves together to bring into manifestation an expression of the Church Universal, also to be known as The Church of Antioch, to proclaim and give witness to the world of this faith, by which:

1. We affirm that God is Love, Power, Truth, and Light; that His Law of Good rules the world; that all His sons shall one day reach His feet, however far they stray. We hold the Fatherhood of God, the Brotherhood of man. We know that we serve Him best, when best we serve our brother;

2. We place our faith in God, the Holy and All-Glorious Trinity, who dwelleth in the spirit of man;

3. And in the eternal and indwelling Christ, the Lord of Love and Wisdom, the first-born of every creature, Who leads us to the glory of the Father, Who is Himself the Way, the Truth, and the Life, without whose Way there is no going, without whose Truth there is no knowing, without whose Life there is no living;

4. We give recognition and allegiance to the Law of Good which rules the world, and

5. We strive toward that Wisdom which leads to the Fulfillment of Life, without discriminating against any Source that would reveal a further measure of that Wisdom.

Notes: *This statement is taken from the church's constitution. Because it contains essential doctrinal statements, the preamble to the constitution is also reproduced here.*

*   *   *

AN ACT OF GNOSIS (ECCLESIA GNOSTICA)

We know Thee
Thou eternal thought
immovable, unchangeable, unlimited and unconditioned
remaining unchanged in essential essence
while forever thinking the mystery of the universe
manifesting three extensions of cosmic power
creation, preservation and destruction -
Thou, Lord of all.

We know Thee

Father
Thou secret, supreme and ineffable Maker
unchanging in essence
yet ever-changing in appearance and manifestation
visualizing as an act of consciousness the mystery of
   creation
and by an act of will absorbed into life -
Creator.

We know Thee
Son
Thou Word, Thou Logos
divine manifestation of the Lord
alone-begotten of the great stillness
begotten by an act of consciousness alone
coming to the flesh to destroy incarnate error -
Sustainer.

We know Thee
Holy Spirit
Thou giver of life and goodness
principle of love, beauty and compassion
remaining here on earth to guide and care for us
Thou, with the Father and the Son
art the wholeness upon which the manifested universe is
   erected -
and Destroyed.

We know you
Messengers
custodians of the essential wisdom of the race
preachers of the great Law
containing within yourselves spiritual insight and courage
living and laboring unselfishly
mediating between the supreme source and its creation
dedicated to the advancement of all.
We look to the absorption of the self
into the universal Will
and thus liberation
from the infinite chain of attainment.

Notes: *Not from a creedal tradition, the Ecclesia Gnostica includes this Act of Gnosis [knowledge] in its major liturgy. Within the service it functions similarly to a creed in the more orthodox liturgical traditions. Within gnosticism, the emphasis is not placed on creedal assent, but on the gaining of cosmic wisdom by the individual members.*

*   *   *

STATEMENT OF FAITH (FEDERATION OF ST. THOMAS CHRISTIAN CHURCHES)

We believe in the True Light which enlightens all in the Holy One, the Lord Jesus Christ, who brought salvation to us from the Father by the power of the Holy Spirit.

We believe that we must make a personal committment to the Lord Jesus as the Savior of our lives and the Chief Bishop of the Church.

We receive the ancient priesthood by Apostolic Succession from the Lord Jesus, Our King of Kings and Lord of Lords.

We acknowledge the Levitical Order in our deacons.

We celebrate the Aaronic and the Melchizedek orders combined in our presbyters and bishops.

We look to the Universal Divine Gnosis and the life of the world to come. We believe that the gifts of the Holy Spirit and regeneration are necessary for spiritual growth.

Blessings eternal be upon the Sons and Daughters of Light in Christ Jesus.

Amen.

Notes: *This church is gnostic in its teachings, placing its faith in the "True Light" which brought the "Universal Divine Gnosis" (wisdom).*

* * *

ABRIDGEMENT OF DOCTRINE (INTERNATIONAL LIBERAL CATHOLIC CHURCH)

1. GOD IS—immanent, eternal, and transcendent. "In Him we live, and move, and have our being." (Acts 17:28)

2. God manifests in the universe under a triplicity expressed as the Father, the Son and the Holy Spirit—co-equal and co-eternal.

3. Man, created in the image and likeness of God, is divine in essence, an unfolding spiritual intelligence. Sharing in God's nature, he cannot cease to be, and his future is one whose glory and splendor are without limits.

4. Christ ever lives as a mighty spiritual Presence in the world, guiding and sustaining His people. The divinity manifest in Him is gradually being unfolded in man, until he shall become "unto a perfect man, unto the measure of the stature of the fulness of Christ." (Eph. 4:13)

5. The world is a stage of a Divine Plan in which the soul of man, by expressing himself in varied earthly experiences, continually unfolds his God-given potential. This evolution or spiritual development follows the inviolable law of causality. "Be not deceived; God is not mocked: for whatsoever a man soweth, that shall he also reap." (Gal. 6:7)

6. Man is a link in a vast chain of lives, from the lowest to the highest. As he helps those below him, he receives help from those above him on the ladder of lives, thus receiving the "free gift of Grace." A Communion of Saints and Ministry of Angels function to help mankind evolve.

7. Man has ethical responsibilities to himself and to his fellow men. "Thou shalt love the Lord thy God with all thy heart, and with all thy soul, and with all thy mind. This is the first great commandment. And the second is like unto it, thou shalt love thy neighbor as thy-self. On these two commandments hang all the law and the prophets." (Matt. 22:37-40)

8. It is the duty of man to discern the Divine Light in himself and others: that Light "which lighteth every man that cometh into the world." (John 1:9) Because men are sons of God, they are inseparably linked together as brothers. That which harms one harms the entire brotherhood. Service to humanity and the conscious alignment of the personality with the soul's high aspirations are the laws of spiritual growth.

9. The seven Sacraments of the Church have been instituted by the Christ, outward and visible signs of inward and spiritual grace, as potent aids for the unfoldment of the divine character of man—altruism, selflessness, creativity, wisdom, compassion and nobility. Christ, the Living Head of His Church, is the true Minister of the Sacraments wherein deacons, priests and bishops function as His channels of blessing and grace to mankind.

Notes: *This statement is derived from that of the Liberal Catholic Church, Province of the United States.*

* * *

SUMMARY OF DOCTRINE (LIBERAL CATHOLIC CHURCH, PROVINCE OF THE UNITED STATES)

1. The existence of God, infinite, eternal, transcendent and immanent. He is the one existence from which all other existences are derived. "In him we live and move and have our being." (Acts xvii, 28).

2. The manifestation of God in the universe under a triplicity called in the Christian religion, Father, Son and Holy Spirit; three Persons in one God, co-equal, co-eternal, the Son "alone-born" of the Father, the Spirit proceeding from the Father and the Son. The Father, the source of all; the Son, "The Word who was made flesh and dwelt among us"; the Holy Spirit, the life-giver, the inspirer and sanctifier.

3. Man, made in the image of God, is himself divine in essence—a spark of the divine fire. Sharing God's nature, he cannot cease to exist, therefore he is eternal and his future is one whose glory and splendour have no limit.

4. Christ ever lives as a mighty spiritual presence in the world, guiding and sustaining his people. The divinity that was manifest in him is gradually being unfolded in every man, until each shall come "unto a perfect man, unto the measure of the stature of the fulness of Christ." (Eph. iv, 13).

5. The world is the theatre of an ordered plan, according to which the spirit of man, by repeatedly expressing himself in varying conditions of life and experience, continually unfolds his powers. That evolution or spiritual unfoldment takes place under an inviolable law of cause and effect. "Whatsoever a man soweth, that shall he also reap." (Gal. vi, 7). His doings in each physical incarnation largely determine his experience after death in the intermediate world (or world of purgation) and the heavenly world and greatly influence the circumstances of his next birth. Man is a link in a vast chain of life extending from

SUMMARY OF DOCTRINE (LIBERAL CATHOLIC CHURCH, PROVINCE OF THE UNITED STATES) (continued)

the highest to the lowest. As he helps those below him, so also he is helped by those who stand above him on the ladder of lives, receiving thus a "free gift of grace." There is a "communion of saints" of "just men made perfect" or holy ones, who help mankind. There is a ministry of angels.

6. Man has ethical duties to himself and to others. "Thou shalt love the Lord thy God with all thy heart and with all thy soul and with all thy mind and with all thy strength. This is the first and great commandment, and the second is like unto it: Thou shalt love thy neighbor as thyself. On these two commandments hang all the law and the prophets." (Matt. 22, 37-40)

   It is the duty of man to learn to discern the divine light in himself and others—that light "which lighteth every man" (St. John i, 9). Because men are sons of God they are brothers and inseparably linked together. That which harms one harms the entire brotherhood. Hence a man owes it as a duty to the God within himself and others: first, to endeavor constantly to live up to the highest that is in him, thereby enabling that God within himself to become more perfectly manifest, and, secondly, to recognize the fact of that brotherhood by constant effort towards unselfishness, love, consideration for, and service of, his fellowmen. Service of humanity and the sacrifice of the lower self to the higher are laws of spiritual growth.

7. Christ instituted various sacraments in which "an inward and spiritual grace" is given unto us through "an outward and visible sign." There are seven of these rites which may be ranked as sacraments, namely, Baptism, Confirmation, the Holy Eucharist, Absolution, Holy Unction, Holy Matrimony, Holy Orders.

Notes: *Both the Liberal Catholic Church, Province of the United States, and the International Liberal Catholic Church have the same summary statement of doctrine, and those Liberal Catholic jurisdictions that have not written a separate doctrinal statement accept the content if not the wording of this document. Individual members do not have to accept the statement, but it is considered the embodiment of "the distinctive contribution of the Liberal Catholic Church to Christian thought." Candidates for ordination must be in agreement with the statement.*

* * *

WHAT WE BELIEVE (NEW ORDER OF GLASTONBURY)

The New Order of Glastonbury is a mystically-oriented ecumenical religious Order. We espouse the following Principles:

1. To encourage the recognition that God, the Eternal Spirit, is One.

2. To encourage the recognition of the Triune Aspects of God as manifested in the Creator; The Son, the Cosmic Christ; and the Holy Spirit, the Comforter.

3. To encourage the recognition that the Son, the Cosmic Christ, is also the Light that shines in every human heart.

4. To encourage the celebration and preservation of the Christian Sacraments: Baptism; Confirmation; Holy Eucharist; Marriage; Holy Orders; Absolution; and Anointing for Healing.

5. To uphold and share the Apostolic Succession of the Western Christian Church and the Eastern Christian Church.

6. To provide pastoral care, the application of spiritual and Christian ideas and ideals to matters of life.

7. To encourage the study of the Bible, Comparative Religion, Philosophy and the other Spiritual Arts and Sciences.

8. To encourage the understanding of the life of Christ and human evolution.

9. To encourage the development of the gifts of the Spirit and the fruits of the Spirit.

10. To encourage the recognition that the spiritual can never be put into a rigid mold and so there will be diversities of emphasis, practice, and theology.

11. To encourage the expression of these principles in daily life, through practice and service to others.

* * *

SUMMARY OF BELIEF (OLD HOLY CATHOLIC CHURCH, PROVINCE OF NORTH AMERICA)

We believe that God is the creator of heaven and earth. We believe that He seeks one-ness with man that man might dwell in Him and He in man. Although God may not be understood by the finite mind, He can be experienced. We believe that during the celebration of the sacrifice of the Holy Eucharist, we become at-one with the Christ and unite our hearts and minds with Him, so that His will becomes our will.

We believe that Jesus Christ is God and man and that He is true and eternal. As we truly accept Him as our Saviour we become co-heirs with Him as sons of God. That He and He alone offers us the way, the Truth, and the Life and that no person comes unto the Father save by Christ.

We believe that the Holy Spirit is GOD and that He dwells among men and seeks to guide and instruct them that they might direct their affairs heavenward.

We believe that the church is the body of God. It is the community of the faithful and is governed by Jesus Christ. This body of God is composed of all baptized Christians who regularly participate in public worship.

We believe in the right of private judgement for members both lay and clergy in matters of doctrine as long as the judgement is in harmony with that of the undivided Catholic Church.

The Church's doctrinal position in all matters of faith and practice shall be in accordance with the Holy Scriptures, the Ecumenical Creeds, and the Holy Apostolic Tradition. We further accept, because they conform to the above, the doctrines embodied in the official liturgy of the church, its catechism, and the constitution and Canons of this church.

Notes: *Of the several juridictions in the Liberal Catholic orb, the Old Holy Catholic Church has the most orthodox Christian statement.*

. * * *

"I AM" Groups

TENETS (CHURCH UNIVERSAL AND TRIUMPHANT)

I. FOUNDATION, HEAD, AND MEMBERS OF THE CHURCH UNIVERSAL AND TRIUMPHANT

We proclaim the Church Universal and Triumphant, founded by Almighty God upon the rock of the Christ consciousness, to be the true Church of Jesus the Christ, Guautama the Buddha, and all who have ever become one with the Christ and the I AM THAT I AM in the ritual of the ascension.

We declare Jesus the Christ to be the head of this Church, and we accept the one anointed by the Lord to be the Vicar of Christ as his representative on earth. We declare Gautama the Buddha to be the Lord of the World, and we accept the ones anointed by the hierarchy to be the messengers of the Great White Brotherhood as his representatives on earth.

We recognize the members of this Church to be those in heaven and on earth who have retained the essential flame of the way of the Christ and the way of the Buddha, having the cosmic cube within the heart, those who are one in heart, mind, and soul as the body of God on earth and in heaven.

We recognize affiliates of this Church to be those who show forth the quickening of that flame and that cube by allegiance and obedience to the ascended hierarchy, the Vicar of Christ, and the Messengers by becoming Communicants of this congregation, by regularly partaking of the sacraments and meeting their obligations to God and man in invocation to light, in service to life, and in fulfillment of the law of the tithe.

II. THE GOD FLAME, THE SOUL

We acknowledge and adore the one supreme God, the Creator of heaven and earth, and the individualization of the God flame in the I AM Presence as the I AM THAT I AM, the Source of life for each individual soul. We give allegiance to the Word that was made flesh, the only begotten of the Father, the eternal Logos, who is the universal Christ individualized as the Christed Self of the sons and daughters of God and the children of God.

We acknowledge the Kingdoms of the Elohim, the Archangels, and the Ascended Masters to be the manifestation of the Sacred Trinity of power, wisdom, and love—of Father, Son, and Holy Spirit—throughout the cosmos. And we acknowledge the Divine Mother, both in Spirit and in Matter, as the Mater-realization of the Trinity in the God flame.

We define the soul as the living potential of God and the purpose of the soul's evolution and its descent into the planes of Matter as the proving of the law of being through the correct exercise of free will, self-mastery in time and space, the balancing of karma, the fulfillment of dharma, including discipleship on the path of Christic and Buddhic initiation, followed by the return to the plane of Spirit through the union with the I AM Presence that was demonstrated by Jesus and Gautama in the ritual of the ascension.

III. ASCENDED MASTERS, HIERARCHY, THE GREAT WHITE BROTHERHOOD

Inasmuch as we acknowledge the goal of life to be the ascension, we recognize those who have attained that goal to be ascended masters (those who have ascended out of the planes of Matter, the kingdoms of this world, having mastered time and space); and we declare them to be the true teachers of mankind, inhabitants of the planes of Spirit (the kingdom of heaven), living masters in God's cosmic consciousness whose presence with and among us we affirm to be the communion of the Holy Spirit.

We therefore acknowledge the law of hierarchy in the ascending scale of being, from the lowest unto the highest, from the least in the kingdom unto the greatest, as individualizations of the God flame unfolding aspects of the identity of the one flame of life that is God. And we affirm our allegiance on earth and in heaven and our conscious cooperation with the cause of the fraternity of ascended and unascended beings known as the Great White Brotherhood.

IV. SACRED SCRIPTURES, PROGRESSIVE REVELATION, THE MESSENGERS

We accept the message of salvation and the statement of cosmic law contained in all of the sacred scriptures of the world according to the interpretation of the Holy Spirit given to the messengers Mark L. Prophet and Elizabeth Clare Prophet.

We accept the progressive revelation of God as dictated through his emissaries, the ascended masters, to their messengers Mark L. Prophet and Elizabeth Clare Prophet and their appointed successors. We accept this revelation as the word of God, The Everlasting Gospel, and the prophecy of the two witnesses (Rev. 11) set forth as sacred scripture for the two-thousand-year dispensation of Aquarius.

V. THE PATH OF BECOMING THE CHRIST AND THE BUDDHA

We accept the way of the Christ and the Buddha as the path of initiation defined by the messengers Mark I. Prophet and Elizabeth Clare Prophet according to the teachings of the ascended masters in the Holy Spirit's interpretation of the sacred scriptures of the world, the via dolorosa and the Eightfold Path, the words and works, the life and example of Jesus and Gautama, their profound teaching and their demonstration of many signs and wonders to their disciples.

We find in the lives of Jesus and Gautama examples of the life lived in God which we are compelled by the living flame to emulate. Above all, we find therein the calling to fulfill the promise which Jesus gave when he said, "He that believeth on me, the works that I do shall he do also; and greater works than these shall he do; because I go unto my Father," and of Gautama, who has said of man, "He may grow—oh, wondrous maturity—into the consciousness of becoming a true Buddha, an aspiring one, one who seeks by the process of budding to become a cosmic flower in the garden of God."

Therefore in obedience to the flame of living love we accept the cross of white fire of Jesus and Gautama as the sign of our attainment of the Christ consciousness, our enlightenment through the Buddhic consciousness, and our soul's victory through God Self-awareness over sin, disease, and death.

VI. MASCULINE AND FEMININE RAY, FATHER AND MOTHER OF THE CHURCH

As Jesus proclaimed himself to be the Son of God, thereby defining his mission to set the example of the Christ as the Real Self of every man and woman, so we accept our calling in the Aquarian age to be the challenge of defining our identity in and as the Mother—Mother as the feminine counterpart of God the Father, Mother as the materialization of the God flame, and Mother as the mastery within us of the planes of Matter.

We understand the raising-up of the feminine ray to be the challenge of the Aquarian age and the balancing of that ray with its masculine counterpart to be the fusion within being of the energies of the Father-Mother God for the birth of the Cosmic Christ and the advent of the Holy Spirit. To fulfill the goal of balancing the masculine and feminine rays of being for the fullness of the Holy Spirit to dwell in us bodily, we earnestly aspire to demonstrate the mastery of the energies of the chakras as centers of God Self-awareness through the recitation of Mary's Scriptural Rosary for the New Age, Jesus' "Watch with Me," and other meditations and invocations as shall be set forth from time to time by the Vicar of Christ and the Messenger.

We accept the example of the Virgin Mary in her ensoulment of the Mother ray as the supreme definition of our own opportunity to prove the Mother as the God flame where we are. Therefore, we do accept Mary not only as the Mother of the Word incarnate in Jesus and in all mankind, but also as the Mother of the Church, and her flame—anchored in the heart of the Mother of the Flame, her appointed representative on earth—nourishing and sustaining all life evolving in the planes of Matter.

We accept the flaming consciousness of Saint Germain, Hierarch of the Seventh Ray of the Holy Spirit and master of the Aquarian dispensation, as the open door to mankind's freedom in this age; and we do accept the Protector of Mary as the Father of the Church and the

example of God-freedom to all life through whose heart and mind we demonstrate self-mastery on the masculine ray even as the messenger Mark L. Prophet lived to the utmost the perfection of the fatherhood of God.

We accept and adore God in heaven and on earth in the planes of Spirit and in the planes of Matter, and God within the threefold flame anchored in the heart as Father, as Mother, as Christed Self in son and daughter and as Holy Spirit. And through the paths of Christic initiation and Buddhic attainment and enlightenment, we diligently pursue the converging of every aspect of the identity of God in the fiery core of being that is the I AM Presence.

VII. BAPTISM OF THE HOLY SPIRIT, FORGIVENESS OF SIN, BALANCE OF KARMA

We acknowledge the baptism of the Holy Spirit as the action of the sacred fire, and specifically of the violet flame, which is the power to forgive (hold in abeyance) the weight of sin and to transmute (transform) the misqualified energies of mankind's karma (cause-effect sequences in Matter) into the purified and perfected energies of the Holy Spirit.

We recognize this baptism of fire, prophesied by John the Baptist, as a dispensation of the Cosmic Christ implemented through the consciousness of Saint Germain as an altogether necessary component of our salvation in this age. Therefore do we vow to offer in the Spirit of Harmony daily invocations to Almighty God in the name of the Christ for the release of the violet flame as the action of Saint Germain's consciousness of God-freedom to a planet and a people. We acknowledge that this form of application results in (1) the transmutation of the records of sin, disease, and death and, when reinforced by active, selfless service to God and man, the fulfillment of the soul's divine plan and the obligations of sacred labor, in (2) the balancing of any and all karma necessary for the soul's liberation from the wheel of rebirth and its reunion with the I AM Presence in the ritual of the ascension.

VIII. CHILDREN OF GOD, SONS AND DAUGHTERS OF GOD

We recognize all mankind as children of the one God who become communicants of the one flame of the Holy Spirit when they acknowledge, adore, and give allegiance to the flame of God as the I AM THAT I AM, personified as the universal Christ, and, when they bow before the true nature of their own being, as the I AM Presence, personified in the individual Christ Self.

We recognize the sons and daughters of God to be those who have passed certain initiations on the path by entering into the God consciousness and accepting the responsibility for being, consciousness, energy, action and interaction in the planes of Spirit and Matter.

We define the creation of God to be the individualization of the God flame as twin flames of the masculine and feminine rays of the Godhead. Thus sons and daughters of God and children of God, as living souls clothed upon with spirals of God's consciousness, are endowed with the flame of life anchored in the heart known in the planes of Spirit and Matter as the threefold flame of the Christ. This flame distinguishes them from the children of the wicked one—soulless beings without flame or God-awareness whom Jesus described in his parable of the tares among the wheat.

IX. EIGHT SACRAMENTS, DEFENSE OF CONSCIOUSNESS

We accept and we agree to participate in, as we are able, the ritual of the eight sacraments of the rays as taught by the Vicar of Christ and administered by him and the ministers of the Church Universal and Triumphant.

We promise to watch and pray earnestly for the coming of the kingdom of God into manifestation on earth as it is in heaven and to hold perpetually within our hearts the surrender of the Lord Jesus made in the Garden of Gethsemane, "Nevertheless, not my will, but thine be done."

We pledge to defend the citadel of consciousness against all forms of evil and animal magnetism originating in the carnal mind; this defense we shall pursue most diligently through the methods of invocation, meditation, prayer, and decree taught by the ascended masters and the messengers and through the study and application of the teachings and example of the entire Spirit of the Great White Brotherhood.

In the name of Jesus the Christ and Gautama the Buddha, we vow to serve with Michael the Archangel, the Defender of the Faith, and the hosts of the Lord to defend the souls of all mankind against the deceptions and divisions of the laggards and the fallen ones and the entire luciferian rebellion.

X. FREE WILL, ANTICHRIST, ARMAGEDDON

We recognize, in the words of Jesus, that "in a universe of absolute good will and perfection, it must be recognized that the freedom to choose, known as free will, has permitted mankind to depart from the perfection of God and to act as a creator in his own domain." We recognize that by the misguided use of free will, many souls have elected to follow the path of the denial of the Real Self as God and, through pride, rebellion, ego ambition, and selfishness, have taken the way of Antichrist and united, albeit unwittingly, with the forces of the dragon, the beast, the false prophet, and the great whore abroad in the world. Thus, having placed themselves outside the circumference of God's awareness of all that is real, these souls, by their denial of the Christ and the Buddha, may, as an alternative to the ascension, pass through the second death as the result of the final judgment before the Court of the Sacred Fire and the Four and Twenty Elders.

Therefore in defense of the freedom, the light, the individuality, and the victory of all souls, we do accept the calling given to the body of God on earth to challenge every form of evil, the energy veil, or maya—personal and impersonal, embodied or disembodied. And we accept our responsibility as sons and daughters of God to pursue the calling of the Christed ones to expand the flame of life, truth, and love in the hearts of all mankind.

We understand that because of the presence in the universe of these fallen ones, influencing and being influenced by the Liar and his lie, there is now going on within the soul of a cosmos and within the universe the Battle of Armageddon betwixt the forces of light and darkness. We acknowledge the supremacy of the light and of the Christed ones in the Battle of Armageddon and pledge our lives and our flames—heart, head, and hand—to the drawing of souls into the flame of God-reality, the I AM Presence, and the true teachings of Jesus the Christ, Gautama the Buddha, and the entire Spirit of the Great White Brotherhood. Therefore our ultimate dedication is to individual self-mastery and the ascension in the light for ourselves and for every man, woman, and child upon the planet.

XI. SELFLESSNESS, SACRIFICE, SURRENDER

We accept the path of selflessness, the sacrifice of the lesser self, and the surrender of all aspects of the human consciousness to the Divine Self as the goal of the path we have chosen as we serve step by step, measure by measure, to replace every aspect of mortality with immortality, every aspect of the corruptible nature with the Incorruptible One, every aspect of the human consciousness with the divine.

XII. LAW OF THE TITHE

Understanding the law of the tithe to be the law of the abundant life, understanding Jesus' admonishment on giving freely as we have freely received, understanding the mission of the Christed ones in the words of Jesus "I am come that they might have life, and that they might have it more abundantly," we do therefore pledge our tithe in support of the Church Universal and Triumphant as one-tenth of our supply.

Notes: *The Church Universal and Triumphant's summary clearly distinguishes its position from other "I AM" groups. While its teachings have consistently departed from traditional Christianity, the church has retained the strongest attachment to Christian symbols of the several "I AM" organizations.*

*   *   *

THE DECLARATION OF FAITH (SANCTUARY OF THE MASTER'S PRESENCE)

I believe in God, The Mighty "I AM", God Presence within all life, and in the Holy Christ Self, through which the Will of God manifests in the world of Form.

I believe in the Eternal Three-fold Power of the Holy Spirit, which is the Divine Essence of all Being.

I believe in the Universal Brotherhood of man, and in the fellowship and communion of the Great White Brotherhood and Hierarchy of Heaven, with man.

I believe in the forgiveness of all transgressions against the Law of Life, through love; the purification of the human soul through the conscious recognition and use of the Sacred Fire; the ascension into Christ Perfection through the mastery of substance and energy in thought, feeling and desire, and I believe in Life Everlasting through the Light of God that never fails to produce perfection when called into action through Divine Love.

Miscellaneous Theosophical Groups

THE CREED [CHRISTIAN COMMUNITY (ANTHROPOSOPHICAL SOCIETY)]

An Almighty Being of God, spiritual-physical, is the Foundation of existence, of the heavens and the earth, Who goes before His creatures like a Father.

Christ, through whom men attain the re-animation of the dying earth existence, is to this divine Being as the Son, born in eternity.

In Jesus the Christ entered as man into the earthly world. The birth of Jesus upon earth is a working of the Holy Spirit, Who, that He might spiritually heal the sickness of sin upon the bodily nature of mankind, prepared the Son of Mary to be the vehicle of the Christ.

The Christ Jesus suffered under Pontius Pilate, the death of the Cross and was lowered into the grave of the earth.

In death he became the Helper of the souls of the dead who had lost their divine nature.

Then He overcame death, after three days.

Since that time He is the Lord of the heavenly forces upon earth and lives the Fulfiller of the deeds of the Father, the Ground of the World.

He will in time unite for the advancement of the world with those whom through their bearing He can wrest from the death of matter.

Through Him can the Healing Spirit Work.

Communities whose members feel the Christ within them may feel themselves united in a Church to which all men who are aware of the health-bringing power of the Christ.

They may hope for the Overcoming of the sickness of sin, for the continuance of man's being and for the preservation of their life, destined for eternity.

Notes: *The Creed is taken from the liturgy of the community, the Act of the Consecration of Man. It is recited by the priest(ess) after the Gospel lesson is read. Before reciting it, the officiant takes off his/her stole, signifying that the words are spoken in a non-priestly capacity, thus allowing freedom to those in the congregation unprepared to accept the statement. While this creed follows the format of the Apostles' Creed, its content consistently departs from that of the older creed in numerous, if often subtle, ways. The Creed deals with the physicality of God, uses the abstract phrase "the Christ," and ignores the concept of "resurrection of the body" while addressing the escape from the "death of matter."*

Chapter 19

Magick Family

Ritual Magick

THE AQUARIAN MANIFESTO [AQUARIAN ANTI-DEFAMATION LEAGUE (AMERICAN GNOSTIC CHURCH)]

All Sentient Beings have the Right to worship Who, What, Where, When, Why and How they wish, provided that they do not violate the similar Rights of others. All Sentient Beings have, as well, the Right (some would say Duty) to develop their Talents mental, physical, psychic and others to the highest degree possible; subject as always to the equal Rights of others. It is in this complex interplay of Rights that the Children of the Aquarian Age may be distinguished from their ancestors of previous Ages.

According to Astrological Tradition, the term "Aquarian Age" implies a time in which there is increased concern with the ways in which the individual can live by his or her own lights, while guaranteeing the same Freedom to all others. All those, therefore, who work for the greater Evolution of Consciousness and Freedom may be justly called "Aquarians," regardless of the day or year of their actual birth.

Aquarians—Neo-Pagan, Neo Christian, Agnostic or of any Faith—are by definition tolerant of ALL Pro-Life Beliefs and Organizations. They do not proclaim the existence of any One True Right-And-Only Way, but rather that every Sentient Being must find her or his own Path.

We will NOT, however, in the name of Tolerance or any other Ideal allow ourselves to be persecuted or exterminated by Anti Life individuals or organizations, whether political or religious.

As Aquarians we do NOT, in our religious services, magical rituals, psychic activities or in our private lives, engage in the commission or encouragement of Felony-Crimes With Victims, (as defined by Civil Law and modern Sociological Research). We do NOT, therefore, engage in Ritual Murder, Rape, Maiming, Torture of Animals, Grand Larceny, or other Heinous Crimes, and we will no longer quietly accept accusations that we do so.

Neither do Aquarians use their Talents whether we call them "psychic," "magical," "spiritual," "paranormal," or whatever—to achieve ends or through means that, if done physically would constitute such Felony-Crimes With Victims. Accusations in this area will not go uncountered either.

We know full well that the New Witchburners are seeking to once again light the Stakes of Persecution with the Fires of Bigotry and Hate. Equally well do we know that, despite our innumerable differences with one another, the Time has come for us to stand Together against the forces of Fear and Oppression. The very survival of ourselves, our children and our planet depend upon the outcome of our present struggles.

The Aquarian Anti-Defamation League will exist for the purpose of defending Aquarian Individuals and Ideals from those Witchburners who would destroy them. We shall attempt to use whatever means exist to preserve, protect and defend our Religious, Civil, Economic, and Human Rights, as well as our Reputations, from ALL those who would slander, libel, defame, suppress or otherwise persecute us for our Beliefs.

We shall no longer Allow self righteous followers of Anti Life Beliefs to prevent us from the free exercise of our Human and Constitutional Rights. We shall no longer allow anyone with impunity to publically accuse us of being "Satanists," "Devil Worshippers," "Charlatans," "Lunatics" or any other loaded terms of Slander and Libel designed to denigrate, defame or prevent us from the peaceful and legal spreading of our Beliefs. We shall no longer hesitate to bring Civil and/or Criminal charges against our would be Inquisitors whenever possible, no matter how wealthy or powerful they may be.

Aquarians Together—Witches, Warlocks, and Wizards, Psychics, Priests and Parapsychologists, Mystics, Mediums and Magicians, Astrologers, Diviners and Occultists of both Sexes and all Races, many Faiths and Traditions, Ages and Nationalities, hereby agree upon our Battle Cry as we declare War upon those who would persecute us!

NEVER AGAIN THE BURNING!!

Notes: *Written by P. E. Isaac Bonewits and issued in 1973 for the short-lived Aquarian Anti-Defamation League, the*

THE AQUARIAN MANIFESTO [AQUARIAN ANTI-DEFAMATION LEAGUE (AMERICAN GNOSTIC CHURCH)] (continued)

Aquarian Manifesto has been seen as a civil rights declaration for Pagans and ceremonial magicians in general. At least one group, the American Gnostic Church, has adopted it as part of its official teachings.

*　　　*　　　*

STATEMENT BY THE ORDER OF THELEMA

THE ORDER OF THELEMA is a small group of occultists basing its practices upon THE BOOK OF THE LAW as revealed to the Master Therion. We came to an acceptance of this book through a personal encounter with the divine forces which gave rise to the authorship of it. We believe that we are being directed by the agents of the Goddess Nuit; and that we are among Her Chosen.

We believe that on an ultimate or noumenal level, all reality is a Unity: Thus we are Pantheistic on the level of mystical attainment. However, on the phenomenal level of reality, we find that Godhead has refracted Itself into multi-aspect Deity: Thus we are Polytheistic on the Magickal level of attainment. We have chosen to accept the God and Goddess forms of ancient Egypt as the most adequate pattern of the interrelated functions of Godhead.

Among our immediate activities are studies in practical Magick, techniques of Yoga (Hatha and Kundalini), and metaphysics. Some of our members have been long-time practitioners of Wicca-Craft; and as a result, we partake of the celebration of Life and Nature.

We believe that for too long, groups following the various paths of wisdom and power have been in conflict over minor points of doctrine (tragic because all doctrines eventually resolve themselves into one), or petty jealousies. Our real enemy is and always has been ignorance and superstition. We are syncretic in our beliefs, and we try to absorb the wisdom that is freely given by others; and we freely offer what insights we might have.

Notes: *This statement defines the use of Egyptian mythical symbols by the Order of Thelema, which understands reality on both a mystical and magical level. "Thelema" is the Greek word for "will." Master Therion is one of the magical names assumed by Aleister Crowley.*

*　　　*　　　*

LIBER LXXVII (ORDO TEMPLI ORIENTIS)

Oz: "the law of the strong: this is our law and the joy of the world."—*AL.11.21*

"Do what thou wilt shall be the whole of the law."—*AL.1.40.*

"thou hast no right but to do thy will. Do that, and no other shall say nay."—*AL.1.42-3.*

"Every man and every woman is a star."—*AL.1.3.*

There is no god but man.

1. Man has the right to live by his own law—
   to live in the way that he wills to do:
   to work as he will:
   to play as he will:
   to rest as he will:
   to die when and how he will.

2. Man has the right to eat what he will:
   to drink what he will:
   to dwell where he will:
   to move as he will on the face of the earth.

3. Man has the right to think what he will:
   to speak what he will:
   to write what he will:
   to draw, paint, carve, etch, mould, build as he will.
   to dress as he will:

4. Man has the right to love as he will:—
   "take your fill and will of love as ye will,
   when, where, and with whom ye will."—*AL.1.51.*

5. Man has the right to kill those who would thwart these rights.

"the slaves shall serve."—*AL.11.58.*

"Love is the law, love under will."—*AL.1.57.*

Notes: *Each member of the Ordo Templi Orientis (O.T.O.), at one point in his/her career in the order, is responsible for the publication and distribution of multiple copies of Liber LXXVII (also known as Liber Oz), which states the basic principles of the thelemic world view. It is used by all branches of the O.T.O. as well as other groups that rely heavily upon the writing of Aleister Crowley. The text of Liber Oz consists of quotations taken from* The Book of the Law, *also known as Liber AL, the bible of the O.T.O.*

*　　　*　　　*

THE CONFESSION FROM THE GNOSTIC MASS OF THE ORDO TEMPLI ORIENTIS

I believe in one secret and ineffable LORD; and in one Star in the Company of Stars of whose fire we are created, and to which we shall return; and in one Father of Life, Mystery of Mystery, in His name CHAOS, the sole viceregent of the Sun upon the Earth; and in one Air the nourisher of all that breathes.

And I believe in one Earth, the Mother of us all, and in one Womb wherein all men are begotten, and wherein they shall rest, Mystery of Mystery, in Her name BABALON.

And I believe in the Serpent and the Lion, Mystery of Mystery, in His name BAPHOMET.

And I believe in one Gnostic and Catholic Church of Light, Life, Love and Liberty, the Word of whose Law is THELEMA.

And I believe in the communion of Saints.

And, forasmuch as meat and drink are transmuted in us daily into spiritual substance, I believe in the Miracle of the Mass.

And I confess one Baptism of Wisdom, whereby we accomplish the Miracle of Incarnation.

And I confess my life one, individual, and eternal that was, and is, and is to come.

Notes: *Where possible, members of the Ordo Templi Orientis (O.T.O.) gather weekly for the Gnostic Mass, a magical ritual based upon the Roman Catholic mass, but completely rewritten to embody the symbolism of thelemic magick. The confession is difficult to decipher apart from some understanding of the thelemic world view and the unique meaning given some ancient symbols. The cryptic language of the confession revolves around sex magick.*

*　　*　　*

Witchcraft and Neo-Paganism

PRINCIPLES OF WICCAN BELIEF (AMERICAN COUNCIL OF WITCHES)

1. We practice Rites to attune ourselves with the natural rhythm of life forces marked by the Phases of the Moon and the Seasonal Quarters and Cross Quarters.

2. We recognize that our intelligence gives us a unique responsibility toward our environment. We seek to live in harmony with Nature, in ecological balance offering fulfillment to life and consciousness with an evolutionary concept.

3. We acknowledge a depth of power far greater than is apparent to the average person. Because it is far greater than ordinary, it is sometimes called "supernatural," but we see it as lying within that which is naturally potential to all.

4. We conceive the Creative Power in the Universe as manifesting through polarity—as masculine and feminine—and that this same Creative Power lives in all people, and functions through the interaction of the masculine and feminine. We value neither above the other, knowing each to be supportive of the other. We value Sex as pleasure, as the symbol and embodiment of life, and as one of the sources of energies used in magical practice and religious worship.

5. We recognize both outer worlds and inner or psychological worlds—sometimes known as the Spiritual World, the collective Unconscious, the Inner Planes, etc.—and we see the interaction of these two dimensions as the basis for paranormal phenomena and magical exercises. We neglect neither dimension for the other, seeing both as necessary for our fulfillment.

6. We do not recognize any authoritarian hierarchy, but do honor those who teach, respect those who share their greater knowledge and wisdom, and acknowledge those who have courageously given of themselves in leadership.

7. We see religion, magick, and wisdom-in-living as being united in the way one views the world and lives within it—a world-view and philosophy-of-life, which we identify as Witchcraft, the Wiccan way.

8. Calling oneself a "Witch" does not make a witch—but neither does heredity itself, or the collecting of titles, degrees, and initiations. A Witch seeks to control the forces within him/herself that make life possible in order to live wisely and well without harm to others, and in harmony with Nature.

9. We acknowledge that it is the affirmation and fulfillment of life, in a continuation of evolution and development of consciousness, that gives meaning to the Universe we know, and to our personal role in it.

10. Our only animosity toward Christianity, or toward any other religion or philosophy-of-life, is to the extent that its institutions have claimed to be "the only way" and have sought to deny freedom to others and to suppress other ways of religious practice and belief.

11. As American Witches, we are not threatened by debates on the history of the Craft, the origins of various terms, the legitimacy of various aspects of different traditions. We are concerned with the present, and our future.

12. We do not accept the concept of "absolute evil," nor do we worship any entity known as "Satan" or "the devil" as defined by the Christian tradition. We do not seek power through the suffering of others, nor do we accept the concept that personal benefit can be only derived by denial to another.

13. We acknowledge that we seek within Nature for that which is contributory to our health and well-being.

Notes: *In the early 1970s some witches attempted to organize a national fellowship based on a conciliar model. During the American Council of Witches' brief existence, it adopted a statement which has been the main artifact surviving the organization. The statement is still occasionally used.*

The Principles acknowledge the basic masculine-feminine polarity in the universe, the pleasurableness of sex, magical power as natural and creative, and a oneness with nature. The Principles deny any relationship to Satanism and attempt to mediate the arguments concerning the various Wiccan "traditions."

*　　*　　*

WHAT IS A NEO-PAGAN? (AQUARIAN TABERNACLE CHURCH)

The term "pagan" comes from the Latin "paganus," which simply meant "country dweller." Today, most people who define themselves as Pagans use the word as a general term for "native and natural religions, usually polytheistic, and their members."

In simple terms Paganism is a positive, natural-based religion, preaching brotherly love and harmony with all life-forms. Its origins are found in early human development of religion; animistic deities gradually being refined to become a main God or Goddess of All Nature. This God or Goddess—bearing different names at different times and in different places—can be compared to the

WHAT IS A NEO-PAGAN? (AQUARIAN TABERNACLE CHURCH) (continued)

Jesus and Mary figures of Christianity. Paganism is *not* anti-Christian; it is simply *pre*-Christian.

Most Pagans (of various persuasions) seem to agree that their similarities are often of more importance than their specific doctrinal distinctions or ethnic focuses. Some of these common beliefs may include:

1. *The idea that divinity is immanent (internal) as well as transcendent (external).* This is often phrased as "Thou art God" and "Thou art Goddess."

2. *The belief that divinity is just as likely to manifest itself as female.* This has resulted in a large number of women being attracted to the faiths and joining the clergy.

3. *A belief in a multiplicity of "gods" and "goddesses,"* whether as individual deities or as facets of one or a few archetypes. This leads to multi-valued logic systems and increased tolerance towards other religions.

4. *A respect and love for nature as divine in Her own right.* This makes ecological awareness and activity a religious duty.

5. *A distaste for monolithic religious organizations and a distrust of would-be messiahs and gurus.* This makes Pagans hard to organize, even "for their own good," and leads to constant schisming, mutation and growth in the movements.

6. *The firm conviction that human beings were meant to lead lives filled with joy, love, pleasure and humor.* The traditional western concepts of sin, guilt and divine retribution are seen as sad misunderstandings of natural growth experiences.

7. *A simple set of ethics and morality based on the avoidance of actual harm to other people* (and some extend this to some or all living beings and the planet as a whole).

8. *The knowledge that with proper training and intent, human minds and hearts are fully capable of performing all the magic and miracles they are ever likely to need,* through the use of natural psychic powers.

9. *A belief in the importance of celebrating the solar, lunar and other cycles of our lives.* This has led to the investigation and revival of many ancient customs and the invention of some new ones.

10. *A minimum amount of dogma and a maximum amount of eclecticism.* Pagans are reluctant to accept any idea without personally investigating it, and are willing to use any concept they find useful, regardless of its origins.

11. *A strong faith in the ability of people to solve their current problems on all levels, public and private.* This leads to . . .

12. *A strong commitment to personal and universal growth, evolution and balance.* Pagans are expected to be making continuous efforts in these directions.

13. *A belief that one can progress far towards achieving such growth, evolution and balance through the carefully planned alteration of one's "normal" state of consciousness,* using both ancient and modern methods of aiding concentration, meditation, reprogramming and ecstacy.

14. *The knowledge that human interdependence implies community cooperation.* Pagans are encouraged to use their talents to actually help each other as well as the community at large.

15. *An awareness that if they are to achieve any of their goals, they must practice what they preach.* This leads to a concern with making one's lifestyle consistent with one's proclaimed beliefs.

Notes: *This statement, not a creed in any formal sense, is one of several documents attempting to summarize not only the perspective of the Aquarian Tabernacle Church, but also that of Neo-Paganism in general. This statement is the product of a community that has tolerated a wide variety of belief while retaining some sense of a commonly held core of belief in such concepts as the divine nature of individuals, polytheism, the astrological cycles, and the joyful life.*

*　　*　　*

A VIKING MANIFESTO [ASATRU FREE ASSEMBLY (VIKING BROTHERHOOD)]

The Viking Brotherhood is a body dedicated to preserving, promoting, and practicing the Norse religion as it was epitomized during the Viking Age, and to furthering the moral and ethical values of courage, individualism, and independence which characterized the Viking way of life.

We believe in the existence of several gods and goddesses, the chief of whom is Odin, the father of the gods and the god of war, poetry, and magic. Thor is also a warrior, but his aspect is more that of the toiler or worker. Balder represents the gentle and refined in Norse culture, Freyr is the god of growth and fertility, and Loki is a mischievous and traitorous god who often runs afoul of the other gods. The goddess Friggs is Odin's wife, Freye is the female counterpart of Freyr, Hels watches over the dead in Hel, and there are other lesser deities.

We believe that those who lead a life in accordance with the precepts of Norse Paganism and who die the death of a hero in battle will be received into Valhalla, the Hall of the Slain. Here they will make wassail and fight until the great last battle, Ragnerok. Those who do not die a worthy death will go down to Hel, a gloomy and cheerless place.

We believe in the existence of other supernatural entities besides our gods, to include Valkyries, the "Choosers of the Slain," female beings who bear the body of the fallen hero to Valhalla.

Because of our set of values we do not "worship" our gods in the usual sense of the word. We do not bend our knee even to Odin, or petition him, or otherwise deny our individuality and personal sovereignty. The gods are for us intelligent personifications of the forces of the Universe and examples for those who follow the Viking Way, not masters or superentities into which one becomes absorbed.

We see a cosmos in conflict - a Universe in which collectivism in its many forms, from communism to fascism to Christianity and a myriad others, threatens to destroy forever the individuality which we Vikings cherish so much. It is our historical role to oppose as best we can this trend toward collectivism in whatever guise it may appear.

We believe in heroism, which to us means not only courage and strength but also a sense of what is honorable and worthy of a hero.

We believe in nature not because it is fashionable to do so or because we are nature mystics, but because our spiritual forebearers were wild and untamed men who were educated in wild and untamed places - the tumultous seas and the forbidding forests. The wilderness has traditionally been the refuge of free men.

Finally, we affirm that the Viking Way is open to all regardless of their race or the country of their origin, for it is the mind and the heart which identify one as a Viking, not any superficial factor.

Notes: *This is one of a series of manifestos produced by Pagan groups in the 1970s. The Viking Brotherhood, now known as the Asatru Free Assembly, published its statement of Norse Paganism in 1972.*

* * *

MANIFESTO (ATLANTION WICCA)

HISTORY OF ATLANTION WICCA: Atlantion Wicca is based on teachings and dedicated to the memory of Elizabeth Sawyer, the Witch of Edmonton. For her part in the Craft she was hanged at Tyburn, England, on Thursday, April 19, 1621. The reason for her execution was that she by the use of diabolical help and out of malice did Witch to death one Agnes Ratcleife, a neighbor of hers. These were the charges brought down on her by the courts with no mention given to the help she gave the local farmers with their crops, the numerous babies she delivered, and the fevers she lowered when many were drawn to death's doors by the filth they were forced to live in during the seventeenth century. We however remember the babies, the crops, and the fevers, and we try to teach others to do the same.

REGULATIONS OF ATLANTION WICCA: Atlantion Wicca has as its rule book a "Book of Shadows" consisting of almost two hundred laws, many of which cannot be found in existing books. Rituals for conducting the various Sabbats, Esbats, New Moon and Full Moon Ceremonies together with the various rituals for Opening and Closing the Circle, Initiations, etc.

GENERAL VIEWS OF ATLANTION WICCA: We of Atlantion Wicca believe that nothing should be done to reflect a bad image of the Craft, for all of us have been reincarnated and we realize all too well what can happen when the Christians decide to raise up in force to squelch the Pagans. It is with this thought in mind that we forbid the use of drugs, sacrificing of any kind, orgies, public nudity while representing the sect, and in general any other type of behavior that might reflect an adverse reaction to the sect.

GOALS OF ATLANTION WICCA: Our goal is to set up in the Central New York area several working covens based on the tradition handed down to us by our ancestors. We wish to work with the serious student of the Craft and help him or her to find the right path to our Beloved Lady. We encourage inquiries, write editorials for local newspapers, and we are trying to present to the public what we feel is the true image of the Craft. We are trying to wash the ideas out of people's minds put there by movies like Rosemary's Baby and Simon King of the Witches, and by news stories like those written on the Charles Manson case. We are trying to prevent another Inquisition brought on by ignorance of the masses. We are trying to obtain freedom of religion laws for those of the Craft so that we may all be free to worship how, when, and where we want. We are trying to make contact with other members of the Craft, and other Pagan groups through joining groups like the Themis Council, and by having our names listed in various newsletters directed toward Craft and Pagan groups.

Notes: *This short-lived Wiccan group published its statement in 1972.*

* * *

THE FIREBEAR MANIFESTO (BROTHERS OF THE EARTH)

The feminist covens have achieved an incredible depth of experience these past years. They have described a vision of people drawn together to celebrate the life and life-images around them in themselves, their groups, their worlds, and the Cosmos. Women working and playing together to find new levels in power and awareness of self, and with others. They redefine the robotic roles which they have been handed as to who they are and how they must be. They meet in the nude or clothed, they worship the Goddess and Nature, their work is personal and political; they discover and revel in the celebration of womanspiritflesh.

I am the being called Firebear.

I seek the birthing place of the New Man, so that I may join him again to throw off the false shackles of civilization. To feel the natural beast joyously howl from inside—to greet the dawn as Osiris, consort to Her,—to live in the cities and towns, but with the wiliness and wisdom of Coyote, the Trickster—to respect the WoodGod Pan, to call upon the SwiftHealer Hermes, to marvel at the ArtistOracle Apollo, and to worship the grandeur of GrandFather Sky.

I have visions.

I am in a dark wood. Around a low fire I sit with other men like myself. We are dressed or not, but in some way adorned to reflect our powers and true ways. We have all journeyed together, and journey still, away from the vampiric influences of staid culture and conventional mind-sets. We realize, like our shaman brothers, that we must see the world as new each day. We realize that there

THE FIREBEAR MANIFESTO (BROTHERS OF THE EARTH) (continued)

are worlds we ignore, yet that does not mean they are beyond our reach.

In this circle we discover and channel the eternal power of mensynergy. It comes first from finding out how we make ourselves smaller and smaller, day by day. We are brought up to yield to authority, yet it keeps us short of our own authenticity. We have power over our bodies and minds that we have never realized and step-by-step we can learn to heal ourselves. We build armor around ourselves and other men, making them alien to us instead of embracing them as one flesh with us.

"Man is not a body only. The heart, the spirit, is man. And this spirit is an entire star, out of which he is built. If, therefore, a man is perfect in his heart, nothing in the whole light of Nature is hidden from him . . . The first step in the operation of these sciences is this: to beget the spirit from the inner firmament by means of the imagination."—Paracelsus (16th c. hermetic)

How do we develop our power-from-within?

We gather in a circle, arms around bodies, and gather our auras of light to heal. We visualize ourselves and our loved ones and those in need as filled with the power that can be man's, our wills united. We invoke the powers of the deep forest, the red lion, the piercing moon.

We gather in the comfort of our castles and discuss the power and vision of our true dreams: the dreams that we yearn for during the days, and the dreams that come unbidden to us in the nights. We gather in the fields to play, to feel the exhilaration and dance of fun and movement and energy awaken in and between our men-flesh. We feel the natural joy of cooperative and supportive activity with our kind. Our collective body learns from the individuals within it. No one shall have power over another, even in games of competition, because we play to play, and to be together; not to beat an enemy, for there is no enemy except the chains we place on ourselves from within.

We gather to work on our anger, too. We are not good, we are not bad, we simply are, and to ignore the dark and inner parts that brood inside or that simmer below the surface is to whip the beast until it turns on us and rends us. So we tell our tales, every man jack of us, so that the importance of the beasts can be seen, and the power transformed and turned back into its natural place.

We gather to learn how to use the strength that Nature-Spirit gave us. We learn to harness ourselves and our arts in a spirit of experimentation and care, so that we can bring our power-from-within to bear naturally—not with fear and violence, but with strength, should we need to nurture and defend. And we will build a community to empower ourselves and those we love.

We gather to learn that we haven't really seen the world but only our illusion of it, and that we have a place and a reason to be here. "Man is an organ in the body of the universe." (the Hermetic tradition)

And most of all, *we gather in a spirit of awareness and knowledge and celebration of the spirit-that-moves-in-all-things, and the joy of our hearts and flesh in this world, and the harmony of it all.* We tell our stories and write our rituals and bring the full power of pageantry, theatre, play, and healing to create magick that will be with us within our circle and throughout our mundane lives.

"Now again we see that all is unbegun. The only danger is not going far enough. If we go deep enough, we reach common life, the shared experiences of man, the world of possibility. If we do not go deep enough, if we live and write half-way, there are obscurity, vulgarity, the slang of fashion, and several kinds of death."—Muriel Rukeyser

Notes: *This unofficial statement was printed in the periodical of the Brothers of the Earth, a Neo-Pagan group celebrating men's mysteries. It is a positive response to the feminist aspect of Neo-Paganism, and while unofficial, it summarizes the most common perspectives and opinions expressed by those affiliated with the Brothers of the Earth.*

*   *   *

MAJOR BELIEFS OF CELTIC WICCA (CHURCH AND SCHOOL OF WICCA)

1. God is the overseeing intelligence that created the universe and the side.

2. The ultimate aim of each individual is to reach the sphere of God.

   To reach the sphere of God, all evil must be removed from the soul or spirit. Basic training in good and evil is received on earth and continues in the side. The lowest level in the side, 'guides,' are learning to give unselfishly of their time and effort to help those on earth. When each level is adequately mastered, the soul or spirit progresses. Several complete lifetimes in any given level may be required to master it. Long discussions can be heard in coven meetings on the number of levels of progression on earth and in the side. The number generally accepted is ten levels on each side of the invisible barrier. Progression on earth is divided into ten steps, called in Celtic Wicca levels ten through one.

3. As on earth, so in the side.

   There is a similarity in the two sides of the invisible barrier. The side is organized in a rational way. Rather than one being who attends to every detail on earth, there is a realistic delegation of God's responsibility and authority through the ten levels. It should be recognized that the directions from on high are imperfectly transmitted through the levels in the side; you must temper your messages from the side by the use of your own intelligence.

4. Hell is within the mind of man.

   Wicca does not believe in a hell to which souls are assigned when they've been naughty on earth. Hell is here on earth. It is inside you. The frustration of being unable to get or to do something, the temptation to take the easy road that will harm someone, and the fears of having your errors catch up with you: these things cause regret, and when they are allowed to rule the life, this regret becomes hell with sleepless nights and mind-torturing dreams.

5. Good is external.

It consists in helping the less fortunate with love, understanding, and consideration. One of the basics of Wicca is helping: first within the coven and then, with the coven's agreement, outside. This help is not the giving of conscience money to the less fortunate. It is the help which a person, animal, or plant needs to develop naturally and to become in tune with its place in the scheme of natural development. When you give money, you develop dependence. When you give help, you develop character.

6. Evil in the soul must be eliminated for progression to the higher levels.

Wicca is not an organization of social workers; but, in common with other philosophies, it does require its followers to conscientiously help in diminishing evil. First you must set your house in order by refusing to perpetrate evil acts. In Wicca you take only your own conscience into account. When you knowingly defraud someone of his rights, your own conscience is troubled and you have added spots of soil on your soul. The only way to expurgate these spots is to make restitution to the one who was defrauded. As you develop, you perceive that acts which in yesteryear seem irreproachable turn reproachable and then evil. This remembrance of past acts and your changed opinion of them is the surest sign of your development.

7. Reincarnation is for those who have not progressed far enough on earth.

We have noted before that progression is by learning and selflessness. A spirit is rewarded for its learning by progressing to the next level; conversely it is returned to the previous level when its learning is incomplete.

8. All must live in harmony with nature.

Until the time when we all live on chemicals, you will rely on nature to supply the the majority of your needs. All living things have a soul, from the minutest bacteria to man. These souls can feel, and they respond to the stimulus of their environment.

9. The development and care of the earthplane shell is a sacred duty.

The earthplane shell, your body, should be kept in the best possible physical shape because most illnesses slow or even reverse soul development. The God of Wicca loves all. Your earthplane shell is the most perfectly developed of all the shells on earth and is a manifestation of God's love. Your body is not to be ritually deformed by circumcision or tattooing or silicone injections, and is to be kept naked or minimally bound up on all possible occasions. The Greeks were the last nation to practice Wicca tenets with regard to the beauty of the body. Naked Olympian athletes, their tanned bodies perfected, trained, and glistening, must have been a wonderful sight. When the soul becomes a spirit, the body literally becomes a shell. It can be burnt or used to the best advantage of those left on earth.

10. Power is available from the human mind and from the spirits.

These two sorts of power are different and must be used correctly and with understanding.

a. Mind or raised power is obtained by the concentration of as many persons as possible on the one thought that will result in the desired goal. Wicca believe that thoughts have power. Experimenters at Duke University have photographed thoughts. It is also a fact that by careful concentration pendulums can be made to swing or the roll of the dice altered.

b. Spirit power is called down to help Wicca in tasks that are beyond the capability of thought power. The main area where the spirit is used is in prediction. This requires that the mind be made blank so that the spirits can communicate.

11. Good begets good; evil begets evil.

There is a reaction to all positive and negative thoughts and deeds. The world is gradually admitting that positive thinking gets good results. Many corporations led by hard-headed businessmen are giving their executives courses in positive thinking. This is of course a manifestation of raised power, affecting the minds of others telepathically. Wicca have known and used these effects for thousands of years. It has been found that when the power is used for self-gain a terrible toll is exacted because the evil use draws evil to the practitioner.

12. The development level of souls and spirits is presently degrading.

The constant pleas of the old Wicca for fertility have been answered. The over-population of the world proceeds apace, and with this overpopulation more and more souls are called from the side. These souls are taken from the less developed spirits of the higher primates; consequently we are seeing a lowering of the development level throughout the system.

SUMMARY

Celtic Wicca believes in:

1. An overseeing God who delegates authority throughout the universe.

2. The development cycle wherein the souls of elemental living things are developed upward through man and thence through the side to the sphere of God. Reincarnation is a result of incomplete development.

3. The rationality of the system. Everything is basically simple and not run by magic.

4. Hell does not exist except as it is envisioned within ourselves.

5. Good is giving help. Evil must be diminished. Good begets good and evil begets evil.

MAJOR BELIEFS OF CELTIC WICCA (CHURCH AND SCHOOL OF WICCA) (continued)

6. Each must live in harmony with those above and below himself on the scale (both on the earthplane and in the side).

7. There are two sorts of power: spirit and thought. Each has its respective uses. Wicca uses both.

8. The present system is degrading. We must help it to improve.

Notes: *This statement, which draws heavily on nineteenth-century ritual magic, has been published in a number of sources by one of the larger Wiccan organizations. The Church and School of Wicca believes in a form of reincarnation for those who have not yet progressed to a suitable condition to advance to higher things. The group is unique among Wiccan groups for its silence on the Mother deity.*

* * *

DOGMA AND DOCTRINE (CHURCH OF SEVEN ARROWS)

DOGMA

1. Each Being is, as a Spirit, a Living Medicine Wheel of Infinite Beauty, Capability, and Power; and Each is a Mirror of Every Other, Including Creator.

   Source(s): Directly stated in the Mythos, though one might also develop a similar Idea from looking at the Basic Principles and Operational Laws of Magical Technology in conjunction with an Idea that Before the Beginning, Creator was the Only ISness.

2. A Being (Spirit) Cannot be Destroyed, though its Condition can be Changed, even into such a Condition that It may Attempt to Not-Exist, or to seem to Not-Exist, or be Led to Think it is Not-Existing or is Capable of Not-Existing.

   Sources(s): Basically derived from the Mythos-statement of Each Being's Likeness (Reflection) of Creator, taken in conjunction with Creator's Apparent Omnipotence and Eternalness, though the results of the Past-Life Researches at Church Of Seven Arrows give strong support to the Dogma-position.

3. The Universe exists in a state of Patterned Change, with Defined Realms of Authorities and Responsibilities for Each of the Beings Therein.

   Source(s): Derived from the Mythos-descriptions of the Creations of the Realms and Contents, the Creations of Earth's Species-forms, and of Grandmother's Assignment of a Specific Function to Human-Species, though direct Observation of Earth's Ecology (Life-System) would give rise to a similar Idea, as do the Past-Life Researches at Church Of Seven Arrows.

4. Though the Right of any Being to Exist be Fully Established by Its Existing, this does Not Automatically Establish the Acceptability or "Rightness" of a Particular Manifest or Form Chosen by that Being for a Particular Time or Place.

   Source(s): Derived from the Mythos-descriptions of the Creations and Assignments of Position or Function, plus the History-records of Errors-of-Manifest and the Resulting World-Changes or Cleansings, and further supported by the results of the Past-Life Researches at Church Of Seven Arrows.

5. Bodies, of Whatever Nature, be but Masks Housing the Spirit(s) Within.

   Source(s): Directly from the Mythos-statement that Everything in the Universe has Spirit, and supported by the results of Shamanic entries into, and observations of, the Internal Operations of the Sub-Atomic, Atomic, Molecular, Continental, and Planetary-scale Realms.

6. The Basic Purpose of Humanity be to Lead the Beings of Earth in Harmonious Song to the Ear of Creator.

   Source(s): Directly stated in the Mythos-account of the Creation of Human-species.

7. There is No Single Path of Religious or Spiritual Practice that be Proper for Every Person or Being or Place.

   Source(s): Derived from the Mythos-descriptions of a Variety of Realms, Authorities, and Responsibilities, and given support by the Past-Life Researches at Church Of Seven Arrows, plus Shamanic Explorations into the various Realms of the Cosmogony.

8. As Above, so Below.— which is to say that the Basic Principles and Mechanics of the Universe are the Same for the Material as for the Spiritual, even though They may Manifest Differently in the Material than They Manifest in the Spiritual.

   Source(s): Derived from the Mythos-Idea of Singleness of Purpose and Direction in the Creation, plus the Mythos-statement of the "Reflection"-Nature of Beings, though Evidential Support arises from the Experiential Workability of the Idea when it is Applied as a Basic Principle in Magical, Mystical, and Religious Technologies.

In Summary, a Seeker deciding to become Fully Initiate in the Path of Church Of Seven Arrows will be Required to have a "Working Knowledge" of the Mythos and Cosmogony used by Church Of Seven Arrows as given in earlier chapters, *Plus* being Required to have Examined the Dogmas given above using the Procedures given earlier in this chapter, *And* Found Them Acceptable as Truths by which to Live as an Initiate Practitioner of the Way of the Church Of Seven Arrows.

DOCTRINE

1. Remember Always that Your Basic Purpose be to Live in Growth and Happiness that Your Life may Sound Harmonious in the Ear of Creator.

   Commentary: To the extent that an Individual Focusses On, and Progresses Toward, such Personal Goal, the Mythos-Described "Human Problems" will be Remedied and Fulfillment of the Mythos-Given Purpose for Humankind will be Furthered.

2. Know and Live in Accord With Natural Law, being Ever Mindful to Keep Nature's Balances, both Within and Without Yourself.

Commentary: Doing Thusly will Minimize the chances of Ill-Health and other causes for Unhappiness and Internal Disharmonies, Plus "Leading" (by Example!) Other Beings to do Likewise, thus Contributing toward Fulfillment of Humankind's Function and Purpose within Earth's Ecology.

3. Study the Sciences, both Ancient and Modern, Learning their Proper Uses in Benefitting both Yourself and Others.

Commentary: By such Means, the Mythos-Described "Ignorances" of the Human Spirit can be Remedied on an Individual Level, the Individual thereby Enabled to Understand and Carry Out more Effectively her/his Basic Function and Purpose.

4. Know and Be Yourself; You Have a Right to Be Here and Follow Your Own Path so long as you Hinder None Other in Their Doing Likewise.

Commentary: This Self-Knowing, in combination with the Carrying Out of #2 above, will Greatly Promote Your Carrying Out of #1; and the "Non-Interference" Policy regarding Others allows Them the "space" to do Likewise with Their Lives, thus Promoting Fulfillment of the General (Humankind and Others') Functions and Purposes as given per the Mythos.

5. Know and Understand the Powers and Guardians, Using their Aid and Worshipping as You will, Letting Others do Likewise, even though You May Not Understand Their Ways.

Commentary: The "Know and Understand . . . " is part of Remedying the Mythos-Described "Ignorance" of the Human Spirit; the "Using their Aid" is a means of Further Gaining Understanding (to the same End); and the "Letting Others . . . " of course Promotes Harmony AND the Others' Development as They may (as Individuals in Their Own Right) Require.

6. Make No Self-Destructive Agreements, and Let No Other Use You for Their Self-Destruction.

Commentary: NOT to be Equated with Physical-Body Loss or Destruction!!! Self-Destruction, insofar as it Requires Restriction of Awareness, Understanding, and/or Ability-Usage when Considered Relative Spirits, is Clearly Contrary to Fulfillment of Humankind's Function and Purpose in Creator's-Nephew's-Grandmother's Designs as Described in the Mythos.

7. Do Not Cage any Human or Other Free Being.

Commentary: "Cage" Relative Spirits relates to the Forcible Prohibiting or Inhibiting of Growth in Awareness, Understanding, and/or Ability-Development, something Clearly Contrary to the Mythos-Given "Leadership"-Adjuration. (Suppressed Beings do Not Make Joyous and/or Harmonious Song!!!)

8. Take No Life Except for Food or Self-Preservation—and That Only with Proper Respect and Consideration.

Commentary: Given the Observable "Food-Chain" Physical Hierarchy, the Killing of Bodies seems part of Grandmother's Design if issues of Food are involved; however, in view of Spiritual Considerations (such as "Everything has Spirit."), there are matters of Acknowledgement and Communications in Being-to-Being Relationships to be Handled.

And given the Rights and Authorities and so forth Considerations as they relate to Interferences ("NON-Authorized" per Mythos, etc.!) and Suppressions, the Protection of one's Rights May Sometimes Require the Discorporation of some Other Being by way of "Instruction"; however, even so, the matters of Acknowledgement and Communications in Being-to-Being Relationships need to be Handled.

9. Love Whom You Will so long as Your Agreed-Upon Obligations to Home and Community be Fulfilled.

Commentary: This is Specific Application of Doctrines 1, 4, 6, and 7 to some of the Situations and Problems of Human Interactions arising in the Cultural Situation we face in Modern America (and in any other Culture that "sets about" to "standardize" the Spirits of its Inhabitants!).

10. Never Use the Ancient Sciences of Magic and Religion to Harm Others lest Like or Greater Harm Befall You – Except that in Cases of Direct and Mortal Threat which You Did Nothing to Provoke, You May Use Any Means Available in Self-Defense.

11. Use the Ancient Sciences of Magic and Religion when Needful, but Never for Purposes of Show, Pride, or Vainglory.

12. Set No Material Price nor Tribute for Your Use of the Ancient Sciences of Magic and Religion for the Benefit of Others.

Notes: *The complete belief system of the Church of Seven Arrows is found in volume two of its publication,* Shaman's Notes. *It consists of a lengthy statement of the church's underlying Mythos and Cosmology as well as the Dogma and Doctrine. Dogma is defined as those unalterable basic ideas and/or beliefs individuals must hold if they are on a spiritual path. If they reject the dogma, they are, in fact, not on that path. Doctrine, on the other hand, are statements of "work-a-day" applications of the dogma. Doctrine is subject to change, but only in line with the dogma. Reproduced here are the Dogma, complete with explanatory statements, and the Doctrine.*

* * *

DELPHIAN MANIFESTO (DELPHIC COVEN)

OUR FAITH:

As Wicca Traditionals, we are Celtic in that we take our muse from the Cauldron of Kerridwen, and will at length become as the radiant browed Taliesin. We have a Horned God and a Moon Goddess. We visualize the Horned One as a Big Horn Sheep, or a stag with a tremendous horn spread, white as snow and brazen shod. Fleet of foot, wild and untamed in a primeval forest, He is also Lord of the Sun, as well as Saturnian shadows. The giver of wisdom

DELPHIAN MANIFESTO (DELPHIC COVEN) (continued)

and dispenser of judgements. We associate Him with pine trees and cones, Juniper, Sage, Indian Paint Brush, wild sun flowers and all pungent spices.

Our Lady of the Moon and also the sea is associated with white cats, horses, rabbits and all Taurian creatures. Also with various trees and flowers: aspen, plum, apple, wild roses and Shooting Star. Sweet smelling herbs are Her domain. She is the Foam Born Spirit that moves upon the surface of the waters, the rippling laughter of a creek, the Eternal Mother.

We also have Greco-Egyptian leanings, with a strong affinity for the ancient shrine of Apollo in Delphi, Apollo being a God of the arts. A coven totem is the Owl of Athena, patroness of wisdom. We feel a calling to the temples of the Egyptian Mysteries as well. There is an emphasis on Bast, the Cat Goddess, and Hathor, the horned Cow Goddess, and Thoth, the Ibis headed God of wisdom. Also Isis, the Mother Goddess, and the Great Cat Ra who destroyed the dragon of darkness. The cat is another coven totem.

PHILOSOPHY:

Can be summed in the words of Diogenes Laertius— ". . . for a man (or woman) living amid immortal gods, is in no respect like a mortal being." The dragon of darkness is the great fetter of ignorance which we must overcome through educational enlightenment, communication, and involvement with others who are like minded.

We believe that physical death is by no means the end of life, but the opening of another more beautiful chapter when one has completed his or her earthly incarnations and fulfilled his or her Karmic responsibilities.

WAY OF LIFE:

We believe that our great unfoldment lies in freedom of expression . . . the arts in all forms. This leads to freedom of thought, imagination, and then to freedom of spirit. Members of our coven may have any style or design they wish for robes, any fabric, any color, as long as it is a solid color. The same goes for Craft tools. Whenever possible we encourage members to make with their own hands the necessary items, and to embellish them as they desire. Development of psychic ability follows this freedom. This involves card reading, precognitive dreams, astrology, visions and mediumistic development. Candles and incenses are used to promote the proper state of mind, much as the hypnotic vapors of the chasm aided the trance condition of the Delphic Pythoness. Ritual baths are required, as it was in bygone days when seekers who wished to enter the Delphic Temple were required first to bathe in the Sacred Spring of Castalia. Since the cosmic Life-Force is manifest in all living things, these also are sacred. The Earth is a living breathing thing to be reverenced and looked after, as are all the lesser creatures. Therefore, we must do our part to preserve it from ecological destruction. Our magics are those of the Earth. Blessed Be.

Notes: *This statement was issued in 1972.*

MANIFESTO OF THE GEORGIANS (GEORGIAN CHURCH)

The aims and purposes of the Georgians shall be:

1. To worship the Gods of the Old Religion.
2. To aid the members to progress and improve themselves mentally, physically, and spiritually.
3. To work Magick for the benefit of members and any others who may seek our aid for right purposes.
4. To aid others in learning the Craft who truly desire the knowledge of the Craft for proper reasons.
5. To combat the untruths, and to spread the truth about the Craft to those outside the Craft.
6. To work for peace, harmony, and unity among the various branches of the Craft.
7. To work for a better understanding of, and a better relationship between Man and Nature.

Notes: *This church, named for George Patterson, its founder, published its manifesto in 1973.*

* * *

THE BLESSING PRAYER, DECLARATION OF FAITH OF THE BRITISH TRADITIONS, AND THE ORDAINS (NEW WICCAN CHURCH)

THE BLESSING PRAYER

In the name of Dryghtyn,
(Dryghtyn is old Anglo-Saxon for "Great Lord")

The Ancient Providence
(The one who provided for all creation. "Providence" means "Fate" or "Fortune.")

which was from the beginning,
(the Dryghtyn has always existed, every thing else, even the Gods, came after it)

and is for all eternity,
(the Dryghtyn will never cease to exist)

male and female
(the Dryghtyn is bisexual and can create by itself)

the original source of all things
(the Dryghtyn divided itself into the Goddess and the God and they, in turn, created everything else)

All knowing
(the Dryghtyn knows everything - the Goddess knows half of everything and the God knows the other half)

all pervading
(the Dryghtyn is every where, all the time)

all powerful
(the Dryghtyn possesses all the power in the universe; it can do absolutely anything)

Changeless

(this is a great mystery, for, even though the Dryghtyn divided itself it neither gains nor loses any in any way, thus it remains forever a unity and complete)

Eternal
(perhaps the Goddess and the God will recombine some day - we do not know - but the Dryghtyn will always exist)

The Dryghtyn is the one creator that all great world religions worship. The Jews call it Elohim (later replaced by the lesser YHWH); the Moslems call it Allah; the Chinese call it the Tao; the Egyptians called it Ptah; the Sioux call it Wakan Tonka ("Great Spirit"); the Sikh call it Akal ("True Name"); the Hindu call it Brahma; and the ancient Germans called it the Drichtin. The Italian Witches (the Strega) believe the creator was female to begin with and divided off a portion of herself and changed it into the God. Some English Witches have adopted this idea from "Aradia, Gospel of the Witches," a Strega book, but it is not the original English belief. Keltic mythology has numerous different Gods and creation stories, so it is impossible to state a single Theology for the Keltic Witches. Christians believe in the three parts of the Creator (Father, Son and Holy Spirit), but do not believe in the Creator itself. Wicca believe in the Creator and its two parts. Wicca are therefore monotheists, and Christians are not.

The Lady of the Moon
(The Goddess)

The Lord of Death and Resurrection
(The God)

The Mighty Ones of the Four quarters, the Kings of the Elements
(the Lords of the Watchtowers)

The Mighty Dead
(Those who have evolved to the point that they no longer incarnate, such as Merlyn, and Apollonius of Tyana.)

DECLARATION OF FAITH OF THE BRITISH TRADITIONS

We, the undersigned, being Witches of various British Traditions, in recognition of our common origin and similarity of religious practice, do ordain and declare these articles to strengthen our religion, emphasize our uniformity of belief, and to demonstrate to the people and governments of this planet our serious dedication to the worship of the Gods. Witchcraft is composed of numerous traditions, but it is ONE religion. Therefore, we do declare:

Article I. That we are Wicca and our religion is Witchcraft.

Article II. That we give due worship to the Gods, and obey their will.

Article III. That we worship both the Goddess of the Moon and her consort, the God of Death and Resurrection.

Article IV. That the Art is the secret of the Gods and may only be used in earnest and never for show or vain glory.

Article V. That we will never do anything to disgrace the Gods, the Mighty Ones, the religion or its members.

Article VI. That we will never do anything which will bring us into unfavorable contact with the Law of the Land, or any of our persecutors.

Article VII. That a Wicca (Witch) is a proper person who has been validly initiated within a Magic Circle by a Witch of the opposite sex who has the authority to perform the initiation.

Article VIII. That the power may only be passed from woman to man and man to woman, and that a man shall never initiate a man and a woman shall never initiate a woman.

Article IX. That we will ever keep secret and never reveal: the secrets of the religion; the identity, rank or residence of any Wicca without their expressed permission; the location of any secret meeting place of the Wicca; the identity of any person attending such a meeting be they Wicca or not; the secret writings of the Craft or the methods of working magic.

Article X. That we will celebrate our Mysteries in secret and never permit a cowan (non-witch) to observe or participate in our secret ceremonies, rituals or rites.

Article XI. That we will never use magic to kill or injure anyone except in self defense.

Article XII. That we will never use magic to take revenge against anyone.

Article XIII. That we will never curse anyone.

Article XIV. That we will never kill or injure any living thing as a sacrifice or offering to the Gods. This prohibition does not include pricking the finger as demanded at initiation.

Article XV. That we do not believe in the divinity of Jesus Christ and that we do not mock or parody Christianity.

Article XVI. That we do not believe in the existence of Satan or the devil nor do we worship him.

All this we do declare by the Gods and our past lives and our hope of future ones to come.

So mote it be.

THE ORDAINS

May the blessings of the Goddess and the God be on all who keep these laws which are ordained and the curses of both the God and the Goddess be upon all who break them.

So be it ordained: The law was made and ordained of old. The Law was made for the Wicca to advise and help them in their need. The Wicca shall give due worship to the Gods and obey their will, which they ordain, for it was made for the good of the Wicca as the worship of Wicca is good for the Gods, for the Gods ever love the Wicca. As a man loveth a woman, so the Gods love man. And it is necessary that the circle which is the temple of the Gods should be duly cast and purified, that it may be a fit place for the Gods to enter. And the Wicca shall be properly prepared and purified to enter into the presence of the Gods. With love and worship in their hearts, they shall raise the power from their bodies to give power to the Gods, as has been taught of old. For in this way only may man have communion with the Gods, for the Gods cannot help man without the help of man.

Let each High Priestess govern her coven with justice and love, with the help of the High Priest and the Elders, always heeding the advice of the messenger of the Gods if he comes.

And the High Priestess shall rule her coven as the representative of the Goddess, and the High Priest shall support her as the representative of the God. And the High Priestess shall choose whom she will, be he of sufficient rank, to be her High Priest. For, as the God himself kissed her feet in the fivefold salute, laying his power at the feet of the Goddess because of her youth and beauty, her sweetness and kindness, her wisdom and justice, and her generosity. So he resigned all his power to her. But the High Priestess should ever mind that all power comes from him, it is only lent, to be used wisely and justly. And the greatest virtue of a High Priestess be that she recognize that youth is necessary to the representative of the Goddess, so will she gracefully retire in favor of a younger woman should the coven so decide in council. For a true High Priestess realizes that gracefully surrendering the place of pride is one of the greatest virtues, and that thereby will she return to that place of pride in another life, with greater power and beauty.

She will heed all complaints of all brothers and strive to settle all differences among them. So be it ordained. If there be any quarrel or dispute among the Brethren, the High Priestess shall straight away convene the Elders and inquire into the matter and they shall hear both sides, first alone, then together, and they shall decide justly no favoring one side on the other. But it must ever be recognized that there will always be people who will ever strive to force others to do as they will. Such as these are not necessarily evil and they oft have good ideas and such ideas should be talked over in council. But if they will not agree with their Brothers or if they say I will not work under this High Priestess. To those who must ever be chief there is one answer. Avoid the coven or seek another one, or make a coven of your own, taking with you those who will go. Ever recognizing there are people who can never agree to work under others but at the same time, there are some people who cannot rule justly. To those who cannot, justly the answer be those who cannot bear your rule will leave with out you. For none may come to meeting with those whom they are at variance. So if either cannot agree, get hence, for the craft must ever survive. It has ever been the Law of the Brethren to avoid disputes. Any of the third may claim to found a new coven because they live over a

league from the Covenstead or are about to do so. Any one living within the covendom and wishing to form a new coven shall tell the Elders of their intention and on the instant avoid their dwelling and remove to the new covendom. Members of the old coven may join the new one when it is formed, but if they do, they must utterly avoid the Old Coven. The Elders of the old and new covens should meet in peace and brotherly love to decide the new boundaries. Those of the craft who live outside both covendoms may join either coven but not both. All may, if the Elders agree, meet for the great festivals if it be truly in peace and brotherly love. But splitting the coven oft means strife, so for this reason these laws were made of old and may the curse of the Gods be on any who disregard them.

In the old day when witches extended far, we were free and worshipped in the great temples. But in these unhappy times we must celebrate our sacred mysteries in secret! So be it ordained, that none but the Wicca may see our mysteries, for our enemies are many and torture loosens the tongue of man. So be it ordained that no coven shall know where the next coven bide, or who its members be, save only the priest and priestess and messenger. And there shall be no communication between them, save by the messenger of the Gods. And only if it be safe may the covens meet in some safe place for the great festivals, and while there, none shall say whence they have come, nor give their true names. To this end that any be tortured, in their agony they may not tell what they do not know.

So be it ordained, that no one shall tell any one not of the craft, who be of the Wicca, nor give any names or where they bide, or in any way tell anything which can betray any of us to our foes. Nor may he tell where the Covendom be, or the Covenstead, or where the meetings be. And if any break these laws, even under torture, the curse of the Gods shall be upon them, that they may never be reborn on earth but remain where they belong, in the hell of the Christians.

If any speak of the craft, say "Speak not to me of such, it frightens me, it is evil luck to speak of it." For this reason, they have their spies everywhere. These speak as if they were well affected to us, as if they would come to our meetings, saying, "My mother used to worship the Old Ones. I would I could go myself." To such as these, ever deny all knowledge. But to others, say, it is foolish to talk of witches flying through the air. To do so they must be light as thistledown. And men say witches be blear eyed, old crones, so what pleasure can there be at a meeting such as folks. And say, "Many wise men say there be no such creatures." Ever make it a jest.

It is not forbidden to say as Christians do, "There be witchcraft in the land," because our oppressors of old make it hereby not to believe in witchcraft and so a crime to deny it which thereby puts you under suspicion. But ever you say, I know not of it here. Perchance there may be, but far off, I know not where. But ever speak of them as old crones, consorting with the devil and riding through the air. And ever say, "But how may they ride through the air if they are not light as thistledown."

But the curse of the Gods be upon any who cast suspicion on any of the brotherhood, or who speaks of any real meeting place where any abide.

Ever remember that you are the hidden children of the Gods, so never do aught to disgrace them. Never boast, never threaten, never say you wish ill to anyone. So be it ordained: In the olden days we could use the Art against any who ill treated the Brotherhood. But in these evil days, we must not do so for our enemies have devised a burning pit of everlasting fire into which they say their god casts all the people who worship him, except the very few who are released by their priests spells and masses. And this be chiefly by giving monies and rich gifts to receive his favor for their god is ever in need of money. But as the Gods need our aid to make fertile man and crops, so the god of the Christians is ever in need of man's help to search out and destroy us. Their priests ever tell them that any who help us are damned to this hell forever, so men be mad with the terror of it. But they make men believe that they may escape this hell if they give us over to the tormentors so for this reason all be forever saying, thinking, "If I catch one of the Wicca, I shall escape the fiery pit." So for this reason, we have our hidels and men search long and not finding any, say, "There be none, or if there are, they are in a far country." But when one of our oppressors dies, or even is sick, ever is the cry, "This is witches malice," and the hunt is up again and even though they slay ten of their own to one of ours, still they care not, for they have countless thousands, while we are few indeed. So be it ordained that none shall use the art in any way to do ill to any, however much they injure us. Harm none, and now times many believe we exist not. So be it ordained that this law shall ever continue to help us in our plight. No one however great an injury or injustice they receive, may use the art in any way to do ill or harm to any. But they may after consult with all, use the art to restrain the Christians from harming us or taxing others, but only to permit or constrain them. To this end men will say, "Such a one is a mighty searcher out and persecutor of old women whom they deem to be witches, and none has done him skith, so it is proof they cannot or more truly there are none." For all know full well that many folk have died because someone had a grudge against them, or were persecuted because they had money or goods to seize, or because they had none to bribe the searchers. And many have died because they were scolding old women. So much that men now say that only old women are witches. And this is to our advantage and turns suspicion away from us. In England and Scotland it is now many a year since a witch has died the death. But any misuse of the power might raise the persecution again. So never break this law, however much you are tempted and never consent to it being broken in the least. If you know it is being broken, you must work strongly against it. And any High Priestess who consents to its breach must immediately be deposed for it is the blood of the Brethren they endanger. No good, if it is safe and only if it is safe, and keep strictly to the old law.

So be it ordained: Keep a book in your own hand of write. Let brethren copy what they will, but never let this book out of your hand and never keep the writings of another, for if it be found in their hand of write, they will be taken and tortured. Each shall guard his own writings and destroy them whenever danger threatens. Learn as much as you may by heart and when danger is past rewrite your book. For this reason, if any die, destroy their book if they have not been able to, for, if it be found, it is clear proof against them, for our oppressors know that you may not be a witch alone, so all their kin and friends be in danger of arrest. Therefore destroy everything not necessary. If your book is found on you, it is clear proof against you. The same with the working tools. Let them be as ordinary things that many have in their houses. Let the pentacles be of wax that they may be melted or broken at once. Have no sword lest your rank allows you one. Have no names or signs or anything. Write the names and signs in ink before consecrating them and wash it off immediately after. Do not bigrave them lest they cause discovery; let the colors of the hilts tell which is which.

If you are arrested you may be tortured. Keep all thought of the craft from your mind. Say you had bad dreams, that a devil caused you to write this without your knowledge. Think to yourself, "I know nothing, I remember nothing, I have forgotten it all." Drive this into your mind. If the torture be too great to bear say, "I will confess, I cannot bear this torment, what do you want me to say, tell me and I will say it." If they try to make you tell of the Brotherhood, do not. But if they try to make you speak of the impossible, such as flying through the air, consorting with the devil, sacrificing children or eating mens flesh, say I had bad dreams, I was not myself, I was crazed. Not all magistrates are bad, if there be an excuse they may show mercy. If you have confessed to aught, deny it afterwards. Say you babbled under torture, you know not what you said. If you are condemned, fear not. The Brotherhood is powerful, they will help you to escape if you are steadfast. But if you betray aught, there is no hope in this life or that to come. If you go steadfast to the pyre, drugs will reach you, you will feel naught. You but go to the ecstasy of the Goddess.

If the craft have any appendage, let all guard it and help to keep it clear and good for the craft. And let all justly guard all monies of the craft. And if any brother truly wrought it, it is right they have their pay, if it be just, and this be not taking money for the art, but for good and honest work.

And ever the Christians say, "the laborer is worthy of his hire," but if any brother work willingly for the good of the craft, without pay, it is to their greater honor. Never accept money for the use of the art, for money ever smeareth the taker. It is sorcerers and conjurors and priests of the Christians who ever accept money for the use of their arts. And they sell dwale, and evil love spells and pardons, to let men escape from their sins. Be not as these. If you accept no money, you will be free from temptation to use the art for evil causes. All may use the art for their advantage or for the advantage of the craft only if it harm none. But ever let the coven debate this at length. Only if all are satisfied and none are harmed, may the Art be used. If it is not possible to achieve your ends one way, perchance the aim may be achieved by acting in a different way so as to harm none. May the curse of the Gods be upon any who break this law. So be it ordained. It is

763

THE BLESSING PRAYER, DECLARATION OF FAITH OF THE BRITISH TRADITIONS, AND THE ORDAINS (NEW WICCAN CHURCH) (continued)

judged lawful if any of the craft need a house or land and none will sell, to incline the owner's mind so as to be willing to sell, providing it harms him not in any way and the full price is paid without haggling. Never bargain or cheapen anything while you live by the Art.

So be it ordained. Let the Craft keep books with the names of all herbs which are good, and all cures, so all may learn. But keep another book with all the Bales (poisons) and spices (aphrodisiacs) and let only the Elders and other trustworthy people have this knowledge.

So be it ordained. Remember the Art is the secret of the Gods and only may be used in earnest and never for show or vain glory. Magicians and Christians may taunt us [and] say, "You have no power. Do magic before our eyes, then only will we believe," seeking to cause us to betray our Art before them. Heed them not. For the Art is Holy and may only be used in need. And the curse of the Gods be upon any who break this law.

It is ever the way with women and men also that they ever seek new love, nor should we reprove them for this, But it may be found a disadvantage to the Craft, as many a time it has happened that a High Priest or High Priestess impelled by love has departed with their love, that is they have left the coven. Now if a High Priestess wishes to resign, she may do so in full coven, and the resignation is valid. But if they should run off without resigning, who may know if they may not return in a few months? So the law is, if a High Priestess leaves her Coven, she be taken back and all be as before. Meanwhile, if she has a deputy, that deputy shall act as High Priestess for as long as the High Priestess is away. If she returns not at the end of a year and a day, then shall the coven elect a new High Priestess. Unless there is good reason to the contrary, the person who has done the work shall reap the benefit of the reward, maiden and deputy of the High Priestess.

It is the old law and the most important of all laws that no one may do anything which will endanger any of the craft, or bring them into contact with the law of the land or any persecutors.

In any dispute between the brethren, no one may invoke any laws but those of the craft, or any tribunal but that of the Priestess, Priest, and Elders.

So be it ordained. Order and discipline must be kept. The High Priestess or the High Priest may and should punish all faults. To this end, all of the craft must receive correction willingly. All, properly prepared, the culprit kneeling shall be told his fault and his sentence pronounced. Punishment shall be the scourge, followed by something amusing. The culprit must acknowledge the justice of the punishment by kissing the hand of the Priestess on receiving sentence and again thanking for punishment received.

Notes: *The beliefs of the New Wiccan Church, a West Coast Wiccan fellowship of covens, are found in three documents. The first, The Blessing Prayer, reproduced here with a church-produced commentary following each phrase, is considered equivalent to the Apostles' Creed for the Christian Church. The Declaration of Faith, written in the early 1970s, summarizes the beliefs of the New Wiccan Church and other covens who trace their origins to the British Gardnerian tradition. The declaration was "distilled" from the last and most lengthy document, The Ordains. The three documents emphasize a polytheistic belief with central worship directed to the Goddess and her consort, the God; the necessary role of both men and women in ritual duties; and the proper use of magical power.*

*   *   *

BASIC PRINCIPLES [TEMPLE OF THE GODDESS WITHIN (MATILDA JOSLYN GAGE COVEN)]

AMONG OUR BASIC PRINCIPLES ARE:

1. We believe in the primary importance of a distinctly feminist perspective in our religion and our goals for a better world.

2. We believe in worshipping the Goddess as the primary Deity and as an expression of the life-force of the universe; we believe the male principle is a "complementary" but not superior force.

3. We believe that all members of the Matilda Joslyn Gage Coven should be like-minded; we believe that coven members should share a unity of purpose and agreement about goals, so that coven members can work together easily and happily.

4. We believe our coven must be experimental and eclectic, finding a tradition of Feminist Wicce among the varieties of Wicca (Wicce) that exist and flourish.

5. We believe in the necessity of taking public action, as a coven and as individuals, as relates to our feminist goals.

6. We believe in the necessity of taking private actions consistent with our feminist goals.

7. We believe that feminist men can enter into coven ceremonies, subject to the consensus of coven members.

8. We believe the Matilda Joslyn Gage Coven is a teaching coven; we believe that new members may join us at the Equinoxes and Solstices, and that continuing members are learning more about feminist spirituality.

9. We believe that we as witches are seeking wisdom.

10. We believe that Wicce is a religion of love.

11. We believe that the power we achieve must be used towards the betterment and care of this entire planet.

12. We believe that we must work with Nature.

Notes: *Within the larger Wiccan/Neo-Pagan community, feminist Wicce (Witchcraft) forms a significant part. The Matilda Joslyn Gage Coven of Sacramento, California, was an early feminist coven formed in the summer of 1977. It has since disbanded but some of its impulse flowed into the Temple of the Goddess Within, now located in Oakland, California. While promoting a feminist perspective, the* *oven was not anti-male and recognized the male aspect of he deity.*

* * *

Satanism

THE 9 SATANIC STATEMENTS (CHURCH OF SATAN)

1. Satan represents indulgence, instead of abstinence!

2. Satan represents vital existence, instead of spiritual pipe dreams!

3. Satan represents undefiled wisdom, instead of hypocritical self-deceit!

4. Satan represents kindness to those who deserve it, instead of love wasted on ingrates!

5. Satan represents vengeance, instead of turning the other cheek!

6. Satan represents responsibility to the responsible, instead of concern for psychic vampires!

7. Satan represents man as just another animal, sometimes better, more often worse than those that walk on all fours, who because of his "divine spiritual and intellectual development" has become the most vicious animal of all!

8. Satan represents all of the so-called sins, as they all lead to physical or mental gratification!

9. Satan has been the best friend the church has ever had, as he has kept it in business all these years!

The record speaks for itself — SATAN RULES THE EARTH!

REGIE SATANAS!   HAIL SATAN!

Notes: *These nine statements, which summarize the basic stance of Satanists toward the world, were written by Anton LaVey, founder of the Church of Satan. They have been accepted by other Satanic groups, especially those composed of former members of the Church of Satan. Widely circulated as a basic manifesto, The 9 Satanic Statements opened LaVey's first book,* The Satanic Bible.

Chapter 20
Middle Eastern Family

Main Line Judaism

THE THIRTEEN PRINCIPLES OF THE FAITH
(RABBI MOSES MAIMONIDES)

1. I believe with perfect faith that the Creator, blessed be his name, is the Author and Guide of everything that has been created, and that he alone has made, does make, and will make all things.

2. I believe with perfect faith that the Creator, blessed be his name, is a Unity, and that there is no unity in any manner like unto his, and that he alone is our God, who was, is, and will be.

3. I believe with perfect faith that the Creator, blessed be his name, is not a body, and that he is free from all the accidents of matter, and that he has not any form whatsoever.

4. I believe with perfect faith that the Creator, blessed be his name, is the first and the last.

5. I believe with perfect faith that to the Creator, blessed be his name, and to him alone, it is right to pray, and that it is not right to pray to any being besides him.

6. I believe with perfect faith that all the words of the prophets are true.

7. I believe with perfect faith that the prophecy of Moses our teacher, peace be unto him, was true, and that he was the chief of the prophets, both of those that preceded and of those that followed him.

8. I believe with perfect faith that the whole Law, now in our possession, is the same that was given to Moses our teacher, peace be unto him.

9. I believe with perfect faith that this Law will not be changed, and that there will never be any other law from the Creator, blessed be his name.

10. I believe with perfect faith that the Creator, blessed be his name, knows every deed of the children of men, and all their thoughts, as it is said, It is he that fashioneth the hearts of them all, that giveth heed to all their deeds.

11. I believe with perfect faith that the Creator, blessed be his name, rewards those that keep his commandments, and punishes those that transgress them.

12. I believe with perfect faith in the coming of the Messiah, and, though he tarry, I will wait daily for his coming.

13. I believe with perfect faith that there will be a resurrection of the dead at the time when it shall please the Creator, blessed be his name, and exalted be the remembrance of him for ever and ever.

For thy salvation I hope, O Lord! I hope, O Lord, for thy salvation! O Lord, for thy salvation I hope!

For thy salvation I hope, O Lord! I hope, O Lord, for thy salvation! O Lord, for thy salvation I hope!

Notes: *Judaism is generally viewed as a religion of deed rather than creed. While there are numerous writings concerning Judaism, only rarely have there been attempts to summarize the faith in a creed-like statement. One interesting attempt to assemble a set of such credos from a variety of individual Jews (though collected in the cause of Reconstructionism) can be found in Ira Eisenstein's* Varieties of Jewish Belief *(New York: Reconstructionist Press, 1966). Of course, the Shema provides a basic statement of the Jewish perspective in the midst of a Pagan world: "Hear O Israel, the Lord is our God, the Lord is One." That sentence (which has slightly variant renderings in English) is taken from the Scripture, Deuteronomy 6:4. Beyond the Shema, only one statement has received wide acknowledgement as a perceptive synopsis of Jewish belief—the twelfth-century "creed" of Rabbi Moses Maimonides.*

The Thirteen Principles of the Faith is the single most acceptable summary of the common beliefs of religious Jews. Maimonides was a twelfth-century rabbi residing in Egypt who is remembered for his codification of Jewish law. The text reproduced here is from an Orthodox Jewish morning prayer liturgy. It is noteworthy that in the early nineteenth century, when South Carolina Jews issued a statement of their Reform position, they revised Maimonides' creed.

THE FUNDAMENTAL BELIEFS OF JUDAISM (GERMAN RABBINICAL ASSOCIATION, 1897)

1) Judaism teaches the unity of the human race. We all have one Father, one God has created us.

2) Judaism commands: "Love thy neighbor as thyself," and declares this command of all-embracing love to be the fundamental principle of Jewish religion. It therefore forbids every sort of animosity, envy, malevolence, or unkindness towards any one of whatsoever race, nationality, or religion. It demands justice and righteousness and forbids injustice, improbity, fraud, taking unfair advantage of the need, the heedlessness, and the inexperience of a fellow-man, as well as usury, and the usurious employment of the powers of a fellow-man.

3) Judaism demands consideration for the life, health, powers, and possessions of one's neighbor. It therefore forbids injuring a fellow-man by force, or cunning, or in any other iniquitous manner depriving him of his property, or leaving him helplessly exposed to unlawful attacks.

4) Judaism commands holding a fellow-man's honor as sacred as one's own. It therefore forbids degrading him by evil reports. vexing him with ridicule, or mortifying him.

5) Judaism commands respect for the religious conviction of others. It therefore forbids aspersion or disrespectful treatment of the religious customs and symbols of other religions.

6) Judaism commands the practice of charity towards all, clothing the naked, feeding the hungry, nursing the sick, comforting those that mourn. It therefore forbids limiting our care to ourselves and our families, and withholding sympathy when our neighbors suffer.

7) Judaism commands respect for labor; each in his place shall take part by means of physical or mental labor, in the work of the community, and strive for the blessings of life by busy, creative activity. It therefore demands the cultivation, development, and active employment of all our powers and capabilities. On the other hand, it forbids inactive enjoyment of life and idleness confident of support by others.

8) Judaism commands absolute truthfulness: our yea shall be yea, our nay, nay. It therefore forbids distortion of truth, deceit, hypocrisy, double dealing and dissimulation.

9) Judaism commands walking humbly with God and in modesty among men. It therefore forbids self-conceit, arrogance, pride, presumptuousness, boasting and disparagement of the merits of others.

10) Judaism demands peaceableness, placability, mildness, benevolence. It therefore commands the return of good for evil, to suffer rather than inflict injury. It therefore forbids taking revenge, nursing hatred, bearing a grudge, abandoning even an adversary in his helplessness.

11) Judaism commands chastity and sanctity of marriage. It therefore forbids dissoluteness, license, and relaxation of family ties.

12) Judaism commands the conscientious observance of the laws of the state, respect for obedience to the government. It therefore forbids rebellion against governmental ordinances and evasion of the law.

13) Judaism commands the promotion of the welfare of one's fellow-men, the service of individuals and communities in accordance with one's ability. It therefore forbids slothful indifference to the common weal and selfish exclusion from the societies instituted for charitable purposes and for the betterment of mankind.

14) Judaism commands that its adherents shall love the state, and willingly sacrifice property and life for its honor, welfare and liberty.

15) Judaism commands sanctification of the name of God through acts and it bids us exert ourselves to hasten the time in which men shall be united in the love of God and the love of one another.

Notes: *In 1897, the leaders of the several branches of German Judaism adopted a statement. Typical of the manner in which many approach Judaism (as a religion in which deed is more important than belief), the statement emphasizes the commandments of Judaism while limiting theological considerations to the affirmation of one Creator God.*

* * *

A STATEMENT OF JEWISH DOCTRINE FROM *RELIGIOUS BODIES IN AMERICA* (1936)

The Jewish religion is a way of life and has no formulated creed, or articles of faith, the acceptance of which brings redemption or salvation to the believer, or divergence from which involves separation from the Jewish congregation. On the other hand, it has certain teachings, sometimes called doctrines or dogmas, which have been at all times considered obligatory on the adherents of the Jewish religion.

The unity of God.—The fundamental doctrine of the Jewish religion is that God is One. At all times the religion of the Jew vigorously protested against any infringement of this dogma of pure monotheism, whether by the dualism of the East or by the Trinitarianism of the West. It never permitted the attributes of justice and of love to divide the Godhead into different powers or personalities. God is a Spirit without limitations of form, eternal, noncorporeal, unique, omniscient, omnipotent, and one. "Hear, O Israel: The Lord our God, the Lord is One" is the declaration of faith which the Jew pronounces daily and breathes it even in his hour of death. God is the Creator of the world. He is also the preserver of the world, its ruler, and the arbiter of its destiny. He was God from the very beginning, and the worship of other gods is a rebellion against the universal God beside whom there is no other. "Look unto Me, and be ye saved, all the ends of the earth; for I am God and there is none else." (Isaiah, xlv, 22). He is the God of righteousness, mercy, love, and holiness; the ideal of moral perfection. God is "our Father, our Redeemer for everlasting" (Isaiah, lxiii, 16); He is not remote from mortal man in his need, but He is rather, as Jewish sages have put it "near, nearer than any other help or sympathy can be," who "appears to each according to his capacity or temporary need." A Jew cannot compromise with idolatry or polytheism; indeed he is enjoined to give his life rather than to renounce the purity of his religion.

The world and man.—The world is a cosmic unit and it is good. The Holy One created and sustains the earth and the heaven, light and darkness, life and death; and the world is ruled by everlasting wisdom and kindness. There is no cosmic force for evil, no principle of evil in creation. There is no inherent impurity in the flesh or in matter, and man is not subject to Satan. There is no original sin; sin is the erring from the right path. The crown and the acme of God's creation is man. He is capable of perfection without the aid of an extraneous being, and, being born free, is able to choose between good and evil, and is endowed with intelligence; "God created man in His own image" and made him "but little lower than the angels." From one man did all the races of the earth descend, and thus they constitute one family. This doctrine of the unity of the human family is a corollary of the doctrine of the unity of God. The One God is in direct relation with man, all men, there being no mediator between God and man, and all men may attain to immortality through following the good life; for immortality, the Jewish religion teaches, is the reward of human righteousness. There is in this respect no distinction between its own adherents and those of other faiths. As one ancient teacher exclaims: "I call heaven and earth to witness that whether it be Jew or gentile, man or woman, manservant or maidservant, according to their acts does the divine spirit rest upon them."

The future of mankind and Israel.—The perfection of humanity through the unfolding of the divine powers in man is the aim of history. There is to be a divine kingdom of truth and righteousness on this earth. Daily the Jew concludes his prayers by declaring his hope to behold speedily the time when God, in the glory of His might, will be manifested, and the abominations will be removed from the earth and idolatry utterly cut off, and He will perfect the world as the kingdom of the Almighty, and all flesh will call upon His name. This kingdom is the hope of mankind and the goal toward which it is striving. Whether or not this universal kingdom of God will be preceded by the day of God or by a universal judgment when "all that work wickedness shall be stubble," Jewish religion teaches the coming on this earth of a social order of human perfection and bliss, of peace without end, when none shall hurt or destroy, and when the earth shall be full of the knowledge of the Lord (Isaiah chapters ix, xi); this is the Messianic era.

Israel is a unique people that shall never cease (Jeremiah xxxi, 36). It is not claimed that this people is better than others or that it possesses a special share of the divine love; but it is affirmed, and the Jew daily declares this faith in his prayers, that God has brought them near to His great name, to give thanks unto Him, and to proclaim His unity. In this sense Israel is called a "kingdom of priests and a holy nation" (Exodus xix, 6), selected or assigned by God for His special purpose. Because of this duty they are taken to task more severely than others: "You only have I known of all the families of the earth, therefore I will visit upon you all your iniquities" (Amos iii, 2). It is a widespread Jewish interpretation that the Servant of the Lord described in Isaiah refers not to an individual but to the Jewish people as a group. Israel is God's witness (Isaiah xli-xliii), testifying to His existence and His unity. The duty of Israel, its imperishability and restoration (Deuteronomy xxx, 1-4) and the blessed future that awaits mankind, are doctrines of the Jewish religion.

The Law.—The belief in the unity of God, in the future hope of the world, and in the other doctrines is of no value unless one lives in accordance with the requirements of the beliefs. The emphasis is not on belief, but on righteous conduct. What is required is service of the Lord, a just system of human conduct in accordance with statutes and ordinances, "which if a man do, he shall live by them." The duty of man, created in the image of God, is to order his life entirely in accordance with the will of God, and only by so doing can he attain perfection and fulfill his destiny. And what does God desire of man? That was definitely conveyed to him. Already the first man, Adam, had received divine revelation for his conduct and for that of his descendants; others followed, until Moses received the full revelation, all the commandments and the statutes and the ordinances, which should govern the life of man and lead him to moral and religious perfection. This revelation, as contained in the Five Books of Moses, constitutes the Law of Moses, the Law, the Torah, the Written Law, and it must be understood in the light of Jewish tradition, the Oral Law. This Torah of divine origin, which will not be changed, is the foundation of the Jewish faith; and that the Jew must order his life in accordance with the Torah has always been a basic principle of the Jewish religion. To fear God and to keep His commandments is the whole duty of man.

The Torah, written and oral, preeminently emphasizes the principle of justice; other principles stressed are purity and truth, optimism and hope, joy and thanksgiving, holiness and the love of God. Righteousness and compassionate love are demanded for the fatherless, the widow, the oppressed, the stranger, and even the criminal; charity is *zedakah,* justice to the needy; and compassion is required even for the dumb animal. Further, a man's life must be permeated by purity of heart and built on truth. For, "the seal of the Holy One is truth" and "upon truth rests the world." Hope and optimism are other requirements, and hope is but rarely deferred to the world to come, but a man must rather wait for the moral and spiritual advancement of mankind in this world. At times this world is declared to be "like a vestibule in which one prepares for the palace," nevertheless, "one hour devoted to repentance and good deeds in this world is more valuable than the entire life of the world to come." A man should "rejoice before the Lord" and gratefully enjoy his gifts and fill other hearts with joy and thanksgiving: asceticism is discouraged. The whole life of man is holy, for the "Lord our God is holy," and man's life should be motivated by the love of God. Twice daily a Jew recites the *Shema',* a

A STATEMENT OF JEWISH DOCTRINE FROM *RELIGIOUS BODIES IN AMERICA* (1936) (continued)

declaration which contains the words "Thou shalt love the Lord thy God with all thy heart and with all thy soul and with all thy might." It implies the purest motives for action, specifically serving the Lord, not from fear but rather out of love and for the sake of God and the glorification of His name; the doing of good, not in view of any reward, but for its own sake: and the love of man and the most unselfish devotion and the willing surrender of one's life itself whenever the cause of God demands.

Other fundamental teachings of the law, written and oral, are freedom of will and human responsibility, divine providence, retribution, resurrection of the dead, the power of repentance and of prayer. Man is free, the choice between good and evil having been left to him as a participant of God's spirit; man is responsible for his own actions. In close relation with the doctrine of divine providence stands that of retribution—that God rewards the righteous and punishes transgressors. The doctrine of the soul's immortality and of a future life in which retribution shall take place is plainly set forth in the Talmud, and the belief in the resurrection of the dead is closely connected with the doctrines of immortality and of retribution in the hereafter. Emphasis is laid on the power of repentance to avert from man the evil which threatens and to procure for him God's grace, and on the efficacy of the prayer "of all that call upon Him in truth." There is no need for any mediator when one prays to God, "for the Lord is nigh unto all them that call upon Him." He hears great and small alike.

The Torah emphasizes the need of study and education. It imposes a duty upon every father to instruct his children and upon the community to provide for the general instruction of old and young. The law sanctifies labor and makes the teaching of a trade whereby one may earn his living a duty upon the father and upon the communal authorities. Each man is enjoined to build a home and to contribute to the welfare of human society; celibacy, except under rare circumstances, is unlawful. Systematic care of the poor is a duty of a community. Love of one's country and loyalty to his government is enjoined upon every Jew, and he is solemnly adjured to seek the peace of his country and to pray for the welfare of its government.

Side by side with these universal principles of conduct the Torah surrounds the Jewish people with numerous laws and rites. Some laws, also called testimonies, have been given to make Israel testify to God's miraculous guidance, such as the festive seasons of the year; others, called signs, are tokens of the covenant between God and Israel, such as circumcision and the Sabbath; and still others, also called statutes, are divine marks of distinction—special means to preserve Israel and its group life. The covenant at Sinai made Israel a society "of priests and a holy nation" and laws were given to them designed to preserve the priestly character of the nation. Some of these appeal to the human reason while others do not, but even those which human intelligence is unable to grasp, are, through belief in their divine origin, vouchsafed the same high religious importance. Judaism is bound up with the Jewish people. "Ye

shall be holy unto Me: for I the Lord am holy, and have set you apart from the peoples, that ye should be Mine" (Leviticus xx. 26). These particularistic religious obligations of the Torah, written and oral, enabled the small Jewish people to resist the disintegrating forces of the idolatry and error which surrounded them, and encouraged the Jews to live by the principle, ascribed by the early rabbis to Abraham, "let all the world stand on the one side, I side with God and shall win in the end." The laws gave the Jews the strength to withstand the persecutions of the nations and the vicissitudes of time, and to fight for the truth amidst a hostile world. The Jewish religion knows of no sacraments, in the sense of rites by which a person is brought in bodily relationship to God; but the whole life of the Jew, even his commonest acts, are invested with religious obligations and meanings, and they are regarded as a sign of merit; as the rabbis have put it, "The Holy One, blessed be He, was pleased to bestow merit upon Israel and therefore heaped upon them laws and commandments." A pious man is "eager in the pursuit of religious obligations" and they fill the life of the Jew with a higher joy.

The Jewish religion in its relation to other faiths.—The Jewish religion enjoins upon its adherents the application of one law for Jew and members of other faiths, home-born or stranger; "Ye shall have one manner of law, as well for the stranger as for the home-born" (Numbers xxiv, 22). The harsh expressions found sometimes in ancient Jewish lore, concerning the heathen and the laws against him, are directed against the moral depravity ascribed to the heathen because of his unchastity and violence; he is always under grave suspicion of immoral conduct. The Jewish religion recognizes two classes of proselytes—"a proselyte of the gate" is one who abandons idolatry and accepts instead the seven Noachian laws of humanity, while "a proselyte of righteousness" is one who submits to the Abrahamic rite and becomes a full member of the House of Israel. No distinction whatever is drawn between a born Jew and a proselyte of righteousness. In former centuries, the Jews carried on an extensive proselytizing propaganda; later the world conditions prevented it. But whether as a result of that interference or not, proselytizing activities have since been neglected. In the fullness of time, however, the prophetic promises of the universal recognition of God will be fulfilled, and as the Jew expresses it in his prayers on New Year's Day, "God will reign in His glory over the whole universe and all the living shall say, the Lord, God of Israel, is King, and His kingdom ruleth over all."

Notes: *This statement was prepared for the United States Bureau of the Census for its 1936 (and last) edition of* Religious Bodies in America *by Dr. H. S. Linfield of the Jewish Statistical Bureau. It varied in no substantial manner from the statement appearing in the 1926 edition; it can thus be construed as representing the concensus of opinion of the major branches of American Judaism prior to World War II. It avoids mention of those issues that most differentiate Reform, Orthodox, and Conservative Jewish congregations. The statement mentions the "restoration" of Israel in passing, and ends with an affirmative paragraph on proselytization. It was written shortly before the Reform* congregations adopted a new statement, the Columbus Platform.

* * *

FROM THE *CONSTITUTION* [UNITED SYNAGOGUE OF AMERICA (1916) (CONSERVATIVE JUDAISM)]

The objects of said corporation shall be: The advancement of the cause of Judaism in America and the maintenance of Jewish tradition in its historical continuity; to assert and establish loyalty to the Torah and its historical exposition; to further the observance of the Sabbath and the Dietary Laws: to preserve in the service the reference to Israel's past and the hopes for Israel's restoration; to maintain the traditional character of the liturgy, with Hebrew as the language of prayer; to foster Jewish religious life in the home, as expressed in traditional observances; to encourage the establishment of Jewish religious schools, in the curricula of which the study of the Hebrew language and literature shall be given a prominent place, both as the key to the true understanding of Judaism, and as a bond holding together the scattered communities of Israel throughout the world. It shall be the aim of the United Synagogue of America, while not endorsing the innovations introduced by any of its constituent bodies, to embrace all elements essentially loyal to traditional Judaism and in sympathy with the purposes outlined above.

Notes: *In their constitution, Conservative Jewish leaders stated their objectives in such a manner as to distinguish them from both the Reform and Orthodox communities.*

* * *

PREAMBLE TO THE CONSTITUTION [WORLD COUNCIL OF SYNAGOGUES (1959) (CONSERVATIVE JUDAISM)]

Moved by an abiding faith in God, a deep love for His Torah, and a profound concern for the future of Judaism, the Jewish people, and all mankind, and

Keenly conscious of the responsibility which has fallen upon our generation, having experienced the nadir of disaster and having witnessed the miracle of deliverance, to preserve, enrich and transmit to coming generations our precious legacy of faith, learning, piety and wisdom and the ideals of universal peace, justice, and brotherhood, and

Desirous of strengthening Jewish life throughout the world, without impairing the essential, traditional autonomy of every Jewish community.

We, the representatives of like-minded congregations from different climes and continents, do hereby establish the World Council of Synagogues for the following purposes:

To foster the Jewish tradition in its historic continuity;

To promote the study of Torah and the observance of mitzvot;

To advocate the centrality and preeminence of the synagogue in the life of the Jewish people;

To further the study of the Hebrew language as the repository of our sacred literature and our accumulated spiritual and cultural heritage, and as the most potent cultural bond among Jews throughout the world;

To deepen our dedication to the prophetic ideal of creating in the land of our fathers a Jewish community which shall pattern its life by the ideals and teachings of the Torah, and which shall seek to be "a light unto the nations"; and,

To relate the ideals and practices of Judaism to contemporary life and thought to the end that mankind's spiritual and ethical aspirations may be enhanced and God's Kingdom may be established on this earth.

Notes: *The World Council of Synagogues, a worldwide organization of Conservative Jews in which American Jews play an important role, provided a recent statement of the unique Conservative Jewish traditional perspective.*

* * *

PRINCIPLES ADOPTED BY THE ORTHODOX JEWISH CONGREGATIONAL UNION OF AMERICA (1898) (ORTHODOX JUDAISM)

This Conference of delegates from Jewish congregations in the United States and the Dominion of Canada is convened to advance the interests of positive Biblical Rabbinical and Historical Judaism.

We are assembled not as a synod, and, therefore, we have no legislative authority to amend religious questions, but as a representative body, which by organization and cooperation will endeavor to advance the interests of Judaism in America.

We favor the convening of a Jewish Synod specifically authorized by congregations to meet, to be composed of men who must be certified Rabbis, and

a. Elders in official position (cf. Numbers XI:16);

b. Men of wisdom and understanding, and known amongst us (cf. Deut. I:13);

c. Able men, God-fearing men, men of truth, hating profit (cf. Exodus XVIII:21).

We believe in the Divine revelation of the Bible, and we declare that the prophets in no way discountenanced ceremonial duty, but only condemned the personal life of those who observed ceremonial law, but disregarded the moral. Ceremonial law is not optative; it is obligatory.

We affirm our adherence to the acknowledged codes of our Rabbis and the thirteen principles of Maimonides.

We believe that in our dispersion we are to be united with our brethren of alien faith in all that devolves upon men as citizens; but that religiously in rites, ceremonies, ideals and doctrines, we are separate, and must remain separate in accordance with the Divine declaration: 'I have separated you from the nations to be Mine.' (Lev. XX:26.)

And further, to prevent misunderstanding concerning Judaism, we reaffirm our belief in the coming of a personal

PRINCIPLES ADOPTED BY THE ORTHODOX JEWISH CONGREGATIONAL UNION OF AMERICA (1898) (ORTHODOX JUDAISM) (continued)

Messiah and we protest against the admission of proselytes into the fold of Judaism without *millah* (circumcision) and *tebilah* (immersion).

We protest against intermarriage between Jew and Gentile; we protest against the idea that we are merely a religious sect, and maintain that we are a nation, though temporarily without a national home, and

Furthermore, that the restoration to Zion is the legitimate aspiration of scattered Israel, in no way conflicting with our loyalty to the land in which we dwell or may dwell at any time.

Notes: *In July 1898 delegates from approximately 100 Orthodox congregations met in New York City to form the Orthodox Jewish Congregational Union of America, now known as the Union of Orthodox Jewish Congregations, the largest of the Orthodox Jewish bodies in America. During the meeting, a set of principles representative of the Orthodox position, as opposed to the recently published Reform Pittsburgh Platform, was adopted, though the delegates understood clearly the limitations of any statement they might issue. The statement remains a strong assertion of the traditional Orthodox perspective.*

* * *

CRITERIA OF JEWISH LOYALTY [JEWISH RECONSTRUCTIONIST FOUNDATION (RECONSTRUCTIONIST JUDAISM)]

1) We want Judaism to help us overcome temptation, doubt and discouragement.

2) We want Judaism to imbue us with a sense of responsibility for the righteous use of the blessings wherewith God endowed us.

3) We want the Jew so to be trusted that his yea will be taken as yea and his nay as nay.

4) We want to learn how to utilize our leisure to best advantage physically, intellectually and spiritually.

5) We want the Jewish home to live up to its traditional standards of virtue and piety.

6) We want the Jewish upbringing of our children to further their moral and spiritual growth, and to enable them to accept with joy their heritage as Jews.

7) We want the synagogue to enable us to worship God in sincerity and in truth.

8) We want our religious traditions to be interpreted in terms of understandable experience and to be made relevant to our present day needs.

9) We want to participate in the upbuilding of Eretz Yisrael as a means to the renaissance of the Jewish spirit.

10) We want Judaism to find rich, manifold and ever new expression in philosophy, in letters and in the arts.

11) We want all forms of Jewish organization to make for spiritual purpose and ethical endeavor.

12) We want the unity of Israel throughout the world to be fostered through mutual help in time of need and through cooperation in the furtherance of Judaism at all times.

13) We want Judaism to function as a potent influence for justice, freedom and peace in the life of men and nations.

Notes: *This Reconstructionist Jewish statement functions in a manner somewhat analogous to articles of faith. Following theorist Mordecai Kaplan's idea of Judaism as a religious civilization, the Reconstructionist Sabbath Prayer Book asserts: "In view of the changed conditions in Jewish life, the criterion of loyalty to Judaism can no longer be the acceptance of a creed, but the experience of the need to have one's life enriched by the Jewish heritage."*

* * *

ARTICLES OF FAITH [THE REFORM SOCIETY OF ISRAELITES (1825) (REFORM JUDAISM)]

1. I believe with a perfect faith, that God Almighty (blessed be His name!) is the Creator and Governor of all Creation; and that He alone has made, does make and will make all things.

2. I believe with a perfect faith that the Creator (blessed be His name!) is only one unity; to which there is no resemblance and that He alone has been, is and will be God.

3. I believe with a perfect faith that the Creator (blessed be His name!) is not corporeal; nor to be comprehended by any understanding capable of comprehending only what is corporeal; and that there is nothing like Him in the universe.

4. I believe with a perfect faith that the Creator (blessed be His name!) is the only true object of adoration, and that no other being whatsoever ought to be worshipped.

5. I believe with a perfect faith that the soul of man is breathed into him by God and is therefore immortal.

6. I believe with a perfect faith that the Creator (blessed be His name!) knows all things, and that He will reward those who observe His commands, and punish those who transgress them.

7. I believe with a perfect faith that the laws of God, as delivered by Moses in the Ten Commandments, are the only true foundation of piety toward the Almighty, and of morality among men.

8. I believe with a perfect faith, that morality is essentially connected with religion, and that good faith toward all mankind, is among the most acceptable offerings to the Deity.

9. I believe with a perfect faith, that the love of God is the highest duty of his creatures, and that the pure and upright heart is the chosen temple of Jehovah.

10. I believe with a perfect faith that the Creator (blessed be His name!) is the only true Redeemer of all His children, and that He will spread the worship of His name over the whole earth.

Notes: *Among the earliest documents of American Reform Judaism is the 1825 statement issued by the Reform party associated with the synagogue in Charleston, South Carolina. The articles are based upon the traditional creed-like formulation of Jewish belief written by Maimonides, now adapted to the new Reform concerns.*

* * *

PITTSBURGH PLATFORM [CENTRAL CONFERENCE OF AMERICAN RABBIS (1885) (REFORM JUDAISM)]

First—We recognize in every religion an attempt to grasp the Infinite, and in every mode, source, or book or revelation held sacred in any religious system, the consciousness of the indwelling of God in man. We hold that Judaism presents the highest conception of the God idea as taught in our holy Scriptures and developed and spiritualized by the Jewish teachers, in accordance with the moral and philosophical progress of their respective ages. We maintain that Judaism preserved and defended, midst continual struggles and trials and under enforced isolation, this God idea as the central religious truth for the human race.

Second—We recognize in the Bible the record of the consecration of the Jewish people to its mission as priest of the one God, and value it as the most potent instrument of religious and moral instruction. We hold that the modern discoveries of scientific researches in the domains of nature and history are not antagonistic to the doctrines of Judaism, the Bible reflecting the primitive ideas of its own age, and at times clothing its conception of Divine Providence and justice, dealing with man in miraculous narratives.

Third—We recognize in the Mosaic legislation a system of training the Jewish people for its mission during its national life in Palestine, and to-day we accept as binding only the moral laws, and maintain only such ceremonies as elevate and sanctify our lives, but reject all such as are not adapted to the views and habits of modern civilization.

Fourth—We hold that all such Mosaic and rabbinical laws as regulate diet, priestly purity, and dress, originated in ages and under the influence of ideas altogether foreign to our present mental and spiritual state. They fail to impress the modern Jew with a spirit of priestly holiness: their observance in our days is apt rather to obstruct than to further modern spiritual elevation.

Fifth—We recognize, in the modern era of universal culture of heart and intellect, the approaching of the realization of Israel's great Messianic hope for the establishment of the kingdom of truth, justice, and peace among all men. We consider ourselves no longer a nation, but a religious community, and therefore expect neither a return to Palestine, nor a sacrificial worship under the sons of Aaron, nor the restoration of any of the laws concerning the Jewish state.

Sixth—We recognize in Judaism a progressive religion, ever striving to be in accord with the postulates of reason. We are convinced of the utmost necessity of preserving the historical identity with our great past. Christianity and Islam being daughter religions of Judaism, we appreciate their providential mission to aid in the spreading of monotheistic and moral truth. We acknowledge that the spirit of broad humanity of our age is our ally in the fulfillment of our mission, and therefore, we extend the hand of fellowship to all who operate with us in the establishment of the reign of truth and righteousness among men.

Seventh—We reassert the doctrine of Judaism, that the soul of man is immortal, grounding this belief on the divine nature of the human spirit, which forever finds bliss in righteousness and misery in wickedness. We reject as ideas not rooted in Judaism the beliefs both in bodily resurrection and in Gehenna and Eden (Hell and Paradise) as abodes for everlasting punishment or reward.

Eighth—In full accordance with the spirit of Mosaic legislation, which strives to regulate the relation between rich and poor, we deem it our duty to participate in the great task of modern times, to solve on the basis of justice and righteousness, the problems presented by the contrasts and evils of the present organization of society.

Notes: *The debates over Reform Judaism led to the formation of a rabbinical association, the Central Conference of American Rabbis, in 1889. In 1885, a group of prominent Reform rabbis, led by Issac M. Wise, drew up and adopted the Pittsburgh Platform and in 1889 presented it to the Central Conference. Though never officially adopted by the Conference, the document was generally assumed to be a statement of the Conference's position.*

The Platform affirms some of Reform Judaism's most controversial ideas such as the abandonment of many of the laws of the Mosaic code and hope for a Messianic kingdom among all people. It is reflective of the early non-Zionist position of the Reform movement, declaring a loss of expectation of any return to Palestine by the Jewish people. This position was reversed in the Columbus Platform of 1937.

* * *

COLUMBUS PLATFORM [CENTRAL CONFERENCE OF AMERICAN RABBIS (1937) (REFORM JUDAISM)]

1. JUDAISM AND ITS FOUNDATIONS

1. NATURE OF JUDAISM. Judaism is the historical religious experience of the Jewish people. Though growing out of Jewish life, its message is universal, aiming at the union and perfection of mankind under the sovereignty of God. Reform Judaism recognizes the principle of progressive development in religion and consciously applies this principle to spiritual as well as to cultural and social life.

COLUMBUS PLATFORM [CENTRAL CONFERENCE OF
  AMERICAN RABBIS (1937) (REFORM
  JUDAISM)] (continued)

Judaism welcomes all truth, whether written in the pages of Scripture or deciphered from the records of nature. The new discoveries of science, while replacing the older scientific views underlying our sacred literature, do not conflict with the essential spirit of religion as manifested in the consecration of man's will, heart and mind to the service of God and of humanity.

2. GOD. The heart of Judaism and its chief contribution to religion is the doctrine of the One, living God, Who rules the world through law and love. In Him all existence has its creative source and mankind its ideal of conduct. Though transcending time and space, He is the indwelling Presence of the world. We worship Him as the Lord of the Universe and as our merciful Father.

3. MAN. Judaism affirms that man is created in the Divine image. His spirit is immortal. He is an active co-worker with God. As a child of God, he is endowed with moral freedom and is charged with the responsibility of overcoming evil and striving after ideal ends.

4. TORAH. God reveals Himself not only in the majesty, beauty and orderliness of nature, but also in the vision and moral striving of the human spirit. Revelation is a continuous process, confined to no one group and to no one age. Yet the people of Israel, through its prophets and sages, achieved unique insight in the realm of religious truth. The Torah, both written and oral, enshrines Israel's ever-growing consciousness of God and of the moral law. It preserves the historical precedents, sanctions and norms of Jewish life, and seeks to mold it in the patterns of goodness and of holiness. Being products of historical processes, certain of its laws have lost their binding force with the passing of the conditions that called them forth. But as a depository of permanent spiritual ideals, the Torah remains the dynamic source of the life of Israel. Each age has the obligation to adapt the teaching of the Torah to its needs in consonance with the genius of Judaism.

5. ISRAEL. Judaism is the soul of which Israel is the body. Living in all parts of the world, Israel has been held together by the ties of a common history, and above all, by the heritage of faith. Though we recognize in the group-loyalty of Jews who have become estranged from our religious tradition a bond which still unites them with us, we maintain that it is by its religion and for its religion that the Jewish people have lived. The non-Jew who accepts our faith is welcome as a full member of the Jewish community.

In all lands where our people live, they assume and seek to share loyally the full duties and responsibilities of citizenship and to create seats of Jewish knowledge and religion. In the rehabilitation of Palestine, the land hallowed by memories and hopes, we behold the promise of renewed life for many of our brethren. We affirm the obligation of all Jewry to aid in its upbuilding as a Jewish homeland by endeavoring to make it not only a haven of refuge for the oppressed but also a center of Jewish culture and spiritual life.

Throughout the ages it has been Israel's mission to witness to the Divine in the face of every form of paganism and materialism. We regard it as our historic task to cooperate with all men in the establishment of the kingdom of God, of universal brotherhood, justice, truth and peace on earth. This is our Messianic Goal.

II. ETHICS

6. ETHICS AND RELIGION. In Judaism religion and morality blend into an indissoluble unity. Seeking God means to strive after holiness, righteousness and goodness. The love of God is incomplete without the love of one's fellowmen. Judaism emphasizes the kinship of the human race, the sanctity and worth of human life and personality and the right of the individual to freedom and to the pursuit of his chosen vocation. Justice to all, irrespective of race, sect or class is the inalienable right and the inescapable obligation of all. The state and organized government exist in order to further these ends.

7. SOCIAL JUSTICE. Judaism seeks the attainment of a just society by the application of its teachings to the economic order, to industry and commerce, and to national and international affairs. It aims at the elimination of man-made misery and suffering, poverty and degradation, of tyranny and slavery, of social inequality and prejudice, of ill-will and strife. It advocates the promotion of harmonious relations between warring classes on the basis of equity and justice, and the creation of conditions under which human personality may flourish. It pleads for the safeguarding of childhood against exploitation. It champions the cause of all who work and of their right to an adequate standard of living, as prior to the rights of property. Judaism emphasizes the duty of charity, and strives for a social order which will protect men against disabilities of old age, sickness and unemployment.

8. PEACE. Judaism, from the days of the prophets, has proclaimed to mankind the ideal of universal peace. The spiritual and physical disarmament of all nations has been one of its essential teachings. It abhors all violence and relies upon moral education, love and sympathy to secure human progress. It regards justice as the foundation of the well-being of nations and the condition of enduring peace. It urges organized international action for disarmament, collective security and world peace.

III. RELIGIOUS PRACTICE

9. THE RELIGIOUS LIFE. Jewish life is marked by consecration to these ideas of Judaism. It calls for faithful participation in the life of the Jewish community as it finds expression in home, synagogue

and school and in all other agencies that enrich Jewish life and promote its welfare.

The Home has been and must continue to be a stronghold of Jewish life hallowed by the spirit of love and reverence, by moral discipline and religious observance and worship.

The Synagogue is the oldest and most democratic institution in Jewish life. It is the prime communal agency by which Judaism is fostered and preserved. It links the Jews of each community and unites them with all Israel.

The perpetuation of Judaism as a living force depends upon religious knowledge and upon the education of each new generation in our rich cultural and spiritual heritage.

Prayer is the voice of religion, the language of faith and aspiration. It directs man's heart and mind Godward, voices the needs and hopes of the community and reaches out after goals which invest life with supreme value. To deepen the spiritual life of our people, we must cultivate the traditional habit of communion with God through prayer in both home and synagogue.

Judaism as a way of life requires, in addition to its moral and spiritual demands, the preservation of the Sabbath, festivals and Holy Days, the retention and development of such customs, symbols and ceremonies as possess inspirational value, the cultivation of distinctive forms of religious art and music and the use of Hebrew, together with the vernacular, in our worship and instruction.

These timeless aims and ideals of our faith we present to a confused and troubled world. We call upon our fellow Jews to rededicate themselves to them and, in harmony with all men, hopefully and courageously to continue Israel's eternal quest after God and His kingdom.

Notes: *The Columbus Platform replaced the earlier Pittsburgh Platform (1885), the prime positional statement of Reform Judaism. Among the most important changes in this new document, Zionism (the return of Jews to Palestine) was affirmed. The Platform also welcomed non-Jews to accept the Jewish faith.*

* * *

Black Judaism

THE TWELVE PRINCIPLES OF THE DOCTRINES OF ISRAEL WITH SCRIPTURAL PROOF [COMMANDMENT KEEPERS CONGREGATION OF THE LIVING GOD (BLACK JEWS)]

Principle No. 1. *The New Creation.*—Gen. 1:1, 5; Ez. 14:6; Isa. 28:11, 12; Ez. 36:26, 28; Ez. 14:26, 31; Jer. 31:31; Joel 2:28-39; Mal. 1:2

Principle No. 2. *The Observance of All the Laws of God, Given to Us Through Moses Our Teacher.*—Gen. 2:1, 3; Ex. 31:18, 32, 15, 16; Deut. 29:29; Isa. 58:13, 14; Dan. 7:25; Ez. 8:16; Num. 15:32, 33; Psalm 1:1, 4; Ez. 46:1

Principle No. 3. *Divine Healing.*—Ex. 23:25; Ex. 15:26; Psalm 103:1, 3; Isa. 53:4, 5; Psalm 41:2, 4; Jer. 8:22; 2 Chron. 30:20; Psalm 107:20; Hos. 7:1

Principle No. 4. *The Administration of Feet Washing and All the Rites of the Passover.*—Gen. 18:3; Gen. 19:2; 43:24; 34:32

Principle No. 5. *Tithes and Offerings; the Early Duty of the People of God.*—Gen. 14:18, 20; 28:20, 22; Lev. 27:30, 32; Mal. 3:8, 12; Neh. 10:37, 39; Deut. 14:21; Hag. 1:1, 6

Principle No. 6. *The Eating of Koshered Foods According to Israel's Law.*—Lev. 11:1, 12; Deut. 14:2, 3; Isa. 65:4-5; 66:17

Principle No. 7. *Everlasting Life.*—Gen. 5:24; 2 Kings 2:11; Hos. 13:13, 14; Psalm 49:6, 9; 118:17; Prov. 7:1, 3, 23; 6:23

Principle No. 8. *Absolute Holiness According to the Law of God.*—Gen. 17:1; Exod. 3:5; Deut. 14:2; Ex. 19:6; Lev. 10:10; 20:7; Psalm 86:2; Isaiah 6:3; 35:8

Principle No. 9. *The Resurrection of the Dead (Black Israel).*—Hos. 13:13, 14; Ezra 37:11, 12; Job 14:5-14, 15; 19:26; Isaiah 35:10; Ezek. 37

Principle No. 10. *The Restoration of Israel.*—Isa. 1:26; Jer. 30:17, 18; 27:22; Joel 2:25; Isa. 11:10, 11, 12; Jer. 31:31, 34

Principle No. 11. *The Coming of the Messiah.*—Deut. 18:15, 18, 19; Mal. 3:1; Isa. 41:2, 3, 4; Isa. 9:6, 7

Principle No. 12. *The Theocratic Age.*—Gen. 49:9-10; Isa. 11:1; 5:9-10

Notes: *These principles were "codified" by Rabbi Arthur Wentworth Matthew, the founder of the Commandment Keepers, a black Jewish synagogue in New York City.*

* * *

BLACK CHRISTIAN NATIONALIST CREED (PAN AFRICAN ORTHODOX CHRISTIAN CHURCH)

I Believe, that human society stands under the judgement of one God, revealed to all and known by many names. His creative power is visible in the mysteries of the universe, in the revolutionary Holy Spirit which will not long permit men to endure injustice nor to wear the shackles of bondage, in the rage of the powerless when they struggle to be free, and in the violence and conflict which even now threaten to level the hills and the mountains.

I Believe that Jesus, the Black Messiah, was a revolutionary leader, sent by God to rebuild the Black Nation Israel and to liberate Black People from powerlessness and from the oppression, brutality, and exploitation of the white gentile world.

I Believe that the revolutionary spirit of God, embodied in the Black Messiah, is born anew in each generation and that Black Christian Nationalists constitute the living remnant of God's Chosen People in this day, and are

BLACK CHRISTIAN NATIONALIST CREED (PAN AFRICAN ORTHODOX CHRISTIAN CHURCH) (continued)

charged by him with responsibility for the Liberation of Black People.

I Believe that both my survival and my salvation depend upon my willingness to reject INDIVIDUALISM and so I commit my life to the Liberation Struggle of Black People and accept the values, ethics, morals and program of the Black Nation, defined by that struggle, and taught by the Pan-African Orthodox Christian Church.

Notes: *The Pan African Orthodox Christian Church is a Christian church with a creedal statement very much in line with the nationalism of Black Judaism, which has always had an ambivalent relationship to traditional Christianity.*

* * *

Miscellaneous Jewish Groups

I BELIEVE (RABBI JOSEPH H. GELBERMAN, LITTLE SYNAGOGUE)

1. I believe that most of my beliefs are not necessarily in harmony with the truth, as I believe with P.P. Quimby, that man is made up of beliefs and truths.

2. I believe that there is an eleventh commandment which states: *Thou shalt have purpose.*

3. I believe that my purpose in life is to be *totally alive,* i.e., to express the basic principles inherent in the five letters of the word *alive:* to be Aware, to be Loving, to be Intuitive, to be Victorious, to be Enthusiastic about every nuance of life.

4. I believe in the separation of Rabbi and Synagogue. Like the Talmudic Rabbis we should never have an employer-employee relationship with any congregation.

5. I believe that there is a special purpose for my life: twice I have been miraculously saved.

6. I believe that whatever I am, I have chosen to be that way.

7. I believe that the purpose of my life is to grow in four ways simultaneously: physically, emotionally, intellectually and spiritually.

8. I believe that my Karma in life is to be Jewish i.e. to be a joyous Jew.

9. I believe in reincarnation, who I was and who I shall be are already combined in that which I am now.

10. I believe in the partnership with God as the mystery of Creation. It is I and God that can and will finish the creation.

11. I believe in the joy of life though I'm not always happy. *Joy* and *Happiness* are two different concepts. Joy is inner centered, happiness is outer centered.

12. I believe in the importance of tradition, therefore, my basic philosophy of life is: *Never instead, always in addition.*

13. I believe that my aim in life is not to become a saint, certainly not a sinner, but a sage. I'm not a machine, ergo, not programmed, but respond spontaneously to each situation as it happens with wisdom and justice.

14. I believe that the Kabbalah wisdom is an integral part of Torah and my religion and therefore it is to be shared with all who are willing to pursue it.

15. I believe that I am responsible for the actions of my life and therefore, as a responsible person, can transmute my erroneous ways to the will of God.

16. I believe that there is a part of God's soul in me which I call Neshamah which yearns to be Godlike and thus try to overcome doubt, discouragement and temptation.

17. I believe that it is important for me to express daily my gratitude to my parents who imbued in me the love of Torah — wisdom, a sense of responsibility and a sense of virtue and piety.

18. I believe in the concept of Kitov — that life is basically good and therefore I am to search for the joy and goodness in life.

19. I believe that being created in the image of God means that I am meant to express my Godlikeness in terms of loving all my fellow beings regardless of race, creed or nationality.

20. I believe that:

    I am the reality of things that seem

    I am the waking who am called the dream

    I am the utmost height there is to climb

    I am stability, all else will pass

    I am eternity encircling time

    Kill me, none may, conquer me, nothing can

    I am God's soul fused in the heart of man

21. Finally, I believe in Interfaith as a means to reach out to my fellow beings and tell them: *Please trust me, hold my hand and let's walk together to the mountain of the Lord and listen to His words addressed to each one of us: 'You are all my beloved children and I love all of you.'*

Notes: *Rabbi Joseph H. Gelberman of the Little Synagogue has attempted to build a Judaism that draws upon Hassidic, New Thought, and New Age traditions and is open to non-Jewish religion. In the opening paragraph of this personal statement, he refers to Phineas Parkhurst Quimby, the New England mental healer often cited as the founder of New Thought.*

* * *

AFFIRMATIONS FOR HUMANISTIC JEWS (SHERWIN T. WINE, SOCIETY FOR HUMANISTIC JUDAISM)

Humanistic Jews want to bring their beliefs and their behavior together and to find their integrity. They are eager to affirm:

That they are disciples of the Secular Revolution.

That the Secular Revolution was good for the Jews.

That reason is the best method for the discovery of truth.

That morality derives from human needs and is the defense of human dignity.

That the universe is indifferent to the desires and aspirations of human beings.

That people must ultimately rely on people.

That Jewish history is a testimony to the absence of God and the necessity of human self-esteem.

That Jewish identity is valuable because it connects them to that history.

That Jewish personality flows from that history — and not from official texts that seek to describe it.

That Jewish identity serves individual dignity — and not the reverse.

That the Jewish people is an international family that has its center in Israel and its roots in the Diaspora.

That the humanistic Gentile has a positive role to play in the life of the Jewish people.

Notes: *These affirmations were written by Rabbi Sherwin T. Wine, head of the Humanistic congregation in suburban Detroit, Michigan. Although not an official document, the statement expresses the secular religiosity of the Society for Humanistic Judaism.*

*   *   *

FUNDAMENTALS (SOCIETY OF JEWISH SCIENCE)

1. The Jewish faith is the only faith we acknowledge. Jewish Science is the application of the Jewish Faith to the practices of life.

2. We believe wholeheartedly in the efficacy of prayer. We believe that no prayer, when properly offered, goes unanswered.

3. We shall endeavor every day of our lives to keep serene; to check all tendencies to violence and anger; to keep calm even in the face of unpleasant and discouraging circumstances.

4. We shall strive to be cheerful every day of our lives. The Talmud says that the Divine Presence departs from one who is in gloom. It is God's design that man should find joy and cheer in his existence on this earth.

5. We shall seek to cultivate an attitude of love and good-will towards everyone. We shall make no room in our heart for hatred or bitterness. The world was created on a plan of divine love, and to admit thoughts of hatred or malice is to violate the plan of God.

6. We shall cultivate a disposition to contentment, envying no one, and praising God for the good he has already bestowed upon us. Contentment is the greatest friend of happiness; envy, its greatest enemy.

7. We shall make conscious effort to banish worry and fear from our lives. We regard these two as the greatest enemies of mankind and give them no place in our consciousness.

8. We shall trust in God's goodness in every circumstance of our life.

9. We believe that death is an elevation to eternal life, and not a cessation of existence.

10. We believe that God is the Source of Health and the Restorer of Health.

11. In these fundamentals, we, in Jewish Science, profess our wholehearted belief in the efficacy of prayer; we acknowledge the duty of keeping serene and cheerful, of cherishing good-will and contentment, of banishing worry and fear; we declare our trust in God's goodness and love; we profess our assurance of immortality because we have faith in God's loving-kindness and the everlastingness of His creations.

Notes: *Rabbi Joshua Lichtenstein attempted to build a metaphysical Judaism that would function in the Jewish community much as Christian Science did in the larger context of American society. In his basic textbook, he outlined a declaration of the ideals by which Jewish Scientists (metaphysicians) were to govern their lives day by day.*

Islam

THE FUNDAMENTAL ARTICLES OF FAITH IN ISLAM [HAMMUDAH ABD AL-ATI (SUNNI ISLAM)]

A faithful Muslim believes in the following principal articles of faith:

1. He believes in One God, Supreme and Eternal, Infinite and Mighty, Merciful and Compassionate, Creator and Provider. This belief, in order to be effective, requires complete trust and hope in God, submission to His Will and reliance on His aid. It secures man's dignity and saves him from fear and despair, from wrong and confusion. The reader is invited to see the meaning of Islam as explained above.

2. He believes in all the messengers of God without any discrimination between them. Every known nation had a warner or messenger from God. These messengers were great teachers of the good and true champions of the right. They were chosen by God to teach mankind and deliver His Divine message. They were sent at different times of history and every known nation had one messenger or more. During certain periods two or more messengers were sent by God at the same time to the same nation. The Holy Qur'an mentions the names of twenty-five of them, and a Muslim believes in them all and accepts them as authorized messengers of God. They were, with the exception of Muhammad, known as "national" or local messengers. But their message, their religion, was basically the same and was called ISLAM; because it came from One and the Same Source, namely, God, to serve one and the same purpose, and

that is to guide humanity to the Straight Path of God. All the messengers with no exception whatsoever were mortals, human beings, endowed with Divine revelations and appointed by God to perform certain tasks. Among them Muhammad stands as the Last Messenger and the crowning glory of the foundation of prophethood. This is not an arbitrary attitude, nor is it just a convenient belief. Like all the other Islamic beliefs, it is an authentic and logical truth. Also, it may be useful to mention here the names of some of the great messengers like Noah and Abraham, Ishmael and Moses, Jesus and Muhammad, may the peace and blessings of God be upon them all. The Qur'an says:

"Say you: 'We believe in God, and the revelation given to us, and to Abraham, Ishmael, Isaac, Jacob and the Tribes; and that which was given to Moses and Jesus, and that which was given to all prophets from their Lord. We make no difference between one and another of them, and we bow to God (in Islam).'" (Qur'an 2:136, cf. 3:84; 4:163-165; 6:84-87)

3. A true Muslim believes, as a result of article number two, in all the scriptures and revelations of God. They were the guiding light which the messengers received to show their respective peoples the Right Path of God. In the Qur'an a special reference is made to the books of Abraham, Moses, David and Jesus. But long before the revelation of the Qur'an to Muhammad some of those books and revelations had been lost or interpolated, some neglected or concealed. The only authentic and complete book of God in existence today is the Qur'an. In principle a Muslim believes in the previous books and revelations. But where are their complete and original versions? They could be still at the bottom of the Dead Sea, and there may be more Scrolls to be discovered. Or perhaps more information about them will become available when the Christian and Jewish archaeologists reveal to the public the complete original findings of their continued excavations in the Holy Land. For a Muslim, there is no problem of that kind. The Qur'an is in his hand complete and authentic. Nothing of it is missing and no more of it is expected. Its authenticity is beyond doubt, and no serious scholar or thinker has ventured to question its genuineness. The Qur'an was made so by God Who revealed it and made it incumbent upon Himself to protect it against interpolation and corruption of all kinds. Thus it is given to the Muslims as the standard or criterion by which all the other books are judged. So whatever agrees with the Qur'an is accepted as Divine truth, and whatever differs from the Qur'an is either rejected or suspended. God says: "Verily We have, without doubt, sent down the Qur'an; and We will assuredly guard it (from corruption). (Qur'an 15:9; Cf. 2:75-79; 5:13-14 and 41. See also references in (2) above.)

4. A true Muslim believes in the angels of God. They are purely spiritual and splendid beings whose nature requires no food or drink or sleep. They have no physical desires of any kind nor material needs, but spend their days and nights in the service of God. There are many of them, and each one is charged with a certain duty. If we cannot see the angels with our naked eyes, it does not necessarily deny their actual existence. There are many things in the world that are invisible to the eye or inaccessible to the senses, yet we do believe in their existence. There are places we have never seen and things like gas and ether that we could not see with our naked eyes, smell or touch or taste or hear; yet we do acknowledge their existence. Belief in the angels originates from the Islamic principle that knowledge and truth are not entirely confined to the sensory knowledge or sensory perception alone. (Qur'an 16:49-50; 21:19-20. See also references in (2) above.)

5. A true Muslim believes in the Last Day of Judgement. This world will come to an end some day, and the dead will rise to stand for their final and fair trial. Everything we do in this world, every intention we have, every move we make, every thought we entertain, and every word we say, all are counted and kept in accurate records. On the Day of Judgement they will be brought up. People with good records will be generously rewarded and warmly welcomed to the Heaven of God, and those with bad records will be severely punished and cast into Hell. The real nature of Heaven and Hell and the exact description of them are known to God only. There are descriptions of Heaven and Hell in the Qur'an and the Traditions of Muhammad but they should not be taken literally. In Heaven, said Muhammad, there are things which no eye has ever seen, no ear has ever heard, and no mind has ever conceived. However, the Muslim believes that there definitely will be compensation and reward for the good deeds, and punishment for the evil ones. That is the Day of Justice and final settlement of all accounts.

If some people think that they are shrewd enough and can get away with their wrong doings, just as they sometimes escape the penalty of the mundane laws, they are wrong, they will not be able to do so on the Day of Judgement. They will be caught right on the spot defenceless, without any lawyer or counsel to stand in their behalf. All their deeds are visible to God and counted by His agents. Also, if some pious people do good deeds to please God and seem to get no appreciation or acknowledgement in this temporary world, they will eventually receive full compensation and be widely acknowledged on That Day. Absolute Justice will be done to all.

Belief in the Day of Judgement is the final relieving answer to many complicated problems of our world. There are people who commit sins, neglect God and indulge in immoral activities, yet they seem to be "superficially" successful in business and prosperous in life. And there are virtuous and God-minded people, yet they seem to be getting less rewards for their sincere efforts and more suffering in the present world. This is puzzling and incompatible with the Justice of God. If the guilty people can escape the mundane law unharmed and, on top of that, be more prosperous, what is, then, left for the virtuous people? What will promote the cause of morality and goodness? There must be some way to reward goodness and arrest evil. If this is not done here on this earth—and we know it is not done regularly or immediately—it has to be done some day, and that is the Day of Judgement. This is not to condone injustice or tolerate mischief in this world, but is to warn the deviants from the Right Path and remind them that the Justice of God shall run its full course sooner or later. (See, for example, the previous references of the Qur'an.)

6. A true Muslim believes in the timeless knowledge of God and in His power to plan and execute His plans. God is not indifferent to this world nor is He neutral to it. His knowledge and power are in action at all times to keep order in His vast domain and maintain full command over His creation. He is Wise and Loving, and whatever He does must have a good motive and a meaningful purpose. If this is established in our minds, we should accept with good Faith all that He does, although we may fail to understand it fully, or even think it is bad. We should have strong Faith in Him and accept whatever He does because our knowledge is limited and our thinking is based on individual or personal considerations, whereas His knowledge is limitless and He plans on a universal basis.

This does not in any way make man fatalist or predestinarian. It simply draws the demarcation line between what is God's concern and what is man's responsibility. Because we are by nature finite and limited, we have a finite and limited degree of power and freedom. We cannot do everything, and He graciously holds us responsible only for the things we do. The things which we cannot do, or things which He Himself does, are not in the realm of our responsibility. He is Just and has given us limited power to match our finite nature and limited responsibility. On the other hand, the timeless knowledge and power of God to execute His plans do not prevent us from making our own plans in our own limited sphere of power. On the contrary, He exhorts us to think, to plan and to make sound choices, but if things do not happen the way we wanted or planned them, we should not lose Faith or surrender ourselves to mental strains and shattering worries. We should try again and again, and if the results are not satisfactory, then we know that we have tried our best and cannot be held responsible for the results, because what is beyond our capacity and responsibility is the affair of God alone. Muslims call this article of Faith the belief in "Qudaa" and "Qadar", which simply means, in other words, that the Timeless Knowledge of God anticipates events, and that events take place according to the exact Knowledge of God. (Qur'an, for example, 18:29; 41:46; 53:33-62; 54:49; 65:3; 76:30-31.)

7. A true Muslim believes that God's creation is meaningful and that life has a sublime purpose beyond the physical needs and material activities of man. The purpose of life is to worship God. This does not simply mean that we have to spend our entire lives in constant seclusion and absolute meditation. To worship God is to know Him; to love Him; to obey His commandments; to enforce His law in every aspect of life; to serve His cause by doing the right and shunning the evil; and to be just to Him, to ourselves, and to our fellow human beings. To worship God is to "live" life not to run away from it. In brief, to worship God is to imbue ourselves with His Supreme Attributes. This is by no means a simple statement, nor is it an over-simplification of the matter. It is most comprehensive and conclusive. So if life has a purpose and if man is created to serve that purpose, then he cannot escape the responsibility. He cannot deny his existence or ignore the vital role he has to play. When God charges him with any responsibility, He provides him with all the required assistance. He endows him with intelligence and power to choose his course of conduct. Man, thus, is strongly recommended by God to exert his utmost to fully serve the purpose of his existence. Should he fail to do that, or misuse his life or neglect his duties, he shall be responsible to God for his wrong deeds. (See, for example, the Qur'an 51:56-58.)

8. A true Muslim believes that man enjoys an especially high-ranking status in the hierarchy of all the known creatures. He occupies this distinguished position because he alone is gifted with rational faculties and spiritual aspirations as well as powers of action. But the more his rank excels, the more his responsibility grows. He occupies the position of God's viceroy on earth. The person who is appointed by God to be His active agent, must necessarily have some power and authority, and be, at least potentially, endowed with honour and integrity. And this is the status of man in Islam; not a condemned race from birth to death, but a dignified being potentially capable of good and noble achievements. The fact that God chose His messengers from the human race shows that man is trustworthy and capable, and that he can acquire immense treasures of goodness. (Qur'an 2:30-34; 6:165; 7:11; 17:70-72 and 90-95.)

9. A true Muslim believes that every person is born "Muslim." This means that the very course of birth takes place in accordance with the Will of God, in realization of His plans and in submission to His Commands. It also means that every person is endowed with spiritual potentialities and intellectual inclinations that can make him a good Muslim, if he has the right access to Islam and is left to develop his innate nature. Many people can readily accept Islam if it is properly presented to them, because it is the Divine formula for those who want to satisfy their moral and spiritual needs as well as their natural aspirations and want to lead a constructive and

THE FUNDAMENTAL ARTICLES OF FAITH IN ISLAM
[HAMMUDAH ABD AL-ATI (SUNNI ISLAM)] (continued)

sound life whether personal or social, national or international; whether spiritual or socio-economic. This is so because Islam is the universal religion of God, the Maker of human nature, Who knows what is best for human nature. (Qur'an 30:30; 64:1-3; 82:6-8.)

10. A true Muslim believes that every person is born free from sin and good, like a blank book. When the person reaches the age of maturity he becomes accountable for his deeds and intentions, if his development is normal and if he is sane. Man is not only free from sin until he commits sin, but he is also free to do things according to his plans on his own responsibility. This dual freedom: freedom from sin and freedom to do effective things, clears the Muslim's conscience from the heavy pressure of Inherited Sin. It relieves his soul and mind from the unnecessary strains of the Doctrine of Original Sin.

This Islamic concept of freedom is based upon the principle of God's justice and the individual's direct responsibility to God. Each person must bear his own burden and be responsible for his own actions, because no one can expiate for another's sin. Thus, a Muslim believes that if Adam had committed the First Sin, it was his own responsibility to expiate for that sin. To assume that God was unable to forgive Adam and had to make somebody else expiate for his sin, or to assume that Adam did not pray for pardon or prayed for it but it was not granted, would be extremely illogical and contrary to God's mercy and justice as well as to His attribute of forgiveness and power to forgive. To assume the said hypothesis, would be an audacious defiance of common sense and flagrant violation of the very concept of God. (See the reference in article 9 above, and Qur'an 41:46; 45:15; 53:31-42; 74:38.)

On this rational basis as well as on the authority of the Qur'an a Muslim believes that Adam realized what he had committed and prayed to God for pardon, like any other sensible sinner would. It is also on the same basis, a Muslim believes, that God the Forgiving and Merciful granted Adam pardon. (Qur'an 2:35-37; 20:117-122.) Hence, a Muslim cannot possibly accept the doctrine that Adam with the whole human race had been condemned and unforgiven until Jesus came to expiate for their sins. Consequently, a Muslim cannot entrtain the romantic story of Jesus' death on the cross just to do away with all human sins once and for all.

Here the reader must be cautioned against any wrong conclusions. A Muslim does not believe in the crucifixion of Jesus by his enemies because the basis of this doctrine of crucifixion is contrary to Divine mercy and justice as much as it is to human logic and dignity. Such a disbelief in the doctrine does not in any way devaluate the Muslim's reverence for Jesus, or degrade the high status of Jesus in Islam, or even shake the Muslim's belief in Jesus as a distinguished

prophet of God. On the contrary, by rejecting this doctrine the Muslim accepts Jesus but only with more esteem and higher respect, and looks upon his original message as an essential part of Islam. So let it be stated, again, that to be a Muslim a person must accept and respect all the prophets of God without any discrimination. The general status of Jesus in Islam will be further discussed in a later chapter.

11. A true Muslim believes that man must work out his salvation through the guidance of God. This means that in order to attain salvation a person must combine Faith and action, belief and practice. Faith without action is as insufficient as action without Faith. In other words, no one can attain salvation until his Faith in God becomes dynamic in his life and his beliefs are translated into reality. This is in complete harmony with the other Islamic articles of Faith. It shows that God does not accept lip service, and that no true believer can be indifferent as far as the practical requirements of Faith are concerned. It also shows that no one can act on behalf of another or intercede between him and God. (See, for example, the Qur'an 10:9-10; 18:30; 103:1-3.)

12. A true Muslim believes that God does not hold any person responsible until He has shown him the Right Way. This is why God has sent many messengers and revelations, and made it clear that there would be no punishment before issuing a guidance and sounding the alarm. So, a person who has never come across any Divine revelations or messenger, or a person who is insane is not held responsible to God for failing to obey the Divine instructions. Such a person will be responsible only for not doing what his sound common sense tells him to be good and right. But the person who knowingly and intentionally violates the Law of God or deviates from His Right Path will be punished for his wrong deeds. (Qur'an 4:165; 5:16 & 21; 17:15.)

This point is very important for every Muslim. There are many people in the world who have not heard of Islam and have no way of knowing about it. Such people may be honest and may become good Muslims, if they find their way to Islam. If they do not know and have no way of knowing, they will not be responsible for failing to be Muslims. Instead, the Muslims who can present Islam to such people will be the ones responsible for failing to invite them to Islam and show them what Islam is. This calls upon every Muslim throughout the globe not only to preach Islam in words but to live according to it and let others see it in action and practice. (See, for example, the Qur'an 3:104; 16:125.)

13. A true Muslim believes that in human nature, which God created, there is more good than evil, and the probability of successful reform is greater than the probability of hopeless failure. This belief is derived from the fact that God has tasked man with certain assignments and sent messengers with revelations for his guidance. If man were by nature a hopeless case, impossible to reform, and without expectation of any

good from him, how could God with His absolute wisdom assign him responsibilities and invite him to do or shun certain things? How could God do that, if it were all in vain? The fact that God cares for man and takes a stand in his interest proves that man is neither helpless nor hopeless, but is more appreciative of and inclined to good than otherwise. Surely with sound Faith in God and due confidence in man miracles can be worked out, even in our own times. To understand this properly, one has to carefully study the relevant passages in the Qur'an and reflect on their meanings.

14. A true Muslim believes that Faith is not complete when it is followed blindly or accepted unquestioningly unless the professor of such a faith is fully satisfied. If Faith is to inspire action, and if Faith and action are to lead to salvation, then Faith must be founded on unshakeable convictions without any deception or compulsion. In other words, the person who calls himself a Muslim because of his family traditions, or accepts Islam out of fear or under coercion or blind imitation is not a complete Muslim in the sight of God. A Muslim must build his Faith on well-grounded convictions beyond any reasonable doubt and above uncertainty. If he is not certain about his Faith, he is invited by God to search in the open book of Nature, to use his reasoning powers, and to reflect on the teachings of the Qur'an. He must search for the indisputable truth until he finds it, and he will certainly find it, if he is capable and serious enough. (See, for example, the Qur'an 2:170; 43:22-24.)

This is why Islam demands sound convictions and opposes blind imitation. Every person who is duly qualified as a genuine and earnest thinker is enjoined by Islam to employ his faculties to the fullest extent. But if a person is unqualified or uncertain of himself, he should pursue his thinking only as far as his limits can take him. It will be quite in order for such a person to rely only on the authentic sources of religion, which are sufficient in themselves, without applying to them any critical questioning of which he is incapable. The point is that no one can call himself a true Muslim unless his Faith is based on strong convictions and his mind is clear from doubts. Because Islam is complete only when it is based on strong convictions and freedom of choice, it cannot be forced upon anybody, for God will not accept this forced faith. Nor will He consider it a true Islam if it does not develop from within or originate from free and sound convictions. And because Islam insures freedom of belief many non-Muslim groups lived and still live in the Islamic countries enjoying full freedom of belief and conscience. Muslims take this attitude because Islam forbids compulsion in religion. It is the light which must radiate from within, because in Islam no one can make up another's mind. This does not exempt the parents from responsibility for their children. Nor does it condone their being indifferent to the spiritual welfare of their dependents. In fact, they should do everything possible to help theirs build a strong inspiring faith.

To establish Faith on sound grounds, there are various parallel avenues. There is the Spiritual approach which is based mainly on the Qur'an and the Traditions of Muhammad. There is also the rational approach which eventually leads to Faith in the Supreme Being. This is not to say that the Spiritual approach lacks sound rationality. Nor is the rational approach deprived of inspiring spirituality. Both approaches, in fact, overlap one another and may well become in a state of lively interaction. Now if a person is sufficiently equipped with sound rational qualities, he may resort to the rational approach or to the Spiritual approach or to both, and may be confident that his conclusion will be right. But if a person is incapable of profound inquiry or is uncertain of his reasoning powers, he may confine himself to the Spiritual approach and be contented with the knowledge he can derive from the authentic sources of religion. The point is that whether one uses the Spiritual approach or the rational technique or both, one will in the end come to Faith in God. All these avenues are equally important and accepted by Islam, and, when properly channelled, lead to the same end, namely, Faith in the Supreme Being.

15. A true Muslim believes that the Qur'an is the word of God revealed to Muhammad through the agency of the Angel Gabriel. The Qur'an was revealed from God piece by piece on various occasions to answer certain questions, solve certain problems, settle certain disputes, and to be man's best guide to the truth of God and eternal happiness. Every letter in the Qur'an is the word of God, and every sound in it is the true echo of God's voice. The Qur'an is the First and most authentic Source of Islam. It was revealed in Arabic. It is still and will remain in its original and complete Arabic version, because God has made it His concern to preserve the Qur'an, to make it always the best guide for man, and to safeguard it against corruption. (See, for example, the Qur'an 4:82; 15:9; 17:9; 41:41-44; 42:7, 52-53.)

In testimony to God's conservation, the Qur'an is the only Scripture in human history that has been preserved in its complete and original version without the slightest change in style or even punctuations. The history of recording the Qur'an, compiling its chapters and conserving its text is beyond any doubt not only in the minds of Muslims but also in the minds of honest and serious scholars. This is a historical fact which no scholar from any faith—who respects his knowledge and integrity—has ever questioned. As a matter of fact, it is Muhammad's standing miracle that if all mankind were to work together they could not produce the like of one Qur'anic chapter. (Qur'an 2:22-24; 11:13-14; 17:88-89.)

16. A true Muslim believes in a clear distinction between the Qur'an and the Traditions of Muhammad. The Qur'an is the word of God whereas the Traditions of

Muhammad are the practical interpretations of the Qur'an. The role of Muhammad was to convey the Qur'an as he received it, to interpret it, and to practise it fully. His interpretations and practises produced what is known as the Traditions of Muhammad. They are considered the Second Source of Islam and must be in complete harmony with the First Source, namely, the Qur'an, which is the Standard and the Criterion. If there be any contradiction or inconsistency between any of the Traditions and the Qur'an, the Muslim adheres to the Qur'an alone and regards everything else as open to question because no genuine Tradition of Muhammad can ever disagree with the Qur'an or be opposed to it.

REMARKS

In this discussion of the cardinal articles of Faith in Islam, I have deliberately differed from the Traditional view on the subject. I did not confine them to five or six articles. Instead, I tried to include as many Principles as was possible. But it should be pointed out here that all the articles of Faith mentioned above are based upon and derived from the teachings of the Qur'an and the Traditions of Muhammad. I could have quoted more verses from the Qur'an and many parts of the Traditions to show the foundation of these articles of Faith. This was not done because of the limitations of space. However, the Qur'an and the Traditions of Muhammad are available references for any detailed study.

I have also kept to a minimum the use of Western terminology and technical language like predestination, fatalism, free will and so on. This was done deliberately because I wanted to avoid confusion and technicalities. Most of the technical terms used in religion among non-Arabic speaking people lead to misunderstanding, when applied to Islam, and give wrong impressions. I realize that I could not serve the purpose of this work if foreign religious terms were adopted and applied to Islam. If I were to use the alien religious terminology here, I would have had to add many qualifications and comments to clarify the picture of Islam. This also would have required much more space which I could not possibly afford under the circumstances. So, I tried to explain things in ordinary simple language, and this same course will be followed in the remainder of the book.

Notes: *Like Judaism, Islam has not produced creedal statements in any profusion. Translated from the Arabic, Islam's basic creedal statement is as follows: "There is no God but Allah. Muhammad is His Messenger." There are also five beliefs commonly presented as Articles of Faith in North American Islamic literature. For Sunni Muslims, these are: 1) Belief in the Unity of God; 2) Belief in God's Angels; 3) Belief in Books of God; 4) Belief in God's Prophets; 5) Belief in Life after Death. These articles have been expanded upon in the Fundamental Articles of Faith in Islam. This statement of Islamic belief written by Hammudah Abd Al-Ati, director of the Canadian Islamic Center in Edmonton, Alberta, was included in his book*

Islam in Focus. The book is popular among North American Sunni Muslims and has been reprinted on several occasions. In the remarks at the end of the Articles, the author explains his method in producing them.

* * *

ARTICLES OF FAITH [SAIYADUL ULAMA (SHI'A ISLAM)]

ARTICLES OF FAITH

The fundamental principles of Islam are five:

1. *Tauhid* i.e. Belief in the Unity of God.
2. *'Adl* i.e. Belief in Divine Justice.
3. *Nubuwat* i.e. Belief in the Apostles of God.
4. *Imamat* i.e. Belief in the viceregents of the Prophet.
5. *Ma'ad* i.e. Belief in the Day of Judgement.

Let us take one by one in regular sequence. Tauhid comes first. This is the foundation stone of religion. It draws attention towards God Who is the Creator and the Central Figure for the entire humanity. God is the Creator. Man is His creation. This leads to the idea that all men are equal by right of birth, and answerable to their Creator for their acts. They cannot freely indulge in their passions and work at cross-purposes. By virtue of this faith the entire humanity is strung into one thread. Differences of race, country, caste and colour are shed. All being subject to the same Power should act in conformity and have common religious outlook. The Creator is Omnipotent and Omnipresent. Minutest movements of man cannot escape His notice; man should therefore beware of neglecting His laws and should not be elated at his unobserved misdeed. Certainly it is noted by Him Who alone has the power to reward and to punish. He is the Sole Master. His pleasure should be the chief concern of man and he should dread to incur His displeasure. He is the Mightiest. Man should not be awed by the might of any earthly soul. God alone can help man achieve his object—no task, however difficult should therefore be deemed unsurmountable. He alone is the Prop of the weak. One should not despair of one's weakness. This faith leads to the conception of a vast human brotherhood every unit of which should be imbued with the feeling of unity and equality among them and should jointly and individually march towards the common goal for all, set by Him and should strictly observe religious tenets and always pray for His aid in joint or individual undertakings. People of such faith will have self-respect enough not to humble themselves before any material power and confidence enough never to despair. These are the qualities that become great people for their march onward.

DIVINE JUSTICE ('ADL)

It is part and parcel of the faith in the Unity of God. God's acts are all just and good. There can be no shadow of evil in His acts. Every act of His is full of wisdom and foresight. The justness of His actions demands justice from man in his acts. He has made man master of his acts. This is a gift from Him to man. Man should utilize this gift with the utmost propriety. The opposite of justice is tyranny. Tyrants override God's Law and God has condemned them.

The faith in the justness of God's actions cements the foundations of the mutual rights of the members of the vast human brotherhood stated above. None of the members of that society would look down upon the others. They would know that differences of positions in this world are ephemeral and that in the eye of God all are equal. He will reward and punish the rich and the poor alike for their good and bad deeds—Wealth or poverty of man in this world would not weigh with Him in meeting out justice. This faith creates in man the feeling of performing his duties justly and to weigh his deeds.

God does not countenance extremes. Moderation is perfection. Belief in Divine Justice teaches moderation to man. Those who do not overstep the limits of moderation can rightly be called just and they are Muslims in the true sense of the word.

THE INSTITUTION OF PROPHETS (NUBUWAT)

Belief in the prophets is the third essential of Islam. A Prophet is the vice-regent of God on earth. He communicates God's commands to man. No one has a right to question those commands or criticise a Prophet's decisions. A prophet is the best model of all that is good in character and standard. Human weaknesses like partiality, selfishness, egotism and hankering after position are to a great extent mastered by His true adherents and in this lies the secret of the well being of humanity. He is infallible.

IMAMAT

A prophet like any man is mortal. If after the demise of a prophet man is left without a guide the evils a man is prone to will raise their heads again. All the order that the Prophet had brought about will be disrupted. Appointment of Imams checks this disruption. Man knows that after the death of a prophet there is a central figure to help him stick to the right path. An Imam is a model of perfection himself and well versed in Divine Law. Like a prophet is also infallible. Loyalty to the Imam is as essential as loyalty to the Prophet. He alone becomes the central figure after the death of the Prophet.

There comes a time, like the present, when access to the Imam is an impossibility. The recognised scholars who have mastered the teachings of the Prophet and Imams, the successors of the Prophet, are then to be approached and the instructions and orders given by them according to the Qur'an and Sunnat to be strictly followed. The order set up in pursuance of such instructions will be the Islamic order.

The arrangement stated above is sufficient proof that Islam admits the necessity of a central figure. The status, however, of this central figure is not ethical but Divine. His sway will be on the hearts of his followers who will always hold God to be the real Sovereign and the worldly formed kingdom to be nothing.

Of course loyalty to the earthly ruler cannot be avoided. Necessities for the protection of life, property and for maintenance of peace demand it. But this ruler can neither be Eternal nor Divine.

Islam lays down no foundation for material rule. It makes arrangements for the perfection of man and shapes people who may be counted model men under the guidance of the Prophet, his nominated successors and scholars of religion.

RESURRECTION

Having made all arrangements for the guidance of man reward to those who obey the guides and punishment to those who disobey is the demand of God's justice; otherwise there can be no difference between the pious and the impious. The Day fixed for this is called the Day of Judgment.

The above essentials show that they are so well-connected links of Divine arrangement that if any of them is suppressed the entire edifice will tumble down.

The aim of all the essentials is to recognise the absolute Sovereignty of God and not to humble our selves by paying homage to any material power.

Notes: *There are five Articles of Faith commonly presented in North American Islamic literature. For the Shi'a Muslim, these are: 1) Belief in the Unity of God; 2) Belief in Divine Justice; 3) Belief in the Apostles of God; 4) Belief in the Vice-regents of the Prophet; 5) Belief in the Day of Judgment. These articles have been expanded upon by Saiyadul Ulama in his pamphlet* What Is Islam?, *which has circulated particularly among Indian- and Pakistani-American Shi'a Muslims. The prime point of difference between Sunni and Shi'a is over the doctrine of the imans, or vice-regents, of the Prophet.*

* * *

Sufism

PURPOSE (PROSPEROS)

A. "To bear witness in an age of material greatness to the primacy of the spiritual; to interpret the importance of spiritual dimensions in practical affairs and common concerns, and to spell out what free man can do to act effectively in the present world crisis."

B. "To give man a new identity (actually show him how to recognize his only true identity) and to develop and channel this concept beyond his presently cognized equipment and resources."

C. "To foster and develop spiritually-motivated action in social and civil life."

Notes: *Prosperos is one of several groups that found inspiration in the work of Georgei Gurdjieff, the mystical teacher who brought his own brand of Sufism to the West in the early twentieth century.*

THE OBJECTS OF THE SUFI ORDER AND SUFI THOUGHTS (SUFI ORDER)

THE OBJECTS OF THE SUFI ORDER

1. To realize and spread the knowledge of unity, the religion of love and wisdom, so that the bias of faiths and beliefs may of itself fall away, the human heart may overflow with love, and all hatred caused by distinctions and differences may be rooted out:

2. To discover the light and power latent in man, the secret of all religion, the power of mysticism, and the essence of philosophy, without interfering with customs or belief.

3. To help bring the world's two opposite poles, East and West, closer together by the interchange of thought and ideals, that the Universal Brotherhood may form of itself, and man may see with man beyond the narrow national and racial boundaries.

SUFI THOUGHTS

1. There is one God, the Eternal, the Only Being; none else exists save He.

2. There is one Master, the Guiding Spirit of all souls, who constantly leads His followers towards the light.

3. There is one Holy Book, the sacred manuscript of nature, the only scripture which can enlighten the reader.

4. There is one Religion, the unswerving progress in the right direction toward the ideal, which fulfils the life's purpose of every soul.

5. There is one Law, the Law of Reciprocity, which can be observed by a selfless conscience together with a sense of awakened justice.

6. There is one Brotherhood, the human Brotherhood, which unites the children of earth indiscriminately in the Fatherhood of God.

7. There is one Moral Principle, the love which springs forth from self-denial, and blooms in deeds of beneficence.

8. There is one Object of Praise, the beauty which uplifts the heart of its worshipper through all aspects from the seen to the unseen.

9. There is one Truth, the true knowledge of our being within and without, which is the essence of all wisdom.

10. There is one Path, the annihilation of the false ego in the real, which raises the mortal to immortality and in which resides all perfection.

Notes: *Most of the mystically-oriented Sufi groups operating in the United States are small, function on a very informal level, and do not publish statements. Through its brief declarations, the Sufi Order attempts to state in words the order's ideal of oneness, which is captured most fully in the individual's spiritual life.*

Black Islam

OUR BELIEFS (AHMADIYYA ANJUMAN ISHAAT ISLAM, LAHORE, INC.)

(1) That there is no God but Allah and Muhammad is His Messenger.

(2) After the Holy Prophet (peace be upon him), Allah has completely barred the appearance of a prophet, old or new.

(3) After the Holy Prophet, Gabriel can never descend and bring Prophetic Revelation *(Wahy Nubuwwah)* to any person.

(4) If Gabriel were to descend with one word of Prophetic Revelation *(Wahy Nubuwwah)* on any person, it would contradict the two complementary verses:

"This day have I perfected your Religion for you" (5:5); "He is the Messenger of Allah and the Last of the prophets."

(5) The Holy Prophet also said: "I am Muhammad and I am Ahmad and I am al-'Aqib (the one who comes last) after whom there can be no prophet." (Al-Bukhari: Kitab al-Manaqib)

(6) In the light of the above Islamic fundamentals, the Holy Founder of the Ahmadiyya Movement never claimed to be a *Nabi,* but the God-Ordained Mujaddid ("The Promised Messiah") of the 14th Islamic Century, having been expressly raised to re-establish the predominance of Islam in the world.

(7) He named his followers 'Ahmadi' after the Holy Prophet's *Jamali* (beatific) name 'Ahmad'.

(8) He proclaimed that no verse of the Holy Qur'-an has been abrogated nor shall ever be abrogated.

(9) All the Companions of the Holy Prophet and the Imams are venerable.

(10) It is spiritually conducive to our Faith to accept the revivalist Islamic missions of *all Mujaddids (Renovators).*

(11) *Any one who declares his faith in the* Kalimah (Muslim formula of faith—*la ilaha ilallahu Muhammadur Rasulullah)* is a Muslim.

Notes: *This creed clearly distinguishes (in articles 5 and 6) the Ahmadiyya Anjuman Ishaat, Lahore, from the Ahmadiyya Movement of Islam, the other group following the teachings of Mizra Ghulam Ahmad. The Ahmadiyya Anjuman Ishaat, Lahore, does not recognize Ahmad as a prophet (and hence equal to Muhammad), but merely as a "mujaddid," (literally, a "restorer of Islam"), a promised messiah, one of several figures who have appeared to revive Islam when it was at a low point in its development.*

BELIEFS OF THE AHMADIYYA MOVEMENT OF ISLAM

(1) We believe that God exists and to assert His existence is to assert a most important truth.

(2) We believe that God is ONE, without an equal in heaven or in earth. Everything else is His creation, dependent upon Him and His subsistence. He is without son or daughter or father or mother or wife or brother. He is one and unique.

(3) We believe that God is Holy, free from all imperfections and possessed of all perfections. There is no imperfection which may be found in Him and no perfection which may not be found in Him. His power and knowledge are unlimited. He encompasses everything and there is nothing which encompasses Him. He is the First, the Last, the Manifest, the Hidden, the Creator, the Master. He is the Loving, the Enduring. His actions are willed, not constrained or determined. He rules today as He ever ruled before. His attributes are eternal.

(4) We believe that angels are a part of God's creation. As the Quran has it, angels do what they are bidden to do. They have been created in His wisdom to carry out certain duties. Their existence is real and references to them in the Holy Book are not metaphorical. They depend on God as do all men and all other creatures.

(5) We believe that God speaks to His chosen Servants and reveals to them His Purpose. Revelation comes in words. Man lives by revelation and through it comes to have contact with God. The words in which revelation comes are unique in their power and wisdom. Their wisdom may not be revealed at once. A mine may be exhausted but not the wisdom of revelation. Revelation brings us divine ordinances, laws, and exhortations. It also brings us knowledge of the unseen and of important spiritual truths. It conveys to us the approval of God as well as His disapproval and displeasure, His love as well as His warnings. God communicates with man through revelation. The communications vary with circumstances and with the recipients. Of all divine communications the most perfect, the most complete, the most comprehensive is the Holy Quran. The Holy Quran is to last for ever. It cannot be superseded by any future revelation.

(6) We also believe that when darkness prevails in the world and man sinks deep in sin and evil, it becomes difficult for him to rise again without the help of God. Then out of His mercy and beneficence God chooses one of His own loving, loyal servants, charges him with the duty to lead and guide other men. As the Quran says, not a people but have had a warner sent to them (35:25). God has sent Messengers to every people. Through them God has revealed His Will and His Purpose. Those who turn away from them ruin themselves, those who turn to them earn the love and pleasure of God.

(7) We also believe that divine messengers belong to different spiritual ranks and contribute in different degrees to the fulfilment of the ultimate Divine Design. The greatest of all messengers is the Holy Prophet MUHAMMAD (on whom the peace and the blessings of God). He is the chief of all men, messenger to them all. The revelation he received was addressed to all mankind. The whole of this earth was a mosque for him. Time came when his message spread to lands and climes beyond Arabia. People forsook gods of their own conception and began to believe in the ONE and only God that the Holy Prophet Muhammad taught them to believe. The coming of the Holy Prophet marked an unparalleled spiritual revolution. Justice began to reign instead of injustice, kindness instead of cruelty. If Moses and Jesus had existed in the time of the Holy Prophet Muhammad they would have had to believe in him and to follow him.

(8) We also believe that God hears our prayers and helps us out of difficulties. He is a living God, His living character being evident in all things at all times. God continues His benevolent interest in His servants and His creatures. When they need His help He turns to them with His help. If they forget Him, He reminds them of Himself and of His concern for them. "I am near indeed; I answer the prayer of every supplicant when he supplicates to Me. Let them, therefore, harken unto Me and believe in Me, so that they may go aright." (2:187).

(9) We also believe that from time to time God determines and designs the course of events in special ways. Events of this world are not determined entirely by unchanging laws called the Laws of Nature. For, besides these ordinary laws there are special laws through which God manifests Himself. It is these special laws which bring to us evidence of the Will, the Power and Love of God. Too many there are who deny this. They would believe in nothing besides the laws of nature. Yet laws of nature are not all the laws we have. Laws of nature are themselves governed by the wider Laws of God. Through these laws, God helps His chosen servants. Through them He destroys His enemies. Moses could not have triumphed over a cruel and mighty enemy, but for the special laws of God. The Holy Prophet Muhammad could not have triumphed over Arabs determined to put an end to him and his mission except for the laws of God, which worked on his side. In everything that he encountered, God helped the Holy Prophet. At last with 10,000 followers he re-entered the valley of Mecca out of which 10 years before he had to flee for his life. Laws of nature cannot account for these events.

(10) We also believe that death is not the end of everything. Man survives death. He has to account for what he does in this life, in life hereafter. The Power of God guarantees human survival.

(11) We believe, that unless forgiven out of His infinite Mercy, unbelievers go to Hell. The object of Hell is

not to give pain to the inmates but only to reform them. In Hell unbelievers and enemies of God spend their days in wail and woe and continue so until the Mercy of God encompasses the evil-doers and their evil. Truly did the Holy Prophet say, "A time will come when Hell will be emptied of all sinners." (Tafsir-ul-Maalam-ut-tanzil).

(12) Similarly we believe that those who believe in God and the Prophets, the angels and the books, who accept the guidance which comes from God, and walk in humility and abjure excesses of all kinds, will all go to a place called Heaven. Peace and pleasure will reign here and God will be present to all. Low desires will disappear. Men will have attained ever-lasting life and become an image of their Creator.

Notes: *This statement emphasizes the beliefs the Ahmadiyya hold that are identical to those of orthodox Islam. The statement does not cover those beliefs that have led to the denunciation of the Ahmadiyya Movement of Islam by the majority of Muslims, primarily the elevation of founder Hazrat Mirza Ghulam Ahmad to the status of a Prophet. The beliefs enunciated by Ahmad are also affirmed by the Ahmadiyya Anjuman Ishaat Islam, Lahore, Inc., the other branch of the Ahmadiyya movement.*

*   *   *

THE MUSLIM PROGRAM [AMERICAN MUSLIM MISSION (NATION OF ISLAM)]

WHAT THE MUSLIMS BELIEVE

1. WE BELIEVE in the One God Whose proper Name is Allah.

2. WE BELIEVE in the Holy Qur-an and in the Scriptures of all the Prophets of God.

3. WE BELIEVE in the truth of the Bible but we believe that it has been tampered with and must be reinterpreted so that mankind will not be snared by the falsehoods that have added to it.

4. WE BELIEVE in Allah's Prophets and the Scriptures they brought to the people.

5. WE BELIEVE in the resurrection of the dead—not in physical resurrection—but in mental resurrection. We believe that the so-called Negroes are most in need of mental resurrection: therefore, they will be resurrected first.

   Furthermore, we believe we are the people of God's choice, as it has been written, that God would choose the rejected and the despised. We can find no other persons fitting this description in these last days more than the so-called Negroes in America. We believe in the resurrection of the righteous.

6. WE BELIEVE in the judgment; we believe this first judgment will take place as God revealed, in America . . .

7. WE BELIEVE this is the time in history for the separation of the so-called Negroes and the so-called white Americans. We believe the black man should be freed in name as well as in fact. By this we mean that he should be freed from the names imposed upon him by his former slave masters. Names which identified him as being the slave master's slave. We believe that if we are free indeed, we should go in our own people's names—the black peoples of the earth.

8. WE BELIEVE in justice for all, whether in God or not; we believe as others, that we are due equal justice as human beings. We believe in equality—as a nation—of equals. We do not believe that we are equal with our slave masters in the status of "freed slaves."

   We recognize and respect American citizens as independent peoples and we respect their laws which govern this nation.

9. WE BELIEVE that the offer of integration is hypocritical and is made by those who are trying to deceive the black peoples into believing that their 400-year-old enemies of freedom, justice and equality are, all of a sudden, their "friends." Furthermore, we believe that such deception is intended to prevent black people from realizing that the time in history has arrived for the separation from the whites of this nation.

   If the white people are truthful about their professed frienship toward the so-called Negro, they can prove it by dividing up America with their slaves.

   We do not believe that America will ever be able to furnish enough jobs for her own millions of unemployed, in addition to jobs for the 20,000,000 black people as well.

10. WE BELIEVE that we who declared ourselves to be righteous Muslims, should not participate in wars which take the lives of humans. We do not believe this nation should force us to take part in such wars, for we have nothing to gain from it unless America agrees to give us the necessary territory wherein we may have something to fight for.

11. WE BELIEVE our women should be respected and protected as the women of other nationalities are respected and protected.

12. WE BELIEVE that Allah (God) appeared in the Person of Master W. Fard Muhammad, July, 1930; the long-awaited "Messiah" of the Christians and the "Mahdi" of the Muslims.

    We believe further and lastly that Allah is God and besides HIM there is no God and He will bring about a universal government of peace wherein we all can live in peace together.

WHAT THE MUSLIMS WANT

This is the question asked most frequently by both the whites and the blacks. The answers to this question I shall state as simply as possible.

1. We want freedom. We want a full and complete freedom.

2. We want justice. Equal justice under the law. We want justice applied equally to all, regardless of creed or class or color.

3. We want equality of opportunity. We want equal membership in society with the best in civilized society.

4. We want our people in America whose parents or grandparents were descendants from slaves, to be allowed to establish a separate state or territory of their own—either on this continent or elsewhere. We believe that our former slave masters are obligated to provide such land and that the area must be fertile and minerally rich. We believe that our former slave masters are obligated to maintain and supply our needs in this separate territory for the next 20 to 25 years—until we are able to produce and supply our own needs.

Since we cannot get along with them in peace and equality, after giving them 400 years of our sweat and blood and receiving in return some of the worst treatment human beings have ever experienced, we believe our contributions to this land and the suffering forced upon us by white America, justifies our demand for complete separation in a state or territory of our own.

5. We want freedom for all Believers of Islam now held in federal prisons. We want freedom for all black men and women now under death sentence in innumerable prisons in the North as well as the South.

We want every black man and woman to have the freedom to accept or reject being separated from the slave master's children and establish a land of their own.

We know that the above plan for the solution of the black and white conflict is the best and only answer to the problem between two people.

6. We want an immediate end to the police brutality and mob attacks against the so-called Negro throughout the United States.

We believe that the Federal government should intercede to see that black men and women tried in white courts receive justice in accordance with the laws of the land—or allow us to build a new nation for ourselves, dedicated to justice, freedom and liberty.

7. As long as we are not allowed to establish a state or territory of our own, we demand not only equal justice under the laws of the United States, but equal employment opportunities—NOW!

We do not believe that after 400 years of free or nearly free labor, sweat and blood, which has helped America become rich and powerful, that so many thousands of black people should have to subsist on relief, charity or live in poor houses.

8. We want the government of the United States to exempt our people from ALL taxation as long as we are deprived of equal justice under the laws of the land.

9. We want equal education—but separate schools up to 16 for boys and 18 for girls on the condition that the girls be sent to women's colleges and universities. We want all black children educated, taught and trained by their own teachers.

Under such schooling system we believe we will make a better nation of people. The United States government should provide, free, all necessary text books and equipment, schools and college buildings. The Muslim teachers shall be left free to teach and train their people in the way of righteousness, decency and self respect.

10. We believe that intermarriage or race mixing should be prohibited. We want the religion of Islam taught without hinderance or suppression.

These are some of the things that we, the Muslims, want for our people in North America.

Notes: *The Muslim Program, divided into two segments, What the Muslims Believe and What the Muslim Wants, details the assumptions upon which the Nation of Islam was built in the 1960s. In the 1970s, The Muslim Program was largely abandoned by the American Muslim Mission as it moved toward orthodox Sunni Muslim belief. However, the Program remains central to the several Nation of Islam factions such as the one led by Louis Farrakhan. The crucial element in the Program, which separates the Nation of Islam from orthodox Islam, is item 12 concerning the appearance of Allah as Master W. Fard Muhammad.*

* * *

Zoroastrianism

THE MAZDAZNAN CONFESSION (MAZDAZNAN MOVEMENT)

I am a Mazdaznan who worships but one God, who is in me and I am in Him.

I recognize all things throughout time and space with their diverse causations to be the result of Infinite thought.

I acknowledge all things in matter to be the means to an end and not the end of the Intelligence of God. I realize matter to be the result of the operations of God's intelligence through substance co-existent with intelligence through Infinite Thought.

I see in the countenance of man the male creative principle of God the Father, and in the woman I recognize the pro-creative female principle of God the Mother, and in the child I realize the perpetuative principle of destiny as Our Savior through life, and add that these three images of God constitute the one Holy Family, reproduced and multiplied into the greater Family of God and the Congregation of Gods with its endless chain of associations.

I confess all the painful in matter to be the result of obstinacy on the part of substance through its processes of

THE MAZDAZNAN CONFESSION (MAZDAZNAN MOVEMENT) (continued)

creations and evolutions, declining to yield to the peaceful operations of intelligence, thus introducing repulsion and impelling resistance.

I hold that all misunderstanding through the processes of creation and evolution is to be eliminated through the application of the higher intelligence, and that for this reason man must take up his work where the Spirit of God left to our care.

I join the sentiments of our Blessed Mother as expressed through the ideal of Ainyahita, that *I am here upon this earth to reclaim the earth, to turn the deserts into a paradise, a paradise most suitable unto God and His associates to dwell therein.*

I declare with Our Father of the pure faith through the *reality* of His Holy One, Zarathushtra, to stand for *Good Thought, Good Word, Good Deed.*

I agree with the saving power of the sonship of God through the incarnation of Christ in his command, *Love thy neighbor as thyself.*

I confide in the power of God. I shall set aside the useless and hold to the good. By the direction of perfect wisdom I shall choose the better part.

I deny the bonds of ancestral relation through sickness, sin and sorrow and sever myself from the pre-natal influence of inherited tendencies, and herewith annul association with evil, error and illusion.

I shall no longer recall to my mind my offenses nor the offenses of forefathers, but exercise all the attributes and endowments of my birthright which come to me through the blessings of *Mazda*, without measure and abundantly, that I may thus verify the words of God, *I shall remember their sins no more*, and continue to bear in mind, *What man soweth that he shall reap!*

I shall follow the *still small voice* in all its directions as coming from the realm of God, that by right living I may always demonstrate the full Truth through the health of the body and most ably perform my duty in a spirit of obedience—prove the power of mind through reason, logic, consideration, discrimination and deduction—have assurance of soul communion, comfort in spirit and the joys of life everlasting.

I shall conduct my life in a way that the knife shall never need be resorted to and herbal medicines never need to pass my lips, but in their stead holy spells through the formulas of invocations and prayers exemplify the perfect life in God on earth.

I shall ever laud creation and through the objects thereof worship the Lord God Mazda, and in all things of Nature, whether great or small the creature, behold the face of my Creator.

With mine eyes lifted beyond the mountain tops and my heart fixed by the burning fire of love I shall daily join in harmonious accord the prayer of the faithful worshipers— the prayer thrice spoken distinctly and with the presence of mind fixed upon the meaning of every word—the prayer that heals the body and assures tranquility to the mind— the prayer that gives solace to the soul and whispers to the spirit, *Peace*,—the prayer breathed in tuneful measure with fervor, zeal and the spirit of assurance, *on one single expiration.*

May Mazda be rejoiced and His Associates continue to be victorious. May obstinacy in this home be destroyed through the Virtue of Obedience, discord by Peace, avarice by Generosity, vanity by Wisdom, false witness by Truthfulness, that the Immortals may long bless it with maintenance and friendly help.—Never the splendor of Prosperity or Progeny be distinguished, that we may shine with purity and see Thee face to face, O Mazda, attaining attributes leading unto worlds without end. May peace come to one and all, and may there be given to this country purity, dominion, profit, majesty and splendor. This is my wish. Be it so.

Notes: *The oldest of the American Zoroastrian groups, the Mazdaznan Movement, has issued a confession.*

* * *

Bahaism

SUMMARY OF BAHA'I TEACHINGS OF THE BAHA'I WORLD FAITH

1. The oneness of mankind.
2. Independent investigation of truth.
3. The foundation of all religions is one.
4. Religion must be the cause of unity.
5. Religion must be in accord with science and reason.
6. Equality between men and women.
7. Prejudice of all kinds must be forgotten.
8. Universal peace.
9. Universal education.
10. Spiritual solution of the economic problem.
11. A universal language.
12. An international tribunal.

Notes: *The Baha'i World Faith accepts the writings of Baha'u'llah and Abdu'l-Baha as sacred texts. While the Bahais have no creed, they have frequently attempted to summarize the teachings. In one such summary circulated by the Bahais and reproduced here, twelve principles are listed. This list should not be taken as exhaustive. Other lists with varying numbers of items have also been circulated.*

Chapter 21
Eastern Family

Hinduism

THE SUPREME COMMAND (ANANDA MARGA YOGA SOCIETY)

He who performs Sadhana twice a day regularly, the thought of Paramapurusa will certainly arise in his mind at the time of death, his liberation is a sure guarantee—therefore every Ananda Margii will have to perform Sadhana twice a day invariably—verily is this the command of the Lord. Without Yama and Niyama, Sadhana is an impossibility; hence the Lord's command is also to follow Yama and Niyama. Disobedience to this command is nothing but to throw oneself into the tortures of animal life for crores of years. That no one should undergo torments such as this, that he might be enabled to enjoy the eternal blessedness under the loving shelter of the Lord, it is the bounden-duty of every Ananda Margii to endeavour to bring all to the path of bliss. Verily is this a part and parcel of Sadhana to lead others along the path of righteousness.

—Shrii Shrii A'nandanu'rti

Notes: *This statement comes from an aggressively missionary Hindu organization as a guiding document for all members.*

*   *   *

A SHORT STATEMENT OF THE PHILOSOPHY OF KRISHNA CONSCIOUSNESS (INTERNATIONAL SOCIETY OF KRISHNA CONSCIOUSNESS)

1. By cultivating a bona fide spiritual science, we can be free from anxiety and achieve pure, unending, blissful consciousness in this lifetime.

2. We are not our bodies but eternal spirit souls, parts and parcels of God (Krsna).

3. Krsna is the eternal, all-knowing, omnipresent, all-powerful, and all-attractive Personality of Godhead, the sustaining energy of the entire cosmic creation, and the seed-giving father of all living beings.

4. The Absolute Truth is present in all the world's great scriptures, particularly the ancient Vedic literatures, whose *Bhagavad-gita* records God's actual words.

5. We should learn the Vedic knowledge from a genuine spiritual master—one who has no selfish motives and whose mind is firmly fixed on Krsna.

6. Before we eat, we should offer to the Lord the food that sustains us. Then Krsna becomes the offering and purifies us.

7. We should offer to Krsna all that we do and do nothing for our own sense gratification.

8. The recommended way to achieve mature love of God in this age of Kali (quarrel) is to chant the Lord's holy names. For most people it is easiest to chant the Hare Krsna *mantra*.

   Hare Krsna, Hare Krsna, Krsna Krsna, Hare Hare
   Hare Rama, Hare Rama, Rama Rama, Hare Hare.

Notes: *Members of the International Society of Krisha Consciousness (ISKCON), the Hare Krishna movement, are believers in a personal deity to which they give daily devotion. The repetition of the Hare Krishna mantra is an important daily duty of disciples. The statement of philosophy has been published in every issue of the society's major periodical,* Back to Godhead, *for many years.*

*   *   *

AIMS AND TENETS (YOGODA SAT-SANGA MOVEMENT) AND AIMS AND IDEALS (SELF-REALIZATION FELLOWSHIP)

AIMS AND TENETS

1. Universal all-round education, and establishment of educational institutions for the development of man's physical, mental and spiritual natures.

2. Contacting Cosmic Consciousness—the ever-new, ever-existing, ever-conscious Bliss-God—through the scientific technique of concentration and meditation taught by the Masters of all ages.

3. Attaining bodily health through the "Yogoda" technique of recharging the body-battery from inner life-energy.

4. Intelligently maintaining the physical body on unadulterated foods, including a large percentage of raw fruits, vegetables and nuts.

5. Physical, mental and spiritual healing.

6. Establishing, by a scientific system of realization, the absolute basic harmony and oneness of Christianity, Hindu Yoga teachings, and all true religions.

7. Serving all mankind as one's larger Self.

8. Demonstrating the superiority of mind over body, and of soul over mind.

9. Fighting the Satan of Ignorance—man's common enemy.

10. Establishing a spiritual unity between all nations.

11. Overcoming evil by good; overcoming sorrow by joy; overcoming cruelty by kindness.

12. Realization of the purpose of life as being the evolution from human consciousness into divine consciousness, through individual struggle.

13. Realization of the truth that human life is given to man to afford him opportunity to manifest his inner divine qualities, and not for physical pleasure nor selfish gratifications.

14. Furthering the cultural and spiritual understanding between East and West, and the constructive exchange of the distinctive features of their civilizations.

15. Uniting science and religion through study and practical realization of the unity of their underlying principles.

AIMS AND IDEALS

To disseminate among the nations a knowledge of definite scientific techniques for attaining direct personal experience of God.

To teach that the purpose of life is the evolution, through self-effort, of man's limited mortal consciousness into God Consciousness; and to this end to establish Self-Realization Fellowship temples for God-communion throughout the world, and to encourage the establishment of individual temples of God in the homes and in the hearts of men.

To reveal the complete harmony and basic oneness of original Christianity as taught by Jesus Christ and original Yoga as taught by Bhagavan Krishna; and to show that these principles of truth are the common scientific foundation of all true religions.

To point out the one divine highway to which all paths of true religious beliefs eventually lead: the highway of daily, scientific, devotional meditation on God.

To liberate man from his threefold suffering: physical disease, mental inharmonies, and spiritual ignorance.

To encourage "plain living and high thinking"; and to spread a spirit of brotherhood among all peoples by teaching the eternal basis of their unity: kinship with God.

To demonstrate the superiority of mind over body, of soul over mind.

To overcome evil by good, sorrow by joy, cruelty by kindness, ignorance by wisdom.

To unite science and religion through realization of the unity of their underlying principles.

To advocate cultural and spiritual understanding between East and West and the exchange of their finest distinctive features.

To serve mankind as one's larger Self.

Notes: *Shortly after Paramahansa Yogananda arrived in the United States in the 1920s, he circulated a statement concerning the organization he had founded, then called the Yogoda Sat-Sanga. In more recent years, that statement has undergone revision and emerged as the Aims and Ideals of the organization under its current name, the Self-Realization Fellowship. The older statement makes several references to the "kriya yoga" system taught by Yogananda, a "scientific system of realization." These references have been deleted from the more recent statement.*

* * *

THE ETERNAL TRUTHS (SELF-REVELATION CHURCH OF ABSOLUTE MONISM)

I AM AN ABSOLUTE MONIST. I BELIEVE:

"Truth is one; men call it by various names."

"God, Brahman, is Consciousness-Existence-Bliss Absolute."

"Everything is the manifestation of God, the divine Reality."

"The soul of man is of identical nature with the God of the universe."

"Realize thyself."

"By the realization of one's own self, the absolute Self is realized."

"God is the light of the heavens and the earth."

"He who realizes God becomes one with God."

"I am that I am."

"I and my Father are one."

"I am Brahman, the absolute Self."

Notes: *A Westernized branch of the Vedanta movement, the Self-Revelation Church of Absolute Monism has attempted to render the basic affirmation of the Vedanta philosophy in a set of brief statements.*

* * *

MEMBERSHIP STATEMENT OF SRI RAM ASHRAMA

All members should study and manifest the following five resolutions:

1. The will to neither kill nor injure.

2. The will always to speak the truth and to act truthfully.

3. The will always to remain honest and not to pilfer.

4. The will to direct all bodily and mental energies toward reality.

5. The resolution not to take gifts or seek rewards with the idea of piling them up for personal gain.

All members should study and follow these eight steps or principles:

1. Yama - firm determination to lead life in the light of truth.

2. Niyama - firm activity of mind and body to lead life toward truth by way of these five methods:

   a) Cleanliness of body and mind.

   b) Contentment.

   c) Critical examination of senses.

   d) Study of physics, metaphysics, and psychology.

   e) Realization of the oneness of individual existence with universal existence; complete self-surrender.

3. Asana - physical, biological, chemical, and bio-chemical exercising for the purpose of refining mind and body to study Truth.

4. Pranayama - the control of enerty or prana.

5. Pratyahara - displacement of psychic energy from the lower regions and its sublimation to higher purposes.

6. Dharana - fixation of attention on a particular object or idea with the aim of steadying the mind and making it absolutely fit and pliant.

7. Dhyana - continuous meditation and focusing of attention on that particular object or idea.

8. Samadhi - transformation of all attention into that particular object.

Three other principles to be followed by all members on the Path:

1. To be devoted and dedicated to the practice of Vichara as taught by Sri Bhagavan Ramana Maharshi.

2. Non-violence, or Ahimsa—to abstain from causing pain at any time, in any way, however small in mind, word or body, to any living thing, including oneself, is non-violence. All other abstinences and observances lead up to it and have to be brought into action before full non-violence can be attained. It is said that they exist only for the sake of non-violence, and further, that without non-violence, their practice is fruitless.

3. Truth or Satya—According to testimony of the inner faculties and senses, to show things as they are with the aim of doing good in friendly words and without deceit is Truth.

Notes: *In its constitution, the Sri Ram Ashrama has a lengthy statement in the section on membership which delineates basic concepts and teachings. In essence, this statement presents the ashrama's consensus on matters of belief and practice. The various items are part of the common teachings of yogic philosophy.*

* * *

PLEDGE AND DASASHRAM DISCIPLINES (TEMPLE OF COSMIC RELIGION)

PLEDGE

On this day we take the pledge that we dedicate our lives for Universal peace, to bridge the east and west and to bring understanding among people through the message of love and wisdom of all sages and saints.

"We live as one family with Prem (Love Divine) in the name of God Who is our Father". Let this be the meditation for the whole world. If every one meditates on this thought, God will certainly bless His children with happiness and peace.

Let the whole world have one ideal which the great sages of the Himalayas taught and that is, "Sarve Jananam sukhino bhavanthu", let all people be happy. Let there be peace in the world, peace above and peace within. Om Shantih Shantih Shantih

We work for this, day and night through:

1. Establishing Dasashram branches all over the world to teach the message of the sages and saints of east and west.

2. Through installing the Image of the Lord of Love (Panduranga) as the symbol of the holy east.

3. We initiate people for spiritual training in eternal religion (Sanatana Dharma) to serve God and saints through humanity.

4. Our ideas of peace extends not only to humanity but to all animals, the plant kingdom and the whole creation of God.

   (1) Bhuta-daya (compassion) to all creatures

   (2) Kshama (forgiveness)

   (3) Dharma (Divine Law)

   (4) Prema (Love Divine)

   (5) Satya (truth)

   (6) Jnana (wisdom)

   (7) Seva (service)

   (8) Shanti (peace)

These are the eight "Daivi Sampat" or divine attributes which makes man perfect. This comes through the realization of God or God-realization will come by developing these divine qualities.

   Shoucha (inner and outer purity)

   Shraddha (unflinching faith in God and Guru)

   Sadhana (spiritual discipline)

These three make man eligible for Grace of God and the Grace of God brings love and peace ineffeble which is the be-all and end-all of our existence.

The technique to reach this state is NAMA (chanting of the name divine) and PREMA (yoga of Love divine)

PLEDGE AND DASASHRAM DISCIPLINES (TEMPLE OF COSMIC RELIGION) (continued)

which includes Hatha yoga, Raja yoga, Dhyana yoga, Bhakti yoga and Karma yoga or the yoga of knowledge, the yoga of mediation, the yoga of devotion and the yoga of selfless service, yoga for health and purification of Nadis and yoga of psychological self-discipline.

God bless all with His supreme love.

Om and Prem, Sant Keshavadas

DASASHRAM DISCIPLINES

1. We belong to Sanatana Vedic Hindu Dharma.

2. We have faith in the Vedas, Vedanta or Upanishads Brahmasutras, Bhagavad Gifa, Mahabharata, Ramayana; Eighteen Puranas, Manusmruti and all spiritual literature that is not against the Sanatana Vedic Scriptures.

3. We believe Mother India to be the Karma-Bhumi; Ganges water to be most Holy Water; Cow is to be worshipped as the mother and non-killing of any animal consciously, as our Great Dharma. We believe Mother as God, Father as God, Guru as God and Guest as God and we strive to realise God in everything and Everywhere.

4. We consider Gayatri as the greatest of all Mantras and "OM" as our symbol of God.

5. We believe in worshipping God through images and rituals, but always with the knowledge to realise God in us and in everything.

6. Sanatana Dharma is the Eternal and Ancient wisdom of God and this is a Way of Life Divine.

7. As an outer symbol of our inner conviction we wear:

 (a) "OM" symbol

 (b) White clothes (Sattwa Guna)

 (c) Tulsi or Rudrakshi beads &

 (d) Nam or Holy mark and Vibhuti the holy ashes.

8. We believe in Brahma, Vishnu and Siva as the three aspects of ONE GOD and We worship all Gods described in our Scriptures as the manifestation of one God.

9. We believe in the Doctrine of Incarnation of God and the Doctrine of Reincarnation of man.

10. We believe Gnana, Karma and Bhakti-Yogas to be the greatest of all the yogas, the others being the practical preparatory Yoga which lead towards the three major yogas. We call the integration of the three major yogas as "Prema Yoga" and practise it.

"Love born of wisdom practised in selfless service could solve all problems of Humanity."

Notes: *Embedded in these two guiding documents for the members of the Temple of Cosmic Religion are the basic beliefs espoused by the temple and its leader, Sant Keshavadas.*

WHAT DO WE BELIEVE? (TEMPLE OF KRIYA YOGA)

1. There is only one ultimate law, and that law is God.

2. There is only one spirit, and that spirit is God.

3. There is only one love, and that love is God.

4. The universe is meaningful and you have your rightful place in it.

5. Illumination and fulfillment are possible in this lifetime.

Notes: *This brief statement presents several affirmations that undergird the extensive teaching program of the Temple of Kriya Yoga.*

*   *   *

UNIVERSAL UNDERSTANDING (YASODHARA ASHRAM SOCIETY)

God is universal, yet man has followed many paths in seeking him. Outwardly these ways of search differ, owing to their various traditions and to the separate historical and cultural circumstances in which each has arisen. At its finest, each religion is suited to answer the spiritual, emotional and psychological needs of the particular people or group among whom it has developed.

In the past, unfortunately, these inevitable differences between creeds have become hardened and exaggerated by man-made laws and doctrines, so that the various religious movements have helped to divide men rather than to unite them.

Yet underlying all religions there are certain universal and ethical concepts; all religions advocate—as fundamental principles—truth, love, selflessness, and moderation. They are also alike in making use of certain essential spiritual practices, such as prayer, chanting and meditation.

Now, in an age when the spiritual and physical perils of mankind loom larger than ever before, and ignorance has gained its maximum destructive power, it is necessary that religion should unite rather than divide, and that the ideal of brotherhood in spiritual understanding should at last be put into practice. This can come about only when the unwisdom of religious exclusiveness is recognized, and the adherents of all creeds are willing to cultivate spiritual companionship in freedom and universal tolerance.

Yasodhara Ashram aims to provide a setting in which people — no matter what their religious affiliation, or lack of affiliation — who are conscious of this pressing need for spiritual unity, may come together in the search for universal principles and unifying practices; and yet remain free in their personal search for spiritual enlightenment.

Notes: *This statement gives expression to a popular Hindu notion about the universal essence of religion.*

Sikhism

INITIATION INSTRUCTIONS FOR THE RUHANI SATSANG

Before the living Master (an adept in the science of the Sound Current or Word), gives Initation, he wishes that every prospective initiate abide by the following instructions:

I. To cultivate and develop the five cardinal virtues which constitute the bedrock of spirituality. These are:

1. *Ahimsa* or Non-injury to all living creatures, and more so to fellow beings, by thoughts, words and deeds—the injunction in this behalf being: "Injure not a human heart for it is the seat of God." We must have respect for others' feelings and tolerance for others' opinions.

2. *Satayam* or Truthfulness: As God is Truth, we must practice Truth in all our dealings. If Truth resides in every heart, it must manifest itself in life and action. "Be true to thyself and it must follow as night the day, thou canst not be false to any man." We must therefore avoid falsehood at all costs. It includes, besides downright lies, hypocrisy and dishonesty, *suppresso veri* (suppression of truth), and *suggestio falsi* (suggestions of false ideas).

3. *Brahmcharya* or life of Chastity: It includes continence in thoughts, words and deeds. We must not cast covetous eyes on others nor entertain impure thoughts within, for "Chastity is life and sexuality is death." If we want to tread the Path of Life Eternal, we must be chaste and clean both within and without.

4. *Prem* or love for all living creatures and more so for all human beings. Let there be hatred for none. The entire manifestation is the handiwork of God and must therefore be loved and respected. "He who does not know love, cannot know God."

5. *Nishkam Seva* or Selfless Service to all living creatures in sorrow and distress. If one limb of the body is in torture, the other limbs can have no rest.

    "Service before self" should therefore be our motto in life.

II. To practice these three purities - in Diet, Livelihood and Conduct.

1. *Ahar* or Diet. What we eat goes to constitute the body and the mind. "Sound mind in a sound body" is a well known aphorism. We can neither have one nor the other with unwholesome diet. A strictly vegetarian diet consisting of vegetables and fruits, both fresh and dried, cereals, dairy products like milk, cream, butter, cheese, yogurt, etc., is essential for all aspirants for Truth. We must, therefore avoid meat, meat juices, fish, fowl, eggs both fertile and unfertile, or anything containing any of these ingredients in any form or in any degree. Every action has a reaction and flesh eating involves contracting fresh Karmas and thus helps to keep the inexorable Karmic wheel in motion for we have to reap what we sow. We cannot have roses if we sow thistles.

    The above prohibitions apply equally to all kinds of Alcohlic drinks, intoxicants, opiates and narcotic drugs, as they tend to dull our consciousness and make one morbid.

    "The body is the temple of living God" and it must, therefore, be kept scrupulously clean.

    Any prospective candidate for initiation should therefore try vegetarian for at least three to six months, to ensure that he or she can adhere to it, when put on the Path.

2. *Vibar* or Livelihood: Closely associated with diet, are the means of livelihood. There are no short-cuts in spirituality. The end here does not justify the means, as it may be construed to do so, anywhere else. The ignoble means to earn one's living, do contaminate one's diet, the very source of life itself. So an honest living by the sweat of one's brow is essential in this line. The life plant has therefore to be nurtured with pure water, to make it sound and healthy, a fit instrument for the efflorescence of spirituality.

3. *Achar* or Conduct. The above remarks apply equally to one's conduct in life. Every thought, every word and every deed, good or bad, leaves an indelible imprint on the mind and has to be accounted for. Hence the necessity for right thoughts, right aspirations and right conduct, all of which constitute the hedge around the tender sapling of spirituality. The details in this behalf have been dealt with under the five virtues discussed above.

III. *Satsang* or Association with Truth: The guidance of the Living Master is of supreme importance. A Master is a Master indeed, a Master in all three phases of life: A Guru or Master on the physical plane, sharing our joys and sorrows, guiding affectionately each one of us in our wordly affairs, and above all imparting spiritual instructions: a Guru Dev or Radiant Form of the Master on Astral and Causal regions helping the spirit in meditation at each place and Sat Guru or Master of Truth or Truth itself in the Beyond.

The importance of attending Satsangs or spiritual gatherings can not be over emphasised. Theory always preceeds practice. It is but necessary to understand clearly the teaching of the Master in all their bearings, before starting spiritual practice. The Master is the be-all and end-all on the spiritual path. He, however, does not ask for blind faith, though experimental faith is necessary for the purpose, to start with. He emphatically expresses: "Believe not the words of the Master, unless you see the Reality yourself" or at least have some experience of it yourself.

IV. Spirituality: It is a path of love, discipline and self control. After the initial spiritual experience given at the time of Initiation, the rest depends on relentless regular practice as enjoined by the Master. Daily practice with loving faith, in all sincerity and humility, is the cornerstone round which each disciple must turn, so as to make progress on the Path. Love for the Master means implicit obedience to His commandments.

V. To Eschew All Symbolism and Rituals: The observance of religious practices, rites and rituals, keeping fasts and vigils, going on pilgrimages, etc., and doing breathing exercises are the elementary steps only which go to create in you a desire for turning to or meeting God. You have made best use of them when you are put on the way back to God, which is the science of the Word or the Sound Current and is one for all humanity. A devotee of this science need not indulge in the elementary steps. In short, all acts involving physical labor belong to the realm of the physical world while we have to rise above the body and bodily consciousness to get contact with the primal manifestations of the Godhead: Light and Sound. You cannot pray God with hands. "God is Spirit and can only be worshiped in spirit."

VI. Record of Conduct and Progress: Every seeker after God is enjoined to maintain a strictly impartial record of his daily conduct, so as to find out his weaknesses and try to weed them out one by one; to note his/her progress on the Path and the various difficulties and shortcomings in the way. The diary so maintained is to be sent to the Master every four months for further guidance. For this purpose regular forms are available and can be obtained from the nearest center.

VII. Application for Initiation: Every true aspirant for spiritual science, who can adhere to the above, after preliminary abstinence in diet for about three to six months, can put in an application on the form prescribed for the purpose, giving his brief life sketch, age, marital status and the like along with a copy of his or her photograph. All applications for Initiation are to be forwarded to the nearest representative of the Master for His approval, and instructions in Initiation are given only after the Master authorizes them. The place and time of Initiation are communicated in each case by the representative.

VIII. Ruhani Satsang or Path of the Masters: The science of the living Masters is the most ancient and the most perfect science the world has ever seen. It is the most natural and the easiest to follow, and can be followed by men of all ages. Married life, avocation, caste and creed, social and religious beliefs, poverty or illiteracy, etc., are no bars. It is an inner science of the soul and consists in contacting the soul with the Oversoul, with the help and guidance of the spiritual adept, well versed in the theory and the practice of *Para Vidya* or the Science of the Beyond and capable of granting some first-hand spiritual experience at the very first sitting. Nothing is to be taken on trust or make-believe. Miracles, spiritual healings, psychic phenomena, fortunetelling, akashic records and worldly desires are all to be left aside, for these are positive hindrances on the Path. The entire energy is to be conserved for internal progress.

Seek ye first the Kingdom of God, and all things shall be added unto you.

This is the highest Truth that has been taught from hoary antiquity by sages and seers since the day of creation. It is unalterable and shall remain so. God, Godway and Godman can never suffer any change and shall ever remain eternal.

Notes: *The single representative statement from among Sikh groups derives from one of the "Sant Mat" organizations which, because they retain a living guru, are not considered true Sikhs by the more orthodox. Since the death of Kirpal Singh, founder and leader of Ruhani Satsang, three organizations have claimed to be led by his successor—the Kirpal Light Satsang, the Sant Bani Ashram, and the Sawan Kirpal Ruhani Mission. Each offers the same instructions to new initiates.*

*   *   *

Buddhism

SUMMARY OF BUDDHA'S DHARMA (DWIGHT GODDARD)

INTRODUCTION

The Buddha's Dharma ought not to be considered as a system of philosophic or intellectual thought, much less as a system of ethical idealism. Strictly speaking, even less is it a religion based upon authority. It is simply a way of life which Buddha called the Eightfold Noble Path and the Middle Way, and which he said would lead him who followed it to emancipation of body, to enlightenment of mind, to tranquillity of spirit, to highest Samadhi. That is, it is a system of mind-control leading to highest perfect cognition. He did not make it up—it is the record of his own experience under the Bodhitree, when he himself attained Enlightenment.

The summary is introduced by what is known as the Twelve Nirdanas, or the Chain of Simultaneous Dependent Originations *(paticca-samutpada)*. Then he taught the Four Noble Truths upon which he based the Eightfold Noble Path. These are all briefly summarized.

THE TWELVE NIRDANAS

1. Because of Ignorance *(avidya)* the principle of individuation as discriminated from Enlightenment which is the principle of unity and sameness the primal unity becomes divided into thinking, thinker and discriminated thoughts by reason of which there appear the "formations" of karma.

2. Because of these "forms" *(samsara)*, the principle of consciousness emerges.

3. Because of the principle of consciousness *(vijnana)*, mentality and body emerge.

4. Because of mentality and body *(nama-rupa)*, the six sense minds and organs appear.

5. Because of the six sense minds and organs *(shadaya-tana)*, sensations and perceptions arise.

6. Because of sensations and perceptions *(spasha)*, feelings and discriminations arise.

7. Because of feelings and sensations *(vedana)*, thirst and craving arise.

8. Because of thirst and craving *(trishna)*, grasping and clinging appear.

9. Because of grasping and clinging *(upadana)*, conception takes place.

10. Because of conception *(bhava)*, the continuing process of existence goes on.

11. Because of the continuing process of existence *(jeti)*, growth, sickness, old age, decay and death take place.

12. Because of sickness, old age and death *(jana-mara-na)*, "sorrow, lamentation, pain, grief and despair arise. Thus arises the whole mass of suffering." In all this

> "No doer of the deeds is found,
> No one who ever reaps their fruit.
> Empty phenomena are there.
> Thus does the world roll on.
> No god, no Brahma, can be found,
> No maker of this wheel of life.
> Empty phenomena are there,
> Dependent upon conditions all."

THE FOUR NOBLE TRUTHS

1. The universality of suffering.
2. The cause of suffering rooted in desire.
3. By ending desire, suffering comes to an end.
4. The way to end desire and hence to end suffering, is to follow the Eightfold Noble Path.

THE EIGHTFOLD NOBLE PATH

1. RIGHT IDEAS: The Twelve Nirdanas and the Four Noble Truths. Not only should one understand them but he should make them the basis of all his thinking and understanding of life, he should make them the basis for a life of patient and humble acceptance and submission.

2. RIGHT RESOLUTION: He should make it the purpose of his life to follow the Noble Path. In loyalty to this purpose he should be willing to give up anything that is contrary to it, or which hinders his progress. He should be willing to pay any cost of comfort, or self denial, or effort, in order to attain its goal. He should not do this for any selfish motive but that he might devote the merit of its attainment to all

animate life. And finally he should make his great Vow *(Pranadana)* not to enter Nirvana until all others may enter with him.

3. RIGHT SPEECH: Speech is the connecting link between thought and action; words often obscure the Truth within one's own mind, and often give a false impression to those that hear them. It is important therefore, that one should restrain his speech. It should always be characterized by wisdom and kindness. Undue loudness, over emphasis, and excitement should be avoided. Speech should not be prompted by prejudice, fear, anger, nor infatuation, nor self-interest. Careless, idle and flippant words should be avoided. All invidious distinctions, and discriminations, and dogmatic assertions and negations, should be avoided. Words that are liable to cause hard feelings, such as repeating scandal, mean or angry words, words that deceive or cause misunderstandings, or that tend to arouse passion and lust, should never be uttered. In general speech should be limited to asking and answering necessary questions, and because speech is so easily conditioned by crowd psychology, all formal speech before groups, audiences and crowds should be avoided.

4. RIGHT BEHAVIOR. Besides behaving according to the general rules of propriety, one should be especially careful to keep the Five Precepts:—Not to kill but to practice kindness and harmlessness toward all animate life. Not to steal or covet what does not belong to one, but to practice charity and going without things oneself. Not to commit adultery but to practice purity of mind and sexual self-control. Not to lie but to practice honesty and sincerity in thought, word and deed. Not to partake of alcoholic drinks or drugs, or anything that weakens one's mind-control, but to practice abstinence and self-control.

The reason that Buddha made keeping the Precepts so important was not so much for ethical reasons as for its bearing on mind development and its goal of the attainment of highest cognition and enlightenment. One can not progress toward this high goal if he is living a wicked or self-indulgent life. Even the keeping of the Precepts is only a beginning, for as disciples advance on the Path and undertake the homeless life, there are five other Precepts that must also be observed, namely: Not to use ointments or condiments and not to eat between meals. Not to wear jewelry or expensive clothes, but to practice humility. Not to sleep on soft beds but to resist all tendency to sloth and sleepiness. Not to attend entertainments, dances, concerts or to take part in games of chance; keeping the mind at all times under strict control. Not to have anything to do with money or precious things, but to practice poverty.

5. RIGHT VOCATION. One must not engage in any business or profession that involves cruelty or injustice to either men or animals. His life must be free from acquisitiveness, deceit or dishonesty. He must have nothing to do with war, gambling,

prostitution. It must be a life of service rather than a life of profit and indulgence. For those who wish to devote their entire attention to attaining enlightenment it must be a Homeless Life, free from all dependence or responsibility for property, family life or society.

The ideal life, therefore, for one who has resolved to follow the Noble Path is the Homeless Life. But before one is willing and able to do this, he should come as near to it as possible while living the ordinary life of a householder. Being engaged in the family, social and economical life of the world, he will often find it difficult to do much more than keep the Precepts, but as he advances on the Path he can at least in part observe the other precepts, and as fast as it becomes possible, he can separate from his family and business, and undertake to live more simply and abstemiously and devote more time to his devotional practices. If there is any personal or family property it should gradually be disposed of, so that being free from family and property responsibilities, he may more exclusively undertake the Homeless Life.

In cutting himself off from all relations and responsibilities with the household and worldly life, the Homeless Brother does so with the single purpose of devoting himself to the attainment of enlightenment and Buddhahood, not for selfish reasons but that he may share his attainment and merit with whoever may need his instruction or help. In making his decision to follow the Homeless Life he does so in perfect faith that the Lay Brothers and other Homeless Brothers will take good care of him.

Some may think that this homeless, mendicant life might have been possible and rewarding under the primitive and simple conditions of patriarchical life, but that it would be impossible and foolish and futile under the more complex conditions of our modern, acquisitive, comfort-seeking, excitement-loving conditions, founded as they are upon scientific materialism and enforced by conventions, laws, courts and police. If we count one's comfort and convenience important, it probably is. But are they of first importance? Is not enlightenment, the ending of suffering, the attainment of peace, of far more importance? If they are then any discipline, any deprivation, any inconvenience, any suffering even, is fully warranted. It would be different if there was any easier method known, but Buddha, who was perfectly enlightened, presented it as the only possible Path. Is it not for us who are seeking enlightenment and peace of mind, and who are following Buddha, to have faith in his Noble Path and give it a fair trial? It is noticeable, however, that doubt as to its reasonableness and possibility is not voiced by those who have tried it but by those whose habits and comforts would be curtailed and interfered with.

The Buddha's Dharma is too deep and inclusive to be translated into writing and even less to be completely understood and fully realized by the study of the Scriptures alone. It must be carried out into practice, systematically, earnestly, persistently. The source of all truth is within one's own mind and heart, by the practice of Dhyana, it issues forth in unutterable treasures of compassion and wisdom.

But more significant than that, it is by means of dhyana practised by free minds in undisturbed solitude that the deeper realizations of Truth issue forth spontaneously in unseen spiritual ways to implant intimations and seeds of faith and hope in the minds of others. Thus one, who in the midst of the world's unrest, craving and suffering, has found wisdom and peace, radiates from his being a serenity and compassion and wisdom that emancipates and enlightens others. He is already a Buddha. Being one with Buddha in the blissful peace of Samadhi, he will be radiating compassion and wisdom toward this Saha world of suffering and drawing in to his peace the world's woe. He has learned the secret of the Dharma breathing—going forth, drawing in—in eternal rhythm.

6. RIGHT EFFORT. As one advances along the Path, he needs something more than ethical Precepts to guide and activate his progress, namely, he needs spiritual ideals. To meet this need, the Dharma presents Six Paramitas: (1) Dana Paramita. One should cherish a spirit of unselfish charity and good will that will prompt him to the giving of material gifts for the relief of need and suffering, being especially thoughtful of the needs of the Homeless Brothers, and always remembering that the greatest gift is the gift of the Dharma. (2) Sila Paramita. This same spirit of good-will towards others, the clearing sense of his oneness with all sentient beings, will first prompt him to greater sincerity and fidelity in keeping the Precepts himself for their sakes. Next it will lead him to ignore and forget his own comfort and convenience in offering wherever needed the more intangible gifts of compassion and sympathy and personal service. (3) Kshanti Paramita. This Paramita of humility and patience will help him to bear without complaint, the acts of others without fear or malice or anger. It will help him to bear the common ills of life, the difficulties of the Path and the burden of his karma. It will keep him free from both elation or discouragement as he meets the extremes of success or failure, and will help him to always maintain an equitable spirit of serenity and peacefulness. (4) Virya Paramita. This Paramita of zeal and perseverance will keep one from becoming indolent, careless and changeable. This Paramita is not intended so much to prompt one to outward acts of charity and propaganda as it is wholly concerned with these inner states of mind that affect one's control of mind and attainment of highest cognition and unceasing compassion. The results of behavior are not all outward and apparent; they also affect one's inner habits and dispositions and are surely

registered in one's karma. One does not truly attain until he becomes earnest and faithful in both outward behavior and inner states of mind. Therefore, one should be earnest and persevering and faithful in cherishing right ideas, right purposes, right effort, right devotional practices, right vows. (5) Dhyana Paramita. This Paramita of tranquility prompts one to practice one-pointedness of mind. One should always keep his mind concentrated on the task in hand, undistracted by thoughts of policy, or its relation to one's selfish advantage or comfort. It will often prompt one to a course far different from the old competitive, acquisitive, exciting habits of the worldly life. One must often disregard personal comfort and advantage in an effort to be truly sympathetic and charitable. But so long as one acts from motives of sympathy and kindness the mind will be undisturbed by consequences, and so long as one has no desires, he will be undisturbed by conditions. So long as the mind is free from greed, anger, fear and egoism, it rests in peace. The mind should be trained, therefore, to be concentrated on spiritual ends. (6) Prajna Paramita. This Paramita prompts one to be yielding to the suggestions of wisdom. Thus far we have been considering aspects of spiritual behavior that are more or less under the control of one's own mind, but now in this Wisdom Paramita, we should cease from all self-direction of will and effort and, remaining tranquil in spirit, should yield ourselves in effortless ways, a free channel for the flow of mingled wisdom and compassion.

7. RIGHT MINDFULNESS. This stage of the Noble Path is the culmination of the intellective process and the connecting link with the intuitive process. The goal to be reached is the establishment of a habit of looking at things truthfully, at their meaning and significance rather than at their discriminated appearances, and relations. This is quite different and an advance from the instinctive reactions of the will-to-live, to enjoy, to propagate. It is also quite different and a further advance beyond the habit of considering things by their differences and relations. The senses can give one sensations and perceptions which the lower mind unites and names and discriminates, but they have little value in truth. Things seem real but they are not, they seem good and bad, big and little, right and wrong, but they are not. They often seem necessary but they are not. This consciously discriminated stream of appearances is only food for the higher intellectual mind to digest and assimilate, which by doing enables one to cognize more truthfully the realness or falsity of these first impressions. But the conclusions of the intellectual mind are not final for it can only arrive at a knowledge of relations among things which we think are true. If one is to gain an immediate awareness of Truth, he must transcend the intellectual mind, also. To make the highest and best use of the intellectual mind, however, it is necessary to first practice "recollective mindfulness," which is the Seventh Stage of the Noble Path.

The Seventh Stage is usually translated, Mindfulness. It consists in recollecting and mediating upon the conclusions of the intellectual mind, seeking to understand their true meaning and significance.

8. RIGHT DHYANA. The Eighth Stage of the Noble Path is called in Sanskrit, Dhyana. It is a difficult word to translate into English because of its unfamiliar content of meaning. The nearest term is "concentration of mind" although in Pali this stage is named, "rapture." There are, thus, two aspects to it: the first is its active aspect of concentration, the second is a passive aspect of realization, or rapture. Having tranquillized the mind by the practice of the Seventh Stage of Mindfulness, to practice the Eighth Stage of Dhyana, one should sit quietly with empty and tranquil mind, but with attentive and concentrated mind, keeping the mind fixed on its pure essence. If attention wavers and vagrant thoughts arise, one should humbly and patiently regulate the mind anew, again and again, stopping all thinking, realizing Truth itself.

In doing this breathing plays an important part. Right breathing consists in breathing gently, deliberately, evenly. Think of it as filling the whole body to the top of the head, then gently pressing it downward to the abdomen, let it quietly pass away. Ordinarily we think of its course as being in a straight line, up and down, but it is better to think of it as a circle or loop always moving in one direction—upward to the head, downward to the abdomen, upward to the head and so on. Then forgetting the breathing, think of this circle moving more and more slowly and growing smaller and smaller until it comes to rest at a point between the eyes, the "wisdom eye" of the ancient, between the pineal and pituitary glands of the moderns. Hold the attention there, realizing its perfect balance and emptiness and silence.

At first it may be advisable to hold some simple thought conception in mind, such as counting the out-going breaths, or repeating Buddha's name, or some "koan" puzzle that can only be solved intuitively. But *avoid thinking about them*, keeping the mind fixed on its pure essence. In the primitive days of Buddhism, masters encouraged their disciples to keep in mind the abhorrent and painful aspects of the body, and the empty and transitory nature of all component things; but in later times and Western lands, not liking to think of disgusting and negative things, we more often go to the other extreme and think of the beautiful, noble and rewarding things of life, of wisdom and compassion and purity and solitude and joy and peace. But the right way is to avoid both extremes, keeping the mind fixed on its pure essence, unperturbed by any differentiations whatever.

In the course of this discipline, various psychic effects appear—colors, sounds, visions, raptures, etc., and beginners are apt to become elated or discouraged by them, and to measure their success or failure by their appearing or not appearing. But this is all wrong. All these transitory psychic experiences should be ignored and forgotten; they are only milestones on the path and will be left behind as we move upward toward emancipation and enlightenment and perfect equanimity. The goal is not some entrancing rapture, or indescribable vision; it is highest perfect Wisdom and a great heart of Compassion and blissful Peace. Then ceasing all thought, realize its unceasing calm and silence.

THE FOUR JNANAS, OR HOLY STATES

1. COMPASSION. As the mind progresses towards Enlightenment, it becomes aware of clearing insight and sensitiveness as to the essential unity of all animate life, and there awakens within him a great heart of compassion and sympathy drawing all animate life together, harmonizing differences, unifying all dualisms.

2. JOY. With the disappearing of all sense of difference between self and others and all dualisms, the heart becomes filled with a great rapture of gladness and joy.

3. PEACE. Gradually as the difference between suffering and happiness fades away, this feeling of gladness and joy is transmuted into perfect tranquillity and peacefulness.

4. EQUANIMITY. Gradually even the conception of difference and likeness vanishes and all notions of even joy and peace drop out of sight, and the mind abides in the blissful peace of perfect Equanimity.

THE TEN BODHISATTVA STAGES

For a long time the above Four Holy States engrossed the attention of the Pali Scriptures and Southern Buddhists, but gradually there appeared among Northern Buddhists and in the Sanskrit Scriptures a new vision of the goal of the Buddha's Noble Path. The enjoyment of the Four Raptures for one's self to their culmination in Nirvana, seemed less worthy and satisfying, and meditation on the deeper implications of the Buddha's Dharma, led the great Mahayana Masters to the vision of the Ten Stages of Bodhisattvahood.

1. *Premudita*. Based upon the perfect practice of the Dana Paramita, the Bodhisattva enters the stage of gladness and Joy.

2. *Vimala*. Based upon the Sila Paramita, the Bodhisattva enters upon the perfect practice of purity wherein there is neither joy nor the absence of joy but the mind abides in perfect Peace.

3. *Prabhakari*. Based upon the perfect practice of the Kshanti Paramita, the Bodhisattva enters upon the stage of self-luminous humility in which there is absent even the conception of joy or peace—the stage

of perfect Equanimity, of effortless, self-shining patience.

4. *Archismati*. Based upon the perfect practice of the Virya Paramita, the Bodhisattva enters upon the stage wherein there is conviction and purpose and zeal and determination and perseverance. It is the stage of unceasing, in-drawing, effortless "Energy."

5. *Sudurgaya*. Based upon the perfect practice of the Dhyana Paramita, the Bodhisattva enters upon the overcoming stage of self-mastery and the attainment of tranquillity that is based upon unshakable confidence.

6. *Abhimukhi*. Based upon the perfect practice of the Prajna Paramita, the Bodhisattva enters upon the realization stage of Samadhi. While still being in touch with the passions and discriminations of the Saha world, he turns his mind inward by his faculty of intuitive insight to the realization of the intrinsic emptiness and silence of the mind's pure essence.

7. *Durangama*. The Bodhisattva, having attained highest Samadhi, leaves behind all remembrance of discriminations and wholly abiding in the Mind's Pure Essence, he attains within his mind a "turning about" from which he never again recedes. It is the stage of "far-going."

8. *Acala*. This is the "immovable stage," in which the Bodhisattva attains the Samapatti graces and transcendental powers. Having attained a clear understanding of all inner and outer conditions, his mind accepting things as they are, he neither desires to return to the world or to enter Nirvana. He has no desire or purpose except to live a pure life of *anutpatika-dharma-kshanti-gocaya*—a life of patient submissive acceptance.

9. *Sadhumati*. This is the state of perfect identity with *anuttara-samyak-sambodhi*—highest perfect Wisdom. In this state the Bodhisattva has passed beyond all thought of individuation, or discrimination, or integration; he has passed beyond all dualisms, all incompleteness, and is abiding in perfect balance and equanimity realizing the blissful peace of unceasing Samadhi. But still he retains in mind a memory of the world's ignorance and suffering, unreal as it is in fact, but untainted and undisturbed by it, his mind overflowing with compassion, he goes forth in wisdom and love for its emancipation and enlightenment.

10. *Dharmamaga*. In this highest state, the Bodhisattva becomes wholly identified with the Great Truth Cloud and, like a cloud saturated with Truth and Compassion, he becomes Tathagata, his life perfectly integrated with the lives of all, and goes forth to sprinkle the rain of the Good Law by which the seed of enlightenment takes root in the minds of all sentient beings and in the long last brings them to Buddhahood.

NIRVANA

In the more primitive type of Buddhism as still held in Ceylon and Burma, the end of the Path is the attainment of Arhatship and, when life passes, to Nirvana. What then is Nirvana? The root meaning of the word is the extinguishment of a fire when the fuel is all consumed. That is, in Southern Buddhism, when the fires of earthly passion die down, and the disciple becomes an Arhat, free from all desire, and life passes, he is said to have attained Nirvana, or Parinirvana. In Northern Buddhism, Nirvana has a more philosophic meaning: it means the state where not only the fires of earthly passion have died down and earthly life has passed, but all karmaic desire for individual life is extinguished and the disciple has passed into the unitive life of Buddhahood.

The term *pratyakabuddha,* as used by both schools, means a disciple or an arhat who is selfishly desiring Nirvana for his own satisfaction. Such a disciple, according to the Mahayana school has ceased to follow the Path at the seventh stage of Bodhisattvahood and "passes to his nirvana." But after a Bodhisattva attains the eighth stage there is, thereafter, "no more recension," and he goes on to the attainment of highest perfect Wisdom which constrains him, instead of passing to Nirvana, to return to the Saha world of Ignorance and suffering for its liberation and enlightenment. Hence the saying in the Lankavatara Sutra: "For Buddhas there is no Nirvana."

The question may be asked, how, in this world of ignorance, suffering and death, we are to recognize these "returning" Buddhas and Tathagatas? Please recall that Bodhisattvas as they attain the ninth and tenth stages of Bodhisattvahood lose all individuation as human personalities to become identified with Buddhahood in the Great Truth Cloud, and as "formless" Tathagatas attain boundless potentiality and command of skillful means and transcendental powers of self-mastery and efficiency, and as the integrating principle of Buddhahood, are able to take any form they think best, or to be present wherever there is need to support and to draw all sentient beings to enlightenment and Buddhahood. By our practice of Dhyana, as we attain moments of intuitive Samadhi, we integrate our lives with this ever present Buddha-nature, and when we attain highest perfect Samadhi, we become one with all the Buddhas, enjoying their blissful peace, and becoming able ourselves to return to this Saha-world of suffering for its emancipation and enlightenment.

American and European Buddhists, before they can commonly attain Enlightenment and Buddhahood, will need their own method for practicing the Eighth Stage of the Noble Path, but such a Right Method can not be formulated until the Buddha that is taking form within our own minds, comes. Some among us must first attain the Seventh and Eighth of the Bodhisattva Stages and himself have experienced the Durangama Samadhi of "Far-going" and the Acala Samadhi of "No-recension" before he will be worthy of being employed as a skillful device and convenient means for formulating such a Right Method for practicing the Eighth Stage of the Noble Path. "When He comes, we shall be like Him, for we shall see Him as He is." "Even so come, Lord Maitreya!"

Notes: *Dwight Goddard was a prominent early twentieth-century American Buddhist convert. He prepared a massive compilation of Buddhist texts for an English-speaking audience in* A Buddhist Bible *(1932, 1938). At the end of the volume he compiled a variety of brief statements. Together, these statements outline the Buddhist path and are used by almost all branches of Buddhism. That section of the book is reproduced here along with Goddard's introduction and commentary on the eightfold path (about which different Buddhists have the most marked disagreement).*

*   *   *

Theravada Buddhism

THE NATURE AND PURPOSE (NEO-DHARMA)

The world view of Neo-Dharma can be summarized into four major concepts:

1. The universe is regulated by impartial and unchanging laws.

2. Knowledge of these laws is acquired by insight and by unprejudiced reasoning in the light of one's experiences—not by faith in scriptures or mystical revelations.

3. Moral law, like physical law, is inherent in the workings of nature. Greed, hatred and egotism result in proportionate amounts of unhappiness for one who is responsible for such motivations.

4. This three-dimensional realm of space, time and matter is not the only level of existence. The concrete world of sense perception is a reality, but it is not the only possible dimension of reality.

Since human actions are nearly always the results of their preceding mental conditions, good and evil are best defined as being states of mind rather than types of behavior. Therefore, Neo-Dharma advocates maturation and improvement of one's personality by means of five practices:

1. Development of wisdom and understanding—that is, progressive development of one's intellectual faculties for the sake of better understanding life.

2. Development of insight into one's own personality and awareness of one's conscious and subconscious motivations.

3. Purification of the mind—that is, removal of greed, hatred, fear, egotism, lethargy, etc.

4. Discipline of the mind and body.

5. Cultivation of four states of mind—friendship, kindness, compassion and equanimity.

The beliefs and practices of Neo-Dharma are closer to those of Theravada Buddhism than to any other religious or philosophical institution, and it is from the original teachings of Buddha that the above principles have been derived. "Dharma" is the name for the teaching or gospel

THE NATURE AND PURPOSE (NEO-DHARMA) (continued)

of Buddha, and Neo-Dharma is in agreement with the basic teachings of the Dharma.

Notes: *Founded in 1960, Neo-Dharma is possibly the oldest Theravada Buddhist group in America. This statement attempts to interpret its teachings without recourse to the special vocabulary of Buddhism, which has become more familiar to the public since the early 1960s when this statement was composed.*

* * *

Japanese Buddhism

PROFESSION OF FAITH (BUDDHIST CHURCHES OF AMERICA)

I. We affirm our faith in Amida Buddha, whose infinite light of wisdom and compassion shines on all corners of the universe.

II. We feel deeply that our hearts are dark with ignorance and passions, that even our good acts are tainted with the poison of selfishness and that by ourselves we are incapable of true goodness.

III. We are firmly determined to seek the spirit of Amida's Primal Vow which embraces all and forsakes none, which frees us from the world of impermanence and assures our birth into the Pure Land.

IV. We rely wholeheartedly on Amida's grace and, renouncing all good works contrived by self-power, we depend for our enlightenment on faith in Other Power.

V. We rejoice that this grace is accorded freely and equally to us as well as all other living beings, and this joy pervades our every thought and act.

VI. We recite NAMU AMIDA BUTSU in gratitude for the great Compassionate Vow.

VII. We regard all things with profound thankfulness, and whether suffering or happiness comes to us, we are content in the realization that Amida's grace is always with us.

VIII. We search within ourselves by the light of Amida's Compassion and find that we have drowned in the ocean of selfish desires, that we have lost our way in the pursuit of power and gain. Though we have entered the company of the faithful, we are pained that true joy does not brighten our hearts.

IX. We treasure the Dharma and long to hear it again and again until we are fired with zeal to practice it. We strive to avoid the sinners' way and to model our conduct on that of virtuous people. We desire the company of good friends who follow the same Way, and we wish to be good friends to all who need us. We are resolved to persevere unceasingly in the aspiration for enlightenment and in gratitude for Amida's grace.

X. We resolve to do our daily tasks with the same whole-hearted reverence as if they were religious duties. We devote ourselves to being good members of our families, good workers in our jobs, and good citizens of our country. In this we seek no reward and simply act as our gratitude prompts us.

XI. The power of NAMU AMIDA BUTSU clears the path before us, gives us courage, frees us from evil influences, and brings countless good influences to bless us. It casts the light of infinite love and insight onto the road of our life.

Notes: *Only one Buddhist group has attempted to render its teachings into a creed-like formula. The Buddhist Churches of America is the largest Buddhist organization in North America. Its Profession describes its form of Pure Land Buddhism from Japan.*

* * *

THREE PRINCIPLES (GEDATSU CHURCH OF AMERICA)

We shall observe the teachings of Gedatsu Kongo and pledge utmost effort to live the life of Gedatsu.

We shall endeavour in every way to return appreciation and gratitude for all.

We shall rely upon the Law of Karma and firmly establish peace of mind in our daily lives as it stands.

Notes: *This creed-like statement, the Three Principles, is found in the ritual book of the Gedatsu Church and repeated weekly by members during worship.*

* * *

GOLDEN CHAIN AFFIRMATION, PLEDGE, AND CREED (JODO MISSION)

GOLDEN CHAIN

I am a link in Lord Buddha's golden chain of love that stretches around the world. I must keep my link bright and strong.

I will try to be kind and gentle to every living thing, and protect all who are weaker than myself.

I will try to think pure and beautiful thoughts, to say pure and beautiful words, and to do pure and beautiful deeds, knowing that on what I do now depends my happiness or misery.

May every link in Lord Buddha's golden chain of love become bright and strong, and may we all attain Perfect Peace.

PLEDGE

To the Buddha who promised to be present in His Teaching, We pledge our loyalty and devotion. We dedicate our thoughts, words and deeds to his Service and to the Way of life He laid down for us. We resolve to follow his Example and to have reverence for our religion, respect for our parents and teachers, and love for all forms of life.

THE CREED

We thank the Lord Buddha for showing to us the Way of Freedom.

We will endeavor to walk in His Noble Path every day of our lives.

Notes: *Common to many Japanese Buddhist groups are three brief documents that affirm basic Buddhist beliefs. Rendered into English by the several Japanese-American organizations, the Golden Chain Affirmation, Pledge, and Creed appear in hymnals and ritual books with minor variations in wording. The text reproduced here comes from that used by the Jodo Mission, but it can also be found in the material of such other groups as the Buddhist Churches in America and the Soto [Zen] Mission. These three items are repeated by Japanese Buddhists much as the Apostles' Creed or Nicene Creed are repeated by Christians. In the text of the Golden Chain Affirmation, Nichiren Buddhists add a threefold repetition of their mantra, "Namu Myoho Renge Kyo." The Shingon Mission alters the text of the Creed and terms it The Promise.*

*   *   *

THE PROMISE (SHINGON MISSION)

We thank the Lord Buddha and the Saviour Kobo-daishi for showing us the Way of finding peace. We will endeavor to walk in the Noble Path They showed us, everyday of our lives.

Namu Sakyamuni Butsu

Namu Daishi Henjo Kongo

Notes: *The text of what is termed The Creed by other Japanese Buddhist groups is called The Promise in the songbook of the Shingon Buddhists. It varies significantly from the standard text used by other Japanese Buddhists in its addition of a reference to Shingon Buddhism's founder, Kobo-daishi, who is ranked with Buddha.*

*   *   *

Chinese Buddhism

THE ORDER OF THE UNIVERSE AND THE TWELVE THEOREMS OF THE UNIQUE PRINCIPLE (EAST WEST FOUNDATION)

THE ORDER OF THE UNIVERSE

1. That which has a face has a back. (Negation of the law of identity and contradiction in space.)

2. That which has a beginning has an end. (Negation of the above in time.)

3. There is nothing identical in the universe. (Negation of the law of identity.)

4. The bigger the face, the bigger the back. (Negation of the law of the exclusive middle.)

5. All antagonisms are complementary, for example, beginning-end, front-back, justice-injustice, freedom-slavery, happiness-unhappiness, rise-fall, expansion-contraction, love-hate. (Negation of formal logic.)

6. All antagonisms can be classified in two categories—Yin and Yang—and they are complementary. (Foundation of universal dialectic logic.)

7. Yin and Yang are the two arms of Infinity, Absolute Oneness, God, or the Infinite pure expansion.

TWELVE THEOREMS OF THE UNIQUE PRINCIPLE

1. Yin and Yang are the two poles of the infinite pure expansion.

2. Yin and Yang are produced infinitely, continuously, and forever from the infinite pure expansion itself.

3. Yin is centrifugal; Yang is centripetal. Yin, centrifugal, produces expansion, lightness, cold, etc. Yang, centripetal, produces constriction, weight, heat, light, etc.

4. Yin attracts Yang; Yang attracts Yin.

5. All things and phenomena are composed of Yin and Yang in different proportions.

6. All things and phenomena are constantly changing their Yin and Yang components. Everything is restless.

7. There is nothing completely Yin or completely Yang. All is relative.

8. There is nothing neuter. There is always Yin or Yang in excess.

9. Affinity or force of attraction between things is proportional to the difference of Yin and Yang in them.

10. Yin expels Yin; Yang expels Yang. Expulsion or attraction between two things Yin or Yang is in inverse proportion to the difference of their Yin or Yang force.

11. Yin produces Yang; Yang produces Yin in the extremity.

12. Everything is Yang at its center and Yin at its periphery (surface).

Notes: *These two sets of statements summarize the basic teachings of Michio Kushi, founder of the East West Foundation. The principles, drawn from Chinese philosophy, also form the basis for the natural medical system, macrobiotics, which Kushi advocates.*

*   *   *

Tibetan Buddhism

FUNDAMENTAL PRINCIPLES (PANSOPHIC INSTITUTE)

1) The philosophic dualism so deeply ingrained in the mind of Man (responsible for Man's original mental

development) is today seen to be only an illusion. There are no absolutes of good and evil, or any other dichotomies.

2) However, Man possesses inherent qualities of honesty, justice and courage. Without needing to fear awesome Deities, it is possible to apply these qualities to the basic ethical code without hypocrisy, thereby ceasing to cause harm to oneself or other beings.

3) It is only reasonable to strive to live according to these values, and to desire such conduct from others. But to discipline the self it is necessary to defeat greed, anger and sloth, Man's three main enemies to progress.

4) Life is a process of evolution, both of physical form and of individual spirit or consciousness. By the defeat of greed, anger and sloth, and the cultivation of honesty, justice and courage, the evolution of Mankind as a whole and of the individual is hastened.

5) If the emotions are mastered and one's mind is made calm, efforts can be directed toward the increase of awareness. This results in an expanded understanding of life and one's relationship to the cosmos and the all-pervading Divine Consciousness which ensouls it.

6) These principles represent the Path from the darkness of spiritual ignorance to the state of Enlightenment (Illumination). They are symbolized as a reality through the lives of humanity's great spiritual Masters. Each individual can develop the innate divinity in his or her own nature.

7) Such development brings FREEDOM from karma or fate, the results of previous thoughts, desires and actions. If one who is so freed then chooses to work for the similar freedom of others, the evolution of Mankind (and through Man all life) is hastened. This is the Bodhisattva or Savior Ideal: the dedication to assist in the eventual Enlightenment of all beings.

Notes: *The principles of the Pansophic Institute attempt to state the basics of Tibetan Buddhism without resorting to the technical Tibetan terminology commonly employed by followers.*

* * *

Shinto and the Japanese New Religions

DAILY TEACHING (KONKO KYO)

1. On this day, pray with a sincere heart. The divine favor depends on your own heart.

2. Remember the universe is your eternal home.

3. Have faith. To have faith is to keep Kami in your heart.

4. Since man is the master of all things, let his faith be in harmony with the way of the universe.

5. Food is bestowed as a blessing for the life of man.

6. Instead of worrying, have faith in Kami.

7. Pray for health. Make your body strong, for it is the basis of all things.

8. With a grateful heart, receive your food.

9. Suffering is a divine favor in disguise.

10. To have faith is to live fully day to day.

11. All men are brothers as children of Kami.

12. A peaceful home is rooted in faith.

13. The birth of a child derives not from your own strength, but from the blessing of Kami.

14. As you love your own children, understand Kami's love for you.

15. Do not give yourself over to selfish desires.

16. Overeating and overdrinking is the cause of hunger.

17. Pray first and then seek treatment for your illness; then, you will receive the divine favor.

18. You need not practice religious austerities, just pursue your occupation diligently.

19. Faith is not simply listening to words of instructions; let it be an expression from the heart.

20. Treat every man with respect. If you treat any man lightly, you will not receive the divine favor.

21. A heart of love is the heart of Kami.

22. Now hear the sound of the opening of the universe and be awakened.

23. Training in faith is as gradual as the progress of your studies.

24. Maintain your faith even under favorable conditions.

25. Open your spiritual eyes without depending on your physical eyes.

26. Your lifetime is a training period of faith.

27. You should not break the bond with Kami. Kami will keep the bond with you.

28. Enrich your faith. You must have faith now and always.

29. You should do whatever you do with sincerity.

30. Faith is like a sacred fire. Hand it down from generation to generation, without losing it.

31. Without faith, the world would be dark.

* * *

KYO JI (FUNDAMENTAL TEACHINGS) (MAHIKARI OF AMERICA)

1. The three spiritual worlds, the Divine, the Astral, and the present (Physical) worlds, are not subjects pertaining to ideology and philosophy.

   They, in reality exist and are closely connected as air is to life. They are infinite and omnipresent sources of spiritual energy and of the emanation of Divine Light.

Hence, they are above religion, beyond the influence of races or religious dominations made by human intelligence. They are determined by the Divine Law which is the arrangement for eternal flourishment of the universe and are full of wonder.

Motosu Hajimari Kamu, the Creator, is the source of Power which unites and administers all for the eternal flourishment of His creatures. He is the master of mankind, all spirits and materials.

He is the source of Spiritual Wisdom, and manifests as the Cosmic Will, Light, and Absolute Power to shine upon the universe.

Moses, Buddha, Jesus, Confusis, and Mencius were the holy messengers of God, Su no Kami. There are no religious denominations in the Divine World.

2. It is the great destiny for mankind to build a holy century of Divine (heavenly) Civilization that is to come by complying with His great love and the Divine understanding of truth. This is the supreme order for mankind.

Regardless of religious denominations, all man should practice what is written in this book at all times, as this is the origin of the "practice of truth".

This righteous way of devotion to Su no Kami is not intended for Mahikari Bunmei Kyodan only, but for all human beings. This is *SU-KYO* (to respect the original Divine Teachings).

3. All seemingly truthful and pseudo-teachings have come to an end as well as salvation by a weak, white, passive light. Now the time has come to perceive quietly and directly, the true light of God and to master the Divine Light.

Experience this for yourself because it is the first appearance of the Divine Law prophesied by Buddha and Jesus.

This is the history of mankind and the sublime moment of religious renaissance. Present teachings are old and deteriorating or they are disguised or provisional.

The dawning of the Spiritual Civilization has come . . . a true, new civilization for the restoration of theocracy and the achievement of the Divine Administration.

This will be the final opportunity for the door of heaven to open up for mankind.

This is an era for SUMEI GODO (unification of the five great religious) and YOSUKA (to transmit the power of Su no Kami). It is time for us to become evangelists for the Divine teaching.

4. The earth is originally one; the world is one; the origin of mankind is one; the root of all religious is one.

Become heralds for the coming civilization of

MI RO KU, ME SHI A
5 6 7, 3 4 5

the Cross (+ = Kami, God) civilization and SANJUJI (triple cross) civilization.

Grow as a child of God and become a *TANE BITO* (seed person) for the coming Holy Century. Practice MAHIKARI NO WAZA and cultivate your soul. This is the secret Art to overcome religious divisions. Elevate your soul and master *SEIHO* (Divine Theory) obediently.

Become an instrument for the Divine Administration and be His disciples. This will be the most fruitful epoch for mankind.

5. The time for mankind to trifle with ideological existence of God is over. Time of meaningless prayers are over. It is time for mankind to realize the pragmatism of *SU KYO* (to respect the original Divine Teachings) in their daily living.

These prayers are the foundation for all religions. God allows all human beings to participate in His Plan through prayer, practicing and performing Mahikari no waza.

This is a marvelous method to revive the essence of all teachings and religions of the world. It is possible to actualize perfect health; free from disease and poverty and to enjoy harmonious love and peace. All mankind will be profoundly moved after witnessing such miracles.

It is man's responsibility, a supreme duty to God, to create a world where each and every man may enjoy true happiness.

* * *

GOREIGEN (DIVINE MAXIM) (SHINREIKYO)

The path to God as taught by Shinreikyo is nothing else but the universal law which applies to the three existences of past, present and future.

All that takes place in the universe is based on this unique principle. True happiness and lasting prosperity become a reality to those who abide by this law, while the fate of all earthly things is ultimate destruction if this rigid law is resisted. Disaster brought by disease and calamity is no exception. Therefore, the divine teachings of Shinreikyo are the only teachings that every living person should pursue. All that is asked of its followers is to practise the teachings of Shinreikyo with deep faith.

Chapter 22
Unclassified Christian Churches

BASIS OF FELLOWSHIP (CHRISTIAN CATHOLIC CHURCH)

FIRST — That we recognize the infallible inspiration and sufficiency of the Holy Scriptures as the rule of faith and practice.

SECOND — That we recognize that no persons can be members of the Church who have not repented of their sins and have not trusted in Christ for Salvation.

THIRD — That such persons must also be able to make a good profession, and declare that they do know, in their own hearts, that they have truly repented, and are truly trusting Christ, and have the witness, in a measure, of the Holy Spirit.

FOURTH — That all other questions of every kind shall be held to be matters of opinion and not matters that are essential to Church unity.

Notes: *The Christian Catholic Church is best known for the emphasis upon spiritual healing practiced by its founder, John Alexander Dowie. This brief statement is reflective of the ecumenical spirit of the church.*

*   *   *

DOCTRINE (CHRISTIAN UNION)

Seven cardinal principles are considered essential to the organization.

I. The Oneness of the Church of Christ.

II. Christ the Only Head.

III. The Bible the Only Rule of Faith and Practice.

IV. Good Fruits the Only Condition of Fellowship.

V. Christian Union Without Controversy.

VI. Each Local Church Governs Itself.

VII. Partisan Political Preaching Discountenanced.

In addition to these principles the position taken by The Christian Union on the fundamental doctrines of the Word of God is as follows:

1. The Bible is infallible, the inspired and authoritative Word of God.

2. There is one God, eternally existent in three persons—Father, Son, and Holy Spirit.

3. We believe in: the Deity of Christ, His conception by the Holy Spirit and His virgin birth; His sinless life, miracles, and vicarious and atoning death; His bodily resurrection and ascension to the right hand of the Father; His personal return in power and glory.

4. Salvation is wholly of grace but conditioned upon repentance toward God and faith toward Jesus Christ. Regeneration and justification follow the meeting of these conditions.

5. The Holy Spirit indwells believers, gives power for service and holy living, guides into truth, produces the fruits of Christian character; and carries on toward perfection the sanctification of believers.

6. We believe in the resurrection to immortality of the bodies of believers at the return of the Lord Jesus which shall be changed so they shall be literal, spiritual, and immortal bodies like unto Christ's own glorious body.

7. We believe that man was created by God and not by any accidental or spontaneous, or self propagated occurrence, action, method, or process. As a result of his fall, death passed upon all men and sin entered into the world. Therefore condemnation rests upon each person who has reached the age and development with which comes accountability before God, and he is lost forever, except he be born again.

8. The church of Christ is composed of all Spirit regenerated believers.

Thus it can be seen that The Christian Union is committed to a conservative and fundamental interpretation of the Christian Faith.

Notes: *The Christian Union has as its main objectives: 1) the promotion of fellowship among God's people; 2) the proclamation of the gospel at home and abroad; and 3) the declaration of the "whole Council of God" for the edification of believers. In keeping with these goals, the doctrinal principles are held to a summary of the fundamentals. Emphasis is placed on Christianity as a life to be lived.*

OUR MESSAGE [FAMILY OF LOVE (CHILDREN OF GOD)]

I. OUR SAMPLE PROVES OUR SERMON

1. WE ARE HERE TO PREACH NOT A 50% OR A 70%, BUT A TOTAL, 100% LIVING FOR GOD: Living in a totally new society, loving one another and having the truth. Our message will go over the whole world. They have heard from the church that Jesus saves, but they don't want any part of churchianity. But they will hear about Jesus from you because you will be living it.

2. YOU WILL BE A LIVING EXAMPLE OF THE TRUTH. You are preaching it in the greatest way of preaching—by living it! Jesus' last prayer for His disciples was that "they may be one . . . that the world may believe . . . and know that Thou (God) hath sent Me." In other words, Jesus was saying that this unity with each other and God is the sample that will prove to the world the reality of His Message.

3. IT'S TRUE WHEN IT COMES TO THE FINAL SHOWDOWN THAT ONLY THE MIRACLE-WORKING POWER OF THE HOLY SPIRIT of God Himself can really do the job of winning their hearts but they must see Him doing it through us first of all! They must see this miracle-working power at work in our lives, as a genuine living sample and proof that the sermon can happen!

4. JESUS NOT ONLY PREACHED HIS MESSAGE, BUT HE LIVED IT! He was not only the Living Word, the Sermon, but He was also the Living Work, the Sample. For He said He had not only "spoken unto them", but He also had "done the works that none other man did."

5. HOWEVER, DON'T PUT THE CART BEFORE THE HORSE, THE SAMPLE BEFORE THE SERMON: remember, the words are the cause and the kids and Colonies are the effect!

6. COLONY LIVING IS NOT OUR MAIN MESSAGE. It's just a sample that proves the words.

7. WITNESSING HIS WONDER-WORKING WORDS TO THE WORLD IS OUR MAIN TASK, and our main motive should be to obey God and get the message out. But remember, the sample sells the sales talk. You are product and proof that it works! So, "Let your light so shine before men that they may see your good works, and glorify your Father which is in heaven."

II. OUR MESSAGE OF LOVE AND DISCIPLESHIP

8. OUR MESSAGE OF LOVE IS TAKEN FROM OUR REVOLUTIONARY HAND-BOOK, THE BIBLE, and is simply that "God so loved the world that He gave His only begotten Son (Jesus), that whosoever believeth in Him should not perish but have everlasting life."

9. "FOR ALL HAVE SINNED and come short of the glory of God." "There is none righteous, no, not one." "All we like sheep have gone astray, and the Lord hath laid on Him the iniquity of us all."

10. "THE WAGES OF SIN IS DEATH, BUT THE GIFT OF GOD IS ETERNAL LIFE through Jesus Christ our Lord." "Not by works of righteousness which we have done, but according to His mercy He saved us."

11. "FOR BY GRACE ARE YE SAVED, THROUGH FAITH, and that not of yourselves; it is the gift of God: not of works, lest any man should boast." "If we confess our sins, He is faithful and just to forgive us." "Believe on the Lord Jesus Christ, and thou shalt be saved."

12. "YE SHALL RECEIVE POWER after that the Holy Ghost is come upon you, and ye shall be witnesses unto Me."

13. WE ALSO BELIEVE THAT ALL THOSE WHO WISH TO BE JESUS' DISCIPLES SHOULD: "Go . . . into all the world and preach the Gospel to every creature!" "Go out into the highways and hedges and compel them to come in!" "Sell all that thou hast and give to the poor . . . and come follow Me!"

14. "HE THAT FORSAKETH NOT ALL THAT HE HATH, CANNOT BE MY DISCIPLE." "Seek ye first the Kingdom of God and His righteousness and all these things shall be added unto you." "Warn the wicked of his wicked way to save his life."

15. "ALL THAT BELIEVED WERE TOGETHER AND HAD ALL THINGS COMMON." "And they continued steadfastly in the Apostles' doctrine and fellowship, and in breaking of bread, and prayers." "And daily in the temple and in every house, they ceased not to teach and preach Jesus Christ."

16. SO THERE'S NOTHING NEW ABOUT OUR MESSAGE—GOD'S MESSAGE THROUGH US! IT'S THE SAME MESSAGE JESUS PREACHED, the same message His disciples preached; but they not only preached it—they also lived it, just like we're doing. That's the difference! The scribes and pharisees were preaching it, but they weren't practising it.

17. THAT'S THE DIFFERENCE BETWEEN THE CHURCHES AND US! Jesus said to the common people, "The scribes and pharisees (the church leaders) sit in Moses' seat: All therefore they bid you observe, that observe and do, but do not ye after their works: for they say and do not." And that goes for today's churches too!

III. OUR MESSAGE OF DOOM AND JUDGMENT AGAINST THIS WORLD'S SYSTEMS

18. IN EVERY AGE GOD HAD HIS LAST PROPHET who gave them God's last words. Today they are being given it through us, before God gives it to them.

19. THE MESSAGE OF JEREMIAH, the Prophet of Doom, was revealed to us in December of 1961,

when I was very ill, and God said this was to be our message from now on—the Doomsday, End-Time Warning Message. We are to become as a red flashing warning light to the World, a sombre warning of serious danger ahead.

20. AS WITH JEREMIAH, GOD HAS "SET THEE OVER THE NATIONS and over the kingdoms to root out, and to pull down, and to destroy and to throw down their idols with the spiritual weapons of God's Word) and to build and to plant (God's spiritual kingdom in the hearts of men)."

21. "AND I (GOD) WILL UTTER MY JUDG-MENTS AGAINST THEM (through you) touching all their wickedness who have forsaken Me and have burned incense unto other gods and worshipped the works of their own hands." "But if they will not obey (our warnings), I will utterly pluck up and destroy that nation, saith the Lord!"

22. GOD HAS ALSO CALLED US, EVEN AS HE DID THE PROPHET EZEKIEL, TO BE WATCHMEN unto the House of Israel, those who were supposed to be His Church; therefore we're to hear His Words and give them warning from the Lord.

23. AS HE TOLD EZEKIEL, GOD HAS TOLD US: "Son of man, I have made thee a watchman unto the House of Israel: therefore hear the word at My mouth and give them warning from Me. When I say unto the wicked, Thou shalt surely die; and thou givest him not warning, nor speakest to warn the wicked from his wicked way, to save his life; the same wicked man shall die in his iniquity; but his blood will I require at thine hand. Yet if thou warn the wicked, and he turn not from his wickedness, nor from his wicked way, he shall die in his iniquity; but thou hast delivered thy soul."

24. OUR MAIN WITNESS (WHICH INCLUDES BOTH OUR WAY OF LIFE AND OUR SER-MON) IS THAT WE ARE AGAINST THE SYS-TEM; that is 95% of our witness. It is a damning witness against them. By the System, I'm not talking about the legal laws—I'm talking about the damnable Satanic principles of which the damned System is built, its laws of selfishness and do your own thing and keep on living just as you did, refusing any change.

IV. A TWO-FOLD MESSAGE

25. OUR MESSAGE IS TO "FEAR GOD AND GIVE GLORY TO HIM; for the hour of His Judgment is come: and worship Him that made Heaven, and earth, and the sea, and the fountains of waters."

26. IN OTHER WORDS, WE TELL PEOPLE TO FOLLOW GOD OR RECEIVE HIS JUDG-MENTS. So in a way our message is two-fold: against the rebellious System and for God's Sheep.

27. OUR MAJOR JOB IS TO STAND UP AS GOD'S STRONGEST WITNESSES before both the Church and the whole world and to explain to them what's happening and to lead and encourage and feed God's Children to the very End!

28. WE'RE THE MIGHTY ARMY OF CHRISTIAN SOLDIERS FIGHTING A RELENTLESS WAR FOR THE TRUTH AND LOVE OF GOD, AGAINST THE CONFUSION OF BABYLON— the anti-God, anti-Christ Systems of this world, whether Godless educations, Christless religions, vicious economics, or the hellish wars of the traditions, boundaries and prejudices of selfish, greedy and Godless man.

V. WHY WE PREACH REVOLUTION, NOT REFORMATION

29. IT IS IMPOSSIBLE, AS JESUS SAID, TO RE-FORM THE OLD, FOR THEY WILL NOT ACCEPT IT and in the attempt the bottle will be broken and the contents lost.

30. THE OLD RELIGIOUS AND ECONOMIC SYS-TEMS CANNOT BE PATCHED UP, for they are tattered, threadbare, and rotten and must be cast upon the fires of His Judgment that He may create "a new Heaven and a new earth" in which "old things are passed away and all things are become new."

31. SO IT IS ALWAYS NECESSARY TO ROOT OUT, PULL DOWN, DESTROY and throw down the old in order to build and to plant the new; there just isn't room for both.

32. THERE IS NO SUCH THING AS THE PEACE-FUL COEXISTENCE OF GOOD AND EVIL! I came not to bring peace, but a sword! One or the other has to conquer. One or the other has to be destroyed that the other might live. Ye cannot serve God and Mammon. "Ye cannot serve two masters."

33. YE CANNOT BELONG TO BOTH THE SYS-TEM AND THE REVOLUTION, the forces of reaction and the forces of change! It's impossible: as Jesus said, you'll either hate the one, and love the other, or hold to the one and despise the other. You'll either stay in the System or drop out. There's no such thing as hanging somewhere in between, suspended between Heaven and Hell in some kind of compromiser's limbo!

34. YOU'VE GOTTA DROP OUT IF YOU'RE GON-NA LIVE, or else you'll die with the old, and the worn out System will collapse on top of you!

35. HOWEVER, WE ARE NOT TALKING ABOUT PHYSICAL, VIOLENT REVOLUTION that doesn't do anything but a lot of damage, and that doesn't change the hearts of the System one tiny little bit, but just creates another System where things are just as bad, if not worse.

36. WE'RE TALKING ABOUT A SPIRITUALLY VIOLENT REVOLUTION that absolutely rends your heart right out completely and gives you a new Spirit, the Holy Ghost of God! "A new heart also will I give you, and a new spirit will I put within you."

OUR MESSAGE [FAMILY OF LOVE (CHILDREN OF GOD)] (continued)

37. WHEN JESUS WENT SAYING, "REPENT, for the Kingdom of heaven is at hand". He was saying "Revolt, revolute, have a Revolution!"

38. THE BIBLICAL WORD "REPENT" COMES FROM THE GREEK WORD "METANOIA", which means a complete change of mind or a total turning around and going in the opposite direction or to "revolute"—so repentance is a revolution. It means to change your direction—change everything.

39. CHANGE YOUR WAY OF LIVING—not just your so-called heart, but your whole life and the way you live and the way you work! That's a Revolution!

40. THAT'S WHAT JESUS PREACHED! And that's the kind of Revolution we've got! For, "the Kingdom of Heaven suffereth violence, and the violent take it by force."

VI. DELIVERING THE MESSAGE

41. THE TRUTH FEEDS SOME AND CHOKES OTHERS. To some we're like a lion; to others, like a lamb. To the wolves we're as lions; to the sheep we're as lambs. There are times to roar and times to bleat. Just please, pray God you'll know the difference!

42. HIS WORD NEVER CHANGES, Christ doesn't change, but God keeps moving every day.

43. IT MAY BE THE SAME MESSAGE, BUT IT IS VARIED EVERY DAY TO SUIT THE NEED and adapt to the situation. As Paul himself conceded, we must become all things to all men in order that we might win some.

44. THEREFORE, THERE ARE CERTAINLY DIFFERENCES IN APPROACHES—To the Roman as a Roman, to the Jew as a Jew, to the Greek as a Greek, and to the Japanese as a Japanese. It's a matter of communication in order to make our message understandable and our witness comprehensible and our lives interpretable in the terms, language and even gestures that they understand.

45. BUT LIKE THE MESSAGE OF EVERY TRUE PROPHET OF GOD, THE TRUTH OFTEN HURTS, and no matter how lovingly you present it, some people may resent it bitterly and blame you for what God said! So use lots of love and wisdom. Be very cautious and try not to take one side or the other—we're on God's side!

46. SOME OF THESE LETTERS ARE HIGHLY CONTROVERSIAL. But they have to get out; people have to know the truth, and we have to obey the Lord! But you don't have to convince them. Leave the decision to them.

VII. REACTION TO OUR MESSAGE

47. A. ENEMIES: FOR A WHILE WE WILL BE BIG NEWS AND GET PATTED ON THE BACK FOR OUR GOOD WORK converting the radicals and dopers, but soon they will realise what a threat we are to their children and to their System. We are a kind of Communist that their kids have not been conditioned against—Christian Communists!

48. THEY CAN TELL THEIR KIDS THAT WE ARE WRONG and evil and a Marxist Communist front, but their kids will know better.

49. THE COMMUNISTS TODAY SAY "JESUS WAS A VIOLENT REVOLUTIONARY." This is the ammunition that the leaders of Moloch (education) and Baal (church) will use against us to link us with the violent, physical revolutionaries and turn their followers, the common people, against us; and eventually their leaders will pull a Mt 12:14: "Then the Pharisees went out and held a council against him, how they might destroy him".

50. BUT ALL THOSE THAT DO LIFT EVEN A FINGER AGAINST ONE OF THE HAIRS OF THY HEADS SHALL PERISH. So ridiculous are those nincompoops who fight God's Children.

51. B. VAST MAJORITY (silent majority): The thousands to whom He had preached, had healed, and fed were seldom to be counted on for loyalty or faithfulness or genuine discipleship.

52. THE VAST MAJORITY COULDN'T CARE LESS; they're not even interested, except when you attract their attention momentarily, as Jesus did with His miracles.

53. THE VAST MAJORITY ARE ALWAYS WRONG, that is, in the world at large! And they can usually easily be swayed by a very wicked minority of enemies, as the religious leaders did when they persuaded the crowds that Jesus, Who fed and healed them, should be crucified. They'll do it to us someday too, and, in a measure, already have upon occasion.

54. C. SHEEP: DURING JESUS' 3 1/2 YEARS OF PUBLIC MINISTRY THE NUMBER OF TRUE DISCIPLES OR GENUINE FOLLOWERS WAS FEW—about 12 to 70, to be exact. The true followers, the true disciples, willing to forsake all, truly follow His teaching and truly obey His Words will always be the infinitesimal minority. "Because straight is the gate and narrow is the way which leadeth unto Life and few there be that find it."

55. VERY FEW MEN ARE SO IDEALISTIC AS TO BE WILLING TO GIVE UP THEIR OWN SINS IN ORDER TO PLEASE GOD that they might try to save their fellowman! —Only a few! God help us to find those few!

56. A PROPHECY: FOR THEY CRY UNTO ME AND CALL UPON ME IN THEIR DISTRESS AND THEIR HUNGER, for they are as sheep having no shepherd and they are scattered abroad throughout all the earth.

57. THEREFORE, I HAVE GIVEN THEM A SHEPHERD that shall guide them into the fold of the True Shepherd.

58. MY VOICE SHALL THEY HEED THROUGH MY SERVANT DAVID! For My sheep hear My

Voice and know My Voice, and they follow Me, and the Voice of the stranger they will not follow.

Notes: *Originally issued in 1975, this document summarizes the message, without mention of the more controversial teachings, of this early Jesus People group. Emphasis is placed upon the apocalyptic aspect of the message, with little hope being offered for the world and a call for revolution. Scriptural references and cross references to other writings of the Children of God have been deleted.*

* * *

THE AFFIRMATIONS (FREE CHURCH OF BERKELEY)

God is not dead.

God is bread.

The bread is rising.

Bread means revolution.

God means revolution.

Murder is no revolution.

Revolution is love.

Win with love.

The radical Jesus is winning.

The world is coming to a beginning.

The whole world is watching.

Organize for a new world.

Wash off your brother's blood.

Burn out the mark of the Beast.

Join the freedom meal.

Plant the people's park.

The asphalt church is marching.

The guerrilla church is recruiting.

The people's church is striking.

The submarine church is surfacing.

The war is over.

The war is over.

The war is over.

The Liberated Zone is at hand.

Notes: *The Free Church of Berkeley was an expression of the radical Protestant Christianity of the 1960s. It developed its own liturgy, one part of which was the Freedom Meal, the church's equivalent to the Lord's Supper. The Affirmations is taken from that liturgy and serves as a poetic summary of the church's activist stance.*

* * *

ARTICLES OF FAITH (MOUNT ZION SANCTUARY)

I. THE SCRIPTURES.

We believe the Holy Bible contains the divine revelation of the eternal GOD; that it is the expression of His will to man; written by holy men of old, divinely moved and inspired by the Holy Spirit; and is the divinely appointed standard and guide to our faith and practice. II. Peter 1:20-21; II. Tim. 3:15-17; Rom. 16:25-27; Psa. 119:105.

II. THE TRUE GOD.

We believe there is one God—eternal, immortal, invisible, omniscient, omnipotent and omnipresent: the Supreme and Omnipotent Creator and Ruler of the universe. Gen. 1 and 2; Psa. 90:2; I. Tim. 1:17; Eph. 4:6.

III. THE LORD JESUS CHRIST.

We believe that Jesus is the Christ, the son of the living God; that He was in the beginning with God; that all things were created by Him, and without Him was not anything made that was made. John 1:1-14; Heb. 1:1-3; Luke 3:22; Matt. 16:15-16; John 17:1, 20-26.

IV. INCARNATION AND VIRGIN BIRTH.

We believe that Christ, the Son, was in the beginning with God, the Father, and became, by voluntary consent party to the marvelous plan of redemption, conceived by the determinate counsel and foreknowledge of God before the world was; and that the child, Jesus, immaculately conceived of the Holy Spirit and born of the Virgin Mary, was the physical body thus prepared for the incarnation of the Christ, the Son of the living God, manifested in the flesh, that He might destroy the works of the devil, and do the will of God on the earth, in executing the plan of redemption for fallen man. Isa. 9:6; Luke 1:26-38; Heb. 10:5-7; I. John 3:8.

V. THE HOLY SPIRIT.

We believe that the Holy Spirit, the Comforter, proceeding from God, the Father, is the executive power of God, by which the Church is born again, taught, instructed, inspired, energized and empowered for its God-given ministry; and that every believer is commanded to be filled therewith. John 14:15-18; 15:26; 16:7-11; 3:3-8; Eph. 5:18; Acts 1:8; Luke 24:49; Acts 2:1-4.

VI. THE FALL OF MAN.

We believe man was created holy, and in his holy estate enjoyed the personal presence and fellowship of his Creator with unspeakable Edenic happiness; but by willful and voluntary transgression, he fell from his Edenic bliss, and under just condemnation was banished therefrom, to suffer the death of separation from God, and become a bond-slave to Satan, without defense or excuse. Gen. 3:1-24; Rom. 5:12-19; I. Cor. 15:21-22.

VII. THE ATONEMENT.

We believe in the sacrificial death and vicarious atonement of the Lord Jesus Christ, for man's sin; that "He was wounded for our transgressions, He was bruised for our iniquities: the chastisement of our peace was upon Him; and with His stripes we are healed;" that, "being justified freely by His blood, we are saved from wrath through Him." Rom. 5:9; Isa. 53:5; John 3:14-17; I. Peter 2:24; 3:18; Heb. 9:28.

VIII. THE RESURRECTION AND ASCENSION

We believe in the triumphant bodily resurrection of Jesus Christ, and His glorious ascension with the same body, glorified, into heaven, to the right hand of the Majesty on high, where He ever lives as our High Priest, making

ARTICLES OF FAITH (MOUNT ZION SANCTUARY) (continued)

intercession for us. Matt. 28:1-6; Luke 24:36-48; Heb. 7:22-28; Acts 1:9-11; Eph. 4:8-10.

IX. JUSTIFICATION.

We believe Jesus Christ was delivered for our offenses, and raised for our justification; that being justified by faith in His death and resurrection, we have peace with God through our Lord Jesus Christ; by Whom we have now received the atonement. Rom. 4:25; 5:1-9.

X. SANCTIFICATION AND HOLINESS.

We believe it is the privilege of every believer to be sanctified wholly, spirit, soul and body; that we are sanctified only in the proportion that we live and obey the Word of God; that we are sanctified and made holy as we obey the Truth, "Thy Word is Truth." We are commanded to be holy as He is holy; for "without holiness no man shall see the Lord." I. Thess. 5:23; John 17:17-19; Lev. 20:7; Matt. 5:48; Heb. 12:14.

XI. DIVINE HEALING.

We believe divine healing is a part of the atonement, and is a Gospel privilege, which has never been withdrawn from the believing Church. Isa. 53:6; Matt. 8:17; Heb. 13:8; Matt. 28:18-20.

XII. WATER BAPTISM.

We believe that immersion, which symbolizes death, burial and resurrection of the believer, is the only Scriptural mode of water baptism; demonstrated by the baptised of our Lord Jesus Christ — being baptised in this manner; leaving us an example that we should follow in His steps. Rom. 6:3-5; Matt. 3:13-17: I. Peter 2:21.

XIII. THE SABBATH DAY.

We believe the Seventh Day is still the sabbath of the Lord our God; that He has never changed, nor authorized anyone else to change His holy day from the Seventh to any other day. We find no authority anywhere in the Scriptures for the first day observance, nor any evidence of the first day resurrection, upon which the erroneous claim for the first day Sabbath observance is based. Psa. 89:34; Deut. 4:2; Prov. 30:6; Rev. 22:14, 18, 19.

XIV. SECOND COMING.

We believe the second coming of our Lord Jesus is very near; that it will be personal, literal, pre-millennial; that He is coming to reign on the earth; and that the saints will reign with Him a thousand years; and of the increase of His government and peace there will be no end. Acts 1:9-11; James 5:7-8; Rev. 1:7; Isa. 9:6-7; Rev. 20:4; 5:10.

XV. THE CHRISTIAN CHURCH.

We believe the Christian Church, built upon the foundation of the Apostles and Prophets, and Jesus Christ the Chief Cornerstone, is a body of born again believers, who follow Christ, as their perfect example in all things; and His teachings as their infallible guide; and are as thoroughly detached and separate from the world as was He! walking in holiness of life and character; that its work and ministry is supported financially, on the Bible plan of tithes and freewill offerings. Num. 18:20-21; Mal. 3:8-12.

XVI. PLEDGE TO FEDERAL GOVERNMENT.

We believe that the Constitution of the United States is largely, if not entirely, an inspired document; and we pledge our loyalty to the Constitutional Government of the U.S.A., and to non-combatant service in time of war. Rom. 13:1-10; Ex. 20:13.

*   *   *

Homosexually Oriented Churches

DECLARATION OF FAITH, THE PROCLAMATION OF FAITH, AND THE MANIFESTO [COMMUNITY OF THE LOVE OF CHRIST (EVANGELICAL CATHOLIC)]

DECLARATION OF FAITH

We believe in God, Creator of all, of the heavens and of the earth, Who goes before creation as our common Parent, calling us to Choose Life!—and to God's deeds we testify:

God calls the worlds into being, creates persons in God's own image and sets before us the Way of Life.

God seeks in holy love to liberate all people from sin and alienation.

Christ, through Whom humanity attains New Life, is the Word of God spoken in eternity: Whom in the alone-born of God, Jesus of Nazareth, has come to us as our Messiah and Liberator, entering our humanity by the conception of the Holy Spirit in the virgin Mary, and sharing our common lot conquered sin and reconciles the world to God. Jesus suffered the death of the cross.

After three days, Christ Jesus rose from the dead.

Jesus bestows upon us the Holy Spirit, regenerating and sanctifying persons, creating and renewing Community in the love of Christ: binding in covenant faithful people of all ages, sexes, races and tongues.

The Holy Spirit of God, sent through Jesus, calls us into the Church-Community to accept the cost and joy of discipleship: to be Jesus' friends in the service of the people; to preach the Gospel to all peoples in the world; to bring the Good News to the poor; to proclaim liberty to the captives, new vision to the unseeing, freedom to those in bondage, liberation to the oppressed, the time of the Lord to all; to share in Jesus' Baptism and eat at Jesus' Table until Christ comes again; to join in Jesus' suffering and victory.

The Bible is the divinely inspired Word of God, spoken by the Holy Spirit through prophets and apostles; interpreted by the Holy Spirit given to women and men in the Church-Community of Jesus: and is our guide in faith and discipline as the pointer to the inward Word of God, the Light which enlightens every person who comes into the world.

Jesus promises to all who have faith liberation from the bondage of sin and oppression, fullness of grace and strength for the struggle for justice and peace through the Spirit; Jesus' own Presence in our midst in trial and rejoicing, and eternal life in God's Kingdom, the liberated Community which has no end. Amen.

THE PROCLAMATION OF FAITH

Praising and offering thanks, truly we proclaim:

The One God, Sovereign and Eternal, Who Creates, Redeems and Sustains all, is the Foundation of the heavens and the earth and all that dwell therein, Who calls us to Choose Life. God is One: and Faith and Charity are joined eternally. Therefore, to the deeds of God we testify:

God calls the worlds into being, creates us in the divine image and likeness, and sets before us the Way of Life, seeking in Holy Love to liberate all people from alienation, sin and hatred.

In Jesus of Nazareth, the Eternal Word of God has come to us and shared our common lot, as foretold by the Prophets: in the fulness of time entering our humanity by the Work of the Holy Spirit Who, that God might spiritually heal the separation of sin, prepared the Son of Mary to be the vehicle of the Word, so that Jesus Christ is fully human and fully Divine, both natures maintained in perfect union so that there is One Christ, our Sovereign Saviour, Who overcame sin, sickness and death, and reconciled the earth to God. In the days of Pontius Pilate, Jesus Christ suffered the death of the Cross and was buried; and after three days, by the Power of God, overcame death.

Christ bestows upon us the Paraclete, the Spirit of Light, of Truth and of Love. In Jesus Christ all glory is given to the One Eternal God through the Holy Spirit; Who unites, for the advancement of humanity and the earth in the Reign of God, with those who through Faith are wrested from the principalities and powers, the rule of evil in the world: binding in covenant the Mystical Body of Christ, the blessed company of all faithful people even from the foundation of the world.

Through Holy Spirit, the Wisdom of God, Jesus Christ calls us to accept the cost and joy of discipleship in the journey from darkness to the Light: to share in Christ's Baptism and eat at Christ's Table.

Christ promises to all who bear Faith liberation from the bondage of sin and fulness of grace; the Presence of the Holy Spirit through trial and rejoicing; and eternal life in the Community of Love, the New Jerusalem, the Reign and Dominion of God which has no end and in the Light of which we walk. Amen.

MANIFESTO

The People's Church Collective is a community within the revolutionary Movement which relates to the radical tradition of Jesus, the Prophets & the Church of Liberation: an ecumenical voluntary association for the spiritual renewal, consecration and transformation of Humanity & the World. The Work to which we are called is the Celebration of Life! the maximal actualization of the creative potential of the Whole Person and of all Life, the realization of ultimate personal freedom and personal responsibility in Community in harmonious relationship with one another.

As Jesus our Brother & Liberator said: "I Am come that they might have Life and have it more abundantly." (John 10:10). We are called upon to bring the Life More Abundant to all and thus to realize the Universal Free Community of Sister/Brotherhood in the Creative Life.

Explore in action, in the Service of the People, in the Movement for Liberation: and you come face to face with the God of the Universe, the Power behind nature, history and freedom. Explore, in contemplation, the inner life: and you find the God of the human heart, the Beingness beyond space and time. God is there in the midst of the world and in the inner person: and God is One.

Has not the Community of Love—the Kingdom of God—been promised to the poor & lowly, and was not the Liberator of the world a Carpenter & a Convict?

We come together to restore the apostolic revolution of transforming Love meaningfully for contemporary Humanity; to Serve the People and do the Work of the renewed Christ-Teaching in our Age for the spiritual realization & actualization of All—both now and in generations yet unborn—; to fulfill the need of our Age for Jesuene Discipleship (a free & revolutionary Christianity: "Yes, a Christian revolutionary. And not a revolutionary who happens to be a Christian or in spite of being a Christian, but revolutionary because Christian."—Eric Gill) bearing witness, in a time of technological greatness to the primacy of the Creative Spirit; to unify the learning of the Age with Christ and the Christ with the learning of the Age and thus to bring about the beautiful non-violent free Community of Love.

Members of the P.C.C. covenant with the Community in the words of the ancient initiate's vow: "I have beheld a Spark of the Divine Humanity. That Spark, the Christ within, must be nurtured, as the flickering ember is shielded from the driving rain, even at the cost of my life."

The real Church, the Church of Liberation, has no self-interest but Humanity & the World. It claims to be Universal, and therefore it is set over against each and every society in which it finds itself as an international conspiracy for the Life More Abundant, in accord with Jesus Charter given to it: "to bring the Good News to the poor: to proclaim liberty to the captives, new vision to the unseeing, freedom to those in bondage, liberation to the oppressed, the Time of Liberation to All." (Luke 4:18-19)

Jesus our Brother is Christ and Liberator, who died, who rose, who comes again in the ever-present Now! The Cross must be raised again at the center of the People's struggle for a transformed world, and not merely on the steeple of the church. Jesus was not crucified in a cathedral between two candles, but on a cross between two political prisoners (mis-translated "thief" by theologians); at the town garbage-heap, at a cross-roads so cosmopolitan that they had to write his title in Hebrew & Latin & Greek: at the kind of place where cynics talk smut & thieves curse & soldiers gamble. That is where Jesus died, and that is what Jesus died about: and that is where the church ought to be & what the church ought to be about—the bringing into being a transformed world, the beautiful non-violent free Community of sister/brotherhood in the Creative Life. Walk down the streets of the city and take a moment out

DECLARATION OF FAITH, THE PROCLAMATION OF FAITH, AND THE MANIFESTO [COMMUNITY OF THE LOVE OF CHRIST (EVANGELICAL CATHOLIC)] (continued)

to talk to adolescent runaways, youth without homes, street-people, students; to the aged, largely discarded by an affluent society; to Women & Gay males oppressed by the bureaucratic structures & ideology of a patriarchal sexist society; to Black, Amer-Indian & Third World people oppressed by the institutions & ideology of a racist society; to Workers thrown out of work & on the dole due to technological advance used for profit rather than for humane ends & the internal contradictions of a capitalist society in its death-throes; to war-resisters, peacemakers & radicals who rightly feel the institutional church has betrayed the revolutionary Gospel: look at the parallel oppression of Gay people, ethnic minorities & political dissenters in state-socialist nations: and know in your gut the alienation of a world-wide cross-section of the People.

It is precisely in this time & place that we are called by the Spirit to participate in the revolutionary life-style of Love & Service of the People taught by Jesus our Brother & Liberator.

Even in the present hostile environment, as much as possible, we are called to live, in a concrete way, those changes we wish to see in Humanity & a new society. This means we must work for inward transformation while developing the Way of Life of the new society: "forming the structure of the new society within the shell of the old" (IWW).

This is the work of the universal androgynous Community of sister/brotherhood in the Creative Life, an already existing Principle of Truth in Christ on the spiritu-al/archetypal level and one to be brought into external manifestation through the revolutionary struggle of the People in the Creative Spirit. Humanity begins where the State ends. You cannot serve God & Mammon, Christ & the State. Let Humanity begin!

Serve the People and thus serve Christ who is known inwardly—personally/outwardly in the People collective-ly:

"Now who so despised and lost, but what shall be my
    Saviour?
Is there one yet sick and suffering in the whole world? or
    deformed, condemned, degraded?
Thither hastening, I am at rest—for this one can absolve
    me.
O, I am greedy of love—all, all are beautiful to me!
You are my deliverers every one—from death, from sin,
    from evil—
I float, I dissolve in you!
O bars of self, you cannot shut me now.
O frailest child, O blackest criminal,
Whoe'er you are I never can repay you—though the world
    despise you, you are glorious to me;
For you have saved me from myself,
You delivered me when I was in prison—
I passed through you into heaven,
You were my Christ to me."—Edward Carpenter

"In the secret quarters, in the underground, in Greenwich Village, Saint Germain, among the campus students planning sit-ins and freedom rides, in the hidden quarters of Africa, wherever change is initiated, in the midst of changes, in the march to the sea, in the picket lines in front of embassies, the worth of the world is proclaimed. In the invisible lofts where the anarchists and pacifists defy money and the structures of society, where the lies are being examined and reversed, lies which are the allies of death, in these places is the poetry which is the language of God." (from a 1962 P.C.C. brochure: quotation from Judith Malina & Julian Beck)

The only effective Work of the Gospel today is to be found in a Community serving the People with that "poetry which is the language of God," a Community of non-violent revolutionary Love & Action, affirming that the revolution is New Life for all Humanity and taking up the claims of the Good News for this age, claims which have been largely abandoned by the institutional church since its sell-out to the State in the IVth century c.e.

Jesus Teaching calls us to comfort the afflicted and afflict the comfortable: but in the ages of its sell-out to the State, the institutional church has been more concerned with comforting the comfortable & so has added to the affliction of the already oppressed. In Nazi Germany the institutional church sold out & went under. Its identity was not with the oppressed but with the oppressor. Then an alternative Community, a "Confessing Church" stood up & made its witness in its own blood. Is it possible that such a time will come to us? Is it possible that now is that time?

Looking at the world-crisis today, the People's Church Collective responds: Yes! "Now is the time of choice! Now is the day of liberation!" (2 Cor. 6:2) Therefore, we come together to do the Work of Jesus' revolution—a truly humanistic revolution— in our time, proclaiming the Creative Spirit in transforming Love and Serving the People (vide. Matt. 25:31-46; Acts 2:44-6)

Faith divorced from a revolutionary commitment to social liberation is a mockery! (*vide.* James 2:1-26) The determination of the Movemental Church, of which the P.C.C. is only one manifestation, is to be those people of a new order who live by the values and revolutionary priority of Jesus and the Community of Liberating Love which is motivated by the Creative Spirit, even in the midst of the hostility and oppression of the State. We wish to serve the People by proclaiming the Good News of Liberation in the Christ, by articulating the ethical demands of discipleship, by working for peace, freedom and human dignity for all, and by serving in day-to-day needs as they arise and as we are able.

Notes: *Over the years the Community of the Love of Christ (Evangelical Catholic) has issued various statements that embody the Church's belief as it relates both to the historical Christian tradition and to contemporary social issues. All of the statements have been written and/or edited to eliminate sexist (non-inclusive) language. Distinctive emphases of the community are seen in the inclusion of phrases such as "the image of God in all persons," "liberation," "the beautiful* *non-violent free community of sister/brotherhood," and "the radical tradition of Jesus."*

* * *

PREAMBLE TO THE CONSTITUTION (GAY ATHEISTS LEAGUE OF AMERICA)

Because Atheism recognizes the supremacy of *reason,* and bases its ethics on the experience of living, independent of any arbitrary authority, creed, dogma or ritual; and

Because the primary source of hostility against Lesbians and Gay males has been organized religion, resulting in:

—an irrational hatred and suppression of same-sex affectional and sexual preferences, which, when unfettered by dogma, are natural, beautiful and healthy expressions of love, which should be encouraged rather than discouraged; and

—the harassment and incarceration by governments of Lesbians and Gay males; and

—denial to Lesbians and Gay males of the right to equal access to government programs, which they are compelled to support; and

—discrimination against Lesbians and Gay males in jobs, housing, and public accommodations; and

Because, in spite of religion's longstanding practice of suppressing same-sex affectional and sexual preference, many Lesbians and Gay males, reluctant to interpret the world rationally, have felt compelled by the pervasive and irrational forces of religion to form their own religious groups, loosely based upon the established religious organizations, but which change the religious dogma so that ancient myths and teachings, which are clearly anti-Lesbian and anti-Gay male, are ignored, while the remainder of the myths and teachings are adhered to:

We hereby adopt this constitution of the GAY ATHEISTS LEAGUE OF AMERICA with the following purposes:

(1) To provide a forum where Lesbian and Gay male Atheists can meet, and can exchange and disseminate ideas;

(2) To counterbalance the predominance, within the Lesbian and Gay male movement, of religiously-oriented organizations;

(3) To work toward the complete separation of church and state, and, in particular, to oppose the influence of religious conditioning, and the tax-free institutions which support such conditioning, on legislators, judges, and law enforcement agents when they pass, interpret and enforce the laws that affect the lives of Lesbians and Gay males;

(4) To promote a positive image of Lesbians and Gay males, and of the virtues of Atheism as a philosophical stance of freedom from the mind-control of religion, a stance that holds that women and men can be ethical without the influence and intervention of superstition.

Notes: *Frequently reprinted, this statement presents the league's rationale.*

* * *

DOCTRINE, SACRAMENTS, RITES (METROPOLITAN COMMUNITY CHURCH)

DOCTRINE: Christianity is the revelation of God in Jesus Christ and is the religion set forth in the Scriptures. Jesus Christ is foretold in the Old Testament, presented in the New Testament, and proclaimed by the Christian Church in every age and in every land.

Founded in the interest of offering a church home to all who confess and believe, the Universal Fellowship of Metropolitan Community Churches moves in the mainstream of Christianity.

Our faith is based upon the principles outlined in the historic creeds: Apostles and Nicene.

We believe:

1. In one triune God, omnipotent, omnipresent and omniscient, of one substance and of three persons: God - our Parent-Creator; Jesus Christ the only begotten son of God, God in flesh, human; and the Holy Spirit - God as our Sustainer.

2. That the Bible is the divinely inspired Word of God, showing forth God to every person through the law and the prophets, and finally, completely and ultimately on earth in the being of Jesus Christ.

3. That Jesus . . . the Christ . . . historically recorded as living some 2,000 years before this writing is God incarnate, of human birth, fully God and fully human, and that by being one with God, Jesus has demonstrated once and forever that all people are likewise Children of God, being spiritually made in God's image.

4. That the Holy Spirit is God making known God's love and interest to all people. The Holy Spirit is God, available to and working through all who are willing to place their welfare in God's keeping.

5. Every person is justified by Grace to God through faith in Jesus Christ.

6. We are saved from loneliness, despair and degradation through God's gift of grace, as was declared by our Saviour. Such grace is not earned, but is a pure gift from a God of pure love. We further commend the community of the faithful to a life of prayer; to seek genuine forgiveness for unkind, thoughtless and unloving acts; and to a committed life of Christian service.

7. The Church serves to bring all people to God through Christ. To this end, it shall arrange for regular services of worship, prayer, interpretation of the Scriptures, and edification through the teaching and preaching of the Word.

DOCTRINE, SACRAMENTS, RITES (METROPOLITAN COMMUNITY CHURCH) (continued)

SACRAMENTS: THIS CHURCH EMBRACES TWO HOLY SACRAMENTS:

1. BAPTISM by water and the Spirit, as recorded in the Scriptures, shall be a sign of the dedication of each life to God and God's service. Through the words and acts of this sacrament, the recipient is identified as God's own Child.

2. HOLY COMMUNION is the partaking of blessed bread and fruit of the vine in accordance with the words of Jesus, our Sovereign: "This is my body . . . this is my blood." (Matthew 26:26-28). All who believe, confess and repent and seek God's love through Christ, after examining their consciences, may freely participate in the communal meal, signifying their desire to be received into community with Jesus Christ, to be saved by Jesus Christ's sacrifice, to participate in Jesus Christ's resurrection, and to commit their lives anew to the service of Jesus Christ.

RITES: The Rites of the Church as performed by its duly authorized ministers shall consist of the following:

1. The RITE OF ORDINATION is the setting apart of duly qualified persons for the professional ministry of this church. It is evidenced by the laying on of hands by authorized ordained clergy, pursuant to these By-Laws.

2. The RITE OF ATTAINING MEMBERSHIP IN THE CHURCH, Mission or Study Group, shall be conducted by the pastor, interim pastor or worship coordinator before a local congregation at any regular worship service. After completing classes for instruction in the beliefs and doctrines of the church, a baptized Christian may become a member in good standing of the local church group through a letter of transfer from a recognized Christian body or through affirmation of faith.

3. The RITE OF HOLY UNION and the RITE OF HOLY MATRIMONY are the spiritual joining of two persons in a manner fitting and proper by a duly authorized clergy of the Church. After both persons have been counseled and apprised of their responsibilities one towards the other, this rite of conferring God's blessing may be performed.

4. The RITE OF FUNERAL OR MEMORIAL SERVICE is to be fittingly conducted by the ministers of the Church for the deceased.

5. The RITE OF LAYING ON OF HANDS or prayer for the healing of the sick in mind, body or spirit is to be conducted by the ministers of the Church, at their discretion, upon request.

6. The RITE OF BLESSING may be conducted by the ministers of the Church for persons, things and relationships, when deemed appropriate by the minister. This includes the dedication of a church building to the glory of God.

Notes: *This document is taken from Article II of the church's constitution.*

*　　*　　*

SIX PRECEPTS (TAYU FELLOWSHIP)

1) I will Confront Ignorance, Seek Understanding, Love Innocence.

2) I will accept nothing for which I am not willing and able to pay.

3) I will create the most fulfilling existence of which I am capable.

4) I will harm nothing in Creation without its consent.

5) I will love Myself, I will love Others also.

6) I will Satisfy Needs, Surrender Desires, Expect Surprises.

Notes: *According to the Tayu Fellowship, members live by these six precepts.*

Chapter 23
Unclassified Religious Groups

SUMMARY OF DOCTRINES (CHURCH OF THE NEW SONG)

1. The DOCTRINE OF FREEDOM OF RELIGION to develop and enjoy peacefully the faith of the people on Earth and *spaceforth,* whether they be in prison or out personally (see Mizan 304.54-63).

2. The DOCTRINE OF THE CLARITY to help make their faith more clear and in harmony with nature, and thus *inverse* the process of pollution which the population of the Earth has committed against the environment of this planet (see Mizan 102.04-05).

3. The DOCTRINE OF THE DEMOCRATIZATION OF SCRIPTURES to *guide themselves* closer to the truth among all the religions in the world (see Mizan 108.75 and 400.29 and 201.02-05 and 304.11).

4. The DOCTRINE OF THE INFIXUS combining both the Doctrine of the Clarity and the Democratization of Scriptures to accomplish the *inversal* of pollution more readily and improve world relations synergetically (see Mizan 102.04-05 and 108.75 and 400.29 and 304.11 and 201.02-05).

5. The DOCTRINE OF HEALTHESIS which is that everybody on Earth is at least entitled to (1) something to eat, (2) somewhere to sleep, (3) somebody to love, and (4) something to wear including the Sacrament of Ascorbation (at least 500 to 1000 milligrams of Vitamin C per day with any other supplements for health and depollution as prescribed through *The Complete Book of Vitamins* published by Rodale Press, Emmaus, Pennsylvania, United States of America, 1977) to *genetically* aid the difficult process of thinking less split-mindedly and more synergetically, since lack of ascorbate in humanity has been one of the causes of the split-mindedness on Earth thus far, because, unlike other animals on this planet, the human body does not yet manufacture its own ascorbation within, so it must be taken to eat from external sources. Remember, your body is your home; don't junk it up (see Mizan 107.81 and 401.96-97).

6. The DOCTRINE OF SYNERGY OF SPEECH to say what is on your mind and *develop* freedom of honesty, rather than remain all pent-up with it or frustrated by it (see Mizan 108.11-15 and 102.06).

7. The DOCTRINE OF SEMINARS to meet in groups and deal with their problems by connecting up their ideas with reality through the *resocializing process of faith exchanging and synergetical considerations* toward an Apocalyptic future as promised in scripture (see Mizan 304.64-97).

8. The DOCTRINE OF ACOLIGHTS to help free themselves of past errors and immutual circumstances by candidly selecting an acolight partner and working together justly with him or her, instead of having to sneak around or circumvent procedures for good companionship or the consensual validating experience necessary *to form a more perfect union* in harmony with nature (see Mizan 403.97 and 401.31 and 106.26 and 401.52).

9. The DOCTRINE OF LOVEPARTNERSHIP which can be developed into *synergetical marriage* or Sacred Unity for people who fall in love with each other and want to become each other's spouse in terms of law as mizanically outlined (see Mizan 400.93-94 and 106.21).

10. The DOCTRINE OF BIOMENTOLOGY to study *how* two or more things can work together more justly (that is, synergetically) and to share this research for truth in relations with others both personally and professionally (see Mizan 108.61 and 403.65-66 and 304.87).

11. The DOCTRINE OF FREEDOM OF RESOCIALIZATION including the Apocalyptic Unifactions to give people a *new start* and biomentally develop *synergetical relations* between Adam and Eve today as a daily resocial experience of applied mizanic law (see Mizan 400.83-88 and 402.57-60 and 102.01 and 105.14-15 and 107.40).

12. The DOCTRINE OF JUSTICE BY SYNERGY BETWEEN FACTS AND LAW for the healing of the nations worldwide eventually and the historical enjoyment of Gridarian Democracy to *coordinate*

our energies and glorify our species in space and time, hopefully contacting other worlds as a United World Ourselves (see Mizan 401.01-99 and 304.88-89).

*   *   *

THE 21 PRECEPTS (PERFECT LIBERTY KYODAN)

1. Life is art.
2. Man's life is a succession of self-expressions.
3. Man is a manifestation of God.
4. Man suffers if he fails to express himself.
5. Man loses his true self when swayed by feelings and emotion.
6. Man's true self is revealed when his ego is effaced.
7. All things exist in mutual relationship to one another.
8. Live radiantly as the sun.
9. All men are equal.
10. Strive for creating mutual happiness.
11. Have true faith in God.
12. There is a way (function) peculiar to every "name" (existence).
13. There is a way for men, and there is another for women.
14. All is for world peace.
15. All is a mirror.
16. All things progress and develop.
17. Comprehend what is most essential.
18. At every moment man stands at the crossroads of good and evil.
19. Act when your intuition dictates.
20. Live in perfect unity of mind and matter.
21. Live in Perfect Liberty.

Acknowledgments

Grateful acknowledgment is due to the
following publishers for use of their material.

"Account of Our Religion, Doctrine and Faith [Hutterite Brethren]." Reprinted from *Baptist Confessions of Faith,* edited by William L. Lumpkin (copyright © 1959, Valley Forge: Judson Press; reprinted by permission of the publisher), pp. 40-41.

"Affirmations for Humanistic Jews [Sherwin T. Wine, Society for Humanistic Judaism]." Reprinted from *Judaism Beyond God: A Radical New Way to Be Jewish* by Sherwin T. Wine (copyright © 1985 by Sherwin T. Wine; reprinted by permission of the Society for Humanistic Judaism, 28611 W. Twelve Mile Rd., Farmington Hills, Mich. 48018), Society for Humanistic Judaism, 1985, p. 244.

Confessions [of the General Church of the New Jerusalem]. Reprinted from *Liturgy and Hymnal for the Use of the General Church of the New Jerusalem* (copyright 1916, 1921, 1939, and 1966 by the General Church of the New Jerusalem; reprinted by permission of the publisher), General Church of the New Jerusalem, 1966, pp. 217-20.

"The Creed [Church of Eductivism]." Reprinted from the bulletin of the Association of International Dianologists (copyright © 1970 by: The Church of Spiritual Freedoms; reprinted by permission of the publisher), 1970.

"Dogma" and "Doctrine [Church of Seven Arrows]." Reprinted from *Shaman's Notes 2: Structure of Complete Belief-Systems* (copyright 1985 by Church of Seven Arrows; reprinted by permission of the publisher), Church of Seven Arrows, 1985, pp. 14-26.

"I Believe [Rabbi Joseph H. Gelberman, Little Synagogue]." Reprinted from *To Be . . . Fully Alive: A Collection of Essays for Life Enhancement on the Spiritual and Psychological Potential of Man* by Dr. Joseph H. Gelberman (copyright © 1983 by Dr. Joseph H. Gelberman; reprinted by permission of the publisher), Coleman Graphics, 1983, pp. xxiii-xxv.

"Our Message [Family of Love (Children of God)]." Reprinted from *The Basic Mo Letters* by Moses David (© Children of God, 1976), Children of God, 1976, pp. 27-31.

"Principles of Miracles [Miracles Experiences, Inc.]." Reprinted from *A Course in Miracles* (copyright © 1975 by the Foundation for Inner Peace; reprinted by permission of the publisher), Foundation for Inner Peace, 1975, pp. 1-4.

"Statement of Principles" and "Affirmations of the Ethical Movement [American Ethical Union]." Reprinted from *Ethical Perspectives: Statements by the Ethical Culture Movement* (© 1972 New York Society for Ethical Culture; reprinted by permission of the publisher), New York Society for Ethical Culture, 1972.

"The Theological Declaration of Barmen." Reprinted from *The Church's Confession Under Hitler* by Arthur C. Cochrane, Westminster Press, 1962, pp. 237-42.

Creed/Organization Name and Keyword Index

Creed names are indicated by italic type, while organizations
and religious traditions appear in regular type.

A

D

I

J

N

Q

R

Name and Keyword Index

Y

Z